Make a Difference

Youth Bible

New Living Translation

BroadStreet
PUBLISHING

new living
TRANSLATION.

BroadStreet Publishing® Group, LLC
Savage, Minnesota, USA
BroadStreetPublishing.com

Make a Difference Youth Bible

9781424562411 (hardcover)
9781424562428 (ebook)

Cover and interior design by 2K/DENMARK and Ken Castor
Make a Difference Youth Bible logo design by Garborg Design Works Inc.

Printed in China
24 25 26 27 28 5 4 3 2 1

Table of Contents

A Note to Readers

The *Holy Bible,* New Living Translation, was first published in 1996. It quickly became one of the most popular Bible translations in the English-speaking world. While the NLT's influence was rapidly growing, the Bible Translation Committee determined that an additional investment in scholarly review and text refinement could make it even better. So shortly after its initial publication, the committee began an eight-year process with the purpose of increasing the level of the NLT's precision without sacrificing its easy-to-understand quality. This second-generation text was completed in 2004, with minor changes subsequently introduced in 2007, 2013, and 2015.

The goal of any Bible translation is to convey the meaning and content of the ancient Hebrew, Aramaic, and Greek texts as accurately as possible to contemporary readers. The challenge for our translators was to create a text that would communicate as clearly and powerfully to today's readers as the original texts did to readers and listeners in the ancient biblical world. The resulting translation is easy to read and understand, while also accurately communicating the meaning and content of the original biblical texts. The NLT is a general-purpose text especially good for study, devotional reading, and reading aloud in worship services.

We believe that the New Living Translation—which combines the latest biblical scholarship with a clear, dynamic writing style—will communicate God's word powerfully to all who read it. We publish it with the prayer that God will use it to speak his timeless truth to the church and the world in a fresh, new way.

The Publishers

Introduction to the New Living Translation

Translation Philosophy and Methodology

English Bible translations tend to be governed by one of two general translation theories. The first theory has been called "formal-equivalence," "literal," or "word-for-word" translation. According to this theory, the translator attempts to render each word of the original language into English and seeks to preserve the original syntax and sentence structure as much as possible in translation. The second theory has been called "dynamic-equivalence," "functional-equivalence," or "thought-for-thought" translation. The goal of this translation theory is to produce in English the closest natural equivalent of the message expressed by the original-language text, both in meaning and in style.

Both of these translation theories have their strengths. A formal-equivalence translation preserves aspects of the original text—including ancient idioms, term consistency, and original-language syntax—that are valuable for scholars and professional study. It allows a reader to trace formal elements of the original-language text through the English translation. A dynamic-equivalence translation, on the other hand, focuses on translating the message of the original-language text. It ensures that the meaning of the text is readily apparent to the contemporary reader. This allows the message to come through with immediacy, without requiring the reader to struggle with foreign idioms and awkward syntax. It also facilitates serious study of the text's message and clarity in both devotional and public reading.

The pure application of either of these translation philosophies would create translations at opposite ends of the translation spectrum. But in reality, all translations contain a mixture of these two philosophies. A purely formal-equivalence translation would be unintelligible in English, and a purely dynamic-equivalence translation would risk being unfaithful to the original. That is why translations shaped by dynamic-equivalence theory are usually quite literal when the original text is relatively clear, and the translations shaped by formal-equivalence theory are sometimes quite dynamic when the original text is obscure.

The translators of the New Living Translation set out to render the message of the original texts of Scripture into clear, contemporary English. As they did so, they kept the concerns of both formal-equivalence and dynamic-equivalence in mind. On the one hand, they translated as simply and literally as possible when that approach yielded an accurate, clear, and natural English text. Many words and phrases were rendered literally and consistently into English, preserving essential literary and rhetorical devices, ancient metaphors, and word choices that give structure to the text and provide echoes of meaning from one passage to the next.

On the other hand, the translators rendered the message more dynamically when the literal rendering was hard to understand, was misleading, or yielded archaic or foreign wording. They clarified difficult metaphors and terms to aid in the reader's understanding. The translators first struggled with the meaning of the words and phrases in the ancient context; then they rendered the message into clear, natural English. Their goal was to be both faithful to the ancient texts and eminently readable. The result is a translation that is both exegetically accurate and idiomatically powerful.

Translation Process and Team

To produce an accurate translation of the Bible into contemporary English, the translation team needed the skills necessary to enter into the thought patterns of the ancient authors and then to render their ideas, connotations, and effects into clear, contemporary English. To begin this process, qualified biblical scholars were needed to interpret the meaning of the original text and to check it against our base English translation. In order to guard against personal and theological biases, the scholars needed to represent a diverse group of evangelicals who would employ the best exegetical tools. Then to work alongside the scholars, skilled English stylists were needed to shape the text into clear, contemporary English.

With these concerns in mind, the Bible Translation Committee recruited teams of scholars that represented a broad spectrum of denominations, theological perspectives, and backgrounds within the worldwide evangelical community. (A list of these scholars can be found online.) Each book of the Bible was assigned to three different scholars with proven expertise in the book or group of books to be reviewed. Each of these scholars made a thorough review of a base translation and submitted suggested revisions to the appropriate Senior Translator. The Senior Translator then reviewed and summarized these suggestions and proposed a first-draft revision of the base text. This draft served as the basis for several additional phases of exegetical and stylistic committee review. Then the Bible Translation Committee jointly reviewed and approved every verse of the final translation.

Throughout the translation and editing process, the Senior Translators and their scholar teams were given a chance to review the editing done by the team of stylists. This ensured that exegetical errors would not be introduced late in the process and that the entire Bible Translation Committee was happy with the final result. By choosing a team of qualified scholars and skilled stylists and by setting up a process that allowed their interaction throughout the process, the New Living Translation has been refined to preserve the essential formal elements of the original biblical texts, while also creating a clear, understandable English text.

The New Living Translation was first published in 1996. Shortly after its initial publication, the Bible Translation Committee began a process of further committee review and translation refinement. The purpose of this continued revision was to increase the level of precision without sacrificing the text's easy-to-understand quality. This second-edition text was completed in 2004, with minor changes subsequently introduced in 2007, 2013, and 2015.

Written to Be Read Aloud

It is evident in Scripture that the biblical documents were written to be read aloud, often in public worship (see Nehemiah 8; Luke 4:16-20; 1 Timothy 4:13; Revelation 1:3). It is still the case today that more people will hear the Bible read aloud in church than are likely to read it for themselves. Therefore, a new translation must communicate with clarity and power when it is read publicly. Clarity was a primary goal for the NLT translators, not only to facilitate private reading and understanding, but also to ensure that it would be excellent for public reading and make an immediate and powerful impact on any listener.

The Texts behind the New Living Translation

The Old Testament translators used the Masoretic Text of the Hebrew Bible as represented in *Biblia Hebraica Stuttgartensia* (1977), with its extensive system of textual notes; this is an update of Rudolf Kittel's *Biblia Hebraica* (Stuttgart, 1937). The translators also further compared the Dead Sea Scrolls, the Septuagint and other Greek manuscripts, the Samaritan Pentateuch, the Syriac Peshitta, the Latin Vulgate, and any other versions or manuscripts that shed light on the meaning of difficult passages.

The New Testament translators used the two standard editions of the Greek New Testament: the *Greek New Testament*, published by the United Bible Societies (UBS, fourth revised edition, 1993), and *Novum Testamentum Graece*, edited by Nestle and Aland (NA, twenty-seventh edition, 1993). These two editions, which have the same text but differ in punctuation and textual notes, represent, for the most part, the best in modern textual scholarship. However, in cases where strong textual or other scholarly evidence supported the decision, the translators sometimes chose to differ from the UBS and NA Greek texts and followed variant readings found in other ancient witnesses. Significant textual variants of this sort are always noted in the textual notes of the New Living Translation.

Translation Issues

The translators have made a conscious effort to provide a text that can be easily understood by the typical reader of modern English. To this end, we sought to use only vocabulary and language structures in common use today. We avoided using language likely to become quickly dated or that reflects only a narrow subdialect of English, with the goal of making the New Living Translation as broadly useful and timeless as possible.

But our concern for readability goes beyond the concerns of vocabulary and sentence structure. We are also concerned about historical and cultural barriers to understanding the Bible, and we have sought to translate terms shrouded in history and culture in ways that can be immediately understood. To this end:

- We have converted ancient weights and measures (for example, "ephah" [a unit of dry volume] or "cubit" [a unit of length]) to modern English (American) equivalents, since the ancient measures are not generally meaningful to today's readers. Then in the textual footnotes we offer the literal Hebrew, Aramaic, or Greek measures, along with modern metric equivalents.

- Instead of translating ancient currency values literally, we have expressed them in common terms that communicate the message. For example, in the Old Testament, "ten shekels of silver" becomes "ten pieces of silver" to convey the intended message. In the New Testament, we have often translated the "denarius" as "the normal daily wage" to facilitate understanding. Then a footnote offers: "Greek *a denarius*, the payment for a full day's labor." In general, we give a clear English rendering and then state the literal Hebrew, Aramaic, or Greek in a textual footnote.

- Since the names of Hebrew months are unknown to most contemporary readers, and since the Hebrew lunar calendar fluctuates from year to year in relation to the solar calendar used today, we have looked for clear ways to communicate the time of year the Hebrew months (such as Abib) refer to. When an expanded or interpretive rendering is given in the text, a textual note gives the literal rendering. Where it is possible to define a specific ancient date in terms of our modern calendar, we use modern dates in the text. A textual footnote then gives the literal Hebrew date and states the rationale for our rendering. For example, Ezra 6:15 pinpoints the date when the postexilic Temple was completed in Jerusalem: "the third day of the month Adar." This was during the sixth year of King Darius's reign (that is, 515 B.C.). We have translated that date as March 12, with a footnote giving the Hebrew and identifying the year as 515 B.C.

- Since ancient references to the time of day differ from our modern methods of denoting time, we have used renderings that are instantly understandable to the modern reader. Accordingly, we have rendered specific times of day by using approximate equivalents in terms of our common "o'clock" system. On occasion, translations such as "at dawn the next morning" or "as the sun was setting" have been used when the biblical reference is more general.

- When the meaning of a proper name (or a wordplay inherent in a proper name) is relevant to the message of the text, its meaning is often illuminated with a textual footnote. For example, in Exodus 2:10 the text reads: "The princess named him Moses, for she explained, 'I lifted him out of the water.'" The accompanying footnote reads: "*Moses* sounds like a Hebrew term that means 'to lift out.'"

  Sometimes, when the actual meaning of a name is clear, that meaning is included in parentheses within the text itself. For example, the text at Genesis 16:11 reads: "You are to name him Ishmael *(which means 'God hears')*, for the LORD has heard your cry of distress." Since the original hearers and readers would have instantly understood the meaning of the name "Ishmael," we have provided modern readers with the same information so they can experience the text in a similar way.

- Many words and phrases carry a great deal of cultural meaning that was obvious to the original readers but needs explanation in our own culture. For example, the phrase "they beat their breasts" (Luke 23:48) in ancient times meant that people were very upset, often in mourning. In our translation we chose to translate this phrase dynamically for clarity: "They went home *in deep sorrow*." Then we included a footnote with the literal Greek, which reads: "Greek *went home beating their breasts*." In other similar cases, however, we have sometimes chosen to illuminate the existing literal expression to make it immediately understandable. For example, here we might have expanded the literal Greek phrase to read: "They went home beating their breasts *in sorrow*." If we had done this, we would not have included a textual footnote, since the literal Greek clearly appears in translation.

- Metaphorical language is sometimes difficult for contemporary readers to understand, so at times we have chosen to translate or illuminate the meaning of a metaphor. For example, the ancient poet writes, "Your neck is *like* the tower of

David" (Song of Songs 4:4). We have rendered it "Your neck is *as beautiful as* the tower of David" to clarify the intended positive meaning of the simile. Another example comes in Ecclesiastes 12:3, which can be literally rendered: "Remember him . . . when the grinding women cease because they are few, and the women who look through the windows see dimly." We have rendered it: "Remember him before your teeth—your few remaining servants—stop grinding; and before your eyes—the women looking through the windows—see dimly." We clarified such metaphors only when we believed a typical reader might be confused by the literal text.

- When the content of the original language text is poetic in character, we have rendered it in English poetic form. We sought to break lines in ways that clarify and highlight the relationships between phrases of the text. Hebrew poetry often uses parallelism, a literary form where a second phrase (or in some instances a third or fourth) echoes the initial phrase in some way. In Hebrew parallelism, the subsequent parallel phrases continue, while also furthering and sharpening, the thought expressed in the initial line or phrase. Whenever possible, we sought to represent these parallel phrases in natural poetic English.

- The Greek term *hoi Ioudaioi* is literally translated "the Jews" in many English translations. In the Gospel of John, however, this term doesn't always refer to the Jewish people generally. In some contexts, it refers more particularly to the Jewish religious leaders. We have attempted to capture the meaning in these different contexts by using terms such as "the people" (with a footnote: Greek *the Jewish people*) or "the Jewish leaders," where appropriate.

- One challenge we faced was how to translate accurately the ancient biblical text that was originally written in a context where male-oriented terms were used to refer to humanity generally. We needed to respect the nature of the ancient context while also trying to make the translation clear to a modern audience that tends to read male-oriented language as applying only to males. Often the original text, though using masculine nouns and pronouns, clearly intends that the message be applied to both men and women. A typical example is found in the New Testament letters, where the believers are called "brothers" (*adelphoi*). Yet it is clear from the content of these letters that they were addressed to all the believers—male and female. Thus, we have usually translated this Greek word as "brothers and sisters" in order to represent the historical situation more accurately.

  We have also been sensitive to passages where the text applies generally to human beings or to the human condition. In some instances we have used plural pronouns (they, them) in place of the masculine singular (he, him). For example, a traditional rendering of Proverbs 22:6 is: "Train up a child in the way he should go, and when he is old he will not turn from it." We have rendered it: "Direct your children onto the right path, and when they are older, they will not leave it." At times, we have also replaced third person pronouns with the second person to ensure clarity. A traditional rendering of Proverbs 26:27 is: "He who digs a pit will fall into it, and he who rolls a stone, it will come back on him." We have rendered it: "If you set a trap for others, you will get caught in it yourself. If you roll a boulder down on others, it will crush you instead."

  We should emphasize, however, that all masculine nouns and pronouns used to represent God (for example, "Father") have been maintained without exception. All decisions of this kind have been driven by the concern to reflect accurately the intended meaning of the original texts of Scripture.

Lexical Consistency in Terminology

For the sake of clarity, we have translated certain original-language terms consistently, especially within synoptic passages and for commonly repeated rhetorical phrases, and within certain word categories such as divine names and non-theological technical terminology (e.g., liturgical, legal, cultural, zoological, and botanical terms). For theological terms, we have allowed a greater semantic range of acceptable English words or phrases for a single Hebrew or Greek word. We have avoided some theological terms that are not readily understood by many modern readers. For example, we avoided using words such as "justification" and "sanctification," which are carryovers from Latin translations. In place of these words, we have provided renderings such as "made right with God" and "made holy."

The Spelling of Proper Names

Many individuals in the Bible, especially the Old Testament, are known by more than one name (e.g., Uzziah/Azariah). For the sake of clarity, we have tried to use a single spelling for any one individual, footnoting the literal spelling whenever we differ from it. This is especially helpful in delineating the kings of Israel and Judah. King Joash/Jehoash of Israel has been consistently called Jehoash, while King Joash/Jehoash of Judah is called Joash. A similar distinction has been used to distinguish between Joram/Jehoram of Israel and Joram/Jehoram of Judah. All such decisions were made with the goal of clarifying the text for the reader. When the ancient biblical writers clearly had a theological purpose in their choice of a variant name (e.g., Esh-baal/Ishbosheth), the different names have been maintained with an explanatory footnote.

For the names Jacob and Israel, which are used interchangeably for both the individual patriarch and the nation, we generally render it "Israel" when it refers to the nation and "Jacob" when it refers to the individual. When our rendering of the name differs from the underlying Hebrew text, we provide a textual footnote, which includes this explanation: "The names 'Jacob' and 'Israel' are often interchanged throughout the Old Testament, referring sometimes to the individual patriarch and sometimes to the nation."

The Rendering of Divine Names

In the Old Testament, all appearances of *'el*, *'elohim*, or *'eloah* have been translated "God," except where the context demands the translation "god(s)." We have generally rendered the tetragrammaton (*YHWH*) consistently as "the LORD," utilizing a form with small capitals that is common among English translations. This will distinguish it from the name *'adonai*, which we render "Lord." When *'adonai* and *YHWH* appear together, we have rendered it "Sovereign LORD." When *'elohim* and *YHWH* appear together, we have rendered it "LORD God." When *YH* (the short form of *YHWH*) and *YHWH* appear together, we have rendered it "LORD GOD." When *YHWH* appears with the term *tseba'oth*, we have rendered it "LORD of Heaven's Armies" to translate the meaning of the name. In a few cases, we have utilized the transliteration, *Yahweh*, when the personal character of the name is being invoked in contrast to another divine name or the name of some other god (for example, see Exodus 3:15; 6:2-3).

In the Gospels and Acts, the Greek word *christos* has normally been translated as "Messiah" when the context assumes a Jewish audience. When a Gentile audience can be assumed (which is consistently the case in the Epistles and Revelation), *christos* has been translated as "Christ." The Greek word *kurios* is consistently translated "Lord," except that it is translated "LORD" wherever the New Testament text explicitly quotes from the Old Testament, and the text there has it in small capitals.

Textual Footnotes

The New Living Translation provides several kinds of textual footnotes, all designated in the text with an asterisk:

- When for the sake of clarity the NLT renders a difficult or potentially confusing phrase dynamically, we generally give the literal rendering in a textual footnote. This allows the reader to see the literal source of our dynamic rendering and how our translation relates to other more literal translations. These notes are prefaced with "Hebrew," "Aramaic," or "Greek," identifying the language of the underlying source text. For example, in Acts 2:42 we translated the literal "breaking of bread" (from the Greek) as "the Lord's Supper" to clarify that this verse refers to the ceremonial practice of the church rather than just an ordinary meal. Then we attached a footnote to "the Lord's Supper," which reads: "Greek *the breaking of bread*."

- Textual footnotes are also used to show alternative renderings, prefaced with the word "Or." These normally occur for passages where an aspect of the meaning is debated. On occasion, we also provide notes on words or phrases that represent a departure from long-standing tradition. These notes are prefaced with "Traditionally rendered." For example, the footnote to the translation "serious skin disease" at Leviticus 13:2 says: "Traditionally rendered *leprosy*. The Hebrew word used throughout this passage is used to describe various skin diseases."

- When our translators follow a textual variant that differs significantly from our standard Hebrew or Greek texts (listed earlier), we document that difference with a footnote. We also footnote cases when the NLT excludes a passage that is included in the Greek text known as the *Textus Receptus* (and familiar to readers through its translation in the King James Version). In such cases, we offer a translation of the excluded text in a footnote, even though it is generally recognized as a later addition to the Greek text and not part of the original Greek New Testament.

- All Old Testament passages that are quoted in the New Testament are identified by a textual footnote at the New Testament location. When the New Testament clearly quotes from the Greek translation of the Old Testament, and when it differs significantly in wording from the Hebrew text, we also place a textual footnote at the Old Testament location. This note includes a rendering of the Greek version, along with a cross-reference to the New Testament passage(s) where it is cited (for example, see notes on Psalms 8:2; 53:3; Proverbs 3:12).

- Some textual footnotes provide cultural and historical information on places, things, and people in the Bible that are probably obscure to modern readers. Such notes should aid the reader in understanding the message of the text. For example, in Acts 12:1, "King Herod" is named in this translation as "King Herod Agrippa" and is identified in a footnote as being "the nephew of Herod Antipas and a grandson of Herod the Great."

- When the meaning of a proper name (or a wordplay inherent in a proper name) is relevant to the meaning of the text, it is either illuminated with a textual footnote or included within parentheses in the text itself. For example, the footnote concerning the name "Eve" at Genesis 3:20 reads: "*Eve* sounds like a Hebrew term that means 'to give life.'" This wordplay in the Hebrew illuminates the meaning of the text, which goes on to say that Eve "would be the mother of all who live."

AS WE SUBMIT this translation for publication, we recognize that any translation of the Scriptures is subject to limitations and imperfections. Anyone who has attempted to communicate the richness of God's word into another language will realize it is impossible to make a perfect translation. Recognizing these limitations, we sought God's guidance and wisdom throughout this project. Now we pray that he will accept our efforts and use this translation for the benefit of the church and of all people.

We pray that the New Living Translation will overcome some of the barriers of history, culture, and language that have kept people from reading and understanding God's word. We hope that readers unfamiliar with the Bible will find the words clear and easy to understand and that readers well versed in the Scriptures will gain a fresh perspective. We pray that readers will gain insight and wisdom for living, but most of all that they will meet the God of the Bible and be forever changed by knowing him.

The Bible Translation Committee

A complete list of the translators can be found at tyndale.com/nlt/scholars.

Introduction to the *Make a Difference Youth Bible*

Our world needs you. It's a mess out there, and God has called you to take initiative, to do something, to change the world because Jesus created you to do so. The *Make a Difference Youth Bible* helps you walk with Jesus in such a way that you are encouraged to see the opportunities you have to bring his good news to a world in desperate need.

God's Word is "alive and powerful" (Hebrews 4:12)! Even so, maybe you think of the Bible as boring or irrelevant. The *Make a Difference Youth Bible* is a reminder that this "book" isn't just a relic of history. This "book" is transforming lives today and will be doing so tomorrow.

The Bible is made up of sixty-six life-changing pieces of literature. Each one, on its own, deserves a lifetime of devotion. From the longest (Psalms with 150 chapters) to the shortest (a battle between 2 John and 3 John), from the craziest (maybe Ezekiel) to the wisest (maybe Ecclesiastes), from the most epic (maybe Jonah) to the most depressing (maybe Lamentations), the Bible draws you into relationship with God—your Creator, your Sustainer, your Savior.

In our day, reading a Bible so that you can see the story arc of God's work in your life means that you have to overcome two problems: First, you may have to break through the barrier that many people have with simply "reading." The Bible is not meant to be read like the latest young adult fiction book—binged quickly and then discarded for the next interesting series. The Bible is also not to be approached like a textbook or manual, using only study formulas that often fail to engage most people into the story of Scripture. These approaches can leave many people unconvinced about the transformative nature of God's Word.

The second obstacle you might have to overcome is that many people are under the impression that the Bible is mostly for thinking, but you want to be doing! There is a popular rumor that the Bible is just for Bible study or personal devotions. Interestingly, that's not how the Bible was primarily used for most of its existence. The Bible was written not just for deep, individual meditation but more so for radical, world-changing action. In fact, it could be argued that the inward work of God's Word will compel you to be motivated outwardly, sharing God's message and love to others.

Jesus is not passive. He's passionate, and he's proactive. He doesn't want you to be lethargic about him or apathetic about people any longer. He wants to change you, and he wants to change the world through you.

A disciple is an active learner. Our world needs more active learners of Jesus—people who are intentionally seeking him in a radical relationship, searching for his life around every corner and in every person.

The Bible will help kick you into that world-changing gear where God operates. This earth needs more people pursuing their radical, God-created purpose. People like you.

Through Difference Maker challenges (sometimes quirky, sometimes serious, always deep), story arcs, questions, and prayers, the *Make a Difference Youth Bible* is meant to help you discover ways to grow closer to Jesus daily and do something as a result.

This Bible prompts action steps you can take—steps which are meant to help you put the Word of God into play. No more keeping the Bible on the bench (or shelf or unused app...). This *Make a Difference Youth Bible* is more than just a quiet-time devotional study. It's meant to be a loud-time, get-out-of-your-chair-and-do-something-to-change-the-world resource.

User Guide

Book introductions
The introductions to the Bible's sixty-six books will highlight the effect that each book can have on your faith and actions.

Prayer boxes
Reflective prayers will encourage you to let God's Word dwell within you for life-changing devotion.

Question boxes
Thought-provoking questions will prompt you to dig deep into your faith and stand strongly in Jesus.

Single-column New Living Translation
This easy-to-read format will help you follow the message of God's Word.

Difference Maker challenges
Action-step boxes help you deepen your commitment to Jesus and boldly change the world.

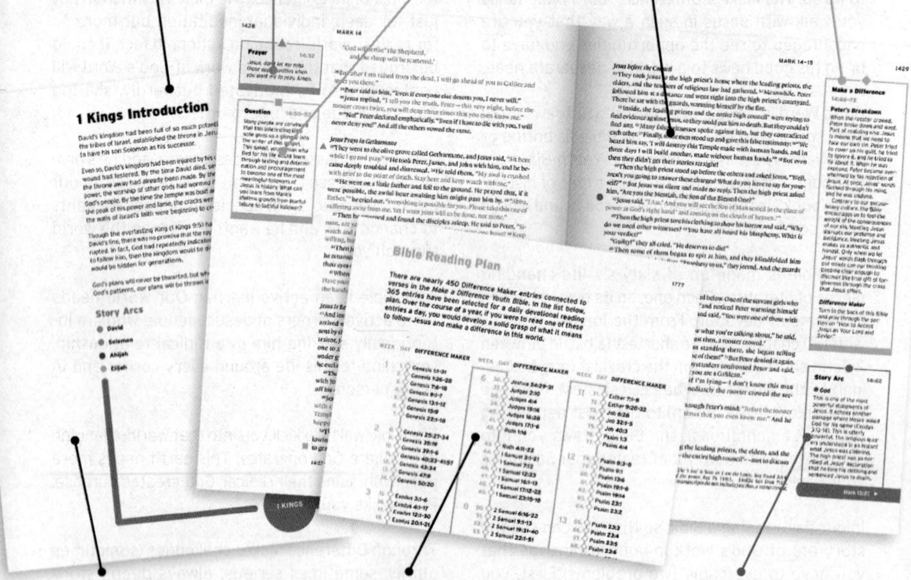

Wide margins
There is intentional room for you to mark up your favorite passages and creatively draw and journal as you go through God's Word. Many pages have prompts to encourage note-taking.

Appendixes
These entries, written by nationally trusted youth ministry workers, will help you commit your life to Jesus, jump into a devotional reading plan, and follow his call to make a difference in the world.

Story Arc entries and graphics
These entry points will pull you into the larger "expanded universe" of Scripture. The running red line will help you see how the entire Bible is connected through Jesus.

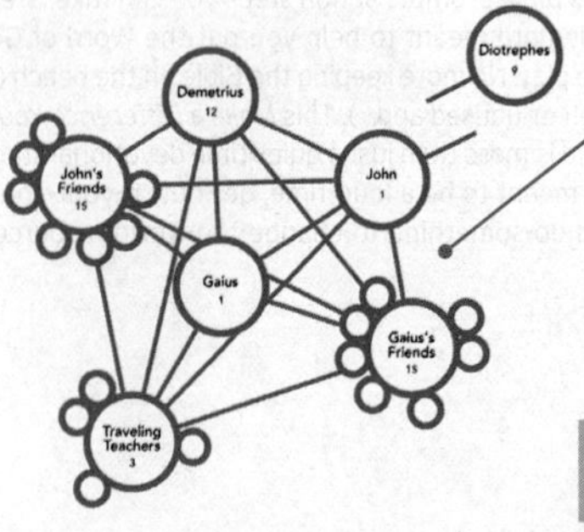

Church Network graphics
Real relationships with real people in real places are personally mentioned in several of the New Testament letters. To represent the remarkable interconnectivity of the early church, "hub network" visuals help readers understand the importance of community to the mission of Jesus. In the graphics, larger circles represent a specific person or church, smaller circles represent multiple people or groups, lines show connections between groups, and broken lines show struggling relationships.

The *Make a Difference Youth Bible* invites you to discover how Jesus is at work to restore the world. From the first page of the Bible to the last, God wants you to be involved in his story. Through this resource, allow God to empower you with inner strength through his Spirit. May Christ make his home in your heart as you trust in him. May your roots grow down into God's love and keep you strong. May you experience the love of Christ, though it is too great to understand fully. May you lead a life worthy of your calling, for you have been called (Ephesians 3:14–4:1).

Dr. Ken Castor, General Editor

About the General Editor

After over thirty years of serving in next-generation ministry in the US and Canada, Dr. Ken Castor is balding in his hairline but still bold in his faith. He holds degrees from Taylor University, Regent College, and Trinity Western University. Ken is the blue letters editor of the award-winning *Jesus-Centered Bible* and has authored numerous next-gen discipleship resources like *Grow Down: How to Build a Jesus-Centered Faith* and *Make a Difference: 365 World-Changing Devotions*. He enjoys living in Minnesota with his brilliantly witty and slightly freezing family.

Make a Difference Youth Bible Contributors

The following selected team of youth ministry influencers and Bible scholars contributed to entries throughout the *Make a Difference Youth Bible*.

Bill Allison, Michael Baker, Dr. Jeff Baxter, Zane Black, Dan Boal, Collin Carroll, Tim Ciccone, Jeremy Donovan, Brandon Early, Dr. Dean Erickson, Heather Flies, James Grout, Micah Hegerle, Bob Lenz, Nathan Lyke, Erin Maroney, David Martin, Dr. Steve McCready, Jonathan Meyer, Brad Mock, Tony Myles, Ginny Olson, Ryan Tarman, Emma Teal, Chris Theule-VanDam, Luke Trouten, Sharon Van Vlymen, Erik Williams, and Dr. Justin Winzenburg.

The
OLD TESTAMENT

OLD TESTAMENT INTRODUCTION

Jesus took them through the writings of Moses and all the prophets, explaining from all the Scriptures the things concerning himself.
Luke 24:27

Imagine that conversation. What sorts of things did Jesus say about himself as he walked through each of the parts of Scripture? Did he point to Genesis 1:1 or Genesis 3:15? Did he explain Leviticus 23? Did he rejoice as he referred to Psalm 22 or Isaiah 53? Did he light up when he thought of Ezekiel 34 or Micah 5:2?

Jesus knew the Old Testament was about him. Do you? Do you see the first two-thirds of the Bible as being about Jesus? Or do you see the Old Testament as "old" and irrelevant? Let's face it: while twenty-first-century Western Christians don't seem to naturally gravitate toward the Old Testament, the New Testament writers themselves deeply loved and deeply valued the Old Testament.

The apostle Paul wrote, "All Scripture is inspired by God [literally, "God breathed"] and is useful to teach us what is true and to make us realize what is wrong in our lives. It corrects us when we are wrong and teaches us to do what is right. God uses it to prepare and equip his people to do every good work" (2 Timothy 3:16-17). Ironically, when Paul talked about "all Scripture," he was talking about what we know as the Old Testament.

Where is this kind of passion and appreciation for the Old Testament today? Part of the problem is that we run into a mental roadblock before we even start to read. It's that word *Old* in front of the word *Testament* on the title page. Too often the connotations of the word *old* are things like "passé" and "not relevant" and "boring." Even before we begin reading the Bible, the word *old* puts a very unhelpful lens on the way we read and interact with the God of the Old Testament.

Even so, the God of the Old Testament is the very same God of the New Testament. You will never fully understand the New Testament without a working knowledge of the Old Testament. The Bible is the God-breathed Word of God. In other words, the greatest commentary on the Bible is the Bible.

As followers of Jesus, we must allow the Old Testament to inform our understanding of the New Testament, and the New Testament must inform our understanding of the Old Testament. This is sound hermeneutics (that is, the interpretation of the Bible).

Need more proof? The resurrected Jesus Christ said this to his disciples: "'When I was with you before, I told you that everything written *about me* in the law of Moses and the prophets and in the Psalms must be fulfilled.' Then he opened their minds to understand the Scriptures" (Luke 24:44-45, emphasis added).

As you dive into the first two-thirds of the Bible, may Jesus open your mind to understand both the Old Testament and New Testament Scriptures so that you might know God's personal and compelling call for your life.

Genesis Introduction

In the beginning, God created. Here is an understatement: God made a difference. He altered the circumstance. He created a better outcome. He took nothing and made something. He took chaos and made life. He spoke his creative, artistic vision into being. From the moment he acted, everything changed forever.

God created humans to be like him. We learn this in Genesis, the book of beginning. Reflecting God's creative desire to see "good," Genesis tells us that God created people so they could have a special and close relationship with him. The Bible calls this unique God-human relationship a "covenant." He also created people so they could seize opportunities to have a creative, positive effect on this world. It was what God called Adam and Eve to do. It was what he led Noah to do. It was the long-term vision he gave to Abraham and Sarah. It was the struggle he gave to Isaac and Jacob. Thankfully, it was what Joseph, the creative ruler of Egypt, did.

Genesis is also the origin of unraveling. Even though humans were created to be creative, Genesis tells the story of how people failed to follow God's model for their lives. As a result, they brought harm upon themselves, their communities, and their world. In this sad reality, however, Genesis sets the stage for the dramatic story: humans need someone to stand up and make a difference in this chaotic world. The covenant theme runs throughout the Old Testament.

You are part of this life-changing story arc, a story that spans untold thousands of years through the actions of countless difference makers along the way. You are invited to dive into this history, God's history, and become an active participant in the re-creation of this world.

Don't miss this major truth: ultimately, Genesis points to the story of how humanity came to need a Savior, Jesus, the greatest difference maker of them all.

Story Arcs

- **Adam and Eve: The First Humans**
- **Noah**
- **Abram and Sarai**
- **Melchizedek**
- **The Twelve Tribes**
- **Jacob → Israel**
- **Joseph**

Genesis

The Account of Creation

1 In the beginning God created the heavens and the earth.* 2The earth
was formless and empty, and darkness covered the deep waters. And the
Spirit of God was hovering over the surface of the waters.

3Then God said, "Let there be light," and there was light. 4And God saw
that the light was good. Then he separated the light from the darkness.
5God called the light "day" and the darkness "night."
And evening passed and morning came, marking the first day.

6Then God said, "Let there be a space between the waters, to separate the
waters of the heavens from the waters of the earth." 7And that is what
happened. God made this space to separate the waters of the earth from
the waters of the heavens. 8God called the space "sky."
And evening passed and morning came, marking the second day.

9Then God said, "Let the waters beneath the sky flow together into one
place, so dry ground may appear." And that is what happened. 10God
called the dry ground "land" and the waters "seas." And God saw that
it was good. 11Then God said, "Let the land sprout with vegetation—
every sort of seed-bearing plant, and trees that grow seed-bearing
fruit. These seeds will then produce the kinds of plants and trees from
which they came." And that is what happened. 12The land produced
vegetation—all sorts of seed-bearing plants, and trees with seed-
bearing fruit. Their seeds produced plants and trees of the same kind.
And God saw that it was good.
13And evening passed and morning came, marking the third day.

14Then God said, "Let lights appear in the sky to separate the day from
the night. Let them be signs to mark the seasons, days, and years. 15Let
these lights in the sky shine down on the earth." And that is what
happened. 16God made two great lights—the larger one to govern the
day, and the smaller one to govern the night. He also made the stars.
17God set these lights in the sky to light the earth, 18to govern the day
and night, and to separate the light from the darkness. And God saw
that it was good.
19And evening passed and morning came, marking the fourth day.

20Then God said, "Let the waters swarm with fish and other life. Let the
skies be filled with birds of every kind." 21So God created great sea
creatures and every living thing that scurries and swarms in the water,

Make a Difference 1:1-31

God's Word

The Bible describes the earth as a void, shrouded in darkness, with no form or substance. Over this emptiness, God's Spirit was "hovering." Then he spoke, and everything changed. He separated day from night, parted land from water, and made vegetation different from creatures. He made us. The effect God made was good—so very good. It's what he created people to do: to make a difference. Everything that follows this first chapter of the Bible is the story of how God speaks life into the chaos and how humanity is called to follow God's lead.

Difference Maker

Set yourself on a journey to "hover" over all the words of Scripture. Ask God to make a difference in your life so that you can make a difference in the lives of others.

1:1 Or *In the beginning when God created the heavens and the earth,* ... Or *When God began to create the heavens and the earth,* ...

and every sort of bird—each producing offspring of the same kind. And
God saw that it was good. 22 Then God blessed them, saying, "Be fruitful
and multiply. Let the fish fill the seas, and let the birds multiply on the
earth."
23 And evening passed and morning came, marking the fifth day.

24 Then God said, "Let the earth produce every sort of animal, each
producing offspring of the same kind—livestock, small animals
that scurry along the ground, and wild animals." And that is what
happened. 25 God made all sorts of wild animals, livestock, and small
animals, each able to produce offspring of the same kind. And God saw
that it was good.
26 Then God said, "Let us make human beings* in our image, to be
like us. They will reign over the fish in the sea, the birds in the sky, the
livestock, all the wild animals on the earth,* and the small animals that
scurry along the ground."

27 So God created human beings* in his own image.
In the image of God he created them;
male and female he created them.

28 Then God blessed them and said, "Be fruitful and multiply. Fill the
earth and govern it. Reign over the fish in the sea, the birds in the sky,
and all the animals that scurry along the ground."
29 Then God said, "Look! I have given you every seed-bearing plant
throughout the earth and all the fruit trees for your food. 30 And I have
given every green plant as food for all the wild animals, the birds in the
sky, and the small animals that scurry along the ground—everything
that has life." And that is what happened.
31 Then God looked over all he had made, and he saw that it was very
good!
And evening passed and morning came, marking the sixth day.

2 So the creation of the heavens and the earth and everything in them
was completed. 2 On the seventh day God had finished his work of
creation, so he rested* from all his work. 3 And God blessed the seventh
day and declared it holy, because it was the day when he rested from all
his work of creation.

4 This is the account of the creation of the heavens and the earth.

The Man and Woman in Eden

When the LORD God made the earth and the heavens, 5 neither wild plants
nor grains were growing on the earth. For the LORD God had not yet sent rain
to water the earth, and there were no people to cultivate the soil. 6 Instead,
springs* came up from the ground and watered all the land. 7 Then the LORD
God formed the man from the dust of the ground. He breathed the breath of
life into the man's nostrils, and the man became a living person.
8 Then the LORD God planted a garden in Eden in the east, and there he

1:26a Or *man;* Hebrew reads *adam.* 1:26b As in Syriac version; Hebrew reads *all the earth.*
1:27 Or *the man;* Hebrew reads *ha-adam.* 2:2 Or *ceased;* also in 2:3. 2:6 Or *mist.*

Make a Difference

1:26-28

Imago Dei

An image is a reflection of the original. It has traits that resemble another, like a mirror or a picture. It is an amazing announcement when the Bible declares that humans were created in God's image. *Imago Dei* is a Latin term that describes how people were made in the "image of God"—reflections of the Creator.

All God's characteristics, desires, and abilities are on display in each of us. His compassion, strength, wisdom, love, creativity, joy, and wonder are embedded in who we are. He endowed us with world-changing authority and entrusted us with life-giving responsibility. God made us to be his very representatives on earth.

Difference Maker

Write down at least five ways that you, as a human, created in the *imago Dei*, look and act like a representative of God.

Prayer **1:27**

Dear Jesus, let everything I do today be as a representative of you. Let me not be a distraction but let my words and actions reveal who you are. Amen.

Question **1:31**

Why do you think at the end of each day God calls his creation "good," but he calls *all* of creation "very good" the sixth day?

placed the man he had made. 9 The LORD God made all sorts of trees grow
up from the ground—trees that were beautiful and that produced delicious
fruit. In the middle of the garden he placed the tree of life and the tree of the
knowledge of good and evil.
10 A river flowed from the land of Eden, watering the garden and then
dividing into four branches. 11 The first branch, called the Pishon, flowed
around the entire land of Havilah, where gold is found. 12 The gold of that
land is exceptionally pure; aromatic resin and onyx stone are also found
there. 13 The second branch, called the Gihon, flowed around the entire land
of Cush. 14 The third branch, called the Tigris, flowed east of the land of As-
shur. The fourth branch is called the Euphrates.
15 The LORD God placed the man in the Garden of Eden to tend and watch
over it. 16 But the LORD God warned him, "You may freely eat the fruit of
every tree in the garden—17 except the tree of the knowledge of good and
evil. If you eat its fruit, you are sure to die."
18 Then the LORD God said, "It is not good for the man to be alone. I will
make a helper who is just right for him." 19 So the LORD God formed from the
ground all the wild animals and all the birds of the sky. He brought them to
the man* to see what he would call them, and the man chose a name for each
one. 20 He gave names to all the livestock, all the birds of the sky, and all the
wild animals. But still there was no helper just right for him.
21 So the LORD God caused the man to fall into a deep sleep. While the
man slept, the LORD God took out one of the man's ribs* and closed up the
opening. 22 Then the LORD God made a woman from the rib, and he brought
her to the man.
23 "At last!" the man exclaimed.

"This one is bone from my bone,
and flesh from my flesh!
She will be called 'woman,'
because she was taken from 'man.'"

24 This explains why a man leaves his father and mother and is joined to
his wife, and the two are united into one.
25 Now the man and his wife were both naked, but they felt no shame.

The Man and Woman Sin

3 The serpent was the shrewdest of all the wild animals the LORD God
had made. One day he asked the woman, "Did God really say you must
not eat the fruit from any of the trees in the garden?"
2 "Of course we may eat fruit from the trees in the garden," the woman
replied. 3 "It's only the fruit from the tree in the middle of the garden that
we are not allowed to eat. God said, 'You must not eat it or even touch it; if
you do, you will die.'"
4 "You won't die!" the serpent replied to the woman. 5 "God knows that
your eyes will be opened as soon as you eat it, and you will be like God,
knowing both good and evil."
6 The woman was convinced. She saw that the tree was beautiful and its
fruit looked delicious, and she wanted the wisdom it would give her. So she

Question 2:15

What kind of difference did God want humanity to make before sin entered the world? What kind of a difference does he want us to make now?

Question 2:18

A few moments ago, all of creation was "very good," then we see something is "not good." Why do you think being alone is something God doesn't want for his creation?

2:19 Or *Adam,* and so throughout the chapter. **2:21** Or *took a part of the man's side.*

took some of the fruit and ate it. Then she gave some to her husband, who
was with her, and he ate it, too. 7 At that moment their eyes were opened,
and they suddenly felt shame at their nakedness. So they sewed fig leaves
together to cover themselves.

8 When the cool evening breezes were blowing, the man* and his wife
heard the LORD God walking about in the garden. So they hid from the
LORD God among the trees. 9 Then the LORD God called to the man, "Where
are you?"

10 He replied, "I heard you walking in the garden, so I hid. I was afraid
because I was naked."

11 "Who told you that you were naked?" the LORD God asked. "Have you
eaten from the tree whose fruit I commanded you not to eat?"

12 The man replied, "It was the woman you gave me who gave me the fruit,
and I ate it."

13 Then the LORD God asked the woman, "What have you done?"

"The serpent deceived me," she replied. "That's why I ate it."

14 Then the LORD God said to the serpent,

> "Because you have done this, you are cursed
>   more than all animals, domestic and wild.
> You will crawl on your belly,
>   groveling in the dust as long as you live.
> 15 And I will cause hostility between you and the woman,
>   and between your offspring and her offspring.
> He will strike* your head,
>   and you will strike his heel."

16 Then he said to the woman,

> "I will sharpen the pain of your pregnancy,
>   and in pain you will give birth.
> And you will desire to control your husband,
>   but he will rule over you.*"

17 And to the man he said,

> "Since you listened to your wife and ate from the tree
>   whose fruit I commanded you not to eat,
> the ground is cursed because of you.
>   All your life you will struggle to scratch
>   a living from it.
> 18 It will grow thorns and thistles for you,
>   though you will eat of its grains.
> 19 By the sweat of your brow
>   will you have food to eat
> until you return to the ground
>   from which you were made.
> For you were made from dust,
>   and to dust you will return."

Story Arc **3:1-24**

Adam and Eve: The First Humans

The first people to make a difference in this world made a huge mistake that had life-altering consequences. They probably wished they could have had a do-over. Adam and Eve were asked to walk with God and take care of creation, but they messed that up. Since then, every human has fallen into the same pattern. Still, God invites each person to join him on a redemptive story line in which he himself acts to change the outcome of death and destruction and despair into a knowable truth, one of life and abundance and repair. In fact, God promised that one day, one of Eve's descendants would destroy the serpent (that is, Satan) by striking his head (v. 15). This is the Bible's very first glimpse of God's promise to send his Son, Jesus Christ, to die on the cross for the sins of the world, which would forever destroy the power of sin and death.

Gen 6:1-9 ►

3:8 Or *Adam,* and so throughout the chapter. 3:15 Or *bruise;* also in 3:15b. 3:16 Or *And though you will have desire for your husband, / he will rule over you.*

Paradise Lost: God's Judgment
20 Then the man—Adam—named his wife Eve, because she would be the
mother of all who live.* 21 And the LORD God made clothing from animal
skins for Adam and his wife.
22 Then the LORD God said, "Look, the human beings* have become like us,
knowing both good and evil. What if they reach out, take fruit from the tree
of life, and eat it? Then they will live forever!" 23 So the LORD God banished
them from the Garden of Eden, and he sent Adam out to cultivate the ground
from which he had been made. 24 After sending them out, the LORD God sta-
tioned mighty cherubim to the east of the Garden of Eden. And he placed a
flaming sword that flashed back and forth to guard the way to the tree of life.

Cain and Abel
4 Now Adam* had sexual relations with his wife, Eve, and she became
pregnant. When she gave birth to Cain, she said, "With the LORD's help,
I have produced* a man!" 2 Later she gave birth to his brother and named
him Abel.
When they grew up, Abel became a shepherd, while Cain cultivated the
ground. 3 When it was time for the harvest, Cain presented some of his crops as
a gift to the LORD. 4 Abel also brought a gift—the best portions of the firstborn
lambs from his flock. The LORD accepted Abel and his gift, 5 but he did not
accept Cain and his gift. This made Cain very angry, and he looked dejected.
6 "Why are you so angry?" the LORD asked Cain. "Why do you look so de-
jected? 7 You will be accepted if you do what is right. But if you refuse to do
what is right, then watch out! Sin is crouching at the door, eager to control
you. But you must subdue it and be its master."
8 One day Cain suggested to his brother, "Let's go out into the fields."* And
while they were in the field, Cain attacked his brother, Abel, and killed him.
9 Afterward the LORD asked Cain, "Where is your brother? Where is Abel?"
"I don't know," Cain responded. "Am I my brother's guardian?"
10 But the LORD said, "What have you done? Listen! Your brother's blood
cries out to me from the ground! 11 Now you are cursed and banished from
the ground, which has swallowed your brother's blood. 12 No longer will the
ground yield good crops for you, no matter how hard you work! From now
on you will be a homeless wanderer on the earth."
13 Cain replied to the LORD, "My punishment* is too great for me to bear!
14 You have banished me from the land and from your presence; you have
made me a homeless wanderer. Anyone who finds me will kill me!"
15 The LORD replied, "No, for I will give a sevenfold punishment to anyone
who kills you." Then the LORD put a mark on Cain to warn anyone who
might try to kill him. 16 So Cain left the LORD's presence and settled in the
land of Nod,* east of Eden.

The Descendants of Cain
17 Cain had sexual relations with his wife, and she became pregnant and gave
birth to Enoch. Then Cain founded a city, which he named Enoch, after his
son. 18 Enoch had a son named Irad. Irad became the father of* Mehujael.

Question 4:7

What sin is tempting you to rebel against God and mess things up? What is God asking you to do about it?

3:20 *Eve* sounds like a Hebrew term that means "to give life." 3:22 Or *the man;* Hebrew reads *ha-adam.* 4:1a Or *the man;* also in 4:25. 4:1b Or *I have acquired. Cain* sounds like a Hebrew term that can mean "produce" or "acquire." 4:8 As in Samaritan Pentateuch, Greek and Syriac versions, and Latin Vulgate; Masoretic Text lacks *"Let's go out into the fields."* 4:13 Or *My sin.* 4:16 *Nod* means "wandering." 4:18 Or *the ancestor of,* and so throughout the verse.

Mehujael became the father of Methushael. Methushael became the father
of Lamech.
19 Lamech married two women. The first was named Adah, and the second
was Zillah. 20 Adah gave birth to Jabal, who was the first of those who raise
livestock and live in tents. 21 His brother's name was Jubal, the first of all who
play the harp and flute. 22 Lamech's other wife, Zillah, gave birth to a son
named Tubal-cain. He became an expert in forging tools of bronze and iron.
Tubal-cain had a sister named Naamah. 23 One day Lamech said to his wives,

"Adah and Zillah, hear my voice;
listen to me, you wives of Lamech.
I have killed a man who attacked me,
a young man who wounded me.
24 If someone who kills Cain is punished seven times,
then the one who kills me will be punished seventy-seven times!"

The Birth of Seth

25 Adam had sexual relations with his wife again, and she gave birth to an-
other son. She named him Seth,* for she said, "God has granted me another
son in place of Abel, whom Cain killed." 26 When Seth grew up, he had a
son and named him Enosh. At that time people first began to worship the
LORD by name.

The Descendants of Adam

5 This is the written account of the descendants of Adam. When God cre-
ated human beings,* he made them to be like himself. 2 He created them
male and female, and he blessed them and called them "human."

3 When Adam was 130 years old, he became the father of a son who was
just like him—in his very image. He named his son Seth. 4 After the
birth of Seth, Adam lived another 800 years, and he had other sons and
daughters. 5 Adam lived 930 years, and then he died.
6 When Seth was 105 years old, he became the father of* Enosh. 7 After the
birth of* Enosh, Seth lived another 807 years, and he had other sons and
daughters. 8 Seth lived 912 years, and then he died.
9 When Enosh was 90 years old, he became the father of Kenan. 10 After the
birth of Kenan, Enosh lived another 815 years, and he had other sons
and daughters. 11 Enosh lived 905 years, and then he died.
12 When Kenan was 70 years old, he became the father of Mahalalel. 13 After
the birth of Mahalalel, Kenan lived another 840 years, and he had other
sons and daughters. 14 Kenan lived 910 years, and then he died.
15 When Mahalalel was 65 years old, he became the father of Jared. 16 After
the birth of Jared, Mahalalel lived another 830 years, and he had other
sons and daughters. 17 Mahalalel lived 895 years, and then he died.
18 When Jared was 162 years old, he became the father of Enoch. 19 After the
birth of Enoch, Jared lived another 800 years, and he had other sons and
daughters. 20 Jared lived 962 years, and then he died.
21 When Enoch was 65 years old, he became the father of Methuselah.

4:25 *Seth* probably means "granted"; the name may also mean "appointed." 5:1 Or *man;* Hebrew reads *adam;* similarly in 5:2. 5:6 Or *the ancestor of;* also in 5:9, 12, 15, 18, 21, 25. 5:7 Or *the birth of this ancestor of;* also in 5:10, 13, 16, 19, 22, 26.

22 After the birth of Methuselah, Enoch lived in close fellowship with
God for another 300 years, and he had other sons and daughters.
23 Enoch lived 365 years, 24 walking in close fellowship with God. Then
one day he disappeared, because God took him.
25 When Methuselah was 187 years old, he became the father of Lamech.
26 After the birth of Lamech, Methuselah lived another 782 years, and he
had other sons and daughters. 27 Methuselah lived 969 years, and then
he died.
28 When Lamech was 182 years old, he became the father of a son. 29 Lamech
named his son Noah, for he said, "May he bring us relief* from our work
and the painful labor of farming this ground that the LORD has cursed."
30 After the birth of Noah, Lamech lived another 595 years, and he had
other sons and daughters. 31 Lamech lived 777 years, and then he died.
32 After Noah was 500 years old, he became the father of Shem, Ham, and
Japheth.

A World Gone Wrong

6 Then the people began to multiply on the earth, and daughters were
born to them. 2 The sons of God saw the beautiful women* and took
any they wanted as their wives. 3 Then the LORD said, "My Spirit will not put
up with* humans for such a long time, for they are only mortal flesh. In the
future, their normal lifespan will be no more than 120 years."
4 In those days, and for some time after, giant Nephilites lived on the earth,
for whenever the sons of God had intercourse with women, they gave birth
to children who became the heroes and famous warriors of ancient times.
5 The LORD observed the extent of human wickedness on the earth, and he
saw that everything they thought or imagined was consistently and totally
evil. 6 So the LORD was sorry he had ever made them and put them on the
earth. It broke his heart. 7 And the LORD said, "I will wipe this human race
I have created from the face of the earth. Yes, and I will destroy every living
thing—all the people, the large animals, the small animals that scurry along
the ground, and even the birds of the sky. I am sorry I ever made them." 8 But
Noah found favor with the LORD.

The Story of Noah

9 This is the account of Noah and his family. Noah was a righteous man, the
only blameless person living on earth at the time, and he walked in close
fellowship with God. 10 Noah was the father of three sons: Shem, Ham, and
Japheth.
11 Now God saw that the earth had become corrupt and was filled with
violence. 12 God observed all this corruption in the world, for everyone on
earth was corrupt. 13 So God said to Noah, "I have decided to destroy all living
creatures, for they have filled the earth with violence. Yes, I will wipe them
all out along with the earth!
14 "Build a large boat* from cypress wood* and waterproof it with tar, in-
side and out. Then construct decks and stalls throughout its interior. 15 Make
the boat 450 feet long, 75 feet wide, and 45 feet high.* 16 Leave an 18-inch

5:29 *Noah* sounds like a Hebrew term that can mean "relief" or "comfort." 6:2 Hebrew *daughters of men;* also in 6:4. 6:3 Greek version reads *will not remain in.* 6:14a Traditionally rendered *an ark.* 6:14b Or *gopher wood.* 6:15 Hebrew *300 cubits* [138 meters] *long, 50 cubits* [23 meters] *wide, and 30 cubits* [13.8 meters] *high.*

Prayer 5:23-24

Dear Jesus, as I begin reading the Bible, please help me to become someone like Enoch who was faithful to walk with you. Amen.

Story Arc 6:1-9

Noah

In verses 6:1-8, we get a glimpse at God's heart...and it is broken. The creation he loved and called "very good" was now wicked, and every thought of the human heart was "consistently and totally evil" (v. 5). God's goal is to walk in close fellowship with humans. We are designed to have this close relationship with God. He walked in the garden with Adam and Eve. He walked in close fellowship with Enoch. In the midst of a depraved world, God walked in close relationship with Noah.

Gen 11:29-30 ►

Make a Difference

7:6-18

Restoration

God has always been the one to help his people when they sin. He helped Adam and Eve clothe themselves after they sinned. Later, he "closed the door" for Noah, his family, and species of every kind so that they could be saved and restart the world (v. 16). When people sin, God works to restore what sin has broken. God is always making a difference in people's lives when they sin, and he uses those stories to help others discover his restorative work. In fact, God wants to use your story to help others know he wants to restore them too.

Difference Maker

Write a short story that shows how sin and brokenness entered your world and how God has been at work restoring your life. Share that with someone who needs their story restored.

opening* below the roof all the way around the boat. Put the door on the side,
and build three decks inside the boat—lower, middle, and upper.
17 "Look! I am about to cover the earth with a flood that will destroy every
living thing that breathes. Everything on earth will die. 18 But I will con-
firm my covenant with you. So enter the boat—you and your wife and your
sons and their wives. 19 Bring a pair of every kind of animal—a male and a
female—into the boat with you to keep them alive during the flood. 20 Pairs
of every kind of bird, and every kind of animal, and every kind of small ani-
mal that scurries along the ground, will come to you to be kept alive. 21 And
be sure to take on board enough food for your family and for all the animals."
22 So Noah did everything exactly as God had commanded him.

The Flood Covers the Earth

7 When everything was ready, the LORD said to Noah, "Go into the boat
with all your family, for among all the people of the earth, I can see that
you alone are righteous. 2 Take with you seven pairs—male and female—of
each animal I have approved for eating and for sacrifice,* and take one pair
of each of the others. 3 Also take seven pairs of every kind of bird. There must
be a male and a female in each pair to ensure that all life will survive on the
earth after the flood. 4 Seven days from now I will make the rains pour down
on the earth. And it will rain for forty days and forty nights, until I have
wiped from the earth all the living things I have created."
5 So Noah did everything as the LORD commanded him.
6 Noah was 600 years old when the flood covered the earth. 7 He went on
board the boat to escape the flood—he and his wife and his sons and their
wives. 8 With them were all the various kinds of animals—those approved
for eating and for sacrifice and those that were not—along with all the birds
and the small animals that scurry along the ground. 9 They entered the boat
in pairs, male and female, just as God had commanded Noah. 10 After seven
days, the waters of the flood came and covered the earth.
11 When Noah was 600 years old, on the seventeenth day of the second
month, all the underground waters erupted from the earth, and the rain
fell in mighty torrents from the sky. 12 The rain continued to fall for forty
days and forty nights.
13 That very day Noah had gone into the boat with his wife and his sons—
Shem, Ham, and Japheth—and their wives. 14 With them in the boat were
pairs of every kind of animal—domestic and wild, large and small—along
with birds of every kind. 15 Two by two they came into the boat, representing
every living thing that breathes. 16 A male and female of each kind entered,
just as God had commanded Noah. Then the LORD closed the door behind
them.
17 For forty days the floodwaters grew deeper, covering the ground and
lifting the boat high above the earth. 18 As the waters rose higher and higher
above the ground, the boat floated safely on the surface. 19 Finally, the water
covered even the highest mountains on the earth, 20 rising more than twenty-
two feet* above the highest peaks. 21 All the living things on earth died—
birds, domestic animals, wild animals, small animals that scurry along the
ground, and all the people. 22 Everything that breathed and lived on dry land
died. 23 God wiped out every living thing on the earth—people, livestock,

6:16 Hebrew *an opening of 1 cubit* [46 centimeters]. 7:2 Hebrew *of each clean animal;* similarly in 7:8. 7:20 Hebrew *15 cubits* [6.9 meters].

small animals that scurry along the ground, and the birds of the sky. All were destroyed. The only people who survived were Noah and those with him in the boat. 24 And the floodwaters covered the earth for 150 days.

The Flood Recedes

8 But God remembered Noah and all the wild animals and livestock with him in the boat. He sent a wind to blow across the earth, and the floodwaters began to recede. 2 The underground waters stopped flowing, and the torrential rains from the sky were stopped. 3 So the floodwaters gradually receded from the earth. After 150 days, 4 exactly five months from the time the flood began,* the boat came to rest on the mountains of Ararat. 5 Two and a half months later,* as the waters continued to go down, other mountain peaks became visible.

6 After another forty days, Noah opened the window he had made in the boat 7 and released a raven. The bird flew back and forth until the floodwaters on the earth had dried up. 8 He also released a dove to see if the water had receded and it could find dry ground. 9 But the dove could find no place to land because the water still covered the ground. So it returned to the boat, and Noah held out his hand and drew the dove back inside. 10 After waiting another seven days, Noah released the dove again. 11 This time the dove returned to him in the evening with a fresh olive leaf in its beak. Then Noah knew that the floodwaters were almost gone. 12 He waited another seven days and then released the dove again. This time it did not come back.

13 Noah was now 601 years old. On the first day of the new year, ten and a half months after the flood began,* the floodwaters had almost dried up from the earth. Noah lifted back the covering of the boat and saw that the surface of the ground was drying. 14 Two more months went by,* and at last the earth was dry!

15 Then God said to Noah, 16 "Leave the boat, all of you—you and your wife, and your sons and their wives. 17 Release all the animals—the birds, the livestock, and the small animals that scurry along the ground—so they can be fruitful and multiply throughout the earth."

18 So Noah, his wife, and his sons and their wives left the boat. 19 And all of the large and small animals and birds came out of the boat, pair by pair.

20 Then Noah built an altar to the LORD, and there he sacrificed as burnt offerings the animals and birds that had been approved for that purpose.* 21 And the LORD was pleased with the aroma of the sacrifice and said to himself, "I will never again curse the ground because of the human race, even though everything they think or imagine is bent toward evil from childhood. I will never again destroy all living things. 22 As long as the earth remains, there will be planting and harvest, cold and heat, summer and winter, day and night."

God Confirms His Covenant

9 Then God blessed Noah and his sons and told them, "Be fruitful and multiply. Fill the earth. 2 All the animals of the earth, all the birds of the sky, all the small animals that scurry along the ground, and all the fish in the sea will look on you with fear and terror. I have placed them in your

8:4 Hebrew *on the seventeenth day of the seventh month;* see 7:11. 8:5 Hebrew *On the first day of the tenth month;* see 7:11 and note on 8:4. 8:13 Hebrew *On the first day of the first month;* see 7:11. 8:14 Hebrew *The twenty-seventh day of the second month arrived;* see note on 8:13. 8:20 Hebrew *every clean animal and every clean bird.*

Make a Difference 9:1-7

Give Respect

Talk about starting over! God instructed Noah using the same words he used with Adam in Genesis 2. Here in Genesis 9:1-7, God again reaffirmed his desire for humanity to fill the earth with people, use the earth and its creatures according to their needs, and treat other humans with great respect and dignity because they are the best of God's creative work. Many people feel like they are worthless because other humans don't affirm and recognize their value. As we follow God, we learn that our responsibility is to uphold the dignity, beauty, uniqueness, and value of every person, and in so doing, we make a difference in their life.

Difference Maker

Go out of your way to treat everyone around you with dignity and respect today. Note how they respond to you.

Question 9:12-17

The rainbow is a covenant sign (or promise) that God made with people and his creation. It means that God promises to care for people and that people promise to follow God's commands. When was the last time you saw a rainbow and remembered God's promise?

power. [3]I have given them to you for food, just as I have given you grain and
vegetables. [4]But you must never eat any meat that still has the lifeblood in it.
[5]"And I will require the blood of anyone who takes another person's life. If
a wild animal kills a person, it must die. And anyone who murders a fellow
human must die. [6]If anyone takes a human life, that person's life will also
be taken by human hands. For God made human beings* in his own image.
[7]Now be fruitful and multiply, and repopulate the earth."
[8]Then God told Noah and his sons, [9]"I hereby confirm my covenant with you
and your descendants, [10]and with all the animals that were on the boat with
you—the birds, the livestock, and all the wild animals—every living creature
on earth. [11]Yes, I am confirming my covenant with you. Never again will flood-
waters kill all living creatures; never again will a flood destroy the earth."
[12]Then God said, "I am giving you a sign of my covenant with you and with
all living creatures, for all generations to come. [13]I have placed my rainbow
in the clouds. It is the sign of my covenant with you and with all the earth.
[14]When I send clouds over the earth, the rainbow will appear in the clouds,
[15]and I will remember my covenant with you and with all living creatures.
Never again will the floodwaters destroy all life. [16]When I see the rainbow
in the clouds, I will remember the eternal covenant between God and every
living creature on earth." [17]Then God said to Noah, "Yes, this rainbow is the
sign of the covenant I am confirming with all the creatures on earth."

Noah's Sons

[18]The sons of Noah who came out of the boat with their father were Shem,
Ham, and Japheth. (Ham is the father of Canaan.) [19]From these three sons
of Noah came all the people who now populate the earth.
[20]After the flood, Noah began to cultivate the ground, and he planted a
vineyard. [21]One day he drank some wine he had made, and he became drunk
and lay naked inside his tent. [22]Ham, the father of Canaan, saw that his father
was naked and went outside and told his brothers. [23]Then Shem and Japheth
took a robe, held it over their shoulders, and backed into the tent to cover
their father. As they did this, they looked the other way so they would not
see him naked.
[24]When Noah woke up from his stupor, he learned what Ham, his youn-
gest son, had done. [25]Then he cursed Canaan, the son of Ham:

"May Canaan be cursed!
  May he be the lowest of servants to his relatives."

[26]Then Noah said,

"May the LORD, the God of Shem, be blessed,
  and may Canaan be his servant!
[27] May God expand the territory of Japheth!
May Japheth share the prosperity of Shem,*
  and may Canaan be his servant."

[28]Noah lived another 350 years after the great flood. [29]He lived 950 years,
and then he died.

9:6 Or *man;* Hebrew reads *ha-adam.* 9:27 Hebrew *May he live in the tents of Shem.*

10 This is the account of the families of Shem, Ham, and Japheth, the three sons of Noah. Many children were born to them after the great flood.

Descendants of Japheth

2 The descendants of Japheth were Gomer, Magog, Madai, Javan, Tubal, Meshech, and Tiras.
3 The descendants of Gomer were Ashkenaz, Riphath, and Togarmah.
4 The descendants of Javan were Elishah, Tarshish, Kittim, and Rodanim.*
5 Their descendants became the seafaring peoples that spread out to
various lands, each identified by its own language, clan, and national
identity.

Descendants of Ham

6 The descendants of Ham were Cush, Mizraim, Put, and Canaan.
7 The descendants of Cush were Seba, Havilah, Sabtah, Raamah, and Sabteca. The descendants of Raamah were Sheba and Dedan.
8 Cush was also the ancestor of Nimrod, who was the first heroic
warrior on earth. 9 Since he was the greatest hunter in the world,* his
name became proverbial. People would say, "This man is like Nimrod,
the greatest hunter in the world." 10 He built his kingdom in the land
of Babylonia,* with the cities of Babylon, Erech, Akkad, and Calneh.
11 From there he expanded his territory to Assyria,* building the cities
of Nineveh, Rehoboth-ir, Calah, 12 and Resen (the great city located
between Nineveh and Calah).
13 Mizraim was the ancestor of the Ludites, Anamites, Lehabites,
Naphtuhites, 14 Pathrusites, Casluhites, and the Caphtorites, from
whom the Philistines came.*
15 Canaan's oldest son was Sidon, the ancestor of the Sidonians. Canaan
was also the ancestor of the Hittites,* 16 Jebusites, Amorites, Girgashites,
17 Hivites, Arkites, Sinites, 18 Arvadites, Zemarites, and Hamathites. The
Canaanite clans eventually spread out, 19 and the territory of Canaan
extended from Sidon in the north to Gerar and Gaza in the south, and
east as far as Sodom, Gomorrah, Admah, and Zeboiim, near Lasha.
20 These were the descendants of Ham, identified by clan, language, territory, and national identity.

Descendants of Shem

21 Sons were also born to Shem, the older brother of Japheth.* Shem was the ancestor of all the descendants of Eber.
22 The descendants of Shem were Elam, Asshur, Arphaxad, Lud, and Aram.
23 The descendants of Aram were Uz, Hul, Gether, and Mash.
24 Arphaxad was the father of Shelah,* and Shelah was the father of Eber.
25 Eber had two sons. The first was named Peleg (which means "division"), for during his lifetime the people of the world were divided into different language groups. His brother's name was Joktan.

10:4 As in some Hebrew manuscripts and Greek version (see also 1 Chr 1:7); most Hebrew manuscripts read *Dodanim.* 10:9 Hebrew *a great hunter before the LORD;* also in 10:9b. 10:10 Hebrew *Shinar.* 10:11 Or *From that land Assyria went out.* 10:14 Hebrew *Casluhites, from whom the Philistines came, and Caphtorites.* Compare Jer 47:4; Amos 9:7. 10:15 Hebrew *ancestor of Heth.* 10:21 Or *Shem, whose older brother was Japheth.* 10:24 Greek version reads *Arphaxad was the father of Cainan, Cainan was the father of Shelah.* Compare Luke 3:36.

Question 10:32

All the people on earth today come from one of these three families! How does this influence the way you see people from other cultures?

Question 11:4

Why would this building project upset the Lord, and how can you avoid a similar mistake in your life?

26 Joktan was the ancestor of Almodad, Sheleph, Hazarmaveth, Jerah,
27 Hadoram, Uzal, Diklah, 28 Obal, Abimael, Sheba, 29 Ophir, Havilah,
and Jobab. All these were descendants of Joktan. 30 The territory they
occupied extended from Mesha all the way to Sephar in the eastern
mountains.
31 These were the descendants of Shem, identified by clan, language, terri-
tory, and national identity.

Conclusion

32 These are the clans that descended from Noah's sons, arranged by nation
according to their lines of descent. All the nations of the earth descended
from these clans after the great flood.

The Tower of Babel

11 At one time all the people of the world spoke the same language and
used the same words. 2 As the people migrated to the east, they found
a plain in the land of Babylonia* and settled there.
3 They began saying to each other, "Let's make bricks and harden them
with fire." (In this region bricks were used instead of stone, and tar was used
for mortar.) 4 Then they said, "Come, let's build a great city for ourselves with
a tower that reaches into the sky. This will make us famous and keep us from
being scattered all over the world."
5 But the LORD came down to look at the city and the tower the people were
building. 6 "Look!" he said. "The people are united, and they all speak the
same language. After this, nothing they set out to do will be impossible for
them! 7 Come, let's go down and confuse the people with different languages.
Then they won't be able to understand each other."
8 In that way, the LORD scattered them all over the world, and they stopped
building the city. 9 That is why the city was called Babel,* because that is
where the LORD confused the people with different languages. In this way
he scattered them all over the world.

The Line of Descent from Shem to Abram

10 This is the account of Shem's family.

Two years after the great flood, when Shem was 100 years old, he became
the father of* Arphaxad. 11 After the birth of* Arphaxad, Shem lived
another 500 years and had other sons and daughters.
12 When Arphaxad was 35 years old, he became the father of Shelah. 13 After
the birth of Shelah, Arphaxad lived another 403 years and had other
sons and daughters.*
14 When Shelah was 30 years old, he became the father of Eber. 15 After the
birth of Eber, Shelah lived another 403 years and had other sons and
daughters.
16 When Eber was 34 years old, he became the father of Peleg. 17 After the

11:2 Hebrew *Shinar.* 11:9 Or *Babylon. Babel* sounds like a Hebrew term that means "confusion." 11:10 Or *the ancestor of;* also in 11:12, 14, 16, 18, 20, 22, 24. 11:11 Or *the birth of this ancestor of;* also in 11:13, 15, 17, 19, 21, 23, 25. 11:12-13 Greek version reads *12 When Arphaxad was 135 years old, he became the father of Cainan. 13 After the birth of Cainan, Arphaxad lived another 430 years and had other sons and daughters, and then he died. When Cainan was 130 years old, he became the father of Shelah. After the birth of Shelah, Cainan lived another 330 years and had other sons and daughters, and then he died.* Compare Luke 3:35-36.

birth of Peleg, Eber lived another 430 years and had other sons and
daughters.
18 When Peleg was 30 years old, he became the father of Reu. 19 After the
birth of Reu, Peleg lived another 209 years and had other sons and
daughters.
20 When Reu was 32 years old, he became the father of Serug. 21 After the
birth of Serug, Reu lived another 207 years and had other sons and
daughters.
22 When Serug was 30 years old, he became the father of Nahor. 23 After the
birth of Nahor, Serug lived another 200 years and had other sons and
daughters.
24 When Nahor was 29 years old, he became the father of Terah. 25 After the
birth of Terah, Nahor lived another 119 years and had other sons and
daughters.
26 After Terah was 70 years old, he became the father of Abram, Nahor, and
Haran.

The Family of Terah

27 This is the account of Terah's family. Terah was the father of Abram, Na-
hor, and Haran; and Haran was the father of Lot. 28 But Haran died in Ur of
the Chaldeans, the land of his birth, while his father, Terah, was still living.
29 Meanwhile, Abram and Nahor both married. The name of Abram's wife
was Sarai, and the name of Nahor's wife was Milcah. (Milcah and her sister
Iscah were daughters of Nahor's brother Haran.) 30 But Sarai was unable to
become pregnant and had no children.
31 One day Terah took his son Abram, his daughter-in-law Sarai (his son
Abram's wife), and his grandson Lot (his son Haran's child) and moved away
from Ur of the Chaldeans. He was headed for the land of Canaan, but they
stopped at Haran and settled there. 32 Terah lived for 205 years* and died
while still in Haran.

The Call of Abram

12 The LORD had said to Abram, "Leave your native country, your rela-
tives, and your father's family, and go to the land that I will show
you. 2 I will make you into a great nation. I will bless you and make you
famous, and you will be a blessing to others. 3 I will bless those who bless
you and curse those who treat you with contempt. All the families on earth
will be blessed through you."
4 So Abram departed as the LORD had instructed, and Lot went with him.
Abram was seventy-five years old when he left Haran. 5 He took his wife, Sa-
rai, his nephew Lot, and all his wealth—his livestock and all the people he
had taken into his household at Haran—and headed for the land of Canaan.
When they arrived in Canaan, 6 Abram traveled through the land as far as
Shechem. There he set up camp beside the oak of Moreh. At that time, the
area was inhabited by Canaanites.
7 Then the LORD appeared to Abram and said, "I will give this land to your
descendants.*" And Abram built an altar there and dedicated it to the LORD,
who had appeared to him. 8 After that, Abram traveled south and set up camp
in the hill country, with Bethel to the west and Ai to the east. There he built

11:32 Some ancient versions read *145 years*; compare 11:26 and 12:4. 12:7 Hebrew *seed*.

Prayer 12:4

Lord, no matter my age, help me obey your commands with as much faith as Abraham did. Amen.

Story Arc 11:29–30

● Abram and Sarai

Abram was a direct descendant of Shem, whose children gave birth to many nations. Sadly, it seemed like no nation would ever come from Abram because his wife, Sarai, was unable to have children.

God had other plans. He chose Abram and Sarai to give birth to the nation of Israel. Even though they were old, they had faith that God would keep his promise to give them children. Later, God would change their names to Abraham ("Father of Many") and Sarah ("Princess") (17:5, 15), which are the perfect names! Through their family line, Jesus, the King of kings, would enable all who believe in him to become sons and daughters of God. Through their offspring, all nations will be blessed (12:3).

Gen 14:18-20 ►

another altar and dedicated it to the LORD, and he worshiped the LORD.
9 Then Abram continued traveling south by stages toward the Negev.

Abram and Sarai in Egypt

10 At that time a severe famine struck the land of Canaan, forcing Abram to
go down to Egypt, where he lived as a foreigner. 11 As he was approaching the
border of Egypt, Abram said to his wife, Sarai, "Look, you are a very beautiful
woman. 12 When the Egyptians see you, they will say, 'This is his wife. Let's
kill him; then we can have her!' 13 So please tell them you are my sister. Then
they will spare my life and treat me well because of their interest in you."
14 And sure enough, when Abram arrived in Egypt, everyone noticed Sa-
rai's beauty. 15 When the palace officials saw her, they sang her praises to
Pharaoh, their king, and Sarai was taken into his palace. 16 Then Pharaoh
gave Abram many gifts because of her—sheep, goats, cattle, male and female
donkeys, male and female servants, and camels.
17 But the LORD sent terrible plagues upon Pharaoh and his household
because of Sarai, Abram's wife. 18 So Pharaoh summoned Abram and accused
him sharply. "What have you done to me?" he demanded. "Why didn't you
tell me she was your wife? 19 Why did you say, 'She is my sister,' and allow me
to take her as my wife? Now then, here is your wife. Take her and get out of
here!" 20 Pharaoh ordered some of his men to escort them, and he sent Abram
out of the country, along with his wife and all his possessions.

Abram and Lot Separate

13 So Abram left Egypt and traveled north into the Negev, along with
his wife and Lot and all that they owned. 2 (Abram was very rich in
livestock, silver, and gold.) 3 From the Negev, they continued traveling by
stages toward Bethel, and they pitched their tents between Bethel and Ai,
where they had camped before. 4 This was the same place where Abram had
built the altar, and there he worshiped the LORD again.
5 Lot, who was traveling with Abram, had also become very wealthy with
flocks of sheep and goats, herds of cattle, and many tents. 6 But the land
could not support both Abram and Lot with all their flocks and herds living
so close together. 7 So disputes broke out between the herdsmen of Abram
and Lot. (At that time Canaanites and Perizzites were also living in the land.)
8 Finally Abram said to Lot, "Let's not allow this conflict to come between
us or our herdsmen. After all, we are close relatives! 9 The whole countryside
is open to you. Take your choice of any section of the land you want, and we
will separate. If you want the land to the left, then I'll take the land on the
right. If you prefer the land on the right, then I'll go to the left."
10 Lot took a long look at the fertile plains of the Jordan Valley in the direc-
tion of Zoar. The whole area was well watered everywhere, like the garden of
the LORD or the beautiful land of Egypt. (This was before the LORD destroyed
Sodom and Gomorrah.) 11 Lot chose for himself the whole Jordan Valley to the
east of them. He went there with his flocks and servants and parted company
with his uncle Abram. 12 So Abram settled in the land of Canaan, and Lot
moved his tents to a place near Sodom and settled among the cities of the
plain. 13 But the people of this area were extremely wicked and constantly
sinned against the LORD.
14 After Lot had gone, the LORD said to Abram, "Look as far as you can see

Make a Difference

13:1-12

Blessing Others

Abraham was wealthy (v. 2). When his younger brother died, it fell to Abraham to care for his nephew, Lot, as an adoptive father. Over the years, the two men grew in friendship, love, respect, and wealth. However, when the land could no longer sustain their business, they decided under duress to part ways (v. 7). It was a hard but necessary family and business decision.

Abraham was entitled to decide what part of the land he wanted, yet Abraham loved Lot and knew that God would be faithful to sustain them both no matter what land they chose. Abraham allowed Lot to choose the "well-watered" land of the valley of the river Jordan, a perfect spot for someone with many sheep and goats. As a result, God blessed Abraham for his generosity to his nephew and his faith that God would sustain and prosper him.

Difference Maker

Pick a family member you love and do something generous for them.

Question **13:14-17**

The Lord showed Abraham the land that he would be giving to Abraham and to his descendants. As you think about the rest of the story of the Bible, what important role did this land play in God's plan for humanity?

in every direction—north and south, east and west. 15 I am giving all this
land, as far as you can see, to you and your descendants* as a permanent
possession. 16 And I will give you so many descendants that, like the dust of
the earth, they cannot be counted! 17 Go and walk through the land in every
direction, for I am giving it to you."

18 So Abram moved his camp to Hebron and settled near the oak grove
belonging to Mamre. There he built another altar to the LORD.

Abram Rescues Lot

14 About this time war broke out in the region. King Amraphel of Babylonia,* King Arioch of Ellasar, King Kedorlaomer of Elam, and King
Tidal of Goiim 2 fought against King Bera of Sodom, King Birsha of Gomor-
rah, King Shinab of Admah, King Shemeber of Zeboiim, and the king of
Bela (also called Zoar).

3 This second group of kings joined forces in Siddim Valley (that is, the
valley of the Dead Sea*). 4 For twelve years they had been subject to King
Kedorlaomer, but in the thirteenth year they rebelled against him.

5 One year later Kedorlaomer and his allies arrived and defeated the
Rephaites at Ashteroth-karnaim, the Zuzites at Ham, the Emites at Shaveh-
kiriathaim, 6 and the Horites at Mount Seir, as far as El-paran at the edge of
the wilderness. 7 Then they turned back and came to En-mishpat (now called
Kadesh) and conquered all the territory of the Amalekites, and also the Am-
orites living in Hazazon-tamar.

8 Then the rebel kings of Sodom, Gomorrah, Admah, Zeboiim, and Bela
(also called Zoar) prepared for battle in the valley of the Dead Sea.* 9 They
fought against King Kedorlaomer of Elam, King Tidal of Goiim, King Amra-
phel of Babylonia, and King Arioch of Ellasar—four kings against five. 10 As
it happened, the valley of the Dead Sea was filled with tar pits. And as the
army of the kings of Sodom and Gomorrah fled, some fell into the tar pits,
while the rest escaped into the mountains. 11 The victorious invaders then
plundered Sodom and Gomorrah and headed for home, taking with them all
the spoils of war and the food supplies. 12 They also captured Lot—Abram's
nephew who lived in Sodom—and carried off everything he owned.

13 But one of Lot's men escaped and reported everything to Abram the
Hebrew, who was living near the oak grove belonging to Mamre the Amorite.
Mamre and his relatives, Eshcol and Aner, were Abram's allies.

14 When Abram heard that his nephew Lot had been captured, he mobi-
lized the 318 trained men who had been born into his household. Then he
pursued Kedorlaomer's army until he caught up with them at Dan. 15 There
he divided his men and attacked during the night. Kedorlaomer's army fled,
but Abram chased them as far as Hobah, north of Damascus. 16 Abram recov-
ered all the goods that had been taken, and he brought back his nephew Lot
with his possessions and all the women and other captives.

Melchizedek Blesses Abram

17 After Abram returned from his victory over Kedorlaomer and all his allies,
the king of Sodom went out to meet him in the valley of Shaveh (that is, the
King's Valley).

18 And Melchizedek, the king of Salem and a priest of God Most High,*

Story Arc **14:18-20**

● Melchizedek

Melchizedek was called a "priest of God Most High" (v. 18). A priest is someone chosen by God to be his representative among people. He was also called the "king of Salem" (v. 18), which means king of "peace." This is the first time Melchizedek appears in the Bible, but it isn't the last. Hundreds of years later, David referenced him in Psalm 110:4. He was also mentioned again in Hebrews 5:6 as a priest and a king who had the ability to judge and rule nations as well as represent the people before God.

One day, God would choose another man as his final representative to all people for all time: Jesus Christ, God's very own Son. The book of Hebrews tells us that Jesus is a "High Priest in the order of Melchizedek" (5:10). This means Jesus is worthy to rule and judge nations and worthy to be God's representative before all people.

Gen 29:32-30:24 ►

13:15 Hebrew *seed;* also in 13:16. 14:1 Hebrew *Shinar;* also in 14:9. 14:3 Hebrew *Salt Sea.* 14:8 Hebrew *Siddim Valley* (see 14:3); also in 14:10. 14:18 Hebrew *El-Elyon;* also in 14:19, 20, 22.

Make a Difference 15:9

God's Promise

This chapter is one wild scene: halved animals, smoking pots, a fiery torch, and big promises about descendants and nations. As bizarre as it might seem to us today, this display was a fairly common way to solidify deals, and this was how God chose to seal a contractual agreement with Abram. The shocking visual of this contract indicated that what happened to the animals would happen to the one who broke the contract. As was customary, both parties would usually walk through the halved animals as a sign that they would keep the contract...or else.

In a fascinating twist, however, God chose to walk through the animals for both of them (v. 17). It seems that God did this because he knew that Abram and his descendants wouldn't be able to keep the demands of the contract. By this action, God did two remarkable things: (1) he promised to be faithful to his people, and (2) he promised to take the consequence of their sin upon himself.

Difference Maker

What agreement have you made with God? What do you need to do to uphold your end of the contract?

brought Abram some bread and wine. 19 Melchizedek blessed Abram with
this blessing:

"Blessed be Abram by God Most High,
Creator of heaven and earth.
20 And blessed be God Most High,
who has defeated your enemies for you."

Then Abram gave Melchizedek a tenth of all the goods he had recovered.
21 The king of Sodom said to Abram, "Give back my people who were cap-
tured. But you may keep for yourself all the goods you have recovered."
22 Abram replied to the king of Sodom, "I solemnly swear to the LORD,
God Most High, Creator of heaven and earth, 23 that I will not take so much
as a single thread or sandal thong from what belongs to you. Otherwise you
might say, 'I am the one who made Abram rich.' 24 I will accept only what my
young warriors have already eaten, and I request that you give a fair share of
the goods to my allies—Aner, Eshcol, and Mamre."

The LORD's Covenant Promise to Abram

15 Some time later, the LORD spoke to Abram in a vision and said to
him, "Do not be afraid, Abram, for I will protect you, and your re-
ward will be great."
2 But Abram replied, "O Sovereign LORD, what good are all your blessings
when I don't even have a son? Since you've given me no children, Eliezer of
Damascus, a servant in my household, will inherit all my wealth. 3 You have
given me no descendants of my own, so one of my servants will be my heir."
4 Then the LORD said to him, "No, your servant will not be your heir, for
you will have a son of your own who will be your heir." 5 Then the LORD took
Abram outside and said to him, "Look up into the sky and count the stars if
you can. That's how many descendants you will have!"
6 And Abram believed the LORD, and the LORD counted him as righteous
because of his faith.
7 Then the LORD told him, "I am the LORD who brought you out of Ur of
the Chaldeans to give you this land as your possession."
8 But Abram replied, "O Sovereign LORD, how can I be sure that I will ac-
tually possess it?"
9 The LORD told him, "Bring me a three-year-old heifer, a three-year-old
female goat, a three-year-old ram, a turtledove, and a young pigeon." 10 So
Abram presented all these to him and killed them. Then he cut each animal
down the middle and laid the halves side by side; he did not, however, cut
the birds in half. 11 Some vultures swooped down to eat the carcasses, but
Abram chased them away.
12 As the sun was going down, Abram fell into a deep sleep, and a terrifying
darkness came down over him. 13 Then the LORD said to Abram, "You can be
sure that your descendants will be strangers in a foreign land, where they
will be oppressed as slaves for 400 years. 14 But I will punish the nation that
enslaves them, and in the end they will come away with great wealth. 15 (As
for you, you will die in peace and be buried at a ripe old age.) 16 After four
generations your descendants will return here to this land, for the sins of
the Amorites do not yet warrant their destruction."

17 After the sun went down and darkness fell, Abram saw a smoking firepot
and a flaming torch pass between the halves of the carcasses. 18 So the LORD
made a covenant with Abram that day and said, "I have given this land to
your descendants, all the way from the border of Egypt* to the great Euphra-
tes River— 19 the land now occupied by the Kenites, Kenizzites, Kadmonites,
20 Hittites, Perizzites, Rephaites, 21 Amorites, Canaanites, Girgashites, and
Jebusites."

The Birth of Ishmael

16 Now Sarai, Abram's wife, had not been able to bear children for
him. But she had an Egyptian servant named Hagar. 2 So Sarai said
to Abram, "The LORD has prevented me from having children. Go and sleep
with my servant. Perhaps I can have children through her." And Abram
agreed with Sarai's proposal. 3 So Sarai, Abram's wife, took Hagar the Egyp-
tian servant and gave her to Abram as a wife. (This happened ten years after
Abram had settled in the land of Canaan.)
4 So Abram had sexual relations with Hagar, and she became pregnant.
But when Hagar knew she was pregnant, she began to treat her mistress,
Sarai, with contempt. 5 Then Sarai said to Abram, "This is all your fault! I put
my servant into your arms, but now that she's pregnant she treats me with
contempt. The LORD will show who's wrong—you or me!"
6 Abram replied, "Look, she is your servant, so deal with her as you see fit."
Then Sarai treated Hagar so harshly that she finally ran away.
7 The angel of the LORD found Hagar beside a spring of water in the wilder-
ness, along the road to Shur. 8 The angel said to her, "Hagar, Sarai's servant,
where have you come from, and where are you going?"
"I'm running away from my mistress, Sarai," she replied.
9 The angel of the LORD said to her, "Return to your mistress, and submit
to her authority." 10 Then he added, "I will give you more descendants than
you can count."
11 And the angel also said, "You are now pregnant and will give birth to a
son. You are to name him Ishmael (which means 'God hears'), for the LORD
has heard your cry of distress. 12 This son of yours will be a wild man, as un-
tamed as a wild donkey! He will raise his fist against everyone, and everyone
will be against him. Yes, he will live in open hostility against all his relatives."
13 Thereafter, Hagar used another name to refer to the LORD, who had
spoken to her. She said, "You are the God who sees me."* She also said, "Have
I truly seen the One who sees me?" 14 So that well was named Beer-lahai-roi
(which means "well of the Living One who sees me"). It can still be found
between Kadesh and Bered.
15 So Hagar gave Abram a son, and Abram named him Ishmael. 16 Abram
was eighty-six years old when Ishmael was born.

Abram Is Named Abraham

17 When Abram was ninety-nine years old, the LORD appeared to him
and said, "I am El-Shaddai—'God Almighty.' Serve me faithfully
and live a blameless life. 2 I will make a covenant with you, by which I will
guarantee to give you countless descendants."
3 At this, Abram fell face down on the ground. Then God said to him,

15:18 Hebrew *the river of Egypt,* referring either to an eastern branch of the Nile River or to the Brook of Egypt in the Sinai (see Num 34:5). 16:13 Hebrew *El-roi.*

Question 16:2

Why do you think people get impatient with God, and how can you grow in patience as you wait for God to work?

4“This is my covenant with you: I will make you the father of a multitude
of nations! 5What’s more, I am changing your name. It will no longer be
Abram. Instead, you will be called Abraham,* for you will be the father of
many nations. 6I will make you extremely fruitful. Your descendants will
become many nations, and kings will be among them!
7“I will confirm my covenant with you and your descendants* after you,
from generation to generation. This is the everlasting covenant: I will always
be your God and the God of your descendants after you. 8And I will give the
entire land of Canaan, where you now live as a foreigner, to you and your
descendants. It will be their possession forever, and I will be their God.”

The Mark of the Covenant

9Then God said to Abraham, “Your responsibility is to obey the terms of
the covenant. You and all your descendants have this continual responsibil-
ity. 10This is the covenant that you and your descendants must keep: Each
male among you must be circumcised. 11You must cut off the flesh of your
foreskin as a sign of the covenant between me and you. 12From generation
to generation, every male child must be circumcised on the eighth day after
his birth. This applies not only to members of your family but also to the
servants born in your household and the foreign-born servants whom you
have purchased. 13All must be circumcised. Your bodies will bear the mark
of my everlasting covenant. 14Any male who fails to be circumcised will be
cut off from the covenant family for breaking the covenant.”

Sarai Is Named Sarah

15Then God said to Abraham, “Regarding Sarai, your wife—her name will
no longer be Sarai. From now on her name will be Sarah.* 16And I will bless
her and give you a son from her! Yes, I will bless her richly, and she will
become the mother of many nations. Kings of nations will be among her
descendants.”
17Then Abraham bowed down to the ground, but he laughed to himself in
disbelief. “How could I become a father at the age of 100?” he thought. “And
how can Sarah have a baby when she is ninety years old?” 18So Abraham said
to God, “May Ishmael live under your special blessing!”
19But God replied, “No—Sarah, your wife, will give birth to a son for you.
You will name him Isaac,* and I will confirm my covenant with him and his
descendants as an everlasting covenant. 20As for Ishmael, I will bless him
also, just as you have asked. I will make him extremely fruitful and multi-
ply his descendants. He will become the father of twelve princes, and I will
make him a great nation. 21But my covenant will be confirmed with Isaac,
who will be born to you and Sarah about this time next year.” 22When God
had finished speaking, he left Abraham.
23On that very day Abraham took his son, Ishmael, and every male in his
household, including those born there and those he had bought. Then he cir-
cumcised them, cutting off their foreskins, just as God had told him. 24Abra-
ham was ninety-nine years old when he was circumcised, 25and Ishmael, his
son, was thirteen. 26Both Abraham and his son, Ishmael, were circumcised

17:5 *Abram* means “exalted father”; *Abraham* sounds like a Hebrew term that means “father of many.” **17:7** Hebrew *seed;* also in 17:7b, 8, 9, 10, 19. **17:15** *Sarai* and *Sarah* both mean “princess”; the change in spelling may reflect the difference in dialect between Ur and Canaan. **17:19** *Isaac* means “he laughs.”

on that same day, 27 along with all the other men and boys of the household, whether they were born there or bought as servants. All were circumcised with him.

> **Prayer** 18:14
>
> *Lord, thank you for always keeping your promises. Even when I don't understand how or why or when, I should know that you will come through in your way, in your purpose, and in your timing. Strengthen my faith in you today. Amen.*

A Son Is Promised to Sarah

18 The LORD appeared again to Abraham near the oak grove belonging
to Mamre. One day Abraham was sitting at the entrance to his tent
during the hottest part of the day. 2 He looked up and noticed three men
standing nearby. When he saw them, he ran to meet them and welcomed
them, bowing low to the ground.
3 "My lord," he said, "if it pleases you, stop here for a while. 4 Rest in the
shade of this tree while water is brought to wash your feet. 5 And since you've
honored your servant with this visit, let me prepare some food to refresh you
before you continue on your journey."
"All right," they said. "Do as you have said."
6 So Abraham ran back to the tent and said to Sarah, "Hurry! Get three
large measures* of your best flour, knead it into dough, and bake some
bread." 7 Then Abraham ran out to the herd and chose a tender calf and gave
it to his servant, who quickly prepared it. 8 When the food was ready, Abra-
ham took some yogurt and milk and the roasted meat, and he served it to
the men. As they ate, Abraham waited on them in the shade of the trees.
9 "Where is Sarah, your wife?" the visitors asked.
"She's inside the tent," Abraham replied.
10 Then one of them said, "I will return to you about this time next year,
and your wife, Sarah, will have a son!"
Sarah was listening to this conversation from the tent. 11 Abraham and
Sarah were both very old by this time, and Sarah was long past the age of
having children. 12 So she laughed silently to herself and said, "How could a
worn-out woman like me enjoy such pleasure, especially when my master—
my husband—is also so old?"
13 Then the LORD said to Abraham, "Why did Sarah laugh? Why did she
say, 'Can an old woman like me have a baby?' 14 Is anything too hard for the
LORD? I will return about this time next year, and Sarah will have a son."
15 Sarah was afraid, so she denied it, saying, "I didn't laugh."
But the LORD said, "No, you did laugh."

Abraham Intercedes for Sodom

16 Then the men got up from their meal and looked out toward Sodom. As
they left, Abraham went with them to send them on their way.
17 "Should I hide my plan from Abraham?" the LORD asked. 18 "For Abra-
ham will certainly become a great and mighty nation, and all the nations of
the earth will be blessed through him. 19 I have singled him out so that he
will direct his sons and their families to keep the way of the LORD by doing
what is right and just. Then I will do for Abraham all that I have promised."
20 So the LORD told Abraham, "I have heard a great outcry from Sodom and
Gomorrah, because their sin is so flagrant. 21 I am going down to see if their
actions are as wicked as I have heard. If not, I want to know."
22 The other men turned and headed toward Sodom, but the LORD re-
mained with Abraham. 23 Abraham approached him and said, "Will you

18:6 Hebrew *3 seahs,* about half a bushel or 22 liters.

sweep away both the righteous and the wicked? 24 Suppose you find fifty
righteous people living there in the city—will you still sweep it away and not
spare it for their sakes? 25 Surely you wouldn't do such a thing, destroying the
righteous along with the wicked. Why, you would be treating the righteous
and the wicked exactly the same! Surely you wouldn't do that! Should not
the Judge of all the earth do what is right?"

26 And the LORD replied, "If I find fifty righteous people in Sodom, I will
spare the entire city for their sake."

27 Then Abraham spoke again. "Since I have begun, let me speak further
to my Lord, even though I am but dust and ashes. 28 Suppose there are only
forty-five righteous people rather than fifty? Will you destroy the whole
city for lack of five?"

And the LORD said, "I will not destroy it if I find forty-five righteous
people there."

29 Then Abraham pressed his request further. "Suppose there are only
forty?"

And the LORD replied, "I will not destroy it for the sake of the forty."

30 "Please don't be angry, my Lord," Abraham pleaded. "Let me speak—
suppose only thirty righteous people are found?"

And the LORD replied, "I will not destroy it if I find thirty."

31 Then Abraham said, "Since I have dared to speak to the Lord, let me
continue—suppose there are only twenty?"

And the LORD replied, "Then I will not destroy it for the sake of the
twenty."

32 Finally, Abraham said, "Lord, please don't be angry with me if I speak
one more time. Suppose only ten are found there?"

And the LORD replied, "Then I will not destroy it for the sake of the ten."

33 When the LORD had finished his conversation with Abraham, he went
on his way, and Abraham returned to his tent.

Sodom and Gomorrah Destroyed

19 That evening the two angels came to the entrance of the city of Sod-
om. Lot was sitting there, and when he saw them, he stood up to
meet them. Then he welcomed them and bowed with his face to the ground.
2 "My lords," he said, "come to my home to wash your feet, and be my guests
for the night. You may then get up early in the morning and be on your
way again."

"Oh no," they replied. "We'll just spend the night out here in the city
square."

3 But Lot insisted, so at last they went home with him. Lot prepared a
feast for them, complete with fresh bread made without yeast, and they ate.
4 But before they retired for the night, all the men of Sodom, young and old,
came from all over the city and surrounded the house. 5 They shouted to Lot,
"Where are the men who came to spend the night with you? Bring them out
to us so we can have sex with them!"

6 So Lot stepped outside to talk to them, shutting the door behind him.
7 "Please, my brothers," he begged, "don't do such a wicked thing. 8 Look, I
have two virgin daughters. Let me bring them out to you, and you can do
with them as you wish. But please, leave these men alone, for they are my
guests and are under my protection."

9“Stand back!” they shouted. “This fellow came to town as an outsider,
and now he’s acting like our judge! We’ll treat you far worse than those other
men!” And they lunged toward Lot to break down the door.
10But the two angels* reached out, pulled Lot into the house, and bolted
the door. 11Then they blinded all the men, young and old, who were at the
door of the house, so they gave up trying to get inside.
12Meanwhile, the angels questioned Lot. “Do you have any other relatives
here in the city?” they asked. “Get them out of this place—your sons-in-law,
sons, daughters, or anyone else. 13For we are about to destroy this city com-
pletely. The outcry against this place is so great it has reached the LORD, and
he has sent us to destroy it.”
14So Lot rushed out to tell his daughters’ fiancés, “Quick, get out of the
city! The LORD is about to destroy it.” But the young men thought he was
only joking.
15At dawn the next morning the angels became insistent. “Hurry,” they
said to Lot. “Take your wife and your two daughters who are here. Get out
right now, or you will be swept away in the destruction of the city!”
16When Lot still hesitated, the angels seized his hand and the hands of his
wife and two daughters and rushed them to safety outside the city, for the
LORD was merciful. 17When they were safely out of the city, one of the angels
ordered, “Run for your lives! And don’t look back or stop anywhere in the
valley! Escape to the mountains, or you will be swept away!”
18“Oh no, my lord!” Lot begged. 19“You have been so gracious to me and
saved my life, and you have shown such great kindness. But I cannot go to
the mountains. Disaster would catch up to me there, and I would soon die.
20See, there is a small village nearby. Please let me go there instead; don’t you
see how small it is? Then my life will be saved.”
21“All right,” the angel said, “I will grant your request. I will not destroy
the little village. 22But hurry! Escape to it, for I can do nothing until you ar-
rive there.” (This explains why that village was known as Zoar, which means
“little place.”)
23Lot reached the village just as the sun was rising over the horizon. 24Then
the LORD rained down fire and burning sulfur from the sky on Sodom and
Gomorrah. 25He utterly destroyed them, along with the other cities and vil-
lages of the plain, wiping out all the people and every bit of vegetation. 26But
Lot’s wife looked back as she was following behind him, and she turned into
a pillar of salt.
27Abraham got up early that morning and hurried out to the place where
he had stood in the LORD’s presence. 28He looked out across the plain toward
Sodom and Gomorrah and watched as columns of smoke rose from the cities
like smoke from a furnace.
29But God had listened to Abraham’s request and kept Lot safe, removing
him from the disaster that engulfed the cities on the plain.

Lot and His Daughters

30Afterward Lot left Zoar because he was afraid of the people there, and he
went to live in a cave in the mountains with his two daughters. 31One day
the older daughter said to her sister, “There are no men left anywhere in
this entire area, so we can’t get married like everyone else. And our father

19:10 Hebrew *men;* also in 19:12, 16.

Question 19:16

This is a very scary story. Do you think God has ever pulled you away from evil when you were tempted to linger? What do you learn about how God wants to work in our lives?

will soon be too old to have children. 32 Come, let's get him drunk with wine,
and then we will have sex with him. That way we will preserve our family
line through our father."

33 So that night they got him drunk with wine, and the older daughter
went in and had intercourse with her father. He was unaware of her lying
down or getting up again.

34 The next morning the older daughter said to her younger sister, "I had
sex with our father last night. Let's get him drunk with wine again tonight,
and you go in and have sex with him. That way we will preserve our family
line through our father." 35 So that night they got him drunk with wine again,
and the younger daughter went in and had intercourse with him. As before,
he was unaware of her lying down or getting up again.

36 As a result, both of Lot's daughters became pregnant by their own father.
37 When the older daughter gave birth to a son, she named him Moab.* He
became the ancestor of the nation now known as the Moabites. 38 When the
younger daughter gave birth to a son, she named him Ben-ammi.* He became
the ancestor of the nation now known as the Ammonites.

Abraham Deceives Abimelech

20 Abraham moved south to the Negev and lived for a while between
Kadesh and Shur, and then he moved on to Gerar. While living there
as a foreigner, 2 Abraham introduced his wife, Sarah, by saying, "She is my
sister." So King Abimelech of Gerar sent for Sarah and had her brought to
him at his palace.

3 But that night God came to Abimelech in a dream and told him, "You are
a dead man, for that woman you have taken is already married!"

4 But Abimelech had not slept with her yet, so he said, "Lord, will you
destroy an innocent nation? 5 Didn't Abraham tell me, 'She is my sister'? And
she herself said, 'Yes, he is my brother.' I acted in complete innocence! My
hands are clean."

6 In the dream God responded, "Yes, I know you are innocent. That's why
I kept you from sinning against me, and why I did not let you touch her.
7 Now return the woman to her husband, and he will pray for you, for he is
a prophet. Then you will live. But if you don't return her to him, you can be
sure that you and all your people will die."

8 Abimelech got up early the next morning and quickly called all his ser-
vants together. When he told them what had happened, his men were ter-
rified. 9 Then Abimelech called for Abraham. "What have you done to us?"
he demanded. "What crime have I committed that deserves treatment like
this, making me and my kingdom guilty of this great sin? No one should
ever do what you have done! 10 Whatever possessed you to do such a thing?"

11 Abraham replied, "I thought, 'This is a godless place. They will want
my wife and will kill me to get her.' 12 And she really is my sister, for we both
have the same father, but different mothers. And I married her. 13 When God
called me to leave my father's home and to travel from place to place, I told
her, 'Do me a favor. Wherever we go, tell the people that I am your brother.'"

14 Then Abimelech took some of his sheep and goats, cattle, and male and
female servants, and he presented them to Abraham. He also returned his
wife, Sarah, to him. 15 Then Abimelech said, "Look over my land and choose

19:37 *Moab* sounds like a Hebrew term that means "from father." **19:38** *Ben-ammi* means "son of my kinsman."

any place where you would like to live." 16 And he said to Sarah, "Look, I am
giving your 'brother' 1,000 pieces of silver* in the presence of all these wit-
nesses. This is to compensate you for any wrong I may have done to you. This
will settle any claim against me, and your reputation is cleared."
17 Then Abraham prayed to God, and God healed Abimelech, his wife, and
his female servants, so they could have children. 18 For the LORD had caused
all the women to be infertile because of what happened with Abraham's
wife, Sarah.

The Birth of Isaac

21 The LORD kept his word and did for Sarah exactly what he had prom-
ised. 2 She became pregnant, and she gave birth to a son for Abraham
in his old age. This happened at just the time God had said it would. 3 And
Abraham named their son Isaac. 4 Eight days after Isaac was born, Abraham
circumcised him as God had commanded. 5 Abraham was 100 years old when
Isaac was born.
6 And Sarah declared, "God has brought me laughter.* All who hear about
this will laugh with me. 7 Who would have said to Abraham that Sarah would
nurse a baby? Yet I have given Abraham a son in his old age!"

Hagar and Ishmael Are Sent Away

8 When Isaac grew up and was about to be weaned, Abraham prepared a
huge feast to celebrate the occasion. 9 But Sarah saw Ishmael—the son of
Abraham and her Egyptian servant Hagar—making fun of her son, Isaac.*
10 So she turned to Abraham and demanded, "Get rid of that slave woman
and her son. He is not going to share the inheritance with my son, Isaac. I
won't have it!"
11 This upset Abraham very much because Ishmael was his son. 12 But God
told Abraham, "Do not be upset over the boy and your servant. Do whatever
Sarah tells you, for Isaac is the son through whom your descendants will be
counted. 13 But I will also make a nation of the descendants of Hagar's son
because he is your son, too."
14 So Abraham got up early the next morning, prepared food and a con-
tainer of water, and strapped them on Hagar's shoulders. Then he sent
her away with their son, and she wandered aimlessly in the wilderness of
Beersheba.
15 When the water was gone, she put the boy in the shade of a bush. 16 Then
she went and sat down by herself about a hundred yards* away. "I don't want
to watch the boy die," she said, as she burst into tears.
17 But God heard the boy crying, and the angel of God called to Hagar
from heaven, "Hagar, what's wrong? Do not be afraid! God has heard the
boy crying as he lies there. 18 Go to him and comfort him, for I will make a
great nation from his descendants."
19 Then God opened Hagar's eyes, and she saw a well full of water. She
quickly filled her water container and gave the boy a drink.
20 And God was with the boy as he grew up in the wilderness. He became
a skillful archer, 21 and he settled in the wilderness of Paran. His mother ar-
ranged for him to marry a woman from the land of Egypt.

20:16 Hebrew *1,000 [shekels] of silver,* about 25 pounds or 11.4 kilograms in weight. 21:6 The name *Isaac* means "he laughs." 21:9 As in Greek version and Latin Vulgate; Hebrew lacks *of her son, Isaac.* 21:16 Hebrew *a bowshot.*

Write your notes in this space

Make a Difference

22:1-18

Holding On

As you think about all that you have, it's important to remember God is the one who gave it to you. When he asks for it, we have to trust that he is able to not only give it back but also give us something even better. It's all a matter of faith. When God asks us to give up something, will God still do all that he promised even if we can't see how he'll do it? The answer is always yes. As a result, whatever God asks of us, our answer should also always be yes.

Difference Maker

Make a list of the top five most frequently used things that would be difficult for you to give back to God. From that list, pick one to surrender for one day. As you do, see how God works in your life.

Question **22:8**

In what ways has Jesus become the ultimate "sheep" that God provides?

Abraham's Covenant with Abimelech

22 About this time, Abimelech came with Phicol, his army commander, to visit
Abraham. "God is obviously with you, helping you in everything you do,"
Abimelech said. 23 "Swear to me in God's name that you will never deceive
me, my children, or any of my descendants. I have been loyal to you, so now
swear that you will be loyal to me and to this country where you are living
as a foreigner."

24 Abraham replied, "Yes, I swear to it!" 25 Then Abraham complained to
Abimelech about a well that Abimelech's servants had taken by force from
Abraham's servants.

26 "This is the first I've heard of it," Abimelech answered. "I have no idea
who is responsible. You have never complained about this before."

27 Abraham then gave some of his sheep, goats, and cattle to Abimelech,
and they made a treaty. 28 But Abraham also took seven additional female
lambs and set them off by themselves. 29 Abimelech asked, "Why have you
set these seven apart from the others?"

30 Abraham replied, "Please accept these seven lambs to show your agree-
ment that I dug this well." 31 Then he named the place Beersheba (which
means "well of the oath"), because that was where they had sworn the oath.

32 After making their covenant at Beersheba, Abimelech left with Phicol,
the commander of his army, and they returned home to the land of the Phi-
listines. 33 Then Abraham planted a tamarisk tree at Beersheba, and there he
worshiped the LORD, the Eternal God.* 34 And Abraham lived as a foreigner
in Philistine country for a long time.

Abraham's Faith Tested

22 Some time later, God tested Abraham's faith. "Abraham!" God called.
"Yes," he replied. "Here I am."

2 "Take your son, your only son—yes, Isaac, whom you love so much—and
go to the land of Moriah. Go and sacrifice him as a burnt offering on one of
the mountains, which I will show you."

3 The next morning Abraham got up early. He saddled his donkey and took
two of his servants with him, along with his son, Isaac. Then he chopped
wood for a fire for a burnt offering and set out for the place God had told
him about. 4 On the third day of their journey, Abraham looked up and saw
the place in the distance. 5 "Stay here with the donkey," Abraham told the
servants. "The boy and I will travel a little farther. We will worship there,
and then we will come right back."

6 So Abraham placed the wood for the burnt offering on Isaac's shoulders,
while he himself carried the fire and the knife. As the two of them walked
on together, 7 Isaac turned to Abraham and said, "Father?"

"Yes, my son?" Abraham replied.

"We have the fire and the wood," the boy said, "but where is the sheep
for the burnt offering?"

8 "God will provide a sheep for the burnt offering, my son," Abraham an-
swered. And they both walked on together.

9 When they arrived at the place where God had told him to go, Abraham
built an altar and arranged the wood on it. Then he tied his son, Isaac, and
laid him on the altar on top of the wood. 10 And Abraham picked up the knife

21:33 Hebrew *El-Olam*.

to kill his son as a sacrifice. 11 At that moment the angel of the LORD called to
him from heaven, "Abraham! Abraham!"
"Yes," Abraham replied. "Here I am!"
12 "Don't lay a hand on the boy!" the angel said. "Do not hurt him in any
way, for now I know that you truly fear God. You have not withheld from
me even your son, your only son."
13 Then Abraham looked up and saw a ram caught by its horns in a thicket.
So he took the ram and sacrificed it as a burnt offering in place of his son.
14 Abraham named the place Yahweh-Yireh (which means "the LORD will pro-
vide"). To this day, people still use that name as a proverb: "On the mountain
of the LORD it will be provided."
15 Then the angel of the LORD called again to Abraham from heaven.
16 "This is what the LORD says: Because you have obeyed me and have not
withheld even your son, your only son, I swear by my own name that 17 I
will certainly bless you. I will multiply your descendants* beyond number,
like the stars in the sky and the sand on the seashore. Your descendants will
conquer the cities of their enemies. 18 And through your descendants all the
nations of the earth will be blessed—all because you have obeyed me."
19 Then they returned to the servants and traveled back to Beersheba,
where Abraham continued to live.
20 Soon after this, Abraham heard that Milcah, his brother Nahor's wife,
had borne Nahor eight sons. 21 The oldest was named Uz, the next oldest
was Buz, followed by Kemuel (the ancestor of the Arameans), 22 Kesed, Hazo,
Pildash, Jidlaph, and Bethuel. 23 (Bethuel became the father of Rebekah.) In
addition to these eight sons from Milcah, 24 Nahor had four other children
from his concubine Reumah. Their names were Tebah, Gaham, Tahash, and
Maacah.

The Burial of Sarah

23 When Sarah was 127 years old, 2 she died at Kiriath-arba (now called
Hebron) in the land of Canaan. There Abraham mourned and wept
for her.
3 Then, leaving her body, he said to the Hittite elders, 4 "Here I am, a
stranger and a foreigner among you. Please sell me a piece of land so I can
give my wife a proper burial."
5 The Hittites replied to Abraham, 6 "Listen, my lord, you are an honored
prince among us. Choose the finest of our tombs and bury her there. No one
here will refuse to help you in this way."
7 Then Abraham bowed low before the Hittites 8 and said, "Since you are
willing to help me in this way, be so kind as to ask Ephron son of Zohar 9 to
let me buy his cave at Machpelah, down at the end of his field. I will pay
the full price in the presence of witnesses, so I will have a permanent burial
place for my family."
10 Ephron was sitting there among the others, and he answered Abraham
as the others listened, speaking publicly before all the Hittite elders of the
town. 11 "No, my lord," he said to Abraham, "please listen to me. I will give
you the field and the cave. Here in the presence of my people, I give it to you.
Go and bury your dead."
12 Abraham again bowed low before the citizens of the land, 13 and he

22:17 Hebrew *seed;* also in 22:17b, 18.

replied to Ephron as everyone listened. "No, listen to me. I will buy it from
you. Let me pay the full price for the field so I can bury my dead there."
14 Ephron answered Abraham, 15 "My lord, please listen to me. The land is
worth 400 pieces* of silver, but what is that between friends? Go ahead and
bury your dead."
16 So Abraham agreed to Ephron's price and paid the amount he had
suggested—400 pieces of silver, weighed according to the market standard.
The Hittite elders witnessed the transaction.
17 So Abraham bought the plot of land belonging to Ephron at Machpe-
lah, near Mamre. This included the field itself, the cave that was in it, and
all the surrounding trees. 18 It was transferred to Abraham as his permanent
possession in the presence of the Hittite elders at the city gate. 19 Then Abra-
ham buried his wife, Sarah, there in Canaan, in the cave of Machpelah, near
Mamre (also called Hebron). 20 So the field and the cave were transferred from
the Hittites to Abraham for use as a permanent burial place.

A Wife for Isaac

24 Abraham was now a very old man, and the LORD had blessed him
in every way. 2 One day Abraham said to his oldest servant, the man
in charge of his household, "Take an oath by putting your hand under my
thigh. 3 Swear by the LORD, the God of heaven and earth, that you will not
allow my son to marry one of these local Canaanite women. 4 Go instead to
my homeland, to my relatives, and find a wife there for my son Isaac."
5 The servant asked, "But what if I can't find a young woman who is will-
ing to travel so far from home? Should I then take Isaac there to live among
your relatives in the land you came from?"
6 "No!" Abraham responded. "Be careful never to take my son there. 7 For
the LORD, the God of heaven, who took me from my father's house and my
native land, solemnly promised to give this land to my descendants.* He will
send his angel ahead of you, and he will see to it that you find a wife there for
my son. 8 If she is unwilling to come back with you, then you are free from
this oath of mine. But under no circumstances are you to take my son there."
9 So the servant took an oath by putting his hand under the thigh of his
master, Abraham. He swore to follow Abraham's instructions. 10 Then he
loaded ten of Abraham's camels with all kinds of expensive gifts from his
master, and he traveled to distant Aram-naharaim. There he went to the
town where Abraham's brother Nahor had settled. 11 He made the camels
kneel beside a well just outside the town. It was evening, and the women
were coming out to draw water.
12 "O LORD, God of my master, Abraham," he prayed. "Please give me suc-
cess today, and show unfailing love to my master, Abraham. 13 See, I am stand-
ing here beside this spring, and the young women of the town are coming
out to draw water. 14 This is my request. I will ask one of them, 'Please give
me a drink from your jug.' If she says, 'Yes, have a drink, and I will water your
camels, too!'—let her be the one you have selected as Isaac's wife. This is how
I will know that you have shown unfailing love to my master."
15 Before he had finished praying, he saw a young woman named Rebekah
coming out with her water jug on her shoulder. She was the daughter of Be-
thuel, who was the son of Abraham's brother Nahor and his wife, Milcah.

23:15 Hebrew *400 shekels,* about 10 pounds or 4.6 kilograms in weight; also in 23:16.
24:7 Hebrew *seed;* also in 24:60.

16 Rebekah was very beautiful and old enough to be married, but she was
still a virgin. She went down to the spring, filled her jug, and came up again.
17 Running over to her, the servant said, "Please give me a little drink of water
from your jug."
18 "Yes, my lord," she answered, "have a drink." And she quickly lowered
her jug from her shoulder and gave him a drink. 19 When she had given him
a drink, she said, "I'll draw water for your camels, too, until they have had
enough to drink." 20 So she quickly emptied her jug into the watering trough
and ran back to the well to draw water for all his camels.
21 The servant watched her in silence, wondering whether or not the LORD
had given him success in his mission. 22 Then at last, when the camels had
finished drinking, he took out a gold ring for her nose and two large gold
bracelets* for her wrists.
23 "Whose daughter are you?" he asked. "And please tell me, would your
father have any room to put us up for the night?"
24 "I am the daughter of Bethuel," she replied. "My grandparents are Na-
hor and Milcah. 25 Yes, we have plenty of straw and feed for the camels, and
we have room for guests."
26 The man bowed low and worshiped the LORD. 27 "Praise the LORD, the
God of my master, Abraham," he said. "The LORD has shown unfailing love
and faithfulness to my master, for he has led me straight to my master's
relatives."
28 The young woman ran home to tell her family everything that had hap-
pened. 29 Now Rebekah had a brother named Laban, who ran out to meet
the man at the spring. 30 He had seen the nose-ring and the bracelets on his
sister's wrists, and had heard Rebekah tell what the man had said. So he
rushed out to the spring, where the man was still standing beside his cam-
els. 31 Laban said to him, "Come and stay with us, you who are blessed by the
LORD! Why are you standing here outside the town when I have a room all
ready for you and a place prepared for the camels?"
32 So the man went home with Laban, and Laban unloaded the camels, gave
him straw for their bedding, fed them, and provided water for the man and
the camel drivers to wash their feet. 33 Then food was served. But Abraham's
servant said, "I don't want to eat until I have told you why I have come."
"All right," Laban said, "tell us."
34 "I am Abraham's servant," he explained. 35 "And the LORD has greatly
blessed my master; he has become a wealthy man. The LORD has given him
flocks of sheep and goats, herds of cattle, a fortune in silver and gold, and
many male and female servants and camels and donkeys.
36 "When Sarah, my master's wife, was very old, she gave birth to my mas-
ter's son, and my master has given him everything he owns. 37 And my master
made me take an oath. He said, 'Do not allow my son to marry one of these
local Canaanite women. 38 Go instead to my father's house, to my relatives,
and find a wife there for my son.'
39 "But I said to my master, 'What if I can't find a young woman who is
willing to go back with me?' 40 He responded, 'The LORD, in whose pres-
ence I have lived, will send his angel with you and will make your mission
successful. Yes, you must find a wife for my son from among my relatives,
from my father's family. 41 Then you will have fulfilled your obligation. But

24:22 Hebrew *a gold nose-ring weighing a beka* [0.2 ounces or 6 grams] *and two gold bracelets weighing 10 [shekels]* [4 ounces or 114 grams].

Why this matters!

Prayer **24:42**

Jesus, let me be an answer to someone else's prayer today. Give me the eyes to see the needs around me and the ability to meet them. Amen.

Question **24:58**

Rebekah agreed to leave her family and follow Abraham's servant to become the wife of Isaac, whom she had not met. How can you follow Jesus faithfully without having all the answers?

if you go to my relatives and they refuse to let her go with you, you will be
free from my oath.'
42 "So today when I came to the spring, I prayed this prayer: 'O LORD, God of
my master, Abraham, please give me success on this mission. 43 See, I am stand-
ing here beside this spring. This is my request. When a young woman comes to
draw water, I will say to her, "Please give me a little drink of water from your
jug." 44 If she says, "Yes, have a drink, and I will draw water for your camels,
too," let her be the one you have selected to be the wife of my master's son.'
45 "Before I had finished praying in my heart, I saw Rebekah coming out
with her water jug on her shoulder. She went down to the spring and drew
water. So I said to her, 'Please give me a drink.' 46 She quickly lowered her jug
from her shoulder and said, 'Yes, have a drink, and I will water your camels,
too!' So I drank, and then she watered the camels.
47 "Then I asked, 'Whose daughter are you?' She replied, 'I am the daughter
of Bethuel, and my grandparents are Nahor and Milcah.' So I put the ring
on her nose, and the bracelets on her wrists.
48 "Then I bowed low and worshiped the LORD. I praised the LORD, the
God of my master, Abraham, because he had led me straight to my master's
niece to be his son's wife. 49 So tell me—will you or won't you show unfail-
ing love and faithfulness to my master? Please tell me yes or no, and then
I'll know what to do next."
50 Then Laban and Bethuel replied, "The LORD has obviously brought you
here, so there is nothing we can say. 51 Here is Rebekah; take her and go. Yes,
let her be the wife of your master's son, as the LORD has directed."
52 When Abraham's servant heard their answer, he bowed down to the
ground and worshiped the LORD. 53 Then he brought out silver and gold
jewelry and clothing and presented them to Rebekah. He also gave expen-
sive presents to her brother and mother. 54 Then they ate their meal, and the
servant and the men with him stayed there overnight.

But early the next morning, Abraham's servant said, "Send me back to my master."

55 "But we want Rebekah to stay with us at least ten days," her brother and
mother said. "Then she can go."
56 But he said, "Don't delay me. The LORD has made my mission successful;
now send me back so I can return to my master."
57 "Well," they said, "we'll call Rebekah and ask her what she thinks." 58 So
they called Rebekah. "Are you willing to go with this man?" they asked her.

And she replied, "Yes, I will go."

59 So they said good-bye to Rebekah and sent her away with Abraham's
servant and his men. The woman who had been Rebekah's childhood nurse
went along with her. 60 They gave her this blessing as she parted:

"Our sister, may you become
the mother of many millions!
May your descendants be strong
and conquer the cities of their enemies."

61 Then Rebekah and her servant girls mounted the camels and followed the
man. So Abraham's servant took Rebekah and went on his way.
62 Meanwhile, Isaac, whose home was in the Negev, had returned from

Beer-lahai-roi. 63 One evening as he was walking and meditating in the fields,
he looked up and saw the camels coming. 64 When Rebekah looked up and
saw Isaac, she quickly dismounted from her camel. 65 "Who is that man walk-
ing through the fields to meet us?" she asked the servant.
And he replied, "It is my master." So Rebekah covered her face with her
veil. 66 Then the servant told Isaac everything he had done.
67 And Isaac brought Rebekah into his mother Sarah's tent, and she became
his wife. He loved her deeply, and she was a special comfort to him after the
death of his mother.

The Death of Abraham

25 Abraham married another wife, whose name was Keturah. 2 She
gave birth to Zimran, Jokshan, Medan, Midian, Ishbak, and Shu-
ah. 3 Jokshan was the father of Sheba and Dedan. Dedan's descendants were
the Asshurites, Letushites, and Leummites. 4 Midian's sons were Ephah,
Epher, Hanoch, Abida, and Eldaah. These were all descendants of Abraham
through Keturah.
5 Abraham gave everything he owned to his son Isaac. 6 But before he died,
he gave gifts to the sons of his concubines and sent them off to a land in the
east, away from Isaac.
7 Abraham lived for 175 years, 8 and he died at a ripe old age, having lived
a long and satisfying life. He breathed his last and joined his ancestors in
death. 9 His sons Isaac and Ishmael buried him in the cave of Machpelah, near
Mamre, in the field of Ephron son of Zohar the Hittite. 10 This was the field
Abraham had purchased from the Hittites and where he had buried his wife
Sarah. 11 After Abraham's death, God blessed his son Isaac, who settled near
Beer-lahai-roi in the Negev.

Ishmael's Descendants

12 This is the account of the family of Ishmael, the son of Abraham through
Hagar, Sarah's Egyptian servant. 13 Here is a list, by their names and clans, of
Ishmael's descendants: The oldest was Nebaioth, followed by Kedar, Adbeel,
Mibsam, 14 Mishma, Dumah, Massa, 15 Hadad, Tema, Jetur, Naphish, and Ked-
emah. 16 These twelve sons of Ishmael became the founders of twelve tribes
named after them, listed according to the places they settled and camped.
17 Ishmael lived for 137 years. Then he breathed his last and joined his ances-
tors in death. 18 Ishmael's descendants occupied the region from Havilah to
Shur, which is east of Egypt in the direction of Asshur. There they lived in
open hostility toward all their relatives.*

The Births of Esau and Jacob

19 This is the account of the family of Isaac, the son of Abraham. 20 When Isaac
was forty years old, he married Rebekah, the daughter of Bethuel the Ara-
mean from Paddan-aram and the sister of Laban the Aramean.
21 Isaac pleaded with the LORD on behalf of his wife, because she was un-
able to have children. The LORD answered Isaac's prayer, and Rebekah be-
came pregnant with twins. 22 But the two children struggled with each other
in her womb. So she went to ask the LORD about it. "Why is this happening
to me?" she asked.

25:18 The meaning of the Hebrew is uncertain.

23 And the LORD told her, "The sons in your womb will become two nations. From the very beginning, the two nations will be rivals. One nation will be stronger than the other; and your older son will serve your younger son."

24 And when the time came to give birth, Rebekah discovered that she did indeed have twins! 25 The first one was very red at birth and covered with thick hair like a fur coat. So they named him Esau.* 26 Then the other twin was born with his hand grasping Esau's heel. So they named him Jacob.* Isaac was sixty years old when the twins were born.

Esau Sells His Birthright

27 As the boys grew up, Esau became a skillful hunter. He was an outdoorsman, but Jacob had a quiet temperament, preferring to stay at home. 28 Isaac loved Esau because he enjoyed eating the wild game Esau brought home, but Rebekah loved Jacob.

29 One day when Jacob was cooking some stew, Esau arrived home from the wilderness exhausted and hungry. 30 Esau said to Jacob, "I'm starved! Give me some of that red stew!" (This is how Esau got his other name, Edom, which means "red.")

31 "All right," Jacob replied, "but trade me your rights as the firstborn son."

32 "Look, I'm dying of starvation!" said Esau. "What good is my birthright to me now?"

33 But Jacob said, "First you must swear that your birthright is mine." So Esau swore an oath, thereby selling all his rights as the firstborn to his brother, Jacob.

34 Then Jacob gave Esau some bread and lentil stew. Esau ate the meal, then got up and left. He showed contempt for his rights as the firstborn.

Isaac Deceives Abimelech

26 A severe famine now struck the land, as had happened before in Abraham's time. So Isaac moved to Gerar, where Abimelech, king of the Philistines, lived.

2 The LORD appeared to Isaac and said, "Do not go down to Egypt, but do as I tell you. 3 Live here as a foreigner in this land, and I will be with you and bless you. I hereby confirm that I will give all these lands to you and your descendants,* just as I solemnly promised Abraham, your father. 4 I will cause your descendants to become as numerous as the stars of the sky, and I will give them all these lands. And through your descendants all the nations of the earth will be blessed. 5 I will do this because Abraham listened to me and obeyed all my requirements, commands, decrees, and instructions." 6 So Isaac stayed in Gerar.

7 When the men who lived there asked Isaac about his wife, Rebekah, he said, "She is my sister." He was afraid to say, "She is my wife." He thought, "They will kill me to get her, because she is so beautiful." 8 But some time later, Abimelech, king of the Philistines, looked out his window and saw Isaac caressing Rebekah.

9 Immediately, Abimelech called for Isaac and exclaimed, "She is obviously your wife! Why did you say, 'She is my sister'?"

"Because I was afraid someone would kill me to get her from me," Isaac replied.

25:25 *Esau* sounds like a Hebrew term that means "hair." 25:26 *Jacob* sounds like the Hebrew words for "heel" and "deceiver." 26:3 Hebrew *seed;* also in 26:4, 24.

Make a Difference

25:27-34

Inheritance

Would you choose a bowl of soup at the cost of your entire inheritance? Without realizing it, you might be making impatient choices like that more often than you think.

Jesus promised that all his followers have a special inheritance waiting for them (1 Peter 1:3-4). Still, waiting can be hard to do! Perhaps you are tempted like Esau to abandon a future gift to satisfy an immediate need. While you may not know the full extent of your inheritance, you can rest assured that nothing in this world could even come close to being as satisfying as receiving the fullness of God's promises in his time.

Difference Maker

Place up to twenty dollars in an envelope and write three things on the outside: (1) the date, (2) "Genesis 25:32," and (3) "Do not open for twelve months." Put the envelope in a safe place. Every time you are tempted to spend that money on something, put a tally mark on the envelope. At the end of twelve months, use that money to bless someone else.

10“How could you do this to us?” Abimelech exclaimed. “One of my people
might easily have taken your wife and slept with her, and you would have
made us guilty of great sin.”
11Then Abimelech issued a public proclamation: “Anyone who touches
this man or his wife will be put to death!”

Conflict over Water Rights

12When Isaac planted his crops that year, he harvested a hundred times more
grain than he planted, for the LORD blessed him. 13He became a very rich
man, and his wealth continued to grow. 14He acquired so many flocks of
sheep and goats, herds of cattle, and servants that the Philistines became jeal-
ous of him. 15So the Philistines filled up all of Isaac’s wells with dirt. These
were the wells that had been dug by the servants of his father, Abraham.
16Finally, Abimelech ordered Isaac to leave the country. “Go somewhere
else,” he said, “for you have become too powerful for us.”
17So Isaac moved away to the Gerar Valley, where he set up their tents and
settled down. 18He reopened the wells his father had dug, which the Phi-
listines had filled in after Abraham’s death. Isaac also restored the names
Abraham had given them.
19Isaac’s servants also dug in the Gerar Valley and discovered a well of fresh
water. 20But then the shepherds from Gerar came and claimed the spring.
“This is our water,” they said, and they argued over it with Isaac’s herdsmen.
So Isaac named the well Esek (which means “argument”). 21Isaac’s men then
dug another well, but again there was a dispute over it. So Isaac named it Sit-
nah (which means “hostility”). 22Abandoning that one, Isaac moved on and
dug another well. This time there was no dispute over it, so Isaac named the
place Rehoboth (which means “open space”), for he said, “At last the LORD
has created enough space for us to prosper in this land.”
23From there Isaac moved to Beersheba, 24where the LORD appeared to
him on the night of his arrival. “I am the God of your father, Abraham,” he
said. “Do not be afraid, for I am with you and will bless you. I will multiply
your descendants, and they will become a great nation. I will do this because
of my promise to Abraham, my servant.” 25Then Isaac built an altar there
and worshiped the LORD. He set up his camp at that place, and his servants
dug another well.

Isaac’s Covenant with Abimelech

26One day King Abimelech came from Gerar with his adviser, Ahuzzath, and
also Phicol, his army commander. 27“Why have you come here?” Isaac asked.
“You obviously hate me, since you kicked me off your land.”
28They replied, “We can plainly see that the LORD is with you. So we want
to enter into a sworn treaty with you. Let’s make a covenant. 29Swear that
you will not harm us, just as we have never troubled you. We have always
treated you well, and we sent you away from us in peace. And now look how
the LORD has blessed you!”
30So Isaac prepared a covenant feast to celebrate the treaty, and they ate
and drank together. 31Early the next morning, they each took a solemn oath
not to interfere with each other. Then Isaac sent them home again, and they
left him in peace.
32That very day Isaac’s servants came and told him about a new well they

had dug. "We've found water!" they exclaimed. 33 So Isaac named the well
Shibah (which means "oath"). And to this day the town that grew up there
is called Beersheba (which means "well of the oath").
34 At the age of forty, Esau married two Hittite wives: Judith, the daughter
of Beeri, and Basemath, the daughter of Elon. 35 But Esau's wives made life
miserable for Isaac and Rebekah.

Jacob Steals Esau's Blessing

27 One day when Isaac was old and turning blind, he called for Esau,
his older son, and said, "My son."
"Yes, Father?" Esau replied.
2 "I am an old man now," Isaac said, "and I don't know when I may die.
3 Take your bow and a quiver full of arrows, and go out into the open country
to hunt some wild game for me. 4 Prepare my favorite dish, and bring it here
for me to eat. Then I will pronounce the blessing that belongs to you, my
firstborn son, before I die."
5 But Rebekah overheard what Isaac had said to his son Esau. So when Esau
left to hunt for the wild game, 6 she said to her son Jacob, "Listen. I overheard
your father say to Esau, 7 'Bring me some wild game and prepare me a deli-
cious meal. Then I will bless you in the LORD's presence before I die.' 8 Now,
my son, listen to me. Do exactly as I tell you. 9 Go out to the flocks, and bring
me two fine young goats. I'll use them to prepare your father's favorite dish.
10 Then take the food to your father so he can eat it and bless you before he dies."
11 "But look," Jacob replied to Rebekah, "my brother, Esau, is a hairy man,
and my skin is smooth. 12 What if my father touches me? He'll see that I'm
trying to trick him, and then he'll curse me instead of blessing me."
13 But his mother replied, "Then let the curse fall on me, my son! Just do
what I tell you. Go out and get the goats for me!"
14 So Jacob went out and got the young goats for his mother. Rebekah took
them and prepared a delicious meal, just the way Isaac liked it. 15 Then she
took Esau's favorite clothes, which were there in the house, and gave them
to her younger son, Jacob. 16 She covered his arms and the smooth part of his
neck with the skin of the young goats. 17 Then she gave Jacob the delicious
meal, including freshly baked bread.
18 So Jacob took the food to his father. "My father?" he said.
"Yes, my son," Isaac answered. "Who are you—Esau or Jacob?"
19 Jacob replied, "It's Esau, your firstborn son. I've done as you told me.
Here is the wild game. Now sit up and eat it so you can give me your blessing."
20 Isaac asked, "How did you find it so quickly, my son?"
"The LORD your God put it in my path!" Jacob replied.
21 Then Isaac said to Jacob, "Come closer so I can touch you and make
sure that you really are Esau." 22 So Jacob went closer to his father, and Isaac
touched him. "The voice is Jacob's, but the hands are Esau's," Isaac said. 23 But
he did not recognize Jacob, because Jacob's hands felt hairy just like Esau's.
So Isaac prepared to bless Jacob. 24 "But are you really my son Esau?" he asked.
"Yes, I am," Jacob replied.
25 Then Isaac said, "Now, my son, bring me the wild game. Let me eat it,
and then I will give you my blessing." So Jacob took the food to his father,
and Isaac ate it. He also drank the wine that Jacob served him. 26 Then Isaac
said to Jacob, "Please come a little closer and kiss me, my son."

27 So Jacob went over and kissed him. And when Isaac caught the smell of
his clothes, he was finally convinced, and he blessed his son. He said, "Ah! The
smell of my son is like the smell of the outdoors, which the LORD has blessed!

28 "From the dew of heaven
and the richness of the earth,
may God always give you abundant harvests of grain
and bountiful new wine.
29 May many nations become your servants,
and may they bow down to you.
May you be the master over your brothers,
and may your mother's sons bow down to you.
All who curse you will be cursed,
and all who bless you will be blessed."

30 As soon as Isaac had finished blessing Jacob, and almost before Jacob
had left his father, Esau returned from his hunt. 31 Esau prepared a delicious
meal and brought it to his father. Then he said, "Sit up, my father, and eat
my wild game so you can give me your blessing."

32 But Isaac asked him, "Who are you?"

Esau replied, "It's your son, your firstborn son, Esau."

33 Isaac began to tremble uncontrollably and said, "Then who just served
me wild game? I have already eaten it, and I blessed him just before you came.
And yes, that blessing must stand!"

34 When Esau heard his father's words, he let out a loud and bitter cry.
"Oh my father, what about me? Bless me, too!" he begged.

35 But Isaac said, "Your brother was here, and he tricked me. He has taken
away your blessing."

36 Esau exclaimed, "No wonder his name is Jacob, for now he has cheated
me twice.* First he took my rights as the firstborn, and now he has stolen my
blessing. Oh, haven't you saved even one blessing for me?"

37 Isaac said to Esau, "I have made Jacob your master and have declared that
all his brothers will be his servants. I have guaranteed him an abundance of
grain and wine—what is left for me to give you, my son?"

38 Esau pleaded, "But do you have only one blessing? Oh my father, bless
me, too!" Then Esau broke down and wept.

39 Finally, his father, Isaac, said to him,

"You will live away from the richness of the earth,
and away from the dew of the heaven above.
40 You will live by your sword,
and you will serve your brother.
But when you decide to break free,
you will shake his yoke from your neck."

Jacob Flees to Paddan-Aram

41 From that time on, Esau hated Jacob because their father had given Jacob
the blessing. And Esau began to scheme: "I will soon be mourning my fa-
ther's death. Then I will kill my brother, Jacob."

Question 27:36

In Genesis 32:22-32, alone in his camp, Jacob wrestled with God until daybreak. Then God changed Jacob's name to *Israel*. *Jacob* means "supplanter," or one who deceives to get his way. *Israel* means "wrestles with God" or "triumphant with God." By wrestling with God throughout his life, Jacob would undergo a total transformation of identity that would redeem his past. What wrestling do you need to do with God so that he will change your identity and redeem your past?

27:36 *Jacob* sounds like the Hebrew words for "heel" and "deceiver."

Prayer **28:16-17**

Lord, let me see your awesome presence in the places I otherwise consider ordinary. Amen.

42 But Rebekah heard about Esau's plans. So she sent for Jacob and told him, "Listen, Esau is consoling himself by plotting to kill you. 43 So listen carefully, my son. Get ready and flee to my brother, Laban, in Haran. 44 Stay there with him until your brother cools off. 45 When he calms down and forgets what you have done to him, I will send for you to come back. Why should I lose both of you in one day?"

46 Then Rebekah said to Isaac, "I'm sick and tired of these local Hittite women! I would rather die than see Jacob marry one of them."

28

So Isaac called for Jacob, blessed him, and said, "You must not marry any of these Canaanite women. 2 Instead, go at once to Paddan-aram, to the house of your grandfather Bethuel, and marry one of your uncle Laban's daughters. 3 May God Almighty* bless you and give you many children. And may your descendants multiply and become many nations! 4 May God pass on to you and your descendants* the blessings he promised to Abraham. May you own this land where you are now living as a foreigner, for God gave this land to Abraham."

5 So Isaac sent Jacob away, and he went to Paddan-aram to stay with his uncle Laban, his mother's brother, the son of Bethuel the Aramean.

6 Esau knew that his father, Isaac, had blessed Jacob and sent him to Paddan-aram to find a wife, and that he had warned Jacob, "You must not marry a Canaanite woman." 7 He also knew that Jacob had obeyed his parents and gone to Paddan-aram. 8 It was now very clear to Esau that his father did not like the local Canaanite women. 9 So Esau visited his uncle Ishmael's family and married one of Ishmael's daughters, in addition to the wives he already had. His new wife's name was Mahalath. She was the sister of Nebaioth and the daughter of Ishmael, Abraham's son.

Jacob's Dream at Bethel

10 Meanwhile, Jacob left Beersheba and traveled toward Haran. 11 At sundown he arrived at a good place to set up camp and stopped there for the night. Jacob found a stone to rest his head against and lay down to sleep. 12 As he slept, he dreamed of a stairway that reached from the earth up to heaven. And he saw the angels of God going up and down the stairway.

13 At the top of the stairway stood the LORD, and he said, "I am the LORD, the God of your grandfather Abraham, and the God of your father, Isaac. The ground you are lying on belongs to you. I am giving it to you and your descendants. 14 Your descendants will be as numerous as the dust of the earth! They will spread out in all directions—to the west and the east, to the north and the south. And all the families of the earth will be blessed through you and your descendants. 15 What's more, I am with you, and I will protect you wherever you go. One day I will bring you back to this land. I will not leave you until I have finished giving you everything I have promised you."

16 Then Jacob awoke from his sleep and said, "Surely the LORD is in this place, and I wasn't even aware of it!" 17 But he was also afraid and said, "What an awesome place this is! It is none other than the house of God, the very gateway to heaven!"

18 The next morning Jacob got up very early. He took the stone he had rested his head against, and he set it upright as a memorial pillar. Then he

28:3 Hebrew *El-Shaddai.* 28:4 Hebrew *seed;* also in 28:13, 14.

poured olive oil over it. 19 He named that place Bethel (which means "house
of God"), although it was previously called Luz.
20 Then Jacob made this vow: "If God will indeed be with me and protect
me on this journey, and if he will provide me with food and clothing, 21 and if
I return safely to my father's home, then the LORD will certainly be my God.
22 And this memorial pillar I have set up will become a place for worshiping
God, and I will present to God a tenth of everything he gives me."

Jacob Arrives at Paddan-Aram

29 Then Jacob hurried on, finally arriving in the land of the east. 2 He
saw a well in the distance. Three flocks of sheep and goats lay in an
open field beside it, waiting to be watered. But a heavy stone covered the
mouth of the well.
3 It was the custom there to wait for all the flocks to arrive before removing
the stone and watering the animals. Afterward the stone would be placed
back over the mouth of the well. 4 Jacob went over to the shepherds and
asked, "Where are you from, my friends?"
"We are from Haran," they answered.
5 "Do you know a man there named Laban, the grandson of Nahor?" he
asked.
"Yes, we do," they replied.
6 "Is he doing well?" Jacob asked.
"Yes, he's well," they answered. "Look, here comes his daughter Rachel
with the flock now."
7 Jacob said, "Look, it's still broad daylight—too early to round up the
animals. Why don't you water the sheep and goats so they can get back out
to pasture?"
8 "We can't water the animals until all the flocks have arrived," they re-
plied. "Then the shepherds move the stone from the mouth of the well, and
we water all the sheep and goats."
9 Jacob was still talking with them when Rachel arrived with her father's
flock, for she was a shepherd. 10 And because Rachel was his cousin—the
daughter of Laban, his mother's brother—and because the sheep and goats
belonged to his uncle Laban, Jacob went over to the well and moved the stone
from its mouth and watered his uncle's flock. 11 Then Jacob kissed Rachel,
and he wept aloud. 12 He explained to Rachel that he was her cousin on her
father's side—the son of her aunt Rebekah. So Rachel quickly ran and told
her father, Laban.
13 As soon as Laban heard that his nephew Jacob had arrived, he ran out
to meet him. He embraced and kissed him and brought him home. When
Jacob had told him his story, 14 Laban exclaimed, "You really are my own
flesh and blood!"

Jacob Marries Leah and Rachel

After Jacob had stayed with Laban for about a month, 15 Laban said to him,
"You shouldn't work for me without pay just because we are relatives. Tell
me how much your wages should be."
16 Now Laban had two daughters. The older daughter was named Leah,
and the younger one was Rachel. 17 There was no sparkle in Leah's eyes,* but

29:17 Or *Leah had dull eyes,* or *Leah had soft eyes.* The meaning of the Hebrew is uncertain.

Rachel had a beautiful figure and a lovely face. 18 Since Jacob was in love
with Rachel, he told her father, "I'll work for you for seven years if you'll
give me Rachel, your younger daughter, as my wife."
19 "Agreed!" Laban replied. "I'd rather give her to you than to anyone else.
Stay and work with me." 20 So Jacob worked seven years to pay for Rachel. But
his love for her was so strong that it seemed to him but a few days.
21 Finally, the time came for him to marry her. "I have fulfilled my agree-
ment," Jacob said to Laban. "Now give me my wife so I can sleep with her."
22 So Laban invited everyone in the neighborhood and prepared a wedding
feast. 23 But that night, when it was dark, Laban took Leah to Jacob, and he
slept with her. 24 (Laban had given Leah a servant, Zilpah, to be her maid.)
25 But when Jacob woke up in the morning—it was Leah! "What have you
done to me?" Jacob raged at Laban. "I worked seven years for Rachel! Why
have you tricked me?"
26 "It's not our custom here to marry off a younger daughter ahead of the
firstborn," Laban replied. 27 "But wait until the bridal week is over; then
we'll give you Rachel, too—provided you promise to work another seven
years for me."
28 So Jacob agreed to work seven more years. A week after Jacob had mar-
ried Leah, Laban gave him Rachel, too. 29 (Laban gave Rachel a servant, Bil-
hah, to be her maid.) 30 So Jacob slept with Rachel, too, and he loved her
much more than Leah. He then stayed and worked for Laban the additional
seven years.

Jacob's Many Children

31 When the LORD saw that Leah was unloved, he enabled her to have chil-
dren, but Rachel could not conceive. 32 So Leah became pregnant and gave
birth to a son. She named him Reuben,* for she said, "The LORD has noticed
my misery, and now my husband will love me."
33 She soon became pregnant again and gave birth to another son. She
named him Simeon,* for she said, "The LORD heard that I was unloved and
has given me another son."
34 Then she became pregnant a third time and gave birth to another son.
He was named Levi,* for she said, "Surely this time my husband will feel
affection for me, since I have given him three sons!"
35 Once again Leah became pregnant and gave birth to another son. She
named him Judah,* for she said, "Now I will praise the LORD!" And then she
stopped having children.

30 When Rachel saw that she wasn't having any children for Jacob, she
became jealous of her sister. She pleaded with Jacob, "Give me chil-
dren, or I'll die!"
2 Then Jacob became furious with Rachel. "Am I God?" he asked. "He's the
one who has kept you from having children!"
3 Then Rachel told him, "Take my maid, Bilhah, and sleep with her. She
will bear children for me,* and through her I can have a family, too." 4 So Ra-
chel gave her servant, Bilhah, to Jacob as a wife, and he slept with her. 5 Bilhah

29:32 *Reuben* means "Look, a son!" It also sounds like the Hebrew for "He has seen my misery." 29:33 *Simeon* probably means "one who hears." 29:34 *Levi* sounds like a Hebrew term that means "being attached" or "feeling affection for." 29:35 *Judah* is related to the Hebrew term for "praise." 30:3 Hebrew *bear children on my knees.*

Story Arc 29:32-30:24

The Twelve Tribes

The verses to follow describe Jacob's complicated family. Each one of Jacob's children (along with Joseph's two sons) would become the heads of twelve families that would comprise the nation of Israel. Eventually, as their numbers grew into the tens of thousands and more, they would be known as tribes. This is why genealogies in the Old Testament were so important. They helped people track their family heritage to Abraham and, therefore, to God's promise that he made in Genesis 15. They also become an important aspect of how God instructs Joshua to divide the promised land of Israel into livable sections based on the needs of the family groups (Numbers 32). What difference does it make that this important and dysfunctional lineage becomes a major part of Jesus' story (Matthew 1:1)?

Gen 32:28 ►

became pregnant and presented him with a son. 6 Rachel named him Dan,*
for she said, "God has vindicated me! He has heard my request and given me
a son." 7 Then Bilhah became pregnant again and gave Jacob a second son.
8 Rachel named him Naphtali,* for she said, "I have struggled hard with my
sister, and I'm winning!"
9 Meanwhile, Leah realized that she wasn't getting pregnant anymore,
so she took her servant, Zilpah, and gave her to Jacob as a wife. 10 Soon Zil-
pah presented him with a son. 11 Leah named him Gad,* for she said, "How
fortunate I am!" 12 Then Zilpah gave Jacob a second son. 13 And Leah named
him Asher,* for she said, "What joy is mine! Now the other women will cel-
ebrate with me."
14 One day during the wheat harvest, Reuben found some mandrakes
growing in a field and brought them to his mother, Leah. Rachel begged
Leah, "Please give me some of your son's mandrakes."
15 But Leah angrily replied, "Wasn't it enough that you stole my husband?
Now will you steal my son's mandrakes, too?"
Rachel answered, "I will let Jacob sleep with you tonight if you give me
some of the mandrakes."
16 So that evening, as Jacob was coming home from the fields, Leah went
out to meet him. "You must come and sleep with me tonight!" she said. "I
have paid for you with some mandrakes that my son found." So that night
he slept with Leah. 17 And God answered Leah's prayers. She became pregnant
again and gave birth to a fifth son for Jacob. 18 She named him Issachar,* for
she said, "God has rewarded me for giving my servant to my husband as a
wife." 19 Then Leah became pregnant again and gave birth to a sixth son for
Jacob. 20 She named him Zebulun,* for she said, "God has given me a good
reward. Now my husband will treat me with respect, for I have given him six
sons." 21 Later she gave birth to a daughter and named her Dinah.
22 Then God remembered Rachel's plight and answered her prayers by
enabling her to have children. 23 She became pregnant and gave birth to a son.
"God has removed my disgrace," she said. 24 And she named him Joseph,* for
she said, "May the LORD add yet another son to my family."

Jacob's Wealth Increases

25 Soon after Rachel had given birth to Joseph, Jacob said to Laban, "Please
release me so I can go home to my own country. 26 Let me take my wives and
children, for I have earned them by serving you, and let me be on my way.
You certainly know how hard I have worked for you."
27 "Please listen to me," Laban replied. "I have become wealthy, for* the
LORD has blessed me because of you. 28 Tell me how much I owe you. What-
ever it is, I'll pay it."
29 Jacob replied, "You know how hard I've worked for you, and how your
flocks and herds have grown under my care. 30 You had little indeed before I
came, but your wealth has increased enormously. The LORD has blessed you
through everything I've done. But now, what about me? When can I start
providing for my own family?"
31 "What wages do you want?" Laban asked again.

30:6 *Dan* means "he judged" or "he vindicated." 30:8 *Naphtali* means "my struggle." 30:11 *Gad* means "good fortune." 30:13 *Asher* means "happy." 30:18 *Issachar* sounds like a Hebrew term that means "reward." 30:20 *Zebulun* probably means "honor." 30:24 *Joseph* means "may he add." 30:27 Or *I have learned by divination that.*

Jacob replied, "Don't give me anything. Just do this one thing, and I'll con-
tinue to tend and watch over your flocks. 32 Let me inspect your flocks today
and remove all the sheep and goats that are speckled or spotted, along with
all the black sheep. Give these to me as my wages. 33 In the future, when you
check on the animals you have given me as my wages, you'll see that I have
been honest. If you find in my flock any goats without speckles or spots, or
any sheep that are not black, you will know that I have stolen them from you."

34 "All right," Laban replied. "It will be as you say." 35 But that very day La-
ban went out and removed the male goats that were streaked and spotted, all
the female goats that were speckled and spotted or had white patches, and
all the black sheep. He placed them in the care of his own sons, 36 who took
them a three-days' journey from where Jacob was. Meanwhile, Jacob stayed
and cared for the rest of Laban's flock.

37 Then Jacob took some fresh branches from poplar, almond, and plane
trees and peeled off strips of bark, making white streaks on them. 38 Then he
placed these peeled branches in the watering troughs where the flocks came
to drink, for that was where they mated. 39 And when they mated in front of
the white-streaked branches, they gave birth to young that were streaked,
speckled, and spotted. 40 Jacob separated those lambs from Laban's flock. And
at mating time he turned the flock to face Laban's animals that were streaked
or black. This is how he built his own flock instead of increasing Laban's.

41 Whenever the stronger females were ready to mate, Jacob would place
the peeled branches in the watering troughs in front of them. Then they
would mate in front of the branches. 42 But he didn't do this with the weaker
ones, so the weaker lambs belonged to Laban, and the stronger ones were
Jacob's. 43 As a result, Jacob became very wealthy, with large flocks of sheep
and goats, female and male servants, and many camels and donkeys.

Jacob Flees from Laban

31 But Jacob soon learned that Laban's sons were grumbling about
him. "Jacob has robbed our father of everything!" they said. "He
has gained all his wealth at our father's expense." 2 And Jacob began to notice
a change in Laban's attitude toward him.

3 Then the LORD said to Jacob, "Return to the land of your father and
grandfather and to your relatives there, and I will be with you."

4 So Jacob called Rachel and Leah out to the field where he was watching
his flock. 5 He said to them, "I have noticed that your father's attitude toward
me has changed. But the God of my father has been with me. 6 You know how
hard I have worked for your father, 7 but he has cheated me, changing my
wages ten times. But God has not allowed him to do me any harm. 8 For if he
said, 'The speckled animals will be your wages,' the whole flock began to pro-
duce speckled young. And when he changed his mind and said, 'The striped
animals will be your wages,' then the whole flock produced striped young.
9 In this way, God has taken your father's animals and given them to me.

10 "One time during the mating season, I had a dream and saw that the male
goats mating with the females were streaked, speckled, and spotted. 11 Then in
my dream, the angel of God said to me, 'Jacob!' And I replied, 'Yes, here I am.'

12 "The angel said, 'Look up, and you will see that only the streaked,
speckled, and spotted males are mating with the females of your flock. For
I have seen how Laban has treated you. 13 I am the God who appeared to you

at Bethel,* the place where you anointed the pillar of stone and made your
vow to me. Now get ready and leave this country and return to the land of
your birth.'"
14 Rachel and Leah responded, "That's fine with us! We won't inherit any
of our father's wealth anyway. 15 He has reduced our rights to those of foreign
women. And after he sold us, he wasted the money you paid him for us. 16 All
the wealth God has given you from our father legally belongs to us and our
children. So go ahead and do whatever God has told you."
17 So Jacob put his wives and children on camels, 18 and he drove all his
livestock in front of him. He packed all the belongings he had acquired in
Paddan-aram and set out for the land of Canaan, where his father, Isaac,
lived. 19 At the time they left, Laban was some distance away, shearing his
sheep. Rachel stole her father's household idols and took them with her.
20 Jacob outwitted Laban the Aramean, for they set out secretly and never
told Laban they were leaving. 21 So Jacob took all his possessions with him
and crossed the Euphrates River,* heading for the hill country of Gilead.

Laban Pursues Jacob

22 Three days later, Laban was told that Jacob had fled. 23 So he gathered a
group of his relatives and set out in hot pursuit. He caught up with Jacob
seven days later in the hill country of Gilead. 24 But the previous night God
had appeared to Laban the Aramean in a dream and told him, "I'm warning
you—leave Jacob alone!"
25 Laban caught up with Jacob as he was camped in the hill country of
Gilead, and he set up his camp not far from Jacob's. 26 "What do you mean by
deceiving me like this?" Laban demanded. "How dare you drag my daugh-
ters away like prisoners of war? 27 Why did you slip away secretly? Why
did you deceive me? And why didn't you say you wanted to leave? I would
have given you a farewell feast, with singing and music, accompanied by
tambourines and harps. 28 Why didn't you let me kiss my daughters and
grandchildren and tell them good-bye? You have acted very foolishly! 29 I
could destroy you, but the God of your father appeared to me last night
and warned me, 'Leave Jacob alone!' 30 I can understand your feeling that
you must go, and your intense longing for your father's home. But why
have you stolen my gods?"
31 "I rushed away because I was afraid," Jacob answered. "I thought you
would take your daughters from me by force. 32 But as for your gods, see if
you can find them, and let the person who has taken them die! And if you
find anything else that belongs to you, identify it before all these relatives of
ours, and I will give it back!" But Jacob did not know that Rachel had stolen
the household idols.
33 Laban went first into Jacob's tent to search there, then into Leah's, and
then the tents of the two servant wives—but he found nothing. Finally, he
went into Rachel's tent. 34 But Rachel had taken the household idols and hid-
den them in her camel saddle, and now she was sitting on them. When La-
ban had thoroughly searched her tent without finding them, 35 she said to
her father, "Please, sir, forgive me if I don't get up for you. I'm having my
monthly period." So Laban continued his search, but he could not find the
household idols.

31:13 As in Greek version and an Aramaic Targum; Hebrew reads *the God of Bethel.*
31:21 Hebrew *the river.*

Remember to take notes!

[36]Then Jacob became very angry, and he challenged Laban. "What's my
crime?" he demanded. "What have I done wrong to make you chase after
me as though I were a criminal? [37]You have rummaged through everything
I own. Now show me what you found that belongs to you! Set it out here in
front of us, before our relatives, for all to see. Let them judge between us!
[38]"For twenty years I have been with you, caring for your flocks. In all
that time your sheep and goats never miscarried. In all those years I never
used a single ram of yours for food. [39]If any were attacked and killed by wild
animals, I never showed you the carcass and asked you to reduce the count
of your flock. No, I took the loss myself! You made me pay for every stolen
animal, whether it was taken in broad daylight or in the dark of night.
[40]"I worked for you through the scorching heat of the day and through
cold and sleepless nights. [41]Yes, for twenty years I slaved in your house! I
worked for fourteen years earning your two daughters, and then six more
years for your flock. And you changed my wages ten times! [42]In fact, if the
God of my father had not been on my side—the God of Abraham and the
fearsome God of Isaac*—you would have sent me away empty-handed. But
God has seen your abuse and my hard work. That is why he appeared to you
last night and rebuked you!"

Jacob's Treaty with Laban

[43]Then Laban replied to Jacob, "These women are my daughters, these chil-
dren are my grandchildren, and these flocks are my flocks—in fact, every-
thing you see is mine. But what can I do now about my daughters and their
children? [44]So come, let's make a covenant, you and I, and it will be a witness
to our commitment."
[45]So Jacob took a stone and set it up as a monument. [46]Then he told his
family members, "Gather some stones." So they gathered stones and piled
them in a heap. Then Jacob and Laban sat down beside the pile of stones to
eat a covenant meal. [47]To commemorate the event, Laban called the place
Jegar-sahadutha (which means "witness pile" in Aramaic), and Jacob called
it Galeed (which means "witness pile" in Hebrew).
[48]Then Laban declared, "This pile of stones will stand as a witness to re-
mind us of the covenant we have made today." This explains why it was
called Galeed—"Witness Pile." [49]But it was also called Mizpah (which means
"watchtower"), for Laban said, "May the LORD keep watch between us to
make sure that we keep this covenant when we are out of each other's sight.
[50]If you mistreat my daughters or if you marry other wives, God will see it
even if no one else does. He is a witness to this covenant between us.
[51]"See this pile of stones," Laban continued, "and see this monument I
have set between us. [52]They stand between us as witnesses of our vows. I will
never pass this pile of stones to harm you, and you must never pass these
stones or this monument to harm me. [53]I call on the God of our ancestors—
the God of your grandfather Abraham and the God of my grandfather Na-
hor—to serve as a judge between us."
So Jacob took an oath before the fearsome God of his father, Isaac,* to
respect the boundary line. [54]Then Jacob offered a sacrifice to God there on
the mountain and invited everyone to a covenant feast. After they had eaten,
they spent the night on the mountain.

31:42 Or *and the Fear of Isaac.* **31:53** Or *the Fear of his father, Isaac.*

55*Laban got up early the next morning, and he kissed his grandchildren
and his daughters and blessed them. Then he left and returned home.

32 1*As Jacob started on his way again, angels of God came to meet him.
2When Jacob saw them, he exclaimed, "This is God's camp!" So he
named the place Mahanaim.*

Jacob Sends Gifts to Esau

3Then Jacob sent messengers ahead to his brother, Esau, who was living in
the region of Seir in the land of Edom. 4He told them, "Give this message
to my master Esau: 'Humble greetings from your servant Jacob. Until now
I have been living with Uncle Laban, 5and now I own cattle, donkeys, flocks
of sheep and goats, and many servants, both men and women. I have sent
these messengers to inform my lord of my coming, hoping that you will be
friendly to me.'"

6After delivering the message, the messengers returned to Jacob and re-
ported, "We met your brother, Esau, and he is already on his way to meet
you—with an army of 400 men!" 7Jacob was terrified at the news. He di-
vided his household, along with the flocks and herds and camels, into two
groups. 8He thought, "If Esau meets one group and attacks it, perhaps the
other group can escape."

9Then Jacob prayed, "O God of my grandfather Abraham, and God of my
father, Isaac—O LORD, you told me, 'Return to your own land and to your
relatives.' And you promised me, 'I will treat you kindly.' 10I am not wor-
thy of all the unfailing love and faithfulness you have shown to me, your
servant. When I left home and crossed the Jordan River, I owned nothing
except a walking stick. Now my household fills two large camps! 11O LORD,
please rescue me from the hand of my brother, Esau. I am afraid that he is
coming to attack me, along with my wives and children. 12But you prom-
ised me, 'I will surely treat you kindly, and I will multiply your descendants
until they become as numerous as the sands along the seashore—too many
to count.'"

13Jacob stayed where he was for the night. Then he selected these gifts
from his possessions to present to his brother, Esau: 14200 female goats,
20 male goats, 200 ewes, 20 rams, 1530 female camels with their young,
40 cows, 10 bulls, 20 female donkeys, and 10 male donkeys. 16He divided
these animals into herds and assigned each to different servants. Then he
told his servants, "Go ahead of me with the animals, but keep some distance
between the herds."

17He gave these instructions to the men leading the first group: "When
my brother, Esau, meets you, he will ask, 'Whose servants are you? Where
are you going? Who owns these animals?' 18You must reply, 'They belong to
your servant Jacob, but they are a gift for his master Esau. Look, he is com-
ing right behind us.'"

19Jacob gave the same instructions to the second and third herdsmen and
to all who followed behind the herds: "You must say the same thing to Esau
when you meet him. 20And be sure to say, 'Look, your servant Jacob is right
behind us.'"

Jacob thought, "I will try to appease him by sending gifts ahead of me.

31:55 Verse 31:55 is numbered 32:1 in Hebrew text. 32:1 Verses 32:1-32 are numbered 32:2-33 in Hebrew text. 32:2 *Mahanaim* means "two camps."

How God is at work here

When I see him in person, perhaps he will be friendly to me." 21 So the gifts
were sent on ahead, while Jacob himself spent that night in the camp.

Jacob Wrestles with God

22 During the night Jacob got up and took his two wives, his two servant
wives, and his eleven sons and crossed the Jabbok River with them. 23 After
taking them to the other side, he sent over all his possessions.
24 This left Jacob all alone in the camp, and a man came and wrestled with
him until the dawn began to break. 25 When the man saw that he would not
win the match, he touched Jacob's hip and wrenched it out of its socket.
26 Then the man said, "Let me go, for the dawn is breaking!"
But Jacob said, "I will not let you go unless you bless me."
27 "What is your name?" the man asked.
He replied, "Jacob."
28 "Your name will no longer be Jacob," the man told him. "From now on
you will be called Israel,* because you have fought with God and with men
and have won."
29 "Please tell me your name," Jacob said.
"Why do you want to know my name?" the man replied. Then he blessed
Jacob there.
30 Jacob named the place Peniel (which means "face of God"), for he said,
"I have seen God face to face, yet my life has been spared." 31 The sun was ris-
ing as Jacob left Peniel,* and he was limping because of the injury to his hip.
32 (Even today the people of Israel don't eat the tendon near the hip socket
because of what happened that night when the man strained the tendon
of Jacob's hip.)

Jacob and Esau Make Peace

33 Then Jacob looked up and saw Esau coming with his 400 men. So
he divided the children among Leah, Rachel, and his two servant
wives. 2 He put the servant wives and their children at the front, Leah and
her children next, and Rachel and Joseph last. 3 Then Jacob went on ahead.
As he approached his brother, he bowed to the ground seven times before
him. 4 Then Esau ran to meet him and embraced him, threw his arms around
his neck, and kissed him. And they both wept.
5 Then Esau looked at the women and children and asked, "Who are these
people with you?"
"These are the children God has graciously given to me, your servant,"
Jacob replied. 6 Then the servant wives came forward with their children
and bowed before him. 7 Next came Leah with her children, and they bowed
before him. Finally, Joseph and Rachel came forward and bowed before
him.
8 "And what were all the flocks and herds I met as I came?" Esau asked.
Jacob replied, "They are a gift, my lord, to ensure your friendship."
9 "My brother, I have plenty," Esau answered. "Keep what you have for
yourself."
10 But Jacob insisted, "No, if I have found favor with you, please accept this
gift from me. And what a relief to see your friendly smile. It is like seeing
the face of God! 11 Please take this gift I have brought you, for God has been

32:28 *Jacob* sounds like the Hebrew words for "heel" and "deceiver." *Israel* means "God fights."
32:31 Hebrew *Penuel,* a variant spelling of Peniel.

Story Arc 32:28

Jacob → Israel

Names are powerful descriptors that carry meaning and help us understand important characteristics of people, places, and things. You may have already noticed how many people in Genesis were given names related to the experiences of their parents, or you may have noticed that Abraham, Isaac, and Jacob named locations in order to describe how God was at work in those places.

In this passage, God himself deliberately gave Jacob a new name and with it a new identity (see the Question Box for Genesis 27:36). The meaning of this new name would be the defining characteristic of God's chosen people, the Israelites.

As you read the rest of the Bible, notice how the Israelites both wrestled with God and discovered that God fought their battles and brought victory to their lives.

Gen 37:2-36 ►

very gracious to me. I have more than enough.” And because Jacob insisted,
Esau finally accepted the gift.
12“Well,” Esau said, “let’s be going. I will lead the way.”
13But Jacob replied, “You can see, my lord, that some of the children are
very young, and the flocks and herds have their young, too. If they are driven
too hard, even for one day, all the animals could die. 14Please, my lord, go
ahead of your servant. We will follow slowly, at a pace that is comfortable
for the livestock and the children. I will meet you at Seir.”
15“All right,” Esau said, “but at least let me assign some of my men to
guide and protect you.”
Jacob responded, “That’s not necessary. It’s enough that you’ve received
me warmly, my lord!”
16So Esau turned around and started back to Seir that same day. 17Jacob,
on the other hand, traveled on to Succoth. There he built himself a house
and made shelters for his livestock. That is why the place was named Succoth
(which means “shelters”).
18Later, having traveled all the way from Paddan-aram, Jacob arrived safely
at the town of Shechem, in the land of Canaan. There he set up camp outside
the town. 19Jacob bought the plot of land where he camped from the family
of Hamor, the father of Shechem, for 100 pieces of silver.* 20And there he built
an altar and named it El-Elohe-Israel.*

Revenge against Shechem

34 One day Dinah, the daughter of Jacob and Leah, went to visit some of
the young women who lived in the area. 2But when the local prince,
Shechem son of Hamor the Hivite, saw Dinah, he seized her and raped her.
3But then he fell in love with her, and he tried to win her affection with
tender words. 4He said to his father, Hamor, “Get me this young girl. I want
to marry her.”
5Soon Jacob heard that Shechem had defiled his daughter, Dinah. But
since his sons were out in the fields herding his livestock, he said nothing
until they returned. 6Hamor, Shechem’s father, came to discuss the matter
with Jacob. 7Meanwhile, Jacob’s sons had come in from the field as soon as
they heard what had happened. They were shocked and furious that their
sister had been raped. Shechem had done a disgraceful thing against Jacob’s
family,* something that should never be done.
8Hamor tried to speak with Jacob and his sons. “My son Shechem is truly
in love with your daughter,” he said. “Please let him marry her. 9In fact, let’s
arrange other marriages, too. You give us your daughters for our sons, and
we will give you our daughters for your sons. 10And you may live among us;
the land is open to you! Settle here and trade with us. And feel free to buy
property in the area.”
11Then Shechem himself spoke to Dinah’s father and brothers. “Please be
kind to me, and let me marry her,” he begged. “I will give you whatever you
ask. 12No matter what dowry or gift you demand, I will gladly pay it—just
give me the girl as my wife.”
13But since Shechem had defiled their sister, Dinah, Jacob’s sons re-
sponded deceitfully to Shechem and his father, Hamor. 14They said to them,
“We couldn’t possibly allow this, because you’re not circumcised. It would

33:19 Hebrew *100 kesitahs;* the value or weight of the kesitah is no longer known. **33:20** *El-Elohe-Israel* means “God, the God of Israel.” **34:7** Hebrew *a disgraceful thing in Israel.*

be a disgrace for our sister to marry a man like you! 15 But here is a solution. If every man among you will be circumcised like we are, 16 then we will give you our daughters, and we'll take your daughters for ourselves. We will live among you and become one people. 17 But if you don't agree to be circumcised, we will take her and be on our way."

18 Hamor and his son Shechem agreed to their proposal. 19 Shechem wasted no time in acting on this request, for he wanted Jacob's daughter desperately. Shechem was a highly respected member of his family, 20 and he went with his father, Hamor, to present this proposal to the leaders at the town gate.

21 "These men are our friends," they said. "Let's invite them to live here among us and trade freely. Look, the land is large enough to hold them. We can take their daughters as wives and let them marry ours. 22 But they will consider staying here and becoming one people with us only if all of our men are circumcised, just as they are. 23 But if we do this, all their livestock and possessions will eventually be ours. Come, let's agree to their terms and let them settle here among us."

24 So all the men in the town council agreed with Hamor and Shechem, and every male in the town was circumcised. 25 But three days later, when their wounds were still sore, two of Jacob's sons, Simeon and Levi, who were Dinah's full brothers, took their swords and entered the town without opposition. Then they slaughtered every male there, 26 including Hamor and his son Shechem. They killed them with their swords, then took Dinah from Shechem's house and returned to their camp.

27 Meanwhile, the rest of Jacob's sons arrived. Finding the men slaughtered, they plundered the town because their sister had been defiled there. 28 They seized all the flocks and herds and donkeys—everything they could lay their hands on, both inside the town and outside in the fields. 29 They looted all their wealth and plundered their houses. They also took all their little children and wives and led them away as captives.

30 Afterward Jacob said to Simeon and Levi, "You have ruined me! You've made me stink among all the people of this land—among all the Canaanites and Perizzites. We are so few that they will join forces and crush us. I will be ruined, and my entire household will be wiped out!"

31 "But why should we let him treat our sister like a prostitute?" they retorted angrily.

Jacob's Return to Bethel

35 Then God said to Jacob, "Get ready and move to Bethel and settle there. Build an altar there to the God who appeared to you when you fled from your brother, Esau."

2 So Jacob told everyone in his household, "Get rid of all your pagan idols, purify yourselves, and put on clean clothing. 3 We are now going to Bethel, where I will build an altar to the God who answered my prayers when I was in distress. He has been with me wherever I have gone."

4 So they gave Jacob all their pagan idols and earrings, and he buried them under the great tree near Shechem. 5 As they set out, a terror from God spread over the people in all the towns of that area, so no one attacked Jacob's family.

6 Eventually, Jacob and his household arrived at Luz (also called Bethel)

in Canaan. 7 Jacob built an altar there and named the place El-bethel (which
means "God of Bethel"), because God had appeared to him there when he
was fleeing from his brother, Esau.
8 Soon after this, Rebekah's old nurse, Deborah, died. She was buried be-
neath the oak tree in the valley below Bethel. Ever since, the tree has been
called Allon-bacuth (which means "oak of weeping").
9 Now that Jacob had returned from Paddan-aram, God appeared to him
again at Bethel. God blessed him, 10 saying, "Your name is Jacob, but you will
not be called Jacob any longer. From now on your name will be Israel."* So
God renamed him Israel.
11 Then God said, "I am El-Shaddai—'God Almighty.' Be fruitful and
multiply. You will become a great nation, even many nations. Kings will
be among your descendants! 12 And I will give you the land I once gave to
Abraham and Isaac. Yes, I will give it to you and your descendants after you."
13 Then God went up from the place where he had spoken to Jacob.
14 Jacob set up a stone pillar to mark the place where God had spoken to
him. Then he poured wine over it as an offering to God and anointed the pil-
lar with olive oil. 15 And Jacob named the place Bethel (which means "house
of God"), because God had spoken to him there.

The Deaths of Rachel and Isaac

16 Leaving Bethel, Jacob and his clan moved on toward Ephrath. But Rachel
went into labor while they were still some distance away. Her labor pains
were intense. 17 After a very hard delivery, the midwife finally exclaimed,
"Don't be afraid—you have another son!" 18 Rachel was about to die, but with
her last breath she named the baby Ben-oni (which means "son of my sor-
row"). The baby's father, however, called him Benjamin (which means "son
of my right hand"). 19 So Rachel died and was buried on the way to Ephrath
(that is, Bethlehem). 20 Jacob set up a stone monument over Rachel's grave,
and it can be seen there to this day.
21 Then Jacob* traveled on and camped beyond Migdal-eder. 22 While he
was living there, Reuben had intercourse with Bilhah, his father's concubine,
and Jacob soon heard about it.

These are the names of the twelve sons of Jacob:

23 The sons of Leah were Reuben (Jacob's oldest son), Simeon, Levi, Judah,
Issachar, and Zebulun.
24 The sons of Rachel were Joseph and Benjamin.
25 The sons of Bilhah, Rachel's servant, were Dan and Naphtali.
26 The sons of Zilpah, Leah's servant, were Gad and Asher.

These are the names of the sons who were born to Jacob at Paddan-aram.

27 So Jacob returned to his father, Isaac, in Mamre, which is near Kiriath-
arba (now called Hebron), where Abraham and Isaac had both lived as for-
eigners. 28 Isaac lived for 180 years. 29 Then he breathed his last and died at
a ripe old age, joining his ancestors in death. And his sons, Esau and Jacob,
buried him.

35:10 *Jacob* sounds like the Hebrew words for "heel" and "deceiver." *Israel* means "God fights." **35:21** Hebrew *Israel;* also in 35:22a. The names "Jacob" and "Israel" are often interchanged throughout the Old Testament, referring sometimes to the individual patriarch and sometimes to the nation.

Make a Difference 35:19

Fruitful

When Rachel died during childbirth, she was buried on the way to Ephrath, which means "fruitful." Ephrath is also known as Bethlehem. Maybe you've heard of it? That's the very same town where Jesus would be born.

In the midst of immense challenges, God was preparing for an incredible blessing. In life, God sometimes uses hardships to accomplish some of his greatest works. Sometimes it seems that nothing good could come from the difficulties you face. Even in these times, God, who is able to do immeasurably more than you can ask or imagine, could be at work creating a bounty of blessings for you.

Difference Maker

Listen to someone talk about one of their greatest hardships, and ask God to help you see how he has made a way for fruitful blessing to come for them or for others as a result.

Descendants of Esau

36 This is the account of the descendants of Esau (also known as Edom).
2 Esau married two young women from Canaan: Adah, the daugh-
ter of Elon the Hittite; and Oholibamah, the daughter of Anah and grand-
daughter of Zibeon the Hivite. 3 He also married his cousin Basemath, who
was the daughter of Ishmael and the sister of Nebaioth. 4 Adah gave birth to
a son named Eliphaz for Esau. Basemath gave birth to a son named Reuel.
5 Oholibamah gave birth to sons named Jeush, Jalam, and Korah. All these
sons were born to Esau in the land of Canaan.

6 Esau took his wives, his children, and his entire household, along with
his livestock and cattle—all the wealth he had acquired in the land of Ca-
naan—and moved away from his brother, Jacob. 7 There was not enough
land to support them both because of all the livestock and possessions they
had acquired. 8 So Esau (also known as Edom) settled in the hill country
of Seir.

9 This is the account of Esau's descendants, the Edomites, who lived in
the hill country of Seir.

10 These are the names of Esau's sons: Eliphaz, the son of Esau's wife Adah;
and Reuel, the son of Esau's wife Basemath.
11 The descendants of Eliphaz were Teman, Omar, Zepho, Gatam, and
Kenaz. 12 Timna, the concubine of Esau's son Eliphaz, gave birth to a son
named Amalek. These are the descendants of Esau's wife Adah.
13 The descendants of Reuel were Nahath, Zerah, Shammah, and Mizzah.
These are the descendants of Esau's wife Basemath.
14 Esau also had sons through Oholibamah, the daughter of Anah and
granddaughter of Zibeon. Their names were Jeush, Jalam, and Korah.

15 These are the descendants of Esau who became the leaders of various
clans:

The descendants of Esau's oldest son, Eliphaz, became the leaders of the
clans of Teman, Omar, Zepho, Kenaz, 16 Korah, Gatam, and Amalek.
These are the clan leaders in the land of Edom who descended from
Eliphaz. All these were descendants of Esau's wife Adah.
17 The descendants of Esau's son Reuel became the leaders of the clans of
Nahath, Zerah, Shammah, and Mizzah. These are the clan leaders in the
land of Edom who descended from Reuel. All these were descendants of
Esau's wife Basemath.
18 The descendants of Esau and his wife Oholibamah became the leaders
of the clans of Jeush, Jalam, and Korah. These are the clan leaders who
descended from Esau's wife Oholibamah, the daughter of Anah.
19 These are the clans descended from Esau (also known as Edom), identified
by their clan leaders.

Original Peoples of Edom

20 These are the names of the tribes that descended from Seir the Horite. They
lived in the land of Edom: Lotan, Shobal, Zibeon, Anah, 21 Dishon, Ezer, and
Dishan. These were the Horite clan leaders, the descendants of Seir, who
lived in the land of Edom.

22 The descendants of Lotan were Hori and Hemam. Lotan's sister was named Timna.
23 The descendants of Shobal were Alvan, Manahath, Ebal, Shepho, and Onam.
24 The descendants of Zibeon were Aiah and Anah. (This is the Anah who discovered the hot springs in the wilderness while he was grazing his father's donkeys.)
25 The descendants of Anah were his son, Dishon, and his daughter, Oholibamah.
26 The descendants of Dishon* were Hemdan, Eshban, Ithran, and Keran.
27 The descendants of Ezer were Bilhan, Zaavan, and Akan.
28 The descendants of Dishan were Uz and Aran.
29 So these were the leaders of the Horite clans: Lotan, Shobal, Zibeon, Anah,
30 Dishon, Ezer, and Dishan. The Horite clans are named after their clan leaders, who lived in the land of Seir.

Rulers of Edom

31 These are the kings who ruled in the land of Edom before any king ruled over the Israelites*:

32 Bela son of Beor, who ruled in Edom from his city of Dinhabah.
33 When Bela died, Jobab son of Zerah from Bozrah became king in his place.
34 When Jobab died, Husham from the land of the Temanites became king in his place.
35 When Husham died, Hadad son of Bedad became king in his place and ruled from the city of Avith. He was the one who defeated the Midianites in the land of Moab.
36 When Hadad died, Samlah from the city of Masrekah became king in his place.
37 When Samlah died, Shaul from the city of Rehoboth-on-the-River became king in his place.
38 When Shaul died, Baal-hanan son of Acbor became king in his place.
39 When Baal-hanan son of Acbor died, Hadad* became king in his place and ruled from the city of Pau. His wife was Mehetabel, the daughter of Matred and granddaughter of Me-zahab.

40 These are the names of the leaders of the clans descended from Esau,
who lived in the places named for them: Timna, Alvah, Jetheth, 41 Oholi-
bamah, Elah, Pinon, 42 Kenaz, Teman, Mibzar, 43 Magdiel, and Iram. These
are the leaders of the clans of Edom, listed according to their settlements in the land they occupied. They all descended from Esau, the ancestor of the Edomites.

Joseph's Dreams

37 So Jacob settled again in the land of Canaan, where his father had lived as a foreigner.

2 This is the account of Jacob and his family. When Joseph was seventeen

36:26 Hebrew *Dishan,* a variant spelling of Dishon; compare 36:21, 28. 36:31 Or *before an Israelite king ruled over them.* 36:39 As in some Hebrew manuscripts, Samaritan Pentateuch, and Syriac version (see also 1 Chr 1:50); most Hebrew manuscripts read *Hadar.*

Patterns I see in this text

Patterns I see in this text

years old, he often tended his father's flocks. He worked for his half brothers,
the sons of his father's wives Bilhah and Zilpah. But Joseph reported to his
father some of the bad things his brothers were doing.
3 Jacob* loved Joseph more than any of his other children because Joseph had
been born to him in his old age. So one day Jacob had a special gift made for
Joseph—a beautiful robe.* 4 But his brothers hated Joseph because their father
loved him more than the rest of them. They couldn't say a kind word to him.
5 One night Joseph had a dream, and when he told his brothers about it,
they hated him more than ever. 6 "Listen to this dream," he said. 7 "We were
out in the field, tying up bundles of grain. Suddenly my bundle stood up,
and your bundles all gathered around and bowed low before mine!"
8 His brothers responded, "So you think you will be our king, do you? Do
you actually think you will reign over us?" And they hated him all the more
because of his dreams and the way he talked about them.
9 Soon Joseph had another dream, and again he told his brothers about
it. "Listen, I have had another dream," he said. "The sun, moon, and eleven
stars bowed low before me!"
10 This time he told the dream to his father as well as to his brothers, but
his father scolded him. "What kind of dream is that?" he asked. "Will your
mother and I and your brothers actually come and bow to the ground before
you?" 11 But while his brothers were jealous of Joseph, his father wondered
what the dreams meant.
12 Soon after this, Joseph's brothers went to pasture their father's flocks at
Shechem. 13 When they had been gone for some time, Jacob said to Joseph,
"Your brothers are pasturing the sheep at Shechem. Get ready, and I will
send you to them."
"I'm ready to go," Joseph replied.
14 "Go and see how your brothers and the flocks are getting along," Jacob
said. "Then come back and bring me a report." So Jacob sent him on his way,
and Joseph traveled to Shechem from their home in the valley of Hebron.
15 When he arrived there, a man from the area noticed him wandering
around the countryside. "What are you looking for?" he asked.
16 "I'm looking for my brothers," Joseph replied. "Do you know where they
are pasturing their sheep?"
17 "Yes," the man told him. "They have moved on from here, but I heard
them say, 'Let's go on to Dothan.'" So Joseph followed his brothers to Dothan
and found them there.

Joseph Sold into Slavery

18 When Joseph's brothers saw him coming, they recognized him in the dis-
tance. As he approached, they made plans to kill him. 19 "Here comes the
dreamer!" they said. 20 "Come on, let's kill him and throw him into one of
these cisterns. We can tell our father, 'A wild animal has eaten him.' Then
we'll see what becomes of his dreams!"
21 But when Reuben heard of their scheme, he came to Joseph's rescue.
"Let's not kill him," he said. 22 "Why should we shed any blood? Let's just
throw him into this empty cistern here in the wilderness. Then he'll die
without our laying a hand on him." Reuben was secretly planning to rescue
Joseph and return him to his father.

37:3a Hebrew *Israel;* also in 37:13. See note on 35:21. 37:3b Traditionally rendered *a coat of many colors.* The exact meaning of the Hebrew is uncertain.

Story Arc **37:2–36**

● Joseph

Joseph didn't have it easy. You can imagine the difficulty of living a life knowing your older brothers (who already had a reputation for being murderous) were jealous of you and growing in their hatred of you.

Joseph grew to learn that God had a plan to use his brothers' deceitfulness to save the entire family from an impending famine... and the entire world from an impending punishment for sin.

God often takes terrible circumstances and uses them for his redeeming purposes. Thousands of years later, the murderous and lying people of Jerusalem were jealous and growing in their hatred of Jesus, chanting the words, "Crucify him" (Luke 23:21). Remarkably, however, what people intended for evil, God intended to use as the primary way to save all people once and for all from the evil effects of sin in the world.

Exod 2:10 ▶

23 So when Joseph arrived, his brothers ripped off the beautiful robe he was
wearing. 24 Then they grabbed him and threw him into the cistern. Now the
cistern was empty; there was no water in it. 25 Then, just as they were sitting
down to eat, they looked up and saw a caravan of camels in the distance
coming toward them. It was a group of Ishmaelite traders taking a load of
gum, balm, and aromatic resin from Gilead down to Egypt.

26 Judah said to his brothers, "What will we gain by killing our brother?
We'd have to cover up the crime.* 27 Instead of hurting him, let's sell him to
those Ishmaelite traders. After all, he is our brother—our own flesh and
blood!" And his brothers agreed. 28 So when the Ishmaelites, who were Mid-
ianite traders, came by, Joseph's brothers pulled him out of the cistern and
sold him to them for twenty pieces* of silver. And the traders took him to
Egypt.

29 Some time later, Reuben returned to get Joseph out of the cistern. When
he discovered that Joseph was missing, he tore his clothes in grief. 30 Then
he went back to his brothers and lamented, "The boy is gone! What will I
do now?"

31 Then the brothers killed a young goat and dipped Joseph's robe in its
blood. 32 They sent the beautiful robe to their father with this message: "Look
at what we found. Doesn't this robe belong to your son?"

33 Their father recognized it immediately. "Yes," he said, "it is my son's
robe. A wild animal must have eaten him. Joseph has clearly been torn to
pieces!" 34 Then Jacob tore his clothes and dressed himself in burlap. He
mourned deeply for his son for a long time. 35 His family all tried to comfort
him, but he refused to be comforted. "I will go to my grave* mourning for
my son," he would say, and then he would weep.

36 Meanwhile, the Midianite traders* arrived in Egypt, where they sold
Joseph to Potiphar, an officer of Pharaoh, the king of Egypt. Potiphar was
captain of the palace guard.

Judah and Tamar

38 About this time, Judah left home and moved to Adullam, where he
stayed with a man named Hirah. 2 There he saw a Canaanite woman,
the daughter of Shua, and he married her. When he slept with her, 3 she be-
came pregnant and gave birth to a son, and he named the boy Er. 4 Then she
became pregnant again and gave birth to another son, and she named him
Onan. 5 And when she gave birth to a third son, she named him Shelah. At
the time of Shelah's birth, they were living at Kezib.

6 In the course of time, Judah arranged for his firstborn son, Er, to marry a
young woman named Tamar. 7 But Er was a wicked man in the LORD's sight,
so the LORD took his life. 8 Then Judah said to Er's brother Onan, "Go and
marry Tamar, as our law requires of the brother of a man who has died. You
must produce an heir for your brother."

9 But Onan was not willing to have a child who would not be his own heir.
So whenever he had intercourse with his brother's wife, he spilled the semen
on the ground. This prevented her from having a child who would belong
to his brother. 10 But the LORD considered it evil for Onan to deny a child to
his dead brother. So the LORD took Onan's life, too.

37:26 Hebrew *cover his blood.* 37:28 Hebrew *20 [shekels],* about 8 ounces or 228 grams in weight. 37:35 Hebrew *go down to Sheol.* 37:36 Hebrew *the Medanites.* The relationship between the Midianites and Medanites is unclear; compare 37:28. See also 25:2.

11 Then Judah said to Tamar, his daughter-in-law, "Go back to your parents' home and remain a widow until my son Shelah is old enough to marry you." (But Judah didn't really intend to do this because he was afraid Shelah would also die, like his two brothers.) So Tamar went back to live in her father's home.

12 Some years later Judah's wife died. After the time of mourning was over, Judah and his friend Hirah the Adullamite went up to Timnah to supervise the shearing of his sheep. 13 Someone told Tamar, "Look, your father-in-law is going up to Timnah to shear his sheep."

14 Tamar was aware that Shelah had grown up, but no arrangements had been made for her to come and marry him. So she changed out of her widow's clothing and covered herself with a veil to disguise herself. Then she sat beside the road at the entrance to the village of Enaim, which is on the road to Timnah. 15 Judah noticed her and thought she was a prostitute, since she had covered her face. 16 So he stopped and propositioned her. "Let me have sex with you," he said, not realizing that she was his own daughter-in-law.

"How much will you pay to have sex with me?" Tamar asked.

17 "I'll send you a young goat from my flock," Judah promised.

"But what will you give me to guarantee that you will send the goat?" she asked.

18 "What kind of guarantee do you want?" he replied.

She answered, "Leave me your identification seal and its cord and the walking stick you are carrying." So Judah gave them to her. Then he had intercourse with her, and she became pregnant. 19 Afterward she went back home, took off her veil, and put on her widow's clothing as usual.

20 Later Judah asked his friend Hirah the Adullamite to take the young goat to the woman and to pick up the things he had given her as his guarantee. But Hirah couldn't find her. 21 So he asked the men who lived there, "Where can I find the shrine prostitute who was sitting beside the road at the entrance to Enaim?"

"We've never had a shrine prostitute here," they replied.

22 So Hirah returned to Judah and told him, "I couldn't find her anywhere, and the men of the village claim they've never had a shrine prostitute there."

23 "Then let her keep the things I gave her," Judah said. "I sent the young goat as we agreed, but you couldn't find her. We'd be the laughingstock of the village if we went back again to look for her."

24 About three months later, Judah was told, "Tamar, your daughter-in-law, has acted like a prostitute. And now, because of this, she's pregnant."

"Bring her out, and let her be burned!" Judah demanded.

25 But as they were taking her out to kill her, she sent this message to her father-in-law: "The man who owns these things made me pregnant. Look closely. Whose seal and cord and walking stick are these?"

26 Judah recognized them immediately and said, "She is more righteous than I am, because I didn't arrange for her to marry my son Shelah." And Judah never slept with Tamar again.

27 When the time came for Tamar to give birth, it was discovered that she was carrying twins. 28 While she was in labor, one of the babies reached out his hand. The midwife grabbed it and tied a scarlet string around the child's wrist, announcing, "This one came out first." 29 But then he pulled back his hand, and out came his brother! "What!" the midwife exclaimed. "How did

you break out first?" So he was named Perez.* 30 Then the baby with the scarlet string on his wrist was born, and he was named Zerah.*

Joseph in Potiphar's House

39 When Joseph was taken to Egypt by the Ishmaelite traders, he was purchased by Potiphar, an Egyptian officer. Potiphar was captain of the guard for Pharaoh, the king of Egypt.

2 The LORD was with Joseph, so he succeeded in everything he did as he served in the home of his Egyptian master. 3 Potiphar noticed this and realized that the LORD was with Joseph, giving him success in everything he did. 4 This pleased Potiphar, so he soon made Joseph his personal attendant. He put him in charge of his entire household and everything he owned. 5 From the day Joseph was put in charge of his master's household and property, the LORD began to bless Potiphar's household for Joseph's sake. All his household affairs ran smoothly, and his crops and livestock flourished. 6 So Potiphar gave Joseph complete administrative responsibility over everything he owned. With Joseph there, he didn't worry about a thing—except what kind of food to eat!

Joseph was a very handsome and well-built young man, 7 and Potiphar's wife soon began to look at him lustfully. "Come and sleep with me," she demanded.

8 But Joseph refused. "Look," he told her, "my master trusts me with everything in his entire household. 9 No one here has more authority than I do. He has held back nothing from me except you, because you are his wife. How could I do such a wicked thing? It would be a great sin against God."

10 She kept putting pressure on Joseph day after day, but he refused to sleep with her, and he kept out of her way as much as possible. 11 One day, however, no one else was around when he went in to do his work. 12 She came and grabbed him by his cloak, demanding, "Come on, sleep with me!" Joseph tore himself away, but he left his cloak in her hand as he ran from the house.

13 When she saw that she was holding his cloak and he had fled, 14 she called out to her servants. Soon all the men came running. "Look!" she said. "My husband has brought this Hebrew slave here to make fools of us! He came into my room to rape me, but I screamed. 15 When he heard me scream, he ran outside and got away, but he left his cloak behind with me."

16 She kept the cloak with her until her husband came home. 17 Then she told him her story. "That Hebrew slave you've brought into our house tried to come in and fool around with me," she said. 18 "But when I screamed, he ran outside, leaving his cloak with me!"

Joseph Put in Prison

19 Potiphar was furious when he heard his wife's story about how Joseph had treated her. 20 So he took Joseph and threw him into the prison where the king's prisoners were held, and there he remained. 21 But the LORD was with Joseph in the prison and showed him his faithful love. And the LORD made Joseph a favorite with the prison warden. 22 Before long, the warden put Joseph in charge of all the other prisoners and over everything that happened in the prison. 23 The warden had no more worries, because Joseph took care of everything. The LORD was with him and caused everything he did to succeed.

38:29 *Perez* means "breaking out." **38:30** *Zerah* means "scarlet" or "brightness."

Make a Difference

39:1-6

Favored

Receiving God's favor doesn't mean a person is God's favorite. It simply means God sees their faithfulness and turns his attention toward them. Usually, someone who has found favor with God is someone who exemplifies personal integrity and faith in God's promises. Joseph found favor because he was honest in his handling of Potiphar's household and he trusted God's promise to be with him. For Joseph, being found in God's favor was part of God's plan to honor Joseph and use him to make a difference in the years to come.

This is important information for all who desire for God to use them to make a difference. You already have his favor as a follower of Jesus, but you should seek to keep yourself in a position to receive more of God's favor for his greater purposes. We do this by loving God, obeying his commands, and having full faith in his promises.

Difference Maker

Make a list of your regular responsibilities in your household and be consistent, honest, and quick to attend to them to bless your family.

Prayer **40:6**

Jesus, give me strength to act with integrity in my hardships so that I may always be able to attend to the needs of others who are also suffering. Amen.

Joseph Interprets Two Dreams

40 Some time later, Pharaoh's chief cup-bearer and chief baker of-
fended their royal master. 2 Pharaoh became angry with these two
officials, 3 and he put them in the prison where Joseph was, in the palace of
the captain of the guard. 4 They remained in prison for quite some time, and
the captain of the guard assigned them to Joseph, who looked after them.
5 While they were in prison, Pharaoh's cup-bearer and baker each had a
dream one night, and each dream had its own meaning. 6 When Joseph saw
them the next morning, he noticed that they both looked upset. 7 "Why do
you look so worried today?" he asked them.
8 And they replied, "We both had dreams last night, but no one can tell
us what they mean."
"Interpreting dreams is God's business," Joseph replied. "Go ahead and
tell me your dreams."
9 So the chief cup-bearer told Joseph his dream first. "In my dream," he
said, "I saw a grapevine in front of me. 10 The vine had three branches that
began to bud and blossom, and soon it produced clusters of ripe grapes. 11 I
was holding Pharaoh's wine cup in my hand, so I took a cluster of grapes and
squeezed the juice into the cup. Then I placed the cup in Pharaoh's hand."
12 "This is what the dream means," Joseph said. "The three branches repre-
sent three days. 13 Within three days Pharaoh will lift you up and restore you
to your position as his chief cup-bearer. 14 And please remember me and do
me a favor when things go well for you. Mention me to Pharaoh, so he might
let me out of this place. 15 For I was kidnapped from my homeland, the land
of the Hebrews, and now I'm here in prison, but I did nothing to deserve it."
16 When the chief baker saw that Joseph had given the first dream such a
positive interpretation, he said to Joseph, "I had a dream, too. In my dream
there were three baskets of white pastries stacked on my head. 17 The top
basket contained all kinds of pastries for Pharaoh, but the birds came and
ate them from the basket on my head."
18 "This is what the dream means," Joseph told him. "The three baskets
also represent three days. 19 Three days from now Pharaoh will lift you up and
impale your body on a pole. Then birds will come and peck away at your flesh."
20 Pharaoh's birthday came three days later, and he prepared a banquet
for all his officials and staff. He summoned* his chief cup-bearer and chief
baker to join the other officials. 21 He then restored the chief cup-bearer to
his former position, so he could again hand Pharaoh his cup. 22 But Pharaoh
impaled the chief baker, just as Joseph had predicted when he interpreted
his dream. 23 Pharaoh's chief cup-bearer, however, forgot all about Joseph,
never giving him another thought.

Pharaoh's Dreams

41 Two full years later, Pharaoh dreamed that he was standing on the
bank of the Nile River. 2 In his dream he saw seven fat, healthy cows
come up out of the river and begin grazing in the marsh grass. 3 Then he
saw seven more cows come up behind them from the Nile, but these were
scrawny and thin. These cows stood beside the fat cows on the riverbank.
4 Then the scrawny, thin cows ate the seven healthy, fat cows! At this point
in the dream, Pharaoh woke up.

40:20 Hebrew *He lifted up the head of.*

5But he fell asleep again and had a second dream. This time he saw seven
heads of grain, plump and beautiful, growing on a single stalk. 6Then seven
more heads of grain appeared, but these were shriveled and withered by
the east wind. 7And these thin heads swallowed up the seven plump, well-
formed heads! Then Pharaoh woke up again and realized it was a dream.

8The next morning Pharaoh was very disturbed by the dreams. So he
called for all the magicians and wise men of Egypt. When Pharaoh told them
his dreams, not one of them could tell him what they meant.

9Finally, the king's chief cup-bearer spoke up. "Today I have been re-
minded of my failure," he told Pharaoh. 10"Some time ago, you were angry
with the chief baker and me, and you imprisoned us in the palace of the
captain of the guard. 11One night the chief baker and I each had a dream, and
each dream had its own meaning. 12There was a young Hebrew man with us
in the prison who was a slave of the captain of the guard. We told him our
dreams, and he told us what each of our dreams meant. 13And everything
happened just as he had predicted. I was restored to my position as cup-
bearer, and the chief baker was executed and impaled on a pole."

14Pharaoh sent for Joseph at once, and he was quickly brought from the
prison. After he shaved and changed his clothes, he went in and stood before
Pharaoh. 15Then Pharaoh said to Joseph, "I had a dream last night, and no
one here can tell me what it means. But I have heard that when you hear
about a dream you can interpret it."

16"It is beyond my power to do this," Joseph replied. "But God can tell you
what it means and set you at ease."

17So Pharaoh told Joseph his dream. "In my dream," he said, "I was stand-
ing on the bank of the Nile River, 18and I saw seven fat, healthy cows come up
out of the river and begin grazing in the marsh grass. 19But then I saw seven
sick-looking cows, scrawny and thin, come up after them. I've never seen
such sorry-looking animals in all the land of Egypt. 20These thin, scrawny
cows ate the seven fat cows. 21But afterward you wouldn't have known it, for
they were still as thin and scrawny as before! Then I woke up.

22"In my dream I also saw seven heads of grain, full and beautiful, growing
on a single stalk. 23Then seven more heads of grain appeared, but these were
blighted, shriveled, and withered by the east wind. 24And the shriveled heads
swallowed the seven healthy heads. I told these dreams to the magicians, but
no one could tell me what they mean."

25Joseph responded, "Both of Pharaoh's dreams mean the same thing. God
is telling Pharaoh in advance what he is about to do. 26The seven healthy cows
and the seven healthy heads of grain both represent seven years of prosper-
ity. 27The seven thin, scrawny cows that came up later and the seven thin
heads of grain, withered by the east wind, represent seven years of famine.

28"This will happen just as I have described it, for God has revealed to
Pharaoh in advance what he is about to do. 29The next seven years will be
a period of great prosperity throughout the land of Egypt. 30But afterward
there will be seven years of famine so great that all the prosperity will be
forgotten in Egypt. Famine will destroy the land. 31This famine will be so
severe that even the memory of the good years will be erased. 32As for having
two similar dreams, it means that these events have been decreed by God,
and he will soon make them happen.

33"Therefore, Pharaoh should find an intelligent and wise man and put

Make a Difference

40:23–41:57

Humility

Can you imagine going from being a prisoner to being the second most powerful person in a country? A drastic change in circumstances can change you radically. Think about how you are affected when something in your plan or schedule goes wrong or surprises you. It can be tempting to react with feelings and anxieties that don't represent your identity in God. The key to maintaining your integrity in the midst of change is to remember the Lord every day. God is the one who gives and who takes away—all for his greater plan. Putting his plan above yours in every circumstance is a true act of humility.

Difference Maker

Write a letter of thanks to God and detail all your hopes and dreams. Then end it with "Your will be done." Put it somewhere you will find it in the years ahead.

him in charge of the entire land of Egypt. 34 Then Pharaoh should appoint supervisors over the land and let them collect one-fifth of all the crops during the seven good years. 35 Have them gather all the food produced in the good years that are just ahead and bring it to Pharaoh's storehouses. Store it away, and guard it so there will be food in the cities. 36 That way there will be enough to eat when the seven years of famine come to the land of Egypt. Otherwise this famine will destroy the land."

Joseph Made Ruler of Egypt

37 Joseph's suggestions were well received by Pharaoh and his officials. 38 So Pharaoh asked his officials, "Can we find anyone else like this man so obviously filled with the spirit of God?" 39 Then Pharaoh said to Joseph, "Since God has revealed the meaning of the dreams to you, clearly no one else is as intelligent or wise as you are. 40 You will be in charge of my court, and all my people will take orders from you. Only I, sitting on my throne, will have a rank higher than yours."

41 Pharaoh said to Joseph, "I hereby put you in charge of the entire land of Egypt." 42 Then Pharaoh removed his signet ring from his hand and placed it on Joseph's finger. He dressed him in fine linen clothing and hung a gold chain around his neck. 43 Then he had Joseph ride in the chariot reserved for his second-in-command. And wherever Joseph went, the command was shouted, "Kneel down!" So Pharaoh put Joseph in charge of all Egypt. 44 And Pharaoh said to him, "I am Pharaoh, but no one will lift a hand or foot in the entire land of Egypt without your approval."

45 Then Pharaoh gave Joseph a new Egyptian name, Zaphenath-paneah.* He also gave him a wife, whose name was Asenath. She was the daughter of Potiphera, the priest of On.* So Joseph took charge of the entire land of Egypt. 46 He was thirty years old when he began serving in the court of Pharaoh, the king of Egypt. And when Joseph left Pharaoh's presence, he inspected the entire land of Egypt.

47 As predicted, for seven years the land produced bumper crops. 48 During those years, Joseph gathered all the crops grown in Egypt and stored the grain from the surrounding fields in the cities. 49 He piled up huge amounts of grain like sand on the seashore. Finally, he stopped keeping records because there was too much to measure.

50 During this time, before the first of the famine years, two sons were born to Joseph and his wife, Asenath, the daughter of Potiphera, the priest of On. 51 Joseph named his older son Manasseh,* for he said, "God has made me forget all my troubles and everyone in my father's family." 52 Joseph named his second son Ephraim,* for he said, "God has made me fruitful in this land of my grief."

53 At last the seven years of bumper crops throughout the land of Egypt came to an end. 54 Then the seven years of famine began, just as Joseph had predicted. The famine also struck all the surrounding countries, but throughout Egypt there was plenty of food. 55 Eventually, however, the famine spread throughout the land of Egypt as well. And when the people cried out to Pharaoh for food, he told them, "Go to Joseph, and do whatever he tells you." 56 So with severe famine everywhere, Joseph opened up the storehouses

41:45a *Zaphenath-paneah* probably means "God speaks and lives." **41:45b** Greek version reads *of Heliopolis;* also in 41:50. **41:51** *Manasseh* sounds like a Hebrew term that means "causing to forget." **41:52** *Ephraim* sounds like a Hebrew term that means "fruitful."

and distributed grain to the Egyptians, for the famine was severe throughout the land of Egypt. 57 And people from all around came to Egypt to buy grain from Joseph because the famine was severe throughout the world.

Joseph's Brothers Go to Egypt

42 When Jacob heard that grain was available in Egypt, he said to his sons, "Why are you standing around looking at one another? 2 I have heard there is grain in Egypt. Go down there, and buy enough grain to keep us alive. Otherwise we'll die."

3 So Joseph's ten older brothers went down to Egypt to buy grain. 4 But Jacob wouldn't let Joseph's younger brother, Benjamin, go with them, for fear some harm might come to him. 5 So Jacob's* sons arrived in Egypt along with others to buy food, for the famine was in Canaan as well.

6 Since Joseph was governor of all Egypt and in charge of selling grain to all the people, it was to him that his brothers came. When they arrived, they bowed before him with their faces to the ground. 7 Joseph recognized his brothers instantly, but he pretended to be a stranger and spoke harshly to them. "Where are you from?" he demanded.

"From the land of Canaan," they replied. "We have come to buy food."

8 Although Joseph recognized his brothers, they didn't recognize him. 9 And he remembered the dreams he'd had about them many years before. He said to them, "You are spies! You have come to see how vulnerable our land has become."

10 "No, my lord!" they exclaimed. "Your servants have simply come to buy food. 11 We are all brothers—members of the same family. We are honest men, sir! We are not spies!"

12 "Yes, you are!" Joseph insisted. "You have come to see how vulnerable our land has become."

13 "Sir," they said, "there are actually twelve of us. We, your servants, are all brothers, sons of a man living in the land of Canaan. Our youngest brother is back there with our father right now, and one of our brothers is no longer with us."

14 But Joseph insisted, "As I said, you are spies! 15 This is how I will test your story. I swear by the life of Pharaoh that you will never leave Egypt unless your youngest brother comes here! 16 One of you must go and get your brother. I'll keep the rest of you here in prison. Then we'll find out whether or not your story is true. By the life of Pharaoh, if it turns out that you don't have a younger brother, then I'll know you are spies."

17 So Joseph put them all in prison for three days. 18 On the third day Joseph said to them, "I am a God-fearing man. If you do as I say, you will live. 19 If you really are honest men, choose one of your brothers to remain in prison. The rest of you may go home with grain for your starving families. 20 But you must bring your youngest brother back to me. This will prove that you are telling the truth, and you will not die." To this they agreed.

21 Speaking among themselves, they said, "Clearly we are being punished because of what we did to Joseph long ago. We saw his anguish when he pleaded for his life, but we wouldn't listen. That's why we're in this trouble."

22 "Didn't I tell you not to sin against the boy?" Reuben asked. "But you wouldn't listen. And now we have to answer for his blood!"

42:5 Hebrew *Israel's.* See note on 35:21.

Question 42:7

How would you have responded to your family in this situation? What would have been your thoughts?

23 Of course, they didn't know that Joseph understood them, for he had
been speaking to them through an interpreter. 24 Now he turned away from
them and began to weep. When he regained his composure, he spoke to
them again. Then he chose Simeon from among them and had him tied up
right before their eyes.
25 Joseph then ordered his servants to fill the men's sacks with grain, but
he also gave secret instructions to return each brother's payment at the top of
his sack. He also gave them supplies for their journey home. 26 So the brothers
loaded their donkeys with the grain and headed for home.
27 But when they stopped for the night and one of them opened his sack to
get grain for his donkey, he found his money in the top of his sack. 28 "Look!"
he exclaimed to his brothers. "My money has been returned; it's here in my
sack!" Then their hearts sank. Trembling, they said to each other, "What
has God done to us?"
29 When the brothers came to their father, Jacob, in the land of Canaan,
they told him everything that had happened to them. 30 "The man who is
governor of the land spoke very harshly to us," they told him. "He accused
us of being spies scouting the land. 31 But we said, 'We are honest men, not
spies. 32 We are twelve brothers, sons of one father. One brother is no longer
with us, and the youngest is at home with our father in the land of Canaan.'
33 "Then the man who is governor of the land told us, 'This is how I will
find out if you are honest men. Leave one of your brothers here with me,
and take grain for your starving families and go on home. 34 But you must
bring your youngest brother back to me. Then I will know you are honest
men and not spies. Then I will give you back your brother, and you may
trade freely in the land.'"
35 As they emptied out their sacks, there in each man's sack was the bag of
money he had paid for the grain! The brothers and their father were terrified
when they saw the bags of money. 36 Jacob exclaimed, "You are robbing me
of my children! Joseph is gone! Simeon is gone! And now you want to take
Benjamin, too. Everything is going against me!"
37 Then Reuben said to his father, "You may kill my two sons if I don't
bring Benjamin back to you. I'll be responsible for him, and I promise to
bring him back."
38 But Jacob replied, "My son will not go down with you. His brother Jo-
seph is dead, and he is all I have left. If anything should happen to him on
your journey, you would send this grieving, white-haired man to his grave.*"

The Brothers Return to Egypt

43 But the famine continued to ravage the land of Canaan. 2 When the
grain they had brought from Egypt was almost gone, Jacob said to
his sons, "Go back and buy us a little more food."
3 But Judah said, "The man was serious when he warned us, 'You won't see
my face again unless your brother is with you.' 4 If you send Benjamin with
us, we will go down and buy more food. 5 But if you don't let Benjamin go,
we won't go either. Remember, the man said, 'You won't see my face again
unless your brother is with you.'"
6 "Why were you so cruel to me?" Jacob* moaned. "Why did you tell him
you had another brother?"

42:38 Hebrew *to Sheol.* 43:6 Hebrew *Israel;* also in 43:11. See note on 35:21.

7 “The man kept asking us questions about our family,” they replied. “He
asked, ‘Is your father still alive? Do you have another brother?’ So we an-
swered his questions. How could we know he would say, ‘Bring your brother
down here’?”
8 Judah said to his father, “Send the boy with me, and we will be on our way.
Otherwise we will all die of starvation—and not only we, but you and our
little ones. 9 I personally guarantee his safety. You may hold me responsible
if I don’t bring him back to you. Then let me bear the blame forever. 10 If we
hadn’t wasted all this time, we could have gone and returned twice by now.”
11 So their father, Jacob, finally said to them, “If it can’t be avoided, then at
least do this. Pack your bags with the best products of this land. Take them
down to the man as gifts—balm, honey, gum, aromatic resin, pistachio nuts,
and almonds. 12 Also take double the money that was put back in your sacks,
as it was probably someone’s mistake. 13 Then take your brother, and go back
to the man. 14 May God Almighty* give you mercy as you go before the man,
so that he will release Simeon and let Benjamin return. But if I must lose
my children, so be it.”
15 So the men packed Jacob’s gifts and double the money and headed off
with Benjamin. They finally arrived in Egypt and presented themselves to
Joseph. 16 When Joseph saw Benjamin with them, he said to the manager of
his household, “These men will eat with me this noon. Take them inside the
palace. Then go slaughter an animal, and prepare a big feast.” 17 So the man
did as Joseph told him and took them into Joseph’s palace.
18 The brothers were terrified when they saw that they were being taken
into Joseph’s house. “It’s because of the money someone put in our sacks last
time we were here,” they said. “He plans to pretend that we stole it. Then he
will seize us, make us slaves, and take our donkeys.”

A Feast at Joseph’s Palace

19 The brothers approached the manager of Joseph’s household and spoke
to him at the entrance to the palace. 20 “Sir,” they said, “we came to Egypt
once before to buy food. 21 But as we were returning home, we stopped
for the night and opened our sacks. Then we discovered that each man’s
money—the exact amount paid—was in the top of his sack! Here it is; we
have brought it back with us. 22 We also have additional money to buy more
food. We have no idea who put our money in our sacks.”
23 “Relax. Don’t be afraid,” the household manager told them. “Your God,
the God of your father, must have put this treasure into your sacks. I know
I received your payment.” Then he released Simeon and brought him out
to them.
24 The manager then led the men into Joseph’s palace. He gave them water
to wash their feet and provided food for their donkeys. 25 They were told
they would be eating there, so they prepared their gifts for Joseph’s arrival
at noon.
26 When Joseph came home, they gave him the gifts they had brought him,
then bowed low to the ground before him. 27 After greeting them, he asked,
“How is your father, the old man you spoke about? Is he still alive?”
28 “Yes,” they replied. “Our father, your servant, is alive and well.” And
they bowed low again.

43:14 Hebrew *El-Shaddai.*

Things to reflect on

Make a Difference
43:34

Honoring Others

You have more power and influence than you may realize. You have the power to bless others, honor them, celebrate their existence, and enjoy their presence. When you give someone recognition for their value, skills, contributions, or personal importance, you are using your power for the benefit of other people.

When Joseph gave Benjamin five times the portion of food than the other brothers received, he was honoring Benjamin in two ways. First, he honored Benjamin as his father's youngest son, who held a special place in his father's heart. Second, after being separated for all these years, Joseph honored Benjamin as his brother, restored to him again! Joseph was telling everyone in attendance at the feast that Benjamin was the guest of honor. This act certainly elevated Benjamin's sense of worth among his other siblings.

Difference Maker

Use your words to give honor and praise to someone in a public place. This act of kindness will boost their self-esteem and encourage others to recognize this person's value too.

29 Then Joseph looked at his brother Benjamin, the son of his own mother.
"Is this your youngest brother, the one you told me about?" Joseph asked.
"May God be gracious to you, my son." 30 Then Joseph hurried from the room
because he was overcome with emotion for his brother. He went into his
private room, where he broke down and wept. 31 After washing his face, he
came back out, keeping himself under control. Then he ordered, "Bring
out the food!"
32 The waiters served Joseph at his own table, and his brothers were served
at a separate table. The Egyptians who ate with Joseph sat at their own table,
because Egyptians despise Hebrews and refuse to eat with them. 33 Joseph
told each of his brothers where to sit, and to their amazement, he seated
them according to age, from oldest to youngest. 34 And Joseph filled their
plates with food from his own table, giving Benjamin five times as much as
he gave the others. So they feasted and drank freely with him.

Joseph's Silver Cup

44 When his brothers were ready to leave, Joseph gave these instruc-
tions to his palace manager: "Fill each of their sacks with as much
grain as they can carry, and put each man's money back into his sack. 2 Then
put my personal silver cup at the top of the youngest brother's sack, along
with the money for his grain." So the manager did as Joseph instructed him.
3 The brothers were up at dawn and were sent on their journey with their
loaded donkeys. 4 But when they had gone only a short distance and were
barely out of the city, Joseph said to his palace manager, "Chase after them and
stop them. When you catch up with them, ask them, 'Why have you repaid
my kindness with such evil? 5 Why have you stolen my master's silver cup,*
which he uses to predict the future? What a wicked thing you have done!'"
6 When the palace manager caught up with the men, he spoke to them as
he had been instructed.
7 "What are you talking about?" the brothers responded. "We are your
servants and would never do such a thing! 8 Didn't we return the money we
found in our sacks? We brought it back all the way from the land of Canaan.
Why would we steal silver or gold from your master's house? 9 If you find
his cup with any one of us, let that man die. And all the rest of us, my lord,
will be your slaves."
10 "That's fair," the man replied. "But only the one who stole the cup will
be my slave. The rest of you may go free."
11 They all quickly took their sacks from the backs of their donkeys and
opened them. 12 The palace manager searched the brothers' sacks, from the
oldest to the youngest. And the cup was found in Benjamin's sack! 13 When
the brothers saw this, they tore their clothing in despair. Then they loaded
their donkeys again and returned to the city.
14 Joseph was still in his palace when Judah and his brothers arrived,
and they fell to the ground before him. 15 "What have you done?" Joseph
demanded. "Don't you know that a man like me can predict the future?"
16 Judah answered, "Oh, my lord, what can we say to you? How can we
explain this? How can we prove our innocence? God is punishing us for our
sins. My lord, we have all returned to be your slaves—all of us, not just our
brother who had your cup in his sack."

44:5 As in Greek version; Hebrew lacks this phrase.

17“No,” Joseph said. “I would never do such a thing! Only the man who
stole the cup will be my slave. The rest of you may go back to your father
in peace.”

Judah Speaks for His Brothers

18Then Judah stepped forward and said, “Please, my lord, let your servant
say just one word to you. Please, do not be angry with me, even though you
are as powerful as Pharaoh himself.

19“My lord, previously you asked us, your servants, ‘Do you have a father
or a brother?’ 20And we responded, ‘Yes, my lord, we have a father who is an
old man, and his youngest son is a child of his old age. His full brother is
dead, and he alone is left of his mother’s children, and his father loves him
very much.’

21“And you said to us, ‘Bring him here so I can see him with my own eyes.’
22But we said to you, ‘My lord, the boy cannot leave his father, for his father
would die.’ 23But you told us, ‘Unless your youngest brother comes with you,
you will never see my face again.’

24“So we returned to your servant, our father, and told him what you had
said. 25Later, when he said, ‘Go back again and buy us more food,’ 26we re-
plied, ‘We can’t go unless you let our youngest brother go with us. We’ll
never get to see the man’s face unless our youngest brother is with us.’

27“Then my father said to us, ‘As you know, my wife had two sons, 28and
one of them went away and never returned. Doubtless he was torn to pieces
by some wild animal. I have never seen him since. 29Now if you take his
brother away from me, and any harm comes to him, you will send this griev-
ing, white-haired man to his grave.*’

30“And now, my lord, I cannot go back to my father without the boy. Our
father’s life is bound up in the boy’s life. 31If he sees that the boy is not with
us, our father will die. We, your servants, will indeed be responsible for send-
ing that grieving, white-haired man to his grave. 32My lord, I guaranteed to
my father that I would take care of the boy. I told him, ‘If I don’t bring him
back to you, I will bear the blame forever.’

33“So please, my lord, let me stay here as a slave instead of the boy, and
let the boy return with his brothers. 34For how can I return to my father if
the boy is not with me? I couldn’t bear to see the anguish this would cause
my father!”

Joseph Reveals His Identity

45 Joseph could stand it no longer. There were many people in the
room, and he said to his attendants, “Out, all of you!” So he was
alone with his brothers when he told them who he was. 2Then he broke down
and wept. He wept so loudly the Egyptians could hear him, and word of it
quickly carried to Pharaoh’s palace.

3“I am Joseph!” he said to his brothers. “Is my father still alive?” But his
brothers were speechless! They were stunned to realize that Joseph was
standing there in front of them. 4“Please, come closer,” he said to them. So
they came closer. And he said again, “I am Joseph, your brother, whom you
sold into slavery in Egypt. 5But don’t be upset, and don’t be angry with your-
selves for selling me to this place. It was God who sent me here ahead of you

44:29 Hebrew *to Sheol;* also in 44:31.

Question 44:33

Years before, Judah sold his brother Joseph into slavery for his own personal gain (37:26-27), yet here we see Judah offer himself up to stay in Egypt as a slave in the place of his brother Benjamin. What do you think changed in Judah’s life to make him someone who now was willing to lay down his life for his brother? What would need to change in you before you would be willing to sacrifice yourself for someone else?

Prayer 45:5

Jesus, allow me to see your greater purposes and plans and my role in them. Amen.

to preserve your lives. 6 This famine that has ravaged the land for two years will last five more years, and there will be neither plowing nor harvesting. 7 God has sent me ahead of you to keep you and your families alive and to preserve many survivors.* 8 So it was God who sent me here, not you! And he is the one who made me an adviser* to Pharaoh—the manager of his entire palace and the governor of all Egypt.

9 "Now hurry back to my father and tell him, 'This is what your son Joseph says: God has made me master over all the land of Egypt. So come down to me immediately! 10 You can live in the region of Goshen, where you can be near me with all your children and grandchildren, your flocks and herds, and everything you own. 11 I will take care of you there, for there are still five years of famine ahead of us. Otherwise you, your household, and all your animals will starve.'"

12 Then Joseph added, "Look! You can see for yourselves, and so can my brother Benjamin, that I really am Joseph! 13 Go tell my father of my honored position here in Egypt. Describe for him everything you have seen, and then bring my father here quickly." 14 Weeping with joy, he embraced Benjamin, and Benjamin did the same. 15 Then Joseph kissed each of his brothers and wept over them, and after that they began talking freely with him.

Pharaoh Invites Jacob to Egypt

16 The news soon reached Pharaoh's palace: "Joseph's brothers have arrived!" Pharaoh and his officials were all delighted to hear this.

17 Pharaoh said to Joseph, "Tell your brothers, 'This is what you must do: Load your pack animals, and hurry back to the land of Canaan. 18 Then get your father and all of your families, and return here to me. I will give you the very best land in Egypt, and you will eat from the best that the land produces.'"

19 Then Pharaoh said to Joseph, "Tell your brothers, 'Take wagons from the land of Egypt to carry your little children and your wives, and bring your father here. 20 Don't worry about your personal belongings, for the best of all the land of Egypt is yours.'"

21 So the sons of Jacob* did as they were told. Joseph provided them with wagons, as Pharaoh had commanded, and he gave them supplies for the journey. 22 And he gave each of them new clothes—but to Benjamin he gave five changes of clothes and 300 pieces* of silver. 23 He also sent his father ten male donkeys loaded with the finest products of Egypt, and ten female donkeys loaded with grain and bread and other supplies he would need on his journey.

24 So Joseph sent his brothers off, and as they left, he called after them, "Don't quarrel about all this along the way!" 25 And they left Egypt and returned to their father, Jacob, in the land of Canaan.

26 "Joseph is still alive!" they told him. "And he is governor of all the land of Egypt!" Jacob was stunned at the news—he couldn't believe it. 27 But when they repeated to Jacob everything Joseph had told them, and when he saw the wagons Joseph had sent to carry him, their father's spirits revived.

28 Then Jacob exclaimed, "It must be true! My son Joseph is alive! I must go and see him before I die."

45:7 Or *and to save you with an extraordinary rescue.* The meaning of the Hebrew is uncertain. 45:8 Hebrew *a father.* 45:21 Hebrew *Israel;* also in 45:28. See note on 35:21. 45:22 Hebrew *300 [shekels],* about 7.5 pounds or 3.4 kilograms in weight.

Jacob's Journey to Egypt

46 So Jacob* set out for Egypt with all his possessions. And when he
came to Beersheba, he offered sacrifices to the God of his father,
Isaac. 2 During the night God spoke to him in a vision. "Jacob! Jacob!" he
called.

"Here I am," Jacob replied.

3 "I am God,* the God of your father," the voice said. "Do not be afraid to
go down to Egypt, for there I will make your family into a great nation. 4 I
will go with you down to Egypt, and I will bring you back again. You will
die in Egypt, but Joseph will be with you to close your eyes."

5 So Jacob left Beersheba, and his sons took him to Egypt. They carried him
and their little ones and their wives in the wagons Pharaoh had provided
for them. 6 They also took all their livestock and all the personal belongings
they had acquired in the land of Canaan. So Jacob and his entire family went
to Egypt—7 sons and grandsons, daughters and granddaughters—all his
descendants.

8 These are the names of the descendants of Israel—the sons of Jacob—
who went to Egypt:

Reuben was Jacob's oldest son. 9 The sons of Reuben were Hanoch, Pallu,
Hezron, and Carmi.
10 The sons of Simeon were Jemuel, Jamin, Ohad, Jakin, Zohar, and Shaul.
(Shaul's mother was a Canaanite woman.)
11 The sons of Levi were Gershon, Kohath, and Merari.
12 The sons of Judah were Er, Onan, Shelah, Perez, and Zerah (though
Er and Onan had died in the land of Canaan). The sons of Perez were
Hezron and Hamul.
13 The sons of Issachar were Tola, Puah,* Jashub,* and Shimron.
14 The sons of Zebulun were Sered, Elon, and Jahleel.
15 These were the sons of Leah and Jacob who were born in Paddan-aram, in
addition to their daughter, Dinah. The number of Jacob's descendants (male
and female) through Leah was thirty-three.

16 The sons of Gad were Zephon,* Haggi, Shuni, Ezbon, Eri, Arodi, and Areli.
17 The sons of Asher were Imnah, Ishvah, Ishvi, and Beriah. Their sister was
Serah. Beriah's sons were Heber and Malkiel.
18 These were the sons of Zilpah, the servant given to Leah by her father, La-
ban. The number of Jacob's descendants through Zilpah was sixteen.

19 The sons of Jacob's wife Rachel were Joseph and Benjamin.
20 Joseph's sons, born in the land of Egypt, were Manasseh and Ephraim.
Their mother was Asenath, daughter of Potiphera, the priest of On.*
21 Benjamin's sons were Bela, Beker, Ashbel, Gera, Naaman, Ehi, Rosh,
Muppim, Huppim, and Ard.
22 These were the sons of Rachel and Jacob. The number of Jacob's descen-
dants through Rachel was fourteen.

46:1 Hebrew *Israel;* also in 46:29, 30. See note on 35:21. **46:3** Hebrew *I am El.* **46:13a** As in Syriac version and Samaritan Pentateuch (see also 1 Chr 7:1); Hebrew reads *Puvah.* **46:13b** As in some Greek manuscripts and Samaritan Pentateuch (see also Num 26:24; 1 Chr 7:1); Hebrew reads *Iob.* **46:16** As in Greek version and Samaritan Pentateuch (see also Num 26:15); Hebrew reads *Ziphion.* **46:20** Greek version reads *of Heliopolis.*

Your thoughts can go here

Make a Difference 47:9

Leaving a Legacy

No matter what age you are, the question of what kind of legacy you want to leave behind is worth answering because it can direct the steps of your life.

Deception was the hallmark of Jacob's life until his radical wrestling match with God. Here at the end, we encounter a profoundly different man. No longer was he scheming, lying, and working the system to make his circumstances turn out in his favor. Instead, he "blessed" Pharaoh. In chapter 49, he also blessed his children. Powerfully, Jacob's lasting legacy wouldn't be as someone who spoke lies that destroyed but as someone who spoke words that gave life and built people up.

Difference Maker

What kind of legacy do you want to leave, and what actions must you take for that legacy to happen? Make a list of those legacy actions and try a couple of them out today.

23 The son of Dan was Hushim.
24 The sons of Naphtali were Jahzeel, Guni, Jezer, and Shillem.
25 These were the sons of Bilhah, the servant given to Rachel by her father,
Laban. The number of Jacob's descendants through Bilhah was seven.

26 The total number of Jacob's direct descendants who went with him to
Egypt, not counting his sons' wives, was sixty-six. 27 In addition, Joseph
had two sons* who were born in Egypt. So altogether, there were seventy*
members of Jacob's family in the land of Egypt.

Jacob's Family Arrives in Goshen

28 As they neared their destination, Jacob sent Judah ahead to meet Joseph
and get directions to the region of Goshen. And when they finally arrived
there, 29 Joseph prepared his chariot and traveled to Goshen to meet his fa-
ther, Jacob. When Joseph arrived, he embraced his father and wept, holding
him for a long time. 30 Finally, Jacob said to Joseph, "Now I am ready to die,
since I have seen your face again and know you are still alive."
31 And Joseph said to his brothers and to his father's entire family, "I will
go to Pharaoh and tell him, 'My brothers and my father's entire family have
come to me from the land of Canaan. 32 These men are shepherds, and they
raise livestock. They have brought with them their flocks and herds and
everything they own.'"
33 Then he said, "When Pharaoh calls for you and asks you about your occu-
pation, 34 you must tell him, 'We, your servants, have raised livestock all our
lives, as our ancestors have always done.' When you tell him this, he will let
you live here in the region of Goshen, for the Egyptians despise shepherds."

Jacob Blesses Pharaoh

47 Then Joseph went to see Pharaoh and told him, "My father and my
brothers have arrived from the land of Canaan. They have come with
all their flocks and herds and possessions, and they are now in the region
of Goshen."
2 Joseph took five of his brothers with him and presented them to Pharaoh.
3 And Pharaoh asked the brothers, "What is your occupation?"
They replied, "We, your servants, are shepherds, just like our ancestors.
4 We have come to live here in Egypt for a while, for there is no pasture for
our flocks in Canaan. The famine is very severe there. So please, we request
permission to live in the region of Goshen."
5 Then Pharaoh said to Joseph, "Now that your father and brothers have
joined you here, 6 choose any place in the entire land of Egypt for them to live.
Give them the best land of Egypt. Let them live in the region of Goshen. And
if any of them have special skills, put them in charge of my livestock, too."
7 Then Joseph brought in his father, Jacob, and presented him to Pharaoh.
And Jacob blessed Pharaoh.
8 "How old are you?" Pharaoh asked him.
9 Jacob replied, "I have traveled this earth for 130 hard years. But my life
has been short compared to the lives of my ancestors." 10 Then Jacob blessed
Pharaoh again before leaving his court.

46:27a Greek version reads *nine sons,* probably including Joseph's grandsons through Ephraim and Manasseh (see 1 Chr 7:14-20). **46:27b** Greek version reads *seventy-five;* see note on Exod 1:5.

[11] So Joseph assigned the best land of Egypt—the region of Rameses—to his father and his brothers, and he settled them there, just as Pharaoh had commanded. [12] And Joseph provided food for his father and his brothers in amounts appropriate to the number of their dependents, including the smallest children.

Joseph's Leadership in the Famine

[13] Meanwhile, the famine became so severe that all the food was used up, and people were starving throughout the lands of Egypt and Canaan. [14] By selling grain to the people, Joseph eventually collected all the money in Egypt and Canaan, and he put the money in Pharaoh's treasury. [15] When the people of Egypt and Canaan ran out of money, all the Egyptians came to Joseph. "Our money is gone!" they cried. "But please give us food, or we will die before your very eyes!"

[16] Joseph replied, "Since your money is gone, bring me your livestock. I will give you food in exchange for your livestock." [17] So they brought their livestock to Joseph in exchange for food. In exchange for their horses, flocks of sheep and goats, herds of cattle, and donkeys, Joseph provided them with food for another year.

[18] But that year ended, and the next year they came again and said, "We cannot hide the truth from you, my lord. Our money is gone, and all our livestock and cattle are yours. We have nothing left to give but our bodies and our land. [19] Why should we die before your very eyes? Buy us and our land in exchange for food; we offer our land and ourselves as slaves for Pharaoh. Just give us grain so we may live and not die, and so the land does not become empty and desolate."

[20] So Joseph bought all the land of Egypt for Pharaoh. All the Egyptians sold him their fields because the famine was so severe, and soon all the land belonged to Pharaoh. [21] As for the people, he made them all slaves,* from one end of Egypt to the other. [22] The only land he did not buy was the land belonging to the priests. They received an allotment of food directly from Pharaoh, so they didn't need to sell their land.

[23] Then Joseph said to the people, "Look, today I have bought you and your land for Pharaoh. I will provide you with seed so you can plant the fields. [24] Then when you harvest it, one-fifth of your crop will belong to Pharaoh. You may keep the remaining four-fifths as seed for your fields and as food for you, your households, and your little ones."

[25] "You have saved our lives!" they exclaimed. "May it please you, my lord, to let us be Pharaoh's servants." [26] Joseph then issued a decree still in effect in the land of Egypt, that Pharaoh should receive one-fifth of all the crops grown on his land. Only the land belonging to the priests was not given to Pharaoh.

[27] Meanwhile, the people of Israel settled in the region of Goshen in Egypt. There they acquired property, and they were fruitful, and their population grew rapidly. [28] Jacob lived for seventeen years after his arrival in Egypt, so he lived 147 years in all.

[29] As the time of his death drew near, Jacob* called for his son Joseph and said to him, "Please do me this favor. Put your hand under my thigh and swear that you will treat me with unfailing love by honoring this last request: Do not bury me in Egypt. [30] When I die, please take my body out of Egypt and bury me with my ancestors."

47:21 As in Greek version and Samaritan Pentateuch; Hebrew reads *he moved them all into the towns.* **47:29** Hebrew *Israel;* also in 47:31b. See note on 35:21.

So Joseph promised, "I will do as you ask."
31 "Swear that you will do it," Jacob insisted. So Joseph gave his oath, and
Jacob bowed humbly at the head of his bed.*

Jacob Blesses Manasseh and Ephraim

48 One day not long after this, word came to Joseph, "Your father is
failing rapidly." So Joseph went to visit his father, and he took with
him his two sons, Manasseh and Ephraim.
2 When Joseph arrived, Jacob was told, "Your son Joseph has come to see
you." So Jacob* gathered his strength and sat up in his bed.
3 Jacob said to Joseph, "God Almighty* appeared to me at Luz in the land
of Canaan and blessed me. 4 He said to me, 'I will make you fruitful, and I
will multiply your descendants. I will make you a multitude of nations. And
I will give this land of Canaan to your descendants* after you as an ever-
lasting possession.'
5 "Now I am claiming as my own sons these two boys of yours, Ephraim
and Manasseh, who were born here in the land of Egypt before I arrived.
They will be my sons, just as Reuben and Simeon are. 6 But any children born
to you in the future will be your own, and they will inherit land within the
territories of their brothers Ephraim and Manasseh.
7 "Long ago, as I was returning from Paddan-aram,* Rachel died in the land
of Canaan. We were still on the way, some distance from Ephrath (that is, Beth-
lehem). So with great sorrow I buried her there beside the road to Ephrath."
8 Then Jacob looked over at the two boys. "Are these your sons?" he asked.
9 "Yes," Joseph told him, "these are the sons God has given me here in
Egypt."
And Jacob said, "Bring them closer to me, so I can bless them."
10 Jacob was half blind because of his age and could hardly see. So Joseph
brought the boys close to him, and Jacob kissed and embraced them. 11 Then
Jacob said to Joseph, "I never thought I would see your face again, but now
God has let me see your children, too!"
12 Joseph moved the boys, who were at their grandfather's knees, and he
bowed with his face to the ground. 13 Then he positioned the boys in front
of Jacob. With his right hand he directed Ephraim toward Jacob's left hand,
and with his left hand he put Manasseh at Jacob's right hand. 14 But Jacob
crossed his arms as he reached out to lay his hands on the boys' heads. He put
his right hand on the head of Ephraim, though he was the younger boy, and
his left hand on the head of Manasseh, though he was the firstborn. 15 Then
he blessed Joseph and said,

"May the God before whom my grandfather Abraham
  and my father, Isaac, walked—
the God who has been my shepherd
  all my life, to this very day,
16 the Angel who has redeemed me from all harm—
  may he bless these boys.
May they preserve my name

47:31 Greek version reads *and Israel bowed in worship as he leaned on his staff.* Compare Heb 11:21. 48:2 Hebrew *Israel;* also in 48:8, 10, 11, 13, 14, 21. See note on 35:21. 48:3 Hebrew *El-Shaddai.* 48:4 Hebrew *seed;* also in 48:19. 48:7 Hebrew *Paddan,* referring to Paddan-aram; compare Gen 35:9.

and the names of Abraham and Isaac.
And may their descendants multiply greatly
throughout the earth."

17 But Joseph was upset when he saw that his father placed his right hand
on Ephraim's head. So Joseph lifted it to move it from Ephraim's head to
Manasseh's head. 18 "No, my father," he said. "This one is the firstborn. Put
your right hand on his head."
19 But his father refused. "I know, my son; I know," he replied. "Manasseh
will also become a great people, but his younger brother will become even
greater. And his descendants will become a multitude of nations."
20 So Jacob blessed the boys that day with this blessing: "The people of Is-
rael will use your names when they give a blessing. They will say, 'May God
make you as prosperous as Ephraim and Manasseh.'" In this way, Jacob put
Ephraim ahead of Manasseh.
21 Then Jacob said to Joseph, "Look, I am about to die, but God will be
with you and will take you back to Canaan, the land of your ancestors. 22 And
beyond what I have given your brothers, I am giving you an extra portion of
the land* that I took from the Amorites with my sword and bow."

Jacob's Last Words to His Sons

49 Then Jacob called together all his sons and said, "Gather around me, and I will tell you what will happen to each of you in the days to come.

2 "Come and listen, you sons of Jacob;
listen to Israel, your father.

3 "Reuben, you are my firstborn, my strength,
the child of my vigorous youth.
You are first in rank and first in power.
4 But you are as unruly as a flood,
and you will be first no longer.
For you went to bed with my wife;
you defiled my marriage couch.

5 "Simeon and Levi are two of a kind;
their weapons are instruments of violence.
6 May I never join in their meetings;
may I never be a party to their plans.
For in their anger they murdered men,
and they crippled oxen just for sport.
7 A curse on their anger, for it is fierce;
a curse on their wrath, for it is cruel.
I will scatter them among the descendants of Jacob;
I will disperse them throughout Israel.

8 "Judah, your brothers will praise you.
You will grasp your enemies by the neck.

48:22 Or *an extra ridge of land*. The meaning of the Hebrew is uncertain.

Reflect on this passage

Prayer 49:9-10

Jesus, Lion of Judah, you reign forever. Be the ruler of my life. Amen.

All your relatives will bow before you.
9 Judah, my son, is a young lion
that has finished eating its prey.
Like a lion he crouches and lies down;
like a lioness—who dares to rouse him?
10 The scepter will not depart from Judah,
nor the ruler's staff from his descendants,*
until the coming of the one to whom it belongs,*
the one whom all nations will honor.
11 He ties his foal to a grapevine,
the colt of his donkey to a choice vine.
He washes his clothes in wine,
his robes in the blood of grapes.
12 His eyes are darker than wine,
and his teeth are whiter than milk.

13 "Zebulun will settle by the seashore
and will be a harbor for ships;
his borders will extend to Sidon.

14 "Issachar is a sturdy donkey,
resting between two saddlepacks.*
15 When he sees how good the countryside is
and how pleasant the land,
he will bend his shoulder to the load
and submit himself to hard labor.

16 "Dan will govern his people,
like any other tribe in Israel.
17 Dan will be a snake beside the road,
a poisonous viper along the path
that bites the horse's hooves
so its rider is thrown off.
18 I trust in you for salvation, O LORD!

19 "Gad will be attacked by marauding bands,
but he will attack them when they retreat.

20 "Asher will dine on rich foods
and produce food fit for kings.

21 "Naphtali is a doe set free
that bears beautiful fawns.

22 "Joseph is the foal of a wild donkey,
the foal of a wild donkey at a spring—
one of the wild donkeys on the ridge.*

49:10a Hebrew *from between his feet.* **49:10b** Or *until tribute is brought to him and the peoples obey;* traditionally rendered *until Shiloh comes.* **49:14** Or *sheepfolds,* or *hearths.* **49:22** Or *Joseph is a fruitful tree, / a fruitful tree beside a spring. / His branches reach over the wall.* The meaning of the Hebrew is uncertain.

23 Archers attacked him savagely;
they shot at him and harassed him.
24 But his bow remained taut,
and his arms were strengthened
by the hands of the Mighty One of Jacob,
by the Shepherd, the Rock of Israel.
25 May the God of your father help you;
may the Almighty bless you
with the blessings of the heavens above,
and blessings of the watery depths below,
and blessings of the breasts and womb.
26 May my fatherly blessings on you
surpass the blessings of my ancestors,*
reaching to the heights of the eternal hills.
May these blessings rest on the head of Joseph,
who is a prince among his brothers.

27 "Benjamin is a ravenous wolf,
devouring his enemies in the morning
and dividing his plunder in the evening."

28 These are the twelve tribes of Israel, and this is what their father said as he told his sons good-bye. He blessed each one with an appropriate message.

Jacob's Death and Burial

29 Then Jacob instructed them, "Soon I will die and join my ancestors. Bury
me with my father and grandfather in the cave in the field of Ephron the
Hittite.
30 This is the cave in the field of Machpelah, near Mamre in Canaan,
that Abraham bought from Ephron the Hittite as a permanent burial site.
31 There Abraham and his wife Sarah are buried. There Isaac and his wife,
Rebekah, are buried. And there I buried Leah.
32 It is the plot of land and the
cave that my grandfather Abraham bought from the Hittites."

33 When Jacob had finished this charge to his sons, he drew his feet into the bed, breathed his last, and joined his ancestors in death.

50 Joseph threw himself on his father and wept over him and kissed
him.
2 Then Joseph told the physicians who served him to embalm
his father's body; so Jacob* was embalmed.
3 The embalming process took
the usual forty days. And the Egyptians mourned his death for seventy days.
4 When the period of mourning was over, Joseph approached Pharaoh's
advisers and said, "Please do me this favor and speak to Pharaoh on my be-
half.
5 Tell him that my father made me swear an oath. He said to me, 'Listen,
I am about to die. Take my body back to the land of Canaan, and bury me in
the tomb I prepared for myself.' So please allow me to go and bury my father.
After his burial, I will return without delay."
6 Pharaoh agreed to Joseph's request. "Go and bury your father, as he made
you promise," he said.
7 So Joseph went up to bury his father. He was ac-
companied by all of Pharaoh's officials, all the senior members of Pharaoh's
household, and all the senior officers of Egypt.
8 Joseph also took his entire

49:26 Or *of the ancient mountains.* 50:2 Hebrew *Israel.* See note on 35:21.

Make a Difference

50:20

God's Got This

Throughout the book of Genesis, however, there is a truthful message: no matter what a person's most evil intentions may be, no matter what Satan's most ruinous plans are, no matter how many mistakes people make, God's got this! God is able to make whatever was intended for evil turn out for good.

You can look to the pain experienced by Adam, Noah, Abraham, Isaac, Jacob, and Joseph. You can look all the way through their family line, all the way through the whole Old Testament until you get to Jesus. You can be reminded that ever since the beginning of time, God has had—and still has—the power and the desire to make good out of what sin has made bad.

Difference Maker

Who or what has cause you the greatest pain? Put your hands out with your palms up in surrender to God, and invite Jesus to somehow weave a restorative story out of that pain.

household and his brothers and their households. But they left their little
children and flocks and herds in the land of Goshen. 9 A great number of
chariots and charioteers accompanied Joseph.
10 When they arrived at the threshing floor of Atad, near the Jordan River,
they held a very great and solemn memorial service, with a seven-day pe-
riod of mourning for Joseph's father. 11 The local residents, the Canaanites,
watched them mourning at the threshing floor of Atad. Then they renamed
that place (which is near the Jordan) Abel-mizraim,* for they said, "This is a
place of deep mourning for these Egyptians."
12 So Jacob's sons did as he had commanded them. 13 They carried his body
to the land of Canaan and buried him in the cave in the field of Machpelah,
near Mamre. This is the cave that Abraham had bought as a permanent burial
site from Ephron the Hittite.

Joseph Reassures His Brothers

14 After burying Jacob, Joseph returned to Egypt with his brothers and all
who had accompanied him to his father's burial. 15 But now that their father
was dead, Joseph's brothers became fearful. "Now Joseph will show his anger
and pay us back for all the wrong we did to him," they said.
16 So they sent this message to Joseph: "Before your father died, he in-
structed us 17 to say to you: 'Please forgive your brothers for the great wrong
they did to you—for their sin in treating you so cruelly.' So we, the servants
of the God of your father, beg you to forgive our sin." When Joseph received
the message, he broke down and wept. 18 Then his brothers came and threw
themselves down before Joseph. "Look, we are your slaves!" they said.
19 But Joseph replied, "Don't be afraid of me. Am I God, that I can pun-
ish you? 20 You intended to harm me, but God intended it all for good. He
brought me to this position so I could save the lives of many people. 21 No,
don't be afraid. I will continue to take care of you and your children." So he
reassured them by speaking kindly to them.

The Death of Joseph

22 So Joseph and his brothers and their families continued to live in Egypt.
Joseph lived to the age of 110. 23 He lived to see three generations of descen-
dants of his son Ephraim, and he lived to see the birth of the children of
Manasseh's son Makir, whom he claimed as his own.*
24 "Soon I will die," Joseph told his brothers, "but God will surely come to
help you and lead you out of this land of Egypt. He will bring you back to
the land he solemnly promised to give to Abraham, to Isaac, and to Jacob."
25 Then Joseph made the sons of Israel swear an oath, and he said, "When
God comes to help you and lead you back, you must take my bones with
you." 26 So Joseph died at the age of 110. The Egyptians embalmed him, and
his body was placed in a coffin in Egypt.

50:11 *Abel-mizraim* means "mourning of the Egyptians." **50:23** Hebrew *who were born on Joseph's knees.*

Exodus Introduction

At the end of Genesis, Jacob (whom the Lord called "Israel") and his family had settled in Egypt. Those were good years, and the family increased rapidly in its numbers. After many generations, the Israelites had become so numerous and so powerful that they were threatening to overwhelm the Egyptians. Therefore, the pharaoh of Egypt forced the Israelites into harsh slavery. Unlike the pharaoh who had welcomed Jacob's family in the book of Genesis, this pharaoh was cruel to Israel. He opposed God's people, killed their babies, and oppressed them severely.

Thankfully, God wasn't done working (and never is). He called a man named Moses to stand in the gap between both cultures so that the Israelites could leave behind a life of slavery and tangibly step into all the promises God had given to their forefathers (Abraham, Isaac, and Jacob).

Exodus chronicles Israel's first "baby steps" of trusting the Lord together. Exodus is a book of growing pains as Israel learns God's name, marvels at God's abilities, hears God's commands, and throws tantrums in tired frustration. Exodus is an epic story that paves the way for a long journey of faith and salvation through life's dramatic moments, painful times, mundane routines, and hopeful future. Ultimately, Exodus is about how God plans to rescue his people through the proclamation of his Word and the Passover sacrifice he provides.

Read this book expectantly. Expect to see God. Expect to hear God. Expect to be wrecked in his presence. Then expect to see his plan of salvation.

Story Arcs

- **Moses**
- **Aaron**
- **Miriam**
- **Joshua**
- **Bezalel**
- **Oholiab**

Exodus

Question **1:17**

To whom do the midwives show more allegiance: Pharaoh or God? If you were presented with a choice today to follow the pressure of the world around you or to follow God, what do you think your tendency would be?

The Israelites in Egypt

1 These are the names of the sons of Israel (that is, Jacob) who moved to
Egypt with their father, each with his family: 2 Reuben, Simeon, Levi,
Judah, 3 Issachar, Zebulun, Benjamin, 4 Dan, Naphtali, Gad, and Asher. 5 In
all, Jacob had seventy* descendants in Egypt, including Joseph, who was
already there.

6 In time, Joseph and all of his brothers died, ending that entire genera-
tion. 7 But their descendants, the Israelites, had many children and grand-
children. In fact, they multiplied so greatly that they became extremely
powerful and filled the land.

8 Eventually, a new king came to power in Egypt who knew nothing about
Joseph or what he had done. 9 He said to his people, "Look, the people of
Israel now outnumber us and are stronger than we are. 10 We must make a
plan to keep them from growing even more. If we don't, and if war breaks
out, they will join our enemies and fight against us. Then they will escape
from the country.*"

11 So the Egyptians made the Israelites their slaves. They appointed
brutal slave drivers over them, hoping to wear them down with crushing
labor. They forced them to build the cities of Pithom and Rameses as sup-
ply centers for the king. 12 But the more the Egyptians oppressed them,
the more the Israelites multiplied and spread, and the more alarmed the
Egyptians became. 13 So the Egyptians worked the people of Israel without
mercy. 14 They made their lives bitter, forcing them to mix mortar and
make bricks and do all the work in the fields. They were ruthless in all
their demands.

15 Then Pharaoh, the king of Egypt, gave this order to the Hebrew mid-
wives, Shiphrah and Puah: 16 "When you help the Hebrew women as they
give birth, watch as they deliver.* If the baby is a boy, kill him; if it is a girl,
let her live." 17 But because the midwives feared God, they refused to obey
the king's orders. They allowed the boys to live, too.

18 So the king of Egypt called for the midwives. "Why have you done this?"
he demanded. "Why have you allowed the boys to live?"

19 "The Hebrew women are not like the Egyptian women," the midwives
replied. "They are more vigorous and have their babies so quickly that we
cannot get there in time."

20 So God was good to the midwives, and the Israelites continued to mul-
tiply, growing more and more powerful. 21 And because the midwives feared
God, he gave them families of their own.

22 Then Pharaoh gave this order to all his people: "Throw every newborn
Hebrew boy into the Nile River. But you may let the girls live."

1:5 Dead Sea Scrolls and Greek version read *seventy-five;* see notes on Gen 46:27. **1:10** Or *will take the country.* **1:16** Hebrew *look upon the two stones;* perhaps the reference is to a birthstool.

The Birth of Moses

2 About this time, a man and woman from the tribe of Levi got married.
2 The woman became pregnant and gave birth to a son. She saw that
he was a special baby and kept him hidden for three months. 3 But when
she could no longer hide him, she got a basket made of papyrus reeds and
waterproofed it with tar and pitch. She put the baby in the basket and laid
it among the reeds along the bank of the Nile River. 4 The baby's sister then
stood at a distance, watching to see what would happen to him.
5 Soon Pharaoh's daughter came down to bathe in the river, and her atten-
dants walked along the riverbank. When the princess saw the basket among
the reeds, she sent her maid to get it for her. 6 When the princess opened it,
she saw the baby. The little boy was crying, and she felt sorry for him. "This
must be one of the Hebrew children," she said.
7 Then the baby's sister approached the princess. "Should I go and find one
of the Hebrew women to nurse the baby for you?" she asked.
8 "Yes, do!" the princess replied. So the girl went and called the baby's
mother.
9 "Take this baby and nurse him for me," the princess told the baby's
mother. "I will pay you for your help." So the woman took her baby home
and nursed him.
10 Later, when the boy was older, his mother brought him back to Pharaoh's
daughter, who adopted him as her own son. The princess named him Moses,*
for she explained, "I lifted him out of the water."

Moses Escapes to Midian

11 Many years later, when Moses had grown up, he went out to visit his own
people, the Hebrews, and he saw how hard they were forced to work. Dur-
ing his visit, he saw an Egyptian beating one of his fellow Hebrews. 12 After
looking in all directions to make sure no one was watching, Moses killed the
Egyptian and hid the body in the sand.
13 The next day, when Moses went out to visit his people again, he saw two
Hebrew men fighting. "Why are you beating up your friend?" Moses said to
the one who had started the fight.
14 The man replied, "Who appointed you to be our prince and judge? Are
you going to kill me as you killed that Egyptian yesterday?"
Then Moses was afraid, thinking, "Everyone knows what I did." 15 And
sure enough, Pharaoh heard what had happened, and he tried to kill Moses.
But Moses fled from Pharaoh and went to live in the land of Midian.
When Moses arrived in Midian, he sat down beside a well. 16 Now the priest
of Midian had seven daughters who came as usual to draw water and fill the
water troughs for their father's flocks. 17 But some other shepherds came
and chased them away. So Moses jumped up and rescued the girls from the
shepherds. Then he drew water for their flocks.
18 When the girls returned to Reuel, their father, he asked, "Why are you
back so soon today?"
19 "An Egyptian rescued us from the shepherds," they answered. "And then
he drew water for us and watered our flocks."
20 "Then where is he?" their father asked. "Why did you leave him there?
Invite him to come and eat with us."

2:10 *Moses* sounds like a Hebrew term that means "to lift out."

Story Arc 2:10

● Moses

For over four hundred years, the Jewish people had multiplied into a powerful population within Egypt. The Egyptian rulers, fearful of the Israelites, began treating God's people ruthlessly. In an alarming move, the Egyptian ruler ordered the killing of the Hebrew baby boys. Moses' mother tried to hide him, but in desperation, she eventually had to launch a radical plan, which would lead to Moses being raised by the same royal family that was oppressing the Jews.

When Moses grew older, he chose to live as a Jew instead of in a life of privilege (Acts 7:22-23, 35-36; Hebrews 11:24-26). This included standing up for his people when he saw them abused and eventually becoming God's chosen representative to rescue his people.

Moses was by no means perfect. He had moments of doubt, of weakness, and of regrettable rage. Despite Moses' imperfections, in so many intentional ways, God used Moses to set the stage for Jesus. Moses worked wonders, proclaimed God's commands, and shepherded God's people to salvation. Moses spoke with God face-to-face and was transfigured. Through God's power, he controlled waters and provided food for the masses. Moses looked to the promised land, confident that God would do what he promised to do: save his people.

Exod 7:1-13 ►

Make a Difference 3:1-6

Fully Lit

As a shepherd, Moses was probably used to seeing a lot of surprising things. Even so, he probably hadn't seen a fire in a bush that didn't burn up. How long did he look at it before his brain began to register that there was something unique about this visual? This was a holy moment on holy ground. God was demonstrating his glory and his mission. He was inviting Moses to understand and participate.

Difference Maker

Right now, slow yourself down to connect with God in a holy moment. Imagine being in Moses' sandals as he looked at the bush. Imagine the moments that followed. Let the Holy Spirit fire you up for the mission he has for you.

Prayer 3:14

Lord, I'd like to get to know you for who you are. Thank you for inviting me to know you. Amen.

21 Moses accepted the invitation, and he settled there with him. In time,
Reuel gave Moses his daughter Zipporah to be his wife. 22 Later she gave birth
to a son, and Moses named him Gershom,* for he explained, "I have been a
foreigner in a foreign land."
23 Years passed, and the king of Egypt died. But the Israelites continued
to groan under their burden of slavery. They cried out for help, and their cry
rose up to God. 24 God heard their groaning, and he remembered his covenant
promise to Abraham, Isaac, and Jacob. 25 He looked down on the people of
Israel and knew it was time to act.*

Moses and the Burning Bush

3 One day Moses was tending the flock of his father-in-law, Jethro,* the
priest of Midian. He led the flock far into the wilderness and came to Si-
nai,* the mountain of God. 2 There the angel of the LORD appeared to him in a
blazing fire from the middle of a bush. Moses stared in amazement. Though
the bush was engulfed in flames, it didn't burn up. 3 "This is amazing," Moses
said to himself. "Why isn't that bush burning up? I must go see it."
4 When the LORD saw Moses coming to take a closer look, God called to
him from the middle of the bush, "Moses! Moses!"
"Here I am!" Moses replied.
5 "Do not come any closer," the LORD warned. "Take off your sandals, for
you are standing on holy ground. 6 I am the God of your father*—the God of
Abraham, the God of Isaac, and the God of Jacob." When Moses heard this,
he covered his face because he was afraid to look at God.
7 Then the LORD told him, "I have certainly seen the oppression of my
people in Egypt. I have heard their cries of distress because of their harsh
slave drivers. Yes, I am aware of their suffering. 8 So I have come down to
rescue them from the power of the Egyptians and lead them out of Egypt
into their own fertile and spacious land. It is a land flowing with milk and
honey—the land where the Canaanites, Hittites, Amorites, Perizzites,
Hivites, and Jebusites now live. 9 Look! The cry of the people of Israel has
reached me, and I have seen how harshly the Egyptians abuse them. 10 Now
go, for I am sending you to Pharaoh. You must lead my people Israel out of
Egypt."
11 But Moses protested to God, "Who am I to appear before Pharaoh? Who
am I to lead the people of Israel out of Egypt?"
12 God answered, "I will be with you. And this is your sign that I am the
one who has sent you: When you have brought the people out of Egypt, you
will worship God at this very mountain."
13 But Moses protested, "If I go to the people of Israel and tell them, 'The
God of your ancestors has sent me to you,' they will ask me, 'What is his
name?' Then what should I tell them?"
14 God replied to Moses, "I AM WHO I AM.* Say this to the people of Israel:
I AM has sent me to you." 15 God also said to Moses, "Say this to the people of
Israel: Yahweh,* the God of your ancestors—the God of Abraham, the God
of Isaac, and the God of Jacob—has sent me to you.

2:22 *Gershom* sounds like a Hebrew term that means "a foreigner there." 2:25 Or *and acknowledged his obligation to help them.* 3:1a Moses' father-in-law went by two names, Jethro and Reuel. 3:1b Hebrew *Horeb,* another name for Sinai. 3:6 Greek version reads *your fathers.* 3:14 Or *I WILL BE WHAT I WILL BE.* 3:15 *Yahweh* (also in 3:16) is a transliteration of the proper name *YHWH* that is sometimes rendered "Jehovah"; in this translation it is usually rendered "the LORD" (note the use of small capitals).

This is my eternal name,
my name to remember for all generations.

16"Now go and call together all the elders of Israel. Tell them, 'Yahweh, the
God of your ancestors—the God of Abraham, Isaac, and Jacob—has appeared
to me. He told me, "I have been watching closely, and I see how the Egyptians
are treating you. 17 I have promised to rescue you from your oppression in
Egypt. I will lead you to a land flowing with milk and honey—the land where
the Canaanites, Hittites, Amorites, Perizzites, Hivites, and Jebusites now live."'
18"The elders of Israel will accept your message. Then you and the elders
must go to the king of Egypt and tell him, 'The LORD, the God of the He-
brews, has met with us. So please let us take a three-day journey into the
wilderness to offer sacrifices to the LORD, our God.'
19"But I know that the king of Egypt will not let you go unless a mighty
hand forces him.* 20 So I will raise my hand and strike the Egyptians, perform-
ing all kinds of miracles among them. Then at last he will let you go. 21 And
I will cause the Egyptians to look favorably on you. They will give you gifts
when you go so you will not leave empty-handed. 22 Every Israelite woman
will ask for articles of silver and gold and fine clothing from her Egyptian
neighbors and from the foreign women in their houses. You will dress your
sons and daughters with these, stripping the Egyptians of their wealth."

Signs of the LORD's Power

4 But Moses protested again, "What if they won't believe me or listen to
me? What if they say, 'The LORD never appeared to you'?"
2 Then the LORD asked him, "What is that in your hand?"
"A shepherd's staff," Moses replied.
3"Throw it down on the ground," the LORD told him. So Moses threw
down the staff, and it turned into a snake! Moses jumped back.
4 Then the LORD told him, "Reach out and grab its tail." So Moses reached
out and grabbed it, and it turned back into a shepherd's staff in his hand.
5"Perform this sign," the LORD told him. "Then they will believe that the
LORD, the God of their ancestors—the God of Abraham, the God of Isaac,
and the God of Jacob—really has appeared to you."
6 Then the LORD said to Moses, "Now put your hand inside your cloak." So
Moses put his hand inside his cloak, and when he took it out again, his hand
was white as snow with a severe skin disease.* 7"Now put your hand back
into your cloak," the LORD said. So Moses put his hand back in, and when
he took it out again, it was as healthy as the rest of his body.
8 The LORD said to Moses, "If they do not believe you and are not convinced
by the first miraculous sign, they will be convinced by the second sign. 9 And
if they don't believe you or listen to you even after these two signs, then take
some water from the Nile River and pour it out on the dry ground. When you
do, the water from the Nile will turn to blood on the ground."
10 But Moses pleaded with the LORD, "O Lord, I'm not very good with
words. I never have been, and I'm not now, even though you have spoken to
me. I get tongue-tied, and my words get tangled."
11 Then the LORD asked Moses, "Who makes a person's mouth? Who de-
cides whether people speak or do not speak, hear or do not hear, see or do

3:19 As in Greek and Latin versions; Hebrew reads *will not let you go, not by a mighty hand.*
4:6 Or *with leprosy.* The Hebrew word used here can describe various skin diseases.

Question **4:3**

Even in the presence of God, Moses was still startled by the snake. What profound lessons can you draw from where Moses put his focus?

Make a Difference

4:1–17

Mumbling Truth

We all need to be called out, don't we? Moses believed he wouldn't be able to speak well on God's behalf because he didn't see himself as qualified for the job. Keep in mind that he was well studied in all the wisdom of the Egyptians (Acts 7:22). Sadly now, for whatever reasons, Moses felt like he fell short. It could be that forty years of speaking to sheep all day had made him lose his confidence with people, or perhaps he had become intimidated by how wise and confident his old Egyptian leaders and peers were.

When insecurity hits, you might tend to mumble or stutter your way through your anxiety, but remember this amazing truth: you are qualified because God has called you. Your greatest ability is your availability to let God work in you. Clear your throat, take a deep breath, and speak out what he has put on your heart.

Difference Maker

Find a quiet space and listen to God speaking to you. Write down what the Lord instructs you to do. Pray for boldness to trust him.

Question **4:20**

God used an ordinary shepherding tool to do something extraordinary. What has God put in your hands that he could use?

not see? Is it not I, the LORD? [12]Now go! I will be with you as you speak, and I will instruct you in what to say."

[13]But Moses again pleaded, "Lord, please! Send anyone else."

[14]Then the LORD became angry with Moses. "All right," he said. "What about your brother, Aaron the Levite? I know he speaks well. And look! He is on his way to meet you now. He will be delighted to see you. [15]Talk to him, and put the words in his mouth. I will be with both of you as you speak, and I will instruct you both in what to do. [16]Aaron will be your spokesman to the people. He will be your mouthpiece, and you will stand in the place of God for him, telling him what to say. [17]And take your shepherd's staff with you, and use it to perform the miraculous signs I have shown you."

Moses Returns to Egypt

[18]So Moses went back home to Jethro, his father-in-law. "Please let me return to my relatives in Egypt," Moses said. "I don't even know if they are still alive."

"Go in peace," Jethro replied.

[19]Before Moses left Midian, the LORD said to him, "Return to Egypt, for all those who wanted to kill you have died."

[20]So Moses took his wife and sons, put them on a donkey, and headed back to the land of Egypt. In his hand he carried the staff of God.

[21]And the LORD told Moses, "When you arrive back in Egypt, go to Pharaoh and perform all the miracles I have empowered you to do. But I will harden his heart so he will refuse to let the people go. [22]Then you will tell him, 'This is what the LORD says: Israel is my firstborn son. [23]I commanded you, "Let my son go, so he can worship me." But since you have refused, I will now kill your firstborn son!'"

[24]On the way to Egypt, at a place where Moses and his family had stopped for the night, the LORD confronted him and was about to kill him. [25]But Moses' wife, Zipporah, took a flint knife and circumcised her son. She touched his feet* with the foreskin and said, "Now you are a bridegroom of blood to me." [26](When she said "a bridegroom of blood," she was referring to the circumcision.) After that, the LORD left him alone.

[27]Now the LORD had said to Aaron, "Go out into the wilderness to meet Moses." So Aaron went and met Moses at the mountain of God, and he embraced him. [28]Moses then told Aaron everything the LORD had commanded him to say. And he told him about the miraculous signs the LORD had commanded him to perform.

[29]Then Moses and Aaron returned to Egypt and called all the elders of Israel together. [30]Aaron told them everything the LORD had told Moses, and Moses performed the miraculous signs as they watched. [31]Then the people of Israel were convinced that the LORD had sent Moses and Aaron. When they heard that the LORD was concerned about them and had seen their misery, they bowed down and worshiped.

Moses and Aaron Speak to Pharaoh

5 After this presentation to Israel's leaders, Moses and Aaron went and spoke to Pharaoh. They told him, "This is what the LORD, the God of Israel, says: Let my people go so they may hold a festival in my honor in the wilderness."

4:25 The Hebrew word for "feet" may refer here to the male sex organ.

2 “Is that so?” retorted Pharaoh. “And who is the LORD? Why should I listen
to him and let Israel go? I don’t know the LORD, and I will not let Israel go.”
3 But Aaron and Moses persisted. “The God of the Hebrews has met with
us,” they declared. “So let us take a three-day journey into the wilderness so
we can offer sacrifices to the LORD our God. If we don’t, he will kill us with
a plague or with the sword.”
4 Pharaoh replied, “Moses and Aaron, why are you distracting the people
from their tasks? Get back to work! 5 Look, there are many of your people in
the land, and you are stopping them from their work.”

Question 5:2

Who is the Lord? Pharaoh’s question is the ultimate question that every human must deal with. Imagine being asked this question. How would you answer?

Making Bricks without Straw

6 That same day Pharaoh sent this order to the Egyptian slave drivers and
the Israelite foremen: 7 “Do not supply any more straw for making bricks.
Make the people get it themselves! 8 But still require them to make the same
number of bricks as before. Don’t reduce the quota. They are lazy. That’s
why they are crying out, ‘Let us go and offer sacrifices to our God.’ 9 Load
them down with more work. Make them sweat! That will teach them to
listen to lies!”
10 So the slave drivers and foremen went out and told the people: “This is
what Pharaoh says: I will not provide any more straw for you. 11 Go and get
it yourselves. Find it wherever you can. But you must produce just as many
bricks as before!” 12 So the people scattered throughout the land of Egypt in
search of stubble to use as straw.
13 Meanwhile, the Egyptian slave drivers continued to push hard. “Meet
your daily quota of bricks, just as you did when we provided you with straw!”
they demanded. 14 Then they whipped the Israelite foremen they had put in
charge of the work crews. “Why haven’t you met your quotas either yesterday
or today?” they demanded.
15 So the Israelite foremen went to Pharaoh and pleaded with him. “Please
don’t treat your servants like this,” they begged. 16 “We are given no straw,
but the slave drivers still demand, ‘Make bricks!’ We are being beaten, but
it isn’t our fault! Your own people are to blame!”
17 But Pharaoh shouted, “You’re just lazy! Lazy! That’s why you’re saying,
‘Let us go and offer sacrifices to the LORD.’ 18 Now get back to work! No straw
will be given to you, but you must still produce the full quota of bricks.”
19 The Israelite foremen could see that they were in serious trouble when
they were told, “You must not reduce the number of bricks you make each
day.” 20 As they left Pharaoh’s court, they confronted Moses and Aaron, who
were waiting outside for them. 21 The foremen said to them, “May the LORD
judge and punish you for making us stink before Pharaoh and his officials.
You have put a sword into their hands, an excuse to kill us!”
22 Then Moses went back to the LORD and protested, “Why have you
brought all this trouble on your own people, Lord? Why did you send me?
23 Ever since I came to Pharaoh as your spokesman, he has been even more
brutal to your people. And you have done nothing to rescue them!”

Promises of Deliverance

6 Then the LORD told Moses, “Now you will see what I will do to Pharaoh.
When he feels the force of my strong hand, he will let the people go. In
fact, he will force them to leave his land!”

Prayer **6:12**

Lord, it is surprising to see Moses feel so inadequate here. So many people have this same feeling of not being good enough. Even so, you used Moses mightily because you called him to do your will. Would you show me that no matter how I feel, you can do infinitely more than I can ask or imagine? Amen.

2 And God said to Moses, "I am Yahweh—'the LORD.'* 3 I appeared to Abra-
ham, to Isaac, and to Jacob as El-Shaddai—'God Almighty'*—but I did not
reveal my name, Yahweh, to them. 4 And I reaffirmed my covenant with
them. Under its terms, I promised to give them the land of Canaan, where
they were living as foreigners. 5 You can be sure that I have heard the groans
of the people of Israel, who are now slaves to the Egyptians. And I am well
aware of my covenant with them.

6 "Therefore, say to the people of Israel: 'I am the LORD. I will free you
from your oppression and will rescue you from your slavery in Egypt. I will
redeem you with a powerful arm and great acts of judgment. 7 I will claim
you as my own people, and I will be your God. Then you will know that I am
the LORD your God who has freed you from your oppression in Egypt. 8 I will
bring you into the land I swore to give to Abraham, Isaac, and Jacob. I will
give it to you as your very own possession. I am the LORD!'"

9 So Moses told the people of Israel what the LORD had said, but they re-
fused to listen anymore. They had become too discouraged by the brutality
of their slavery.

10 Then the LORD said to Moses, 11 "Go back to Pharaoh, the king of Egypt,
and tell him to let the people of Israel leave his country."

12 "But LORD!" Moses objected. "My own people won't listen to me any-
more. How can I expect Pharaoh to listen? I'm such a clumsy speaker!*"

13 But the LORD spoke to Moses and Aaron and gave them orders for the
Israelites and for Pharaoh, the king of Egypt. The LORD commanded Moses
and Aaron to lead the people of Israel out of Egypt.

The Ancestors of Moses and Aaron

14 These are the ancestors of some of the clans of Israel:

The sons of Reuben, Israel's oldest son, were Hanoch, Pallu, Hezron, and Carmi. Their descendants became the clans of Reuben.

15 The sons of Simeon were Jemuel, Jamin, Ohad, Jakin, Zohar, and Shaul. (Shaul's mother was a Canaanite woman.) Their descendants became the clans of Simeon.

16 These are the descendants of Levi, as listed in their family records:

The sons of Levi were Gershon, Kohath, and Merari. (Levi lived to be 137 years old.)

17 The descendants of Gershon included Libni and Shimei, each of whom became the ancestor of a clan.

18 The descendants of Kohath included Amram, Izhar, Hebron, and Uzziel. (Kohath lived to be 133 years old.)

19 The descendants of Merari included Mahli and Mushi.

These are the clans of the Levites, as listed in their family records.

20 Amram married his father's sister Jochebed, and she gave birth to his sons, Aaron and Moses. (Amram lived to be 137 years old.)

21 The sons of Izhar were Korah, Nepheg, and Zicri.

6:2 *Yahweh* is a transliteration of the proper name *YHWH* that is sometimes rendered "Jehovah"; in this translation it is usually rendered "the LORD" (note the use of small capitals). 6:3 *El-Shaddai,* which means "God Almighty," is the name for God used in Gen 17:1; 28:3; 35:11; 43:14; 48:3. 6:12 Hebrew *I have uncircumcised lips;* also in 6:30.

22 The sons of Uzziel were Mishael, Elzaphan, and Sithri.
23 Aaron married Elisheba, the daughter of Amminadab and sister of Nahshon, and she gave birth to his sons, Nadab, Abihu, Eleazar, and Ithamar.
24 The sons of Korah were Assir, Elkanah, and Abiasaph. Their descendants became the clans of Korah.
25 Eleazar son of Aaron married one of the daughters of Putiel, and she gave birth to his son, Phinehas.
These are the ancestors of the Levite families, listed according to their clans.

26 The Aaron and Moses named in this list are the same ones to whom the
LORD said, "Lead the people of Israel out of the land of Egypt like an army."
27 It was Moses and Aaron who spoke to Pharaoh, the king of Egypt, about
leading the people of Israel out of Egypt.
28 When the LORD spoke to Moses in the land of Egypt, 29 he said to him, "I
am the LORD! Tell Pharaoh, the king of Egypt, everything I am telling you."
30 But Moses argued with the LORD, saying, "I can't do it! I'm such a clumsy
speaker! Why should Pharaoh listen to me?"

Aaron's Staff Becomes a Serpent

7 Then the LORD said to Moses, "Pay close attention to this. I will make
you seem like God to Pharaoh, and your brother, Aaron, will be your
prophet. 2 Tell Aaron everything I command you, and Aaron must command
Pharaoh to let the people of Israel leave his country. 3 But I will make Pha-
raoh's heart stubborn so I can multiply my miraculous signs and wonders
in the land of Egypt. 4 Even then Pharaoh will refuse to listen to you. So I
will bring down my fist on Egypt. Then I will rescue my forces—my people,
the Israelites—from the land of Egypt with great acts of judgment. 5 When
I raise my powerful hand and bring out the Israelites, the Egyptians will
know that I am the LORD."
6 So Moses and Aaron did just as the LORD had commanded them. 7 Moses
was eighty years old, and Aaron was eighty-three when they made their de-
mands to Pharaoh.
8 Then the LORD said to Moses and Aaron, 9 "Pharaoh will demand, 'Show
me a miracle.' When he does this, say to Aaron, 'Take your staff and throw it
down in front of Pharaoh, and it will become a serpent.*'"
10 So Moses and Aaron went to Pharaoh and did what the LORD had com-
manded them. Aaron threw down his staff before Pharaoh and his officials,
and it became a serpent! 11 Then Pharaoh called in his own wise men and
sorcerers, and these Egyptian magicians did the same thing with their magic.
12 They threw down their staffs, which also became serpents! But then Aaron's
staff swallowed up their staffs. 13 Pharaoh's heart, however, remained hard.
He still refused to listen, just as the LORD had predicted.

A Plague of Blood

14 Then the LORD said to Moses, "Pharaoh's heart is stubborn,* and he still
refuses to let the people go. 15 So go to Pharaoh in the morning as he goes
down to the river. Stand on the bank of the Nile and meet him there. Be sure
to take along the staff that turned into a snake. 16 Then announce to him, 'The

7:9 Hebrew *tannin,* which elsewhere refers to a sea monster. Greek version translates it "dragon." 7:14 Hebrew *heavy.*

Prayer **7:7**

Lord, I want to serve you, trust you, and make a difference for you no matter how young or old I am. Prepare me for what's ahead as I get to know you better today. Amen.

Story Arc **7:1-13**

Aaron

Aaron might, at first glance, seem to be God's plan B. God had asked Moses to speak to Pharaoh. When Moses kept worrying and arguing about his insecurities, God instructed Aaron to support his brother (4:16). Still the Lord had intended all along to invite Aaron into the inner circle of history.

Sadly, Aaron was not always a consistent leader. He actually did a number of horrible things, like the time he created a golden calf for everyone to worship (Exodus 32) and the time he foolishly led a mutiny against Moses (Numbers 12).

The Lord still used Aaron's presence to spread the message Moses shared. God also used Aaron to explain how God's people should follow the Lord. His role as the first high priest in the tabernacle helped the people deal with their sins. This religious system pointed to how God would forgive sin through sacrifices—something that Jesus would later fulfill in becoming the once-and-for-all sacrifice on the cross (Hebrews 4:15; 7:27).

Exod 15:20-21 ►

LORD, the God of the Hebrews, has sent me to tell you, "Let my people go, so
they can worship me in the wilderness." Until now, you have refused to listen
to him. 17 So this is what the LORD says: "I will show you that I am the LORD."
Look! I will strike the water of the Nile with this staff in my hand, and the
river will turn to blood. 18 The fish in it will die, and the river will stink. The
Egyptians will not be able to drink any water from the Nile.'"

19 Then the LORD said to Moses: "Tell Aaron, 'Take your staff and raise
your hand over the waters of Egypt—all its rivers, canals, ponds, and all
the reservoirs. Turn all the water to blood. Everywhere in Egypt the water
will turn to blood, even the water stored in wooden bowls and stone pots.'"

20 So Moses and Aaron did just as the LORD commanded them. As Pha-
raoh and all of his officials watched, Aaron raised his staff and struck the
water of the Nile. Suddenly, the whole river turned to blood! 21 The fish in the
river died, and the water became so foul that the Egyptians couldn't drink it.
There was blood everywhere throughout the land of Egypt. 22 But again the
magicians of Egypt used their magic, and they, too, turned water into blood.
So Pharaoh's heart remained hard. He refused to listen to Moses and Aaron,
just as the LORD had predicted. 23 Pharaoh returned to his palace and put the
whole thing out of his mind. 24 Then all the Egyptians dug along the river-
bank to find drinking water, for they couldn't drink the water from the Nile.

25 Seven days passed from the time the LORD struck the Nile.

A Plague of Frogs

8 1* Then the LORD said to Moses, "Go back to Pharaoh and announce to
him, 'This is what the LORD says: Let my people go, so they can worship
me. 2 If you refuse to let them go, I will send a plague of frogs across your
entire land. 3 The Nile River will swarm with frogs. They will come up out of
the river and into your palace, even into your bedroom and onto your bed!
They will enter the houses of your officials and your people. They will even
jump into your ovens and your kneading bowls. 4 Frogs will jump on you,
your people, and all your officials.'"

5* Then the LORD said to Moses, "Tell Aaron, 'Raise the staff in your hand
over all the rivers, canals, and ponds of Egypt, and bring up frogs over all
the land.'" 6 So Aaron raised his hand over the waters of Egypt, and frogs
came up and covered the whole land! 7 But the magicians were able to do
the same thing with their magic. They, too, caused frogs to come up on the
land of Egypt.

8 Then Pharaoh summoned Moses and Aaron and begged, "Plead with the
LORD to take the frogs away from me and my people. I will let your people
go, so they can offer sacrifices to the LORD."

9 "You set the time!" Moses replied. "Tell me when you want me to pray
for you, your officials, and your people. Then you and your houses will be
rid of the frogs. They will remain only in the Nile River."

10 "Do it tomorrow," Pharaoh said.

"All right," Moses replied, "it will be as you have said. Then you will know
that there is no one like the LORD our God. 11 The frogs will leave you and
your houses, your officials, and your people. They will remain only in the
Nile River."

12 So Moses and Aaron left Pharaoh's palace, and Moses cried out to the LORD

8:1 Verses 8:1-4 are numbered 7:26-29 in Hebrew text. 8:5 Verses 8:5-32 are numbered 8:1-28 in Hebrew text.

about the frogs he had inflicted on Pharaoh. 13 And the LORD did just what
Moses had predicted. The frogs in the houses, the courtyards, and the fields all
died. 14 The Egyptians piled them into great heaps, and a terrible stench filled
the land. 15 But when Pharaoh saw that relief had come, he became stubborn.*
He refused to listen to Moses and Aaron, just as the LORD had predicted.

A Plague of Gnats

16 So the LORD said to Moses, "Tell Aaron, 'Raise your staff and strike the
ground. The dust will turn into swarms of gnats throughout the land of
Egypt.'" 17 So Moses and Aaron did just as the LORD had commanded them.
When Aaron raised his hand and struck the ground with his staff, gnats
infested the entire land, covering the Egyptians and their animals. All the
dust in the land of Egypt turned into gnats. 18 Pharaoh's magicians tried to
do the same thing with their secret arts, but this time they failed. And the
gnats covered everyone, people and animals alike.

19 "This is the finger of God!" the magicians exclaimed to Pharaoh. But
Pharaoh's heart remained hard. He wouldn't listen to them, just as the LORD
had predicted.

A Plague of Flies

20 Then the LORD told Moses, "Get up early in the morning and stand in
Pharaoh's way as he goes down to the river. Say to him, 'This is what the
LORD says: Let my people go, so they can worship me. 21 If you refuse, then
I will send swarms of flies on you, your officials, your people, and all the
houses. The Egyptian homes will be filled with flies, and the ground will be
covered with them. 22 But this time I will spare the region of Goshen, where
my people live. No flies will be found there. Then you will know that I am
the LORD and that I am present even in the heart of your land. 23 I will make
a clear distinction between* my people and your people. This miraculous
sign will happen tomorrow.'"

24 And the LORD did just as he had said. A thick swarm of flies filled Pha-
raoh's palace and the houses of his officials. The whole land of Egypt was
thrown into chaos by the flies.

25 Pharaoh called for Moses and Aaron. "All right! Go ahead and offer sac-
rifices to your God," he said. "But do it here in this land."

26 But Moses replied, "That wouldn't be right. The Egyptians detest the
sacrifices that we offer to the LORD our God. Look, if we offer our sacrifices
here where the Egyptians can see us, they will stone us. 27 We must take a
three-day trip into the wilderness to offer sacrifices to the LORD our God,
just as he has commanded us."

28 "All right, go ahead," Pharaoh replied. "I will let you go into the wilder-
ness to offer sacrifices to the LORD your God. But don't go too far away. Now
hurry and pray for me."

29 Moses answered, "As soon as I leave you, I will pray to the LORD, and
tomorrow the swarms of flies will disappear from you and your officials
and all your people. But I am warning you, Pharaoh, don't lie to us again
and refuse to let the people go to sacrifice to the LORD."

30 So Moses left Pharaoh's palace and pleaded with the LORD to remove
all the flies. 31 And the LORD did as Moses asked and caused the swarms of

Question 8:19

What do you think it would take for someone who doesn't believe in God to admit that he exists?

8:15 Hebrew *made his heart heavy;* also in 8:32. **8:23** As in Greek and Latin versions; Hebrew reads *I will set redemption between.*

flies to disappear from Pharaoh, his officials, and his people. Not a single
fly remained. 32 But Pharaoh again became stubborn and refused to let the
people go.

A Plague against Livestock

9 "Go back to Pharaoh," the LORD commanded Moses. "Tell him, 'This is
what the LORD, the God of the Hebrews, says: Let my people go, so they
can worship me. 2 If you continue to hold them and refuse to let them go,
3 the hand of the LORD will strike all your livestock—your horses, donkeys,
camels, cattle, sheep, and goats—with a deadly plague. 4 But the LORD will
again make a distinction between the livestock of the Israelites and that of
the Egyptians. Not a single one of Israel's animals will die! 5 The LORD has
already set the time for the plague to begin. He has declared that he will
strike the land tomorrow.'"

6 And the LORD did just as he had said. The next morning all the livestock
of the Egyptians died, but the Israelites didn't lose a single animal. 7 Pharaoh
sent his officials to investigate, and they discovered that the Israelites had
not lost a single animal! But even so, Pharaoh's heart remained stubborn,*
and he still refused to let the people go.

A Plague of Festering Boils

8 Then the LORD said to Moses and Aaron, "Take handfuls of soot from a brick
kiln, and have Moses toss it into the air while Pharaoh watches. 9 The ashes
will spread like fine dust over the whole land of Egypt, causing festering
boils to break out on people and animals throughout the land."

10 So they took soot from a brick kiln and went and stood before Pharaoh.
As Pharaoh watched, Moses threw the soot into the air, and boils broke out
on people and animals alike. 11 Even the magicians were unable to stand be-
fore Moses, because the boils had broken out on them and all the Egyptians.
12 But the LORD hardened Pharaoh's heart, and just as the LORD had predicted
to Moses, Pharaoh refused to listen.

A Plague of Hail

13 Then the LORD said to Moses, "Get up early in the morning and stand be-
fore Pharaoh. Tell him, 'This is what the LORD, the God of the Hebrews, says:
Let my people go, so they can worship me. 14 If you don't, I will send more
plagues on you* and your officials and your people. Then you will know that
there is no one like me in all the earth. 15 By now I could have lifted my hand
and struck you and your people with a plague to wipe you off the face of the
earth. 16 But I have spared you for a purpose—to show you my power* and to
spread my fame throughout the earth. 17 But you still lord it over my people
and refuse to let them go. 18 So tomorrow at this time I will send a hailstorm
more devastating than any in all the history of Egypt. 19 Quick! Order your
livestock and servants to come in from the fields to find shelter. Any person
or animal left outside will die when the hail falls.'"

20 Some of Pharaoh's officials were afraid because of what the LORD had
said. They quickly brought their servants and livestock in from the fields.
21 But those who paid no attention to the word of the LORD left theirs out
in the open.

9:7 Hebrew *heavy.* 9:14 Hebrew *on your heart.* 9:16 Greek version reads *to display my power in you;* compare Rom 9:17.

22 Then the LORD said to Moses, "Lift your hand toward the sky so hail may fall on the people, the livestock, and all the plants throughout the land of Egypt."

23 So Moses lifted his staff toward the sky, and the LORD sent thunder and hail, and lightning flashed toward the earth. The LORD sent a tremendous hailstorm against all the land of Egypt. 24 Never in all the history of Egypt had there been a storm like that, with such devastating hail and continuous lightning. 25 It left all of Egypt in ruins. The hail struck down everything in the open field—people, animals, and plants alike. Even the trees were destroyed. 26 The only place without hail was the region of Goshen, where the people of Israel lived.

27 Then Pharaoh quickly summoned Moses and Aaron. "This time I have sinned," he confessed. "The LORD is the righteous one, and my people and I are wrong. 28 Please beg the LORD to end this terrifying thunder and hail. We've had enough. I will let you go; you don't need to stay any longer."

29 "All right," Moses replied. "As soon as I leave the city, I will lift my hands and pray to the LORD. Then the thunder and hail will stop, and you will know that the earth belongs to the LORD. 30 But I know that you and your officials still do not fear the LORD God."

31 (All the flax and barley were ruined by the hail, because the barley had formed heads and the flax was budding. 32 But the wheat and the emmer wheat were spared, because they had not yet sprouted from the ground.)

33 So Moses left Pharaoh's court and went out of the city. When he lifted his hands to the LORD, the thunder and hail stopped, and the downpour ceased. 34 But when Pharaoh saw that the rain, hail, and thunder had stopped, he and his officials sinned again, and Pharaoh again became stubborn.* 35 Because his heart was hard, Pharaoh refused to let the people leave, just as the LORD had predicted through Moses.

A Plague of Locusts

10 Then the LORD said to Moses, "Return to Pharaoh and make your demands again. I have made him and his officials stubborn* so I can display my miraculous signs among them. 2 I've also done it so you can tell your children and grandchildren about how I made a mockery of the Egyptians and about the signs I displayed among them—and so you will know that I am the LORD."

3 So Moses and Aaron went to Pharaoh and said, "This is what the LORD, the God of the Hebrews, says: How long will you refuse to submit to me? Let my people go, so they can worship me. 4 If you refuse, watch out! For tomorrow I will bring a swarm of locusts on your country. 5 They will cover the land so that you won't be able to see the ground. They will devour what little is left of your crops after the hailstorm, including all the trees growing in the fields. 6 They will overrun your palaces and the homes of your officials and all the houses in Egypt. Never in the history of Egypt have your ancestors seen a plague like this one!" And with that, Moses turned and left Pharaoh.

7 Pharaoh's officials now came to Pharaoh and appealed to him. "How long will you let this man hold us hostage? Let the men go to worship the LORD their God! Don't you realize that Egypt lies in ruins?"

8 So Moses and Aaron were brought back to Pharaoh. "All right," he told

Prayer **10:3**

Lord, it's hard to understand why some people seem to get away with not honoring you. I will trust your timing for how you deal with them. In the meantime, I promise to follow you as genuinely as I know how. Amen.

9:34 Hebrew *made his heart heavy.* 10:1 Hebrew *have made his heart and his officials' hearts heavy.*

them, "go and worship the LORD your God. But who exactly will be going with you?"

[9]Moses replied, "We will all go—young and old, our sons and daughters, and our flocks and herds. We must all join together in celebrating a festival to the LORD."

[10]Pharaoh retorted, "The LORD will certainly need to be with you if I let you take your little ones! I can see through your evil plan. [11]Never! Only the men may go and worship the LORD, since that is what you requested." And Pharaoh threw them out of the palace.

[12]Then the LORD said to Moses, "Raise your hand over the land of Egypt to bring on the locusts. Let them cover the land and devour every plant that survived the hailstorm."

[13]So Moses raised his staff over Egypt, and the LORD caused an east wind to blow over the land all that day and through the night. When morning arrived, the east wind had brought the locusts. [14]And the locusts swarmed over the whole land of Egypt, settling in dense swarms from one end of the country to the other. It was the worst locust plague in Egyptian history, and there has never been another one like it. [15]For the locusts covered the whole country and darkened the land. They devoured every plant in the fields and all the fruit on the trees that had survived the hailstorm. Not a single leaf was left on the trees and plants throughout the land of Egypt.

[16]Pharaoh quickly summoned Moses and Aaron. "I have sinned against the LORD your God and against you," he confessed. [17]"Forgive my sin, just this once, and plead with the LORD your God to take away this death from me."

[18]So Moses left Pharaoh's court and pleaded with the LORD. [19]The LORD responded by shifting the wind, and the strong west wind blew the locusts into the Red Sea.* Not a single locust remained in all the land of Egypt. [20]But the LORD hardened Pharaoh's heart again, so he refused to let the people go.

A Plague of Darkness

[21]Then the LORD said to Moses, "Lift your hand toward heaven, and the land of Egypt will be covered with a darkness so thick you can feel it." [22]So Moses lifted his hand to the sky, and a deep darkness covered the entire land of Egypt for three days. [23]During all that time the people could not see each other, and no one moved. But there was light as usual where the people of Israel lived.

[24]Finally, Pharaoh called for Moses. "Go and worship the LORD," he said. "But leave your flocks and herds here. You may even take your little ones with you."

[25]"No," Moses said, "you must provide us with animals for sacrifices and burnt offerings to the LORD our God. [26]All our livestock must go with us, too; not a hoof can be left behind. We must choose our sacrifices for the LORD our God from among these animals. And we won't know how we are to worship the LORD until we get there."

[27]But the LORD hardened Pharaoh's heart once more, and he would not let them go. [28]"Get out of here!" Pharaoh shouted at Moses. "I'm warning you. Never come back to see me again! The day you see my face, you will die!"

[29]"Very well," Moses replied. "I will never see your face again."

10:19 Hebrew *sea of reeds.*

Death for Egypt's Firstborn

11 Then the LORD said to Moses, "I will strike Pharaoh and the land of Egypt with one more blow. After that, Pharaoh will let you leave this country. In fact, he will be so eager to get rid of you that he will force you all to leave. 2 Tell all the Israelite men and women to ask their Egyptian neighbors for articles of silver and gold." 3 (Now the LORD had caused the Egyptians to look favorably on the people of Israel. And Moses was considered a very great man in the land of Egypt, respected by Pharaoh's officials and the Egyptian people alike.)

4 Moses had announced to Pharaoh, "This is what the LORD says: At midnight tonight I will pass through the heart of Egypt. 5 All the firstborn sons will die in every family in Egypt, from the oldest son of Pharaoh, who sits on his throne, to the oldest son of his lowliest servant girl who grinds the flour. Even the firstborn of all the livestock will die. 6 Then a loud wail will rise throughout the land of Egypt, a wail like no one has heard before or will ever hear again. 7 But among the Israelites it will be so peaceful that not even a dog will bark. Then you will know that the LORD makes a distinction between the Egyptians and the Israelites. 8 All the officials of Egypt will run to me and fall to the ground before me. 'Please leave!' they will beg. 'Hurry! And take all your followers with you.' Only then will I go!" Then, burning with anger, Moses left Pharaoh.

9 Now the LORD had told Moses earlier, "Pharaoh will not listen to you, but then I will do even more mighty miracles in the land of Egypt." 10 Moses and Aaron performed these miracles in Pharaoh's presence, but the LORD hardened Pharaoh's heart, and he wouldn't let the Israelites leave the country.

The First Passover

12 While the Israelites were still in the land of Egypt, the LORD gave the following instructions to Moses and Aaron: 2 "From now on, this month will be the first month of the year for you. 3 Announce to the whole community of Israel that on the tenth day of this month each family must choose a lamb or a young goat for a sacrifice, one animal for each household. 4 If a family is too small to eat a whole animal, let them share with another family in the neighborhood. Divide the animal according to the size of each family and how much they can eat. 5 The animal you select must be a one-year-old male, either a sheep or a goat, with no defects.

6 "Take special care of this chosen animal until the evening of the fourteenth day of this first month. Then the whole assembly of the community of Israel must slaughter their lamb or young goat at twilight. 7 They are to take some of the blood and smear it on the sides and top of the doorframes of the houses where they eat the animal. 8 That same night they must roast the meat over a fire and eat it along with bitter salad greens and bread made without yeast. 9 Do not eat any of the meat raw or boiled in water. The whole animal—including the head, legs, and internal organs—must be roasted over a fire. 10 Do not leave any of it until the next morning. Burn whatever is not eaten before morning.

11 "These are your instructions for eating this meal: Be fully dressed,* wear your sandals, and carry your walking stick in your hand. Eat the meal with urgency, for this is the LORD's Passover. 12 On that night I will pass through

12:11 Hebrew *Bind up your loins.*

Question **11:3**

God stirred the people of Egypt to look favorably on the Israelites and on Moses in particular. What does this teach you about the ultimate source and purpose of a good reputation?

Make a Difference

12:1-30

Passover

God didn't want anyone in any future generation to forget how he had saved his people from slavery. This is why, to this day, the Jewish people share the Passover meal, a traditional meal filled with symbolism.

Think about the last meal Jesus shared with his disciples before his crucifixion. During that meal, which, in God's deliberate timing, happened to be the Passover meal, Jesus instructed his followers to remember his sacrifice for them whenever they celebrated that meal. Remarkably, by his death on the cross, Jesus was fulfilling the complete meaning of salvation through the Passover lamb (Luke 22:7-20).

The Passover meal should be celebrated and practiced today because it helps us enter into an experience that reminds us of the salvation God has provided.

Difference Maker

Look up what a traditional Passover (or "Seder") meal entails, from the preparation of the home to the unique food. Imagine what something formal like this could look like for you and some of your friends to take part in. The next time Passover comes around on the calendar, organize the experience and walk through the symbolism as God intended.

Question 12:26

This is the key to next-generation ministry. Are you modeling this kind of practice in your life so that others will ask, "Why are you doing this?" How can you be ready to give an answer?

the land of Egypt and strike down every firstborn son and firstborn male
animal in the land of Egypt. I will execute judgment against all the gods
of Egypt, for I am the LORD! 13 But the blood on your doorposts will serve
as a sign, marking the houses where you are staying. When I see the blood,
I will pass over you. This plague of death will not touch you when I strike
the land of Egypt.
14 "This is a day to remember. Each year, from generation to generation,
you must celebrate it as a special festival to the LORD. This is a law for all time.
15 For seven days the bread you eat must be made without yeast. On the first
day of the festival, remove every trace of yeast from your homes. Anyone who
eats bread made with yeast during the seven days of the festival will be cut off
from the community of Israel. 16 On the first day of the festival and again on the
seventh day, all the people must observe an official day for holy assembly. No
work of any kind may be done on these days except in the preparation of food.
17 "Celebrate this Festival of Unleavened Bread, for it will remind you that
I brought your forces out of the land of Egypt on this very day. This festival
will be a permanent law for you; celebrate this day from generation to generation.
18 The bread you eat must be made without yeast from the evening
of the fourteenth day of the first month until the evening of the twenty-first
day of that month. 19 During those seven days, there must be no trace of yeast
in your homes. Anyone who eats anything made with yeast during this week
will be cut off from the community of Israel. These regulations apply both to
the foreigners living among you and to the native-born Israelites. 20 During
those days you must not eat anything made with yeast. Wherever you live,
eat only bread made without yeast."
21 Then Moses called all the elders of Israel together and said to them,
"Go, pick out a lamb or young goat for each of your families, and slaughter
the Passover animal. 22 Drain the blood into a basin. Then take a bundle of
hyssop branches and dip it into the blood. Brush the hyssop across the top
and sides of the doorframes of your houses. And no one may go out through
the door until morning. 23 For the LORD will pass through the land to strike
down the Egyptians. But when he sees the blood on the top and sides of the
doorframe, the LORD will pass over your home. He will not permit his death
angel to enter your house and strike you down.
24 "Remember, these instructions are a permanent law that you and your
descendants must observe forever. 25 When you enter the land the LORD has
promised to give you, you will continue to observe this ceremony. 26 Then
your children will ask, 'What does this ceremony mean?' 27 And you will reply,
'It is the Passover sacrifice to the LORD, for he passed over the houses of
the Israelites in Egypt. And though he struck the Egyptians, he spared our
families.'" When Moses had finished speaking, all the people bowed down
to the ground and worshiped.
28 So the people of Israel did just as the LORD had commanded through
Moses and Aaron. 29 And that night at midnight, the LORD struck down all
the firstborn sons in the land of Egypt, from the firstborn son of Pharaoh,
who sat on his throne, to the firstborn son of the prisoner in the dungeon.
Even the firstborn of their livestock were killed. 30 Pharaoh and all his officials
and all the people of Egypt woke up during the night, and loud wailing
was heard throughout the land of Egypt. There was not a single house where
someone had not died.

Israel's Exodus from Egypt

31 Pharaoh sent for Moses and Aaron during the night. "Get out!" he ordered.
"Leave my people—and take the rest of the Israelites with you! Go and wor-
ship the LORD as you have requested. 32 Take your flocks and herds, as you
said, and be gone. Go, but bless me as you leave." 33 All the Egyptians urged
the people of Israel to get out of the land as quickly as possible, for they
thought, "We will all die!"

34 The Israelites took their bread dough before yeast was added. They
wrapped their kneading boards in their cloaks and carried them on their
shoulders. 35 And the people of Israel did as Moses had instructed; they asked
the Egyptians for clothing and articles of silver and gold. 36 The LORD caused
the Egyptians to look favorably on the Israelites, and they gave the Israelites
whatever they asked for. So they stripped the Egyptians of their wealth!

37 That night the people of Israel left Rameses and started for Succoth.
There were about 600,000 men,* plus all the women and children. 38 A rabble
of non-Israelites went with them, along with great flocks and herds of live-
stock. 39 For bread they baked flat cakes from the dough without yeast they
had brought from Egypt. It was made without yeast because the people were
driven out of Egypt in such a hurry that they had no time to prepare the
bread or other food.

40 The people of Israel had lived in Egypt* for 430 years. 41 In fact, it was
on the last day of the 430th year that all the LORD's forces left the land. 42 On
this night the LORD kept his promise to bring his people out of the land of
Egypt. So this night belongs to him, and it must be commemorated every
year by all the Israelites, from generation to generation.

Instructions for the Passover

43 Then the LORD said to Moses and Aaron, "These are the instructions for
the festival of Passover. No outsiders are allowed to eat the Passover meal.
44 But any slave who has been purchased may eat it if he has been circumcised.
45 Temporary residents and hired servants may not eat it. 46 Each Passover
lamb must be eaten in one house. Do not carry any of its meat outside, and do
not break any of its bones. 47 The whole community of Israel must celebrate
this Passover festival.

48 "If there are foreigners living among you who want to celebrate the
LORD's Passover, let all their males be circumcised. Only then may they cel-
ebrate the Passover with you like any native-born Israelite. But no uncircum-
cised male may ever eat the Passover meal. 49 This instruction applies to
everyone, whether a native-born Israelite or a foreigner living among you."

50 So all the people of Israel followed all the LORD's commands to Moses
and Aaron. 51 On that very day the LORD brought the people of Israel out of
the land of Egypt like an army.

Dedication of the Firstborn

13 Then the LORD said to Moses, 2 "Dedicate to me every firstborn
among the Israelites. The first offspring to be born, of both humans
and animals, belongs to me."

3 So Moses said to the people, "This is a day to remember forever—the day
you left Egypt, the place of your slavery. Today the LORD has brought you out

12:37 Or *fighting men;* Hebrew reads *men on foot.* 12:40 Samaritan Pentateuch reads *in Canaan and Egypt;* Greek version reads *in Egypt and Canaan.*

Question 13:21

God wanted to show his own people that he would rescue them and guide them through life. What point does God want you to see here in terms of your own walk of faith?

by the power of his mighty hand. (Remember, eat no food containing yeast.) 4 On this day in early spring, in the month of Abib,* you have been set free. 5 You must celebrate this event in this month each year after the LORD brings you into the land of the Canaanites, Hittites, Amorites, Hivites, and Jebusites. (He swore to your ancestors that he would give you this land—a land flowing with milk and honey.) 6 For seven days the bread you eat must be made without yeast. Then on the seventh day, celebrate a feast to the LORD. 7 Eat bread without yeast during those seven days. In fact, there must be no yeast bread or any yeast at all found within the borders of your land during this time.

8 "On the seventh day you must explain to your children, 'I am celebrating what the LORD did for me when I left Egypt.' 9 This annual festival will be a visible sign to you, like a mark branded on your hand or your forehead. Let it remind you always to recite this teaching of the LORD: 'With a strong hand, the LORD rescued you from Egypt.'* 10 So observe the decree of this festival at the appointed time each year.

11 "This is what you must do when the LORD fulfills the promise he swore to you and to your ancestors. When he gives you the land where the Canaanites now live, 12 you must present all firstborn sons and firstborn male animals to the LORD, for they belong to him. 13 A firstborn donkey may be bought back from the LORD by presenting a lamb or young goat in its place. But if you do not buy it back, you must break its neck. However, you must buy back every firstborn son.

14 "And in the future, your children will ask you, 'What does all this mean?' Then you will tell them, 'With the power of his mighty hand, the LORD brought us out of Egypt, the place of our slavery. 15 Pharaoh stubbornly refused to let us go, so the LORD killed all the firstborn males throughout the land of Egypt, both people and animals. That is why I now sacrifice all the firstborn males to the LORD—except that the firstborn sons are always bought back.' 16 This ceremony will be like a mark branded on your hand or your forehead. It is a reminder that the power of the LORD's mighty hand brought us out of Egypt."

Israel's Wilderness Detour

17 When Pharaoh finally let the people go, God did not lead them along the main road that runs through Philistine territory, even though that was the shortest route to the Promised Land. God said, "If the people are faced with a battle, they might change their minds and return to Egypt." 18 So God led them in a roundabout way through the wilderness toward the Red Sea.* Thus the Israelites left Egypt like an army ready for battle.*

19 Moses took the bones of Joseph with him, for Joseph had made the sons of Israel swear to do this. He said, "God will certainly come to help you. When he does, you must take my bones with you from this place."

20 The Israelites left Succoth and camped at Etham on the edge of the wilderness. 21 The LORD went ahead of them. He guided them during the day with a pillar of cloud, and he provided light at night with a pillar of fire. This allowed them to travel by day or by night. 22 And the LORD did not remove the pillar of cloud or pillar of fire from its place in front of the people.

13:4 Hebrew *On this day in the month of Abib.* This first month of the ancient Hebrew lunar calendar usually occurs within the months of March and April. **13:9** Or *Let it remind you always to keep the instructions of the LORD on the tip of your tongue, because with a strong hand, the LORD rescued you from Egypt.* **13:18a** Hebrew *sea of reeds.* **13:18b** Greek version reads *left Egypt in the fifth generation.*

14 Then the LORD gave these instructions to Moses: 2"Order the Israel-
ites to turn back and camp by Pi-hahiroth between Migdol and the
sea. Camp there along the shore, across from Baal-zephon. 3Then Pharaoh
will think, 'The Israelites are confused. They are trapped in the wilderness!'
4And once again I will harden Pharaoh's heart, and he will chase after you.*
I have planned this in order to display my glory through Pharaoh and his
whole army. After this the Egyptians will know that I am the LORD!" So the
Israelites camped there as they were told.

The Egyptians Pursue Israel

5When word reached the king of Egypt that the Israelites had fled, Pharaoh
and his officials changed their minds. "What have we done, letting all those
Israelite slaves get away?" they asked. 6So Pharaoh harnessed his chariot
and called up his troops. 7He took with him 600 of Egypt's best chariots,
along with the rest of the chariots of Egypt, each with its commander. 8The
LORD hardened the heart of Pharaoh, the king of Egypt, so he chased after
the people of Israel, who had left with fists raised in defiance. 9The Egyp-
tians chased after them with all the forces in Pharaoh's army—all his horses
and chariots, his charioteers, and his troops. The Egyptians caught up with
the people of Israel as they were camped beside the shore near Pi-hahiroth,
across from Baal-zephon.

10As Pharaoh approached, the people of Israel looked up and panicked
when they saw the Egyptians overtaking them. They cried out to the LORD,
11and they said to Moses, "Why did you bring us out here to die in the wilder-
ness? Weren't there enough graves for us in Egypt? What have you done to
us? Why did you make us leave Egypt? 12Didn't we tell you this would happen
while we were still in Egypt? We said, 'Leave us alone! Let us be slaves to the
Egyptians. It's better to be a slave in Egypt than a corpse in the wilderness!'"

13But Moses told the people, "Don't be afraid. Just stand still and watch
the LORD rescue you today. The Egyptians you see today will never be seen
again. 14The LORD himself will fight for you. Just stay calm."

Escape through the Red Sea

15Then the LORD said to Moses, "Why are you crying out to me? Tell the people
to get moving! 16Pick up your staff and raise your hand over the sea. Divide
the water so the Israelites can walk through the middle of the sea on dry
ground. 17And I will harden the hearts of the Egyptians, and they will charge
in after the Israelites. My great glory will be displayed through Pharaoh and
his troops, his chariots, and his charioteers. 18When my glory is displayed
through them, all Egypt will see my glory and know that I am the LORD!"

19Then the angel of God, who had been leading the people of Israel, moved
to the rear of the camp. The pillar of cloud also moved from the front and
stood behind them. 20The cloud settled between the Egyptian and Israelite
camps. As darkness fell, the cloud turned to fire, lighting up the night. But
the Egyptians and Israelites did not approach each other all night.

21Then Moses raised his hand over the sea, and the LORD opened up a path
through the water with a strong east wind. The wind blew all that night,
turning the seabed into dry land. 22So the people of Israel walked through
the middle of the sea on dry ground, with walls of water on each side!

14:4 Hebrew *after them.*

Prayer **14:14**

Lord, I know you will fight for me as I put my trust in you. Show me how to take this step of faith. Amen.

23 Then the Egyptians—all of Pharaoh's horses, chariots, and chari-
oteers—chased them into the middle of the sea. 24 But just before dawn the
LORD looked down on the Egyptian army from the pillar of fire and cloud,
and he threw their forces into total confusion. 25 He twisted* their chariot
wheels, making their chariots difficult to drive. "Let's get out of here—away
from these Israelites!" the Egyptians shouted. "The LORD is fighting for
them against Egypt!"

26 When all the Israelites had reached the other side, the LORD said to
Moses, "Raise your hand over the sea again. Then the waters will rush back
and cover the Egyptians and their chariots and charioteers." 27 So as the
sun began to rise, Moses raised his hand over the sea, and the water rushed
back into its usual place. The Egyptians tried to escape, but the LORD swept
them into the sea. 28 Then the waters returned and covered all the chariots
and charioteers—the entire army of Pharaoh. Of all the Egyptians who had
chased the Israelites into the sea, not a single one survived.

29 But the people of Israel had walked through the middle of the sea on
dry ground, as the water stood up like a wall on both sides. 30 That is how the
LORD rescued Israel from the hand of the Egyptians that day. And the Israel-
ites saw the bodies of the Egyptians washed up on the seashore. 31 When the
people of Israel saw the mighty power that the LORD had unleashed against
the Egyptians, they were filled with awe before him. They put their faith in
the LORD and in his servant Moses.

A Song of Deliverance

15 Then Moses and the people of Israel sang this song to the LORD:

"I will sing to the LORD,
for he has triumphed gloriously;
he has hurled both horse and rider
into the sea.
2 The LORD is my strength and my song;
he has given me victory.
This is my God, and I will praise him—
my father's God, and I will exalt him!
3 The LORD is a warrior;
Yahweh* is his name!
4 Pharaoh's chariots and army
he has hurled into the sea.
The finest of Pharaoh's officers
are drowned in the Red Sea.*
5 The deep waters gushed over them;
they sank to the bottom like a stone.

6 "Your right hand, O LORD,
is glorious in power.
Your right hand, O LORD,
smashes the enemy.

14:25 As in Greek version, Samaritan Pentateuch, and Syriac version; Hebrew reads *He removed.* 15:3 *Yahweh* is a transliteration of the proper name *YHWH* that is sometimes rendered "Jehovah"; in this translation it is usually rendered "the LORD" (note the use of small capitals). 15:4 Hebrew *sea of reeds;* also in 15:22.

7 In the greatness of your majesty,
you overthrow those who rise against you.
You unleash your blazing fury;
it consumes them like straw.
8 At the blast of your breath,
the waters piled up!
The surging waters stood straight like a wall;
in the heart of the sea the deep waters became hard.

9 "The enemy boasted, 'I will chase them
and catch up with them.
I will plunder them
and consume them.
I will flash my sword;
my powerful hand will destroy them.'
10 But you blew with your breath,
and the sea covered them.
They sank like lead
in the mighty waters.

11 "Who is like you among the gods, O LORD—
glorious in holiness,
awesome in splendor,
performing great wonders?
12 You raised your right hand,
and the earth swallowed our enemies.

13 "With your unfailing love you lead
the people you have redeemed.
In your might, you guide them
to your sacred home.
14 The peoples hear and tremble;
anguish grips those who live in Philistia.
15 The leaders of Edom are terrified;
the nobles of Moab tremble.
All who live in Canaan melt away;
16 terror and dread fall upon them.
The power of your arm
makes them lifeless as stone
until your people pass by, O LORD,
until the people you purchased pass by.
17 You will bring them in and plant them on your own mountain—
the place, O LORD, reserved for your own dwelling,
the sanctuary, O Lord, that your hands have established.
18 The LORD will reign forever and ever!"

19 When Pharaoh's horses, chariots, and charioteers rushed into the sea, the
LORD brought the water crashing down on them. But the people of Israel
had walked through the middle of the sea on dry ground!
20 Then Miriam the prophet, Aaron's sister, took a tambourine and led

Story Arc **15:20-21**

● Miriam

The first time we see Miriam's name in the Bible is here, when she led the women of Israel in praising God. As the sea crushed Pharaoh's army, Miriam took a tambourine and led all the women of Israel in a song.

The first time Miriam likely appears in the Bible, however, is back in the second chapter of Exodus. Miriam was probably the same sister who looked out for Moses when he was born (Exodus 2:4; Numbers 26:59; 1 Chronicles 6:3). While Miriam (like Aaron) wasn't always a supportive sibling to Moses (Numbers 12), her legacy as an influential prophetess who led people to worship the Lord is profound.

Significantly, Jesus was born to a mother named Mary (an equivalent of the Hebrew Miriam), who likewise led the first worship song about the Savior rescuing his people (Luke 1:46-55).

Exod 17:9 ►

all the women as they played their tambourines and danced. 21 And Miriam sang this song:

"Sing to the LORD,
  for he has triumphed gloriously;
he has hurled both horse and rider
  into the sea."

Bitter Water at Marah

22 Then Moses led the people of Israel away from the Red Sea, and they moved out into the desert of Shur. They traveled in this desert for three days without finding any water. 23 When they came to the oasis of Marah, the water was too bitter to drink. So they called the place Marah (which means "bitter").

24 Then the people complained and turned against Moses. "What are we going to drink?" they demanded. 25 So Moses cried out to the LORD for help, and the LORD showed him a piece of wood. Moses threw it into the water, and this made the water good to drink.

It was there at Marah that the LORD set before them the following decree as a standard to test their faithfulness to him. 26 He said, "If you will listen carefully to the voice of the LORD your God and do what is right in his sight, obeying his commands and keeping all his decrees, then I will not make you suffer any of the diseases I sent on the Egyptians; for I am the LORD who heals you."

27 After leaving Marah, the Israelites traveled on to the oasis of Elim, where they found twelve springs and seventy palm trees. They camped there beside the water.

Manna and Quail from Heaven

16 Then the whole community of Israel set out from Elim and journeyed into the wilderness of Sin,* between Elim and Mount Sinai. They arrived there on the fifteenth day of the second month, one month after leaving the land of Egypt.* 2 There, too, the whole community of Israel complained about Moses and Aaron.

3 "If only the LORD had killed us back in Egypt," they moaned. "There we sat around pots filled with meat and ate all the bread we wanted. But now you have brought us into this wilderness to starve us all to death."

4 Then the LORD said to Moses, "Look, I'm going to rain down food from heaven for you. Each day the people can go out and pick up as much food as they need for that day. I will test them in this to see whether or not they will follow my instructions. 5 On the sixth day they will gather food, and when they prepare it, there will be twice as much as usual."

6 So Moses and Aaron said to all the people of Israel, "By evening you will realize it was the LORD who brought you out of the land of Egypt. 7 In the morning you will see the glory of the LORD, because he has heard your complaints, which are against him, not against us. What have we done that you should complain about us?" 8 Then Moses added, "The LORD will give you meat to eat in the evening and bread to satisfy you in the morning, for he has heard all your complaints against him. What have we done? Yes, your complaints are against the LORD, not against us."

16:1a The geographical name *Sin* is related to *Sinai* and should not be confused with the English word *sin.* **16:1b** The Exodus had occurred on the fifteenth day of the first month (see Num 33:3).

[9]Then Moses said to Aaron, "Announce this to the entire community of Israel: 'Present yourselves before the LORD, for he has heard your complaining.'" [10]And as Aaron spoke to the whole community of Israel, they looked out toward the wilderness. There they could see the awesome glory of the LORD in the cloud.

[11]Then the LORD said to Moses, [12]"I have heard the Israelites' complaints. Now tell them, 'In the evening you will have meat to eat, and in the morning you will have all the bread you want. Then you will know that I am the LORD your God.'"

[13]That evening vast numbers of quail flew in and covered the camp. And the next morning the area around the camp was wet with dew. [14]When the dew evaporated, a flaky substance as fine as frost blanketed the ground. [15]The Israelites were puzzled when they saw it. "What is it?" they asked each other. They had no idea what it was.

And Moses told them, "It is the food the LORD has given you to eat. [16]These are the LORD's instructions: Each household should gather as much as it needs. Pick up two quarts* for each person in your tent."

[17]So the people of Israel did as they were told. Some gathered a lot, some only a little. [18]But when they measured it out,* everyone had just enough. Those who gathered a lot had nothing left over, and those who gathered only a little had enough. Each family had just what it needed.

[19]Then Moses told them, "Do not keep any of it until morning." [20]But some of them didn't listen and kept some of it until morning. But by then it was full of maggots and had a terrible smell. Moses was very angry with them.

[21]After this the people gathered the food morning by morning, each family according to its need. And as the sun became hot, the flakes they had not picked up melted and disappeared. [22]On the sixth day, they gathered twice as much as usual—four quarts* for each person instead of two. Then all the leaders of the community came and asked Moses for an explanation. [23]He told them, "This is what the LORD commanded: Tomorrow will be a day of complete rest, a holy Sabbath day set apart for the LORD. So bake or boil as much as you want today, and set aside what is left for tomorrow."

[24]So they put some aside until morning, just as Moses had commanded. And in the morning the leftover food was wholesome and good, without maggots or odor. [25]Moses said, "Eat this food today, for today is a Sabbath day dedicated to the LORD. There will be no food on the ground today. [26]You may gather the food for six days, but the seventh day is the Sabbath. There will be no food on the ground that day."

[27]Some of the people went out anyway on the seventh day, but they found no food. [28]The LORD asked Moses, "How long will these people refuse to obey my commands and instructions? [29]They must realize that the Sabbath is the LORD's gift to you. That is why he gives you a two-day supply on the sixth day, so there will be enough for two days. On the Sabbath day you must each stay in your place. Do not go out to pick up food on the seventh day." [30]So the people did not gather any food on the seventh day.

[31]The Israelites called the food manna.* It was white like coriander seed, and it tasted like honey wafers.

[32]Then Moses said, "This is what the LORD has commanded: Fill a two-quart container with manna to preserve it for your descendants. Then later

16:16 Hebrew *1 omer* [2.2 liters]; also in 16:32, 33. 16:18 Hebrew *measured it with an omer.* 16:22 Hebrew *2 omers* [4.4 liters]. 16:31 *Manna* means "What is it?" See 16:15.

Question 16:15

How is God providing for you each day? Check out John 6. What does Jesus want us to recognize about God in this passage in Exodus and about himself in John 6?

generations will be able to see the food I gave you in the wilderness when I
set you free from Egypt."
33 Moses said to Aaron, "Get a jar and fill it with two quarts of manna. Then
put it in a sacred place before the LORD to preserve it for all future genera-
tions." 34 Aaron did just as the LORD had commanded Moses. He eventually
placed it in the Ark of the Covenant—in front of the stone tablets inscribed
with the terms of the covenant.* 35 So the people of Israel ate manna for forty
years until they arrived at the land where they would settle. They ate manna
until they came to the border of the land of Canaan.
36 The container used to measure the manna was an omer, which was one-
tenth of an ephah; it held about two quarts.*

Water from the Rock

17 At the LORD's command, the whole community of Israel left the
wilderness of Sin* and moved from place to place. Eventually they
camped at Rephidim, but there was no water there for the people to drink.
2 So once more the people complained against Moses. "Give us water to
drink!" they demanded.
"Quiet!" Moses replied. "Why are you complaining against me? And why
are you testing the LORD?"
3 But tormented by thirst, they continued to argue with Moses. "Why did
you bring us out of Egypt? Are you trying to kill us, our children, and our
livestock with thirst?"
4 Then Moses cried out to the LORD, "What should I do with these people?
They are ready to stone me!"
5 The LORD said to Moses, "Walk out in front of the people. Take your staff,
the one you used when you struck the water of the Nile, and call some of the
elders of Israel to join you. 6 I will stand before you on the rock at Mount Si-
nai.* Strike the rock, and water will come gushing out. Then the people will
be able to drink." So Moses struck the rock as he was told, and water gushed
out as the elders looked on.
7 Moses named the place Massah (which means "test") and Meribah (which
means "arguing") because the people of Israel argued with Moses and tested
the LORD by saying, "Is the LORD here with us or not?"

Israel Defeats the Amalekites

8 While the people of Israel were still at Rephidim, the warriors of Amalek
attacked them. 9 Moses commanded Joshua, "Choose some men to go out and
fight the army of Amalek for us. Tomorrow, I will stand at the top of the hill,
holding the staff of God in my hand."
10 So Joshua did what Moses had commanded and fought the army of
Amalek. Meanwhile, Moses, Aaron, and Hur climbed to the top of a nearby
hill. 11 As long as Moses held up the staff in his hand, the Israelites had the
advantage. But whenever he dropped his hand, the Amalekites gained the
advantage. 12 Moses' arms soon became so tired he could no longer hold them
up. So Aaron and Hur found a stone for him to sit on. Then they stood on each
side of Moses, holding up his hands. So his hands held steady until sunset.
13 As a result, Joshua overwhelmed the army of Amalek in battle.

Story Arc **17:9**

● Joshua

There are a lot of people named after Joshua in the world and rightfully so. The Joshua we read about in the Bible was a faithful student and aide to Moses, fought battles as a fierce warrior, spoke courage when others spoke fear, led the people into the promised land, and let it be known in his final days that his household would serve no one other than God. Simply put, Joshua was willing to do what the Lord asked of him—so he changed the world.

The best takeaway from Joshua's story isn't admiration, however, but inspiration. The world is broken, and God is looking for faithful men and women of all ages to join him in restoring it. Just as Joshua grew from one role to the next, so might the Lord bring you through small moments into larger ones. In everything, you get to step completely into whatever and wherever God has for you today. Be strong and courageous, for the Lord your God is with you.

Exod 31:1-11 ▶

16:34 Hebrew *He placed it in front of the Testimony;* see note on 25:16. 16:36 Hebrew *An omer is one-tenth of an ephah.* 17:1 The geographical name *Sin* is related to *Sinai* and should not be confused with the English word *sin.* 17:6 Hebrew *Horeb,* another name for Sinai.

14 After the victory, the LORD instructed Moses, "Write this down on a
scroll as a permanent reminder, and read it aloud to Joshua: I will erase the
memory of Amalek from under heaven." 15 Moses built an altar there and
named it Yahweh-Nissi (which means "the LORD is my banner"). 16 He said,
"They have raised their fist against the LORD's throne, so now* the LORD will
be at war with Amalek generation after generation."

Jethro's Visit to Moses

18 Moses' father-in-law, Jethro, the priest of Midian, heard about
everything God had done for Moses and his people, the Israelites.
He heard especially about how the LORD had rescued them from Egypt.
2 Earlier, Moses had sent his wife, Zipporah, and his two sons back to
Jethro, who had taken them in. 3 (Moses' first son was named Gershom,* for
Moses had said when the boy was born, "I have been a foreigner in a foreign
land." 4 His second son was named Eliezer,* for Moses had said, "The God of
my ancestors was my helper; he rescued me from the sword of Pharaoh.")
5 Jethro, Moses' father-in-law, now came to visit Moses in the wilderness. He
brought Moses' wife and two sons with him, and they arrived while Moses
and the people were camped near the mountain of God. 6 Jethro had sent a
message to Moses, saying, "I, Jethro, your father-in-law, am coming to see
you with your wife and your two sons."
7 So Moses went out to meet his father-in-law. He bowed low and kissed
him. They asked about each other's welfare and then went into Moses' tent.
8 Moses told his father-in-law everything the LORD had done to Pharaoh
and Egypt on behalf of Israel. He also told about all the hardships they had
experienced along the way and how the LORD had rescued his people from
all their troubles. 9 Jethro was delighted when he heard about all the good
things the LORD had done for Israel as he rescued them from the hand of
the Egyptians.
10 "Praise the LORD," Jethro said, "for he has rescued you from the Egyp-
tians and from Pharaoh. Yes, he has rescued Israel from the powerful hand
of Egypt! 11 I know now that the LORD is greater than all other gods, because
he rescued his people from the oppression of the proud Egyptians."
12 Then Jethro, Moses' father-in-law, brought a burnt offering and sacri-
fices to God. Aaron and all the elders of Israel came out and joined him in a
sacrificial meal in God's presence.

Jethro's Wise Advice

13 The next day, Moses took his seat to hear the people's disputes against each
other. They waited before him from morning till evening.
14 When Moses' father-in-law saw all that Moses was doing for the people,
he asked, "What are you really accomplishing here? Why are you trying to do
all this alone while everyone stands around you from morning till evening?"
15 Moses replied, "Because the people come to me to get a ruling from God.
16 When a dispute arises, they come to me, and I am the one who settles the
case between the quarreling parties. I inform the people of God's decrees
and give them his instructions."
17 "This is not good!" Moses' father-in-law exclaimed. 18 "You're going to
wear yourself out—and the people, too. This job is too heavy a burden for

17:16 Or *Hands have been lifted up to the LORD's throne, and now.* **18:3** *Gershom* sounds like a Hebrew term that means "a foreigner there." **18:4** *Eliezer* means "God is my helper."

Make a Difference

18:13-26

Delegate

At some point in your life, you will likely feel overwhelmed by your responsibilities. That's how Moses felt here. As Israel's leader, people were clamoring for Moses' attention and decisions and resources and rulings. Naturally, Moses hit a limit in his capacity and was getting tired of dealing with every need or argument the people had.

That was when Moses' father-in-law, Jethro, suggested he delegate. "This job is too heavy a burden for you to handle all by yourself," he told Moses (v. 18). He advised Moses to select other capable people and equip them to share the load of responsibility. Moses listened to his father-in-law and began restructuring things more efficiently so that more could be accomplished and so that he could lead more effectively.

Difference Maker

Choose a big task that helps people (like cleaning someone's house or raising money for a project). Ask some friends to help and delegate responsibilities so that, together, you accomplish the task.

Question **19:8**

Notice that God's people said they would do "everything" the Lord commanded. What would "everything" mean for you?

you to handle all by yourself. 19 Now listen to me, and let me give you a word of advice, and may God be with you. You should continue to be the people's representative before God, bringing their disputes to him. 20 Teach them God's decrees, and give them his instructions. Show them how to conduct their lives. 21 But select from all the people some capable, honest men who fear God and hate bribes. Appoint them as leaders over groups of one thousand, one hundred, fifty, and ten. 22 They should always be available to solve the people's common disputes, but have them bring the major cases to you. Let the leaders decide the smaller matters themselves. They will help you carry the load, making the task easier for you. 23 If you follow this advice, and if God commands you to do so, then you will be able to endure the pressures, and all these people will go home in peace."

24 Moses listened to his father-in-law's advice and followed his suggestions. 25 He chose capable men from all over Israel and appointed them as leaders over the people. He put them in charge of groups of one thousand, one hundred, fifty, and ten. 26 These men were always available to solve the people's common disputes. They brought the major cases to Moses, but they took care of the smaller matters themselves.

27 Soon after this, Moses said good-bye to his father-in-law, who returned to his own land.

The Lord Reveals Himself at Sinai

19 Exactly two months after the Israelites left Egypt,* they arrived in the wilderness of Sinai. 2 After breaking camp at Rephidim, they came to the wilderness of Sinai and set up camp there at the base of Mount Sinai.

3 Then Moses climbed the mountain to appear before God. The Lord called to him from the mountain and said, "Give these instructions to the family of Jacob; announce it to the descendants of Israel: 4 'You have seen what I did to the Egyptians. You know how I carried you on eagles' wings and brought you to myself. 5 Now if you will obey me and keep my covenant, you will be my own special treasure from among all the peoples on earth; for all the earth belongs to me. 6 And you will be my kingdom of priests, my holy nation.' This is the message you must give to the people of Israel."

7 So Moses returned from the mountain and called together the elders of the people and told them everything the Lord had commanded him. 8 And all the people responded together, "We will do everything the Lord has commanded." So Moses brought the people's answer back to the Lord.

9 Then the Lord said to Moses, "I will come to you in a thick cloud, Moses, so the people themselves can hear me when I speak with you. Then they will always trust you."

Moses told the Lord what the people had said. 10 Then the Lord told Moses, "Go down and prepare the people for my arrival. Consecrate them today and tomorrow, and have them wash their clothing. 11 Be sure they are ready on the third day, for on that day the Lord will come down on Mount Sinai as all the people watch. 12 Mark off a boundary all around the mountain. Warn the people, 'Be careful! Do not go up on the mountain or even touch its boundaries. Anyone who touches the mountain will certainly be put to death. 13 No hand may touch the person or animal that crosses the boundary;

19:1 Hebrew *In the third month after the Israelites left Egypt, on the very day,* i.e., two lunar months to the day after leaving Egypt. Compare Num 33:3.

instead, stone them or shoot them with arrows. They must be put to death.'
However, when the ram's horn sounds a long blast, then the people may go
up on the mountain.*"

14 So Moses went down to the people. He consecrated them for worship,
and they washed their clothes. 15 He told them, "Get ready for the third day,
and until then abstain from having sexual intercourse."

16 On the morning of the third day, thunder roared and lightning flashed,
and a dense cloud came down on the mountain. There was a long, loud blast
from a ram's horn, and all the people trembled. 17 Moses led them out from
the camp to meet with God, and they stood at the foot of the mountain. 18 All
of Mount Sinai was covered with smoke because the LORD had descended
on it in the form of fire. The smoke billowed into the sky like smoke from
a brick kiln, and the whole mountain shook violently. 19 As the blast of the
ram's horn grew louder and louder, Moses spoke, and God thundered his
reply. 20 The LORD came down on the top of Mount Sinai and called Moses
to the top of the mountain. So Moses climbed the mountain.

21 Then the LORD told Moses, "Go back down and warn the people not to
break through the boundaries to see the LORD, or they will die. 22 Even the
priests who regularly come near to the LORD must purify themselves so that
the LORD does not break out and destroy them."

23 "But LORD," Moses protested, "the people cannot come up to Mount
Sinai. You already warned us. You told me, 'Mark off a boundary all around
the mountain to set it apart as holy.'"

24 But the LORD said, "Go down and bring Aaron back up with you. In the
meantime, do not let the priests or the people break through to approach
the LORD, or he will break out and destroy them."

25 So Moses went down to the people and told them what the LORD had
said.

Ten Commandments for the Covenant Community

20 Then God gave the people all these instructions*:

2 "I am the LORD your God, who rescued you from the land
of Egypt, the place of your slavery.
3 "You must not have any other god but me.
4 "You must not make for yourself an idol of any kind or an image of
anything in the heavens or on the earth or in the sea. 5 You must not
bow down to them or worship them, for I, the LORD your God, am a
jealous God who will not tolerate your affection for any other gods.
I lay the sins of the parents upon their children; the entire family is
affected—even children in the third and fourth generations of those
who reject me. 6 But I lavish unfailing love for a thousand generations
on those* who love me and obey my commands.
7 "You must not misuse the name of the LORD your God. The LORD will
not let you go unpunished if you misuse his name.
8 "Remember to observe the Sabbath day by keeping it holy. 9 You have
six days each week for your ordinary work, 10 but the seventh day is a
Sabbath day of rest dedicated to the LORD your God. On that day no
one in your household may do any work. This includes you, your sons

19:13 Or *up to the mountain.* 20:1 Hebrew *all these words.* 20:6 Hebrew *for thousands of those.*

Make a Difference

20:1–21

Safety Bars

If you've ever been on a roller coaster, you know that one of your greatest resources is the safety bar. Someone could argue that this feature "constricts you" or "keeps you down," but this bar is actually provided so you can experience the ride in the way it's intended to be enjoyed. Without it, you'd surely die.

The Ten Commandments are the safety bar for life. God provided them to spare us from hurting ourselves or others. These ten safety bars keep us in place by telling us (1) how there is one true God (2) so we don't get distracted by false ideas of God or (3) treat him flippantly. You can (4) grow this relationship with God by prioritizing it, (5) including when you honor your family. This means (6) you don't have to live in anger or (7) let lust destroy your life. You also won't experience life to the fullest if you (8) steal from others or (9) stir up a mess of lies or (10) envy what others have. Rather than being constricting, these safety bars free us to enjoy the ups and downs of the ride of life.

Difference Maker

Write down a personal action step for each of the Ten Commandments.

and daughters, your male and female servants, your livestock, and
any foreigners living among you. 11 For in six days the LORD made the
heavens, the earth, the sea, and everything in them; but on the seventh
day he rested. That is why the LORD blessed the Sabbath day and set it
apart as holy.
12 "Honor your father and mother. Then you will live a long, full life in the
land the LORD your God is giving you.
13 "You must not murder.
14 "You must not commit adultery.
15 "You must not steal.
16 "You must not testify falsely against your neighbor.
17 "You must not covet your neighbor's house. You must not covet your
neighbor's wife, male or female servant, ox or donkey, or anything else
that belongs to your neighbor."

18 When the people heard the thunder and the loud blast of the ram's horn,
and when they saw the flashes of lightning and the smoke billowing from
the mountain, they stood at a distance, trembling with fear.
19 And they said to Moses, "You speak to us, and we will listen. But don't
let God speak directly to us, or we will die!"
20 "Don't be afraid," Moses answered them, "for God has come in this way
to test you, and so that your fear of him will keep you from sinning!"
21 As the people stood in the distance, Moses approached the dark cloud
where God was.

Proper Use of Altars

22 And the LORD said to Moses, "Say this to the people of Israel: You saw for
yourselves that I spoke to you from heaven. 23 Remember, you must not make
any idols of silver or gold to rival me.
24 "Build for me an altar made of earth, and offer your sacrifices to me—
your burnt offerings and peace offerings, your sheep and goats, and your
cattle. Build my altar wherever I cause my name to be remembered, and I
will come to you and bless you. 25 If you use stones to build my altar, use only
natural, uncut stones. Do not shape the stones with a tool, for that would
make the altar unfit for holy use. 26 And do not approach my altar by going
up steps. If you do, someone might look up under your clothing and see
your nakedness.

Fair Treatment of Slaves

21 "These are the regulations you must present to Israel.
2 "If you buy a Hebrew slave, he may serve for no more than six
years. Set him free in the seventh year, and he will owe you nothing for his free-
dom. 3 If he was single when he became your slave, he shall leave single. But if
he was married before he became a slave, then his wife must be freed with him.
4 "If his master gave him a wife while he was a slave and they had sons or
daughters, then only the man will be free in the seventh year, but his wife
and children will still belong to his master. 5 But the slave may declare, 'I love
my master, my wife, and my children. I don't want to go free.' 6 If he does this,
his master must present him before God.* Then his master must take him to

21:6 Or *before the judges.*

the door or doorpost and publicly pierce his ear with an awl. After that, the slave will serve his master for life.

7"When a man sells his daughter as a slave, she will not be freed at the end of six years as the men are. 8If she does not satisfy her owner, he must allow her to be bought back again. But he is not allowed to sell her to foreigners, since he is the one who broke the contract with her. 9But if the slave's owner arranges for her to marry his son, he may no longer treat her as a slave but as a daughter.

10"If a man who has married a slave wife takes another wife for himself, he must not neglect the rights of the first wife to food, clothing, and sexual intimacy. 11If he fails in any of these three obligations, she may leave as a free woman without making any payment.

Cases of Personal Injury

12"Anyone who assaults and kills another person must be put to death. 13But if it was simply an accident permitted by God, I will appoint a place of refuge where the slayer can run for safety. 14However, if someone deliberately kills another person, then the slayer must be dragged even from my altar and be put to death.

15"Anyone who strikes father or mother must be put to death.

16"Kidnappers must be put to death, whether they are caught in possession of their victims or have already sold them as slaves.

17"Anyone who dishonors* father or mother must be put to death.

18"Now suppose two men quarrel, and one hits the other with a stone or fist, and the injured person does not die but is confined to bed. 19If he is later able to walk outside again, even with a crutch, the assailant will not be punished but must compensate his victim for lost wages and provide for his full recovery.

20"If a man beats his male or female slave with a club and the slave dies as a result, the owner must be punished. 21But if the slave recovers within a day or two, then the owner shall not be punished, since the slave is his property.

22"Now suppose two men are fighting, and in the process they accidentally strike a pregnant woman so she gives birth prematurely.* If no further injury results, the man who struck the woman must pay the amount of compensation the woman's husband demands and the judges approve. 23But if there is further injury, the punishment must match the injury: a life for a life, 24an eye for an eye, a tooth for a tooth, a hand for a hand, a foot for a foot, 25a burn for a burn, a wound for a wound, a bruise for a bruise.

26"If a man hits his male or female slave in the eye and the eye is blinded, he must let the slave go free to compensate for the eye. 27And if a man knocks out the tooth of his male or female slave, he must let the slave go free to compensate for the tooth.

28"If an ox* gores a man or woman to death, the ox must be stoned, and its flesh may not be eaten. In such a case, however, the owner will not be held liable. 29But suppose the ox had a reputation for goring, and the owner had been informed but failed to keep it under control. If the ox then kills someone, it must be stoned, and the owner must also be put to death. 30However, the dead person's relatives may accept payment to compensate for the

21:17 Greek version reads *Anyone who speaks disrespectfully of.* Compare Matt 15:4; Mark 7:10. 21:22 Or *so she has a miscarriage;* Hebrew reads *so her children come out.* 21:28 Or *bull,* or *cow;* also in 21:29-36.

loss of life. The owner of the ox may redeem his life by paying whatever is
demanded.

31 “The same regulation applies if the ox gores a boy or a girl. 32 But if the ox
gores a slave, either male or female, the animal’s owner must pay the slave’s
owner thirty silver coins,* and the ox must be stoned.

33 “Suppose someone digs or uncovers a pit and fails to cover it, and then
an ox or a donkey falls into it. 34 The owner of the pit must pay full compen-
sation to the owner of the animal, but then he gets to keep the dead animal.

35 “If someone’s ox injures a neighbor’s ox and the injured ox dies, then
the two owners must sell the live ox and divide the price equally between
them. They must also divide the dead animal. 36 But if the ox had a reputa-
tion for goring, yet its owner failed to keep it under control, he must pay full
compensation—a live ox for the dead one—but he may keep the dead ox.

Protection of Property

22 1* “If someone steals an ox* or sheep and then kills or sells it, the
thief must pay back five oxen for each ox stolen, and four sheep for
each sheep stolen.

2* “If a thief is caught in the act of breaking into a house and is struck
and killed in the process, the person who killed the thief is not guilty of
murder. 3 But if it happens in daylight, the one who killed the thief is guilty
of murder.

“A thief who is caught must pay in full for everything he stole. If he can-
not pay, he must be sold as a slave to pay for his theft. 4 If someone steals an
ox or a donkey or a sheep and it is found in the thief’s possession, then the
thief must pay double the value of the stolen animal.

5 “If an animal is grazing in a field or vineyard and the owner lets it stray
into someone else’s field to graze, then the animal’s owner must pay com-
pensation from the best of his own grain or grapes.

6 “If you are burning thornbushes and the fire gets out of control and
spreads into another person’s field, destroying the sheaves or the uncut grain
or the whole crop, the one who started the fire must pay for the lost crop.

7 “Suppose someone leaves money or goods with a neighbor for safe-
keeping, and they are stolen from the neighbor’s house. If the thief is caught,
the compensation is double the value of what was stolen. 8 But if the thief
is not caught, the neighbor must appear before God,* who will determine
if he stole the property.

9 “Suppose there is a dispute between two people who both claim to own
a particular ox, donkey, sheep, article of clothing, or any lost property. Both
parties must come before God, and the person whom God declares* guilty
must pay double compensation to the other.

10 “Now suppose someone leaves a donkey, ox, sheep, or any other animal
with a neighbor for safekeeping, but it dies or is injured or is taken away,
and no one sees what happened. 11 The neighbor must then take an oath in
the presence of the LORD. If the LORD confirms that the neighbor did not
steal the property, the owner must accept the verdict, and no payment will
be required. 12 But if the animal was indeed stolen, the guilty person must

21:32 Hebrew *30 shekels of silver,* about 12 ounces or 342 grams in weight. **22:1a** Verse 22:1 is numbered 21:37 in Hebrew text. **22:1b** Or *bull,* or *cow;* also in 22:4, 9, 10. **22:2** Verses 22:2-31 are numbered 22:1-30 in Hebrew text. **22:8** Or *before the judges.* **22:9** Or *before the judges, and the person whom the judges declare.*

pay compensation to the owner. 13 If it was torn to pieces by a wild animal,
the remains of the carcass must be shown as evidence, and no compensation
will be required.
14 "If someone borrows an animal from a neighbor and it is injured or
dies when the owner is absent, the person who borrowed it must pay full
compensation. 15 But if the owner was present, no compensation is required.
And no compensation is required if the animal was rented, for this loss is
covered by the rental fee.

Social Responsibility

16 "If a man seduces a virgin who is not engaged to anyone and has sex with
her, he must pay the customary bride price and marry her. 17 But if her father
refuses to let him marry her, the man must still pay him an amount equal to
the bride price of a virgin.
18 "You must not allow a sorceress to live.
19 "Anyone who has sexual relations with an animal must certainly be put
to death.
20 "Anyone who sacrifices to any god other than the LORD must be destroyed.*
21 "You must not mistreat or oppress foreigners in any way. Remember,
you yourselves were once foreigners in the land of Egypt.
22 "You must not exploit a widow or an orphan. 23 If you exploit them in
any way and they cry out to me, then I will certainly hear their cry. 24 My anger
will blaze against you, and I will kill you with the sword. Then your wives
will be widows and your children fatherless.
25 "If you lend money to any of my people who are in need, do not charge
interest as a money lender would. 26 If you take your neighbor's cloak as se-
curity for a loan, you must return it before sunset. 27 This coat may be the
only blanket your neighbor has. How can a person sleep without it? If you
do not return it and your neighbor cries out to me for help, then I will hear,
for I am merciful.
28 "You must not dishonor God or curse any of your rulers.
29 "You must not hold anything back when you give me offerings from
your crops and your wine.
"You must give me your firstborn sons.
30 "You must also give me the firstborn of your cattle, sheep, and goats.
But leave the newborn animal with its mother for seven days; then give it
to me on the eighth day.
31 "You must be my holy people. Therefore, do not eat any animal that has
been torn up and killed by wild animals. Throw it to the dogs.

A Call for Justice

23 "You must not pass along false rumors. You must not cooperate with
evil people by lying on the witness stand.
2 "You must not follow the crowd in doing wrong. When you are called
to testify in a dispute, do not be swayed by the crowd to twist justice. 3 And
do not slant your testimony in favor of a person just because that person
is poor.
4 "If you come upon your enemy's ox or donkey that has strayed away, take

22:20 The Hebrew term used here refers to the complete consecration of things or people to the LORD, either by destroying them or by giving them as an offering.

Prayer **22:23**

Lord, you care for everyone and especially have a heart for widows and orphans. Show me how I can love those whom you care about so much. Amen.

Question **23:2**

Are you ever tempted to follow the crowd in doing wrong? How does God see this as an act of injustice?

it back to its owner. 5If you see that the donkey of someone who hates you has collapsed under its load, do not walk by. Instead, stop and help.

6"In a lawsuit, you must not deny justice to the poor.

7"Be sure never to charge anyone falsely with evil. Never sentence an innocent or blameless person to death, for I never declare a guilty person to be innocent.

8"Take no bribes, for a bribe makes you ignore something that you clearly see. A bribe makes even a righteous person twist the truth.

9"You must not oppress foreigners. You know what it's like to be a foreigner, for you yourselves were once foreigners in the land of Egypt.

10"Plant and harvest your crops for six years, 11but let the land be renewed and lie uncultivated during the seventh year. Then let the poor among you harvest whatever grows on its own. Leave the rest for wild animals to eat. The same applies to your vineyards and olive groves.

12"You have six days each week for your ordinary work, but on the seventh day you must stop working. This gives your ox and your donkey a chance to rest. It also allows your slaves and the foreigners living among you to be refreshed.

13"Pay close attention to all my instructions. You must not call on the name of any other gods. Do not even speak their names.

Three Annual Festivals

14"Each year you must celebrate three festivals in my honor. 15First, celebrate the Festival of Unleavened Bread. For seven days the bread you eat must be made without yeast, just as I commanded you. Celebrate this festival annually at the appointed time in early spring, in the month of Abib,* for that is the anniversary of your departure from Egypt. No one may appear before me without an offering.

16"Second, celebrate the Festival of Harvest,* when you bring me the first crops of your harvest.

"Finally, celebrate the Festival of the Final Harvest* at the end of the harvest season, when you have harvested all the crops from your fields. 17At these three times each year, every man in Israel must appear before the Sovereign, the LORD.

18"You must not offer the blood of my sacrificial offerings together with any baked goods containing yeast. And do not leave the fat from the festival offerings until the next morning.

19"As you harvest your crops, bring the very best of the first harvest to the house of the LORD your God.

"You must not cook a young goat in its mother's milk.

A Promise of the LORD's Presence

20"See, I am sending an angel before you to protect you on your journey and lead you safely to the place I have prepared for you. 21Pay close attention to him, and obey his instructions. Do not rebel against him, for he is my representative, and he will not forgive your rebellion. 22But if you are careful to obey him, following all my instructions, then I will be an enemy to your

23:15 Hebrew *appointed time in the month of Abib.* This first month of the ancient Hebrew lunar calendar usually occurs within the months of March and April. **23:16a** Or *Festival of Weeks.* This was later called the Festival of Pentecost (see Acts 2:1). It is celebrated today as Shavuot (or Shabuoth). **23:16b** Or *Festival of Ingathering.* This was later called the Festival of Shelters or Festival of Tabernacles (see Lev 23:33-36). It is celebrated today as Sukkot (or Succoth).

enemies, and I will oppose those who oppose you. 23 For my angel will go before you and bring you into the land of the Amorites, Hittites, Perizzites, Canaanites, Hivites, and Jebusites, so you may live there. And I will destroy them completely. 24 You must not worship the gods of these nations or serve them in any way or imitate their evil practices. Instead, you must utterly destroy them and smash their sacred pillars.

25 "You must serve only the LORD your God. If you do, I* will bless you with food and water, and I will protect you from illness. 26 There will be no miscarriages or infertility in your land, and I will give you long, full lives.

27 "I will send my terror ahead of you and create panic among all the people whose lands you invade. I will make all your enemies turn and run. 28 I will send terror* ahead of you to drive out the Hivites, Canaanites, and Hittites. 29 But I will not drive them out in a single year, because the land would become desolate and the wild animals would multiply and threaten you. 30 I will drive them out a little at a time until your population has increased enough to take possession of the land. 31 And I will fix your boundaries from the Red Sea to the Mediterranean Sea,* and from the eastern wilderness to the Euphrates River.* I will hand over to you the people now living in the land, and you will drive them out ahead of you.

32 "Make no treaties with them or their gods. 33 They must not live in your land, or they will cause you to sin against me. If you serve their gods, you will be caught in the trap of idolatry."

Israel Accepts the LORD's Covenant

24 Then the LORD instructed Moses: "Come up here to me, and bring along Aaron, Nadab, Abihu, and seventy of Israel's elders. All of you must worship from a distance. 2 Only Moses is allowed to come near to the LORD. The others must not come near, and none of the other people are allowed to climb up the mountain with him."

3 Then Moses went down to the people and repeated all the instructions and regulations the LORD had given him. All the people answered with one voice, "We will do everything the LORD has commanded."

4 Then Moses carefully wrote down all the LORD's instructions. Early the next morning Moses got up and built an altar at the foot of the mountain. He also set up twelve pillars, one for each of the twelve tribes of Israel. 5 Then he sent some of the young Israelite men to present burnt offerings and to sacrifice bulls as peace offerings to the LORD. 6 Moses drained half the blood from these animals into basins. The other half he splattered against the altar. 7 Then he took the Book of the Covenant and read it aloud to the people. Again they all responded, "We will do everything the LORD has commanded. We will obey."

8 Then Moses took the blood from the basins and splattered it over the people, declaring, "Look, this blood confirms the covenant the LORD has made with you in giving you these instructions."

9 Then Moses, Aaron, Nadab, Abihu, and the seventy elders of Israel climbed up the mountain. 10 There they saw the God of Israel. Under his feet there seemed to be a surface of brilliant blue lapis lazuli, as clear as the sky itself. 11 And though these nobles of Israel gazed upon God, he did not

23:25 As in Greek and Latin versions; Hebrew reads *he.* 23:28 Often rendered *the hornet.* The meaning of the Hebrew is uncertain. 23:31a Hebrew *from the sea of reeds to the sea of the Philistines.* 23:31b Hebrew *from the wilderness to the river.*

Make a Difference

24:9–11

With Union

In a remarkable scene, Moses and several other of Israel's leaders shared a communion meal with the Lord. As they focused on the Lord together, "they saw the God of Israel" (v. 10).

Communion is a compound word. It simply means "with" + "union." To have communion with God means to be united in relationship and direction of life. Moses and the other leaders were able to gaze upon God, in awe of his presence, because they were in union with him and one another.

This moment was a glimpse of the personal conversations Jesus would have with his disciples about communion. The Israelites looked forward to a physical promised land, where God would dwell among them. Today, we can have an eternal relationship in which Immanuel ("God with us") dwells with us now and forever.

Difference Maker

The next time you take communion in your church, remember this scene in Exodus 24. Invite your friends to take communion seriously, united together in the presence of God.

Question **25:9**

Why might God be specific about how his people learn to connect with him? What do you think happens when people invent their own ways of connecting with God? How does John 14:6 relate to this question?

destroy them. In fact, they ate a covenant meal, eating and drinking in his presence!
12 Then the LORD said to Moses, "Come up to me on the mountain. Stay there, and I will give you the tablets of stone on which I have inscribed the instructions and commands so you can teach the people." 13 So Moses and his assistant Joshua set out, and Moses climbed up the mountain of God.
14 Moses told the elders, "Stay here and wait for us until we come back. Aaron and Hur are here with you. If anyone has a dispute while I am gone, consult with them."
15 Then Moses climbed up the mountain, and the cloud covered it. 16 And the glory of the LORD settled down on Mount Sinai, and the cloud covered it for six days. On the seventh day the LORD called to Moses from inside the cloud. 17 To the Israelites at the foot of the mountain, the glory of the LORD appeared at the summit like a consuming fire. 18 Then Moses disappeared into the cloud as he climbed higher up the mountain. He remained on the mountain forty days and forty nights.

Offerings for the Tabernacle

25 The LORD said to Moses, 2 "Tell the people of Israel to bring me their sacred offerings. Accept the contributions from all whose hearts are moved to offer them. 3 Here is a list of sacred offerings you may accept from them:

gold, silver, and bronze;
4 blue, purple, and scarlet thread;
fine linen and goat hair for cloth;
5 tanned ram skins and fine goatskin leather;
acacia wood;
6 olive oil for the lamps;
spices for the anointing oil and the fragrant incense;
7 onyx stones, and other gemstones to be set in the ephod and the priest's chestpiece.

8 "Have the people of Israel build me a holy sanctuary so I can live among them. 9 You must build this Tabernacle and its furnishings exactly according to the pattern I will show you.

Plans for the Ark of the Covenant

10 "Have the people make an Ark of acacia wood—a sacred chest 45 inches long, 27 inches wide, and 27 inches high.* 11 Overlay it inside and outside with pure gold, and run a molding of gold all around it. 12 Cast four gold rings and attach them to its four feet, two rings on each side. 13 Make poles from acacia wood, and overlay them with gold. 14 Insert the poles into the rings at the sides of the Ark to carry it. 15 These carrying poles must stay inside the rings; never remove them. 16 When the Ark is finished, place inside it the stone tablets inscribed with the terms of the covenant,* which I will give to you.
17 "Then make the Ark's cover—the place of atonement—from pure gold.

25:10 Hebrew *2.5 cubits* [115 centimeters] *long, 1.5 cubits* [69 centimeters] *wide, and 1.5 cubits high.* 25:16 Hebrew *Place inside the Ark the Testimony;* similarly in 25:21. The Hebrew word for "testimony" refers to the terms of the LORD's covenant with Israel as written on stone tablets, and also to the covenant itself.

It must be 45 inches long and 27 inches wide.* 18 Then make two cherubim from hammered gold, and place them on the two ends of the atonement cover. 19 Mold the cherubim on each end of the atonement cover, making it all of one piece of gold. 20 The cherubim will face each other and look down on the atonement cover. With their wings spread above it, they will protect it. 21 Place inside the Ark the stone tablets inscribed with the terms of the covenant, which I will give to you. Then put the atonement cover on top of the Ark. 22 I will meet with you there and talk to you from above the atonement cover between the gold cherubim that hover over the Ark of the Covenant.* From there I will give you my commands for the people of Israel.

Plans for the Table

23 "Then make a table of acacia wood, 36 inches long, 18 inches wide, and 27 inches high.* 24 Overlay it with pure gold and run a gold molding around the edge. 25 Decorate it with a 3-inch border* all around, and run a gold molding along the border. 26 Make four gold rings for the table and attach them at the four corners next to the four legs. 27 Attach the rings near the border to hold the poles that are used to carry the table. 28 Make these poles from acacia wood, and overlay them with gold. 29 Make special containers of pure gold for the table—bowls, ladles, pitchers, and jars—to be used in pouring out liquid offerings. 30 Place the Bread of the Presence on the table to remain before me at all times.

Plans for the Lampstand

31 "Make a lampstand of pure, hammered gold. Make the entire lampstand and its decorations of one piece—the base, center stem, lamp cups, buds, and petals. 32 Make it with six branches going out from the center stem, three on each side. 33 Each of the six branches will have three lamp cups shaped like almond blossoms, complete with buds and petals. 34 Craft the center stem of the lampstand with four lamp cups shaped like almond blossoms, complete with buds and petals. 35 There will also be an almond bud beneath each pair of branches where the six branches extend from the center stem. 36 The almond buds and branches must all be of one piece with the center stem, and they must be hammered from pure gold. 37 Then make the seven lamps for the lampstand, and set them so they reflect their light forward. 38 The lamp snuffers and trays must also be made of pure gold. 39 You will need 75 pounds* of pure gold for the lampstand and its accessories.

40 "Be sure that you make everything according to the pattern I have shown you here on the mountain.

Plans for the Tabernacle

26 "Make the Tabernacle from ten curtains of finely woven linen. Decorate the curtains with blue, purple, and scarlet thread and with skillfully embroidered cherubim. 2 These ten curtains must all be exactly the same size—42 feet long and 6 feet wide.* 3 Join five of these curtains together to make one long curtain, then join the other five into a second long curtain. 4 Put loops of blue yarn along the edge of the last curtain in each set. 5 The

25:17 Hebrew *2.5 cubits* [115 centimeters] *long and 1.5 cubits* [69 centimeters] *wide.* **25:22** Or *Ark of the Testimony.* **25:23** Hebrew *2 cubits* [92 centimeters] *long, 1 cubit* [46 centimeters] *wide, and 1.5 cubits* [69 centimeters] *high.* **25:25** Hebrew *a border of a handbreadth* [8 centimeters]. **25:39** Hebrew *1 talent* [34 kilograms]. **26:2** Hebrew *28 cubits* [12.9 meters] *long and 4 cubits* [1.8 meters] *wide.*

fifty loops along the edge of one curtain are to match the fifty loops along the edge of the other curtain. 6 Then make fifty gold clasps and fasten the long curtains together with the clasps. In this way, the Tabernacle will be made of one continuous piece.

7 “Make eleven curtains of goat-hair cloth to serve as a tent covering for the Tabernacle. 8 These eleven curtains must all be exactly the same size—45 feet long and 6 feet wide.* 9 Join five of these curtains together to make one long curtain, and join the other six into a second long curtain. Allow 3 feet of material from the second set of curtains to hang over the front* of the sacred tent. 10 Make fifty loops for one edge of each large curtain. 11 Then make fifty bronze clasps, and fasten the loops of the long curtains with the clasps. In this way, the tent covering will be made of one continuous piece. 12 The remaining 3 feet* of this tent covering will be left to hang over the back of the Tabernacle. 13 Allow 18 inches* of remaining material to hang down over each side, so the Tabernacle is completely covered. 14 Complete the tent covering with a protective layer of tanned ram skins and a layer of fine goatskin leather.

15 “For the framework of the Tabernacle, construct frames of acacia wood. 16 Each frame must be 15 feet high and 27 inches wide,* 17 with two pegs under each frame. Make all the frames identical. 18 Make twenty of these frames to support the curtains on the south side of the Tabernacle. 19 Also make forty silver bases—two bases under each frame, with the pegs fitting securely into the bases. 20 For the north side of the Tabernacle, make another twenty frames, 21 with their forty silver bases, two bases under each frame. 22 Make six frames for the rear—the west side of the Tabernacle—23 along with two additional frames to reinforce the rear corners of the Tabernacle. 24 These corner frames will be matched at the bottom and firmly attached at the top with a single ring, forming a single corner unit. Make both of these corner units the same way. 25 So there will be eight frames at the rear of the Tabernacle, set in sixteen silver bases—two bases under each frame.

26 “Make crossbars of acacia wood to link the frames, five crossbars for the north side of the Tabernacle 27 and five for the south side. Also make five crossbars for the rear of the Tabernacle, which will face west. 28 The middle crossbar, attached halfway up the frames, will run all the way from one end of the Tabernacle to the other. 29 Overlay the frames with gold, and make gold rings to hold the crossbars. Overlay the crossbars with gold as well.

30 “Set up this Tabernacle according to the pattern you were shown on the mountain.

31 “For the inside of the Tabernacle, make a special curtain of finely woven linen. Decorate it with blue, purple, and scarlet thread and with skillfully embroidered cherubim. 32 Hang this curtain on gold hooks attached to four posts of acacia wood. Overlay the posts with gold, and set them in four silver bases. 33 Hang the inner curtain from clasps, and put the Ark of the Covenant* in the room behind it. This curtain will separate the Holy Place from the Most Holy Place.

34 “Then put the Ark’s cover—the place of atonement—on top of the Ark of the Covenant inside the Most Holy Place. 35 Place the table outside the

26:8 Hebrew *30 cubits* [13.8 meters] *long and 4 cubits* [1.8 meters] *wide.* **26:9** Hebrew *Double over the sixth sheet at the front.* **26:12** Hebrew *The half sheet that is left over.* **26:13** Hebrew *1 cubit* [46 centimeters]. **26:16** Hebrew *10 cubits* [4.6 meters] *high and 1.5 cubits* [69 centimeters] *wide.* **26:33** Or *Ark of the Testimony;* also in 26:34.

inner curtain on the north side of the Tabernacle, and place the lampstand
across the room on the south side.
36 "Make another curtain for the entrance to the sacred tent. Make it of
finely woven linen and embroider it with exquisite designs, using blue,
purple, and scarlet thread. 37 Craft five posts from acacia wood. Overlay them
with gold, and hang the curtain from them with gold hooks. Cast five bronze
bases for the posts.

Plans for the Altar of Burnt Offering

27 "Using acacia wood, construct a square altar 7½ feet wide, 7½ feet
long, and 4½ feet high.* 2 Make horns for each of its four corners
so that the horns and altar are all one piece. Overlay the altar with bronze.
3 Make ash buckets, shovels, basins, meat forks, and firepans, all of bronze.
4 Make a bronze grating for it, and attach four bronze rings at its four cor-
ners. 5 Install the grating halfway down the side of the altar, under the ledge.
6 For carrying the altar, make poles from acacia wood, and overlay them with
bronze. 7 Insert the poles through the rings on the two sides of the altar. 8 The
altar must be hollow, made from planks. Build it just as you were shown on
the mountain.

Plans for the Courtyard

9 "Then make the courtyard for the Tabernacle, enclosed with curtains made
of finely woven linen. On the south side, make the curtains 150 feet long.*
10 They will be held up by twenty posts set securely in twenty bronze bases.
Hang the curtains with silver hooks and rings. 11 Make the curtains the same
on the north side—150 feet of curtains held up by twenty posts set securely
in bronze bases. Hang the curtains with silver hooks and rings. 12 The cur-
tains on the west end of the courtyard will be 75 feet long,* supported by ten
posts set into ten bases. 13 The east end of the courtyard, the front, will also
be 75 feet long. 14 The courtyard entrance will be on the east end, flanked by
two curtains. The curtain on the right side will be 22½ feet long,* supported
by three posts set into three bases. 15 The curtain on the left side will also be
22½ feet long, supported by three posts set into three bases.
16 "For the entrance to the courtyard, make a curtain that is 30 feet long.*
Make it from finely woven linen, and decorate it with beautiful embroidery
in blue, purple, and scarlet thread. Support it with four posts, each securely
set in its own base. 17 All the posts around the courtyard must have silver rings
and hooks and bronze bases. 18 So the entire courtyard will be 150 feet long
and 75 feet wide, with curtain walls 7½ feet high,* made from finely woven
linen. The bases for the posts will be made of bronze.
19 "All the articles used in the rituals of the Tabernacle, including all the
tent pegs used to support the Tabernacle and the courtyard curtains, must
be made of bronze.

Light for the Tabernacle

20 "Command the people of Israel to bring you pure oil of pressed olives for
the light, to keep the lamps burning continually. 21 The lampstand will stand

27:1 Hebrew *5 cubits* [2.3 meters] *wide, 5 cubits long, a square, and 3 cubits* [1.4 meters] *high.* 27:9 Hebrew *100 cubits* [46 meters]; also in 27:11. 27:12 Hebrew *50 cubits* [23 meters]; also in 27:13. 27:14 Hebrew *15 cubits* [6.9 meters]; also in 27:15. 27:16 Hebrew *20 cubits* [9.2 meters]. 27:18 Hebrew *100 cubits* [46 meters] *long and 50 by 50* [23 meters] *wide and 5 cubits* [2.3 meters] *high.*

What God is saying to us

Question 28:2

The Lord gave instructions for specific clothing for Aaron to set him apart as the high priest for Israel. Read Colossians 3:12 and consider this: How does God ask us to dress in a way that sets us apart?

in the Tabernacle, in front of the inner curtain that shields the Ark of the Covenant.* Aaron and his sons must keep the lamps burning in the LORD's presence all night. This is a permanent law for the people of Israel, and it must be observed from generation to generation.

Clothing for the Priests

28 "Call for your brother, Aaron, and his sons, Nadab, Abihu, Eleazar, and Ithamar. Set them apart from the rest of the people of Israel so they may minister to me and be my priests. 2 Make sacred garments for Aaron that are glorious and beautiful. 3 Instruct all the skilled craftsmen whom I have filled with the spirit of wisdom. Have them make garments for Aaron that will distinguish him as a priest set apart for my service. 4 These are the garments they are to make: a chestpiece, an ephod, a robe, a patterned tunic, a turban, and a sash. They are to make these sacred garments for your brother, Aaron, and his sons to wear when they serve me as priests. 5 So give them fine linen cloth, gold thread, and blue, purple, and scarlet thread.

Design of the Ephod

6 "The craftsmen must make the ephod of finely woven linen and skillfully embroider it with gold and with blue, purple, and scarlet thread. 7 It will consist of two pieces, front and back, joined at the shoulders with two shoulder-pieces. 8 The decorative sash will be made of the same materials: finely woven linen embroidered with gold and with blue, purple, and scarlet thread.

9 "Take two onyx stones, and engrave on them the names of the tribes of Israel. 10 Six names will be on each stone, arranged in the order of the births of the original sons of Israel. 11 Engrave these names on the two stones in the same way a jeweler engraves a seal. Then mount the stones in settings of gold filigree. 12 Fasten the two stones on the shoulder-pieces of the ephod as a reminder that Aaron represents the people of Israel. Aaron will carry these names on his shoulders as a constant reminder whenever he goes before the LORD. 13 Make the settings of gold filigree, 14 then braid two cords of pure gold and attach them to the filigree settings on the shoulders of the ephod.

Design of the Chestpiece

15 "Then, with great skill and care, make a chestpiece to be worn for seeking a decision from God.* Make it to match the ephod, using finely woven linen embroidered with gold and with blue, purple, and scarlet thread. 16 Make the chestpiece of a single piece of cloth folded to form a pouch nine inches* square. 17 Mount four rows of gemstones* on it. The first row will contain a red carnelian, a pale-green peridot, and an emerald. 18 The second row will contain a turquoise, a blue lapis lazuli, and a white moonstone. 19 The third row will contain an orange jacinth, an agate, and a purple amethyst. 20 The fourth row will contain a blue-green beryl, an onyx, and a green jasper. All these stones will be set in gold filigree. 21 Each stone will represent one of the twelve sons of Israel, and the name of that tribe will be engraved on it like a seal.

22 "To attach the chestpiece to the ephod, make braided cords of pure gold thread. 23 Then make two gold rings and attach them to the top corners of the

27:21 Hebrew *in the Tent of Meeting, outside the inner curtain that is in front of the Testimony.* See note on 25:16. **28:15** Hebrew *a chestpiece for decision.* **28:16** Hebrew *1 span* [23 centimeters]. **28:17** The identification of some of these gemstones is uncertain.

chestpiece. 24Tie the two gold cords to the two rings on the chestpiece. 25Tie the other ends of the cords to the gold settings on the shoulder-pieces of the ephod. 26Then make two more gold rings and attach them to the inside edges of the chestpiece next to the ephod. 27And make two more gold rings and attach them to the front of the ephod, below the shoulder-pieces, just above the knot where the decorative sash is fastened to the ephod. 28Then attach the bottom rings of the chestpiece to the rings on the ephod with blue cords. This will hold the chestpiece securely to the ephod above the decorative sash.

29"In this way, Aaron will carry the names of the tribes of Israel on the sacred chestpiece* over his heart when he goes into the Holy Place. This will be a continual reminder that he represents the people when he comes before the LORD. 30Insert the Urim and Thummim into the sacred chestpiece so they will be carried over Aaron's heart when he goes into the LORD's presence. In this way, Aaron will always carry over his heart the objects used to determine the LORD's will for his people whenever he goes in before the LORD.

Additional Clothing for the Priests

31"Make the robe that is worn with the ephod from a single piece of blue cloth, 32with an opening for Aaron's head in the middle of it. Reinforce the opening with a woven collar* so it will not tear. 33Make pomegranates out of blue, purple, and scarlet yarn, and attach them to the hem of the robe, with gold bells between them. 34The gold bells and pomegranates are to alternate all around the hem. 35Aaron will wear this robe whenever he ministers before the LORD, and the bells will tinkle as he goes in and out of the LORD's presence in the Holy Place. If he wears it, he will not die.

36"Next make a medallion of pure gold, and engrave it like a seal with these words: HOLY TO THE LORD. 37Attach the medallion with a blue cord to the front of Aaron's turban, where it must remain. 38Aaron must wear it on his forehead so he may take on himself any guilt of the people of Israel when they consecrate their sacred offerings. He must always wear it on his forehead so the LORD will accept the people.

39"Weave Aaron's patterned tunic from fine linen cloth. Fashion the turban from this linen as well. Also make a sash, and decorate it with colorful embroidery.

40"For Aaron's sons, make tunics, sashes, and special head coverings that are glorious and beautiful. 41Clothe your brother, Aaron, and his sons with these garments, and then anoint and ordain them. Consecrate them so they can serve as my priests. 42Also make linen undergarments for them, to be worn next to their bodies, reaching from their hips to their thighs. 43These must be worn whenever Aaron and his sons enter the Tabernacle* or approach the altar in the Holy Place to perform their priestly duties. Then they will not incur guilt and die. This is a permanent law for Aaron and all his descendants after him.

Dedication of the Priests

29 "This is the ceremony you must follow when you consecrate Aaron and his sons to serve me as priests: Take a young bull and two rams with no defects. 2Then, using choice wheat flour and no yeast, make loaves of bread, thin cakes mixed with olive oil, and wafers spread with oil. 3Place

28:29 Hebrew *the chestpiece for decision;* also in 28:30. See 28:15. 28:32 The meaning of the Hebrew is uncertain. 28:43 Hebrew *Tent of Meeting.*

them all in a single basket, and present them at the entrance of the Tabernacle, along with the young bull and the two rams.

[4]"Present Aaron and his sons at the entrance of the Tabernacle,* and wash them with water. [5]Dress Aaron in his priestly garments—the tunic, the robe worn with the ephod, the ephod itself, and the chestpiece. Then wrap the decorative sash of the ephod around him. [6]Place the turban on his head, and fasten the sacred medallion to the turban. [7]Then anoint him by pouring the anointing oil over his head. [8]Next present his sons, and dress them in their tunics. [9]Wrap the sashes around the waists of Aaron and his sons, and put their special head coverings on them. Then the right to the priesthood will be theirs by law forever. In this way, you will ordain Aaron and his sons.

[10]"Bring the young bull to the entrance of the Tabernacle, where Aaron and his sons will lay their hands on its head. [11]Then slaughter the bull in the LORD's presence at the entrance of the Tabernacle. [12]Put some of its blood on the horns of the altar with your finger, and pour out the rest at the base of the altar. [13]Take all the fat around the internal organs, the long lobe of the liver, and the two kidneys and the fat around them, and burn it all on the altar. [14]Then take the rest of the bull, including its hide, meat, and dung, and burn it outside the camp as a sin offering.

[15]"Next Aaron and his sons must lay their hands on the head of one of the rams. [16]Then slaughter the ram, and splatter its blood against all sides of the altar. [17]Cut the ram into pieces, and wash off the internal organs and the legs. Set them alongside the head and the other pieces of the body, [18]then burn the entire animal on the altar. This is a burnt offering to the LORD; it is a pleasing aroma, a special gift presented to the LORD.

[19]"Now take the other ram, and have Aaron and his sons lay their hands on its head. [20]Then slaughter it, and apply some of its blood to the right earlobes of Aaron and his sons. Also put it on the thumbs of their right hands and the big toes of their right feet. Splatter the rest of the blood against all sides of the altar. [21]Then take some of the blood from the altar and some of the anointing oil, and sprinkle it on Aaron and his sons and on their garments. In this way, they and their garments will be set apart as holy.

[22]"Since this is the ram for the ordination of Aaron and his sons, take the fat of the ram, including the fat of the broad tail, the fat around the internal organs, the long lobe of the liver, and the two kidneys and the fat around them, along with the right thigh. [23]Then take one round loaf of bread, one thin cake mixed with olive oil, and one wafer from the basket of bread without yeast that was placed in the LORD's presence. [24]Put all these in the hands of Aaron and his sons to be lifted up as a special offering to the LORD. [25]Afterward take the various breads from their hands, and burn them on the altar along with the burnt offering. It is a pleasing aroma to the LORD, a special gift for him. [26]Then take the breast of Aaron's ordination ram, and lift it up in the LORD's presence as a special offering to him. Then keep it as your own portion.

[27]"Set aside the portions of the ordination ram that belong to Aaron and his sons. This includes the breast and the thigh that were lifted up before the LORD as a special offering. [28]In the future, whenever the people of Israel lift up a peace offering, a portion of it must be set aside for Aaron and his descendants. This is their permanent right, and it is a sacred offering from the Israelites to the LORD.

29:4 Hebrew *Tent of Meeting;* also in 29:10, 11, 30, 32, 42, 44.

29 “Aaron’s sacred garments must be preserved for his descendants who succeed him, and they will wear them when they are anointed and ordained. 30 The descendant who succeeds him as high priest will wear these clothes for seven days as he ministers in the Tabernacle and the Holy Place.

31 “Take the ram used in the ordination ceremony, and boil its meat in a sacred place. 32 Then Aaron and his sons will eat this meat, along with the bread in the basket, at the Tabernacle entrance. 33 They alone may eat the meat and bread used for their purification* in the ordination ceremony. No one else may eat them, for these things are set apart and holy. 34 If any of the ordination meat or bread remains until the morning, it must be burned. It may not be eaten, for it is holy.

35 “This is how you will ordain Aaron and his sons to their offices, just as I have commanded you. The ordination ceremony will go on for seven days. 36 Each day you must sacrifice a young bull as a sin offering to purify them, making them right with the LORD.* Afterward, cleanse the altar by purifying it*; make it holy by anointing it with oil. 37 Purify the altar, and consecrate it every day for seven days. After that, the altar will be absolutely holy, and whatever touches it will become holy.

38 “These are the sacrifices you are to offer regularly on the altar. Each day, offer two lambs that are a year old, 39 one in the morning and the other in the evening. 40 With one of them, offer two quarts of choice flour mixed with one quart of pure oil of pressed olives; also, offer one quart of wine* as a liquid offering. 41 Offer the other lamb in the evening, along with the same offerings of flour and wine as in the morning. It will be a pleasing aroma, a special gift presented to the LORD.

42 “These burnt offerings are to be made each day from generation to generation. Offer them in the LORD’s presence at the Tabernacle entrance; there I will meet with you and speak with you. 43 I will meet the people of Israel there, in the place made holy by my glorious presence. 44 Yes, I will consecrate the Tabernacle and the altar, and I will consecrate Aaron and his sons to serve me as priests. 45 Then I will live among the people of Israel and be their God, 46 and they will know that I am the LORD their God. I am the one who brought them out of the land of Egypt so that I could live among them. I am the LORD their God.

Prayer 29:45

Lord, all throughout your Bible, you tell your people that you want to live among them. Then you sent Jesus to do just that. God, come live in me and in my family and friends through your Holy Spirit today. I want you to dwell among us. Amen.

Plans for the Incense Altar

30 “Then make another altar of acacia wood for burning incense. 2 Make it 18 inches square and 36 inches high,* with horns at the corners carved from the same piece of wood as the altar itself. 3 Overlay the top, sides, and horns of the altar with pure gold, and run a gold molding around the entire altar. 4 Make two gold rings, and attach them on opposite sides of the altar below the gold molding to hold the carrying poles. 5 Make the poles of acacia wood and overlay them with gold. 6 Place the incense altar just outside the inner curtain that shields the Ark of the Covenant,* in front of the Ark’s cover—the place of atonement—that covers the tablets inscribed with the terms of the covenant.* I will meet with you there.

7 “Every morning when Aaron maintains the lamps, he must burn fragrant

29:33 Or *their atonement.* **29:36a** Or *to make atonement.* **29:36b** Or *by making atonement for it;* similarly in 29:37. **29:40** Hebrew *1⁄10 [of an ephah]* [2.2 liters] *of choice flour . . . 1⁄4 of a hin* [1 liter] *of pure oil . . . 1⁄4 of a hin of wine.* **30:2** Hebrew *1 cubit* [46 centimeters] *long and 1 cubit wide, a square, and 2 cubits* [92 centimeters] *high.* **30:6a** Or *Ark of the Testimony;* also in 30:26. **30:6b** Hebrew *that covers the Testimony;* see note on 25:16.

incense on the altar. 8 And each evening when he lights the lamps, he must
again burn incense in the LORD's presence. This must be done from genera-
tion to generation. 9 Do not offer any unholy incense on this altar, or any
burnt offerings, grain offerings, or liquid offerings.

10 "Once a year Aaron must purify* the altar by smearing its horns with
blood from the offering made to purify the people from their sin. This will be
a regular, annual event from generation to generation, for this is the LORD's
most holy altar."

Money for the Tabernacle

11 Then the LORD said to Moses, 12 "Whenever you take a census of the people
of Israel, each man who is counted must pay a ransom for himself to the
LORD. Then no plague will strike the people as you count them. 13 Each per-
son who is counted must give a small piece of silver as a sacred offering to
the LORD. (This payment is half a shekel,* based on the sanctuary shekel,
which equals twenty gerahs.) 14 All who have reached their twentieth birth-
day must give this sacred offering to the LORD. 15 When this offering is given
to the LORD to purify your lives, making you right with him,* the rich must
not give more than the specified amount, and the poor must not give less.
16 Receive this ransom money from the Israelites, and use it for the care of
the Tabernacle.* It will bring the Israelites to the LORD's attention, and it
will purify your lives."

Plans for the Washbasin

17 Then the LORD said to Moses, 18 "Make a bronze washbasin with a bronze
stand. Place it between the Tabernacle and the altar, and fill it with water.
19 Aaron and his sons will wash their hands and feet there. 20 They must
wash with water whenever they go into the Tabernacle to appear before the
LORD and when they approach the altar to burn up their special gifts to the
LORD—or they will die! 21 They must always wash their hands and feet, or
they will die. This is a permanent law for Aaron and his descendants, to be
observed from generation to generation."

The Anointing Oil

22 Then the LORD said to Moses, 23 "Collect choice spices—12½ pounds of
pure myrrh, 6¼ pounds of fragrant cinnamon, 6¼ pounds of fragrant
calamus,* 24 and 12½ pounds of cassia*—as measured by the weight of the
sanctuary shekel. Also get one gallon of olive oil.* 25 Like a skilled incense
maker, blend these ingredients to make a holy anointing oil. 26 Use this sacred
oil to anoint the Tabernacle, the Ark of the Covenant, 27 the table and all its
utensils, the lampstand and all its accessories, the incense altar, 28 the altar of
burnt offering and all its utensils, and the washbasin with its stand. 29 Conse-
crate them to make them absolutely holy. After this, whatever touches them
will also become holy.

30 "Anoint Aaron and his sons also, consecrating them to serve me as
priests. 31 And say to the people of Israel, 'This holy anointing oil is reserved
for me from generation to generation. 32 It must never be used to anoint

30:10 Or *make atonement for;* also in 30:10b. **30:13** Or *0.2 ounces* [6 grams]. **30:15** Or *to make atonement for your lives;* similarly in 30:16. **30:16** Hebrew *Tent of Meeting;* also in 30:18, 20, 26, 36. **30:23** Hebrew *500 [shekels]* [5.7 kilograms] *of pure myrrh, 250 [shekels]* [2.9 kilograms] *of fragrant cinnamon, 250 [shekels] of fragrant calamus.* **30:24a** Hebrew *500 [shekels]* [5.7 kilograms] *of cassia.* **30:24b** Hebrew *1 hin* [3.8 liters] *of olive oil.*

anyone else, and you must never make any blend like it for yourselves. It is
holy, and you must treat it as holy. 33 Anyone who makes a blend like it or
anoints someone other than a priest will be cut off from the community.'"

The Incense

34 Then the LORD said to Moses, "Gather fragrant spices—resin droplets,
mollusk shell, and galbanum—and mix these fragrant spices with pure
frankincense, weighed out in equal amounts. 35 Using the usual techniques
of the incense maker, blend the spices together and sprinkle them with salt
to produce a pure and holy incense. 36 Grind some of the mixture into a very
fine powder and put it in front of the Ark of the Covenant,* where I will meet
with you in the Tabernacle. You must treat this incense as most holy. 37 Never
use this formula to make this incense for yourselves. It is reserved for the
LORD, and you must treat it as holy. 38 Anyone who makes incense like this
for personal use will be cut off from the community."

Craftsmen: Bezalel and Oholiab

31 Then the LORD said to Moses, 2 "Look, I have specifically chosen Bez-
alel son of Uri, grandson of Hur, of the tribe of Judah. 3 I have filled
him with the Spirit of God, giving him great wisdom, ability, and expertise
in all kinds of crafts. 4 He is a master craftsman, expert in working with gold,
silver, and bronze. 5 He is skilled in engraving and mounting gemstones and
in carving wood. He is a master at every craft!

6 "And I have personally appointed Oholiab son of Ahisamach, of the tribe
of Dan, to be his assistant. Moreover, I have given special skill to all the gifted
craftsmen so they can make all the things I have commanded you to make:

7 the Tabernacle;*
the Ark of the Covenant;*
the Ark's cover—the place of atonement;
all the furnishings of the Tabernacle;
8 the table and its utensils;
the pure gold lampstand with all its accessories;
the incense altar;
9 the altar of burnt offering with all its utensils;
the washbasin with its stand;
10 the beautifully stitched garments—the sacred garments for Aaron
the priest, and the garments for his sons to wear as they minister as
priests;
11 the anointing oil;
the fragrant incense for the Holy Place.

The craftsmen must make everything as I have commanded you."

Instructions for the Sabbath

12 The LORD then gave these instructions to Moses: 13 "Tell the people of
Israel: 'Be careful to keep my Sabbath day, for the Sabbath is a sign of the
covenant between me and you from generation to generation. It is given so
you may know that I am the LORD, who makes you holy. 14 You must keep

30:36 Hebrew *in front of the Testimony;* see note on 25:16. 31:7a Hebrew *the Tent of Meeting.*
31:7b Hebrew *the Ark of the Testimony.*

Question 31:13

Every seven days, God wants people to have a day of rest and restoration with him and one another. Do you view Sabbath as a "have-to" day or a "get-to" day? As an option or a necessity? How could you make Sabbath a meaningful experience in the way God intended it to be?

Story Arc 31:1–11

● Bezalel

When you think of a leader God uses, you might consider those who are up front giving speeches or decisive point people who make command decisions. Bezalel is a different example of someone who reveals the creativity God puts into those whom he chooses to use. The Lord supernaturally gifted Bezalel and other craftsmen to make what was needed in the building of the tabernacle. This means that God recognized this kind of job to be just as important as any other role, which is why he enabled it through the Holy Spirit. By being creative for the Lord, they were able to tell his story to everyone in a powerful way.

In a similar way, consider that God has given you skill sets to help others connect to the life-changing message of Jesus.

Exod 38:22-23 ►

the Sabbath day, for it is a holy day for you. Anyone who desecrates it must
be put to death; anyone who works on that day will be cut off from the
community. 15 You have six days each week for your ordinary work, but the
seventh day must be a Sabbath day of complete rest, a holy day dedicated to
the LORD. Anyone who works on the Sabbath must be put to death. 16 The
people of Israel must keep the Sabbath day by observing it from generation
to generation. This is a covenant obligation for all time. 17 It is a permanent
sign of my covenant with the people of Israel. For in six days the LORD
made heaven and earth, but on the seventh day he stopped working and
was refreshed.'"

18 When the LORD finished speaking with Moses on Mount Sinai, he gave
him the two stone tablets inscribed with the terms of the covenant,* written
by the finger of God.

The Gold Calf

32 When the people saw how long it was taking Moses to come back
down the mountain, they gathered around Aaron. "Come on," they
said, "make us some gods who can lead us. We don't know what happened
to this fellow Moses, who brought us here from the land of Egypt."

2 So Aaron said, "Take the gold rings from the ears of your wives and sons
and daughters, and bring them to me."

3 All the people took the gold rings from their ears and brought them to
Aaron. 4 Then Aaron took the gold, melted it down, and molded it into the
shape of a calf. When the people saw it, they exclaimed, "O Israel, these are
the gods who brought you out of the land of Egypt!"

5 Aaron saw how excited the people were, so he built an altar in front of
the calf. Then he announced, "Tomorrow will be a festival to the LORD!"

6 The people got up early the next morning to sacrifice burnt offerings
and peace offerings. After this, they celebrated with feasting and drinking,
and they indulged in pagan revelry.

7 The LORD told Moses, "Quick! Go down the mountain! Your people
whom you brought from the land of Egypt have corrupted themselves. 8 How
quickly they have turned away from the way I commanded them to live! They
have melted down gold and made a calf, and they have bowed down and
sacrificed to it. They are saying, 'These are your gods, O Israel, who brought
you out of the land of Egypt.'"

9 Then the LORD said, "I have seen how stubborn and rebellious these
people are. 10 Now leave me alone so my fierce anger can blaze against them,
and I will destroy them. Then I will make you, Moses, into a great nation."

11 But Moses tried to pacify the LORD his God. "O LORD!" he said. "Why
are you so angry with your own people whom you brought from the land of
Egypt with such great power and such a strong hand? 12 Why let the Egyp-
tians say, 'Their God rescued them with the evil intention of slaughtering
them in the mountains and wiping them from the face of the earth'? Turn
away from your fierce anger. Change your mind about this terrible disaster
you have threatened against your people! 13 Remember your servants Abra-
ham, Isaac, and Jacob.* You bound yourself with an oath to them, saying, 'I
will make your descendants as numerous as the stars of heaven. And I will

31:18 Hebrew *the two tablets of the Testimony;* see note on 25:16. **32:13** Hebrew *Israel.* The names "Jacob" and "Israel" are often interchanged throughout the Old Testament, referring sometimes to the individual patriarch and sometimes to the nation.

give them all of this land that I have promised to your descendants, and they
will possess it forever.'"
[14]So the LORD changed his mind about the terrible disaster he had threat-
ened to bring on his people.
[15]Then Moses turned and went down the mountain. He held in his hands
the two stone tablets inscribed with the terms of the covenant.* They were
inscribed on both sides, front and back. [16]These tablets were God's work; the
words on them were written by God himself.
[17]When Joshua heard the boisterous noise of the people shouting below
them, he exclaimed to Moses, "It sounds like war in the camp!"
[18]But Moses replied, "No, it's not a shout of victory nor the wailing of
defeat. I hear the sound of a celebration."
[19]When they came near the camp, Moses saw the calf and the dancing, and
he burned with anger. He threw the stone tablets to the ground, smashing
them at the foot of the mountain. [20]He took the calf they had made and
burned it. Then he ground it into powder, threw it into the water, and forced
the people to drink it.
[21]Finally, he turned to Aaron and demanded, "What did these people do
to you to make you bring such terrible sin upon them?"
[22]"Don't get so upset, my lord," Aaron replied. "You yourself know how evil
these people are. [23]They said to me, 'Make us gods who will lead us. We don't
know what happened to this fellow Moses, who brought us here from the
land of Egypt.' [24]So I told them, 'Whoever has gold jewelry, take it off.' When
they brought it to me, I simply threw it into the fire—and out came this calf!"
[25]Moses saw that Aaron had let the people get completely out of control,
much to the amusement of their enemies.* [26]So he stood at the entrance to
the camp and shouted, "All of you who are on the LORD's side, come here
and join me." And all the Levites gathered around him.
[27]Moses told them, "This is what the LORD, the God of Israel, says: Each
of you, take your swords and go back and forth from one end of the camp
to the other. Kill everyone—even your brothers, friends, and neighbors."
[28]The Levites obeyed Moses' command, and about 3,000 people died that day.
[29]Then Moses told the Levites, "Today you have ordained yourselves* for
the service of the LORD, for you obeyed him even though it meant killing
your own sons and brothers. Today you have earned a blessing."

Moses Intercedes for Israel

▲ [30]The next day Moses said to the people, "You have committed a terrible sin,
but I will go back up to the LORD on the mountain. Perhaps I will be able to
obtain forgiveness* for your sin."
[31]So Moses returned to the LORD and said, "Oh, what a terrible sin these
people have committed. They have made gods of gold for themselves. [32]But
now, if you will only forgive their sin—but if not, erase my name from the
record you have written!"
[33]But the LORD replied to Moses, "No, I will erase the name of everyone
who has sinned against me. [34]Now go, lead the people to the place I told you
about. Look! My angel will lead the way before you. And when I come to call
the people to account, I will certainly hold them responsible for their sins."

32:15 Hebrew *the two tablets of the Testimony;* see note on 25:16. **32:25** Or *out of control, and they mocked anyone who opposed them.* The meaning of the Hebrew is uncertain. **32:29** As in Greek and Latin versions; Hebrew reads *Today ordain yourselves.* **32:30** Or *to make atonement.*

Prayer **32:30**

Lord, it's so easy to get distracted by man-made things. Show me the difference between these things and the things of you and remind me of the joy of fixing my eyes on you. Amen.

Make a Difference

33:7-11

God's Friend

Moses talked to God "as one speaks to a friend" (v. 11). Moses did not treat God like he was some distant cosmic force to be manipulated. Moses didn't just reach out to God when he needed something. Moses didn't ignore God when life was fine. Moses treated God like a friend, and God treated Moses the same way.

God is relational. God wants a face-to-face relationship with you. God wants to have conversation with you and share his heart with you. God wants to be your friend who sticks closer to you than a brother (Proverbs 18:24).

God made this friendship possible by coming to earth to dwell with you. Jesus referred to himself as a friend of sinners (Luke 7:34). Jesus called his disciples his friends (John 15:15).

Difference Maker

Today, practice praying with the Lord as your closest friend. Invite God into the regular routines of your day. In everything you do, hang out with God. Share your hopes and dreams, your concerns and passions with him. Let God share his with you.

Question **33:16**

Recognizing the presence of God in your life will set you apart from others. What will you do with this reality and responsibility?

35 Then the LORD sent a great plague upon the people because they had
worshiped the calf Aaron had made.

33 The LORD said to Moses, "Get going, you and the people you brought
up from the land of Egypt. Go up to the land I swore to give to Abra-
ham, Isaac, and Jacob. I told them, 'I will give this land to your descendants.'
2 And I will send an angel before you to drive out the Canaanites, Amorites,
Hittites, Perizzites, Hivites, and Jebusites. 3 Go up to this land that flows
with milk and honey. But I will not travel among you, for you are a stubborn
and rebellious people. If I did, I would surely destroy you along the way."
4 When the people heard these stern words, they went into mourning and
stopped wearing their jewelry and fine clothes. 5 For the LORD had told Moses
to tell them, "You are a stubborn and rebellious people. If I were to travel
with you for even a moment, I would destroy you. Remove your jewelry and
fine clothes while I decide what to do with you." 6 So from the time they left
Mount Sinai,* the Israelites wore no more jewelry or fine clothes.
7 It was Moses' practice to take the Tent of Meeting* and set it up some
distance from the camp. Everyone who wanted to make a request of the LORD
would go to the Tent of Meeting outside the camp.
8 Whenever Moses went out to the Tent of Meeting, all the people would
get up and stand in the entrances of their own tents. They would all watch
Moses until he disappeared inside. 9 As he went into the tent, the pillar of
cloud would come down and hover at its entrance while the LORD spoke with
Moses. 10 When the people saw the cloud standing at the entrance of the tent,
they would stand and bow down in front of their own tents. 11 Inside the Tent
of Meeting, the LORD would speak to Moses face to face, as one speaks to a
friend. Afterward Moses would return to the camp, but the young man who
assisted him, Joshua son of Nun, would remain behind in the Tent of Meeting.

Moses Sees the LORD's Glory

12 One day Moses said to the LORD, "You have been telling me, 'Take these
people up to the Promised Land.' But you haven't told me whom you will
send with me. You have told me, 'I know you by name, and I look favorably
on you.' 13 If it is true that you look favorably on me, let me know your ways
so I may understand you more fully and continue to enjoy your favor. And
remember that this nation is your very own people."
14 The LORD replied, "I will personally go with you, Moses, and I will give
you rest—everything will be fine for you."
15 Then Moses said, "If you don't personally go with us, don't make us leave
this place. 16 How will anyone know that you look favorably on me—on me
and on your people—if you don't go with us? For your presence among us
sets your people and me apart from all other people on the earth."
17 The LORD replied to Moses, "I will indeed do what you have asked, for
I look favorably on you, and I know you by name."
18 Moses responded, "Then show me your glorious presence."
19 The LORD replied, "I will make all my goodness pass before you, and I
will call out my name, Yahweh,* before you. For I will show mercy to anyone

33:6 Hebrew *Horeb,* another name for Sinai. 33:7 This "Tent of Meeting" is different from the Tabernacle described in chapters 26 and 36. 33:19 *Yahweh* is a transliteration of the proper name *YHWH* that is sometimes rendered "Jehovah"; in this translation it is usually rendered "the LORD" (note the use of small capitals).

I choose, and I will show compassion to anyone I choose. 20 But you may
not look directly at my face, for no one may see me and live." 21 The LORD
continued, "Look, stand near me on this rock. 22 As my glorious presence
passes by, I will hide you in the crevice of the rock and cover you with my
hand until I have passed by. 23 Then I will remove my hand and let you see
me from behind. But my face will not be seen."

A New Copy of the Covenant

34 Then the LORD told Moses, "Chisel out two stone tablets like the first
ones. I will write on them the same words that were on the tablets
you smashed. 2 Be ready in the morning to climb up Mount Sinai and present
yourself to me on the top of the mountain. 3 No one else may come with you.
In fact, no one is to appear anywhere on the mountain. Do not even let the
flocks or herds graze near the mountain."

4 So Moses chiseled out two tablets of stone like the first ones. Early in the
morning he climbed Mount Sinai as the LORD had commanded him, and he
carried the two stone tablets in his hands.

5 Then the LORD came down in a cloud and stood there with him; and
he called out his own name, Yahweh.* 6 The LORD passed in front of Moses,
calling out,

"Yahweh!* The LORD!
The God of compassion and mercy!
I am slow to anger
and filled with unfailing love and faithfulness.
7 I lavish unfailing love to a thousand generations.*
I forgive iniquity, rebellion, and sin.
But I do not excuse the guilty.
I lay the sins of the parents upon their children and
grandchildren;
the entire family is affected—
even children in the third and fourth generations."

8 Moses immediately threw himself to the ground and worshiped. 9 And he
said, "O Lord, if it is true that I have found favor with you, then please travel
with us. Yes, this is a stubborn and rebellious people, but please forgive our
iniquity and our sins. Claim us as your own special possession."

10 The LORD replied, "Listen, I am making a covenant with you in the pres-
ence of all your people. I will perform miracles that have never been per-
formed anywhere in all the earth or in any nation. And all the people around
you will see the power of the LORD—the awesome power I will display for
you. 11 But listen carefully to everything I command you today. Then I will
go ahead of you and drive out the Amorites, Canaanites, Hittites, Perizzites,
Hivites, and Jebusites.

12 "Be very careful never to make a treaty with the people who live in the
land where you are going. If you do, you will follow their evil ways and be
trapped. 13 Instead, you must break down their pagan altars, smash their sa-
cred pillars, and cut down their Asherah poles. 14 You must worship no other

34:5 *Yahweh* is a transliteration of the proper name *YHWH* that is sometimes rendered "Jehovah"; in this translation it is usually rendered "the LORD" (note the use of small capitals).
34:6 See note on 34:5. **34:7** Hebrew *for thousands.*

Question 34:29

If spending time with God could transform you, then how much time are you really willing to spend with him?

gods, for the LORD, whose very name is Jealous, is a God who is jealous about his relationship with you.

15 "You must not make a treaty of any kind with the people living in the land. They lust after their gods, offering sacrifices to them. They will invite you to join them in their sacrificial meals, and you will go with them. 16 Then you will accept their daughters, who sacrifice to other gods, as wives for your sons. And they will seduce your sons to commit adultery against me by worshiping other gods. 17 You must not make any gods of molten metal for yourselves.

18 "You must celebrate the Festival of Unleavened Bread. For seven days the bread you eat must be made without yeast, just as I commanded you. Celebrate this festival annually at the appointed time in early spring, in the month of Abib,* for that is the anniversary of your departure from Egypt.

19 "The firstborn of every animal belongs to me, including the firstborn males* from your herds of cattle and your flocks of sheep and goats. 20 A firstborn donkey may be bought back from the LORD by presenting a lamb or young goat in its place. But if you do not buy it back, you must break its neck. However, you must buy back every firstborn son.

"No one may appear before me without an offering.

21 "You have six days each week for your ordinary work, but on the seventh day you must stop working, even during the seasons of plowing and harvest.

22 "You must celebrate the Festival of Harvest* with the first crop of the wheat harvest, and celebrate the Festival of the Final Harvest* at the end of the harvest season. 23 Three times each year every man in Israel must appear before the Sovereign, the LORD, the God of Israel. 24 I will drive out the other nations ahead of you and expand your territory, so no one will covet and conquer your land while you appear before the LORD your God three times each year.

25 "You must not offer the blood of my sacrificial offerings together with any baked goods containing yeast. And none of the meat of the Passover sacrifice may be kept over until the next morning.

26 "As you harvest your crops, bring the very best of the first harvest to the house of the LORD your God.

"You must not cook a young goat in its mother's milk."

27 Then the LORD said to Moses, "Write down all these instructions, for they represent the terms of the covenant I am making with you and with Israel."

28 Moses remained there on the mountain with the LORD forty days and forty nights. In all that time he ate no bread and drank no water. And the LORD* wrote the terms of the covenant—the Ten Commandments*—on the stone tablets.

29 When Moses came down Mount Sinai carrying the two stone tablets inscribed with the terms of the covenant,* he wasn't aware that his face had become radiant because he had spoken to the LORD. 30 So when Aaron and the people of Israel saw the radiance of Moses' face, they were afraid to come near him.

34:18 Hebrew *appointed time in the month of Abib.* This first month of the ancient Hebrew lunar calendar usually occurs within the months of March and April. **34:19** As in Greek version; the meaning of the Hebrew word is uncertain. **34:22a** Hebrew *Festival of Weeks;* compare 23:16. This was later called the Festival of Pentecost. It is celebrated today as Shavuot (or Shabuoth). **34:22b** Or *Festival of Ingathering.* This was later called the Festival of Shelters or Festival of Tabernacles (see Lev 23:33-36). It is celebrated today as Sukkot (or Succoth). **34:28a** Hebrew *he.* **34:28b** Hebrew *the ten words.* **34:29** Hebrew *the two tablets of the Testimony;* see note on 25:16.

31 But Moses called out to them and asked Aaron and all the leaders of the
community to come over, and he talked with them. 32 Then all the people of
Israel approached him, and Moses gave them all the instructions the LORD
had given him on Mount Sinai. 33 When Moses finished speaking with them,
he covered his face with a veil. 34 But whenever he went into the Tent of Meet-
ing to speak with the LORD, he would remove the veil until he came out
again. Then he would give the people whatever instructions the LORD had
given him, 35 and the people of Israel would see the radiant glow of his face.
So he would put the veil over his face until he returned to speak with the
LORD.

Instructions for the Sabbath

35 Then Moses called together the whole community of Israel and told
them, "These are the instructions the LORD has commanded you to
follow. 2 You have six days each week for your ordinary work, but the seventh
day must be a Sabbath day of complete rest, a holy day dedicated to the LORD.
Anyone who works on that day must be put to death. 3 You must not even
light a fire in any of your homes on the Sabbath."

Offerings for the Tabernacle

4 Then Moses said to the whole community of Israel, "This is what the LORD
has commanded: 5 Take a sacred offering for the LORD. Let those with gener-
ous hearts present the following gifts to the LORD:

gold, silver, and bronze;
6 blue, purple, and scarlet thread;
fine linen and goat hair for cloth;
7 tanned ram skins and fine goatskin leather;
acacia wood;
8 olive oil for the lamps;
spices for the anointing oil and the fragrant incense;
9 onyx stones, and other gemstones to be set in the ephod and the priest's chestpiece.

10 "Come, all of you who are gifted craftsmen. Construct everything that
the LORD has commanded:

11 the Tabernacle and its sacred tent, its covering, clasps, frames, crossbars, posts, and bases;
12 the Ark and its carrying poles;
the Ark's cover—the place of atonement;
the inner curtain to shield the Ark;
13 the table, its carrying poles, and all its utensils;
the Bread of the Presence;
14 for light, the lampstand, its accessories, the lamp cups, and the olive oil for lighting;
15 the incense altar and its carrying poles;
the anointing oil and fragrant incense;
the curtain for the entrance of the Tabernacle;
16 the altar of burnt offering;

Make a Difference

35:30-35

Excel

Jesus sees your unique role. You are a part of his body, working to bring good change to this world. You have a significant and strategic role to play in God's mission on this earth. He loves seeing you use the gifts that he has given you to make a difference around you for his glory.

This passage (35:30-35) makes it clear that the Lord enjoys gifting people differently so that each person can love him completely and serve others fully according to their unique abilities. When each person draws upon the excellence of the Lord to use their distinctive gifts to serve one another, then the world is built anew.

Difference Maker

Grab a friend. Together, identify and affirm the unique things that each of you does well. Then dream up a mission project that you could do together using your gifts.

the bronze grating of the altar and its carrying poles and utensils;
the washbasin with its stand;
17 the curtains for the walls of the courtyard;
the posts and their bases;
the curtain for the entrance to the courtyard;
18 the tent pegs of the Tabernacle and courtyard and their ropes;
19 the beautifully stitched garments for the priests to wear while
ministering in the Holy Place—the sacred garments for Aaron the
priest, and the garments for his sons to wear as they minister as
priests."

20 So the whole community of Israel left Moses and returned to their tents.
21 All whose hearts were stirred and whose spirits were moved came and
brought their sacred offerings to the LORD. They brought all the materials
needed for the Tabernacle,* for the performance of its rituals, and for the sa-
cred garments. 22 Both men and women came, all whose hearts were willing.
They brought to the LORD their offerings of gold—brooches, earrings, rings
from their fingers, and necklaces. They presented gold objects of every kind
as a special offering to the LORD. 23 All those who owned the following items
willingly brought them: blue, purple, and scarlet thread; fine linen and goat
hair for cloth; and tanned ram skins and fine goatskin leather. 24 And all who
had silver and bronze objects gave them as a sacred offering to the LORD. And
those who had acacia wood brought it for use in the project.
25 All the women who were skilled in sewing and spinning prepared blue,
purple, and scarlet thread, and fine linen cloth. 26 All the women who were
willing used their skills to spin the goat hair into yarn. 27 The leaders brought
onyx stones and the special gemstones to be set in the ephod and the priest's
chestpiece. 28 They also brought spices and olive oil for the light, the anoint-
ing oil, and the fragrant incense. 29 So the people of Israel—every man and
woman who was eager to help in the work the LORD had given them through
Moses—brought their gifts and gave them freely to the LORD.
30 Then Moses told the people of Israel, "The LORD has specifically chosen
Bezalel son of Uri, grandson of Hur, of the tribe of Judah. 31 The LORD has
filled Bezalel with the Spirit of God, giving him great wisdom, ability, and
expertise in all kinds of crafts. 32 He is a master craftsman, expert in work-
ing with gold, silver, and bronze. 33 He is skilled in engraving and mounting
gemstones and in carving wood. He is a master at every craft. 34 And the LORD
has given both him and Oholiab son of Ahisamach, of the tribe of Dan, the
ability to teach their skills to others. 35 The LORD has given them special skills
as engravers, designers, embroiderers in blue, purple, and scarlet thread
on fine linen cloth, and weavers. They excel as craftsmen and as designers.

36 "The LORD has gifted Bezalel, Oholiab, and the other skilled crafts-
men with wisdom and ability to perform any task involved in build-
ing the sanctuary. Let them construct and furnish the Tabernacle, just as the
LORD has commanded."
2 So Moses summoned Bezalel and Oholiab and all the others who were
specially gifted by the LORD and were eager to get to work. 3 Moses gave
them the materials donated by the people of Israel as sacred offerings for

35:21 Hebrew *Tent of Meeting.*

the completion of the sanctuary. But the people continued to bring addi-
tional gifts each morning. 4 Finally the craftsmen who were working on the
sanctuary left their work. 5 They went to Moses and reported, "The people
have given more than enough materials to complete the job the LORD has
commanded us to do!"

6 So Moses gave the command, and this message was sent throughout the
camp: "Men and women, don't prepare any more gifts for the sanctuary.
We have enough!" So the people stopped bringing their sacred offerings.
7 Their contributions were more than enough to complete the whole project.

Building the Tabernacle

8 The skilled craftsmen made ten curtains of finely woven linen for the
Tabernacle. Then Bezalel* decorated the curtains with blue, purple, and
scarlet thread and with skillfully embroidered cherubim. 9 All ten curtains
were exactly the same size—42 feet long and 6 feet wide.* 10 Five of these
curtains were joined together to make one long curtain, and the other five
were joined to make a second long curtain. 11 He made fifty loops of blue
yarn and put them along the edge of the last curtain in each set. 12 The fifty
loops along the edge of one curtain matched the fifty loops along the edge
of the other curtain. 13 Then he made fifty gold clasps and fastened the long
curtains together with the clasps. In this way, the Tabernacle was made of
one continuous piece.

14 He made eleven curtains of goat-hair cloth to serve as a tent covering for
the Tabernacle. 15 These eleven curtains were all exactly the same size—45 feet
long and 6 feet wide.* 16 Bezalel joined five of these curtains together to make
one long curtain, and the other six were joined to make a second long curtain.
17 He made fifty loops for the edge of each large curtain. 18 He also made fifty
bronze clasps to fasten the long curtains together. In this way, the tent cover-
ing was made of one continuous piece. 19 He completed the tent covering with
a layer of tanned ram skins and a layer of fine goatskin leather.

20 For the framework of the Tabernacle, Bezalel constructed frames of
acacia wood. 21 Each frame was 15 feet high and 27 inches wide,* 22 with two
pegs under each frame. All the frames were identical. 23 He made twenty of
these frames to support the curtains on the south side of the Tabernacle.
24 He also made forty silver bases—two bases under each frame, with the
pegs fitting securely into the bases. 25 For the north side of the Tabernacle,
he made another twenty frames, 26 with their forty silver bases, two bases
under each frame. 27 He made six frames for the rear—the west side of the
Tabernacle—28 along with two additional frames to reinforce the rear cor-
ners of the Tabernacle. 29 These corner frames were matched at the bottom
and firmly attached at the top with a single ring, forming a single corner
unit. Both of these corner units were made the same way. 30 So there were
eight frames at the rear of the Tabernacle, set in sixteen silver bases—two
bases under each frame.

31 Then he made crossbars of acacia wood to link the frames, five crossbars
for the north side of the Tabernacle 32 and five for the south side. He also
made five crossbars for the rear of the Tabernacle, which faced west. 33 He
made the middle crossbar to attach halfway up the frames; it ran all the

36:8 Hebrew *he;* also in 36:16, 20, 35. See 37:1. **36:9** Hebrew *28 cubits* [12.9 meters] *long and 4 cubits* [1.8 meters] *wide.* **36:15** Hebrew *30 cubits* [13.8 meters] *long and 4 cubits* [1.8 meters] *wide.* **36:21** Hebrew *10 cubits* [4.6 meters] *high and 1.5 cubits* [69 centimeters] *wide.*

way from one end of the Tabernacle to the other. 34 He overlaid the frames
with gold and made gold rings to hold the crossbars. Then he overlaid the
crossbars with gold as well.
35 For the inside of the Tabernacle, Bezalel made a special curtain of finely
woven linen. He decorated it with blue, purple, and scarlet thread and with
skillfully embroidered cherubim. 36 For the curtain, he made four posts of
acacia wood and four gold hooks. He overlaid the posts with gold and set
them in four silver bases.
37 Then he made another curtain for the entrance to the sacred tent. He
made it of finely woven linen and embroidered it with exquisite designs
using blue, purple, and scarlet thread. 38 This curtain was hung on gold
hooks attached to five posts. The posts with their decorated tops and hooks
were overlaid with gold, and the five bases were cast from bronze.

Building the Ark of the Covenant

37 Next Bezalel made the Ark of acacia wood—a sacred chest 45 inches
long, 27 inches wide, and 27 inches high.* 2 He overlaid it inside and
outside with pure gold, and he ran a molding of gold all around it. 3 He cast
four gold rings and attached them to its four feet, two rings on each side.
4 Then he made poles from acacia wood and overlaid them with gold. 5 He
inserted the poles into the rings at the sides of the Ark to carry it.
6 Then he made the Ark's cover—the place of atonement—from pure gold.
It was 45 inches long and 27 inches wide.* 7 He made two cherubim from
hammered gold and placed them on the two ends of the atonement cover.
8 He molded the cherubim on each end of the atonement cover, making it
all of one piece of gold. 9 The cherubim faced each other and looked down
on the atonement cover. With their wings spread above it, they protected it.

Building the Table

10 Then Bezalel* made the table of acacia wood, 36 inches long, 18 inches wide,
and 27 inches high.* 11 He overlaid it with pure gold and ran a gold molding
around the edge. 12 He decorated it with a 3-inch border* all around, and he
ran a gold molding along the border. 13 Then he cast four gold rings for the
table and attached them at the four corners next to the four legs. 14 The rings
were attached near the border to hold the poles that were used to carry the
table. 15 He made these poles from acacia wood and overlaid them with gold.
16 Then he made special containers of pure gold for the table—bowls, ladles,
jars, and pitchers—to be used in pouring out liquid offerings.

Building the Lampstand

17 Then Bezalel made the lampstand of pure, hammered gold. He made the en-
tire lampstand and its decorations of one piece—the base, center stem, lamp
cups, buds, and petals. 18 The lampstand had six branches going out from the
center stem, three on each side. 19 Each of the six branches had three lamp cups
shaped like almond blossoms, complete with buds and petals. 20 The center
stem of the lampstand was crafted with four lamp cups shaped like almond
blossoms, complete with buds and petals. 21 There was an almond bud beneath

37:1 Hebrew *2.5 cubits* [115 centimeters] *long, 1.5 cubits* [69 centimeters] *wide, and 1.5 cubits high.* **37:6** Hebrew *2.5 cubits* [115 centimeters] *long and 1.5 cubits* [69 centimeters] *wide.* **37:10a** Hebrew *he;* also in 37:17, 25. **37:10b** Hebrew *2 cubits* [92 centimeters] *long, 1 cubit* [46 centimeters] *wide, and 1.5 cubits* [69 centimeters] *high.* **37:12** Hebrew *a border of a handbreadth* [8 centimeters].

each pair of branches where the six branches extended from the center stem,
all made of one piece. 22 The almond buds and branches were all of one piece
with the center stem, and they were hammered from pure gold.
23 He also made seven lamps for the lampstand, lamp snuffers, and trays,
all of pure gold. 24 The entire lampstand, along with its accessories, was made
from 75 pounds* of pure gold.

Building the Incense Altar

25 Then Bezalel made the incense altar of acacia wood. It was 18 inches square
and 36 inches high,* with horns at the corners carved from the same piece
of wood as the altar itself. 26 He overlaid the top, sides, and horns of the altar
with pure gold, and he ran a gold molding around the entire altar. 27 He made
two gold rings and attached them on opposite sides of the altar below the
gold molding to hold the carrying poles. 28 He made the poles of acacia wood
and overlaid them with gold.
29 Then he made the sacred anointing oil and the fragrant incense, using
the techniques of a skilled incense maker.

Building the Altar of Burnt Offering

38 Next Bezalel* used acacia wood to construct the square altar of burnt
offering. It was 7½ feet wide, 7½ feet long, and 4½ feet high.* 2 He
made horns for each of its four corners so that the horns and altar were all one
piece. He overlaid the altar with bronze. 3 Then he made all the altar utensils
of bronze—the ash buckets, shovels, basins, meat forks, and firepans. 4 Next
he made a bronze grating and installed it halfway down the side of the altar,
under the ledge. 5 He cast four rings and attached them to the corners of the
bronze grating to hold the carrying poles. 6 He made the poles from acacia
wood and overlaid them with bronze. 7 He inserted the poles through the
rings on the sides of the altar. The altar was hollow and was made from planks.

Building the Washbasin

8 Bezalel made the bronze washbasin and its bronze stand from bronze mirrors donated by the women who served at the entrance of the Tabernacle.*

Building the Courtyard

9 Then Bezalel made the courtyard, which was enclosed with curtains made
of finely woven linen. On the south side the curtains were 150 feet long.*
10 They were held up by twenty posts set securely in twenty bronze bases.
He hung the curtains with silver hooks and rings. 11 He made a similar set of
curtains for the north side—150 feet of curtains held up by twenty posts set
securely in bronze bases. He hung the curtains with silver hooks and rings.
12 The curtains on the west end of the courtyard were 75 feet long,* hung with
silver hooks and rings and supported by ten posts set into ten bases. 13 The
east end, the front, was also 75 feet long.
14 The courtyard entrance was on the east end, flanked by two curtains.
The curtain on the right side was 22½ feet long* and was supported by three
posts set into three bases. 15 The curtain on the left side was also 22½ feet long

Drop your brilliant thoughts here

37:24 Hebrew *1 talent* [34 kilograms]. 37:25 Hebrew *1 cubit* [46 centimeters] *long and 1 cubit wide, a square, and 2 cubits* [92 centimeters] *high.* 38:1a Hebrew *he;* also in 38:8, 9. 38:1b Hebrew *5 cubits* [2.3 meters] *wide, 5 cubits long, a square, and 3 cubits* [1.4 meters] *high.* 38:8 Hebrew *Tent of Meeting;* also in 38:30. 38:9 Hebrew *100 cubits* [46 meters]; also in 38:11. 38:12 Hebrew *50 cubits* [23 meters]; also in 38:13. 38:14 Hebrew *15 cubits* [6.9 meters]; also in 38:15.

and was supported by three posts set into three bases. 16 All the curtains used
in the courtyard were made of finely woven linen. 17 Each post had a bronze
base, and all the hooks and rings were silver. The tops of the posts of the
courtyard were overlaid with silver, and the rings to hold up the curtains
were made of silver.

18 He made the curtain for the entrance to the courtyard of finely woven
linen, and he decorated it with beautiful embroidery in blue, purple, and
scarlet thread. It was 30 feet long, and its height was 7½ feet,* just like the
curtains of the courtyard walls. 19 It was supported by four posts, each set
securely in its own bronze base. The tops of the posts were overlaid with
silver, and the hooks and rings were also made of silver.

20 All the tent pegs used in the Tabernacle and courtyard were made of
bronze.

Inventory of Materials

21 This is an inventory of the materials used in building the Tabernacle of the
Covenant.* The Levites compiled the figures, as Moses directed, and Ithamar
son of Aaron the priest served as recorder. 22 Bezalel son of Uri, grandson of
Hur, of the tribe of Judah, made everything just as the LORD had commanded
Moses. 23 He was assisted by Oholiab son of Ahisamach, of the tribe of Dan,
a craftsman expert at engraving, designing, and embroidering with blue,
purple, and scarlet thread on fine linen cloth.

24 The people brought special offerings of gold totaling 2,193 pounds,* as
measured by the weight of the sanctuary shekel. This gold was used through-
out the Tabernacle.

25 The whole community of Israel gave 7,545 pounds* of silver, as measured
by the weight of the sanctuary shekel. 26 This silver came from the tax collected
from each man registered in the census. (The tax is one beka, which is half a
shekel,* based on the sanctuary shekel.) The tax was collected from 603,550
men who had reached their twentieth birthday. 27 The hundred bases for the
frames of the sanctuary walls and for the posts supporting the inner curtain
required 7,500 pounds of silver, about 75 pounds for each base.* 28 The remain-
ing 45 pounds* of silver was used to make the hooks and rings and to overlay
the tops of the posts.

29 The people also brought as special offerings 5,310 pounds* of bronze,
30 which was used for casting the bases for the posts at the entrance to the
Tabernacle, and for the bronze altar with its bronze grating and all the
altar utensils. 31 Bronze was also used to make the bases for the posts that
supported the curtains around the courtyard, the bases for the curtain at
the entrance of the courtyard, and all the tent pegs for the Tabernacle and
the courtyard.

Clothing for the Priests

39 The craftsmen made beautiful sacred garments of blue, purple, and
scarlet cloth—clothing for Aaron to wear while ministering in the
Holy Place, just as the LORD had commanded Moses.

Story Arc **38:22-23**

Oholiab

Oholiab was gifted by God to do the unique work of crafting the holy items that people would use to connect with God. He served with Bezalel (Exodus 31:6) as a sort of employee. This means that while Bezalel got most of the recognized credit, Oholiab also invested himself substantially to help accomplish much of the work. There isn't any record of him complaining about this, but he simply walked faithfully to be used for the glory of God.

You may not get the same time in the spotlight that others do, but that doesn't make your work any less important. It can be challenging to do something knowing you might not get the glory, but it can also be very freeing and become a real joy. The goal is not to glorify yourself but to let God change the world through you so that everyone glorifies God.

Lev 8:1-15 ►

38:18 Hebrew *20 cubits* [9.2 meters] *long and 5 cubits* [2.3 meters] *high.* **38:21** Hebrew *the Tabernacle, the Tabernacle of the Testimony.* **38:24** Hebrew *29 talents and 730 shekels* [994 kilograms]. Each shekel weighed about 0.4 ounces or 11 grams. **38:25** Hebrew *100 talents and 1,775 shekels* [3,420 kilograms]. **38:26** Or *0.2 ounces* [6 grams]. **38:27** Hebrew *100 talents* [3,400 kilograms] *of silver, 1 talent* [34 kilograms] *for each base.* **38:28** Hebrew *1,775 [shekels]* [20.2 kilograms]. **38:29** Hebrew *70 talents and 2,400 shekels* [2,407 kilograms].

Making the Ephod

2 Bezalel* made the ephod of finely woven linen and embroidered it with
gold and with blue, purple, and scarlet thread. 3 He made gold thread by
hammering out thin sheets of gold and cutting it into fine strands. With
great skill and care, he worked it into the fine linen with the blue, purple,
and scarlet thread.

4 The ephod consisted of two pieces, front and back, joined at the shoul-
ders with two shoulder-pieces. 5 The decorative sash was made of the same
materials: finely woven linen embroidered with gold and with blue, purple,
and scarlet thread, just as the LORD had commanded Moses. 6 They mounted
the two onyx stones in settings of gold filigree. The stones were engraved
with the names of the tribes of Israel, just as a seal is engraved. 7 He fastened
these stones on the shoulder-pieces of the ephod as a reminder that the priest
represents the people of Israel. All this was done just as the LORD had com-
manded Moses.

Making the Chestpiece

8 Bezalel made the chestpiece with great skill and care. He made it to match
the ephod, using finely woven linen embroidered with gold and with blue,
purple, and scarlet thread. 9 He made the chestpiece of a single piece of cloth
folded to form a pouch nine inches* square. 10 They mounted four rows of
gemstones* on it. The first row contained a red carnelian, a pale-green peri-
dot, and an emerald. 11 The second row contained a turquoise, a blue lapis
lazuli, and a white moonstone. 12 The third row contained an orange jacinth,
an agate, and a purple amethyst. 13 The fourth row contained a blue-green
beryl, an onyx, and a green jasper. All these stones were set in gold filigree.
14 Each stone represented one of the twelve sons of Israel, and the name of
that tribe was engraved on it like a seal.

15 To attach the chestpiece to the ephod, they made braided cords of pure
gold thread. 16 They also made two settings of gold filigree and two gold
rings and attached them to the top corners of the chestpiece. 17 They tied
the two gold cords to the rings on the chestpiece. 18 They tied the other
ends of the cords to the gold settings on the shoulder-pieces of the ephod.
19 Then they made two more gold rings and attached them to the inside
edges of the chestpiece next to the ephod. 20 Then they made two more gold
rings and attached them to the front of the ephod, below the shoulder-
pieces, just above the knot where the decorative sash was fastened to the
ephod. 21 They attached the bottom rings of the chestpiece to the rings on
the ephod with blue cords. In this way, the chestpiece was held securely
to the ephod above the decorative sash. All this was done just as the LORD
had commanded Moses.

Additional Clothing for the Priests

22 Bezalel made the robe that is worn with the ephod from a single piece
of blue woven cloth, 23 with an opening for Aaron's head in the middle of
it. The opening was reinforced with a woven collar* so it would not tear.
24 They made pomegranates of blue, purple, and scarlet yarn, and attached
them to the hem of the robe. 25 They also made bells of pure gold and placed

39:2 Hebrew *He;* also in 39:8, 22. **39:9** Hebrew *1 span* [23 centimeters]. **39:10** The identification of some of these gemstones is uncertain. **39:23** The meaning of the Hebrew is uncertain.

Prayer 39:43

Lord, you have put people in my life who can examine me and make sure I'm on the right path. Soften my heart toward them, even when they say something I may not immediately want to hear. Amen.

them between the pomegranates along the hem of the robe, 26 with bells
and pomegranates alternating all around the hem. This robe was to be worn
whenever the priest ministered before the LORD, just as the LORD had commanded Moses.

27 They made tunics for Aaron and his sons from fine linen cloth. 28 The turban and the special head coverings were made of fine linen, and the undergarments were also made of finely woven linen. 29 The sashes were made of finely woven linen and embroidered with blue, purple, and scarlet thread, just as the LORD had commanded Moses.

30 Finally, they made the sacred medallion—the badge of holiness—of pure gold. They engraved it like a seal with these words: HOLY TO THE LORD.
31 They attached the medallion with a blue cord to Aaron's turban, just as the
LORD had commanded Moses.

Moses Inspects the Work

32 And so at last the Tabernacle* was finished. The Israelites had done everything just as the LORD had commanded Moses. 33 And they brought the entire Tabernacle to Moses:

the sacred tent with all its furnishings, clasps, frames, crossbars, posts, and bases;
34 the tent coverings of tanned ram skins and fine goatskin leather;
the inner curtain to shield the Ark;
35 the Ark of the Covenant* and its carrying poles;
the Ark's cover—the place of atonement;
36 the table and all its utensils;
the Bread of the Presence;
37 the pure gold lampstand with its symmetrical lamp cups, all its accessories, and the olive oil for lighting;
38 the gold altar;
the anointing oil and fragrant incense;
the curtain for the entrance of the sacred tent;
39 the bronze altar;
the bronze grating and its carrying poles and utensils;
the washbasin with its stand;
40 the curtains for the walls of the courtyard;
the posts and their bases;
the curtain for the entrance to the courtyard;
the ropes and tent pegs;
all the furnishings to be used in worship at the Tabernacle;
41 the beautifully stitched garments for the priests to wear while ministering in the Holy Place—the sacred garments for Aaron the priest, and the garments for his sons to wear as they minister as priests.

42 So the people of Israel followed all of the LORD's instructions to Moses.
43 Then Moses inspected all their work. When he found it had been done just
as the LORD had commanded him, he blessed them.

39:32 Hebrew *the Tabernacle, the Tent of Meeting;* also in 39:40. 39:35 Or *Ark of the Testimony.*

The Tabernacle Completed

40 Then the LORD said to Moses, 2 "Set up the Tabernacle* on the first
day of the new year.* 3 Place the Ark of the Covenant* inside, and
install the inner curtain to enclose the Ark within the Most Holy Place. 4 Then
bring in the table, and arrange the utensils on it. And bring in the lampstand,
and set up the lamps.

5 "Place the gold incense altar in front of the Ark of the Covenant. Then
hang the curtain at the entrance of the Tabernacle. 6 Place the altar of burnt
offering in front of the Tabernacle entrance. 7 Set the washbasin between
the Tabernacle* and the altar, and fill it with water. 8 Then set up the court-
yard around the outside of the tent, and hang the curtain for the courtyard
entrance.

9 "Take the anointing oil and anoint the Tabernacle and all its furnishings
to consecrate them and make them holy. 10 Anoint the altar of burnt offering
and its utensils to consecrate them. Then the altar will become absolutely
holy. 11 Next anoint the washbasin and its stand to consecrate them.

12 "Present Aaron and his sons at the entrance of the Tabernacle, and wash
them with water. 13 Dress Aaron with the sacred garments and anoint him,
consecrating him to serve me as a priest. 14 Then present his sons and dress
them in their tunics. 15 Anoint them as you did their father, so they may also
serve me as priests. With their anointing, Aaron's descendants are set apart
for the priesthood forever, from generation to generation."

16 Moses proceeded to do everything just as the LORD had commanded
him. 17 So the Tabernacle was set up on the first day of the first month of the
second year. 18 Moses erected the Tabernacle by setting down its bases, insert-
ing the frames, attaching the crossbars, and setting up the posts. 19 Then he
spread the coverings over the Tabernacle framework and put on the protec-
tive layers, just as the LORD had commanded him.

20 He took the stone tablets inscribed with the terms of the covenant and
placed them* inside the Ark. Then he attached the carrying poles to the Ark,
and he set the Ark's cover—the place of atonement—on top of it. 21 Then he
brought the Ark of the Covenant into the Tabernacle and hung the inner
curtain to shield it from view, just as the LORD had commanded him.

22 Next Moses placed the table in the Tabernacle, along the north side of
the Holy Place, just outside the inner curtain. 23 And he arranged the Bread
of the Presence on the table before the LORD, just as the LORD had com-
manded him.

24 He set the lampstand in the Tabernacle across from the table on the
south side of the Holy Place. 25 Then he lit the lamps in the LORD's presence,
just as the LORD had commanded him. 26 He also placed the gold incense
altar in the Tabernacle, in the Holy Place in front of the inner curtain. 27 On
it he burned the fragrant incense, just as the LORD had commanded him.

28 He hung the curtain at the entrance of the Tabernacle, 29 and he placed
the altar of burnt offering near the Tabernacle entrance. On it he offered a
burnt offering and a grain offering, just as the LORD had commanded him.

30 Next Moses placed the washbasin between the Tabernacle and the altar.
He filled it with water so the priests could wash themselves. 31 Moses and

40:2a Hebrew *the Tabernacle, the Tent of Meeting;* also in 40:6, 29. **40:2b** Hebrew *the first day of the first month.* This day of the ancient Hebrew lunar calendar occurred in March or April. **40:3** Or *Ark of the Testimony;* also in 40:5, 21. **40:7** Hebrew *Tent of Meeting;* also in 40:12, 22, 24, 26, 30, 32, 34, 35. **40:20** Hebrew *He placed the Testimony;* see note on 25:16.

Question 40:36

If you were truly to follow God wherever he leads, when would you be most excited? When would you be most nervous?

Aaron and Aaron's sons used water from it to wash their hands and feet.
32 Whenever they approached the altar and entered the Tabernacle, they
washed themselves, just as the LORD had commanded Moses.
33 Then he hung the curtains forming the courtyard around the Tabernacle
and the altar. And he set up the curtain at the entrance of the courtyard. So
at last Moses finished the work.

The LORD's Glory Fills the Tabernacle

34 Then the cloud covered the Tabernacle, and the glory of the LORD filled the
Tabernacle. 35 Moses could no longer enter the Tabernacle because the cloud
had settled down over it, and the glory of the LORD filled the Tabernacle.
36 Now whenever the cloud lifted from the Tabernacle, the people of Israel
would set out on their journey, following it. 37 But if the cloud did not rise,
they remained where they were until it lifted. 38 The cloud of the LORD hov-
ered over the Tabernacle during the day, and at night fire glowed inside the
cloud so the whole family of Israel could see it. This continued throughout
all their journeys.

Leviticus Introduction

The book of Leviticus is so...*Levitical*. At first glance, it seems to be just a bunch of rules and regulations and religious rituals. It's no secret: people in our day who aspire to read the Bible often get stuck—and stop reading altogether—when they get to Leviticus.

However, when the New Testament speaks about the Old Testament, it makes interesting comments like, "All Scripture is inspired by God and is useful to teach us what is true and to make us realize what is wrong in our lives. It corrects us when we are wrong and teaches us to do what is right" (2 Timothy 3:16). That's right. *All* Scripture is God breathed, including the book of Leviticus.

Evidently, we must be missing something when we read Leviticus, right? The greatest Bible commentator ever is Jesus. What did Jesus say about the book of Leviticus? Jesus quoted Leviticus when he was confronted with a pivotal question:

> "Teacher, which is the most important commandment in the law of Moses?"
>
> Jesus replied, "'You must love the LORD your God with all your heart, all your soul, and all your mind.' This is the first and greatest commandment. A second is equally important: *'Love your neighbor as yourself.'*" (Matthew 22:36–39, emphasis added)

Did you get that? "Love your neighbor as yourself" is a specific instruction directly from the "rules" of Leviticus. According to Jesus, the entire law of God, which includes the book of Leviticus, is about loving God and loving people. If you miss that Leviticus is about learning to love God with everything you are and then letting God's love overflow from your life to others, then, according to Jesus, you will miss the whole point of Leviticus.

Think about that for a moment. Instead of reading Leviticus like it's a bunch of irrelevant, outdated, archaic laws for Jews of antiquity, perhaps we should read it (and the rest of the Old Testament) through Jesus' lens of loving God and loving people.

Let Jesus inform the way you read the book of Leviticus. As you read this book, mark every place you see that is about loving God and loving people. If you do this, you'll begin to see how Leviticus reveals the way of Jesus throughout the fabric of its pages.

Story Arc

- **Aaron**

Leviticus

Procedures for the Burnt Offering

1 The LORD called to Moses from the Tabernacle* and said to him, 2“Give
the following instructions to the people of Israel. When you present an
animal as an offering to the LORD, you may take it from your herd of cattle
or your flock of sheep and goats.
3“If the animal you present as a burnt offering is from the herd, it must
be a male with no defects. Bring it to the entrance of the Tabernacle so you*
may be accepted by the LORD. 4Lay your hand on the animal's head, and the
LORD will accept its death in your place to purify you, making you right with
him.* 5Then slaughter the young bull in the LORD's presence, and Aaron's
sons, the priests, will present the animal's blood by splattering it against all
sides of the altar that stands at the entrance to the Tabernacle. 6Then skin
the animal and cut it into pieces. 7The sons of Aaron the priest will build a
wood fire on the altar. 8They will arrange the pieces of the offering, including
the head and fat, on the wood burning on the altar. 9But the internal organs
and the legs must first be washed with water. Then the priest will burn the
entire sacrifice on the altar as a burnt offering. It is a special gift, a pleasing
aroma to the LORD.
10“If the animal you present as a burnt offering is from the flock, it may
be either a sheep or a goat, but it must be a male with no defects. 11Slaughter
the animal on the north side of the altar in the LORD's presence, and Aaron's
sons, the priests, will splatter its blood against all sides of the altar. 12Then
cut the animal in pieces, and the priests will arrange the pieces of the offer-
ing, including the head and fat, on the wood burning on the altar. 13But the
internal organs and the legs must first be washed with water. Then the priest
will burn the entire sacrifice on the altar as a burnt offering. It is a special
gift, a pleasing aroma to the LORD.
14“If you present a bird as a burnt offering to the LORD, choose either a
turtledove or a young pigeon. 15The priest will take the bird to the altar,
wring off its head, and burn it on the altar. But first he must drain its blood
against the side of the altar. 16The priest must also remove the crop and the
feathers* and throw them in the ashes on the east side of the altar. 17Then,
grasping the bird by its wings, the priest will tear the bird open, but without
tearing it apart. Then he will burn it as a burnt offering on the wood burning
on the altar. It is a special gift, a pleasing aroma to the LORD.

Procedures for the Grain Offering

2 “When you present grain as an offering to the LORD, the offering must
consist of choice flour. You are to pour olive oil on it, sprinkle it with
frankincense, 2and bring it to Aaron's sons, the priests. The priest will
scoop out a handful of the flour moistened with oil, together with all the

Make a Difference 1:1-4

In Your Place

The sacrificial sheep or goat accepts death on your behalf and makes you right with the Lord. The book of Leviticus is ultimately an invitation to accept what Jesus has done for you on the cross. The most important thing you could ever do is believe that Jesus has deliberately chosen to die in your place to cleanse you from your sin. It is as if your hand was laid on Jesus' head and the Lord has accepted his substitutionary death. By allowing Jesus to take your sins, you are made right with the Lord!

Difference Maker

Accept Jesus! Go to the back of this Bible and read "How to Accept Jesus as Your Lord and Savior."

Question 1:9

Read Romans 12:1-2 and 2 Corinthians 2:15-16. Why would the aroma of an offering be pleasing to the Lord?

1:1 Hebrew *Tent of Meeting;* also in 1:3, 5. 1:3 Or *it.* 1:4 Or *to make atonement for you.* 1:16 Or *the crop and its contents.* The meaning of the Hebrew is uncertain.

frankincense, and burn this representative portion on the altar. It is a special
gift, a pleasing aroma to the LORD. 3 The rest of the grain offering will then
be given to Aaron and his sons. This offering will be considered a most holy
part of the special gifts presented to the LORD.
4 "If your offering is a grain offering baked in an oven, it must be made of
choice flour, but without any yeast. It may be presented in the form of thin
cakes mixed with olive oil or wafers spread with olive oil. 5 If your grain of-
fering is cooked on a griddle, it must be made of choice flour mixed with
olive oil but without any yeast. 6 Break it in pieces and pour olive oil on it;
it is a grain offering. 7 If your grain offering is prepared in a pan, it must be
made of choice flour and olive oil.
8 "No matter how a grain offering for the LORD has been prepared, bring
it to the priest, who will present it at the altar. 9 The priest will take a repre-
sentative portion of the grain offering and burn it on the altar. It is a special
gift, a pleasing aroma to the LORD. 10 The rest of the grain offering will then
be given to Aaron and his sons as their food. This offering will be considered
a most holy part of the special gifts presented to the LORD.
11 "Do not use yeast in preparing any of the grain offerings you present
to the LORD, because no yeast or honey may be burned as a special gift pre-
sented to the LORD. 12 You may add yeast and honey to an offering of the
first crops of your harvest, but these must never be offered on the altar as
a pleasing aroma to the LORD. 13 Season all your grain offerings with salt
to remind you of God's eternal covenant. Never forget to add salt to your
grain offerings.
14 "If you present a grain offering to the LORD from the first portion of your
harvest, bring fresh grain that is coarsely ground and roasted on a fire. 15 Put
olive oil on this grain offering, and sprinkle it with frankincense. 16 The priest
will take a representative portion of the grain moistened with oil, together
with all the frankincense, and burn it as a special gift presented to the LORD.

Procedures for the Peace Offering

3 "If you present an animal from the herd as a peace offering to the LORD,
it may be a male or a female, but it must have no defects. 2 Lay your hand
on the animal's head, and slaughter it at the entrance of the Tabernacle.*
Then Aaron's sons, the priests, will splatter its blood against all sides of the
altar. 3 The priest must present part of this peace offering as a special gift
to the LORD. This includes all the fat around the internal organs, 4 the two
kidneys and the fat around them near the loins, and the long lobe of the liver.
These must be removed with the kidneys, 5 and Aaron's sons will burn them
on top of the burnt offering on the wood burning on the altar. It is a special
gift, a pleasing aroma to the LORD.
6 "If you present an animal from the flock as a peace offering to the LORD,
it may be a male or a female, but it must have no defects. 7 If you present a
sheep as your offering, bring it to the LORD, 8 lay your hand on its head, and
slaughter it in front of the Tabernacle. Aaron's sons will then splatter the
sheep's blood against all sides of the altar. 9 The priest must present the fat
of this peace offering as a special gift to the LORD. This includes the fat of the
broad tail cut off near the backbone, all the fat around the internal organs,
10 the two kidneys and the fat around them near the loins, and the long lobe

3:2 Hebrew *Tent of Meeting;* also in 3:8, 13.

Make a Difference

3:6–8

Once for All

The book of Leviticus gives a lot of attention to five types of sacrificial offerings: burnt offerings, grain offerings, peace offerings, sin offerings, and guilt offerings. Each offering had its own procedures and purposes for dealing with a wide range of ways that people fell short of God's standards. The goal was to set up a system that covered people's shortcomings so that they could express their heart's desire to be right with the Lord. Even so, the system also proved that there were no offerings people could ever make to cover their deficiencies with God fully. In other words, the offerings didn't save people. Only God has the power to forgive sin and offer salvation.

Difference Maker

Challenge yourself a bit. Read Hebrews 10:1–18 and compare the inadequacy of the sacrificial system to the fullness of salvation God offers through Jesus Christ. How would you explain to someone the difference between the old system and what Jesus accomplished on the cross?

of the liver. These must be removed with the kidneys, [11]and the priest will
burn them on the altar. It is a special gift of food presented to the LORD.
[12]"If you present a goat as your offering, bring it to the LORD, [13]lay your
hand on its head, and slaughter it in front of the Tabernacle. Aaron's sons
will then splatter the goat's blood against all sides of the altar. [14]The priest
must present part of this offering as a special gift to the LORD. This includes
all the fat around the internal organs, [15]the two kidneys and the fat around
them near the loins, and the long lobe of the liver. These must be removed
with the kidneys, [16]and the priest will burn them on the altar. It is a special
gift of food, a pleasing aroma to the LORD. All the fat belongs to the LORD.
[17]"You must never eat any fat or blood. This is a permanent law for you,
and it must be observed from generation to generation, wherever you live."

Procedures for the Sin Offering

4 Then the LORD said to Moses, [2]"Give the following instructions to the
people of Israel. This is how you are to deal with those who sin unin-
tentionally by doing anything that violates one of the LORD's commands.
[3]"If the high priest* sins, bringing guilt upon the entire community, he
must give a sin offering for the sin he has committed. He must present to the
LORD a young bull with no defects. [4]He must bring the bull to the LORD at
the entrance of the Tabernacle,* lay his hand on the bull's head, and slaughter
it before the LORD. [5]The high priest will then take some of the bull's blood
into the Tabernacle, [6]dip his finger in the blood, and sprinkle it seven times
before the LORD in front of the inner curtain of the sanctuary. [7]The priest will
then put some of the blood on the horns of the altar for fragrant incense that
stands in the LORD's presence inside the Tabernacle. He will pour out the rest
of the bull's blood at the base of the altar for burnt offerings at the entrance
of the Tabernacle. [8]Then the priest must remove all the fat of the bull to be
offered as a sin offering. This includes all the fat around the internal organs,
[9]the two kidneys and the fat around them near the loins, and the long lobe
of the liver. He must remove these along with the kidneys, [10]just as he does
with cattle offered as a peace offering, and burn them on the altar of burnt
offerings. [11]But he must take whatever is left of the bull—its hide, meat,
head, legs, internal organs, and dung—[12]and carry it away to a place outside
the camp that is ceremonially clean, the place where the ashes are dumped.
There, on the ash heap, he will burn it on a wood fire.
[13]"If the entire Israelite community sins by violating one of the LORD's
commands, but the people don't realize it, they are still guilty. [14]When they
become aware of their sin, the people must bring a young bull as an offer-
ing for their sin and present it before the Tabernacle. [15]The elders of the
community must then lay their hands on the bull's head and slaughter it
before the LORD. [16]The high priest will then take some of the bull's blood
into the Tabernacle, [17]dip his finger in the blood, and sprinkle it seven times
before the LORD in front of the inner curtain. [18]He will then put some of the
blood on the horns of the altar for fragrant incense that stands in the LORD's
presence inside the Tabernacle. He will pour out the rest of the blood at the
base of the altar for burnt offerings at the entrance of the Tabernacle. [19]Then
the priest must remove all the animal's fat and burn it on the altar, [20]just as
he does with the bull offered as a sin offering for the high priest. Through

4:3 Hebrew *the anointed priest;* also in 4:5, 16. **4:4** Hebrew *Tent of Meeting;* also in 4:5, 7, 14, 16, 18.

this process, the priest will purify the people, making them right with the LORD,* and they will be forgiven. 21 Then the priest must take what is left of the bull and carry it outside the camp and burn it there, just as is done with the sin offering for the high priest. This offering is for the sin of the entire congregation of Israel.

22 "If one of Israel's leaders sins by violating one of the commands of the LORD his God but doesn't realize it, he is still guilty. 23 When he becomes aware of his sin, he must bring as his offering a male goat with no defects. 24 He must lay his hand on the goat's head and slaughter it at the place where burnt offerings are slaughtered before the LORD. This is an offering for his sin. 25 Then the priest will dip his finger in the blood of the sin offering and put it on the horns of the altar for burnt offerings. He will pour out the rest of the blood at the base of the altar. 26 Then he must burn all the goat's fat on the altar, just as he does with the peace offering. Through this process, the priest will purify the leader from his sin, making him right with the LORD, and he will be forgiven.

27 "If any of the common people sin by violating one of the LORD's commands, but they don't realize it, they are still guilty. 28 When they become aware of their sin, they must bring as an offering for their sin a female goat with no defects. 29 They must lay a hand on the head of the sin offering and slaughter it at the place where burnt offerings are slaughtered. 30 Then the priest will dip his finger in the blood and put it on the horns of the altar for burnt offerings. He will pour out the rest of the blood at the base of the altar. 31 Then he must remove all the goat's fat, just as he does with the fat of the peace offering. He will burn the fat on the altar, and it will be a pleasing aroma to the LORD. Through this process, the priest will purify the people, making them right with the LORD, and they will be forgiven.

32 "If the people bring a sheep as their sin offering, it must be a female with no defects. 33 They must lay a hand on the head of the sin offering and slaughter it at the place where burnt offerings are slaughtered. 34 Then the priest will dip his finger in the blood of the sin offering and put it on the horns of the altar for burnt offerings. He will pour out the rest of the blood at the base of the altar. 35 Then he must remove all the sheep's fat, just as he does with the fat of a sheep presented as a peace offering. He will burn the fat on the altar on top of the special gifts presented to the LORD. Through this process, the priest will purify the people from their sin, making them right with the LORD, and they will be forgiven.

Sins Requiring a Sin Offering

5 "If you are called to testify about something you have seen or that you know about, it is sinful to refuse to testify, and you will be punished for your sin.

2 "Or suppose you unknowingly touch something that is ceremonially unclean, such as the carcass of an unclean animal. When you realize what you have done, you must admit your defilement and your guilt. This is true whether it is a wild animal, a domestic animal, or an animal that scurries along the ground.

3 "Or suppose you unknowingly touch something that makes a person unclean. When you realize what you have done, you must admit your guilt.

4 "Or suppose you make a foolish vow of any kind, whether its purpose

4:20 Or *will make atonement for the people;* similarly in 4:26, 31, 35.

How this passage impacts me

Prayer **5:10**

Lord, thank you that because of what Jesus has done on the cross, my sins can be forgiven, and I can be made right with you. Amen.

is for good or for bad. When you realize its foolishness, you must admit
your guilt.
5 "When you become aware of your guilt in any of these ways, you must con-
fess your sin. 6 Then you must bring to the LORD as the penalty for your sin a
female from the flock, either a sheep or a goat. This is a sin offering with which
the priest will purify you from your sin, making you right with the LORD.*
7 "But if you cannot afford to bring a sheep, you may bring to the LORD two
turtledoves or two young pigeons as the penalty for your sin. One of the birds
will be for a sin offering, and the other for a burnt offering. 8 You must bring
them to the priest, who will present the first bird as the sin offering. He will
wring its neck but without severing its head from the body. 9 Then he will
sprinkle some of the blood of the sin offering against the sides of the altar,
and the rest of the blood will be drained out at the base of the altar. This is
an offering for sin. 10 The priest will then prepare the second bird as a burnt
offering, following all the procedures that have been prescribed. Through
this process the priest will purify you from your sin, making you right with
the LORD, and you will be forgiven.
11 "If you cannot afford to bring two turtledoves or two young pigeons,
you may bring two quarts* of choice flour for your sin offering. Since it is an
offering for sin, you must not moisten it with olive oil or put any frankin-
cense on it. 12 Take the flour to the priest, who will scoop out a handful as a
representative portion. He will burn it on the altar on top of the special gifts
presented to the LORD. It is an offering for sin. 13 Through this process, the
priest will purify those who are guilty of any of these sins, making them right
with the LORD, and they will be forgiven. The rest of the flour will belong to
the priest, just as with the grain offering."

Procedures for the Guilt Offering

14 Then the LORD said to Moses, 15 "If one of you commits a sin by uninten-
tionally defiling the LORD's sacred property, you must bring a guilt offering
to the LORD. The offering must be your own ram with no defects, or you
may buy one of equal value with silver, as measured by the weight of the
sanctuary shekel.* 16 You must make restitution for the sacred property you
have harmed by paying for the loss, plus an additional 20 percent. When you
give the payment to the priest, he will purify you with the ram sacrificed as
a guilt offering, making you right with the LORD, and you will be forgiven.
17 "Suppose you sin by violating one of the LORD's commands. Even if you
are unaware of what you have done, you are guilty and will be punished for
your sin. 18 For a guilt offering, you must bring to the priest your own ram
with no defects, or you may buy one of equal value. Through this process the
priest will purify you from your unintentional sin, making you right with
the LORD, and you will be forgiven. 19 This is a guilt offering, for you have
been guilty of an offense against the LORD."

Sins Requiring a Guilt Offering

6 1 *Then the LORD said to Moses, 2 "Suppose one of you sins against your
associate and is unfaithful to the LORD. Suppose you cheat in a deal
involving a security deposit, or you steal or commit fraud, 3 or you find lost

5:6 Or *will make atonement for you for your sin;* similarly in 5:10, 13, 16, 18. 5:11 Hebrew *1/10 of an ephah* [2.2 liters]. 5:15 Each shekel was about 0.4 ounces or 11 grams in weight. 6:1 Verses 6:1-7 are numbered 5:20-26 in Hebrew text.

property and lie about it, or you lie while swearing to tell the truth, or you
commit any other such sin. 4If you have sinned in any of these ways, you are
guilty. You must give back whatever you stole, or the money you took by ex-
tortion, or the security deposit, or the lost property you found, 5or anything
obtained by swearing falsely. You must make restitution by paying the full
price plus an additional 20 percent to the person you have harmed. On the
same day you must present a guilt offering. 6As a guilt offering to the LORD,
you must bring to the priest your own ram with no defects, or you may buy
one of equal value. 7Through this process, the priest will purify you before
the LORD, making you right with him,* and you will be forgiven for any of
these sins you have committed."

Further Instructions for the Burnt Offering

8*Then the LORD said to Moses, 9"Give Aaron and his sons the following
instructions regarding the burnt offering. The burnt offering must be left
on top of the altar until the next morning, and the fire on the altar must be
kept burning all night. 10In the morning, after the priest on duty has put on
his official linen clothing and linen undergarments, he must clean out the
ashes of the burnt offering and put them beside the altar. 11Then he must
take off these garments, change back into his regular clothes, and carry the
ashes outside the camp to a place that is ceremonially clean. 12Meanwhile, the
fire on the altar must be kept burning; it must never go out. Each morning
the priest will add fresh wood to the fire and arrange the burnt offering on
it. He will then burn the fat of the peace offerings on it. 13Remember, the fire
must be kept burning on the altar at all times. It must never go out.

Further Instructions for the Grain Offering

14"These are the instructions regarding the grain offering. Aaron's sons must
present this offering to the LORD in front of the altar. 15The priest on duty
will take from the grain offering a handful of the choice flour moistened with
olive oil, together with all the frankincense. He will burn this representative
portion on the altar as a pleasing aroma to the LORD. 16Aaron and his sons
may eat the rest of the flour, but it must be baked without yeast and eaten in
a sacred place within the courtyard of the Tabernacle.* 17Remember, it must
never be prepared with yeast. I have given it to the priests as their share of the
special gifts presented to me. Like the sin offering and the guilt offering, it is
most holy. 18Any of Aaron's male descendants may eat from the special gifts
presented to the LORD. This is their permanent right from generation to gen-
eration. Anyone or anything that touches these offerings will become holy."

Procedures for the Ordination Offering

19Then the LORD said to Moses, 20"On the day Aaron and his sons are
anointed, they must present to the LORD the standard grain offering of two
quarts* of choice flour, half to be offered in the morning and half to be of-
fered in the evening. 21It must be carefully mixed with olive oil and cooked
on a griddle. Then slice* this grain offering and present it as a pleasing aroma
to the LORD. 22In each generation, the high priest* who succeeds Aaron must

Question 6:13

Have you noticed in these chapters how purposeful and intricate the procedures are for sacrificial offerings? Because of Jesus, we don't have to rely on this sort of system to be made right with God. Still, we can develop rhythms in our routines that keep the fire of faith burning, so to speak. What kind of patterns or practices could you develop in your life to keep the fire of your faith going at all times?

6:7 Or *will make atonement for you before the LORD.* **6:8** Verses 6:8-30 are numbered 6:1-23 in Hebrew text. **6:16** Hebrew *Tent of Meeting;* also in 6:26, 30. **6:20** Hebrew $\frac{1}{10}$ *of an ephah* [2.2 liters]. **6:21** The meaning of this Hebrew term is uncertain. **6:22** Hebrew *the anointed priest.*

prepare this same offering. It belongs to the LORD and must be burned up completely. This is a permanent law. 23 All such grain offerings of a priest must be burned up entirely. None of it may be eaten."

Further Instructions for the Sin Offering

24 Then the LORD said to Moses, 25 "Give Aaron and his sons the following instructions regarding the sin offering. The animal given as an offering for sin is a most holy offering, and it must be slaughtered in the LORD's presence at the place where the burnt offerings are slaughtered. 26 The priest who offers the sacrifice as a sin offering must eat his portion in a sacred place within the courtyard of the Tabernacle. 27 Anyone or anything that touches the sacrificial meat will become holy. If any of the sacrificial blood spatters on a person's clothing, the soiled garment must be washed in a sacred place. 28 If a clay pot is used to boil the sacrificial meat, it must then be broken. If a bronze pot is used, it must be scoured and thoroughly rinsed with water. 29 Any male from a priest's family may eat from this offering; it is most holy. 30 But the offering for sin may not be eaten if its blood was brought into the Tabernacle as an offering for purification* in the Holy Place. It must be completely burned with fire.

Further Instructions for the Guilt Offering

7 "These are the instructions for the guilt offering. It is most holy. 2 The animal sacrificed as a guilt offering must be slaughtered at the place where the burnt offerings are slaughtered, and its blood must be splattered against all sides of the altar. 3 The priest will then offer all its fat on the altar, including the fat of the broad tail, the fat around the internal organs, 4 the two kidneys and the fat around them near the loins, and the long lobe of the liver. These are to be removed with the kidneys, 5 and the priests will burn them on the altar as a special gift presented to the LORD. This is the guilt offering. 6 Any male from a priest's family may eat the meat. It must be eaten in a sacred place, for it is most holy.

7 "The same instructions apply to both the guilt offering and the sin offering. Both belong to the priest who uses them to purify someone, making that person right with the LORD.* 8 In the case of the burnt offering, the priest may keep the hide of the sacrificed animal. 9 Any grain offering that has been baked in an oven, prepared in a pan, or cooked on a griddle belongs to the priest who presents it. 10 All other grain offerings, whether made of dry flour or flour moistened with olive oil, are to be shared equally among all the priests, the descendants of Aaron.

Further Instructions for the Peace Offering

11 "These are the instructions regarding the different kinds of peace offerings that may be presented to the LORD. 12 If you present your peace offering as an expression of thanksgiving, the usual animal sacrifice must be accompanied by various kinds of bread made without yeast—thin cakes mixed with olive oil, wafers spread with oil, and cakes made of choice flour mixed with olive oil. 13 This peace offering of thanksgiving must also be accompanied by loaves of bread made with yeast. 14 One of each kind of bread must be presented as a gift to the LORD. It will then belong to the priest who splatters the blood

6:30 Or *an offering to make atonement.* **7:7** Or *to make atonement.*

What I want to remember

of the peace offering against the altar. 15 The meat of the peace offering of
thanksgiving must be eaten on the same day it is offered. None of it may be
saved for the next morning.

16 "If you bring an offering to fulfill a vow or as a voluntary offering, the
meat must be eaten on the same day the sacrifice is offered, but whatever
is left over may be eaten on the second day. 17 Any meat left over until the
third day must be completely burned up. 18 If any of the meat from the peace
offering is eaten on the third day, the person who presented it will not be
accepted by the LORD. You will receive no credit for offering it. By then the
meat will be contaminated; if you eat it, you will be punished for your sin.

19 "Meat that touches anything ceremonially unclean may not be eaten; it
must be completely burned up. The rest of the meat may be eaten, but only
by people who are ceremonially clean. 20 If you are ceremonially unclean
and you eat meat from a peace offering that was presented to the LORD, you
will be cut off from the community. 21 If you touch anything that is unclean
(whether it is human defilement or an unclean animal or any other unclean,
detestable thing) and then eat meat from a peace offering presented to the
LORD, you will be cut off from the community."

The Forbidden Blood and Fat

22 Then the LORD said to Moses, 23 "Give the following instructions to the
people of Israel. You must never eat fat, whether from cattle, sheep, or goats.
24 The fat of an animal found dead or torn to pieces by wild animals must
never be eaten, though it may be used for any other purpose. 25 Anyone who
eats fat from an animal presented as a special gift to the LORD will be cut off
from the community. 26 No matter where you live, you must never consume
the blood of any bird or animal. 27 Anyone who consumes blood will be cut
off from the community."

A Portion for the Priests

28 Then the LORD said to Moses, 29 "Give the following instructions to the
people of Israel. When you present a peace offering to the LORD, bring part
of it as a gift to the LORD. 30 Present it to the LORD with your own hands as
a special gift to the LORD. Bring the fat of the animal, together with the
breast, and lift up the breast as a special offering to the LORD. 31 Then the
priest will burn the fat on the altar, but the breast will belong to Aaron and
his descendants. 32 Give the right thigh of your peace offering to the priest
as a gift. 33 The right thigh must always be given to the priest who offers the
blood and the fat of the peace offering. 34 For I have reserved the breast of the
special offering and the right thigh of the sacred offering for the priests. It
is the permanent right of Aaron and his descendants to share in the peace
offerings brought by the people of Israel. 35 This is their rightful share. The
special gifts presented to the LORD have been reserved for Aaron and his
descendants from the time they were set apart to serve the LORD as priests.
36 On the day they were anointed, the LORD commanded the Israelites to
give these portions to the priests as their permanent share from generation
to generation."

37 These are the instructions for the burnt offering, the grain offering, the
sin offering, and the guilt offering, as well as the ordination offering and the
peace offering. 38 The LORD gave these instructions to Moses on Mount Sinai

when he commanded the Israelites to present their offerings to the LORD in the wilderness of Sinai.

Ordination of the Priests

8 Then the LORD said to Moses, 2"Bring Aaron and his sons, along with their sacred garments, the anointing oil, the bull for the sin offering, the two rams, and the basket of bread made without yeast, 3and call the entire community of Israel together at the entrance of the Tabernacle.*"

4So Moses followed the LORD's instructions, and the whole community assembled at the Tabernacle entrance. 5Moses announced to them, "This is what the LORD has commanded us to do!" 6Then he presented Aaron and his sons and washed them with water. 7He put the official tunic on Aaron and tied the sash around his waist. He dressed him in the robe, placed the ephod on him, and attached the ephod securely with its decorative sash. 8Then Moses placed the chestpiece on Aaron and put the Urim and the Thummim inside it. 9He placed the turban on Aaron's head and attached the gold medallion—the badge of holiness—to the front of the turban, just as the LORD had commanded him.

10Then Moses took the anointing oil and anointed the Tabernacle and everything in it, making them holy. 11He sprinkled the oil on the altar seven times, anointing it and all its utensils, as well as the washbasin and its stand, making them holy. 12Then he poured some of the anointing oil on Aaron's head, anointing him and making him holy for his work. 13Next Moses presented Aaron's sons. He clothed them in their tunics, tied their sashes around them, and put their special head coverings on them, just as the LORD had commanded him.

14Then Moses presented the bull for the sin offering. Aaron and his sons laid their hands on the bull's head, 15and Moses slaughtered it. Moses took some of the blood, and with his finger he put it on the four horns of the altar to purify it. He poured out the rest of the blood at the base of the altar. Through this process, he made the altar holy by purifying it.* 16Then Moses took all the fat around the internal organs, the long lobe of the liver, and the two kidneys and the fat around them, and he burned it all on the altar. 17He took the rest of the bull, including its hide, meat, and dung, and burned it on a fire outside the camp, just as the LORD had commanded him.

18Then Moses presented the ram for the burnt offering. Aaron and his sons laid their hands on the ram's head, 19and Moses slaughtered it. Then Moses took the ram's blood and splattered it against all sides of the altar. 20Then he cut the ram into pieces, and he burned the head, some of its pieces, and the fat on the altar. 21After washing the internal organs and the legs with water, Moses burned the entire ram on the altar as a burnt offering. It was a pleasing aroma, a special gift presented to the LORD, just as the LORD had commanded him.

22Then Moses presented the other ram, which was the ram of ordination. Aaron and his sons laid their hands on the ram's head, 23and Moses slaughtered it. Then Moses took some of its blood and applied it to the lobe of Aaron's right ear, the thumb of his right hand, and the big toe of his right foot. 24Next Moses presented Aaron's sons and applied some of the blood to the lobes of their right ears, the thumbs of their right hands, and the big

Story Arc **8:1–15**

● Aaron

Aaron became the first high priest of Israel. His garments and instruments for the sacrificial system set him apart for the holy responsibility of making people right with the Lord. He would repeatedly need to enter into the presence of God as a mediator between God and his sinful people.

This practice led by Aaron established a living illustration of our need for the Savior. This is why it is so profound when Jesus is called the "great High Priest," the only Mediator who himself becomes the holy sacrifice to cover our sin and make us right with God (Hebrews 10:21-22).

Num 1:1 ►

8:3 Hebrew *Tent of Meeting;* also in 8:4, 31, 33, 35. 8:15 Or *by making atonement for it;* or *that offerings for purification might be made on it.*

toes of their right feet. He then splattered the rest of the blood against all sides of the altar.

25 Next Moses took the fat, including the fat of the broad tail, the fat around the internal organs, the long lobe of the liver, and the two kidneys and the fat around them, along with the right thigh. 26 On top of these he placed a thin cake of bread made without yeast, a cake of bread mixed with olive oil, and a wafer spread with olive oil. All these were taken from the basket of bread made without yeast that was placed in the LORD's presence. 27 He put all these in the hands of Aaron and his sons, and he lifted these gifts as a special offering to the LORD. 28 Moses then took all the offerings back from them and burned them on the altar on top of the burnt offering. This was the ordination offering. It was a pleasing aroma, a special gift presented to the LORD. 29 Then Moses took the breast and lifted it up as a special offering to the LORD. This was Moses' portion of the ram of ordination, just as the LORD had commanded him.

30 Next Moses took some of the anointing oil and some of the blood that was on the altar, and he sprinkled them on Aaron and his garments and on his sons and their garments. In this way, he made Aaron and his sons and their garments holy.

31 Then Moses said to Aaron and his sons, "Boil the remaining meat of the offerings at the Tabernacle entrance, and eat it there, along with the bread that is in the basket of offerings for the ordination, just as I commanded when I said, 'Aaron and his sons will eat it.' 32 Any meat or bread that is left over must then be burned up. 33 You must not leave the Tabernacle entrance for seven days, for that is when the ordination ceremony will be completed. 34 Everything we have done today was commanded by the LORD in order to purify you, making you right with him.* 35 Now stay at the entrance of the Tabernacle day and night for seven days, and do everything the LORD requires. If you fail to do this, you will die, for this is what the LORD has commanded." 36 So Aaron and his sons did everything the LORD had commanded through Moses.

The Priests Begin Their Work

9 After the ordination ceremony, on the eighth day, Moses called together Aaron and his sons and the elders of Israel. 2 He said to Aaron, "Take a young bull for a sin offering and a ram for a burnt offering, both without defects, and present them to the LORD. 3 Then tell the Israelites, 'Take a male goat for a sin offering, and take a calf and a lamb, both a year old and without defects, for a burnt offering. 4 Also take a bull* and a ram for a peace offering and flour moistened with olive oil for a grain offering. Present all these offerings to the LORD because the LORD will appear to you today.'"

5 So the people presented all these things at the entrance of the Tabernacle,* just as Moses had commanded. Then the whole community came forward and stood before the LORD. 6 And Moses said, "This is what the LORD has commanded you to do so that the glory of the LORD may appear to you."

7 Then Moses said to Aaron, "Come to the altar and sacrifice your sin offering and your burnt offering to purify yourself and the people. Then present the offerings of the people to purify them, making them right with the LORD,* just as he has commanded."

8:34 Or *to make atonement for you.* 9:4 Or *cow;* also in 9:18, 19. 9:5 Hebrew *Tent of Meeting;* also in 9:23. 9:7 Or *to make atonement for them.*

8 So Aaron went to the altar and slaughtered the calf as a sin offering for
himself. 9 His sons brought him the blood, and he dipped his finger in it and
put it on the horns of the altar. He poured out the rest of the blood at the
base of the altar. 10 Then he burned on the altar the fat, the kidneys, and the
long lobe of the liver from the sin offering, just as the LORD had commanded
Moses. 11 The meat and the hide, however, he burned outside the camp.
12 Next Aaron slaughtered the animal for the burnt offering. His sons
brought him the blood, and he splattered it against all sides of the altar.
13 Then they handed him each piece of the burnt offering, including the
head, and he burned them on the altar. 14 Then he washed the internal or-
gans and the legs and burned them on the altar along with the rest of the
burnt offering.
15 Next Aaron presented the offerings of the people. He slaughtered the
people's goat and presented it as an offering for their sin, just as he had first
done with the offering for his own sin. 16 Then he presented the burnt of-
fering and sacrificed it in the prescribed way. 17 He also presented the grain
offering, burning a handful of the flour mixture on the altar, in addition to
the regular burnt offering for the morning.
18 Then Aaron slaughtered the bull and the ram for the people's peace
offering. His sons brought him the blood, and he splattered it against all
sides of the altar. 19 Then he took the fat of the bull and the ram—the fat of
the broad tail and from around the internal organs—along with the kidneys
and the long lobes of the livers. 20 He placed these fat portions on top of the
breasts of these animals and burned them on the altar. 21 Aaron then lifted up
the breasts and right thighs as a special offering to the LORD, just as Moses
had commanded.
22 After that, Aaron raised his hands toward the people and blessed them.
Then, after presenting the sin offering, the burnt offering, and the peace
offering, he stepped down from the altar. 23 Then Moses and Aaron went
into the Tabernacle, and when they came back out, they blessed the people
again, and the glory of the LORD appeared to the whole community. 24 Fire
blazed forth from the LORD's presence and consumed the burnt offering and
the fat on the altar. When the people saw this, they shouted with joy and fell
face down on the ground.

The Sin of Nadab and Abihu

10 Aaron's sons Nadab and Abihu put coals of fire in their incense burn-
ers and sprinkled incense over them. In this way, they disobeyed the
LORD by burning before him the wrong kind of fire, different than he had
commanded. 2 So fire blazed forth from the LORD's presence and burned
them up, and they died there before the LORD.
3 Then Moses said to Aaron, "This is what the LORD meant when he said,

'I will display my holiness
through those who come near me.
I will display my glory
before all the people.'"

And Aaron was silent.
4 Then Moses called for Mishael and Elzaphan, Aaron's cousins, the sons

of Aaron's uncle Uzziel. He said to them, "Come forward and carry away the bodies of your relatives from in front of the sanctuary to a place outside the camp." 5 So they came forward and picked them up by their garments and carried them out of the camp, just as Moses had commanded.

6 Then Moses said to Aaron and his sons Eleazar and Ithamar, "Do not show grief by leaving your hair uncombed* or by tearing your clothes. If you do, you will die, and the LORD's anger will strike the whole community of Israel. However, the rest of the Israelites, your relatives, may mourn because of the LORD's fiery destruction of Nadab and Abihu. 7 But you must not leave the entrance of the Tabernacle* or you will die, for you have been anointed with the LORD's anointing oil." So they did as Moses commanded.

Instructions for Priestly Conduct

8 Then the LORD said to Aaron, 9 "You and your descendants must never drink wine or any other alcoholic drink before going into the Tabernacle. If you do, you will die. This is a permanent law for you, and it must be observed from generation to generation. 10 You must distinguish between what is sacred and what is common, between what is ceremonially unclean and what is clean. 11 And you must teach the Israelites all the decrees that the LORD has given them through Moses."

12 Then Moses said to Aaron and his remaining sons, Eleazar and Ithamar, "Take what is left of the grain offering after a portion has been presented as a special gift to the LORD, and eat it beside the altar. Make sure it contains no yeast, for it is most holy. 13 You must eat it in a sacred place, for it has been given to you and your descendants as your portion of the special gifts presented to the LORD. These are the commands I have been given. 14 But the breast and thigh that were lifted up as a special offering may be eaten in any place that is ceremonially clean. These parts have been given to you and your descendants as your portion of the peace offerings presented by the people of Israel. 15 You must lift up the thigh and breast as a special offering to the LORD, along with the fat of the special gifts. These parts will belong to you and your descendants as your permanent right, just as the LORD has commanded."

16 Moses then asked them what had happened to the goat of the sin offering. When he discovered it had been burned up, he became very angry with Eleazar and Ithamar, Aaron's remaining sons. 17 "Why didn't you eat the sin offering in the sacred area?" he demanded. "It is a holy offering! The LORD has given it to you to remove the guilt of the community and to purify the people, making them right with the LORD.* 18 Since the animal's blood was not brought into the Holy Place, you should have eaten the meat in the sacred area as I ordered you."

19 Then Aaron answered Moses, "Today my sons presented both their sin offering and their burnt offering to the LORD. And yet this tragedy has happened to me. If I had eaten the people's sin offering on such a tragic day as this, would the LORD have been pleased?" 20 And when Moses heard this, he was satisfied.

Ceremonially Clean and Unclean Animals

11 Then the LORD said to Moses and Aaron, 2 "Give the following instructions to the people of Israel.

"Of all the land animals, these are the ones you may use for food. 3 You

10:6 Or *by uncovering your heads.* **10:7** Hebrew *Tent of Meeting;* also in 10:9. **10:17** Or *to make atonement for the people before the LORD.*

Question 10:9

Why do you think God set up such strict behavioral expectations for those who served as priests? Read 1 Peter 2:9 and Revelation 5:9-10. What implications does the concept of the priesthood of all believers have for followers of Jesus?

may eat any animal that has completely split hooves and chews the cud. 4 You may not, however, eat the following animals* that have split hooves or that chew the cud, but not both. The camel chews the cud but does not have split hooves, so it is ceremonially unclean for you. 5 The hyrax* chews the cud but does not have split hooves, so it is unclean. 6 The hare chews the cud but does not have split hooves, so it is unclean. 7 The pig has evenly split hooves but does not chew the cud, so it is unclean. 8 You may not eat the meat of these animals or even touch their carcasses. They are ceremonially unclean for you.

9 "Of all the marine animals, these are ones you may use for food. You may eat anything from the water if it has both fins and scales, whether taken from salt water or from streams. 10 But you must never eat animals from the sea or from rivers that do not have both fins and scales. They are detestable to you. This applies both to little creatures that live in shallow water and to all creatures that live in deep water. 11 They will always be detestable to you. You must never eat their meat or even touch their dead bodies. 12 Any marine animal that does not have both fins and scales is detestable to you.

13 "These are the birds that are detestable to you. You must never eat them: the griffon vulture, the bearded vulture, the black vulture, 14 the kite, falcons of all kinds, 15 ravens of all kinds, 16 the eagle owl, the short-eared owl, the seagull, hawks of all kinds, 17 the little owl, the cormorant, the great owl, 18 the barn owl, the desert owl, the Egyptian vulture, 19 the stork, herons of all kinds, the hoopoe, and the bat.

20 "You must not eat winged insects that walk along the ground; they are detestable to you. 21 You may, however, eat winged insects that walk along the ground and have jointed legs so they can jump. 22 The insects you are permitted to eat include all kinds of locusts, bald locusts, crickets, and grasshoppers. 23 All other winged insects that walk along the ground are detestable to you.

24 "The following creatures will make you ceremonially unclean. If any of you touch their carcasses, you will be defiled until evening. 25 If you pick up their carcasses, you must wash your clothes, and you will remain defiled until evening.

26 "Any animal that has split hooves that are not evenly divided or that does not chew the cud is unclean for you. If you touch the carcass of such an animal, you will be defiled. 27 Of the animals that walk on all fours, those that have paws are unclean. If you touch the carcass of such an animal, you will be defiled until evening. 28 If you pick up its carcass, you must wash your clothes, and you will remain defiled until evening. These animals are unclean for you.

29 "Of the small animals that scurry along the ground, these are unclean for you: the mole rat, the rat, large lizards of all kinds, 30 the gecko, the monitor lizard, the common lizard, the sand lizard, and the chameleon. 31 All these small animals are unclean for you. If any of you touch the dead body of such an animal, you will be defiled until evening. 32 If such an animal dies and falls on something, that object will be unclean. This is true whether the object is made of wood, cloth, leather, or burlap. Whatever its use, you must dip it in water, and it will remain defiled until evening. After that, it will be ceremonially clean and may be used again.

33 "If such an animal falls into a clay pot, everything in the pot will be

11:4 The identification of some of the animals, birds, and insects in this chapter is uncertain.
11:5 Or *coney,* or *rock badger.*

defiled, and the pot must be smashed. 34 If the water from such a container spills on any food, the food will be defiled. And any beverage in such a container will be defiled. 35 Any object on which the carcass of such an animal falls will be defiled. If it is an oven or hearth, it must be destroyed, for it is defiled, and you must treat it accordingly.

36 "However, if the carcass of such an animal falls into a spring or a cistern, the water will still be clean. But anyone who touches the carcass will be defiled. 37 If the carcass falls on seed grain to be planted in the field, the seed will still be considered clean. 38 But if the seed is wet when the carcass falls on it, the seed will be defiled.

39 "If an animal you are permitted to eat dies and you touch its carcass, you will be defiled until evening. 40 If you eat any of its meat or carry away its carcass, you must wash your clothes, and you will remain defiled until evening.

41 "All small animals that scurry along the ground are detestable, and you must never eat them. 42 This includes all animals that slither along on their bellies, as well as those with four legs and those with many feet. All such animals that scurry along the ground are detestable, and you must never eat them. 43 Do not defile yourselves by touching them. You must not make yourselves ceremonially unclean because of them. 44 For I am the LORD your God. You must consecrate yourselves and be holy, because I am holy. So do not defile yourselves with any of these small animals that scurry along the ground. 45 For I, the LORD, am the one who brought you up from the land of Egypt, that I might be your God. Therefore, you must be holy because I am holy.

46 "These are the instructions regarding land animals, birds, marine creatures, and animals that scurry along the ground. 47 By these instructions you will know what is unclean and clean, and which animals may be eaten and which may not be eaten."

Purification after Childbirth

12 The LORD said to Moses, 2 "Give the following instructions to the people of Israel. If a woman becomes pregnant and gives birth to a son, she will be ceremonially unclean for seven days, just as she is unclean during her menstrual period. 3 On the eighth day the boy's foreskin must be circumcised. 4 After waiting thirty-three days, she will be purified from the bleeding of childbirth. During this time of purification, she must not touch anything that is set apart as holy. And she must not enter the sanctuary until her time of purification is over. 5 If a woman gives birth to a daughter, she will be ceremonially unclean for two weeks, just as she is unclean during her menstrual period. After waiting sixty-six days, she will be purified from the bleeding of childbirth.

6 "When the time of purification is completed for either a son or a daughter, the woman must bring a one-year-old lamb for a burnt offering and a young pigeon or turtledove for a purification offering. She must bring her offerings to the priest at the entrance of the Tabernacle.* 7 The priest will then present them to the LORD to purify her.* Then she will be ceremonially clean again after her bleeding at childbirth. These are the instructions for a woman after the birth of a son or a daughter.

8 "If a woman cannot afford to bring a lamb, she must bring two turtledoves

12:6 Hebrew *Tent of Meeting.* 12:7 Or *to make atonement for her;* also in 12:8.

Question 11:47

How dedicated do you think you would have been to follow all these instructions? What difficult thing is God asking you to do to stay "clean" in your faith in him?

Make a Difference 12:8

Connections to Jesus

Notice the requirement here for a new mom who cannot afford to bring a lamb for sacrifice. The Lord provided a way for poor moms to dedicate themselves and their children faithfully to God. This is noteworthy because Mary brought this very offering after Jesus was born (Luke 2:24).

Difference Maker

Even though the book of Leviticus is complicated, it is full of connection points to Jesus. On a piece of paper, take a moment to list as many links as you can make between the details of this book and the life of Jesus, the Lamb of God.

or two young pigeons. One will be for the burnt offering and the other for the purification offering. The priest will sacrifice them to purify her, and she will be ceremonially clean."

Serious Skin Diseases

13 The LORD said to Moses and Aaron, 2"If anyone has a swelling or a rash or discolored skin that might develop into a serious skin disease,* that person must be brought to Aaron the priest or to one of his sons.* 3The priest will examine the affected area of the skin. If the hair in the affected area has turned white and the problem appears to be more than skin-deep, it is a serious skin disease, and the priest who examines it must pronounce the person ceremonially unclean.

4"But if the affected area of the skin is only a white discoloration and does not appear to be more than skin-deep, and if the hair on the spot has not turned white, the priest will quarantine the person for seven days. 5On the seventh day the priest will make another examination. If he finds the affected area has not changed and the problem has not spread on the skin, the priest will quarantine the person for seven more days. 6On the seventh day the priest will make another examination. If he finds the affected area has faded and has not spread, the priest will pronounce the person ceremonially clean. It was only a rash. The person's clothing must be washed, and the person will be ceremonially clean. 7But if the rash continues to spread after the person has been examined by the priest and has been pronounced clean, the infected person must return to be examined again. 8If the priest finds that the rash has spread, he must pronounce the person ceremonially unclean, for it is indeed a skin disease.

9"Anyone who develops a serious skin disease must go to the priest for an examination. 10If the priest finds a white swelling on the skin, and some hair on the spot has turned white, and there is an open sore in the affected area, 11it is a chronic skin disease, and the priest must pronounce the person ceremonially unclean. In such cases the person need not be quarantined, for it is obvious that the skin is defiled by the disease.

12"Now suppose the disease has spread all over the person's skin, covering the body from head to foot. 13When the priest examines the infected person and finds that the disease covers the entire body, he will pronounce the person ceremonially clean. Since the skin has turned completely white, the person is clean. 14But if any open sores appear, the infected person will be pronounced ceremonially unclean. 15The priest must make this pronouncement as soon as he sees an open sore, since open sores indicate the presence of a skin disease. 16However, if the open sores heal and turn white like the rest of the skin, the person must return to the priest 17for another examination. If the affected areas have indeed turned white, the priest will then pronounce the person ceremonially clean by declaring, 'You are clean!'

18"If anyone has a boil on the skin that has started to heal, 19but a white swelling or a reddish white spot develops in its place, that person must go to the priest to be examined. 20If the priest examines it and finds it to be more than skin-deep, and if the hair in the affected area has turned white, the priest must pronounce the person ceremonially unclean. The boil has become a serious skin disease. 21But if the priest finds no white hair on the

13:2a Traditionally rendered *leprosy.* The Hebrew word used throughout this passage is used to describe various skin diseases. **13:2b** Or *one of his descendants.*

affected area and the problem appears to be no more than skin-deep and
has faded, the priest must quarantine the person for seven days. 22 If during
that time the affected area spreads on the skin, the priest must pronounce
the person ceremonially unclean, because it is a serious disease. 23 But if the
area grows no larger and does not spread, it is merely the scar from the boil,
and the priest will pronounce the person ceremonially clean.
24 "If anyone has suffered a burn on the skin and the burned area
changes color, becoming either reddish white or shiny white, 25 the priest
must examine it. If he finds that the hair in the affected area has turned
white and the problem appears to be more than skin-deep, a skin disease
has broken out in the burn. The priest must then pronounce the person
ceremonially unclean, for it is clearly a serious skin disease. 26 But if the
priest finds no white hair on the affected area and the problem appears
to be no more than skin-deep and has faded, the priest must quarantine
the infected person for seven days. 27 On the seventh day the priest must
examine the person again. If the affected area has spread on the skin, the
priest must pronounce that person ceremonially unclean, for it is clearly
a serious skin disease. 28 But if the affected area has not changed or spread
on the skin and has faded, it is simply a swelling from the burn. The priest
will then pronounce the person ceremonially clean, for it is only the scar
from the burn.
29 "If anyone, either a man or woman, has a sore on the head or chin,
30 the priest must examine it. If he finds it is more than skin-deep and has
fine yellow hair on it, the priest must pronounce the person ceremonially
unclean. It is a scabby sore of the head or chin. 31 If the priest examines the
scabby sore and finds that it is only skin-deep but there is no black hair
on it, he must quarantine the person for seven days. 32 On the seventh day
the priest must examine the sore again. If he finds that the scabby sore has
not spread, and there is no yellow hair on it, and it appears to be only skin-
deep, 33 the person must shave off all hair except the hair on the affected
area. Then the priest must quarantine the person for another seven days.
34 On the seventh day he will examine the sore again. If it has not spread
and appears to be no more than skin-deep, the priest will pronounce the
person ceremonially clean. The person's clothing must be washed, and the
person will be ceremonially clean. 35 But if the scabby sore begins to spread
after the person is pronounced clean, 36 the priest must do another exami-
nation. If he finds that the sore has spread, the priest does not need to look
for yellow hair. The infected person is ceremonially unclean. 37 But if the
color of the scabby sore does not change and black hair has grown on it, it
has healed. The priest will then pronounce the person ceremonially clean.
38 "If anyone, either a man or woman, has shiny white patches on the
skin, 39 the priest must examine the affected area. If he finds that the shiny
patches are only pale white, this is a harmless skin rash, and the person is
ceremonially clean.
40 "If a man loses his hair and his head becomes bald, he is still ceremoni-
ally clean. 41 And if he loses hair on his forehead, he simply has a bald fore-
head; he is still clean. 42 However, if a reddish white sore appears on the bald
area on top of his head or on his forehead, this is a skin disease. 43 The priest
must examine him, and if he finds swelling around the reddish white sore
anywhere on the man's head and it looks like a skin disease, 44 the man is

What God wants people to know

Question 14:2

In Luke 5, Jesus healed a man suffering with leprosy. He then instructed the man to follow the purification ceremonies for those who had been healed of skin diseases (v. 14). What do you learn from this example about Jesus' respect for the religious laws in Leviticus?

indeed infected with a skin disease and is unclean. The priest must pro-
nounce him ceremonially unclean because of the sore on his head.
45"Those who suffer from a serious skin disease must tear their clothing
and leave their hair uncombed.* They must cover their mouth and call out,
'Unclean! Unclean!' 46As long as the serious disease lasts, they will be ceremo-
nially unclean. They must live in isolation in their place outside the camp.

Treatment of Contaminated Clothing

47"Now suppose mildew* contaminates some woolen or linen cloth-
ing, 48woolen or linen fabric, the hide of an animal, or anything made of
leather. 49If the contaminated area in the clothing, the animal hide, the fab-
ric, or the leather article has turned greenish or reddish, it is contaminated
with mildew and must be shown to the priest. 50After examining the affected
spot, the priest will put the article in quarantine for seven days. 51On the
seventh day the priest must inspect it again. If the contaminated area has
spread, the clothing or fabric or leather is clearly contaminated by a serious
mildew and is ceremonially unclean. 52The priest must burn the item—
the clothing, the woolen or linen fabric, or piece of leather—for it has been
contaminated by a serious mildew. It must be completely destroyed by fire.
53"But if the priest examines it and finds that the contaminated area has
not spread in the clothing, the fabric, or the leather, 54the priest will order the
object to be washed and then quarantined for seven more days. 55Then the
priest must examine the object again. If he finds that the contaminated area
has not changed color after being washed, even if it did not spread, the object
is defiled. It must be completely burned up, whether the contaminated spot*
is on the inside or outside. 56But if the priest examines it and finds that the
contaminated area has faded after being washed, he must cut the spot from
the clothing, the fabric, or the leather. 57If the spot later reappears on the
clothing, the fabric, or the leather article, the mildew is clearly spreading,
and the contaminated object must be burned up. 58But if the spot disappears
from the clothing, the fabric, or the leather article after it has been washed,
it must be washed again; then it will be ceremonially clean.
59"These are the instructions for dealing with mildew that contaminates
woolen or linen clothing or fabric or anything made of leather. This is how
the priest will determine whether these items are ceremonially clean or
unclean."

Cleansing from Skin Diseases

14 And the LORD said to Moses, 2"The following instructions are for
those seeking ceremonial purification from a skin disease.* Those
who have been healed must be brought to the priest, 3who will examine
them at a place outside the camp. If the priest finds that someone has been
healed of a serious skin disease, 4he will perform a purification ceremony,
using two live birds that are ceremonially clean, a stick of cedar,* some scarlet
yarn, and a hyssop branch. 5The priest will order that one bird be slaughtered
over a clay pot filled with fresh water. 6He will take the live bird, the cedar
stick, the scarlet yarn, and the hyssop branch, and dip them into the blood

13:45 Or *and uncover their heads.* 13:47 Traditionally rendered *leprosy.* The Hebrew term used throughout this passage is the same term used for the various skin diseases described in 13:1-46. 13:55 The meaning of the Hebrew is uncertain. 14:2 Traditionally rendered *leprosy;* see note on 13:2a. 14:4 Or *juniper;* also in 14:6, 49, 51.

of the bird that was slaughtered over the fresh water. 7 The priest will then
sprinkle the blood of the dead bird seven times on the person being purified
of the skin disease. When the priest has purified the person, he will release
the live bird in the open field to fly away.
8 "The persons being purified must then wash their clothes, shave off all
their hair, and bathe themselves in water. Then they will be ceremonially
clean and may return to the camp. However, they must remain outside their
tents for seven days. 9 On the seventh day they must again shave all the hair
from their heads, including the hair of the beard and eyebrows. They must
also wash their clothes and bathe themselves in water. Then they will be
ceremonially clean.
10 "On the eighth day each person being purified must bring two male
lambs and a one-year-old female lamb, all with no defects, along with a grain
offering of six quarts* of choice flour moistened with olive oil, and a cup* of
olive oil. 11 Then the officiating priest will present that person for purifica-
tion, along with the offerings, before the LORD at the entrance of the Tab-
ernacle.* 12 The priest will take one of the male lambs and the olive oil and
present them as a guilt offering, lifting them up as a special offering before
the LORD. 13 He will then slaughter the male lamb in the sacred area where
sin offerings and burnt offerings are slaughtered. As with the sin offering,
the guilt offering belongs to the priest. It is a most holy offering. 14 The priest
will then take some of the blood of the guilt offering and apply it to the lobe
of the right ear, the thumb of the right hand, and the big toe of the right foot
of the person being purified.
15 "Then the priest will pour some of the olive oil into the palm of his own
left hand. 16 He will dip his right finger into the oil in his palm and sprinkle
some of it with his finger seven times before the LORD. 17 The priest will then
apply some of the oil in his palm over the blood from the guilt offering that
is on the lobe of the right ear, the thumb of the right hand, and the big toe
of the right foot of the person being purified. 18 The priest will apply the oil
remaining in his hand to the head of the person being purified. Through
this process, the priest will purify* the person before the LORD.
19 "Then the priest must present the sin offering to purify the person who
was cured of the skin disease. After that, the priest will slaughter the burnt
offering 20 and offer it on the altar along with the grain offering. Through
this process, the priest will purify the person who was healed, and the person
will be ceremonially clean.
21 "But anyone who is too poor and cannot afford these offerings may bring
one male lamb for a guilt offering, to be lifted up as a special offering for pu-
rification. The person must also bring two quarts* of choice flour moistened
with olive oil for the grain offering and a cup of olive oil. 22 The offering must
also include two turtledoves or two young pigeons, whichever the person
can afford. One of the pair must be used for the sin offering and the other
for a burnt offering. 23 On the eighth day of the purification ceremony, the
person being purified must bring the offerings to the priest in the LORD's
presence at the entrance of the Tabernacle. 24 The priest will take the lamb
for the guilt offering, along with the olive oil, and lift them up as a special
offering to the LORD. 25 Then the priest will slaughter the lamb for the guilt

14:10a Hebrew *3/10 of an ephah* [6.6 liters]. **14:10b** Hebrew *1 log* [0.3 liters]; also in 14:21. **14:11** Hebrew *Tent of Meeting;* also in 14:23. **14:18** Or *will make atonement for;* similarly in 14:19, 20, 21, 29, 31, 53. **14:21** Hebrew *1/10 of an ephah* [2.2 liters].

offering. He will take some of its blood and apply it to the lobe of the right
ear, the thumb of the right hand, and the big toe of the right foot of the
person being purified.
26 “The priest will also pour some of the olive oil into the palm of his own
left hand. 27 He will dip his right finger into the oil in his palm and sprinkle
some of it seven times before the LORD. 28 The priest will then apply some of
the oil in his palm over the blood from the guilt offering that is on the lobe
of the right ear, the thumb of the right hand, and the big toe of the right
foot of the person being purified. 29 The priest will apply the oil remaining
in his hand to the head of the person being purified. Through this process,
the priest will purify the person before the LORD.
30 “Then the priest will offer the two turtledoves or the two young pigeons,
whichever the person can afford. 31 One of them is for a sin offering and the
other for a burnt offering, to be presented along with the grain offering.
Through this process, the priest will purify the person before the LORD.
32 These are the instructions for purification for those who have recovered
from a serious skin disease but who cannot afford to bring the offerings
normally required for the ceremony of purification.”

Treatment of Contaminated Houses

33 Then the LORD said to Moses and Aaron, 34 “When you arrive in Canaan,
the land I am giving you as your own possession, I may contaminate some
of the houses in your land with mildew.* 35 The owner of such a house must
then go to the priest and say, ‘It appears that my house has some kind of
mildew.’ 36 Before the priest goes in to inspect the house, he must have the
house emptied so nothing inside will be pronounced ceremonially unclean.
37 Then the priest will go in and examine the mildew on the walls. If he finds
greenish or reddish streaks and the contamination appears to go deeper than
the wall’s surface, 38 the priest will step outside the door and put the house
in quarantine for seven days. 39 On the seventh day the priest must return for
another inspection. If he finds that the mildew on the walls of the house has
spread, 40 the priest must order that the stones from those areas be removed.
The contaminated material will then be taken outside the town to an area
designated as ceremonially unclean. 41 Next the inside walls of the entire
house must be scraped thoroughly and the scrapings dumped in the unclean
place outside the town. 42 Other stones will be brought in to replace the ones
that were removed, and the walls will be replastered.
43 “But if the mildew reappears after all the stones have been replaced and
the house has been scraped and replastered, 44 the priest must return and
inspect the house again. If he finds that the mildew has spread, the walls
are clearly contaminated with a serious mildew, and the house is defiled.
45 It must be torn down, and all its stones, timbers, and plaster must be car-
ried out of town to the place designated as ceremonially unclean. 46 Those
who enter the house during the period of quarantine will be ceremonially
unclean until evening, 47 and all who sleep or eat in the house must wash
their clothing.
48 “But if the priest returns for his inspection and finds that the mildew
has not reappeared in the house after the fresh plastering, he will pronounce
it clean because the mildew is clearly gone. 49 To purify the house the priest

14:34 Traditionally rendered *leprosy;* see note on 13:47.

must take two birds, a stick of cedar, some scarlet yarn, and a hyssop branch.
50 He will slaughter one of the birds over a clay pot filled with fresh water.
51 He will take the cedar stick, the hyssop branch, the scarlet yarn, and the
live bird, and dip them into the blood of the slaughtered bird and into the
fresh water. Then he will sprinkle the house seven times. 52 When the priest
has purified the house in exactly this way, 53 he will release the live bird in
the open fields outside the town. Through this process, the priest will purify
the house, and it will be ceremonially clean.
54 "These are the instructions for dealing with serious skin diseases,*
including scabby sores; 55 and mildew,* whether on clothing or in a house;
56 and a swelling on the skin, a rash, or discolored skin. 57 This procedure
will determine whether a person or object is ceremonially clean or unclean.
"These are the instructions regarding skin diseases and mildew."

Please write on this page!

Bodily Discharges

15 The LORD said to Moses and Aaron, 2 "Give the following instruc-
tions to the people of Israel.
"Any man who has a bodily discharge is ceremonially unclean. 3 This
defilement is caused by his discharge, whether the discharge continues or
stops. In either case the man is unclean. 4 Any bed on which the man with the
discharge lies and anything on which he sits will be ceremonially unclean.
5 So if you touch the man's bed, you must wash your clothes and bathe your-
self in water, and you will remain unclean until evening. 6 If you sit where
the man with the discharge has sat, you must wash your clothes and bathe
yourself in water, and you will remain unclean until evening. 7 If you touch
the man with the discharge, you must wash your clothes and bathe yourself
in water, and you will remain unclean until evening. 8 If the man spits on
you, you must wash your clothes and bathe yourself in water, and you will
remain unclean until evening. 9 Any saddle blanket on which the man rides
will be ceremonially unclean. 10 If you touch anything that was under the
man, you will be unclean until evening. You must wash your clothes and
bathe yourself in water, and you will remain unclean until evening. 11 If the
man touches you without first rinsing his hands, you must wash your clothes
and bathe yourself in water, and you will remain unclean until evening.
12 Any clay pot the man touches must be broken, and any wooden utensil he
touches must be rinsed with water.
13 "When the man with the discharge is healed, he must count off seven
days for the period of purification. Then he must wash his clothes and bathe
himself in fresh water, and he will be ceremonially clean. 14 On the eighth
day he must get two turtledoves or two young pigeons and come before the
LORD at the entrance of the Tabernacle* and give his offerings to the priest.
15 The priest will offer one bird for a sin offering and the other for a burnt
offering. Through this process, the priest will purify* the man before the
LORD for his discharge.
16 "Whenever a man has an emission of semen, he must bathe his entire
body in water, and he will remain ceremonially unclean until the next eve-
ning.* 17 Any clothing or leather with semen on it must be washed in water,
and it will remain unclean until evening. 18 After a man and a woman have

14:54 Traditionally rendered *leprosy;* see note on 13:2a. **14:55** Traditionally rendered *leprosy;* see note on 13:47. **15:14** Hebrew *Tent of Meeting;* also in 15:29. **15:15** Or *will make atonement for;* also in 15:30. **15:16** Hebrew *until evening;* also in 15:18.

sexual intercourse, they must each bathe in water, and they will remain unclean until the next evening.

19 “Whenever a woman has her menstrual period, she will be ceremonially unclean for seven days. Anyone who touches her during that time will be unclean until evening. 20 Anything on which the woman lies or sits during the time of her period will be unclean. 21 If any of you touch her bed, you must wash your clothes and bathe yourself in water, and you will remain unclean until evening. 22 If you touch any object she has sat on, you must wash your clothes and bathe yourself in water, and you will remain unclean until evening. 23 This includes her bed or any other object she has sat on; you will be unclean until evening if you touch it. 24 If a man has sexual intercourse with her and her blood touches him, her menstrual impurity will be transmitted to him. He will remain unclean for seven days, and any bed on which he lies will be unclean.

25 “If a woman has a flow of blood for many days that is unrelated to her menstrual period, or if the blood continues beyond the normal period, she is ceremonially unclean. As during her menstrual period, the woman will be unclean as long as the discharge continues. 26 Any bed she lies on and any object she sits on during that time will be unclean, just as during her normal menstrual period. 27 If any of you touch these things, you will be ceremonially unclean. You must wash your clothes and bathe yourself in water, and you will remain unclean until evening.

28 “When the woman's bleeding stops, she must count off seven days. Then she will be ceremonially clean. 29 On the eighth day she must bring two turtledoves or two young pigeons and present them to the priest at the entrance of the Tabernacle. 30 The priest will offer one for a sin offering and the other for a burnt offering. Through this process, the priest will purify her before the LORD for the ceremonial impurity caused by her bleeding.

31 “This is how you will guard the people of Israel from ceremonial uncleanness. Otherwise they would die, for their impurity would defile my Tabernacle that stands among them. 32 These are the instructions for dealing with anyone who has a bodily discharge—a man who is unclean because of an emission of semen 33 or a woman during her menstrual period. It applies to any man or woman who has a bodily discharge, and to a man who has sexual intercourse with a woman who is ceremonially unclean.”

The Day of Atonement

16 The LORD spoke to Moses after the death of Aaron's two sons, who died after they entered the LORD's presence and burned the wrong kind of fire before him. 2 The LORD said to Moses, “Warn your brother, Aaron, not to enter the Most Holy Place behind the inner curtain whenever he chooses; if he does, he will die. For the Ark's cover—the place of atonement—is there, and I myself am present in the cloud above the atonement cover.

3 “When Aaron enters the sanctuary area, he must follow these instructions fully. He must bring a young bull for a sin offering and a ram for a burnt offering. 4 He must put on his linen tunic and the linen undergarments worn next to his body. He must tie the linen sash around his waist and put the linen turban on his head. These are sacred garments, so he must bathe himself in water before he puts them on. 5 Aaron must take

from the community of Israel two male goats for a sin offering and a ram
for a burnt offering.
6"Aaron will present his own bull as a sin offering to purify himself and his
family, making them right with the LORD.* 7Then he must take the two male
goats and present them to the LORD at the entrance of the Tabernacle.* 8He
is to cast sacred lots to determine which goat will be reserved as an offering
to the LORD and which will carry the sins of the people to the wilderness of
Azazel. 9Aaron will then present as a sin offering the goat chosen by lot for
the LORD. 10The other goat, the scapegoat chosen by lot to be sent away, will
be kept alive, standing before the LORD. When it is sent away to Azazel in
the wilderness, the people will be purified and made right with the LORD.*
11"Aaron will present his own bull as a sin offering to purify himself and
his family, making them right with the LORD. After he has slaughtered the
bull as a sin offering, 12he will fill an incense burner with burning coals
from the altar that stands before the LORD. Then he will take two hand-
fuls of fragrant powdered incense and will carry the burner and the incense
behind the inner curtain. 13There in the LORD's presence he will put the
incense on the burning coals so that a cloud of incense will rise over the Ark's
cover—the place of atonement—that rests on the Ark of the Covenant.* If
he follows these instructions, he will not die. 14Then he must take some of
the blood of the bull, dip his finger in it, and sprinkle it on the east side of
the atonement cover. He must sprinkle blood seven times with his finger in
front of the atonement cover.
15"Then Aaron must slaughter the first goat as a sin offering for the people
and carry its blood behind the inner curtain. There he will sprinkle the goat's
blood over the atonement cover and in front of it, just as he did with the
bull's blood. 16Through this process, he will purify* the Most Holy Place,
and he will do the same for the entire Tabernacle, because of the defiling sin
and rebellion of the Israelites. 17No one else is allowed inside the Tabernacle
when Aaron enters it for the purification ceremony in the Most Holy Place.
No one may enter until he comes out again after purifying himself, his fam-
ily, and all the congregation of Israel, making them right with the LORD.
18"Then Aaron will come out to purify the altar that stands before the
LORD. He will do this by taking some of the blood from the bull and the goat
and putting it on each of the horns of the altar. 19Then he must sprinkle the
blood with his finger seven times over the altar. In this way, he will cleanse
it from Israel's defilement and make it holy.
20"When Aaron has finished purifying the Most Holy Place and the Tab-
ernacle and the altar, he must present the live goat. 21He will lay both of his
hands on the goat's head and confess over it all the wickedness, rebellion,
and sins of the people of Israel. In this way, he will transfer the people's sins
to the head of the goat. Then a man specially chosen for the task will drive
the goat into the wilderness. 22As the goat goes into the wilderness, it will
carry all the people's sins upon itself into a desolate land.
23"When Aaron goes back into the Tabernacle, he must take off the linen
garments he was wearing when he entered the Most Holy Place, and he must

Prayer **16:10**

Jesus, you are truly the GOAT (greatest of all time)! You have taken our sin upon yourself and carried it away. Thank you for being the scapegoat, chosen to stand before the Lord to purify us and make us right with God. Amen.

16:6 Or *to make atonement for himself and his family;* similarly in 16:11, 17b, 24, 34. 16:7 Hebrew *Tent of Meeting;* also in 16:16, 17, 20, 23, 33. 16:10 Or *wilderness, it will make atonement for the people.* 16:13 Hebrew *that is above the Testimony.* The Hebrew word for "testimony" refers to the terms of the LORD's covenant with Israel as written on stone tablets, which were kept in the Ark, and also to the covenant itself. 16:16 Or *make atonement for;* similarly in 16:17a, 18, 20, 27, 33.

> **Question** 16:1-34
>
> The Day of Atonement was established by God as a "permanent law" to be celebrated by future generations (v. 34). The Day of Atonement was the most significant ritual of sacrifice. Without it, all other offerings and efforts to be made right with God were invalid. Something (or someone) had to take sin away for us. How does the Day of Atonement reveal Jesus as the permanent sacrifice on our behalf?

leave the garments there. 24 Then he must bathe himself with water in a sa-
cred place, put on his regular garments, and go out to sacrifice a burnt offer-
ing for himself and a burnt offering for the people. Through this process, he
will purify himself and the people, making them right with the LORD. 25 He
must then burn all the fat of the sin offering on the altar.

26 "The man chosen to drive the scapegoat into the wilderness of Azazel
must wash his clothes and bathe himself in water. Then he may return to
the camp.

27 "The bull and the goat presented as sin offerings, whose blood Aaron
takes into the Most Holy Place for the purification ceremony, will be carried
outside the camp. The animals' hides, internal organs, and dung are all to be
burned. 28 The man who burns them must wash his clothes and bathe himself
in water before returning to the camp.

29 "On the tenth day of the appointed month in early autumn,* you
must deny yourselves.* Neither native-born Israelites nor foreigners liv-
ing among you may do any kind of work. This is a permanent law for you.
30 On that day offerings of purification will be made for you,* and you will
be purified in the LORD's presence from all your sins. 31 It will be a Sabbath
day of complete rest for you, and you must deny yourselves. This is a per-
manent law for you. 32 In future generations, the purification* ceremony
will be performed by the priest who has been anointed and ordained to
serve as high priest in place of his ancestor Aaron. He will put on the holy
linen garments 33 and purify the Most Holy Place, the Tabernacle, the altar,
the priests, and the entire congregation. 34 This is a permanent law for you,
to purify the people of Israel from their sins, making them right with the
LORD once each year."

Moses followed all these instructions exactly as the LORD had commanded
him.

Prohibitions against Eating Blood

17 Then the LORD said to Moses, 2 "Give the following instructions to
Aaron and his sons and all the people of Israel. This is what the LORD
has commanded.

3 "If any native Israelite sacrifices a bull* or a lamb or a goat anywhere
inside or outside the camp 4 instead of bringing it to the entrance of the Tab-
ernacle* to present it as an offering to the LORD, that person will be as guilty
as a murderer.* Such a person has shed blood and will be cut off from the
community. 5 The purpose of this rule is to stop the Israelites from sacrificing
animals in the open fields. It will ensure that they bring their sacrifices to the
priest at the entrance of the Tabernacle, so he can present them to the LORD
as peace offerings. 6 Then the priest will be able to splatter the blood against
the LORD's altar at the entrance of the Tabernacle, and he will burn the fat
as a pleasing aroma to the LORD. 7 The people must no longer be unfaithful
to the LORD by offering sacrifices to the goat idols.* This is a permanent law
for them, to be observed from generation to generation.

8 "Give them this command as well. If any native Israelite or foreigner
living among you offers a burnt offering or a sacrifice 9 but does not bring it

16:29a Hebrew *On the tenth day of the seventh month.* This day in the ancient Hebrew lunar calendar occurred in September or October. **16:29b** Or *must fast;* also in 16:31. **16:30** Or *atonement will be made for you, to purify you.* **16:32** Or *atonement.* **17:3** Or *cow.* **17:4a** Hebrew *Tent of Meeting;* also in 17:5, 6, 9. **17:4b** Hebrew *will be guilty of blood.* **17:7** Or *goat demons.*

to the entrance of the Tabernacle to offer it to the LORD, that person will be
cut off from the community.
10"And if any native Israelite or foreigner living among you eats or drinks
blood in any form, I will turn against that person and cut him off from the
community of your people, 11 for the life of the body is in its blood. I have
given you the blood on the altar to purify you, making you right with the
LORD.* It is the blood, given in exchange for a life, that makes purification
possible. 12That is why I have said to the people of Israel, 'You must never eat
or drink blood—neither you nor the foreigners living among you.'
13"And if any native Israelite or foreigner living among you goes hunting
and kills an animal or bird that is approved for eating, he must drain its
blood and cover it with earth. 14The life of every creature is in its blood. That
is why I have said to the people of Israel, 'You must never eat or drink blood,
for the life of any creature is in its blood.' So whoever consumes blood will
be cut off from the community.
15"And if any native-born Israelites or foreigners eat the meat of an ani-
mal that died naturally or was torn up by wild animals, they must wash
their clothes and bathe themselves in water. They will remain ceremonially
unclean until evening, but then they will be clean. 16But if they do not wash
their clothes and bathe themselves, they will be punished for their sin."

Forbidden Sexual Practices

18 Then the LORD said to Moses, 2"Give the following instructions to
the people of Israel. I am the LORD your God. 3So do not act like the
people in Egypt, where you used to live, or like the people of Canaan, where
I am taking you. You must not imitate their way of life. 4You must obey all
my regulations and be careful to obey my decrees, for I am the LORD your
God. 5If you obey my decrees and my regulations, you will find life through
them. I am the LORD.
6"You must never have sexual relations with a close relative, for I am the
LORD.
7"Do not violate your father by having sexual relations with your mother.
She is your mother; you must not have sexual relations with her.
8"Do not have sexual relations with any of your father's wives, for this
would violate your father.
9"Do not have sexual relations with your sister or half sister, whether she
is your father's daughter or your mother's daughter, whether she was born
into your household or someone else's.
10"Do not have sexual relations with your granddaughter, whether she
is your son's daughter or your daughter's daughter, for this would violate
yourself.
11"Do not have sexual relations with your stepsister, the daughter of any
of your father's wives, for she is your sister.
12"Do not have sexual relations with your father's sister, for she is your
father's close relative.
13"Do not have sexual relations with your mother's sister, for she is your
mother's close relative.
14"Do not violate your uncle, your father's brother, by having sexual rela-
tions with his wife, for she is your aunt.

Make a Difference

18:1-5

Don't Copy Culture

"You must not imitate their way of life" (v. 3). In terms of sexual activity, God does not want his people to copy the customs and behaviors of the culture around them. Too often, the practices of society run contrary to God's design. That certainly was the case for Israel, both while they were living in Egypt and as they were wandering in the desert. Leviticus 18:26 states clearly that God's people must not commit any of the "detestable sins" mentioned in this chapter but rather obey God's commands about sexual activity.

Difference Maker

Pray about these questions: In what ways have you imitated the sexual practices or thoughts of the society around you? What course-direction changes do you need to make? How could you prepare yourself for the way God designed sex in the confines of marriage between a man and woman?

17:11 Or *to make atonement for you.*

15 “Do not have sexual relations with your daughter-in-law; she is your
son’s wife, so you must not have sexual relations with her.
16 “Do not have sexual relations with your brother’s wife, for this would
violate your brother.
17 “Do not have sexual relations with both a woman and her daughter. And
do not take* her granddaughter, whether her son’s daughter or her daugh-
ter’s daughter, and have sexual relations with her. They are close relatives,
and this would be a wicked act.
18 “While your wife is living, do not marry her sister and have sexual rela-
tions with her, for they would be rivals.
19 “Do not have sexual relations with a woman during her period of men-
strual impurity.
20 “Do not defile yourself by having sexual intercourse with your neigh-
bor’s wife.
21 “Do not permit any of your children to be offered as a sacrifice to Molech,
for you must not bring shame on the name of your God. I am the LORD.
22 “Do not practice homosexuality, having sex with another man as with
a woman. It is a detestable sin.
23 “A man must not defile himself by having sex with an animal. And a
woman must not offer herself to a male animal to have intercourse with it.
This is a perverse act.
24 “Do not defile yourselves in any of these ways, for the people I am driv-
ing out before you have defiled themselves in all these ways. 25 Because the
entire land has become defiled, I am punishing the people who live there. I
will cause the land to vomit them out. 26 You must obey all my decrees and
regulations. You must not commit any of these detestable sins. This applies
both to native-born Israelites and to the foreigners living among you.
27 “All these detestable activities are practiced by the people of the land
where I am taking you, and this is how the land has become defiled. 28 So do
not defile the land and give it a reason to vomit you out, as it will vomit out
the people who live there now. 29 Whoever commits any of these detestable
sins will be cut off from the community of Israel. 30 So obey my instructions,
and do not defile yourselves by committing any of these detestable practices
that were committed by the people who lived in the land before you. I am
the LORD your God.”

Holiness in Personal Conduct

19 The LORD also said to Moses, 2 “Give the following instructions to the
entire community of Israel. You must be holy because I, the LORD
your God, am holy.
3 “Each of you must show great respect for your mother and father, and
you must always observe my Sabbath days of rest. I am the LORD your God.
4 “Do not put your trust in idols or make metal images of gods for your-
selves. I am the LORD your God.
5 “When you sacrifice a peace offering to the LORD, offer it properly so
you* will be accepted by God. 6 The sacrifice must be eaten on the same day
you offer it or on the next day. Whatever is left over until the third day must
be completely burned up. 7 If any of the sacrifice is eaten on the third day,
it will be contaminated, and I will not accept it. 8 Anyone who eats it on the

18:17 Or *do not marry.* 19:5 Or *it.*

third day will be punished for defiling what is holy to the LORD and will be cut off from the community.

9 "When you harvest the crops of your land, do not harvest the grain along
the edges of your fields, and do not pick up what the harvesters drop. 10 It is the
same with your grape crop—do not strip every last bunch of grapes from
the vines, and do not pick up the grapes that fall to the ground. Leave them
for the poor and the foreigners living among you. I am the LORD your God.

11 "Do not steal.

"Do not deceive or cheat one another.

12 "Do not bring shame on the name of your God by using it to swear falsely. I am the LORD.

13 "Do not defraud or rob your neighbor.

"Do not make your hired workers wait until the next day to receive their pay.

14 "Do not insult the deaf or cause the blind to stumble. You must fear your God; I am the LORD.

15 "Do not twist justice in legal matters by favoring the poor or being partial to the rich and powerful. Always judge people fairly.

16 "Do not spread slanderous gossip among your people.*

"Do not stand idly by when your neighbor's life is threatened. I am the LORD.

17 "Do not nurse hatred in your heart for any of your relatives.* Confront people directly so you will not be held guilty for their sin.

18 "Do not seek revenge or bear a grudge against a fellow Israelite, but love your neighbor as yourself. I am the LORD.

19 "You must obey all my decrees.

"Do not mate two different kinds of animals. Do not plant your field with two different kinds of seed. Do not wear clothing woven from two different kinds of thread.

20 "If a man has sex with a slave girl whose freedom has never been pur-
chased but who is committed to become another man's wife, he must pay
full compensation to her master. But since she is not a free woman, neither
the man nor the woman will be put to death. 21 The man, however, must
bring a ram as a guilt offering and present it to the LORD at the entrance of
the Tabernacle.* 22 The priest will then purify him* before the LORD with the
ram of the guilt offering, and the man's sin will be forgiven.

23 "When you enter the land and plant fruit trees, leave the fruit un-
harvested for the first three years and consider it forbidden.* Do not eat it.
24 In the fourth year the entire crop must be consecrated to the LORD as a
celebration of praise. 25 Finally, in the fifth year you may eat the fruit. If you
follow this pattern, your harvest will increase. I am the LORD your God.

26 "Do not eat meat that has not been drained of its blood.

"Do not practice fortune-telling or witchcraft.

27 "Do not trim off the hair on your temples or trim your beards.

28 "Do not cut your bodies for the dead, and do not mark your skin with tattoos. I am the LORD.

29 "Do not defile your daughter by making her a prostitute, or the land will be filled with prostitution and wickedness.

19:16 Hebrew *Do not act as a merchant toward your own people.* 19:17 Hebrew *for your brother.* 19:21 Hebrew *Tent of Meeting.* 19:22 Or *make atonement for him.* 19:23 Hebrew *consider it uncircumcised.*

Make a Difference 19:14

Can You See?

Stop and hear this. The Lord cares deeply for those who have lost the most basic of human abilities. It surprises many people to hear that the Old Testament was ahead of its time in terms of promoting access and respect for those who were physically disadvantaged. The Lord elevates those with physical disabilities to a high status in society, and he calls others to serve them with honor.

Stop and see this. The Lord himself came to the aid of those with physical limitations. If someone who is deaf is mocked, the Lord takes it personally—very personally. If someone who is blind is ridiculed, God says we are messing with him directly. Jesus himself said that the way we treat people who are in disadvantaged situations is how we treat him (Matthew 25:31-46). He will not stand by idly as we mock, neglect, or create difficulties for those who have physical impairments.

Difference Maker

Sign up for an introductory course that teaches sign language or braille so that you can empathize more with someone who has a hearing or visual impairment.

Question 19:18

What does it mean to love your neighbor as yourself?

30 "Keep my Sabbath days of rest, and show reverence toward my sanctu-
ary. I am the LORD.
31 "Do not defile yourselves by turning to mediums or to those who consult
the spirits of the dead. I am the LORD your God.
32 "Stand up in the presence of the elderly, and show respect for the aged.
Fear your God. I am the LORD.
33 "Do not take advantage of foreigners who live among you in your land.
34 Treat them like native-born Israelites, and love them as you love yourself.
Remember that you were once foreigners living in the land of Egypt. I am
the LORD your God.
35 "Do not use dishonest standards when measuring length, weight, or
volume. 36 Your scales and weights must be accurate. Your containers for
measuring dry materials or liquids must be accurate.* I am the LORD your
God who brought you out of the land of Egypt.
37 "You must be careful to keep all of my decrees and regulations by put-
ting them into practice. I am the LORD."

Punishments for Disobedience

20 The LORD said to Moses, 2 "Give the people of Israel these instruc-
tions, which apply both to native Israelites and to the foreigners
living in Israel.
"If any of them offer their children as a sacrifice to Molech, they must be put
to death. The people of the community must stone them to death. 3 I myself will
turn against them and cut them off from the community, because they have
defiled my sanctuary and brought shame on my holy name by offering their
children to Molech. 4 And if the people of the community ignore those who
offer their children to Molech and refuse to execute them, 5 I myself will turn
against them and their families and will cut them off from the community. This
will happen to all who commit spiritual prostitution by worshiping Molech.
6 "I will also turn against those who commit spiritual prostitution by put-
ting their trust in mediums or in those who consult the spirits of the dead. I
will cut them off from the community. 7 So set yourselves apart to be holy, for
I am the LORD your God. 8 Keep all my decrees by putting them into practice,
for I am the LORD who makes you holy.
9 "Anyone who dishonors* father or mother must be put to death. Such a
person is guilty of a capital offense.
10 "If a man commits adultery with his neighbor's wife, both the man and
the woman who have committed adultery must be put to death.
11 "If a man violates his father by having sex with one of his father's wives,
both the man and the woman must be put to death, for they are guilty of a
capital offense.
12 "If a man has sex with his daughter-in-law, both must be put to death.
They have committed a perverse act and are guilty of a capital offense.
13 "If a man practices homosexuality, having sex with another man as with
a woman, both men have committed a detestable act. They must both be put
to death, for they are guilty of a capital offense.
14 "If a man marries both a woman and her mother, he has committed a
wicked act. The man and both women must be burned to death to wipe out
such wickedness from among you.

19:36 Hebrew *Use an honest ephah* [a dry measure] *and an honest hin* [a liquid measure].
20:9 Greek version reads *Anyone who speaks disrespectfully of.* Compare Matt 15:4; Mark 7:10.

Make a Difference

19:32

Respect Age

God loves the elderly. He loves their long stories and deeply ingrained smiles. He loves their rascally outlook and feisty concern for the world. He loves their wrinkles and wisdom and wit. He loves people who have aged like good wine, without whining, of course. He loves those young-hearted warriors who have lived through generations, through wars, through terrors, through changing economies, through different leaders, and who still stay simple and focused on what is right and true.

God seems to believe that someone who has lived a long life has earned the right to be respected. The years haven't always been easy on them. For every ring of the tree, they have borne the weight of joys and sorrows, jubilation and loss. Their memories are both sweet and bitter. The Lord knows every fiber of their being, and he loves them with every fiber of his being.

Difference Maker

Do something that shows respect for an older person, such as sending a thank-you note, extending an invitation to lunch, offering to do yard work, going fishing, or simply sitting down for a long conversation.

15 "If a man has sex with an animal, he must be put to death, and the ani-
mal must be killed.
16 "If a woman presents herself to a male animal to have intercourse with
it, she and the animal must both be put to death. You must kill both, for they
are guilty of a capital offense.
17 "If a man marries his sister, the daughter of either his father or his
mother, and they have sexual relations, it is a shameful disgrace. They must
be publicly cut off from the community. Since the man has violated his sister,
he will be punished for his sin.
18 "If a man has sexual relations with a woman during her menstrual pe-
riod, both of them must be cut off from the community, for together they
have exposed the source of her blood flow.
19 "Do not have sexual relations with your aunt, whether your mother's
sister or your father's sister. This would dishonor a close relative. Both par-
ties are guilty and will be punished for their sin.
20 "If a man has sex with his uncle's wife, he has violated his uncle. Both the
man and woman will be punished for their sin, and they will die childless.
21 "If a man marries his brother's wife, it is an act of impurity. He has vio-
lated his brother, and the guilty couple will remain childless.
22 "You must keep all my decrees and regulations by putting them into
practice; otherwise the land to which I am bringing you as your new home
will vomit you out. 23 Do not live according to the customs of the people I
am driving out before you. It is because they do these shameful things that I
detest them. 24 But I have promised you, 'You will possess their land because
I will give it to you as your possession—a land flowing with milk and honey.'
I am the LORD your God, who has set you apart from all other people.
25 "You must therefore make a distinction between ceremonially clean and
unclean animals, and between clean and unclean birds. You must not defile
yourselves by eating any unclean animal or bird or creature that scurries
along the ground. I have identified them as being unclean for you. 26 You
must be holy because I, the LORD, am holy. I have set you apart from all other
people to be my very own.
27 "Men and women among you who act as mediums or who consult the
spirits of the dead must be put to death by stoning. They are guilty of a
capital offense."

Instructions for the Priests

21 The LORD said to Moses, "Give the following instructions to the
priests, the descendants of Aaron.
"A priest must not make himself ceremonially unclean by touching the
dead body of a relative. 2 The only exceptions are his closest relatives—his
mother or father, son or daughter, brother, 3 or his virgin sister who depends
on him because she has no husband. 4 But a priest must not defile himself and
make himself unclean for someone who is related to him only by marriage.
5 "The priests must not shave their heads or trim their beards or cut their
bodies. 6 They must be set apart as holy to their God and must never bring
shame on the name of God. They must be holy, for they are the ones who
present the special gifts to the LORD, gifts of food for their God.
7 "Priests may not marry a woman defiled by prostitution, and they may
not marry a woman who is divorced from her husband, for the priests are set

Prayer **20:26**

Lord, help me be holy because you are holy. Set me apart as your very own so that I can represent you to others. Amen.

apart as holy to their God. 8 You must treat them as holy because they offer
up food to your God. You must consider them holy because I, the LORD, am
holy, and I make you holy.
9 "If a priest's daughter defiles herself by becoming a prostitute, she also
defiles her father's holiness, and she must be burned to death.
10 "The high priest has the highest rank of all the priests. The anointing oil
has been poured on his head, and he has been ordained to wear the priestly
garments. He must never leave his hair uncombed* or tear his clothing. 11 He
must not defile himself by going near a dead body. He may not make himself
ceremonially unclean even for his father or mother. 12 He must not defile the
sanctuary of his God by leaving it to attend to a dead person, for he has been
made holy by the anointing oil of his God. I am the LORD.
13 "The high priest may marry only a virgin. 14 He may not marry a widow,
a woman who is divorced, or a woman who has defiled herself by prostitu-
tion. She must be a virgin from his own clan, 15 so that he will not dishonor
his descendants among his clan, for I am the LORD who makes him holy."
16 Then the LORD said to Moses, 17 "Give the following instructions to
Aaron: In all future generations, none of your descendants who has any de-
fect will qualify to offer food to his God. 18 No one who has a defect qualifies,
whether he is blind, lame, disfigured, deformed, 19 or has a broken foot or
arm, 20 or is hunchbacked or dwarfed, or has a defective eye, or skin sores or
scabs, or damaged testicles. 21 No descendant of Aaron who has a defect may
approach the altar to present special gifts to the LORD. Since he has a defect,
he may not approach the altar to offer food to his God. 22 However, he may
eat from the food offered to God, including the holy offerings and the most
holy offerings. 23 Yet because of his physical defect, he may not enter the room
behind the inner curtain or approach the altar, for this would defile my holy
places. I am the LORD who makes them holy."
24 So Moses gave these instructions to Aaron and his sons and to all the
Israelites.

22 The LORD said to Moses, 2 "Tell Aaron and his sons to be very careful
with the sacred gifts that the Israelites set apart for me, so they do
not bring shame on my holy name. I am the LORD. 3 Give them the follow-
ing instructions.

"In all future generations, if any of your descendants is ceremonially unclean when he approaches the sacred offerings that the people of Israel consecrate to the LORD, he must be cut off from my presence. I am the LORD.
4 "If any of Aaron's descendants has a skin disease* or any kind of discharge
that makes him ceremonially unclean, he may not eat from the sacred of-
ferings until he has been pronounced clean. He also becomes unclean by
touching a corpse, or by having an emission of semen, 5 or by touching a small
animal that is unclean, or by touching someone who is ceremonially unclean
for any reason. 6 The man who is defiled in any of these ways will remain
unclean until evening. He may not eat from the sacred offerings until he has
bathed himself in water. 7 When the sun goes down, he will be ceremonially
clean again and may eat from the sacred offerings, for this is his food. 8 He
may not eat an animal that has died a natural death or has been torn apart
by wild animals, for this would defile him. I am the LORD.

21:10 Or *never uncover his head.* **22:4** Traditionally rendered *leprosy;* see note on 13:2a.

[9]"The priests must follow my instructions carefully. Otherwise they will
be punished for their sin and will die for violating my instructions. I am the
LORD who makes them holy.

[10]"No one outside a priest's family may eat the sacred offerings. Even
guests and hired workers in a priest's home are not allowed to eat them.
[11]However, if the priest buys a slave for himself, the slave may eat from the
sacred offerings. And if his slaves have children, they also may share his food.
[12]If a priest's daughter marries someone outside the priestly family, she may
no longer eat the sacred offerings. [13]But if she becomes a widow or is divorced
and has no children to support her, and she returns to live in her father's
home as in her youth, she may eat her father's food again. Otherwise, no one
outside a priest's family may eat the sacred offerings.

[14]"Any such person who eats the sacred offerings without realizing it must
pay the priest for the amount eaten, plus an additional 20 percent. [15]The
priests must not let the Israelites defile the sacred offerings brought to the
LORD [16]by allowing unauthorized people to eat them. This would bring
guilt upon them and require them to pay compensation. I am the LORD
who makes them holy."

Worthy and Unworthy Offerings

[17]And the LORD said to Moses, [18]"Give Aaron and his sons and all the Isra-
elites these instructions, which apply both to native Israelites and to the
foreigners living among you.

"If you present a gift as a burnt offering to the LORD, whether it is to
fulfill a vow or is a voluntary offering, [19]you* will be accepted only if your
offering is a male animal with no defects. It may be a bull, a ram, or a male
goat. [20]Do not present an animal with defects, because the LORD will not
accept it on your behalf.

[21]"If you present a peace offering to the LORD from the herd or the flock,
whether it is to fulfill a vow or is a voluntary offering, you must offer a per-
fect animal. It may have no defect of any kind. [22]You must not offer an animal
that is blind, crippled, or injured, or that has a wart, a skin sore, or scabs.
Such animals must never be offered on the altar as special gifts to the LORD.
[23]If a bull* or lamb has a leg that is too long or too short, it may be offered as
a voluntary offering, but it may not be offered to fulfill a vow. [24]If an animal
has damaged testicles or is castrated, you may not offer it to the LORD. You
must never do this in your own land, [25]and you must not accept such an ani-
mal from foreigners and then offer it as a sacrifice to your God. Such animals
will not be accepted on your behalf, for they are mutilated or defective."

[26]And the LORD said to Moses, [27]"When a calf or lamb or goat is born, it
must be left with its mother for seven days. From the eighth day on, it will
be acceptable as a special gift to the LORD. [28]But you must not slaughter a
mother animal and her offspring on the same day, whether from the herd or
the flock. [29]When you bring a thanksgiving offering to the LORD, sacrifice it
properly so you will be accepted. [30]Eat the entire sacrificial animal on the day
it is presented. Do not leave any of it until the next morning. I am the LORD.

[31]"You must faithfully keep all my commands by putting them into prac-
tice, for I am the LORD. [32]Do not bring shame on my holy name, for I will
display my holiness among the people of Israel. I am the LORD who makes

22:19 Or *it.* **22:23** Or *cow.*

Question **22:9**

Why is it so important to God that those who serve as priests should follow his instructions carefully? What could go wrong if the priests were not carefully following God?

Make a Difference

23:15–22

The Harvest of Pentecost

Fifty days after the Passover celebration, Israel was instructed to celebrate a "Festival of Harvest." This festival marked Israel's expectation that the Lord would provide an abundant harvest of crops and a blessing of fruitfulness in life.

In Jesus' day, in the Greek language, this fiftieth day of celebration became known as "Pentecost." It was on that day, fifty days after Jesus' Passover death on the cross, that God poured out his Holy Spirit on his people as an abundant, overflowing harvest (Acts 2). This event changed the history of the entire world.

Difference Maker

Read Acts 2 through the lens of the Festival of Harvest in Leviticus 23. How does the instruction for this celebration change the way you understand what God did for those early Christians on Pentecost? How does this affect your expectations of what God will do in your life?

you holy. 33 It was I who rescued you from the land of Egypt, that I might be your God. I am the LORD."

The Appointed Festivals

23 The LORD said to Moses, 2 "Give the following instructions to the people of Israel. These are the LORD's appointed festivals, which you are to proclaim as official days for holy assembly.

3 "You have six days each week for your ordinary work, but the seventh day is a Sabbath day of complete rest, an official day for holy assembly. It is the LORD's Sabbath day, and it must be observed wherever you live.

4 "In addition to the Sabbath, these are the LORD's appointed festivals, the official days for holy assembly that are to be celebrated at their proper times each year.

Passover and the Festival of Unleavened Bread

5 "The LORD's Passover begins at sundown on the fourteenth day of the first month.* 6 On the next day, the fifteenth day of the month, you must begin celebrating the Festival of Unleavened Bread. This festival to the LORD continues for seven days, and during that time the bread you eat must be made without yeast. 7 On the first day of the festival, all the people must stop their ordinary work and observe an official day for holy assembly. 8 For seven days you must present special gifts to the LORD. On the seventh day the people must again stop all their ordinary work to observe an official day for holy assembly."

Celebration of First Harvest

9 Then the LORD said to Moses, 10 "Give the following instructions to the people of Israel. When you enter the land I am giving you and you harvest its first crops, bring the priest a bundle of grain from the first cutting of your grain harvest. 11 On the day after the Sabbath, the priest will lift it up before the LORD so it may be accepted on your behalf. 12 On that same day you must sacrifice a one-year-old male lamb with no defects as a burnt offering to the LORD. 13 With it you must present a grain offering consisting of four quarts* of choice flour moistened with olive oil. It will be a special gift, a pleasing aroma to the LORD. You must also offer one quart* of wine as a liquid offering. 14 Do not eat any bread or roasted grain or fresh kernels on that day until you bring this offering to your God. This is a permanent law for you, and it must be observed from generation to generation wherever you live.

The Festival of Harvest

15 "From the day after the Sabbath—the day you bring the bundle of grain to be lifted up as a special offering—count off seven full weeks. 16 Keep counting until the day after the seventh Sabbath, fifty days later. Then present an offering of new grain to the LORD. 17 From wherever you live, bring two loaves of bread to be lifted up before the LORD as a special offering. Make these loaves from four quarts of choice flour, and bake them with yeast. They will be an offering to the LORD from the first of your crops. 18 Along with the bread, present seven one-year-old male lambs with no defects, one young

23:5 This day in the ancient Hebrew lunar calendar occurred in late March, April, or early May. **23:13a** Hebrew *2/10 of an ephah* [4.4 liters]; also in 23:17. **23:13b** Hebrew *1/4 of a hin* [1 liter].

bull, and two rams as burnt offerings to the LORD. These burnt offerings,
together with the grain offerings and liquid offerings, will be a special gift,
a pleasing aroma to the LORD. 19 Then you must offer one male goat as a sin
offering and two one-year-old male lambs as a peace offering.
20 "The priest will lift up the two lambs as a special offering to the LORD,
together with the loaves representing the first of your crops. These offer-
ings, which are holy to the LORD, belong to the priests. 21 That same day will
be proclaimed an official day for holy assembly, a day on which you do no
ordinary work. This is a permanent law for you, and it must be observed
from generation to generation wherever you live.*
22 "When you harvest the crops of your land, do not harvest the grain along
the edges of your fields, and do not pick up what the harvesters drop. Leave it
for the poor and the foreigners living among you. I am the LORD your God."

The Festival of Trumpets

23 The LORD said to Moses, 24 "Give the following instructions to the people
of Israel. On the first day of the appointed month in early autumn,* you are
to observe a day of complete rest. It will be an official day for holy assembly,
a day commemorated with loud blasts of a trumpet. 25 You must do no ordi-
nary work on that day. Instead, you are to present special gifts to the LORD."

The Day of Atonement

26 Then the LORD said to Moses, 27 "Be careful to celebrate the Day of Atone-
ment on the tenth day of that same month—nine days after the Festival of
Trumpets.* You must observe it as an official day for holy assembly, a day to
deny yourselves* and present special gifts to the LORD. 28 Do no work dur-
ing that entire day because it is the Day of Atonement, when offerings of
purification are made for you, making you right with* the LORD your God.
29 All who do not deny themselves that day will be cut off from God's people.
30 And I will destroy anyone among you who does any work on that day. 31 You
must not do any work at all! This is a permanent law for you, and it must
be observed from generation to generation wherever you live. 32 This will
be a Sabbath day of complete rest for you, and on that day you must deny
yourselves. This day of rest will begin at sundown on the ninth day of the
month and extend until sundown on the tenth day."

The Festival of Shelters

33 And the LORD said to Moses, 34 "Give the following instructions to the
people of Israel. Begin celebrating the Festival of Shelters* on the fifteenth
day of the appointed month—five days after the Day of Atonement.* This
festival to the LORD will last for seven days. 35 On the first day of the festival
you must proclaim an official day for holy assembly, when you do no or-
dinary work. 36 For seven days you must present special gifts to the LORD.

23:21 This celebration, called the Festival of Harvest or the Festival of Weeks, was later called the Festival of Pentecost (see Acts 2:1). It is celebrated today as Shavuot (or Shabuoth). **23:24** Hebrew *On the first day of the seventh month.* This day in the ancient Hebrew lunar calendar occurred in September or October. This festival is celebrated today as Rosh Hashanah, the Jewish new year. **23:27a** Hebrew *on the tenth day of the seventh month;* see 23:24 and the note there. This day in the ancient Hebrew lunar calendar occurred in September or October. It is celebrated today as Yom Kippur. **23:27b** Or *to fast;* similarly in 23:29, 32. **23:28** Or *when atonement is made for you before.* **23:34a** Or *Festival of Booths,* or *Festival of Tabernacles.* This was earlier called the Festival of the Final Harvest or Festival of Ingathering (see Exod 23:16b). It is celebrated today as Sukkot (or Succoth). **23:34b** Hebrew *on the fifteenth day of the seventh month;* see 23:27a and the note there.

Prayer 23:43

Lord Jesus, thank you that you took on flesh and made a "shelter" among us. Amen.

Question 24:3

What difference does it make that the holy bread was lit by the lampstand? What implications does this have for you as the "light of the world" (Matthew 5:14) who shines on Jesus, the Bread of Life (John 6:35)?

The eighth day is another holy day on which you present your special gifts to the LORD. This will be a solemn occasion, and no ordinary work may be done that day.

37 ("These are the LORD's appointed festivals. Celebrate them each year as official days for holy assembly by presenting special gifts to the LORD—burnt offerings, grain offerings, sacrifices, and liquid offerings—each on its proper day. 38 These festivals must be observed in addition to the LORD's regular Sabbath days, and the offerings are in addition to your personal gifts, the offerings you give to fulfill your vows, and the voluntary offerings you present to the LORD.)

39 "Remember that this seven-day festival to the LORD—the Festival of Shelters—begins on the fifteenth day of the appointed month,* after you have harvested all the produce of the land. The first day and the eighth day of the festival will be days of complete rest. 40 On the first day gather branches from magnificent trees*—palm fronds, boughs from leafy trees, and willows that grow by the streams. Then celebrate with joy before the LORD your God for seven days. 41 You must observe this festival to the LORD for seven days every year. This is a permanent law for you, and it must be observed in the appointed month* from generation to generation. 42 For seven days you must live outside in little shelters. All native-born Israelites must live in shelters. 43 This will remind each new generation of Israelites that I made their ancestors live in shelters when I rescued them from the land of Egypt. I am the LORD your God."

44 So Moses gave the Israelites these instructions regarding the annual festivals of the LORD.

Pure Oil and Holy Bread

24 The LORD said to Moses, 2 "Command the people of Israel to bring you pure oil of pressed olives for the light, to keep the lamps burning continually. 3 This is the lampstand that stands in the Tabernacle, in front of the inner curtain that shields the Ark of the Covenant.* Aaron must keep the lamps burning in the LORD's presence all night. This is a permanent law for you, and it must be observed from generation to generation. 4 Aaron and the priests must tend the lamps on the pure gold lampstand continually in the LORD's presence.

5 "You must bake twelve flat loaves of bread from choice flour, using four quarts* of flour for each loaf. 6 Place the bread before the LORD on the pure gold table, and arrange the loaves in two stacks, with six loaves in each stack. 7 Put some pure frankincense near each stack to serve as a representative offering, a special gift presented to the LORD. 8 Every Sabbath day this bread must be laid out before the LORD as a gift from the Israelites; it is an ongoing expression of the eternal covenant. 9 The loaves of bread will belong to Aaron and his descendants, who must eat them in a sacred place, for they are most holy. It is the permanent right of the priests to claim this portion of the special gifts presented to the LORD."

An Example of Just Punishment

10 One day a man who had an Israelite mother and an Egyptian father came out of his tent and got into a fight with one of the Israelite men. 11 During

23:39 Hebrew *on the fifteenth day of the seventh month.* 23:40 Or *gather fruit from majestic trees.* 23:41 Hebrew *the seventh month.* 24:3 Hebrew *in the Tent of Meeting, outside the inner curtain of the Testimony;* see note on 16:13. 24:5 Hebrew *2/10 of an ephah* [4.4 liters].

the fight, this son of an Israelite woman blasphemed the Name of the LORD*
with a curse. So the man was brought to Moses for judgment. His mother was
Shelomith, the daughter of Dibri of the tribe of Dan. 12 They kept the man
in custody until the LORD's will in the matter should become clear to them.
13 Then the LORD said to Moses, 14 "Take the blasphemer outside the camp,
and tell all those who heard the curse to lay their hands on his head. Then
let the entire community stone him to death. 15 Say to the people of Israel:
Those who curse their God will be punished for their sin. 16 Anyone who
blasphemes the Name of the LORD must be stoned to death by the whole
community of Israel. Any native-born Israelite or foreigner among you who
blasphemes the Name of the LORD must be put to death.
17 "Anyone who takes another person's life must be put to death.
18 "Anyone who kills another person's animal must pay for it in full—a
live animal for the animal that was killed.
19 "Anyone who injures another person must be dealt with according to
the injury inflicted—20 a fracture for a fracture, an eye for an eye, a tooth
for a tooth. Whatever anyone does to injure another person must be paid
back in kind.
21 "Whoever kills an animal must pay for it in full, but whoever kills an-
other person must be put to death.
22 "This same standard applies both to native-born Israelites and to the
foreigners living among you. I am the LORD your God."
23 After Moses gave all these instructions to the Israelites, they took the
blasphemer outside the camp and stoned him to death. The Israelites did
just as the LORD had commanded Moses.

The Sabbath Year

25 While Moses was on Mount Sinai, the LORD said to him, 2 "Give the
following instructions to the people of Israel. When you have en-
tered the land I am giving you, the land itself must observe a Sabbath rest
before the LORD every seventh year. 3 For six years you may plant your fields
and prune your vineyards and harvest your crops, 4 but during the seventh
year the land must have a Sabbath year of complete rest. It is the LORD's
Sabbath. Do not plant your fields or prune your vineyards during that year.
5 And don't store away the crops that grow on their own or gather the grapes
from your unpruned vines. The land must have a year of complete rest. 6 But
you may eat whatever the land produces on its own during its Sabbath. This
applies to you, your male and female servants, your hired workers, and the
temporary residents who live with you. 7 Your livestock and the wild animals
in your land will also be allowed to eat what the land produces.

The Year of Jubilee

8 "In addition, you must count off seven Sabbath years, seven sets of seven
years, adding up to forty-nine years in all. 9 Then on the Day of Atonement
in the fiftieth year,* blow the ram's horn loud and long throughout the land.
10 Set this year apart as holy, a time to proclaim freedom throughout the land
for all who live there. It will be a jubilee year for you, when each of you may
return to the land that belonged to your ancestors and return to your own
clan. 11 This fiftieth year will be a jubilee for you. During that year you must

24:11 Hebrew *the Name;* also in 24:16b. 25:9 Hebrew *on the tenth day of the seventh month, on the Day of Atonement;* see 23:27a and the note there.

Make a Difference

25:1-55

Jubilee

God set up a remarkable system of restoration by declaring a year of Jubilee. If anything in society got out of order during a fifty-year period, it was supposed to be redeemed during the year of Jubilee. If someone lost their property or got stuck in debt, the Jubilee provided a system in which they would receive another chance. If a family had become dependent on others, the Jubilee helped them get back on their feet. If someone had wronged someone else in business, the Jubilee corrected injustices.

It was as close to a perfect economic and justice system imaginable. The problem, however, is that there is hardly any evidence that the people of Israel were faithfully able to follow the redemptive practices of the Jubilee. It seems that it may have been too good of a standard for sinful people to follow.

Difference Maker

Challenge yourself to dig into this description of the Jubilee year and understand how it worked. Ask God to examine any areas of your life where you have become out of order and ask God to help you make the necessary changes to restore you through a Jubilee-style life over the next year.

not plant your fields or store away any of the crops that grow on their own,
and don't gather the grapes from your unpruned vines. 12 It will be a jubilee
year for you, and you must keep it holy. But you may eat whatever the land
produces on its own. 13 In the Year of Jubilee each of you may return to the
land that belonged to your ancestors.

14 "When you make an agreement with your neighbor to buy or sell prop-
erty, you must not take advantage of each other. 15 When you buy land from
your neighbor, the price you pay must be based on the number of years since
the last jubilee. The seller must set the price by taking into account the num-
ber of years remaining until the next Year of Jubilee. 16 The more years until
the next jubilee, the higher the price; the fewer years, the lower the price.
After all, the person selling the land is actually selling you a certain number
of harvests. 17 Show your fear of God by not taking advantage of each other.
I am the LORD your God.

18 "If you want to live securely in the land, follow my decrees and obey
my regulations. 19 Then the land will yield large crops, and you will eat your
fill and live securely in it. 20 But you might ask, 'What will we eat during the
seventh year, since we are not allowed to plant or harvest crops that year?'
21 Be assured that I will send my blessing for you in the sixth year, so the land
will produce a crop large enough for three years. 22 When you plant your
fields in the eighth year, you will still be eating from the large crop of the
sixth year. In fact, you will still be eating from that large crop when the new
crop is harvested in the ninth year.

Redemption of Property

23 "The land must never be sold on a permanent basis, for the land belongs to
me. You are only foreigners and tenant farmers working for me.

24 "With every purchase of land you must grant the seller the right to buy
it back. 25 If one of your fellow Israelites falls into poverty and is forced to sell
some family land, then a close relative should buy it back for him. 26 If there
is no close relative to buy the land, but the person who sold it gets enough
money to buy it back, 27 he then has the right to redeem it from the one who
bought it. The price of the land will be discounted according to the number
of years until the next Year of Jubilee. In this way the original owner can then
return to the land. 28 But if the original owner cannot afford to buy back the
land, it will remain with the new owner until the next Year of Jubilee. In the
jubilee year, the land must be returned to the original owners so they can
return to their family land.

29 "Anyone who sells a house inside a walled town has the right to buy it
back for a full year after its sale. During that year, the seller retains the right
to buy it back. 30 But if it is not bought back within a year, the sale of the house
within the walled town cannot be reversed. It will become the permanent
property of the buyer. It will not be returned to the original owner in the
Year of Jubilee. 31 But a house in a village—a settlement without fortified
walls—will be treated like property in the countryside. Such a house may
be bought back at any time, and it must be returned to the original owner
in the Year of Jubilee.

32 "The Levites always have the right to buy back a house they have sold
within the towns allotted to them. 33 And any property that is sold by the
Levites—all houses within the Levitical towns—must be returned in the

Year of Jubilee. After all, the houses in the towns reserved for the Levites are the only property they own in all Israel. 34 The open pastureland around the Levitical towns may never be sold. It is their permanent possession.

Redemption of the Poor and Enslaved

35 "If one of your fellow Israelites falls into poverty and cannot support himself, support him as you would a foreigner or a temporary resident and allow him to live with you. 36 Do not charge interest or make a profit at his expense. Instead, show your fear of God by letting him live with you as your relative. 37 Remember, do not charge interest on money you lend him or make a profit on food you sell him. 38 I am the LORD your God, who brought you out of the land of Egypt to give you the land of Canaan and to be your God.

39 "If one of your fellow Israelites falls into poverty and is forced to sell himself to you, do not treat him as a slave. 40 Treat him instead as a hired worker or as a temporary resident who lives with you, and he will serve you only until the Year of Jubilee. 41 At that time he and his children will no longer be obligated to you, and they will return to their clans and go back to the land originally allotted to their ancestors. 42 The people of Israel are my servants, whom I brought out of the land of Egypt, so they must never be sold as slaves. 43 Show your fear of God by not treating them harshly.

44 "However, you may purchase male and female slaves from among the nations around you. 45 You may also purchase the children of temporary residents who live among you, including those who have been born in your land. You may treat them as your property, 46 passing them on to your children as a permanent inheritance. You may treat them as slaves, but you must never treat your fellow Israelites this way.

47 "Suppose a foreigner or temporary resident becomes rich while living among you. If any of your fellow Israelites fall into poverty and are forced to sell themselves to such a foreigner or to a member of his family, 48 they still retain the right to be bought back, even after they have been purchased. They may be bought back by a brother, 49 an uncle, or a cousin. In fact, anyone from the extended family may buy them back. They may also redeem themselves if they have prospered. 50 They will negotiate the price of their freedom with the person who bought them. The price will be based on the number of years from the time they were sold until the next Year of Jubilee—whatever it would cost to hire a worker for that period of time. 51 If many years still remain until the jubilee, they will repay the proper proportion of what they received when they sold themselves. 52 If only a few years remain until the Year of Jubilee, they will repay a small amount for their redemption. 53 The foreigner must treat them as workers hired on a yearly basis. You must not allow a foreigner to treat any of your fellow Israelites harshly. 54 If any Israelites have not been bought back by the time the Year of Jubilee arrives, they and their children must be set free at that time. 55 For the people of Israel belong to me. They are my servants, whom I brought out of the land of Egypt. I am the LORD your God.

Blessings for Obedience

26 "Do not make idols or set up carved images, or sacred pillars, or sculptured stones in your land so you may worship them. I am the LORD your God. 2 You must keep my Sabbath days of rest and show reverence for my sanctuary. I am the LORD.

Question **25:35**

This instruction assumes that you might be more willing to help a stranger than to help your own family member. Why is it sometimes easier to help someone you don't know than to help someone you do know?

Prayer **26:12**

Thank you, Jesus, for walking among us. Amen.

3 “If you follow my decrees and are careful to obey my commands, 4 I will
send you the seasonal rains. The land will then yield its crops, and the trees
of the field will produce their fruit. 5 Your threshing season will overlap
with the grape harvest, and your grape harvest will overlap with the season
of planting grain. You will eat your fill and live securely in your own land.
6 “I will give you peace in the land, and you will be able to sleep with no
cause for fear. I will rid the land of wild animals and keep your enemies
out of your land. 7 In fact, you will chase down your enemies and slaughter
them with your swords. 8 Five of you will chase a hundred, and a hundred of
you will chase ten thousand! All your enemies will fall beneath your sword.
9 “I will look favorably upon you, making you fertile and multiplying
your people. And I will fulfill my covenant with you. 10 You will have such a
surplus of crops that you will need to clear out the old grain to make room
for the new harvest! 11 I will live among you, and I will not despise you. 12 I
will walk among you; I will be your God, and you will be my people. 13 I am
the LORD your God, who brought you out of the land of Egypt so you would
no longer be their slaves. I broke the yoke of slavery from your neck so you
can walk with your heads held high.

Punishments for Disobedience

14 “However, if you do not listen to me or obey all these commands, 15 and
if you break my covenant by rejecting my decrees, treating my regulations
with contempt, and refusing to obey my commands, 16 I will punish you. I
will bring sudden terrors upon you—wasting diseases and burning fevers
that will cause your eyes to fail and your life to ebb away. You will plant your
crops in vain because your enemies will eat them. 17 I will turn against you,
and you will be defeated by your enemies. Those who hate you will rule over
you, and you will run even when no one is chasing you!
18 “And if, in spite of all this, you still disobey me, I will punish you seven
times over for your sins. 19 I will break your proud spirit by making the skies
as unyielding as iron and the earth as hard as bronze. 20 All your work will
be for nothing, for your land will yield no crops, and your trees will bear
no fruit.
21 “If even then you remain hostile toward me and refuse to obey me, I
will inflict disaster on you seven times over for your sins. 22 I will send wild
animals that will rob you of your children and destroy your livestock. Your
numbers will dwindle, and your roads will be deserted.
23 “And if you fail to learn the lesson and continue your hostility toward
me, 24 then I myself will be hostile toward you. I will personally strike you
with calamity seven times over for your sins. 25 I will send armies against
you to carry out the curse of the covenant you have broken. When you run
to your towns for safety, I will send a plague to destroy you there, and you
will be handed over to your enemies. 26 I will destroy your food supply, so
that ten women will need only one oven to bake bread for their families.
They will ration your food by weight, and though you have food to eat, you
will not be satisfied.
27 “If in spite of all this you still refuse to listen and still remain hostile
toward me, 28 then I will give full vent to my hostility. I myself will punish
you seven times over for your sins. 29 Then you will eat the flesh of your own
sons and daughters. 30 I will destroy your pagan shrines and knock down your

places of worship. I will leave your lifeless corpses piled on top of your lifeless
idols,* and I will despise you. 31 I will make your cities desolate and destroy
your places of pagan worship. I will take no pleasure in your offerings that
should be a pleasing aroma to me. 32 Yes, I myself will devastate your land,
and your enemies who come to occupy it will be appalled at what they see.
33 I will scatter you among the nations and bring out my sword against you.
Your land will become desolate, and your cities will lie in ruins. 34 Then at last
the land will enjoy its neglected Sabbath years as it lies desolate while you
are in exile in the land of your enemies. Then the land will finally rest and
enjoy the Sabbaths it missed. 35 As long as the land lies in ruins, it will enjoy
the rest you never allowed it to take every seventh year while you lived in it.

36 "And for those of you who survive, I will demoralize you in the land of
your enemies. You will live in such fear that the sound of a leaf driven by the
wind will send you fleeing. You will run as though fleeing from a sword, and
you will fall even when no one pursues you. 37 Though no one is chasing you,
you will stumble over each other as though fleeing from a sword. You will
have no power to stand up against your enemies. 38 You will die among the
foreign nations and be devoured in the land of your enemies. 39 Those of you
who survive will waste away in your enemies' lands because of their sins and
the sins of their ancestors.

40 "But at last my people will confess their sins and the sins of their ances-
tors for betraying me and being hostile toward me. 41 When I have turned
their hostility back on them and brought them to the land of their enemies,
then at last their stubborn hearts will be humbled, and they will pay for
their sins. 42 Then I will remember my covenant with Jacob and my covenant
with Isaac and my covenant with Abraham, and I will remember the land.
43 For the land must be abandoned to enjoy its years of Sabbath rest as it lies
deserted. At last the people will pay for their sins, for they have continually
rejected my regulations and despised my decrees.

44 "But despite all this, I will not utterly reject or despise them while they
are in exile in the land of their enemies. I will not cancel my covenant with
them by wiping them out, for I am the LORD their God. 45 For their sakes I
will remember my ancient covenant with their ancestors, whom I brought
out of the land of Egypt in the sight of all the nations, that I might be their
God. I am the LORD."

46 These are the decrees, regulations, and instructions that the LORD gave
through Moses on Mount Sinai as evidence of the relationship between him-
self and the Israelites.

Redemption of Gifts Offered to the LORD

27 The LORD said to Moses, 2 "Give the following instructions to the
people of Israel. If anyone makes a special vow to dedicate someone
to the LORD by paying the value of that person, 3 here is the scale of values to
be used. A man between the ages of twenty and sixty is valued at fifty shek-
els* of silver, as measured by the sanctuary shekel. 4 A woman of that age is
valued at thirty shekels* of silver. 5 A boy between the ages of five and twenty
is valued at twenty shekels of silver; a girl of that age is valued at ten shekels*
of silver. 6 A boy between the ages of one month and five years is valued at

26:30 The Hebrew term (literally *round things*) probably alludes to dung. 27:3 Or *20 ounces* [570 grams]. 27:4 Or *12 ounces* [342 grams]. 27:5 Or *A boy . . . 8 ounces* [228 grams] *of silver; a girl . . . 4 ounces* [114 grams].

five shekels of silver; a girl of that age is valued at three shekels* of silver. 7 A
man older than sixty is valued at fifteen shekels of silver; a woman of that
age is valued at ten shekels* of silver. 8 If you desire to make such a vow but
cannot afford to pay the required amount, take the person to the priest. He
will determine the amount for you to pay based on what you can afford.

9 "If your vow involves giving an animal that is acceptable as an offering
to the LORD, any gift to the LORD will be considered holy. 10 You may not ex-
change or substitute it for another animal—neither a good animal for a bad
one nor a bad animal for a good one. But if you do exchange one animal for
another, then both the original animal and its substitute will be considered
holy. 11 If your vow involves an unclean animal—one that is not acceptable
as an offering to the LORD—then you must bring the animal to the priest.
12 He will assess its value, and his assessment will be final, whether high or
low. 13 If you want to buy back the animal, you must pay the value set by the
priest, plus 20 percent.

14 "If someone dedicates a house to the LORD, the priest will come to assess
its value. The priest's assessment will be final, whether high or low. 15 If the
person who dedicated the house wants to buy it back, he must pay the value
set by the priest, plus 20 percent. Then the house will again be his.

16 "If someone dedicates to the LORD a piece of his family property, its value
will be assessed according to the amount of seed required to plant it—fifty
shekels of silver for a field planted with five bushels of barley seed.* 17 If the
field is dedicated to the LORD in the Year of Jubilee, then the entire assess-
ment will apply. 18 But if the field is dedicated after the Year of Jubilee, the
priest will assess the land's value in proportion to the number of years left
until the next Year of Jubilee. Its assessed value is reduced each year. 19 If the
person who dedicated the field wants to buy it back, he must pay the value
set by the priest, plus 20 percent. Then the field will again be legally his.
20 But if he does not want to buy it back, and it is sold to someone else, the
field can no longer be bought back. 21 When the field is released in the Year of
Jubilee, it will be holy, a field specially set apart* for the LORD. It will become
the property of the priests.

22 "If someone dedicates to the LORD a field he has purchased but which is
not part of his family property, 23 the priest will assess its value based on the
number of years left until the next Year of Jubilee. On that day he must give
the assessed value of the land as a sacred donation to the LORD. 24 In the Year
of Jubilee the field must be returned to the person from whom he purchased
it, the one who inherited it as family property. 25 (All the payments must
be measured by the weight of the sanctuary shekel,* which equals twenty
gerahs.)

26 "You may not dedicate a firstborn animal to the LORD, for the first-
born of your cattle, sheep, and goats already belong to him. 27 However, you
may buy back the firstborn of a ceremonially unclean animal by paying the
priest's assessment of its worth, plus 20 percent. If you do not buy it back,
the priest will sell it at its assessed value.

28 "However, anything specially set apart for the LORD—whether a person,

27:6 Or *A boy . . . 2 ounces* [57 grams] *of silver; a girl . . . 1.2 ounces* [34 grams]. **27:7** Or *A man . . . 6 ounces* [171 grams] *of silver; a woman . . . 4 ounces* [114 grams]. **27:16** Hebrew *50 shekels* [20 ounces or 570 grams] *of silver for a homer* [220 liters] *of barley seed.* **27:21** The Hebrew term used here refers to the complete consecration of things or people to the LORD, either by destroying them or by giving them as an offering; also in 27:28, 29. **27:25** Each shekel was about 0.4 ounces [11 grams] in weight.

an animal, or family property—must never be sold or bought back. Anything
devoted in this way has been set apart as holy, and it belongs to the LORD.
29 No person specially set apart for destruction may be bought back. Such a
person must be put to death.
30 "One-tenth of the produce of the land, whether grain from the fields
or fruit from the trees, belongs to the LORD and must be set apart to him
as holy. 31 If you want to buy back the LORD's tenth of the grain or fruit, you
must pay its value, plus 20 percent. 32 Count off every tenth animal from
your herds and flocks and set them apart for the LORD as holy. 33 You may not
pick and choose between good and bad animals, and you may not substitute
one for another. But if you do exchange one animal for another, then both
the original animal and its substitute will be considered holy and cannot
be bought back."
34 These are the commands that the LORD gave through Moses on Mount
Sinai for the Israelites.

Make a Difference

27:30

The One-Tenth Habit

Leviticus wraps up with a final challenge that God's people should tithe. In other words, as a sign of his people's thankfulness and faithfulness, God wants them to offer the first one-tenth of their produce (or income) as a holy offering to the Lord.

Today, Christians continue this habit by giving to their local church community to support missions and relief work. By combining our resources, we are able to spread the good news and help care for people in the name of Jesus.

Difference Maker

Make it your habit to tithe 10 percent of anything you earn to honor your relationship with the Lord.

Numbers Introduction

The book of Numbers has a bit of a misleading name. *Numbers* is a Latin title given to this book some fifteen hundred years after it was written. This title comes from the census numbers that are included in chapters 1 and 26. The Romans, who spoke Latin, loved a good census.

However, the Hebraic name for this book was *In the Wilderness*. That's a much more engaging title! The ancient Hebraic title reflects the narrative nature of this book much more accurately than "Numbers." After all, this is not just a ledger of accounting but also an epic journal of the wandering experiences of God's people, who struggled to follow the Lord for forty years in the wilderness after leaving Egypt.

Does a talking donkey sound like a boring mathematics problem? Does Moses performing miracles sound like equation solving? Does an anxiety attack due to a fear of giants sound like a geometry lecture? Does Aaron's shepherd staff turning into an almond factory seem like a monotonous drone of data? Does the annoying whining of the mobs sound like a statistical sheet? Does Joshua's young, bold faith sound like a routine attendance chart?

The book of Numbers adds up to a riveting story of how God multiplies blessing on his people when they make him the center of their lives. It is also a shocking account of the outcomes that result when people subtract God from the practices of their lives. Read this book with your eyes and heart open to discovering the dramatic plans God intends to accomplish through you just as he worked through Israel.

Story Arcs

- **Moses**
- **Joshua and Caleb**
- **Aaron**
- **Jesus**
- **Joshua**

Numbers

Registration of Israel's Troops

1 A year after Israel's departure from Egypt, the LORD spoke to Moses in
the Tabernacle* in the wilderness of Sinai. On the first day of the second
month* of that year he said, 2 "From the whole community of Israel, record the
names of all the warriors by their clans and families. List all the men 3 twenty
years old or older who are able to go to war. You and Aaron must register the
troops, 4 and you will be assisted by one family leader from each tribe.
5 "These are the tribes and the names of the leaders who will assist you:

	Tribe	*Leader*
	Reuben	Elizur son of Shedeur
6	Simeon	Shelumiel son of Zurishaddai
7	Judah	Nahshon son of Amminadab
8	Issachar	Nethanel son of Zuar
9	Zebulun	Eliab son of Helon
10	Ephraim son of Joseph	Elishama son of Ammihud
	Manasseh son of Joseph	Gamaliel son of Pedahzur
11	Benjamin	Abidan son of Gideoni
12	Dan	Ahiezer son of Ammishaddai
13	Asher	Pagiel son of Ocran
14	Gad	Eliasaph son of Deuel
15	Naphtali	Ahira son of Enan

16 These are the chosen leaders of the community, the leaders of their ances-
tral tribes, the heads of the clans of Israel."
17 So Moses and Aaron called together these chosen leaders, 18 and they
assembled the whole community of Israel on that very day.* All the people
were registered according to their ancestry by their clans and families. The
men of Israel who were twenty years old or older were listed one by one,
19 just as the LORD had commanded Moses. So Moses recorded their names
in the wilderness of Sinai.
20-21 This is the number of men twenty years old or older who were able
to go to war, as their names were listed in the records of their clans and
families*:

	Tribe	*Number*
	Reuben (Jacob's* oldest son)	46,500
22-23	Simeon	59,300

1:1a Hebrew *the Tent of Meeting.* 1:1b This day in the ancient Hebrew lunar calendar occurred in April or May. 1:18 Hebrew *on the first day of the second month;* see 1:1. 1:20-21a In the Hebrew text, this sentence (*This is the number of men twenty years old or older who were able to go to war, as their names were listed in the records of their clans and families*) is repeated in 1:22, 24, 26, 28, 30, 32, 34, 36, 38, 40, 42. 1:20-21b Hebrew *Israel's.* The names "Jacob" and "Israel" are often interchanged throughout the Old Testament, referring sometimes to the individual patriarch and sometimes to the nation.

Story Arc **1:1**

Moses

The Lord spoke with Moses in a personal way so that Moses would change the world. Through Moses, God set up a nation with a system to bring salvation for all humanity. Every time Moses spoke with the Lord, remarkable things happened. As you read this book, look for the difference that Moses' personal relationship with the Lord made.

Num 14:5-30 ►

Question 1:2-46

Israel's exodus from Egypt wasn't a small thing. Over six hundred thousand men of fighting age were counted among Israel's population. On top of that number were hundreds of thousands of women, older men, and children. Some have estimated there were well over two million people in the nation of Israel at the time. Imagine traveling through a desert with this many people. What kind of resources and organization would you need to manage all of this?

24-25	Gad	45,650
26-27	Judah	74,600
28-29	Issachar	54,400
30-31	Zebulun	57,400
32-33	Ephraim son of Joseph	40,500
34-35	Manasseh son of Joseph	32,200
36-37	Benjamin	35,400
38-39	Dan	62,700
40-41	Asher	41,500
42-43	Naphtali	53,400

44 These were the men registered by Moses and Aaron and the twelve leaders
of Israel, all listed according to their ancestral descent. 45 They were regis-
tered by families—all the men of Israel who were twenty years old or older
and able to go to war. 46 The total number was 603,550.
47 But this total did not include the Levites. 48 For the LORD had said to
Moses, 49 "Do not include the tribe of Levi in the registration; do not count
them with the rest of the Israelites. 50 Put the Levites in charge of the Tab-
ernacle of the Covenant,* along with all its furnishings and equipment.
They must carry the Tabernacle and all its furnishings as you travel, and
they must take care of it and camp around it. 51 Whenever it is time for the
Tabernacle to move, the Levites will take it down. And when it is time to
stop, they will set it up again. But any unauthorized person who goes too
near the Tabernacle must be put to death. 52 Each tribe of Israel will camp
in a designated area with its own family banner. 53 But the Levites will camp
around the Tabernacle of the Covenant to protect the community of Israel
from the LORD's anger. The Levites are responsible to stand guard around
the Tabernacle."
54 So the Israelites did everything just as the LORD had commanded Moses.

Organization for Israel's Camp

2 Then the LORD gave these instructions to Moses and Aaron: 2 "When
the Israelites set up camp, each tribe will be assigned its own area. The
tribal divisions will camp beneath their family banners on all four sides of
the Tabernacle,* but at some distance from it.
3-4 "The divisions of Judah, Issachar, and Zebulun are to camp toward the
sunrise on the east side of the Tabernacle, beneath their family banners.
These are the names of the tribes, their leaders, and the numbers of their
registered troops:

	Tribe	*Leader*	*Number*
	Judah	Nahshon son of Amminadab	74,600
5-6	Issachar	Nethanel son of Zuar	54,400
7-8	Zebulun	Eliab son of Helon	57,400

9 So the total of all the troops on Judah's side of the camp is 186,400. These
three tribes are to lead the way whenever the Israelites travel to a new
campsite.
10-11 "The divisions of Reuben, Simeon, and Gad are to camp on the south

1:50 Or *Tabernacle of the Testimony;* also in 1:53. 2:2 Hebrew *the Tent of Meeting;* also in 2:17.

side of the Tabernacle, beneath their family banners. These are the names of the tribes, their leaders, and the numbers of their registered troops:

	Tribe	Leader	Number
	Reuben	Elizur son of Shedeur	46,500
12-13	Simeon	Shelumiel son of Zurishaddai	59,300
14-15	Gad	Eliasaph son of Deuel*	45,650

16 So the total of all the troops on Reuben's side of the camp is 151,450. These three tribes will be second in line whenever the Israelites travel.

17 "Then the Tabernacle, carried by the Levites, will set out from the middle of the camp. All the tribes are to travel in the same order that they camp, each in position under the appropriate family banner.

18-19 "The divisions of Ephraim, Manasseh, and Benjamin are to camp on the west side of the Tabernacle, beneath their family banners. These are the names of the tribes, their leaders, and the numbers of their registered troops:

	Tribe	Leader	Number
	Ephraim	Elishama son of Ammihud	40,500
20-21	Manasseh	Gamaliel son of Pedahzur	32,200
22-23	Benjamin	Abidan son of Gideoni	35,400

24 So the total of all the troops on Ephraim's side of the camp is 108,100. These three tribes will be third in line whenever the Israelites travel.

25-26 "The divisions of Dan, Asher, and Naphtali are to camp on the north side of the Tabernacle, beneath their family banners. These are the names of the tribes, their leaders, and the numbers of their registered troops:

	Tribe	Leader	Number
	Dan	Ahiezer son of Ammishaddai	62,700
27-28	Asher	Pagiel son of Ocran	41,500
29-30	Naphtali	Ahira son of Enan	53,400

31 So the total of all the troops on Dan's side of the camp is 157,600. These three tribes will be last, marching under their banners whenever the Israelites travel."

32 In summary, the troops of Israel listed by their families totaled 603,550.
33 But as the LORD had commanded, the Levites were not included in this
registration. 34 So the people of Israel did everything as the LORD had com-
manded Moses. Each clan and family set up camp and marched under their
banners exactly as the LORD had instructed them.

Prayer 2:34

Lord Jesus, empower me to do what you want me to do today. Amen.

Levites Appointed for Service

3 This is the family line of Aaron and Moses as it was recorded when the
LORD spoke to Moses on Mount Sinai: 2 The names of Aaron's sons were
Nadab (the oldest), Abihu, Eleazar, and Ithamar. 3 These sons of Aaron were
anointed and ordained to minister as priests. 4 But Nadab and Abihu died
in the LORD's presence in the wilderness of Sinai when they burned before
the LORD the wrong kind of fire, different than he had commanded. Since

2:14-15 As in many Hebrew manuscripts, Samaritan Pentateuch, and Latin Vulgate (see also 1:14); most Hebrew manuscripts read *son of Reuel.*

Question 3:12

The Levites were set aside for a purpose: to perform sacred duties to help Israel remain close to the Lord. Today, in what ways are there similar callings for ministry workers commissioned for service to God?

they had no sons, this left only Eleazar and Ithamar to serve as priests with their father, Aaron.

5 Then the LORD said to Moses, 6 "Call forward the tribe of Levi, and present them to Aaron the priest to serve as his assistants. 7 They will serve Aaron and the whole community, performing their sacred duties in and around the Tabernacle.* 8 They will also maintain all the furnishings of the sacred tent,* serving in the Tabernacle on behalf of all the Israelites. 9 Assign the Levites to Aaron and his sons. They have been given from among all the people of Israel to serve as their assistants. 10 Appoint Aaron and his sons to carry out the duties of the priesthood. But any unauthorized person who goes too near the sanctuary must be put to death."

11 And the LORD said to Moses, 12 "Look, I have chosen the Levites from among the Israelites to serve as substitutes for all the firstborn sons of the people of Israel. The Levites belong to me, 13 for all the firstborn males are mine. On the day I struck down all the firstborn sons of the Egyptians, I set apart for myself all the firstborn in Israel, both of people and of animals. They are mine; I am the LORD."

Registration of the Levites

14 The LORD spoke again to Moses in the wilderness of Sinai. He said, 15 "Record the names of the members of the tribe of Levi by their families and clans. List every male who is one month old or older." 16 So Moses listed them, just as the LORD had commanded.

17 Levi had three sons, whose names were Gershon, Kohath, and Merari.
18 The clans descended from Gershon were named after two of his descendants, Libni and Shimei.
19 The clans descended from Kohath were named after four of his descendants, Amram, Izhar, Hebron, and Uzziel.
20 The clans descended from Merari were named after two of his descendants, Mahli and Mushi.
These were the Levite clans, listed according to their family groups.

21 The descendants of Gershon were composed of the clans descended from Libni and Shimei. 22 There were 7,500 males one month old or older among these Gershonite clans. 23 They were assigned the area to the west of the Tabernacle for their camp. 24 The leader of the Gershonite clans was Eliasaph son of Lael. 25 These two clans were responsible to care for the Tabernacle, including the sacred tent with its layers of coverings, the curtain at its entrance, 26 the curtains of the courtyard that surrounded the Tabernacle and altar, the curtain at the courtyard entrance, the ropes, and all the equipment related to their use.

27 The descendants of Kohath were composed of the clans descended from Amram, Izhar, Hebron, and Uzziel. 28 There were 8,600* males one month old or older among these Kohathite clans. They were responsible for the care of the sanctuary, 29 and they were assigned the area south of the Tabernacle for their camp. 30 The leader of the Kohathite clans was Elizaphan son of Uzziel. 31 These four clans were responsible for the care of the Ark, the table, the lampstand, the altars, the various articles used in the sanctuary,

3:7 Hebrew *around the Tent of Meeting, doing service at the Tabernacle.* 3:8 Hebrew *the Tent of Meeting;* also in 3:25. 3:28 Some Greek manuscripts read *8,300;* see total in 3:39.

the inner curtain, and all the equipment related to their use. 32 Eleazar, son
of Aaron the priest, was the chief administrator over all the Levites, with
special responsibility for the oversight of the sanctuary.
33 The descendants of Merari were composed of the clans descended from
Mahli and Mushi. 34 There were 6,200 males one month old or older among
these Merarite clans. 35 They were assigned the area north of the Tabernacle
for their camp. The leader of the Merarite clans was Zuriel son of Abihail.
36 These two clans were responsible for the care of the frames supporting the
Tabernacle, the crossbars, the pillars, the bases, and all the equipment related
to their use. 37 They were also responsible for the posts of the courtyard and
all their bases, pegs, and ropes.
38 The area in front of the Tabernacle, in the east toward the sunrise,* was
reserved for the tents of Moses and of Aaron and his sons, who had the final
responsibility for the sanctuary on behalf of the people of Israel. Anyone other
than a priest or Levite who went too near the sanctuary was to be put to death.
39 When Moses and Aaron counted the Levite clans at the LORD's com-
mand, the total number was 22,000 males one month old or older.

Redeeming the Firstborn Sons

40 Then the LORD said to Moses, "Now count all the firstborn sons in Israel
who are one month old or older, and make a list of their names. 41 The Levites
must be reserved for me as substitutes for the firstborn sons of Israel; I am
the LORD. And the Levites' livestock must be reserved for me as substitutes
for the firstborn livestock of the whole nation of Israel."
42 So Moses counted the firstborn sons of the people of Israel, just as the
LORD had commanded. 43 The number of firstborn sons who were one month
old or older was 22,273.
44 Then the LORD said to Moses, 45 "Take the Levites as substitutes for the
firstborn sons of the people of Israel. And take the livestock of the Levites as
substitutes for the firstborn livestock of the people of Israel. The Levites be-
long to me; I am the LORD. 46 There are 273 more firstborn sons of Israel than
there are Levites. To redeem these extra firstborn sons, 47 collect five pieces
of silver* for each of them (each piece weighing the same as the sanctuary
shekel, which equals twenty gerahs). 48 Give the silver to Aaron and his sons
as the redemption price for the extra firstborn sons."
49 So Moses collected the silver for redeeming the firstborn sons of Israel
who exceeded the number of Levites. 50 He collected 1,365 pieces of silver* on
behalf of these firstborn sons of Israel (each piece weighing the same as the
sanctuary shekel). 51 And Moses gave the silver for the redemption to Aaron
and his sons, just as the LORD had commanded.

Duties of the Kohathite Clan

4 Then the LORD said to Moses and Aaron, 2 "Record the names of the
members of the clans and families of the Kohathite division of the tribe
of Levi. 3 List all the men between the ages of thirty and fifty who are eligible
to serve in the Tabernacle.*
4 "The duties of the Kohathites at the Tabernacle will relate to the most
sacred objects. 5 When the camp moves, Aaron and his sons must enter the

3:38 Hebrew *toward the sunrise, in front of the Tent of Meeting.* 3:47 Hebrew *5 shekels* [2 ounces or 57 grams]. 3:50 Hebrew *1,365 [shekels] of silver* [34 pounds or 15.5 kilograms]. 4:3 Hebrew *the Tent of Meeting;* also in 4:4, 15, 23, 25, 28, 30, 31, 33, 35, 37, 39, 41, 43, 47.

Question 4:22

It is true that an accountant would love reading different sections of the book of Numbers. Why do you think there are so many exact lists recorded in this book? Why are these details important? What difference does this precision make?

Tabernacle first to take down the inner curtain and cover the Ark of the Covenant* with it. 6 Then they must cover the inner curtain with fine goatskin leather and spread over that a single piece of blue cloth. Finally, they must put the carrying poles of the Ark in place.

7 "Next they must spread a blue cloth over the table where the Bread of the Presence is displayed, and on the cloth they will place the bowls, ladles, jars, pitchers, and the special bread. 8 They must spread a scarlet cloth over all of this, and finally a covering of fine goatskin leather on top of the scarlet cloth. Then they must insert the carrying poles into the table.

9 "Next they must cover the lampstand with a blue cloth, along with its lamps, lamp snuffers, trays, and special jars of olive oil. 10 Then they must cover the lampstand and its accessories with fine goatskin leather and place the bundle on a carrying frame.

11 "Next they must spread a blue cloth over the gold incense altar and cover this cloth with fine goatskin leather. Then they must attach the carrying poles to the altar. 12 They must take all the remaining furnishings of the sanctuary and wrap them in a blue cloth, cover them with fine goatskin leather, and place them on the carrying frame.

13 "They must remove the ashes from the altar for sacrifices and cover the altar with a purple cloth. 14 All the altar utensils—the firepans, meat forks, shovels, basins, and all the containers—must be placed on the cloth, and a covering of fine goatskin leather must be spread over them. Finally, they must put the carrying poles in place. 15 The camp will be ready to move when Aaron and his sons have finished covering the sanctuary and all the sacred articles. The Kohathites will come and carry these things to the next destination. But they must not touch the sacred objects, or they will die. So these are the things from the Tabernacle that the Kohathites must carry.

16 "Eleazar son of Aaron the priest will be responsible for the oil of the lampstand, the fragrant incense, the daily grain offering, and the anointing oil. In fact, Eleazar will be responsible for the entire Tabernacle and everything in it, including the sanctuary and its furnishings."

17 Then the LORD said to Moses and Aaron, 18 "Do not let the Kohathite clans be destroyed from among the Levites! 19 This is what you must do so they will live and not die when they approach the most sacred objects. Aaron and his sons must always go in with them and assign a specific duty or load to each person. 20 The Kohathites must never enter the sanctuary to look at the sacred objects for even a moment, or they will die."

Duties of the Gershonite Clan

21 And the LORD said to Moses, 22 "Record the names of the members of the clans and families of the Gershonite division of the tribe of Levi. 23 List all the men between the ages of thirty and fifty who are eligible to serve in the Tabernacle.

24 "These Gershonite clans will be responsible for general service and carrying loads. 25 They must carry the curtains of the Tabernacle, the Tabernacle itself with its coverings, the outer covering of fine goatskin leather, and the curtain for the Tabernacle entrance. 26 They are also to carry the curtains for the courtyard walls that surround the Tabernacle and altar, the curtain across the courtyard entrance, the ropes, and all the equipment related to their use.

4:5 Or *Ark of the Testimony.*

The Gershonites are responsible for all these items. 27 Aaron and his sons will direct the Gershonites regarding all their duties, whether it involves moving the equipment or doing other work. They must assign the Gershonites responsibility for the loads they are to carry. 28 So these are the duties assigned to the Gershonite clans at the Tabernacle. They will be directly responsible to Ithamar son of Aaron the priest.

Duties of the Merarite Clan

29 "Now record the names of the members of the clans and families of the Merarite division of the tribe of Levi. 30 List all the men between the ages of thirty and fifty who are eligible to serve in the Tabernacle.

31 "Their only duty at the Tabernacle will be to carry loads. They will carry the frames of the Tabernacle, the crossbars, the posts, and the bases; 32 also the posts for the courtyard walls with their bases, pegs, and ropes; and all the accessories and everything else related to their use. Assign the various loads to each man by name. 33 So these are the duties of the Merarite clans at the Tabernacle. They are directly responsible to Ithamar son of Aaron the priest."

Summary of the Registration

34 So Moses, Aaron, and the other leaders of the community listed the members of the Kohathite division by their clans and families. 35 The list included all the men between thirty and fifty years of age who were eligible for service in the Tabernacle, 36 and the total number came to 2,750. 37 So this was the total of all those from the Kohathite clans who were eligible to serve at the Tabernacle. Moses and Aaron listed them, just as the LORD had commanded through Moses.

38 The Gershonite division was also listed by its clans and families. 39 The list included all the men between thirty and fifty years of age who were eligible for service in the Tabernacle, 40 and the total number came to 2,630. 41 So this was the total of all those from the Gershonite clans who were eligible to serve at the Tabernacle. Moses and Aaron listed them, just as the LORD had commanded.

42 The Merarite division was also listed by its clans and families. 43 The list included all the men between thirty and fifty years of age who were eligible for service in the Tabernacle, 44 and the total number came to 3,200. 45 So this was the total of all those from the Merarite clans who were eligible for service. Moses and Aaron listed them, just as the LORD had commanded through Moses.

46 So Moses, Aaron, and the leaders of Israel listed all the Levites by their clans and families. 47 All the men between thirty and fifty years of age who were eligible for service in the Tabernacle and for its transportation 48 numbered 8,580. 49 When their names were recorded, as the LORD had commanded through Moses, each man was assigned his task and told what to carry.

And so the registration was completed, just as the LORD had commanded Moses.

Purity in Israel's Camp

5 The LORD gave these instructions to Moses: 2 "Command the people of Israel to remove from the camp anyone who has a skin disease* or a discharge, or who has become ceremonially unclean by touching a dead person.

5:2 Traditionally rendered *leprosy.* The Hebrew word used here describes various skin diseases.

Make a Difference

5:6–8

What to Do If…

While still wandering in the desert, Israel established a remarkable system to deal with injustice. The focus was on opportunities for reconciliation. The system protected those who were wronged by giving them the right to receive compensation for the hurt caused by the wrong action. The system also provided for those who had committed the wrong by giving them the right to seek reconciliation.

Difference Maker

Think of a wrong you have committed against someone. Have you followed the guidelines in these verses for making up for your sin? What steps do you need to take to make things right?

3This command applies to men and women alike. Remove them so they will
not defile the camp in which I live among them." 4So the Israelites did as
the LORD had commanded Moses and removed such people from the camp.
5Then the LORD said to Moses, 6"Give the following instructions to the
people of Israel: If any of the people—men or women—betray the LORD by
doing wrong to another person, they are guilty. 7They must confess their
sin and make full restitution for what they have done, adding an additional
20 percent and returning it to the person who was wronged. 8But if the per-
son who was wronged is dead, and there are no near relatives to whom res-
titution can be made, the payment belongs to the LORD and must be given
to the priest. Those who are guilty must also bring a ram as a sacrifice, and
they will be purified and made right with the LORD.* 9All the sacred offerings
that the Israelites bring to a priest will belong to him. 10Each priest may keep
all the sacred donations that he receives."

Protecting Marital Faithfulness

11And the LORD said to Moses, 12"Give the following instructions to the
people of Israel.
"Suppose a man's wife goes astray, and she is unfaithful to her husband
13and has sex with another man, but neither her husband nor anyone else
knows about it. She has defiled herself, even though there was no witness
and she was not caught in the act. 14If her husband becomes jealous and is
suspicious of his wife and needs to know whether or not she has defiled
herself, 15the husband must bring his wife to the priest. He must also bring
an offering of two quarts* of barley flour to be presented on her behalf. Do
not mix it with olive oil or frankincense, for it is a jealousy offering—an
offering to prove whether or not she is guilty.
16"The priest will then present her to stand trial before the LORD. 17He
must take some holy water in a clay jar and pour into it dust he has taken
from the Tabernacle floor. 18When the priest has presented the woman before
the LORD, he must unbind her hair and place in her hands the offering of
proof—the jealousy offering to determine whether her husband's suspicions
are justified. The priest will stand before her, holding the jar of bitter water
that brings a curse to those who are guilty. 19The priest will then put the
woman under oath and say to her, 'If no other man has had sex with you,
and you have not gone astray and defiled yourself while under your hus-
band's authority, may you be immune from the effects of this bitter water
that brings on the curse. 20But if you have gone astray by being unfaithful to
your husband, and have defiled yourself by having sex with another man—'
21"At this point the priest must put the woman under oath by saying,
'May the people know that the LORD's curse is upon you when he makes you
infertile, causing your womb to shrivel* and your abdomen to swell. 22Now
may this water that brings the curse enter your body and cause your abdo-
men to swell and your womb to shrivel.*' And the woman will be required
to say, 'Yes, let it be so.' 23And the priest will write these curses on a piece of
leather and wash them off into the bitter water. 24He will make the woman
drink the bitter water that brings on the curse. When the water enters her
body, it will cause bitter suffering if she is guilty.

5:8 Or *bring a ram for atonement, which will make atonement for them.* 5:15 Hebrew *1/10 of an ephah* [2.2 liters]. 5:21 Hebrew *when he causes your thigh to waste away.* 5:22 Hebrew *and your thigh to waste away.*

25 "The priest will take the jealousy offering from the woman's hand, lift
it up before the LORD, and carry it to the altar. 26 He will take a handful of
the flour as a token portion and burn it on the altar, and he will require the
woman to drink the water. 27 If she has defiled herself by being unfaithful
to her husband, the water that brings on the curse will cause bitter suffer-
ing. Her abdomen will swell and her womb will shrink,* and her name will
become a curse among her people. 28 But if she has not defiled herself and
is pure, then she will be unharmed and will still be able to have children.
29 "This is the ritual law for dealing with suspicion. If a woman goes astray
and defiles herself while under her husband's authority, 30 or if a man be-
comes jealous and is suspicious that his wife has been unfaithful, the hus-
band must present his wife before the LORD, and the priest will apply this
entire ritual law to her. 31 The husband will be innocent of any guilt in this
matter, but his wife will be held accountable for her sin."

Nazirite Laws

6 Then the LORD said to Moses, 2 "Give the following instructions to the
people of Israel.
"If any of the people, either men or women, take the special vow of a Naz-
irite, setting themselves apart to the LORD in a special way, 3 they must give
up wine and other alcoholic drinks. They must not use vinegar made from
wine or from other alcoholic drinks, they must not drink fresh grape juice,
and they must not eat grapes or raisins. 4 As long as they are bound by their
Nazirite vow, they are not allowed to eat or drink anything that comes from
a grapevine—not even the grape seeds or skins.
5 "They must never cut their hair throughout the time of their vow, for
they are holy and set apart to the LORD. Until the time of their vow has been
fulfilled, they must let their hair grow long. 6 And they must not go near a
dead body during the entire period of their vow to the LORD. 7 Even if the
dead person is their own father, mother, brother, or sister, they must not
defile themselves, for the hair on their head is the symbol of their separation
to God. 8 This requirement applies as long as they are set apart to the LORD.
9 "If someone falls dead beside them, the hair they have dedicated will
be defiled. They must wait for seven days and then shave their heads. Then
they will be cleansed from their defilement. 10 On the eighth day they must
bring two turtledoves or two young pigeons to the priest at the entrance of
the Tabernacle.* 11 The priest will offer one of the birds for a sin offering and
the other for a burnt offering. In this way, he will purify them* from the guilt
they incurred through contact with the dead body. Then they must reaffirm
their commitment and let their hair begin to grow again. 12 The days of their
vow that were completed before their defilement no longer count. They
must rededicate themselves to the LORD as a Nazirite for the full term of
their vow, and each must bring a one-year-old male lamb for a guilt offering.
13 "This is the ritual law for Nazirites. At the conclusion of their time of
separation as Nazirites, they must each go to the entrance of the Tabernacle
14 and offer their sacrifices to the LORD: a one-year-old male lamb without
defect for a burnt offering, a one-year-old female lamb without defect for
a sin offering, a ram without defect for a peace offering, 15 a basket of bread
made without yeast—cakes of choice flour mixed with olive oil and wafers

5:27 Hebrew *and her thigh will waste away.* 6:10 Hebrew *the Tent of Meeting;* also in 6:13, 18.
6:11 Or *make atonement for them.*

spread with olive oil—along with their prescribed grain offerings and liquid
offerings. 16 The priest will present these offerings before the LORD: first the
sin offering and the burnt offering; 17 then the ram for a peace offering, along
with the basket of bread made without yeast. The priest must also present
the prescribed grain offering and liquid offering to the LORD.
18 "Then the Nazirites will shave their heads at the entrance of the Tab-
ernacle. They will take the hair that had been dedicated and place it on the
fire beneath the peace-offering sacrifice. 19 After the Nazirite's head has been
shaved, the priest will take for each of them the boiled shoulder of the ram,
and he will take from the basket a cake and a wafer made without yeast. He
will put them all into the Nazirite's hands. 20 Then the priest will lift them up
as a special offering before the LORD. These are holy portions for the priest,
along with the breast of the special offering and the thigh of the sacred of-
fering that are lifted up before the LORD. After this ceremony the Nazirites
may again drink wine.
21 "This is the ritual law of the Nazirites, who vow to bring these offerings
to the LORD. They may also bring additional offerings if they can afford it.
And they must be careful to do whatever they vowed when they set them-
selves apart as Nazirites."

The Priestly Blessing

22 Then the LORD said to Moses, 23 "Tell Aaron and his sons to bless the people
of Israel with this special blessing:

24 'May the LORD bless you
and protect you.
25 May the LORD smile on you
and be gracious to you.
26 May the LORD show you his favor
and give you his peace.'

27 Whenever Aaron and his sons bless the people of Israel in my name, I my-
self will bless them."

Offerings of Dedication

7 On the day Moses set up the Tabernacle, he anointed it and set it apart
as holy. He also anointed and set apart all its furnishings and the altar
with its utensils. 2 Then the leaders of Israel—the tribal leaders who had
registered the troops—came and brought their offerings. 3 Together they
brought six large wagons and twelve oxen. There was a wagon for every
two leaders and an ox for each leader. They presented these to the LORD in
front of the Tabernacle.
4 Then the LORD said to Moses, 5 "Receive their gifts, and use these oxen
and wagons for transporting the Tabernacle.* Distribute them among the
Levites according to the work they have to do." 6 So Moses took the wagons
and oxen and presented them to the Levites. 7 He gave two wagons and four
oxen to the Gershonite division for their work, 8 and he gave four wagons and
eight oxen to the Merarite division for their work. All their work was done
under the leadership of Ithamar son of Aaron the priest. 9 But he gave none

7:5 Hebrew *the Tent of Meeting;* also in 7:89.

Make a Difference

6:22–27

God's Favor

Maybe you've heard this "priestly blessing" at the end of a church service? God gave this poetic blessing to Aaron and his sons so that they would proclaim God's favor over the people. God wanted his people to desire that everyone receive God's blessing, not just a select few. God also wanted to bless people personally and sincerely with his comforting heart and the glory of his own name.

Difference Maker

Unpack every line of this blessing. Which line is most comforting to you? Which one do you most need? Run this blessing through your mind again and again until you've memorized it. Then look for an opportunity to boldly ask if you could pray this blessing over a friend.

of the wagons or oxen to the Kohathite division, since they were required to
carry the sacred objects of the Tabernacle on their shoulders.
10 The leaders also presented dedication gifts for the altar at the time it was
anointed. They each placed their gifts before the altar. 11 The LORD said to
Moses, "Let one leader bring his gift each day for the dedication of the altar."

12 On the first day Nahshon son of Amminadab, leader of the tribe of Judah,
presented his offering.
13 His offering consisted of a silver platter weighing 3¼ pounds and a
silver basin weighing 1¾ pounds* (as measured by the weight of the
sanctuary shekel). These were both filled with grain offerings of choice
flour moistened with olive oil. 14 He also brought a gold container
weighing four ounces,* which was filled with incense. 15 He brought a
young bull, a ram, and a one-year-old male lamb for a burnt offering,
16 and a male goat for a sin offering. 17 For a peace offering he brought
two bulls, five rams, five male goats, and five one-year-old male lambs.
This was the offering brought by Nahshon son of Amminadab.

18 On the second day Nethanel son of Zuar, leader of the tribe of Issachar,
presented his offering.
19 His offering consisted of a silver platter weighing 3¼ pounds and
a silver basin weighing 1¾ pounds (as measured by the weight of the
sanctuary shekel). These were both filled with grain offerings of choice
flour moistened with olive oil. 20 He also brought a gold container
weighing four ounces, which was filled with incense. 21 He brought a
young bull, a ram, and a one-year-old male lamb for a burnt offering,
22 and a male goat for a sin offering. 23 For a peace offering he brought
two bulls, five rams, five male goats, and five one-year-old male lambs.
This was the offering brought by Nethanel son of Zuar.

24 On the third day Eliab son of Helon, leader of the tribe of Zebulun, pre-
sented his offering.
25 His offering consisted of a silver platter weighing 3¼ pounds and
a silver basin weighing 1¾ pounds (as measured by the weight of the
sanctuary shekel). These were both filled with grain offerings of choice
flour moistened with olive oil. 26 He also brought a gold container
weighing four ounces, which was filled with incense. 27 He brought a
young bull, a ram, and a one-year-old male lamb for a burnt offering,
28 and a male goat for a sin offering. 29 For a peace offering he brought
two bulls, five rams, five male goats, and five one-year-old male lambs.
This was the offering brought by Eliab son of Helon.

30 On the fourth day Elizur son of Shedeur, leader of the tribe of Reuben,
presented his offering.
31 His offering consisted of a silver platter weighing 3¼ pounds and
a silver basin weighing 1¾ pounds (as measured by the weight of the
sanctuary shekel). These were both filled with grain offerings of choice
flour moistened with olive oil. 32 He also brought a gold container

7:13 Hebrew *silver platter weighing 130 [shekels]* [1.5 kilograms] *and a silver basin weighing 70 shekels* [800 grams]; also in 7:19, 25, 31, 37, 43, 49, 55, 61, 67, 73, 79, 85. **7:14** Hebrew *10 [shekels]* [114 grams]; also in 7:20, 26, 32, 38, 44, 50, 56, 62, 68, 74, 80, 86.

weighing four ounces, which was filled with incense. 33 He brought a
young bull, a ram, and a one-year-old male lamb for a burnt offering,
34 and a male goat for a sin offering. 35 For a peace offering he brought
two bulls, five rams, five male goats, and five one-year-old male lambs.
This was the offering brought by Elizur son of Shedeur.

36 On the fifth day Shelumiel son of Zurishaddai, leader of the tribe of Simeon, presented his offering.

37 His offering consisted of a silver platter weighing 3¼ pounds and
a silver basin weighing 1¾ pounds (as measured by the weight of the
sanctuary shekel). These were both filled with grain offerings of choice
flour moistened with olive oil. 38 He also brought a gold container
weighing four ounces, which was filled with incense. 39 He brought a
young bull, a ram, and a one-year-old male lamb for a burnt offering,
40 and a male goat for a sin offering. 41 For a peace offering he brought
two bulls, five rams, five male goats, and five one-year-old male lambs.
This was the offering brought by Shelumiel son of Zurishaddai.

42 On the sixth day Eliasaph son of Deuel, leader of the tribe of Gad, presented his offering.

43 His offering consisted of a silver platter weighing 3¼ pounds and
a silver basin weighing 1¾ pounds (as measured by the weight of the
sanctuary shekel). These were both filled with grain offerings of choice
flour moistened with olive oil. 44 He also brought a gold container
weighing four ounces, which was filled with incense. 45 He brought a
young bull, a ram, and a one-year-old male lamb for a burnt offering,
46 and a male goat for a sin offering. 47 For a peace offering he brought
two bulls, five rams, five male goats, and five one-year-old male lambs.
This was the offering brought by Eliasaph son of Deuel.

48 On the seventh day Elishama son of Ammihud, leader of the tribe of Ephraim, presented his offering.

49 His offering consisted of a silver platter weighing 3¼ pounds and
a silver basin weighing 1¾ pounds (as measured by the weight of the
sanctuary shekel). These were both filled with grain offerings of choice
flour moistened with olive oil. 50 He also brought a gold container
weighing four ounces, which was filled with incense. 51 He brought a
young bull, a ram, and a one-year-old male lamb for a burnt offering,
52 and a male goat for a sin offering. 53 For a peace offering he brought
two bulls, five rams, five male goats, and five one-year-old male lambs.
This was the offering brought by Elishama son of Ammihud.

54 On the eighth day Gamaliel son of Pedahzur, leader of the tribe of Manasseh, presented his offering.

55 His offering consisted of a silver platter weighing 3¼ pounds and
a silver basin weighing 1¾ pounds (as measured by the weight of the
sanctuary shekel). These were both filled with grain offerings of choice
flour moistened with olive oil. 56 He also brought a gold container
weighing four ounces, which was filled with incense. 57 He brought a
young bull, a ram, and a one-year-old male lamb for a burnt offering,

58 and a male goat for a sin offering. 59 For a peace offering he brought two bulls, five rams, five male goats, and five one-year-old male lambs. This was the offering brought by Gamaliel son of Pedahzur.

60 On the ninth day Abidan son of Gideoni, leader of the tribe of Benjamin, presented his offering.

61 His offering consisted of a silver platter weighing 3¼ pounds and a silver basin weighing 1¾ pounds (as measured by the weight of the sanctuary shekel). These were both filled with grain offerings of choice flour moistened with olive oil. 62 He also brought a gold container weighing four ounces, which was filled with incense. 63 He brought a young bull, a ram, and a one-year-old male lamb for a burnt offering, 64 and a male goat for a sin offering. 65 For a peace offering he brought two bulls, five rams, five male goats, and five one-year-old male lambs. This was the offering brought by Abidan son of Gideoni.

66 On the tenth day Ahiezer son of Ammishaddai, leader of the tribe of Dan, presented his offering.

67 His offering consisted of a silver platter weighing 3¼ pounds and a silver basin weighing 1¾ pounds (as measured by the weight of the sanctuary shekel). These were both filled with grain offerings of choice flour moistened with olive oil. 68 He also brought a gold container weighing four ounces, which was filled with incense. 69 He brought a young bull, a ram, and a one-year-old male lamb for a burnt offering, 70 and a male goat for a sin offering. 71 For a peace offering he brought two bulls, five rams, five male goats, and five one-year-old male lambs. This was the offering brought by Ahiezer son of Ammishaddai.

72 On the eleventh day Pagiel son of Ocran, leader of the tribe of Asher, presented his offering.

73 His offering consisted of a silver platter weighing 3¼ pounds and a silver basin weighing 1¾ pounds (as measured by the weight of the sanctuary shekel). These were both filled with grain offerings of choice flour moistened with olive oil. 74 He also brought a gold container weighing four ounces, which was filled with incense. 75 He brought a young bull, a ram, and a one-year-old male lamb for a burnt offering, 76 and a male goat for a sin offering. 77 For a peace offering he brought two bulls, five rams, five male goats, and five one-year-old male lambs. This was the offering brought by Pagiel son of Ocran.

78 On the twelfth day Ahira son of Enan, leader of the tribe of Naphtali, presented his offering.

79 His offering consisted of a silver platter weighing 3¼ pounds and a silver basin weighing 1¾ pounds (as measured by the weight of the sanctuary shekel). These were both filled with grain offerings of choice flour moistened with olive oil. 80 He also brought a gold container weighing four ounces, which was filled with incense. 81 He brought a young bull, a ram, and a one-year-old male lamb for a burnt offering, 82 and a male goat for a sin offering. 83 For a peace offering he brought

Highlights from the text

Question **7:89**

The Lord spoke to Moses in the tabernacle. What do you think this conversation was like? If God spoke with you today, what might he talk about?

two bulls, five rams, five male goats, and five one-year-old male lambs.
This was the offering brought by Ahira son of Enan.

84 So this was the dedication offering brought by the leaders of Israel at the
time the altar was anointed: twelve silver platters, twelve silver basins, and
twelve gold incense containers. 85 Each silver platter weighed 3¼ pounds,
and each silver basin weighed 1¾ pounds. The total weight of the silver was
60 pounds* (as measured by the weight of the sanctuary shekel). 86 Each of
the twelve gold containers that was filled with incense weighed four ounces
(as measured by the weight of the sanctuary shekel). The total weight of
the gold was three pounds.* 87 Twelve young bulls, twelve rams, and twelve
one-year-old male lambs were donated for the burnt offerings, along with
their prescribed grain offerings. Twelve male goats were brought for the
sin offerings. 88 Twenty-four bulls, sixty rams, sixty male goats, and sixty
one-year-old male lambs were donated for the peace offerings. This was the
dedication offering for the altar after it was anointed.
89 Whenever Moses went into the Tabernacle to speak with the LORD, he
heard the voice speaking to him from between the two cherubim above the
Ark's cover—the place of atonement—that rests on the Ark of the Covenant.*
The LORD spoke to him from there.

Preparing the Lamps

8 The LORD said to Moses, 2 "Give Aaron the following instructions: When
you set up the seven lamps in the lampstand, place them so their light
shines forward in front of the lampstand." 3 So Aaron did this. He set up
the seven lamps so they reflected their light forward, just as the LORD had
commanded Moses. 4 The entire lampstand, from its base to its decorative
blossoms, was made of beaten gold. It was built according to the exact design
the LORD had shown Moses.

The Levites Dedicated

5 Then the LORD said to Moses, 6 "Now set the Levites apart from the rest of
the people of Israel and make them ceremonially clean. 7 Do this by sprin-
kling them with the water of purification, and have them shave their entire
body and wash their clothing. Then they will be ceremonially clean. 8 Have
them bring a young bull and a grain offering of choice flour moistened with
olive oil, along with a second young bull for a sin offering. 9 Then assemble
the whole community of Israel, and present the Levites at the entrance of the
Tabernacle.* 10 When you present the Levites before the LORD, the people of
Israel must lay their hands on them. 11 Raising his hands, Aaron must then
present the Levites to the LORD as a special offering from the people of Israel,
thus dedicating them to the LORD's service.

12 "Next the Levites will lay their hands on the heads of the young bulls.
Present one as a sin offering and the other as a burnt offering to the LORD,
to purify the Levites and make them right with the LORD.* 13 Then have the
Levites stand in front of Aaron and his sons, and raise your hands and present
them as a special offering to the LORD. 14 In this way, you will set the Levites
apart from the rest of the people of Israel, and the Levites will belong to me.

7:85 Hebrew *2,400 [shekels]* [27.6 kilograms]. **7:86** Hebrew *120 [shekels]* [1.4 kilograms]. **7:89** Or *Ark of the Testimony.* **8:9** Hebrew *the Tent of Meeting;* also in 8:15, 19, 22, 24, 26. **8:12** Or *to make atonement for the Levites.*

15 After this, they may go into the Tabernacle to do their work, because you
have purified them and presented them as a special offering.
16 "Of all the people of Israel, the Levites are reserved for me. I have claimed
them for myself in place of all the firstborn sons of the Israelites; I have
taken the Levites as their substitutes. 17 For all the firstborn males among the
people of Israel are mine, both of people and of animals. I set them apart for
myself on the day I struck down all the firstborn sons of the Egyptians. 18 Yes,
I have claimed the Levites in place of all the firstborn sons of Israel. 19 And
of all the Israelites, I have assigned the Levites to Aaron and his sons. They
will serve in the Tabernacle on behalf of the Israelites and make sacrifices
to purify* the people so no plague will strike them when they approach the
sanctuary."
20 So Moses, Aaron, and the whole community of Israel dedicated the Le-
vites, carefully following all the LORD's instructions to Moses. 21 The Levites
purified themselves from sin and washed their clothes, and Aaron lifted
them up and presented them to the LORD as a special offering. He then of-
fered a sacrifice to purify them and make them right with the LORD.* 22 After
that the Levites went into the Tabernacle to perform their duties, assisting
Aaron and his sons. So they carried out all the commands that the LORD gave
Moses concerning the Levites.
23 The LORD also instructed Moses, 24 "This is the rule the Levites must
follow: They must begin serving in the Tabernacle at the age of twenty-five,
25 and they must retire at the age of fifty. 26 After retirement they may assist
their fellow Levites by serving as guards at the Tabernacle, but they may not
officiate in the service. This is how you must assign duties to the Levites."

The Second Passover

9 A year after Israel's departure from Egypt, the LORD spoke to Moses in
the wilderness of Sinai. In the first month* of that year he said, 2 "Tell
the Israelites to celebrate the Passover at the prescribed time, 3 at twilight
on the fourteenth day of the first month.* Be sure to follow all my decrees
and regulations concerning this celebration."
4 So Moses told the people to celebrate the Passover 5 in the wilderness of
Sinai as twilight fell on the fourteenth day of the month. And they celebrated
the festival there, just as the LORD had commanded Moses. 6 But some of the
men had been ceremonially defiled by touching a dead body, so they could
not celebrate the Passover that day. They came to Moses and Aaron that day
7 and said, "We have become ceremonially unclean by touching a dead body.
But why should we be prevented from presenting the LORD's offering at the
proper time with the rest of the Israelites?"
8 Moses answered, "Wait here until I have received instructions for you
from the LORD."
9 This was the LORD's reply to Moses. 10 "Give the following instructions
to the people of Israel: If any of the people now or in future generations are
ceremonially unclean at Passover time because of touching a dead body, or if
they are on a journey and cannot be present at the ceremony, they may still
celebrate the LORD's Passover. 11 They must offer the Passover sacrifice one

8:19 Or *make atonement for.* **8:21** Or *then made atonement for them to purify them.* **9:1** The first month of the ancient Hebrew lunar calendar usually occurs within the months of March and April. **9:3** This day in the ancient Hebrew lunar calendar occurred in late March, April, or early May.

Prayer **9:23**

Lord, let this be reflective of me. Let me be so flexible with my priorities and commitments that I could follow you wherever and whenever you choose to lead me. Amen.

month later, at twilight on the fourteenth day of the second month.* They must eat the Passover lamb at that time with bitter salad greens and bread made without yeast. 12 They must not leave any of the lamb until the next morning, and they must not break any of its bones. They must follow all the normal regulations concerning the Passover.

13 "But those who neglect to celebrate the Passover at the regular time, even though they are ceremonially clean and not away on a trip, will be cut off from the community of Israel. If they fail to present the LORD's offering at the proper time, they will suffer the consequences of their guilt. 14 And if foreigners living among you want to celebrate the Passover to the LORD, they must follow these same decrees and regulations. The same laws apply both to native-born Israelites and to the foreigners living among you."

The Fiery Cloud

15 On the day the Tabernacle was set up, the cloud covered it.* But from evening until morning the cloud over the Tabernacle looked like a pillar of fire. 16 This was the regular pattern—at night the cloud that covered the Tabernacle had the appearance of fire. 17 Whenever the cloud lifted from over the sacred tent, the people of Israel would break camp and follow it. And wherever the cloud settled, the people of Israel would set up camp. 18 In this way, they traveled and camped at the LORD's command wherever he told them to go. Then they remained in their camp as long as the cloud stayed over the Tabernacle. 19 If the cloud remained over the Tabernacle for a long time, the Israelites stayed and performed their duty to the LORD. 20 Sometimes the cloud would stay over the Tabernacle for only a few days, so the people would stay for only a few days, as the LORD commanded. Then at the LORD's command they would break camp and move on. 21 Sometimes the cloud stayed only overnight and lifted the next morning. But day or night, when the cloud lifted, the people broke camp and moved on. 22 Whether the cloud stayed above the Tabernacle for two days, a month, or a year, the people of Israel stayed in camp and did not move on. But as soon as it lifted, they broke camp and moved on. 23 So they camped or traveled at the LORD's command, and they did whatever the LORD told them through Moses.

The Silver Trumpets

10 Now the LORD said to Moses, 2 "Make two trumpets of hammered silver for calling the community to assemble and for signaling the breaking of camp. 3 When both trumpets are blown, everyone must gather before you at the entrance of the Tabernacle.* 4 But if only one trumpet is blown, then only the leaders—the heads of the clans of Israel—must present themselves to you.

5 "When you sound the signal to move on, the tribes camped on the east side of the Tabernacle must break camp and move forward. 6 When you sound the signal a second time, the tribes camped on the south will follow. You must sound short blasts as the signal for moving on. 7 But when you call the people to an assembly, blow the trumpets with a different signal. 8 Only the priests, Aaron's descendants, are allowed to blow the trumpets. This is a permanent law for you, to be observed from generation to generation.

9 "When you arrive in your own land and go to war against your enemies

9:11 This day in the ancient Hebrew lunar calendar occurred in late April, May, or early June.
9:15 Hebrew *covered the Tabernacle, the Tent of the Testimony.* **10:3** Hebrew *Tent of Meeting.*

who attack you, sound the alarm with the trumpets. Then the LORD your
God will remember you and rescue you from your enemies. 10 Blow the trum-
pets in times of gladness, too, sounding them at your annual festivals and
at the beginning of each month. And blow the trumpets over your burnt
offerings and peace offerings. The trumpets will remind your God of his
covenant with you. I am the LORD your God."

The Israelites Leave Sinai

11 In the second year after Israel's departure from Egypt—on the twentieth
day of the second month*—the cloud lifted from the Tabernacle of the Cov-
enant.* 12 So the Israelites set out from the wilderness of Sinai and traveled
on from place to place until the cloud stopped in the wilderness of Paran.

13 When the people set out for the first time, following the instructions
the LORD had given through Moses, 14 Judah's troops led the way. They
marched behind their banner, and their leader was Nahshon son of Am-
minadab. 15 They were joined by the troops of the tribe of Issachar, led by
Nethanel son of Zuar, 16 and the troops of the tribe of Zebulun, led by Eliab
son of Helon.

17 Then the Tabernacle was taken down, and the Gershonite and Merarite
divisions of the Levites were next in the line of march, carrying the Taber-
nacle with them. 18 Reuben's troops went next, marching behind their ban-
ner. Their leader was Elizur son of Shedeur. 19 They were joined by the troops
of the tribe of Simeon, led by Shelumiel son of Zurishaddai, 20 and the troops
of the tribe of Gad, led by Eliasaph son of Deuel.

21 Next came the Kohathite division of the Levites, carrying the sacred
objects from the Tabernacle. Before they arrived at the next camp, the Tab-
ernacle would already be set up at its new location. 22 Ephraim's troops went
next, marching behind their banner. Their leader was Elishama son of Am-
mihud. 23 They were joined by the troops of the tribe of Manasseh, led by
Gamaliel son of Pedahzur, 24 and the troops of the tribe of Benjamin, led by
Abidan son of Gideoni.

25 Dan's troops went last, marching behind their banner and serving as
the rear guard for all the tribal camps. Their leader was Ahiezer son of Am-
mishaddai. 26 They were joined by the troops of the tribe of Asher, led by
Pagiel son of Ocran, 27 and the troops of the tribe of Naphtali, led by Ahira
son of Enan.

28 This was the order in which the Israelites marched, division by division.

29 One day Moses said to his brother-in-law, Hobab son of Reuel the Mid-
ianite, "We are on our way to the place the LORD promised us, for he said,
'I will give it to you.' Come with us and we will treat you well, for the LORD
has promised wonderful blessings for Israel!"

30 But Hobab replied, "No, I will not go. I must return to my own land
and family."

31 "Please don't leave us," Moses pleaded. "You know the places in the
wilderness where we should camp. Come, be our guide. 32 If you do, we'll
share with you all the blessings the LORD gives us."

33 They marched for three days after leaving the mountain of the LORD,
with the Ark of the LORD's Covenant moving ahead of them to show them
where to stop and rest. 34 As they moved on each day, the cloud of the LORD

10:11a This day in the ancient Hebrew lunar calendar occurred in late April, May, or early June. 10:11b Or *Tabernacle of the Testimony.*

Make a Difference

11:1–14

Heart Murmur

A heart murmur is the sound of blood flowing through the heart valves abnormally. Instead of the normal heartbeat, the heart makes a murmuring noise because something has become turbulent within it.

The people of Israel had developed a sort of heart murmur in their relationship with God. Life was difficult. They hadn't eaten well. Food was scarce. They thought about the melons and onions and cucumbers they had eaten in Egypt, and their hearts began to desire them, their mouths salivating. They were tired of constantly traveling. They were nervous about the future. They were hurt by their past. They had some issues.

Even so, God had done so much for them. Why were the people so prone to complain? God provided them rescue from slavery, water in the desert, miracles all around, and one of the most compelling heroes in all of history—Moses. It's remarkable that even though the people had received so much from God, they wouldn't stop complaining. They were "murmuring" about their hardship.

Difference Maker

Listen to the rhythm of your own heart and consider whether you are in rhythm with the Lord. Spend some time praying about the condition of your heart with God.

Question **11:13**

Look at Luke 9:10-17. How is this moment in the book of Numbers similar to the disciples' questioning how Jesus would feed the crowd of over five thousand people? What does Jesus

hovered over them. 35 And whenever the Ark set out, Moses would shout,
"Arise, O LORD, and let your enemies be scattered! Let them flee before you!"
36 And when the Ark was set down, he would say, "Return, O LORD, to the
countless thousands of Israel!"

The People Complain to Moses

11 Soon the people began to complain about their hardship, and the
LORD heard everything they said. Then the LORD's anger blazed
against them, and he sent a fire to rage among them, and he destroyed some
of the people in the outskirts of the camp. 2 Then the people screamed to
Moses for help, and when he prayed to the LORD, the fire stopped. 3 After
that, the area was known as Taberah (which means "the place of burning"),
because fire from the LORD had burned among them there.
4 Then the foreign rabble who were traveling with the Israelites began
to crave the good things of Egypt. And the people of Israel also began to
complain. "Oh, for some meat!" they exclaimed. 5 "We remember the fish we
used to eat for free in Egypt. And we had all the cucumbers, melons, leeks,
onions, and garlic we wanted. 6 But now our appetites are gone. All we ever
see is this manna!"
7 The manna looked like small coriander seeds, and it was pale yellow like
gum resin. 8 The people would go out and gather it from the ground. They
made flour by grinding it with hand mills or pounding it in mortars. Then
they boiled it in a pot and made it into flat cakes. These cakes tasted like
pastries baked with olive oil. 9 The manna came down on the camp with the
dew during the night.
10 Moses heard all the families standing in the doorways of their tents
whining, and the LORD became extremely angry. Moses was also very aggra-
vated. 11 And Moses said to the LORD, "Why are you treating me, your servant,
so harshly? Have mercy on me! What did I do to deserve the burden of all
these people? 12 Did I give birth to them? Did I bring them into the world?
Why did you tell me to carry them in my arms like a mother carries a nursing
baby? How can I carry them to the land you swore to give their ancestors?
13 Where am I supposed to get meat for all these people? They keep whining
to me, saying, 'Give us meat to eat!' 14 I can't carry all these people by myself!
The load is far too heavy! 15 If this is how you intend to treat me, just go ahead
and kill me. Do me a favor and spare me this misery!"

Moses Chooses Seventy Leaders

16 Then the LORD said to Moses, "Gather before me seventy men who are
recognized as elders and leaders of Israel. Bring them to the Tabernacle* to
stand there with you. 17 I will come down and talk to you there. I will take
some of the Spirit that is upon you, and I will put the Spirit upon them also.
They will bear the burden of the people along with you, so you will not have
to carry it alone.
18 "And say to the people, 'Purify yourselves, for tomorrow you will have
meat to eat. You were whining, and the LORD heard you when you cried,
"Oh, for some meat! We were better off in Egypt!" Now the LORD will give
you meat, and you will have to eat it. 19 And it won't be for just a day or two,
or for five or ten or even twenty. 20 You will eat it for a whole month until you

11:16 Hebrew *the Tent of Meeting.*

gag and are sick of it. For you have rejected the LORD, who is here among you, and you have whined to him, saying, "Why did we ever leave Egypt?"'"

21 But Moses responded to the LORD, "There are 600,000 foot soldiers here with me, and yet you say, 'I will give them meat for a whole month!' 22 Even if we butchered all our flocks and herds, would that satisfy them? Even if we caught all the fish in the sea, would that be enough?"

23 Then the LORD said to Moses, "Has my arm lost its power? Now you will see whether or not my word comes true!"

24 So Moses went out and reported the LORD's words to the people. He gathered the seventy elders and stationed them around the Tabernacle.* 25 And the LORD came down in the cloud and spoke to Moses. Then he gave the seventy elders the same Spirit that was upon Moses. And when the Spirit rested upon them, they prophesied. But this never happened again.

26 Two men, Eldad and Medad, had stayed behind in the camp. They were listed among the elders, but they had not gone out to the Tabernacle. Yet the Spirit rested upon them as well, so they prophesied there in the camp. 27 A young man ran and reported to Moses, "Eldad and Medad are prophesying in the camp!"

28 Joshua son of Nun, who had been Moses' assistant since his youth, protested, "Moses, my master, make them stop!"

29 But Moses replied, "Are you jealous for my sake? I wish that all the LORD's people were prophets and that the LORD would put his Spirit upon them all!" 30 Then Moses returned to the camp with the elders of Israel.

The LORD Sends Quail

31 Now the LORD sent a wind that brought quail from the sea and let them fall all around the camp. For miles in every direction there were quail flying about three feet above the ground.* 32 So the people went out and caught quail all that day and throughout the night and all the next day, too. No one gathered less than fifty bushels*! They spread the quail all around the camp to dry. 33 But while they were gorging themselves on the meat—while it was still in their mouths—the anger of the LORD blazed against the people, and he struck them with a severe plague. 34 So that place was called Kibroth-hattaavah (which means "graves of gluttony") because there they buried the people who had craved meat from Egypt. 35 From Kibroth-hattaavah the Israelites traveled to Hazeroth, where they stayed for some time.

The Complaints of Miriam and Aaron

12 While they were at Hazeroth, Miriam and Aaron criticized Moses because he had married a Cushite woman. 2 They said, "Has the LORD spoken only through Moses? Hasn't he spoken through us, too?" But the LORD heard them. 3 (Now Moses was very humble—more humble than any other person on earth.)

4 So immediately the LORD called to Moses, Aaron, and Miriam and said, "Go out to the Tabernacle,* all three of you!" So the three of them went to the Tabernacle. 5 Then the LORD descended in the pillar of cloud and stood at the entrance of the Tabernacle.* "Aaron and Miriam!" he called, and they stepped forward. 6 And the LORD said to them, "Now listen to what I say:

11:24 Hebrew *the tent;* also in 11:26. **11:31** Or *there were quail about 3 feet* [2 cubits or 92 centimeters] *deep on the ground.* **11:32** Hebrew *10 homers* [2.2 kiloliters]. **12:4** Hebrew *the Tent of Meeting.* **12:5** Hebrew *the tent;* also in 12:10.

hope you will notice about his identity through this comparison?

Prayer **11:29**

Lord, give me this kind of confidence so that I will rejoice when others are filled with your Spirit. Amen.

Make a Difference **12:3**

Humble Leadership

Why should you show love to people who criticize you unfairly? You should because that's what Jesus would have done. In fact, it's what he did. There were days when he was exhausted, exasperated, fed up, weary, lonely, and upset, but he still kept serving. There were days when people ridiculed him and defamed his name. Still, he didn't give up being humble and gentle and patient and forgiving because of his intense love for people.

In this passage, Moses practiced a remarkable humility. Even as those closest to him criticized him, he presented a resilience. He reflected Ephesians 4:2, which says, "Always be humble and gentle. Be patient with each other, making allowance for each other's faults because of your love." Notice that because of Moses' humble attitude, the Lord himself ended up advocating for him.

Difference Maker

Think of somebody you struggle to get along with and take even the smallest of steps toward extending this person a loving attitude today.

Prayer 12:8

Lord, please give me even just a fraction of the face-to-face relationship you had with Moses. Speak clearly to me and let me be trustworthy. Amen.

"If there were prophets among you,
I, the LORD, would reveal myself in visions.
I would speak to them in dreams.
7 But not with my servant Moses.
Of all my house, he is the one I trust.
8 I speak to him face to face,
clearly, and not in riddles!
He sees the LORD as he is.
So why were you not afraid
to criticize my servant Moses?"

9 The LORD was very angry with them, and he departed. 10 As the cloud
moved from above the Tabernacle, there stood Miriam, her skin as white as
snow from leprosy.* When Aaron saw what had happened to her, 11 he cried
out to Moses, "Oh, my master! Please don't punish us for this sin we have so
foolishly committed. 12 Don't let her be like a stillborn baby, already decayed
at birth."
13 So Moses cried out to the LORD, "O God, I beg you, please heal her!"
14 But the LORD said to Moses, "If her father had done nothing more than
spit in her face, wouldn't she be defiled for seven days? So keep her outside
the camp for seven days, and after that she may be accepted back."
15 So Miriam was kept outside the camp for seven days, and the people
waited until she was brought back before they traveled again. 16 Then they
left Hazeroth and camped in the wilderness of Paran.

Twelve Scouts Explore Canaan

13 The LORD now said to Moses, 2 "Send out men to explore the land
of Canaan, the land I am giving to the Israelites. Send one leader
from each of the twelve ancestral tribes." 3 So Moses did as the LORD com-
manded him. He sent out twelve men, all tribal leaders of Israel, from their
camp in the wilderness of Paran. 4 These were the tribes and the names of
their leaders:

	Tribe	*Leader*
	Reuben	Shammua son of Zaccur
5	Simeon	Shaphat son of Hori
6	Judah	Caleb son of Jephunneh
7	Issachar	Igal son of Joseph
8	Ephraim	Hoshea son of Nun
9	Benjamin	Palti son of Raphu
10	Zebulun	Gaddiel son of Sodi
11	Manasseh son of Joseph	Gaddi son of Susi
12	Dan	Ammiel son of Gemalli
13	Asher	Sethur son of Michael
14	Naphtali	Nahbi son of Vophsi
15	Gad	Geuel son of Maki

16 These are the names of the men Moses sent out to explore the land. (Moses
called Hoshea son of Nun by the name Joshua.)

12:10 Or *with a skin disease.* The Hebrew word used here can describe various skin diseases.

17 Moses gave the men these instructions as he sent them out to explore the
land: "Go north through the Negev into the hill country. 18 See what the land
is like, and find out whether the people living there are strong or weak, few
or many. 19 See what kind of land they live in. Is it good or bad? Do their towns
have walls, or are they unprotected like open camps? 20 Is the soil fertile or
poor? Are there many trees? Do your best to bring back samples of the crops
you see." (It happened to be the season for harvesting the first ripe grapes.)
21 So they went up and explored the land from the wilderness of Zin as far
as Rehob, near Lebo-hamath. 22 Going north, they passed through the Negev
and arrived at Hebron, where Ahiman, Sheshai, and Talmai—all descendants
of Anak—lived. (The ancient town of Hebron was founded seven years before
the Egyptian city of Zoan.) 23 When they came to the valley of Eshcol, they
cut down a branch with a single cluster of grapes so large that it took two of
them to carry it on a pole between them! They also brought back samples of
the pomegranates and figs. 24 That place was called the valley of Eshcol (which
means "cluster"), because of the cluster of grapes the Israelite men cut there.

The Scouting Report

25 After exploring the land for forty days, the men returned 26 to Moses, Aaron,
and the whole community of Israel at Kadesh in the wilderness of Paran.
They reported to the whole community what they had seen and showed
them the fruit they had taken from the land. 27 This was their report to Moses:
"We entered the land you sent us to explore, and it is indeed a bountiful
country—a land flowing with milk and honey. Here is the kind of fruit it
produces. 28 But the people living there are powerful, and their towns are
large and fortified. We even saw giants there, the descendants of Anak! 29 The
Amalekites live in the Negev, and the Hittites, Jebusites, and Amorites live
in the hill country. The Canaanites live along the coast of the Mediterranean
Sea* and along the Jordan Valley."
30 But Caleb tried to quiet the people as they stood before Moses. "Let's go
at once to take the land," he said. "We can certainly conquer it!"
31 But the other men who had explored the land with him disagreed. "We
can't go up against them! They are stronger than we are!" 32 So they spread this
bad report about the land among the Israelites: "The land we traveled through
and explored will devour anyone who goes to live there. All the people we saw
were huge. 33 We even saw giants* there, the descendants of Anak. Next to them
we felt like grasshoppers, and that's what they thought, too!"

The People Rebel

14 Then the whole community began weeping aloud, and they cried all
night. 2 Their voices rose in a great chorus of protest against Moses
and Aaron. "If only we had died in Egypt, or even here in the wilderness!"
they complained. 3 "Why is the LORD taking us to this country only to have
us die in battle? Our wives and our little ones will be carried off as plunder!
Wouldn't it be better for us to return to Egypt?" 4 Then they plotted among
themselves, "Let's choose a new leader and go back to Egypt!"
5 Then Moses and Aaron fell face down on the ground before the whole
community of Israel. 6 Two of the men who had explored the land, Joshua
son of Nun and Caleb son of Jephunneh, tore their clothing. 7 They said to

13:29 Hebrew *the sea.* 13:33 Hebrew *nephilim.*

Question 13:28

What "giant" obstacles are obscuring your ability to see what God will do in your life?

Story Arc 14:5-30

Joshua and Caleb

Joshua and Caleb offer a counternarrative to the stuck perspective of the generation around them. Instead of conforming to the trends of waning faith, they knew the Lord was with them. Therefore, there was nothing to fear.

As a result of their faith, only Joshua and Caleb were permitted to enter the holy land. God forbid everyone else over the age of twenty to enter Abraham's land (vv. 29-30). The nation of Israel had to wait forty years until God allowed them to cross the Jordan and take possession of the land. God chose to work in the next generation, with Joshua and Caleb at the helm, rather than to work through a weak, stubborn generation.

What kind of resilience does it take to stand against the trends of weak faith?

Num 18:1-32 ►

all the people of Israel, "The land we traveled through and explored is a
wonderful land! 8And if the LORD is pleased with us, he will bring us safely
into that land and give it to us. It is a rich land flowing with milk and honey.
9Do not rebel against the LORD, and don't be afraid of the people of the land.
They are only helpless prey to us! They have no protection, but the LORD is
with us! Don't be afraid of them!"

10But the whole community began to talk about stoning Joshua and Caleb.
Then the glorious presence of the LORD appeared to all the Israelites at the
Tabernacle.* 11And the LORD said to Moses, "How long will these people
treat me with contempt? Will they never believe me, even after all the mi-
raculous signs I have done among them? 12I will disown them and destroy
them with a plague. Then I will make you into a nation greater and mightier
than they are!"

Moses Intercedes for the People

13But Moses objected. "What will the Egyptians think when they hear about
it?" he asked the LORD. "They know full well the power you displayed in res-
cuing your people from Egypt. 14Now if you destroy them, the Egyptians will
send a report to the inhabitants of this land, who have already heard that you
live among your people. They know, LORD, that you have appeared to your
people face to face and that your pillar of cloud hovers over them. They know
that you go before them in the pillar of cloud by day and the pillar of fire by
night. 15Now if you slaughter all these people with a single blow, the nations
that have heard of your fame will say, 16'The LORD was not able to bring them
into the land he swore to give them, so he killed them in the wilderness.'

17"Please, Lord, prove that your power is as great as you have claimed. For
you said, 18'The LORD is slow to anger and filled with unfailing love, forgiv-
ing every kind of sin and rebellion. But he does not excuse the guilty. He lays
the sins of the parents upon their children; the entire family is affected—
even children in the third and fourth generations.' 19In keeping with your
magnificent, unfailing love, please pardon the sins of this people, just as you
have forgiven them ever since they left Egypt."

20Then the LORD said, "I will pardon them as you have requested. 21But as
surely as I live, and as surely as the earth is filled with the LORD's glory, 22not
one of these people will ever enter that land. They have all seen my glorious
presence and the miraculous signs I performed both in Egypt and in the
wilderness, but again and again they have tested me by refusing to listen to
my voice. 23They will never even see the land I swore to give their ancestors.
None of those who have treated me with contempt will ever see it. 24But my
servant Caleb has a different attitude than the others have. He has remained
loyal to me, so I will bring him into the land he explored. His descendants
will possess their full share of that land. 25Now turn around, and don't go on
toward the land where the Amalekites and Canaanites live. Tomorrow you
must set out for the wilderness in the direction of the Red Sea.*"

The LORD Punishes the Israelites

26Then the LORD said to Moses and Aaron, 27"How long must I put up with
this wicked community and its complaints about me? Yes, I have heard the
complaints the Israelites are making against me. 28Now tell them this: 'As

14:10 Hebrew *the Tent of Meeting.* **14:25** Hebrew *sea of reeds.*

surely as I live, declares the LORD, I will do to you the very things I heard
you say. 29 You will all drop dead in this wilderness! Because you complained
against me, every one of you who is twenty years old or older and was in-
cluded in the registration will die. 30 You will not enter and occupy the land
I swore to give you. The only exceptions will be Caleb son of Jephunneh and
Joshua son of Nun.

31 "'You said your children would be carried off as plunder. Well, I will
bring them safely into the land, and they will enjoy what you have despised.
32 But as for you, you will drop dead in this wilderness. 33 And your children
will be like shepherds, wandering in the wilderness for forty years. In this
way, they will pay for your faithlessness, until the last of you lies dead in
the wilderness.

34 "'Because your men explored the land for forty days, you must wander
in the wilderness for forty years—a year for each day, suffering the conse-
quences of your sins. Then you will discover what it is like to have me for an
enemy.' 35 I, the LORD, have spoken! I will certainly do these things to every
member of the community who has conspired against me. They will be de-
stroyed here in this wilderness, and here they will die!"

36 The ten men Moses had sent to explore the land—the ones who incited
rebellion against the LORD with their bad report—37 were struck dead with
a plague before the LORD. 38 Of the twelve who had explored the land, only
Joshua and Caleb remained alive.

39 When Moses reported the LORD's words to all the Israelites, the people
were filled with grief. 40 Then they got up early the next morning and went
to the top of the range of hills. "Let's go," they said. "We realize that we have
sinned, but now we are ready to enter the land the LORD has promised us."

41 But Moses said, "Why are you now disobeying the LORD's orders to re-
turn to the wilderness? It won't work. 42 Do not go up into the land now.
You will only be crushed by your enemies because the LORD is not with you.
43 When you face the Amalekites and Canaanites in battle, you will be slaugh-
tered. The LORD will abandon you because you have abandoned the LORD."

44 But the people defiantly pushed ahead toward the hill country, even
though neither Moses nor the Ark of the LORD's Covenant left the camp.
45 Then the Amalekites and the Canaanites who lived in those hills came
down and attacked them and chased them back as far as Hormah.

Laws concerning Offerings

15 Then the LORD told Moses, 2 "Give the following instructions to the
people of Israel.

"When you finally settle in the land I am giving you, 3 you will offer spe-
cial gifts as a pleasing aroma to the LORD. These gifts may take the form
of a burnt offering, a sacrifice to fulfill a vow, a voluntary offering, or an
offering at any of your annual festivals, and they may be taken from your
herds of cattle or your flocks of sheep and goats. 4 When you present these
offerings, you must also give the LORD a grain offering of two quarts* of
choice flour mixed with one quart* of olive oil. 5 For each lamb offered as a
burnt offering or a special sacrifice, you must also present one quart of wine
as a liquid offering.

6 "If the sacrifice is a ram, give a grain offering of four quarts* of choice

15:4a Hebrew *1/10 of an ephah* [2.2 liters]. **15:4b** Hebrew *1/4 of a hin* [1 liter]; also in 15:5.
15:6a Hebrew *2/10 of an ephah* [4.4 liters].

What I will do next

flour mixed with a third of a gallon* of olive oil, 7 and give a third of a gal-
lon of wine as a liquid offering. This will be a pleasing aroma to the LORD.
8 "When you present a young bull as a burnt offering or as a sacrifice to
fulfill a vow or as a peace offering to the LORD, 9 you must also give a grain
offering of six quarts* of choice flour mixed with two quarts* of olive oil,
10 and give two quarts of wine as a liquid offering. This will be a special gift,
a pleasing aroma to the LORD.
11 "Each sacrifice of a bull, ram, lamb, or young goat should be prepared
in this way. 12 Follow these instructions with each offering you present. 13 All
of you native-born Israelites must follow these instructions when you offer
a special gift as a pleasing aroma to the LORD. 14 And if any foreigners visit
you or live among you and want to present a special gift as a pleasing aroma
to the LORD, they must follow these same procedures. 15 Native-born Isra-
elites and foreigners are equal before the LORD and are subject to the same
decrees. This is a permanent law for you, to be observed from generation to
generation. 16 The same instructions and regulations will apply both to you
and to the foreigners living among you."
17 Then the LORD said to Moses, 18 "Give the following instructions to the
people of Israel.
"When you arrive in the land where I am taking you, 19 and you eat the
crops that grow there, you must set some aside as a sacred offering to the
LORD. 20 Present a cake from the first of the flour you grind, and set it aside
as a sacred offering, as you do with the first grain from the threshing floor.
21 Throughout the generations to come, you are to present a sacred offering
to the LORD each year from the first of your ground flour.
22 "But suppose you unintentionally fail to carry out all these commands
that the LORD has given you through Moses. 23 And suppose your descen-
dants in the future fail to do everything the LORD has commanded through
Moses. 24 If the mistake was made unintentionally, and the community was
unaware of it, the whole community must present a young bull for a burnt
offering as a pleasing aroma to the LORD. It must be offered along with its
prescribed grain offering and liquid offering and with one male goat for a
sin offering. 25 With it the priest will purify the whole community of Israel,
making them right with the LORD,* and they will be forgiven. For it was
an unintentional sin, and they have corrected it with their offerings to the
LORD—the special gift and the sin offering. 26 The whole community of Is-
rael will be forgiven, including the foreigners living among you, for all the
people were involved in the sin.
27 "If one individual commits an unintentional sin, the guilty person must
bring a one-year-old female goat for a sin offering. 28 The priest will sacrifice
it to purify* the guilty person before the LORD, and that person will be for-
given. 29 These same instructions apply both to native-born Israelites and to
the foreigners living among you.
30 "But those who brazenly violate the LORD's will, whether native-born
Israelites or foreigners, have blasphemed the LORD, and they must be cut
off from the community. 31 Since they have treated the LORD's word with
contempt and deliberately disobeyed his command, they must be completely
cut off and suffer the punishment for their guilt."

15:6b Hebrew *1/3 of a hin* [1.3 liters]; also in 15:7. **15:9a** Hebrew *3/10 of an ephah* [6.6 liters]. **15:9b** Hebrew *1/2 of a hin* [2 liters]; also in 15:10. **15:25** Or *will make atonement for the whole community of Israel.* **15:28** Or *to make atonement for.*

Penalty for Breaking the Sabbath
32 One day while the people of Israel were in the wilderness, they discovered
a man gathering wood on the Sabbath day. 33 The people who found him
doing this took him before Moses, Aaron, and the rest of the community.
34 They held him in custody because they did not know what to do with him.
35 Then the LORD said to Moses, "The man must be put to death! The whole
community must stone him outside the camp." 36 So the whole community
took the man outside the camp and stoned him to death, just as the LORD
had commanded Moses.

Question 15:40

The tassels seem like a strange command here. What is the point of these tassels? What difference were they supposed to make? What kind of reminders can you set for yourself to help you grow in your walk with the Lord?

Tassels on Clothing
37 Then the LORD said to Moses, 38 "Give the following instructions to the
people of Israel: Throughout the generations to come you must make tassels
for the hems of your clothing and attach them with a blue cord. 39 When you
see the tassels, you will remember and obey all the commands of the LORD in-
stead of following your own desires and defiling yourselves, as you are prone
to do. 40 The tassels will help you remember that you must obey all my com-
mands and be holy to your God. 41 I am the LORD your God who brought you
out of the land of Egypt that I might be your God. I am the LORD your God!"

Korah's Rebellion
16 One day Korah son of Izhar, a descendant of Kohath son of Levi,
conspired with Dathan and Abiram, the sons of Eliab, and On son
of Peleth, from the tribe of Reuben. 2 They incited a rebellion against Moses,
along with 250 other leaders of the community, all prominent members of
the assembly. 3 They united against Moses and Aaron and said, "You have
gone too far! The whole community of Israel has been set apart by the LORD,
and he is with all of us. What right do you have to act as though you are
greater than the rest of the LORD's people?"
4 When Moses heard what they were saying, he fell face down on the
ground. 5 Then he said to Korah and his followers, "Tomorrow morning the
LORD will show us who belongs to him* and who is holy. The LORD will allow
only those whom he selects to enter his own presence. 6 Korah, you and all
your followers must prepare your incense burners. 7 Light fires in them to-
morrow, and burn incense before the LORD. Then we will see whom the LORD
chooses as his holy one. You Levites are the ones who have gone too far!"
8 Then Moses spoke again to Korah: "Now listen, you Levites! 9 Does it
seem insignificant to you that the God of Israel has chosen you from among
all the community of Israel to be near him so you can serve in the LORD's
Tabernacle and stand before the people to minister to them? 10 Korah, he
has already given this special ministry to you and your fellow Levites. Are
you now demanding the priesthood as well? 11 The LORD is the one you and
your followers are really revolting against! For who is Aaron that you are
complaining about him?"
12 Then Moses summoned Dathan and Abiram, the sons of Eliab, but they
replied, "We refuse to come before you! 13 Isn't it enough that you brought
us out of Egypt, a land flowing with milk and honey, to kill us here in this
wilderness, and that you now treat us like your subjects? 14 What's more,
you haven't brought us into another land flowing with milk and honey. You

16:5 Greek version reads *God has visited and knows those who are his.* Compare 2 Tim 2:19.

haven't given us a new homeland with fields and vineyards. Are you trying
to fool these men?* We will not come."

15 Then Moses became very angry and said to the LORD, "Do not accept
their grain offerings! I have not taken so much as a donkey from them, and
I have never hurt a single one of them." 16 And Moses said to Korah, "You and
all your followers must come here tomorrow and present yourselves before
the LORD. Aaron will also be here. 17 You and each of your 250 followers must
prepare an incense burner and put incense on it, so you can all present them
before the LORD. Aaron will also bring his incense burner."

18 So each of these men prepared an incense burner, lit the fire, and placed
incense on it. Then they all stood at the entrance of the Tabernacle* with
Moses and Aaron. 19 Meanwhile, Korah had stirred up the entire community
against Moses and Aaron, and they all gathered at the Tabernacle entrance.
Then the glorious presence of the LORD appeared to the whole community,
20 and the LORD said to Moses and Aaron, 21 "Get away from all these people
so that I may instantly destroy them!"

22 But Moses and Aaron fell face down on the ground. "O God," they
pleaded, "you are the God who gives breath to all creatures. Must you be
angry with all the people when only one man sins?"

23 And the LORD said to Moses, 24 "Then tell all the people to get away from
the tents of Korah, Dathan, and Abiram."

25 So Moses got up and rushed over to the tents of Dathan and Abiram,
followed by the elders of Israel. 26 "Quick!" he told the people. "Get away
from the tents of these wicked men, and don't touch anything that belongs
to them. If you do, you will be destroyed for their sins." 27 So all the people
stood back from the tents of Korah, Dathan, and Abiram. Then Dathan and
Abiram came out and stood at the entrances of their tents, together with
their wives and children and little ones.

28 And Moses said, "This is how you will know that the LORD has sent me
to do all these things that I have done—for I have not done them on my own.
29 If these men die a natural death, or if nothing unusual happens, then the
LORD has not sent me. 30 But if the LORD does something entirely new and
the ground opens its mouth and swallows them and all their belongings,
and they go down alive into the grave,* then you will know that these men
have shown contempt for the LORD."

31 He had hardly finished speaking the words when the ground suddenly
split open beneath them. 32 The earth opened its mouth and swallowed the
men, along with their households and all their followers who were standing
with them, and everything they owned. 33 So they went down alive into the
grave, along with all their belongings. The earth closed over them, and they
all vanished from among the people of Israel. 34 All the people around them
fled when they heard their screams. "The earth will swallow us, too!" they
cried. 35 Then fire blazed forth from the LORD and burned up the 250 men
who were offering incense.

36* And the LORD said to Moses, 37 "Tell Eleazar son of Aaron the priest
to pull all the incense burners from the fire, for they are holy. Also tell him
to scatter the burning coals. 38 Take the incense burners of these men who
have sinned at the cost of their lives, and hammer the metal into a thin sheet

16:14 Hebrew *Are you trying to put out the eyes of these men?* **16:18** Hebrew *the Tent of Meeting;* also in 16:19, 42, 43, 50. **16:30** Hebrew *into Sheol;* also in 16:33. **16:36** Verses 16:36-50 are numbered 17:1-15 in Hebrew text.

> **Question** 16:48
>
> How does Jesus do for us eternally what Aaron does for the people in this moment?

to overlay the altar. Since these burners were used in the LORD's presence,
they have become holy. Let them serve as a warning to the people of Israel."
39 So Eleazar the priest collected the 250 bronze incense burners that had
been used by the men who died in the fire, and the bronze was hammered
into a thin sheet to overlay the altar. 40 This would warn the Israelites that no
unauthorized person—no one who was not a descendant of Aaron—should
ever enter the LORD's presence to burn incense. If anyone did, the same thing
would happen to him as happened to Korah and his followers. So the LORD's
instructions to Moses were carried out.

41 But the very next morning the whole community of Israel began mut-
tering again against Moses and Aaron, saying, "You have killed the LORD's
people!" 42 As the community gathered to protest against Moses and Aaron,
they turned toward the Tabernacle and saw that the cloud had covered it,
and the glorious presence of the LORD appeared.

43 Moses and Aaron came and stood in front of the Tabernacle, 44 and the
LORD said to Moses, 45 "Get away from all these people so that I can instantly
destroy them!" But Moses and Aaron fell face down on the ground.

46 And Moses said to Aaron, "Quick, take an incense burner and place burn-
ing coals on it from the altar. Lay incense on it, and carry it out among the
people to purify them and make them right with the LORD.* The LORD's
anger is blazing against them—the plague has already begun."

47 Aaron did as Moses told him and ran out among the people. The plague
had already begun to strike down the people, but Aaron burned the incense
and purified* the people. 48 He stood between the dead and the living, and
the plague stopped. 49 But 14,700 people died in that plague, in addition to
those who had died in the affair involving Korah. 50 Then because the plague
had stopped, Aaron returned to Moses at the entrance of the Tabernacle.

The Budding of Aaron's Staff

17 1* Then the LORD said to Moses, 2 "Tell the people of Israel to bring
you twelve wooden staffs, one from each leader of Israel's ancestral
tribes, and inscribe each leader's name on his staff. 3 Inscribe Aaron's name
on the staff of the tribe of Levi, for there must be one staff for the leader of
each ancestral tribe. 4 Place these staffs in the Tabernacle in front of the Ark
containing the tablets of the Covenant,* where I meet with you. 5 Buds will
sprout on the staff belonging to the man I choose. Then I will finally put an
end to the people's murmuring and complaining against you."

6 So Moses gave the instructions to the people of Israel, and each of the
twelve tribal leaders, including Aaron, brought Moses a staff. 7 Moses placed
the staffs in the LORD's presence in the Tabernacle of the Covenant.* 8 When
he went into the Tabernacle of the Covenant the next day, he found that
Aaron's staff, representing the tribe of Levi, had sprouted, budded, blos-
somed, and produced ripe almonds!

9 When Moses brought all the staffs out from the LORD's presence, he showed
them to the people. Each man claimed his own staff. 10 And the LORD said to
Moses: "Place Aaron's staff permanently before the Ark of the Covenant*
to serve as a warning to rebels. This should put an end to their complaints

16:46 Or *to make atonement for them.* **16:47** Or *and made atonement for.* **17:1** Verses 17:1-13 are numbered 17:16-28 in Hebrew text. **17:4** Hebrew *in the Tent of Meeting before the Testimony.* The Hebrew word for "testimony" refers to the terms of the LORD's covenant with Israel as written on stone tablets, which were kept in the Ark, and also to the covenant itself. **17:7** Or *Tabernacle of the Testimony;* also in 17:8. **17:10** Hebrew *before the Testimony;* see note on 17:4.

against me and prevent any further deaths." 11 So Moses did as the LORD com-
manded him.
12 Then the people of Israel said to Moses, "Look, we are doomed! We are
dead! We are ruined! 13 Everyone who even comes close to the Tabernacle of
the LORD dies. Are we all doomed to die?"

Duties of Priests and Levites

18 Then the LORD said to Aaron: "You, your sons, and your relatives
from the tribe of Levi will be held responsible for any offenses related
to the sanctuary. But you and your sons alone will be held responsible for
violations connected with the priesthood.
2 "Bring your relatives of the tribe of Levi—your ancestral tribe—to assist
you and your sons as you perform the sacred duties in front of the Tabernacle
of the Covenant.* 3 But as the Levites go about all their assigned duties at the
Tabernacle, they must be careful not to go near any of the sacred objects or
the altar. If they do, both you and they will die. 4 The Levites must join you
in fulfilling their responsibilities for the care and maintenance of the Tab-
ernacle,* but no unauthorized person may assist you.
5 "You yourselves must perform the sacred duties inside the sanctuary
and at the altar. If you follow these instructions, the LORD's anger will never
again blaze against the people of Israel. 6 I myself have chosen your fellow
Levites from among the Israelites to be your special assistants. They are a gift
to you, dedicated to the LORD for service in the Tabernacle. 7 But you and your
sons, the priests, must personally handle all the priestly rituals associated
with the altar and with everything behind the inner curtain. I am giving you
the priesthood as your special privilege of service. Any unauthorized person
who comes too near the sanctuary will be put to death."

Support for the Priests and Levites

8 The LORD gave these further instructions to Aaron: "I myself have put you
in charge of all the holy offerings that are brought to me by the people of Is-
rael. I have given all these consecrated offerings to you and your sons as your
permanent share. 9 You are allotted the portion of the most holy offerings
that is not burned on the fire. This portion of all the most holy offerings—
including the grain offerings, sin offerings, and guilt offerings—will be
most holy, and it belongs to you and your sons. 10 You must eat it as a most
holy offering. All the males may eat of it, and you must treat it as most holy.
11 "All the sacred offerings and special offerings presented to me when
the Israelites lift them up before the altar also belong to you. I have given
them to you and to your sons and daughters as your permanent share. Any
member of your family who is ceremonially clean may eat of these offerings.
12 "I also give you the harvest gifts brought by the people as offerings to the
LORD—the best of the olive oil, new wine, and grain. 13 All the first crops of
their land that the people present to the LORD belong to you. Any member
of your family who is ceremonially clean may eat this food.
14 "Everything in Israel that is specially set apart for the LORD* also be-
longs to you.
15 "The firstborn of every mother, whether human or animal, that is offered

Story Arc **18:1-32**

● Aaron

Aaron and his family were set aside to serve as a priesthood for Israel. Their role was a special privilege of service. They had the serious responsibility of representing the Lord to the people and representing the people to the Lord. They were to follow the Lord's commands meticulously so that they could present offerings and teach God's law without blame.

What challenges would you have if you were asked to be a part of this priesthood? How would you respond if the Lord told you that, because of Jesus, you are part of a kingdom of priests? (See Revelation 1:6.)

Num 21:4-9 ►

18:2 Or *Tabernacle of the Testimony.* 18:4 Hebrew *the Tent of Meeting;* also in 18:6, 21, 22, 23, 31. 18:14 The Hebrew term used here refers to the complete consecration of things or people to the LORD, either by destroying them or by giving them as an offering.

to the LORD will be yours. But you must always redeem your firstborn sons
and the firstborn of ceremonially unclean animals. 16 Redeem them when they
are one month old. The redemption price is five pieces of silver* (as measured
by the weight of the sanctuary shekel, which equals twenty gerahs).
17 "However, you may not redeem the firstborn of cattle, sheep, or goats.
They are holy and have been set apart for the LORD. Sprinkle their blood on
the altar, and burn their fat as a special gift, a pleasing aroma to the LORD.
18 The meat of these animals will be yours, just like the breast and right thigh
that are presented by lifting them up as a special offering before the altar.
19 Yes, I am giving you all these holy offerings that the people of Israel bring to
the LORD. They are for you and your sons and daughters, to be eaten as your
permanent share. This is an eternal and unbreakable covenant* between the
LORD and you, and it also applies to your descendants."
20 And the LORD said to Aaron, "You priests will receive no allotment of
land or share of property among the people of Israel. I am your share and
your allotment. 21 As for the tribe of Levi, your relatives, I will compensate
them for their service in the Tabernacle. Instead of an allotment of land, I
will give them the tithes from the entire land of Israel.
22 "From now on, no Israelites except priests or Levites may approach the
Tabernacle. If they come too near, they will be judged guilty and will die.
23 Only the Levites may serve at the Tabernacle, and they will be held re-
sponsible for any offenses against it. This is a permanent law for you, to be
observed from generation to generation. The Levites will receive no allot-
ment of land among the Israelites, 24 because I have given them the Israelites'
tithes, which have been presented as sacred offerings to the LORD. This will
be the Levites' share. That is why I said they would receive no allotment of
land among the Israelites."
25 The LORD also told Moses, 26 "Give these instructions to the Levites:
When you receive from the people of Israel the tithes I have assigned as your
allotment, give a tenth of the tithes you receive—a tithe of the tithe—to the
LORD as a sacred offering. 27 The LORD will consider this offering to be your
harvest offering, as though it were the first grain from your own threshing
floor or wine from your own winepress. 28 You must present one-tenth of the
tithe received from the Israelites as a sacred offering to the LORD. This is the
LORD's sacred portion, and you must present it to Aaron the priest. 29 Be sure
to give to the LORD the best portions of the gifts given to you.
30 "Also, give these instructions to the Levites: When you present the best
part as your offering, it will be considered as though it came from your own
threshing floor or winepress. 31 You Levites and your families may eat this food
anywhere you wish, for it is your compensation for serving in the Tabernacle.
32 You will not be considered guilty for accepting the LORD's tithes if you give
the best portion to the priests. But be careful not to treat the holy gifts of the
people of Israel as though they were common. If you do, you will die."

The Water of Purification

19 The LORD said to Moses and Aaron, 2 "Here is another legal require-
ment commanded by the LORD: Tell the people of Israel to bring you
a red heifer, a perfect animal that has no defects and has never been yoked to
a plow. 3 Give it to Eleazar the priest, and it will be taken outside the camp

18:16 Hebrew 5 *shekels* [2 ounces or 57 grams] *of silver.* 18:19 Hebrew *a covenant of salt.*

and slaughtered in his presence. 4Eleazar will take some of its blood on his finger and sprinkle it seven times toward the front of the Tabernacle.* 5As Eleazar watches, the heifer must be burned—its hide, meat, blood, and dung. 6Eleazar the priest must then take a stick of cedar,* a hyssop branch, and some scarlet yarn and throw them into the fire where the heifer is burning.

7"Then the priest must wash his clothes and bathe himself in water. Afterward he may return to the camp, though he will remain ceremonially unclean until evening. 8The man who burns the animal must also wash his clothes and bathe himself in water, and he, too, will remain unclean until evening. 9Then someone who is ceremonially clean will gather up the ashes of the heifer and deposit them in a purified place outside the camp. They will be kept there for the community of Israel to use in the water for the purification ceremony. This ceremony is performed for the removal of sin. 10The man who gathers up the ashes of the heifer must also wash his clothes, and he will remain ceremonially unclean until evening. This is a permanent law for the people of Israel and any foreigners who live among them.

11"All those who touch a dead human body will be ceremonially unclean for seven days. 12They must purify themselves on the third and seventh days with the water of purification; then they will be purified. But if they do not do this on the third and seventh days, they will continue to be unclean even after the seventh day. 13All those who touch a dead body and do not purify themselves in the proper way defile the LORD's Tabernacle, and they will be cut off from the community of Israel. Since the water of purification was not sprinkled on them, their defilement continues.

14"This is the ritual law that applies when someone dies inside a tent: All those who enter that tent and those who were inside when the death occurred will be ceremonially unclean for seven days. 15Any open container in the tent that was not covered with a lid is also defiled. 16And if someone in an open field touches the corpse of someone who was killed with a sword or who died a natural death, or if someone touches a human bone or a grave, that person will be defiled for seven days.

17"To remove the defilement, put some of the ashes from the burnt purification offering in a jar, and pour fresh water over them. 18Then someone who is ceremonially clean must take a hyssop branch and dip it into the water. That person must sprinkle the water on the tent, on all the furnishings in the tent, and on the people who were in the tent; also on the person who touched a human bone, or touched someone who was killed or who died naturally, or touched a grave. 19On the third and seventh days the person who is ceremonially clean must sprinkle the water on those who are defiled. Then on the seventh day the people being cleansed must wash their clothes and bathe themselves, and that evening they will be cleansed of their defilement.

20"But those who become defiled and do not purify themselves will be cut off from the community, for they have defiled the sanctuary of the LORD. Since the water of purification has not been sprinkled on them, they remain defiled. 21This is a permanent law for the people. Those who sprinkle the water of purification must afterward wash their clothes, and anyone who then touches the water used for purification will remain defiled until evening. 22Anything and anyone that a defiled person touches will be ceremonially unclean until evening."

19:4 Hebrew *the Tent of Meeting.* **19:6** Or *juniper.*

Moses Strikes the Rock

20 In the first month of the year,* the whole community of Israel ar-
rived in the wilderness of Zin and camped at Kadesh. While they
were there, Miriam died and was buried.
2There was no water for the people to drink at that place, so they rebelled
against Moses and Aaron. 3The people blamed Moses and said, "If only we
had died in the LORD's presence with our brothers! 4Why have you brought
the congregation of the LORD's people into this wilderness to die, along with
all our livestock? 5Why did you make us leave Egypt and bring us here to this
terrible place? This land has no grain, no figs, no grapes, no pomegranates,
and no water to drink!"
6Moses and Aaron turned away from the people and went to the entrance
of the Tabernacle,* where they fell face down on the ground. Then the glori-
ous presence of the LORD appeared to them, 7and the LORD said to Moses,
8"You and Aaron must take the staff and assemble the entire community. As
the people watch, speak to the rock over there, and it will pour out its water.
You will provide enough water from the rock to satisfy the whole community
and their livestock."
9So Moses did as he was told. He took the staff from the place where it was
kept before the LORD. 10Then he and Aaron summoned the people to come
and gather at the rock. "Listen, you rebels!" he shouted. "Must we bring you
water from this rock?" 11Then Moses raised his hand and struck the rock
twice with the staff, and water gushed out. So the entire community and
their livestock drank their fill.
12But the LORD said to Moses and Aaron, "Because you did not trust me
enough to demonstrate my holiness to the people of Israel, you will not lead
them into the land I am giving them!" 13This place was known as the waters
of Meribah (which means "arguing") because there the people of Israel ar-
gued with the LORD, and there he demonstrated his holiness among them.

Question 20:12

Moses and Aaron got caught in a predicament in which they tried to do the right thing but with the wrong attitude. Have you ever struggled with this? Why is it sinful to do the "right" thing with an angry attitude?

Edom Refuses Israel Passage

14While Moses was at Kadesh, he sent ambassadors to the king of Edom with
this message:

"This is what your relatives, the people of Israel, say: You know all the
hardships we have been through. 15Our ancestors went down to Egypt,
and we lived there a long time, and we and our ancestors were brutally
mistreated by the Egyptians. 16But when we cried out to the LORD, he
heard us and sent an angel who brought us out of Egypt. Now we are
camped at Kadesh, a town on the border of your land. 17Please let us
travel through your land. We will be careful not to go through your
fields and vineyards. We won't even drink water from your wells. We
will stay on the king's road and never leave it until we have passed
through your territory."

18But the king of Edom said, "Stay out of my land, or I will meet you with
an army!"
19The Israelites answered, "We will stay on the main road. If our livestock

20:1 The first month of the ancient Hebrew lunar calendar usually occurs within the months of March and April. The number of years since leaving Egypt is not specified. 20:6 Hebrew *the Tent of Meeting.*

Prayer 20:26

Lord, let me be ready to take the responsibility of leadership when it is my turn. Prepare me to be ready to pass it on to the next generation when it is theirs. Amen.

Story Arc 21:4-9

● Jesus

In this wild account, the people were complaining against God and Moses. Consequently, God let poisonous snakes bite them! When the people realized their sin, they begged for mercy. At this point, God asked Moses to fashion a bronze snake and lift it up on a pole. Scripture indicates that anyone who looked to the snake that was lifted up would be healed.

Weird? Or witty? God wanted the people to take seriously their sin and the source of their mess. God also wanted the people to look up to something that represented all their sin and all their mess and to place their trust in the salvation that God provides.

It is fascinating when, fifteen hundred years later, Jesus compared himself to the snake lifted up. In John 3:14-15, Jesus indicated that anyone who looks to him as he is lifted up (on the cross) will be saved.

Num 27:12-23 ▸

drink your water, we will pay for it. Just let us pass through your country.
That's all we ask."
20 But the king of Edom replied, "Stay out! You may not pass through our
land." With that he mobilized his army and marched out against them with
an imposing force. 21 Because Edom refused to allow Israel to pass through
their country, Israel was forced to turn around.

The Death of Aaron

22 The whole community of Israel left Kadesh and arrived at Mount Hor.
23 There, on the border of the land of Edom, the LORD said to Moses and
Aaron, 24 "The time has come for Aaron to join his ancestors in death. He will
not enter the land I am giving the people of Israel, because the two of you rebelled against my instructions concerning the water at Meribah. 25 Now take
▲ Aaron and his son Eleazar up Mount Hor. 26 There you will remove Aaron's
priestly garments and put them on Eleazar, his son. Aaron will die there
and join his ancestors."
27 So Moses did as the LORD commanded. The three of them went up
Mount Hor together as the whole community watched. 28 At the summit,
Moses removed the priestly garments from Aaron and put them on Eleazar,
Aaron's son. Then Aaron died there on top of the mountain, and Moses and
Eleazar went back down. 29 When the people realized that Aaron had died,
all Israel mourned for him thirty days.

Victory over the Canaanites

21 The Canaanite king of Arad, who lived in the Negev, heard that the
Israelites were approaching on the road through Atharim. So he attacked the Israelites and took some of them as prisoners. 2 Then the people
of Israel made this vow to the LORD: "If you will hand these people over to
us, we will completely destroy* all their towns." 3 The LORD heard the Israelites' request and gave them victory over the Canaanites. The Israelites
completely destroyed them and their towns, and the place has been called
Hormah* ever since.

The Bronze Snake

4 Then the people of Israel set out from Mount Hor, taking the road to the
Red Sea* to go around the land of Edom. But the people grew impatient
with the long journey, 5 and they began to speak against God and Moses.
"Why have you brought us out of Egypt to die here in the wilderness?" they
complained. "There is nothing to eat here and nothing to drink. And we
hate this horrible manna!"
6 So the LORD sent poisonous snakes among the people, and many were
bitten and died. 7 Then the people came to Moses and cried out, "We have
sinned by speaking against the LORD and against you. Pray that the LORD
will take away the snakes." So Moses prayed for the people.
8 Then the LORD told him, "Make a replica of a poisonous snake and attach
● it to a pole. All who are bitten will live if they simply look at it!" 9 So Moses
made a snake out of bronze and attached it to a pole. Then anyone who was
bitten by a snake could look at the bronze snake and be healed!

21:2 The Hebrew term used here refers to the complete consecration of things or people to the LORD, either by destroying them or by giving them as an offering; also in 21:3. 21:3 *Hormah* means "destruction." 21:4 Hebrew *sea of reeds.*

Israel's Journey to Moab
10 The Israelites traveled next to Oboth and camped there. 11 Then they went
on to Iye-abarim, in the wilderness on the eastern border of Moab. 12 From
there they traveled to the valley of Zered Brook and set up camp. 13 Then they
moved out and camped on the far side of the Arnon River, in the wilderness
adjacent to the territory of the Amorites. The Arnon is the boundary line be-
tween the Moabites and the Amorites. 14 For this reason *The Book of the Wars of
the LORD* speaks of "the town of Waheb in the area of Suphah, and the ravines
of the Arnon River, 15 and the ravines that extend as far as the settlement of
Ar on the border of Moab."

16 From there the Israelites traveled to Beer,* which is the well where the
LORD said to Moses, "Assemble the people, and I will give them water."
17 There the Israelites sang this song:

"Spring up, O well!
  Yes, sing its praises!
18 Sing of this well,
  which princes dug,
which great leaders hollowed out
  with their scepters and staffs."

Then the Israelites left the wilderness and proceeded on through Mat-
tanah, 19 Nahaliel, and Bamoth. 20 After that they went to the valley in Moab
where Pisgah Peak overlooks the wasteland.*

Victory over Sihon and Og
21 The Israelites sent ambassadors to King Sihon of the Amorites with this
message:

22 "Let us travel through your land. We will be careful not to go through
your fields and vineyards. We won't even drink water from your wells. We
will stay on the king's road until we have passed through your territory."

23 But King Sihon refused to let them cross his territory. Instead, he mobi-
lized his entire army and attacked Israel in the wilderness, engaging them
in battle at Jahaz. 24 But the Israelites slaughtered them with their swords
and occupied their land from the Arnon River to the Jabbok River. They
went only as far as the Ammonite border because the boundary of the Am-
monites was fortified.*
25 So Israel captured all the towns of the Amorites and settled in them,
including the city of Heshbon and its surrounding villages. 26 Heshbon had
been the capital of King Sihon of the Amorites. He had defeated a former
Moabite king and seized all his land as far as the Arnon River. 27 Therefore,
the ancient poets wrote this about him:

"Come to Heshbon and let it be rebuilt!
  Let the city of Sihon be restored.
28 A fire flamed forth from Heshbon,
  a blaze from the city of Sihon.

21:16 *Beer* means "well." **21:20** Or *overlooks Jeshimon.* **21:24** Or *because the terrain of the Ammonite frontier was rugged;* Hebrew reads *because the boundary of the Ammonites was strong.*

It burned the city of Ar in Moab;
it destroyed the rulers of the Arnon heights.
29 What sorrow awaits you, O people of Moab!
You are finished, O worshipers of Chemosh!
Chemosh has left his sons as refugees,
his daughters as captives of Sihon, the Amorite king.
30 We have utterly destroyed them,
from Heshbon to Dibon.
We have completely wiped them out
as far away as Nophah and Medeba.*"

31 So the people of Israel occupied the territory of the Amorites. 32 After
Moses sent men to explore the Jazer area, they captured all the towns in the
region and drove out the Amorites who lived there. 33 Then they turned and
marched up the road to Bashan, but King Og of Bashan and all his people
attacked them at Edrei. 34 The LORD said to Moses, "Do not be afraid of him,
for I have handed him over to you, along with all his people and his land.
Do the same to him as you did to King Sihon of the Amorites, who ruled in
Heshbon." 35 And Israel killed King Og, his sons, and all his subjects; not a
single survivor remained. Then Israel occupied their land.

Balak Sends for Balaam

22 Then the people of Israel traveled to the plains of Moab and camped
east of the Jordan River, across from Jericho. 2 Balak son of Zippor,
the Moabite king, had seen everything the Israelites did to the Amorites.
3 And when the people of Moab saw how many Israelites there were, they
were terrified. 4 The king of Moab said to the elders of Midian, "This mob
will devour everything in sight, like an ox devours grass in the field!"

So Balak, king of Moab, 5 sent messengers to call Balaam son of Beor, who
was living in his native land of Pethor* near the Euphrates River.* His mes-
sage said:

> "Look, a vast horde of people has arrived from Egypt. They cover the
> face of the earth and are threatening me. 6 Please come and curse these
> people for me because they are too powerful for me. Then perhaps I
> will be able to conquer them and drive them from the land. I know that
> blessings fall on any people you bless, and curses fall on people you
> curse."

7 Balak's messengers, who were elders of Moab and Midian, set out with
money to pay Balaam to place a curse upon Israel.* They went to Balaam
and delivered Balak's message to him. 8 "Stay here overnight," Balaam said.
"In the morning I will tell you whatever the LORD directs me to say." So the
officials from Moab stayed there with Balaam.

9 That night God came to Balaam and asked him, "Who are these men
visiting you?"

10 Balaam said to God, "Balak son of Zippor, king of Moab, has sent me
this message: 11 'Look, a vast horde of people has arrived from Egypt, and

21:30 Or *until fire spread to Medeba.* The meaning of the Hebrew is uncertain. **22:5a** Or *who was at Pethor in the land of the Amavites.* **22:5b** Hebrew *the river.* **22:7** Hebrew *set out with the money of divination in their hand.*

they cover the face of the earth. Come and curse these people for me. Then
perhaps I will be able to stand up to them and drive them from the land.'"
12 But God told Balaam, "Do not go with them. You are not to curse these
people, for they have been blessed!"
13 The next morning Balaam got up and told Balak's officials, "Go on
home! The LORD will not let me go with you."
14 So the Moabite officials returned to King Balak and reported, "Balaam
refused to come with us." 15 Then Balak tried again. This time he sent a
larger number of even more distinguished officials than those he had sent
the first time. 16 They went to Balaam and delivered this message to him:

"This is what Balak son of Zippor says: Please don't let anything stop
you from coming to help me. 17 I will pay you very well and do whatever
you tell me. Just come and curse these people for me!"

18 But Balaam responded to Balak's messengers, "Even if Balak were to give
me his palace filled with silver and gold, I would be powerless to do anything
against the will of the LORD my God. 19 But stay here one more night, and I
will see if the LORD has anything else to say to me."
20 That night God came to Balaam and told him, "Since these men have
come for you, get up and go with them. But do only what I tell you to do."

Balaam and His Donkey

21 So the next morning Balaam got up, saddled his donkey, and started off
with the Moabite officials. 22 But God was angry that Balaam was going, so
he sent the angel of the LORD to stand in the road to block his way. As Balaam
and two servants were riding along, 23 Balaam's donkey saw the angel of the
LORD standing in the road with a drawn sword in his hand. The donkey
bolted off the road into a field, but Balaam beat it and turned it back onto
the road. 24 Then the angel of the LORD stood at a place where the road nar-
rowed between two vineyard walls. 25 When the donkey saw the angel of the
LORD, it tried to squeeze by and crushed Balaam's foot against the wall. So
Balaam beat the donkey again. 26 Then the angel of the LORD moved farther
down the road and stood in a place too narrow for the donkey to get by at
all. 27 This time when the donkey saw the angel, it lay down under Balaam.
In a fit of rage Balaam beat the animal again with his staff.
28 Then the LORD gave the donkey the ability to speak. "What have I done
to you that deserves your beating me three times?" it asked Balaam.
29 "You have made me look like a fool!" Balaam shouted. "If I had a sword
with me, I would kill you!"
30 "But I am the same donkey you have ridden all your life," the donkey
answered. "Have I ever done anything like this before?"
"No," Balaam admitted.
31 Then the LORD opened Balaam's eyes, and he saw the angel of the LORD
standing in the roadway with a drawn sword in his hand. Balaam bowed his
head and fell face down on the ground before him.
32 "Why did you beat your donkey those three times?" the angel of the
LORD demanded. "Look, I have come to block your way because you are
stubbornly resisting me. 33 Three times the donkey saw me and shied away;
otherwise, I would certainly have killed you by now and spared the donkey."

Question 22:28

Why did God talk to Balaam through a donkey? What does this reveal to you about the creativity of God? What does this reveal to you about the stubbornness of humans?

Prayer **23:9**

Lord, set us apart in such a way that others will be introduced to your glory. Amen.

34 Then Balaam confessed to the angel of the LORD, "I have sinned. I didn't
realize you were standing in the road to block my way. I will return home if
you are against my going."
35 But the angel of the LORD told Balaam, "Go with these men, but say
only what I tell you to say." So Balaam went on with Balak's officials.
36 When King Balak heard that Balaam was on the way, he went out to
meet him at a Moabite town on the Arnon River at the farthest border
of his land.
37 "Didn't I send you an urgent invitation? Why didn't you come right
away?" Balak asked Balaam. "Didn't you believe me when I said I would
reward you richly?"
38 Balaam replied, "Look, now I have come, but I have no power to say
whatever I want. I will speak only the message that God puts in my mouth."
39 Then Balaam accompanied Balak to Kiriath-huzoth, 40 where the king
sacrificed cattle and sheep. He sent portions of the meat to Balaam and
the officials who were with him. 41 The next morning Balak took Balaam
up to Bamoth-baal. From there he could see some of the people of Israel
spread out below him.

Balaam Blesses Israel

23 Then Balaam said to King Balak, "Build me seven altars here, and
prepare seven young bulls and seven rams for me to sacrifice." 2 Ba-
lak followed his instructions, and the two of them sacrificed a young bull
and a ram on each altar.
3 Then Balaam said to Balak, "Stand here by your burnt offerings, and I
will go to see if the LORD will respond to me. Then I will tell you whatever
he reveals to me." So Balaam went alone to the top of a bare hill, 4 and God
met him there. Balaam said to him, "I have prepared seven altars and have
sacrificed a young bull and a ram on each altar."
5 The LORD gave Balaam a message for King Balak. Then he said, "Go back
to Balak and give him my message."
6 So Balaam returned and found the king standing beside his burnt
offerings with all the officials of Moab. 7 This was the message Balaam
delivered:

"Balak summoned me to come from Aram;
  the king of Moab brought me from the eastern hills.
'Come,' he said, 'curse Jacob for me!
  Come and announce Israel's doom.'
8 But how can I curse those
  whom God has not cursed?
How can I condemn those
  whom the LORD has not condemned?
9 I see them from the cliff tops;
  I watch them from the hills.
I see a people who live by themselves,
  set apart from other nations.
10 Who can count Jacob's descendants, as numerous
    as dust?
  Who can count even a fourth of Israel's people?

Let me die like the righteous;
let my life end like theirs."

11 Then King Balak demanded of Balaam, "What have you done to me? I
brought you to curse my enemies. Instead, you have blessed them!"
12 But Balaam replied, "I will speak only the message that the LORD puts
in my mouth."

Balaam's Second Message

13 Then King Balak told him, "Come with me to another place. There you will
see another part of the nation of Israel, but not all of them. Curse at least that
many!" 14 So Balak took Balaam to the plateau of Zophim on Pisgah Peak.
He built seven altars there and offered a young bull and a ram on each altar.
15 Then Balaam said to the king, "Stand here by your burnt offerings while
I go over there to meet the LORD."
16 And the LORD met Balaam and gave him a message. Then he said, "Go
back to Balak and give him my message."
17 So Balaam returned and found the king standing beside his burnt of-
ferings with all the officials of Moab. "What did the LORD say?" Balak asked
eagerly.
18 This was the message Balaam delivered:

"Rise up, Balak, and listen!
Hear me, son of Zippor.
19 God is not a man, so he does not lie.
He is not human, so he does not change his mind.
Has he ever spoken and failed to act?
Has he ever promised and not carried it through?
20 Listen, I received a command to bless;
God has blessed, and I cannot reverse it!
21 No misfortune is in his plan for Jacob;
no trouble is in store for Israel.
For the LORD their God is with them;
he has been proclaimed their king.
22 God brought them out of Egypt;
for them he is as strong as a wild ox.
23 No curse can touch Jacob;
no magic has any power against Israel.
For now it will be said of Jacob,
'What wonders God has done for Israel!'
24 These people rise up like a lioness,
like a majestic lion rousing itself.
They refuse to rest
until they have feasted on prey,
drinking the blood of the slaughtered!"

25 Then Balak said to Balaam, "Fine, but if you won't curse them, at least
don't bless them!"
26 But Balaam replied to Balak, "Didn't I tell you that I can do only what
the LORD tells me?"

Question 23:19

Describe the differences between God and humans. If we choose to follow God, what implications does this have for how we live our everyday lives? What implications does it have for you personally?

Question 24:13

Balaam doesn't always get things right regarding his strange interactions with the Lord. What does Balaam get right here?

Balaam's Third Message

27 Then King Balak said to Balaam, "Come, I will take you to one more place. Perhaps it will please God to let you curse them from there."

28 So Balak took Balaam to the top of Mount Peor, overlooking the waste-
land.* 29 Balaam again told Balak, "Build me seven altars, and prepare seven
young bulls and seven rams for me to sacrifice." 30 So Balak did as Balaam
ordered and offered a young bull and a ram on each altar.

24 By now Balaam realized that the LORD was determined to bless Israel, so he did not resort to divination as before. Instead, he turned
and looked out toward the wilderness, 2 where he saw the people of Israel
camped, tribe by tribe. Then the Spirit of God came upon him, 3 and this is
the message he delivered:

"This is the message of Balaam son of Beor,
the message of the man whose eyes see clearly,
4 the message of one who hears the words of God,
who sees a vision from the Almighty,
who bows down with eyes wide open:
5 How beautiful are your tents, O Jacob;
how lovely are your homes, O Israel!
6 They spread before me like palm groves,*
like gardens by the riverside.
They are like tall trees planted by the LORD,
like cedars beside the waters.
7 Water will flow from their buckets;
their offspring have all they need.
Their king will be greater than Agag;
their kingdom will be exalted.
8 God brought them out of Egypt;
for them he is as strong as a wild ox.
He devours all the nations that oppose him,
breaking their bones in pieces,
shooting them with arrows.
9 Like a lion, Israel crouches and lies down;
like a lioness, who dares to arouse her?
Blessed is everyone who blesses you, O Israel,
and cursed is everyone who curses you."

10 King Balak flew into a rage against Balaam. He angrily clapped his hands
and shouted, "I called you to curse my enemies! Instead, you have blessed
them three times. 11 Now get out of here! Go back home! I promised to reward
you richly, but the LORD has kept you from your reward."

12 Balaam told Balak, "Don't you remember what I told your messengers?
I said, 13 'Even if Balak were to give me his palace filled with silver and gold,
I would be powerless to do anything against the will of the LORD.' I told you
that I could say only what the LORD says! 14 Now I am returning to my own
people. But first let me tell you what the Israelites will do to your people
in the future."

23:28 Or *overlooking Jeshimon.* 24:6 Or *like a majestic valley.*

Balaam's Final Messages

15 This is the message Balaam delivered:

"This is the message of Balaam son of Beor,
the message of the man whose eyes see clearly,
16 the message of one who hears the words of God,
who has knowledge from the Most High,
who sees a vision from the Almighty,
who bows down with eyes wide open:
17 I see him, but not here and now.
I perceive him, but far in the distant future.
A star will rise from Jacob;
a scepter will emerge from Israel.
It will crush the heads of Moab's people,
cracking the skulls* of the people of Sheth.
18 Edom will be taken over,
and Seir, its enemy, will be conquered,
while Israel marches on in triumph.
19 A ruler will rise in Jacob
who will destroy the survivors of Ir."

20 Then Balaam looked over toward the people of Amalek and delivered this message:

"Amalek was the greatest of nations,
but its destiny is destruction!"

21 Then he looked over toward the Kenites and delivered this message:

"Your home is secure;
your nest is set in the rocks.
22 But the Kenites will be destroyed
when Assyria* takes you captive."

23 Balaam concluded his messages by saying:

"Alas, who can survive
unless God has willed it?
24 Ships will come from the coasts of Cyprus*;
they will oppress Assyria and afflict Eber,
but they, too, will be utterly destroyed."

25 Then Balaam left and returned home, and Balak also went on his way.

Moab Seduces Israel

25 While the Israelites were camped at Acacia Grove,* some of the men
defiled themselves by having* sexual relations with local Moabite
women. 2 These women invited them to attend sacrifices to their gods, so

24:17 As in Samaritan Pentateuch; the meaning of the Hebrew word is uncertain. **24:22** Hebrew *Asshur;* also in 24:24. **24:24** Hebrew *Kittim.* **25:1a** Hebrew *Shittim.* **25:1b** As in Greek version; Hebrew reads *some of the men began having.*

the Israelites feasted with them and worshiped the gods of Moab. 3In this
way, Israel joined in the worship of Baal of Peor, causing the LORD's anger
to blaze against his people.
4The LORD issued the following command to Moses: "Seize all the ring-
leaders and execute them before the LORD in broad daylight, so his fierce
anger will turn away from the people of Israel."
5So Moses ordered Israel's judges, "Each of you must put to death the men
under your authority who have joined in worshiping Baal of Peor."
6Just then one of the Israelite men brought a Midianite woman into his tent,
right before the eyes of Moses and all the people, as everyone was weeping at
the entrance of the Tabernacle.* 7When Phinehas son of Eleazar and grandson
of Aaron the priest saw this, he jumped up and left the assembly. He took a
spear 8and rushed after the man into his tent. Phinehas thrust the spear all
the way through the man's body and into the woman's stomach. So the plague
against the Israelites was stopped, 9but not before 24,000 people had died.
10Then the LORD said to Moses, 11"Phinehas son of Eleazar and grandson
of Aaron the priest has turned my anger away from the Israelites by being
as zealous among them as I was. So I stopped destroying all Israel as I had
intended to do in my zealous anger. 12Now tell him that I am making my
special covenant of peace with him. 13In this covenant, I give him and his
descendants a permanent right to the priesthood, for in his zeal for me, his
God, he purified the people of Israel, making them right with me.*"
14The Israelite man killed with the Midianite woman was named Zimri
son of Salu, the leader of a family from the tribe of Simeon. 15The woman's
name was Cozbi; she was the daughter of Zur, the leader of a Midianite clan.
16Then the LORD said to Moses, 17"Attack the Midianites and destroy them,
18because they assaulted you with deceit and tricked you into worshiping
Baal of Peor, and because of Cozbi, the daughter of a Midianite leader, who
was killed at the time of the plague because of what happened at Peor."

The Second Registration of Israel's Troops

26 After the plague had ended,* the LORD said to Moses and to Elea-
zar son of Aaron the priest, 2"From the whole community of Israel,
record the names of all the warriors by their families. List all the men twenty
years old or older who are able to go to war."
3So there on the plains of Moab beside the Jordan River, across from Jer-
icho, Moses and Eleazar the priest issued these instructions to the leaders
of Israel: 4"List all the men of Israel twenty years old and older, just as the
LORD commanded Moses."
This is the record of all the descendants of Israel who came out of Egypt.

The Tribe of Reuben

5These were the clans descended from the sons of Reuben, Jacob's* oldest
son:
The Hanochite clan, named after their ancestor Hanoch.
The Palluite clan, named after their ancestor Pallu.
6 The Hezronite clan, named after their ancestor Hezron.
The Carmite clan, named after their ancestor Carmi.

25:6 Hebrew *the Tent of Meeting.* 25:13 Or *he made atonement for the people of Israel.* 26:1 The initial phrase in verse 26:1 is numbered 25:19 in Hebrew text. 26:5 Hebrew *Israel's;* see note on 1:20-21b.

[7]These were the clans of Reuben. Their registered troops numbered 43,730.
[8]Pallu was the ancestor of Eliab, [9]and Eliab was the father of Nemuel,
Dathan, and Abiram. This Dathan and Abiram are the same community lead-
ers who conspired with Korah against Moses and Aaron, rebelling against
the LORD. [10]But the earth opened up its mouth and swallowed them with
Korah, and fire devoured 250 of their followers. This served as a warning to
the entire nation of Israel. [11]However, the sons of Korah did not die that day.

The Tribe of Simeon

[12]These were the clans descended from the sons of Simeon:
The Jemuelite clan, named after their ancestor Jemuel.*
The Jaminite clan, named after their ancestor Jamin.
The Jakinite clan, named after their ancestor Jakin.
[13] The Zoharite clan, named after their ancestor Zohar.*
The Shaulite clan, named after their ancestor Shaul.

[14]These were the clans of Simeon. Their registered troops numbered 22,200.

The Tribe of Gad

[15]These were the clans descended from the sons of Gad:
The Zephonite clan, named after their ancestor Zephon.
The Haggite clan, named after their ancestor Haggi.
The Shunite clan, named after their ancestor Shuni.
[16] The Oznite clan, named after their ancestor Ozni.
The Erite clan, named after their ancestor Eri.
[17] The Arodite clan, named after their ancestor Arodi.*
The Arelite clan, named after their ancestor Areli.

[18]These were the clans of Gad. Their registered troops numbered 40,500.

The Tribe of Judah

[19]Judah had two sons, Er and Onan, who had died in the land of Canaan.
[20]These were the clans descended from Judah's surviving sons:
The Shelanite clan, named after their ancestor Shelah.
The Perezite clan, named after their ancestor Perez.
The Zerahite clan, named after their ancestor Zerah.

[21]These were the subclans descended from the Perezites:
The Hezronites, named after their ancestor Hezron.
The Hamulites, named after their ancestor Hamul.

[22]These were the clans of Judah. Their registered troops numbered 76,500.

The Tribe of Issachar

[23]These were the clans descended from the sons of Issachar:
The Tolaite clan, named after their ancestor Tola.
The Puite clan, named after their ancestor Puah.*

26:12 As in Syriac version (see also Gen 46:10; Exod 6:15); Hebrew reads *Nemuelite . . . Nemuel.* 26:13 As in parallel texts at Gen 46:10 and Exod 6:15; Hebrew reads *Zerahite . . . Zerah.* 26:17 As in Samaritan Pentateuch and Greek and Syriac versions (see also Gen 46:16); Hebrew reads *Arod.* 26:23 As in Samaritan Pentateuch, Greek and Syriac versions, and Latin Vulgate (see also 1 Chr 7:1); Hebrew reads *The Punite clan, named after its ancestor Puvah.*

Encouragements from these verses

24 The Jashubite clan, named after their ancestor Jashub.
The Shimronite clan, named after their ancestor Shimron.

25 These were the clans of Issachar. Their registered troops numbered 64,300.

The Tribe of Zebulun

26 These were the clans descended from the sons of Zebulun:
The Seredite clan, named after their ancestor Sered.
The Elonite clan, named after their ancestor Elon.
The Jahleelite clan, named after their ancestor Jahleel.

27 These were the clans of Zebulun. Their registered troops numbered 60,500.

The Tribe of Manasseh

28 Two clans were descended from Joseph through Manasseh and Ephraim.

29 These were the clans descended from Manasseh:
The Makirite clan, named after their ancestor Makir.
The Gileadite clan, named after their ancestor Gilead, Makir's son.

30 These were the subclans descended from the Gileadites:
The Iezerites, named after their ancestor Iezer.
The Helekites, named after their ancestor Helek.
31 The Asrielites, named after their ancestor Asriel.
The Shechemites, named after their ancestor Shechem.
32 The Shemidaites, named after their ancestor Shemida.
The Hepherites, named after their ancestor Hepher.
33 (One of Hepher's descendants, Zelophehad, had no sons, but his daughters' names were Mahlah, Noah, Hoglah, Milcah, and Tirzah.)

34 These were the clans of Manasseh. Their registered troops numbered 52,700.

The Tribe of Ephraim

35 These were the clans descended from the sons of Ephraim:
The Shuthelahite clan, named after their ancestor Shuthelah.
The Bekerite clan, named after their ancestor Beker.
The Tahanite clan, named after their ancestor Tahan.

36 This was the subclan descended from the Shuthelahites:
The Eranites, named after their ancestor Eran.

37 These were the clans of Ephraim. Their registered troops numbered 32,500.

These clans of Manasseh and Ephraim were all descendants of Joseph.

The Tribe of Benjamin

38 These were the clans descended from the sons of Benjamin:
The Belaite clan, named after their ancestor Bela.
The Ashbelite clan, named after their ancestor Ashbel.
The Ahiramite clan, named after their ancestor Ahiram.

39 The Shuphamite clan, named after their ancestor Shupham.*
The Huphamite clan, named after their ancestor Hupham.

40 These were the subclans descended from the Belaites:
The Ardites, named after their ancestor Ard.*
The Naamites, named after their ancestor Naaman.

41 These were the clans of Benjamin. Their registered troops numbered 45,600.

The Tribe of Dan
42 These were the clans descended from the sons of Dan:
The Shuhamite clan, named after their ancestor Shuham.

43 These were the Shuhamite clans of Dan. Their registered troops numbered 64,400.

The Tribe of Asher
44 These were the clans descended from the sons of Asher:
The Imnite clan, named after their ancestor Imnah.
The Ishvite clan, named after their ancestor Ishvi.
The Beriite clan, named after their ancestor Beriah.

45 These were the subclans descended from the Beriites:
The Heberites, named after their ancestor Heber.
The Malkielites, named after their ancestor Malkiel.

46 Asher also had a daughter named Serah.

47 These were the clans of Asher. Their registered troops numbered 53,400.

The Tribe of Naphtali
48 These were the clans descended from the sons of Naphtali:
The Jahzeelite clan, named after their ancestor Jahzeel.
The Gunite clan, named after their ancestor Guni.
49 The Jezerite clan, named after their ancestor Jezer.
The Shillemite clan, named after their ancestor Shillem.

50 These were the clans of Naphtali. Their registered troops numbered 45,400.

Results of the Registration
51 In summary, the registered troops of all Israel numbered 601,730.
52 Then the LORD said to Moses, 53 "Divide the land among the tribes, and
distribute the grants of land in proportion to the tribes' populations, as
indicated by the number of names on the list. 54 Give the larger tribes more
land and the smaller tribes less land, each group receiving a grant in pro-
portion to the size of its population. 55 But you must assign the land by lot,
and give land to each ancestral tribe according to the number of names on

26:39 As in some Hebrew manuscripts, Samaritan Pentateuch, Greek and Syriac versions, and Latin Vulgate; most Hebrew manuscripts read *Shephupham.* **26:40** As in Samaritan Pentateuch, some Greek manuscripts, and Latin Vulgate; Hebrew lacks *named after their ancestor Ard.*

Questions I want to ask

Question 27:7

In this passage, what do you learn about the dignity and rights of women in Israel's ancient system of justice and government?

the list. 56 Each grant of land must be assigned by lot among the larger and
smaller tribal groups."

The Tribe of Levi

57 This is the record of the Levites who were counted according to their clans:
The Gershonite clan, named after their ancestor Gershon.
The Kohathite clan, named after their ancestor Kohath.
The Merarite clan, named after their ancestor Merari.

58 The Libnites, the Hebronites, the Mahlites, the Mushites, and the Korahites
were all subclans of the Levites.
Now Kohath was the ancestor of Amram, 59 and Amram's wife was named
Jochebed. She also was a descendant of Levi, born among the Levites in the
land of Egypt. Amram and Jochebed became the parents of Aaron, Moses,
and their sister, Miriam. 60 To Aaron were born Nadab, Abihu, Eleazar, and
Ithamar. 61 But Nadab and Abihu died when they burned before the LORD
the wrong kind of fire, different than he had commanded.
62 The men from the Levite clans who were one month old or older num-
bered 23,000. But the Levites were not included in the registration of the
rest of the people of Israel because they were not given an allotment of land
when it was divided among the Israelites.
63 So these are the results of the registration of the people of Israel as con-
ducted by Moses and Eleazar the priest on the plains of Moab beside the
Jordan River, across from Jericho. 64 Not one person on this list had been
among those listed in the previous registration taken by Moses and Aaron
in the wilderness of Sinai. 65 For the LORD had said of them, "They will all die
in the wilderness." Not one of them survived except Caleb son of Jephunneh
and Joshua son of Nun.

The Daughters of Zelophehad

27 One day a petition was presented by the daughters of Zelophe-
had—Mahlah, Noah, Hoglah, Milcah, and Tirzah. Their father,
Zelophehad, was a descendant of Hepher son of Gilead, son of Makir, son
of Manasseh, son of Joseph. 2 These women stood before Moses, Eleazar the
priest, the tribal leaders, and the entire community at the entrance of the
Tabernacle.* 3 "Our father died in the wilderness," they said. "He was not
among Korah's followers, who rebelled against the LORD; he died because
of his own sin. But he had no sons. 4 Why should the name of our father dis-
appear from his clan just because he had no sons? Give us property along
with the rest of our relatives."
5 So Moses brought their case before the LORD. 6 And the LORD replied to
Moses, 7 "The claim of the daughters of Zelophehad is legitimate. You must
give them a grant of land along with their father's relatives. Assign them the
property that would have been given to their father.
8 "And give the following instructions to the people of Israel: If a man
dies and has no son, then give his inheritance to his daughters. 9 And if
he has no daughter either, transfer his inheritance to his brothers. 10 If he
has no brothers, give his inheritance to his father's brothers. 11 But if his
father has no brothers, give his inheritance to the nearest relative in his

27:2 Hebrew *the Tent of Meeting.*

clan. This is a legal requirement for the people of Israel, just as the LORD
commanded Moses."

Joshua Chosen to Lead Israel

12 One day the LORD said to Moses, "Climb one of the mountains east of the
river,* and look out over the land I have given the people of Israel. 13 After
you have seen it, you will die like your brother, Aaron, 14 for you both rebelled
against my instructions in the wilderness of Zin. When the people of Is-
rael rebelled, you failed to demonstrate my holiness to them at the waters."
(These are the waters of Meribah at Kadesh* in the wilderness of Zin.)
15 Then Moses said to the LORD, 16 "O LORD, you are the God who gives
breath to all creatures. Please appoint a new man as leader for the commu-
nity. 17 Give them someone who will guide them wherever they go and will
lead them into battle, so the community of the LORD will not be like sheep
without a shepherd."
18 The LORD replied, "Take Joshua son of Nun, who has the Spirit in him,
and lay your hands on him. 19 Present him to Eleazar the priest before the
whole community, and publicly commission him to lead the people. 20 Trans-
fer some of your authority to him so the whole community of Israel will obey
him. 21 When direction from the LORD is needed, Joshua will stand before
Eleazar the priest, who will use the Urim—one of the sacred lots cast before
the LORD—to determine his will. This is how Joshua and the rest of the com-
munity of Israel will determine everything they should do."
22 So Moses did as the LORD commanded. He presented Joshua to Eleazar
the priest and the whole community. 23 Moses laid his hands on him and
commissioned him to lead the people, just as the LORD had commanded
through Moses.

The Daily Offerings

28 The LORD said to Moses, 2 "Give these instructions to the people of
Israel: The offerings you present as special gifts are a pleasing aroma
to me; they are my food. See to it that they are brought at the appointed times
and offered according to my instructions.
3 "Say to the people: This is the special gift you must present to the LORD as
your daily burnt offering. You must offer two one-year-old male lambs with
no defects. 4 Sacrifice one lamb in the morning and the other in the evening.
5 With each lamb you must offer a grain offering of two quarts* of choice
flour mixed with one quart* of pure oil of pressed olives. 6 This is the regular
burnt offering instituted at Mount Sinai as a special gift, a pleasing aroma
to the LORD. 7 Along with it you must present the proper liquid offering of
one quart of alcoholic drink with each lamb, poured out in the Holy Place
as an offering to the LORD. 8 Offer the second lamb in the evening with the
same grain offering and liquid offering. It, too, is a special gift, a pleasing
aroma to the LORD.

The Sabbath Offerings

9 "On the Sabbath day, sacrifice two one-year-old male lambs with no defects.
They must be accompanied by a grain offering of four quarts* of choice flour

27:12 Or *the mountains of Abarim.* **27:14** Hebrew *waters of Meribath-kadesh.* **28:5a** Hebrew *1/10 of an ephah* [2.2 liters]; also in 28:13, 21, 29. **28:5b** Hebrew *1/4 of a hin* [1 liter]; also in 28:7. **28:9** Hebrew *2/10 of an ephah* [4.4 liters]; also in 28:12, 20, 28.

Story Arc **27:12-23**

● Joshua

Moses received a sneak peek of the land that the Lord had promised to Abraham and that he was providing to the nation of Israel. With a mixture of emotions, knowing that he would not be permitted to enter the land, Moses pleaded with the Lord to anoint a new leader who would guide God's people "so the community of the LORD will not be like sheep without a shepherd" (v. 17).

To this request, the Lord answered with Joshua. Moses then publicly commissioned Joshua to take his role of leadership. Moses deliberately laid his hands on Joshua as a symbol of transferring the responsibility of God's call to the next generation.

Succeeding Moses, one of the most important leaders the world has ever seen, would not be an easy task. What does it take for one generation to assume the responsibility of ministry from a prior generation?

Deut 3:21-28 ►

Question 28:16-25

Read through these instructions for the Lord's Passover. Be sure to go back to Exodus 12 to remember the events of the first Passover. What difference did God want this celebration to make every year?

moistened with olive oil, and a liquid offering. 10 This is the burnt offering to be presented each Sabbath day, in addition to the regular burnt offering and its accompanying liquid offering.

The Monthly Offerings

11 "On the first day of each month, present an extra burnt offering to the LORD of two young bulls, one ram, and seven one-year-old male lambs, all with no defects. 12 These must be accompanied by grain offerings of choice flour moistened with olive oil—six quarts* with each bull, four quarts with the ram, 13 and two quarts with each lamb. This burnt offering will be a special gift, a pleasing aroma to the LORD. 14 You must also present a liquid offering with each sacrifice: two quarts* of wine for each bull, a third of a gallon* for the ram, and one quart* for each lamb. Present this monthly burnt offering on the first day of each month throughout the year.

15 "On the first day of each month, you must also offer one male goat for a sin offering to the LORD. This is in addition to the regular burnt offering and its accompanying liquid offering.

Offerings for the Passover

16 "On the fourteenth day of the first month,* you must celebrate the LORD's Passover. 17 On the following day—the fifteenth day of the month—a joyous, seven-day festival will begin, but no bread made with yeast may be eaten. 18 The first day of the festival will be an official day for holy assembly, and no ordinary work may be done on that day. 19 As a special gift you must present a burnt offering to the LORD—two young bulls, one ram, and seven one-year-old male lambs, all with no defects. 20 These will be accompanied by grain offerings of choice flour moistened with olive oil—six quarts with each bull, four quarts with the ram, 21 and two quarts with each of the seven lambs. 22 You must also offer a male goat as a sin offering to purify yourselves and make yourselves right with the LORD.* 23 Present these offerings in addition to your regular morning burnt offering. 24 On each of the seven days of the festival, this is how you must prepare the food offering that is presented as a special gift, a pleasing aroma to the LORD. These will be offered in addition to the regular burnt offerings and liquid offerings. 25 The seventh day of the festival will be another official day for holy assembly, and no ordinary work may be done on that day.

Offerings for the Festival of Harvest

26 "At the Festival of Harvest,* when you present the first of your new grain to the LORD, you must call an official day for holy assembly, and you may do no ordinary work on that day. 27 Present a special burnt offering on that day as a pleasing aroma to the LORD. It will consist of two young bulls, one ram, and seven one-year-old male lambs. 28 These will be accompanied by grain offerings of choice flour moistened with olive oil—six quarts with each bull, four quarts with the ram, 29 and two quarts with each of the seven lambs. 30 Also, offer one male goat to purify yourselves and make yourselves right with the LORD. 31 Prepare these special burnt offerings, along with their

28:12 Hebrew *3⁄10 of an ephah* [6.6 liters]; also in 28:20, 28. **28:14a** Hebrew *½ of a hin* [2 liters]. **28:14b** Hebrew *⅓ of a hin* [1.3 liters]. **28:14c** Hebrew *¼ of a hin* [1 liter]. **28:16** This day in the ancient Hebrew lunar calendar occurred in late March, April, or early May. **28:22** Or *to make atonement for yourselves;* also in 28:30. **28:26** Hebrew *Festival of Weeks.* This was later called the Festival of Pentecost (see Acts 2:1). It is celebrated today as Shavuot (or Shabuoth).

liquid offerings, in addition to the regular burnt offering and its accompanying grain offering. Be sure that all the animals you sacrifice have no defects.

Offerings for the Festival of Trumpets

29 "Celebrate the Festival of Trumpets each year on the first day of the appointed month in early autumn.* You must call an official day for holy assembly, and you may do no ordinary work. 2 On that day you must present a burnt offering as a pleasing aroma to the LORD. It will consist of one young bull, one ram, and seven one-year-old male lambs, all with no defects. 3 These must be accompanied by grain offerings of choice flour moistened with olive oil—six quarts* with the bull, four quarts* with the ram, 4 and two quarts* with each of the seven lambs. 5 In addition, you must sacrifice a male goat as a sin offering to purify yourselves and make yourselves right with the LORD.* 6 These special sacrifices are in addition to your regular monthly and daily burnt offerings, and they must be given with their prescribed grain offerings and liquid offerings. These offerings are given as a special gift to the LORD, a pleasing aroma to him.

Offerings for the Day of Atonement

7 "Ten days later, on the tenth day of the same month,* you must call another holy assembly. On that day, the Day of Atonement, the people must go without food and must do no ordinary work. 8 You must present a burnt offering as a pleasing aroma to the LORD. It will consist of one young bull, one ram, and seven one-year-old male lambs, all with no defects. 9 These offerings must be accompanied by the prescribed grain offerings of choice flour moistened with olive oil—six quarts of choice flour with the bull, four quarts of choice flour with the ram, 10 and two quarts of choice flour with each of the seven lambs. 11 You must also sacrifice one male goat for a sin offering. This is in addition to the sin offering of atonement and the regular daily burnt offering with its grain offering, and their accompanying liquid offerings.

Offerings for the Festival of Shelters

12 "Five days later, on the fifteenth day of the same month,* you must call another holy assembly of all the people, and you may do no ordinary work on that day. It is the beginning of the Festival of Shelters,* a seven-day festival to the LORD. 13 On the first day of the festival, you must present a burnt offering as a special gift, a pleasing aroma to the LORD. It will consist of thirteen young bulls, two rams, and fourteen one-year-old male lambs, all with no defects. 14 Each of these offerings must be accompanied by a grain offering of choice flour moistened with olive oil—six quarts for each of the thirteen bulls, four quarts for each of the two rams, 15 and two quarts for each of the fourteen lambs. 16 You must also sacrifice a male goat as a sin offering, in addition to

29:1 Hebrew *the first day of the seventh month.* This day in the ancient Hebrew lunar calendar occurred in September or October. This festival is celebrated today as Rosh Hashanah, the Jewish new year. **29:3a** Hebrew *3/10 of an ephah* [6.6 liters]; also in 29:9, 14. **29:3b** Hebrew *2/10 of an ephah* [4.4 liters]; also in 29:9, 14. **29:4** Hebrew *1/10 of an ephah* [2.2 liters]; also in 29:10, 15. **29:5** Or *to make atonement for yourselves.* **29:7** Hebrew *On the tenth day of the seventh month;* see 29:1 and the note there. This day in the ancient Hebrew lunar calendar occurred in September or October. It is celebrated today as Yom Kippur. **29:12a** Hebrew *On the fifteenth day of the seventh month;* see 29:1, 7 and the notes there. This day in the ancient Hebrew lunar calendar occurred in late September, October, or early November. **29:12b** Or *Festival of Booths,* or *Festival of Tabernacles.* This was earlier called the Festival of the Final Harvest or Festival of Ingathering (see Exod 23:16b). It is celebrated today as Sukkot (or Succoth).

the regular burnt offering with its accompanying grain offering and liquid
offering.

17 “On the second day of this seven-day festival, sacrifice twelve young
bulls, two rams, and fourteen one-year-old male lambs, all with no defects.
18 Each of these offerings of bulls, rams, and lambs must be accompanied by
its prescribed grain offering and liquid offering. 19 You must also sacrifice a
male goat as a sin offering, in addition to the regular burnt offering with its
accompanying grain offering and liquid offering.

20 “On the third day of the festival, sacrifice eleven young bulls, two rams,
and fourteen one-year-old male lambs, all with no defects. 21 Each of these
offerings of bulls, rams, and lambs must be accompanied by its prescribed
grain offering and liquid offering. 22 You must also sacrifice a male goat as a
sin offering, in addition to the regular burnt offering with its accompanying
grain offering and liquid offering.

23 “On the fourth day of the festival, sacrifice ten young bulls, two rams,
and fourteen one-year-old male lambs, all with no defects. 24 Each of these
offerings of bulls, rams, and lambs must be accompanied by its prescribed
grain offering and liquid offering. 25 You must also sacrifice a male goat as a
sin offering, in addition to the regular burnt offering with its accompanying
grain offering and liquid offering.

26 “On the fifth day of the festival, sacrifice nine young bulls, two rams,
and fourteen one-year-old male lambs, all with no defects. 27 Each of these
offerings of bulls, rams, and lambs must be accompanied by its prescribed
grain offering and liquid offering. 28 You must also sacrifice a male goat as a
sin offering, in addition to the regular burnt offering with its accompanying
grain offering and liquid offering.

29 “On the sixth day of the festival, sacrifice eight young bulls, two rams,
and fourteen one-year-old male lambs, all with no defects. 30 Each of these
offerings of bulls, rams, and lambs must be accompanied by its prescribed
grain offering and liquid offering. 31 You must also sacrifice a male goat as a
sin offering, in addition to the regular burnt offering with its accompanying
grain offering and liquid offering.

32 “On the seventh day of the festival, sacrifice seven young bulls, two rams,
and fourteen one-year-old male lambs, all with no defects. 33 Each of these
offerings of bulls, rams, and lambs must be accompanied by its prescribed
grain offering and liquid offering. 34 You must also sacrifice one male goat as
a sin offering, in addition to the regular burnt offering with its accompany-
ing grain offering and liquid offering.

35 “On the eighth day of the festival, proclaim another holy day. You must
do no ordinary work on that day. 36 You must present a burnt offering as a
special gift, a pleasing aroma to the LORD. It will consist of one young bull,
one ram, and seven one-year-old male lambs, all with no defects. 37 Each of
these offerings must be accompanied by its prescribed grain offering and
liquid offering. 38 You must also sacrifice one male goat as a sin offering, in
addition to the regular burnt offering with its accompanying grain offering
and liquid offering.

39 “You must present these offerings to the LORD at your annual festivals.
These are in addition to the sacrifices and offerings you present in connec-
tion with vows, or as voluntary offerings, burnt offerings, grain offerings,
liquid offerings, or peace offerings.”

40*So Moses gave all of these instructions to the people of Israel as the
LORD had commanded him.

Laws concerning Vows

30 1*Then Moses summoned the leaders of the tribes of Israel and told
them, "This is what the LORD has commanded: 2A man who makes a
vow to the LORD or makes a pledge under oath must never break it. He must
do exactly what he said he would do.
3"If a young woman makes a vow to the LORD or a pledge under oath while
she is still living at her father's home, 4and her father hears of the vow or
pledge and does not object to it, then all her vows and pledges will stand.
5But if her father refuses to let her fulfill the vow or pledge on the day he
hears of it, then all her vows and pledges will become invalid. The LORD will
forgive her because her father would not let her fulfill them.
6"Now suppose a young woman makes a vow or binds herself with an
impulsive pledge and later marries. 7If her husband learns of her vow or
pledge and does not object on the day he hears of it, her vows and pledges
will stand. 8But if her husband refuses to accept her vow or impulsive pledge
on the day he hears of it, he nullifies her commitments, and the LORD will
forgive her. 9If, however, a woman is a widow or is divorced, she must fulfill
all her vows and pledges.
10"But suppose a woman is married and living in her husband's home
when she makes a vow or binds herself with a pledge. 11If her husband hears
of it and does not object to it, her vow or pledge will stand. 12But if her hus-
band refuses to accept it on the day he hears of it, her vow or pledge will
be nullified, and the LORD will forgive her. 13So her husband may either
confirm or nullify any vows or pledges she makes to deny herself. 14But if he
does not object on the day he hears of it, then he is agreeing to all her vows
and pledges. 15If he waits more than a day and then tries to nullify a vow or
pledge, he will be punished for her guilt."
16These are the regulations the LORD gave Moses concerning relationships
between a man and his wife, and between a father and a young daughter
who still lives at home.

Question 30:16

In a world that doesn't value integrity and promises, how do Israel's standards for living a holy life stand out?

Conquest of the Midianites

31 Then the LORD said to Moses, 2"On behalf of the people of Israel,
take revenge on the Midianites for leading them into idolatry. After
that, you will die and join your ancestors."
3So Moses said to the people, "Choose some men, and arm them to fight
the LORD's war of revenge against Midian. 4From each tribe of Israel, send
1,000 men into battle." 5So they chose 1,000 men from each tribe of Israel, a
total of 12,000 men armed for battle. 6Then Moses sent them out, 1,000 men
from each tribe, and Phinehas son of Eleazar the priest led them into battle.
They carried along the holy objects of the sanctuary and the trumpets for
sounding the charge. 7They attacked Midian as the LORD had commanded
Moses, and they killed all the men. 8All five of the Midianite kings—Evi,
Rekem, Zur, Hur, and Reba—died in the battle. They also killed Balaam
son of Beor with the sword.
9Then the Israelite army captured the Midianite women and children and

29:40 Verse 29:40 is numbered 30:1 in Hebrew text. 30:1 Verses 30:1-16 are numbered 30:2-17 in Hebrew text.

seized their cattle and flocks and all their wealth as plunder. 10 They burned
all the towns and villages where the Midianites had lived. 11 After they had
gathered the plunder and captives, both people and animals, 12 they brought
them all to Moses and Eleazar the priest, and to the whole community of
Israel, which was camped on the plains of Moab beside the Jordan River,
across from Jericho. 13 Moses, Eleazar the priest, and all the leaders of the
community went to meet them outside the camp. 14 But Moses was furious
with all the generals and captains* who had returned from the battle.

15 "Why have you let all the women live?" he demanded. 16 "These are the
very ones who followed Balaam's advice and caused the people of Israel to
rebel against the LORD at Mount Peor. They are the ones who caused the
plague to strike the LORD's people. 17 So kill all the boys and all the women
who have had intercourse with a man. 18 Only the young girls who are vir-
gins may live; you may keep them for yourselves. 19 And all of you who have
killed anyone or touched a dead body must stay outside the camp for seven
days. You must purify yourselves and your captives on the third and seventh
days. 20 Purify all your clothing, too, and everything made of leather, goat
hair, or wood."

21 Then Eleazar the priest said to the men who were in the battle, "The
LORD has given Moses this legal requirement: 22 Anything made of gold,
silver, bronze, iron, tin, or lead—23 that is, all metals that do not burn—
must be passed through fire in order to be made ceremonially pure. These
metal objects must then be further purified with the water of purification.
But everything that burns must be purified by the water alone. 24 On the
seventh day you must wash your clothes and be purified. Then you may
return to the camp."

Division of the Plunder

25 And the LORD said to Moses, 26 "You and Eleazar the priest and the fam-
ily leaders of each tribe are to make a list of all the plunder taken in the
battle, including the people and animals. 27 Then divide the plunder into
two parts, and give half to the men who fought the battle and half to the
rest of the people. 28 From the army's portion, first give the LORD his share
of the plunder—one of every 500 of the prisoners and of the cattle, donkeys,
sheep, and goats. 29 Give this share of the army's half to Eleazar the priest as
an offering to the LORD. 30 From the half that belongs to the people of Israel,
take one of every fifty of the prisoners and of the cattle, donkeys, sheep,
goats, and other animals. Give this share to the Levites, who are in charge of
maintaining the LORD's Tabernacle." 31 So Moses and Eleazar the priest did
as the LORD commanded Moses.

32 The plunder remaining from everything the fighting men had taken
totaled 675,000 sheep and goats, 33 72,000 cattle, 34 61,000 donkeys, 35 and
32,000 virgin girls.

36 Half of the plunder was given to the fighting men. It totaled 337,500
sheep and goats, 37 of which 675 were the LORD's share; 38 36,000 cattle, of
which 72 were the LORD's share; 39 30,500 donkeys, of which 61 were the
LORD's share; 40 and 16,000 virgin girls, of whom 32 were the LORD's share.
41 Moses gave all the LORD's share to Eleazar the priest, just as the LORD had
directed him.

31:14 Hebrew *the commanders of thousands, and the commanders of hundreds;* also in 31:48, 52, 54.

42 Half of the plunder belonged to the people of Israel, and Moses sepa-
rated it from the half belonging to the fighting men. 43 It totaled 337,500
sheep and goats, 44 36,000 cattle, 45 30,500 donkeys, 46 and 16,000 virgin girls.
47 From the half-share given to the people, Moses took one of every fifty pris-
oners and animals and gave them to the Levites, who maintained the LORD's
Tabernacle. All this was done as the LORD had commanded Moses.

48 Then all the generals and captains came to Moses 49 and said, "We, your
servants, have accounted for all the men who went out to battle under our
command; not one of us is missing! 50 So we are presenting the items of gold
we captured as an offering to the LORD from our share of the plunder—
armbands, bracelets, rings, earrings, and necklaces. This will purify our lives
before the LORD and make us right with him.*"

51 So Moses and Eleazar the priest received the gold from all the military
commanders—all kinds of jewelry and crafted objects. 52 In all, the gold that
the generals and captains presented as a gift to the LORD weighed about
420 pounds.* 53 All the fighting men had taken some of the plunder for them-
selves. 54 So Moses and Eleazar the priest accepted the gifts from the generals
and captains and brought the gold to the Tabernacle* as a reminder to the
LORD that the people of Israel belong to him.

The Tribes East of the Jordan

32 The tribes of Reuben and Gad owned vast numbers of livestock. So
when they saw that the lands of Jazer and Gilead were ideally suited
for their flocks and herds, 2 they came to Moses, Eleazar the priest, and the
other leaders of the community. They said, 3 "Notice the towns of Ataroth,
Dibon, Jazer, Nimrah, Heshbon, Elealeh, Sibmah,* Nebo, and Beon. 4 The
LORD has conquered this whole area for the community of Israel, and it is
ideally suited for all our livestock. 5 If we have found favor with you, please
let us have this land as our property instead of giving us land across the
Jordan River."

6 "Do you intend to stay here while your brothers go across and do all the
fighting?" Moses asked the men of Gad and Reuben. 7 "Why do you want to
discourage the rest of the people of Israel from going across to the land the
LORD has given them? 8 Your ancestors did the same thing when I sent them
from Kadesh-barnea to explore the land. 9 After they went up to the valley
of Eshcol and explored the land, they discouraged the people of Israel from
entering the land the LORD was giving them. 10 Then the LORD was very angry
with them, and he vowed, 11 'Of all those I rescued from Egypt, no one who is
twenty years old or older will ever see the land I swore to give to Abraham,
Isaac, and Jacob, for they have not obeyed me wholeheartedly. 12 The only
exceptions are Caleb son of Jephunneh the Kenizzite and Joshua son of Nun,
for they have wholeheartedly followed the LORD.'

13 "The LORD was angry with Israel and made them wander in the wilder-
ness for forty years until the entire generation that sinned in the LORD's
sight had died. 14 But here you are, a brood of sinners, doing exactly the same
thing! You are making the LORD even angrier with Israel. 15 If you turn away
from him like this and he abandons them again in the wilderness, you will
be responsible for destroying this entire nation!"

31:50 Or *will make atonement for our lives before the LORD.* **31:52** Hebrew *16,750 shekels* [191 kilograms]. **31:54** Hebrew *the Tent of Meeting.* **32:3** As in Samaritan Pentateuch and Greek version (see also 32:38); Hebrew reads *Sebam.*

Prayer **32:12**

Lord, let this be said of me. Let others see that I have walked wholeheartedly with you throughout my life. Amen.

16 But they approached Moses and said, “We simply want to build pens for our livestock and fortified towns for our wives and children. 17 Then we will arm ourselves and lead our fellow Israelites into battle until we have brought them safely to their land. Meanwhile, our families will stay in the fortified towns we build here, so they will be safe from any attacks by the local people. 18 We will not return to our homes until all the people of Israel have received their portions of land. 19 But we do not claim any of the land on the other side of the Jordan. We would rather live here on the east side and accept this as our grant of land.”

20 Then Moses said, “If you keep your word and arm yourselves for the LORD’s battles, 21 and if your troops cross the Jordan and keep fighting until the LORD has driven out his enemies, 22 then you may return when the LORD has conquered the land. You will have fulfilled your duty to the LORD and to the rest of the people of Israel. And the land on the east side of the Jordan will be your property from the LORD. 23 But if you fail to keep your word, then you will have sinned against the LORD, and you may be sure that your sin will find you out. 24 Go ahead and build towns for your families and pens for your flocks, but do everything you have promised.”

25 Then the men of Gad and Reuben replied, “We, your servants, will follow your instructions exactly. 26 Our children, wives, flocks, and cattle will stay here in the towns of Gilead. 27 But all who are able to bear arms will cross over to fight for the LORD, just as you have said.”

28 So Moses gave orders to Eleazar the priest, Joshua son of Nun, and the leaders of the clans of Israel. 29 He said, “The men of Gad and Reuben who are armed for battle must cross the Jordan with you to fight for the LORD. If they do, give them the land of Gilead as their property when the land is conquered. 30 But if they refuse to arm themselves and cross over with you, then they must accept land with the rest of you in the land of Canaan.”

31 The tribes of Gad and Reuben said again, “We are your servants, and we will do as the LORD has commanded! 32 We will cross the Jordan into Canaan fully armed to fight for the LORD, but our property will be here on this side of the Jordan.”

33 So Moses assigned land to the tribes of Gad, Reuben, and half the tribe of Manasseh son of Joseph. He gave them the territory of King Sihon of the Amorites and the land of King Og of Bashan—the whole land with its cities and surrounding lands.

34 The descendants of Gad built the towns of Dibon, Ataroth, Aroer, 35 Atroth-shophan, Jazer, Jogbehah, 36 Beth-nimrah, and Beth-haran. These were all fortified towns with pens for their flocks.

37 The descendants of Reuben built the towns of Heshbon, Elealeh, Kiriathaim, 38 Nebo, Baal-meon, and Sibmah. They changed the names of some of the towns they conquered and rebuilt.

39 Then the descendants of Makir of the tribe of Manasseh went to Gilead and conquered it, and they drove out the Amorites living there. 40 So Moses gave Gilead to the Makirites, descendants of Manasseh, and they settled there. 41 The people of Jair, another clan of the tribe of Manasseh, captured many of the towns in Gilead and changed the name of that region to the Towns of Jair.* 42 Meanwhile, a man named Nobah captured the town of Kenath and its surrounding villages, and he renamed that area Nobah after himself.

32:41 Hebrew *Havvoth-jair.*

Remembering Israel's Journey

33 This is the route the Israelites followed as they marched out of Egypt
under the leadership of Moses and Aaron. 2 At the LORD's direction,
Moses kept a written record of their progress. These are the stages of their
march, identified by the different places where they stopped along the way.
3 They set out from the city of Rameses in early spring—on the fifteenth
day of the first month*—on the morning after the first Passover celebration.
The people of Israel left defiantly, in full view of all the Egyptians. 4 Meanwhile, the Egyptians were burying all their firstborn sons, whom the LORD
had killed the night before. The LORD had defeated the gods of Egypt that
night with great acts of judgment!

5 After leaving Rameses, the Israelites set up camp at Succoth.
6 Then they left Succoth and camped at Etham on the edge of the wilderness.
7 They left Etham and turned back toward Pi-hahiroth, opposite Baal-zephon, and camped near Migdol.
8 They left Pi-hahiroth* and crossed the Red Sea* into the wilderness beyond. Then they traveled for three days into the Etham wilderness and camped at Marah.
9 They left Marah and camped at Elim, where there were twelve springs of water and seventy palm trees.
10 They left Elim and camped beside the Red Sea.*
11 They left the Red Sea and camped in the wilderness of Sin.*
12 They left the wilderness of Sin and camped at Dophkah.
13 They left Dophkah and camped at Alush.
14 They left Alush and camped at Rephidim, where there was no water for the people to drink.
15 They left Rephidim and camped in the wilderness of Sinai.
16 They left the wilderness of Sinai and camped at Kibroth-hattaavah.
17 They left Kibroth-hattaavah and camped at Hazeroth.
18 They left Hazeroth and camped at Rithmah.
19 They left Rithmah and camped at Rimmon-perez.
20 They left Rimmon-perez and camped at Libnah.
21 They left Libnah and camped at Rissah.
22 They left Rissah and camped at Kehelathah.
23 They left Kehelathah and camped at Mount Shepher.
24 They left Mount Shepher and camped at Haradah.
25 They left Haradah and camped at Makheloth.
26 They left Makheloth and camped at Tahath.
27 They left Tahath and camped at Terah.
28 They left Terah and camped at Mithcah.
29 They left Mithcah and camped at Hashmonah.
30 They left Hashmonah and camped at Moseroth.
31 They left Moseroth and camped at Bene-jaakan.
32 They left Bene-jaakan and camped at Hor-haggidgad.
33 They left Hor-haggidgad and camped at Jotbathah.

Question **33:2**

Why is it important to be able to tell the story of what God has done?

33:3 This day in the ancient Hebrew lunar calendar occurred in late March, April, or early May. **33:8a** As in many Hebrew manuscripts, Samaritan Pentateuch, and Latin Vulgate (see also 33:7); most Hebrew manuscripts read *left from in front of Hahiroth.* **33:8b** Hebrew *the sea.* **33:10** Hebrew *sea of reeds;* also in 33:11. **33:11** The geographical name *Sin* is related to *Sinai* and should not be confused with the English word *sin.*

Question 34:2

To many people, this may seem like an unimportant section. After considering God's plan for salvation through Jesus Christ, why is this description of the boundaries of the promised land so important?

34 They left Jotbathah and camped at Abronah.
35 They left Abronah and camped at Ezion-geber.
36 They left Ezion-geber and camped at Kadesh in the wilderness of Zin.
37 They left Kadesh and camped at Mount Hor, at the border of Edom.
38 While they were at the foot of Mount Hor, Aaron the priest was
directed by the LORD to go up the mountain, and there he died. This
happened in midsummer, on the first day of the fifth month* of the
fortieth year after Israel's departure from Egypt. 39 Aaron was 123 years
old when he died there on Mount Hor.
40 At that time the Canaanite king of Arad, who lived in the Negev in the land of Canaan, heard that the people of Israel were approaching his land.
41 Meanwhile, the Israelites left Mount Hor and camped at Zalmonah.
42 Then they left Zalmonah and camped at Punon.
43 They left Punon and camped at Oboth.
44 They left Oboth and camped at Iye-abarim on the border of Moab.
45 They left Iye-abarim* and camped at Dibon-gad.
46 They left Dibon-gad and camped at Almon-diblathaim.
47 They left Almon-diblathaim and camped in the mountains east of the river,* near Mount Nebo.
48 They left the mountains east of the river and camped on the plains of
Moab beside the Jordan River, across from Jericho. 49 Along the Jordan
River they camped from Beth-jeshimoth as far as the meadows of
Acacia* on the plains of Moab.

50 While they were camped near the Jordan River on the plains of Moab
opposite Jericho, the LORD said to Moses, 51 "Give the following instructions
to the people of Israel: When you cross the Jordan River into the land of
Canaan, 52 you must drive out all the people living there. You must destroy
all their carved and molten images and demolish all their pagan shrines.
53 Take possession of the land and settle in it, because I have given it to you
to occupy. 54 You must distribute the land among the clans by sacred lot and
in proportion to their size. A larger portion of land will be allotted to each of
the larger clans, and a smaller portion will be allotted to each of the smaller
clans. The decision of the sacred lot is final. In this way, the portions of land
will be divided among your ancestral tribes. 55 But if you fail to drive out the
people who live in the land, those who remain will be like splinters in your
eyes and thorns in your sides. They will harass you in the land where you
live. 56 And I will do to you what I had planned to do to them."

Boundaries of the Land

34 Then the LORD said to Moses, 2 "Give these instructions to the Isra-
elites: When you come into the land of Canaan, which I am giving
you as your special possession, these will be the boundaries. 3 The southern
portion of your country will extend from the wilderness of Zin, along the
edge of Edom. The southern boundary will begin on the east at the Dead
Sea.* 4 It will then run south past Scorpion Pass* in the direction of Zin. Its

33:38 This day in the ancient Hebrew lunar calendar occurred in July or August. 33:45 As in 33:44; Hebrew reads *Iyim*, another name for Iye-abarim. 33:47 Or *the mountains of Abarim;* also in 33:48. 33:49 Hebrew *as far as Abel-shittim.* 34:3 Hebrew *Salt Sea;* also in 34:12. 34:4 Or *the ascent of Akrabbim.*

southernmost point will be Kadesh-barnea, from which it will go to Hazar-
addar, and on to Azmon. 5 From Azmon the boundary will turn toward the
Brook of Egypt and end at the Mediterranean Sea.*
6 "Your western boundary will be the coastline of the Mediterranean Sea.
7 "Your northern boundary will begin at the Mediterranean Sea and run
east to Mount Hor, 8 then to Lebo-hamath, and on through Zedad 9 and Ziph-
ron to Hazar-enan. This will be your northern boundary.
10 "The eastern boundary will start at Hazar-enan and run south to She-
pham, 11 then down to Riblah on the east side of Ain. From there the bound-
ary will run down along the eastern edge of the Sea of Galilee,* 12 and then
along the Jordan River to the Dead Sea. These are the boundaries of your
land."

13 Then Moses told the Israelites, "This territory is the homeland you are
to divide among yourselves by sacred lot. The LORD has commanded that the
land be divided among the nine and a half remaining tribes. 14 The families
of the tribes of Reuben, Gad, and half the tribe of Manasseh have already
received their grants of land 15 on the east side of the Jordan River, across
from Jericho toward the sunrise."

Leaders to Divide the Land

16 And the LORD said to Moses, 17 "Eleazar the priest and Joshua son of Nun
are the men designated to divide the grants of land among the people. 18 En-
list one leader from each tribe to help them with the task. 19 These are the
tribes and the names of the leaders:

	Tribe	*Leader*
	Judah	Caleb son of Jephunneh
20	Simeon	Shemuel son of Ammihud
21	Benjamin	Elidad son of Kislon
22	Dan	Bukki son of Jogli
23	Manasseh son of Joseph	Hanniel son of Ephod
24	Ephraim son of Joseph	Kemuel son of Shiphtan
25	Zebulun	Elizaphan son of Parnach
26	Issachar	Paltiel son of Azzan
27	Asher	Ahihud son of Shelomi
28	Naphtali	Pedahel son of Ammihud

29 These are the men the LORD has appointed to divide the grants of land in
Canaan among the Israelites."

Towns for the Levites

35 While Israel was camped beside the Jordan on the plains of Moab
across from Jericho, the LORD said to Moses, 2 "Command the
people of Israel to give to the Levites from their property certain towns to
live in, along with the surrounding pasturelands. 3 These towns will be for
the Levites to live in, and the surrounding lands will provide pasture for
their cattle, flocks, and other livestock. 4 The pastureland assigned to the
Levites around these towns will extend 1,500 feet* from the town walls in
every direction. 5 Measure off 3,000 feet* outside the town walls in every

34:5 Hebrew *the sea;* also in 34:6, 7. **34:11** Hebrew *Sea of Kinnereth.* **35:4** Hebrew *1,000 cubits* [460 meters]. **35:5** Hebrew *2,000 cubits* [920 meters].

Question 35:11

People often have the impression that God's rules were harsh. However, the Lord set up an ingenious system of reconciliation for people who had committed the worst of crimes. How does God's desire to restore people challenge you to offer second chances to people?

direction—east, south, west, north—with the town at the center. This area
will serve as the larger pastureland for the towns.
6 “Six of the towns you give the Levites will be cities of refuge, where a
person who has accidentally killed someone can flee for safety. In addition,
give them forty-two other towns. 7 In all, forty-eight towns with the sur-
rounding pastureland will be given to the Levites. 8 These towns will come
from the property of the people of Israel. The larger tribes will give more
towns to the Levites, while the smaller tribes will give fewer. Each tribe will
give property in proportion to the size of its land.”

Cities of Refuge

9 The LORD said to Moses, 10 “Give the following instructions to the people
of Israel.
“When you cross the Jordan into the land of Canaan, 11 designate cities
of refuge to which people can flee if they have killed someone accidentally.
12 These cities will be places of protection from a dead person's relatives who
want to avenge the death. The slayer must not be put to death before being
tried by the community. 13 Designate six cities of refuge for yourselves, 14 three
on the east side of the Jordan River and three on the west in the land of
Canaan. 15 These cities are for the protection of Israelites, foreigners living
among you, and traveling merchants. Anyone who accidentally kills some-
one may flee there for safety.
16 “But if someone strikes and kills another person with a piece of iron, it
is murder, and the murderer must be executed. 17 Or if someone with a stone
in his hand strikes and kills another person, it is murder, and the murderer
must be put to death. 18 Or if someone strikes and kills another person with
a wooden object, it is murder, and the murderer must be put to death. 19 The
victim's nearest relative is responsible for putting the murderer to death.
When they meet, the avenger must put the murderer to death. 20 So if some-
one hates another person and waits in ambush, then pushes him or throws
something at him and he dies, it is murder. 21 Or if someone hates another
person and hits him with a fist and he dies, it is murder. In such cases, the
avenger must put the murderer to death when they meet.
22 “But suppose someone pushes another person without having shown
previous hostility, or throws something that unintentionally hits another
person, 23 or accidentally drops a huge stone on someone, though they were
not enemies, and the person dies. 24 If this should happen, the community
must follow these regulations in making a judgment between the slayer and
the avenger, the victim's nearest relative: 25 The community must protect the
slayer from the avenger and must escort the slayer back to live in the city of
refuge to which he fled. There he must remain until the death of the high
priest, who was anointed with the sacred oil.
26 “But if the slayer ever leaves the limits of the city of refuge, 27 and the
avenger finds him outside the city and kills him, it will not be considered
murder. 28 The slayer should have stayed inside the city of refuge until the
death of the high priest. But after the death of the high priest, the slayer may
return to his own property. 29 These are legal requirements for you to observe
from generation to generation, wherever you may live.
30 “All murderers must be put to death, but only if evidence is presented by
more than one witness. No one may be put to death on the testimony of only

one witness. 31 Also, you must never accept a ransom payment for the life of
someone judged guilty of murder and subject to execution; murderers must
always be put to death. 32 And never accept a ransom payment from someone
who has fled to a city of refuge, allowing a slayer to return to his property
before the death of the high priest. 33 This will ensure that the land where
you live will not be polluted, for murder pollutes the land. And no sacrifice
except the execution of the murderer can purify the land from murder.*
34 You must not defile the land where you live, for I live there myself. I am
the LORD, who lives among the people of Israel."

Women Who Inherit Property

36 Then the heads of the clans of Gilead—descendants of Makir, son
of Manasseh, son of Joseph—came to Moses and the family leaders
of Israel with a petition. 2 They said, "Sir, the LORD instructed you to divide
the land by sacred lot among the people of Israel. You were told by the LORD
to give the grant of land owned by our brother Zelophehad to his daugh-
ters. 3 But if they marry men from another tribe, their grants of land will go
with them to the tribe into which they marry. In this way, the total area of
our tribal land will be reduced. 4 Then when the Year of Jubilee comes, their
portion of land will be added to that of the new tribe, causing it to be lost
forever to our ancestral tribe."

5 So Moses gave the Israelites this command from the LORD: "The claim
of the men of the tribe of Joseph is legitimate. 6 This is what the LORD com-
mands concerning the daughters of Zelophehad: Let them marry anyone
they like, as long as it is within their own ancestral tribe. 7 None of the ter-
ritorial land may pass from tribe to tribe, for all the land given to each tribe
must remain within the tribe to which it was first allotted. 8 The daughters
throughout the tribes of Israel who are in line to inherit property must
marry within their tribe, so that all the Israelites will keep their ancestral
property. 9 No grant of land may pass from one tribe to another; each tribe
of Israel must keep its allotted portion of land."

10 The daughters of Zelophehad did as the LORD commanded Moses.
11 Mahlah, Tirzah, Hoglah, Milcah, and Noah all married cousins on their
father's side. 12 They married into the clans of Manasseh son of Joseph. Thus,
their inheritance of land remained within their ancestral tribe.

13 These are the commands and regulations that the LORD gave to the
people of Israel through Moses while they were camped on the plains of
Moab beside the Jordan River, across from Jericho.

35:33 Or *can make atonement for murder.*

Make a Difference

35:34

Live among the Land

We see a glimpse of it often. In the brilliance of millions of stars. The intricate dance of leaves in the wind. The sparkle of wonder in someone's eye. The deep pausing breath during a treasured moment. The hopeful spring of a child's step. This is how the world was created to be. This is how we were created to live in the world. Beautiful.

Sadly, we also see the exact opposite. Stars obscured. Creation spoiled. The snarled brow of anger. The mourning of loss. The shattering of innocence. This is how many people perceive the world to be. Contaminated.

We need Jesus because he is the one who created this world to be beautiful. He is ready to re-create it, and he wants to begin his re-creative work in us (Ephesians 4:23-24).

Difference Maker

Invite some people to look at the world with fresh eyes today. Take a moment together to notice the beauty that is inherent in your region. Then imagine what this land would be like if people fully followed God's patterns. Take time to pray, asking God to re-create hearts in your area.

Prayer **36:13**

Lord Jesus, teach me to love your commands. As I follow your ways, your Spirit will help me become freer to make this world the place you created it to be. Amen.

Deuteronomy Introduction

Take a moment to think about a good childhood memory: perhaps a fun vacation, a time you accomplished a really big goal, or a time you remember simply being very happy. You probably have other childhood memories that aren't as fun to recall: a time you were injured, a fight with a good friend, or maybe the death of someone you loved very much. Some memories remind us that life can be very good. Other memories can bring sadness or a sense of loss.

The book of Deuteronomy was written to the nation of Israel as the people were preparing to enter the land that God had promised to their ancestors several generations earlier. This book was written by Moses, who had been the leader of the Israelites for forty years. He wanted to remind them of many things that had happened to them and their parents, both terrible things and the miraculous. This was more than a history lesson or a moment to reminisce. This was an opportunity to learn from past successes and failures. Moses wanted this young generation of Israelites to remember the presence and work of God throughout their family history. He wanted to remind them so they could make better choices than their parents.

Moses also knew these would be his final words as the leader of Israel. Moses had been disobedient to a command God had given, so another man named Joshua would now lead the people as they moved into the new land they would call home. Final words are important, and Moses chose his carefully. He used his final words to call the Israelites to be unique, to live so differently that the other nations around them would know and believe that the God of the Israelites was unlike any other god. Through Moses, God was instructing his people to be difference makers.

Story Arcs

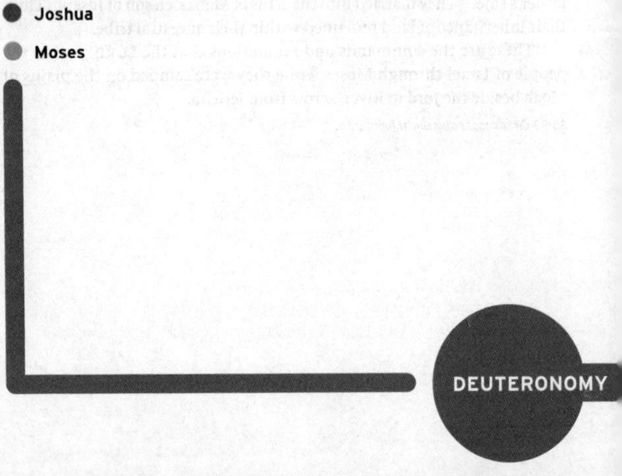

Deuteronomy

Introduction to Moses' First Address

1 These are the words that Moses spoke to all the people of Israel while
they were in the wilderness east of the Jordan River. They were camped
in the Jordan Valley* near Suph, between Paran on one side and Tophel, La-
ban, Hazeroth, and Di-zahab on the other.
2 Normally it takes only eleven days to travel from Mount Sinai* to Kadesh-
barnea, going by way of Mount Seir. 3 But forty years after the Israelites left
Egypt, on the first day of the eleventh month,* Moses addressed the people
of Israel, telling them everything the LORD had commanded him to say.
4 This took place after he had defeated King Sihon of the Amorites, who ruled
in Heshbon, and at Edrei had defeated King Og of Bashan, who ruled in
Ashtaroth.
5 While the Israelites were in the land of Moab east of the Jordan River,
Moses carefully explained the LORD's instructions as follows.

The Command to Leave Sinai

6 "When we were at Mount Sinai, the LORD our God said to us, 'You have
stayed at this mountain long enough. 7 It is time to break camp and move on.
Go to the hill country of the Amorites and to all the neighboring regions—
the Jordan Valley, the hill country, the western foothills,* the Negev, and the
coastal plain. Go to the land of the Canaanites and to Lebanon, and all the
way to the great Euphrates River. 8 Look, I am giving all this land to you! Go
in and occupy it, for it is the land the LORD swore to give to your ancestors
Abraham, Isaac, and Jacob, and to all their descendants.'"

Moses Appoints Leaders from Each Tribe

9 Moses continued, "At that time I told you, 'You are too great a burden for
me to carry all by myself. 10 The LORD your God has increased your popula-
tion, making you as numerous as the stars! 11 And may the LORD, the God
of your ancestors, multiply you a thousand times more and bless you as he
promised! 12 But you are such a heavy load to carry! How can I deal with all
your problems and bickering? 13 Choose some well-respected men from each
tribe who are known for their wisdom and understanding, and I will appoint
them as your leaders.'
14 "Then you responded, 'Your plan is a good one.' 15 So I took the wise and
respected men you had selected from your tribes and appointed them to
serve as judges and officials over you. Some were responsible for a thousand
people, some for a hundred, some for fifty, and some for ten.
16 "At that time I instructed the judges, 'You must hear the cases of your
fellow Israelites and the foreigners living among you. Be perfectly fair in

Make a Difference 1:3

Trust God

What was supposed to be an eleven-day trip ended up taking forty years. How is that even possible? It happened because the generation of Israelites who were rescued from slavery in Egypt demonstrated a serious lack of faith when it came to entering the land God had already promised them. Instead of believing that he would help them defeat anyone who stood in the way of his promises, the people decided, out of fear, to walk around for forty years and live as nomads (people constantly on the move without a place to call home).

Difference Maker

Decide in your heart that you will trust God's promises and boldly follow his lead throughout your whole life.

1:1 Hebrew *the Arabah;* also in 1:7. 1:2 Hebrew *Horeb,* another name for Sinai; also in 1:6, 19. 1:3 Hebrew *In the fortieth year, on the first day of the eleventh month.* This day in the ancient Hebrew lunar calendar occurred in January or February. 1:7 Hebrew *the Shephelah.*

your decisions 17 and impartial in your judgments. Hear the cases of those
who are poor as well as those who are rich. Don't be afraid of anyone's anger,
for the decision you make is God's decision. Bring me any cases that are too
difficult for you, and I will handle them.'
18 "At that time I gave you instructions about everything you were to do.

Scouts Explore the Land

19 "Then, just as the LORD our God commanded us, we left Mount Sinai
and traveled through the great and terrifying wilderness, as you yourselves
remember, and headed toward the hill country of the Amorites. When we
arrived at Kadesh-barnea, 20 I said to you, 'You have now reached the hill
country of the Amorites that the LORD our God is giving us. 21 Look! He has
placed the land in front of you. Go and occupy it as the LORD, the God of
your ancestors, has promised you. Don't be afraid! Don't be discouraged!'
22 "But you all came to me and said, 'First, let's send out scouts to explore
the land for us. They will advise us on the best route to take and which towns
we should enter.'
23 "This seemed like a good idea to me, so I chose twelve scouts, one from
each of your tribes. 24 They headed for the hill country and came to the val-
ley of Eshcol and explored it. 25 They picked some of its fruit and brought it
back to us. And they reported, 'The land the LORD our God has given us is
indeed a good land.'

Israel's Rebellion against the LORD

26 "But you rebelled against the command of the LORD your God and refused
to go in. 27 You complained in your tents and said, 'The LORD must hate us.
That's why he has brought us here from Egypt—to hand us over to the Am-
orites to be slaughtered. 28 Where can we go? Our brothers have demoralized
us with their report. They tell us, "The people of the land are taller and more
powerful than we are, and their towns are large, with walls rising high into
the sky! We even saw giants there—the descendants of Anak!"'
29 "But I said to you, 'Don't be shocked or afraid of them! 30 The LORD your
God is going ahead of you. He will fight for you, just as you saw him do in
Egypt. 31 And you saw how the LORD your God cared for you all along the way
as you traveled through the wilderness, just as a father cares for his child.
Now he has brought you to this place.'
32 "But even after all he did, you refused to trust the LORD your God, 33 who
goes before you looking for the best places to camp, guiding you with a pillar
of fire by night and a pillar of cloud by day.
34 "When the LORD heard your complaining, he became very angry. So he
solemnly swore, 35 'Not one of you from this wicked generation will live to see
the good land I swore to give your ancestors, 36 except Caleb son of Jephun-
neh. He will see this land because he has followed the LORD completely. I will
give to him and his descendants some of the very land he explored during
his scouting mission.'
37 "And the LORD was also angry with me because of you. He said to me,
'Moses, not even you will enter the Promised Land! 38 Instead, your assistant,
Joshua son of Nun, will lead the people into the land. Encourage him, for he
will lead Israel as they take possession of it. 39 I will give the land to your little
ones—your innocent children. You were afraid they would be captured, but

they will be the ones who occupy it. 40 As for you, turn around now and go
on back through the wilderness toward the Red Sea.*'
41 "Then you confessed, 'We have sinned against the LORD! We will go
into the land and fight for it, as the LORD our God has commanded us.' So
your men strapped on their weapons, thinking it would be easy to attack
the hill country.
42 "But the LORD told me to tell you, 'Do not attack, for I am not with you.
If you go ahead on your own, you will be crushed by your enemies.'
43 "This is what I told you, but you would not listen. Instead, you again
rebelled against the LORD's command and arrogantly went into the hill
country to fight. 44 But the Amorites who lived there came out against you
like a swarm of bees. They chased and battered you all the way from Seir to
Hormah. 45 Then you returned and wept before the LORD, but he refused to
listen. 46 So you stayed there at Kadesh for a long time.

Remembering Israel's Wanderings

2 "Then we turned around and headed back across the wilderness toward
the Red Sea,* just as the LORD had instructed me, and we wandered
around in the region of Mount Seir for a long time.
2 "Then at last the LORD said to me, 3 'You have been wandering around
in this hill country long enough; turn to the north. 4 Give these orders to the
people: "You will pass through the country belonging to your relatives the
Edomites, the descendants of Esau, who live in Seir. The Edomites will feel
threatened, so be careful. 5 Do not bother them, for I have given them all the hill
country around Mount Seir as their property, and I will not give you even one
square foot of their land. 6 If you need food to eat or water to drink, pay them
for it. 7 For the LORD your God has blessed you in everything you have done. He
has watched your every step through this great wilderness. During these forty
years, the LORD your God has been with you, and you have lacked nothing."'
8 "So we bypassed the territory of our relatives, the descendants of Esau,
who live in Seir. We avoided the road through the Arabah Valley that comes
up from Elath and Ezion-geber.
"Then as we turned north along the desert route through Moab, 9 the
LORD warned us, 'Do not bother the Moabites, the descendants of Lot, or
start a war with them. I have given them Ar as their property, and I will not
give you any of their land.'"
10 (A race of giants called the Emites had once lived in the area of Ar. They
were as strong and numerous and tall as the Anakites, another race of giants.
11 Both the Emites and the Anakites are also known as the Rephaites, though
the Moabites call them Emites. 12 In earlier times the Horites had lived in Seir,
but they were driven out and displaced by the descendants of Esau, just as
Israel drove out the people of Canaan when the LORD gave Israel their land.)
13 Moses continued, "Then the LORD said to us, 'Get moving. Cross the
Zered Brook.' So we crossed the brook.
14 "Thirty-eight years passed from the time we first left Kadesh-barnea
until we finally crossed the Zered Brook! By then, all the men old enough
to fight in battle had died in the wilderness, as the LORD had vowed would
happen. 15 The LORD struck them down until they had all been eliminated
from the community.

1:40 Hebrew *sea of reeds.* 2:1 Hebrew *sea of reeds.*

Write your notes in this space

[16]"When all the men of fighting age had died, [17]the LORD said to me,
[18]'Today you will cross the border of Moab at Ar [19]and enter the land of the Ammonites, the descendants of Lot. But do not bother them or start a war with them. I have given the land of Ammon to them as their property, and I will not give you any of their land.'"

[20](That area was once considered the land of the Rephaites, who had lived
there, though the Ammonites call them Zamzummites. [21]They were also as
strong and numerous and tall as the Anakites. But the LORD destroyed them
so the Ammonites could occupy their land. [22]He had done the same for the
descendants of Esau who lived in Seir, for he destroyed the Horites so they could settle there in their place. The descendants of Esau live there to this
day. [23]A similar thing happened when the Caphtorites from Crete* invaded
and destroyed the Avvites, who had lived in villages in the area of Gaza.)

[24]Moses continued, "Then the LORD said, 'Now get moving! Cross the Arnon Gorge. Look, I will hand over to you Sihon the Amorite, king of Heshbon, and I will give you his land. Attack him and begin to occupy the land.
[25]Beginning today I will make people throughout the earth terrified because of you. When they hear reports about you, they will tremble with dread and fear.'"

Victory over Sihon of Heshbon

[26]Moses continued, "From the wilderness of Kedemoth I sent ambassadors to King Sihon of Heshbon with this proposal of peace:

> [27]'Let us travel through your land. We will stay on the main road and
> won't turn off into the fields on either side. [28]Sell us food to eat and
> water to drink, and we will pay for it. All we want is permission to pass
> through your land. [29]The descendants of Esau who live in Seir allowed
> us to go through their country, and so did the Moabites, who live in Ar. Let us pass through until we cross the Jordan into the land the LORD our God is giving us.'

[30]"But King Sihon of Heshbon refused to allow us to pass through, because the LORD your God made Sihon stubborn and defiant so he could help you defeat him, as he has now done.

[31]"Then the LORD said to me, 'Look, I have begun to hand King Sihon and his land over to you. Begin now to conquer and occupy his land.'

[32]"Then King Sihon declared war on us and mobilized his forces at Jahaz.
[33]But the LORD our God handed him over to us, and we crushed him, his
sons, and all his people. [34]We conquered all his towns and completely destroyed* everyone—men, women, and children. Not a single person was
spared. [35]We took all the livestock as plunder for ourselves, along with anything of value from the towns we ransacked.

[36]"The LORD our God also helped us conquer Aroer on the edge of the Arnon Gorge, and the town in the gorge, and the whole area as far as Gilead.
No town had walls too strong for us. [37]However, we avoided the land of the Ammonites all along the Jabbok River and the towns in the hill country—all the places the LORD our God had commanded us to leave alone.

2:23 Hebrew *from Caphtor.* 2:34 The Hebrew term used here refers to the complete consecration of things or people to the LORD, either by destroying them or by giving them as an offering.

Victory over Og of Bashan

3 "Next we turned and headed for the land of Bashan, where King Og and
his entire army attacked us at Edrei. 2 But the LORD told me, 'Do not be
afraid of him, for I have given you victory over Og and his entire army, and
I will give you all his land. Treat him just as you treated King Sihon of the
Amorites, who ruled in Heshbon.'
3 "So the LORD our God handed King Og and all his people over to us,
and we killed them all. Not a single person survived. 4 We conquered all
sixty of his towns—the entire Argob region in his kingdom of Bashan. Not
a single town escaped our conquest. 5 These towns were all fortified with
high walls and barred gates. We also took many unwalled villages at the
same time. 6 We completely destroyed* the kingdom of Bashan, just as we
had destroyed King Sihon of Heshbon. We destroyed all the people in every
town we conquered—men, women, and children alike. 7 But we kept all the
livestock for ourselves and took plunder from all the towns.
8 "So we took the land of the two Amorite kings east of the Jordan River—
all the way from the Arnon Gorge to Mount Hermon. 9 (Mount Hermon is
called Sirion by the Sidonians, and the Amorites call it Senir.) 10 We had now
conquered all the cities on the plateau and all Gilead and Bashan, as far as
the towns of Salecah and Edrei, which were part of Og's kingdom in Bashan.
11 (King Og of Bashan was the last survivor of the giant Rephaites. His bed
was made of iron and was more than thirteen feet long and six feet wide.* It
can still be seen in the Ammonite city of Rabbah.)

Land Division East of the Jordan

12 "When we took possession of this land, I gave to the tribes of Reuben and
Gad the territory beyond Aroer along the Arnon Gorge, plus half of the hill
country of Gilead with its towns. 13 Then I gave the rest of Gilead and all of
Bashan—Og's former kingdom—to the half-tribe of Manasseh. (This entire
Argob region of Bashan used to be known as the land of the Rephaites. 14 Jair,
a leader from the tribe of Manasseh, conquered the whole Argob region in
Bashan, all the way to the border of the Geshurites and Maacathites. Jair
renamed this region after himself, calling it the Towns of Jair,* as it is still
known today.) 15 I gave Gilead to the clan of Makir. 16 But I also gave part of
Gilead to the tribes of Reuben and Gad. The area I gave them extended from
the middle of the Arnon Gorge in the south to the Jabbok River on the Am-
monite frontier. 17 They also received the Jordan Valley, all the way from the
Sea of Galilee down to the Dead Sea,* with the Jordan River serving as the
western boundary. To the east were the slopes of Pisgah.
18 "At that time I gave this command to the tribes that would live east of
the Jordan: 'Although the LORD your God has given you this land as your
property, all your fighting men must cross the Jordan ahead of your Isra-
elite relatives, armed and ready to assist them. 19 Your wives, children, and
numerous livestock, however, may stay behind in the towns I have given you.
20 When the LORD has given security to the rest of the Israelites, as he has to
you, and when they occupy the land the LORD your God is giving them across
the Jordan River, then you may all return here to the land I have given you.'

3:6 The Hebrew term used here refers to the complete consecration of things or people to the LORD, either by destroying them or by giving them as an offering; also in 3:6b. **3:11** Hebrew *9 cubits* [4.1 meters] *long and 4 cubits* [1.8 meters] *wide.* **3:14** Hebrew *Havvoth-jair.* **3:17** Hebrew *from Kinnereth to the Sea of the Arabah, the Salt Sea.*

Why this matters!

Moses Forbidden to Enter the Land

21 “At that time I gave Joshua this charge: ‘You have seen for yourself every-
thing the LORD your God has done to these two kings. He will do the same
to all the kingdoms on the west side of the Jordan. 22 Do not be afraid of the
nations there, for the LORD your God will fight for you.’

23 “At that time I pleaded with the LORD and said, 24 ‘O Sovereign LORD,
you have only begun to show your greatness and the strength of your hand
to me, your servant. Is there any god in heaven or on earth who can perform
such great and mighty deeds as you do? 25 Please let me cross the Jordan to
see the wonderful land on the other side, the beautiful hill country and the
Lebanon mountains.’

26 “But the LORD was angry with me because of you, and he would not
listen to me. ‘That’s enough!’ he declared. ‘Speak of it no more. 27 But go up
to Pisgah Peak, and look over the land in every direction. Take a good look,
but you may not cross the Jordan River. 28 Instead, commission Joshua and
encourage and strengthen him, for he will lead the people across the Jordan.
He will give them all the land you now see before you as their possession.’
29 So we stayed in the valley near Beth-peor.

Moses Urges Israel to Obey

4 “And now, Israel, listen carefully to these decrees and regulations that I
am about to teach you. Obey them so that you may live, so you may enter
and occupy the land that the LORD, the God of your ancestors, is giving you.
2 Do not add to or subtract from these commands I am giving you. Just obey
the commands of the LORD your God that I am giving you.

3 “You saw for yourself what the LORD did to you at Baal-peor. There the
LORD your God destroyed everyone who had worshiped Baal, the god of
Peor. 4 But all of you who were faithful to the LORD your God are still alive
today—every one of you.

5 “Look, I now teach you these decrees and regulations just as the LORD my
God commanded me, so that you may obey them in the land you are about to
enter and occupy. 6 Obey them completely, and you will display your wisdom
and intelligence among the surrounding nations. When they hear all these
decrees, they will exclaim, ‘How wise and prudent are the people of this
great nation!’ 7 For what great nation has a god as near to them as the LORD
our God is near to us whenever we call on him? 8 And what great nation has
decrees and regulations as righteous and fair as this body of instructions
that I am giving you today?

9 “But watch out! Be careful never to forget what you yourself have seen.
Do not let these memories escape from your mind as long as you live! And
be sure to pass them on to your children and grandchildren. 10 Never forget
the day when you stood before the LORD your God at Mount Sinai,* where
he told me, ‘Summon the people before me, and I will personally instruct
them. Then they will learn to fear me as long as they live, and they will teach
their children to fear me also.’

11 “You came near and stood at the foot of the mountain, while flames from
the mountain shot into the sky. The mountain was shrouded in black clouds
and deep darkness. 12 And the LORD spoke to you from the heart of the fire.
You heard the sound of his words but didn’t see his form; there was only a

Story Arc **3:21-28**

● Joshua

God appointed Joshua to be Moses’ successor and to lead the new generation of Israelites into the promised land. Joshua was a perfect choice for this role, in part because he was one of only two leaders who believed forty years earlier that if the people would trust God’s promises, they would have nothing to fear as they entered the new land. The people chose instead to walk away from the promise of a new land to call their own and wander through the wilderness for about forty years. Because Joshua trusted God, it is fitting that he would fill the leadership void and take a new generation of Israelites across the Jordan River and into the promised land. What lesson do you see in this generational handoff of leadership?

Deut 32:48-52 ►

4:10 Hebrew *Horeb,* another name for Sinai; also in 4:15.

voice. 13 He proclaimed his covenant—the Ten Commandments*—which he
commanded you to keep, and which he wrote on two stone tablets. 14 It was at
that time that the LORD commanded me to teach you his decrees and regula-
tions so you would obey them in the land you are about to enter and occupy.

A Warning against Idolatry

15 "But be very careful! You did not see the LORD's form on the day he spoke
to you from the heart of the fire at Mount Sinai. 16 So do not corrupt your-
selves by making an idol in any form—whether of a man or a woman, 17 an
animal on the ground, a bird in the sky, 18 a small animal that scurries along
the ground, or a fish in the deepest sea. 19 And when you look up into the sky
and see the sun, moon, and stars—all the forces of heaven—don't be seduced
into worshiping them. The LORD your God gave them to all the peoples of
the earth. 20 Remember that the LORD rescued you from the iron-smelting
furnace of Egypt in order to make you his very own people and his special
possession, which is what you are today.

21 "But the LORD was angry with me because of you. He vowed that I would
not cross the Jordan River into the good land the LORD your God is giving
you as your special possession. 22 You will cross the Jordan to occupy the land,
but I will not. Instead, I will die here on the east side of the river. 23 So be care-
ful not to break the covenant the LORD your God has made with you. Do not
make idols of any shape or form, for the LORD your God has forbidden this.
24 The LORD your God is a devouring fire; he is a jealous God.

25 "In the future, when you have children and grandchildren and have
lived in the land a long time, do not corrupt yourselves by making idols of
any kind. This is evil in the sight of the LORD your God and will arouse his
anger.

26 "Today I call on heaven and earth as witnesses against you. If you break
my covenant, you will quickly disappear from the land you are crossing the
Jordan to occupy. You will live there only a short time; then you will be ut-
terly destroyed. 27 For the LORD will scatter you among the nations, where
only a few of you will survive. 28 There, in a foreign land, you will worship
idols made from wood and stone—gods that neither see nor hear nor eat
nor smell. 29 But from there you will search again for the LORD your God.
And if you search for him with all your heart and soul, you will find him.

30 "In the distant future, when you are suffering all these things, you will
finally return to the LORD your God and listen to what he tells you. 31 For the
LORD your God is a merciful God; he will not abandon you or destroy you or
forget the solemn covenant he made with your ancestors.

There Is Only One God

32 "Now search all of history, from the time God created people on the earth
until now, and search from one end of the heavens to the other. Has anything
as great as this ever been seen or heard before? 33 Has any nation ever heard
the voice of God* speaking from fire—as you did—and survived? 34 Has any
other god dared to take a nation for himself out of another nation by means
of trials, miraculous signs, wonders, war, a strong hand, a powerful arm, and
terrifying acts? Yet that is what the LORD your God did for you in Egypt,
right before your eyes.

4:13 Hebrew *the ten words.* 4:33 Or *voice of a god.*

Make a Difference 4:1-2

Obedience

It's very easy to try to change a rule when we don't like obeying it. We sometimes make a sinful choice, feel guilty about it, and then try to downplay the seriousness of it so that we don't have to deal with the uncomfortable guilt. However, feeling guilty, in this case, is good. When we are disobedient and make sinful choices, we feel bad about it because the Holy Spirit prompts our hearts to respond with regret and remorse. To ignore that feeling or to decide that the feeling should not have any effect on us is to ignore an important part of what it means to be a child of God. When we disobey God, we turn our hearts away from him and toward something else. This posture makes it hard for God to show us how to be difference makers.

Difference Maker

Identify any area of disobedience in your life, confess that to God, and ask him to forgive you. Then receive his unconditional forgiveness and let him know you are ready to make a difference wherever and whenever he calls you.

Question **5:1**

Why do you think these ten commands were given in such a dramatic way?

35"He showed you these things so you would know that the LORD is God and there is no other. 36He let you hear his voice from heaven so he could instruct you. He let you see his great fire here on earth so he could speak to you from it. 37Because he loved your ancestors, he chose to bless their descendants, and he personally brought you out of Egypt with a great display of power. 38He drove out nations far greater than you, so he could bring you in and give you their land as your special possession, as it is today.

39"So remember this and keep it firmly in mind: The LORD is God both in heaven and on earth, and there is no other. 40If you obey all the decrees and commands I am giving you today, all will be well with you and your children. I am giving you these instructions so you will enjoy a long life in the land the LORD your God is giving you for all time."

Eastern Cities of Refuge

41Then Moses set apart three cities of refuge east of the Jordan River. 42Anyone who killed another person unintentionally, without previous hostility, could flee there to live in safety. 43These were the cities: Bezer on the wilderness plateau for the tribe of Reuben; Ramoth in Gilead for the tribe of Gad; Golan in Bashan for the tribe of Manasseh.

Introduction to Moses' Second Address

44This is the body of instruction that Moses presented to the Israelites. 45These are the laws, decrees, and regulations that Moses gave to the people of Israel when they left Egypt, 46and as they camped in the valley near Beth-peor east of the Jordan River. (This land was formerly occupied by the Amorites under King Sihon, who ruled from Heshbon. But Moses and the Israelites destroyed him and his people when they came up from Egypt. 47Israel took possession of his land and that of King Og of Bashan—the two Amorite kings east of the Jordan. 48So Israel conquered the entire area from Aroer at the edge of the Arnon Gorge all the way to Mount Sirion,* also called Mount Hermon. 49And they conquered the eastern bank of the Jordan River as far south as the Dead Sea,* below the slopes of Pisgah.)

Ten Commandments for the Covenant Community

5 Moses called all the people of Israel together and said, "Listen carefully, Israel. Hear the decrees and regulations I am giving you today, so you may learn them and obey them!

2"The LORD our God made a covenant with us at Mount Sinai.* 3The LORD did not make this covenant with our ancestors, but with all of us who are alive today. 4At the mountain the LORD spoke to you face to face from the heart of the fire. 5I stood as an intermediary between you and the LORD, for you were afraid of the fire and did not want to approach the mountain. He spoke to me, and I passed his words on to you. This is what he said:

6"I am the LORD your God, who rescued you from the land of Egypt, the place of your slavery.

7"You must not have any other god but me.

8"You must not make for yourself an idol of any kind, or an image of anything in the heavens or on the earth or in the sea. 9You must not

4:48 As in Syriac version (see also 3:9); Hebrew reads *Mount Sion.* **4:49** Hebrew *took the Arabah on the east side of the Jordan as far as the sea of the Arabah.* **5:2** Hebrew *Horeb,* another name for Sinai.

bow down to them or worship them, for I, the LORD your God, am a
jealous God who will not tolerate your affection for any other gods.
I lay the sins of the parents upon their children; the entire family is
affected—even children in the third and fourth generations of those
who reject me. 10 But I lavish unfailing love for a thousand generations
on those* who love me and obey my commands.
11 "You must not misuse the name of the LORD your God. The LORD will
not let you go unpunished if you misuse his name.
12 "Observe the Sabbath day by keeping it holy, as the LORD your God has
commanded you. 13 You have six days each week for your ordinary work,
14 but the seventh day is a Sabbath day of rest dedicated to the LORD
your God. On that day no one in your household may do any work. This includes you, your sons and daughters, your male and female servants, your oxen and donkeys and other livestock, and any foreigners living among you. All your male and female servants must rest as you do.
15 Remember that you were once slaves in Egypt, but the LORD your God
brought you out with his strong hand and powerful arm. That is why the LORD your God has commanded you to rest on the Sabbath day.
16 "Honor your father and mother, as the LORD your God commanded you. Then you will live a long, full life in the land the LORD your God is giving you.
17 "You must not murder.
18 "You must not commit adultery.
19 "You must not steal.
20 "You must not testify falsely against your neighbor.
21 "You must not covet your neighbor's wife. You must not covet your neighbor's house or land, male or female servant, ox or donkey, or anything else that belongs to your neighbor.

22 "The LORD spoke these words to all of you assembled there at the foot of the mountain. He spoke with a loud voice from the heart of the fire, surrounded by clouds and deep darkness. This was all he said at that time, and he wrote his words on two stone tablets and gave them to me.
23 "But when you heard the voice from the heart of the darkness, while the
mountain was blazing with fire, all your tribal leaders and elders came to me.
24 They said, 'Look, the LORD our God has shown us his glory and greatness,
and we have heard his voice from the heart of the fire. Today we have seen
that God can speak to us humans, and yet we live! 25 But now, why should we
risk death again? If the LORD our God speaks to us again, we will certainly
die and be consumed by this awesome fire. 26 Can any living thing hear the
voice of the living God from the heart of the fire as we did and yet survive?
27 Go yourself and listen to what the LORD our God says. Then come and tell
us everything he tells you, and we will listen and obey.'
28 "The LORD heard the request you made to me. And he said, 'I have heard
what the people said to you, and they are right. 29 Oh, that they would always
have hearts like this, that they might fear me and obey all my commands!
If they did, they and their descendants would prosper forever. 30 Go and
tell them, "Return to your tents." 31 But you stand here with me so I can
give you all my commands, decrees, and regulations. You must teach them

5:10 Hebrew *for thousands of those.*

Make a Difference 5:11

The Name

God's name is too often tossed about like a dirty rag in a garage. If we slam our thumb in the door or if we get some frustrating news, we launch his name into the air like a ballistic missile fueled by our irritation. If someone cuts us off in a line or in traffic, we grab the Lord's name and throw it back in reaction. If we get a juicy morsel of gossip or some unexpected news, we erupt in a barrage of flippant repetitions of his name. Sadly, we use various mutations of the name of Jesus—frequently laced with the vulgar power of profanity.

This needs to stop. We wouldn't want our own name discarded in the mud, cast carelessly about, and coupled with cursing. How can we dare do that with God's name? Importantly, out of the Ten Commandments, God placed the honor of his name as number three. We must not misuse God's name but rather seek to honor it in all that we do.

Difference Maker

Put Deuteronomy 5:11 into action today. Check yourself and gently remind others. As much as you are able, make a difference in how others talk about Jesus.

Make a Difference 5:16

Parents

Honor for parents ultimately honors God. It also will have long-term benefits for the child.

Difference Maker

Reach out to your mom or dad (or another significant mentor figure in your life) in a way that would meaningfully show them respect, gratitude, and love.

to the people so they can obey them in the land I am giving them as their
possession.'"
32 So Moses told the people, "You must be careful to obey all the commands
of the LORD your God, following his instructions in every detail. 33 Stay on the
path that the LORD your God has commanded you to follow. Then you will
live long and prosperous lives in the land you are about to enter and occupy.

A Call for Wholehearted Commitment

6 "These are the commands, decrees, and regulations that the LORD your
God commanded me to teach you. You must obey them in the land you
are about to enter and occupy, 2 and you and your children and grandchildren
must fear the LORD your God as long as you live. If you obey all his decrees
and commands, you will enjoy a long life. 3 Listen closely, Israel, and be care-
ful to obey. Then all will go well with you, and you will have many children
in the land flowing with milk and honey, just as the LORD, the God of your
ancestors, promised you.
4 "Listen, O Israel! The LORD is our God, the LORD alone.* 5 And you must
love the LORD your God with all your heart, all your soul, and all your
strength. 6 And you must commit yourselves wholeheartedly to these com-
mands that I am giving you today. 7 Repeat them again and again to your
children. Talk about them when you are at home and when you are on the
road, when you are going to bed and when you are getting up. 8 Tie them to
your hands and wear them on your forehead as reminders. 9 Write them on
the doorposts of your house and on your gates.
10 "The LORD your God will soon bring you into the land he swore to give
you when he made a vow to your ancestors Abraham, Isaac, and Jacob. It is a
land with large, prosperous cities that you did not build. 11 The houses will
be richly stocked with goods you did not produce. You will draw water from
cisterns you did not dig, and you will eat from vineyards and olive trees you
did not plant. When you have eaten your fill in this land, 12 be careful not to
forget the LORD, who rescued you from slavery in the land of Egypt. 13 You
must fear the LORD your God and serve him. When you take an oath, you
must use only his name.
14 "You must not worship any of the gods of neighboring nations, 15 for the
LORD your God, who lives among you, is a jealous God. His anger will flare
up against you, and he will wipe you from the face of the earth. 16 You must
not test the LORD your God as you did when you complained at Massah.
17 You must diligently obey the commands of the LORD your God—all the
laws and decrees he has given you. 18 Do what is right and good in the LORD's
sight, so all will go well with you. Then you will enter and occupy the good
land that the LORD swore to give your ancestors. 19 You will drive out all the
enemies living in the land, just as the LORD said you would.
20 "In the future your children will ask you, 'What is the meaning of these
laws, decrees, and regulations that the LORD our God has commanded us
to obey?'
21 "Then you must tell them, 'We were Pharaoh's slaves in Egypt, but the
LORD brought us out of Egypt with his strong hand. 22 The LORD did mi-
raculous signs and wonders before our eyes, dealing terrifying blows against
Egypt and Pharaoh and all his people. 23 He brought us out of Egypt so he

6:4 Or *The LORD our God is one LORD;* or *The LORD our God, the LORD is one;* or *The LORD is our God, the LORD is one.*

Prayer 6:4

God, I believe that you are the one true God. Help me to love you today with all my heart, soul, and strength. Amen.

Make a Difference

6:5–9

Teach Kids

One of the greatest differences you could make is to help the next generation follow Jesus. God wants us to be intentional about sharing faith with kids in every circumstance of our lives. Whether you have siblings, nieces, or nephews, or you are just around kids at church, the call to share faith with children is given to everyone.

Following Jesus is not just a Sunday morning activity. We follow him and demonstrate our faith to younger people when we are hanging out at home, commuting to work, praying before bedtime, or eating breakfast in the morning. In every activity and every place are opportunities to grow in Jesus and inspire younger people to do the same.

Difference Maker

Tie a string around your wrist (loosely, of course—don't cut off your circulation!) to remind yourself to help kids (maybe in a local church ministry) learn about Jesus.

could give us this land he had sworn to give our ancestors. 24 And the LORD
our God commanded us to obey all these decrees and to fear him so he can
continue to bless us and preserve our lives, as he has done to this day. 25 For
we will be counted as righteous when we obey all the commands the LORD
our God has given us.'

The Privilege of Holiness

7 "When the LORD your God brings you into the land you are about to
enter and occupy, he will clear away many nations ahead of you: the Hit-
tites, Girgashites, Amorites, Canaanites, Perizzites, Hivites, and Jebusites.
These seven nations are greater and more numerous than you. 2 When the
LORD your God hands these nations over to you and you conquer them, you
must completely destroy* them. Make no treaties with them and show them
no mercy. 3 You must not intermarry with them. Do not let your daughters
and sons marry their sons and daughters, 4 for they will lead your children
away from me to worship other gods. Then the anger of the LORD will burn
against you, and he will quickly destroy you. 5 This is what you must do.
You must break down their pagan altars and shatter their sacred pillars. Cut
down their Asherah poles and burn their idols. 6 For you are a holy people,
who belong to the LORD your God. Of all the people on earth, the LORD your
God has chosen you to be his own special treasure.
7 "The LORD did not set his heart on you and choose you because you were
more numerous than other nations, for you were the smallest of all nations!
8 Rather, it was simply that the LORD loves you, and he was keeping the oath
he had sworn to your ancestors. That is why the LORD rescued you with such
a strong hand from your slavery and from the oppressive hand of Pharaoh,
king of Egypt. 9 Understand, therefore, that the LORD your God is indeed
God. He is the faithful God who keeps his covenant for a thousand genera-
tions and lavishes his unfailing love on those who love him and obey his
commands. 10 But he does not hesitate to punish and destroy those who reject
him. 11 Therefore, you must obey all these commands, decrees, and regula-
tions I am giving you today.
12 "If you listen to these regulations and faithfully obey them, the LORD
your God will keep his covenant of unfailing love with you, as he promised
with an oath to your ancestors. 13 He will love you and bless you, and he will
give you many children. He will give fertility to your land and your animals.
When you arrive in the land he swore to give your ancestors, you will have
large harvests of grain, new wine, and olive oil, and great herds of cattle,
sheep, and goats. 14 You will be blessed above all the nations of the earth.
None of your men or women will be childless, and all your livestock will
bear young. 15 And the LORD will protect you from all sickness. He will not
let you suffer from the terrible diseases you knew in Egypt, but he will inflict
them on all your enemies!
16 "You must destroy all the nations the LORD your God hands over to you.
Show them no mercy, and do not worship their gods, or they will trap you.
17 Perhaps you will think to yourselves, 'How can we ever conquer these na-
tions that are so much more powerful than we are?' 18 But don't be afraid of
them! Just remember what the LORD your God did to Pharaoh and to all the
land of Egypt. 19 Remember the great terrors the LORD your God sent against

7:2 The Hebrew term used here refers to the complete consecration of things or people to the LORD, either by destroying them or by giving them as an offering; also in 7:26.

Make a Difference 7:6

Share Your Testimony

How do you typically care for and value things that you "treasure"? You might put those things in a safe place, away from potential harm, or perhaps in a highly visible place because seeing that treasure makes you happy.

You are God's special treasure. Imagine God caring for you, protecting you, admiring you, and giving you a place of importance. When he thinks about you, he smiles. That's true even if you make a mistake or really blow it when trying to live by his commands. Being treasured by the one who can have all the treasure in the world is an amazing truth.

Difference Maker

If you have a chance to tell a friend about God, be sure that this is part of the story. God cherishes those who are his children. We are valued beyond measure by the God of the universe. When he thinks about us and looks at us, he smiles. This might be a truth about God that your friend has never considered.

Prayer **8:3**

God, please shape me to be a person who always trusts you at your word. Amen.

them. You saw it all with your own eyes! And remember the miraculous signs
and wonders, and the strong hand and powerful arm with which he brought
you out of Egypt. The LORD your God will use this same power against all
the people you fear. 20 And then the LORD your God will send terror* to drive
out the few survivors still hiding from you!

21 "No, do not be afraid of those nations, for the LORD your God is among
you, and he is a great and awesome God. 22 The LORD your God will drive
those nations out ahead of you little by little. You will not clear them away
all at once, otherwise the wild animals would multiply too quickly for you.
23 But the LORD your God will hand them over to you. He will throw them
into complete confusion until they are destroyed. 24 He will put their kings
in your power, and you will erase their names from the face of the earth. No
one will be able to stand against you, and you will destroy them all.

25 "You must burn their idols in fire, and you must not covet the silver or
gold that covers them. You must not take it or it will become a trap to you, for
it is detestable to the LORD your God. 26 Do not bring any detestable objects
into your home, for then you will be destroyed, just like them. You must
utterly detest such things, for they are set apart for destruction.

A Call to Remember and Obey

8 "Be careful to obey all the commands I am giving you today. Then you
will live and multiply, and you will enter and occupy the land the LORD
swore to give your ancestors. 2 Remember how the LORD your God led you
through the wilderness for these forty years, humbling you and testing you
to prove your character, and to find out whether or not you would obey his
commands. 3 Yes, he humbled you by letting you go hungry and then feeding
you with manna, a food previously unknown to you and your ancestors. He
did it to teach you that people do not live by bread alone; rather, we live by
every word that comes from the mouth of the LORD. 4 For all these forty years
your clothes didn't wear out, and your feet didn't blister or swell. 5 Think
about it: Just as a parent disciplines a child, the LORD your God disciplines
you for your own good.

6 "So obey the commands of the LORD your God by walking in his ways
and fearing him. 7 For the LORD your God is bringing you into a good land
of flowing streams and pools of water, with fountains and springs that gush
out in the valleys and hills. 8 It is a land of wheat and barley; of grapevines,
fig trees, and pomegranates; of olive oil and honey. 9 It is a land where food
is plentiful and nothing is lacking. It is a land where iron is as common as
stone, and copper is abundant in the hills. 10 When you have eaten your fill,
be sure to praise the LORD your God for the good land he has given you.

11 "But that is the time to be careful! Beware that in your plenty you do
not forget the LORD your God and disobey his commands, regulations, and
decrees that I am giving you today. 12 For when you have become full and pros-
perous and have built fine homes to live in, 13 and when your flocks and herds
have become very large and your silver and gold have multiplied along with
everything else, be careful! 14 Do not become proud at that time and forget
the LORD your God, who rescued you from slavery in the land of Egypt. 15 Do
not forget that he led you through the great and terrifying wilderness with
its poisonous snakes and scorpions, where it was so hot and dry. He gave

7:20 Often rendered *the hornet.* The meaning of the Hebrew is uncertain.

you water from the rock! 16 He fed you with manna in the wilderness, a food
unknown to your ancestors. He did this to humble you and test you for your
own good. 17 He did all this so you would never say to yourself, 'I have achieved
this wealth with my own strength and energy.' 18 Remember the LORD your
God. He is the one who gives you power to be successful, in order to fulfill
the covenant he confirmed to your ancestors with an oath.
19 "But I assure you of this: If you ever forget the LORD your God and fol-
low other gods, worshiping and bowing down to them, you will certainly be
destroyed. 20 Just as the LORD has destroyed other nations in your path, you
also will be destroyed if you refuse to obey the LORD your God.

Victory by God's Grace

9 "Listen, O Israel! Today you are about to cross the Jordan River to take
over the land belonging to nations much greater and more powerful
than you. They live in cities with walls that reach to the sky! 2 The people are
strong and tall—descendants of the famous Anakite giants. You've heard the
saying, 'Who can stand up to the Anakites?' 3 But recognize today that the
LORD your God is the one who will cross over ahead of you like a devouring
fire to destroy them. He will subdue them so that you will quickly conquer
them and drive them out, just as the LORD has promised.
4 "After the LORD your God has done this for you, don't say in your hearts,
'The LORD has given us this land because we are such good people!' No, it is
because of the wickedness of the other nations that he is pushing them out
of your way. 5 It is not because you are so good or have such integrity that you
are about to occupy their land. The LORD your God will drive these nations
out ahead of you only because of their wickedness, and to fulfill the oath he
swore to your ancestors Abraham, Isaac, and Jacob. 6 You must recognize that
the LORD your God is not giving you this good land because you are good,
for you are not—you are a stubborn people.

Remembering the Gold Calf

7 "Remember and never forget how angry you made the LORD your God out
in the wilderness. From the day you left Egypt until now, you have been
constantly rebelling against him. 8 Even at Mount Sinai* you made the LORD
so angry he was ready to destroy you. 9 This happened when I was on the
mountain receiving the tablets of stone inscribed with the words of the
covenant that the LORD had made with you. I was there for forty days and
forty nights, and all that time I ate no food and drank no water. 10 The LORD
gave me the two tablets on which God had written with his own finger all
the words he had spoken to you from the heart of the fire when you were
assembled at the mountain.
11 "At the end of the forty days and nights, the LORD handed me the two
stone tablets inscribed with the words of the covenant. 12 Then the LORD
said to me, 'Get up! Go down immediately, for the people you brought out
of Egypt have corrupted themselves. How quickly they have turned away
from the way I commanded them to live! They have melted gold and made
an idol for themselves!'
13 "The LORD also said to me, 'I have seen how stubborn and rebellious
these people are. 14 Leave me alone so I may destroy them and erase their

9:8 Hebrew *Horeb,* another name for Sinai.

Make a Difference

9:7-17

False Gods

In this chapter, Moses used one of the worst stories from the Israelites' past to remind them that the promised land they were about to enter was not a reward for their good behavior but rather a gracious gift from the God who loved them and was willing to forgive their pride and rebellion. He reminded them that the older generation had made an idol out of gold so they could worship a "god" that was in the image of a young cow.

It would be easy to look at this story and say, "The Israelites were crazy to betray God and choose to worship a golden statue instead." However, we have to be careful because we are often prone to make the same grave error. We sometimes desire to have a "god" that we can see and control. The God of the Israelites is the God of this universe, and he will never be okay with his beloved children turning their affections to a lesser, false god.

Difference Maker

Making a difference in this world begins with acknowledging that there is no god that we can create that will be greater than the God who created us. If you can find any idols in your life, decide today to turn your back on them and your face toward God.

name from under heaven. Then I will make a mighty nation of your descen-
dants, a nation larger and more powerful than they are.'
15 "So while the mountain was blazing with fire I turned and came down,
holding in my hands the two stone tablets inscribed with the terms of the
covenant. 16 There below me I could see that you had sinned against the LORD
your God. You had melted gold and made a calf idol for yourselves. How
quickly you had turned away from the path the LORD had commanded you
to follow! 17 So I took the stone tablets and threw them to the ground, smash-
ing them before your eyes.
18 "Then, as before, I threw myself down before the LORD for forty days
and nights. I ate no bread and drank no water because of the great sin you
had committed by doing what the LORD hated, provoking him to anger. 19 I
feared that the furious anger of the LORD, which turned him against you,
would drive him to destroy you. But again he listened to me. 20 The LORD
was so angry with Aaron that he wanted to destroy him, too. But I prayed
for Aaron, and the LORD spared him. 21 I took your sin—the calf you had
made—and I melted it down in the fire and ground it into fine dust. Then I
threw the dust into the stream that flows down the mountain.
22 "You also made the LORD angry at Taberah,* Massah,* and Kibroth-
hattaavah.* 23 And at Kadesh-barnea the LORD sent you out with this com-
mand: 'Go up and take over the land I have given you.' But you rebelled
against the command of the LORD your God and refused to put your trust
in him or obey him. 24 Yes, you have been rebelling against the LORD as long
as I have known you.
25 "That is why I threw myself down before the LORD for forty days and
nights—for the LORD said he would destroy you. 26 I prayed to the LORD and
said, 'O Sovereign LORD, do not destroy them. They are your own people.
They are your special possession, whom you redeemed from Egypt by your
mighty power and your strong hand. 27 Please overlook the stubbornness and
the awful sin of these people, and remember instead your servants Abraham,
Isaac, and Jacob. 28 If you destroy these people, the Egyptians will say, "The
Israelites died because the LORD wasn't able to bring them to the land he
had promised to give them." Or they might say, "He destroyed them because
he hated them; he deliberately took them into the wilderness to slaughter
them." 29 But they are your people and your special possession, whom you
brought out of Egypt by your great strength and powerful arm.'

A New Copy of the Covenant

10 "At that time the LORD said to me, 'Chisel out two stone tablets like
the first ones. Also make a wooden Ark—a sacred chest to store them
in. Come up to me on the mountain, 2 and I will write on the tablets the same
words that were on the ones you smashed. Then place the tablets in the Ark.'
3 "So I made an Ark of acacia wood and cut two stone tablets like the first
two. Then I went up the mountain with the tablets in my hand. 4 Once again
the LORD wrote the Ten Commandments* on the tablets and gave them to
me. They were the same words the LORD had spoken to you from the heart
of the fire on the day you were assembled at the foot of the mountain. 5 Then
I turned and came down the mountain and placed the tablets in the Ark of

9:22a *Taberah* means "place of burning." See Num 11:1-3. 9:22b *Massah* means "place of testing." See Exod 17:1-7. 9:22c *Kibroth-hattaavah* means "graves of gluttony." See Num 11:31-34. 10:4 Hebrew *the ten words.*

the Covenant, which I had made, just as the LORD commanded me. And the
tablets are still there in the Ark."
6(The people of Israel set out from the wells of the people of Jaakan* and
traveled to Moserah, where Aaron died and was buried. His son Eleazar min-
istered as high priest in his place. 7Then they journeyed to Gudgodah, and
from there to Jotbathah, a land with many brooks and streams. 8At that time
the LORD set apart the tribe of Levi to carry the Ark of the LORD's Covenant,
and to stand before the LORD as his ministers, and to pronounce blessings in
his name. These are their duties to this day. 9That is why the Levites have no
share of property or possession of land among the other Israelite tribes. The
LORD himself is their special possession, as the LORD your God told them.)
10"As for me, I stayed on the mountain in the LORD's presence for forty
days and nights, as I had done the first time. And once again the LORD lis-
tened to my pleas and agreed not to destroy you. 11Then the LORD said to
me, 'Get up and resume the journey, and lead the people to the land I swore
to give to their ancestors, so they may take possession of it.'

A Call to Love and Obedience

12"And now, Israel, what does the LORD your God require of you? He requires
only that you fear the LORD your God, and live in a way that pleases him,
and love him and serve him with all your heart and soul. 13And you must
always obey the LORD's commands and decrees that I am giving you today
for your own good.
14"Look, the highest heavens and the earth and everything in it all belong
to the LORD your God. 15Yet the LORD chose your ancestors as the objects of
his love. And he chose you, their descendants, above all other nations, as is
evident today. 16Therefore, change your hearts* and stop being stubborn.
17"For the LORD your God is the God of gods and Lord of lords. He is
the great God, the mighty and awesome God, who shows no partiality and
cannot be bribed. 18He ensures that orphans and widows receive justice.
He shows love to the foreigners living among you and gives them food and
clothing. 19So you, too, must show love to foreigners, for you yourselves were
once foreigners in the land of Egypt. 20You must fear the LORD your God and
worship him and cling to him. Your oaths must be in his name alone. 21He
alone is your God, the only one who is worthy of your praise, the one who has
done these mighty miracles that you have seen with your own eyes. 22When
your ancestors went down into Egypt, there were only seventy of them. But
now the LORD your God has made you as numerous as the stars in the sky!

11 "You must love the LORD your God and always obey his require-
ments, decrees, regulations, and commands. 2Keep in mind that I am
not talking now to your children, who have never experienced the discipline
of the LORD your God or seen his greatness and his strong hand and powerful
arm. 3They didn't see the miraculous signs and wonders he performed in
Egypt against Pharaoh and all his land. 4They didn't see what the LORD did
to the armies of Egypt and to their horses and chariots—how he drowned
them in the Red Sea* as they were chasing you. He destroyed them, and they
have not recovered to this very day!
5"Your children didn't see how the LORD cared for you in the wilderness

10:6 Or *set out from Beeroth of Bene-jaakan.* 10:16 Hebrew *circumcise the foreskin of your hearts.*
11:4 Hebrew *sea of reeds.*

Make a Difference

10:12-22

Yet

Of the entirety of his creation, God's greatest joy is reserved for his chosen people. Regardless of how much God possesses, his most esteemed treasure is humanity.

To Nicodemus, Jesus said, "This is how God loved the world: He gave his one and only Son, so that everyone who believes in him will not perish but have eternal life" (John 3:16). In other words, people were in a state of perishing, yet because of his deep love for his people, God chose to initiate the process by which his people could be reclaimed.

In the whole of the Bible, it is clear that God is holy, yet he has chosen to offer forgiveness to people (Romans 3:23-24). The Psalms resound with wonder as they recognize that creation is so marvelous, yet God gives humankind his utmost affection (Psalm 8:5). Isaiah reveals that humanity has gone astray, yet the Suffering Servant of God will carry humanity's weakness, sorrow, and punishment (Isaiah 53:4-6). The *yet* of God is a wonderful gift indeed.

Difference Maker

Take a few moments and allow yourself to be overcome by the *yet* of God in your own life.

Prayer **11:19**

God, please give me power to live a life that younger children can look to as an example. Let me be one who puts you first and joins your mission to make a difference in this world. Amen.

until you arrived here. 6They didn't see what he did to Dathan and Abiram
(the sons of Eliab, a descendant of Reuben) when the earth opened its mouth
in the Israelite camp and swallowed them, along with their households and
tents and every living thing that belonged to them. 7But you have seen the
LORD perform all these mighty deeds with your own eyes!

The Blessings of Obedience

8"Therefore, be careful to obey every command I am giving you today, so
you may have strength to go in and take over the land you are about to enter.
9If you obey, you will enjoy a long life in the land the LORD swore to give to
your ancestors and to you, their descendants—a land flowing with milk
and honey! 10For the land you are about to enter and take over is not like
the land of Egypt from which you came, where you planted your seed and
made irrigation ditches with your foot as in a vegetable garden. 11Rather,
the land you will soon take over is a land of hills and valleys with plenty of
rain—12a land that the LORD your God cares for. He watches over it through
each season of the year!

13"If you carefully obey the commands I am giving you today, and if you
love the LORD your God and serve him with all your heart and soul, 14then
he will send the rains in their proper seasons—the early and late rains—so
you can bring in your harvests of grain, new wine, and olive oil. 15He will
give you lush pastureland for your livestock, and you yourselves will have
all you want to eat.

16"But be careful. Don't let your heart be deceived so that you turn away
from the LORD and serve and worship other gods. 17If you do, the LORD's
anger will burn against you. He will shut up the sky and hold back the rain,
and the ground will fail to produce its harvests. Then you will quickly die
in that good land the LORD is giving you.

18"So commit yourselves wholeheartedly to these words of mine. Tie them
to your hands and wear them on your forehead as reminders. 19Teach them
to your children. Talk about them when you are at home and when you are
on the road, when you are going to bed and when you are getting up. 20Write
them on the doorposts of your house and on your gates, 21so that as long as
the sky remains above the earth, you and your children may flourish in the
land the LORD swore to give your ancestors.

22"Be careful to obey all these commands I am giving you. Show love to the
LORD your God by walking in his ways and holding tightly to him. 23Then
the LORD will drive out all the nations ahead of you, though they are much
greater and stronger than you, and you will take over their land. 24Wherever
you set foot, that land will be yours. Your frontiers will stretch from the
wilderness in the south to Lebanon in the north, and from the Euphrates
River in the east to the Mediterranean Sea in the west.* 25No one will be able
to stand against you, for the LORD your God will cause the people to fear and
dread you, as he promised, wherever you go in the whole land.

26"Look, today I am giving you the choice between a blessing and a curse!
27You will be blessed if you obey the commands of the LORD your God that
I am giving you today. 28But you will be cursed if you reject the commands
of the LORD your God and turn away from him and worship gods you have
not known before.

11:24 Hebrew *to the western sea.*

29“When the LORD your God brings you into the land and helps you take
possession of it, you must pronounce the blessing at Mount Gerizim and the
curse at Mount Ebal. 30(These two mountains are west of the Jordan River
in the land of the Canaanites who live in the Jordan Valley,* near the town
of Gilgal, not far from the oaks of Moreh.) 31For you are about to cross the
Jordan River to take over the land the LORD your God is giving you. When
you take that land and are living in it, 32you must be careful to obey all the
decrees and regulations I am giving you today.

The LORD’s Chosen Place for Worship

12 “These are the decrees and regulations you must be careful to obey
when you live in the land that the LORD, the God of your ancestors,
is giving you. You must obey them as long as you live.

2“When you drive out the nations that live there, you must destroy all the
places where they worship their gods—high on the mountains, up on the
hills, and under every green tree. 3Break down their altars and smash their
sacred pillars. Burn their Asherah poles and cut down their carved idols.
Completely erase the names of their gods!

4“Do not worship the LORD your God in the way these pagan peoples wor-
ship their gods. 5Rather, you must seek the LORD your God at the place of
worship he himself will choose from among all the tribes—the place where
his name will be honored. 6There you will bring your burnt offerings, your
sacrifices, your tithes, your sacred offerings, your offerings to fulfill a vow,
your voluntary offerings, and your offerings of the firstborn animals of your
herds and flocks. 7There you and your families will feast in the presence
of the LORD your God, and you will rejoice in all you have accomplished
because the LORD your God has blessed you.

8“Your pattern of worship will change. Today all of you are doing as you
please, 9because you have not yet arrived at the place of rest, the land the
LORD your God is giving you as your special possession. 10But you will soon
cross the Jordan River and live in the land the LORD your God is giving you.
When he gives you rest from all your enemies and you’re living safely in the
land, 11you must bring everything I command you—your burnt offerings,
your sacrifices, your tithes, your sacred offerings, and your offerings to fulfill
a vow—to the designated place of worship, the place the LORD your God
chooses for his name to be honored.

12“You must celebrate there in the presence of the LORD your God with
your sons and daughters and all your servants. And remember to include
the Levites who live in your towns, for they will receive no allotment of land
among you. 13Be careful not to sacrifice your burnt offerings just anywhere
you like. 14You may do so only at the place the LORD will choose within one
of your tribal territories. There you must offer your burnt offerings and do
everything I command you.

15“But you may butcher your animals and eat their meat in any town
whenever you want. You may freely eat the animals with which the LORD
your God blesses you. All of you, whether ceremonially clean or unclean,
may eat that meat, just as you now eat gazelle and deer. 16But you must not
consume the blood. You must pour it out on the ground like water.

17“But you may not eat your offerings in your hometown—neither the

11:30 Hebrew *the Arabah.*

tithe of your grain and new wine and olive oil, nor the firstborn of your flocks and herds, nor any offering to fulfill a vow, nor your voluntary offerings, nor your sacred offerings. 18You must eat these in the presence of the LORD your God at the place he will choose. Eat them there with your children, your servants, and the Levites who live in your towns, celebrating in the presence of the LORD your God in all you do. 19And be very careful never to neglect the Levites as long as you live in your land.

20“When the LORD your God expands your territory as he has promised, and you have the urge to eat meat, you may freely eat meat whenever you want. 21It might happen that the designated place of worship—the place the LORD your God chooses for his name to be honored—is a long way from your home. If so, you may butcher any of the cattle, sheep, or goats the LORD has given you, and you may freely eat the meat in your hometown, as I have commanded you. 22Anyone, whether ceremonially clean or unclean, may eat that meat, just as you do now with gazelle and deer. 23But never consume the blood, for the blood is the life, and you must not consume the lifeblood with the meat. 24Instead, pour out the blood on the ground like water. 25Do not consume the blood, so that all may go well with you and your children after you, because you will be doing what pleases the LORD.

26“Take your sacred gifts and your offerings given to fulfill a vow to the place the LORD chooses. 27You must offer the meat and blood of your burnt offerings on the altar of the LORD your God. The blood of your other sacrifices must be poured out on the altar of the LORD your God, but you may eat the meat. 28Be careful to obey all my commands, so that all will go well with you and your children after you, because you will be doing what is good and pleasing to the LORD your God.

29“When the LORD your God goes ahead of you and destroys the nations and you drive them out and live in their land, 30do not fall into the trap of following their customs and worshiping their gods. Do not inquire about their gods, saying, ‘How do these nations worship their gods? I want to follow their example.’ 31You must not worship the LORD your God the way the other nations worship their gods, for they perform for their gods every detestable act that the LORD hates. They even burn their sons and daughters as sacrifices to their gods.

32*“So be careful to obey all the commands I give you. You must not add anything to them or subtract anything from them.

A Warning against Idolatry

13 1*“Suppose there are prophets among you or those who dream dreams about the future, and they promise you signs or miracles, 2and the predicted signs or miracles occur. If they then say, ‘Come, let us worship other gods’—gods you have not known before—3do not listen to them. The LORD your God is testing you to see if you truly love him with all your heart and soul. 4Serve only the LORD your God and fear him alone. Obey his commands, listen to his voice, and cling to him. 5The false prophets or visionaries who try to lead you astray must be put to death, for they encourage rebellion against the LORD your God, who redeemed you from slavery and brought you out of the land of Egypt. Since they try to lead you astray

12:32 Verse 12:32 is numbered 13:1 in Hebrew text. 13:1 Verses 13:1-18 are numbered 13:2-19 in Hebrew text.

from the way the LORD your God commanded you to live, you must put them
to death. In this way you will purge the evil from among you.
6 "Suppose someone secretly entices you—even your brother, your son
or daughter, your beloved wife, or your closest friend—and says, 'Let us go
worship other gods'—gods that neither you nor your ancestors have known.
7 They might suggest that you worship the gods of peoples who live nearby or
who come from the ends of the earth. 8 But do not give in or listen. Have no
pity, and do not spare or protect them. 9 You must put them to death! Strike
the first blow yourself, and then all the people must join in. 10 Stone the guilty
ones to death because they have tried to draw you away from the LORD your
God, who rescued you from the land of Egypt, the place of slavery. 11 Then all
Israel will hear about it and be afraid, and no one will act so wickedly again.
12 "When you begin living in the towns the LORD your God is giving you,
you may hear 13 that scoundrels among you are leading their fellow citizens
astray by saying, 'Let us go worship other gods'—gods you have not known
before. 14 In such cases, you must examine the facts carefully. If you find that
the report is true and such a detestable act has been committed among you,
15 you must attack that town and completely destroy* all its inhabitants, as
well as all the livestock. 16 Then you must pile all the plunder in the middle
of the open square and burn it. Burn the entire town as a burnt offering to
the LORD your God. That town must remain a ruin forever; it may never be
rebuilt. 17 Keep none of the plunder that has been set apart for destruction.
Then the LORD will turn from his fierce anger and be merciful to you. He
will have compassion on you and make you a large nation, just as he swore
to your ancestors.
18 "The LORD your God will be merciful only if you listen to his voice and
keep all his commands that I am giving you today, doing what pleases him.

Ceremonially Clean and Unclean Animals

14 "Since you are the people of the LORD your God, never cut yourselves
or shave the hair above your foreheads in mourning for the dead.
2 You have been set apart as holy to the LORD your God, and he has chosen
you from all the nations of the earth to be his own special treasure.
3 "You must not eat any detestable animals that are ceremonially unclean.
4 These are the animals* you may eat: the ox, the sheep, the goat, 5 the deer,
the gazelle, the roe deer, the wild goat, the addax, the antelope, and the
mountain sheep.
6 "You may eat any animal that has completely split hooves and chews
the cud, 7 but if the animal doesn't have both, it may not be eaten. So you
may not eat the camel, the hare, or the hyrax.* They chew the cud but do
not have split hooves, so they are ceremonially unclean for you. 8 And you
may not eat the pig. It has split hooves but does not chew the cud, so it is
ceremonially unclean for you. You may not eat the meat of these animals or
even touch their carcasses.
9 "Of all the marine animals, you may eat whatever has both fins and scales.
10 You may not, however, eat marine animals that do not have both fins and
scales. They are ceremonially unclean for you.

Make a Difference 13:18

Stand Out

Chapters 12 through 14 are a reminder that God wants us to be different—not just different for the sake of being different but, rather, unique in comparison to the culture around us. Sometimes this is called being "set apart." If a person who loves God looks exactly like one who does not, what difference would that make?

Being a difference maker means being distinct from those who have chosen to live their lives without God. In the book of Acts, we discover that people who saw the way early Christians behaved knew they were different. These Christians were caring for those whom no one else even wanted to go near. In many places around the world today, Christians stand out as those who go to unpopular places to care for uncared-for people by doing unappealing acts of service.

Difference Maker

What would it take for you to "stand out" as a difference maker? Do something selflessly this week to care for and serve someone whom others ignore. If anyone notices your actions, give the credit to the God who has called you to serve others.

13:15 The Hebrew term used here refers to the complete consecration of things or people to the LORD, either by destroying them or by giving them as an offering; similarly in 13:17.
14:4 The identification of some of the animals and birds listed in this chapter is uncertain.
14:7 Or *coney*, or *rock badger*.

11 "You may eat any bird that is ceremonially clean. 12 These are the birds you may not eat: the griffon vulture, the bearded vulture, the black vulture, 13 the kite, the falcon, buzzards of all kinds, 14 ravens of all kinds, 15 the eagle owl, the short-eared owl, the seagull, hawks of all kinds, 16 the little owl, the great owl, the barn owl, 17 the desert owl, the Egyptian vulture, the cormorant, 18 the stork, herons of all kinds, the hoopoe, and the bat.

19 "All winged insects that walk along the ground are ceremonially unclean for you and may not be eaten. 20 But you may eat any winged bird or insect that is ceremonially clean.

21 "You must not eat anything that has died a natural death. You may give it to a foreigner living in your town, or you may sell it to a stranger. But do not eat it yourselves, for you are set apart as holy to the LORD your God.

"You must not cook a young goat in its mother's milk.

The Giving of Tithes

22 "You must set aside a tithe of your crops—one-tenth of all the crops you harvest each year. 23 Bring this tithe to the designated place of worship—the place the LORD your God chooses for his name to be honored—and eat it there in his presence. This applies to your tithes of grain, new wine, olive oil, and the firstborn males of your flocks and herds. Doing this will teach you always to fear the LORD your God.

24 "Now when the LORD your God blesses you with a good harvest, the place of worship he chooses for his name to be honored might be too far for you to bring the tithe. 25 If so, you may sell the tithe portion of your crops and herds, put the money in a pouch, and go to the place the LORD your God has chosen. 26 When you arrive, you may use the money to buy any kind of food you want—cattle, sheep, goats, wine, or other alcoholic drink. Then feast there in the presence of the LORD your God and celebrate with your household. 27 And do not neglect the Levites in your town, for they will receive no allotment of land among you.

28 "At the end of every third year, bring the entire tithe of that year's harvest and store it in the nearest town. 29 Give it to the Levites, who will receive no allotment of land among you, as well as to the foreigners living among you, the orphans, and the widows in your towns, so they can eat and be satisfied. Then the LORD your God will bless you in all your work.

Release for Debtors

15 "At the end of every seventh year you must cancel the debts of everyone who owes you money. 2 This is how it must be done. Everyone must cancel the loans they have made to their fellow Israelites. They must not demand payment from their neighbors or relatives, for the LORD's time of release has arrived. 3 This release from debt, however, applies only to your fellow Israelites—not to the foreigners living among you.

4 "There should be no poor among you, for the LORD your God will greatly bless you in the land he is giving you as a special possession. 5 You will receive this blessing if you are careful to obey all the commands of the LORD your God that I am giving you today. 6 The LORD your God will bless you as he has promised. You will lend money to many nations but will never need to borrow. You will rule many nations, but they will not rule over you.

7 "But if there are any poor Israelites in your towns when you arrive in the

land the LORD your God is giving you, do not be hard-hearted or tightfisted
toward them. 8 Instead, be generous and lend them whatever they need. 9 Do
not be mean-spirited and refuse someone a loan because the year for can-
celing debts is close at hand. If you refuse to make the loan and the needy
person cries out to the LORD, you will be considered guilty of sin. 10 Give
generously to the poor, not grudgingly, for the LORD your God will bless
you in everything you do. 11 There will always be some in the land who are
poor. That is why I am commanding you to share freely with the poor and
with other Israelites in need.

Release for Hebrew Slaves

12 "If a fellow Hebrew sells himself or herself to be your servant* and serves
you for six years, in the seventh year you must set that servant free.

13 "When you release a male servant, do not send him away empty-handed.
14 Give him a generous farewell gift from your flock, your threshing floor,
and your winepress. Share with him some of the bounty with which the
LORD your God has blessed you. 15 Remember that you were once slaves in
the land of Egypt and the LORD your God redeemed you! That is why I am
giving you this command.

16 "But suppose your servant says, 'I will not leave you,' because he loves
you and your family, and he has done well with you. 17 In that case, take an
awl and push it through his earlobe into the door. After that, he will be your
servant for life. And do the same for your female servants.

18 "You must not consider it a hardship when you release your servants.
Remember that for six years they have given you services worth double the
wages of hired workers, and the LORD your God will bless you in all you do.

Sacrificing Firstborn Male Animals

19 "You must set aside for the LORD your God all the firstborn males from
your flocks and herds. Do not use the firstborn of your herds to work your
fields, and do not shear the firstborn of your flocks. 20 Instead, you and your
family must eat these animals in the presence of the LORD your God each
year at the place he chooses. 21 But if this firstborn animal has any defect, such
as lameness or blindness, or if anything else is wrong with it, you must not
sacrifice it to the LORD your God. 22 Instead, use it for food for your family in
your hometown. Anyone, whether ceremonially clean or unclean, may eat
it, just as anyone may eat a gazelle or deer. 23 But you must not consume the
blood. You must pour it out on the ground like water.

Passover and the Festival of Unleavened Bread

16 "In honor of the LORD your God, celebrate the Passover each year
in the early spring, in the month of Abib,* for that was the month
in which the LORD your God brought you out of Egypt by night. 2 Your
Passover sacrifice may be from either the flock or the herd, and it must be
sacrificed to the LORD your God at the designated place of worship—the
place he chooses for his name to be honored. 3 Eat it with bread made with-
out yeast. For seven days the bread you eat must be made without yeast, as
when you escaped from Egypt in such a hurry. Eat this bread—the bread

Prayer **15:8**

Jesus, you have asked me to be like you. Please lead me to be radically openhanded. Amen.

15:12 Or *If a Hebrew man or woman is sold to you.* 16:1 Hebrew *Observe the month of Abib, and keep the Passover unto the LORD your God.* Abib, the first month of the ancient Hebrew lunar calendar, usually occurs within the months of March and April.

Make a Difference 16:17

Give

No one goes to heaven because they put money in the offering plate at church. Giving to church was never about following a rule or paying a price of membership. It has always been about the attitude of the heart. The Bible talks about tithing, when a person gives back to the Lord a tenth of what the Lord has blessed them with. The Bible also talks about laying down one's whole life for God and for others because of all Jesus has done on our behalf.

Our gifts to God are a sign of gratitude for all God's blessing. These gifts are to be personal and related to the blessings the Lord has given us. To appear before God without a heart of thanksgiving shows a lack of forethought and respect. We give because he first has given to us.

Difference Maker

Out of the response of your heart for all Jesus has done, give some of your time or talent or money to your local church.

of suffering—so that as long as you live you will remember the day you
departed from Egypt. 4 Let no yeast be found in any house throughout
your land for those seven days. And when you sacrifice the Passover lamb
on the evening of the first day, do not let any of the meat remain until the
next morning.
5 "You may not sacrifice the Passover in just any of the towns that the LORD
your God is giving you. 6 You must offer it only at the designated place of
worship—the place the LORD your God chooses for his name to be honored.
Sacrifice it there in the evening as the sun goes down on the anniversary of
your exodus from Egypt. 7 Roast the lamb and eat it in the place the LORD
your God chooses. Then you may go back to your tents the next morning.
8 For the next six days you may not eat any bread made with yeast. On the
seventh day proclaim another holy day in honor of the LORD your God, and
no work may be done on that day.

The Festival of Harvest

9 "Count off seven weeks from when you first begin to cut the grain at the
time of harvest. 10 Then celebrate the Festival of Harvest* to honor the LORD
your God. Bring him a voluntary offering in proportion to the blessings
you have received from him. 11 This is a time to celebrate before the LORD
your God at the designated place of worship he will choose for his name to
be honored. Celebrate with your sons and daughters, your male and female
servants, the Levites from your towns, and the foreigners, orphans, and wid-
ows who live among you. 12 Remember that you were once slaves in Egypt,
so be careful to obey all these decrees.

The Festival of Shelters

13 "You must observe the Festival of Shelters* for seven days at the end of the
harvest season, after the grain has been threshed and the grapes have been
pressed. 14 This festival will be a happy time of celebrating with your sons
and daughters, your male and female servants, and the Levites, foreigners,
orphans, and widows from your towns. 15 For seven days you must celebrate
this festival to honor the LORD your God at the place he chooses, for it is he
who blesses you with bountiful harvests and gives you success in all your
work. This festival will be a time of great joy for all.
16 "Each year every man in Israel must celebrate these three festivals: the
Festival of Unleavened Bread, the Festival of Harvest, and the Festival of
Shelters. On each of these occasions, all men must appear before the LORD
your God at the place he chooses, but they must not appear before the LORD
without a gift for him. 17 All must give as they are able, according to the bless-
ings given to them by the LORD your God.

Justice for the People

18 "Appoint judges and officials for yourselves from each of your tribes in
all the towns the LORD your God is giving you. They must judge the people
fairly. 19 You must never twist justice or show partiality. Never accept a bribe,
for bribes blind the eyes of the wise and corrupt the decisions of the godly.

16:10 Hebrew *Festival of Weeks;* also in 16:16. This was later called the Festival of Pentecost (see Acts 2:1). It is celebrated today as Shavuot (or Shabuoth). 16:13 Or *Festival of Booths,* or *Festival of Tabernacles;* also in 16:16. This was earlier called the Festival of the Final Harvest or Festival of Ingathering (see Exod 23:16b). It is celebrated today as Sukkot (or Succoth).

20 Let true justice prevail, so you may live and occupy the land that the LORD
your God is giving you.
21 "You must never set up a wooden Asherah pole beside the altar you build
for the LORD your God. 22 And never set up sacred pillars for worship, for the
LORD your God hates them.

17 "Never sacrifice sick or defective cattle, sheep, or goats to the LORD
your God, for he detests such gifts.
2 "When you begin living in the towns the LORD your God is giving you,
a man or woman among you might do evil in the sight of the LORD your
God and violate the covenant. 3 For instance, they might serve other gods
or worship the sun, the moon, or any of the stars—the forces of heaven—
which I have strictly forbidden. 4 When you hear about it, investigate the
matter thoroughly. If it is true that this detestable thing has been done in
Israel, 5 then the man or woman who has committed such an evil act must be
taken to the gates of the town and stoned to death. 6 But never put a person
to death on the testimony of only one witness. There must always be two
or three witnesses. 7 The witnesses must throw the first stones, and then all
the people may join in. In this way, you will purge the evil from among you.
8 "Suppose a case arises in a local court that is too hard for you to decide—
for instance, whether someone is guilty of murder or only of manslaughter,
or a difficult lawsuit, or a case involving different kinds of assault. Take such
legal cases to the place the LORD your God will choose, 9 and present them
to the Levitical priests or the judge on duty at that time. They will hear the
case and declare the verdict. 10 You must carry out the verdict they announce
and the sentence they prescribe at the place the LORD chooses. You must do
exactly what they say. 11 After they have interpreted the law and declared their
verdict, the sentence they impose must be fully executed; do not modify it
in any way. 12 Anyone arrogant enough to reject the verdict of the judge or
of the priest who represents the LORD your God must die. In this way you
will purge the evil from Israel. 13 Then everyone else will hear about it and
be afraid to act so arrogantly.

Guidelines for a King

14 "You are about to enter the land the LORD your God is giving you. When
you take it over and settle there, you may think, 'We should select a king to
rule over us like the other nations around us.' 15 If this happens, be sure to
select as king the man the LORD your God chooses. You must appoint a fellow
Israelite; he may not be a foreigner.
16 "The king must not build up a large stable of horses for himself or send
his people to Egypt to buy horses, for the LORD has told you, 'You must never
return to Egypt.' 17 The king must not take many wives for himself, because
they will turn his heart away from the LORD. And he must not accumulate
large amounts of wealth in silver and gold for himself.
18 "When he sits on the throne as king, he must copy for himself this body
of instruction on a scroll in the presence of the Levitical priests. 19 He must al-
ways keep that copy with him and read it daily as long as he lives. That way he
will learn to fear the LORD his God by obeying all the terms of these instruc-
tions and decrees. 20 This regular reading will prevent him from becoming
proud and acting as if he is above his fellow citizens. It will also prevent him

Question 17:19

Based on God's guidelines for anyone who would be the earthly king of the Israelites, what would you conclude are the qualities you should look for in spiritual leaders in the church?

from turning away from these commands in the smallest way. And it will
ensure that he and his descendants will reign for many generations in Israel.

Gifts for the Priests and Levites

18 "Remember that the Levitical priests—that is, the whole of the tribe
of Levi—will receive no allotment of land among the other tribes in
Israel. Instead, the priests and Levites will eat from the special gifts given
to the LORD, for that is their share. 2They will have no land of their own
among the Israelites. The LORD himself is their special possession, just as
he promised them.
3"These are the parts the priests may claim as their share from the cattle,
sheep, and goats that the people bring as offerings: the shoulder, the cheeks,
and the stomach. 4You must also give to the priests the first share of the
grain, the new wine, the olive oil, and the wool at shearing time. 5For the
LORD your God chose the tribe of Levi out of all your tribes to minister in
the LORD's name forever.
6"Suppose a Levite chooses to move from his town in Israel, wherever he is
living, to the place the LORD chooses for worship. 7He may minister there in
the name of the LORD his God, just like all his fellow Levites who are serving
the LORD there. 8He may eat his share of the sacrifices and offerings, even if
he also receives support from his family.

A Call to Holy Living

9"When you enter the land the LORD your God is giving you, be very care-
ful not to imitate the detestable customs of the nations living there. 10For
example, never sacrifice your son or daughter as a burnt offering.* And
do not let your people practice fortune-telling, or use sorcery, or interpret
omens, or engage in witchcraft, 11or cast spells, or function as mediums or
psychics, or call forth the spirits of the dead. 12Anyone who does these things
is detestable to the LORD. It is because the other nations have done these
detestable things that the LORD your God will drive them out ahead of you.
13But you must be blameless before the LORD your God. 14The nations you
are about to displace consult sorcerers and fortune-tellers, but the LORD your
God forbids you to do such things."

True and False Prophets

15Moses continued, "The LORD your God will raise up for you a prophet
like me from among your fellow Israelites. You must listen to him. 16For
this is what you yourselves requested of the LORD your God when you were
assembled at Mount Sinai.* You said, 'Don't let us hear the voice of the LORD
our God anymore or see this blazing fire, for we will die.'
17"Then the LORD said to me, 'What they have said is right. 18I will raise
up a prophet like you from among their fellow Israelites. I will put my words
in his mouth, and he will tell the people everything I command him. 19I will
personally deal with anyone who will not listen to the messages the prophet
proclaims on my behalf. 20But any prophet who falsely claims to speak in my
name or who speaks in the name of another god must die.'
21"But you may wonder, 'How will we know whether or not a proph-
ecy is from the LORD?' 22If the prophet speaks in the LORD's name but his

18:10 Or *never make your son or daughter pass through the fire.* **18:16** Hebrew *Horeb,* another name for Sinai.

Make a Difference 18:9

Imitate Jesus

To imitate someone is to follow him or her as your model for living. God told the Israelites not to imitate the ways of the nations around them. This was especially true when it came to the way they worshiped. Other nations' destructive forms of worship were detestable in God's eyes, and he didn't want his people to resemble those who practiced it in any way.

Generations later the apostle Paul repeated this warning in Romans 12:2. He said that Christ followers should not "copy the behavior and customs of this world." In other words, he was saying don't merely blend in. Instead, through Jesus, God transforms us into a new person with a new way of thinking. This makes it possible to increasingly know and understand God's will for our lives.

Difference Maker

God has called his children to be distinct in the way they worship. You can honor this command by worshiping only God and imitating his Son, Jesus. Get to know the way of Jesus by reading about him in any of the Gospel accounts (Matthew, Mark, Luke, and John).

prediction does not happen or come true, you will know that the LORD did
not give that message. That prophet has spoken without my authority and
need not be feared.

Cities of Refuge

19 "When the LORD your God destroys the nations whose land he is
giving you, you will take over their land and settle in their towns
and homes. 2 Then you must set apart three cities of refuge in the land the
LORD your God is giving you. 3 Survey the territory,* and divide the land the
LORD your God is giving you into three districts, with one of these cities in
each district. Then anyone who has killed someone can flee to one of the
cities of refuge for safety.

4 "If someone kills another person unintentionally, without previous hos-
tility, the slayer may flee to any of these cities to live in safety. 5 For example,
suppose someone goes into the forest with a neighbor to cut wood. And
suppose one of them swings an ax to chop down a tree, and the ax head flies
off the handle, killing the other person. In such cases, the slayer may flee to
one of the cities of refuge to live in safety.

6 "If the distance to the nearest city of refuge is too far, an enraged avenger
might be able to chase down and kill the person who caused the death. Then
the slayer would die unfairly, since he had never shown hostility toward
the person who died. 7 That is why I am commanding you to set aside three
cities of refuge.

8 "And if the LORD your God enlarges your territory, as he swore to your
ancestors, and gives you all the land he promised them, 9 you must des-
ignate three additional cities of refuge. (He will give you this land if you
are careful to obey all the commands I have given you—if you always love
the LORD your God and walk in his ways.) 10 That way you will prevent the
death of innocent people in the land the LORD your God is giving you as
your special possession. You will not be held responsible for the death of
innocent people.

11 "But suppose someone is hostile toward a neighbor and deliberately
ambushes and murders him and then flees to one of the cities of refuge.
12 In that case, the elders of the murderer's hometown must send agents to
the city of refuge to bring him back and hand him over to the dead person's
avenger to be put to death. 13 Do not feel sorry for that murderer! Purge from
Israel the guilt of murdering innocent people; then all will go well with you.

Concern for Justice

14 "When you arrive in the land the LORD your God is giving you as your spe-
cial possession, you must never steal anyone's land by moving the boundary
markers your ancestors set up to mark their property.

15 "You must not convict anyone of a crime on the testimony of only one
witness. The facts of the case must be established by the testimony of two
or three witnesses.

16 "If a malicious witness comes forward and accuses someone of a crime,
17 then both the accuser and accused must appear before the LORD by coming
to the priests and judges in office at that time. 18 The judges must investi-
gate the case thoroughly. If the accuser has brought false charges against his

Question 19:1-7

Why do you think God commanded that multiple "cities of refuge" be established for his people? What does that tell you about the nature of God?

19:3 Or *Keep the roads in good repair.*

fellow Israelite, 19 you must impose on the accuser the sentence he intended
for the other person. In this way, you will purge such evil from among you.
20 Then the rest of the people will hear about it and be afraid to do such an
evil thing. 21 You must show no pity for the guilty! Your rule should be life
for life, eye for eye, tooth for tooth, hand for hand, foot for foot.

Regulations concerning War

20 "When you go out to fight your enemies and you face horses and
chariots and an army greater than your own, do not be afraid. The
LORD your God, who brought you out of the land of Egypt, is with you!
2 When you prepare for battle, the priest must come forward to speak to the
troops. 3 He will say to them, 'Listen to me, all you men of Israel! Do not be
afraid as you go out to fight your enemies today! Do not lose heart or panic
or tremble before them. 4 For the LORD your God is going with you! He will
fight for you against your enemies, and he will give you victory!'

5 "Then the officers of the army must address the troops and say, 'Has
anyone here just built a new house but not yet dedicated it? If so, you may
go home! You might be killed in the battle, and someone else would dedicate
your house. 6 Has anyone here just planted a vineyard but not yet eaten any of
its fruit? If so, you may go home! You might die in battle, and someone else
would eat the first fruit. 7 Has anyone here just become engaged to a woman
but not yet married her? Well, you may go home and get married! You might
die in the battle, and someone else would marry her.'

8 "Then the officers will also say, 'Is anyone here afraid or worried? If
you are, you may go home before you frighten anyone else.' 9 When the
officers have finished speaking to their troops, they will appoint the unit
commanders.

10 "As you approach a town to attack it, you must first offer its people terms
for peace. 11 If they accept your terms and open the gates to you, then all the
people inside will serve you in forced labor. 12 But if they refuse to make peace
and prepare to fight, you must attack the town. 13 When the LORD your God
hands the town over to you, use your swords to kill every man in the town.
14 But you may keep for yourselves all the women, children, livestock, and
other plunder. You may enjoy the plunder from your enemies that the LORD
your God has given you.

15 "But these instructions apply only to distant towns, not to the towns
of the nations in the land you will enter. 16 In those towns that the LORD
your God is giving you as a special possession, destroy every living thing.
17 You must completely destroy* the Hittites, Amorites, Canaanites, Periz-
zites, Hivites, and Jebusites, just as the LORD your God has commanded you.
18 This will prevent the people of the land from teaching you to imitate their
detestable customs in the worship of their gods, which would cause you to
sin deeply against the LORD your God.

19 "When you are attacking a town and the war drags on, you must not
cut down the trees with your axes. You may eat the fruit, but do not cut
down the trees. Are the trees your enemies, that you should attack them?
20 You may only cut down trees that you know are not valuable for food.
Use them to make the equipment you need to attack the enemy town until
it falls.

20:17 The Hebrew term used here refers to the complete consecration of things or people to the LORD, either by destroying them or by giving them as an offering.

Cleansing for Unsolved Murder

21 "When you are in the land the LORD your God is giving you, someone may be found murdered in a field, and you don't know who committed the murder. 2 In such a case, your elders and judges must measure the distance from the site of the crime to the nearby towns. 3 When the nearest town has been determined, that town's elders must select from the herd a heifer that has never been trained or yoked to a plow. 4 They must lead it down to a valley that has not been plowed or planted and that has a stream running through it. There in the valley they must break the heifer's neck. 5 Then the Levitical priests must step forward, for the LORD your God has chosen them to minister before him and to pronounce blessings in the LORD's name. They are to decide all legal and criminal cases.

6 "The elders of the town must wash their hands over the heifer whose neck was broken. 7 Then they must say, 'Our hands did not shed this person's blood, nor did we see it happen. 8 O LORD, forgive your people Israel whom you have redeemed. Do not charge your people with the guilt of murdering an innocent person.' Then they will be absolved of the guilt of this person's blood. 9 By following these instructions, you will do what is right in the LORD's sight and will cleanse the guilt of murder from your community.

Marriage to a Captive Woman

10 "Suppose you go out to war against your enemies and the LORD your God hands them over to you, and you take some of them as captives. 11 And suppose you see among the captives a beautiful woman, and you are attracted to her and want to marry her. 12 If this happens, you may take her to your home, where she must shave her head, cut her nails, 13 and change the clothes she was wearing when she was captured. She will stay in your home, but let her mourn for her father and mother for a full month. Then you may marry her, and you will be her husband and she will be your wife. 14 But if you marry her and she does not please you, you must let her go free. You may not sell her or treat her as a slave, for you have humiliated her.

Rights of the Firstborn

15 "Suppose a man has two wives, but he loves one and not the other, and both have given him sons. And suppose the firstborn son is the son of the wife he does not love. 16 When the man divides his inheritance, he may not give the larger inheritance to his younger son, the son of the wife he loves, as if he were the firstborn son. 17 He must recognize the rights of his oldest son, the son of the wife he does not love, by giving him a double portion. He is the first son of his father's virility, and the rights of the firstborn belong to him.

Dealing with a Rebellious Son

18 "Suppose a man has a stubborn and rebellious son who will not obey his father or mother, even though they discipline him. 19 In such a case, the father and mother must take the son to the elders as they hold court at the town gate. 20 The parents must say to the elders, 'This son of ours is stubborn and rebellious and refuses to obey. He is a glutton and a drunkard.' 21 Then all the men of his town must stone him to death. In this way, you will purge this evil from among you, and all Israel will hear about it and be afraid.

Question **21:8-9**

God's instructions, given through Moses, included a ceremony to deal with any unsolved murder. The ceremony called for people who were innocent of the killing to cleanse themselves and then call upon God to forgive the whole nation of Israel. Obviously, the whole nation did not commit the murder, but God wanted to remind his people that they were not just a group of individuals. The entire nation was a living representation of God for other nations to see. They were interconnected.

What eternal truths do you see in this?

Various Regulations

22“If someone has committed a crime worthy of death and is executed and
hung on a tree,* 23the body must not remain hanging from the tree over-
night. You must bury the body that same day, for anyone who is hung* is
cursed in the sight of God. In this way, you will prevent the defilement of the
land the LORD your God is giving you as your special possession.

22 “If you see your neighbor’s ox or sheep or goat wandering away,
don’t ignore your responsibility.* Take it back to its owner. 2If its
owner does not live nearby or you don’t know who the owner is, take it to
your place and keep it until the owner comes looking for it. Then you must
return it. 3Do the same if you find your neighbor’s donkey, clothing, or any-
thing else your neighbor loses. Don’t ignore your responsibility.
4“If you see that your neighbor’s donkey or ox has collapsed on the road,
do not look the other way. Go and help your neighbor get it back on its feet!
5“A woman must not put on men’s clothing, and a man must not wear
women’s clothing. Anyone who does this is detestable in the sight of the
LORD your God.
6“If you happen to find a bird’s nest in a tree or on the ground, and there
are young ones or eggs in it with the mother sitting in the nest, do not take
the mother with the young. 7You may take the young, but let the mother go,
so that you may prosper and enjoy a long life.
8“When you build a new house, you must build a railing around the edge
of its flat roof. That way you will not be considered guilty of murder if some-
one falls from the roof.
9“You must not plant any other crop between the rows of your vineyard.
If you do, you are forbidden to use either the grapes from the vineyard or
the other crop.
10“You must not plow with an ox and a donkey harnessed together.
11“You must not wear clothing made of wool and linen woven together.
12“You must put four tassels on the hem of the cloak with which you cover
yourself—on the front, back, and sides.

Regulations for Sexual Purity

13“Suppose a man marries a woman, but after sleeping with her, he turns
against her 14and publicly accuses her of shameful conduct, saying, ‘When I
married this woman, I discovered she was not a virgin.’ 15Then the woman’s
father and mother must bring the proof of her virginity to the elders as they
hold court at the town gate. 16Her father must say to them, ‘I gave my daugh-
ter to this man to be his wife, and now he has turned against her. 17He has
accused her of shameful conduct, saying, “I discovered that your daughter
was not a virgin.” But here is the proof of my daughter’s virginity.’ Then they
must spread her bed sheet before the elders. 18The elders must then take the
man and punish him. 19They must also fine him 100 pieces of silver,* which
he must pay to the woman’s father because he publicly accused a virgin of
Israel of shameful conduct. The woman will then remain the man’s wife,
and he may never divorce her.
20“But suppose the man’s accusations are true, and he can show that she

21:22 Or *impaled on a pole;* similarly in 21:23. 21:23 Greek version reads *for everyone who is hung on a tree.* Compare Gal 3:13. 22:1 Hebrew *don’t hide yourself;* similarly in 22:3. 22:19 Hebrew *100 [shekels] of silver,* about 2.5 pounds or 1.1 kilograms in weight.

Remember to take notes!

was not a virgin. 21 The woman must be taken to the door of her father's
home, and there the men of the town must stone her to death, for she has
committed a disgraceful crime in Israel by being promiscuous while living
in her parents' home. In this way, you will purge this evil from among you.
22 "If a man is discovered committing adultery, both he and the woman
must die. In this way, you will purge Israel of such evil.
23 "Suppose a man meets a young woman, a virgin who is engaged to be
married, and he has sexual intercourse with her. If this happens within a
town, 24 you must take both of them to the gates of that town and stone them
to death. The woman is guilty because she did not scream for help. The man
must die because he violated another man's wife. In this way, you will purge
this evil from among you.
25 "But if the man meets the engaged woman out in the country, and he
rapes her, then only the man must die. 26 Do nothing to the young woman;
she has committed no crime worthy of death. She is as innocent as a murder
victim. 27 Since the man raped her out in the country, it must be assumed that
she screamed, but there was no one to rescue her.
28 "Suppose a man has intercourse with a young woman who is a virgin
but is not engaged to be married. If they are discovered, 29 he must pay her
father fifty pieces of silver.* Then he must marry the young woman because
he violated her, and he may never divorce her as long as he lives.
30 *"A man must not marry his father's former wife, for this would violate
his father.

Regulations concerning Worship

23 1 *"If a man's testicles are crushed or his penis is cut off, he may not
be admitted to the assembly of the LORD.
2 "If a person is illegitimate by birth, neither he nor his descendants for
ten generations may be admitted to the assembly of the LORD.
3 "No Ammonite or Moabite or any of their descendants for ten genera-
tions may be admitted to the assembly of the LORD. 4 These nations did not
welcome you with food and water when you came out of Egypt. Instead,
they hired Balaam son of Beor from Pethor in distant Aram-naharaim to
curse you. 5 But the LORD your God refused to listen to Balaam. He turned
the intended curse into a blessing because the LORD your God loves you. 6 As
long as you live, you must never promote the welfare and prosperity of the
Ammonites or Moabites.
7 "Do not detest the Edomites or the Egyptians, because the Edomites are
your relatives and you lived as foreigners among the Egyptians. 8 The third
generation of Edomites and Egyptians may enter the assembly of the LORD.

Miscellaneous Regulations

9 "When you go to war against your enemies, be sure to stay away from any-
thing that is impure.
10 "Any man who becomes ceremonially defiled because of a nocturnal
emission must leave the camp and stay away all day. 11 Toward evening he
must bathe himself, and at sunset he may return to the camp.
12 "You must have a designated area outside the camp where you can go to

22:29 Hebrew *50 [shekels] of silver,* about 1.25 pounds or 570 grams in weight.
22:30 Verse 22:30 is numbered 23:1 in Hebrew text. 23:1 Verses 23:1-25 are numbered 23:2-26 in Hebrew text.

Question 23:23

Moses instructed the people to be very careful about fulfilling any vows that they made voluntarily. Making a vow to someone else is like also creating a contract with God. Why do you think that is true?

relieve yourself. [13]Each of you must have a spade as part of your equipment. Whenever you relieve yourself, dig a hole with the spade and cover the excrement. [14]The camp must be holy, for the LORD your God moves around in your camp to protect you and to defeat your enemies. He must not see any shameful thing among you, or he will turn away from you.

[15]"If slaves should escape from their masters and take refuge with you, you must not hand them over to their masters. [16]Let them live among you in any town they choose, and do not oppress them.

[17]"No Israelite, whether man or woman, may become a temple prostitute. [18]When you are bringing an offering to fulfill a vow, you must not bring to the house of the LORD your God any offering from the earnings of a prostitute, whether a man* or a woman, for both are detestable to the LORD your God.

[19]"Do not charge interest on the loans you make to a fellow Israelite, whether you loan money, or food, or anything else. [20]You may charge interest to foreigners, but you may not charge interest to Israelites, so that the LORD your God may bless you in everything you do in the land you are about to enter and occupy.

[21]"When you make a vow to the LORD your God, be prompt in fulfilling whatever you promised him. For the LORD your God demands that you promptly fulfill all your vows, or you will be guilty of sin. [22]However, it is not a sin to refrain from making a vow. [23]But once you have voluntarily made a vow, be careful to fulfill your promise to the LORD your God.

[24]"When you enter your neighbor's vineyard, you may eat your fill of grapes, but you must not carry any away in a basket. [25]And when you enter your neighbor's field of grain, you may pluck the heads of grain with your hand, but you must not harvest it with a sickle.

24

"Suppose a man marries a woman but she does not please him. Having discovered something wrong with her, he writes a document of divorce, hands it to her, and sends her away from his house. [2]When she leaves his house, she is free to marry another man. [3]But if the second husband also turns against her, writes a document of divorce, hands it to her, and sends her away, or if he dies, [4]the first husband may not marry her again, for she has been defiled. That would be detestable to the LORD. You must not bring guilt upon the land the LORD your God is giving you as a special possession.

[5]"A newly married man must not be drafted into the army or be given any other official responsibilities. He must be free to spend one year at home, bringing happiness to the wife he has married.

[6]"It is wrong to take a set of millstones, or even just the upper millstone, as security for a loan, for the owner uses it to make a living.

[7]"If anyone kidnaps a fellow Israelite and treats him as a slave or sells him, the kidnapper must die. In this way, you will purge the evil from among you.

[8]"In all cases involving serious skin diseases,* be careful to follow the instructions of the Levitical priests; obey all the commands I have given them. [9]Remember what the LORD your God did to Miriam as you were coming from Egypt.

[10]"If you lend anything to your neighbor, do not enter his house to pick up the item he is giving as security. [11]You must wait outside while he goes in and brings it out to you. [12]If your neighbor is poor and gives you his cloak as

23:18 Hebrew *a dog.* **24:8** Traditionally rendered *leprosy.* The Hebrew word used here can describe various skin diseases.

security for a loan, do not keep the cloak overnight. 13 Return the cloak to its owner by sunset so he can stay warm through the night and bless you, and the LORD your God will count you as righteous.

14 "Never take advantage of poor and destitute laborers, whether they are fellow Israelites or foreigners living in your towns. 15 You must pay them their wages each day before sunset because they are poor and are counting on it. If you don't, they might cry out to the LORD against you, and it would be counted against you as sin.

16 "Parents must not be put to death for the sins of their children, nor children for the sins of their parents. Those deserving to die must be put to death for their own crimes.

17 "True justice must be given to foreigners living among you and to orphans, and you must never accept a widow's garment as security for her debt. 18 Always remember that you were slaves in Egypt and that the LORD your God redeemed you from your slavery. That is why I have given you this command.

19 "When you are harvesting your crops and forget to bring in a bundle of grain from your field, don't go back to get it. Leave it for the foreigners, orphans, and widows. Then the LORD your God will bless you in all you do. 20 When you beat the olives from your olive trees, don't go over the boughs twice. Leave the remaining olives for the foreigners, orphans, and widows. 21 When you gather the grapes in your vineyard, don't glean the vines after they are picked. Leave the remaining grapes for the foreigners, orphans, and widows. 22 Remember that you were slaves in the land of Egypt. That is why I am giving you this command.

25 "Suppose two people take a dispute to court, and the judges declare that one is right and the other is wrong. 2 If the person in the wrong is sentenced to be flogged, the judge must command him to lie down and be beaten in his presence with the number of lashes appropriate to the crime. 3 But never give more than forty lashes; more than forty lashes would publicly humiliate your neighbor.

4 "You must not muzzle an ox to keep it from eating as it treads out the grain.

5 "If two brothers are living together on the same property and one of them dies without a son, his widow may not be married to anyone from outside the family. Instead, her husband's brother should marry her and have intercourse with her to fulfill the duties of a brother-in-law. 6 The first son she bears to him will be considered the son of the dead brother, so that his name will not be forgotten in Israel.

7 "But if the man refuses to marry his brother's widow, she must go to the town gate and say to the elders assembled there, 'My husband's brother refuses to preserve his brother's name in Israel—he refuses to fulfill the duties of a brother-in-law by marrying me.' 8 The elders of the town will then summon him and talk with him. If he still refuses and says, 'I don't want to marry her,' 9 the widow must walk over to him in the presence of the elders, pull his sandal from his foot, and spit in his face. Then she must declare, 'This is what happens to a man who refuses to provide his brother with children.' 10 Ever afterward in Israel his family will be referred to as 'the family of the man whose sandal was pulled off'!

Make a Difference

24:14-22

Fairness

God's compassion for the poor is evident throughout the Bible. Moses instructed the people to treat the poor among them with fairness. If anyone hired someone who was poor, they were to pay that person a fair wage. This is an especially important command because in that day (and today as well), poor people were used as cheap labor and rarely got paid the full wage for their work. The Israelites were supposed to be distinct from the nations around them. Caring for the poor was one of the ways they would stand out.

Difference Maker

As a representative of the compassionate God of this world, will you be one who opposes injustice wherever you see it? Ask God to show you some of the people around you who are defenseless and treated unfairly. Do whatever you can to help them and restore their dignity.

Question **26:10**

What can you learn from this chapter about tithing?

11“If two Israelite men get into a fight and the wife of one tries to rescue her husband by grabbing the testicles of the other man, 12you must cut off her hand. Show her no pity.

13“You must use accurate scales when you weigh out merchandise, 14and you must use full and honest measures. 15Yes, always use honest weights and measures, so that you may enjoy a long life in the land the LORD your God is giving you. 16All who cheat with dishonest weights and measures are detestable to the LORD your God.

17“Never forget what the Amalekites did to you as you came from Egypt. 18They attacked you when you were exhausted and weary, and they struck down those who were straggling behind. They had no fear of God. 19Therefore, when the LORD your God has given you rest from all your enemies in the land he is giving you as a special possession, you must destroy the Amalekites and erase their memory from under heaven. Never forget this!

Harvest Offerings and Tithes

26 “When you enter the land the LORD your God is giving you as a special possession and you have conquered it and settled there, 2put some of the first produce from each crop you harvest into a basket and bring it to the designated place of worship—the place the LORD your God chooses for his name to be honored. 3Go to the priest in charge at that time and say to him, ‘With this gift I acknowledge to the LORD your God that I have entered the land he swore to our ancestors he would give us.’ 4The priest will then take the basket from your hand and set it before the altar of the LORD your God.

5“You must then say in the presence of the LORD your God, ‘My ancestor Jacob was a wandering Aramean who went to live as a foreigner in Egypt. His family arrived few in number, but in Egypt they became a large and mighty nation. 6When the Egyptians oppressed and humiliated us by making us their slaves, 7we cried out to the LORD, the God of our ancestors. He heard our cries and saw our hardship, toil, and oppression. 8So the LORD brought us out of Egypt with a strong hand and powerful arm, with overwhelming terror, and with miraculous signs and wonders. 9He brought us to this place and gave us this land flowing with milk and honey! 10And now, O LORD, I have brought you the first portion of the harvest you have given me from the ground.’ Then place the produce before the LORD your God, and bow to the ground in worship before him. 11Afterward you may go and celebrate because of all the good things the LORD your God has given to you and your household. Remember to include the Levites and the foreigners living among you in the celebration.

12“Every third year you must offer a special tithe of your crops. In this year of the special tithe you must give your tithes to the Levites, foreigners, orphans, and widows, so that they will have enough to eat in your towns. 13Then you must declare in the presence of the LORD your God, ‘I have taken the sacred gift from my house and have given it to the Levites, foreigners, orphans, and widows, just as you commanded me. I have not violated or forgotten any of your commands. 14I have not eaten any of it while in mourning; I have not handled it while I was ceremonially unclean; and I have not offered any of it to the dead. I have obeyed the LORD my God and have done everything you commanded me. 15Now look down from your holy dwelling place in heaven and bless your people Israel and the land you swore to our ancestors to give us—a land flowing with milk and honey.'

A Call to Obey the LORD's Commands

16 "Today the LORD your God has commanded you to obey all these decrees
and regulations. So be careful to obey them wholeheartedly. 17 You have de-
clared today that the LORD is your God. And you have promised to walk in his
ways, and to obey his decrees, commands, and regulations, and to do every-
thing he tells you. 18 The LORD has declared today that you are his people,
his own special treasure, just as he promised, and that you must obey all his
commands. 19 And if you do, he will set you high above all the other nations
he has made. Then you will receive praise, honor, and renown. You will be a
nation that is holy to the LORD your God, just as he promised."

The Altar on Mount Ebal

27 Then Moses and the leaders of Israel gave this charge to the people:
"Obey all these commands that I am giving you today. 2 When you
cross the Jordan River and enter the land the LORD your God is giving you,
set up some large stones and coat them with plaster. 3 Write this whole body
of instruction on them when you cross the river to enter the land the LORD
your God is giving you—a land flowing with milk and honey, just as the
LORD, the God of your ancestors, promised you. 4 When you cross the Jor-
dan, set up these stones at Mount Ebal and coat them with plaster, as I am
commanding you today.

5 "Then build an altar there to the LORD your God, using natural, uncut
stones. You must not shape the stones with an iron tool. 6 Build the altar
of uncut stones, and use it to offer burnt offerings to the LORD your God.
7 Also sacrifice peace offerings on it, and celebrate by feasting there before
the LORD your God. 8 You must clearly write all these instructions on the
stones coated with plaster."

9 Then Moses and the Levitical priests addressed all Israel as follows: "O Is-
rael, be quiet and listen! Today you have become the people of the LORD your
God. 10 So you must obey the LORD your God by keeping all these commands
and decrees that I am giving you today."

Curses from Mount Ebal

11 That same day Moses also gave this charge to the people: 12 "When you
cross the Jordan River, the tribes of Simeon, Levi, Judah, Issachar, Joseph,
and Benjamin must stand on Mount Gerizim to proclaim a blessing over the
people. 13 And the tribes of Reuben, Gad, Asher, Zebulun, Dan, and Naphtali
must stand on Mount Ebal to proclaim a curse.

14 "Then the Levites will shout to all the people of Israel:

15 'Cursed is anyone who carves or casts an idol and secretly sets it up.
These idols, the work of craftsmen, are detestable to the LORD.'
And all the people will reply, 'Amen.'

16 'Cursed is anyone who dishonors father or mother.'
And all the people will reply, 'Amen.'

Make a Difference

28:1–14

If-Then

God told his people that if they took his commands seriously and obeyed them in every way, then they would be blessed. He even listed many examples of the kinds of blessings they could expect if they obeyed his commands.

This sounds like a pretty good deal. All we have to do to get blessings is honor and obey God's commands. It really is that simple. However, we have a natural human tendency to begin thinking more about the blessings. We start to think of all the things we might get and forget that the first command here is to obey. The obedience is the point. The blessings are results of God's pleasure with our faithful living. He wants us to pay attention to his commands because he knows that is what will give us meaningful lives.

Difference Maker

Read Matthew 5:1-11. Jesus also taught about the blessings that come from an obedient and faithful life. When God blesses you for your obedience and careful attention to your life, enjoy the blessing because the obedient life is for your good.

17 'Cursed is anyone who steals property from a neighbor by moving a
boundary marker.'
And all the people will reply, 'Amen.'

18 'Cursed is anyone who leads a blind person astray on the road.'
And all the people will reply, 'Amen.'

19 'Cursed is anyone who denies justice to foreigners, orphans, or widows.'
And all the people will reply, 'Amen.'

20 'Cursed is anyone who has sexual intercourse with one of his father's
wives, for he has violated his father.'
And all the people will reply, 'Amen.'

21 'Cursed is anyone who has sexual intercourse with an animal.'
And all the people will reply, 'Amen.'

22 'Cursed is anyone who has sexual intercourse with his sister, whether
she is the daughter of his father or his mother.'
And all the people will reply, 'Amen.'

23 'Cursed is anyone who has sexual intercourse with his mother-in-law.'
And all the people will reply, 'Amen.'

24 'Cursed is anyone who attacks a neighbor in secret.'
And all the people will reply, 'Amen.'

25 'Cursed is anyone who accepts payment to kill an innocent person.'
And all the people will reply, 'Amen.'

26 'Cursed is anyone who does not affirm and obey the terms of these
instructions.'
And all the people will reply, 'Amen.'

Blessings for Obedience

28 "If you fully obey the LORD your God and carefully keep all his com-
mands that I am giving you today, the LORD your God will set you
high above all the nations of the world. 2 You will experience all these bless-
ings if you obey the LORD your God:

3 Your towns and your fields
will be blessed.
4 Your children and your crops
will be blessed.
The offspring of your herds and flocks
will be blessed.
5 Your fruit baskets and breadboards
will be blessed.
6 Wherever you go and whatever you do,
you will be blessed.

7 "The LORD will conquer your enemies when they attack you. They will
attack you from one direction, but they will scatter from you in seven!
8 "The LORD will guarantee a blessing on everything you do and will fill
your storehouses with grain. The LORD your God will bless you in the land
he is giving you.
9 "If you obey the commands of the LORD your God and walk in his ways,
the LORD will establish you as his holy people as he swore he would do.
10 Then all the nations of the world will see that you are a people claimed by
the LORD, and they will stand in awe of you.
11 "The LORD will give you prosperity in the land he swore to your ances-
tors to give you, blessing you with many children, numerous livestock, and
abundant crops. 12 The LORD will send rain at the proper time from his rich
treasury in the heavens and will bless all the work you do. You will lend to
many nations, but you will never need to borrow from them. 13 If you listen
to these commands of the LORD your God that I am giving you today, and if
you carefully obey them, the LORD will make you the head and not the tail,
and you will always be on top and never at the bottom. 14 You must not turn
away from any of the commands I am giving you today, nor follow after other
gods and worship them.

Curses for Disobedience

15 "But if you refuse to listen to the LORD your God and do not obey all the
commands and decrees I am giving you today, all these curses will come and
overwhelm you:

16 Your towns and your fields
    will be cursed.
17 Your fruit baskets and breadboards
    will be cursed.
18 Your children and your crops
    will be cursed.
The offspring of your herds and flocks
    will be cursed.
19 Wherever you go and whatever you do,
    you will be cursed.

20 "The LORD himself will send on you curses, confusion, and frustration in
everything you do, until at last you are completely destroyed for doing evil and
abandoning me. 21 The LORD will afflict you with diseases until none of you
are left in the land you are about to enter and occupy. 22 The LORD will strike
you with wasting diseases, fever, and inflammation, with scorching heat and
drought, and with blight and mildew. These disasters will pursue you until you
die. 23 The skies above will be as unyielding as bronze, and the earth beneath
will be as hard as iron. 24 The LORD will change the rain that falls on your land
into powder, and dust will pour down from the sky until you are destroyed.
25 "The LORD will cause you to be defeated by your enemies. You will at-
tack your enemies from one direction, but you will scatter from them in
seven! You will be an object of horror to all the kingdoms of the earth. 26 Your
corpses will be food for all the scavenging birds and wild animals, and no
one will be there to chase them away.

27 “The LORD will afflict you with the boils of Egypt and with tumors, scurvy, and the itch, from which you cannot be cured. 28 The LORD will strike you with madness, blindness, and panic. 29 You will grope around in broad daylight like a blind person groping in the darkness, but you will not find your way. You will be oppressed and robbed continually, and no one will come to save you.

30 “You will be engaged to a woman, but another man will sleep with her. You will build a house, but someone else will live in it. You will plant a vineyard, but you will never enjoy its fruit. 31 Your ox will be butchered before your eyes, but you will not eat a single bite of the meat. Your donkey will be taken from you, never to be returned. Your sheep and goats will be given to your enemies, and no one will be there to help you. 32 You will watch as your sons and daughters are taken away as slaves. Your heart will break for them, but you won’t be able to help them. 33 A foreign nation you have never heard about will eat the crops you worked so hard to grow. You will suffer under constant oppression and harsh treatment. 34 You will go mad because of all the tragedy you see around you. 35 The LORD will cover your knees and legs with incurable boils. In fact, you will be covered from head to foot.

36 “The LORD will exile you and your king to a nation unknown to you and your ancestors. There in exile you will worship gods of wood and stone! 37 You will become an object of horror, ridicule, and mockery among all the nations to which the LORD sends you.

38 “You will plant much but harvest little, for locusts will eat your crops. 39 You will plant vineyards and care for them, but you will not drink the wine or eat the grapes, for worms will destroy the vines. 40 You will grow olive trees throughout your land, but you will never use the olive oil, for the fruit will drop before it ripens. 41 You will have sons and daughters, but you will lose them, for they will be led away into captivity. 42 Swarms of insects will destroy your trees and crops.

43 “The foreigners living among you will become stronger and stronger, while you become weaker and weaker. 44 They will lend money to you, but you will not lend to them. They will be the head, and you will be the tail!

45 “If you refuse to listen to the LORD your God and to obey the commands and decrees he has given you, all these curses will pursue and overtake you until you are destroyed. 46 These horrors will serve as a sign and warning among you and your descendants forever. 47 If you do not serve the LORD your God with joy and enthusiasm for the abundant benefits you have received, 48 you will serve your enemies whom the LORD will send against you. You will be left hungry, thirsty, naked, and lacking in everything. The LORD will put an iron yoke on your neck, oppressing you harshly until he has destroyed you.

49 “The LORD will bring a distant nation against you from the end of the earth, and it will swoop down on you like a vulture. It is a nation whose language you do not understand, 50 a fierce and heartless nation that shows no respect for the old and no pity for the young. 51 Its armies will devour your livestock and crops, and you will be destroyed. They will leave you no grain, new wine, olive oil, calves, or lambs, and you will starve to death. 52 They will attack your cities until all the fortified walls in your land—the walls you trusted to protect you—are knocked down. They will attack all the towns in the land the LORD your God has given you.

53“The siege and terrible distress of the enemy’s attack will be so severe
that you will eat the flesh of your own sons and daughters, whom the LORD
your God has given you. 54The most tenderhearted man among you will
have no compassion for his own brother, his beloved wife, and his surviving
children. 55He will refuse to share with them the flesh he is devouring—the
flesh of one of his own children—because he has nothing else to eat during
the siege and terrible distress that your enemy will inflict on all your towns.
56The most tender and delicate woman among you—so delicate she would
not so much as touch the ground with her foot—will be selfish toward the
husband she loves and toward her own son or daughter. 57She will hide from
them the afterbirth and the new baby she has borne, so that she herself can
secretly eat them. She will have nothing else to eat during the siege and ter-
rible distress that your enemy will inflict on all your towns.
58“If you refuse to obey all the words of instruction that are written in
this book, and if you do not fear the glorious and awesome name of the
LORD your God, 59then the LORD will overwhelm you and your children
with indescribable plagues. These plagues will be intense and without relief,
making you miserable and unbearably sick. 60He will afflict you with all the
diseases of Egypt that you feared so much, and you will have no relief. 61The
LORD will afflict you with every sickness and plague there is, even those not
mentioned in this Book of Instruction, until you are destroyed. 62Though
you become as numerous as the stars in the sky, few of you will be left because
you would not listen to the LORD your God.
63“Just as the LORD has found great pleasure in causing you to prosper
and multiply, the LORD will find pleasure in destroying you. You will be torn
from the land you are about to enter and occupy. 64For the LORD will scatter
you among all the nations from one end of the earth to the other. There you
will worship foreign gods that neither you nor your ancestors have known,
gods made of wood and stone! 65There among those nations you will find no
peace or place to rest. And the LORD will cause your heart to tremble, your
eyesight to fail, and your soul to despair. 66Your life will constantly hang in
the balance. You will live night and day in fear, unsure if you will survive.
67In the morning you will say, ‘If only it were night!’ And in the evening
you will say, ‘If only it were morning!’ For you will be terrified by the awful
horrors you see around you. 68Then the LORD will send you back to Egypt in
ships, to a destination I promised you would never see again. There you will
offer to sell yourselves to your enemies as slaves, but no one will buy you.”

29 1*These are the terms of the covenant the LORD commanded Moses
to make with the Israelites while they were in the land of Moab, in
addition to the covenant he had made with them at Mount Sinai.*

Moses Reviews the Covenant

2*Moses summoned all the Israelites and said to them, “You have seen with
your own eyes everything the LORD did in the land of Egypt to Pharaoh and
to all his servants and to his whole country—3all the great tests of strength,
the miraculous signs, and the amazing wonders. 4But to this day the LORD
has not given you minds that understand, nor eyes that see, nor ears that
hear! 5For forty years I led you through the wilderness, yet your clothes and

29:1a Verse 29:1 is numbered 28:69 in Hebrew text. **29:1b** Hebrew *Horeb,* another name for Sinai. **29:2** Verses 29:2-29 are numbered 29:1-28 in Hebrew text.

How God is at work here

Question 29:19

Hearing a warning is one thing, but if the warning does not cause you to act differently, it doesn't really matter that you heard it. How does God feel about those who hear but do nothing?

sandals did not wear out. 6 You ate no bread and drank no wine or other
alcoholic drink, but he provided for you so you would know that he is the
LORD your God.
7 "When we came here, King Sihon of Heshbon and King Og of Bashan
came out to fight against us, but we defeated them. 8 We took their land and
gave it to the tribes of Reuben and Gad and to the half-tribe of Manasseh as
their grant of land.
9 "Therefore, obey the terms of this covenant so that you will prosper in
everything you do. 10 All of you—tribal leaders, elders, officers, all the men
of Israel—are standing today in the presence of the LORD your God. 11 Your
little ones and your wives are with you, as well as the foreigners living among
you who chop your wood and carry your water. 12 You are standing here today
to enter into the covenant of the LORD your God. The LORD is making this
covenant, including the curses. 13 By entering into the covenant today, he
will establish you as his people and confirm that he is your God, just as he
promised you and as he swore to your ancestors Abraham, Isaac, and Jacob.
14 "But you are not the only ones with whom I am making this covenant
with its curses. 15 I am making this covenant both with you who stand here
today in the presence of the LORD our God, and also with the future genera-
tions who are not standing here today.
16 "You remember how we lived in the land of Egypt and how we trav-
eled through the lands of enemy nations as we left. 17 You have seen their
detestable practices and their idols* made of wood, stone, silver, and gold.
18 I am making this covenant with you so that no one among you—no man,
woman, clan, or tribe—will turn away from the LORD our God to worship
these gods of other nations, and so that no root among you bears bitter and
poisonous fruit.
19 "Those who hear the warnings of this curse should not congratulate
themselves, thinking, 'I am safe, even though I am following the desires
of my own stubborn heart.' This would lead to utter ruin! 20 The LORD will
never pardon such people. Instead his anger and jealousy will burn against
them. All the curses written in this book will come down on them, and the
LORD will erase their names from under heaven. 21 The LORD will separate
them from all the tribes of Israel, to pour out on them all the curses of the
covenant recorded in this Book of Instruction.
22 "Then the generations to come, both your own descendants and the
foreigners who come from distant lands, will see the devastation of the land
and the diseases the LORD inflicts on it. 23 They will exclaim, 'The whole
land is devastated by sulfur and salt. It is a wasteland with nothing planted
and nothing growing, not even a blade of grass. It is like the cities of Sod-
om and Gomorrah, Admah and Zeboiim, which the LORD destroyed in his
intense anger.'
24 "And all the surrounding nations will ask, 'Why has the LORD done this
to this land? Why was he so angry?'
25 "And the answer will be, 'This happened because the people of the land
abandoned the covenant that the LORD, the God of their ancestors, made
with them when he brought them out of the land of Egypt. 26 Instead, they
turned away to serve and worship gods they had not known before, gods that
were not from the LORD. 27 That is why the LORD's anger has burned against

29:17 The Hebrew term (literally *round things*) probably alludes to dung.

this land, bringing down on it every curse recorded in this book. 28In great
anger and fury the LORD uprooted his people from their land and banished
them to another land, where they still live today!'
29"The LORD our God has secrets known to no one. We are not account-
able for them, but we and our children are accountable forever for all that
he has revealed to us, so that we may obey all the terms of these instructions.

A Call to Return to the LORD

30 "In the future, when you experience all these blessings and curses
I have listed for you, and when you are living among the nations to
which the LORD your God has exiled you, take to heart all these instructions.
2If at that time you and your children return to the LORD your God, and if
you obey with all your heart and all your soul all the commands I have given
you today, 3then the LORD your God will restore your fortunes. He will have
mercy on you and gather you back from all the nations where he has scattered
you. 4Even though you are banished to the ends of the earth,* the LORD your
God will gather you from there and bring you back again. 5The LORD your
God will return you to the land that belonged to your ancestors, and you will
possess that land again. Then he will make you even more prosperous and
numerous than your ancestors!
6"The LORD your God will change your heart* and the hearts of all your
descendants, so that you will love him with all your heart and soul and so you
may live! 7The LORD your God will inflict all these curses on your enemies
and on those who hate and persecute you. 8Then you will again obey the
LORD and keep all his commands that I am giving you today.
9"The LORD your God will then make you successful in everything you do.
He will give you many children and numerous livestock, and he will cause
your fields to produce abundant harvests, for the LORD will again delight
in being good to you as he was to your ancestors. 10The LORD your God will
delight in you if you obey his voice and keep the commands and decrees
written in this Book of Instruction, and if you turn to the LORD your God
with all your heart and soul.

The Choice of Life or Death

11"This command I am giving you today is not too difficult for you, and it is
not beyond your reach. 12It is not kept in heaven, so distant that you must
ask, 'Who will go up to heaven and bring it down so we can hear it and obey?'
13It is not kept beyond the sea, so far away that you must ask, 'Who will cross
the sea to bring it to us so we can hear it and obey?' 14No, the message is very
close at hand; it is on your lips and in your heart so that you can obey it.
15"Now listen! Today I am giving you a choice between life and death, be-
tween prosperity and disaster. 16For I command you this day to love the LORD
your God and to keep his commands, decrees, and regulations by walking in
his ways. If you do this, you will live and multiply, and the LORD your God
will bless you and the land you are about to enter and occupy.
17"But if your heart turns away and you refuse to listen, and if you are
drawn away to serve and worship other gods, 18then I warn you now that you
will certainly be destroyed. You will not live a long, good life in the land you
are crossing the Jordan to occupy.

30:4 Hebrew *of the heavens*. 30:6 Hebrew *circumcise your heart*.

Make a Difference

30:1-10

Heart Change

Moses looked into the future here and saw a time when the descendants of the Israelites would be driven out of the promised land. They would be scattered and mixed in with all the other nations. They would be disobedient, and the blessings of God would not be available to them any longer. What a sad prediction about their future.

The good news is they already knew the pathway back to God and his blessing. At that future moment, they could confess to God that they had been sinful and rebellious. They could cry out for his mercy. Most importantly, they could begin living in relationship with God again. When they did, God would change their hearts. This means that no matter how far one wandered from God, when they chose to live by his commands again, the relationship would be restored.

Difference Maker

Is there someone you consider to be too far from God? Continue to pray for that person. Ask God to change his or her heart. He is the God who can do the impossible.

Question **30:15**

In 30:15-20, God has clearly given his people the choice to honor or disgrace him by following or turning their backs on his commands. We get to choose which path we walk down. What appears to be the ultimate end of each path?

19“Today I have given you the choice between life and death, between
blessings and curses. Now I call on heaven and earth to witness the choice
you make. Oh, that you would choose life, so that you and your descendants
might live! 20You can make this choice by loving the LORD your God, obeying
him, and committing yourself firmly to him. This* is the key to your life. And
if you love and obey the LORD, you will live long in the land the LORD swore
to give your ancestors Abraham, Isaac, and Jacob.”

Joshua Becomes Israel's Leader

31 When Moses had finished giving these instructions* to all the people
of Israel, 2he said, “I am now 120 years old, and I am no longer able to
lead you. The LORD has told me, ‘You will not cross the Jordan River.’ 3But
the LORD your God himself will cross over ahead of you. He will destroy the
nations living there, and you will take possession of their land. Joshua will
lead you across the river, just as the LORD promised.
4“The LORD will destroy the nations living in the land, just as he destroyed
Sihon and Og, the kings of the Amorites. 5The LORD will hand over to you the
people who live there, and you must deal with them as I have commanded
you. 6So be strong and courageous! Do not be afraid and do not panic before
them. For the LORD your God will personally go ahead of you. He will neither
fail you nor abandon you.”
7Then Moses called for Joshua, and as all Israel watched, he said to him,
“Be strong and courageous! For you will lead these people into the land
that the LORD swore to their ancestors he would give them. You are the one
who will divide it among them as their grants of land. 8Do not be afraid or
discouraged, for the LORD will personally go ahead of you. He will be with
you; he will neither fail you nor abandon you.”

Public Reading of the Book of Instruction

9So Moses wrote this entire body of instruction in a book and gave it to the
priests, who carried the Ark of the LORD's Covenant, and to the elders of Israel.
10Then Moses gave them this command: “At the end of every seventh year, the
Year of Release, during the Festival of Shelters, 11you must read this Book of
Instruction to all the people of Israel when they assemble before the LORD your
God at the place he chooses. 12Call them all together—men, women, children,
and the foreigners living in your towns—so they may hear this Book of In-
struction and learn to fear the LORD your God and carefully obey all the terms
of these instructions. 13Do this so that your children who have not known
these instructions will hear them and will learn to fear the LORD your God.
Do this as long as you live in the land you are crossing the Jordan to occupy.”

Israel's Disobedience Predicted

14Then the LORD said to Moses, “The time has come for you to die. Call
Joshua and present yourselves at the Tabernacle,* so that I may commission
him there.” So Moses and Joshua went and presented themselves at the Tab-
ernacle. 15And the LORD appeared to them in a pillar of cloud that stood at
the entrance to the sacred tent.
16The LORD said to Moses, “You are about to die and join your ancestors.
After you are gone, these people will begin to worship foreign gods, the

30:20 Or *He.* **31:1** As in Dead Sea Scrolls and Greek version; Masoretic Text reads *Moses went and spoke.* **31:14** Hebrew *Tent of Meeting;* also in 31:14b.

Make a Difference **31:6**

B = S + C

Be strong and courageous. Notice the command here. Don't just be strong and don't just be courageous. Be strong *and* courageous. This is what the Lord told Joshua as he was about to take a huge leadership role. The responsibility must have been overwhelming. Moses, Mr. Miracle Man, who had led Israel for forty years, had passed the baton to Joshua. Everyone must have wondered, *Will Joshua be able to lead us like Moses did?*

The Lord can enable anyone to do anything he wants them to do. God is calling you to make a difference in the world. Trust him to work through you today. He is with you when you are following his lead in your life.

Difference Maker

What do you believe God has called you to do but you have struggled to take the initiative to get started? Apply this verse to your life today.

Question **31:10**

Moses instructed the people to gather regularly and have a leader read aloud this entire Book of Instruction (Deuteronomy). Do you see the wisdom in that? Do you think it would be wise to set aside regular time in your life to read the Bible?

gods of the land where they are going. They will abandon me and break
my covenant that I have made with them. 17 Then my anger will blaze forth
against them. I will abandon them, hiding my face from them, and they will
be devoured. Terrible trouble will come down on them, and on that day they
will say, 'These disasters have come down on us because God is no longer
among us!' 18 At that time I will hide my face from them on account of all
the evil they commit by worshiping other gods.

19 "So write down the words of this song, and teach it to the people of
Israel. Help them learn it, so it may serve as a witness for me against them.
20 For I will bring them into the land I swore to give their ancestors—a land
flowing with milk and honey. There they will become prosperous, eat all the
food they want, and become fat. But they will begin to worship other gods;
they will despise me and break my covenant. 21 And when great disasters
come down on them, this song will stand as evidence against them, for it
will never be forgotten by their descendants. I know the intentions of these
people, even now before they have entered the land I swore to give them."

22 So that very day Moses wrote down the words of the song and taught
it to the Israelites.

23 Then the LORD commissioned Joshua son of Nun with these words: "Be
strong and courageous, for you must bring the people of Israel into the land
I swore to give them. I will be with you."

24 When Moses had finished writing this entire body of instruction in
a book, 25 he gave this command to the Levites who carried the Ark of the
LORD's Covenant: 26 "Take this Book of Instruction and place it beside the Ark
of the Covenant of the LORD your God, so it may remain there as a witness
against the people of Israel. 27 For I know how rebellious and stubborn you
are. Even now, while I am still alive and am here with you, you have rebelled
against the LORD. How much more rebellious will you be after my death!

28 "Now summon all the elders and officials of your tribes, so that I can
speak to them directly and call heaven and earth to witness against them. 29 I
know that after my death you will become utterly corrupt and will turn from
the way I have commanded you to follow. In the days to come, disaster will
come down on you, for you will do what is evil in the LORD's sight, making
him very angry with your actions."

The Song of Moses

30 So Moses recited this entire song publicly to the assembly of Israel:

32

1 "Listen, O heavens, and I will speak!
Hear, O earth, the words that I say!
2 Let my teaching fall on you like rain;
let my speech settle like dew.
Let my words fall like rain on tender grass,
like gentle showers on young plants.
3 I will proclaim the name of the LORD;
how glorious is our God!
4 He is the Rock; his deeds are perfect.
Everything he does is just and fair.
He is a faithful God who does no wrong;
how just and upright he is!

5 “But they have acted corruptly toward him;
when they act so perversely,
are they really his children?*
They are a deceitful and twisted generation.
6 Is this the way you repay the LORD,
you foolish and senseless people?
Isn’t he your Father who created you?
Has he not made you and established you?
7 Remember the days of long ago;
think about the generations past.
Ask your father, and he will inform you.
Inquire of your elders, and they will tell you.
8 When the Most High assigned lands to the nations,
when he divided up the human race,
he established the boundaries of the peoples
according to the number in his heavenly court.*

9 “For the people of Israel belong to the LORD;
Jacob is his special possession.
10 He found them in a desert land,
in an empty, howling wasteland.
He surrounded them and watched over them;
he guarded them as he would guard his own eyes.*
11 Like an eagle that rouses her chicks
and hovers over her young,
so he spread his wings to take them up
and carried them safely on his pinions.
12 The LORD alone guided them;
they followed no foreign gods.
13 He let them ride over the highlands
and feast on the crops of the fields.
He nourished them with honey from the rock
and olive oil from the stony ground.
14 He fed them yogurt from the herd
and milk from the flock,
together with the fat of lambs.
He gave them choice rams from Bashan, and goats,
together with the choicest wheat.
You drank the finest wine,
made from the juice of grapes.

15 “But Israel* soon became fat and unruly;
the people grew heavy, plump, and stuffed!
Then they abandoned the God who had made them;
they made light of the Rock of their salvation.
16 They stirred up his jealousy by worshiping foreign gods;
they provoked his fury with detestable deeds.

32:5 The meaning of the Hebrew is uncertain. 32:8 As in Dead Sea Scrolls, which read *the number of the sons of God,* and Greek version, which reads *the number of the angels of God;* Masoretic Text reads *the number of the sons of Israel.* 32:10 Hebrew *as the pupil of his eye.* 32:15 Hebrew *Jeshurun,* a term of endearment for Israel.

17 They offered sacrifices to demons, which are not God,
to gods they had not known before,
to new gods only recently arrived,
to gods their ancestors had never feared.
18 You neglected the Rock who had fathered you;
you forgot the God who had given you birth.

19 “The LORD saw this and drew back,
provoked to anger by his own sons and daughters.
20 He said, ‘I will abandon them;
then see what becomes of them.
For they are a twisted generation,
children without integrity.
21 They have roused my jealousy by worshiping things
that are not God;
they have provoked my anger with their
useless idols.
Now I will rouse their jealousy through people
who are not even a people;
I will provoke their anger through the foolish Gentiles.
22 For my anger blazes forth like fire
and burns to the depths of the grave.*
It devours the earth and all its crops
and ignites the foundations of the mountains.
23 I will heap disasters upon them
and shoot them down with my arrows.
24 I will weaken them with famine,
burning fever, and deadly disease.
I will send the fangs of wild beasts
and poisonous snakes that glide in the dust.
25 Outside, the sword will bring death,
and inside, terror will strike
both young men and young women,
both infants and the aged.
26 I would have annihilated them,
wiping out even the memory of them.
27 But I feared the taunt of Israel’s enemy,
who might misunderstand and say,
“Our own power has triumphed!
The LORD had nothing to do with this!”’

28 “But Israel is a senseless nation;
the people are foolish, without understanding.
29 Oh, that they were wise and could understand this!
Oh, that they might know their fate!
30 How could one person chase a thousand of them,
and two people put ten thousand to flight,
unless their Rock had sold them,
unless the LORD had given them up?

32:22 Hebrew *of Sheol.*

Patterns I see in this text

Question **32:39**

Why is this perspective about God, even if it is unsettling, a healthy one for humans?

31 But the rock of our enemies is not like our Rock,
as even they recognize.*
32 Their vine grows from the vine of Sodom,
from the vineyards of Gomorrah.
Their grapes are poison,
and their clusters are bitter.
33 Their wine is the venom of serpents,
the deadly poison of cobras.

34 "The LORD says, 'Am I not storing up these things,
sealing them away in my treasury?
35 I will take revenge; I will pay them back.
In due time their feet will slip.
Their day of disaster will arrive,
and their destiny will overtake them.'

36 "Indeed, the LORD will give justice to his people,
and he will change his mind about* his servants,
when he sees their strength is gone
and no one is left, slave or free.
37 Then he will ask, 'Where are their gods,
the rocks they fled to for refuge?
38 Where now are those gods,
who ate the fat of their sacrifices
and drank the wine of their offerings?
Let those gods arise and help you!
Let them provide you with shelter!
39 Look now; I myself am he!
There is no other god but me!
I am the one who kills and gives life;
I am the one who wounds and heals;
no one can be rescued from my powerful hand!
40 Now I raise my hand to heaven
and declare, "As surely as I live,
41 when I sharpen my flashing sword
and begin to carry out justice,
I will take revenge on my enemies
and repay those who reject me.
42 I will make my arrows drunk with blood,
and my sword will devour flesh—
the blood of the slaughtered and the captives,
and the heads of the enemy leaders."'

43 "Rejoice with him, you heavens,
and let all of God's angels worship him.*
Rejoice with his people, you Gentiles,
and let all the angels be strengthened in him.*

32:31 The meaning of the Hebrew is uncertain. Greek version reads *our enemies are fools.* 32:36 Or *will take revenge for.* 32:43a As in Dead Sea Scrolls and Greek version; Masoretic Text lacks the first two lines. Compare Heb 1:6. 32:43b As in Greek version; Hebrew text lacks this sentence. Compare Rom 15:10.

Story Arc **32:48–52**

● Moses

God's authority and power were given to Moses, and he used them to lead his people to freedom from their oppressors. He had faithfully led a people who lacked faith and, eventually, brought a whole new generation right to the border of the land God had promised them generations earlier.

For all the good he did as a leader, Moses also had moments when his human failures made a mark. In a moment of anger and frustration, he disobeyed God's command, and the consequence was that he would not be allowed to lead his people the final steps of their journey into the promised land.

In this final scene of his life, God led Moses to a place where he could view the promised land from a distance. He died within sight of the destination he had been moving toward for forty years.

During Moses' lifetime, God used him to do mighty and miraculous things. We all have weaknesses and failures, but God desires to use each one of us, making the most of our unique abilities and strengths. Our job is simply to obey.

Josh 1:1 ►

For he will avenge the blood of his children*;
he will take revenge against his enemies.
He will repay those who hate him*
and cleanse his people's land."

44 So Moses came with Joshua* son of Nun and recited all the words of this
song to the people.
45 When Moses had finished reciting all these words to the people of Israel,
46 he added: "Take to heart all the words of warning I have given you today.
Pass them on as a command to your children so they will obey every word of
these instructions. 47 These instructions are not empty words—they are your
life! By obeying them you will enjoy a long life in the land you will occupy
when you cross the Jordan River."

Moses' Death Foretold

48 That same day the LORD said to Moses, 49 "Go to Moab, to the mountains
east of the river,* and climb Mount Nebo, which is across from Jericho. Look
out across the land of Canaan, the land I am giving to the people of Israel
as their own special possession. 50 Then you will die there on the mountain.
You will join your ancestors, just as Aaron, your brother, died on Mount
Hor and joined his ancestors. 51 For both of you betrayed me with the Israel-
ites at the waters of Meribah at Kadesh* in the wilderness of Zin. You failed
to demonstrate my holiness to the people of Israel there. 52 So you will see
the land from a distance, but you may not enter the land I am giving to the
people of Israel."

Moses Blesses the People

33 This is the blessing that Moses, the man of God, gave to the people of Israel before his death:

2 "The LORD came from Mount Sinai
and dawned upon us* from Mount Seir;
he shone forth from Mount Paran
and came from Meribah-kadesh
with flaming fire at his right hand.*
3 Indeed, he loves his people;*
all his holy ones are in his hands.
They follow in his steps
and accept his teaching.
4 Moses gave us the LORD's instruction,
the special possession of the people of Israel.*
5 The LORD became king in Israel*—
when the leaders of the people assembled,
when the tribes of Israel gathered as one."

32:43c As in Dead Sea Scrolls and Greek version; Masoretic Text reads *his servants.* **32:43d** As in Dead Sea Scrolls and Greek version; Masoretic Text lacks this line. **32:44** Hebrew *Hoshea,* a variant name for Joshua. **32:49** Hebrew *the mountains of Abarim.* **32:51** Hebrew *waters of Meribath-kadesh.* **33:2a** As in Greek and Syriac versions; Hebrew reads *upon them.* **33:2b** Or *came from myriads of holy ones, from the south, from his mountain slopes.* The meaning of the Hebrew is uncertain. **33:3** As in Greek version; Hebrew reads *Indeed, lover of the peoples.* **33:4** Hebrew *of Jacob.* The names "Jacob" and "Israel" are often interchanged throughout the Old Testament, referring sometimes to the individual patriarch and sometimes to the nation. **33:5** Hebrew *in Jeshurun,* a term of endearment for Israel.

Make a Difference

33:1-29

God's Love

Before Moses' death, he spoke a blessing over each of the twelve tribes of Israel. He introduced these verbal blessings by reminding the whole nation that God loves and takes care of his people. He also described the people of God as those who follow his path and accept his teaching. This description of the people of God is still true today.

God's call on the church today is to put him first and follow his teaching. Those who faithfully pursue a life with God always put him above anything and anyone. Becoming a difference maker requires submission to God's plans and obedience to his commands.

Difference Maker

God has given you unique gifts and talents. There is no one else exactly like you. With the power of the Holy Spirit, you can walk the path laid out for you. With humility you can submit yourself to the teachings and commands of God. You are not alone, so go make a difference.

6 Moses said this about the tribe of Reuben:*

"Let the tribe of Reuben live and not die out,
though they are few in number."

7 Moses said this about the tribe of Judah:

"O LORD, hear the cry of Judah
and bring them together as a people.
Give them strength to defend their cause;
help them against their enemies!"

8 Moses said this about the tribe of Levi:

"O LORD, you have given your Thummim and Urim—the sacred lots—
to your faithful servants the Levites.*
You put them to the test at Massah
and struggled with them at the waters of Meribah.
9 The Levites obeyed your word
and guarded your covenant.
They were more loyal to you
than to their own parents.
They ignored their relatives
and did not acknowledge their own children.
10 They teach your regulations to Jacob;
they give your instructions to Israel.
They present incense before you
and offer whole burnt offerings on the altar.
11 Bless the ministry of the Levites, O LORD,
and accept all the work of their hands.
Hit their enemies where it hurts the most;
strike down their foes so they never rise again."

12 Moses said this about the tribe of Benjamin:

"The people of Benjamin are loved by the LORD
and live in safety beside him.
He surrounds them continuously
and preserves them from every harm."

13 Moses said this about the tribes of Joseph:

"May their land be blessed by the LORD
with the precious gift of dew from the heavens
and water from beneath the earth;
14 with the rich fruit that grows in the sun,
and the rich harvest produced each month;
15 with the finest crops of the ancient mountains,
and the abundance from the everlasting hills;

33:6 Hebrew lacks *Moses said this about the tribe of Reuben.* 33:8 As in Greek version; Hebrew lacks *the Levites.*

16 with the best gifts of the earth and its bounty,
and the favor of the one who appeared in the burning bush.
May these blessings rest on Joseph's head,
crowning the brow of the prince among his brothers.
17 Joseph has the majesty of a young bull;
he has the horns of a wild ox.
He will gore distant nations,
even to the ends of the earth.
This is my blessing for the multitudes of Ephraim
and the thousands of Manasseh."

18 Moses said this about the tribes of Zebulun and Issachar*:

"May the people of Zebulun prosper in their travels.
May the people of Issachar prosper at home in their tents.
19 They summon the people to the mountain
to offer proper sacrifices there.
They benefit from the riches of the sea
and the hidden treasures in the sand."

20 Moses said this about the tribe of Gad:

"Blessed is the one who enlarges Gad's territory!
Gad is poised there like a lion
to tear off an arm or a head.
21 The people of Gad took the best land for themselves;
a leader's share was assigned to them.
When the leaders of the people were assembled,
they carried out the LORD's justice
and obeyed his regulations for Israel."

22 Moses said this about the tribe of Dan:

"Dan is a lion's cub,
leaping out from Bashan."

23 Moses said this about the tribe of Naphtali:

"O Naphtali, you are rich in favor
and full of the LORD's blessings;
may you possess the west and the south."

24 Moses said this about the tribe of Asher:

"May Asher be blessed above other sons;
may he be esteemed by his brothers;
may he bathe his feet in olive oil.

33:18 Hebrew lacks *and Issachar.*

Highlights from the text

Question 34:9

Joshua was given the spirit of wisdom as the leadership mantle was passed from Moses to him. The people were aware of the influence of Moses on the life of Joshua, so they followed Joshua and obeyed his commands as well. What can you learn about true leadership from this one profound verse?

Question 34:10

What would it mean to know God "face to face"? How much more meaning does this phrase have considering that Jesus came in the flesh to share life with us?

25 May the bolts of your gates be of iron and bronze;
may you be secure all your days."

26 "There is no one like the God of Israel.*
He rides across the heavens to help you,
across the skies in majestic splendor.
27 The eternal God is your refuge,
and his everlasting arms are under you.
He drives out the enemy before you;
he cries out, 'Destroy them!'
28 So Israel will live in safety,
prosperous Jacob in security,
in a land of grain and new wine,
while the heavens drop down dew.
29 How blessed you are, O Israel!
Who else is like you, a people saved by the LORD?
He is your protecting shield
and your triumphant sword!
Your enemies will cringe before you,
and you will stomp on their backs!"

The Death of Moses

34 Then Moses went up to Mount Nebo from the plains of Moab and
climbed Pisgah Peak, which is across from Jericho. And the LORD
showed him the whole land, from Gilead as far as Dan; 2 all the land of Naph-
tali; the land of Ephraim and Manasseh; all the land of Judah, extending to
the Mediterranean Sea*; 3 the Negev; the Jordan Valley with Jericho—the city
of palms—as far as Zoar. 4 Then the LORD said to Moses, "This is the land I
promised on oath to Abraham, Isaac, and Jacob when I said, 'I will give it to
your descendants.' I have now allowed you to see it with your own eyes, but
you will not enter the land."
5 So Moses, the servant of the LORD, died there in the land of Moab, just
as the LORD had said. 6 The LORD buried him* in a valley near Beth-peor in
Moab, but to this day no one knows the exact place. 7 Moses was 120 years old
when he died, yet his eyesight was clear, and he was as strong as ever. 8 The
people of Israel mourned for Moses on the plains of Moab for thirty days,
until the customary period of mourning was over.
9 Now Joshua son of Nun was full of the spirit of wisdom, for Moses had
laid his hands on him. So the people of Israel obeyed him, doing just as the
LORD had commanded Moses.
10 There has never been another prophet in Israel like Moses, whom the
LORD knew face to face. 11 The LORD sent him to perform all the miraculous
signs and wonders in the land of Egypt against Pharaoh, and all his servants,
and his entire land. 12 With mighty power, Moses performed terrifying acts
in the sight of all Israel.

33:26 Hebrew *of Jeshurun,* a term of endearment for Israel. **34:2** Hebrew *the western sea.* **34:6** Hebrew *He buried him;* Samaritan Pentateuch and some Greek manuscripts read *They buried him.*

Joshua Introduction

When young Joshua left Egypt with Caleb and the other Israelites, he had no idea it would take him forty years to arrive at the doorstep of the promised land. Through years of rebellion and disobedience, the people of Israel wandered around the Sinai Peninsula under Moses' leadership. Now, the people were worn down, afraid, and homeless. The book of Joshua is the story of what happened when over one million people began looking to Joshua for leadership after his mentor, Moses, died. Was he afraid? Yes! Who wouldn't be?

From a young age, Joshua loved being in the presence of God (Exodus 33:11). He was there when Moses went way up the mountain to receive the Ten Commandments (Exodus 24:13-14). He was ready to fight when others were afraid (Numbers 14:6-9). He made some tough choices that were the right decisions but weren't always the popular ones (Numbers 14:10).

His great faith and courage in those younger years set the stage for the common theme that you will see over and over in the pages that follow: "Be strong and courageous! Do not be afraid or discouraged. For the LORD your God is with you wherever you go" (Joshua 1:9).

Imagine the difference that theme could make in your life. As you dive into this book, get ready for some heroic battles and some challenging setbacks. Near the end of the story, don't miss the question that Joshua asks the people (24:15): Will you and your household serve the Lord?

Story Arcs

- **Joshua**
- **Rahab**
- **Caleb**

Joshua

Prayer 1:6-9

Lord Jesus, make me strong. Make me courageous. Let me not be afraid. Let me stand tall in the confidence of your power and presence. Amen.

The LORD's Charge to Joshua

1 After the death of Moses the LORD's servant, the LORD spoke to Joshua
son of Nun, Moses' assistant. He said, 2"Moses my servant is dead.
Therefore, the time has come for you to lead these people, the Israelites,
across the Jordan River into the land I am giving them. 3I promise you what
I promised Moses: 'Wherever you set foot, you will be on land I have given
you—4from the Negev wilderness in the south to the Lebanon mountains in
the north, from the Euphrates River in the east to the Mediterranean Sea* in
the west, including all the land of the Hittites.' 5No one will be able to stand
against you as long as you live. For I will be with you as I was with Moses. I
will not fail you or abandon you.
6"Be strong and courageous, for you are the one who will lead these people
to possess all the land I swore to their ancestors I would give them. 7Be strong
and very courageous. Be careful to obey all the instructions Moses gave you.
Do not deviate from them, turning either to the right or to the left. Then you
will be successful in everything you do. 8Study this Book of Instruction con-
tinually. Meditate on it day and night so you will be sure to obey everything
written in it. Only then will you prosper and succeed in all you do. 9This is
my command—be strong and courageous! Do not be afraid or discouraged.
For the LORD your God is with you wherever you go."

Joshua's Charge to the Israelites

10Joshua then commanded the officers of Israel, 11"Go through the camp and
tell the people to get their provisions ready. In three days you will cross the
Jordan River and take possession of the land the LORD your God is giving you."
12Then Joshua called together the tribes of Reuben, Gad, and the half-tribe
of Manasseh. He told them, 13"Remember what Moses, the servant of the
LORD, commanded you: 'The LORD your God is giving you a place of rest. He
has given you this land.' 14Your wives, children, and livestock may remain
here in the land Moses assigned to you on the east side of the Jordan River.
But your strong warriors, fully armed, must lead the other tribes across the
Jordan to help them conquer their territory. Stay with them 15until the LORD
gives them rest, as he has given you rest, and until they, too, possess the land
the LORD your God is giving them. Only then may you return and settle here
on the east side of the Jordan River in the land that Moses, the servant of the
LORD, assigned to you."
16They answered Joshua, "We will do whatever you command us, and we
will go wherever you send us. 17We will obey you just as we obeyed Moses.
And may the LORD your God be with you as he was with Moses. 18Anyone
who rebels against your orders and does not obey your words and everything
you command will be put to death. So be strong and courageous!"

Story Arc 1:1

● Joshua

Joshua is one of the greatest figures in all the Bible. He stepped out of the shadow of the mighty Moses and into the visionary leadership of Israel as they entered the promised land. Joshua's strength and courage came from his dependance on the Lord. In the pages ahead, look for Joshua's faithfulness as a template for how you can live out your faith.

Josh 2:1-24 ►

1:4 Hebrew *the Great Sea.*

Rahab Protects the Spies

2 Then Joshua secretly sent out two spies from the Israelite camp at Aca-
cia Grove.* He instructed them, "Scout out the land on the other side
of the Jordan River, especially around Jericho." So the two men set out and
came to the house of a prostitute named Rahab and stayed there that night.
2 But someone told the king of Jericho, "Some Israelites have come here
tonight to spy out the land." 3 So the king of Jericho sent orders to Rahab:
"Bring out the men who have come into your house, for they have come here
to spy out the whole land."
4 Rahab had hidden the two men, but she replied, "Yes, the men were here
earlier, but I didn't know where they were from. 5 They left the town at dusk,
as the gates were about to close. I don't know where they went. If you hurry,
you can probably catch up with them." 6 (Actually, she had taken them up to
the roof and hidden them beneath bundles of flax she had laid out.) 7 So the
king's men went looking for the spies along the road leading to the shallow
crossings of the Jordan River. And as soon as the king's men had left, the
gate of Jericho was shut.
8 Before the spies went to sleep that night, Rahab went up on the roof to
talk with them. 9 "I know the LORD has given you this land," she told them.
"We are all afraid of you. Everyone in the land is living in terror. 10 For we have
heard how the LORD made a dry path for you through the Red Sea* when
you left Egypt. And we know what you did to Sihon and Og, the two Amo-
rite kings east of the Jordan River, whose people you completely destroyed.*
11 No wonder our hearts have melted in fear! No one has the courage to fight
after hearing such things. For the LORD your God is the supreme God of the
heavens above and the earth below.
12 "Now swear to me by the LORD that you will be kind to me and my family
since I have helped you. Give me some guarantee that 13 when Jericho is con-
quered, you will let me live, along with my father and mother, my brothers
and sisters, and all their families."
14 "We offer our own lives as a guarantee for your safety," the men agreed.
"If you don't betray us, we will keep our promise and be kind to you when
the LORD gives us the land."
15 Then, since Rahab's house was built into the town wall, she let them
down by a rope through the window. 16 "Escape to the hill country," she told
them. "Hide there for three days from the men searching for you. Then,
when they have returned, you can go on your way."
17 Before they left, the men told her, "We will be bound by the oath we
have taken only if you follow these instructions. 18 When we come into the
land, you must leave this scarlet rope hanging from the window through
which you let us down. And all your family members—your father, mother,
brothers, and all your relatives—must be here inside the house. 19 If they go
out into the street and are killed, it will not be our fault. But if anyone lays a
hand on people inside this house, we will accept the responsibility for their
death. 20 If you betray us, however, we are not bound by this oath in any way."
21 "I accept your terms," she replied. And she sent them on their way, leav-
ing the scarlet rope hanging from the window.
22 The spies went up into the hill country and stayed there three days. The

2:1 Hebrew *Shittim*. **2:10a** Hebrew *sea of reeds*. **2:10b** The Hebrew term used here refers to the complete consecration of things or people to the LORD, either by destroying them or by giving them as an offering.

Story Arc **2:1-24**

● Rahab

Here is the unexpected introduction of Rahab, one of the most important people in all Scripture. Until the day she encountered the people of God, she was a woman with a very questionable profession. She was not an Israelite. She had not been following the Lord. Despite her past, when she had a chance to side with God, she took the chance. She protected God's people (by hanging a scarlet-colored rope from her window so that the Israelite spies could escape), so God protected Rahab and her family. From that moment onward, Rahab was invited into the central vein of the Lord's good news. She was welcomed into the fold of God's people. Fourteen hundred years later, she would become the great-ancestor to the Messiah (Matthew 1:5). As you read this chapter, consider what Rahab's remarkable story teaches us about God.

Josh 14:6-15 ►

Question 3:5

Why is taking time to prepare for God to do great things an essential aspect to your life with God?

men who were chasing them searched everywhere along the road, but they
finally returned without success.
23Then the two spies came down from the hill country, crossed the Jordan
River, and reported to Joshua all that had happened to them. 24"The LORD
has given us the whole land," they said, "for all the people in the land are
terrified of us."

The Israelites Cross the Jordan

3 Early the next morning Joshua and all the Israelites left Acacia Grove*
and arrived at the banks of the Jordan River, where they camped before
crossing. 2Three days later the Israelite officers went through the camp,
3giving these instructions to the people: "When you see the Levitical priests
carrying the Ark of the Covenant of the LORD your God, move out from
your positions and follow them. 4Since you have never traveled this way
before, they will guide you. Stay about half a mile* behind them, keeping
a clear distance between you and the Ark. Make sure you don't come any
closer."
5Then Joshua told the people, "Purify yourselves, for tomorrow the LORD
will do great wonders among you."
6In the morning Joshua said to the priests, "Lift up the Ark of the Covenant and lead the people across the river." And so they started out and went
ahead of the people.
7The LORD told Joshua, "Today I will begin to make you a great leader
in the eyes of all the Israelites. They will know that I am with you, just as I
was with Moses. 8Give this command to the priests who carry the Ark of the
Covenant: 'When you reach the banks of the Jordan River, take a few steps
into the river and stop there.'"
9So Joshua told the Israelites, "Come and listen to what the LORD your God
says. 10Today you will know that the living God is among you. He will surely
drive out the Canaanites, Hittites, Hivites, Perizzites, Girgashites, Amorites,
and Jebusites ahead of you. 11Look, the Ark of the Covenant, which belongs
to the Lord of the whole earth, will lead you across the Jordan River! 12Now
choose twelve men from the tribes of Israel, one from each tribe. 13The priests
will carry the Ark of the LORD, the Lord of all the earth. As soon as their feet
touch the water, the flow of water will be cut off upstream, and the river will
stand up like a wall."
14So the people left their camp to cross the Jordan, and the priests who
were carrying the Ark of the Covenant went ahead of them. 15It was the harvest season, and the Jordan was overflowing its banks. But as soon as the
feet of the priests who were carrying the Ark touched the water at the river's
edge, 16the water above that point began backing up a great distance away at
a town called Adam, which is near Zarethan. And the water below that point
flowed on to the Dead Sea* until the riverbed was dry. Then all the people
crossed over near the town of Jericho.
17Meanwhile, the priests who were carrying the Ark of the LORD's Covenant stood on dry ground in the middle of the riverbed as the people passed
by. They waited there until the whole nation of Israel had crossed the Jordan
on dry ground.

3:1 Hebrew *Shittim.* 3:4 Hebrew *about 2,000 cubits* [920 meters]. 3:16 Hebrew *the sea of the Arabah, the Salt Sea.*

Memorials to the Jordan Crossing

4 When all the people had crossed the Jordan, the LORD said to Joshua,
2“Now choose twelve men, one from each tribe. 3Tell them, ‘Take twelve
stones from the very place where the priests are standing in the middle of
the Jordan. Carry them out and pile them up at the place where you will
camp tonight.’”
4So Joshua called together the twelve men he had chosen—one from each
of the tribes of Israel. 5He told them, “Go into the middle of the Jordan, in
front of the Ark of the LORD your God. Each of you must pick up one stone
and carry it out on your shoulder—twelve stones in all, one for each of the
twelve tribes of Israel. 6We will use these stones to build a memorial. In the
future your children will ask you, ‘What do these stones mean?’ 7Then you
can tell them, ‘They remind us that the Jordan River stopped flowing when
the Ark of the LORD’s Covenant went across.’ These stones will stand as a
memorial among the people of Israel forever.”
8So the men did as Joshua had commanded them. They took twelve stones
from the middle of the Jordan River, one for each tribe, just as the LORD had
told Joshua. They carried them to the place where they camped for the night
and constructed the memorial there.
9Joshua also set up another pile of twelve stones in the middle of the Jor-
dan, at the place where the priests who carried the Ark of the Covenant were
standing. And they are there to this day.
10The priests who were carrying the Ark stood in the middle of the river
until all of the LORD’s commands that Moses had given to Joshua were car-
ried out. Meanwhile, the people hurried across the riverbed. 11And when
everyone was safely on the other side, the priests crossed over with the Ark
of the LORD as the people watched.
12The armed warriors from the tribes of Reuben, Gad, and the half-tribe
of Manasseh led the Israelites across the Jordan, just as Moses had directed.
13These armed men—about 40,000 strong—were ready for battle, and the
LORD was with them as they crossed over to the plains of Jericho.
14That day the LORD made Joshua a great leader in the eyes of all the Is-
raelites, and for the rest of his life they revered him as much as they had
revered Moses.
15The LORD had said to Joshua, 16“Command the priests carrying the Ark
of the Covenant* to come up out of the riverbed.” 17So Joshua gave the com-
mand. 18As soon as the priests carrying the Ark of the LORD’s Covenant came
up out of the riverbed and their feet were on high ground, the water of the
Jordan returned and overflowed its banks as before.
19The people crossed the Jordan on the tenth day of the first month.* Then
they camped at Gilgal, just east of Jericho. 20It was there at Gilgal that Joshua
piled up the twelve stones taken from the Jordan River.
21Then Joshua said to the Israelites, “In the future your children will ask,
‘What do these stones mean?’ 22Then you can tell them, ‘This is where the Is-
raelites crossed the Jordan on dry ground.’ 23For the LORD your God dried up
the river right before your eyes, and he kept it dry until you were all across,
just as he did at the Red Sea* when he dried it up until we had all crossed over.
24He did this so all the nations of the earth might know that the LORD’s hand
is powerful, and so you might fear the LORD your God forever.”

4:16 Hebrew *Ark of the Testimony.* **4:19** This day in the ancient Hebrew lunar calendar occurred in late March, April, or early May. **4:23** Hebrew *sea of reeds.*

Make a Difference

4:1-8

Marker

The Israelites took twelve large stones from the middle of the Jordan and then piled them up into a memorial. They did this so that in the future, their children would ask them about the stones. This was a strategic way to help the coming generations discover what God had done for them.

Difference Maker

What “marker” could you create that might prompt someone younger than you to ask a question that would lead to a discovery of God?

Question 5:13

Whose side is God on? Do you expect him to be on yours? Are you going to be on God's side?

5 When all the Amorite kings west of the Jordan and all the Canaanite
kings who lived along the Mediterranean coast* heard how the LORD
had dried up the Jordan River so the people of Israel could cross, they lost
heart and were paralyzed with fear because of them.

Israel Reestablishes Covenant Ceremonies

2 At that time the LORD told Joshua, "Make flint knives and circumcise this
second generation of Israelites.*" 3 So Joshua made flint knives and circum-
cised the entire male population of Israel at Gibeath-haaraloth.*
4 Joshua had to circumcise them because all the men who were old enough to
fight in battle when they left Egypt had died in the wilderness. 5 Those who left
Egypt had all been circumcised, but none of those born after the Exodus, dur-
ing the years in the wilderness, had been circumcised. 6 The Israelites had trav-
eled in the wilderness for forty years until all the men who were old enough
to fight in battle when they left Egypt had died. For they had disobeyed the
LORD, and the LORD vowed he would not let them enter the land he had sworn
to give us—a land flowing with milk and honey. 7 So Joshua circumcised their
sons—those who had grown up to take their fathers' places—for they had not
been circumcised on the way to the Promised Land. 8 After all the males had
been circumcised, they rested in the camp until they were healed.
9 Then the LORD said to Joshua, "Today I have rolled away the shame of
your slavery in Egypt." So that place has been called Gilgal* to this day.
10 While the Israelites were camped at Gilgal on the plains of Jericho, they
celebrated Passover on the evening of the fourteenth day of the first month.*
11 The very next day they began to eat unleavened bread and roasted grain
harvested from the land. 12 No manna appeared on the day they first ate from
the crops of the land, and it was never seen again. So from that time on the
Israelites ate from the crops of Canaan.

The LORD's Commander Confronts Joshua

13 When Joshua was near the town of Jericho, he looked up and saw a man
standing in front of him with sword in hand. Joshua went up to him and
demanded, "Are you friend or foe?"
14 "Neither one," he replied. "I am the commander of the LORD's army."
At this, Joshua fell with his face to the ground in reverence. "I am at your
command," Joshua said. "What do you want your servant to do?"
15 The commander of the LORD's army replied, "Take off your sandals, for
the place where you are standing is holy." And Joshua did as he was told.

The Fall of Jericho

6 Now the gates of Jericho were tightly shut because the people were
afraid of the Israelites. No one was allowed to go out or in. 2 But the
LORD said to Joshua, "I have given you Jericho, its king, and all its strong
warriors. 3 You and your fighting men should march around the town once
a day for six days. 4 Seven priests will walk ahead of the Ark, each carrying
a ram's horn. On the seventh day you are to march around the town seven
times, with the priests blowing the horns. 5 When you hear the priests give
one long blast on the rams' horns, have all the people shout as loud as they

5:1 Hebrew *along the sea.* 5:2 Or *circumcise the Israelites a second time.* 5:3 *Gibeath-haaraloth* means "hill of foreskins." 5:9 *Gilgal* sounds like the Hebrew word *galal,* meaning "to roll." 5:10 This day in the ancient Hebrew lunar calendar occurred in late March, April, or early May.

can. Then the walls of the town will collapse, and the people can charge straight into the town."

6 So Joshua called together the priests and said, "Take up the Ark of the LORD's Covenant, and assign seven priests to walk in front of it, each carrying a ram's horn." 7 Then he gave orders to the people: "March around the town, and the armed men will lead the way in front of the Ark of the LORD."

8 After Joshua spoke to the people, the seven priests with the rams' horns started marching in the presence of the LORD, blowing the horns as they marched. And the Ark of the LORD's Covenant followed behind them. 9 Some of the armed men marched in front of the priests with the horns and some behind the Ark, with the priests continually blowing the horns. 10 "Do not shout; do not even talk," Joshua commanded. "Not a single word from any of you until I tell you to shout. Then shout!" 11 So the Ark of the LORD was carried around the town once that day, and then everyone returned to spend the night in the camp.

12 Joshua got up early the next morning, and the priests again carried the Ark of the LORD. 13 The seven priests with the rams' horns marched in front of the Ark of the LORD, blowing their horns. Again the armed men marched both in front of the priests with the horns and behind the Ark of the LORD. All this time the priests were blowing their horns. 14 On the second day they again marched around the town once and returned to the camp. They followed this pattern for six days.

15 On the seventh day the Israelites got up at dawn and marched around the town as they had done before. But this time they went around the town seven times. 16 The seventh time around, as the priests sounded the long blast on their horns, Joshua commanded the people, "Shout! For the LORD has given you the town! 17 Jericho and everything in it must be completely destroyed* as an offering to the LORD. Only Rahab the prostitute and the others in her house will be spared, for she protected our spies.

18 "Do not take any of the things set apart for destruction, or you yourselves will be completely destroyed, and you will bring trouble on the camp of Israel. 19 Everything made from silver, gold, bronze, or iron is sacred to the LORD and must be brought into his treasury."

20 When the people heard the sound of the rams' horns, they shouted as loud as they could. Suddenly, the walls of Jericho collapsed, and the Israelites charged straight into the town and captured it. 21 They completely destroyed everything in it with their swords—men and women, young and old, cattle, sheep, goats, and donkeys.

22 Meanwhile, Joshua said to the two spies, "Keep your promise. Go to the prostitute's house and bring her out, along with all her family."

23 The men who had been spies went in and brought out Rahab, her father, mother, brothers, and all the other relatives who were with her. They moved her whole family to a safe place near the camp of Israel.

24 Then the Israelites burned the town and everything in it. Only the things made from silver, gold, bronze, or iron were kept for the treasury of the LORD's house. 25 So Joshua spared Rahab the prostitute and her relatives who were with her in the house, because she had hidden the spies Joshua sent to Jericho. And she lives among the Israelites to this day.

26 At that time Joshua invoked this curse:

6:17 The Hebrew term used here refers to the complete consecration of things or people to the LORD, either by destroying them or by giving them as an offering; similarly in 6:18, 21.

Question 6:27

The two phrases of this verse go together: "The LORD was with Joshua," and Joshua's "reputation spread throughout the land." Why does this matter? What problems might arise if your reputation spread but the Lord wasn't with you?

"May the curse of the LORD fall on anyone
who tries to rebuild the town of Jericho.
At the cost of his firstborn son,
he will lay its foundation.
At the cost of his youngest son,
he will set up its gates."

27 So the LORD was with Joshua, and his reputation spread throughout the land.

Ai Defeats the Israelites

7 But Israel violated the instructions about the things set apart for the LORD.* A man named Achan had stolen some of these dedicated things, so the LORD was very angry with the Israelites. Achan was the son of Carmi, a descendant of Zimri* son of Zerah, of the tribe of Judah.
2 Joshua sent some of his men from Jericho to spy out the town of Ai, east
of Bethel, near Beth-aven. 3 When they returned, they told Joshua, "There's no need for all of us to go up there; it won't take more than two or three thousand men to attack Ai. Since there are so few of them, don't make all our people struggle to go up there."
4 So approximately 3,000 warriors were sent, but they were soundly de-
feated. The men of Ai 5 chased the Israelites from the town gate as far as the quarries,* and they killed about thirty-six who were retreating down the slope. The Israelites were paralyzed with fear at this turn of events, and their courage melted away.
6 Joshua and the elders of Israel tore their clothing in dismay, threw dust
on their heads, and bowed face down to the ground before the Ark of the
LORD until evening. 7 Then Joshua cried out, "Oh, Sovereign LORD, why did you bring us across the Jordan River if you are going to let the Amorites kill
us? If only we had been content to stay on the other side! 8 Lord, what can I
say now that Israel has fled from its enemies? 9 For when the Canaanites and all the other people living in the land hear about it, they will surround us and wipe our name off the face of the earth. And then what will happen to the honor of your great name?"
10 But the LORD said to Joshua, "Get up! Why are you lying on your face
like this? 11 Israel has sinned and broken my covenant! They have stolen some of the things that I commanded must be set apart for me. And they have not only stolen them but have lied about it and hidden the things among their
own belongings. 12 That is why the Israelites are running from their enemies in defeat. For now Israel itself has been set apart for destruction. I will not remain with you any longer unless you destroy the things among you that were set apart for destruction.
13 "Get up! Command the people to purify themselves in preparation for tomorrow. For this is what the LORD, the God of Israel, says: Hidden among you, O Israel, are things set apart for the LORD. You will never defeat your enemies until you remove these things from among you.
14 "In the morning you must present yourselves by tribes, and the LORD

7:1a The Hebrew term used here refers to the complete consecration of things or people to the LORD, either by destroying them or by giving them as an offering; similarly in 7:11, 12, 13, 15. 7:1b As in parallel text at 1 Chr 2:6; Hebrew reads *Zabdi.* Also in 7:17, 18. 7:5 Or *as far as Shebarim.*

will point out the tribe to which the guilty man belongs. That tribe must
come forward with its clans, and the LORD will point out the guilty clan. That
clan will then come forward, and the LORD will point out the guilty family.
Finally, each member of the guilty family must come forward one by one.
15 The one who has stolen what was set apart for destruction will himself be
burned with fire, along with everything he has, for he has broken the cov-
enant of the LORD and has done a horrible thing in Israel."

Achan's Sin

16 Early the next morning Joshua brought the tribes of Israel before the LORD,
and the tribe of Judah was singled out. 17 Then the clans of Judah came for-
ward, and the clan of Zerah was singled out. Then the families of Zerah came
forward, and the family of Zimri was singled out. 18 Every member of Zimri's
family was brought forward person by person, and Achan was singled out.

19 Then Joshua said to Achan, "My son, give glory to the LORD, the God of
Israel, by telling the truth. Make your confession and tell me what you have
done. Don't hide it from me."

20 Achan replied, "It is true! I have sinned against the LORD, the God of
Israel. 21 Among the plunder I saw a beautiful robe from Babylon,* 200 silver
coins,* and a bar of gold weighing more than a pound.* I wanted them so
much that I took them. They are hidden in the ground beneath my tent,
with the silver buried deeper than the rest."

22 So Joshua sent some men to make a search. They ran to the tent and
found the stolen goods hidden there, just as Achan had said, with the silver
buried beneath the rest. 23 They took the things from the tent and brought
them to Joshua and all the Israelites. Then they laid them on the ground in
the presence of the LORD.

24 Then Joshua and all the Israelites took Achan, the silver, the robe, the bar
of gold, his sons, daughters, cattle, donkeys, sheep, goats, tent, and every-
thing he had, and they brought them to the valley of Achor. 25 Then Joshua
said to Achan, "Why have you brought trouble on us? The LORD will now
bring trouble on you." And all the Israelites stoned Achan and his family
and burned their bodies. 26 They piled a great heap of stones over Achan,
which remains to this day. That is why the place has been called the Valley
of Trouble* ever since. So the LORD was no longer angry.

The Israelites Defeat Ai

8 Then the LORD said to Joshua, "Do not be afraid or discouraged. Take all
your fighting men and attack Ai, for I have given you the king of Ai, his
people, his town, and his land. 2 You will destroy them as you destroyed Jer-
icho and its king. But this time you may keep the plunder and the livestock
for yourselves. Set an ambush behind the town."

3 So Joshua and all the fighting men set out to attack Ai. Joshua chose
30,000 of his best warriors and sent them out at night 4 with these orders:
"Hide in ambush close behind the town and be ready for action. 5 When
our main army attacks, the men of Ai will come out to fight as they did be-
fore, and we will run away from them. 6 We will let them chase us until we
have drawn them away from the town. For they will say, 'The Israelites are

7:21a Hebrew *Shinar.* **7:21b** Hebrew *200 shekels of silver,* about 5 pounds or 2.3 kilograms in weight. **7:21c** Hebrew *50 shekels,* about 20 ounces or 570 grams in weight. **7:26** Hebrew *valley of Achor.*

Prayer 7:1-26

Lord, Achan's sin was a big deal, and it messed up a lot of things for all God's people. God, convict me of my sin. Don't let me be flippant about my disobedience. Please forgive me and cleanse me of unrighteousness. Amen.

running away from us as they did before.' Then, while we are running from them, 7 you will jump up from your ambush and take possession of the town, for the LORD your God will give it to you. 8 Set the town on fire, as the LORD has commanded. You have your orders."

9 So they left and went to the place of ambush between Bethel and the west side of Ai. But Joshua remained among the people in the camp that night. 10 Early the next morning Joshua roused his men and started toward Ai, accompanied by the elders of Israel. 11 All the fighting men who were with Joshua marched in front of the town and camped on the north side of Ai, with a valley between them and the town. 12 That night Joshua sent about 5,000 men to lie in ambush between Bethel and Ai, on the west side of the town. 13 So they stationed the main army north of the town and the ambush west of the town. Joshua himself spent that night in the valley.

14 When the king of Ai saw the Israelites across the valley, he and all his army hurried out early in the morning and attacked the Israelites at a place overlooking the Jordan Valley.* But he didn't realize there was an ambush behind the town. 15 Joshua and the Israelite army fled toward the wilderness as though they were badly beaten. 16 Then all the men in the town were called out to chase after them. In this way, they were lured away from the town. 17 There was not a man left in Ai or Bethel* who did not chase after the Israelites, and the town was left wide open.

18 Then the LORD said to Joshua, "Point the spear in your hand toward Ai, for I will hand the town over to you." Joshua did as he was commanded. 19 As soon as Joshua gave this signal, all the men in ambush jumped up from their position and poured into the town. They quickly captured it and set it on fire.

20 When the men of Ai looked behind them, smoke from the town was filling the sky, and they had nowhere to go. For the Israelites who had fled in the direction of the wilderness now turned on their pursuers. 21 When Joshua and all the other Israelites saw that the ambush had succeeded and that smoke was rising from the town, they turned and attacked the men of Ai. 22 Meanwhile, the Israelites who were inside the town came out and attacked the enemy from the rear. So the men of Ai were caught in the middle, with Israelite fighters on both sides. Israel attacked them, and not a single person survived or escaped. 23 Only the king of Ai was taken alive and brought to Joshua.

24 When the Israelite army finished chasing and killing all the men of Ai in the open fields, they went back and finished off everyone inside. 25 So the entire population of Ai, including men and women, was wiped out that day—12,000 in all. 26 For Joshua kept holding out his spear until everyone who had lived in Ai was completely destroyed.* 27 Only the livestock and the treasures of the town were not destroyed, for the Israelites kept these as plunder for themselves, as the LORD had commanded Joshua. 28 So Joshua burned the town of Ai,* and it became a permanent mound of ruins, desolate to this very day.

29 Joshua impaled the king of Ai on a sharpened pole and left him there until evening. At sunset the Israelites took down the body, as Joshua commanded, and threw it in front of the town gate. They piled a great heap of stones over him that can still be seen today.

8:14 Hebrew *the Arabah.* 8:17 Some manuscripts lack *or Bethel.* 8:26 The Hebrew term used here refers to the complete consecration of things or people to the LORD, either by destroying them or by giving them as an offering. 8:28 *Ai* means "ruin."

The LORD's Covenant Renewed

30 Then Joshua built an altar to the LORD, the God of Israel, on Mount Ebal. 31 He followed the commands that Moses the LORD's servant had written in the Book of Instruction: "Make me an altar from stones that are uncut and have not been shaped with iron tools."* Then on the altar they presented burnt offerings and peace offerings to the LORD. 32 And as the Israelites watched, Joshua copied onto the stones of the altar* the instructions Moses had given them.

33 Then all the Israelites—foreigners and native-born alike—along with the elders, officers, and judges, were divided into two groups. One group stood in front of Mount Gerizim, the other in front of Mount Ebal. Each group faced the other, and between them stood the Levitical priests carrying the Ark of the LORD's Covenant. This was all done according to the commands that Moses, the servant of the LORD, had previously given for blessing the people of Israel.

34 Joshua then read to them all the blessings and curses Moses had written in the Book of Instruction. 35 Every word of every command that Moses had ever given was read to the entire assembly of Israel, including the women and children and the foreigners who lived among them.

The Gibeonites Deceive Israel

9 Now all the kings west of the Jordan River heard about what had happened. These were the kings of the Hittites, Amorites, Canaanites, Perizzites, Hivites, and Jebusites, who lived in the hill country, in the western foothills,* and along the coast of the Mediterranean Sea* as far north as the Lebanon mountains. 2 These kings combined their armies to fight as one against Joshua and the Israelites.

3 But when the people of Gibeon heard what Joshua had done to Jericho and Ai, 4 they resorted to deception to save themselves. They sent ambassadors to Joshua, loading their donkeys with weathered saddlebags and old, patched wineskins. 5 They put on worn-out, patched sandals and ragged clothes. And the bread they took with them was dry and moldy. 6 When they arrived at the camp of Israel at Gilgal, they told Joshua and the men of Israel, "We have come from a distant land to ask you to make a peace treaty with us."

7 The Israelites replied to these Hivites, "How do we know you don't live nearby? For if you do, we cannot make a treaty with you."

8 They replied, "We are your servants."

"But who are you?" Joshua demanded. "Where do you come from?"

9 They answered, "Your servants have come from a very distant country. We have heard of the might of the LORD your God and of all he did in Egypt. 10 We have also heard what he did to the two Amorite kings east of the Jordan River—King Sihon of Heshbon and King Og of Bashan (who lived in Ashtaroth). 11 So our elders and all our people instructed us, 'Take supplies for a long journey. Go meet with the people of Israel and tell them, "We are your servants; please make a treaty with us."'

12 "This bread was hot from the ovens when we left our homes. But now, as you can see, it is dry and moldy. 13 These wineskins were new when we filled them, but now they are old and split open. And our clothing and sandals are worn out from our very long journey."

8:31 Exod 20:25; Deut 27:5-6. 8:32 Hebrew *onto the stones.* 9:1a Hebrew *the Shephelah.* 9:1b Hebrew *the Great Sea.*

Make a Difference

8:30-32

Written on Stone?

Joshua copied the instructions Moses had given them directly onto the altar where Israel will offer sacrifices to the Lord. This was the law written on stone to remind people to follow the commands of God.

What's interesting, though, is that the Lord doesn't want his commands to remain stuck on stone. Actually, God always wanted his law written in people's hearts. In Ezekiel 11:19-20 the Lord promised to "take away their stony, stubborn heart and give them a tender, responsive heart, so they will obey my decrees." In Jeremiah 31:33, the Lord promised, "I will put my instructions deep within them, and I will write them on their hearts. I will be their God, and they will be my people."

Difference Maker

Find a verse in the Bible, like Joshua 1:9, to learn by heart. Go over it again and again until you memorize it in your mind and allow it to make a difference in your heart.

14 So the Israelites examined their food, but they did not consult the LORD.
15 Then Joshua made a peace treaty with them and guaranteed their safety, and
the leaders of the community ratified their agreement with a binding oath.
16 Three days after making the treaty, they learned that these people actu-
ally lived nearby! 17 The Israelites set out at once to investigate and reached
their towns in three days. The names of these towns were Gibeon, Kephirah,
Beeroth, and Kiriath-jearim. 18 But the Israelites did not attack the towns,
for the Israelite leaders had made a vow to them in the name of the LORD,
the God of Israel.

The people of Israel grumbled against their leaders because of the treaty.
19 But the leaders replied, "Since we have sworn an oath in the presence of
the LORD, the God of Israel, we cannot touch them. 20 This is what we must
do. We must let them live, for divine anger would come upon us if we broke
our oath. 21 Let them live." So they made them woodcutters and water carriers
for the entire community, as the Israelite leaders directed.
22 Joshua called together the Gibeonites and said, "Why did you lie to us?
Why did you say that you live in a distant land when you live right here
among us? 23 May you be cursed! From now on you will always be servants
who cut wood and carry water for the house of my God."
24 They replied, "We did it because we—your servants—were clearly told
that the LORD your God commanded his servant Moses to give you this entire
land and to destroy all the people living in it. So we feared greatly for our
lives because of you. That is why we have done this. 25 Now we are at your
mercy—do to us whatever you think is right."
26 So Joshua did not allow the people of Israel to kill them. 27 But that day he
made the Gibeonites the woodcutters and water carriers for the community
of Israel and for the altar of the LORD—wherever the LORD would choose to
build it. And that is what they do to this day.

Israel Defeats the Southern Armies

10 Adoni-zedek, king of Jerusalem, heard that Joshua had captured
and completely destroyed* Ai and killed its king, just as he had de-
stroyed the town of Jericho and killed its king. He also learned that the Gib-
eonites had made peace with Israel and were now their allies. 2 He and his
people became very afraid when they heard all this because Gibeon was a
large town—as large as the royal cities and larger than Ai. And the Gibeonite
men were strong warriors.
3 So King Adoni-zedek of Jerusalem sent messengers to several other kings:
Hoham of Hebron, Piram of Jarmuth, Japhia of Lachish, and Debir of Eglon.
4 "Come and help me destroy Gibeon," he urged them, "for they have made
peace with Joshua and the people of Israel." 5 So these five Amorite kings
combined their armies for a united attack. They moved all their troops into
place and attacked Gibeon.
6 The men of Gibeon quickly sent messengers to Joshua at his camp in
Gilgal. "Don't abandon your servants now!" they pleaded. "Come at once!
Save us! Help us! For all the Amorite kings who live in the hill country have
joined forces to attack us."
7 So Joshua and his entire army, including his best warriors, left Gilgal and
set out for Gibeon. 8 "Do not be afraid of them," the LORD said to Joshua, "for

10:1 The Hebrew term used here refers to the complete consecration of things or people to the LORD, either by destroying them or by giving them as an offering; also in 10:28, 35, 37, 39, 40.

I have given you victory over them. Not a single one of them will be able to
stand up to you."
[9]Joshua traveled all night from Gilgal and took the Amorite armies by
surprise. [10]The LORD threw them into a panic, and the Israelites slaugh-
tered great numbers of them at Gibeon. Then the Israelites chased the enemy
along the road to Beth-horon, killing them all along the way to Azekah and
Makkedah. [11]As the Amorites retreated down the road from Beth-horon, the
LORD destroyed them with a terrible hailstorm from heaven that continued
until they reached Azekah. The hail killed more of the enemy than the Isra-
elites killed with the sword.
[12]On the day the LORD gave the Israelites victory over the Amorites, Joshua
prayed to the LORD in front of all the people of Israel. He said,

"Let the sun stand still over Gibeon,
and the moon over the valley of Aijalon."

[13]So the sun stood still and the moon stayed in place until the nation of Israel
had defeated its enemies.
Is this event not recorded in *The Book of Jashar**? The sun stayed in the
middle of the sky, and it did not set as on a normal day.* [14]There has never
been a day like this one before or since, when the LORD answered such a
prayer. Surely the LORD fought for Israel that day!
[15]Then Joshua and the Israelite army returned to their camp at Gilgal.

Prayer 10:12-13

What can't you do, Lord? Forgive my small faith. Help my faith! Amen.

Joshua Kills the Five Southern Kings

[16]During the battle the five kings escaped and hid in a cave at Makkedah.
[17]When Joshua heard that they had been found, [18]he issued this command:
"Cover the opening of the cave with large rocks, and place guards at the
entrance to keep the kings inside. [19]The rest of you continue chasing the
enemy and cut them down from the rear. Don't give them a chance to get
back to their towns, for the LORD your God has given you victory over them."
[20]So Joshua and the Israelite army continued the slaughter and completely
crushed the enemy. They totally wiped out the five armies except for a tiny
remnant that managed to reach their fortified towns. [21]Then the Israelites
returned safely to Joshua in the camp at Makkedah. After that, no one dared
to speak even a word against Israel.
[22]Then Joshua said, "Remove the rocks covering the opening of the cave,
and bring the five kings to me." [23]So they brought the five kings out of the
cave—the kings of Jerusalem, Hebron, Jarmuth, Lachish, and Eglon. [24]When
they brought them out, Joshua told the commanders of his army, "Come and
put your feet on the kings' necks." And they did as they were told.
[25]"Don't ever be afraid or discouraged," Joshua told his men. "Be strong
and courageous, for the LORD is going to do this to all of your enemies."
[26]Then Joshua killed each of the five kings and impaled them on five sharp-
ened poles, where they hung until evening.
[27]As the sun was going down, Joshua gave instructions for the bodies of
the kings to be taken down from the poles and thrown into the cave where
they had been hiding. Then they covered the opening of the cave with a pile
of large rocks, which remains to this very day.

10:13a Or *The Book of the Upright.* **10:13b** Or *did not set for about a whole day.*

Israel Destroys the Southern Towns

28 That same day Joshua captured and destroyed the town of Makkedah. He
killed everyone in it, including the king, leaving no survivors. He destroyed
them all, and he killed the king of Makkedah as he had killed the king of
Jericho. 29 Then Joshua and the Israelites went to Libnah and attacked it.
30 There, too, the LORD gave them the town and its king. He killed everyone
in it, leaving no survivors. Then Joshua killed the king of Libnah as he had
killed the king of Jericho.

31 From Libnah, Joshua and the Israelites went to Lachish and attacked
it. 32 Here again, the LORD gave them Lachish. Joshua took it on the second
day and killed everyone in it, just as he had done at Libnah. 33 During the
attack on Lachish, King Horam of Gezer arrived with his army to help
defend the town. But Joshua's men killed him and his army, leaving no
survivors.

34 Then Joshua and the Israelite army went on to Eglon and attacked
it. 35 They captured it that day and killed everyone in it. He completely
destroyed everyone, just as he had done at Lachish. 36 From Eglon, Joshua
and the Israelite army went up to Hebron and attacked it. 37 They captured
the town and killed everyone in it, including its king, leaving no survivors.
They did the same thing to all of its surrounding villages. And just as he
had done at Eglon, he completely destroyed the entire population.

38 Then Joshua and the Israelites turned back and attacked Debir. 39 He
captured the town, its king, and all of its surrounding villages. He com-
pletely destroyed everyone in it, leaving no survivors. He did to Debir
and its king just what he had done to Hebron and to Libnah and its king.

40 So Joshua conquered the whole region—the kings and people of the
hill country, the Negev, the western foothills,* and the mountain slopes.
He completely destroyed everyone in the land, leaving no survivors, just
as the LORD, the God of Israel, had commanded. 41 Joshua slaughtered
them from Kadesh-barnea to Gaza and from the region around the town
of Goshen up to Gibeon. 42 Joshua conquered all these kings and their
land in a single campaign, for the LORD, the God of Israel, was fighting
for his people.

43 Then Joshua and the Israelite army returned to their camp at Gilgal.

Israel Defeats the Northern Armies

11 When King Jabin of Hazor heard what had happened, he sent mes-
sages to the following kings: King Jobab of Madon; the king of
Shimron; the king of Acshaph; 2 all the kings of the northern hill country;
the kings in the Jordan Valley south of Galilee*; the kings in the Galilean
foothills*; the kings of Naphoth-dor on the west; 3 the kings of Canaan, both
east and west; the kings of the Amorites, the Hittites, the Perizzites, the Jebu-
sites in the hill country, and the Hivites in the towns on the slopes of Mount
Hermon in the land of Mizpah.

4 All these kings came out to fight. Their combined armies formed a vast
horde. And with all their horses and chariots, they covered the landscape
like the sand on the seashore. 5 The kings joined forces and established their
camp around the water near Merom to fight against Israel.

6 Then the LORD said to Joshua, "Do not be afraid of them. By this time

10:40 Hebrew *the Shephelah.* 11:2a Hebrew *in the Arabah south of Kinnereth.* 11:2b Hebrew *the Shephelah;* also in 11:16.

tomorrow I will hand all of them over to Israel as dead men. Then you must
cripple their horses and burn their chariots."
7 So Joshua and all his fighting men traveled to the water near Merom and
attacked suddenly. 8 And the LORD gave them victory over their enemies. The
Israelites chased them as far as Greater Sidon and Misrephoth-maim, and
eastward into the valley of Mizpah, until not one enemy warrior was left
alive. 9 Then Joshua crippled the horses and burned all the chariots, as the
LORD had instructed.
10 Joshua then turned back and captured Hazor and killed its king. (Ha-
zor had at one time been the capital of all these kingdoms.) 11 The Israelites
completely destroyed* every living thing in the city, leaving no survivors. Not
a single person was spared. And then Joshua burned the city.
12 Joshua slaughtered all the other kings and their people, completely
destroying them, just as Moses, the servant of the LORD, had commanded.
13 But the Israelites did not burn any of the towns built on mounds except
Hazor, which Joshua burned. 14 And the Israelites took all the plunder and
livestock of the ravaged towns for themselves. But they killed all the people,
leaving no survivors. 15 As the LORD had commanded his servant Moses, so
Moses commanded Joshua. And Joshua did as he was told, carefully obeying
all the commands that the LORD had given to Moses.
16 So Joshua conquered the entire region—the hill country, the entire Ne-
gev, the whole area around the town of Goshen, the western foothills, the
Jordan Valley,* the mountains of Israel, and the Galilean foothills. 17 The Is-
raelite territory now extended all the way from Mount Halak, which leads
up to Seir in the south, as far north as Baal-gad at the foot of Mount Her-
mon in the valley of Lebanon. Joshua killed all the kings of those territories,
18 waging war for a long time to accomplish this. 19 No one in this region made
peace with the Israelites except the Hivites of Gibeon. All the others were
defeated. 20 For the LORD hardened their hearts and caused them to fight the
Israelites. So they were completely destroyed without mercy, as the LORD
had commanded Moses.
21 During this period Joshua destroyed all the descendants of Anak, who
lived in the hill country of Hebron, Debir, Anab, and the entire hill country
of Judah and Israel. He killed them all and completely destroyed their towns.
22 None of the descendants of Anak were left in all the land of Israel, though
some still remained in Gaza, Gath, and Ashdod.
23 So Joshua took control of the entire land, just as the LORD had instructed
Moses. He gave it to the people of Israel as their special possession, dividing
the land among the tribes. So the land finally had rest from war.

Question 11:23

What if the Lord had not given this land to the people of Israel? What if God had never promised this land to Abraham? What effect does this land and this people have on the overarching story of Jesus? What difference does this land and this people make to your faith?

Kings Defeated East of the Jordan

12 These are the kings east of the Jordan River who had been killed by
the Israelites and whose land was taken. Their territory extended
from the Arnon Gorge to Mount Hermon and included all the land east of
the Jordan Valley.*
2 King Sihon of the Amorites, who lived in Heshbon, was defeated. His
kingdom included Aroer, on the edge of the Arnon Gorge, and extended from
the middle of the Arnon Gorge to the Jabbok River, which serves as a border

11:11 The Hebrew term used here refers to the complete consecration of things or people to the LORD, either by destroying them or by giving them as an offering; also in 11:12, 20, 21. 11:16 Hebrew *the Shephelah, the Arabah.* 12:1 Hebrew *the Arabah;* also in 12:3, 8.

for the Ammonites. This territory included the southern half of the terri-
tory of Gilead. 3 Sihon also controlled the Jordan Valley and regions to the
east—from as far north as the Sea of Galilee to as far south as the Dead Sea,*
including the road to Beth-jeshimoth and southward to the slopes of Pisgah.
4 King Og of Bashan, the last of the Rephaites, lived at Ashtaroth and Ed-
rei. 5 He ruled a territory stretching from Mount Hermon to Salecah in the
north and to all of Bashan in the east, and westward to the borders of the
kingdoms of Geshur and Maacah. This territory included the northern half
of Gilead, as far as the boundary of King Sihon of Heshbon.
6 Moses, the servant of the LORD, and the Israelites had destroyed the
people of King Sihon and King Og. And Moses gave their land as a posses-
sion to the tribes of Reuben, Gad, and the half-tribe of Manasseh.

Kings Defeated West of the Jordan

7 The following is a list of the kings that Joshua and the Israelite armies de-
feated on the west side of the Jordan, from Baal-gad in the valley of Lebanon
to Mount Halak, which leads up to Seir. (Joshua gave this land to the tribes of
Israel as their possession, 8 including the hill country, the western foothills,*
the Jordan Valley, the mountain slopes, the Judean wilderness, and the Ne-
gev. The people who lived in this region were the Hittites, the Amorites,
the Canaanites, the Perizzites, the Hivites, and the Jebusites.) These are the
kings Israel defeated:

9 The king of Jericho
The king of Ai, near Bethel
10 The king of Jerusalem
The king of Hebron
11 The king of Jarmuth
The king of Lachish
12 The king of Eglon
The king of Gezer
13 The king of Debir
The king of Geder
14 The king of Hormah
The king of Arad
15 The king of Libnah
The king of Adullam
16 The king of Makkedah
The king of Bethel
17 The king of Tappuah
The king of Hepher
18 The king of Aphek
The king of Lasharon
19 The king of Madon
The king of Hazor
20 The king of Shimron-meron
The king of Acshaph
21 The king of Taanach
The king of Megiddo

12:3 Hebrew *from the Sea of Kinnereth to the Sea of the Arabah, which is the Salt Sea.* 12:8 Hebrew *the Shephelah.*

22 The king of Kedesh
The king of Jokneam in Carmel
23 The king of Dor in the town of Naphoth-dor*
The king of Goyim in Gilgal*
24 The king of Tirzah.

In all, thirty-one kings were defeated.

The Land Yet to Be Conquered

13 When Joshua was an old man, the LORD said to him, "You are grow-
ing old, and much land remains to be conquered. 2This is the ter-
ritory that remains: all the regions of the Philistines and the Geshurites,
3and the larger territory of the Canaanites, extending from the stream of
Shihor on the border of Egypt, northward to the boundary of Ekron. It
includes the territory of the five Philistine rulers of Gaza, Ashdod, Ashke-
lon, Gath, and Ekron. The land of the Avvites 4in the south also remains to
be conquered. In the north, the following area has not yet been conquered:
all the land of the Canaanites, including Mearah (which belongs to the Si-
donians), stretching northward to Aphek on the border of the Amorites;
5the land of the Gebalites and all of the Lebanon mountain area to the
east, from Baal-gad below Mount Hermon to Lebo-hamath; 6and all the
hill country from Lebanon to Misrephoth-maim, including all the land
of the Sidonians.

"I myself will drive these people out of the land ahead of the Israelites. So
be sure to give this land to Israel as a special possession, just as I have com-
manded you. 7Include all this territory as Israel's possession when you divide
this land among the nine tribes and the half-tribe of Manasseh."

The Land Divided East of the Jordan

8Half the tribe of Manasseh and the tribes of Reuben and Gad had already
received their grants of land on the east side of the Jordan, for Moses, the
servant of the LORD, had previously assigned this land to them.

9Their territory extended from Aroer on the edge of the Arnon Gorge
(including the town in the middle of the gorge) to the plain beyond
Medeba, as far as Dibon. 10It also included all the towns of King Sihon
of the Amorites, who had reigned in Heshbon, and extended as far
as the borders of Ammon. 11It included Gilead, the territory of the
kingdoms of Geshur and Maacah, all of Mount Hermon, all of Bashan
as far as Salecah, 12and all the territory of King Og of Bashan, who had
reigned in Ashtaroth and Edrei. King Og was the last of the Rephaites,
for Moses had attacked them and driven them out. 13But the Israelites
failed to drive out the people of Geshur and Maacah, so they continue
to live among the Israelites to this day.

An Allotment for the Tribe of Levi

14Moses did not assign any allotment of land to the tribe of Levi. Instead,
as the LORD had promised them, their allotment came from the offerings
burned on the altar to the LORD, the God of Israel.

12:23a Hebrew *Naphath-dor,* a variant spelling of Naphoth-dor. **12:23b** Greek version reads *Goyim in Galilee.*

Things to reflect on

The Land Given to the Tribe of Reuben

15 Moses had assigned the following area to the clans of the tribe of
Reuben.

16 Their territory extended from Aroer on the edge of the Arnon
Gorge (including the town in the middle of the gorge) to the
plain beyond Medeba. 17 It included Heshbon and the other towns
on the plain—Dibon, Bamoth-baal, Beth-baal-meon, 18 Jahaz,
Kedemoth, Mephaath, 19 Kiriathaim, Sibmah, Zereth-shahar on
the hill above the valley, 20 Beth-peor, the slopes of Pisgah, and
Beth-jeshimoth.
21 The land of Reuben also included all the towns of the plain and
the entire kingdom of Sihon. Sihon was the Amorite king who had
reigned in Heshbon and was killed by Moses along with the leaders of
Midian—Evi, Rekem, Zur, Hur, and Reba—princes living in the region
who were allied with Sihon. 22 The Israelites had also killed Balaam son
of Beor, who used magic to tell the future. 23 The Jordan River marked
the western boundary for the tribe of Reuben. The towns and their
surrounding villages in this area were given as a homeland to the clans
of the tribe of Reuben.

The Land Given to the Tribe of Gad

24 Moses had assigned the following area to the clans of the tribe of Gad.

25 Their territory included Jazer, all the towns of Gilead, and half of
the land of Ammon, as far as the town of Aroer just west of* Rabbah.
26 It extended from Heshbon to Ramath-mizpeh and Betonim,
and from Mahanaim to the territory of Lo-debar.* 27 In the valley
were Beth-haram, Beth-nimrah, Succoth, Zaphon, and the rest of
the kingdom of King Sihon of Heshbon. The western boundary
ran along the Jordan River, extended as far north as the tip of the
Sea of Galilee,* and then turned eastward. 28 The towns and their
surrounding villages in this area were given as a homeland to the
clans of the tribe of Gad.

The Land Given to the Half-Tribe of Manasseh

29 Moses had assigned the following area to the clans of the half-tribe of
Manasseh.

30 Their territory extended from Mahanaim, including all of Bashan, all
the former kingdom of King Og, and the sixty towns of Jair in Bashan.
31 It also included half of Gilead and King Og's royal cities of Ashtaroth
and Edrei. All this was given to the clans of the descendants of Makir,
who was Manasseh's son.

32 These are the allotments Moses had made while he was on the plains of
Moab, across the Jordan River, east of Jericho. 33 But Moses gave no allotment
of land to the tribe of Levi, for the LORD, the God of Israel, had promised
that he himself would be their allotment.

13:25 Hebrew *in front of.* 13:26 Hebrew *Li-debir,* apparently a variant spelling of Lo-debar (compare 2 Sam 9:4; 17:27; Amos 6:13). 13:27 Hebrew *Sea of Kinnereth.*

The Land Divided West of the Jordan

14 The remaining tribes of Israel received land in Canaan as allotted by
Eleazar the priest, Joshua son of Nun, and the tribal leaders. 2These
nine and a half tribes received their grants of land by means of sacred lots, in
accordance with the LORD's command through Moses. 3Moses had already
given a grant of land to the two and a half tribes on the east side of the Jordan
River, but he had given the Levites no such allotment. 4The descendants of
Joseph had become two separate tribes—Manasseh and Ephraim. And the
Levites were given no land at all, only towns to live in with surrounding
pasturelands for their livestock and all their possessions. 5So the land was
distributed in strict accordance with the LORD's commands to Moses.

Caleb Requests His Land

6A delegation from the tribe of Judah, led by Caleb son of Jephunneh the
Kenizzite, came to Joshua at Gilgal. Caleb said to Joshua, "Remember what
the LORD said to Moses, the man of God, about you and me when we were at
Kadesh-barnea. 7I was forty years old when Moses, the servant of the LORD,
sent me from Kadesh-barnea to explore the land of Canaan. I returned and
gave an honest report, 8but my brothers who went with me frightened the
people from entering the Promised Land. For my part, I wholeheartedly fol-
lowed the LORD my God. 9So that day Moses solemnly promised me, 'The
land of Canaan on which you were just walking will be your grant of land
and that of your descendants forever, because you wholeheartedly followed
the LORD my God.'

10"Now, as you can see, the LORD has kept me alive and well as he promised
for all these forty-five years since Moses made this promise—even while Is-
rael wandered in the wilderness. Today I am eighty-five years old. 11I am as
strong now as I was when Moses sent me on that journey, and I can still travel
and fight as well as I could then. 12So give me the hill country that the LORD
promised me. You will remember that as scouts we found the descendants
of Anak living there in great, walled towns. But if the LORD is with me, I will
drive them out of the land, just as the LORD said."

13So Joshua blessed Caleb son of Jephunneh and gave Hebron to him as
his portion of land. 14Hebron still belongs to the descendants of Caleb son
of Jephunneh the Kenizzite because he wholeheartedly followed the LORD,
the God of Israel. 15(Previously Hebron had been called Kiriath-arba. It had
been named after Arba, a great hero of the descendants of Anak.)

And the land had rest from war.

The Land Given to the Tribe of Judah

15 The allotment for the clans of the tribe of Judah reached southward
to the border of Edom, as far south as the wilderness of Zin.

2The southern boundary began at the south bay of the Dead Sea,* 3ran
south of Scorpion Pass* into the wilderness of Zin, and then went south
of Kadesh-barnea to Hezron. Then it went up to Addar, where it turned
toward Karka. 4From there it passed to Azmon until it finally reached
the Brook of Egypt, which it followed to the Mediterranean Sea.* This
was their* southern boundary.

15:2 Hebrew *the Salt Sea;* also in 15:5. 15:3 Hebrew *Akrabbim.* 15:4a Hebrew *the sea;* also in 15:11. 15:4b Hebrew *your.*

Story Arc **14:6-15**

Caleb

At eighty-five years old, after the exodus from Egypt and the wandering in the desert, Caleb was still strong and able to fight. Even more significantly, he was still wholeheartedly following the Lord. Caleb had quite a long testimony! Here he gave Joshua his eyewitness account from an experience when the Lord had given some instructions to Moses. With tremendous faith in God, Caleb had held on to those instructions for forty-five years. What testimony can you give about what God has done? What have you seen God do that you can remind others about?

Judg 3:7-11 ►

5 The eastern boundary extended along the Dead Sea to the mouth
of the Jordan River.
The northern boundary began at the bay where the Jordan River
empties into the Dead Sea, 6 went up from there to Beth-hoglah,
then proceeded north of Beth-arabah to the Stone of Bohan. (Bohan
was Reuben's son.) 7 From that point it went through the valley of
Achor to Debir, turning north toward Gilgal, which is across from the
slopes of Adummim on the south side of the valley. From there the
boundary extended to the springs at En-shemesh and on to En-rogel.
8 The boundary then passed through the valley of Ben-Hinnom, along
the southern slopes of the Jebusites, where the city of Jerusalem is
located. Then it went west to the top of the mountain above the valley
of Hinnom, and on up to the northern end of the valley of Rephaim.
9 From there the boundary extended from the top of the mountain to
the spring at the waters of Nephtoah,* and from there to the towns
on Mount Ephron. Then it turned toward Baalah (that is, Kiriath-
jearim). 10 The boundary circled west of Baalah to Mount Seir, passed
along to the town of Kesalon on the northern slope of Mount Jearim,
and went down to Beth-shemesh and on to Timnah. 11 The boundary
then proceeded to the slope of the hill north of Ekron, where it turned
toward Shikkeron and Mount Baalah. It passed Jabneel and ended at
the Mediterranean Sea.
12 The western boundary was the shoreline of the Mediterranean Sea.*

These are the boundaries for the clans of the tribe of Judah.

The Land Given to Caleb

13 The LORD commanded Joshua to assign some of Judah's territory to Caleb
son of Jephunneh. So Caleb was given the town of Kiriath-arba (that is, He-
bron), which had been named after Anak's ancestor. 14 Caleb drove out the
three groups of Anakites—the descendants of Sheshai, Ahiman, and Talmai,
the sons of Anak.
15 From there he went to fight against the people living in the town of
Debir (formerly called Kiriath-sepher). 16 Caleb said, "I will give my daugh-
ter Acsah in marriage to the one who attacks and captures Kiriath-sepher."
17 Othniel, the son of Caleb's brother Kenaz, was the one who conquered it,
so Acsah became Othniel's wife.
18 When Acsah married Othniel, she urged him* to ask her father for a
field. As she got down off her donkey, Caleb asked her, "What's the matter?"
19 She said, "Give me another gift. You have already given me land in the
Negev; now please give me springs of water, too." So Caleb gave her the upper
and lower springs.

The Towns Allotted to Judah

20 This was the homeland allocated to the clans of the tribe of Judah.

21 The towns of Judah situated along the borders of Edom in the
extreme south were Kabzeel, Eder, Jagur, 22 Kinah, Dimonah, Adadah,
23 Kedesh, Hazor, Ithnan, 24 Ziph, Telem, Bealoth, 25 Hazor-hadattah,

15:9 Or *the spring at Me-nephtoah.* **15:12** Hebrew *the Great Sea;* also in 15:47. **15:18** Some Greek manuscripts read *he urged her.*

Kerioth-hezron (that is, Hazor), 26 Amam, Shema, Moladah, 27 Hazar-
gaddah, Heshmon, Beth-pelet, 28 Hazar-shual, Beersheba, Biziothiah,
29 Baalah, Iim, Ezem, 30 Eltolad, Kesil, Hormah, 31 Ziklag, Madmannah,
Sansannah, 32 Lebaoth, Shilhim, Ain, and Rimmon—twenty-nine towns
with their surrounding villages.

33 The following towns situated in the western foothills* were
also given to Judah: Eshtaol, Zorah, Ashnah, 34 Zanoah, En-gannim,
Tappuah, Enam, 35 Jarmuth, Adullam, Socoh, Azekah, 36 Shaaraim,
Adithaim, Gederah, and Gederothaim—fourteen towns with their
surrounding villages.

37 Also included were Zenan, Hadashah, Migdal-gad, 38 Dilean,
Mizpeh, Joktheel, 39 Lachish, Bozkath, Eglon, 40 Cabbon, Lahmam,
Kitlish, 41 Gederoth, Beth-dagon, Naamah, and Makkedah—sixteen
towns with their surrounding villages.

42 Besides these, there were Libnah, Ether, Ashan, 43 Iphtah, Ashnah,
Nezib, 44 Keilah, Aczib, and Mareshah—nine towns with their
surrounding villages.

45 The territory of the tribe of Judah also included Ekron and its
surrounding settlements and villages. 46 From Ekron the boundary
extended west and included the towns near Ashdod with their
surrounding villages. 47 It also included Ashdod with its surrounding
settlements and villages and Gaza with its settlements and villages, as
far as the Brook of Egypt and along the coast of the Mediterranean Sea.

48 Judah also received the following towns in the hill country:
Shamir, Jattir, Socoh, 49 Dannah, Kiriath-sannah (that is, Debir), 50 Anab,
Eshtemoh, Anim, 51 Goshen, Holon, and Giloh—eleven towns with
their surrounding villages.

52 Also included were the towns of Arab, Dumah, Eshan, 53 Janim,
Beth-tappuah, Aphekah, 54 Humtah, Kiriath-arba (that is, Hebron), and
Zior—nine towns with their surrounding villages.

55 Besides these, there were Maon, Carmel, Ziph, Juttah, 56 Jezreel,
Jokdeam, Zanoah, 57 Kain, Gibeah, and Timnah—ten towns with their
surrounding villages.

58 In addition, there were Halhul, Beth-zur, Gedor, 59 Maarath, Beth-
anoth, and Eltekon—six towns with their surrounding villages.

60 There were also Kiriath-baal (that is, Kiriath-jearim) and Rabbah—
two towns with their surrounding villages.

61 In the wilderness there were the towns of Beth-arabah, Middin,
Secacah, 62 Nibshan, the City of Salt, and En-gedi—six towns with their
surrounding villages.

63 But the tribe of Judah could not drive out the Jebusites, who lived in
the city of Jerusalem, so the Jebusites live there among the people of Judah
to this day.

The Land Given to Ephraim and West Manasseh

16 The allotment for the descendants of Joseph extended from the
Jordan River near Jericho, east of the springs of Jericho, through
the wilderness and into the hill country of Bethel. 2 From Bethel (that

15:33 Hebrew *the Shephelah*.

Your thoughts can go here

Question 17:1

Chapters 13 through 19 recount how Joshua divided up the land among the tribes of Israel. Look through the land mentioned in these chapters. What are some of the important places that God used throughout the Bible to change the world?

is, Luz)* it ran over to Ataroth in the territory of the Arkites. 3Then it
descended westward to the territory of the Japhletites as far as Lower
Beth-horon, then to Gezer and over to the Mediterranean Sea.*

4This was the homeland allocated to the families of Joseph's sons, Manasseh
and Ephraim.

The Land Given to Ephraim

5The following territory was given to the clans of the tribe of Ephraim.

The boundary of their homeland began at Ataroth-addar in the east.
From there it ran to Upper Beth-horon, 6then on to the Mediterranean
Sea. From Micmethath on the north, the boundary curved eastward
past Taanath-shiloh to the east of Janoah. 7From Janoah it turned
southward to Ataroth and Naarah, touched Jericho, and ended at
the Jordan River. 8From Tappuah the boundary extended westward,
following the Kanah Ravine to the Mediterranean Sea. This is the
homeland allocated to the clans of the tribe of Ephraim.

9In addition, some towns with their surrounding villages in the
territory allocated to the half-tribe of Manasseh were set aside for the
tribe of Ephraim. 10They did not drive the Canaanites out of Gezer,
however, so the people of Gezer live as slaves among the people of
Ephraim to this day.

The Land Given to West Manasseh

17 The next allotment of land was given to the half-tribe of Manasseh, the descendants of Joseph's older son. Makir, the firstborn son of Manasseh, was the father of Gilead. Because his descendants were experienced soldiers, the regions of Gilead and Bashan on the east side of the Jordan had already been given to them.
2So the allotment on the
west side of the Jordan was for the remaining families within the clans
of the tribe of Manasseh: Abiezer, Helek, Asriel, Shechem, Hepher, and
Shemida. These clans represent the male descendants of Manasseh son
of Joseph.

3However, Zelophehad, a descendant of Hepher son of Gilead, son of Ma-
kir, son of Manasseh, had no sons. He had only daughters, whose names
were Mahlah, Noah, Hoglah, Milcah, and Tirzah. 4These women came to
Eleazar the priest, Joshua son of Nun, and the Israelite leaders and said,
"The LORD commanded Moses to give us a grant of land along with the
men of our tribe."

So Joshua gave them a grant of land along with their uncles, as the LORD
had commanded. 5As a result, Manasseh's total allocation came to ten parcels
of land, in addition to the land of Gilead and Bashan across the Jordan River,
6because the female descendants of Manasseh received a grant of land along
with the male descendants. (The land of Gilead was given to the rest of the
male descendants of Manasseh.)

7The boundary of the tribe of Manasseh extended from the border of
Asher to Micmethath, near Shechem. Then the boundary went south

16:2 As in Greek version (also see 18:13); Hebrew reads *From Bethel to Luz.* 16:3 Hebrew *the sea;* also in 16:6, 8.

from Micmethath to the settlement near the spring of Tappuah. [8]The
land surrounding Tappuah belonged to Manasseh, but the town of
Tappuah itself, on the border of Manasseh's territory, belonged to
the tribe of Ephraim. [9]From the spring of Tappuah, the boundary
of Manasseh followed the Kanah Ravine to the Mediterranean Sea.*
Several towns south of the ravine were inside Manasseh's territory, but
they actually belonged to the tribe of Ephraim. [10]In general, however,
the land south of the ravine belonged to Ephraim, and the land north
of the ravine belonged to Manasseh. Manasseh's boundary ran along
the northern side of the ravine and ended at the Mediterranean Sea.
North of Manasseh was the territory of Asher, and to the east was the
territory of Issachar.

[11]The following towns within the territory of Issachar and Asher,
however, were given to Manasseh: Beth-shan,* Ibleam, Dor (that
is, Naphoth-dor),* Endor, Taanach, and Megiddo, each with their
surrounding settlements.

[12]But the descendants of Manasseh were unable to occupy these towns
because the Canaanites were determined to stay in that region. [13]Later, how-
ever, when the Israelites became strong enough, they forced the Canaanites
to work as slaves. But they did not drive them out of the land.

[14]The descendants of Joseph came to Joshua and asked, "Why have you
given us only one portion of land as our homeland when the LORD has
blessed us with so many people?"

[15]Joshua replied, "If there are so many of you, and if the hill country of
Ephraim is not large enough for you, clear out land for yourselves in the
forest where the Perizzites and Rephaites live."

[16]The descendants of Joseph responded, "It's true that the hill country
is not large enough for us. But all the Canaanites in the lowlands have iron
chariots, both those in Beth-shan and its surrounding settlements and those
in the valley of Jezreel. They are too strong for us."

[17]Then Joshua said to the tribes of Ephraim and Manasseh, the descen-
dants of Joseph, "Since you are so large and strong, you will be given more
than one portion. [18]The forests of the hill country will be yours as well. Clear
as much of the land as you wish, and take possession of its farthest corners.
And you will drive out the Canaanites from the valleys, too, even though
they are strong and have iron chariots."

The Allotments of the Remaining Land

18 Now that the land was under Israelite control, the entire community
of Israel gathered at Shiloh and set up the Tabernacle.* [2]But there
remained seven tribes who had not yet been allotted their grants of land.

[3]Then Joshua asked them, "How long are you going to wait before taking
possession of the remaining land the LORD, the God of your ancestors, has
given to you? [4]Select three men from each tribe, and I will send them out to
explore the land and map it out. They will then return to me with a written
report of their proposed divisions of their new homeland. [5]Let them divide
the land into seven sections, excluding Judah's territory in the south and

17:9 Hebrew *the sea;* also in 17:10. 17:11a Hebrew *Beth-shean,* a variant spelling of Beth-shan; also in 17:16. 17:11b The meaning of the Hebrew here is uncertain. 18:1 Hebrew *Tent of Meeting.*

Joseph's territory in the north. 6 And when you record the seven divisions of
the land and bring them to me, I will cast sacred lots in the presence of the
LORD our God to assign land to each tribe.

7 "The Levites, however, will not receive any allotment of land. Their role
as priests of the LORD is their allotment. And the tribes of Gad, Reuben,
and the half-tribe of Manasseh won't receive any more land, for they have
already received their grant of land, which Moses, the servant of the LORD,
gave them on the east side of the Jordan River."

8 As the men started on their way to map out the land, Joshua commanded
them, "Go and explore the land and write a description of it. Then return to
me, and I will assign the land to the tribes by casting sacred lots here in the
presence of the LORD at Shiloh." 9 The men did as they were told and mapped
the entire territory into seven sections, listing the towns in each section. They
made a written record and then returned to Joshua in the camp at Shiloh.
10 And there at Shiloh, Joshua cast sacred lots in the presence of the LORD to
determine which tribe should have each section.

The Land Given to Benjamin

11 The first allotment of land went to the clans of the tribe of Benjamin. It lay
between the territory assigned to the tribes of Judah and Joseph.

12 The northern boundary of Benjamin's land began at the Jordan River,
went north of the slope of Jericho, then west through the hill country
and the wilderness of Beth-aven. 13 From there the boundary went south
to Luz (that is, Bethel) and proceeded down to Ataroth-addar on the hill
that lies south of Lower Beth-horon.

14 The boundary then made a turn and swung south along the
western edge of the hill facing Beth-horon, ending at the village of
Kiriath-baal (that is, Kiriath-jearim), a town belonging to the tribe of
Judah. This was the western boundary.

15 The southern boundary began at the outskirts of Kiriath-jearim.
From that western point it ran* to the spring at the waters of Nephtoah,*
16 and down to the base of the mountain beside the valley of Ben-
Hinnom, at the northern end of the valley of Rephaim. From there it
went down the valley of Hinnom, crossing south of the slope where the
Jebusites lived, and continued down to En-rogel. 17 From En-rogel the
boundary proceeded in a northerly direction and came to En-shemesh
and on to Geliloth (which is across from the slopes of Adummim). Then
it went down to the Stone of Bohan. (Bohan was Reuben's son.) 18 From
there it passed along the north side of the slope overlooking the Jordan
Valley.* The border then went down into the valley, 19 ran past the north
slope of Beth-hoglah, and ended at the north bay of the Dead Sea,*
which is the southern end of the Jordan River. This was the southern
boundary.

20 The eastern boundary was the Jordan River.

These were the boundaries of the homeland allocated to the clans of the
tribe of Benjamin.

18:15a Or *From there it went to Mozah.* The meaning of the Hebrew is uncertain. **18:15b** Or *the spring at Me-nephtoah.* **18:18** Hebrew *overlooking the Arabah,* or *overlooking Beth-arabah.* **18:19** Hebrew *Salt Sea.*

Reflect on this passage

The Towns Given to Benjamin
21 These were the towns given to the clans of the tribe of Benjamin.

Jericho, Beth-hoglah, Emek-keziz, 22 Beth-arabah, Zemaraim, Bethel,
23 Avvim, Parah, Ophrah, 24 Kephar-ammoni, Ophni, and Geba—twelve
towns with their surrounding villages. 25 Also Gibeon, Ramah, Beeroth,
26 Mizpah, Kephirah, Mozah, 27 Rekem, Irpeel, Taralah, 28 Zela, Haeleph,
the Jebusite town (that is, Jerusalem), Gibeah, and Kiriath-jearim*—
fourteen towns with their surrounding villages.

This was the homeland allocated to the clans of the tribe of Benjamin.

The Land Given to Simeon
19 The second allotment of land went to the clans of the tribe of Simeon. Their homeland was surrounded by Judah's territory.

2 Simeon's homeland included Beersheba, Sheba, Moladah, 3 Hazar-
shual, Balah, Ezem, 4 Eltolad, Bethul, Hormah, 5 Ziklag, Beth-marcaboth,
Hazar-susah, 6 Beth-lebaoth, and Sharuhen—thirteen towns with
their surrounding villages. 7 It also included Ain, Rimmon, Ether, and
Ashan—four towns with their villages, 8 including all the surrounding
villages as far south as Baalath-beer (also known as Ramah of the Negev).

This was the homeland allocated to the clans of the tribe of Simeon. 9 Their
allocation of land came from part of what had been given to Judah because
Judah's territory was too large for them. So the tribe of Simeon received an
allocation within the territory of Judah.

The Land Given to Zebulun
10 The third allotment of land went to the clans of the tribe of Zebulun.

The boundary of Zebulun's homeland started at Sarid. 11 From there it
went west, going past Maralah, touching Dabbesheth, and proceeding
to the brook east of Jokneam. 12 In the other direction, the boundary
went east from Sarid to the border of Kisloth-tabor, and from there to
Daberath and up to Japhia. 13 Then it continued east to Gath-hepher, Eth-
kazin, and Rimmon and turned toward Neah. 14 The northern boundary
of Zebulun passed Hannathon and ended at the valley of Iphtah-el. 15 The
towns in these areas included Kattath, Nahalal, Shimron, Idalah, and
Bethlehem—twelve towns with their surrounding villages.

16 The homeland allocated to the clans of the tribe of Zebulun included these
towns and their surrounding villages.

The Land Given to Issachar
17 The fourth allotment of land went to the clans of the tribe of Issachar.

18 Its boundaries included the following towns: Jezreel, Kesulloth,
Shunem, 19 Hapharaim, Shion, Anaharath, 20 Rabbith, Kishion, Ebez,

18:28 As in Greek version; Hebrew reads *Kiriath*.

[21]Remeth, En-gannim, En-haddah, and Beth-pazzez. [22]The boundary
also touched Tabor, Shahazumah, and Beth-shemesh, ending at the
Jordan River—sixteen towns with their surrounding villages.

[23]The homeland allocated to the clans of the tribe of Issachar included these towns and their surrounding villages.

The Land Given to Asher

[24]The fifth allotment of land went to the clans of the tribe of Asher.

[25]Its boundaries included these towns: Helkath, Hali, Beten, Acshaph,
[26]Allammelech, Amad, and Mishal. The boundary on the west touched
Carmel and Shihor-libnath, [27]then it turned east toward Beth-dagon,
and ran as far as Zebulun in the valley of Iphtah-el, going north to Beth-
emek and Neiel. It then continued north to Cabul, [28]Abdon,* Rehob,
Hammon, Kanah, and as far as Greater Sidon. [29]Then the boundary
turned toward Ramah and the fortress of Tyre, where it turned toward
Hosah and came to the Mediterranean Sea.* The territory also included
Mehebel, Aczib, [30]Ummah, Aphek, and Rehob—twenty-two towns
with their surrounding villages.

[31]The homeland allocated to the clans of the tribe of Asher included these towns and their surrounding villages.

The Land Given to Naphtali

[32]The sixth allotment of land went to the clans of the tribe of Naphtali.

[33]Its boundary ran from Heleph, from the oak at Zaanannim, and
extended across to Adami-nekeb, Jabneel, and as far as Lakkum, ending
at the Jordan River. [34]The western boundary ran past Aznoth-tabor,
then to Hukkok, and touched the border of Zebulun in the south, the
border of Asher on the west, and the Jordan River* on the east. [35]The
fortified towns included in this territory were Ziddim, Zer, Hammath,
Rakkath, Kinnereth, [36]Adamah, Ramah, Hazor, [37]Kedesh, Edrei,
En-hazor, [38]Yiron, Migdal-el, Horem, Beth-anath, and Beth-shemesh—
nineteen towns with their surrounding villages.

[39]The homeland allocated to the clans of the tribe of Naphtali included these towns and their surrounding villages.

The Land Given to Dan

[40]The seventh allotment of land went to the clans of the tribe of Dan.

[41]The land allocated as their homeland included the following towns:
Zorah, Eshtaol, Ir-shemesh, [42]Shaalabbin, Aijalon, Ithlah, [43]Elon,
Timnah, Ekron, [44]Eltekeh, Gibbethon, Baalath, [45]Jehud, Bene-berak,
Gath-rimmon, [46]Me-jarkon, Rakkon, and the territory across from Joppa.
[47]But the tribe of Dan had trouble taking possession of their land,*

19:28 As in some Hebrew manuscripts (see also 21:30); most Hebrew manuscripts read *Ebron.* **19:29** Hebrew *the sea.* **19:34** Hebrew *and Judah at the Jordan River.* **19:47a** Or *had trouble holding on to their land.*

so they attacked the town of Laish.* They captured it, slaughtered
its people, and settled there. They renamed the town Dan after their
ancestor.

48 The homeland allocated to the clans of the tribe of Dan included these
towns and their surrounding villages.

The Land Given to Joshua

49 After all the land was divided among the tribes, the Israelites gave a piece
of land to Joshua as his allocation. 50 For the LORD had said he could have any
town he wanted. He chose Timnath-serah in the hill country of Ephraim.
He rebuilt the town and lived there.

51 These are the territories that Eleazar the priest, Joshua son of Nun, and
the tribal leaders allocated as grants of land to the tribes of Israel by casting
sacred lots in the presence of the LORD at the entrance of the Tabernacle* at
Shiloh. So the division of the land was completed.

The Cities of Refuge

20 The LORD said to Joshua, 2 "Now tell the Israelites to designate the
cities of refuge, as I instructed Moses. 3 Anyone who kills another
person accidentally and unintentionally can run to one of these cities; they
will be places of refuge from relatives seeking revenge for the person who
was killed.

4 "Upon reaching one of these cities, the one who caused the death will
appear before the elders at the city gate and present his case. They must
allow him to enter the city and give him a place to live among them. 5 If the
relatives of the victim come to avenge the killing, the leaders must not re-
lease the slayer to them, for he killed the other person unintentionally and
without previous hostility. 6 But the slayer must stay in that city and be tried
by the local assembly, which will render a judgment. And he must continue
to live in that city until the death of the high priest who was in office at the
time of the accident. After that, he is free to return to his own home in the
town from which he fled."

7 The following cities were designated as cities of refuge: Kedesh of Galilee,
in the hill country of Naphtali; Shechem, in the hill country of Ephraim; and
Kiriath-arba (that is, Hebron), in the hill country of Judah. 8 On the east side
of the Jordan River, across from Jericho, the following cities were designated:
Bezer, in the wilderness plain of the tribe of Reuben; Ramoth in Gilead, in
the territory of the tribe of Gad; and Golan in Bashan, in the land of the
tribe of Manasseh. 9 These cities were set apart for all the Israelites as well as
the foreigners living among them. Anyone who accidentally killed another
person could take refuge in one of these cities. In this way, they could escape
being killed in revenge prior to standing trial before the local assembly.

The Towns Given to the Levites

21 Then the leaders of the tribe of Levi came to consult with Eleazar
the priest, Joshua son of Nun, and the leaders of the other tribes of
Israel. 2 They came to them at Shiloh in the land of Canaan and said, "The
LORD commanded Moses to give us towns to live in and pasturelands for our

19:47b Hebrew *Leshem,* a variant spelling of Laish. **19:51** Hebrew *Tent of Meeting.*

Question **20:1-9**

The Lord instructed Israel to establish cities of refuge to provide shelter and redemption and protection for those in trouble. What does this teach you about the expectations God places on his followers?

livestock." 3 So by the command of the LORD the people of Israel gave the Le-
vites the following towns and pasturelands out of their own grants of land.

4 The descendants of Aaron, who were members of the Kohathite clan
within the tribe of Levi, were allotted thirteen towns that were originally
assigned to the tribes of Judah, Simeon, and Benjamin. 5 The other families
of the Kohathite clan were allotted ten towns from the tribes of Ephraim,
Dan, and the half-tribe of Manasseh.

6 The clan of Gershon was allotted thirteen towns from the tribes of Issa-
char, Asher, Naphtali, and the half-tribe of Manasseh in Bashan.

7 The clan of Merari was allotted twelve towns from the tribes of Reuben,
Gad, and Zebulun.

8 So the Israelites obeyed the LORD's command to Moses and assigned
these towns and pasturelands to the Levites by casting sacred lots.

9 The Israelites gave the following towns from the tribes of Judah and Sim-
eon 10 to the descendants of Aaron, who were members of the Kohathite clan
within the tribe of Levi, since the sacred lot fell to them first: 11 Kiriath-arba
(that is, Hebron), in the hill country of Judah, along with its surrounding
pasturelands. (Arba was an ancestor of Anak.) 12 But the open fields beyond
the town and the surrounding villages were given to Caleb son of Jephun-
neh as his possession.

13 The following towns with their pasturelands were given to the descen-
dants of Aaron the priest: Hebron (a city of refuge for those who accidentally
killed someone), Libnah, 14 Jattir, Eshtemoa, 15 Holon, Debir, 16 Ain, Juttah,
and Beth-shemesh—nine towns from these two tribes.

17 From the tribe of Benjamin the priests were given the following towns
with their pasturelands: Gibeon, Geba, 18 Anathoth, and Almon—four
towns. 19 So in all, thirteen towns with their pasturelands were given to the
priests, the descendants of Aaron.

20 The rest of the Kohathite clan from the tribe of Levi was allotted the
following towns and pasturelands from the tribe of Ephraim: 21 Shechem in
the hill country of Ephraim (a city of refuge for those who accidentally killed
someone), Gezer, 22 Kibzaim, and Beth-horon—four towns.

23 The following towns and pasturelands were allotted to the priests from the
tribe of Dan: Eltekeh, Gibbethon, 24 Aijalon, and Gath-rimmon—four towns.

25 The half-tribe of Manasseh allotted the following towns with their
pasturelands to the priests: Taanach and Gath-rimmon—two towns. 26 So
in all, ten towns with their pasturelands were given to the rest of the Ko-
hathite clan.

27 The descendants of Gershon, another clan within the tribe of Levi, re-
ceived the following towns with their pasturelands from the half-tribe of
Manasseh: Golan in Bashan (a city of refuge for those who accidentally killed
someone) and Be-eshterah—two towns.

28 From the tribe of Issachar they received the following towns with their
pasturelands: Kishion, Daberath, 29 Jarmuth, and En-gannim—four towns.

30 From the tribe of Asher they received the following towns with their
pasturelands: Mishal, Abdon, 31 Helkath, and Rehob—four towns.

32 From the tribe of Naphtali they received the following towns with their
pasturelands: Kedesh in Galilee (a city of refuge for those who accidentally
killed someone), Hammoth-dor, and Kartan—three towns. 33 So in all, thir-
teen towns with their pasturelands were allotted to the clan of Gershon.

34 The rest of the Levites—the Merari clan—were given the following towns with their pasturelands from the tribe of Zebulun: Jokneam, Kartah, 35 Dimnah, and Nahalal—four towns.

36 From the tribe of Reuben they received the following towns with their pasturelands: Bezer, Jahaz,* 37 Kedemoth, and Mephaath—four towns.

38 From the tribe of Gad they received the following towns with their pasturelands: Ramoth in Gilead (a city of refuge for those who accidentally killed someone), Mahanaim, 39 Heshbon, and Jazer—four towns. 40 So in all, twelve towns were allotted to the clan of Merari.

41 The total number of towns and pasturelands within Israelite territory given to the Levites came to forty-eight. 42 Every one of these towns had pasturelands surrounding it.

43 So the LORD gave to Israel all the land he had sworn to give their ancestors, and they took possession of it and settled there. 44 And the LORD gave them rest on every side, just as he had solemnly promised their ancestors. None of their enemies could stand against them, for the LORD helped them conquer all their enemies. 45 Not a single one of all the good promises the LORD had given to the family of Israel was left unfulfilled; everything he had spoken came true.

Question 21:45

How does God set an example of faithfulness for us?

The Eastern Tribes Return Home

22 Then Joshua called together the tribes of Reuben, Gad, and the half-tribe of Manasseh. 2 He told them, "You have done as Moses, the servant of the LORD, commanded you, and you have obeyed every order I have given you. 3 During all this time you have not deserted the other tribes. You have been careful to obey the commands of the LORD your God right up to the present day. 4 And now the LORD your God has given the other tribes rest, as he promised them. So go back home to the land that Moses, the servant of the LORD, gave you as your possession on the east side of the Jordan River. 5 But be very careful to obey all the commands and the instructions that Moses gave to you. Love the LORD your God, walk in all his ways, obey his commands, hold firmly to him, and serve him with all your heart and all your soul." 6 So Joshua blessed them and sent them away, and they went home.

7 Moses had given the land of Bashan, east of the Jordan River, to the half-tribe of Manasseh. (The other half of the tribe was given land west of the Jordan.) As Joshua sent them away and blessed them, 8 he said to them, "Go back to your homes with the great wealth you have taken from your enemies—the vast herds of livestock, the silver, gold, bronze, and iron, and the large supply of clothing. Share the plunder with your relatives."

9 So the men of Reuben, Gad, and the half-tribe of Manasseh left the rest of Israel at Shiloh in the land of Canaan. They started the journey back to their own land of Gilead, the territory that belonged to them according to the LORD's command through Moses.

The Eastern Tribes Build an Altar

10 But while they were still in Canaan, and when they came to a place called Geliloth* near the Jordan River, the men of Reuben, Gad, and the half-tribe of Manasseh stopped to build a large and imposing altar.

11 The rest of Israel heard that the people of Reuben, Gad, and the half-tribe

21:36 Hebrew *Jahzah,* a variant spelling of Jahaz. 22:10 Or *to the circle of stones;* similarly in 22:11.

of Manasseh had built an altar at Geliloth at the edge of the land of Canaan,
on the west side of the Jordan River. 12So the whole community of Israel
gathered at Shiloh and prepared to go to war against them. 13First, however,
they sent a delegation led by Phinehas son of Eleazar, the priest, to talk with
the tribes of Reuben, Gad, and the half-tribe of Manasseh. 14In this delega-
tion were ten leaders of Israel, one from each of the ten tribes, and each the
head of his family within the clans of Israel.
15When they arrived in the land of Gilead, they said to the tribes of Reu-
ben, Gad, and the half-tribe of Manasseh, 16"The whole community of the
LORD demands to know why you are betraying the God of Israel. How
could you turn away from the LORD and build an altar for yourselves in
rebellion against him? 17Was our sin at Peor not enough? To this day we are
not fully cleansed of it, even after the plague that struck the entire com-
munity of the LORD. 18And yet today you are turning away from following
the LORD. If you rebel against the LORD today, he will be angry with all of
us tomorrow.
19"If you need the altar because the land you possess is defiled, then join us
in the LORD's land, where the Tabernacle of the LORD is situated, and share
our land with us. But do not rebel against the LORD or against us by building
an altar other than the one true altar of the LORD our God. 20Didn't divine
anger fall on the entire community of Israel when Achan, a member of the
clan of Zerah, sinned by stealing the things set apart for the LORD*? He was
not the only one who died because of his sin."
21Then the people of Reuben, Gad, and the half-tribe of Manasseh an-
swered the heads of the clans of Israel: 22"The LORD, the Mighty One, is God!
The LORD, the Mighty One, is God! He knows the truth, and may Israel know
it, too! We have not built the altar in treacherous rebellion against the LORD.
If we have done so, do not spare our lives this day. 23If we have built an altar
for ourselves to turn away from the LORD or to offer burnt offerings or grain
offerings or peace offerings, may the LORD himself punish us.
24"The truth is, we have built this altar because we fear that in the future
your descendants will say to ours, 'What right do you have to worship the
LORD, the God of Israel? 25The LORD has placed the Jordan River as a bar-
rier between our people and you people of Reuben and Gad. You have no
claim to the LORD.' So your descendants may prevent our descendants from
worshiping the LORD.
26"So we decided to build the altar, not for burnt offerings or sacrifices,
27but as a memorial. It will remind our descendants and your descendants
that we, too, have the right to worship the LORD at his sanctuary with our
burnt offerings, sacrifices, and peace offerings. Then your descendants will
not be able to say to ours, 'You have no claim to the LORD.'
28"If they say this, our descendants can reply, 'Look at this copy of the
LORD's altar that our ancestors made. It is not for burnt offerings or sacri-
fices; it is a reminder of the relationship both of us have with the LORD.' 29Far
be it from us to rebel against the LORD or turn away from him by building
our own altar for burnt offerings, grain offerings, or sacrifices. Only the altar
of the LORD our God that stands in front of the Tabernacle may be used for
that purpose."
30When Phinehas the priest and the leaders of the community—the

22:20 The Hebrew term used here refers to the complete consecration of things or people to the LORD, either by destroying them or by giving them as an offering.

heads of the clans of Israel—heard this from the tribes of Reuben, Gad, and
the half-tribe of Manasseh, they were satisfied. 31 Phinehas son of Eleazar,
the priest, replied to them, "Today we know the LORD is among us because
you have not committed this treachery against the LORD as we thought.
Instead, you have rescued Israel from being destroyed by the hand of the
LORD."
32 Then Phinehas son of Eleazar, the priest, and the other leaders left the
tribes of Reuben and Gad in Gilead and returned to the land of Canaan to
tell the Israelites what had happened. 33 And all the Israelites were satis-
fied and praised God and spoke no more of war against Reuben and Gad.
34 The people of Reuben and Gad named the altar "Witness,"* for they
said, "It is a witness between us and them that the LORD is our God, too."

Joshua's Final Words to Israel

23 The years passed, and the LORD had given the people of Israel rest
from all their enemies. Joshua, who was now very old, 2 called to-
gether all the elders, leaders, judges, and officers of Israel. He said to them,
"I am now a very old man. 3 You have seen everything the LORD your God
has done for you during my lifetime. The LORD your God has fought for you
against your enemies. 4 I have allotted to you as your homeland all the land
of the nations yet unconquered, as well as the land of those we have already
conquered—from the Jordan River to the Mediterranean Sea* in the west.
5 This land will be yours, for the LORD your God will himself drive out all
the people living there now. You will take possession of their land, just as
the LORD your God promised you.
6 "So be very careful to follow everything Moses wrote in the Book of In-
struction. Do not deviate from it, turning either to the right or to the left.
7 Make sure you do not associate with the other people still remaining in the
land. Do not even mention the names of their gods, much less swear by them
or serve them or worship them. 8 Rather, cling tightly to the LORD your God
as you have done until now.
9 "For the LORD has driven out great and powerful nations for you, and
no one has yet been able to defeat you. 10 Each one of you will put to flight a
thousand of the enemy, for the LORD your God fights for you, just as he has
promised. 11 So be very careful to love the LORD your God.
12 "But if you turn away from him and cling to the customs of the survivors
of these nations remaining among you, and if you intermarry with them,
13 then know for certain that the LORD your God will no longer drive them
out of your land. Instead, they will be a snare and a trap to you, a whip for
your backs and thorny brambles in your eyes, and you will vanish from this
good land the LORD your God has given you.
14 "Soon I will die, going the way of everything on earth. Deep in your
hearts you know that every promise of the LORD your God has come true.
Not a single one has failed! 15 But as surely as the LORD your God has given
you the good things he promised, he will also bring disaster on you if you
disobey him. He will completely destroy you from this good land he has
given you. 16 If you break the covenant of the LORD your God by worshiping
and serving other gods, his anger will burn against you, and you will quickly
vanish from the good land he has given you."

22:34 Some manuscripts lack this word. 23:4 Hebrew *the Great Sea.*

Question 22:34

The people gave this altar the name "Witness" because it was a witness to how Israel was rescued from destruction. Where else can you find "witness" as a difference-making theme in the Bible?

Make a Difference 23:6

Be Careful to Follow

God's idea of effective leadership has less to do with accomplishments and more to do with unwavering commitment to the Lord. Joshua's final words to Israel focused not on the conquering of land, not on his military accolades, and not on his great oratory skills. His final words to God's people reiterated what it meant to follow the Lord.

Jesus said something very similar in some of his last words to his followers: "Teach these new disciples to obey all the commands I have given you" (Matthew 28:20).

Difference Maker

What would have to change in your life to follow *all* the commands Jesus gave? What would it look like to never deviate from his instructions?

Prayer 24:15

God, looking ahead into my future, I declare this to you today: as for me and my house, we will serve the Lord. Amen.

The LORD's Covenant Renewed

24 Then Joshua summoned all the tribes of Israel to Shechem, includ-
ing their elders, leaders, judges, and officers. So they came and pre-
sented themselves to God.
2 Joshua said to the people, "This is what the LORD, the God of Israel, says:
Long ago your ancestors, including Terah, the father of Abraham and Nahor,
lived beyond the Euphrates River,* and they worshiped other gods. 3 But I
took your ancestor Abraham from the land beyond the Euphrates and led
him into the land of Canaan. I gave him many descendants through his son
Isaac. 4 To Isaac I gave Jacob and Esau. To Esau I gave the mountains of Seir,
while Jacob and his children went down into Egypt.
5 "Then I sent Moses and Aaron, and I brought terrible plagues on Egypt;
and afterward I brought you out as a free people. 6 But when your ances-
tors arrived at the Red Sea,* the Egyptians chased after you with chariots
and charioteers. 7 When your ancestors cried out to the LORD, I put darkness
between you and the Egyptians. I brought the sea crashing down on the
Egyptians, drowning them. With your very own eyes you saw what I did.
Then you lived in the wilderness for many years.
8 "Finally, I brought you into the land of the Amorites on the east side of
the Jordan. They fought against you, but I destroyed them before you. I gave
you victory over them, and you took possession of their land. 9 Then Balak
son of Zippor, king of Moab, started a war against Israel. He summoned
Balaam son of Beor to curse you, 10 but I would not listen to him. Instead, I
made Balaam bless you, and so I rescued you from Balak.
11 "When you crossed the Jordan River and came to Jericho, the men of Jer-
icho fought against you, as did the Amorites, the Perizzites, the Canaanites,
the Hittites, the Girgashites, the Hivites, and the Jebusites. But I gave you
victory over them. 12 And I sent terror* ahead of you to drive out the two kings
of the Amorites. It was not your swords or bows that brought you victory.
13 I gave you land you had not worked on, and I gave you towns you did not
build—the towns where you are now living. I gave you vineyards and olive
groves for food, though you did not plant them.
14 "So fear the LORD and serve him wholeheartedly. Put away forever the
idols your ancestors worshiped when they lived beyond the Euphrates River
and in Egypt. Serve the LORD alone. 15 But if you refuse to serve the LORD,
then choose today whom you will serve. Would you prefer the gods your
ancestors served beyond the Euphrates? Or will it be the gods of the Amo-
rites in whose land you now live? But as for me and my family, we will serve
the LORD."
16 The people replied, "We would never abandon the LORD and serve other
gods. 17 For the LORD our God is the one who rescued us and our ancestors from
slavery in the land of Egypt. He performed mighty miracles before our very
eyes. As we traveled through the wilderness among our enemies, he preserved
us. 18 It was the LORD who drove out the Amorites and the other nations liv-
ing here in the land. So we, too, will serve the LORD, for he alone is our God."
19 Then Joshua warned the people, "You are not able to serve the LORD,
for he is a holy and jealous God. He will not forgive your rebellion and your
sins. 20 If you abandon the LORD and serve other gods, he will turn against
you and destroy you, even though he has been so good to you."

24:2 Hebrew *the river;* also in 24:3, 14, 15. 24:6 Hebrew *sea of reeds.* 24:12 Often rendered *the hornet.* The meaning of the Hebrew is uncertain.

21 But the people answered Joshua, "No, we will serve the LORD!"
22 "You are a witness to your own decision," Joshua said. "You have chosen
to serve the LORD."
"Yes," they replied, "we are witnesses to what we have said."
23 "All right then," Joshua said, "destroy the idols among you, and turn
your hearts to the LORD, the God of Israel."
24 The people said to Joshua, "We will serve the LORD our God. We will
obey him alone."
25 So Joshua made a covenant with the people that day at Shechem, com-
mitting them to follow the decrees and regulations of the LORD. 26 Joshua
recorded these things in the Book of God's Instructions. As a reminder of
their agreement, he took a huge stone and rolled it beneath the terebinth
tree beside the Tabernacle of the LORD.
27 Joshua said to all the people, "This stone has heard everything the LORD
said to us. It will be a witness to testify against you if you go back on your
word to God."
28 Then Joshua sent all the people away to their own homelands.

Leaders Buried in the Promised Land

29 After this, Joshua son of Nun, the servant of the LORD, died at the age of
110. 30 They buried him in the land he had been allocated, at Timnath-serah
in the hill country of Ephraim, north of Mount Gaash.
31 The people of Israel served the LORD throughout the lifetime of Joshua
and of the elders who outlived him—those who had personally experienced
all that the LORD had done for Israel.
32 The bones of Joseph, which the Israelites had brought along with them
when they left Egypt, were buried at Shechem, in the plot of land Jacob had
bought from the sons of Hamor for 100 pieces of silver.* This land was located
in the territory allotted to the descendants of Joseph.
33 Eleazar son of Aaron also died. He was buried in the hill country of
Ephraim, in the town of Gibeah, which had been given to his son Phinehas.

24:32 Hebrew *100 kesitahs;* the value or weight of the kesitah is no longer known.

Make a Difference

24:29-31

Legacy

When Joshua died, the Scriptures make a remarkable comment. The Bible says that throughout his lifetime, "the people of Israel served the LORD" (v. 31). Long after Joshua died, the way that he lived his life encouraged people to continue following after God. He left a remarkably good legacy for the generations to come.

If you could look ahead many years into the future, what kind of legacy would you like to have left on this earth? One way of thinking about this is to consider what kind of words you would like others to speak about you at your funeral or what phrase you'd like written on your epitaph (the message that is etched on your tombstone). This isn't a morbid thought about death. Rather, it is a proactive thought about your life.

How will you have lived? What stories do you want people to tell? Do you want others to follow in your footsteps? What difference do you want to have made in this world? Living in the light of our legacy should cause us to live for eternity rather than for the fleeting pleasures of this world.

Difference Maker

Write an epitaph for yourself that you would be proud to have etched on your tombstone.

Judges Introduction

The book of Judges cycles through miracles and pain. It is not only a book of epic, can't-miss moments but also a book of heartbreak and tragedy. You will read numerous stories of God showing up to save Israel using "judges"—although it might be helpful to think of these heroes as rulers or military leaders rather than robed figures with gavels and law degrees. Most notably, though, you will read shocking accounts of a historic rebellion by the people of Israel as they turned their backs on God time and time again.

A cycle is a sequence of actions that are repeated again and again. Maybe you get stuck in cycles in your life—doing or experiencing things in the same order...over and over and over. Maybe you find yourself in the same cycle every day—wake up, eat something, do schoolwork, play video games, go to sleep, repeat!

In the pages ahead, take a close look at the painful cycle that people got stuck in: they turned their backs on God (sin), so God allowed them to suffer the consequences of their actions (judgment) until the people cried for help (repentance), and God delivered them (salvation). This same pattern—or cycle—happens several times throughout the book, and every time, God was faithful to save the people.

Is it so different for you today? If you are anything like the people in Judges, you probably want God's favor, you probably want God's salvation, but you also probably want to do things your own way. In essence, even if you want to follow God, you choose to turn your back on God. The book of Judges is a graphic narrative that, at times, is hard to read, yet it is filled with miraculous stories that show both the commitment and character of God, who desires to save and be in relationship with the people.

Story Arcs

- **Othniel**
- **Ehud**
- **Gideon**
- **Jotham**
- **Samson → Rescuer!**

Judges

Judah and Simeon Conquer the Land

1 After the death of Joshua, the Israelites asked the LORD, "Which tribe
should go first to attack the Canaanites?"
2 The LORD answered, "Judah, for I have given them victory over the land."
3 The men of Judah said to their relatives from the tribe of Simeon, "Join
with us to fight against the Canaanites living in the territory allotted to us.
Then we will help you conquer your territory." So the men of Simeon went
with Judah.
4 When the men of Judah attacked, the LORD gave them victory over the
Canaanites and Perizzites, and they killed 10,000 enemy warriors at the town
of Bezek.
5 While at Bezek they encountered King Adoni-bezek and fought
against him, and the Canaanites and Perizzites were defeated.
6 Adoni-bezek
escaped, but the Israelites soon captured him and cut off his thumbs and
big toes.
7 Adoni-bezek said, "I once had seventy kings with their thumbs and big
toes cut off, eating scraps from under my table. Now God has paid me back
for what I did to them." They took him to Jerusalem, and he died there.
8 The men of Judah attacked Jerusalem and captured it, killing all its
people and setting the city on fire.
9 Then they went down to fight the Canaanites living in the hill country, the Negev, and the western foothills.*
10 Judah marched against the Canaanites in Hebron (formerly called Kiriath-arba), defeating the forces of Sheshai, Ahiman, and Talmai.
11 From there they went to fight against the people living in the town of
Debir (formerly called Kiriath-sepher).
12 Caleb said, "I will give my daughter Acsah in marriage to the one who attacks and captures Kiriath-sepher."
13 Othniel, the son of Caleb's younger brother, Kenaz, was the one who conquered it, so Acsah became Othniel's wife.
14 When Acsah married Othniel, she urged him* to ask her father for a
field. As she got down off her donkey, Caleb asked her, "What's the matter?"
15 She said, "Let me have another gift. You have already given me land in
the Negev; now please give me springs of water, too." So Caleb gave her the
upper and lower springs.
16 When the tribe of Judah left Jericho—the city of palms—the Kenites,
who were descendants of Moses' father-in-law, traveled with them into the
wilderness of Judah. They settled among the people there, near the town of
Arad in the Negev.
17 Then Judah joined with Simeon to fight against the Canaanites living in
Zephath, and they completely destroyed* the town. So the town was named
Hormah.*
18 In addition, Judah captured the towns of Gaza, Ashkelon, and
Ekron, along with their surrounding territories.

1:9 Hebrew *the Shephelah.* 1:14 Greek version and Latin Vulgate read *he urged her.* 1:17a The Hebrew term used here refers to the complete consecration of things or people to the LORD, either by destroying them or by giving them as an offering. 1:17b *Hormah* means "destruction."

Make a Difference 1:19

"The LORD Was With..."

God was with the people of Judah. Because of this, they were able to live the life God called them to. What would your life look like if this could be said of you?

If we zoom forward in the narrative of Scripture, we know that when Jesus left the earth, the Holy Spirit—the great Counselor—came to be with God's people. The good news for us is that if we have said yes to following Jesus, then we know that the Holy Spirit is with us—that God is with us.

The key focus in this story is that the people from Judah answered the call to be obedient to God, and because of this, God was with them and blessed them. It's the same with us today. When we take a step of obedience toward God, we, too, can experience God's presence in our lives.

Difference Maker

In what situation in your life can you follow the Holy Spirit's lead to be a blessing to someone? What can you do to help them know the Holy Spirit is with you?

Israel Fails to Conquer the Land

19The LORD was with the people of Judah, and they took possession of the
hill country. But they failed to drive out the people living in the plains, who
had iron chariots. 20The town of Hebron was given to Caleb as Moses had
promised. And Caleb drove out the people living there, who were descen-
dants of the three sons of Anak.

21The tribe of Benjamin, however, failed to drive out the Jebusites, who
were living in Jerusalem. So to this day the Jebusites live in Jerusalem
among the people of Benjamin.

22The descendants of Joseph attacked the town of Bethel, and the LORD
was with them. 23They sent men to scout out Bethel (formerly known as
Luz). 24They confronted a man coming out of the town and said to him,
"Show us a way into the town, and we will have mercy on you." 25So he
showed them a way in, and they killed everyone in the town except that man
and his family. 26Later the man moved to the land of the Hittites, where he
built a town. He named it Luz, which is its name to this day.

27The tribe of Manasseh failed to drive out the people living in Beth-
shan,* Taanach, Dor, Ibleam, Megiddo, and all their surrounding settle-
ments, because the Canaanites were determined to stay in that region.
28When the Israelites grew stronger, they forced the Canaanites to work as
slaves, but they never did drive them completely out of the land.

29The tribe of Ephraim failed to drive out the Canaanites living in Gezer,
so the Canaanites continued to live there among them.

30The tribe of Zebulun failed to drive out the residents of Kitron and Na-
halol, so the Canaanites continued to live among them. But the Canaanites
were forced to work as slaves for the people of Zebulun.

31The tribe of Asher failed to drive out the residents of Acco, Sidon, Ah-
lab, Aczib, Helbah, Aphik, and Rehob. 32Instead, the people of Asher moved
in among the Canaanites, who controlled the land, for they failed to drive
them out.

33Likewise, the tribe of Naphtali failed to drive out the residents of
Beth-shemesh and Beth-anath. Instead, they moved in among the Ca-
naanites, who controlled the land. Nevertheless, the people of Beth-
shemesh and Beth-anath were forced to work as slaves for the people
of Naphtali.

34As for the tribe of Dan, the Amorites forced them back into the hill
country and would not let them come down into the plains. 35The Amorites
were determined to stay in Mount Heres, Aijalon, and Shaalbim, but when
the descendants of Joseph became stronger, they forced the Amorites to
work as slaves. 36The boundary of the Amorites ran from Scorpion Pass* to
Sela and continued upward from there.

The LORD's Messenger Comes to Bokim

2 The angel of the LORD went up from Gilgal to Bokim and said to the
Israelites, "I brought you out of Egypt into this land that I swore to give
your ancestors, and I said I would never break my covenant with you. 2For
your part, you were not to make any covenants with the people living in this
land; instead, you were to destroy their altars. But you disobeyed my com-
mand. Why did you do this? 3So now I declare that I will no longer drive out

1:27 Hebrew *Beth-shean,* a variant spelling of Beth-shan. **1:36** Hebrew *Akrabbim.*

the people living in your land. They will be thorns in your sides,* and their
gods will be a constant temptation to you."
4 When the angel of the LORD finished speaking to all the Israelites, the
people wept loudly. 5 So they called the place Bokim (which means "weep-
ing"), and they offered sacrifices there to the LORD.

The Death of Joshua

6 After Joshua sent the people away, each of the tribes left to take possession
of the land allotted to them. 7 And the Israelites served the LORD throughout
the lifetime of Joshua and the leaders who outlived him—those who had
seen all the great things the LORD had done for Israel.
8 Joshua son of Nun, the servant of the LORD, died at the age of 110. 9 They
buried him in the land he had been allocated, at Timnath-serah* in the hill
country of Ephraim, north of Mount Gaash.

Israel Disobeys the LORD

10 After that generation died, another generation grew up who did not
acknowledge the LORD or remember the mighty things he had done for
Israel.
11 The Israelites did evil in the LORD's sight and served the images of Baal.
12 They abandoned the LORD, the God of their ancestors, who had brought
them out of Egypt. They went after other gods, worshiping the gods of the
people around them. And they angered the LORD. 13 They abandoned the
LORD to serve Baal and the images of Ashtoreth. 14 This made the LORD burn
with anger against Israel, so he handed them over to raiders who stole their
possessions. He turned them over to their enemies all around, and they were
no longer able to resist them. 15 Every time Israel went out to battle, the LORD
fought against them, causing them to be defeated, just as he had warned.
And the people were in great distress.

The LORD Rescues His People

16 Then the LORD raised up judges to rescue the Israelites from their attack-
ers. 17 Yet Israel did not listen to the judges but prostituted themselves by
worshiping other gods. How quickly they turned away from the path of their
ancestors, who had walked in obedience to the LORD's commands.
18 Whenever the LORD raised up a judge over Israel, he was with that judge
and rescued the people from their enemies throughout the judge's lifetime.
For the LORD took pity on his people, who were burdened by oppression and
suffering. 19 But when the judge died, the people returned to their corrupt
ways, behaving worse than those who had lived before them. They went after
other gods, serving and worshiping them. And they refused to give up their
evil practices and stubborn ways.
20 So the LORD burned with anger against Israel. He said, "Because these
people have violated my covenant, which I made with their ancestors, and
have ignored my commands, 21 I will no longer drive out the nations that
Joshua left unconquered when he died. 22 I did this to test Israel—to see
whether or not they would follow the ways of the LORD as their ancestors
did." 23 That is why the LORD left those nations in place. He did not quickly
drive them out or allow Joshua to conquer them all.

2:3 Hebrew *They will be in your sides;* compare Num 33:55. 2:9 As in parallel text at Josh 24:30; Hebrew reads *Timnath-heres,* a variant spelling of Timnath-serah.

Make a Difference 2:10

Generational Trouble

Why are we so easily drawn away from God and toward things that hurt us? Why do we secretly adore things that leave us empty, unfulfilled, and worse off?

Those questions are the sad story of the book of Judges. A people who once experienced God in spectacular, personal ways became a people far from God, not knowing his presence, not following his patterns. Generation after generation grew more disgusting and more depraved than the one before it. People grew further and further removed from God, less and less aware of right and wrong, more confused and less secure.

One of the most significant things we can do today is pray for our generation to have the courage to turn from darkness and to walk toward the light of Jesus.

Difference Maker

Grab some friends and set aside time to pray for your generation today.

Question 2:12

Isn't it interesting that God experiences different emotions–for example anger (vv. 12, 14, 20) and pity (v. 18). How are these godly emotions different from when you experience similar feelings? (Hint: God's holiness has something to do with it.)

Question 2:22

What are some instances in your life when you felt like your own faith was being tested?

The Nations Left in Canaan

3 These are the nations that the LORD left in the land to test those Israelites who had not experienced the wars of Canaan. 2He did this to teach warfare to generations of Israelites who had no experience in battle. 3These are the nations: the Philistines (those living under the five Philistine rulers), all the Canaanites, the Sidonians, and the Hivites living in the mountains of Lebanon from Mount Baal-hermon to Lebo-hamath. 4These people were left to test the Israelites—to see whether they would obey the commands the LORD had given to their ancestors through Moses.

5So the people of Israel lived among the Canaanites, Hittites, Amorites, Perizzites, Hivites, and Jebusites, 6and they intermarried with them. Israelite sons married their daughters, and Israelite daughters were given in marriage to their sons. And the Israelites served their gods.

Othniel Becomes Israel's Judge

7The Israelites did evil in the LORD's sight. They forgot about the LORD their God, and they served the images of Baal and the Asherah poles. 8Then the LORD burned with anger against Israel, and he turned them over to King Cushan-rishathaim of Aram-naharaim.* And the Israelites served Cushan-rishathaim for eight years.

9But when the people of Israel cried out to the LORD for help, the LORD raised up a rescuer to save them. His name was Othniel, the son of Caleb's younger brother, Kenaz. 10The Spirit of the LORD came upon him, and he became Israel's judge. He went to war against King Cushan-rishathaim of Aram, and the LORD gave Othniel victory over him. 11So there was peace in the land for forty years. Then Othniel son of Kenaz died.

Ehud Becomes Israel's Judge

12Once again the Israelites did evil in the LORD's sight, and the LORD gave King Eglon of Moab control over Israel because of their evil. 13Eglon enlisted the Ammonites and Amalekites as allies, and then he went out and defeated Israel, taking possession of Jericho, the city of palms. 14And the Israelites served Eglon of Moab for eighteen years.

15But when the people of Israel cried out to the LORD for help, the LORD again raised up a rescuer to save them. His name was Ehud son of Gera, a left-handed man of the tribe of Benjamin. The Israelites sent Ehud to deliver their tribute money to King Eglon of Moab. 16So Ehud made a double-edged dagger that was about a foot* long, and he strapped it to his right thigh, keeping it hidden under his clothing. 17He brought the tribute money to Eglon, who was very fat.

18After delivering the payment, Ehud started home with those who had helped carry the tribute. 19But when Ehud reached the stone idols near Gilgal, he turned back. He came to Eglon and said, "I have a secret message for you."

So the king commanded his servants, "Be quiet!" and he sent them all out of the room.

20Ehud walked over to Eglon, who was sitting alone in a cool upstairs room. And Ehud said, "I have a message from God for you!" As King Eglon rose from his seat, 21Ehud reached with his left hand, pulled out the dagger

3:8 *Aram-naharaim* means "Aram of the two rivers," thought to have been located between the Euphrates and Balih Rivers in northwestern Mesopotamia. 3:16 Hebrew *gomed,* the length of which is uncertain.

Story Arc 3:7-11

Othniel

Here is the first example of the painful cycle in the book of Judges—the Israelites did evil in the eyes of the Lord (v. 7), the Lord judged them (v. 8), the people cried out for help (v. 9), and God delivered them (v. 10). We see another example of how God's Spirit was with a judge—Othniel. God raised up Othniel to be the rescuer in this situation. Because of Othniel's faithfulness, God used him to bring about God's glory. What followed was forty years of peace.

Story Arc 3:12-30

Ehud

The story of Ehud is fascinating...and quite graphic. Again, the cycle of Judges was played out—the people sinned, God judged, the people cried out, and God delivered.

This time God raised up Ehud, a left-handed swordsman. The significance of Ehud's left-handedness was specifically related to how God used him to deliver the people. In these ancient days, it would have been considered really strange to be left-handed. Even if someone was born with a tendency to be left-handed, they would have learned to be right-handed to avoid being shunned by the community around them. Left-handedness was so rare that the palace guards would not have even considered that Ehud would be carrying a sword strapped to the right side of his body.

Judg 6:11 ►

strapped to his right thigh, and plunged it into the king's belly. 22 The dagger
went so deep that the handle disappeared beneath the king's fat. So Ehud did
not pull out the dagger, and the king's bowels emptied.* 23 Then Ehud closed
and locked the doors of the room and escaped down the latrine.*
24 After Ehud was gone, the king's servants returned and found the doors
to the upstairs room locked. They thought he might be using the latrine
in the room, 25 so they waited. But when the king didn't come out after a
long delay, they became concerned and got a key. And when they opened the
doors, they found their master dead on the floor.
26 While the servants were waiting, Ehud escaped, passing the stone idols
on his way to Seirah. 27 When he arrived in the hill country of Ephraim, Ehud
sounded a call to arms. Then he led a band of Israelites down from the hills.
28 "Follow me," he said, "for the LORD has given you victory over Moab your
enemy." So they followed him. And the Israelites took control of the shallow
crossings of the Jordan River across from Moab, preventing anyone from
crossing.
29 They attacked the Moabites and killed about 10,000 of their strongest
and most able-bodied warriors. Not one of them escaped. 30 So Moab was
conquered by Israel that day, and there was peace in the land for eighty years.

Shamgar Becomes Israel's Judge

31 After Ehud, Shamgar son of Anath rescued Israel. He once killed 600 Phi-
listines with an ox goad.

Deborah Becomes Israel's Judge

4 After Ehud's death, the Israelites again did evil in the LORD's sight. 2 So
the LORD turned them over to King Jabin of Hazor, a Canaanite king.
The commander of his army was Sisera, who lived in Harosheth-haggoyim.
3 Sisera, who had 900 iron chariots, ruthlessly oppressed the Israelites for
twenty years. Then the people of Israel cried out to the LORD for help.
4 Deborah, the wife of Lappidoth, was a prophet who was judging Israel at
that time. 5 She would sit under the Palm of Deborah, between Ramah and
Bethel in the hill country of Ephraim, and the Israelites would go to her for
judgment. 6 One day she sent for Barak son of Abinoam, who lived in Kedesh
in the land of Naphtali. She said to him, "This is what the LORD, the God
of Israel, commands you: Call out 10,000 warriors from the tribes of Naph-
tali and Zebulun at Mount Tabor. 7 And I will call out Sisera, commander of
Jabin's army, along with his chariots and warriors, to the Kishon River. There
I will give you victory over him."
8 Barak told her, "I will go, but only if you go with me."
9 "Very well," she replied, "I will go with you. But you will receive no honor
in this venture, for the LORD's victory over Sisera will be at the hands of a
woman." So Deborah went with Barak to Kedesh. 10 At Kedesh, Barak called
together the tribes of Zebulun and Naphtali, and 10,000 warriors went up
with him. Deborah also went with him.
11 Now Heber the Kenite, a descendant of Moses' brother-in-law* Hobab,
had moved away from the other members of his tribe and pitched his tent
by the oak of Zaanannim near Kedesh.
12 When Sisera was told that Barak son of Abinoam had gone up to Mount

3:22 Or *and it came out behind.* 3:23 Or *and went out through the porch;* the meaning of the Hebrew is uncertain. 4:11 Or *father-in-law.*

Make a Difference 4:4

Deborah

God raised up a prophetess named Deborah to bring about deliverance. Throughout Judges 4 and 5, we see several examples of Deborah's faithfulness and confidence in the Lord. She was surrounded by men who were timid in their faith, but all along, she pointed them back to the work God was doing (v. 14). Her vision of what God would do can be seen at the end of Deborah's song and prayer in 5:31, when she said, "May those who love you rise like the sun in all its power."

Difference Maker

Read through Deborah's song in Judges 5 and pick out ways that you, too, can be faithful in your relationship with God like she was.

Tabor, [13] he called for all 900 of his iron chariots and all of his warriors, and
they marched from Harosheth-haggoyim to the Kishon River.
[14] Then Deborah said to Barak, "Get ready! This is the day the LORD will
give you victory over Sisera, for the LORD is marching ahead of you." So Barak
led his 10,000 warriors down the slopes of Mount Tabor into battle. [15] When
Barak attacked, the LORD threw Sisera and all his chariots and warriors into a
panic. Sisera leaped down from his chariot and escaped on foot. [16] Then Barak
chased the chariots and the enemy army all the way to Harosheth-haggoyim,
killing all of Sisera's warriors. Not a single one was left alive.
[17] Meanwhile, Sisera ran to the tent of Jael, the wife of Heber the Kenite,
because Heber's family was on friendly terms with King Jabin of Hazor. [18] Jael
went out to meet Sisera and said to him, "Come into my tent, sir. Come in.
Don't be afraid." So he went into her tent, and she covered him with a blanket.
[19] "Please give me some water," he said. "I'm thirsty." So she gave him some
milk from a leather bag and covered him again.
[20] "Stand at the door of the tent," he told her. "If anybody comes and asks
you if there is anyone here, say no."
[21] But when Sisera fell asleep from exhaustion, Jael quietly crept up to
him with a hammer and tent peg in her hand. Then she drove the tent peg
through his temple and into the ground, and so he died.
[22] When Barak came looking for Sisera, Jael went out to meet him. She
said, "Come, and I will show you the man you are looking for." So he fol-
lowed her into the tent and found Sisera lying there dead, with the tent peg
through his temple.
[23] So on that day Israel saw God defeat Jabin, the Canaanite king. [24] And
from that time on Israel became stronger and stronger against King Jabin
until they finally destroyed him.

The Song of Deborah

5 On that day Deborah and Barak son of Abinoam sang this song:

[2] "Israel's leaders took charge,
and the people gladly followed.
Praise the LORD!

[3] "Listen, you kings!
Pay attention, you mighty rulers!
For I will sing to the LORD.
I will make music to the LORD, the God of Israel.

[4] "LORD, when you set out from Seir
and marched across the fields of Edom,
the earth trembled,
and the cloudy skies poured down rain.
[5] The mountains quaked in the presence of the LORD,
the God of Mount Sinai—
in the presence of the LORD,
the God of Israel.

[6] "In the days of Shamgar son of Anath,
and in the days of Jael,

people avoided the main roads,
and travelers stayed on winding pathways.
7 There were few people left in the villages of Israel*—
until Deborah arose as a mother for Israel.
8 When Israel chose new gods,
war erupted at the city gates.
Yet not a shield or spear could be seen
among forty thousand warriors in Israel!
9 My heart is with the commanders of Israel,
with those who volunteered for war.
Praise the LORD!

10 "Consider this, you who ride on fine donkeys,
you who sit on fancy saddle blankets,
and you who walk along the road.
11 Listen to the village musicians*
gathered at the watering holes.
They recount the righteous victories of the LORD
and the victories of his villagers in Israel.
Then the people of the LORD
marched down to the city gates.

12 "Wake up, Deborah, wake up!
Wake up, wake up, and sing a song!
Arise, Barak!
Lead your captives away, son of Abinoam!

13 "Down from Tabor marched the few against the nobles.
The people of the LORD marched down against mighty warriors.
14 They came down from Ephraim—
a land that once belonged to the Amalekites;
they followed you, Benjamin, with your troops.
From Makir the commanders marched down;
from Zebulun came those who carry a commander's staff.
15 The princes of Issachar were with Deborah and Barak.
They followed Barak, rushing into the valley.
But in the tribe of Reuben
there was great indecision.*
16 Why did you sit at home among the sheepfolds—
to hear the shepherds whistle for their flocks?
Yes, in the tribe of Reuben
there was great indecision.
17 Gilead remained east of the Jordan.
And why did Dan stay home?
Asher sat unmoved at the seashore,
remaining in his harbors.
18 But Zebulun risked his life,
as did Naphtali, on the heights of the battlefield.

5:7 The meaning of the Hebrew is uncertain. 5:11 The meaning of the Hebrew is uncertain.
5:15 As in some Hebrew manuscripts and Syriac version, which read *searchings of heart;* Masoretic Text reads *resolve of heart.*

What God is saying to us

19 "The kings of Canaan came and fought,
at Taanach near Megiddo's springs,
but they carried off no silver treasures.
20 The stars fought from heaven.
The stars in their orbits fought against Sisera.
21 The Kishon River swept them away—
that ancient torrent, the Kishon.
March on with courage, my soul!
22 Then the horses' hooves hammered the ground,
the galloping, galloping of Sisera's mighty steeds.
23 'Let the people of Meroz be cursed,' said the angel
of the LORD.
'Let them be utterly cursed,
because they did not come to help the LORD—
to help the LORD against the mighty warriors.'

24 "Most blessed among women is Jael,
the wife of Heber the Kenite.
May she be blessed above all women who live in tents.
25 Sisera asked for water,
and she gave him milk.
In a bowl fit for nobles,
she brought him yogurt.
26 Then with her left hand she reached for a tent peg,
and with her right hand for the workman's hammer.
She struck Sisera with the hammer, crushing his head.
With a shattering blow, she pierced his temples.
27 He sank, he fell,
he lay still at her feet.
And where he sank,
there he died.

28 "From the window Sisera's mother looked out.
Through the window she watched for his return, saying,
'Why is his chariot so long in coming?
Why don't we hear the sound of chariot wheels?'

29 "Her wise women answer,
and she repeats these words to herself:
30 'They must be dividing the captured plunder—
with a woman or two for every man.
There will be colorful robes for Sisera,
and colorful, embroidered robes for me.
Yes, the plunder will include
colorful robes embroidered on both sides.'

31 "LORD, may all your enemies die like Sisera!
But may those who love you rise like the sun in all its power!"

Then there was peace in the land for forty years.

Gideon Becomes Israel's Judge

6 The Israelites did evil in the LORD's sight. So the LORD handed them over
to the Midianites for seven years. 2The Midianites were so cruel that the
Israelites made hiding places for themselves in the mountains, caves, and
strongholds. 3Whenever the Israelites planted their crops, marauders from
Midian, Amalek, and the people of the east would attack Israel, 4camping
in the land and destroying crops as far away as Gaza. They left the Israelites
with nothing to eat, taking all the sheep, goats, cattle, and donkeys. 5These
enemy hordes, coming with their livestock and tents, were as thick as locusts;
they arrived on droves of camels too numerous to count. And they stayed
until the land was stripped bare. 6So Israel was reduced to starvation by the
Midianites. Then the Israelites cried out to the LORD for help.

7When they cried out to the LORD because of Midian, 8the LORD sent a
prophet to the Israelites. He said, "This is what the LORD, the God of Is-
rael, says: I brought you up out of slavery in Egypt. 9I rescued you from the
Egyptians and from all who oppressed you. I drove out your enemies and
gave you their land. 10I told you, 'I am the LORD your God. You must not
worship the gods of the Amorites, in whose land you now live.' But you have
not listened to me."

11Then the angel of the LORD came and sat beneath the great tree at Oph-
rah, which belonged to Joash of the clan of Abiezer. Gideon son of Joash
was threshing wheat at the bottom of a winepress to hide the grain from
the Midianites. 12The angel of the LORD appeared to him and said, "Mighty
hero, the LORD is with you!"

13"Sir," Gideon replied, "if the LORD is with us, why has all this happened
to us? And where are all the miracles our ancestors told us about? Didn't
they say, 'The LORD brought us up out of Egypt'? But now the LORD has
abandoned us and handed us over to the Midianites."

14Then the LORD turned to him and said, "Go with the strength you have,
and rescue Israel from the Midianites. I am sending you!"

15"But Lord," Gideon replied, "how can I rescue Israel? My clan is the
weakest in the whole tribe of Manasseh, and I am the least in my entire
family!"

16The LORD said to him, "I will be with you. And you will destroy the
Midianites as if you were fighting against one man."

17Gideon replied, "If you are truly going to help me, show me a sign to
prove that it is really the LORD speaking to me. 18Don't go away until I come
back and bring my offering to you."

He answered, "I will stay here until you return."

19Gideon hurried home. He cooked a young goat, and with a basket* of
flour he baked some bread without yeast. Then, carrying the meat in a basket
and the broth in a pot, he brought them out and presented them to the angel,
who was under the great tree.

20The angel of God said to him, "Place the meat and the unleavened bread
on this rock, and pour the broth over it." And Gideon did as he was told.
21Then the angel of the LORD touched the meat and bread with the tip of
the staff in his hand, and fire flamed up from the rock and consumed all he
had brought. And the angel of the LORD disappeared.

22When Gideon realized that it was the angel of the LORD, he cried out,

6:19 Hebrew *an ephah* [20 quarts or 22 liters].

Story Arc **6:11**

Gideon

Starting in Judges 6, God raised up Gideon to deliver the people out of the hands of the Midianites. Gideon's story is found in Judges 6-8, and in it, Gideon destroyed his family idols (6:27) because they did not honor God, used a fleece to determine God's will (6:36-37), and defeated 135,000 Midianites with just 300 soldiers. God was faithful to Gideon in a way that was remarkable.

God was patient with Gideon, and it is a good thing. Gideon was not convinced that God really wanted to use him to save Israel. Gideon asked God several times to prove that God indeed wanted to use Gideon (read the story of the fleece in 6:36-40).

God has done the same for us today. His faithfulness is displayed in the life, death, and resurrection of Jesus Christ. In Jesus' death and resurrection, we see the ultimate example of God's faithfulness to us—and this is good news for us!

Judg 9:1-21 ►

Question 6:40

Was Gideon's doubt connected more to God or to himself and the fickle people around him? What do you think? Have you ever experienced this sort of doubt?

"Oh, Sovereign LORD, I'm doomed! I have seen the angel of the LORD face
to face!"
23 "It is all right," the LORD replied. "Do not be afraid. You will not die."
24 And Gideon built an altar to the LORD there and named it Yahweh-Shalom
(which means "the LORD is peace"). The altar remains in Ophrah in the land
of the clan of Abiezer to this day.

25 That night the LORD said to Gideon, "Take the second bull from your
father's herd, the one that is seven years old. Pull down your father's altar
to Baal, and cut down the Asherah pole standing beside it. 26 Then build an
altar to the LORD your God here on this hilltop sanctuary, laying the stones
carefully. Sacrifice the bull as a burnt offering on the altar, using as fuel the
wood of the Asherah pole you cut down."

27 So Gideon took ten of his servants and did as the LORD had commanded.
But he did it at night because he was afraid of the other members of his
father's household and the people of the town.

28 Early the next morning, as the people of the town began to stir, someone
discovered that the altar of Baal had been broken down and that the Asherah
pole beside it had been cut down. In their place a new altar had been built,
and on it were the remains of the bull that had been sacrificed. 29 The people
said to each other, "Who did this?" And after asking around and making a
careful search, they learned that it was Gideon, the son of Joash.

30 "Bring out your son," the men of the town demanded of Joash. "He must
die for destroying the altar of Baal and for cutting down the Asherah pole."

31 But Joash shouted to the mob that confronted him, "Why are you de-
fending Baal? Will you argue his case? Whoever pleads his case will be put
to death by morning! If Baal truly is a god, let him defend himself and de-
stroy the one who broke down his altar!" 32 From then on Gideon was called
Jerub-baal, which means "Let Baal defend himself," because he broke down
Baal's altar.

Gideon Asks for a Sign

33 Soon afterward the armies of Midian, Amalek, and the people of the
east formed an alliance against Israel and crossed the Jordan, camping in
the valley of Jezreel. 34 Then the Spirit of the LORD clothed Gideon with
power. He blew a ram's horn as a call to arms, and the men of the clan of
Abiezer came to him. 35 He also sent messengers throughout Manasseh,
Asher, Zebulun, and Naphtali, summoning their warriors, and all of them
responded.

36 Then Gideon said to God, "If you are truly going to use me to rescue
Israel as you promised, 37 prove it to me in this way. I will put a wool fleece
on the threshing floor tonight. If the fleece is wet with dew in the morning
but the ground is dry, then I will know that you are going to help me rescue
Israel as you promised." 38 And that is just what happened. When Gideon got
up early the next morning, he squeezed the fleece and wrung out a whole
bowlful of water.

39 Then Gideon said to God, "Please don't be angry with me, but let me
make one more request. Let me use the fleece for one more test. This time
let the fleece remain dry while the ground around it is wet with dew." 40 So
that night God did as Gideon asked. The fleece was dry in the morning, but
the ground was covered with dew.

Gideon Defeats the Midianites

7 So Jerub-baal (that is, Gideon) and his army got up early and went as
far as the spring of Harod. The armies of Midian were camped north of
them in the valley near the hill of Moreh. 2 The LORD said to Gideon, "You
have too many warriors with you. If I let all of you fight the Midianites, the
Israelites will boast to me that they saved themselves by their own strength.
3 Therefore, tell the people, 'Whoever is timid or afraid may leave this moun-
tain* and go home.'" So 22,000 of them went home, leaving only 10,000 who
were willing to fight.

4 But the LORD told Gideon, "There are still too many! Bring them down
to the spring, and I will test them to determine who will go with you and
who will not." 5 When Gideon took his warriors down to the water, the
LORD told him, "Divide the men into two groups. In one group put all
those who cup water in their hands and lap it up with their tongues like
dogs. In the other group put all those who kneel down and drink with their
mouths in the stream." 6 Only 300 of the men drank from their hands. All
the others got down on their knees and drank with their mouths in the
stream.

7 The LORD told Gideon, "With these 300 men I will rescue you and give
you victory over the Midianites. Send all the others home." 8 So Gideon col-
lected the provisions and rams' horns of the other warriors and sent them
home. But he kept the 300 men with him.

The Midianite camp was in the valley just below Gideon. 9 That night the
LORD said, "Get up! Go down into the Midianite camp, for I have given you
victory over them! 10 But if you are afraid to attack, go down to the camp with
your servant Purah. 11 Listen to what the Midianites are saying, and you will
be greatly encouraged. Then you will be eager to attack."

So Gideon took Purah and went down to the edge of the enemy camp.
12 The armies of Midian, Amalek, and the people of the east had settled in the
valley like a swarm of locusts. Their camels were like grains of sand on the
seashore—too many to count! 13 Gideon crept up just as a man was telling
his companion about a dream. The man said, "I had this dream, and in my
dream a loaf of barley bread came tumbling down into the Midianite camp.
It hit a tent, turned it over, and knocked it flat!"

14 His companion answered, "Your dream can mean only one thing—God
has given Gideon son of Joash, the Israelite, victory over Midian and all its
allies!"

15 When Gideon heard the dream and its interpretation, he bowed in wor-
ship before the LORD.* Then he returned to the Israelite camp and shouted,
"Get up! For the LORD has given you victory over the Midianite hordes!" 16 He
divided the 300 men into three groups and gave each man a ram's horn and
a clay jar with a torch in it.

17 Then he said to them, "Keep your eyes on me. When I come to the edge
of the camp, do just as I do. 18 As soon as I and those with me blow the rams'
horns, blow your horns, too, all around the entire camp, and shout, 'For the
LORD and for Gideon!'"

19 It was just after midnight,* after the changing of the guard, when Gid-
eon and the 100 men with him reached the edge of the Midianite camp.

7:3 Hebrew *may leave Mount Gilead.* The identity of Mount Gilead is uncertain in this context. It is perhaps used here as another name for Mount Gilboa. 7:15 As in Greek version; Hebrew reads *he bowed.* 7:19 Hebrew *at the beginning of the second watch.*

Make a Difference

8:1-3

Gideon's Patient Words

Gideon found himself in a heated conversation. He was in a discussion with the Ephraimites (the people who fought with Gideon). They were angry and jealous that they had not received the recognition they felt they deserved.

Gideon could have returned their anger with more anger, but instead, he made a wise choice by complimenting them (vv. 2-3), and in doing so, he gave them the recognition they were hoping for. He also pointed the glory straight toward God and not to himself or the Ephraimites.

Proverbs 15:1 brings a good reminder in situations like these: "A gentle answer deflects anger, but harsh words make tempers flare."

Difference Maker

We all find ourselves in situations where it would be very easy to return angry words with more anger. The next time you find yourself in this situation, remember Gideon's example and follow Scripture's lead and, instead of an angry response, give a gentle and wise answer. You never know what God will do!

Suddenly, they blew the rams' horns and broke their clay jars. 20 Then all
three groups blew their horns and broke their jars. They held the blazing
torches in their left hands and the horns in their right hands, and they all
shouted, "A sword for the LORD and for Gideon!"
21 Each man stood at his position around the camp and watched as all the
Midianites rushed around in a panic, shouting as they ran to escape. 22 When
the 300 Israelites blew their rams' horns, the LORD caused the warriors in
the camp to fight against each other with their swords. Those who were
not killed fled to places as far away as Beth-shittah near Zererah and to the
border of Abel-meholah near Tabbath.
23 Then Gideon sent for the warriors of Naphtali, Asher, and Manasseh,
who joined in chasing the army of Midian. 24 Gideon also sent messengers
throughout the hill country of Ephraim, saying, "Come down to attack the
Midianites. Cut them off at the shallow crossings of the Jordan River at
Beth-barah."
So all the men of Ephraim did as they were told. 25 They captured Oreb and
Zeeb, the two Midianite commanders, killing Oreb at the rock of Oreb, and
Zeeb at the winepress of Zeeb. And they continued to chase the Midianites.
Afterward the Israelites brought the heads of Oreb and Zeeb to Gideon, who
was by the Jordan River.

Gideon Kills Zebah and Zalmunna

8 Then the people of Ephraim asked Gideon, "Why have you treated us
this way? Why didn't you send for us when you first went out to fight
the Midianites?" And they argued heatedly with Gideon.
2 But Gideon replied, "What have I accomplished compared to you? Aren't
even the leftover grapes of Ephraim's harvest better than the entire crop of
my little clan of Abiezer? 3 God gave you victory over Oreb and Zeeb, the
commanders of the Midianite army. What have I accomplished compared
to that?" When the men of Ephraim heard Gideon's answer, their anger
subsided.
4 Gideon then crossed the Jordan River with his 300 men, and though
exhausted, they continued to chase the enemy. 5 When they reached Succoth,
Gideon asked the leaders of the town, "Please give my warriors some food.
They are very tired. I am chasing Zebah and Zalmunna, the kings of Midian."
6 But the officials of Succoth replied, "Catch Zebah and Zalmunna first,
and then we will feed your army."
7 So Gideon said, "After the LORD gives me victory over Zebah and Zalmunna,
I will return and tear your flesh with the thorns and briers from
the wilderness."
8 From there Gideon went up to Peniel* and again asked for food, but he
got the same answer. 9 So he said to the people of Peniel, "After I return in
victory, I will tear down this tower."
10 By this time Zebah and Zalmunna were in Karkor with about 15,000
warriors—all that remained of the allied armies of the east, for 120,000 had
already been killed. 11 Gideon circled around by the caravan route east of
Nobah and Jogbehah, taking the Midianite army by surprise. 12 Zebah and
Zalmunna, the two Midianite kings, fled, but Gideon chased them down
and captured all their warriors.

8:8 Hebrew *Penuel,* a variant spelling of Peniel; also in 8:9, 17.

13 After this, Gideon returned from the battle by way of Heres Pass. 14 There
he captured a young man from Succoth and demanded that he write down
the names of all the seventy-seven officials and elders in the town. 15 Gideon
then returned to Succoth and said to the leaders, "Here are Zebah and Zal-
munna. When we were here before, you taunted me, saying, 'Catch Zebah
and Zalmunna first, and then we will feed your exhausted army.'" 16 Then
Gideon took the elders of the town and taught them a lesson, punishing
them with thorns and briers from the wilderness. 17 He also tore down the
tower of Peniel and killed all the men in the town.
18 Then Gideon asked Zebah and Zalmunna, "The men you killed at Ta-
bor—what were they like?"
"Like you," they replied. "They all had the look of a king's son."
19 "They were my brothers, the sons of my own mother!" Gideon ex-
claimed. "As surely as the LORD lives, I wouldn't kill you if you hadn't killed
them."
20 Turning to Jether, his oldest son, he said, "Kill them!" But Jether did not
draw his sword, for he was only a boy and was afraid.
21 Then Zebah and Zalmunna said to Gideon, "Be a man! Kill us yourself!"
So Gideon killed them both and took the royal ornaments from the necks
of their camels.

Gideon's Sacred Ephod

22 Then the Israelites said to Gideon, "Be our ruler! You and your son and
your grandson will be our rulers, for you have rescued us from Midian."
23 But Gideon replied, "I will not rule over you, nor will my son. The LORD
will rule over you! 24 However, I do have one request—that each of you give
me an earring from the plunder you collected from your fallen enemies."
(The enemies, being Ishmaelites, all wore gold earrings.)
25 "Gladly!" they replied. They spread out a cloak, and each one threw in
a gold earring he had gathered from the plunder. 26 The weight of the gold
earrings was forty-three pounds,* not including the royal ornaments and
pendants, the purple clothing worn by the kings of Midian, or the chains
around the necks of their camels.
27 Gideon made a sacred ephod from the gold and put it in Ophrah, his
hometown. But soon all the Israelites prostituted themselves by worshiping
it, and it became a trap for Gideon and his family.
28 That is the story of how the people of Israel defeated Midian, which
never recovered. Throughout the rest of Gideon's lifetime—about forty
years—there was peace in the land.
29 Then Gideon* son of Joash returned home. 30 He had seventy sons born
to him, for he had many wives. 31 He also had a concubine in Shechem, who
gave birth to a son, whom he named Abimelech. 32 Gideon died when he was
very old, and he was buried in the grave of his father, Joash, at Ophrah in the
land of the clan of Abiezer.
33 As soon as Gideon died, the Israelites prostituted themselves by wor-
shiping the images of Baal, making Baal-berith their god. 34 They forgot the
LORD their God, who had rescued them from all their enemies surrounding
them. 35 Nor did they show any loyalty to the family of Jerub-baal (that is,
Gideon), despite all the good he had done for Israel.

Prayer **8:34**

Lord Jesus, my heart breaks for my generation. Don't let us forget you and walk away from you. Restore us to relationship with you. Amen.

8:26 Hebrew *1,700 [shekels]* [19.4 kilograms]. 8:29 Hebrew *Jerub-baal;* see 6:32.

Abimelech Rules over Shechem

9 One day Gideon's* son Abimelech went to Shechem to visit his uncles—
his mother's brothers. He said to them and to the rest of his mother's
family, 2 "Ask the leading citizens of Shechem whether they want to be ruled
by all seventy of Gideon's sons or by one man. And remember that I am your
own flesh and blood!"
3 So Abimelech's uncles gave his message to all the citizens of Shechem
on his behalf. And after listening to this proposal, the people of Shechem
decided in favor of Abimelech because he was their relative. 4 They gave
him seventy silver coins from the temple of Baal-berith, which he used
to hire some reckless troublemakers who agreed to follow him. 5 He went to
his father's home at Ophrah, and there, on one stone, they killed all seventy
of his half brothers, the sons of Gideon.* But the youngest brother, Jotham,
escaped and hid.
6 Then all the leading citizens of Shechem and Beth-millo called a meeting
under the oak beside the pillar* at Shechem and made Abimelech their king.

Jotham's Parable

7 When Jotham heard about this, he climbed to the top of Mount Gerizim
and shouted,

"Listen to me, citizens of Shechem!
Listen to me if you want God to listen to you!
8 Once upon a time the trees decided to choose a king.
First they said to the olive tree,
'Be our king!'
9 But the olive tree refused, saying,
'Should I quit producing the olive oil
that blesses both God and people,
just to wave back and forth over the trees?'

10 "Then they said to the fig tree,
'You be our king!'
11 But the fig tree also refused, saying,
'Should I quit producing my sweet fruit
just to wave back and forth over the trees?'

12 "Then they said to the grapevine,
'You be our king!'
13 But the grapevine also refused, saying,
'Should I quit producing the wine
that cheers both God and people,
just to wave back and forth over the trees?'

14 "Then all the trees finally turned to the thornbush and said,
'Come, you be our king!'
15 And the thornbush replied to the trees,
'If you truly want to make me your king,
come and take shelter in my shade.

9:1 Hebrew *Jerub-baal's* (see 6:32); also in 9:2, 24. 9:5 Hebrew *Jerub-baal* (see 6:32); also in 9:16, 19, 28, 57. 9:6 The meaning of the Hebrew is uncertain.

Story Arc 9:1-21

● Jotham

Jotham had a small but important part of the story in Judges 9. He was the youngest son of Gideon (also referred to as Jerub-Baal). Keep in mind that Gideon had seventy sons according to Scripture. Jotham escaped the wrath of one of his older brothers (Abimelech), and he took a stand against the evil his brother was committing. He delivered what is known as the parable of the trees, which essentially condemned Abimelech and his evil intentions.

There are likely situations in your life when God has called you to take a stand. Can you think of a few? There is no doubt that when we take a stand for God—perhaps it is standing up for a vulnerable person in your life or deciding to have a godly standard in your thoughts, words, and conduct—it can be challenging, maybe even risky. Keep in mind that God is with you even in challenging situations.

Judg 13:24 ►

If not, let fire come out from me
  and devour the cedars of Lebanon.'"

16 Jotham continued, "Now make sure you have acted honorably and in
good faith by making Abimelech your king, and that you have done right
by Gideon and all of his descendants. Have you treated him with the honor
he deserves for all he accomplished? 17 For he fought for you and risked his
life when he rescued you from the Midianites. 18 But today you have revolted
against my father and his descendants, killing his seventy sons on one stone.
And you have chosen his slave woman's son, Abimelech, to be your king just
because he is your relative.
19 "If you have acted honorably and in good faith toward Gideon and his
descendants today, then may you find joy in Abimelech, and may he find
joy in you. 20 But if you have not acted in good faith, then may fire come
out from Abimelech and devour the leading citizens of Shechem and Beth-
millo; and may fire come out from the citizens of Shechem and Beth-millo
and devour Abimelech!"
21 Then Jotham escaped and lived in Beer because he was afraid of his
brother Abimelech.

Shechem Rebels against Abimelech

22 After Abimelech had ruled over Israel for three years, 23 God sent a spirit
that stirred up trouble between Abimelech and the leading citizens of She-
chem, and they revolted. 24 God was punishing Abimelech for murdering
Gideon's seventy sons, and the citizens of Shechem for supporting him in
this treachery of murdering his brothers. 25 The citizens of Shechem set an
ambush for Abimelech on the hilltops and robbed everyone who passed that
way. But someone warned Abimelech about their plot.
26 One day Gaal son of Ebed moved to Shechem with his brothers and
gained the confidence of the leading citizens of Shechem. 27 During the an-
nual harvest festival at Shechem, held in the temple of the local god, the
wine flowed freely, and everyone began cursing Abimelech. 28 "Who is Abim-
elech?" Gaal shouted. "He's not a true son of Shechem,* so why should we
be his servants? He's merely the son of Gideon, and this Zebul is merely his
deputy. Serve the true sons of Hamor, the founder of Shechem. Why should
we serve Abimelech? 29 If I were in charge here, I would get rid of Abimelech.
I would say* to him, 'Get some soldiers, and come out and fight!'"
30 But when Zebul, the leader of the city, heard what Gaal was saying, he
was furious. 31 He sent messengers to Abimelech in Arumah,* telling him,
"Gaal son of Ebed and his brothers have come to live in Shechem, and now
they are inciting the city to rebel against you. 32 Come by night with an army
and hide out in the fields. 33 In the morning, as soon as it is daylight, attack
the city. When Gaal and those who are with him come out against you, you
can do with them as you wish."
34 So Abimelech and all his men went by night and split into four groups,
stationing themselves around Shechem. 35 Gaal was standing at the city gates
when Abimelech and his army came out of hiding. 36 When Gaal saw them,
he said to Zebul, "Look, there are people coming down from the hilltops!"
Zebul replied, "It's just the shadows on the hills that look like men."

9:28 Hebrew *Who is Shechem?* **9:29** As in Greek version; Hebrew reads *And he said.* **9:31** Or *in secret;* Hebrew reads *in Tormah;* compare 9:41.

37 But again Gaal said, "No, people are coming down from the hills.* And
another group is coming down the road past the Diviners' Oak.*"
38 Then Zebul turned on him and asked, "Now where is that big mouth
of yours? Wasn't it you that said, 'Who is Abimelech, and why should we be
his servants?' The men you mocked are right outside the city! Go out and
fight them!"
39 So Gaal led the leading citizens of Shechem into battle against Abim-
elech. 40 But Abimelech chased him, and many of Shechem's men were
wounded and fell along the road as they retreated to the city gate. 41 Abim-
elech returned to Arumah, and Zebul drove Gaal and his brothers out of
Shechem.
42 The next day the people of Shechem went out into the fields to battle.
When Abimelech heard about it, 43 he divided his men into three groups
and set an ambush in the fields. When Abimelech saw the people coming
out of the city, he and his men jumped up from their hiding places and at-
tacked them. 44 Abimelech and his group stormed the city gate to keep the
men of Shechem from getting back in, while Abimelech's other two groups
cut them down in the fields. 45 The battle went on all day before Abimelech
finally captured the city. He killed the people, leveled the city, and scattered
salt all over the ground.
46 When the leading citizens who lived in the tower of Shechem heard
what had happened, they ran and hid in the temple of Baal-berith.* 47 Some-
one reported to Abimelech that the citizens had gathered in the temple,
48 so he led his forces to Mount Zalmon. He took an ax and chopped some
branches from a tree, then put them on his shoulder. "Quick, do as I have
done!" he told his men. 49 So each of them cut down some branches, follow-
ing Abimelech's example. They piled the branches against the walls of the
temple and set them on fire. So all the people who had lived in the tower of
Shechem died—about 1,000 men and women.
50 Then Abimelech attacked the town of Thebez and captured it. 51 But
there was a strong tower inside the town, and all the men and women—the
entire population—fled to it. They barricaded themselves in and climbed up
to the roof of the tower. 52 Abimelech followed them to attack the tower. But
as he prepared to set fire to the entrance, 53 a woman on the roof dropped a
millstone that landed on Abimelech's head and crushed his skull.
54 He quickly said to his young armor bearer, "Draw your sword and kill
me! Don't let it be said that a woman killed Abimelech!" So the young man
ran him through with his sword, and he died. 55 When Abimelech's men saw
that he was dead, they disbanded and returned to their homes.
56 In this way, God punished Abimelech for the evil he had done against
his father by murdering his seventy brothers. 57 God also punished the
men of Shechem for all their evil. So the curse of Jotham son of Gideon
was fulfilled.

Tola Becomes Israel's Judge

10 After Abimelech died, Tola son of Puah, son of Dodo, was the next
person to rescue Israel. He was from the tribe of Issachar but lived
in the town of Shamir in the hill country of Ephraim. 2 He judged Israel for
twenty-three years. When he died, he was buried in Shamir.

9:37a Or *the center of the land.* **9:37b** Hebrew *Elon-meonenim.* **9:46** Hebrew *El-berith,* another name for Baal-berith; compare 9:4.

Jair Becomes Israel's Judge

3 After Tola died, Jair from Gilead judged Israel for twenty-two years. 4 His
thirty sons rode around on thirty donkeys, and they owned thirty towns in
the land of Gilead, which are still called the Towns of Jair.* 5 When Jair died,
he was buried in Kamon.

The Ammonites Oppress Israel

6 Again the Israelites did evil in the LORD's sight. They served the images
of Baal and Ashtoreth, and the gods of Aram, Sidon, Moab, Ammon, and
Philistia. They abandoned the LORD and no longer served him at all. 7 So
the LORD burned with anger against Israel, and he turned them over to the
Philistines and the Ammonites, 8 who began to oppress them that year. For
eighteen years they oppressed all the Israelites east of the Jordan River in
the land of the Amorites (that is, in Gilead). 9 The Ammonites also crossed
to the west side of the Jordan and attacked Judah, Benjamin, and Ephraim.
The Israelites were in great distress. 10 Finally, they cried out to the LORD
for help, saying, "We have sinned against you because we have abandoned
you as our God and have served the images of Baal."
11 The LORD replied, "Did I not rescue you from the Egyptians, the Amo-
rites, the Ammonites, the Philistines, 12 the Sidonians, the Amalekites, and
the Maonites? When they oppressed you, you cried out to me for help, and I
rescued you. 13 Yet you have abandoned me and served other gods. So I will
not rescue you anymore. 14 Go and cry out to the gods you have chosen! Let
them rescue you in your hour of distress!"
15 But the Israelites pleaded with the LORD and said, "We have sinned.
Punish us as you see fit, only rescue us today from our enemies." 16 Then
the Israelites put aside their foreign gods and served the LORD. And he was
grieved by their misery.
17 At that time the armies of Ammon had gathered for war and were
camped in Gilead, and the people of Israel assembled and camped at Mizpah.
18 The leaders of Gilead said to each other, "Whoever attacks the Ammonites
first will become ruler over all the people of Gilead."

Jephthah Becomes Israel's Judge

11 Now Jephthah of Gilead was a great warrior. He was the son of Gil-
ead, but his mother was a prostitute. 2 Gilead's wife also had several
sons, and when these half brothers grew up, they chased Jephthah off the
land. "You will not get any of our father's inheritance," they said, "for you
are the son of a prostitute." 3 So Jephthah fled from his brothers and lived
in the land of Tob. Soon he had a band of worthless rebels following him.
4 At about this time, the Ammonites began their war against Israel. 5 When
the Ammonites attacked, the elders of Gilead sent for Jephthah in the land
of Tob. 6 The elders said, "Come and be our commander! Help us fight the
Ammonites!"
7 But Jephthah said to them, "Aren't you the ones who hated me and drove
me from my father's house? Why do you come to me now when you're in
trouble?"
8 "Because we need you," the elders replied. "If you lead us in battle against
the Ammonites, we will make you ruler over all the people of Gilead."

Question 10:16

God "was grieved by their misery." Here we see the *character* of God come out. This is an example of a holy emotion that caused God to act in such a way that the people were saved. Have you ever been in a situation where you were filled with compassion for someone else and *had* to act?

10:4 Hebrew *Havvoth-jair.*

Prayer 11:23

God, help me see the ways you are moving around me and join you in your work in the world. Amen.

9 Jephthah said to the elders, "Let me get this straight. If I come with you and if the LORD gives me victory over the Ammonites, will you really make me ruler over all the people?"

10 "The LORD is our witness," the elders replied. "We promise to do whatever you say."

11 So Jephthah went with the elders of Gilead, and the people made him their ruler and commander of the army. At Mizpah, in the presence of the LORD, Jephthah repeated what he had said to the elders.

12 Then Jephthah sent messengers to the king of Ammon, asking, "Why have you come out to fight against my land?"

13 The king of Ammon answered Jephthah's messengers, "When the Israelites came out of Egypt, they stole my land from the Arnon River to the Jabbok River and all the way to the Jordan. Now then, give back the land peaceably."

14 Jephthah sent this message back to the Ammonite king:

15 "This is what Jephthah says: Israel did not steal any land from Moab
or Ammon. 16 When the people of Israel arrived at Kadesh on their
journey from Egypt after crossing the Red Sea,* 17 they sent messengers
to the king of Edom asking for permission to pass through his land. But their request was denied. Then they asked the king of Moab for similar permission, but he wouldn't let them pass through either. So the people of Israel stayed in Kadesh.

18 "Finally, they went around Edom and Moab through the wilderness. They traveled along Moab's eastern border and camped on the other side of the Arnon River. But they never once crossed the Arnon River into Moab, for the Arnon was the border of Moab.

19 "Then Israel sent messengers to King Sihon of the Amorites, who
ruled from Heshbon, asking for permission to cross through his land
to get to their destination. 20 But King Sihon didn't trust Israel to pass
through his land. Instead, he mobilized his army at Jahaz and attacked
them. 21 But the LORD, the God of Israel, gave his people victory over
King Sihon. So Israel took control of all the land of the Amorites, who
lived in that region, 22 from the Arnon River to the Jabbok River, and
from the eastern wilderness to the Jordan.

23 "So you see, it was the LORD, the God of Israel, who took away
the land from the Amorites and gave it to Israel. Why, then, should
we give it back to you? 24 You keep whatever your god Chemosh gives
you, and we will keep whatever the LORD our God gives us. 25 Are
you any better than Balak son of Zippor, king of Moab? Did he try to make a case against Israel for disputed land? Did he go to war against them?

26 "Israel has been living here for 300 years, inhabiting Heshbon and
its surrounding settlements, all the way to Aroer and its settlements,
and in all the towns along the Arnon River. Why have you made no
effort to recover it before now? 27 Therefore, I have not sinned against
you. Rather, you have wronged me by attacking me. Let the LORD, who is judge, decide today which of us is right—Israel or Ammon."

28 But the king of Ammon paid no attention to Jephthah's message.

11:16 Hebrew *sea of reeds.*

Jephthah's Vow

29 At that time the Spirit of the LORD came upon Jephthah, and he went
throughout the land of Gilead and Manasseh, including Mizpah in Gilead,
and from there he led an army against the Ammonites. 30 And Jephthah made
a vow to the LORD. He said, "If you give me victory over the Ammonites, 31 I
will give to the LORD whatever comes out of my house to meet me when I
return in triumph. I will sacrifice it as a burnt offering."

32 So Jephthah led his army against the Ammonites, and the LORD gave
him victory. 33 He crushed the Ammonites, devastating about twenty towns
from Aroer to an area near Minnith and as far away as Abel-keramim. In this
way Israel defeated the Ammonites.

34 When Jephthah returned home to Mizpah, his daughter came out to
meet him, playing on a tambourine and dancing for joy. She was his one and
only child; he had no other sons or daughters. 35 When he saw her, he tore his
clothes in anguish. "Oh, my daughter!" he cried out. "You have completely
destroyed me! You've brought disaster on me! For I have made a vow to the
LORD, and I cannot take it back."

36 And she said, "Father, if you have made a vow to the LORD, you must
do to me what you have vowed, for the LORD has given you a great victory
over your enemies, the Ammonites. 37 But first let me do this one thing: Let
me go up and roam in the hills and weep with my friends for two months,
because I will die a virgin."

38 "You may go," Jephthah said. And he sent her away for two months. She
and her friends went into the hills and wept because she would never have
children. 39 When she returned home, her father kept the vow he had made,
and she died a virgin.

So it has become a custom in Israel 40 for young Israelite women to go away
for four days each year to lament the fate of Jephthah's daughter.

Ephraim Fights with Jephthah

12 Then the people of Ephraim mobilized an army and crossed over the
Jordan River to Zaphon. They sent this message to Jephthah: "Why
didn't you call for us to help you fight against the Ammonites? We are going
to burn down your house with you in it!"

2 Jephthah replied, "I summoned you at the beginning of the dispute, but
you refused to come! You failed to help us in our struggle against Ammon.
3 So when I realized you weren't coming, I risked my life and went to battle
without you, and the LORD gave me victory over the Ammonites. So why
have you now come to fight me?"

4 The people of Ephraim responded, "You men of Gilead are nothing more
than fugitives from Ephraim and Manasseh." So Jephthah gathered all the
men of Gilead and attacked the men of Ephraim and defeated them.

5 Jephthah captured the shallow crossings of the Jordan River, and when-
ever a fugitive from Ephraim tried to go back across, the men of Gilead would
challenge him. "Are you a member of the tribe of Ephraim?" they would ask.
If the man said, "No, I'm not," 6 they would tell him to say "Shibboleth." If he
was from Ephraim, he would say "Sibboleth," because people from Ephraim
cannot pronounce the word correctly. Then they would take him and kill
him at the shallow crossings of the Jordan. In all, 42,000 Ephraimites were
killed at that time.

Make a Difference 12:7

A Tale of Two Lists

The curious story of Jephthah began with God calling him to rescue the people of Israel. Jephthah was known as a "great warrior" (11:1) and a wise military strategist. His greatest moment happened when he called upon the Lord to bless him. The Lord honored his request and gave him supernatural strength. That is amazing!

Despite this, the story of Jephthah was not all good. He made a rash vow to the Lord, which would eventually have tragic consequences (11:30-31, 34-35). His pride would lead to the death of his daughter and the people turning from God.

Pride can get in the way of a lot of good things in our lives and, eventually, can separate us from following God's will. The message of Scripture is clear for all of us: seek to follow the Lord in all you do—always pointing toward God's glory instead of your own.

Difference Maker

Make a list of the victories God has given you in life and another list of big mistakes you have made. Ask God to refine you and make the victory list more significant than the mistake list.

Question 12:8-15

Which one of these three difference makers would you have most liked to meet: Ibzan (v. 8), Elon (v. 11), or Abdon (v. 13)?

7Jephthah judged Israel for six years. When he died, he was buried in one
of the towns of Gilead.

Ibzan Becomes Israel's Judge

8After Jephthah died, Ibzan from Bethlehem judged Israel. 9He had thirty
sons and thirty daughters. He sent his daughters to marry men outside his
clan, and he brought in thirty young women from outside his clan to marry
his sons. Ibzan judged Israel for seven years. 10When he died, he was buried
at Bethlehem.

Elon Becomes Israel's Judge

11After Ibzan died, Elon from the tribe of Zebulun judged Israel for ten years.
12When he died, he was buried at Aijalon in Zebulun.

Abdon Becomes Israel's Judge

13After Elon died, Abdon son of Hillel, from Pirathon, judged Israel. 14He had
forty sons and thirty grandsons, who rode on seventy donkeys. He judged
Israel for eight years. 15When he died, he was buried at Pirathon in Ephraim,
in the hill country of the Amalekites.

The Birth of Samson

13 Again the Israelites did evil in the LORD's sight, so the LORD handed
them over to the Philistines, who oppressed them for forty years.
2In those days a man named Manoah from the tribe of Dan lived in the town
of Zorah. His wife was unable to become pregnant, and they had no children.
3The angel of the LORD appeared to Manoah's wife and said, "Even though
you have been unable to have children, you will soon become pregnant and
give birth to a son. 4So be careful; you must not drink wine or any other alco-
holic drink nor eat any forbidden food.* 5You will become pregnant and give
birth to a son, and his hair must never be cut. For he will be dedicated to God
as a Nazirite from birth. He will begin to rescue Israel from the Philistines."
6The woman ran and told her husband, "A man of God appeared to me!
He looked like one of God's angels, terrifying to see. I didn't ask where he
was from, and he didn't tell me his name. 7But he told me, 'You will become
pregnant and give birth to a son. You must not drink wine or any other al-
coholic drink nor eat any forbidden food. For your son will be dedicated to
God as a Nazirite from the moment of his birth until the day of his death.'"
8Then Manoah prayed to the LORD, saying, "Lord, please let the man of
God come back to us again and give us more instructions about this son
who is to be born."
9God answered Manoah's prayer, and the angel of God appeared once
again to his wife as she was sitting in the field. But her husband, Manoah,
was not with her. 10So she quickly ran and told her husband, "The man who
appeared to me the other day is here again!"
11Manoah ran back with his wife and asked, "Are you the man who spoke
to my wife the other day?"
"Yes," he replied, "I am."
12So Manoah asked him, "When your words come true, what kind of rules
should govern the boy's life and work?"

13:4 Hebrew *any unclean thing;* also in 13:7, 14.

13 The angel of the LORD replied, "Be sure your wife follows the instructions I gave her. 14 She must not eat grapes or raisins, drink wine or any other alcoholic drink, or eat any forbidden food."

15 Then Manoah said to the angel of the LORD, "Please stay here until we can prepare a young goat for you to eat."

16 "I will stay," the angel of the LORD replied, "but I will not eat anything. However, you may prepare a burnt offering as a sacrifice to the LORD." (Manoah didn't realize it was the angel of the LORD.)

17 Then Manoah asked the angel of the LORD, "What is your name? For when all this comes true, we want to honor you."

18 "Why do you ask my name?" the angel of the LORD replied. "It is too wonderful for you to understand."

19 Then Manoah took a young goat and a grain offering and offered it on a rock as a sacrifice to the LORD. And as Manoah and his wife watched, the LORD did an amazing thing. 20 As the flames from the altar shot up toward the sky, the angel of the LORD ascended in the fire. When Manoah and his wife saw this, they fell with their faces to the ground.

21 The angel did not appear again to Manoah and his wife. Manoah finally realized it was the angel of the LORD, 22 and he said to his wife, "We will certainly die, for we have seen God!"

23 But his wife said, "If the LORD were going to kill us, he wouldn't have accepted our burnt offering and grain offering. He wouldn't have appeared to us and told us this wonderful thing and done these miracles."

24 When her son was born, she named him Samson. And the LORD blessed him as he grew up. 25 And the Spirit of the LORD began to stir him while he lived in Mahaneh-dan, which is located between the towns of Zorah and Eshtaol.

Samson's Riddle

14 One day when Samson was in Timnah, one of the Philistine women caught his eye. 2 When he returned home, he told his father and mother, "A young Philistine woman in Timnah caught my eye. I want to marry her. Get her for me."

3 His father and mother objected. "Isn't there even one woman in our tribe or among all the Israelites you could marry?" they asked. "Why must you go to the pagan Philistines to find a wife?"

But Samson told his father, "Get her for me! She looks good to me." 4 His father and mother didn't realize the LORD was at work in this, creating an opportunity to work against the Philistines, who ruled over Israel at that time.

5 As Samson and his parents were going down to Timnah, a young lion suddenly attacked Samson near the vineyards of Timnah. 6 At that moment the Spirit of the LORD came powerfully upon him, and he ripped the lion's jaws apart with his bare hands. He did it as easily as if it were a young goat. But he didn't tell his father or mother about it. 7 When Samson arrived in Timnah, he talked with the woman and was very pleased with her.

8 Later, when he returned to Timnah for the wedding, he turned off the path to look at the carcass of the lion. And he found that a swarm of bees had made some honey in the carcass. 9 He scooped some of the honey into his hands and ate it along the way. He also gave some to his father and mother,

Question 14:1

Samson allowed a distraction to catch his eye. In this case, it was a Philistine woman who later in the narrative will lead Samson away from God's plan. We all have distractions that come at us every day in many ways. What catches your eye that leads you away from God?

Story Arc 13:24

Samson → Rescuer!

The story of Samson is one of the most well-known stories in the Bible. When we read the story of Samson in Judges 13-16, we find out that Samson was a Nazarite, killed a lion with his bare hands, killed one thousand Philistines with a donkey's jawbone, tore off an iron gate, was betrayed by Delilah, and killed thousands of Philistines in one last mighty act. Oh, and he was very, very strong—supernaturally strong!

Another very interesting fact about Samson is that his life, in many ways, was a precursor to Jesus. They both have so much in common: Samson's birth was announced by an angel (Judges 13:3) just like Jesus' birth was foretold by an angel (Luke 1); Samson's mother was not able to have children yet became miraculously pregnant with him (Judges 13:24) similar to the way Jesus was born to a virgin mother (Luke 1); Samson was a Nazarite, and Jesus was from Nazareth; and Samson was a savior of Israel similar to how Jesus was called to save God's people (Matthew 1).

Ruth 2:1-23 ►

and they ate it. But he didn't tell them he had taken the honey from the
carcass of the lion.
10 As his father was making final arrangements for the marriage, Samson
threw a party at Timnah, as was the custom for elite young men. 11 When the
bride's parents* saw him, they selected thirty young men from the town to
be his companions.
12 Samson said to them, "Let me tell you a riddle. If you solve my riddle
during these seven days of the celebration, I will give you thirty fine
linen robes and thirty sets of festive clothing. 13 But if you can't solve it,
then you must give me thirty fine linen robes and thirty sets of festive
clothing."

"All right," they agreed, "let's hear your riddle."
14 So he said:

"Out of the one who eats came something to eat;
  out of the strong came something sweet."

Three days later they were still trying to figure it out. 15 On the fourth* day
they said to Samson's wife, "Entice your husband to explain the riddle for
us, or we will burn down your father's house with you in it. Did you invite
us to this party just to make us poor?"
16 So Samson's wife came to him in tears and said, "You don't love me;
you hate me! You have given my people a riddle, but you haven't told me
the answer."

"I haven't even given the answer to my father or mother," he replied. "Why
should I tell you?" 17 So she cried whenever she was with him and kept it up
for the rest of the celebration. At last, on the seventh day he told her the an-
swer because she was tormenting him with her nagging. Then she explained
the riddle to the young men.
18 So before sunset of the seventh day, the men of the town came to Sam-
son with their answer:

"What is sweeter than honey?
  What is stronger than a lion?"

Samson replied, "If you hadn't plowed with my heifer, you wouldn't have
solved my riddle!"
19 Then the Spirit of the LORD came powerfully upon him. He went down
to the town of Ashkelon, killed thirty men, took their belongings, and gave
their clothing to the men who had solved his riddle. But Samson was furious
about what had happened, and he went back home to live with his father
and mother. 20 So his wife was given in marriage to the man who had been
Samson's best man at the wedding.

Samson's Vengeance on the Philistines

15 Later on, during the wheat harvest, Samson took a young goat as a
present to his wife. He said, "I'm going into my wife's room to sleep
with her," but her father wouldn't let him in.
2 "I truly thought you must hate her," her father explained, "so I gave her

14:11 Hebrew *they.* 14:15 As in Greek version; Hebrew reads *seventh.*

in marriage to your best man. But look, her younger sister is even more beau-
tiful than she is. Marry her instead."
3 Samson said, "This time I cannot be blamed for everything I am going to
do to you Philistines." 4 Then he went out and caught 300 foxes. He tied their
tails together in pairs, and he fastened a torch to each pair of tails. 5 Then he
lit the torches and let the foxes run through the grain fields of the Philistines.
He burned all their grain to the ground, including the sheaves and the uncut
grain. He also destroyed their vineyards and olive groves.
6 "Who did this?" the Philistines demanded.
"Samson," was the reply, "because his father-in-law from Timnah gave
Samson's wife to be married to his best man." So the Philistines went and
got the woman and her father and burned them to death.
7 "Because you did this," Samson vowed, "I won't rest until I take my re-
venge on you!" 8 So he attacked the Philistines with great fury and killed
many of them. Then he went to live in a cave in the rock of Etam.
9 The Philistines retaliated by setting up camp in Judah and spreading
out near the town of Lehi. 10 The men of Judah asked the Philistines, "Why
are you attacking us?"
The Philistines replied, "We've come to capture Samson. We've come to
pay him back for what he did to us."
11 So 3,000 men of Judah went down to get Samson at the cave in the rock
of Etam. They said to Samson, "Don't you realize the Philistines rule over
us? What are you doing to us?"
But Samson replied, "I only did to them what they did to me."
12 But the men of Judah told him, "We have come to tie you up and hand
you over to the Philistines."
"All right," Samson said. "But promise that you won't kill me yourselves."
13 "We will only tie you up and hand you over to the Philistines," they
replied. "We won't kill you." So they tied him up with two new ropes and
brought him up from the rock.
14 As Samson arrived at Lehi, the Philistines came shouting in triumph.
But the Spirit of the LORD came powerfully upon Samson, and he snapped
the ropes on his arms as if they were burnt strands of flax, and they fell
from his wrists. 15 Then he found the jawbone of a recently killed donkey.
He picked it up and killed 1,000 Philistines with it. 16 Then Samson said,

"With the jawbone of a donkey,
  I've piled them in heaps!
With the jawbone of a donkey,
  I've killed a thousand men!"

17 When he finished his boasting, he threw away the jawbone; and the place
was named Jawbone Hill.*
18 Samson was now very thirsty, and he cried out to the LORD, "You have
accomplished this great victory by the strength of your servant. Must I now
die of thirst and fall into the hands of these pagans?" 19 So God caused water
to gush out of a hollow in the ground at Lehi, and Samson was revived as he
drank. Then he named that place "The Spring of the One Who Cried Out,"*
and it is still in Lehi to this day.

Make a Difference 15:16

Samson, the Poet?

Interestingly, there are two times when the brutish Samson tried his hand at poetry (14:14 and 15:16), and in both cases, there is much to be desired by his verse. Still, we have to applaud Samson for trying to give in to his creative side, right? (Even if what he was saying is quite graphic!)

What sort of creative expressions do you enjoy? Is it poetry, art, music, or other activities? The difference-maker moment comes when we do our best to honor God with our gifts (or even lack of gifts) in everything we do. Enjoy giving these things to God.

Difference Maker

Do something artistic today. Think outside the box of what you would normally do and create. Unlike Samson, though, use the talent and ideas God gives you to encourage people rather than mess with them.

15:17 Hebrew *Ramath-lehi.* **15:19** Hebrew *En-hakkore.*

20 Samson judged Israel for twenty years during the period when the Philistines dominated the land.

Samson Carries Away Gaza's Gates

16 One day Samson went to the Philistine town of Gaza and spent the night with a prostitute. 2 Word soon spread* that Samson was there, so the men of Gaza gathered together and waited all night at the town gates. They kept quiet during the night, saying to themselves, "When the light of morning comes, we will kill him."

3 But Samson stayed in bed only until midnight. Then he got up, took hold of the doors of the town gate, including the two posts, and lifted them up, bar and all. He put them on his shoulders and carried them all the way to the top of the hill across from Hebron.

Samson and Delilah

4 Some time later Samson fell in love with a woman named Delilah, who lived in the valley of Sorek. 5 The rulers of the Philistines went to her and said, "Entice Samson to tell you what makes him so strong and how he can be overpowered and tied up securely. Then each of us will give you 1,100 pieces* of silver."

6 So Delilah said to Samson, "Please tell me what makes you so strong and what it would take to tie you up securely."

7 Samson replied, "If I were tied up with seven new bowstrings that have not yet been dried, I would become as weak as anyone else."

8 So the Philistine rulers brought Delilah seven new bowstrings, and she tied Samson up with them. 9 She had hidden some men in one of the inner rooms of her house, and she cried out, "Samson! The Philistines have come to capture you!" But Samson snapped the bowstrings as a piece of string snaps when it is burned by a fire. So the secret of his strength was not discovered.

10 Afterward Delilah said to him, "You've been making fun of me and telling me lies! Now please tell me how you can be tied up securely."

11 Samson replied, "If I were tied up with brand-new ropes that had never been used, I would become as weak as anyone else."

12 So Delilah took new ropes and tied him up with them. The men were hiding in the inner room as before, and again Delilah cried out, "Samson! The Philistines have come to capture you!" But again Samson snapped the ropes from his arms as if they were thread.

13 Then Delilah said, "You've been making fun of me and telling me lies! Now tell me how you can be tied up securely."

Samson replied, "If you were to weave the seven braids of my hair into the fabric on your loom and tighten it with the loom shuttle, I would become as weak as anyone else."

So while he slept, Delilah wove the seven braids of his hair into the fabric. 14 Then she tightened it with the loom shuttle.* Again she cried out, "Samson! The Philistines have come to capture you!" But Samson woke up, pulled back the loom shuttle, and yanked his hair away from the loom and the fabric.

16:2 As in Greek and Syriac versions and Latin Vulgate; Hebrew lacks *Word soon spread.* **16:5** Hebrew *1,100 [shekels],* about 28 pounds or 12.5 kilograms in weight. **16:13-14** As in Greek version and Latin Vulgate; Hebrew lacks *I would become as weak as anyone else. / So while he slept, Delilah wove the seven braids of his hair into the fabric. 14 Then she tightened it with the loom shuttle.*

[15]Then Delilah pouted, "How can you tell me, 'I love you,' when you don't share your secrets with me? You've made fun of me three times now, and you still haven't told me what makes you so strong!" [16]She tormented him with her nagging day after day until he was sick to death of it.

[17]Finally, Samson shared his secret with her. "My hair has never been cut," he confessed, "for I was dedicated to God as a Nazirite from birth. If my head were shaved, my strength would leave me, and I would become as weak as anyone else."

[18]Delilah realized he had finally told her the truth, so she sent for the Philistine rulers. "Come back one more time," she said, "for he has finally told me his secret." So the Philistine rulers returned with the money in their hands. [19]Delilah lulled Samson to sleep with his head in her lap, and then she called in a man to shave off the seven locks of his hair. In this way she began to bring him down,* and his strength left him.

[20]Then she cried out, "Samson! The Philistines have come to capture you!"

When he woke up, he thought, "I will do as before and shake myself free." But he didn't realize the LORD had left him.

[21]So the Philistines captured him and gouged out his eyes. They took him to Gaza, where he was bound with bronze chains and forced to grind grain in the prison.

[22]But before long, his hair began to grow back.

Samson's Final Victory

[23]The Philistine rulers held a great festival, offering sacrifices and praising their god, Dagon. They said, "Our god has given us victory over our enemy Samson!"

[24]When the people saw him, they praised their god, saying, "Our god has delivered our enemy to us! The one who killed so many of us is now in our power!"

[25]Half drunk by now, the people demanded, "Bring out Samson so he can amuse us!" So he was brought from the prison to amuse them, and they had him stand between the pillars supporting the roof.

[26]Samson said to the young servant who was leading him by the hand, "Place my hands against the pillars that hold up the temple. I want to rest against them." [27]Now the temple was completely filled with people. All the Philistine rulers were there, and there were about 3,000 men and women on the roof who were watching as Samson amused them.

[28]Then Samson prayed to the LORD, "Sovereign LORD, remember me again. O God, please strengthen me just one more time. With one blow let me pay back the Philistines for the loss of my two eyes." [29]Then Samson put his hands on the two center pillars that held up the temple. Pushing against them with both hands, [30]he prayed, "Let me die with the Philistines." And the temple crashed down on the Philistine rulers and all the people. So he killed more people when he died than he had during his entire lifetime.

[31]Later his brothers and other relatives went down to get his body. They took him back home and buried him between Zorah and Eshtaol, where his father, Manoah, was buried. Samson had judged Israel for twenty years.

16:19 Or *she began to torment him.* Greek version reads *He began to grow weak.*

Make a Difference

16:28

Samson, the Dysfunctional Hero

Samson lived a life that was at times impulsive and irresponsible. The story of his life is filled with dysfunction, yet he was still considered a faithful champion (Hebrews 11:32).

There are many lessons from the life of Samson that we could examine, but at the very least, we see how God used a struggling person to bring about God's glory in the world. This is good news for those of us who have also fallen short and struggle at times (like Samson) to live holy lives. Perfection is not necessarily required for God to use us (although that would be nice). Obedience and faithfulness are the prerequisites.

Difference Maker

What are some areas in your life that you need to turn over to God in an act of obedience? Pray right now and give those things to God.

Micah's Idols

17 There was a man named Micah, who lived in the hill country of
Ephraim. 2One day he said to his mother, "I heard you place a curse
on the person who stole 1,100 pieces* of silver from you. Well, I have the
money. I was the one who took it."
"The LORD bless you for admitting it," his mother replied. 3He returned
the money to her, and she said, "I now dedicate these silver coins to the LORD.
In honor of my son, I will have an image carved and an idol cast."
4So when he returned the money to his mother, she took 200 silver coins
and gave them to a silversmith, who made them into an image and an idol.
And these were placed in Micah's house. 5Micah set up a shrine for the idol,
and he made a sacred ephod and some household idols. Then he installed
one of his sons as his personal priest.
6In those days Israel had no king; all the people did whatever seemed
right in their own eyes.
7One day a young Levite, who had been living in Bethlehem in Judah, ar-
rived in that area. 8He had left Bethlehem in search of another place to live,
and as he traveled, he came to the hill country of Ephraim. He happened to
stop at Micah's house as he was traveling through. 9"Where are you from?"
Micah asked him.
He replied, "I am a Levite from Bethlehem in Judah, and I am looking
for a place to live."
10"Stay here with me," Micah said, "and you can be a father and priest to
me. I will give you ten pieces of silver* a year, plus a change of clothes and
your food." 11The Levite agreed to this, and the young man became like one
of Micah's sons.
12So Micah installed the Levite as his personal priest, and he lived in Mi-
cah's house. 13"I know the LORD will bless me now," Micah said, "because I
have a Levite serving as my priest."

Idolatry in the Tribe of Dan

18 Now in those days Israel had no king. And the tribe of Dan was
trying to find a place where they could settle, for they had not yet
moved into the land assigned to them when the land was divided among
the tribes of Israel. 2So the men of Dan chose from their clans five capable
warriors from the towns of Zorah and Eshtaol to scout out a land for them
to settle in.
When these warriors arrived in the hill country of Ephraim, they came
to Micah's house and spent the night there. 3While at Micah's house, they
recognized the young Levite's accent, so they went over and asked him, "Who
brought you here, and what are you doing in this place? Why are you here?"
4He told them about his agreement with Micah and that he had been hired
as Micah's personal priest.
5Then they said, "Ask God whether or not our journey will be successful."
6"Go in peace," the priest replied. "For the LORD is watching over your
journey."
7So the five men went on to the town of Laish, where they noticed the
people living carefree lives, like the Sidonians; they were peaceful and secure.*

17:2 Hebrew *1,100 [shekels]*, about 28 pounds or 12.5 kilograms in weight. 17:10 Hebrew *10 [shekels] of silver*, about 4 ounces or 114 grams in weight. 18:7 The meaning of the Hebrew is uncertain.

Make a Difference

17:1–6

The Absent Judges

For the rest of the book of Judges, the "judges" are absent. They're missing in action. Instead of rescuers, this final section names the people who led the Israelites further and further away from God—especially into painful idolatry (worshiping other gods) and, eventually, civil war.

Is it so different in our world today? There is a repeated phrase used in this final section: "All the people did whatever seemed right in their own eyes" (17:6; 21:25). We could certainly apply this phrase to much of humanity across the world even now.

Look, we need a King. We need a Savior. We need our God—and despite our rebellious nature, he has blessed us with the gift of his Son, Jesus Christ, who invites each of us into a relationship that is filled with an abundant life (John 10:10).

Difference Maker

Choose to follow Christ. Learn the painful lessons from the people of Israel during the time of the Judges and, instead, make God your King and let him rule your life. Turn to the back of this Bible and pray through the section on "How to Accept Jesus as Your Lord and Savior."

Prayer 17:6

God, help me to do what is right in your eyes—even when things are difficult. Help me, God, especially in times when I lack a strong person to guide me on earth. Help me to follow you. Amen.

The people were also wealthy because their land was very fertile. And they
lived a great distance from Sidon and had no allies nearby.
8 When the men returned to Zorah and Eshtaol, their relatives asked them,
"What did you find?"
9 The men replied, "Come on, let's attack them! We have seen the land,
and it is very good. What are you waiting for? Don't hesitate to go and take
possession of it. 10 When you get there, you will find the people living care-
free lives. God has given us a spacious and fertile land, lacking in nothing!"
11 So 600 men from the tribe of Dan, armed with weapons of war, set out
from Zorah and Eshtaol. 12 They camped at a place west of Kiriath-jearim
in Judah, which is called Mahaneh-dan* to this day. 13 Then they went on
from there into the hill country of Ephraim and came to the house of Micah.
14 The five men who had scouted out the land around Laish explained to
the others, "These buildings contain a sacred ephod, as well as some house-
hold idols, a carved image, and a cast idol. What do you think you should
do?" 15 Then the five men turned off the road and went over to Micah's house,
where the young Levite lived, and greeted him kindly. 16 As the 600 armed
warriors from the tribe of Dan stood at the entrance of the gate, 17 the five
scouts entered the shrine and removed the carved image, the sacred ephod,
the household idols, and the cast idol. Meanwhile, the priest was standing
at the gate with the 600 armed warriors.
18 When the priest saw the men carrying all the sacred objects out of Mi-
cah's shrine, he said, "What are you doing?"
19 "Be quiet and come with us," they said. "Be a father and priest to all of
us. Isn't it better to be a priest for an entire tribe and clan of Israel than for
the household of just one man?"
20 The young priest was quite happy to go with them, so he took along the
sacred ephod, the household idols, and the carved image. 21 They turned and
started on their way again, placing their children, livestock, and possessions
in front of them.
22 When the people from the tribe of Dan were quite a distance from
Micah's house, the people who lived near Micah came chasing after them.
23 They were shouting as they caught up with them. The men of Dan turned
around and said to Micah, "What's the matter? Why have you called these
men together and chased after us like this?"
24 "What do you mean, 'What's the matter?'" Micah replied. "You've taken
away all the gods I have made, and my priest, and I have nothing left!"
25 The men of Dan said, "Watch what you say! There are some short-
tempered men around here who might get angry and kill you and your fam-
ily." 26 So the men of Dan continued on their way. When Micah saw that there
were too many of them for him to attack, he turned around and went home.
27 Then, with Micah's idols and his priest, the men of Dan came to the
town of Laish, whose people were peaceful and secure. They attacked with
swords and burned the town to the ground. 28 There was no one to rescue the
people, for they lived a great distance from Sidon and had no allies nearby.
This happened in the valley near Beth-rehob.

Then the people of the tribe of Dan rebuilt the town and lived there.
29 They renamed the town Dan after their ancestor, Israel's son, but it had
originally been called Laish.

18:12 *Mahaneh-dan* means "the camp of Dan."

30 Then they set up the carved image, and they appointed Jonathan son of
Gershom, son of Moses,* as their priest. This family continued as priests for
the tribe of Dan until the Exile. 31 So Micah's carved image was worshiped
by the tribe of Dan as long as the Tabernacle of God remained at Shiloh.

The Levite and His Concubine

19 Now in those days Israel had no king. There was a man from the
tribe of Levi living in a remote area of the hill country of Ephraim.
One day he brought home a woman from Bethlehem in Judah to be his con-
cubine. 2 But she became angry with him* and returned to her father's home
in Bethlehem.

After about four months, 3 her husband set out for Bethlehem to speak
personally to her and persuade her to come back. He took with him a servant
and a pair of donkeys. When he arrived at* her father's house, her father saw
him and welcomed him. 4 Her father urged him to stay awhile, so he stayed
three days, eating, drinking, and sleeping there.

5 On the fourth day the man was up early, ready to leave, but the woman's
father said to his son-in-law, "Have something to eat before you go." 6 So the
two men sat down together and had something to eat and drink. Then the
woman's father said, "Please stay another night and enjoy yourself." 7 The
man got up to leave, but his father-in-law kept urging him to stay, so he
finally gave in and stayed the night.

8 On the morning of the fifth day he was up early again, ready to leave, and
again the woman's father said, "Have something to eat; then you can leave
later this afternoon." So they had another day of feasting. 9 Later, as the man
and his concubine and servant were preparing to leave, his father-in-law
said, "Look, it's almost evening. Stay the night and enjoy yourself. Tomorrow
you can get up early and be on your way."

10 But this time the man was determined to leave. So he took his two
saddled donkeys and his concubine and headed in the direction of Jebus
(that is, Jerusalem). 11 It was late in the day when they neared Jebus, and the
man's servant said to him, "Let's stop at this Jebusite town and spend the
night there."

12 "No," his master said, "we can't stay in this foreign town where there
are no Israelites. Instead, we will go on to Gibeah. 13 Come on, let's try to get
as far as Gibeah or Ramah, and we'll spend the night in one of those towns."
14 So they went on. The sun was setting as they came to Gibeah, a town in the
land of Benjamin, 15 so they stopped there to spend the night. They rested in
the town square, but no one took them in for the night.

16 That evening an old man came home from his work in the fields. He
was from the hill country of Ephraim, but he was living in Gibeah, where
the people were from the tribe of Benjamin. 17 When he saw the travelers
sitting in the town square, he asked them where they were from and where
they were going.

18 "We have been in Bethlehem in Judah," the man replied. "We are on
our way to a remote area in the hill country of Ephraim, which is my home.
I traveled to Bethlehem, and now I'm returning home.* But no one has taken

18:30 As in an ancient Hebrew tradition, some Greek manuscripts, and Latin Vulgate; Masoretic Text reads *son of Manasseh.* 19:2 Or *she was unfaithful to him.* 19:3 As in Greek version; Hebrew reads *When she brought him to.* 19:18 As in Greek version (see also 19:29); Hebrew reads *now I'm going to the Tabernacle of the* LORD.

us in for the night, 19 even though we have everything we need. We have
straw and feed for our donkeys and plenty of bread and wine for ourselves."
20 "You are welcome to stay with me," the old man said. "I will give you
anything you might need. But whatever you do, don't spend the night in the
square." 21 So he took them home with him and fed the donkeys. After they
washed their feet, they ate and drank together.
22 While they were enjoying themselves, a crowd of troublemakers from
the town surrounded the house. They began beating at the door and shout-
ing to the old man, "Bring out the man who is staying with you so we can
have sex with him."
23 The old man stepped outside to talk to them. "No, my brothers, don't
do such an evil thing. For this man is a guest in my house, and such a thing
would be shameful. 24 Here, take my virgin daughter and this man's concu-
bine. I will bring them out to you, and you can abuse them and do whatever
you like. But don't do such a shameful thing to this man."
25 But they wouldn't listen to him. So the Levite took hold of his concubine
and pushed her out the door. The men of the town abused her all night,
taking turns raping her until morning. Finally, at dawn they let her go. 26 At
daybreak the woman returned to the house where her husband was staying.
She collapsed at the door of the house and lay there until it was light.
27 When her husband opened the door to leave, there lay his concubine
with her hands on the threshold. 28 He said, "Get up! Let's go!" But there was
no answer.* So he put her body on his donkey and took her home.
29 When he got home, he took a knife and cut his concubine's body into
twelve pieces. Then he sent one piece to each tribe throughout all the ter-
ritory of Israel.
30 Everyone who saw it said, "Such a horrible crime has not been commit-
ted in all the time since Israel left Egypt. Think about it! What are we going
to do? Who's going to speak up?"

Israel's War with Benjamin

20 Then all the Israelites were united as one man, from Dan in the north
to Beersheba in the south, including those from across the Jordan
in the land of Gilead. The entire community assembled in the presence of
the LORD at Mizpah. 2 The leaders of all the people and all the tribes of Is-
rael—400,000 warriors armed with swords—took their positions in the
assembly of the people of God. 3 (Word soon reached the land of Benjamin
that the other tribes had gone up to Mizpah.) The Israelites then asked how
this terrible crime had happened.
4 The Levite, the husband of the woman who had been murdered, said,
"My concubine and I came to spend the night in Gibeah, a town that belongs
to the people of Benjamin. 5 That night some of the leading citizens of Gib-
eah surrounded the house, planning to kill me, and they raped my concubine
until she was dead. 6 So I cut her body into twelve pieces and sent the pieces
throughout the territory assigned to Israel, for these men have committed a
terrible and shameful crime. 7 Now then, all of you—the entire community
of Israel—must decide here and now what should be done about this!"
8 And all the people rose to their feet in unison and declared, "None of us
will return home! No, not even one of us! 9 Instead, this is what we will do

Prayer **19:30**

Chapter 19 describes depravity at its worst. Disgusting. Sad. Hopeless. Verse 30 erupts with despair. The people desperately needed a Savior. They needed an Advocate who could rescue them. *Jesus, we need you! I need you! Let me not become intertwined with sin and fear and mess. Amen.*

19:28 Greek version adds *for she was dead.*

to Gibeah; we will draw lots to decide who will attack it. 10 One-tenth of the
men* from each tribe will be chosen to supply the warriors with food, and the
rest of us will take revenge on Gibeah* of Benjamin for this shameful thing
they have done in Israel." 11 So all the Israelites were completely united, and
they gathered together to attack the town.

12 The Israelites sent messengers to the tribe of Benjamin, saying, "What a
terrible thing has been done among you! 13 Give up those evil men, those trouble-
makers from Gibeah, so we can execute them and purge Israel of this evil."

But the people of Benjamin would not listen. 14 Instead, they came from
their towns and gathered at Gibeah to fight the Israelites. 15 In all, 26,000
of their warriors armed with swords arrived in Gibeah to join the 700 elite
troops who lived there. 16 Among Benjamin's elite troops, 700 were left-
handed, and each of them could sling a rock and hit a target within a hairs-
breadth without missing. 17 Israel had 400,000 experienced soldiers armed
with swords, not counting Benjamin's warriors.

18 Before the battle the Israelites went to Bethel and asked God, "Which
tribe should go first to attack the people of Benjamin?"

The LORD answered, "Judah is to go first."

19 So the Israelites left early the next morning and camped near Gibeah.
20 Then they advanced toward Gibeah to attack the men of Benjamin. 21 But
Benjamin's warriors, who were defending the town, came out and killed
22,000 Israelites on the battlefield that day.

22 But the Israelites encouraged each other and took their positions again
at the same place they had fought the previous day. 23 For they had gone up to
Bethel and wept in the presence of the LORD until evening. They had asked
the LORD, "Should we fight against our relatives from Benjamin again?"

And the LORD had said, "Go out and fight against them."

24 So the next day they went out again to fight against the men of Benja-
min, 25 but the men of Benjamin killed another 18,000 Israelites, all of whom
were experienced with the sword.

26 Then all the Israelites went up to Bethel and wept in the presence of the
LORD and fasted until evening. They also brought burnt offerings and peace
offerings to the LORD. 27 The Israelites went up seeking direction from the
LORD. (In those days the Ark of the Covenant of God was in Bethel, 28 and
Phinehas son of Eleazar and grandson of Aaron was the priest.) The Isra-
elites asked the LORD, "Should we fight against our relatives from Benjamin
again, or should we stop?"

The LORD said, "Go! Tomorrow I will hand them over to you."

29 So the Israelites set an ambush all around Gibeah. 30 They went out on
the third day and took their positions at the same place as before. 31 When the
men of Benjamin came out to attack, they were drawn away from the town.
And as they had done before, they began to kill the Israelites. About thirty
Israelites died in the open fields and along the roads, one leading to Bethel
and the other leading back to Gibeah.

32 Then the warriors of Benjamin shouted, "We're defeating them as we
did before!" But the Israelites had planned in advance to run away so that
the men of Benjamin would chase them along the roads and be drawn away
from the town.

33 When the main group of Israelite warriors reached Baal-tamar, they

20:10a Hebrew *10 men from every hundred, 100 men from every thousand, and 1,000 men from every 10,000.* **20:10b** Hebrew *Geba,* in this case a variant spelling of Gibeah; also in 20:33.

turned and took up their positions. Meanwhile, the Israelites hiding in am-
bush to the west* of Gibeah jumped up to fight. 34 There were 10,000 elite
Israelite troops who advanced against Gibeah. The fighting was so heavy
that Benjamin didn't realize the impending disaster. 35 So the LORD helped
Israel defeat Benjamin, and that day the Israelites killed 25,100 of Benja-
min's warriors, all of whom were experienced swordsmen. 36 Then the men
of Benjamin saw that they were beaten.

The Israelites had retreated from Benjamin's warriors in order to give
those hiding in ambush more room to maneuver against Gibeah. 37 Then
those who were hiding rushed in from all sides and killed everyone in the
town. 38 They had arranged to send up a large cloud of smoke from the town
as a signal. 39 When the Israelites saw the smoke, they turned and attacked
Benjamin's warriors.

By that time Benjamin's warriors had killed about thirty Israelites, and
they shouted, "We're defeating them as we did in the first battle!" 40 But
when the warriors of Benjamin looked behind them and saw the smoke ris-
ing into the sky from every part of the town, 41 the men of Israel turned and
attacked. At this point the men of Benjamin became terrified, because they
realized disaster was close at hand. 42 So they turned around and fled before
the Israelites toward the wilderness. But they couldn't escape the battle,
and the people who came out of the nearby towns were also killed.* 43 The
Israelites surrounded the men of Benjamin and chased them relentlessly,
finally overtaking them east of Gibeah.* 44 That day 18,000 of Benjamin's
strongest warriors died in battle. 45 The survivors fled into the wilderness
toward the rock of Rimmon, but Israel killed 5,000 of them along the road.
They continued the chase until they had killed another 2,000 near Gidom.

46 So that day the tribe of Benjamin lost 25,000 strong warriors armed with
swords, 47 leaving only 600 men who escaped to the rock of Rimmon, where
they lived for four months. 48 And the Israelites returned and slaughtered
every living thing in all the towns—the people, the livestock, and everything
they found. They also burned down all the towns they came to.

Israel Provides Wives for Benjamin

21 The Israelites had vowed at Mizpah, "We will never give our daugh-
ters in marriage to a man from the tribe of Benjamin." 2 Now the
people went to Bethel and sat in the presence of God until evening, weeping
loudly and bitterly. 3 "O LORD, God of Israel," they cried out, "why has this
happened in Israel? Now one of our tribes is missing from Israel!"

4 Early the next morning the people built an altar and presented their
burnt offerings and peace offerings on it. 5 Then they said, "Who among
the tribes of Israel did not join us at Mizpah when we held our assembly
in the presence of the LORD?" At that time they had taken a solemn oath
in the LORD's presence, vowing that anyone who refused to come would be
put to death.

6 The Israelites felt sorry for their brother Benjamin and said, "Today one
of the tribes of Israel has been cut off. 7 How can we find wives for the few
who remain, since we have sworn by the LORD not to give them our daugh-
ters in marriage?"

20:33 As in Greek and Syriac versions and Latin Vulgate; Hebrew reads *hiding in the open space.* **20:42** Or *battle, for the people from the nearby towns also came out and killed them.* **20:43** The meaning of the Hebrew is uncertain.

Drop your brilliant thoughts here

Make a Difference

21:25

The Sad Final Words of the Book of Judges

The story of Judges ends worse than it began: "In those days Israel had no king; all the people did whatever seemed right in their own eyes." The downward cycle of the book of Judges is incredibly sad. In twenty-one chapters, spanning a few hundred years, the people became stuck in a pattern of falling away from the Lord. Even so, God wasn't stuck. He had a plan!

Thankfully, there are more books after Judges. In the next book, for instance, Ruth paved the way for David, who paved the way for Jesus. In the book after that, Samuel emerged as Israel's last historical judge (1 Samuel 7:15) and first major prophet who prepared people for a king and stirred their longing for the Savior.

Difference Maker

Don't stop now! Keep going in God's story of redemption. Don't let your life get stuck like the lives of those in the book of Judges. Take a step to discover the hope and faith found in the next few biblical books.

8 So they asked, "Who among the tribes of Israel did not join us at Miz-
pah when we assembled in the presence of the LORD?" And they discovered
that no one from Jabesh-gilead had attended the assembly. 9 For after they
counted all the people, no one from Jabesh-gilead was present.
10 So the assembly sent 12,000 of their best warriors to Jabesh-gilead with
orders to kill everyone there, including women and children. 11 "This is
what you are to do," they said. "Completely destroy* all the males and every
woman who is not a virgin." 12 Among the residents of Jabesh-gilead they
found 400 young virgins who had never slept with a man, and they brought
them to the camp at Shiloh in the land of Canaan.
13 The Israelite assembly sent a peace delegation to the remaining people
of Benjamin who were living at the rock of Rimmon. 14 Then the men of
Benjamin returned to their homes, and the 400 women of Jabesh-gilead who
had been spared were given to them as wives. But there were not enough
women for all of them.
15 The people felt sorry for Benjamin because the LORD had made this gap
among the tribes of Israel. 16 So the elders of the assembly asked, "How can
we find wives for the few who remain, since the women of the tribe of Ben-
jamin are dead? 17 There must be heirs for the survivors so that an entire tribe
of Israel is not wiped out. 18 But we cannot give them our own daughters in
marriage because we have sworn with a solemn oath that anyone who does
this will fall under God's curse."
19 Then they thought of the annual festival of the LORD held in Shiloh,
south of Lebonah and north of Bethel, along the east side of the road that
goes from Bethel to Shechem. 20 They told the men of Benjamin who still
needed wives, "Go and hide in the vineyards. 21 When you see the young
women of Shiloh come out for their dances, rush out from the vineyards,
and each of you can take one of them home to the land of Benjamin to be your
wife! 22 And when their fathers and brothers come to us in protest, we will tell
them, 'Please be sympathetic. Let them have your daughters, for we didn't
find wives for all of them when we destroyed Jabesh-gilead. And you are not
guilty of breaking the vow since you did not actually give your daughters to
them in marriage.'"
23 So the men of Benjamin did as they were told. Each man caught one
of the women as she danced in the celebration and carried her off to be his
wife. They returned to their own land, and they rebuilt their towns and lived
in them.
24 Then the people of Israel departed by tribes and families, and they re-
turned to their own homes.
25 In those days Israel had no king; all the people did whatever seemed
right in their own eyes.

21:11 The Hebrew term used here refers to the complete consecration of things or people to the LORD, either by destroying them or by giving them as an offering.

Ruth Introduction

The book of Ruth is the shortest book of the first half of the Old Testament. At first, it seems like an insignificant story of obscure characters surrounded by the massive historical epics of Joshua, Judges, and 1 and 2 Samuel. However, the book of Ruth will not allow itself to be overlooked. Not only is this book profoundly refreshing after slogging through the twenty-one bloodthirsty and vulgar chapters of Judges, but it also is the stage setter for the redemption of the entire world.

This book helps readers of the Bible become familiar with Bethlehem, a small and seemingly inconsequential shepherding town in Judah that will eventually become the birthplace of royalty.

We are introduced to Naomi, who wanted people to call her Mara (meaning "bitter") because of her deep sadness resulting from the deaths of her husband and sons. We are introduced to her daughter-in-law Ruth, a foreigner widowed too young, who would become the great-grandmother of a king. We are introduced to Boaz, who stands out as good and righteous even though he lived "in the days when the Judges ruled in Israel" (Ruth 1:1). Finally, we are introduced to David, whose name is the last word of this profound little book.

The book of Ruth wants us to "see" what's really going on. In the midst of the anxious upheavals of the times, here is a reminder that those who live by faith are a part of a prevailing backdrop of God's action in the world. There is a theme of "witness." Do you see this? We are all witnesses today of what God is doing! If you look through the muck and mire of misery in this world, you'll see Ruth's name included in the remarkable genealogical record of Jesus, who is called the Messiah (Matthew 1:5).

Story Arc

Ruth

RUTH

Ruth

Elimelech Moves His Family to Moab

1 In the days when the judges ruled in Israel, a severe famine came upon
the land. So a man from Bethlehem in Judah left his home and went to
live in the country of Moab, taking his wife and two sons with him. 2 The
man's name was Elimelech, and his wife was Naomi. Their two sons were
Mahlon and Kilion. They were Ephrathites from Bethlehem in the land of
Judah. And when they reached Moab, they settled there.
3 Then Elimelech died, and Naomi was left with her two sons. 4 The two
sons married Moabite women. One married a woman named Orpah, and the
other a woman named Ruth. But about ten years later, 5 both Mahlon and
Kilion died. This left Naomi alone, without her two sons or her husband.

Naomi and Ruth Return

6 Then Naomi heard in Moab that the LORD had blessed his people in Judah
by giving them good crops again. So Naomi and her daughters-in-law got
ready to leave Moab to return to her homeland. 7 With her two daughters-
in-law she set out from the place where she had been living, and they took
the road that would lead them back to Judah.
8 But on the way, Naomi said to her two daughters-in-law, "Go back to
your mothers' homes. And may the LORD reward you for your kindness to
your husbands and to me. 9 May the LORD bless you with the security of an-
other marriage." Then she kissed them good-bye, and they all broke down
and wept.
10 "No," they said. "We want to go with you to your people."
11 But Naomi replied, "Why should you go on with me? Can I still give
birth to other sons who could grow up to be your husbands? 12 No, my
daughters, return to your parents' homes, for I am too old to marry again.
And even if it were possible, and I were to get married tonight and bear
sons, then what? 13 Would you wait for them to grow up and refuse to
marry someone else? No, of course not, my daughters! Things are far more
bitter for me than for you, because the LORD himself has raised his fist
against me."
14 And again they wept together, and Orpah kissed her mother-in-law
good-bye. But Ruth clung tightly to Naomi. 15 "Look," Naomi said to her,
"your sister-in-law has gone back to her people and to her gods. You should
do the same."
16 But Ruth replied, "Don't ask me to leave you and turn back. Wherever
you go, I will go; wherever you live, I will live. Your people will be my people,
and your God will be my God. 17 Wherever you die, I will die, and there I will
be buried. May the LORD punish me severely if I allow anything but death
to separate us!" 18 When Naomi saw that Ruth was determined to go with
her, she said nothing more.

Make a Difference 1:16

Walk with Others

This verse has been used in countless weddings as an indication of deep commitment in the joyous occasion of marriage. "Wherever you go, I will go; wherever you live, I will live." However, this statement was actually the determined commitment of one very sad young woman to her very sad mother-in-law. Having lost their husbands, both Ruth and Naomi were widows who chose to lean on one another for support. This raises a question to us today whether we are willing to take our sadness, our weakness, our fears, and our uncertainties and offer commitment to walk with someone who is going through the same sort of circumstances.

Difference Maker

Do you know someone who is going through a difficult time and needs you by their side? What could you do for them?

19 So the two of them continued on their journey. When they came to Beth-
lehem, the entire town was excited by their arrival. "Is it really Naomi?" the
women asked.
20 "Don't call me Naomi," she responded. "Instead, call me Mara,* for the
Almighty has made life very bitter for me. 21 I went away full, but the LORD
has brought me home empty. Why call me Naomi when the LORD has caused
me to suffer* and the Almighty has sent such tragedy upon me?"
22 So Naomi returned from Moab, accompanied by her daughter-in-law
Ruth, the young Moabite woman. They arrived in Bethlehem in late spring,
at the beginning of the barley harvest.

Ruth Works in Boaz's Field

2 Now there was a wealthy and influential man in Bethlehem named
Boaz, who was a relative of Naomi's husband, Elimelech.
2 One day Ruth the Moabite said to Naomi, "Let me go out into the har-
vest fields to pick up the stalks of grain left behind by anyone who is kind
enough to let me do it."
Naomi replied, "All right, my daughter, go ahead." 3 So Ruth went out to
gather grain behind the harvesters. And as it happened, she found herself
working in a field that belonged to Boaz, the relative of her father-in-law,
Elimelech.
4 While she was there, Boaz arrived from Bethlehem and greeted the har-
vesters. "The LORD be with you!" he said.
"The LORD bless you!" the harvesters replied.
5 Then Boaz asked his foreman, "Who is that young woman over there?
Who does she belong to?"
6 And the foreman replied, "She is the young woman from Moab who came
back with Naomi. 7 She asked me this morning if she could gather grain
behind the harvesters. She has been hard at work ever since, except for a few
minutes' rest in the shelter."
8 Boaz went over and said to Ruth, "Listen, my daughter. Stay right here
with us when you gather grain; don't go to any other fields. Stay right behind
the young women working in my field. 9 See which part of the field they are
harvesting, and then follow them. I have warned the young men not to treat
you roughly. And when you are thirsty, help yourself to the water they have
drawn from the well."
10 Ruth fell at his feet and thanked him warmly. "What have I done to
deserve such kindness?" she asked. "I am only a foreigner."
11 "Yes, I know," Boaz replied. "But I also know about everything you have
done for your mother-in-law since the death of your husband. I have heard
how you left your father and mother and your own land to live here among
complete strangers. 12 May the LORD, the God of Israel, under whose wings
you have come to take refuge, reward you fully for what you have done."
13 "I hope I continue to please you, sir," she replied. "You have comforted
me by speaking so kindly to me, even though I am not one of your workers."
14 At mealtime Boaz called to her, "Come over here, and help yourself to
some food. You can dip your bread in the sour wine." So she sat with his har-
vesters, and Boaz gave her some roasted grain to eat. She ate all she wanted
and still had some left over.

1:20 *Naomi* means "pleasant"; *Mara* means "bitter." 1:21 Or *has testified against me.*

Question **2:12**

If you believe what Boaz believed about God, how would that make a difference in your own actions toward others?

Story Arc **2:1-23**

● **Ruth**

Ruth was willing to follow behind the harvesters and collect whatever scraps of grain that were left behind. There was a system in Israel, instituted by the Lord, to leave unpicked grain in the fields so that the poor and the foreigners living in the land could gather food (Leviticus 23:22). As a humble foreigner, Ruth was thankful to gather whatever scraps were leftover for her. Boaz was so impressed by Ruth's humble determination that he invited her to walk alongside everyone else in the harvest. Her attitude was echoed later in the firm humility of a Gentile woman who simply wanted to "eat the scraps that fall" from Jesus' power (Matthew 15:21-28). Like how Boaz offered a compassionate invitation to Ruth, Jesus was impressed by the resolute faith that he saw, and he granted the woman inclusion in the "harvest."

1 Sam 1:2-22 ►

Make a Difference 2:20

Contrasting Kindness

Naomi noticed that Boaz showed kindness to Ruth. How did Boaz avoid all the dysfunction of his culture and peers? He lived "in the days when the judges ruled in Israel" (1:1). "In those days, Israel had no king; all the people did whatever seemed right in their own eyes" (Judges 21:25). If you read the book of Judges, you'll see appalling sin after sin. Boaz stood out because he somehow avoided being wrapped up in the tidal waves of violence, hatred, and sexual deviance all around him. Maybe you feel that you are sometimes surrounded by a violent, hateful, hypersexualized culture. How can you stand out?

Difference Maker

Read through the four chapters of the book of Ruth and pick out one way to be like Boaz in the way you live your life.

15 When Ruth went back to work again, Boaz ordered his young men, "Let
her gather grain right among the sheaves without stopping her. 16 And pull
out some heads of barley from the bundles and drop them on purpose for
her. Let her pick them up, and don't give her a hard time!"

17 So Ruth gathered barley there all day, and when she beat out the grain
that evening, it filled an entire basket.* 18 She carried it back into town and
showed it to her mother-in-law. Ruth also gave her the roasted grain that
was left over from her meal.

19 "Where did you gather all this grain today?" Naomi asked. "Where did
you work? May the LORD bless the one who helped you!"

So Ruth told her mother-in-law about the man in whose field she had
worked. She said, "The man I worked with today is named Boaz."

20 "May the LORD bless him!" Naomi told her daughter-in-law. "He is
showing his kindness to us as well as to your dead husband.* That man is
one of our closest relatives, one of our family redeemers."

21 Then Ruth* said, "What's more, Boaz even told me to come back and stay
with his harvesters until the entire harvest is completed."

22 "Good!" Naomi exclaimed. "Do as he said, my daughter. Stay with his
young women right through the whole harvest. You might be harassed in
other fields, but you'll be safe with him."

23 So Ruth worked alongside the women in Boaz's fields and gathered
grain with them until the end of the barley harvest. Then she continued
working with them through the wheat harvest in early summer. And all the
while she lived with her mother-in-law.

Ruth at the Threshing Floor

3 One day Naomi said to Ruth, "My daughter, it's time that I found a per-
manent home for you, so that you will be provided for. 2 Boaz is a close
relative of ours, and he's been very kind by letting you gather grain with his
young women. Tonight he will be winnowing barley at the threshing floor.
3 Now do as I tell you—take a bath and put on perfume and dress in your
nicest clothes. Then go to the threshing floor, but don't let Boaz see you until
he has finished eating and drinking. 4 Be sure to notice where he lies down;
then go and uncover his feet and lie down there. He will tell you what to do."

5 "I will do everything you say," Ruth replied. 6 So she went down
to the threshing floor that night and followed the instructions of her
mother-in-law.

7 After Boaz had finished eating and drinking and was in good spirits, he
lay down at the far end of the pile of grain and went to sleep. Then Ruth came
quietly, uncovered his feet, and lay down. 8 Around midnight Boaz suddenly
woke up and turned over. He was surprised to find a woman lying at his feet!
9 "Who are you?" he asked.

"I am your servant Ruth," she replied. "Spread the corner of your covering
over me, for you are my family redeemer."

10 "The LORD bless you, my daughter!" Boaz exclaimed. "You are show-
ing even more family loyalty now than you did before, for you have not
gone after a younger man, whether rich or poor. 11 Now don't worry about a
thing, my daughter. I will do what is necessary, for everyone in town knows
you are a virtuous woman. 12 But while it's true that I am one of your family

2:17 Hebrew *it was about an ephah* [20 quarts or 22 liters]. 2:20 Hebrew *to the living and to the dead.* 2:21 Hebrew *Ruth the Moabite.*

redeemers, there is another man who is more closely related to you than I
am. 13 Stay here tonight, and in the morning I will talk to him. If he is will-
ing to redeem you, very well. Let him marry you. But if he is not willing,
then as surely as the LORD lives, I will redeem you myself! Now lie down
here until morning."
14 So Ruth lay at Boaz's feet until the morning, but she got up before it was
light enough for people to recognize each other. For Boaz had said, "No one
must know that a woman was here at the threshing floor." 15 Then Boaz said
to her, "Bring your cloak and spread it out." He measured six scoops* of bar-
ley into the cloak and placed it on her back. Then he* returned to the town.
16 When Ruth went back to her mother-in-law, Naomi asked, "What hap-
pened, my daughter?"
Ruth told Naomi everything Boaz had done for her, 17 and she added, "He
gave me these six scoops of barley and said, 'Don't go back to your mother-
in-law empty-handed.'"
18 Then Naomi said to her, "Just be patient, my daughter, until we hear
what happens. The man won't rest until he has settled things today."

Boaz Marries Ruth

4 Boaz went to the town gate and took a seat there. Just then the family
redeemer he had mentioned came by, so Boaz called out to him, "Come
over here and sit down, friend. I want to talk to you." So they sat down to-
gether. 2 Then Boaz called ten leaders from the town and asked them to sit as
witnesses. 3 And Boaz said to the family redeemer, "You know Naomi, who
came back from Moab. She is selling the land that belonged to our relative
Elimelech. 4 I thought I should speak to you about it so that you can redeem
it if you wish. If you want the land, then buy it here in the presence of these
witnesses. But if you don't want it, let me know right away, because I am next
in line to redeem it after you."
The man replied, "All right, I'll redeem it."
5 Then Boaz told him, "Of course, your purchase of the land from Naomi
also requires that you marry Ruth, the Moabite widow. That way she can
have children who will carry on her husband's name and keep the land in
the family."
6 "Then I can't redeem it," the family redeemer replied, "because this
might endanger my own estate. You redeem the land; I cannot do it."
7 Now in those days it was the custom in Israel for anyone transferring a
right of purchase to remove his sandal and hand it to the other party. This
publicly validated the transaction. 8 So the other family redeemer drew off
his sandal as he said to Boaz, "You buy the land."
9 Then Boaz said to the elders and to the crowd standing around, "You are
witnesses that today I have bought from Naomi all the property of Elim-
elech, Kilion, and Mahlon. 10 And with the land I have acquired Ruth, the
Moabite widow of Mahlon, to be my wife. This way she can have a son to carry
on the family name of her dead husband and to inherit the family property
here in his hometown. You are all witnesses today."
11 Then the elders and all the people standing in the gate replied, "We are
witnesses! May the LORD make this woman who is coming into your home
like Rachel and Leah, from whom all the nation of Israel descended! May you

3:15a Hebrew *six measures,* an unknown quantity. **3:15b** Most Hebrew manuscripts read *he;* many Hebrew manuscripts, Syriac version, and Latin Vulgate read *she.*

Make a Difference

4:11–22

Future Witness to Jesus

A witness is someone who sees something and then testifies about what they have seen. Here, the people witnessed the marriage of Boaz and Ruth, who would soon give birth to a son in Bethlehem. This chapter is significant in that it sets the stage for another birth in Bethlehem one thousand years later, when angels sang and shepherds witnessed the Savior born for them (Luke 2:11). Before his ascension, Jesus said his followers were to be "witnesses" around the world for him (Acts 1:8).

Difference Maker

In what ways could you be a witness for Jesus today?

Prayer 4:22

Lord, let me follow you faithfully in my lifetime so that generations from now, the world will be changed by those who follow after me. Amen.

prosper in Ephrathah and be famous in Bethlehem. 12And may the LORD give
you descendants by this young woman who will be like those of our ancestor
Perez, the son of Tamar and Judah."

The Descendants of Boaz

13So Boaz took Ruth into his home, and she became his wife. When he slept
with her, the LORD enabled her to become pregnant, and she gave birth to
a son. 14Then the women of the town said to Naomi, "Praise the LORD, who
has now provided a redeemer for your family! May this child be famous in
Israel. 15May he restore your youth and care for you in your old age. For he
is the son of your daughter-in-law who loves you and has been better to you
than seven sons!"

16Naomi took the baby and cuddled him to her breast. And she cared for
him as if he were her own. 17The neighbor women said, "Now at last Naomi
has a son again!" And they named him Obed. He became the father of Jesse
and the grandfather of David.

18This is the genealogical record of their ancestor Perez:

Perez was the father of Hezron.
19 Hezron was the father of Ram.
Ram was the father of Amminadab.
20 Amminadab was the father of Nahshon.
Nahshon was the father of Salmon.*
21 Salmon was the father of Boaz.
Boaz was the father of Obed.
22 Obed was the father of Jesse.
Jesse was the father of David.

4:20 As in some Greek manuscripts (see also 4:21); Hebrew reads *Salma.*

1 Samuel Introduction

You could read this story as an epic tale of a nation trying to fight its way out of the dark ages. The time of the Judges was a rather horrific period for the people of Israel. Death, despair, and division nearly destroyed them. Despite this, God raised up a final judge, Samuel, to begin to solidify a more permanent identity for the people of Israel in the midst of the gruesome realities of their day.

Alternatively, you could read this story as an epic tale of friendship forged in a world more familiar with betrayals and backstabbing. Jonathan, the son of the maniacal King Saul, and David, the son of the faithful shepherd Jesse, encouraged and equipped one another to live for God. Despite circumstances that should have ripped them apart, both honored and treasured one another above themselves.

Then again, you could read this story as a combination of both of those things. This book is the story of how God began tilling the soil in preparation for the ultimate King, his one and only Son, Jesus, the friend of sinners. God raised up Samuel, the great judge and prophet, to raise up David, the great warrior and shepherd, upon whose kingdom the reign of Jesus would be raised up on the cross.

Story Arcs

- Hannah
- Samuel
- Jonathan
- David

1 Samuel

Elkanah and His Family

1 There was a man named Elkanah who lived in Ramah in the region of
Zuph* in the hill country of Ephraim. He was the son of Jeroham, son
of Elihu, son of Tohu, son of Zuph, of Ephraim. 2 Elkanah had two wives,
Hannah and Peninnah. Peninnah had children, but Hannah did not.
3 Each year Elkanah would travel to Shiloh to worship and sacrifice to the
LORD of Heaven's Armies at the Tabernacle. The priests of the LORD at that
time were the two sons of Eli—Hophni and Phinehas. 4 On the days Elka-
nah presented his sacrifice, he would give portions of the meat to Peninnah
and each of her children. 5 And though he loved Hannah, he would give her
only one choice portion* because the LORD had given her no children. 6 So
Peninnah would taunt Hannah and make fun of her because the LORD had
kept her from having children. 7 Year after year it was the same—Peninnah
would taunt Hannah as they went to the Tabernacle.* Each time, Hannah
would be reduced to tears and would not even eat.
8 "Why are you crying, Hannah?" Elkanah would ask. "Why aren't you
eating? Why be downhearted just because you have no children? You have
me—isn't that better than having ten sons?"

Hannah's Prayer for a Son

9 Once after a sacrificial meal at Shiloh, Hannah got up and went to pray.
Eli the priest was sitting at his customary place beside the entrance of the
Tabernacle.* 10 Hannah was in deep anguish, crying bitterly as she prayed
to the LORD. 11 And she made this vow: "O LORD of Heaven's Armies, if
you will look upon my sorrow and answer my prayer and give me a son,
then I will give him back to you. He will be yours for his entire lifetime,
and as a sign that he has been dedicated to the LORD, his hair will never
be cut.*"
12 As she was praying to the LORD, Eli watched her. 13 Seeing her lips mov-
ing but hearing no sound, he thought she had been drinking. 14 "Must you
come here drunk?" he demanded. "Throw away your wine!"
15 "Oh no, sir!" she replied. "I haven't been drinking wine or anything
stronger. But I am very discouraged, and I was pouring out my heart to the
LORD. 16 Don't think I am a wicked woman! For I have been praying out of
great anguish and sorrow."
17 "In that case," Eli said, "go in peace! May the God of Israel grant the
request you have asked of him."
18 "Oh, thank you, sir!" she exclaimed. Then she went back and began to
eat again, and she was no longer sad.

Story Arc **1:2-22**

Hannah

In her grief, Hannah trusted in God. She poured out her heart to the Lord. Her husband didn't understand her. Eli, the high priest, misjudged her. However, the Lord remembered her prayer and set in motion a string of events that would change the world forever. Soon she gave birth to Samuel, the one who would prepare the way for King David. It was Hannah's outpouring of prayer that ignited God's plan. From Hannah's example, what do you learn about the difference prayer makes in God's orchestration of the world?

1 Sam 1:19-28 ►

1:1 As in Greek version; Hebrew reads *in Ramathaim-zophim;* compare 1:19. 1:5 Or *And because he loved Hannah, he would give her a choice portion.* The meaning of the Hebrew is uncertain. 1:7 Hebrew *the house of the LORD;* also in 1:24. 1:9 Hebrew *the Temple of the LORD.* 1:11 Some manuscripts add *He will drink neither wine nor intoxicants.*

Samuel's Birth and Dedication
19 The entire family got up early the next morning and went to worship the
LORD once more. Then they returned home to Ramah. When Elkanah slept
with Hannah, the LORD remembered her plea, 20 and in due time she gave
birth to a son. She named him Samuel,* for she said, "I asked the LORD for
him."
21 The next year Elkanah and his family went on their annual trip to offer
a sacrifice to the LORD and to keep his vow. 22 But Hannah did not go. She
told her husband, "Wait until the boy is weaned. Then I will take him to the
Tabernacle and leave him there with the LORD permanently.*"
23 "Whatever you think is best," Elkanah agreed. "Stay here for now, and
may the LORD help you keep your promise.*" So she stayed home and nursed
the boy until he was weaned.
24 When the child was weaned, Hannah took him to the Tabernacle in Shi-
loh. They brought along a three-year-old bull* for the sacrifice and a basket*
of flour and some wine. 25 After sacrificing the bull, they brought the boy to
Eli. 26 "Sir, do you remember me?" Hannah asked. "I am the very woman who
stood here several years ago praying to the LORD. 27 I asked the LORD to give
me this boy, and he has granted my request. 28 Now I am giving him to the
LORD, and he will belong to the LORD his whole life." And they* worshiped
the LORD there.

Hannah's Prayer of Praise
2 Then Hannah prayed:

"My heart rejoices in the LORD!
The LORD has made me strong.*
Now I have an answer for my enemies;
I rejoice because you rescued me.
2 No one is holy like the LORD!
There is no one besides you;
there is no Rock like our God.

3 "Stop acting so proud and haughty!
Don't speak with such arrogance!
For the LORD is a God who knows what you have done;
he will judge your actions.
4 The bow of the mighty is now broken,
and those who stumbled are now strong.
5 Those who were well fed are now starving,
and those who were starving are now full.
The childless woman now has seven children,
and the woman with many children wastes away.
6 The LORD gives both death and life;
he brings some down to the grave* but raises others up.
7 The LORD makes some poor and others rich;
he brings some down and lifts others up.

1:20 *Samuel* sounds like the Hebrew term for "asked of God" or "heard by God." 1:22 Some manuscripts add *I will offer him as a Nazirite for all time.* 1:23 As in Dead Sea Scrolls and Greek version; Masoretic Text reads *may the LORD keep his promise.* 1:24a As in Dead Sea Scrolls, Greek and Syriac versions; Masoretic Text reads *three bulls.* 1:24b Hebrew *and an ephah* [20 quarts or 22 liters]. 1:28 Hebrew *he.* 2:1 Hebrew *has exalted my horn.* 2:6 Hebrew *to Sheol.*

Prayer **2:2**

There is no one besides you, Lord! There is no one holy, no one strong, no one strategic, no one powerful like the Lord God! Amen.

Story Arc **1:19–28**

● Samuel
The greatest leader since Joshua and Moses, Samuel grew to put fear into the hearts and minds of the people of Israel and the surrounding enemies, yet this powerful man's life was truly shaped in the simple prayers of a humble, broken woman. Samuel carried his mother's grieving heart with him his entire life. He also carried her faithfulness to the Lord. There have been few who have lived who bore the burdens of leadership the way that Samuel did, so faithfully and true.

1 Sam 13:2 ►

Question 2:25

First Timothy 2:5 says, "There is one God and one Mediator who can reconcile God and humanity—the man Christ Jesus." How does Eli's question point to Jesus?

8 He lifts the poor from the dust
and the needy from the garbage dump.
He sets them among princes,
placing them in seats of honor.
For all the earth is the LORD's,
and he has set the world in order.

9 "He will protect his faithful ones,
but the wicked will disappear in darkness.
No one will succeed by strength alone.
10 Those who fight against the LORD will be shattered.
He thunders against them from heaven;
the LORD judges throughout the earth.
He gives power to his king;
he increases the strength* of his anointed one."

11 Then Elkanah returned home to Ramah without Samuel. And the boy
served the LORD by assisting Eli the priest.

Eli's Wicked Sons

12 Now the sons of Eli were scoundrels who had no respect for the LORD 13 or
for their duties as priests. Whenever anyone offered a sacrifice, Eli's sons
would send over a servant with a three-pronged fork. While the meat of the
sacrificed animal was still boiling, 14 the servant would stick the fork into
the pot and demand that whatever it brought up be given to Eli's sons. All
the Israelites who came to worship at Shiloh were treated this way. 15 Some-
times the servant would come even before the animal's fat had been burned
on the altar. He would demand raw meat before it had been boiled so that it
could be used for roasting.

16 The man offering the sacrifice might reply, "Take as much as you want,
but the fat must be burned first." Then the servant would demand, "No,
give it to me now, or I'll take it by force." 17 So the sin of these young men
was very serious in the LORD's sight, for they treated the LORD's offerings
with contempt.

18 But Samuel, though he was only a boy, served the LORD. He wore a linen
garment like that of a priest.* 19 Each year his mother made a small coat for
him and brought it to him when she came with her husband for the sacrifice.
20 Before they returned home, Eli would bless Elkanah and his wife and say,
"May the LORD give you other children to take the place of this one she gave
to the LORD.*" 21 And the LORD blessed Hannah, and she conceived and gave
birth to three sons and two daughters. Meanwhile, Samuel grew up in the
presence of the LORD.

22 Now Eli was very old, but he was aware of what his sons were doing
to the people of Israel. He knew, for instance, that his sons were seducing
the young women who assisted at the entrance of the Tabernacle.* 23 Eli
said to them, "I have been hearing reports from all the people about the
wicked things you are doing. Why do you keep sinning? 24 You must stop,
my sons! The reports I hear among the LORD's people are not good. 25 If

2:10 Hebrew *he exalts the horn.* 2:18 Hebrew *He wore a linen ephod.* 2:20 As in Dead Sea Scrolls and Greek version; Masoretic Text reads *this one he requested of the LORD.* 2:22 Hebrew *Tent of Meeting.* Some manuscripts lack this entire sentence.

someone sins against another person, God* can mediate for the guilty
party. But if someone sins against the LORD, who can intercede?" But Eli's
sons wouldn't listen to their father, for the LORD was already planning to
put them to death.
26 Meanwhile, the boy Samuel grew taller and grew in favor with the LORD
and with the people.

A Warning for Eli's Family

27 One day a man of God came to Eli and gave him this message from the
LORD: "I revealed myself* to your ancestors when they were Pharaoh's slaves
in Egypt. 28 I chose your ancestor Aaron* from among all the tribes of Israel to
be my priest, to offer sacrifices on my altar, to burn incense, and to wear the
priestly vest* as he served me. And I assigned the sacrificial offerings to you
priests. 29 So why do you scorn my sacrifices and offerings? Why do you give
your sons more honor than you give me—for you and they have become fat
from the best offerings of my people Israel!
30 "Therefore, the LORD, the God of Israel, says: I promised that your
branch of the tribe of Levi* would always be my priests. But I will honor those
who honor me, and I will despise those who think lightly of me. 31 The time
is coming when I will put an end to your family, so it will no longer serve as
my priests. All the members of your family will die before their time. None
will reach old age. 32 You will watch with envy as I pour out prosperity on the
people of Israel. But no members of your family will ever live out their days.
33 The few not cut off from serving at my altar will survive, but only so their
eyes can go blind and their hearts break, and their children will die a violent
death.* 34 And to prove that what I have said will come true, I will cause your
two sons, Hophni and Phinehas, to die on the same day!
35 "Then I will raise up a faithful priest who will serve me and do what I de-
sire. I will establish his family, and they will be priests to my anointed kings
forever. 36 Then all of your surviving family will bow before him, begging for
money and food. 'Please,' they will say, 'give us jobs among the priests so we
will have enough to eat.'"

The LORD Speaks to Samuel

3 Meanwhile, the boy Samuel served the LORD by assisting Eli. Now in
those days messages from the LORD were very rare, and visions were
quite uncommon.
2 One night Eli, who was almost blind by now, had gone to bed. 3 The lamp
of God had not yet gone out, and Samuel was sleeping in the Tabernacle*
near the Ark of God. 4 Suddenly the LORD called out, "Samuel!"
"Yes?" Samuel replied. "What is it?" 5 He got up and ran to Eli. "Here I
am. Did you call me?"
"I didn't call you," Eli replied. "Go back to bed." So he did.
6 Then the LORD called out again, "Samuel!"
Again Samuel got up and went to Eli. "Here I am. Did you call me?"
"I didn't call you, my son," Eli said. "Go back to bed."
7 Samuel did not yet know the LORD because he had never had a message

2:25 Or *the judges.* 2:27 As in Greek and Syriac versions; Hebrew reads *Did I reveal myself.* 2:28a Hebrew *your father.* 2:28b Hebrew *an ephod.* 2:30 Hebrew *that your house and your father's house.* 2:33 As in Dead Sea Scrolls and Greek version, which read *die by the sword;* Masoretic Text reads *die like mortals.* 3:3 Hebrew *the Temple of the LORD.*

from the LORD before. 8 So the LORD called a third time, and once more Samuel got up and went to Eli. “Here I am. Did you call me?”

Then Eli realized it was the LORD who was calling the boy. 9 So he said to Samuel, “Go and lie down again, and if someone calls again, say, ‘Speak, LORD, your servant is listening.’” So Samuel went back to bed.

10 And the LORD came and called as before, “Samuel! Samuel!”

And Samuel replied, “Speak, your servant is listening.”

11 Then the LORD said to Samuel, “I am about to do a shocking thing in Israel. 12 I am going to carry out all my threats against Eli and his family, from beginning to end. 13 I have warned him that judgment is coming upon his family forever, because his sons are blaspheming God* and he hasn’t disciplined them. 14 So I have vowed that the sins of Eli and his sons will never be forgiven by sacrifices or offerings.”

Samuel Speaks for the LORD

15 Samuel stayed in bed until morning, then got up and opened the doors of the Tabernacle* as usual. He was afraid to tell Eli what the LORD had said to him. 16 But Eli called out to him, “Samuel, my son.”

“Here I am,” Samuel replied.

17 “What did the LORD say to you? Tell me everything. And may God strike you and even kill you if you hide anything from me!” 18 So Samuel told Eli everything; he didn’t hold anything back. “It is the LORD’s will,” Eli replied. “Let him do what he thinks best.”

19 As Samuel grew up, the LORD was with him, and everything Samuel said proved to be reliable. 20 And all Israel, from Dan in the north to Beersheba in the south, knew that Samuel was confirmed as a prophet of the LORD. 21 The LORD continued to appear at Shiloh and gave messages to Samuel there at the Tabernacle. 4:1 And Samuel’s words went out to all the people of Israel.

The Philistines Capture the Ark

4 At that time Israel was at war with the Philistines. The Israelite army was camped near Ebenezer, and the Philistines were at Aphek. 2 The Philistines attacked and defeated the army of Israel, killing 4,000 men. 3 After the battle was over, the troops retreated to their camp, and the elders of Israel asked, “Why did the LORD allow us to be defeated by the Philistines?” Then they said, “Let’s bring the Ark of the Covenant of the LORD from Shiloh. If we carry it into battle with us, it* will save us from our enemies.”

4 So they sent men to Shiloh to bring the Ark of the Covenant of the LORD of Heaven’s Armies, who is enthroned between the cherubim. Hophni and Phinehas, the sons of Eli, were also there with the Ark of the Covenant of God. 5 When all the Israelites saw the Ark of the Covenant of the LORD coming into the camp, their shout of joy was so loud it made the ground shake!

6 “What’s going on?” the Philistines asked. “What’s all the shouting about in the Hebrew camp?” When they were told it was because the Ark of the LORD had arrived, 7 they panicked. “The gods have* come into their camp!” they cried. “This is a disaster! We have never had to face anything like this before! 8 Help! Who can save us from these mighty gods of Israel? They are the same gods who destroyed the Egyptians with plagues when Israel was

3:13 As in Greek version; Hebrew reads *his sons have made themselves contemptible.* 3:15 Hebrew *the house of the LORD.* 4:3 Or *he.* 4:7 Or *A god has.*

Make a Difference

3:1–21

Listen

There isn’t anything magical about prayer. You can’t say any special formula that will twist God’s arm or trick him into doing what you want him to do. God will never say, “Oh, you got me there. You said the secret password.” Prayer is much simpler than that. It’s about matching what is on your heart with what’s on God’s heart. No tricks. Just a relationship.

Samuel, as a boy, learned to listen for God’s voice. Imagine the difference this would make if people approached God with this attitude. Instead of clamoring with a list of demands and troubles or rather than ignoring God altogether, what if you spent some time in silence, listening for God to speak?

Difference Maker

In a posture of prayer, begin your time with God by stating Samuel’s words, “Speak, your servant is listening” (v. 10). Then take several minutes to listen to what the Lord would like to tell you.

Question 3:19

Could this be said of you as you are getting older?

in the wilderness. 9 Fight as never before, Philistines! If you don't, we will
become the Hebrews' slaves just as they have been ours! Stand up like men
and fight!"
10 So the Philistines fought desperately, and Israel was defeated again. The
slaughter was great; 30,000 Israelite soldiers died that day. The survivors
turned and fled to their tents. 11 The Ark of God was captured, and Hophni
and Phinehas, the two sons of Eli, were killed.

The Death of Eli

12 A man from the tribe of Benjamin ran from the battlefield and arrived
at Shiloh later that same day. He had torn his clothes and put dust on his
head to show his grief. 13 Eli was waiting beside the road to hear the news
of the battle, for his heart trembled for the safety of the Ark of God. When
the messenger arrived and told what had happened, an outcry resounded
throughout the town.
14 "What is all the noise about?" Eli asked.
The messenger rushed over to Eli, 15 who was ninety-eight years old and
blind. 16 He said to Eli, "I have just come from the battlefield—I was there
this very day."
"What happened, my son?" Eli demanded.
17 "Israel has been defeated by the Philistines," the messenger replied.
"The people have been slaughtered, and your two sons, Hophni and Phine-
has, were also killed. And the Ark of God has been captured."
18 When the messenger mentioned what had happened to the Ark of God,
Eli fell backward from his seat beside the gate. He broke his neck and died,
for he was old and overweight. He had been Israel's judge for forty years.
19 Eli's daughter-in-law, the wife of Phinehas, was pregnant and near her
time of delivery. When she heard that the Ark of God had been captured and
that her father-in-law and husband were dead, she went into labor and gave
birth. 20 She died in childbirth, but before she passed away the midwives tried
to encourage her. "Don't be afraid," they said. "You have a baby boy!" But
she did not answer or pay attention to them.
21 She named the child Ichabod (which means "Where is the glory?"), for
she said, "Israel's glory is gone." She named him this because the Ark of God
had been captured and because her father-in-law and husband were dead.
22 Then she said, "The glory has departed from Israel, for the Ark of God has
been captured."

The Ark in Philistia

5 After the Philistines captured the Ark of God, they took it from the
battleground at Ebenezer to the town of Ashdod. 2 They carried the Ark
of God into the temple of Dagon and placed it beside an idol of Dagon. 3 But
when the citizens of Ashdod went to see it the next morning, Dagon had
fallen with his face to the ground in front of the Ark of the LORD! So they
took Dagon and put him in his place again. 4 But the next morning the same
thing happened—Dagon had fallen face down before the Ark of the LORD
again. This time his head and hands had broken off and were lying in the
doorway. Only the trunk of his body was left intact. 5 That is why to this day
neither the priests of Dagon nor anyone who enters the temple of Dagon in
Ashdod will step on its threshold.

Question 5:4

Dagon's temple was closed for business! Only the Lord is God. There is no other. What competing powers of this world would you like God to confront like this?

6 Then the LORD's heavy hand struck the people of Ashdod and the nearby
villages with a plague of tumors.* 7 When the people realized what was hap-
pening, they cried out, "We can't keep the Ark of the God of Israel here any
longer! He is against us! We will all be destroyed along with Dagon, our god."
8 So they called together the rulers of the Philistine towns and asked, "What
should we do with the Ark of the God of Israel?"

The rulers discussed it and replied, "Move it to the town of Gath." So they
moved the Ark of the God of Israel to Gath. 9 But when the Ark arrived at
Gath, the LORD's heavy hand fell on its men, young and old; he struck them
with a plague of tumors, and there was a great panic.

10 So they sent the Ark of God to the town of Ekron, but when the people of
Ekron saw it coming they cried out, "They are bringing the Ark of the God of
Israel here to kill us, too!" 11 The people summoned the Philistine rulers again
and begged them, "Please send the Ark of the God of Israel back to its own
country, or it* will kill us all." For the deadly plague from God had already
begun, and great fear was sweeping across the town. 12 Those who didn't
die were afflicted with tumors; and the cry from the town rose to heaven.

The Philistines Return the Ark

6 The Ark of the LORD remained in Philistine territory seven months in
all. 2 Then the Philistines called in their priests and diviners and asked
them, "What should we do about the Ark of the LORD? Tell us how to return
it to its own country."

3 "Send the Ark of the God of Israel back with a gift," they were told. "Send
a guilt offering so the plague will stop. Then, if you are healed, you will know
it was his hand that caused the plague."

4 "What sort of guilt offering should we send?" they asked.

And they were told, "Since the plague has struck both you and your five
rulers, make five gold tumors and five gold rats, just like those that have
ravaged your land. 5 Make these things to show honor to the God of Israel.
Perhaps then he will stop afflicting you, your gods, and your land. 6 Don't
be stubborn and rebellious as Pharaoh and the Egyptians were. By the time
God was finished with them, they were eager to let Israel go.

7 "Now build a new cart, and find two cows that have just given birth to
calves. Make sure the cows have never been yoked to a cart. Hitch the cows
to the cart, but shut their calves away from them in a pen. 8 Put the Ark of
the LORD on the cart, and beside it place a chest containing the gold rats and
gold tumors you are sending as a guilt offering. Then let the cows go wher-
ever they want. 9 If they cross the border of our land and go to Beth-shemesh,
we will know it was the LORD who brought this great disaster upon us. If
they don't, we will know it was not his hand that caused the plague. It came
simply by chance."

10 So these instructions were carried out. Two cows were hitched to the
cart, and their newborn calves were shut up in a pen. 11 Then the Ark of the
LORD and the chest containing the gold rats and gold tumors were placed on
the cart. 12 And sure enough, without veering off in other directions, the cows
went straight along the road toward Beth-shemesh, lowing as they went.
The Philistine rulers followed them as far as the border of Beth-shemesh.

13 The people of Beth-shemesh were harvesting wheat in the valley, and

5:6 Greek version and Latin Vulgate read *tumors; and rats appeared in their land, and death and destruction were throughout the city.* **5:11** Or *he.*

when they saw the Ark, they were overjoyed! 14 The cart came into the field of
a man named Joshua and stopped beside a large rock. So the people broke up
the wood of the cart for a fire and killed the cows and sacrificed them to the
LORD as a burnt offering. 15 Several men of the tribe of Levi lifted the Ark of
the LORD and the chest containing the gold rats and gold tumors from the
cart and placed them on the large rock. Many sacrifices and burnt offerings
were offered to the LORD that day by the people of Beth-shemesh. 16 The five
Philistine rulers watched all this and then returned to Ekron that same day.
17 The five gold tumors sent by the Philistines as a guilt offering to the
LORD were gifts from the rulers of Ashdod, Gaza, Ashkelon, Gath, and Ek-
ron. 18 The five gold rats represented the five Philistine towns and their sur-
rounding villages, which were controlled by the five rulers. The large rock*
at Beth-shemesh, where they set the Ark of the LORD, still stands in the field
of Joshua as a witness to what happened there.

The Ark Moved to Kiriath-Jearim

19 But the LORD killed seventy men* from Beth-shemesh because they looked
into the Ark of the LORD. And the people mourned greatly because of what
the LORD had done. 20 "Who is able to stand in the presence of the LORD, this
holy God?" they cried out. "Where can we send the Ark from here?"
21 So they sent messengers to the people at Kiriath-jearim and told them,
"The Philistines have returned the Ark of the LORD. Come here and get it!"

7 So the men of Kiriath-jearim came to get the Ark of the LORD. They took
it to the hillside home of Abinadab and ordained Eleazar, his son, to be
in charge of it. 2 The Ark remained in Kiriath-jearim for a long time—twenty
years in all. During that time all Israel mourned because it seemed the LORD
had abandoned them.

Samuel Leads Israel to Victory

3 Then Samuel said to all the people of Israel, "If you want to return to the
LORD with all your hearts, get rid of your foreign gods and your images of
Ashtoreth. Turn your hearts to the LORD and obey him alone; then he will
rescue you from the Philistines." 4 So the Israelites got rid of their images of
Baal and Ashtoreth and worshiped only the LORD.
5 Then Samuel told them, "Gather all of Israel to Mizpah, and I will pray
to the LORD for you." 6 So they gathered at Mizpah and, in a great ceremony,
drew water from a well and poured it out before the LORD. They also went
without food all day and confessed that they had sinned against the LORD.
(It was at Mizpah that Samuel became Israel's judge.)
7 When the Philistine rulers heard that Israel had gathered at Mizpah,
they mobilized their army and advanced. The Israelites were badly fright-
ened when they learned that the Philistines were approaching. 8 "Don't
stop pleading with the LORD our God to save us from the Philistines!" they
begged Samuel. 9 So Samuel took a young lamb and offered it to the LORD
as a whole burnt offering. He pleaded with the LORD to help Israel, and the
LORD answered him.

6:18 As in some Hebrew manuscripts and Greek version; most Hebrew manuscripts read *great meadow* or *Abel-haggedolah*. **6:19** As in a few Hebrew manuscripts; most Hebrew manuscripts read *70 men, 50,000 men*. Perhaps the text should be understood to read *the LORD killed 70 men and 50 oxen.*

Question 6:18

The theme of "witness" runs throughout the Bible. Why is being a witness so important to the story of God's work in our world?

Make a Difference 7:3

Challenge Accepted

Samuel laid down a challenge to the people of Israel. He offered a choice, much like Joshua's ultimatum in Joshua 24. Basically, Samuel declared, "Turn your hearts to the LORD and obey him alone," or they would suffer the consequences on their own without him.

On this occasion, Israel responded positively, but based on upcoming behaviors, it is unclear if the people were more interested in returning to the Lord or in being rescued. This is the tension of the person who cries out to God. The reward is great, but eventually people really must become more interested in pursuing God rather than pursuing salvation. In pursuing God, there is salvation, but in pursuing salvation more than we pursue God, we are still lost.

Difference Maker

Would you rather have a reward, or would you rather have a relationship with God? Write down the reasons for your choice.

Make a Difference **7:12**

Ebenezer

Before Scrooge ruined this name, an *Ebenezer* was simply a marker, a monument dedicated to a moment when the Lord significantly affected something. Here, Samuel took a large stone and placed it between two towns as a visual reminder that the Lord had helped the people to this point.

Difference Maker

Think of something significant that God has done for you. Then set up some kind of an "Ebenezer" to remind you of God's help. Put the visual marker somewhere you will see it regularly.

10 Just as Samuel was sacrificing the burnt offering, the Philistines arrived
to attack Israel. But the LORD spoke with a mighty voice of thunder from
heaven that day, and the Philistines were thrown into such confusion that
the Israelites defeated them. 11 The men of Israel chased them from Mizpah
to a place below Beth-car, slaughtering them all along the way.
12 Samuel then took a large stone and placed it between the towns of Mizpah and Jeshanah.* He named it Ebenezer (which means "the stone of help"),
for he said, "Up to this point the LORD has helped us!"
13 So the Philistines were subdued and didn't invade Israel again for some
time. And throughout Samuel's lifetime, the LORD's powerful hand was
raised against the Philistines. 14 The Israelite villages near Ekron and Gath
that the Philistines had captured were restored to Israel, along with the rest
of the territory that the Philistines had taken. And there was peace between
Israel and the Amorites in those days.
15 Samuel continued as Israel's judge for the rest of his life. 16 Each year he
traveled around, setting up his court first at Bethel, then at Gilgal, and then
at Mizpah. He judged the people of Israel at each of these places. 17 Then he
would return to his home at Ramah, and he would hear cases there, too. And
Samuel built an altar to the LORD at Ramah.

Israel Requests a King

8 As Samuel grew old, he appointed his sons to be judges over Israel. 2 Joel
and Abijah, his oldest sons, held court in Beersheba. 3 But they were not
like their father, for they were greedy for money. They accepted bribes and
perverted justice.
4 Finally, all the elders of Israel met at Ramah to discuss the matter with
Samuel. 5 "Look," they told him, "you are now old, and your sons are not like
you. Give us a king to judge us like all the other nations have."
6 Samuel was displeased with their request and went to the LORD for guidance. 7 "Do everything they say to you," the LORD replied, "for they are rejecting me, not you. They don't want me to be their king any longer. 8 Ever
since I brought them from Egypt they have continually abandoned me and
followed other gods. And now they are giving you the same treatment. 9 Do
as they ask, but solemnly warn them about the way a king will reign over
them."

Samuel Warns against a Kingdom

10 So Samuel passed on the LORD's warning to the people who were asking
him for a king. 11 "This is how a king will reign over you," Samuel said. "The
king will draft your sons and assign them to his chariots and his charioteers,
making them run before his chariots. 12 Some will be generals and captains
in his army,* some will be forced to plow in his fields and harvest his crops,
and some will make his weapons and chariot equipment. 13 The king will
take your daughters from you and force them to cook and bake and make
perfumes for him. 14 He will take away the best of your fields and vineyards
and olive groves and give them to his own officials. 15 He will take a tenth of
your grain and your grape harvest and distribute it among his officers and
attendants. 16 He will take your male and female slaves and demand the finest
of your cattle* and donkeys for his own use. 17 He will demand a tenth of your

7:12 As in Greek and Syriac versions; Hebrew reads *Shen.* 8:12 Hebrew *commanders of thousands and commanders of fifties.* 8:16 As in Greek version; Hebrew reads *young men.*

flocks, and you will be his slaves. 18When that day comes, you will beg for relief from this king you are demanding, but then the LORD will not help you."

19But the people refused to listen to Samuel's warning. "Even so, we still want a king," they said. 20"We want to be like the nations around us. Our king will judge us and lead us into battle."

21So Samuel repeated to the LORD what the people had said, 22and the LORD replied, "Do as they say, and give them a king." Then Samuel agreed and sent the people home.

Saul Meets Samuel

9 There was a wealthy, influential man named Kish from the tribe of Benjamin. He was the son of Abiel, son of Zeror, son of Becorath, son of Aphiah, of the tribe of Benjamin. 2His son Saul was the most handsome man in Israel—head and shoulders taller than anyone else in the land.

3One day Kish's donkeys strayed away, and he told Saul, "Take a servant with you, and go look for the donkeys." 4So Saul took one of the servants and traveled through the hill country of Ephraim, the land of Shalishah, the Shaalim area, and the entire land of Benjamin, but they couldn't find the donkeys anywhere.

5Finally, they entered the region of Zuph, and Saul said to his servant, "Let's go home. By now my father will be more worried about us than about the donkeys!"

6But the servant said, "I've just thought of something! There is a man of God who lives here in this town. He is held in high honor by all the people because everything he says comes true. Let's go find him. Perhaps he can tell us which way to go."

7"But we don't have anything to offer him," Saul replied. "Even our food is gone, and we don't have a thing to give him."

8"Well," the servant said, "I have one small silver piece.* We can at least offer it to the man of God and see what happens!" 9(In those days if people wanted a message from God, they would say, "Let's go and ask the seer," for prophets used to be called seers.)

10"All right," Saul agreed, "let's try it!" So they started into the town where the man of God lived.

11As they were climbing the hill to the town, they met some young women coming out to draw water. So Saul and his servant asked, "Is the seer here today?"

12"Yes," they replied. "Stay right on this road. He is at the town gates. He has just arrived to take part in a public sacrifice up at the place of worship. 13Hurry and catch him before he goes up there to eat. The guests won't begin eating until he arrives to bless the food."

14So they entered the town, and as they passed through the gates, Samuel was coming out toward them to go up to the place of worship.

15Now the LORD had told Samuel the previous day, 16"About this time tomorrow I will send you a man from the land of Benjamin. Anoint him to be the leader of my people, Israel. He will rescue them from the Philistines, for I have looked down on my people in mercy and have heard their cry."

17When Samuel saw Saul, the LORD said, "That's the man I told you about! He will rule my people."

9:8 Hebrew *¼ shekel of silver,* about 0.1 ounces or 3 grams in weight.

Prayer 8:20

Almighty God, let me be faithful to you and you alone. Let me desire to be like you and not like everyone else. Amen.

Question 9:2

In what ways did Saul check all the boxes of the world's definition of someone with great leadership potential? How would you compare this with God's definition in 1 Samuel 16:7?

Question 9:15

Read what Paul said about Jesus in Acts 28:20. How does Jesus ultimately fulfill what King Saul could not?

18 Just then Saul approached Samuel at the gateway and asked, "Can you
please tell me where the seer's house is?"
19 "I am the seer!" Samuel replied. "Go up to the place of worship ahead
of me. We will eat there together, and in the morning I'll tell you what you
want to know and send you on your way. 20 And don't worry about those
donkeys that were lost three days ago, for they have been found. And I am
here to tell you that you and your family are the focus of all Israel's hopes."
21 Saul replied, "But I'm only from the tribe of Benjamin, the smallest tribe
in Israel, and my family is the least important of all the families of that tribe!
Why are you talking like this to me?"
22 Then Samuel brought Saul and his servant into the hall and placed
them at the head of the table, honoring them above the thirty special guests.
23 Samuel then instructed the cook to bring Saul the finest cut of meat, the
piece that had been set aside for the guest of honor. 24 So the cook brought
in the meat and placed it before Saul. "Go ahead and eat it," Samuel said.
"I was saving it for you even before I invited these others!" So Saul ate with
Samuel that day.
25 When they came down from the place of worship and returned to town,
Samuel took Saul up to the roof of the house and prepared a bed for him
there.* 26 At daybreak the next morning, Samuel called to Saul, "Get up! It's
time you were on your way." So Saul got ready, and he and Samuel left the
house together. 27 When they reached the edge of town, Samuel told Saul to
send his servant on ahead. After the servant was gone, Samuel said, "Stay
here, for I have received a special message for you from God."

Samuel Anoints Saul as King

10 Then Samuel took a flask of olive oil and poured it over Saul's head.
He kissed Saul and said, "I am doing this because the LORD has ap-
pointed you to be the ruler over Israel, his special possession.* 2 When you
leave me today, you will see two men beside Rachel's tomb at Zelzah, on the
border of Benjamin. They will tell you that the donkeys have been found
and that your father has stopped worrying about them and is now worried
about you. He is asking, 'Have you seen my son?'
3 "When you get to the oak of Tabor, you will see three men coming toward
you who are on their way to worship God at Bethel. One will be bringing
three young goats, another will have three loaves of bread, and the third will
be carrying a wineskin full of wine. 4 They will greet you and offer you two
of the loaves, which you are to accept.
5 "When you arrive at Gibeah of God,* where the garrison of the Philis-
tines is located, you will meet a band of prophets coming down from the
place of worship. They will be playing a harp, a tambourine, a flute, and a
lyre, and they will be prophesying. 6 At that time the Spirit of the LORD will
come powerfully upon you, and you will prophesy with them. You will be
changed into a different person. 7 After these signs take place, do what must
be done, for God is with you. 8 Then go down to Gilgal ahead of me. I will join
you there to sacrifice burnt offerings and peace offerings. You must wait for
seven days until I arrive and give you further instructions."

9:25 As in Greek version; Hebrew reads *and talked with him there.* **10:1** Greek version reads *over Israel. And you will rule over the LORD's people and save them from their enemies around them. This will be the sign to you that the LORD has appointed you to be leader over his special possession.* **10:5** Hebrew *Gibeath-haelohim.*

Samuel's Signs Are Fulfilled

9 As Saul turned and started to leave, God gave him a new heart, and all Sam-
uel's signs were fulfilled that day. 10 When Saul and his servant arrived at
Gibeah, they saw a group of prophets coming toward them. Then the Spirit
of God came powerfully upon Saul, and he, too, began to prophesy. 11 When
those who knew Saul heard about it, they exclaimed, "What? Is even Saul a
prophet? How did the son of Kish become a prophet?"
12 And one of those standing there said, "Can anyone become a prophet,
no matter who his father is?"* So that is the origin of the saying "Is even
Saul a prophet?"
13 When Saul had finished prophesying, he went up to the place of wor-
ship. 14 "Where have you been?" Saul's uncle asked him and his servant.

"We were looking for the donkeys," Saul replied, "but we couldn't find them. So we went to Samuel to ask him where they were."

15 "Oh? And what did he say?" his uncle asked.
16 "He told us that the donkeys had already been found," Saul replied. But
Saul didn't tell his uncle what Samuel said about the kingdom.

Saul Is Acclaimed King

17 Later Samuel called all the people of Israel to meet before the LORD at Miz-
pah. 18 And he said, "This is what the LORD, the God of Israel, has declared:
I brought you from Egypt and rescued you from the Egyptians and from all
of the nations that were oppressing you. 19 But though I have rescued you
from your misery and distress, you have rejected your God today and have
said, 'No, we want a king instead!' Now, therefore, present yourselves before
the LORD by tribes and clans."
20 So Samuel brought all the tribes of Israel before the LORD, and the
tribe of Benjamin was chosen by lot. 21 Then he brought each family of
the tribe of Benjamin before the LORD, and the family of the Matrites was
chosen. And finally Saul son of Kish was chosen from among them. But
when they looked for him, he had disappeared! 22 So they asked the LORD,
"Where is he?"
And the LORD replied, "He is hiding among the baggage." 23 So they found
him and brought him out, and he stood head and shoulders above anyone else.
24 Then Samuel said to all the people, "This is the man the LORD has chosen
as your king. No one in all Israel is like him!"

And all the people shouted, "Long live the king!"

25 Then Samuel told the people what the rights and duties of a king were.
He wrote them down on a scroll and placed it before the LORD. Then Samuel
sent the people home again.
26 When Saul returned to his home at Gibeah, a group of men whose hearts
God had touched went with him. 27 But there were some scoundrels who
complained, "How can this man save us?" And they scorned him and refused
to bring him gifts. But Saul ignored them.

[Nahash, king of the Ammonites, had been grievously oppressing the people of Gad and Reuben who lived east of the Jordan River. He gouged out the right eye of each of the Israelites living there, and he didn't allow anyone to come and rescue them. In fact, of all the Israelites east of the Jordan, there wasn't a single one whose right eye Nahash had not gouged out.

10:12 Hebrew *said, "Who is their father?"*

Prayer **10:9**

Lord, examine my heart and do for me what you did for Saul here. Amen.

But there were 7,000 men who had escaped from the Ammonites, and they
had settled in Jabesh-gilead.]*

Saul Defeats the Ammonites

11 About a month later,* King Nahash of Ammon led his army against
the Israelite town of Jabesh-gilead. But all the citizens of Jabesh
asked for peace. "Make a treaty with us, and we will be your servants," they
pleaded.
2"All right," Nahash said, "but only on one condition. I will gouge out the
right eye of every one of you as a disgrace to all Israel!"
3"Give us seven days to send messengers throughout Israel!" replied the
elders of Jabesh. "If no one comes to save us, we will agree to your terms."
4When the messengers came to Gibeah of Saul and told the people about
their plight, everyone broke into tears. 5Saul had been plowing a field with
his oxen, and when he returned to town, he asked, "What's the matter? Why
is everyone crying?" So they told him about the message from Jabesh.
6Then the Spirit of God came powerfully upon Saul, and he became very
angry. 7He took two oxen and cut them into pieces and sent the messengers
to carry them throughout Israel with this message: "This is what will happen
to the oxen of anyone who refuses to follow Saul and Samuel into battle!"
And the LORD made the people afraid of Saul's anger, and all of them came
out together as one. 8When Saul mobilized them at Bezek, he found that
there were 300,000 men from Israel and 30,000* men from Judah.
9So Saul sent the messengers back to Jabesh-gilead to say, "We will res-
cue you by noontime tomorrow!" There was great joy throughout the town
when that message arrived!
10The men of Jabesh then told their enemies, "Tomorrow we will come
out to you, and you can do to us whatever you wish." 11But before dawn the
next morning, Saul arrived, having divided his army into three detachments.
He launched a surprise attack against the Ammonites and slaughtered them
the whole morning. The remnant of their army was so badly scattered that
no two of them were left together.
12Then the people exclaimed to Samuel, "Now where are those men who
said, 'Why should Saul rule over us?' Bring them here, and we will kill them!"
13But Saul replied, "No one will be executed today, for today the LORD
has rescued Israel!"
14Then Samuel said to the people, "Come, let us all go to Gilgal to renew
the kingdom." 15So they all went to Gilgal, and in a solemn ceremony be-
fore the LORD they made Saul king. Then they offered peace offerings to the
LORD, and Saul and all the Israelites were filled with joy.

Samuel's Farewell Address

12 Then Samuel addressed all Israel: "I have done as you asked and
given you a king. 2Your king is now your leader. I stand here before
you—an old, gray-haired man—and my sons serve you. I have served as
your leader from the time I was a boy to this very day. 3Now testify against
me in the presence of the LORD and before his anointed one. Whose ox or
donkey have I stolen? Have I ever cheated any of you? Have I ever oppressed

10:27 This paragraph, which is not included in the Masoretic Text, is found in Dead Sea Scroll 4QSam[a]. 11:1 As in Dead Sea Scroll 4QSam[a] and Greek version; Masoretic Text lacks *About a month later.* 11:8 Dead Sea Scrolls and Greek version read *70,000.*

you? Have I ever taken a bribe and perverted justice? Tell me and I will make
right whatever I have done wrong.”
4 “No,” they replied, “you have never cheated or oppressed us, and you
have never taken even a single bribe.”
5 “The LORD and his anointed one are my witnesses today,” Samuel de-
clared, “that my hands are clean.”
“Yes, he is a witness,” they replied.
6 “It was the LORD who appointed Moses and Aaron,” Samuel continued.
“He brought your ancestors out of the land of Egypt. 7 Now stand here quietly
before the LORD as I remind you of all the great things the LORD has done for
you and your ancestors.
8 “When the Israelites were* in Egypt and cried out to the LORD, he sent
Moses and Aaron to rescue them from Egypt and to bring them into this
land. 9 But the people soon forgot about the LORD their God, so he handed
them over to Sisera, the commander of Hazor’s army, and also to the Philis-
tines and to the king of Moab, who fought against them.
10 “Then they cried to the LORD again and confessed, ‘We have sinned by
turning away from the LORD and worshiping the images of Baal and Ashto-
reth. But we will worship you and you alone if you will rescue us from our
enemies.’ 11 Then the LORD sent Gideon,* Bedan,* Jephthah, and Samuel* to
save you, and you lived in safety.
12 “But when you were afraid of Nahash, the king of Ammon, you came to
me and said that you wanted a king to reign over you, even though the LORD
your God was already your king. 13 All right, here is the king you have chosen.
You asked for him, and the LORD has granted your request.
14 “Now if you fear and worship the LORD and listen to his voice, and if you
do not rebel against the LORD’s commands, then both you and your king will
show that you recognize the LORD as your God. 15 But if you rebel against the
LORD’s commands and refuse to listen to him, then his hand will be as heavy
upon you as it was upon your ancestors.
16 “Now stand here and see the great thing the LORD is about to do. 17 You
know that it does not rain at this time of the year during the wheat harvest. I
will ask the LORD to send thunder and rain today. Then you will realize how
wicked you have been in asking the LORD for a king!”
18 So Samuel called to the LORD, and the LORD sent thunder and rain that
day. And all the people were terrified of the LORD and of Samuel. 19 “Pray to
the LORD your God for us, or we will die!” they all said to Samuel. “For now
we have added to our sins by asking for a king.”
20 “Don’t be afraid,” Samuel reassured them. “You have certainly done
wrong, but make sure now that you worship the LORD with all your heart,
and don’t turn your back on him. 21 Don’t go back to worshiping worthless
idols that cannot help or rescue you—they are totally useless! 22 The LORD
will not abandon his people, because that would dishonor his great name.
For it has pleased the LORD to make you his very own people.
23 “As for me, I will certainly not sin against the LORD by ending my prayers
for you. And I will continue to teach you what is good and right. 24 But be
sure to fear the LORD and faithfully serve him. Think of all the wonderful

12:8 Hebrew *When Jacob was.* The names “Jacob” and “Israel” are often interchanged throughout the Old Testament, referring sometimes to the individual patriarch and sometimes to the nation. 12:11a Hebrew *Jerub-baal,* another name for Gideon; see Judg 6:32. 12:11b Greek and Syriac versions read *Barak.* 12:11c Greek and Syriac versions read *Samson.*

Question 12:1-25

How do Samuel’s “farewell” comments resonate with Jesus’ final words to his disciples before he ascends into heaven in Acts 1:8?

Question 12:16

Are you on the lookout today for the great things the Lord is about to do? What do you need to change in your own life so that you will become more aware of what God is doing?

Prayer 12:20

Lord, I worship you with all my heart and will not turn my back on you. Thank you for making me one of your people. I’m humbled to be called your own. Amen.

Make a Difference 12:23

Keep Praying

Are you one who tells someone, “I’ll pray for you,” but then forgets to do it? Here in his farewell remarks to the people of Israel, Samuel promised that he would certainly keep praying for them. He promised to keep engaging in their lives so that they would do what is good and continue to fear the Lord. Samuel was concerned for how God’s people were going to live, so he committed to lift his heart to the Lord on their behalf.

Difference Maker

Whom have you recently told that you would pray for them? Go ahead. Pray for them. Right now.

things he has done for you. 25 But if you continue to sin, you and your king will be swept away."

Continued War with Philistia

13 Saul was thirty* years old when he became king, and he reigned for forty-two years.*

2 Saul selected 3,000 special troops from the army of Israel and sent the rest of the men home. He took 2,000 of the chosen men with him to Micmash and the hill country of Bethel. The other 1,000 went with Saul's son Jonathan to Gibeah in the land of Benjamin.

3 Soon after this, Jonathan attacked and defeated the garrison of Philistines at Geba. The news spread quickly among the Philistines. So Saul blew the ram's horn throughout the land, saying, "Hebrews, hear this! Rise up in revolt!" 4 All Israel heard the news that Saul had destroyed the Philistine garrison at Geba and that the Philistines now hated the Israelites more than ever. So the entire Israelite army was summoned to join Saul at Gilgal.

5 The Philistines mustered a mighty army of 3,000* chariots, 6,000 charioteers, and as many warriors as the grains of sand on the seashore! They camped at Micmash east of Beth-aven. 6 The men of Israel saw what a tight spot they were in; and because they were hard pressed by the enemy, they tried to hide in caves, thickets, rocks, holes, and cisterns. 7 Some of them crossed the Jordan River and escaped into the land of Gad and Gilead.

Saul's Disobedience and Samuel's Rebuke

Meanwhile, Saul stayed at Gilgal, and his men were trembling with fear. 8 Saul waited there seven days for Samuel, as Samuel had instructed him earlier, but Samuel still didn't come. Saul realized that his troops were rapidly slipping away. 9 So he demanded, "Bring me the burnt offering and the peace offerings!" And Saul sacrificed the burnt offering himself.

10 Just as Saul was finishing with the burnt offering, Samuel arrived. Saul went out to meet and welcome him, 11 but Samuel said, "What is this you have done?"

Saul replied, "I saw my men scattering from me, and you didn't arrive when you said you would, and the Philistines are at Micmash ready for battle. 12 So I said, 'The Philistines are ready to march against us at Gilgal, and I haven't even asked for the LORD's help!' So I felt compelled to offer the burnt offering myself before you came."

13 "How foolish!" Samuel exclaimed. "You have not kept the command the LORD your God gave you. Had you kept it, the LORD would have established your kingdom over Israel forever. 14 But now your kingdom must end, for the LORD has sought out a man after his own heart. The LORD has already appointed him to be the leader of his people, because you have not kept the LORD's command."

Israel's Military Disadvantage

15 Samuel then left Gilgal and went on his way, but the rest of the troops went with Saul to meet the army. They went up from Gilgal to Gibeah in the

Story Arc 13:2

Jonathan

The future king of Israel, Jonathan. That's surely what his father, Saul, must have called him. He was, after all, the prince. He was also a mighty warrior and a loyal, trustworthy man. When his father began to compromise his commitment to the Lord, Jonathan showed unwavering allegiance to God. When Jonathan learned that the Lord had rejected Saul's kingdom in favor of another (13:14), he stayed true to his faith even then. Look ahead at Jonathan's story in 1 Samuel. What impresses you about his humility and integrity in such tumultuous times?

1 Sam 16:1-23 ►

13:1a As in a few Greek manuscripts; the number is missing in the Hebrew. 13:1b Hebrew *reigned . . . and two;* the number is incomplete in the Hebrew. Compare Acts 13:21. 13:5 As in Greek and Syriac versions; Hebrew reads *30,000.*

land of Benjamin.* When Saul counted the men who were still with him, he
found only 600 were left! 16 Saul and Jonathan and the troops with them were
staying at Geba in the land of Benjamin. The Philistines set up their camp
at Micmash. 17 Three raiding parties soon left the camp of the Philistines.
One went north toward Ophrah in the land of Shual, 18 another went west
to Beth-horon, and the third moved toward the border above the valley of
Zeboim near the wilderness.

19 There were no blacksmiths in the land of Israel in those days. The Phi-
listines wouldn't allow them for fear they would make swords and spears
for the Hebrews. 20 So whenever the Israelites needed to sharpen their plow-
shares, picks, axes, or sickles,* they had to take them to a Philistine black-
smith. 21 The charges were as follows: a quarter of an ounce* of silver for
sharpening a plowshare or a pick, and an eighth of an ounce* for sharpening
an ax or making the point of an ox goad. 22 So on the day of the battle none
of the people of Israel had a sword or spear, except for Saul and Jonathan.

23 The pass at Micmash had meanwhile been secured by a contingent of
the Philistine army.

Jonathan's Daring Plan

14 One day Jonathan said to his armor bearer, "Come on, let's go over
to where the Philistines have their outpost." But Jonathan did not
tell his father what he was doing.

2 Meanwhile, Saul and his 600 men were camped on the outskirts of Gib-
eah, around the pomegranate tree* at Migron. 3 Among Saul's men was Ahi-
jah the priest, who was wearing the ephod, the priestly vest. Ahijah was the
son of Ichabod's brother Ahitub, son of Phinehas, son of Eli, the priest of the
LORD who had served at Shiloh.

No one realized that Jonathan had left the Israelite camp. 4 To reach the
Philistine outpost, Jonathan had to go down between two rocky cliffs that
were called Bozez and Seneh. 5 The cliff on the north was in front of Micmash,
and the one on the south was in front of Geba. 6 "Let's go across to the outpost
of those pagans," Jonathan said to his armor bearer. "Perhaps the LORD will
help us, for nothing can hinder the LORD. He can win a battle whether he
has many warriors or only a few!"

7 "Do what you think is best," the armor bearer replied. "I'm with you
completely, whatever you decide."

8 "All right, then," Jonathan told him. "We will cross over and let them
see us. 9 If they say to us, 'Stay where you are or we'll kill you,' then we will
stop and not go up to them. 10 But if they say, 'Come on up and fight,' then
we will go up. That will be the LORD's sign that he will help us defeat them."

11 When the Philistines saw them coming, they shouted, "Look! The He-
brews are crawling out of their holes!" 12 Then the men from the outpost
shouted to Jonathan, "Come on up here, and we'll teach you a lesson!"

"Come on, climb right behind me," Jonathan said to his armor bearer, "for
the LORD will help us defeat them!"

13 So they climbed up using both hands and feet, and the Philistines fell
before Jonathan, and his armor bearer killed those who came behind them.

Question 14:6

What inspires you about Jonathan's faith here? How would you compare your own faith in God to Jonathan's?

13:15 As in Greek version; Hebrew reads *Samuel then left Gilgal and went to Gibeah in the land of Benjamin.* **13:20** As in Greek version; Hebrew reads *or plowshares.* **13:21a** Hebrew *1 pim* [8 grams]. **13:21b** Hebrew *⅓ [of a shekel]* [4 grams]. **14:2** Or *around the rock of Rimmon;* compare Judg 20:45, 47; 21:13.

[14]They killed some twenty men in all, and their bodies were scattered over about half an acre.*

[15]Suddenly, panic broke out in the Philistine army, both in the camp and in the field, including even the outposts and raiding parties. And just then an earthquake struck, and everyone was terrified.

Israel Defeats the Philistines

[16]Saul's lookouts in Gibeah of Benjamin saw a strange sight—the vast army of Philistines began to melt away in every direction.* [17]"Call the roll and find out who's missing," Saul ordered. And when they checked, they found that Jonathan and his armor bearer were gone.

[18]Then Saul shouted to Ahijah, "Bring the ephod here!" For at that time Ahijah was wearing the ephod in front of the Israelites.* [19]But while Saul was talking to the priest, the confusion in the Philistine camp grew louder and louder. So Saul said to the priest, "Never mind; let's get going!"*

[20]Then Saul and all his men rushed out to the battle and found the Philistines killing each other. There was terrible confusion everywhere. [21]Even the Hebrews who had previously gone over to the Philistine army revolted and joined in with Saul, Jonathan, and the rest of the Israelites. [22]Likewise, the men of Israel who were hiding in the hill country of Ephraim joined the chase when they saw the Philistines running away. [23]So the LORD saved Israel that day, and the battle continued to rage even beyond Beth-aven.

Saul's Foolish Oath

[24]Now the men of Israel were pressed to exhaustion that day, because Saul had placed them under an oath, saying, "Let a curse fall on anyone who eats before evening—before I have full revenge on my enemies." So no one ate anything all day, [25]even though they had all found honeycomb on the ground in the forest. [26]They didn't dare touch the honey because they all feared the oath they had taken.

[27]But Jonathan had not heard his father's command, and he dipped the end of his stick into a piece of honeycomb and ate the honey. After he had eaten it, he felt refreshed.* [28]But one of the men saw him and said, "Your father made the army take a strict oath that anyone who eats food today will be cursed. That is why everyone is weary and faint."

[29]"My father has made trouble for us all!" Jonathan exclaimed. "A command like that only hurts us. See how refreshed I am now that I have eaten this little bit of honey. [30]If the men had been allowed to eat freely from the food they found among our enemies, think how many more Philistines we could have killed!"

[31]They chased and killed the Philistines all day from Micmash to Aijalon, growing more and more faint. [32]That evening they rushed for the battle plunder and butchered the sheep, goats, cattle, and calves, but they ate them without draining the blood. [33]Someone reported to Saul, "Look, the men are sinning against the LORD by eating meat that still has blood in it."

"That is very wrong," Saul said. "Find a large stone and roll it over here. [34]Then go out among the troops and tell them, 'Bring the cattle, sheep, and

14:14 Hebrew *half a yoke;* a "yoke" was the amount of land plowed by a pair of yoked oxen in one day. **14:16** As in Greek version; Hebrew reads *they went and there.* **14:18** As in some Greek manuscripts; Hebrew reads *"Bring the Ark of God." For at that time the Ark of God was with the Israelites.* **14:19** Hebrew *Withdraw your hand.* **14:27** Or *his eyes brightened;* similarly in 14:29.

goats here to me. Kill them here, and drain the blood before you eat them. Do not sin against the LORD by eating meat with the blood still in it.'"

So that night all the troops brought their animals and slaughtered them
there. 35 Then Saul built an altar to the LORD; it was the first of the altars he
built to the LORD.
36 Then Saul said, "Let's chase the Philistines all night and plunder them
until sunrise. Let's destroy every last one of them."

His men replied, "We'll do whatever you think is best."

But the priest said, "Let's ask God first."
37 So Saul asked God, "Should we go after the Philistines? Will you help us
defeat them?" But God made no reply that day.
38 Then Saul said to the leaders, "Something's wrong! I want all my army
commanders to come here. We must find out what sin was committed today.
39 I vow by the name of the LORD who rescued Israel that the sinner will
surely die, even if it is my own son Jonathan!" But no one would tell him
what the trouble was.
40 Then Saul said, "Jonathan and I will stand over here, and all of you stand
over there."

And the people responded to Saul, "Whatever you think is best."
41 Then Saul prayed, "O LORD, God of Israel, please show us who is guilty
and who is innocent.*" Then they cast sacred lots, and Jonathan and Saul
were chosen as the guilty ones, and the people were declared innocent.
42 Then Saul said, "Now cast lots again and choose between me and Jona-
than." And Jonathan was shown to be the guilty one.
43 "Tell me what you have done," Saul demanded of Jonathan.

"I tasted a little honey," Jonathan admitted. "It was only a little bit on the end of my stick. Does that deserve death?"
44 "Yes, Jonathan," Saul said, "you must die! May God strike me and even
kill me if you do not die for this."
45 But the people broke in and said to Saul, "Jonathan has won this great
victory for Israel. Should he die? Far from it! As surely as the LORD lives, not
one hair on his head will be touched, for God helped him do a great deed
today." So the people rescued Jonathan, and he was not put to death.
46 Then Saul called back the army from chasing the Philistines, and the
Philistines returned home.

Saul's Military Successes

47 Now when Saul had secured his grasp on Israel's throne, he fought against
his enemies in every direction—against Moab, Ammon, Edom, the kings of
Zobah, and the Philistines. And wherever he turned, he was victorious.* 48 He
performed great deeds and conquered the Amalekites, saving Israel from all
those who had plundered them.
49 Saul's sons included Jonathan, Ishbosheth,* and Malkishua. He also had
two daughters: Merab, who was older, and Michal. 50 Saul's wife was Ahin-
oam, the daughter of Ahimaaz. The commander of Saul's army was Abner,
the son of Saul's uncle Ner. 51 Saul's father, Kish, and Abner's father, Ner,
were both sons of Abiel.
52 The Israelites fought constantly with the Philistines throughout Saul's

Question **14:45**

The people stepped in to rescue Jonathan, who was being threatened by King Saul, his father. Can you think of someone or some people who need a large group to step in to rescue them? What could you do about this?

14:41 Greek version adds *If the fault is with me or my son Jonathan, respond with Urim; but if the men of Israel are at fault, respond with Thummim.* **14:47** As in Greek version; Hebrew reads *he acted wickedly.* **14:49** Hebrew *Ishvi*, a variant name for Ishbosheth; also known as Esh-baal.

lifetime. So whenever Saul observed a young man who was brave and strong,
he drafted him into his army.

Saul Defeats the Amalekites

15 One day Samuel said to Saul, "It was the LORD who told me to anoint
you as king of his people, Israel. Now listen to this message from
the LORD! 2 This is what the LORD of Heaven's Armies has declared: I have
decided to settle accounts with the nation of Amalek for opposing Israel
when they came from Egypt. 3 Now go and completely destroy* the entire
Amalekite nation—men, women, children, babies, cattle, sheep, goats, cam-
els, and donkeys."

4 So Saul mobilized his army at Telaim. There were 200,000 soldiers from
Israel and 10,000 men from Judah. 5 Then Saul and his army went to a town
of the Amalekites and lay in wait in the valley. 6 Saul sent this warning to the
Kenites: "Move away from where the Amalekites live, or you will die with
them. For you showed kindness to all the people of Israel when they came
up from Egypt." So the Kenites packed up and left.

7 Then Saul slaughtered the Amalekites from Havilah all the way to Shur,
east of Egypt. 8 He captured Agag, the Amalekite king, but completely de-
stroyed everyone else. 9 Saul and his men spared Agag's life and kept the best
of the sheep and goats, the cattle, the fat calves, and the lambs—everything,
in fact, that appealed to them. They destroyed only what was worthless or
of poor quality.

The LORD Rejects Saul

10 Then the LORD said to Samuel, 11 "I am sorry that I ever made Saul king, for
he has not been loyal to me and has refused to obey my command." Samuel was
so deeply moved when he heard this that he cried out to the LORD all night.

12 Early the next morning Samuel went to find Saul. Someone told him,
"Saul went to the town of Carmel to set up a monument to himself; then he
went on to Gilgal."

13 When Samuel finally found him, Saul greeted him cheerfully. "May the
LORD bless you," he said. "I have carried out the LORD's command!"

14 "Then what is all the bleating of sheep and goats and the lowing of cattle
I hear?" Samuel demanded.

15 "It's true that the army spared the best of the sheep, goats, and cattle,"
Saul admitted. "But they are going to sacrifice them to the LORD your God.
We have destroyed everything else."

16 Then Samuel said to Saul, "Stop! Listen to what the LORD told me last
night!"

"What did he tell you?" Saul asked.

17 And Samuel told him, "Although you may think little of yourself, are you
not the leader of the tribes of Israel? The LORD has anointed you king of Is-
rael. 18 And the LORD sent you on a mission and told you, 'Go and completely
destroy the sinners, the Amalekites, until they are all dead.' 19 Why haven't
you obeyed the LORD? Why did you rush for the plunder and do what was
evil in the LORD's sight?"

20 "But I did obey the LORD," Saul insisted. "I carried out the mission he

15:3 The Hebrew term used here refers to the complete consecration of things or people to the LORD, either by destroying them or by giving them as an offering; also in 15:8, 9, 15, 18, 20, 21.

gave me. I brought back King Agag, but I destroyed everyone else. 21 Then my
troops brought in the best of the sheep, goats, cattle, and plunder to sacrifice
to the LORD your God in Gilgal."
22 But Samuel replied,

"What is more pleasing to the LORD:
    your burnt offerings and sacrifices
    or your obedience to his voice?
Listen! Obedience is better than sacrifice,
    and submission is better than offering the fat of rams.
23 Rebellion is as sinful as witchcraft,
    and stubbornness as bad as worshiping idols.
So because you have rejected the command of the LORD,
    he has rejected you as king."

Saul Pleads for Forgiveness

24 Then Saul admitted to Samuel, "Yes, I have sinned. I have disobeyed your
instructions and the LORD's command, for I was afraid of the people and did
what they demanded. 25 But now, please forgive my sin and come back with
me so that I may worship the LORD."
26 But Samuel replied, "I will not go back with you! Since you have rejected
the LORD's command, he has rejected you as king of Israel."
27 As Samuel turned to go, Saul tried to hold him back and tore the hem
of his robe. 28 And Samuel said to him, "The LORD has torn the kingdom of
Israel from you today and has given it to someone else—one who is better
than you. 29 And he who is the Glory of Israel will not lie, nor will he change
his mind, for he is not human that he should change his mind!"
30 Then Saul pleaded again, "I know I have sinned. But please, at least
honor me before the elders of my people and before Israel by coming back
with me so that I may worship the LORD your God." 31 So Samuel finally
agreed and went back with him, and Saul worshiped the LORD.

Question 15:29

This verse contains an amazing description of God. What stands out to you here? How can you reflect these characteristics in your own life?

Samuel Executes King Agag

32 Then Samuel said, "Bring King Agag to me." Agag arrived full of hope, for
he thought, "Surely the worst is over, and I have been spared!"* 33 But Samuel
said, "As your sword has killed the sons of many mothers, now your mother
will be childless." And Samuel cut Agag to pieces before the LORD at Gilgal.
34 Then Samuel went home to Ramah, and Saul returned to his house
at Gibeah of Saul. 35 Samuel never went to meet with Saul again, but he
mourned constantly for him. And the LORD was sorry he had ever made
Saul king of Israel.

Samuel Anoints David as King

16 Now the LORD said to Samuel, "You have mourned long enough for
Saul. I have rejected him as king of Israel, so fill your flask with olive
oil and go to Bethlehem. Find a man named Jesse who lives there, for I have
selected one of his sons to be my king."
2 But Samuel asked, "How can I do that? If Saul hears about it, he will
kill me."

15:32 Dead Sea Scrolls and Greek version read *Agag arrived hesitantly, for he thought, "Surely this is the bitterness of death."*

Make a Difference

16:1-13

What God Looks At

Three thousand years ago, Israel was searching for a king. The Lord told the prophet Samuel to anoint a king from the family of Jesse, a shepherd from Bethlehem. When Jesse's oldest son, Eliab, was presented to Samuel, the prophet was convinced he had the "looks" of the next king, but the Lord gave Samuel a bit of a rebuke. God sees things differently than we are initially inclined to see. The Lord is concerned about something other than good looks. He cares about our hearts.

Difference Maker

Don't take a selfie for the entire next week. Instead, take pictures that highlight others doing good things.

Story Arc 16:1-23

● David

In this passage we are delving deeply into two of the most significant aspects of the story of the Bible. One is the town of Bethlehem—a little shepherding outlet that would become the pinpoint of God's plan of salvation for the world. The other is a teenager named David—a little shepherd who wrote masterful praise songs and slew fearsome enemies of the flock. In this way, the shepherd-king, the son of Jesse, the grandchild of Ruth and Boaz, was anointed God's servant for the nation of Israel.

A thousand years later, another King in the lineage of David would be born. He, too, did not appear majestic (Isaiah 53:2), but he would rise to shepherd God's people to salvation.

2 Sam 5:7 ►

"Take a heifer with you," the LORD replied, "and say that you have come
to make a sacrifice to the LORD. 3 Invite Jesse to the sacrifice, and I will show
you which of his sons to anoint for me."

4 So Samuel did as the LORD instructed. When he arrived at Bethlehem,
the elders of the town came trembling to meet him. "What's wrong?" they
asked. "Do you come in peace?"

5 "Yes," Samuel replied. "I have come to sacrifice to the LORD. Purify yourselves and come with me to the sacrifice." Then Samuel performed the purification rite for Jesse and his sons and invited them to the sacrifice, too.

6 When they arrived, Samuel took one look at Eliab and thought, "Surely
this is the LORD's anointed!"

7 But the LORD said to Samuel, "Don't judge by his appearance or height,
for I have rejected him. The LORD doesn't see things the way you see them.
People judge by outward appearance, but the LORD looks at the heart."

8 Then Jesse told his son Abinadab to step forward and walk in front of
Samuel. But Samuel said, "This is not the one the LORD has chosen." 9 Next
Jesse summoned Shimea,* but Samuel said, "Neither is this the one the LORD
has chosen." 10 In the same way all seven of Jesse's sons were presented to
Samuel. But Samuel said to Jesse, "The LORD has not chosen any of these."
11 Then Samuel asked, "Are these all the sons you have?"

"There is still the youngest," Jesse replied. "But he's out in the fields
watching the sheep and goats."

"Send for him at once," Samuel said. "We will not sit down to eat until
he arrives."

12 So Jesse sent for him. He was dark and handsome, with beautiful eyes.

And the LORD said, "This is the one; anoint him."

13 So as David stood there among his brothers, Samuel took the flask of
olive oil he had brought and anointed David with the oil. And the Spirit
of the LORD came powerfully upon David from that day on. Then Samuel
returned to Ramah.

David Serves in Saul's Court

14 Now the Spirit of the LORD had left Saul, and the LORD sent a tormenting
spirit* that filled him with depression and fear.

15 Some of Saul's servants said to him, "A tormenting spirit from God is
troubling you. 16 Let us find a good musician to play the harp whenever the
tormenting spirit troubles you. He will play soothing music, and you will
soon be well again."

17 "All right," Saul said. "Find me someone who plays well, and bring him
here."

18 One of the servants said to Saul, "One of Jesse's sons from Bethlehem is
a talented harp player. Not only that—he is a brave warrior, a man of war,
and has good judgment. He is also a fine-looking young man, and the LORD
is with him."

19 So Saul sent messengers to Jesse to say, "Send me your son David, the
shepherd." 20 Jesse responded by sending David to Saul, along with a young
goat, a donkey loaded with bread, and a wineskin full of wine.

21 So David went to Saul and began serving him. Saul loved David very
much, and David became his armor bearer.

16:9 Hebrew *Shammah,* a variant spelling of Shimea; compare 1 Chr 2:13; 20:7. 16:14 Or *an evil spirit;* also in 16:15, 16, 23.

22 Then Saul sent word to Jesse asking, "Please let David remain in my
service, for I am very pleased with him."
23 And whenever the tormenting spirit from God troubled Saul, David
would play the harp. Then Saul would feel better, and the tormenting spirit
would go away.

Goliath Challenges the Israelites

17 The Philistines now mustered their army for battle and camped
between Socoh in Judah and Azekah at Ephes-dammim. 2 Saul
countered by gathering his Israelite troops near the valley of Elah. 3 So the
Philistines and Israelites faced each other on opposite hills, with the valley
between them.
4 Then Goliath, a Philistine champion from Gath, came out of the Philis-
tine ranks to face the forces of Israel. He was over nine feet* tall! 5 He wore a
bronze helmet, and his bronze coat of mail weighed 125 pounds.* 6 He also
wore bronze leg armor, and he carried a bronze javelin on his shoulder. 7 The
shaft of his spear was as heavy and thick as a weaver's beam, tipped with an
iron spearhead that weighed 15 pounds.* His armor bearer walked ahead of
him carrying a shield.
8 Goliath stood and shouted a taunt across to the Israelites. "Why are you
all coming out to fight?" he called. "I am the Philistine champion, but you
are only the servants of Saul. Choose one man to come down here and fight
me! 9 If he kills me, then we will be your slaves. But if I kill him, you will
be our slaves! 10 I defy the armies of Israel today! Send me a man who will
fight me!" 11 When Saul and the Israelites heard this, they were terrified and
deeply shaken.

Jesse Sends David to Saul's Camp

12 Now David was the son of a man named Jesse, an Ephrathite from Beth-
lehem in the land of Judah. Jesse was an old man at that time, and he had
eight sons. 13 Jesse's three oldest sons—Eliab, Abinadab, and Shimea*—had
already joined Saul's army to fight the Philistines. 14 David was the youngest
son. David's three oldest brothers stayed with Saul's army, 15 but David went
back and forth so he could help his father with the sheep in Bethlehem.
16 For forty days, every morning and evening, the Philistine champion
strutted in front of the Israelite army.
17 One day Jesse said to David, "Take this basket* of roasted grain and these
ten loaves of bread, and carry them quickly to your brothers. 18 And give
these ten cuts of cheese to their captain. See how your brothers are getting
along, and bring back a report on how they are doing.*" 19 David's brothers
were with Saul and the Israelite army at the valley of Elah, fighting against
the Philistines.
20 So David left the sheep with another shepherd and set out early the next
morning with the gifts, as Jesse had directed him. He arrived at the camp just
as the Israelite army was leaving for the battlefield with shouts and battle
cries. 21 Soon the Israelite and Philistine forces stood facing each other, army
against army. 22 David left his things with the keeper of supplies and hurried

17:4 Hebrew *6 cubits and 1 span* [which totals about 9.75 feet or 3 meters]; Dead Sea Scrolls and Greek version read *4 cubits and 1 span* [which totals about 6.75 feet or 2 meters]. 17:5 Hebrew *5,000 shekels* [57 kilograms]. 17:7 Hebrew *600 shekels* [6.8 kilograms]. 17:13 Hebrew *Shammah,* a variant spelling of Shimea; compare 1 Chr 2:13; 20:7. 17:17 Hebrew *ephah* [20 quarts or 22 liters]. 17:18 Hebrew *and take their pledge.*

Question 16:22

As a boy, David served a king with his skills. Why do you think our society today so often keeps young people from having significant opportunities of leadership and ministry?

Make a Difference
17:12–22

You Can Do More Than You Think

It was remarkable for David, a teenager, to slay Goliath. It wasn't just how he did it, with a slingshot and a rock, but also that he did it at all. The fate of an entire nation was in his arm. Even so, this wasn't the first time David had done the remarkable. He had already killed lions and bears that had tried to attack his sheep. He had already been anointed as the next king, and he had the guts to stand up to the current one face-to-face.

David, as a young man, also managed the family business. When he was instructed by his dad to bring supplies to his brothers at the battle lines, David had the authority to put another employee in charge while he was away. Perhaps our society doesn't champion young people enough. Perhaps we don't challenge ourselves enough either. We can do more than we think we can do, especially if God is with us.

Difference Maker

Tackle a higher-level responsibility today that you have not previously felt encouraged to do.

Question 17:26

While other people are focused on fear of a person, David was focused on the fear of God. That changed his perspective on events. What fears do you have that would pale in comparison to a proper fear of God?

Prayer 17:33

Lord, give me the grit of faith that David had. Don't let my young age stop me from doing great things for you. Amen.

Question 17:40

There was nothing wrong with Saul's armor; it just wasn't what David was used to using. David used his five smooth stones instead. What unique skill sets of yours might God use that are different from the skills God used in previous generations?

out to the ranks to greet his brothers. 23 As he was talking with them, Goliath, the Philistine champion from Gath, came out from the Philistine ranks. Then David heard him shout his usual taunt to the army of Israel.

24 As soon as the Israelite army saw him, they began to run away in fright.
25 "Have you seen the giant?" the men asked. "He comes out each day to defy Israel. The king has offered a huge reward to anyone who kills him. He will give that man one of his daughters for a wife, and the man's entire family will be exempted from paying taxes!"

26 David asked the soldiers standing nearby, "What will a man get for killing this Philistine and ending his defiance of Israel? Who is this pagan Philistine anyway, that he is allowed to defy the armies of the living God?"

27 And these men gave David the same reply. They said, "Yes, that is the reward for killing him."

28 But when David's oldest brother, Eliab, heard David talking to the men, he was angry. "What are you doing around here anyway?" he demanded. "What about those few sheep you're supposed to be taking care of? I know about your pride and deceit. You just want to see the battle!"

29 "What have I done now?" David replied. "I was only asking a question!"
30 He walked over to some others and asked them the same thing and received the same answer. 31 Then David's question was reported to King Saul, and the king sent for him.

David Kills Goliath

32 "Don't worry about this Philistine," David told Saul. "I'll go fight him!"

33 "Don't be ridiculous!" Saul replied. "There's no way you can fight this Philistine and possibly win! You're only a boy, and he's been a man of war since his youth."

34 But David persisted. "I have been taking care of my father's sheep and goats," he said. "When a lion or a bear comes to steal a lamb from the flock,
35 I go after it with a club and rescue the lamb from its mouth. If the animal turns on me, I catch it by the jaw and club it to death. 36 I have done this to both lions and bears, and I'll do it to this pagan Philistine, too, for he has defied the armies of the living God! 37 The LORD who rescued me from the claws of the lion and the bear will rescue me from this Philistine!"

Saul finally consented. "All right, go ahead," he said. "And may the LORD be with you!"

38 Then Saul gave David his own armor—a bronze helmet and a coat of mail. 39 David put it on, strapped the sword over it, and took a step or two to see what it was like, for he had never worn such things before.

"I can't go in these," he protested to Saul. "I'm not used to them." So David took them off again. 40 He picked up five smooth stones from a stream and put them into his shepherd's bag. Then, armed only with his shepherd's staff and sling, he started across the valley to fight the Philistine.

41 Goliath walked out toward David with his shield bearer ahead of him,
42 sneering in contempt at this ruddy-faced boy. 43 "Am I a dog," he roared at David, "that you come at me with a stick?" And he cursed David by the names of his gods. 44 "Come over here, and I'll give your flesh to the birds and wild animals!" Goliath yelled.

45 David replied to the Philistine, "You come to me with sword, spear, and javelin, but I come to you in the name of the LORD of Heaven's Armies—the

God of the armies of Israel, whom you have defied. 46Today the LORD will
conquer you, and I will kill you and cut off your head. And then I will give
the dead bodies of your men to the birds and wild animals, and the whole
world will know that there is a God in Israel! 47And everyone assembled here
will know that the LORD rescues his people, but not with sword and spear.
This is the LORD's battle, and he will give you to us!"
48As Goliath moved closer to attack, David quickly ran out to meet him.
49Reaching into his shepherd's bag and taking out a stone, he hurled it with
his sling and hit the Philistine in the forehead. The stone sank in, and Goli-
ath stumbled and fell face down on the ground.
50So David triumphed over the Philistine with only a sling and a stone, for
he had no sword. 51Then David ran over and pulled Goliath's sword from its
sheath. David used it to kill him and cut off his head.

Israel Routs the Philistines

When the Philistines saw that their champion was dead, they turned and
ran. 52Then the men of Israel and Judah gave a great shout of triumph and
rushed after the Philistines, chasing them as far as Gath* and the gates of
Ekron. The bodies of the dead and wounded Philistines were strewn all
along the road from Shaaraim, as far as Gath and Ekron. 53Then the Isra-
elite army returned and plundered the deserted Philistine camp. 54(David
took the Philistine's head to Jerusalem, but he stored the man's armor in
his own tent.)
55As Saul watched David go out to fight the Philistine, he asked Abner, the
commander of his army, "Abner, whose son is this young man?"

"I really don't know," Abner declared.
56"Well, find out who he is!" the king told him.
57As soon as David returned from killing Goliath, Abner brought him to
Saul with the Philistine's head still in his hand. 58"Tell me about your father,
young man," Saul said.

And David replied, "His name is Jesse, and we live in Bethlehem."

Saul Becomes Jealous of David

18 After David had finished talking with Saul, he met Jonathan, the
king's son. There was an immediate bond between them, for Jona-
than loved David. 2From that day on Saul kept David with him and wouldn't
let him return home. 3And Jonathan made a solemn pact with David, because
he loved him as he loved himself. 4Jonathan sealed the pact by taking off his
robe and giving it to David, together with his tunic, sword, bow, and belt.
5Whatever Saul asked David to do, David did it successfully. So Saul made
him a commander over the men of war, an appointment that was welcomed
by the people and Saul's officers alike.
6When the victorious Israelite army was returning home after David had
killed the Philistine, women from all the towns of Israel came out to meet
King Saul. They sang and danced for joy with tambourines and cymbals.*
7This was their song:

"Saul has killed his thousands,
and David his ten thousands!"

17:52 As in some Greek manuscripts; Hebrew reads *a valley*. 18:6 The type of instrument represented by the word *cymbals* is uncertain.

Make a Difference

18:6–16

Rot

Three thousand years ago there was a chart-topping pop song that must have gotten stuck in King Saul's mind and driven him mad. The lyrics weren't too deep, really, just regular boy-band type of stuff. Regardless, they must have irritated Saul over and over and over again. The words from 1 Samuel 18 went like this: "Saul has killed his thousands, and David his ten thousands!" (v. 7). Saul didn't like that song.

King Saul began to envy this young warrior named David. What David had (faith, fame, talent, good looks, pictures on magazine covers?), Saul once had but had lost. Saul must have thought, *If I can't have it, then David can't have it anymore either.*

The Bible says that the song "made Saul very angry" (v. 8). He heard the song, he looked at David, and he looked at himself and became malcontent. Jealousy, not God, took control of the way he looked at his life, so he "kept a jealous eye on David" (v. 9).

Difference Maker

Think about something you are specifically jealous about and give it to the Lord in prayer right now.

Question 18:14

What difference does a close walk with God have on the failures of Saul and the successes of David?

8This made Saul very angry. "What's this?" he said. "They credit David
with ten thousands and me with only thousands. Next they'll be making
him their king!" 9So from that time on Saul kept a jealous eye on David.
10The very next day a tormenting spirit* from God overwhelmed Saul,
and he began to rave in his house like a madman. David was playing the
harp, as he did each day. But Saul had a spear in his hand, 11and he suddenly
hurled it at David, intending to pin him to the wall. But David escaped
him twice.
12Saul was then afraid of David, for the LORD was with David and had
turned away from Saul. 13Finally, Saul sent him away and appointed him
commander over 1,000 men, and David faithfully led his troops into
battle.
14David continued to succeed in everything he did, for the LORD was with
him. 15When Saul recognized this, he became even more afraid of him. 16But
all Israel and Judah loved David because he was so successful at leading his
troops into battle.

David Marries Saul's Daughter

17One day Saul said to David, "I am ready to give you my older daughter,
Merab, as your wife. But first you must prove yourself to be a real warrior by
fighting the LORD's battles." For Saul thought, "I'll send him out against the
Philistines and let them kill him rather than doing it myself."
18"Who am I, and what is my family in Israel that I should be the king's
son-in-law?" David exclaimed. "My father's family is nothing!" 19So* when
the time came for Saul to give his daughter Merab in marriage to David, he
gave her instead to Adriel, a man from Meholah.
20In the meantime, Saul's daughter Michal had fallen in love with David,
and Saul was delighted when he heard about it. 21"Here's another chance to
see him killed by the Philistines!" Saul said to himself. But to David he said,
"Today you have a second chance to become my son-in-law!"
22Then Saul told his men to say to David, "The king really likes you, and
so do we. Why don't you accept the king's offer and become his son-in-law?"
23When Saul's men said these things to David, he replied, "How can a
poor man from a humble family afford the bride price for the daughter
of a king?"
24When Saul's men reported this back to the king, 25he told them, "Tell
David that all I want for the bride price is 100 Philistine foreskins! Vengeance
on my enemies is all I really want." But what Saul had in mind was that David
would be killed in the fight.
26David was delighted to accept the offer. Before the time limit expired,
27he and his men went out and killed 200 Philistines. Then David fulfilled
the king's requirement by presenting all their foreskins to him. So Saul gave
his daughter Michal to David to be his wife.
28When Saul realized that the LORD was with David and how much his
daughter Michal loved him, 29Saul became even more afraid of him, and he
remained David's enemy for the rest of his life.
30Every time the commanders of the Philistines attacked, David was more
successful against them than all the rest of Saul's officers. So David's name
became very famous.

18:10 Or *an evil spirit.* 18:19 Or *But.*

Saul Tries to Kill David

19 Saul now urged his servants and his son Jonathan to assassinate
David. But Jonathan, because of his strong affection for David, 2 told
him what his father was planning. "Tomorrow morning," he warned him,
"you must find a hiding place out in the fields. 3 I'll ask my father to go out
there with me, and I'll talk to him about you. Then I'll tell you everything
I can find out."
4 The next morning Jonathan spoke with his father about David, saying
many good things about him. "The king must not sin against his servant
David," Jonathan said. "He's never done anything to harm you. He has al-
ways helped you in any way he could. 5 Have you forgotten about the time
he risked his life to kill the Philistine giant and how the LORD brought a
great victory to all Israel as a result? You were certainly happy about it then.
Why should you murder an innocent man like David? There is no reason
for it at all!"
6 So Saul listened to Jonathan and vowed, "As surely as the LORD lives,
David will not be killed."
7 Afterward Jonathan called David and told him what had happened. Then
he brought David to Saul, and David served in the court as before.
8 War broke out again after that, and David led his troops against the Phi-
listines. He attacked them with such fury that they all ran away.
9 But one day when Saul was sitting at home, with spear in hand, the tor-
menting spirit* from the LORD suddenly came upon him again. As David
played his harp, 10 Saul hurled his spear at David. But David dodged out of
the way, and leaving the spear stuck in the wall, he fled and escaped into
the night.

Michal Saves David's Life

11 Then Saul sent troops to watch David's house. They were told to kill David
when he came out the next morning. But Michal, David's wife, warned him,
"If you don't escape tonight, you will be dead by morning." 12 So she helped
him climb out through a window, and he fled and escaped. 13 Then she took
an idol* and put it in his bed, covered it with blankets, and put a cushion of
goat's hair at its head.
14 When the troops came to arrest David, she told them he was sick and
couldn't get out of bed.
15 But Saul sent the troops back to get David. He ordered, "Bring him to
me in his bed so I can kill him!" 16 But when they came to carry David out,
they discovered that it was only an idol in the bed with a cushion of goat's
hair at its head.
17 "Why have you betrayed me like this and let my enemy escape?" Saul
demanded of Michal.
"I had to," Michal replied. "He threatened to kill me if I didn't help him."
18 So David escaped and went to Ramah to see Samuel, and he told him all
that Saul had done to him. Then Samuel took David with him to live at Nai-
oth. 19 When the report reached Saul that David was at Naioth in Ramah, 20 he
sent troops to capture him. But when they arrived and saw Samuel leading
a group of prophets who were prophesying, the Spirit of God came upon
Saul's men, and they also began to prophesy. 21 When Saul heard what had

19:9 Or *evil spirit.* **19:13** Hebrew *teraphim;* also in 19:16.

Make a Difference

19:1–10

Don't Throw Back

For a second time, King Saul threw a spear at David. For a second time, David didn't throw one back.

There is too much retaliation in our world today. When people who say they are followers of God throw grenades of hurtful words and actions back into the mix, the world stumbles even further into the chaos of battle. No one needs Christians to add to the agitation that already exists. Retribution and followers of Jesus do not make a redeeming recipe for the world.

Even if anger is justified, what our world needs is individuals, armed with the hope of Jesus, who will patiently but confidently sow peace. Become a person who sows the seeds of peace today. Resolve to be a refreshing presence amid the strife.

Difference Maker

Whom are you tempted to retaliate against today? Ask God for the fortitude not to take revenge.

Question 20:17

How does Jonathan live out the second greatest commandment—love your neighbor as yourself?

happened, he sent other troops, but they, too, prophesied! The same thing
happened a third time. 22 Finally, Saul himself went to Ramah and arrived
at the great well in Secu. "Where are Samuel and David?" he demanded.
"They are at Naioth in Ramah," someone told him.
23 But on the way to Naioth in Ramah the Spirit of God came even upon
Saul, and he, too, began to prophesy all the way to Naioth! 24 He tore off his
clothes and lay naked on the ground all day and all night, prophesying in
the presence of Samuel. The people who were watching exclaimed, "What?
Is even Saul a prophet?"

Jonathan Helps David

20 David now fled from Naioth in Ramah and found Jonathan. "What
have I done?" he exclaimed. "What is my crime? How have I of-
fended your father that he is so determined to kill me?"
2 "That's not true!" Jonathan protested. "You're not going to die. He al-
ways tells me everything he's going to do, even the little things. I know my
father wouldn't hide something like this from me. It just isn't so!"
3 Then David took an oath before Jonathan and said, "Your father knows
perfectly well about our friendship, so he has said to himself, 'I won't tell
Jonathan—why should I hurt him?' But I swear to you that I am only a step
away from death! I swear it by the LORD and by your own soul!"
4 "Tell me what I can do to help you," Jonathan exclaimed.
5 David replied, "Tomorrow we celebrate the new moon festival. I've al-
ways eaten with the king on this occasion, but tomorrow I'll hide in the
field and stay there until the evening of the third day. 6 If your father asks
where I am, tell him I asked permission to go home to Bethlehem for an an-
nual family sacrifice. 7 If he says, 'Fine!' you will know all is well. But if he is
angry and loses his temper, you will know he is determined to kill me. 8 Show
me this loyalty as my sworn friend—for we made a solemn pact before the
LORD—or kill me yourself if I have sinned against your father. But please
don't betray me to him!"
9 "Never!" Jonathan exclaimed. "You know that if I had the slightest no-
tion my father was planning to kill you, I would tell you at once."
10 Then David asked, "How will I know whether or not your father is angry?"
11 "Come out to the field with me," Jonathan replied. And they went out
there together. 12 Then Jonathan told David, "I promise by the LORD, the God
of Israel, that by this time tomorrow, or the next day at the latest, I will talk
to my father and let you know at once how he feels about you. If he speaks
favorably about you, I will let you know. 13 But if he is angry and wants you
killed, may the LORD strike me and even kill me if I don't warn you so you can
escape and live. May the LORD be with you as he used to be with my father.
14 And may you treat me with the faithful love of the LORD as long as I live.
But if I die, 15 treat my family with this faithful love, even when the LORD
destroys all your enemies from the face of the earth."
16 So Jonathan made a solemn pact with David,* saying, "May the LORD
destroy all your enemies!" 17 And Jonathan made David reaffirm his vow of
friendship again, for Jonathan loved David as he loved himself.
18 Then Jonathan said, "Tomorrow we celebrate the new moon festival.
You will be missed when your place at the table is empty. 19 The day after

20:16 Hebrew *with the house of David.*

tomorrow, toward evening, go to the place where you hid before, and wait
there by the stone pile.* 20 I will come out and shoot three arrows to the side
of the stone pile as though I were shooting at a target. 21 Then I will send a
boy to bring the arrows back. If you hear me tell him, 'They're on this side,'
then you will know, as surely as the LORD lives, that all is well, and there is
no trouble. 22 But if I tell him, 'Go farther—the arrows are still ahead of you,'
then it will mean that you must leave immediately, for the LORD is sending
you away. 23 And may the LORD make us keep our promises to each other, for
he has witnessed them."

24 So David hid himself in the field, and when the new moon festival began,
the king sat down to eat. 25 He sat at his usual place against the wall, with
Jonathan sitting opposite him* and Abner beside him. But David's place was
empty. 26 Saul didn't say anything about it that day, for he said to himself,
"Something must have made David ceremonially unclean." 27 But when Da-
vid's place was empty again the next day, Saul asked Jonathan, "Why hasn't
the son of Jesse been here for the meal either yesterday or today?"

28 Jonathan replied, "David earnestly asked me if he could go to Beth-
lehem. 29 He said, 'Please let me go, for we are having a family sacrifice. My
brother demanded that I be there. So please let me get away to see my broth-
ers.' That's why he isn't here at the king's table."

30 Saul boiled with rage at Jonathan. "You stupid son of a whore!"* he
swore at him. "Do you think I don't know that you want him to be king in
your place, shaming yourself and your mother? 31 As long as that son of Jesse
is alive, you'll never be king. Now go and get him so I can kill him!"

32 "But why should he be put to death?" Jonathan asked his father. "What
has he done?" 33 Then Saul hurled his spear at Jonathan, intending to kill
him. So at last Jonathan realized that his father was really determined to
kill David.

34 Jonathan left the table in fierce anger and refused to eat on that second
day of the festival, for he was crushed by his father's shameful behavior to-
ward David.

35 The next morning, as agreed, Jonathan went out into the field and took
a young boy with him to gather his arrows. 36 "Start running," he told the boy,
"so you can find the arrows as I shoot them." So the boy ran, and Jonathan
shot an arrow beyond him. 37 When the boy had almost reached the arrow,
Jonathan shouted, "The arrow is still ahead of you. 38 Hurry, hurry, don't
wait." So the boy quickly gathered up the arrows and ran back to his master.
39 He, of course, suspected nothing; only Jonathan and David understood the
signal. 40 Then Jonathan gave his bow and arrows to the boy and told him to
take them back to town.

41 As soon as the boy was gone, David came out from where he had been
hiding near the stone pile.* Then David bowed three times to Jonathan with
his face to the ground. Both of them were in tears as they embraced each
other and said good-bye, especially David.

42 At last Jonathan said to David, "Go in peace, for we have sworn loyalty to
each other in the LORD's name. The LORD is the witness of a bond between us
and our children forever." Then David left, and Jonathan returned to the town.*

Prayer **20:42**

Lord, give me the opportunity and ability to have a friendship this deep. Amen.

20:19 Hebrew *the stone Ezel.* The meaning of the Hebrew is uncertain. 20:25 As in Greek version; Hebrew reads *with Jonathan standing.* 20:30 Hebrew *You son of a perverse and rebellious woman.* 20:41 As in Greek version; Hebrew reads *near the south edge.* 20:42 This sentence is numbered 21:1 in Hebrew text.

Question 22:1-4

David's family had seen Samuel anoint David as the future king. Now, in this dangerous setting, as David was fleeing for his life and hiding himself in a cave, what must his family have been struggling with? In what ways do you struggle to see God's plans working themselves out in your own life?

David Runs from Saul

21 1*David went to the town of Nob to see Ahimelech the priest. Ahim-
elech trembled when he saw him. “Why are you alone?” he asked.
“Why is no one with you?”
2“The king has sent me on a private matter,” David said. “He told me not
to tell anyone why I am here. I have told my men where to meet me later.
3Now, what is there to eat? Give me five loaves of bread or anything else
you have.”
4“We don't have any regular bread,” the priest replied. “But there is the
holy bread, which you can have if your young men have not slept with any
women recently.”
5“Don't worry,” David replied. “I never allow my men to be with women
when we are on a campaign. And since they stay clean even on ordinary trips,
how much more on this one!”
6Since there was no other food available, the priest gave him the holy
bread—the Bread of the Presence that was placed before the LORD in the
Tabernacle. It had just been replaced that day with fresh bread.
7Now Doeg the Edomite, Saul's chief herdsman, was there that day, having
been detained before the LORD.*
8David asked Ahimelech, “Do you have a spear or sword? The king's busi-
ness was so urgent that I didn't even have time to grab a weapon!”
9“I only have the sword of Goliath the Philistine, whom you killed in the
valley of Elah,” the priest replied. “It is wrapped in a cloth behind the ephod.
Take that if you want it, for there is nothing else here.”
“There is nothing like it!” David replied. “Give it to me!”
10So David escaped from Saul and went to King Achish of Gath. 11But the
officers of Achish were unhappy about his being there. “Isn't this David,
the king of the land?” they asked. “Isn't he the one the people honor with
dances, singing,

‘Saul has killed his thousands,
and David his ten thousands’?”

12David heard these comments and was very afraid of what King Achish of
Gath might do to him. 13So he pretended to be insane, scratching on doors
and drooling down his beard.
14Finally, King Achish said to his men, “Must you bring me a madman?
15We already have enough of them around here! Why should I let someone
like this be my guest?”

David at the Cave of Adullam

22 So David left Gath and escaped to the cave of Adullam. Soon his
brothers and all his other relatives joined him there. 2Then others
began coming—men who were in trouble or in debt or who were just
discontented—until David was the captain of about 400 men.
3Later David went to Mizpeh in Moab, where he asked the king, “Please
allow my father and mother to live here with you until I know what God is
going to do for me.” 4So David's parents stayed in Moab with the king during
the entire time David was living in his stronghold.

21:1 Verses 21:1-15 are numbered 21:2-16 in Hebrew text. **21:7** The meaning of the Hebrew is uncertain.

5One day the prophet Gad told David, "Leave the stronghold and return
to the land of Judah." So David went to the forest of Hereth.
6The news of his arrival in Judah soon reached Saul. At the time, the
king was sitting beneath the tamarisk tree on the hill at Gibeah, holding
his spear and surrounded by his officers.
7"Listen here, you men of Benjamin!" Saul shouted to his officers when
he heard the news. "Has that son of Jesse promised every one of you fields
and vineyards? Has he promised to make you all generals and captains in
his army?* 8Is that why you have conspired against me? For not one of you
told me when my own son made a solemn pact with the son of Jesse. You're
not even sorry for me. Think of it! My own son—encouraging him to kill
me, as he is trying to do this very day!"
9Then Doeg the Edomite, who was standing there with Saul's men,
spoke up. "When I was at Nob," he said, "I saw the son of Jesse talk-
ing to the priest, Ahimelech son of Ahitub. 10Ahimelech consulted the
LORD for him. Then he gave him food and the sword of Goliath the Phi-
listine."

The Slaughter of the Priests

11King Saul immediately sent for Ahimelech and all his family, who served
as priests at Nob. 12When they arrived, Saul shouted at him, "Listen to me,
you son of Ahitub!"

"What is it, my king?" Ahimelech asked.

13"Why have you and the son of Jesse conspired against me?" Saul de-
manded. "Why did you give him food and a sword? Why have you con-
sulted God for him? Why have you encouraged him to kill me, as he is
trying to do this very day?"
14"But sir," Ahimelech replied, "is anyone among all your servants as
faithful as David, your son-in-law? Why, he is the captain of your body-
guard and a highly honored member of your household! 15This was cer-
tainly not the first time I had consulted God for him! May the king not
accuse me and my family in this matter, for I knew nothing at all of any
plot against you."
16"You will surely die, Ahimelech, along with your entire family!" the
king shouted. 17And he ordered his bodyguards, "Kill these priests of the
LORD, for they are allies and conspirators with David! They knew he was
running away from me, but they didn't tell me!" But Saul's men refused
to kill the LORD's priests.
18Then the king said to Doeg, "You do it." So Doeg the Edomite turned
on them and killed them that day, eighty-five priests in all, still wearing
their priestly garments. 19Then he went to Nob, the town of the priests,
and killed the priests' families—men and women, children and babies—
and all the cattle, donkeys, sheep, and goats.
20Only Abiathar, one of the sons of Ahimelech, escaped and fled to Da-
vid. 21When he told David that Saul had killed the priests of the LORD,
22David exclaimed, "I knew it! When I saw Doeg the Edomite there that
day, I knew he was sure to tell Saul. Now I have caused the death of all your
father's family. 23Stay here with me, and don't be afraid. I will protect you
with my own life, for the same person wants to kill us both."

22:7 Hebrew *commanders of thousands and commanders of hundreds?*

Make a Difference

23:15-18

A True Friend

Jonathan is impressive. Putting his own life at risk, Jonathan went to find David and encouraged him to stay strong in his faith in the Lord. No matter how stressful, how difficult, how anxious the situation became, Jonathan cared most that David would trust in God.

Do you have friends like that? Are you a friend like that to others? Do your friendships place other priorities ahead of putting God first?

Difference Maker

Focus on friendships today that will help you make God your number one priority.

David Protects the Town of Keilah

23 One day news came to David that the Philistines were at Keilah stealing grain from the threshing floors. 2 David asked the LORD, "Should I go and attack them?"

"Yes, go and save Keilah," the LORD told him.

3 But David's men said, "We're afraid even here in Judah. We certainly don't want to go to Keilah to fight the whole Philistine army!"

4 So David asked the LORD again, and again the LORD replied, "Go down to Keilah, for I will help you conquer the Philistines."

5 So David and his men went to Keilah. They slaughtered the Philistines and took all their livestock and rescued the people of Keilah. 6 Now when Abiathar son of Ahimelech fled to David at Keilah, he brought the ephod with him.

7 Saul soon learned that David was at Keilah. "Good!" he exclaimed. "We've got him now! God has handed him over to me, for he has trapped himself in a walled town!" 8 So Saul mobilized his entire army to march to Keilah and besiege David and his men.

9 But David learned of Saul's plan and told Abiathar the priest to bring the ephod and ask the LORD what he should do. 10 Then David prayed, "O LORD, God of Israel, I have heard that Saul is planning to come and destroy Keilah because I am here. 11 Will the leaders of Keilah betray me to him?* And will Saul actually come as I have heard? O LORD, God of Israel, please tell me."

And the LORD said, "He will come."

12 Again David asked, "Will the leaders of Keilah betray me and my men to Saul?"

And the LORD replied, "Yes, they will betray you."

David Hides in the Wilderness

13 So David and his men—about 600 of them now—left Keilah and began roaming the countryside. Word soon reached Saul that David had escaped, so he didn't go to Keilah after all. 14 David now stayed in the strongholds of the wilderness and in the hill country of Ziph. Saul hunted him day after day, but God didn't let Saul find him.

15 One day near Horesh, David received the news that Saul was on the way to Ziph to search for him and kill him. 16 Jonathan went to find David and encouraged him to stay strong in his faith in God. 17 "Don't be afraid," Jonathan reassured him. "My father will never find you! You are going to be the king of Israel, and I will be next to you, as my father, Saul, is well aware." 18 So the two of them renewed their solemn pact before the LORD. Then Jonathan returned home, while David stayed at Horesh.

19 But now the men of Ziph went to Saul in Gibeah and betrayed David to him. "We know where David is hiding," they said. "He is in the strongholds of Horesh on the hill of Hakilah, which is in the southern part of Jeshimon. 20 Come down whenever you're ready, O king, and we will catch him and hand him over to you!"

21 "The LORD bless you," Saul said. "At last someone is concerned about me! 22 Go and check again to be sure of where he is staying and who has seen him there, for I know that he is very crafty. 23 Discover his hiding places, and come back when you are sure. Then I'll go with you. And if he is in the area at

23:11 Some manuscripts lack the first sentence of 23:11.

all, I'll track him down, even if I have to search every hiding place in Judah!"
24 So the men of Ziph returned home ahead of Saul.
Meanwhile, David and his men had moved into the wilderness of Maon
in the Arabah Valley south of Jeshimon. 25 When David heard that Saul and
his men were searching for him, he went even farther into the wilderness to
the great rock, and he remained there in the wilderness of Maon. But Saul
kept after him in the wilderness.
26 Saul and David were now on opposite sides of a mountain. Just as Saul
and his men began to close in on David and his men, 27 an urgent message
reached Saul that the Philistines were raiding Israel again. 28 So Saul quit
chasing David and returned to fight the Philistines. Ever since that time, the
place where David was camped has been called the Rock of Escape.* 29*David
then went to live in the strongholds of En-gedi.

Question 24:15

Read John 15:26 and 16:7-15. What did David understand about how God is our Advocate?

David Spares Saul's Life

24 1*After Saul returned from fighting the Philistines, he was told that
David had gone into the wilderness of En-gedi. 2 So Saul chose 3,000
elite troops from all Israel and went to search for David and his men near
the rocks of the wild goats.
3 At the place where the road passes some sheepfolds, Saul went into a
cave to relieve himself. But as it happened, David and his men were hiding
farther back in that very cave!
4 "Now's your opportunity!" David's men whispered to him. "Today the
LORD is telling you, 'I will certainly put your enemy into your power, to do
with as you wish.'" So David crept forward and cut off a piece of the hem
of Saul's robe.
5 But then David's conscience began bothering him because he had cut
Saul's robe. 6 He said to his men, "The LORD forbid that I should do this to
my lord the king. I shouldn't attack the LORD's anointed one, for the LORD
himself has chosen him." 7 So David restrained his men and did not let them
kill Saul.
After Saul had left the cave and gone on his way, 8 David came out and
shouted after him, "My lord the king!" And when Saul looked around, Da-
vid bowed low before him.
9 Then he shouted to Saul, "Why do you listen to the people who say I am
trying to harm you? 10 This very day you can see with your own eyes it isn't
true. For the LORD placed you at my mercy back there in the cave. Some of
my men told me to kill you, but I spared you. For I said, 'I will never harm
the king—he is the LORD's anointed one.' 11 Look, my father, at what I have
in my hand. It is a piece of the hem of your robe! I cut it off, but I didn't kill
you. This proves that I am not trying to harm you and that I have not sinned
against you, even though you have been hunting for me to kill me.
12 "May the LORD judge between us. Perhaps the LORD will punish you
for what you are trying to do to me, but I will never harm you. 13 As that old
proverb says, 'From evil people come evil deeds.' So you can be sure I will
never harm you. 14 Who is the king of Israel trying to catch anyway? Should he
spend his time chasing one who is as worthless as a dead dog or a single flea?
15 May the LORD therefore judge which of us is right and punish the guilty
one. He is my advocate, and he will rescue me from your power!"

23:28 Hebrew *Sela-hammahlekoth.* **23:29** Verse 23:29 is numbered 24:1 in Hebrew text.
24:1 Verses 24:1-22 are numbered 24:2-23 in Hebrew text.

Question 24:17

Read Proverbs 25:21 and Romans 12:17-21. What are some practical ways that you could repay evil with good?

16 When David had finished speaking, Saul called back, "Is that really you,
my son David?" Then he began to cry. 17 And he said to David, "You are a
better man than I am, for you have repaid me good for evil. 18 Yes, you have
been amazingly kind to me today, for when the LORD put me in a place where
you could have killed me, you didn't do it. 19 Who else would let his enemy
get away when he had him in his power? May the LORD reward you well for
the kindness you have shown me today. 20 And now I realize that you are
surely going to be king, and that the kingdom of Israel will flourish under
your rule. 21 Now swear to me by the LORD that when that happens you will
not kill my family and destroy my line of descendants!"
22 So David promised this to Saul with an oath. Then Saul went home, but
David and his men went back to their stronghold.

The Death of Samuel

25 Now Samuel died, and all Israel gathered for his funeral. They buried him at his house in Ramah.

Nabal Angers David

Then David moved down to the wilderness of Maon.* 2 There was a wealthy
man from Maon who owned property near the town of Carmel. He had 3,000
sheep and 1,000 goats, and it was sheep-shearing time. 3 This man's name was
Nabal, and his wife, Abigail, was a sensible and beautiful woman. But Nabal,
a descendant of Caleb, was crude and mean in all his dealings.
4 When David heard that Nabal was shearing his sheep, 5 he sent ten of his
young men to Carmel with this message for Nabal: 6 "Peace and prosperity to
you, your family, and everything you own! 7 I am told that it is sheep-shearing
time. While your shepherds stayed among us near Carmel, we never harmed
them, and nothing was ever stolen from them. 8 Ask your own men, and they
will tell you this is true. So would you be kind to us, since we have come at
a time of celebration? Please share any provisions you might have on hand
with us and with your friend David." 9 David's young men gave this message
to Nabal in David's name, and they waited for a reply.
10 "Who is this fellow David?" Nabal sneered to the young men. "Who
does this son of Jesse think he is? There are lots of servants these days who
run away from their masters. 11 Should I take my bread and my water and my
meat that I've slaughtered for my shearers and give it to a band of outlaws
who come from who knows where?"
12 So David's young men returned and told him what Nabal had said. 13 "Get
your swords!" was David's reply as he strapped on his own. Then 400 men
started off with David, and 200 remained behind to guard their equipment.
14 Meanwhile, one of Nabal's servants went to Abigail and told her, "David
sent messengers from the wilderness to greet our master, but he screamed
insults at them. 15 These men have been very good to us, and we never suffered any harm from them. Nothing was stolen from us the whole time they
were with us. 16 In fact, day and night they were like a wall of protection to us
and the sheep. 17 You need to know this and figure out what to do, for there is
going to be trouble for our master and his whole family. He's so ill-tempered
that no one can even talk to him!"
18 Abigail wasted no time. She quickly gathered 200 loaves of bread, two

25:1 As in Greek version (see also 25:2); Hebrew reads *Paran*.

wineskins full of wine, five sheep that had been slaughtered, nearly a bushel*
of roasted grain, 100 clusters of raisins, and 200 fig cakes. She packed them on
donkeys 19 and said to her servants, "Go on ahead. I will follow you shortly."
But she didn't tell her husband Nabal what she was doing.
20 As she was riding her donkey into a mountain ravine, she saw David and
his men coming toward her. 21 David had just been saying, "A lot of good it
did to help this fellow. We protected his flocks in the wilderness, and noth-
ing he owned was lost or stolen. But he has repaid me evil for good. 22 May
God strike me and kill me* if even one man of his household is still alive
tomorrow morning!"

Abigail Intercedes for Nabal

23 When Abigail saw David, she quickly got off her donkey and bowed low
before him. 24 She fell at his feet and said, "I accept all blame in this matter,
my lord. Please listen to what I have to say. 25 I know Nabal is a wicked and
ill-tempered man; please don't pay any attention to him. He is a fool, just as
his name suggests.* But I never even saw the young men you sent.
26 "Now, my lord, as surely as the LORD lives and you yourself live, since
the LORD has kept you from murdering and taking vengeance into your own
hands, let all your enemies and those who try to harm you be as cursed as
Nabal is. 27 And here is a present that I, your servant, have brought to you and
your young men. 28 Please forgive me if I have offended you in any way. The
LORD will surely reward you with a lasting dynasty, for you are fighting the
LORD's battles. And you have not done wrong throughout your entire life.
29 "Even when you are chased by those who seek to kill you, your life is
safe in the care of the LORD your God, secure in his treasure pouch! But the
lives of your enemies will disappear like stones shot from a sling! 30 When the
LORD has done all he promised and has made you leader of Israel, 31 don't let
this be a blemish on your record. Then your conscience won't have to bear
the staggering burden of needless bloodshed and vengeance. And when the
LORD has done these great things for you, please remember me, your servant!"
32 David replied to Abigail, "Praise the LORD, the God of Israel, who has
sent you to meet me today! 33 Thank God for your good sense! Bless you for
keeping me from murder and from carrying out vengeance with my own
hands. 34 For I swear by the LORD, the God of Israel, who has kept me from
hurting you, that if you had not hurried out to meet me, not one of Nabal's
men would still be alive tomorrow morning." 35 Then David accepted her
present and told her, "Return home in peace. I have heard what you said.
We will not kill your husband."
36 When Abigail arrived home, she found that Nabal was throwing a big
party and was celebrating like a king. He was very drunk, so she didn't tell
him anything about her meeting with David until dawn the next day. 37 In the
morning when Nabal was sober, his wife told him what had happened. As a
result he had a stroke,* and he lay paralyzed on his bed like a stone. 38 About
ten days later, the LORD struck him, and he died.

David Marries Abigail

39 When David heard that Nabal was dead, he said, "Praise the LORD, who
has avenged the insult I received from Nabal and has kept me from doing

25:18 Hebrew *5 seahs* [36.5 liters]. **25:22** As in Greek version; Hebrew reads *May God strike and kill the enemies of David.* **25:25** The name *Nabal* means "fool." **25:37** Hebrew *his heart failed him.*

Make a Difference

25:2-35

Excuse for Sin?

Unfortunately, the wear and tear of turmoil seemed to be getting to David. Here, his ethics and integrity were beginning to show some cracks. He was strained and frantic. He was getting run down. If it hadn't been for Abigail's intervention here, David would have been guilty of a huge mistake.

Slipping into sin was understandable considering all the stress David was under, right? Well, can we ever really excuse sin just because life is difficult? Just because someone has a bad day or month, does that mean it is okay for them to compromise their soul? Is anyone ever allowed to sin just because they're stressed out?

Difference Maker

Identify some of the sins you permit yourself to do when you are tired or angry or stressed out. Pray that God will send good people into your life at just the right times to help you avoid making some big mistakes.

Question **26:6**

David was a bit of a social media king. He had a huge network of people following him from many different regions with many different backgrounds. Why did all these different people follow David? What did they see in him that they didn't see in King Saul?

it myself. Nabal has received the punishment for his sin." Then David sent
messengers to Abigail to ask her to become his wife.
40 When the messengers arrived at Carmel, they told Abigail, "David has
sent us to take you back to marry him."
41 She bowed low to the ground and responded, "I, your servant, would be
happy to marry David. I would even be willing to become a slave, washing
the feet of his servants!" 42 Quickly getting ready, she took along five of her
servant girls as attendants, mounted her donkey, and went with David's
messengers. And so she became his wife. 43 David also married Ahinoam from
Jezreel, making both of them his wives. 44 Saul, meanwhile, had given his
daughter Michal, David's wife, to a man from Gallim named Palti son of
Laish.

David Spares Saul Again

26 Now some men from Ziph came to Saul at Gibeah to tell him, "Da-
vid is hiding on the hill of Hakilah, which overlooks Jeshimon."
2 So Saul took 3,000 of Israel's elite troops and went to hunt him down in
the wilderness of Ziph. 3 Saul camped along the road beside the hill of Ha-
kilah, near Jeshimon, where David was hiding. When David learned that
Saul had come after him into the wilderness, 4 he sent out spies to verify the
report of Saul's arrival.
5 David slipped over to Saul's camp one night to look around. Saul and
Abner son of Ner, the commander of his army, were sleeping inside a ring
formed by the slumbering warriors. 6 "Who will volunteer to go in there
with me?" David asked Ahimelech the Hittite and Abishai son of Zeruiah,
Joab's brother.
"I'll go with you," Abishai replied. 7 So David and Abishai went right into
Saul's camp and found him asleep, with his spear stuck in the ground beside
his head. Abner and the soldiers were lying asleep around him.
8 "God has surely handed your enemy over to you this time!" Abishai whis-
pered to David. "Let me pin him to the ground with one thrust of the spear;
I won't need to strike twice!"
9 "No!" David said. "Don't kill him. For who can remain innocent after
attacking the LORD's anointed one? 10 Surely the LORD will strike Saul down
someday, or he will die of old age or in battle. 11 The LORD forbid that I should
kill the one he has anointed! But take his spear and that jug of water beside
his head, and then let's get out of here!"
12 So David took the spear and jug of water that were near Saul's head.
Then he and Abishai got away without anyone seeing them or even waking
up, because the LORD had put Saul's men into a deep sleep.
13 David climbed the hill opposite the camp until he was at a safe distance.
14 Then he shouted down to the soldiers and to Abner son of Ner, "Wake up,
Abner!"
"Who is it?" Abner demanded.
15 "Well, Abner, you're a great man, aren't you?" David taunted. "Where in
all Israel is there anyone as mighty? So why haven't you guarded your master
the king when someone came to kill him? 16 This isn't good at all! I swear by
the LORD that you and your men deserve to die, because you failed to protect
your master, the LORD's anointed! Look around! Where are the king's spear
and the jug of water that were beside his head?"

17 Saul recognized David's voice and called out, "Is that you, my son
David?"
And David replied, "Yes, my lord the king. 18 Why are you chasing me?
What have I done? What is my crime? 19 But now let my lord the king listen
to his servant. If the LORD has stirred you up against me, then let him accept
my offering. But if this is simply a human scheme, then may those involved
be cursed by the LORD. For they have driven me from my home, so I can no
longer live among the LORD's people, and they have said, 'Go, worship pagan
gods.' 20 Must I die on foreign soil, far from the presence of the LORD? Why
has the king of Israel come out to search for a single flea? Why does he hunt
me down like a partridge on the mountains?"
21 Then Saul confessed, "I have sinned. Come back home, my son, and I
will no longer try to harm you, for you valued my life today. I have been a
fool and very, very wrong."
22 "Here is your spear, O king," David replied. "Let one of your young men
come over and get it. 23 The LORD gives his own reward for doing good and
for being loyal, and I refused to kill you even when the LORD placed you in
my power, for you are the LORD's anointed one. 24 Now may the LORD value
my life, even as I have valued yours today. May he rescue me from all my
troubles."
25 And Saul said to David, "Blessings on you, my son David. You will do
many heroic deeds, and you will surely succeed." Then David went away,
and Saul returned home.

David among the Philistines

27 But David kept thinking to himself, "Someday Saul is going to get
me. The best thing I can do is escape to the Philistines. Then Saul will
stop hunting for me in Israelite territory, and I will finally be safe."
2 So David took his 600 men and went over and joined Achish son of
Maoch, the king of Gath. 3 David and his men and their families settled
there with Achish at Gath. David brought his two wives along with him—
Ahinoam from Jezreel and Abigail, Nabal's widow from Carmel. 4 Word soon
reached Saul that David had fled to Gath, so he stopped hunting for him.
5 One day David said to Achish, "If it is all right with you, we would rather
live in one of the country towns instead of here in the royal city."
6 So Achish gave him the town of Ziklag (which still belongs to the kings
of Judah to this day), 7 and they lived there among the Philistines for a year
and four months.
8 David and his men spent their time raiding the Geshurites, the Girzites,
and the Amalekites—people who had lived near Shur, toward the land of
Egypt, since ancient times. 9 David did not leave one person alive in the vil-
lages he attacked. He took the sheep, goats, cattle, donkeys, camels, and
clothing before returning home to see King Achish.
10 "Where did you make your raid today?" Achish would ask.
And David would reply, "Against the south of Judah, the Jerahmeelites,
and the Kenites."
11 No one was left alive to come to Gath and tell where he had really been.
This happened again and again while he was living among the Philistines.
12 Achish believed David and thought to himself, "By now the people of Israel
must hate him bitterly. Now he will have to stay here and serve me forever!"

Question 26:24

In what ways was Saul fighting God, and in what ways was David trusting God?

Saul Consults a Medium

28 About that time the Philistines mustered their armies for another
war with Israel. King Achish told David, "You and your men will be
expected to join me in battle."
2 "Very well!" David agreed. "Now you will see for yourself what we can do."
Then Achish told David, "I will make you my personal bodyguard for life."
3 Meanwhile, Samuel had died, and all Israel had mourned for him. He
was buried in Ramah, his hometown. And Saul had banned from the land of
Israel all mediums and those who consult the spirits of the dead.
4 The Philistines set up their camp at Shunem, and Saul gathered all the
army of Israel and camped at Gilboa. 5 When Saul saw the vast Philistine
army, he became frantic with fear. 6 He asked the LORD what he should do,
but the LORD refused to answer him, either by dreams or by sacred lots* or
by the prophets. 7 Saul then said to his advisers, "Find a woman who is a
medium, so I can go and ask her what to do."
His advisers replied, "There is a medium at Endor."
8 So Saul disguised himself by wearing ordinary clothing instead of his
royal robes. Then he went to the woman's home at night, accompanied by
two of his men.
"I have to talk to a man who has died," he said. "Will you call up his spirit
for me?"
9 "Are you trying to get me killed?" the woman demanded. "You know
that Saul has outlawed all the mediums and all who consult the spirits of
the dead. Why are you setting a trap for me?"
10 But Saul took an oath in the name of the LORD and promised, "As surely
as the LORD lives, nothing bad will happen to you for doing this."
11 Finally, the woman said, "Well, whose spirit do you want me to call up?"
"Call up Samuel," Saul replied.
12 When the woman saw Samuel, she screamed, "You've deceived me! You
are Saul!"
13 "Don't be afraid!" the king told her. "What do you see?"
"I see a god* coming up out of the earth," she said.
14 "What does he look like?" Saul asked.
"He is an old man wrapped in a robe," she replied. Saul realized it was
Samuel, and he fell to the ground before him.
15 "Why have you disturbed me by calling me back?" Samuel asked Saul.
"Because I am in deep trouble," Saul replied. "The Philistines are at war
with me, and God has left me and won't reply by prophets or dreams. So I
have called for you to tell me what to do."
16 But Samuel replied, "Why ask me, since the LORD has left you and has
become your enemy? 17 The LORD has done just as he said he would. He has
torn the kingdom from you and given it to your rival, David. 18 The LORD
has done this to you today because you refused to carry out his fierce anger
against the Amalekites. 19 What's more, the LORD will hand you and the army
of Israel over to the Philistines tomorrow, and you and your sons will be here
with me. The LORD will bring down the entire army of Israel in defeat."
20 Saul fell full length on the ground, paralyzed with fright because of
Samuel's words. He was also faint with hunger, for he had eaten nothing
all day and all night.

28:6 Hebrew *by Urim*. 28:13 Or *gods*.

21 When the woman saw how distraught he was, she said, "Sir, I obeyed your command at the risk of my life. 22 Now do what I say, and let me give you a little something to eat so you can regain your strength for the trip back."

23 But Saul refused to eat anything. Then his advisers joined the woman in urging him to eat, so he finally yielded and got up from the ground and sat on the couch.

24 The woman had been fattening a calf, so she hurried out and killed it. She took some flour, kneaded it into dough and baked unleavened bread.
25 She brought the meal to Saul and his advisers, and they ate it. Then they went out into the night.

The Philistines Reject David

29 The entire Philistine army now mobilized at Aphek, and the Israelites camped at the spring in Jezreel. 2 As the Philistine rulers were leading out their troops in groups of hundreds and thousands, David and his men marched at the rear with King Achish. 3 But the Philistine commanders demanded, "What are these Hebrews doing here?"

And Achish told them, "This is David, the servant of King Saul of Israel. He's been with me for years, and I've never found a single fault in him from the day he arrived until today."

4 But the Philistine commanders were angry. "Send him back to the town you've given him!" they demanded. "He can't go into the battle with us. What if he turns against us in battle and becomes our adversary? Is there any better way for him to reconcile himself with his master than by handing our heads over to him? 5 Isn't this the same David about whom the women of Israel sing in their dances,

'Saul has killed his thousands,
and David his ten thousands'?"

6 So Achish finally summoned David and said to him, "I swear by the LORD that you have been a trustworthy ally. I think you should go with me into battle, for I've never found a single flaw in you from the day you arrived until today. But the other Philistine rulers won't hear of it. 7 Please don't upset them, but go back quietly."

8 "What have I done to deserve this treatment?" David demanded. "What have you ever found in your servant, that I can't go and fight the enemies of my lord the king?"

9 But Achish insisted, "As far as I'm concerned, you're as perfect as an angel of God. But the Philistine commanders are afraid to have you with them in the battle. 10 Now get up early in the morning, and leave with your men as soon as it gets light."

11 So David and his men headed back into the land of the Philistines, while the Philistine army went on to Jezreel.

David Destroys the Amalekites

30 Three days later, when David and his men arrived home at their town of Ziklag, they found that the Amalekites had made a raid into the Negev and Ziklag; they had crushed Ziklag and burned it to the

Question 29:5

This song, one of the greatest hits of ancient Israel, followed David around. The enemies of Israel knew this song. The people of Israel knew this song. King Saul knew this song. How did this song help spread the news about what God was doing through David? How can songs spread the news about what God is doing through his people today?

Prayer **30:6**

Jesus, give me the strength to boldly stand for you in this important moment of history. Amen.

ground. 2They had carried off the women and children and everyone else
but without killing anyone.
3When David and his men saw the ruins and realized what had happened
to their families, 4they wept until they could weep no more. 5David's two
wives, Ahinoam from Jezreel and Abigail, the widow of Nabal from Carmel,
were among those captured. 6David was now in great danger because all his
men were very bitter about losing their sons and daughters, and they began
to talk of stoning him. But David found strength in the LORD his God.
7Then he said to Abiathar the priest, "Bring me the ephod!" So Abiathar
brought it. 8Then David asked the LORD, "Should I chase after this band of
raiders? Will I catch them?"
And the LORD told him, "Yes, go after them. You will surely recover everything that was taken from you!"
9So David and his 600 men set out, and they came to the brook Besor. 10But
200 of the men were too exhausted to cross the brook, so David continued
the pursuit with 400 men.
11Along the way they found an Egyptian man in a field and brought him to
David. They gave him some bread to eat and water to drink. 12They also gave
him part of a fig cake and two clusters of raisins, for he hadn't had anything
to eat or drink for three days and nights. Before long his strength returned.
13"To whom do you belong, and where do you come from?" David asked
him.
"I am an Egyptian—the slave of an Amalekite," he replied. "My master
abandoned me three days ago because I was sick. 14We were on our way back
from raiding the Kerethites in the Negev, the territory of Judah, and the land
of Caleb, and we had just burned Ziklag."
15"Will you lead me to this band of raiders?" David asked.
The young man replied, "If you take an oath in God's name that you will not kill me or give me back to my master, then I will guide you to them."
16So he led David to them, and they found the Amalekites spread out
across the fields, eating and drinking and dancing with joy because of the
vast amount of plunder they had taken from the Philistines and the land of
Judah. 17David and his men rushed in among them and slaughtered them
throughout that night and the entire next day until evening. None of the
Amalekites escaped except 400 young men who fled on camels. 18David got
back everything the Amalekites had taken, and he rescued his two wives.
19Nothing was missing: small or great, son or daughter, nor anything else
that had been taken. David brought everything back. 20He also recovered all
the flocks and herds, and his men drove them ahead of the other livestock.
"This plunder belongs to David!" they said.
21Then David returned to the brook Besor and met up with the 200 men
who had been left behind because they were too exhausted to go with him.
They went out to meet David and his men, and David greeted them joyfully.
22But some evil troublemakers among David's men said, "They didn't go
with us, so they can't have any of the plunder we recovered. Give them their
wives and children, and tell them to be gone."
23But David said, "No, my brothers! Don't be selfish with what the LORD
has given us. He has kept us safe and helped us defeat the band of raiders
that attacked us. 24Who will listen when you talk like this? We share and
share alike—those who go to battle and those who guard the equipment."

25 From then on David made this a decree and regulation for Israel, and it is
still followed today.
26 When he arrived at Ziklag, David sent part of the plunder to the elders
of Judah, who were his friends. "Here is a present for you, taken from the
LORD's enemies," he said.
27 The gifts were sent to the people of the following towns David had vis-
ited: Bethel, Ramoth-negev, Jattir, 28 Aroer, Siphmoth, Eshtemoa, 29 Racal,*
the towns of the Jerahmeelites, the towns of the Kenites, 30 Hormah, Bor-
ashan, Athach, 31 Hebron, and all the other places David and his men had
visited.

The Death of Saul

31 Now the Philistines attacked Israel, and the men of Israel fled be-
fore them. Many were slaughtered on the slopes of Mount Gilboa.
2 The Philistines closed in on Saul and his sons, and they killed three of his
sons—Jonathan, Abinadab, and Malkishua. 3 The fighting grew very fierce
around Saul, and the Philistine archers caught up with him and wounded
him severely.
4 Saul groaned to his armor bearer, "Take your sword and kill me before
these pagan Philistines come to run me through and taunt and torture me."
But his armor bearer was afraid and would not do it. So Saul took his own
sword and fell on it. 5 When his armor bearer realized that Saul was dead, he
fell on his own sword and died beside the king. 6 So Saul, his three sons, his
armor bearer, and his troops all died together that same day.
7 When the Israelites on the other side of the Jezreel Valley and beyond
the Jordan saw that the Israelite army had fled and that Saul and his sons
were dead, they abandoned their towns and fled. So the Philistines moved
in and occupied their towns.
8 The next day, when the Philistines went out to strip the dead, they found
the bodies of Saul and his three sons on Mount Gilboa. 9 So they cut off Saul's
head and stripped off his armor. Then they proclaimed the good news of
Saul's death in their pagan temple and to the people throughout the land of
Philistia. 10 They placed his armor in the temple of the Ashtoreths, and they
fastened his body to the wall of the city of Beth-shan.
11 But when the people of Jabesh-gilead heard what the Philistines had
done to Saul, 12 all their mighty warriors traveled through the night to Beth-
shan and took the bodies of Saul and his sons down from the wall. They
brought them to Jabesh, where they burned the bodies. 13 Then they took
their bones and buried them beneath the tamarisk tree at Jabesh, and they
fasted for seven days.

30:29 Greek version reads *Carmel.*

Question 31:4

Saul's story ended tragically. Going back through his story, where did Saul go wrong? How can we avoid making a similar type of mess of our own lives?

2 Samuel Introduction

You are about to join David as he stepped into his anointing as king. His journey as king was packed with beautiful moments when he represented why he was a man after God's own heart. You'll find moments when he represented the heart of God in stories like his encounter with Jonathan's son, Mephibosheth. You're also going to find stories full of battles and betrayals. You'll encounter a dysfunctional family with all kinds of heartbreaking sins. This is a book that will show you how completely imperfect King David was in his journey. Honestly, you're going to find reasons to question how a man like David could ever be considered "a man after God's own heart" (1 Samuel 13:14).

With all the craziness you're about to read, look deeply into King David's repentance. Pay attention to his relationship with God. Even though David's life was a bit of a roller coaster, you will find a trustworthy track. In the middle of the twists and turns of King David's life, you will notice a deep love between King David and our heavenly Father.

His story is a wonderful example to us that we don't have to be perfect to love God and be loved by him. Remember, God knew everything David would do before he ever anointed him king as a shepherd boy. David was a man after God's own heart because of his heart for God. Nothing you're about to read could ever change the deep love God had for David just as nothing you could ever do will change God's deep love for you.

Story Arcs

- **Zion**
- **Nathan**
- **Bathsheba**

2 Samuel

David Learns of Saul's Death

1 After the death of Saul, David returned from his victory over the Am-
alekites and spent two days in Ziklag. 2 On the third day a man arrived
from Saul's army camp. He had torn his clothes and put dirt on his head to
show that he was in mourning. He fell to the ground before David in deep
respect.
3 "Where have you come from?" David asked.
"I escaped from the Israelite camp," the man replied.
4 "What happened?" David demanded. "Tell me how the battle went."
The man replied, "Our entire army fled from the battle. Many of the men
are dead, and Saul and his son Jonathan are also dead."
5 "How do you know Saul and Jonathan are dead?" David demanded of
the young man.
6 The man answered, "I happened to be on Mount Gilboa, and there was
Saul leaning on his spear with the enemy chariots and charioteers closing in
on him. 7 When he turned and saw me, he cried out for me to come to him.
'How can I help?' I asked him.
8 "He responded, 'Who are you?'
"'I am an Amalekite,' I told him.
9 "Then he begged me, 'Come over here and put me out of my misery, for
I am in terrible pain and want to die.'
10 "So I killed him," the Amalekite told David, "for I knew he couldn't live.
Then I took his crown and his armband, and I have brought them here to
you, my lord."
11 David and his men tore their clothes in sorrow when they heard the
news. 12 They mourned and wept and fasted all day for Saul and his son Jon-
athan, and for the LORD's army and the nation of Israel, because they had
died by the sword that day.
13 Then David said to the young man who had brought the news, "Where
are you from?"
And he replied, "I am a foreigner, an Amalekite, who lives in your land."
14 "Why were you not afraid to kill the LORD's anointed one?" David
asked.
15 Then David said to one of his men, "Kill him!" So the man thrust his
sword into the Amalekite and killed him. 16 "You have condemned yourself,"
David said, "for you yourself confessed that you killed the LORD's anointed
one."

David's Song for Saul and Jonathan

17 Then David composed a funeral song for Saul and Jonathan, 18 and he com-
manded that it be taught to the people of Judah. It is known as the Song of
the Bow, and it is recorded in *The Book of Jashar.**

1:18 Or *The Book of the Upright.*

Question 1:26

Have you ever lost a family member or a good friend? What does this song reveal about the loss David felt?

19 Your pride and joy, O Israel, lies dead on the hills!
Oh, how the mighty heroes have fallen!
20 Don't announce the news in Gath,
don't proclaim it in the streets of Ashkelon,
or the daughters of the Philistines will rejoice
and the pagans will laugh in triumph.

21 O mountains of Gilboa,
let there be no dew or rain upon you,
nor fruitful fields producing offerings of grain.*
For there the shield of the mighty heroes was defiled;
the shield of Saul will no longer be anointed with oil.
22 The bow of Jonathan was powerful,
and the sword of Saul did its mighty work.
They shed the blood of their enemies
and pierced the bodies of mighty heroes.

23 How beloved and gracious were Saul and Jonathan!
They were together in life and in death.
They were swifter than eagles,
stronger than lions.
24 O women of Israel, weep for Saul,
for he dressed you in luxurious scarlet clothing,
in garments decorated with gold.

25 Oh, how the mighty heroes have fallen in battle!
Jonathan lies dead on the hills.
26 How I weep for you, my brother Jonathan!
Oh, how much I loved you!
And your love for me was deep,
deeper than the love of women!

27 Oh, how the mighty heroes have fallen!
Stripped of their weapons, they lie dead.

David Anointed King of Judah

2 After this, David asked the LORD, "Should I move back to one of the
towns of Judah?"

"Yes," the LORD replied.

Then David asked, "Which town should I go to?"

"To Hebron," the LORD answered.

2 David's two wives were Ahinoam from Jezreel and Abigail, the widow of
Nabal from Carmel. So David and his wives 3 and his men and their families
all moved to Judah, and they settled in the villages near Hebron. 4 Then the
men of Judah came to David and anointed him king over the people of Judah.

When David heard that the men of Jabesh-gilead had buried Saul, 5 he sent
them this message: "May the LORD bless you for being so loyal to your master
Saul and giving him a decent burial. 6 May the LORD be loyal to you in return
and reward you with his unfailing love! And I, too, will reward you for what

1:21 The meaning of the Hebrew is uncertain.

you have done. 7 Now that Saul is dead, I ask you to be my strong and loyal
subjects like the people of Judah, who have anointed me as their new king."

Ishbosheth Proclaimed King of Israel

8 But Abner son of Ner, the commander of Saul's army, had already gone to
Mahanaim with Saul's son Ishbosheth.* 9 There he proclaimed Ishbosheth
king over Gilead, Jezreel, Ephraim, Benjamin, the land of the Ashurites,
and all the rest of Israel.
10 Ishbosheth, Saul's son, was forty years old when he became king, and
he ruled from Mahanaim for two years. Meanwhile, the people of Judah
remained loyal to David. 11 David made Hebron his capital, and he ruled as
king of Judah for seven and a half years.

War between Israel and Judah

12 One day Abner led Ishbosheth's troops from Mahanaim to Gibeon. 13 About
the same time, Joab son of Zeruiah led David's troops out and met them at
the pool of Gibeon. The two groups sat down there, facing each other from
opposite sides of the pool.
14 Then Abner suggested to Joab, "Let's have a few of our warriors fight
hand to hand here in front of us."
"All right," Joab agreed. 15 So twelve men were chosen to fight from each
side—twelve men of Benjamin representing Ishbosheth son of Saul, and
twelve representing David. 16 Each one grabbed his opponent by the hair and
thrust his sword into the other's side so that all of them died. So this place at
Gibeon has been known ever since as the Field of Swords.*
17 A fierce battle followed that day, and Abner and the men of Israel were
defeated by the forces of David.

The Death of Asahel

18 Joab, Abishai, and Asahel—the three sons of Zeruiah—were among Da-
vid's forces that day. Asahel could run like a gazelle, 19 and he began chas-
ing Abner. He pursued him relentlessly, not stopping for anything. 20 When
Abner looked back and saw him coming, he called out, "Is that you, Asahel?"
"Yes, it is," he replied.
21 "Go fight someone else!" Abner warned. "Take on one of the younger
men, and strip him of his weapons." But Asahel kept right on chasing Abner.
22 Again Abner shouted to him, "Get away from here! I don't want to kill
you. How could I ever face your brother Joab again?"
23 But Asahel refused to turn back, so Abner thrust the butt end of his
spear through Asahel's stomach, and the spear came out through his back.
He stumbled to the ground and died there. And everyone who came by that
spot stopped and stood still when they saw Asahel lying there.
24 When Joab and Abishai found out what had happened, they set out after
Abner. The sun was just going down as they arrived at the hill of Ammah
near Giah, along the road to the wilderness of Gibeon. 25 Abner's troops from
the tribe of Benjamin regrouped there at the top of the hill to take a stand.
26 Abner shouted down to Joab, "Must we always be killing each other?
Don't you realize that bitterness is the only result? When will you call off
your men from chasing their Israelite brothers?"

2:8 *Ishbosheth* is another name for Esh-baal. **2:16** Hebrew *Helkath-hazzurim.*

Question **2:10**

Ishbosheth, one of Saul's sons who had survived his father's reign, was proclaimed king in the northern region of Israel. David, meanwhile, had been anointed king of Judah (2:4). In essence, the kingdom that Samuel and Saul had united split into two kingdoms after Saul was killed. The situation remained like this for the next seven and a half years. If you were David, how discouraged would you be? In what ways do you think you would have struggled to believe God's promise that your throne would be established over all of Israel?

[27] Then Joab said, "God only knows what would have happened if you
hadn't spoken, for we would have chased you all night if necessary." [28] So
Joab blew the ram's horn, and his men stopped chasing the troops of Israel.
[29] All that night Abner and his men retreated through the Jordan Valley.*
They crossed the Jordan River, traveling all through the morning,* and
didn't stop until they arrived at Mahanaim.
[30] Meanwhile, Joab and his men also returned home. When Joab counted his
casualties, he discovered that only 19 men were missing in addition to Asahel.
[31] But 360 of Abner's men had been killed, all from the tribe of Benjamin. [32] Joab
and his men took Asahel's body to Bethlehem and buried him there in his
father's tomb. Then they traveled all night and reached Hebron at daybreak.

Question 3:1

Through years of war between northern tribes of Israel (which supported Saul's son Ishbosheth) and the tribe of Judah (which supported David), the outcome became clearer. David grew in strength while Saul's dynasty started to crack. Eventually, Ishbosheth's greatest general, Abner, realized that he should have been supporting David's claim to the throne over all of Israel (3:9). For a moment, put yourself in the mind of one of the common people of Israel. Do you think you could have discerned which king to follow? How can you know who is the right leader to follow when the world is so divided?

3 That was the beginning of a long war between those who were loyal to
Saul and those loyal to David. As time passed David became stronger
and stronger, while Saul's dynasty became weaker and weaker.

David's Sons Born in Hebron

[2] These are the sons who were born to David in Hebron:

The oldest was Amnon, whose mother was Ahinoam from Jezreel.
[3] The second was Daniel,* whose mother was Abigail, the widow of Nabal from Carmel.
The third was Absalom, whose mother was Maacah, the daughter of Talmai, king of Geshur.
[4] The fourth was Adonijah, whose mother was Haggith.
The fifth was Shephatiah, whose mother was Abital.
[5] The sixth was Ithream, whose mother was Eglah, David's wife.

These sons were all born to David in Hebron.

Abner Joins Forces with David

[6] As the war between the house of Saul and the house of David went on, Abner
became a powerful leader among those loyal to Saul. [7] One day Ishbosheth,*
Saul's son, accused Abner of sleeping with one of his father's concubines, a
woman named Rizpah, daughter of Aiah.
[8] Abner was furious. "Am I some Judean dog to be kicked around like this?"
he shouted. "After all I have done for your father, Saul, and his family and
friends by not handing you over to David, is this my reward—that you find
fault with me about this woman? [9] May God strike me and even kill me if
I don't do everything I can to help David get what the LORD has promised
him! [10] I'm going to take Saul's kingdom and give it to David. I will establish
the throne of David over Israel as well as Judah, all the way from Dan in the
north to Beersheba in the south." [11] Ishbosheth didn't dare say another word
because he was afraid of what Abner might do.
[12] Then Abner sent messengers to David, saying, "Doesn't the entire land
belong to you? Make a solemn pact with me, and I will help turn over all of
Israel to you."

2:29a Hebrew *the Arabah.* **2:29b** Or *continued on through the Bithron.* The meaning of the Hebrew is uncertain. **3:3** As in parallel text at 1 Chr 3:1 (see also Greek version, which reads *Daluia,* and possible support by Dead Sea Scrolls); Hebrew reads *Kileab.* **3:7** *Ishbosheth* is another name for Esh-baal.

13"All right," David replied, "but I will not negotiate with you unless you
bring back my wife Michal, Saul's daughter, when you come."
14David then sent this message to Ishbosheth, Saul's son: "Give me back
my wife Michal, for I bought her with the lives* of 100 Philistines."
15So Ishbosheth took Michal away from her husband, Palti* son of Laish.
16Palti followed along behind her as far as Bahurim, weeping as he went.
Then Abner told him, "Go back home!" So Palti returned.
17Meanwhile, Abner had consulted with the elders of Israel. "For some
time now," he told them, "you have wanted to make David your king.
18Now is the time! For the LORD has said, 'I have chosen David to save my
people Israel from the hands of the Philistines and from all their other
enemies.'" 19Abner also spoke with the men of Benjamin. Then he went to
Hebron to tell David that all the people of Israel and Benjamin had agreed
to support him.
20When Abner and twenty of his men came to Hebron, David entertained
them with a great feast. 21Then Abner said to David, "Let me go and call an
assembly of all Israel to support my lord the king. They will make a covenant
with you to make you their king, and you will rule over everything your heart
desires." So David sent Abner safely on his way.

Joab Murders Abner

22But just after David had sent Abner away in safety, Joab and some of David's
troops returned from a raid, bringing much plunder with them. 23When Joab
arrived, he was told that Abner had just been there visiting the king and had
been sent away in safety.
24Joab rushed to the king and demanded, "What have you done? What do
you mean by letting Abner get away? 25You know perfectly well that he came
to spy on you and find out everything you're doing!"
26Joab then left David and sent messengers to catch up with Abner, asking
him to return. They found him at the well of Sirah and brought him back,
though David knew nothing about it. 27When Abner arrived back at Hebron,
Joab took him aside at the gateway as if to speak with him privately. But
then he stabbed Abner in the stomach and killed him in revenge for killing
his brother Asahel.
28When David heard about it, he declared, "I vow by the LORD that I and
my kingdom are forever innocent of this crime against Abner son of Ner.
29Joab and his family are the guilty ones. May the family of Joab be cursed
in every generation with a man who has open sores or leprosy* or who walks
on crutches* or dies by the sword or begs for food!"
30So Joab and his brother Abishai killed Abner because Abner had killed
their brother Asahel at the battle of Gibeon.

David Mourns Abner's Death

31Then David said to Joab and all those who were with him, "Tear your
clothes and put on burlap. Mourn for Abner." And King David himself
walked behind the procession to the grave. 32They buried Abner in Hebron,
and the king and all the people wept at his graveside. 33Then the king sang
this funeral song for Abner:

3:14 Hebrew *the foreskins.* 3:15 As in 1 Sam 25:44; Hebrew reads *Paltiel,* a variant spelling of Palti. 3:29a Or *or a contagious skin disease.* The Hebrew word used here can describe various skin diseases. 3:29b Or *who is effeminate;* Hebrew reads *who handles a spindle.*

"Should Abner have died as fools die?
34 Your hands were not bound;
your feet were not chained.
No, you were murdered—
the victim of a wicked plot."

All the people wept again for Abner. 35 David had refused to eat anything on the day of the funeral, and now everyone begged him to eat. But David had made a vow, saying, "May God strike me and even kill me if I eat anything before sundown."

36 This pleased the people very much. In fact, everything the king did
pleased them! 37 So everyone in Judah and all Israel understood that David
was not responsible for Abner's murder.

38 Then King David said to his officials, "Don't you realize that a great
commander has fallen today in Israel? 39 And even though I am the anointed
king, these two sons of Zeruiah—Joab and Abishai—are too strong for me to control. So may the LORD repay these evil men for their evil deeds."

The Murder of Ishbosheth

4 When Ishbosheth,* Saul's son, heard about Abner's death at Hebron, he
lost all courage, and all Israel became paralyzed with fear. 2 Now there
were two brothers, Baanah and Recab, who were captains of Ishbosheth's raiding parties. They were sons of Rimmon, a member of the tribe of Benjamin who lived in Beeroth. The town of Beeroth is now part of Benjamin's
territory 3 because the original people of Beeroth fled to Gittaim, where they
still live as foreigners.

4 (Saul's son Jonathan had a son named Mephibosheth,* who was crippled as a child. He was five years old when the report came from Jezreel that Saul and Jonathan had been killed in battle. When the child's nurse heard the news, she picked him up and fled. But as she hurried away, she dropped him, and he became crippled.)

5 One day Recab and Baanah, the sons of Rimmon from Beeroth, went
to Ishbosheth's house around noon as he was taking his midday rest. 6 The
doorkeeper, who had been sifting wheat, became drowsy and fell asleep. So
Recab and Baanah slipped past her.* 7 They went into the house and found
Ishbosheth sleeping on his bed. They struck and killed him and cut off his head. Then, taking his head with them, they fled across the Jordan Valley*
through the night. 8 When they arrived at Hebron, they presented Ishbo-
sheth's head to David. "Look!" they exclaimed to the king. "Here is the head of Ishbosheth, the son of your enemy Saul who tried to kill you. Today the LORD has given my lord the king revenge on Saul and his entire family!"

9 But David said to Recab and Baanah, "The LORD, who saves me from all
my enemies, is my witness. 10 Someone once told me, 'Saul is dead,' thinking
he was bringing me good news. But I seized him and killed him at Ziklag.
That's the reward I gave him for his news! 11 How much more should I reward
evil men who have killed an innocent man in his own house and on his own bed? Shouldn't I hold you responsible for his blood and rid the earth of you?"

12 So David ordered his young men to kill them, and they did. They

4:1 *Ishbosheth* is another name for Esh-baal. **4:4** *Mephibosheth* is another name for Merib-baal. **4:6** As in Greek version; Hebrew reads *So they went into the house pretending to fetch wheat, but they stabbed him in the stomach. Then Recab and Baanah escaped.* **4:7** Hebrew *the Arabah.*

cut off their hands and feet and hung their bodies beside the pool in Hebron. Then they took Ishbosheth's head and buried it in Abner's tomb in Hebron.

David Becomes King of All Israel

5 Then all the tribes of Israel went to David at Hebron and told him, "We
are your own flesh and blood. 2 In the past,* when Saul was our king,
you were the one who really led the forces of Israel. And the LORD told you,
'You will be the shepherd of my people Israel. You will be Israel's leader.'"
3 So there at Hebron, King David made a covenant before the LORD with
all the elders of Israel. And they anointed him king of Israel.
4 David was thirty years old when he began to reign, and he reigned forty
years in all. 5 He had reigned over Judah from Hebron for seven years and
six months, and from Jerusalem he reigned over all Israel and Judah for
thirty-three years.

David Captures Jerusalem

6 David then led his men to Jerusalem to fight against the Jebusites, the original inhabitants of the land who were living there. The Jebusites taunted
David, saying, "You'll never get in here! Even the blind and lame could keep
you out!" For the Jebusites thought they were safe. 7 But David captured the
fortress of Zion, which is now called the City of David.
8 On the day of the attack, David said to his troops, "I hate those 'lame' and
'blind' Jebusites.* Whoever attacks them should strike by going into the city
through the water tunnel.*" That is the origin of the saying, "The blind and
the lame may not enter the house."*
9 So David made the fortress his home, and he called it the City of David.
He extended the city, starting at the supporting terraces* and working inward. 10 And David became more and more powerful, because the LORD God
of Heaven's Armies was with him.
11 Then King Hiram of Tyre sent messengers to David, along with cedar
timber and carpenters and stonemasons, and they built David a palace. 12 And
David realized that the LORD had confirmed him as king over Israel and had
blessed his kingdom for the sake of his people Israel.
13 After moving from Hebron to Jerusalem, David married more concubines and wives, and they had more sons and daughters. 14 These are the
names of David's sons who were born in Jerusalem: Shammua, Shobab, Nathan, Solomon, 15 Ibhar, Elishua, Nepheg, Japhia, 16 Elishama, Eliada, and
Eliphelet.

David Conquers the Philistines

17 When the Philistines heard that David had been anointed king of Israel,
they mobilized all their forces to capture him. But David was told they were
coming, so he went into the stronghold. 18 The Philistines arrived and spread
out across the valley of Rephaim. 19 So David asked the LORD, "Should I go
out to fight the Philistines? Will you hand them over to me?"
The LORD replied to David, "Yes, go ahead. I will certainly hand them
over to you."

5:2 Or *For some time.* **5:8a** Or *Those 'lame' and 'blind' Jebusites hate me.* **5:8b** Or *with scaling hooks.* The meaning of the Hebrew is uncertain. **5:8c** The meaning of this saying is uncertain. **5:9** Hebrew *the millo.* The meaning of the Hebrew is uncertain.

Question **5:2**

This is a profound verse revealing David's calling as the one true king of Israel. Embedded in his calling is this idea of David as a shepherd-king. What's the difference between Saul's kingdom and David's shepherd-kingdom?

Story Arc **5:7**

● Zion

This historically seismic event shook the world forever. This is the location where Melchizedek was the king and high priest (Genesis 14:18; Hebrews 7). This is where the Lord tested Abraham's faith and provided a substitutionary sacrifice in place of Isaac (Genesis 22). This was also the place where the Lord told Abraham he would be the father of many nations and that from his family would come one who would bless the entire world (Genesis 22:18).

Now, in this moment, David captured the "fortress of Zion." By establishing the "City of David" here, the stage was set for Jesus to become the great High Priest (Hebrews 7) in the order of Melchizedek and King of kings in the lineage of Judah and David. Of course, Jesus also became the substitutionary sacrifice in our place (Romans 3:25; Hebrews 7:27).

2 Sam 7:1-17 ►

Question 5:24

What do you think this sounded like? Also, how does this passage relate to John 3:5-8?

Prayer 6:14

Dear Jesus, I can be bold today because you are with me. No matter what circumstances I find myself in today, let me dance in your steps, sing out your songs, and see with your vision. Amen.

[20]So David went to Baal-perazim and defeated the Philistines there. "The LORD did it!" David exclaimed. "He burst through my enemies like a raging flood!" So he named that place Baal-perazim (which means "the Lord who bursts through"). [21]The Philistines had abandoned their idols there, so David and his men confiscated them.

[22]But after a while the Philistines returned and again spread out across the valley of Rephaim. [23]And again David asked the LORD what to do. "Do not attack them straight on," the LORD replied. "Instead, circle around behind and attack them near the poplar* trees. [24]When you hear a sound like marching feet in the tops of the poplar trees, be on the alert! That will be the signal that the LORD is moving ahead of you to strike down the Philistine army." [25]So David did what the LORD commanded, and he struck down the Philistines all the way from Gibeon* to Gezer.

Moving the Ark to Jerusalem

6 Then David again gathered all the elite troops in Israel, 30,000 in all. [2]He led them to Baalah of Judah* to bring back the Ark of God, which bears the name of the LORD of Heaven's Armies,* who is enthroned between the cherubim. [3]They placed the Ark of God on a new cart and brought it from Abinadab's house, which was on a hill. Uzzah and Ahio, Abinadab's sons, were guiding the cart [4]that carried the Ark of God.* Ahio walked in front of the Ark. [5]David and all the people of Israel were celebrating before the LORD, singing songs* and playing all kinds of musical instruments—lyres, harps, tambourines, castanets, and cymbals.

[6]But when they arrived at the threshing floor of Nacon, the oxen stumbled, and Uzzah reached out his hand and steadied the Ark of God. [7]Then the LORD's anger was aroused against Uzzah, and God struck him dead because of this.* So Uzzah died right there beside the Ark of God.

[8]David was angry because the LORD's anger had burst out against Uzzah. He named that place Perez-uzzah (which means "to burst out against Uzzah"), as it is still called today.

[9]David was now afraid of the LORD, and he asked, "How can I ever bring the Ark of the LORD back into my care?" [10]So David decided not to move the Ark of the LORD into the City of David. Instead, he took it to the house of Obed-edom of Gath. [11]The Ark of the LORD remained there in Obed-edom's house for three months, and the LORD blessed Obed-edom and his entire household.

[12]Then King David was told, "The LORD has blessed Obed-edom's household and everything he has because of the Ark of God." So David went there and brought the Ark of God from the house of Obed-edom to the City of David with a great celebration. [13]After the men who were carrying the Ark of the LORD had gone six steps, David sacrificed a bull and a fattened calf. [14]And David danced before the LORD with all his might, wearing a priestly garment.* [15]So David and all the people of Israel brought up the Ark of the LORD with shouts of joy and the blowing of rams' horns.

5:23 Or *aspen,* or *balsam;* also in 5:24. The exact identification of this tree is uncertain. 5:25 As in Greek version (see also 1 Chr 14:16); Hebrew reads *Geba.* 6:2a Hebrew *Baale of Judah,* another name for Kiriath-jearim; compare 1 Chr 13:6. 6:2b Or *the Ark of God where the Name is proclaimed—the name of the LORD of Heaven's Armies.* 6:4 As in Dead Sea Scrolls and some Greek manuscripts; Masoretic Text reads *[4]and they brought it from Abinadab's house, which was on a hill, with the Ark of God.* 6:5 As in Dead Sea Scrolls and Greek version (see also 1 Chr 13:8); Masoretic Text reads *before the LORD with all manner of cypress wood.* 6:7 As in Dead Sea Scrolls; Masoretic Text reads *because of his irreverence.* 6:14 Hebrew *a linen ephod.*

Michal's Contempt for David

16 But as the Ark of the LORD entered the City of David, Michal, the daughter
of Saul, looked down from her window. When she saw King David leaping
and dancing before the LORD, she was filled with contempt for him.
17 They brought the Ark of the LORD and set it in its place inside the special
tent David had prepared for it. And David sacrificed burnt offerings and
peace offerings to the LORD. 18 When he had finished his sacrifices, David
blessed the people in the name of the LORD of Heaven's Armies. 19 Then he
gave to every Israelite man and woman in the crowd a loaf of bread, a cake
of dates,* and a cake of raisins. Then all the people returned to their homes.
20 When David returned home to bless his own family, Michal, the daugh-
ter of Saul, came out to meet him. She said in disgust, "How distinguished
the king of Israel looked today, shamelessly exposing himself to the servant
girls like any vulgar person might do!"
21 David retorted to Michal, "I was dancing before the LORD, who chose
me above your father and all his family! He appointed me as the leader of
Israel, the people of the LORD, so I celebrate before the LORD. 22 Yes, and I
am willing to look even more foolish than this, even to be humiliated in
my own eyes! But those servant girls you mentioned will indeed think I
am distinguished!" 23 So Michal, the daughter of Saul, remained childless
throughout her entire life.

The LORD's Covenant Promise to David

7 When King David was settled in his palace and the LORD had given him
rest from all the surrounding enemies, 2 the king summoned Nathan the
prophet. "Look," David said, "I am living in a beautiful cedar palace,* but the
Ark of God is out there in a tent!"
3 Nathan replied to the king, "Go ahead and do whatever you have in mind,
for the LORD is with you."
4 But that same night the LORD said to Nathan,
5 "Go and tell my servant David, 'This is what the LORD has declared:
Are you the one to build a house for me to live in? 6 I have never lived
in a house, from the day I brought the Israelites out of Egypt until this
very day. I have always moved from one place to another with a tent
and a Tabernacle as my dwelling. 7 Yet no matter where I have gone with
the Israelites, I have never once complained to Israel's tribal leaders, the
shepherds of my people Israel. I have never asked them, "Why haven't
you built me a beautiful cedar house?"'
8 "Now go and say to my servant David, 'This is what the LORD of
Heaven's Armies has declared: I took you from tending sheep in the
pasture and selected you to be the leader of my people Israel. 9 I have
been with you wherever you have gone, and I have destroyed all your
enemies before your eyes. Now I will make your name as famous as
anyone who has ever lived on the earth! 10 And I will provide a homeland
for my people Israel, planting them in a secure place where they will
never be disturbed. Evil nations won't oppress them as they've done in
the past, 11 starting from the time I appointed judges to rule my people
Israel. And I will give you rest from all your enemies.

6:19 Or *a portion of meat.* The meaning of the Hebrew is uncertain. 7:2 Hebrew *a house of cedar.*

Make a Difference

6:16-22

Fool for Christ

David's wife was upset that David had made a fool of himself (and her!) by dancing so ridiculously in worship (v. 16). David was unapologetic to his wife. "Yes, and I am willing to look even more foolish than this!" he replied (v. 22).

A thousand years later, the apostle Paul proclaimed, "Our dedication to Christ makes us look like fools" (1 Corinthians 4:10). Also, Paul taught, God chooses "things the world considers foolish in order to shame those who think they are wise" (1 Corinthians 1:27).

Difference Maker

Do something "foolish" for God today. Dance in worship. Do a chore no one asked you to do. Give money to a charity. Smile and say hello to someone (and mean it).

Story Arc **7:1-17**

Nathan

The prophet Nathan would become one of David's most trusted advisers. His wisdom and discernment were instrumental to David's decision to wait to build a temple for the Lord (vv. 12-13). Nathan would also be instrumental in anointing David's son Solomon as the next king (1 Kings 1:34). However, it is what would happen in between these events that would be even more significant. Look ahead to 2 Samuel 12 to see how Nathan confronted the sin of the most famous king in the world—and helped him repent.

2 Sam 11:1-5 ►

Prayer 7:22

Who is like you, O Lord? Let me never take you for granted. Amen.

"'Furthermore, the LORD declares that he will make a house for
you—a dynasty of kings! 12 For when you die and are buried with your
ancestors, I will raise up one of your descendants, your own offspring,
and I will make his kingdom strong. 13 He is the one who will build a
house—a temple—for my name. And I will secure his royal throne
forever. 14 I will be his father, and he will be my son. If he sins, I will
correct and discipline him with the rod, like any father would do.
15 But my favor will not be taken from him as I took it from Saul,
whom I removed from your sight. 16 Your house and your kingdom
will continue before me* for all time, and your throne will be secure
forever.'"

17 So Nathan went back to David and told him everything the LORD had said
in this vision.

David's Prayer of Thanks

18 Then King David went in and sat before the LORD and prayed,

"Who am I, O Sovereign LORD, and what is my family, that you have
brought me this far? 19 And now, Sovereign LORD, in addition to
everything else, you speak of giving your servant a lasting dynasty!
Do you deal with everyone this way, O Sovereign LORD?*
20 "What more can I say to you? You know what your servant is really
like, Sovereign LORD. 21 Because of your promise and according to your
will, you have done all these great things and have made them known
to your servant.
22 "How great you are, O Sovereign LORD! There is no one like you.
We have never even heard of another God like you! 23 What other nation
on earth is like your people Israel? What other nation, O God, have
you redeemed from slavery to be your own people? You made a great
name for yourself when you redeemed your people from Egypt. You
performed awesome miracles and drove out the nations and gods that
stood in their way.* 24 You made Israel your very own people forever,
and you, O LORD, became their God.
25 "And now, O LORD God, I am your servant; do as you have promised
concerning me and my family. Confirm it as a promise that will last
forever. 26 And may your name be honored forever so that everyone will
say, 'The LORD of Heaven's Armies is God over Israel!' And may the
house of your servant David continue before you forever.
27 "O LORD of Heaven's Armies, God of Israel, I have been bold
enough to pray this prayer to you because you have revealed all this to
your servant, saying, 'I will build a house for you—a dynasty of kings!'
28 For you are God, O Sovereign LORD. Your words are truth, and you
have promised these good things to your servant. 29 And now, may it
please you to bless the house of your servant, so that it may continue
forever before you. For you have spoken, and when you grant a blessing
to your servant, O Sovereign LORD, it is an eternal blessing!"

7:16 As in Greek version and some Hebrew manuscripts; Masoretic Text reads *before you.* **7:19** Or *This is your instruction for all humanity, O Sovereign LORD.* **7:23** As in Greek version (see also 1 Chr 17:21); Hebrew reads *You made a name for yourself and awesome miracles for your land in the sight of your people, whom you redeemed from Egypt, the nations and their gods.*

David's Military Victories

8 After this, David defeated and subdued the Philistines by conquering
Gath, their largest town.* 2 David also conquered the land of Moab. He
made the people lie down on the ground in a row, and he measured them off
in groups with a length of rope. He measured off two groups to be executed
for every one group to be spared. The Moabites who were spared became
David's subjects and paid him tribute money.
3 David also destroyed the forces of Hadadezer son of Rehob, king of
Zobah, when Hadadezer marched out to strengthen his control along the
Euphrates River. 4 David captured 1,000 chariots, 7,000 charioteers,* and
20,000 foot soldiers. He crippled all the chariot horses except enough for
100 chariots.
5 When Arameans from Damascus arrived to help King Hadadezer, David
killed 22,000 of them. 6 Then he placed several army garrisons in Damascus,
the Aramean capital, and the Arameans became David's subjects and paid
him tribute money. So the LORD made David victorious wherever he went.
7 David brought the gold shields of Hadadezer's officers to Jerusalem,
8 along with a large amount of bronze from Hadadezer's towns of Tebah*
and Berothai.
9 When King Toi of Hamath heard that David had destroyed the entire
army of Hadadezer, 10 he sent his son Joram to congratulate King David for
his successful campaign. Hadadezer and Toi had been enemies and were
often at war. Joram presented David with many gifts of silver, gold, and
bronze.
11 King David dedicated all these gifts to the LORD, as he did with the silver
and gold from the other nations he had defeated—12 from Edom,* Moab,
Ammon, Philistia, and Amalek—and from Hadadezer son of Rehob, king
of Zobah.
13 So David became even more famous when he returned from destroying
18,000 Edomites* in the Valley of Salt. 14 He placed army garrisons through-
out Edom, and all the Edomites became David's subjects. In fact, the LORD
made David victorious wherever he went.
15 So David reigned over all Israel and did what was just and right for all
his people. 16 Joab son of Zeruiah was commander of the army. Jehoshaphat
son of Ahilud was the royal historian. 17 Zadok son of Ahitub and Ahimelech
son of Abiathar were the priests. Seraiah was the court secretary. 18 Bena-
iah son of Jehoiada was captain of the king's bodyguard.* And David's sons
served as priestly leaders.*

David's Kindness to Mephibosheth

9 One day David asked, "Is anyone in Saul's family still alive—anyone
to whom I can show kindness for Jonathan's sake?" 2 He summoned a
man named Ziba, who had been one of Saul's servants. "Are you Ziba?" the
king asked.

8:1 Hebrew *by conquering Metheg-ammah,* a name that means "the bridle," possibly referring to the size of the town or the tribute money taken from it. Compare 1 Chr 18:1. **8:4** As in Dead Sea Scrolls and Greek version (see also 1 Chr 18:4); Masoretic Text reads *captured 1,700 charioteers.* **8:8** As in some Greek manuscripts (see also 1 Chr 18:8); Hebrew reads *Betah.* **8:12** As in a few Hebrew manuscripts and Greek and Syriac versions (see also 8:14; 1 Chr 18:11); most Hebrew manuscripts read *Aram.* **8:13** As in a few Hebrew manuscripts and Greek and Syriac versions (see also 8:14; 1 Chr 18:12); most Hebrew manuscripts read *Arameans.* **8:18a** Hebrew *of the Kerethites and Pelethites.* **8:18b** Hebrew *David's sons were priests;* compare parallel text at 1 Chr 18:17.

Make a Difference

9:1-13

Invited to the Table

In a remarkable gesture of respect and dignity, David invited one of Saul's grandsons, Mephibosheth, to regularly eat at his table as if he were one of David's own sons. David, you'll remember, had fled for his life for years while Saul hunted him down and tried to kill him. To honor one of Saul's grandsons like this was astonishing. In addition, Mephibosheth's feet had been permanently damaged when Saul was killed. A king in those days would typically not have invited someone with a crippling disability as a guest at the royal table.

Difference Maker

Like Mephibosheth, we, crippled in our sin, are invited to sit restored at God's table. Could you invite to lunch or dinner someone whom others would normally not invite?

"Yes sir, I am," Ziba replied.
3 The king then asked him, "Is anyone still alive from Saul's family? If so,
I want to show God's kindness to them."
Ziba replied, "Yes, one of Jonathan's sons is still alive. He is crippled in
both feet."
4 "Where is he?" the king asked.
"In Lo-debar," Ziba told him, "at the home of Makir son of Ammiel."
5 So David sent for him and brought him from Makir's home. 6 His name
was Mephibosheth*; he was Jonathan's son and Saul's grandson. When he
came to David, he bowed low to the ground in deep respect. David said,
"Greetings, Mephibosheth."
Mephibosheth replied, "I am your servant."
7 "Don't be afraid!" David said. "I intend to show kindness to you because
of my promise to your father, Jonathan. I will give you all the property that
once belonged to your grandfather Saul, and you will eat here with me at
the king's table!"
8 Mephibosheth bowed respectfully and exclaimed, "Who is your servant,
that you should show such kindness to a dead dog like me?"
9 Then the king summoned Saul's servant Ziba and said, "I have given your
master's grandson everything that belonged to Saul and his family. 10 You
and your sons and servants are to farm the land for him to produce food for
your master's household.* But Mephibosheth, your master's grandson, will
eat here at my table." (Ziba had fifteen sons and twenty servants.)
11 Ziba replied, "Yes, my lord the king; I am your servant, and I will do
all that you have commanded." And from that time on, Mephibosheth ate
regularly at David's table,* like one of the king's own sons.
12 Mephibosheth had a young son named Mica. From then on, all the mem-
bers of Ziba's household were Mephibosheth's servants. 13 And Mephibo-
sheth, who was crippled in both feet, lived in Jerusalem and ate regularly
at the king's table.

David Defeats the Ammonites

10 Some time after this, King Nahash* of the Ammonites died, and his
son Hanun became king. 2 David said, "I am going to show loyalty
to Hanun just as his father, Nahash, was always loyal to me." So David sent
ambassadors to express sympathy to Hanun about his father's death.
But when David's ambassadors arrived in the land of Ammon, 3 the Am-
monite commanders said to Hanun, their master, "Do you really think these
men are coming here to honor your father? No! David has sent them to spy
out the city so they can come in and conquer it!" 4 So Hanun seized David's
ambassadors and shaved off half of each man's beard, cut off their robes at
the buttocks, and sent them back to David in shame.
5 When David heard what had happened, he sent messengers to tell the
men, "Stay at Jericho until your beards grow out, and then come back." For
they felt deep shame because of their appearance.
6 When the people of Ammon realized how seriously they had angered
David, they sent and hired 20,000 Aramean foot soldiers from the lands of
Beth-rehob and Zobah, 1,000 from the king of Maacah, and 12,000 from the

9:6 *Mephibosheth* is another name for Merib-baal. 9:10 As in Greek version; Hebrew reads *your master's grandson.* 9:11 As in Greek version; Hebrew reads *my table.* 10:1 As in parallel text at 1 Chr 19:1; Hebrew reads *the king.*

land of Tob. 7 When David heard about this, he sent Joab and all his warriors
to fight them. 8 The Ammonite troops came out and drew up their battle
lines at the entrance of the city gate, while the Arameans from Zobah and
Rehob and the men from Tob and Maacah positioned themselves to fight
in the open fields.
9 When Joab saw that he would have to fight on both the front and the
rear, he chose some of Israel's elite troops and placed them under his per-
sonal command to fight the Arameans in the fields. 10 He left the rest of the
army under the command of his brother Abishai, who was to attack the Am-
monites. 11 "If the Arameans are too strong for me, then come over and help
me," Joab told his brother. "And if the Ammonites are too strong for you, I
will come and help you. 12 Be courageous! Let us fight bravely for our people
and the cities of our God. May the LORD's will be done."
13 When Joab and his troops attacked, the Arameans began to run away.
14 And when the Ammonites saw the Arameans running, they ran from
Abishai and retreated into the city. After the battle was over, Joab returned
to Jerusalem.
15 The Arameans now realized that they were no match for Israel. So when
they regrouped, 16 they were joined by additional Aramean troops sum-
moned by Hadadezer from the other side of the Euphrates River.* These
troops arrived at Helam under the command of Shobach, the commander
of Hadadezer's forces.
17 When David heard what was happening, he mobilized all Israel, crossed
the Jordan River, and led the army to Helam. The Arameans positioned
themselves in battle formation and fought against David. 18 But again the
Arameans fled from the Israelites. This time David's forces killed 700 chari-
oteers and 40,000 foot soldiers,* including Shobach, the commander of their
army. 19 When all the kings allied with Hadadezer saw that they had been
defeated by Israel, they surrendered to Israel and became their subjects. After
that, the Arameans were afraid to help the Ammonites.

David and Bathsheba

11 In the spring of the year,* when kings normally go out to war, Da-
vid sent Joab and the Israelite army to fight the Ammonites. They
destroyed the Ammonite army and laid siege to the city of Rabbah. However,
David stayed behind in Jerusalem.
2 Late one afternoon, after his midday rest, David got out of bed and was
walking on the roof of the palace. As he looked out over the city, he noticed
a woman of unusual beauty taking a bath. 3 He sent someone to find out
who she was, and he was told, "She is Bathsheba, the daughter of Eliam
and the wife of Uriah the Hittite." 4 Then David sent messengers to get her;
and when she came to the palace, he slept with her. She had just completed
the purification rites after having her menstrual period. Then she returned
home. 5 Later, when Bathsheba discovered that she was pregnant, she sent
David a message, saying, "I'm pregnant."
6 Then David sent word to Joab: "Send me Uriah the Hittite." So Joab sent
him to David. 7 When Uriah arrived, David asked him how Joab and the army
were getting along and how the war was progressing. 8 Then he told Uriah,

10:16 Hebrew *the river.* 10:18 As in some Greek manuscripts (see also 1 Chr 19:18); Hebrew reads *charioteers.* 11:1 Hebrew *At the turn of the year.* The first day of the year in the ancient Hebrew lunar calendar occurred in March or April.

Question 11:1

David wasn't doing his job. How can a lazy and overly comfortable attitude create the opportunity for sin?

Story Arc 11:1–5

● Bathsheba

Does it surprise you that Bathsheba, the wife of Uriah the Hittite, appears later in Jesus' genealogy (Matthew 1:6)? Bathsheba's story in the Bible doesn't make anyone feel good. Even so, God's redemption of this tragically sinful episode in David's life is inspirational. Bathsheba went on to become the mother of Solomon, the wisest and most powerful king Israel would have. That is, of course, until Jesus was born.

1 Kgs 1:1 ►

Question 11:1–27

David fell into a downward cycle of manipulation and deception as his soul grew sicker. This chapter should humble us and make us angry. The cascading sin that started with his lazy posture (v. 1) gave way to murderous treachery. How is it that David, a man after God's own heart (1 Samuel 13:14), could fall so deeply into sin?

"Go on home and relax.*" David even sent a gift to Uriah after he had left the
palace. 9 But Uriah didn't go home. He slept that night at the palace entrance
with the king's palace guard.

10 When David heard that Uriah had not gone home, he summoned him
and asked, "What's the matter? Why didn't you go home last night after
being away for so long?"

11 Uriah replied, "The Ark and the armies of Israel and Judah are living in
tents,* and Joab and my master's men are camping in the open fields. How
could I go home to wine and dine and sleep with my wife? I swear that I
would never do such a thing."

12 "Well, stay here today," David told him, "and tomorrow you may return
to the army." So Uriah stayed in Jerusalem that day and the next. 13 Then
David invited him to dinner and got him drunk. But even then he couldn't
get Uriah to go home to his wife. Again he slept at the palace entrance with
the king's palace guard.

David Arranges for Uriah's Death

14 So the next morning David wrote a letter to Joab and gave it to Uriah to de-
liver. 15 The letter instructed Joab, "Station Uriah on the front lines where the
battle is fiercest. Then pull back so that he will be killed." 16 So Joab assigned
Uriah to a spot close to the city wall where he knew the enemy's strongest
men were fighting. 17 And when the enemy soldiers came out of the city to
fight, Uriah the Hittite was killed along with several other Israelite soldiers.

18 Then Joab sent a battle report to David. 19 He told his messenger, "Report
all the news of the battle to the king. 20 But he might get angry and ask, 'Why
did the troops go so close to the city? Didn't they know there would be shoot-
ing from the walls? 21 Wasn't Abimelech son of Gideon* killed at Thebez by a
woman who threw a millstone down on him from the wall? Why would you
get so close to the wall?' Then tell him, 'Uriah the Hittite was killed, too.'"

22 So the messenger went to Jerusalem and gave a complete report to David.
23 "The enemy came out against us in the open fields," he said. "And as we
chased them back to the city gate, 24 the archers on the wall shot arrows at us.
Some of the king's men were killed, including Uriah the Hittite."

25 "Well, tell Joab not to be discouraged," David said. "The sword devours
this one today and that one tomorrow! Fight harder next time, and conquer
the city!"

26 When Uriah's wife heard that her husband was dead, she mourned
for him. 27 When the period of mourning was over, David sent for her and
brought her to the palace, and she became one of his wives. Then she gave
birth to a son. But the LORD was displeased with what David had done.

Nathan Rebukes David

12 So the LORD sent Nathan the prophet to tell David this story: "There
were two men in a certain town. One was rich, and one was poor.
2 The rich man owned a great many sheep and cattle. 3 The poor man owned
nothing but one little lamb he had bought. He raised that little lamb, and
it grew up with his children. It ate from the man's own plate and drank
from his cup. He cuddled it in his arms like a baby daughter. 4 One day a

11:8 Hebrew *and wash your feet,* an expression that may also have a connotation of ritualistic washing. 11:11 Or *at Succoth.* 11:21 Hebrew *son of Jerub-besheth.* Jerub-besheth is a variation on the name Jerub-baal, which is another name for Gideon; see Judg 6:32.

guest arrived at the home of the rich man. But instead of killing an animal from his own flock or herd, he took the poor man's lamb and killed it and prepared it for his guest."

5 David was furious. "As surely as the LORD lives," he vowed, "any man who would do such a thing deserves to die! 6 He must repay four lambs to the poor man for the one he stole and for having no pity."

7 Then Nathan said to David, "You are that man! The LORD, the God of Israel, says: I anointed you king of Israel and saved you from the power of Saul. 8 I gave you your master's house and his wives and the kingdoms of Israel and Judah. And if that had not been enough, I would have given you much, much more. 9 Why, then, have you despised the word of the LORD and done this horrible deed? For you have murdered Uriah the Hittite with the sword of the Ammonites and stolen his wife. 10 From this time on, your family will live by the sword because you have despised me by taking Uriah's wife to be your own.

11 "This is what the LORD says: Because of what you have done, I will cause your own household to rebel against you. I will give your wives to another man before your very eyes, and he will go to bed with them in public view. 12 You did it secretly, but I will make this happen to you openly in the sight of all Israel."

David Confesses His Guilt

▲ 13 Then David confessed to Nathan, "I have sinned against the LORD."

Nathan replied, "Yes, but the LORD has forgiven you, and you won't die for this sin. 14 Nevertheless, because you have shown utter contempt for the word of the LORD* by doing this, your child will die."

15 After Nathan returned to his home, the LORD sent a deadly illness to the child of David and Uriah's wife. 16 David begged God to spare the child. He went without food and lay all night on the bare ground. 17 The elders of his household pleaded with him to get up and eat with them, but he refused.

18 Then on the seventh day the child died. David's advisers were afraid to tell him. "He wouldn't listen to reason while the child was ill," they said. "What drastic thing will he do when we tell him the child is dead?"

19 When David saw them whispering, he realized what had happened. "Is the child dead?" he asked.

"Yes," they replied, "he is dead."

20 Then David got up from the ground, washed himself, put on lotions,* and changed his clothes. He went to the Tabernacle and worshiped the LORD. After that, he returned to the palace and was served food and ate.

21 His advisers were amazed. "We don't understand you," they told him. "While the child was still living, you wept and refused to eat. But now that the child is dead, you have stopped your mourning and are eating again."

22 David replied, "I fasted and wept while the child was alive, for I said, 'Perhaps the LORD will be gracious to me and let the child live.' 23 But why should I fast when he is dead? Can I bring him back again? I will go to him one day, but he cannot return to me."

24 Then David comforted Bathsheba, his wife, and slept with her. She became pregnant and gave birth to a son, and David* named him Solomon.

12:14 As in Dead Sea Scrolls; Masoretic Text reads *the enemies of the LORD.* 12:20 Hebrew *anointed himself.* 12:24 Hebrew *he;* an alternate Hebrew reading and some Hebrew manuscripts read *she.*

Prayer **12:13**

Lord, I have sinned against you. Have mercy on me. Cleanse me. Create a new heart within me. Amen.

The LORD loved the child 25 and sent word through Nathan the prophet that
they should name him Jedidiah (which means "beloved of the LORD"), as the
LORD had commanded.*

David Captures Rabbah

26 Meanwhile, Joab was fighting against Rabbah, the capital of Ammon, and
he captured the royal fortifications.* 27 Joab sent messengers to tell David,
"I have fought against Rabbah and captured its water supply.* 28 Now bring
the rest of the army and capture the city. Otherwise, I will capture it and get
credit for the victory."
29 So David gathered the rest of the army and went to Rabbah, and he
fought against it and captured it. 30 David removed the crown from the
king's head,* and it was placed on his own head. The crown was made of
gold and set with gems, and it weighed seventy-five pounds.* David took a
vast amount of plunder from the city. 31 He also made slaves of the people
of Rabbah and forced them to labor with* saws, iron picks, and iron axes,
and to work in the brick kilns.* That is how he dealt with the people of all
the Ammonite towns. Then David and all the army returned to Jerusalem.

The Rape of Tamar

13 Now David's son Absalom had a beautiful sister named Tamar. And
Amnon, her half brother, fell desperately in love with her. 2 Amnon
became so obsessed with Tamar that he became ill. She was a virgin, and
Amnon thought he could never have her.
3 But Amnon had a very crafty friend—his cousin Jonadab. He was the son of
David's brother Shimea.* 4 One day Jonadab said to Amnon, "What's the trouble?
Why should the son of a king look so dejected morning after morning?"
So Amnon told him, "I am in love with Tamar, my brother Absalom's
sister."
5 "Well," Jonadab said, "I'll tell you what to do. Go back to bed and pretend
you are ill. When your father comes to see you, ask him to let Tamar come
and prepare some food for you. Tell him you'll feel better if she prepares it
as you watch and feeds you with her own hands."
6 So Amnon lay down and pretended to be sick. And when the king came
to see him, Amnon asked him, "Please let my sister Tamar come and cook
my favorite dish* as I watch. Then I can eat it from her own hands." 7 So Da-
vid agreed and sent Tamar to Amnon's house to prepare some food for him.
8 When Tamar arrived at Amnon's house, she went to the place where he
was lying down so he could watch her mix some dough. Then she baked
his favorite dish for him. 9 But when she set the serving tray before him,
he refused to eat. "Everyone get out of here," Amnon told his servants. So
they all left.
10 Then he said to Tamar, "Now bring the food into my bedroom and feed
it to me here." So Tamar took his favorite dish to him. 11 But as she was feed-
ing him, he grabbed her and demanded, "Come to bed with me, my darling
sister."

12:25 As in Greek version; Hebrew reads *because of the LORD.* 12:26 Or *the royal city.* 12:27 Or *captured the city of water.* 12:30a Or *from the head of Milcom* (as in Greek version). Milcom, also called Molech, was the god of the Ammonites. 12:30b Hebrew *1 talent* [34 kilograms]. 12:31a Hebrew *He also brought out the people [of Rabbah] and put them under.* 12:31b Hebrew *and he made them pass through the brick kilns.* 13:3 Hebrew *Shimeah* (also in 13:32), a variant spelling of Shimea; compare 1 Chr 2:13. 13:6 Or *a couple of cakes;* also in 13:8, 10.

12"No, my brother!" she cried. "Don't be foolish! Don't do this to me! Such
wicked things aren't done in Israel. 13Where could I go in my shame? And
you would be called one of the greatest fools in Israel. Please, just speak to
the king about it, and he will let you marry me."
14But Amnon wouldn't listen to her, and since he was stronger than she was,
he raped her. 15Then suddenly Amnon's love turned to hate, and he hated her
even more than he had loved her. "Get out of here!" he snarled at her.
16"No, no!" Tamar cried. "Sending me away now is worse than what you've
already done to me."

But Amnon wouldn't listen to her. 17He shouted for his servant and de-
manded, "Throw this woman out, and lock the door behind her!"
18So the servant put her out and locked the door behind her. She was wear-
ing a long, beautiful robe,* as was the custom in those days for the king's
virgin daughters. 19But now Tamar tore her robe and put ashes on her head.
And then, with her face in her hands, she went away crying.
20Her brother Absalom saw her and asked, "Is it true that Amnon has been
with you? Well, my sister, keep quiet for now, since he's your brother. Don't
you worry about it." So Tamar lived as a desolate woman in her brother Ab-
salom's house.
21When King David heard what had happened, he was very angry.* 22And
though Absalom never spoke to Amnon about this, he hated Amnon deeply
because of what he had done to his sister.

Absalom's Revenge on Amnon

23Two years later, when Absalom's sheep were being sheared at Baal-hazor
near Ephraim, Absalom invited all the king's sons to come to a feast. 24He
went to the king and said, "My sheep-shearers are now at work. Would the
king and his servants please come to celebrate the occasion with me?"
25The king replied, "No, my son. If we all came, we would be too much
of a burden on you." Absalom pressed him, but the king would not come,
though he gave Absalom his blessing.
26"Well, then," Absalom said, "if you can't come, how about sending my
brother Amnon with us?"

"Why Amnon?" the king asked. 27But Absalom kept on pressing the king
until he finally agreed to let all his sons attend, including Amnon. So Absa-
lom prepared a feast fit for a king.*
28Absalom told his men, "Wait until Amnon gets drunk; then at my signal,
kill him! Don't be afraid. I'm the one who has given the command. Take
courage and do it!" 29So at Absalom's signal they murdered Amnon. Then
the other sons of the king jumped on their mules and fled.
30As they were on the way back to Jerusalem, this report reached David:
"Absalom has killed all the king's sons; not one is left alive!" 31The king got
up, tore his robe, and threw himself on the ground. His advisers also tore
their clothes in horror and sorrow.
32But just then Jonadab, the son of David's brother Shimea, arrived and
said, "No, don't believe that all the king's sons have been killed! It was only
Amnon! Absalom has been plotting this ever since Amnon raped his sister

13:18 Or *a robe with sleeves,* or *an ornamented robe.* The meaning of the Hebrew is uncertain. **13:21** Dead Sea Scrolls and Greek version add *But he did not punish his son Amnon, because he loved him, for he was his firstborn.* **13:27** As in Greek and Latin versions (compare also Dead Sea Scrolls); the Hebrew text lacks this sentence.

How this passage impacts me

Tamar. 33 No, my lord the king, your sons aren't all dead! It was only Amnon." 34 Meanwhile Absalom escaped.

Then the watchman on the Jerusalem wall saw a great crowd coming down the hill on the road from the west. He ran to tell the king, "I see a crowd of people coming from the Horonaim road along the side of the hill."*

35 "Look!" Jonadab told the king. "There they are now! The king's sons are coming, just as I said."

36 They soon arrived, weeping and sobbing, and the king and all his servants wept bitterly with them. 37 And David mourned many days for his son Amnon.

Absalom fled to his grandfather, Talmai son of Ammihud, the king of Geshur. 38 He stayed there in Geshur for three years. 39 And King David,* now reconciled to Amnon's death, longed to be reunited with his son Absalom.*

Joab Arranges for Absalom's Return

14 Joab realized how much the king longed to see Absalom. 2 So he sent for a woman from Tekoa who had a reputation for great wisdom. He said to her, "Pretend you are in mourning; wear mourning clothes and don't put on lotions.* Act like a woman who has been mourning for the dead for a long time. 3 Then go to the king and tell him the story I am about to tell you." Then Joab told her what to say.

4 When the woman from Tekoa approached* the king, she bowed with her face to the ground in deep respect and cried out, "O king! Help me!"

5 "What's the trouble?" the king asked.

"Alas, I am a widow!" she replied. "My husband is dead. 6 My two sons had a fight out in the field. And since no one was there to stop it, one of them was killed. 7 Now the rest of the family is demanding, 'Let us have your son. We will execute him for murdering his brother. He doesn't deserve to inherit his family's property.' They want to extinguish the only coal I have left, and my husband's name and family will disappear from the face of the earth."

8 "Leave it to me," the king told her. "Go home, and I'll see to it that no one touches him."

9 "Oh, thank you, my lord the king," the woman from Tekoa replied. "If you are criticized for helping me, let the blame fall on me and on my father's house, and let the king and his throne be innocent."

10 "If anyone objects," the king said, "bring him to me. I can assure you he will never harm you again!"

11 Then she said, "Please swear to me by the LORD your God that you won't let anyone take vengeance against my son. I want no more bloodshed."

"As surely as the LORD lives," he replied, "not a hair on your son's head will be disturbed!"

12 "Please allow me to ask one more thing of my lord the king," she said.

"Go ahead and speak," he responded.

13 She replied, "Why don't you do as much for the people of God as you have promised to do for me? You have convicted yourself in making this

13:34 As in Greek version; Hebrew lacks this sentence. **13:39a** Dead Sea Scrolls and Greek version read *And the spirit of the king.* **13:39b** Or *no longer felt a need to go out after Absalom.* **14:2** Hebrew *don't anoint yourself with oil.* **14:4** As in many Hebrew manuscripts and Greek and Syriac versions; Masoretic Text reads *spoke to.*

decision, because you have refused to bring home your own banished son.
[14] All of us must die eventually. Our lives are like water spilled out on the
ground, which cannot be gathered up again. But God does not just sweep
life away; instead, he devises ways to bring us back when we have been sepa-
rated from him.
[15] "I have come to plead with my lord the king because people have threat-
ened me. I said to myself, 'Perhaps the king will listen to me [16] and rescue us
from those who would cut us off from the inheritance* God has given us.
[17] Yes, my lord the king will give us peace of mind again.' I know that you
are like an angel of God in discerning good from evil. May the LORD your
God be with you."
[18] "I must know one thing," the king replied, "and tell me the truth."
"Yes, my lord the king," she responded.
[19] "Did Joab put you up to this?"
And the woman replied, "My lord the king, how can I deny it? Nobody
can hide anything from you. Yes, Joab sent me and told me what to say.
[20] He did it to place the matter before you in a different light. But you are
as wise as an angel of God, and you understand everything that happens
among us!"
[21] So the king sent for Joab and told him, "All right, go and bring back the
young man Absalom."
[22] Joab bowed with his face to the ground in deep respect and said, "At
last I know that I have gained your approval, my lord the king, for you have
granted me this request!"
[23] Then Joab went to Geshur and brought Absalom back to Jerusalem.
[24] But the king gave this order: "Absalom may go to his own house, but he
must never come into my presence." So Absalom did not see the king.

Absalom Reconciled to David

[25] Now Absalom was praised as the most handsome man in all Israel. He was
flawless from head to foot. [26] He cut his hair only once a year, and then only
because it was so heavy. When he weighed it out, it came to five pounds!*
[27] He had three sons and one daughter. His daughter's name was Tamar, and
she was very beautiful.
[28] Absalom lived in Jerusalem for two years, but he never got to see the
king. [29] Then Absalom sent for Joab to ask him to intercede for him, but
Joab refused to come. Absalom sent for him a second time, but again Joab
refused to come. [30] So Absalom said to his servants, "Go and set fire to Joab's
barley field, the field next to mine." So they set his field on fire, as Absalom
had commanded.
[31] Then Joab came to Absalom at his house and demanded, "Why did your
servants set my field on fire?"
[32] And Absalom replied, "Because I wanted you to ask the king why he
brought me back from Geshur if he didn't intend to see me. I might as well
have stayed there. Let me see the king; if he finds me guilty of anything,
then let him kill me."
[33] So Joab told the king what Absalom had said. Then at last David sum-
moned Absalom, who came and bowed low before the king, and the king
kissed him.

14:16 Or *the property;* or *the people.* **14:26** Hebrew *200 shekels* [2.3 kilograms] *by the royal standard.*

Question **14:14**

Chapters 13 and 14 are disgusting. Here we realize that God longs to work redemption for anyone who has walked away. "God does not just sweep life away; instead, he devises ways to bring us back when we have been separated from him." How does this surprising comment from this surprising woman sum up the essence of the gospel?

Question 15:1-6

Absalom stole the hearts of people. What a sad commentary on the fickle condition of the human heart. This scene causes us to ask, "Who will my heart always be allegiant to?"

Absalom's Rebellion

15 After this, Absalom bought a chariot and horses, and he hired fifty
bodyguards to run ahead of him. 2 He got up early every morning
and went out to the gate of the city. When people brought a case to the king
for judgment, Absalom would ask where in Israel they were from, and they
would tell him their tribe. 3 Then Absalom would say, "You've really got a
strong case here! It's too bad the king doesn't have anyone to hear it. 4 I wish
I were the judge. Then everyone could bring their cases to me for judgment,
and I would give them justice!"

5 When people tried to bow before him, Absalom wouldn't let them. Instead, he took them by the hand and kissed them. 6 Absalom did this with
everyone who came to the king for judgment, and so he stole the hearts of
all the people of Israel.

7 After four years,* Absalom said to the king, "Let me go to Hebron to offer
a sacrifice to the LORD and fulfill a vow I made to him. 8 For while your servant was at Geshur in Aram, I promised to sacrifice to the LORD in Hebron*
if he would bring me back to Jerusalem."

9 "All right," the king told him. "Go and fulfill your vow."

So Absalom went to Hebron. 10 But while he was there, he sent secret messengers to all the tribes of Israel to stir up a rebellion against the king. "As
soon as you hear the ram's horn," his message read, "you are to say, 'Absalom
has been crowned king in Hebron.'" 11 He took 200 men from Jerusalem with
him as guests, but they knew nothing of his intentions. 12 While Absalom was
offering the sacrifices, he sent for Ahithophel, one of David's counselors who
lived in Giloh. Soon many others also joined Absalom, and the conspiracy
gained momentum.

David Escapes from Jerusalem

13 A messenger soon arrived in Jerusalem to tell David, "All Israel has joined
Absalom in a conspiracy against you!"

14 "Then we must flee at once, or it will be too late!" David urged his men.
"Hurry! If we get out of the city before Absalom arrives, both we and the city
of Jerusalem will be spared from disaster."

15 "We are with you," his advisers replied. "Do what you think is best."

16 So the king and all his household set out at once. He left no one behind
except ten of his concubines to look after the palace. 17 The king and all his
people set out on foot, pausing at the last house 18 to let all the king's men
move past to lead the way. There were 600 men from Gath who had come
with David, along with the king's bodyguard.*

19 Then the king turned and said to Ittai, a leader of the men from Gath,
"Why are you coming with us? Go on back to King Absalom, for you are a
guest in Israel, a foreigner in exile. 20 You arrived only recently, and should I
force you today to wander with us? I don't even know where we will go. Go
on back and take your kinsmen with you, and may the LORD show you his
unfailing love and faithfulness.*"

21 But Ittai said to the king, "I vow by the LORD and by your own life that I
will go wherever my lord the king goes, no matter what happens—whether
it means life or death."

15:7 As in Greek and Syriac versions; Hebrew reads *forty years.* 15:8 As in some Greek manuscripts; Hebrew lacks *in Hebron.* 15:18 Hebrew *the Kerethites and Pelethites.* 15:20 As in Greek version; Hebrew reads *and may unfailing love and faithfulness go with you.*

22 David replied, "All right, come with us." So Ittai and all his men and
their families went along.
23 Everyone cried loudly as the king and his followers passed by. They
crossed the Kidron Valley and then went out toward the wilderness.
24 Zadok and all the Levites also came along, carrying the Ark of the
Covenant of God. They set down the Ark of God, and Abiathar offered
sacrifices* until everyone had passed out of the city.
25 Then the king instructed Zadok to take the Ark of God back into the
city. "If the LORD sees fit," David said, "he will bring me back to see the Ark
and the Tabernacle* again. 26 But if he is through with me, then let him do
what seems best to him."
27 The king also told Zadok the priest, "Look,* here is my plan. You and
Abiathar* should return quietly to the city with your son Ahimaaz and Abi-
athar's son Jonathan. 28 I will stop at the shallows of the Jordan River* and
wait there for a report from you." 29 So Zadok and Abiathar took the Ark of
God back to the city and stayed there.
30 David walked up the road to the Mount of Olives, weeping as he went. His
head was covered and his feet were bare as a sign of mourning. And the people
who were with him covered their heads and wept as they climbed the hill.
31 When someone told David that his adviser Ahithophel was now backing Ab-
salom, David prayed, "O LORD, let Ahithophel give Absalom foolish advice!"
32 When David reached the summit of the Mount of Olives where people
worshiped God, Hushai the Arkite was waiting there for him. Hushai had
torn his clothing and put dirt on his head as a sign of mourning. 33 But David
told him, "If you go with me, you will only be a burden. 34 Return to Jerusa-
lem and tell Absalom, 'I will now be your adviser, O king, just as I was your
father's adviser in the past.' Then you can frustrate and counter Ahithophel's
advice. 35 Zadok and Abiathar, the priests, will be there. Tell them about the
plans being made in the king's palace, 36 and they will send their sons Ahim-
aaz and Jonathan to tell me what is going on."
37 So David's friend Hushai returned to Jerusalem, getting there just as
Absalom arrived.

David and Ziba

16 When David had gone a little beyond the summit of the Mount of
Olives, Ziba, the servant of Mephibosheth,* was waiting there for
him. He had two donkeys loaded with 200 loaves of bread, 100 clusters of
raisins, 100 bunches of summer fruit, and a wineskin full of wine.
2 "What are these for?" the king asked Ziba.

Ziba replied, "The donkeys are for the king's people to ride on, and the
bread and summer fruit are for the young men to eat. The wine is for those
who become exhausted in the wilderness."
3 "And where is Mephibosheth, Saul's grandson?" the king asked him.

"He stayed in Jerusalem," Ziba replied. "He said, 'Today I will get back
the kingdom of my grandfather Saul.'"
4 "In that case," the king told Ziba, "I give you everything Mephibosheth
owns."

15:24 Or *Abiathar went up.* 15:25 Hebrew *and his dwelling place.* 15:27a As in Greek version; Hebrew reads *Are you a seer?* or *Do you see?* 15:27b Hebrew lacks *and Abiathar;* compare 15:29. 15:28 Hebrew *at the crossing points of the wilderness.* 16:1 *Mephibosheth* is another name for Merib-baal.

Make a Difference

15:25–26

Not My Will

Though his life was crashing down around him, though his own had betrayed him, though none of his closest followers seemed to understand, David trusted the outcomes to the Lord. In essence, he was saying, "I want the Lord's will to be done, not mine."

In the same area, a thousand years later, Jesus would pray these words in the garden of Gethsemane: "Father, if you are willing, please take this cup of suffering away from me. Yet I want your will to be done, not mine" (Luke 22:42).

Difference Maker

Stop everything right now and pray for something that you want to happen. Then offer it to the Lord by saying, "I want your will to be done, not mine."

Question **15:30**

Compare the events of 2 Samuel 15:13 and 15:25-30 with Luke 22:39-51. What do these moments reveal to you about the depth of passion Jesus has for you?

Prayer **16:12**

Lord, in the face of opposition, help me. Give me courage not to worry about those who don't like me or who are mistreating me. Let me look to you for my confidence and strength. Amen.

"I bow before you," Ziba replied. "May I always be pleasing to you, my
lord the king."

Shimei Curses David

5As King David came to Bahurim, a man came out of the village cursing them.
It was Shimei son of Gera, from the same clan as Saul's family. 6He threw stones
at the king and the king's officers and all the mighty warriors who surrounded
him. 7"Get out of here, you murderer, you scoundrel!" he shouted at David.
8"The LORD is paying you back for all the bloodshed in Saul's clan. You stole
his throne, and now the LORD has given it to your son Absalom. At last you
will taste some of your own medicine, for you are a murderer!"

9"Why should this dead dog curse my lord the king?" Abishai son of Zer-
uiah demanded. "Let me go over and cut off his head!"

10"No!" the king said. "Who asked your opinion, you sons of Zeruiah! If
the LORD has told him to curse me, who are you to stop him?"

11Then David said to Abishai and to all his servants, "My own son is try-
ing to kill me. Doesn't this relative of Saul* have even more reason to do
so? Leave him alone and let him curse, for the LORD has told him to do it.
12And perhaps the LORD will see that I am being wronged* and will bless
me because of these curses today." 13So David and his men continued down
the road, and Shimei kept pace with them on a nearby hillside, cursing and
throwing stones and dirt at David.

14The king and all who were with him grew weary along the way, so they
rested when they reached the Jordan River.*

Ahithophel Advises Absalom

15Meanwhile, Absalom and all the army of Israel arrived at Jerusalem, ac-
companied by Ahithophel. 16When David's friend Hushai the Arkite arrived,
he went immediately to see Absalom. "Long live the king!" he exclaimed.
"Long live the king!"

17"Is this the way you treat your friend David?" Absalom asked him. "Why
aren't you with him?"

18"I'm here because I belong to the man who is chosen by the LORD and by
all the men of Israel," Hushai replied. 19"And anyway, why shouldn't I serve
you? Just as I was your father's adviser, now I will be your adviser!"

20Then Absalom turned to Ahithophel and asked him, "What should I
do next?"

21Ahithophel told him, "Go and sleep with your father's concubines, for he
has left them here to look after the palace. Then all Israel will know that you
have insulted your father beyond hope of reconciliation, and they will throw
their support to you." 22So they set up a tent on the palace roof where everyone
could see it, and Absalom went in and had sex with his father's concubines.

23Absalom followed Ahithophel's advice, just as David had done. For every
word Ahithophel spoke seemed as wise as though it had come directly from
the mouth of God.

17 Now Ahithophel urged Absalom, "Let me choose 12,000 men to start
out after David tonight. 2I will catch up with him while he is weary
and discouraged. He and his troops will panic, and everyone will run away.

16:11 Hebrew *this Benjaminite.* **16:12** As in Greek and Syriac versions; Hebrew reads *see my iniquity.* **16:14** As in Greek version (see also 17:16); Hebrew reads *when they reached their destination.*

Then I will kill only the king, 3and I will bring all the people back to you as
a bride returns to her husband. After all, it is only one man's life that you
seek.* Then you will be at peace with all the people." 4This plan seemed good
to Absalom and to all the elders of Israel.

Hushai Counters Ahithophel's Advice

5But then Absalom said, "Bring in Hushai the Arkite. Let's see what he thinks
about this." 6When Hushai arrived, Absalom told him what Ahithophel had
said. Then he asked, "What is your opinion? Should we follow Ahithophel's
advice? If not, what do you suggest?"

7"Well," Hushai replied to Absalom, "this time Ahithophel has made
a mistake. 8You know your father and his men; they are mighty warriors.
Right now they are as enraged as a mother bear who has been robbed of
her cubs. And remember that your father is an experienced man of war. He
won't be spending the night among the troops. 9He has probably already
hidden in some pit or cave. And when he comes out and attacks and a few
of your men fall, there will be panic among your troops, and the word will
spread that Absalom's men are being slaughtered. 10Then even the bravest
soldiers, though they have the heart of a lion, will be paralyzed with fear.
For all Israel knows what a mighty warrior your father is and how coura-
geous his men are.

11"I recommend that you mobilize the entire army of Israel, bringing
them from as far away as Dan in the north and Beersheba in the south. That
way you will have an army as numerous as the sand on the seashore. And I
advise that you personally lead the troops. 12When we find David, we'll fall
on him like dew that falls on the ground. Then neither he nor any of his men
will be left alive. 13And if David were to escape into some town, you will have
all Israel there at your command. Then we can take ropes and drag the walls
of the town into the nearest valley until every stone is torn down."

14Then Absalom and all the men of Israel said, "Hushai's advice is better
than Ahithophel's." For the LORD had determined to defeat the counsel of
Ahithophel, which really was the better plan, so that he could bring disaster
on Absalom!

Hushai Warns David to Escape

15Hushai told Zadok and Abiathar, the priests, what Ahithophel had said to
Absalom and the elders of Israel and what he himself had advised instead.
16"Quick!" he told them. "Find David and urge him not to stay at the shal-
lows of the Jordan River* tonight. He must go across at once into the wilder-
ness beyond. Otherwise he will die and his entire army with him."

17Jonathan and Ahimaaz had been staying at En-rogel so as not to be seen
entering and leaving the city. Arrangements had been made for a servant girl
to bring them the message they were to take to King David. 18But a boy spot-
ted them at En-rogel, and he told Absalom about it. So they quickly escaped
to Bahurim, where a man hid them down inside a well in his courtyard. 19The
man's wife put a cloth over the top of the well and scattered grain on it to
dry in the sun; so no one suspected they were there.

20When Absalom's men arrived, they asked her, "Have you seen Ahimaaz
and Jonathan?"

17:3 As in Greek version; Hebrew reads *like the return of all is the man whom you seek.*
17:16 Hebrew *at the crossing points of the wilderness.*

The woman replied, "They were here, but they crossed over the brook." Absalom's men looked for them without success and returned to Jerusalem.

21 Then the two men crawled out of the well and hurried on to King David. "Quick!" they told him, "cross the Jordan tonight!" And they told him how Ahithophel had advised that he be captured and killed. 22 So David and all the people with him went across the Jordan River during the night, and they were all on the other bank before dawn.

23 When Ahithophel realized that his advice had not been followed, he saddled his donkey, went to his hometown, set his affairs in order, and hanged himself. He died there and was buried in the family tomb.

24 David soon arrived at Mahanaim. By now, Absalom had mobilized the entire army of Israel and was leading his troops across the Jordan River. 25 Absalom had appointed Amasa as commander of his army, replacing Joab, who had been commander under David. (Amasa was Joab's cousin. His father was Jether,* an Ishmaelite.* His mother, Abigail daughter of Nahash, was the sister of Joab's mother, Zeruiah.) 26 Absalom and the Israelite army set up camp in the land of Gilead.

27 When David arrived at Mahanaim, he was warmly greeted by Shobi son of Nahash, who came from Rabbah of the Ammonites, and by Makir son of Ammiel from Lo-debar, and by Barzillai of Gilead from Rogelim. 28 They brought sleeping mats, cooking pots, serving bowls, wheat and barley, flour and roasted grain, beans, lentils, 29 honey, butter, sheep, goats, and cheese for David and those who were with him. For they said, "You must all be very hungry and tired and thirsty after your long march through the wilderness."

Absalom's Defeat and Death

18 David now mustered the men who were with him and appointed generals and captains* to lead them. 2 He sent the troops out in three groups, placing one group under Joab, one under Joab's brother Abishai son of Zeruiah, and one under Ittai, the man from Gath. The king told his troops, "I am going out with you."

3 But his men objected strongly. "You must not go," they urged. "If we have to turn and run—and even if half of us die—it will make no difference to Absalom's troops; they will be looking only for you. You are worth 10,000 of us,* and it is better that you stay here in the town and send help if we need it."

4 "If you think that's the best plan, I'll do it," the king answered. So he stood alongside the gate of the town as all the troops marched out in groups of hundreds and of thousands.

5 And the king gave this command to Joab, Abishai, and Ittai: "For my sake, deal gently with young Absalom." And all the troops heard the king give this order to his commanders.

6 So the battle began in the forest of Ephraim, 7 and the Israelite troops were beaten back by David's men. There was a great slaughter that day, and 20,000 men laid down their lives. 8 The battle raged all across the countryside, and more men died because of the forest than were killed by the sword.

9 During the battle, Absalom happened to come upon some of David's men. He tried to escape on his mule, but as he rode beneath the thick branches

17:25a Hebrew *Ithra,* a variant spelling of Jether. **17:25b** As in some Greek manuscripts (see also 1 Chr 2:17); Hebrew reads *an Israelite.* **18:1** Hebrew *appointed commanders of thousands and commanders of hundreds.* **18:3** As in two Hebrew manuscripts and some Greek and Latin manuscripts; most Hebrew manuscripts read *Now there are 10,000 like us.*

of a great tree, his hair* got caught in the tree. His mule kept going and left
him dangling in the air. 10 One of David's men saw what had happened and
told Joab, "I saw Absalom dangling from a great tree."
11 "What?" Joab demanded. "You saw him there and didn't kill him? I
would have rewarded you with ten pieces of silver* and a hero's belt!"
12 "I would not kill the king's son for even a thousand pieces of silver,*" the
man replied to Joab. "We all heard the king say to you and Abishai and Ittai,
'For my sake, please spare young Absalom.' 13 And if I had betrayed the king
by killing his son—and the king would certainly find out who did it—you
yourself would be the first to abandon me."
14 "Enough of this nonsense," Joab said. Then he took three daggers and
plunged them into Absalom's heart as he dangled, still alive, in the great tree.
15 Ten of Joab's young armor bearers then surrounded Absalom and killed him.
16 Then Joab blew the ram's horn, and his men returned from chasing the
army of Israel. 17 They threw Absalom's body into a deep pit in the forest and
piled a great heap of stones over it. And all Israel fled to their homes.
18 During his lifetime, Absalom had built a monument to himself in the
King's Valley, for he said, "I have no son to carry on my name." He named
the monument after himself, and it is known as Absalom's Monument to
this day.

David Mourns Absalom's Death

19 Then Zadok's son Ahimaaz said, "Let me run to the king with the good
news that the LORD has rescued him from his enemies."
20 "No," Joab told him, "it wouldn't be good news to the king that his son
is dead. You can be my messenger another time, but not today."
21 Then Joab said to a man from Ethiopia,* "Go tell the king what you have
seen." The man bowed and ran off.
22 But Ahimaaz continued to plead with Joab, "Whatever happens, please
let me go, too."
"Why should you go, my son?" Joab replied. "There will be no reward
for your news."
23 "Yes, but let me go anyway," he begged.
Joab finally said, "All right, go ahead." So Ahimaaz took the less demand-
ing route by way of the plain and ran to Mahanaim ahead of the Ethiopian.
24 While David was sitting between the inner and outer gates of the town,
the watchman climbed to the roof of the gateway by the wall. As he looked,
he saw a lone man running toward them. 25 He shouted the news down to
David, and the king replied, "If he is alone, he has news."
As the messenger came closer, 26 the watchman saw another man running
toward them. He shouted down, "Here comes another one!"
The king replied, "He also will have news."
27 "The first man runs like Ahimaaz son of Zadok," the watchman said.
"He is a good man and comes with good news," the king replied.
28 Then Ahimaaz cried out to the king, "Everything is all right!" He bowed
before the king with his face to the ground and said, "Praise to the LORD
your God, who has handed over the rebels who dared to stand against my
lord the king."

18:9 Hebrew *his head.* 18:11 Hebrew *10 [shekels] of silver,* about 4 ounces or 114 grams in weight. 18:12 Hebrew *1,000 [shekels] of silver,* about 25 pounds or 11.4 kilograms in weight. 18:21 Hebrew *from Cush;* similarly in 18:23, 31, 32.

What I want to remember

Question 18:33

Even though Absalom had caused so much anguish and so much destruction, David was still overcome with grief at his death. Have you ever felt this way—where the pain in your heart paralyzes you and bursts from your soul? What does the deep grief of David reveal about the heart of God for all people?

Question 19:6

This is an outcome of dysfunctional relationships. Do you know anyone like this? How could you help get some support for someone with this problem?

29 “What about young Absalom?” the king demanded. “Is he all right?”
Ahimaaz replied, “When Joab told me to come, there was a lot of commo-
tion. But I didn't know what was happening.”
30 “Wait here,” the king told him. So Ahimaaz stepped aside.
31 Then the man from Ethiopia arrived and said, “I have good news for my
lord the king. Today the LORD has rescued you from all those who rebelled
against you.”
32 “What about young Absalom?” the king demanded. “Is he all right?”
And the Ethiopian replied, “May all of your enemies, my lord the king,
both now and in the future, share the fate of that young man!”
33 *The king was overcome with emotion. He went up to the room over the
gateway and burst into tears. And as he went, he cried, “O my son Absalom!
My son, my son Absalom! If only I had died instead of you! O Absalom, my
son, my son.”

Joab Rebukes the King

19 1 *Word soon reached Joab that the king was weeping and mourn-
ing for Absalom. 2 As all the people heard of the king's deep grief
for his son, the joy of that day's victory was turned into deep sadness. 3 They
crept back into the town that day as though they were ashamed and had
deserted in battle. 4 The king covered his face with his hands and kept on
crying, “O my son Absalom! O Absalom, my son, my son!”
5 Then Joab went to the king's room and said to him, “We saved your life
today and the lives of your sons, your daughters, and your wives and concu-
bines. Yet you act like this, making us feel ashamed of ourselves. 6 You seem
to love those who hate you and hate those who love you. You have made it
clear today that your commanders and troops mean nothing to you. It seems
that if Absalom had lived and all of us had died, you would be pleased. 7 Now
go out there and congratulate your troops, for I swear by the LORD that if
you don't go out, not a single one of them will remain here tonight. Then
you will be worse off than ever before.”
8 So the king went out and took his seat at the town gate, and as the news
spread throughout the town that he was there, everyone went to him.
Meanwhile, the Israelites who had supported Absalom fled to their
homes. 9 And throughout all the tribes of Israel there was much discussion
and argument going on. The people were saying, “The king rescued us from
our enemies and saved us from the Philistines, but Absalom chased him out
of the country. 10 Now Absalom, whom we anointed to rule over us, is dead.
Why not ask David to come back and be our king again?”
11 Then King David sent Zadok and Abiathar, the priests, to say to the el-
ders of Judah, “Why are you the last ones to welcome back the king into his
palace? For I have heard that all Israel is ready. 12 You are my relatives, my own
tribe, my own flesh and blood! So why are you the last ones to welcome back
the king?” 13 And David told them to tell Amasa, “Since you are my own flesh
and blood, like Joab, may God strike me and even kill me if I do not appoint
you as commander of my army in his place.”
14 Then Amasa* convinced all the men of Judah, and they responded unani-
mously. They sent word to the king, “Return to us, and bring back all who
are with you.”

18:33 Verse 18:33 is numbered 19:1 in Hebrew text. 19:1 Verses 19:1-43 are numbered 19:2-44 in Hebrew text. 19:14 Or *David;* Hebrew reads *he.*

David's Return to Jerusalem

15 So the king started back to Jerusalem. And when he arrived at the Jordan
River, the people of Judah came to Gilgal to meet him and escort him across the
river. 16 Shimei son of Gera, the man from Bahurim in Benjamin, hurried across
with the men of Judah to welcome King David. 17 A thousand other men from
the tribe of Benjamin were with him, including Ziba, the chief servant of the
house of Saul, and Ziba's fifteen sons and twenty servants. They rushed down to
the Jordan to meet the king. 18 They crossed the shallows of the Jordan to bring
the king's household across the river, helping him in every way they could.

David's Mercy to Shimei

As the king was about to cross the river, Shimei fell down before him. 19 "My
lord the king, please forgive me," he pleaded. "Forget the terrible thing your
servant did when you left Jerusalem. May the king put it out of his mind. 20 I
know how much I sinned. That is why I have come here today, the very first
person in all Israel* to greet my lord the king."

21 Then Abishai son of Zeruiah said, "Shimei should die, for he cursed the
LORD's anointed king!"

22 "Who asked your opinion, you sons of Zeruiah!" David exclaimed. "Why
have you become my adversary* today? This is not a day for execution, for
today I am once again the king of Israel!" 23 Then, turning to Shimei, David
vowed, "Your life will be spared."

David's Kindness to Mephibosheth

24 Now Mephibosheth,* Saul's grandson, came down from Jerusalem to meet
the king. He had not cared for his feet, trimmed his beard, or washed his
clothes since the day the king left Jerusalem. 25 "Why didn't you come with
me, Mephibosheth?" the king asked him.

26 Mephibosheth replied, "My lord the king, my servant Ziba deceived me.
I told him, 'Saddle my donkey* so I can go with the king.' For as you know I
am crippled. 27 Ziba has slandered me by saying that I refused to come. But
I know that my lord the king is like an angel of God, so do what you think
is best. 28 All my relatives and I could expect only death from you, my lord,
but instead you have honored me by allowing me to eat at your own table!
What more can I ask?"

29 "You've said enough," David replied. "I've decided that you and Ziba
will divide your land equally between you."

30 "Give him all of it," Mephibosheth said. "I am content just to have you
safely back again, my lord the king!"

David's Kindness to Barzillai

31 Barzillai of Gilead had come down from Rogelim to escort the king across
the Jordan. 32 He was very old—eighty years of age—and very wealthy. He
was the one who had provided food for the king during his stay in Maha-
naim. 33 "Come across with me and live in Jerusalem," the king said to Bar-
zillai. "I will take care of you there."

34 "No," he replied, "I am far too old to go with the king to Jerusalem. 35 I am
eighty years old today, and I can no longer enjoy anything. Food and wine are

19:20 Hebrew *in the house of Joseph.* **19:22** Or *my prosecutor.* **19:24** *Mephibosheth* is another name for Merib-baal. **19:26** As in Greek, Syriac, and Latin versions; Hebrew reads *I will saddle a donkey for myself.*

Make a Difference

19:31-40

Kindness

In 2 Samuel 19:31-40, David's kindness to an eighty-year-old man named Barzillai marked a refreshingly encouraging note in the midst of several overwhelmingly depressing chapters.

Difference Maker

Practice serving people all day long through acts of politeness and kindness. Trust that the Lord will bless you and others as you serve.

no longer tasty, and I cannot hear the singers as they sing. I would only be a
burden to my lord the king. 36 Just to go across the Jordan River with the king is
all the honor I need! 37 Then let me return again to die in my own town, where
my father and mother are buried. But here is your servant, my son Kimham.
Let him go with my lord the king and receive whatever you want to give him."
38 "Good," the king agreed. "Kimham will go with me, and I will help him
in any way you would like. And I will do for you anything you want." 39 So all
the people crossed the Jordan with the king. After David had blessed Barzil-
lai and kissed him, Barzillai returned to his own home.
40 The king then crossed over to Gilgal, taking Kimham with him. All the
troops of Judah and half the troops of Israel escorted the king on his way.

An Argument over the King

41 But all the men of Israel complained to the king, "The men of Judah stole
the king and didn't give us the honor of helping take you, your household,
and all your men across the Jordan."
42 The men of Judah replied, "The king is one of our own kinsmen. Why
should this make you angry? We haven't eaten any of the king's food or re-
ceived any special favors!"
43 "But there are ten tribes in Israel," the others replied. "So we have ten
times as much right to the king as you do. What right do you have to treat us
with such contempt? Weren't we the first to speak of bringing him back to
be our king again?" The argument continued back and forth, and the men
of Judah spoke even more harshly than the men of Israel.

The Revolt of Sheba

20 There happened to be a troublemaker there named Sheba son of
Bicri, a man from the tribe of Benjamin. Sheba blew a ram's horn
and began to chant:

"Down with the dynasty of David!
  We have no interest in the son of Jesse.
Come on, you men of Israel,
  back to your homes!"

2 So all the men of Israel deserted David and followed Sheba son of Bic-
ri. But the men of Judah stayed with their king and escorted him from the
Jordan River to Jerusalem.
3 When David came to his palace in Jerusalem, he took the ten concubines
he had left to look after the palace and placed them in seclusion. Their needs
were provided for, but he no longer slept with them. So each of them lived
like a widow until she died.
4 Then the king told Amasa, "Mobilize the army of Judah within three
days, and report back at that time." 5 So Amasa went out to notify Judah, but
it took him longer than the time he had been given.
6 Then David said to Abishai, "Sheba son of Bicri is going to hurt us more
than Absalom did. Quick, take my troops and chase after him before he gets
into a fortified town where we can't reach him."
7 So Abishai and Joab,* together with the king's bodyguard* and all the

20:7a Hebrew *So Joab's men.* 20:7b Hebrew *the Kerethites and Pelethites;* also in 20:23.

mighty warriors, set out from Jerusalem to go after Sheba. 8 As they arrived
at the great stone in Gibeon, Amasa met them. Joab was wearing his military
tunic with a dagger strapped to his belt. As he stepped forward to greet Am-
asa, he slipped the dagger from its sheath.*
9 "How are you, my cousin?" Joab said and took him by the beard with his
right hand as though to kiss him. 10 Amasa didn't notice the dagger in his left
hand, and Joab stabbed him in the stomach with it so that his insides gushed
out onto the ground. Joab did not need to strike again, and Amasa soon died.
Joab and his brother Abishai left him lying there and continued after Sheba.
11 One of Joab's young men shouted to Amasa's troops, "If you are for Joab
and David, come and follow Joab." 12 But Amasa lay in his blood in the middle
of the road, and Joab's man saw that everyone was stopping to stare at him.
So he pulled him off the road into a field and threw a cloak over him. 13 With
Amasa's body out of the way, everyone went on with Joab to capture Sheba
son of Bicri.
14 Meanwhile, Sheba traveled through all the tribes of Israel and eventu-
ally came to the town of Abel-beth-maacah. All the members of his own clan,
the Bicrites,* assembled for battle and followed him into the town. 15 When
Joab's forces arrived, they attacked Abel-beth-maacah. They built a siege ramp
against the town's fortifications and began battering down the wall. 16 But a
wise woman in the town called out to Joab, "Listen to me, Joab. Come over here
so I can talk to you." 17 As he approached, the woman asked, "Are you Joab?"
"I am," he replied.
So she said, "Listen carefully to your servant."
"I'm listening," he said.
18 Then she continued, "There used to be a saying, 'If you want to settle
an argument, ask advice at the town of Abel.' 19 I am one who is peace loving
and faithful in Israel. But you are destroying an important town in Israel.*
Why do you want to devour what belongs to the LORD?"
20 And Joab replied, "Believe me, I don't want to devour or destroy your
town! 21 That's not my purpose. All I want is a man named Sheba son of Bicri
from the hill country of Ephraim, who has revolted against King David. If
you hand over this one man to me, I will leave the town in peace."
"All right," the woman replied, "we will throw his head over the wall to
you." 22 Then the woman went to all the people with her wise advice, and
they cut off Sheba's head and threw it out to Joab. So he blew the ram's horn
and called his troops back from the attack. They all returned to their homes,
and Joab returned to the king at Jerusalem.
23 Now Joab was the commander of the army of Israel. Benaiah son of Je-
hoiada was captain of the king's bodyguard. 24 Adoniram* was in charge of
forced labor. Jehoshaphat son of Ahilud was the royal historian. 25 Sheva was
the court secretary. Zadok and Abiathar were the priests. 26 And Ira, a descen-
dant of Jair, was David's personal priest.

David Avenges the Gibeonites

21 There was a famine during David's reign that lasted for three years, so
David asked the LORD about it. And the LORD said, "The famine has
come because Saul and his family are guilty of murdering the Gibeonites."

20:8 Hebrew *As he stepped forward, it fell out.* 20:14 As in Greek and Latin versions; Hebrew reads *All the Berites.* 20:19 Hebrew *a town that is a mother in Israel.* 20:24 As in Greek version (see also 1 Kgs 4:6; 5:14); Hebrew reads *Adoram.*

What God wants people to know

Question 21:15-17

David's season of life was changing through these later chapters of 2 Samuel. He was no longer a young man. As he grew older and as he struggled with sin and painful events, he struggled to keep his childlike faith. So much of his vibrant faith was wrapped up in being youthful and full of ability. Later, as he became a very weathered man, David's faith needed to adapt. The question all of us must face as we go through the seasons of life is this: As we grow older, how can we keep the vibrancy of faith that we more easily experience when we are young?

2 So the king summoned the Gibeonites. They were not part of Israel but
were all that was left of the nation of the Amorites. The people of Israel had
sworn not to kill them, but Saul, in his zeal for Israel and Judah, had tried to
wipe them out. 3 David asked them, "What can I do for you? How can I make
amends so that you will bless the LORD's people again?"
4 "Well, money can't settle this matter between us and the family of
Saul," the Gibeonites replied. "Neither can we demand the life of anyone
in Israel."
"What can I do then?" David asked. "Just tell me and I will do it for you."
5 Then they replied, "It was Saul who planned to destroy us, to keep us
from having any place at all in the territory of Israel. 6 So let seven of Saul's
sons be handed over to us, and we will execute them before the LORD at Gib-
eon, on the mountain of the LORD.*"
"All right," the king said, "I will do it." 7 The king spared Jonathan's son
Mephibosheth,* who was Saul's grandson, because of the oath David and
Jonathan had sworn before the LORD. 8 But he gave them Saul's two sons
Armoni and Mephibosheth, whose mother was Rizpah daughter of Aiah.
He also gave them the five sons of Saul's daughter Merab,* the wife of Adriel
son of Barzillai from Meholah. 9 The men of Gibeon executed them on the
mountain before the LORD. So all seven of them died together at the begin-
ning of the barley harvest.
10 Then Rizpah daughter of Aiah, the mother of two of the men, spread
burlap on a rock and stayed there the entire harvest season. She prevented
the scavenger birds from tearing at their bodies during the day and stopped
wild animals from eating them at night. 11 When David learned what Rizpah,
Saul's concubine, had done, 12 he went to the people of Jabesh-gilead and
retrieved the bones of Saul and his son Jonathan. (When the Philistines had
killed Saul and Jonathan on Mount Gilboa, the people of Jabesh-gilead stole
their bodies from the public square of Beth-shan, where the Philistines had
hung them.) 13 So David obtained the bones of Saul and Jonathan, as well as
the bones of the men the Gibeonites had executed.
14 Then the king ordered that they bury the bones in the tomb of Kish,
Saul's father, at the town of Zela in the land of Benjamin. After that, God
ended the famine in the land.

Battles against Philistine Giants

15 Once again the Philistines were at war with Israel. And when David and his
men were in the thick of battle, David became weak and exhausted. 16 Ishbi-
benob was a descendant of the giants*; his bronze spearhead weighed more
than seven pounds,* and he was armed with a new sword. He had cornered
David and was about to kill him. 17 But Abishai son of Zeruiah came to Da-
vid's rescue and killed the Philistine. Then David's men declared, "You are
not going out to battle with us again! Why risk snuffing out the light of
Israel?"
18 After this, there was another battle against the Philistines at Gob. As they
fought, Sibbecai from Hushah killed Saph, another descendant of the giants.
19 During another battle at Gob, Elhanan son of Jair* from Bethlehem

21:6 As in Greek version (see also 21:9); Hebrew reads *at Gibeah of Saul, the chosen of the LORD.* **21:7** *Mephibosheth* is another name for Merib-baal. **21:8** As in a few Hebrew and Greek manuscripts and Syriac version (see also 1 Sam 18:19); most Hebrew manuscripts read *Michal.* **21:16a** Or *a descendant of the Rapha;* also in 21:18, 20, 22. **21:16b** Hebrew *300 [shekels]* [3.4 kilograms]. **21:19a** As in parallel text at 1 Chr 20:5; Hebrew reads *son of Jaare-oregim.*

killed the brother of Goliath of Gath.* The handle of his spear was as thick as a weaver's beam!

20 In another battle with the Philistines at Gath, they encountered a huge man* with six fingers on each hand and six toes on each foot, twenty-four in all, who was also a descendant of the giants. 21 But when he defied and taunted Israel, he was killed by Jonathan, the son of David's brother Shimea.*

22 These four Philistines were descendants of the giants of Gath, but David and his warriors killed them.

David's Song of Praise

22 David sang this song to the LORD on the day the LORD rescued him from all his enemies and from Saul. 2 He sang:

"The LORD is my rock, my fortress, and my savior;
3 my God is my rock, in whom I find protection.
He is my shield, the power that saves me,
and my place of safety.
He is my refuge, my savior,
the one who saves me from violence.
4 I called on the LORD, who is worthy of praise,
and he saved me from my enemies.

5 "The waves of death overwhelmed me;
floods of destruction swept over me.
6 The grave* wrapped its ropes around me;
death laid a trap in my path.
7 But in my distress I cried out to the LORD;
yes, I cried to my God for help.
He heard me from his sanctuary;
my cry reached his ears.

8 "Then the earth quaked and trembled.
The foundations of the heavens shook;
they quaked because of his anger.
9 Smoke poured from his nostrils;
fierce flames leaped from his mouth.
Glowing coals blazed forth from him.
10 He opened the heavens and came down;
dark storm clouds were beneath his feet.
11 Mounted on a mighty angelic being,* he flew,
soaring* on the wings of the wind.
12 He shrouded himself in darkness,
veiling his approach with dense rain clouds.
13 A great brightness shone around him,
and burning coals* blazed forth.
14 The LORD thundered from heaven;
the voice of the Most High resounded.

21:19b As in parallel text at 1 Chr 20:5; Hebrew reads *killed Goliath of Gath.* **21:20** As in parallel text at 1 Chr 20:6; Hebrew reads *a Midianite.* **21:21** As in parallel text at 1 Chr 20:7; Hebrew reads *Shimei,* a variant spelling of Shimea. **22:6** Hebrew *Sheol.* **22:11a** Hebrew *a cherub.* **22:11b** As in some Hebrew manuscripts (see also Ps 18:10); other Hebrew manuscripts read *appearing.* **22:13** Or *and lightning bolts.*

Make a Difference

22:1-51

The Lord Is Our Savior

This beautiful prayer of David is nearly identical to Psalm 18. At the end of his life, he affirmed a truth he had always known: the Lord was his Savior.

The fact that you are reading this Bible shows that you understand this truth in one way or another too. Keep challenging yourself to be changed by God every day for the rest of your life. Don't ever stop this pursuit.

Like David, at some point in your life, maybe you have recognized your need for God. You've probably had some ups and downs in your walk with Jesus, but today you know you need him to be the primary focus of your life. Right now is a new opportunity to give your life to Jesus afresh. Commit today to discover who he is and what he wants for you. Continue to learn about what he has done and what he is doing for you while you continue to look for him, call out to him, and follow him.

Difference Maker

Take a moment to pray through the section in the back of the Bible titled "How to Accept Jesus as Your Lord and Savior."

15 He shot arrows and scattered his enemies;
his lightning flashed, and they were confused.
16 Then at the command of the LORD,
at the blast of his breath,
the bottom of the sea could be seen,
and the foundations of the earth were laid bare.

17 "He reached down from heaven and rescued me;
he drew me out of deep waters.
18 He rescued me from my powerful enemies,
from those who hated me and were too strong for me.
19 They attacked me at a moment when I was in distress,
but the LORD supported me.
20 He led me to a place of safety;
he rescued me because he delights in me.
21 The LORD rewarded me for doing right;
he restored me because of my innocence.
22 For I have kept the ways of the LORD;
I have not turned from my God to follow evil.
23 I have followed all his regulations;
I have never abandoned his decrees.
24 I am blameless before God;
I have kept myself from sin.
25 The LORD rewarded me for doing right.
He has seen my innocence.

26 "To the faithful you show yourself faithful;
to those with integrity you show integrity.
27 To the pure you show yourself pure,
but to the crooked you show yourself shrewd.
28 You rescue the humble,
but your eyes watch the proud and humiliate them.
29 O LORD, you are my lamp.
The LORD lights up my darkness.
30 In your strength I can crush an army;
with my God I can scale any wall.

31 "God's way is perfect.
All the LORD's promises prove true.
He is a shield for all who look to him for protection.
32 For who is God except the LORD?
Who but our God is a solid rock?
33 God is my strong fortress,
and he makes my way perfect.
34 He makes me as surefooted as a deer,
enabling me to stand on mountain heights.
35 He trains my hands for battle;
he strengthens my arm to draw a bronze bow.
36 You have given me your shield of victory;
your help* has made me great.

22:36 As in Dead Sea Scrolls; Masoretic Text reads *your answering.*

37 You have made a wide path for my feet
to keep them from slipping.

38 "I chased my enemies and destroyed them;
I did not stop until they were conquered.
39 I consumed them;
I struck them down so they did not get up;
they fell beneath my feet.
40 You have armed me with strength for the battle;
you have subdued my enemies under my feet.
41 You placed my foot on their necks.
I have destroyed all who hated me.
42 They looked for help, but no one came to their rescue.
They even cried to the LORD, but he refused to answer.
43 I ground them as fine as the dust of the earth;
I trampled them* in the gutter like dirt.

44 "You gave me victory over my accusers.
You preserved me as the ruler over nations;
people I don't even know now serve me.
45 Foreign nations cringe before me;
as soon as they hear of me, they submit.
46 They all lose their courage
and come trembling* from their strongholds.

47 "The LORD lives! Praise to my Rock!
May God, the Rock of my salvation, be exalted!
48 He is the God who pays back those who harm me;
he brings down the nations under me
49 and delivers me from my enemies.
You hold me safe beyond the reach of my enemies;
you save me from violent opponents.
50 For this, O LORD, I will praise you among the nations;
I will sing praises to your name.
51 You give great victories to your king;
you show unfailing love to your anointed,
to David and all his descendants forever."

David's Last Words

23 These are the last words of David:

"David, the son of Jesse, speaks—
David, the man who was raised up so high,
David, the man anointed by the God of Jacob,
David, the sweet psalmist of Israel.*

2 "The Spirit of the LORD speaks through me;
his words are upon my tongue.

Prayer **23:2**

May this be true of me, Lord. Amen.

22:43 As in Dead Sea Scrolls (see also Ps 18:42); Masoretic Text reads *I crushed and trampled them.* 22:46 As in parallel text at Ps 18:45; Hebrew reads *come girding themselves.* 23:1 Or *the favorite subject of the songs of Israel;* or *the favorite of the Strong One of Israel.*

3 The God of Israel spoke.
The Rock of Israel said to me:
'The one who rules righteously,
who rules in the fear of God,
4 is like the light of morning at sunrise,
like a morning without clouds,
like the gleaming of the sun
on new grass after rain.'

5 "Is it not my family God has chosen?
Yes, he has made an everlasting covenant with me.
His agreement is arranged and guaranteed in every detail.
He will ensure my safety and success.
6 But the godless are like thorns to be thrown away,
for they tear the hand that touches them.
7 One must use iron tools to chop them down;
they will be totally consumed by fire."

David's Mightiest Warriors

8 These are the names of David's mightiest warriors. The first was Jashobeam
the Hacmonite,* who was leader of the Three*—the three mightiest warriors
among David's men. He once used his spear to kill 800 enemy warriors in
a single battle.*

9 Next in rank among the Three was Eleazar son of Dodai, a descendant
of Ahoah. Once Eleazar and David stood together against the Philistines
when the entire Israelite army had fled. 10 He killed Philistines until his
hand was too tired to lift his sword, and the LORD gave him a great victory
that day. The rest of the army did not return until it was time to collect
the plunder!

11 Next in rank was Shammah son of Agee from Harar. One time the Phi-
listines gathered at Lehi and attacked the Israelites in a field full of lentils.
The Israelite army fled, 12 but Shammah* held his ground in the middle of
the field and beat back the Philistines. So the LORD brought about a great
victory.

13 Once during the harvest, when David was at the cave of Adullam, the
Philistine army was camped in the valley of Rephaim. The Three (who were
among the Thirty—an elite group among David's fighting men) went down
to meet him there. 14 David was staying in the stronghold at the time, and a
Philistine detachment had occupied the town of Bethlehem.

15 David remarked longingly to his men, "Oh, how I would love some of
that good water from the well by the gate in Bethlehem." 16 So the Three
broke through the Philistine lines, drew some water from the well by the
gate in Bethlehem, and brought it back to David. But he refused to drink
it. Instead, he poured it out as an offering to the LORD. 17 "The LORD forbid
that I should drink this!" he exclaimed. "This water is as precious as the
blood of these men* who risked their lives to bring it to me." So David did
not drink it. These are examples of the exploits of the Three.

23:8a As in parallel text at 1 Chr 11:11; Hebrew reads *Josheb-basshebeth the Tahkemonite.* **23:8b** As in Greek and Latin versions (see also 1 Chr 11:11); the meaning of the Hebrew is uncertain. **23:8c** As in some Greek manuscripts (see also 1 Chr 11:11); the meaning of the Hebrew is uncertain, though it might be rendered *the Three. It was Adino the Eznite who killed 800 men at one time.* **23:12** Hebrew *he.* **23:17** Hebrew *Shall I drink the blood of these men?*

Please write on this page!

David's Thirty Mighty Men
18 Abishai son of Zeruiah, the brother of Joab, was the leader of the Thirty.* He once used his spear to kill 300 enemy warriors in a single battle. It was by such feats that he became as famous as the Three.
19 Abishai was the most famous of the Thirty* and was their commander, though he was not one of the Three.

20 There was also Benaiah son of Jehoiada, a valiant warrior* from Kabzeel. He did many heroic deeds, which included killing two champions* of Moab. Another time, on a snowy day, he chased a lion down into a pit and killed it.
21 Once, armed only with a club, he killed an imposing Egyptian warrior who was armed with a spear. Benaiah wrenched the spear from the Egyptian's hand and killed him with it.
22 Deeds like these made Benaiah as famous as the Three mightiest warriors.
23 He was more honored than the other members of the Thirty, though he was not one of the Three. And David made him captain of his bodyguard.

24 Other members of the Thirty included:

Asahel, Joab's brother;
Elhanan son of Dodo from Bethlehem;
25 Shammah from Harod;
Elika from Harod;
26 Helez from Pelon*;
Ira son of Ikkesh from Tekoa;
27 Abiezer from Anathoth;
Sibbecai* from Hushah;
28 Zalmon from Ahoah;
Maharai from Netophah;
29 Heled* son of Baanah from Netophah;
Ithai* son of Ribai from Gibeah (in the land of Benjamin);
30 Benaiah from Pirathon;
Hurai* from Nahale-gaash*;
31 Abi-albon from Arabah;
Azmaveth from Bahurim;
32 Eliahba from Shaalbon;
the sons of Jashen;
Jonathan
33 son of Shagee* from Harar;
Ahiam son of Sharar from Harar;
34 Eliphelet son of Ahasbai from Maacah;
Eliam son of Ahithophel from Giloh;
35 Hezro from Carmel;
Paarai from Arba;
36 Igal son of Nathan from Zobah;
Bani from Gad;
37 Zelek from Ammon;
Naharai from Beeroth, the armor bearer of Joab son of Zeruiah;

23:18 As in a few Hebrew manuscripts and Syriac version; most Hebrew manuscripts read *the Three.* **23:19** As in Syriac version; Hebrew reads *the Three.* **23:20a** Or *son of Jehoiada, son of Ish-hai.* **23:20b** Hebrew *two of Ariel.* **23:26** As in parallel text at 1 Chr 11:27 (see also 1 Chr 27:10); Hebrew reads *from Palti.* **23:27** As in some Greek manuscripts (see also 1 Chr 11:29); Hebrew reads *Mebunnai.* **23:29a** As in some Hebrew manuscripts (see also 1 Chr 11:30); most Hebrew manuscripts read *Heleb.* **23:29b** As in parallel text at 1 Chr 11:31; Hebrew reads *Ittai.* **23:30a** As in some Greek manuscripts (see also 1 Chr 11:32); Hebrew reads *Hiddai.* **23:30b** Or *from the ravines of Gaash.* **23:33** As in parallel text at 1 Chr 11:34; Hebrew reads *Jonathan, Shammah;* some Greek manuscripts read *Jonathan son of Shammah.*

38 Ira from Jattir;
Gareb from Jattir;
39 Uriah the Hittite.

There were thirty-seven in all.

David Takes a Census

24 Once again the anger of the LORD burned against Israel, and he
caused David to harm them by taking a census. "Go and count the
people of Israel and Judah," the LORD told him.
2 So the king said to Joab and the commanders* of the army, "Take a cen-
sus of all the tribes of Israel—from Dan in the north to Beersheba in the
south—so I may know how many people there are."
3 But Joab replied to the king, "May the LORD your God let you live to see a
hundred times as many people as there are now! But why, my lord the king,
do you want to do this?"
4 But the king insisted that they take the census, so Joab and the command-
ers of the army went out to count the people of Israel. 5 First they crossed the
Jordan and camped at Aroer, south of the town in the valley, in the direction
of Gad. Then they went on to Jazer, 6 then to Gilead in the land of Tahtim-
hodshi* and to Dan-jaan and around to Sidon. 7 Then they came to the for-
tress of Tyre, and all the towns of the Hivites and Canaanites. Finally, they
went south to Judah* as far as Beersheba.
8 Having gone through the entire land for nine months and twenty days,
they returned to Jerusalem. 9 Joab reported the number of people to the king.
There were 800,000 capable warriors in Israel who could handle a sword,
and 500,000 in Judah.

Judgment for David's Sin

10 But after he had taken the census, David's conscience began to bother him.
And he said to the LORD, "I have sinned greatly by taking this census. Please
forgive my guilt, LORD, for doing this foolish thing."
11 The next morning the word of the LORD came to the prophet Gad, who
was David's seer. This was the message: 12 "Go and say to David, 'This is what
the LORD says: I will give you three choices. Choose one of these punish-
ments, and I will inflict it on you.'"
13 So Gad came to David and asked him, "Will you choose three* years of
famine throughout your land, three months of fleeing from your enemies,
or three days of severe plague throughout your land? Think this over and
decide what answer I should give the LORD who sent me."
14 "I'm in a desperate situation!" David replied to Gad. "But let us fall into
the hands of the LORD, for his mercy is great. Do not let me fall into human
hands."
15 So the LORD sent a plague upon Israel that morning, and it lasted for
three days.* A total of 70,000 people died throughout the nation, from Dan
in the north to Beersheba in the south. 16 But as the angel was preparing to
destroy Jerusalem, the LORD relented and said to the death angel, "Stop! That

Make a Difference

24:10-14

The Goodness of a Guilty Conscience

Look back on your last twenty-four hours. Would you say that your words and actions reflected Jesus? Did your decisions suggest someone who is letting Jesus make a difference in their life? Don't worry. Everyone is guilty of messing up (Romans 3:23). Every person has a shoe-shaped hole in the bottom of their face because they keep putting their foot where their mouth is. At some point, everyone allows their hands to commit wrong things, their words to spit venom, or their brains to entertain sins.

This world needs you to set a different pattern. Like David here at the end of 2 Samuel, let God wrestle with your conscience. Let yourself grow in discomfort with areas of your life that are off target with God. Let your soul be kicked back into alignment with the Lord's patterns for your life.

Difference Maker

Live well today. Watch your mouth, your hands, and your mind. Watch the change that happens in your heart and in the people around you as you live for God.

24:2 As in Greek version (see also 24:4 and 1 Chr 21:2); Hebrew reads *Joab the commander.* **24:6** Greek version reads *to Gilead and to Kadesh in the land of the Hittites.* **24:7** Or *they went to the Negev of Judah.* **24:13** As in Greek version (see also 1 Chr 21:12); Hebrew reads *seven.* **24:15** Hebrew *for the designated time.*

is enough!" At that moment the angel of the LORD was by the threshing floor
of Araunah the Jebusite.
17 When David saw the angel, he said to the LORD, "I am the one who has
sinned and done wrong! But these people are as innocent as sheep—what
have they done? Let your anger fall against me and my family."

David Builds an Altar

18 That day Gad came to David and said to him, "Go up and build an altar to
the LORD on the threshing floor of Araunah the Jebusite."
19 So David went up to do what the LORD had commanded him. 20 When
Araunah saw the king and his men coming toward him, he came and bowed
before the king with his face to the ground. 21 "Why have you come, my lord
the king?" Araunah asked.
David replied, "I have come to buy your threshing floor and to build an
altar to the LORD there, so that he will stop the plague."
22 "Take it, my lord the king, and use it as you wish," Araunah said to Da-
vid. "Here are oxen for the burnt offering, and you can use the threshing
boards and ox yokes for wood to build a fire on the altar. 23 I will give it all
to you, Your Majesty, and may the LORD your God accept your sacrifice."
24 But the king replied to Araunah, "No, I insist on buying it, for I will not
present burnt offerings to the LORD my God that have cost me nothing." So
David paid him fifty pieces of silver* for the threshing floor and the oxen.
25 David built an altar there to the LORD and sacrificed burnt offerings
and peace offerings. And the LORD answered his prayer for the land, and the
plague on Israel was stopped.

24:24 Hebrew *50 shekels of silver,* about 20 ounces or 570 grams in weight.

Question 24:25

Thankfully, the difficult second half of 2 Samuel ends with a foundation of hope. In the same place where Melchizedek had blessed Abraham (Genesis 14:18-20) and where God had provided a sacrifice for Isaac and promised to bless the entire world through one of Abraham's offspring (Genesis 22), David built an altar. This site, owned by Araunah the Jebusite, was where David prayed for forgiveness and where God agreed to heal the land. It was this very site that would become the foundation of Solomon's Temple and where Jesus would spend so much of his life and ministry. How does this knowledge help you see the Lord's hand in orchestrating the events of his gospel throughout the pages of the Bible?

1 Kings Introduction

David's kingdom had been full of so much potential. He had solidified the tribes of Israel, established the throne in Jerusalem, and arranged to have his son Solomon as his successor.

Even so, David's kingdom had been injured by his unfaithfulness—and the wound had festered. By the time David died, several attempts to steal the throne away had already been made. By the time Solomon rose to power, the worship of other gods had wormed its way into the fabric of God's people. By the time the temple was built and Solomon had reached the peak of his power and fame, the cracks were beginning to show, and the walls of Israel's faith were beginning to crumble.

Though the everlasting King (1 Kings 9:5) had been promised through David's line, there was no promise that the royal throne would go uninterrupted. In fact, God had repeatedly indicated that if the people refused to follow him, then the kingdom would be dismantled, and David's reign would be hidden for generations.

God's plans will never be thwarted, but when we fail to live according to God's patterns, our plans will be thrown into disarray.

Story Arcs

- **David**
- **Solomon**
- **Ahijah**
- **Elijah**

1 Kings

David in His Old Age

1 King David was now very old, and no matter how many blankets covered
him, he could not keep warm. 2 So his advisers told him, "Let us find a
young virgin to wait on you and look after you, my lord. She will lie in your
arms and keep you warm."
3 So they searched throughout the land of Israel for a beautiful girl, and
they found Abishag from Shunem and brought her to the king. 4 The girl
was very beautiful, and she looked after the king and took care of him. But
the king had no sexual relations with her.

Adonijah Claims the Throne

5 About that time David's son Adonijah, whose mother was Haggith, began
boasting, "I will make myself king." So he provided himself with chariots
and charioteers and recruited fifty men to run in front of him. 6 Now his
father, King David, had never disciplined him at any time, even by asking,
"Why are you doing that?" Adonijah had been born next after Absalom, and
he was very handsome.
7 Adonijah took Joab son of Zeruiah and Abiathar the priest into his con-
fidence, and they agreed to help him become king. 8 But Zadok the priest,
Benaiah son of Jehoiada, Nathan the prophet, Shimei, Rei, and David's per-
sonal bodyguard refused to support Adonijah.
9 Adonijah went to the Stone of Zoheleth* near the spring of En-rogel,
where he sacrificed sheep, cattle, and fattened calves. He invited all his
brothers—the other sons of King David—and all the royal officials of Ju-
dah. 10 But he did not invite Nathan the prophet or Benaiah or the king's
bodyguard or his brother Solomon.
11 Then Nathan went to Bathsheba, Solomon's mother, and asked her,
"Haven't you heard that Haggith's son, Adonijah, has made himself king,
and our lord David doesn't even know about it? 12 If you want to save your
own life and the life of your son Solomon, follow my advice. 13 Go at once to
King David and say to him, 'My lord the king, didn't you make a vow and
say to me, "Your son Solomon will surely be the next king and will sit on
my throne"? Why then has Adonijah become king?' 14 And while you are
still talking with him, I will come and confirm everything you have said."
15 So Bathsheba went into the king's bedroom. (He was very old now, and
Abishag was taking care of him.) 16 Bathsheba bowed down before the king.
"What can I do for you?" he asked her.
17 She replied, "My lord, you made a vow before the LORD your God when
you said to me, 'Your son Solomon will surely be the next king and will
sit on my throne.' 18 But instead, Adonijah has made himself king, and my
lord the king does not even know about it. 19 He has sacrificed many cattle,

Story Arc 1:1

David

The young man who had slain Goliath had lived a long life mixed with godliness and sin. The first chapter of 1 Kings emphasizes that David was now "very old" (vv. 1, 15) and that his monarchy was compromised with immorality. In David's later years, the kingdom had grown restless and lost confidence. There had been several close calls to the end of David's life and reign. Here, in David's old age, one of his sons, Adonijah, began to threaten to make himself king. This scene set in motion the gut-wrenching conspiracies and power plays and throne intrigue that make up 1 and 2 Kings. As you read these books, consider what lessons this historical reality teaches us about the legacy we could have as we get older.

1 Kgs 1:28-40 ►

1:9 Or *to the Serpent's Stone;* Greek version supports reading *Zoheleth* as a proper name.

fattened calves, and sheep, and he has invited all the king's sons to attend the celebration. He also invited Abiathar the priest and Joab, the commander of the army. But he did not invite your servant Solomon. [20] And now, my lord the king, all Israel is waiting for you to announce who will become king after you. [21] If you do not act, my son Solomon and I will be treated as criminals as soon as my lord the king has died."

[22] While she was still speaking with the king, Nathan the prophet arrived. [23] The king's officials told him, "Nathan the prophet is here to see you."

Nathan went in and bowed before the king with his face to the ground. [24] Nathan asked, "My lord the king, have you decided that Adonijah will be the next king and that he will sit on your throne? [25] Today he has sacrificed many cattle, fattened calves, and sheep, and he has invited all the king's sons to attend the celebration. He also invited the commanders of the army and Abiathar the priest. They are feasting and drinking with him and shouting, 'Long live King Adonijah!' [26] But he did not invite me or Zadok the priest or Benaiah or your servant Solomon. [27] Has my lord the king really done this without letting any of his officials know who should be the next king?"

David Makes Solomon King

[28] King David responded, "Call Bathsheba!" So she came back in and stood before the king. [29] And the king repeated his vow: "As surely as the LORD lives, who has rescued me from every danger, [30] your son Solomon will be the next king and will sit on my throne this very day, just as I vowed to you before the LORD, the God of Israel."

[31] Then Bathsheba bowed down with her face to the ground before the king and exclaimed, "May my lord King David live forever!"

[32] Then King David ordered, "Call Zadok the priest, Nathan the prophet, and Benaiah son of Jehoiada." When they came into the king's presence, [33] the king said to them, "Take Solomon and my officials down to Gihon Spring. Solomon is to ride on my own mule. [34] There Zadok the priest and Nathan the prophet are to anoint him king over Israel. Blow the ram's horn and shout, 'Long live King Solomon!' [35] Then escort him back here, and he will sit on my throne. He will succeed me as king, for I have appointed him to be ruler over Israel and Judah."

[36] "Amen!" Benaiah son of Jehoiada replied. "May the LORD, the God of my lord the king, decree that it happen. [37] And may the LORD be with Solomon as he has been with you, my lord the king, and may he make Solomon's reign even greater than yours!"

[38] So Zadok the priest, Nathan the prophet, Benaiah son of Jehoiada, and the king's bodyguard* took Solomon down to Gihon Spring, with Solomon riding on King David's own mule. [39] There Zadok the priest took the flask of olive oil from the sacred tent and anointed Solomon with the oil. Then they sounded the ram's horn and all the people shouted, "Long live King Solomon!" [40] And all the people followed Solomon into Jerusalem, playing flutes and shouting for joy. The celebration was so joyous and noisy that the earth shook with the sound.

[41] Adonijah and his guests heard the celebrating and shouting just as they were finishing their banquet. When Joab heard the sound of the ram's horn, he asked, "What's going on? Why is the city in such an uproar?"

Story Arc 1:28-40

Solomon

As Solomon was anointed king by Zadok and Nathan, he was placed on a donkey and rode into Jerusalem. As he rode, the crowds shouted, "Long live King Solomon!" and celebrated so loudly that "the earth shook with the sound" (vv. 39-40).

A thousand years later, in Luke 19:36-40, Jesus would enter Jerusalem riding on a donkey. The crowds would rejoice so loudly that someone asked Jesus to quiet them down. Jesus then declared, "If they kept quiet, the stones along the road would burst into cheers!" (v. 40).

With a friend, try to describe the story arc of God's plan through the connections and comparisons of Solomon and Jesus.

1 Kgs 11:29-39 ►

1:38 Hebrew *the Kerethites and Pelethites;* also in 1:44.

42 And while he was still speaking, Jonathan son of Abiathar the priest ar-
rived. "Come in," Adonijah said to him, "for you are a good man. You must
have good news."
43 "Not at all!" Jonathan replied. "Our lord King David has just declared
Solomon king! 44 The king sent him down to Gihon Spring with Zadok the
priest, Nathan the prophet, and Benaiah son of Jehoiada, protected by the
king's bodyguard. They had him ride on the king's own mule, 45 and Zadok
and Nathan have anointed him at Gihon Spring as the new king. They have
just returned, and the whole city is celebrating and rejoicing. That's what all
the noise is about. 46 What's more, Solomon is now sitting on the royal throne
as king. 47 And all the royal officials have gone to King David and congratu-
lated him, saying, 'May your God make Solomon's fame even greater than
your own, and may Solomon's reign be even greater than yours!' Then the
king bowed his head in worship as he lay in his bed, 48 and he said, 'Praise
the LORD, the God of Israel, who today has chosen a successor to sit on my
throne while I am still alive to see it.'"
49 Then all of Adonijah's guests jumped up in panic from the banquet table
and quickly scattered. 50 Adonijah was afraid of Solomon, so he rushed to the
sacred tent and grabbed on to the horns of the altar. 51 Word soon reached
Solomon that Adonijah had seized the horns of the altar in fear, and that
he was pleading, "Let King Solomon swear today that he will not kill me!"
52 Solomon replied, "If he proves himself to be loyal, not a hair on his head
will be touched. But if he makes trouble, he will die." 53 So King Solomon
summoned Adonijah, and they brought him down from the altar. He came
and bowed respectfully before King Solomon, who dismissed him, saying,
"Go on home."

David's Final Instructions to Solomon

2 As the time of King David's death approached, he gave this charge to
his son Solomon:
2 "I am going where everyone on earth must someday go. Take courage and
be a man. 3 Observe the requirements of the LORD your God, and follow all
his ways. Keep the decrees, commands, regulations, and laws written in the
Law of Moses so that you will be successful in all you do and wherever you go.
4 If you do this, then the LORD will keep the promise he made to me. He told
me, 'If your descendants live as they should and follow me faithfully with
all their heart and soul, one of them will always sit on the throne of Israel.'
5 "And there is something else. You know what Joab son of Zeruiah did
to me when he murdered my two army commanders, Abner son of Ner and
Amasa son of Jether. He pretended that it was an act of war, but it was done
in a time of peace,* staining his belt and sandals with innocent blood.* 6 Do
with him what you think best, but don't let him grow old and go to his
grave in peace.*
7 "Be kind to the sons of Barzillai of Gilead. Make them permanent guests
at your table, for they took care of me when I fled from your brother Absalom.
8 "And remember Shimei son of Gera, the man from Bahurim in Benjamin.
He cursed me with a terrible curse as I was fleeing to Mahanaim. When he
came down to meet me at the Jordan River, I swore by the LORD that I would

Question 2:1-4

Everyone must die. The question on David's mind at the end of his life was whether everyone in his kingdom would continue to follow God. For this reason, David gave his final instructions to Solomon—instructions to help Solomon be successful in all he would do by keeping God's commands. Of all the things David wanted Solomon to be sure to accomplish, this was the most important. Where do you put this on your list of priorities for yourself?

2:5a Or *He murdered them during a time of peace as revenge for deaths they had caused in time of war.* **2:5b** As in some Greek and Old Latin manuscripts; Hebrew reads *with the blood of war.* **2:6** Hebrew *don't let his white head go down to Sheol in peace.*

not kill him. 9But that oath does not make him innocent. You are a wise man,
and you will know how to arrange a bloody death for him.*"
10Then David died and was buried with his ancestors in the City of David.
11David had reigned over Israel for forty years, seven of them in Hebron and
thirty-three in Jerusalem. 12Solomon became king and sat on the throne of
David his father, and his kingdom was firmly established.

Solomon Establishes His Rule

13One day Adonijah, whose mother was Haggith, came to see Bathsheba, Sol-
omon's mother. "Have you come with peaceful intentions?" she asked him.
"Yes," he said, "I come in peace. 14In fact, I have a favor to ask of you."
"What is it?" she asked.
15He replied, "As you know, the kingdom was rightfully mine; all Israel
wanted me to be the next king. But the tables were turned, and the kingdom
went to my brother instead; for that is the way the LORD wanted it. 16So now
I have just one favor to ask of you. Please don't turn me down."
"What is it?" she asked.
17He replied, "Speak to King Solomon on my behalf, for I know he will do
anything you request. Ask him to let me marry Abishag, the girl from Shunem."
18"All right," Bathsheba replied. "I will speak to the king for you."
19So Bathsheba went to King Solomon to speak on Adonijah's behalf. The
king rose from his throne to meet her, and he bowed down before her. When
he sat down on his throne again, the king ordered that a throne be brought
for his mother, and she sat at his right hand.
20"I have one small request to make of you," she said. "I hope you won't
turn me down."
"What is it, my mother?" he asked. "You know I won't refuse you."
21"Then let your brother Adonijah marry Abishag, the girl from Shunem,"
she replied.
22"How can you possibly ask me to give Abishag to Adonijah?" King Sol-
omon demanded. "You might as well ask me to give him the kingdom! You
know that he is my older brother, and that he has Abiathar the priest and
Joab son of Zeruiah on his side."
23Then King Solomon made a vow before the LORD: "May God strike me
and even kill me if Adonijah has not sealed his fate with this request. 24The
LORD has confirmed me and placed me on the throne of my father, David;
he has established my dynasty as he promised. So as surely as the LORD lives,
Adonijah will die this very day!" 25So King Solomon ordered Benaiah son of
Jehoiada to execute him, and Adonijah was put to death.
26Then the king said to Abiathar the priest, "Go back to your home in
Anathoth. You deserve to die, but I will not kill you now, because you car-
ried the Ark of the Sovereign LORD for David my father and you shared all
his hardships." 27So Solomon deposed Abiathar from his position as priest
of the LORD, thereby fulfilling the prophecy the LORD had given at Shiloh
concerning the descendants of Eli.
28Joab had not joined Absalom's earlier rebellion, but he had joined Ado-
nijah's rebellion. So when Joab heard about Adonijah's death, he ran to the
sacred tent of the LORD and grabbed on to the horns of the altar. 29When this
was reported to King Solomon, he sent Benaiah son of Jehoiada to execute him.

2:9 Hebrew *how to bring his white head down to Sheol in blood.*

30 Benaiah went to the sacred tent of the LORD and said to Joab, "The king
orders you to come out!"

But Joab answered, "No, I will die here."

So Benaiah returned to the king and told him what Joab had said.

31 "Do as he said," the king replied. "Kill him there beside the altar and
bury him. This will remove the guilt of Joab's senseless murders from me
and from my father's family. 32 The LORD will repay him* for the murders of
two men who were more righteous and better than he. For my father knew
nothing about the deaths of Abner son of Ner, commander of the army of
Israel, and of Amasa son of Jether, commander of the army of Judah. 33 May
their blood be on Joab and his descendants forever, and may the LORD grant
peace forever to David, his descendants, his dynasty, and his throne."

34 So Benaiah son of Jehoiada returned to the sacred tent and killed Joab,
and he was buried at his home in the wilderness. 35 Then the king appointed
Benaiah to command the army in place of Joab, and he installed Zadok the
priest to take the place of Abiathar.

36 The king then sent for Shimei and told him, "Build a house here in Je-
rusalem and live there. But don't step outside the city to go anywhere else.
37 On the day you so much as cross the Kidron Valley, you will surely die; and
your blood will be on your own head."

38 Shimei replied, "Your sentence is fair; I will do whatever my lord the
king commands." So Shimei lived in Jerusalem for a long time.

39 But three years later two of Shimei's slaves ran away to King Achish son
of Maacah of Gath. When Shimei learned where they were, 40 he saddled
his donkey and went to Gath to search for them. When he found them, he
brought them back to Jerusalem.

41 Solomon heard that Shimei had left Jerusalem and had gone to Gath
and returned. 42 So the king sent for Shimei and demanded, "Didn't I make
you swear by the LORD and warn you not to go anywhere else or you would
surely die? And you replied, 'The sentence is fair; I will do as you say.' 43 Then
why haven't you kept your oath to the LORD and obeyed my command?"

44 The king also said to Shimei, "You certainly remember all the wicked
things you did to my father, David. May the LORD now bring that evil on
your own head. 45 But may I, King Solomon, receive the LORD's blessings,
and may one of David's descendants always sit on this throne in the presence
of the LORD." 46 Then, at the king's command, Benaiah son of Jehoiada took
Shimei outside and killed him.

So the kingdom was now firmly in Solomon's grip.

Solomon Asks for Wisdom

3 Solomon made an alliance with Pharaoh, the king of Egypt, and mar-
ried one of his daughters. He brought her to live in the City of David
until he could finish building his palace and the Temple of the LORD and
the wall around the city. 2 At that time the people of Israel sacrificed their
offerings at local places of worship, for a temple honoring the name of the
LORD had not yet been built.

3 Solomon loved the LORD and followed all the decrees of his father, David,
except that Solomon, too, offered sacrifices and burned incense at the local
places of worship. 4 The most important of these places of worship was at

2:32 Hebrew *will return his blood on his own head.*

Highlights from the text

Prayer 3:10

Lord Jesus, kick my mind into gear. Give me wisdom that will be relevant and active for everything I will face today. Amen.

Gibeon, so the king went there and sacrificed 1,000 burnt offerings. 5 That
night the LORD appeared to Solomon in a dream, and God said, "What do
you want? Ask, and I will give it to you!"
6 Solomon replied, "You showed great and faithful love to your servant my
father, David, because he was honest and true and faithful to you. And you
have continued to show this great and faithful love to him today by giving
him a son to sit on his throne.
7 "Now, O LORD my God, you have made me king instead of my father, Da-
vid, but I am like a little child who doesn't know his way around. 8 And here
I am in the midst of your own chosen people, a nation so great and numer-
ous they cannot be counted! 9 Give me an understanding heart so that I can
govern your people well and know the difference between right and wrong.
For who by himself is able to govern this great people of yours?"
10 The Lord was pleased that Solomon had asked for wisdom. 11 So God
replied, "Because you have asked for wisdom in governing my people with
justice and have not asked for a long life or wealth or the death of your
enemies—12 I will give you what you asked for! I will give you a wise and
understanding heart such as no one else has had or ever will have! 13 And I
will also give you what you did not ask for—riches and fame! No other king
in all the world will be compared to you for the rest of your life! 14 And if you
follow me and obey my decrees and my commands as your father, David, did,
I will give you a long life."
15 Then Solomon woke up and realized it had been a dream. He returned
to Jerusalem and stood before the Ark of the Lord's Covenant, where he sac-
rificed burnt offerings and peace offerings. Then he invited all his officials
to a great banquet.

Solomon Judges Wisely

16 Some time later two prostitutes came to the king to have an argument
settled. 17 "Please, my lord," one of them began, "this woman and I live in
the same house. I gave birth to a baby while she was with me in the house.
18 Three days later this woman also had a baby. We were alone; there were
only two of us in the house.
19 "But her baby died during the night when she rolled over on it. 20 Then
she got up in the night and took my son from beside me while I was asleep.
She laid her dead child in my arms and took mine to sleep beside her. 21 And
in the morning when I tried to nurse my son, he was dead! But when I looked
more closely in the morning light, I saw that it wasn't my son at all."
22 Then the other woman interrupted, "It certainly was your son, and the
living child is mine."

"No," the first woman said, "the living child is mine, and the dead one is
yours." And so they argued back and forth before the king.
23 Then the king said, "Let's get the facts straight. Both of you claim the
living child is yours, and each says that the dead one belongs to the other.
24 All right, bring me a sword." So a sword was brought to the king.
25 Then he said, "Cut the living child in two, and give half to one woman
and half to the other!"
26 Then the woman who was the real mother of the living child, and who
loved him very much, cried out, "Oh no, my lord! Give her the child—please
do not kill him!"

But the other woman said, "All right, he will be neither yours nor mine; divide him between us!"

27 Then the king said, "Do not kill the child, but give him to the woman who wants him to live, for she is his mother!"

28 When all Israel heard the king's decision, the people were in awe of the king, for they saw the wisdom God had given him for rendering justice.

Solomon's Officials and Governors

4 King Solomon now ruled over all Israel, 2 and these were his high officials:

Azariah son of Zadok was the priest.
3 Elihoreph and Ahijah, the sons of Shisha, were court secretaries.
Jehoshaphat son of Ahilud was the royal historian.
4 Benaiah son of Jehoiada was commander of the army.
Zadok and Abiathar were priests.
5 Azariah son of Nathan was in charge of the district governors.
Zabud son of Nathan, a priest, was a trusted adviser to the king.
6 Ahishar was manager of the palace property.
Adoniram son of Abda was in charge of forced labor.

7 Solomon also had twelve district governors who were over all Israel. They
were responsible for providing food for the king's household. Each of them
arranged provisions for one month of the year. 8 These are the names of the
twelve governors:

Ben-hur, in the hill country of Ephraim.
9 Ben-deker, in Makaz, Shaalbim, Beth-shemesh, and Elon-bethhanan.
10 Ben-hesed, in Arubboth, including Socoh and all the land of Hepher.
11 Ben-abinadab, in all of Naphoth-dor.* (He was married to Taphath, one of Solomon's daughters.)
12 Baana son of Ahilud, in Taanach and Megiddo, all of Beth-shan* near Zarethan below Jezreel, and all the territory from Beth-shan to Abel-meholah and over to Jokmeam.
13 Ben-geber, in Ramoth-gilead, including the Towns of Jair (named for Jair of the tribe of Manasseh*) in Gilead, and in the Argob region of Bashan, including sixty large fortified towns with bronze bars on their gates.
14 Ahinadab son of Iddo, in Mahanaim.
15 Ahimaaz, in Naphtali. (He was married to Basemath, another of Solomon's daughters.)
16 Baana son of Hushai, in Asher and in Aloth.
17 Jehoshaphat son of Paruah, in Issachar.
18 Shimei son of Ela, in Benjamin.
19 Geber son of Uri, in the land of Gilead,* including the territories of King Sihon of the Amorites and King Og of Bashan.
There was also one governor over the land of Judah.*

4:11 Hebrew *Naphath-dor,* a variant spelling of Naphoth-dor. **4:12** Hebrew *Beth-shean,* a variant spelling of Beth-shan; also in 4:12b. **4:13** Hebrew *Jair son of Manasseh;* compare 1 Chr 2:22. **4:19a** Greek version reads *of Gad;* compare 4:13. **4:19b** As in some Greek manuscripts; Hebrew lacks *of Judah.* The meaning of the Hebrew is uncertain.

Question 4:29-34

First Kings 4:29-34 reveals just how wise Solomon was. Which of the areas of Solomon's wisdom stands out to you the most? In what areas of wisdom would you like to increase in the years ahead?

Solomon's Prosperity and Wisdom

[20]The people of Judah and Israel were as numerous as the sand on the sea-
shore. They were very contented, with plenty to eat and drink. [21]*Solomon
ruled over all the kingdoms from the Euphrates River* in the north to the
land of the Philistines and the border of Egypt in the south. The conquered
peoples of those lands sent tribute money to Solomon and continued to serve
him throughout his lifetime.

[22]The daily food requirements for Solomon's palace were 150 bushels of
choice flour and 300 bushels of meal*; [23]also 10 oxen from the fattening pens,
20 pasture-fed cattle, 100 sheep or goats, as well as deer, gazelles, roe deer,
and choice poultry.*

[24]Solomon's dominion extended over all the kingdoms west of the Eu-
phrates River, from Tiphsah to Gaza. And there was peace on all his borders.
[25]During the lifetime of Solomon, all of Judah and Israel lived in peace and
safety. And from Dan in the north to Beersheba in the south, each family had
its own home and garden.*

[26]Solomon had 4,000* stalls for his chariot horses, and he had 12,000
horses.*

[27]The district governors faithfully provided food for King Solomon and
his court; each made sure nothing was lacking during the month assigned
to him. [28]They also brought the necessary barley and straw for the royal
horses in the stables.

[29]God gave Solomon very great wisdom and understanding, and knowl-
edge as vast as the sands of the seashore. [30]In fact, his wisdom exceeded that
of all the wise men of the East and the wise men of Egypt. [31]He was wiser than
anyone else, including Ethan the Ezrahite and the sons of Mahol—Heman,
Calcol, and Darda. His fame spread throughout all the surrounding nations.
[32]He composed some 3,000 proverbs and wrote 1,005 songs. [33]He could speak
with authority about all kinds of plants, from the great cedar of Lebanon to
the tiny hyssop that grows from cracks in a wall. He could also speak about
animals, birds, small creatures, and fish. [34]And kings from every nation sent
their ambassadors to listen to the wisdom of Solomon.

Preparations for Building the Temple

5 [1]*King Hiram of Tyre had always been a loyal friend of David. When
Hiram learned that David's son Solomon was the new king of Israel, he
sent ambassadors to congratulate him.

[2]Then Solomon sent this message back to Hiram:

[3]"You know that my father, David, was not able to build a Temple to
honor the name of the LORD his God because of the many wars waged
against him by surrounding nations. He could not build until the LORD
gave him victory over all his enemies. [4]But now the LORD my God has
given me peace on every side; I have no enemies, and all is well. [5]So I
am planning to build a Temple to honor the name of the LORD my God,
just as he had instructed my father, David. For the LORD told him, 'Your

4:21a Verses 4:21-34 are numbered 5:1-14 in Hebrew text. **4:21b** Hebrew *the river;* also in 4:24. **4:22** Hebrew *30 cors* [6.6 kiloliters] *of choice flour and 60 cors* [13.2 kiloliters] *of meal.* **4:23** Or *and fattened geese.* **4:25** Hebrew *each family lived under its own grapevine and under its own fig tree.* **4:26a** As in some Greek manuscripts (see also 2 Chr 9:25); Hebrew reads *40,000.* **4:26b** Or *12,000 charioteers.* **5:1** Verses 5:1-18 are numbered 5:15-32 in Hebrew text.

son, whom I will place on your throne, will build the Temple to honor my name.’

6“Therefore, please command that cedars from Lebanon be cut for me. Let my men work alongside yours, and I will pay your men whatever wages you ask. As you know, there is no one among us who can cut timber like you Sidonians!”

7When Hiram received Solomon’s message, he was very pleased and said, “Praise the LORD today for giving David a wise son to be king of the great nation of Israel.” 8Then he sent this reply to Solomon:

“I have received your message, and I will supply all the cedar and cypress timber you need. 9My servants will bring the logs from the Lebanon mountains to the Mediterranean Sea* and make them into rafts and float them along the coast to whatever place you choose. Then we will break the rafts apart so you can carry the logs away. You can pay me by supplying me with food for my household.”

10So Hiram supplied as much cedar and cypress timber as Solomon desired. 11In return, Solomon sent him an annual payment of 100,000 bushels* of wheat for his household and 110,000 gallons* of pure olive oil. 12So the LORD gave wisdom to Solomon, just as he had promised. And Hiram and Solomon made a formal alliance of peace.

13Then King Solomon conscripted a labor force of 30,000 men from all Israel. 14He sent them to Lebanon in shifts, 10,000 every month, so that each man would be one month in Lebanon and two months at home. Adoniram was in charge of this labor force. 15Solomon also had 70,000 common laborers, 80,000 quarry workers in the hill country, 16and 3,600* foremen to supervise the work. 17At the king’s command, they quarried large blocks of high-quality stone and shaped them to make the foundation of the Temple. 18Men from the city of Gebal helped Solomon’s and Hiram’s builders prepare the timber and stone for the Temple.

Solomon Builds the Temple

6 It was in midspring, in the month of Ziv,* during the fourth year of Solomon’s reign, that he began to construct the Temple of the LORD. This was 480 years after the people of Israel were rescued from their slavery in the land of Egypt.

2The Temple that King Solomon built for the LORD was 90 feet long, 30 feet wide, and 45 feet high.* 3The entry room at the front of the Temple was 30 feet* wide, running across the entire width of the Temple. It projected outward 15 feet* from the front of the Temple. 4Solomon also made narrow recessed windows throughout the Temple.

5He built a complex of rooms against the outer walls of the Temple, all the way around the sides and rear of the building. 6The complex was three

Question 6:1

Four hundred eighty years is a long time to pursue a goal. The Lord had promised to reside with the nation of Israel, so Solomon built him a home where the Lord promised to "live among the Israelites" and "never abandon" them (v. 13). Which is more impressive: that Israel was able to accomplish this goal after nearly five centuries or that God desired to dwell among them?

5:9 Hebrew *the sea.* **5:11a** Hebrew *20,000 cors* [4,400 kiloliters]. **5:11b** As in Greek version, which reads *20,000 baths* [420 kiloliters] (see also 2 Chr 2:10); Hebrew reads *20 cors,* about 1,000 gallons or 4.4 kiloliters in volume. **5:16** As in some Greek manuscripts (see also 2 Chr 2:2, 18); Hebrew reads *3,300.* **6:1** Hebrew *It was in the month of Ziv, which is the second month.* This month of the ancient Hebrew lunar calendar usually occurs within the months of April and May. **6:2** Hebrew *60 cubits* [27.6 meters] *long, 20 cubits* [9.2 meters] *wide, and 30 cubits* [13.8 meters] *high.* **6:3a** Hebrew *20 cubits* [9.2 meters]; also in 6:16, 20. **6:3b** Hebrew *10 cubits* [4.6 meters].

stories high, the bottom floor being 7½ feet wide, the second floor 9 feet
wide, and the top floor 10½ feet wide.* The rooms were connected to the
walls of the Temple by beams resting on ledges built out from the wall. So
the beams were not inserted into the walls themselves.

7 The stones used in the construction of the Temple were finished at the
quarry, so there was no sound of hammer, ax, or any other iron tool at the
building site.

8 The entrance to the bottom floor* was on the south side of the Temple.
There were winding stairs going up to the second floor, and another flight
of stairs between the second and third floors. 9 After completing the Temple
structure, Solomon put in a ceiling made of cedar beams and planks. 10 As
already stated, he built a complex of rooms along the sides of the building,
attached to the Temple walls by cedar timbers. Each story of the complex was
7½ feet* high.

11 Then the LORD gave this message to Solomon: 12 "Concerning this Temple
you are building, if you keep all my decrees and regulations and obey all my
commands, I will fulfill through you the promise I made to your father, David.
13 I will live among the Israelites and will never abandon my people Israel."

The Temple's Interior

14 So Solomon finished building the Temple. 15 The entire inside, from floor
to ceiling, was paneled with wood. He paneled the walls and ceilings with
cedar, and he used planks of cypress for the floors. 16 He partitioned off an
inner sanctuary—the Most Holy Place—at the far end of the Temple. It was
30 feet deep and was paneled with cedar from floor to ceiling. 17 The main
room of the Temple, outside the Most Holy Place, was 60 feet* long. 18 Cedar
paneling completely covered the stone walls throughout the Temple, and the
paneling was decorated with carvings of gourds and open flowers.

19 He prepared the inner sanctuary at the far end of the Temple, where the
Ark of the LORD's Covenant would be placed. 20 This inner sanctuary was 30 feet
long, 30 feet wide, and 30 feet high. He overlaid the inside with solid gold.
He also overlaid the altar made of cedar.* 21 Then Solomon overlaid the rest of
the Temple's interior with solid gold, and he made gold chains to protect the
entrance* to the Most Holy Place. 22 So he finished overlaying the entire Temple
with gold, including the altar that belonged to the Most Holy Place.

23 He made two cherubim of wild olive* wood, each 15 feet* tall, and placed
them in the inner sanctuary. 24 The wingspan of each of the cherubim was
15 feet, each wing being 7½ feet* long. 25 The two cherubim were identical
in shape and size; 26 each was 15 feet tall. 27 He placed them side by side in the
inner sanctuary of the Temple. Their outspread wings reached from wall to
wall, while their inner wings touched at the center of the room. 28 He overlaid
the two cherubim with gold.

29 He decorated all the walls of the inner sanctuary and the main room
with carvings of cherubim, palm trees, and open flowers. 30 He overlaid the
floor in both rooms with gold.

31 For the entrance to the inner sanctuary, he made double doors of wild

6:6 Hebrew *the bottom floor being 5 cubits* [2.3 meters] *wide, the second floor 6 cubits* [2.8 meters] *wide, and the top floor 7 cubits* [3.2 meters] *wide.* **6:8** As in Greek version; Hebrew reads *middle floor.* **6:10** Hebrew *5 cubits* [2.3 meters]. **6:17** Hebrew *40 cubits* [18.4 meters]. **6:20** Or *overlaid the altar with cedar.* The meaning of the Hebrew is uncertain. **6:21** Or *to draw curtains across.* The meaning of the Hebrew is uncertain. **6:23a** Or *pine;* Hebrew reads *oil tree;* also in 6:31, 33. **6:23b** Hebrew *10 cubits* [4.6 meters]; also in 6:24, 26. **6:24** Hebrew *5 cubits* [2.3 meters].

Question 7:13-50

Solomon commissioned a man named Huram, a skilled bronze worker, to furnish all the important elements of the interior of the temple, where the Lord would choose to dwell. This was a significant and sacred work of ministry. What sort of significant and sacred work might the Lord be preparing you to do through the skill sets he is developing in you?

olive wood with five-sided doorposts.* 32 These double doors were decorated
with carvings of cherubim, palm trees, and open flowers. The doors, includ-
ing the decorations of cherubim and palm trees, were overlaid with gold.
33 Then he made four-sided doorposts of wild olive wood for the entrance
to the Temple. 34 There were two folding doors of cypress wood, and each door
was hinged to fold back upon itself. 35 These doors were decorated with carv-
ings of cherubim, palm trees, and open flowers—all overlaid evenly with gold.
36 The walls of the inner courtyard were built so that there was one layer
of cedar beams between every three layers of finished stone.
37 The foundation of the LORD's Temple was laid in midspring, in the
month of Ziv,* during the fourth year of Solomon's reign. 38 The entire build-
ing was completed in every detail by midautumn, in the month of Bul,* dur-
ing the eleventh year of his reign. So it took seven years to build the Temple.

Solomon Builds His Palace

7 Solomon also built a palace for himself, and it took him thirteen years
to complete the construction.
2 One of Solomon's buildings was called the Palace of the Forest of Leb-
anon. It was 150 feet long, 75 feet wide, and 45 feet high.* There were four
rows of cedar pillars, and great cedar beams rested on the pillars. 3 The hall
had a cedar roof. Above the beams on the pillars were forty-five side rooms,*
arranged in three tiers of fifteen each. 4 On each end of the long hall were
three rows of windows facing each other. 5 All the doorways and doorposts*
had rectangular frames and were arranged in sets of three, facing each other.
6 Solomon also built the Hall of Pillars, which was 75 feet long and 45 feet
wide.* There was a porch in front, along with a canopy supported by pillars.
7 Solomon also built the throne room, known as the Hall of Justice, where
he sat to hear legal matters. It was paneled with cedar from floor to ceiling.*
8 Solomon's living quarters surrounded a courtyard behind this hall, and
they were constructed the same way. He also built similar living quarters
for Pharaoh's daughter, whom he had married.
9 From foundation to eaves, all these buildings were built from huge
blocks of high-quality stone, cut with saws and trimmed to exact measure
on all sides. 10 Some of the huge foundation stones were 15 feet long, and
some were 12 feet* long. 11 The blocks of high-quality stone used in the walls
were also cut to measure, and cedar beams were also used. 12 The walls of the
great courtyard were built so that there was one layer of cedar beams between
every three layers of finished stone, just like the walls of the inner courtyard
of the LORD's Temple with its entry room.

Furnishings for the Temple

13 King Solomon then asked for a man named Huram* to come from Tyre.
14 He was half Israelite, since his mother was a widow from the tribe of

6:31 The meaning of the Hebrew is uncertain. **6:37** Hebrew *was laid in the month of Ziv.* This month of the ancient Hebrew lunar calendar usually occurs within the months of April and May. **6:38** Hebrew *by the month of Bul, which is the eighth month.* This month of the ancient Hebrew lunar calendar usually occurs within the months of October and November. **7:2** Hebrew *100 cubits* [46 meters] *long, 50 cubits* [23 meters] *wide, and 30 cubits* [13.8 meters] *high.* **7:3** Or *45 rafters,* or *45 beams,* or *45 pillars.* The architectural details in 7:2-6 can be interpreted in many different ways. **7:5** Greek version reads *windows.* **7:6** Hebrew *50 cubits* [23 meters] *long and 30 cubits* [13.8 meters] *wide.* **7:7** As in Syriac version and Latin Vulgate; Hebrew reads *from floor to floor.* **7:10** Hebrew *10 cubits* [4.6 meters] . . . *8 cubits* [3.7 meters]. **7:13** Hebrew *Hiram* (also in 7:40, 45); compare 2 Chr 2:13. This is not the same person mentioned in 5:1.

Naphtali, and his father had been a craftsman in bronze from Tyre. Huram
was extremely skillful and talented in any work in bronze, and he came to
do all the metal work for King Solomon.
15 Huram cast two bronze pillars, each 27 feet tall and 18 feet in circumfer-
ence.* 16 For the tops of the pillars he cast bronze capitals, each 7½ feet* tall.
17 Each capital was decorated with seven sets of latticework and interwoven
chains. 18 He also encircled the latticework with two rows of pomegranates
to decorate the capitals over the pillars. 19 The capitals on the columns inside
the entry room were shaped like water lilies, and they were six feet* tall.
20 The capitals on the two pillars had 200 pomegranates in two rows around
them, beside the rounded surface next to the latticework. 21 Huram set the
pillars at the entrance of the Temple, one toward the south and one toward
the north. He named the one on the south Jakin, and the one on the north
Boaz.* 22 The capitals on the pillars were shaped like water lilies. And so the
work on the pillars was finished.

23 Then Huram cast a great round basin, 15 feet across from rim to rim,
called the Sea. It was 7½ feet deep and about 45 feet in circumference.* 24 It
was encircled just below its rim by two rows of decorative gourds. There
were about six gourds per foot* all the way around, and they were cast as
part of the basin.

25 The Sea was placed on a base of twelve bronze oxen,* all facing outward.
Three faced north, three faced west, three faced south, and three faced east,
and the Sea rested on them. 26 The walls of the Sea were about three inches*
thick, and its rim flared out like a cup and resembled a water lily blossom.
It could hold about 11,000 gallons* of water.

27 Huram also made ten bronze water carts, each 6 feet long, 6 feet wide,
and 4½ feet tall.* 28 They were constructed with side panels braced with cross-
bars. 29 Both the panels and the crossbars were decorated with carved lions,
oxen, and cherubim. Above and below the lions and oxen were wreath deco-
rations. 30 Each of these carts had four bronze wheels and bronze axles. There
were supporting posts for the bronze basins at the corners of the carts; these
supports were decorated on each side with carvings of wreaths. 31 The top of
each cart had a rounded frame for the basin. It projected 1½ feet* above the
cart's top like a round pedestal, and its opening was 2¼ feet* across; it was
decorated on the outside with carvings of wreaths. The panels of the carts
were square, not round. 32 Under the panels were four wheels that were con-
nected to axles that had been cast as one unit with the cart. The wheels were
2¼ feet in diameter 33 and were similar to chariot wheels. The axles, spokes,
rims, and hubs were all cast from molten bronze.

34 There were handles at each of the four corners of the carts, and these,
too, were cast as one unit with the cart. 35 Around the top of each cart was a
rim nine inches wide.* The corner supports and side panels were cast as one
unit with the cart. 36 Carvings of cherubim, lions, and palm trees decorated
the panels and corner supports wherever there was room, and there were

7:15 Hebrew *18 cubits* [8.3 meters] *tall and 12 cubits* [5.5 meters] *in circumference.* 7:16 Hebrew *5 cubits* [2.3 meters]. 7:19 Hebrew *4 cubits* [1.8 meters]; also in 7:38. 7:21 *Jakin* probably means "he establishes"; *Boaz* probably means "in him is strength." 7:23 Hebrew *10 cubits* [4.6 meters] *across. . . . 5 cubits* [2.3 meters] *deep and 30 cubits* [13.8 meters] *in circumference.* 7:24 Or *20 gourds per meter;* Hebrew reads *10 per cubit.* 7:25 Hebrew *12 oxen;* compare 2 Kgs 16:17, which specifies *bronze oxen.* 7:26a Hebrew *a handbreadth* [8 centimeters]. 7:26b Hebrew *2,000 baths* [42 kiloliters]. 7:27 Hebrew *4 cubits* [1.8 meters] *long, 4 cubits wide, and 3 cubits* [1.4 meters] *high.* 7:31a Hebrew *a cubit* [46 centimeters]. 7:31b Hebrew *1½ cubits* [69 centimeters]; also in 7:32. 7:35 Hebrew *half a cubit wide* [23 centimeters].

wreaths all around. 37 All ten water carts were the same size and were made
alike, for each was cast from the same mold.
38 Huram also made ten smaller bronze basins, one for each cart. Each
basin was six feet across and could hold 220 gallons* of water. 39 He set five
water carts on the south side of the Temple and five on the north side. The
great bronze basin called the Sea was placed near the southeast corner of
the Temple. 40 He also made the necessary washbasins, shovels, and bowls.
So at last Huram completed everything King Solomon had assigned him
to make for the Temple of the LORD:

41 the two pillars;
the two bowl-shaped capitals on top of the pillars;
the two networks of interwoven chains that decorated the capitals;
42 the 400 pomegranates that hung from the chains on the capitals (two
rows of pomegranates for each of the chain networks that decorated
the capitals on top of the pillars);
43 the ten water carts holding the ten basins;
44 the Sea and the twelve oxen under it;
45 the ash buckets, the shovels, and the bowls.

Huram made all these things of burnished bronze for the Temple of the
LORD, just as King Solomon had directed. 46 The king had them cast in clay
molds in the Jordan Valley between Succoth and Zarethan. 47 Solomon did
not weigh all these things because there were so many; the weight of the
bronze could not be measured.
48 Solomon also made all the furnishings of the Temple of the LORD:

the gold altar;
the gold table for the Bread of the Presence;
49 the lampstands of solid gold, five on the south and five on the north, in
front of the Most Holy Place;
the flower decorations, lamps, and tongs—all of gold;
50 the small bowls, lamp snuffers, bowls, ladles, and incense burners—all
of solid gold;
the doors for the entrances to the Most Holy Place and the main room of
the Temple, with their fronts overlaid with gold.

51 So King Solomon finished all his work on the Temple of the LORD. Then he
brought all the gifts his father, David, had dedicated—the silver, the gold, and
the various articles—and he stored them in the treasuries of the LORD's Temple.

The Ark Brought to the Temple

8 Solomon then summoned to Jerusalem the elders of Israel and all the
heads of the tribes—the leaders of the ancestral families of the Israelites.
They were to bring the Ark of the LORD's Covenant to the Temple from its
location in the City of David, also known as Zion. 2 So all the men of Israel
assembled before King Solomon at the annual Festival of Shelters, which is
held in early autumn in the month of Ethanim.*

7:38 Hebrew *40 baths* [840 liters]. 8:2 Hebrew *at the festival in the month Ethanim, which is the seventh month.* The Festival of Shelters began on the fifteenth day of the seventh month of the ancient Hebrew lunar calendar. This day occurred in late September, October, or early November.

What I will do next

3 When all the elders of Israel arrived, the priests picked up the Ark. 4 The
priests and Levites brought up the Ark of the LORD along with the special
tent* and all the sacred items that had been in it. 5 There, before the Ark, King
Solomon and the entire community of Israel sacrificed so many sheep, goats,
and cattle that no one could keep count!

6 Then the priests carried the Ark of the LORD's Covenant into the inner
sanctuary of the Temple—the Most Holy Place—and placed it beneath the
wings of the cherubim. 7 The cherubim spread their wings over the Ark,
forming a canopy over the Ark and its carrying poles. 8 These poles were so
long that their ends could be seen from the Holy Place, which is in front of
the Most Holy Place, but not from the outside. They are still there to this day.
9 Nothing was in the Ark except the two stone tablets that Moses had placed
in it at Mount Sinai,* where the LORD made a covenant with the people of
Israel when they left the land of Egypt.

10 When the priests came out of the Holy Place, a thick cloud filled the
Temple of the LORD. 11 The priests could not continue their service because
of the cloud, for the glorious presence of the LORD filled the Temple of the
LORD.

Solomon Praises the LORD

12 Then Solomon prayed, "O LORD, you have said that you would live in a
thick cloud of darkness. 13 Now I have built a glorious Temple for you, a place
where you can live forever!*"

14 Then the king turned around to the entire community of Israel stand-
ing before him and gave this blessing: 15 "Praise the LORD, the God of Israel,
who has kept the promise he made to my father, David. For he told my fa-
ther, 16 'From the day I brought my people Israel out of Egypt, I have never
chosen a city among any of the tribes of Israel as the place where a Temple
should be built to honor my name. But I have chosen David to be king over
my people Israel.'"

17 Then Solomon said, "My father, David, wanted to build this Temple to
honor the name of the LORD, the God of Israel. 18 But the LORD told him, 'You
wanted to build the Temple to honor my name. Your intention is good, 19 but
you are not the one to do it. One of your own sons will build the Temple to
honor me.'

20 "And now the LORD has fulfilled the promise he made, for I have become
king in my father's place, and now I sit on the throne of Israel, just as the
LORD promised. I have built this Temple to honor the name of the LORD, the
God of Israel. 21 And I have prepared a place there for the Ark, which contains
the covenant that the LORD made with our ancestors when he brought them
out of Egypt."

Solomon's Prayer of Dedication

22 Then Solomon stood before the altar of the LORD in front of the entire
community of Israel. He lifted his hands toward heaven, 23 and he prayed,

> "O LORD, God of Israel, there is no God like you in all of heaven above
> or on the earth below. You keep your covenant and show unfailing love

8:4 Hebrew *the Tent of Meeting;* i.e., the tent mentioned in 2 Sam 6:17 and 1 Chr 16:1.
8:9 Hebrew *at Horeb,* another name for Sinai. 8:13 Some Greek texts add the line *Is this not written in the Book of Jashar?*

to all who walk before you in wholehearted devotion. [24]You have kept your promise to your servant David, my father. You made that promise with your own mouth, and with your own hands you have fulfilled it today.

[25]"And now, O LORD, God of Israel, carry out the additional promise you made to your servant David, my father. For you said to him, 'If your descendants guard their behavior and faithfully follow me as you have done, one of them will always sit on the throne of Israel.' [26]Now, O God of Israel, fulfill this promise to your servant David, my father.

[27]"But will God really live on earth? Why, even the highest heavens cannot contain you. How much less this Temple I have built! [28]Nevertheless, listen to my prayer and my plea, O LORD my God. Hear the cry and the prayer that your servant is making to you today. [29]May you watch over this Temple night and day, this place where you have said, 'My name will be there.' May you always hear the prayers I make toward this place. [30]May you hear the humble and earnest requests from me and your people Israel when we pray toward this place. Yes, hear us from heaven where you live, and when you hear, forgive.

[31]"If someone wrongs another person and is required to take an oath of innocence in front of your altar in this Temple, [32]then hear from heaven and judge between your servants—the accuser and the accused. Punish the guilty as they deserve. Acquit the innocent because of their innocence.

[33]"If your people Israel are defeated by their enemies because they have sinned against you, and if they turn to you and acknowledge your name and pray to you here in this Temple, [34]then hear from heaven and forgive the sin of your people Israel and return them to this land you gave their ancestors.

[35]"If the skies are shut up and there is no rain because your people have sinned against you, and if they pray toward this Temple and acknowledge your name and turn from their sins because you have punished them, [36]then hear from heaven and forgive the sins of your servants, your people Israel. Teach them to follow the right path, and send rain on your land that you have given to your people as their special possession.

[37]"If there is a famine in the land or a plague or crop disease or attacks of locusts or caterpillars, or if your people's enemies are in the land besieging their towns—whatever disaster or disease there is—[38]and if your people Israel pray about their troubles, raising their hands toward this Temple, [39]then hear from heaven where you live, and forgive. Give your people what their actions deserve, for you alone know each human heart. [40]Then they will fear you as long as they live in the land you gave to our ancestors.

[41]"In the future, foreigners who do not belong to your people Israel will hear of you. They will come from distant lands because of your name, [42]for they will hear of your great name and your strong hand and your powerful arm. And when they pray toward this Temple, [43]then hear from heaven where you live, and grant what they ask of you. In this way, all the people of the earth will come to know and fear you,

Make a Difference 8:27

Dwell on Earth

Would God really live on earth? What a great question! Solomon was in awe that the Lord, who cannot be contained even in the heavens, would choose to make his dwelling in a building that Solomon constructed. Who was he, and what was this building, that God should choose to dwell among them?

The same awe is due today. We are the "temple" of the Holy Spirit, but can we really contain God? Would God really choose to live among us? The answer is, humbly and boldly, yes! Because God chooses to do so, he will.

Difference Maker

What is different about you as a result of knowing that Jesus chose to make his dwelling among us and that his Spirit chooses to dwell within you?

Prayer **8:58**

Lord, today, no matter what I face, give me the desire to do your will. Amen.

just as your own people Israel do. They, too, will know that this Temple
I have built honors your name.
44 "If your people go out where you send them to fight their enemies,
and if they pray to the LORD by turning toward this city you have
chosen and toward this Temple I have built to honor your name, 45 then
hear their prayers from heaven and uphold their cause.
46 "If they sin against you—and who has never sinned?—you might
become angry with them and let their enemies conquer them and take
them captive to their land far away or near. 47 But in that land of exile,
they might turn to you in repentance and pray, 'We have sinned, done
evil, and acted wickedly.' 48 If they turn to you with their whole heart
and soul in the land of their enemies and pray toward the land you
gave to their ancestors—toward this city you have chosen, and toward
this Temple I have built to honor your name— 49 then hear their
prayers and their petition from heaven where you live, and uphold
their cause. 50 Forgive your people who have sinned against you.
Forgive all the offenses they have committed against you. Make their
captors merciful to them, 51 for they are your people—your special
possession—whom you brought out of the iron-smelting furnace of
Egypt.
52 "May your eyes be open to my requests and to the requests of your
people Israel. May you hear and answer them whenever they cry out to
you. 53 For when you brought our ancestors out of Egypt, O Sovereign
LORD, you told your servant Moses that you had set Israel apart from all
the nations of the earth to be your own special possession."

The Dedication of the Temple

54 When Solomon finished making these prayers and petitions to the LORD,
he stood up in front of the altar of the LORD, where he had been kneeling
with his hands raised toward heaven. 55 He stood and in a loud voice blessed
the entire congregation of Israel:
56 "Praise the LORD who has given rest to his people Israel, just as he prom-
ised. Not one word has failed of all the wonderful promises he gave through
his servant Moses. 57 May the LORD our God be with us as he was with our
ancestors; may he never leave us or abandon us. 58 May he give us the desire to
do his will in everything and to obey all the commands, decrees, and regula-
tions that he gave our ancestors. 59 And may these words that I have prayed
in the presence of the LORD be before him constantly, day and night, so that
the LORD our God may give justice to me and to his people Israel, according
to each day's needs. 60 Then people all over the earth will know that the LORD
alone is God and there is no other. 61 And may you be completely faithful to
the LORD our God. May you always obey his decrees and commands, just as
you are doing today."
62 Then the king and all Israel with him offered sacrifices to the LORD.
63 Solomon offered to the LORD a peace offering of 22,000 cattle and 120,000
sheep and goats. And so the king and all the people of Israel dedicated the
Temple of the LORD.
64 That same day the king consecrated the central area of the courtyard
in front of the LORD's Temple. He offered burnt offerings, grain offerings,
and the fat of peace offerings there, because the bronze altar in the LORD's

presence was too small to hold all the burnt offerings, grain offerings, and
the fat of the peace offerings.
65 Then Solomon and all Israel celebrated the Festival of Shelters* in the
presence of the LORD our God. A large congregation had gathered from as far
away as Lebo-hamath in the north and the Brook of Egypt in the south. The
celebration went on for fourteen days in all—seven days for the dedication
of the altar and seven days for the Festival of Shelters.* 66 After the festival
was over,* Solomon sent the people home. They blessed the king and went to
their homes joyful and glad because the LORD had been good to his servant
David and to his people Israel.

The LORD's Response to Solomon

9 So Solomon finished building the Temple of the LORD, as well as the
royal palace. He completed everything he had planned to do. 2 Then the
LORD appeared to Solomon a second time, as he had done before at Gibeon.
3 The LORD said to him,

"I have heard your prayer and your petition. I have set this Temple
apart to be holy—this place you have built where my name will be
honored forever. I will always watch over it, for it is dear to my heart.
4 "As for you, if you will follow me with integrity and godliness,
as David your father did, obeying all my commands, decrees, and
regulations, 5 then I will establish the throne of your dynasty over Israel
forever. For I made this promise to your father, David: 'One of your
descendants will always sit on the throne of Israel.'
6 "But if you or your descendants abandon me and disobey the
commands and decrees I have given you, and if you serve and worship
other gods, 7 then I will uproot Israel from this land that I have given
them. I will reject this Temple that I have made holy to honor my name.
I will make Israel an object of mockery and ridicule among the nations.
8 And though this Temple is impressive now, all who pass by will be
appalled and will gasp in horror. They will ask, 'Why did the LORD do
such terrible things to this land and to this Temple?'
9 "And the answer will be, 'Because his people abandoned the
LORD their God, who brought their ancestors out of Egypt, and they
worshiped other gods instead and bowed down to them. That is why
the LORD has brought all these disasters on them.'"

Solomon's Agreement with Hiram

10 It took Solomon twenty years to build the LORD's Temple and his own royal
palace. At the end of that time, 11 he gave twenty towns in the land of Galilee
to King Hiram of Tyre. (Hiram had previously provided all the cedar and cy-
press timber and gold that Solomon had requested.) 12 But when Hiram came
from Tyre to see the towns Solomon had given him, he was not at all pleased
with them. 13 "What kind of towns are these, my brother?" he asked. So Hi-
ram called that area Cabul (which means "worthless"), as it is still known
today. 14 Nevertheless, Hiram paid* Solomon 9,000 pounds* of gold.

8:65a Hebrew *the festival;* see note on 8:2. **8:65b** Hebrew *seven days and seven days, fourteen days;* compare parallel text at 2 Chr 7:8-10. **8:66** Hebrew *On the eighth day,* probably referring to the day following the seven-day Festival of Shelters; compare parallel text at 2 Chr 7:9-10. **9:14a** Or *For Hiram had paid.* **9:14b** Hebrew *120 talents* [4,000 kilograms].

Question 10:1–13

The queen of Sheba went to great lengths to study and learn from Solomon. Do you know someone who is wise? If you took the initiative to spend some time with them, what questions would you want to ask? What would you want to learn?

Solomon's Many Achievements

15 This is the account of the forced labor that King Solomon conscripted to
build the LORD's Temple, the royal palace, the supporting terraces,* the wall
of Jerusalem, and the cities of Hazor, Megiddo, and Gezer. 16 (Pharaoh, the
king of Egypt, had attacked and captured Gezer, killing the Canaanite popu-
lation and burning it down. He gave the city to his daughter as a wedding gift
when she married Solomon. 17 So Solomon rebuilt the city of Gezer.) He also
built up the towns of Lower Beth-horon, 18 Baalath, and Tamar* in the wilder-
ness within his land. 19 He built towns as supply centers and constructed
towns where his chariots and horses* could be stationed. He built everything
he desired in Jerusalem and Lebanon and throughout his entire realm.

20 There were still some people living in the land who were not Israelites,
including Amorites, Hittites, Perizzites, Hivites, and Jebusites. 21 These were
descendants of the nations whom the people of Israel had not completely
destroyed.* So Solomon conscripted them as slaves, and they serve as forced
laborers to this day. 22 But Solomon did not conscript any of the Israelites for
forced labor. Instead, he assigned them to serve as fighting men, government
officials, officers and captains in his army, commanders of his chariots, and
charioteers. 23 Solomon appointed 550 of them to supervise the people work-
ing on his various projects.

24 Solomon moved his wife, Pharaoh's daughter, from the City of David
to the new palace he had built for her. Then he constructed the supporting
terraces.

25 Three times each year Solomon presented burnt offerings and peace
offerings on the altar he had built for the LORD. He also burned incense to
the LORD. And so he finished the work of building the Temple.

26 King Solomon also built a fleet of ships at Ezion-geber, a port near Elath*
in the land of Edom, along the shore of the Red Sea.* 27 Hiram sent experi-
enced crews of sailors to sail the ships with Solomon's men. 28 They sailed to
Ophir and brought back to Solomon some sixteen tons* of gold.

Visit of the Queen of Sheba

10 When the queen of Sheba heard of Solomon's fame, which brought
honor to the name of the LORD,* she came to test him with hard ques-
tions. 2 She arrived in Jerusalem with a large group of attendants and a great
caravan of camels loaded with spices, large quantities of gold, and precious
jewels. When she met with Solomon, she talked with him about everything
she had on her mind. 3 Solomon had answers for all her questions; nothing
was too hard for the king to explain to her. 4 When the queen of Sheba real-
ized how very wise Solomon was, and when she saw the palace he had built,
5 she was overwhelmed. She was also amazed at the food on his tables, the
organization of his officials and their splendid clothing, the cup-bearers, and
the burnt offerings Solomon made at the Temple of the LORD.

6 She exclaimed to the king, "Everything I heard in my country about your
achievements* and wisdom is true! 7 I didn't believe what was said until I

9:15 Hebrew *the millo;* also in 9:24. The meaning of the Hebrew is uncertain. **9:18** An alternate reading in the Masoretic Text reads *Tadmor.* **9:19** Or *and charioteers.* **9:21** The Hebrew term used here refers to the complete consecration of things or people to the LORD, either by destroying them or by giving them as an offering. **9:26a** As in Greek version (see also 2 Kgs 14:22; 16:6); Hebrew reads *Eloth,* a variant spelling of Elath. **9:26b** Hebrew *sea of reeds.* **9:28** Hebrew *420 talents* [14 metric tons]. **10:1** Or *which was due to the name of the* LORD. The meaning of the Hebrew is uncertain. **10:6** Hebrew *your words.*

arrived here and saw it with my own eyes. In fact, I had not heard the half
of it! Your wisdom and prosperity are far beyond what I was told. 8 How
happy your people* must be! What a privilege for your officials to stand
here day after day, listening to your wisdom! 9 Praise the LORD your God,
who delights in you and has placed you on the throne of Israel. Because of
the LORD's eternal love for Israel, he has made you king so you can rule with
justice and righteousness."

10 Then she gave the king a gift of 9,000 pounds* of gold, great quantities
of spices, and precious jewels. Never again were so many spices brought in
as those the queen of Sheba gave to King Solomon.

11 (In addition, Hiram's ships brought gold from Ophir, and they also
brought rich cargoes of red sandalwood* and precious jewels. 12 The king
used the sandalwood to make railings for the Temple of the LORD and the
royal palace, and to construct lyres and harps for the musicians. Never before
or since has there been such a supply of sandalwood.)

13 King Solomon gave the queen of Sheba whatever she asked for, besides
all the customary gifts he had so generously given. Then she and all her at-
tendants returned to their own land.

Solomon's Wealth and Splendor

14 Each year Solomon received about 25 tons* of gold. 15 This did not include
the additional revenue he received from merchants and traders, all the kings
of Arabia, and the governors of the land.

16 King Solomon made 200 large shields of hammered gold, each weighing
more than fifteen pounds.* 17 He also made 300 smaller shields of hammered
gold, each weighing nearly four pounds.* The king placed these shields in
the Palace of the Forest of Lebanon.

18 Then the king made a huge throne, decorated with ivory and overlaid
with fine gold. 19 The throne had six steps and a rounded back. There were
armrests on both sides of the seat, and the figure of a lion stood on each side
of the throne. 20 There were also twelve other lions, one standing on each end
of the six steps. No other throne in all the world could be compared with it!

21 All of King Solomon's drinking cups were solid gold, as were all the
utensils in the Palace of the Forest of Lebanon. They were not made of silver,
for silver was considered worthless in Solomon's day!

22 The king had a fleet of trading ships of Tarshish that sailed with Hiram's
fleet. Once every three years the ships returned, loaded with gold, silver,
ivory, apes, and peacocks.*

23 So King Solomon became richer and wiser than any other king on earth.
24 People from every nation came to consult him and to hear the wisdom God
had given him. 25 Year after year everyone who visited brought him gifts of
silver and gold, clothing, weapons, spices, horses, and mules.

26 Solomon built up a huge force of chariots and horses.* He had 1,400 char-
iots and 12,000 horses. He stationed some of them in the chariot cities and
some near him in Jerusalem. 27 The king made silver as plentiful in Jerusalem
as stone. And valuable cedar timber was as common as the sycamore-fig trees
that grow in the foothills of Judah.* 28 Solomon's horses were imported from

10:8 Greek and Syriac versions and Latin Vulgate read *your wives.* 10:10 Hebrew *120 talents* [4,000 kilograms]. 10:11 Hebrew *almug wood;* also in 10:12. 10:14 Hebrew *666 talents* [23 metric tons]. 10:16 Hebrew *600 [shekels] of gold* [6.8 kilograms]. 10:17 Hebrew *3 minas* [1.8 kilograms]. 10:22 Or *and baboons.* 10:26 Or *charioteers;* also in 10:26b. 10:27 Hebrew *the Shephelah.*

Egypt* and from Cilicia*; the king's traders acquired them from Cilicia at the standard price. 29 At that time chariots from Egypt could be purchased for 600 pieces of silver,* and horses for 150 pieces of silver.* They were then exported to the kings of the Hittites and the kings of Aram.

Solomon's Many Wives

11 Now King Solomon loved many foreign women. Besides Pharaoh's daughter, he married women from Moab, Ammon, Edom, Sidon, and from among the Hittites. 2 The LORD had clearly instructed the people of Israel, "You must not marry them, because they will turn your hearts to their gods." Yet Solomon insisted on loving them anyway. 3 He had 700 wives of royal birth and 300 concubines. And in fact, they did turn his heart away from the LORD.

4 In Solomon's old age, they turned his heart to worship other gods instead of being completely faithful to the LORD his God, as his father, David, had been. 5 Solomon worshiped Ashtoreth, the goddess of the Sidonians, and Molech,* the detestable god of the Ammonites. 6 In this way, Solomon did what was evil in the LORD's sight; he refused to follow the LORD completely, as his father, David, had done.

7 On the Mount of Olives, east of Jerusalem,* he even built a pagan shrine for Chemosh, the detestable god of Moab, and another for Molech, the detestable god of the Ammonites. 8 Solomon built such shrines for all his foreign wives to use for burning incense and sacrificing to their gods.

9 The LORD was very angry with Solomon, for his heart had turned away from the LORD, the God of Israel, who had appeared to him twice. 10 He had warned Solomon specifically about worshiping other gods, but Solomon did not listen to the LORD's command. 11 So now the LORD said to him, "Since you have not kept my covenant and have disobeyed my decrees, I will surely tear the kingdom away from you and give it to one of your servants. 12 But for the sake of your father, David, I will not do this while you are still alive. I will take the kingdom away from your son. 13 And even so, I will not take away the entire kingdom; I will let him be king of one tribe, for the sake of my servant David and for the sake of Jerusalem, my chosen city."

Solomon's Adversaries

14 Then the LORD raised up Hadad the Edomite, a member of Edom's royal family, to be Solomon's adversary. 15 Years before, David had defeated Edom. Joab, his army commander, had stayed to bury some of the Israelite soldiers who had died in battle. While there, they killed every male in Edom. 16 Joab and the army of Israel had stayed there for six months, killing them.

17 But Hadad and a few of his father's royal officials escaped and headed for Egypt. (Hadad was just a boy at the time.) 18 They set out from Midian and went to Paran, where others joined them. Then they traveled to Egypt and went to Pharaoh, who gave them a home, food, and some land. 19 Pharaoh grew very fond of Hadad, and he gave him his wife's sister in marriage—the sister of Queen Tahpenes. 20 She bore him a son named Genubath. Tahpenes raised him* in Pharaoh's palace among Pharaoh's own sons.

10:28a Possibly *Muzur,* a district near Cilicia; also in 10:29. **10:28b** Hebrew *Kue,* probably another name for Cilicia. **10:29a** Hebrew *600 [shekels] of silver,* about 15 pounds or 6.8 kilograms in weight. **10:29b** Hebrew *150 [shekels],* about 3.8 pounds or 1.7 kilograms in weight. **11:5** Hebrew *Milcom,* a variant spelling of Molech; also in 11:33. **11:7** Hebrew *On the mountain east of Jerusalem.* **11:20** As in Greek version; Hebrew reads *weaned him.*

Make a Difference

11:1–13

Shiny Lures

Solomon had incredible wisdom and wealth. The question was this: Which would win, wisdom or wealth? In 11:3, we learn that wealth eventually won over Solomon's heart. He became "rich" with possessions, "rich" with fame, and "rich" with women—a scenario the Lord had specifically warned him against. As a result, Solomon's heart was lured, and he was snagged away from the Lord. As he grew older, he also grew further away from God and, astonishingly, began to worship other gods. The sad irony of Solomon's story is that even all his wisdom did not keep him from the entrapment of his wealth.

Difference Maker

What do you own that could lure you away from wisdom and from God? Figure out how you could avoid that temptation today.

21 When the news reached Hadad in Egypt that David and his commander Joab were both dead, he said to Pharaoh, "Let me return to my own country."
22 "Why?" Pharaoh asked him. "What do you lack here that makes you want to go home?"

"Nothing," he replied. "But even so, please let me return home."
23 God also raised up Rezon son of Eliada as Solomon's adversary. Rezon had fled from his master, King Hadadezer of Zobah,
24 and had become the leader of a gang of rebels. After David conquered Hadadezer, Rezon and his men fled to Damascus, where he became king.
25 Rezon was Israel's bitter adversary for the rest of Solomon's reign, and he made trouble, just as Hadad did. Rezon hated Israel intensely and continued to reign in Aram.

Jeroboam Rebels against Solomon

26 Another rebel leader was Jeroboam son of Nebat, one of Solomon's own officials. He came from the town of Zeredah in Ephraim, and his mother was Zeruah, a widow.
27 This is the story behind his rebellion. Solomon was rebuilding the supporting terraces* and repairing the walls of the city of his father, David.
28 Jeroboam was a very capable young man, and when Solomon saw how industrious he was, he put him in charge of the labor force from the tribes of Ephraim and Manasseh, the descendants of Joseph.
29 One day as Jeroboam was leaving Jerusalem, the prophet Ahijah from Shiloh met him along the way. Ahijah was wearing a new cloak. The two of them were alone in a field,
30 and Ahijah took hold of the new cloak he was wearing and tore it into twelve pieces.
31 Then he said to Jeroboam, "Take ten of these pieces, for this is what the LORD, the God of Israel, says: 'I am about to tear the kingdom from the hand of Solomon, and I will give ten of the tribes to you!
32 But I will leave him one tribe for the sake of my servant David and for the sake of Jerusalem, which I have chosen out of all the tribes of Israel.
33 For Solomon has* abandoned me and worshiped Ashtoreth, the goddess of the Sidonians; Chemosh, the god of Moab; and Molech, the god of the Ammonites. He has not followed my ways and done what is pleasing in my sight. He has not obeyed my decrees and regulations as David his father did.
34 "'But I will not take the entire kingdom from Solomon at this time. For the sake of my servant David, the one whom I chose and who obeyed my commands and decrees, I will keep Solomon as leader for the rest of his life.
35 But I will take the kingdom away from his son and give ten of the tribes to you.
36 His son will have one tribe so that the descendants of David my servant will continue to reign, shining like a lamp in Jerusalem, the city I have chosen to be the place for my name.
37 And I will place you on the throne of Israel, and you will rule over all that your heart desires.
38 If you listen to what I tell you and follow my ways and do whatever I consider to be right, and if you obey my decrees and commands, as my servant David did, then I will always be with you. I will establish an enduring dynasty for you as I did for David, and I will give Israel to you.
39 Because of Solomon's sin I will punish the descendants of David—though not forever.'"
40 Solomon tried to kill Jeroboam, but he fled to King Shishak of Egypt and stayed there until Solomon died.

11:27 Hebrew *the millo.* The meaning of the Hebrew is uncertain. 11:33 As in Greek, Syriac, and Latin Vulgate; Hebrew reads *For they have.*

Story Arc **11:29–39**

● Ahijah

Through the prophet Ahijah, God told Jeroboam that because of Solomon's sin, the nation would be ripped in two. Jeroboam was to take ten tribes of Israel and form a Northern Kingdom (Israel) while the Lord would keep one tribe (Judah) in the south to reign in Jerusalem, "shining like a lamp" and continuing the reign of David (v. 36). God used Ahijah's words and work to reveal to us that God will carry out his plans and promises even when leaders fail.

1 Kgs 17:1 ►

Summary of Solomon's Reign

41 The rest of the events in Solomon's reign, including all his deeds and his
wisdom, are recorded in *The Book of the Acts of Solomon.* 42 Solomon ruled in Jeru-
salem over all Israel for forty years. 43 When he died, he was buried in the City
of David, named for his father. Then his son Rehoboam became the next king.

The Northern Tribes Revolt

12 Rehoboam went to Shechem, where all Israel had gathered to make
him king. 2 When Jeroboam son of Nebat heard of this, he returned
from Egypt,* for he had fled to Egypt to escape from King Solomon. 3 The
leaders of Israel summoned him, and Jeroboam and the whole assembly of
Israel went to speak with Rehoboam. 4 "Your father was a hard master," they
said. "Lighten the harsh labor demands and heavy taxes that your father
imposed on us. Then we will be your loyal subjects."

5 Rehoboam replied, "Give me three days to think this over. Then come
back for my answer." So the people went away.

6 Then King Rehoboam discussed the matter with the older men who
had counseled his father, Solomon. "What is your advice?" he asked. "How
should I answer these people?"

7 The older counselors replied, "If you are willing to be a servant to these
people today and give them a favorable answer, they will always be your
loyal subjects."

8 But Rehoboam rejected the advice of the older men and instead asked
the opinion of the young men who had grown up with him and were now
his advisers. 9 "What is your advice?" he asked them. "How should I answer
these people who want me to lighten the burdens imposed by my father?"

10 The young men replied, "This is what you should tell those complainers
who want a lighter burden: 'My little finger is thicker than my father's waist!
11 Yes, my father laid heavy burdens on you, but I'm going to make them even
heavier! My father beat you with whips, but I will beat you with scorpions!'"

12 Three days later Jeroboam and all the people returned to hear Re-
hoboam's decision, just as the king had ordered. 13 But Rehoboam spoke
harshly to the people, for he rejected the advice of the older counselors 14 and
followed the counsel of his younger advisers. He told the people, "My father
laid heavy burdens on you, but I'm going to make them even heavier! My
father beat you with whips, but I will beat you with scorpions!"

15 So the king paid no attention to the people. This turn of events was the
will of the LORD, for it fulfilled the LORD's message to Jeroboam son of Nebat
through the prophet Ahijah from Shiloh.

16 When all Israel realized that the king had refused to listen to them, they
responded,

"Down with the dynasty of David!
    We have no interest in the son of Jesse.
Back to your homes, O Israel!
    Look out for your own house, O David!"

So the people of Israel returned home. 17 But Rehoboam continued to rule
over the Israelites who lived in the towns of Judah.

12:2 As in Greek version and Latin Vulgate (see also 2 Chr 10:2); Hebrew reads *he lived in Egypt.*

18 King Rehoboam sent Adoniram,* who was in charge of forced labor, to
restore order, but the people of Israel stoned him to death. When this news
reached King Rehoboam, he quickly jumped into his chariot and fled to
Jerusalem. 19 And to this day the northern tribes of Israel have refused to be
ruled by a descendant of David.

20 When the people of Israel learned of Jeroboam's return from Egypt, they
called an assembly and made him king over all Israel. So only the tribe of
Judah remained loyal to the family of David.

Shemaiah's Prophecy

21 When Rehoboam arrived at Jerusalem, he mobilized the men of Judah and
the tribe of Benjamin—180,000 select troops—to fight against the men of
Israel and to restore the kingdom to himself.

22 But God said to Shemaiah, the man of God, 23 "Say to Rehoboam son of
Solomon, king of Judah, and to all the people of Judah and Benjamin, and
to the rest of the people, 24 'This is what the LORD says: Do not fight against
your relatives, the Israelites. Go back home, for what has happened is my
doing!'" So they obeyed the message of the LORD and went home, as the
LORD had commanded.

Jeroboam Makes Gold Calves

25 Jeroboam then built up the city of Shechem in the hill country of Ephraim,
and it became his capital. Later he went and built up the town of Peniel.*

26 Jeroboam thought to himself, "Unless I am careful, the kingdom will re-
turn to the dynasty of David. 27 When these people go to Jerusalem to offer sac-
rifices at the Temple of the LORD, they will again give their allegiance to King
Rehoboam of Judah. They will kill me and make him their king instead."

28 So on the advice of his counselors, the king made two gold calves. He
said to the people,* "It is too much trouble for you to worship in Jerusalem.
Look, Israel, these are the gods who brought you out of Egypt!"

29 He placed these calf idols in Bethel and in Dan—at either end of his
kingdom. 30 But this became a great sin, for the people worshiped the idols,
traveling as far north as Dan to worship the one there.

31 Jeroboam also erected buildings at the pagan shrines and ordained
priests from the common people—those who were not from the priestly
tribe of Levi. 32 And Jeroboam instituted a religious festival in Bethel, held on
the fifteenth day of the eighth month,* in imitation of the annual Festival of
Shelters in Judah. There at Bethel he himself offered sacrifices to the calves
he had made, and he appointed priests for the pagan shrines he had made.
33 So on the fifteenth day of the eighth month, a day that he himself had
designated, Jeroboam offered sacrifices on the altar at Bethel. He instituted
a religious festival for Israel, and he went up to the altar to burn incense.

A Prophet Denounces Jeroboam

13 At the LORD's command, a man of God from Judah went to Bethel,
arriving there just as Jeroboam was approaching the altar to burn
incense. 2 Then at the LORD's command, he shouted, "O altar, altar! This is

12:18 As in some Greek manuscripts and Syriac version (see also 4:6; 5:14); Hebrew reads *Adoram.* 12:25 Hebrew *Penuel,* a variant spelling of Peniel. 12:28 Hebrew *to them.* 12:32 This day of the ancient Hebrew lunar calendar occurred in late October or early November, exactly one month after the annual Festival of Shelters in Judah (see Lev 23:34).

Question 12:28

Didn't Jeroboam remember his history lessons? When Israel made a golden calf to worship in the wilderness, God was furious (Exodus 32). Now, here, they made *two* golden calves. Why do you think we struggle to learn from the sins of prior generations? What mistakes are in your family's heritage that you should be sure not to repeat?

what the LORD says: A child named Josiah will be born into the dynasty of David. On you he will sacrifice the priests from the pagan shrines who come here to burn incense, and human bones will be burned on you." 3 That same day the man of God gave a sign to prove his message. He said, "The LORD has promised to give this sign: This altar will split apart, and its ashes will be poured out on the ground."

4 When King Jeroboam heard the man of God speaking against the altar at Bethel, he pointed at him and shouted, "Seize that man!" But instantly the king's hand became paralyzed in that position, and he couldn't pull it back. 5 At the same time a wide crack appeared in the altar, and the ashes poured out, just as the man of God had predicted in his message from the LORD.

6 The king cried out to the man of God, "Please ask the LORD your God to restore my hand again!" So the man of God prayed to the LORD, and the king's hand was restored and he could move it again.

7 Then the king said to the man of God, "Come to the palace with me and have something to eat, and I will give you a gift."

8 But the man of God said to the king, "Even if you gave me half of everything you own, I would not go with you. I would not eat or drink anything in this place. 9 For the LORD gave me this command: 'You must not eat or drink anything while you are there, and do not return to Judah by the same way you came.'" 10 So he left Bethel and went home another way.

11 As it happened, there was an old prophet living in Bethel, and his sons* came home and told him what the man of God had done in Bethel that day. They also told their father what the man had said to the king. 12 The old prophet asked them, "Which way did he go?" So they showed their father* which road the man of God had taken. 13 "Quick, saddle the donkey," the old man said. So they saddled the donkey for him, and he mounted it.

14 Then he rode after the man of God and found him sitting under a great tree. The old prophet asked him, "Are you the man of God who came from Judah?"

"Yes, I am," he replied.

15 Then he said to the man of God, "Come home with me and eat some food."

16 "No, I cannot," he replied. "I am not allowed to eat or drink anything here in this place. 17 For the LORD gave me this command: 'You must not eat or drink anything while you are there, and do not return to Judah by the same way you came.'"

18 But the old prophet answered, "I am a prophet, too, just as you are. And an angel gave me this command from the LORD: 'Bring him home with you so he can have something to eat and drink.'" But the old man was lying to him. 19 So they went back together, and the man of God ate and drank at the prophet's home.

20 Then while they were sitting at the table, a command from the LORD came to the old prophet. 21 He cried out to the man of God from Judah, "This is what the LORD says: You have defied the word of the LORD and have disobeyed the command the LORD your God gave you. 22 You came back to this place and ate and drank where he told you not to eat or drink. Because of this, your body will not be buried in the grave of your ancestors."

13:11 As in Greek version; Hebrew reads *son.* **13:12** As in Greek version; Hebrew reads *They had seen.*

[23]After the man of God had finished eating and drinking, the old prophet
saddled his own donkey for him, [24]and the man of God started off again. But
as he was traveling along, a lion came out and killed him. His body lay there
on the road, with the donkey and the lion standing beside it. [25]People who
passed by saw the body lying in the road and the lion standing beside it, and
they went and reported it in Bethel, where the old prophet lived.
[26]When the prophet heard the report, he said, "It is the man of God who
disobeyed the LORD's command. The LORD has fulfilled his word by causing
the lion to attack and kill him."
[27]Then the prophet said to his sons, "Saddle a donkey for me." So they
saddled a donkey, [28]and he went out and found the body lying in the road.
The donkey and lion were still standing there beside it, for the lion had not
eaten the body nor attacked the donkey. [29]So the prophet laid the body of
the man of God on the donkey and took it back to the town to mourn over
him and bury him. [30]He laid the body in his own grave, crying out in grief,
"Oh, my brother!"
[31]Afterward the prophet said to his sons, "When I die, bury me in the
grave where the man of God is buried. Lay my bones beside his bones. [32]For
the message the LORD told him to proclaim against the altar in Bethel and
against the pagan shrines in the towns of Samaria will certainly come
true."
[33]But even after this, Jeroboam did not turn from his evil ways. He con-
tinued to choose priests from the common people. He appointed anyone
who wanted to become a priest for the pagan shrines. [34]This became a great
sin and resulted in the utter destruction of Jeroboam's dynasty from the
face of the earth.

Ahijah's Prophecy against Jeroboam

14 At that time Jeroboam's son Abijah became very sick. [2]So Jeroboam
told his wife, "Disguise yourself so that no one will recognize you as
my wife. Then go to the prophet Ahijah at Shiloh—the man who told me I
would become king. [3]Take him a gift of ten loaves of bread, some cakes, and
a jar of honey, and ask him what will happen to the boy."
[4]So Jeroboam's wife went to Ahijah's home at Shiloh. He was an old man
now and could no longer see. [5]But the LORD had told Ahijah, "Jeroboam's
wife will come here, pretending to be someone else. She will ask you about
her son, for he is very sick. Give her the answer I give you."
[6]So when Ahijah heard her footsteps at the door, he called out, "Come
in, wife of Jeroboam! Why are you pretending to be someone else?" Then
he told her, "I have bad news for you. [7]Give your husband, Jeroboam, this
message from the LORD, the God of Israel: 'I promoted you from the ranks
of the common people and made you ruler over my people Israel. [8]I ripped
the kingdom away from the family of David and gave it to you. But you
have not been like my servant David, who obeyed my commands and fol-
lowed me with all his heart and always did whatever I wanted. [9]You have
done more evil than all who lived before you. You have made other gods
for yourself and have made me furious with your gold calves. And since
you have turned your back on me, [10]I will bring disaster on your dynasty
and will destroy every one of your male descendants, slave and free alike,
anywhere in Israel. I will burn up your royal dynasty as one burns up trash

Make a Difference

14:1-18

Age Well

At the beginning of the book of 1 Kings, David had become a feeble, old man with a feeble, old faith in God. The prophet Ahijah stood in contrast to that, however. Like David, he had become an old man. Ahijah had even lost his eyesight (v. 4), yet his discernment was as sharp as ever. He spoke with the authority of the Lord. Ahijah's grit of faith kept him renewed in his soul even as his body began to fail him.

Difference Maker

Look ahead through the years of your life. What practices do you need to put into place now so that you can be sure to be strong and sharp in your faith in your old age?

until it is all gone. 11 The members of Jeroboam's family who die in the
city will be eaten by dogs, and those who die in the field will be eaten by
vultures. I, the LORD, have spoken.'"

12 Then Ahijah said to Jeroboam's wife, "Go on home, and when you enter
the city, the child will die. 13 All Israel will mourn for him and bury him. He
is the only member of your family who will have a proper burial, for this
child is the only good thing that the LORD, the God of Israel, sees in the
entire family of Jeroboam.

14 "In addition, the LORD will raise up a king over Israel who will destroy
the family of Jeroboam. This will happen today, even now! 15 Then the LORD
will shake Israel like a reed whipped about in a stream. He will uproot the
people of Israel from this good land that he gave their ancestors and will
scatter them beyond the Euphrates River,* for they have angered the LORD
with the Asherah poles they have set up for worship. 16 He will abandon Israel
because Jeroboam sinned and made Israel sin along with him."

17 So Jeroboam's wife returned to Tirzah, and the child died just as she
walked through the door of her home. 18 And all Israel buried him and
mourned for him, as the LORD had promised through the prophet Ahijah.

19 The rest of the events in Jeroboam's reign, including all his wars and
how he ruled, are recorded in *The Book of the History of the Kings of Israel.* 20 Jer-
oboam reigned in Israel twenty-two years. When Jeroboam died, his son
Nadab became the next king.

Rehoboam Rules in Judah

21 Meanwhile, Rehoboam son of Solomon was king in Judah. He was forty-
one years old when he became king, and he reigned seventeen years in Je-
rusalem, the city the LORD had chosen from among all the tribes of Israel
as the place to honor his name. Rehoboam's mother was Naamah, an Am-
monite woman.

22 During Rehoboam's reign, the people of Judah did what was evil in the
LORD's sight, provoking his anger with their sin, for it was even worse than
that of their ancestors. 23 For they also built for themselves pagan shrines and
set up sacred pillars and Asherah poles on every high hill and under every
green tree. 24 There were even male and female shrine prostitutes throughout
the land. The people imitated the detestable practices of the pagan nations
the LORD had driven from the land ahead of the Israelites.

25 In the fifth year of King Rehoboam's reign, King Shishak of Egypt came
up and attacked Jerusalem. 26 He ransacked the treasuries of the LORD's
Temple and the royal palace; he stole everything, including all the gold
shields Solomon had made. 27 King Rehoboam later replaced them with
bronze shields as substitutes, and he entrusted them to the care of the
commanders of the guard who protected the entrance to the royal palace.
28 Whenever the king went to the Temple of the LORD, the guards would also
take the shields and then return them to the guardroom.

29 The rest of the events in Rehoboam's reign and everything he did are re-
corded in *The Book of the History of the Kings of Judah.* 30 There was constant war
between Rehoboam and Jeroboam. 31 When Rehoboam died, he was buried
among his ancestors in the City of David. His mother was Naamah, an Am-
monite woman. Then his son Abijam* became the next king.

14:15 Hebrew *the river.* 14:31 Also known as *Abijah.*

Abijam Rules in Judah

15 Abijam* began to rule over Judah in the eighteenth year of Jerobo-
am's reign in Israel. 2 He reigned in Jerusalem three years. His mother
was Maacah, the granddaughter of Absalom.*
3 He committed the same sins as his father before him, and he was not
faithful to the LORD his God, as his ancestor David had been. 4 But for Da-
vid's sake, the LORD his God allowed his descendants to continue ruling,
shining like a lamp, and he gave Abijam a son to rule after him in Jerusalem.
5 For David had done what was pleasing in the LORD's sight and had obeyed
the LORD's commands throughout his life, except in the affair concerning
Uriah the Hittite.
6 There was war between Abijam and Jeroboam* throughout Abijam's
reign. 7 The rest of the events in Abijam's reign and everything he did are
recorded in *The Book of the History of the Kings of Judah.* There was constant
war between Abijam and Jeroboam. 8 When Abijam died, he was buried in
the City of David. Then his son Asa became the next king.

Asa Rules in Judah

9 Asa began to rule over Judah in the twentieth year of Jeroboam's reign in
Israel. 10 He reigned in Jerusalem forty-one years. His grandmother* was
Maacah, the granddaughter of Absalom.
11 Asa did what was pleasing in the LORD's sight, as his ancestor David had
done. 12 He banished the male and female shrine prostitutes from the land
and got rid of all the idols* his ancestors had made. 13 He even deposed his
grandmother Maacah from her position as queen mother because she had
made an obscene Asherah pole. He cut down her obscene pole and burned it
in the Kidron Valley. 14 Although the pagan shrines were not removed, Asa's
heart remained completely faithful to the LORD throughout his life. 15 He
brought into the Temple of the LORD the silver and gold and the various
items that he and his father had dedicated.
16 There was constant war between King Asa of Judah and King Baasha of
Israel. 17 King Baasha of Israel invaded Judah and fortified Ramah in order
to prevent anyone from entering or leaving King Asa's territory in Judah.
18 Asa responded by removing all the silver and gold that was left in the
treasuries of the Temple of the LORD and the royal palace. He sent it with
some of his officials to Ben-hadad son of Tabrimmon, son of Hezion, the
king of Aram, who was ruling in Damascus, along with this message:

> 19 "Let there be a treaty* between you and me like the one between your
> father and my father. See, I am sending you a gift of silver and gold.
> Break your treaty with King Baasha of Israel so that he will leave me
> alone."

20 Ben-hadad agreed to King Asa's request and sent the commanders of his
army to attack the towns of Israel. They conquered the towns of Ijon, Dan,
Abel-beth-maacah, and all Kinnereth, and all the land of Naphtali. 21 As soon
as Baasha of Israel heard what was happening, he abandoned his project of

Question 15:11

This is a refreshing line after so much sin. Why is it so difficult to do what is pleasing in the Lord's sight when everyone else is doing what feels right in their own sight?

15:1 Also known as *Abijah.* **15:2** Hebrew *Abishalom* (also in 15:10), a variant spelling of Absalom; compare 2 Chr 11:20. **15:6** As in a few Hebrew and Greek manuscripts; most Hebrew manuscripts read *between Rehoboam and Jeroboam.* **15:10** Or *The queen mother;* Hebrew reads *His mother* (also in 15:13); compare 15:2. **15:12** The Hebrew term (literally *round things*) probably alludes to dung. **15:19** As in Greek version; Hebrew reads *There is a treaty.*

fortifying Ramah and withdrew to Tirzah. 22 Then King Asa sent an order
throughout Judah, requiring that everyone, without exception, help to carry
away the building stones and timbers that Baasha had been using to fortify
Ramah. Asa used these materials to fortify the town of Geba in Benjamin
and the town of Mizpah.
23 The rest of the events in Asa's reign—the extent of his power, everything
he did, and the names of the cities he built—are recorded in *The Book of the
History of the Kings of Judah.* In his old age his feet became diseased. 24 When
Asa died, he was buried with his ancestors in the City of David.
Then Jehoshaphat, Asa's son, became the next king.

Nadab Rules in Israel

25 Nadab son of Jeroboam began to rule over Israel in the second year of King
Asa's reign in Judah. He reigned in Israel two years. 26 But he did what was
evil in the LORD's sight and followed the example of his father, continuing
the sins that Jeroboam had led Israel to commit.
27 Then Baasha son of Ahijah, from the tribe of Issachar, plotted against
Nadab and assassinated him while he and the Israelite army were laying
siege to the Philistine town of Gibbethon. 28 Baasha killed Nadab in the third
year of King Asa's reign in Judah, and he became the next king of Israel.
29 He immediately slaughtered all the descendants of King Jeroboam, so
that not one of the royal family was left, just as the LORD had promised
concerning Jeroboam by the prophet Ahijah from Shiloh. 30 This was done
because Jeroboam had provoked the anger of the LORD, the God of Israel, by
the sins he had committed and the sins he had led Israel to commit.
31 The rest of the events in Nadab's reign and everything he did are re-
corded in *The Book of the History of the Kings of Israel.*

Baasha Rules in Israel

32 There was constant war between King Asa of Judah and King Baasha of
Israel. 33 Baasha son of Ahijah began to rule over all Israel in the third year
of King Asa's reign in Judah. Baasha reigned in Tirzah twenty-four years.
34 But he did what was evil in the LORD's sight and followed the example
of Jeroboam, continuing the sins that Jeroboam had led Israel to commit.

16 This message from the LORD was delivered to King Baasha by the
prophet Jehu son of Hanani: 2 "I lifted you out of the dust to make
you ruler of my people Israel, but you have followed the evil example of Jer-
oboam. You have provoked my anger by causing my people Israel to sin. 3 So
now I will destroy you and your family, just as I destroyed the descendants of
Jeroboam son of Nebat. 4 The members of Baasha's family who die in the city
will be eaten by dogs, and those who die in the field will be eaten by vultures."
5 The rest of the events in Baasha's reign and the extent of his power are
recorded in *The Book of the History of the Kings of Israel.* 6 When Baasha died, he
was buried in Tirzah. Then his son Elah became the next king.
7 The message from the LORD against Baasha and his family came through
the prophet Jehu son of Hanani. It was delivered because Baasha had done
what was evil in the LORD's sight (just as the family of Jeroboam had done),
and also because Baasha had destroyed the family of Jeroboam. The LORD's
anger was provoked by Baasha's sins.

Elah Rules in Israel
8 Elah son of Baasha began to rule over Israel in the twenty-sixth year of King
Asa's reign in Judah. He reigned in the city of Tirzah for two years.
9 Then Zimri, who commanded half of the royal chariots, made plans to
kill him. One day in Tirzah, Elah was getting drunk at the home of Arza, the
supervisor of the palace. 10 Zimri walked in and struck him down and killed
him. This happened in the twenty-seventh year of King Asa's reign in Judah.
Then Zimri became the next king.
11 Zimri immediately killed the entire royal family of Baasha, leaving
him not even a single male child. He even destroyed distant relatives and
friends. 12 So Zimri destroyed the dynasty of Baasha as the LORD had prom-
ised through the prophet Jehu. 13 This happened because of all the sins Baa-
sha and his son Elah had committed, and because of the sins they led Israel
to commit. They provoked the anger of the LORD, the God of Israel, with
their worthless idols.
14 The rest of the events in Elah's reign and everything he did are recorded
in *The Book of the History of the Kings of Israel.*

Zimri Rules in Israel
15 Zimri began to rule over Israel in the twenty-seventh year of King Asa's
reign in Judah, but his reign in Tirzah lasted only seven days. The army of
Israel was then attacking the Philistine town of Gibbethon. 16 When they
heard that Zimri had committed treason and had assassinated the king,
that very day they chose Omri, commander of the army, as the new king of
Israel. 17 So Omri led the entire army of Israel up from Gibbethon to attack
Tirzah, Israel's capital. 18 When Zimri saw that the city had been taken, he
went into the citadel of the palace and burned it down over himself and died
in the flames. 19 For he, too, had done what was evil in the LORD's sight. He
followed the example of Jeroboam in all the sins he had committed and led
Israel to commit.
20 The rest of the events in Zimri's reign and his conspiracy are recorded
in *The Book of the History of the Kings of Israel.*

Omri Rules in Israel
21 But now the people of Israel were split into two factions. Half the people
tried to make Tibni son of Ginath their king, while the other half supported
Omri. 22 But Omri's supporters defeated the supporters of Tibni. So Tibni was
killed, and Omri became the next king.
23 Omri began to rule over Israel in the thirty-first year of King Asa's reign
in Judah. He reigned twelve years in all, six of them in Tirzah. 24 Then Omri
bought the hill now known as Samaria from its owner, Shemer, for 150 pounds
of silver.* He built a city on it and called the city Samaria in honor of Shemer.
25 But Omri did what was evil in the LORD's sight, even more than any of
the kings before him. 26 He followed the example of Jeroboam son of Nebat in
all the sins he had committed and led Israel to commit. The people provoked
the anger of the LORD, the God of Israel, with their worthless idols.
27 The rest of the events in Omri's reign, the extent of his power, and every-
thing he did are recorded in *The Book of the History of the Kings of Israel.* 28 When
Omri died, he was buried in Samaria. Then his son Ahab became the next king.

16:24 Hebrew *for 2 talents* [68 kilograms] *of silver.*

Encouragements from these verses

Ahab Rules in Israel

29 Ahab son of Omri began to rule over Israel in the thirty-eighth year of King
Asa's reign in Judah. He reigned in Samaria twenty-two years. 30 But Ahab
son of Omri did what was evil in the LORD's sight, even more than any of the
kings before him. 31 And as though it were not enough to follow the sinful
example of Jeroboam, he married Jezebel, the daughter of King Ethbaal of
the Sidonians, and he began to bow down in worship of Baal. 32 First Ahab
built a temple and an altar for Baal in Samaria. 33 Then he set up an Asherah
pole. He did more to provoke the anger of the LORD, the God of Israel, than
any of the other kings of Israel before him.

34 It was during his reign that Hiel, a man from Bethel, rebuilt Jericho.
When he laid its foundations, it cost him the life of his oldest son, Abiram.
And when he completed it and set up its gates, it cost him the life of his
youngest son, Segub.* This all happened according to the message from the
LORD concerning Jericho spoken by Joshua son of Nun.

Elijah Fed by Ravens

17 Now Elijah, who was from Tishbe in Gilead, told King Ahab, "As
surely as the LORD, the God of Israel, lives—the God I serve—there
will be no dew or rain during the next few years until I give the word!"

2 Then the LORD said to Elijah, 3 "Go to the east and hide by Kerith Brook,
near where it enters the Jordan River. 4 Drink from the brook and eat what
the ravens bring you, for I have commanded them to bring you food."

5 So Elijah did as the LORD told him and camped beside Kerith Brook, east
of the Jordan. 6 The ravens brought him bread and meat each morning and
evening, and he drank from the brook. 7 But after a while the brook dried
up, for there was no rainfall anywhere in the land.

The Widow at Zarephath

8 Then the LORD said to Elijah, 9 "Go and live in the village of Zarephath, near
the city of Sidon. I have instructed a widow there to feed you."

10 So he went to Zarephath. As he arrived at the gates of the village, he saw
a widow gathering sticks, and he asked her, "Would you please bring me a
little water in a cup?" 11 As she was going to get it, he called to her, "Bring
me a bite of bread, too."

12 But she said, "I swear by the LORD your God that I don't have a single
piece of bread in the house. And I have only a handful of flour left in the jar
and a little cooking oil in the bottom of the jug. I was just gathering a few
sticks to cook this last meal, and then my son and I will die."

13 But Elijah said to her, "Don't be afraid! Go ahead and do just what you've
said, but make a little bread for me first. Then use what's left to prepare a
meal for yourself and your son. 14 For this is what the LORD, the God of Israel,
says: There will always be flour and olive oil left in your containers until the
time when the LORD sends rain and the crops grow again!"

15 So she did as Elijah said, and she and Elijah and her family continued to
eat for many days. 16 There was always enough flour and olive oil left in the
containers, just as the LORD had promised through Elijah.

17 Some time later the woman's son became sick. He grew worse and worse,

Story Arc 17:1

Elijah

The powerful prophet Elijah entered the story just as the wickedness of Ahab was introduced (16:30). Elijah's first act was to tell Ahab that the Lord, the God of Israel, lives and that the God who lives, the one whom Elijah served, was going to demonstrate his authority over Ahab's god, Baal, by halting the rain and dew for a few years. This alarming act established that God considered the battle of thrones of 1 Kings a battle of spiritual warfare. God anointed Elijah to be the deliverer of his messages in word and action.

2 Kgs 1:3 ►

16:34 An ancient Hebrew scribal tradition reads *He killed his oldest son when he laid its foundations, and he killed his youngest son when he set up its gates.*

and finally he died. 18 Then she said to Elijah, "O man of God, what have you
done to me? Have you come here to point out my sins and kill my son?"
19 But Elijah replied, "Give me your son." And he took the child's body
from her arms, carried him up the stairs to the room where he was staying,
and laid the body on his bed. 20 Then Elijah cried out to the LORD, "O LORD
my God, why have you brought tragedy to this widow who has opened her
home to me, causing her son to die?"
21 And he stretched himself out over the child three times and cried out to
the LORD, "O LORD my God, please let this child's life return to him." 22 The
LORD heard Elijah's prayer, and the life of the child returned, and he revived!
23 Then Elijah brought him down from the upper room and gave him to his
mother. "Look!" he said. "Your son is alive!"
24 Then the woman told Elijah, "Now I know for sure that you are a man
of God, and that the LORD truly speaks through you."

The Contest on Mount Carmel

18 Later on, in the third year of the drought, the LORD said to Elijah,
"Go and present yourself to King Ahab. Tell him that I will soon send
rain!" 2 So Elijah went to appear before Ahab.
Meanwhile, the famine had become very severe in Samaria. 3 So Ahab
summoned Obadiah, who was in charge of the palace. (Obadiah was a de-
voted follower of the LORD. 4 Once when Jezebel had tried to kill all the
LORD's prophets, Obadiah had hidden 100 of them in two caves. He put fifty
prophets in each cave and supplied them with food and water.) 5 Ahab said
to Obadiah, "We must check every spring and valley in the land to see if we
can find enough grass to save at least some of my horses and mules." 6 So they
divided the land between them. Ahab went one way by himself, and Obadiah
went another way by himself.
7 As Obadiah was walking along, he suddenly saw Elijah coming toward
him. Obadiah recognized him at once and bowed low to the ground before
him. "Is it really you, my lord Elijah?" he asked.
8 "Yes, it is," Elijah replied. "Now go and tell your master, 'Elijah is here.'"
9 "Oh, sir," Obadiah protested, "what harm have I done to you that you are
sending me to my death at the hands of Ahab? 10 For I swear by the LORD your
God that the king has searched every nation and kingdom on earth from end
to end to find you. And each time he was told, 'Elijah isn't here,' King Ahab
forced the king of that nation to swear to the truth of his claim. 11 And now
you say, 'Go and tell your master, "Elijah is here."' 12 But as soon as I leave you,
the Spirit of the LORD will carry you away to who knows where. When Ahab
comes and cannot find you, he will kill me. Yet I have been a true servant of
the LORD all my life. 13 Has no one told you, my lord, about the time when
Jezebel was trying to kill the LORD's prophets? I hid 100 of them in two caves
and supplied them with food and water. 14 And now you say, 'Go and tell your
master, "Elijah is here."' Sir, if I do that, Ahab will certainly kill me."
15 But Elijah said, "I swear by the LORD Almighty, in whose presence I
stand, that I will present myself to Ahab this very day."
16 So Obadiah went to tell Ahab that Elijah had come, and Ahab went out
to meet Elijah. 17 When Ahab saw him, he exclaimed, "So, is it really you, you
troublemaker of Israel?"
18 "I have made no trouble for Israel," Elijah replied. "You and your family

Question 17:8-24

As you read 1 Kings 17:8-24, see how a widow miraculously fed Elijah. Sadly, when her son got sick and died, she began to doubt God's work in her life. Elijah earnestly prayed, and her son was raised back to life! What does God want to declare through this story?

Prayer 18:21

Lord, you are God, so let me follow you and you alone. Amen.

Question 18:27

What do you think of Elijah's taunting of those who worshiped Baal? Why was God okay with this kind of behavior in this circumstance?

are the troublemakers, for you have refused to obey the commands of the LORD and have worshiped the images of Baal instead. 19 Now summon all Israel to join me at Mount Carmel, along with the 450 prophets of Baal and the 400 prophets of Asherah who are supported by Jezebel.*"

20 So Ahab summoned all the people of Israel and the prophets to Mount Carmel. 21 Then Elijah stood in front of them and said, "How much longer will you waver, hobbling between two opinions? If the LORD is God, follow him! But if Baal is God, then follow him!" But the people were completely silent.

22 Then Elijah said to them, "I am the only prophet of the LORD who is left, but Baal has 450 prophets. 23 Now bring two bulls. The prophets of Baal may choose whichever one they wish and cut it into pieces and lay it on the wood of their altar, but without setting fire to it. I will prepare the other bull and lay it on the wood on the altar, but not set fire to it. 24 Then call on the name of your god, and I will call on the name of the LORD. The god who answers by setting fire to the wood is the true God!" And all the people agreed.

25 Then Elijah said to the prophets of Baal, "You go first, for there are many of you. Choose one of the bulls, and prepare it and call on the name of your god. But do not set fire to the wood."

26 So they prepared one of the bulls and placed it on the altar. Then they called on the name of Baal from morning until noontime, shouting, "O Baal, answer us!" But there was no reply of any kind. Then they danced, hobbling around the altar they had made.

27 About noontime Elijah began mocking them. "You'll have to shout louder," he scoffed, "for surely he is a god! Perhaps he is daydreaming, or is relieving himself.* Or maybe he is away on a trip, or is asleep and needs to be wakened!"

28 So they shouted louder, and following their normal custom, they cut themselves with knives and swords until the blood gushed out. 29 They raved all afternoon until the time of the evening sacrifice, but still there was no sound, no reply, no response.

30 Then Elijah called to the people, "Come over here!" They all crowded around him as he repaired the altar of the LORD that had been torn down. 31 He took twelve stones, one to represent each of the tribes of Israel,* 32 and he used the stones to rebuild the altar in the name of the LORD. Then he dug a trench around the altar large enough to hold about three gallons.* 33 He piled wood on the altar, cut the bull into pieces, and laid the pieces on the wood.*

Then he said, "Fill four large jars with water, and pour the water over the offering and the wood."

34 After they had done this, he said, "Do the same thing again!" And when they were finished, he said, "Now do it a third time!" So they did as he said, 35 and the water ran around the altar and even filled the trench.

36 At the usual time for offering the evening sacrifice, Elijah the prophet walked up to the altar and prayed, "O LORD, God of Abraham, Isaac, and Jacob,* prove today that you are God in Israel and that I am your servant. Prove that I have done all this at your command. 37 O LORD, answer me!

18:19 Hebrew *who eat at Jezebel's table.* **18:27** Or *is busy somewhere else,* or *is engaged in business.* **18:31** Hebrew *each of the tribes of the sons of Jacob to whom the LORD had said, "Your name will be Israel."* **18:32** Hebrew *2 seahs* [14.6 liters] *of seed.* **18:33** Verse 18:34 in the Hebrew text begins here. **18:36** Hebrew *and Israel.* The names "Jacob" and "Israel" are often interchanged throughout the Old Testament, referring sometimes to the individual patriarch and sometimes to the nation.

Answer me so these people will know that you, O LORD, are God and that
you have brought them back to yourself."
38 Immediately the fire of the LORD flashed down from heaven and
burned up the young bull, the wood, the stones, and the dust. It even licked
up all the water in the trench! 39 And when all the people saw it, they fell
face down on the ground and cried out, "The LORD—he is God! Yes, the
LORD is God!"
40 Then Elijah commanded, "Seize all the prophets of Baal. Don't let a
single one escape!" So the people seized them all, and Elijah took them down
to the Kishon Valley and killed them there.

Elijah Prays for Rain

41 Then Elijah said to Ahab, "Go get something to eat and drink, for I hear a
mighty rainstorm coming!"
42 So Ahab went to eat and drink. But Elijah climbed to the top of Mount
Carmel and bowed low to the ground and prayed with his face between his
knees.
43 Then he said to his servant, "Go and look out toward the sea."
The servant went and looked, then returned to Elijah and said, "I didn't
see anything."
Seven times Elijah told him to go and look. 44 Finally the seventh time, his
servant told him, "I saw a little cloud about the size of a man's hand rising
from the sea."
Then Elijah shouted, "Hurry to Ahab and tell him, 'Climb into your char-
iot and go back home. If you don't hurry, the rain will stop you!'"
45 And soon the sky was black with clouds. A heavy wind brought a terrific
rainstorm, and Ahab left quickly for Jezreel. 46 Then the LORD gave special
strength to Elijah. He tucked his cloak into his belt* and ran ahead of Ahab's
chariot all the way to the entrance of Jezreel.

Elijah Flees to Sinai

19 When Ahab got home, he told Jezebel everything Elijah had done,
including the way he had killed all the prophets of Baal. 2 So Jezebel
sent this message to Elijah: "May the gods strike me and even kill me if by
this time tomorrow I have not killed you just as you killed them."
3 Elijah was afraid and fled for his life. He went to Beersheba, a town in
Judah, and he left his servant there. 4 Then he went on alone into the wilder-
ness, traveling all day. He sat down under a solitary broom tree and prayed
that he might die. "I have had enough, LORD," he said. "Take my life, for I
am no better than my ancestors who have already died."
5 Then he lay down and slept under the broom tree. But as he was sleeping,
an angel touched him and told him, "Get up and eat!" 6 He looked around
and there beside his head was some bread baked on hot stones and a jar of
water! So he ate and drank and lay down again.
7 Then the angel of the LORD came again and touched him and said, "Get
up and eat some more, or the journey ahead will be too much for you."
8 So he got up and ate and drank, and the food gave him enough strength
to travel forty days and forty nights to Mount Sinai,* the mountain of God.
9 There he came to a cave, where he spent the night.

18:46 Hebrew *He bound up his loins.* **19:8** Hebrew *to Horeb,* another name for Sinai.

The LORD Speaks to Elijah

But the LORD said to him, "What are you doing here, Elijah?"
10 Elijah replied, "I have zealously served the LORD God Almighty. But the
people of Israel have broken their covenant with you, torn down your altars,
and killed every one of your prophets. I am the only one left, and now they
are trying to kill me, too."
11 "Go out and stand before me on the mountain," the LORD told him. And as
Elijah stood there, the LORD passed by, and a mighty windstorm hit the moun-
tain. It was such a terrible blast that the rocks were torn loose, but the LORD
was not in the wind. After the wind there was an earthquake, but the LORD
was not in the earthquake. 12 And after the earthquake there was a fire, but
the LORD was not in the fire. And after the fire there was the sound of a gentle
whisper. 13 When Elijah heard it, he wrapped his face in his cloak and went out
and stood at the entrance of the cave.
And a voice said, "What are you doing here, Elijah?"
14 He replied again, "I have zealously served the LORD God Almighty. But
the people of Israel have broken their covenant with you, torn down your
altars, and killed every one of your prophets. I am the only one left, and now
they are trying to kill me, too."
15 Then the LORD told him, "Go back the same way you came, and travel
to the wilderness of Damascus. When you arrive there, anoint Hazael to be
king of Aram. 16 Then anoint Jehu grandson of Nimshi* to be king of Israel,
and anoint Elisha son of Shaphat from the town of Abel-meholah to replace
you as my prophet. 17 Anyone who escapes from Hazael will be killed by Jehu,
and those who escape Jehu will be killed by Elisha! 18 Yet I will preserve 7,000
others in Israel who have never bowed down to Baal or kissed him!"

The Call of Elisha

19 So Elijah went and found Elisha son of Shaphat plowing a field. There were
twelve teams of oxen in the field, and Elisha was plowing with the twelfth
team. Elijah went over to him and threw his cloak across his shoulders and
then walked away. 20 Elisha left the oxen standing there, ran after Elijah,
and said to him, "First let me go and kiss my father and mother good-bye,
and then I will go with you!"
Elijah replied, "Go on back, but think about what I have done to you."
21 So Elisha returned to his oxen and slaughtered them. He used the
wood from the plow to build a fire to roast their flesh. He passed around
the meat to the townspeople, and they all ate. Then he went with Elijah as
his assistant.

Ben-Hadad Attacks Samaria

20 About that time King Ben-hadad of Aram mobilized his army, sup-
ported by the chariots and horses of thirty-two allied kings. They
went to besiege Samaria, the capital of Israel, and launched attacks against it.
2 Ben-hadad sent messengers into the city to relay this message to King Ahab
of Israel: "This is what Ben-hadad says: 3 'Your silver and gold are mine, and
so are your wives and the best of your children!'"
4 "All right, my lord the king," Israel's king replied. "All that I have is yours!"
5 Soon Ben-hadad's messengers returned again and said, "This is what

19:16 Hebrew *descendant of Nimshi;* compare 2 Kgs 9:2, 14.

Make a Difference

19:9–13

If God Wants

If God wants to, of course he could crash our party and force us to listen. Instead, he would rather get our attention through a gentle whisper. It's God's way of being gentle on our fragile hearts and ears. God's voice of wrath could tear the skin from our bones; his words could destroy us. On the other hand, God's voice of grace can create us. His breath could mend our tissue back together, and his words could give us new life—if he wants.

Do we want it? Are we willing to listen to his gentle whisper? If yes, then God will call out gently. If no, then God might eventually need to clap his hands and thunder his voice in our direction.

Difference Maker

Set aside uncrowded time today to listen for God's voice.

Question **19:18**

Just when you think you are alone in following God, the reality is that there are thousands of others also committed to the Lord. Perhaps you need the reminder that the Lord has many people you aren't aware of who have never bowed to another god and who are faithful to him. Where could you go to be among some others who are also following God this week?

Ben-hadad says: 'I have already demanded that you give me your silver, gold,
wives, and children. [6]But about this time tomorrow I will send my officials
to search your palace and the homes of your officials. They will take away
everything you consider valuable!'"

[7]Then Ahab summoned all the elders of the land and said to them, "Look
how this man is stirring up trouble! I already agreed with his demand that
I give him my wives and children and silver and gold."

[8]"Don't give in to any more demands," all the elders and the people
advised.

[9]So Ahab told the messengers from Ben-hadad, "Say this to my lord the
king: 'I will give you everything you asked for the first time, but I cannot
accept this last demand of yours.'" So the messengers returned to Ben-hadad
with that response.

[10]Then Ben-hadad sent this message to Ahab: "May the gods strike me and
even kill me if there remains enough dust from Samaria to provide even a
handful for each of my soldiers."

[11]The king of Israel sent back this answer: "A warrior putting on his sword
for battle should not boast like a warrior who has already won."

[12]Ahab's reply reached Ben-hadad and the other kings as they were drink-
ing in their tents.* "Prepare to attack!" Ben-hadad commanded his officers.
So they prepared to attack the city.

Ahab's Victory over Ben-Hadad

[13]Then a certain prophet came to see King Ahab of Israel and told him, "This
is what the LORD says: Do you see all these enemy forces? Today I will hand
them all over to you. Then you will know that I am the LORD."

[14]Ahab asked, "How will he do it?"

And the prophet replied, "This is what the LORD says: The troops of the
provincial commanders will do it."

"Should we attack first?" Ahab asked.

"Yes," the prophet answered.

[15]So Ahab mustered the troops of the 232 provincial commanders. Then he
called out the rest of the army of Israel, some 7,000 men. [16]About noontime,
as Ben-hadad and the thirty-two allied kings were still in their tents drink-
ing themselves into a stupor, [17]the troops of the provincial commanders
marched out of the city as the first contingent.

As they approached, Ben-hadad's scouts reported to him, "Some troops
are coming from Samaria."

[18]"Take them alive," Ben-hadad commanded, "whether they have come
for peace or for war."

[19]But Ahab's provincial commanders and the entire army had now come
out to fight. [20]Each Israelite soldier killed his Aramean opponent, and sud-
denly the entire Aramean army panicked and fled. The Israelites chased
them, but King Ben-hadad and a few of his charioteers escaped on horses.
[21]However, the king of Israel destroyed the other horses and chariots and
slaughtered the Arameans.

[22]Afterward the prophet said to King Ahab, "Get ready for another at-
tack. Begin making plans now, for the king of Aram will come back next
spring.*"

20:12 Or *in Succoth;* also in 20:16. 20:22 Hebrew *at the turn of the year;* similarly in 20:26. The first day of the year in the ancient Hebrew lunar calendar occurred in March or April.

Ben-Hadad's Second Attack

23 After their defeat, Ben-hadad's officers said to him, "The Israelite gods
are gods of the hills; that is why they won. But we can beat them easily
on the plains. 24 Only this time replace the kings with field commanders!
25 Recruit another army like the one you lost. Give us the same number of
horses, chariots, and men, and we will fight against them on the plains.
There's no doubt that we will beat them." So King Ben-hadad did as they
suggested.

26 The following spring he called up the Aramean army and marched out
against Israel, this time at Aphek. 27 Israel then mustered its army, set up
supply lines, and marched out for battle. But the Israelite army looked like
two little flocks of goats in comparison to the vast Aramean forces that filled
the countryside!

28 Then the man of God went to the king of Israel and said, "This is what
the LORD says: The Arameans have said, 'The LORD is a god of the hills and
not of the plains.' So I will defeat this vast army for you. Then you will know
that I am the LORD."

29 The two armies camped opposite each other for seven days, and on the
seventh day the battle began. The Israelites killed 100,000 Aramean foot
soldiers in one day. 30 The rest fled into the town of Aphek, but the wall fell
on them and killed another 27,000. Ben-hadad fled into the town and hid
in a secret room.

31 Ben-hadad's officers said to him, "Sir, we have heard that the kings of
Israel are merciful. So let's humble ourselves by wearing burlap around our
waists and putting ropes on our heads, and surrender to the king of Israel.
Then perhaps he will let you live."

32 So they put on burlap and ropes, and they went to the king of Israel and
begged, "Your servant Ben-hadad says, 'Please let me live!'"

The king of Israel responded, "Is he still alive? He is my brother!"

33 The men took this as a good sign and quickly picked up on his words.
"Yes," they said, "your brother Ben-hadad!"

"Go and get him," the king of Israel told them. And when Ben-hadad arrived, Ahab invited him up into his chariot.

34 Ben-hadad told him, "I will give back the towns my father took from
your father, and you may establish places of trade in Damascus, as my father
did in Samaria."

Then Ahab said, "I will release you under these conditions." So they made a new treaty, and Ben-hadad was set free.

A Prophet Condemns Ahab

35 Meanwhile, the LORD instructed one of the group of prophets to say to
another man, "Hit me!" But the man refused to hit the prophet. 36 Then the
prophet told him, "Because you have not obeyed the voice of the LORD, a
lion will kill you as soon as you leave me." And when he had gone, a lion did
attack and kill him.

37 Then the prophet turned to another man and said, "Hit me!" So he
struck the prophet and wounded him.

38 The prophet placed a bandage over his eyes to disguise himself and then
waited beside the road for the king. 39 As the king passed by, the prophet
called out to him, "Sir, I was in the thick of battle, and suddenly a man

brought me a prisoner. He said, 'Guard this man; if for any reason he gets away, you will either die or pay a fine of seventy-five pounds* of silver!'
40 But while I was busy doing something else, the prisoner disappeared!"

"Well, it's your own fault," the king replied. "You have brought the judgment on yourself."

41 Then the prophet quickly pulled the bandage from his eyes, and the king of Israel recognized him as one of the prophets.
42 The prophet said to him, "This is what the LORD says: Because you have spared the man I said must be destroyed,* now you must die in his place, and your people will die instead of his people."
43 So the king of Israel went home to Samaria angry and sullen.

Question 21:1

Read the whole story about Naboth's vineyard in this chapter. There are many lessons to be learned here. What would you say are the three most important?

Naboth's Vineyard

21 Now there was a man named Naboth, from Jezreel, who owned a vineyard in Jezreel beside the palace of King Ahab of Samaria.
2 One day Ahab said to Naboth, "Since your vineyard is so convenient to my palace, I would like to buy it to use as a vegetable garden. I will give you a better vineyard in exchange, or if you prefer, I will pay you for it."

3 But Naboth replied, "The LORD forbid that I should give you the inheritance that was passed down by my ancestors."

4 So Ahab went home angry and sullen because of Naboth's answer. The king went to bed with his face to the wall and refused to eat!

5 "What's the matter?" his wife Jezebel asked him. "What's made you so upset that you're not eating?"

6 "I asked Naboth to sell me his vineyard or trade it, but he refused!" Ahab told her.

7 "Are you the king of Israel or not?" Jezebel demanded. "Get up and eat something, and don't worry about it. I'll get you Naboth's vineyard!"

8 So she wrote letters in Ahab's name, sealed them with his seal, and sent them to the elders and other leaders of the town where Naboth lived.
9 In her letters she commanded: "Call the citizens together for a time of fasting, and give Naboth a place of honor.
10 And then seat two scoundrels across from him who will accuse him of cursing God and the king. Then take him out and stone him to death."

11 So the elders and other town leaders followed the instructions Jezebel had written in the letters.
12 They called for a fast and put Naboth at a prominent place before the people.
13 Then the two scoundrels came and sat down across from him. And they accused Naboth before all the people, saying, "He cursed God and the king." So he was dragged outside the town and stoned to death.
14 The town leaders then sent word to Jezebel, "Naboth has been stoned to death."

15 When Jezebel heard the news, she said to Ahab, "You know the vineyard Naboth wouldn't sell you? Well, you can have it now! He's dead!"
16 So Ahab immediately went down to the vineyard of Naboth to claim it.

17 But the LORD said to Elijah,*
18 "Go down to meet King Ahab of Israel, who rules in Samaria. He will be at Naboth's vineyard in Jezreel, claiming it for himself.
19 Give him this message: 'This is what the LORD says: Wasn't it enough that you killed Naboth? Must you rob him, too? Because you have

20:39 Hebrew *1 talent* [34 kilograms]. **20:42** The Hebrew term used here refers to the complete consecration of things or people to the LORD, either by destroying them or by giving them as an offering. **21:17** Hebrew *Elijah the Tishbite;* also in 21:28.

done this, dogs will lick your blood at the very place where they licked the
blood of Naboth!'"
20"So, my enemy, you have found me!" Ahab exclaimed to Elijah.
"Yes," Elijah answered, "I have come because you have sold yourself to
what is evil in the LORD's sight. 21So now the LORD says,* 'I will bring disaster
on you and consume you. I will destroy every one of your male descendants,
slave and free alike, anywhere in Israel! 22I am going to destroy your family
as I did the family of Jeroboam son of Nebat and the family of Baasha son
of Ahijah, for you have made me very angry and have led Israel into sin.'
23"And regarding Jezebel, the LORD says, 'Dogs will eat Jezebel's body at
the plot of land in Jezreel.*'
24"The members of Ahab's family who die in the city will be eaten by dogs,
and those who die in the field will be eaten by vultures."
25(No one else so completely sold himself to what was evil in the LORD's
sight as Ahab did under the influence of his wife Jezebel. 26His worst outrage
was worshiping idols* just as the Amorites had done—the people whom the
LORD had driven out from the land ahead of the Israelites.)
27But when Ahab heard this message, he tore his clothing, dressed in bur-
lap, and fasted. He even slept in burlap and went about in deep mourning.
28Then another message from the LORD came to Elijah: 29"Do you see
how Ahab has humbled himself before me? Because he has done this, I will
not do what I promised during his lifetime. It will happen to his sons; I will
destroy his dynasty."

Jehoshaphat and Ahab

22 For three years there was no war between Aram and Israel. 2Then
during the third year, King Jehoshaphat of Judah went to visit King
Ahab of Israel. 3During the visit, the king of Israel said to his officials, "Do
you realize that the town of Ramoth-gilead belongs to us? And yet we've
done nothing to recapture it from the king of Aram!"
4Then he turned to Jehoshaphat and asked, "Will you join me in battle to
recover Ramoth-gilead?"
Jehoshaphat replied to the king of Israel, "Why, of course! You and I are
as one. My troops are your troops, and my horses are your horses." 5Then
Jehoshaphat added, "But first let's find out what the LORD says."
6So the king of Israel summoned the prophets, about 400 of them, and
asked them, "Should I go to war against Ramoth-gilead, or should I hold
back?"
They all replied, "Yes, go right ahead! The Lord will give the king victory."
7But Jehoshaphat asked, "Is there not also a prophet of the LORD here?
We should ask him the same question."
8The king of Israel replied to Jehoshaphat, "There is one more man who
could consult the LORD for us, but I hate him. He never prophesies anything
but trouble for me! His name is Micaiah son of Imlah."
Jehoshaphat replied, "That's not the way a king should talk! Let's hear
what he has to say."
9So the king of Israel called one of his officials and said, "Quick! Bring
Micaiah son of Imlah."

21:21 As in Greek version; Hebrew lacks *So now the LORD says.* 21:23 As in several Hebrew manuscripts, Syriac, and Latin Vulgate (see also 2 Kgs 9:26, 36); most Hebrew manuscripts read *at the city wall.* 21:26 The Hebrew term (literally *round things*) probably alludes to dung.

Micaiah Prophesies against Ahab
10King Ahab of Israel and King Jehoshaphat of Judah, dressed in their royal
robes, were sitting on thrones at the threshing floor near the gate of Samaria.
All of Ahab's prophets were prophesying there in front of them. 11One of
them, Zedekiah son of Kenaanah, made some iron horns and proclaimed,
"This is what the LORD says: With these horns you will gore the Arameans
to death!"
12All the other prophets agreed. "Yes," they said, "go up to Ramoth-gilead
and be victorious, for the LORD will give the king victory!"
13Meanwhile, the messenger who went to get Micaiah said to him, "Look,
all the prophets are promising victory for the king. Be sure that you agree
with them and promise success."
14But Micaiah replied, "As surely as the LORD lives, I will say only what
the LORD tells me to say."
15When Micaiah arrived before the king, Ahab asked him, "Micaiah,
should we go to war against Ramoth-gilead, or should we hold back?"
Micaiah replied sarcastically, "Yes, go up and be victorious, for the LORD
will give the king victory!"
16But the king replied sharply, "How many times must I demand that you
speak only the truth to me when you speak for the LORD?"
17Then Micaiah told him, "In a vision I saw all Israel scattered on the
mountains, like sheep without a shepherd. And the LORD said, 'Their mas-
ter has been killed.* Send them home in peace.'"
18"Didn't I tell you?" the king of Israel exclaimed to Jehoshaphat. "He
never prophesies anything but trouble for me."
19Then Micaiah continued, "Listen to what the LORD says! I saw the LORD
sitting on his throne with all the armies of heaven around him, on his right
and on his left. 20And the LORD said, 'Who can entice Ahab to go into battle
against Ramoth-gilead so he can be killed?'
"There were many suggestions, 21and finally a spirit approached the LORD
and said, 'I can do it!'
22"'How will you do this?' the LORD asked.
"And the spirit replied, 'I will go out and inspire all of Ahab's prophets
to speak lies.'
"'You will succeed,' said the LORD. 'Go ahead and do it.'
23"So you see, the LORD has put a lying spirit in the mouths of all your
prophets. For the LORD has pronounced your doom."
24Then Zedekiah son of Kenaanah walked up to Micaiah and slapped him
across the face. "Since when did the Spirit of the LORD leave me to speak to
you?" he demanded.
25And Micaiah replied, "You will find out soon enough when you are try-
ing to hide in some secret room!"
26"Arrest him!" the king of Israel ordered. "Take him back to Amon, the
governor of the city, and to my son Joash. 27Give them this order from the
king: 'Put this man in prison, and feed him nothing but bread and water
until I return safely from the battle!'"
28But Micaiah replied, "If you return safely, it will mean that the LORD has
not spoken through me!" Then he added to those standing around, "Every-
one mark my words!"

22:17 Hebrew *These people have no master.*

Make a Difference

22:10-28

Only God's Words

The prophet Micaiah gives us a great character study in confidence and moral conviction. Here he confronted King Jehoshaphat of Judah and King Ahab of Israel and four hundred of Ahab's angry prophets. Talk about standing up to pressure!

It is clear that Micaiah didn't do this in his own strength, however. Micaiah committed himself to say only what the Lord told him to say. When pressed to speak the Lord's words, Micaiah gave them a vision of "Israel scattered on the mountains, like sheep without a shepherd" (v. 17).

Clearly, Micaiah was speaking on behalf of the Lord. The kings and prophets who heard him were incensed and ordered him arrested. He would be in good company. Jesus would later repeat this same heartbreaking vision (Matthew 9:36), and he would have the same moral fortitude when pressured to speak (John 12:49).

Difference Maker

What kind of pressure are you facing that goes against your faith? Study Micaiah's courage in this chapter and ask the Lord to ground you with the same conviction as this prophet.

The Death of Ahab

29 So King Ahab of Israel and King Jehoshaphat of Judah led their armies
against Ramoth-gilead. 30 The king of Israel said to Jehoshaphat, "As we go
into battle, I will disguise myself so no one will recognize me, but you wear
your royal robes." So the king of Israel disguised himself, and they went
into battle.

31 Meanwhile, the king of Aram had issued these orders to his thirty-two
chariot commanders: "Attack only the king of Israel. Don't bother with any-
one else!" 32 So when the Aramean chariot commanders saw Jehoshaphat
in his royal robes, they went after him. "There is the king of Israel!" they
shouted. But when Jehoshaphat called out, 33 the chariot commanders real-
ized he was not the king of Israel, and they stopped chasing him.

34 An Aramean soldier, however, randomly shot an arrow at the Israelite
troops and hit the king of Israel between the joints of his armor. "Turn the
horses* and get me out of here!" Ahab groaned to the driver of his chariot.
"I'm badly wounded!"

35 The battle raged all that day, and the king remained propped up in his
chariot facing the Arameans. The blood from his wound ran down to the
floor of his chariot, and as evening arrived he died. 36 Just as the sun was
setting, the cry ran through his troops: "We're done for! Run for your lives!"

37 So the king died, and his body was taken to Samaria and buried there.
38 Then his chariot was washed beside the pool of Samaria, and dogs came
and licked his blood at the place where the prostitutes bathed,* just as the
LORD had promised.

39 The rest of the events in Ahab's reign and everything he did, including
the story of the ivory palace and the towns he built, are recorded in *The Book
of the History of the Kings of Israel.* 40 So Ahab died, and his son Ahaziah became
the next king.

Jehoshaphat Rules in Judah

41 Jehoshaphat son of Asa began to rule over Judah in the fourth year of King
Ahab's reign in Israel. 42 Jehoshaphat was thirty-five years old when he be-
came king, and he reigned in Jerusalem twenty-five years. His mother was
Azubah, the daughter of Shilhi.

43 Jehoshaphat was a good king, following the example of his father, Asa.
He did what was pleasing in the LORD's sight. *During his reign, however,
he failed to remove all the pagan shrines, and the people still offered sac-
rifices and burned incense there. 44 Jehoshaphat also made peace with the
king of Israel.

45 The rest of the events in Jehoshaphat's reign, the extent of his power,
and the wars he waged are recorded in *The Book of the History of the Kings of Ju-
dah.* 46 He banished from the land the rest of the male and female shrine pros-
titutes, who still continued their practices from the days of his father, Asa.

47 (There was no king in Edom at that time, only a deputy.)

48 Jehoshaphat also built a fleet of trading ships* to sail to Ophir for gold. But
the ships never set sail, for they met with disaster in their home port of Ezion-
geber. 49 At one time Ahaziah son of Ahab had proposed to Jehoshaphat, "Let
my men sail with your men in the ships." But Jehoshaphat refused the request.

22:34 Hebrew *Turn your hand.* 22:38 Or *his blood, and the prostitutes bathed [in it];* or *his blood, and they washed his armor.* 22:43 Verses 22:43b-53 are numbered 22:44-54 in Hebrew text. 22:48 Hebrew *fleet of ships of Tarshish.*

[50] When Jehoshaphat died, he was buried with his ancestors in the City of
David. Then his son Jehoram became the next king.

Ahaziah Rules in Israel

[51] Ahaziah son of Ahab began to rule over Israel in the seventeenth year of
King Jehoshaphat's reign in Judah. He reigned in Samaria two years. [52] But
he did what was evil in the LORD's sight, following the example of his father
and mother and the example of Jeroboam son of Nebat, who had led Israel to
sin. [53] He served Baal and worshiped him, provoking the anger of the LORD,
the God of Israel, just as his father had done.

Question 22:53

The last verse of 1 Kings draws out the spiritual muddle that God's people had gotten themselves into. If you could summarize how they got to this point, what would you say? How could they have avoided this mess?

2 Kings Introduction

The battle of thrones and spiritual warfare continues in this sequel to 1 Kings. The story opens with God's people still in turmoil. The story ends with God's people in even greater turmoil. The pages go back and forth between the soulless Northern Kingdom (Israel) and the nauseating roller coaster of the Southern Kingdom (Judah).

Still, all along the way, through the generations of unfaithful rulers and populations, the Lord raised up great prophets and priests and powerful kings to remind the people that he was still there, that he was still in charge, and that he would still work out his plan of salvation.

Some of the greatest stories in Scripture happened unexpectedly with the turn of a page in 2 Kings. There are stories of chariots of fire, of the dead coming to life, of bears mauling boys, of struggling souls, of inspiring young kings, of frightening madmen (and madwomen!). This is not a book for the faint of heart nor the queasy of stomach. You might need a bottle of antacids next to you as you try to digest some of the worst that humanity dishes up.

You will also see God's redemptive story arc through the promise and potential of the people who choose to follow the Lord. Let that be the filter of your heart as you work your way through this gut-wrenchingly, incredibly surprising account of God's people.

Story Arcs

- **Elijah**
- **Elisha**
- **Joash**
- **Jehoiada**
- **Hezekiah**
- **Isaiah**
- **Josiah**
- **Jesus**

2 Kings

Elijah Confronts King Ahaziah

1 After King Ahab's death, the land of Moab rebelled against Israel.
2 One day Israel's new king, Ahaziah, fell through the latticework of
an upper room at his palace in Samaria and was seriously injured. So he sent
messengers to the temple of Baal-zebub, the god of Ekron, to ask whether
he would recover.
3 But the angel of the LORD told Elijah, who was from Tishbe, "Go and
confront the messengers of the king of Samaria and ask them, 'Is there no
God in Israel? Why are you going to Baal-zebub, the god of Ekron, to ask
whether the king will recover? 4 Now, therefore, this is what the LORD says:
You will never leave the bed you are lying on; you will surely die.'" So Elijah
went to deliver the message.
5 When the messengers returned to the king, he asked them, "Why have
you returned so soon?"
6 They replied, "A man came up to us and told us to go back to the king and
give him this message. 'This is what the LORD says: Is there no God in Israel?
Why are you sending men to Baal-zebub, the god of Ekron, to ask whether
you will recover? Therefore, because you have done this, you will never leave
the bed you are lying on; you will surely die.'"
7 "What sort of man was he?" the king demanded. "What did he look like?"
8 They replied, "He was a hairy man,* and he wore a leather belt around
his waist."
"Elijah from Tishbe!" the king exclaimed.
9 Then he sent an army captain with fifty soldiers to arrest him. They found
him sitting on top of a hill. The captain said to him, "Man of God, the king
has commanded you to come down with us."
10 But Elijah replied to the captain, "If I am a man of God, let fire come
down from heaven and destroy you and your fifty men!" Then fire fell from
heaven and killed them all.
11 So the king sent another captain with fifty men. The captain said to him,
"Man of God, the king demands that you come down at once."
12 Elijah replied, "If I am a man of God, let fire come down from heaven
and destroy you and your fifty men!" And again the fire of God fell from
heaven and killed them all.
13 Once more the king sent a third captain with fifty men. But this time
the captain went up the hill and fell to his knees before Elijah. He pleaded
with him, "O man of God, please spare my life and the lives of these, your
fifty servants. 14 See how the fire from heaven came down and destroyed the
first two groups. But now please spare my life!"
15 Then the angel of the LORD said to Elijah, "Go down with him, and don't
be afraid of him." So Elijah got up and went with him to the king.

1:8 Or *He was wearing clothing made of hair.*

Story Arc **1:3**

● Elijah

Many people consider Elijah to be the most powerful prophet to have lived. He battled hundreds of wizards of Baal, he performed astonishing miracles, and he raised a child from the dead. He also spent much of his life confronting and escaping the extremely wicked rulers of the Northern Kingdom (Israel), King Ahab and his wife, Jezebel. Most incredibly, perhaps, Elijah had a direct encounter with the Lord that echoed the personal face-to-face conversations that Moses had with God.

It is significant, then, that Jesus met with both Moses and Elijah during an incredible moment witnessed by three of Jesus' disciples—an event we now call the transfiguration. Take a moment to turn in your Bible to Matthew 17 to read about and imagine this incredible face-to-face conversation among Moses, Elijah, and the One they both had been looking forward to.

2 Kgs 2:1 ►

16 And Elijah said to the king, "This is what the LORD says: Why did you send messengers to Baal-zebub, the god of Ekron, to ask whether you will recover? Is there no God in Israel to answer your question? Therefore, because you have done this, you will never leave the bed you are lying on; you will surely die."

17 So Ahaziah died, just as the LORD had promised through Elijah. Since Ahaziah did not have a son to succeed him, his brother Joram* became the next king. This took place in the second year of the reign of Jehoram son of Jehoshaphat, king of Judah.

18 The rest of the events in Ahaziah's reign and everything he did are recorded in *The Book of the History of the Kings of Israel.*

Elijah Taken into Heaven

2 When the LORD was about to take Elijah up to heaven in a whirlwind, Elijah and Elisha were traveling from Gilgal. 2 And Elijah said to Elisha, "Stay here, for the LORD has told me to go to Bethel."

But Elisha replied, "As surely as the LORD lives and you yourself live, I will never leave you!" So they went down together to Bethel.

3 The group of prophets from Bethel came to Elisha and asked him, "Did you know that the LORD is going to take your master away from you today?"

"Of course I know," Elisha answered. "But be quiet about it."

4 Then Elijah said to Elisha, "Stay here, for the LORD has told me to go to Jericho."

But Elisha replied again, "As surely as the LORD lives and you yourself live, I will never leave you." So they went on together to Jericho.

5 Then the group of prophets from Jericho came to Elisha and asked him, "Did you know that the LORD is going to take your master away from you today?"

"Of course I know," Elisha answered. "But be quiet about it."

6 Then Elijah said to Elisha, "Stay here, for the LORD has told me to go to the Jordan River."

But again Elisha replied, "As surely as the LORD lives and you yourself live, I will never leave you." So they went on together.

7 Fifty men from the group of prophets also went and watched from a distance as Elijah and Elisha stopped beside the Jordan River. 8 Then Elijah folded his cloak together and struck the water with it. The river divided, and the two of them went across on dry ground!

9 When they came to the other side, Elijah said to Elisha, "Tell me what I can do for you before I am taken away."

And Elisha replied, "Please let me inherit a double share of your spirit and become your successor."

10 "You have asked a difficult thing," Elijah replied. "If you see me when I am taken from you, then you will get your request. But if not, then you won't."

11 As they were walking along and talking, suddenly a chariot of fire appeared, drawn by horses of fire. It drove between the two men, separating them, and Elijah was carried by a whirlwind into heaven. 12 Elisha saw it and cried out, "My father! My father! I see the chariots and charioteers of Israel!" And as they disappeared from sight, Elisha tore his clothes in distress.

1:17 Hebrew *Jehoram,* a variant spelling of Joram.

Question **2:9**

Would you be bold enough to ask for something like this from your mentor? How does a request like this show respect for someone who paved the trail before you?

Story Arc **2:1**

Elisha

Elisha was Elijah's go-to guy. In 1 Kings 19, Elijah put his cloak across Elisha's shoulders to indicate that Elijah was choosing him to be his apprentice. In 2 Kings 2, Elijah left his cloak on the ground when he was taken up into heaven. Soon after, people began to take note that "Elijah's spirit rests upon Elisha!" (v. 15).

You'll find that Elisha was cut from the same cloth as Elijah. They both had the same sarcastic wit. They both were powerful prophets, confronting kings and wicked strongmen. They both performed healings and wonders not seen since Moses and Joshua's days. Their great miracles wouldn't be seen again until Jesus walked the same paths hundreds of years later.

What can we learn from the apprenticeship that Elijah and Elisha had? How did Elijah's investment in Elisha affect the younger man? Whom do you have as a mentor in your life—and what kind of an effect are they having on you?

2 Kgs 11:1-3 ►

13Elisha picked up Elijah's cloak, which had fallen when he was taken up.
Then Elisha returned to the bank of the Jordan River. 14He struck the water
with Elijah's cloak and cried out, "Where is the LORD, the God of Elijah?"
Then the river divided, and Elisha went across.
15When the group of prophets from Jericho saw from a distance what
happened, they exclaimed, "Elijah's spirit rests upon Elisha!" And they went
to meet him and bowed to the ground before him. 16"Sir," they said, "just
say the word and fifty of our strongest men will search the wilderness for
your master. Perhaps the Spirit of the LORD has left him on some mountain
or in some valley."
"No," Elisha said, "don't send them." 17But they kept urging him until
they shamed him into agreeing, and he finally said, "All right, send them."
So fifty men searched for three days but did not find Elijah. 18Elisha was
still at Jericho when they returned. "Didn't I tell you not to go?" he asked.

Elisha's First Miracles

19One day the leaders of the town of Jericho visited Elisha. "We have a prob-
lem, my lord," they told him. "This town is located in pleasant surroundings,
as you can see. But the water is bad, and the land is unproductive."
20Elisha said, "Bring me a new bowl with salt in it." So they brought it to
him. 21Then he went out to the spring that supplied the town with water
and threw the salt into it. And he said, "This is what the LORD says: I have
purified this water. It will no longer cause death or infertility.*" 22And the
water has remained pure ever since, just as Elisha said.
23Elisha left Jericho and went up to Bethel. As he was walking along the
road, a group of boys from the town began mocking and making fun of him.
"Go away, baldy!" they chanted. "Go away, baldy!" 24Elisha turned around
and looked at them, and he cursed them in the name of the LORD. Then two
bears came out of the woods and mauled forty-two of them. 25From there
Elisha went to Mount Carmel and finally returned to Samaria.

War between Israel and Moab

3 Ahab's son Joram* began to rule over Israel in the eighteenth year of
King Jehoshaphat's reign in Judah. He reigned in Samaria twelve years.
2He did what was evil in the LORD's sight, but not to the same extent as his
father and mother. He at least tore down the sacred pillar of Baal that his
father had set up. 3Nevertheless, he continued in the sins that Jeroboam son
of Nebat had committed and led the people of Israel to commit.
4King Mesha of Moab was a sheep breeder. He used to pay the king of Israel
an annual tribute of 100,000 lambs and the wool of 100,000 rams. 5But after
Ahab's death, the king of Moab rebelled against the king of Israel. 6So King
Joram promptly mustered the army of Israel and marched from Samaria.
7On the way, he sent this message to King Jehoshaphat of Judah: "The king
of Moab has rebelled against me. Will you join me in battle against him?"
And Jehoshaphat replied, "Why, of course! You and I are as one. My troops
are your troops, and my horses are your horses." 8Then Jehoshaphat asked,
"What route will we take?"
"We will attack from the wilderness of Edom," Joram replied.
9The king of Edom and his troops joined them, and all three armies

2:21 Or *or make the land unproductive;* Hebrew reads *or barrenness.* 3:1 Hebrew *Jehoram,* a variant spelling of Joram; also in 3:6.

Make a Difference

2:23-24

Insulting a Holy Man

When a gang of boys started insulting Elisha, calling him "baldy," he cursed them. Then two bears came out and mauled forty-two of them! The lesson here just might be that you shouldn't insult a prophet of God.

Could the lesson be even more profound? Jesus was infinitely more powerful than even Elisha. When people hurled insults at him, he had every right to respond in righteous wrath. No one should be allowed to insult the Son of God—the Messiah, the Almighty, the Holy One—and live. In spite of this, Jesus responded to the insults by opening his arms and taking the consequence of their sin upon himself.

Isaiah predicted that the Messiah would be "treated harshly" yet never say a word in response, and Isaiah predicted he would be "led like a lamb to the slaughter. And as a sheep is silent before the shearers, he did not open his mouth" (Isaiah 53:7). Though he could have called down curses upon his mockers, he carried their sins.

Difference Maker

Read through Elisha's ministry and take note of some similarities to and differences from Jesus. Then take a few minutes to praise the Lord for his good plan (Isaiah 53).

traveled along a roundabout route through the wilderness for seven days. But there was no water for the men or their animals.

10 "What should we do?" the king of Israel cried out. "The LORD has brought the three of us here to let the king of Moab defeat us."

11 But King Jehoshaphat of Judah asked, "Is there no prophet of the LORD with us? If there is, we can ask the LORD what to do through him."

One of King Joram's officers replied, "Elisha son of Shaphat is here. He used to be Elijah's personal assistant.*"

12 Jehoshaphat said, "Yes, the LORD speaks through him." So the king of Israel, King Jehoshaphat of Judah, and the king of Edom went to consult with Elisha.

13 "Why are you coming to me?"* Elisha asked the king of Israel. "Go to the pagan prophets of your father and mother!"

But King Joram of Israel said, "No! For it was the LORD who called us three kings here—only to be defeated by the king of Moab!"

14 Elisha replied, "As surely as the LORD Almighty lives, whom I serve, I wouldn't even bother with you except for my respect for King Jehoshaphat of Judah. 15 Now bring me someone who can play the harp."

While the harp was being played, the power* of the LORD came upon Elisha, 16 and he said, "This is what the LORD says: This dry valley will be filled with pools of water! 17 You will see neither wind nor rain, says the LORD, but this valley will be filled with water. You will have plenty for yourselves and your cattle and other animals. 18 But this is only a simple thing for the LORD, for he will make you victorious over the army of Moab! 19 You will conquer the best of their towns, even the fortified ones. You will cut down all their good trees, stop up all their springs, and ruin all their good land with stones."

20 The next day at about the time when the morning sacrifice was offered, water suddenly appeared! It was flowing from the direction of Edom, and soon there was water everywhere.

21 Meanwhile, when the people of Moab heard about the three armies marching against them, they mobilized every man who was old enough to strap on a sword, and they stationed themselves along their border. 22 But when they got up the next morning, the sun was shining across the water, making it appear red to the Moabites—like blood. 23 "It's blood!" the Moabites exclaimed. "The three armies must have attacked and killed each other! Let's go, men of Moab, and collect the plunder!"

24 But when the Moabites arrived at the Israelite camp, the army of Israel rushed out and attacked them until they turned and ran. The army of Israel chased them into the land of Moab, destroying everything as they went.* 25 They destroyed the towns, covered their good land with stones, stopped up all the springs, and cut down all the good trees. Finally, only Kir-hareseth and its stone walls were left, but men with slings surrounded and attacked it.

26 When the king of Moab saw that he was losing the battle, he led 700 of his swordsmen in a desperate attempt to break through the enemy lines near the king of Edom, but they failed. 27 Then the king of Moab took his oldest son, who would have been the next king, and sacrificed him as a burnt offering on the wall. So there was great anger against Israel,* and the Israelites withdrew and returned to their own land.

3:11 Hebrew *He used to pour water on the hands of Elijah.* 3:13 Hebrew *What is there in common between you and me?* 3:15 Hebrew *the hand.* 3:24 The meaning of the Hebrew is uncertain. 3:27 Or *So Israel's anger was great.* The meaning of the Hebrew is uncertain.

Elisha Helps a Poor Widow

4 One day the widow of a member of the group of prophets came to Eli-
sha and cried out, "My husband who served you is dead, and you know
how he feared the LORD. But now a creditor has come, threatening to take
my two sons as slaves."
2 "What can I do to help you?" Elisha asked. "Tell me, what do you have
in the house?"
"Nothing at all, except a flask of olive oil," she replied.
3 And Elisha said, "Borrow as many empty jars as you can from your friends
and neighbors. 4 Then go into your house with your sons and shut the door
behind you. Pour olive oil from your flask into the jars, setting each one
aside when it is filled."
5 So she did as she was told. Her sons kept bringing jars to her, and she
filled one after another. 6 Soon every container was full to the brim!
"Bring me another jar," she said to one of her sons.
"There aren't any more!" he told her. And then the olive oil stopped
flowing.
7 When she told the man of God what had happened, he said to her, "Now
sell the olive oil and pay your debts, and you and your sons can live on what
is left over."

Elisha and the Woman from Shunem

8 One day Elisha went to the town of Shunem. A wealthy woman lived there,
and she urged him to come to her home for a meal. After that, whenever he
passed that way, he would stop there for something to eat.
9 She said to her husband, "I am sure this man who stops in from time to
time is a holy man of God. 10 Let's build a small room for him on the roof and
furnish it with a bed, a table, a chair, and a lamp. Then he will have a place
to stay whenever he comes by."
11 One day Elisha returned to Shunem, and he went up to this upper room
to rest. 12 He said to his servant Gehazi, "Tell the woman from Shunem I want
to speak to her." When she appeared, 13 Elisha said to Gehazi, "Tell her, 'We
appreciate the kind concern you have shown us. What can we do for you? Can
we put in a good word for you to the king or to the commander of the army?'"
"No," she replied, "my family takes good care of me."
14 Later Elisha asked Gehazi, "What can we do for her?"
Gehazi replied, "She doesn't have a son, and her husband is an old man."
15 "Call her back again," Elisha told him. When the woman returned, Eli-
sha said to her as she stood in the doorway, 16 "Next year at this time you will
be holding a son in your arms!"
"No, my lord!" she cried. "O man of God, don't deceive me and get my
hopes up like that."
17 But sure enough, the woman soon became pregnant. And at that time
the following year she had a son, just as Elisha had said.
18 One day when her child was older, he went out to help his father, who
was working with the harvesters. 19 Suddenly he cried out, "My head hurts!
My head hurts!"
His father said to one of the servants, "Carry him home to his mother."
20 So the servant took him home, and his mother held him on her lap. But
around noontime he died. 21 She carried him up and laid him on the bed of

Questions I want to ask

Question 4:8-27

When the woman fell to the ground and grabbed hold of Elisha's feet, Gehazi tried to remove her for being disrespectful. Elisha had compassion on her and instructed him, "Leave her alone. She is deeply troubled" (v. 27). How can you learn from Elisha's example? When people are suffering and become undignified in their actions, what sorts of things could you do to show compassion?

Question 4:32-37

Compare this story of Elisha's with Luke 7:11-20. What reasons did people have for asking if Jesus was the Messiah they had been expecting?

the man of God, then shut the door and left him there.
22 She sent a message
to her husband: "Send one of the servants and a donkey so that I can hurry
to the man of God and come right back."
23 "Why go today?" he asked. "It is neither a new moon festival nor a
Sabbath."
But she said, "It will be all right."
24 So she saddled the donkey and said to the servant, "Hurry! Don't slow
down unless I tell you to."
25 As she approached the man of God at Mount Carmel, Elisha saw her in
the distance. He said to Gehazi, "Look, the woman from Shunem is coming.
26 Run out to meet her and ask her, 'Is everything all right with you, your
husband, and your child?'"
"Yes," the woman told Gehazi, "everything is fine."
27 But when she came to the man of God at the mountain, she fell to the
ground before him and caught hold of his feet. Gehazi began to push her
away, but the man of God said, "Leave her alone. She is deeply troubled, but
the LORD has not told me what it is."
28 Then she said, "Did I ask you for a son, my lord? And didn't I say, 'Don't
deceive me and get my hopes up'?"
29 Then Elisha said to Gehazi, "Get ready to travel*; take my staff and go!
Don't talk to anyone along the way. Go quickly and lay the staff on the child's
face."
30 But the boy's mother said, "As surely as the LORD lives and you yourself
live, I won't go home unless you go with me." So Elisha returned with her.
31 Gehazi hurried on ahead and laid the staff on the child's face, but nothing happened. There was no sign of life. He returned to meet Elisha and told
him, "The child is still dead."
32 When Elisha arrived, the child was indeed dead, lying there on the
prophet's bed.
33 He went in alone and shut the door behind him and prayed
to the LORD.
34 Then he lay down on the child's body, placing his mouth on
the child's mouth, his eyes on the child's eyes, and his hands on the child's
hands. And as he stretched out on him, the child's body began to grow warm
again!
35 Elisha got up, walked back and forth across the room once, and then
stretched himself out again on the child. This time the boy sneezed seven
times and opened his eyes!
36 Then Elisha summoned Gehazi. "Call the child's mother!" he said. And
when she came in, Elisha said, "Here, take your son!"
37 She fell at his feet
and bowed before him, overwhelmed with gratitude. Then she took her son
in her arms and carried him downstairs.

Miracles during a Famine

38 Elisha now returned to Gilgal, and there was a famine in the land. One
day as the group of prophets was seated before him, he said to his servant,
"Put a large pot on the fire, and make some stew for the rest of the group."
39 One of the young men went out into the field to gather herbs and came
back with a pocketful of wild gourds. He shredded them and put them into
the pot without realizing they were poisonous.
40 Some of the stew was served
to the men. But after they had eaten a bite or two they cried out, "Man of
God, there's poison in this stew!" So they would not eat it.

4:29 Hebrew *Bind up your loins.*

41 Elisha said, "Bring me some flour." Then he threw it into the pot and
said, "Now it's all right; go ahead and eat." And then it did not harm them.
42 One day a man from Baal-shalishah brought the man of God a sack of
fresh grain and twenty loaves of barley bread made from the first grain of
his harvest. Elisha said, "Give it to the people so they can eat."
43 "What?" his servant exclaimed. "Feed a hundred people with only this?"
But Elisha repeated, "Give it to the people so they can eat, for this is what
the LORD says: Everyone will eat, and there will even be some left over!"
44 And when they gave it to the people, there was plenty for all and some left
over, just as the LORD had promised.

The Healing of Naaman

5 The king of Aram had great admiration for Naaman, the commander of
his army, because through him the LORD had given Aram great victories.
But though Naaman was a mighty warrior, he suffered from leprosy.*
2 At this time Aramean raiders had invaded the land of Israel, and among
their captives was a young girl who had been given to Naaman's wife as a
maid. 3 One day the girl said to her mistress, "I wish my master would go to
see the prophet in Samaria. He would heal him of his leprosy."
4 So Naaman told the king what the young girl from Israel had said. 5 "Go
and visit the prophet," the king of Aram told him. "I will send a letter of
introduction for you to take to the king of Israel." So Naaman started out,
carrying as gifts 750 pounds of silver, 150 pounds of gold,* and ten sets of
clothing. 6 The letter to the king of Israel said: "With this letter I present my
servant Naaman. I want you to heal him of his leprosy."
7 When the king of Israel read the letter, he tore his clothes in dismay and
said, "Am I God, that I can give life and take it away? Why is this man ask-
ing me to heal someone with leprosy? I can see that he's just trying to pick
a fight with me."
8 But when Elisha, the man of God, heard that the king of Israel had torn his
clothes in dismay, he sent this message to him: "Why are you so upset? Send
Naaman to me, and he will learn that there is a true prophet here in Israel."
9 So Naaman went with his horses and chariots and waited at the door of
Elisha's house. 10 But Elisha sent a messenger out to him with this message:
"Go and wash yourself seven times in the Jordan River. Then your skin will
be restored, and you will be healed of your leprosy."
11 But Naaman became angry and stalked away. "I thought he would cer-
tainly come out to meet me!" he said. "I expected him to wave his hand over
the leprosy and call on the name of the LORD his God and heal me! 12 Aren't
the rivers of Damascus, the Abana and the Pharpar, better than any of the
rivers of Israel? Why shouldn't I wash in them and be healed?" So Naaman
turned and went away in a rage.
13 But his officers tried to reason with him and said, "Sir,* if the prophet
had told you to do something very difficult, wouldn't you have done it? So
you should certainly obey him when he says simply, 'Go and wash and be
cured!'" 14 So Naaman went down to the Jordan River and dipped himself
seven times, as the man of God had instructed him. And his skin became as
healthy as the skin of a young child, and he was healed!

5:1 Or *from a contagious skin disease.* The Hebrew word used here and throughout this passage can describe various skin diseases. **5:5** Hebrew *10 talents* [340 kilograms] *of silver, 6,000 [shekels]* [68 kilograms] *of gold.* **5:13** Hebrew *My father.*

Make a Difference

5:1–15

Childlike Faith

Naaman was a great general for a neighboring nation, but he was suffering from a skin disease. There was a little girl who served his wife as a maid (v. 2). She urged him to go see Elisha to be healed. When he went to see Elisha, Naaman was instructed by Elisha's messenger to wash himself seven times in the Jordan River, and then he would be healed. Naaman was skeptical and upset at the instructions, but his officers pleaded with him to obey Elisha. Therefore, Naaman went down to the Jordan River and dipped himself into the water seven times. His skin became as healthy as the skin of a young child, and he was healed.

From this experience, Naaman learned that there is "no God in all the world except in Israel" (v. 15). If he had been observant, he would have also learned that he should have the faith of a child (vv. 2–3) and not a skeptical, arrogant adult.

Difference Maker

Read Matthew 18:1–7 and examine the childlikeness of your own faith.

15 Then Naaman and his entire party went back to find the man of God. They stood before him, and Naaman said, "Now I know that there is no God in all the world except in Israel. So please accept a gift from your servant."

16 But Elisha replied, "As surely as the LORD lives, whom I serve, I will not accept any gifts." And though Naaman urged him to take the gift, Elisha refused.

17 Then Naaman said, "All right, but please allow me to load two of my mules with earth from this place, and I will take it back home with me. From now on I will never again offer burnt offerings or sacrifices to any other god except the LORD. 18 However, may the LORD pardon me in this one thing: When my master the king goes into the temple of the god Rimmon to worship there and leans on my arm, may the LORD pardon me when I bow, too."

19 "Go in peace," Elisha said. So Naaman started home again.

The Greed of Gehazi

20 But Gehazi, the servant of Elisha, the man of God, said to himself, "My master should not have let this Aramean get away without accepting any of his gifts. As surely as the LORD lives, I will chase after him and get something from him." 21 So Gehazi set off after Naaman.

When Naaman saw Gehazi running after him, he climbed down from his chariot and went to meet him. "Is everything all right?" Naaman asked.

22 "Yes," Gehazi said, "but my master has sent me to tell you that two young prophets from the hill country of Ephraim have just arrived. He would like 75 pounds* of silver and two sets of clothing to give to them."

23 "By all means, take twice as much* silver," Naaman insisted. He gave him two sets of clothing, tied up the money in two bags, and sent two of his servants to carry the gifts for Gehazi. 24 But when they arrived at the citadel,* Gehazi took the gifts from the servants and sent the men back. Then he went and hid the gifts inside the house.

25 When he went in to his master, Elisha asked him, "Where have you been, Gehazi?"

"I haven't been anywhere," he replied.

26 But Elisha asked him, "Don't you realize that I was there in spirit when Naaman stepped down from his chariot to meet you? Is this the time to receive money and clothing, olive groves and vineyards, sheep and cattle, and male and female servants? 27 Because you have done this, you and your descendants will suffer from Naaman's leprosy forever." When Gehazi left the room, he was covered with leprosy; his skin was white as snow.

The Floating Ax Head

6 One day the group of prophets came to Elisha and told him, "As you can see, this place where we meet with you is too small. 2 Let's go down to the Jordan River, where there are plenty of logs. There we can build a new place for us to meet."

"All right," he told them, "go ahead."

3 "Please come with us," someone suggested.

"I will," he said. 4 So he went with them.

When they arrived at the Jordan, they began cutting down trees. 5 But as one of them was cutting a tree, his ax head fell into the river. "Oh, sir!" he cried. "It was a borrowed ax!"

5:22 Hebrew *1 talent* [34 kilograms]. 5:23 Hebrew *take 2 talents* [150 pounds or 68 kilograms]. 5:24 Hebrew *the Ophel.*

6 "Where did it fall?" the man of God asked. When he showed him the
place, Elisha cut a stick and threw it into the water at that spot. Then the
ax head floated to the surface. 7 "Grab it," Elisha said. And the man reached
out and grabbed it.

Elisha Traps the Arameans

8 When the king of Aram was at war with Israel, he would confer with his
officers and say, "We will mobilize our forces at such and such a place."

9 But immediately Elisha, the man of God, would warn the king of Israel,
"Do not go near that place, for the Arameans are planning to mobilize their
troops there." 10 So the king of Israel would send word to the place indicated
by the man of God. Time and again Elisha warned the king, so that he would
be on the alert there.

11 The king of Aram became very upset over this. He called his officers together and demanded, "Which of you is the traitor? Who has been informing
the king of Israel of my plans?"

12 "It's not us, my lord the king," one of the officers replied. "Elisha, the
prophet in Israel, tells the king of Israel even the words you speak in the
privacy of your bedroom!"

13 "Go and find out where he is," the king commanded, "so I can send
troops to seize him."

And the report came back: "Elisha is at Dothan." 14 So one night the king of
Aram sent a great army with many chariots and horses to surround the city.

15 When the servant of the man of God got up early the next morning and
went outside, there were troops, horses, and chariots everywhere. "Oh, sir,
what will we do now?" the young man cried to Elisha.

16 "Don't be afraid!" Elisha told him. "For there are more on our side
than on theirs!" 17 Then Elisha prayed, "O LORD, open his eyes and let him
see!" The LORD opened the young man's eyes, and when he looked up, he
saw that the hillside around Elisha was filled with horses and chariots
of fire.

18 As the Aramean army advanced toward him, Elisha prayed, "O LORD,
please make them blind." So the LORD struck them with blindness as Elisha had asked.

19 Then Elisha went out and told them, "You have come the wrong way!
This isn't the right city! Follow me, and I will take you to the man you are
looking for." And he led them to the city of Samaria.

20 As soon as they had entered Samaria, Elisha prayed, "O LORD, now open
their eyes and let them see." So the LORD opened their eyes, and they discovered that they were in the middle of Samaria.

21 When the king of Israel saw them, he shouted to Elisha, "My father,
should I kill them? Should I kill them?"

22 "Of course not!" Elisha replied. "Do we kill prisoners of war? Give them
food and drink and send them home again to their master."

23 So the king made a great feast for them and then sent them home to their
master. After that, the Aramean raiders stayed away from the land of Israel.

Ben-Hadad Besieges Samaria

24 Some time later, however, King Ben-hadad of Aram mustered his entire
army and besieged Samaria. 25 As a result, there was a great famine in the city.

Question 6:15-20

Elisha prayed that his servant would have his eyes opened to see. As a result, the young man saw chariots of fire filling the landscape. Ironically, then, Elisha prayed that the enemy troops would be struck with blindness. What followed was an amusing scene of surprising wit demonstrating how ingenious and powerful God is. If God could do this through Elisha, in what unexpected, creative ways could God use you today?

The siege lasted so long that a donkey's head sold for eighty pieces of silver, and a cup of dove's dung sold for five pieces* of silver.

26 One day as the king of Israel was walking along the wall of the city, a woman called to him, "Please help me, my lord the king!"

27 He answered, "If the LORD doesn't help you, what can I do? I have neither food from the threshing floor nor wine from the press to give you." 28 But then the king asked, "What is the matter?"

She replied, "This woman said to me: 'Come on, let's eat your son today, then we will eat my son tomorrow.' 29 So we cooked my son and ate him. Then the next day I said to her, 'Kill your son so we can eat him,' but she has hidden her son."

30 When the king heard this, he tore his clothes in despair. And as the king walked along the wall, the people could see that he was wearing burlap under his robe next to his skin. 31 "May God strike me and even kill me if I don't separate Elisha's head from his shoulders this very day," the king vowed.

32 Elisha was sitting in his house with the elders of Israel when the king sent a messenger to summon him. But before the messenger arrived, Elisha said to the elders, "A murderer has sent a man to cut off my head. When he arrives, shut the door and keep him out. We will soon hear his master's steps following him."

33 While Elisha was still saying this, the messenger arrived. And the king* said, "All this misery is from the LORD! Why should I wait for the LORD any longer?"

7 Elisha replied, "Listen to this message from the LORD! This is what the LORD says: By this time tomorrow in the markets of Samaria, six quarts of choice flour will cost only one piece of silver,* and twelve quarts of barley grain will cost only one piece of silver.*"

2 The officer assisting the king said to the man of God, "That couldn't happen even if the LORD opened the windows of heaven!"

But Elisha replied, "You will see it happen with your own eyes, but you won't be able to eat any of it!"

Outcasts Visit the Enemy Camp

3 Now there were four men with leprosy* sitting at the entrance of the city gates. "Why should we sit here waiting to die?" they asked each other. 4 "We will starve if we stay here, but with the famine in the city, we will starve if we go back there. So we might as well go out and surrender to the Aramean army. If they let us live, so much the better. But if they kill us, we would have died anyway."

5 So at twilight they set out for the camp of the Arameans. But when they came to the edge of the camp, no one was there! 6 For the Lord had caused the Aramean army to hear the clatter of speeding chariots and the galloping of horses and the sounds of a great army approaching. "The king of Israel has hired the Hittites and Egyptians* to attack us!" they cried to one another.

6:25 Hebrew *sold for 80 [shekels]* [2 pounds or 0.9 kilograms] *of silver, and ¼ of a cab* [0.3 liters] *of dove's dung sold for 5 [shekels]* [2 ounces or 57 grams]. *Dove's dung* may be a variety of wild vegetable. 6:33 Hebrew *he.* 7:1a Hebrew *1 seah* [7.3 liters] *of choice flour will cost 1 shekel* [0.4 ounces or 11 grams]; also in 7:16, 18. 7:1b Hebrew *2 seahs* [14.6 liters] *of barley grain will cost 1 shekel* [0.4 ounces or 11 grams]; also in 7:16, 18. 7:3 Or *with a contagious skin disease.* The Hebrew word used here and throughout this passage can describe various skin diseases. 7:6 Possibly *and the people of Muzur,* a district near Cilicia.

7 So they panicked and ran into the night, abandoning their tents, horses,
donkeys, and everything else, as they fled for their lives.
8 When the men with leprosy arrived at the edge of the camp, they went
into one tent after another, eating and drinking wine; and they carried off
silver and gold and clothing and hid it. 9 Finally, they said to each other, "This
is not right. This is a day of good news, and we aren't sharing it with anyone!
If we wait until morning, some calamity will certainly fall upon us. Come
on, let's go back and tell the people at the palace."
10 So they went back to the city and told the gatekeepers what had hap-
pened. "We went out to the Aramean camp," they said, "and no one was
there! The horses and donkeys were tethered and the tents were all in order,
but there wasn't a single person around!" 11 Then the gatekeepers shouted
the news to the people in the palace.

Prayer **7:9**

Lord Jesus, help me be so changed by your good news that I can't help but share it with others. Amen.

Israel Plunders the Camp

12 The king got out of bed in the middle of the night and told his officers, "I
know what has happened. The Arameans know we are starving, so they have
left their camp and have hidden in the fields. They are expecting us to leave
the city, and then they will take us alive and capture the city."
13 One of his officers replied, "We had better send out scouts to check into
this. Let them take five of the remaining horses. If something happens to
them, it will be no worse than if they stay here and die with the rest of us."
14 So two chariots with horses were prepared, and the king sent scouts to
see what had happened to the Aramean army. 15 They went all the way to the
Jordan River, following a trail of clothing and equipment that the Arameans
had thrown away in their mad rush to escape. The scouts returned and told
the king about it. 16 Then the people of Samaria rushed out and plundered
the Aramean camp. So it was true that six quarts of choice flour were sold
that day for one piece of silver, and twelve quarts of barley grain were sold
for one piece of silver, just as the LORD had promised. 17 The king appointed
his officer to control the traffic at the gate, but he was knocked down and
trampled to death as the people rushed out.

So everything happened exactly as the man of God had predicted when
the king came to his house. 18 The man of God had said to the king, "By this
time tomorrow in the markets of Samaria, six quarts of choice flour will
cost one piece of silver, and twelve quarts of barley grain will cost one piece
of silver."
19 The king's officer had replied, "That couldn't happen even if the LORD
opened the windows of heaven!" And the man of God had said, "You will see
it happen with your own eyes, but you won't be able to eat any of it!" 20 And
so it was, for the people trampled him to death at the gate!

The Woman from Shunem Returns Home

8 Elisha had told the woman whose son he had brought back to life, "Take
your family and move to some other place, for the LORD has called for
a famine on Israel that will last for seven years." 2 So the woman did as the
man of God instructed. She took her family and settled in the land of the
Philistines for seven years.
3 After the famine ended she returned from the land of the Philistines, and
she went to see the king about getting back her house and land. 4 As she came

Question 8:1-6

The woman whose son had been brought back to life became an unexpected witness. She was asked to tell her story to the king. Her testimony was personal and true. It was what she had experienced, told from her perspective, without embellishment or additional information. She simply told the king what she had seen. If someone asked you to share what you had seen God do (even if it wasn't as dramatic as the woman's testimony), what would you say?

in, the king was talking with Gehazi, the servant of the man of God. The king
had just said, "Tell me some stories about the great things Elisha has done."
5 And Gehazi was telling the king about the time Elisha had brought a boy
back to life. At that very moment, the mother of the boy walked in to make
her appeal to the king about her house and land.
"Look, my lord the king!" Gehazi exclaimed. "Here is the woman now,
and this is her son—the very one Elisha brought back to life!"
6 "Is this true?" the king asked her. And she told him the story. So he di-
rected one of his officials to see that everything she had lost was restored to
her, including the value of any crops that had been harvested during her
absence.

Hazael Murders Ben-Hadad

7 Elisha went to Damascus, the capital of Aram, where King Ben-hadad lay
sick. When someone told the king that the man of God had come, 8 the king
said to Hazael, "Take a gift to the man of God. Then tell him to ask the LORD,
'Will I recover from this illness?'"
9 So Hazael loaded down forty camels with the finest products of Damas-
cus as a gift for Elisha. He went to him and said, "Your servant Ben-hadad,
the king of Aram, has sent me to ask, 'Will I recover from this illness?'"
10 And Elisha replied, "Go and tell him, 'You will surely recover.' But ac-
tually the LORD has shown me that he will surely die!" 11 Elisha stared at
Hazael* with a fixed gaze until Hazael became uneasy.* Then the man of
God started weeping.
12 "What's the matter, my lord?" Hazael asked him.
Elisha replied, "I know the terrible things you will do to the people of
Israel. You will burn their fortified cities, kill their young men with the
sword, dash their little children to the ground, and rip open their pregnant
women!"
13 Hazael responded, "How could a nobody like me* ever accomplish such
great things?"
Elisha answered, "The LORD has shown me that you are going to be the
king of Aram."
14 When Hazael left Elisha and went back, the king asked him, "What did
Elisha tell you?"
And Hazael replied, "He told me that you will surely recover."
15 But the next day Hazael took a blanket, soaked it in water, and held it
over the king's face until he died. Then Hazael became the next king of Aram.

Jehoram Rules in Judah

16 Jehoram son of King Jehoshaphat of Judah began to rule over Judah in the
fifth year of the reign of Joram son of Ahab, king of Israel. 17 Jehoram was
thirty-two years old when he became king, and he reigned in Jerusalem eight
years. 18 But Jehoram followed the example of the kings of Israel and was as
wicked as King Ahab, for he had married one of Ahab's daughters. So Jeho-
ram did what was evil in the LORD's sight. 19 But the LORD did not want to
destroy Judah, for he had promised his servant David that his descendants
would continue to rule, shining like a lamp forever.
20 During Jehoram's reign, the Edomites revolted against Judah and

8:11a Hebrew *He stared at him.* **8:11b** The meaning of the Hebrew is uncertain. **8:13** Hebrew *a dog.*

crowned their own king. 21 So Jehoram* went with all his chariots to attack
the town of Zair.* The Edomites surrounded him and his chariot command-
ers, but he went out at night and attacked them* under cover of darkness.
But Jehoram's army deserted him and fled to their homes. 22 So Edom has
been independent from Judah to this day. The town of Libnah also revolted
about that same time.
23 The rest of the events in Jehoram's reign and everything he did are re-
corded in *The Book of the History of the Kings of Judah.* 24 When Jehoram died,
he was buried with his ancestors in the City of David. Then his son Ahaziah
became the next king.

Ahaziah Rules in Judah

25 Ahaziah son of Jehoram began to rule over Judah in the twelfth year of the
reign of Joram son of Ahab, king of Israel.
26 Ahaziah was twenty-two years old when he became king, and he reigned
in Jerusalem one year. His mother was Athaliah, a granddaughter of King
Omri of Israel. 27 Ahaziah followed the evil example of King Ahab's family.
He did what was evil in the LORD's sight, just as Ahab's family had done, for
he was related by marriage to the family of Ahab.
28 Ahaziah joined Joram son of Ahab in his war against King Hazael of
Aram at Ramoth-gilead. When the Arameans wounded King Joram in the
battle, 29 he returned to Jezreel to recover from the wounds he had received
at Ramoth.* Because Joram was wounded, King Ahaziah of Judah went to
Jezreel to visit him.

Jehu Anointed King of Israel

9 Meanwhile, Elisha the prophet had summoned a member of the group
of prophets. "Get ready to travel,"* he told him, "and take this flask of
olive oil with you. Go to Ramoth-gilead, 2 and find Jehu son of Jehoshaphat,
son of Nimshi. Call him into a private room away from his friends, 3 and pour
the oil over his head. Say to him, 'This is what the LORD says: I anoint you to
be the king over Israel.' Then open the door and run for your life!"
4 So the young prophet did as he was told and went to Ramoth-gilead.
5 When he arrived there, he found Jehu sitting around with the other army
officers. "I have a message for you, Commander," he said.
"For which one of us?" Jehu asked.
"For you, Commander," he replied.
6 So Jehu left the others and went into the house. Then the young prophet
poured the oil over Jehu's head and said, "This is what the LORD, the God
of Israel, says: I anoint you king over the LORD's people, Israel. 7 You are to
destroy the family of Ahab, your master. In this way, I will avenge the mur-
der of my prophets and all the LORD's servants who were killed by Jezebel.
8 The entire family of Ahab must be wiped out. I will destroy every one of
his male descendants, slave and free alike, anywhere in Israel. 9 I will destroy
the family of Ahab as I destroyed the families of Jeroboam son of Nebat and
of Baasha son of Ahijah. 10 Dogs will eat Ahab's wife Jezebel at the plot of
land in Jezreel, and no one will bury her." Then the young prophet opened
the door and ran.

8:21a Hebrew *Joram,* a variant spelling of Jehoram; also in 8:23, 24. **8:21b** Greek version reads *Seir.* **8:21c** Or *he went out and escaped.* The meaning of the Hebrew is uncertain. **8:29** Hebrew *Ramah,* a variant spelling of Ramoth. **9:1** Hebrew *Bind up your loins.*

Question **9:14**

Meaningfully, Jehu led a portion of the revolt against King Ahab's family line at the land that had belonged to Naboth (1 Kings 21). What does this tell you about how God demonstrates that he is a righteous judge—who works in his own timing?

11 Jehu went back to his fellow officers, and one of them asked him, "What
did that madman want? Is everything all right?"
"You know how a man like that babbles on," Jehu replied.
12 "You're hiding something," they said. "Tell us."
So Jehu told them, "He said to me, 'This is what the LORD says: I have
anointed you to be king over Israel.'"
13 Then they quickly spread out their cloaks on the bare steps and blew the
ram's horn, shouting, "Jehu is king!"

Jehu Kills Joram and Ahaziah

14 So Jehu son of Jehoshaphat, son of Nimshi, led a conspiracy against King Jo-
ram. (Now Joram had been with the army at Ramoth-gilead, defending Israel
against the forces of King Hazael of Aram. 15 But King Joram* was wounded
in the fighting and returned to Jezreel to recover from his wounds.) So Jehu
told the men with him, "If you want me to be king, don't let anyone leave
town and go to Jezreel to report what we have done."
16 Then Jehu got into a chariot and rode to Jezreel to find King Joram,
who was lying there wounded. King Ahaziah of Judah was there, too, for
he had gone to visit him. 17 The watchman on the tower of Jezreel saw Jehu
and his company approaching, so he shouted to Joram, "I see a company of
troops coming!"
"Send out a rider to ask if they are coming in peace," King Joram ordered.
18 So a horseman went out to meet Jehu and said, "The king wants to know
if you are coming in peace."
Jehu replied, "What do you know about peace? Fall in behind me!"
The watchman called out to the king, "The messenger has met them, but
he's not returning."
19 So the king sent out a second horseman. He rode up to them and said,
"The king wants to know if you come in peace."
Again Jehu answered, "What do you know about peace? Fall in behind me!"
20 The watchman exclaimed, "The messenger has met them, but he isn't re-
turning either! It must be Jehu son of Nimshi, for he's driving like a madman."
21 "Quick! Get my chariot ready!" King Joram commanded.
Then King Joram of Israel and King Ahaziah of Judah rode out in their
chariots to meet Jehu. They met him at the plot of land that had belonged to
Naboth of Jezreel. 22 King Joram demanded, "Do you come in peace, Jehu?"
Jehu replied, "How can there be peace as long as the idolatry and witch-
craft of your mother, Jezebel, are all around us?"
23 Then King Joram turned the horses around* and fled, shouting to King
Ahaziah, "Treason, Ahaziah!" 24 But Jehu drew his bow and shot Joram be-
tween the shoulders. The arrow pierced his heart, and he sank down dead in
his chariot.
25 Jehu said to Bidkar, his officer, "Throw him into the plot of land that
belonged to Naboth of Jezreel. Do you remember when you and I were riding
along behind his father, Ahab? The LORD pronounced this message against
him: 26 'I solemnly swear that I will repay him here on this plot of land, says
the LORD, for the murder of Naboth and his sons that I saw yesterday.' So
throw him out on Naboth's property, just as the LORD said."
27 When King Ahaziah of Judah saw what was happening, he fled along

9:15 Hebrew *Jehoram,* a variant spelling of Joram; also in 9:17, 21, 22, 23, 24. **9:23** Hebrew *turned his hands.*

the road to Beth-haggan. Jehu rode after him, shouting, "Shoot him, too!" So
they shot Ahaziah* in his chariot at the Ascent of Gur, near Ibleam. He was
able to go on as far as Megiddo, but he died there. 28 His servants took him by
chariot to Jerusalem, where they buried him with his ancestors in the City
of David. 29 Ahaziah had become king over Judah in the eleventh year of the
reign of Joram son of Ahab.

The Death of Jezebel

30 When Jezebel, the queen mother, heard that Jehu had come to Jezreel,
she painted her eyelids and fixed her hair and sat at a window. 31 When Jehu
entered the gate of the palace, she shouted at him, "Have you come in peace,
you murderer? You're just like Zimri, who murdered his master!"*

32 Jehu looked up and saw her at the window and shouted, "Who is on my
side?" And two or three eunuchs looked out at him. 33 "Throw her down!"
Jehu yelled. So they threw her out the window, and her blood spattered
against the wall and on the horses. And Jehu trampled her body under his
horses' hooves.

34 Then Jehu went into the palace and ate and drank. Afterward he said,
"Someone go and bury this cursed woman, for she is the daughter of a king."
35 But when they went out to bury her, they found only her skull, her feet,
and her hands.

36 When they returned and told Jehu, he stated, "This fulfills the message
from the LORD, which he spoke through his servant Elijah from Tishbe: 'At
the plot of land in Jezreel, dogs will eat Jezebel's body. 37 Her remains will
be scattered like dung on the plot of land in Jezreel, so that no one will be
able to recognize her.'"

Jehu Kills Ahab's Family

10 Ahab had seventy sons living in the city of Samaria. So Jehu wrote
letters and sent them to Samaria, to the elders and officials of the
city,* and to the guardians of King Ahab's sons. He said, 2 "The king's sons
are with you, and you have at your disposal chariots, horses, a fortified city,
and weapons. As soon as you receive this letter, 3 select the best qualified of
your master's sons to be your king, and prepare to fight for Ahab's dynasty."

4 But they were paralyzed with fear and said, "We've seen that two kings
couldn't stand against this man! What can we do?"

5 So the palace and city administrators, together with the elders and the
guardians of the king's sons, sent this message to Jehu: "We are your servants
and will do anything you tell us. We will not make anyone king; do whatever
you think is best."

6 Jehu responded with a second letter: "If you are on my side and are going
to obey me, bring the heads of your master's sons to me at Jezreel by this time
tomorrow." Now the seventy sons of the king were being cared for by the
leaders of Samaria, where they had been raised since childhood. 7 When the
letter arrived, the leaders killed all seventy of the king's sons. They placed
their heads in baskets and presented them to Jehu at Jezreel.

8 A messenger went to Jehu and said, "They have brought the heads of
the king's sons."

9:27 As in Greek and Syriac versions; Hebrew lacks *So they shot Ahaziah.* **9:31** See 1 Kgs 16:9-10, where Zimri killed his master, King Elah. **10:1** As in some Greek manuscripts and Latin Vulgate (see also 10:6); Hebrew reads *of Jezreel.*

So Jehu ordered, "Pile them in two heaps at the entrance of the city gate, and leave them there until morning."

9 In the morning he went out and spoke to the crowd that had gathered around them. "You are not to blame," he told them. "I am the one who conspired against my master and killed him. But who killed all these? 10 You can be sure that the message of the LORD that was spoken concerning Ahab's family will not fail. The LORD declared through his servant Elijah that this would happen." 11 Then Jehu killed all who were left of Ahab's relatives living in Jezreel and all his important officials, his personal friends, and his priests. So Ahab was left without a single survivor.

12 Then Jehu set out for Samaria. Along the way, while he was at Beth-eked of the Shepherds, 13 he met some relatives of King Ahaziah of Judah. "Who are you?" he asked them.

And they replied, "We are relatives of King Ahaziah. We are going to visit the sons of King Ahab and the sons of the queen mother."

14 "Take them alive!" Jehu shouted to his men. And they captured all forty-two of them and killed them at the well of Beth-eked. None of them escaped.

15 When Jehu left there, he met Jehonadab son of Recab, who was coming to meet him. After they had greeted each other, Jehu said to him, "Are you as loyal to me as I am to you?"

"Yes, I am," Jehonadab replied.

"If you are," Jehu said, "then give me your hand." So Jehonadab put out his hand, and Jehu helped him into the chariot. 16 Then Jehu said, "Now come with me, and see how devoted I am to the LORD." So Jehonadab rode along with him.

17 When Jehu arrived in Samaria, he killed everyone who was left there from Ahab's family, just as the LORD had promised through Elijah.

Jehu Kills the Priests of Baal

18 Then Jehu called a meeting of all the people of the city and said to them, "Ahab's worship of Baal was nothing compared to the way I will worship him! 19 Therefore, summon all the prophets and worshipers of Baal, and call together all his priests. See to it that every one of them comes, for I am going to offer a great sacrifice to Baal. Anyone who fails to come will be put to death." But Jehu's cunning plan was to destroy all the worshipers of Baal.

20 Then Jehu ordered, "Prepare a solemn assembly to worship Baal!" So they did. 21 He sent messengers throughout all Israel summoning those who worshiped Baal. They all came—not a single one remained behind—and they filled the temple of Baal from one end to the other. 22 And Jehu instructed the keeper of the wardrobe, "Be sure that every worshiper of Baal wears one of these robes." So robes were given to them.

23 Then Jehu went into the temple of Baal with Jehonadab son of Recab. Jehu said to the worshipers of Baal, "Make sure no one who worships the LORD is here—only those who worship Baal." 24 So they were all inside the temple to offer sacrifices and burnt offerings. Now Jehu had stationed eighty of his men outside the building and had warned them, "If you let anyone escape, you will pay for it with your own life."

25 As soon as Jehu had finished sacrificing the burnt offering, he commanded his guards and officers, "Go in and kill all of them. Don't let a single one escape!" So they killed them all with their swords, and the guards and

officers dragged their bodies outside.* Then Jehu's men went into the inner-
most fortress* of the temple of Baal. 26 They dragged out the sacred pillar*
used in the worship of Baal and burned it. 27 They smashed the sacred pil-
lar and wrecked the temple of Baal, converting it into a public toilet, as it
remains to this day.
28 In this way, Jehu destroyed every trace of Baal worship from Israel. 29 He
did not, however, destroy the gold calves at Bethel and Dan, with which Jer-
oboam son of Nebat had caused Israel to sin.
30 Nonetheless the LORD said to Jehu, "You have done well in following
my instructions to destroy the family of Ahab. Therefore, your descendants
will be kings of Israel down to the fourth generation." 31 But Jehu did not
obey the Law of the LORD, the God of Israel, with all his heart. He refused to
turn from the sins that Jeroboam had led Israel to commit.

The Death of Jehu

32 At about that time the LORD began to cut down the size of Israel's territory.
King Hazael conquered several sections of the country 33 east of the Jordan
River, including all of Gilead, Gad, Reuben, and Manasseh. He conquered
the area from the town of Aroer by the Arnon Gorge to as far north as Gil-
ead and Bashan.
34 The rest of the events in Jehu's reign—everything he did and all his
achievements—are recorded in *The Book of the History of the Kings of Israel.*
35 When Jehu died, he was buried in Samaria. Then his son Jehoahaz
became the next king. 36 In all, Jehu reigned over Israel from Samaria for
twenty-eight years.

Queen Athaliah Rules in Judah

11 When Athaliah, the mother of King Ahaziah of Judah, learned that
her son was dead, she began to destroy the rest of the royal fam-
ily. 2 But Ahaziah's sister Jehosheba, the daughter of King Jehoram,* took
Ahaziah's infant son, Joash, and stole him away from among the rest of the
king's children, who were about to be killed. She put Joash and his nurse in
a bedroom, and they hid him from Athaliah, so the child was not murdered.
3 Joash remained hidden in the Temple of the LORD for six years while Ath-
aliah ruled over the land.

Revolt against Athaliah

4 In the seventh year of Athaliah's reign, Jehoiada the priest summoned the
commanders, the Carite mercenaries, and the palace guards to come to the
Temple of the LORD. He made a solemn pact with them and made them
swear an oath of loyalty there in the LORD's Temple; then he showed them
the king's son.
5 Jehoiada told them, "This is what you must do. A third of you who are
on duty on the Sabbath are to guard the royal palace itself. 6 Another third of
you are to stand guard at the Sur Gate. And the final third must stand guard
behind the palace guard. These three groups will all guard the palace. 7 The
other two units who are off duty on the Sabbath must stand guard for the
king at the LORD's Temple. 8 Form a bodyguard around the king and keep

10:25a Or *and they left their bodies lying there;* or *and they threw them out into the outermost court.* **10:25b** Hebrew *city.* **10:26** As in Greek and Syriac versions and Latin Vulgate; Hebrew reads *sacred pillars.* **11:2** Hebrew *Joram,* a variant spelling of Jehoram.

Question 10:31

God used Jehu mightily to right some wrongs in Israel. Still, Jehu did not obey the law of the Lord with his heart. He continued some of the sinful habits and dismissal of the Lord so common in his day. Why do you think people throughout history refuse to make their lives right with God even when they know they should?

Story Arc 11:1-3

● **Joash**

Multiple times throughout the Bible, significant children were rescued by thoughtful family members and protected by God. Here, Joash was whisked away and hidden in the temple, where he lived for six years while Queen Athaliah hunted down and murdered the rest of the royal family.

The story of the Bible often reveals how, in impossible circumstances, God would protect a remnant to carry on his plan of salvation. Joash would go on to become king when he was seven years old (v. 21). He repaired the temple and reformed religious practices in Judah. Perhaps more significantly, though he wasn't always perfect, he "did what was pleasing in the LORD's sight" for the next forty years of his life (12:1-2).

What kind of story is God going to weave in your life? What has God set you apart to accomplish? No matter what, he wants you to live your life in a way that fits his plan of salvation (for you and for others).

2 Kgs 11:4-21 ►

your weapons in hand. Kill anyone who tries to break through. Stay with
the king wherever he goes."
9 So the commanders did everything as Jehoiada the priest ordered. The
commanders took charge of the men reporting for duty that Sabbath, as
well as those who were going off duty. They brought them all to Jehoiada
the priest, 10 and he supplied them with the spears and small shields that had
once belonged to King David and were stored in the Temple of the LORD.
11 The palace guards stationed themselves around the king, with their weap-
ons ready. They formed a line from the south side of the Temple around to
the north side and all around the altar.
12 Then Jehoiada brought out Joash, the king's son, placed the crown on
his head, and presented him with a copy of God's laws.* They anointed him
and proclaimed him king, and everyone clapped their hands and shouted,
"Long live the king!"

The Death of Athaliah

13 When Athaliah heard the noise made by the palace guards and the people,
she hurried to the LORD's Temple to see what was happening. 14 When she
arrived, she saw the newly crowned king standing in his place of authority
by the pillar, as was the custom at times of coronation. The commanders
and trumpeters were surrounding him, and people from all over the land
were rejoicing and blowing trumpets. When Athaliah saw all this, she tore
her clothes in despair and shouted, "Treason! Treason!"
15 Then Jehoiada the priest ordered the commanders who were in charge of
the troops, "Take her to the soldiers in front of the Temple,* and kill anyone
who tries to rescue her." For the priest had said, "She must not be killed in the
Temple of the LORD." 16 So they seized her and led her out to the gate where
horses enter the palace grounds, and she was killed there.

Jehoiada's Religious Reforms

17 Then Jehoiada made a covenant between the LORD and the king and the
people that they would be the LORD's people. He also made a covenant be-
tween the king and the people. 18 And all the people of the land went over to the
temple of Baal and tore it down. They demolished the altars and smashed the
idols to pieces, and they killed Mattan the priest of Baal in front of the altars.
Jehoiada the priest stationed guards at the Temple of the LORD. 19 Then the
commanders, the Carite mercenaries, the palace guards, and all the people of
the land escorted the king from the Temple of the LORD. They went through
the gate of the guards and into the palace, and the king took his seat on the
royal throne. 20 So all the people of the land rejoiced, and the city was peaceful
because Athaliah had been killed at the king's palace.
21 *Joash* was seven years old when he became king.

Joash Repairs the Temple

12 1 *Joash* began to rule over Judah in the seventh year of King Jehu's
reign in Israel. He reigned in Jerusalem forty years. His mother
was Zibiah from Beersheba. 2 All his life Joash did what was pleasing in the

Story Arc **11:4–21**

Jehoiada

Jehoiada was the high priest of Judah and the brother-in-law of King Ahaziah, and he just happened to save the line of David. After Ahaziah was killed, his mother, Queen Athaliah, ruthlessly hunted down the rest of the royal family. Athaliah was the daughter of the wicked rulers in northern Israel (King Ahab and Queen Jezebel). Jehoiada, sensing the plot, hid the youngest of Ahaziah's sons, a one-year-old named Joash, until there was a significant-enough movement to revolt against the queen. Jehoiada kept Joash hidden in the temple of the Lord for six years.

Jehoiada went on to help Joash restore much of Judah's commitment to the Lord and to bring religious reforms to the land. Second Chronicles 24:15 notes that Jehoiada lived a faithful life to the age of one hundred thirty and was buried with honor due to kings.

How does someone develop the type of deep resiliency that Jehoiada exhibited during his long lifetime?

2 Kgs 18:1-8 ►

11:12 Or *a copy of the covenant.* 11:15 Or *Bring her out from between the ranks;* or *Take her out of the Temple precincts.* The meaning of the Hebrew is uncertain. 11:21a Verse 11:21 is numbered 12:1 in Hebrew text. 11:21b Hebrew *Jehoash,* a variant spelling of Joash. 12:1a Verses 12:1-21 are numbered 12:2-22 in Hebrew text. 12:1b Hebrew *Jehoash,* a variant spelling of Joash; also in 12:2, 4, 6, 7, 18.

LORD's sight because Jehoiada the priest instructed him. 3 Yet even so, he
did not destroy the pagan shrines, and the people still offered sacrifices and
burned incense there.
4 One day King Joash said to the priests, "Collect all the money brought as
a sacred offering to the LORD's Temple, whether it is a regular assessment, a
payment of vows, or a voluntary gift. 5 Let the priests take some of that money
to pay for whatever repairs are needed at the Temple."
6 But by the twenty-third year of Joash's reign, the priests still had not re-
paired the Temple. 7 So King Joash called for Jehoiada and the other priests
and asked them, "Why haven't you repaired the Temple? Don't use any more
money for your own needs. From now on, it must all be spent on Temple re-
pairs." 8 So the priests agreed not to accept any more money from the people,
and they also agreed to let others take responsibility for repairing the Temple.
9 Then Jehoiada the priest bored a hole in the lid of a large chest and set it
on the right-hand side of the altar at the entrance of the Temple of the LORD.
The priests guarding the entrance put all of the people's contributions into
the chest. 10 Whenever the chest became full, the court secretary and the high
priest counted the money that had been brought to the LORD's Temple and put
it into bags. 11 Then they gave the money to the construction supervisors, who
used it to pay the people working on the LORD's Temple—the carpenters, the
builders, 12 the masons, and the stonecutters. They also used the money to buy
the timber and the finished stone needed for repairing the LORD's Temple, and
they paid any other expenses related to the Temple's restoration.
13 The money brought to the Temple was not used for making silver bowls,
lamp snuffers, basins, trumpets, or other articles of gold or silver for the
Temple of the LORD. 14 It was paid to the workmen, who used it for the Temple
repairs. 15 No accounting of this money was required from the construction
supervisors, because they were honest and trustworthy men. 16 However, the
money that was contributed for guilt offerings and sin offerings was not
brought into the LORD's Temple. It was given to the priests for their own use.

The End of Joash's Reign

17 About this time King Hazael of Aram went to war against Gath and cap-
tured it. Then he turned to attack Jerusalem. 18 King Joash collected all the
sacred objects that Jehoshaphat, Jehoram, and Ahaziah, the previous kings
of Judah, had dedicated, along with what he himself had dedicated. He sent
them all to Hazael, along with all the gold in the treasuries of the LORD's
Temple and the royal palace. So Hazael called off his attack on Jerusalem.
19 The rest of the events in Joash's reign and everything he did are recorded
in *The Book of the History of the Kings of Judah.*
20 Joash's officers plotted against him and assassinated him at Beth-millo
on the road to Silla. 21 The assassins were Jozacar* son of Shimeath and Je-
hozabad son of Shomer—both trusted advisers. Joash was buried with his
ancestors in the City of David. Then his son Amaziah became the next king.

Jehoahaz Rules in Israel

13 Jehoahaz son of Jehu began to rule over Israel in the twenty-third
year of King Joash's reign in Judah. He reigned in Samaria seventeen
years. 2 But he did what was evil in the LORD's sight. He followed the example

12:21 As in Greek and Syriac versions; Hebrew reads *Jozabad.*

Question 13:20-21

When Elisha died, there seems to have been very little commotion. It certainly wasn't the big dramatic scene of Elijah's "death," when a chariot of fire appeared and carried him by a whirlwind into heaven (2 Kings 2:11). No, the people simply buried Elisha.

Then, when some Israelites decided to quickly bury a man in Elisha's tomb, something strange happened. When the man's corpse touched Elisha's bones, "the dead man revived and jumped to his feet!" (13:21).

What does this odd story reveal to you about what God can do? Likewise, what does it reveal to you about what God can do through his people? How does this affect your faith in God in terms of your own life?

of Jeroboam son of Nebat, continuing the sins that Jeroboam had led Israel
to commit. 3 So the LORD was very angry with Israel, and he allowed King
Hazael of Aram and his son Ben-hadad to defeat them repeatedly.
4 Then Jehoahaz prayed for the LORD's help, and the LORD heard his
prayer, for he could see how severely the king of Aram was oppressing
Israel. 5 So the LORD provided someone to rescue the Israelites from the
tyranny of the Arameans. Then Israel lived in safety again as they had in
former days.
6 But they continued to sin, following the evil example of Jeroboam. They
also allowed the Asherah pole in Samaria to remain standing. 7 Finally, Je-
hoahaz's army was reduced to 50 charioteers, 10 chariots, and 10,000 foot
soldiers. The king of Aram had killed the others, trampling them like dust
under his feet.
8 The rest of the events in Jehoahaz's reign—everything he did and the
extent of his power—are recorded in *The Book of the History of the Kings of Is-
rael.* 9 When Jehoahaz died, he was buried in Samaria. Then his son Jehoash*
became the next king.

Jehoash Rules in Israel

10 Jehoash son of Jehoahaz began to rule over Israel in the thirty-seventh year
of King Joash's reign in Judah. He reigned in Samaria sixteen years. 11 But he
did what was evil in the LORD's sight. He refused to turn from the sins that
Jeroboam son of Nebat had led Israel to commit.
12 The rest of the events in Jehoash's reign and everything he did, includ-
ing the extent of his power and his war with King Amaziah of Judah, are
recorded in *The Book of the History of the Kings of Israel.* 13 When Jehoash died,
he was buried in Samaria with the kings of Israel. Then his son Jeroboam II
became the next king.

Elisha's Final Prophecy

14 When Elisha was in his last illness, King Jehoash of Israel visited him and
wept over him. "My father! My father! I see the chariots and charioteers of
Israel!" he cried.
15 Elisha told him, "Get a bow and some arrows." And the king did as he
was told. 16 Elisha told him, "Put your hand on the bow," and Elisha laid his
own hands on the king's hands.
17 Then he commanded, "Open that eastern window," and he opened it.
Then he said, "Shoot!" So he shot an arrow. Elisha proclaimed, "This is the
LORD's arrow, an arrow of victory over Aram, for you will completely conquer
the Arameans at Aphek."
18 Then he said, "Now pick up the other arrows and strike them against
the ground." So the king picked them up and struck the ground three times.
19 But the man of God was angry with him. "You should have struck the
ground five or six times!" he exclaimed. "Then you would have beaten Aram
until it was entirely destroyed. Now you will be victorious only three times."
20 Then Elisha died and was buried.
Groups of Moabite raiders used to invade the land each spring. 21 Once
when some Israelites were burying a man, they spied a band of these raid-
ers. So they hastily threw the corpse into the tomb of Elisha and fled. But as

13:9 Hebrew *Joash,* a variant spelling of Jehoash; also in 13:10, 12, 13, 14, 25.

soon as the body touched Elisha's bones, the dead man revived and jumped
to his feet!
22 King Hazael of Aram had oppressed Israel during the entire reign of
King Jehoahaz. 23 But the LORD was gracious and merciful to the people of
Israel, and they were not totally destroyed. He pitied them because of his
covenant with Abraham, Isaac, and Jacob. And to this day he still has not
completely destroyed them or banished them from his presence.
24 King Hazael of Aram died, and his son Ben-hadad became the next king.
25 Then Jehoash son of Jehoahaz recaptured from Ben-hadad son of Hazael
the towns that had been taken from Jehoash's father, Jehoahaz. Jehoash de-
feated Ben-hadad on three occasions, and he recovered the Israelite towns.

Amaziah Rules in Judah

14 Amaziah son of Joash began to rule over Judah in the second year of
the reign of King Jehoash* of Israel. 2 Amaziah was twenty-five years
old when he became king, and he reigned in Jerusalem twenty-nine years.
His mother was Jehoaddin from Jerusalem. 3 Amaziah did what was pleasing
in the LORD's sight, but not like his ancestor David. Instead, he followed the
example of his father, Joash. 4 Amaziah did not destroy the pagan shrines,
and the people still offered sacrifices and burned incense there.
5 When Amaziah was well established as king, he executed the officials
who had assassinated his father. 6 However, he did not kill the children of
the assassins, for he obeyed the command of the LORD as written by Moses
in the Book of the Law: "Parents must not be put to death for the sins of their
children, nor children for the sins of their parents. Those deserving to die
must be put to death for their own crimes."*
7 Amaziah also killed 10,000 Edomites in the Valley of Salt. He also con-
quered Sela and changed its name to Joktheel, as it is called to this day.
8 One day Amaziah sent messengers with this challenge to Israel's king Jeho-
ash, the son of Jehoahaz and grandson of Jehu: "Come and meet me in battle!"*
9 But King Jehoash of Israel replied to King Amaziah of Judah with this
story: "Out in the Lebanon mountains, a thistle sent a message to a mighty
cedar tree: 'Give your daughter in marriage to my son.' But just then a wild
animal of Lebanon came by and stepped on the thistle, crushing it!
10 "You have indeed defeated Edom, and you are proud of it. But be content
with your victory and stay at home! Why stir up trouble that will only bring
disaster on you and the people of Judah?"
11 But Amaziah refused to listen, so King Jehoash of Israel mobilized his army
against King Amaziah of Judah. The two armies drew up their battle lines at
Beth-shemesh in Judah. 12 Judah was routed by the army of Israel, and its army
scattered and fled for home. 13 King Jehoash of Israel captured Judah's king,
Amaziah son of Joash and grandson of Ahaziah, at Beth-shemesh. Then he
marched to Jerusalem, where he demolished 600 feet* of Jerusalem's wall, from
the Ephraim Gate to the Corner Gate. 14 He carried off all the gold and silver and
all the articles from the Temple of the LORD. He also seized the treasures from
the royal palace, along with hostages, and then returned to Samaria.
15 The rest of the events in Jehoash's reign and everything he did, includ-
ing the extent of his power and his war with King Amaziah of Judah, are
recorded in *The Book of the History of the Kings of Israel.* 16 When Jehoash died,

14:1 Hebrew *Joash,* a variant spelling of Jehoash; also in 14:13, 23, 27. 14:6 Deut 24:16.
14:8 Hebrew *Come, let us look one another in the face.* 14:13 Hebrew *400 cubits* [180 meters].

Question 14:3–4

Amaziah mostly did what was pleasing in the Lord's sight like his dad, Joash. However, he failed to destroy the pagan shrines where people sacrificed to other gods. Why do people so easily compromise their faith?

he was buried in Samaria with the kings of Israel. And his son Jeroboam II
became the next king.
17 King Amaziah of Judah lived for fifteen years after the death of King
Jehoash of Israel. 18 The rest of the events in Amaziah's reign are recorded in
The Book of the History of the Kings of Judah.
19 There was a conspiracy against Amaziah's life in Jerusalem, and he fled
to Lachish. But his enemies sent assassins after him, and they killed him
there. 20 They brought his body back to Jerusalem on a horse, and he was
buried with his ancestors in the City of David.
21 All the people of Judah had crowned Amaziah's sixteen-year-old son,
Uzziah,* as king in place of his father, Amaziah. 22 After his father's death,
Uzziah rebuilt the town of Elath and restored it to Judah.

Jeroboam II Rules in Israel

23 Jeroboam II, the son of Jehoash, began to rule over Israel in the fifteenth
year of King Amaziah's reign in Judah. He reigned in Samaria forty-one
years. 24 He did what was evil in the LORD's sight. He refused to turn from
the sins that Jeroboam son of Nebat had led Israel to commit. 25 Jeroboam II
recovered the territories of Israel between Lebo-hamath and the Dead Sea,*
just as the LORD, the God of Israel, had promised through Jonah son of Amit-
tai, the prophet from Gath-hepher.
26 For the LORD saw the bitter suffering of everyone in Israel, and that
there was no one in Israel, slave or free, to help them. 27 And because the
LORD had not said he would blot out the name of Israel completely, he used
Jeroboam II, the son of Jehoash, to save them.
28 The rest of the events in the reign of Jeroboam II and everything he
did—including the extent of his power, his wars, and how he recovered for
Israel both Damascus and Hamath, which had belonged to Judah*—are re-
corded in *The Book of the History of the Kings of Israel.* 29 When Jeroboam II died,
he was buried in Samaria* with the kings of Israel. Then his son Zechariah
became the next king.

Uzziah Rules in Judah

15 Uzziah* son of Amaziah began to rule over Judah in the twenty-
seventh year of the reign of King Jeroboam II of Israel. 2 He was six-
teen years old when he became king, and he reigned in Jerusalem fifty-two
years. His mother was Jecoliah from Jerusalem.
3 He did what was pleasing in the LORD's sight, just as his father, Ama-
ziah, had done. 4 But he did not destroy the pagan shrines, and the people
still offered sacrifices and burned incense there. 5 The LORD struck the king
with leprosy,* which lasted until the day he died. He lived in isolation in a
separate house. The king's son Jotham was put in charge of the royal palace,
and he governed the people of the land.
6 The rest of the events in Uzziah's reign and everything he did are re-
corded in *The Book of the History of the Kings of Judah.* 7 When Uzziah died, he
was buried with his ancestors in the City of David. And his son Jotham be-
came the next king.

Make a Difference

15:1-5

Generational Patterns

Stupid pagan shrines. There seems to be a pattern here. Amaziah had done just what his father, King Joash, had done. Now, Uzziah did what was pleasing in the Lord's sight just as his father, Amaziah, had done. Despite this, like the two men before him, Uzziah also failed to destroy the pagan shrines.

Difference Maker

Consider what this pattern teaches you about how easy it is to mirror the faith of our parents. Then identify one generational pattern in your family that should be continued and one pattern that should be changed.

14:21 Hebrew *Azariah,* a variant spelling of Uzziah. 14:25 Hebrew *the sea of the Arabah.* 14:28 Or *to Yaudi.* The meaning of the Hebrew is uncertain. 14:29 As in some Greek manuscripts; Hebrew lacks *he was buried in Samaria.* 15:1 Hebrew *Azariah,* a variant spelling of Uzziah; also in 15:6, 7, 8, 17, 23, 27. 15:5 Or *with a contagious skin disease.* The Hebrew word used here and throughout this passage can describe various skin diseases.

Zechariah Rules in Israel

8 Zechariah son of Jeroboam II began to rule over Israel in the thirty-eighth
year of King Uzziah's reign in Judah. He reigned in Samaria six months.
9 Zechariah did what was evil in the LORD's sight, as his ancestors had done.
He refused to turn from the sins that Jeroboam son of Nebat had led Israel
to commit. 10 Then Shallum son of Jabesh conspired against Zechariah, as-
sassinated him in public,* and became the next king.

11 The rest of the events in Zechariah's reign are recorded in *The Book of the
History of the Kings of Israel.* 12 So the LORD's message to Jehu came true: "Your
descendants will be kings of Israel down to the fourth generation."

Shallum Rules in Israel

13 Shallum son of Jabesh began to rule over Israel in the thirty-ninth year of
King Uzziah's reign in Judah. Shallum reigned in Samaria only one month.
14 Then Menahem son of Gadi went to Samaria from Tirzah and assassinated
him, and he became the next king.

15 The rest of the events in Shallum's reign, including his conspiracy, are
recorded in *The Book of the History of the Kings of Israel.*

Menahem Rules in Israel

16 At that time Menahem destroyed the town of Tappuah* and all the sur-
rounding countryside as far as Tirzah, because its citizens refused to surren-
der the town. He killed the entire population and ripped open the pregnant
women.

17 Menahem son of Gadi began to rule over Israel in the thirty-ninth
year of King Uzziah's reign in Judah. He reigned in Samaria ten years.
18 But Menahem did what was evil in the LORD's sight. During his entire
reign, he refused to turn from the sins that Jeroboam son of Nebat had led
Israel to commit.

19 Then King Tiglath-pileser* of Assyria invaded the land. But Menahem
paid him thirty-seven tons* of silver to gain his support in tightening his
grip on royal power. 20 Menahem extorted the money from the rich of Is-
rael, demanding that each of them pay fifty pieces* of silver to the king of
Assyria. So the king of Assyria turned from attacking Israel and did not stay
in the land.

21 The rest of the events in Menahem's reign and everything he did are
recorded in *The Book of the History of the Kings of Israel.* 22 When Menahem died,
his son Pekahiah became the next king.

Pekahiah Rules in Israel

23 Pekahiah son of Menahem began to rule over Israel in the fiftieth year of
King Uzziah's reign in Judah. He reigned in Samaria two years. 24 But Pek-
ahiah did what was evil in the LORD's sight. He refused to turn from the sins
that Jeroboam son of Nebat had led Israel to commit.

25 Then Pekah son of Remaliah, the commander of Pekahiah's army, con-
spired against him. With fifty men from Gilead, Pekah assassinated the king,
along with Argob and Arieh, in the citadel of the palace at Samaria. And
Pekah reigned in his place.

15:10 Or *at Ibleam.* **15:16** As in some Greek manuscripts; Hebrew reads *Tiphsah.* **15:19a** Hebrew *Pul,* another name for Tiglath-pileser. **15:19b** Hebrew *1,000 talents* [34 metric tons]. **15:20** Hebrew *50 shekels* [20 ounces or 570 grams].

Question 15:34

What difference does it make if God's people mix some other religious beliefs into their commitment to God?

26 The rest of the events in Pekahiah's reign and everything he did are re-
corded in *The Book of the History of the Kings of Israel.*

Pekah Rules in Israel

27 Pekah son of Remaliah began to rule over Israel in the fifty-second year
of King Uzziah's reign in Judah. He reigned in Samaria twenty years. 28 But
Pekah did what was evil in the LORD's sight. He refused to turn from the sins
that Jeroboam son of Nebat had led Israel to commit.
29 During Pekah's reign, King Tiglath-pileser of Assyria attacked Israel
again, and he captured the towns of Ijon, Abel-beth-maacah, Janoah, Ke-
desh, and Hazor. He also conquered the regions of Gilead, Galilee, and all
of Naphtali, and he took the people to Assyria as captives. 30 Then Hoshea
son of Elah conspired against Pekah and assassinated him. He began to rule
over Israel in the twentieth year of Jotham son of Uzziah.
31 The rest of the events in Pekah's reign and everything he did are recorded
in *The Book of the History of the Kings of Israel.*

Jotham Rules in Judah

32 Jotham son of Uzziah began to rule over Judah in the second year of King
Pekah's reign in Israel. 33 He was twenty-five years old when he became
king, and he reigned in Jerusalem sixteen years. His mother was Jerusha,
the daughter of Zadok.
■ 34 Jotham did what was pleasing in the LORD's sight. He did everything
his father, Uzziah, had done. 35 But he did not destroy the pagan shrines, and
the people still offered sacrifices and burned incense there. He rebuilt the
upper gate of the Temple of the LORD.
36 The rest of the events in Jotham's reign and everything he did are re-
corded in *The Book of the History of the Kings of Judah.* 37 In those days the LORD
began to send King Rezin of Aram and King Pekah of Israel to attack Judah.
38 When Jotham died, he was buried with his ancestors in the City of David.
And his son Ahaz became the next king.

Ahaz Rules in Judah

16 Ahaz son of Jotham began to rule over Judah in the seventeenth year
of King Pekah's reign in Israel. 2 Ahaz was twenty years old when
he became king, and he reigned in Jerusalem sixteen years. He did not do
what was pleasing in the sight of the LORD his God, as his ancestor David
had done. 3 Instead, he followed the example of the kings of Israel, even
sacrificing his own son in the fire.* In this way, he followed the detestable
practices of the pagan nations the LORD had driven from the land ahead of
the Israelites. 4 He offered sacrifices and burned incense at the pagan shrines
and on the hills and under every green tree.
5 Then King Rezin of Aram and King Pekah of Israel came up to attack
Jerusalem. They besieged Ahaz but could not conquer him. 6 At that time
the king of Edom* recovered the town of Elath for Edom.* He drove out
the people of Judah and sent Edomites* to live there, as they do to this day.
7 King Ahaz sent messengers to King Tiglath-pileser of Assyria with this

16:3 Or *even making his son pass through the fire.* 16:6a As in Latin Vulgate; Hebrew reads *Rezin king of Aram.* 16:6b As in Latin Vulgate; Hebrew reads *Aram.* 16:6c As in Greek version, Latin Vulgate, and an alternate reading of the Masoretic Text; the other alternate reads *Arameans.*

message: "I am your servant and your vassal.* Come up and rescue me from
the attacking armies of Aram and Israel." 8 Then Ahaz took the silver and
gold from the Temple of the LORD and the palace treasury and sent it as a
payment to the Assyrian king. 9 So the king of Assyria attacked the Aramean
capital of Damascus and led its population away as captives, resettling them
in Kir. He also killed King Rezin.
10 King Ahaz then went to Damascus to meet with King Tiglath-pileser
of Assyria. While he was there, he took special note of the altar. Then he
sent a model of the altar to Uriah the priest, along with its design in full
detail. 11 Uriah followed the king's instructions and built an altar just like it,
and it was ready before the king returned from Damascus. 12 When the king
returned, he inspected the altar and made offerings on it. 13 He presented a
burnt offering and a grain offering, he poured out a liquid offering, and he
sprinkled the blood of peace offerings on the altar.
14 Then King Ahaz removed the old bronze altar from its place in front of
the LORD's Temple, between the entrance and the new altar, and placed it
on the north side of the new altar. 15 He told Uriah the priest, "Use the new
altar* for the morning sacrifices of burnt offering, the evening grain offer-
ing, the king's burnt offering and grain offering, and the burnt offerings of
all the people, as well as their grain offerings and liquid offerings. Sprinkle
the blood from all the burnt offerings and sacrifices on the new altar. The
bronze altar will be for my personal use only." 16 Uriah the priest did just as
King Ahaz commanded him.
17 Then the king removed the side panels and basins from the portable
water carts. He also removed the great bronze basin called the Sea from the
backs of the bronze oxen and placed it on the stone pavement. 18 In deference
to the king of Assyria, he also removed the canopy that had been constructed
inside the palace for use on the Sabbath day,* as well as the king's outer en-
trance to the Temple of the LORD.
19 The rest of the events in Ahaz's reign and everything he did are recorded
in *The Book of the History of the Kings of Judah.* 20 When Ahaz died, he was buried
with his ancestors in the City of David. Then his son Hezekiah became the
next king.

Hoshea Rules in Israel

17 Hoshea son of Elah began to rule over Israel in the twelfth year of
King Ahaz's reign in Judah. He reigned in Samaria nine years. 2 He
did what was evil in the LORD's sight, but not to the same extent as the kings
of Israel who ruled before him.
3 King Shalmaneser of Assyria attacked King Hoshea, so Hoshea was forced
to pay heavy tribute to Assyria. 4 But Hoshea stopped paying the annual trib-
ute and conspired against the king of Assyria by asking King So of Egypt* to
help him shake free of Assyria's power. When the king of Assyria discovered
this treachery, he seized Hoshea and put him in prison.

Samaria Falls to Assyria

5 Then the king of Assyria invaded the entire land, and for three years he
besieged the city of Samaria. 6 Finally, in the ninth year of King Hoshea's
reign, Samaria fell, and the people of Israel were exiled to Assyria. They were

16:7 Hebrew *your son.* **16:15** Hebrew *the great altar.* **16:18** The meaning of the Hebrew is uncertain. **17:4** Or *by asking the king of Egypt at Sais.*

Make a Difference

17:5-18

Compromised Commitment

Take a moment and read 17:5-18. Despite the Lord's warnings, the people of Israel sinned anyway. Despite all that God had done for them, the people still compromised their commitment to him. They became so sick in their faith that some people even sacrificed their own sons and daughters to other gods (v. 17)! As a result, disaster came upon the people, and they were exiled to the kingdom of Assyria.

Difference Maker

In what areas of your life are you compromising your faith? Even if this sin doesn't feel like a big deal now, it could fester and become a major problem down the line (for you or for the next generations). What could you do today to change some of the compromised commitments you have made?

settled in colonies in Halah, along the banks of the Habor River in Gozan, and in the cities of the Medes.

7 This disaster came upon the people of Israel because they worshiped other gods. They sinned against the LORD their God, who had brought them safely out of Egypt and had rescued them from the power of Pharaoh, the king of Egypt. 8 They had followed the practices of the pagan nations the LORD had driven from the land ahead of them, as well as the practices the kings of Israel had introduced. 9 The people of Israel had also secretly done many things that were not pleasing to the LORD their God. They built pagan shrines for themselves in all their towns, from the smallest outpost to the largest walled city. 10 They set up sacred pillars and Asherah poles at the top of every hill and under every green tree. 11 They offered sacrifices on all the hilltops, just like the nations the LORD had driven from the land ahead of them. So the people of Israel had done many evil things, arousing the LORD's anger. 12 Yes, they worshiped idols,* despite the LORD's specific and repeated warnings.

13 Again and again the LORD had sent his prophets and seers to warn both Israel and Judah: "Turn from all your evil ways. Obey my commands and decrees—the entire law that I commanded your ancestors to obey, and that I gave you through my servants the prophets."

14 But the Israelites would not listen. They were as stubborn as their ancestors who had refused to believe in the LORD their God. 15 They rejected his decrees and the covenant he had made with their ancestors, and they despised all his warnings. They worshiped worthless idols, so they became worthless themselves. They followed the example of the nations around them, disobeying the LORD's command not to imitate them.

16 They rejected all the commands of the LORD their God and made two calves from metal. They set up an Asherah pole and worshiped Baal and all the forces of heaven. 17 They even sacrificed their own sons and daughters in the fire.* They consulted fortune-tellers and practiced sorcery and sold themselves to evil, arousing the LORD's anger.

18 Because the LORD was very angry with Israel, he swept them away from his presence. Only the tribe of Judah remained in the land. 19 But even the people of Judah refused to obey the commands of the LORD their God, for they followed the evil practices that Israel had introduced. 20 The LORD rejected all the descendants of Israel. He punished them by handing them over to their attackers until he had banished Israel from his presence.

21 For when the LORD* tore Israel away from the kingdom of David, they chose Jeroboam son of Nebat as their king. But Jeroboam drew Israel away from following the LORD and made them commit a great sin. 22 And the people of Israel persisted in all the evil ways of Jeroboam. They did not turn from these sins 23 until the LORD finally swept them away from his presence, just as all his prophets had warned. So Israel was exiled from their land to Assyria, where they remain to this day.

Foreigners Settle in Israel

24 The king of Assyria transported groups of people from Babylon, Cuthah, Avva, Hamath, and Sepharvaim and resettled them in the towns of Samaria, replacing the people of Israel. They took possession of Samaria and lived in its

17:12 The Hebrew term (literally *round things*) probably alludes to dung. 17:17 Or *They even made their sons and daughters pass through the fire.* 17:21 Hebrew *he;* compare 1 Kgs 11:31-32.

towns. 25But since these foreign settlers did not worship the LORD when they
first arrived, the LORD sent lions among them, which killed some of them.
26So a message was sent to the king of Assyria: "The people you have sent
to live in the towns of Samaria do not know the religious customs of the God
of the land. He has sent lions among them to destroy them because they have
not worshiped him correctly."
27The king of Assyria then commanded, "Send one of the exiled priests
back to Samaria. Let him live there and teach the new residents the religious
customs of the God of the land." 28So one of the priests who had been exiled
from Samaria returned to Bethel and taught the new residents how to worship the LORD.

29But these various groups of foreigners also continued to worship their
own gods. In town after town where they lived, they placed their idols at the
pagan shrines that the people of Samaria had built. 30Those from Babylon
worshiped idols of their god Succoth-benoth. Those from Cuthah worshiped
their god Nergal. And those from Hamath worshiped Ashima. 31The Avvites
worshiped their gods Nibhaz and Tartak. And the people from Sepharvaim
even burned their own children as sacrifices to their gods Adrammelech
and Anammelech.
32These new residents worshiped the LORD, but they also appointed from
among themselves all sorts of people as priests to offer sacrifices at their
places of worship. 33And though they worshiped the LORD, they continued to
follow their own gods according to the religious customs of the nations from
which they came. 34And this is still going on today. They continue to follow
their former practices instead of truly worshiping the LORD and obeying the
decrees, regulations, instructions, and commands he gave the descendants
of Jacob, whose name he changed to Israel.
35For the LORD had made a covenant with the descendants of Jacob and
commanded them: "Do not worship any other gods or bow before them or
serve them or offer sacrifices to them. 36But worship only the LORD, who
brought you out of Egypt with great strength and a powerful arm. Bow down
to him alone, and offer sacrifices only to him. 37Be careful at all times to obey
the decrees, regulations, instructions, and commands that he wrote for you.
You must not worship other gods. 38Do not forget the covenant I made with
you, and do not worship other gods. 39You must worship only the LORD your
God. He is the one who will rescue you from all your enemies."
40But the people would not listen and continued to follow their former
practices. 41So while these new residents worshiped the LORD, they also worshiped their idols. And to this day their descendants do the same.

Hezekiah Rules in Judah

18 Hezekiah son of Ahaz began to rule over Judah in the third year of
King Hoshea's reign in Israel. 2He was twenty-five years old when he
became king, and he reigned in Jerusalem twenty-nine years. His mother was
Abijah,* the daughter of Zechariah. 3He did what was pleasing in the LORD's
sight, just as his ancestor David had done. 4He removed the pagan shrines,
smashed the sacred pillars, and cut down the Asherah poles. He broke up
the bronze serpent that Moses had made, because the people of Israel had
been offering sacrifices to it. The bronze serpent was called Nehushtan.*

18:2 As in parallel text at 2 Chr 29:1; Hebrew reads *Abi*, a variant spelling of Abijah. 18:4 *Nehushtan* sounds like the Hebrew terms that mean "snake," "bronze," and "unclean thing."

Story Arc **18:1-8**

● Hezekiah

After all the sin and devastation, how refreshing is verse 3? King Hezekiah brought tremendous revival to the land. He trusted the Lord and carefully obeyed God's commands (vv. 5-6). He was a successful king in a time when smaller kingdoms, like the wayward Israel to the north, were being overrun by conquering empires. While Hezekiah brought reform, he was supported by epic prophets like Isaiah and Micah and Hosea, who were busy warning people to repent and follow the Lord's patterns.

Sadly though, in some ways, Hezekiah outlived his faith. After the Lord healed him of a boil and a deadly disease (see also Isaiah 38), Hezekiah took his newfound health for granted and became prideful about all the wealth and power of his kingdom. Without giving the Lord credit, Hezekiah seemed to have become inwardly focused and puffed up. In this way, perhaps, Hezekiah did live "just as his ancestor David had done" (2 Kings 18:3). David's apathetic faith as king brought down the future of the kingdom. Hezekiah's did the same.

Watch out for the pride of ego and apathy of faith that can creep into your life.

2 Kgs 19:5-7 ►

5 Hezekiah trusted in the LORD, the God of Israel. There was no one like him among all the kings of Judah, either before or after his time. 6 He remained faithful to the LORD in everything, and he carefully obeyed all the commands the LORD had given Moses. 7 So the LORD was with him, and Hezekiah was successful in everything he did. He revolted against the king of Assyria and refused to pay him tribute. 8 He also conquered the Philistines as far distant as Gaza and its territory, from their smallest outpost to their largest walled city.

9 During the fourth year of Hezekiah's reign, which was the seventh year of King Hoshea's reign in Israel, King Shalmaneser of Assyria attacked the city of Samaria and began a siege against it. 10 Three years later, during the sixth year of King Hezekiah's reign and the ninth year of King Hoshea's reign in Israel, Samaria fell. 11 At that time the king of Assyria exiled the Israelites to Assyria and placed them in colonies in Halah, along the banks of the Habor River in Gozan, and in the cities of the Medes. 12 For they refused to listen to the LORD their God and obey him. Instead, they violated his covenant—all the laws that Moses the LORD's servant had commanded them to obey.

Assyria Invades Judah

13 In the fourteenth year of King Hezekiah's reign,* King Sennacherib of Assyria came to attack the fortified towns of Judah and conquered them. 14 King Hezekiah sent this message to the king of Assyria at Lachish: "I have done wrong. I will pay whatever tribute money you demand if you will only withdraw." The king of Assyria then demanded a settlement of more than eleven tons of silver and one ton of gold.* 15 To gather this amount, King Hezekiah used all the silver stored in the Temple of the LORD and in the palace treasury. 16 Hezekiah even stripped the gold from the doors of the LORD's Temple and from the doorposts he had overlaid with gold, and he gave it all to the Assyrian king.

17 Nevertheless, the king of Assyria sent his commander in chief, his field commander, and his chief of staff* from Lachish with a huge army to confront King Hezekiah in Jerusalem. The Assyrians took up a position beside the aqueduct that feeds water into the upper pool, near the road leading to the field where cloth is washed.* 18 They summoned King Hezekiah, but the king sent these officials to meet with them: Eliakim son of Hilkiah, the palace administrator; Shebna the court secretary; and Joah son of Asaph, the royal historian.

Sennacherib Threatens Jerusalem

19 Then the Assyrian king's chief of staff told them to give this message to Hezekiah:

> "This is what the great king of Assyria says: What are you trusting in that makes you so confident? 20 Do you think that mere words can substitute for military skill and strength? Who are you counting on, that you have rebelled against me? 21 On Egypt? If you lean on Egypt, it will be like a reed that splinters beneath your weight and pierces your hand. Pharaoh, the king of Egypt, is completely unreliable!
>
> 22 "But perhaps you will say to me, 'We are trusting in the LORD

18:13 The fourteenth year of Hezekiah's reign was 701 B.C. **18:14** Hebrew *300 talents* [10 metric tons] *of silver and 30 talents* [1 metric ton] *of gold.* **18:17a** Or *the rabshakeh;* also in 18:19, 26, 27, 28, 37. **18:17b** Or *bleached.*

our God!' But isn't he the one who was insulted by Hezekiah? Didn't
Hezekiah tear down his shrines and altars and make everyone in Judah
and Jerusalem worship only at the altar here in Jerusalem?
23"I'll tell you what! Strike a bargain with my master, the king of
Assyria. I will give you 2,000 horses if you can find that many men to
ride on them! 24With your tiny army, how can you think of challenging
even the weakest contingent of my master's troops, even with the
help of Egypt's chariots and charioteers? 25What's more, do you think
we have invaded your land without the LORD's direction? The LORD
himself told us, 'Attack this land and destroy it!'"

26Then Eliakim son of Hilkiah, Shebna, and Joah said to the Assyrian chief
of staff, "Please speak to us in Aramaic, for we understand it well. Don't speak
in Hebrew,* for the people on the wall will hear."
27But Sennacherib's chief of staff replied, "Do you think my master sent
this message only to you and your master? He wants all the people to hear
it, for when we put this city under siege, they will suffer along with you.
They will be so hungry and thirsty that they will eat their own dung and
drink their own urine."
28Then the chief of staff stood and shouted in Hebrew to the people on
the wall, "Listen to this message from the great king of Assyria! 29This is
what the king says: Don't let Hezekiah deceive you. He will never be able to
rescue you from my power. 30Don't let him fool you into trusting in the LORD
by saying, 'The LORD will surely rescue us. This city will never fall into the
hands of the Assyrian king!'
31"Don't listen to Hezekiah! These are the terms the king of Assyria is
offering: Make peace with me—open the gates and come out. Then each of
you can continue eating from your own grapevine and fig tree and drinking
from your own well. 32Then I will arrange to take you to another land like
this one—a land of grain and new wine, bread and vineyards, olive groves
and honey. Choose life instead of death!
"Don't listen to Hezekiah when he tries to mislead you by saying, 'The
LORD will rescue us!' 33Have the gods of any other nations ever saved their
people from the king of Assyria? 34What happened to the gods of Hamath
and Arpad? And what about the gods of Sepharvaim, Hena, and Ivvah? Did
any god rescue Samaria from my power? 35What god of any nation has ever
been able to save its people from my power? So what makes you think that
the LORD can rescue Jerusalem from me?"
36But the people were silent and did not utter a word because Hezekiah
had commanded them, "Do not answer him."
37Then Eliakim son of Hilkiah, the palace administrator; Shebna the court
secretary; and Joah son of Asaph, the royal historian, went back to Hezekiah.
They tore their clothes in despair, and they went in to see the king and told
him what the Assyrian chief of staff had said.

Hezekiah Seeks the LORD's Help

19 When King Hezekiah heard their report, he tore his clothes and
put on burlap and went into the Temple of the LORD. 2And he
sent Eliakim the palace administrator, Shebna the court secretary, and

18:26 Hebrew *in the dialect of Judah;* also in 18:28.

Write your notes in this space

the leading priests, all dressed in burlap, to the prophet Isaiah son of
Amoz. 3They told him, "This is what King Hezekiah says: Today is a day
of trouble, insults, and disgrace. It is like when a child is ready to be born,
but the mother has no strength to deliver the baby. 4But perhaps the LORD
your God has heard the Assyrian chief of staff,* sent by the king to defy
the living God, and will punish him for his words. Oh, pray for those of
us who are left!"

5After King Hezekiah's officials delivered the king's message to Isaiah,
6the prophet replied, "Say to your master, 'This is what the LORD says: Do
not be disturbed by this blasphemous speech against me from the Assyrian
king's messengers. 7Listen! I myself will move against him,* and the king will
receive a message that he is needed at home. So he will return to his land,
where I will have him killed with a sword.'"

8Meanwhile, the Assyrian chief of staff left Jerusalem and went to consult
the king of Assyria, who had left Lachish and was attacking Libnah.

9Soon afterward King Sennacherib received word that King Tirhakah
of Ethiopia* was leading an army to fight against him. Before leaving to
meet the attack, he sent messengers back to Hezekiah in Jerusalem with
this message:

10"This message is for King Hezekiah of Judah. Don't let your God, in
whom you trust, deceive you with promises that Jerusalem will not
be captured by the king of Assyria. 11You know perfectly well what
the kings of Assyria have done wherever they have gone. They have
completely destroyed everyone who stood in their way! Why should you
be any different? 12Have the gods of other nations rescued them—such
nations as Gozan, Haran, Rezeph, and the people of Eden who were in
Tel-assar? My predecessors destroyed them all! 13What happened to the
king of Hamath and the king of Arpad? What happened to the kings of
Sepharvaim, Hena, and Ivvah?"

14After Hezekiah received the letter from the messengers and read it, he
went up to the LORD's Temple and spread it out before the LORD. 15And
Hezekiah prayed this prayer before the LORD: "O LORD, God of Israel, you
are enthroned between the mighty cherubim! You alone are God of all the
kingdoms of the earth. You alone created the heavens and the earth. 16Bend
down, O LORD, and listen! Open your eyes, O LORD, and see! Listen to Sen-
nacherib's words of defiance against the living God.

17"It is true, LORD, that the kings of Assyria have destroyed all these na-
tions. 18And they have thrown the gods of these nations into the fire and
burned them. But of course the Assyrians could destroy them! They were not
gods at all—only idols of wood and stone shaped by human hands. 19Now,
O LORD our God, rescue us from his power; then all the kingdoms of the
earth will know that you alone, O LORD, are God."

Isaiah Predicts Judah's Deliverance

20Then Isaiah son of Amoz sent this message to Hezekiah: "This is what the
LORD, the God of Israel, says: I have heard your prayer about King Sennach-
erib of Assyria. 21And the LORD has spoken this word against him:

19:4 Or *the rabshakeh;* also in 19:8. 19:7 Hebrew *I will put a spirit in him.* 19:9 Hebrew *of Cush.*

Story Arc **19:5-7**

● Isaiah

When the Assyrian emperor mocked and threatened Hezekiah, he reached out to the prophet Isaiah, who essentially assured him, "We're all good, King. Don't worry." Isaiah proclaimed a powerful message in those years. It was a message of good news to the poor but judgment for those who refused to humble themselves before the Lord. When King Hezekiah and the people presented themselves in a posture of mercy and humility, Isaiah's message was one of rescue and salvation (Isaiah 61). When, however, people rejected the patterns of God, Isaiah's message was frightful (Isaiah 24). Go to the book of Isaiah and read through his messages for the nations. What consistent story arc of Scripture do you see embedded in Isaiah's words?

2 Kgs 22:1-2 ►

"The virgin daughter of Zion
despises you and laughs at you.
The daughter of Jerusalem
shakes her head in derision as you flee.

22 "Whom have you been defying and ridiculing?
Against whom did you raise your voice?
At whom did you look with such haughty eyes?
It was the Holy One of Israel!
23 By your messengers you have defied the Lord.
You have said, 'With my many chariots
I have conquered the highest mountains—
yes, the remotest peaks of Lebanon.
I have cut down its tallest cedars
and its finest cypress trees.
I have reached its farthest corners
and explored its deepest forests.
24 I have dug wells in many foreign lands
and refreshed myself with their water.
With the sole of my foot
I stopped up all the rivers of Egypt!'

25 "But have you not heard?
I decided this long ago.
Long ago I planned it,
and now I am making it happen.
I planned for you to crush fortified cities
into heaps of rubble.
26 That is why their people have so little power
and are so frightened and confused.
They are as weak as grass,
as easily trampled as tender green shoots.
They are like grass sprouting on a housetop,
scorched before it can grow lush and tall.

27 "But I know you well—
where you stay
and when you come and go.
I know the way you have raged against me.
28 And because of your raging against me
and your arrogance, which I have heard for myself,
I will put my hook in your nose
and my bit in your mouth.
I will make you return
by the same road on which you came."

29 Then Isaiah said to Hezekiah, "Here is the proof that what I say is true:

"This year you will eat only what grows up by itself,
and next year you will eat what springs up from that.

Prayer 20:2

Lord, you are a healer who gives mercy to the brokenhearted, so let me be brokenhearted. Amen.

But in the third year you will plant crops and harvest them;
you will tend vineyards and eat their fruit.
30 And you who are left in Judah,
who have escaped the ravages of the siege,
will put roots down in your own soil
and will grow up and flourish.
31 For a remnant of my people will spread out from Jerusalem,
a group of survivors from Mount Zion.
The passionate commitment of the LORD of Heaven's Armies*
will make this happen!

32 "And this is what the LORD says about the king of Assyria:

"His armies will not enter Jerusalem.
They will not even shoot an arrow at it.
They will not march outside its gates with their shields
nor build banks of earth against its walls.
33 The king will return to his own country
by the same road on which he came.
He will not enter this city,
says the LORD.
34 For my own honor and for the sake of my servant David,
I will defend this city and protect it."

35 That night the angel of the LORD went out to the Assyrian camp and
killed 185,000 Assyrian soldiers. When the surviving Assyrians* woke up
the next morning, they found corpses everywhere. 36 Then King Sennacherib
of Assyria broke camp and returned to his own land. He went home to his
capital of Nineveh and stayed there.
37 One day while he was worshiping in the temple of his god Nisroch, his
sons* Adrammelech and Sharezer killed him with their swords. They then
escaped to the land of Ararat, and another son, Esarhaddon, became the
next king of Assyria.

Hezekiah's Sickness and Recovery

20 About that time Hezekiah became deathly ill, and the prophet Isaiah
son of Amoz went to visit him. He gave the king this message: "This
is what the LORD says: Set your affairs in order, for you are going to die. You
will not recover from this illness."
2 When Hezekiah heard this, he turned his face to the wall and prayed to
the LORD, 3 "Remember, O LORD, how I have always been faithful to you and
have served you single-mindedly, always doing what pleases you." Then he
broke down and wept bitterly.
4 But before Isaiah had left the middle courtyard,* this message came to him
from the LORD: 5 "Go back to Hezekiah, the leader of my people. Tell him,
'This is what the LORD, the God of your ancestor David, says: I have heard
your prayer and seen your tears. I will heal you, and three days from now you

19:31 As in Greek and Syriac versions, Latin Vulgate, and an alternate reading of the Masoretic Text (see also Isa 37:32); the other alternate reads *the LORD.* 19:35 Hebrew *When they.* 19:37 As in Greek version and an alternate reading of the Masoretic Text (see also Isa 37:38); the other alternate reading lacks *his sons.* 20:4 As in Greek version and an alternate reading in the Masoretic Text; the other alternate reads *the middle of the city.*

will get out of bed and go to the Temple of the LORD. 6 I will add fifteen years
to your life, and I will rescue you and this city from the king of Assyria. I will
defend this city for my own honor and for the sake of my servant David.'"
7 Then Isaiah said, "Make an ointment from figs." So Hezekiah's servants
spread the ointment over the boil, and Hezekiah recovered!
8 Meanwhile, Hezekiah had said to Isaiah, "What sign will the LORD give
to prove that he will heal me and that I will go to the Temple of the LORD
three days from now?"
9 Isaiah replied, "This is the sign from the LORD to prove that he will do as
he promised. Would you like the shadow on the sundial to go forward ten
steps or backward ten steps?*"
10 "The shadow always moves forward," Hezekiah replied, "so that would
be easy. Make it go ten steps backward instead." 11 So Isaiah the prophet asked
the LORD to do this, and he caused the shadow to move ten steps backward
on the sundial* of Ahaz!

Envoys from Babylon

12 Soon after this, Merodach-baladan* son of Baladan, king of Babylon, sent
Hezekiah his best wishes and a gift, for he had heard that Hezekiah had
been very sick. 13 Hezekiah received the Babylonian envoys and showed them
everything in his treasure-houses—the silver, the gold, the spices, and the
aromatic oils. He also took them to see his armory and showed them every-
thing in his royal treasuries! There was nothing in his palace or kingdom
that Hezekiah did not show them.
14 Then Isaiah the prophet went to King Hezekiah and asked him, "What
did those men want? Where were they from?"
Hezekiah replied, "They came from the distant land of Babylon."
15 "What did they see in your palace?" Isaiah asked.
"They saw everything," Hezekiah replied. "I showed them everything I
own—all my royal treasuries."
16 Then Isaiah said to Hezekiah, "Listen to this message from the LORD:
17 The time is coming when everything in your palace—all the treasures
stored up by your ancestors until now—will be carried off to Babylon. Noth-
ing will be left, says the LORD. 18 Some of your very own sons will be taken
away into exile. They will become eunuchs who will serve in the palace of
Babylon's king."
19 Then Hezekiah said to Isaiah, "This message you have given me from
the LORD is good." For the king was thinking, "At least there will be peace
and security during my lifetime."
20 The rest of the events in Hezekiah's reign, including the extent of his
power and how he built a pool and dug a tunnel* to bring water into the city,
are recorded in *The Book of the History of the Kings of Judah.* 21 Hezekiah died,
and his son Manasseh became the next king.

Manasseh Rules in Judah

21 Manasseh was twelve years old when he became king, and he reigned
in Jerusalem fifty-five years. His mother was Hephzibah. 2 He did
what was evil in the LORD's sight, following the detestable practices of the

20:9 Or *The shadow on the sundial has gone forward ten steps; do you want it to go backward ten steps?*
20:11 Hebrew *the steps.* **20:12** As in some Hebrew manuscripts and Greek and Syriac versions
(see also Isa 39:1); Masoretic Text reads *Berodach-baladan.* **20:20** Hebrew *watercourse.*

pagan nations that the LORD had driven from the land ahead of the Isra-
elites. 3 He rebuilt the pagan shrines his father, Hezekiah, had destroyed.
He constructed altars for Baal and set up an Asherah pole, just as King Ahab
of Israel had done. He also bowed before all the powers of the heavens and
worshiped them.

4 He built pagan altars in the Temple of the LORD, the place where the
LORD had said, "My name will remain in Jerusalem forever." 5 He built these
altars for all the powers of the heavens in both courtyards of the LORD's
Temple. 6 Manasseh also sacrificed his own son in the fire.* He practiced sor-
cery and divination, and he consulted with mediums and psychics. He did
much that was evil in the LORD's sight, arousing his anger.

7 Manasseh even made a carved image of Asherah and set it up in the
Temple, the very place where the LORD had told David and his son Solomon:
"My name will be honored forever in this Temple and in Jerusalem—the
city I have chosen from among all the tribes of Israel. 8 If the Israelites will be
careful to obey my commands—all the laws my servant Moses gave them—I
will not send them into exile from this land that I gave their ancestors."
9 But the people refused to listen, and Manasseh led them to do even more
evil than the pagan nations that the LORD had destroyed when the people
of Israel entered the land.

10 Then the LORD said through his servants the prophets: 11 "King Ma-
nasseh of Judah has done many detestable things. He is even more wicked
than the Amorites, who lived in this land before Israel. He has caused the
people of Judah to sin with his idols.* 12 So this is what the LORD, the God of
Israel, says: I will bring such disaster on Jerusalem and Judah that the ears of
those who hear about it will tingle with horror. 13 I will judge Jerusalem by
the same standard I used for Samaria and the same measure* I used for the
family of Ahab. I will wipe away the people of Jerusalem as one wipes a dish
and turns it upside down. 14 Then I will reject even the remnant of my own
people who are left, and I will hand them over as plunder for their enemies.
15 For they have done great evil in my sight and have angered me ever since
their ancestors came out of Egypt."

16 Manasseh also murdered many innocent people until Jerusalem was
filled from one end to the other with innocent blood. This was in addition
to the sin that he caused the people of Judah to commit, leading them to do
evil in the LORD's sight.

17 The rest of the events in Manasseh's reign and everything he did, includ-
ing the sins he committed, are recorded in *The Book of the History of the Kings of
Judah*. 18 When Manasseh died, he was buried in the palace garden, the garden
of Uzza. Then his son Amon became the next king.

Amon Rules in Judah

19 Amon was twenty-two years old when he became king, and he reigned in
Jerusalem two years. His mother was Meshullemeth, the daughter of Haruz
from Jotbah. 20 He did what was evil in the LORD's sight, just as his father,
Manasseh, had done. 21 He followed the example of his father, worshiping
the same idols his father had worshiped. 22 He abandoned the LORD, the God
of his ancestors, and he refused to follow the LORD's ways.

21:6 Or *also made his son pass through the fire.* **21:11** The Hebrew term (literally *round things*) probably alludes to dung; also in 21:21. **21:13** Hebrew *the same plumb line I used for Samaria and the same plumb bob.*

23 Then Amon's own officials conspired against him and assassinated him in his palace. 24 But the people of the land killed all those who had conspired against King Amon, and they made his son Josiah the next king.

25 The rest of the events in Amon's reign and what he did are recorded in *The Book of the History of the Kings of Judah.* 26 He was buried in his tomb in the garden of Uzza. Then his son Josiah became the next king.

Josiah Rules in Judah

22 Josiah was eight years old when he became king, and he reigned in Jerusalem thirty-one years. His mother was Jedidah, the daughter of Adaiah from Bozkath. 2 He did what was pleasing in the LORD's sight and followed the example of his ancestor David. He did not turn away from doing what was right.

3 In the eighteenth year of his reign, King Josiah sent Shaphan son of Azaliah and grandson of Meshullam, the court secretary, to the Temple of the LORD. He told him, 4 "Go to Hilkiah the high priest and have him count the money the gatekeepers have collected from the people at the LORD's Temple. 5 Entrust this money to the men assigned to supervise the restoration of the LORD's Temple. Then they can use it to pay workers to repair the Temple. 6 They will need to hire carpenters, builders, and masons. Also have them buy the timber and the finished stone needed to repair the Temple. 7 But don't require the construction supervisors to keep account of the money they receive, for they are honest and trustworthy men."

Hilkiah Discovers God's Law

8 Hilkiah the high priest said to Shaphan the court secretary, "I have found the Book of the Law in the LORD's Temple!" Then Hilkiah gave the scroll to Shaphan, and he read it.

9 Shaphan went to the king and reported, "Your officials have turned over the money collected at the Temple of the LORD to the workers and supervisors at the Temple." 10 Shaphan also told the king, "Hilkiah the priest has given me a scroll." So Shaphan read it to the king.

11 When the king heard what was written in the Book of the Law, he tore his clothes in despair. 12 Then he gave these orders to Hilkiah the priest, Ahikam son of Shaphan, Acbor son of Micaiah, Shaphan the court secretary, and Asaiah the king's personal adviser: 13 "Go to the Temple and speak to the LORD for me and for the people and for all Judah. Inquire about the words written in this scroll that has been found. For the LORD's great anger is burning against us because our ancestors have not obeyed the words in this scroll. We have not been doing everything it says we must do."

14 So Hilkiah the priest, Ahikam, Acbor, Shaphan, and Asaiah went to the New Quarter* of Jerusalem to consult with the prophet Huldah. She was the wife of Shallum son of Tikvah, son of Harhas, the keeper of the Temple wardrobe.

15 She said to them, "The LORD, the God of Israel, has spoken! Go back and tell the man who sent you, 16 'This is what the LORD says: I am going to bring disaster on this city* and its people. All the words written in the scroll that the king of Judah has read will come true. 17 For my people have abandoned me and offered sacrifices to pagan gods, and I am very angry with them for

22:14 Or *the Second Quarter,* a newer section of Jerusalem. Hebrew reads *the Mishneh.*
22:16 Hebrew *this place;* also in 22:19, 20.

Question **22:8**

Notice in the following verses the huge difference the Word of God made! What kind of changes would occur in the community around you if people rediscovered the Word of God?

Story Arc **22:1–2**

Josiah

After the mess Manasseh left and the turmoil of the throne in the years that followed, it is astonishing that the young Josiah was able to live wholeheartedly for the Lord. He became king when he was eight years old and reigned for thirty-one years.

When the high priest rediscovered the book of the law (which many people think may have been the book of Deuteronomy and might have been lost or purposefully hidden during Manasseh's reign), Josiah was gutted by God's Word. In fact, the Scripture made such a huge difference in his soul that he decided to reform himself and the entire kingdom. Second Kings 23:25 speaks of his legacy: "Never before had there been a king like Josiah, who turned to the LORD with all his heart and soul and strength, obeying all the laws of Moses."

2 Kgs 25:27-30 ►

Question **23:2**

Isaiah 55:11 proclaims that everywhere the Lord sent out his Word, fruitfulness would be the result. The Word of God will prosper everywhere it goes. Here's a question for you: Have you spent time with the Bible in such a way that God's Word will enter your heart and mind and soul?

everything they have done. My anger will burn against this place, and it will
not be quenched.'
18 "But go to the king of Judah who sent you to seek the LORD and tell him:
'This is what the LORD, the God of Israel, says concerning the message you
have just heard: 19 You were sorry and humbled yourself before the LORD
when you heard what I said against this city and its people—that this land
would be cursed and become desolate. You tore your clothing in despair and
wept before me in repentance. And I have indeed heard you, says the LORD.
20 So I will not send the promised disaster until after you have died and been
buried in peace. You will not see the disaster I am going to bring on this city.'"
So they took her message back to the king.

Josiah's Religious Reforms

23 Then the king summoned all the elders of Judah and Jerusalem.
2 And the king went up to the Temple of the LORD with all the people
of Judah and Jerusalem, along with the priests and the prophets—all the
people from the least to the greatest. There the king read to them the entire
Book of the Covenant that had been found in the LORD's Temple. 3 The king
took his place of authority beside the pillar and renewed the covenant in the
LORD's presence. He pledged to obey the LORD by keeping all his commands,
laws, and decrees with all his heart and soul. In this way, he confirmed all
the terms of the covenant that were written in the scroll, and all the people
pledged themselves to the covenant.
4 Then the king instructed Hilkiah the high priest and the priests of the
second rank and the Temple gatekeepers to remove from the LORD's Temple
all the articles that were used to worship Baal, Asherah, and all the powers
of the heavens. The king had all these things burned outside Jerusalem on
the terraces of the Kidron Valley, and he carried the ashes away to Bethel.
5 He did away with the idolatrous priests, who had been appointed by the
previous kings of Judah, for they had offered sacrifices at the pagan shrines
throughout Judah and even in the vicinity of Jerusalem. They had also of-
fered sacrifices to Baal, and to the sun, the moon, the constellations, and to
all the powers of the heavens. 6 The king removed the Asherah pole from the
LORD's Temple and took it outside Jerusalem to the Kidron Valley, where he
burned it. Then he ground the ashes of the pole to dust and threw the dust
over the graves of the people. 7 He also tore down the living quarters of the
male and female shrine prostitutes that were inside the Temple of the LORD,
where the women wove coverings for the Asherah pole.
8 Josiah brought to Jerusalem all the priests who were living in other
towns of Judah. He also defiled the pagan shrines, where they had offered
sacrifices—all the way from Geba to Beersheba. He destroyed the shrines
at the entrance to the gate of Joshua, the governor of Jerusalem. This gate
was located to the left of the city gate as one enters the city. 9 The priests who
had served at the pagan shrines were not allowed to serve at* the LORD's
altar in Jerusalem, but they were allowed to eat unleavened bread with the
other priests.
10 Then the king defiled the altar of Topheth in the valley of Ben-Hinnom,
so no one could ever again use it to sacrifice a son or daughter in the fire* as
an offering to Molech. 11 He removed from the entrance of the LORD's Temple

23:9 Hebrew *did not come up to.* **23:10** Or *to make a son or daughter pass through the fire.*

the horse statues that the former kings of Judah had dedicated to the sun. They were near the quarters of Nathan-melech the eunuch, an officer of the court.* The king also burned the chariots dedicated to the sun.

12 Josiah tore down the altars that the kings of Judah had built on the palace roof above the upper room of Ahaz. The king destroyed the altars that Manasseh had built in the two courtyards of the LORD's Temple. He smashed them to bits* and scattered the pieces in the Kidron Valley. 13 The king also desecrated the pagan shrines east of Jerusalem, to the south of the Mount of Corruption, where King Solomon of Israel had built shrines for Ashtoreth, the detestable goddess of the Sidonians; and for Chemosh, the detestable god of the Moabites; and for Molech,* the vile god of the Ammonites. 14 He smashed the sacred pillars and cut down the Asherah poles. Then he desecrated these places by scattering human bones over them.

15 The king also tore down the altar at Bethel—the pagan shrine that Jeroboam son of Nebat had made when he caused Israel to sin. He burned down the shrine and ground it to dust, and he burned the Asherah pole. 16 Then Josiah turned around and noticed several tombs in the side of the hill. He ordered that the bones be brought out, and he burned them on the altar at Bethel to desecrate it. (This happened just as the LORD had promised through the man of God when Jeroboam stood beside the altar at the festival.)

Then Josiah turned and looked up at the tomb of the man of God* who had predicted these things. 17 "What is that monument over there?" Josiah asked.

And the people of the town told him, "It is the tomb of the man of God who came from Judah and predicted the very things that you have just done to the altar at Bethel!"

18 Josiah replied, "Leave it alone. Don't disturb his bones." So they did not burn his bones or those of the old prophet from Samaria.

19 Then Josiah demolished all the buildings at the pagan shrines in the towns of Samaria, just as he had done at Bethel. They had been built by the various kings of Israel and had made the LORD* very angry. 20 He executed the priests of the pagan shrines on their own altars, and he burned human bones on the altars to desecrate them. Finally, he returned to Jerusalem.

Josiah Celebrates Passover

21 King Josiah then issued this order to all the people: "You must celebrate the Passover to the LORD your God, as required in this Book of the Covenant." 22 There had not been a Passover celebration like that since the time when the judges ruled in Israel, nor throughout all the years of the kings of Israel and Judah. 23 But in the eighteenth year of King Josiah's reign, this Passover was celebrated to the LORD in Jerusalem.

24 Josiah also got rid of the mediums and psychics, the household gods, the idols,* and every other kind of detestable practice, both in Jerusalem and throughout the land of Judah. He did this in obedience to the laws written in the scroll that Hilkiah the priest had found in the LORD's Temple. 25 Never before had there been a king like Josiah, who turned to the LORD with all his heart and soul and strength, obeying all the laws of Moses. And there has never been a king like him since.

23:11 The meaning of the Hebrew is uncertain. 23:12 Or *He quickly removed them.* 23:13 Hebrew *Milcom,* a variant spelling of Molech. 23:16 As in Greek version; Hebrew lacks *when Jeroboam stood beside the altar at the festival. Then Josiah turned and looked up at the tomb of the man of God.* 23:19 As in Greek and Syriac versions and Latin Vulgate; Hebrew lacks *the LORD.* 23:24 The Hebrew term (literally *round things*) probably alludes to dung.

Prayer 23:25

Lord, give me this sort of depth of faith and passion for you. Amen.

26 Even so, the LORD was very angry with Judah because of all the wicked
things Manasseh had done to provoke him. 27 For the LORD said, "I will also
banish Judah from my presence just as I have banished Israel. And I will
reject my chosen city of Jerusalem and the Temple where my name was to
be honored."

28 The rest of the events in Josiah's reign and all his deeds are recorded in
The Book of the History of the Kings of Judah.

29 While Josiah was king, Pharaoh Neco, king of Egypt, went to the Eu-
phrates River to help the king of Assyria. King Josiah and his army marched
out to fight him,* but King Neco* killed him when they met at Megiddo.
30 Josiah's officers took his body back in a chariot from Megiddo to Jerusa-
lem and buried him in his own tomb. Then the people of the land anointed
Josiah's son Jehoahaz and made him the next king.

Jehoahaz Rules in Judah

31 Jehoahaz was twenty-three years old when he became king, and he reigned
in Jerusalem three months. His mother was Hamutal, the daughter of Jer-
emiah from Libnah. 32 He did what was evil in the LORD's sight, just as his
ancestors had done.

33 Pharaoh Neco put Jehoahaz in prison at Riblah in the land of Hamath
to prevent him from ruling* in Jerusalem. He also demanded that Judah pay
7,500 pounds of silver and 75 pounds of gold* as tribute.

Jehoiakim Rules in Judah

34 Pharaoh Neco then installed Eliakim, another of Josiah's sons, to reign in
place of his father, and he changed Eliakim's name to Jehoiakim. Jehoahaz
was taken to Egypt as a prisoner, where he died.

35 In order to get the silver and gold demanded as tribute by Pharaoh Neco,
Jehoiakim collected a tax from the people of Judah, requiring them to pay
in proportion to their wealth.

36 Jehoiakim was twenty-five years old when he became king, and he
reigned in Jerusalem eleven years. His mother was Zebidah, the daughter
of Pedaiah from Rumah. 37 He did what was evil in the LORD's sight, just as
his ancestors had done.

24 During Jehoiakim's reign, King Nebuchadnezzar of Babylon in-
vaded the land of Judah. Jehoiakim surrendered and paid him
tribute for three years but then rebelled. 2 Then the LORD sent bands of
Babylonian,* Aramean, Moabite, and Ammonite raiders against Judah to
destroy it, just as the LORD had promised through his prophets. 3 These
disasters happened to Judah because of the LORD's command. He had de-
cided to banish Judah from his presence because of the many sins of Ma-
nasseh, 4 who had filled Jerusalem with innocent blood. The LORD would
not forgive this.

5 The rest of the events in Jehoiakim's reign and all his deeds are recorded
in *The Book of the History of the Kings of Judah.* 6 When Jehoiakim died, his son
Jehoiachin became the next king.

7 The king of Egypt did not venture out of his country after that, for the

23:29a Or *Josiah went out to meet him.* **23:29b** Hebrew *he.* **23:33a** The meaning of the Hebrew is uncertain. **23:33b** Hebrew *100 talents* [3,400 kilograms] *of silver and 1 talent* [34 kilograms] *of gold.* **24:2** Or *Chaldean.*

king of Babylon captured the entire area formerly claimed by Egypt—from
the Brook of Egypt to the Euphrates River.

Jehoiachin Rules in Judah

8 Jehoiachin was eighteen years old when he became king, and he reigned
in Jerusalem three months. His mother was Nehushta, the daughter of El-
nathan from Jerusalem. 9 Jehoiachin did what was evil in the LORD's sight,
just as his father had done.

10 During Jehoiachin's reign, the officers of King Nebuchadnezzar of Bab-
ylon came up against Jerusalem and besieged it. 11 Nebuchadnezzar himself
arrived at the city during the siege. 12 Then King Jehoiachin, along with the
queen mother, his advisers, his commanders, and his officials, surrendered
to the Babylonians.

In the eighth year of Nebuchadnezzar's reign, he took Jehoiachin prisoner.
13 As the LORD had said beforehand, Nebuchadnezzar carried away all the
treasures from the LORD's Temple and the royal palace. He stripped away*
all the gold objects that King Solomon of Israel had placed in the Temple.
14 King Nebuchadnezzar took all of Jerusalem captive, including all the com-
manders and the best of the soldiers, craftsmen, and artisans—10,000 in all.
Only the poorest people were left in the land.

15 Nebuchadnezzar led King Jehoiachin away as a captive to Babylon, along
with the queen mother, his wives and officials, and all Jerusalem's elite. 16 He
also exiled 7,000 of the best troops and 1,000 craftsmen and artisans, all of
whom were strong and fit for war. 17 Then the king of Babylon installed Mat-
taniah, Jehoiachin's* uncle, as the next king, and he changed Mattaniah's
name to Zedekiah.

Zedekiah Rules in Judah

18 Zedekiah was twenty-one years old when he became king, and he reigned
in Jerusalem eleven years. His mother was Hamutal, the daughter of Jere-
miah from Libnah. 19 But Zedekiah did what was evil in the LORD's sight,
just as Jehoiakim had done. 20 These things happened because of the LORD's
anger against the people of Jerusalem and Judah, until he finally banished
them from his presence and sent them into exile.

The Fall of Jerusalem

Zedekiah rebelled against the king of Babylon.

25 So on January 15,* during the ninth year of Zedekiah's reign, King
Nebuchadnezzar of Babylon led his entire army against Jerusa-
lem. They surrounded the city and built siege ramps against its walls.
2 Jerusalem was kept under siege until the eleventh year of King Zede-
kiah's reign.

3 By July 18 in the eleventh year of Zedekiah's reign,* the famine in the city
had become very severe, and the last of the food was entirely gone. 4 Then
a section of the city wall was broken down. Since the city was surrounded

24:13 Or *He cut apart.* **24:17** Hebrew *his.* **25:1** Hebrew *on the tenth day of the tenth month,* of the ancient Hebrew lunar calendar. A number of events in 2 Kings can be cross-checked with dates in surviving Babylonian records and related accurately to our modern calendar. This day was January 15, 588 B.C. **25:3** Hebrew *By the ninth day of the [fourth] month* [in the eleventh year of Zedekiah's reign] (compare Jer 39:2; 52:6 and the notes there). This day was July 18, 586 B.C.; also see note on 25:1.

Why this matters!

Question 25:8–11

Why was this such an incredibly devastating event? Why did it seem that the Lord had been defeated in Jerusalem? What was the real story behind the scenes?

by the Babylonians,* the soldiers waited for nightfall and escaped* through
the gate between the two walls behind the king's garden. Then they headed
toward the Jordan Valley.*
5 But the Babylonian* troops chased the king and overtook him on the
plains of Jericho, for his men had all deserted him and scattered. 6 They cap-
tured the king and took him to the king of Babylon at Riblah, where they
pronounced judgment upon Zedekiah. 7 They made Zedekiah watch as they
slaughtered his sons. Then they gouged out Zedekiah's eyes, bound him in
bronze chains, and led him away to Babylon.

The Temple Destroyed

8 On August 14 of that year,* which was the nineteenth year of King Nebuchad-
nezzar's reign, Nebuzaradan, the captain of the guard and an official of the
Babylonian king, arrived in Jerusalem. 9 He burned down the Temple of the
LORD, the royal palace, and all the houses of Jerusalem. He destroyed all the im-
portant buildings* in the city. 10 Then he supervised the entire Babylonian army
as they tore down the walls of Jerusalem on every side. 11 Then Nebuzaradan,
the captain of the guard, took as exiles the rest of the people who remained in
the city, the defectors who had declared their allegiance to the king of Babylon,
and the rest of the population. 12 But the captain of the guard allowed some of
the poorest people to stay behind to care for the vineyards and fields.
13 The Babylonians broke up the bronze pillars in front of the LORD's
Temple, the bronze water carts, and the great bronze basin called the Sea,
and they carried all the bronze away to Babylon. 14 They also took all the ash
buckets, shovels, lamp snuffers, ladles, and all the other bronze articles used
for making sacrifices at the Temple. 15 The captain of the guard also took the in-
cense burners and basins, and all the other articles made of pure gold or silver.
16 The weight of the bronze from the two pillars, the Sea, and the water
carts was too great to be measured. These things had been made for the
LORD's Temple in the days of Solomon. 17 Each of the pillars was 27 feet* tall.
The bronze capital on top of each pillar was 7½ feet* high and was decorated
with a network of bronze pomegranates all the way around.
18 Nebuzaradan, the captain of the guard, took with him as prisoners Se-
raiah the high priest, Zephaniah the priest of the second rank, and the three
chief gatekeepers. 19 And from among the people still hiding in the city, he
took an officer who had been in charge of the Judean army; five of the king's
personal advisers; the army commander's chief secretary, who was in charge
of recruitment; and sixty other citizens. 20 Nebuzaradan, the captain of the
guard, took them all to the king of Babylon at Riblah. 21 And there at Riblah,
in the land of Hamath, the king of Babylon had them all put to death. So the
people of Judah were sent into exile from their land.

Gedaliah Governs in Judah

22 Then King Nebuchadnezzar appointed Gedaliah son of Ahikam and
grandson of Shaphan as governor over the people he had left in Judah.

25:4a Or *the Chaldeans;* also in 25:13, 25, 26. **25:4b** As in Greek version (see also Jer 39:4; 52:7); Hebrew lacks *escaped.* **25:4c** Hebrew *the Arabah.* **25:5** Or *Chaldean;* also in 25:10, 24. **25:8** Hebrew *On the seventh day of the fifth month,* of the ancient Hebrew lunar calendar. This day was August 14, 586 B.C.; also see note on 25:1. **25:9** Or *destroyed the houses of all the important people.* **25:17a** Hebrew *18 cubits* [8.3 meters]. **25:17b** As in parallel texts at 1 Kgs 7:16, 2 Chr 3:15, and Jer 52:22, all of which read *5 cubits* [2.3 meters]; Hebrew reads *3 cubits,* which is 4.5 feet or 1.4 meters.

23 When all the army commanders and their men learned that the king of
Babylon had appointed Gedaliah as governor, they went to see him at Miz-
pah. These included Ishmael son of Nethaniah, Johanan son of Kareah, Se-
raiah son of Tanhumeth the Netophathite, Jezaniah* son of the Maacathite,
and all their men.
24 Gedaliah vowed to them that the Babylonian officials meant them no
harm. "Don't be afraid of them. Live in the land and serve the king of Bab-
ylon, and all will go well for you," he promised.
25 But in midautumn of that year,* Ishmael son of Nethaniah and grandson
of Elishama, who was a member of the royal family, went to Mizpah with
ten men and killed Gedaliah. He also killed all the Judeans and Babylonians
who were with him at Mizpah.
26 Then all the people of Judah, from the least to the greatest, as well as
the army commanders, fled in panic to Egypt, for they were afraid of what
the Babylonians would do to them.

Hope for Israel's Royal Line

27 In the thirty-seventh year of the exile of King Jehoiachin of Judah, Evil-
merodach ascended to the Babylonian throne. He was kind to* Jehoiachin
and released him* from prison on April 2 of that year.* 28 He spoke kindly to
Jehoiachin and gave him a higher place than all the other exiled kings in
Babylon. 29 He supplied Jehoiachin with new clothes to replace his prison
garb and allowed him to dine in the king's presence for the rest of his life.
30 So the king gave him a regular food allowance as long as he lived.

25:23 As in parallel text at Jer 40:8; Hebrew reads *Jaazaniah,* a variant spelling of Jezaniah. **25:25** Hebrew *in the seventh month,* of the ancient Hebrew lunar calendar. This month occurred within the months of October and November 586 B.C.; also see note on 25:1. **25:27a** Hebrew *He raised the head of.* **25:27b** As in some Hebrew manuscripts and Greek and Syriac versions (see also Jer 52:31); Masoretic Text lacks *released him.* **25:27c** Hebrew *on the twenty-seventh day of the twelfth month,* of the ancient Hebrew lunar calendar. This day was April 2, 561 B.C.; also see note on 25:1.

Story Arc 25:27-30

● Jesus

This book ends on an interesting note. Throughout 2 Kings, it appears as if the royal line of David could be wiped out. This is significant because the story arc of God, his promises of salvation through a Messiah in the line of David, could be destroyed. Despite these threats, here, at the end of this account of sin and destruction and intrigue and betrayal and violence, is a glimmer of hope. With King Jehoiachin, even though he was divested of true power, the line of David still survived. A remnant of royalty was kept alive. Several hundred years later, Jehoiachin's name is mentioned again: in Matthew's account of the lineage of the Messiah, Jesus Christ (Matthew 1:12)!

As you consider the overarching promise of salvation, even in the midst of human disruption and destruction, how do you see God orchestrating his plan?

1 Chr 1:1-2:15 ►

1 Chronicles Introduction

Do you like remakes—when a movie or series of movies is remade with different actors and adjusted story lines? The books of Chronicles are a retelling of the stories of the books of Samuel and Kings. Why was this needed? The exile changed everything! As you read in 2 Kings, Israel's story ended with the destruction of Jerusalem and the exile of God's people to Babylon. Daniel tells the story of one of those exiles in Babylon and the challenges the exiles faced in a land that did not worship the one true God—Yahweh.

The books of Samuel and Kings were written in the exile to answer the question: What went wrong? Idolatry was the chief cause—worshiping false gods rather than the one true God. Chronicles was written after the exile, after Zerubbabel, Ezra, and Nehemiah led the Israelites back to Israel to remake their country and reestablish their capital city of Jerusalem. Now the question had changed from "What went wrong?" to "What did David and the good kings do right that allowed the Israelites to live in the promised land for 350 years before exile?"

First Chronicles starts with genealogies to connect this version of the story with history. It then tells stories of David's greatness, emphasizing God's work in David's life and victories. The greatest accomplishment was David's plan to build the temple. He gathered the materials and organized every detail because of his love for God. He desired that Israel replace the tent and tabernacle with a permanent temple worthy of the one true God. The building of that temple would be left to Solomon in 2 Chronicles.

Story Arcs

- **Adam → David**
- **David**
- **Asaph**
- **Nathan**
- **Solomon**

1 Chronicles

From Adam to Noah's Sons

1 The descendants of Adam were Seth, Enosh, 2 Kenan, Mahalalel, Jared,
3 Enoch, Methuselah, Lamech, 4 and Noah.

The sons of Noah were* Shem, Ham, and Japheth.

Descendants of Japheth

5 The descendants of Japheth were Gomer, Magog, Madai, Javan, Tubal, Meshech, and Tiras.

6 The descendants of Gomer were Ashkenaz, Riphath,* and Togarmah.

7 The descendants of Javan were Elishah, Tarshish, Kittim, and Rodanim.

Descendants of Ham

8 The descendants of Ham were Cush, Mizraim,* Put, and Canaan.

9 The descendants of Cush were Seba, Havilah, Sabtah, Raamah, and
Sabteca. The descendants of Raamah were Sheba and Dedan. 10 Cush
was also the ancestor of Nimrod, who was the first heroic warrior on
earth.

11 Mizraim was the ancestor of the Ludites, Anamites, Lehabites,
Naphtuhites, 12 Pathrusites, Casluhites, and the Caphtorites, from
whom the Philistines came.*

13 Canaan's oldest son was Sidon, the ancestor of the Sidonians.
Canaan was also the ancestor of the Hittites,* 14 Jebusites, Amorites,
Girgashites, 15 Hivites, Arkites, Sinites, 16 Arvadites, Zemarites, and
Hamathites.

Descendants of Shem

17 The descendants of Shem were Elam, Asshur, Arphaxad, Lud, and Aram.

The descendants of Aram were* Uz, Hul, Gether, and Mash.*

18 Arphaxad was the father of Shelah.

Shelah was the father of Eber.

19 Eber had two sons. The first was named Peleg (which means "division"),
for during his lifetime the people of the world were divided into
different language groups. His brother's name was Joktan.

20 Joktan was the ancestor of Almodad, Sheleph, Hazarmaveth, Jerah,
21 Hadoram, Uzal, Diklah, 22 Obal,* Abimael, Sheba, 23 Ophir, Havilah,
and Jobab. All these were descendants of Joktan.

1:4 As in Greek version (see also Gen 5:3-32); Hebrew lacks *The sons of Noah were.* 1:6 As in some Hebrew manuscripts and Greek version (see also Gen 10:3); most Hebrew manuscripts read *Diphath.* 1:8 Or *Egypt;* also in 1:11. 1:12 Hebrew *Casluhites, from whom the Philistines came, Caphtorites.* See Jer 47:4; Amos 9:7. 1:13 Hebrew *ancestor of Heth.* 1:17a As in one Hebrew manuscript and some Greek manuscripts (see also Gen 10:23); most Hebrew manuscripts lack *The descendants of Aram were.* 1:17b As in parallel text at Gen 10:23; Hebrew reads *and Meshech.* 1:22 As in some Hebrew manuscripts and Syriac version (see also Gen 10:28); most Hebrew manuscripts read *Ebal.*

Story Arc **1:1-2:15**

● Adam → David

Sometimes the Bible reveals God's plan of salvation for humanity by listing different lines of ancestry. Look through the lineage lists and the many names in these first several chapters of 1 Chronicles. What names do you recognize? Can you spot the story arc of Scripture through these names? If you look ahead to the list of names in Matthew 1:1-16 or Luke 3:23-38, how do these lists mark a midway point in God's grand plan and set the stage for what will happen next?

1 Chr 11:1-2 ►

24 So this is the family line descended from Shem: Arphaxad, Shelah,*
25 Eber, Peleg, Reu, 26 Serug, Nahor, Terah, 27 and Abram, later known
as Abraham.

Descendants of Abraham

28 The sons of Abraham were Isaac and Ishmael. 29 These are their
genealogical records:

The sons of Ishmael were Nebaioth (the oldest), Kedar, Adbeel, Mibsam,
30 Mishma, Dumah, Massa, Hadad, Tema, 31 Jetur, Naphish, and
Kedemah. These were the sons of Ishmael.

32 The sons of Keturah, Abraham's concubine, were Zimran, Jokshan, Medan, Midian, Ishbak, and Shuah.

The sons of Jokshan were Sheba and Dedan.

33 The sons of Midian were Ephah, Epher, Hanoch, Abida, and Eldaah.

All these were descendants of Abraham through his concubine Keturah.

Descendants of Isaac

34 Abraham was the father of Isaac. The sons of Isaac were Esau and Israel.*

Descendants of Esau

35 The sons of Esau were Eliphaz, Reuel, Jeush, Jalam, and Korah.

36 The descendants of Eliphaz were Teman, Omar, Zepho,* Gatam, Kenaz, and Amalek, who was born to Timna.*

37 The descendants of Reuel were Nahath, Zerah, Shammah, and Mizzah.

Original Peoples of Edom

38 The descendants of Seir were Lotan, Shobal, Zibeon, Anah, Dishon, Ezer, and Dishan.

39 The descendants of Lotan were Hori and Hemam.* Lotan's sister was named Timna.

40 The descendants of Shobal were Alvan,* Manahath, Ebal, Shepho,* and Onam.

The descendants of Zibeon were Aiah and Anah.

41 The son of Anah was Dishon.

The descendants of Dishon were Hemdan,* Eshban, Ithran, and Keran.

42 The descendants of Ezer were Bilhan, Zaavan, and Akan.*

The descendants of Dishan* were Uz and Aran.

Rulers of Edom

43 These are the kings who ruled in the land of Edom before any king ruled over the Israelites*:

1:24 Some Greek manuscripts read *Arphaxad, Cainan, Shelah.* See notes on Gen 10:24; 11:12-13. **1:34** *Israel* is the name that God gave to Jacob. **1:36a** As in many Hebrew manuscripts and a few Greek manuscripts (see also Gen 36:11); most Hebrew manuscripts read *Zephi.* **1:36b** As in some Greek manuscripts (see also Gen 36:12); Hebrew reads *Kenaz, Timna, and Amalek.* **1:39** As in parallel text at Gen 36:22; Hebrew reads *and Homam.* **1:40a** As in many Hebrew manuscripts and a few Greek manuscripts (see also Gen 36:23); most Hebrew manuscripts read *Alian.* **1:40b** As in some Hebrew manuscripts (see also Gen 36:23); most Hebrew manuscripts read *Shephi.* **1:41** As in many Hebrew manuscripts and some Greek manuscripts (see also Gen 36:26); most Hebrew manuscripts read *Hamran.* **1:42a** As in many Hebrew and Greek manuscripts (see also Gen 36:27); most Hebrew manuscripts read *Jaakan.* **1:42b** Hebrew *Dishon;* compare 1:38 and parallel text at Gen 36:28. **1:43** Or *before an Israelite king ruled over them.*

Bela son of Beor, who ruled from his city of Dinhabah.
44 When Bela died, Jobab son of Zerah from Bozrah became king in his place.
45 When Jobab died, Husham from the land of the Temanites became king in his place.
46 When Husham died, Hadad son of Bedad became king in his place and ruled from the city of Avith. He was the one who destroyed the Midianite army in the land of Moab.
47 When Hadad died, Samlah from the city of Masrekah became king in his place.
48 When Samlah died, Shaul from the city of Rehoboth-on-the-River became king in his place.
49 When Shaul died, Baal-hanan son of Acbor became king in his place.
50 When Baal-hanan died, Hadad became king in his place and ruled from the city of Pau.* His wife was Mehetabel, the daughter of Matred and
granddaughter of Me-zahab. 51 Then Hadad died.

The clan leaders of Edom were Timna, Alvah,* Jetheth, 52 Oholibamah,
Elah, Pinon, 53 Kenaz, Teman, Mibzar, 54 Magdiel, and Iram. These are the clan leaders of Edom.

Descendants of Israel

2 The sons of Israel* were Reuben, Simeon, Levi, Judah, Issachar,
Zebulun, 2 Dan, Joseph, Benjamin, Naphtali, Gad, and Asher.

Descendants of Judah

3 Judah had three sons from Bathshua, a Canaanite woman. Their names were Er, Onan, and Shelah. But the LORD saw that the oldest son, Er,
was a wicked man, so he killed him. 4 Later Judah had twin sons from
Tamar, his widowed daughter-in-law. Their names were Perez and Zerah. So Judah had five sons in all.
5 The sons of Perez were Hezron and Hamul.
6 The sons of Zerah were Zimri, Ethan, Heman, Calcol, and Darda*—five in all.
7 The son of Carmi (a descendant of Zimri) was Achan,* who brought disaster on Israel by taking plunder that had been set apart for the LORD.*
8 The son of Ethan was Azariah.

From Judah's Grandson Hezron to David

9 The sons of Hezron were Jerahmeel, Ram, and Caleb.*
10 Ram was the father of Amminadab.
Amminadab was the father of Nahshon, a leader of Judah.
11 Nahshon was the father of Salmon.*
Salmon was the father of Boaz.

Question 2:1-15

Talk about a list of difference makers! Give yourself a challenge. Pick out some key names in 2:1-15 and go through the Old Testament to study them. How do their stories fit into God's ultimate plan to redeem humanity? Where do you fit in these lists?

1:50 As in many Hebrew manuscripts, some Greek manuscripts, Syriac version, and Latin Vulgate (see also Gen 36:39); most Hebrew manuscripts read *Pai.* 1:51 As in an alternate reading of the Masoretic Text (see also Gen 36:40); the other alternate reads *Aliah.* 2:1 *Israel* is the name that God gave to Jacob. 2:6 As in many Hebrew manuscripts, some Greek manuscripts, and Syriac version (see also 1 Kgs 4:31); Hebrew reads *Dara.* 2:7a Hebrew *Achar;* compare Josh 7:1. *Achar* means "disaster." 2:7b The Hebrew term used here refers to the complete consecration of things or people to the LORD, either by destroying them or by giving them as an offering. 2:9 Hebrew *Kelubai,* a variant spelling of Caleb; compare 2:18. 2:11 As in Greek version (see also Ruth 4:20); Hebrew reads *Salma.*

12 Boaz was the father of Obed.
Obed was the father of Jesse.
13 Jesse's first son was Eliab, his second was Abinadab, his third was
Shimea, 14 his fourth was Nethanel, his fifth was Raddai, 15 his sixth was
Ozem, and his seventh was David.
16 Their sisters were named Zeruiah and Abigail. Zeruiah had three
sons named Abishai, Joab, and Asahel. 17 Abigail married a man named
Jether, an Ishmaelite, and they had a son named Amasa.

Other Descendants of Hezron

18 Hezron's son Caleb had sons from his wife Azubah and from Jerioth.*
Her sons were named Jesher, Shobab, and Ardon. 19 After Azubah died,
Caleb married Ephrathah,* and they had a son named Hur. 20 Hur was
the father of Uri. Uri was the father of Bezalel.
21 When Hezron was sixty years old, he married Gilead's sister, the
daughter of Makir. They had a son named Segub. 22 Segub was the
father of Jair, who ruled twenty-three towns in the land of Gilead.
23 (But Geshur and Aram captured the Towns of Jair* and also took
Kenath and its sixty surrounding villages.) All these were descendants
of Makir, the father of Gilead.
24 Soon after Hezron died in the town of Caleb-ephrathah, his wife Abijah
gave birth to a son named Ashhur (the father of* Tekoa).

Descendants of Hezron's Son Jerahmeel

25 The sons of Jerahmeel, the oldest son of Hezron, were Ram (the
firstborn), Bunah, Oren, Ozem, and Ahijah. 26 Jerahmeel had a second
wife named Atarah. She was the mother of Onam.
27 The sons of Ram, the oldest son of Jerahmeel, were Maaz, Jamin, and
Eker.
28 The sons of Onam were Shammai and Jada.
The sons of Shammai were Nadab and Abishur.
29 The sons of Abishur and his wife Abihail were Ahban and Molid.
30 The sons of Nadab were Seled and Appaim. Seled died without children,
31 but Appaim had a son named Ishi. The son of Ishi was Sheshan.
Sheshan had a descendant named Ahlai.
32 The sons of Jada, Shammai's brother, were Jether and Jonathan. Jether
died without children, 33 but Jonathan had two sons named Peleth and
Zaza.
These were all descendants of Jerahmeel.
34 Sheshan had no sons, though he did have daughters. He also had an
Egyptian servant named Jarha. 35 Sheshan gave one of his daughters
to be the wife of Jarha, and they had a son named Attai.
36 Attai was the father of Nathan.
Nathan was the father of Zabad.
37 Zabad was the father of Ephlal.
Ephlal was the father of Obed.
38 Obed was the father of Jehu.
Jehu was the father of Azariah.

2:18 Or *Caleb had a daughter named Jerioth from his wife, Azubah.* The meaning of the Hebrew is uncertain. 2:19 Hebrew *Ephrath,* a variant spelling of Ephrathah; compare 2:50 and 4:4. 2:23 Or *captured Havvoth-jair.* 2:24 Or *the founder of;* also in 2:42, 45, 49.

39 Azariah was the father of Helez.
Helez was the father of Eleasah.
40 Eleasah was the father of Sismai.
Sismai was the father of Shallum.
41 Shallum was the father of Jekamiah.
Jekamiah was the father of Elishama.

Descendants of Hezron's Son Caleb

42 The descendants of Caleb, the brother of Jerahmeel, included Mesha
(the firstborn), who became the father of Ziph. Caleb's descendants also
included the sons of Mareshah, the father of Hebron.*
43 The sons of Hebron were Korah, Tappuah, Rekem, and Shema. 44 Shema
was the father of Raham. Raham was the father of Jorkeam. Rekem was
the father of Shammai. 45 The son of Shammai was Maon. Maon was the
father of Beth-zur.
46 Caleb's concubine Ephah gave birth to Haran, Moza, and Gazez. Haran
was the father of Gazez.
47 The sons of Jahdai were Regem, Jotham, Geshan, Pelet, Ephah, and
Shaaph.
48 Another of Caleb's concubines, Maacah, gave birth to Sheber and
Tirhanah. 49 She also gave birth to Shaaph (the father of Madmannah)
and Sheva (the father of Macbenah and Gibea). Caleb also had a
daughter named Acsah.
50 These were all descendants of Caleb.

Descendants of Caleb's Son Hur

The sons of Hur, the oldest son of Caleb's wife Ephrathah, were Shobal
(the founder of Kiriath-jearim), 51 Salma (the founder of Bethlehem),
and Hareph (the founder of Beth-gader).
52 The descendants of Shobal (the founder of Kiriath-jearim) were Haroeh,
half the Manahathites, 53 and the families of Kiriath-jearim—the
Ithrites, Puthites, Shumathites, and Mishraites, from whom came the
people of Zorah and Eshtaol.
54 The descendants of Salma were the people of Bethlehem, the
Netophathites, Atroth-beth-joab, the other half of the Manahathites,
the Zorites, 55 and the families of scribes living at Jabez—the Tirathites,
Shimeathites, and Sucathites. All these were Kenites who descended
from Hammath, the father of the family of Recab.*

Descendants of David

3 These are the sons of David who were born in Hebron:

The oldest was Amnon, whose mother was Ahinoam from Jezreel.
The second was Daniel, whose mother was Abigail from Carmel.
2 The third was Absalom, whose mother was Maacah, the daughter
of Talmai, king of Geshur.
The fourth was Adonijah, whose mother was Haggith.
3 The fifth was Shephatiah, whose mother was Abital.
The sixth was Ithream, whose mother was Eglah, David's wife.

2:42 Or *who founded Hebron.* The meaning of the Hebrew is uncertain. **2:55** Or *the founder of Beth-recab.*

Remember to take notes!

[4]These six sons were born to David in Hebron, where he reigned seven and
a half years.

Then David reigned another thirty-three years in Jerusalem. [5]The sons
born to David in Jerusalem included Shammua,* Shobab, Nathan, and Sol-
omon. Their mother was Bathsheba,* the daughter of Ammiel. [6]David also
had nine other sons: Ibhar, Elishua,* Elpelet,* [7]Nogah, Nepheg, Japhia,
[8]Elishama, Eliada, and Eliphelet.

[9]These were the sons of David, not including his sons born to his concu-
bines. Their sister was named Tamar.

Descendants of Solomon

[10]The descendants of Solomon were Rehoboam, Abijah, Asa, Jehoshaphat,
[11]Jehoram,* Ahaziah, Joash, [12]Amaziah, Uzziah,* Jotham, [13]Ahaz,
Hezekiah, Manasseh, [14]Amon, and Josiah.

[15]The sons of Josiah were Johanan (the oldest), Jehoiakim (the second), Zedekiah (the third), and Jehoahaz* (the fourth).

[16]The successors of Jehoiakim were his son Jehoiachin and his brother Zedekiah.*

Descendants of Jehoiachin

[17]The sons of Jehoiachin,* who was taken prisoner by the Babylonians,
were Shealtiel, [18]Malkiram, Pedaiah, Shenazzar, Jekamiah, Hoshama,
and Nedabiah.

[19]The sons of Pedaiah were Zerubbabel and Shimei.

The sons of Zerubbabel were Meshullam and Hananiah. (Their sister
was Shelomith.) [20]His five other sons were Hashubah, Ohel, Berekiah,
Hasadiah, and Jushab-hesed.

[21]The sons of Hananiah were Pelatiah and Jeshaiah. Jeshaiah's son was Rephaiah. Rephaiah's son was Arnan. Arnan's son was Obadiah. Obadiah's son was Shecaniah.

[22]The descendants of Shecaniah were Shemaiah and his sons, Hattush, Igal, Bariah, Neariah, and Shaphat—six in all.

[23]The sons of Neariah were Elioenai, Hizkiah, and Azrikam—three in all.

[24]The sons of Elioenai were Hodaviah, Eliashib, Pelaiah, Akkub, Johanan, Delaiah, and Anani—seven in all.

Other Descendants of Judah

4 The descendants of Judah were Perez, Hezron, Carmi, Hur, and Shobal.

[2]Shobal's son Reaiah was the father of Jahath. Jahath was the father of Ahumai and Lahad. These were the families of the Zorathites.

[3]The descendants of* Etam were Jezreel, Ishma, Idbash, their sister
Hazzelelponi, [4]Penuel (the father of* Gedor), and Ezer (the father

3:5a As in Syriac version (see also 14:4; 2 Sam 5:14); Hebrew reads *Shimea.* **3:5b** Hebrew *Bathshua,* a variant spelling of Bathsheba. **3:6a** As in some Hebrew and Greek manuscripts (see also 14:5-7 and 2 Sam 5:15); most Hebrew manuscripts read *Elishama.* **3:6b** Hebrew *Eliphelet;* compare parallel text at 14:5-7. **3:11** Hebrew *Joram,* a variant spelling of Jehoram. **3:12** Hebrew *Azariah,* a variant spelling of Uzziah. **3:15** Hebrew *Shallum,* another name for Jehoahaz. **3:16** Hebrew *The sons of Jehoiakim were his son Jeconiah* [a variant spelling of Jehoiachin] *and his son Zedekiah.* **3:17** Hebrew *Jeconiah,* a variant spelling of Jehoiachin. **4:3** As in Greek version; Hebrew reads *father of.* The meaning of the Hebrew is uncertain. **4:4** Or *the founder of;* also in 4:5, 12, 14, 17, 18, and perhaps other instances where the text reads *the father of.*

of Hushah). These were the descendants of Hur (the firstborn of
Ephrathah), the ancestor of Bethlehem.
5 Ashhur (the father of Tekoa) had two wives, named Helah and Naarah.
6 Naarah gave birth to Ahuzzam, Hepher, Temeni, and Haahashtari.
7 Helah gave birth to Zereth, Izhar,* Ethnan, 8 and Koz, who became the
ancestor of Anub, Zobebah, and all the families of Aharhel son of Harum.
9 There was a man named Jabez who was more honorable than any of his
brothers. His mother named him Jabez* because his birth had been so
painful. 10 He was the one who prayed to the God of Israel, "Oh, that you
would bless me and expand my territory! Please be with me in all that I
do, and keep me from all trouble and pain!" And God granted him his
request.
11 Kelub (the brother of Shuhah) was the father of Mehir. Mehir was
the father of Eshton. 12 Eshton was the father of Beth-rapha, Paseah,
and Tehinnah. Tehinnah was the father of Ir-nahash. These were the
descendants of Recah.
13 The sons of Kenaz were Othniel and Seraiah. Othniel's sons were
Hathath and Meonothai.* 14 Meonothai was the father of Ophrah.
Seraiah was the father of Joab, the founder of the Valley of Craftsmen,*
so called because they were craftsmen.
15 The sons of Caleb son of Jephunneh were Iru, Elah, and Naam. The son
of Elah was Kenaz.
16 The sons of Jehallelel were Ziph, Ziphah, Tiria, and Asarel.
17 The sons of Ezrah were Jether, Mered, Epher, and Jalon. One of Mered's
wives became* the mother of Miriam, Shammai, and Ishbah (the father
of Eshtemoa). 18 He married a woman from Judah, who became the
mother of Jered (the father of Gedor), Heber (the father of Soco), and
Jekuthiel (the father of Zanoah). Mered also married Bithia, a daughter
of Pharaoh, and she bore him children.
19 Hodiah's wife was the sister of Naham. One of her sons was the father
of Keilah the Garmite, and another was the father of Eshtemoa the
Maacathite.
20 The sons of Shimon were Amnon, Rinnah, Ben-hanan, and Tilon.
The descendants of Ishi were Zoheth and Ben-zoheth.

Descendants of Judah's Son Shelah

21 Shelah was one of Judah's sons. The descendants of Shelah were Er (the
father of Lecah); Laadah (the father of Mareshah); the families of linen
workers at Beth-ashbea; 22 Jokim; the men of Cozeba; and Joash and
Saraph, who ruled over Moab and Jashubi-lehem. These names all come
from ancient records. 23 They were the pottery makers who lived in
Netaim and Gederah. They lived there and worked for the king.

Descendants of Simeon

24 The sons of Simeon were Jemuel,* Jamin, Jarib, Zohar,* and Shaul.
25 The descendants of Shaul were Shallum, Mibsam, and Mishma.

4:7 As in an alternate reading in the Masoretic Text (see also Latin Vulgate); the other alternate and the Greek version read *Zohar.* **4:9** *Jabez* sounds like a Hebrew word meaning "distress" or "pain." **4:13** As in some Greek manuscripts and Latin Vulgate; Hebrew lacks *and Meonothai.* **4:14** Or *Joab, the father of Ge-harashim.* **4:17** Or *Jether's wife became;* Hebrew reads *She became.* **4:24a** As in Syriac version (see also Gen 46:10; Exod 6:15); Hebrew reads *Nemuel.* **4:24b** As in parallel texts at Gen 46:10 and Exod 6:15; Hebrew reads *Zerah.*

Make a Difference 4:9

Jabez and His Bold Prayer

This commentary about a man named Jabez is unique in the first several chapters of 1 Chronicles. In contrast to the more ordinary lists of names (such as, "The descendants of [person] were [person], [person], and [person]"), the lists are momentarily interrupted to highlight an obscure individual who is not mentioned anywhere else in the Bible. By the time the writer of 1 Chronicles penned these lists, Jabez had developed a legacy as a man who had been more honorable than those around him. He was especially remembered, however, for his bold prayer to the God of Israel: "Bless me and expand my territory! Please be with me in all that I do, and keep me from all trouble and pain!" It is noted that "God granted him his request" (v. 10). Then the writer of 1 Chronicles went right back to the typical lineage listings.

Difference Maker

Being careful about the legacy you will leave, pray the same prayer that Jabez prayed.

26 The descendants of Mishma were Hammuel, Zaccur, and Shimei.
27 Shimei had sixteen sons and six daughters, but none of his brothers
had large families. So Simeon's tribe never grew as large as the tribe
of Judah.
28 They lived in Beersheba, Moladah, Hazar-shual, 29 Bilhah, Ezem, Tolad,
30 Bethuel, Hormah, Ziklag, 31 Beth-marcaboth, Hazar-susim, Beth-biri,
and Shaaraim. These towns were under their control until the time
of King David. 32 Their descendants also lived in Etam, Ain, Rimmon,
Token, and Ashan—five towns 33 and their surrounding villages as far
away as Baalath.* This was their territory, and these names are listed in
their genealogical records.
34 Other descendants of Simeon included Meshobab, Jamlech, Joshah son
of Amaziah, 35 Joel, Jehu son of Joshibiah, son of Seraiah, son of Asiel,
36 Elioenai, Jaakobah, Jeshohaiah, Asaiah, Adiel, Jesimiel, Benaiah, 37 and
Ziza son of Shiphi, son of Allon, son of Jedaiah, son of Shimri, son of
Shemaiah.

38 These were the names of some of the leaders of Simeon's wealthy clans.
Their families grew, 39 and they traveled to the region of Gerar,* in the east
part of the valley, seeking pastureland for their flocks. 40 They found lush
pastures there, and the land was spacious, quiet, and peaceful.

Some of Ham's descendants had been living in that region. 41 But during
the reign of King Hezekiah of Judah, these leaders of Simeon invaded the
region and completely destroyed* the homes of the descendants of Ham
and of the Meunites. No trace of them remains today. They killed everyone
who lived there and took the land for themselves, because they wanted its
good pastureland for their flocks. 42 Five hundred of these invaders from
the tribe of Simeon went to Mount Seir, led by Pelatiah, Neariah, Rephaiah,
and Uzziel—all sons of Ishi. 43 They destroyed the few Amalekites who had
survived, and they have lived there ever since.

Descendants of Reuben

5 The oldest son of Israel* was Reuben. But since he dishonored his fa-
ther by sleeping with one of his father's concubines, his birthright was
given to the sons of his brother Joseph. For this reason, Reuben is not listed
in the genealogical records as the firstborn son. 2 The descendants of Judah
became the most powerful tribe and provided a ruler for the nation,* but the
birthright belonged to Joseph.

3 The sons of Reuben, the oldest son of Israel, were Hanoch, Pallu, Hezron,
and Carmi.
4 The descendants of Joel were Shemaiah, Gog, Shimei, 5 Micah, Reaiah,
Baal, 6 and Beerah. Beerah was the leader of the Reubenites when they
were taken into captivity by King Tiglath-pileser* of Assyria.
7 Beerah's* relatives are listed in their genealogical records by their clans:
Jeiel (the leader), Zechariah, 8 and Bela son of Azaz, son of Shema, son
of Joel.

4:33 As in some Greek manuscripts (see also Josh 19:8); Hebrew reads *Baal*. 4:39 As in Greek version; Hebrew reads *Gedor*. 4:41 The Hebrew term used here refers to the complete consecration of things or people to the LORD, either by destroying them or by giving them as an offering. 5:1 *Israel* is the name that God gave to Jacob. 5:2 Or *and from Judah came a prince.* 5:6 Hebrew *Tilgath-pilneser,* a variant spelling of Tiglath-pileser; also in 5:26. 5:7 Hebrew *His.*

The Reubenites lived in the area that stretches from Aroer to Nebo and
Baal-meon. 9 And since they had so many livestock in the land of Gilead,
they spread east toward the edge of the desert that stretches to the
Euphrates River.
10 During the reign of Saul, the Reubenites defeated the Hagrites in battle.
Then they moved into the Hagrite settlements all along the eastern
edge of Gilead.

Descendants of Gad

11 Next to the Reubenites, the descendants of Gad lived in the land of
Bashan as far east as Salecah. 12 Joel was the leader in the land of Bashan,
and Shapham was second-in-command, followed by Janai and Shaphat.
13 Their relatives, the leaders of seven other clans, were Michael,
Meshullam, Sheba, Jorai, Jacan, Zia, and Eber. 14 These were all
descendants of Abihail son of Huri, son of Jaroah, son of Gilead, son of
Michael, son of Jeshishai, son of Jahdo, son of Buz. 15 Ahi son of Abdiel,
son of Guni, was the leader of their clans.

16 The Gadites lived in the land of Gilead, in Bashan and its villages, and
throughout all the pasturelands of Sharon. 17 All of these were listed in the
genealogical records during the days of King Jotham of Judah and King
Jeroboam of Israel.

The Tribes East of the Jordan

18 There were 44,760 capable warriors in the armies of Reuben, Gad, and
the half-tribe of Manasseh. They were all skilled in combat and armed with
shields, swords, and bows. 19 They waged war against the Hagrites, the Je-
turites, the Naphishites, and the Nodabites. 20 They cried out to God during
the battle, and he answered their prayer because they trusted in him. So the
Hagrites and all their allies were defeated. 21 The plunder taken from the
Hagrites included 50,000 camels, 250,000 sheep and goats, 2,000 donkeys,
and 100,000 captives. 22 Many of the Hagrites were killed in the battle because
God was fighting against them. The people of Reuben, Gad, and Manasseh
lived in their land until they were taken into exile.
23 The half-tribe of Manasseh was very large and spread through the land from
Bashan to Baal-hermon, Senir, and Mount Hermon. 24 These were the leaders
of their clans: Epher,* Ishi, Eliel, Azriel, Jeremiah, Hodaviah, and Jahdiel. These
men had a great reputation as mighty warriors and leaders of their clans.
25 But these tribes were unfaithful to the God of their ancestors. They wor-
shiped the gods of the nations that God had destroyed. 26 So the God of Israel
caused King Pul of Assyria (also known as Tiglath-pileser) to invade the land
and take away the people of Reuben, Gad, and the half-tribe of Manasseh as
captives. The Assyrians exiled them to Halah, Habor, Hara, and the Gozan
River, where they remain to this day.

The Priestly Line

6 1*The sons of Levi were Gershon, Kohath, and Merari.
2 The descendants of Kohath included Amram, Izhar, Hebron, and
Uzziel.

5:24 As in Greek version and Latin Vulgate; Hebrew reads *and Epher.* 6:1 Verses 6:1-15 are numbered 5:27-41 in Hebrew text.

Question 5:18–26

Notice the contrast between those who trusted in God and those who turned to false gods (v. 25). What does this teach you about trusting anyone or anything rather than God?

3 The children of Amram were Aaron, Moses, and Miriam.
The sons of Aaron were Nadab, Abihu, Eleazar, and Ithamar.
4 Eleazar was the father of Phinehas.
Phinehas was the father of Abishua.
5 Abishua was the father of Bukki.
Bukki was the father of Uzzi.
6 Uzzi was the father of Zerahiah.
Zerahiah was the father of Meraioth.
7 Meraioth was the father of Amariah.
Amariah was the father of Ahitub.
8 Ahitub was the father of Zadok.
Zadok was the father of Ahimaaz.
9 Ahimaaz was the father of Azariah.
Azariah was the father of Johanan.
10 Johanan was the father of Azariah, the high priest at the Temple*
built by Solomon in Jerusalem.
11 Azariah was the father of Amariah.
Amariah was the father of Ahitub.
12 Ahitub was the father of Zadok.
Zadok was the father of Shallum.
13 Shallum was the father of Hilkiah.
Hilkiah was the father of Azariah.
14 Azariah was the father of Seraiah.
Seraiah was the father of Jehozadak, 15 who went into exile when the
LORD sent the people of Judah and Jerusalem into captivity under
Nebuchadnezzar.

The Levite Clans

16* The sons of Levi were Gershon,* Kohath, and Merari.
17 The descendants of Gershon included Libni and Shimei.
18 The descendants of Kohath included Amram, Izhar, Hebron, and
Uzziel.
19 The descendants of Merari included Mahli and Mushi.

The following were the Levite clans, listed according to their ancestral descent:

20 The descendants of Gershon included Libni, Jahath, Zimmah, 21 Joah,
Iddo, Zerah, and Jeatherai.
22 The descendants of Kohath included Amminadab, Korah, Assir,
23 Elkanah, Abiasaph,* Assir, 24 Tahath, Uriel, Uzziah, and Shaul.
25 The descendants of Elkanah included Amasai, Ahimoth, 26 Elkanah,
Zophai, Nahath, 27 Eliab, Jeroham, Elkanah, and Samuel.*
28 The sons of Samuel were Joel* (the older) and Abijah (the second).
29 The descendants of Merari included Mahli, Libni, Shimei, Uzzah,
30 Shimea, Haggiah, and Asaiah.

6:10 Hebrew *the house.* 6:16a Verses 6:16-81 are numbered 6:1-66 in Hebrew text. 6:16b Hebrew *Gershom,* a variant spelling of Gershon (see 6:1); also in 6:17, 20, 43, 62, 71. 6:23 Hebrew *Ebiasaph,* a variant spelling of Abiasaph (also in 6:37); compare parallel text at Exod 6:24. 6:27 As in some Greek manuscripts (see also 6:33-34); Hebrew lacks *and Samuel.* 6:28 As in some Greek manuscripts and the Syriac version (see also 6:33 and 1 Sam 8:2); Hebrew lacks *Joel.*

The Temple Musicians

31 David assigned the following men to lead the music at the house of the LORD after the Ark was placed there. 32 They ministered with music at the Tabernacle* until Solomon built the Temple of the LORD in Jerusalem. They carried out their work, following all the regulations handed down to them. 33 These are the men who served, along with their sons:

Heman the musician was from the clan of Kohath. His genealogy was traced back through Joel, Samuel, 34 Elkanah, Jeroham, Eliel, Toah,
35 Zuph, Elkanah, Mahath, Amasai, 36 Elkanah, Joel, Azariah, Zephaniah,
37 Tahath, Assir, Abiasaph, Korah, 38 Izhar, Kohath, Levi, and Israel.*
39 Heman's first assistant was Asaph from the clan of Gershon.* Asaph's genealogy was traced back through Berekiah, Shimea, 40 Michael,
Baaseiah, Malkijah, 41 Ethni, Zerah, Adaiah, 42 Ethan, Zimmah, Shimei,
43 Jahath, Gershon, and Levi.
44 Heman's second assistant was Ethan from the clan of Merari. Ethan's genealogy was traced back through Kishi, Abdi, Malluch, 45 Hashabiah,
Amaziah, Hilkiah, 46 Amzi, Bani, Shemer, 47 Mahli, Mushi, Merari, and Levi.

48 Their fellow Levites were appointed to various other tasks in the Tabernacle, the house of God.

Aaron's Descendants

49 Only Aaron and his descendants served as priests. They presented the offerings on the altar of burnt offering and the altar of incense, and they performed all the other duties related to the Most Holy Place. They made atonement for Israel by doing everything that Moses, the servant of God, had commanded them.

50 The descendants of Aaron were Eleazar, Phinehas, Abishua, 51 Bukki,
Uzzi, Zerahiah, 52 Meraioth, Amariah, Ahitub, 53 Zadok, and Ahimaaz.

Territory for the Levites

54 This is a record of the towns and territory assigned by means of sacred lots to the descendants of Aaron, who were from the clan of Kohath. 55 This
territory included Hebron and its surrounding pasturelands in Judah, 56 but
the fields and outlying areas belonging to the city were given to Caleb son of
Jephunneh. 57 So the descendants of Aaron were given the following towns, each with its pasturelands: Hebron (a city of refuge),* Libnah, Jattir, Eshte-
moa, 58 Holon,* Debir, 59 Ain,* Juttah,* and Beth-shemesh. 60 And from the ter-
ritory of Benjamin they were given Gibeon,* Geba, Alemeth, and Anathoth, each with its pasturelands. So thirteen towns were given to the descendants
of Aaron. 61 The remaining descendants of Kohath received ten towns from the territory of the half-tribe of Manasseh by means of sacred lots.

Question 6:31

In these first chapters, when commentary notes interrupt the genealogy lists, you should always wonder why. In this case, what important practice did the writer of 1 Chronicles want the readers to emphasize?

6:32 Hebrew *the Tabernacle, the Tent of Meeting.* **6:38** *Israel* is the name that God gave to Jacob. **6:39** Hebrew lacks *from the clan of Gershon;* see 6:43. **6:57** As in parallel text at Josh 21:13; Hebrew reads *were given the cities of refuge: Hebron, and the following towns, each with its pasturelands.* **6:58** As in parallel text at Josh 21:15; Masoretic Text reads *Hilez;* other manuscripts read *Hilen.* **6:59a** As in parallel text at Josh 21:16; Hebrew reads *Ashan.* **6:59b** As in Syriac version (see also Josh 21:16); Hebrew lacks *Juttah.* **6:60** As in parallel text at Josh 21:17; Hebrew lacks *Gibeon.*

62 The descendants of Gershon received by sacred lots thirteen towns from
the territories of Issachar, Asher, Naphtali, and from the Bashan area of Ma-
nasseh, east of the Jordan.
63 The descendants of Merari received by sacred lots twelve towns from
the territories of Reuben, Gad, and Zebulun.
64 So the people of Israel assigned all these towns and pasturelands to the
Levites. 65 The towns in the territories of Judah, Simeon, and Benjamin, men-
tioned above, were assigned to them by means of sacred lots.
66 The descendants of Kohath were given the following towns from the
territory of Ephraim, each with its pasturelands: 67 Shechem (a city of refuge
in the hill country of Ephraim),* Gezer, 68 Jokmeam, Beth-horon, 69 Aijalon,
and Gath-rimmon. 70 The remaining descendants of Kohath were assigned
the towns of Aner and Bileam from the territory of the half-tribe of Manas-
seh, each with its pasturelands.
71 The descendants of Gershon received the towns of Golan (in Bashan)
and Ashtaroth from the territory of the half-tribe of Manasseh, each with its
pasturelands. 72 From the territory of Issachar, they were given Kedesh, Dab-
erath, 73 Ramoth, and Anem, each with its pasturelands. 74 From the territory
of Asher, they received Mashal, Abdon, 75 Hukok, and Rehob, each with its
pasturelands. 76 From the territory of Naphtali, they were given Kedesh in
Galilee, Hammon, and Kiriathaim, each with its pasturelands.
77 The remaining descendants of Merari received the towns of Jokneam, Kar-
tah,* Rimmon,* and Tabor from the territory of Zebulun, each with its pasture-
lands. 78 From the territory of Reuben, east of the Jordan River opposite Jericho,
they received Bezer (a desert town), Jahaz,* 79 Kedemoth, and Mephaath, each
with its pasturelands. 80 And from the territory of Gad, they received Ramoth
in Gilead, Mahanaim, 81 Heshbon, and Jazer, each with its pasturelands.

Descendants of Issachar

7 The four sons of Issachar were Tola, Puah, Jashub, and Shimron.
2 The sons of Tola were Uzzi, Rephaiah, Jeriel, Jahmai, Ibsam, and
Shemuel. Each of them was the leader of an ancestral clan. At the time
of King David, the total number of mighty warriors listed in the records
of these clans was 22,600.
3 The son of Uzzi was Izrahiah. The sons of Izrahiah were Michael,
Obadiah, Joel, and Isshiah. These five became the leaders of clans. 4 All
of them had many wives and many sons, so the total number of men
available for military service among their descendants was 36,000.
5 The total number of mighty warriors from all the clans of the tribe of
Issachar was 87,000. All of them were listed in their genealogical records.

Descendants of Benjamin

6 Three of Benjamin's sons were Bela, Beker, and Jediael.
7 The five sons of Bela were Ezbon, Uzzi, Uzziel, Jerimoth, and Iri. Each of
them was the leader of an ancestral clan. The total number of mighty
warriors from these clans was 22,034, as listed in their genealogical
records.

6:66-67 As in parallel text at Josh 21:21; Hebrew text reads *were given the cities of refuge: Shechem in the hill country of Ephraim, and the following towns, each with its pasturelands.* **6:77a** As in Greek version (see also Josh 21:34); Hebrew lacks *Jokneam, Kartah.* **6:77b** As in Greek version (see also Josh 19:13); Hebrew reads *Rimmono.* **6:78** Hebrew *Jahzah,* a variant spelling of Jahaz.

How God is at work here

8 The sons of Beker were Zemirah, Joash, Eliezer, Elioenai, Omri,
Jeremoth, Abijah, Anathoth, and Alemeth. 9 Each of them was the
leader of an ancestral clan. The total number of mighty warriors and
leaders from these clans was 20,200, as listed in their genealogical
records.
10 The son of Jediael was Bilhan. The sons of Bilhan were Jeush, Benjamin,
Ehud, Kenaanah, Zethan, Tarshish, and Ahishahar. 11 Each of them was
the leader of an ancestral clan. From these clans the total number of
mighty warriors ready for war was 17,200.
12 The sons of Ir were Shuppim and Huppim. Hushim was the son of Aher.

Descendants of Naphtali

13 The sons of Naphtali were Jahzeel,* Guni, Jezer, and Shillem.* They were
all descendants of Jacob's concubine Bilhah.

Descendants of Manasseh

14 The descendants of Manasseh through his Aramean concubine included
Asriel. She also bore Makir, the father of Gilead. 15 Makir found wives
for* Huppim and Shuppim. Makir had a sister named Maacah. One of
his descendants was Zelophehad, who had only daughters.
16 Makir's wife, Maacah, gave birth to a son whom she named Peresh. His
brother's name was Sheresh. The sons of Peresh were Ulam and Rakem.
17 The son of Ulam was Bedan. All these were considered Gileadites,
descendants of Makir son of Manasseh.
18 Makir's sister Hammoleketh gave birth to Ishhod, Abiezer, and Mahlah.
19 The sons of Shemida were Ahian, Shechem, Likhi, and Aniam.

Descendants of Ephraim

20 The descendants of Ephraim were Shuthelah, Bered, Tahath, Eleadah,
Tahath, 21 Zabad, Shuthelah, Ezer, and Elead. These two were killed
trying to steal livestock from the local farmers near Gath. 22 Their father,
Ephraim, mourned for them a long time, and his relatives came to
comfort him. 23 Afterward Ephraim slept with his wife, and she became
pregnant and gave birth to a son. Ephraim named him Beriah* because
of the tragedy his family had suffered. 24 He had a daughter named
Sheerah. She built the towns of Lower and Upper Beth-horon and
Uzzen-sheerah.
25 The descendants of Ephraim included Rephah, Resheph, Telah, Tahan,
26 Ladan, Ammihud, Elishama, 27 Nun, and Joshua.

28 The descendants of Ephraim lived in the territory that included Bethel
and its surrounding towns to the south, Naaran to the east, Gezer and its
villages to the west, and Shechem and its surrounding villages to the north
as far as Ayyah and its towns. 29 Along the border of Manasseh were the towns
of Beth-shan,* Taanach, Megiddo, Dor, and their surrounding villages. The
descendants of Joseph son of Israel* lived in these towns.

7:13a As in parallel text at Gen 46:24; Hebrew reads *Jahziel,* a variant spelling of Jahzeel. **7:13b** As in some Hebrew and Greek manuscripts (see also Gen 46:24; Num 26:49); most Hebrew manuscripts read *Shallum.* **7:15** Or *Makir took a wife from.* The meaning of the Hebrew is uncertain. **7:23** *Beriah* sounds like a Hebrew term meaning "tragedy" or "misfortune." **7:29a** Hebrew *Beth-shean,* a variant spelling of Beth-shan. **7:29b** *Israel* is the name that God gave to Jacob.

Descendants of Asher

30 The sons of Asher were Imnah, Ishvah, Ishvi, and Beriah. They had a sister named Serah.

31 The sons of Beriah were Heber and Malkiel (the father of Birzaith).

32 The sons of Heber were Japhlet, Shomer, and Hotham. They had a sister named Shua.

33 The sons of Japhlet were Pasach, Bimhal, and Ashvath.

34 The sons of Shomer were Ahi,* Rohgah, Hubbah, and Aram.

35 The sons of his brother Helem* were Zophah, Imna, Shelesh, and Amal.

36 The sons of Zophah were Suah, Harnepher, Shual, Beri, Imrah, 37 Bezer, Hod, Shamma, Shilshah, Ithran,* and Beera.

38 The sons of Jether were Jephunneh, Pispah, and Ara.

39 The sons of Ulla were Arah, Hanniel, and Rizia.

40 Each of these descendants of Asher was the head of an ancestral clan. They were all select men—mighty warriors and outstanding leaders. The total number of men available for military service was 26,000, as listed in their genealogical records.

Descendants of Benjamin

8 Benjamin's first son was Bela, the second was Ashbel, the third was Aharah, 2 the fourth was Nohah, and the fifth was Rapha.

3 The sons of Bela were Addar, Gera, Abihud,* 4 Abishua, Naaman, Ahoah, 5 Gera, Shephuphan, and Huram.

6 The sons of Ehud, leaders of the clans living at Geba, were exiled to Manahath. 7 Ehud's sons were Naaman, Ahijah, and Gera. Gera, who led them into exile, was the father of Uzza and Ahihud.*

8 After Shaharaim divorced his wives Hushim and Baara, he had children in the land of Moab. 9 His wife Hodesh gave birth to Jobab, Zibia, Mesha, Malcam, 10 Jeuz, Sakia, and Mirmah. These sons all became the leaders of clans.

11 Shaharaim's wife Hushim had already given birth to Abitub and Elpaal. 12 The sons of Elpaal were Eber, Misham, Shemed (who built the towns of Ono and Lod and their nearby villages), 13 Beriah, and Shema. They were the leaders of the clans living in Aijalon, and they drove out the inhabitants of Gath.

14 Ahio, Shashak, Jeremoth, 15 Zebadiah, Arad, Eder, 16 Michael, Ishpah, and Joha were the sons of Beriah.

17 Zebadiah, Meshullam, Hizki, Heber, 18 Ishmerai, Izliah, and Jobab were the sons of Elpaal.

19 Jakim, Zicri, Zabdi, 20 Elienai, Zillethai, Eliel, 21 Adaiah, Beraiah, and Shimrath were the sons of Shimei.

22 Ishpan, Eber, Eliel, 23 Abdon, Zicri, Hanan, 24 Hananiah, Elam, Anthothijah, 25 Iphdeiah, and Penuel were the sons of Shashak.

26 Shamsherai, Shehariah, Athaliah, 27 Jaareshiah, Elijah, and Zicri were the sons of Jeroham.

28 These were the leaders of the ancestral clans; they were listed in their genealogical records, and they all lived in Jerusalem.

7:34 Or *The sons of Shomer, his brother, were.* 7:35 Possibly another name for *Hotham;* compare 7:32. 7:37 Possibly another name for *Jether;* compare 7:38. 8:3 Possibly *Gera the father of Ehud;* compare 8:6. 8:7 Or *Gera, that is Heglam, was the father of Uzza and Ahihud.*

Patterns I see in this text

The Family of Saul

29 Jeiel* (the father of* Gibeon) lived in the town of Gibeon. His wife's
name was Maacah, 30 and his oldest son was named Abdon. Jeiel's other
sons were Zur, Kish, Baal, Ner,* Nadab, 31 Gedor, Ahio, Zechariah,* 32 and
Mikloth, who was the father of Shimeam.* All these families lived near
each other in Jerusalem.

33 Ner was the father of Kish.
Kish was the father of Saul.
Saul was the father of Jonathan, Malkishua, Abinadab, and
Esh-baal.
34 Jonathan was the father of Merib-baal.
Merib-baal was the father of Micah.
35 Micah was the father of Pithon, Melech, Tahrea,* and Ahaz.
36 Ahaz was the father of Jadah.*
Jadah was the father of Alemeth, Azmaveth, and Zimri.
Zimri was the father of Moza.
37 Moza was the father of Binea.
Binea was the father of Rephaiah.*
Rephaiah was the father of Eleasah.
Eleasah was the father of Azel.

38 Azel had six sons: Azrikam, Bokeru, Ishmael, Sheariah, Obadiah, and
Hanan. These were the sons of Azel.
39 Azel's brother Eshek had three sons: the first was Ulam, the second
was Jeush, and the third was Eliphelet. 40 Ulam's sons were all
mighty warriors and expert archers. They had many sons and
grandsons—150 in all.

All these were descendants of Benjamin.

9 So all Israel was listed in the genealogical records in *The Book of the Kings of Israel.*

The Returning Exiles

The people of Judah were exiled to Babylon because they were unfaithful to
the LORD. 2 The first of the exiles to return to their property in their former
towns were priests, Levites, Temple servants, and other Israelites. 3 Some
of the people from the tribes of Judah, Benjamin, Ephraim, and Manasseh
came and settled in Jerusalem.

4 One family that returned was that of Uthai son of Ammihud, son of
Omri, son of Imri, son of Bani, a descendant of Perez son of Judah.
5 Others returned from the Shilonite clan, including Asaiah (the oldest)
and his sons.
6 From the Zerahite clan, Jeuel returned with his relatives.
In all, 690 families from the tribe of Judah returned.

8:29a As in some Greek manuscripts (see also 9:35); Hebrew lacks *Jeiel.* 8:29b Or *the founder of.* 8:30 As in some Greek manuscripts (see also 9:36); Hebrew lacks *Ner.* 8:31 As in parallel text at 9:37; Hebrew reads *Zeker,* a variant spelling of Zechariah. 8:32 As in parallel text at 9:38; Hebrew reads *Shimeah,* a variant spelling of Shimeam. 8:35 As in parallel text at 9:41; Hebrew reads *Tarea,* a variant spelling of Tahrea. 8:36 As in parallel text at 9:42; Hebrew reads *Jehoaddah,* a variant spelling of Jadah. 8:37 As in parallel text at 9:43; Hebrew reads *Raphah,* a variant spelling of Rephaiah.

7 From the tribe of Benjamin came Sallu son of Meshullam, son of
Hodaviah, son of Hassenuah; 8 Ibneiah son of Jeroham; Elah son of
Uzzi, son of Micri; and Meshullam son of Shephatiah, son of Reuel,
son of Ibnijah.
9 These men were all leaders of clans, and they were listed in their genealogical records. In all, 956 families from the tribe of Benjamin returned.

The Returning Priests

10 Among the priests who returned were Jedaiah, Jehoiarib, Jakin,
11 Azariah son of Hilkiah, son of Meshullam, son of Zadok, son of
Meraioth, son of Ahitub. Azariah was the chief officer of the house
of God.
12 Other returning priests were Adaiah son of Jeroham, son of Pashhur,
son of Malkijah, and Maasai son of Adiel, son of Jahzerah, son of
Meshullam, son of Meshillemith, son of Immer.
13 In all, 1,760 priests returned. They were heads of clans and very able men.
They were responsible for ministering at the house of God.

The Returning Levites

14 The Levites who returned were Shemaiah son of Hasshub, son of
Azrikam, son of Hashabiah, a descendant of Merari; 15 Bakbakkar;
Heresh; Galal; Mattaniah son of Mica, son of Zicri, son of Asaph;
16 Obadiah son of Shemaiah, son of Galal, son of Jeduthun; and Berekiah
son of Asa, son of Elkanah, who lived in the area of Netophah.
17 The gatekeepers who returned were Shallum, Akkub, Talmon, Ahiman,
and their relatives. Shallum was the chief gatekeeper. 18 Prior to this
time, they were responsible for the King's Gate on the east side. These
men served as gatekeepers for the camps of the Levites. 19 Shallum was
the son of Kore, a descendant of Abiasaph,* from the clan of Korah.
He and his relatives, the Korahites, were responsible for guarding
the entrance to the sanctuary, just as their ancestors had guarded the
Tabernacle in the camp of the LORD.

20 Phinehas son of Eleazar had been in charge of the gatekeepers in
earlier times, and the LORD had been with him. 21 And later Zechariah
son of Meshelemiah was responsible for guarding the entrance to the
Tabernacle.*

22 In all, there were 212 gatekeepers in those days, and they were listed
according to the genealogies in their villages. David and Samuel the seer
had appointed their ancestors because they were reliable men. 23 These
gatekeepers and their descendants, by their divisions, were responsible for
guarding the entrance to the house of the LORD when that house was a tent.
24 The gatekeepers were stationed on all four sides—east, west, north, and
south. 25 Their relatives in the villages came regularly to share their duties
for seven-day periods.

26 The four chief gatekeepers, all Levites, were trusted officials, for they
were responsible for the rooms and treasuries at the house of God. 27 They
would spend the night around the house of God, since it was their duty to
guard it and to open the gates every morning.

9:19 Hebrew *Ebiasaph,* a variant spelling of Abiasaph; compare Exod 6:24. 9:21 Hebrew *Tent of Meeting.*

[28]Some of the gatekeepers were assigned to care for the various articles
used in worship. They checked them in and out to avoid any loss. [29]Others
were responsible for the furnishings, the items in the sanctuary, and the sup-
plies, such as choice flour, wine, olive oil, frankincense, and spices. [30]But it
was the priests who blended the spices. [31]Mattithiah, a Levite and the oldest
son of Shallum the Korahite, was entrusted with baking the bread used in
the offerings. [32]And some members of the clan of Kohath were in charge of
preparing the bread to be set on the table each Sabbath day.

[33]The musicians, all prominent Levites, lived at the Temple. They were
exempt from other responsibilities since they were on duty at all hours. [34]All
these men lived in Jerusalem. They were the heads of Levite families and
were listed as prominent leaders in their genealogical records.

King Saul's Family Tree

[35]Jeiel (the father of* Gibeon) lived in the town of Gibeon. His wife's
name was Maacah, [36]and his oldest son was named Abdon. Jeiel's other
sons were Zur, Kish, Baal, Ner, Nadab, [37]Gedor, Ahio, Zechariah, and
Mikloth. [38]Mikloth was the father of Shimeam. All these families lived
near each other in Jerusalem.
39 Ner was the father of Kish.
Kish was the father of Saul.
Saul was the father of Jonathan, Malkishua, Abinadab, and Esh-baal.
40 Jonathan was the father of Merib-baal.
Merib-baal was the father of Micah.
41 The sons of Micah were Pithon, Melech, Tahrea, and Ahaz.*
42 Ahaz was the father of Jadah.*
Jadah was the father of Alemeth, Azmaveth, and Zimri.
Zimri was the father of Moza.
43 Moza was the father of Binea.
Binea's son was Rephaiah.
Rephaiah's son was Eleasah.
Eleasah's son was Azel.
[44]Azel had six sons, whose names were Azrikam, Bokeru, Ishmael,
Sheariah, Obadiah, and Hanan. These were the sons of Azel.

The Death of King Saul

10 Now the Philistines attacked Israel, and the men of Israel fled before
them. Many were slaughtered on the slopes of Mount Gilboa. [2]The
Philistines closed in on Saul and his sons, and they killed three of his sons—
Jonathan, Abinadab, and Malkishua. [3]The fighting grew very fierce around
Saul, and the Philistine archers caught up with him and wounded him.

[4]Saul groaned to his armor bearer, "Take your sword and kill me before
these pagan Philistines come to taunt and torture me."

But his armor bearer was afraid and would not do it. So Saul took his own
sword and fell on it. [5]When his armor bearer realized that Saul was dead,
he fell on his own sword and died. [6]So Saul and his three sons died there
together, bringing his dynasty to an end.

[7]When all the Israelites in the Jezreel Valley saw that their army had fled

Question **10:1-14**

This account of King Saul's death is nearly identical to the account in 1 Samuel 31. This reminds us that these six historical books (1 and 2 Samuel, 1 and 2 Kings, and 1 and 2 Chronicles) offer intriguing insight into the struggle to establish a flourishing nation and the subsequent struggle of identity that follows. If someone were to ask you what difference it makes to know this history, how would you answer?

9:35 Or *the founder of.* **9:41** As in Syriac version and Latin Vulgate (see also 8:35); Hebrew lacks *and Ahaz.* **9:42** As in some Hebrew manuscripts and Greek version (see also 8:36); Hebrew reads *Jarah.*

Question 10:10

The first real story after nine chapters of genealogies in 1 Chronicles is a story of shocking, grotesque failure! What point is the writer of 1 Chronicles hoping you, the reader, will understand in chapter 10?

Prayer 11:5

Lord, upon this rock of Zion, you changed the course of history for all eternity. Thank you for your grand plan. Amen.

and that Saul and his sons were dead, they abandoned their towns and fled.
So the Philistines moved in and occupied their towns.
8 The next day, when the Philistines went out to strip the dead, they found
the bodies of Saul and his sons on Mount Gilboa. 9 So they stripped off Saul's
armor and cut off his head. Then they proclaimed the good news of Saul's
death before their idols and to the people throughout the land of Philistia.
10 They placed his armor in the temple of their gods, and they fastened his
head to the temple of Dagon.
11 But when everyone in Jabesh-gilead heard about everything the Phi-
listines had done to Saul, 12 all their mighty warriors brought the bodies of
Saul and his sons back to Jabesh. Then they buried their bones beneath the
great tree at Jabesh, and they fasted for seven days.
13 So Saul died because he was unfaithful to the LORD. He failed to obey
the LORD's command, and he even consulted a medium 14 instead of asking
the LORD for guidance. So the LORD killed him and turned the kingdom
over to David son of Jesse.

David Becomes King of All Israel

11 Then all Israel gathered before David at Hebron and told him, "We
are your own flesh and blood. 2 In the past,* even when Saul was king,
you were the one who really led the forces of Israel. And the LORD your God
told you, 'You will be the shepherd of my people Israel. You will be the leader
of my people Israel.'"
3 So there at Hebron, David made a covenant before the LORD with all the
elders of Israel. And they anointed him king of Israel, just as the LORD had
promised through Samuel.

David Captures Jerusalem

4 Then David and all Israel went to Jerusalem (or Jebus, as it used to be called),
where the Jebusites, the original inhabitants of the land, were living. 5 The
people of Jebus taunted David, saying, "You'll never get in here!" But David
captured the fortress of Zion, which is now called the City of David.
6 David had said to his troops, "Whoever is first to attack the Jebusites will
become the commander of my armies!" And Joab, the son of David's sister
Zeruiah, was first to attack, so he became the commander of David's armies.
7 David made the fortress his home, and that is why it is called the City of
David. 8 He extended the city from the supporting terraces* to the surround-
ing area, while Joab rebuilt the rest of Jerusalem. 9 And David became more
and more powerful, because the LORD of Heaven's Armies was with him.

David's Mightiest Warriors

10 These are the leaders of David's mighty warriors. Together with all Israel,
they decided to make David their king, just as the LORD had promised con-
cerning Israel.
11 Here is the record of David's mightiest warriors: The first was Jasho-
beam the Hacmonite, who was leader of the Three—the mightiest warriors
among David's men.* He once used his spear to kill 300 enemy warriors in
a single battle.

Story Arc 11:1-2

● David

Even though Saul had been king, it was David who had truly been leading Israel. He had shepherded God's flock. How did David's shepherding reign prepare the way for Jesus to arrive on Mount Zion a thousand years later?

1 Chr 16:37 ►

11:2 Or *For some time.* 11:8 Hebrew *the millo.* The meaning of the Hebrew is uncertain. 11:11 As in some Greek manuscripts (see also 2 Sam 23:8); Hebrew reads *leader of the Thirty,* or *leader of the captains.*

[12]Next in rank among the Three was Eleazar son of Dodai,* a descendant
of Ahoah. [13]He was with David when the Philistines gathered for battle at
Pas-dammim and attacked the Israelites in a field full of barley. The Israelite
army fled, [14]but Eleazar and David* held their ground in the middle of the
field and beat back the Philistines. So the LORD saved them by giving them
a great victory.

[15]Once when David was at the rock near the cave of Adullam, the Philistine
army was camped in the valley of Rephaim. The Three (who were among the
Thirty—an elite group among David's fighting men) went down to meet
him there. [16]David was staying in the stronghold at the time, and a Philistine
detachment had occupied the town of Bethlehem.

[17]David remarked longingly to his men, "Oh, how I would love some of
that good water from the well by the gate in Bethlehem." [18]So the Three
broke through the Philistine lines, drew some water from the well by the
gate in Bethlehem, and brought it back to David. But David refused to drink
it. Instead, he poured it out as an offering to the LORD. [19]"God forbid that I
should drink this!" he exclaimed. "This water is as precious as the blood of
these men* who risked their lives to bring it to me." So David did not drink
it. These are examples of the exploits of the Three.

David's Thirty Mighty Men

[20]Abishai, the brother of Joab, was the leader of the Thirty.* He once used his
spear to kill 300 enemy warriors in a single battle. It was by such feats that he
became as famous as the Three. [21]Abishai was the most famous of the Thirty
and was their commander, though he was not one of the Three.

[22]There was also Benaiah son of Jehoiada, a valiant warrior from Kab-
zeel. He did many heroic deeds, which included killing two champions*
of Moab. Another time, on a snowy day, he chased a lion down into a pit
and killed it. [23]Once, armed only with a club, he killed an Egyptian war-
rior who was 7½ feet* tall and who was armed with a spear as thick as a
weaver's beam. Benaiah wrenched the spear from the Egyptian's hand and
killed him with it. [24]Deeds like these made Benaiah as famous as the three
mightiest warriors. [25]He was more honored than the other members of the
Thirty, though he was not one of the Three. And David made him captain
of his bodyguard.

[26]David's mighty warriors also included:

Asahel, Joab's brother;
Elhanan son of Dodo from Bethlehem;
27 Shammah from Harod;*
Helez from Pelon;
28 Ira son of Ikkesh from Tekoa;
Abiezer from Anathoth;
29 Sibbecai from Hushah;
Zalmon* from Ahoah;
30 Maharai from Netophah;
Heled son of Baanah from Netophah;

11:12 As in parallel text at 2 Sam 23:9 (see also 1 Chr 27:4); Hebrew reads *Dodo,* a variant spelling of Dodai. 11:14 Hebrew *they.* 11:19 Hebrew *Shall I drink the lifeblood of these men?* 11:20 As in Syriac version; Hebrew reads *the Three;* also in 11:21. 11:22 Or *two sons of Ariel.* 11:23 Hebrew *5 cubits* [2.3 meters]. 11:27 As in parallel text at 2 Sam 23:25; Hebrew reads *Shammoth from Haror.* 11:29 As in parallel text at 2 Sam 23:28; Hebrew reads *Ilai.*

Question 12:2

The heroes listed in chapters 11 and 12 all line up behind David. Even exceptionally gifted warriors from Saul's family served David. What was it about David's leadership in those early days before he was king that so inspired people? What can you model in your life from David's example?

31 Ithai son of Ribai from Gibeah (in the land of Benjamin);
Benaiah from Pirathon;
32 Hurai from near Nahale-gaash*;
Abi-albon* from Arabah;
33 Azmaveth from Bahurim*;
Eliahba from Shaalbon;
34 the sons of Jashen* from Gizon;
Jonathan son of Shagee from Harar;
35 Ahiam son of Sharar* from Harar;
Eliphal son of Ur;
36 Hepher from Mekerah;
Ahijah from Pelon;
37 Hezro from Carmel;
Paarai* son of Ezbai;
38 Joel, the brother of Nathan;
Mibhar son of Hagri;
39 Zelek from Ammon;
Naharai from Beeroth, the armor bearer of Joab son of Zeruiah;
40 Ira from Jattir;
Gareb from Jattir;
41 Uriah the Hittite;
Zabad son of Ahlai;
42 Adina son of Shiza, the Reubenite leader who had thirty men with him;
43 Hanan son of Maacah;
Joshaphat from Mithna;
44 Uzzia from Ashtaroth;
Shama and Jeiel, the sons of Hotham, from Aroer;
45 Jediael son of Shimri;
Joha, his brother, from Tiz;
46 Eliel from Mahavah;
Jeribai and Joshaviah, the sons of Elnaam;
Ithmah from Moab;
47 Eliel and Obed;
Jaasiel from Zobah.*

Warriors Join David's Army

12 The following men joined David at Ziklag while he was hiding from
Saul son of Kish. They were among the warriors who fought beside
David in battle. 2 All of them were expert archers, and they could shoot ar-
rows or sling stones with their left hand as well as their right. They were all
relatives of Saul from the tribe of Benjamin. 3 Their leader was Ahiezer son
of Shemaah from Gibeah; his brother Joash was second-in-command. These
were the other warriors:

Jeziel and Pelet, sons of Azmaveth;
Beracah;
Jehu from Anathoth;

11:32a Or *from the ravines of Gaash.* 11:32b As in parallel text at 2 Sam 23:31; Hebrew reads *Abiel.* 11:33 As in parallel text at 2 Sam 23:31; Hebrew reads *Baharum.* 11:34 As in parallel text at 2 Sam 23:32; Hebrew reads *sons of Hashem.* 11:35 As in parallel text at 2 Sam 23:33; Hebrew reads *son of Sacar.* 11:37 As in parallel text at 2 Sam 23:35; Hebrew reads *Naarai.* 11:47 Or *the Mezobaite.*

4 Ishmaiah from Gibeon, a famous warrior and leader among the Thirty;
*Jeremiah, Jahaziel, Johanan, and Jozabad from Gederah;
5 Eluzai, Jerimoth, Bealiah, Shemariah, and Shephatiah from Haruph;
6 Elkanah, Isshiah, Azarel, Joezer, and Jashobeam, who were Korahites;
7 Joelah and Zebadiah, sons of Jeroham from Gedor.

8 Some brave and experienced warriors from the tribe of Gad also defected
to David while he was at the stronghold in the wilderness. They were ex-
pert with both shield and spear, as fierce as lions and as swift as deer on the
mountains.

9 Ezer was their leader.
Obadiah was second.
Eliab was third.
10 Mishmannah was fourth.
Jeremiah was fifth.
11 Attai was sixth.
Eliel was seventh.
12 Johanan was eighth.
Elzabad was ninth.
13 Jeremiah was tenth.
Macbannai was eleventh.

14 These warriors from Gad were army commanders. The weakest among
them could take on a hundred regular troops, and the strongest could take
on a thousand! 15 These were the men who crossed the Jordan River during
its seasonal flooding at the beginning of the year and drove out all the people
living in the lowlands on both the east and west banks.
16 Others from Benjamin and Judah came to David at the stronghold. 17 Da-
vid went out to meet them and said, "If you have come in peace to help me,
we are friends. But if you have come to betray me to my enemies when I am
innocent, then may the God of our ancestors see it and punish you."
18 Then the Spirit came upon Amasai, the leader of the Thirty, and he said,

"We are yours, David!
We are on your side, son of Jesse.
Peace and prosperity be with you,
and success to all who help you,
for your God is the one who helps you."

So David let them join him, and he made them officers over his troops.
19 Some men from Manasseh defected from the Israelite army and joined
David when he set out with the Philistines to fight against Saul. But as it
turned out, the Philistine rulers refused to let David and his men go with
them. After much discussion, they sent them back, for they said, "It will
cost us our heads if David switches loyalties to Saul and turns against us."
20 Here is a list of the men from Manasseh who defected to David as he was
returning to Ziklag: Adnah, Jozabad, Jediael, Michael, Jozabad, Elihu, and
Zillethai. Each commanded 1,000 troops from the tribe of Manasseh. 21 They

12:4 Verses 12:4b-40 are numbered 12:5-41 in Hebrew text.

Make a Difference

12:32

Understand the Times

Does it ever feel to you like the world is out of control? Do you have a sense of anxiety about the trends of society? Do you worry about the blowing winds of culture, how quickly people's opinions change?

The men of Issachar "understood the signs of the times and knew the best course of action for Israel to take." These people were able to look around at their current events and discern what was really going on. In other words, they could interpret the pressures of the world and interpret God's will.

Difference Maker

Instead of worrying about current events, take a step back and observe them. What trends do you see? What recurring themes and patterns are there? What agendas and manipulations are creating chaos? Finally, from what you already know about God's plans, how can you stand firmly rooted in God's course of action in the midst of it all?

helped David chase down bands of raiders, for they were all brave and able
warriors who became commanders in his army. 22 Day after day more men
joined David until he had a great army, like the army of God.

23 These are the numbers of armed warriors who joined David at Hebron.
They were all eager to see David become king instead of Saul, just as the
LORD had promised.

24 From the tribe of Judah, there were 6,800 warriors armed with shields and spears.
25 From the tribe of Simeon, there were 7,100 brave warriors.
26 From the tribe of Levi, there were 4,600 warriors. 27 This included
Jehoiada, leader of the family of Aaron, who had 3,700 under his
command. 28 This also included Zadok, a brave young warrior, with
22 members of his family who were all officers.
29 From the tribe of Benjamin, Saul's relatives, there were 3,000 warriors. Most of the men from Benjamin had remained loyal to Saul until this time.
30 From the tribe of Ephraim, there were 20,800 brave warriors, each highly respected in his own clan.
31 From the half-tribe of Manasseh west of the Jordan, 18,000 men were designated by name to help David become king.
32 From the tribe of Issachar, there were 200 leaders of the tribe with their relatives. All these men understood the signs of the times and knew the best course for Israel to take.
33 From the tribe of Zebulun, there were 50,000 skilled warriors. They were fully armed and prepared for battle and completely loyal to David.
34 From the tribe of Naphtali, there were 1,000 officers and 37,000 warriors armed with shields and spears.
35 From the tribe of Dan, there were 28,600 warriors, all prepared for battle.
36 From the tribe of Asher, there were 40,000 trained warriors, all prepared for battle.
37 From the east side of the Jordan River—where the tribes of Reuben and Gad and the half-tribe of Manasseh lived—there were 120,000 troops armed with every kind of weapon.

38 All these men came in battle array to Hebron with the single purpose
of making David the king over all Israel. In fact, everyone in Israel agreed
that David should be their king. 39 They feasted and drank with David for
three days, for preparations had been made by their relatives for their arrival.
40 And people from as far away as Issachar, Zebulun, and Naphtali brought
food on donkeys, camels, mules, and oxen. Vast supplies of flour, fig cakes,
clusters of raisins, wine, olive oil, cattle, sheep, and goats were brought to
the celebration. There was great joy throughout the land of Israel.

David Attempts to Move the Ark

13 David consulted with all his officials, including the generals and
captains of his army.* 2 Then he addressed the entire assembly of Is-
rael as follows: "If you approve and if it is the will of the LORD our God, let us

13:1 Hebrew *the commanders of thousands and of hundreds.*

send messages to all the Israelites throughout the land, including the priests
and Levites in their towns and pasturelands. Let us invite them to come and
join us. 3It is time to bring back the Ark of our God, for we neglected it dur-
ing the reign of Saul."
4The whole assembly agreed to this, for the people could see it was the
right thing to do. 5So David summoned all Israel, from the Shihor Brook of
Egypt in the south all the way to the town of Lebo-hamath in the north, to
join in bringing the Ark of God from Kiriath-jearim. 6Then David and all
Israel went to Baalah of Judah (also called Kiriath-jearim) to bring back the
Ark of God, which bears the name* of the LORD who is enthroned between
the cherubim. 7They placed the Ark of God on a new cart and brought it
from Abinadab's house. Uzzah and Ahio were guiding the cart. 8David and
all Israel were celebrating before God with all their might, singing songs
and playing all kinds of musical instruments—lyres, harps, tambourines,
cymbals, and trumpets.
9But when they arrived at the threshing floor of Nacon,* the oxen
stumbled, and Uzzah reached out his hand to steady the Ark. 10Then the
LORD's anger was aroused against Uzzah, and he struck him dead because
he had laid his hand on the Ark. So Uzzah died there in the presence of God.
11David was angry because the LORD's anger had burst out against Uzzah.
He named that place Perez-uzzah (which means "to burst out against Uz-
zah"), as it is still called today.
12David was now afraid of God, and he asked, "How can I ever bring the
Ark of God back into my care?" 13So David did not move the Ark into the City
of David. Instead, he took it to the house of Obed-edom of Gath. 14The Ark of
God remained there in Obed-edom's house for three months, and the LORD
blessed the household of Obed-edom and everything he owned.

David's Palace and Family

14 Then King Hiram of Tyre sent messengers to David, along with cedar
timber, and stonemasons and carpenters to build him a palace. 2And
David realized that the LORD had confirmed him as king over Israel and had
greatly blessed his kingdom for the sake of his people Israel.
3Then David married more wives in Jerusalem, and they had more sons
and daughters. 4These are the names of David's sons who were born in Jeru-
salem: Shammua, Shobab, Nathan, Solomon, 5Ibhar, Elishua, Elpelet, 6No-
gah, Nepheg, Japhia, 7Elishama, Eliada,* and Eliphelet.

David Conquers the Philistines

8When the Philistines heard that David had been anointed king over all Is-
rael, they mobilized all their forces to capture him. But David was told they
were coming, so he marched out to meet them. 9The Philistines arrived and
made a raid in the valley of Rephaim. 10So David asked God, "Should I go out
to fight the Philistines? Will you hand them over to me?"
The LORD replied, "Yes, go ahead. I will hand them over to you."
11So David and his troops went up to Baal-perazim and defeated the Philis-
tines there. "God did it!" David exclaimed. "He used me to burst through my
enemies like a raging flood!" So they named that place Baal-perazim (which

13:6 Or *the Ark of God, where the Name is proclaimed—the name.* 13:9 As in parallel text at 2 Sam 6:6; Hebrew reads *Kidon.* 14:7 Hebrew *Beeliada,* a variant spelling of Eliada; compare 3:8 and parallel text at 2 Sam 5:16.

Question 13:3

Notice how David prioritized God's throne, the ark, after Saul prioritized his own kingdom. What things have you prioritized that get in the way of making God the first focus of your life?

Prayer 14:11

Lord, you are more powerful than anything or anyone. Let me walk courageously today, for you will burst through anything that stands against your plan. Amen.

Question 15:13

How does life go when you don't follow God?

means "the Lord who bursts through"). 12 The Philistines had abandoned
their gods there, so David gave orders to burn them.
13 But after a while the Philistines returned and raided the valley again.
14 And once again David asked God what to do. "Do not attack them straight
on," God replied. "Instead, circle around behind and attack them near the
poplar* trees. 15 When you hear a sound like marching feet in the tops of the
poplar trees, go out and attack! That will be the signal that God is moving
ahead of you to strike down the Philistine army." 16 So David did what God
commanded, and they struck down the Philistine army all the way from
Gibeon to Gezer.
17 So David's fame spread everywhere, and the LORD caused all the nations
to fear David.

Preparing to Move the Ark

15 David now built several buildings for himself in the City of David.
He also prepared a place for the Ark of God and set up a special tent
for it. 2 Then he commanded, "No one except the Levites may carry the Ark
of God. The LORD has chosen them to carry the Ark of the LORD and to serve
him forever."
3 Then David summoned all Israel to Jerusalem to bring the Ark of the
LORD to the place he had prepared for it. 4 This is the number of the descen-
dants of Aaron (the priests) and the Levites who were called together:

5 From the clan of Kohath, 120, with Uriel as their leader.
6 From the clan of Merari, 220, with Asaiah as their leader.
7 From the clan of Gershon,* 130, with Joel as their leader.
8 From the descendants of Elizaphan, 200, with Shemaiah as their leader.
9 From the descendants of Hebron, 80, with Eliel as their leader.
10 From the descendants of Uzziel, 112, with Amminadab as their leader.

11 Then David summoned the priests, Zadok and Abiathar, and these Levite
leaders: Uriel, Asaiah, Joel, Shemaiah, Eliel, and Amminadab. 12 He said to
them, "You are the leaders of the Levite families. You must purify yourselves
and all your fellow Levites, so you can bring the Ark of the LORD, the God of
Israel, to the place I have prepared for it. 13 Because you Levites did not carry
the Ark the first time, the anger of the LORD our God burst out against us.
We failed to ask God how to move it properly." 14 So the priests and the Levites
purified themselves in order to bring the Ark of the LORD, the God of Israel,
to Jerusalem. 15 Then the Levites carried the Ark of God on their shoulders
with its carrying poles, just as the LORD had instructed Moses.
16 David also ordered the Levite leaders to appoint a choir of Levites who were
singers and musicians to sing joyful songs to the accompaniment of harps,
lyres, and cymbals. 17 So the Levites appointed Heman son of Joel along with
his fellow Levites: Asaph son of Berekiah, and Ethan son of Kushaiah from the
clan of Merari. 18 The following men were chosen as their assistants: Zechariah,
Jaaziel,* Shemiramoth, Jehiel, Unni, Eliab, Benaiah, Maaseiah, Mattithiah,
Eliphelehu, Mikneiah, and the gatekeepers—Obed-edom and Jeiel.

14:14 Or *aspen,* or *balsam;* also in 14:15. The exact identification of this tree is uncertain. **15:7** Hebrew *Gershom,* a variant spelling of Gershon. **15:18** As in several Hebrew manuscripts and Greek version (see also parallel lists in 15:20; 16:5); Masoretic Text reads *Zechariah ben Jaaziel.*

19 The musicians Heman, Asaph, and Ethan were chosen to sound the
bronze cymbals. 20 Zechariah, Aziel, Shemiramoth, Jehiel, Unni, Eliab, Maa-
seiah, and Benaiah were chosen to play the harps.* 21 Mattithiah, Eliphelehu,
Mikneiah, Obed-edom, Jeiel, and Azaziah were chosen to play the lyres.*
22 Kenaniah, the head Levite, was chosen as the choir leader because of his skill.
23 Berekiah and Elkanah were chosen to guard* the Ark. 24 Shebaniah, Josh-
aphat, Nethanel, Amasai, Zechariah, Benaiah, and Eliezer—all of whom
were priests—were chosen to blow the trumpets as they marched in front
of the Ark of God. Obed-edom and Jehiah were chosen to guard the Ark.

Moving the Ark to Jerusalem

25 Then David and the elders of Israel and the generals of the army* went
to the house of Obed-edom to bring the Ark of the LORD's Covenant up to
Jerusalem with a great celebration. 26 And because God was clearly helping
the Levites as they carried the Ark of the LORD's Covenant, they sacrificed
seven bulls and seven rams.
27 David was dressed in a robe of fine linen, as were all the Levites who
carried the Ark, and also the singers, and Kenaniah the choir leader. David
was also wearing a priestly garment.* 28 So all Israel brought up the Ark of
the LORD's Covenant with shouts of joy, the blowing of rams' horns and
trumpets, the crashing of cymbals, and loud playing on harps and lyres.
29 But as the Ark of the LORD's Covenant entered the City of David, Michal,
the daughter of Saul, looked down from her window. When she saw King
David skipping about and laughing with joy, she was filled with contempt
for him.

16 They brought the Ark of God and placed it inside the special tent
David had prepared for it. And they presented burnt offerings and
peace offerings to God. 2 When he had finished his sacrifices, David blessed
the people in the name of the LORD. 3 Then he gave to every man and woman
in all Israel a loaf of bread, a cake of dates,* and a cake of raisins.
4 David appointed the following Levites to lead the people in worship
before the Ark of the LORD—to invoke his blessings, to give thanks, and to
praise the LORD, the God of Israel. 5 Asaph, the leader of this group, sounded
the cymbals. Second to him was Zechariah, followed by Jeiel, Shemiramoth,
Jehiel, Mattithiah, Eliab, Benaiah, Obed-edom, and Jeiel. They played the
harps and lyres. 6 The priests, Benaiah and Jahaziel, played the trumpets
regularly before the Ark of God's Covenant.

David's Song of Praise

7 On that day David gave to Asaph and his fellow Levites this song of thanks-
giving to the LORD:

8 Give thanks to the LORD and proclaim his greatness.
  Let the whole world know what he has done.
9 Sing to him; yes, sing his praises.
  Tell everyone about his wonderful deeds.

Question 15:29

This is a shortened version of 2 Samuel 6:16-23. The reader is expected to remember the longer version. The point here is that David was not ashamed of his enthusiasm for God; he expressed it openly even if it bothered others. How could you be more like David and less like Michal here?

Make a Difference

16:7-36

What He Has Done

Stop. In the margins of this page or on a napkin or a blank piece of paper, brainstorm all the things that God has done for you. Just start listing whatever comes to your mind. Think of things both large and small, grand and intricate, massive in scale and microscopic to the eye, beautiful and strange, wonderful and surprising, overwhelmingly powerful and perplexingly gentle. Think of things he has promised and things he has fulfilled. Think of things he has said. Think of songs he has written and dances he has led. Think of meals he has prepared and sacrifices he has made. Think of the authority he has used and the hope he has shown. How could you begin to give thanks for all these wonderful blessings? How could you begin to tell the world about what God has done?

Difference Maker

Using the list you have made and the creative talent God has given you, create a work of art, a poem, or a song that proclaims the greatness of God.

15:20 Hebrew adds *according to Alamoth,* which is probably a musical term. The meaning of the Hebrew is uncertain. 15:21 Hebrew adds *according to the Sheminith,* which is probably a musical term. The meaning of the Hebrew is uncertain. 15:23 Hebrew *chosen as gatekeepers for;* also in 15:24. 15:25 Hebrew *the commanders of thousands.* 15:27 Hebrew *a linen ephod.* 16:3 Or *a portion of meat.* The meaning of the Hebrew is uncertain.

Question **16:24**

On your social media accounts, what could you post about God's glorious deeds?

Make a Difference

16:34

Words from Thanksgiving

The Bible often uses other words that are derived from a heart of thanksgiving. An attitude of gratitude causes people to erupt in thankful expressions. For instance, in 1 Chronicles 16:8-36, David overflowed with thanksgiving, which created in him a litany of other words too: *sing, praise, tell, miracles, generations, glory, deeds, wonderful, name, nations, good, joy, rejoice, remember, seek, LORD, strength, dwelling, worthy, worship, endures, splendor, holy, tremble, heavens, salvation, everlasting, people, shout, amen.*

Difference Maker

Give thanks to God right now. Use David's prayer to prompt the overflow of your words.

10 Exult in his holy name;
rejoice, you who worship the LORD.
11 Search for the LORD and for his strength;
continually seek him.
12 Remember the wonders he has performed,
his miracles, and the rulings he has given,
13 you children of his servant Israel,
you descendants of Jacob, his chosen ones.

14 He is the LORD our God.
His justice is seen throughout the land.
15 Remember his covenant forever—
the commitment he made to a thousand generations.
16 This is the covenant he made with Abraham
and the oath he swore to Isaac.
17 He confirmed it to Jacob as a decree,
and to the people of Israel as a never-ending covenant:
18 "I will give you the land of Canaan
as your special possession."

19 He said this when you were few in number,
a tiny group of strangers in Canaan.
20 They wandered from nation to nation,
from one kingdom to another.
21 Yet he did not let anyone oppress them.
He warned kings on their behalf:
22 "Do not touch my chosen people,
and do not hurt my prophets."

23 Let the whole earth sing to the LORD!
Each day proclaim the good news that he saves.
24 Publish his glorious deeds among the nations.
Tell everyone about the amazing things he does.
25 Great is the LORD! He is most worthy of praise!
He is to be feared above all gods.
26 The gods of other nations are mere idols,
but the LORD made the heavens!
27 Honor and majesty surround him;
strength and joy fill his dwelling.

28 O nations of the world, recognize the LORD,
recognize that the LORD is glorious and strong.
29 Give to the LORD the glory he deserves!
Bring your offering and come into his presence.
Worship the LORD in all his holy splendor.
30 Let all the earth tremble before him.
The world stands firm and cannot be shaken.

31 Let the heavens be glad, and the earth rejoice!
Tell all the nations, "The LORD reigns!"

32 Let the sea and everything in it shout his praise!
Let the fields and their crops burst out with joy!
33 Let the trees of the forest sing for joy before the LORD,
for he is coming to judge the earth.
34 Give thanks to the LORD, for he is good!
His faithful love endures forever.
35 Cry out, "Save us, O God of our salvation!
Gather and rescue us from among the nations,
so we can thank your holy name
and rejoice and praise you."

36 Praise the LORD, the God of Israel,
who lives from everlasting to everlasting!

And all the people shouted "Amen!" and praised the LORD.

Worship at Jerusalem and Gibeon

37 David arranged for Asaph and his fellow Levites to serve regularly before
the Ark of the LORD's Covenant, doing whatever needed to be done each day.
38 This group included Obed-edom (son of Jeduthun), Hosah, and sixty-eight
other Levites as gatekeepers.
39 Meanwhile, David stationed Zadok the priest and his fellow priests at
the Tabernacle of the LORD at the place of worship in Gibeon, where they
continued to minister before the LORD. 40 They sacrificed the regular burnt
offerings to the LORD each morning and evening on the altar set aside for
that purpose, obeying everything written in the Law of the LORD, as he had
commanded Israel. 41 David also appointed Heman, Jeduthun, and the others
chosen by name to give thanks to the LORD, for "his faithful love endures
forever." 42 They used their trumpets, cymbals, and other instruments to
accompany their songs of praise to God.* And the sons of Jeduthun were
appointed as gatekeepers.
43 Then all the people returned to their homes, and David turned and went
home to bless his own family.

The LORD's Covenant Promise to David

17 When David was settled in his palace, he summoned Nathan the
prophet. "Look," David said, "I am living in a beautiful cedar palace,*
but the Ark of the LORD's Covenant is out there under a tent!"
2 Nathan replied to David, "Do whatever you have in mind, for God is
with you."
3 But that same night God said to Nathan,

4 "Go and tell my servant David, 'This is what the LORD has declared:
You are not the one to build a house for me to live in. 5 I have never
lived in a house, from the day I brought the Israelites out of Egypt
until this very day. My home has always been a tent, moving from one
place to another in a Tabernacle. 6 Yet no matter where I have gone
with the Israelites, I have never once complained to Israel's leaders,

16:42 Or *to accompany the sacred music;* or *to accompany singing to God.* 17:1 Hebrew *a house of cedar.*

Story Arc **16:37**

Asaph

Worship is central to the story of God's redemptive plan for humanity. One of the key shapers of worship in the Bible was a man named Asaph. He and his team wrote many of the psalms and helped lead Israel through some of its most vibrant experiences of worship. David entrusted this responsibility to Asaph and others because God wants people to work together, sharing the joy of serving the Lord and equipping one another.

Story Arc **17:1-15**

Nathan

Before Nathan's prophetic confrontation with David, the two men were trusted friends. Here, Nathan was excited to help David build a house for God. In his excitement, Nathan actually got a little ahead of God's plans, so God let him know there were bigger plans in the works. Nathan came to realize that David wanted to build God a house but that God intended to build David a dynasty that would change the world.

1 Chr 22:5-19 ►

the shepherds of my people. I have never asked them, "Why haven't
you built me a beautiful cedar house?"'

7"Now go and say to my servant David, 'This is what the LORD of
Heaven's Armies has declared: I took you from tending sheep in the
pasture and selected you to be the leader of my people Israel. 8I have
been with you wherever you have gone, and I have destroyed all your
enemies before your eyes. Now I will make your name as famous as
anyone who has ever lived on the earth! 9And I will provide a homeland
for my people Israel, planting them in a secure place where they will
never be disturbed. Evil nations won't oppress them as they've done in
the past, 10starting from the time I appointed judges to rule my people
Israel. And I will defeat all your enemies.

"'Furthermore, I declare that the LORD will build a house for you—
a dynasty of kings! 11For when you die and join your ancestors, I will
raise up one of your descendants, one of your sons, and I will make his
kingdom strong. 12He is the one who will build a house—a temple—
for me. And I will secure his throne forever. 13I will be his father, and
he will be my son. I will never take my favor from him as I took it
from the one who ruled before you. 14I will confirm him as king over
my house and my kingdom for all time, and his throne will be secure
forever.'"

15So Nathan went back to David and told him everything the LORD had said
in this vision.

David's Prayer of Thanks

16Then King David went in and sat before the LORD and prayed,

"Who am I, O LORD God, and what is my family, that you have brought
me this far? 17And now, O God, in addition to everything else, you speak
of giving your servant a lasting dynasty! You speak as though I were
someone very great,* O LORD God!

18"What more can I say to you about the way you have honored me?
You know what your servant is really like. 19For the sake of your servant,
O LORD, and according to your will, you have done all these great things
and have made them known.

20"O LORD, there is no one like you. We have never even heard of
another God like you! 21What other nation on earth is like your people
Israel? What other nation, O God, have you redeemed from slavery to
be your own people? You made a great name for yourself when you
redeemed your people from Egypt. You performed awesome miracles
and drove out the nations that stood in their way. 22You chose Israel to
be your very own people forever, and you, O LORD, became their God.

23"And now, O LORD, I am your servant; do as you have promised
concerning me and my family. May it be a promise that will last forever.
24And may your name be established and honored forever so that
everyone will say, 'The LORD of Heaven's Armies, the God of Israel, is
Israel's God!' And may the house of your servant David continue before
you forever.

17:17 The meaning of the Hebrew is uncertain.

25“O my God, I have been bold enough to pray to you because
you have revealed to your servant that you will build a house for
him—a dynasty of kings! 26For you are God, O LORD. And you have
promised these good things to your servant. 27And now, it has pleased
you to bless the house of your servant, so that it will continue forever
before you. For when you grant a blessing, O LORD, it is an eternal
blessing!”

David's Military Victories

18 After this, David defeated and subdued the Philistines by conquering
Gath and its surrounding towns. 2David also conquered the land of
Moab, and the Moabites who were spared became David's subjects and paid
him tribute money.
3David also destroyed the forces of Hadadezer, king of Zobah, as far as
Hamath,* when Hadadezer marched out to strengthen his control along
the Euphrates River. 4David captured 1,000 chariots, 7,000 charioteers, and
20,000 foot soldiers. He crippled all the chariot horses except enough for
100 chariots.
5When Arameans from Damascus arrived to help King Hadadezer, David
killed 22,000 of them. 6Then he placed several army garrisons* in Damas-
cus, the Aramean capital, and the Arameans became David's subjects and
paid him tribute money. So the LORD made David victorious wherever he
went.
7David brought the gold shields of Hadadezer's officers to Jerusalem,
8along with a large amount of bronze from Hadadezer's towns of Tebah*
and Cun. Later Solomon melted the bronze and molded it into the great
bronze basin called the Sea, the pillars, and the various bronze articles used
at the Temple.
9When King Toi* of Hamath heard that David had destroyed the entire
army of King Hadadezer of Zobah, 10he sent his son Joram* to congratu-
late King David for his successful campaign. Hadadezer and Toi had been
enemies and were often at war. Joram presented David with many gifts of
gold, silver, and bronze.
11King David dedicated all these gifts to the LORD, along with the silver
and gold he had taken from the other nations—from Edom, Moab, Ammon,
Philistia, and Amalek.
12Abishai son of Zeruiah destroyed 18,000 Edomites in the Valley of Salt.
13He placed army garrisons in Edom, and all the Edomites became David's
subjects. In fact, the LORD made David victorious wherever he went.
14So David reigned over all Israel and did what was just and right for all
his people. 15Joab son of Zeruiah was commander of the army. Jehoshaphat
son of Ahilud was the royal historian. 16Zadok son of Ahitub and Ahimelech*
son of Abiathar were the priests. Seraiah* was the court secretary. 17Bena-
iah son of Jehoiada was captain of the king's bodyguard.* And David's sons
served as the king's chief assistants.

18:3 The meaning of the Hebrew is uncertain. **18:6** As in Greek version and Latin Vulgate (see also 2 Sam 8:6); Hebrew lacks *several army garrisons.* **18:8** Hebrew reads *Tibhath,* a variant spelling of Tebah; compare parallel text at 2 Sam 8:8. **18:9** As in parallel text at 2 Sam 8:9; Hebrew reads *Tou;* also in 18:10. **18:10** As in parallel text at 2 Sam 8:10; Hebrew reads *Hadoram,* a variant spelling of Joram. **18:16a** As in some Hebrew manuscripts, Syriac version, and Latin Vulgate (see also 2 Sam 8:17); most Hebrew manuscripts read *Abimelech.* **18:16b** As in parallel text at 2 Sam 8:17; Hebrew reads *Shavsha.* **18:17** Hebrew *of the Kerethites and Pelethites.*

Things to reflect on

David Defeats the Ammonites

19 Some time after this, King Nahash of the Ammonites died, and his son Hanun* became king. 2 David said, "I am going to show loyalty to Hanun because his father, Nahash, was always loyal to me." So David sent messengers to express sympathy to Hanun about his father's death.

But when David's ambassadors arrived in the land of Ammon, 3 the Ammonite commanders said to Hanun, "Do you really think these men are coming here to honor your father? No! David has sent them to spy out the land so they can come in and conquer it!" 4 So Hanun seized David's ambassadors and shaved them, cut off their robes at the buttocks, and sent them back to David in shame.

5 When David heard what had happened to the men, he sent messengers to tell them, "Stay at Jericho until your beards grow out, and then come back." For they felt deep shame because of their appearance.

6 When the people of Ammon realized how seriously they had angered David, Hanun and the Ammonites sent 75,000 pounds* of silver to hire chariots and charioteers from Aram-naharaim, Aram-maacah, and Zobah. 7 They also hired 32,000 chariots and secured the support of the king of Maacah and his army. These forces camped at Medeba, where they were joined by the Ammonite troops that Hanun had recruited from his own towns. 8 When David heard about this, he sent Joab and all his warriors to fight them. 9 The Ammonite troops came out and drew up their battle lines at the entrance of the city, while the other kings positioned themselves to fight in the open fields.

10 When Joab saw that he would have to fight on both the front and the rear, he chose some of Israel's elite troops and placed them under his personal command to fight the Arameans in the fields. 11 He left the rest of the army under the command of his brother Abishai, who was to attack the Ammonites. 12 "If the Arameans are too strong for me, then come over and help me," Joab told his brother. "And if the Ammonites are too strong for you, I will help you. 13 Be courageous! Let us fight bravely for our people and the cities of our God. May the LORD's will be done."

14 When Joab and his troops attacked, the Arameans began to run away. 15 And when the Ammonites saw the Arameans running, they also ran from Abishai and retreated into the city. Then Joab returned to Jerusalem.

16 The Arameans now realized that they were no match for Israel, so they sent messengers and summoned additional Aramean troops from the other side of the Euphrates River.* These troops were under the command of Shobach,* the commander of Hadadezer's forces.

17 When David heard what was happening, he mobilized all Israel, crossed the Jordan River, and positioned his troops in battle formation. Then David engaged the Arameans in battle, and they fought against him. 18 But again the Arameans fled from the Israelites. This time David's forces killed 7,000 charioteers and 40,000 foot soldiers, including Shobach, the commander of their army. 19 When Hadadezer's allies saw that they had been defeated by Israel, they surrendered to David and became his subjects. After that, the Arameans were no longer willing to help the Ammonites.

19:1 As in parallel text at 2 Sam 10:1; Hebrew lacks *Hanun.* **19:6** Hebrew *1,000 talents* [34,000 kilograms]. **19:16a** Hebrew *the river.* **19:16b** As in parallel text at 2 Sam 10:16; Hebrew reads *Shophach;* also in 19:18.

David Captures Rabbah

20 In the spring of the year,* when kings normally go out to war, Joab
led the Israelite army in successful attacks against the land of the
Ammonites. In the process he laid siege to the city of Rabbah, attacking and
destroying it. However, David stayed behind in Jerusalem.
2Then David went to Rabbah and removed the crown from the king's
head,* and it was placed on his own head. The crown was made of gold and
set with gems, and he found that it weighed seventy-five pounds.* David
took a vast amount of plunder from the city. 3He also made slaves of the
people of Rabbah and forced them to labor with saws, iron picks, and iron
axes.* That is how David dealt with the people of all the Ammonite towns.
Then David and all the army returned to Jerusalem.

Battles against Philistine Giants

4After this, war broke out with the Philistines at Gezer. As they fought,
Sibbecai from Hushah killed Saph,* a descendant of the giants,* and so the
Philistines were subdued.
5During another battle with the Philistines, Elhanan son of Jair killed
Lahmi, the brother of Goliath of Gath. The handle of Lahmi's spear was as
thick as a weaver's beam!
6In another battle with the Philistines at Gath, they encountered a huge
man with six fingers on each hand and six toes on each foot, twenty-four
in all, who was also a descendant of the giants. 7But when he defied and
taunted Israel, he was killed by Jonathan, the son of David's brother Shimea.
8These Philistines were descendants of the giants of Gath, but David and
his warriors killed them.

David Takes a Census

21 Satan rose up against Israel and caused David to take a census of the
people of Israel. 2So David said to Joab and the commanders of the
army, "Take a census of all the people of Israel—from Beersheba in the south to
Dan in the north—and bring me a report so I may know how many there are."
3But Joab replied, "May the LORD increase the number of his people a
hundred times over! But why, my lord the king, do you want to do this? Are
they not all your servants? Why must you cause Israel to sin?"
4But the king insisted that they take the census, so Joab traveled through-
out all Israel to count the people. Then he returned to Jerusalem 5and re-
ported the number of people to David. There were 1,100,000 warriors in
all Israel who could handle a sword, and 470,000 in Judah. 6But Joab did
not include the tribes of Levi and Benjamin in the census because he was so
distressed at what the king had made him do.

Judgment for David's Sin

7God was very displeased with the census, and he punished Israel for it.
8Then David said to God, "I have sinned greatly by taking this census. Please
forgive my guilt for doing this foolish thing."

20:1 Hebrew *At the turn of the year.* The first day of the year in the ancient Hebrew lunar calendar occurred in March or April. 20:2a Or *from the head of Milcom* (as in Greek version and Latin Vulgate). Milcom, also called Molech, was the god of the Ammonites. 20:2b Hebrew *1 talent* [34 kilograms]. 20:3 As in parallel text at 2 Sam 12:31; Hebrew reads *and cut them with saws, iron picks, and saws.* 20:4a As in parallel text at 2 Sam 21:18; Hebrew reads *Sippai.* 20:4b Hebrew *descendant of the Rephaites;* also in 20:6, 8.

Question 20:1

This phrase, "when kings normally go out to war," recalls the fuller account of David's sin with Bathsheba and the murder of Uriah (see 2 Samuel 11). While that story line is omitted here, the writer was triggering its memory by this phrasing. First Chronicles as a book is focused on telling the good news of God's long-range plan. How can a focus on sin derail our ability to see God's work?

Question 21:1-17

This is such an interesting verse: "Satan rose up against Israel." Compare this verse to the complication of 2 Samuel 24:1 (if you dare). It seems that God allowed David to be tempted by Satan with all the ability to win, but David trusted his own strength—the number of his troops—and failed the temptation. Eventually, David confessed and owned his responsibility (1 Chronicles 21:17). What lessons of faith can you learn in this awkward passage?

9 Then the LORD spoke to Gad, David's seer. This was the message: 10 "Go and say to David, 'This is what the LORD says: I will give you three choices. Choose one of these punishments, and I will inflict it on you.'"

11 So Gad came to David and said, "These are the choices the LORD has given you. 12 You may choose three years of famine, three months of destruction by the sword of your enemies, or three days of severe plague as the angel of the LORD brings devastation throughout the land of Israel. Decide what answer I should give the LORD who sent me."

13 "I'm in a desperate situation!" David replied to Gad. "But let me fall into the hands of the LORD, for his mercy is very great. Do not let me fall into human hands."

14 So the LORD sent a plague upon Israel, and 70,000 people died as a result. 15 And God sent an angel to destroy Jerusalem. But just as the angel was preparing to destroy it, the LORD relented and said to the death angel, "Stop! That is enough!" At that moment the angel of the LORD was standing by the threshing floor of Araunah* the Jebusite.

16 David looked up and saw the angel of the LORD standing between heaven and earth with his sword drawn, reaching out over Jerusalem. So David and the leaders of Israel put on burlap to show their deep distress and fell face down on the ground. 17 And David said to God, "I am the one who called for the census! I am the one who has sinned and done wrong! But these people are as innocent as sheep—what have they done? O LORD my God, let your anger fall against me and my family, but do not destroy your people."

David Builds an Altar

18 Then the angel of the LORD told Gad to instruct David to go up and build an altar to the LORD on the threshing floor of Araunah the Jebusite. 19 So David went up to do what the LORD had commanded him through Gad. 20 Araunah, who was busy threshing wheat at the time, turned and saw the angel there. His four sons, who were with him, ran away and hid. 21 When Araunah saw David approaching, he left his threshing floor and bowed before David with his face to the ground.

22 David said to Araunah, "Let me buy this threshing floor from you at its full price. Then I will build an altar to the LORD there, so that he will stop the plague."

23 "Take it, my lord the king, and use it as you wish," Araunah said to David. "I will give the oxen for the burnt offerings, and the threshing boards for wood to build a fire on the altar, and the wheat for the grain offering. I will give it all to you."

24 But King David replied to Araunah, "No, I insist on buying it for the full price. I will not take what is yours and give it to the LORD. I will not present burnt offerings that have cost me nothing!" 25 So David gave Araunah 600 pieces of gold* in payment for the threshing floor.

26 David built an altar there to the LORD and sacrificed burnt offerings and peace offerings. And when David prayed, the LORD answered him by sending fire from heaven to burn up the offering on the altar. 27 Then the LORD spoke to the angel, who put the sword back into its sheath.

28 When David saw that the LORD had answered his prayer, he offered sacrifices there at Araunah's threshing floor. 29 At that time the Tabernacle of the

21:15 As in parallel text at 2 Sam 24:16; Hebrew reads *Ornan,* another name for Araunah; also in 21:18-28. 21:25 Hebrew *600 shekels of gold,* about 15 pounds or 6.8 kilograms in weight.

LORD and the altar of burnt offering that Moses had made in the wilderness
were located at the place of worship in Gibeon. 30But David was not able to
go there to inquire of God, because he was terrified by the drawn sword of
the angel of the LORD.

22 Then David said, "This will be the location for the Temple of the
LORD God and the place of the altar for Israel's burnt offerings!"

Preparations for the Temple
2So David gave orders to call together the foreigners living in Israel, and he
assigned them the task of preparing finished stone for building the Temple
of God. 3David provided large amounts of iron for the nails that would be
needed for the doors in the gates and for the clamps, and he gave more
bronze than could be weighed. 4He also provided innumerable cedar logs,
for the men of Tyre and Sidon had brought vast amounts of cedar to David.
5David said, "My son Solomon is still young and inexperienced. And since
the Temple to be built for the LORD must be a magnificent structure, famous
and glorious throughout the world, I will begin making preparations for
it now." So David collected vast amounts of building materials before his
death.
6Then David sent for his son Solomon and instructed him to build a
Temple for the LORD, the God of Israel. 7"My son, I wanted to build a Temple
to honor the name of the LORD my God," David told him. 8"But the LORD
said to me, 'You have killed many men in the battles you have fought. And
since you have shed so much blood in my sight, you will not be the one to
build a Temple to honor my name. 9But you will have a son who will be a
man of peace. I will give him peace with his enemies in all the surrounding
lands. His name will be Solomon,* and I will give peace and quiet to Israel
during his reign. 10He is the one who will build a Temple to honor my name.
He will be my son, and I will be his father. And I will secure the throne of his
kingdom over Israel forever.'
11"Now, my son, may the LORD be with you and give you success as you
follow his directions in building the Temple of the LORD your God. 12And
may the LORD give you wisdom and understanding, that you may obey the
Law of the LORD your God as you rule over Israel. 13For you will be successful
if you carefully obey the decrees and regulations that the LORD gave to Israel
through Moses. Be strong and courageous; do not be afraid or lose heart!
14"I have worked hard to provide materials for building the Temple of the
LORD—nearly 4,000 tons of gold, 40,000 tons of silver,* and so much iron
and bronze that it cannot be weighed. I have also gathered timber and stone
for the walls, though you may need to add more. 15You have a large number
of skilled stonemasons and carpenters and craftsmen of every kind. 16You
have expert goldsmiths and silversmiths and workers of bronze and iron.
Now begin the work, and may the LORD be with you!"
17Then David ordered all the leaders of Israel to assist Solomon in this
project. 18"The LORD your God is with you," he declared. "He has given you
peace with the surrounding nations. He has handed them over to me, and
they are now subject to the LORD and his people. 19Now seek the LORD your

Story Arc **22:5–19**

● **Solomon**

David gave instructions to his son Solomon to build a house for the Lord. This is a fulfillment of God's conversation with Nathan and David in 1 Chronicles 17:11-12. David's primary instruction to Solomon, therefore, was this: "Seek the LORD your God with all your heart and soul" (22:19). This is the whole purpose of God dwelling among humanity—that we may seek him while he is near.

2 Chr 1:1 ►

22:9 *Solomon* sounds like and is probably derived from the Hebrew word for "peace."
22:14 Hebrew *100,000 talents* [3,400 metric tons] *of gold, 1,000,000 talents* [34,000 metric tons] *of silver.*

Question 23:1-5

During the transfer of power from David to Solomon (v. 1), worship played a central role. Dedication to and focus on the Lord was what had made David's reign so successful, and it was what would make Solomon's successful. The real difference maker in our own lives is in our devotion to and worship of God. How have you worshiped God recently? How will you worship him in the week ahead?

God with all your heart and soul. Build the sanctuary of the LORD God so that you can bring the Ark of the LORD's Covenant and the holy vessels of God into the Temple built to honor the LORD's name."

Duties of the Levites

23 When David was an old man, he appointed his son Solomon to
be king over Israel. 2 David summoned all the leaders of Israel, to-
gether with the priests and Levites. 3 All the Levites who were thirty years
old or older were counted, and the total came to 38,000. 4 Then David said,
"From all the Levites, 24,000 will supervise the work at the Temple of the
LORD. Another 6,000 will serve as officials and judges. 5 Another 4,000 will
work as gatekeepers, and 4,000 will praise the LORD with the musical in-
struments I have made." 6 Then David divided the Levites into divisions
named after the clans descended from the three sons of Levi—Gershon,
Kohath, and Merari.

The Gershonites

7 The Gershonite family units were defined by their lines of descent from
Libni* and Shimei, the sons of Gershon. 8 Three of the descendants of
Libni were Jehiel (the family leader), Zetham, and Joel. 9 These were the
leaders of the family of Libni.
Three of the descendants of Shimei were Shelomoth, Haziel, and Haran.
10 Four other descendants of Shimei were Jahath, Ziza,* Jeush, and
Beriah. 11 Jahath was the family leader, and Ziza was next. Jeush and
Beriah were counted as a single family because neither had many sons.

The Kohathites

12 Four of the descendants of Kohath were Amram, Izhar, Hebron, and
Uzziel.
13 The sons of Amram were Aaron and Moses. Aaron and his descendants
were set apart to dedicate the most holy things, to offer sacrifices in the
LORD's presence, to serve the LORD, and to pronounce blessings in his
name forever.
14 As for Moses, the man of God, his sons were included with the
tribe of Levi. 15 The sons of Moses were Gershom and Eliezer. 16 The
descendants of Gershom included Shebuel, the family leader. 17 Eliezer
had only one son, Rehabiah, the family leader. Rehabiah had numerous
descendants.
18 The descendants of Izhar included Shelomith, the family leader.
19 The descendants of Hebron included Jeriah (the family leader), Amariah
(the second), Jahaziel (the third), and Jekameam (the fourth).
20 The descendants of Uzziel included Micah (the family leader) and
Isshiah (the second).

The Merarites

21 The descendants of Merari included Mahli and Mushi.
The sons of Mahli were Eleazar and Kish. 22 Eleazar died with no sons,
only daughters. His daughters married their cousins, the sons of Kish.
23 Three of the descendants of Mushi were Mahli, Eder, and Jerimoth.

23:7 Hebrew *Ladan* (also in 23:8, 9), a variant spelling of Libni; compare 6:17. 23:10 As in Greek version and Latin Vulgate (see also 23:11); Hebrew reads *Zina*.

24 These were the descendants of Levi by clans, the leaders of their family
groups, registered carefully by name. Each had to be twenty years old or older
to qualify for service in the house of the LORD. 25 For David said, "The LORD,
the God of Israel, has given us peace, and he will always live in Jerusalem.
26 Now the Levites will no longer need to carry the Tabernacle and its furnish-
ings from place to place." 27 In accordance with David's final instructions, all
the Levites twenty years old or older were registered for service.

28 The work of the Levites was to assist the priests, the descendants of Aaron,
as they served at the house of the LORD. They also took care of the courtyards
and side rooms, helped perform the ceremonies of purification, and served in
many other ways in the house of God. 29 They were in charge of the sacred bread
that was set out on the table, the choice flour for the grain offerings, the wafers
made without yeast, the cakes cooked in olive oil, and the other mixed breads.
They were also responsible to check all the weights and measures. 30 And each
morning and evening they stood before the LORD to sing songs of thanks and
praise to him. 31 They assisted with the burnt offerings that were presented to
the LORD on Sabbath days, at new moon celebrations, and at all the appointed
festivals. The required number of Levites served in the LORD's presence at all
times, following all the procedures they had been given.

32 And so, under the supervision of the priests, the Levites watched over
the Tabernacle and the Temple* and faithfully carried out their duties of
service at the house of the LORD.

Duties of the Priests

24 This is how Aaron's descendants, the priests, were divided into
groups for service. The sons of Aaron were Nadab, Abihu, Eleazar,
and Ithamar. 2 But Nadab and Abihu died before their father, and they had
no sons. So only Eleazar and Ithamar were left to carry on as priests.

3 With the help of Zadok, who was a descendant of Eleazar, and of Ahim-
elech, who was a descendant of Ithamar, David divided Aaron's descendants
into groups according to their various duties. 4 Eleazar's descendants were
divided into sixteen groups and Ithamar's into eight, for there were more
family leaders among the descendants of Eleazar.

5 All tasks were assigned to the various groups by means of sacred lots so that
no preference would be shown, for there were many qualified officials serving
God in the sanctuary from among the descendants of both Eleazar and Itha-
mar. 6 Shemaiah son of Nethanel, a Levite, acted as secretary and wrote down
the names and assignments in the presence of the king, the officials, Zadok
the priest, Ahimelech son of Abiathar, and the family leaders of the priests
and Levites. The descendants of Eleazar and Ithamar took turns casting lots.

7 The first lot fell to Jehoiarib.
The second lot fell to Jedaiah.
8 The third lot fell to Harim.
The fourth lot fell to Seorim.
9 The fifth lot fell to Malkijah.
The sixth lot fell to Mijamin.
10 The seventh lot fell to Hakkoz.
The eighth lot fell to Abijah.

23:32 Hebrew *the Tent of Meeting and the sanctuary.*

11 The ninth lot fell to Jeshua.
The tenth lot fell to Shecaniah.
12 The eleventh lot fell to Eliashib.
The twelfth lot fell to Jakim.
13 The thirteenth lot fell to Huppah.
The fourteenth lot fell to Jeshebeab.
14 The fifteenth lot fell to Bilgah.
The sixteenth lot fell to Immer.
15 The seventeenth lot fell to Hezir.
The eighteenth lot fell to Happizzez.
16 The nineteenth lot fell to Pethahiah.
The twentieth lot fell to Jehezkel.
17 The twenty-first lot fell to Jakin.
The twenty-second lot fell to Gamul.
18 The twenty-third lot fell to Delaiah.
The twenty-fourth lot fell to Maaziah.

19 Each group carried out its appointed duties in the house of the LORD according to the procedures established by their ancestor Aaron in obedience to the commands of the LORD, the God of Israel.

Family Leaders among the Levites
20 These were the other family leaders descended from Levi:

From the descendants of Amram, the leader was Shebuel.*
From the descendants of Shebuel, the leader was Jehdeiah.
21 From the descendants of Rehabiah, the leader was Isshiah.
22 From the descendants of Izhar, the leader was Shelomith.*
From the descendants of Shelomith, the leader was Jahath.
23 From the descendants of Hebron, Jeriah was the leader,* Amariah was second, Jahaziel was third, and Jekameam was fourth.
24 From the descendants of Uzziel, the leader was Micah.
From the descendants of Micah, the leader was Shamir,
25 along with Isshiah, the brother of Micah.
From the descendants of Isshiah, the leader was Zechariah.
26 From the descendants of Merari, the leaders were Mahli and Mushi.
From the descendants of Jaaziah, the leader was Beno.
27 From the descendants of Merari through Jaaziah, the leaders were Beno, Shoham, Zaccur, and Ibri.
28 From the descendants of Mahli, the leader was Eleazar, though he had no sons.
29 From the descendants of Kish, the leader was Jerahmeel.
30 From the descendants of Mushi, the leaders were Mahli, Eder, and Jerimoth.

These were the descendants of Levi in their various families.
31 Like the descendants of Aaron, they were assigned to their duties by means of sacred lots, without regard to age or rank. Lots were drawn in the presence

24:20 Hebrew *Shubael* (also in 24:20b), a variant spelling of Shebuel; compare 23:16 and 26:24. 24:22 Hebrew *Shelomoth* (also in 24:22b), a variant spelling of Shelomith; compare 23:18. 24:23 Hebrew *From the descendants of Jeriah;* compare 23:19.

of King David, Zadok, Ahimelech, and the family leaders of the priests and the Levites.

Duties of the Musicians

25 David and the army commanders then appointed men from the families of Asaph, Heman, and Jeduthun to proclaim God's messages to the accompaniment of lyres, harps, and cymbals. Here is a list of their names and their work:

2 From the sons of Asaph, there were Zaccur, Joseph, Nethaniah, and Asarelah. They worked under the direction of their father, Asaph, who proclaimed God's messages by the king's orders.
3 From the sons of Jeduthun, there were Gedaliah, Zeri, Jeshaiah, Shimei,* Hashabiah, and Mattithiah, six in all. They worked under the direction of their father, Jeduthun, who proclaimed God's messages to the accompaniment of the lyre, offering thanks and praise to the LORD.
4 From the sons of Heman, there were Bukkiah, Mattaniah, Uzziel, Shubael,* Jerimoth, Hananiah, Hanani, Eliathah, Giddalti, Romamti-ezer, Joshbekashah, Mallothi, Hothir, and Mahazioth.
5 All these were the sons of Heman, the king's seer, for God had honored him with fourteen sons and three daughters.

6 All these men were under the direction of their fathers as they made music at the house of the LORD. Their responsibilities included the playing of cymbals, harps, and lyres at the house of God. Asaph, Jeduthun, and Heman reported directly to the king.
7 They and their families were all trained in making music before the LORD, and each of them—288 in all—was an accomplished musician.
8 The musicians were appointed to their term of service by means of sacred lots, without regard to whether they were young or old, teacher or student.

9 The first lot fell to Joseph of the Asaph clan and twelve of his sons and relatives.*
The second lot fell to Gedaliah and twelve of his sons and relatives.
10 The third lot fell to Zaccur and twelve of his sons and relatives.
11 The fourth lot fell to Zeri* and twelve of his sons and relatives.
12 The fifth lot fell to Nethaniah and twelve of his sons and relatives.
13 The sixth lot fell to Bukkiah and twelve of his sons and relatives.
14 The seventh lot fell to Asarelah* and twelve of his sons and relatives.
15 The eighth lot fell to Jeshaiah and twelve of his sons and relatives.
16 The ninth lot fell to Mattaniah and twelve of his sons and relatives.
17 The tenth lot fell to Shimei and twelve of his sons and relatives.
18 The eleventh lot fell to Uzziel* and twelve of his sons and relatives.
19 The twelfth lot fell to Hashabiah and twelve of his sons and relatives.
20 The thirteenth lot fell to Shubael and twelve of his sons and relatives.

Question **25:2**

Asaph equipped his sons to write psalms and lead in worship. Equipping the next generation to lead in faith is one of the most important aspects of what it means to follow God. Who are you helping to grow in faith? What skills and passions do you have that you could pass on to the next generation?

25:3 As in one Hebrew manuscript and some Greek manuscripts (see also 25:17); most Hebrew manuscripts lack *Shimei.* **25:4** Hebrew *Shebuel,* a variant spelling of Shubael; compare 25:20. **25:9** As in Greek version; Hebrew lacks *and twelve of his sons and relatives.* **25:11** Hebrew *Izri,* a variant spelling of Zeri; compare 25:3. **25:14** Hebrew *Jesarelah,* a variant spelling of Asarelah; compare 25:2. **25:18** Hebrew *Azarel,* a variant spelling of Uzziel; compare 25:4.

Question 26:14

This description of a gatekeeper named Zechariah is unusual in the lists of names throughout 2 Chronicles. What does someone need to do during their lifetime to get a reputation like this?

21 The fourteenth lot fell to Mattithiah and twelve of his sons and relatives.
22 The fifteenth lot fell to Jerimoth* and twelve of his sons and relatives.
23 The sixteenth lot fell to Hananiah and twelve of his sons and relatives.
24 The seventeenth lot fell to Joshbekashah* and twelve of his sons and relatives.
25 The eighteenth lot fell to Hanani and twelve of his sons and relatives.
26 The nineteenth lot fell to Mallothi and twelve of his sons and relatives.
27 The twentieth lot fell to Eliathah and twelve of his sons and relatives.
28 The twenty-first lot fell to Hothir and twelve of his sons and relatives.
29 The twenty-second lot fell to Giddalti and twelve of his sons and relatives.
30 The twenty-third lot fell to Mahazioth and twelve of his sons and relatives.
31 The twenty-fourth lot fell to Romamti-ezer and twelve of his sons and relatives.

Duties of the Gatekeepers

26 These are the divisions of the gatekeepers:

From the Korahites, there was Meshelemiah son of Kore, of the
family of Abiasaph.* 2 The sons of Meshelemiah were Zechariah (the
oldest), Jediael (the second), Zebadiah (the third), Jathniel (the fourth),
3 Elam (the fifth), Jehohanan (the sixth), and Eliehoenai (the seventh).
4 The sons of Obed-edom, also gatekeepers, were Shemaiah (the oldest),
Jehozabad (the second), Joah (the third), Sacar (the fourth), Nethanel
(the fifth), 5 Ammiel (the sixth), Issachar (the seventh), and Peullethai
(the eighth). God had richly blessed Obed-edom.
6 Obed-edom's son Shemaiah had sons with great ability who earned
positions of great authority in the clan. 7 Their names were Othni,
Rephael, Obed, and Elzabad. Their relatives, Elihu and Semakiah, were
also very capable men.
8 All of these descendants of Obed-edom, including their sons and
grandsons—sixty-two of them in all—were very capable men, well
qualified for their work.
9 Meshelemiah's eighteen sons and relatives were also very capable men.

10 Hosah, of the Merari clan, appointed Shimri as the leader among his
sons, though he was not the oldest. 11 His other sons included Hilkiah
(the second), Tebaliah (the third), and Zechariah (the fourth). Hosah's
sons and relatives, who served as gatekeepers, numbered thirteen in all.

12 These divisions of the gatekeepers were named for their family leaders,
and like the other Levites, they served at the house of the LORD. 13 They were
assigned by families for guard duty at the various gates, without regard to
age or training, for it was all decided by means of sacred lots.
14 The responsibility for the east gate went to Meshelemiah* and his group.

25:22 Hebrew *Jeremoth,* a variant spelling of Jerimoth; compare 25:4. 25:24 Hebrew *Joshbekasha,* a variant spelling of Joshbekashah; compare 25:4. 26:1 As in Greek version (see also Exod 6:24); Hebrew reads *Asaph.* 26:14 Hebrew *Shelemiah,* a variant spelling of Meshelemiah; compare 26:2.

The north gate was assigned to his son Zechariah, a man of unusual wisdom.
15 The south gate went to Obed-edom, and his sons were put in charge of
the storehouse. 16 Shuppim and Hosah were assigned the west gate and the
gateway leading up to the Temple.* Guard duties were divided evenly. 17 Six
Levites were assigned each day to the east gate, four to the north gate, four
to the south gate, and two pairs at the storehouse. 18 Six were assigned each
day to the west gate, four to the gateway leading up to the Temple, and two
to the courtyard.*

19 These were the divisions of the gatekeepers from the clans of Korah
and Merari.

Treasurers and Other Officials

20 Other Levites, led by Ahijah, were in charge of the treasuries of the house
of God and the treasuries of the gifts dedicated to the LORD. 21 From the
family of Libni* in the clan of Gershon, Jehiel* was the leader. 22 The sons of
Jehiel, Zetham and his brother Joel, were in charge of the treasuries of the
house of the LORD.

23 These are the leaders that descended from Amram, Izhar, Hebron, and
Uzziel:

24 From the clan of Amram, Shebuel was a descendant of Gershom son of
Moses. He was the chief officer of the treasuries. 25 His relatives through
Eliezer were Rehabiah, Jeshaiah, Joram, Zicri, and Shelomoth.

26 Shelomoth and his relatives were in charge of the treasuries
containing the gifts that King David, the family leaders, and the
generals and captains* and other officers of the army had dedicated to
the LORD. 27 These men dedicated some of the plunder they had gained
in battle to maintain the house of the LORD. 28 Shelomoth* and his
relatives also cared for the gifts dedicated to the LORD by Samuel the
seer, Saul son of Kish, Abner son of Ner, and Joab son of Zeruiah. All the
other dedicated gifts were in their care, too.

29 From the clan of Izhar came Kenaniah. He and his sons were given
administrative responsibilities* over Israel as officials and judges.

30 From the clan of Hebron came Hashabiah. He and his relatives—1,700
capable men—were put in charge of the Israelite lands west of the
Jordan River. They were responsible for all matters related to the things
of the LORD and the service of the king in that area.

31 Also from the clan of Hebron came Jeriah,* who was the leader of
the Hebronites according to the genealogical records. (In the fortieth
year of David's reign, a search was made in the records, and capable
men from the clan of Hebron were found at Jazer in the land of Gilead.)
32 There were 2,700 capable men among the relatives of Jeriah. King
David sent them to the east side of the Jordan River and put them in
charge of the tribes of Reuben and Gad and the half-tribe of Manasseh.
They were responsible for all matters related to God and to the king.

26:16 Or *the gate of Shalleketh on the upper road* (also in 26:18). The meaning of the Hebrew is uncertain. **26:18** Or *the colonnade.* The meaning of the Hebrew is uncertain. **26:21a** Hebrew *Ladan,* a variant spelling of Libni; compare 6:17. **26:21b** Hebrew *Jehieli* (also in 26:22), a variant spelling of Jehiel; compare 23:8. **26:26** Hebrew *the commanders of thousands and of hundreds.* **26:28** Hebrew *Shelomith,* a variant spelling of Shelomoth. **26:29** Or *were given outside work;* or *were given work away from the Temple area.* **26:31** Hebrew *Jerijah,* a variant spelling of Jeriah; compare 23:19.

Military Commanders and Divisions

27 This is the list of Israelite generals and captains,* and their officers, who served the king by supervising the army divisions that were on duty each month of the year. Each division served for one month and had 24,000 troops.

2 Jashobeam son of Zabdiel was commander of the first division of
24,000 troops, which was on duty during the first month. 3 He was a
descendant of Perez and was in charge of all the army officers for the first month.
4 Dodai, a descendant of Ahoah, was commander of the second division of 24,000 troops, which was on duty during the second month. Mikloth was his chief officer.
5 Benaiah son of Jehoiada the priest was commander of the third division
of 24,000 troops, which was on duty during the third month. 6 This was
the Benaiah who commanded David's elite military group known as the Thirty. His son Ammizabad was his chief officer.
7 Asahel, the brother of Joab, was commander of the fourth division of 24,000 troops, which was on duty during the fourth month. Asahel was succeeded by his son Zebadiah.
8 Shammah* the Izrahite was commander of the fifth division of 24,000 troops, which was on duty during the fifth month.
9 Ira son of Ikkesh from Tekoa was commander of the sixth division of 24,000 troops, which was on duty during the sixth month.
10 Helez, a descendant of Ephraim from Pelon, was commander of the seventh division of 24,000 troops, which was on duty during the seventh month.
11 Sibbecai, a descendant of Zerah from Hushah, was commander of the eighth division of 24,000 troops, which was on duty during the eighth month.
12 Abiezer from Anathoth in the territory of Benjamin was commander of the ninth division of 24,000 troops, which was on duty during the ninth month.
13 Maharai, a descendant of Zerah from Netophah, was commander of the tenth division of 24,000 troops, which was on duty during the tenth month.
14 Benaiah from Pirathon in Ephraim was commander of the eleventh division of 24,000 troops, which was on duty during the eleventh month.
15 Heled,* a descendant of Othniel from Netophah, was commander of the twelfth division of 24,000 troops, which was on duty during the twelfth month.

Leaders of the Tribes

16 The following were the tribes of Israel and their leaders:

Tribe	*Leader*
Reuben	Eliezer son of Zicri
Simeon	Shephatiah son of Maacah

27:1 Hebrew *commanders of thousands and of hundreds.* 27:8 Hebrew *Shamhuth,* a variant spelling of Shammah; compare 11:27 and 2 Sam 23:25. 27:15 Hebrew *Heldai,* a variant spelling of Heled; compare 11:30 and 2 Sam 23:29.

17 Levi . . . . Hashabiah son of Kemuel
Aaron (the priests) . . . . Zadok
18 Judah . . . . Elihu (a brother of David)
Issachar . . . . Omri son of Michael
19 Zebulun . . . . Ishmaiah son of Obadiah
Naphtali . . . . Jeremoth son of Azriel
20 Ephraim . . . . Hoshea son of Azaziah
Manasseh (west) . . . . Joel son of Pedaiah
21 Manasseh in Gilead (east) . . . . Iddo son of Zechariah
Benjamin . . . . Jaasiel son of Abner
22 Dan . . . . Azarel son of Jeroham

These were the leaders of the tribes of Israel.
23 When David took his census, he did not count those who were younger
than twenty years of age, because the LORD had promised to make the Isra-
elites as numerous as the stars in heaven. 24 Joab son of Zeruiah began the
census but never finished it because* the anger of God fell on Israel. The total
number was never recorded in King David's official records.

Officials of David's Kingdom

25 Azmaveth son of Adiel was in charge of the palace treasuries.
Jonathan son of Uzziah was in charge of the regional treasuries throughout the towns, villages, and fortresses of Israel.
26 Ezri son of Kelub was in charge of the field workers who farmed the king's lands.
27 Shimei from Ramah was in charge of the king's vineyards.
Zabdi from Shepham was responsible for the grapes and the supplies of wine.
28 Baal-hanan from Geder was in charge of the king's olive groves and sycamore-fig trees in the foothills of Judah.*
Joash was responsible for the supplies of olive oil.
29 Shitrai from Sharon was in charge of the cattle on the Sharon Plain.
Shaphat son of Adlai was responsible for the cattle in the valleys.
30 Obil the Ishmaelite was in charge of the camels.
Jehdeiah from Meronoth was in charge of the donkeys.
31 Jaziz the Hagrite was in charge of the king's flocks of sheep and goats.
All these officials were overseers of King David's property.

32 Jonathan, David's uncle, was a wise counselor to the king, a man of great
insight, and a scribe. Jehiel the Hacmonite was responsible for teaching the
king's sons. 33 Ahithophel was the royal adviser. Hushai the Arkite was the
king's friend. 34 Ahithophel was succeeded by Jehoiada son of Benaiah and
by Abiathar. Joab was commander of the king's army.

David's Instructions to Solomon

28 David summoned all the officials of Israel to Jerusalem—the lead-
ers of the tribes, the commanders of the army divisions, the other
generals and captains,* the overseers of the royal property and livestock,
the palace officials, the mighty men, and all the other brave warriors in the

27:24 Or *never finished it, and yet.* 27:28 Hebrew *the Shephelah.* 28:1 Hebrew *the commanders of thousands and commanders of hundreds.*

Your thoughts can go here

kingdom. 2David rose to his feet and said: "My brothers and my people! It
was my desire to build a Temple where the Ark of the LORD's Covenant,
God's footstool, could rest permanently. I made the necessary preparations
for building it, 3but God said to me, 'You must not build a Temple to honor
my name, for you are a warrior and have shed much blood.'
4"Yet the LORD, the God of Israel, has chosen me from among all my fa-
ther's family to be king over Israel forever. For he has chosen the tribe of
Judah to rule, and from among the families of Judah he chose my father's
family. And from among my father's sons the LORD was pleased to make me
king over all Israel. 5And from among my sons—for the LORD has given me
many—he chose Solomon to succeed me on the throne of Israel and to rule
over the LORD's kingdom. 6He said to me, 'Your son Solomon will build my
Temple and its courtyards, for I have chosen him as my son, and I will be his
father. 7And if he continues to obey my commands and regulations as he does
now, I will make his kingdom last forever.'
8"So now, with God as our witness, and in the sight of all Israel—the
LORD's assembly—I give you this charge. Be careful to obey all the com-
mands of the LORD your God, so that you may continue to possess this good
land and leave it to your children as a permanent inheritance.
9"And Solomon, my son, learn to know the God of your ancestors inti-
mately. Worship and serve him with your whole heart and a willing mind.
For the LORD sees every heart and knows every plan and thought. If you seek
him, you will find him. But if you forsake him, he will reject you forever.
10So take this seriously. The LORD has chosen you to build a Temple as his
sanctuary. Be strong, and do the work."
11Then David gave Solomon the plans for the Temple and its surround-
ings, including the entry room, the storerooms, the upstairs rooms, the inner
rooms, and the inner sanctuary—which was the place of atonement. 12David
also gave Solomon all the plans he had in mind* for the courtyards of the
LORD's Temple, the outside rooms, the treasuries, and the rooms for the
gifts dedicated to the LORD. 13The king also gave Solomon the instructions
concerning the work of the various divisions of priests and Levites in the
Temple of the LORD. And he gave specifications for the items in the Temple
that were to be used for worship.
14David gave instructions regarding how much gold and silver should be
used to make the items needed for service. 15He told Solomon the amount
of gold needed for the gold lampstands and lamps, and the amount of silver
for the silver lampstands and lamps, depending on how each would be used.
16He designated the amount of gold for the table on which the Bread of the
Presence would be placed and the amount of silver for other tables.
17David also designated the amount of gold for the solid gold meat hooks
used to handle the sacrificial meat and for the basins, pitchers, and dishes,
as well as the amount of silver for every dish. 18He designated the amount
of refined gold for the altar of incense. Finally, he gave him a plan for the
LORD's "chariot"—the gold cherubim* whose wings were stretched out over
the Ark of the LORD's Covenant. 19"Every part of this plan," David told Sol-
omon, "was given to me in writing from the hand of the LORD.*"
20Then David continued, "Be strong and courageous, and do the work.
Don't be afraid or discouraged, for the LORD God, my God, is with you. He

28:12 Or *the plans of the spirit that was with him.* 28:18 Hebrew *for the gold cherub chariot.*
28:19 Or *was written under the direction of the LORD.*

Make a Difference
28:7-10

Know God

David's instructions to Solomon were less about what he wanted his son to accomplish and more about whom he wanted Solomon to acknowledge. David wanted Solomon to live his life focused on God. He wanted Solomon to know God intimately.

Knowing God personally is a major theme of the entire Bible. Throughout the lists of ancestry (which have been so prominent in this book of 1 Chronicles), the fact that people can know God intimately, face-to-face, on a personal level, is the life-changing message that God wants us to acknowledge. From Adam to Abraham to Moses to David, God wants people to know him. From David to Solomon to Ezekiel to Hosea to Jesus, God's goal is that people would realize that God wants to dwell among them. Solomon's job as king can be summed up in this: know God!

Difference Maker

Make God the most important relationship of your life. If you have never done so, invite God into your life. You can turn to the back of this Bible and pray through the section called "How to Accept Jesus as Your Lord and Savior."

Prayer **28:20**

Lord, give me courage to stand tall in faith and love, even in the midst of threats. Your gospel turns the world upside down. Use me to make a difference in this world for you. Amen.

will not fail you or forsake you. He will see to it that all the work related to the Temple of the LORD is finished correctly. [21] The various divisions of priests and Levites will serve in the Temple of God. Others with skills of every kind will volunteer, and the officials and the entire nation are at your command."

Gifts for Building the Temple

29 Then King David turned to the entire assembly and said, "My son Solomon, whom God has clearly chosen as the next king of Israel, is still young and inexperienced. The work ahead of him is enormous, for the Temple he will build is not for mere mortals—it is for the LORD God himself! [2] Using every resource at my command, I have gathered as much as I could for building the Temple of my God. Now there is enough gold, silver, bronze, iron, and wood, as well as great quantities of onyx, other precious stones, costly jewels, and all kinds of fine stone and marble.

[3] "And now, because of my devotion to the Temple of my God, I am giving all of my own private treasures of gold and silver to help in the construction. This is in addition to the building materials I have already collected for his holy Temple. [4] I am donating more than 112 tons of gold* from Ophir and 262 tons of refined silver* to be used for overlaying the walls of the buildings [5] and for the other gold and silver work to be done by the craftsmen. Now then, who will follow my example and give offerings to the LORD today?"

[6] Then the family leaders, the leaders of the tribes of Israel, the generals and captains of the army,* and the king's administrative officers all gave willingly. [7] For the construction of the Temple of God, they gave about 188 tons of gold,* 10,000 gold coins,* 375 tons of silver,* 675 tons of bronze,* and 3,750 tons of iron.* [8] They also contributed numerous precious stones, which were deposited in the treasury of the house of the LORD under the care of Jehiel, a descendant of Gershon. [9] The people rejoiced over the offerings, for they had given freely and wholeheartedly to the LORD, and King David was filled with joy.

David's Prayer of Praise

[10] Then David praised the LORD in the presence of the whole assembly:

"O LORD, the God of our ancestor Israel,* may you be praised forever and ever! [11] Yours, O LORD, is the greatness, the power, the glory, the victory, and the majesty. Everything in the heavens and on earth is yours, O LORD, and this is your kingdom. We adore you as the one who is over all things. [12] Wealth and honor come from you alone, for you rule over everything. Power and might are in your hand, and at your discretion people are made great and given strength.

[13] "O our God, we thank you and praise your glorious name! [14] But who am I, and who are my people, that we could give anything to you? Everything we have has come from you, and we give you only what you first gave us! [15] We are here for only a moment, visitors and strangers

29:4a Hebrew *3,000 talents* [102 metric tons] *of gold.* **29:4b** Hebrew *7,000 talents* [238 metric tons] *of silver.* **29:6** Hebrew *the commanders of thousands and commanders of hundreds.* **29:7a** Hebrew *5,000 talents* [170 metric tons] *of gold.* **29:7b** Hebrew *10,000 darics* [a Persian coin] *of gold,* about 185 pounds or 84 kilograms in weight. **29:7c** Hebrew *10,000 talents* [340 metric tons] *of silver.* **29:7d** Hebrew *18,000 talents* [612 metric tons] *of bronze.* **29:7e** Hebrew *100,000 talents* [3,400 metric tons] *of iron.* **29:10** *Israel* is the name that God gave to Jacob.

Prayer 29:18

Lord, let me thrive in life by trusting in your love every day. Amen.

in the land as our ancestors were before us. Our days on earth are like
a passing shadow, gone so soon without a trace.
16 "O LORD our God, even this material we have gathered to build a
Temple to honor your holy name comes from you! It all belongs to you!
17 I know, my God, that you examine our hearts and rejoice when you
find integrity there. You know I have done all this with good motives,
and I have watched your people offer their gifts willingly and joyously.
18 "O LORD, the God of our ancestors Abraham, Isaac, and Israel, make
your people always want to obey you. See to it that their love for you
never changes. 19 Give my son Solomon the wholehearted desire to obey
all your commands, laws, and decrees, and to do everything necessary
to build this Temple, for which I have made these preparations."

20 Then David said to the whole assembly, "Give praise to the LORD your
God!" And the entire assembly praised the LORD, the God of their ancestors,
and they bowed low and knelt before the LORD and the king.

Solomon Named as King

21 The next day they brought 1,000 bulls, 1,000 rams, and 1,000 male lambs
as burnt offerings to the LORD. They also brought liquid offerings and many
other sacrifices on behalf of all Israel. 22 They feasted and drank in the LORD's
presence with great joy that day.

And again they crowned David's son Solomon as their new king. They
anointed him before the LORD as their leader, and they anointed Zadok as
priest. 23 So Solomon took the throne of the LORD in place of his father, Da-
vid, and he succeeded in everything, and all Israel obeyed him. 24 All the
officials, the warriors, and the sons of King David pledged their loyalty to
King Solomon. 25 And the LORD exalted Solomon in the sight of all Israel, and
he gave Solomon greater royal splendor than any king in Israel before him.

Summary of David's Reign

26 So David son of Jesse reigned over all Israel. 27 He reigned over Israel for
forty years, seven of them in Hebron and thirty-three in Jerusalem. 28 He died
at a ripe old age, having enjoyed long life, wealth, and honor. Then his son
Solomon ruled in his place.

29 All the events of King David's reign, from beginning to end, are written
in *The Record of Samuel the Seer, The Record of Nathan the Prophet,* and *The Record
of Gad the Seer.* 30 These accounts include the mighty deeds of his reign and
everything that happened to him and to Israel and to all the surrounding
kingdoms.

2 Chronicles Introduction

Have you ever heard two people from opposite teams tell the story of a game? The winner tells the story as if it were a huge triumph while the loser tells the story as if it were an utter defeat. Both stories are true and factual, historically accurate, but they are told from two different perspectives. This is the difference between the story of Israel in 1 and 2 Samuel through 1 and 2 Kings and the story in 1 and 2 Chronicles.

The books of Samuel and Kings told the story of Israel from the loser's perspective, asking, "What went wrong?" Chronicles tells the story from the winner's perspective of the restored people of Israel back in the promised land. They were now asking, "What did David and the good kings do right that allowed us to live in the promised land for 350 years before exile?"

What made the difference? Continual turning to God for help and instruction is the answer. When the good kings put God first and listened to the prophets and priests, the people enjoyed blessing and victory. When the bad kings neglected God and sought their own glory and false gods, failure and defeat were inevitable. In 2 Chronicles, the focus will be on the difference makers—those who put God first in their lives and enjoyed victory and peace for God's people.

Story Arcs

- **Solomon**
- **The Mount**
- **Micaiah**
- **Elijah**
- **Jehosheba**
- **Jehoiada**
- **Hezekiah**
- **Isaiah**
- **Josiah**
- **Jeremiah**

2 Chronicles

Question 1:7

If God had asked you this question, what would you have asked God for?

Solomon Asks for Wisdom

1 Solomon son of David took firm control of his kingdom, for the LORD his God was with him and made him very powerful.

2 Solomon called together all the leaders of Israel—the generals and captains of the army,* the judges, and all the political and clan leaders. 3 Then he led the entire assembly to the place of worship in Gibeon, for God's Tabernacle* was located there. (This was the Tabernacle that Moses, the LORD's servant, had made in the wilderness.)

4 David had already moved the Ark of God from Kiriath-jearim to the tent he had prepared for it in Jerusalem. 5 But the bronze altar made by Bezalel son of Uri and grandson of Hur was there* at Gibeon in front of the Tabernacle of the LORD. So Solomon and the people gathered in front of it to consult the LORD.* 6 There in front of the Tabernacle, Solomon went up to the bronze altar in the LORD's presence and sacrificed 1,000 burnt offerings on it.

7 That night God appeared to Solomon and said, "What do you want? Ask, and I will give it to you!"

8 Solomon replied to God, "You showed great and faithful love to David, my father, and now you have made me king in his place. 9 O LORD God, please continue to keep your promise to David my father, for you have made me king over a people as numerous as the dust of the earth! 10 Give me the wisdom and knowledge to lead them properly,* for who could possibly govern this great people of yours?"

11 God said to Solomon, "Because your greatest desire is to help your people, and you did not ask for wealth, riches, fame, or even the death of your enemies or a long life, but rather you asked for wisdom and knowledge to properly govern my people— 12 I will certainly give you the wisdom and knowledge you requested. But I will also give you wealth, riches, and fame such as no other king has had before you or will ever have in the future!"

13 Then Solomon returned to Jerusalem from the Tabernacle at the place of worship in Gibeon, and he reigned over Israel.

14 Solomon built up a huge force of chariots and horses.* He had 1,400 chariots and 12,000 horses. He stationed some of them in the chariot cities and some near him in Jerusalem. 15 The king made silver and gold as plentiful in Jerusalem as stone. And valuable cedar timber was as common as the sycamore-fig trees that grow in the foothills of Judah.* 16 Solomon's horses were imported from Egypt* and from Cilicia*; the king's traders acquired them from Cilicia at the standard price. 17 At that time chariots from Egypt could be purchased for 600 pieces of silver,* and horses for 150 pieces

Story Arc 1:1

● **Solomon**

The key to understanding the reign of Solomon is here in this verse. First, he was the son of David. It was through David that the Lord promised his eternal plan. Second, the Lord was with Solomon. It was the Lord who made Solomon powerful. It is God who makes all the difference in the trajectory of our lives. Notice in this book what happens when Solomon no longer wants the Lord with him.

2 Chr 3:1 ►

1:2 Hebrew *the commanders of thousands and of hundreds.* **1:3** Hebrew *Tent of Meeting;* also in 1:6, 13. **1:5a** As in Greek version and Latin Vulgate, and some Hebrew manuscripts; Masoretic Text reads *he placed.* **1:5b** Hebrew *to consult him.* **1:10** Hebrew *to go out and come in before this people.* **1:14** Or *charioteers;* also in 1:14b. **1:15** Hebrew *the Shephelah.* **1:16a** Possibly *Muzur,* a district near Cilicia; also in 1:17. **1:16b** Hebrew *Kue,* probably another name for Cilicia. **1:17a** Hebrew *600 [shekels] of silver,* about 15 pounds or 6.8 kilograms in weight.

of silver.* They were then exported to the kings of the Hittites and the kings
of Aram.

Preparations for Building the Temple

2 1*Solomon decided to build a Temple to honor the name of the LORD,
and also a royal palace for himself. 2*He enlisted a force of 70,000 la-
borers, 80,000 men to quarry stone in the hill country, and 3,600 foremen.
3Solomon also sent this message to King Hiram* at Tyre:

"Send me cedar logs as you did for my father, David, when he was
building his palace. 4I am about to build a Temple to honor the name
of the LORD my God. It will be a place set apart to burn fragrant incense
before him, to display the special sacrificial bread, and to sacrifice burnt
offerings each morning and evening, on the Sabbaths, at new moon
celebrations, and at the other appointed festivals of the LORD our God.
He has commanded Israel to do these things forever.
5"This must be a magnificent Temple because our God is greater
than all other gods. 6But who can really build him a worthy home? Not
even the highest heavens can contain him! So who am I to consider
building a Temple for him, except as a place to burn sacrifices to him?
7"So send me a master craftsman who can work with gold, silver,
bronze, and iron, as well as with purple, scarlet, and blue cloth. He
must be a skilled engraver who can work with the craftsmen of Judah
and Jerusalem who were selected by my father, David.
8"Also send me cedar, cypress, and red sandalwood* logs from
Lebanon, for I know that your men are without equal at cutting timber
in Lebanon. I will send my men to help them. 9An immense amount of
timber will be needed, for the Temple I am going to build will be very
large and magnificent. 10In payment for your woodcutters, I will send
100,000 bushels of crushed wheat, 100,000 bushels of barley,* 110,000
gallons of wine, and 110,000 gallons of olive oil.*"

11King Hiram sent this letter of reply to Solomon:

"It is because the LORD loves his people that he has made you their
king! 12Praise the LORD, the God of Israel, who made the heavens and
the earth! He has given King David a wise son, gifted with skill and
understanding, who will build a Temple for the LORD and a royal palace
for himself.
13"I am sending you a master craftsman named Huram-abi, who
is extremely talented. 14His mother is from the tribe of Dan in Israel,
and his father is from Tyre. He is skillful at making things from gold,
silver, bronze, and iron, and he also works with stone and wood. He
can work with purple, blue, and scarlet cloth and fine linen. He is also
an engraver and can follow any design given to him. He will work with
your craftsmen and those appointed by my lord David, your father.

Prayer **2:7**

God, serving you does not mean I have to become a pastor or missionary, but it does mean I get to use my skills and talents for your glory. Let me become a type of "master craftsman" in whatever area of life you call me to serve. Amen.

1:17b Hebrew *150 [shekels]*, about 3.8 pounds or 1.7 kilograms in weight. 2:1 Verse 2:1 is numbered 1:18 in Hebrew text. 2:2 Verses 2:2-18 are numbered 2:1-17 in Hebrew text. 2:3 Hebrew *Huram*, a variant spelling of Hiram; also in 2:11. 2:8 Or *juniper;* Hebrew reads *algum*, perhaps a variant spelling of *almug;* compare 9:10-11 and parallel text at 1 Kgs 10:11-12. 2:10a Hebrew *20,000 cors* [4,400 kiloliters] *of crushed wheat, 20,000 cors of barley.* 2:10b Hebrew *20,000 baths* [420 kiloliters] *of wine, and 20,000 baths of olive oil.*

15 "Send along the wheat, barley, olive oil, and wine that my lord
has mentioned. 16 We will cut whatever timber you need from the
Lebanon mountains and will float the logs in rafts down the coast of
the Mediterranean Sea* to Joppa. From there you can transport the
logs up to Jerusalem."

17 Solomon took a census of all foreigners in the land of Israel, like the
census his father had taken, and he counted 153,600. 18 He assigned 70,000
of them as common laborers, 80,000 as quarry workers in the hill country,
and 3,600 as foremen.

Solomon Builds the Temple

3 So Solomon began to build the Temple of the LORD in Jerusalem on
Mount Moriah, where the LORD had appeared to David, his father. The
Temple was built on the threshing floor of Araunah* the Jebusite, the site
that David had selected. 2 The construction began in midspring,* during the
fourth year of Solomon's reign.

3 These are the dimensions Solomon used for the foundation of the Temple
of God (using the old standard of measurement).* It was 90 feet long and
30 feet wide.* 4 The entry room at the front of the Temple was 30 feet* wide,
running across the entire width of the Temple, and 30 feet* high. He overlaid
the inside with pure gold.

5 He paneled the main room of the Temple with cypress wood, overlaid
it with fine gold, and decorated it with carvings of palm trees and chains.
6 He decorated the walls of the Temple with beautiful jewels and with gold
from the land of Parvaim. 7 He overlaid the beams, thresholds, walls, and
doors throughout the Temple with gold, and he carved figures of cherubim
on the walls.

8 He made the Most Holy Place 30 feet wide, corresponding to the width
of the Temple, and 30 feet deep. He overlaid its interior with 23 tons* of
fine gold. 9 The gold nails that were used weighed 20 ounces* each. He also
overlaid the walls of the upper rooms with gold.

10 He made two figures shaped like cherubim, overlaid them with gold,
and placed them in the Most Holy Place. 11 The total wingspan of the two
cherubim standing side by side was 30 feet. One wing of the first figure was
7½ feet* long, and it touched the Temple wall. The other wing, also 7½ feet
long, touched one of the wings of the second figure. 12 In the same way, the
second figure had one wing 7½ feet long that touched the opposite wall. The
other wing, also 7½ feet long, touched the wing of the first figure. 13 So the
wingspan of the two cherubim side by side was 30 feet. They stood on their
feet and faced out toward the main room of the Temple.

14 Across the entrance of the Most Holy Place he hung a curtain made of
fine linen, decorated with blue, purple, and scarlet thread and embroidered
with figures of cherubim.

2:16 Hebrew *the sea.* 3:1 Hebrew reads *Ornan,* a variant spelling of Araunah; compare 2 Sam 24:16. 3:2 Hebrew *on the second [day] of the second month.* This day of the ancient Hebrew lunar calendar occurred in April or May. 3:3a The "old standard of measurement" was a cubit equal to 18 inches [46 centimeters]. The new standard was a cubit of approximately 21 inches [53 centimeters]. 3:3b Hebrew *60 cubits* [27.6 meters] *long and 20 cubits* [9.2 meters] *wide.* 3:4a Hebrew *20 cubits* [9.2 meters]; also in 3:8, 11, 13. 3:4b As in some Greek and Syriac manuscripts, which read *20 cubits* [9.2 meters]; Hebrew reads *120 [cubits],* which is 180 feet or 55 meters. 3:8 Hebrew *600 talents* [20.4 metric tons]. 3:9 Hebrew *50 shekels* [570 grams]. 3:11 Hebrew *5 cubits* [2.3 meters]; also in 3:11b, 12, 15.

Story Arc **3:1**

The Mount

The location where Solomon built the temple is central to God's entire plan to save the world. Take a moment to go back to this same mountain in Genesis 22—the place where "the LORD will provide" a substitutionary sacrifice to save humanity (v. 11). Take a look at this same "threshing floor" in 2 Samuel 24:15-25—the spot where David offered to take the consequence of sin upon himself so that others wouldn't need to face the wrath of God. It was on this spot that the Lord chose to dwell and to provide the ultimate substitutionary sacrifice for all time.

2 Chr 18:6-27 ►

15 For the front of the Temple, he made two pillars that were 27 feet* tall,
each topped by a capital extending upward another 7½ feet. 16 He made a
network of interwoven chains* and used them to decorate the tops of the
pillars. He also made 100 decorative pomegranates and attached them to the
chains. 17 Then he set up the two pillars at the entrance of the Temple, one to
the south of the entrance and the other to the north. He named the one on
the south Jakin, and the one on the north Boaz.*

Question 4:11

Why do you think Solomon and his master craftsman, Huram-abi, paid such meticulous attention to every detail of the temple? Do you think God pays that much attention to you?

Furnishings for the Temple

4 Solomon* also made a bronze altar 30 feet long, 30 feet wide, and 15 feet
high.* 2 Then he cast a great round basin, 15 feet across from rim to rim,
called the Sea. It was 7½ feet deep and about 45 feet in circumference.* 3 It
was encircled just below its rim by two rows of figures that resembled oxen.
There were about six oxen per foot* all the way around, and they were cast
as part of the basin.

4 The Sea was placed on a base of twelve bronze oxen, all facing outward.
Three faced north, three faced west, three faced south, and three faced east,
and the Sea rested on them. 5 The walls of the Sea were about three inches*
thick, and its rim flared out like a cup and resembled a water lily blossom.
It could hold about 16,500 gallons* of water.

6 He also made ten smaller basins for washing the utensils for the burnt
offerings. He set five on the south side and five on the north. But the priests
washed themselves in the Sea.

7 He then cast ten gold lampstands according to the specifications that
had been given, and he put them in the Temple. Five were placed against
the south wall, and five were placed against the north wall.

8 He also built ten tables and placed them in the Temple, five along the
south wall and five along the north wall. Then he molded 100 gold basins.

9 He then built a courtyard for the priests, and also the large outer court-
yard. He made doors for the courtyard entrances and overlaid them with
bronze. 10 The great bronze basin called the Sea was placed near the southeast
corner of the Temple.

11 Huram-abi also made the necessary washbasins, shovels, and bowls.
So at last Huram-abi completed everything King Solomon had assigned
him to make for the Temple of God:

12 the two pillars;
the two bowl-shaped capitals on top of the pillars;
the two networks of interwoven chains that decorated the capitals;
13 the 400 pomegranates that hung from the chains on the capitals (two
rows of pomegranates for each of the chain networks that decorated
the capitals on top of the pillars);
14 the water carts holding the basins;
15 the Sea and the twelve oxen under it;
16 the ash buckets, the shovels, the meat hooks, and all the related articles.

3:15 As in Syriac version (see also 1 Kgs 7:15; 2 Kgs 25:17; Jer 52:21), which reads *18 cubits* [8.3 meters]; Hebrew reads *35 cubits,* which is 52.5 feet or 16.5 meters. **3:16** Hebrew *He made chains in the inner sanctuary.* The meaning of the Hebrew is uncertain. **3:17** *Jakin* probably means "he establishes"; *Boaz* probably means "in him is strength." **4:1a** Or *Huram-abi;* Hebrew reads *He.* **4:1b** Hebrew *20 cubits* [9.2 meters] *long, 20 cubits wide, and 10 cubits* [4.6 meters] *high.* **4:2** Hebrew *10 cubits* [4.6 meters] *across . . . 5 cubits* [2.3 meters] *deep and 30 cubits* [13.8 meters] *in circumference.* **4:3** Or *20 oxen per meter;* Hebrew reads *10 per cubit.* **4:5a** Hebrew *a handbreadth* [8 centimeters]. **4:5b** Hebrew *3,000 baths* [63 kiloliters].

Prayer 5:2

Lord, like the ark of the covenant, may there be nothing in my heart except for your Word. Amen.

Huram-abi made all these things of burnished bronze for the Temple of the
LORD, just as King Solomon had directed. 17 The king had them cast in clay
molds in the Jordan Valley between Succoth and Zarethan.* 18 Solomon used
such great quantities of bronze that its weight could not be determined.
19 Solomon also made all the furnishings for the Temple of God:

the gold altar;
the tables for the Bread of the Presence;
20 the lampstands and their lamps of solid gold, to burn in front of the Most Holy Place as prescribed;
21 the flower decorations, lamps, and tongs—all of the purest gold;
22 the lamp snuffers, bowls, ladles, and incense burners—all of solid gold;
the doors for the entrances to the Most Holy Place and the main room of the Temple, overlaid with gold.

5 So Solomon finished all his work on the Temple of the LORD. Then he
brought all the gifts his father, David, had dedicated—the silver, the
gold, and the various articles—and he stored them in the treasuries of the
Temple of God.

The Ark Brought to the Temple

2 Solomon then summoned to Jerusalem the elders of Israel and all the heads
of tribes—the leaders of the ancestral families of Israel. They were to bring
the Ark of the LORD's Covenant to the Temple from its location in the City
of David, also known as Zion. 3 So all the men of Israel assembled before
the king at the annual Festival of Shelters, which is held in early autumn.*
4 When all the elders of Israel arrived, the Levites picked up the Ark. 5 The
priests and Levites brought up the Ark along with the special tent* and all
the sacred items that had been in it. 6 There, before the Ark, King Solomon
and the entire community of Israel sacrificed so many sheep, goats, and cattle
that no one could keep count!
7 Then the priests carried the Ark of the LORD's Covenant into the inner
sanctuary of the Temple—the Most Holy Place—and placed it beneath the
wings of the cherubim. 8 The cherubim spread their wings over the Ark,
forming a canopy over the Ark and its carrying poles. 9 These poles were so
long that their ends could be seen from the Holy Place,* which is in front of
the Most Holy Place, but not from the outside. They are still there to this day.
10 Nothing was in the Ark except the two stone tablets that Moses had placed
in it at Mount Sinai,* where the LORD made a covenant with the people of
Israel when they left Egypt.
11 Then the priests left the Holy Place. All the priests who were present had
purified themselves, whether or not they were on duty that day. 12 And the Le-
vites who were musicians—Asaph, Heman, Jeduthun, and all their sons and
brothers—were dressed in fine linen robes and stood at the east side of the
altar playing cymbals, lyres, and harps. They were joined by 120 priests who
were playing trumpets. 13 The trumpeters and singers performed together

4:17 As in parallel text at 1 Kgs 7:46; Hebrew reads *Zeredah*. 5:3 Hebrew *at the festival that is in the seventh month*. The Festival of Shelters began on the fifteenth day of the seventh month of the ancient Hebrew lunar calendar. This day occurred in late September, October, or early November. 5:5 Hebrew *the Tent of Meeting*; i.e., the tent mentioned in 2 Sam 6:17 and 1 Chr 16:1. 5:9 As in some Hebrew manuscripts and Greek version (see also 1 Kgs 8:8); Masoretic Text reads *from the Ark*. 5:10 Hebrew *Horeb*, another name for Sinai.

in unison to praise and give thanks to the LORD. Accompanied by trumpets,
cymbals, and other instruments, they raised their voices and praised the
LORD with these words:

"He is good!
His faithful love endures forever!"

At that moment a thick cloud filled the Temple of the LORD. [14]The priests
could not continue their service because of the cloud, for the glorious pres-
ence of the LORD filled the Temple of God.

Solomon Praises the LORD

6 Then Solomon prayed, "O LORD, you have said that you would live in a
thick cloud of darkness. [2]Now I have built a glorious Temple for you, a
place where you can live forever!"
[3]Then the king turned around to the entire community of Israel standing
before him and gave this blessing: [4]"Praise the LORD, the God of Israel, who
has kept the promise he made to my father, David. For he told my father,
[5]'From the day I brought my people out of the land of Egypt, I have never
chosen a city among any of the tribes of Israel as the place where a Temple
should be built to honor my name. Nor have I chosen a king to lead my
people Israel. [6]But now I have chosen Jerusalem as the place for my name
to be honored, and I have chosen David to be king over my people Israel.'"
[7]Then Solomon said, "My father, David, wanted to build this Temple to
honor the name of the LORD, the God of Israel. [8]But the LORD told him, 'You
wanted to build the Temple to honor my name. Your intention is good, [9]but
you are not the one to do it. One of your own sons will build the Temple to
honor me.'
[10]"And now the LORD has fulfilled the promise he made, for I have become
king in my father's place, and now I sit on the throne of Israel, just as the
LORD promised. I have built this Temple to honor the name of the LORD, the
God of Israel. [11]There I have placed the Ark, which contains the covenant that
the LORD made with the people of Israel."

Solomon's Prayer of Dedication

[12]Then Solomon stood before the altar of the LORD in front of the entire
community of Israel, and he lifted his hands in prayer. [13]Now Solomon had
made a bronze platform 7½ feet long, 7½ feet wide, and 4½ feet high* and
had placed it at the center of the Temple's outer courtyard. He stood on the
platform, and then he knelt in front of the entire community of Israel and
lifted his hands toward heaven. [14]He prayed,

"O LORD, God of Israel, there is no God like you in all of heaven and
earth. You keep your covenant and show unfailing love to all who walk
before you in wholehearted devotion. [15]You have kept your promise to
your servant David, my father. You made that promise with your own
mouth, and with your own hands you have fulfilled it today.
[16]"And now, O LORD, God of Israel, carry out the additional promise
you made to your servant David, my father. For you said to him, 'If your

6:13 Hebrew *5 cubits* [2.3 meters] *long, 5 cubits wide, and 3 cubits* [1.4 meters] *high.*

Question 6:18

"Will God really live on earth among people?" Why would he do that? Not even the highest heavens can contain God. What could the answers to these questions teach us about how a person could become the temple of God's Spirit (1 Corinthians 6:19)?

descendants guard their behavior and faithfully follow my Law as you
have done, one of them will always sit on the throne of Israel.' 17 Now,
O LORD, God of Israel, fulfill this promise to your servant David.
18 "But will God really live on earth among people? Why, even the
highest heavens cannot contain you. How much less this Temple I have
built! 19 Nevertheless, listen to my prayer and my plea, O LORD my God.
Hear the cry and the prayer that your servant is making to you. 20 May
you watch over this Temple day and night, this place where you have
said you would put your name. May you always hear the prayers I make
toward this place. 21 May you hear the humble and earnest requests from
me and your people Israel when we pray toward this place. Yes, hear us
from heaven where you live, and when you hear, forgive.
22 "If someone wrongs another person and is required to take an oath
of innocence in front of your altar at this Temple, 23 then hear from
heaven and judge between your servants—the accuser and the accused.
Pay back the guilty as they deserve. Acquit the innocent because of
their innocence.
24 "If your people Israel are defeated by their enemies because they
have sinned against you, and if they turn back and acknowledge your
name and pray to you here in this Temple, 25 then hear from heaven and
forgive the sin of your people Israel and return them to this land you
gave to them and to their ancestors.
26 "If the skies are shut up and there is no rain because your people
have sinned against you, and if they pray toward this Temple and
acknowledge your name and turn from their sins because you have
punished them, 27 then hear from heaven and forgive the sins of your
servants, your people Israel. Teach them to follow the right path, and
send rain on your land that you have given to your people as their
special possession.
28 "If there is a famine in the land or a plague or crop disease or
attacks of locusts or caterpillars, or if your people's enemies are in
the land besieging their towns—whatever disaster or disease there
is—29 and if your people Israel pray about their troubles or sorrow,
raising their hands toward this Temple, 30 then hear from heaven
where you live, and forgive. Give your people what their actions
deserve, for you alone know each human heart. 31 Then they will fear
you and walk in your ways as long as they live in the land you gave to
our ancestors.
32 "In the future, foreigners who do not belong to your people Israel
will hear of you. They will come from distant lands when they hear of
your great name and your strong hand and your powerful arm. And
when they pray toward this Temple, 33 then hear from heaven where
you live, and grant what they ask of you. In this way, all the people
of the earth will come to know and fear you, just as your own people
Israel do. They, too, will know that this Temple I have built honors
your name.
34 "If your people go out where you send them to fight their enemies,
and if they pray to you by turning toward this city you have chosen and
toward this Temple I have built to honor your name, 35 then hear their
prayers from heaven and uphold their cause.

36 "If they sin against you—and who has never sinned?—you might
become angry with them and let their enemies conquer them and take
them captive to a foreign land far away or near. 37 But in that land of
exile, they might turn to you in repentance and pray, 'We have sinned,
done evil, and acted wickedly.' 38 If they turn to you with their whole
heart and soul in the land of their captivity and pray toward the land
you gave to their ancestors—toward this city you have chosen, and
toward this Temple I have built to honor your name— 39 then hear their
prayers and their petitions from heaven where you live, and uphold
their cause. Forgive your people who have sinned against you.

40 "O my God, may your eyes be open and your ears attentive to all the
prayers made to you in this place.

41 "And now arise, O LORD God, and enter your resting place,
along with the Ark, the symbol of your power.
May your priests, O LORD God, be clothed with salvation;
may your loyal servants rejoice in your goodness.
42 O LORD God, do not reject the king you have anointed.
Remember your unfailing love for your servant David."

The Dedication of the Temple

7 When Solomon finished praying, fire flashed down from heaven and
burned up the burnt offerings and sacrifices, and the glorious presence
of the LORD filled the Temple. 2 The priests could not enter the Temple of
the LORD because the glorious presence of the LORD filled it. 3 When all the
people of Israel saw the fire coming down and the glorious presence of the
LORD filling the Temple, they fell face down on the ground and worshiped
and praised the LORD, saying,

"He is good!
His faithful love endures forever!"

4 Then the king and all the people offered sacrifices to the LORD. 5 King
Solomon offered a sacrifice of 22,000 cattle and 120,000 sheep and goats.
And so the king and all the people dedicated the Temple of God. 6 The
priests took their assigned positions, and so did the Levites who were sing-
ing, "His faithful love endures forever!" They accompanied the singing
with music from the instruments King David had made for praising the
LORD. Across from the Levites, the priests blew the trumpets, while all
Israel stood.

7 Solomon then consecrated the central area of the courtyard in front of
the LORD's Temple. He offered burnt offerings and the fat of peace offerings
there, because the bronze altar he had built could not hold all the burnt of-
ferings, grain offerings, and sacrificial fat.

8 For the next seven days Solomon and all Israel celebrated the Festival of
Shelters.* A large congregation had gathered from as far away as Lebo-hamath
in the north and the Brook of Egypt in the south. 9 On the eighth day they
had a closing ceremony, for they had celebrated the dedication of the altar for
seven days and the Festival of Shelters for seven days. 10 Then at the end of the

7:8 Hebrew *the festival* (also in 7:9); see note on 5:3.

Make a Difference

7:11-22

Created to Pray

Three thousand years ago, King Solomon was finishing one of the wonders of the world. The temple in Jerusalem was an architectural masterpiece. People traveled from around the world to visit this structure and worship the God of Israel. As it was nearing completion, the Lord wanted to put things into perspective for King Solomon and the people of Israel. As great as the building was, he knew that they would struggle to keep their focus on him. God told them that he would do certain things (or, better said, withhold from doing things) to get back their attention. Then, if they turned their eyes once again to him, he promised to restore their grandeur. When you find yourself losing focus on God, do not forget that he will try to get your attention. When he does, turn your eyes to him.

Difference Maker

Attend to God. Pray to him today. Repent, asking him to forgive your sins.

Question **8:4**

Ministry is not just what happens at the church building. Often, ministry happens in the everyday aspects of life in our local communities. King Solomon made a difference even when he was not in the spotlight of the temple by rebuilding struggling villages and supply centers. What does this teach us about the ways our churches could make a difference in our cities and towns today?

celebration,* Solomon sent the people home. They were all joyful and glad because the LORD had been so good to David and to Solomon and to his people Israel.

The LORD's Response to Solomon

11 So Solomon finished the Temple of the LORD, as well as the royal palace. He
completed everything he had planned to do in the construction of the Temple
and the palace. 12 Then one night the LORD appeared to Solomon and said,

"I have heard your prayer and have chosen this Temple as the place
for making sacrifices. 13 At times I might shut up the heavens so that
no rain falls, or command grasshoppers to devour your crops, or send
plagues among you. 14 Then if my people who are called by my name
will humble themselves and pray and seek my face and turn from their
wicked ways, I will hear from heaven and will forgive their sins and
restore their land. 15 My eyes will be open and my ears attentive to every
prayer made in this place. 16 For I have chosen this Temple and set it
apart to be holy—a place where my name will be honored forever. I will
always watch over it, for it is dear to my heart.

17 "As for you, if you faithfully follow me as David your father did,
obeying all my commands, decrees, and regulations, 18 then I will establish
the throne of your dynasty. For I made this covenant with your father,
David, when I said, 'One of your descendants will always rule over Israel.'

19 "But if you or your descendants abandon me and disobey the
decrees and commands I have given you, and if you serve and worship
other gods, 20 then I will uproot the people from this land that I have
given them. I will reject this Temple that I have made holy to honor
my name. I will make it an object of mockery and ridicule among the
nations. 21 And though this Temple is impressive now, all who pass by
will be appalled. They will ask, 'Why did the LORD do such terrible
things to this land and to this Temple?'

22 "And the answer will be, 'Because his people abandoned the LORD,
the God of their ancestors, who brought them out of Egypt, and they
worshiped other gods instead and bowed down to them. That is why he
has brought all these disasters on them.'"

Solomon's Many Achievements

8 It took Solomon twenty years to build the LORD's Temple and his own
royal palace. At the end of that time, 2 Solomon turned his attention to
rebuilding the towns that King Hiram* had given him, and he settled Isra-
elites in them.

3 Solomon also fought against the town of Hamath-zobah and conquered
it. 4 He rebuilt Tadmor in the wilderness and built towns in the region of
Hamath as supply centers. 5 He fortified the towns of Upper Beth-horon and
Lower Beth-horon, rebuilding their walls and installing barred gates. 6 He
also rebuilt Baalath and other supply centers and constructed towns where
his chariots and horses* could be stationed. He built everything he desired
in Jerusalem and Lebanon and throughout his entire realm.

7:10 Hebrew *Then on the twenty-third day of the seventh month.* This day of the ancient Hebrew lunar calendar occurred in October or early November. **8:2** Hebrew *Huram,* a variant spelling of Hiram; also in 8:18. **8:6** Or *and charioteers.*

7There were still some people living in the land who were not Israelites,
including the Hittites, Amorites, Perizzites, Hivites, and Jebusites. 8These
were descendants of the nations whom the people of Israel had not de-
stroyed. So Solomon conscripted them for his labor force, and they serve
as forced laborers to this day. 9But Solomon did not conscript any of the
Israelites for his labor force. Instead, he assigned them to serve as fighting
men, officers in his army, commanders of his chariots, and charioteers.
10King Solomon appointed 250 of them to supervise the people.

11Solomon moved his wife, Pharaoh's daughter, from the City of David to
the new palace he had built for her. He said, "My wife must not live in King
David's palace, for the Ark of the LORD has been there, and it is holy ground."

12Then Solomon presented burnt offerings to the LORD on the altar he
had built for him in front of the entry room of the Temple. 13He offered the
sacrifices for the Sabbaths, the new moon festivals, and the three annual
festivals—the Passover celebration, the Festival of Harvest,* and the Festival
of Shelters—as Moses had commanded.

14In assigning the priests to their duties, Solomon followed the regula-
tions of his father, David. He also assigned the Levites to lead the people
in praise and to assist the priests in their daily duties. And he assigned the
gatekeepers to their gates by their divisions, following the commands of
David, the man of God. 15Solomon did not deviate in any way from David's
commands concerning the priests and Levites and the treasuries.

16So Solomon made sure that all the work related to building the Temple
of the LORD was carried out, from the day its foundation was laid to the day
of its completion.

17Later Solomon went to Ezion-geber and Elath,* ports along the shore of
the Red Sea* in the land of Edom. 18Hiram sent him ships commanded by his
own officers and manned by experienced crews of sailors. These ships sailed
to Ophir with Solomon's men and brought back to Solomon almost seventeen
tons* of gold.

Question 9:1

In Matthew 12:42, Jesus suggested that the people of Israel should have received him the way that the queen of Sheba received Solomon. What did the queen of Sheba do here that impressed Jesus so much? How can we receive Jesus in this same way today?

Visit of the Queen of Sheba

9 When the queen of Sheba heard of Solomon's fame, she came to Jerusa-
lem to test him with hard questions. She arrived with a large group of
attendants and a great caravan of camels loaded with spices, large quantities
of gold, and precious jewels. When she met with Solomon, she talked with
him about everything she had on her mind. 2Solomon had answers for all
her questions; nothing was too hard for him to explain to her. 3When the
queen of Sheba realized how wise Solomon was, and when she saw the palace
he had built, 4she was overwhelmed. She was also amazed at the food on
his tables, the organization of his officials and their splendid clothing, the
cup-bearers and their robes, and the burnt offerings* Solomon made at the
Temple of the LORD.

5She exclaimed to the king, "Everything I heard in my country about your
achievements* and wisdom is true! 6I didn't believe what was said until I arrived
here and saw it with my own eyes. In fact, I had not heard the half of your great
wisdom! It is far beyond what I was told. 7How happy your people must be!

8:13 Or *Festival of Weeks.* **8:17a** As in Greek version (see also 2 Kgs 14:22; 16:6); Hebrew reads *Eloth,* a variant spelling of Elath. **8:17b** As in parallel text at 1 Kgs 9:26; Hebrew reads *the sea.* **8:18** Hebrew *450 talents* [15.3 metric tons]. **9:4** As in Greek and Syriac versions (see also 1 Kgs 10:5); Hebrew reads *and the ascent.* **9:5** Hebrew *your words.*

What a privilege for your officials to stand here day after day, listening to your
wisdom! 8 Praise the LORD your God, who delights in you and has placed you
on the throne as king to rule for him. Because God loves Israel and desires this
kingdom to last forever, he has made you king over them so you can rule with
justice and righteousness."

9 Then she gave the king a gift of 9,000 pounds* of gold, great quantities
of spices, and precious jewels. Never before had there been spices as fine as
those the queen of Sheba gave to King Solomon.

10 (In addition, the crews of Hiram and Solomon brought gold from Ophir,
and they also brought red sandalwood* and precious jewels. 11 The king used
the sandalwood to make steps* for the Temple of the LORD and the royal
palace, and to construct lyres and harps for the musicians. Never before had
such beautiful things been seen in Judah.)

12 King Solomon gave the queen of Sheba whatever she asked for—gifts
of greater value than the gifts she had given him. Then she and all her at-
tendants returned to their own land.

Solomon's Wealth and Splendor

13 Each year Solomon received about 25 tons* of gold. 14 This did not include
the additional revenue he received from merchants and traders. All the kings
of Arabia and the governors of the provinces also brought gold and silver
to Solomon.

15 King Solomon made 200 large shields of hammered gold, each weigh-
ing more than 15 pounds.* 16 He also made 300 smaller shields of hammered
gold, each weighing more than 7½ pounds.* The king placed these shields
in the Palace of the Forest of Lebanon.

17 Then the king made a huge throne, decorated with ivory and overlaid
with pure gold. 18 The throne had six steps, with a footstool of gold. There were
armrests on both sides of the seat, and the figure of a lion stood on each side
of the throne. 19 There were also twelve other lions, one standing on each end
of the six steps. No other throne in all the world could be compared with it!

20 All of King Solomon's drinking cups were solid gold, as were all the
utensils in the Palace of the Forest of Lebanon. They were not made of silver,
for silver was considered worthless in Solomon's day!

21 The king had a fleet of trading ships of Tarshish manned by the sailors
sent by Hiram.* Once every three years the ships returned, loaded with gold,
silver, ivory, apes, and peacocks.*

22 So King Solomon became richer and wiser than any other king on earth.
23 Kings from every nation came to consult him and to hear the wisdom God
had given him. 24 Year after year everyone who visited brought him gifts of
silver and gold, clothing, weapons, spices, horses, and mules.

25 Solomon had 4,000 stalls for his horses and chariots, and he had 12,000
horses.* He stationed some of them in the chariot cities, and some near him
in Jerusalem. 26 He ruled over all the kings from the Euphrates River* in the
north to the land of the Philistines and the border of Egypt in the south.
27 The king made silver as plentiful in Jerusalem as stone. And valuable cedar

9:9 Hebrew *120 talents* [4,000 kilograms]. **9:10** Hebrew *algum wood* (also in 9:11); perhaps a variant spelling of *almug.* Compare parallel text at 1 Kgs 10:11-12. **9:11** Or *gateways.* The meaning of the Hebrew is uncertain. **9:13** Hebrew *666 talents* [23 metric tons]. **9:15** Hebrew *600 [shekels] of hammered gold* [6.8 kilograms]. **9:16** Hebrew *300 [shekels] of gold* [3.4 kilograms]. **9:21a** Hebrew *Huram,* a variant spelling of Hiram. **9:21b** Or *and baboons.* **9:25** Or *12,000 charioteers.* **9:26** Hebrew *the river.*

timber was as common as the sycamore-fig trees that grow in the foothills
of Judah.* 28 Solomon's horses were imported from Egypt* and many other
countries.

Summary of Solomon's Reign
29 The rest of the events of Solomon's reign, from beginning to end, are re-
corded in *The Record of Nathan the Prophet,* and *The Prophecy of Ahijah from Shi-
loh,* and also in *The Visions of Iddo the Seer,* concerning Jeroboam son of Nebat.
30 Solomon ruled in Jerusalem over all Israel for forty years. 31 When he died,
he was buried in the City of David, named for his father. Then his son Re-
hoboam became the next king.

The Northern Tribes Revolt
10 Rehoboam went to Shechem, where all Israel had gathered to make
him king. 2 When Jeroboam son of Nebat heard of this, he returned
from Egypt, for he had fled to Egypt to escape from King Solomon. 3 The
leaders of Israel summoned him, and Jeroboam and all Israel went to speak
with Rehoboam. 4 "Your father was a hard master," they said. "Lighten the
harsh labor demands and heavy taxes that your father imposed on us. Then
we will be your loyal subjects."
5 Rehoboam replied, "Come back in three days for my answer." So the
people went away.
6 Then King Rehoboam discussed the matter with the older men who
had counseled his father, Solomon. "What is your advice?" he asked. "How
should I answer these people?"
7 The older counselors replied, "If you are good to these people and do
your best to please them and give them a favorable answer, they will always
be your loyal subjects."
8 But Rehoboam rejected the advice of the older men and instead asked
the opinion of the young men who had grown up with him and were now
his advisers. 9 "What is your advice?" he asked them. "How should I answer
these people who want me to lighten the burdens imposed by my father?"
10 The young men replied, "This is what you should tell those complainers
who want a lighter burden: 'My little finger is thicker than my father's waist!
11 Yes, my father laid heavy burdens on you, but I'm going to make them even
heavier! My father beat you with whips, but I will beat you with scorpions!'"
12 Three days later Jeroboam and all the people returned to hear Re-
hoboam's decision, just as the king had ordered. 13 But Rehoboam spoke
harshly to them, for he rejected the advice of the older counselors 14 and fol-
lowed the counsel of his younger advisers. He told the people, "My father
laid* heavy burdens on you, but I'm going to make them even heavier! My
father beat you with whips, but I will beat you with scorpions!"
15 So the king paid no attention to the people. This turn of events was the
will of God, for it fulfilled the LORD's message to Jeroboam son of Nebat
through the prophet Ahijah from Shiloh.
16 When all Israel realized* that the king had refused to listen to them,
they responded,

9:27 Hebrew *the Shephelah.* **9:28** Possibly *Muzur,* a district near Cilicia. **10:14** As in Greek version and many Hebrew manuscripts (see also 1 Kgs 12:14); Masoretic Text reads *I will lay.* **10:16** As in Syriac version, Latin Vulgate, and many Hebrew manuscripts (see also 1 Kgs 12:16); Masoretic Text lacks *realized.*

Reflect on this passage

"Down with the dynasty of David!
We have no interest in the son of Jesse.
Back to your homes, O Israel!
Look out for your own house, O David!"

So all the people of Israel returned home. 17 But Rehoboam continued to
rule over the Israelites who lived in the towns of Judah.
18 King Rehoboam sent Adoniram,* who was in charge of forced labor, to
restore order, but the people of Israel stoned him to death. When this news
reached King Rehoboam, he quickly jumped into his chariot and fled to
Jerusalem. 19 And to this day the northern tribes of Israel have refused to be
ruled by a descendant of David.

Shemaiah's Prophecy

11 When Rehoboam arrived at Jerusalem, he mobilized the men of Ju-
dah and Benjamin—180,000 select troops—to fight against Israel
and to restore the kingdom to himself.
2 But the LORD said to Shemaiah, the man of God, 3 "Say to Rehoboam son
of Solomon, king of Judah, and to all the Israelites in Judah and Benjamin:
4 'This is what the LORD says: Do not fight against your relatives. Go back
home, for what has happened is my doing!'" So they obeyed the message of
the LORD and did not fight against Jeroboam.

Rehoboam Fortifies Judah

5 Rehoboam remained in Jerusalem and fortified various towns for the de-
fense of Judah. 6 He built up Bethlehem, Etam, Tekoa, 7 Beth-zur, Soco, Adul-
lam, 8 Gath, Mareshah, Ziph, 9 Adoraim, Lachish, Azekah, 10 Zorah, Aijalon,
and Hebron. These became the fortified towns of Judah and Benjamin. 11 Re-
hoboam strengthened their defenses and stationed commanders in them,
and he stored supplies of food, olive oil, and wine. 12 He also put shields and
spears in these towns as a further safety measure. So only Judah and Benjamin
remained under his control.
13 But all the priests and Levites living among the northern tribes of Israel
sided with Rehoboam. 14 The Levites even abandoned their pasturelands and
property and moved to Judah and Jerusalem, because Jeroboam and his sons
would not allow them to serve the LORD as priests. 15 Jeroboam appointed
his own priests to serve at the pagan shrines, where they worshiped the goat
and calf idols he had made. 16 From all the tribes of Israel, those who sincerely
wanted to worship the LORD, the God of Israel, followed the Levites to Jerusa-
lem, where they could offer sacrifices to the LORD, the God of their ancestors.
17 This strengthened the kingdom of Judah, and for three years they supported
Rehoboam son of Solomon, for during those years they faithfully followed in
the footsteps of David and Solomon.

Rehoboam's Family

18 Rehoboam married his cousin Mahalath, the daughter of David's son Jeri-
moth and of Abihail, the daughter of Eliab son of Jesse. 19 Mahalath had three
sons—Jeush, Shemariah, and Zaham.
20 Later Rehoboam married another cousin, Maacah, the granddaughter

10:18 Hebrew *Hadoram*, a variant spelling of Adoniram; compare 1 Kgs 4:6; 5:14; 12:18.

Make a Difference

10:16-19

Editorial Note on Your Life

The foolish actions of Jeroboam and the pressures of civil war led to an interesting editorial note in verse 19. Perhaps the question for the readers of 2 Chronicles is whether the northern tribes of Israel would ever again align themselves with the promised king of Judah.

This is actually the most important editorial comment on anyone's life. Will we align ourselves with the promised King of kings and Lord of lords born to a descendant of Judah in the line of David in the town of Bethlehem? How we answer that question determines whether we reject God's redemptive work in this world.

Difference Maker

Align yourself with Jesus. If you've never done so, accept Jesus into your life today. Turn to the back of this Bible and pray through the section called "How to Accept Jesus as Your Lord and Savior."

Question **11:16**

Sometimes sincere followers of God get caught up in geopolitical events. Their goal, in the midst of all the stress and mess, is to just try to do their best to worship the Lord. During political anxiety in your culture, how could you set an example for others that focuses on God?

of Absalom. Maacah gave birth to Abijah, Attai, Ziza, and Shelomith. 21 Re-
hoboam loved Maacah more than any of his other wives and concubines.
In all, he had eighteen wives and sixty concubines, and they gave birth to
twenty-eight sons and sixty daughters.
22 Rehoboam appointed Maacah's son Abijah as leader among the princes,
making it clear that he would be the next king. 23 Rehoboam also wisely gave
responsibilities to his other sons and stationed some of them in the fortified
towns throughout the land of Judah and Benjamin. He provided them with
generous provisions, and he found many wives for them.

Egypt Invades Judah

12 But when Rehoboam was firmly established and strong, he aban-
doned the Law of the LORD, and all Israel followed him in this sin.
2 Because they were unfaithful to the LORD, King Shishak of Egypt came up
and attacked Jerusalem in the fifth year of King Rehoboam's reign. 3 He came
with 1,200 chariots, 60,000 horses,* and a countless army of foot soldiers, in-
cluding Libyans, Sukkites, and Ethiopians.* 4 Shishak conquered Judah's forti-
fied towns and then advanced to attack Jerusalem.
5 The prophet Shemaiah then met with Rehoboam and Judah's leaders, who
had all fled to Jerusalem because of Shishak. Shemaiah told them, "This is what
the LORD says: You have abandoned me, so I am abandoning you to Shishak."
6 Then the leaders of Israel and the king humbled themselves and said,
"The LORD is right in doing this to us!"
7 When the LORD saw their change of heart, he gave this message to She-
maiah: "Since the people have humbled themselves, I will not completely
destroy them and will soon give them some relief. I will not use Shishak to
pour out my anger on Jerusalem. 8 But they will become his subjects, so they
will know the difference between serving me and serving earthly rulers."
9 So King Shishak of Egypt came up and attacked Jerusalem. He ransacked
the treasuries of the LORD's Temple and the royal palace; he stole everything,
including all the gold shields Solomon had made. 10 King Rehoboam later
replaced them with bronze shields as substitutes, and he entrusted them
to the care of the commanders of the guard who protected the entrance to
the royal palace. 11 Whenever the king went to the Temple of the LORD, the
guards would also take the shields and then return them to the guardroom.
12 Because Rehoboam humbled himself, the LORD's anger was turned away,
and he did not destroy him completely. There were still some good things
in the land of Judah.

Summary of Rehoboam's Reign

13 King Rehoboam firmly established himself in Jerusalem and continued
to rule. He was forty-one years old when he became king, and he reigned
seventeen years in Jerusalem, the city the LORD had chosen from among all
the tribes of Israel as the place to honor his name. Rehoboam's mother was
Naamah, a woman from Ammon. 14 But he was an evil king, for he did not
seek the LORD with all his heart.
15 The rest of the events of Rehoboam's reign, from beginning to end, are
recorded in *The Record of Shemaiah the Prophet* and *The Record of Iddo the Seer,*
which are part of the genealogical record. Rehoboam and Jeroboam were

Question 12:1

Often, when we get comfortable, we can forget (or choose not) to follow the Lord. What comfortable patterns do you have in your life that actually lead you away from faithfulness to God?

12:3a Or *charioteers,* or *horsemen.* 12:3b Hebrew *and Cushites.*

Prayer 13:12

Dear Jesus, don't let me do stupid things today. Get those things out of my life and let me follow your commands. Amen.

continually at war with each other. 16 When Rehoboam died, he was buried
in the City of David. Then his son Abijah became the next king.

Abijah's War with Jeroboam

13 Abijah began to rule over Judah in the eighteenth year of Jeroboam's
reign in Israel. 2 He reigned in Jerusalem three years. His mother was
Maacah,* the daughter of Uriel from Gibeah.

Then war broke out between Abijah and Jeroboam. 3 Judah, led by
King Abijah, fielded 400,000 select warriors, while Jeroboam mustered
800,000 select troops from Israel.

4 When the army of Judah arrived in the hill country of Ephraim, Abijah
stood on Mount Zemaraim and shouted to Jeroboam and all Israel: "Listen
to me! 5 Don't you realize that the LORD, the God of Israel, made a lasting
covenant* with David, giving him and his descendants the throne of Israel
forever? 6 Yet Jeroboam son of Nebat, a mere servant of David's son Solomon,
rebelled against his master. 7 Then a whole gang of scoundrels joined him,
defying Solomon's son Rehoboam when he was young and inexperienced
and could not stand up to them.

8 "Do you really think you can stand against the kingdom of the LORD that
is led by the descendants of David? You may have a vast army, and you have
those gold calves that Jeroboam made as your gods. 9 But you have chased
away the priests of the LORD (the descendants of Aaron) and the Levites, and
you have appointed your own priests, just like the pagan nations. You let any-
one become a priest these days! Whoever comes to be dedicated with a young
bull and seven rams can become a priest of these so-called gods of yours!

10 "But as for us, the LORD is our God, and we have not abandoned him.
Only the descendants of Aaron serve the LORD as priests, and the Levites alone
may help them in their work. 11 They present burnt offerings and fragrant
incense to the LORD every morning and evening. They place the Bread of the
Presence on the holy table, and they light the gold lampstand every evening.
We are following the instructions of the LORD our God, but you have aban-
doned him. 12 So you see, God is with us. He is our leader. His priests blow
their trumpets and lead us into battle against you. O people of Israel, do not
fight against the LORD, the God of your ancestors, for you will not succeed!"

13 Meanwhile, Jeroboam had secretly sent part of his army around behind
the men of Judah to ambush them. 14 When Judah realized that they were
being attacked from the front and the rear, they cried out to the LORD for
help. Then the priests blew the trumpets, 15 and the men of Judah began to
shout. At the sound of their battle cry, God defeated Jeroboam and all Israel
and routed them before Abijah and the army of Judah.

16 The Israelite army fled from Judah, and God handed them over to Ju-
dah in defeat. 17 Abijah and his army inflicted heavy losses on them; 500,000
of Israel's select troops were killed that day. 18 So Judah defeated Israel on
that occasion because they trusted in the LORD, the God of their ancestors.
19 Abijah and his army pursued Jeroboam's troops and captured some of his
towns, including Bethel, Jeshanah, and Ephron, along with their surround-
ing villages.

20 So Jeroboam of Israel never regained his power during Abijah's lifetime,
and finally the LORD struck him down and he died. 21 Meanwhile, Abijah of

13:2 As in most Greek manuscripts and Syriac version (see also 2 Chr 11:20-21; 1 Kgs 15:2); Hebrew reads *Micaiah,* a variant spelling of Maacah. 13:5 Hebrew *a covenant of salt.*

Judah grew more and more powerful. He married fourteen wives and had
twenty-two sons and sixteen daughters.
22 The rest of the events of Abijah's reign, including his words and deeds,
are recorded in *The Commentary of Iddo the Prophet.*

Early Years of Asa's Reign

14 1* When Abijah died, he was buried in the City of David. Then his son
Asa became the next king. There was peace in the land for ten years.
2* Asa did what was pleasing and good in the sight of the LORD his God. 3 He
removed the foreign altars and the pagan shrines. He smashed the sacred
pillars and cut down the Asherah poles. 4 He commanded the people of Ju-
dah to seek the LORD, the God of their ancestors, and to obey his law and
his commands. 5 Asa also removed the pagan shrines, as well as the incense
altars from every one of Judah's towns. So Asa's kingdom enjoyed a period
of peace. 6 During those peaceful years, he was able to build up the fortified
towns throughout Judah. No one tried to make war against him at this time,
for the LORD was giving him rest from his enemies.
7 Asa told the people of Judah, "Let us build towns and fortify them with
walls, towers, gates, and bars. The land is still ours because we sought the
LORD our God, and he has given us peace on every side." So they went ahead
with these projects and brought them to completion.
8 King Asa had an army of 300,000 warriors from the tribe of Judah, armed
with large shields and spears. He also had an army of 280,000 warriors from
the tribe of Benjamin, armed with small shields and bows. Both armies were
composed of well-trained fighting men.
9 Once an Ethiopian* named Zerah attacked Judah with an army of
1,000,000 men* and 300 chariots. They advanced to the town of Mareshah,
10 so Asa deployed his armies for battle in the valley north of Mareshah.*
11 Then Asa cried out to the LORD his God, "O LORD, no one but you can help
the powerless against the mighty! Help us, O LORD our God, for we trust
in you alone. It is in your name that we have come against this vast horde.
O LORD, you are our God; do not let mere men prevail against you!"
12 So the LORD defeated the Ethiopians* in the presence of Asa and the
army of Judah, and the enemy fled. 13 Asa and his army pursued them as far
as Gerar, and so many Ethiopians fell that they were unable to rally. They
were destroyed by the LORD and his army, and the army of Judah carried off
a vast amount of plunder.
14 While they were at Gerar, they attacked all the towns in that area, and
terror from the LORD came upon the people there. As a result, a vast amount
of plunder was taken from these towns, too. 15 They also attacked the camps
of herdsmen and captured many sheep, goats, and camels before finally
returning to Jerusalem.

Asa's Religious Reforms

15 Then the Spirit of God came upon Azariah son of Oded, 2 and he went
out to meet King Asa as he was returning from the battle. "Listen to
me, Asa!" he shouted. "Listen, all you people of Judah and Benjamin! The

14:1 Verse 14:1 is numbered 13:23 in Hebrew text. 14:2 Verses 14:2-15 are numbered 14:1-14 in Hebrew text. 14:9a Hebrew *a Cushite.* 14:9b Or *an army of thousands and thousands;* Hebrew reads *an army of a thousand thousands.* 14:10 As in Greek version; Hebrew reads *valley of Zephathah near Mareshah.* 14:12 Hebrew *Cushites;* also in 14:13.

Question 14:2

Can this be said of you?

Question 15:2

In what ways is Azariah's message the theme of 2 Chronicles? In what ways could it be the theme for your life?

LORD will stay with you as long as you stay with him! Whenever you seek
him, you will find him. But if you abandon him, he will abandon you. 3 For a
long time Israel was without the true God, without a priest to teach them, and
without the Law to instruct them. 4 But whenever they were in trouble and
turned to the LORD, the God of Israel, and sought him out, they found him.
5 "During those dark times, it was not safe to travel. Problems troubled
the people of every land. 6 Nation fought against nation, and city against city,
for God was troubling them with every kind of problem. 7 But as for you, be
strong and courageous, for your work will be rewarded."
8 When Asa heard this message from Azariah the prophet,* he took courage
and removed all the detestable idols from the land of Judah and Benjamin
and in the towns he had captured in the hill country of Ephraim. And he
repaired the altar of the LORD, which stood in front of the entry room of
the LORD's Temple.
9 Then Asa called together all the people of Judah and Benjamin, along
with the people of Ephraim, Manasseh, and Simeon who had settled among
them. For many from Israel had moved to Judah during Asa's reign when
they saw that the LORD his God was with him. 10 The people gathered at Je-
rusalem in late spring,* during the fifteenth year of Asa's reign.
11 On that day they sacrificed to the LORD 700 cattle and 7,000 sheep and
goats from the plunder they had taken in the battle. 12 Then they entered into
a covenant to seek the LORD, the God of their ancestors, with all their heart
and soul. 13 They agreed that anyone who refused to seek the LORD, the God of
Israel, would be put to death—whether young or old, man or woman. 14 They
shouted out their oath of loyalty to the LORD with trumpets blaring and rams'
horns sounding. 15 All in Judah were happy about this covenant, for they had
entered into it with all their heart. They earnestly sought after God, and they
found him. And the LORD gave them rest from their enemies on every side.
16 King Asa even deposed his grandmother* Maacah from her position as
queen mother because she had made an obscene Asherah pole. He cut down
her obscene pole, broke it up, and burned it in the Kidron Valley. 17 Although
the pagan shrines were not removed from Israel, Asa's heart remained com-
pletely faithful throughout his life. 18 He brought into the Temple of God the
silver and gold and the various items that he and his father had dedicated.
19 So there was no more war until the thirty-fifth year of Asa's reign.

Final Years of Asa's Reign

16 In the thirty-sixth year of Asa's reign, King Baasha of Israel invaded
Judah and fortified Ramah in order to prevent anyone from entering
or leaving King Asa's territory in Judah.
2 Asa responded by removing the silver and gold from the treasuries of the
Temple of the LORD and the royal palace. He sent it to King Ben-hadad of
Aram, who was ruling in Damascus, along with this message:

> 3 "Let there be a treaty* between you and me like the one between your
> father and my father. See, I am sending you silver and gold. Break your
> treaty with King Baasha of Israel so that he will leave me alone."

15:8 As in Syriac version and Latin Vulgate (see also 15:1); Hebrew reads *from Oded the prophet.* 15:10 Hebrew *in the third month.* This month of the ancient Hebrew lunar calendar usually occurs within the months of May and June. 15:16 Hebrew *his mother.* 16:3 As in Greek version; Hebrew reads *There is a treaty.*

4 Ben-hadad agreed to King Asa's request and sent the commanders of his
army to attack the towns of Israel. They conquered the towns of Ijon, Dan,
Abel-beth-maacah,* and all the store cities in Naphtali. 5 As soon as Baasha
of Israel heard what was happening, he abandoned his project of fortifying
Ramah and stopped all work on it. 6 Then King Asa called out all the men of
Judah to carry away the building stones and timbers that Baasha had been
using to fortify Ramah. Asa used these materials to fortify the towns of Geba
and Mizpah.
7 At that time Hanani the seer came to King Asa and told him, "Because
you have put your trust in the king of Aram instead of in the LORD your God,
you missed your chance to destroy the army of the king of Aram. 8 Don't you
remember what happened to the Ethiopians* and Libyans and their vast
army, with all of their chariots and charioteers?* At that time you relied on
the LORD, and he handed them over to you. 9 The eyes of the LORD search the
whole earth in order to strengthen those whose hearts are fully committed
to him. What a fool you have been! From now on you will be at war."
10 Asa became so angry with Hanani for saying this that he threw him into
prison and put him in stocks. At that time Asa also began to oppress some
of his people.

Summary of Asa's Reign

11 The rest of the events of Asa's reign, from beginning to end, are recorded
in *The Book of the Kings of Judah and Israel.* 12 In the thirty-ninth year of his
reign, Asa developed a serious foot disease. Yet even with the severity of his
disease, he did not seek the LORD's help but turned only to his physicians.
13 So he died in the forty-first year of his reign. 14 He was buried in the tomb
he had carved out for himself in the City of David. He was laid on a bed
perfumed with sweet spices and fragrant ointments, and the people built a
huge funeral fire in his honor.

Jehoshaphat Rules in Judah

17 Then Jehoshaphat, Asa's son, became the next king. He strengthened
Judah to stand against any attack from Israel. 2 He stationed troops in
all the fortified towns of Judah, and he assigned additional garrisons to the
land of Judah and to the towns of Ephraim that his father, Asa, had captured.
3 The LORD was with Jehoshaphat because he followed the example of
his father's early years* and did not worship the images of Baal. 4 He sought
his father's God and obeyed his commands instead of following the evil
practices of the kingdom of Israel. 5 So the LORD established Jehoshaphat's
control over the kingdom of Judah. All the people of Judah brought gifts
to Jehoshaphat, so he became very wealthy and highly esteemed. 6 He was
deeply committed to* the ways of the LORD. He removed the pagan shrines
and Asherah poles from Judah.
7 In the third year of his reign Jehoshaphat sent his officials to teach in
all the towns of Judah. These officials included Ben-hail, Obadiah, Zecha-
riah, Nethanel, and Micaiah. 8 He sent Levites along with them, including
Shemaiah, Nethaniah, Zebadiah, Asahel, Shemiramoth, Jehonathan, Ado-
nijah, Tobijah, and Tob-adonijah. He also sent out the priests Elishama and

16:4 As in parallel text at 1 Kgs 15:20; Hebrew reads *Abel-maim,* another name for Abel-beth-maacah. **16:8a** Hebrew *Cushites.* **16:8b** Or *and horsemen?* **17:3** Some Hebrew manuscripts read *the example of his father, David.* **17:6** Hebrew *His heart was courageous in.*

Question **16:9**

God searches the entire world "in order to strengthen those whose hearts are fully committed to him." When God searches in your community, will he see you as someone he will strengthen? Why or why not?

Make a Difference

17:3–6

Following Your Father's Faith

This is an interesting devotional moment for those who have had a father who fell into sin. Many dads don't expect to fail. Often, when their children are first born, dads commit themselves to being good role models for their sons and daughters. Sadly, over time, many fathers fall away from that passion and fall into sin.

The Bible is full of examples of next-generation leaders who had to make a choice: Will I be like my dad when he was younger and full of vibrant faith or like my dad when he was older and fell into sin? Jehoshaphat decided to live a life of faith similar to the way his dad had lived in his younger years. This greatly pleased the Lord.

Difference Maker

You can choose today to be a person of faithfulness. Just because someone else falls into sin doesn't mean that you must also.

> **Question** 18:1-2
>
> Watch out! The person you date and eventually marry will make a difference for better or worse. Jehoshaphat's whole family was led away from the Lord due to his son's marriage into the family of Ahab. Would you say your dating practices reflect a pattern that will lead you away from God or closer to God?

Jehoram. 9 They took copies of the Book of the Law of the LORD and traveled
around through all the towns of Judah, teaching the people.
10 Then the fear of the LORD fell over all the surrounding kingdoms so that
none of them wanted to declare war on Jehoshaphat. 11 Some of the Philis-
tines brought him gifts and silver as tribute, and the Arabs brought 7,700
rams and 7,700 male goats.
12 So Jehoshaphat became more and more powerful and built fortresses
and storage cities throughout Judah. 13 He stored numerous supplies in Ju-
dah's towns and stationed an army of seasoned troops at Jerusalem. 14 His
army was enrolled according to ancestral clans.

From Judah there were 300,000 troops organized in units of 1,000, under the
command of Adnah. 15 Next in command was Jehohanan, who commanded
280,000 troops. 16 Next was Amasiah son of Zicri, who volunteered for the
LORD's service, with 200,000 troops under his command.
17 From Benjamin there were 200,000 troops equipped with bows and
shields. They were under the command of Eliada, a veteran soldier. 18 Next
in command was Jehozabad, who commanded 180,000 armed men.

19 These were the troops stationed in Jerusalem to serve the king, besides
those Jehoshaphat stationed in the fortified towns throughout Judah.

Jehoshaphat and Ahab

18 Jehoshaphat enjoyed great riches and high esteem, and he made an
alliance with Ahab of Israel by having his son marry Ahab's daughter.
2 A few years later he went to Samaria to visit Ahab, who prepared a great
banquet for him and his officials. They butchered great numbers of sheep,
goats, and cattle for the feast. Then Ahab enticed Jehoshaphat to join forces
with him to recover Ramoth-gilead.
3 "Will you go with me to Ramoth-gilead?" King Ahab of Israel asked King
Jehoshaphat of Judah.
Jehoshaphat replied, "Why, of course! You and I are as one, and my troops
are your troops. We will certainly join you in battle." 4 Then Jehoshaphat
added, "But first let's find out what the LORD says."
5 So the king of Israel summoned the prophets, 400 of them, and asked
them, "Should we go to war against Ramoth-gilead, or should I hold back?"
They all replied, "Yes, go right ahead! God will give the king victory."
6 But Jehoshaphat asked, "Is there not also a prophet of the LORD here?
We should ask him the same question."
7 The king of Israel replied to Jehoshaphat, "There is one more man who
could consult the LORD for us, but I hate him. He never prophesies anything
but trouble for me! His name is Micaiah son of Imlah."
Jehoshaphat replied, "That's not the way a king should talk! Let's hear
what he has to say."
8 So the king of Israel called one of his officials and said, "Quick! Bring
Micaiah son of Imlah."

Micaiah Prophesies against Ahab

9 King Ahab of Israel and King Jehoshaphat of Judah, dressed in their royal
robes, were sitting on thrones at the threshing floor near the gate of Samaria.

All of Ahab's prophets were prophesying there in front of them. 10 One of them,
Zedekiah son of Kenaanah, made some iron horns and proclaimed, "This is
what the LORD says: With these horns you will gore the Arameans to death!"
11 All the other prophets agreed. "Yes," they said, "go up to Ramoth-gilead
and be victorious, for the LORD will give the king victory!"
12 Meanwhile, the messenger who went to get Micaiah said to him, "Look,
all the prophets are promising victory for the king. Be sure that you agree
with them and promise success."
13 But Micaiah replied, "As surely as the LORD lives, I will say only what
my God says."
14 When Micaiah arrived before the king, Ahab asked him, "Micaiah,
should we go to war against Ramoth-gilead, or should I hold back?"
Micaiah replied sarcastically, "Yes, go up and be victorious, for you will
have victory over them!"
15 But the king replied sharply, "How many times must I demand that you
speak only the truth to me when you speak for the LORD?"
16 Then Micaiah told him, "In a vision I saw all Israel scattered on the
mountains, like sheep without a shepherd. And the LORD said, 'Their mas-
ter has been killed.* Send them home in peace.'"
17 "Didn't I tell you?" the king of Israel exclaimed to Jehoshaphat. "He
never prophesies anything but trouble for me."
18 Then Micaiah continued, "Listen to what the LORD says! I saw the LORD
sitting on his throne with all the armies of heaven around him, on his right
and on his left. 19 And the LORD said, 'Who can entice King Ahab of Israel to
go into battle against Ramoth-gilead so he can be killed?'
"There were many suggestions, 20 and finally a spirit approached the LORD
and said, 'I can do it!'
"'How will you do this?' the LORD asked.
21 "And the spirit replied, 'I will go out and inspire all of Ahab's prophets
to speak lies.'
"'You will succeed,' said the LORD. 'Go ahead and do it.'
22 "So you see, the LORD has put a lying spirit in the mouths of your
prophets. For the LORD has pronounced your doom."
23 Then Zedekiah son of Kenaanah walked up to Micaiah and slapped him
across the face. "Since when did the Spirit of the LORD leave me to speak to
you?" he demanded.
24 And Micaiah replied, "You will find out soon enough when you are try-
ing to hide in some secret room!"
25 "Arrest him!" the king of Israel ordered. "Take him back to Amon, the
governor of the city, and to my son Joash. 26 Give them this order from the
king: 'Put this man in prison, and feed him nothing but bread and water
until I return safely from the battle!'"
27 But Micaiah replied, "If you return safely, it will mean that the LORD has
not spoken through me!" Then he added to those standing around, "Every-
one mark my words!"

The Death of Ahab

28 So King Ahab of Israel and King Jehoshaphat of Judah led their armies
against Ramoth-gilead. 29 The king of Israel said to Jehoshaphat, "As we go

Story Arc **18:6-27**

● Micaiah

Micaiah was a bold and somewhat sarcastic follower of God. He stood powerfully against a mob that opposed him. He remained steadfast to the Lord even though his life was threatened. He did not retaliate even as he was struck across the face and arrested. His strength came from one simple truth: he spoke the words of the Lord.

2 Chr 21:12-15 ►

18:16 Hebrew *These people have no master.*

Question 19:2

From these words of Jehu, son of Hanani, what can you learn about how God wants you to live?

into battle, I will disguise myself so no one will recognize me, but you wear your royal robes." So the king of Israel disguised himself, and they went into battle.
30 Meanwhile, the king of Aram had issued these orders to his chariot commanders: "Attack only the king of Israel! Don't bother with anyone else."
31 So when the Aramean chariot commanders saw Jehoshaphat in his royal robes, they went after him. "There is the king of Israel!" they shouted. But Jehoshaphat called out, and the LORD saved him. God helped him by turning the attackers away from him.
32 As soon as the chariot commanders realized he was not the king of Israel, they stopped chasing him.
33 An Aramean soldier, however, randomly shot an arrow at the Israelite troops and hit the king of Israel between the joints of his armor. "Turn the horses* and get me out of here!" Ahab groaned to the driver of the chariot. "I'm badly wounded!"
34 The battle raged all that day, and the king of Israel propped himself up in his chariot facing the Arameans. In the evening, just as the sun was setting, he died.

Jehoshaphat Appoints Judges

19 When King Jehoshaphat of Judah arrived safely home in Jerusalem,
2 Jehu son of Hanani the seer went out to meet him. "Why should you help the wicked and love those who hate the LORD?" he asked the king. "Because of what you have done, the LORD is very angry with you.
3 Even so, there is some good in you, for you have removed the Asherah poles throughout the land, and you have committed yourself to seeking God."
4 Jehoshaphat lived in Jerusalem, but he went out among the people, traveling from Beersheba to the hill country of Ephraim, encouraging the people to return to the LORD, the God of their ancestors.
5 He appointed judges throughout the nation in all the fortified towns,
6 and he said to them, "Always think carefully before pronouncing judgment. Remember that you do not judge to please people but to please the LORD. He will be with you when you render the verdict in each case.
7 Fear the LORD and judge with integrity, for the LORD our God does not tolerate perverted justice, partiality, or the taking of bribes."
8 In Jerusalem, Jehoshaphat appointed some of the Levites and priests and clan leaders in Israel to serve as judges* for cases involving the LORD's regulations and for civil disputes.
9 These were his instructions to them: "You must always act in the fear of the LORD, with faithfulness and an undivided heart.
10 Whenever a case comes to you from fellow citizens in an outlying town, whether a murder case or some other violation of God's laws, commands, decrees, or regulations, you must warn them not to sin against the LORD, so that he will not be angry with you and them. Do this and you will not be guilty.
11 "Amariah the high priest will have final say in all cases involving the LORD. Zebadiah son of Ishmael, a leader from the tribe of Judah, will have final say in all civil cases. The Levites will assist you in making sure that justice is served. Take courage as you fulfill your duties, and may the LORD be with those who do what is right."

18:33 Hebrew *Turn your hand.* **19:8** As in Greek version; the meaning of the Hebrew is uncertain.

War with Surrounding Nations

20 After this, the armies of the Moabites, Ammonites, and some of the
Meunites* declared war on Jehoshaphat. 2 Messengers came and told
Jehoshaphat, "A vast army from Edom* is marching against you from beyond
the Dead Sea.* They are already at Hazazon-tamar." (This was another name
for En-gedi.)
3 Jehoshaphat was terrified by this news and begged the LORD for guid-
ance. He also ordered everyone in Judah to begin fasting. 4 So people from all
the towns of Judah came to Jerusalem to seek the LORD's help.
5 Jehoshaphat stood before the community of Judah and Jerusalem in
front of the new courtyard at the Temple of the LORD. 6 He prayed, "O LORD,
God of our ancestors, you alone are the God who is in heaven. You are ruler
of all the kingdoms of the earth. You are powerful and mighty; no one can
stand against you! 7 O our God, did you not drive out those who lived in this
land when your people Israel arrived? And did you not give this land forever
to the descendants of your friend Abraham? 8 Your people settled here and
built this Temple to honor your name. 9 They said, 'Whenever we are faced
with any calamity such as war,* plague, or famine, we can come to stand in
your presence before this Temple where your name is honored. We can cry
out to you to save us, and you will hear us and rescue us.'
10 "And now see what the armies of Ammon, Moab, and Mount Seir are
doing. You would not let our ancestors invade those nations when Israel left
Egypt, so they went around them and did not destroy them. 11 Now see how
they reward us! For they have come to throw us out of your land, which you
gave us as an inheritance. 12 O our God, won't you stop them? We are power-
less against this mighty army that is about to attack us. We do not know what
to do, but we are looking to you for help."
13 As all the men of Judah stood before the LORD with their little ones,
wives, and children, 14 the Spirit of the LORD came upon one of the men
standing there. His name was Jahaziel son of Zechariah, son of Benaiah,
son of Jeiel, son of Mattaniah, a Levite who was a descendant of Asaph.
15 He said, "Listen, all you people of Judah and Jerusalem! Listen, King
Jehoshaphat! This is what the LORD says: Do not be afraid! Don't be dis-
▲ couraged by this mighty army, for the battle is not yours, but God's. 16 To-
morrow, march out against them. You will find them coming up through
the ascent of Ziz at the end of the valley that opens into the wilderness of
Jeruel. 17 But you will not even need to fight. Take your positions; then stand
still and watch the LORD's victory. He is with you, O people of Judah and Je-
rusalem. Do not be afraid or discouraged. Go out against them tomorrow,
for the LORD is with you!"
18 Then King Jehoshaphat bowed low with his face to the ground. And
all the people of Judah and Jerusalem did the same, worshiping the LORD.
19 Then the Levites from the clans of Kohath and Korah stood to praise the
LORD, the God of Israel, with a very loud shout.
20 Early the next morning the army of Judah went out into the wilderness
of Tekoa. On the way Jehoshaphat stopped and said, "Listen to me, all you
people of Judah and Jerusalem! Believe in the LORD your God, and you will
be able to stand firm. Believe in his prophets, and you will succeed."

Prayer **20:16**

Lord, give me courage to face what is ahead, trusting that this battle belongs to you and that I am on your side. Amen.

20:1 As in some Greek manuscripts (see also 26:7); Hebrew repeats *Ammonites.* **20:2a** As in one Hebrew manuscript; most Hebrew manuscripts and ancient versions read *Aram.* **20:2b** Hebrew *the sea.* **20:9** Or *sword of judgment;* or *sword, judgment.*

Question 20:21

The military strategy here was to have the worship leaders on the front lines of battle. What difference would it make in your life if you made worship the first priority in your struggles?

[21] After consulting the people, the king appointed singers to walk ahead of the army, singing to the LORD and praising him for his holy splendor. This is what they sang:

"Give thanks to the LORD;
his faithful love endures forever!"

[22] At the very moment they began to sing and give praise, the LORD caused
the armies of Ammon, Moab, and Mount Seir to start fighting among them-
selves. [23] The armies of Moab and Ammon turned against their allies from
Mount Seir and killed every one of them. After they had destroyed the army
of Seir, they began attacking each other. [24] So when the army of Judah ar-
rived at the lookout point in the wilderness, all they saw were dead bodies lying on the ground as far as they could see. Not a single one of the enemy had escaped.

[25] King Jehoshaphat and his men went out to gather the plunder. They found vast amounts of equipment, clothing,* and other valuables—more than they could carry. There was so much plunder that it took them three
days just to collect it all! [26] On the fourth day they gathered in the Valley
of Blessing,* which got its name that day because the people praised and thanked the LORD there. It is still called the Valley of Blessing today.

[27] Then all the men returned to Jerusalem, with Jehoshaphat leading
them, overjoyed that the LORD had given them victory over their enemies.
[28] They marched into Jerusalem to the music of harps, lyres, and trumpets,
and they proceeded to the Temple of the LORD.

[29] When all the surrounding kingdoms heard that the LORD himself had
fought against the enemies of Israel, the fear of God came over them. [30] So
Jehoshaphat's kingdom was at peace, for his God had given him rest on every side.

Summary of Jehoshaphat's Reign

[31] So Jehoshaphat ruled over the land of Judah. He was thirty-five years old when he became king, and he reigned in Jerusalem twenty-five years. His mother was Azubah, the daughter of Shilhi.

[32] Jehoshaphat was a good king, following the ways of his father, Asa. He
did what was pleasing in the LORD's sight. [33] During his reign, however, he
failed to remove all the pagan shrines, and the people never fully committed themselves to follow the God of their ancestors.

[34] The rest of the events of Jehoshaphat's reign, from beginning to end, are recorded in *The Record of Jehu Son of Hanani,* which is included in *The Book of the Kings of Israel.*

[35] Some time later King Jehoshaphat of Judah made an alliance with King
Ahaziah of Israel, who was very wicked.* [36] Together they built a fleet of trad-
ing ships* at the port of Ezion-geber. [37] Then Eliezer son of Dodavahu from
Mareshah prophesied against Jehoshaphat. He said, "Because you have allied yourself with King Ahaziah, the LORD will destroy your work." So the ships met with disaster and never put out to sea.*

20:25 As in some Hebrew manuscripts and Latin Vulgate; most Hebrew manuscripts read *corpses.* **20:26** Hebrew *valley of Beracah.* **20:35** Or *who made him do what was wicked.* **20:36** Hebrew *fleet of ships that could go to Tarshish.* **20:37** Hebrew *never set sail for Tarshish.*

Jehoram Rules in Judah

21 When Jehoshaphat died, he was buried with his ancestors in the City
of David. Then his son Jehoram became the next king.
2 Jehoram's brothers—the other sons of Jehoshaphat—were Azariah, Je-
hiel, Zechariah, Azariahu, Michael, and Shephatiah; all these were the sons
of Jehoshaphat king of Judah.* 3 Their father had given each of them valuable
gifts of silver, gold, and costly items, and also some of Judah's fortified towns.
However, he designated Jehoram as the next king because he was the oldest.
4 But when Jehoram had become solidly established as king, he killed all his
brothers and some of the other leaders of Judah.
5 Jehoram was thirty-two years old when he became king, and he reigned in
Jerusalem eight years. 6 But Jehoram followed the example of the kings of Israel
and was as wicked as King Ahab, for he had married one of Ahab's daughters.
So Jehoram did what was evil in the LORD's sight. 7 But the LORD did not want
to destroy David's dynasty, for he had made a covenant with David and prom-
ised that his descendants would continue to rule, shining like a lamp forever.
8 During Jehoram's reign, the Edomites revolted against Judah and crowned
their own king. 9 So Jehoram went out with his full army and all his chariots.
The Edomites surrounded him and his chariot commanders, but he went out
at night and attacked them* under cover of darkness. 10 Even so, Edom has been
independent from Judah to this day. The town of Libnah also revolted about
that same time. All this happened because Jehoram had abandoned the LORD,
the God of his ancestors. 11 He had built pagan shrines in the hill country of
Judah and had led the people of Jerusalem and Judah to give themselves to
pagan gods and to go astray.
12 Then Elijah the prophet wrote Jehoram this letter:

"This is what the LORD, the God of your ancestor David, says: You
have not followed the good example of your father, Jehoshaphat, or
your grandfather King Asa of Judah. 13 Instead, you have been as evil as
the kings of Israel. You have led the people of Jerusalem and Judah to
worship idols, just as King Ahab did in Israel. And you have even killed
your own brothers, men who were better than you. 14 So now the LORD is
about to strike you, your people, your children, your wives, and all that is
yours with a heavy blow. 15 You yourself will suffer with a severe intestinal
disease that will get worse each day until your bowels come out."

16 Then the LORD stirred up the Philistines and the Arabs, who lived near
the Ethiopians,* to attack Jehoram. 17 They marched against Judah, broke
down its defenses, and carried away everything of value in the royal palace,
including the king's sons and his wives. Only his youngest son, Ahaziah,*
was spared.
18 After all this, the LORD struck Jehoram with an incurable intestinal disease.
19 The disease grew worse and worse, and at the end of two years it caused his
bowels to come out, and he died in agony. His people did not build a great
funeral fire to honor him as they had done for his ancestors.
20 Jehoram was thirty-two years old when he became king, and he reigned

21:2 Masoretic Text reads *of Israel;* also in 21:4. The author of Chronicles sees Judah as representative of the true Israel. (Some Hebrew manuscripts, Greek and Syriac versions, and Latin Vulgate read *of Judah.*) **21:9** Or *he went out and escaped.* The meaning of the Hebrew is uncertain. **21:16** Hebrew *the Cushites.* **21:17** Hebrew *Jehoahaz,* a variant spelling of Ahaziah; compare 22:1.

Story Arc **21:12-15**

● Elijah

Elijah's life was marked by confronting wicked kings, especially King Ahab in the northern tribes of Israel. Here, in his later years, he wrote a frightening letter to Jehoram, the king of Judah. Jehoram was as wicked as Ahab, his father-in-law (21:6). Jehoram had all his brothers killed and built pagan shrines throughout the land. Then Elijah passed on word to the wicked king that God would strike him with a nasty and humiliating disease. Hundreds of years later, when Jesus was speaking out against the sins of rulers and performing miraculous signs, many people began to wonder if he was Elijah reborn (see Malachi 4:5-6 and Matthew 16:13-16).

2 Chr 22:10-12 ►

in Jerusalem eight years. No one was sorry when he died. They buried him in
the City of David, but not in the royal cemetery.

Ahaziah Rules in Judah

22 Then the people of Jerusalem made Ahaziah, Jehoram's youngest
son, their next king, since the marauding bands who came with
the Arabs* had killed all the older sons. So Ahaziah son of Jehoram reigned
as king of Judah.
2 Ahaziah was twenty-two* years old when he became king, and he reigned
in Jerusalem one year. His mother was Athaliah, a granddaughter of King
Omri. 3 Ahaziah also followed the evil example of King Ahab's family, for
his mother encouraged him in doing wrong. 4 He did what was evil in the
LORD's sight, just as Ahab's family had done. They even became his advisers
after the death of his father, and they led him to ruin.
5 Following their evil advice, Ahaziah joined Joram,* the son of King Ahab
of Israel, in his war against King Hazael of Aram at Ramoth-gilead. When the
Arameans* wounded Joram in the battle, 6 he returned to Jezreel to recover
from the wounds he had received at Ramoth.* Because Joram was wounded,
King Ahaziah* of Judah went to Jezreel to visit him.
7 But God had decided that this visit would be Ahaziah's downfall. While
he was there, Ahaziah went out with Joram to meet Jehu grandson of Nim-
shi,* whom the LORD had appointed to destroy the dynasty of Ahab.
8 While Jehu was executing judgment against the family of Ahab, he hap-
pened to meet some of Judah's officials and Ahaziah's relatives* who were
traveling with Ahaziah. So Jehu killed them all. 9 Then Jehu's men searched
for Ahaziah, and they found him hiding in the city of Samaria. They brought
him to Jehu, who killed him. Ahaziah was given a decent burial because the
people said, "He was the grandson of Jehoshaphat—a man who sought the
LORD with all his heart." But none of the surviving members of Ahaziah's
family was capable of ruling the kingdom.

Queen Athaliah Rules in Judah

10 When Athaliah, the mother of King Ahaziah of Judah, learned that her son
was dead, she began to destroy the rest of Judah's royal family. 11 But Ahazi-
ah's sister Jehosheba,* the daughter of King Jehoram, took Ahaziah's infant
son, Joash, and stole him away from among the rest of the king's children,
who were about to be killed. She put Joash and his nurse in a bedroom. In
this way, Jehosheba, wife of Jehoiada the priest and sister of Ahaziah, hid the
child so that Athaliah could not murder him. 12 Joash remained hidden in the
Temple of God for six years while Athaliah ruled over the land.

Revolt against Athaliah

23 In the seventh year of Athaliah's reign, Jehoiada the priest decided
to act. He summoned his courage and made a pact with five army

22:1 Or *marauding bands of Arabs.* 22:2 As in some Greek manuscripts and Syriac version (see also 2 Kgs 8:26); Hebrew reads *forty-two.* 22:5a Hebrew *Jehoram,* a variant spelling of Joram; also in 22:6, 7. 22:5b As in two Hebrew manuscripts and Latin Vulgate (see also 2 Kgs 8:28); Masoretic Text reads *the archers.* 22:6a Hebrew *Ramah,* a variant spelling of Ramoth. 22:6b As in some Hebrew manuscripts, Greek and Syriac versions, and Latin Vulgate (see also 2 Kgs 8:29); most Hebrew manuscripts read *Azariah.* 22:7 Hebrew *descendant of Nimshi;* compare 2 Kgs 9:2, 14. 22:8 As in Greek version (see also 2 Kgs 10:13); Hebrew reads *and sons of the brothers of Ahaziah.* 22:11 As in parallel text at 2 Kgs 11:2; Hebrew lacks *Ahaziah's sister* and reads *Jehoshabeath* [a variant spelling of Jehosheba].

Story Arc **22:10-12**

● Jehosheba

In a murderous climate, a brave woman named Jehosheba rescued her nephew Joash. The queen was slaughtering the royal family, wanting to destroy the line of David and take sole possession of the throne for herself. When Jehosheba realized that the royal infant, Joash, was in line to be executed, she hid him away. For the next six years, she and her husband, Jehoiada, kept the boy safe while the queen devastated the kingdom.

Do you know people who have so much resiliency that they would risk their lives for the sake of others? What gives them such a brave conviction?

Story Arc **23:1-11**

● Jehoiada

Jehoiada was the husband to Jehosheba (22:11). Because of the murderous behaviors of his mother-in-law, Queen Athaliah, Jehoiada became the mastermind of a patiently planned revolt against her. While he was not the king, he was the true orchestrator of the revival of faith in chapters 23-24 of 2 Chronicles. The Spirit of the Lord was leading him, enabling him to become one of the most significant leaders God's people had ever seen. His story ends with a dramatic statement in 24:15-16. He lived to a very old age and was buried among the kings.

Do you know an older person who has lived their life faithfully for the Lord? Sit down with them to listen to their story and to the conviction of their faith.

2 Chr 29:3 ►

commanders: Azariah son of Jeroham, Ishmael son of Jehohanan, Azariah
son of Obed, Maaseiah son of Adaiah, and Elishaphat son of Zicri. 2 These
men traveled secretly throughout Judah and summoned the Levites and
clan leaders in all the towns to come to Jerusalem. 3 They all gathered at the
Temple of God, where they made a solemn pact with Joash, the young king.

Jehoiada said to them, "Here is the king's son! The time has come for him
to reign! The LORD has promised that a descendant of David will be our king.
4 This is what you must do. When you priests and Levites come on duty on
the Sabbath, a third of you will serve as gatekeepers. 5 Another third will go
over to the royal palace, and the final third will be at the Foundation Gate.
Everyone else should stay in the courtyards of the LORD's Temple. 6 Remem-
ber, only the priests and Levites on duty may enter the Temple of the LORD,
for they are set apart as holy. The rest of the people must obey the LORD's
instructions and stay outside. 7 You Levites, form a bodyguard around the
king and keep your weapons in hand. Kill anyone who tries to enter the
Temple. Stay with the king wherever he goes."

8 So the Levites and all the people of Judah did everything as Jehoiada the
priest ordered. The commanders took charge of the men reporting for duty
that Sabbath, as well as those who were going off duty. Jehoiada the priest did
not let anyone go home after their shift ended. 9 Then Jehoiada supplied the
commanders with the spears and the large and small shields that had once be-
longed to King David and were stored in the Temple of God. 10 He stationed all
the people around the king, with their weapons ready. They formed a line from
the south side of the Temple around to the north side and all around the altar.

11 Then Jehoiada and his sons brought out Joash, the king's son, placed
the crown on his head, and presented him with a copy of God's laws.* They
anointed him and proclaimed him king, and everyone shouted, "Long live
the king!"

The Death of Athaliah

12 When Athaliah heard the noise of the people running and the shouts of
praise to the king, she hurried to the LORD's Temple to see what was hap-
pening. 13 When she arrived, she saw the newly crowned king standing in his
place of authority by the pillar at the Temple entrance. The commanders and
trumpeters were surrounding him, and people from all over the land were
rejoicing and blowing trumpets. Singers with musical instruments were
leading the people in a great celebration. When Athaliah saw all this, she
tore her clothes in despair and shouted, "Treason! Treason!"

14 Then Jehoiada the priest ordered the commanders who were in charge of
the troops, "Take her to the soldiers in front of the Temple,* and kill anyone
who tries to rescue her." For the priest had said, "She must not be killed in
the Temple of the LORD." 15 So they seized her and led her out to the entrance
of the Horse Gate on the palace grounds, and they killed her there.

Jehoiada's Religious Reforms

16 Then Jehoiada made a covenant between himself and the king and the
people that they would be the LORD's people. 17 And all the people went over to
the temple of Baal and tore it down. They demolished the altars and smashed
the idols, and they killed Mattan the priest of Baal in front of the altars.

23:11 Or *a copy of the covenant.* **23:14** Or *Bring her out from between the ranks;* or *Take her out of the Temple precincts.* The meaning of the Hebrew is uncertain.

18 Jehoiada now put the priests and Levites in charge of the Temple of
the LORD, following all the directions given by David. He also commanded
them to present burnt offerings to the LORD, as prescribed by the Law of
Moses, and to sing and rejoice as David had instructed. 19 He also stationed
gatekeepers at the gates of the LORD's Temple to keep out those who for any
reason were ceremonially unclean.

20 Then the commanders, nobles, rulers, and all the people of the land
escorted the king from the Temple of the LORD. They went through the
upper gate and into the palace, and they seated the king on the royal throne.
21 So all the people of the land rejoiced, and the city was peaceful because
Athaliah had been killed.

Joash Repairs the Temple

24 Joash was seven years old when he became king, and he reigned
in Jerusalem forty years. His mother was Zibiah from Beersheba.
2 Joash did what was pleasing in the LORD's sight throughout the lifetime
of Jehoiada the priest. 3 Jehoiada chose two wives for Joash, and he had sons
and daughters.

4 At one point Joash decided to repair and restore the Temple of the LORD.
5 He summoned the priests and Levites and gave them these instructions:
"Go to all the towns of Judah and collect the required annual offerings, so
that we can repair the Temple of your God. Do not delay!" But the Levites
did not act immediately.

6 So the king called for Jehoiada the high priest and asked him, "Why
haven't you demanded that the Levites go out and collect the Temple taxes
from the towns of Judah and from Jerusalem? Moses, the servant of the
LORD, levied this tax on the community of Israel in order to maintain the
Tabernacle of the Covenant.*"

7 Over the years the followers of wicked Athaliah had broken into the
Temple of God, and they had used all the dedicated things from the Temple
of the LORD to worship the images of Baal.

8 So now the king ordered a chest to be made and set outside the gate lead-
ing to the Temple of the LORD. 9 Then a proclamation was sent throughout
Judah and Jerusalem, telling the people to bring to the LORD the tax that
Moses, the servant of God, had required of the Israelites in the wilderness.
10 This pleased all the leaders and the people, and they gladly brought their
money and filled the chest with it.

11 Whenever the chest became full, the Levites would carry it to the king's
officials. Then the court secretary and an officer of the high priest would
come and empty the chest and take it back to the Temple again. This went
on day after day, and a large amount of money was collected. 12 The king
and Jehoiada gave the money to the construction supervisors, who hired
masons and carpenters to restore the Temple of the LORD. They also hired
metalworkers, who made articles of iron and bronze for the LORD's Temple.

13 The men in charge of the renovation worked hard and made steady
progress. They restored the Temple of God according to its original design
and strengthened it. 14 When all the repairs were finished, they brought the
remaining money to the king and Jehoiada. It was used to make various
articles for the Temple of the LORD—articles for worship services and for

24:6 Hebrew *Tent of the Testimony.*

burnt offerings, including ladles and other articles made of gold and silver.
And the burnt offerings were sacrificed continually in the Temple of the
LORD during the lifetime of Jehoiada the priest.
15 Jehoiada lived to a very old age, finally dying at 130. 16 He was buried
among the kings in the City of David, because he had done so much good in
Israel for God and his Temple.

Jehoiada's Reforms Reversed

17 But after Jehoiada's death, the leaders of Judah came and bowed before
King Joash and persuaded him to listen to their advice. 18 They decided to
abandon the Temple of the LORD, the God of their ancestors, and they wor-
shiped Asherah poles and idols instead! Because of this sin, divine anger fell
on Judah and Jerusalem. 19 Yet the LORD sent prophets to bring them back
to him. The prophets warned them, but still the people would not listen.
20 Then the Spirit of God came upon Zechariah son of Jehoiada the priest.
He stood before the people and said, "This is what God says: Why do you
disobey the LORD's commands and keep yourselves from prospering? You
have abandoned the LORD, and now he has abandoned you!"
21 Then the leaders plotted to kill Zechariah, and King Joash ordered that
they stone him to death in the courtyard of the LORD's Temple. 22 That was
how King Joash repaid Jehoiada for his loyalty—by killing his son. Zech-
ariah's last words as he died were, "May the LORD see what they are doing
and avenge my death!"

The End of Joash's Reign

23 In the spring of the year* the Aramean army marched against Joash. They
invaded Judah and Jerusalem and killed all the leaders of the nation. Then
they sent all the plunder back to their king in Damascus. 24 Although the
Arameans attacked with only a small army, the LORD helped them conquer
the much larger army of Judah. The people of Judah had abandoned the
LORD, the God of their ancestors, so judgment was carried out against Joash.
25 The Arameans withdrew, leaving Joash severely wounded. But his own
officials plotted to kill him for murdering the son* of Jehoiada the priest.
They assassinated him as he lay in bed. Then he was buried in the City of
David, but not in the royal cemetery. 26 The assassins were Jozacar,* the son of
an Ammonite woman named Shimeath, and Jehozabad, the son of a Moab-
ite woman named Shomer.*
27 The account of the sons of Joash, the prophecies about him, and the
record of his restoration of the Temple of God are written in *The Commentary
on the Book of the Kings.* His son Amaziah became the next king.

Amaziah Rules in Judah

25 Amaziah was twenty-five years old when he became king, and he
reigned in Jerusalem twenty-nine years. His mother was Jehoaddin*
from Jerusalem. 2 Amaziah did what was pleasing in the LORD's sight, but not
wholeheartedly.
3 When Amaziah was well established as king, he executed the officials

Question 24:20-22

In a very sad moment, Zechariah, the son of the respected Jehoiada, was killed for confronting the sinful practices of the people. Why do the masses so quickly sway from doing what is right to doing what is wrong?

24:23 Hebrew *At the turn of the year.* The first day of the year in the ancient Hebrew lunar calendar occurred in March or April. 24:25 As in Greek version and Latin Vulgate; Hebrew reads *sons.* 24:26a As in parallel text at 2 Kgs 12:21; Hebrew reads *Zabad.* 24:26b As in parallel text at 2 Kgs 12:21; Hebrew reads *Shimrith,* a variant spelling of Shomer. 25:1 As in parallel text at 2 Kgs 14:2; Hebrew reads *Jehoaddan,* a variant spelling of Jehoaddin.

who had assassinated his father. 4 However, he did not kill the children of the assassins, for he obeyed the command of the LORD as written by Moses in the Book of the Law: "Parents must not be put to death for the sins of their children, nor children for the sins of their parents. Those deserving to die must be put to death for their own crimes."*

5 Then Amaziah organized the army, assigning generals and captains* for all Judah and Benjamin. He took a census and found that he had an army of 300,000 select troops, twenty years old and older, all trained in the use of spear and shield. 6 He also paid about 7,500 pounds* of silver to hire 100,000 experienced fighting men from Israel.

7 But a man of God came to him and said, "Your Majesty, do not hire troops from Israel, for the LORD is not with Israel. He will not help those people of Ephraim! 8 If you let them go with your troops into battle, you will be defeated by the enemy no matter how well you fight. God will overthrow you, for he has the power to help you or to trip you up."

9 Amaziah asked the man of God, "But what about all that silver I paid to hire the army of Israel?"

The man of God replied, "The LORD is able to give you much more than this!" 10 So Amaziah discharged the hired troops and sent them back to Ephraim. This made them very angry with Judah, and they returned home in a great rage.

11 Then Amaziah summoned his courage and led his army to the Valley of Salt, where they killed 10,000 Edomite troops from Seir. 12 They captured another 10,000 and took them to the top of a cliff and threw them off, dashing them to pieces on the rocks below.

13 Meanwhile, the hired troops that Amaziah had sent home raided several of the towns of Judah between Samaria and Beth-horon. They killed 3,000 people and carried off great quantities of plunder.

14 When King Amaziah returned from slaughtering the Edomites, he brought with him idols taken from the people of Seir. He set them up as his own gods, bowed down in front of them, and offered sacrifices to them! 15 This made the LORD very angry, and he sent a prophet to ask, "Why do you turn to gods who could not even save their own people from you?"

16 But the king interrupted him and said, "Since when have I made you the king's counselor? Be quiet now before I have you killed!"

So the prophet stopped with this warning: "I know that God has determined to destroy you because you have done this and have refused to accept my counsel."

17 After consulting with his advisers, King Amaziah of Judah sent this challenge to Israel's king Jehoash,* the son of Jehoahaz and grandson of Jehu: "Come and meet me in battle!"*

18 But King Jehoash of Israel replied to King Amaziah of Judah with this story: "Out in the Lebanon mountains, a thistle sent a message to a mighty cedar tree: 'Give your daughter in marriage to my son.' But just then a wild animal of Lebanon came by and stepped on the thistle, crushing it!

19 "You are saying, 'I have defeated Edom,' and you are very proud of it. But my advice is to stay at home. Why stir up trouble that will only bring disaster on you and the people of Judah?"

25:4 Deut 24:16. 25:5 Hebrew *commanders of thousands and commanders of hundreds.* 25:6 Hebrew *100 talents* [3,400 kilograms]. 25:17a Hebrew *Joash,* a variant spelling of Jehoash; also in 25:18, 21, 23, 25. 25:17b Hebrew *Come, let us look one another in the face.*

20 But Amaziah refused to listen, for God was determined to destroy him
for turning to the gods of Edom. 21 So King Jehoash of Israel mobilized his
army against King Amaziah of Judah. The two armies drew up their battle
lines at Beth-shemesh in Judah. 22 Judah was routed by the army of Israel, and
its army scattered and fled for home. 23 King Jehoash of Israel captured Ju-
dah's king, Amaziah son of Joash and grandson of Ahaziah, at Beth-shemesh.
Then he brought him to Jerusalem, where he demolished 600 feet* of Jeru-
salem's wall, from the Ephraim Gate to the Corner Gate. 24 He carried off all
the gold and silver and all the articles from the Temple of God that had been
in the care of Obed-edom. He also seized the treasures of the royal palace,
along with hostages, and then returned to Samaria.

25 King Amaziah of Judah lived for fifteen years after the death of King Je-
hoash of Israel. 26 The rest of the events in Amaziah's reign, from beginning
to end, are recorded in *The Book of the Kings of Judah and Israel.*

27 After Amaziah turned away from the LORD, there was a conspiracy
against his life in Jerusalem, and he fled to Lachish. But his enemies sent
assassins after him, and they killed him there. 28 They brought his body back
on a horse, and he was buried with his ancestors in the City of David.*

Uzziah Rules in Judah

26 All the people of Judah had crowned Amaziah's sixteen-year-old
son, Uzziah, as king in place of his father. 2 After his father's death,
Uzziah rebuilt the town of Elath* and restored it to Judah.

3 Uzziah was sixteen years old when he became king, and he reigned in
Jerusalem fifty-two years. His mother was Jecoliah from Jerusalem. 4 He did
what was pleasing in the LORD's sight, just as his father, Amaziah, had done.
5 Uzziah sought God during the days of Zechariah, who taught him to fear
God.* And as long as the king sought guidance from the LORD, God gave
him success.

6 Uzziah declared war on the Philistines and broke down the walls of Gath,
Jabneh, and Ashdod. Then he built new towns in the Ashdod area and in
other parts of Philistia. 7 God helped him in his wars against the Philistines,
his battles with the Arabs of Gur,* and his wars with the Meunites. 8 The Me-
unites* paid annual tribute to him, and his fame spread even to Egypt, for
he had become very powerful.

9 Uzziah built fortified towers in Jerusalem at the Corner Gate, at the
Valley Gate, and at the angle in the wall. 10 He also constructed forts in the
wilderness and dug many water cisterns, because he kept great herds of live-
stock in the foothills of Judah* and on the plains. He was also a man who
loved the soil. He had many workers who cared for his farms and vineyards,
both on the hillsides and in the fertile valleys.

11 Uzziah had an army of well-trained warriors, ready to march into battle,
unit by unit. This army had been mustered and organized by Jeiel, the sec-
retary of the army, and his assistant, Maaseiah. They were under the direc-
tion of Hananiah, one of the king's officials. 12 These regiments of mighty
warriors were commanded by 2,600 clan leaders. 13 The army consisted of

Prayer 26:4

Lord, help me listen to the wise and faithful advice of the pastors and mentors that you've put in my life. Amen.

25:23 Hebrew *400 cubits* [180 meters]. **25:28** As in some Hebrew manuscripts and other ancient versions (see also 2 Kgs 14:20); most Hebrew manuscripts read *the city of Judah.* **26:2** As in Greek version (see also 2 Kgs 14:22; 16:6); Hebrew reads *Eloth,* a variant spelling of Elath. **26:5** As in Syriac and Greek versions; Hebrew reads *who instructed him in divine visions.* **26:7** As in Greek version; Hebrew reads *Gur-baal.* **26:8** As in Greek version; Hebrew reads *Ammonites.* Compare 26:7. **26:10** Hebrew *the Shephelah.*

307,500 men, all elite troops. They were prepared to assist the king against
any enemy.
14 Uzziah provided the entire army with shields, spears, helmets, coats of
mail, bows, and sling stones. 15 And he built structures on the walls of Jerusa-
lem, designed by experts to protect those who shot arrows and hurled large
stones* from the towers and the corners of the wall. His fame spread far and
wide, for the LORD gave him marvelous help, and he became very powerful.

Uzziah's Sin and Punishment

16 But when he had become powerful, he also became proud, which led to his
downfall. He sinned against the LORD his God by entering the sanctuary of
the LORD's Temple and personally burning incense on the incense altar. 17 Az-
ariah the high priest went in after him with eighty other priests of the LORD,
all brave men. 18 They confronted King Uzziah and said, "It is not for you,
Uzziah, to burn incense to the LORD. That is the work of the priests alone,
the descendants of Aaron who are set apart for this work. Get out of the
sanctuary, for you have sinned. The LORD God will not honor you for this!"
19 Uzziah, who was holding an incense burner, became furious. But as
he was standing there raging at the priests before the incense altar in the
LORD's Temple, leprosy* suddenly broke out on his forehead. 20 When Az-
ariah the high priest and all the other priests saw the leprosy, they rushed
him out. And the king himself was eager to get out because the LORD had
struck him. 21 So King Uzziah had leprosy until the day he died. He lived in
isolation in a separate house, for he was excluded from the Temple of the
LORD. His son Jotham was put in charge of the royal palace, and he governed
the people of the land.
22 The rest of the events of Uzziah's reign, from beginning to end, are
recorded by the prophet Isaiah son of Amoz. 23 When Uzziah died, he was
buried with his ancestors; his grave was in a nearby burial field belonging to
the kings, for the people said, "He had leprosy." And his son Jotham became
the next king.

Jotham Rules in Judah

27 Jotham was twenty-five years old when he became king, and he
reigned in Jerusalem sixteen years. His mother was Jerusha, the
daughter of Zadok.
2 Jotham did what was pleasing in the LORD's sight. He did everything
his father, Uzziah, had done, except that Jotham did not sin by entering
the Temple of the LORD. But the people continued in their corrupt ways.
3 Jotham rebuilt the upper gate of the Temple of the LORD. He also did
extensive rebuilding on the wall at the hill of Ophel. 4 He built towns in the
hill country of Judah and constructed fortresses and towers in the wooded
areas. 5 Jotham went to war against the Ammonites and conquered them.
Over the next three years he received from them an annual tribute of 7,500
pounds* of silver, 50,000 bushels of wheat, and 50,000 bushels of barley.*
6 King Jotham became powerful because he was careful to live in obedience
to the LORD his God.

26:15 Or *to shoot arrows and hurl large stones.* **26:19** Or *a contagious skin disease.* The Hebrew word used here and throughout this passage can describe various skin diseases. **27:5a** Hebrew *100 talents* [3,400 kilograms]. **27:5b** Hebrew *10,000 cors* [2,200 kiloliters] *of wheat, and 10,000 cors of barley.*

7 The rest of the events of Jotham's reign, including all his wars and other
activities, are recorded in *The Book of the Kings of Israel and Judah.* 8 He was
twenty-five years old when he became king, and he reigned in Jerusalem
sixteen years. 9 When Jotham died, he was buried in the City of David. And
his son Ahaz became the next king.

Ahaz Rules in Judah

28 Ahaz was twenty years old when he became king, and he reigned
in Jerusalem sixteen years. He did not do what was pleasing in the
sight of the LORD, as his ancestor David had done. 2 Instead, he followed
the example of the kings of Israel. He cast metal images for the worship of
Baal. 3 He offered sacrifices in the valley of Ben-Hinnom, even sacrificing his
own sons in the fire.* In this way, he followed the detestable practices of the
pagan nations the LORD had driven from the land ahead of the Israelites.
4 He offered sacrifices and burned incense at the pagan shrines and on the
hills and under every green tree.

5 Because of all this, the LORD his God allowed the king of Aram to defeat
Ahaz and to exile large numbers of his people to Damascus. The armies of the
king of Israel also defeated Ahaz and inflicted many casualties on his army.
6 In a single day Pekah son of Remaliah, Israel's king, killed 120,000 of Ju-
dah's troops, all of them experienced warriors, because they had abandoned
the LORD, the God of their ancestors. 7 Then Zicri, a warrior from Ephraim,
killed Maaseiah, the king's son; Azrikam, the king's palace commander; and
Elkanah, the king's second-in-command. 8 The armies of Israel captured
200,000 women and children from Judah and seized tremendous amounts
of plunder, which they took back to Samaria.

9 But a prophet of the LORD named Oded was there in Samaria when the
army of Israel returned home. He went out to meet them and said, "The
LORD, the God of your ancestors, was angry with Judah and let you defeat
them. But you have gone too far, killing them without mercy, and all heaven
is disturbed. 10 And now you are planning to make slaves of these people
from Judah and Jerusalem. What about your own sins against the LORD your
God? 11 Listen to me and return these prisoners you have taken, for they are
your own relatives. Watch out, because now the LORD's fierce anger has been
turned against you!"

12 Then some of the leaders of Israel*—Azariah son of Jehohanan, Ber-
ekiah son of Meshillemoth, Jehizkiah son of Shallum, and Amasa son of
Hadlai—agreed with this and confronted the men returning from battle.
13 "You must not bring the prisoners here!" they declared. "We cannot afford
to add to our sins and guilt. Our guilt is already great, and the LORD's fierce
anger is already turned against Israel."

14 So the warriors released the prisoners and handed over the plunder in
the sight of the leaders and all the people. 15 Then the four men just men-
tioned by name came forward and distributed clothes from the plunder to
the prisoners who were naked. They provided clothing and sandals to wear,
gave them enough food and drink, and dressed their wounds with olive
oil. They put those who were weak on donkeys and took all the prisoners
back to their own people in Jericho, the city of palms. Then they returned
to Samaria.

28:3 Or *even making his sons pass through the fire.* **28:12** Hebrew *Ephraim,* referring to the northern kingdom of Israel.

Question 28:9

Look through these chapters about compromised kings. What recurring themes do you notice in their behaviors? What message did the Lord continually put before them (like he did here through his prophet Oded)? If you were to filter your own life through these two questions, what would God have to say to you?

Ahaz Closes the Temple

16 At that time King Ahaz of Judah asked the king of Assyria for help. 17 The
armies of Edom had again invaded Judah and taken captives. 18 And the Phi-
listines had raided towns located in the foothills of Judah* and in the Negev
of Judah. They had already captured and occupied Beth-shemesh, Aijalon,
Gederoth, Soco with its villages, Timnah with its villages, and Gimzo with
its villages. 19 The LORD was humbling Judah because of King Ahaz of Judah,*
for he had encouraged his people to sin and had been utterly unfaithful to
the LORD.
20 So when King Tiglath-pileser* of Assyria arrived, he attacked Ahaz in-
stead of helping him. 21 Ahaz took valuable items from the LORD's Temple,
the royal palace, and from the homes of his officials and gave them to the
king of Assyria as tribute. But this did not help him.
22 Even during this time of trouble, King Ahaz continued to reject the
LORD. 23 He offered sacrifices to the gods of Damascus who had defeated
him, for he said, "Since these gods helped the kings of Aram, they will help
me, too, if I sacrifice to them." But instead, they led to his ruin and the ruin
of all Judah.
24 The king took the various articles from the Temple of God and broke
them into pieces. He shut the doors of the LORD's Temple so that no one
could worship there, and he set up altars to pagan gods in every corner of
Jerusalem. 25 He made pagan shrines in all the towns of Judah for offering
sacrifices to other gods. In this way, he aroused the anger of the LORD, the
God of his ancestors.
26 The rest of the events of Ahaz's reign and everything he did, from begin-
ning to end, are recorded in *The Book of the Kings of Judah and Israel.* 27 When
Ahaz died, he was buried in Jerusalem but not in the royal cemetery of the
kings of Judah. Then his son Hezekiah became the next king.

Hezekiah Rules in Judah

29 Hezekiah was twenty-five years old when he became the king of
Judah, and he reigned in Jerusalem twenty-nine years. His mother
was Abijah, the daughter of Zechariah. 2 He did what was pleasing in the
LORD's sight, just as his ancestor David had done.

Hezekiah Reopens the Temple

3 In the very first month of the first year of his reign, Hezekiah reopened
the doors of the Temple of the LORD and repaired them. 4 He summoned
the priests and Levites to meet him at the courtyard east of the Temple. 5 He
said to them, "Listen to me, you Levites! Purify yourselves, and purify the
Temple of the LORD, the God of your ancestors. Remove all the defiled things
from the sanctuary. 6 Our ancestors were unfaithful and did what was evil
in the sight of the LORD our God. They abandoned the LORD and his dwell-
ing place; they turned their backs on him. 7 They also shut the doors to the
Temple's entry room, and they snuffed out the lamps. They stopped burning
incense and presenting burnt offerings at the sanctuary of the God of Israel.
8 "That is why the LORD's anger has fallen upon Judah and Jerusalem. He

Story Arc **29:3**

Hezekiah

The new king of Judah, Hezekiah, started his kingdom right. The first thing Hezekiah did was purify the temple. He rededicated the nation and its practices to the Lord (29:10, 30). He observed the Passover (30:2) to restart the country, just as Moses and Joshua had done. It is noteworthy that during this time, "God's hand was on the people," and he gave them "one heart to obey the orders of the king and his officials" (30:12).

Sometimes, we need to restart the direction of our lives by going back to those things that helped us become right with God in the first place. What practices of faith do you need to go back to in order to revive your commitment to God?

2 Chr 32:20 ►

28:18 Hebrew *the Shephelah.* 28:19 Masoretic Text reads *of Israel;* also in 28:23, 27. The author of Chronicles sees Judah as representative of the true Israel. (Some Hebrew manuscripts and Greek version read *of Judah.*) 28:20 Hebrew *Tilgath-pilneser,* a variant spelling of Tiglath-pileser.

has made them an object of dread, horror, and ridicule, as you can see with
your own eyes. 9 Because of this, our fathers have been killed in battle, and
our sons and daughters and wives have been captured. 10 But now I will make
a covenant with the LORD, the God of Israel, so that his fierce anger will turn
away from us. 11 My sons, do not neglect your duties any longer! The LORD
has chosen you to stand in his presence, to minister to him, and to lead the
people in worship and present offerings to him."
12 Then these Levites got right to work:

From the clan of Kohath: Mahath son of Amasai and Joel son of Azariah.
From the clan of Merari: Kish son of Abdi and Azariah son of Jehallelel.
From the clan of Gershon: Joah son of Zimmah and Eden son of Joah.
13 From the family of Elizaphan: Shimri and Jeiel.
From the family of Asaph: Zechariah and Mattaniah.
14 From the family of Heman: Jehiel and Shimei.
From the family of Jeduthun: Shemaiah and Uzziel.

15 These men called together their fellow Levites, and they all purified
themselves. Then they began to cleanse the Temple of the LORD, just as the
king had commanded. They were careful to follow all the LORD's instruc-
tions in their work. 16 The priests went into the sanctuary of the Temple of
the LORD to cleanse it, and they took out to the Temple courtyard all the
defiled things they found. From there the Levites carted it all out to the
Kidron Valley.
17 They began the work in early spring, on the first day of the new year,*
and in eight days they had reached the entry room of the LORD's Temple.
Then they purified the Temple of the LORD itself, which took another eight
days. So the entire task was completed in sixteen days.

The Temple Rededication

18 Then the Levites went to King Hezekiah and gave him this report: "We
have cleansed the entire Temple of the LORD, the altar of burnt offering with
all its utensils, and the table of the Bread of the Presence with all its utensils.
19 We have also recovered all the items discarded by King Ahaz when he was
unfaithful and closed the Temple. They are now in front of the altar of the
LORD, purified and ready for use."
20 Early the next morning King Hezekiah gathered the city officials and
went to the Temple of the LORD. 21 They brought seven bulls, seven rams,
and seven male lambs as a burnt offering, together with seven male goats
as a sin offering for the kingdom, for the Temple, and for Judah. The king
commanded the priests, who were descendants of Aaron, to sacrifice the
animals on the altar of the LORD.
22 So they killed the bulls, and the priests took the blood and sprinkled
it on the altar. Next they killed the rams and sprinkled their blood on the
altar. And finally, they did the same with the male lambs. 23 The male goats
for the sin offering were then brought before the king and the assembly of
people, who laid their hands on them. 24 The priests then killed the goats as
a sin offering and sprinkled their blood on the altar to make atonement for

29:17 Hebrew *on the first day of the first month.* This day in the ancient Hebrew lunar calendar occurred in March or early April, 715 B.C.

the sins of all Israel. The king had specifically commanded that this burnt
offering and sin offering should be made for all Israel.
[25]King Hezekiah then stationed the Levites at the Temple of the LORD
with cymbals, lyres, and harps. He obeyed all the commands that the LORD
had given to King David through Gad, the king's seer, and the prophet Na-
than. [26]The Levites then took their positions around the Temple with the
instruments of David, and the priests took their positions with the trumpets.
[27]Then Hezekiah ordered that the burnt offering be placed on the altar. As
the burnt offering was presented, songs of praise to the LORD were begun,
accompanied by the trumpets and other instruments of David, the former
king of Israel. [28]The entire assembly worshiped the LORD as the singers sang
and the trumpets blew, until all the burnt offerings were finished. [29]Then the
king and everyone with him bowed down in worship. [30]King Hezekiah and
the officials ordered the Levites to praise the LORD with the psalms written
by David and by Asaph the seer. So they offered joyous praise and bowed
down in worship.
[31]Then Hezekiah declared, "Now that you have consecrated yourselves to
the LORD, bring your sacrifices and thanksgiving offerings to the Temple of
the LORD." So the people brought their sacrifices and thanksgiving offerings,
and all whose hearts were willing brought burnt offerings, too. [32]The people
brought to the LORD 70 bulls, 100 rams, and 200 male lambs for burnt of-
ferings. [33]They also brought 600 cattle and 3,000 sheep and goats as sacred
offerings.
[34]But there were too few priests to prepare all the burnt offerings. So their
relatives the Levites helped them until the work was finished and more
priests had been purified, for the Levites had been more conscientious about
purifying themselves than the priests had been. [35]There was an abundance
of burnt offerings, along with the usual liquid offerings, and a great deal of
fat from the many peace offerings.
So the Temple of the LORD was restored to service. [36]And Hezekiah and
all the people rejoiced because of what God had done for the people, for
everything had been accomplished so quickly.

Preparations for Passover

30 King Hezekiah now sent word to all Israel and Judah, and he wrote
letters of invitation to the people of Ephraim and Manasseh. He
asked everyone to come to the Temple of the LORD at Jerusalem to celebrate
the Passover of the LORD, the God of Israel. [2]The king, his officials, and all
the community of Jerusalem decided to celebrate Passover a month later
than usual.* [3]They were unable to celebrate it at the prescribed time because
not enough priests could be purified by then, and the people had not yet
assembled at Jerusalem.
[4]This plan for keeping the Passover seemed right to the king and all the
people. [5]So they sent a proclamation throughout all Israel, from Beersheba
in the south to Dan in the north, inviting everyone to come to Jerusalem to
celebrate the Passover of the LORD, the God of Israel. The people had not
been celebrating it in great numbers as required in the Law.
[6]At the king's command, runners were sent throughout Israel and Judah.
They carried letters that said:

30:2 Hebrew *in the second month.* Passover was normally observed in the first month (of the ancient Hebrew lunar calendar).

"O people of Israel, return to the LORD, the God of Abraham, Isaac,
and Israel,* so that he will return to the few of us who have survived
the conquest of the Assyrian kings. 7 Do not be like your ancestors and
relatives who abandoned the LORD, the God of their ancestors, and
became an object of derision, as you yourselves can see. 8 Do not be
stubborn, as they were, but submit yourselves to the LORD. Come to his
Temple, which he has set apart as holy forever. Worship the LORD your
God so that his fierce anger will turn away from you.
9 "For if you return to the LORD, your relatives and your children will
be treated mercifully by their captors, and they will be able to return to
this land. For the LORD your God is gracious and merciful. If you return
to him, he will not continue to turn his face from you."

Celebration of Passover

10 The runners went from town to town throughout Ephraim and Manasseh
and as far as the territory of Zebulun. But most of the people just laughed
at the runners and made fun of them. 11 However, some people from Asher,
Manasseh, and Zebulun humbled themselves and went to Jerusalem.
12 At the same time, God's hand was on the people in the land of Judah,
giving them all one heart to obey the orders of the king and his officials, who
were following the word of the LORD. 13 So a huge crowd assembled at Jeru-
salem in midspring* to celebrate the Festival of Unleavened Bread. 14 They
set to work and removed the pagan altars from Jerusalem. They took away
all the incense altars and threw them into the Kidron Valley.
15 On the fourteenth day of the second month, one month later than usual,*
the people slaughtered the Passover lamb. This shamed the priests and Le-
vites, so they purified themselves and brought burnt offerings to the Temple
of the LORD. 16 Then they took their places at the Temple as prescribed in the
Law of Moses, the man of God. The Levites brought the sacrificial blood to
the priests, who then sprinkled it on the altar.
17 Since many of the people had not purified themselves, the Levites had
to slaughter their Passover lamb for them, to set them apart for the LORD.
18 Most of those who came from Ephraim, Manasseh, Issachar, and Zebulun
had not purified themselves. But King Hezekiah prayed for them, and they
were allowed to eat the Passover meal anyway, even though this was contrary
to the requirements of the Law. For Hezekiah said, "May the LORD, who is
good, pardon those 19 who decide to follow the LORD, the God of their ances-
tors, even though they are not properly cleansed for the ceremony." 20 And
the LORD listened to Hezekiah's prayer and healed the people.
21 So the people of Israel who were present in Jerusalem joyously cele-
brated the Festival of Unleavened Bread for seven days. Each day the Levites
and priests sang to the LORD, accompanied by loud instruments.* 22 Heze-
kiah encouraged all the Levites regarding the skill they displayed as they
served the LORD. The celebration continued for seven days. Peace offerings
were sacrificed, and the people gave thanks to the LORD, the God of their
ancestors.
23 The entire assembly then decided to continue the festival another seven

30:6 *Israel* is the name that God gave to Jacob. **30:13** Hebrew *in the second month.* The second month of the ancient Hebrew lunar calendar usually occurs within the months of April and May. **30:15** Hebrew *On the fourteenth day of the second month.* Passover normally began on the fourteenth day of the first month (see Lev 23:5). **30:21** Or *sang to the LORD with all their strength.*

Make a Difference

30:4-11

Runners

Hezekiah's celebration of Passover and of the work of God meant that he needed people to run from town to town to proclaim the good news and call people back to God (v. 6). Sadly, most people in most towns just made fun of them and thought the runners were foolish.

However, a few heard what the runners had to say and were changed by their message. These people decided to go to Jerusalem to see for themselves all that God was doing (v. 11).

Difference Maker

Are you willing to be a runner for God, even if people think you (and the life-changing message you carry) are foolish? If you were to share God's good news, what would you say?

Prayer **30:26**

Lord, let my heart come alive with joy before you today. Amen.

days, so they celebrated joyfully for another week. 24 King Hezekiah gave the
people 1,000 bulls and 7,000 sheep and goats for offerings, and the officials
donated 1,000 bulls and 10,000 sheep and goats. Meanwhile, many more
priests purified themselves.
25 The entire assembly of Judah rejoiced, including the priests, the Levites,
all who came from the land of Israel, the foreigners who came to the festival,
and all those who lived in Judah. 26 There was great joy in the city, for Jerusa-
lem had not seen a celebration like this one since the days of Solomon, King
David's son. 27 Then the priests and Levites stood and blessed the people, and
God heard their prayer from his holy dwelling in heaven.

Hezekiah's Religious Reforms

31 When the festival ended, the Israelites who attended went to all
the towns of Judah, Benjamin, Ephraim, and Manasseh, and they
smashed all the sacred pillars, cut down the Asherah poles, and removed
the pagan shrines and altars. After this, the Israelites returned to their own
towns and homes.
2 Hezekiah then organized the priests and Levites into divisions to offer
the burnt offerings and peace offerings, and to worship and give thanks
and praise to the LORD at the gates of the Temple. 3 The king also made a
personal contribution of animals for the daily morning and evening burnt
offerings, the weekly Sabbath festivals, the monthly new moon festivals,
and the annual festivals as prescribed in the Law of the LORD. 4 In addition,
he required the people in Jerusalem to bring a portion of their goods to
the priests and Levites, so they could devote themselves fully to the Law
of the LORD.
5 When the people of Israel heard these requirements, they responded gen-
erously by bringing the first share of their grain, new wine, olive oil, honey,
and all the produce of their fields. They brought a large quantity—a tithe
of all they produced. 6 The people who had moved to Judah from Israel, and
the people of Judah themselves, brought in the tithes of their cattle, sheep,
and goats and a tithe of the things that had been dedicated to the LORD their
God, and they piled them up in great heaps. 7 They began piling them up in
late spring, and the heaps continued to grow until early autumn.* 8 When
Hezekiah and his officials came and saw these huge piles, they thanked the
LORD and his people Israel!
9 "Where did all this come from?" Hezekiah asked the priests and Levites.
10 And Azariah the high priest, from the family of Zadok, replied, "Since
the people began bringing their gifts to the LORD's Temple, we have had
enough to eat and plenty to spare. The LORD has blessed his people, and all
this is left over."
11 Hezekiah ordered that storerooms be prepared in the Temple of the
LORD. When this was done, 12 the people faithfully brought all the gifts,
tithes, and other items dedicated for use in the Temple. Conaniah the Le-
vite was put in charge, assisted by his brother Shimei. 13 The supervisors
under them were Jehiel, Azaziah, Nahath, Asahel, Jerimoth, Jozabad, Eliel,
Ismakiah, Mahath, and Benaiah. These appointments were made by King
Hezekiah and Azariah, the chief official in the Temple of God.

31:7 Hebrew *in the third month . . . until the seventh month.* The third month of the ancient Hebrew lunar calendar usually occurs within the months of May and June; the seventh month usually occurs within September and October.

[14]Kore son of Imnah the Levite, who was the gatekeeper at the East Gate,
was put in charge of distributing the voluntary offerings given to God, the
gifts, and the things that had been dedicated to the LORD. [15]His faithful as-
sistants were Eden, Miniamin, Jeshua, Shemaiah, Amariah, and Shecaniah.
They distributed the gifts among the families of priests in their towns by
their divisions, dividing the gifts fairly among old and young alike. [16]They
distributed the gifts to all males three years old or older, regardless of their
place in the genealogical records. The distribution went to all who would
come to the LORD's Temple to perform their daily duties according to their
divisions. [17]They distributed gifts to the priests who were listed by their
families in the genealogical records, and to the Levites twenty years old or
older who were listed according to their jobs and their divisions. [18]Food al-
lotments were also given to the families of all those listed in the genealogical
records, including their little babies, wives, sons, and daughters. For they
had all been faithful in purifying themselves.

[19]As for the priests, the descendants of Aaron, who were living in the open
villages around the towns, men were appointed by name to distribute por-
tions to every male among the priests and to all the Levites listed in the
genealogical records.

[20]In this way, King Hezekiah handled the distribution throughout all
Judah, doing what was pleasing and good in the sight of the LORD his God.
[21]In all that he did in the service of the Temple of God and in his efforts to
follow God's laws and commands, Hezekiah sought his God wholeheartedly.
As a result, he was very successful.

Question 31:18–21

One of the ways Hezekiah revived the nation was to revive the livelihood of the people. Here he reformed the distribution of food and daily supplies. What does this teach you about the type of ministry that is pleasing to the Lord?

Assyria Invades Judah

32 After Hezekiah had faithfully carried out this work, King Sennach-
erib of Assyria invaded Judah. He laid siege to the fortified towns,
giving orders for his army to break through their walls. [2]When Hezekiah
realized that Sennacherib also intended to attack Jerusalem, [3]he consulted
with his officials and military advisers, and they decided to stop the flow of
the springs outside the city. [4]They organized a huge work crew to stop the
flow of the springs, cutting off the brook that ran through the fields. For they
said, "Why should the kings of Assyria come here and find plenty of water?"

[5]Then Hezekiah worked hard at repairing all the broken sections of the
wall, erecting towers, and constructing a second wall outside the first. He
also reinforced the supporting terraces* in the City of David and manufac-
tured large numbers of weapons and shields. [6]He appointed military officers
over the people and assembled them before him in the square at the city gate.
Then Hezekiah encouraged them by saying: [7]"Be strong and courageous!
Don't be afraid or discouraged because of the king of Assyria or his mighty
army, for there is a power far greater on our side! [8]He may have a great army,
but they are merely men. We have the LORD our God to help us and to fight
our battles for us!" Hezekiah's words greatly encouraged the people.

Sennacherib Threatens Jerusalem

[9]While King Sennacherib of Assyria was still besieging the town of Lachish,
he sent his officers to Jerusalem with this message for Hezekiah and all the
people in the city:

32:5 Hebrew *the millo.* The meaning of the Hebrew is uncertain.

10"This is what King Sennacherib of Assyria says: What are you trusting
in that makes you think you can survive my siege of Jerusalem?
11Hezekiah has said, 'The LORD our God will rescue us from the king of
Assyria.' Surely Hezekiah is misleading you, sentencing you to death by
famine and thirst! 12Don't you realize that Hezekiah is the very person
who destroyed all the LORD's shrines and altars? He commanded Judah
and Jerusalem to worship only at the altar at the Temple and to offer
sacrifices on it alone.
13"Surely you must realize what I and the other kings of Assyria
before me have done to all the people of the earth! Were any of the gods
of those nations able to rescue their people from my power? 14Which of
their gods was able to rescue its people from the destructive power of
my predecessors? What makes you think your God can rescue you from
me? 15Don't let Hezekiah deceive you! Don't let him fool you like this!
I say it again—no god of any nation or kingdom has ever yet been able
to rescue his people from me or my ancestors. How much less will your
God rescue you from my power!"

16And Sennacherib's officers further mocked the LORD God and his ser-
vant Hezekiah, heaping insult upon insult. 17The king also sent letters scorn-
ing the LORD, the God of Israel. He wrote, "Just as the gods of all the other
nations failed to rescue their people from my power, so the God of Hezekiah
will also fail." 18The Assyrian officials who brought the letters shouted this
in Hebrew* to the people gathered on the walls of the city, trying to terrify
them so it would be easier to capture the city. 19These officers talked about
the God of Jerusalem as though he were one of the pagan gods, made by
human hands.
20Then King Hezekiah and the prophet Isaiah son of Amoz cried out in
prayer to God in heaven. 21And the LORD sent an angel who destroyed the
Assyrian army with all its commanders and officers. So Sennacherib was
forced to return home in disgrace to his own land. And when he entered
the temple of his god, some of his own sons killed him there with a sword.
22That is how the LORD rescued Hezekiah and the people of Jerusalem
from King Sennacherib of Assyria and from all the others who threatened
them. So there was peace throughout the land. 23From then on King Hez-
ekiah became highly respected among all the surrounding nations, and
many gifts for the LORD arrived at Jerusalem, with valuable presents for
King Hezekiah, too.

Hezekiah's Sickness and Recovery

24About that time Hezekiah became deathly ill. He prayed to the LORD,
who healed him and gave him a miraculous sign. 25But Hezekiah did not
respond appropriately to the kindness shown him, and he became proud.
So the LORD's anger came against him and against Judah and Jerusalem.
26Then Hezekiah humbled himself and repented of his pride, as did the
people of Jerusalem. So the LORD's anger did not fall on them during Hez-
ekiah's lifetime.
27Hezekiah was very wealthy and highly honored. He built special trea-
sury buildings for his silver, gold, precious stones, and spices, and for his

Story Arc **32:20**

● Isaiah

Isaiah joined with Hezekiah to cry out to the Lord. God's people learned that day that, even in the face of seemingly superior enemies, the Lord is stronger. God's followers can be strong and courageous, knowing that the Lord will work out his plan for good. Isaiah's story throughout the historical books and in the book that bears his name gives testimony to the Lord's unrivaled power.

2 Chr 34:3 ►

32:18 Hebrew *in the dialect of Judah.*

shields and other valuable items. 28 He also constructed many storehouses for his grain, new wine, and olive oil; and he made many stalls for his cattle and pens for his flocks of sheep and goats. 29 He built many towns and acquired vast flocks and herds, for God had given him great wealth. 30 He blocked up the upper spring of Gihon and brought the water down through a tunnel to the west side of the City of David. And so he succeeded in everything he did.

31 However, when ambassadors arrived from Babylon to ask about the remarkable events that had taken place in the land, God withdrew from Hezekiah in order to test him and to see what was really in his heart.

Summary of Hezekiah's Reign

32 The rest of the events in Hezekiah's reign and his acts of devotion are recorded in *The Vision of the Prophet Isaiah Son of Amoz,* which is included in *The Book of the Kings of Judah and Israel.* 33 When Hezekiah died, he was buried in the upper area of the royal cemetery, and all Judah and Jerusalem honored him at his death. And his son Manasseh became the next king.

Manasseh Rules in Judah

33 Manasseh was twelve years old when he became king, and he reigned in Jerusalem fifty-five years. 2 He did what was evil in the LORD's sight, following the detestable practices of the pagan nations that the LORD had driven from the land ahead of the Israelites. 3 He rebuilt the pagan shrines his father, Hezekiah, had broken down. He constructed altars for the images of Baal and set up Asherah poles. He also bowed before all the powers of the heavens and worshiped them.

4 He built pagan altars in the Temple of the LORD, the place where the LORD had said, "My name will remain in Jerusalem forever." 5 He built these altars for all the powers of the heavens in both courtyards of the LORD's Temple. 6 Manasseh also sacrificed his own sons in the fire* in the valley of Ben-Hinnom. He practiced sorcery, divination, and witchcraft, and he consulted with mediums and psychics. He did much that was evil in the LORD's sight, arousing his anger.

7 Manasseh even took a carved idol he had made and set it up in God's Temple, the very place where God had told David and his son Solomon: "My name will be honored forever in this Temple and in Jerusalem—the city I have chosen from among all the tribes of Israel. 8 If the Israelites will be careful to obey my commands—all the laws, decrees, and regulations given through Moses—I will not send them into exile from this land that I set aside for your ancestors." 9 But Manasseh led the people of Judah and Jerusalem to do even more evil than the pagan nations that the LORD had destroyed when the people of Israel entered the land.

10 The LORD spoke to Manasseh and his people, but they ignored all his warnings. 11 So the LORD sent the commanders of the Assyrian armies, and they took Manasseh prisoner. They put a ring through his nose, bound him in bronze chains, and led him away to Babylon. 12 But while in deep distress, Manasseh sought the LORD his God and sincerely humbled himself before the God of his ancestors. 13 And when he prayed, the LORD listened to him and was moved by his request. So the LORD brought Manasseh back to Jerusalem and to his kingdom. Then Manasseh finally realized that the LORD alone is God!

33:6 Or *also made his sons pass through the fire.*

Prayer **33:13**

Lord, don't let it take the destruction of my life for me to realize that you alone are God. Amen.

14 After this Manasseh rebuilt the outer wall of the City of David, from
west of the Gihon Spring in the Kidron Valley to the Fish Gate, and continu-
ing around the hill of Ophel. He built the wall very high. And he stationed
his military officers in all of the fortified towns of Judah. 15 Manasseh also
removed the foreign gods and the idol from the LORD's Temple. He tore
down all the altars he had built on the hill where the Temple stood and all
the altars that were in Jerusalem, and he dumped them outside the city.
16 Then he restored the altar of the LORD and sacrificed peace offerings and
thanksgiving offerings on it. He also encouraged the people of Judah to
worship the LORD, the God of Israel. 17 However, the people still sacrificed
at the pagan shrines, though only to the LORD their God.

18 The rest of the events of Manasseh's reign, his prayer to God, and the
words the seers spoke to him in the name of the LORD, the God of Israel, are
recorded in *The Book of the Kings of Israel.* 19 Manasseh's prayer, the account of
the way God answered him, and an account of all his sins and unfaithfulness
are recorded in *The Record of the Seers.** It includes a list of the locations where
he built pagan shrines and set up Asherah poles and idols before he humbled
himself and repented. 20 When Manasseh died, he was buried in his palace.
Then his son Amon became the next king.

Amon Rules in Judah

21 Amon was twenty-two years old when he became king, and he reigned in
Jerusalem two years. 22 He did what was evil in the LORD's sight, just as his
father, Manasseh, had done. He worshiped and sacrificed to all the idols his
father had made. 23 But unlike his father, he did not humble himself before
the LORD. Instead, Amon sinned even more.

24 Then Amon's own officials conspired against him and assassinated him
in his palace. 25 But the people of the land killed all those who had conspired
against King Amon, and they made his son Josiah the next king.

Josiah Rules in Judah

34 Josiah was eight years old when he became king, and he reigned in
Jerusalem thirty-one years. 2 He did what was pleasing in the LORD's
sight and followed the example of his ancestor David. He did not turn away
from doing what was right.

3 During the eighth year of his reign, while he was still young, Josiah began
to seek the God of his ancestor David. Then in the twelfth year he began to
purify Judah and Jerusalem, destroying all the pagan shrines, the Asherah
poles, and the carved idols and cast images. 4 He ordered that the altars of
Baal be demolished and that the incense altars which stood above them be
broken down. He also made sure that the Asherah poles, the carved idols,
and the cast images were smashed and scattered over the graves of those who
had sacrificed to them. 5 He burned the bones of the pagan priests on their
own altars, and so he purified Judah and Jerusalem.

6 He did the same thing in the towns of Manasseh, Ephraim, and Simeon,
even as far as Naphtali, and in the regions* all around them. 7 He destroyed
the pagan altars and the Asherah poles, and he crushed the idols into dust.
He cut down all the incense altars throughout the land of Israel. Finally, he
returned to Jerusalem.

33:19 Or *The Record of Hozai.* 34:6 As in Syriac version; Hebrew reads *in their temples,* or *in their ruins.* The meaning of the Hebrew is uncertain.

Story Arc **34:3**

● Josiah

Josiah was eight years old when he became king. Throughout his thirty-one-year reign, he did what was pleasing to the Lord though what he did when he was sixteen years old is most important. While he was a teenager, he made the choice to "seek the God of his ancestor David." He made a personal decision to follow God. He owned his faith and committed the course of his life to the Lord.

You, too, can commit yourself to seeking the Lord. If you have not done so yet, take this opportunity to ask the Lord to come into your life. You can turn to the back of this Bible and pray through the section titled "How to Accept Jesus as Your Lord and Savior."

2 Chr 35:25 ►

[8]In the eighteenth year of his reign, after he had purified the land and the
Temple, Josiah appointed Shaphan son of Azaliah, Maaseiah the governor of
Jerusalem, and Joah son of Joahaz, the royal historian, to repair the Temple
of the LORD his God. [9]They gave Hilkiah the high priest the money that
had been collected by the Levites who served as gatekeepers at the Temple
of God. The gifts were brought by people from Manasseh, Ephraim, and
from all the remnant of Israel, as well as from all Judah, Benjamin, and the
people of Jerusalem.
[10]He entrusted the money to the men assigned to supervise the restora-
tion of the LORD's Temple. Then they paid the workers who did the repairs
and renovation of the Temple. [11]They hired carpenters and builders, who
purchased finished stone for the walls and timber for the rafters and beams.
They restored what earlier kings of Judah had allowed to fall into ruin.
[12]The workers served faithfully under the leadership of Jahath and Oba-
diah, Levites of the Merarite clan, and Zechariah and Meshullam, Levites of
the Kohathite clan. Other Levites, all of whom were skilled musicians, [13]were
put in charge of the laborers of the various trades. Still others assisted as
secretaries, officials, and gatekeepers.

Hilkiah Discovers God's Law

[14]While they were bringing out the money collected at the LORD's Temple,
Hilkiah the priest found the Book of the Law of the LORD that was written by
Moses. [15]Hilkiah said to Shaphan the court secretary, "I have found the Book
of the Law in the LORD's Temple!" Then Hilkiah gave the scroll to Shaphan.
[16]Shaphan took the scroll to the king and reported, "Your officials are
doing everything they were assigned to do. [17]The money that was collected
at the Temple of the LORD has been turned over to the supervisors and
workmen." [18]Shaphan also told the king, "Hilkiah the priest has given me a
scroll." So Shaphan read it to the king.
[19]When the king heard what was written in the Law, he tore his clothes
in despair. [20]Then he gave these orders to Hilkiah, Ahikam son of Shaphan,
Acbor son of Micaiah,* Shaphan the court secretary, and Asaiah the king's
personal adviser: [21]"Go to the Temple and speak to the LORD for me and for
all the remnant of Israel and Judah. Inquire about the words written in the
scroll that has been found. For the LORD's great anger has been poured out
on us because our ancestors have not obeyed the word of the LORD. We have
not been doing everything this scroll says we must do."
[22]So Hilkiah and the other men went to the New Quarter* of Jerusalem to
consult with the prophet Huldah. She was the wife of Shallum son of Tikvah,
son of Harhas,* the keeper of the Temple wardrobe.
[23]She said to them, "The LORD, the God of Israel, has spoken! Go back
and tell the man who sent you, [24]'This is what the LORD says: I am going to
bring disaster on this city* and its people. All the curses written in the scroll
that was read to the king of Judah will come true. [25]For my people have
abandoned me and offered sacrifices to pagan gods, and I am very angry
with them for everything they have done. My anger will be poured out on
this place, and it will not be quenched.'
[26]"But go to the king of Judah who sent you to seek the LORD and tell him:

34:20 As in parallel text at 2 Kgs 22:12; Hebrew reads *Abdon son of Micah.* **34:22a** Or *the Second Quarter,* a newer section of Jerusalem. Hebrew reads *the Mishneh.* **34:22b** As in parallel text at 2 Kgs 22:14; Hebrew reads *son of Tokhath, son of Hasrah.* **34:24** Hebrew *this place;* also in 34:27, 28.

Question 34:14

Do you know anyone who has strayed so far from God that they need to rediscover his Word? How could you pray for them or help them to remember the life that can be found in the Bible?

Question 34:29

Read Deuteronomy 17:19. This is exactly what a king is supposed to do. Why does true reform of our lives and communities need to start with the Word of God?

'This is what the LORD, the God of Israel, says concerning the message you have just heard: 27 You were sorry and humbled yourself before God when you heard his words against this city and its people. You humbled yourself and tore your clothing in despair and wept before me in repentance. And I have indeed heard you, says the LORD. 28 So I will not send the promised disaster until after you have died and been buried in peace. You yourself will not see the disaster I am going to bring on this city and its people.'"

So they took her message back to the king.

Josiah's Religious Reforms

29 Then the king summoned all the elders of Judah and Jerusalem. 30 And the king went up to the Temple of the LORD with all the people of Judah and Jerusalem, along with the priests and the Levites—all the people from the greatest to the least. There the king read to them the entire Book of the Covenant that had been found in the LORD's Temple. 31 The king took his place of authority beside the pillar and renewed the covenant in the LORD's presence. He pledged to obey the LORD by keeping all his commands, laws, and decrees with all his heart and soul. He promised to obey all the terms of the covenant that were written in the scroll. 32 And he required everyone in Jerusalem and the people of Benjamin to make a similar pledge. The people of Jerusalem did so, renewing their covenant with God, the God of their ancestors.

33 So Josiah removed all detestable idols from the entire land of Israel and required everyone to worship the LORD their God. And throughout the rest of his lifetime, they did not turn away from the LORD, the God of their ancestors.

Josiah Celebrates Passover

35 Then Josiah announced that the Passover of the LORD would be celebrated in Jerusalem, and so the Passover lamb was slaughtered on the fourteenth day of the first month.* 2 Josiah also assigned the priests to their duties and encouraged them in their work at the Temple of the LORD. 3 He issued this order to the Levites, who were to teach all Israel and who had been set apart to serve the LORD: "Put the holy Ark in the Temple that was built by Solomon son of David, the king of Israel. You no longer need to carry it back and forth on your shoulders. Now spend your time serving the LORD your God and his people Israel. 4 Report for duty according to the family divisions of your ancestors, following the directions of King David of Israel and the directions of his son Solomon.

5 "Then stand in the sanctuary at the place appointed for your family division and help the families assigned to you as they bring their offerings to the Temple. 6 Slaughter the Passover lambs, purify yourselves, and prepare to help those who come. Follow all the directions that the LORD gave through Moses."

7 Then Josiah provided 30,000 lambs and young goats for the people's Passover offerings, along with 3,000 cattle, all from the king's own flocks and herds. 8 The king's officials also made willing contributions to the people, priests, and Levites. Hilkiah, Zechariah, and Jehiel, the administrators of God's Temple, gave the priests 2,600 lambs and young goats and 300 cattle as Passover offerings. 9 The Levite leaders—Conaniah and his brothers

35:1 This day in the ancient Hebrew lunar calendar was April 5, 622 B.C.

Shemaiah and Nethanel, as well as Hashabiah, Jeiel, and Jozabad—gave
5,000 lambs and young goats and 500 cattle to the Levites for their Passover
offerings.
10 When everything was ready for the Passover celebration, the priests and
the Levites took their places, organized by their divisions, as the king had
commanded. 11 The Levites then slaughtered the Passover lambs and pre-
sented the blood to the priests, who sprinkled the blood on the altar while
the Levites prepared the animals. 12 They divided the burnt offerings among
the people by their family groups, so they could offer them to the LORD as
prescribed in the Book of Moses. They did the same with the cattle. 13 Then
they roasted the Passover lambs as prescribed; and they boiled the holy offer-
ings in pots, kettles, and pans, and brought them out quickly so the people
could eat them.
14 Afterward the Levites prepared Passover offerings for themselves and for
the priests—the descendants of Aaron—because the priests had been busy
from morning till night offering the burnt offerings and the fat portions.
The Levites took responsibility for all these preparations.
15 The musicians, descendants of Asaph, were in their assigned places, fol-
lowing the commands that had been given by David, Asaph, Heman, and
Jeduthun, the king's seer. The gatekeepers guarded the gates and did not
need to leave their posts of duty, for their Passover offerings were prepared
for them by their fellow Levites.
16 The entire ceremony for the LORD's Passover was completed that day.
All the burnt offerings were sacrificed on the altar of the LORD, as King Jo-
siah had commanded. 17 All the Israelites present in Jerusalem celebrated
Passover and the Festival of Unleavened Bread for seven days. 18 Never since
the time of the prophet Samuel had there been such a Passover. None of the
kings of Israel had ever kept a Passover as Josiah did, involving all the priests
and Levites, all the people of Jerusalem, and people from all over Judah and
Israel. 19 This Passover was celebrated in the eighteenth year of Josiah's reign.

Josiah Dies in Battle

20 After Josiah had finished restoring the Temple, King Neco of Egypt led
his army up from Egypt to do battle at Carchemish on the Euphrates River,
and Josiah and his army marched out to fight him.* 21 But King Neco sent
messengers to Josiah with this message:

> "What do you want with me, king of Judah? I have no quarrel with you today! I am on my way to fight another nation, and God has told me to hurry! Do not interfere with God, who is with me, or he will destroy you."

22 But Josiah refused to listen to Neco, to whom God had indeed spoken,
and he would not turn back. Instead, he disguised himself and led his army
into battle on the plain of Megiddo. 23 But the enemy archers hit King Josiah
with their arrows and wounded him. He cried out to his men, "Take me from
the battle, for I am badly wounded!"
24 So they lifted Josiah out of his chariot and placed him in another chariot.
Then they brought him back to Jerusalem, where he died. He was buried

35:20 Or *Josiah went out to meet him.*

Make a Difference

35:1-19

Passover

The celebration of Passover once again played a central role in God's people getting right with the Lord. Passover started on the night that the Lord provided a sacrifice to rescue his people (Exodus 12), and it played the central role in the death of Christ, whose sacrifice rescued all people though the forgiveness of sin.

Difference Maker

Explore the connections between the celebration of Passover (see Exodus 12) and the significance of Jesus' work on the cross during Passover (see John 1:29; Luke 22-23; Hebrews 10).

there in the royal cemetery. And all Judah and Jerusalem mourned for him.
25 The prophet Jeremiah composed funeral songs for Josiah, and to this day
choirs still sing these sad songs about his death. These songs of sorrow have
become a tradition and are recorded in *The Book of Laments.*
26 The rest of the events of Josiah's reign and his acts of devotion (carried
out according to what was written in the Law of the LORD), 27 from beginning
to end—all are recorded in *The Book of the Kings of Israel and Judah.*

Jehoahaz Rules in Judah

36 Then the people of the land took Josiah's son Jehoahaz and made
him the next king in Jerusalem.
2 Jehoahaz* was twenty-three years old when he became king, and he
reigned in Jerusalem three months.
3 Then he was deposed by the king of Egypt, who demanded that Judah
pay 7,500 pounds of silver and 75 pounds of gold* as tribute.

Jehoiakim Rules in Judah

4 The king of Egypt then installed Eliakim, the brother of Jehoahaz, as the
next king of Judah and Jerusalem, and he changed Eliakim's name to Jehoi-
akim. Then Neco took Jehoahaz to Egypt as a prisoner.
5 Jehoiakim was twenty-five years old when he became king, and he
reigned in Jerusalem eleven years. He did what was evil in the sight of the
LORD his God.
6 Then King Nebuchadnezzar of Babylon came to Jerusalem and captured
it, and he bound Jehoiakim in bronze chains and led him away to Babylon.
7 Nebuchadnezzar also took some of the treasures from the Temple of the
LORD, and he placed them in his palace* in Babylon.
8 The rest of the events in Jehoiakim's reign, including all the evil things
he did and everything found against him, are recorded in *The Book of the Kings
of Israel and Judah.* Then his son Jehoiachin became the next king.

Jehoiachin Rules in Judah

9 Jehoiachin was eighteen* years old when he became king, and he reigned
in Jerusalem three months and ten days. Jehoiachin did what was evil in
the LORD's sight.
10 In the spring of the year* King Nebuchadnezzar took Jehoiachin to
Babylon. Many treasures from the Temple of the LORD were also taken to
Babylon at that time. And Nebuchadnezzar installed Jehoiachin's uncle,*
Zedekiah, as the next king in Judah and Jerusalem.

Zedekiah Rules in Judah

11 Zedekiah was twenty-one years old when he became king, and he reigned
in Jerusalem eleven years. 12 But Zedekiah did what was evil in the sight of the
LORD his God, and he refused to humble himself when the prophet Jeremiah
spoke to him directly from the LORD. 13 He also rebelled against King Neb-
uchadnezzar, even though he had taken an oath of loyalty in God's name.

36:2 Hebrew *Joahaz,* a variant spelling of Jehoahaz; also in 36:4. 36:3 Hebrew *100 talents* [3,400 kilograms] *of silver and 1 talent* [34 kilograms] *of gold.* 36:7 Or *temple.* 36:9 As in one Hebrew manuscript, some Greek manuscripts, and Syriac version (see also 2 Kgs 24:8); most Hebrew manuscripts read *eight.* 36:10a Hebrew *At the turn of the year.* The first day of this year in the ancient Hebrew lunar calendar was April 13, 597 B.C. 36:10b As in parallel text at 2 Kgs 24:17; Hebrew reads *brother,* or *relative.*

Story Arc **35:25**

Jeremiah

An important and often overlooked aspect of worship is lament—a cry of sorrow or anguish. Here, the influential prophet Jeremiah composed funeral songs for King Josiah. It was appropriate that he would be the one to write these, for Jeremiah was known as the Weeping Prophet. The book of the Bible that bears his name is threaded with themes of lament and sadness. The biblical book of Lamentations (not the collection of funeral songs mentioned in this verse) also echoes the hurting soul of one who wants the restoration of life and the patterns of God.

Neh 1:1-11 ►

Zedekiah was a hard and stubborn man, refusing to turn to the LORD, the
God of Israel.
14 Likewise, all the leaders of the priests and the people became more and
more unfaithful. They followed all the pagan practices of the surrounding
nations, desecrating the Temple of the LORD that had been consecrated in
Jerusalem.
15 The LORD, the God of their ancestors, repeatedly sent his prophets to
warn them, for he had compassion on his people and his Temple. 16 But the
people mocked these messengers of God and despised their words. They
scoffed at the prophets until the LORD's anger could no longer be restrained
and nothing could be done.

The Fall of Jerusalem

17 So the LORD brought the king of Babylon against them. The Babylonians*
killed Judah's young men, even chasing after them into the Temple. They had
no pity on the people, killing both young men and young women, the old
and the infirm. God handed all of them over to Nebuchadnezzar. 18 The king
took home to Babylon all the articles, large and small, used in the Temple of
God, and the treasures from both the LORD's Temple and from the palace of
the king and his officials. 19 Then his army burned the Temple of God, tore
down the walls of Jerusalem, burned all the palaces, and completely destroyed
everything of value.* 20 The few who survived were taken as exiles to Babylon,
and they became servants to the king and his sons until the kingdom of Persia came to power.
21 So the message of the LORD spoken through Jeremiah was fulfilled. The
land finally enjoyed its Sabbath rest, lying desolate until the seventy years
were fulfilled, just as the prophet had said.

Cyrus Allows the Exiles to Return

22 In the first year of King Cyrus of Persia,* the LORD fulfilled the prophecy
he had given through Jeremiah.* He stirred the heart of Cyrus to put this
proclamation in writing and to send it throughout his kingdom:

23 "This is what King Cyrus of Persia says:

"The LORD, the God of heaven, has given me all the kingdoms of the earth. He has appointed me to build him a Temple at Jerusalem, which is in Judah. Any of you who are his people may go there for this task. And may the LORD your God be with you!"

36:17 Or *Chaldeans.* **36:19** Or *destroyed all the valuable articles from the Temple.* **36:22a** The first year of Cyrus's reign over Babylon was 538 B.C. **36:22b** See Jer 25:11-12; 29:10.

Question 36:21

The Lord caused Sabbath (a seventy-year-long Sabbath) for the land because the people would not choose it. Read Leviticus 26:40-45 and consider this: Why does the Lord want rest and restoration as a regular rhythm in our lives?

Prayer 36:23

Lord, may you be with us! Amen.

Ezra Introduction

Imagine being stuck, far away from home, hopeless in a distant place, when all of a sudden, God moves heaven and earth to help you get home again. This is the story of the book of Ezra. It is a book of great relief and great rejoicing but also great struggle. It is a book about how God's people were rescued from a distant land (Babylon) and brought back to their hometown (Jerusalem). However, they had to learn to resettle in the midst of enemies and hard realities. The book of Ezra is better than an epic movie because it shows that God is in control of our lives and wants us to love and live for him.

The major themes of this book are extraordinary:

First, the book of Ezra shows that God is in control even when all seems lost. The fact that this ragtag group of people was allowed to return home and rebuild is astonishing. Only God could make this happen.

Second, God moves in the hearts of leaders so they can do extraordinary things. This book contains some heroic actions from some bold difference makers. For instance, God stirred a man named Zerubbabel to lead thousands of people back home, and about sixty years later, God stirred a man named Ezra to give an eyewitness account of how it was all working out.

Third, God enabled his people to rebuild the temple. This led to a huge celebration through which the instructions of God were reestablished and people returned to lifestyles that worshiped the Lord.

Fourth, the book of Ezra shows that God protects his people. It wasn't easy. The tribes around them grew angry. Despite this, as his people followed him, the Lord kept them safe.

Fifth, God challenges people to live for him. Although there were several times when the people turned their backs on him, God was still gracious and forgiving when they made mistakes. The book ends with some tension as the people struggled to stay pure to God's desires.

Ezra

Cyrus Allows the Exiles to Return

1 In the first year of King Cyrus of Persia,* the LORD fulfilled the prophecy
he had given through Jeremiah.* He stirred the heart of Cyrus to put this
proclamation in writing and to send it throughout his kingdom:

Question 1:1

How has God been moving in your heart to take action for him? Be specific and take action.

2 "This is what King Cyrus of Persia says:
"The LORD, the God of heaven, has given me all the kingdoms of
the earth. He has appointed me to build him a Temple at Jerusalem,
which is in Judah. 3 Any of you who are his people may go to Jerusalem
in Judah to rebuild this Temple of the LORD, the God of Israel, who
lives in Jerusalem. And may your God be with you! 4 Wherever this
Jewish remnant is found, let their neighbors contribute toward their
expenses by giving them silver and gold, supplies for the journey,
and livestock, as well as a voluntary offering for the Temple of God
in Jerusalem."

5 Then God stirred the hearts of the priests and Levites and the leaders of
the tribes of Judah and Benjamin to go to Jerusalem to rebuild the Temple
of the LORD. 6 And all their neighbors assisted by giving them articles of sil-
ver and gold, supplies for the journey, and livestock. They gave them many
valuable gifts in addition to all the voluntary offerings.
7 King Cyrus himself brought out the articles that King Nebuchadnez-
zar had taken from the LORD's Temple in Jerusalem and had placed in the
temple of his own gods. 8 Cyrus directed Mithredath, the treasurer of Per-
sia, to count these items and present them to Sheshbazzar, the leader of the
exiles returning to Judah.* 9 This is a list of the items that were returned:

	gold basins	30
	silver basins	1,000
	silver incense burners*	29
10	gold bowls	30
	silver bowls	410
	other items	1,000

11 In all, there were 5,400 articles of gold and silver. Sheshbazzar brought all of these along when the exiles went from Babylon to Jerusalem.

Exiles Who Returned with Zerubbabel

2 Here is the list of the Jewish exiles of the provinces who returned
from their captivity. King Nebuchadnezzar had deported them to Bab-
ylon, but now they returned to Jerusalem and the other towns in Judah

1:1a The first year of Cyrus's reign over Babylon was 538 B.C. **1:1b** See Jer 25:11-12; 29:10. **1:8** Hebrew *Sheshbazzar, the prince of Judah.* **1:9** The meaning of this Hebrew word is uncertain.

where they originally lived. 2 Their leaders were Zerubbabel, Jeshua, Ne-
hemiah, Seraiah, Reelaiah, Mordecai, Bilshan, Mispar, Bigvai, Rehum, and
Baanah.

This is the number of the men of Israel who returned from exile:

3	The family of Parosh	2,172
4	The family of Shephatiah	372
5	The family of Arah	775
6	The family of Pahath-moab (descendants of Jeshua and Joab)	2,812
7	The family of Elam	1,254
8	The family of Zattu	945
9	The family of Zaccai	760
10	The family of Bani	642
11	The family of Bebai	623
12	The family of Azgad	1,222
13	The family of Adonikam	666
14	The family of Bigvai	2,056
15	The family of Adin	454
16	The family of Ater (descendants of Hezekiah)	98
17	The family of Bezai	323
18	The family of Jorah	112
19	The family of Hashum	223
20	The family of Gibbar	95
21	The people of Bethlehem	123
22	The people of Netophah	56
23	The people of Anathoth	128
24	The people of Beth-azmaveth*	42
25	The people of Kiriath-jearim,* Kephirah, and Beeroth	743
26	The people of Ramah and Geba	621
27	The people of Micmash	122
28	The people of Bethel and Ai	223
29	The citizens of Nebo	52
30	The citizens of Magbish	156
31	The citizens of West Elam*	1,254
32	The citizens of Harim	320
33	The citizens of Lod, Hadid, and Ono	725
34	The citizens of Jericho	345
35	The citizens of Senaah	3,630

36 These are the priests who returned from exile:

	The family of Jedaiah (through the line of Jeshua)	973
37	The family of Immer	1,052
38	The family of Pashhur	1,247
39	The family of Harim	1,017

40 These are the Levites who returned from exile:

	The families of Jeshua and Kadmiel (descendants of Hodaviah)	74
41	The singers of the family of Asaph	128

2:24 As in parallel text at Neh 7:28; Hebrew reads *Azmaveth.* 2:25 As in some Hebrew manuscripts and Greek version (see also Neh 7:29); Hebrew reads *Kiriath-arim.* 2:31 Or *of the other Elam.*

42 The gatekeepers of the families of Shallum, Ater,
Talmon, Akkub, Hatita, and Shobai 139

43 The descendants of the following Temple servants returned from exile:
Ziha, Hasupha, Tabbaoth,
44 Keros, Siaha, Padon,
45 Lebanah, Hagabah, Akkub,
46 Hagab, Shalmai,* Hanan,
47 Giddel, Gahar, Reaiah,
48 Rezin, Nekoda, Gazzam,
49 Uzza, Paseah, Besai,
50 Asnah, Meunim, Nephusim,
51 Bakbuk, Hakupha, Harhur,
52 Bazluth, Mehida, Harsha,
53 Barkos, Sisera, Temah,
54 Neziah, and Hatipha.

55 The descendants of these servants of King Solomon returned from exile:
Sotai, Hassophereth, Peruda,
56 Jaalah, Darkon, Giddel,
57 Shephatiah, Hattil, Pokereth-hazzebaim, and Ami.

58 In all, the Temple servants and the descendants of Solomon's servants numbered 392.

59 Another group returned at this time from the towns of Tel-melah, Tel-
harsha, Kerub, Addan, and Immer. However, they could not prove that they
or their families were descendants of Israel. 60 This group included the fami-
lies of Delaiah, Tobiah, and Nekoda—a total of 652 people.
61 Three families of priests—Hobaiah, Hakkoz, and Barzillai—also re-
turned. (This Barzillai had married a woman who was a descendant of
Barzillai of Gilead, and he had taken her family name.) 62 They searched
for their names in the genealogical records, but they were not found, so
they were disqualified from serving as priests. 63 The governor told them
not to eat the priests' share of food from the sacrifices until a priest could
consult the LORD about the matter by using the Urim and Thummim—the
sacred lots.
64 So a total of 42,360 people returned to Judah, 65 in addition to 7,337
servants and 200 singers, both men and women. 66 They took with them
736 horses, 245 mules, 67 435 camels, and 6,720 donkeys.
68 When they arrived at the Temple of the LORD in Jerusalem, some of
the family leaders made voluntary offerings toward the rebuilding of God's
Temple on its original site, 69 and each leader gave as much as he could. The
total of their gifts came to 61,000 gold coins,* 6,250 pounds* of silver, and
100 robes for the priests.
70 So the priests, the Levites, the singers, the gatekeepers, the Temple ser-
vants, and some of the common people settled in villages near Jerusalem.
The rest of the people returned to their own towns throughout Israel.

2:46 As in an alternate reading of the Masoretic Text (see also Neh 7:48); the other alternate reads *Shamlai*. 2:69a Hebrew *61,000 darics of gold*, about 1,100 pounds or 500 kilograms in weight. 2:69b Hebrew *5,000 minas* [3,000 kilograms].

Make a Difference 2:70

Use Your Gift

This chapter lists lots of people with all different abilities, talents, and gifts. They all gave as they could to help rebuild the temple of God so everyone could serve God inside and outside the temple. Some were like pastors, worship leaders, greeters at the door, and others serving the people. There were also masons, carpenters, tradesmen, shippers (3:7), prophets (5:1), and many others of various skills. In all, there were more than forty thousand people who returned to the land of Israel (2:64).

Difference Maker

What gifts and abilities do you have? Make a list. How could you use them to serve God and make a difference in the lives of others?

The Altar Is Rebuilt

3 In early autumn,* when the Israelites had settled in their towns, all the
people assembled in Jerusalem with a unified purpose. 2 Then Jeshua
son of Jehozadak* joined his fellow priests and Zerubbabel son of Shealtiel
with his family in rebuilding the altar of the God of Israel. They wanted to
sacrifice burnt offerings on it, as instructed in the Law of Moses, the man of
God. 3 Even though the people were afraid of the local residents, they rebuilt
the altar at its old site. Then they began to sacrifice burnt offerings on the
altar to the LORD each morning and evening.

4 They celebrated the Festival of Shelters as prescribed in the Law, sacrific-
ing the number of burnt offerings specified for each day of the festival. 5 They
also offered the regular burnt offerings and the offerings required for the
new moon celebrations and the annual festivals as prescribed by the LORD.
The people also gave voluntary offerings to the LORD. 6 Fifteen days before
the Festival of Shelters began,* the priests had begun to sacrifice burnt offer-
ings to the LORD. This was even before they had started to lay the foundation
of the LORD's Temple.

The People Begin to Rebuild the Temple

7 Then the people hired masons and carpenters and bought cedar logs from
the people of Tyre and Sidon, paying them with food, wine, and olive oil.
The logs were brought down from the Lebanon mountains and floated along
the coast of the Mediterranean Sea* to Joppa, for King Cyrus had given per-
mission for this.

8 The construction of the Temple of God began in midspring,* during the
second year after they arrived in Jerusalem. The work force was made up of
everyone who had returned from exile, including Zerubbabel son of Shealtiel,
Jeshua son of Jehozadak and his fellow priests, and all the Levites. The Le-
vites who were twenty years old or older were put in charge of rebuilding the
LORD's Temple. 9 The workers at the Temple of God were supervised by Jeshua
with his sons and relatives, and Kadmiel and his sons, all descendants of Hod-
aviah.* They were helped in this task by the Levites of the family of Henadad.

10 When the builders completed the foundation of the LORD's Temple, the
priests put on their robes and took their places to blow their trumpets. And
the Levites, descendants of Asaph, clashed their cymbals to praise the LORD,
just as King David had prescribed. 11 With praise and thanks, they sang this
song to the LORD:

"He is so good!
His faithful love for Israel endures forever!"

Then all the people gave a great shout, praising the LORD because the foundation of the LORD's Temple had been laid.

3:1 Hebrew *In the seventh month.* The year is not specified, so it may have been during Cyrus's first year (538 B.C.) or second year (537 B.C.). The seventh month of the ancient Hebrew lunar calendar occurred within the months of September/October 538 B.C. and October/November 537 B.C. 3:2 Hebrew *Jozadak,* a variant spelling of Jehozadak; also in 3:8. 3:6 Hebrew *On the first day of the seventh month.* This day in the ancient Hebrew lunar calendar occurred in September or October. The Festival of Shelters began on the fifteenth day of the seventh month. 3:7 Hebrew *the sea.* 3:8 Hebrew *in the second month.* This month in the ancient Hebrew lunar calendar occurred within the months of April and May 536 B.C. 3:9 Hebrew *sons of Judah* (i.e., *bene Yehudah*). *Bene* might also be read here as the proper name Binnui; *Yehudah* is probably another name for Hodaviah. Compare 2:40; Neh 7:43; 1 Esdras 5:58.

12But many of the older priests, Levites, and other leaders who had seen the first Temple wept aloud when they saw the new Temple's foundation. The others, however, were shouting for joy. 13The joyful shouting and weeping mingled together in a loud noise that could be heard far in the distance.

Question 3:12

Have you ever had a moment in your life when you felt both sadness and happiness at the same time? What did this look like for you, and how did you handle this?

Enemies Oppose the Rebuilding

4 The enemies of Judah and Benjamin heard that the exiles were rebuilding a Temple to the LORD, the God of Israel. 2So they approached Zerubbabel and the other leaders and said, "Let us build with you, for we worship your God just as you do. We have sacrificed to him ever since King Esarhaddon of Assyria brought us here."

3But Zerubbabel, Jeshua, and the other leaders of Israel replied, "You may have no part in this work. We alone will build the Temple for the LORD, the God of Israel, just as King Cyrus of Persia commanded us."

4Then the local residents tried to discourage and frighten the people of Judah to keep them from their work. 5They bribed agents to work against them and to frustrate their plans. This went on during the entire reign of King Cyrus of Persia and lasted until King Darius of Persia took the throne.*

Later Opposition under Xerxes and Artaxerxes

6Years later when Xerxes* began his reign, the enemies of Judah wrote a letter of accusation against the people of Judah and Jerusalem.

7Even later, during the reign of King Artaxerxes of Persia,* the enemies of Judah, led by Bishlam, Mithredath, and Tabeel, sent a letter to Artaxerxes in the Aramaic language, and it was translated for the king.

8*Rehum the governor and Shimshai the court secretary wrote the letter, telling King Artaxerxes about the situation in Jerusalem. 9They greeted the king for all their colleagues—the judges and local leaders, the people of Tarpel, the Persians, the Babylonians, and the people of Erech and Susa (that is, Elam). 10They also sent greetings from the rest of the people whom the great and noble Ashurbanipal* had deported and relocated in Samaria and throughout the neighboring lands of the province west of the Euphrates River.* 11This is a copy of their letter:

"To King Artaxerxes, from your loyal subjects in the province west of the Euphrates River.

12"The king should know that the Jews who came here to Jerusalem from Babylon are rebuilding this rebellious and evil city. They have already laid the foundation and will soon finish its walls. 13And the king should know that if this city is rebuilt and its walls are completed, it will be much to your disadvantage, for the Jews will then refuse to pay their tribute, customs, and tolls to you.

14"Since we are your loyal subjects* and do not want to see the king dishonored in this way, we have sent the king this information. 15We suggest that a search be made in your ancestors' records, where you will

4:5 Darius reigned 521–486 B.C. **4:6** Hebrew *Ahasuerus,* another name for Xerxes. He reigned 486–465 B.C. **4:7** Artaxerxes reigned 465–424 B.C. **4:8** The original text of 4:8–6:18 is in Aramaic. **4:10a** Aramaic *Osnappar,* another name for Ashurbanipal. **4:10b** Aramaic *the province beyond the river;* also in 4:11, 16, 17, 20. **4:14** Aramaic *Since we eat the salt of the palace.*

Make a Difference 5:2

Get Help

These two men, Zerubbabel and Jeshua, were dedicated and resilient! Even though there was opposition, nothing was going to get in the way of rebuilding the temple. They were focused on worshiping God, and they weren't alone. They had support from some powerful prophets, Haggai and Zechariah.

We all need a team. Who is on your spiritual team? Who is going to help you be resilient?

Difference Maker

Ask an adult to support you on your journey with Jesus so that you remain resilient in the calling God has for you.

discover what a rebellious city this has been in the past. In fact, it was destroyed because of its long and troublesome history of revolt against the kings and countries who controlled it.
16 We declare to the king that if this city is rebuilt and its walls are completed, the province west of the Euphrates River will be lost to you."

17 Then King Artaxerxes sent this reply:

"To Rehum the governor, Shimshai the court secretary, and their colleagues living in Samaria and throughout the province west of the Euphrates River. Greetings.

18 "The letter you sent has been translated and read to me.
19 I ordered a search of the records and have found that Jerusalem has indeed been a hotbed of insurrection against many kings. In fact, rebellion and revolt are normal there!
20 Powerful kings have ruled over Jerusalem and the entire province west of the Euphrates River, receiving tribute, customs, and tolls.
21 Therefore, issue orders to have these men stop their work. That city must not be rebuilt except at my express command.
22 Be diligent, and don't neglect this matter, for we must not permit the situation to harm the king's interests."

23 When this letter from King Artaxerxes was read to Rehum, Shimshai, and their colleagues, they hurried to Jerusalem. Then, with a show of strength, they forced the Jews to stop building.

The Rebuilding Resumes

24 So the work on the Temple of God in Jerusalem had stopped, and it remained at a standstill until the second year of the reign of King Darius of Persia.*

5 At that time the prophets Haggai and Zechariah son of Iddo prophesied to the Jews in Judah and Jerusalem. They prophesied in the name of the God of Israel who was over them.
2 Zerubbabel son of Shealtiel and Jeshua son of Jehozadak* responded by starting again to rebuild the Temple of God in Jerusalem. And the prophets of God were with them and helped them.
3 But Tattenai, governor of the province west of the Euphrates River,* and Shethar-bozenai and their colleagues soon arrived in Jerusalem and asked, "Who gave you permission to rebuild this Temple and restore this structure?"
4 They also asked for* the names of all the men working on the Temple.
5 But because their God was watching over them, the leaders of the Jews were not prevented from building until a report was sent to Darius and he returned his decision.

Tattenai's Letter to King Darius

6 This is a copy of the letter that Tattenai the governor, Shethar-bozenai, and the other officials of the province west of the Euphrates River sent to King Darius:

4:24 The second year of Darius's reign was 520 B.C. The narrative started in 4:1-5 is resumed at verse 24. 5:2 Aramaic *Jozadak,* a variant spelling of Jehozadak. 5:3 Aramaic *the province beyond the river;* also in 5:6. 5:4 As in one Hebrew manuscript and Greek and Syriac versions; Masoretic Text reads *Then we told them.*

7 “To King Darius. Greetings.
8 “The king should know that we went to the construction site of the
Temple of the great God in the province of Judah. It is being rebuilt
with specially prepared stones, and timber is being laid in its walls. The
work is going forward with great energy and success.
9 “We asked the leaders, ‘Who gave you permission to rebuild this
Temple and restore this structure?’ 10 And we demanded their names so
that we could tell you who the leaders were.
11 “This was their answer: ‘We are the servants of the God of heaven
and earth, and we are rebuilding the Temple that was built here many
years ago by a great king of Israel. 12 But because our ancestors angered
the God of heaven, he abandoned them to King Nebuchadnezzar
of Babylon,* who destroyed this Temple and exiled the people to
Babylonia. 13 However, King Cyrus of Babylon,* during the first year
of his reign, issued a decree that the Temple of God should be rebuilt.
14 King Cyrus returned the gold and silver cups that Nebuchadnezzar
had taken from the Temple of God in Jerusalem and had placed in
the temple of Babylon. These cups were taken from that temple and
presented to a man named Sheshbazzar, whom King Cyrus appointed
as governor of Judah. 15 The king instructed him to return the cups to
their place in Jerusalem and to rebuild the Temple of God there on its
original site. 16 So this Sheshbazzar came and laid the foundations of the
Temple of God in Jerusalem. The people have been working on it ever
since, though it is not yet completed.’
17 “Therefore, if it pleases the king, we request that a search be made
in the royal archives of Babylon to discover whether King Cyrus ever
issued a decree to rebuild God’s Temple in Jerusalem. And then let the
king send us his decision in this matter.”

Darius Approves the Rebuilding

6 So King Darius issued orders that a search be made in the Babylonian archives, which were stored in the treasury. 2 But it was at the fortress at Ecbatana in the province of Media that a scroll was found. This is what it said:

“Memorandum:
3 “In the first year of King Cyrus’s reign, a decree was sent out
concerning the Temple of God at Jerusalem.
“Let the Temple be rebuilt on the site where Jews used to offer their
sacrifices, using the original foundations. Its height will be ninety
feet, and its width will be ninety feet.* 4 Every three layers of specially
prepared stones will be topped by a layer of timber. All expenses will
be paid by the royal treasury. 5 Furthermore, the gold and silver cups,
which were taken to Babylon by Nebuchadnezzar from the Temple of
God in Jerusalem, must be returned to Jerusalem and put back where
they belong. Let them be taken back to the Temple of God.”

5:12 Aramaic *Nebuchadnezzar the Chaldean.* **5:13** King Cyrus of Persia is here identified as the king of Babylon because Persia had conquered the Babylonian Empire. **6:3** Aramaic *Its height will be 60 cubits* [27.6 meters], *and its width will be 60 cubits.* It is commonly held that this verse should be emended to read: “Its height will be 30 cubits [45 feet or 13.8 meters], its length will be 60 cubits [90 feet or 27.6 meters], and its width will be 20 cubits [30 feet or 9.2 meters]”; compare 1 Kgs 6:2. The emendation regarding the width is supported by the Syriac version.

[6]So King Darius sent this message:

"Now therefore, Tattenai, governor of the province west of the
Euphrates River,* and Shethar-bozenai, and your colleagues and other
officials west of the Euphrates River—stay away from there! [7]Do not
disturb the construction of the Temple of God. Let it be rebuilt on its
original site, and do not hinder the governor of Judah and the elders
of the Jews in their work.

[8]"Moreover, I hereby decree that you are to help these elders of
the Jews as they rebuild this Temple of God. You must pay the full
construction costs, without delay, from my taxes collected in the province
west of the Euphrates River so that the work will not be interrupted.

[9]"Give the priests in Jerusalem whatever is needed in the way of
young bulls, rams, and male lambs for the burnt offerings presented to
the God of heaven. And without fail, provide them with as much wheat,
salt, wine, and olive oil as they need each day. [10]Then they will be able to
offer acceptable sacrifices to the God of heaven and pray for the welfare
of the king and his sons.

[11]"Those who violate this decree in any way will have a beam pulled
from their house. Then they will be lifted up and impaled on it, and
their house will be reduced to a pile of rubble.* [12]May the God who has
chosen the city of Jerusalem as the place to honor his name destroy any
king or nation that violates this command and destroys this Temple.

"I, Darius, have issued this decree. Let it be obeyed with all diligence."

The Temple's Dedication

[13]Tattenai, governor of the province west of the Euphrates River, and Shethar-bozenai and their colleagues complied at once with the command of King
Darius. [14]So the Jewish elders continued their work, and they were greatly
encouraged by the preaching of the prophets Haggai and Zechariah son of Iddo. The Temple was finally finished, as had been commanded by the God of Israel and decreed by Cyrus, Darius, and Artaxerxes, the kings of Persia.
[15]The Temple was completed on March 12,* during the sixth year of King Darius's reign.

[16]The Temple of God was then dedicated with great joy by the people of Israel, the priests, the Levites, and the rest of the people who had returned from
exile. [17]During the dedication ceremony for the Temple of God, 100 young bulls, 200 rams, and 400 male lambs were sacrificed. And 12 male goats were presented as a sin offering for the twelve tribes of Israel. [18]Then the priests
and Levites were divided into their various divisions to serve at the Temple of God in Jerusalem, as prescribed in the Book of Moses.

Celebration of Passover

[19]On April 21* the returned exiles celebrated Passover. [20]The priests and Levites had purified themselves and were ceremonially clean. So they

6:6 Aramaic *the province beyond the river;* also in 6:6b, 8, 13. 6:11 Aramaic *a dunghill.* 6:15 Aramaic *on the third day of the month Adar,* of the ancient Hebrew lunar calendar. A number of events in Ezra can be cross-checked with dates in surviving Persian records and related accurately to our modern calendar. This day was March 12, 515 B.C. 6:19 Hebrew *On the fourteenth day of the first month,* of the ancient Hebrew lunar calendar. This day was April 21, 515 B.C.; also see note on 6:15.

slaughtered the Passover lamb for all the returned exiles, for their fellow priests, and for themselves. 21 The Passover meal was eaten by the people of Israel who had returned from exile and by the others in the land who had turned from their corrupt practices to worship the LORD, the God of Israel. 22 Then they celebrated the Festival of Unleavened Bread for seven days. There was great joy throughout the land because the LORD had caused the king of Assyria* to be favorable to them, so that he helped them to rebuild the Temple of God, the God of Israel.

Ezra Arrives in Jerusalem

7 Many years later, during the reign of King Artaxerxes of Persia,* there was a man named Ezra. He was the son* of Seraiah, son of Azariah, son of Hilkiah, 2 son of Shallum, son of Zadok, son of Ahitub, 3 son of Amariah, son of Azariah, son* of Meraioth, 4 son of Zerahiah, son of Uzzi, son of Bukki, 5 son of Abishua, son of Phinehas, son of Eleazar, son of Aaron the high priest.* 6 This Ezra was a scribe who was well versed in the Law of Moses, which the LORD, the God of Israel, had given to the people of Israel. He came up to Jerusalem from Babylon, and the king gave him everything he asked for, because the gracious hand of the LORD his God was on him. 7 Some of the people of Israel, as well as some of the priests, Levites, singers, gatekeepers, and Temple servants, traveled up to Jerusalem with him in the seventh year of King Artaxerxes' reign.

8 Ezra arrived in Jerusalem in August* of that year. 9 He had arranged to leave Babylon on April 8, the first day of the new year,* and he arrived at Jerusalem on August 4,* for the gracious hand of his God was on him. 10 This was because Ezra had determined to study and obey the Law of the LORD and to teach those decrees and regulations to the people of Israel.

Question 7:10

Ezra was determined to study the Word of God and share it with others. What a great example this is for us. What changes would you need to make to set this kind of example for your friends and family?

Artaxerxes' Letter to Ezra

11 King Artaxerxes had given a copy of the following letter to Ezra, the priest and scribe who studied and taught the commands and decrees of the LORD to Israel:

> 12*"From Artaxerxes, the king of kings, to Ezra the priest, the teacher of the law of the God of heaven. Greetings.
>
> 13 "I decree that any of the people of Israel in my kingdom, including the priests and Levites, may volunteer to return to Jerusalem with you. 14 I and my council of seven hereby instruct you to conduct an inquiry into the situation in Judah and Jerusalem, based on your God's law, which is in your hand. 15 We also commission you to take with you silver and gold, which we are freely presenting as an offering to the God of Israel who lives in Jerusalem.
>
> 16 "Furthermore, you are to take any silver and gold that you may obtain from the province of Babylon, as well as the voluntary offerings

6:22 King Darius of Persia is here identified as the king of Assyria because Persia had conquered the Babylonian Empire, which included the earlier Assyrian Empire. 7:1a Artaxerxes reigned 465–424 B.C. 7:1b Or *descendant;* see 1 Chr 6:14. 7:3 Or *descendant;* see 1 Chr 6:6-10. 7:5 Or *the first priest.* 7:8 Hebrew *in the fifth month.* This month in the ancient Hebrew lunar calendar occurred within the months of August and September 458 B.C. 7:9a Hebrew *on the first day of the first month,* of the ancient Hebrew lunar calendar. This day was April 8, 458 B.C.; also see note on 6:15. 7:9b Hebrew *on the first day of the fifth month,* of the ancient Hebrew lunar calendar. This day was August 4, 458 B.C.; also see note on 6:15. 7:12 The original text of 7:12-26 is in Aramaic.

of the people and the priests that are presented for the Temple of their
God in Jerusalem. 17 These donations are to be used specifically for the
purchase of bulls, rams, male lambs, and the appropriate grain offerings
and liquid offerings, all of which will be offered on the altar of the
Temple of your God in Jerusalem. 18 Any silver and gold that is left over
may be used in whatever way you and your colleagues feel is the will of
your God.

19 "But as for the cups we are entrusting to you for the service of the
Temple of your God, deliver them all to the God of Jerusalem. 20 If you
need anything else for your God's Temple or for any similar needs, you
may take it from the royal treasury.

21 "I, Artaxerxes the king, hereby send this decree to all the treasurers
in the province west of the Euphrates River*: 'You are to give Ezra,
the priest and teacher of the law of the God of heaven, whatever he
requests of you. 22 You are to give him up to 7,500 pounds* of silver,
500 bushels* of wheat, 550 gallons of wine, 550 gallons of olive oil,* and
an unlimited supply of salt. 23 Be careful to provide whatever the God of
heaven demands for his Temple, for why should we risk bringing God's
anger against the realm of the king and his sons? 24 I also decree that no
priest, Levite, singer, gatekeeper, Temple servant, or other worker in
this Temple of God will be required to pay tribute, customs, or tolls of
any kind.'

25 "And you, Ezra, are to use the wisdom your God has given you to
appoint magistrates and judges who know your God's laws to govern all
the people in the province west of the Euphrates River. Teach the law to
anyone who does not know it. 26 Anyone who refuses to obey the law of
your God and the law of the king will be punished immediately, either
by death, banishment, confiscation of goods, or imprisonment."

Ezra Praises the Lord

27 Praise the LORD, the God of our ancestors, who made the king want to
beautify the Temple of the LORD in Jerusalem! 28 And praise him for dem-
onstrating such unfailing love to me by honoring me before the king, his
council, and all his mighty nobles! I felt encouraged because the gracious
hand of the LORD my God was on me. And I gathered some of the leaders of
Israel to return with me to Jerusalem.

Exiles Who Returned with Ezra

8 Here is a list of the family leaders and the genealogies of those who came
with me from Babylon during the reign of King Artaxerxes:

2 From the family of Phinehas: Gershom.
From the family of Ithamar: Daniel.
From the family of David: Hattush, 3 a descendant of Shecaniah.
From the family of Parosh: Zechariah and 150 other men were registered.
4 From the family of Pahath-moab: Eliehoenai son of Zerahiah and 200 other men.

7:21 Aramaic *the province beyond the river;* also in 7:25. 7:22a Aramaic *100 talents* [3,400 kilograms]. 7:22b Aramaic *100 cors* [22 kiloliters]. 7:22c Aramaic *100 baths* [2.1 kiloliters] *of wine, 100 baths of olive oil.*

5 From the family of Zattu*: Shecaniah son of Jahaziel and 300 other men.
6 From the family of Adin: Ebed son of Jonathan and 50 other men.
7 From the family of Elam: Jeshaiah son of Athaliah and 70 other men.
8 From the family of Shephatiah: Zebadiah son of Michael and 80 other men.
9 From the family of Joab: Obadiah son of Jehiel and 218 other men.
10 From the family of Bani*: Shelomith son of Josiphiah and 160 other men.
11 From the family of Bebai: Zechariah son of Bebai and 28 other men.
12 From the family of Azgad: Johanan son of Hakkatan and 110 other men.
13 From the family of Adonikam, who came later*: Eliphelet, Jeuel, Shemaiah, and 60 other men.
14 From the family of Bigvai: Uthai, Zaccur,* and 70 other men.

Ezra's Journey to Jerusalem

15 I assembled the exiles at the Ahava Canal, and we camped there for three
days while I went over the lists of the people and the priests who had arrived.
I found that not one Levite had volunteered to come along. 16 So I sent for
Eliezer, Ariel, Shemaiah, Elnathan, Jarib, Elnathan, Nathan, Zechariah, and
Meshullam, who were leaders of the people. I also sent for Joiarib and Elna-
than, who were men of discernment. 17 I sent them to Iddo, the leader of the
Levites at Casiphia, to ask him and his relatives and the Temple servants to
send us ministers for the Temple of God at Jerusalem.

18 Since the gracious hand of our God was on us, they sent us a man named
Sherebiah, along with eighteen of his sons and brothers. He was a very astute
man and a descendant of Mahli, who was a descendant of Levi son of Israel.*
19 They also sent Hashabiah, together with Jeshaiah from the descendants of
Merari, and twenty of his sons and brothers, 20 and 220 Temple servants. The
Temple servants were assistants to the Levites—a group of Temple workers
first instituted by King David and his officials. They were all listed by name.

21 And there by the Ahava Canal, I gave orders for all of us to fast and
humble ourselves before our God. We prayed that he would give us a safe
journey and protect us, our children, and our goods as we traveled. 22 For I
was ashamed to ask the king for soldiers and horsemen* to accompany us
and protect us from enemies along the way. After all, we had told the king,
"Our God's hand of protection is on all who worship him, but his fierce anger
rages against those who abandon him." 23 So we fasted and earnestly prayed
that our God would take care of us, and he heard our prayer.

24 I appointed twelve leaders of the priests—Sherebiah, Hashabiah, and
ten other priests—25 to be in charge of transporting the silver, the gold, the
gold bowls, and the other items that the king, his council, his officials, and
all the people of Israel had presented for the Temple of God. 26 I weighed the
treasure as I gave it to them and found the totals to be as follows:

24 tons* of silver,
7,500 pounds* of silver articles,
7,500 pounds of gold,

Question 8:21-23

Ezra ordered everyone to fast and humble themselves before God. Fasting is giving something up for a time (usually food) in order to focus the mind and heart on God. Why did Ezra order his men to do this at this moment? When would fasting be appropriate for you to do?

8:5 As in some Greek manuscripts (see also 1 Esdras 8:32); Hebrew lacks *Zattu.* 8:10 As in some Greek manuscripts (see also 1 Esdras 8:36); Hebrew lacks *Bani.* 8:13 Or *who were the last of his family.* 8:14 As in Greek and Syriac versions and an alternate reading of the Masoretic Text; the other alternate reads *Zabbud.* 8:18 *Israel* is the name that God gave to Jacob. 8:22 Or *charioteers.* 8:26a Hebrew *650 talents* [22 metric tons]. 8:26b Hebrew *100 talents* [3,400 kilograms]; also in 8:26c.

Prayer **9:9**

Lord, thank you for the kindness you have shown me and for never leaving me even when things are difficult. Amen.

27 20 gold bowls, equal in value to 1,000 gold coins,*
2 fine articles of polished bronze, as precious as gold.

28 And I said to these priests, "You and these treasures have been set apart
as holy to the LORD. This silver and gold is a voluntary offering to the LORD,
the God of our ancestors. 29 Guard these treasures well until you present them
to the leading priests, the Levites, and the leaders of Israel, who will weigh
them at the storerooms of the LORD's Temple in Jerusalem." 30 So the priests
and the Levites accepted the task of transporting these treasures of silver and
gold to the Temple of our God in Jerusalem.
31 We broke camp at the Ahava Canal on April 19* and started off to Jerusa-
lem. And the gracious hand of our God protected us and saved us from en-
emies and bandits along the way. 32 So we arrived safely in Jerusalem, where
we rested for three days.
33 On the fourth day after our arrival, the silver, gold, and other valuables
were weighed at the Temple of our God and entrusted to Meremoth son of
Uriah the priest and to Eleazar son of Phinehas, along with Jozabad son of
Jeshua and Noadiah son of Binnui—both of whom were Levites. 34 Every-
thing was accounted for by number and weight, and the total weight was
officially recorded.
35 Then the exiles who had come out of captivity sacrificed burnt offerings
to the God of Israel. They presented twelve bulls for all the people of Israel,
as well as ninety-six rams and seventy-seven male lambs. They also offered
twelve male goats as a sin offering. All this was given as a burnt offering to
the LORD. 36 The king's decrees were delivered to his highest officers and the
governors of the province west of the Euphrates River,* who then cooperated
by supporting the people and the Temple of God.

Ezra's Prayer concerning Intermarriage

9 When these things had been done, the Jewish leaders came to me and said,
"Many of the people of Israel, and even some of the priests and Levites,
have not kept themselves separate from the other peoples living in the land.
They have taken up the detestable practices of the Canaanites, Hittites, Periz-
zites, Jebusites, Ammonites, Moabites, Egyptians, and Amorites. 2 For the men
of Israel have married women from these people and have taken them as wives
for their sons. So the holy race has become polluted by these mixed marriages.
Worse yet, the leaders and officials have led the way in this outrage."
3 When I heard this, I tore my cloak and my shirt, pulled hair from my
head and beard, and sat down utterly shocked. 4 Then all who trembled at
the words of the God of Israel came and sat with me because of this outrage
committed by the returned exiles. And I sat there utterly appalled until the
time of the evening sacrifice.
5 At the time of the sacrifice, I stood up from where I had sat in mourning
with my clothes torn. I fell to my knees and lifted my hands to the LORD my
God. 6 I prayed,

"O my God, I am utterly ashamed; I blush to lift up my face to you. For
our sins are piled higher than our heads, and our guilt has reached

8:27 Hebrew *1,000 darics,* about 19 pounds or 8.6 kilograms in weight. 8:31 Hebrew *on the twelfth day of the first month,* of the ancient Hebrew lunar calendar. This day was April 19, 458 B.C.; also see note on 6:15. 8:36 Hebrew *the province beyond the river.*

to the heavens. 7From the days of our ancestors until now, we have
been steeped in sin. That is why we and our kings and our priests have
been at the mercy of the pagan kings of the land. We have been killed,
captured, robbed, and disgraced, just as we are today.
8"But now we have been given a brief moment of grace, for the LORD
our God has allowed a few of us to survive as a remnant. He has given
us security in this holy place. Our God has brightened our eyes and
granted us some relief from our slavery. 9For we were slaves, but in
his unfailing love our God did not abandon us in our slavery. Instead,
he caused the kings of Persia to treat us favorably. He revived us so we
could rebuild the Temple of our God and repair its ruins. He has given
us a protective wall in Judah and Jerusalem.
10"And now, O our God, what can we say after all of this? For once
again we have abandoned your commands! 11Your servants the
prophets warned us when they said, 'The land you are entering to
possess is totally defiled by the detestable practices of the people living
there. From one end to the other, the land is filled with corruption.
12Don't let your daughters marry their sons! Don't take their daughters
as wives for your sons. Don't ever promote the peace and prosperity of
those nations. If you follow these instructions, you will be strong and
will enjoy the good things the land produces, and you will leave this
prosperity to your children forever.'
13"Now we are being punished because of our wickedness and our
great guilt. But we have actually been punished far less than we deserve,
for you, our God, have allowed some of us to survive as a remnant. 14But
even so, we are again breaking your commands and intermarrying with
people who do these detestable things. Won't your anger be enough
to destroy us, so that even this little remnant no longer survives?
15O LORD, God of Israel, you are just. We come before you in our guilt as
nothing but an escaped remnant, though in such a condition none of us
can stand in your presence."

The People Confess Their Sin

10 While Ezra prayed and made this confession, weeping and lying
face down on the ground in front of the Temple of God, a very
large crowd of people from Israel—men, women, and children—gathered
and wept bitterly with him. 2Then Shecaniah son of Jehiel, a descendant
of Elam, said to Ezra, "We have been unfaithful to our God, for we have
married these pagan women of the land. But in spite of this there is hope
for Israel. 3Let us now make a covenant with our God to divorce our pagan
wives and to send them away with their children. We will follow the advice
given by you and by the others who respect the commands of our God. Let
it be done according to the Law of God. 4Get up, for it is your duty to tell us
how to proceed in setting things straight. We are behind you, so be strong
and take action."
5So Ezra stood up and demanded that the leaders of the priests and the
Levites and all the people of Israel swear that they would do as Shecaniah had
said. And they all swore a solemn oath. 6Then Ezra left the front of the Temple
of God and went to the room of Jehohanan son of Eliashib. He spent the night*

10:6 As in parallel text at 1 Esdras 9:2; Hebrew reads *He went.*

Prayer **10:1**

Lord, please forgive me for the times when I have failed to live for you, when I have turned to things that I know are against you, and when I have not trusted you. Thank you for your forgiveness and love. Amen.

Make a Difference

10:1–17

Keep Going

God brilliantly used Ezra. He led displaced exiles back home to Jerusalem, helped to rebuild the nation's infrastructure, and established a new beginning for the people of Israel. While Ezra's heart was full, it was also heavy. There was still so much to be done. He felt so burdened and tired. That's when a friend spoke to him with these empowering words: "Get up...We are behind you...Be strong...Take action" (v. 4).

Jesus wants to keep making a difference in you every day so that you can keep making a difference in the world around you every day. Jesus also wants you to know the support of a good church and of good friends who want to empower you to keep going.

Difference Maker

Take some time right now to pray for the difference Jesus will make in you and the difference he will make in the lives of others through you. Pray that God will supply you with good friends who will encourage you to keep going even when you grow weary.

there without eating or drinking anything. He was still in mourning because
of the unfaithfulness of the returned exiles.

7 Then a proclamation was made throughout Judah and Jerusalem that all
the exiles should come to Jerusalem. 8 Those who failed to come within three
days would, if the leaders and elders so decided, forfeit all their property and
be expelled from the assembly of the exiles.

9 Within three days, all the people of Judah and Benjamin had gathered
in Jerusalem. This took place on December 19,* and all the people were
sitting in the square before the Temple of God. They were trembling both
because of the seriousness of the matter and because it was raining. 10 Then
Ezra the priest stood and said to them: "You have committed a terrible
sin. By marrying pagan women, you have increased Israel's guilt. 11 So now
confess your sin to the LORD, the God of your ancestors, and do what he
demands. Separate yourselves from the people of the land and from these
pagan women."

12 Then the whole assembly raised their voices and answered, "Yes, you are
right; we must do as you say!" 13 Then they added, "This isn't something that
can be done in a day or two, for many of us are involved in this extremely
sinful affair. And this is the rainy season, so we cannot stay out here much
longer. 14 Let our leaders act on behalf of us all. Let everyone who has a pagan
wife come at a scheduled time, accompanied by the leaders and judges of
his city, so that the fierce anger of our God concerning this affair may be
turned away from us."

15 Only Jonathan son of Asahel and Jahzeiah son of Tikvah opposed this
course of action, and they were supported by Meshullam and Shabbethai
the Levite.

16 So this was the plan they followed. Ezra selected leaders to represent
their families, designating each of the representatives by name. On Decem-
ber 29,* the leaders sat down to investigate the matter. 17 By March 27, the
first day of the new year,* they had finished dealing with all the men who
had married pagan wives.

Those Guilty of Intermarriage

18 These are the priests who had married pagan wives:
From the family of Jeshua son of Jehozadak* and his brothers: Maaseiah,
Eliezer, Jarib, and Gedaliah. 19 They vowed to divorce their wives,
and they each acknowledged their guilt by offering a ram as a guilt
offering.
20 From the family of Immer: Hanani and Zebadiah.
21 From the family of Harim: Maaseiah, Elijah, Shemaiah, Jehiel, and
Uzziah.
22 From the family of Pashhur: Elioenai, Maaseiah, Ishmael, Nethanel,
Jozabad, and Elasah.

23 These are the Levites who were guilty: Jozabad, Shimei, Kelaiah (also
called Kelita), Pethahiah, Judah, and Eliezer.

10:9 Hebrew *on the twentieth day of the ninth month,* of the ancient Hebrew lunar calendar. This day was December 19, 458 B.C.; also see note on 6:15. **10:16** Hebrew *On the first day of the tenth month,* of the ancient Hebrew lunar calendar. This day was December 29, 458 B.C.; also see note on 6:15. **10:17** Hebrew *By the first day of the first month,* of the ancient Hebrew lunar calendar. This day was March 27, 457 B.C.; also see note on 6:15. **10:18** Hebrew *Jozadak,* a variant spelling of Jehozadak.

[24]This is the singer who was guilty: Eliashib.

These are the gatekeepers who were guilty: Shallum, Telem, and Uri.

[25]These are the other people of Israel who were guilty:
From the family of Parosh: Ramiah, Izziah, Malkijah, Mijamin, Eleazar, Hashabiah,* and Benaiah.
[26]From the family of Elam: Mattaniah, Zechariah, Jehiel, Abdi, Jeremoth, and Elijah.
[27]From the family of Zattu: Elioenai, Eliashib, Mattaniah, Jeremoth, Zabad, and Aziza.
[28]From the family of Bebai: Jehohanan, Hananiah, Zabbai, and Athlai.
[29]From the family of Bani: Meshullam, Malluch, Adaiah, Jashub, Sheal, and Jeremoth.
[30]From the family of Pahath-moab: Adna, Kelal, Benaiah, Maaseiah, Mattaniah, Bezalel, Binnui, and Manasseh.
[31]From the family of Harim: Eliezer, Ishijah, Malkijah, Shemaiah,
Shimeon, [32]Benjamin, Malluch, and Shemariah.
[33]From the family of Hashum: Mattenai, Mattattah, Zabad, Eliphelet, Jeremai, Manasseh, and Shimei.
[34]From the family of Bani: Maadai, Amram, Uel, [35]Benaiah, Bedeiah,
Keluhi, [36]Vaniah, Meremoth, Eliashib, [37]Mattaniah, Mattenai, and
Jaasu.
[38]From the family of Binnui*: Shimei, [39]Shelemiah, Nathan, Adaiah,
[40]Macnadebai, Shashai, Sharai, [41]Azarel, Shelemiah, Shemariah,
[42]Shallum, Amariah, and Joseph.
[43]From the family of Nebo: Jeiel, Mattithiah, Zabad, Zebina, Jaddai, Joel, and Benaiah.

[44]Each of these men had a pagan wife, and some even had children by these wives.*

10:25 As in parallel text at 1 Esdras 9:26; Hebrew reads *Malkijah.* **10:37-38** As in Greek version; Hebrew reads *Jaasu,* [38]*Bani, Binnui.* **10:44** Or *and they sent them away with their children.* The meaning of the Hebrew is uncertain.

What God is saying to us

Nehemiah Introduction

Every family has a value that's important to them. It's usually symbolized in objects or traditions, like a special item that's passed from one generation to the next or certain colors that represent a favorite sports team everyone cheers for. The symbolic item and the deep value become intertwined.

Now, think about how you'd feel if your family's assets were suddenly destroyed. You could all certainly try to press on, but everyone would sense that something was different anytime you came together. The absence of those meaningful things would feel like the absence of the value.

This is when Nehemiah's part of God's story speaks to us. Like his counterpart Ezra, Nehemiah lived when the Jewish people were released from being captives in the foreign land of Persia. After more than fifty thousand people made it back to their home territory, they realized (and sent word) back to Nehemiah that the walls of Jerusalem were in shambles. To the outside world, this may have seemed inconsequential; however, to the Jews missing their homeland, this was devastating. They had lost everything once before. Now, with no protection, they knew they'd be open to outside influence and attack once again. Their special value of being "God's people" was intertwined with the city and the temple of Jerusalem—and Jerusalem was vulnerable.

Nehemiah heard this alarming news while still working for the Persian king as a cupbearer. As he literally taste tested (and poison tested) anything the most powerful man in the land drank, God used the unique trust and tension of this relationship to position Nehemiah into a leadership role. Nehemiah was allowed to help rebuild Jerusalem and reset the identity of God's people.

This book challenges us to live our lives on mission. Like Nehemiah, we learn to live with integrity in our everyday responsibilities yet with God's great passion and vision for this world.

Story Arcs

- **Nehemiah**
- **Ezra**
- **Zerubbabel and Jeshua**

NEHEMIAH

Nehemiah

1 These are the memoirs of Nehemiah son of Hacaliah.

Nehemiah's Concern for Jerusalem

In late autumn, in the month of Kislev, in the twentieth year of King Artaxer-
xes' reign,* I was at the fortress of Susa. 2 Hanani, one of my brothers, came
to visit me with some other men who had just arrived from Judah. I asked
them about the Jews who had returned there from captivity and about how
things were going in Jerusalem.
3 They said to me, "Things are not going well for those who returned to
the province of Judah. They are in great trouble and disgrace. The wall of
Jerusalem has been torn down, and the gates have been destroyed by fire."
4 When I heard this, I sat down and wept. In fact, for days I mourned,
fasted, and prayed to the God of heaven. 5 Then I said,

"O Lord, God of heaven, the great and awesome God who keeps his
covenant of unfailing love with those who love him and obey his
commands, 6 listen to my prayer! Look down and see me praying night
and day for your people Israel. I confess that we have sinned against
you. Yes, even my own family and I have sinned! 7 We have sinned
terribly by not obeying the commands, decrees, and regulations that
you gave us through your servant Moses.
8 "Please remember what you told your servant Moses: 'If you are
unfaithful to me, I will scatter you among the nations. 9 But if you
return to me and obey my commands and live by them, then even if
you are exiled to the ends of the earth,* I will bring you back to the
place I have chosen for my name to be honored.'
10 "The people you rescued by your great power and strong hand are
your servants. 11 O Lord, please hear my prayer! Listen to the prayers
of those of us who delight in honoring you. Please grant me success
today by making the king favorable to me.* Put it into his heart to be
kind to me."

In those days I was the king's cup-bearer.

Nehemiah Goes to Jerusalem

2 Early the following spring, in the month of Nisan,* during the twen-
tieth year of King Artaxerxes' reign, I was serving the king his wine.
I had never before appeared sad in his presence. 2 So the king asked me,

1:1 Hebrew *In the month of Kislev of the twentieth year.* A number of dates in the book of Nehemiah can be cross-checked with dates in surviving Persian records and related accurately to our modern calendar. This month of the ancient Hebrew lunar calendar occurred within the months of November and December 446 B.C. The *twentieth year* probably refers to the reign of King Artaxerxes I; compare 2:1; 5:14. 1:9 Hebrew *of the heavens.* 1:11 Hebrew *today in the sight of this man.* 2:1 Hebrew *In the month of Nisan.* This month of the ancient Hebrew lunar calendar occurred within the months of April and May 445 B.C.

Story Arc **1:1-11**

● Nehemiah

Nehemiah had an important job in a challenging season. In the autumn, when he heard about the terrible condition of Jerusalem, he sat down to weep, to mourn, and to seek God. He didn't jump up in anger but rooted himself in his relationship with the Lord for several months. It was during this time between seasons, during these winter months, during the everyday moments while he served as the cupbearer for the king, that Nehemiah became equipped for the significant events that would unfold.

If you want to be a person of influence, be affected by what affects God and serve in anticipation of what God will call you to do in his timing.

Neh 8:1-9 ▶

Make a Difference

2:1-8

Bold Request

Nehemiah did the same task on this day that he did every day, but the king noticed something was different in Nehemiah's spirit. This alone reveals how well the king had grown to know and trust him. Nehemiah lived with integrity, and the king recognized him for it. When Nehemiah was given the opportunity to approach the king with a personal request, he addressed his boss with honor before speaking what was on his heart. Nehemiah wasn't manipulative or conniving. He simply lived out God's story every day because God lived in his own story.

What if you lived with integrity and faithfully cared for the people who are in authority around you? The goal isn't to manipulate situations so you can get a yes to your next big ask but to live and treat others the best way possible. Perhaps in doing so you'll model to them how to step into God's story through your story.

Difference Maker

Pick one person who is in a position of authority in your life and come up with a way you could address them with honor the next time you greet them.

"Why are you looking so sad? You don't look sick to me. You must be deeply troubled."

Then I was terrified, 3 but I replied, "Long live the king! How can I not
be sad? For the city where my ancestors are buried is in ruins, and the gates
have been destroyed by fire."

4 The king asked, "Well, how can I help you?"

With a prayer to the God of heaven, 5 I replied, "If it please the king, and if
you are pleased with me, your servant, send me to Judah to rebuild the city
where my ancestors are buried."

6 The king, with the queen sitting beside him, asked, "How long will you
be gone? When will you return?" After I told him how long I would be gone,
the king agreed to my request.

7 I also said to the king, "If it please the king, let me have letters addressed
to the governors of the province west of the Euphrates River,* instructing
them to let me travel safely through their territories on my way to Judah.
8 And please give me a letter addressed to Asaph, the manager of the king's
forest, instructing him to give me timber. I will need it to make beams for
the gates of the Temple fortress, for the city walls, and for a house for myself." And the king granted these requests, because the gracious hand of
God was on me.

9 When I came to the governors of the province west of the Euphrates
River, I delivered the king's letters to them. The king, I should add, had sent
along army officers and horsemen* to protect me. 10 But when Sanballat the
Horonite and Tobiah the Ammonite official heard of my arrival, they were
very displeased that someone had come to help the people of Israel.

Nehemiah Inspects Jerusalem's Wall

11 So I arrived in Jerusalem. Three days later, 12 I slipped out during the night,
taking only a few others with me. I had not told anyone about the plans God
had put in my heart for Jerusalem. We took no pack animals with us except
the donkey I was riding. 13 After dark I went out through the Valley Gate, past
the Jackal's Well,* and over to the Dung Gate to inspect the broken walls and
burned gates. 14 Then I went to the Fountain Gate and to the King's Pool, but
my donkey couldn't get through the rubble. 15 So, though it was still dark, I
went up the Kidron Valley* instead, inspecting the wall before I turned back
and entered again at the Valley Gate.

16 The city officials did not know I had been out there or what I was doing,
for I had not yet said anything to anyone about my plans. I had not yet spoken to the Jewish leaders—the priests, the nobles, the officials, or anyone else
in the administration. 17 But now I said to them, "You know very well what
trouble we are in. Jerusalem lies in ruins, and its gates have been destroyed
by fire. Let us rebuild the wall of Jerusalem and end this disgrace!" 18 Then I
told them about how the gracious hand of God had been on me, and about
my conversation with the king.

They replied at once, "Yes, let's rebuild the wall!" So they began the good work.

19 But when Sanballat, Tobiah, and Geshem the Arab heard of our plan,
they scoffed contemptuously. "What are you doing? Are you rebelling
against the king?" they asked.

2:7 Hebrew *the province beyond the river;* also in 2:9. 2:9 Or *charioteers.* 2:13 Or *Serpent's Well.* 2:15 Hebrew *the valley.*

20 I replied, "The God of heaven will help us succeed. We, his servants, will start rebuilding this wall. But you have no share, legal right, or historic claim in Jerusalem."

Rebuilding the Wall of Jerusalem

3 Then Eliashib the high priest and the other priests started to rebuild at the Sheep Gate. They dedicated it and set up its doors, building the wall as far as the Tower of the Hundred, which they dedicated, and the Tower of Hananel. 2 People from the town of Jericho worked next to them, and beyond them was Zaccur son of Imri.

3 The Fish Gate was built by the sons of Hassenaah. They laid the beams, set up its doors, and installed its bolts and bars. 4 Meremoth son of Uriah and grandson of Hakkoz repaired the next section of wall. Beside him were Meshullam son of Berekiah and grandson of Meshezabel, and then Zadok son of Baana. 5 Next were the people from Tekoa, though their leaders refused to work with the construction supervisors.

6 The Old City Gate* was repaired by Joiada son of Paseah and Meshullam son of Besodeiah. They laid the beams, set up its doors, and installed its bolts and bars. 7 Next to them were Melatiah from Gibeon, Jadon from Meronoth, people from Gibeon, and people from Mizpah, the headquarters of the governor of the province west of the Euphrates River.* 8 Next was Uzziel son of Harhaiah, a goldsmith by trade, who also worked on the wall. Beyond him was Hananiah, a manufacturer of perfumes. They left out a section of Jerusalem as they built the Broad Wall.*

9 Rephaiah son of Hur, the leader of half the district of Jerusalem, was next to them on the wall. 10 Next Jedaiah son of Harumaph repaired the wall across from his own house, and next to him was Hattush son of Hashabneiah. 11 Then came Malkijah son of Harim and Hasshub son of Pahath-moab, who repaired another section of the wall and the Tower of the Ovens. 12 Shallum son of Hallohesh and his daughters repaired the next section. He was the leader of the other half of the district of Jerusalem.

13 The Valley Gate was repaired by the people from Zanoah, led by Hanun. They set up its doors and installed its bolts and bars. They also repaired the 1,500 feet* of wall to the Dung Gate.

14 The Dung Gate was repaired by Malkijah son of Recab, the leader of the Beth-hakkerem district. He rebuilt it, set up its doors, and installed its bolts and bars.

15 The Fountain Gate was repaired by Shallum* son of Col-hozeh, the leader of the Mizpah district. He rebuilt it, roofed it, set up its doors, and installed its bolts and bars. Then he repaired the wall of the pool of Siloam* near the king's garden, and he rebuilt the wall as far as the stairs that descend from the City of David. 16 Next to him was Nehemiah son of Azbuk, the leader of half the district of Beth-zur. He rebuilt the wall from a place across from the tombs of David's family as far as the water reservoir and the House of the Warriors.

17 Next to him, repairs were made by a group of Levites working under the supervision of Rehum son of Bani. Then came Hashabiah, the leader of half

Prayer **3:1**

Lord, like the people in this chapter who helped Nehemiah, surround me with people who will help me become a person of God and do what you have asked of me. Help me also encourage and inspire them. Amen.

3:6 Or *The Mishneh Gate,* or *The Jeshanah Gate.* **3:7** Hebrew *the province beyond the river.* **3:8** Or *They fortified Jerusalem up to the Broad Wall.* **3:13** Hebrew *1,000 cubits* [460 meters]. **3:15a** As in Syriac version; Hebrew reads *Shallun.* **3:15b** Hebrew *pool of Shelah,* another name for the pool of Siloam.

Question 3:28-30

Why might Nehemiah have put people to work on a section of the city wall that was closest to where they lived or worked (vv. 28-30)? In what ways is God similarly daring you to challenge the people around you to serve God where they live?

Make a Difference

4:1-5

Mocking Criticism

You probably have a Sanballat (vv. 1-2) or Tobiah (v. 3) in your life—people who enjoy taunting you and others you care about. Maybe they do it with smiles on their faces, but there's a poisonous sarcasm in their spirits. They can even make you feel insecure and nervous whenever they show up. If they aren't around you today, they may show up tomorrow.

Take a cue from Nehemiah and acknowledge the attack while also continuing to work and grow in what God has shown you. In doing so, you're mocking criticism through faithfulness. You don't need to attend every taunting you're invited to.

Difference Maker

Decide today what you'll do the next time someone gives you a hard time. Pray and ask God for his wisdom so you follow his lead and not your emotions.

the district of Keilah, who supervised the building of the wall on behalf of
his own district. [18]Next down the line were his countrymen led by Binnui*
son of Henadad, the leader of the other half of the district of Keilah.
[19]Next to them, Ezer son of Jeshua, the leader of Mizpah, repaired an-
other section of wall across from the ascent to the armory near the angle in
the wall. [20]Next to him was Baruch son of Zabbai, who zealously repaired
an additional section from the angle to the door of the house of Eliashib
the high priest. [21]Meremoth son of Uriah and grandson of Hakkoz rebuilt
another section of the wall extending from the door of Eliashib's house to
the end of the house.
[22]The next repairs were made by the priests from the surrounding region.
[23]After them, Benjamin and Hasshub repaired the section across from their
house, and Azariah son of Maaseiah and grandson of Ananiah repaired the
section across from his house. [24]Next was Binnui son of Henadad, who re-
built another section of the wall from Azariah's house to the angle and the
corner. [25]Palal son of Uzai carried on the work from a point opposite the
angle and the tower that projects up from the king's upper house beside
the court of the guard. Next to him were Pedaiah son of Parosh, [26]with the
Temple servants living on the hill of Ophel, who repaired the wall as far
as a point across from the Water Gate to the east and the projecting tower.
[27]Then came the people of Tekoa, who repaired another section across from
the great projecting tower and over to the wall of Ophel.
[28]Above the Horse Gate, the priests repaired the wall. Each one repaired
the section immediately across from his own house. [29]Next Zadok son of
Immer also rebuilt the wall across from his own house, and beyond him
was Shemaiah son of Shecaniah, the gatekeeper of the East Gate. [30]Next
Hananiah son of Shelemiah and Hanun, the sixth son of Zalaph, repaired
another section, while Meshullam son of Berekiah rebuilt the wall across
from where he lived. [31]Malkijah, one of the goldsmiths, repaired the wall as
far as the housing for the Temple servants and merchants, across from the
Inspection Gate. Then he continued as far as the upper room at the corner.
[32]The other goldsmiths and merchants repaired the wall from that corner
to the Sheep Gate.

Enemies Oppose the Rebuilding

4 [1]*Sanballat was very angry when he learned that we were rebuilding
the wall. He flew into a rage and mocked the Jews, [2]saying in front of
his friends and the Samarian army officers, "What does this bunch of poor,
feeble Jews think they're doing? Do they think they can build the wall in a
single day by just offering a few sacrifices?* Do they actually think they can
make something of stones from a rubbish heap—and charred ones at that?"
[3]Tobiah the Ammonite, who was standing beside him, remarked, "That
stone wall would collapse if even a fox walked along the top of it!"
[4]Then I prayed, "Hear us, our God, for we are being mocked. May their
scoffing fall back on their own heads, and may they themselves become cap-
tives in a foreign land! [5]Do not ignore their guilt. Do not blot out their sins,
for they have provoked you to anger here in front of* the builders."

3:18 As in a few Hebrew manuscripts, some Greek manuscripts, and Syriac version (see also 3:24; 10:9); most Hebrew manuscripts read *Bavvai.* **4:1** Verses 4:1-6 are numbered 3:33-38 in Hebrew text. **4:2** The meaning of the Hebrew is uncertain. **4:5** Or *for they have thrown insults in the face of.*

6At last the wall was completed to half its height around the entire city,
for the people had worked with enthusiasm.
7*But when Sanballat and Tobiah and the Arabs, Ammonites, and Ash-
dodites heard that the work was going ahead and that the gaps in the wall
of Jerusalem were being repaired, they were furious. 8They all made plans
to come and fight against Jerusalem and throw us into confusion. 9But we
prayed to our God and guarded the city day and night to protect ourselves.
10Then the people of Judah began to complain, "The workers are getting
tired, and there is so much rubble to be moved. We will never be able to build
the wall by ourselves."
11Meanwhile, our enemies were saying, "Before they know what's hap-
pening, we will swoop down on them and kill them and end their work."
12The Jews who lived near the enemy came and told us again and again,
"They will come from all directions and attack us!"* 13So I placed armed
guards behind the lowest parts of the wall in the exposed areas. I stationed
the people to stand guard by families, armed with swords, spears, and bows.
14Then as I looked over the situation, I called together the nobles and the
rest of the people and said to them, "Don't be afraid of the enemy! Remember
the Lord, who is great and glorious, and fight for your brothers, your sons,
your daughters, your wives, and your homes!"
15When our enemies heard that we knew of their plans and that God had
frustrated them, we all returned to our work on the wall. 16But from then
on, only half my men worked while the other half stood guard with spears,
shields, bows, and coats of mail. The leaders stationed themselves behind
the people of Judah 17who were building the wall. The laborers carried on
their work with one hand supporting their load and one hand holding a
weapon. 18All the builders had a sword belted to their side. The trumpeter
stayed with me to sound the alarm.
19Then I explained to the nobles and officials and all the people, "The
work is very spread out, and we are widely separated from each other along
the wall. 20When you hear the blast of the trumpet, rush to wherever it is
sounding. Then our God will fight for us!"
21We worked early and late, from sunrise to sunset. And half the men
were always on guard. 22I also told everyone living outside the walls to stay
in Jerusalem. That way they and their servants could help with guard duty
at night and work during the day. 23During this time, none of us—not I,
nor my relatives, nor my servants, nor the guards who were with me—ever
took off our clothes. We carried our weapons with us at all times, even when
we went for water.*

Nehemiah Defends the Oppressed

5 About this time some of the men and their wives raised a cry of protest
against their fellow Jews. 2They were saying, "We have such large fami-
lies. We need more food to survive."
3Others said, "We have mortgaged our fields, vineyards, and homes to get
food during the famine."
4And others said, "We have had to borrow money on our fields and vine-
yards to pay our taxes. 5We belong to the same family as those who are

4:7 Verses 4:7-23 are numbered 4:1-17 in Hebrew text. 4:12 The meaning of the Hebrew is uncertain. 4:23 Or *Each carried his weapon in his right hand.* Hebrew reads *Each his weapon the water.* The meaning of the Hebrew is uncertain.

Make a Difference

4:6-23

The Good Fight

Movies have shown us what happens when an ancient village is attacked and the townspeople rise up to fight for each other. They draw their swords, raise their shields, and give rousing speeches. Nehemiah and the people around him had their own version of this as they began protecting each other more intentionally to keep everyone safe while continuing their project. He even divided the men up to rotate in shifts so that everyone always had both a tool and a sword on them, and no one ever changed out of their clothes (vv. 15-18, 23).

God may not ever call you to do this exact thing, but he does call you to the same value. We don't just fight the good fight for ourselves but for each other. God puts us into relationships with others to help them just as they can help us. This is what Jesus established the church to do (Hebrews 10:24-25).

Difference Maker

If you and your friends were all in with God and each other today, what would be different about tomorrow?

Question **5:14**

What do you think of Nehemiah's example not to eat better food than everyone else did? How does it challenge you?

Prayer **5:19**

Lord, when I do something good, let that be between the two of us versus me getting credit for it. I trust you when I serve you. Amen.

wealthy, and our children are just like theirs. Yet we must sell our children
into slavery just to get enough money to live. We have already sold some of
our daughters, and we are helpless to do anything about it, for our fields and
vineyards are already mortgaged to others."
6 When I heard their complaints, I was very angry. 7 After thinking it over,
I spoke out against these nobles and officials. I told them, "You are hurting
your own relatives by charging interest when they borrow money!" Then I
called a public meeting to deal with the problem.
8 At the meeting I said to them, "We are doing all we can to redeem our
Jewish relatives who have had to sell themselves to pagan foreigners, but you
are selling them back into slavery again. How often must we redeem them?"
And they had nothing to say in their defense.
9 Then I pressed further, "What you are doing is not right! Should you not
walk in the fear of our God in order to avoid being mocked by enemy na-
tions? 10 I myself, as well as my brothers and my workers, have been lending
the people money and grain, but now let us stop this business of charging
interest. 11 You must restore their fields, vineyards, olive groves, and homes to
them this very day. And repay the interest you charged when you lent them
money, grain, new wine, and olive oil."
12 They replied, "We will give back everything and demand nothing more
from the people. We will do as you say." Then I called the priests and made
the nobles and officials swear to do what they had promised.
13 I shook out the folds of my robe and said, "If you fail to keep your prom-
ise, may God shake you like this from your homes and from your property!"
The whole assembly responded, "Amen," and they praised the LORD. And
the people did as they had promised.
14 For the entire twelve years that I was governor of Judah—from the
twentieth year to the thirty-second year of the reign of King Artaxerxes*—
neither I nor my officials drew on our official food allowance. 15 The former
governors, in contrast, had laid heavy burdens on the people, demanding
a daily ration of food and wine, besides forty pieces* of silver. Even their
assistants took advantage of the people. But because I feared God, I did
not act that way.
16 I also devoted myself to working on the wall and refused to acquire any
land. And I required all my servants to spend time working on the wall. 17 I
asked for nothing, even though I regularly fed 150 Jewish officials at my
table, besides all the visitors from other lands! 18 The provisions I paid for
each day included one ox, six choice sheep or goats, and a large number of
poultry. And every ten days we needed a large supply of all kinds of wine. Yet
I refused to claim the governor's food allowance because the people already
carried a heavy burden.

19 Remember, O my God, all that I have done for these people, and bless
me for it.

Continued Opposition to Rebuilding

6 Sanballat, Tobiah, Geshem the Arab, and the rest of our enemies found
out that I had finished rebuilding the wall and that no gaps remained—
though we had not yet set up the doors in the gates. 2 So Sanballat and

5:14 That is, 445–433 B.C. 5:15 Hebrew *40 shekels* [1 pound or 456 grams].

Geshem sent a message asking me to meet them at one of the villages* in
the plain of Ono.
But I realized they were plotting to harm me, 3 so I replied by sending this
message to them: "I am engaged in a great work, so I can't come. Why should
I stop working to come and meet with you?"
4 Four times they sent the same message, and each time I gave the same
reply. 5 The fifth time, Sanballat's servant came with an open letter in his
hand, 6 and this is what it said:

"There is a rumor among the surrounding nations, and Geshem* tells me it is true, that you and the Jews are planning to rebel and that is why you are building the wall. According to his reports, you plan to be their king. 7 He also reports that you have appointed prophets in Jerusalem to proclaim about you, 'Look! There is a king in Judah!'

"You can be very sure that this report will get back to the king, so I suggest that you come and talk it over with me."

8 I replied, "There is no truth in any part of your story. You are making
up the whole thing."
9 They were just trying to intimidate us, imagining that they could dis-
courage us and stop the work. So I continued the work with even greater
determination.*
10 Later I went to visit Shemaiah son of Delaiah and grandson of Mehet-
abel, who was confined to his home. He said, "Let us meet together inside
the Temple of God and bolt the doors shut. Your enemies are coming to kill
you tonight."
11 But I replied, "Should someone in my position run from danger? Should
someone in my position enter the Temple to save his life? No, I won't do it!"
12 I realized that God had not spoken to him, but that he had uttered this
prophecy against me because Tobiah and Sanballat had hired him. 13 They
were hoping to intimidate me and make me sin. Then they would be able
to accuse and discredit me.

14 Remember, O my God, all the evil things that Tobiah and Sanballat have done. And remember Noadiah the prophet and all the prophets like her who have tried to intimidate me.

The Builders Complete the Wall

15 So on October 2* the wall was finished—just fifty-two days after we had
begun. 16 When our enemies and the surrounding nations heard about it,
they were frightened and humiliated. They realized this work had been done
with the help of our God.
17 During those fifty-two days, many letters went back and forth between
Tobiah and the nobles of Judah. 18 For many in Judah had sworn allegiance
to him because his father-in-law was Shecaniah son of Arah, and his son
Jehohanan was married to the daughter of Meshullam son of Berekiah.
19 They kept telling me about Tobiah's good deeds, and then they told him

6:2 As in Greek version; Hebrew reads *at Kephirim.* 6:6 Hebrew *Gashmu,* a variant spelling of Geshem. 6:9 As in Greek version; Hebrew reads *But now to strengthen my hands.* 6:15 Hebrew *on the twenty-fifth day of the month Elul,* of the ancient Hebrew lunar calendar. This day was October 2, 445 B.C.; also see note on 1:1.

Make a Difference

6:15–19

Until the End

There came a moment when all the hard work reached its end. To get there, the people fought long battles and undertook huge tasks amid fatigue and discouragement. Because of their efforts, the job was now finished within fewer than two months (which is interesting, especially when you realize Nehemiah had prayed for four months before talking with the king).

At some point in your life, you will be tempted to quit before you have completed the task God has given you. Look at what the people of Israel did to overcome their quitting points. Likewise, plan to serve and be faithful until the end. The thick skin you'll need comes by keeping your heart tender before God.

Difference Maker

Think of something you've quit doing because you got tired of doing it. Read Galatians 6:9 and pray about any steps God would have you take.

everything I said. And Tobiah kept sending threatening letters to intimidate me.

7 After the wall was finished and I had set up the doors in the gates, the
gatekeepers, singers, and Levites were appointed. 2 I gave the responsi-
bility of governing Jerusalem to my brother Hanani, along with Hananiah,
the commander of the fortress, for he was a faithful man who feared God
more than most. 3 I said to them, "Do not leave the gates open during the
hottest part of the day.* And even while the gatekeepers are on duty, have
them shut and bar the doors. Appoint the residents of Jerusalem to act as
guards, everyone on a regular watch. Some will serve at sentry posts and
some in front of their own homes."

Nehemiah Registers the People

4 At that time the city was large and spacious, but the population was small,
and none of the houses had been rebuilt. 5 So my God gave me the idea to
call together all the nobles and leaders of the city, along with the ordinary
citizens, for registration. I had found the genealogical record of those who
had first returned to Judah. This is what was written there:

6 Here is the list of the Jewish exiles of the provinces who returned from
their captivity. King Nebuchadnezzar had deported them to Babylon,
but now they returned to Jerusalem and the other towns in Judah
where they originally lived. 7 Their leaders were Zerubbabel, Jeshua,
Nehemiah, Seraiah,* Reelaiah,* Nahamani, Mordecai, Bilshan, Mispar,*
Bigvai, Rehum,* and Baanah.

This is the number of the men of Israel who returned from exile:

8 The family of Parosh 2,172
9 The family of Shephatiah 372
10 The family of Arah 652
11 The family of Pahath-moab (descendants of Jeshua and Joab) . . . 2,818
12 The family of Elam 1,254
13 The family of Zattu 845
14 The family of Zaccai 760
15 The family of Bani* 648
16 The family of Bebai 628
17 The family of Azgad 2,322
18 The family of Adonikam 667
19 The family of Bigvai 2,067
20 The family of Adin 655
21 The family of Ater (descendants of Hezekiah) 98
22 The family of Hashum 328
23 The family of Bezai 324
24 The family of Jorah* 112
25 The family of Gibbar* 95

7:3 Or *Keep the gates of Jerusalem closed until the sun is hot.* 7:7a As in parallel text at Ezra 2:2; Hebrew reads *Azariah.* 7:7b As in parallel text at Ezra 2:2; Hebrew reads *Raamiah.* 7:7c As in parallel text at Ezra 2:2; Hebrew reads *Mispereth.* 7:7d As in parallel text at Ezra 2:2; Hebrew reads *Nehum.* 7:15 As in parallel text at Ezra 2:10; Hebrew reads *Binnui.* 7:24 As in parallel text at Ezra 2:18; Hebrew reads *Hariph.* 7:25 As in parallel text at Ezra 2:20; Hebrew reads *Gibeon.*

26	The people of Bethlehem and Netophah	188
27	The people of Anathoth	128
28	The people of Beth-azmaveth	42
29	The people of Kiriath-jearim, Kephirah, and Beeroth	743
30	The people of Ramah and Geba	621
31	The people of Micmash	122
32	The people of Bethel and Ai	123
33	The people of West Nebo*	52
34	The citizens of West Elam*	1,254
35	The citizens of Harim	320
36	The citizens of Jericho	345
37	The citizens of Lod, Hadid, and Ono	721
38	The citizens of Senaah	3,930

39 These are the priests who returned from exile:

	The family of Jedaiah (through the line of Jeshua)	973
40	The family of Immer	1,052
41	The family of Pashhur	1,247
42	The family of Harim	1,017

43 These are the Levites who returned from exile:

	The families of Jeshua and Kadmiel (descendants of Hodaviah*)	74
44	The singers of the family of Asaph	148
45	The gatekeepers of the families of Shallum, Ater, Talmon, Akkub, Hatita, and Shobai	138

46 The descendants of the following Temple servants returned from exile:

Ziha, Hasupha, Tabbaoth,
47 Keros, Siaha,* Padon,
48 Lebanah, Hagabah, Shalmai,
49 Hanan, Giddel, Gahar,
50 Reaiah, Rezin, Nekoda,
51 Gazzam, Uzza, Paseah,
52 Besai, Meunim, Nephusim,*
53 Bakbuk, Hakupha, Harhur,
54 Bazluth,* Mehida, Harsha,
55 Barkos, Sisera, Temah,
56 Neziah, and Hatipha.

57 The descendants of these servants of King Solomon returned from exile:

Sotai, Hassophereth, Peruda,*
58 Jaalah,* Darkon, Giddel,
59 Shephatiah, Hattil, Pokereth-hazzebaim, and Ami.*

7:33 Or *of the other Nebo.* 7:34 Or *of the other Elam.* 7:43 As in parallel text at Ezra 2:40; Hebrew reads *Hodevah.* 7:47 As in parallel text at Ezra 2:44; Hebrew reads *Sia.* 7:52 As in parallel text at Ezra 2:50; Hebrew reads *Nephushesim.* 7:54 As in parallel text at Ezra 2:52; Hebrew reads *Bazlith.* 7:57 As in parallel text at Ezra 2:55; Hebrew reads *Sotai, Sophereth, Perida.* 7:58 As in parallel text at Ezra 2:56; Hebrew reads *Jaala.* 7:59 As in parallel text at Ezra 2:57; Hebrew reads *Amon.*

Drop your brilliant thoughts here

60 In all, the Temple servants and the descendants of Solomon's servants
numbered 392.

61 Another group returned at this time from the towns of Tel-melah,
Tel-harsha, Kerub, Addan,* and Immer. However, they could not prove that
they or their families were descendants of Israel. 62 This group included
the families of Delaiah, Tobiah, and Nekoda—a total of 642 people.
63 Three families of priests—Hobaiah, Hakkoz, and Barzillai—also
returned. (This Barzillai had married a woman who was a descendant of
Barzillai of Gilead, and he had taken her family name.) 64 They searched
for their names in the genealogical records, but they were not found, so
they were disqualified from serving as priests. 65 The governor told them
not to eat the priests' share of food from the sacrifices until a priest could
consult the LORD about the matter by using the Urim and Thummim—
the sacred lots.
66 So a total of 42,360 people returned to Judah, 67 in addition to 7,337
servants and 245 singers, both men and women. 68 They took with them
736 horses, 245 mules,* 69 435 camels, and 6,720 donkeys.
70 Some of the family leaders gave gifts for the work. The governor
gave to the treasury 1,000 gold coins,* 50 gold basins, and 530 robes for
the priests. 71 The other leaders gave to the treasury a total of 20,000
gold coins* and some 2,750 pounds* of silver for the work. 72 The rest of
the people gave 20,000 gold coins, about 2,500 pounds* of silver, and
67 robes for the priests.
73 So the priests, the Levites, the gatekeepers, the singers, the Temple
servants, and some of the common people settled near Jerusalem. The
rest of the people returned to their own towns throughout Israel.

Ezra Reads the Law

8 In October,* when the Israelites had settled in their towns, 8:1 all the
people assembled with a unified purpose at the square just inside the
Water Gate. They asked Ezra the scribe to bring out the Book of the Law of
Moses, which the LORD had given for Israel to obey.
2 So on October 8* Ezra the priest brought the Book of the Law before
the assembly, which included the men and women and all the children old
enough to understand. 3 He faced the square just inside the Water Gate from
early morning until noon and read aloud to everyone who could understand.
All the people listened closely to the Book of the Law.
4 Ezra the scribe stood on a high wooden platform that had been made
for the occasion. To his right stood Mattithiah, Shema, Anaiah, Uriah, Hil-
kiah, and Maaseiah. To his left stood Pedaiah, Mishael, Malkijah, Hashum,
Hashbaddanah, Zechariah, and Meshullam. 5 Ezra stood on the platform in
full view of all the people. When they saw him open the book, they all rose
to their feet.

7:61 As in parallel text at Ezra 2:59; Hebrew reads *Addon.* 7:68 As in some Hebrew manuscripts (see also Ezra 2:66); most Hebrew manuscripts lack this verse. Verses 7:69-73 are numbered 7:68-72 in Hebrew text. 7:70 Hebrew *1,000 darics of gold,* about 19 pounds or 8.6 kilograms in weight. 7:71a Hebrew *20,000 darics of gold,* about 375 pounds or 170 kilograms in weight; also in 7:72. 7:71b Hebrew *2,200 minas* [1,300 kilograms]. 7:72 Hebrew *2,000 minas* [1,200 kilograms]. 7:73 Hebrew *In the seventh month.* This month of the ancient Hebrew lunar calendar occurred within the months of October and November 445 B.C. 8:2 Hebrew *on the first day of the seventh month,* of the ancient Hebrew lunar calendar. This day was October 8, 445 B.C.; also see note on 1:1.

6 Then Ezra praised the LORD, the great God, and all the people chanted, "Amen! Amen!" as they lifted their hands. Then they bowed down and worshiped the LORD with their faces to the ground.

7 The Levites—Jeshua, Bani, Sherebiah, Jamin, Akkub, Shabbethai, Hodiah, Maaseiah, Kelita, Azariah, Jozabad, Hanan, and Pelaiah—then instructed the people in the Law while everyone remained in their places. 8 They read from the Book of the Law of God and clearly explained the meaning of what was being read, helping the people understand each passage.

9 Then Nehemiah the governor, Ezra the priest and scribe, and the Levites who were interpreting for the people said to them, "Don't mourn or weep on such a day as this! For today is a sacred day before the LORD your God." For the people had all been weeping as they listened to the words of the Law.

10 And Nehemiah* continued, "Go and celebrate with a feast of rich foods and sweet drinks, and share gifts of food with people who have nothing prepared. This is a sacred day before our Lord. Don't be dejected and sad, for the joy of the LORD is your strength!"

11 And the Levites, too, quieted the people, telling them, "Hush! Don't weep! For this is a sacred day." 12 So the people went away to eat and drink at a festive meal, to share gifts of food, and to celebrate with great joy because they had heard God's words and understood them.

The Festival of Shelters

13 On October 9* the family leaders of all the people, together with the priests and Levites, met with Ezra the scribe to go over the Law in greater detail. 14 As they studied the Law, they discovered that the LORD had commanded through Moses that the Israelites should live in shelters during the festival to be held that month.* 15 He had said that a proclamation should be made throughout their towns and in Jerusalem, telling the people to go to the hills to get branches from olive, wild olive,* myrtle, palm, and other leafy trees. They were to use these branches to make shelters in which they would live during the festival, as prescribed in the Law.

16 So the people went out and cut branches and used them to build shelters on the roofs of their houses, in their courtyards, in the courtyards of God's Temple, or in the squares just inside the Water Gate and the Ephraim Gate. 17 So everyone who had returned from captivity lived in these shelters during the festival, and they were all filled with great joy! The Israelites had not celebrated like this since the days of Joshua* son of Nun.

18 Ezra read from the Book of the Law of God on each of the seven days of the festival. Then on the eighth day they held a solemn assembly, as was required by law.

The People Confess Their Sins

9 On October 31* the people assembled again, and this time they fasted and dressed in burlap and sprinkled dust on their heads. 2 Those of Israelite descent separated themselves from all foreigners as they confessed

8:10 Hebrew *he.* 8:13 Hebrew *On the second day,* of the seventh month of the ancient Hebrew lunar calendar. This day was October 9, 445 B.C.; also see notes on 1:1 and 8:2. 8:14 Hebrew *in the seventh month.* This month of the ancient Hebrew lunar calendar usually occurs within the months of September and October. See Lev 23:39-43. 8:15 Or *pine;* Hebrew reads *oil tree.* 8:17 Hebrew *Jeshua,* a variant spelling of Joshua. 9:1 Hebrew *On the twenty-fourth day of that same month,* the seventh month of the ancient Hebrew lunar calendar. This day was October 31, 445 B.C.; also see notes on 1:1 and 8:2.

Story Arc **8:1-9**

Ezra

For all the physical work Nehemiah organized, Ezra was his counterpart in guiding the people back to God. He was on-site in Jerusalem before Nehemiah and helped the people rebuild the temple so they could worship the Lord together. Now the people wanted Ezra to remind them of what mattered by having him read the book of the law (God's written words) aloud to them.

The real key was in whether the people would then also obey it. It's one thing to hear God's wisdom and commands through sermons, Bible studies, and small group gatherings, but it's another thing to cooperate with that wisdom instead of pushing back on it. Ezra modeled what it means not only to share the truth but also to show people what living it out looks like.

What aspects of Ezra's pattern of Bible study and accountability could you implement in your own life?

Neh 12:1 ►

Question 9:9

How might knowing the history of God's people and God's actions with his people help you know how to act and live today?

their own sins and the sins of their ancestors. 3 They remained standing in
place for three hours* while the Book of the Law of the LORD their God was
read aloud to them. Then for three more hours they confessed their sins
and worshiped the LORD their God. 4 The Levites—Jeshua, Bani, Kadmiel,
Shebaniah, Bunni, Sherebiah, Bani, and Kenani—stood on the stairway of
the Levites and cried out to the LORD their God with loud voices.

5 Then the leaders of the Levites—Jeshua, Kadmiel, Bani, Hashabneiah,
Sherebiah, Hodiah, Shebaniah, and Pethahiah—called out to the people:
"Stand up and praise the LORD your God, for he lives from everlasting to
everlasting!" Then they prayed:

"May your glorious name be praised! May it be exalted above all blessing
and praise!

6 "You alone are the LORD. You made the skies and the heavens and all
the stars. You made the earth and the seas and everything in them. You
preserve them all, and the angels of heaven worship you.

7 "You are the LORD God, who chose Abram and brought him from
Ur of the Chaldeans and renamed him Abraham. 8 When he had proved
himself faithful, you made a covenant with him to give him and his
descendants the land of the Canaanites, Hittites, Amorites, Perizzites,
Jebusites, and Girgashites. And you have done what you promised, for
you are always true to your word.

9 "You saw the misery of our ancestors in Egypt, and you heard their
cries from beside the Red Sea.* 10 You displayed miraculous signs and
wonders against Pharaoh, his officials, and all his people, for you knew
how arrogantly they were treating our ancestors. You have a glorious
reputation that has never been forgotten. 11 You divided the sea for your
people so they could walk through on dry land! And then you hurled
their enemies into the depths of the sea. They sank like stones beneath
the mighty waters. 12 You led our ancestors by a pillar of cloud during
the day and a pillar of fire at night so that they could find their way.

13 "You came down at Mount Sinai and spoke to them from heaven.
You gave them regulations and instructions that were just, and decrees
and commands that were good. 14 You instructed them concerning your
holy Sabbath. And you commanded them, through Moses your servant,
to obey all your commands, decrees, and instructions.

15 "You gave them bread from heaven when they were hungry and
water from the rock when they were thirsty. You commanded them to
go and take possession of the land you had sworn to give them.

16 "But our ancestors were proud and stubborn, and they paid no
attention to your commands. 17 They refused to obey and did not
remember the miracles you had done for them. Instead, they became
stubborn and appointed a leader to take them back to their slavery
in Egypt.* But you are a God of forgiveness, gracious and merciful,
slow to become angry, and rich in unfailing love. You did not abandon
them, 18 even when they made an idol shaped like a calf and said, 'This
is your god who brought you out of Egypt!' They committed terrible
blasphemies.

19 "But in your great mercy you did not abandon them to die in the

9:3 Hebrew *for a quarter of a day.* 9:9 Hebrew *sea of reeds.* 9:17 As in Greek version; Hebrew reads *in their rebellion.*

wilderness. The pillar of cloud still led them forward by day, and the
pillar of fire showed them the way through the night. 20 You sent your
good Spirit to instruct them, and you did not stop giving them manna
from heaven or water for their thirst. 21 For forty years you sustained
them in the wilderness, and they lacked nothing. Their clothes did not
wear out, and their feet did not swell!

22 "Then you helped our ancestors conquer kingdoms and nations,
and you placed your people in every corner of the land.* They took over
the land of King Sihon of Heshbon and the land of King Og of Bashan.
23 You made their descendants as numerous as the stars in the sky and
brought them into the land you had promised to their ancestors.

24 "They went in and took possession of the land. You subdued whole
nations before them. Even the Canaanites, who inhabited the land, were
powerless! Your people could deal with these nations and their kings as
they pleased. 25 Our ancestors captured fortified cities and fertile land.
They took over houses full of good things, with cisterns already dug and
vineyards and olive groves and fruit trees in abundance. So they ate until
they were full and grew fat and enjoyed themselves in all your blessings.

26 "But despite all this, they were disobedient and rebelled against
you. They turned their backs on your Law, they killed your prophets
who warned them to return to you, and they committed terrible
blasphemies. 27 So you handed them over to their enemies, who made
them suffer. But in their time of trouble they cried to you, and you
heard them from heaven. In your great mercy, you sent them liberators
who rescued them from their enemies.

28 "But as soon as they were at peace, your people again committed
evil in your sight, and once more you let their enemies conquer them.
Yet whenever your people turned and cried to you again for help, you
listened once more from heaven. In your wonderful mercy, you rescued
them many times!

29 "You warned them to return to your Law, but they became proud
and obstinate and disobeyed your commands. They did not follow
your regulations, by which people will find life if only they obey. They
stubbornly turned their backs on you and refused to listen. 30 In your
love, you were patient with them for many years. You sent your Spirit,
who warned them through the prophets. But still they wouldn't listen!
So once again you allowed the peoples of the land to conquer them.
31 But in your great mercy, you did not destroy them completely or
abandon them forever. What a gracious and merciful God you are!

32 "And now, our God, the great and mighty and awesome God,
who keeps his covenant of unfailing love, do not let all the hardships
we have suffered seem insignificant to you. Great trouble has come
upon us and upon our kings and leaders and priests and prophets
and ancestors—all of your people—from the days when the kings of
Assyria first triumphed over us until now. 33 Every time you punished us
you were being just. We have sinned greatly, and you gave us only what
we deserved. 34 Our kings, leaders, priests, and ancestors did not obey
your Law or listen to the warnings in your commands and laws. 35 Even
while they had their own kingdom, they did not serve you, though you

9:22 The meaning of the Hebrew is uncertain.

Make a Difference

10:28–29

A Rough Vow

A covenant has consequences built into it. If a person who made a covenant falls short, they have already agreed to the penalties for breaking the vow.

Just like the Israelites, we have to determine if we're willing to accept the consequences from God if we rebel. Keep in mind that in Ezra's day, the situation was discouraging. People were spiritually lazy, God's law was widely disregarded, and public and private morality were at low levels.

By making this solemn promise, these leaders took ownership of a holy fear. This careful vow helped them stay obedient. In a day when many people wanted to simply pray that everything would go smoothly, these people, instead, wanted to be shaped by a gritty faith, a fortitude of soul, determined to follow the Lord.

Difference Maker

Write down the names of three other people in your life who can help hold you accountable and remind you to stay true. Reach out to them and ask them to remind you each week to be faithful to the Lord.

showered your goodness on them. You gave them a large, fertile land,
but they refused to turn from their wickedness.
36"So now today we are slaves in the land of plenty that you gave our
ancestors for their enjoyment! We are slaves here in this good land. 37The
lush produce of this land piles up in the hands of the kings whom you
have set over us because of our sins. They have power over us and our
livestock. We serve them at their pleasure, and we are in great misery."

The People Agree to Obey

38*The people responded, "In view of all this,* we are making a solemn prom-
ise and putting it in writing. On this sealed document are the names of our
leaders and Levites and priests."

10

1*The document was ratified and sealed with the following
names:

The governor:
Nehemiah son of Hacaliah, and also Zedekiah.
2The following priests:
Seraiah, Azariah, Jeremiah, 3Pashhur, Amariah, Malkijah, 4Hattush,
Shebaniah, Malluch, 5Harim, Meremoth, Obadiah, 6Daniel, Ginnethon,
Baruch, 7Meshullam, Abijah, Mijamin, 8Maaziah, Bilgai, and Shemaiah.
These were the priests.
9The following Levites:
Jeshua son of Azaniah, Binnui from the family of Henadad, Kadmiel,
10and their fellow Levites: Shebaniah, Hodiah, Kelita, Pelaiah, Hanan,
11Mica, Rehob, Hashabiah, 12Zaccur, Sherebiah, Shebaniah, 13Hodiah,
Bani, and Beninu.
14The following leaders:
Parosh, Pahath-moab, Elam, Zattu, Bani, 15Bunni, Azgad, Bebai,
16Adonijah, Bigvai, Adin, 17Ater, Hezekiah, Azzur, 18Hodiah, Hashum,
Bezai, 19Hariph, Anathoth, Nebai, 20Magpiash, Meshullam, Hezir,
21Meshezabel, Zadok, Jaddua, 22Pelatiah, Hanan, Anaiah, 23Hoshea,
Hananiah, Hasshub, 24Hallohesh, Pilha, Shobek, 25Rehum, Hashabnah,
Maaseiah, 26Ahiah, Hanan, Anan, 27Malluch, Harim, and Baanah.

The Vow of the People

28Then the rest of the people—the priests, Levites, gatekeepers, singers,
Temple servants, and all who had separated themselves from the pagan
people of the land in order to obey the Law of God, together with their wives,
sons, daughters, and all who were old enough to understand—29joined their
leaders and bound themselves with an oath. They swore a curse on them-
selves if they failed to obey the Law of God as issued by his servant Moses.
They solemnly promised to carefully follow all the commands, regulations,
and decrees of the LORD our Lord:

30"We promise not to let our daughters marry the pagan people of the
land, and not to let our sons marry their daughters.
31"We also promise that if the people of the land should bring any

9:38a Verse 9:38 is numbered 10:1 in Hebrew text. **9:38b** Or *In spite of all this.* **10:1** Verses 10:1-39 are numbered 10:2-40 in Hebrew text.

merchandise or grain to be sold on the Sabbath or on any other holy day,
we will refuse to buy it. Every seventh year we will let our land rest, and
we will cancel all debts owed to us.
32 "In addition, we promise to obey the command to pay the annual
Temple tax of one-eighth of an ounce of silver* for the care of the
Temple of our God. 33 This will provide for the Bread of the Presence;
for the regular grain offerings and burnt offerings; for the offerings
on the Sabbaths, the new moon celebrations, and the annual festivals;
for the holy offerings; and for the sin offerings to make atonement
for Israel. It will provide for everything necessary for the work of the
Temple of our God.
34 "We have cast sacred lots to determine when—at regular times
each year—the families of the priests, Levites, and the common people
should bring wood to God's Temple to be burned on the altar of the
LORD our God, as is written in the Law.
35 "We promise to bring the first part of every harvest to the LORD's
Temple year after year—whether it be a crop from the soil or from our
fruit trees. 36 We agree to give God our oldest sons and the firstborn of
all our herds and flocks, as prescribed in the Law. We will present them
to the priests who minister in the Temple of our God. 37 We will store
the produce in the storerooms of the Temple of our God. We will bring
the best of our flour and other grain offerings, the best of our fruit,
and the best of our new wine and olive oil. And we promise to bring to
the Levites a tenth of everything our land produces, for it is the Levites
who collect the tithes in all our rural towns.
38 "A priest—a descendant of Aaron—will be with the Levites as they
receive these tithes. And a tenth of all that is collected as tithes will be
delivered by the Levites to the Temple of our God and placed in the
storerooms. 39 The people and the Levites must bring these offerings
of grain, new wine, and olive oil to the storerooms and place them in
the sacred containers near the ministering priests, the gatekeepers, and
the singers.
"We promise together not to neglect the Temple of our God."

The People Occupy Jerusalem

11 The leaders of the people were living in Jerusalem, the holy city. A
tenth of the people from the other towns of Judah and Benjamin
were chosen by sacred lots to live there, too, while the rest stayed where they
were. 2 And the people commended everyone who volunteered to resettle
in Jerusalem.
3 Here is a list of the names of the provincial officials who came to live in
Jerusalem. (Most of the people, priests, Levites, Temple servants, and de-
scendants of Solomon's servants continued to live in their own homes in the
various towns of Judah, 4 but some of the people from Judah and Benjamin
resettled in Jerusalem.)

From the tribe of Judah:
Athaiah son of Uzziah, son of Zechariah, son of Amariah, son of
Shephatiah, son of Mahalalel, of the family of Perez. 5 Also Maaseiah

10:32 Hebrew *tax of ⅓ of a shekel* [4 grams].

Make a Difference 11:1

Pioneers versus Settlers

For a city to exist and be great, it requires both pioneers and settlers. For more than seventy years, Jerusalem had been nothing more than an abandoned ruin. With a new temple and rebuilt walls, it was ready to reset—if only people would see the opportunity to jump in. By setting an example of pioneering, the leaders hoped that others would soon join the movement.

Not everyone will be a pioneer. Some need to see a value or goal lived out in their lives before they'll decide to join in and make it something to champion. Before others will live out the genuine life in Jesus that we hope they will, we must first genuinely live it out in our own lives. Being a pioneer of faith means that even in your fears and uncertainties, you will be willing to step forward and let God grow you through the process.

Difference Maker

Pray about a value that others might consider embracing if they see it in you. Then take a step in living out that value.

son of Baruch, son of Col-hozeh, son of Hazaiah, son of Adaiah, son
of Joiarib, son of Zechariah, of the family of Shelah.* 6 There were
468 descendants of Perez who lived in Jerusalem—all outstanding men.

7 From the tribe of Benjamin:
Sallu son of Meshullam, son of Joed, son of Pedaiah, son of Kolaiah,
son of Maaseiah, son of Ithiel, son of Jeshaiah. 8 After him were Gabbai
and Sallai and a total of 928 relatives. 9 Their chief officer was Joel
son of Zicri, who was assisted by Judah son of Hassenuah, second-in-command over the city.

10 From the priests:
Jedaiah son of Joiarib; Jakin; 11 and Seraiah son of Hilkiah, son
of Meshullam, son of Zadok, son of Meraioth, son of Ahitub, the
supervisor of the Temple of God. 12 Also 822 of their associates, who
worked at the Temple. Also Adaiah son of Jeroham, son of Pelaliah, son
of Amzi, son of Zechariah, son of Pashhur, son of Malkijah, 13 along with
242 of his associates, who were heads of their families. Also Amashsai
son of Azarel, son of Ahzai, son of Meshillemoth, son of Immer, 14 and
128 of his* outstanding associates. Their chief officer was Zabdiel son
of Haggedolim.

15 From the Levites:
Shemaiah son of Hasshub, son of Azrikam, son of Hashabiah, son
of Bunni. 16 Also Shabbethai and Jozabad, who were in charge of the
work outside the Temple of God. 17 Also Mattaniah son of Mica, son of
Zabdi, a descendant of Asaph, who led in thanksgiving and prayer. Also
Bakbukiah, who was Mattaniah's assistant, and Abda son of Shammua,
son of Galal, son of Jeduthun. 18 In all, there were 284 Levites in the
holy city.

19 From the gatekeepers:
Akkub, Talmon, and 172 of their associates, who guarded the gates.

20 The other priests, Levites, and the rest of the Israelites lived wherever
their family inheritance was located in any of the towns of Judah. 21 The
Temple servants, however, whose leaders were Ziha and Gishpa, all lived
on the hill of Ophel.

22 The chief officer of the Levites in Jerusalem was Uzzi son of Bani, son
of Hashabiah, son of Mattaniah, son of Mica, a descendant of Asaph, whose
family served as singers at God's Temple. 23 Their daily responsibilities were
carried out according to the terms of a royal command.

24 Pethahiah son of Meshezabel, a descendant of Zerah son of Judah, was
the royal adviser in all matters of public administration.

25 As for the surrounding villages with their open fields, some of the
people of Judah lived in Kiriath-arba with its settlements, Dibon with its
settlements, and Jekabzeel with its villages. 26 They also lived in Jeshua, Moladah, Beth-pelet, 27 Hazar-shual, Beersheba with its settlements, 28 Ziklag,
and Meconah with its settlements. 29 They also lived in En-rimmon, Zorah,
Jarmuth, 30 Zanoah, and Adullam with their surrounding villages. They also
lived in Lachish with its nearby fields and Azekah with its surrounding villages. So the people of Judah were living all the way from Beersheba in the
south to the valley of Hinnom.

11:5 Hebrew *son of the Shilonite.* **11:14** As in Greek version; Hebrew reads *their.*

31 Some of the people of Benjamin lived at Geba, Micmash, Aija, and Bethel
with its settlements. 32 They also lived in Anathoth, Nob, Ananiah, 33 Hazor,
Ramah, Gittaim, 34 Hadid, Zeboim, Neballat, 35 Lod, Ono, and the Valley of
Craftsmen.* 36 Some of the Levites who lived in Judah were sent to live with
the tribe of Benjamin.

A History of the Priests and Levites

12 Here is the list of the priests and Levites who returned with Zerubbabel son of Shealtiel and Jeshua the high priest:

Seraiah, Jeremiah, Ezra,
2 Amariah, Malluch, Hattush,
3 Shecaniah, Harim,* Meremoth,
4 Iddo, Ginnethon,* Abijah,
5 Miniamin, Moadiah,* Bilgah,
6 Shemaiah, Joiarib, Jedaiah,
7 Sallu, Amok, Hilkiah, and Jedaiah.
These were the leaders of the priests and their associates in the days of Jeshua.

8 The Levites who returned with them were Jeshua, Binnui, Kadmiel, Sher-
ebiah, Judah, and Mattaniah, who with his associates was in charge of the
songs of thanksgiving. 9 Their associates, Bakbukiah and Unni, stood op-
posite them during the service.

10 Jeshua the high priest was the father of Joiakim.
Joiakim was the father of Eliashib.
Eliashib was the father of Joiada.
11 Joiada was the father of Johanan.*
Johanan was the father of Jaddua.

12 Now when Joiakim was high priest, the family leaders of the priests were
as follows:

Meraiah was leader of the family of Seraiah.
Hananiah was leader of the family of Jeremiah.
13 Meshullam was leader of the family of Ezra.
Jehohanan was leader of the family of Amariah.
14 Jonathan was leader of the family of Malluch.*
Joseph was leader of the family of Shecaniah.*
15 Adna was leader of the family of Harim.
Helkai was leader of the family of Meremoth.*
16 Zechariah was leader of the family of Iddo.
Meshullam was leader of the family of Ginnethon.
17 Zicri was leader of the family of Abijah.
There was also a* leader of the family of Miniamin.

11:35 Or *and Ge-harashim.* **12:3** Hebrew *Rehum;* compare 7:42; 12:15; Ezra 2:39. **12:4** As in some Hebrew manuscripts and Latin Vulgate (see also 12:16); most Hebrew manuscripts read *Ginnethoi.* **12:5** Hebrew *Mijamin, Maadiah;* compare 12:17. **12:11** Hebrew *Jonathan;* compare 12:22. **12:14a** As in Greek version (see also 10:4; 12:2); Hebrew reads *Malluchi.* **12:14b** As in many Hebrew manuscripts, some Greek manuscripts, and Syriac version (see also 12:3); most Hebrew manuscripts read *Shebaniah.* **12:15** As in some Greek manuscripts (see also 12:3); Hebrew reads *Meraioth.* **12:17** Hebrew lacks the name of this family leader.

Story Arc **12:1**

● Zerubbabel and Jeshua

People like Zerubbabel and Jeshua were some of the most important difference makers in history. In the middle of the crushing disappointment of seeing the city in ruins, these two (and others like them) used whatever influence they had to help the Jewish exiles have a place to worship and live in.

Again, don't write this off as a mere construction project in history. These servant leaders helped create space for people to accurately learn and relearn who God is. Without their efforts, the foundation would not have been laid for people to find salvation in Jesus centuries later, for he taught in the temple and ministered all around Jerusalem. Never doubt that what you do today will carry on into future generations and influence those who come after you.

Esth 2:5-6 ►

Piltai was leader of the family of Moadiah.
18 Shammua was leader of the family of Bilgah.
Jehonathan was leader of the family of Shemaiah.
19 Mattenai was leader of the family of Joiarib.
Uzzi was leader of the family of Jedaiah.
20 Kallai was leader of the family of Sallu.*
Eber was leader of the family of Amok.
21 Hashabiah was leader of the family of Hilkiah.
Nethanel was leader of the family of Jedaiah.

22 A record of the Levite families was kept during the years when Eliashib,
Joiada, Johanan, and Jaddua served as high priest. Another record of the
priests was kept during the reign of Darius the Persian.* 23 A record of the
heads of the Levite families was kept in *The Book of History* down to the days
of Johanan, the grandson* of Eliashib.
24 These were the family leaders of the Levites: Hashabiah, Sherebiah,
Jeshua, Binnui,* Kadmiel, and other associates, who stood opposite them
during the ceremonies of praise and thanksgiving, one section responding
to the other, as commanded by David, the man of God. 25 This included Mat-
taniah, Bakbukiah, and Obadiah.

Meshullam, Talmon, and Akkub were the gatekeepers in charge of the
storerooms at the gates. 26 These all served in the days of Joiakim son of
Jeshua, son of Jehozadak,* and in the days of Nehemiah the governor and
of Ezra the priest and scribe.

Dedication of Jerusalem's Wall

27 For the dedication of the new wall of Jerusalem, the Levites throughout the
land were asked to come to Jerusalem to assist in the ceremonies. They were
to take part in the joyous occasion with their songs of thanksgiving and with
the music of cymbals, harps, and lyres. 28 The singers were brought together
from the region around Jerusalem and from the villages of the Netopha-
thites. 29 They also came from Beth-gilgal and the rural areas near Geba and
Azmaveth, for the singers had built their own settlements around Jerusalem.
30 The priests and Levites first purified themselves; then they purified the
people, the gates, and the wall.
31 I led the leaders of Judah to the top of the wall and organized two large
choirs to give thanks. One of the choirs proceeded southward* along the top
of the wall to the Dung Gate. 32 Hoshaiah and half the leaders of Judah fol-
lowed them, 33 along with Azariah, Ezra, Meshullam, 34 Judah, Benjamin,
Shemaiah, and Jeremiah. 35 Then came some priests who played trumpets, in-
cluding Zechariah son of Jonathan, son of Shemaiah, son of Mattaniah, son of
Micaiah, son of Zaccur, a descendant of Asaph. 36 And Zechariah's colleagues
were Shemaiah, Azarel, Milalai, Gilalai, Maai, Nethanel, Judah, and Hanani.
They used the musical instruments prescribed by David, the man of God.
Ezra the scribe led this procession. 37 At the Fountain Gate they went straight
up the steps on the ascent of the city wall toward the City of David. They
passed the house of David and then proceeded to the Water Gate on the east.

12:20 Hebrew *Sallai;* compare 12:7. 12:22 *Darius the Persian* is probably Darius II, who reigned 423–404 B.C., or possibly Darius III, who reigned 336–331 B.C. 12:23 Hebrew *descendant;* compare 12:10-11. 12:24 Hebrew *son of* (i.e., *ben*), which should probably be read here as the proper name Binnui; compare Ezra 3:9 and the note there. 12:26 Hebrew *Jozadak,* a variant spelling of Jehozadak. 12:31 Hebrew *to the right.*

38The second choir giving thanks went northward* around the other way
to meet them. I followed them, together with the other half of the people,
along the top of the wall past the Tower of the Ovens to the Broad Wall,
39then past the Ephraim Gate to the Old City Gate,* past the Fish Gate and the
Tower of Hananel, and on to the Tower of the Hundred. Then we continued
on to the Sheep Gate and stopped at the Guard Gate.
40The two choirs that were giving thanks then proceeded to the Temple
of God, where they took their places. So did I, together with the group of
leaders who were with me. 41We went together with the trumpet-playing
priests—Eliakim, Maaseiah, Miniamin, Micaiah, Elioenai, Zechariah, and
Hananiah—42and the singers—Maaseiah, Shemaiah, Eleazar, Uzzi, Jeho-
hanan, Malkijah, Elam, and Ezer. They played and sang loudly under the
direction of Jezrahiah the choir director.
43Many sacrifices were offered on that joyous day, for God had given the
people cause for great joy. The women and children also participated in the
celebration, and the joy of the people of Jerusalem could be heard far away.

Provisions for Temple Worship

44On that day men were appointed to be in charge of the storerooms for the
offerings, the first part of the harvest, and the tithes. They were responsible
to collect from the fields outside the towns the portions required by the Law
for the priests and Levites. For all the people of Judah took joy in the priests
and Levites and their work. 45They performed the service of their God and
the service of purification, as commanded by David and his son Solomon,
and so did the singers and the gatekeepers. 46The custom of having choir di-
rectors to lead the choirs in hymns of praise and thanksgiving to God began
long ago in the days of David and Asaph. 47So now, in the days of Zerubbabel
and of Nehemiah, all Israel brought a daily supply of food for the singers,
the gatekeepers, and the Levites. The Levites, in turn, gave a portion of what
they received to the priests, the descendants of Aaron.

Nehemiah's Various Reforms

13 On that same day, as the Book of Moses was being read to the people,
the passage was found that said no Ammonite or Moabite should
ever be permitted to enter the assembly of God.* 2For they had not provided
the Israelites with food and water in the wilderness. Instead, they hired Ba-
laam to curse them, though our God turned the curse into a blessing. 3When
this passage of the Law was read, all those of foreign descent were immedi-
ately excluded from the assembly.
4Before this had happened, Eliashib the priest, who had been appointed
as supervisor of the storerooms of the Temple of our God and who was also
a relative of Tobiah, 5had converted a large storage room and placed it at
Tobiah's disposal. The room had previously been used for storing the grain
offerings, the frankincense, various articles for the Temple, and the tithes
of grain, new wine, and olive oil (which were prescribed for the Levites, the
singers, and the gatekeepers), as well as the offerings for the priests.
6I was not in Jerusalem at that time, for I had returned to King Artaxerxes
of Babylon in the thirty-second year of his reign,* though I later asked his

Prayer **13:1**

Lord, as I read about things that happened in the past, help me to understand how to apply it all today. I want to understand the deepest meaning of your truth and apply it. Amen.

12:38 Hebrew *to the left.* 12:39 Or *the Mishneh Gate,* or *the Jeshanah Gate.* 13:1 See Deut 23:3-6.
13:6 King Artaxerxes of Persia is here identified as the king of Babylon because Persia had conquered the Babylonian Empire. The thirty-second year of Artaxerxes was 433 B.C.

Question 13:13

What opportunities might someone with a good reputation have that others won't? What are situations they might not get invited into because of their good reputation?

permission to return. 7 When I arrived back in Jerusalem, I learned about
Eliashib's evil deed in providing Tobiah with a room in the courtyards of the
Temple of God. 8 I became very upset and threw all of Tobiah's belongings out
of the room. 9 Then I demanded that the rooms be purified, and I brought
back the articles for God's Temple, the grain offerings, and the frankincense.

10 I also discovered that the Levites had not been given their prescribed
portions of food, so they and the singers who were to conduct the worship
services had all returned to work their fields. 11 I immediately confronted the
leaders and demanded, "Why has the Temple of God been neglected?" Then
I called all the Levites back again and restored them to their proper duties.
12 And once more all the people of Judah began bringing their tithes of grain,
new wine, and olive oil to the Temple storerooms.

13 I assigned supervisors for the storerooms: Shelemiah the priest, Zadok
the scribe, and Pedaiah, one of the Levites. And I appointed Hanan son of
Zaccur and grandson of Mattaniah as their assistant. These men had an ex-
cellent reputation, and it was their job to make honest distributions to their
fellow Levites.

14 Remember this good deed, O my God, and do not forget all that I have
faithfully done for the Temple of my God and its services.

15 In those days I saw men of Judah treading out their winepresses on the
Sabbath. They were also bringing in grain, loading it on donkeys, and bring-
ing their wine, grapes, figs, and all sorts of produce to Jerusalem to sell on
the Sabbath. So I rebuked them for selling their produce on that day. 16 Some
men from Tyre, who lived in Jerusalem, were bringing in fish and all kinds
of merchandise. They were selling it on the Sabbath to the people of Ju-
dah—and in Jerusalem at that!

17 So I confronted the nobles of Judah. "Why are you profaning the Sab-
bath in this evil way?" I asked. 18 "Wasn't it just this sort of thing that your
ancestors did that caused our God to bring all this trouble upon us and our
city? Now you are bringing even more wrath upon Israel by permitting the
Sabbath to be desecrated in this way!"

19 Then I commanded that the gates of Jerusalem should be shut as dark-
ness fell every Friday evening,* not to be opened until the Sabbath ended.
I sent some of my own servants to guard the gates so that no merchandise
could be brought in on the Sabbath day. 20 The merchants and tradesmen
with a variety of wares camped outside Jerusalem once or twice. 21 But I spoke
sharply to them and said, "What are you doing out here, camping around the
wall? If you do this again, I will arrest you!" And that was the last time they
came on the Sabbath. 22 Then I commanded the Levites to purify themselves
and to guard the gates in order to preserve the holiness of the Sabbath.

Remember this good deed also, O my God! Have compassion on me
according to your great and unfailing love.

23 About the same time I realized that some of the men of Judah had mar-
ried women from Ashdod, Ammon, and Moab. 24 Furthermore, half their
children spoke the language of Ashdod or of some other people and could

13:19 Hebrew *on the day before the Sabbath.*

not speak the language of Judah at all. 25 So I confronted them and called
down curses on them. I beat some of them and pulled out their hair. I made
them swear in the name of God that they would not let their children intermarry with the pagan people of the land.

26 "Wasn't this exactly what led King Solomon of Israel into sin?" I demanded. "There was no king from any nation who could compare to him,
and God loved him and made him king over all Israel. But even he was led into
sin by his foreign wives. 27 How could you even think of committing this sinful deed and acting unfaithfully toward God by marrying foreign women?"
28 One of the sons of Joiada son of Eliashib the high priest had married a
daughter of Sanballat the Horonite, so I banished him from my presence.

29 Remember them, O my God, for they have defiled the priesthood and
the solemn vows of the priests and Levites.

30 So I purged out everything foreign and assigned tasks to the priests
and Levites, making certain that each knew his work. 31 I also made sure that
the supply of wood for the altar and the first portions of the harvest were
brought at the proper times.

Remember this in my favor, O my God.

Esther Introduction

The book of Esther is filled with drama, romance, and plot twists. Esther found herself in a situation where she had to risk her life to save the entire Jewish population. She made a bold decision that made a huge difference in her life, her family, and her people.

Long before we meet Esther, the Jewish people have been exiled from their homes in Judah and Israel. By the time Esther was a teenager, the Persian Empire had absorbed all the scattered lands where the Jewish people lived. Now the Persian Empire was threatening to kill every single one of them. God's people desperately needed an advocate. They needed a rescuer. They needed someone to speak up for them and mediate on their behalf.

It was not a coincidence that Esther found herself in just the right place at just the right time. God appointed her for "just such a time as this" (Esther 4:14). Because of her bold actions, hundreds of thousands of people were saved.

You may find it interesting that this book is unique in the Bible because it doesn't mention God's name. The goal of this book is to document this specific time in history because it marked such a significant deliverance of the Jewish people. This moment became known as the Festival of Purim. While God's name isn't mentioned in this book, God's sovereignty is woven through each page. It is clear that the story of Esther demonstrates what God's sovereignty looks like. As you read this book, enjoy the many ways that God orchestrated events to accomplish his good plans.

Story Arcs

- **Mordecai**
- **Esther**

Esther

The King's Banquet

1 These events happened in the days of King Xerxes,* who reigned over
127 provinces stretching from India to Ethiopia.* 2 At that time Xerxes
ruled his empire from his royal throne at the fortress of Susa. 3 In the third
year of his reign, he gave a banquet for all his nobles and officials. He invited
all the military officers of Persia and Media as well as the princes and nobles
of the provinces. 4 The celebration lasted 180 days—a tremendous display of
the opulent wealth of his empire and the pomp and splendor of his majesty.
5 When it was all over, the king gave a banquet for all the people, from the
greatest to the least, who were in the fortress of Susa. It lasted for seven days
and was held in the courtyard of the palace garden. 6 The courtyard was beau-
tifully decorated with white cotton curtains and blue hangings, which were
fastened with white linen cords and purple ribbons to silver rings embedded
in marble pillars. Gold and silver couches stood on a mosaic pavement of
porphyry, marble, mother-of-pearl, and other costly stones.
7 Drinks were served in gold goblets of many designs, and there was an
abundance of royal wine, reflecting the king's generosity. 8 By edict of the
king, no limits were placed on the drinking, for the king had instructed all
his palace officials to serve each man as much as he wanted.
9 At the same time, Queen Vashti gave a banquet for the women in the
royal palace of King Xerxes.

Queen Vashti Deposed

10 On the seventh day of the feast, when King Xerxes was in high spirits be-
cause of the wine, he told the seven eunuchs who attended him—Mehuman,
Biztha, Harbona, Bigtha, Abagtha, Zethar, and Carcas—11 to bring Queen
Vashti to him with the royal crown on her head. He wanted the nobles and
all the other men to gaze on her beauty, for she was a very beautiful woman.
12 But when they conveyed the king's order to Queen Vashti, she refused to
come. This made the king furious, and he burned with anger.
13 He immediately consulted with his wise advisers, who knew all the Per-
sian laws and customs, for he always asked their advice. 14 The names of these
men were Carshena, Shethar, Admatha, Tarshish, Meres, Marsena, and Me-
mucan—seven nobles of Persia and Media. They met with the king regularly
and held the highest positions in the empire.
15 "What must be done to Queen Vashti?" the king demanded. "What pen-
alty does the law provide for a queen who refuses to obey the king's orders,
properly sent through his eunuchs?"
16 Memucan answered the king and his nobles, "Queen Vashti has wronged
not only the king but also every noble and citizen throughout your empire.
17 Women everywhere will begin to despise their husbands when they learn

1:1a Hebrew *Ahasuerus,* another name for Xerxes; also throughout the book of Esther. Xerxes reigned 486–465 B.C. 1:1b Hebrew *to Cush.*

that Queen Vashti has refused to appear before the king. 18 Before this day
is out, the wives of all the king's nobles throughout Persia and Media will
hear what the queen did and will start treating their husbands the same way.
There will be no end to their contempt and anger.
19 "So if it please the king, we suggest that you issue a written decree, a
law of the Persians and Medes that cannot be revoked. It should order that
Queen Vashti be forever banished from the presence of King Xerxes, and
that the king should choose another queen more worthy than she. 20 When
this decree is published throughout the king's vast empire, husbands every-
where, whatever their rank, will receive proper respect from their wives!"
21 The king and his nobles thought this made good sense, so he followed
Memucan's counsel. 22 He sent letters to all parts of the empire, to each prov-
ince in its own script and language, proclaiming that every man should be
the ruler of his own home and should say whatever he pleases.*

Esther Becomes Queen

2 But after Xerxes' anger had subsided, he began thinking about Vashti
and what she had done and the decree he had made. 2 So his personal
attendants suggested, "Let us search the empire to find beautiful young
virgins for the king. 3 Let the king appoint agents in each province to bring
these beautiful young women into the royal harem at the fortress of Susa.
Hegai, the king's eunuch in charge of the harem, will see that they are all
given beauty treatments. 4 After that, the young woman who most pleases the
king will be made queen instead of Vashti." This advice was very appealing
to the king, so he put the plan into effect.
5 At that time there was a Jewish man in the fortress of Susa whose name
was Mordecai son of Jair. He was from the tribe of Benjamin and was a
descendant of Kish and Shimei. 6 His family* had been among those who,
with King Jehoiachin* of Judah, had been exiled from Jerusalem to Bab-
ylon by King Nebuchadnezzar. 7 This man had a very beautiful and lovely
young cousin, Hadassah, who was also called Esther. When her father and
mother died, Mordecai adopted her into his family and raised her as his
own daughter.
8 As a result of the king's decree, Esther, along with many other young
women, was brought to the king's harem at the fortress of Susa and placed
in Hegai's care. 9 Hegai was very impressed with Esther and treated her kindly.
He quickly ordered a special menu for her and provided her with beauty
treatments. He also assigned her seven maids specially chosen from the king's
palace, and he moved her and her maids into the best place in the harem.
10 Esther had not told anyone of her nationality and family background,
because Mordecai had directed her not to do so. 11 Every day Mordecai would
take a walk near the courtyard of the harem to find out about Esther and
what was happening to her.
12 Before each young woman was taken to the king's bed, she was given
the prescribed twelve months of beauty treatments—six months with oil
of myrrh, followed by six months with special perfumes and ointments.
13 When it was time for her to go to the king's palace, she was given her choice
of whatever clothing or jewelry she wanted to take from the harem. 14 That
evening she was taken to the king's private rooms, and the next morning she

1:22 Or *and should speak in the language of his own people.* 2:6a Hebrew *He.* 2:6b Hebrew *Jeconiah,* a variant spelling of Jehoiachin.

Story Arc **2:5–6**

● Mordecai

Mordecai was a Jewish man from the tribe of Benjamin. Because the Jewish people were taken hostage and exiled from their land, he lived in Susa, the capital of the Persian Empire. His great-grandfather Kish had been brought into captivity by King Nebuchadnezzar. Now, in Persia, Mordecai remained committed to his faith even though it was not a popular choice. There was tremendous tension for the Jews in Persia. It was not safe to be Jewish in that culture. Still, Mordecai did not waver in who he was, and he did not back down from the consequences of his unpopular heritage. What can you learn about integrity and faith from the story of Mordecai throughout the book of Esther?

Esth 2:7-20 ►

was brought to the second harem,* where the king's wives lived. There she would be under the care of Shaashgaz, the king's eunuch in charge of the concubines. She would never go to the king again unless he had especially enjoyed her and requested her by name.

15 Esther was the daughter of Abihail, who was Mordecai's uncle. (Mordecai had adopted his younger cousin Esther.) When it was Esther's turn to go to the king, she accepted the advice of Hegai, the eunuch in charge of the harem. She asked for nothing except what he suggested, and she was admired by everyone who saw her.

16 Esther was taken to King Xerxes at the royal palace in early winter* of
the seventh year of his reign. 17 And the king loved Esther more than any of
the other young women. He was so delighted with her that he set the royal
crown on her head and declared her queen instead of Vashti. 18 To celebrate
the occasion, he gave a great banquet in Esther's honor for all his nobles and officials, declaring a public holiday for the provinces and giving generous gifts to everyone.

19 Even after all the young women had been transferred to the second
harem* and Mordecai had become a palace official,* 20 Esther continued to
keep her family background and nationality a secret. She was still following Mordecai's directions, just as she did when she lived in his home.

Mordecai's Loyalty to the King

21 One day as Mordecai was on duty at the king's gate, two of the king's eunuchs, Bigthana* and Teresh—who were guards at the door of the king's private quarters—became angry at King Xerxes and plotted to assassinate
him. 22 But Mordecai heard about the plot and gave the information to Queen
Esther. She then told the king about it and gave Mordecai credit for the re-
port. 23 When an investigation was made and Mordecai's story was found to
be true, the two men were impaled on a sharpened pole. This was all recorded in *The Book of the History of King Xerxes' Reign.*

Haman's Plot against the Jews

3 Some time later King Xerxes promoted Haman son of Hammedatha the Agagite over all the other nobles, making him the most powerful official
in the empire. 2 All the king's officials would bow down before Haman to show him respect whenever he passed by, for so the king had commanded. But Mordecai refused to bow down or show him respect.

3 Then the palace officials at the king's gate asked Mordecai, "Why are you
disobeying the king's command?" 4 They spoke to him day after day, but still
he refused to comply with the order. So they spoke to Haman about this to see if he would tolerate Mordecai's conduct, since Mordecai had told them he was a Jew.

5 When Haman saw that Mordecai would not bow down or show him re-
spect, he was filled with rage. 6 He had learned of Mordecai's nationality, so he
decided it was not enough to lay hands on Mordecai alone. Instead, he looked for a way to destroy all the Jews throughout the entire empire of Xerxes.

2:14 Or *to another part of the harem.* **2:16** Hebrew *in the tenth month, the month of Tebeth.* A number of dates in the book of Esther can be cross-checked with dates in surviving Persian records and related accurately to our modern calendar. This month of the ancient Hebrew lunar calendar occurred within the months of December 479 B.C. and January 478 B.C. **2:19a** The meaning of the Hebrew is uncertain. **2:19b** Hebrew *and Mordecai was sitting in the gate of the king.* **2:21** Hebrew *Bigthan;* compare 6:2.

Question 2:21–23

Mordecai's job at the gate was probably a low-level position. He likely had no access to the king to warn him of the assassination plot. He was, however, connected to the new queen. The problem was that if Mordecai told Esther and she told the king, then everyone would soon know that Queen Esther was Jewish. If Mordecai told Esther, he would put her life at risk. Even so, if Mordecai did not tell her, the king would surely die. If you were Mordecai, what would you have done?

Story Arc 2:7–20

Esther

How can that be? How can an orphan and Jew exiled in a foreign, hostile land become the queen of Persia? Simple. God orchestrated this one! Esther found favor with the Persian court. She was admired for her wisdom and beauty. The other women did everything to be seen, grabbing the best clothing, perfumes, and accessories to make themselves more attractive, while Esther won the heart of the king through her humble courage and by listening to good advice. Esther became a difference maker because she humbled herself and trusted God. Through the favor she found with King Xerxes, she was able to make some bold moves that stopped some powerful adversaries from committing genocide against her people.

Job 1:1–22 ►

Question 3:7

As a Jew, Mordecai would have been taught to only bow to the Lord God of Israel. What would you have done in this circumstance? Are there any moments when you are tempted to bow to things other than God?

Make a Difference
4:1–14

Step Up, Girl!

Mordecai gave Esther the challenge of her life. She had to step up to save her people. Esther faced a dilemma in which she had to do something drastic. If she broke the law and went to the king uninvited, she could get herself killed by offending the most powerful man on earth. Still, Esther was emboldened because she knew that the timing of this problem was not an accident. She knew that she had been placed in this position for "just such a time as this" to rescue the Jewish people (v. 14). No pressure, right?

Difference Maker

Look for a "just such a time as this" moment in your life. Is there something in your life that God has orchestrated to put you right where you need to be at just the right time?

7 So in the month of April,* during the twelfth year of King Xerxes' reign,
lots were cast in Haman's presence (the lots were called *purim*) to determine
the best day and month to take action. And the day selected was March 7,
nearly a year later.*
8 Then Haman approached King Xerxes and said, "There is a certain race
of people scattered through all the provinces of your empire who keep them-
selves separate from everyone else. Their laws are different from those of any
other people, and they refuse to obey the laws of the king. So it is not in the
king's interest to let them live. 9 If it please the king, issue a decree that they
be destroyed, and I will give 10,000 large sacks* of silver to the government
administrators to be deposited in the royal treasury."
10 The king agreed, confirming his decision by removing his signet ring
from his finger and giving it to Haman son of Hammedatha the Agagite,
the enemy of the Jews. 11 The king said, "The money and the people are both
yours to do with as you see fit."
12 So on April 17* the king's secretaries were summoned, and a decree was
written exactly as Haman dictated. It was sent to the king's highest officers,
the governors of the respective provinces, and the nobles of each province in
their own scripts and languages. The decree was written in the name of King
Xerxes and sealed with the king's signet ring. 13 Dispatches were sent by swift
messengers into all the provinces of the empire, giving the order that all Jews—
young and old, including women and children—must be killed, slaughtered,
and annihilated on a single day. This was scheduled to happen on March 7 of the
next year.* The property of the Jews would be given to those who killed them.
14 A copy of this decree was to be issued as law in every province and pro-
claimed to all peoples, so that they would be ready to do their duty on the
appointed day. 15 At the king's command, the decree went out by swift mes-
sengers, and it was also proclaimed in the fortress of Susa. Then the king and
Haman sat down to drink, but the city of Susa fell into confusion.

Mordecai Requests Esther's Help

4 When Mordecai learned about all that had been done, he tore his
clothes, put on burlap and ashes, and went out into the city, crying with
a loud and bitter wail. 2 He went as far as the gate of the palace, for no one
was allowed to enter the palace gate while wearing clothes of mourning.
3 And as news of the king's decree reached all the provinces, there was great
mourning among the Jews. They fasted, wept, and wailed, and many people
lay in burlap and ashes.
4 When Queen Esther's maids and eunuchs came and told her about Mor-
decai, she was deeply distressed. She sent clothing to him to replace the
burlap, but he refused it. 5 Then Esther sent for Hathach, one of the king's
eunuchs who had been appointed as her attendant. She ordered him to go to
Mordecai and find out what was troubling him and why he was in mourning.
6 So Hathach went out to Mordecai in the square in front of the palace gate.

3:7a Hebrew *in the first month, the month of Nisan.* This month of the ancient Hebrew lunar calendar occurred within the months of April and May 474 B.C.; also see note on 2:16. 3:7b As in 3:13, which reads *the thirteenth day of the twelfth month, the month of Adar;* Hebrew reads *in the twelfth month,* of the ancient Hebrew lunar calendar. The date selected was March 7, 473 B.C.; also see note on 2:16. 3:9 Hebrew *10,000 talents,* about 375 tons or 340 metric tons in weight. 3:12 Hebrew *On the thirteenth day of the first month,* of the ancient Hebrew lunar calendar. This day was April 17, 474 B.C.; also see note on 2:16. 3:13 Hebrew *on the thirteenth day of the twelfth month, the month of Adar,* of the ancient Hebrew lunar calendar. The date selected was March 7, 473 B.C.; also see note on 2:16.

7 Mordecai told him the whole story, including the exact amount of money
Haman had promised to pay into the royal treasury for the destruction of the
Jews. 8 Mordecai gave Hathach a copy of the decree issued in Susa that called
for the death of all Jews. He asked Hathach to show it to Esther and explain
the situation to her. He also asked Hathach to direct her to go to the king
to beg for mercy and plead for her people. 9 So Hathach returned to Esther
with Mordecai's message.
10 Then Esther told Hathach to go back and relay this message to Mor-
decai: 11 "All the king's officials and even the people in the provinces know
that anyone who appears before the king in his inner court without being
invited is doomed to die unless the king holds out his gold scepter. And the
king has not called for me to come to him for thirty days." 12 So Hathach* gave
Esther's message to Mordecai.
13 Mordecai sent this reply to Esther: "Don't think for a moment that be-
cause you're in the palace you will escape when all other Jews are killed. 14 If
you keep quiet at a time like this, deliverance and relief for the Jews will arise
from some other place, but you and your relatives will die. Who knows if
perhaps you were made queen for just such a time as this?"
15 Then Esther sent this reply to Mordecai: 16 "Go and gather together all
the Jews of Susa and fast for me. Do not eat or drink for three days, night
or day. My maids and I will do the same. And then, though it is against the
law, I will go in to see the king. If I must die, I must die." 17 So Mordecai went
away and did everything as Esther had ordered him.

Esther's Request to the King

5 On the third day of the fast, Esther put on her royal robes and entered
the inner court of the palace, just across from the king's hall. The king
was sitting on his royal throne, facing the entrance. 2 When he saw Queen
Esther standing there in the inner court, he welcomed her and held out the
gold scepter to her. So Esther approached and touched the end of the scepter.
3 Then the king asked her, "What do you want, Queen Esther? What is your
request? I will give it to you, even if it is half the kingdom!"
4 And Esther replied, "If it please the king, let the king and Haman come
today to a banquet I have prepared for the king."
5 The king turned to his attendants and said, "Tell Haman to come quickly
to a banquet, as Esther has requested." So the king and Haman went to Es-
ther's banquet.
6 And while they were drinking wine, the king said to Esther, "Now tell
me what you really want. What is your request? I will give it to you, even if
it is half the kingdom!"
7 Esther replied, "This is my request and deepest wish. 8 If I have found
favor with the king, and if it pleases the king to grant my request and do
what I ask, please come with Haman tomorrow to the banquet I will prepare
for you. Then I will explain what this is all about."

Haman's Plan to Kill Mordecai

9 Haman was a happy man as he left the banquet! But when he saw Mordecai
sitting at the palace gate, not standing up or trembling nervously before him,
Haman became furious. 10 However, he restrained himself and went on home.

4:12 As in Greek version; Hebrew reads *they.*

Make a Difference

4:15–5:8

To the Death

Esther knew the risk. The law prohibited an uninvited guest from visiting the king. She chose to act because her life and the lives of every Jew in Persia were at risk. First, she called for God's people to fast in order to demonstrate dependency on God in the narrative of herself and her people. She relied on God for her next step but was willing to die as a result of her action.

In all, Esther committed to three days of fasting (5:1). Then on the last day of the fast, she went to the king. She did not stall or find other excuses not to go. She could have found reasons to put it off and let doubt and fear stop her, but her time spent praying and fasting gave her confidence, peace, and a perspective that God would work all things for his glory.

Difference Maker

Prayer and fasting were Esther's prerequisites before action. Without God's guidance, Esther knew she would be acting in her own strength and wisdom. If you are going to make a difference, dedicate yourself to prayer and fasting before acting.

Question 6:1

What if we deliberately watched for what God was doing? Throughout the book of Esther, it is clear that God was doing amazing things. Take a few minutes and "scroll" through Esther and imagine posting an image and caption on social media every time God did something. For instance, look at 6:1-2. Do you think it was a coincidence that King Xerxes was struggling to sleep and just so happened to ask for this particular reading material? Do you think perhaps God was up to something here?

Make a Difference 7:1-8

Defining Moment

This was the opportunity she had prepared for. This was her defining moment. Her words and the way she delivered them would determine the fate of her life and of every Jewish person in Persia. There was no turning back! Esther needed to request that the king provide her and her people with safety. She was careful and discerning and shrewd. As a result, the king listened and responded in her favor.

Difference Maker

Confronting people is not easy. The way you approach a conflict will determine the outcome greatly. Read Esther 7 and imagine what could have happened if Esther started with accusing Haman or if the king refused her. Think of situations in your life in which you led conflict with accusations and how that worked for you. How could the situation have been different?

Then Haman gathered together his friends and Zeresh, his wife, 11 and
boasted to them about his great wealth and his many children. He bragged
about the honors the king had given him and how he had been promoted
over all the other nobles and officials.
12 Then Haman added, "And that's not all! Queen Esther invited only me
and the king himself to the banquet she prepared for us. And she has invited
me to dine with her and the king again tomorrow!" 13 Then he added, "But
this is all worth nothing as long as I see Mordecai the Jew just sitting there
at the palace gate."
14 So Haman's wife, Zeresh, and all his friends suggested, "Set up a sharp-
ened pole that stands seventy-five feet* tall, and in the morning ask the king
to impale Mordecai on it. When this is done, you can go on your merry way
to the banquet with the king." This pleased Haman, and he ordered the
pole set up.

The King Honors Mordecai

6 That night the king had trouble sleeping, so he ordered an attendant
to bring the book of the history of his reign so it could be read to him.
2 In those records he discovered an account of how Mordecai had exposed
the plot of Bigthana and Teresh, two of the eunuchs who guarded the door
to the king's private quarters. They had plotted to assassinate King Xerxes.
3 "What reward or recognition did we ever give Mordecai for this?" the
king asked.
His attendants replied, "Nothing has been done for him."
4 "Who is that in the outer court?" the king inquired. As it happened,
Haman had just arrived in the outer court of the palace to ask the king to
impale Mordecai on the pole he had prepared.
5 So the attendants replied to the king, "Haman is out in the court."
"Bring him in," the king ordered. 6 So Haman came in, and the king said,
"What should I do to honor a man who truly pleases me?"
Haman thought to himself, "Whom would the king wish to honor more
than me?" 7 So he replied, "If the king wishes to honor someone, 8 he should
bring out one of the king's own royal robes, as well as a horse that the king
himself has ridden—one with a royal emblem on its head. 9 Let the robes
and the horse be handed over to one of the king's most noble officials. And
let him see that the man whom the king wishes to honor is dressed in the
king's robes and led through the city square on the king's horse. Have the
official shout as they go, 'This is what the king does for someone he wishes
to honor!'"
10 "Excellent!" the king said to Haman. "Quick! Take the robes and my
horse, and do just as you have said for Mordecai the Jew, who sits at the gate
of the palace. Leave out nothing you have suggested!"
11 So Haman took the robes and put them on Mordecai, placed him on
the king's own horse, and led him through the city square, shouting, "This
is what the king does for someone he wishes to honor!" 12 Afterward Mor-
decai returned to the palace gate, but Haman hurried home dejected and
completely humiliated.
13 When Haman told his wife, Zeresh, and all his friends what had hap-
pened, his wise advisers and his wife said, "Since Mordecai—this man who

5:14 Hebrew *50 cubits* [23 meters].

has humiliated you—is of Jewish birth, you will never succeed in your plans against him. It will be fatal to continue opposing him."

14 While they were still talking, the king's eunuchs arrived and quickly took Haman to the banquet Esther had prepared.

The King Executes Haman

7 So the king and Haman went to Queen Esther's banquet. 2 On this second occasion, while they were drinking wine, the king again said to Esther, "Tell me what you want, Queen Esther. What is your request? I will give it to you, even if it is half the kingdom!"

3 Queen Esther replied, "If I have found favor with the king, and if it pleases the king to grant my request, I ask that my life and the lives of my people will be spared. 4 For my people and I have been sold to those who would kill, slaughter, and annihilate us. If we had merely been sold as slaves, I could remain quiet, for that would be too trivial a matter to warrant disturbing the king."

5 "Who would do such a thing?" King Xerxes demanded. "Who would be so presumptuous as to touch you?"

6 Esther replied, "This wicked Haman is our adversary and our enemy." Haman grew pale with fright before the king and queen. 7 Then the king jumped to his feet in a rage and went out into the palace garden.

Haman, however, stayed behind to plead for his life with Queen Esther, for he knew that the king intended to kill him. 8 In despair he fell on the couch where Queen Esther was reclining, just as the king was returning from the palace garden.

The king exclaimed, "Will he even assault the queen right here in the palace, before my very eyes?" And as soon as the king spoke, his attendants covered Haman's face, signaling his doom.

9 Then Harbona, one of the king's eunuchs, said, "Haman has set up a sharpened pole that stands seventy-five feet* tall in his own courtyard. He intended to use it to impale Mordecai, the man who saved the king from assassination."

"Then impale Haman on it!" the king ordered. 10 So they impaled Haman on the pole he had set up for Mordecai, and the king's anger subsided.

A Decree to Help the Jews

8 On that same day King Xerxes gave the property of Haman, the enemy of the Jews, to Queen Esther. Then Mordecai was brought before the king, for Esther had told the king how they were related. 2 The king took off his signet ring—which he had taken back from Haman—and gave it to Mordecai. And Esther appointed Mordecai to be in charge of Haman's property.

3 Then Esther went again before the king, falling down at his feet and begging him with tears to stop the evil plot devised by Haman the Agagite against the Jews. 4 Again the king held out the gold scepter to Esther. So she rose and stood before him.

5 Esther said, "If it please the king, and if I have found favor with him, and if he thinks it is right, and if I am pleasing to him, let there be a decree that reverses the orders of Haman son of Hammedatha the Agagite, who ordered

7:9 Hebrew 50 *cubits* [23 meters].

Make a Difference **7:6**

Name It

In this life-and-death chess match, Esther used all her skills and wisdom to outwit her opponent, Haman. Still, she had to be prepared. Haman was a crafty creature, looking to destroy the Jewish people. She had to watch every step.

In 1 Peter 5:8-9, Peter wrote, "Stay alert! Watch out for your great enemy, the devil. He prowls around like a roaring lion, looking for someone to devour. Stand firm against him, and be strong in your faith." Jesus told his followers to "be as shrewd as snakes and harmless as doves" (Matthew 10:16). As followers of Jesus, it is important to name our adversary, understand his methods, and be on the lookout for him.

Difference Maker

As followers of Jesus, it is important for us to recognize that we also have an adversary who wants to destroy our faith and get our eyes off Jesus. Naming him allows us to see him and understand how to fight against his tactics.

Make a Difference

9:3-4

Make Him Famous

Deuteronomy 14:2 tells us that the Jewish nation had been "set apart as holy" and that the Lord had chosen them "from all the nations of the earth to be his own special treasure." God was never going to give up on his people. He placed Esther and Mordecai in positions of influence to protect his people. Because of their faithfulness, God gave them favor to make highly important decisions in high levels of leadership. Remember, Esther was an orphan in a foreign land, and Mordecai worked as a lower-level gatekeeper for the king. Through their right choices to honor God, they gained influence, protected their people, and made God famous for all to see.

Difference Maker

How could your consistent faith and bold actions make God famous?

that Jews throughout all the king's provinces should be destroyed. 6 For how
can I endure to see my people and my family slaughtered and destroyed?"
7 Then King Xerxes said to Queen Esther and Mordecai the Jew, "I have
given Esther the property of Haman, and he has been impaled on a pole
because he tried to destroy the Jews. 8 Now go ahead and send a message to
the Jews in the king's name, telling them whatever you want, and seal it with
the king's signet ring. But remember that whatever has already been written
in the king's name and sealed with his signet ring can never be revoked."
9 So on June 25* the king's secretaries were summoned, and a decree was
written exactly as Mordecai dictated. It was sent to the Jews and to the high-
est officers, the governors, and the nobles of all the 127 provinces stretching
from India to Ethiopia.* The decree was written in the scripts and languages
of all the peoples of the empire, including that of the Jews. 10 The decree was
written in the name of King Xerxes and sealed with the king's signet ring.
Mordecai sent the dispatches by swift messengers, who rode fast horses es-
pecially bred for the king's service.
11 The king's decree gave the Jews in every city authority to unite to defend
their lives. They were allowed to kill, slaughter, and annihilate anyone of any
nationality or province who might attack them or their children and wives,
and to take the property of their enemies. 12 The day chosen for this event
throughout all the provinces of King Xerxes was March 7 of the next year.*
13 A copy of this decree was to be issued as law in every province and pro-
claimed to all peoples, so that the Jews would be ready to take revenge on
their enemies on the appointed day. 14 So urged on by the king's command,
the messengers rode out swiftly on fast horses bred for the king's service.
The same decree was also proclaimed in the fortress of Susa.
15 Then Mordecai left the king's presence, wearing the royal robe of blue
and white, the great crown of gold, and an outer cloak of fine linen and
purple. And the people of Susa celebrated the new decree. 16 The Jews were
filled with joy and gladness and were honored everywhere. 17 In every prov-
ince and city, wherever the king's decree arrived, the Jews rejoiced and had
a great celebration and declared a public festival and holiday. And many of
the people of the land became Jews themselves, for they feared what the
Jews might do to them.

The Victory of the Jews

9 So on March 7* the two decrees of the king were put into effect. On that
day, the enemies of the Jews had hoped to overpower them, but quite
the opposite happened. It was the Jews who overpowered their enemies.
2 The Jews gathered in their cities throughout all the king's provinces to at-
tack anyone who tried to harm them. But no one could make a stand against
them, for everyone was afraid of them. 3 And all the nobles of the provinces,
the highest officers, the governors, and the royal officials helped the Jews
for fear of Mordecai. 4 For Mordecai had been promoted in the king's palace,
and his fame spread throughout all the provinces as he became more and
more powerful.

8:9a Hebrew *on the twenty-third day of the third month, the month of Sivan,* of the ancient Hebrew lunar calendar. This day was June 25, 474 B.C.; also see note on 2:16. 8:9b Hebrew *to Cush.* 8:12 Hebrew *the thirteenth day of the twelfth month, the month of Adar,* of the ancient Hebrew lunar calendar. The date selected was March 7, 473 B.C.; also see note on 2:16. 9:1 Hebrew *on the thirteenth day of the twelfth month, the month of Adar,* of the ancient Hebrew lunar calendar. This day was March 7, 473 B.C.; also see note on 2:16.

5 So the Jews went ahead on the appointed day and struck down their en-
emies with the sword. They killed and annihilated their enemies and did as
they pleased with those who hated them. 6 In the fortress of Susa itself, the
Jews killed 500 men. 7 They also killed Parshandatha, Dalphon, Aspatha,
8 Poratha, Adalia, Aridatha, 9 Parmashta, Arisai, Aridai, and Vaizatha—10 the
ten sons of Haman son of Hammedatha, the enemy of the Jews. But they
did not take any plunder.
11 That very day, when the king was informed of the number of people
killed in the fortress of Susa, 12 he called for Queen Esther. He said, "The
Jews have killed 500 men in the fortress of Susa alone, as well as Haman's
ten sons. If they have done that here, what has happened in the rest of the
provinces? But now, what more do you want? It will be granted to you; tell
me and I will do it."
13 Esther responded, "If it please the king, give the Jews in Susa permission
to do again tomorrow as they have done today, and let the bodies of Haman's
ten sons be impaled on a pole."
14 So the king agreed, and the decree was announced in Susa. And they
impaled the bodies of Haman's ten sons. 15 Then the Jews at Susa gathered to-
gether on March 8* and killed 300 more men, and again they took no plunder.
16 Meanwhile, the other Jews throughout the king's provinces had gath-
ered together to defend their lives. They gained relief from all their enemies,
killing 75,000 of those who hated them. But they did not take any plunder.
17 This was done throughout the provinces on March 7, and on March 8 they
rested,* celebrating their victory with a day of feasting and gladness. 18 (The
Jews at Susa killed their enemies on March 7 and again on March 8, then
rested on March 9,* making that their day of feasting and gladness.) 19 So
to this day, rural Jews living in remote villages celebrate an annual festival
and holiday on the appointed day in late winter,* when they rejoice and send
gifts of food to each other.

The Festival of Purim

20 Mordecai recorded these events and sent letters to the Jews near and far,
throughout all the provinces of King Xerxes, 21 calling on them to celebrate
an annual festival on these two days.* 22 He told them to celebrate these days
with feasting and gladness and by giving gifts of food to each other and
presents to the poor. This would commemorate a time when the Jews gained
relief from their enemies, when their sorrow was turned into gladness and
their mourning into joy.
23 So the Jews accepted Mordecai's proposal and adopted this annual cus-
tom. 24 Haman son of Hammedatha the Agagite, the enemy of the Jews, had
plotted to crush and destroy them on the date determined by casting lots (the
lots were called *purim*). 25 But when Esther came before the king, he issued a
decree causing Haman's evil plot to backfire, and Haman and his sons were
impaled on a sharpened pole. 26 That is why this celebration is called Purim,
because it is the ancient word for casting lots.

9:15 Hebrew *the fourteenth day of the month of Adar,* of the ancient Hebrew lunar calendar. This day was March 8, 473 B.C.; also see note on 2:16. **9:17** Hebrew *on the thirteenth day of the month of Adar, and on the fourteenth day they rested.* These days were March 7 and 8, 473 B.C.; also see note on 2:16. **9:18** Hebrew *killed their enemies on the thirteenth day and the fourteenth day, and then rested on the fifteenth day,* of the Hebrew month of Adar. **9:19** Hebrew *on the fourteenth day of the month of Adar.* This day of the ancient Hebrew lunar calendar occurs in February or March. **9:21** Hebrew *on the fourteenth and fifteenth days of Adar,* of the ancient Hebrew lunar calendar.

Make a Difference

9:20-32

Purim

The most important celebration in the book of Esther is the annual Festival of Purim. It is named after Haman's failed attempt to kill the Jews in Persia. Haman had tried to pick a date to kill the Jews by casting lots (the lots were called *purim*). Instead, because of Esther and Mordecai, the king issued a decree that caused Haman's evil plots to backfire. As a result, the Jews had victory over Haman and seventy-five thousand of their enemies. The book of Esther was written so every one of God's people would not forget the orchestrated events that led up to that day.

Difference Maker

Whether we recognize this truth or not, God is always present and working. Take a piece of paper and write out a timeline of your life. Along the way, look for how God has been at work orchestrating events.

Prayer **10:3**

God, help me be like Mordecai in my actions. Let me work for the good of the people around me. Amen.

So because of Mordecai's letter and because of what they had experienced,
27 the Jews throughout the realm agreed to inaugurate this tradition and to
pass it on to their descendants and to all who became Jews. They declared
they would never fail to celebrate these two prescribed days at the appointed
time each year. 28 These days would be remembered and kept from genera-
tion to generation and celebrated by every family throughout the provinces
and cities of the empire. This Festival of Purim would never cease to be cel-
ebrated among the Jews, nor would the memory of what happened ever die
out among their descendants.

29 Then Queen Esther, the daughter of Abihail, along with Mordecai the
Jew, wrote another letter putting the queen's full authority behind Morde-
cai's letter to establish the Festival of Purim. 30 Letters wishing peace and
security were sent to the Jews throughout the 127 provinces of the empire of
Xerxes. 31 These letters established the Festival of Purim—an annual celebra-
tion of these days at the appointed time, decreed by both Mordecai the Jew
and Queen Esther. (The people decided to observe this festival, just as they
had decided for themselves and their descendants to establish the times of
fasting and mourning.) 32 So the command of Esther confirmed the practices
of Purim, and it was all written down in the records.

The Greatness of Xerxes and Mordecai

10 King Xerxes imposed a tribute throughout his empire, even to the
distant coastlands. 2 His great achievements and the full account of
the greatness of Mordecai, whom the king had promoted, are recorded in
The Book of the History of the Kings of Media and Persia. 3 Mordecai the Jew became
the prime minister, with authority next to that of King Xerxes himself. He
was very great among the Jews, who held him in high esteem, because he
continued to work for the good of his people and to speak up for the welfare
of all their descendants.

Job Introduction

We know the Bible talks about God. We know there are some great sayings in the Bible that have some good advice. We know it is a good thing to read the Bible. Even so, sometimes we can get stuck approaching the Bible like it is a textbook. While the Bible was made for digging and discovering more about who God is and how we can live our lives for him, we have to come to terms with the fact that the Bible pushes us to know God by engaging in God's living and active Word. That's when God helps us grow in our relationship with him.

The book of Job is a look at an incredibly difficult journey of going from knowing about God to knowing God. Job did everything in life to please God, but when everything was stripped away, he questioned God. You will find several of his friends who tried to come up with answers, mostly pointing at Job and saying he must have sinned. That just wasn't the case.

"Why do bad things happen?" or "Why do bad things happen to good people?" Have you ever asked those questions? I am sure you have at least thought them. The book of Job will not satisfy your need for an answer. God has reasons for allowing pain, but he may not reveal what those reasons are. Sure, sin is the reason why there is any pain at all, but Job lost everything, and his friends sat with him and tried to figure out what Job did to deserve all his pain. God had called Job "blameless" and "a man of complete integrity" (Job 1:1), so how could this happen?

James 1:2 tells us, "When troubles of any kind come your way, consider it an opportunity for great joy." Digging into the book of Job is all about discovering our faith. It's hard to hear in the moment, but when we look back at difficult seasons in our life, we can often see God's hand at work and how we are better because of them. This is not to discount any pain you have suffered but to encourage you to see that God is good, in good times and hard times. In those difficult seasons, try to look inside yourself and see if you are trusting your Creator even though things don't make sense.

Job demanded a response from God, and God responded by telling Job to trust in him. We can bring our honest thoughts and struggles to God. He is okay with that. He is big enough to handle our struggle. Ultimately, however, the book of Job is all about God's invitation not to know *about* him but to know him and trust him personally.

Story Arc

● **Job**

Job

> **Question** 1:7
>
> Do you think people are aware that Satan is patrolling the earth, watching everything going on? In 1 Peter 5:8, we are told that Satan prowls around like a lion looking for someone to devour. If people actually stopped to realize this, how might they live differently?

Prologue

1 There once was a man named Job who lived in the land of Uz. He was blameless—a man of complete integrity. He feared God and stayed away from evil. 2 He had seven sons and three daughters. 3 He owned 7,000 sheep, 3,000 camels, 500 teams of oxen, and 500 female donkeys. He also had many servants. He was, in fact, the richest person in that entire area.

4 Job's sons would take turns preparing feasts in their homes, and they would also invite their three sisters to celebrate with them. 5 When these celebrations ended—sometimes after several days—Job would purify his children. He would get up early in the morning and offer a burnt offering for each of them. For Job said to himself, "Perhaps my children have sinned and have cursed God in their hearts." This was Job's regular practice.

Job's First Test

6 One day the members of the heavenly court* came to present themselves before the LORD, and the Accuser, Satan,* came with them. 7 "Where have you come from?" the LORD asked Satan.

Satan answered the LORD, "I have been patrolling the earth, watching everything that's going on."

8 Then the LORD asked Satan, "Have you noticed my servant Job? He is the finest man in all the earth. He is blameless—a man of complete integrity. He fears God and stays away from evil."

9 Satan replied to the LORD, "Yes, but Job has good reason to fear God. 10 You have always put a wall of protection around him and his home and his property. You have made him prosper in everything he does. Look how rich he is! 11 But reach out and take away everything he has, and he will surely curse you to your face!"

12 "All right, you may test him," the LORD said to Satan. "Do whatever you want with everything he possesses, but don't harm him physically." So Satan left the LORD's presence.

13 One day when Job's sons and daughters were feasting at the oldest brother's house, 14 a messenger arrived at Job's home with this news: "Your oxen were plowing, with the donkeys feeding beside them, 15 when the Sabeans raided us. They stole all the animals and killed all the farmhands. I am the only one who escaped to tell you."

16 While he was still speaking, another messenger arrived with this news: "The fire of God has fallen from heaven and burned up your sheep and all the shepherds. I am the only one who escaped to tell you."

17 While he was still speaking, a third messenger arrived with this news: "Three bands of Chaldean raiders have stolen your camels and killed your servants. I am the only one who escaped to tell you."

1:6a Hebrew *the sons of God.* 1:6b Hebrew *and the satan;* similarly throughout this chapter.

18 While he was still speaking, another messenger arrived with this news:
"Your sons and daughters were feasting in their oldest brother's home.
19 Suddenly, a powerful wind swept in from the wilderness and hit the house
on all sides. The house collapsed, and all your children are dead. I am the only
one who escaped to tell you."
20 Job stood up and tore his robe in grief. Then he shaved his head and fell
to the ground to worship. 21 He said,

"I came naked from my mother's womb,
 and I will be naked when I leave.
The LORD gave me what I had,
 and the LORD has taken it away.
Praise the name of the LORD!"

22 In all of this, Job did not sin by blaming God.

Job's Second Test

2 One day the members of the heavenly court* came again to present
themselves before the LORD, and the Accuser, Satan,* came with them.
2 "Where have you come from?" the LORD asked Satan.
Satan answered the LORD, "I have been patrolling the earth, watching
everything that's going on."
3 Then the LORD asked Satan, "Have you noticed my servant Job? He is the
finest man in all the earth. He is blameless—a man of complete integrity.
He fears God and stays away from evil. And he has maintained his integrity,
even though you urged me to harm him without cause."
4 Satan replied to the LORD, "Skin for skin! A man will give up everything
he has to save his life. 5 But reach out and take away his health, and he will
surely curse you to your face!"
6 "All right, do with him as you please," the LORD said to Satan. "But spare
his life." 7 So Satan left the LORD's presence, and he struck Job with terrible
boils from head to foot.
8 Job scraped his skin with a piece of broken pottery as he sat among the
ashes. 9 His wife said to him, "Are you still trying to maintain your integrity?
Curse God and die."
10 But Job replied, "You talk like a foolish woman. Should we accept only
good things from the hand of God and never anything bad?" So in all this,
Job said nothing wrong.

Job's Three Friends Share His Anguish

11 When three of Job's friends heard of the tragedy he had suffered, they got
together and traveled from their homes to comfort and console him. Their
names were Eliphaz the Temanite, Bildad the Shuhite, and Zophar the Naa-
mathite. 12 When they saw Job from a distance, they scarcely recognized him.
Wailing loudly, they tore their robes and threw dust into the air over their
heads to show their grief. 13 Then they sat on the ground with him for seven
days and nights. No one said a word to Job, for they saw that his suffering
was too great for words.

2:1a Hebrew *the sons of God.* 2:1b Hebrew *and the satan;* similarly throughout this chapter.

Question **2:10**

What is the answer to Job's question to his wife?

Story Arc **1:1-22**

● Job

Job was so distraught over the tragedies that affected his life and family that he tore his robe in grief. He shaved his head in mourning. He then fell to the ground—to worship!

Job's life teaches us that worship is not just an experience that makes us feel better. Worship is less about how we feel and more about praising the name of the Lord. What if worship were also an experience in which you could grieve? What if you could lament through worship? What if you could fall to your knees with nothing to give God but yourself? What if all you had was your raw, uncovered soul, so you offered that to the Lord? Job's example is later echoed by Jesus' agonizing prayer the night before he is crucified (Luke 22:39-44). In this way, Job's story challenges us to lift up any moment, even overwhelming suffering, to God.

Ps 22:1-31 ►

Job's First Speech

3 At last Job spoke, and he cursed the day of his birth. 2 He said:

3 "Let the day of my birth be erased,
and the night I was conceived.
4 Let that day be turned to darkness.
Let it be lost even to God on high,
and let no light shine on it.
5 Let the darkness and utter gloom claim that day for its own.
Let a black cloud overshadow it,
and let the darkness terrify it.
6 Let that night be blotted off the calendar,
never again to be counted among the days of the year,
never again to appear among the months.
7 Let that night be childless.
Let it have no joy.
8 Let those who are experts at cursing—
whose cursing could rouse Leviathan*—
curse that day.
9 Let its morning stars remain dark.
Let it hope for light, but in vain;
may it never see the morning light.
10 Curse that day for failing to shut my mother's womb,
for letting me be born to see all this trouble.

11 "Why wasn't I born dead?
Why didn't I die as I came from the womb?
12 Why was I laid on my mother's lap?
Why did she nurse me at her breasts?
13 Had I died at birth, I would now be at peace.
I would be asleep and at rest.
14 I would rest with the world's kings and prime ministers,
whose great buildings now lie in ruins.
15 I would rest with princes, rich in gold,
whose palaces were filled with silver.
16 Why wasn't I buried like a stillborn child,
like a baby who never lives to see the light?
17 For in death the wicked cause no trouble,
and the weary are at rest.
18 Even captives are at ease in death,
with no guards to curse them.
19 Rich and poor are both there,
and the slave is free from his master.

20 "Oh, why give light to those in misery,
and life to those who are bitter?
21 They long for death, and it won't come.
They search for death more eagerly than for hidden
treasure.

3:8 The identification of Leviathan is disputed, ranging from an earthly creature to a mythical sea monster in ancient literature.

22 They're filled with joy when they finally die,
and rejoice when they find the grave.
23 Why is life given to those with no future,
those God has surrounded with difficulties?
24 I cannot eat for sighing;
my groans pour out like water.
25 What I always feared has happened to me.
What I dreaded has come true.
26 I have no peace, no quietness.
I have no rest; only trouble comes."

Eliphaz's First Response to Job

4 Then Eliphaz the Temanite replied to Job:

2 "Will you be patient and let me say a word?
For who could keep from speaking out?

3 "In the past you have encouraged many people;
you have strengthened those who were weak.
4 Your words have supported those who were falling;
you encouraged those with shaky knees.
5 But now when trouble strikes, you lose heart.
You are terrified when it touches you.
6 Doesn't your reverence for God give you
confidence?
Doesn't your life of integrity give you hope?

7 "Stop and think! Do the innocent die?
When have the upright been destroyed?
8 My experience shows that those who plant trouble
and cultivate evil will harvest the same.
9 A breath from God destroys them.
They vanish in a blast of his anger.
10 The lion roars and the wildcat snarls,
but the teeth of strong lions will be broken.
11 The fierce lion will starve for lack of prey,
and the cubs of the lioness will be scattered.

12 "This truth was given to me in secret,
as though whispered in my ear.
13 It came to me in a disturbing vision at night,
when people are in a deep sleep.
14 Fear gripped me,
and my bones trembled.
15 A spirit* swept past my face,
and my hair stood on end.*
16 The spirit stopped, but I couldn't see its shape.
There was a form before my eyes.
In the silence I heard a voice say,

4:15a Or *wind;* also in 4:16. **4:15b** Or *its wind sent shivers up my spine.*

Question 3:26

The Bible at times is raw with human emotion. When he lost his worldly possessions, children, and health, Job fell into a deep depression and despair. Does it comfort you or does it bother you to know that a righteous person can suffer emotionally like this?

Question 4:3

Job's friend reminded him of his track record. Could someone say this about you? This is quite a legacy Job had. What would it take, if you were to start today, to develop this kind of difference in your lifetime?

17 'Can a mortal be innocent before God?
Can anyone be pure before the Creator?'

18 "If God does not trust his own angels
and has charged his messengers with foolishness,
19 how much less will he trust people made of clay!
They are made of dust, crushed as easily as a moth.
20 They are alive in the morning but dead by evening,
gone forever without a trace.
21 Their tent-cords are pulled and the tent collapses,
and they die in ignorance.

Eliphaz's Response Continues

5 1 "Cry for help, but will anyone answer you?
Which of the angels* will help you?
2 Surely resentment destroys the fool,
and jealousy kills the simple.
3 I have seen that fools may be successful for the moment,
but then comes sudden disaster.
4 Their children are abandoned far from help;
they are crushed in court with no one to defend them.
5 The hungry devour their harvest,
even when it is guarded by brambles.*
The thirsty pant after their wealth.*
6 But evil does not spring from the soil,
and trouble does not sprout from the earth.
7 People are born for trouble
as readily as sparks fly up from a fire.

8 "If I were you, I would go to God
and present my case to him.
9 He does great things too marvelous to understand.
He performs countless miracles.
10 He gives rain for the earth
and water for the fields.
11 He gives prosperity to the poor
and protects those who suffer.
12 He frustrates the plans of schemers
so the work of their hands will not succeed.
13 He traps the wise in their own cleverness
so their cunning schemes are thwarted.
14 They find it is dark in the daytime,
and they grope at noon as if it were night.
15 He rescues the poor from the cutting words of the strong,
and rescues them from the clutches of the powerful.
16 And so at last the poor have hope,
and the snapping jaws of the wicked are shut.

5:1 Hebrew *the holy ones.* **5:5a** The meaning of the Hebrew for this phrase is uncertain.
5:5b As in Greek and Syriac versions; Hebrew reads *A snare snatches their wealth.*

17 "But consider the joy of those corrected by God!
Do not despise the discipline of the Almighty when you sin.
18 For though he wounds, he also bandages.
He strikes, but his hands also heal.
19 From six disasters he will rescue you;
even in the seventh, he will keep you from evil.
20 He will save you from death in time of famine,
from the power of the sword in time of war.
21 You will be safe from slander
and have no fear when destruction comes.
22 You will laugh at destruction and famine;
wild animals will not terrify you.
23 You will be at peace with the stones of the field,
and its wild animals will be at peace with you.
24 You will know that your home is safe.
When you survey your possessions, nothing will be missing.
25 You will have many children;
your descendants will be as plentiful as grass!
26 You will go to the grave at a ripe old age,
like a sheaf of grain harvested at the proper time!

27 "We have studied life and found all this to be true.
Listen to my counsel, and apply it to yourself."

Question 5:17

Nothing Eliphaz said was necessarily wrong, but what was wrong about his approach to his friend in a time like this?

Job's Second Speech: A Response to Eliphaz

6 Then Job spoke again:

2 "If my misery could be weighed
and my troubles be put on the scales,
3 they would outweigh all the sands of the sea.
That is why I spoke impulsively.
4 For the Almighty has struck me down with his arrows.
Their poison infects my spirit.
God's terrors are lined up against me.
5 Don't I have a right to complain?
Don't wild donkeys bray when they find no grass,
and oxen bellow when they have no food?
6 Don't people complain about unsalted food?
Does anyone want the tasteless white of an egg?*
7 My appetite disappears when I look at it;
I gag at the thought of eating it!

8 "Oh, that I might have my request,
that God would grant my desire.
9 I wish he would crush me.
I wish he would reach out his hand and kill me.
10 At least I can take comfort in this:
Despite the pain,
I have not denied the words of the Holy One.

6:6 Or *the tasteless juice of the mallow plant?*

Make a Difference 6:26

Words

When someone is desperately hurting, words of rational challenge can sometimes feel like further blows. Job needed compassion, not rationality! He challenged his friends to suffer with him instead of confronting him.

When someone is desperately hurting, don't be quick to speak. Instead, be quick to listen. Don't be quick to offer your opinions. This is wise advice in a world that doesn't give attention to others. The skill of listening shows a heart that cares for people. Listening to someone shows a person they are valued, important, and worth the time. This could simply be life-changing.

Difference Maker

Go twenty-four hours without talking about yourself (unless you absolutely must). As much as possible, ask friends and family open-ended questions and give them your undivided, caring attention.

11 But I don't have the strength to endure.
I have nothing to live for.
12 Do I have the strength of a stone?
Is my body made of bronze?
13 No, I am utterly helpless,
without any chance of success.

14 "One should be kind to a fainting friend,
but you accuse me without any fear of the Almighty.*
15 My brothers, you have proved as unreliable as a seasonal brook
that overflows its banks in the spring
16 when it is swollen with ice and melting snow.
17 But when the hot weather arrives, the water disappears.
The brook vanishes in the heat.
18 The caravans turn aside to be refreshed,
but there is nothing to drink, so they die.
19 The caravans from Tema search for this water;
the travelers from Sheba hope to find it.
20 They count on it but are disappointed.
When they arrive, their hopes are dashed.
21 You, too, have given no help.
You have seen my calamity, and you are afraid.
22 But why? Have I ever asked you for a gift?
Have I begged for anything of yours for myself?
23 Have I asked you to rescue me from my enemies,
or to save me from ruthless people?
24 Teach me, and I will keep quiet.
Show me what I have done wrong.
25 Honest words can be painful,
but what do your criticisms amount to?
26 Do you think your words are convincing
when you disregard my cry of desperation?
27 You would even send an orphan into slavery*
or sell a friend.
28 Look at me!
Would I lie to your face?
29 Stop assuming my guilt,
for I have done no wrong.
30 Do you think I am lying?
Don't I know the difference between right and wrong?

7 1 "Is not all human life a struggle?
Our lives are like that of a hired hand,
2 like a worker who longs for the shade,
like a servant waiting to be paid.
3 I, too, have been assigned months of futility,
long and weary nights of misery.
4 Lying in bed, I think, 'When will it be morning?'
But the night drags on, and I toss till dawn.

6:14 Or *friend, / or he might lose his fear of the Almighty.* **6:27** Hebrew *even gamble over an orphan.*

5 My body is covered with maggots and scabs.
My skin breaks open, oozing with pus.

Job Cries Out to God

6 "My days fly faster than a weaver's shuttle.
They end without hope.
7 O God, remember that my life is but a breath,
and I will never again feel happiness.
8 You see me now, but not for long.
You will look for me, but I will be gone.
9 Just as a cloud dissipates and vanishes,
those who die* will not come back.
10 They are gone forever from their home—
never to be seen again.

11 "I cannot keep from speaking.
I must express my anguish.
My bitter soul must complain.
12 Am I a sea monster or a dragon
that you must place me under guard?
13 I think, 'My bed will comfort me,
and sleep will ease my misery,'
14 but then you shatter me with dreams
and terrify me with visions.
15 I would rather be strangled—
rather die than suffer like this.
16 I hate my life and don't want to go on living.
Oh, leave me alone for my few remaining days.

17 "What are people, that you should make so much of us,
that you should think of us so often?
18 For you examine us every morning
and test us every moment.
19 Why won't you leave me alone,
at least long enough for me to swallow!
20 If I have sinned, what have I done to you,
O watcher of all humanity?
Why make me your target?
Am I a burden to you?*
21 Why not just forgive my sin
and take away my guilt?
For soon I will lie down in the dust and die.
When you look for me, I will be gone."

Bildad's First Response to Job

8 Then Bildad the Shuhite replied to Job:

2 "How long will you go on like this?
You sound like a blustering wind.

7:9 Hebrew *who go down to Sheol.* 7:20 As in Greek version; Hebrew reads *target, so that I am a burden to myself?*

Question 8:4

Jesus also encountered this attitude—where people were convinced someone must have sinned for a person to be in their troubled condition (for example, see John 9:2). How does Jesus' response to this kind of attitude support Job?

Question 9:2

What is the answer to this question? Find a couple of verses in the Bible that could help you answer this.

3 Does God twist justice?
Does the Almighty twist what is right?
4 Your children must have sinned against him,
so their punishment was well deserved.
5 But if you pray to God
and seek the favor of the Almighty,
6 and if you are pure and live with integrity,
he will surely rise up and restore your happy home.
7 And though you started with little,
you will end with much.

8 "Just ask the previous generation.
Pay attention to the experience of our ancestors.
9 For we were born but yesterday and know nothing.
Our days on earth are as fleeting as a shadow.
10 But those who came before us will teach you.
They will teach you the wisdom of old.

11 "Can papyrus reeds grow tall without a marsh?
Can marsh grass flourish without water?
12 While they are still flowering, not ready to be cut,
they begin to wither more quickly than grass.
13 The same happens to all who forget God.
The hopes of the godless evaporate.
14 Their confidence hangs by a thread.
They are leaning on a spider's web.
15 They cling to their home for security, but it won't last.
They try to hold it tight, but it will not endure.
16 The godless seem like a lush plant growing in the sunshine,
its branches spreading across the garden.
17 Its roots grow down through a pile of stones;
it takes hold on a bed of rocks.
18 But when it is uprooted,
it's as though it never existed!
19 That's the end of its life,
and others spring up from the earth to replace it.

20 "But look, God will not reject a person of integrity,
nor will he lend a hand to the wicked.
21 He will once again fill your mouth with laughter
and your lips with shouts of joy.
22 Those who hate you will be clothed with shame,
and the home of the wicked will be destroyed."

Job's Third Speech: A Response to Bildad

9 Then Job spoke again:

2 "Yes, I know all this is true in principle.
But how can a person be declared innocent in God's sight?

3 If someone wanted to take God to court,*
would it be possible to answer him even once in a thousand times?
4 For God is so wise and so mighty.
Who has ever challenged him successfully?

5 "Without warning, he moves the mountains,
overturning them in his anger.
6 He shakes the earth from its place,
and its foundations tremble.
7 If he commands it, the sun won't rise
and the stars won't shine.
8 He alone has spread out the heavens
and marches on the waves of the sea.
9 He made all the stars—the Bear and Orion,
the Pleiades and the constellations of the southern sky.
10 He does great things too marvelous to understand.
He performs countless miracles.

11 "Yet when he comes near, I cannot see him.
When he moves by, I do not see him go.
12 If he snatches someone in death, who can stop him?
Who dares to ask, 'What are you doing?'
13 And God does not restrain his anger.
Even the monsters of the sea* are crushed beneath his feet.

14 "So who am I, that I should try to answer God
or even reason with him?
15 Even if I were right, I would have no defense.
I could only plead for mercy.
16 And even if I summoned him and he responded,
I'm not sure he would listen to me.
17 For he attacks me with a storm
and repeatedly wounds me without cause.
18 He will not let me catch my breath,
but fills me instead with bitter sorrows.
19 If it's a question of strength, he's the strong one.
If it's a matter of justice, who dares to summon him* to court?
20 Though I am innocent, my own mouth would pronounce me guilty.
Though I am blameless, it* would prove me wicked.

21 "I am innocent,
but it makes no difference to me—
I despise my life.
22 Innocent or wicked, it is all the same to God.
That's why I say, 'He destroys both the blameless and the wicked.'
23 When a plague* sweeps through,
he laughs at the death of the innocent.

9:3 Or *If God wanted to take someone to court.* 9:13 Hebrew *the helpers of Rahab,* the name of a mythical sea monster that represents chaos in ancient literature. 9:19 As in Greek version; Hebrew reads *me.* 9:20 Or *he.* 9:23 Or *disaster.*

Prayer 9:33

Thank you, Jesus, that you are the Mediator between God and humans! You are the one who brings us together! Amen. (See 1 Timothy 2:5.)

24 The whole earth is in the hands of the wicked,
and God blinds the eyes of the judges.
If he's not the one who does it, who is?

25 "My life passes more swiftly than a runner.
It flees away without a glimpse of happiness.
26 It disappears like a swift papyrus boat,
like an eagle swooping down on its prey.
27 If I decided to forget my complaints,
to put away my sad face and be cheerful,
28 I would still dread all the pain,
for I know you will not find me innocent, O God.
29 Whatever happens, I will be found guilty.
So what's the use of trying?
30 Even if I were to wash myself with soap
and clean my hands with lye,
31 you would plunge me into a muddy ditch,
and my own filthy clothing would hate me.

32 "God is not a mortal like me,
so I cannot argue with him or take him to trial.
33 If only there were a mediator between us,
someone who could bring us together.
34 The mediator could make God stop beating me,
and I would no longer live in terror of his punishment.
35 Then I could speak to him without fear,
but I cannot do that in my own strength.

Job Frames His Plea to God

10 1 "I am disgusted with my life.
Let me complain freely.
My bitter soul must complain.
2 I will say to God, 'Don't simply condemn me—
tell me the charge you are bringing against me.
3 What do you gain by oppressing me?
Why do you reject me, the work of your own hands,
while smiling on the schemes of the wicked?
4 Are your eyes like those of a human?
Do you see things only as people see them?
5 Is your lifetime only as long as ours?
Is your life so short
6 that you must quickly probe for my guilt
and search for my sin?
7 Although you know I am not guilty,
no one can rescue me from your hands.

8 "'You formed me with your hands; you made me,
yet now you completely destroy me.
9 Remember that you made me from dust—
will you turn me back to dust so soon?

10 You guided my conception
and formed me in the womb.*
11 You clothed me with skin and flesh,
and you knit my bones and sinews together.
12 You gave me life and showed me your unfailing love.
My life was preserved by your care.

13 "'Yet your real motive—
your true intent—
14 was to watch me, and if I sinned,
you would not forgive my guilt.
15 If I am guilty, too bad for me;
and even if I'm innocent, I can't hold my head high,
because I am filled with shame and misery.
16 And if I hold my head high, you hunt me like a lion
and display your awesome power against me.
17 Again and again you witness against me.
You pour out your growing anger on me
and bring fresh armies against me.

18 "'Why, then, did you deliver me from my mother's
womb?
Why didn't you let me die at birth?
19 It would be as though I had never existed,
going directly from the womb to the grave.
20 I have only a few days left, so leave me alone,
that I may have a moment of comfort
21 before I leave—never to return—
for the land of darkness and utter gloom.
22 It is a land as dark as midnight,
a land of gloom and confusion,
where even the light is dark as midnight.'"

Zophar's First Response to Job

11 Then Zophar the Naamathite replied to Job:

2 "Shouldn't someone answer this torrent of words?
Is a person proved innocent just by a lot of talking?
3 Should I remain silent while you babble on?
When you mock God, shouldn't someone make you
ashamed?
4 You claim, 'My beliefs are pure,'
and 'I am clean in the sight of God.'
5 If only God would speak;
if only he would tell you what he thinks!
6 If only he would tell you the secrets of wisdom,
for true wisdom is not a simple matter.
Listen! God is doubtless punishing you
far less than you deserve!

Question 10:18

Total despair—have you ever felt this way? Do you know anyone who has? Why do you think God's Word has moments like this, when the most troubling, raw reality of humanity is on full display?

Question 11:2

Job was hurting, yet his friend treated him rudely. Read 2 Corinthians 1:3-5. How was Job's friend doing the opposite of what God calls us to do for someone who is suffering?

10:10 Hebrew *You poured me out like milk / and curdled me like cheese.*

7 "Can you solve the mysteries of God?
Can you discover everything about the Almighty?
8 Such knowledge is higher than the heavens—
and who are you?
It is deeper than the underworld*—
what do you know?
9 It is broader than the earth
and wider than the sea.
10 If God comes and puts a person in prison
or calls the court to order, who can stop him?
11 For he knows those who are false,
and he takes note of all their sins.
12 An empty-headed person won't become wise
any more than a wild donkey can bear a human
child.*

13 "If only you would prepare your heart
and lift up your hands to him in prayer!
14 Get rid of your sins,
and leave all iniquity behind you.
15 Then your face will brighten with innocence.
You will be strong and free of fear.
16 You will forget your misery;
it will be like water flowing away.
17 Your life will be brighter than the noonday.
Even darkness will be as bright as morning.
18 Having hope will give you courage.
You will be protected and will rest in safety.
19 You will lie down unafraid,
and many will look to you for help.
20 But the wicked will be blinded.
They will have no escape.
Their only hope is death."

Job's Fourth Speech: A Response to Zophar

12 Then Job spoke again:

2 "You people really know everything, don't you?
And when you die, wisdom will die with you!
3 Well, I know a few things myself—
and you're no better than I am.
Who doesn't know these things you've been saying?
4 Yet my friends laugh at me,
for I call on God and expect an answer.
I am a just and blameless man,
yet they laugh at me.
5 People who are at ease mock those in trouble.
They give a push to people who are stumbling.
6 But robbers are left in peace,

11:8 Hebrew *than Sheol.* **11:12** Or *than a wild male donkey can bear a tame colt.*

Make a Difference 12:4

Doubt

Is it okay to doubt God? We struggle as humans to trust anyone completely, including God. At times we're not sure God is really watching out for us, or we don't feel God cares about us. Maybe we wonder why God allows tragedy to happen in our lives or even in the world at large. We are disappointed that God doesn't seem more real. Doubt is normal. Still, is it okay?

The Bible is filled with doubt. Gideon, for one, was a pessimist when it came to God in his life (Judges 6). The Psalms echo with cries of bewilderment and despair. Martha was distressed that Jesus didn't arrive when she wanted him to (John 11:21). Peter and the disciples failed miserably on more than a few occasions. Here, Job expected God to answer, but God seemed to be silent.

Doubt can be a sign that we are trying to work out our faith in real life. When we lift our doubt to God, it reveals our faith. God honors the heart that trusts its deepest doubts to him.

Difference Maker

Trust whatever doubt you have to the Lord in prayer today.

and those who provoke God live in safety—
though God keeps them in his power.*

7 "Just ask the animals, and they will teach you.
Ask the birds of the sky, and they will tell you.
8 Speak to the earth, and it will instruct you.
Let the fish in the sea speak to you.
9 For they all know
that my disaster* has come from the hand of the LORD.
10 For the life of every living thing is in his hand,
and the breath of every human being.
11 The ear tests the words it hears
just as the mouth distinguishes between foods.
12 Wisdom belongs to the aged,
and understanding to the old.

13 "But true wisdom and power are found in God;
counsel and understanding are his.
14 What he destroys cannot be rebuilt.
When he puts someone in prison, there is no escape.
15 If he holds back the rain, the earth becomes a desert.
If he releases the waters, they flood the earth.
16 Yes, strength and wisdom are his;
deceivers and deceived are both in his power.
17 He leads counselors away, stripped of good judgment;
wise judges become fools.
18 He removes the royal robe of kings.
They are led away with ropes around their waist.
19 He leads priests away, stripped of status;
he overthrows those with long years in power.
20 He silences the trusted adviser
and removes the insight of the elders.
21 He pours disgrace upon princes
and disarms the strong.

22 "He uncovers mysteries hidden in darkness;
he brings light to the deepest gloom.
23 He builds up nations, and he destroys them.
He expands nations, and he abandons them.
24 He strips kings of understanding
and leaves them wandering in a pathless wasteland.
25 They grope in the darkness without a light.
He makes them stagger like drunkards.

Job Wants to Argue His Case with God

13 1 "Look, I have seen all this with my own eyes
and heard it with my own ears, and now I understand.
2 I know as much as you do.
You are no better than I am.

12:6 Or *safety—those who try to manipulate God.* The meaning of the Hebrew is uncertain.
12:9 Hebrew *that this.*

3 As for me, I would speak directly to the Almighty.
I want to argue my case with God himself.
4 As for you, you smear me with lies.
As physicians, you are worthless quacks.
5 If only you could be silent!
That's the wisest thing you could do.
6 Listen to my charge;
pay attention to my arguments.

7 "Are you defending God with lies?
Do you make your dishonest arguments for his sake?
8 Will you slant your testimony in his favor?
Will you argue God's case for him?
9 What will happen when he finds out what you are doing?
Can you fool him as easily as you fool people?
10 No, you will be in trouble with him
if you secretly slant your testimony in his favor.
11 Doesn't his majesty terrify you?
Doesn't your fear of him overwhelm you?
12 Your platitudes are as valuable as ashes.
Your defense is as fragile as a clay pot.

13 "Be silent now and leave me alone.
Let me speak, and I will face the consequences.
14 Why should I put myself in mortal danger*
and take my life in my own hands?
15 God might kill me, but I have no other hope.*
I am going to argue my case with him.
16 But this is what will save me—I am not godless.
If I were, I could not stand before him.

17 "Listen closely to what I am about to say.
Hear me out.
18 I have prepared my case;
I will be proved innocent.
19 Who can argue with me over this?
And if you prove me wrong, I will remain silent and die.

Job Asks How He Has Sinned

20 "O God, grant me these two things,
and then I will be able to face you.
21 Remove your heavy hand from me,
and don't terrify me with your awesome presence.
22 Now summon me, and I will answer!
Or let me speak to you, and you reply.
23 Tell me, what have I done wrong?
Show me my rebellion and my sin.
24 Why do you turn away from me?
Why do you treat me as your enemy?

13:14 Hebrew *Why should I take my flesh in my teeth.* 13:15 An alternate reading in the Masoretic Text reads *God might kill me, but I hope in him.*

25 Would you terrify a leaf blown by the wind?
Would you chase dry straw?

26 "You write bitter accusations against me
and bring up all the sins of my youth.
27 You put my feet in stocks.
You examine all my paths.
You trace all my footprints.
28 I waste away like rotting wood,
like a moth-eaten coat.

14

1 "How frail is humanity!
How short is life, how full of trouble!
2 We blossom like a flower and then wither.
Like a passing shadow, we quickly disappear.
3 Must you keep an eye on such a frail creature
and demand an accounting from me?
4 Who can bring purity out of an impure person?
No one!
5 You have decided the length of our lives.
You know how many months we will live,
and we are not given a minute longer.
6 So leave us alone and let us rest!
We are like hired hands, so let us finish our work in peace.

7 "Even a tree has more hope!
If it is cut down, it will sprout again
and grow new branches.
8 Though its roots have grown old in the earth
and its stump decays,
9 at the scent of water it will bud
and sprout again like a new seedling.

10 "But when people die, their strength is gone.
They breathe their last, and then where are they?
11 As water evaporates from a lake
and a river disappears in drought,
12 people are laid to rest and do not rise again.
Until the heavens are no more, they will not wake up
nor be roused from their sleep.

13 "I wish you would hide me in the grave*
and forget me there until your anger has passed.
But mark your calendar to think of me again!
14 Can the dead live again?
If so, this would give me hope through all my years of struggle,
and I would eagerly await the release of death.
15 You would call and I would answer,
and you would yearn for me, your handiwork.

Prayer **14:14**

Lord, the answer to Job's question is "Yes, the dead can live again!" There is hope! Thank you that the resurrection of Jesus proves that the sting of death will be broken. Amen. (See 1 Corinthians 15:55-57.)

14:13 Hebrew *in Sheol.*

16 For then you would guard my steps,
instead of watching for my sins.
17 My sins would be sealed in a pouch,
and you would cover my guilt.

18 "But instead, as mountains fall and crumble
and as rocks fall from a cliff,
19 as water wears away the stones
and floods wash away the soil,
so you destroy people's hope.
20 You always overpower them, and they pass from the scene.
You disfigure them in death and send them away.
21 They never know if their children grow up in honor
or sink to insignificance.
22 They suffer painfully;
their life is full of trouble."

Eliphaz's Second Response to Job

15 Then Eliphaz the Temanite replied:

2 "A wise man wouldn't answer with such empty talk!
You are nothing but a windbag.
3 The wise don't engage in empty chatter.
What good are such words?
4 Have you no fear of God,
no reverence for him?
5 Your sins are telling your mouth what to say.
Your words are based on clever deception.
6 Your own mouth condemns you, not I.
Your own lips testify against you.

7 "Were you the first person ever born?
Were you born before the hills were made?
8 Were you listening at God's secret council?
Do you have a monopoly on wisdom?
9 What do you know that we don't?
What do you understand that we do not?
10 On our side are aged, gray-haired men
much older than your father!

11 "Is God's comfort too little for you?
Is his gentle word not enough?
12 What has taken away your reason?
What has weakened your vision,*
13 that you turn against God
and say all these evil things?
14 Can any mortal be pure?
Can anyone born of a woman be just?

15:12 Or *Why do your eyes flash with anger;* Hebrew reads *Why do your eyes blink.*

15 Look, God does not even trust the angels.*
Even the heavens are not absolutely pure in his sight.
16 How much less pure is a corrupt and sinful person
with a thirst for wickedness!

17 "If you will listen, I will show you.
I will answer you from my own experience.
18 And it is confirmed by the reports of wise men
who have heard the same thing from their fathers—
19 from those to whom the land was given
long before any foreigners arrived.

20 "The wicked writhe in pain throughout their lives.
Years of trouble are stored up for the ruthless.
21 The sound of terror rings in their ears,
and even on good days they fear the attack of the
destroyer.
22 They dare not go out into the darkness
for fear they will be murdered.
23 They wander around, saying, 'Where can I find bread?'*
They know their day of destruction is near.
24 That dark day terrifies them.
They live in distress and anguish,
like a king preparing for battle.
25 For they shake their fists at God,
defying the Almighty.
26 Holding their strong shields,
they defiantly charge against him.

27 "These wicked people are heavy and prosperous;
their waists bulge with fat.
28 But their cities will be ruined.
They will live in abandoned houses
that are ready to tumble down.
29 Their riches will not last,
and their wealth will not endure.
Their possessions will no longer spread across the horizon.

30 "They will not escape the darkness.
The burning sun will wither their shoots,
and the breath of God will destroy them.
31 Let them no longer fool themselves by trusting in empty
riches,
for emptiness will be their only reward.
32 They will be cut down in the prime of life;
their branches will never again be green.
33 They will be like a vine whose grapes are harvested too early,
like an olive tree that loses its blossoms before the fruit
can form.

15:15 Hebrew *the holy ones.* **15:23** Greek version reads *He is appointed to be food for a vulture.*

How this passage impacts me

34 For the godless are barren.
Their homes, enriched through bribery,
will burn.
35 They conceive trouble and give birth to evil.
Their womb produces deceit."

Job's Fifth Speech: A Response to Eliphaz

16 Then Job spoke again:

2 "I have heard all this before.
What miserable comforters you are!
3 Won't you ever stop blowing hot air?
What makes you keep on talking?
4 I could say the same things if you were in my place.
I could spout off criticism and shake my head
at you.
5 But if it were me, I would encourage you.
I would try to take away your grief.
6 Instead, I suffer if I defend myself,
and I suffer no less if I refuse to speak.

7 "O God, you have ground me down
and devastated my family.
8 As if to prove I have sinned, you've reduced me to skin
and bones.
My gaunt flesh testifies against me.
9 God hates me and angrily tears me apart.
He snaps his teeth at me
and pierces me with his eyes.
10 People jeer and laugh at me.
They slap my cheek in contempt.
A mob gathers against me.
11 God has handed me over to sinners.
He has tossed me into the hands of the wicked.

12 "I was living quietly until he shattered me.
He took me by the neck and broke me in pieces.
Then he set me up as his target,
13 and now his archers surround me.
His arrows pierce me without mercy.
The ground is wet with my blood.*
14 Again and again he smashes against me,
charging at me like a warrior.
15 I wear burlap to show my grief.
My pride lies in the dust.
16 My eyes are red with weeping;
dark shadows circle my eyes.
17 Yet I have done no wrong,
and my prayer is pure.

16:13 Hebrew *my gall.*

18 "O earth, do not conceal my blood.
Let it cry out on my behalf.
19 Even now my witness is in heaven.
My advocate is there on high.
20 My friends scorn me,
but I pour out my tears to God.
21 I need someone to mediate between God and me,
as a person mediates between friends.
22 For soon I must go down that road
from which I will never return.

Job Continues to Defend His Innocence

17 1 "My spirit is crushed,
and my life is nearly snuffed out.
The grave is ready to receive me.
2 I am surrounded by mockers.
I watch how bitterly they taunt me.

3 "You must defend my innocence, O God,
since no one else will stand up for me.
4 You have closed their minds to understanding,
but do not let them triumph.
5 They betray their friends for their own advantage,
so let their children faint with hunger.

6 "God has made a mockery of me among the people;
they spit in my face.
7 My eyes are swollen with weeping,
and I am but a shadow of my former self.
8 The virtuous are horrified when they see me.
The innocent rise up against the ungodly.
9 The righteous keep moving forward,
and those with clean hands become stronger and stronger.

10 "As for all of you, come back with a better argument,
though I still won't find a wise man among you.
11 My days are over.
My hopes have disappeared.
My heart's desires are broken.
12 These men say that night is day;
they claim that the darkness is light.
13 What if I go to the grave*
and make my bed in darkness?
14 What if I call the grave my father,
and the maggot my mother or my sister?
15 Where then is my hope?
Can anyone find it?
16 No, my hope will go down with me to the grave.
We will rest together in the dust!"

17:13 Hebrew *to Sheol;* also in 17:16.

Prayer **16:21**

Lord, I need someone to speak on my behalf, to plead for mercy, to stand up for me when no one else will or when no one else can. I can't save myself! Lord Jesus, thank you for being my Advocate. Thank you for coming to my defense even though I don't deserve it. Thank you for offering me peace with God because of what you have done for me. Amen. (See Romans 5.)

Prayer **17:3**

No one else will stand up for me. Only you, God, can defend me. Amen.

Bildad's Second Response to Job

18 Then Bildad the Shuhite replied:

2 "How long before you stop talking?
Speak sense if you want us to answer!
3 Do you think we are mere animals?
Do you think we are stupid?
4 You may tear out your hair in anger,
but will that destroy the earth?
Will it make the rocks tremble?

5 "Surely the light of the wicked will be snuffed out.
The sparks of their fire will not glow.
6 The light in their tent will grow dark.
The lamp hanging above them will be quenched.
7 The confident stride of the wicked will be shortened.
Their own schemes will be their downfall.
8 The wicked walk into a net.
They fall into a pit.
9 A trap grabs them by the heel.
A snare holds them tight.
10 A noose lies hidden on the ground.
A rope is stretched across their path.

11 "Terrors surround the wicked
and trouble them at every step.
12 Hunger depletes their strength,
and calamity waits for them to stumble.
13 Disease eats their skin;
death devours their limbs.
14 They are torn from the security of their homes
and are brought down to the king of terrors.
15 The homes of the wicked will burn down;
burning sulfur rains on their houses.
16 Their roots will dry up,
and their branches will wither.
17 All memory of their existence will fade from the earth;
no one will remember their names.
18 They will be thrust from light into darkness,
driven from the world.
19 They will have neither children nor grandchildren,
nor any survivor in the place where they lived.
20 People in the west are appalled at their fate;
people in the east are horrified.
21 They will say, 'This was the home of a wicked person,
the place of one who rejected God.'"

Job's Sixth Speech: A Response to Bildad

19 Then Job spoke again:

2 "How long will you torture me?
How long will you try to crush me with your words?
3 You have already insulted me ten times.
You should be ashamed of treating me so badly.
4 Even if I have sinned,
that is my concern, not yours.
5 You think you're better than I am,
using my humiliation as evidence of my sin.
6 But it is God who has wronged me,
capturing me in his net.*

7 "I cry out, 'Help!' but no one answers me.
I protest, but there is no justice.
8 God has blocked my way so I cannot move.
He has plunged my path into darkness.
9 He has stripped me of my honor
and removed the crown from my head.
10 He has demolished me on every side, and I am finished.
He has uprooted my hope like a fallen tree.
11 His fury burns against me;
he counts me as an enemy.
12 His troops advance.
They build up roads to attack me.
They camp all around my tent.

13 "My relatives stay far away,
and my friends have turned against me.
14 My family is gone,
and my close friends have forgotten me.
15 My servants and maids consider me a stranger.
I am like a foreigner to them.
16 When I call my servant, he doesn't come;
I have to plead with him!
17 My breath is repulsive to my wife.
I am rejected by my own family.
18 Even young children despise me.
When I stand to speak, they turn their backs on me.
19 My close friends detest me.
Those I loved have turned against me.
20 I have been reduced to skin and bones
and have escaped death by the skin of my teeth.

21 "Have mercy on me, my friends, have mercy,
for the hand of God has struck me.
22 Must you also persecute me, like God does?
Haven't you chewed me up enough?

19:6 Or *for I am like a city under siege.*

What I want to remember

Question 19:25-27

In his isolation and misery, Job declared the hope that resides deep in his soul: "I know that my Redeemer lives." As you read 19:25-27, what inspires you about Job's continued faith despite all that he had been through, and what inspires you about God?

23 "Oh, that my words could be recorded.
Oh, that they could be inscribed on a monument,
24 carved with an iron chisel and filled with lead,
engraved forever in the rock.

25 "But as for me, I know that my Redeemer lives,
and he will stand upon the earth at last.
26 And after my body has decayed,
yet in my body I will see God!*
27 I will see him for myself.
Yes, I will see him with my own eyes.
I am overwhelmed at the thought!

28 "How dare you go on persecuting me,
saying, 'It's his own fault'?
29 You should fear punishment yourselves,
for your attitude deserves punishment.
Then you will know that there is indeed a judgment."

Zophar's Second Response to Job

20 Then Zophar the Naamathite replied:

2 "I must reply
because I am greatly disturbed.
3 I've had to endure your insults,
but now my spirit prompts me to reply.

4 "Don't you realize that from the beginning of time,
ever since people were first placed on the earth,
5 the triumph of the wicked has been short lived
and the joy of the godless has been only temporary?
6 Though the pride of the godless reaches to the heavens
and their heads touch the clouds,
7 yet they will vanish forever,
thrown away like their own dung.
Those who knew them will ask,
'Where are they?'
8 They will fade like a dream and not be found.
They will vanish like a vision in the night.
9 Those who once saw them will see them no more.
Their families will never see them again.
10 Their children will beg from the poor,
for they must give back their stolen riches.
11 Though they are young,
their bones will lie in the dust.

12 "They enjoyed the sweet taste of wickedness,
letting it melt under their tongue.
13 They savored it,

19:26 Or *without my body I will see God.* The meaning of the Hebrew is uncertain.

holding it long in their mouths.
14 But suddenly the food in their bellies turns sour,
a poisonous venom in their stomach.
15 They will vomit the wealth they swallowed.
God won't let them keep it down.
16 They will suck the poison of cobras.
The viper will kill them.
17 They will never again enjoy streams of olive oil
or rivers of milk and honey.
18 They will give back everything they worked for.
Their wealth will bring them no joy.
19 For they oppressed the poor and left them destitute.
They foreclosed on their homes.
20 They were always greedy and never satisfied.
Nothing remains of all the things they dreamed about.
21 Nothing is left after they finish gorging themselves.
Therefore, their prosperity will not endure.

22 "In the midst of plenty, they will run into trouble
and be overcome by misery.
23 May God give them a bellyful of trouble.
May God rain down his anger upon them.
24 When they try to escape an iron weapon,
a bronze-tipped arrow will pierce them.
25 The arrow is pulled from their back,
and the arrowhead glistens with blood.*
The terrors of death are upon them.
26 Their treasures will be thrown into deepest darkness.
A wildfire will devour their goods,
consuming all they have left.
27 The heavens will reveal their guilt,
and the earth will testify against them.
28 A flood will sweep away their house.
God's anger will descend on them in torrents.
29 This is the reward that God gives the wicked.
It is the inheritance decreed by God."

Job's Seventh Speech: A Response to Zophar

21 Then Job spoke again:

2 "Listen closely to what I am saying.
That's one consolation you can give me.
3 Bear with me, and let me speak.
After I have spoken, you may resume mocking me.

4 "My complaint is with God, not with people.
I have good reason to be so impatient.
5 Look at me and be stunned.
Put your hand over your mouth in shock.

20:25 Hebrew *with gall.*

Question 21:4

God's Word gives voice to the very doubts people have, even doubts about God. The book of Job is extraordinary that way. Reading this dialogue between Job and his friends lets us sit in the discontent of people struggling with the tension of God's sovereignty in the midst of trouble. Does it surprise you how remarkably honest the Bible is? Why or why not?

6 When I think about what I am saying, I shudder.
My body trembles.

7 "Why do the wicked prosper,
growing old and powerful?
8 They live to see their children grow up and settle down,
and they enjoy their grandchildren.
9 Their homes are safe from every fear,
and God does not punish them.
10 Their bulls never fail to breed.
Their cows bear calves and never miscarry.
11 They let their children frisk about like lambs.
Their little ones skip and dance.
12 They sing with tambourine and harp.
They celebrate to the sound of the flute.
13 They spend their days in prosperity,
then go down to the grave* in peace.
14 And yet they say to God, 'Go away.
We want no part of you and your ways.
15 Who is the Almighty, and why should we obey him?
What good will it do us to pray?'
16 (They think their prosperity is of their own doing,
but I will have nothing to do with that kind of thinking.)

17 "Yet the light of the wicked never seems to be extinguished.
Do they ever have trouble?
Does God distribute sorrows to them in anger?
18 Are they driven before the wind like straw?
Are they carried away by the storm like chaff?
Not at all!

19 "'Well,' you say, 'at least God will punish their children!'
But I say he should punish the ones who sin,
so that they understand his judgment.
20 Let them see their destruction with their own eyes.
Let them drink deeply of the anger of the Almighty.
21 For they will not care what happens to their family
after they are dead.

22 "But who can teach a lesson to God,
since he judges even the most powerful?
23 One person dies in prosperity,
completely comfortable and secure,
24 the picture of good health,
vigorous and fit.
25 Another person dies in bitter poverty,
never having tasted the good life.
26 But both are buried in the same dust,
both eaten by the same maggots.

21:13 Hebrew *to Sheol.*

27 "Look, I know what you're thinking.
I know the schemes you plot against me.
28 You will tell me of rich and wicked people
whose houses have vanished because of their sins.
29 But ask those who have been around,
and they will tell you the truth.
30 Evil people are spared in times of calamity
and are allowed to escape disaster.
31 No one criticizes them openly
or pays them back for what they have done.
32 When they are carried to the grave,
an honor guard keeps watch at their tomb.
33 A great funeral procession goes to the cemetery.
Many pay their respects as the body is laid to rest,
and the earth gives sweet repose.

34 "How can your empty clichés comfort me?
All your explanations are lies!"

Eliphaz's Third Response to Job

22 Then Eliphaz the Temanite replied:

2 "Can a person do anything to help God?
Can even a wise person be helpful to him?
3 Is it any advantage to the Almighty if you are righteous?
Would it be any gain to him if you were perfect?
4 Is it because you're so pious that he accuses you
and brings judgment against you?
5 No, it's because of your wickedness!
There's no limit to your sins.

6 "For example, you must have lent money to your friend
and demanded clothing as security.
Yes, you stripped him to the bone.
7 You must have refused water for the thirsty
and food for the hungry.
8 You probably think the land belongs to the powerful
and only the privileged have a right to it!
9 You must have sent widows away empty-handed
and crushed the hopes of orphans.
10 That is why you are surrounded by traps
and tremble from sudden fears.
11 That is why you cannot see in the darkness,
and waves of water cover you.

12 "God is so great—higher than the heavens,
higher than the farthest stars.
13 But you reply, 'That's why God can't see what I am
doing!
How can he judge through the thick darkness?

Question 22:5

His friends were getting increasingly frustrated that Job was still petitioning God so personally and directly. Job's very persistent faith was an assault on their neatly controlled theology. Before Job's struggle, all their understanding about God fit into a nice box. Job's raw, humble-yet-bold relationship with God during his struggles strained the confines of their small faith. How does the book of Job expand your view of how God walks with you through the good and bad times of life?

14 For thick clouds swirl about him, and he cannot see us.
He is way up there, walking on the vault of heaven.'

15 "Will you continue on the old paths
where evil people have walked?
16 They were snatched away in the prime of life,
the foundations of their lives washed away.
17 For they said to God, 'Leave us alone!
What can the Almighty do to us?'
18 Yet he was the one who filled their homes with good things,
so I will have nothing to do with that kind of thinking.

19 "The righteous will be happy to see the wicked destroyed,
and the innocent will laugh in contempt.
20 They will say, 'See how our enemies have been destroyed.
The last of them have been consumed in the fire.'

21 "Submit to God, and you will have peace;
then things will go well for you.
22 Listen to his instructions,
and store them in your heart.
23 If you return to the Almighty, you will be restored—
so clean up your life.
24 If you give up your lust for money
and throw your precious gold into the river,
25 the Almighty himself will be your treasure.
He will be your precious silver!

26 "Then you will take delight in the Almighty
and look up to God.
27 You will pray to him, and he will hear you,
and you will fulfill your vows to him.
28 You will succeed in whatever you choose to do,
and light will shine on the road ahead of you.
29 If people are in trouble and you say, 'Help them,'
God will save them.
30 Even sinners will be rescued;
they will be rescued because your hands are pure."

Job's Eighth Speech: A Response to Eliphaz

23

Then Job spoke again:

2 "My complaint today is still a bitter one,
and I try hard not to groan aloud.
3 If only I knew where to find God,
I would go to his court.
4 I would lay out my case
and present my arguments.
5 Then I would listen to his reply
and understand what he says to me.

6 Would he use his great power to argue with me?
No, he would give me a fair hearing.
7 Honest people can reason with him,
so I would be forever acquitted by my judge.
8 I go east, but he is not there.
I go west, but I cannot find him.
9 I do not see him in the north, for he is hidden.
I look to the south, but he is concealed.

10 "But he knows where I am going.
And when he tests me, I will come out as pure as gold.
11 For I have stayed on God's paths;
I have followed his ways and not turned aside.
12 I have not departed from his commands,
but have treasured his words more than daily food.
13 But once he has made his decision, who can change his mind?
Whatever he wants to do, he does.
14 So he will do to me whatever he has planned.
He controls my destiny.
15 No wonder I am so terrified in his presence.
When I think of it, terror grips me.
16 God has made me sick at heart;
the Almighty has terrified me.
17 Darkness is all around me;
thick, impenetrable darkness is everywhere.

Job Asks Why the Wicked Are Not Punished

24 1 "Why doesn't the Almighty bring the wicked to judgment?
Why must the godly wait for him in vain?
2 Evil people steal land by moving the boundary markers.
They steal livestock and put them in their own pastures.
3 They take the orphan's donkey
and demand the widow's ox as security for a loan.
4 The poor are pushed off the path;
the needy must hide together for safety.
5 Like wild donkeys in the wilderness,
the poor must spend all their time looking for food,
searching even in the desert for food for their children.
6 They harvest a field they do not own,
and they glean in the vineyards of the wicked.
7 All night they lie naked in the cold,
without clothing or covering.
8 They are soaked by mountain showers,
and they huddle against the rocks for want of a home.

9 "The wicked snatch a widow's child from her breast,
taking the baby as security for a loan.
10 The poor must go about naked, without any clothing.
They harvest food for others while they themselves are starving.

Make a Difference 23:6

Fair Trial

Job believed in God—not as an idea but as a personal being who longs to respond in relationship to people. Job thought that God cared enough for him that he would get a fair trial in God's court. Still, Job didn't assume he deserved anything from God, just that God would treat him fairly. After all, Job knew the Lord is good and just.

By taking his complaint to God, Job was showing his trust in God as the one who could do something about it. Similar to Paul in Philippians 4:6-7, Job demonstrated what it's like to be someone who brings his petition to the one who had the authority to address the problem.

Difference Maker

Ask God to change something that is not good. Take your deepest frustration to him and trust him to be fair.

Question 24:1

Job asked the questions that all humans ask at some point in their lives. If God is all-powerful and if God is all good, why do bad things happen, and why do wicked people prosper? Why do you think God allows the Bible to ask these difficult questions? What does God think will happen if you were honestly to wrestle with these questions?

11 They press out olive oil without being allowed to taste it,
and they tread in the winepress as they suffer from thirst.
12 The groans of the dying rise from the city,
and the wounded cry for help,
yet God ignores their moaning.

13 "Wicked people rebel against the light.
They refuse to acknowledge its ways
or stay in its paths.
14 The murderer rises in the early dawn
to kill the poor and needy;
at night he is a thief.
15 The adulterer waits for the twilight,
saying, 'No one will see me then.'
He hides his face so no one will know him.
16 Thieves break into houses at night
and sleep in the daytime.
They are not acquainted with the light.
17 The black night is their morning.
They ally themselves with the terrors of the darkness.

18 "But they disappear like foam down a river.
Everything they own is cursed,
and they are afraid to enter their own vineyards.
19 The grave* consumes sinners
just as drought and heat consume snow.
20 Their own mothers will forget them.
Maggots will find them sweet to eat.
No one will remember them.
Wicked people are broken like a tree in the storm.
21 They cheat the woman who has no son to help her.
They refuse to help the needy widow.

22 "God, in his power, drags away the rich.
They may rise high, but they have no assurance of life.
23 They may be allowed to live in security,
but God is always watching them.
24 And though they are great now,
in a moment they will be gone like all others,
cut off like heads of grain.
25 Can anyone claim otherwise?
Who can prove me wrong?"

Bildad's Third Response to Job

25 Then Bildad the Shuhite replied:

2 "God is powerful and dreadful.
He enforces peace in the heavens.

24:19 Hebrew *Sheol.*

3 Who is able to count his heavenly army?
Doesn't his light shine on all the earth?
4 How can a mortal be innocent before God?
Can anyone born of a woman be pure?
5 God is more glorious than the moon;
he shines brighter than the stars.
6 In comparison, people are maggots;
we mortals are mere worms."

Job's Ninth Speech: A Response to Bildad

26 Then Job spoke again:

2 "How you have helped the powerless!
How you have saved the weak!
3 How you have enlightened my stupidity!
What wise advice you have offered!
4 Where have you gotten all these wise sayings?
Whose spirit speaks through you?

5 "The dead tremble—
those who live beneath the waters.
6 The underworld* is naked in God's presence.
The place of destruction* is uncovered.
7 God stretches the northern sky over empty space
and hangs the earth on nothing.
8 He wraps the rain in his thick clouds,
and the clouds don't burst with the weight.
9 He covers the face of the moon,*
shrouding it with his clouds.
10 He created the horizon when he separated the waters;
he set the boundary between day and night.
11 The foundations of heaven tremble;
they shudder at his rebuke.
12 By his power the sea grew calm.
By his skill he crushed the great sea monster.*
13 His Spirit made the heavens beautiful,
and his power pierced the gliding serpent.
14 These are just the beginning of all that he does,
merely a whisper of his power.
Who, then, can comprehend the thunder of his power?"

Job's Final Speech

27 Job continued speaking:

2 "I vow by the living God, who has taken away my rights,
by the Almighty who has embittered my soul—
3 As long as I live,
while I have breath from God,

26:6a Hebrew *Sheol.* **26:6b** Hebrew *Abaddon.* **26:9** Or *covers his throne.* **26:12** Hebrew *Rahab,* the name of a mythical sea monster that represents chaos in ancient literature.

Prayer **27:3-4**

Lord Jesus, shape me into an honest person. If I start a lie today, stop me from completing it. Help me speak the truth. Amen.

4 my lips will speak no evil,
and my tongue will speak no lies.
5 I will never concede that you are right;
I will defend my integrity until I die.
6 I will maintain my innocence without wavering.
My conscience is clear for as long as I live.

7 "May my enemy be punished like the wicked,
my adversary like those who do evil.
8 For what hope do the godless have when God cuts them off
and takes away their life?
9 Will God listen to their cry
when trouble comes upon them?
10 Can they take delight in the Almighty?
Can they call to God at any time?
11 I will teach you about God's power.
I will not conceal anything concerning the Almighty.
12 But you have seen all this,
yet you say all these useless things to me.

13 "This is what the wicked will receive from God;
this is their inheritance from the Almighty.
14 They may have many children,
but the children will die in war or starve to death.
15 Those who survive will die of a plague,
and not even their widows will mourn them.

16 "Evil people may have piles of money
and may store away mounds of clothing.
17 But the righteous will wear that clothing,
and the innocent will divide that money.
18 The wicked build houses as fragile as a spider's web,*
as flimsy as a shelter made of branches.
19 The wicked go to bed rich
but wake to find that all their wealth is gone.
20 Terror overwhelms them like a flood,
and they are blown away in the storms of the night.
21 The east wind carries them away, and they are gone.
It sweeps them away.
22 It whirls down on them without mercy.
They struggle to flee from its power.
23 But everyone jeers at them
and mocks them.

Job Speaks of Wisdom and Understanding

28 1 "People know where to mine silver
and how to refine gold.
2 They know where to dig iron from the earth
and how to smelt copper from rock.

27:18 As in Greek and Syriac versions (see also 8:14); Hebrew reads *a moth.*

3 They know how to shine light in the darkness
and explore the farthest regions of the earth
as they search in the dark for ore.
4 They sink a mine shaft into the earth
far from where anyone lives.
They descend on ropes, swinging back and forth.
5 Food is grown on the earth above,
but down below, the earth is melted as by fire.
6 Here the rocks contain precious lapis lazuli,
and the dust contains gold.
7 These are treasures no bird of prey can see,
no falcon's eye observe.
8 No wild animal has walked upon these treasures;
no lion has ever set his paw there.
9 People know how to tear apart flinty rocks
and overturn the roots of mountains.
10 They cut tunnels in the rocks
and uncover precious stones.
11 They dam up the trickling streams
and bring to light the hidden treasures.

12 "But do people know where to find wisdom?
Where can they find understanding?
13 No one knows where to find it,*
for it is not found among the living.
14 'It is not here,' says the ocean.
'Nor is it here,' says the sea.
15 It cannot be bought with gold.
It cannot be purchased with silver.
16 It's worth more than all the gold of Ophir,
greater than precious onyx or lapis lazuli.
17 Wisdom is more valuable than gold and crystal.
It cannot be purchased with jewels mounted in fine gold.
18 Coral and jasper are worthless in trying to get it.
The price of wisdom is far above rubies.
19 Precious peridot from Ethiopia* cannot be exchanged for it.
It's worth more than the purest gold.

20 "But do people know where to find wisdom?
Where can they find understanding?
21 It is hidden from the eyes of all humanity.
Even the sharp-eyed birds in the sky cannot discover it.
22 Destruction* and Death say,
'We've heard only rumors of where wisdom can be found.'

23 "God alone understands the way to wisdom;
he knows where it can be found,

28:13 As in Greek version; Hebrew reads *knows its value.* **28:19** Hebrew *from Cush.* **28:22** Hebrew *Abaddon.*

What God wants people to know

Question 28:28

You can mine the whole earth and still find no wisdom—just rumors of it. Only God knows the way to wisdom. With this in mind, how does "the fear of the Lord" lead us to true wisdom?

24 for he looks throughout the whole earth
and sees everything under the heavens.
25 He decided how hard the winds should blow
and how much rain should fall.
26 He made the laws for the rain
and laid out a path for the lightning.
27 Then he saw wisdom and evaluated it.
He set it in place and examined it thoroughly.
28 And this is what he says to all humanity:
'The fear of the Lord is true wisdom;
to forsake evil is real understanding.'"

Job Speaks of His Former Blessings

29 Job continued speaking:

2 "I long for the years gone by
when God took care of me,
3 when he lit up the way before me
and I walked safely through the darkness.
4 When I was in my prime,
God's friendship was felt in my home.
5 The Almighty was still with me,
and my children were around me.
6 My steps were awash in cream,
and the rocks gushed olive oil for me.

7 "Those were the days when I went to the city gate
and took my place among the honored leaders.
8 The young stepped aside when they saw me,
and even the aged rose in respect at my coming.
9 The princes stood in silence
and put their hands over their mouths.
10 The highest officials of the city stood quietly,
holding their tongues in respect.

11 "All who heard me praised me.
All who saw me spoke well of me.
12 For I assisted the poor in their need
and the orphans who required help.
13 I helped those without hope, and they blessed me.
And I caused the widows' hearts to sing for joy.
14 Everything I did was honest.
Righteousness covered me like a robe,
and I wore justice like a turban.
15 I served as eyes for the blind
and feet for the lame.
16 I was a father to the poor
and assisted strangers who needed help.
17 I broke the jaws of godless oppressors
and plucked their victims from their teeth.

18 "I thought, 'Surely I will die surrounded by my family
after a long, good life.*
19 For I am like a tree whose roots reach the water,
whose branches are refreshed with the dew.
20 New honors are constantly bestowed on me,
and my strength is continually renewed.'

21 "Everyone listened to my advice.
They were silent as they waited for me to speak.
22 And after I spoke, they had nothing to add,
for my counsel satisfied them.
23 They longed for me to speak as people long for rain.
They drank my words like a refreshing spring rain.
24 When they were discouraged, I smiled at them.
My look of approval was precious to them.
25 Like a chief, I told them what to do.
I lived like a king among his troops
and comforted those who mourned.

Job Speaks of His Anguish

30 1 "But now I am mocked by people younger than I,
by young men whose fathers are not worthy to run
with my sheepdogs.
2 A lot of good they are to me—
those worn-out wretches!
3 They are gaunt from poverty and hunger.
They claw the dry ground in desolate wastelands.
4 They pluck wild greens from among the bushes
and eat from the roots of broom trees.
5 They are driven from human society,
and people shout at them as if they were thieves.
6 So now they live in frightening ravines,
in caves and among the rocks.
7 They sound like animals howling among the bushes,
huddled together beneath the nettles.
8 They are nameless fools,
outcasts from society.

9 "And now they mock me with vulgar songs!
They taunt me!
10 They despise me and won't come near me,
except to spit in my face.
11 For God has cut my bowstring.
He has humbled me,
so they have thrown off all restraint.
12 These outcasts oppose me to my face.
They send me sprawling
and lay traps in my path.
13 They block my road

29:18 Hebrew *after I have counted my days like sand.*

Prayer 30:20

Lord, whenever I feel this way, please listen to my heart. I am searching for you. I need you, and I am worried that I am all alone. Please turn your ear to me and comfort me. Amen.

and do everything they can to destroy me.
They know I have no one to help me.
14 They come at me from all directions.
They jump on me when I am down.
15 I live in terror now.
My honor has blown away in the wind,
and my prosperity has vanished like a cloud.

16 "And now my life seeps away.
Depression haunts my days.
17 At night my bones are filled with pain,
which gnaws at me relentlessly.
18 With a strong hand, God grabs my shirt.*
He grips me by the collar of my coat.
19 He has thrown me into the mud.
I'm nothing more than dust and ashes.

20 "I cry to you, O God, but you don't answer.
I stand before you, but you don't even look.
21 You have become cruel toward me.
You use your power to persecute me.
22 You throw me into the whirlwind
and destroy me in the storm.
23 And I know you are sending me to my death—
the destination of all who live.

24 "Surely no one would turn against the needy
when they cry for help in their trouble.
25 Did I not weep for those in trouble?
Was I not deeply grieved for the needy?
26 So I looked for good, but evil came instead.
I waited for the light, but darkness fell.
27 My heart is troubled and restless.
Days of suffering torment me.
28 I walk in gloom, without sunlight.
I stand in the public square and cry for help.
29 Instead, I am considered a brother to jackals
and a companion to owls.
30 My skin has turned dark,
and my bones burn with fever.
31 My harp plays sad music,
and my flute accompanies those who weep.

Job's Final Protest of Innocence

31 1 "I made a covenant with my eyes
not to look with lust at a young woman.
2 For what has God above chosen for us?
What is our inheritance from the Almighty
on high?

30:18 As in Greek version; Hebrew reads *hand, my garment is disfigured.*

3 Isn't it calamity for the wicked
and misfortune for those who do evil?
4 Doesn't he see everything I do
and every step I take?

5 "Have I lied to anyone
or deceived anyone?
6 Let God weigh me on the scales of justice,
for he knows my integrity.
7 If I have strayed from his pathway,
or if my heart has lusted for what my eyes have seen,
or if I am guilty of any other sin,
8 then let someone else eat the crops I have planted.
Let all that I have planted be uprooted.

9 "If my heart has been seduced by a woman,
or if I have lusted for my neighbor's wife,
10 then let my wife serve* another man;
let other men sleep with her.
11 For lust is a shameful sin,
a crime that should be punished.
12 It is a fire that burns all the way to hell.*
It would wipe out everything I own.

13 "If I have been unfair to my male or female servants
when they brought their complaints to me,
14 how could I face God?
What could I say when he questioned me?
15 For God created both me and my servants.
He created us both in the womb.

16 "Have I refused to help the poor,
or crushed the hopes of widows?
17 Have I been stingy with my food
and refused to share it with orphans?
18 No, from childhood I have cared for orphans like a father,
and all my life I have cared for widows.
19 Whenever I saw the homeless without clothes
and the needy with nothing to wear,
20 did they not praise me
for providing wool clothing to keep them warm?

21 "If I raised my hand against an orphan,
knowing the judges would take my side,
22 then let my shoulder be wrenched out of place!
Let my arm be torn from its socket!
23 That would be better than facing God's judgment.
For if the majesty of God opposes me, what hope
is there?

31:10 Hebrew *grind for.* **31:12** Hebrew *to Abaddon.*

Question 31:40

The last phrase of this chapter is such an interesting note: "Job's words are ended." Have you ever talked or argued a really long time with someone and made very little progress? How frustrating is that kind of experience? How do you feel after an exchange like that? What guidance does this little phrase give us regarding conversations like that?

24 "Have I put my trust in money
or felt secure because of my gold?
25 Have I gloated about my wealth
and all that I own?

26 "Have I looked at the sun shining in the skies,
or the moon walking down its silver pathway,
27 and been secretly enticed in my heart
to throw kisses at them in worship?
28 If so, I should be punished by the judges,
for it would mean I had denied the God of heaven.

29 "Have I ever rejoiced when disaster struck my enemies,
or become excited when harm came their way?
30 No, I have never sinned by cursing anyone
or by asking for revenge.

31 "My servants have never said,
'He let others go hungry.'
32 I have never turned away a stranger
but have opened my doors to everyone.

33 "Have I tried to hide my sins like other people do,
concealing my guilt in my heart?
34 Have I feared the crowd
or the contempt of the masses,
so that I kept quiet and stayed indoors?

35 "If only someone would listen to me!
Look, I will sign my name to my defense.
Let the Almighty answer me.
Let my accuser write out the charges against me.
36 I would face the accusation proudly.
I would wear it like a crown.
37 For I would tell him exactly what I have done.
I would come before him like a prince.

38 "If my land accuses me
and all its furrows cry out together,
39 or if I have stolen its crops
or murdered its owners,
40 then let thistles grow on that land instead of wheat,
and weeds instead of barley."

Job's words are ended.

Elihu Responds to Job's Friends

32 Job's three friends refused to reply further to him because he kept insisting on his innocence.
2 Then Elihu son of Barakel the Buzite, of the clan of Ram, became angry.

He was angry because Job refused to admit that he had sinned and that God was right in punishing him. 3 He was also angry with Job's three friends, for they made God* appear to be wrong by their inability to answer Job's arguments. 4 Elihu had waited for the others to speak to Job because they were older than he. 5 But when he saw that they had no further reply, he spoke out angrily. 6 Elihu son of Barakel the Buzite said,

"I am young and you are old,
so I held back from telling you what I think.
7 I thought, 'Those who are older should speak,
for wisdom comes with age.'
8 But there is a spirit* within people,
the breath of the Almighty within them,
that makes them intelligent.
9 Sometimes the elders are not wise.
Sometimes the aged do not understand justice.
10 So listen to me,
and let me tell you what I think.

11 "I have waited all this time,
listening very carefully to your arguments,
listening to you grope for words.
12 I have listened,
but not one of you has refuted Job
or answered his arguments.
13 And don't tell me, 'He is too wise for us.
Only God can convince him.'
14 If Job had been arguing with me,
I would not answer with your kind of logic!
15 You sit there baffled,
with nothing more to say.
16 Should I continue to wait, now that you are silent?
Must I also remain silent?
17 No, I will say my piece.
I will speak my mind.
18 For I am full of pent-up words,
and the spirit within me urges me on.
19 I am like a cask of wine without a vent,
like a new wineskin ready to burst!
20 I must speak to find relief,
so let me give my answers.
21 I won't play favorites
or try to flatter anyone.
22 For if I tried flattery,
my Creator would soon destroy me.

Elihu Presents His Case against Job

33 1 "Listen to my words, Job;
pay attention to what I have to say.

32:3 As in ancient Hebrew scribal tradition; the Masoretic Text reads *Job.* 32:8 Or *Spirit;* also in 32:18.

Make a Difference

32:1-5

Don't Be a Bad Friend

Job's friends were acting like jerks. As the argument carried on, they became increasingly arrogant. They were upset about Job's insistence that he was innocent and that only God could address his suffering.

Here, the young man, Elihu, unleashed an oblivious onslaught toward Job. He claimed he was being respectful of Job by remaining quiet. Now, in his unbridled passion, Elihu couldn't hold back any longer. He had heard enough and wanted to shut Job down. Even though Job had suffered so much, Elihu felt the need to put Job in his place.

Have you ever treated anyone this way? Have you ever felt so right, so correct, that you crushed someone else? Have you ever felt that your friend was so off base, so wrong, that you chewed them out in anger? Well, how did that help? How did your friend feel afterward? How did you feel?

Difference Maker

Romans 12:15 says that we should "weep with those who weep." Today, be a good friend to someone who is suffering. Listen to them. Care for them. Hurt with them. Don't try to fix them. Instead, be a steady reminder that the Lord is present with them in their suffering.

2 Now that I have begun to speak,
let me continue.
3 I speak with all sincerity;
I speak the truth.
4 For the Spirit of God has made me,
and the breath of the Almighty gives me life.
5 Answer me, if you can;
make your case and take your stand.
6 Look, you and I both belong to God.
I, too, was formed from clay.
7 So you don't need to be afraid of me.
I won't come down hard on you.

8 "You have spoken in my hearing,
and I have heard your very words.
9 You said, 'I am pure; I am without sin;
I am innocent; I have no guilt.
10 God is picking a quarrel with me,
and he considers me his enemy.
11 He puts my feet in the stocks
and watches my every move.'

12 "But you are wrong, and I will show you why.
For God is greater than any human being.
13 So why are you bringing a charge against him?
Why say he does not respond to people's complaints?
14 For God speaks again and again,
though people do not recognize it.
15 He speaks in dreams, in visions of the night,
when deep sleep falls on people
as they lie in their beds.
16 He whispers in their ears
and terrifies them with warnings.
17 He makes them turn from doing wrong;
he keeps them from pride.
18 He protects them from the grave,
from crossing over the river of death.

19 "Or God disciplines people with pain on their sickbeds,
with ceaseless aching in their bones.
20 They lose their appetite
for even the most delicious food.
21 Their flesh wastes away,
and their bones stick out.
22 They are at death's door;
the angels of death wait for them.

23 "But if an angel from heaven appears—
a special messenger to intercede for a person
and declare that he is upright—

24 he will be gracious and say,
'Rescue him from the grave,
for I have found a ransom for his life.'
25 Then his body will become as healthy as a child's,
firm and youthful again.
26 When he prays to God,
he will be accepted.
And God will receive him with joy
and restore him to good standing.
27 He will declare to his friends,
'I sinned and twisted the truth,
but it was not worth it.*
28 God rescued me from the grave,
and now my life is filled with light.'

29 "Yes, God does these things
again and again for people.
30 He rescues them from the grave
so they may enjoy the light of life.
31 Mark this well, Job. Listen to me,
for I have more to say.
32 But if you have anything to say, go ahead.
Speak, for I am anxious to see you justified.
33 But if not, then listen to me.
Keep silent and I will teach you wisdom!"

Question 34:7

If you were Job, would you feel supported or thwarted by your young friend, Elihu? Why do you think Elihu talked to Job this way? Why did Elihu struggle to make sense of Job's insistence on innocence before God?

Elihu Accuses Job of Arrogance

34 Then Elihu said:

2 "Listen to me, you wise men.
Pay attention, you who have knowledge.
3 Job said, 'The ear tests the words it hears
just as the mouth distinguishes between foods.'
4 So let us discern for ourselves what is right;
let us learn together what is good.
5 For Job also said, 'I am innocent,
but God has taken away my rights.
6 I am innocent, but they call me a liar.
My suffering is incurable, though I have not sinned.'

7 "Tell me, has there ever been a man like Job,
with his thirst for irreverent talk?
8 He chooses evil people as companions.
He spends his time with wicked men.
9 He has even said, 'Why waste time
trying to please God?'

10 "Listen to me, you who have understanding.
Everyone knows that God doesn't sin!

33:27 Greek version reads *but he* [God] *did not punish me as my sin deserved.*

The Almighty can do no wrong.
11 He repays people according to their deeds.
He treats people as they deserve.
12 Truly, God will not do wrong.
The Almighty will not twist justice.
13 Did someone else put the world in his care?
Who set the whole world in place?
14 If God were to take back his spirit
and withdraw his breath,
15 all life would cease,
and humanity would turn again to dust.

16 "Now listen to me if you are wise.
Pay attention to what I say.
17 Could God govern if he hated justice?
Are you going to condemn the almighty judge?
18 For he says to kings, 'You are wicked,'
and to nobles, 'You are unjust.'
19 He doesn't care how great a person may be,
and he pays no more attention to the rich than
to the poor.
He made them all.
20 In a moment they die.
In the middle of the night they pass away;
the mighty are removed without human hand.

21 "For God watches how people live;
he sees everything they do.
22 No darkness is thick enough
to hide the wicked from his eyes.
23 We don't set the time
when we will come before God in judgment.
24 He brings the mighty to ruin without asking
anyone,
and he sets up others in their place.
25 He knows what they do,
and in the night he overturns and destroys them.
26 He strikes them down because they are wicked,
doing it openly for all to see.
27 For they turned away from following him.
They have no respect for any of his ways.
28 They cause the poor to cry out, catching God's
attention.
He hears the cries of the needy.
29 But if he chooses to remain quiet,
who can criticize him?
When he hides his face, no one can find him,
whether an individual or a nation.
30 He prevents the godless from ruling
so they cannot be a snare to the people.

31 "Why don't people say to God, 'I have sinned,
but I will sin no more'?
32 Or 'I don't know what evil I have done—tell me.
If I have done wrong, I will stop at once'?

33 "Must God tailor his justice to your demands?
But you have rejected him!
The choice is yours, not mine.
Go ahead, share your wisdom with us.
34 After all, bright people will tell me,
and wise people will hear me say,
35 'Job speaks out of ignorance;
his words lack insight.'
36 Job, you deserve the maximum penalty
for the wicked way you have talked.
37 For you have added rebellion to your sin;
you show no respect,
and you speak many angry words against God."

Elihu Reminds Job of God's Justice

35 Then Elihu said:

2 "Do you think it is right for you to claim,
'I am righteous before God'?
3 For you also ask, 'What's in it for me?
What's the use of living a righteous life?'

4 "I will answer you
and all your friends, too.
5 Look up into the sky,
and see the clouds high above you.
6 If you sin, how does that affect God?
Even if you sin again and again,
what effect will it have on him?
7 If you are good, is this some great gift to him?
What could you possibly give him?
8 No, your sins affect only people like yourself,
and your good deeds also affect only humans.

9 "People cry out when they are oppressed.
They groan beneath the power of the mighty.
10 Yet they don't ask, 'Where is God my Creator,
the one who gives songs in the night?
11 Where is the one who makes us smarter than the
animals
and wiser than the birds of the sky?'
12 And when they cry out, God does not answer
because of their pride.
13 But it is wrong to say God doesn't listen,
to say the Almighty isn't concerned.

Please write on this page!

Question 36:2-7

As you read 36:2-7, what do you think is ironic about Elihu's theological statements regarding Job here?

14 You say you can't see him,
but he will bring justice if you will only wait.*
15 You say he does not respond to sinners with anger
and is not greatly concerned about wickedness.*
16 But you are talking nonsense, Job.
You have spoken like a fool."

36

Elihu continued speaking:

2 "Let me go on, and I will show you the truth.
For I have not finished defending God!
3 I will present profound arguments
for the righteousness of my Creator.
4 I am telling you nothing but the truth,
for I am a man of great knowledge.

5 "God is mighty, but he does not despise anyone!
He is mighty in both power and understanding.
6 He does not let the wicked live
but gives justice to the afflicted.
7 He never takes his eyes off the innocent,
but he sets them on thrones with kings
and exalts them forever.
8 If they are bound in chains
and caught up in a web of trouble,
9 he shows them the reason.
He shows them their sins of pride.
10 He gets their attention
and commands that they turn from evil.

11 "If they listen and obey God,
they will be blessed with prosperity throughout their lives.
All their years will be pleasant.
12 But if they refuse to listen to him,
they will cross over the river of death,
dying from lack of understanding.
13 For the godless are full of resentment.
Even when he punishes them,
they refuse to cry out to him for help.
14 They die when they are young,
after wasting their lives in immoral living.
15 But by means of their suffering, he rescues those who suffer.
For he gets their attention through adversity.

16 "God is leading you away from danger, Job,
to a place free from distress.
He is setting your table with the best food.

35:13-14 These verses can also be translated as follows: [13]*Indeed, God doesn't listen to their empty plea; / the Almighty is not concerned. /* [14]*How much less will he listen when you say you don't see him, / and that your case is before him and you're waiting for justice.* **35:15** As in Greek and Latin versions; the meaning of this Hebrew word is uncertain.

17 But you are obsessed with whether the godless will be
judged.
Don't worry, judgment and justice will be upheld.
18 But watch out, or you may be seduced by wealth.*
Don't let yourself be bribed into sin.
19 Could all your wealth*
or all your mighty efforts
keep you from distress?
20 Do not long for the cover of night,
for that is when people will be destroyed.*
21 Be on guard! Turn back from evil,
for God sent this suffering
to keep you from a life of evil.

Elihu Reminds Job of God's Power

22 "Look, God is all-powerful.
Who is a teacher like him?
23 No one can tell him what to do,
or say to him, 'You have done wrong.'
24 Instead, glorify his mighty works,
singing songs of praise.
25 Everyone has seen these things,
though only from a distance.

26 "Look, God is greater than we can understand.
His years cannot be counted.
27 He draws up the water vapor
and then distills it into rain.
28 The rain pours down from the clouds,
and everyone benefits.
29 Who can understand the spreading of the clouds
and the thunder that rolls forth from heaven?
30 See how he spreads the lightning around him
and how it lights up the depths of the sea.
31 By these mighty acts he nourishes* the people,
giving them food in abundance.
32 He fills his hands with lightning bolts
and hurls each at its target.
33 The thunder announces his presence;
the storm announces his indignant anger.*

37 1 "My heart pounds as I think of this.
It trembles within me.
2 Listen carefully to the thunder of God's voice
as it rolls from his mouth.
3 It rolls across the heavens,
and his lightning flashes in every direction.
4 Then comes the roaring of the thunder—

36:18 Or *But don't let your anger lead you to mockery.* 36:19 Or *Could all your cries for help.*
36:16-20 The meaning of the Hebrew in this passage is uncertain. 36:31 Or *he governs.*
36:33 Or *even the cattle know when a storm is coming.* The meaning of the Hebrew is uncertain.

the tremendous voice of his majesty.
He does not restrain it when he speaks.
5 God's voice is glorious in the thunder.
We can't even imagine the greatness of his power.

6 "He directs the snow to fall on the earth
and tells the rain to pour down.
7 Then everyone stops working
so they can watch his power.
8 The wild animals take cover
and stay inside their dens.
9 The stormy wind comes from its chamber,
and the driving winds bring the cold.
10 God's breath sends the ice,
freezing wide expanses of water.
11 He loads the clouds with moisture,
and they flash with his lightning.
12 The clouds churn about at his direction.
They do whatever he commands throughout the earth.
13 He makes these things happen either to punish people
or to show his unfailing love.

14 "Pay attention to this, Job.
Stop and consider the wonderful miracles of God!
15 Do you know how God controls the storm
and causes the lightning to flash from his clouds?
16 Do you understand how he moves the clouds
with wonderful perfection and skill?
17 When you are sweltering in your clothes
and the south wind dies down and everything is still,
18 he makes the skies reflect the heat like a bronze mirror.
Can you do that?

19 "So teach the rest of us what to say to God.
We are too ignorant to make our own arguments.
20 Should God be notified that I want to speak?
Can people even speak when they are confused?*
21 We cannot look at the sun,
for it shines brightly in the sky
when the wind clears away the clouds.
22 So also, golden splendor comes from the mountain of God.*
He is clothed in dazzling splendor.
23 We cannot imagine the power of the Almighty;
but even though he is just and righteous,
he does not destroy us.
24 No wonder people everywhere fear him.
All who are wise show him reverence.*"

37:20 Or *speak without being swallowed up?* **37:22** Or *from the north;* or *from the abode.* **37:24** As in Greek version; Hebrew reads *He is not impressed by the wise.*

The LORD *Challenges Job*

38 Then the LORD answered Job from the whirlwind:

2 "Who is this that questions my wisdom
with such ignorant words?
3 Brace yourself like a man,
because I have some questions for you,
and you must answer them.

4 "Where were you when I laid the foundations of the earth?
Tell me, if you know so much.
5 Who determined its dimensions
and stretched out the surveying line?
6 What supports its foundations,
and who laid its cornerstone
7 as the morning stars sang together
and all the angels* shouted for joy?

8 "Who kept the sea inside its boundaries
as it burst from the womb,
9 and as I clothed it with clouds
and wrapped it in thick darkness?
10 For I locked it behind barred gates,
limiting its shores.
11 I said, 'This far and no farther will you come.
Here your proud waves must stop!'

12 "Have you ever commanded the morning to appear
and caused the dawn to rise in the east?
13 Have you made daylight spread to the ends of the earth,
to bring an end to the night's wickedness?
14 As the light approaches,
the earth takes shape like clay pressed beneath a seal;
it is robed in brilliant colors.*
15 The light disturbs the wicked
and stops the arm that is raised in violence.

16 "Have you explored the springs from which the seas come?
Have you explored their depths?
17 Do you know where the gates of death are located?
Have you seen the gates of utter gloom?
18 Do you realize the extent of the earth?
Tell me about it if you know!

19 "Where does light come from,
and where does darkness go?
20 Can you take each to its home?
Do you know how to get there?

Question **38:1-40:2**

The Lord now joined the conversation. He started by asking a series of questions that were all answered with a resounding no. After Job was mistreated chapter after chapter by his arrogant friends talking about God, would he have felt God's very direct questions as overwhelming, refreshing, or both?

38:7 Hebrew *the sons of God.* **38:14** Or *its features stand out like folds in a robe.*

21 But of course you know all this!
For you were born before it was all created,
and you are so very experienced!

22 "Have you visited the storehouses of the snow
or seen the storehouses of hail?
23 (I have reserved them as weapons for the time of
trouble,
for the day of battle and war.)
24 Where is the path to the source of light?
Where is the home of the east wind?

25 "Who created a channel for the torrents of rain?
Who laid out the path for the lightning?
26 Who makes the rain fall on barren land,
in a desert where no one lives?
27 Who sends rain to satisfy the parched ground
and make the tender grass spring up?

28 "Does the rain have a father?
Who gives birth to the dew?
29 Who is the mother of the ice?
Who gives birth to the frost from the heavens?
30 For the water turns to ice as hard as rock,
and the surface of the water freezes.

31 "Can you direct the movement of the stars—
binding the cluster of the Pleiades
or loosening the cords of Orion?
32 Can you direct the constellations through the
seasons
or guide the Bear with her cubs across the heavens?
33 Do you know the laws of the universe?
Can you use them to regulate the earth?

34 "Can you shout to the clouds
and make it rain?
35 Can you make lightning appear
and cause it to strike as you direct?
36 Who gives intuition to the heart
and instinct to the mind?
37 Who is wise enough to count all the clouds?
Who can tilt the water jars of heaven
38 when the parched ground is dry
and the soil has hardened into clods?

39 "Can you stalk prey for a lioness
and satisfy the young lions' appetites
40 as they lie in their dens
or crouch in the thicket?

41 Who provides food for the ravens
when their young cry out to God
and wander about in hunger?

The LORD's Challenge Continues

39 1 "Do you know when the wild goats give birth?
Have you watched as deer are born in the wild?
2 Do you know how many months they carry their young?
Are you aware of the time of their delivery?
3 They crouch down to give birth to their young
and deliver their offspring.
4 Their young grow up in the open fields,
then leave home and never return.

5 "Who gives the wild donkey its freedom?
Who untied its ropes?
6 I have placed it in the wilderness;
its home is the wasteland.
7 It hates the noise of the city
and has no driver to shout at it.
8 The mountains are its pastureland,
where it searches for every blade of grass.

9 "Will the wild ox consent to being tamed?
Will it spend the night in your stall?
10 Can you hitch a wild ox to a plow?
Will it plow a field for you?
11 Given its strength, can you trust it?
Can you leave and trust the ox to do your work?
12 Can you rely on it to bring home your grain
and deliver it to your threshing floor?

13 "The ostrich flaps her wings grandly,
but they are no match for the feathers of the stork.
14 She lays her eggs on top of the earth,
letting them be warmed in the dust.
15 She doesn't worry that a foot might crush them
or a wild animal might destroy them.
16 She is harsh toward her young,
as if they were not her own.
She doesn't care if they die.
17 For God has deprived her of wisdom.
He has given her no understanding.
18 But whenever she jumps up to run,
she passes the swiftest horse with its rider.

19 "Have you given the horse its strength
or clothed its neck with a flowing mane?
20 Did you give it the ability to leap like a locust?
Its majestic snorting is terrifying!

Question 39:1-30

As you read God's words to Job, which verses amaze you the most? Which aspects of nature do you believe best reveal the truth of God?

Make a Difference 40:3

Humble Response to God

Job responded to God with humility. After chapters of conversation with his frustrating friends, Job's lack of words reflected a deep wisdom in the presence of God. When God spoke, Job chose to cover his mouth with his hand. It's a small moment that changed the course of the rest of his life.

A rudder on a ship makes what seems like a small effect at first. Of all the impressive parts that make a great ship, the rudder is small and doesn't get the attention it deserves. Over time though, the constant influence of that rudder changes the entire course of that massive ship. Though people don't normally think about the rudder, they do notice where the massive ship goes—the direction it takes.

Those who live a life of consistent integrity, who make wise choices and follow God's patterns, can make a difference that lasts for several lifetimes. Perhaps that is why we are still learning from Job thousands of years later.

Difference Maker

Start your day by being silent and listening to God.

21 It paws the earth and rejoices in its strength
when it charges out to battle.
22 It laughs at fear and is unafraid.
It does not run from the sword.
23 The arrows rattle against it,
and the spear and javelin flash.
24 It paws the ground fiercely
and rushes forward into battle when the ram's horn blows.
25 It snorts at the sound of the horn.
It senses the battle in the distance.
It quivers at the captain's commands and the noise of battle.

26 "Is it your wisdom that makes the hawk soar
and spread its wings toward the south?
27 Is it at your command that the eagle rises
to the heights to make its nest?
28 It lives on the cliffs,
making its home on a distant, rocky crag.
29 From there it hunts its prey,
keeping watch with piercing eyes.
30 Its young gulp down blood.
Where there's a carcass, there you'll find it."

40 Then the LORD said to Job,

2 "Do you still want to argue with the Almighty?
You are God's critic, but do you have the answers?"

Job Responds to the LORD

3 Then Job replied to the LORD,

4 "I am nothing—how could I ever find the answers?
I will cover my mouth with my hand.
5 I have said too much already.
I have nothing more to say."

The LORD Challenges Job Again

6 Then the LORD answered Job from the whirlwind:

7 "Brace yourself like a man,
because I have some questions for you,
and you must answer them.

8 "Will you discredit my justice
and condemn me just to prove you are right?
9 Are you as strong as God?
Can you thunder with a voice like his?
10 All right, put on your glory and splendor,
your honor and majesty.

11 Give vent to your anger.
Let it overflow against the proud.
12 Humiliate the proud with a glance;
walk on the wicked where they stand.
13 Bury them in the dust.
Imprison them in the world of the dead.
14 Then even I would praise you,
for your own strength would save you.

15 "Take a look at Behemoth,*
which I made, just as I made you.
It eats grass like an ox.
16 See its powerful loins
and the muscles of its belly.
17 Its tail is as strong as a cedar.
The sinews of its thighs are knit tightly together.
18 Its bones are tubes of bronze.
Its limbs are bars of iron.
19 It is a prime example of God's handiwork,
and only its Creator can threaten it.
20 The mountains offer it their best food,
where all the wild animals play.
21 It lies under the lotus plants,*
hidden by the reeds in the marsh.
22 The lotus plants give it shade
among the willows beside the stream.
23 It is not disturbed by the raging river,
not concerned when the swelling Jordan rushes
around it.
24 No one can catch it off guard
or put a ring in its nose and lead it away.

The LORD's Challenge Continues

41 1*"Can you catch Leviathan* with a hook
or put a noose around its jaw?
2 Can you tie it with a rope through the nose
or pierce its jaw with a spike?
3 Will it beg you for mercy
or implore you for pity?
4 Will it agree to work for you,
to be your slave for life?
5 Can you make it a pet like a bird,
or give it to your little girls to play with?
6 Will merchants try to buy it
to sell it in their shops?
7 Will its hide be hurt by spears
or its head by a harpoon?

40:15 The identification of Behemoth is disputed, ranging from an earthly creature to a mythical sea monster in ancient literature. **40:21** Or *bramble bushes;* also in 40:22. **41:1a** Verses 41:1-8 are numbered 40:25-32 in Hebrew text. **41:1b** The identification of Leviathan is disputed, ranging from an earthly creature to a mythical sea monster in ancient literature.

8 If you lay a hand on it,
you will certainly remember the battle that follows.
You won't try that again!
9*No, it is useless to try to capture it.
The hunter who attempts it will be knocked down.
10 And since no one dares to disturb it,
who then can stand up to me?
11 Who has given me anything that I need to pay back?
Everything under heaven is mine.

12 "I want to emphasize Leviathan's limbs
and its enormous strength and graceful form.
13 Who can strip off its hide,
and who can penetrate its double layer of armor?*
14 Who could pry open its jaws?
For its teeth are terrible!
15 The scales on its back are like* rows of shields
tightly sealed together.
16 They are so close together
that no air can get between them.
17 Each scale sticks tight to the next.
They interlock and cannot be penetrated.

18 "When it sneezes, it flashes light!
Its eyes are like the red of dawn.
19 Lightning leaps from its mouth;
flames of fire flash out.
20 Smoke streams from its nostrils
like steam from a pot heated over burning rushes.
21 Its breath would kindle coals,
for flames shoot from its mouth.

22 "The tremendous strength in Leviathan's neck
strikes terror wherever it goes.
23 Its flesh is hard and firm
and cannot be penetrated.
24 Its heart is hard as rock,
hard as a millstone.
25 When it rises, the mighty are afraid,
gripped by terror.
26 No sword can stop it,
no spear, dart, or javelin.
27 Iron is nothing but straw to that creature,
and bronze is like rotten wood.
28 Arrows cannot make it flee.
Stones shot from a sling are like bits of grass.
29 Clubs are like a blade of grass,
and it laughs at the swish of javelins.

41:9 Verses 41:9-34 are numbered 41:1-26 in Hebrew text. **41:13** As in Greek version; Hebrew reads *its bridle?* **41:15** As in some Greek manuscripts and Latin Vulgate; Hebrew reads *Its pride is in its.*

30 Its belly is covered with scales as sharp as glass.
It plows up the ground as it drags through the mud.

31 "Leviathan makes the water boil with its commotion.
It stirs the depths like a pot of ointment.
32 The water glistens in its wake,
making the sea look white.
33 Nothing on earth is its equal,
no other creature so fearless.
34 Of all the creatures, it is the proudest.
It is the king of beasts."

Job Responds to the LORD

42 Then Job replied to the LORD:

2 "I know that you can do anything,
and no one can stop you.
3 You asked, 'Who is this that questions my wisdom with such ignorance?'
It is I—and I was talking about things I knew nothing about,
things far too wonderful for me.
4 You said, 'Listen and I will speak!
I have some questions for you,
and you must answer them.'
5 I had only heard about you before,
but now I have seen you with my own eyes.
6 I take back everything I said,
and I sit in dust and ashes to show my repentance."

Conclusion: The LORD Blesses Job

7 After the LORD had finished speaking to Job, he said to Eliphaz the Te-
manite: "I am angry with you and your two friends, for you have not spoken
accurately about me, as my servant Job has. 8 So take seven bulls and seven
rams and go to my servant Job and offer a burnt offering for yourselves. My
servant Job will pray for you, and I will accept his prayer on your behalf. I
will not treat you as you deserve, for you have not spoken accurately about
me, as my servant Job has." 9 So Eliphaz the Temanite, Bildad the Shuhite,
and Zophar the Naamathite did as the LORD commanded them, and the
LORD accepted Job's prayer.
10 When Job prayed for his friends, the LORD restored his fortunes. In
fact, the LORD gave him twice as much as before! 11 Then all his brothers,
sisters, and former friends came and feasted with him in his home. And
they consoled him and comforted him because of all the trials the LORD
had brought against him. And each of them brought him a gift of money*
and a gold ring.
12 So the LORD blessed Job in the second half of his life even more than
in the beginning. For now he had 14,000 sheep, 6,000 camels, 1,000 teams
of oxen, and 1,000 female donkeys. 13 He also gave Job seven more sons and
three more daughters. 14 He named his first daughter Jemimah, the second

Question 41:34

Why does God end his comments to Job with this abrupt conversation about a leviathan? Could it have something to do with God's point that humans should not be the arrogant creatures that they often are? How does this idea change your approach to your life today?

Question 42:10

It is noteworthy that Job's fortunes were restored when he prayed for his arrogant friends. Why did God honor Job for doing that? How do you think Job was able not to hold a grudge against his friends?

42:11 Hebrew *a kesitah;* the value or weight of the kesitah is no longer known.

Keziah, and the third Keren-happuch. 15 In all the land no women were as
lovely as the daughters of Job. And their father put them into his will along
with their brothers.

16 Job lived 140 years after that, living to see four generations of his chil-
dren and grandchildren. 17 Then he died, an old man who had lived a long,
full life.

Psalms Introduction

Psalm 1:2-3 declares that those who delight in the Lord "are like trees planted along the riverbank, bearing fruit each season. Their leaves never wither, and they prosper in all they do." These words are the first seeds of thought planted in the longest book of the Bible. The book of Psalms contains 150 chapters, raw and real in life's dirt and abundance, toil and harvest, weeping and reaping.

The New Testament quotes the crop of the psalms nearly eighty times and alludes to its words hundreds more times. Even more profoundly, Jesus frequently took the words of many psalms upon his own identity. It's as if he himself became the soil in which we are to be rooted. These psalms permeated his identity and his work. Jesus personified the very patterns of lament ("My God, my God, why have you abandoned me?"), guidance ("I am the Good Shepherd"), and salvation ("Sit in honor at my right hand"), among other descriptions, so richly evident in the book of Psalms.

Famously, David wrote many of these psalms during times of stress and times of victory. In all, the psalms were ordered seasonally, for preparation, for rhythm, so that people could frequently return to dig deeply into the richness of its soil. No matter what circumstance of life they're in, readers of the psalms can find the raw reality of life at any point of experience in any moment in history.

Story Arcs

- **Jesus**
- **David**
- **Asaph**

Psalms

BOOK ONE (Psalms 1–41)

> **Make a Difference** 1:3
>
> **Rooted Strong**
>
> Take a moment and look outside at a tree. The reason you can see that tree right now is because it is grounded below the surface. The root system, which you can't see (unless some of the stronger roots are breaking through the ground), is equipping that tree to stand tall and flourish. The effort and focus of a tree's growth are downward. The roots supply the nutrition and resources that it needs to thrive.
>
> Likewise, a life rooted into Jesus focuses not on the outward appearance, on what people can see with their eyes, but on the inward growth in Jesus. As a result, though, what people end up seeing is a person standing tall through the winds and trends of culture, a person overflowing with abundant life.
>
> ***Difference Maker***
>
> Find a big tree, sit underneath it, and contemplate the roots beneath you, the trunk standing by you, and the branches and leaves (or springing buds!) above you. How could this visual make a difference in your Christian life?

1 1 Oh, the joys of those who do not
follow the advice of the wicked,
or stand around with sinners,
or join in with mockers.
2 But they delight in the law of the LORD,
meditating on it day and night.
3 They are like trees planted along the riverbank,
bearing fruit each season.
Their leaves never wither,
and they prosper in all they do.

4 But not the wicked!
They are like worthless chaff, scattered by the wind.
5 They will be condemned at the time of judgment.
Sinners will have no place among the godly.
6 For the LORD watches over the path of the godly,
but the path of the wicked leads to destruction.

2 1 Why are the nations so angry?
Why do they waste their time with futile plans?
2 The kings of the earth prepare for battle;
the rulers plot together
against the LORD
and against his anointed one.
3 "Let us break their chains," they cry,
"and free ourselves from slavery to God."

4 But the one who rules in heaven laughs.
The Lord scoffs at them.
5 Then in anger he rebukes them,
terrifying them with his fierce fury.
6 For the Lord declares, "I have placed my chosen king
on the throne
in Jerusalem,* on my holy mountain."

7 The king proclaims the LORD's decree:
"The LORD said to me, 'You are my son.*
Today I have become your Father.*
8 Only ask, and I will give you the nations as your inheritance,
the whole earth as your possession.

2:6 Hebrew *on Zion.* 2:7a Or *Son;* also in 2:12. 2:7b Or *Today I reveal you as my son.*

9 You will break* them with an iron rod
and smash them like clay pots.'"

10 Now then, you kings, act wisely!
Be warned, you rulers of the earth!
11 Serve the LORD with reverent fear,
and rejoice with trembling.
12 Submit to God's royal son,* or he will become angry,
and you will be destroyed in the midst of all your activities—
for his anger flares up in an instant.
But what joy for all who take refuge in him!

3

A psalm of David, regarding the time David fled from his son Absalom.

1 O LORD, I have so many enemies;
so many are against me.
2 So many are saying,
"God will never rescue him!" *Interlude**

3 But you, O LORD, are a shield around me;
you are my glory, the one who holds my head high.
4 I cried out to the LORD,
and he answered me from his holy mountain. *Interlude*

5 I lay down and slept,
yet I woke up in safety,
for the LORD was watching over me.
6 I am not afraid of ten thousand enemies
who surround me on every side.

7 Arise, O LORD!
Rescue me, my God!
Slap all my enemies in the face!
Shatter the teeth of the wicked!
8 Victory comes from you, O LORD.
May you bless your people. *Interlude*

4

For the choir director: A psalm of David, to be accompanied by stringed instruments.

1 Answer me when I call to you,
O God who declares me innocent.
Free me from my troubles.
Have mercy on me and hear my prayer.

2 How long will you people ruin my reputation?
How long will you make groundless accusations?

2:9 Greek version reads *rule.* Compare Rev 2:27. **2:12** The meaning of the Hebrew is uncertain. **3:2** Hebrew *Selah.* The meaning of this word is uncertain, though it is probably a musical or literary term. It is rendered *Interlude* throughout the Psalms.

Make a Difference 4:4

Don't Let the Sun Go Down

Many people prefer to keep letting bitterness step all over their souls instead of trying to stop it. Bitterness seems like a natural fit to hurting hearts. If they have been wronged, the company of resentment is often welcomed. If they have been disappointed, many people invite anger to take up residence in their lives. Once bitterness has taken root, however, it's not much of a stretch to invite retaliation to the party also. No one needs to get special training to become skilled in revenge. With resentment driving the heart, retaliation flows like lava. It wells up without much effort when bitterness kicks in. It's all too easy.

Many people, however, do struggle with forgiveness. To offer forgiveness seems almost like a heavenly pummel on top of bruises. It is a radical, countercultural response to a wrong. Extending reconciliation strains people when they have been wronged because mercy demands that pride be put down and grace be picked up.

Difference Maker

If you face the easy fall into resentment today, write this phrase on the first piece of paper you can find: "Jesus, help me to forgive."

How long will you continue your lies? *Interlude*
3 You can be sure of this:
The LORD set apart the godly for himself.
The LORD will answer when I call to him.

4 Don't sin by letting anger control you.
Think about it overnight and remain silent. *Interlude*
5 Offer sacrifices in the right spirit,
and trust the LORD.

6 Many people say, "Who will show us better times?"
Let your face smile on us, LORD.
7 You have given me greater joy
than those who have abundant harvests of grain and new wine.
8 In peace I will lie down and sleep,
for you alone, O LORD, will keep me safe.

5

For the choir director: A psalm of David, to be accompanied by the flute.

1 O LORD, hear me as I pray;
pay attention to my groaning.
2 Listen to my cry for help, my King and my God,
for I pray to no one but you.
3 Listen to my voice in the morning, LORD.
Each morning I bring my requests to you and wait expectantly.

4 O God, you take no pleasure in wickedness;
you cannot tolerate the sins of the wicked.
5 Therefore, the proud may not stand in your presence,
for you hate all who do evil.
6 You will destroy those who tell lies.
The LORD detests murderers and deceivers.

7 Because of your unfailing love, I can enter your house;
I will worship at your Temple with deepest awe.
8 Lead me in the right path, O LORD,
or my enemies will conquer me.
Make your way plain for me to follow.

9 My enemies cannot speak a truthful word.
Their deepest desire is to destroy others.
Their talk is foul, like the stench from an open grave.
Their tongues are filled with flattery.*
10 O God, declare them guilty.
Let them be caught in their own traps.
Drive them away because of their many sins,
for they have rebelled against you.

5:9 Greek version reads *with lies*. Compare Rom 3:13.

11 But let all who take refuge in you rejoice;
let them sing joyful praises forever.
Spread your protection over them,
that all who love your name may be filled with joy.
12 For you bless the godly, O LORD;
you surround them with your shield of love.

Prayer 6:2

Lord, come to my rescue, please. Amen.

6

*For the choir director: A psalm of David, to be accompanied by an eight-stringed instrument.**

1 O LORD, don't rebuke me in your anger
or discipline me in your rage.
2 Have compassion on me, LORD, for I am weak.
Heal me, LORD, for my bones are in agony.
3 I am sick at heart.
How long, O LORD, until you restore me?

4 Return, O LORD, and rescue me.
Save me because of your unfailing love.
5 For the dead do not remember you.
Who can praise you from the grave?*

6 I am worn out from sobbing.
All night I flood my bed with weeping,
drenching it with my tears.
7 My vision is blurred by grief;
my eyes are worn out because of all my enemies.

8 Go away, all you who do evil,
for the LORD has heard my weeping.
9 The LORD has heard my plea;
the LORD will answer my prayer.
10 May all my enemies be disgraced and terrified.
May they suddenly turn back in shame.

7

A psalm of David, which he sang to the LORD concerning Cush of the tribe of Benjamin.*

1 I come to you for protection, O LORD my God.
Save me from my persecutors—rescue me!
2 If you don't, they will maul me like a lion,
tearing me to pieces with no one to rescue me.
3 O LORD my God, if I have done wrong
or am guilty of injustice,
4 if I have betrayed a friend
or plundered my enemy without cause,
5 then let my enemies capture me.
Let them trample me into the ground
and drag my honor in the dust. *Interlude*

6:TITLE Hebrew *with stringed instruments; according to the sheminith.* 6:5 Hebrew *from Sheol?*
7:TITLE Hebrew *A shiggaion,* probably indicating a musical setting for the psalm.

Make a Difference

8:3–8

Mortals

In some ways our discoveries reveal more about our limitations than our achievements. The more we learn, the more we realize we don't know everything. The more we find, the more we realize the feebleness of our advancement. This is ironic because it is precisely our desire to steal knowledge that led us to disavow the Creator in the first place (Genesis 3). We failed to acknowledge God; will we continue to miss knowing him as well?

Difference Maker

Go outside and look around. Consider the small and large aspects of creation. Explore the universe with a posture of humble awe toward our Creator.

6 Arise, O LORD, in anger!
Stand up against the fury of my enemies!
Wake up, my God, and bring justice!
7 Gather the nations before you.
Rule over them from on high.
8 The LORD judges the nations.
Declare me righteous, O LORD,
for I am innocent, O Most High!
9 End the evil of those who are wicked,
and defend the righteous.
For you look deep within the mind and heart,
O righteous God.

10 God is my shield,
saving those whose hearts are true and right.
11 God is an honest judge.
He is angry with the wicked every day.

12 If a person does not repent,
God* will sharpen his sword;
he will bend and string his bow.
13 He will prepare his deadly weapons
and shoot his flaming arrows.

14 The wicked conceive evil;
they are pregnant with trouble
and give birth to lies.
15 They dig a deep pit to trap others,
then fall into it themselves.
16 The trouble they make for others backfires on them.
The violence they plan falls on their own heads.

17 I will thank the LORD because he is just;
I will sing praise to the name of the LORD Most High.

8

*For the choir director: A psalm of David, to be accompanied by a stringed instrument.**

1 O LORD, our Lord, your majestic name fills the earth!
Your glory is higher than the heavens.
2 You have taught children and infants
to tell of your strength,*
silencing your enemies
and all who oppose you.

3 When I look at the night sky and see the work of your
fingers—
the moon and the stars you set in place—
4 what are mere mortals that you should think about them,

7:12 Hebrew *he.* 8:TITLE Hebrew *according to the gittith.* 8:2 Greek version reads *to give you praise.* Compare Matt 21:16.

human beings that you should care for them?*
5 Yet you made them only a little lower than God*
and crowned them* with glory and honor.
6 You gave them charge of everything you made,
putting all things under their authority—
7 the flocks and the herds
and all the wild animals,
8 the birds in the sky, the fish in the sea,
and everything that swims the ocean currents.

9 O LORD, our Lord, your majestic name fills the earth!

9

For the choir director: A psalm of David, to be sung to the tune "Death of the Son."

1 I will praise you, LORD, with all my heart;
I will tell of all the marvelous things you have done.
2 I will be filled with joy because of you.
I will sing praises to your name, O Most High.

3 My enemies retreated;
they staggered and died when you appeared.
4 For you have judged in my favor;
from your throne you have judged with fairness.
5 You have rebuked the nations and destroyed the wicked;
you have erased their names forever.
6 The enemy is finished, in endless ruins;
the cities you uprooted are now forgotten.

7 But the LORD reigns forever,
executing judgment from his throne.
8 He will judge the world with justice
and rule the nations with fairness.
9 The LORD is a shelter for the oppressed,
a refuge in times of trouble.
10 Those who know your name trust in you,
for you, O LORD, do not abandon those who search
for you.

11 Sing praises to the LORD who reigns in Jerusalem.*
Tell the world about his unforgettable deeds.
12 For he who avenges murder cares for the helpless.
He does not ignore the cries of those who suffer.

13 LORD, have mercy on me.
See how my enemies torment me.
Snatch me back from the jaws of death.

Make a Difference 9:1

With All My Heart

What does it mean to praise God with *all* your heart? Can you use just three out of four chambers? All your ventricles? How about the arteries? The inferior vena cava and pulmonic valve too?

Put your hand over your heart for a moment. Do you feel it pumping? Your heart, your whole heart, right now, is pumping deoxygenated blood from the body in the right atrium and the right ventricle, and your heart is pumping oxygenated blood from the lungs through the left atrium and the left ventricle. The blood that comes into the heart must be pumped out; otherwise the heart would seize up in an attack.

When you receive life from the Lord, you must pump out praise. When someone helps you see what Jesus has done for you, you can't contain that joy and wonder, and you must push it on. The truth of God that fills your heart must circulate within you and come out, or you will seize up.

Difference Maker

Using Psalm 9:1, write a heartfelt thank-you note to God.

8:4 Hebrew *what is man that you should think of him, / the son of man that you should care for him?* 8:5a Or *Yet you made them only a little lower than the angels;* Hebrew reads *Yet you made him* [i.e., man] *a little lower than Elohim.* 8:5b Hebrew *him* [i.e., man]; similarly in 8:6. 9:11 Hebrew *Zion;* also in 9:14.

14 Save me so I can praise you publicly at Jerusalem's
gates,
so I can rejoice that you have rescued me.

15 The nations have fallen into the pit they dug for others.
Their own feet have been caught in the trap they set.
16 The LORD is known for his justice.
The wicked are trapped by their own deeds. *Quiet Interlude**

17 The wicked will go down to the grave.*
This is the fate of all the nations who ignore God.
18 But the needy will not be ignored forever;
the hopes of the poor will not always be crushed.

19 Arise, O LORD!
Do not let mere mortals defy you!
Judge the nations!
20 Make them tremble in fear, O LORD.
Let the nations know they are merely human. *Interlude*

10

1 O LORD, why do you stand so far away?
Why do you hide when I am in trouble?
2 The wicked arrogantly hunt down the poor.
Let them be caught in the evil they plan for others.
3 For they brag about their evil desires;
they praise the greedy and curse the LORD.

4 The wicked are too proud to seek God.
They seem to think that God is dead.
5 Yet they succeed in everything they do.
They do not see your punishment awaiting them.
They sneer at all their enemies.
6 They think, "Nothing bad will ever happen to us!
We will be free of trouble forever!"

7 Their mouths are full of cursing, lies, and threats.*
Trouble and evil are on the tips of their tongues.
8 They lurk in ambush in the villages,
waiting to murder innocent people.
They are always searching for helpless victims.
9 Like lions crouched in hiding,
they wait to pounce on the helpless.
Like hunters they capture the helpless
and drag them away in nets.
10 Their helpless victims are crushed;
they fall beneath the strength of the wicked.
11 The wicked think, "God isn't watching us!
He has closed his eyes and won't even see what
we do!"

9:16 Hebrew *Higgaion Selah.* The meaning of this phrase is uncertain. **9:17** Hebrew *to Sheol.*
10:7 Greek version reads *cursing and bitterness.* Compare Rom 3:14.

12 Arise, O LORD!
Punish the wicked, O God!
Do not ignore the helpless!
13 Why do the wicked get away with despising God?
They think, "God will never call us to account."
14 But you see the trouble and grief they cause.
You take note of it and punish them.
The helpless put their trust in you.
You defend the orphans.

15 Break the arms of these wicked, evil people!
Go after them until the last one is destroyed.
16 The LORD is king forever and ever!
The godless nations will vanish from the land.
17 LORD, you know the hopes of the helpless.
Surely you will hear their cries and comfort them.
18 You will bring justice to the orphans and the oppressed,
so mere people can no longer terrify them.

11 *For the choir director: A psalm of David.*

1 I trust in the LORD for protection.
So why do you say to me,
"Fly like a bird to the mountains for safety!
2 The wicked are stringing their bows
and fitting their arrows on the bowstrings.
They shoot from the shadows
at those whose hearts are right.
3 The foundations of law and order have collapsed.
What can the righteous do?"

4 But the LORD is in his holy Temple;
the LORD still rules from heaven.
He watches everyone closely,
examining every person on earth.
5 The LORD examines both the righteous and the wicked.
He hates those who love violence.
6 He will rain down blazing coals and burning sulfur
on the wicked,
punishing them with scorching winds.
7 For the righteous LORD loves justice.
The virtuous will see his face.

12 *For the choir director: A psalm of David, to be accompanied by an eight-stringed instrument.**

1 Help, O LORD, for the godly are fast disappearing!
The faithful have vanished from the earth!

12:TITLE Hebrew *according to the sheminith.*

Highlights from the text

Prayer 12:3

Lord, unlike the people this psalm talks about, help me be someone who loves my neighbor. Amen.

Make a Difference 13:6

Sing Praise

David didn't have streaming music. How did he even survive? Seriously, how did this guy function without the constant stimulation of media continually rewiring his brain?

Well, David spent some time alone (note: time = days, weeks, months) shepherding flocks in the countryside. To pass his hours, he learned to write songs, play compact instruments, and talk to God. He had sheep—dozens and perhaps hundreds of them. While he sheared wool and killed bears that attacked his flock, he also became an accomplished poet, theologian, musician, and composer. He used his growing skills to turn his heart, again and again, to the Lord.

Difference Maker

Either write a song of praise to God or listen to a song of praise to God. Get that song stuck in your heart and mind and refer to it throughout the day.

Question 14:1

Why are fools the only ones who would say this?

2 Neighbors lie to each other,
speaking with flattering lips and deceitful hearts.
3 May the LORD cut off their flattering lips
and silence their boastful tongues.
4 They say, "We will lie to our hearts' content.
Our lips are our own—who can stop us?"

5 The LORD replies, "I have seen violence done to the helpless,
and I have heard the groans of the poor.
Now I will rise up to rescue them,
as they have longed for me to do."
6 The LORD's promises are pure,
like silver refined in a furnace,
purified seven times over.
7 Therefore, LORD, we know you will protect the oppressed,
preserving them forever from this lying generation,
8 even though the wicked strut about,
and evil is praised throughout the land.

13 *For the choir director: A psalm of David.*

1 O LORD, how long will you forget me? Forever?
How long will you look the other way?
2 How long must I struggle with anguish in my soul,
with sorrow in my heart every day?
How long will my enemy have the upper hand?

3 Turn and answer me, O LORD my God!
Restore the sparkle to my eyes, or I will die.
4 Don't let my enemies gloat, saying, "We have defeated him!"
Don't let them rejoice at my downfall.

5 But I trust in your unfailing love.
I will rejoice because you have rescued me.
6 I will sing to the LORD
because he is good to me.

14 *For the choir director: A psalm of David.*

1 Only fools say in their hearts,
"There is no God."
They are corrupt, and their actions are evil;
not one of them does good!

2 The LORD looks down from heaven
on the entire human race;
he looks to see if anyone is truly wise,
if anyone seeks God.

3 But no, all have turned away;
all have become corrupt.*
No one does good,
not a single one!

4 Will those who do evil never learn?
They eat up my people like bread
and wouldn't think of praying to the LORD.
5 Terror will grip them,
for God is with those who obey him.
6 The wicked frustrate the plans of the oppressed,
but the LORD will protect his people.

7 Who will come from Mount Zion to rescue Israel?
When the LORD restores his people,
Jacob will shout with joy, and Israel will rejoice.

Question 15:1

What is the answer to this question? Why?

15 *A psalm of David.*

1 Who may worship in your sanctuary, LORD?
Who may enter your presence on your holy hill?
2 Those who lead blameless lives and do what is right,
speaking the truth from sincere hearts.
3 Those who refuse to gossip
or harm their neighbors
or speak evil of their friends.
4 Those who despise flagrant sinners,
and honor the faithful followers of the LORD,
and keep their promises even when it hurts.
5 Those who lend money without charging interest,
and who cannot be bribed to lie about the innocent.
Such people will stand firm forever.

16 *A psalm* of David.*

1 Keep me safe, O God,
for I have come to you for refuge.

2 I said to the LORD, "You are my Master!
Every good thing I have comes from you."
3 The godly people in the land
are my true heroes!
I take pleasure in them!
4 Troubles multiply for those who chase after
other gods.
I will not take part in their sacrifices of blood
or even speak the names of their gods.

14:3 Greek version reads *have become useless.* Compare Rom 3:12. 16:TITLE Hebrew *miktam.* This may be a literary or musical term.

5 LORD, you alone are my inheritance, my cup of blessing.
You guard all that is mine.
6 The land you have given me is a pleasant land.
What a wonderful inheritance!

7 I will bless the LORD who guides me;
even at night my heart instructs me.
8 I know the LORD is always with me.
I will not be shaken, for he is right beside me.

9 No wonder my heart is glad, and I rejoice.*
My body rests in safety.
10 For you will not leave my soul among the dead*
or allow your holy one* to rot in the grave.
11 You will show me the way of life,
granting me the joy of your presence
and the pleasures of living with you forever.*

17 *A prayer of David.*

1 O LORD, hear my plea for justice.
Listen to my cry for help.
Pay attention to my prayer,
for it comes from honest lips.
2 Declare me innocent,
for you see those who do right.

3 You have tested my thoughts and examined my heart in the night.
You have scrutinized me and found nothing wrong.
I am determined not to sin in what I say.
4 I have followed your commands,
which keep me from following cruel and evil people.
5 My steps have stayed on your path;
I have not wavered from following you.

6 I am praying to you because I know you will answer, O God.
Bend down and listen as I pray.
7 Show me your unfailing love in wonderful ways.
By your mighty power you rescue
those who seek refuge from their enemies.
8 Guard me as you would guard your own eyes.*
Hide me in the shadow of your wings.
9 Protect me from wicked people who attack me,
from murderous enemies who surround me.
10 They are without pity.
Listen to their boasting!

16:9 Greek version reads *and my tongue shouts his praises.* Compare Acts 2:26. 16:10a Hebrew *in Sheol.* 16:10b Or *your Holy One.* 16:11 Greek version reads *You have shown me the way of life, / and you will fill me with the joy of your presence.* Compare Acts 2:28. 17:8 Hebrew *as the pupil of your eye.*

11 They track me down and surround me,
watching for the chance to throw me to the ground.
12 They are like hungry lions, eager to tear me apart—
like young lions hiding in ambush.

13 Arise, O LORD!
Stand against them, and bring them to their knees!
Rescue me from the wicked with your sword!
14 By the power of your hand, O LORD,
destroy those who look to this world for their reward.
But satisfy the hunger of your treasured ones.
May their children have plenty,
leaving an inheritance for their descendants.
15 Because I am righteous, I will see you.
When I awake, I will see you face to face and be satisfied.

18 *For the choir director: A psalm of David, the servant of the LORD. He sang this song to the LORD on the day the LORD rescued him from all his enemies and from Saul. He sang:*

1 I love you, LORD;
you are my strength.
2 The LORD is my rock, my fortress, and my savior;
my God is my rock, in whom I find protection.
He is my shield, the power that saves me,
and my place of safety.
3 I called on the LORD, who is worthy of praise,
and he saved me from my enemies.

4 The ropes of death entangled me;
floods of destruction swept over me.
5 The grave* wrapped its ropes around me;
death laid a trap in my path.
6 But in my distress I cried out to the LORD;
yes, I prayed to my God for help.
He heard me from his sanctuary;
my cry to him reached his ears.

7 Then the earth quaked and trembled.
The foundations of the mountains shook;
they quaked because of his anger.
8 Smoke poured from his nostrils;
fierce flames leaped from his mouth.
Glowing coals blazed forth from him.
9 He opened the heavens and came down;
dark storm clouds were beneath his feet.
10 Mounted on a mighty angelic being,* he flew,
soaring on the wings of the wind.
11 He shrouded himself in darkness,
veiling his approach with dark rain clouds.

18:5 Hebrew *Sheol.* **18:10** Hebrew *a cherub.*

What I will do next

12 Thick clouds shielded the brightness around him
and rained down hail and burning coals.*
13 The LORD thundered from heaven;
the voice of the Most High resounded
amid the hail and burning coals.
14 He shot his arrows and scattered his enemies;
great bolts of lightning flashed, and they were confused.
15 Then at your command, O LORD,
at the blast of your breath,
the bottom of the sea could be seen,
and the foundations of the earth were laid bare.

16 He reached down from heaven and rescued me;
he drew me out of deep waters.
17 He rescued me from my powerful enemies,
from those who hated me and were too strong for me.
18 They attacked me at a moment when I was in distress,
but the LORD supported me.
19 He led me to a place of safety;
he rescued me because he delights in me.
20 The LORD rewarded me for doing right;
he restored me because of my innocence.
21 For I have kept the ways of the LORD;
I have not turned from my God to follow evil.
22 I have followed all his regulations;
I have never abandoned his decrees.
23 I am blameless before God;
I have kept myself from sin.
24 The LORD rewarded me for doing right.
He has seen my innocence.

25 To the faithful you show yourself faithful;
to those with integrity you show integrity.
26 To the pure you show yourself pure,
but to the crooked you show yourself shrewd.
27 You rescue the humble,
but you humiliate the proud.
28 You light a lamp for me.
The LORD, my God, lights up my darkness.
29 In your strength I can crush an army;
with my God I can scale any wall.

30 God's way is perfect.
All the LORD's promises prove true.
He is a shield for all who look to him for protection.
31 For who is God except the LORD?
Who but our God is a solid rock?
32 God arms me with strength,
and he makes my way perfect.

18:12 Or *and lightning bolts;* also in 18:13.

33 He makes me as surefooted as a deer,
enabling me to stand on mountain heights.
34 He trains my hands for battle;
he strengthens my arm to draw a bronze bow.
35 You have given me your shield of victory.
Your right hand supports me;
your help* has made me great.
36 You have made a wide path for my feet
to keep them from slipping.

37 I chased my enemies and caught them;
I did not stop until they were conquered.
38 I struck them down so they could not get up;
they fell beneath my feet.
39 You have armed me with strength for the battle;
you have subdued my enemies under my feet.
40 You placed my foot on their necks.
I have destroyed all who hated me.
41 They called for help, but no one came to their rescue.
They even cried to the LORD, but he refused to answer.
42 I ground them as fine as dust in the wind.
I swept them into the gutter like dirt.
43 You gave me victory over my accusers.
You appointed me ruler over nations;
people I don't even know now serve me.
44 As soon as they hear of me, they submit;
foreign nations cringe before me.
45 They all lose their courage
and come trembling from their strongholds.

46 The LORD lives! Praise to my Rock!
May the God of my salvation be exalted!
47 He is the God who pays back those who harm me;
he subdues the nations under me
48 and rescues me from my enemies.
You hold me safe beyond the reach of my enemies;
you save me from violent opponents.
49 For this, O LORD, I will praise you among the nations;
I will sing praises to your name.
50 You give great victories to your king;
you show unfailing love to your anointed,
to David and all his descendants forever.

19

For the choir director: A psalm of David.

1 The heavens proclaim the glory of God.
The skies display his craftsmanship.
2 Day after day they continue to speak;

18:35 Hebrew *your humility;* compare 2 Sam 22:36.

Make a Difference

19:1–6

Sky

Look at the sky. What do you see? How far can you see? What is up there? How does what you see change throughout the day? During the day, watch the clouds form and pass by in the atmosphere. If it is rainy, marvel at the science involved. If it is stormy, be humbled by the power of the winds and weather fronts. If it is sunny, feel the warmth of the sun on your skin. Enjoy the light it gives to reveal God's creation. At night, look at the stars. How many are there? Where are they all? Examine the detail of the moon. Think of the importance of its pull on the earth. Look at the sky. What do you learn about God and about what he created you to do?

Difference Maker

Get outside and enjoy what God has made. Let the expanse of the sky cause you to wonder about how great he is and about your role on this earth.

Make a Difference 19:14

Words and Thoughts

What if everything you ever said and thought was pleasing to the Lord? Just think for a moment how radically different, for example, yesterday would have been. If every word that coursed through your brain and crossed over your lips was ordained by God's beauty, how would that have changed the direction of your conversations? How would that have affected what you put your mind to?

Jesus is your Rock, but he is your Redeemer. If you are like many people, in the traps of your words and thoughts, it is so easy to forget that he is there for you. Perhaps if your conversations and quiet times are saturated in God's patterns, then today will bring a new level of recognition of the Lord's firm presence in your life.

Difference Maker

This might feel annoying at first, but choose one hour today when, before you say a word, you write the word down. Use this process as a filter for your mouth and your mind so that everything you say and everything you think will become pleasing to the Lord.

night after night they make him known.
3 They speak without a sound or word;
their voice is never heard.*
4 Yet their message has gone throughout the earth,
and their words to all the world.

God has made a home in the heavens for the sun.
5 It bursts forth like a radiant bridegroom after his wedding.
It rejoices like a great athlete eager to run the race.
6 The sun rises at one end of the heavens
and follows its course to the other end.
Nothing can hide from its heat.

7 The instructions of the LORD are perfect,
reviving the soul.
The decrees of the LORD are trustworthy,
making wise the simple.
8 The commandments of the LORD are right,
bringing joy to the heart.
The commands of the LORD are clear,
giving insight for living.
9 Reverence for the LORD is pure,
lasting forever.
The laws of the LORD are true;
each one is fair.
10 They are more desirable than gold,
even the finest gold.
They are sweeter than honey,
even honey dripping from the comb.
11 They are a warning to your servant,
a great reward for those who obey them.

12 How can I know all the sins lurking in my heart?
Cleanse me from these hidden faults.
13 Keep your servant from deliberate sins!
Don't let them control me.
Then I will be free of guilt
and innocent of great sin.

14 May the words of my mouth
and the meditation of my heart
be pleasing to you,
O LORD, my rock and my redeemer.

20 *For the choir director: A psalm of David.*

1 In times of trouble, may the LORD answer your cry.
May the name of the God of Jacob keep you safe from all harm.

19:3 Or *There is no speech or language where their voice is not heard.*

2 May he send you help from his sanctuary
and strengthen you from Jerusalem.*
3 May he remember all your gifts
and look favorably on your burnt offerings. *Interlude*

4 May he grant your heart's desires
and make all your plans succeed.
5 May we shout for joy when we hear of your victory
and raise a victory banner in the name of our God.
May the LORD answer all your prayers.

6 Now I know that the LORD rescues his anointed king.
He will answer him from his holy heaven
and rescue him by his great power.
7 Some nations boast of their chariots and horses,
but we boast in the name of the LORD our God.
8 Those nations will fall down and collapse,
but we will rise up and stand firm.

9 Give victory to our king, O LORD!
Answer our cry for help.

21 *For the choir director: A psalm of David.*

1 How the king rejoices in your strength, O LORD!
He shouts with joy because you give him victory.
2 For you have given him his heart's desire;
you have withheld nothing he requested. *Interlude*

3 You welcomed him back with success and prosperity.
You placed a crown of finest gold on his head.
4 He asked you to preserve his life,
and you granted his request.
The days of his life stretch on forever.
5 Your victory brings him great honor,
and you have clothed him with splendor and majesty.
6 You have endowed him with eternal blessings
and given him the joy of your presence.
7 For the king trusts in the LORD.
The unfailing love of the Most High will keep him from stumbling.

8 You will capture all your enemies.
Your strong right hand will seize all who hate you.
9 You will throw them in a flaming furnace
when you appear.
The LORD will consume them in his anger;
fire will devour them.
10 You will wipe their children from the face of the earth;

20:2 Hebrew *Zion.*

they will never have descendants.
11 Although they plot against you,
their evil schemes will never succeed.
12 For they will turn and run
when they see your arrows aimed at them.
13 Rise up, O LORD, in all your power.
With music and singing we celebrate your mighty acts.

22

For the choir director: A psalm of David, to be sung to the tune "Doe of the Dawn."

1 My God, my God, why have you abandoned me?
Why are you so far away when I groan for help?
2 Every day I call to you, my God, but you do not answer.
Every night I lift my voice, but I find no relief.

3 Yet you are holy,
enthroned on the praises of Israel.
4 Our ancestors trusted in you,
and you rescued them.
5 They cried out to you and were saved.
They trusted in you and were never disgraced.

6 But I am a worm and not a man.
I am scorned and despised by all!
7 Everyone who sees me mocks me.
They sneer and shake their heads, saying,
8 "Is this the one who relies on the LORD?
Then let the LORD save him!
If the LORD loves him so much,
let the LORD rescue him!"

9 Yet you brought me safely from my mother's womb
and led me to trust you at my mother's breast.
10 I was thrust into your arms at my birth.
You have been my God from the moment I was born.

11 Do not stay so far from me,
for trouble is near,
and no one else can help me.
12 My enemies surround me like a herd of bulls;
fierce bulls of Bashan have hemmed me in!
13 Like lions they open their jaws against me,
roaring and tearing into their prey.
14 My life is poured out like water,
and all my bones are out of joint.
My heart is like wax,
melting within me.
15 My strength has dried up like sunbaked clay.
My tongue sticks to the roof of my mouth.

Story Arc **22:1-31**

● Jesus

Jesus cried out the first words of this psalm while he hung on the cross. It was the epic moment when Jesus took humanity's sin upon his shoulders. It was a cry of utter loss, despair, and separation. It was the worst consequence of humanity's rejection of God, and Jesus took it upon himself. David originally composed this psalm during a remarkably difficult threat to his kingdom. Read this psalm once through with David in mind. Then, considering Jesus' reference to this psalm during his crucifixion, read this psalm again with Jesus in mind.

Ps 51:1-19 ►

You have laid me in the dust and left me for dead.
16 My enemies surround me like a pack of dogs;
an evil gang closes in on me.
They have pierced* my hands and feet.
17 I can count all my bones.
My enemies stare at me and gloat.
18 They divide my garments among themselves
and throw dice* for my clothing.

19 O LORD, do not stay far away!
You are my strength; come quickly to my aid!
20 Save me from the sword;
spare my precious life from these dogs.
21 Snatch me from the lion's jaws
and from the horns of these wild oxen.

22 I will proclaim your name to my brothers and sisters.*
I will praise you among your assembled people.
23 Praise the LORD, all you who fear him!
Honor him, all you descendants of Jacob!
Show him reverence, all you descendants of Israel!
24 For he has not ignored or belittled the suffering of the needy.
He has not turned his back on them,
but has listened to their cries for help.

25 I will praise you in the great assembly.
I will fulfill my vows in the presence of those who worship you.
26 The poor will eat and be satisfied.
All who seek the LORD will praise him.
Their hearts will rejoice with everlasting joy.
27 The whole earth will acknowledge the LORD and return to him.
All the families of the nations will bow down before him.
28 For royal power belongs to the LORD.
He rules all the nations.

29 Let the rich of the earth feast and worship.
Bow before him, all who are mortal,
all whose lives will end as dust.
30 Our children will also serve him.
Future generations will hear about the wonders of the Lord.
31 His righteous acts will be told to those not yet born.
They will hear about everything he has done.

Make a Difference

22:31

Future Generations

Psalm 22 is a messianic lament that is intermingled with hope. Even though the writer, David, was going through terror, his song offered a prayer of blessing for future generations. He envisioned a time when his generation's unselfish faith and sacrifice would produce abundance among the generations that were yet to come.

Those not yet born take a place of importance in David's vision. They are, perhaps, the most important generation to be considered in the foundation being established. David foresaw that those alive today should consider the practice of faith of those yet to be born. One generation is to equip the faith of the next, who, in turn, equips the faith of the next, who, in turn, equips the faith of the next, and so on for generations to come. David believed that how people respond to their circumstances today influences how generations not yet born will respond in the future.

Difference Maker

When you face your next frustrations, consider how your reactions could affect the faith of future generations.

23 *A psalm of David.*

1 The LORD is my shepherd;
I have all that I need.
2 He lets me rest in green meadows;

22:16 As in some Hebrew manuscripts and Greek and Syriac versions; most Hebrew manuscripts read *They are like a lion at.* 22:18 Hebrew *cast lots.* 22:22 Hebrew *my brothers.*

The Difference Psalm 23 Makes

Make a Difference 23:1

Sheep

No offense, but you are a sheep. Just a dumb little lamb. You are a wandering, stinky mess of an animal. A simpleminded, ego-headed, fragile-hearted, bleating lamb.

The Lord, though, is your Shepherd. You are so significant that the Lord has chosen to shepherd your flock. Not some two-bit shepherd, not some random hired hand, not a nomadic wanderer, the Lord alone shepherds you because he thinks you are worth his very life.

Just listen to what your Shepherd does for you. You don't need anyone or anything other than him. The Lord carries you, cleans you up, feeds you full, protects you, guides you, shears you, serves you, nudges you, pokes you, walks with you, hears you, speaks with you, calms you, excites you, instructs you, finds you, gathers you, waters you, mends you, quenches you, rests you, exalts you, lifts you, enjoys you, anoints you, tends to you, offers his life for you, and dwells with you—and he does this for all your life. The Lord is your Shepherd. He is so, so good.

Difference Maker

Every time you are tempted to "need" something else, turn your attention to Jesus instead.

Make a Difference 23:2

Rest

Where is the most restful place you have ever been? A sandy beach with the lapping waves and warm sun? A comfy chair with an ice-cold glass of lemonade after a busy day? If you were a sheep, your answer would be a green meadow with a gentle, warm breeze and a nearby source of fresh water. A good shepherd navigates his sheep toward a place like this. The frantic environment of honking, exhaust-spouting vehicles and noise-ringing appliances and retina-ruining screens and time-rushing schedules is not the proper ecosystem for sheep. Sheep fare better when their rhythm includes intervals of rest.

If a lamb wanders off to create a restful experience without the guidance of the shepherd, however, the lamb will likely soon find itself in a precarious predicament. Rest is the one thing that was not created when God made the world. It was simply embedded into the Lord's shepherding rhythm.

Difference Maker

Set aside time in a comfortable place with a comforting snack, open your Bible to Psalm 23, and let it sink into the rhythm of your soul.

Make a Difference 23:3

GPS

On your phone you can find the location you need to go, and your phone will route you there. You merely follow the GPS navigation, including instructions to change lanes or avoid construction. Many times, you don't even know for sure whether the voice is leading you in the right direction, but you consent to trust the GPS because you believe it knows where you are going.

Where do you need to go in your life? While GPS can only get you so far, Jesus can get you where you were created to be. Are you willing to let him tell you when to turn or when to take an exit? Do you trust yourself to his guidance even if you don't always know all the steps to take? If you do, you will be strengthened by his Spirit to pursue your calling.

Difference Maker

The next time you use your navigation app, consider how it is a metaphor for how you should follow Jesus' direction for your life.

Make a Difference 23:4

Even Though

If you realize that Jesus is there for you, then you can be there for others who find themselves in need today. Once you recognize the comforting presence of your Savior next to you, it is the natural next step to reach out to someone else with the good news about the Good Shepherd.

Jesus has a deep desire to walk with anyone through even the most difficult circumstances. He knows how raw real life can be. He knows that there is not one person who doesn't walk through dark times. Jesus knows this because he came to walk with, to guide, and to shepherd his people. Once you realize his presence in the hardest of circumstances, you notice that his stride carries strength and that his care provides protection. When your fear dissipates, you will want to let others know just how good the Good Shepherd happens to be.

Difference Maker

Reach out to someone who is struggling today. Find a creative way to let them know that Jesus is ready to walk close beside them and that so are you.

Make a Difference 23:5

Feast

Deep-dish pizza. Lobster saturated in garlic butter. Turkey with thick gravy, potatoes on the side, and delicious stuffing. Slow-cooked barbeque pulled pork. Chipotle steak burrito with queso, corn, cheese, sour cream, and extra guacamole. The freshest Caesar salad you've ever had. Rich marble lava cake drizzled with strawberry cream. An unending chocolate fondue fountain with freshly cut fruit and those cool little wooden skewers. Iced tea and lemonade and cappuccinos. Imagine serving after serving after serving placed in front of you. All this doesn't even come close to the sort of attention that your Good Shepherd intends to lavish upon you.

You are worth it to Jesus. He wants you to be overwhelmed by his extravagant love today. Let his abundance disturb your comfort zone, shatter your walled-up insecurities, and cover your brokenness. All that has intended harm against you must cease because your Savior has prepared a meal in your honor.

Difference Maker

Gather the people who are closest to you and share a vibrant feast together. Go overboard with your preparations and planning. Celebrate the life God has given you, and speak about this meal as a metaphor for the table that Jesus offers all of you.

Make a Difference 23:6

Surely

In the old days, when a man fell in love, he courted the woman he wanted to marry—he "pursued" her. This didn't happen in some Neanderthal sort of way nor in a creepy stalker sort of way. No, no, no. When a man fell in love, he tried to win the heart of the woman through gentleness, politeness, good intentions, proven stability, and strength of character. He would have sent her flowers and written her notes (using his actual hand and a pen). He would have sacrificed his own well-being to lift up her life and treasure her.

This is the way Jesus pursues us. His goodness and unfailing love go everywhere we go. He tries to catch our attention with his kindness and his grace. He opens doors and prepares opportunities for us to get to know each other better. Because he follows after us in love, we learn to follow after him in love as well.

Difference Maker

Everywhere you go today, imagine that Jesus is following you, trying to get your attention. Every now and then be sure to pause your activities to allow Jesus to share his life with you.

he leads me beside peaceful streams.
3 He renews my strength.
He guides me along right paths,
bringing honor to his name.
4 Even when I walk
through the darkest valley,*
I will not be afraid,
for you are close beside me.
Your rod and your staff
protect and comfort me.
5 You prepare a feast for me
in the presence of my enemies.
You honor me by anointing my head with oil.
My cup overflows with blessings.
6 Surely your goodness and unfailing love will pursue me
all the days of my life,
and I will live in the house of the LORD
forever.

24

A psalm of David.

1 The earth is the LORD's, and everything in it.
The world and all its people belong to him.
2 For he laid the earth's foundation on the seas
and built it on the ocean depths.

3 Who may climb the mountain of the LORD?
Who may stand in his holy place?
4 Only those whose hands and hearts are pure,
who do not worship idols
and never tell lies.
5 They will receive the LORD's blessing
and have a right relationship with God their savior.
6 Such people may seek you
and worship in your presence, O God of Jacob.* *Interlude*

7 Open up, ancient gates!
Open up, ancient doors,
and let the King of glory enter.
8 Who is the King of glory?
The LORD, strong and mighty;
the LORD, invincible in battle.
9 Open up, ancient gates!
Open up, ancient doors,
and let the King of glory enter.
10 Who is the King of glory?
The LORD of Heaven's Armies—
he is the King of glory. *Interlude*

23:4 Or *the dark valley of death.* 24:6 As in two Hebrew manuscripts and Greek and Syriac versions; most Hebrew manuscripts read *O Jacob.*

25*

A psalm of David.

1 O LORD, I give my life to you.
2 I trust in you, my God!
Do not let me be disgraced,
or let my enemies rejoice in my defeat.
3 No one who trusts in you will ever be disgraced,
but disgrace comes to those who try to deceive
others.

4 Show me the right path, O LORD;
point out the road for me to follow.
5 Lead me by your truth and teach me,
for you are the God who saves me.
All day long I put my hope in you.
6 Remember, O LORD, your compassion and unfailing
love,
which you have shown from long ages past.
7 Do not remember the rebellious sins of my youth.
Remember me in the light of your unfailing love,
for you are merciful, O LORD.

8 The LORD is good and does what is right;
he shows the proper path to those who go astray.
9 He leads the humble in doing right,
teaching them his way.
10 The LORD leads with unfailing love and faithfulness
all who keep his covenant and obey his demands.

11 For the honor of your name, O LORD,
forgive my many, many sins.
12 Who are those who fear the LORD?
He will show them the path they should choose.
13 They will live in prosperity,
and their children will inherit the land.
14 The LORD is a friend to those who fear him.
He teaches them his covenant.
15 My eyes are always on the LORD,
for he rescues me from the traps of my enemies.

16 Turn to me and have mercy,
for I am alone and in deep distress.
17 My problems go from bad to worse.
Oh, save me from them all!
18 Feel my pain and see my trouble.
Forgive all my sins.
19 See how many enemies I have
and how viciously they hate me!

25 This psalm is a Hebrew acrostic poem; each verse begins with a successive letter of the Hebrew alphabet.

Your thoughts can go here

Make a Difference 27:1

Tremble?

What are you afraid of? Why do you hesitate? What stops you from doing what God calls you to do? Is the obstacle confusion, apathy, or perhaps a lack of conviction? Maybe you are tired, hungry, or upset at someone? Perhaps you are struggling with a nagging sin? Do you feel alone in pursuing God's call? Are you worried about how people might respond to you?

What are you afraid of? The Lord is flawlessly focused. God is passionate. He restores your verve for life. He fills your soul. The Lord heals your hurt and forgives your sin. He gives you strength to overcome your weaknesses. He offers companionship and invites you to join others in his mission. The Lord reassures you that he will respond to you with joy and blessing even if others don't. Considering all he provides, what are you afraid of? In the Lord's power, live for Jesus today.

Difference Maker

What are you facing today that causes you concern? What could you do differently, knowing that the presence of Jesus is with you?

20 Protect me! Rescue my life from them!
Do not let me be disgraced, for in you I take refuge.
21 May integrity and honesty protect me,
for I put my hope in you.

22 O God, ransom Israel
from all its troubles.

26 *A psalm of David.*

1 Declare me innocent, O LORD,
for I have acted with integrity;
I have trusted in the LORD without wavering.
2 Put me on trial, LORD, and cross-examine me.
Test my motives and my heart.
3 For I am always aware of your unfailing love,
and I have lived according to your truth.
4 I do not spend time with liars
or go along with hypocrites.
5 I hate the gatherings of those who do evil,
and I refuse to join in with the wicked.
6 I wash my hands to declare my innocence.
I come to your altar, O LORD,
7 singing a song of thanksgiving
and telling of all your wonders.
8 I love your sanctuary, LORD,
the place where your glorious presence dwells.

9 Don't let me suffer the fate of sinners.
Don't condemn me along with murderers.
10 Their hands are dirty with evil schemes,
and they constantly take bribes.
11 But I am not like that; I live with integrity.
So redeem me and show me mercy.
12 Now I stand on solid ground,
and I will publicly praise the LORD.

27 *A psalm of David.*

1 The LORD is my light and my salvation—
so why should I be afraid?
The LORD is my fortress, protecting me from danger,
so why should I tremble?
2 When evil people come to devour me,
when my enemies and foes attack me,
they will stumble and fall.

3 Though a mighty army surrounds me,
my heart will not be afraid.
Even if I am attacked,
I will remain confident.

4 The one thing I ask of the LORD—
the thing I seek most—
is to live in the house of the LORD all the days of my life,
delighting in the LORD's perfections
and meditating in his Temple.
5 For he will conceal me there when troubles come;
he will hide me in his sanctuary.
He will place me out of reach on a high rock.
6 Then I will hold my head high
above my enemies who surround me.
At his sanctuary I will offer sacrifices with shouts of joy,
singing and praising the LORD with music.

7 Hear me as I pray, O LORD.
Be merciful and answer me!
8 My heart has heard you say, "Come and talk with me."
And my heart responds, "LORD, I am coming."
9 Do not turn your back on me.
Do not reject your servant in anger.
You have always been my helper.
Don't leave me now; don't abandon me,
O God of my salvation!
10 Even if my father and mother abandon me,
the LORD will hold me close.

11 Teach me how to live, O LORD.
Lead me along the right path,
for my enemies are waiting for me.
12 Do not let me fall into their hands.
For they accuse me of things I've never done;
with every breath they threaten me with violence.
13 Yet I am confident I will see the LORD's goodness
while I am here in the land of the living.

14 Wait patiently for the LORD.
Be brave and courageous.
Yes, wait patiently for the LORD.

28 *A psalm of David.*

1 I pray to you, O LORD, my rock.
Do not turn a deaf ear to me.
For if you are silent,
I might as well give up and die.

Make a Difference

27:14

In Between

On a scale from one to ten, how antsy do you get when you have to wait? How good are you at waiting? I don't mean waiting for a couple of minutes, but I mean really waiting—like days, weeks, or even months. When is your patience most easily worn out?

Sometimes, you'll need to be patient. Everything significant is not immediate. Some changes take long investment, persistent attention, consistent behavior, and dedicated evidence of your faithfulness. Perhaps you'd like to do only one action, as if you only had to make one motion of a magic wand to make everything around you appear better. However, circumventing true process can produce undesirable side effects.

Some things just take time. Making a difference is a 365-day-a-year endeavor. Your daily commitment to cultivate your heart will harvest huge rewards as time goes on.

Difference Maker

As an illustration of God's long-term work and even though you won't see the benefit for quite a while, put some money in your savings account today. (As an alternative, put some money in someone else's savings!)

2 Listen to my prayer for mercy
as I cry out to you for help,
as I lift my hands toward your holy sanctuary.

3 Do not drag me away with the wicked—
with those who do evil—
those who speak friendly words to their neighbors
while planning evil in their hearts.
4 Give them the punishment they so richly deserve!
Measure it out in proportion to their wickedness.
Pay them back for all their evil deeds!
Give them a taste of what they have done
to others.
5 They care nothing for what the LORD has done
or for what his hands have made.
So he will tear them down,
and they will never be rebuilt!

6 Praise the LORD!
For he has heard my cry for mercy.
7 The LORD is my strength and shield.
I trust him with all my heart.
He helps me, and my heart is filled with joy.
I burst out in songs of thanksgiving.

8 The LORD gives his people strength.
He is a safe fortress for his anointed king.
9 Save your people!
Bless Israel, your special possession.*
Lead them like a shepherd,
and carry them in your arms forever.

29 *A psalm of David.*

1 Honor the LORD, you heavenly beings*;
honor the LORD for his glory and strength.
2 Honor the LORD for the glory of his name.
Worship the LORD in the splendor of his holiness.

3 The voice of the LORD echoes above the sea.
The God of glory thunders.
The LORD thunders over the mighty sea.
4 The voice of the LORD is powerful;
the voice of the LORD is majestic.
5 The voice of the LORD splits the mighty cedars;
the LORD shatters the cedars of Lebanon.
6 He makes Lebanon's mountains skip like a calf;
he makes Mount Hermon* leap like a young wild ox.

28:9 Hebrew *Bless your inheritance.* 29:1 Hebrew *you sons of God.* 29:6 Hebrew *Sirion,* another name for Mount Hermon.

7 The voice of the LORD strikes
with bolts of lightning.
8 The voice of the LORD makes the barren wilderness quake;
the LORD shakes the wilderness of Kadesh.
9 The voice of the LORD twists mighty oaks*
and strips the forests bare.
In his Temple everyone shouts, "Glory!"

10 The LORD rules over the floodwaters.
The LORD reigns as king forever.
11 The LORD gives his people strength.
The LORD blesses them with peace.

Question 30:2

Have you ever done this? Why do you think there are so many psalms of David where he is crying out to God?

30 *A psalm of David. A song for the dedication of the Temple.*

1 I will exalt you, LORD, for you rescued me.
You refused to let my enemies triumph over me.
2 O LORD my God, I cried to you for help,
and you restored my health.
3 You brought me up from the grave,* O LORD.
You kept me from falling into the pit of death.

4 Sing to the LORD, all you godly ones!
Praise his holy name.
5 For his anger lasts only a moment,
but his favor lasts a lifetime!
Weeping may last through the night,
but joy comes with the morning.

6 When I was prosperous, I said,
"Nothing can stop me now!"
7 Your favor, O LORD, made me as secure as a mountain.
Then you turned away from me, and I was shattered.

8 I cried out to you, O LORD.
I begged the Lord for mercy, saying,
9 "What will you gain if I die,
if I sink into the grave?
Can my dust praise you?
Can it tell of your faithfulness?
10 Hear me, LORD, and have mercy on me.
Help me, O LORD."

11 You have turned my mourning into joyful dancing.
You have taken away my clothes of mourning and clothed
me with joy,
12 that I might sing praises to you and not be silent.
O LORD my God, I will give you thanks forever!

29:9 Or *causes the deer to writhe in labor.* 30:3 Hebrew *from Sheol.*

Prayer 31:9

Lord, I pray for everyone who feels this way right now. Restore them, heal them, and give them your presence during their trouble. Amen.

31

For the choir director: A psalm of David.

1 O LORD, I have come to you for protection;
don't let me be disgraced.
Save me, for you do what is right.
2 Turn your ear to listen to me;
rescue me quickly.
Be my rock of protection,
a fortress where I will be safe.
3 You are my rock and my fortress.
For the honor of your name, lead me out of this danger.
4 Pull me from the trap my enemies set for me,
for I find protection in you alone.
5 I entrust my spirit into your hand.
Rescue me, LORD, for you are a faithful God.

6 I hate those who worship worthless idols.
I trust in the LORD.
7 I will be glad and rejoice in your unfailing love,
for you have seen my troubles,
and you care about the anguish of my soul.
8 You have not handed me over to my enemies
but have set me in a safe place.

▲ 9 Have mercy on me, LORD, for I am in distress.
Tears blur my eyes.
My body and soul are withering away.
10 I am dying from grief;
my years are shortened by sadness.
Sin has drained my strength;
I am wasting away from within.
11 I am scorned by all my enemies
and despised by my neighbors—
even my friends are afraid to come near me.
When they see me on the street,
they run the other way.
12 I am ignored as if I were dead,
as if I were a broken pot.
13 I have heard the many rumors about me,
and I am surrounded by terror.
My enemies conspire against me,
plotting to take my life.

14 But I am trusting you, O LORD,
saying, "You are my God!"
15 My future is in your hands.
Rescue me from those who hunt me down relentlessly.
16 Let your favor shine on your servant.
In your unfailing love, rescue me.

17 Don't let me be disgraced, O LORD,
for I call out to you for help.
Let the wicked be disgraced;
let them lie silent in the grave.*
18 Silence their lying lips—
those proud and arrogant lips that accuse the godly.

19 How great is the goodness
you have stored up for those who fear you.
You lavish it on those who come to you for protection,
blessing them before the watching world.
20 You hide them in the shelter of your presence,
safe from those who conspire against them.
You shelter them in your presence,
far from accusing tongues.

21 Praise the LORD,
for he has shown me the wonders of his unfailing love.
He kept me safe when my city was under attack.
22 In panic I cried out,
"I am cut off from the LORD!"
But you heard my cry for mercy
and answered my call for help.

23 Love the LORD, all you godly ones!
For the LORD protects those who are loyal to him,
but he harshly punishes the arrogant.
24 So be strong and courageous,
all you who put your hope in the LORD!

32 *A psalm* of David.*

1 Oh, what joy for those
whose disobedience is forgiven,
whose sin is put out of sight!
2 Yes, what joy for those
whose record the LORD has cleared of guilt,*
whose lives are lived in complete honesty!
3 When I refused to confess my sin,
my body wasted away,
and I groaned all day long.
4 Day and night your hand of discipline was heavy on me.
My strength evaporated like water in the summer heat. *Interlude*

5 Finally, I confessed all my sins to you
and stopped trying to hide my guilt.
I said to myself, "I will confess my rebellion to the LORD."
And you forgave me! All my guilt is gone. *Interlude*

31:17 Hebrew *in Sheol.* 32:TITLE Hebrew *maskil.* This may be a literary or musical term.
32:2 Greek version reads *of sin.* Compare Rom 4:8.

Make a Difference

33:6–9

Start Fresh

Jesus wants you to have a fresh start in this world. In fact, he made this world with you in mind. He made it so that you could breathe in its air, marvel in its sunsets, surf in its waves, and wander in its paths with him. Be confident today in the one who made this world. While most people get caught up in their hectic schedules and busy lives, pause throughout this day to treasure what Jesus created for you and for me.

Difference Maker

With Psalm 33:6–9 in your mind, notice something about this world that you may not have spotted before. Then tell somebody about it.

6 Therefore, let all the godly pray to you while there is still time,
that they may not drown in the floodwaters of judgment.
7 For you are my hiding place;
you protect me from trouble.
You surround me with songs of victory. *Interlude*

8 The LORD says, "I will guide you along the best pathway for your life.
I will advise you and watch over you.
9 Do not be like a senseless horse or mule
that needs a bit and bridle to keep it under control."

10 Many sorrows come to the wicked,
but unfailing love surrounds those who trust the LORD.
11 So rejoice in the LORD and be glad, all you who obey him!
Shout for joy, all you whose hearts are pure!

33

1 Let the godly sing for joy to the LORD;
it is fitting for the pure to praise him.
2 Praise the LORD with melodies on the lyre;
make music for him on the ten-stringed harp.
3 Sing a new song of praise to him;
play skillfully on the harp, and sing with joy.
4 For the word of the LORD holds true,
and we can trust everything he does.
5 He loves whatever is just and good;
the unfailing love of the LORD fills the earth.

6 The LORD merely spoke,
and the heavens were created.
He breathed the word,
and all the stars were born.
7 He assigned the sea its boundaries
and locked the oceans in vast reservoirs.
8 Let the whole world fear the LORD,
and let everyone stand in awe of him.
9 For when he spoke, the world began!
It appeared at his command.

10 The LORD frustrates the plans of the nations
and thwarts all their schemes.
11 But the LORD's plans stand firm forever;
his intentions can never be shaken.

12 What joy for the nation whose God is the LORD,
whose people he has chosen as his inheritance.

13 The LORD looks down from heaven
and sees the whole human race.
14 From his throne he observes
all who live on the earth.

15 He made their hearts,
so he understands everything they do.
16 The best-equipped army cannot save a king,
nor is great strength enough to save a warrior.
17 Don't count on your warhorse to give you victory—
for all its strength, it cannot save you.

18 But the LORD watches over those who fear him,
those who rely on his unfailing love.
19 He rescues them from death
and keeps them alive in times of famine.

20 We put our hope in the LORD.
He is our help and our shield.
21 In him our hearts rejoice,
for we trust in his holy name.
22 Let your unfailing love surround us, LORD,
for our hope is in you alone.

34

* *A psalm of David, regarding the time he pretended to be insane in front of Abimelech, who sent him away.*

1 I will praise the LORD at all times.
I will constantly speak his praises.
2 I will boast only in the LORD;
let all who are helpless take heart.
3 Come, let us tell of the LORD's greatness;
let us exalt his name together.

4 I prayed to the LORD, and he answered me.
He freed me from all my fears.
5 Those who look to him for help will be radiant with joy;
no shadow of shame will darken their faces.
6 In my desperation I prayed, and the LORD listened;
he saved me from all my troubles.
7 For the angel of the LORD is a guard;
he surrounds and defends all who fear him.

8 Taste and see that the LORD is good.
Oh, the joys of those who take refuge in him!
9 Fear the LORD, you his godly people,
for those who fear him will have all they need.
10 Even strong young lions sometimes go hungry,
but those who trust in the LORD will lack no good thing.

11 Come, my children, and listen to me,
and I will teach you to fear the LORD.
12 Does anyone want to live a life
that is long and prosperous?

34 This psalm is a Hebrew acrostic poem; each verse begins with a successive letter of the Hebrew alphabet.

Question 34:6

Have you ever done this? How did the Lord respond?

Question 34:8

What does this mean? What are you going to do about it?

Question 34:18

Here's a challenging question to chew on: If the Lord is close to the brokenhearted, why would you want to be fixed?

13 Then keep your tongue from speaking evil
and your lips from telling lies!
14 Turn away from evil and do good.
Search for peace, and work to maintain it.

15 The eyes of the LORD watch over those who do right;
his ears are open to their cries for help.
16 But the LORD turns his face against those who do evil;
he will erase their memory from the earth.
17 The LORD hears his people when they call to him for help.
He rescues them from all their troubles.
18 The LORD is close to the brokenhearted;
he rescues those whose spirits are crushed.

19 The righteous person faces many troubles,
but the LORD comes to the rescue each time.
20 For the LORD protects the bones of the righteous;
not one of them is broken!

21 Calamity will surely destroy the wicked,
and those who hate the righteous will be punished.
22 But the LORD will redeem those who serve him.
No one who takes refuge in him will be condemned.

35

A psalm of David.

1 O LORD, oppose those who oppose me.
Fight those who fight against me.
2 Put on your armor, and take up your shield.
Prepare for battle, and come to my aid.
3 Lift up your spear and javelin
against those who pursue me.
Let me hear you say,
"I will give you victory!"
4 Bring shame and disgrace on those trying to kill me;
turn them back and humiliate those who want to harm me.
5 Blow them away like chaff in the wind—
a wind sent by the angel of the LORD.
6 Make their path dark and slippery,
with the angel of the LORD pursuing them.
7 I did them no wrong, but they laid a trap for me.
I did them no wrong, but they dug a pit to catch me.
8 So let sudden ruin come upon them!
Let them be caught in the trap they set for me!
Let them be destroyed in the pit they dug for me.

9 Then I will rejoice in the LORD.
I will be glad because he rescues me.
10 With every bone in my body I will praise him:

"LORD, who can compare with you?
Who else rescues the helpless from the strong?
Who else protects the helpless and poor from those who rob them?"

11 Malicious witnesses testify against me.
They accuse me of crimes I know nothing about.
12 They repay me evil for good.
I am sick with despair.
13 Yet when they were ill, I grieved for them.
I denied myself by fasting for them,
but my prayers returned unanswered.
14 I was sad, as though they were my friends or family,
as if I were grieving for my own mother.
15 But they are glad now that I am in trouble;
they gleefully join together against me.
I am attacked by people I don't even know;
they slander me constantly.
16 They mock me and call me names;
they snarl at me.

17 How long, O Lord, will you look on and do nothing?
Rescue me from their fierce attacks.
Protect my life from these lions!
18 Then I will thank you in front of the great assembly.
I will praise you before all the people.
19 Don't let my treacherous enemies rejoice over my defeat.
Don't let those who hate me without cause gloat over
my sorrow.
20 They don't talk of peace;
they plot against innocent people who mind their own business.
21 They shout, "Aha! Aha!
With our own eyes we saw him do it!"

22 O LORD, you know all about this.
Do not stay silent.
Do not abandon me now, O Lord.
23 Wake up! Rise to my defense!
Take up my case, my God and my Lord.
24 Declare me not guilty, O LORD my God, for you give justice.
Don't let my enemies laugh about me in my troubles.
25 Don't let them say, "Look, we got what we wanted!
Now we will eat him alive!"

26 May those who rejoice at my troubles
be humiliated and disgraced.
May those who triumph over me
be covered with shame and dishonor.
27 But give great joy to those who came to my defense.
Let them continually say, "Great is the LORD,
who delights in blessing his servant with peace!"

Make a Difference

37:1-7

Don't Worry

Our world is full of monstrous people who fear nothing other than peace. To be honest, most of us worry about these people and the evil they are capable of unleashing. Instead, what if we were truly to trust the words of the Bible? How would our engagement with the world change? Would our actions be driven by faith and hope and love rather than fear?

Conflict and strife are evident in the raw reality of the words of the Bible. There is, historically and cosmically, a fight launched by forces that want to wreak destruction. In God's power, though, we are called to stand against the world's adversaries without buckling our knees.

After all, why should we be afraid? Whose arm of might and justice will prevail? We choose to join sides with the Mighty Mower of the Yard, the Almighty Trimmer of the Flowers.

Difference Maker

Take some time to attend to the news today without fear. Instead, pray and give courage to your community through the confidence of God.

28 Then I will proclaim your justice,
and I will praise you all day long.

36

For the choir director: A psalm of David, the servant of the LORD.

1 Sin whispers to the wicked, deep within their hearts.*
They have no fear of God at all.
2 In their blind conceit,
they cannot see how wicked they really are.
3 Everything they say is crooked and deceitful.
They refuse to act wisely or do good.
4 They lie awake at night, hatching sinful plots.
Their actions are never good.
They make no attempt to turn from evil.

5 Your unfailing love, O LORD, is as vast as the heavens;
your faithfulness reaches beyond the clouds.
6 Your righteousness is like the mighty mountains,
your justice like the ocean depths.
You care for people and animals alike, O LORD.
7 How precious is your unfailing love, O God!
All humanity finds shelter
in the shadow of your wings.
8 You feed them from the abundance of your own house,
letting them drink from your river of delights.
9 For you are the fountain of life,
the light by which we see.

10 Pour out your unfailing love on those who love you;
give justice to those with honest hearts.
11 Don't let the proud trample me
or the wicked push me around.
12 Look! Those who do evil have fallen!
They are thrown down, never to rise again.

37*

A psalm of David.

1 Don't worry about the wicked
or envy those who do wrong.
2 For like grass, they soon fade away.
Like spring flowers, they soon wither.

3 Trust in the LORD and do good.
Then you will live safely in the land and prosper.
4 Take delight in the LORD,
and he will give you your heart's desires.

36:1 As in some Hebrew manuscripts and Syriac version, which read *in his heart.* Masoretic Text reads *in my heart.* **37** This psalm is a Hebrew acrostic poem; each stanza begins with a successive letter of the Hebrew alphabet.

5 Commit everything you do to the LORD.
Trust him, and he will help you.
6 He will make your innocence radiate like the dawn,
and the justice of your cause will shine like the noonday sun.

7 Be still in the presence of the LORD,
and wait patiently for him to act.
Don't worry about evil people who prosper
or fret about their wicked schemes.

8 Stop being angry!
Turn from your rage!
Do not lose your temper—
it only leads to harm.
9 For the wicked will be destroyed,
but those who trust in the LORD will possess the land.

10 Soon the wicked will disappear.
Though you look for them, they will be gone.
11 The lowly will possess the land
and will live in peace and prosperity.

12 The wicked plot against the godly;
they snarl at them in defiance.
13 But the Lord just laughs,
for he sees their day of judgment coming.

14 The wicked draw their swords
and string their bows
to kill the poor and the oppressed,
to slaughter those who do right.
15 But their swords will stab their own hearts,
and their bows will be broken.

16 It is better to be godly and have little
than to be evil and rich.
17 For the strength of the wicked will be shattered,
but the LORD takes care of the godly.

18 Day by day the LORD takes care of the innocent,
and they will receive an inheritance that lasts forever.
19 They will not be disgraced in hard times;
even in famine they will have more than enough.

20 But the wicked will die.
The LORD's enemies are like flowers in a field—
they will disappear like smoke.

21 The wicked borrow and never repay,
but the godly are generous givers.

Make a Difference 37:7

Take a Deep Breath

Take a deep breath. You really should do this more often. It's cleansing. Oxygen refreshes your brain and strengthens your heart, not to mention all your other organs as well. Pause. Breathe in. Hold. Breathe out. Right now, before tackling any more work or allowing yourself to fall into an endless loop of anxiety, remember to breathe. It is what makes you alive.

A new creation. That's what you are in Jesus.

Breathe. Remember what makes you alive. Don't try to manipulate the events of your life. It was God who first breathed life into you. He now gives you the ability to do the same. With deep yearning, find the rhythm God composed for you. Give all the rises and falls, the notes and beats, the crescendos and melodies of your life to him.

Difference Maker

Commit yourself to silence for at least ten minutes. During that time, lay out your thoughts to God. Then stop thinking for a while, take a deep breath, and just try to be still before God.

22 Those the LORD blesses will possess the land,
but those he curses will die.

23 The LORD directs the steps of the godly.
He delights in every detail of their lives.
24 Though they stumble, they will never fall,
for the LORD holds them by the hand.

25 Once I was young, and now I am old.
Yet I have never seen the godly abandoned
or their children begging for bread.
26 The godly always give generous loans to others,
and their children are a blessing.

27 Turn from evil and do good,
and you will live in the land forever.
28 For the LORD loves justice,
and he will never abandon the godly.

He will keep them safe forever,
but the children of the wicked will die.
29 The godly will possess the land
and will live there forever.

30 The godly offer good counsel;
they teach right from wrong.
31 They have made God's law their own,
so they will never slip from his path.

32 The wicked wait in ambush for the godly,
looking for an excuse to kill them.
33 But the LORD will not let the wicked succeed
or let the godly be condemned when they are put on trial.

34 Put your hope in the LORD.
Travel steadily along his path.
He will honor you by giving you the land.
You will see the wicked destroyed.

35 I have seen wicked and ruthless people
flourishing like a tree in its native soil.
36 But when I looked again, they were gone!
Though I searched for them, I could not find them!

37 Look at those who are honest and good,
for a wonderful future awaits those who love peace.
38 But the rebellious will be destroyed;
they have no future.

39 The LORD rescues the godly;
he is their fortress in times of trouble.

40 The LORD helps them,
rescuing them from the wicked.
He saves them,
and they find shelter in him.

38 *A psalm of David, asking God to remember him.*

1 O LORD, don't rebuke me in your anger
or discipline me in your rage!
2 Your arrows have struck deep,
and your blows are crushing me.
3 Because of your anger, my whole body is sick;
my health is broken because of my sins.
4 My guilt overwhelms me—
it is a burden too heavy to bear.
5 My wounds fester and stink
because of my foolish sins.
6 I am bent over and racked with pain.
All day long I walk around filled with grief.
7 A raging fever burns within me,
and my health is broken.
8 I am exhausted and completely crushed.
My groans come from an anguished heart.

9 You know what I long for, Lord;
you hear my every sigh.
10 My heart beats wildly, my strength fails,
and I am going blind.
11 My loved ones and friends stay away, fearing
my disease.
Even my own family stands at a distance.
12 Meanwhile, my enemies lay traps to kill me.
Those who wish me harm make plans to ruin me.
All day long they plan their treachery.

13 But I am deaf to all their threats.
I am silent before them as one who cannot speak.
14 I choose to hear nothing,
and I make no reply.
15 For I am waiting for you, O LORD.
You must answer for me, O Lord my God.
16 I prayed, "Don't let my enemies gloat over me
or rejoice at my downfall."

17 I am on the verge of collapse,
facing constant pain.
18 But I confess my sins;
I am deeply sorry for what I have done.
19 I have many aggressive enemies;
they hate me without reason.

Encouragements from these verses

20 They repay me evil for good
and oppose me for pursuing good.
21 Do not abandon me, O LORD.
Do not stand at a distance, my God.
22 Come quickly to help me,
O Lord my savior.

39

For Jeduthun, the choir director: A psalm of David.

1 I said to myself, "I will watch what I do
and not sin in what I say.
I will hold my tongue
when the ungodly are around me."
2 But as I stood there in silence—
not even speaking of good things—
the turmoil within me grew worse.
3 The more I thought about it,
the hotter I got,
igniting a fire of words:
4 "LORD, remind me how brief my time on earth will be.
Remind me that my days are numbered—
how fleeting my life is.
5 You have made my life no longer than the width
of my hand.
My entire lifetime is just a moment to you;
at best, each of us is but a breath." *Interlude*

6 We are merely moving shadows,
and all our busy rushing ends in nothing.
We heap up wealth,
not knowing who will spend it.
7 And so, Lord, where do I put my hope?
My only hope is in you.
8 Rescue me from my rebellion.
Do not let fools mock me.
9 I am silent before you; I won't say a word,
for my punishment is from you.
10 But please stop striking me!
I am exhausted by the blows from your hand.
11 When you discipline us for our sins,
you consume like a moth what is precious to us.
Each of us is but a breath. *Interlude*

12 Hear my prayer, O LORD!
Listen to my cries for help!
Don't ignore my tears.
For I am your guest—
a traveler passing through,
as my ancestors were before me.

13 Leave me alone so I can smile again
before I am gone and exist no more.

40 *For the choir director: A psalm of David.*

1 I waited patiently for the LORD to help me,
and he turned to me and heard my cry.
2 He lifted me out of the pit of despair,
out of the mud and the mire.
He set my feet on solid ground
and steadied me as I walked along.
3 He has given me a new song to sing,
a hymn of praise to our God.
Many will see what he has done and be amazed.
They will put their trust in the LORD.

4 Oh, the joys of those who trust the LORD,
who have no confidence in the proud
or in those who worship idols.
5 O LORD my God, you have performed many wonders for us.
Your plans for us are too numerous to list.
You have no equal.
If I tried to recite all your wonderful deeds,
I would never come to the end of them.

6 You take no delight in sacrifices or offerings.
Now that you have made me listen, I finally understand*—
you don't require burnt offerings or sin offerings.
7 Then I said, "Look, I have come.
As is written about me in the Scriptures:
8 I take joy in doing your will, my God,
for your instructions are written on my heart."

9 I have told all your people about your justice.
I have not been afraid to speak out,
as you, O LORD, well know.
10 I have not kept the good news of your justice hidden
in my heart;
I have talked about your faithfulness and saving power.
I have told everyone in the great assembly
of your unfailing love and faithfulness.

11 LORD, don't hold back your tender mercies from me.
Let your unfailing love and faithfulness always protect me.
12 For troubles surround me—
too many to count!
My sins pile up so high
I can't see my way out.

Prayer **40:1**

Dear God, I struggle to be willing to wait for you to act. Help me to trust you. Amen.

40:6 Greek version reads *You have given me a body.* Compare Heb 10:5.

They outnumber the hairs on my head.
  I have lost all courage.

13 Please, LORD, rescue me!
  Come quickly, LORD, and help me.
14 May those who try to destroy me
  be humiliated and put to shame.
May those who take delight in my trouble
  be turned back in disgrace.
15 Let them be horrified by their shame,
  for they said, "Aha! We've got him now!"

16 But may all who search for you
  be filled with joy and gladness in you.
May those who love your salvation
  repeatedly shout, "The LORD is great!"
17 As for me, since I am poor and needy,
  let the Lord keep me in his thoughts.
You are my helper and my savior.
  O my God, do not delay.

41 *For the choir director: A psalm of David.*

1 Oh, the joys of those who are kind to the poor!
  The LORD rescues them when they are in trouble.
2 The LORD protects them
  and keeps them alive.
He gives them prosperity in the land
  and rescues them from their enemies.
3 The LORD nurses them when they are sick
  and restores them to health.

4 "O LORD," I prayed, "have mercy on me.
  Heal me, for I have sinned against you."
5 But my enemies say nothing but evil about me.
  "How soon will he die and be forgotten?"
    they ask.
6 They visit me as if they were my friends,
  but all the while they gather gossip,
  and when they leave, they spread it everywhere.
7 All who hate me whisper about me,
  imagining the worst.
8 "He has some fatal disease," they say.
  "He will never get out of that bed!"
9 Even my best friend, the one I trusted completely,
  the one who shared my food, has turned against me.

10 LORD, have mercy on me.
  Make me well again, so I can pay them back!

11 I know you are pleased with me,
  for you have not let my enemies triumph over me.
12 You have preserved my life because I am innocent;
  you have brought me into your presence forever.

13 Praise the LORD, the God of Israel,
  who lives from everlasting to everlasting.
Amen and amen!

BOOK TWO (Psalms 42–72)

42

For the choir director: A psalm of the descendants of Korah.*

1 As the deer longs for streams of water,
  so I long for you, O God.
2 I thirst for God, the living God.
  When can I go and stand before him?
3 Day and night I have only tears for food,
  while my enemies continually taunt me, saying,
  "Where is this God of yours?"

4 My heart is breaking
  as I remember how it used to be:
I walked among the crowds of worshipers,
  leading a great procession to the house of God,
singing for joy and giving thanks
  amid the sound of a great celebration!

5 Why am I discouraged?
  Why is my heart so sad?
I will put my hope in God!
  I will praise him again—
  my Savior and 6 my God!

Now I am deeply discouraged,
  but I will remember you—
even from distant Mount Hermon, the source of the Jordan,
  from the land of Mount Mizar.
7 I hear the tumult of the raging seas
  as your waves and surging tides sweep over me.
8 But each day the LORD pours his unfailing love upon me,
  and through each night I sing his songs,
  praying to God who gives me life.

9 "O God my rock," I cry,
  "Why have you forgotten me?
Why must I wander around in grief,
  oppressed by my enemies?"

42:TITLE Hebrew *maskil.* This may be a literary or musical term.

Question 42:5

Why are these questions some of the most human of all questions? Why is this answer one of the most hopeful of all answers?

10 Their taunts break my bones.
They scoff, "Where is this God of yours?"

11 Why am I discouraged?
Why is my heart so sad?
I will put my hope in God!
I will praise him again—
my Savior and my God!

43

1 Declare me innocent, O God!
Defend me against these ungodly people.
Rescue me from these unjust liars.
2 For you are God, my only safe haven.
Why have you tossed me aside?
Why must I wander around in grief,
oppressed by my enemies?
3 Send out your light and your truth;
let them guide me.
Let them lead me to your holy mountain,
to the place where you live.
4 There I will go to the altar of God,
to God—the source of all my joy.
I will praise you with my harp,
O God, my God!

5 Why am I discouraged?
Why is my heart so sad?
I will put my hope in God!
I will praise him again—
my Savior and my God!

44

For the choir director: A psalm of the descendants of Korah.*

1 O God, we have heard it with our own ears—
our ancestors have told us
of all you did in their day,
in days long ago:
2 You drove out the pagan nations by your power
and gave all the land to our ancestors.
You crushed their enemies
and set our ancestors free.
3 They did not conquer the land with their swords;
it was not their own strong arm that gave
them victory.
It was your right hand and strong arm
and the blinding light from your face that
helped them,
for you loved them.

44:TITLE Hebrew *maskil.* This may be a literary or musical term.

4 You are my King and my God.
You command victories for Israel.*
5 Only by your power can we push back our enemies;
only in your name can we trample our foes.
6 I do not trust in my bow;
I do not count on my sword to save me.
7 You are the one who gives us victory over our enemies;
you disgrace those who hate us.
8 O God, we give glory to you all day long
and constantly praise your name. *Interlude*

9 But now you have tossed us aside in dishonor.
You no longer lead our armies to battle.
10 You make us retreat from our enemies
and allow those who hate us to plunder our land.
11 You have butchered us like sheep
and scattered us among the nations.
12 You sold your precious people for a pittance,
making nothing on the sale.
13 You let our neighbors mock us.
We are an object of scorn and derision to those around us.
14 You have made us the butt of their jokes;
they shake their heads at us in scorn.
15 We can't escape the constant humiliation;
shame is written across our faces.
16 All we hear are the taunts of our mockers.
All we see are our vengeful enemies.

17 All this has happened though we have not forgotten you.
We have not violated your covenant.
18 Our hearts have not deserted you.
We have not strayed from your path.
19 Yet you have crushed us in the jackal's desert home.
You have covered us with darkness and death.
20 If we had forgotten the name of our God
or spread our hands in prayer to foreign gods,
21 God would surely have known it,
for he knows the secrets of every heart.
22 But for your sake we are killed every day;
we are being slaughtered like sheep.

23 Wake up, O Lord! Why do you sleep?
Get up! Do not reject us forever.
24 Why do you look the other way?
Why do you ignore our suffering and oppression?
25 We collapse in the dust,
lying face down in the dirt.
26 Rise up! Help us!
Ransom us because of your unfailing love.

44:4 Hebrew *for Jacob.* The names "Jacob" and "Israel" are often interchanged throughout the Old Testament, referring sometimes to the individual patriarch and sometimes to the nation.

Questions I want to ask

45

For the choir director: A love song to be sung to the tune "Lilies." A psalm of the descendants of Korah.*

1 Beautiful words stir my heart.
I will recite a lovely poem about the king,
for my tongue is like the pen of a skillful poet.

2 You are the most handsome of all.
Gracious words stream from your lips.
God himself has blessed you forever.
3 Put on your sword, O mighty warrior!
You are so glorious, so majestic!
4 In your majesty, ride out to victory,
defending truth, humility, and justice.
Go forth to perform awe-inspiring deeds!
5 Your arrows are sharp, piercing your enemies' hearts.
The nations fall beneath your feet.

6 Your throne, O God,* endures forever and ever.
You rule with a scepter of justice.
7 You love justice and hate evil.
Therefore God, your God, has anointed you,
pouring out the oil of joy on you more than on
anyone else.
8 Myrrh, aloes, and cassia perfume your robes.
In ivory palaces the music of strings entertains you.
9 Kings' daughters are among your noble women.
At your right side stands the queen,
wearing jewelry of finest gold from Ophir!

10 Listen to me, O royal daughter; take to heart
what I say.
Forget your people and your family far away.
11 For your royal husband delights in your beauty;
honor him, for he is your lord.
12 The princess of Tyre* will shower you with gifts.
The wealthy will beg your favor.
13 The bride, a princess, looks glorious
in her golden gown.
14 In her beautiful robes, she is led to the king,
accompanied by her bridesmaids.
15 What a joyful and enthusiastic procession
as they enter the king's palace!

16 Your sons will become kings like their father.
You will make them rulers over many lands.
17 I will bring honor to your name in every generation.
Therefore, the nations will praise you forever
and ever.

45:TITLE Hebrew *maskil.* This may be a literary or musical term. **45:6** Or *Your divine throne.* **45:12** Hebrew *The daughter of Tyre.*

46 *For the choir director: A song of the descendants of Korah, to be sung by soprano voices.**

1 God is our refuge and strength,
always ready to help in times of trouble.
2 So we will not fear when earthquakes come
and the mountains crumble into the sea.
3 Let the oceans roar and foam.
Let the mountains tremble as the waters surge! *Interlude*

4 A river brings joy to the city of our God,
the sacred home of the Most High.
5 God dwells in that city; it cannot be destroyed.
From the very break of day, God will protect it.
6 The nations are in chaos,
and their kingdoms crumble!
God's voice thunders,
and the earth melts!
7 The LORD of Heaven's Armies is here among us;
the God of Israel* is our fortress. *Interlude*

8 Come, see the glorious works of the LORD:
See how he brings destruction upon the world.
9 He causes wars to end throughout the earth.
He breaks the bow and snaps the spear;
he burns the shields with fire.

10 "Be still, and know that I am God!
I will be honored by every nation.
I will be honored throughout the world."

11 The LORD of Heaven's Armies is here among us;
the God of Israel is our fortress. *Interlude*

47 *For the choir director: A psalm of the descendants of Korah.*

1 Come, everyone! Clap your hands!
Shout to God with joyful praise!
2 For the LORD Most High is awesome.
He is the great King of all the earth.
3 He subdues the nations before us,
putting our enemies beneath our feet.
4 He chose the Promised Land as our inheritance,
the proud possession of Jacob's descendants, whom
he loves. *Interlude*

5 God has ascended with a mighty shout.
The LORD has ascended with trumpets blaring.

46:TITLE Hebrew *according to alamoth.* **46:7** Hebrew *of Jacob;* also in 46:11. See note on 44:4.

Make a Difference 46:3

Selah

Stop whatever else is in your mind right now except for this very moment with God. Halt any distraction. Press pause. This moment right now is an interlude in your life. Let the activities prior to this moment be still. Let the activities that will come after this moment wait. You'll get to them soon enough. They don't need you for the next few minutes. Stop. Quiet your soul. Listen.

Selah is a Hebrew word used dozens of times throughout the Psalms. Scholars think it means something like "interlude" or "quiet break." It is used three times in this psalm alone. It seems to be a moment in the activity of a song when everything pauses. In the vacuum of words and sound, people are encouraged to give reflection to God's mighty work. Likewise, take all your to-do lists and hanging-over-the-head worries and put them aside for a moment. Reflect on this passage from Psalm 46 and then *Selah* for a moment.

Difference Maker

Make a quiet break with God a regular pattern in the hectic activity of your life today.

Prayer **48:1**

God, you are greater than I realize, yet you put my life ahead of your own. In humility, I fall to my knees and find you already there waiting for me. Thank you! Amen.

6 Sing praises to God, sing praises;
sing praises to our King, sing praises!
7 For God is the King over all the earth.
Praise him with a psalm.*
8 God reigns above the nations,
sitting on his holy throne.
9 The rulers of the world have gathered together
with the people of the God of Abraham.
For all the kings of the earth belong to God.
He is highly honored everywhere.

48 *A song. A psalm of the descendants of Korah.*

1 How great is the LORD,
how deserving of praise,
in the city of our God,
which sits on his holy mountain!
2 It is high and magnificent;
the whole earth rejoices to see it!
Mount Zion, the holy mountain,*
is the city of the great King!
3 God himself is in Jerusalem's towers,
revealing himself as its defender.

4 The kings of the earth joined forces
and advanced against the city.
5 But when they saw it, they were stunned;
they were terrified and ran away.
6 They were gripped with terror
and writhed in pain like a woman in labor.
7 You destroyed them like the mighty ships
of Tarshish
shattered by a powerful east wind.

8 We had heard of the city's glory,
but now we have seen it ourselves—
the city of the LORD of Heaven's Armies.
It is the city of our God;
he will make it safe forever. *Interlude*

9 O God, we meditate on your unfailing love
as we worship in your Temple.
10 As your name deserves, O God,
you will be praised to the ends of the earth.
Your strong right hand is filled with victory.
11 Let the people on Mount Zion rejoice.
Let all the towns of Judah be glad
because of your justice.

47:7 Hebrew *maskil.* This may be a literary or musical term. **48:2** Or *Mount Zion, in the far north;* Hebrew reads *Mount Zion, the heights of Zaphon.*

12 Go, inspect the city of Jerusalem.*
Walk around and count the many towers.
13 Take note of the fortified walls,
and tour all the citadels,
that you may describe them
to future generations.
14 For that is what God is like.
He is our God forever and ever,
and he will guide us until we die.

49 *For the choir director: A psalm of the descendants of Korah.*

1 Listen to this, all you people!
Pay attention, everyone in the world!
2 High and low,
rich and poor—listen!
3 For my words are wise,
and my thoughts are filled with insight.
4 I listen carefully to many proverbs
and solve riddles with inspiration from
a harp.

5 Why should I fear when trouble comes,
when enemies surround me?
6 They trust in their wealth
and boast of great riches.
7 Yet they cannot redeem themselves from death*
by paying a ransom to God.
8 Redemption does not come so easily,
for no one can ever pay enough
9 to live forever
and never see the grave.

10 Those who are wise must finally die,
just like the foolish and senseless,
leaving all their wealth behind.
11 The grave* is their eternal home,
where they will stay forever.
They may name their estates after themselves,
12 but their fame will not last.
They will die, just like animals.
13 This is the fate of fools,
though they are remembered as being wise.* *Interlude*

14 Like sheep, they are led to the grave,*
where death will be their shepherd.
In the morning the godly will rule over them.

48:12 Hebrew *Zion.* 49:7 Some Hebrew manuscripts read *no one can redeem the life of another.* 49:11 As in Greek and Syriac versions; Hebrew reads *Their inward [thought].* 49:13 The meaning of the Hebrew is uncertain. 49:14 Hebrew *Sheol;* also in 49:14b, 15.

Question 50:1

To say that the Lord has spoken is an understatement. When the Lord, the Mighty One, speaks, things happen. His word summons everything! What are some other places in the Bible where God speaks? What happens when he does? What might happen if you ask God to speak into your life?

Their bodies will rot in the grave,
far from their grand estates.
15 But as for me, God will redeem my life.
He will snatch me from the power of the grave. *Interlude*

16 So don't be dismayed when the wicked grow rich
and their homes become ever more splendid.
17 For when they die, they take nothing with them.
Their wealth will not follow them into the grave.
18 In this life they consider themselves fortunate
and are applauded for their success.
19 But they will die like all before them
and never again see the light of day.
20 People who boast of their wealth don't understand;
they will die, just like animals.

50 *A psalm of Asaph.*

1 The LORD, the Mighty One, is God,
and he has spoken;
he has summoned all humanity
from where the sun rises to where it sets.
2 From Mount Zion, the perfection of beauty,
God shines in glorious radiance.
3 Our God approaches,
and he is not silent.
Fire devours everything in his way,
and a great storm rages around him.
4 He calls on the heavens above and earth below
to witness the judgment of his people.
5 "Bring my faithful people to me—
those who made a covenant with me by giving
sacrifices."
6 Then let the heavens proclaim his justice,
for God himself will be the judge. *Interlude*

7 "O my people, listen as I speak.
Here are my charges against you, O Israel:
I am God, your God!
8 I have no complaint about your sacrifices
or the burnt offerings you constantly offer.
9 But I do not need the bulls from your barns
or the goats from your pens.
10 For all the animals of the forest are mine,
and I own the cattle on a thousand hills.
11 I know every bird on the mountains,
and all the animals of the field are mine.
12 If I were hungry, I would not tell you,
for all the world is mine and everything in it.

13 Do I eat the meat of bulls?
Do I drink the blood of goats?
14 Make thankfulness your sacrifice to God,
and keep the vows you made to the
Most High.
15 Then call on me when you are in trouble,
and I will rescue you,
and you will give me glory."

16 But God says to the wicked:
"Why bother reciting my decrees
and pretending to obey my covenant?
17 For you refuse my discipline
and treat my words like trash.
18 When you see thieves, you approve of them,
and you spend your time with adulterers.
19 Your mouth is filled with wickedness,
and your tongue is full of lies.
20 You sit around and slander your brother—
your own mother's son.
21 While you did all this, I remained silent,
and you thought I didn't care.
But now I will rebuke you,
listing all my charges against you.
22 Repent, all of you who forget me,
or I will tear you apart,
and no one will help you.
23 But giving thanks is a sacrifice that truly
honors me.
If you keep to my path,
I will reveal to you the salvation of God."

51

For the choir director: A psalm of David, regarding the time Nathan the prophet came to him after David had committed adultery with Bathsheba.

1 Have mercy on me, O God,
because of your unfailing love.
Because of your great compassion,
blot out the stain of my sins.
2 Wash me clean from my guilt.
Purify me from my sin.
3 For I recognize my rebellion;
it haunts me day and night.
4 Against you, and you alone, have I sinned;
I have done what is evil in your sight.
You will be proved right in what you say,
and your judgment against me is just.*
5 For I was born a sinner—
yes, from the moment my mother conceived me.

Story Arc **51:1–19**

David

Read 2 Samuel 11–12 for the context of this psalm, which David wrote after his heart had been skewered by guilt. He had been confronted with the gravity of his sin, and he had broken down. This psalm gives us a remarkable example of confession. It also gives us a remarkable example of a plea for restoration.

Read 1 John 1:9 and then take the opportunity to approach God with that kind of heart.

Ps 73:1 ►

51:4 Greek version reads *and you will win your case in court.* Compare Rom 3:4.

6 But you desire honesty from the womb,*
teaching me wisdom even there.

7 Purify me from my sins,* and I will be clean;
wash me, and I will be whiter than snow.
8 Oh, give me back my joy again;
you have broken me—
now let me rejoice.
9 Don't keep looking at my sins.
Remove the stain of my guilt.
10 Create in me a clean heart, O God.
Renew a loyal spirit within me.
11 Do not banish me from your presence,
and don't take your Holy Spirit* from me.

12 Restore to me the joy of your salvation,
and make me willing to obey you.
13 Then I will teach your ways to rebels,
and they will return to you.
14 Forgive me for shedding blood, O God who saves;
then I will joyfully sing of your forgiveness.
15 Unseal my lips, O Lord,
that my mouth may praise you.

16 You do not desire a sacrifice, or I would offer one.
You do not want a burnt offering.
17 The sacrifice you desire is a broken spirit.
You will not reject a broken and repentant heart, O God.
18 Look with favor on Zion and help her;
rebuild the walls of Jerusalem.
19 Then you will be pleased with sacrifices offered in the
right spirit—
with burnt offerings and whole burnt offerings.
Then bulls will again be sacrificed on your altar.

52

For the choir director: A psalm of David, regarding the time Doeg the Edomite said to Saul, "David has gone to see Ahimelech."*

1 Why do you boast about your crimes, great warrior?
Don't you realize God's justice continues forever?
2 All day long you plot destruction.
Your tongue cuts like a sharp razor;
you're an expert at telling lies.
3 You love evil more than good
and lies more than truth. *Interlude*

4 You love to destroy others with your words,
you liar!

51:6 Or *from the heart;* Hebrew reads *in the inward parts.* **51:7** Hebrew *Purify me with the hyssop branch.* **51:11** Or *your spirit of holiness.* **52:TITLE** Hebrew *maskil.* This may be a literary or musical term.

5 But God will strike you down once and for all.
He will pull you from your home
and uproot you from the land of the living. *Interlude*

6 The righteous will see it and be amazed.
They will laugh and say,
7 "Look what happens to mighty warriors
who do not trust in God.
They trust their wealth instead
and grow more and more bold in their
wickedness."

8 But I am like an olive tree, thriving in the house
of God.
I will always trust in God's unfailing love.
9 I will praise you forever, O God,
for what you have done.
I will trust in your good name
in the presence of your faithful people.

Make a Difference 52:8

Thrive

Even though it is small in size, the olive tree has had a tremendous effect throughout history. It is an evergreen tree that can flower and bear fruit for centuries to come. Its leafy branches are a symbol of abundance and peace, often extended after a violent war between enemies. Olive oil is a useful cooking resource, and it is used symbolically as a sign of blessing in many religious ceremonies and rites of passage around the world.

The olive tree is a metaphor for those who follow God's ways and live daily in his love. Though the world may look upon followers of God as insignificant at first, their lasting significance cannot be disputed. They give shade and refuge in every season of life. The difference they make can be seen for generations to come. They supply this world with a source of abundant life and offer the stability of peace. They provide regular daily care for people and blessing for the major events of life. In other words, followers of Jesus make an incredible difference in this world.

Difference Maker

Which aspect of the olive tree illustration can you put into action for the people around you today?

53 *For the choir director: A meditation; a psalm* of David.*

1 Only fools say in their hearts,
"There is no God."
They are corrupt, and their actions are evil;
not one of them does good!

2 God looks down from heaven
on the entire human race;
he looks to see if anyone is truly wise,
if anyone seeks God.
3 But no, all have turned away;
all have become corrupt.*
No one does good,
not a single one!

4 Will those who do evil never learn?
They eat up my people like bread
and wouldn't think of praying to God.
5 Terror will grip them,
terror like they have never known before.
God will scatter the bones of your enemies.
You will put them to shame, for God has
rejected them.

6 Who will come from Mount Zion to rescue Israel?
When God restores his people,
Jacob will shout with joy, and Israel will rejoice.

53:TITLE Hebrew *According to mahalath; a maskil.* These may be literary or musical terms.
53:3 Greek version reads *have become useless.* Compare Rom 3:12.

54

For the choir director: A psalm of David, regarding the time the Ziphites came and said to Saul, "We know where David is hiding." To be accompanied by stringed instruments.*

1 Come with great power, O God, and rescue me!
Defend me with your might.
2 Listen to my prayer, O God.
Pay attention to my plea.
3 For strangers are attacking me;
violent people are trying to kill me.
They care nothing for God. *Interlude*

4 But God is my helper.
The Lord keeps me alive!
5 May the evil plans of my enemies be turned
against them.
Do as you promised and put an end to them.

6 I will sacrifice a voluntary offering to you;
I will praise your name, O LORD,
for it is good.
7 For you have rescued me from my troubles
and helped me to triumph over my enemies.

55

For the choir director: A psalm of David, to be accompanied by stringed instruments.*

1 Listen to my prayer, O God.
Do not ignore my cry for help!
2 Please listen and answer me,
for I am overwhelmed by my troubles.
3 My enemies shout at me,
making loud and wicked threats.
They bring trouble on me
and angrily hunt me down.

4 My heart pounds in my chest.
The terror of death assaults me.
5 Fear and trembling overwhelm me,
and I can't stop shaking.
6 Oh, that I had wings like a dove;
then I would fly away and rest!
7 I would fly far away
to the quiet of the wilderness. *Interlude*
8 How quickly I would escape—
far from this wild storm of hatred.

9 Confuse them, Lord, and frustrate their plans,
for I see violence and conflict in the city.

54:TITLE Hebrew *maskil.* This may be a literary or musical term. **55:TITLE** Hebrew *maskil.* This may be a literary or musical term.

10 Its walls are patrolled day and night
against invaders,
but the real danger is wickedness within
the city.
11 Everything is falling apart;
threats and cheating are rampant in
the streets.

12 It is not an enemy who taunts me—
I could bear that.
It is not my foes who so arrogantly insult me—
I could have hidden from them.
13 Instead, it is you—my equal,
my companion and close friend.
14 What good fellowship we once enjoyed
as we walked together to the house of God.

15 Let death stalk my enemies;
let the grave* swallow them alive,
for evil makes its home within them.

16 But I will call on God,
and the LORD will rescue me.
17 Morning, noon, and night
I cry out in my distress,
and the LORD hears my voice.
18 He ransoms me and keeps me safe
from the battle waged against me,
though many still oppose me.
19 God, who has ruled forever,
will hear me and humble them. *Interlude*
For my enemies refuse to change their ways;
they do not fear God.

20 As for my companion, he betrayed his friends;
he broke his promises.
21 His words are as smooth as butter,
but in his heart is war.
His words are as soothing as lotion,
but underneath are daggers!

22 Give your burdens to the LORD,
and he will take care of you.
He will not permit the godly to slip and fall.

23 But you, O God, will send the wicked
down to the pit of destruction.
Murderers and liars will die young,
but I am trusting you to save me.

55:15 Hebrew *let Sheol.*

Question **55:22**

What burdens do your friends have that they could be giving to the Lord?

Question 56:13

Compare this with Psalm 55:22. How do these verses support your actions in life?

56

For the choir director: A psalm of David, regarding the time the Philistines seized him in Gath. To be sung to the tune "Dove on Distant Oaks."*

1 O God, have mercy on me,
for people are hounding me.
My foes attack me all day long.
2 I am constantly hounded by those who slander me,
and many are boldly attacking me.
3 But when I am afraid,
I will put my trust in you.
4 I praise God for what he has promised.
I trust in God, so why should I be afraid?
What can mere mortals do to me?

5 They are always twisting what I say;
they spend their days plotting to harm me.
6 They come together to spy on me—
watching my every step, eager to kill me.
7 Don't let them get away with their wickedness;
in your anger, O God, bring them down.

8 You keep track of all my sorrows.*
You have collected all my tears in your bottle.
You have recorded each one in your book.

9 My enemies will retreat when I call to you for help.
This I know: God is on my side!
10 I praise God for what he has promised;
yes, I praise the LORD for what he has promised.
11 I trust in God, so why should I be afraid?
What can mere mortals do to me?

12 I will fulfill my vows to you, O God,
and will offer a sacrifice of thanks for your help.
13 For you have rescued me from death;
you have kept my feet from slipping.
So now I can walk in your presence, O God,
in your life-giving light.

57

For the choir director: A psalm of David, regarding the time he fled from Saul and went into the cave. To be sung to the tune "Do Not Destroy!"*

1 Have mercy on me, O God, have mercy!
I look to you for protection.
I will hide beneath the shadow of your wings
until the danger passes by.
2 I cry out to God Most High,*
to God who will fulfill his purpose for me.
3 He will send help from heaven to rescue me,

56:TITLE Hebrew *miktam*. This may be a literary or musical term. **56:8** Or *my wanderings*.
57:TITLE Hebrew *miktam*. This may be a literary or musical term. **57:2** Hebrew *Elohim-Elyon*.

disgracing those who hound me. *Interlude*
My God will send forth his unfailing love and faithfulness.

4 I am surrounded by fierce lions
who greedily devour human prey—
whose teeth pierce like spears and arrows,
and whose tongues cut like swords.

5 Be exalted, O God, above the highest heavens!
May your glory shine over all the earth.

6 My enemies have set a trap for me.
I am weary from distress.
They have dug a deep pit in my path,
but they themselves have fallen into it. *Interlude*

7 My heart is confident in you, O God;
my heart is confident.
No wonder I can sing your praises!
8 Wake up, my heart!
Wake up, O lyre and harp!
I will wake the dawn with my song.
9 I will thank you, Lord, among all the people.
I will sing your praises among the nations.
10 For your unfailing love is as high as the heavens.
Your faithfulness reaches to the clouds.

11 Be exalted, O God, above the highest heavens.
May your glory shine over all the earth.

58

For the choir director: A psalm of David, to be sung to the tune "Do Not Destroy!"*

1 Justice—do you rulers* know the meaning of the word?
Do you judge the people fairly?
2 No! You plot injustice in your hearts.
You spread violence throughout the land.
3 These wicked people are born sinners;
even from birth they have lied and gone their own way.
4 They spit venom like deadly snakes;
they are like cobras that refuse to listen,
5 ignoring the tunes of the snake charmers,
no matter how skillfully they play.

6 Break off their fangs, O God!
Smash the jaws of these lions, O LORD!
7 May they disappear like water into thirsty ground.
Make their weapons useless in their hands.*

58:TITLE Hebrew *miktam.* This may be a literary or musical term. **58:1** Or *you gods.* **58:7** Or *Let them be trodden down and wither like grass.* The meaning of the Hebrew is uncertain.

Prayer 59:10

May I always stand with you, Lord! Amen.

8 May they be like snails that dissolve into slime,
like a stillborn child who will never see the sun.
9 God will sweep them away, both young and old,
faster than a pot heats over burning thorns.

10 The godly will rejoice when they see injustice avenged.
They will wash their feet in the blood of the wicked.
11 Then at last everyone will say,
"There truly is a reward for those who live for God;
surely there is a God who judges justly here on earth."

59

For the choir director: A psalm of David, regarding the time Saul sent soldiers to watch David's house in order to kill him. To be sung to the tune "Do Not Destroy!"*

1 Rescue me from my enemies, O God.
Protect me from those who have come to destroy me.
2 Rescue me from these criminals;
save me from these murderers.
3 They have set an ambush for me.
Fierce enemies are out there waiting, LORD,
though I have not sinned or offended them.
4 I have done nothing wrong,
yet they prepare to attack me.
Wake up! See what is happening and help me!
5 O LORD God of Heaven's Armies, the God of Israel,
wake up and punish those hostile nations.
Show no mercy to wicked traitors. *Interlude*

6 They come out at night,
snarling like vicious dogs
as they prowl the streets.
7 Listen to the filth that comes from their mouths;
their words cut like swords.
"After all, who can hear us?" they sneer.
8 But LORD, you laugh at them.
You scoff at all the hostile nations.
9 You are my strength; I wait for you to rescue me,
for you, O God, are my fortress.
10 In his unfailing love, my God will stand with me.
He will let me look down in triumph on all my enemies.

11 Don't kill them, for my people soon forget such lessons;
stagger them with your power, and bring them to their knees,
O Lord our shield.
12 Because of the sinful things they say,
because of the evil that is on their lips,
let them be captured by their pride,
their curses, and their lies.

59:TITLE Hebrew *miktam.* This may be a literary or musical term.

13 Destroy them in your anger!
Wipe them out completely!
Then the whole world will know
that God reigns in Israel.* *Interlude*

14 My enemies come out at night,
snarling like vicious dogs
as they prowl the streets.
15 They scavenge for food
but go to sleep unsatisfied.*

16 But as for me, I will sing about your power.
Each morning I will sing with joy about your unfailing love.
For you have been my refuge,
a place of safety when I am in distress.
17 O my Strength, to you I sing praises,
for you, O God, are my refuge,
the God who shows me unfailing love.

60 *For the choir director: A psalm* of David useful for teaching, regarding the time David fought Aram-naharaim and Aram-zobah, and Joab returned and killed 12,000 Edomites in the Valley of Salt. To be sung to the tune "Lily of the Testimony."*

1 You have rejected us, O God, and broken our defenses.
You have been angry with us; now restore us to your favor.
2 You have shaken our land and split it open.
Seal the cracks, for the land trembles.
3 You have been very hard on us,
making us drink wine that sent us reeling.
4 But you have raised a banner for those who fear you—
a rallying point in the face of attack. *Interlude*

5 Now rescue your beloved people.
Answer and save us by your power.
6 God has promised this by his holiness*:
"I will divide up Shechem with joy.
I will measure out the valley of Succoth.
7 Gilead is mine,
and Manasseh, too.
Ephraim, my helmet, will produce my warriors,
and Judah, my scepter, will produce my kings.
8 But Moab, my washbasin, will become my servant,
and I will wipe my feet on Edom
and shout in triumph over Philistia."

9 Who will bring me into the fortified city?
Who will bring me victory over Edom?
10 Have you rejected us, O God?
Will you no longer march with our armies?

59:13 Hebrew *in Jacob.* See note on 44:4. **59:15** Or *and growl if they don't get enough.*
60:TITLE Hebrew *miktam.* This may be a literary or musical term. **60:6** Or *in his sanctuary.*

Make a Difference 62:5

Commit Trust

Today may not make much sense; in fact, it may be a struggle. We may feel blind to the way God is working and wonder what in the world is going on. Partially because trust is so important and partially because our struggles are so real, the Bible reinforces the instruction to trust in God. As difficult as it may be to maintain that focus, it is what we must do. Our daily actions are to be subjected to the eternal scope of the Lord, not to our shortsighted understandings.

God sees our daily toil. He is aware that division and deviousness in this world detract from our ability to live fully. He is aware that the sin and destruction of others hinder our own pursuits. God is fully cognizant that things don't always work out the way we want them to work out. We trust everything we do to him because he is going to use our work to make a difference in the world in which we live.

Difference Maker

Use this question as a filter today: What difference would it make to commit this action to the Lord?

11 Oh, please help us against our enemies,
for all human help is useless.
12 With God's help we will do mighty things,
for he will trample down our foes.

61

For the choir director: A psalm of David, to be accompanied by stringed instruments.

1 O God, listen to my cry!
Hear my prayer!
2 From the ends of the earth,
I cry to you for help
when my heart is overwhelmed.
Lead me to the towering rock of safety,
3 for you are my safe refuge,
a fortress where my enemies cannot reach me.
4 Let me live forever in your sanctuary,
safe beneath the shelter of your wings! *Interlude*

5 For you have heard my vows, O God.
You have given me an inheritance reserved for those who fear your name.
6 Add many years to the life of the king!
May his years span the generations!
7 May he reign under God's protection forever.
May your unfailing love and faithfulness watch over him.
8 Then I will sing praises to your name forever
as I fulfill my vows each day.

62

For Jeduthun, the choir director: A psalm of David.

1 I wait quietly before God,
for my victory comes from him.
2 He alone is my rock and my salvation,
my fortress where I will never be shaken.

3 So many enemies against one man—
all of them trying to kill me.
To them I'm just a broken-down wall
or a tottering fence.
4 They plan to topple me from my high position.
They delight in telling lies about me.
They praise me to my face
but curse me in their hearts. *Interlude*

5 Let all that I am wait quietly before God,
for my hope is in him.
6 He alone is my rock and my salvation,
my fortress where I will not be shaken.

7 My victory and honor come from God alone.
He is my refuge, a rock where no enemy can reach me.
8 O my people, trust in him at all times.
Pour out your heart to him,
for God is our refuge. *Interlude*

9 Common people are as worthless as a puff of wind,
and the powerful are not what they appear to be.
If you weigh them on the scales,
together they are lighter than a breath of air.

10 Don't make your living by extortion
or put your hope in stealing.
And if your wealth increases,
don't make it the center of your life.

11 God has spoken plainly,
and I have heard it many times:
Power, O God, belongs to you;
12 unfailing love, O Lord, is yours.
Surely you repay all people
according to what they have done.

63

A psalm of David, regarding a time when David was in the wilderness of Judah.

1 O God, you are my God;
I earnestly search for you.
My soul thirsts for you;
my whole body longs for you
in this parched and weary land
where there is no water.
2 I have seen you in your sanctuary
and gazed upon your power and glory.
3 Your unfailing love is better than life itself;
how I praise you!
4 I will praise you as long as I live,
lifting up my hands to you in prayer.
5 You satisfy me more than the richest feast.
I will praise you with songs of joy.

6 I lie awake thinking of you,
meditating on you through the night.
7 Because you are my helper,
I sing for joy in the shadow of your wings.
8 I cling to you;
your strong right hand holds me securely.

9 But those plotting to destroy me will come to ruin.
They will go down into the depths of the earth.

Make a Difference 63:1

Seek

Finding Bigfoot has become an obsession for some people. They'll go to great lengths to find the creature, even spending thousands of dollars on camo gear, tracking devices, and all-night surveillance equipment. Some will travel around the continent to pursue alleged sightings.

Tracking Bigfoot certainly isn't a lifestyle that's right for everyone, but pursuing God certainly is. What if we had that much passion in our pursuit of God? God has established a kingdom that offers hope, guidance, restoration, and freedom for anyone who wants to be a part of it.

What might we find if we spent our energy seeking God's kingdom? What if we kept a vigilant eye open for God's reign throughout each day? What if we began to expect to find him rummaging in our life? What if we anticipated spotting him in the community around us?

Perhaps we often miss what God is doing because we are not looking. What people seek defines their lives. It's time to ask ourselves what we seek today.

Difference Maker

Seek God's kingdom throughout your day today. Saturate your thoughts with a search for God's reign in creation, in timing, and in interactions.

10 They will die by the sword
and become the food of jackals.
11 But the king will rejoice in God.
All who swear to tell the truth will praise him,
while liars will be silenced.

64 *For the choir director: A psalm of David.*

1 O God, listen to my complaint.
Protect my life from my enemies' threats.
2 Hide me from the plots of this evil mob,
from this gang of wrongdoers.
3 They sharpen their tongues like swords
and aim their bitter words like arrows.
4 They shoot from ambush at the innocent,
attacking suddenly and fearlessly.
5 They encourage each other to do evil
and plan how to set their traps in secret.
"Who will ever notice?" they ask.
6 As they plot their crimes, they say,
"We have devised the perfect plan!"
Yes, the human heart and mind are cunning.

7 But God himself will shoot them with his arrows,
suddenly striking them down.
8 Their own tongues will ruin them,
and all who see them will shake their heads in scorn.
9 Then everyone will be afraid;
they will proclaim the mighty acts of God
and realize all the amazing things he does.
10 The godly will rejoice in the LORD
and find shelter in him.
And those who do what is right
will praise him.

65 *For the choir director: A song. A psalm of David.*

1 What mighty praise, O God,
belongs to you in Zion.
We will fulfill our vows to you,
2 for you answer our prayers.
All of us must come to you.
3 Though we are overwhelmed by our sins,
you forgive them all.
4 What joy for those you choose to bring near,
those who live in your holy courts.
What festivities await us
inside your holy Temple.

5 You faithfully answer our prayers with awesome deeds,
O God our savior.
You are the hope of everyone on earth,
even those who sail on distant seas.
6 You formed the mountains by your power
and armed yourself with mighty strength.
7 You quieted the raging oceans
with their pounding waves
and silenced the shouting of the nations.
8 Those who live at the ends of the earth
stand in awe of your wonders.
From where the sun rises to where it sets,
you inspire shouts of joy.

9 You take care of the earth and water it,
making it rich and fertile.
The river of God has plenty of water;
it provides a bountiful harvest of grain,
for you have ordered it so.
10 You drench the plowed ground with rain,
melting the clods and leveling the ridges.
You soften the earth with showers
and bless its abundant crops.
11 You crown the year with a bountiful harvest;
even the hard pathways overflow with abundance.
12 The grasslands of the wilderness become
a lush pasture,
and the hillsides blossom with joy.
13 The meadows are clothed with flocks of sheep,
and the valleys are carpeted with grain.
They all shout and sing for joy!

66 *For the choir director: A song. A psalm.*

1 Shout joyful praises to God, all the earth!
2 Sing about the glory of his name!
Tell the world how glorious he is.
3 Say to God, "How awesome are your deeds!
Your enemies cringe before your mighty power.
4 Everything on earth will worship you;
they will sing your praises,
shouting your name in glorious songs." *Interlude*

5 Come and see what our God has done,
what awesome miracles he performs for people!
6 He made a dry path through the Red Sea,*
and his people went across on foot.
There we rejoiced in him.

66:6 Hebrew *the sea.*

Write your notes in this space

Question 66:16

If you were asked what God has done for you, what would you say?

7 For by his great power he rules forever.
He watches every movement of the nations;
let no rebel rise in defiance. *Interlude*

8 Let the whole world bless our God
and loudly sing his praises.
9 Our lives are in his hands,
and he keeps our feet from stumbling.
10 You have tested us, O God;
you have purified us like silver.
11 You captured us in your net
and laid the burden of slavery on our backs.
12 Then you put a leader over us.*
We went through fire and flood,
but you brought us to a place of great abundance.

13 Now I come to your Temple with burnt offerings
to fulfill the vows I made to you—
14 yes, the sacred vows that I made
when I was in deep trouble.
15 That is why I am sacrificing burnt offerings
to you—
the best of my rams as a pleasing aroma,
and a sacrifice of bulls and male goats. *Interlude*

16 Come and listen, all you who fear God,
and I will tell you what he did for me.
17 For I cried out to him for help,
praising him as I spoke.
18 If I had not confessed the sin in my heart,
the Lord would not have listened.
19 But God did listen!
He paid attention to my prayer.
20 Praise God, who did not ignore my prayer
or withdraw his unfailing love from me.

67

For the choir director: A song. A psalm, to be accompanied by stringed instruments.

1 May God be merciful and bless us.
May his face smile with favor on us. *Interlude*

2 May your ways be known throughout the earth,
your saving power among people everywhere.
3 May the nations praise you, O God.
Yes, may all the nations praise you.
4 Let the whole world sing for joy,
because you govern the nations with justice
and guide the people of the whole world. *Interlude*

66:12 Or *You made people ride over our heads.*

5 May the nations praise you, O God.
Yes, may all the nations praise you.
6 Then the earth will yield its harvests,
and God, our God, will richly bless us.
7 Yes, God will bless us,
and people all over the world will fear him.

68 *For the choir director: A song. A psalm of David.*

1 Rise up, O God, and scatter your enemies.
Let those who hate God run for their lives.
2 Blow them away like smoke.
Melt them like wax in a fire.
Let the wicked perish in the presence of God.
3 But let the godly rejoice.
Let them be glad in God's presence.
Let them be filled with joy.
4 Sing praises to God and to his name!
Sing loud praises to him who rides the clouds.*
His name is the LORD—
rejoice in his presence!

5 Father to the fatherless, defender of widows—
this is God, whose dwelling is holy.
6 God places the lonely in families;
he sets the prisoners free and gives them joy.
But he makes the rebellious live in a sun-scorched land.

7 O God, when you led your people out from Egypt,
when you marched through the dry wasteland, *Interlude*
8 the earth trembled, and the heavens poured down rain
before you, the God of Sinai,
before God, the God of Israel.
9 You sent abundant rain, O God,
to refresh the weary land.
10 There your people finally settled,
and with a bountiful harvest, O God,
you provided for your needy people.

11 The Lord gives the word,
and a great army* brings the good news.
12 Enemy kings and their armies flee,
while the women of Israel divide the plunder.
13 Even those who lived among the sheepfolds found treasures—
doves with wings of silver
and feathers of gold.
14 The Almighty scattered the enemy kings
like a blowing snowstorm on Mount Zalmon.

68:4 Or *rides through the deserts.* 68:11 Or *a host of women.*

15 The mountains of Bashan are majestic,
with many peaks stretching high into the sky.
16 Why do you look with envy, O rugged mountains,
at Mount Zion, where God has chosen to live,
where the LORD himself will live forever?

17 Surrounded by unnumbered thousands of chariots,
the Lord came from Mount Sinai into his sanctuary.
18 When you ascended to the heights,
you led a crowd of captives.
You received gifts from the people,
even from those who rebelled against you.
Now the LORD God will live among us there.

19 Praise the Lord; praise God our savior!
For each day he carries us in his arms. *Interlude*
20 Our God is a God who saves!
The Sovereign LORD rescues us from death.

21 But God will smash the heads of his enemies,
crushing the skulls of those who love their guilty ways.
22 The Lord says, "I will bring my enemies down from Bashan;
I will bring them up from the depths of the sea.
23 You, my people, will wash* your feet in their blood,
and even your dogs will get their share!"

24 Your procession has come into view, O God—
the procession of my God and King as he goes into
the sanctuary.
25 Singers are in front, musicians behind;
between them are young women playing tambourines.
26 Praise God, all you people of Israel;
praise the LORD, the source of Israel's life.
27 Look, the little tribe of Benjamin leads the way.
Then comes a great throng of rulers from Judah
and all the rulers of Zebulun and Naphtali.

28 Summon your might, O God.*
Display your power, O God, as you have in the past.
29 The kings of the earth are bringing tribute
to your Temple in Jerusalem.
30 Rebuke these enemy nations—
these wild animals lurking in the reeds,
this herd of bulls among the weaker calves.
Make them bring bars of silver in humble tribute.
Scatter the nations that delight in war.
31 Let Egypt come with gifts of precious metals*;
let Ethiopia* bring tribute to God.

68:23 As in Greek and Syriac versions; Hebrew reads *shatter.* **68:28** As in some Hebrew manuscripts and Greek and Syriac versions; most Hebrew manuscripts read *Your God has commanded your strength.* **68:31a** Or *of rich cloth.* **68:31b** Hebrew *Cush.*

32 Sing to God, you kingdoms of the earth.
Sing praises to the Lord. *Interlude*
33 Sing to the one who rides across the ancient heavens,
his mighty voice thundering from the sky.
34 Tell everyone about God's power.
His majesty shines down on Israel;
his strength is mighty in the heavens.
35 God is awesome in his sanctuary.
The God of Israel gives power and strength to his people.

Praise be to God!

69

For the choir director: A psalm of David, to be sung to the tune "Lilies."

1 Save me, O God,
for the floodwaters are up to my neck.
2 Deeper and deeper I sink into the mire;
I can't find a foothold.
I am in deep water,
and the floods overwhelm me.
3 I am exhausted from crying for help;
my throat is parched.
My eyes are swollen with weeping,
waiting for my God to help me.
4 Those who hate me without cause
outnumber the hairs on my head.
Many enemies try to destroy me with lies,
demanding that I give back what I didn't steal.

5 O God, you know how foolish I am;
my sins cannot be hidden from you.
6 Don't let those who trust in you be ashamed because of me,
O Sovereign LORD of Heaven's Armies.
Don't let me cause them to be humiliated,
O God of Israel.
7 For I endure insults for your sake;
humiliation is written all over my face.
8 Even my own brothers pretend they don't know me;
they treat me like a stranger.

9 Passion for your house has consumed me,
and the insults of those who insult you have fallen
on me.
10 When I weep and fast,
they scoff at me.
11 When I dress in burlap to show sorrow,
they make fun of me.
12 I am the favorite topic of town gossip,
and all the drunks sing about me.

Make a Difference

69:1-36

Helping Someone in Grief

What a gut-wrenching psalm! Why do you think God doesn't just fix grief right away? Could it be that God wants us to find a sense of cherishing in the midst of pain? Could it be that God wants us to learn how to be a good friend who stands alongside someone in their deepest feelings of loss?

In the midst of grief, we see that God loves us. We discover that God is there for us even in our most despairing moments. We find out that God maintains control even though our experiences may feel chaotic. We find out that God can use even the worst pains for eternal good. Imagine standing at the cross on Good Friday. Amid pain, we find Jesus is our anchor.

There are some things that we should not do when someone is grieving. We should not avoid them. We should not say, "I know just what you're going through." We should not try to fix the pain. Instead, we're meant to be friends who stand alongside someone in their grief and pain.

Difference Maker

Here's how to help someone going through grief: Talk to the person about what they have lost. Be present. Say, "Can you tell me more about what this has been like for you?" Love them where they are. Check in with them often.

13 But I keep praying to you, LORD,
hoping this time you will show me favor.
In your unfailing love, O God,
answer my prayer with your sure salvation.
14 Rescue me from the mud;
don't let me sink any deeper!
Save me from those who hate me,
and pull me from these deep waters.
15 Don't let the floods overwhelm me,
or the deep waters swallow me,
or the pit of death devour me.

16 Answer my prayers, O LORD,
for your unfailing love is wonderful.
Take care of me,
for your mercy is so plentiful.
17 Don't hide from your servant;
answer me quickly, for I am in deep trouble!
18 Come and redeem me;
free me from my enemies.

19 You know of my shame, scorn, and disgrace.
You see all that my enemies are doing.
20 Their insults have broken my heart,
and I am in despair.
If only one person would show some pity;
if only one would turn and comfort me.
21 But instead, they give me poison* for food;
they offer me sour wine for my thirst.

22 Let the bountiful table set before them become a snare
and their prosperity become a trap.*
23 Let their eyes go blind so they cannot see,
and make their bodies shake continually.*
24 Pour out your fury on them;
consume them with your burning anger.
25 Let their homes become desolate
and their tents be deserted.
26 To the one you have punished, they add insult to injury;
they add to the pain of those you have hurt.
27 Pile their sins up high,
and don't let them go free.
28 Erase their names from the Book of Life;
don't let them be counted among the righteous.

29 I am suffering and in pain.
Rescue me, O God, by your saving power.

69:21 Or *gall.* **69:22** Greek version reads *Let their bountiful table set before them become a snare, / a trap that makes them think all is well. / Let their blessings cause them to stumble, / and let them get what they deserve.* Compare Rom 11:9. **69:23** Greek version reads *and let their backs be bent forever.* Compare Rom 11:10.

30 Then I will praise God's name with singing,
and I will honor him with thanksgiving.
31 For this will please the LORD more than sacrificing cattle,
more than presenting a bull with its horns and hooves.
32 The humble will see their God at work and be glad.
Let all who seek God's help be encouraged.
33 For the LORD hears the cries of the needy;
he does not despise his imprisoned people.

34 Praise him, O heaven and earth,
the seas and all that move in them.
35 For God will save Jerusalem*
and rebuild the towns of Judah.
His people will live there
and settle in their own land.
36 The descendants of those who obey him will inherit
the land,
and those who love him will live there in safety.

Prayer 70:1

Lord, don't let me be afraid to pray this short prayer whenever I need you. Amen.

70

For the choir director: A psalm of David, asking God to remember him.

1 Please, God, rescue me!
Come quickly, LORD, and help me.
2 May those who try to kill me
be humiliated and put to shame.
May those who take delight in my trouble
be turned back in disgrace.
3 Let them be horrified by their shame,
for they said, "Aha! We've got him now!"
4 But may all who search for you
be filled with joy and gladness in you.
May those who love your salvation
repeatedly shout, "God is great!"
5 But as for me, I am poor and needy;
please hurry to my aid, O God.
You are my helper and my savior;
O LORD, do not delay.

71

1 O LORD, I have come to you for protection;
don't let me be disgraced.
2 Save me and rescue me,
for you do what is right.
Turn your ear to listen to me,
and set me free.
3 Be my rock of safety
where I can always hide.
Give the order to save me,
for you are my rock and my fortress.

69:35 Hebrew *Zion*.

4 My God, rescue me from the power of the wicked,
from the clutches of cruel oppressors.
5 O Lord, you alone are my hope.
I've trusted you, O LORD, from childhood.
6 Yes, you have been with me from birth;
from my mother's womb you have cared for me.
No wonder I am always praising you!

7 My life is an example to many,
because you have been my strength and protection.
8 That is why I can never stop praising you;
I declare your glory all day long.
9 And now, in my old age, don't set me aside.
Don't abandon me when my strength is failing.
10 For my enemies are whispering against me.
They are plotting together to kill me.
11 They say, "God has abandoned him.
Let's go and get him,
for no one will help him now."

12 O God, don't stay away.
My God, please hurry to help me.
13 Bring disgrace and destruction on my accusers.
Humiliate and shame those who want to harm me.
14 But I will keep on hoping for your help;
I will praise you more and more.
15 I will tell everyone about your righteousness.
All day long I will proclaim your saving power,
though I am not skilled with words.*
16 I will praise your mighty deeds, O Sovereign LORD.
I will tell everyone that you alone are just.

17 O God, you have taught me from my earliest childhood,
and I constantly tell others about the wonderful things
you do.
18 Now that I am old and gray,
do not abandon me, O God.
Let me proclaim your power to this new generation,
your mighty miracles to all who come after me.

19 Your righteousness, O God, reaches to the
highest heavens.
You have done such wonderful things.
Who can compare with you, O God?
20 You have allowed me to suffer much hardship,
but you will restore me to life again
and lift me up from the depths of the earth.
21 You will restore me to even greater honor
and comfort me once again.

71:15 Or *though I cannot count it.*

22 Then I will praise you with music on the harp,
because you are faithful to your promises, O my God.
I will sing praises to you with a lyre,
O Holy One of Israel.
23 I will shout for joy and sing your praises,
for you have ransomed me.
24 I will tell about your righteous deeds
all day long,
for everyone who tried to hurt me
has been shamed and humiliated.

72 *A psalm of Solomon.*

1 Give your love of justice to the king, O God,
and righteousness to the king's son.
2 Help him judge your people in the right way;
let the poor always be treated fairly.
3 May the mountains yield prosperity for all,
and may the hills be fruitful.
4 Help him to defend the poor,
to rescue the children of the needy,
and to crush their oppressors.
5 May they fear you* as long as the sun shines,
as long as the moon remains in the sky.
Yes, forever!

6 May the king's rule be refreshing like spring rain on freshly
cut grass,
like the showers that water the earth.
7 May all the godly flourish during his reign.
May there be abundant prosperity until the moon is no more.
8 May he reign from sea to sea,
and from the Euphrates River* to the ends of the earth.
9 Desert nomads will bow before him;
his enemies will fall before him in the dust.
10 The western kings of Tarshish and other distant lands
will bring him tribute.
The eastern kings of Sheba and Seba
will bring him gifts.
11 All kings will bow before him,
and all nations will serve him.

12 He will rescue the poor when they cry to him;
he will help the oppressed, who have no one to defend them.
13 He feels pity for the weak and the needy,
and he will rescue them.
14 He will redeem them from oppression and violence,
for their lives are precious to him.

72:5 Greek version reads *May they endure.* 72:8 Hebrew *the river.*

Why this matters!

15 Long live the king!
  May the gold of Sheba be given to him.
May the people always pray for him
  and bless him all day long.
16 May there be abundant grain throughout the land,
  flourishing even on the hilltops.
May the fruit trees flourish like the trees of Lebanon,
  and may the people thrive like grass in a field.
17 May the king's name endure forever;
  may it continue as long as the sun shines.
May all nations be blessed through him
  and bring him praise.

18 Praise the LORD God, the God of Israel,
  who alone does such wonderful things.
19 Praise his glorious name forever!
  Let the whole earth be filled with his glory.
Amen and amen!

20 (This ends the prayers of David son of Jesse.)

BOOK THREE (Psalms 73–89)

73

A psalm of Asaph.

1 Truly God is good to Israel,
  to those whose hearts are pure.
2 But as for me, I almost lost my footing.
  My feet were slipping, and I was almost gone.
3 For I envied the proud
  when I saw them prosper despite their wickedness.
4 They seem to live such painless lives;
  their bodies are so healthy and strong.
5 They don't have troubles like other people;
  they're not plagued with problems like everyone else.
6 They wear pride like a jeweled necklace
  and clothe themselves with cruelty.
7 These fat cats have everything
  their hearts could ever wish for!
8 They scoff and speak only evil;
  in their pride they seek to crush others.
9 They boast against the very heavens,
  and their words strut throughout the earth.
10 And so the people are dismayed and confused,
  drinking in all their words.
11 "What does God know?" they ask.
  "Does the Most High even know what's happening?"
12 Look at these wicked people—
  enjoying a life of ease while their riches multiply.

Story Arc **73:1**

Asaph

Asaph was one of the main worship leaders for both King David (1 Chronicles 6:39) and King Solomon (2 Chronicles 5:12). He was a prolific Levite who authored numerous psalms focused on God's rule over both the macro (big picture) and micro (personal) aspects of life. Asaph's first words here are a testimony to his faith. What do you notice in this psalm about the genuine nature of Asaph's walk with the Lord?

Prov 1:1 ►

13 Did I keep my heart pure for nothing?
Did I keep myself innocent for no reason?
14 I get nothing but trouble all day long;
every morning brings me pain.

15 If I had really spoken this way to others,
I would have been a traitor to your people.
16 So I tried to understand why the wicked prosper.
But what a difficult task it is!
17 Then I went into your sanctuary, O God,
and I finally understood the destiny of the wicked.
18 Truly, you put them on a slippery path
and send them sliding over the cliff to destruction.
19 In an instant they are destroyed,
completely swept away by terrors.
20 When you arise, O Lord,
you will laugh at their silly ideas
as a person laughs at dreams in the morning.

21 Then I realized that my heart was bitter,
and I was all torn up inside.
22 I was so foolish and ignorant—
I must have seemed like a senseless animal to you.
23 Yet I still belong to you;
you hold my right hand.
24 You guide me with your counsel,
leading me to a glorious destiny.
25 Whom have I in heaven but you?
I desire you more than anything on earth.
26 My health may fail, and my spirit may grow weak,
but God remains the strength of my heart;
he is mine forever.

27 Those who desert him will perish,
for you destroy those who abandon you.
28 But as for me, how good it is to be near God!
I have made the Sovereign LORD my shelter,
and I will tell everyone about the wonderful things you do.

74

A psalm of Asaph.*

1 O God, why have you rejected us so long?
Why is your anger so intense against the sheep of your own pasture?
2 Remember that we are the people you chose long ago,
the tribe you redeemed as your own special possession!
And remember Jerusalem,* your home here on earth.
3 Walk through the awful ruins of the city;
see how the enemy has destroyed your sanctuary.

74:TITLE Hebrew *maskil.* This may be a literary or musical term. 74:2 Hebrew *Mount Zion.*

4 There your enemies shouted their victorious
battle cries;
there they set up their battle standards.
5 They swung their axes
like woodcutters in a forest.
6 With axes and picks,
they smashed the carved paneling.
7 They burned your sanctuary to the ground.
They defiled the place that bears your name.
8 Then they thought, "Let's destroy everything!"
So they burned down all the places where God
was worshiped.

9 We no longer see your miraculous signs.
All the prophets are gone,
and no one can tell us when it will end.
10 How long, O God, will you allow our enemies to
insult you?
Will you let them dishonor your name forever?
11 Why do you hold back your strong right hand?
Unleash your powerful fist and destroy them.

12 You, O God, are my king from ages past,
bringing salvation to the earth.
13 You split the sea by your strength
and smashed the heads of the sea monsters.
14 You crushed the heads of Leviathan*
and let the desert animals eat him.
15 You caused the springs and streams to gush forth,
and you dried up rivers that never run dry.
16 Both day and night belong to you;
you made the starlight* and the sun.
17 You set the boundaries of the earth,
and you made both summer and winter.

18 See how these enemies insult you, LORD.
A foolish nation has dishonored your name.
19 Don't let these wild beasts destroy your turtledoves.
Don't forget your suffering people forever.

20 Remember your covenant promises,
for the land is full of darkness and violence!
21 Don't let the downtrodden be humiliated again.
Instead, let the poor and needy praise your name.

22 Arise, O God, and defend your cause.
Remember how these fools insult you all day long.
23 Don't overlook what your enemies have said
or their growing uproar.

74:14 The identification of Leviathan is disputed, ranging from an earthly creature to a mythical sea monster in ancient literature. **74:16** Or *moon;* Hebrew reads *light.*

75 *For the choir director: A psalm of Asaph. A song to be sung to the tune "Do Not Destroy!"*

1 We thank you, O God!
We give thanks because you are near.
People everywhere tell of your wonderful deeds.

2 God says, "At the time I have planned,
I will bring justice against the wicked.
3 When the earth quakes and its people live in turmoil,
I am the one who keeps its foundations firm. *Interlude*

4 "I warned the proud, 'Stop your boasting!'
I told the wicked, 'Don't raise your fists!
5 Don't raise your fists in defiance at the heavens
or speak with such arrogance.'"
6 For no one on earth—from east or west,
or even from the wilderness—
should raise a defiant fist.*
7 It is God alone who judges;
he decides who will rise and who will fall.
8 For the LORD holds a cup in his hand
that is full of foaming wine mixed with spices.
He pours out the wine in judgment,
and all the wicked must drink it,
draining it to the dregs.

9 But as for me, I will always proclaim what God has done;
I will sing praises to the God of Jacob.
10 For God says, "I will break the strength of the wicked,
but I will increase the power of the godly."

Prayer **75:1**

Lord Jesus, I call on your name. Be near to me now in the reality of my life. Amen.

76 *For the choir director: A psalm of Asaph. A song to be accompanied by stringed instruments.*

1 God is honored in Judah;
his name is great in Israel.
2 Jerusalem* is where he lives;
Mount Zion is his home.
3 There he has broken the fiery arrows of the enemy,
the shields and swords and weapons of war. *Interlude*

4 You are glorious and more majestic
than the everlasting mountains.*
5 Our boldest enemies have been plundered.
They lie before us in the sleep of death.
No warrior could lift a hand against us.
6 At the blast of your breath, O God of Jacob,
their horses and chariots lay still.

75:6 Hebrew *should lift.* **76:2** Hebrew *Salem,* another name for Jerusalem. **76:4** As in Greek version; Hebrew reads *than mountains filled with beasts of prey.*

Make a Difference 78:4

Sharing Truths

Why is it that many who have long ago left the realm of childhood can learn more from children's messages than from all the hymns and sermons of "big church"? Perhaps this is because God is discoverable to children through stories and parables. Children's messages capture the simplistic beauty of Jesus while also drawing us into a more profound life, and adults have an inherent need to share their faith rather than sit on it. Something spectacular happens to people when they see young people come alive with vibrancy of faith and hope and love through Jesus.

Faith should not be reserved to the realm of adulthood. Faith is not yours to keep inside you; rather, it is yours to give to others no matter how young you are. Someone at some point introduced you to a life-changing relationship with God, and now it is your turn to pass on that faith creatively and passionately.

Difference Maker

Connect with the children's ministry director at your local church and ask how you can support children's ministry (either with time or resources or encouragement).

7 No wonder you are greatly feared!
Who can stand before you when your anger explodes?
8 From heaven you sentenced your enemies;
the earth trembled and stood silent before you.
9 You stand up to judge those who do evil, O God,
and to rescue the oppressed of the earth. *Interlude*
10 Human defiance only enhances your glory,
for you use it as a weapon.*

11 Make vows to the LORD your God, and keep them.
Let everyone bring tribute to the Awesome One.
12 For he breaks the pride of princes,
and the kings of the earth fear him.

77

For Jeduthun, the choir director: A psalm of Asaph.

1 I cry out to God; yes, I shout.
Oh, that God would listen to me!
2 When I was in deep trouble,
I searched for the Lord.
All night long I prayed, with hands lifted
toward heaven,
but my soul was not comforted.
3 I think of God, and I moan,
overwhelmed with longing for his help. *Interlude*

4 You don't let me sleep.
I am too distressed even to pray!
5 I think of the good old days,
long since ended,
6 when my nights were filled with joyful songs.
I search my soul and ponder the difference now.
7 Has the Lord rejected me forever?
Will he never again be kind to me?
8 Is his unfailing love gone forever?
Have his promises permanently failed?
9 Has God forgotten to be gracious?
Has he slammed the door on his compassion? *Interlude*
10 And I said, "This is my fate;
the Most High has turned his hand against me."
11 But then I recall all you have done, O LORD;
I remember your wonderful deeds of long ago.
12 They are constantly in my thoughts.
I cannot stop thinking about your mighty works.

13 O God, your ways are holy.
Is there any god as mighty as you?

76:10 The meaning of the Hebrew is uncertain.

14 You are the God of great wonders!
You demonstrate your awesome power among the nations.
15 By your strong arm, you redeemed your people,
the descendants of Jacob and Joseph. *Interlude*

16 When the Red Sea* saw you, O God,
its waters looked and trembled!
The sea quaked to its very depths.
17 The clouds poured down rain;
the thunder rumbled in the sky.
Your arrows of lightning flashed.
18 Your thunder roared from the whirlwind;
the lightning lit up the world!
The earth trembled and shook.
19 Your road led through the sea,
your pathway through the mighty waters—
a pathway no one knew was there!
20 You led your people along that road like a flock of sheep,
with Moses and Aaron as their shepherds.

78 *A psalm* of Asaph.*

1 O my people, listen to my instructions.
Open your ears to what I am saying,
2 for I will speak to you in a parable.
I will teach you hidden lessons from our past—
3 stories we have heard and known,
stories our ancestors handed down to us.
4 We will not hide these truths from our children;
we will tell the next generation
about the glorious deeds of the LORD,
about his power and his mighty wonders.
5 For he issued his laws to Jacob;
he gave his instructions to Israel.
He commanded our ancestors
to teach them to their children,
6 so the next generation might know them—
even the children not yet born—
and they in turn will teach their own children.
7 So each generation should set its hope anew on God,
not forgetting his glorious miracles
and obeying his commands.
8 Then they will not be like their ancestors—
stubborn, rebellious, and unfaithful,
refusing to give their hearts to God.

9 The warriors of Ephraim, though armed with bows,
turned their backs and fled on the day of battle.

77:16 Hebrew *the waters.* **78:TITLE** Hebrew *maskil.* This may be a literary or musical term.

Make a Difference

78:5-7

Generational Vision

Broaden your scope today. As you go about your own business, consider the effect that your actions have not just immediately but also in the long term. Consider the effect your actions have not just on you or on your immediate family or friends but also on those who will come after you.

The scope of vision in the Bible is incredibly forward-thinking. When we make our lives only about the here and now, when we make church or faith about the current benefit, we squander the immensity of influence visualized within Scripture. Our faith was meant to affect generations. Those who came before us passed faith down through the generations, and eventually that faith in Jesus was entrusted to us. Now it is our turn to equip with faith those who follow us so that they not only embrace faith but also are enabled to empower the generations after them to follow Jesus.

Difference Maker

Ask yourself this question: "Am I helping to equip people younger than I am in such a way that they will be able to pass faith on to the generations that follow them?"

10 They did not keep God's covenant
and refused to live by his instructions.
11 They forgot what he had done—
the great wonders he had shown them,
12 the miracles he did for their ancestors
on the plain of Zoan in the land of Egypt.
13 For he divided the sea and led them through,
making the water stand up like walls!
14 In the daytime he led them by a cloud,
and all night by a pillar of fire.
15 He split open the rocks in the wilderness
to give them water, as from a gushing spring.
16 He made streams pour from the rock,
making the waters flow down like a river!

17 Yet they kept on sinning against him,
rebelling against the Most High in the desert.
18 They stubbornly tested God in their hearts,
demanding the foods they craved.
19 They even spoke against God himself, saying,
"God can't give us food in the wilderness.
20 Yes, he can strike a rock so water gushes out,
but he can't give his people bread and meat."
21 When the LORD heard them, he was furious.
The fire of his wrath burned against Jacob.
Yes, his anger rose against Israel,
22 for they did not believe God
or trust him to care for them.
23 But he commanded the skies to open;
he opened the doors of heaven.
24 He rained down manna for them to eat;
he gave them bread from heaven.
25 They ate the food of angels!
God gave them all they could hold.
26 He released the east wind in the heavens
and guided the south wind by his mighty power.
27 He rained down meat as thick as dust—
birds as plentiful as the sand on the seashore!
28 He caused the birds to fall within their camp
and all around their tents.
29 The people ate their fill.
He gave them what they craved.
30 But before they satisfied their craving,
while the meat was yet in their mouths,
31 the anger of God rose against them,
and he killed their strongest men.
He struck down the finest of Israel's young men.

32 But in spite of this, the people kept sinning.
Despite his wonders, they refused to trust him.

33 So he ended their lives in failure,
their years in terror.
34 When God began killing them,
they finally sought him.
They repented and took God seriously.
35 Then they remembered that God was their rock,
that God Most High* was their redeemer.
36 But all they gave him was lip service;
they lied to him with their tongues.
37 Their hearts were not loyal to him.
They did not keep his covenant.
38 Yet he was merciful and forgave their sins
and did not destroy them all.
Many times he held back his anger
and did not unleash his fury!
39 For he remembered that they were merely mortal,
gone like a breath of wind that never returns.

40 Oh, how often they rebelled against him in the wilderness
and grieved his heart in that dry wasteland.
41 Again and again they tested God's patience
and provoked the Holy One of Israel.
42 They did not remember his power
and how he rescued them from their enemies.
43 They did not remember his miraculous signs in Egypt,
his wonders on the plain of Zoan.
44 For he turned their rivers into blood,
so no one could drink from the streams.
45 He sent vast swarms of flies to consume them
and hordes of frogs to ruin them.
46 He gave their crops to caterpillars;
their harvest was consumed by locusts.
47 He destroyed their grapevines with hail
and shattered their sycamore-figs with sleet.
48 He abandoned their cattle to the hail,
their livestock to bolts of lightning.
49 He loosed on them his fierce anger—
all his fury, rage, and hostility.
He dispatched against them
a band of destroying angels.
50 He turned his anger against them;
he did not spare the Egyptians' lives
but ravaged them with the plague.
51 He killed the oldest son in each Egyptian family,
the flower of youth throughout the land of Egypt.*
52 But he led his own people like a flock of sheep,
guiding them safely through the wilderness.
53 He kept them safe so they were not afraid;
but the sea covered their enemies.

78:35 Hebrew *El-Elyon*. **78:51** Hebrew *in the tents of Ham.*

Remember to take notes!

54 He brought them to the border of his holy land,
to this land of hills he had won for them.
55 He drove out the nations before them;
he gave them their inheritance by lot.
He settled the tribes of Israel into their homes.

56 But they kept testing and rebelling against God Most High.
They did not obey his laws.
57 They turned back and were as faithless as their parents.
They were as undependable as a crooked bow.
58 They angered God by building shrines to other gods;
they made him jealous with their idols.
59 When God heard them, he was very angry,
and he completely rejected Israel.
60 Then he abandoned his dwelling at Shiloh,
the Tabernacle where he had lived among the people.
61 He allowed the Ark of his might to be captured;
he surrendered his glory into enemy hands.
62 He gave his people over to be butchered by the sword,
because he was so angry with his own people—his special possession.
63 Their young men were killed by fire;
their young women died before singing their wedding songs.
64 Their priests were slaughtered,
and their widows could not mourn their deaths.

65 Then the Lord rose up as though waking from sleep,
like a warrior aroused from a drunken stupor.
66 He routed his enemies
and sent them to eternal shame.
67 But he rejected Joseph's descendants;
he did not choose the tribe of Ephraim.
68 He chose instead the tribe of Judah,
and Mount Zion, which he loved.
69 There he built his sanctuary as high as the heavens,
as solid and enduring as the earth.
70 He chose his servant David,
calling him from the sheep pens.
71 He took David from tending the ewes and lambs
and made him the shepherd of Jacob's descendants—
God's own people, Israel.
72 He cared for them with a true heart
and led them with skillful hands.

79 *A psalm of Asaph.*

1 O God, pagan nations have conquered your land,
your special possession.
They have defiled your holy Temple
and made Jerusalem a heap of ruins.

2 They have left the bodies of your servants
as food for the birds of heaven.
The flesh of your godly ones
has become food for the wild animals.
3 Blood has flowed like water all around Jerusalem;
no one is left to bury the dead.
4 We are mocked by our neighbors,
an object of scorn and derision to those around us.

5 O LORD, how long will you be angry with us?
Forever?
How long will your jealousy burn like fire?
6 Pour out your wrath on the nations that refuse to
acknowledge you—
on kingdoms that do not call upon your name.
7 For they have devoured your people Israel,*
making the land a desolate wilderness.
8 Do not hold us guilty for the sins of our ancestors!
Let your compassion quickly meet our needs,
for we are on the brink of despair.

9 Help us, O God of our salvation!
Help us for the glory of your name.
Save us and forgive our sins
for the honor of your name.
10 Why should pagan nations be allowed to scoff,
asking, "Where is their God?"
Show us your vengeance against the nations,
for they have spilled the blood of your servants.
11 Listen to the moaning of the prisoners.
Demonstrate your great power by saving those
condemned to die.

12 O Lord, pay back our neighbors seven times
for the scorn they have hurled at you.
13 Then we your people, the sheep of your pasture,
will thank you forever and ever,
praising your greatness from generation to generation.

Question 79:9

Have you invited Jesus to be your Savior? You can turn to the back of the Bible and pray through the section on "How to Accept Jesus as Your Lord and Savior."

80

For the choir director: A psalm of Asaph, to be sung to the tune "Lilies of the Covenant."

1 Please listen, O Shepherd of Israel,
you who lead Joseph's descendants like a flock.
O God, enthroned above the cherubim,
display your radiant glory
2 to Ephraim, Benjamin, and Manasseh.
Show us your mighty power.
Come to rescue us!

79:7 Hebrew *devoured Jacob.* See note on 44:4.

3 Turn us again to yourself, O God.
Make your face shine down upon us.
Only then will we be saved.
4 O LORD God of Heaven's Armies,
how long will you be angry with our prayers?
5 You have fed us with sorrow
and made us drink tears by the bucketful.
6 You have made us the scorn* of neighboring nations.
Our enemies treat us as a joke.

7 Turn us again to yourself, O God of Heaven's Armies.
Make your face shine down upon us.
Only then will we be saved.
8 You brought us from Egypt like a grapevine;
you drove away the pagan nations and transplanted us
into your land.
9 You cleared the ground for us,
and we took root and filled the land.
10 Our shade covered the mountains;
our branches covered the mighty cedars.
11 We spread our branches west to the Mediterranean Sea;
our shoots spread east to the Euphrates River.*
12 But now, why have you broken down our walls
so that all who pass by may steal our fruit?
13 The wild boar from the forest devours it,
and the wild animals feed on it.

14 Come back, we beg you, O God of Heaven's Armies.
Look down from heaven and see our plight.
Take care of this grapevine
15 that you yourself have planted,
this son you have raised for yourself.
16 For we are chopped up and burned by our enemies.
May they perish at the sight of your frown.
17 Strengthen the man you love,
the son of your choice.
18 Then we will never abandon you again.
Revive us so we can call on your name once more.

19 Turn us again to yourself, O LORD God
of Heaven's Armies.
Make your face shine down upon us.
Only then will we be saved.

81

*For the choir director: A psalm of Asaph, to be accompanied by a stringed instrument.**

1 Sing praises to God, our strength.
Sing to the God of Jacob.

80:6 As in Syriac version; Hebrew reads *the strife.* 80:11 Hebrew *west to the sea, . . . east to the river.* 81:TITLE Hebrew *according to the gittith.*

2 Sing! Beat the tambourine.
Play the sweet lyre and the harp.
3 Blow the ram's horn at new moon,
and again at full moon to call a festival!
4 For this is required by the decrees of Israel;
it is a regulation of the God of Jacob.
5 He made it a law for Israel*
when he attacked Egypt to set us free.

I heard an unknown voice say,
6 "Now I will take the load from your shoulders;
I will free your hands from their heavy tasks.
7 You cried to me in trouble, and I saved you;
I answered out of the thundercloud
and tested your faith when there was no water
at Meribah. *Interlude*

8 "Listen to me, O my people, while I give you stern warnings.
O Israel, if you would only listen to me!
9 You must never have a foreign god;
you must not bow down before a false god.
10 For it was I, the LORD your God,
who rescued you from the land of Egypt.
Open your mouth wide, and I will fill it with good
things.

11 "But no, my people wouldn't listen.
Israel did not want me around.
12 So I let them follow their own stubborn desires,
living according to their own ideas.
13 Oh, that my people would listen to me!
Oh, that Israel would follow me, walking in my paths!
14 How quickly I would then subdue their enemies!
How soon my hands would be upon their foes!
15 Those who hate the LORD would cringe before him;
they would be doomed forever.
16 But I would feed you with the finest wheat.
I would satisfy you with wild honey from the rock."

82 *A psalm of Asaph.*

1 God presides over heaven's court;
he pronounces judgment on the heavenly beings:
2 "How long will you hand down unjust decisions
by favoring the wicked? *Interlude*

3 "Give justice to the poor and the orphan;
uphold the rights of the oppressed and the destitute.

Question 82:3

In what creative ways could you obey this verse?

81:5 Hebrew *for Joseph.*

4 Rescue the poor and helpless;
deliver them from the grasp of evil people.
5 But these oppressors know nothing;
they are so ignorant!
They wander about in darkness,
while the whole world is shaken to the core.
6 I say, 'You are gods;
you are all children of the Most High.
7 But you will die like mere mortals
and fall like every other ruler.'"

8 Rise up, O God, and judge the earth,
for all the nations belong to you.

83 *A song. A psalm of Asaph.*

1 O God, do not be silent!
Do not be deaf.
Do not be quiet, O God.
2 Don't you hear the uproar of your enemies?
Don't you see that your arrogant enemies are rising up?
3 They devise crafty schemes against your people;
they conspire against your precious ones.
4 "Come," they say, "let us wipe out Israel as a nation.
We will destroy the very memory of its existence."
5 Yes, this was their unanimous decision.
They signed a treaty as allies against you—
6 these Edomites and Ishmaelites;
Moabites and Hagrites;
7 Gebalites, Ammonites, and Amalekites;
and people from Philistia and Tyre.
8 Assyria has joined them, too,
and is allied with the descendants of Lot. *Interlude*

9 Do to them as you did to the Midianites
and as you did to Sisera and Jabin at the
Kishon River.
10 They were destroyed at Endor,
and their decaying corpses fertilized the soil.
11 Let their mighty nobles die as Oreb and Zeeb did.
Let all their princes die like Zebah and Zalmunna,
12 for they said, "Let us seize for our own use
these pasturelands of God!"
13 O my God, scatter them like tumbleweed,
like chaff before the wind!
14 As a fire burns a forest
and as a flame sets mountains ablaze,
15 chase them with your fierce storm;
terrify them with your tempest.

16 Utterly disgrace them
until they submit to your name, O LORD.
17 Let them be ashamed and terrified forever.
Let them die in disgrace.
18 Then they will learn that you alone are called the LORD,
that you alone are the Most High,
supreme over all the earth.

84 *For the choir director: A psalm of the descendants of Korah, to be accompanied by a stringed instrument.**

1 How lovely is your dwelling place,
O LORD of Heaven's Armies.
2 I long, yes, I faint with longing
to enter the courts of the LORD.
With my whole being, body and soul,
I will shout joyfully to the living God.
3 Even the sparrow finds a home,
and the swallow builds her nest and raises her young
at a place near your altar,
O LORD of Heaven's Armies, my King and my God!
4 What joy for those who can live in your house,
always singing your praises. *Interlude*

5 What joy for those whose strength comes from
the LORD,
who have set their minds on a pilgrimage to Jerusalem.
6 When they walk through the Valley of Weeping,*
it will become a place of refreshing springs.
The autumn rains will clothe it with blessings.
7 They will continue to grow stronger,
and each of them will appear before God in Jerusalem.*

8 O LORD God of Heaven's Armies, hear my prayer.
Listen, O God of Jacob. *Interlude*

9 O God, look with favor upon the king, our shield!
Show favor to the one you have anointed.

10 A single day in your courts
is better than a thousand anywhere else!
I would rather be a gatekeeper in the house of my God
than live the good life in the homes of the wicked.
11 For the LORD God is our sun and our shield.
He gives us grace and glory.
The LORD will withhold no good thing
from those who do what is right.
12 O LORD of Heaven's Armies,
what joy for those who trust in you.

84:TITLE Hebrew *according to the gittith.* **84:6** Or *Valley of Poplars;* Hebrew reads *valley of Baca.*
84:7 Hebrew *Zion.*

Prayer **84:10**

Lord, let the focus of my life be on you. Help me get my priorities in order! Amen.

Question **84:10**

Why is this verse true?

Question 86:1

Would you feel comfortable asking God to do these things for you? What kind of an attitude of heart does it take to be able to approach God with these requests?

85 *For the choir director: A psalm of the descendants of Korah.*

1 LORD, you poured out blessings on your land!
You restored the fortunes of Israel.*
2 You forgave the guilt of your people—
yes, you covered all their sins. *Interlude*
3 You held back your fury.
You kept back your blazing anger.

4 Now restore us again, O God of our salvation.
Put aside your anger against us once more.
5 Will you be angry with us always?
Will you prolong your wrath to all generations?
6 Won't you revive us again,
so your people can rejoice in you?
7 Show us your unfailing love, O LORD,
and grant us your salvation.

8 I listen carefully to what God the LORD is saying,
for he speaks peace to his faithful people.
But let them not return to their foolish ways.
9 Surely his salvation is near to those who fear him,
so our land will be filled with his glory.

10 Unfailing love and truth have met together.
Righteousness and peace have kissed!
11 Truth springs up from the earth,
and righteousness smiles down from heaven.
12 Yes, the LORD pours down his blessings.
Our land will yield its bountiful harvest.
13 Righteousness goes as a herald before him,
preparing the way for his steps.

86 *A prayer of David.*

1 Bend down, O LORD, and hear my prayer;
answer me, for I need your help.
2 Protect me, for I am devoted to you.
Save me, for I serve you and trust you.
You are my God.
3 Be merciful to me, O Lord,
for I am calling on you constantly.
4 Give me happiness, O Lord,
for I give myself to you.
5 O Lord, you are so good, so ready to forgive,
so full of unfailing love for all who ask for your help.
6 Listen closely to my prayer, O LORD;

85:1 Hebrew *of Jacob.* See note on 44:4.

hear my urgent cry.
7 I will call to you whenever I'm in trouble,
and you will answer me.

8 No pagan god is like you, O Lord.
None can do what you do!
9 All the nations you made
will come and bow before you, Lord;
they will praise your holy name.
10 For you are great and perform wonderful deeds.
You alone are God.

11 Teach me your ways, O LORD,
that I may live according to your truth!
Grant me purity of heart,
so that I may honor you.
12 With all my heart I will praise you, O Lord my God.
I will give glory to your name forever,
13 for your love for me is very great.
You have rescued me from the depths of death.*

14 O God, insolent people rise up against me;
a violent gang is trying to kill me.
You mean nothing to them.
15 But you, O Lord,
are a God of compassion and mercy,
slow to get angry
and filled with unfailing love and faithfulness.
16 Look down and have mercy on me.
Give your strength to your servant;
save me, the son of your servant.
17 Send me a sign of your favor.
Then those who hate me will be put to shame,
for you, O LORD, help and comfort me.

87

A song. A psalm of the descendants of Korah.

1 On the holy mountain
stands the city founded by the LORD.
2 He loves the city of Jerusalem
more than any other city in Israel.*
3 O city of God,
what glorious things are said of you! *Interlude*

4 I will count Egypt* and Babylon among those who know me—
also Philistia and Tyre, and even distant Ethiopia.*
They have all become citizens of Jerusalem!

86:13 Hebrew *of Sheol.* **87:2** Hebrew *He loves the gates of Zion more than all the dwellings of Jacob.* See note on 44:4. **87:4a** Hebrew *Rahab,* the name of a mythical sea monster that represents chaos in ancient literature. The name is used here as a poetic name for Egypt. **87:4b** Hebrew *Cush.*

Make a Difference

88:1-18

Anguish

Grief is a deep anguish of the heart, a punch in the soul, a devastating loss to the mind. Grief can show up in your life when you experience the loss of a loved one, the loss of an entire year of a sport because of an injury, or the loss of a pet. Grief can rip you apart when someone close to you gets a divorce or a friend rejects you or a dream gets crushed.

Difference Maker

Think of something that grieves you and, just like the writer of this psalm, cry out to God.

Question **88:14**

This is a psalm of total despair. Is it okay to pray like this? Why would this psalm be allowed to be in the Bible?

5 Regarding Jerusalem* it will be said,
"Everyone enjoys the rights of citizenship there."
And the Most High will personally bless this city.
6 When the LORD registers the nations, he will say,
"They have all become citizens of Jerusalem." *Interlude*

7 The people will play flutes* and sing,
"The source of my life springs from Jerusalem!"

88

For the choir director: A psalm of the descendants of Korah. A song to be sung to the tune "The Suffering of Affliction." A psalm of Heman the Ezrahite.*

1 O LORD, God of my salvation,
I cry out to you by day.
I come to you at night.
2 Now hear my prayer;
listen to my cry.
3 For my life is full of troubles,
and death* draws near.
4 I am as good as dead,
like a strong man with no strength left.
5 They have left me among the dead,
and I lie like a corpse in a grave.
I am forgotten,
cut off from your care.
6 You have thrown me into the lowest pit,
into the darkest depths.
7 Your anger weighs me down;
with wave after wave you have engulfed me. *Interlude*

8 You have driven my friends away
by making me repulsive to them.
I am in a trap with no way of escape.
9 My eyes are blinded by my tears.
Each day I beg for your help, O LORD;
I lift my hands to you for mercy.
10 Are your wonderful deeds of any use to the dead?
Do the dead rise up and praise you? *Interlude*

11 Can those in the grave declare your unfailing love?
Can they proclaim your faithfulness in the place of destruction?*
12 Can the darkness speak of your wonderful deeds?
Can anyone in the land of forgetfulness talk about your righteousness?
13 O LORD, I cry out to you.
I will keep on pleading day by day.
14 O LORD, why do you reject me?
Why do you turn your face from me?

87:5 Hebrew *Zion.* 87:7 Or *will dance.* 88:TITLE Hebrew *maskil.* This may be a literary or musical term. 88:3 Hebrew *Sheol.* 88:11 Hebrew *in Abaddon?*

15 I have been sick and close to death since my youth.
I stand helpless and desperate before your terrors.
16 Your fierce anger has overwhelmed me.
Your terrors have paralyzed me.
17 They swirl around me like floodwaters all day long.
They have engulfed me completely.
18 You have taken away my companions and loved ones.
Darkness is my closest friend.

89

A psalm of Ethan the Ezrahite.*

1 I will sing of the LORD's unfailing love forever!
Young and old will hear of your faithfulness.
2 Your unfailing love will last forever.
Your faithfulness is as enduring as the heavens.

3 The LORD said, "I have made a covenant with David,
my chosen servant.
I have sworn this oath to him:
4 'I will establish your descendants as kings forever;
they will sit on your throne from now until eternity.'" *Interlude*
5 All heaven will praise your great wonders, LORD;
myriads of angels will praise you for your faithfulness.
6 For who in all of heaven can compare with the LORD?
What mightiest angel is anything like the LORD?
7 The highest angelic powers stand in awe of God.
He is far more awesome than all who surround his throne.
8 O LORD God of Heaven's Armies!
Where is there anyone as mighty as you, O LORD?
You are entirely faithful.

9 You rule the oceans.
You subdue their storm-tossed waves.
10 You crushed the great sea monster.*
You scattered your enemies with your mighty arm.
11 The heavens are yours, and the earth is yours;
everything in the world is yours—you created it all.
12 You created north and south.
Mount Tabor and Mount Hermon praise your name.
13 Powerful is your arm!
Strong is your hand!
Your right hand is lifted high in glorious strength.
14 Righteousness and justice are the foundation of your throne.
Unfailing love and truth walk before you as attendants.
15 Happy are those who hear the joyful call to worship,
for they will walk in the light of your presence, LORD.
16 They rejoice all day long in your wonderful reputation.
They exult in your righteousness.

89:TITLE Hebrew *maskil.* This may be a literary or musical term. **89:10** Hebrew *Rahab,* the name of a mythical sea monster that represents chaos in ancient literature.

17 You are their glorious strength.
It pleases you to make us strong.
18 Yes, our protection comes from the LORD,
and he, the Holy One of Israel, has given us our king.

19 Long ago you spoke in a vision to your faithful people.
You said, "I have raised up a warrior.
I have selected him from the common people to
be king.
20 I have found my servant David.
I have anointed him with my holy oil.
21 I will steady him with my hand;
with my powerful arm I will make him strong.
22 His enemies will not defeat him,
nor will the wicked overpower him.
23 I will beat down his adversaries before him
and destroy those who hate him.
24 My faithfulness and unfailing love will be with him,
and by my authority he will grow in power.
25 I will extend his rule over the sea,
his dominion over the rivers.
26 And he will call out to me, 'You are my Father,
my God, and the Rock of my salvation.'
27 I will make him my firstborn son,
the mightiest king on earth.
28 I will love him and be kind to him forever;
my covenant with him will never end.
29 I will preserve an heir for him;
his throne will be as endless as the days of heaven.
30 But if his descendants forsake my instructions
and fail to obey my regulations,
31 if they do not obey my decrees
and fail to keep my commands,
32 then I will punish their sin with the rod,
and their disobedience with beating.
33 But I will never stop loving him
nor fail to keep my promise to him.
34 No, I will not break my covenant;
I will not take back a single word I said.
35 I have sworn an oath to David,
and in my holiness I cannot lie:
36 His dynasty will go on forever;
his kingdom will endure as the sun.
37 It will be as eternal as the moon,
my faithful witness in the sky!" *Interlude*

38 But now you have rejected him and cast him off.
You are angry with your anointed king.
39 You have renounced your covenant with him;
you have thrown his crown in the dust.

40 You have broken down the walls protecting him
and ruined every fort defending him.
41 Everyone who comes along has robbed him,
and he has become a joke to his neighbors.
42 You have strengthened his enemies
and made them all rejoice.
43 You have made his sword useless
and refused to help him in battle.
44 You have ended his splendor
and overturned his throne.
45 You have made him old before his time
and publicly disgraced him. *Interlude*

46 O LORD, how long will this go on?
Will you hide yourself forever?
How long will your anger burn like fire?
47 Remember how short my life is,
how empty and futile this human existence!
48 No one can live forever; all will die.
No one can escape the power of the grave.* *Interlude*

49 Lord, where is your unfailing love?
You promised it to David with a faithful pledge.
50 Consider, Lord, how your servants are disgraced!
I carry in my heart the insults of so many people.
51 Your enemies have mocked me, O LORD;
they mock your anointed king wherever he goes.

52 Praise the LORD forever!
Amen and amen!

BOOK FOUR (Psalms 90–106)

90

A prayer of Moses, the man of God.

1 Lord, through all the generations
you have been our home!
2 Before the mountains were born,
before you gave birth to the earth and the world,
from beginning to end, you are God.

3 You turn people back to dust, saying,
"Return to dust, you mortals!"
4 For you, a thousand years are as a passing day,
as brief as a few night hours.
5 You sweep people away like dreams that disappear.
They are like grass that springs up in the
morning.

89:48 Hebrew *of Sheol.*

How God is at work here

Question 90:12

Why does this psalm ask us to think about how short life is? What difference will that make?

6 In the morning it blooms and flourishes,
but by evening it is dry and withered.
7 We wither beneath your anger;
we are overwhelmed by your fury.
8 You spread out our sins before you—
our secret sins—and you see them all.
9 We live our lives beneath your wrath,
ending our years with a groan.

10 Seventy years are given to us!
Some even live to eighty.
But even the best years are filled with pain and trouble;
soon they disappear, and we fly away.
11 Who can comprehend the power of your anger?
Your wrath is as awesome as the fear you deserve.
12 Teach us to realize the brevity of life,
so that we may grow in wisdom.

13 O LORD, come back to us!
How long will you delay?
Take pity on your servants!
14 Satisfy us each morning with your unfailing love,
so we may sing for joy to the end of our lives.
15 Give us gladness in proportion to our former misery!
Replace the evil years with good.
16 Let us, your servants, see you work again;
let our children see your glory.
17 And may the Lord our God show us his approval
and make our efforts successful.
Yes, make our efforts successful!

91

1 Those who live in the shelter of the Most High
will find rest in the shadow of the Almighty.
2 This I declare about the LORD:
He alone is my refuge, my place of safety;
he is my God, and I trust him.
3 For he will rescue you from every trap
and protect you from deadly disease.
4 He will cover you with his feathers.
He will shelter you with his wings.
His faithful promises are your armor and protection.
5 Do not be afraid of the terrors of the night,
nor the arrow that flies in the day.
6 Do not dread the disease that stalks in darkness,
nor the disaster that strikes at midday.
7 Though a thousand fall at your side,
though ten thousand are dying around you,
these evils will not touch you.
8 Just open your eyes,
and see how the wicked are punished.

9 If you make the LORD your refuge,
if you make the Most High your shelter,
10 no evil will conquer you;
no plague will come near your home.
11 For he will order his angels
to protect you wherever you go.
12 They will hold you up with their hands
so you won't even hurt your foot on a stone.
13 You will trample upon lions and cobras;
you will crush fierce lions and serpents under your feet!

14 The LORD says, "I will rescue those who love me.
I will protect those who trust in my name.
15 When they call on me, I will answer;
I will be with them in trouble.
I will rescue and honor them.
16 I will reward them with a long life
and give them my salvation."

92 *A psalm. A song to be sung on the Sabbath Day.*

1 It is good to give thanks to the LORD,
to sing praises to the Most High.
2 It is good to proclaim your unfailing love in the morning,
your faithfulness in the evening,
3 accompanied by a ten-stringed instrument, a harp,
and the melody of a lyre.

4 You thrill me, LORD, with all you have done for me!
I sing for joy because of what you have done.
5 O LORD, what great works you do!
And how deep are your thoughts.
6 Only a simpleton would not know,
and only a fool would not understand this:
7 Though the wicked sprout like weeds
and evildoers flourish,
they will be destroyed forever.

8 But you, O LORD, will be exalted forever.
9 Your enemies, LORD, will surely perish;
all evildoers will be scattered.
10 But you have made me as strong as a wild ox.
You have anointed me with the finest oil.
11 My eyes have seen the downfall of my enemies;
my ears have heard the defeat of my wicked opponents.
12 But the godly will flourish like palm trees
and grow strong like the cedars of Lebanon.
13 For they are transplanted to the LORD's own house.
They flourish in the courts of our God.

Make a Difference

92:12–14

Flourish

Palm trees in Israel are known as date palms, flourishing for at least five thousand years. They are a symbol of refuge for travelers and an abundant economic resource for fruit, syrups, grains, fibers, and timber. Their leaves were used to celebrate victory, such as when Jesus entered Jerusalem on what has come to be known as Palm Sunday.

Cedar trees were once abundant in Lebanon. They were tall (sometimes 120 feet) and strongly rooted. Their wood was world-renowned for its beautiful red color, for its lightweight yet resilient strength, and for being resistant to decay and repellent to insects. When people choose to root themselves in the patterns of God, they flourish and bless the world like these two types of trees.

Difference Maker

Do one of the following today: sit under a palm tree and enjoy life with God (if you are too far north, look at a picture and drool) or make something with cedar wood, remembering the richness of God at work in your life.

Question 93:4

When would it be helpful in your life for you to remember this?

14 Even in old age they will still produce fruit;
they will remain vital and green.
15 They will declare, "The LORD is just!
He is my rock!
There is no evil in him!"

93

1 The LORD is king! He is robed in majesty.
Indeed, the LORD is robed in majesty and armed with strength.
The world stands firm
and cannot be shaken.

2 Your throne, O LORD, has stood from time immemorial.
You yourself are from the everlasting past.
3 The floods have risen up, O LORD.
The floods have roared like thunder;
the floods have lifted their pounding waves.
4 But mightier than the violent raging of the seas,
mightier than the breakers on the shore—
the LORD above is mightier than these!
5 Your royal laws cannot be changed.
Your reign, O LORD, is holy forever and ever.

94

1 O LORD, the God of vengeance,
O God of vengeance, let your glorious justice shine forth!
2 Arise, O Judge of the earth.
Give the proud what they deserve.
3 How long, O LORD?
How long will the wicked be allowed to gloat?
4 How long will they speak with arrogance?
How long will these evil people boast?
5 They crush your people, LORD,
hurting those you claim as your own.
6 They kill widows and foreigners
and murder orphans.
7 "The LORD isn't looking," they say,
"and besides, the God of Israel* doesn't care."

8 Think again, you fools!
When will you finally catch on?
9 Is he deaf—the one who made your ears?
Is he blind—the one who formed your eyes?
10 He punishes the nations—won't he also punish you?
He knows everything—doesn't he also know what you are doing?
11 The LORD knows people's thoughts;
he knows they are worthless!

12 Joyful are those you discipline, LORD,
those you teach with your instructions.

94:7 Hebrew *of Jacob*. See note on 44:4.

13 You give them relief from troubled times
until a pit is dug to capture the wicked.
14 The LORD will not reject his people;
he will not abandon his special possession.
15 Judgment will again be founded on justice,
and those with virtuous hearts will pursue it.

16 Who will protect me from the wicked?
Who will stand up for me against evildoers?
17 Unless the LORD had helped me,
I would soon have settled in the silence of the grave.
18 I cried out, "I am slipping!"
but your unfailing love, O LORD, supported me.
19 When doubts filled my mind,
your comfort gave me renewed hope and cheer.

20 Can unjust leaders claim that God is on their side—
leaders whose decrees permit injustice?
21 They gang up against the righteous
and condemn the innocent to death.
22 But the LORD is my fortress;
my God is the mighty rock where I hide.
23 God will turn the sins of evil people back on them.
He will destroy them for their sins.
The LORD our God will destroy them.

95

1 Come, let us sing to the LORD!
Let us shout joyfully to the Rock of our salvation.
2 Let us come to him with thanksgiving.
Let us sing psalms of praise to him.
3 For the LORD is a great God,
a great King above all gods.
4 He holds in his hands the depths of the earth
and the mightiest mountains.
5 The sea belongs to him, for he made it.
His hands formed the dry land, too.

6 Come, let us worship and bow down.
Let us kneel before the LORD our maker,
7 for he is our God.
We are the people he watches over,
the flock under his care.

If only you would listen to his voice today!
8 The LORD says, "Don't harden your hearts as Israel did
at Meribah,
as they did at Massah in the wilderness.
9 For there your ancestors tested and tried my patience,
even though they saw everything I did.
10 For forty years I was angry with them, and I said,

Question **95:1-11**

The *Make a Difference Youth Bible* is not meant to be a quiet-time devotional. It is more like a loud time with God! Growing in our faith requires that we *do* something. Read through Psalm 95 and answer this question: What is something from Psalm 95 that you could do today?

'They are a people whose hearts turn away from me.
They refuse to do what I tell them.'
11 So in my anger I took an oath:
'They will never enter my place of rest.'"

96

1 Sing a new song to the LORD!
Let the whole earth sing to the LORD!
2 Sing to the LORD; praise his name.
Each day proclaim the good news that he saves.
3 Publish his glorious deeds among the nations.
Tell everyone about the amazing things he does.
4 Great is the LORD! He is most worthy of praise!
He is to be feared above all gods.
5 The gods of other nations are mere idols,
but the LORD made the heavens!
6 Honor and majesty surround him;
strength and beauty fill his sanctuary.

7 O nations of the world, recognize the LORD;
recognize that the LORD is glorious and strong.
8 Give to the LORD the glory he deserves!
Bring your offering and come into his courts.
9 Worship the LORD in all his holy splendor.
Let all the earth tremble before him.
10 Tell all the nations, "The LORD reigns!"
The world stands firm and cannot be shaken.
He will judge all peoples fairly.

11 Let the heavens be glad, and the earth rejoice!
Let the sea and everything in it shout his praise!
12 Let the fields and their crops burst out with joy!
Let the trees of the forest sing for joy
13 before the LORD, for he is coming!
He is coming to judge the earth.
He will judge the world with justice,
and the nations with his truth.

Make a Difference 96:3

Publish

Let's say for a moment that in the future, you discover the permanent cure for cancer. Then let's imagine that instead of publishing that cure, instead of sharing it and making the cure known, you decide that you will keep it to yourself. Then let's say that you were able to meet yourself in the future and have a blunt conversation. What would you say to yourself?

The Psalms urge people who have discovered the good news to make the good news known to those around them. This is what God has called each one of us to do as well—we are to publish what he has done so those around us can know.

Difference Maker

Brainstorm for a moment: What do you personally know about Jesus? Do you know someone who needs to know these things too?

97

1 The LORD is king!
Let the earth rejoice!
Let the farthest coastlands be glad.
2 Dark clouds surround him.
Righteousness and justice are the foundation of his throne.
3 Fire spreads ahead of him
and burns up all his foes.
4 His lightning flashes out across the world.
The earth sees and trembles.
5 The mountains melt like wax before the LORD,
before the Lord of all the earth.
6 The heavens proclaim his righteousness;
every nation sees his glory.

7 Those who worship idols are disgraced—
all who brag about their worthless gods—
for every god must bow to him.
8 Jerusalem* has heard and rejoiced,
and all the towns of Judah are glad
because of your justice, O LORD!
9 For you, O LORD, are supreme over all the earth;
you are exalted far above all gods.

10 You who love the LORD, hate evil!
He protects the lives of his godly people
and rescues them from the power of the wicked.
11 Light shines on the godly,
and joy on those whose hearts are right.
12 May all who are godly rejoice in the LORD
and praise his holy name!

Prayer 97:11

Jesus, I call on your name today. Be with me in a renewed way. Make me right in your eyes, make me mighty for your plans, and make me a light for this world that you love so much. Amen.

98 *A psalm.*

1 Sing a new song to the LORD,
for he has done wonderful deeds.
His right hand has won a mighty victory;
his holy arm has shown his saving power!
2 The LORD has announced his victory
and has revealed his righteousness to every nation!
3 He has remembered his promise to love and be faithful to Israel.
The ends of the earth have seen the victory of our God.

4 Shout to the LORD, all the earth;
break out in praise and sing for joy!
5 Sing your praise to the LORD with the harp,
with the harp and melodious song,
6 with trumpets and the sound of the ram's horn.
Make a joyful symphony before the LORD, the King!

7 Let the sea and everything in it shout his praise!
Let the earth and all living things join in.
8 Let the rivers clap their hands in glee!
Let the hills sing out their songs of joy
9 before the LORD,
for he is coming to judge the earth.
He will judge the world with justice,
and the nations with fairness.

99
1 The LORD is king!
Let the nations tremble!
He sits on his throne between the cherubim.
Let the whole earth quake!

97:8 Hebrew *Zion.*

Make a Difference

100:3

We Are His

If a committee were to examine every aspect of your day—all your emails and internet traffic, how you spend your money, what you say, what you think—would it be clear that the Lord is your God? Would your actions from an hour ago or an hour from now be in line with someone who follows Jesus?

The irony here is that whether we act like it or not, the Lord already is God. What we think about him or the way that we treat him has nothing to do with whether he is God. Our opinion doesn't change who the Lord is at his very core. What is changeable, what is subject to our opinion and actions, is whether we will acknowledge that the Lord is our God, that we are his people, and that he is our Shepherd.

Difference Maker

Think ahead to one hour from now. What could you do that would offer evidence that the Lord is your God?

2 The LORD sits in majesty in Jerusalem,*
exalted above all the nations.
3 Let them praise your great and awesome name.
Your name is holy!
4 Mighty King, lover of justice,
you have established fairness.
You have acted with justice
and righteousness throughout Israel.*
5 Exalt the LORD our God!
Bow low before his feet, for he is holy!

6 Moses and Aaron were among his priests;
Samuel also called on his name.
They cried to the LORD for help,
and he answered them.
7 He spoke to Israel from the pillar of cloud,
and they followed the laws and decrees
he gave them.
8 O LORD our God, you answered them.
You were a forgiving God to them,
but you punished them when they went wrong.

9 Exalt the LORD our God,
and worship at his holy mountain in Jerusalem,
for the LORD our God is holy!

100 *A psalm of thanksgiving.*

1 Shout with joy to the LORD, all the earth!
2 Worship the LORD with gladness.
Come before him, singing with joy.
3 Acknowledge that the LORD is God!
He made us, and we are his.*
We are his people, the sheep of his pasture.
4 Enter his gates with thanksgiving;
go into his courts with praise.
Give thanks to him and praise his name.
5 For the LORD is good.
His unfailing love continues forever,
and his faithfulness continues to each generation.

101 *A psalm of David.*

1 I will sing of your love and justice, LORD.
I will praise you with songs.
2 I will be careful to live a blameless life—
when will you come to help me?

99:2 Hebrew *Zion.* **99:4** Hebrew *Jacob.* See note on 44:4. **100:3** As in an alternate reading in the Masoretic Text; the other alternate and some ancient versions read *and not we ourselves.*

I will lead a life of integrity
in my own home.
3 I will refuse to look at
anything vile and vulgar.
I hate all who deal crookedly;
I will have nothing to do with them.
4 I will reject perverse ideas
and stay away from every evil.
5 I will not tolerate people who slander their neighbors.
I will not endure conceit and pride.

6 I will search for faithful people
to be my companions.
Only those who are above reproach
will be allowed to serve me.
7 I will not allow deceivers to serve in my house,
and liars will not stay in my presence.
8 My daily task will be to ferret out the wicked
and free the city of the LORD from their grip.

102

A prayer of one overwhelmed with trouble, pouring out problems before the LORD.

1 LORD, hear my prayer!
Listen to my plea!
2 Don't turn away from me
in my time of distress.
Bend down to listen,
and answer me quickly when I call to you.
3 For my days disappear like smoke,
and my bones burn like red-hot coals.
4 My heart is sick, withered like grass,
and I have lost my appetite.
5 Because of my groaning,
I am reduced to skin and bones.
6 I am like an owl in the desert,
like a little owl in a far-off wilderness.
7 I lie awake,
lonely as a solitary bird on the roof.
8 My enemies taunt me day after day.
They mock and curse me.
9 I eat ashes for food.
My tears run down into my drink
10 because of your anger and wrath.
For you have picked me up and thrown me out.
11 My life passes as swiftly as the evening shadows.
I am withering away like grass.

12 But you, O LORD, will sit on your throne forever.
Your fame will endure to every generation.

Make a Difference

100:4

With Thanksgiving

As you look back on your last few years, how would you describe God's work in your life and in the lives of those around you? Are you able to see his faithfulness, even in the difficulties? Are you able to recognize his hands through the ebbs and flows of daily routines? Do you notice those moments when he tried to get your attention? Did you feel him tugging at your heart to respond to others, to care, to love, and to do the right thing in the hard moments? Can you feel him drawing you gently into his presence right now? The Lord loves you. From generation to generation, from season to season, from month to month, and even on this very day, he is faithful to give you his unfailing love.

Difference Maker

Go to the homes of friends and neighbors collecting cans of food for a local food pantry. When someone gives you a can, hand them a thank-you note with Psalm 100:4-5 written on it.

Question 102:18

How will this psalm help future generations praise the Lord? What does this psalm provide that they will need?

13 You will arise and have mercy on Jerusalem*—
and now is the time to pity her,
now is the time you promised to help.
14 For your people love every stone in her walls
and cherish even the dust in her streets.
15 Then the nations will tremble before the LORD.
The kings of the earth will tremble before
his glory.
16 For the LORD will rebuild Jerusalem.
He will appear in his glory.
17 He will listen to the prayers of the destitute.
He will not reject their pleas.

18 Let this be recorded for future generations,
so that a people not yet born will praise the LORD.
19 Tell them the LORD looked down
from his heavenly sanctuary.
He looked down to earth from heaven
20 to hear the groans of the prisoners,
to release those condemned to die.
21 And so the LORD's fame will be celebrated in Zion,
his praises in Jerusalem,
22 when multitudes gather together
and kingdoms come to worship the LORD.

23 He broke my strength in midlife,
cutting short my days.
24 But I cried to him, "O my God, who lives forever,
don't take my life while I am so young!
25 Long ago you laid the foundation of the earth
and made the heavens with your hands.
26 They will perish, but you remain forever;
they will wear out like old clothing.
You will change them like a garment
and discard them.
27 But you are always the same;
you will live forever.
28 The children of your people
will live in security.
Their children's children
will thrive in your presence."

103 *A psalm of David.*

1 Let all that I am praise the LORD;
with my whole heart, I will praise his holy name.
2 Let all that I am praise the LORD;
may I never forget the good things he does for me.

102:13 Hebrew *Zion;* also in 102:16.

3 He forgives all my sins
and heals all my diseases.
4 He redeems me from death
and crowns me with love and tender mercies.
5 He fills my life with good things.
My youth is renewed like the eagle's!

6 The LORD gives righteousness
and justice to all who are treated unfairly.

7 He revealed his character to Moses
and his deeds to the people of Israel.
8 The LORD is compassionate and merciful,
slow to get angry and filled with
unfailing love.
9 He will not constantly accuse us,
nor remain angry forever.
10 He does not punish us for all our sins;
he does not deal harshly with us, as we deserve.
11 For his unfailing love toward those who fear him
is as great as the height of the heavens
above the earth.
12 He has removed our sins as far from us
as the east is from the west.
13 The LORD is like a father to his children,
tender and compassionate to those who fear him.
14 For he knows how weak we are;
he remembers we are only dust.
15 Our days on earth are like grass;
like wildflowers, we bloom and die.
16 The wind blows, and we are gone—
as though we had never been here.
17 But the love of the LORD remains forever
with those who fear him.
His salvation extends to the children's children
18 of those who are faithful to his covenant,
of those who obey his commandments!

19 The LORD has made the heavens his throne;
from there he rules over everything.

20 Praise the LORD, you angels,
you mighty ones who carry out his plans,
listening for each of his commands.
21 Yes, praise the LORD, you armies of angels
who serve him and do his will!
22 Praise the LORD, everything he has created,
everything in all his kingdom.

Let all that I am praise the LORD.

104

1 Let all that I am praise the LORD.

O LORD my God, how great you are!
You are robed with honor and majesty.
2 You are dressed in a robe of light.
You stretch out the starry curtain of the heavens;
3 you lay out the rafters of your home in the rain clouds.
You make the clouds your chariot;
you ride upon the wings of the wind.
4 The winds are your messengers;
flames of fire are your servants.*

5 You placed the world on its foundation
so it would never be moved.
6 You clothed the earth with floods of water,
water that covered even the mountains.
7 At your command, the water fled;
at the sound of your thunder, it hurried away.
8 Mountains rose and valleys sank
to the levels you decreed.
9 Then you set a firm boundary for the seas,
so they would never again cover the earth.

10 You make springs pour water into the ravines,
so streams gush down from the mountains.
11 They provide water for all the animals,
and the wild donkeys quench their thirst.
12 The birds nest beside the streams
and sing among the branches of the trees.
13 You send rain on the mountains from your
heavenly home,
and you fill the earth with the fruit of your labor.
14 You cause grass to grow for the livestock
and plants for people to use.
You allow them to produce food from the earth—
15 wine to make them glad,
olive oil to soothe their skin,
and bread to give them strength.
16 The trees of the LORD are well cared for—
the cedars of Lebanon that he planted.
17 There the birds make their nests,
and the storks make their homes in the cypresses.
18 High in the mountains live the wild goats,
and the rocks form a refuge for the hyraxes.*

19 You made the moon to mark the seasons,
and the sun knows when to set.
20 You send the darkness, and it becomes night,
when all the forest animals prowl about.

104:4 Greek version reads *He sends his angels like the winds, / his servants like flames of fire.* Compare Heb 1:7. **104:18** Or *coneys,* or *rock badgers.*

21 Then the young lions roar for their prey,
stalking the food provided by God.
22 At dawn they slink back
into their dens to rest.
23 Then people go off to their work,
where they labor until evening.

24 O LORD, what a variety of things you have made!
In wisdom you have made them all.
The earth is full of your creatures.
25 Here is the ocean, vast and wide,
teeming with life of every kind,
both large and small.
26 See the ships sailing along,
and Leviathan,* which you made to play in the sea.

27 They all depend on you
to give them food as they need it.
28 When you supply it, they gather it.
You open your hand to feed them,
and they are richly satisfied.
29 But if you turn away from them, they panic.
When you take away their breath,
they die and turn again to dust.
30 When you give them your breath,* life is created,
and you renew the face of the earth.

31 May the glory of the LORD continue forever!
The LORD takes pleasure in all he has made!
32 The earth trembles at his glance;
the mountains smoke at his touch.

33 I will sing to the LORD as long as I live.
I will praise my God to my last breath!
34 May all my thoughts be pleasing to him,
for I rejoice in the LORD.
35 Let all sinners vanish from the face of the earth;
let the wicked disappear forever.

Let all that I am praise the LORD.

Praise the LORD!

105

1 Give thanks to the LORD and proclaim his greatness.
Let the whole world know what he has done.
2 Sing to him; yes, sing his praises.
Tell everyone about his wonderful deeds.
3 Exult in his holy name;
rejoice, you who worship the LORD.

104:26 The identification of Leviathan is disputed, ranging from an earthly creature to a mythical sea monster in ancient literature. **104:30** Or *When you send your Spirit.*

Make a Difference

104:1-35

Staying On Track with God

Psalm 104 is an awe-inspiring ride through the skillful wonder of the earth and sky and oceans. The waters are stretched out like a garment and bursting through the ravines, the mountains are erupting, the seas are teeming with life, the whales are playing games, the lions are depending on God, the birds are nestled in the trees along the streams, the night is active with life, and the day provides for the gathering of food.

Sadly, something disrupts the rhythm of creation at the end of this psalm. The psalmist was jarred from considering God's wondrous work when the shocking vision of the work of humanity entered his mind. The writer's mind was suddenly flooded and defiled by the thought. The murders, the wars, the adultery, the profanity, the abuse, the destruction, the lying, the betrayal, the envy, the arrogance—all this insurrection stood in stark contrast to the beautiful dance of the planet. The point of the psalm is to refuse to step into the fall of creation and instead be reconciled to a waltz with God on the dance floor that he has made.

Difference Maker

Dance in wonder at what God has made. Hike or drive or just sit marveling at the wonder of creation while you pray for humanity to be restored to God.

Make a Difference

105:1–45

God Remembers His Promises

God's house is full of joy. Do you know why? Not one broken promise can be found anywhere within it. Not only does God make promises to those he loves, but he also keeps those promises.

For instance, he told Abraham that one of his future children would become a blessing as numerous as the stars. He promised David that he would have a future son who would rule on his throne forever. He promised Mary that she would have a child who would save the world from its sins. He promised the apostles that he would send the Holy Spirit. He promised also to come again to judge evil and restore his creation. He promised Paul that he would use him to bring the good news of Jesus to people who had never heard of it. He promised he would bring freedom and healing and joy and abundant life. He promised to be with us always, even to the very end of the age.

God's house is full of joy because he keeps his promises.

Difference Maker

Tell people today how God remembers his promises for them.

4 Search for the LORD and for his strength;
continually seek him.
5 Remember the wonders he has performed,
his miracles, and the rulings he has given,
6 you children of his servant Abraham,
you descendants of Jacob, his chosen ones.

7 He is the LORD our God.
His justice is seen throughout the land.
8 He always stands by his covenant—
the commitment he made to a thousand generations.
9 This is the covenant he made with Abraham
and the oath he swore to Isaac.
10 He confirmed it to Jacob as a decree,
and to the people of Israel as a never-ending
covenant:
11 "I will give you the land of Canaan
as your special possession."

12 He said this when they were few in number,
a tiny group of strangers in Canaan.
13 They wandered from nation to nation,
from one kingdom to another.
14 Yet he did not let anyone oppress them.
He warned kings on their behalf:
15 "Do not touch my chosen people,
and do not hurt my prophets."

16 He called for a famine on the land of Canaan,
cutting off its food supply.
17 Then he sent someone to Egypt ahead of them—
Joseph, who was sold as a slave.
18 They bruised his feet with fetters
and placed his neck in an iron collar.
19 Until the time came to fulfill his dreams,*
the LORD tested Joseph's character.
20 Then Pharaoh sent for him and set him free;
the ruler of the nation opened his prison door.
21 Joseph was put in charge of all the king's household;
he became ruler over all the king's possessions.
22 He could instruct* the king's aides as he pleased
and teach the king's advisers.

23 Then Israel arrived in Egypt;
Jacob lived as a foreigner in the land of Ham.
24 And the LORD multiplied the people of Israel
until they became too mighty for their enemies.
25 Then he turned the Egyptians against the Israelites,
and they plotted against the LORD's servants.

105:19 Hebrew *his word.* 105:22 As in Greek and Syriac versions; Hebrew reads *bind* or *imprison.*

26 But the LORD sent his servant Moses,
along with Aaron, whom he had chosen.
27 They performed miraculous signs among the Egyptians,
and wonders in the land of Ham.
28 The LORD blanketed Egypt in darkness,
for they had defied* his commands to let his people go.
29 He turned their water into blood,
poisoning all the fish.
30 Then frogs overran the land
and even invaded the king's bedrooms.
31 When the LORD spoke, flies descended on the Egyptians,
and gnats swarmed across Egypt.
32 He sent them hail instead of rain,
and lightning flashed over the land.
33 He ruined their grapevines and fig trees
and shattered all the trees.
34 He spoke, and hordes of locusts came—
young locusts beyond number.
35 They ate up everything green in the land,
destroying all the crops in their fields.
36 Then he killed the oldest son in each Egyptian home,
the pride and joy of each family.

37 The LORD brought his people out of Egypt, loaded with silver
and gold;
and not one among the tribes of Israel even stumbled.
38 Egypt was glad when they were gone,
for they feared them greatly.
39 The LORD spread a cloud above them as a covering
and gave them a great fire to light the darkness.
40 They asked for meat, and he sent them quail;
he satisfied their hunger with manna—bread from heaven.
41 He split open a rock, and water gushed out
to form a river through the dry wasteland.
42 For he remembered his sacred promise
to his servant Abraham.
43 So he brought his people out of Egypt with joy,
his chosen ones with rejoicing.
44 He gave his people the lands of pagan nations,
and they harvested crops that others had planted.
45 All this happened so they would follow his decrees
and obey his instructions.

Praise the LORD!

106

1 Praise the LORD!

Give thanks to the LORD, for he is good!
His faithful love endures forever.

105:28 As in Greek and Syriac versions; Hebrew reads *had not defied.*

2 Who can list the glorious miracles of the LORD?
Who can ever praise him enough?
3 There is joy for those who deal justly with others
and always do what is right.

4 Remember me, LORD, when you show favor to your people;
come near and rescue me.
5 Let me share in the prosperity of your chosen ones.
Let me rejoice in the joy of your people;
let me praise you with those who are your heritage.

6 Like our ancestors, we have sinned.
We have done wrong! We have acted wickedly!
7 Our ancestors in Egypt
were not impressed by the LORD's miraculous deeds.
They soon forgot his many acts of kindness to them.
Instead, they rebelled against him at the Red Sea.*
8 Even so, he saved them—
to defend the honor of his name
and to demonstrate his mighty power.
9 He commanded the Red Sea* to dry up.
He led Israel across the sea as if it were a desert.
10 So he rescued them from their enemies
and redeemed them from their foes.
11 Then the water returned and covered their enemies;
not one of them survived.
12 Then his people believed his promises.
Then they sang his praise.

13 Yet how quickly they forgot what he had done!
They wouldn't wait for his counsel!
14 In the wilderness their desires ran wild,
testing God's patience in that dry wasteland.
15 So he gave them what they asked for,
but he sent a plague along with it.
16 The people in the camp were jealous of Moses
and envious of Aaron, the LORD's holy priest.
17 Because of this, the earth opened up;
it swallowed Dathan
and buried Abiram and the other rebels.
18 Fire fell upon their followers;
a flame consumed the wicked.

19 The people made a calf at Mount Sinai*;
they bowed before an image made of gold.
20 They traded their glorious God
for a statue of a grass-eating bull.
21 They forgot God, their savior,
who had done such great things in Egypt—

106:7 Hebrew *at the sea, the sea of reeds.* 106:9 Hebrew *sea of reeds;* also in 106:22. 106:19 Hebrew *at Horeb,* another name for Sinai.

22 such wonderful things in the land of Ham,
such awesome deeds at the Red Sea.
23 So he declared he would destroy them.
But Moses, his chosen one, stepped between the LORD
and the people.
He begged him to turn from his anger and not destroy them.

24 The people refused to enter the pleasant land,
for they wouldn't believe his promise to care for them.
25 Instead, they grumbled in their tents
and refused to obey the LORD.
26 Therefore, he solemnly swore
that he would kill them in the wilderness,
27 that he would scatter their descendants* among the nations,
exiling them to distant lands.

28 Then our ancestors joined in the worship of Baal at Peor;
they even ate sacrifices offered to the dead!
29 They angered the LORD with all these things,
so a plague broke out among them.
30 But Phinehas had the courage to intervene,
and the plague was stopped.
31 So he has been regarded as a righteous man
ever since that time.

32 At Meribah, too, they angered the LORD,
causing Moses serious trouble.
33 They made Moses angry,*
and he spoke foolishly.

34 Israel failed to destroy the nations in the land,
as the LORD had commanded them.
35 Instead, they mingled among the pagans
and adopted their evil customs.
36 They worshiped their idols,
which led to their downfall.
37 They even sacrificed their sons
and their daughters to the demons.
38 They shed innocent blood,
the blood of their sons and daughters.
By sacrificing them to the idols of Canaan,
they polluted the land with murder.
39 They defiled themselves by their evil deeds,
and their love of idols was adultery in the LORD's sight.

40 That is why the LORD's anger burned against his people,
and he abhorred his own special possession.
41 He handed them over to pagan nations,
and they were ruled by those who hated them.

106:27 As in Syriac version; Hebrew reads *he would cause their descendants to fall.* 106:33 Hebrew *They embittered his spirit.*

Patterns I see in this text

Make a Difference

107:1-43

For He Is Good

There is so much bad in this world. We are sick and tired of how sick and tired this world is. Still, we keep asking to know more. We are glued to our news sources, looking for more and more bad news. If there is a disaster, the ratings go up, and news providers and advertisers make more money. Even the coverage of bad news is bad.

God is so different—so good. Why don't we gravitate toward the Lord instead of getting sucked into another terrible vortex day after day? Why does the bad entice us more than the good? What's wrong with us that we keep giving undue attention to the bad while ignoring all the good things that are going on around us? Why do we let the one bad tree draw our attention from God in the garden? We sensationalize what is bad when what is good is right before us. Don't give in to bad. Give thanks to the Lord, for he is good.

Difference Maker

Write the words of Psalm 107:1 on a sticky note and stick it to something you will see throughout your day.

42 Their enemies crushed them
and brought them under their cruel power.
43 Again and again he rescued them,
but they chose to rebel against him,
and they were finally destroyed by their sin.
44 Even so, he pitied them in their distress
and listened to their cries.
45 He remembered his covenant with them
and relented because of his unfailing love.
46 He even caused their captors
to treat them with kindness.

47 Save us, O LORD our God!
Gather us back from among the nations,
so we can thank your holy name
and rejoice and praise you.

48 Praise the LORD, the God of Israel,
who lives from everlasting to everlasting!
Let all the people say, "Amen!"

Praise the LORD!

BOOK FIVE (Psalms 107–150)

107 1 Give thanks to the LORD, for he is good!
His faithful love endures forever.
2 Has the LORD redeemed you? Then speak out!
Tell others he has redeemed you from your enemies.
3 For he has gathered the exiles from many lands,
from east and west,
from north and south.*

4 Some wandered in the wilderness,
lost and homeless.
5 Hungry and thirsty,
they nearly died.
6 "LORD, help!" they cried in their trouble,
and he rescued them from their distress.
7 He led them straight to safety,
to a city where they could live.
8 Let them praise the LORD for his great love
and for the wonderful things he has done for them.
9 For he satisfies the thirsty
and fills the hungry with good things.

10 Some sat in darkness and deepest gloom,
imprisoned in iron chains of misery.

107:3 Hebrew *and sea.*

11 They rebelled against the words of God,
scorning the counsel of the Most High.
12 That is why he broke them with hard labor;
they fell, and no one was there to help them.
13 "LORD, help!" they cried in their trouble,
and he saved them from their distress.
14 He led them from the darkness and deepest gloom;
he snapped their chains.
15 Let them praise the LORD for his great love
and for the wonderful things he has done for them.
16 For he broke down their prison gates of bronze;
he cut apart their bars of iron.

17 Some were fools; they rebelled
and suffered for their sins.
18 They couldn't stand the thought of food,
and they were knocking on death's door.
19 "LORD, help!" they cried in their trouble,
and he saved them from their distress.
20 He sent out his word and healed them,
snatching them from the door of death.
21 Let them praise the LORD for his great love
and for the wonderful things he has done for them.
22 Let them offer sacrifices of thanksgiving
and sing joyfully about his glorious acts.

23 Some went off to sea in ships,
plying the trade routes of the world.
24 They, too, observed the LORD's power in action,
his impressive works on the deepest seas.
25 He spoke, and the winds rose,
stirring up the waves.
26 Their ships were tossed to the heavens
and plunged again to the depths;
the sailors cringed in terror.
27 They reeled and staggered like drunkards
and were at their wits' end.
28 "LORD, help!" they cried in their trouble,
and he saved them from their distress.
29 He calmed the storm to a whisper
and stilled the waves.
30 What a blessing was that stillness
as he brought them safely into harbor!
31 Let them praise the LORD for his great love
and for the wonderful things he has done for them.
32 Let them exalt him publicly before the congregation
and before the leaders of the nation.

33 He changes rivers into deserts,
and springs of water into dry, thirsty land.

Question 108:4

Do you have a friend who feels nobody cares about what they are going through or that nobody notices them? Consider these questions: How high is God's love? How far does his faithfulness reach?

34 He turns the fruitful land into salty wastelands,
because of the wickedness of those who live there.
35 But he also turns deserts into pools of water,
the dry land into springs of water.
36 He brings the hungry to settle there
and to build their cities.
37 They sow their fields, plant their vineyards,
and harvest their bumper crops.
38 How he blesses them!
They raise large families there,
and their herds of livestock increase.

39 When they decrease in number and become impoverished
through oppression, trouble, and sorrow,
40 the LORD pours contempt on their princes,
causing them to wander in trackless wastelands.
41 But he rescues the poor from trouble
and increases their families like flocks of sheep.
42 The godly will see these things and be glad,
while the wicked are struck silent.
43 Those who are wise will take all this to heart;
they will see in our history the faithful love of the LORD.

108 *A song. A psalm of David.*

1 My heart is confident in you, O God;
no wonder I can sing your praises with all my heart!
2 Wake up, lyre and harp!
I will wake the dawn with my song.
3 I will thank you, LORD, among all the people.
I will sing your praises among the nations.
4 For your unfailing love is higher than the heavens.
Your faithfulness reaches to the clouds.
5 Be exalted, O God, above the highest heavens.
May your glory shine over all the earth.

6 Now rescue your beloved people.
Answer and save us by your power.
7 God has promised this by his holiness*:
"I will divide up Shechem with joy.
I will measure out the valley of Succoth.
8 Gilead is mine,
and Manasseh, too.
Ephraim, my helmet, will produce my warriors,
and Judah, my scepter, will produce my kings.
9 But Moab, my washbasin, will become my servant,
and I will wipe my feet on Edom
and shout in triumph over Philistia."

108:7 Or *in his sanctuary.*

10 Who will bring me into the fortified city?
Who will bring me victory over Edom?
11 Have you rejected us, O God?
Will you no longer march with our armies?
12 Oh, please help us against our enemies,
for all human help is useless.
13 With God's help we will do mighty things,
for he will trample down our foes.

109 *For the choir director: A psalm of David.*

1 O God, whom I praise,
don't stand silent and aloof
2 while the wicked slander me
and tell lies about me.
3 They surround me with hateful words
and fight against me for no reason.
4 I love them, but they try to destroy me with accusations
even as I am praying for them!
5 They repay evil for good,
and hatred for my love.

6 They say,* "Get an evil person to turn against him.
Send an accuser to bring him to trial.
7 When his case comes up for judgment,
let him be pronounced guilty.
Count his prayers as sins.
8 Let his years be few;
let someone else take his position.
9 May his children become fatherless,
and his wife a widow.
10 May his children wander as beggars
and be driven from* their ruined homes.
11 May creditors seize his entire estate,
and strangers take all he has earned.
12 Let no one be kind to him;
let no one pity his fatherless children.
13 May all his offspring die.
May his family name be blotted out in the next generation.
14 May the LORD never forget the sins of his fathers;
may his mother's sins never be erased from the record.
15 May the LORD always remember these sins,
and may his name disappear from human memory.
16 For he refused all kindness to others;
he persecuted the poor and needy,
and he hounded the brokenhearted to death.
17 He loved to curse others;
now you curse him.

109:6 Hebrew lacks *They say.* **109:10** As in Greek version; Hebrew reads *and seek.*

He never blessed others;
now don't you bless him.
18 Cursing is as natural to him as his clothing,
or the water he drinks,
or the rich food he eats.
19 Now may his curses return and cling to him like clothing;
may they be tied around him like a belt."

20 May those curses become the LORD's punishment
for my accusers who speak evil of me.
21 But deal well with me, O Sovereign LORD,
for the sake of your own reputation!
Rescue me
because you are so faithful and good.
22 For I am poor and needy,
and my heart is full of pain.
23 I am fading like a shadow at dusk;
I am brushed off like a locust.
24 My knees are weak from fasting,
and I am skin and bones.
25 I am a joke to people everywhere;
when they see me, they shake their heads in scorn.

26 Help me, O LORD my God!
Save me because of your unfailing love.
27 Let them see that this is your doing,
that you yourself have done it, LORD.
28 Then let them curse me if they like,
but you will bless me!
When they attack me, they will be disgraced!
But I, your servant, will go right on rejoicing!
29 May my accusers be clothed with disgrace;
may their humiliation cover them like a cloak.
30 But I will give repeated thanks to the LORD,
praising him to everyone.
31 For he stands beside the needy,
ready to save them from those who condemn them.

110 *A psalm of David.*

1 The LORD said to my Lord,*
"Sit in the place of honor at my right hand
until I humble your enemies,
making them a footstool under your feet."

2 The LORD will extend your powerful kingdom from
Jerusalem*;
you will rule over your enemies.

110:1 Or *my lord.* 110:2 Hebrew *Zion.*

3 When you go to war,
your people will serve you willingly.
You are arrayed in holy garments,
and your strength will be renewed each day like the
morning dew.

4 The LORD has taken an oath and will not break his vow:
"You are a priest forever in the order of Melchizedek."

5 The Lord stands at your right hand to protect you.
He will strike down many kings when his anger erupts.
6 He will punish the nations
and fill their lands with corpses;
he will shatter heads over the whole earth.
7 But he himself will be refreshed from brooks along the way.
He will be victorious.

111*

1 Praise the LORD!

I will thank the LORD with all my heart
as I meet with his godly people.
2 How amazing are the deeds of the LORD!
All who delight in him should ponder them.
3 Everything he does reveals his glory and majesty.
His righteousness never fails.
4 He causes us to remember his wonderful works.
How gracious and merciful is our LORD!
5 He gives food to those who fear him;
he always remembers his covenant.
6 He has shown his great power to his people
by giving them the lands of other nations.
7 All he does is just and good,
and all his commandments are trustworthy.
8 They are forever true,
to be obeyed faithfully and with integrity.
9 He has paid a full ransom for his people.
He has guaranteed his covenant with them forever.
What a holy, awe-inspiring name he has!
10 Fear of the LORD is the foundation of true wisdom.
All who obey his commandments will grow in wisdom.

Praise him forever!

112*

1 Praise the LORD!

How joyful are those who fear the LORD
and delight in obeying his commands.

Make a Difference 111:2

Take Delight

Take delight in the Lord. Let God be your definer. Let your will be saturated by his. Let what God wants wholly shape what you want. As you delight in the Lord, the desire of your heart becomes what he wants for your life. When you learn to align your will with his, your desires merge with what God wants to give you. Your heart delights in what God desires, and God delights in giving you what your heart desires.

Does that mean that if you live perfectly in his will, you won't suffer loss or pain today? No, this verse doesn't say that. It also doesn't say that if you are good, you will get a big house and live a trouble-free life and be healthy and wealthy. No one should read that into this verse. Instead, it reveals that if you follow after the Lord, if you do his will and delight in him, then you will receive the desire of your heart: God himself.

Difference Maker

Stop right now to ask God what he desires for you. Then ask him to make that your desire too.

111 This psalm is a Hebrew acrostic poem; after the introductory note of praise, each line begins with a successive letter of the Hebrew alphabet. 112 This psalm is a Hebrew acrostic poem; after the introductory note of praise, each line begins with a successive letter of the Hebrew alphabet.

Make a Difference 113:9

Praise the Lord

Everywhere God's message is this: He has come to fill you with overflowing life. He loves you and wants you to know it in the depths of your being.

Difference Maker

Sing praise to the Lord! It doesn't matter where—the shower, the car, the bus, the sidewalk, the hallway, the elevator, the dinner table, or at the church group. Just sing songs of praise somewhere today.

2 Their children will be successful everywhere;
an entire generation of godly people will be blessed.
3 They themselves will be wealthy,
and their good deeds will last forever.
4 Light shines in the darkness for the godly.
They are generous, compassionate, and righteous.
5 Good comes to those who lend money generously
and conduct their business fairly.
6 Such people will not be overcome by evil.
Those who are righteous will be long remembered.
7 They do not fear bad news;
they confidently trust the LORD to care for them.
8 They are confident and fearless
and can face their foes triumphantly.
9 They share freely and give generously to those in need.
Their good deeds will be remembered forever.
They will have influence and honor.
10 The wicked will see this and be infuriated.
They will grind their teeth in anger;
they will slink away, their hopes thwarted.

113

1 Praise the LORD!

Yes, give praise, O servants of the LORD.
Praise the name of the LORD!
2 Blessed be the name of the LORD
now and forever.
3 Everywhere—from east to west—
praise the name of the LORD.
4 For the LORD is high above the nations;
his glory is higher than the heavens.

5 Who can be compared with the LORD our God,
who is enthroned on high?
6 He stoops to look down
on heaven and on earth.
7 He lifts the poor from the dust
and the needy from the garbage dump.
8 He sets them among princes,
even the princes of his own people!
9 He gives the childless woman a family,
making her a happy mother.

Praise the LORD!

114

1 When the Israelites escaped from Egypt—
when the family of Jacob left that
foreign land—
2 the land of Judah became God's sanctuary,
and Israel became his kingdom.

3 The Red Sea* saw them coming and hurried out of their way!
The water of the Jordan River turned away.
4 The mountains skipped like rams,
the hills like lambs!
5 What's wrong, Red Sea, that made you hurry out
of their way?
What happened, Jordan River, that you turned away?
6 Why, mountains, did you skip like rams?
Why, hills, like lambs?

7 Tremble, O earth, at the presence of the Lord,
at the presence of the God of Jacob.
8 He turned the rock into a pool of water;
yes, a spring of water flowed from solid rock.

115

1 Not to us, O LORD, not to us,
but to your name goes all the glory
for your unfailing love and faithfulness.
2 Why let the nations say,
"Where is their God?"
3 Our God is in the heavens,
and he does as he wishes.
4 Their idols are merely things of silver and gold,
shaped by human hands.
5 They have mouths but cannot speak,
and eyes but cannot see.
6 They have ears but cannot hear,
and noses but cannot smell.
7 They have hands but cannot feel,
and feet but cannot walk,
and throats but cannot make a sound.
8 And those who make idols are just like them,
as are all who trust in them.

9 O Israel, trust the LORD!
He is your helper and your shield.
10 O priests, descendants of Aaron, trust the LORD!
He is your helper and your shield.
11 All you who fear the LORD, trust the LORD!
He is your helper and your shield.

12 The LORD remembers us and will bless us.
He will bless the people of Israel
and bless the priests, the descendants of Aaron.
13 He will bless those who fear the LORD,
both great and lowly.

14 May the LORD richly bless
both you and your children.

114:3 Hebrew *the sea;* also in 114:5.

Prayer **116:6**

Jesus, let my childlike feet find their traction in your footprints. May your Word guide the direction of my life today. Amen.

15 May you be blessed by the LORD,
who made heaven and earth.
16 The heavens belong to the LORD,
but he has given the earth to all humanity.
17 The dead cannot sing praises to the LORD,
for they have gone into the silence of the grave.
18 But we can praise the LORD
both now and forever!

Praise the LORD!

116

1 I love the LORD because he hears my voice
and my prayer for mercy.
2 Because he bends down to listen,
I will pray as long as I have breath!
3 Death wrapped its ropes around me;
the terrors of the grave* overtook me.
I saw only trouble and sorrow.
4 Then I called on the name of the LORD:
"Please, LORD, save me!"
5 How kind the LORD is! How good he is!
So merciful, this God of ours!
6 The LORD protects those of childlike faith;
I was facing death, and he saved me.
7 Let my soul be at rest again,
for the LORD has been good to me.
8 He has saved me from death,
my eyes from tears,
my feet from stumbling.
9 And so I walk in the LORD's presence
as I live here on earth!
10 I believed in you, so I said,
"I am deeply troubled, LORD."
11 In my anxiety I cried out to you,
"These people are all liars!"
12 What can I offer the LORD
for all he has done for me?
13 I will lift up the cup of salvation
and praise the LORD's name for saving me.
14 I will keep my promises to the LORD
in the presence of all his people.

15 The LORD cares deeply
when his loved ones die.
16 O LORD, I am your servant;
yes, I am your servant, born into your household;
you have freed me from my chains.
17 I will offer you a sacrifice of thanksgiving
and call on the name of the LORD.

116:3 Hebrew *of Sheol.*

18 I will fulfill my vows to the LORD
in the presence of all his people—
19 in the house of the LORD
in the heart of Jerusalem.

Praise the LORD!

117

1 Praise the LORD, all you nations.
Praise him, all you people of the earth.
2 For his unfailing love for us is powerful;
the LORD's faithfulness endures forever.

Praise the LORD!

118

1 Give thanks to the LORD, for he is good!
His faithful love endures forever.

2 Let all Israel repeat:
"His faithful love endures forever."
3 Let Aaron's descendants, the priests, repeat:
"His faithful love endures forever."
4 Let all who fear the LORD repeat:
"His faithful love endures forever."

5 In my distress I prayed to the LORD,
and the LORD answered me and set me free.
6 The LORD is for me, so I will have no fear.
What can mere people do to me?
7 Yes, the LORD is for me; he will help me.
I will look in triumph at those who hate me.
8 It is better to take refuge in the LORD
than to trust in people.
9 It is better to take refuge in the LORD
than to trust in princes.

10 Though hostile nations surrounded me,
I destroyed them all with the authority of the LORD.
11 Yes, they surrounded and attacked me,
but I destroyed them all with the authority of the LORD.
12 They swarmed around me like bees;
they blazed against me like a crackling fire.
But I destroyed them all with the authority of the LORD.
13 My enemies did their best to kill me,
but the LORD rescued me.
14 The LORD is my strength and my song;
he has given me victory.
15 Songs of joy and victory are sung in the camp of the godly.
The strong right arm of the LORD has done glorious things!
16 The strong right arm of the LORD is raised in triumph.
The strong right arm of the LORD has done glorious things!

Question 117:1

This is the shortest chapter in the Bible. How could you live this out?

Make a Difference 118:5

Set Free

The Bible is full of times when God's people summoned the Lord for rescue in the midst of distress. For whatever reason, they found themselves in trouble. Sometimes it was stupid and sinful decisions that got them stuck right where they were, and at other times, circumstances beyond their control overwhelmed them. Repeatedly, as these individuals cried out to the Lord, they made this note: "The LORD answered me and set me free."

We don't always know the details of the distress, nor do we always know the details of the rescue either. The trouble and the escape certainly don't always look like what the people expected. Even so, we do know this: God rescues those who call out to him in their time of need.

Difference Maker

If you get yourself stuck today, instead of trying to dig yourself out, start by praying to the Lord for rescue. Then, while placing yourself in his guidance, look for his path of rescue.

17 I will not die; instead, I will live
to tell what the LORD has done.
18 The LORD has punished me severely,
but he did not let me die.

19 Open for me the gates where the righteous enter,
and I will go in and thank the LORD.
20 These gates lead to the presence of the LORD,
and the godly enter there.
21 I thank you for answering my prayer
and giving me victory!

22 The stone that the builders rejected
has now become the cornerstone.
23 This is the LORD's doing,
and it is wonderful to see.
24 This is the day the LORD has made.
We will rejoice and be glad in it.
25 Please, LORD, please save us.
Please, LORD, please give us success.
26 Bless the one who comes in the name of the LORD.
We bless you from the house of the LORD.
27 The LORD is God, shining upon us.
Take the sacrifice and bind it with cords
on the altar.
28 You are my God, and I will praise you!
You are my God, and I will exalt you!

29 Give thanks to the LORD, for he is good!
His faithful love endures forever.

Aleph

119*

1 Joyful are people of integrity,
who follow the instructions of the LORD.
2 Joyful are those who obey his laws
and search for him with all their hearts.
3 They do not compromise with evil,
and they walk only in his paths.
4 You have charged us
to keep your commandments carefully.
5 Oh, that my actions would consistently
reflect your decrees!
6 Then I will not be ashamed
when I compare my life with your commands.
7 As I learn your righteous regulations,
I will thank you by living as I should!
8 I will obey your decrees.
Please don't give up on me!

119 This psalm is a Hebrew acrostic poem; there are twenty-two stanzas, one for each successive letter of the Hebrew alphabet. Each of the eight verses within each stanza begins with the Hebrew letter named in its heading.

Beth

9 How can a young person stay pure?
By obeying your word.
10 I have tried hard to find you—
don't let me wander from your commands.
11 I have hidden your word in my heart,
that I might not sin against you.
12 I praise you, O LORD;
teach me your decrees.
13 I have recited aloud
all the regulations you have given us.
14 I have rejoiced in your laws
as much as in riches.
15 I will study your commandments
and reflect on your ways.
16 I will delight in your decrees
and not forget your word.

Gimel

17 Be good to your servant,
that I may live and obey your word.
18 Open my eyes to see
the wonderful truths in your instructions.
19 I am only a foreigner in the land.
Don't hide your commands from me!
20 I am always overwhelmed
with a desire for your regulations.
21 You rebuke the arrogant;
those who wander from your commands are cursed.
22 Don't let them scorn and insult me,
for I have obeyed your laws.
23 Even princes sit and speak against me,
but I will meditate on your decrees.
24 Your laws please me;
they give me wise advice.

Daleth

25 I lie in the dust;
revive me by your word.
26 I told you my plans, and you answered.
Now teach me your decrees.
27 Help me understand the meaning of your commandments,
and I will meditate on your wonderful deeds.
28 I weep with sorrow;
encourage me by your word.
29 Keep me from lying to myself;
give me the privilege of knowing your instructions.
30 I have chosen to be faithful;
I have determined to live by your regulations.
31 I cling to your laws.

Make a Difference

119:11

Hide

Some people hide things so they won't be found while others hide things so they know where to find them. Which type of hider are you? It is important to bury God's Word deeply in your heart so that you can discover it there. Don't wallow in the shallow end of your heart because life is meant to be lived deeply. Sow the Word of the Lord into your heart. This way, when a relationship calls for deep commitment, you'll find sacrificial love there. When a challenging moment probes the depths of your character, you'll find integrity. When people need a stable leader, you'll find a treasure of endurance. When justice demands an advocate, you'll find God's voice speaking out from within you.

Difference Maker

To help you embed truth in your heart, write this verse out on ten small sticky notes. Then hide the notes in places where you might need the reminder in the coming week.

Make a Difference

119:37

Seeing

It is often said that leaders who make the most significant difference in our world are people who have vision. They see what is, and they envision what could be. They don't waste the focus of their sight on despair, they don't allow their sight to be distracted by sin or selfishness, and they don't develop blurriness or nearsightedness from binge-watching the wrong things.

Leaders who make a significant difference in our world have keen insight into the immediate landscape and crisp foresight of the horizon. They choose to see the God-created potential in humanity, and they help others see it too. A. W. Tozer once wrote, "Faith is the gaze of a soul upon a saving God." In other words, looking and believing are the same thing. What we choose to see reveals what we believe should be the focus of our lives.

Difference Maker

As you use your eyes today, imagine that Jesus is seeing what you see. How would that change the way you look at people? How would that change what you look at?

LORD, don't let me be put to shame!
32 I will pursue your commands,
for you expand my understanding.

He

33 Teach me your decrees, O LORD;
I will keep them to the end.
34 Give me understanding and I will obey your instructions;
I will put them into practice with all my heart.
35 Make me walk along the path of your commands,
for that is where my happiness is found.
36 Give me an eagerness for your laws
rather than a love for money!
37 Turn my eyes from worthless things,
and give me life through your word.*
38 Reassure me of your promise,
made to those who fear you.
39 Help me abandon my shameful ways;
for your regulations are good.
40 I long to obey your commandments!
Renew my life with your goodness.

Waw

41 LORD, give me your unfailing love,
the salvation that you promised me.
42 Then I can answer those who taunt me,
for I trust in your word.
43 Do not snatch your word of truth from me,
for your regulations are my only hope.
44 I will keep on obeying your instructions
forever and ever.
45 I will walk in freedom,
for I have devoted myself to your commandments.
46 I will speak to kings about your laws,
and I will not be ashamed.
47 How I delight in your commands!
How I love them!
48 I honor and love your commands.
I meditate on your decrees.

Zayin

49 Remember your promise to me;
it is my only hope.
50 Your promise revives me;
it comforts me in all my troubles.
51 The proud hold me in utter contempt,
but I do not turn away from your instructions.
52 I meditate on your age-old regulations;
O LORD, they comfort me.

119:37 Some manuscripts read *in your ways.*

53 I become furious with the wicked,
because they reject your instructions.
54 Your decrees have been the theme of my songs
wherever I have lived.
55 I reflect at night on who you are, O LORD;
therefore, I obey your instructions.
56 This is how I spend my life:
obeying your commandments.

Heth

57 LORD, you are mine!
I promise to obey your words!
58 With all my heart I want your blessings.
Be merciful as you promised.
59 I pondered the direction of my life,
and I turned to follow your laws.
60 I will hurry, without delay,
to obey your commands.
61 Evil people try to drag me into sin,
but I am firmly anchored to your instructions.
62 I rise at midnight to thank you
for your just regulations.
63 I am a friend to anyone who fears you—
anyone who obeys your commandments.
64 O LORD, your unfailing love fills the earth;
teach me your decrees.

Teth

65 You have done many good things for me, LORD,
just as you promised.
66 I believe in your commands;
now teach me good judgment and knowledge.
67 I used to wander off until you disciplined me;
but now I closely follow your word.
68 You are good and do only good;
teach me your decrees.
69 Arrogant people smear me with lies,
but in truth I obey your commandments with all my heart.
70 Their hearts are dull and stupid,
but I delight in your instructions.
71 My suffering was good for me,
for it taught me to pay attention to your decrees.
72 Your instructions are more valuable to me
than millions in gold and silver.

Yodh

73 You made me; you created me.
Now give me the sense to follow your commands.
74 May all who fear you find in me a cause for joy,
for I have put my hope in your word.

Make a Difference

119:72

Priorities

Would you rather be incredibly wealthy or have instructions from God? Would you rather have millions upon millions of dollars deposited right into your bank account for you to use in whatever manner you deem fit, or would you like to have God give you instructions on how to live?

The writer of the longest chapter in the Bible played the "Would You Rather" game and felt passionately about his answer. In prayer, he turned to the Lord and made his turn-the-world-upside-down decision.

Difference Maker

Prayerfully filter your goals in life against this verse. Where do your priorities match up, and where do they clash? What could you do today to reinforce your connection to God's purpose for your life?

Prayer **119:73**

Lord, give me the sense to follow your commands. Amen.

Make a Difference
119:96

Perfectionism Falls Short!

No wonder perfectionists are always dissatisfied! Perfect is never good enough. Even if everything were completed to its most excellent potential, it still would fall short. The problem is that perfection sets a bar—a very high bar—that has a limit. Once a person reaches it, if it ever truly can be reached, they still feel incomplete because perfectionism is limited. The enjoyment of perfectionism is limited, the scope of perfectionism is limited, and the lasting effect of perfectionism is limited.

In contrast, God's patterns have no limit. They are boundless. Perfectionists are always dissatisfied because they are chasing the wrong pursuit. God's commands blow right past the limited gratification of perfectionism and open the door to abundant, overflowing life—life that is more fulfilling than you could ever dream any limited human goal could be.

Difference Maker

Make a to-do list. Draw a horizontal line across the middle of a sheet of paper. On the bottom half, list everything important that you think you really need to accomplish, and on the top half, write, "Pursue Jesus." As you work to complete the important bottom items, seek your satisfaction in the one item on the top.

75 I know, O LORD, that your regulations are fair;
you disciplined me because I needed it.
76 Now let your unfailing love comfort me,
just as you promised me, your servant.
77 Surround me with your tender mercies so I may live,
for your instructions are my delight.
78 Bring disgrace upon the arrogant people who lied
about me;
meanwhile, I will concentrate on your commandments.
79 Let me be united with all who fear you,
with those who know your laws.
80 May I be blameless in keeping your decrees;
then I will never be ashamed.

Kaph

81 I am worn out waiting for your rescue,
but I have put my hope in your word.
82 My eyes are straining to see your promises come true.
When will you comfort me?
83 I am shriveled like a wineskin in the smoke,
but I have not forgotten to obey your decrees.
84 How long must I wait?
When will you punish those who persecute me?
85 These arrogant people who hate your instructions
have dug deep pits to trap me.
86 All your commands are trustworthy.
Protect me from those who hunt me down
without cause.
87 They almost finished me off,
but I refused to abandon your commandments.
88 In your unfailing love, spare my life;
then I can continue to obey your laws.

Lamedh

89 Your eternal word, O LORD,
stands firm in heaven.
90 Your faithfulness extends to every generation,
as enduring as the earth you created.
91 Your regulations remain true to this day,
for everything serves your plans.
92 If your instructions hadn't sustained me with joy,
I would have died in my misery.
93 I will never forget your commandments,
for by them you give me life.
94 I am yours; rescue me!
For I have worked hard at obeying your commandments.
95 Though the wicked hide along the way to kill me,
I will quietly keep my mind on your laws.
96 Even perfection has its limits,
but your commands have no limit.

Mem

97 Oh, how I love your instructions!
I think about them all day long.
98 Your commands make me wiser than my enemies,
for they are my constant guide.
99 Yes, I have more insight than my teachers,
for I am always thinking of your laws.
100 I am even wiser than my elders,
for I have kept your commandments.
101 I have refused to walk on any evil path,
so that I may remain obedient to your word.
102 I haven't turned away from your regulations,
for you have taught me well.
103 How sweet your words taste to me;
they are sweeter than honey.
104 Your commandments give me understanding;
no wonder I hate every false way of life.

Nun

105 Your word is a lamp to guide my feet
and a light for my path.
106 I've promised it once, and I'll promise it again:
I will obey your righteous regulations.
107 I have suffered much, O LORD;
restore my life again as you promised.
108 LORD, accept my offering of praise,
and teach me your regulations.
109 My life constantly hangs in the balance,
but I will not stop obeying your instructions.
110 The wicked have set their traps for me,
but I will not turn from your commandments.
111 Your laws are my treasure;
they are my heart's delight.
112 I am determined to keep your decrees
to the very end.

Samekh

113 I hate those with divided loyalties,
but I love your instructions.
114 You are my refuge and my shield;
your word is my source of hope.
115 Get out of my life, you evil-minded people,
for I intend to obey the commands of my God.
116 LORD, sustain me as you promised, that I may live!
Do not let my hope be crushed.
117 Sustain me, and I will be rescued;
then I will meditate continually on your decrees.
118 But you have rejected all who stray from
your decrees.
They are only fooling themselves.

Prayer **119:105**

Lord, guide the steps of my life while I spend time in your word. Amen.

119 You skim off the wicked of the earth like scum;
no wonder I love to obey your laws!
120 I tremble in fear of you;
I stand in awe of your regulations.

Ayin

121 Don't leave me to the mercy of my enemies,
for I have done what is just and right.
122 Please guarantee a blessing for me.
Don't let the arrogant oppress me!
123 My eyes strain to see your rescue,
to see the truth of your promise fulfilled.
124 I am your servant; deal with me in unfailing love,
and teach me your decrees.
125 Give discernment to me, your servant;
then I will understand your laws.
126 LORD, it is time for you to act,
for these evil people have violated your instructions.
127 Truly, I love your commands
more than gold, even the finest gold.
128 Each of your commandments is right.
That is why I hate every false way.

Pe

129 Your laws are wonderful.
No wonder I obey them!
130 The teaching of your word gives light,
so even the simple can understand.
131 I pant with expectation,
longing for your commands.
132 Come and show me your mercy,
as you do for all who love your name.
133 Guide my steps by your word,
so I will not be overcome by evil.
134 Ransom me from the oppression of evil people;
then I can obey your commandments.
135 Look upon me with love;
teach me your decrees.
136 Rivers of tears gush from my eyes
because people disobey your instructions.

Tsadhe

137 O LORD, you are righteous,
and your regulations are fair.
138 Your laws are perfect
and completely trustworthy.
139 I am overwhelmed with indignation,
for my enemies have disregarded your words.
140 Your promises have been thoroughly tested;
that is why I love them so much.

141 I am insignificant and despised,
but I don't forget your commandments.
142 Your justice is eternal,
and your instructions are perfectly true.
143 As pressure and stress bear down on me,
I find joy in your commands.
144 Your laws are always right;
help me to understand them so I may live.

Qoph

145 I pray with all my heart; answer me, LORD!
I will obey your decrees.
146 I cry out to you; rescue me,
that I may obey your laws.
147 I rise early, before the sun is up;
I cry out for help and put my hope in your words.
148 I stay awake through the night,
thinking about your promise.
149 In your faithful love, O LORD, hear my cry;
let me be revived by following your regulations.
150 Lawless people are coming to attack me;
they live far from your instructions.
151 But you are near, O LORD,
and all your commands are true.
152 I have known from my earliest days
that your laws will last forever.

Resh

153 Look upon my suffering and rescue me,
for I have not forgotten your instructions.
154 Argue my case; take my side!
Protect my life as you promised.
155 The wicked are far from rescue,
for they do not bother with your decrees.
156 LORD, how great is your mercy;
let me be revived by following your regulations.
157 Many persecute and trouble me,
yet I have not swerved from your laws.
158 Seeing these traitors makes me sick at heart,
because they care nothing for your word.
159 See how I love your commandments, LORD.
Give back my life because of your unfailing love.
160 The very essence of your words is truth;
all your just regulations will stand forever.

Shin

161 Powerful people harass me without cause,
but my heart trembles only at your word.
162 I rejoice in your word
like one who discovers a great treasure.

Things to reflect on

Make a Difference
119:175

Purpose and Infrastructure

Every building, every society, every product, every family, and every person has some sort of purpose and some sort of infrastructure that supports them. Whether those things or those people have success is directly related to whether the infrastructure serves the purpose. If a building was meant to be fifty stories high and house hundreds of high-tech office spaces, it would be a farce if the infrastructure were made out of wood and a few dial-up modems.

It has been said that the "chief end" of humanity is to glorify God, but humans have often created a dilapidated infrastructure around themselves that has hindered their pursuit of their purpose. The good news is that through Jesus, God has given us the foundation and the resources we need to love the Lord and love our neighbor as ourselves.

Difference Maker

What long-lasting materials do you need to invest your life into today? Choose at least one of the following to build yourself up: reading God's Word, serving others without calling attention to yourself, spending time in prayer, or mentoring a younger person in their walk with God.

163 I hate and abhor all falsehood,
but I love your instructions.
164 I will praise you seven times a day
because all your regulations are just.
165 Those who love your instructions have great peace
and do not stumble.
166 I long for your rescue, LORD,
so I have obeyed your commands.
167 I have obeyed your laws,
for I love them very much.
168 Yes, I obey your commandments and laws
because you know everything I do.

Taw

169 O LORD, listen to my cry;
give me the discerning mind you promised.
170 Listen to my prayer;
rescue me as you promised.
171 Let praise flow from my lips,
for you have taught me your decrees.
172 Let my tongue sing about your word,
for all your commands are right.
173 Give me a helping hand,
for I have chosen to follow your commandments.
174 O LORD, I have longed for your rescue,
and your instructions are my delight.
175 Let me live so I can praise you,
and may your regulations help me.
176 I have wandered away like a lost sheep;
come and find me,
for I have not forgotten your commands.

120

A song for pilgrims ascending to Jerusalem.

1 I took my troubles to the LORD;
I cried out to him, and he answered my prayer.
2 Rescue me, O LORD, from liars
and from all deceitful people.
3 O deceptive tongue, what will God do to you?
How will he increase your punishment?
4 You will be pierced with sharp arrows
and burned with glowing coals.

5 How I suffer in far-off Meshech.
It pains me to live in distant Kedar.
6 I am tired of living
among people who hate peace.
7 I search for peace;
but when I speak of peace, they want war!

121 *A song for pilgrims ascending to Jerusalem.*

1 I look up to the mountains—
does my help come from there?
2 My help comes from the LORD,
who made heaven and earth!

3 He will not let you stumble;
the one who watches over you will
not slumber.
4 Indeed, he who watches over Israel
never slumbers or sleeps.

5 The LORD himself watches over you!
The LORD stands beside you as your
protective shade.
6 The sun will not harm you by day,
nor the moon at night.

7 The LORD keeps you from all harm
and watches over your life.
8 The LORD keeps watch over you as you come
and go,
both now and forever.

Question 121:1

What is the answer to this question? Why?

122 *A song for pilgrims ascending to Jerusalem. A psalm of David.*

1 I was glad when they said to me,
"Let us go to the house of the LORD."
2 And now here we are,
standing inside your gates, O Jerusalem.
3 Jerusalem is a well-built city;
its seamless walls cannot be breached.
4 All the tribes of Israel—the LORD's people—
make their pilgrimage here.
They come to give thanks to the name of the LORD,
as the law requires of Israel.
5 Here stand the thrones where judgment is given,
the thrones of the dynasty of David.

6 Pray for peace in Jerusalem.
May all who love this city prosper.
7 O Jerusalem, may there be peace within your walls
and prosperity in your palaces.
8 For the sake of my family and friends, I will say,
"May you have peace."
9 For the sake of the house of the LORD our God,
I will seek what is best for you, O Jerusalem.

123 *A song for pilgrims ascending to Jerusalem.*

1 I lift my eyes to you,
O God, enthroned in heaven.
2 We keep looking to the LORD our God for his mercy,
just as servants keep their eyes on their master,
as a slave girl watches her mistress for the slightest signal.
3 Have mercy on us, LORD, have mercy,
for we have had our fill of contempt.
4 We have had more than our fill of the scoffing of the proud
and the contempt of the arrogant.

124 *A song for pilgrims ascending to Jerusalem. A psalm of David.*

1 What if the LORD had not been on our side?
Let all Israel repeat:
2 What if the LORD had not been on our side
when people attacked us?
3 They would have swallowed us alive
in their burning anger.
4 The waters would have engulfed us;
a torrent would have overwhelmed us.
5 Yes, the raging waters of their fury
would have overwhelmed our very lives.

6 Praise the LORD,
who did not let their teeth tear us apart!
7 We escaped like a bird from a hunter's trap.
The trap is broken, and we are free!
8 Our help is from the LORD,
who made heaven and earth.

125 *A song for pilgrims ascending to Jerusalem.*

1 Those who trust in the LORD are as secure as Mount Zion;
they will not be defeated but will endure forever.
2 Just as the mountains surround Jerusalem,
so the LORD surrounds his people, both now
and forever.
3 The wicked will not rule the land of the godly,
for then the godly might be tempted to do wrong.
4 O LORD, do good to those who are good,
whose hearts are in tune with you.
5 But banish those who turn to crooked ways, O LORD.
Take them away with those who do evil.

May Israel have peace!

126 *A song for pilgrims ascending to Jerusalem.*

1 When the LORD brought back his exiles to Jerusalem,*
it was like a dream!
2 We were filled with laughter,
and we sang for joy.
And the other nations said,
"What amazing things the LORD has done
for them."
3 Yes, the LORD has done amazing things for us!
What joy!

4 Restore our fortunes, LORD,
as streams renew the desert.
5 Those who plant in tears
will harvest with shouts of joy.
6 They weep as they go to plant their seed,
but they sing as they return with the harvest.

127 *A song for pilgrims ascending to Jerusalem. A psalm of Solomon.*

1 Unless the LORD builds a house,
the work of the builders is wasted.
Unless the LORD protects a city,
guarding it with sentries will do no good.
2 It is useless for you to work so hard
from early morning until late at night,
anxiously working for food to eat;
for God gives rest to his loved ones.

3 Children are a gift from the LORD;
they are a reward from him.
4 Children born to a young man
are like arrows in a warrior's hands.
5 How joyful is the man whose quiver is full of them!
He will not be put to shame when he confronts his accusers
at the city gates.

128 *A song for pilgrims ascending to Jerusalem.*

1 How joyful are those who fear the LORD—
all who follow his ways!
2 You will enjoy the fruit of your labor.
How joyful and prosperous you will be!
3 Your wife will be like a fruitful grapevine,
flourishing within your home.

Prayer **127:1**

Jesus, I have a lot of opportunity to do what you'd like for me to do. Thank you for inviting me into your line of work. Amen.

126:1 Hebrew *Zion.*

Your children will be like vigorous young olive trees
as they sit around your table.
4 That is the LORD's blessing
for those who fear him.

5 May the LORD continually bless you from Zion.
May you see Jerusalem prosper as long as you live.
6 May you live to enjoy your grandchildren.
May Israel have peace!

129 *A song for pilgrims ascending to Jerusalem.*

1 From my earliest youth my enemies have persecuted me.
Let all Israel repeat this:
2 From my earliest youth my enemies have persecuted me,
but they have never defeated me.
3 My back is covered with cuts,
as if a farmer had plowed long furrows.
4 But the LORD is good;
he has cut me free from the ropes of the ungodly.

5 May all who hate Jerusalem*
be turned back in shameful defeat.
6 May they be as useless as grass on a rooftop,
turning yellow when only half grown,
7 ignored by the harvester,
despised by the binder.
8 And may those who pass by
refuse to give them this blessing:
"The LORD bless you;
we bless you in the LORD's name."

130 *A song for pilgrims ascending to Jerusalem.*

1 From the depths of despair, O LORD,
I call for your help.
2 Hear my cry, O Lord.
Pay attention to my prayer.

3 LORD, if you kept a record of our sins,
who, O Lord, could ever survive?
4 But you offer forgiveness,
that we might learn to fear you.

5 I am counting on the LORD;
yes, I am counting on him.
I have put my hope in his word.

129:5 Hebrew *Zion.*

Make a Difference

130:3

Record

Jesus makes you free. Did you know that? He loves you so much that he does not keep a record of your sins. Every time you mess up, he is not going to bring out the Book of Sin with your name on the cover, open to a random page, and say, "Aha! See! I knew you were no good. You're always failing!" That's just not the way of Jesus.

In fact, when you mess up, he might pull out another book that we call the Bible. He might open to a myriad of different passages, like 1 John 1:9, which says, "If we confess our sins to him, he is faithful and just to forgive us our sins and to cleanse us from all wickedness," or Isaiah 43:25, where God said he "will blot out your sins... and will never think of them again." Jesus might even quote from the "love chapter" of the Bible, 1 Corinthians 13, which says that love "keeps no record of being wronged" (v. 5). This is the way of Jesus, and it makes you free.

Difference Maker

Share the good news of Jesus with someone who has sunk into the despair of their mistakes.

6 I long for the Lord
more than sentries long for the dawn,
yes, more than sentries long for the dawn.

7 O Israel, hope in the LORD;
for with the LORD there is unfailing love.
His redemption overflows.
8 He himself will redeem Israel
from every kind of sin.

131 *A song for pilgrims ascending to Jerusalem. A psalm of David.*

1 LORD, my heart is not proud;
my eyes are not haughty.
I don't concern myself with matters too great
or too awesome for me to grasp.
2 Instead, I have calmed and quieted myself,
like a weaned child who no longer cries for its
mother's milk.
Yes, like a weaned child is my soul within me.

3 O Israel, put your hope in the LORD—
now and always.

132 *A song for pilgrims ascending to Jerusalem.*

1 LORD, remember David
and all that he suffered.
2 He made a solemn promise to the LORD.
He vowed to the Mighty One of Israel,*
3 "I will not go home;
I will not let myself rest.
4 I will not let my eyes sleep
nor close my eyelids in slumber
5 until I find a place to build a house
for the LORD,
a sanctuary for the Mighty One of Israel."

6 We heard that the Ark was in Ephrathah;
then we found it in the distant countryside
of Jaar.
7 Let us go to the sanctuary of the LORD;
let us worship at the footstool of his throne.
8 Arise, O LORD, and enter your resting place,
along with the Ark, the symbol of your power.
9 May your priests be clothed in godliness;
may your loyal servants sing for joy.

132:2 Hebrew *of Jacob;* also in 132:5. See note on 44:4.

Make a Difference

133:1–3

Peace Rules

Does anxiety get the best of you at moments throughout your day? Remember that you are called to let peace get the better of you, for who, by worrying, can solve the unresolvable? No one thinks, *Maybe if I worry enough, everything will get better*. No, if you let it, worry will become a mad king over your heart. Peace, not worry, is to reign in your heart.

It is important to recognize that peace comes from Jesus. Peace is the restoration of harmony. It is the reconciliation of relationship. Peace does not look like you, by yourself, trying to hold it all together. Rather, it looks like you and others learning to entrust your lives in harmony together with Jesus.

Difference Maker

Connect with someone today whom you know is anxious. Invite them to share a meal with you or to do something fun together. Let them experience the peace that you have because of what God has done.

10 For the sake of your servant David,
do not reject the king you have anointed.
11 The LORD swore an oath to David
with a promise he will never take back:
"I will place one of your descendants
on your throne.
12 If your descendants obey the terms of my covenant
and the laws that I teach them,
then your royal line
will continue forever and ever."

13 For the LORD has chosen Jerusalem*;
he has desired it for his home.
14 "This is my resting place forever," he said.
"I will live here, for this is the home I desired.
15 I will bless this city and make it prosperous;
I will satisfy its poor with food.
16 I will clothe its priests with godliness;
its faithful servants will sing for joy.
17 Here I will increase the power of David;
my anointed one will be a light for my people.
18 I will clothe his enemies with shame,
but he will be a glorious king."

133 *A song for pilgrims ascending to Jerusalem. A psalm of David.*

1 How wonderful and pleasant it is
when brothers live together in harmony!
2 For harmony is as precious as the anointing oil
that was poured over Aaron's head,
that ran down his beard
and onto the border of his robe.
3 Harmony is as refreshing as the dew from
Mount Hermon
that falls on the mountains of Zion.
And there the LORD has pronounced his blessing,
even life everlasting.

134 *A song for pilgrims ascending to Jerusalem.*

1 Oh, praise the LORD, all you servants of the LORD,
you who serve at night in the house of the LORD.
2 Lift your hands toward the sanctuary,
and praise the LORD.

3 May the LORD, who made heaven and earth,
bless you from Jerusalem.*

132:13 Hebrew *Zion*. 134:3 Hebrew *Zion*.

135

1 Praise the LORD!

Praise the name of the LORD!
Praise him, you who serve the LORD,
2 you who serve in the house of the LORD,
in the courts of the house of our God.

3 Praise the LORD, for the LORD is good;
celebrate his lovely name with music.
4 For the LORD has chosen Jacob for himself,
Israel for his own special treasure.

5 I know the greatness of the LORD—
that our Lord is greater than any other god.
6 The LORD does whatever pleases him
throughout all heaven and earth,
and on the seas and in their depths.
7 He causes the clouds to rise over the whole earth.
He sends the lightning with the rain
and releases the wind from his storehouses.

8 He destroyed the firstborn in each Egyptian home,
both people and animals.
9 He performed miraculous signs and wonders in Egypt
against Pharaoh and all his people.
10 He struck down great nations
and slaughtered mighty kings—
11 Sihon king of the Amorites,
Og king of Bashan,
and all the kings of Canaan.
12 He gave their land as an inheritance,
a special possession to his people Israel.

13 Your name, O LORD, endures forever;
your fame, O LORD, is known to every generation.
14 For the LORD will give justice to his people
and have compassion on his servants.

15 The idols of the nations are merely things of silver
and gold,
shaped by human hands.
16 They have mouths but cannot speak,
and eyes but cannot see.
17 They have ears but cannot hear,
and mouths but cannot breathe.
18 And those who make idols are just like them,
as are all who trust in them.

19 O Israel, praise the LORD!
O priests—descendants of Aaron—praise the LORD!

Question 136:1

What does this psalm model? How could you live out this kind of rhythm today?

20 O Levites, praise the LORD!
All you who fear the LORD, praise
the LORD!
21 The LORD be praised from Zion,
for he lives here in Jerusalem.

Praise the LORD!

136

1 Give thanks to the LORD, for he is good!
His faithful love endures forever.
2 Give thanks to the God of gods.
His faithful love endures forever.
3 Give thanks to the Lord of lords.
His faithful love endures forever.

4 Give thanks to him who alone does mighty miracles.
His faithful love endures forever.
5 Give thanks to him who made the heavens so skillfully.
His faithful love endures forever.
6 Give thanks to him who placed the earth among the waters.
His faithful love endures forever.
7 Give thanks to him who made the heavenly lights—
His faithful love endures forever.
8 the sun to rule the day,
His faithful love endures forever.
9 and the moon and stars to rule the night.
His faithful love endures forever.

10 Give thanks to him who killed the firstborn of Egypt.
His faithful love endures forever.
11 He brought Israel out of Egypt.
His faithful love endures forever.
12 He acted with a strong hand and powerful arm.
His faithful love endures forever.
13 Give thanks to him who parted the Red Sea.*
His faithful love endures forever.
14 He led Israel safely through,
His faithful love endures forever.
15 but he hurled Pharaoh and his army into the Red Sea.
His faithful love endures forever.
16 Give thanks to him who led his people through the wilderness.
His faithful love endures forever.

17 Give thanks to him who struck down mighty kings.
His faithful love endures forever.
18 He killed powerful kings—
His faithful love endures forever.
19 Sihon king of the Amorites,
His faithful love endures forever.

136:13 Hebrew *sea of reeds;* also in 136:15.

20 and Og king of Bashan.
His faithful love endures forever.
21 God gave the land of these kings as an inheritance—
His faithful love endures forever.
22 a special possession to his servant Israel.
His faithful love endures forever.

23 He remembered us in our weakness.
His faithful love endures forever.
24 He saved us from our enemies.
His faithful love endures forever.
25 He gives food to every living thing.
His faithful love endures forever.
26 Give thanks to the God of heaven.
His faithful love endures forever.

137

1 Beside the rivers of Babylon, we sat and wept
as we thought of Jerusalem.*
2 We put away our harps,
hanging them on the branches of poplar trees.
3 For our captors demanded a song from us.
Our tormentors insisted on a joyful hymn:
"Sing us one of those songs of Jerusalem!"
4 But how can we sing the songs of the LORD
while in a pagan land?

5 If I forget you, O Jerusalem,
let my right hand forget how to play the harp.
6 May my tongue stick to the roof of my mouth
if I fail to remember you,
if I don't make Jerusalem my greatest joy.

7 O LORD, remember what the Edomites did
on the day the armies of Babylon captured Jerusalem.
"Destroy it!" they yelled.
"Level it to the ground!"
8 O Babylon, you will be destroyed.
Happy is the one who pays you back
for what you have done to us.
9 Happy is the one who takes your babies
and smashes them against the rocks!

138 *A psalm of David.*

1 I give you thanks, O LORD, with all my heart;
I will sing your praises before the gods.
2 I bow before your holy Temple as I worship.
I praise your name for your unfailing love and faithfulness;

137:1 Hebrew *Zion;* also in 137:3.

for your promises are backed
by all the honor of your name.
3 As soon as I pray, you answer me;
you encourage me by giving me strength.

4 Every king in all the earth will thank you, LORD,
for all of them will hear your words.
5 Yes, they will sing about the LORD's ways,
for the glory of the LORD is very great.
6 Though the LORD is great, he cares for the humble,
but he keeps his distance from the proud.

7 Though I am surrounded by troubles,
you will protect me from the anger of my enemies.
You reach out your hand,
and the power of your right hand saves me.
8 The LORD will work out his plans for my life—
for your faithful love, O LORD, endures forever.
Don't abandon me, for you made me.

139 *For the choir director: A psalm of David.*

1 O LORD, you have examined my heart
and know everything about me.
2 You know when I sit down or stand up.
You know my thoughts even when I'm
far away.
3 You see me when I travel
and when I rest at home.
You know everything I do.
4 You know what I am going to say
even before I say it, LORD.
5 You go before me and follow me.
You place your hand of blessing on my head.
6 Such knowledge is too wonderful for me,
too great for me to understand!

7 I can never escape from your Spirit!
I can never get away from your presence!
8 If I go up to heaven, you are there;
if I go down to the grave,* you are there.
9 If I ride the wings of the morning,
if I dwell by the farthest oceans,
10 even there your hand will guide me,
and your strength will support me.
11 I could ask the darkness to hide me
and the light around me to become night—
12 but even in darkness I cannot hide from you.

139:8 Hebrew *to Sheol.*

To you the night shines as bright as day.
Darkness and light are the same to you.

Highlights from the text

13 You made all the delicate, inner parts of my body
and knit me together in my mother's womb.
14 Thank you for making me so wonderfully complex!
Your workmanship is marvelous—how well I
know it.
15 You watched me as I was being formed in utter seclusion,
as I was woven together in the dark of the womb.
16 You saw me before I was born.
Every day of my life was recorded in your book.
Every moment was laid out
before a single day had passed.

17 How precious are your thoughts about me,* O God.
They cannot be numbered!
18 I can't even count them;
they outnumber the grains of sand!
And when I wake up,
you are still with me!

19 O God, if only you would destroy the wicked!
Get out of my life, you murderers!
20 They blaspheme you;
your enemies misuse your name.
21 O LORD, shouldn't I hate those who hate you?
Shouldn't I despise those who oppose you?
22 Yes, I hate them with total hatred,
for your enemies are my enemies.

23 Search me, O God, and know my heart;
test me and know my anxious thoughts.
24 Point out anything in me that offends you,
and lead me along the path of everlasting life.

140 *For the choir director: A psalm of David.*

1 O LORD, rescue me from evil people.
Protect me from those who are violent,
2 those who plot evil in their hearts
and stir up trouble all day long.
3 Their tongues sting like a snake;
the venom of a viper drips from their lips. *Interlude*

4 O LORD, keep me out of the hands of the wicked.
Protect me from those who are violent,
for they are plotting against me.

139:17 Or *How precious to me are your thoughts.*

The Difference Psalm 139 Makes

Make a Difference 139:1

God Knows You

Remember this truth: You are not forgotten. You are not alone. You are not unseen. You are not unknown. God has taken a remarkable interest in you. He examines you. Like a precision specialist finely tuned to your every joy or fear, God listens and searches and understands what is happening in you and to you. No matter what you are going through today, God knows, and he is close.

David, the writer of Psalm 139, had incredible moments of victory, gut-wrenching moments of failure, endless hours of loneliness, and countless repetitions of everyday routines. Through his experiences, he grew to understand that everything he did throughout each day—every motion and emotion—the Lord knew intimately. Whatever your life is like today, know that God knows all about it. His attention is turned toward you in this very moment.

Difference Maker

Every time you sit down and stand up today, make a note in your mind that God's attention is on you in that very moment. Let that knowledge transform everything you think about and do.

Make a Difference 139:3

God Sees You

Where are you going in the next twenty-four hours? Think about all the places, near or far, that you will pass through. How will you get there? Will the travel be nerve-racking? Whom will you meet? Will the locations be familiar or adventurous? Are you going to a classroom, coffee shop, or office? Gas station, highway, or sidewalk? Hallway, couch, or bathroom? Conversation, speech, or game?

Maybe you have trouble noticing God during a typical day, but God has no problem focusing on you, whether you are a moving blur or a still picture. God sees you when you are far away as clearly as he sees when you are at home. God also has no problem knowing what you're doing or what you're going to do when you are near or far. Jesus knew the thoughts of people (Matthew 9:4) even before they spoke them and even when he wasn't visibly near them (John 1:47-48).

Difference Maker

Realizing that God sees you, choose one positive action to accomplish today that you wouldn't have otherwise done. Then choose one negative habit to avoid.

Make a Difference 139:11

God Is with You

If you could create a high-pressure diving suit and descend to the deepest underwater caves submerged several miles under the most remote surfaces of the ocean, you would still be as near to God as if you were at home asleep in your own bed. You are not alone. *Omnipresent* is the fancy word that people use to state a profound theological reality: God is everywhere.

If you feel alone, maybe this comforts you. If you are trying to hide something, perhaps this gives you the shivers. Even if you rode a rocket past Pluto or if you ran away to the darkest recesses of your soul, still you would find God looking for you there because he is everywhere at all times. There is no place you can go to escape his presence. This is a profound and terrifying truth.

Difference Maker

Jesus goes to great lengths to reach you. Think of someone you know who either feels all alone or is trying to hide. Be bold and make the effort to let them know that Jesus is there for them too.

Make a Difference

139:13

God Made You

It has been said that every stitch of a quilt is made with love. The time and effort that, say, a grandmother puts into making a quilt for her new grandchild is evidence of love. Every stitch is another thought, another prayer, another action of care and compassion for the one she loves.

In the same way, the Lord took the time and effort to stitch you together. Even in the seclusion of your mother's womb, before the day you gasped your first breath, the Lord's heart and hands were forming you. Every time he patiently wove a sinew or precisely measured a cell or miraculously gave a beat to your heart, he thought about you, planned for you, and couldn't help but be consumed with love for you. Every fiber of your being was uniquely patterned and intimately sewn with God's hands. From before you were born, God committed himself to you and loved you.

Difference Maker

Through a prayer, donation, or volunteer work, take a moment to support agencies that celebrate the precious created nature of each individual person (such as a new-life pregnancy agency or an orphanage).

Make a Difference

139:15

God Planned for You

You are not a mistake. God knew you would show up. You didn't surprise him. He was ready for you, and he was looking forward to your arrival. God also was looking forward to how you would live the life he has given to you. He has planned your days with purpose. He has things for you to do and people for you to reach.

Ephesians 2:10 says that you, along with others who follow God, are his masterpiece, created in Christ Jesus to do the good things he planned long ago. He shaped you with incredible attention to detail and with immeasurable value so that you could join him in his good work in this world. You are not a mistake; God made you into a beautiful masterpiece.

Difference Maker

What is something that God created you to do? What step can you take today to pursue that purpose?

Make a Difference

139:17

God Cherishes You

"The very hairs on your head are all numbered," Jesus said. "So don't be afraid" (Luke 12:7). Jesus wants you, just like his first followers, to be empowered by the fact that you are incredibly valuable to God. He wants you to stand with awe-inspiring confidence—a confidence that comes from learning how precious you are in his sight—and to declare with life-changing assurance that God loves you.

In other words, God puts your drawing on his fridge, not because it's perfect but because it came from you. His heart sparkles when you smile, sing, and serve. His hands clap when you create beauty and when you copy his character. His knees bend when you fall, his healing cleanses your wounds, and his power sets you on course to go and play again. He doesn't stop thinking about you—ever.

Difference Maker

Think of a creative way to bring joy to God's heart and let others know how much love he has for them.

Make a Difference

139:23

God Searches You

That cute little magnifying glass icon next to every search bar has tremendous power. Anything that you type next to it, you can search for, and, as long as your device is connected to the internet, it returns millions of hits. A little icon's algorithms are driving the information transfer of the world.

Imagine now that the cute magnifying glass icon was not ruled by some little internet search engine like Google but, instead, owned and operated by God. Then imagine typing your name next to it and hitting enter. What would God's algorithms return on you? Are there any results that might worry you?

The good news about this search process is that Jesus celebrates everyone who comes to him with an open heart. He forgives and cleanses and heals and restores the lives of those who seek him. Come to him today and let his cleansing take effect in your life.

Difference Maker

Type your name in a search engine and pray this question: "Jesus, what results would you like to show up here?"

5 The proud have set a trap to catch me;
they have stretched out a net;
they have placed traps all along the way. *Interlude*

6 I said to the LORD, "You are my God!"
Listen, O LORD, to my cries for mercy!
7 O Sovereign LORD, the strong one who rescued me,
you protected me on the day of battle.
8 LORD, do not let evil people have their way.
Do not let their evil schemes succeed,
or they will become proud. *Interlude*

9 Let my enemies be destroyed
by the very evil they have planned for me.
10 Let burning coals fall down on their heads.
Let them be thrown into the fire
or into watery pits from which they can't escape.
11 Don't let liars prosper here in our land.
Cause great disasters to fall on the violent.

12 But I know the LORD will help those they persecute;
he will give justice to the poor.
13 Surely righteous people are praising your name;
the godly will live in your presence.

141 *A psalm of David.*

1 O LORD, I am calling to you. Please hurry!
Listen when I cry to you for help!
2 Accept my prayer as incense offered to you,
and my upraised hands as an evening offering.

3 Take control of what I say, O LORD,
and guard my lips.
4 Don't let me drift toward evil
or take part in acts of wickedness.
Don't let me share in the delicacies
of those who do wrong.

5 Let the godly strike me!
It will be a kindness!
If they correct me, it is soothing medicine.
Don't let me refuse it.

But I pray constantly
against the wicked and their deeds.
6 When their leaders are thrown down from a cliff,
the wicked will listen to my words and find
them true.

7 Like rocks brought up by a plow,
the bones of the wicked will lie scattered
without burial.*

8 I look to you for help, O Sovereign LORD.
You are my refuge; don't let them kill me.
9 Keep me from the traps they have set for me,
from the snares of those who do wrong.
10 Let the wicked fall into their own nets,
but let me escape.

142 *A psalm* of David, regarding his experience in the cave. A prayer.*

1 I cry out to the LORD;
I plead for the LORD's mercy.
2 I pour out my complaints before him
and tell him all my troubles.
3 When I am overwhelmed,
you alone know the way I should turn.
Wherever I go,
my enemies have set traps for me.
4 I look for someone to come and help me,
but no one gives me a passing thought!
No one will help me;
no one cares a bit what happens to me.
5 Then I pray to you, O LORD.
I say, "You are my place of refuge.
You are all I really want in life.
6 Hear my cry,
for I am very low.
Rescue me from my persecutors,
for they are too strong for me.
7 Bring me out of prison
so I can thank you.
The godly will crowd around me,
for you are good to me."

143 *A psalm of David.*

1 Hear my prayer, O LORD;
listen to my plea!
Answer me because you are faithful and righteous.
2 Don't put your servant on trial,
for no one is innocent before you.
3 My enemy has chased me.
He has knocked me to the ground
and forces me to live in darkness like those in the grave.

141:7 Hebrew *our bones will be scattered at the mouth of Sheol.* **142:TITLE** Hebrew *maskil.* This may be a literary or musical term.

What I will do next

Prayer 143:8

Lord, help me make this psalm my morning prayer. Amen.

4 I am losing all hope;
I am paralyzed with fear.
5 I remember the days of old.
I ponder all your great works
and think about what you have done.
6 I lift my hands to you in prayer.
I thirst for you as parched land thirsts for rain. *Interlude*

7 Come quickly, LORD, and answer me,
for my depression deepens.
Don't turn away from me,
or I will die.
8 Let me hear of your unfailing love each morning,
for I am trusting you.
Show me where to walk,
for I give myself to you.
9 Rescue me from my enemies, LORD;
I run to you to hide me.
10 Teach me to do your will,
for you are my God.
May your gracious Spirit lead me forward
on a firm footing.
11 For the glory of your name, O LORD, preserve my life.
Because of your faithfulness, bring me out of this distress.
12 In your unfailing love, silence all my enemies
and destroy all my foes,
for I am your servant.

144 *A psalm of David.*

1 Praise the LORD, who is my rock.
He trains my hands for war
and gives my fingers skill for battle.
2 He is my loving ally and my fortress,
my tower of safety, my rescuer.
He is my shield, and I take refuge in him.
He makes the nations* submit to me.

3 O LORD, what are human beings that you should notice them,
mere mortals that you should think about them?
4 For they are like a breath of air;
their days are like a passing shadow.

5 Open the heavens, LORD, and come down.
Touch the mountains so they billow smoke.
6 Hurl your lightning bolts and scatter your enemies!
Shoot your arrows and confuse them!

144:2 Some manuscripts read *my people.*

7 Reach down from heaven and rescue me;
rescue me from deep waters,
from the power of my enemies.
8 Their mouths are full of lies;
they swear to tell the truth, but they lie instead.

9 I will sing a new song to you, O God!
I will sing your praises with a ten-stringed harp.
10 For you grant victory to kings!
You rescued your servant David from the fatal sword.
11 Save me!
Rescue me from the power of my enemies.
Their mouths are full of lies;
they swear to tell the truth, but they lie instead.

12 May our sons flourish in their youth
like well-nurtured plants.
May our daughters be like graceful pillars,
carved to beautify a palace.
13 May our barns be filled
with crops of every kind.
May the flocks in our fields multiply by the thousands,
even tens of thousands,
14 and may our oxen be loaded down with produce.
May there be no enemy breaking through our walls,
no going into captivity,
no cries of alarm in our town squares.
15 Yes, joyful are those who live like this!
Joyful indeed are those whose God is the LORD.

145*

A psalm of praise of David.

1 I will exalt you, my God and King,
and praise your name forever and ever.
2 I will praise you every day;
yes, I will praise you forever.
3 Great is the LORD! He is most worthy of praise!
No one can measure his greatness.

4 Let each generation tell its children of your mighty acts;
let them proclaim your power.
5 I will meditate on your majestic, glorious splendor
and your wonderful miracles.
6 Your awe-inspiring deeds will be on every tongue;
I will proclaim your greatness.
7 Everyone will share the story of your wonderful
goodness;
they will sing with joy about your righteousness.

145 This psalm is a Hebrew acrostic poem; each verse (including 13b) begins with a successive letter of the Hebrew alphabet.

Make a Difference

145:8

Slow and Rich

The world is still here, isn't it? God is patient and loving. He initiates and reinitiates love again and again and again. Even though people have repeatedly turned against him, God still desires that no one would perish apart from him. He longs to restore relationship with those he has made. He loves the world so much that he died for every single person. He sacrificed himself for them even while they were rejecting him with their actions. What causes a normal person to react in anger and retaliation causes God to respond with another outburst of grace.

If anyone else offered us this much latitude, this much time, this much empathy and support, we would have no choice but to accept their kindness. How could any of us say no to such an amazing friend?

Difference Maker

Who can benefit from you being gracious and compassionate today? How can you express a slowness in anger and a richness in love toward them?

8 The LORD is merciful and compassionate,
slow to get angry and filled with unfailing love.
9 The LORD is good to everyone.
He showers compassion on all his creation.
10 All of your works will thank you, LORD,
and your faithful followers will praise you.
11 They will speak of the glory of your kingdom;
they will give examples of your power.
12 They will tell about your mighty deeds
and about the majesty and glory of your reign.
13 For your kingdom is an everlasting kingdom.
You rule throughout all generations.

The LORD always keeps his promises;
he is gracious in all he does.*
14 The LORD helps the fallen
and lifts those bent beneath their loads.
15 The eyes of all look to you in hope;
you give them their food as they need it.
16 When you open your hand,
you satisfy the hunger and thirst of every living thing.
17 The LORD is righteous in everything he does;
he is filled with kindness.
18 The LORD is close to all who call on him,
yes, to all who call on him in truth.
19 He grants the desires of those who fear him;
he hears their cries for help and rescues them.
20 The LORD protects all those who love him,
but he destroys the wicked.

21 I will praise the LORD,
and may everyone on earth bless his holy name
forever and ever.

146

1 Praise the LORD!

Let all that I am praise the LORD.
2 I will praise the LORD as long as I live.
I will sing praises to my God with my dying breath.

3 Don't put your confidence in powerful people;
there is no help for you there.
4 When they breathe their last, they return to the earth,
and all their plans die with them.
5 But joyful are those who have the God of Israel* as their helper,
whose hope is in the LORD their God.
6 He made heaven and earth,
the sea, and everything in them.
He keeps every promise forever.

145:13 As in Dead Sea Scrolls and Greek and Syriac versions; the Masoretic Text lacks the final two lines of this verse. 146:5 Hebrew *of Jacob.* See note on 44:4.

7 He gives justice to the oppressed
and food to the hungry.
The LORD frees the prisoners.
8 The LORD opens the eyes of the blind.
The LORD lifts up those who are weighed down.
The LORD loves the godly.
9 The LORD protects the foreigners among us.
He cares for the orphans and widows,
but he frustrates the plans of the wicked.

10 The LORD will reign forever.
He will be your God, O Jerusalem,* throughout
the generations.

Praise the LORD!

147

1 Praise the LORD!

How good to sing praises to our God!
How delightful and how fitting!
2 The LORD is rebuilding Jerusalem
and bringing the exiles back to Israel.
3 He heals the brokenhearted
and bandages their wounds.
4 He counts the stars
and calls them all by name.
5 How great is our Lord! His power is absolute!
His understanding is beyond comprehension!
6 The LORD supports the humble,
but he brings the wicked down into the dust.

7 Sing out your thanks to the LORD;
sing praises to our God with a harp.
8 He covers the heavens with clouds,
provides rain for the earth,
and makes the grass grow in mountain pastures.
9 He gives food to the wild animals
and feeds the young ravens when they cry.
10 He takes no pleasure in the strength of a horse
or in human might.
11 No, the LORD's delight is in those who fear him,
those who put their hope in his unfailing love.

12 Glorify the LORD, O Jerusalem!
Praise your God, O Zion!
13 For he has strengthened the bars of your gates
and blessed your children within your walls.
14 He sends peace across your nation
and satisfies your hunger with the finest wheat.

146:10 Hebrew *Zion.*

Make a Difference

145:18

Called Near

No matter who you are or where you are or what you are with or without today, the Lord is near to you. Whoever you are, call on him today. If you're cool or awkward, just say, "Jesus, I need you." If you're rich or wrecked, just lift up his name and say, "Jesus." Wherever you are, call on him today. If you're lost or found, just reach out and say, "Jesus, will you stand with me?" If you're at home or far away, just speak his name, "Jesus." Whatever you have, call on him. If you have plenty or little, just ask, "Jesus, will you give me what I truly need?" If you have a broken heart or a full one, just whisper, "Jesus."

In each circumstance, he will hear you, and he will do what needs to be done for you. Just be honest about who you are, where you are, and what you have. Don't try to impress or try to trick. Just be yourself and call his name.

Difference Maker

Take a moment to pray about who you are, where you are, and what you have. Ask Jesus to be close to you in each of these areas of your life.

15 He sends his orders to the world—
how swiftly his word flies!
16 He sends the snow like white wool;
he scatters frost upon the ground like ashes.
17 He hurls the hail like stones.*
Who can stand against his freezing cold?
18 Then, at his command, it all melts.
He sends his winds, and the ice thaws.
19 He has revealed his words to Jacob,
his decrees and regulations to Israel.
20 He has not done this for any other nation;
they do not know his regulations.

Praise the LORD!

148

1 Praise the LORD!

Praise the LORD from the heavens!
Praise him from the skies!
2 Praise him, all his angels!
Praise him, all the armies of heaven!
3 Praise him, sun and moon!
Praise him, all you twinkling stars!
4 Praise him, skies above!
Praise him, vapors high above the clouds!
5 Let every created thing give praise to
the LORD,
for he issued his command, and they came
into being.
6 He set them in place forever and ever.
His decree will never be revoked.

7 Praise the LORD from the earth,
you creatures of the ocean depths,
8 fire and hail, snow and clouds,*
wind and weather that obey him,
9 mountains and all hills,
fruit trees and all cedars,
10 wild animals and all livestock,
small scurrying animals and birds,
11 kings of the earth and all people,
rulers and judges of the earth,
12 young men and young women,
old men and children.

13 Let them all praise the name of the LORD.
For his name is very great;
his glory towers over the earth and heaven!
14 He has made his people strong,

147:17 Hebrew *like bread crumbs.* **148:8** Or *mist,* or *smoke.*

honoring his faithful ones—
the people of Israel who are close to him.

Praise the LORD!

149

1 Praise the LORD!

Sing to the LORD a new song.
Sing his praises in the assembly of the faithful.

2 O Israel, rejoice in your Maker.
O people of Jerusalem,* exult in your King.
3 Praise his name with dancing,
accompanied by tambourine and harp.
4 For the LORD delights in his people;
he crowns the humble with victory.
5 Let the faithful rejoice that he honors them.
Let them sing for joy as they lie on their beds.

6 Let the praises of God be in their mouths,
and a sharp sword in their hands—
7 to execute vengeance on the nations
and punishment on the peoples,
8 to bind their kings with shackles
and their leaders with iron chains,
9 to execute the judgment written against them.
This is the glorious privilege of his faithful ones.

Praise the LORD!

150

1 Praise the LORD!

Praise God in his sanctuary;
praise him in his mighty heaven!
2 Praise him for his mighty works;
praise his unequaled greatness!
3 Praise him with a blast of the ram's horn;
praise him with the lyre and harp!
4 Praise him with the tambourine and dancing;
praise him with strings and flutes!
5 Praise him with a clash of cymbals;
praise him with loud clanging cymbals.
6 Let everything that breathes sing praises to the LORD!

Praise the LORD!

149:2 Hebrew *Zion.*

Question 150:6

What is the last line of this psalm? How could you do that today?

Proverbs Introduction

This book is not called *Pronouns*. It is called *Proverbs*. As you read this book, you are the subject who acts with the wisdom that you learn through its teachings. Wisdom is not slothful, lazy, inactive, or dead. Wisdom is productive. Wisdom flashes truth like lightning and reveals reality like a lamp. In the right moment, it makes its way through the race and realigns things to the way God patterned.

The book of Proverbs is all about wisdom but not just the sort of wisdom that helps you do well on a test. This wisdom is proactive, or maybe better said, it is pro-action. Stationary, nondescript living is not an acceptable posture for this type of wisdom. Proverbs does not allow for generic living, just going with the flow, being what culture says you should be, or limiting yourself because someone placed a ceiling on you. Proverbs urges you to search, to treasure, to listen, to learn. Proverbs requires your vigilance.

Will you give this book your steady gaze? Will you tune your ears and concentrate? Nearly every verse of this book deserves a Make a Difference box. Use the space provided to make your own comments and notes. Underline and mark up the pages of this book. Wisdom is granted not to the lazy but to those who deeply desire to act upon God's patterns in their lives.

Story Arc

● **Solomon**

Proverbs

The Purpose of Proverbs

1 These are the proverbs of Solomon, David's son, king of Israel.

2 Their purpose is to teach people wisdom and discipline,
to help them understand the insights of the wise.
3 Their purpose is to teach people to live disciplined and successful lives,
to help them do what is right, just, and fair.
4 These proverbs will give insight to the simple,
knowledge and discernment to the young.

5 Let the wise listen to these proverbs and become even wiser.
Let those with understanding receive guidance
6 by exploring the meaning in these proverbs and parables,
the words of the wise and their riddles.

7 Fear of the LORD is the foundation of true knowledge,
but fools despise wisdom and discipline.

A Father's Exhortation: Acquire Wisdom
8 My child,* listen when your father corrects you.
Don't neglect your mother's instruction.
9 What you learn from them will crown you with grace
and be a chain of honor around your neck.

10 My child, if sinners entice you,
turn your back on them!
11 They may say, "Come and join us.
Let's hide and kill someone!
Just for fun, let's ambush the innocent!
12 Let's swallow them alive, like the grave*;
let's swallow them whole, like those who go down to the pit of death.
13 Think of the great things we'll get!
We'll fill our houses with all the stuff we take.
14 Come, throw in your lot with us;
we'll all share the loot."

15 My child, don't go along with them!
Stay far away from their paths.
16 They rush to commit evil deeds.
They hurry to commit murder.
17 If a bird sees a trap being set,
it knows to stay away.

1:8 Hebrew *My son;* also in 1:10, 15. 1:12 Hebrew *like Sheol.*

Story Arc 1:1

Solomon

Solomon is considered one of the wisest men ever to have lived. In his day, he was known throughout the world for his discernment and judgment, his vision and planning, his ingenuity and insight (1 Kings 10:6). He also was known for his inconsistency and the foolish way he threw his kingdom away through compromising his faith and complicating his reign by marrying hundreds of women who turned his heart away from God (1 Kings 11).

Much of this book's collection of proverbs stems from Solomon's wise advice and from his precautions against foolishness. At this point he seemed to have learned from his mistakes and wanted to pass on to his son the better ways of living.

In the pages to follow, highlight moments of wisdom that stand out to you. The purpose of the proverbs, as Solomon said, is to teach wisdom and discipline that will help you do what is right, just, and fair.

Eccl 2:11 ►

Question 2:1-5

Which one of the action steps in Proverbs 2:1-5 could you implement today? How will you accomplish that?

18 But these people set an ambush for themselves;
they are trying to get themselves killed.
19 Such is the fate of all who are greedy for money;
it robs them of life.

Wisdom Shouts in the Streets

20 Wisdom shouts in the streets.
She cries out in the public square.
21 She calls to the crowds along the main street,
to those gathered in front of the city gate:
22 "How long, you simpletons,
will you insist on being simpleminded?
How long will you mockers relish your mocking?
How long will you fools hate knowledge?
23 Come and listen to my counsel.
I'll share my heart with you
and make you wise.

24 "I called you so often, but you wouldn't come.
I reached out to you, but you paid no attention.
25 You ignored my advice
and rejected the correction I offered.
26 So I will laugh when you are in trouble!
I will mock you when disaster overtakes you—
27 when calamity overtakes you like a storm,
when disaster engulfs you like a cyclone,
and anguish and distress overwhelm you.

28 "When they cry for help, I will not answer.
Though they anxiously search for me, they will not find me.
29 For they hated knowledge
and chose not to fear the LORD.
30 They rejected my advice
and paid no attention when I corrected them.
31 Therefore, they must eat the bitter fruit of living their own way,
choking on their own schemes.
32 For simpletons turn away from me—to death.
Fools are destroyed by their own complacency.
33 But all who listen to me will live in peace,
untroubled by fear of harm."

The Benefits of Wisdom

2 1 My child,* listen to what I say,
and treasure my commands.
2 Tune your ears to wisdom,
and concentrate on understanding.
3 Cry out for insight,
and ask for understanding.
4 Search for them as you would for silver;
seek them like hidden treasures.

2:1 Hebrew *My son.*

5 Then you will understand what it means to fear the LORD,
and you will gain knowledge of God.
6 For the LORD grants wisdom!
From his mouth come knowledge and understanding.
7 He grants a treasure of common sense to the honest.
He is a shield to those who walk with integrity.
8 He guards the paths of the just
and protects those who are faithful to him.

9 Then you will understand what is right, just, and fair,
and you will find the right way to go.
10 For wisdom will enter your heart,
and knowledge will fill you with joy.
11 Wise choices will watch over you.
Understanding will keep you safe.

12 Wisdom will save you from evil people,
from those whose words are twisted.
13 These men turn from the right way
to walk down dark paths.
14 They take pleasure in doing wrong,
and they enjoy the twisted ways of evil.
15 Their actions are crooked,
and their ways are wrong.

16 Wisdom will save you from the immoral woman,
from the seductive words of the promiscuous woman.
17 She has abandoned her husband
and ignores the covenant she made before God.
18 Entering her house leads to death;
it is the road to the grave.*
19 The man who visits her is doomed.
He will never reach the paths of life.

20 So follow the steps of the good,
and stay on the paths of the righteous.
21 For only the godly will live in the land,
and those with integrity will remain in it.
22 But the wicked will be removed from the land,
and the treacherous will be uprooted.

Trusting in the LORD

3 1 My child,* never forget the things I have taught you.
Store my commands in your heart.
2 If you do this, you will live many years,
and your life will be satisfying.
3 Never let loyalty and kindness leave you!
Tie them around your neck as a reminder.
Write them deep within your heart.

2:18 Hebrew *to the spirits of the dead.* 3:1 Hebrew *My son;* also in 3:11, 21.

Make a Difference

3:5–6

Lean

How do you handle making a choice that will dramatically shape your future? Do you get stuck with worry that you might make the wrong decision? When you are at an important juncture in your life, how do you select which way to go? What leads you or guides you when you're in that place?

The Bible encourages you to make decisions based upon what God wants for your life. If you get into the habit of walking with God, then the choices become much clearer. Following God naturally improves your confidence about the direction of your life. Your goal in any decision should be to align yourself with God's will. You should not trust yourself more than you trust God for the future of your life. If you seek God's input, then God will give you the ability and the freedom to make good choices that have a positive effect on your future.

Difference Maker

Lean on something, like a stool or a wall or a desk. As you trust this object to support you, lean on God in prayer for a few minutes. Ask him for his wisdom in any decision you need to make.

4 Then you will find favor with both God and people,
and you will earn a good reputation.

5 Trust in the LORD with all your heart;
do not depend on your own understanding.
6 Seek his will in all you do,
and he will show you which path to take.

7 Don't be impressed with your own wisdom.
Instead, fear the LORD and turn away from evil.
8 Then you will have healing for your body
and strength for your bones.

9 Honor the LORD with your wealth
and with the best part of everything you produce.
10 Then he will fill your barns with grain,
and your vats will overflow with good wine.

11 My child, don't reject the LORD's discipline,
and don't be upset when he corrects you.
12 For the LORD corrects those he loves,
just as a father corrects a child in whom he delights.*

13 Joyful is the person who finds wisdom,
the one who gains understanding.
14 For wisdom is more profitable than silver,
and her wages are better than gold.
15 Wisdom is more precious than rubies;
nothing you desire can compare with her.
16 She offers you long life in her right hand,
and riches and honor in her left.
17 She will guide you down delightful paths;
all her ways are satisfying.
18 Wisdom is a tree of life to those who embrace her;
happy are those who hold her tightly.

19 By wisdom the LORD founded the earth;
by understanding he created the heavens.
20 By his knowledge the deep fountains of the earth burst forth,
and the dew settles beneath the night sky.

21 My child, don't lose sight of common sense and discernment.
Hang on to them,
22 for they will refresh your soul.
They are like jewels on a necklace.
23 They keep you safe on your way,
and your feet will not stumble.
24 You can go to bed without fear;
you will lie down and sleep soundly.

3:12 Greek version reads *loves, / and he punishes those he accepts as his children.* Compare Heb 12:6.

25 You need not be afraid of sudden disaster
or the destruction that comes upon the wicked,
26 for the LORD is your security.
He will keep your foot from being caught in a trap.

27 Do not withhold good from those who deserve it
when it's in your power to help them.
28 If you can help your neighbor now, don't say,
"Come back tomorrow, and then I'll help you."

29 Don't plot harm against your neighbor,
for those who live nearby trust you.
30 Don't pick a fight without reason,
when no one has done you harm.

31 Don't envy violent people
or copy their ways.
32 Such wicked people are detestable to the LORD,
but he offers his friendship to the godly.

33 The LORD curses the house of the wicked,
but he blesses the home of the upright.

34 The LORD mocks the mockers
but is gracious to the humble.*

35 The wise inherit honor,
but fools are put to shame!

A Father's Wise Advice

4 1 My children,* listen when your father corrects you.
Pay attention and learn good judgment,
2 for I am giving you good guidance.
Don't turn away from my instructions.
3 For I, too, was once my father's son,
tenderly loved as my mother's only child.

4 My father taught me,
"Take my words to heart.
Follow my commands, and you will live.
5 Get wisdom; develop good judgment.
Don't forget my words or turn away from them.
6 Don't turn your back on wisdom, for she will
protect you.
Love her, and she will guard you.
7 Getting wisdom is the wisest thing you can do!
And whatever else you do, develop good judgment.
8 If you prize wisdom, she will make you great.
Embrace her, and she will honor you.

3:34 Greek version reads *The LORD opposes the proud / but gives grace to the humble.* Compare Jas 4:6; 1 Pet 5:5. 4:1 Hebrew *My sons.*

Question 3:27

Think of someone who has done good work without much fanfare (like a teacher or a grandparent or a volunteer). How could you honor their trustworthy contributions and encourage their future success?

Make a Difference 4:25

Eyes

You can usually tell when people are afraid or lying or unconfident because their eyes dart all around when you are speaking to them. It's as if they think they're being followed or they're feeling too insecure or too intimidated to look you in the eyes. Such a lack of focused vision causes people to make mistakes, either intentionally or unintentionally, out of chaos or anxiety.

In contrast, those who perseveringly follow Jesus keep steady eyes. A steady gaze on Jesus allows people to notice and absorb his already-focused gaze upon them. Their concentration on their Savior teaches them to walk securely in situations that seem impossible to eye rovers. This is the way of Jesus: keep your eyes secure, sight enabled, vision clear, and steps assured.

Difference Maker

What do you need to do to take the next intentional step in your life to focus on Jesus? Write it down and post it where your eyes will see it throughout the day.

Question 5:1

How could the bluntness of this chapter help people deal with sinful sexual habits?

9 She will place a lovely wreath on your head;
she will present you with a beautiful crown."

10 My child,* listen to me and do as I say,
and you will have a long, good life.
11 I will teach you wisdom's ways
and lead you in straight paths.
12 When you walk, you won't be held back;
when you run, you won't stumble.
13 Take hold of my instructions; don't let them go.
Guard them, for they are the key to life.

14 Don't do as the wicked do,
and don't follow the path of evildoers.
15 Don't even think about it; don't go that way.
Turn away and keep moving.
16 For evil people can't sleep until they've done their evil deed for the day.
They can't rest until they've caused someone to stumble.
17 They eat the food of wickedness
and drink the wine of violence!

18 The way of the righteous is like the first gleam of dawn,
which shines ever brighter until the full light of day.
19 But the way of the wicked is like total darkness.
They have no idea what they are stumbling over.

20 My child, pay attention to what I say.
Listen carefully to my words.
21 Don't lose sight of them.
Let them penetrate deep into your heart,
22 for they bring life to those who find them,
and healing to their whole body.

23 Guard your heart above all else,
for it determines the course of your life.

24 Avoid all perverse talk;
stay away from corrupt speech.

25 Look straight ahead,
and fix your eyes on what lies before you.
26 Mark out a straight path for your feet;
stay on the safe path.
27 Don't get sidetracked;
keep your feet from following evil.

Avoid Immoral Women

5 1 My son, pay attention to my wisdom;
listen carefully to my wise counsel.

4:10 Hebrew *My son;* also in 4:20.

2 Then you will show discernment,
and your lips will express what you've learned.
3 For the lips of an immoral woman are as sweet as honey,
and her mouth is smoother than oil.
4 But in the end she is as bitter as poison,
as dangerous as a double-edged sword.
5 Her feet go down to death;
her steps lead straight to the grave.*
6 For she cares nothing about the path to life.
She staggers down a crooked trail and doesn't realize it.

7 So now, my sons, listen to me.
Never stray from what I am about to say:
8 Stay away from her!
Don't go near the door of her house!
9 If you do, you will lose your honor
and will lose to merciless people all you have achieved.
10 Strangers will consume your wealth,
and someone else will enjoy the fruit of your labor.
11 In the end you will groan in anguish
when disease consumes your body.
12 You will say, "How I hated discipline!
If only I had not ignored all the warnings!
13 Oh, why didn't I listen to my teachers?
Why didn't I pay attention to my instructors?
14 I have come to the brink of utter ruin,
and now I must face public disgrace."

15 Drink water from your own well—
share your love only with your wife.*
16 Why spill the water of your springs in the streets,
having sex with just anyone?*
17 You should reserve it for yourselves.
Never share it with strangers.

18 Let your wife be a fountain of blessing for you.
Rejoice in the wife of your youth.
19 She is a loving deer, a graceful doe.
Let her breasts satisfy you always.
May you always be captivated by her love.
20 Why be captivated, my son, by an immoral woman,
or fondle the breasts of a promiscuous woman?

▲ 21 For the LORD sees clearly what a man does,
examining every path he takes.
22 An evil man is held captive by his own sins;
they are ropes that catch and hold him.
23 He will die for lack of self-control;
he will be lost because of his great foolishness.

5:5 Hebrew *to Sheol.* 5:15 Hebrew *Drink water from your own cistern, / flowing water from your own well.* 5:16 Hebrew *Why spill your springs in the streets, / your streams in the city squares?*

Prayer 5:21

Dear Jesus, I am tugged in multiple directions. Help me drown out the disruptive noise and stay true to you today. Amen.

Lessons for Daily Life

6 1 My child,* if you have put up security for a
friend's debt
or agreed to guarantee the debt of a stranger—
2 if you have trapped yourself by your agreement
and are caught by what you said—
3 follow my advice and save yourself,
for you have placed yourself at your friend's mercy.
Now swallow your pride;
go and beg to have your name erased.
4 Don't put it off; do it now!
Don't rest until you do.
5 Save yourself like a gazelle escaping from a hunter,
like a bird fleeing from a net.

6 Take a lesson from the ants, you lazybones.
Learn from their ways and become wise!
7 Though they have no prince
or governor or ruler to make them work,
8 they labor hard all summer,
gathering food for the winter.
9 But you, lazybones, how long will you sleep?
When will you wake up?
10 A little extra sleep, a little more slumber,
a little folding of the hands to rest—
11 then poverty will pounce on you like a bandit;
scarcity will attack you like an armed robber.

12 What are worthless and wicked people like?
They are constant liars,
13 signaling their deceit with a wink of the eye,
a nudge of the foot, or the wiggle of fingers.
14 Their perverted hearts plot evil,
and they constantly stir up trouble.
15 But they will be destroyed suddenly,
broken in an instant beyond all hope of healing.

16 There are six things the LORD hates—
no, seven things he detests:
17 haughty eyes,
a lying tongue,
hands that kill the innocent,
18 a heart that plots evil,
feet that race to do wrong,
19 a false witness who pours out lies,
a person who sows discord in a family.

20 My son, obey your father's commands,
and don't neglect your mother's instruction.

6:1 Hebrew *My son.*

21 Keep their words always in your heart.
Tie them around your neck.
22 When you walk, their counsel will lead you.
When you sleep, they will protect you.
When you wake up, they will advise you.
23 For their command is a lamp
and their instruction a light;
their corrective discipline
is the way to life.
24 It will keep you from the immoral woman,
from the smooth tongue of a promiscuous woman.
25 Don't lust for her beauty.
Don't let her coy glances seduce you.
26 For a prostitute will bring you to poverty,*
but sleeping with another man's wife will cost you your life.
27 Can a man scoop a flame into his lap
and not have his clothes catch on fire?
28 Can he walk on hot coals
and not blister his feet?
29 So it is with the man who sleeps with another man's wife.
He who embraces her will not go unpunished.

30 Excuses might be found for a thief
who steals because he is starving.
31 But if he is caught, he must pay back seven times what
he stole,
even if he has to sell everything in his house.
32 But the man who commits adultery is an utter fool,
for he destroys himself.
33 He will be wounded and disgraced.
His shame will never be erased.
34 For the woman's jealous husband will be furious,
and he will show no mercy when he takes revenge.
35 He will accept no compensation,
nor be satisfied with a payoff of any size.

Another Warning about Immoral Women

7 1 Follow my advice, my son;
always treasure my commands.
2 Obey my commands and live!
Guard my instructions as you guard your own eyes.*
3 Tie them on your fingers as a reminder.
Write them deep within your heart.

4 Love wisdom like a sister;
make insight a beloved member of your family.
5 Let them protect you from an affair with an immoral
woman,
from listening to the flattery of a promiscuous woman.

Prayer 7:2-3

Jesus, guard my life with wisdom as if your Word were filtered through my eyes. Work in my actions as if your Word were tied to my fingers. Amen.

6:26 Hebrew *to a loaf of bread.* **7:2** Hebrew *as the pupil of your eye.*

6 While I was at the window of my house,
looking through the curtain,
7 I saw some naive young men,
and one in particular who lacked common sense.
8 He was crossing the street near the house of an immoral woman,
strolling down the path by her house.
9 It was at twilight, in the evening,
as deep darkness fell.
10 The woman approached him,
seductively dressed and sly of heart.
11 She was the brash, rebellious type,
never content to stay at home.
12 She is often in the streets and markets,
soliciting at every corner.
13 She threw her arms around him and kissed him,
and with a brazen look she said,
14 "I've just made my peace offerings
and fulfilled my vows.
15 You're the one I was looking for!
I came out to find you, and here you are!
16 My bed is spread with beautiful blankets,
with colored sheets of Egyptian linen.
17 I've perfumed my bed
with myrrh, aloes, and cinnamon.
18 Come, let's drink our fill of love until morning.
Let's enjoy each other's caresses,
19 for my husband is not home.
He's away on a long trip.
20 He has taken a wallet full of money with him
and won't return until later this month.*"

21 So she seduced him with her pretty speech
and enticed him with her flattery.
22 He followed her at once,
like an ox going to the slaughter.
He was like a stag caught in a trap,*
23 awaiting the arrow that would pierce its heart.
He was like a bird flying into a snare,
little knowing it would cost him his life.

24 So listen to me, my sons,
and pay attention to my words.
25 Don't let your hearts stray away toward her.
Don't wander down her wayward path.
26 For she has been the ruin of many;
many men have been her victims.
27 Her house is the road to the grave.*
Her bedroom is the den of death.

7:20 Hebrew *until the moon is full.* 7:22 As in Greek and Syriac versions; Hebrew reads *slaughter, as shackles are for the discipline of a fool.* 7:27 Hebrew *to Sheol.*

Wisdom Calls for a Hearing

8 1 Listen as Wisdom calls out!
Hear as understanding raises her voice!
2 On the hilltop along the road,
she takes her stand at the crossroads.
3 By the gates at the entrance to the town,
on the road leading in, she cries aloud,
4 "I call to you, to all of you!
I raise my voice to all people.
5 You simple people, use good judgment.
You foolish people, show some understanding.
6 Listen to me! For I have important things to tell you.
Everything I say is right,
7 for I speak the truth
and detest every kind of deception.
8 My advice is wholesome.
There is nothing devious or crooked in it.
9 My words are plain to anyone with understanding,
clear to those with knowledge.
10 Choose my instruction rather than silver,
and knowledge rather than pure gold.
11 For wisdom is far more valuable than rubies.
Nothing you desire can compare with it.

12 "I, Wisdom, live together with good judgment.
I know where to discover knowledge and discernment.
13 All who fear the LORD will hate evil.
Therefore, I hate pride and arrogance,
corruption and perverse speech.
14 Common sense and success belong to me.
Insight and strength are mine.
15 Because of me, kings reign,
and rulers make just decrees.
16 Rulers lead with my help,
and nobles make righteous judgments.*

17 "I love all who love me.
Those who search will surely find me.
18 I have riches and honor,
as well as enduring wealth and justice.
19 My gifts are better than gold, even the purest gold,
my wages better than sterling silver!
20 I walk in righteousness,
in paths of justice.
21 Those who love me inherit wealth.
I will fill their treasuries.

22 "The LORD formed me from the beginning,
before he created anything else.

8:16 Some Hebrew manuscripts and Greek version read *and nobles are judges over the earth.*

Your thoughts can go here

23 I was appointed in ages past,
at the very first, before the earth began.
24 I was born before the oceans were created,
before the springs bubbled forth their waters.
25 Before the mountains were formed,
before the hills, I was born—
26 before he had made the earth and fields
and the first handfuls of soil.
27 I was there when he established the heavens,
when he drew the horizon on the oceans.
28 I was there when he set the clouds above,
when he established springs deep in the earth.
29 I was there when he set the limits of the seas,
so they would not spread beyond their boundaries.
And when he marked off the earth's foundations,
30 I was the architect at his side.
I was his constant delight,
rejoicing always in his presence.
31 And how happy I was with the world he created;
how I rejoiced with the human family!

32 "And so, my children,* listen to me,
for all who follow my ways are joyful.
33 Listen to my instruction and be wise.
Don't ignore it.
34 Joyful are those who listen to me,
watching for me daily at my gates,
waiting for me outside my home!
35 For whoever finds me finds life
and receives favor from the LORD.
36 But those who miss me injure themselves.
All who hate me love death."

9 1 Wisdom has built her house;
she has carved its seven columns.
2 She has prepared a great banquet,
mixed the wines, and set the table.
3 She has sent her servants to invite everyone to come.
She calls out from the heights overlooking the city.
4 "Come in with me," she urges the simple.
To those who lack good judgment, she says,
5 "Come, eat my food,
and drink the wine I have mixed.
6 Leave your simple ways behind, and begin to live;
learn to use good judgment."

7 Anyone who rebukes a mocker will get an insult
in return.
Anyone who corrects the wicked will get hurt.

8:32 Hebrew *my sons.*

8 So don't bother correcting mockers;
they will only hate you.
But correct the wise,
and they will love you.
9 Instruct the wise,
and they will be even wiser.
Teach the righteous,
and they will learn even more.

10 Fear of the LORD is the foundation of wisdom.
Knowledge of the Holy One results in good judgment.

11 Wisdom will multiply your days
and add years to your life.
12 If you become wise, you will be the one to benefit.
If you scorn wisdom, you will be the one to suffer.

Folly Calls for a Hearing
13 The woman named Folly is brash.
She is ignorant and doesn't know it.
14 She sits in her doorway
on the heights overlooking the city.
15 She calls out to men going by
who are minding their own business.
16 "Come in with me," she urges the simple.
To those who lack good judgment, she says,
17 "Stolen water is refreshing;
food eaten in secret tastes the best!"
18 But little do they know that the dead are there.
Her guests are in the depths of the grave.*

The Proverbs of Solomon
10 The proverbs of Solomon:

A wise child* brings joy to a father;
a foolish child brings grief to a mother.

2 Tainted wealth has no lasting value,
but right living can save your life.

3 The LORD will not let the godly go hungry,
but he refuses to satisfy the craving of the wicked.

4 Lazy people are soon poor;
hard workers get rich.

5 A wise youth harvests in the summer,
but one who sleeps during harvest is a disgrace.

Question 10:5

Even if this is an annoying proverb, why is it still good advice for a young person?

9:18 Hebrew *in Sheol.* 10:1 Hebrew *son;* also in 10:1b.

Make a Difference 10:17

How to Be a Fool

Here is a time-tested way to guarantee foolishness: don't ever learn anything. Just refuse to do it. If someone corrects you, reject their input. If teachers mark your answers as wrong, just get mad and blame them. If a police officer tells you to use your blinker, just go ahead and swear up a storm and argue. If your friends offer you some constructive feedback, just ignore them.

The word *disciple* means "learn." If you are a disciple of Jesus, that means you are a learner of Jesus. As painful as it may be, learning requires discipline, instruction, and correction. Foolishness requires only ignorance.

Difference Maker

Pick an area of your life that you know needs more discipline. Ask someone to hold you accountable, to correct you when you are wrong, and to help you learn.

6 The godly are showered with blessings;
the words of the wicked conceal violent intentions.

7 We have happy memories of the godly,
but the name of a wicked person rots away.

8 The wise are glad to be instructed,
but babbling fools fall flat on their faces.

9 People with integrity walk safely,
but those who follow crooked paths will be exposed.

10 People who wink at wrong cause trouble,
but a bold reproof promotes peace.*

11 The words of the godly are a life-giving fountain;
the words of the wicked conceal violent intentions.

12 Hatred stirs up quarrels,
but love makes up for all offenses.

13 Wise words come from the lips of people with
understanding,
but those lacking sense will be beaten with a rod.

14 Wise people treasure knowledge,
but the babbling of a fool invites disaster.

15 The wealth of the rich is their fortress;
the poverty of the poor is their destruction.

16 The earnings of the godly enhance their lives,
but evil people squander their money on sin.

17 People who accept discipline are on the pathway to life,
but those who ignore correction will go astray.

18 Hiding hatred makes you a liar;
slandering others makes you a fool.

19 Too much talk leads to sin.
Be sensible and keep your mouth shut.

20 The words of the godly are like sterling silver;
the heart of a fool is worthless.

21 The words of the godly encourage many,
but fools are destroyed by their lack of
common sense.

10:10 As in Greek version; Hebrew reads *but babbling fools fall flat on their faces.*

22 The blessing of the LORD makes a person rich,
and he adds no sorrow with it.

23 Doing wrong is fun for a fool,
but living wisely brings pleasure to the sensible.

24 The fears of the wicked will be fulfilled;
the hopes of the godly will be granted.

25 When the storms of life come, the wicked are whirled away,
but the godly have a lasting foundation.

26 Lazy people irritate their employers,
like vinegar to the teeth or smoke in the eyes.

27 Fear of the LORD lengthens one's life,
but the years of the wicked are cut short.

28 The hopes of the godly result in happiness,
but the expectations of the wicked come to nothing.

29 The way of the LORD is a stronghold to those with integrity,
but it destroys the wicked.

30 The godly will never be disturbed,
but the wicked will be removed from the land.

31 The mouth of the godly person gives wise advice,
but the tongue that deceives will be cut off.

32 The lips of the godly speak helpful words,
but the mouth of the wicked speaks perverse words.

11 1 The LORD detests the use of dishonest scales,
but he delights in accurate weights.

2 Pride leads to disgrace,
but with humility comes wisdom.

3 Honesty guides good people;
dishonesty destroys treacherous people.

4 Riches won't help on the day of judgment,
but right living can save you from death.

5 The godly are directed by honesty;
the wicked fall beneath their load of sin.

6 The godliness of good people rescues them;
the ambition of treacherous people traps them.

Make a Difference 11:17

Kindness

One thing that most certainly affects how anyone feels about themselves is how they treat others. Ironically, by focusing on treating others with kindness, people usually feel built up within themselves. Kindness causes people to stop turning inward and to start living outward. It expands their freedom, their creativity, their joy, and their optimism.

The opposite is also a reality. Cruel treatment of others echoes back to the attacker. Heated anger you throw at someone burns you more than it hurts the targeted person. Hurtful words, despicable harm, shameful acts—they ricochet like shrapnel, rend the hearts of those nearby, and poison the soul of the aggressor. The world hesitates at this thought, but the truth is that kindness has the power to change the world for good.

Difference Maker

Do as many random acts of kindness for others today as you can possibly think of doing. Then rest with confidence and a smile at the end of the day.

Make a Difference 11:25

Generous Ways

Jesus changes lives. It's what he is good at doing. Those who are changed by Jesus change lives too. From one person to the next, there is a passing on of Jesus' generosity, life overflowing with life. Here are just some of the generous ways someone who has been changed by Jesus can live today:

- Leave a 25 percent tip.
- Listen to a friend longer and less distractedly.
- Tutor a younger person in a subject you understand.
- Buy an extra meal and give it to someone.

7 When the wicked die, their hopes die with them,
for they rely on their own feeble strength.

8 The godly are rescued from trouble,
and it falls on the wicked instead.

9 With their words, the godless destroy their friends,
but knowledge will rescue the righteous.

10 The whole city celebrates when the godly succeed;
they shout for joy when the wicked die.

11 Upright citizens are good for a city and make it prosper,
but the talk of the wicked tears it apart.

12 It is foolish to belittle one's neighbor;
a sensible person keeps quiet.

13 A gossip goes around telling secrets,
but those who are trustworthy can keep a confidence.

14 Without wise leadership, a nation falls;
there is safety in having many advisers.

15 There's danger in putting up security for a stranger's debt;
it's safer not to guarantee another person's debt.

16 A gracious woman gains respect,
but ruthless men gain only wealth.

17 Your kindness will reward you,
but your cruelty will destroy you.

18 Evil people get rich for the moment,
but the reward of the godly will last.

19 Godly people find life;
evil people find death.

20 The Lord detests people with crooked hearts,
but he delights in those with integrity.

21 Evil people will surely be punished,
but the children of the godly will go free.

22 A beautiful woman who lacks discretion
is like a gold ring in a pig's snout.

23 The godly can look forward to a reward,
while the wicked can expect only judgment.

24 Give freely and become more wealthy;
be stingy and lose everything.

25 The generous will prosper;
those who refresh others will themselves be refreshed.

26 People curse those who hoard their grain,
but they bless the one who sells in time of need.

27 If you search for good, you will find favor;
but if you search for evil, it will find you!

28 Trust in your money and down you go!
But the godly flourish like leaves in spring.

29 Those who bring trouble on their families inherit
the wind.
The fool will be a servant to the wise.

30 The seeds of good deeds become a tree of life;
a wise person wins friends.*

31 If the righteous are rewarded here on earth,
what will happen to wicked sinners?*

12

1 To learn, you must love discipline;
it is stupid to hate correction.

2 The LORD approves of those who are good,
but he condemns those who plan wickedness.

3 Wickedness never brings stability,
but the godly have deep roots.

4 A worthy wife is a crown for her husband,
but a disgraceful woman is like cancer in his bones.

5 The plans of the godly are just;
the advice of the wicked is treacherous.

6 The words of the wicked are like a murderous
ambush,
but the words of the godly save lives.

7 The wicked die and disappear,
but the family of the godly stands firm.

8 A sensible person wins admiration,
but a warped mind is despised.

11:30 Or *and those who win souls are wise.* **11:31** Greek version reads *If the righteous are barely saved, / what will happen to godless sinners?* Compare 1 Pet 4:18.

- Be the first one to set up and to clean up.
- Look someone in the eyes during a conversation.
- Smile. A lot.

Difference Maker

Choose at least one of the generous ways listed above to put into practice.

Make a Difference 11:30

Plant It Forward

Those who do good things encourage others to do good things too. It really is a simple formula. One person doing something good leads to another person doing something good and so on. Before long, good deeds pile themselves into an expanding difference-making movement. Good deed × good deed × good deed = world change.

Difference Maker

Spend the day doing good things for people. Everywhere you go, intentionally and spontaneously sow kindness into the lives of others.

Make a Difference 12:1

Stupid

Being corrected can feel really annoying. You might even be tempted to get angry with the one who corrects your mistakes. Get over it. Learn from someone's discipline, and do even better next time as a result.

Difference Maker

Find someone you trust and whose advice you would like to have in your life and ask for them to give you some constructive feedback on your plans.

Prayer 12:16

Lord Jesus, don't let me mess up in anger today. Keep my heart cooled by your love. Amen.

9 Better to be an ordinary person with a servant
than to be self-important but have no food.

10 The godly care for their animals,
but the wicked are always cruel.

11 A hard worker has plenty of food,
but a person who chases fantasies has no sense.

12 Thieves are jealous of each other's loot,
but the godly are well rooted and bear their own fruit.

13 The wicked are trapped by their own words,
but the godly escape such trouble.

14 Wise words bring many benefits,
and hard work brings rewards.

15 Fools think their own way is right,
but the wise listen to others.

16 A fool is quick-tempered,
but a wise person stays calm when insulted.

17 An honest witness tells the truth;
a false witness tells lies.

18 Some people make cutting remarks,
but the words of the wise bring healing.

19 Truthful words stand the test of time,
but lies are soon exposed.

20 Deceit fills hearts that are plotting evil;
joy fills hearts that are planning peace!

21 No harm comes to the godly,
but the wicked have their fill of trouble.

22 The LORD detests lying lips,
but he delights in those who tell the truth.

23 The wise don't make a show of their knowledge,
but fools broadcast their foolishness.

24 Work hard and become a leader;
be lazy and become a slave.

25 Worry weighs a person down;
an encouraging word cheers a person up.

26 The godly give good advice to their friends;*
the wicked lead them astray.

27 Lazy people don't even cook the game they catch,
but the diligent make use of everything they find.

28 The way of the godly leads to life;
that path does not lead to death.

13

1 A wise child accepts a parent's discipline;*
a mocker refuses to listen to correction.

2 Wise words will win you a good meal,
but treacherous people have an appetite for
violence.

3 Those who control their tongue will have a long life;
opening your mouth can ruin everything.

4 Lazy people want much but get little,
but those who work hard will prosper.

5 The godly hate lies;
the wicked cause shame and disgrace.

6 Godliness guards the path of the blameless,
but the evil are misled by sin.

7 Some who are poor pretend to be rich;
others who are rich pretend to be poor.

8 The rich can pay a ransom for their lives,
but the poor won't even get threatened.

9 The life of the godly is full of light and joy,
but the light of the wicked will be snuffed out.

10 Pride leads to conflict;
those who take advice are wise.

11 Wealth from get-rich-quick schemes quickly disappears;
wealth from hard work grows over time.

12 Hope deferred makes the heart sick,
but a dream fulfilled is a tree of life.

13 People who despise advice are asking for trouble;
those who respect a command will succeed.

12:26 Or *The godly are cautious in friendship;* or *The godly are freed from evil.* The meaning of the Hebrew is uncertain. **13:1** Hebrew *A wise son accepts his father's discipline.*

Make a Difference 13:3

Accidental Words

It happens in slow motion. You can sense your lips separating, feel your muscles forming, and hear the sounds emerge from your vocal cords, and still, you can't stop the words from screeching out of your mouth, through the red light, and into the intersection. The accident caused by your words can ruin relationships, opportunities, cooperation, and even hope. The debris of your words can shatter people and can be a mess that others need to clean up.

One of the best ways you could positively influence this world is to learn when to speak and what to say when you actually do speak. Those who speak with right words and right timing speak life. Those who speak with harmful words and harmful timing speak only ruin.

Jesus was a master with his words. He was even called the Word by the apostle John. Jesus spoke everything into existence, and even now he speaks truth into your heart and mine. He responded wisely in tricky circumstances, gently in heated moments, and truthfully in the face of sin. He knew just what to say and how to say it so that people would be able to discover God.

Difference Maker

Practice going through the day saying only those things you believe Jesus would want you to say.

Question 13:20

Would you say that the company you keep makes you wiser or more foolish?

14 The instruction of the wise is like a life-giving fountain;
those who accept it avoid the snares of death.

15 A person with good sense is respected;
a treacherous person is headed for destruction.*

16 Wise people think before they act;
fools don't—and even brag about their foolishness.

17 An unreliable messenger stumbles into trouble,
but a reliable messenger brings healing.

18 If you ignore criticism, you will end in poverty and disgrace;
if you accept correction, you will be honored.

19 It is pleasant to see dreams come true,
but fools refuse to turn from evil to attain them.

20 Walk with the wise and become wise;
associate with fools and get in trouble.

21 Trouble chases sinners,
while blessings reward the righteous.

22 Good people leave an inheritance to their grandchildren,
but the sinner's wealth passes to the godly.

23 A poor person's farm may produce much food,
but injustice sweeps it all away.

24 Those who spare the rod of discipline hate their children.
Those who love their children care enough
to discipline them.

25 The godly eat to their hearts' content,
but the belly of the wicked goes hungry.

14

1 A wise woman builds her home,
but a foolish woman tears it down with
her own hands.

2 Those who follow the right path fear the LORD;
those who take the wrong path despise him.

3 A fool's proud talk becomes a rod that beats him,
but the words of the wise keep them safe.

4 Without oxen a stable stays clean,
but you need a strong ox for a large harvest.

13:15 As in Greek version; Hebrew reads *the way of the treacherous is lasting.*

5 An honest witness does not lie;
a false witness breathes lies.

6 A mocker seeks wisdom and never finds it,
but knowledge comes easily to those with
understanding.

7 Stay away from fools,
for you won't find knowledge on their lips.

8 The prudent understand where they are going,
but fools deceive themselves.

9 Fools make fun of guilt,
but the godly acknowledge it and seek
reconciliation.

10 Each heart knows its own bitterness,
and no one else can fully share its joy.

11 The house of the wicked will be destroyed,
but the tent of the godly will flourish.

12 There is a path before each person that seems right,
but it ends in death.

13 Laughter can conceal a heavy heart,
but when the laughter ends, the grief remains.

14 Backsliders get what they deserve;
good people receive their reward.

15 Only simpletons believe everything they're told!
The prudent carefully consider their steps.

16 The wise are cautious* and avoid danger;
fools plunge ahead with reckless confidence.

17 Short-tempered people do foolish things,
and schemers are hated.

18 Simpletons are clothed with foolishness,*
but the prudent are crowned with knowledge.

19 Evil people will bow before good people;
the wicked will bow at the gates of the godly.

20 The poor are despised even by their neighbors,
while the rich have many "friends."

14:16 Hebrew *The wise fear.* **14:18** Or *inherit foolishness.*

Make a Difference 14:17

The Wrong Kind of Difference

Jesus wants you to make a difference in the world. A good difference—not a mixed-up, mangled, messed-up difference. Jesus said to his disciples that their love for each other would prove to the world that they were his followers (John 13:35). Unfortunately, all too often, people who say they follow Jesus end up making the wrong kind of difference in this world.

It would be a terrible thing if those who claimed to follow Jesus demonstrated tempers, idiocy, and conspiracy. People who are quick to anger inevitably do really stupid things, which, in turn, causes them to scheme and worm and twist things for their own protection and gain. It would be terrible for the reputation of Christians to suffer because people who claimed to follow Jesus failed to live with love. Christians are supposed to be a light to the world, reflecting Jesus into the darkness. They are not supposed to be dispensers of darkness themselves.

Difference Maker

What do you see around the corner that is going to trigger your temper? How could you prepare yourself to respond in love?

Make a Difference

14:29

Control Your Anger

Jesus had passion—buckets of it—but somehow, he was able to harness this passion into effective action rather than ineffective anger. Even as the rulers plotted against him, as the mobs rejected him, and as the disciples slept while he wept, Jesus never lost his cool.

His holiness was at his fingertips, his wrath at his disposal, and his creative and destructive capability within the sound of his summons. Still, he kept them sheathed. His anger was only ever righteous, and it was under his control.

Difference Maker

Try taking ten long, slow, deep breaths anytime you get fired up today. As you breathe, pray for God's control in your life.

21 It is a sin to belittle one's neighbor;
blessed are those who help the poor.

22 If you plan to do evil, you will be lost;
if you plan to do good, you will receive unfailing love and faithfulness.

23 Work brings profit,
but mere talk leads to poverty!

24 Wealth is a crown for the wise;
the effort of fools yields only foolishness.

25 A truthful witness saves lives,
but a false witness is a traitor.

26 Those who fear the LORD are secure;
he will be a refuge for their children.

27 Fear of the LORD is a life-giving fountain;
it offers escape from the snares of death.

28 A growing population is a king's glory;
a prince without subjects has nothing.

29 People with understanding control their anger;
a hot temper shows great foolishness.

30 A peaceful heart leads to a healthy body;
jealousy is like cancer in the bones.

31 Those who oppress the poor insult their Maker,
but helping the poor honors him.

32 The wicked are crushed by disaster,
but the godly have a refuge when they die.

33 Wisdom is enshrined in an understanding heart;
wisdom is not* found among fools.

34 Godliness makes a nation great,
but sin is a disgrace to any people.

35 A king rejoices in wise servants
but is angry with those who disgrace him.

15

1 A gentle answer deflects anger,
but harsh words make tempers flare.

14:33 As in Greek and Syriac versions; Hebrew lacks *not*.

2 The tongue of the wise makes knowledge appealing,
but the mouth of a fool belches out foolishness.

3 The LORD is watching everywhere,
keeping his eye on both the evil and the good.

4 Gentle words are a tree of life;
a deceitful tongue crushes the spirit.

5 Only a fool despises a parent's* discipline;
whoever learns from correction is wise.

6 There is treasure in the house of the godly,
but the earnings of the wicked bring trouble.

7 The lips of the wise give good advice;
the heart of a fool has none to give.

8 The LORD detests the sacrifice of the wicked,
but he delights in the prayers of the upright.

9 The LORD detests the way of the wicked,
but he loves those who pursue godliness.

10 Whoever abandons the right path will be severely
disciplined;
whoever hates correction will die.

11 Even Death and Destruction* hold no secrets from
the LORD.
How much more does he know the human heart!

12 Mockers hate to be corrected,
so they stay away from the wise.

13 A glad heart makes a happy face;
a broken heart crushes the spirit.

14 A wise person is hungry for knowledge,
while the fool feeds on trash.

15 For the despondent, every day brings trouble;
for the happy heart, life is a continual feast.

16 Better to have little, with fear for the LORD,
than to have great treasure and inner turmoil.

17 A bowl of vegetables with someone you love
is better than steak with someone you hate.

15:5 Hebrew *father's.* 15:11 Hebrew *Sheol and Abaddon.*

18 A hot-tempered person starts fights;
a cool-tempered person stops them.

19 A lazy person's way is blocked with briers,
but the path of the upright is an open highway.

20 Sensible children bring joy to their father;
foolish children despise their mother.

21 Foolishness brings joy to those with no sense;
a sensible person stays on the right path.

22 Plans go wrong for lack of advice;
many advisers bring success.

23 Everyone enjoys a fitting reply;
it is wonderful to say the right thing at the right time!

24 The path of life leads upward for the wise;
they leave the grave* behind.

25 The LORD tears down the house of the proud,
but he protects the property of widows.

26 The LORD detests evil plans,
but he delights in pure words.

27 Greed brings grief to the whole family,
but those who hate bribes will live.

28 The heart of the godly thinks carefully
before speaking;
the mouth of the wicked overflows with evil words.

29 The LORD is far from the wicked,
but he hears the prayers of the righteous.

30 A cheerful look brings joy to the heart;
good news makes for good health.

31 If you listen to constructive criticism,
you will be at home among the wise.

32 If you reject discipline, you only harm yourself;
but if you listen to correction, you grow in
understanding.

33 Fear of the LORD teaches wisdom;
humility precedes honor.

15:24 Hebrew *Sheol.*

Make a Difference

15:31

Constructive

Have you seen those talent shows where the contestant argues with the judges? Even though the person may have just sung completely off-key or stumbled through their dance, still, they stand there and refuse to accept any avenue for critique.

When someone tells you that you are wrong and they are clearly right, how do you handle it? If a teacher corrects your error, do you make excuses? If a friend points out one of your annoying traits, do you point out two of theirs right back? If an expert shows you a better way, an older person gives you instructions, or a coach tells you to work harder, are you patient and thankful and willing?

Accepting feedback is evidence of godly character. Resisting feedback and reacting negatively to feedback, however, show a lack of maturity. We need to be people who accept feedback in whatever form it comes so we can live looking more and more like Christ.

Difference Maker

Ask a trusted friend to offer you constructive feedback on a recent project, on an assignment, or perhaps on your leadership skills.

16

1 We can make our own plans,
but the LORD gives the right answer.

2 People may be pure in their own eyes,
but the LORD examines their motives.

3 Commit your actions to the LORD,
and your plans will succeed.

4 The LORD has made everything for his own purposes,
even the wicked for a day of disaster.

5 The LORD detests the proud;
they will surely be punished.

6 Unfailing love and faithfulness make atonement for sin.
By fearing the LORD, people avoid evil.

7 When people's lives please the LORD,
even their enemies are at peace with them.

8 Better to have little, with godliness,
than to be rich and dishonest.

9 We can make our plans,
but the LORD determines our steps.

10 The king speaks with divine wisdom;
he must never judge unfairly.

11 The LORD demands accurate scales and balances;
he sets the standards for fairness.

12 A king detests wrongdoing,
for his rule is built on justice.

13 The king is pleased with words from righteous lips;
he loves those who speak honestly.

14 The anger of the king is a deadly threat;
the wise will try to appease it.

15 When the king smiles, there is life;
his favor refreshes like a spring rain.

16 How much better to get wisdom than gold,
and good judgment than silver!

17 The path of the virtuous leads away from evil;
whoever follows that path is safe.

Make a Difference 16:3

Your Plans

If you wanted to rob a bank and you committed this plan to the Lord, would you succeed? Of course not! The whole robbing-the-bank part wouldn't work out because God wouldn't support it. He'd probably hand you back your blueprints and tell you to find a better path.

To commit your plans to God means to hand them over, let him look them over, and work them over until they match his will. He is glad to work with you on any necessary changes (instead of robbing he might suggest investing). If you accept God's revised plans and act on them, then you have shown that you have committed your plans to the Lord. Once this is true, your plans will succeed. In other words, do what God wants you to do today. Make your plan of action in line with God's plan of action, and all will go according to plan.

Difference Maker

Work on your résumé and practice interviewing for the opportunities God has for you in the future. As you do, ask yourself this question: "Do God's plans for me match my plans for me?"

18 Pride goes before destruction,
and haughtiness before a fall.

19 Better to live humbly with the poor
than to share plunder with the proud.

20 Those who listen to instruction will prosper;
those who trust the LORD will be joyful.

21 The wise are known for their understanding,
and pleasant words are persuasive.

22 Discretion is a life-giving fountain to those who possess it,
but discipline is wasted on fools.

23 From a wise mind comes wise speech;
the words of the wise are persuasive.

24 Kind words are like honey—
sweet to the soul and healthy for the body.

25 There is a path before each person that seems right,
but it ends in death.

26 It is good for workers to have an appetite;
an empty stomach drives them on.

27 Scoundrels create trouble;
their words are a destructive blaze.

28 A troublemaker plants seeds of strife;
gossip separates the best of friends.

29 Violent people mislead their companions,
leading them down a harmful path.

30 With narrowed eyes, people plot evil;
with a smirk, they plan their mischief.

31 Gray hair is a crown of glory;
it is gained by living a godly life.

32 Better to be patient than powerful;
better to have self-control than to conquer a city.

33 We may throw the dice,*
but the LORD determines how they fall.

16:33 Hebrew *We may cast lots.*

17 [1] Better a dry crust eaten in peace
than a house filled with feasting—and conflict.

2 A wise servant will rule over the master's disgraceful son
and will share the inheritance of the master's children.

3 Fire tests the purity of silver and gold,
but the LORD tests the heart.

4 Wrongdoers eagerly listen to gossip;
liars pay close attention to slander.

5 Those who mock the poor insult their Maker;
those who rejoice at the misfortune of others will
be punished.

6 Grandchildren are the crowning glory of the aged;
parents* are the pride of their children.

7 Eloquent words are not fitting for a fool;
even less are lies fitting for a ruler.

8 A bribe is like a lucky charm;
whoever gives one will prosper!

9 Love prospers when a fault is forgiven,
but dwelling on it separates close friends.

10 A single rebuke does more for a person of
understanding
than a hundred lashes on the back of a fool.

11 Evil people are eager for rebellion,
but they will be severely punished.

12 It is safer to meet a bear robbed of her cubs
than to confront a fool caught in foolishness.

13 If you repay good with evil,
evil will never leave your house.

14 Starting a quarrel is like opening a floodgate,
so stop before a dispute breaks out.

15 Acquitting the guilty and condemning the innocent—
both are detestable to the LORD.

16 It is senseless to pay to educate a fool,
since he has no heart for learning.

17:6 Hebrew *fathers.*

Reflect on this passage

Prayer **17:27**

Jesus, give me your words and prompt me when to use them. Don't let my mouth get in the way. Amen.

17 A friend is always loyal,
and a brother is born to help in time of need.

18 It's poor judgment to guarantee another person's debt
or put up security for a friend.

19 Anyone who loves to quarrel loves sin;
anyone who trusts in high walls invites disaster.

20 The crooked heart will not prosper;
the lying tongue tumbles into trouble.

21 It is painful to be the parent of a fool;
there is no joy for the father of a rebel.

22 A cheerful heart is good medicine,
but a broken spirit saps a person's strength.

23 The wicked take secret bribes
to pervert the course of justice.

24 Sensible people keep their eyes glued on wisdom,
but a fool's eyes wander to the ends of
the earth.

25 Foolish children* bring grief to their father
and bitterness to the one who gave them birth.

26 It is wrong to punish the godly for being good
or to flog leaders for being honest.

▲ 27 A truly wise person uses few words;
a person with understanding is even-tempered.

28 Even fools are thought wise when they keep silent;
with their mouths shut, they seem intelligent.

18

1 Unfriendly people care only about themselves;
they lash out at common sense.

2 Fools have no interest in understanding;
they only want to air their own opinions.

3 Doing wrong leads to disgrace,
and scandalous behavior brings contempt.

4 Wise words are like deep waters;
wisdom flows from the wise like a bubbling
brook.

17:25 Hebrew *A foolish son.*

5 It is not right to acquit the guilty
or deny justice to the innocent.

6 Fools' words get them into constant quarrels;
they are asking for a beating.

7 The mouths of fools are their ruin;
they trap themselves with their lips.

8 Rumors are dainty morsels
that sink deep into one's heart.

9 A lazy person is as bad as
someone who destroys things.

10 The name of the LORD is a strong fortress;
the godly run to him and are safe.

11 The rich think of their wealth as a strong defense;
they imagine it to be a high wall of safety.

12 Haughtiness goes before destruction;
humility precedes honor.

13 Spouting off before listening to the facts
is both shameful and foolish.

14 The human spirit can endure a sick body,
but who can bear a crushed spirit?

15 Intelligent people are always ready to learn.
Their ears are open for knowledge.

16 Giving a gift can open doors;
it gives access to important people!

17 The first to speak in court sounds right—
until the cross-examination begins.

18 Flipping a coin* can end arguments;
it settles disputes between powerful opponents.

19 An offended friend is harder to win back than a
fortified city.
Arguments separate friends like a gate locked
with bars.

20 Wise words satisfy like a good meal;
the right words bring satisfaction.

18:18 Hebrew *Casting lots.*

Question 18:24

What do you learn about true friendship from this proverb?

Make a Difference 19:2

Eliminate Hurry

Rushing into something with excitement but without understanding is a formula for embarrassing disaster. Hurried mistakes reveal the deficiencies of an undisciplined life.

Difference Maker

Take extra effort to take care of yourself today in order to limit your mistakes. Get good rest, eat healthy, don't rush your attitude, and breathe deeply.

21 The tongue can bring death or life;
those who love to talk will reap the consequences.

22 The man who finds a wife finds a treasure,
and he receives favor from the LORD.

23 The poor plead for mercy;
the rich answer with insults.

24 There are "friends" who destroy each other,
but a real friend sticks closer than a brother.

19

1 Better to be poor and honest
than to be dishonest and a fool.

2 Enthusiasm without knowledge is no good;
haste makes mistakes.

3 People ruin their lives by their own foolishness
and then are angry at the LORD.

4 Wealth makes many "friends";
poverty drives them all away.

5 A false witness will not go unpunished,
nor will a liar escape.

6 Many seek favors from a ruler;
everyone is the friend of a person who
gives gifts!

7 The relatives of the poor despise them;
how much more will their friends avoid them!
Though the poor plead with them,
their friends are gone.

8 To acquire wisdom is to love yourself;
people who cherish understanding will prosper.

9 A false witness will not go unpunished,
and a liar will be destroyed.

10 It isn't right for a fool to live in luxury
or for a slave to rule over princes!

11 Sensible people control their temper;
they earn respect by overlooking wrongs.

12 The king's anger is like a lion's roar,
but his favor is like dew on the grass.

13 A foolish child* is a calamity to a father;
a quarrelsome wife is as annoying as constant dripping.

14 Fathers can give their sons an inheritance of houses and wealth,
but only the LORD can give an understanding wife.

15 Lazy people sleep soundly,
but idleness leaves them hungry.

16 Keep the commandments and keep your life;
despising them leads to death.

17 If you help the poor, you are lending to the LORD—
and he will repay you!

18 Discipline your children while there is hope.
Otherwise you will ruin their lives.

19 Hot-tempered people must pay the penalty.
If you rescue them once, you will have to do it again.

20 Get all the advice and instruction you can,
so you will be wise the rest of your life.

21 You can make many plans,
but the LORD's purpose will prevail.

22 Loyalty makes a person attractive.
It is better to be poor than dishonest.

23 Fear of the LORD leads to life,
bringing security and protection from harm.

24 Lazy people take food in their hand
but don't even lift it to their mouth.

25 If you punish a mocker, the simpleminded will learn
a lesson;
if you correct the wise, they will be all the wiser.

26 Children who mistreat their father or chase away
their mother
are an embarrassment and a public disgrace.

27 If you stop listening to instruction, my child,
you will turn your back on knowledge.

28 A corrupt witness makes a mockery of justice;
the mouth of the wicked gulps down evil.

19:13 Hebrew *son;* also in 19:27.

29 Punishment is made for mockers,
and the backs of fools are made to be beaten.

20

1 Wine produces mockers; alcohol leads to brawls.
Those led astray by drink cannot be wise.

2 The king's fury is like a lion's roar;
to rouse his anger is to risk your life.

3 Avoiding a fight is a mark of honor;
only fools insist on quarreling.

4 Those too lazy to plow in the right season
will have no food at the harvest.

5 Though good advice lies deep within the heart,
a person with understanding will draw it out.

6 Many will say they are loyal friends,
but who can find one who is truly reliable?

7 The godly walk with integrity;
blessed are their children who follow them.

8 When a king sits in judgment, he weighs all
the evidence,
distinguishing the bad from the good.

9 Who can say, "I have cleansed my heart;
I am pure and free from sin"?

10 False weights and unequal measures*—
the LORD detests double standards of every kind.

11 Even children are known by the way they act,
whether their conduct is pure, and whether
it is right.

12 Ears to hear and eyes to see—
both are gifts from the LORD.

13 If you love sleep, you will end in poverty.
Keep your eyes open, and there will be plenty to eat!

14 The buyer haggles over the price, saying, "It's worthless,"
then brags about getting a bargain!

15 Wise words are more valuable
than much gold and many rubies.

20:10 Hebrew *A stone and a stone, an ephah and an ephah.*

16 Get security from someone who guarantees
a stranger's debt.
Get a deposit if he does it for foreigners.*

17 Stolen bread tastes sweet,
but it turns to gravel in the mouth.

18 Plans succeed through good counsel;
don't go to war without wise advice.

19 A gossip goes around telling secrets,
so don't hang around with chatterers.

20 If you insult your father or mother,
your light will be snuffed out in total darkness.

21 An inheritance obtained too early in life
is not a blessing in the end.

22 Don't say, "I will get even for this wrong."
Wait for the LORD to handle the matter.

23 The LORD detests double standards;
he is not pleased by dishonest scales.

24 The LORD directs our steps,
so why try to understand everything along the way?

25 Don't trap yourself by making a rash promise to God
and only later counting the cost.

26 A wise king scatters the wicked like wheat,
then runs his threshing wheel over them.

27 The LORD's light penetrates the human spirit,*
exposing every hidden motive.

28 Unfailing love and faithfulness protect the king;
his throne is made secure through love.

29 The glory of the young is their strength;
the gray hair of experience is the splendor of the old.

30 Physical punishment cleanses away evil;*
such discipline purifies the heart.

21

1 The king's heart is like a stream of water directed
by the LORD;
he guides it wherever he pleases.

20:16 An alternate reading in the Masoretic Text is *for a promiscuous woman.* **20:27** Or *The human spirit is the LORD's light.* **20:30** The meaning of the Hebrew is uncertain.

What God is saying to us

2 People may be right in their own eyes,
but the LORD examines their heart.

3 The LORD is more pleased when we do what is right
and just
than when we offer him sacrifices.

4 Haughty eyes, a proud heart,
and evil actions are all sin.

5 Good planning and hard work lead to prosperity,
but hasty shortcuts lead to poverty.

6 Wealth created by a lying tongue
is a vanishing mist and a deadly trap.*

7 The violence of the wicked sweeps them away,
because they refuse to do what is just.

8 The guilty walk a crooked path;
the innocent travel a straight road.

9 It's better to live alone in the corner of an attic
than with a quarrelsome wife in a lovely home.

10 Evil people desire evil;
their neighbors get no mercy from them.

11 If you punish a mocker, the simpleminded become wise;
if you instruct the wise, they will be all the wiser.

12 The Righteous One* knows what is going on in the homes
of the wicked;
he will bring disaster on them.

13 Those who shut their ears to the cries of the poor
will be ignored in their own time of need.

14 A secret gift calms anger;
a bribe under the table pacifies fury.

15 Justice is a joy to the godly,
but it terrifies evildoers.

16 The person who strays from common sense
will end up in the company of the dead.

17 Those who love pleasure become poor;
those who love wine and luxury will never be rich.

21:6 As in Greek version; Hebrew reads *mist for those who seek death.* 21:12 Or *The righteous man.*

18 The wicked are punished in place of the godly,
and traitors in place of the honest.

19 It's better to live alone in the desert
than with a quarrelsome, complaining wife.

20 The wise have wealth and luxury,
but fools spend whatever they get.

21 Whoever pursues righteousness and unfailing love
will find life, righteousness, and honor.

22 The wise conquer the city of the strong
and level the fortress in which they trust.

23 Watch your tongue and keep your mouth shut,
and you will stay out of trouble.

24 Mockers are proud and haughty;
they act with boundless arrogance.

25 Despite their desires, the lazy will come to ruin,
for their hands refuse to work.

26 Some people are always greedy for more,
but the godly love to give!

27 The sacrifice of an evil person is detestable,
especially when it is offered with wrong motives.

28 A false witness will be cut off,
but a credible witness will be allowed to speak.

29 The wicked bluff their way through,
but the virtuous think before they act.

30 No human wisdom or understanding or plan
can stand against the LORD.

31 The horse is prepared for the day of battle,
but the victory belongs to the LORD.

22 1 Choose a good reputation over great riches;
being held in high esteem is better than silver or gold.

2 The rich and poor have this in common:
The LORD made them both.

3 A prudent person foresees danger and takes precautions.
The simpleton goes blindly on and suffers the consequences.

Question 22:1

What do you want in life? When presented with a choice between things or reputation, which would you choose?

4 True humility and fear of the LORD
lead to riches, honor, and long life.

5 Corrupt people walk a thorny, treacherous road;
whoever values life will avoid it.

6 Direct your children onto the right path,
and when they are older, they will not leave it.

7 Just as the rich rule the poor,
so the borrower is servant to the lender.

8 Those who plant injustice will harvest disaster,
and their reign of terror will come to an end.*

9 Blessed are those who are generous,
because they feed the poor.

10 Throw out the mocker, and fighting goes, too.
Quarrels and insults will disappear.

11 Whoever loves a pure heart and gracious speech
will have the king as a friend.

12 The LORD preserves those with knowledge,
but he ruins the plans of the treacherous.

13 The lazy person claims, "There's a lion out there!
If I go outside, I might be killed!"

14 The mouth of an immoral woman is a dangerous trap;
those who make the LORD angry will fall into it.

15 A youngster's heart is filled with foolishness,
but physical discipline will drive it far away.

16 A person who gets ahead by oppressing the poor
or by showering gifts on the rich will end in poverty.

Sayings of the Wise

17 Listen to the words of the wise;
apply your heart to my instruction.
18 For it is good to keep these sayings in your heart
and always ready on your lips.
19 I am teaching you today—yes, you—
so you will trust in the LORD.
20 I have written thirty sayings* for you,
filled with advice and knowledge.

22:8 The Greek version includes an additional proverb: *God blesses a man who gives cheerfully, / but his worthless deeds will come to an end.* Compare 2 Cor 9:7. 22:20 Or *excellent sayings;* the meaning of the Hebrew is uncertain.

21 In this way, you may know the truth
and take an accurate report to those who sent you.

22 Don't rob the poor just because you can,
or exploit the needy in court.
23 For the LORD is their defender.
He will ruin anyone who ruins them.

24 Don't befriend angry people
or associate with hot-tempered people,
25 or you will learn to be like them
and endanger your soul.

26 Don't agree to guarantee another person's debt
or put up security for someone else.
27 If you can't pay it,
even your bed will be snatched from under you.

28 Don't cheat your neighbor by moving the ancient boundary markers
set up by previous generations.

29 Do you see any truly competent workers?
They will serve kings
rather than working for ordinary people.

23

1 While dining with a ruler,
pay attention to what is put before you.
2 If you are a big eater,
put a knife to your throat;
3 don't desire all the delicacies,
for he might be trying to trick you.

4 Don't wear yourself out trying to get rich.
Be wise enough to know when to quit.
5 In the blink of an eye wealth disappears,
for it will sprout wings
and fly away like an eagle.

6 Don't eat with people who are stingy;
don't desire their delicacies.
7 They are always thinking about how much it costs.*
"Eat and drink," they say, but they don't mean it.
8 You will throw up what little you've eaten,
and your compliments will be wasted.

9 Don't waste your breath on fools,
for they will despise the wisest advice.

23:7 The meaning of the Hebrew is uncertain.

Question 22:24-25

In verses 24-25, what negative difference do hot-tempered friends make in your life?

Question 23:15

How does this verse express the hope of a loving parent? What does this proverb reveal about how your heavenly Father wants to rejoice over you?

10 Don't cheat your neighbor by moving the ancient boundary markers;
don't take the land of defenseless orphans.
11 For their Redeemer* is strong;
he himself will bring their charges against you.

12 Commit yourself to instruction;
listen carefully to words of knowledge.

13 Don't fail to discipline your children.
The rod of punishment won't kill them.
14 Physical discipline
may well save them from death.*

15 My child,* if your heart is wise,
my own heart will rejoice!
16 Everything in me will celebrate
when you speak what is right.

17 Don't envy sinners,
but always continue to fear the LORD.
18 You will be rewarded for this;
your hope will not be disappointed.

19 My child, listen and be wise:
Keep your heart on the right course.
20 Do not carouse with drunkards
or feast with gluttons,
21 for they are on their way to poverty,
and too much sleep clothes them in rags.

22 Listen to your father, who gave you life,
and don't despise your mother when she is old.
23 Get the truth and never sell it;
also get wisdom, discipline, and good judgment.
24 The father of godly children has cause for joy.
What a pleasure to have children who are wise.*
25 So give your father and mother joy!
May she who gave you birth be happy.

26 O my son, give me your heart.
May your eyes take delight in following my ways.
27 A prostitute is a dangerous trap;
a promiscuous woman is as dangerous as falling into a narrow well.
28 She hides and waits like a robber,
eager to make more men unfaithful.

29 Who has anguish? Who has sorrow?
Who is always fighting? Who is always complaining?
Who has unnecessary bruises? Who has bloodshot eyes?

23:11 Or *redeemer.* 23:14 Hebrew *from Sheol.* 23:15 Hebrew *My son;* also in 23:19.
23:24 Hebrew *to have a wise son.*

30 It is the one who spends long hours in the taverns,
trying out new drinks.
31 Don't gaze at the wine, seeing how red it is,
how it sparkles in the cup, how smoothly it
goes down.
32 For in the end it bites like a poisonous snake;
it stings like a viper.
33 You will see hallucinations,
and you will say crazy things.
34 You will stagger like a sailor tossed at sea,
clinging to a swaying mast.
35 And you will say, "They hit me, but I didn't feel it.
I didn't even know it when they beat me up.
When will I wake up
so I can look for another drink?"

24 1 Don't envy evil people
or desire their company.
2 For their hearts plot violence,
and their words always stir up trouble.

3 A house is built by wisdom
and becomes strong through good sense.
4 Through knowledge its rooms are filled
with all sorts of precious riches and valuables.

5 The wise are mightier than the strong,*
and those with knowledge grow stronger and stronger.
6 So don't go to war without wise guidance;
victory depends on having many advisers.

7 Wisdom is too lofty for fools.
Among leaders at the city gate, they have nothing
to say.

8 A person who plans evil
will get a reputation as a troublemaker.
9 The schemes of a fool are sinful;
everyone detests a mocker.

10 If you fail under pressure,
your strength is too small.

11 Rescue those who are unjustly sentenced to die;
save them as they stagger to their death.
12 Don't excuse yourself by saying, "Look, we didn't know."
For God understands all hearts, and he sees you.
He who guards your soul knows you knew.
He will repay all people as their actions deserve.

24:5 As in Greek version; Hebrew reads *A wise man is strength.*

Prayer 24:16

Lord Jesus, give me the resilience to keep getting up when I get knocked down. Let me work with confident determination today and trust you for the long-term results of my actions. Amen.

13 My child,* eat honey, for it is good,
and the honeycomb is sweet to the taste.
14 In the same way, wisdom is sweet to your soul.
If you find it, you will have a bright future,
and your hopes will not be cut short.

15 Don't wait in ambush at the home of the godly,
and don't raid the house where the godly live.
16 The godly may trip seven times, but they will get up again.
But one disaster is enough to overthrow the wicked.

17 Don't rejoice when your enemies fall;
don't be happy when they stumble.
18 For the LORD will be displeased with you
and will turn his anger away from them.

19 Don't fret because of evildoers;
don't envy the wicked.
20 For evil people have no future;
the light of the wicked will be snuffed out.

21 My child, fear the LORD and the king.
Don't associate with rebels,
22 for disaster will hit them suddenly.
Who knows what punishment will come
from the LORD and the king?

More Sayings of the Wise

23 Here are some further sayings of the wise:

It is wrong to show favoritism when passing judgment.
24 A judge who says to the wicked, "You are innocent,"
will be cursed by many people and denounced by the nations.
25 But it will go well for those who convict the guilty;
rich blessings will be showered on them.

26 An honest answer
is like a kiss of friendship.

27 Do your planning and prepare your fields
before building your house.

28 Don't testify against your neighbors without cause;
don't lie about them.
29 And don't say, "Now I can pay them back for what they've done to me!
I'll get even with them!"

30 I walked by the field of a lazy person,
the vineyard of one with no common sense.

24:13 Hebrew *My son;* also in 24:21.

31 I saw that it was overgrown with nettles.
It was covered with weeds,
and its walls were broken down.
32 Then, as I looked and thought about it,
I learned this lesson:
33 A little extra sleep, a little more slumber,
a little folding of the hands to rest—
34 then poverty will pounce on you like a bandit;
scarcity will attack you like an armed robber.

More Proverbs of Solomon

25 These are more proverbs of Solomon, collected by the advisers of King Hezekiah of Judah.

2 It is God's privilege to conceal things
and the king's privilege to discover them.

3 No one can comprehend the height of heaven, the depth
of the earth,
or all that goes on in the king's mind!

4 Remove the impurities from silver,
and the sterling will be ready for the silversmith.
5 Remove the wicked from the king's court,
and his reign will be made secure by justice.

6 Don't demand an audience with the king
or push for a place among the great.
7 It's better to wait for an invitation to the head table
than to be sent away in public disgrace.

Just because you've seen something,
8 don't be in a hurry to go to court.
For what will you do in the end
if your neighbor deals you a shameful defeat?

9 When arguing with your neighbor,
don't betray another person's secret.
10 Others may accuse you of gossip,
and you will never regain your good reputation.

11 Timely advice is lovely,
like golden apples in a silver basket.

12 To one who listens, valid criticism
is like a gold earring or other gold jewelry.

13 Trustworthy messengers refresh like snow
in summer.
They revive the spirit of their employer.

Question 25:21

How does this proverb reflect the way of Jesus?

14 A person who promises a gift but doesn't give it
is like clouds and wind that bring no rain.

15 Patience can persuade a prince,
and soft speech can break bones.

16 Do you like honey?
Don't eat too much, or it will make you sick!

17 Don't visit your neighbors too often,
or you will wear out your welcome.

18 Telling lies about others
is as harmful as hitting them with an ax,
wounding them with a sword,
or shooting them with a sharp arrow.

19 Putting confidence in an unreliable person in times of trouble
is like chewing with a broken tooth or walking on a lame foot.

20 Singing cheerful songs to a person with a heavy heart
is like taking someone's coat in cold weather
or pouring vinegar in a wound.*

21 If your enemies are hungry, give them food to eat.
If they are thirsty, give them water to drink.
22 You will heap burning coals of shame on their heads,
and the LORD will reward you.

23 As surely as a north wind brings rain,
so a gossiping tongue causes anger!

24 It's better to live alone in the corner of an attic
than with a quarrelsome wife in a lovely home.

25 Good news from far away
is like cold water to the thirsty.

26 If the godly give in to the wicked,
it's like polluting a fountain or muddying a spring.

27 It's not good to eat too much honey,
and it's not good to seek honors for yourself.

28 A person without self-control
is like a city with broken-down walls.

26

1 Honor is no more associated with fools
than snow with summer or rain with harvest.

25:20 As in Greek version; Hebrew reads *pouring vinegar on soda.*

2 Like a fluttering sparrow or a darting swallow,
an undeserved curse will not land on its intended victim.

3 Guide a horse with a whip, a donkey with a bridle,
and a fool with a rod to his back!

4 Don't answer the foolish arguments of fools,
or you will become as foolish as they are.

5 Be sure to answer the foolish arguments of fools,
or they will become wise in their own estimation.

6 Trusting a fool to convey a message
is like cutting off one's feet or drinking poison!

7 A proverb in the mouth of a fool
is as useless as a paralyzed leg.

8 Honoring a fool
is as foolish as tying a stone to a slingshot.

9 A proverb in the mouth of a fool
is like a thorny branch brandished by a drunk.

10 An employer who hires a fool or a bystander
is like an archer who shoots at random.

11 As a dog returns to its vomit,
so a fool repeats his foolishness.

12 There is more hope for fools
than for people who think they are wise.

13 The lazy person claims, "There's a lion on the road!
Yes, I'm sure there's a lion out there!"

14 As a door swings back and forth on its hinges,
so the lazy person turns over in bed.

15 Lazy people take food in their hand
but don't even lift it to their mouth.

16 Lazy people consider themselves smarter
than seven wise counselors.

17 Interfering in someone else's argument
is as foolish as yanking a dog's ears.

18 Just as damaging
as a madman shooting a deadly weapon

Make a Difference

26:11

Don't Return to Vomit

This world really needs Jesus because people make so many frustratingly foolish choices. Like dogs that return to their own vomit, some people hurt themselves by revisiting things that disgust their souls. Like vultures that hunt their prey, some people hurt others by repeatedly taking advantage of weaknesses. Like sheep that wander, some people repetitively make wrong choices that end up hurting everyone in their circle of influence.

God did not create people to do stupid things, yet people continually stray from God's patterns, either intentionally or unintentionally. People constantly find themselves humiliated and trapped by the lure of sin's idiocy. Thankfully, Jesus overcame humanity's corrupt absurdity by pursuing the cross, where all the stupidity of sin is collected and destroyed. There Jesus offers his life-giving wisdom and heart-empowering joy in exchange. In this way, the cross of Christ dumbfounds foolish pursuits.

Difference Maker

Don't do something today that you will regret doing. Choose to do something else instead.

19 is someone who lies to a friend
and then says, "I was only joking."

20 Fire goes out without wood,
and quarrels disappear when gossip stops.

21 A quarrelsome person starts fights
as easily as hot embers light charcoal or fire
lights wood.

22 Rumors are dainty morsels
that sink deep into one's heart.

23 Smooth* words may hide a wicked heart,
just as a pretty glaze covers a clay pot.

24 People may cover their hatred with pleasant words,
but they're deceiving you.
25 They pretend to be kind, but don't believe them.
Their hearts are full of many evils.*
26 While their hatred may be concealed by trickery,
their wrongdoing will be exposed in public.

27 If you set a trap for others,
you will get caught in it yourself.
If you roll a boulder down on others,
it will crush you instead.

28 A lying tongue hates its victims,
and flattering words cause ruin.

27 1 Don't brag about tomorrow,
since you don't know what the day
will bring.

2 Let someone else praise you, not your own mouth—
a stranger, not your own lips.

3 A stone is heavy and sand is weighty,
but the resentment caused by a fool is even heavier.

4 Anger is cruel, and wrath is like a flood,
but jealousy is even more dangerous.

5 An open rebuke
is better than hidden love!

6 Wounds from a sincere friend
are better than many kisses from an enemy.

26:23 As in Greek version; Hebrew reads *Burning.* 26:25 Hebrew *seven evils.*

Drop your brilliant thoughts here

7 A person who is full refuses honey,
but even bitter food tastes sweet to the hungry.

8 A person who strays from home
is like a bird that strays from its nest.

9 The heartfelt counsel of a friend
is as sweet as perfume and incense.

10 Never abandon a friend—
either yours or your father's.
When disaster strikes, you won't have to ask your brother for assistance.
It's better to go to a neighbor than to a brother who lives far away.

11 Be wise, my child,* and make my heart glad.
Then I will be able to answer my critics.

12 A prudent person foresees danger and takes precautions.
The simpleton goes blindly on and suffers the consequences.

13 Get security from someone who guarantees a stranger's debt.
Get a deposit if he does it for foreigners.*

14 A loud and cheerful greeting early in the morning
will be taken as a curse!

15 A quarrelsome wife is as annoying
as constant dripping on a rainy day.
16 Stopping her complaints is like trying to stop the wind
or trying to hold something with greased hands.

17 As iron sharpens iron,
so a friend sharpens a friend.

18 As workers who tend a fig tree are allowed to eat the fruit,
so workers who protect their employer's interests will be rewarded.

19 As a face is reflected in water,
so the heart reflects the real person.

20 Just as Death and Destruction* are never satisfied,
so human desire is never satisfied.

21 Fire tests the purity of silver and gold,
but a person is tested by being praised.*

22 You cannot separate fools from their foolishness,
even though you grind them like grain with mortar and pestle.

27:11 Hebrew *my son.* 27:13 As in Greek and Latin versions (see also 20:16); Hebrew reads *for a promiscuous woman.* 27:20 Hebrew *Sheol and Abaddon.* 27:21 Or *by flattery.*

Make a Difference

28:13

No Cover

When you were a kid and did something wrong, maybe you ran to your room and buried yourself under the covers. If you couldn't see out, perhaps your parents couldn't see in. You were covered—or so you thought.

There is an old adage: "Everyone eventually gets caught." Sin, in whatever form, eventually undermines your life. It sneaks up and snatches control of you. It can slowly erode your willpower to do what is right, and if you try to hide, it can twist your perception of truth. No amount of covering conceals your sin.

The irony of covering up wrongs, of course, is that the crime committer always knows—and God always knows too. It is never a secret to everyone. The best way to deal with sin is to expose it. Be honest with God, yourself, and others. Fess up. Change your heart. Let God uncover you in a shower of mercy.

Difference Maker

Confession is not easy, but if there is any concealed sin in your life, turn it over to God right now and take steps to gain freedom from it today.

23 Know the state of your flocks,
and put your heart into caring for your herds,
24 for riches don't last forever,
and the crown might not be passed to the next generation.
25 After the hay is harvested and the new crop appears
and the mountain grasses are gathered in,
26 your sheep will provide wool for clothing,
and your goats will provide the price of a field.
27 And you will have enough goats' milk for yourself,
your family, and your servant girls.

28 1 The wicked run away when no one is chasing them,
but the godly are as bold as lions.

2 When there is moral rot within a nation, its government topples easily.
But wise and knowledgeable leaders bring stability.

3 A poor person who oppresses the poor
is like a pounding rain that destroys the crops.

4 To reject the law is to praise the wicked;
to obey the law is to fight them.

5 Evil people don't understand justice,
but those who follow the LORD understand completely.

6 Better to be poor and honest
than to be dishonest and rich.

7 Young people who obey the law are wise;
those with wild friends bring shame to their parents.*

8 Income from charging high interest rates
will end up in the pocket of someone who is kind to the poor.

9 God detests the prayers
of a person who ignores the law.

10 Those who lead good people along an evil path
will fall into their own trap,
but the honest will inherit good things.

11 Rich people may think they are wise,
but a poor person with discernment can see right through them.

12 When the godly succeed, everyone is glad.
When the wicked take charge, people go into hiding.

28:7 Hebrew *their father.*

13 People who conceal their sins will not prosper,
but if they confess and turn from them, they will receive mercy.

14 Blessed are those who fear to do wrong,*
but the stubborn are headed for serious trouble.

15 A wicked ruler is as dangerous to the poor
as a roaring lion or an attacking bear.

16 A ruler with no understanding will oppress his people,
but one who hates corruption will have a long life.

17 A murderer's tormented conscience will drive him into the grave.
Don't protect him!

18 The blameless will be rescued from harm,
but the crooked will be suddenly destroyed.

19 A hard worker has plenty of food,
but a person who chases fantasies ends up in poverty.

20 The trustworthy person will get a rich reward,
but a person who wants quick riches will get into trouble.

21 Showing partiality is never good,
yet some will do wrong for a mere piece of bread.

22 Greedy people try to get rich quick
but don't realize they're headed for poverty.

23 In the end, people appreciate honest criticism
far more than flattery.

24 Anyone who steals from his father and mother
and says, "What's wrong with that?"
is no better than a murderer.

25 Greed causes fighting;
trusting the LORD leads to prosperity.

26 Those who trust their own insight are foolish,
but anyone who walks in wisdom is safe.

27 Whoever gives to the poor will lack nothing,
but those who close their eyes to poverty will be cursed.

28 When the wicked take charge, people go into hiding.
When the wicked meet disaster, the godly flourish.

28:14 Or *those who fear the* LORD; Hebrew reads *those who fear.*

Make a Difference

28:19

Work

You've heard the stories, right? Some lucky guy strikes it rich in the state lottery only to squander it all away carelessly. All his money didn't stand a chance against all his spending. What once seemed like an endless supply of resources one day leaked away to nothing.

It's great to have dreams and passions. It's wonderful to want to travel and play. It's even okay to pray for an unexpected windfall. Still, ordinarily, to truly obtain the sort of stable life that puts food on the plate and clothes on the back takes healthy planning and hard work. Food doesn't magically appear on the plate, and savings don't miraculously appear in the account. Ask any aging former child superstar or any one-hit musical wonder. The combination of fantastical consumption mixed with a lazy attitude depletes the reservoirs of life.

Difference Maker

Don't procrastinate on any projects today. Finish your to-do list before allowing yourself to play.

29

1 Whoever stubbornly refuses to accept criticism
will suddenly be destroyed beyond recovery.

2 When the godly are in authority, the people rejoice.
But when the wicked are in power, they groan.

3 The man who loves wisdom brings joy to his father,
but if he hangs around with prostitutes, his wealth
is wasted.

4 A just king gives stability to his nation,
but one who demands bribes destroys it.

5 To flatter friends
is to lay a trap for their feet.

6 Evil people are trapped by sin,
but the righteous escape, shouting for joy.

7 The godly care about the rights of the poor;
the wicked don't care at all.

8 Mockers can get a whole town agitated,
but the wise will calm anger.

9 If a wise person takes a fool to court,
there will be ranting and ridicule but no satisfaction.

10 The bloodthirsty hate blameless people,
but the upright seek to help them.*

11 Fools vent their anger,
but the wise quietly hold it back.

12 If a ruler pays attention to liars,
all his advisers will be wicked.

13 The poor and the oppressor have this in common—
the LORD gives sight to the eyes of both.

14 If a king judges the poor fairly,
his throne will last forever.

15 To discipline a child produces wisdom,
but a mother is disgraced by an undisciplined
child.

16 When the wicked are in authority, sin flourishes,
but the godly will live to see their downfall.

29:10 Or *The bloodthirsty hate blameless people, / and they seek to kill the upright;* Hebrew reads *The bloodthirsty hate blameless people; / as for the upright, they seek their life.*

17 Discipline your children, and they will give you peace of mind
and will make your heart glad.

18 When people do not accept divine guidance, they run wild.
But whoever obeys the law is joyful.

19 Words alone will not discipline a servant;
the words may be understood, but they are not heeded.

20 There is more hope for a fool
than for someone who speaks without thinking.

21 A servant pampered from childhood
will become a rebel.

22 An angry person starts fights;
a hot-tempered person commits all kinds of sin.

23 Pride ends in humiliation,
while humility brings honor.

24 If you assist a thief, you only hurt yourself.
You are sworn to tell the truth, but you dare not testify.

25 Fearing people is a dangerous trap,
but trusting the LORD means safety.

26 Many seek the ruler's favor,
but justice comes from the LORD.

27 The righteous despise the unjust;
the wicked despise the godly.

The Sayings of Agur

30 The sayings of Agur son of Jakeh contain this message.*

I am weary, O God;
I am weary and worn out, O God.*
2 I am too stupid to be human,
and I lack common sense.
3 I have not mastered human wisdom,
nor do I know the Holy One.

4 Who but God goes up to heaven and comes back down?
Who holds the wind in his fists?
Who wraps up the oceans in his cloak?
Who has created the whole wide world?
What is his name—and his son's name?
Tell me if you know!

30:1a Or *son of Jakeh from Massa;* or *son of Jakeh, an oracle.* **30:1b** The Hebrew can also be translated *The man declares this to Ithiel, / to Ithiel and to Ucal.*

How this passage impacts me

Question 30:5

If this is true, why do people search for wisdom in places other than God's Word?

5 Every word of God proves true.
He is a shield to all who come to him for protection.
6 Do not add to his words,
or he may rebuke you and expose you as a liar.

7 O God, I beg two favors from you;
let me have them before I die.
8 First, help me never to tell a lie.
Second, give me neither poverty nor riches!
Give me just enough to satisfy my needs.
9 For if I grow rich, I may deny you and say, "Who is the LORD?"
And if I am too poor, I may steal and thus insult God's
holy name.

10 Never slander a worker to the employer,
or the person will curse you, and you will pay for it.

11 Some people curse their father
and do not thank their mother.
12 They are pure in their own eyes,
but they are filthy and unwashed.
13 They look proudly around,
casting disdainful glances.
14 They have teeth like swords
and fangs like knives.
They devour the poor from the earth
and the needy from among humanity.

15 The leech has two suckers
that cry out, "More, more!"*

There are three things that are never satisfied—
no, four that never say, "Enough!":
16 the grave,*
the barren womb,
the thirsty desert,
the blazing fire.

17 The eye that mocks a father
and despises a mother's instructions
will be plucked out by ravens of the valley
and eaten by vultures.

18 There are three things that amaze me—
no, four things that I don't understand:
19 how an eagle glides through the sky,
how a snake slithers on a rock,
how a ship navigates the ocean,
how a man loves a woman.

30:15 Hebrew *two daughters who cry out, "Give, give!"* 30:16 Hebrew *Sheol.*

20 An adulterous woman consumes a man,
then wipes her mouth and says, "What's wrong with that?"

21 There are three things that make the earth tremble—
no, four it cannot endure:
22 a slave who becomes a king,
an overbearing fool who prospers,
23 a bitter woman who finally gets a husband,
a servant girl who supplants her mistress.

24 There are four things on earth that are small but unusually wise:
25 Ants—they aren't strong,
but they store up food all summer.
26 Hyraxes*—they aren't powerful,
but they make their homes among the rocks.
27 Locusts—they have no king,
but they march in formation.
28 Lizards—they are easy to catch,
but they are found even in kings' palaces.

29 There are three things that walk with stately stride—
no, four that strut about:
30 the lion, king of animals, who won't turn aside for anything,
31 the strutting rooster,
the male goat,
a king as he leads his army.

32 If you have been a fool by being proud or plotting evil,
cover your mouth in shame.

33 As the beating of cream yields butter
and striking the nose causes bleeding,
so stirring up anger causes quarrels.

The Sayings of King Lemuel

31 The sayings of King Lemuel contain this message,* which his mother taught him.

2 O my son, O son of my womb,
O son of my vows,
3 do not waste your strength on women,
on those who ruin kings.

4 It is not for kings, O Lemuel, to guzzle wine.
Rulers should not crave alcohol.
5 For if they drink, they may forget the law
and not give justice to the oppressed.
6 Alcohol is for the dying,
and wine for those in bitter distress.

30:26 Or *Coneys,* or *Rock badgers.* **31:1** Or *of Lemuel, king of Massa;* or *of King Lemuel, an oracle.*

Make a Difference 31:8

Speak Up

"What? Did you say something?"

Justice is the process of restoring people to their created relationship with God. Justice fights against whatever it is that unjustly shackles. It gives dignity to those who are being crushed, and it fights for the lives of those who are in danger. It lifts up downtrodden souls, forgives the debts of those who have fallen short, and advocates for those who are trapped in unbreakable cycles. Justice gives more hope to those who hope less. It gives voice to those whose mouths have been silenced. It speaks up and lifts up and rises up on behalf of those who are caught in the despair and oppression of this broken world.

Even so, if you act in justice, it will cost you something. In fact, it *must* cost you something. Justice disturbs your comfort. Justice takes your effort, your compassion, and your determination. Justice takes you. In other words, justice isn't fairness—it is love.

Difference Maker

Think of someone who needs your voice today. Do you know someone who needs an advocate today? Creatively think of a way you could speak up on their behalf.

7 Let them drink to forget their poverty
and remember their troubles no more.

8 Speak up for those who cannot speak for themselves;
ensure justice for those being crushed.
9 Yes, speak up for the poor and helpless,
and see that they get justice.

A Wife of Noble Character

10* Who can find a virtuous and capable wife?
She is more precious than rubies.
11 Her husband can trust her,
and she will greatly enrich his life.
12 She brings him good, not harm,
all the days of her life.

13 She finds wool and flax
and busily spins it.
14 She is like a merchant's ship,
bringing her food from afar.
15 She gets up before dawn to prepare breakfast for
her household
and plan the day's work for her servant girls.

16 She goes to inspect a field and buys it;
with her earnings she plants a vineyard.
17 She is energetic and strong,
a hard worker.
18 She makes sure her dealings are profitable;
her lamp burns late into the night.

19 Her hands are busy spinning thread,
her fingers twisting fiber.
20 She extends a helping hand to the poor
and opens her arms to the needy.
21 She has no fear of winter for her household,
for everyone has warm* clothes.

22 She makes her own bedspreads.
She dresses in fine linen and purple gowns.
23 Her husband is well known at the city gates,
where he sits with the other civic leaders.
24 She makes belted linen garments
and sashes to sell to the merchants.

25 She is clothed with strength and dignity,
and she laughs without fear of the future.
26 When she speaks, her words are wise,
and she gives instructions with kindness.

31:10 Verses 10-31 comprise a Hebrew acrostic poem; each verse begins with a successive letter of the Hebrew alphabet. 31:21 As in Greek and Latin versions; Hebrew reads *scarlet*.

27 She carefully watches everything in her household
and suffers nothing from laziness.

28 Her children stand and bless her.
Her husband praises her:
29 "There are many virtuous and capable women in the world,
but you surpass them all!"

30 Charm is deceptive, and beauty does not last;
but a woman who fears the LORD will be greatly praised.
31 Reward her for all she has done.
Let her deeds publicly declare her praise.

Ecclesiastes Introduction

The name *Ecclesiastes* is a translation of the Hebrew word *Qoheleth*, which means "a collector of sayings" or simply a "preacher" or "teacher." The book does not give specific information about who this *Qoheleth* is, but many scholars have concluded this Teacher is probably Solomon. Ecclesiastes 1:1 identifies "the Teacher" as "King David's son, who ruled in Jerusalem." King Solomon was the son of King David, and he was famous throughout the world for his wisdom.

Throughout this book, the Teacher presented several questions in his search for the purpose of life. His questions and conclusions illustrated his own journey of seeking to understand our existence here on earth. The Teacher described his personal experiences with wisdom, pleasures, folly, and toil and said that "everything is meaningless."

The purpose of Ecclesiastes is to say that there is nothing "under the sun" that can give meaning to life (1:12–17). Regardless of any success or self-satisfaction here on earth, death is waiting at the end. The Teacher's message in Ecclesiastes was that while personal pleasures may be temporarily fulfilling, these things can't offer lasting satisfaction. A God-centered life brings ultimate fulfillment, and our God-honoring pleasures are to be enjoyed as gifts from God.

Story Arc

Ecclesiastes

1 These are the words of the Teacher,* King David's son, who ruled in Jerusalem.

Everything Is Meaningless

2 "Everything is meaningless," says the Teacher, "completely meaningless!"
3 What do people get for all their hard work under the sun? 4 Generations
come and generations go, but the earth never changes. 5 The sun rises and
the sun sets, then hurries around to rise again. 6 The wind blows south, and
then turns north. Around and around it goes, blowing in circles. 7 Rivers
run into the sea, but the sea is never full. Then the water returns again to
the rivers and flows out again to the sea. 8 Everything is wearisome beyond
description. No matter how much we see, we are never satisfied. No matter
how much we hear, we are not content.

9 History merely repeats itself. It has all been done before. Nothing under
the sun is truly new. 10 Sometimes people say, "Here is something new!" But
actually it is old; nothing is ever truly new. 11 We don't remember what hap-
pened in the past, and in future generations, no one will remember what
we are doing now.

The Teacher Speaks: The Futility of Wisdom

12 I, the Teacher, was king of Israel, and I lived in Jerusalem. 13 I devoted myself
to search for understanding and to explore by wisdom everything being
done under heaven. I soon discovered that God has dealt a tragic existence to
the human race. 14 I observed everything going on under the sun, and really,
it is all meaningless—like chasing the wind.

15 What is wrong cannot be made right.
What is missing cannot be recovered.

16 I said to myself, "Look, I am wiser than any of the kings who ruled in Je-
rusalem before me. I have greater wisdom and knowledge than any of them."
17 So I set out to learn everything from wisdom to madness and folly. But I
learned firsthand that pursuing all this is like chasing the wind.

18 The greater my wisdom, the greater my grief.
To increase knowledge only increases sorrow.

The Futility of Pleasure

2 I said to myself, "Come on, let's try pleasure. Let's look for the 'good
things' in life." But I found that this, too, was meaningless. 2 So I said,
"Laughter is silly. What good does it do to seek pleasure?" 3 After much

1:1 Hebrew *Qoheleth;* this term is rendered "the Teacher" throughout this book.

Make a Difference 1:1-11

Make a Difference in Your Life

When you get to the end of your life, you will likely reflect on how you spent your time—the places you traveled to, the people you met, and the highlight reel of memories and experiences you had. At the end of the day, the decisions you make on how you spend your time will determine your future.

Read these first eleven verses of Ecclesiastes. By experience, Solomon grew to understand how feeding our own desires is meaningless in comparison to how God calls us to make a difference with our time. For our life to have true meaning, we need to live a life in pursuit of God, loving him and loving others.

Difference Maker

If your life were over today, how would you feel about how you have spent your time?

Make a Difference 2:1-11

Lasting Joy and Fulfillment

In the first eleven verses of this chapter, notice how the writer tried to find joy in entertainment, large buildings, and wealth, but none could provide everlasting joy. He had everything the world could offer but still did not gain anything everlasting. Only Jesus can give us a joy that can sustain us in any season, even when the Christmas lights are packed up and the holiday high fades away.

Difference Maker

Where and how are you seeking joy?

Make a Difference 2:17

With Him, Our Lives Have Meaning

If we live our life outside of Jesus, it really is meaningless. Acquiring wisdom, working hard, and experiencing pleasure have no long-lasting significance apart from Jesus. When we give our lives to Jesus, he promises to give us eternal life (John 5:24). This promise gives our lives great meaning and purpose!

Difference Maker

Think about your life and the different activities, sports, clubs, and relationships you participate in. What situation in your life seems pointless right now? How can you give that situation to God, trusting that he will give that situation meaning and purpose?

Story Arc 2:11

Solomon

Solomon was most well-known for being a fabulously wise and wealthy king of Israel. When God appeared to Solomon in a dream, God asked Solomon what he most wanted. Solomon asked God for wisdom (1 Kings 3:5-14).

For a long period of his life, Solomon spent his time and used his wisdom in a way that was not honoring to God. The Bible says that he married many women, undertook huge projects, built houses for himself, bought slaves, collected silver and gold, and delighted in anything his own heart desired. Thus, his heart soured. Solomon eventually realized that seeking happiness everywhere but in God was meaningless and that God is ultimately all that matters.

What things are you relying upon for happiness more than you are relying upon God?

Song 1:1 ►

thought, I decided to cheer myself with wine. And while still seeking wisdom, I clutched at foolishness. In this way, I tried to experience the only happiness most people find during their brief life in this world.

4 I also tried to find meaning by building huge homes for myself and by
planting beautiful vineyards. 5 I made gardens and parks, filling them with
all kinds of fruit trees. 6 I built reservoirs to collect the water to irrigate my
many flourishing groves. 7 I bought slaves, both men and women, and others
were born into my household. I also owned large herds and flocks, more
than any of the kings who had lived in Jerusalem before me. 8 I collected
great sums of silver and gold, the treasure of many kings and provinces. I
hired wonderful singers, both men and women, and had many beautiful
concubines. I had everything a man could desire!

9 So I became greater than all who had lived in Jerusalem before me, and
my wisdom never failed me. 10 Anything I wanted, I would take. I denied
myself no pleasure. I even found great pleasure in hard work, a reward for
all my labors. 11 But as I looked at everything I had worked so hard to accom-
plish, it was all so meaningless—like chasing the wind. There was nothing
really worthwhile anywhere.

The Wise and the Foolish

12 So I decided to compare wisdom with foolishness and madness (for who
can do this better than I, the king?*). 13 I thought, "Wisdom is better than
foolishness, just as light is better than darkness. 14 For the wise can see where
they are going, but fools walk in the dark." Yet I saw that the wise and the
foolish share the same fate. 15 Both will die. So I said to myself, "Since I will
end up the same as the fool, what's the value of all my wisdom? This is all
so meaningless!" 16 For the wise and the foolish both die. The wise will not
be remembered any longer than the fool. In the days to come, both will be
forgotten.

17 So I came to hate life because everything done here under the sun is so
troubling. Everything is meaningless—like chasing the wind.

The Futility of Work

18 I came to hate all my hard work here on earth, for I must leave to others
everything I have earned. 19 And who can tell whether my successors will be
wise or foolish? Yet they will control everything I have gained by my skill
and hard work under the sun. How meaningless! 20 So I gave up in despair,
questioning the value of all my hard work in this world.

21 Some people work wisely with knowledge and skill, then must leave
the fruit of their efforts to someone who hasn't worked for it. This, too, is
meaningless, a great tragedy. 22 So what do people get in this life for all their
hard work and anxiety? 23 Their days of labor are filled with pain and grief;
even at night their minds cannot rest. It is all meaningless.

24 So I decided there is nothing better than to enjoy food and drink and to
find satisfaction in work. Then I realized that these pleasures are from the
hand of God. 25 For who can eat or enjoy anything apart from him?* 26 God
gives wisdom, knowledge, and joy to those who please him. But if a sinner
becomes wealthy, God takes the wealth away and gives it to those who please
him. This, too, is meaningless—like chasing the wind.

2:12 The meaning of the Hebrew is uncertain. 2:25 As in Greek and Syriac versions; Hebrew reads *apart from me?*

A Time for Everything

3 [1] For everything there is a season,
a time for every activity under heaven.
[2] A time to be born and a time to die.
A time to plant and a time to harvest.
[3] A time to kill and a time to heal.
A time to tear down and a time to build up.
[4] A time to cry and a time to laugh.
A time to grieve and a time to dance.
[5] A time to scatter stones and a time to gather stones.
A time to embrace and a time to turn away.
[6] A time to search and a time to quit searching.
A time to keep and a time to throw away.
[7] A time to tear and a time to mend.
A time to be quiet and a time to speak.
[8] A time to love and a time to hate.
A time for war and a time for peace.

[9] What do people really get for all their hard work? [10] I have seen the burden
God has placed on us all. [11] Yet God has made everything beautiful for its own
time. He has planted eternity in the human heart, but even so, people cannot
see the whole scope of God's work from beginning to end. [12] So I concluded
there is nothing better than to be happy and enjoy ourselves as long as we
can. [13] And people should eat and drink and enjoy the fruits of their labor,
for these are gifts from God.

[14] And I know that whatever God does is final. Nothing can be added to
it or taken from it. God's purpose is that people should fear him. [15] What is
happening now has happened before, and what will happen in the future
has happened before, because God makes the same things happen over and
over again.

The Injustices of Life

[16] I also noticed that under the sun there is evil in the courtroom. Yes, even
the courts of law are corrupt! [17] I said to myself, "In due season God will judge
everyone, both good and bad, for all their deeds."

[18] I also thought about the human condition—how God proves to people
that they are like animals. [19] For people and animals share the same fate—
both breathe* and both must die. So people have no real advantage over the
animals. How meaningless! [20] Both go to the same place—they came from
dust and they return to dust. [21] For who can prove that the human spirit goes
up and the spirit of animals goes down into the earth? [22] So I saw that there
is nothing better for people than to be happy in their work. That is our lot in
life. And no one can bring us back to see what happens after we die.

4 Again, I observed all the oppression that takes place under the sun. I saw
the tears of the oppressed, with no one to comfort them. The oppressors
have great power, and their victims are helpless. [2] So I concluded that the
dead are better off than the living. [3] But most fortunate of all are those who
are not yet born. For they have not seen all the evil that is done under the sun.

3:19 Or *both have the same spirit.*

Make a Difference
3:1–15

Seasons

By the time we see the leaves begin to change color, summer is gone. The warm days are behind us. Winter is just around the bend. Colder weather is ahead. The falling of the leaves and of the temperatures is all the proof we need that there are different *seasons* to life.

Many of us try to live our lives without seasons. We'd like to have predictability and safety all year long. We forget that change in us, especially when generated by Jesus, produces brilliant opportunities to change the world in which we live.

Difference Maker

Gather some friends and spend a day together outside. Enjoy this season that you are in, right now. Let Jesus' work in you give vibrancy to other seasons as they take their turn.

Prayer 3:8

Lord Jesus, change me through the seasons of my life so that I might bless others. Amen.

4Then I observed that most people are motivated to success because they
envy their neighbors. But this, too, is meaningless—like chasing the wind.

5 “Fools fold their idle hands,
leading them to ruin.”

6And yet,

“Better to have one handful with quietness
than two handfuls with hard work
and chasing the wind.”

The Advantages of Companionship

7I observed yet another example of something meaningless under the sun.
8This is the case of a man who is all alone, without a child or a brother, yet
who works hard to gain as much wealth as he can. But then he asks himself,
“Who am I working for? Why am I giving up so much pleasure now?” It is
all so meaningless and depressing.
9Two people are better off than one, for they can help each other succeed.
10If one person falls, the other can reach out and help. But someone who falls
alone is in real trouble. 11Likewise, two people lying close together can keep
each other warm. But how can one be warm alone? 12A person standing alone
can be attacked and defeated, but two can stand back-to-back and conquer.
Three are even better, for a triple-braided cord is not easily broken.

The Futility of Political Power

13It is better to be a poor but wise youth than an old and foolish king who
refuses all advice. 14Such a youth could rise from poverty and succeed. He
might even become king, though he has been in prison. 15But then everyone
rushes to the side of yet another youth* who replaces him. 16Endless crowds
stand around him,* but then another generation grows up and rejects him,
too. So it is all meaningless—like chasing the wind.

Approaching God with Care

5 1*As you enter the house of God, keep your ears open and your mouth
shut. It is evil to make mindless offerings to God. 2*Don’t make rash
promises, and don’t be hasty in bringing matters before God. After all, God
is in heaven, and you are here on earth. So let your words be few.
3Too much activity gives you restless dreams; too many words make you
a fool.
4When you make a promise to God, don’t delay in following through, for
God takes no pleasure in fools. Keep all the promises you make to him. 5It
is better to say nothing than to make a promise and not keep it. 6Don’t let
your mouth make you sin. And don’t defend yourself by telling the Temple
messenger that the promise you made was a mistake. That would make God
angry, and he might wipe out everything you have achieved.
7Talk is cheap, like daydreams and other useless activities. Fear God
instead.

4:15 Hebrew *the second youth.* **4:16** Hebrew *There is no end to all the people, to all those who are before them.* **5:1** Verse 5:1 is numbered 4:17 in Hebrew text. **5:2** Verses 5:2-20 are numbered 5:1-19 in Hebrew text.

Make a Difference
4:9–12

Better Together

The world measures success based upon scores, awards, and achievements, but Jesus measures success differently. Spiritual success can be measured in the relationships we build with others and how our relationships draw us closer to God. Ecclesiastes 4:9-12 is a passage commonly read at weddings because, in it, Solomon described how two people moving in the same direction can go farther than one person working alone. The cord of three strands illustrates how successful relationships have Jesus at the center, hence the third cord. This idea isn’t just for romantic relationships but can also be applied to every relationship we have. Jesus doesn’t want us to live life alone but wants us to experience community, accountability, and encouragement.

Difference Maker

With whom in your life can you share your struggles, and who can encourage you in your walk with Jesus? Who in your life could use this encouragement?

Question **5:1–3**

Read 5:1-3. The Bible teaches us to use words wisely—whether that be with other people in our lives or with God. In what ways do you find yourself quick with your words, in front of other people and before God? How does this apply to your social media activity? Are you quick to share and hasty in your heart?

The Futility of Wealth
8 Don't be surprised if you see a poor person being oppressed by the powerful
and if justice is being miscarried throughout the land. For every official is
under orders from higher up, and matters of justice get lost in red tape and
bureaucracy. 9 Even the king milks the land for his own profit!*
10 Those who love money will never have enough. How meaningless to
think that wealth brings true happiness! 11 The more you have, the more
people come to help you spend it. So what good is wealth—except perhaps
to watch it slip through your fingers!
12 People who work hard sleep well, whether they eat little or much. But
the rich seldom get a good night's sleep.
13 There is another serious problem I have seen under the sun. Hoarding
riches harms the saver. 14 Money is put into risky investments that turn sour,
and everything is lost. In the end, there is nothing left to pass on to one's
children. 15 We all come to the end of our lives as naked and empty-handed
as on the day we were born. We can't take our riches with us.
16 And this, too, is a very serious problem. People leave this world no better
off than when they came. All their hard work is for nothing—like working
for the wind. 17 Throughout their lives, they live under a cloud—frustrated,
discouraged, and angry.
◆ 18 Even so, I have noticed one thing, at least, that is good. It is good for
people to eat, drink, and enjoy their work under the sun during the short life
God has given them, and to accept their lot in life. 19 And it is a good thing to
receive wealth from God and the good health to enjoy it. To enjoy your work
and accept your lot in life—this is indeed a gift from God. 20 God keeps such
people so busy enjoying life that they take no time to brood over the past.

6 There is another serious tragedy I have seen under the sun, and it weighs
heavily on humanity. 2 God gives some people great wealth and honor
and everything they could ever want, but then he doesn't give them the
chance to enjoy these things. They die, and someone else, even a stranger,
ends up enjoying their wealth! This is meaningless—a sickening tragedy.
3 A man might have a hundred children and live to be very old. But if he
finds no satisfaction in life and doesn't even get a decent burial, it would have
been better for him to be born dead. 4 His birth would have been meaningless,
and he would have ended in darkness. He wouldn't even have had a name,
5 and he would never have seen the sun or known of its existence. Yet he
would have had more peace than in growing up to be an unhappy man. 6 He
might live a thousand years twice over but still not find contentment. And
since he must die like everyone else—well, what's the use?
▲ 7 All people spend their lives scratching for food, but they never seem to
have enough. 8 So are wise people really better off than fools? Do poor people
gain anything by being wise and knowing how to act in front of others?
9 Enjoy what you have rather than desiring what you don't have. Just
dreaming about nice things is meaningless—like chasing the wind.

The Future—Determined and Unknown
10 Everything has already been decided. It was known long ago what each
person would be. So there's no use arguing with God about your destiny.

5:9 The meaning of the Hebrew in verses 8 and 9 is uncertain.

Make a Difference

5:18-20

Gifts from God

Do you have a natural talent, ability, or gift in something? Maybe you are a great chocolate chip cookie baker, an all-star soccer player, or an excellent guitar player. Whatever your talents and abilities, Ecclesiastes 5:18-20 describes how we are to enjoy these things, knowing that they are God-given. If we enjoy our possessions, riches, and talents apart from God, we are not fully giving gratitude to him for what he has given us. Ecclesiastes 5:19 tells us to be happy when God gives us wealth, possessions, and work because they are gifts from him. God wants us to enjoy our lives, and he is deserving of receiving prayers of thanksgiving for all that he has given us.

Difference Maker

What gifts has God given you? Make a list of those things and thank him for them. How can you show him thanksgiving for all that he has given you?

Prayer **6:7**

Dear Lord, help me not to be consumed by jealousy for the things I do not have but rather thankful for the blessings you have given me. Amen.

Question 7:14

When times are good or when times are bad, what does God want you to remember is most important?

11 The more words you speak, the less they mean. So what good are
they?
12 In the few days of our meaningless lives, who knows how our days can
best be spent? Our lives are like a shadow. Who can tell what will happen on
this earth after we are gone?

Wisdom for Life

7 1 A good reputation is more valuable than costly perfume.
And the day you die is better than the day you are born.
2 Better to spend your time at funerals than at parties.
After all, everyone dies—
so the living should take this to heart.
3 Sorrow is better than laughter,
for sadness has a refining influence on us.
4 A wise person thinks a lot about death,
while a fool thinks only about having a good time.

5 Better to be criticized by a wise person
than to be praised by a fool.
6 A fool's laughter is quickly gone,
like thorns crackling in a fire.
This also is meaningless.

7 Extortion turns wise people into fools,
and bribes corrupt the heart.

8 Finishing is better than starting.
Patience is better than pride.

9 Control your temper,
for anger labels you a fool.
10 Don't long for "the good old days."
This is not wise.

11 Wisdom is even better when you have money.
Both are a benefit as you go through life.
12 Wisdom and money can get you almost anything,
but only wisdom can save your life.

13 Accept the way God does things,
for who can straighten what he has made crooked?
14 Enjoy prosperity while you can,
but when hard times strike, realize that both come from God.
Remember that nothing is certain in this life.

The Limits of Human Wisdom

15 I have seen everything in this meaningless life, including the death of good
young people and the long life of wicked people. 16 So don't be too good or
too wise! Why destroy yourself? 17 On the other hand, don't be too wicked

either. Don't be a fool! Why die before your time? 18Pay attention to these
instructions, for anyone who fears God will avoid both extremes.*
19One wise person is stronger than ten leading citizens of a town!
20Not a single person on earth is always good and never sins.
21Don't eavesdrop on others—you may hear your servant curse you. 22For
you know how often you yourself have cursed others.
23I have always tried my best to let wisdom guide my thoughts and actions.
I said to myself, "I am determined to be wise." But it didn't work. 24Wisdom
is always distant and difficult to find. 25I searched everywhere, determined
to find wisdom and to understand the reason for things. I was determined
to prove to myself that wickedness is stupid and that foolishness is madness.
26I discovered that a seductive woman* is a trap more bitter than death.
Her passion is a snare, and her soft hands are chains. Those who are pleasing
to God will escape her, but sinners will be caught in her snare.
27"This is my conclusion," says the Teacher. "I discovered this after look-
ing at the matter from every possible angle. 28Though I have searched repeat-
edly, I have not found what I was looking for. Only one out of a thousand men
is virtuous, but not one woman! 29But I did find this: God created people to
be virtuous, but they have each turned to follow their own downward path."

8 1 How wonderful to be wise,
to analyze and interpret things.
Wisdom lights up a person's face,
softening its harshness.

Obedience to the King

2Obey the king since you vowed to God that you would. 3Don't try to avoid
doing your duty, and don't stand with those who plot evil, for the king can
do whatever he wants. 4His command is backed by great power. No one can
resist or question it. 5Those who obey him will not be punished. Those who
are wise will find a time and a way to do what is right, 6for there is a time
and a way for everything, even when a person is in trouble.
7Indeed, how can people avoid what they don't know is going to happen?
8None of us can hold back our spirit from departing. None of us has the
power to prevent the day of our death. There is no escaping that obligation, that dark battle. And in the face of death, wickedness will certainly
not rescue the wicked.

The Wicked and the Righteous

9I have thought deeply about all that goes on here under the sun, where
people have the power to hurt each other. 10I have seen wicked people buried
with honor. Yet they were the very ones who frequented the Temple and are
now praised* in the same city where they committed their crimes! This, too,
is meaningless. 11When a crime is not punished quickly, people feel it is safe
to do wrong. 12But even though a person sins a hundred times and still lives
a long time, I know that those who fear God will be better off. 13The wicked
will not prosper, for they do not fear God. Their days will never grow long
like the evening shadows.
14And this is not all that is meaningless in our world. In this life, good

7:18 Or *will follow them both.* 7:26 Hebrew *a woman.* 8:10 As in some Hebrew manuscripts and Greek version; many Hebrew manuscripts read *and are forgotten.*

Make a Difference 8:14

Life Isn't Fair

Picture this: A few of your classmates are goofing off in science class. One classmate bumps a beaker, and it falls to the ground and shatters. When your teacher comes to the back of the classroom to inspect the incident, your classmates blame the shattered glass on you even though you were busy working on your classwork. How frustrating and unfair! Sometimes life isn't fair. We get in trouble for things we didn't do, and we see people get let off who we believe deserve punishment.

Solomon described how he saw this happening during his lifetime. He saw the "wicked" succeeding and the "good" receiving what the wicked deserved. As Christians, we know that there's much more to live for than life on earth. Though we might experience unfairness and poor treatment, an eternal relationship with Jesus is much better than temporary fairness.

Difference Maker

Have you ever received unfair treatment or blame for something you believed you didn't deserve? How can you begin having a long-term perspective when it comes to your life and following Jesus?

people are often treated as though they were wicked, and wicked people are
often treated as though they were good. This is so meaningless!
15 So I recommend having fun, because there is nothing better for people
in this world than to eat, drink, and enjoy life. That way they will experi-
ence some happiness along with all the hard work God gives them under
the sun.
16 In my search for wisdom and in my observation of people's burdens
here on earth, I discovered that there is ceaseless activity, day and night. 17 I
realized that no one can discover everything God is doing under the sun.
Not even the wisest people discover everything, no matter what they claim.

Death Comes to All

9 This, too, I carefully explored: Even though the actions of godly and wise
people are in God's hands, no one knows whether God will show them
favor. 2 The same destiny ultimately awaits everyone, whether righteous or
wicked, good or bad,* ceremonially clean or unclean, religious or irreligious.
Good people receive the same treatment as sinners, and people who make
promises to God are treated like people who don't.
3 It seems so wrong that everyone under the sun suffers the same fate.
Already twisted by evil, people choose their own mad course, for they have
no hope. There is nothing ahead but death anyway. 4 There is hope only for
the living. As they say, "It's better to be a live dog than a dead lion!"
5 The living at least know they will die, but the dead know nothing. They
have no further reward, nor are they remembered. 6 Whatever they did in
their lifetime—loving, hating, envying—is all long gone. They no longer
play a part in anything here on earth. 7 So go ahead. Eat your food with joy,
and drink your wine with a happy heart, for God approves of this! 8 Wear fine
clothes, with a splash of cologne!
9 Live happily with the woman you love through all the meaningless
days of life that God has given you under the sun. The wife God gives you
is your reward for all your earthly toil. 10 Whatever you do, do well. For
when you go to the grave,* there will be no work or planning or knowledge
or wisdom.
11 I have observed something else under the sun. The fastest runner doesn't
always win the race, and the strongest warrior doesn't always win the battle.
The wise sometimes go hungry, and the skillful are not necessarily wealthy.
And those who are educated don't always lead successful lives. It is all de-
cided by chance, by being in the right place at the right time.
12 People can never predict when hard times might come. Like fish in a net
or birds in a trap, people are caught by sudden tragedy.

Thoughts on Wisdom and Folly

13 Here is another bit of wisdom that has impressed me as I have watched the
way our world works. 14 There was a small town with only a few people, and
a great king came with his army and besieged it. 15 A poor, wise man knew
how to save the town, and so it was rescued. But afterward no one thought
to thank him. 16 So even though wisdom is better than strength, those who
are wise will be despised if they are poor. What they say will not be appreci-
ated for long.

9:2 As in Greek and Syriac versions and Latin Vulgate; Hebrew lacks *or bad.* 9:10 Hebrew *to Sheol.*

17 Better to hear the quiet words of a wise person
than the shouts of a foolish king.
18 Better to have wisdom than weapons of war,
but one sinner can destroy much that is good.

10

1 As dead flies cause even a bottle of perfume to stink,
so a little foolishness spoils great wisdom
and honor.

2 A wise person chooses the right road;
a fool takes the wrong one.

3 You can identify fools
just by the way they walk down the street!

4 If your boss is angry at you, don't quit!
A quiet spirit can overcome even great mistakes.

The Ironies of Life

5 There is another evil I have seen under the sun. Kings and rulers make a
grave mistake 6 when they give great authority to foolish people and low
positions to people of proven worth. 7 I have even seen servants riding horse-
back like princes—and princes walking like servants!

8 When you dig a well,
you might fall in.
When you demolish an old wall,
you could be bitten by a snake.
9 When you work in a quarry,
stones might fall and crush you.
When you chop wood,
there is danger with each stroke of your ax.

10 Using a dull ax requires great strength,
so sharpen the blade.
That's the value of wisdom;
it helps you succeed.

11 If a snake bites before you charm it,
what's the use of being a snake charmer?

12 Wise words bring approval,
but fools are destroyed by their own words.

13 Fools base their thoughts on foolish assumptions,
so their conclusions will be wicked madness;
14 they chatter on and on.

No one really knows what is going to happen;
no one can predict the future.

Question 9:17

Our culture admires those who fit society's definition of successful, but this verse highlights how much more valuable are the quiet words of the wise. Whom do you turn to for advice? Is that person wise with quiet words, or are they a ruler with loud words?

Prayer 10:4

Lord Jesus, thank you for the example you set for me of what it looks like to be gentle. Please guide me to be calm and gentle when others become angry so their anger may not increase. Amen.

15 Fools are so exhausted by a little work
that they can't even find their way home.

16 What sorrow for the land ruled by a servant,*
the land whose leaders feast in the morning.
17 Happy is the land whose king is a noble leader
and whose leaders feast at the proper time
to gain strength for their work, not to get drunk.

18 Laziness leads to a sagging roof;
idleness leads to a leaky house.

19 A party gives laughter,
wine gives happiness,
and money gives everything!

20 Never make light of the king, even in your thoughts.
And don't make fun of the powerful, even in your own bedroom.
For a little bird might deliver your message
and tell them what you said.

The Uncertainties of Life

11 1 Send your grain across the seas,
and in time, profits will flow back to you.*
2 But divide your investments among many places,*
for you do not know what risks might lie ahead.

3 When clouds are heavy, the rains come down.
Whether a tree falls north or south, it stays where it falls.

4 Farmers who wait for perfect weather never plant.
If they watch every cloud, they never harvest.

5 Just as you cannot understand the path of the wind or the mystery of
a tiny baby growing in its mother's womb,* so you cannot understand the
activity of God, who does all things.
6 Plant your seed in the morning and keep busy all afternoon, for you don't
know if profit will come from one activity or another—or maybe both.

Advice for Young and Old

7 Light is sweet; how pleasant to see a new day dawning.
8 When people live to be very old, let them rejoice in every day of life. But
let them also remember there will be many dark days. Everything still to
come is meaningless.
9 Young people,* it's wonderful to be young! Enjoy every minute of it.
Do everything you want to do; take it all in. But remember that you must
give an account to God for everything you do. 10 So refuse to worry, and keep

10:16 Or *a child.* **11:1** Or *Give generously, / for your gifts will return to you later.* Hebrew reads *Throw your bread on the waters, / for after many days you will find it again.* **11:2** Hebrew *among seven or even eight.* **11:5** Some manuscripts read *Just as you cannot understand how breath comes to a tiny baby in its mother's womb.* **11:9** Hebrew *Young man.*

Make a Difference 11:4

Work for Jesus

It would be so much easier to play another thirty minutes on your game. It would be so much more relaxing to binge-watch for the rest of the afternoon. "Me time" is very alluring, especially when responsibilities hang over your head and needy people wait out in the real world ready to suck the life out of you.

Do you have something you should do today? Did someone ask you to do something for them? What if you just did it? Like, right now? What if, when you did it, you did it really well? What if you kept in your mind that you were doing it for Jesus?

Difference Maker

Write Ecclesiastes 11:4 on a piece of paper and tape it where it will serve as a reminder throughout the day.

Make a Difference 11:9

Follow God's Heart

We can all identify the things in life that bring us great joy and make our hearts happy. For some, it's sitting down with a great book and getting lost in our imaginations. Others love to be outside, enjoying being in God's creation, near the ocean, in the mountains, or in the forests. Whatever it is that you enjoy doing, Solomon said, "Do everything you want to do; take it all in." Even so, remember that God will hold us accountable for whatever we choose to do.

Difference Maker

Write down all the things that bring you joy, then think about how God will hold you accountable for choosing to do those things. Are those things honoring to you, or are they honoring to God?

your body healthy. But remember that youth, with a whole life before you,
is meaningless.

12 Don't let the excitement of youth cause you to forget your Creator.
Honor him in your youth before you grow old and say, "Life is not
pleasant anymore." 2 Remember him before the light of the sun, moon, and
stars is dim to your old eyes, and rain clouds continually darken your sky.
3 Remember him before your legs—the guards of your house—start to
tremble; and before your shoulders—the strong men—stoop. Remember
him before your teeth—your few remaining servants—stop grinding; and
before your eyes—the women looking through the windows—see dimly.
4 Remember him before the door to life's opportunities is closed and the
sound of work fades. Now you rise at the first chirping of the birds, but then
all their sounds will grow faint.
5 Remember him before you become fearful of falling and worry about
danger in the streets; before your hair turns white like an almond tree in
bloom, and you drag along without energy like a dying grasshopper, and
the caperberry no longer inspires sexual desire. Remember him before you
near the grave, your everlasting home, when the mourners will weep at your
funeral.
6 Yes, remember your Creator now while you are young, before the silver
cord of life snaps and the golden bowl is broken. Don't wait until the water
jar is smashed at the spring and the pulley is broken at the well. 7 For then the
dust will return to the earth, and the spirit will return to God who gave it.

Concluding Thoughts about the Teacher

8 "Everything is meaningless," says the Teacher, "completely meaningless."
9 Keep this in mind: The Teacher was considered wise, and he taught the
people everything he knew. He listened carefully to many proverbs, study-
ing and classifying them. 10 The Teacher sought to find just the right words
to express truths clearly.*
11 The words of the wise are like cattle prods—painful but helpful. Their
collected sayings are like a nail-studded stick with which a shepherd* drives
the sheep.
12 But, my child,* let me give you some further advice: Be careful, for writ-
ing books is endless, and much study wears you out.
13 That's the whole story. Here now is my final conclusion: Fear God and
obey his commands, for this is everyone's duty. 14 God will judge us for every-
thing we do, including every secret thing, whether good or bad.

12:10 Or *sought to write what was upright and true.* **12:11** Or *one shepherd.* **12:12** Hebrew *my son.*

Question 12:1

Often, we wait until we are desperate and overwhelmed to reach out to God for help. In this verse, Solomon reminded us to remember God even before the days of trouble come. Think of a difficult and troublesome situation you tried to handle without asking God for help. How did you feel? How would the situation have gone differently if you had sought out God?

Make a Difference
12:13

Wholeness in God

To conclude this book, the Teacher clearly stated its purpose. Ecclesiastes 12:13 tells us that our duty is to fear God and keep his commandments. This reveals the secret to experiencing wholeness in God. Who doesn't want to experience wholeness? We all want to be whole—not broken, upset, or unstable. Fearing God does not mean running from him as if he were a sign of terror or threat but rather being in awe of his majesty, wisdom, and wonder. While we all have desires of our own heart and we are naturally inclined to pursue these desires, Ecclesiastes instructs us to keep God's commandments in order to be a whole person, no longer lacking.

Difference Maker

What desires do you have in your heart? In what ways do those desires help you achieve wholeness in God? In what ways do they hinder you from achieving wholeness?

Song of Songs Introduction

This is not a book for the squeamish. This is a book about love and intimacy. If you don't like kissing or romance, this is a book you may be tempted to avoid. Song of Songs is a blush-inducing conversation between a groom and his bride who are both longing for one another. It is a poetic and provocative and powerful expression of affection.

It can be difficult to believe that Song of Songs is listed in the table of contents of the Bible, sandwiched between the wise musings of Ecclesiastes and the relational prophecies of Isaiah. Song of Songs does not offer historical accounts of battles or kings. It does not offer psalms of praise. It is not written as a rational description of theology or even a call to discipleship. Then what is this book doing here?

Ultimately, Song of Songs is a living parable. The Bible talks about God's people being his "bride." The New Testament frequently describes Jesus as the "groom." The illustration of a "wedding feast" is a common portrait of the kingdom of heaven. In this way, Song of Songs reveals to us just how personal a relationship with God can be. God wants us to know him intimately, personally, and faithfully. God does not want us to desire other gods or idols in our lives, but he desires a deep, mutual, committed relationship with his people. This book, the Song of Songs, helps us understand just how much.

Story Arc

Song of Songs

1 This is Solomon's song of songs, more wonderful than any other.

*Young Woman**

2 Kiss me and kiss me again,
for your love is sweeter than wine.
3 How pleasing is your fragrance;
your name is like the spreading fragrance of scented oils.
No wonder all the young women love you!
4 Take me with you; come, let's run!
The king has brought me into his bedroom.

Young Women of Jerusalem

How happy we are for you, O king.
We praise your love even more than wine.

Young Woman

How right they are to adore you.

5 I am dark but beautiful,
O women of Jerusalem—
dark as the tents of Kedar,
dark as the curtains of Solomon's tents.
6 Don't stare at me because I am dark—
the sun has darkened my skin.
My brothers were angry with me;
they forced me to care for their vineyards,
so I couldn't care for myself—my own vineyard.

7 Tell me, my love, where are you leading your flock today?
Where will you rest your sheep at noon?
For why should I wander like a prostitute*
among your friends and their flocks?

Young Man

8 If you don't know, O most beautiful woman,
follow the trail of my flock,
and graze your young goats by the shepherds' tents.
9 You are as exciting, my darling,
as a mare among Pharaoh's stallions.
10 How lovely are your cheeks;
your earrings set them afire!

1:1 The headings identifying the speakers are not in the original text, though the Hebrew usually gives clues by means of the gender of the person speaking. **1:7** Hebrew *like a veiled woman.*

Story Arc **1:1**

Solomon

Of all the things Solomon wrote, this book is considered to be his greatest song. Why is that? Perhaps it has something to do with how this song reveals the depths of intimate relationship God intended for us: God desires us, so we desire God. We look for one another. We think about one another. We commit ourselves wholeheartedly and personally to one another. The question to ponder, then, is whether we stay committed or whether we will flirt with another lover? God instructed in one of his Ten Commandments, "You must not have any other god but me" (Deuteronomy 5:7).

If only Solomon had lived his life this way. Even with all his wisdom, he struggled and failed to live lovingly committed to one woman. He also struggled and failed to live lovingly committed to God. That struggle makes the raw wisdom and alarming purity of this song so startling—a song of intimacy and commitment reserved for only one.

The ultimate goal of this song is that we pursue God with an intimate desire to be back in a lovingly committed relationship.

Isa 1:1 ►

How lovely is your neck,
enhanced by a string of jewels.
11 We will make for you earrings of gold
and beads of silver.

Young Woman
12 The king is lying on his couch,
enchanted by the fragrance of my perfume.
13 My lover is like a sachet of myrrh
lying between my breasts.
14 He is like a bouquet of sweet henna blossoms
from the vineyards of En-gedi.

Young Man
15 How beautiful you are, my darling,
how beautiful!
Your eyes are like doves.

Young Woman
16 You are so handsome, my love,
pleasing beyond words!
The soft grass is our bed;
17 fragrant cedar branches are the beams of our house,
and pleasant smelling firs are the rafters.

Young Woman
2 1 I am the spring crocus blooming on the Sharon Plain,*
the lily of the valley.

Young Man
2 Like a lily among thistles
is my darling among young women.

Young Woman
3 Like the finest apple tree in the orchard
is my lover among other young men.
I sit in his delightful shade
and taste his delicious fruit.
4 He escorts me to the banquet hall;
it's obvious how much he loves me.
5 Strengthen me with raisin cakes,
refresh me with apples,
for I am weak with love.
6 His left arm is under my head,
and his right arm embraces me.

7 Promise me, O women of Jerusalem,
by the gazelles and wild deer,
not to awaken love until the time is right.*

2:1 Traditionally rendered *I am the rose of Sharon.* Sharon Plain is a region in the coastal plain of Palestine. 2:7 Or *not to awaken love until it is ready.*

8 Ah, I hear my lover coming!
He is leaping over the mountains,
bounding over the hills.
9 My lover is like a swift gazelle
or a young stag.
Look, there he is behind the wall,
looking through the window,
peering into the room.

10 My lover said to me,
"Rise up, my darling!
Come away with me, my fair one!
11 Look, the winter is past,
and the rains are over and gone.
12 The flowers are springing up,
the season of singing birds* has come,
and the cooing of turtledoves fills the air.
13 The fig trees are forming young fruit,
and the fragrant grapevines are blossoming.
Rise up, my darling!
Come away with me, my fair one!"

Young Man

14 My dove is hiding behind the rocks,
behind an outcrop on the cliff.
Let me see your face;
let me hear your voice.
For your voice is pleasant,
and your face is lovely.

Young Women of Jerusalem

15 Catch all the foxes,
those little foxes,
before they ruin the vineyard of love,
for the grapevines are blossoming!

Young Woman

16 My lover is mine, and I am his.
He browses among the lilies.
17 Before the dawn breezes blow
and the night shadows flee,
return to me, my love, like a gazelle
or a young stag on the rugged mountains.*

Young Woman

3 1 One night as I lay in bed, I yearned for my lover.
I yearned for him, but he did not come.
2 So I said to myself, "I will get up and roam the city,
searching in all its streets and squares.

Question 2:16

"My lover is mine, and I am his." This is the essence of Song of Songs. Just as a bride and groom are to commit solely to one another, we, too, enter into a covenant with God. Jesus talks about us as being uniquely his (John 10:14; 15:5). On a scale of one to ten, how well do you know this to be true?

2:12 Or *the season of pruning vines.* 2:17 Or *on the hills of Bether.*

I will search for the one I love."
So I searched everywhere but did not find him.
3 The watchmen stopped me as they made their rounds,
and I asked, "Have you seen the one I love?"
4 Then scarcely had I left them
when I found my love!
I caught and held him tightly,
then I brought him to my mother's house,
into my mother's bed, where I had been conceived.

5 Promise me, O women of Jerusalem,
by the gazelles and wild deer,
not to awaken love until the time is right.*

Young Women of Jerusalem

6 Who is this sweeping in from the wilderness
like a cloud of smoke?
Who is it, fragrant with myrrh and frankincense
and every kind of spice?
7 Look, it is Solomon's carriage,
surrounded by sixty heroic men,
the best of Israel's soldiers.
8 They are all skilled swordsmen,
experienced warriors.
Each wears a sword on his thigh,
ready to defend the king against an attack in the night.
9 King Solomon's carriage is built
of wood imported from Lebanon.
10 Its posts are silver,
its canopy gold;
its cushions are purple.
It was decorated with love
by the young women of Jerusalem.

Young Woman

11 Come out to see King Solomon,
young women of Jerusalem.*
He wears the crown his mother gave him on his wedding day,
his most joyous day.

Young Man

4 1 You are beautiful, my darling,
beautiful beyond words.
Your eyes are like doves
behind your veil.
Your hair falls in waves,
like a flock of goats winding down the slopes of Gilead.
2 Your teeth are as white as sheep,
recently shorn and freshly washed.

3:5 Or *not to awaken love until it is ready.* 3:11 Hebrew *of Zion.*

Your smile is flawless,
each tooth matched with its twin.*
3 Your lips are like scarlet ribbon;
your mouth is inviting.
Your cheeks are like rosy pomegranates
behind your veil.
4 Your neck is as beautiful as the tower of David,
jeweled with the shields of a thousand heroes.
5 Your breasts are like two fawns,
twin fawns of a gazelle grazing among the lilies.
6 Before the dawn breezes blow
and the night shadows flee,
I will hurry to the mountain of myrrh
and to the hill of frankincense.
7 You are altogether beautiful, my darling,
beautiful in every way.

8 Come with me from Lebanon, my bride,
come with me from Lebanon.
Come down* from Mount Amana,
from the peaks of Senir and Hermon,
where the lions have their dens
and leopards live among the hills.

9 You have captured my heart,
my treasure,* my bride.
You hold it hostage with one glance of your eyes,
with a single jewel of your necklace.
10 Your love delights me,
my treasure, my bride.
Your love is better than wine,
your perfume more fragrant than spices.
11 Your lips are as sweet as nectar, my bride.
Honey and milk are under your tongue.
Your clothes are scented
like the cedars of Lebanon.

12 You are my private garden, my treasure, my bride,
a secluded spring, a hidden fountain.
13 Your thighs shelter a paradise of pomegranates
with rare spices—
henna with nard,
14 nard and saffron,
fragrant calamus and cinnamon,
with all the trees of frankincense, myrrh, and aloes,
and every other lovely spice.
15 You are a garden fountain,
a well of fresh water
streaming down from Lebanon's mountains.

4:2 Hebrew *Not one is missing; each has a twin.* 4:8 Or *Look down.* 4:9 Hebrew *my sister;* also in 4:10, 12.

Question 4:9

Did you know that God looks upon you with affection? You have captured his heart! You are his treasure. He delights in you. Knowing this, how are you challenged to live differently today?

Young Woman

16 Awake, north wind!
Rise up, south wind!
Blow on my garden
and spread its fragrance all around.
Come into your garden, my love;
taste its finest fruits.

Young Man

5 1 I have entered my garden, my treasure,*
my bride!
I gather myrrh with my spices
and eat honeycomb with my honey.
I drink wine with my milk.

Young Women of Jerusalem

Oh, lover and beloved, eat and drink!
Yes, drink deeply of your love!

Young Woman

2 I slept, but my heart was awake,
when I heard my lover knocking and calling:
"Open to me, my treasure, my darling,
my dove, my perfect one.
My head is drenched with dew,
my hair with the dampness of the night."

3 But I responded,
"I have taken off my robe.
Should I get dressed again?
I have washed my feet.
Should I get them soiled?"

4 My lover tried to unlatch the door,
and my heart thrilled within me.
5 I jumped up to open the door for my love,
and my hands dripped with perfume.
My fingers dripped with lovely myrrh
as I pulled back the bolt.
6 I opened to my lover,
but he was gone!
My heart sank.
I searched for him
but could not find him anywhere.
I called to him,
but there was no reply.
7 The night watchmen found me
as they made their rounds.
They beat and bruised me

5:1 Hebrew *my sister*; also in 5:2.

and stripped off my veil,
those watchmen on the walls.

8 Make this promise, O women of Jerusalem—
If you find my lover,
tell him I am weak with love.

Young Women of Jerusalem
9 Why is your lover better than all others,
O woman of rare beauty?
What makes your lover so special
that we must promise this?

Young Woman
10 My lover is dark and dazzling,
better than ten thousand others!
11 His head is finest gold,
his wavy hair is black as a raven.
12 His eyes sparkle like doves
beside springs of water;
they are set like jewels
washed in milk.
13 His cheeks are like gardens of spices
giving off fragrance.
His lips are like lilies,
perfumed with myrrh.
14 His arms are like rounded bars of gold,
set with beryl.
His body is like bright ivory,
glowing with lapis lazuli.
15 His legs are like marble pillars
set in sockets of finest gold.
His posture is stately,
like the noble cedars of Lebanon.
16 His mouth is sweetness itself;
he is desirable in every way.
Such, O women of Jerusalem,
is my lover, my friend.

Young Women of Jerusalem
6 1 Where has your lover gone,
O woman of rare beauty?
Which way did he turn
so we can help you find him?

Young Woman
2 My lover has gone down to his garden,
to his spice beds,
to browse in the gardens
and gather the lilies.

What I want to remember

3 I am my lover's, and my lover is mine.
He browses among the lilies.

Young Man

4 You are beautiful, my darling,
like the lovely city of Tirzah.
Yes, as beautiful as Jerusalem,
as majestic as an army with billowing banners.
5 Turn your eyes away,
for they overpower me.
Your hair falls in waves,
like a flock of goats winding down the slopes of Gilead.
6 Your teeth are as white as sheep
that are freshly washed.
Your smile is flawless,
each tooth matched with its twin.*
7 Your cheeks are like rosy pomegranates
behind your veil.

8 Even among sixty queens
and eighty concubines
and countless young women,
9 I would still choose my dove, my perfect one—
the favorite of her mother,
dearly loved by the one who bore her.
The young women see her and praise her;
even queens and royal concubines sing her praises:
10 "Who is this, arising like the dawn,
as fair as the moon,
as bright as the sun,
as majestic as an army with billowing banners?"

Young Woman

11 I went down to the grove of walnut trees
and out to the valley to see the new spring growth,
to see whether the grapevines had budded
or the pomegranates were in bloom.
12 Before I realized it,
my strong desires had taken me to the chariot of a noble man.*

Young Women of Jerusalem

13*Return, return to us, O maid of Shulam.
Come back, come back, that we may see you again.

Young Man

Why do you stare at this young woman of Shulam,
as she moves so gracefully between two lines of dancers?*

6:6 Hebrew *Not one is missing; each has a twin.* 6:12 Or *to the royal chariots of my people,* or *to the chariots of Amminadab.* The meaning of the Hebrew is uncertain. 6:13a Verse 6:13 is numbered 7:1 in Hebrew text. 6:13b Or *as you would at the movements of two armies?* or *as you would at the dance of Mahanaim?* The meaning of the Hebrew is uncertain.

7 1*How beautiful are your sandaled feet,
O queenly maiden.
Your rounded thighs are like jewels,
the work of a skilled craftsman.
2 Your navel is perfectly formed
like a goblet filled with mixed wine.
Between your thighs lies a mound of wheat
bordered with lilies.
3 Your breasts are like two fawns,
twin fawns of a gazelle.
4 Your neck is as beautiful as an ivory tower.
Your eyes are like the sparkling pools in Heshbon
by the gate of Bath-rabbim.
Your nose is as fine as the tower of Lebanon
overlooking Damascus.
5 Your head is as majestic as Mount Carmel,
and the sheen of your hair radiates royalty.
The king is held captive by its tresses.
6 Oh, how beautiful you are!
How pleasing, my love, how full of delights!
7 You are slender like a palm tree,
and your breasts are like its clusters of fruit.
8 I said, "I will climb the palm tree
and take hold of its fruit."
May your breasts be like grape clusters,
and the fragrance of your breath like apples.
9 May your kisses be as exciting as the best wine—

Young Woman

Yes, wine that goes down smoothly for my lover,
flowing gently over lips and teeth.*
10 I am my lover's,
and he claims me as his own.
11 Come, my love, let us go out to the fields
and spend the night among the wildflowers.*
12 Let us get up early and go to the vineyards
to see if the grapevines have budded,
if the blossoms have opened,
and if the pomegranates have bloomed.
There I will give you my love.
13 There the mandrakes give off their fragrance,
and the finest fruits are at our door,
new delights as well as old,
which I have saved for you, my lover.

Young Woman

8 1 Oh, I wish you were my brother,
who nursed at my mother's breasts.
Then I could kiss you no matter who was watching,

7:1 Verses 7:1-13 are numbered 7:2-14 in Hebrew text. 7:9 As in Greek and Syriac versions and Latin Vulgate; Hebrew reads *over lips of sleepers.* 7:11 Or *in the villages.*

What God wants people to know

> **Make a Difference** 8:6
>
> **Till Death**
>
> In wedding ceremonies, a common vow states, "Till death do us part." In other words, the couple promises to stay committed to one another until death separates them. The type of love revealed in Song of Songs is like an unbreakable seal over our hearts. A committed relationship with God provides security that lasts until death. To think, Jesus conquers death! That means a relationship with God is unending.
>
> ***Difference Maker***
>
> If you know someone who has been married a long time, reach out to them and ask them how they've done it. Filter this with God's faithfulness to you for the long haul.

and no one would criticize me.
2 I would bring you to my childhood home,
and there you would teach me.*
I would give you spiced wine to drink,
my sweet pomegranate wine.
3 Your left arm would be under my head,
and your right arm would embrace me.

4 Promise me, O women of Jerusalem,
not to awaken love until the time is right.*

Young Women of Jerusalem

5 Who is this sweeping in from the desert,
leaning on her lover?

Young Woman

I aroused you under the apple tree,
where your mother gave you birth,
where in great pain she delivered you.
6 Place me like a seal over your heart,
like a seal on your arm.
For love is as strong as death,
its jealousy* as enduring as the grave.*
Love flashes like fire,
the brightest kind of flame.
7 Many waters cannot quench love,
nor can rivers drown it.
If a man tried to buy love
with all his wealth,
his offer would be utterly scorned.

The Young Woman's Brothers

8 We have a little sister
too young to have breasts.
What will we do for our sister
if someone asks to marry her?
9 If she is a virgin, like a wall,
we will protect her with a silver tower.
But if she is promiscuous, like a swinging door,
we will block her door with a cedar bar.

Young Woman

10 I was a virgin, like a wall;
now my breasts are like towers.
When my lover looks at me,
he is delighted with what he sees.

11 Solomon has a vineyard at Baal-hamon,
which he leases out to tenant farmers.

8:2 Or *there she will teach me.* **8:4** Or *not to awaken love until it is ready.* **8:6a** Or *its passion.* **8:6b** Hebrew *as Sheol.*

Each of them pays a thousand pieces of silver
for harvesting its fruit.
12 But my vineyard is mine to give,
and Solomon need not pay a thousand pieces of silver.
But I will give two hundred pieces
to those who care for its vines.

Young Man

13 O my darling, lingering in the gardens,
your companions are fortunate to hear your voice.
Let me hear it, too!

Young Woman

14 Come away, my love! Be like a gazelle
or a young stag on the mountains of spices.

Isaiah Introduction

What comes to your mind when you hear the term *prophet*? Maybe your mind jumps to a fortune teller? Maybe you think of some mystical old man on a mountain who can predict upcoming events? While biblical prophets did receive visions from God about the future, being a prophet, at its core, was more about magnifying God's message for people.

Seven hundred years before Jesus was born, the prophet Isaiah lived in a time when there was rampant abuse of power and a lot of spiritual poverty. Still, as Isaiah reminded people, when life is at its darkest and harshest, the light of the world will vividly shine. Isaiah's name means "the Lord is salvation." His message was good news for the poor, hope for the hurting, sight for the blind, freedom for the oppressed (Isaiah 61:1–3). Because of this, Isaiah was not always popular with the powerful ruling classes. He had to persevere through multiple kings, stressful cultural trends, and a lot of adversity. At one point he even had to walk around naked and barefoot (20:3)!

As he endured, Isaiah pointed to the salvation that God offered humanity. Salvation would arrive through a Messiah named Immanuel, meaning "God is with us" (7:14), who himself would be persecuted and pierced for the sins of humanity (52:13–53:12).

Today, it is easy to push aside the need for God in our modern culture. We are tempted to put our faith in things other than Jesus, like a political leader, celebrity influencer, or fill-in-the-blank persona. Like people in Isaiah's day, we are tempted to avoid a dependence on the authority and power of God. However, Isaiah's message was all about magnifying Immanuel and putting God back in the center of our lives. He challenged us to read this book with our eyes and ears open to discovering Jesus.

Story Arcs

- **Isaiah**
- **David**
- **Hezekiah**
- **Jesus**

Isaiah

1 These are the visions that Isaiah son of Amoz saw concerning Judah and Jerusalem. He saw these visions during the years when Uzziah, Jotham, Ahaz, and Hezekiah were kings of Judah.*

A Message for Rebellious Judah

2 Listen, O heavens! Pay attention, earth!
This is what the LORD says:
"The children I raised and cared for
have rebelled against me.
3 Even an ox knows its owner,
and a donkey recognizes its master's care—
but Israel doesn't know its master.
My people don't recognize my care for them."
4 Oh, what a sinful nation they are—
loaded down with a burden of guilt.
They are evil people,
corrupt children who have rejected the LORD.
They have despised the Holy One of Israel
and turned their backs on him.

5 Why do you continue to invite punishment?
Must you rebel forever?
Your head is injured,
and your heart is sick.
6 You are battered from head to foot—
covered with bruises, welts, and infected wounds—
without any soothing ointments or bandages.
7 Your country lies in ruins,
and your towns are burned.
Foreigners plunder your fields before your eyes
and destroy everything they see.
8 Beautiful Jerusalem* stands abandoned
like a watchman's shelter in a vineyard,
like a lean-to in a cucumber field after the harvest,
like a helpless city under siege.
9 If the LORD of Heaven's Armies
had not spared a few of us,*
we would have been wiped out like Sodom,
destroyed like Gomorrah.

1:1 These kings reigned from 792 to 686 B.C. 1:8 Hebrew *The daughter of Zion.* 1:9 Greek version reads *a few of our children.* Compare Rom 9:29.

Story Arc 1:1

Isaiah
Hundreds of years before Jesus, Isaiah persevered through four kings, national upheavals, wars, and personal threats. Through it all, he declared a message that wasn't always popular and wasn't always nice, yet it was constantly filled with hope in the Lord. Isaiah wasn't one to go with the flow of culture. He pointed toward the hope we have in God and called people to join him. Because of his great resolve back then and because of this great book, we are encouraged today to find our identity and trust in Jesus Christ.

Isa 11:1-5 ►

Make a Difference 1:17

Do Good

God enjoys people who do what he created them to do. In fact, God wired people with the desire and ability to do what is good. That means, in a world that has rejected God and, as a result, is struggling with so much bad, people who do what God created them to do become world changers with God's authority and God's ability.

Look around. What problems do you see? What would Jesus do about them? Now ask Jesus to look at you. What potential does he see in you, his follower? What does he want you to do? God rejoices when his people participate in his restorative work for this world. Practice the patterns that God initiated to rescue people from the devastation that is all around them.

Difference Maker

Of the five lines of Isaiah 1:17, which one can you do something about today? What can you do toward that cause? Take immediate action: write it down or tell someone to hold you accountable to do it.

10 Listen to the LORD, you leaders of "Sodom."
Listen to the law of our God, people of "Gomorrah."
11 "What makes you think I want all your sacrifices?"
says the LORD.
"I am sick of your burnt offerings of rams
and the fat of fattened cattle.
I get no pleasure from the blood
of bulls and lambs and goats.
12 When you come to worship me,
who asked you to parade through my courts with
all your ceremony?
13 Stop bringing me your meaningless gifts;
the incense of your offerings disgusts me!
As for your celebrations of the new moon and the Sabbath
and your special days for fasting—
they are all sinful and false.
I want no more of your pious meetings.
14 I hate your new moon celebrations and your annual festivals.
They are a burden to me. I cannot stand them!
15 When you lift up your hands in prayer, I will not look.
Though you offer many prayers, I will not listen,
for your hands are covered with the blood of innocent victims.
16 Wash yourselves and be clean!
Get your sins out of my sight.
Give up your evil ways.
17 Learn to do good.
Seek justice.
Help the oppressed.
Defend the cause of orphans.
Fight for the rights of widows.

18 "Come now, let's settle this,"
says the LORD.
"Though your sins are like scarlet,
I will make them as white as snow.
Though they are red like crimson,
I will make them as white as wool.
19 If you will only obey me,
you will have plenty to eat.
20 But if you turn away and refuse to listen,
you will be devoured by the sword of your enemies.
I, the LORD, have spoken!"

Unfaithful Jerusalem

21 See how Jerusalem, once so faithful,
has become a prostitute.
Once the home of justice and righteousness,
she is now filled with murderers.
22 Once like pure silver,
you have become like worthless slag.

Once so pure,
you are now like watered-down wine.
23 Your leaders are rebels,
the companions of thieves.
All of them love bribes
and demand payoffs,
but they refuse to defend the cause of orphans
or fight for the rights of widows.

24 Therefore, the Lord, the LORD of Heaven's Armies,
the Mighty One of Israel, says,
"I will take revenge on my enemies
and pay back my foes!
25 I will raise my fist against you.
I will melt you down and skim off your slag.
I will remove all your impurities.
26 Then I will give you good judges again
and wise counselors like you used to have.
Then Jerusalem will again be called the Home of Justice
and the Faithful City."

27 Zion will be restored by justice;
those who repent will be revived by righteousness.
28 But rebels and sinners will be completely destroyed,
and those who desert the LORD will be consumed.

29 You will be ashamed of your idol worship
in groves of sacred oaks.
You will blush because you worshiped
in gardens dedicated to idols.
30 You will be like a great tree with withered leaves,
like a garden without water.
31 The strongest among you will disappear like straw;
their evil deeds will be the spark that sets it on fire.
They and their evil works will burn up together,
and no one will be able to put out the fire.

The LORD's Future Reign

2 This is a vision that Isaiah son of Amoz saw concerning Judah and Jerusalem:

2 In the last days, the mountain of the LORD's house
will be the highest of all—
the most important place on earth.
It will be raised above the other hills,
and people from all over the world will stream there
to worship.
3 People from many nations will come and say,
"Come, let us go up to the mountain of the LORD,
to the house of Jacob's God.

There he will teach us his ways,
and we will walk in his paths."
For the LORD's teaching will go out from Zion;
his word will go out from Jerusalem.
4 The LORD will mediate between nations
and will settle international disputes.
They will hammer their swords into plowshares
and their spears into pruning hooks.
Nation will no longer fight against nation,
nor train for war anymore.

A Warning of Judgment

5 Come, descendants of Jacob,
let us walk in the light of the LORD!
6 For the LORD has rejected his people,
the descendants of Jacob,
because they have filled their land with practices from the East
and with sorcerers, as the Philistines do.
They have made alliances with pagans.
7 Israel is full of silver and gold;
there is no end to its treasures.
Their land is full of warhorses;
there is no end to its chariots.
8 Their land is full of idols;
the people worship things they have made
with their own hands.
9 So now they will be humbled,
and all will be brought low—
do not forgive them.
10 Crawl into caves in the rocks.
Hide in the dust
from the terror of the LORD
and the glory of his majesty.
11 Human pride will be brought down,
and human arrogance will be humbled.
Only the LORD will be exalted
on that day of judgment.

12 For the LORD of Heaven's Armies
has a day of reckoning.
He will punish the proud and mighty
and bring down everything that is exalted.
13 He will cut down the tall cedars of Lebanon
and all the mighty oaks of Bashan.
14 He will level all the high mountains
and all the lofty hills.
15 He will break down every high tower
and every fortified wall.
16 He will destroy all the great trading ships*

2:16 Hebrew *every ship of Tarshish.*

and every magnificent vessel.
17 Human pride will be humbled,
and human arrogance will be brought down.
Only the LORD will be exalted
on that day of judgment.

18 Idols will completely disappear.
19 When the LORD rises to shake the earth,
his enemies will crawl into holes in the ground.
They will hide in caves in the rocks
from the terror of the LORD
and the glory of his majesty.
20 On that day of judgment they will abandon the gold
and silver idols
they made for themselves to worship.
They will leave their gods to the rodents and bats,
21 while they crawl away into caverns
and hide among the jagged rocks in the cliffs.
They will try to escape the terror of the LORD
and the glory of his majesty
as he rises to shake the earth.
22 Don't put your trust in mere humans.
They are as frail as breath.
What good are they?

Judgment against Judah

3 1 The Lord, the LORD of Heaven's Armies,
will take away from Jerusalem and Judah
everything they depend on:
every bit of bread
and every drop of water,
2 all their heroes and soldiers,
judges and prophets,
fortune-tellers and elders,
3 army officers and high officials,
advisers, skilled sorcerers, and astrologers.

4 I will make boys their leaders,
and toddlers their rulers.
5 People will oppress each other—
man against man,
neighbor against neighbor.
Young people will insult their elders,
and vulgar people will sneer at the honorable.

6 In those days a man will say to his brother,
"Since you have a coat, you be our leader!
Take charge of this heap of ruins!"
7 But he will reply,
"No! I can't help.

Question 2:22

Isaiah asked a provocative question here: What good are "mere humans"?

Question 3:5

This kind of behavior is a sign that young people have rejected the Lord. How can you be different?

I don't have any extra food or clothes.
Don't put me in charge!"

8 For Jerusalem will stumble,
and Judah will fall,
because they speak out against the LORD and refuse to obey him.
They provoke him to his face.
9 The very look on their faces gives them away.
They display their sin like the people of Sodom
and don't even try to hide it.
They are doomed!
They have brought destruction upon themselves.

10 Tell the godly that all will be well for them.
They will enjoy the rich reward they have earned!
11 But the wicked are doomed,
for they will get exactly what they deserve.

12 Childish leaders oppress my people,
and women rule over them.
O my people, your leaders mislead you;
they send you down the wrong road.

13 The LORD takes his place in court
and presents his case against his people.*
14 The LORD comes forward to pronounce judgment
on the elders and rulers of his people:
"You have ruined Israel, my vineyard.
Your houses are filled with things stolen from the poor.
15 How dare you crush my people,
grinding the faces of the poor into the dust?"
demands the Lord, the LORD of Heaven's Armies.

A Warning to Jerusalem

16 The LORD says, "Beautiful Zion* is haughty:
craning her elegant neck,
flirting with her eyes,
walking with dainty steps,
tinkling her ankle bracelets.
17 So the Lord will send scabs on her head;
the LORD will make beautiful Zion bald."

18 On that day of judgment
the Lord will strip away everything that makes her beautiful:
ornaments, headbands, crescent necklaces,
19 earrings, bracelets, and veils;
20 scarves, ankle bracelets, sashes,
perfumes, and charms;

3:13 As in Greek and Syriac versions; Hebrew reads *against the peoples.* 3:16 Or *The women of Zion* (with corresponding changes to plural forms through verse 24); Hebrew reads *The daughters of Zion;* also in 3:17.

Please write on this page!

21 rings, jewels,
22 party clothes, gowns, capes, and purses;
23 mirrors, fine linen garments,
head ornaments, and shawls.

24 Instead of smelling of sweet perfume, she will stink.
She will wear a rope for a sash,
and her elegant hair will fall out.
She will wear rough burlap instead of rich robes.
Shame will replace her beauty.*
25 The men of the city will be killed with the sword,
and her warriors will die in battle.
26 The gates of Zion will weep and mourn.
The city will be like a ravaged woman,
huddled on the ground.

4 In that day so few men will be left that seven women will fight for each man, saying, "Let us all marry you! We will provide our own food and clothing. Only let us take your name so we won't be mocked as old maids."

A Promise of Restoration

2 But in that day, the branch* of the LORD
will be beautiful and glorious;
the fruit of the land will be the pride and glory
of all who survive in Israel.
3 All who remain in Zion
will be a holy people—
those who survive the destruction of Jerusalem
and are recorded among the living.
4 The Lord will wash the filth from beautiful Zion*
and cleanse Jerusalem of its bloodstains
with the hot breath of fiery judgment.
5 Then the LORD will provide shade for Mount Zion
and all who assemble there.
He will provide a canopy of cloud during the day
and smoke and flaming fire at night,
covering the glorious land.
6 It will be a shelter from daytime heat
and a hiding place from storms and rain.

A Song about the LORD's Vineyard

5 1 Now I will sing for the one I love
a song about his vineyard:
My beloved had a vineyard
on a rich and fertile hill.
2 He plowed the land, cleared its stones,
and planted it with the best vines.
In the middle he built a watchtower
and carved a winepress in the nearby rocks.

3:24 As in Dead Sea Scrolls; Masoretic Text reads *robes / because instead of beauty.* 4:2 Or *the Branch.* 4:4 Or *from the women of Zion;* Hebrew reads *from the daughters of Zion.*

Prayer 5:7

Jesus, you said that you are the vine and we are the branches (John 15:5). Let me remain in you so that I can expect a crop of justice and righteousness. Amen.

Then he waited for a harvest of sweet grapes,
but the grapes that grew were bitter.

3 Now, you people of Jerusalem and Judah,
you judge between me and my vineyard.
4 What more could I have done for my vineyard
that I have not already done?
When I expected sweet grapes,
why did my vineyard give me bitter grapes?

5 Now let me tell you
what I will do to my vineyard:
I will tear down its hedges
and let it be destroyed.
I will break down its walls
and let the animals trample it.
6 I will make it a wild place
where the vines are not pruned and the ground is not hoed,
a place overgrown with briers and thorns.
I will command the clouds
to drop no rain on it.

7 The nation of Israel is the vineyard of the LORD of Heaven's Armies.
The people of Judah are his pleasant garden.
He expected a crop of justice,
but instead he found oppression.
He expected to find righteousness,
but instead he heard cries of violence.

Judah's Guilt and Judgment

8 What sorrow for you who buy up house after house and
field after field,
until everyone is evicted and you live alone in the land.
9 But I have heard the LORD of Heaven's Armies
swear a solemn oath:
"Many houses will stand deserted;
even beautiful mansions will be empty.
10 Ten acres* of vineyard will not produce even six gallons* of wine.
Ten baskets of seed will yield only one basket* of grain."

11 What sorrow for those who get up early in the morning
looking for a drink of alcohol
and spend long evenings drinking wine
to make themselves flaming drunk.
12 They furnish wine and lovely music at their grand parties—
lyre and harp, tambourine and flute—
but they never think about the LORD
or notice what he is doing.

5:10a Hebrew *A ten yoke,* that is, the area of land plowed by ten teams of oxen in one day. **5:10b** Hebrew *a bath* [21 liters]. **5:10c** Hebrew *A homer* [5 bushels or 220 liters] *of seed will yield only an ephah* [20 quarts or 22 liters].

13 So my people will go into exile far away
because they do not know me.
Those who are great and honored will starve,
and the common people will die of thirst.
14 The grave* is licking its lips in anticipation,
opening its mouth wide.
The great and the lowly
and all the drunken mob will be swallowed up.
15 Humanity will be destroyed, and people brought down;
even the arrogant will lower their eyes in humiliation.
16 But the LORD of Heaven's Armies will be exalted by his justice.
The holiness of God will be displayed by his righteousness.
17 In that day lambs will find good pastures,
and fattened sheep and young goats* will feed among
the ruins.

18 What sorrow for those who drag their sins behind them
with ropes made of lies,
who drag wickedness behind them like a cart!
19 They even mock God and say,
"Hurry up and do something!
We want to see what you can do.
Let the Holy One of Israel carry out his plan,
for we want to know what it is."

20 What sorrow for those who say
that evil is good and good is evil,
that dark is light and light is dark,
that bitter is sweet and sweet is bitter.
21 What sorrow for those who are wise in their own eyes
and think themselves so clever.
22 What sorrow for those who are heroes at drinking wine
and boast about all the alcohol they can hold.
23 They take bribes to let the wicked go free,
and they punish the innocent.

24 Therefore, just as fire licks up stubble
and dry grass shrivels in the flame,
so their roots will rot
and their flowers wither.
For they have rejected the law of the LORD of
Heaven's Armies;
they have despised the word of the Holy One of Israel.
25 That is why the LORD's anger burns against his people,
and why he has raised his fist to crush them.
The mountains tremble,
and the corpses of his people litter the streets like garbage.
But even then the LORD's anger is not satisfied.
His fist is still poised to strike!

5:14 Hebrew *Sheol.* **5:17** As in Greek version; Hebrew reads *and strangers.*

Make a Difference

6:1-8

Send Me

Awe-inducing angels called seraphim (meaning "fiery") gathered around the Lord, who was sitting on a throne. The angels sang, "Holy, holy, holy is the LORD of Heaven's Armies! The whole earth is filled with his glory!" (v. 3). Their resounding praise shook the foundations of the temple and filled the sanctuary with smoke.

As Isaiah had this vision, he became certain that his destruction was sealed. How could any human stand in the presence of almighty God? He was overwhelmed until one of the seraphim flew over to Isaiah and touched his lips with a burning coal, telling him, "Your guilt is removed, and your sins are forgiven" (v. 7). Then the Lord wanted to know who would share the message.

Difference Maker

Spend some time with the Lord asking him to prepare you and to send you to share the good news of Jesus with those you will see today.

26 He will send a signal to distant nations far away
and whistle to those at the ends of the earth.
They will come racing toward Jerusalem.
27 They will not get tired or stumble.
They will not stop for rest or sleep.
Not a belt will be loose,
not a sandal strap broken.
28 Their arrows will be sharp
and their bows ready for battle.
Sparks will fly from their horses' hooves,
and the wheels of their chariots will spin like a whirlwind.
29 They will roar like lions,
like the strongest of lions.
Growling, they will pounce on their victims and carry them off,
and no one will be there to rescue them.
30 They will roar over their victims on that day of destruction
like the roaring of the sea.
If someone looks across the land,
only darkness and distress will be seen;
even the light will be darkened by clouds.

Isaiah's Cleansing and Call

6 It was in the year King Uzziah died* that I saw the Lord. He was sitting
on a lofty throne, and the train of his robe filled the Temple. 2 Attending
him were mighty seraphim, each having six wings. With two wings they
covered their faces, with two they covered their feet, and with two they flew.
3 They were calling out to each other,

"Holy, holy, holy is the LORD of Heaven's Armies!
The whole earth is filled with his glory!"

4 Their voices shook the Temple to its foundations, and the entire building
was filled with smoke.
5 Then I said, "It's all over! I am doomed, for I am a sinful man. I have filthy
lips, and I live among a people with filthy lips. Yet I have seen the King, the
LORD of Heaven's Armies."
6 Then one of the seraphim flew to me with a burning coal he had taken
from the altar with a pair of tongs. 7 He touched my lips with it and said,
"See, this coal has touched your lips. Now your guilt is removed, and your
sins are forgiven."
8 Then I heard the Lord asking, "Whom should I send as a messenger to
this people? Who will go for us?"
I said, "Here I am. Send me."
9 And he said, "Yes, go, and say to this people,

'Listen carefully, but do not understand.
Watch closely, but learn nothing.'
10 Harden the hearts of these people.
Plug their ears and shut their eyes.

6:1 King Uzziah died in 740 B.C.

That way, they will not see with their eyes,
nor hear with their ears,
nor understand with their hearts
and turn to me for healing."*

11 Then I said, "Lord, how long will this go on?"
And he replied,

"Until their towns are empty,
their houses are deserted,
and the whole country is a wasteland;
12 until the LORD has sent everyone away,
and the entire land of Israel lies deserted.
13 If even a tenth—a remnant—survive,
it will be invaded again and burned.
But as a terebinth or oak tree leaves a stump when it is cut down,
so Israel's stump will be a holy seed."

A Message for Ahaz

7 When Ahaz, son of Jotham and grandson of Uzziah, was king of Judah,
King Rezin of Syria* and Pekah son of Remaliah, the king of Israel, set
out to attack Jerusalem. However, they were unable to carry out their plan.
2 The news had come to the royal court of Judah: "Syria is allied with Israel*
against us!" So the hearts of the king and his people trembled with fear, like
trees shaking in a storm.
3 Then the LORD said to Isaiah, "Take your son Shear-jashub* and go out
to meet King Ahaz. You will find him at the end of the aqueduct that feeds
water into the upper pool, near the road leading to the field where cloth is
washed.* 4 Tell him to stop worrying. Tell him he doesn't need to fear the
fierce anger of those two burned-out embers, King Rezin of Syria and Pe-
kah son of Remaliah. 5 Yes, the kings of Syria and Israel are plotting against
him, saying, 6 'We will attack Judah and capture it for ourselves. Then we
will install the son of Tabeel as Judah's king.' 7 But this is what the Sovereign
LORD says:

"This invasion will never happen;
it will never take place;
8 for Syria is no stronger than its capital, Damascus,
and Damascus is no stronger than its king, Rezin.
As for Israel, within sixty-five years
it will be crushed and completely destroyed.
9 Israel is no stronger than its capital, Samaria,
and Samaria is no stronger than its king, Pekah son of Remaliah.
Unless your faith is firm,
I cannot make you stand firm."

6:9-10 Greek version reads *And he said, "Go and say to this people, / 'When you hear what I say, you will not understand. / When you see what I do, you will not comprehend.' / For the hearts of these people are hardened, / and their ears cannot hear, and they have closed their eyes— / so their eyes cannot see, / and their ears cannot hear, / and their hearts cannot understand, / and they cannot turn to me and let me heal them."* Compare Matt 13:14-15; Mark 4:12; Luke 8:10; Acts 28:26-27. **7:1** Hebrew *Aram;* also in 7:2, 4, 5, 8. **7:2** Hebrew *Ephraim,* referring to the northern kingdom of Israel; also in 7:5, 8, 9, 17. **7:3a** *Shear-jashub* means "A remnant will return." **7:3b** Or *bleached.*

Make a Difference 7:14

The Advent of Immanuel

The birth of Jesus Christ was such a powerful event that Isaiah explained it as if it were just around the corner. Seven hundred years before Jesus was born, Isaiah already knew it was about to happen. The child was as good as born. His birth was bigger than the past, present, and future itself. That is because his birth was planned outside of time to affect all of time. His birth is the all-time greatest birth.

Isaiah was seeing it happen. He understood it was a birth yet to come, for here in Isaiah 7:14, he declared it as a future event. This child will be born among us; he will be with us. We will know him as "God is with us."

Difference Maker

If possible, volunteer to babysit for someone you know. Consider how Jesus was once a child also.

The Sign of Immanuel

10 Later, the LORD sent this message to King Ahaz: 11 "Ask the LORD your God
for a sign of confirmation, Ahaz. Make it as difficult as you want—as high
as heaven or as deep as the place of the dead.*"
12 But the king refused. "No," he said, "I will not test the LORD like that."
13 Then Isaiah said, "Listen well, you royal family of David! Isn't it enough
to exhaust human patience? Must you exhaust the patience of my God as
well? 14 All right then, the Lord himself will give you the sign. Look! The
virgin* will conceive a child! She will give birth to a son and will call him
Immanuel (which means 'God is with us'). 15 By the time this child is old
enough to choose what is right and reject what is wrong, he will be eating
yogurt* and honey. 16 For before the child is that old, the lands of the two
kings you fear so much will both be deserted.
17 "Then the LORD will bring things on you, your nation, and your family
unlike anything since Israel broke away from Judah. He will bring the king
of Assyria upon you!"
18 In that day the LORD will whistle for the army of southern Egypt and
for the army of Assyria. They will swarm around you like flies and bees.
19 They will come in vast hordes and settle in the fertile areas and also in the
desolate valleys, caves, and thorny places. 20 In that day the Lord will hire a
"razor" from beyond the Euphrates River*—the king of Assyria—and use
it to shave off everything: your land, your crops, and your people.*
21 In that day a farmer will be fortunate to have a cow and two sheep or
goats left. 22 Nevertheless, there will be enough milk for everyone because
so few people will be left in the land. They will eat their fill of yogurt
and honey. 23 In that day the lush vineyards, now worth 1,000 pieces of
silver,* will become patches of briers and thorns. 24 The entire land will
become a vast expanse of briers and thorns, a hunting ground overrun
by wildlife. 25 No one will go to the fertile hillsides where the gardens
once grew, for briers and thorns will cover them. Cattle, sheep, and goats
will graze there.

The Coming Assyrian Invasion

8 Then the LORD said to me, "Make a large signboard and clearly write
this name on it: Maher-shalal-hash-baz.*" 2 I asked Uriah the priest and
Zechariah son of Jeberekiah, both known as honest men, to witness my
doing this.
3 Then I slept with my wife, and she became pregnant and gave birth to a
son. And the LORD said, "Call him Maher-shalal-hash-baz. 4 For before this
child is old enough to say 'Papa' or 'Mama,' the king of Assyria will carry away
both the abundance of Damascus and the riches of Samaria."
5 Then the LORD spoke to me again and said, 6 "My care for the people of
Judah is like the gently flowing waters of Shiloah, but they have rejected
it. They are rejoicing over what will happen to* King Rezin and King Pe-
kah.* 7 Therefore, the Lord will overwhelm them with a mighty flood from
the Euphrates River*—the king of Assyria and all his glory. This flood
will overflow all its channels 8 and sweep into Judah until it is chin deep.

7:11 Hebrew *as deep as Sheol.* 7:14 Or *young woman.* 7:15 Or *curds;* also in 7:22. 7:20a Hebrew *the river.* 7:20b Hebrew *shave off the head, the hair of the legs, and the beard.* 7:23 Hebrew *1,000 [shekels] of silver,* about 25 pounds or 11.4 kilograms in weight. 8:1 *Maher-shalal-hash-baz* means "Swift to plunder and quick to carry away." 8:6a Or *They are rejoicing because of.* 8:6b Hebrew *and the son of Remaliah.* 8:7 Hebrew *the river.*

It will spread its wings, submerging your land from one end to the other,
O Immanuel.

9 "Huddle together, you nations, and be terrified.
Listen, all you distant lands.
Prepare for battle, but you will be crushed!
Yes, prepare for battle, but you will be crushed!
10 Call your councils of war, but they will be worthless.
Develop your strategies, but they will not succeed.
For God is with us!*"

A Call to Trust the LORD

11 The LORD has given me a strong warning not to think like everyone else does. He said,

12 "Don't call everything a conspiracy, like they do,
and don't live in dread of what frightens them.
13 Make the LORD of Heaven's Armies holy in your life.
He is the one you should fear.
He is the one who should make you tremble.
14 He will keep you safe.
But to Israel and Judah
he will be a stone that makes people stumble,
a rock that makes them fall.
And for the people of Jerusalem
he will be a trap and a snare.
15 Many will stumble and fall,
never to rise again.
They will be snared and captured."

16 Preserve the teaching of God;
entrust his instructions to those who follow me.
17 I will wait for the LORD,
who has turned away from the descendants of Jacob.
I will put my hope in him.

18 I and the children the LORD has given me serve as signs and warnings to Israel from the LORD of Heaven's Armies who dwells in his Temple on Mount Zion.

19 Someone may say to you, "Let's ask the mediums and those who consult the spirits of the dead. With their whisperings and mutterings, they will tell us what to do." But shouldn't people ask God for guidance? Should the living seek guidance from the dead?

20 Look to God's instructions and teachings! People who contradict his
word are completely in the dark. 21 They will go from one place to another,
weary and hungry. And because they are hungry, they will rage and curse
their king and their God. They will look up to heaven 22 and down at the
earth, but wherever they look, there will be trouble and anguish and dark
despair. They will be thrown out into the darkness.

8:10 Hebrew *Immanuel!*

Question 8:11

How is this simple verse similar to Romans 12:2? How does God set you apart for his service?

Hope in the Messiah

9 [1]*Nevertheless, that time of darkness and despair will not go on forever. The land of Zebulun and Naphtali will be humbled, but there will be a time in the future when Galilee of the Gentiles, which lies along the road that runs between the Jordan and the sea, will be filled with glory.

2*The people who walk in darkness
will see a great light.
For those who live in a land of deep darkness,*
a light will shine.
3 You will enlarge the nation of Israel,
and its people will rejoice.
They will rejoice before you
as people rejoice at the harvest
and like warriors dividing the plunder.
4 For you will break the yoke of their slavery
and lift the heavy burden from their shoulders.
You will break the oppressor's rod,
just as you did when you destroyed the army of Midian.
5 The boots of the warrior
and the uniforms bloodstained by war
will all be burned.
They will be fuel for the fire.

6 For a child is born to us,
a son is given to us.
The government will rest on his shoulders.
And he will be called:
Wonderful Counselor,* Mighty God,
Everlasting Father, Prince of Peace.
7 His government and its peace
will never end.
He will rule with fairness and justice from the throne
of his ancestor David
for all eternity.
The passionate commitment of the LORD of Heaven's Armies
will make this happen!

The LORD's Anger against Israel

8 The Lord has spoken out against Jacob;
his judgment has fallen upon Israel.
9 And the people of Israel* and Samaria,
who spoke with such pride and arrogance,
will soon know it.
10 They said, "We will replace the broken bricks of our ruins
with finished stone,
and replant the felled sycamore-fig trees with cedars."

9:1 Verse 9:1 is numbered 8:23 in Hebrew text. 9:2a Verses 9:2-21 are numbered 9:1-20 in Hebrew text. 9:2b Greek version reads *a land where death casts its shadow.* Compare Matt 4:16. 9:6 Or *Wonderful, Counselor.* 9:9 Hebrew *of Ephraim,* referring to the northern kingdom of Israel.

11 But the LORD will bring Rezin's enemies against Israel
and stir up all their foes.
12 The Syrians* from the east and the Philistines from the west
will bare their fangs and devour Israel.
But even then the LORD's anger will not be satisfied.
His fist is still poised to strike.

13 For after all this punishment, the people will still
not repent.
They will not seek the LORD of Heaven's Armies.
14 Therefore, in a single day the LORD will destroy both
the head and the tail,
the noble palm branch and the lowly reed.
15 The leaders of Israel are the head,
and the lying prophets are the tail.
16 For the leaders of the people have misled them.
They have led them down the path of destruction.
17 That is why the Lord takes no pleasure in the young men
and shows no mercy even to the widows and orphans.
For they are all wicked hypocrites,
and they all speak foolishness.
But even then the LORD's anger will not be satisfied.
His fist is still poised to strike.

18 This wickedness is like a brushfire.
It burns not only briers and thorns
but also sets the forests ablaze.
Its burning sends up clouds of smoke.
19 The land will be blackened
by the fury of the LORD of Heaven's Armies.
The people will be fuel for the fire,
and no one will spare even his own brother.
20 They will attack their neighbor on the right
but will still be hungry.
They will devour their neighbor on the left
but will not be satisfied.
In the end they will even eat their own children.*
21 Manasseh will feed on Ephraim,
Ephraim will feed on Manasseh,
and both will devour Judah.
But even then the LORD's anger will not be satisfied.
His fist is still poised to strike.

10 1 What sorrow awaits the unjust judges
and those who issue unfair laws.
2 They deprive the poor of justice
and deny the rights of the needy among my people.
They prey on widows
and take advantage of orphans.

9:12 Hebrew *Arameans.* **9:20** Or *eat their own arms.*

Things to reflect on

The Difference Isaiah 9:6 Makes

Make a Difference 9:6a

Child

Back in Isaiah's day, the nation of Assyria struck intense physical distress and spiritual misery upon Israel. Isaiah told the Israelites not to worry because a child would be born. A child. "Hey, don't worry, everyone—a baby is coming." Well, this wasn't just your normal, cute, little, bubble-blowing baby. The power and majesty of this child would be utterly astonishing. Isaiah was not afraid to emphasize this.

Child is the prominent word in Isaiah's prophecy. Upon this child would hinge everything. If you were to take the child out, the entire prophecy falls apart. If this child is not born and does not step into darkness, the entire world collapses. If this child does not make a mark, the world's very soul crumbles. Without this child being born, darkness still reigns, oppression still weighs people down, and despair and struggle and restriction still overwhelm. They always would—if it were not for the amazing capacity of this child to change everything.

Difference Maker

No matter what day or what month it is, give someone a fun, thoughtful, encouraging "Christmas" gift today.

Make a Difference 9:6b

On His Shoulders

Isaiah foresaw that Jesus wouldn't simply rule a local community or write a constitution or enforce laws. This child would rule everything—all of creation. The scope of the responsibility of administration and management and care and livelihood of the entire planet would be upon him. The weight of the world—the consequences of justice and redemption—would rest upon his shoulders. His kingdom would extend beyond borders and jurisdictions (John 18:36). He would have complete authority (Matthew 28:18) and would hold everything together (Colossians 1:15-20), both in heaven and on earth (John 13:3).

The reason the birth of Jesus brings so much joy is because his shoulders are greater than all nations, greater than all powers, greater than all darkness, and greater than all sin both now and forever.

Difference Maker

Speaking of government, consider writing an encouraging note to one of your city, state, or national leaders. Include Isaiah 9:6 in your message as a reminder that Jesus carries the authority of their burdens on his shoulders.

Make a Difference 9:6c

Wonder Counselor

In Isaiah 9:6 are four sets of word pairs that the prophet uses to describe the child who would be born to us. The first is "Wonderful Counselor." By itself in English, this is pretty cool. Still, this title is even more impressive in Hebrew, the language Isaiah used. It is a title of awe. The Hebrew is *Pe-le Yo-w-'es*.

Pe-le means "wonder." In the Old Testament, this word usually refers to God and his miraculous works. He is astonishing and marvelous and indescribable. *Pe-le* hints at the deity of this child who is to be born. It is a word that could even stand alone, and Isaiah 9:6 could be translated, "He will be called Wonder."

Not only will he be called Wonder, but he will also be called Counselor. The Hebrew word *yo-w-'es* means "counselor," "adviser," or "advocate." This child will sit on the throne of the world with wisdom and with judgment. He is a Counselor who needs no other consultants or analysts around him. This child does not need a cabinet to help him make decisions. He himself is the Counselor to whom everyone else will turn.

Difference Maker

Entrust your concerns, worries, and troubles to Jesus today.

Make a Difference **9:6d**

Hero God

The second word pair in Isaiah 9:6 is "Mighty God." How could a child actually be called "Mighty God"—especially in the monotheistic Hebrew worldview? Still, Isaiah says *El-Gibbor*, which is "Mighty God."

El is the Hebrew word for "God." Isaiah never used it in reference to anyone other than the one true God of Israel. For Isaiah to use this title upon a child was absolutely astonishing. The reason people in the future will rejoice, the reason darkness will be destroyed, the reason light is coming into the world is because somehow a child who is God himself will overturn all the consequences of sin and despair and distress and misery.

This God is mighty. *Gibbor* literally means "hero." This child is the hero God. God is going to be the hero of the story. Are you walking in darkness? Don't fear because God will give you light. Are you oppressed? Hang in there, for God is coming to the rescue. Is your soul imprisoned? God will free you. Are you struggling? God will revive you. He is the hero God who comes to save the world.

Difference Maker

If Jesus is the hero God, then, as his follower, do something heroic for someone today.

Make a Difference **9:6e**

Forever Father

The third word pair in Isaiah 9:6 is "Everlasting Father." The Messiah, this child who was to be born, this Son who will carry the weight of the entire world, will also be known as "Father." The Hebrew for this title is *Abbi-'ad*. *Abbi*, or *abba*, means "Father," while *'ad* refers to "endlessness." That means this child will be a Father to his people forever and ever.

When God's children return to God the Father, Isaiah said, they will return to this child. He will stand guard over them, supply their needs, and provide them tenderness and protection and love. He will shepherd them, guide them, and lay his life down for them. All this is not for a brief period of human life; rather, this child will be their Father forever (Isaiah 63:16), a Father who will never abandon his children (Matthew 28:20).

Difference Maker

How would your regular routines today be different if you were to remember that Jesus will be leading you forever?

Make a Difference **9:6f**

Peace Prince

The last word pair in Isaiah 9:6 is "Prince of Peace." *Sur-Shalom*. He will establish a peace that is much more than a temporary cease-fire. His power and rule will launch a new heaven and a new earth. All suffering and frustration and angst and weapons of darkness will be obliterated.

Shalom is the wholeness and fulfillment that only God has. *Shalom* is the purity and the perfection and the knowledge and summary of everything that is right. Isaiah revealed this will come from a child, a child who is the ruler of peace.

This child is going to be one who rules with the power of eternity, a child who is born among us and for us, a child who is too wondrous to describe with just one name. He will be the child who holds titles unimaginable, a child who saves the world, and a child who inaugurates the *shalom* of God.

Difference Maker

Because Jesus is the Prince of Peace, if you are separated from someone because of something you have done, take the necessary steps to make peace with them today.

3 What will you do when I punish you,
when I send disaster upon you from a distant land?
To whom will you turn for help?
Where will your treasures be safe?
4 You will stumble along as prisoners
or lie among the dead.
But even then the LORD's anger will not be satisfied.
His fist is still poised to strike.

Judgment against Assyria

5 "What sorrow awaits Assyria, the rod of my anger.
I use it as a club to express my anger.
6 I am sending Assyria against a godless nation,
against a people with whom I am angry.
Assyria will plunder them,
trampling them like dirt beneath its feet.
7 But the king of Assyria will not understand that he is my tool;
his mind does not work that way.
His plan is simply to destroy,
to cut down nation after nation.
8 He will say,
'Each of my princes will soon be a king.
9 We destroyed Calno just as we did Carchemish.
Hamath fell before us as Arpad did.
And we destroyed Samaria just as we did Damascus.
10 Yes, we have finished off many a kingdom
whose gods were greater than those in Jerusalem and Samaria.
11 So we will defeat Jerusalem and her gods,
just as we destroyed Samaria with hers.'"

12 After the Lord has used the king of Assyria to accomplish his purposes
on Mount Zion and in Jerusalem, he will turn against the king of Assyria
and punish him—for he is proud and arrogant. 13 He boasts,

"By my own powerful arm I have done this.
With my own shrewd wisdom I planned it.
I have broken down the defenses of nations
and carried off their treasures.
I have knocked down their kings like a bull.
14 I have robbed their nests of riches
and gathered up kingdoms as a farmer gathers eggs.
No one can even flap a wing against me
or utter a peep of protest."

15 But can the ax boast greater power than the person who uses it?
Is the saw greater than the person who saws?
Can a rod strike unless a hand moves it?
Can a wooden cane walk by itself?
16 Therefore, the Lord, the LORD of Heaven's Armies,
will send a plague among Assyria's proud troops,

and a flaming fire will consume its glory.
17 The LORD, the Light of Israel, will be a fire;
the Holy One will be a flame.
He will devour the thorns and briers with fire,
burning up the enemy in a single night.
18 The LORD will consume Assyria's glory
like a fire consumes a forest in a fruitful land;
it will waste away like sick people in a plague.
19 Of all that glorious forest, only a few trees will survive—
so few that a child could count them!

Hope for the LORD's People

20 In that day the remnant left in Israel,
the survivors in the house of Jacob,
will no longer depend on allies
who seek to destroy them.
But they will faithfully trust the LORD,
the Holy One of Israel.
21 A remnant will return;*
yes, the remnant of Jacob will return to the Mighty God.
22 But though the people of Israel are as numerous
as the sand of the seashore,
only a remnant of them will return.
The LORD has rightly decided to destroy his people.
23 Yes, the Lord, the LORD of Heaven's Armies,
has already decided to destroy the entire land.*

24 So this is what the Lord, the LORD of Heaven's Armies, says: "O my
people in Zion, do not be afraid of the Assyrians when they oppress you
with rod and club as the Egyptians did long ago. 25 In a little while my anger
against you will end, and then my anger will rise up to destroy them." 26 The
LORD of Heaven's Armies will lash them with his whip, as he did when Gid-
eon triumphed over the Midianites at the rock of Oreb, or when the LORD's
staff was raised to drown the Egyptian army in the sea.

27 In that day the LORD will end the bondage of his people.
He will break the yoke of slavery
and lift it from their shoulders.*

28 Look, the Assyrians are now at Aiath.
They are passing through Migron
and are storing their equipment at Micmash.
29 They are crossing the pass
and are camping at Geba.
Fear strikes the town of Ramah.
All the people of Gibeah, the hometown of Saul,
are running for their lives.

10:21 Hebrew *Shear-jashub;* see 7:3; 8:18. 10:22-23 Greek version reads *only a remnant of them will be saved. / For he will carry out his sentence quickly and with finality and righteousness; / for God will carry out his sentence upon all the world with finality.* Compare Rom 9:27-28. 10:27 As in Greek version; Hebrew reads *The yoke will be broken, / for you have grown so fat.*

Patterns I see in this text

30 Scream in terror,
you people of Gallim!
Shout out a warning to Laishah.
Oh, poor Anathoth!
31 There go the people of Madmenah, all fleeing.
The citizens of Gebim are trying to hide.
32 The enemy stops at Nob for the rest of that day.
He shakes his fist at beautiful Mount Zion, the mountain of Jerusalem.

33 But look! The Lord, the LORD of Heaven's Armies,
will chop down the mighty tree of Assyria with great power!
He will cut down the proud.
That lofty tree will be brought down.
34 He will cut down the forest trees with an ax.
Lebanon will fall to the Mighty One.*

A Branch from David's Line

11 1 Out of the stump of David's family* will grow a shoot—
yes, a new Branch bearing fruit from the old root.
2 And the Spirit of the LORD will rest on him—
the Spirit of wisdom and understanding,
the Spirit of counsel and might,
the Spirit of knowledge and the fear of the LORD.
3 He will delight in obeying the LORD.
He will not judge by appearance
nor make a decision based on hearsay.
4 He will give justice to the poor
and make fair decisions for the exploited.
The earth will shake at the force of his word,
and one breath from his mouth will destroy the wicked.
5 He will wear righteousness like a belt
and truth like an undergarment.

6 In that day the wolf and the lamb will live together;
the leopard will lie down with the baby goat.
The calf and the yearling will be safe with the lion,
and a little child will lead them all.
7 The cow will graze near the bear.
The cub and the calf will lie down together.
The lion will eat hay like a cow.
8 The baby will play safely near the hole of a cobra.
Yes, a little child will put its hand in a nest of deadly snakes without harm.
9 Nothing will hurt or destroy in all my holy mountain,
for as the waters fill the sea,
so the earth will be filled with people who know the LORD.

Story Arc **11:1–5**

David

In the midst of Israel's downfall, even though it would appear that the kingdom of David was finished, Isaiah indicated that one of David's descendants would rise up one day to rule again. How does Jesus fulfill this? What kind of kingdom will he rule?

Isa 37:14-20 ►

10:34 Or *with an ax / as even the mighty trees of Lebanon fall.* 11:1 Hebrew *the stump of the line of Jesse.* Jesse was King David's father.

10 In that day the heir to David's throne*
will be a banner of salvation to all the world.
The nations will rally to him,
and the land where he lives will be a glorious place.*
11 In that day the Lord will reach out his hand a second time
to bring back the remnant of his people—
those who remain in Assyria and northern Egypt;
in southern Egypt, Ethiopia,* and Elam;
in Babylonia,* Hamath, and all the distant coastlands.
12 He will raise a flag among the nations
and assemble the exiles of Israel.
He will gather the scattered people of Judah
from the ends of the earth.

13 Then at last the jealousy between Israel* and Judah will end.
They will not be rivals anymore.
14 They will join forces to swoop down on Philistia to the west.
Together they will attack and plunder the nations to the east.
They will occupy the lands of Edom and Moab,
and Ammon will obey them.
15 The LORD will make a dry path through the gulf of the Red Sea.*
He will wave his hand over the Euphrates River,*
sending a mighty wind to divide it into seven streams
so it can easily be crossed on foot.
16 He will make a highway for the remnant of his people,
the remnant coming from Assyria,
just as he did for Israel long ago
when they returned from Egypt.

Songs of Praise for Salvation

12 1 In that day you will sing:
"I will praise you, O LORD!
You were angry with me, but not any more.
Now you comfort me.
2 See, God has come to save me.
I will trust in him and not be afraid.
The LORD GOD is my strength and my song;
he has given me victory."

3 With joy you will drink deeply
from the fountain of salvation!
4 In that wonderful day you will sing:
"Thank the LORD! Praise his name!
Tell the nations what he has done.
Let them know how mighty he is!
5 Sing to the LORD, for he has done wonderful things.
Make known his praise around the world.

11:10a Hebrew *the root of Jesse.* **11:10b** Greek version reads *In that day the heir to David's throne* [literally *the root of Jesse*] *will come, / and he will rule over the Gentiles. / They will place their hopes on him.* Compare Rom 15:12. **11:11a** Hebrew *in Pathros, Cush.* **11:11b** Hebrew *in Shinar.* **11:13** Hebrew *Ephraim,* referring to the northern kingdom of Israel. **11:15a** Hebrew *will destroy the tongue of the sea of Egypt.* **11:15b** Hebrew *the river.*

Make a Difference 12:4

For His Mighty Power

Anarchy isn't all it's cracked up to be. Or is it? Whatever anarchy is, it is certainly a mess that cannot control itself. Controlled anarchy would be the opposite of anarchy, after all. Anarchy is a void of power and the absence of control. The flames of it spread through terror and false agreements, fear and disasters. What people initially think of as "freedom from authority" quickly devolves into a civil war among power mongers.

Isaiah was concerned about this very thing twenty-seven hundred years ago. Even so, he had a vision. He saw the Servant of the Lord, the Messiah, rising out of the destruction of a nation with the Spirit of the Lord resting on him, defending the poor and the exploited, ruling against the wicked and destroying them with the commissioning of his breath, and overwhelming them with fairness and truth (Isaiah 11-12). Isaiah's fear of the disintegration of society was overcome by the coming King. Aren't you glad someone is actually in control?

Difference Maker

Take some time to pray for the areas of chaos in our world. Pray for people to discover the peace of Jesus in the midst of turmoil.

6 Let all the people of Jerusalem* shout his praise with joy!
For great is the Holy One of Israel who lives among you."

A Message about Babylon

13 Isaiah son of Amoz received this message concerning the destruction of Babylon:

2 "Raise a signal flag on a bare hilltop.
Call up an army against Babylon.
Wave your hand to encourage them
as they march into the palaces of the high and mighty.
3 I, the LORD, have dedicated these soldiers for this task.
Yes, I have called mighty warriors to express my anger,
and they will rejoice when I am exalted."

4 Hear the noise on the mountains!
Listen, as the vast armies march!
It is the noise and shouting of many nations.
The LORD of Heaven's Armies has called this army together.
5 They come from distant countries,
from beyond the farthest horizons.
They are the LORD's weapons to carry out his anger.
With them he will destroy the whole land.

6 Scream in terror, for the day of the LORD has arrived—
the time for the Almighty to destroy.
7 Every arm is paralyzed with fear.
Every heart melts,
8 and people are terrified.
Pangs of anguish grip them,
like those of a woman in labor.
They look helplessly at one another,
their faces aflame with fear.

9 For see, the day of the LORD is coming—
the terrible day of his fury and fierce anger.
The land will be made desolate,
and all the sinners destroyed with it.
10 The heavens will be black above them;
the stars will give no light.
The sun will be dark when it rises,
and the moon will provide no light.

11 "I, the LORD, will punish the world for its evil
and the wicked for their sin.
I will crush the arrogance of the proud
and humble the pride of the mighty.
12 I will make people scarcer than gold—
more rare than the fine gold of Ophir.

12:6 Hebrew *Zion*.

13 For I will shake the heavens.
The earth will move from its place
when the LORD of Heaven's Armies displays his wrath
in the day of his fierce anger."

14 Everyone in Babylon will run about like a hunted gazelle,
like sheep without a shepherd.
They will try to find their own people
and flee to their own land.
15 Anyone who is captured will be cut down—
run through with a sword.
16 Their little children will be dashed to death before their eyes.
Their homes will be sacked, and their wives will be raped.

17 "Look, I will stir up the Medes against Babylon.
They cannot be tempted by silver
or bribed with gold.
18 The attacking armies will shoot down the young men with arrows.
They will have no mercy on helpless babies
and will show no compassion for children."

19 Babylon, the most glorious of kingdoms,
the flower of Chaldean pride,
will be devastated like Sodom and Gomorrah
when God destroyed them.
20 Babylon will never be inhabited again.
It will remain empty for generation after generation.
Nomads will refuse to camp there,
and shepherds will not bed down their sheep.
21 Desert animals will move into the ruined city,
and the houses will be haunted by howling creatures.
Owls will live among the ruins,
and wild goats will go there to dance.
22 Hyenas will howl in its fortresses,
and jackals will make dens in its luxurious palaces.
Babylon's days are numbered;
its time of destruction will soon arrive.

A Taunt for Babylon's King

14 But the LORD will have mercy on the descendants of Jacob. He will
choose Israel as his special people once again. He will bring them
back to settle once again in their own land. And people from many different
nations will come and join them there and unite with the people of Israel.*
2 The nations of the world will help the people of Israel to return, and those
who come to live in the LORD's land will serve them. Those who captured
Israel will themselves be captured, and Israel will rule over its enemies.
3 In that wonderful day when the LORD gives his people rest from sorrow
and fear, from slavery and chains, 4 you will taunt the king of Babylon. You
will say,

14:1 Hebrew *the house of Jacob*. The names "Jacob" and "Israel" are often interchanged throughout the Old Testament, referring sometimes to the individual patriarch and sometimes to the nation.

Highlights from the text

"The mighty man has been destroyed.
Yes, your insolence* is ended.
5 For the LORD has crushed your wicked power
and broken your evil rule.
6 You struck the people with endless blows of rage
and held the nations in your angry grip
with unrelenting tyranny.
7 But finally the earth is at rest and quiet.
Now it can sing again!
8 Even the trees of the forest—
the cypress trees and the cedars of Lebanon—
sing out this joyous song:
'Since you have been cut down,
no one will come now to cut us down!'

9 "In the place of the dead* there is excitement
over your arrival.
The spirits of world leaders and mighty kings long dead
stand up to see you.
10 With one voice they all cry out,
'Now you are as weak as we are!
11 Your might and power were buried with you.*
The sound of the harp in your palace has ceased.
Now maggots are your sheet,
and worms your blanket.'

12 "How you are fallen from heaven,
O shining star, son of the morning!
You have been thrown down to the earth,
you who destroyed the nations of the world.
13 For you said to yourself,
'I will ascend to heaven and set my throne above
God's stars.
I will preside on the mountain of the gods
far away in the north.*
14 I will climb to the highest heavens
and be like the Most High.'
15 Instead, you will be brought down to the place of the dead,
down to its lowest depths.
16 Everyone there will stare at you and ask,
'Can this be the one who shook the earth
and made the kingdoms of the world tremble?
17 Is this the one who destroyed the world
and made it into a wasteland?
Is this the king who demolished the world's greatest cities
and had no mercy on his prisoners?'

18 "The kings of the nations lie in stately glory,
each in his own tomb,

14:4 As in Dead Sea Scrolls; the meaning of the Masoretic Text is uncertain. **14:9** Hebrew *Sheol;* also in 14:15. **14:11** Hebrew *were brought down to Sheol.* **14:13** Or *on the heights of Zaphon.*

19 but you will be thrown out of your grave
like a worthless branch.
Like a corpse trampled underfoot,
you will be dumped into a mass grave
with those killed in battle.
You will descend to the pit.
20 You will not be given a proper burial,
for you have destroyed your nation
and slaughtered your people.
The descendants of such an evil person
will never again receive honor.
21 Kill this man's children!
Let them die because of their father's sins!
They must not rise and conquer the earth,
filling the world with their cities."

22 This is what the LORD of Heaven's Armies says:
"I, myself, have risen against Babylon!
I will destroy its children and its children's children,"
says the LORD.
23 "I will make Babylon a desolate place of owls,
filled with swamps and marshes.
I will sweep the land with the broom of destruction.
I, the LORD of Heaven's Armies, have spoken!"

A Message about Assyria

24 The LORD of Heaven's Armies has sworn this oath:

"It will all happen as I have planned.
It will be as I have decided.
25 I will break the Assyrians when they are in Israel;
I will trample them on my mountains.
My people will no longer be their slaves
nor bow down under their heavy loads.
26 I have a plan for the whole earth,
a hand of judgment upon all the nations.
27 The LORD of Heaven's Armies has spoken—
who can change his plans?
When his hand is raised,
who can stop him?"

A Message about Philistia

28 This message came to me the year King Ahaz died:*

29 Do not rejoice, you Philistines,
that the rod that struck you is broken—
that the king who attacked you is dead.
For from that snake a more poisonous snake will be born,
a fiery serpent to destroy you!

14:28 King Ahaz died in 715 B.C.

Question 14:26

What is God's plan for the whole earth? Where do you fit into this?

30 I will feed the poor in my pasture;
the needy will lie down in peace.
But as for you, I will wipe you out with famine
and destroy the few who remain.
31 Wail at the gates! Weep in the cities!
Melt with fear, you Philistines!
A powerful army comes like smoke from the north.
Each soldier rushes forward eager to fight.

32 What should we tell the Philistine messengers? Tell them,

"The LORD has built Jerusalem*;
its walls will give refuge to his oppressed people."

A Message about Moab

15 This message came to me concerning Moab:

In one night the town of Ar will be leveled,
and the city of Kir will be destroyed.
2 Your people will go to their temple in Dibon to mourn.
They will go to their sacred shrines to weep.
They will wail for the fate of Nebo and Medeba,
shaving their heads in sorrow and cutting off their beards.
3 They will wear burlap as they wander the streets.
From every home and public square will come the
sound of wailing.
4 The people of Heshbon and Elealeh will cry out;
their voices will be heard as far away as Jahaz!
The bravest warriors of Moab will cry out in utter terror.
They will be helpless with fear.

5 My heart weeps for Moab.
Its people flee to Zoar and Eglath-shelishiyah.
Weeping, they climb the road to Luhith.
Their cries of distress can be heard all along the road to Horonaim.
6 Even the waters of Nimrim are dried up!
The grassy banks are scorched.
The tender plants are gone;
nothing green remains.
7 The people grab their possessions
and carry them across the Ravine of Willows.
8 A cry of distress echoes through the land of Moab
from one end to the other—
from Eglaim to Beer-elim.
9 The stream near Dibon* runs red with blood,
but I am still not finished with Dibon!
Lions will hunt down the survivors—
both those who try to escape
and those who remain behind.

14:32 Hebrew *Zion.* 15:9 As in Dead Sea Scrolls, some Greek manuscripts, and Latin Vulgate; Masoretic Text reads *Dimon;* also in 15:9b.

16

1 Send lambs from Sela as tribute
to the ruler of the land.
Send them through the desert
to the mountain of beautiful Zion.
2 The women of Moab are left like homeless birds
at the shallow crossings of the Arnon River.
3 "Help us," they cry.
"Defend us against our enemies.
Protect us from their relentless attack.
Do not betray us now that we have escaped.
4 Let our refugees stay among you.
Hide them from our enemies until the terror is past."

When oppression and destruction have ended
and enemy raiders have disappeared,
5 then God will establish one of David's descendants
as king.
He will rule with mercy and truth.
He will always do what is just
and be eager to do what is right.

6 We have heard about proud Moab—
about its pride and arrogance and rage.
But all that boasting has disappeared.
7 The entire land of Moab weeps.
Yes, everyone in Moab mourns
for the cakes of raisins from Kir-hareseth.
They are all gone now.
8 The farms of Heshbon are abandoned;
the vineyards at Sibmah are deserted.
The rulers of the nations have broken down Moab—
that beautiful grapevine.
Its tendrils spread north as far as the town of Jazer
and trailed eastward into the wilderness.
Its shoots reached so far west
that they crossed over the Dead Sea.*

9 So now I weep for Jazer and the vineyards of Sibmah;
my tears will flow for Heshbon and Elealeh.
There are no more shouts of joy
over your summer fruits and harvest.
10 Gone now is the gladness,
gone the joy of harvest.
There will be no singing in the vineyards,
no more happy shouts,
no treading of grapes in the winepresses.
I have ended all their harvest joys.
11 My heart's cry for Moab is like a lament on a harp.
I am filled with anguish for Kir-hareseth.*

16:8 Hebrew *the sea.* **16:11** Hebrew *Kir-heres*, a variant spelling of Kir-hareseth.

What I will do next

Question 17:10

Do you ever feel like you've put all the effort into something that doesn't work? This verse teaches that in the long run, if you don't follow the Lord, you'll harvest a load of grief and unrelieved pain instead of abundance. What things in your life are you working really hard at right now? Do they fit into God's plan for your life?

12 The people of Moab will worship at their pagan shrines,
but it will do them no good.
They will cry to the gods in their temples,
but no one will be able to save them.

13 The LORD has already said these things about Moab in the past. 14 But
now the LORD says, "Within three years, counting each day,* the glory of
Moab will be ended. From its great population, only a feeble few will be
left alive."

A Message about Damascus and Israel

17 This message came to me concerning Damascus:

"Look, the city of Damascus will disappear!
It will become a heap of ruins.
2 The towns of Aroer will be deserted.
Flocks will graze in the streets and lie down undisturbed,
with no one to chase them away.
3 The fortified towns of Israel* will also be destroyed,
and the royal power of Damascus will end.
All that remains of Syria*
will share the fate of Israel's departed glory,"
declares the LORD of Heaven's Armies.

4 "In that day Israel's* glory will grow dim;
its robust body will waste away.
5 The whole land will look like a grainfield
after the harvesters have gathered the grain.
It will be desolate,
like the fields in the valley of Rephaim after the harvest.
6 Only a few of its people will be left,
like stray olives left on a tree after the harvest.
Only two or three remain in the highest branches,
four or five scattered here and there on the limbs,"
declares the LORD, the God of Israel.

7 Then at last the people will look to their Creator
and turn their eyes to the Holy One of Israel.
8 They will no longer look to their idols for help
or worship what their own hands have made.
They will never again bow down to their Asherah poles
or worship at the pagan shrines they have built.
9 Their largest cities will be like a deserted forest,
like the land the Hivites and Amorites abandoned*
when the Israelites came here so long ago.
It will be utterly desolate.
10 Why? Because you have turned from the God who can save you.

16:14 Hebrew *Within three years, as a servant bound by contract would count them.* 17:3a Hebrew *of Ephraim,* referring to the northern kingdom of Israel. 17:3b Hebrew *Aram.* 17:4 Hebrew *Jacob's.* See note on 14:1. 17:9 As in Greek version; Hebrew reads *like places of the wood and the highest bough.*

You have forgotten the Rock who can hide you.
So you may plant the finest grapevines
and import the most expensive seedlings.
11 They may sprout on the day you set them out;
yes, they may blossom on the very morning you plant them,
but you will never pick any grapes from them.
Your only harvest will be a load of grief and unrelieved pain.

12 Listen! The armies of many nations
roar like the roaring of the sea.
Hear the thunder of the mighty forces
as they rush forward like thundering waves.
13 But though they thunder like breakers on a beach,
God will silence them, and they will run away.
They will flee like chaff scattered by the wind,
like a tumbleweed whirling before a storm.
14 In the evening Israel waits in terror,
but by dawn its enemies are dead.
This is the just reward of those who plunder us,
a fitting end for those who destroy us.

A Message about Ethiopia

18 1 Listen, Ethiopia*—land of fluttering sails*
that lies at the headwaters of the Nile,
2 that sends ambassadors
in swift boats down the river.

Go, swift messengers!
Take a message to a tall, smooth-skinned people,
who are feared far and wide
for their conquests and destruction,
and whose land is divided by rivers.

3 All you people of the world,
everyone who lives on the earth—
when I raise my battle flag on the mountain, look!
When I blow the ram's horn, listen!
4 For the LORD has told me this:
"I will watch quietly from my dwelling place—
as quietly as the heat rises on a summer day,
or as the morning dew forms during the harvest."
5 Even before you begin your attack,
while your plans are ripening like grapes,
the LORD will cut off your new growth with pruning shears.
He will snip off and discard your spreading branches.
6 Your mighty army will be left dead in the fields
for the mountain vultures and wild animals.
The vultures will tear at the corpses all summer.
The wild animals will gnaw at the bones all winter.

18:1a Hebrew *Cush.* 18:1b Or *land of many locusts;* Hebrew reads *land of whirring wings.*

7 At that time the LORD of Heaven's Armies will receive gifts
from this land divided by rivers,
from this tall, smooth-skinned people,
who are feared far and wide for their conquests and destruction.
They will bring the gifts to Jerusalem,*
where the LORD of Heaven's Armies dwells.

A Message about Egypt

19 This message came to me concerning Egypt:

Look! The LORD is advancing against Egypt,
riding on a swift cloud.
The idols of Egypt tremble.
The hearts of the Egyptians melt with fear.

2 "I will make Egyptian fight against Egyptian—
brother against brother,
neighbor against neighbor,
city against city,
province against province.
3 The Egyptians will lose heart,
and I will confuse their plans.
They will plead with their idols for wisdom
and call on spirits, mediums, and those who consult
the spirits of the dead.
4 I will hand Egypt over
to a hard, cruel master.
A fierce king will rule them,"
says the Lord, the LORD of Heaven's Armies.

5 The waters of the Nile will fail to rise and flood the fields.
The riverbed will be parched and dry.
6 The canals of the Nile will dry up,
and the streams of Egypt will stink
with rotting reeds and rushes.
7 All the greenery along the riverbank
and all the crops along the river
will dry up and blow away.
8 The fishermen will lament for lack of work.
Those who cast hooks into the Nile will groan,
and those who use nets will lose heart.
9 There will be no flax for the harvesters,
no thread for the weavers.
10 They will be in despair,
and all the workers will be sick at heart.

11 What fools are the officials of Zoan!
Their best counsel to the king of Egypt is stupid
and wrong.

18:7 Hebrew *to Mount Zion.*

Will they still boast to Pharaoh of their wisdom?
Will they dare brag about all their wise ancestors?
12 Where are your wise counselors, Pharaoh?
Let them tell you what God plans,
what the LORD of Heaven's Armies is going to do to Egypt.
13 The officials of Zoan are fools,
and the officials of Memphis* are deluded.
The leaders of the people
have led Egypt astray.
14 The LORD has sent a spirit of foolishness on them,
so all their suggestions are wrong.
They cause Egypt to stagger
like a drunk in his vomit.
15 There is nothing Egypt can do.
All are helpless—
the head and the tail,
the noble palm branch and the lowly reed.

16In that day the Egyptians will be as weak as women. They will cower in
fear beneath the upraised fist of the LORD of Heaven's Armies. 17Just to speak
the name of Israel will terrorize them, for the LORD of Heaven's Armies has
laid out his plans against them.

18In that day five of Egypt's cities will follow the LORD of Heaven's Armies.
They will even begin to speak Hebrew, the language of Canaan. One of these
cities will be Heliopolis, the City of the Sun.*

19In that day there will be an altar to the LORD in the heart of Egypt, and
there will be a monument to the LORD at its border. 20It will be a sign and a
witness that the LORD of Heaven's Armies is worshiped in the land of Egypt.
When the people cry to the LORD for help against those who oppress them, he
will send them a savior who will rescue them. 21The LORD will make himself
known to the Egyptians. Yes, they will know the LORD and will give their sac-
rifices and offerings to him. They will make a vow to the LORD and will keep
it. 22The LORD will strike Egypt, and then he will bring healing. For the Egyp-
tians will turn to the LORD, and he will listen to their pleas and heal them.

23In that day Egypt and Assyria will be connected by a highway. The Egyp-
tians and Assyrians will move freely between their lands, and they will both
worship God. 24In that day Israel will be the third, along with Egypt and
Assyria, a blessing in the midst of the earth. 25For the LORD of Heaven's Ar-
mies will say, "Blessed be Egypt, my people. Blessed be Assyria, the land I
have made. Blessed be Israel, my special possession!"

A Message about Egypt and Ethiopia

20 In the year when King Sargon of Assyria sent his commander in
chief to capture the Philistine city of Ashdod,* 2the LORD told Isaiah
son of Amoz, "Take off the burlap you have been wearing, and remove your
sandals." Isaiah did as he was told and walked around naked and barefoot.

3Then the LORD said, "My servant Isaiah has been walking around naked
and barefoot for the last three years. This is a sign—a symbol of the terrible
troubles I will bring upon Egypt and Ethiopia.* 4For the king of Assyria

19:13 Hebrew *Noph.* **19:18** Or *will be the City of Destruction.* **20:1** Ashdod was captured by Assyria in 711 B.C. **20:3** Hebrew *Cush;* also in 20:5.

Encouragements from these verses

Prayer 21:3

Lord, give me this kind of holy fear and earnest compassion for the lostness of the world. Amen.

will take away the Egyptians and Ethiopians* as prisoners. He will make
them walk naked and barefoot, both young and old, their buttocks bared,
to the shame of Egypt. [5]Then the Philistines will be thrown into panic, for
they counted on the power of Ethiopia and boasted of their allies in Egypt!
[6]They will say, 'If this can happen to Egypt, what chance do we have? We were
counting on Egypt to protect us from the king of Assyria.'"

A Message about Babylon

21 This message came to me concerning Babylon—the desert by the sea*:

Disaster is roaring down on you from the desert,
like a whirlwind sweeping in from the Negev.
2 I see a terrifying vision:
I see the betrayer betraying,
the destroyer destroying.
Go ahead, you Elamites and Medes,
attack and lay siege.
I will make an end
to all the groaning Babylon caused.
3 My stomach aches and burns with pain.
Sharp pangs of anguish are upon me,
like those of a woman in labor.
I grow faint when I hear what God is planning;
I am too afraid to look.
4 My mind reels and my heart races.
I longed for evening to come,
but now I am terrified of the dark.
5 Look! They are preparing a great feast.
They are spreading rugs for people to sit on.
Everyone is eating and drinking.
But quick! Grab your shields and prepare for battle.
You are being attacked!

6 Meanwhile, the Lord said to me,
"Put a watchman on the city wall.
Let him shout out what he sees.
7 He should look for chariots
drawn by pairs of horses,
and for riders on donkeys and camels.
Let the watchman be fully alert."

8 Then the watchman* called out,
"Day after day I have stood on the watchtower, my lord.
Night after night I have remained at my post.
9 Now at last—look!
Here comes a man in a chariot
with a pair of horses!"

20:4 Hebrew *Cushites.* 21:1 Hebrew *concerning the desert by the sea.* 21:8 As in Dead Sea Scrolls and Syriac version; Masoretic Text reads *a lion.*

Then the watchman said,
"Babylon is fallen, fallen!
All the idols of Babylon
lie broken on the ground!"
10 O my people, threshed and winnowed,
I have told you everything the LORD of Heaven's Armies has said,
everything the God of Israel has told me.

A Message about Edom

11 This message came to me concerning Edom*:

Someone from Edom* keeps calling to me,
"Watchman, how much longer until morning?
When will the night be over?"
12 The watchman replies,
"Morning is coming, but night will soon return.
If you wish to ask again, then come back and ask."

A Message about Arabia

13 This message came to me concerning Arabia:

O caravans from Dedan,
hide in the deserts of Arabia.
14 O people of Tema,
bring water to these thirsty people,
food to these weary refugees.
15 They have fled from the sword,
from the drawn sword,
from the bent bow
and the terrors of battle.

16 The Lord said to me, "Within a year, counting each day,* all the glory of
Kedar will come to an end. 17 Only a few of its courageous archers will survive.
I, the LORD, the God of Israel, have spoken!"

A Message about Jerusalem

22 This message came to me concerning Jerusalem—the Valley of Vision*:

What is happening?
Why is everyone running to the rooftops?
2 The whole city is in a terrible uproar.
What do I see in this reveling city?
Bodies are lying everywhere,
killed not in battle but by famine and disease.
3 All your leaders have fled.
They surrendered without resistance.

21:11a Hebrew *Dumah,* which means "silence" or "stillness." It is a wordplay on the word *Edom.* **21:11b** Hebrew *Seir,* another name for Edom. **21:16** Hebrew *Within a year, as a servant bound by contract would count it.* Some ancient manuscripts read *Within three years,* as in 16:14. **22:1** Hebrew *concerning the Valley of Vision.*

The people tried to slip away,
but they were captured, too.
4 That's why I said, "Leave me alone to weep;
do not try to comfort me.
Let me cry for my people
as I watch them being destroyed."

5 Oh, what a day of crushing defeat!
What a day of confusion and terror
brought by the Lord, the LORD of Heaven's Armies,
upon the Valley of Vision!
The walls of Jerusalem have been broken,
and cries of death echo from the mountainsides.
6 Elamites are the archers,
with their chariots and charioteers.
The men of Kir hold up the shields.
7 Chariots fill your beautiful valleys,
and charioteers storm your gates.
8 Judah's defenses have been stripped away.
You run to the armory* for your weapons.
9 You inspect the breaks in the walls of Jerusalem.*
You store up water in the lower pool.
10 You survey the houses and tear some down
for stone to strengthen the walls.
11 Between the city walls, you build a reservoir
for water from the old pool.
But you never ask for help from the One who did all this.
You never considered the One who planned this long ago.

12 At that time the Lord, the LORD of Heaven's Armies,
called you to weep and mourn.
He told you to shave your heads in sorrow for your sins
and to wear clothes of burlap to show your remorse.
13 But instead, you dance and play;
you slaughter cattle and kill sheep.
You feast on meat and drink wine.
You say, "Let's feast and drink,
for tomorrow we die!"

14 The LORD of Heaven's Armies has revealed this to me: "Till the day you die, you will never be forgiven for this sin." That is the judgment of the Lord, the LORD of Heaven's Armies.

A Message for Shebna

15 This is what the Lord, the LORD of Heaven's Armies, said to me: "Confront Shebna, the palace administrator, and give him this message:

16 "Who do you think you are,
and what are you doing here,

22:8 Hebrew *to the House of the Forest;* see 1 Kgs 7:2-5. 22:9 Hebrew *the city of David.*

building a beautiful tomb for yourself—
a monument high up in the rock?
17 For the LORD is about to hurl you away, mighty man.
He is going to grab you,
18 crumple you into a ball,
and toss you away into a distant, barren land.
There you will die,
and your glorious chariots will be broken and useless.
You are a disgrace to your master!

19 "Yes, I will drive you out of office," says the LORD. "I will pull you down
from your high position. 20 And then I will call my servant Eliakim son of
Hilkiah to replace you. 21 I will dress him in your royal robes and will give
him your title and your authority. And he will be a father to the people of
Jerusalem and Judah. 22 I will give him the key to the house of David—the
highest position in the royal court. When he opens doors, no one will be able
to close them; when he closes doors, no one will be able to open them. 23 He
will bring honor to his family name, for I will drive him firmly in place like
a nail in the wall. 24 They will give him great responsibility, and he will bring
honor to even the lowliest members of his family.*"
25 But the LORD of Heaven's Armies also says: "The time will come when
I will pull out the nail that seemed so firm. It will come out and fall to the
ground. Everything it supports will fall with it. I, the LORD, have spoken!"

A Message about Tyre

23 This message came to me concerning Tyre:

Wail, you trading ships of Tarshish,
for the harbor and houses of Tyre are gone!
The rumors you heard in Cyprus*
are all true.
2 Mourn in silence, you people of the coast
and you merchants of Sidon.
Your traders crossed the sea,*
3 sailing over deep waters.
They brought you grain from Egypt*
and harvests from along the Nile.
You were the marketplace of the world.

4 But now you are put to shame, city of Sidon,
for Tyre, the fortress of the sea, says,*
"Now I am childless;
I have no sons or daughters."
5 When Egypt hears the news about Tyre,
there will be great sorrow.
6 Send word now to Tarshish!
Wail, you people who live in distant lands!

22:24 Hebrew *They will hang on him all the glory of his father's house: its offspring and offshoots, all its lesser vessels, from the bowls to all the jars.* 23:1 Hebrew *Kittim;* also in 23:12. 23:2 As in Dead Sea Scrolls and Greek version; Masoretic Text reads *Those who have gone over the sea have filled you.* 23:3 Hebrew *from Shihor,* a branch of the Nile River. 23:4 Or *for the god of the sea says;* Hebrew reads *for the sea, the fortress of the sea, says.*

Questions I want to ask

7 Is this silent ruin all that is left of your once
joyous city?
What a long history was yours!
Think of all the colonists you sent to
distant places.

8 Who has brought this disaster on Tyre,
that great creator of kingdoms?
Her traders were all princes,
her merchants were nobles.
9 The LORD of Heaven's Armies has done it
to destroy your pride
and bring low all earth's nobility.
10 Come, people of Tarshish,
sweep over the land like the flooding Nile,
for Tyre is defenseless.*
11 The LORD held out his hand over the sea
and shook the kingdoms of the earth.
He has spoken out against Phoenicia,*
ordering that her fortresses be destroyed.
12 He says, "Never again will you rejoice,
O daughter of Sidon, for you have been crushed.
Even if you flee to Cyprus,
you will find no rest."

13 Look at the land of Babylonia*—
the people of that land are gone!
The Assyrians have handed Babylon over
to the wild animals of the desert.
They have built siege ramps against its walls,
torn down its palaces,
and turned it to a heap of rubble.

14 Wail, you ships of Tarshish,
for your harbor is destroyed!

15 For seventy years, the length of a king's life, Tyre will be forgotten. But then the city will come back to life as in the song about the prostitute:

16 Take a harp and walk the streets,
you forgotten harlot.
Make sweet melody and sing your songs
so you will be remembered again.

17 Yes, after seventy years the LORD will revive Tyre. But she will be no different than she was before. She will again be a prostitute to all kingdoms around the world. 18 But in the end her profits will be given to the LORD. Her wealth will not be hoarded but will provide good food and fine clothing for the LORD's priests.

23:10 The meaning of the Hebrew in this verse is uncertain. 23:11 Hebrew *Canaan.* 23:13 Or *Chaldea.*

Destruction of the Earth

24 1 Look! The LORD is about to destroy the earth
and make it a vast wasteland.
He devastates the surface of the earth
and scatters the people.
2 Priests and laypeople,
servants and masters,
maids and mistresses,
buyers and sellers,
lenders and borrowers,
bankers and debtors—none will be spared.
3 The earth will be completely emptied and looted.
The LORD has spoken!

4 The earth mourns and dries up,
and the land wastes away and withers.
Even the greatest people on earth waste away.
5 The earth suffers for the sins of its people,
for they have twisted God's instructions,
violated his laws,
and broken his everlasting covenant.
6 Therefore, a curse consumes the earth.
Its people must pay the price for their sin.
They are destroyed by fire,
and only a few are left alive.
7 The grapevines waste away,
and there is no new wine.
All the merrymakers sigh and mourn.
8 The cheerful sound of tambourines is stilled;
the happy cries of celebration are heard no more.
The melodious chords of the harp are silent.
9 Gone are the joys of wine and song;
alcoholic drink turns bitter in the mouth.
10 The city writhes in chaos;
every home is locked to keep out intruders.
11 Mobs gather in the streets, crying out for wine.
Joy has turned to gloom.
Gladness has been banished from the land.
12 The city is left in ruins,
its gates battered down.
13 Throughout the earth the story is the same—
only a remnant is left,
like the stray olives left on the tree
or the few grapes left on the vine after harvest.

14 But all who are left shout and sing for joy.
Those in the west praise the LORD's majesty.
15 In eastern lands, give glory to the LORD.
In the lands beyond the sea, praise the name of the LORD,
the God of Israel.

Question 24:5

The earth suffers because of sin. How does this make you pray today?

16 We hear songs of praise from the ends of the earth,
songs that give glory to the Righteous One!

But my heart is heavy with grief.
Weep for me, for I wither away.
Deceit still prevails,
and treachery is everywhere.
17 Terror and traps and snares will be your lot,
you people of the earth.
18 Those who flee in terror will fall into a trap,
and those who escape the trap will be caught in a snare.

Destruction falls like rain from the heavens;
the foundations of the earth shake.
19 The earth has broken up.
It has utterly collapsed;
it is violently shaken.
20 The earth staggers like a drunk.
It trembles like a tent in a storm.
It falls and will not rise again,
for the guilt of its rebellion is very heavy.

21 In that day the LORD will punish the gods in the heavens
and the proud rulers of the nations on earth.
22 They will be rounded up and put in prison.
They will be shut up in prison
and will finally be punished.
23 Then the glory of the moon will wane,
and the brightness of the sun will fade,
for the LORD of Heaven's Armies will rule on Mount Zion.
He will rule in great glory in Jerusalem,
in the sight of all the leaders of his people.

Praise for Judgment and Salvation

25 1 O LORD, I will honor and praise your name,
for you are my God.
You do such wonderful things!
You planned them long ago,
and now you have accomplished them.
2 You turn mighty cities into heaps of ruins.
Cities with strong walls are turned to rubble.
Beautiful palaces in distant lands disappear
and will never be rebuilt.
3 Therefore, strong nations will declare your glory;
ruthless nations will fear you.

4 But you are a tower of refuge to the poor, O LORD,
a tower of refuge to the needy in distress.
You are a refuge from the storm
and a shelter from the heat.

For the oppressive acts of ruthless people
are like a storm beating against a wall,
5 or like the relentless heat of the desert.
But you silence the roar of foreign nations.
As the shade of a cloud cools relentless heat,
so the boastful songs of ruthless people are stilled.

6 In Jerusalem,* the LORD of Heaven's Armies
will spread a wonderful feast
for all the people of the world.
It will be a delicious banquet
with clear, well-aged wine and choice meat.
7 There he will remove the cloud of gloom,
the shadow of death that hangs over the earth.
8 He will swallow up death forever!
The Sovereign LORD will wipe away all tears.
He will remove forever all insults and mockery
against his land and people.
The LORD has spoken!

9 In that day the people will proclaim,
"This is our God!
We trusted in him, and he saved us!
This is the LORD, in whom we trusted.
Let us rejoice in the salvation he brings!"
10 For the LORD's hand of blessing will rest on Jerusalem.
But Moab will be crushed.
It will be like straw trampled down and left to rot.
11 God will push down Moab's people
as a swimmer pushes down water with his hands.
He will end their pride
and all their evil works.
12 The high walls of Moab will be demolished.
They will be brought down to the ground,
down into the dust.

Question **25:9**

"This is our God!" Are you proud of what God does for people? Will you boldly proclaim him today?

A Song of Praise to the LORD

26

In that day, everyone in the land of Judah will sing this song:

Our city is strong!
We are surrounded by the walls of God's salvation.
2 Open the gates to all who are righteous;
allow the faithful to enter.
3 You will keep in perfect peace
all who trust in you,
all whose thoughts are fixed on you!
4 Trust in the LORD always,
for the LORD GOD is the eternal Rock.
5 He humbles the proud

25:6 Hebrew *On this mountain;* also in 25:10.

Question 26:8

Here's a reality check: Does this match your desire today?

and brings down the arrogant city.
He brings it down to the dust.
6 The poor and oppressed trample it underfoot,
and the needy walk all over it.

7 But for those who are righteous,
the way is not steep and rough.
You are a God who does what is right,
and you smooth out the path ahead of them.
8 LORD, we show our trust in you by obeying your laws;
our heart's desire is to glorify your name.
9 In the night I search for you;
in the morning* I earnestly seek you.
For only when you come to judge the earth
will people learn what is right.
10 Your kindness to the wicked
does not make them do good.
Although others do right, the wicked keep doing wrong
and take no notice of the LORD's majesty.
11 O LORD, they pay no attention to your upraised fist.
Show them your eagerness to defend your people.
Then they will be ashamed.
Let your fire consume your enemies.

12 LORD, you will grant us peace;
all we have accomplished is really from you.
13 O LORD our God, others have ruled us,
but you alone are the one we worship.
14 Those we served before are dead and gone.
Their departed spirits will never return!
You attacked them and destroyed them,
and they are long forgotten.
15 O LORD, you have made our nation great;
yes, you have made us great.
You have extended our borders,
and we give you the glory!

16 LORD, in distress we searched for you.
We prayed beneath the burden of your discipline.
17 Just as a pregnant woman
writhes and cries out in pain as she gives birth,
so were we in your presence, LORD.
18 We, too, writhe in agony,
but nothing comes of our suffering.
We have not given salvation to the earth,
nor brought life into the world.
19 But those who die in the LORD will live;
their bodies will rise again!
Those who sleep in the earth

26:9 Hebrew *within me.*

will rise up and sing for joy!
For your life-giving light will fall like dew
on your people in the place of the dead!

Restoration for Israel

20 Go home, my people,
and lock your doors!
Hide yourselves for a little while
until the LORD's anger has passed.
21 Look! The LORD is coming from heaven
to punish the people of the earth for their sins.
The earth will no longer hide those who have been killed.
They will be brought out for all to see.

27 In that day the LORD will take his terrible, swift sword and punish
Leviathan,* the swiftly moving serpent, the coiling, writhing ser-
pent. He will kill the dragon of the sea.

2 "In that day,
sing about the fruitful vineyard.
3 I, the LORD, will watch over it,
watering it carefully.
Day and night I will watch so no one can harm it.
4 My anger will be gone.
If I find briers and thorns growing,
I will attack them;
I will burn them up—
5 unless they turn to me for help.
Let them make peace with me;
yes, let them make peace with me."
6 The time is coming when Jacob's descendants will take root.
Israel will bud and blossom
and fill the whole earth with fruit!

7 Has the LORD struck Israel
as he struck her enemies?
Has he punished her
as he punished them?
8 No, but he exiled Israel to call her to account.
She was exiled from her land
as though blown away in a storm from the east.
9 The LORD did this to purge Israel's* wickedness,
to take away all her sin.
As a result, all the pagan altars will be crushed to dust.
No Asherah pole or pagan shrine will be left standing.
10 The fortified towns will be silent and empty,
the houses abandoned, the streets overgrown with weeds.
Calves will graze there,
chewing on twigs and branches.

27:1 The identification of Leviathan is disputed, ranging from an earthly creature to a mythical sea monster in ancient literature. 27:9 Hebrew *Jacob's*. See note on 14:1.

11 The people are like the dead branches of a tree,
broken off and used for kindling beneath the cooking pots.
Israel is a foolish and stupid nation,
for its people have turned away from God.
Therefore, the one who made them
will show them no pity or mercy.

12 Yet the time will come when the LORD will gather them together like
handpicked grain. One by one he will gather them—from the Euphrates
River* in the east to the Brook of Egypt in the west. 13 In that day the great
trumpet will sound. Many who were dying in exile in Assyria and Egypt will
return to Jerusalem to worship the LORD on his holy mountain.

A Message about Samaria

28 1 What sorrow awaits the proud city of Samaria—
the glorious crown of the drunks of Israel.*
It sits at the head of a fertile valley,
but its glorious beauty will fade like a flower.
It is the pride of a people
brought down by wine.
2 For the Lord will send a mighty army against it.
Like a mighty hailstorm and a torrential rain,
they will burst upon it like a surging flood
and smash it to the ground.
3 The proud city of Samaria—
the glorious crown of the drunks of Israel*—
will be trampled beneath its enemies' feet.
4 It sits at the head of a fertile valley,
but its glorious beauty will fade like a flower.
Whoever sees it will snatch it up,
as an early fig is quickly picked and eaten.

5 Then at last the LORD of Heaven's Armies
will himself be Israel's glorious crown.
He will be the pride and joy
of the remnant of his people.
6 He will give a longing for justice
to their judges.
He will give great courage
to their warriors who stand at the gates.

7 Now, however, Israel is led by drunks
who reel with wine and stagger with alcohol.
The priests and prophets stagger with alcohol
and lose themselves in wine.
They reel when they see visions
and stagger as they render decisions.

27:12 Hebrew *the river.* 28:1 Hebrew *What sorrow awaits the crowning glory of the drunks of Ephraim,* referring to Samaria, capital of the northern kingdom of Israel. 28:3 Hebrew *The crowning glory of the drunks of Ephraim;* see note on 28:1.

8 Their tables are covered with vomit;
filth is everywhere.
9 "Who does the LORD think we are?" they ask.
"Why does he speak to us like this?
Are we little children,
just recently weaned?
10 He tells us everything over and over—
one line at a time,
one line at a time,
a little here,
and a little there!"

11 So now God will have to speak to his people
through foreign oppressors who speak a strange language!
12 God has told his people,
"Here is a place of rest;
let the weary rest here.
This is a place of quiet rest."
But they would not listen.
13 So the LORD will spell out his message for them again,
one line at a time,
one line at a time,
a little here,
and a little there,
so that they will stumble and fall.
They will be injured, trapped, and captured.

14 Therefore, listen to this message from the LORD,
you scoffing rulers in Jerusalem.
15 You boast, "We have struck a bargain to cheat death
and have made a deal to dodge the grave.*
The coming destruction can never touch us,
for we have built a strong refuge made of lies and deception."

16 Therefore, this is what the Sovereign LORD says:
"Look! I am placing a foundation stone in Jerusalem,*
a firm and tested stone.
It is a precious cornerstone that is safe to build on.
Whoever believes need never be shaken.*
17 I will test you with the measuring line of justice
and the plumb line of righteousness.
Since your refuge is made of lies,
a hailstorm will knock it down.
Since it is made of deception,
a flood will sweep it away.
18 I will cancel the bargain you made to cheat death,
and I will overturn your deal to dodge the grave.

28:15 Hebrew *Sheol;* also in 28:18. **28:16a** Hebrew *in Zion.* **28:16b** Greek version reads *Look! I am placing a stone in the foundation of Jerusalem* [literally *Zion*], */ a precious cornerstone for its foundation, chosen for great honor. / Anyone who trusts in him will never be disgraced.* Compare Rom 9:33; 1 Pet 2:6.

Why this matters!

When the terrible enemy sweeps through,
you will be trampled into the ground.
19 Again and again that flood will come,
morning after morning,
day and night,
until you are carried away."

This message will bring terror to your people.
20 The bed you have made is too short to lie on.
The blankets are too narrow to cover you.
21 The LORD will come as he did against the Philistines at Mount Perazim
and against the Amorites at Gibeon.
He will come to do a strange thing;
he will come to do an unusual deed:
22 For the Lord, the LORD of Heaven's Armies,
has plainly said that he is determined to crush the whole land.
So scoff no more,
or your punishment will be even greater.

23 Listen to me;
listen, and pay close attention.
24 Does a farmer always plow and never sow?
Is he forever cultivating the soil and never planting?
25 Does he not finally plant his seeds—
black cumin, cumin, wheat, barley, and emmer wheat—
each in its proper way,
and each in its proper place?
26 The farmer knows just what to do,
for God has given him understanding.
27 A heavy sledge is never used to thresh black cumin;
rather, it is beaten with a light stick.
A threshing wheel is never rolled on cumin;
instead, it is beaten lightly with a flail.
28 Grain for bread is easily crushed,
so he doesn't keep on pounding it.
He threshes it under the wheels of a cart,
but he doesn't pulverize it.
29 The LORD of Heaven's Armies is a wonderful teacher,
and he gives the farmer great wisdom.

A Message about Jerusalem

29 1 "What sorrow awaits Ariel,* the City of David.
Year after year you celebrate your feasts.
2 Yet I will bring disaster upon you,
and there will be much weeping and sorrow.
For Jerusalem will become what her name Ariel means—
an altar covered with blood.
3 I will be your enemy,
surrounding Jerusalem and attacking its walls.

29:1 *Ariel* sounds like a Hebrew term that means "hearth" or "altar."

I will build siege towers
and destroy it.
4 Then deep from the earth you will speak;
from low in the dust your words will come.
Your voice will whisper from the ground
like a ghost conjured up from the grave.

5 "But suddenly, your ruthless enemies will be crushed
like the finest of dust.
Your many attackers will be driven away
like chaff before the wind.
Suddenly, in an instant,
6 I, the LORD of Heaven's Armies, will act for you
with thunder and earthquake and great noise,
with whirlwind and storm and consuming fire.
7 All the nations fighting against Jerusalem*
will vanish like a dream!
Those who are attacking her walls
will vanish like a vision in the night.
8 A hungry person dreams of eating
but wakes up still hungry.
A thirsty person dreams of drinking
but is still faint from thirst when morning comes.
So it will be with your enemies,
with those who attack Mount Zion."

9 Are you amazed and incredulous?
Don't you believe it?
Then go ahead and be blind.
You are stupid, but not from wine!
You stagger, but not from liquor!
10 For the LORD has poured out on you a spirit of deep sleep.
He has closed the eyes of your prophets and visionaries.

11 All the future events in this vision are like a sealed book to them. When
you give it to those who can read, they will say, "We can't read it because it
is sealed." 12 When you give it to those who cannot read, they will say, "We
don't know how to read."

13 And so the Lord says,
"These people say they are mine.
They honor me with their lips,
but their hearts are far from me.
And their worship of me
is nothing but man-made rules learned by rote.*
14 Because of this, I will once again astound these hypocrites
with amazing wonders.
The wisdom of the wise will pass away,
and the intelligence of the intelligent will disappear."

29:7 Hebrew *Ariel*. 29:13 Greek version reads *Their worship is a farce, / for they teach man-made ideas as commands from God*. Compare Mark 7:7.

Remember to take notes!

Prayer 29:16

Lord, forgive me for the times I have been arrogant, thinking that my ways were better than yours. Amen.

15 What sorrow awaits those who try to hide their plans from the LORD,
who do their evil deeds in the dark!
"The LORD can't see us," they say.
"He doesn't know what's going on!"
16 How foolish can you be?
He is the Potter, and he is certainly greater than you, the clay!
Should the created thing say of the one who made it,
"He didn't make me"?
Does a jar ever say,
"The potter who made me is stupid"?

17 Soon—and it will not be very long—
the forests of Lebanon will become a fertile field,
and the fertile field will yield bountiful crops.
18 In that day the deaf will hear words read from a book,
and the blind will see through the gloom and darkness.
19 The humble will be filled with fresh joy from the LORD.
The poor will rejoice in the Holy One of Israel.
20 The scoffer will be gone,
the arrogant will disappear,
and those who plot evil will be killed.
21 Those who convict the innocent
by their false testimony will disappear.
A similar fate awaits those who use trickery to pervert justice
and who tell lies to destroy the innocent.

22 That is why the LORD, who redeemed Abraham, says to the people of Israel,*

"My people will no longer be ashamed
or turn pale with fear.
23 For when they see their many children
and all the blessings I have given them,
they will recognize the holiness of the Holy One of Jacob.
They will stand in awe of the God of Israel.
24 Then the wayward will gain understanding,
and complainers will accept instruction.

Judah's Worthless Treaty with Egypt

30 1 "What sorrow awaits my rebellious children,"
says the LORD.
"You make plans that are contrary to mine.
You make alliances not directed by my Spirit,
thus piling up your sins.
2 For without consulting me,
you have gone down to Egypt for help.
You have put your trust in Pharaoh's protection.
You have tried to hide in his shade.
3 But by trusting Pharaoh, you will be humiliated,
and by depending on him, you will be disgraced.

29:22 Hebrew *of Jacob.* See note on 14:1.

4 For though his power extends to Zoan
and his officials have arrived in Hanes,
5 all who trust in him will be ashamed.
He will not help you.
Instead, he will disgrace you."

6 This message came to me concerning the animals in the Negev:

The caravan moves slowly
across the terrible desert to Egypt—
donkeys weighed down with riches
and camels loaded with treasure—
all to pay for Egypt's protection.
They travel through the wilderness,
a place of lionesses and lions,
a place where vipers and poisonous snakes live.
All this, and Egypt will give you nothing in return.
7 Egypt's promises are worthless!
Therefore, I call her Rahab—
the Harmless Dragon.*

A Warning for Rebellious Judah

8 Now go and write down these words.
Write them in a book.
They will stand until the end of time
as a witness
9 that these people are stubborn rebels
who refuse to pay attention to the LORD's instructions.
10 They tell the seers,
"Stop seeing visions!"
They tell the prophets,
"Don't tell us what is right.
Tell us nice things.
Tell us lies.
11 Forget all this gloom.
Get off your narrow path.
Stop telling us about your
'Holy One of Israel.'"

12 This is the reply of the Holy One of Israel:

"Because you despise what I tell you
and trust instead in oppression and lies,
13 calamity will come upon you suddenly—
like a bulging wall that bursts and falls.
In an instant it will collapse
and come crashing down.
14 You will be smashed like a piece of pottery—
shattered so completely that

30:7 Hebrew *Rahab who sits still.* Rahab is the name of a mythical sea monster that represents chaos in ancient literature. The name is used here as a poetic name for Egypt.

Question 30:15

Only by returning to the Lord and resting in him will you be saved. What does it mean to return to and rest in God? How could you do those two things right now?

there won't be a piece big enough
to carry coals from a fireplace
or a little water from the well."

15 This is what the Sovereign LORD,
the Holy One of Israel, says:
"Only in returning to me
and resting in me will you be saved.
In quietness and confidence is your strength.
But you would have none of it.
16 You said, 'No, we will get our help from Egypt.
They will give us swift horses for riding into battle.'
But the only swiftness you are going to see
is the swiftness of your enemies chasing you!
17 One of them will chase a thousand of you.
Five of them will make all of you flee.
You will be left like a lonely flagpole on a hill
or a tattered banner on a distant mountaintop."

Blessings for the LORD's People

18 So the LORD must wait for you to come to him
so he can show you his love and compassion.
For the LORD is a faithful God.
Blessed are those who wait for his help.

19 O people of Zion, who live in Jerusalem,
you will weep no more.
He will be gracious if you ask for help.
He will surely respond to the sound of your cries.
20 Though the Lord gave you adversity for food
and suffering for drink,
he will still be with you to teach you.
You will see your teacher with your own eyes.
21 Your own ears will hear him.
Right behind you a voice will say,
"This is the way you should go,"
whether to the right or to the left.
22 Then you will destroy all your silver idols
and your precious gold images.
You will throw them out like filthy rags,
saying to them, "Good riddance!"

23 Then the LORD will bless you with rain at planting time. There will be
wonderful harvests and plenty of pastureland for your livestock. 24 The oxen
and donkeys that till the ground will eat good grain, its chaff blown away by
the wind. 25 In that day, when your enemies are slaughtered and the towers
fall, there will be streams of water flowing down every mountain and hill.
26 The moon will be as bright as the sun, and the sun will be seven times
brighter—like the light of seven days in one! So it will be when the LORD
begins to heal his people and cure the wounds he gave them.

27 Look! The LORD is coming from far away,
burning with anger,
surrounded by thick, rising smoke.
His lips are filled with fury;
his words consume like fire.
28 His hot breath pours out like a flood
up to the neck of his enemies.
He will sift out the proud nations for destruction.
He will bridle them and lead them away to ruin.

29 But the people of God will sing a song of joy,
like the songs at the holy festivals.
You will be filled with joy,
as when a flutist leads a group of pilgrims
to Jerusalem, the mountain of the LORD—
to the Rock of Israel.
30 And the LORD will make his majestic voice heard.
He will display the strength of his mighty arm.
It will descend with devouring flames,
with cloudbursts, thunderstorms, and huge hailstones.
31 At the LORD's command, the Assyrians will be shattered.
He will strike them down with his royal scepter.
32 And as the LORD strikes them with his rod of punishment,*
his people will celebrate with tambourines and harps.
Lifting his mighty arm, he will fight the Assyrians.
33 Topheth—the place of burning—
has long been ready for the Assyrian king;
the pyre is piled high with wood.
The breath of the LORD, like fire from a volcano,
will set it ablaze.

The Futility of Relying on Egypt

31 1 What sorrow awaits those who look to Egypt for help,
trusting their horses, chariots, and charioteers
and depending on the strength of human armies
instead of looking to the LORD,
the Holy One of Israel.
2 In his wisdom, the LORD will send great disaster;
he will not change his mind.
He will rise against the wicked
and against their helpers.
3 For these Egyptians are mere humans, not God!
Their horses are puny flesh, not mighty spirits!
When the LORD raises his fist against them,
those who help will stumble,
and those being helped will fall.
They will all fall down and die together.

4 But this is what the LORD has told me:

30:32 As in some Hebrew manuscripts and Syriac version; Masoretic Text reads *with the founded rod.*

Question 32:3

How would the world be different if people could see and hear the truth?

"When a strong young lion
stands growling over a sheep it has killed,
it is not frightened by the shouts and noise
of a whole crowd of shepherds.
In the same way, the LORD of Heaven's Armies
will come down and fight on Mount Zion.
5 The LORD of Heaven's Armies will hover over Jerusalem
and protect it like a bird protecting its nest.
He will defend and save the city;
he will pass over it and rescue it."

6 Though you are such wicked rebels, my people, come and return to the
LORD. 7 I know the glorious day will come when each of you will throw away
the gold idols and silver images your sinful hands have made.

8 "The Assyrians will be destroyed,
but not by the swords of men.
The sword of God will strike them,
and they will panic and flee.
The strong young Assyrians
will be taken away as captives.
9 Even the strongest will quake with terror,
and princes will flee when they see your battle flags,"
says the LORD, whose fire burns in Zion,
whose flame blazes from Jerusalem.

Israel's Ultimate Deliverance

32 1 Look, a righteous king is coming!
And honest princes will rule under him.
2 Each one will be like a shelter from the wind
and a refuge from the storm,
like streams of water in the desert
and the shadow of a great rock in a parched land.

3 Then everyone who has eyes will be able to see the truth,
and everyone who has ears will be able to hear it.
4 Even the hotheads will be full of sense and understanding.
Those who stammer will speak out plainly.
5 In that day ungodly fools will not be heroes.
Scoundrels will not be respected.
6 For fools speak foolishness
and make evil plans.
They practice ungodliness
and spread false teachings about the LORD.
They deprive the hungry of food
and give no water to the thirsty.
7 The smooth tricks of scoundrels are evil.
They plot crooked schemes.
They lie to convict the poor,
even when the cause of the poor is just.

8 But generous people plan to do what is generous,
and they stand firm in their generosity.

9 Listen, you women who lie around in ease.
Listen to me, you who are so smug.
10 In a short time—just a little more than a year—
you careless ones will suddenly begin to care.
For your fruit crops will fail,
and the harvest will never take place.
11 Tremble, you women of ease;
throw off your complacency.
Strip off your pretty clothes,
and put on burlap to show your grief.
12 Beat your breasts in sorrow for your bountiful farms
and your fruitful grapevines.
13 For your land will be overgrown with thorns and briers.
Your joyful homes and happy towns will be gone.
14 The palace and the city will be deserted,
and busy towns will be empty.
Wild donkeys will frolic and flocks will graze
in the empty forts* and watchtowers
15 until at last the Spirit is poured out
on us from heaven.
Then the wilderness will become a fertile field,
and the fertile field will yield bountiful crops.

16 Justice will rule in the wilderness
and righteousness in the fertile field.
17 And this righteousness will bring peace.
Yes, it will bring quietness and confidence forever.
18 My people will live in safety, quietly at home.
They will be at rest.
19 Even if the forest should be destroyed
and the city torn down,
20 the LORD will greatly bless his people.
Wherever they plant seed, bountiful crops will spring up.
Their cattle and donkeys will graze freely.

A Message about Assyria

33 1 What sorrow awaits you Assyrians, who have destroyed others*
but have never been destroyed yourselves.
You betray others,
but you have never been betrayed.
When you are done destroying,
you will be destroyed.
When you are done betraying,
you will be betrayed.
2 But LORD, be merciful to us,
for we have waited for you.

32:14 Hebrew *the Ophel.* 33:1 Hebrew *What sorrow awaits you, O destroyer.* The Hebrew text does not specifically name Assyria as the object of the prophecy in this chapter.

Question 33:6

If you had a treasure map that led you on a journey through wilderness and stormy seas and obstacles and difficult decisions, what would you hope to find? How could the "fear of the LORD" be the greatest treasure you could find?

Be our strong arm each day
and our salvation in times of trouble.
3 The enemy runs at the sound of your voice.
When you stand up, the nations flee!
4 Just as caterpillars and locusts strip the fields and vines,
so the fallen army of Assyria will be stripped!

5 Though the LORD is very great and lives in heaven,
he will make Jerusalem* his home of justice and righteousness.
6 In that day he will be your sure foundation,
providing a rich store of salvation, wisdom, and knowledge.
The fear of the LORD will be your treasure.

7 But now your brave warriors weep in public.
Your ambassadors of peace cry in bitter disappointment.
8 Your roads are deserted;
no one travels them anymore.
The Assyrians have broken their peace treaty
and care nothing for the promises they made before witnesses.*
They have no respect for anyone.
9 The land of Israel wilts in mourning.
Lebanon withers with shame.
The plain of Sharon is now a wilderness.
Bashan and Carmel have been plundered.

10 But the LORD says: "Now I will stand up.
Now I will show my power and might.
11 You Assyrians produce nothing but dry grass and stubble.
Your own breath will turn to fire and consume you.
12 Your people will be burned up completely,
like thornbushes cut down and tossed in a fire.
13 Listen to what I have done, you nations far away!
And you that are near, acknowledge my might!"

14 The sinners in Jerusalem shake with fear.
Terror seizes the godless.
"Who can live with this devouring fire?" they cry.
"Who can survive this all-consuming fire?"
15 Those who are honest and fair,
who refuse to profit by fraud,
who stay far away from bribes,
who refuse to listen to those who plot murder,
who shut their eyes to all enticement to do wrong—
16 these are the ones who will dwell on high.
The rocks of the mountains will be their fortress.
Food will be supplied to them,
and they will have water in abundance.

17 Your eyes will see the king in all his splendor,

33:5 Hebrew *Zion;* also in 33:14. 33:8 As in Dead Sea Scrolls; Masoretic Text reads *care nothing for the cities.*

and you will see a land that stretches into
the distance.
18 You will think back to this time of terror, asking,
"Where are the Assyrian officers
who counted our towers?
Where are the bookkeepers
who recorded the plunder taken from our fallen city?"
19 You will no longer see these fierce, violent people
with their strange, unknown language.

20 Instead, you will see Zion as a place of holy festivals.
You will see Jerusalem, a city quiet and secure.
It will be like a tent whose ropes are taut
and whose stakes are firmly fixed.
21 The LORD will be our Mighty One.
He will be like a wide river of protection
that no enemy can cross,
that no enemy ship can sail upon.
22 For the LORD is our judge,
our lawgiver, and our king.
He will care for us and save us.
23 The enemies' sails hang loose
on broken masts with useless tackle.
Their treasure will be divided by the people of God.
Even the lame will take their share!
24 The people of Israel will no longer say,
"We are sick and helpless,"
for the LORD will forgive their sins.

A Message for the Nations

34 1 Come here and listen, O nations of the earth.
Let the world and everything in it hear my words.
2 For the LORD is enraged against the nations.
His fury is against all their armies.
He will completely destroy* them,
dooming them to slaughter.
3 Their dead will be left unburied,
and the stench of rotting bodies will fill the land.
The mountains will flow with their blood.
4 The heavens above will melt away
and disappear like a rolled-up scroll.
The stars will fall from the sky
like withered leaves from a grapevine,
or shriveled figs from a fig tree.

5 And when my sword has finished its work in the heavens,
it will fall upon Edom,
the nation I have marked for destruction.
6 The sword of the LORD is drenched with blood

34:2 The Hebrew term used here refers to the complete consecration of things or people to the LORD, either by destroying them or by giving them as an offering; similarly in 34:5.

and covered with fat—
with the blood of lambs and goats,
with the fat of rams prepared for sacrifice.
Yes, the LORD will offer a sacrifice in the city of Bozrah.
He will make a mighty slaughter in Edom.
7 Even men as strong as wild oxen will die—
the young men alongside the veterans.
The land will be soaked with blood
and the soil enriched with fat.

8 For it is the day of the LORD's revenge,
the year when Edom will be paid back for all it did to Israel.*
9 The streams of Edom will be filled with burning pitch,
and the ground will be covered with fire.
10 This judgment on Edom will never end;
the smoke of its burning will rise forever.
The land will lie deserted from generation to generation.
No one will live there anymore.
11 It will be haunted by the desert owl and the screech owl,
the great owl and the raven.*
For God will measure that land carefully;
he will measure it for chaos and destruction.
12 It will be called the Land of Nothing,
and all its nobles will soon be gone.*
13 Thorns will overrun its palaces;
nettles and thistles will grow in its forts.
The ruins will become a haunt for jackals
and a home for owls.
14 Desert animals will mingle there with hyenas,
their howls filling the night.
Wild goats will bleat at one another among the ruins,
and night creatures* will come there to rest.
15 There the owl will make her nest and lay her eggs.
She will hatch her young and cover them with her wings.
And the buzzards will come,
each one with its mate.

16 Search the book of the LORD,
and see what he will do.
Not one of these birds and animals will be missing,
and none will lack a mate,
for the LORD has promised this.
His Spirit will make it all come true.
17 He has surveyed and divided the land
and deeded it over to those creatures.
They will possess it forever,
from generation to generation.

34:8 Hebrew *to Zion.* **34:11** The identification of some of these birds is uncertain. **34:12** The meaning of the Hebrew is uncertain. **34:14** Hebrew *Lilith,* possibly a reference to a mythical demon of the night.

Hope for Restoration

35 1 Even the wilderness and desert will be glad in those days.
The wasteland will rejoice and blossom with spring crocuses.
2 Yes, there will be an abundance of flowers
and singing and joy!
The deserts will become as green as the mountains of Lebanon,
as lovely as Mount Carmel or the plain of Sharon.
There the LORD will display his glory,
the splendor of our God.
3 With this news, strengthen those who have tired hands,
and encourage those who have weak knees.
4 Say to those with fearful hearts,
"Be strong, and do not fear,
for your God is coming to destroy your enemies.
He is coming to save you."

5 And when he comes, he will open the eyes of the blind
and unplug the ears of the deaf.
6 The lame will leap like a deer,
and those who cannot speak will sing for joy!
Springs will gush forth in the wilderness,
and streams will water the wasteland.
7 The parched ground will become a pool,
and springs of water will satisfy the thirsty land.
Marsh grass and reeds and rushes will flourish
where desert jackals once lived.

8 And a great road will go through that once deserted land.
It will be named the Highway of Holiness.
Evil-minded people will never travel on it.
It will be only for those who walk in God's ways;
fools will never walk there.
9 Lions will not lurk along its course,
nor any other ferocious beasts.
There will be no other dangers.
Only the redeemed will walk on it.
10 Those who have been ransomed by the LORD will return.
They will enter Jerusalem* singing,
crowned with everlasting joy.
Sorrow and mourning will disappear,
and they will be filled with joy and gladness.

Assyria Invades Judah

36 In the fourteenth year of King Hezekiah's reign,* King Sennacherib
of Assyria came to attack the fortified towns of Judah and conquered
them. 2 Then the king of Assyria sent his chief of staff* from Lachish with a
huge army to confront King Hezekiah in Jerusalem. The Assyrians took up
a position beside the aqueduct that feeds water into the upper pool, near the
road leading to the field where cloth is washed.*

35:10 Hebrew *Zion.* **36:1** The fourteenth year of Hezekiah's reign was 701 B.C. **36:2a** Or *the rabshakeh;* also in 36:4, 11, 12, 22. **36:2b** Or *bleached.*

Prayer 35:3

Lord God, help me share the good news of who you are. I pray that your power will strengthen my friends and family who are weakened by their current circumstances. Amen.

3These are the officials who went out to meet with them: Eliakim son of
Hilkiah, the palace administrator; Shebna the court secretary; and Joah son
of Asaph, the royal historian.

Sennacherib Threatens Jerusalem

4Then the Assyrian king's chief of staff told them to give this message to
Hezekiah:

"This is what the great king of Assyria says: What are you trusting
in that makes you so confident? 5Do you think* that mere words can
substitute for military skill and strength? Who are you counting
on, that you have rebelled against me? 6On Egypt? If you lean on
Egypt, it will be like a reed that splinters beneath your weight
and pierces your hand. Pharaoh, the king of Egypt, is completely
unreliable!

7"But perhaps you will say to me, 'We are trusting in the LORD
our God!' But isn't he the one who was insulted by Hezekiah? Didn't
Hezekiah tear down his shrines and altars and make everyone in Judah
and Jerusalem worship only at the altar here in Jerusalem?

8"I'll tell you what! Strike a bargain with my master, the king of
Assyria. I will give you 2,000 horses if you can find that many men to
ride on them! 9With your tiny army, how can you think of challenging
even the weakest contingent of my master's troops, even with the
help of Egypt's chariots and charioteers? 10What's more, do you think
we have invaded your land without the LORD's direction? The LORD
himself told us, 'Attack this land and destroy it!'"

11Then Eliakim, Shebna, and Joah said to the Assyrian chief of staff,
"Please speak to us in Aramaic, for we understand it well. Don't speak in
Hebrew,* for the people on the wall will hear."

12But Sennacherib's chief of staff replied, "Do you think my master sent
this message only to you and your master? He wants all the people to hear
it, for when we put this city under siege, they will suffer along with you.
They will be so hungry and thirsty that they will eat their own dung and
drink their own urine."

13Then the chief of staff stood and shouted in Hebrew to the people on
the wall, "Listen to this message from the great king of Assyria! 14This is
what the king says: Don't let Hezekiah deceive you. He will never be able
to rescue you. 15Don't let him fool you into trusting in the LORD by saying,
'The LORD will surely rescue us. This city will never fall into the hands of
the Assyrian king!'

16"Don't listen to Hezekiah! These are the terms the king of Assyria is
offering: Make peace with me—open the gates and come out. Then each of
you can continue eating from your own grapevine and fig tree and drinking
from your own well. 17Then I will arrange to take you to another land like
this one—a land of grain and new wine, bread and vineyards.

18"Don't let Hezekiah mislead you by saying, 'The LORD will rescue
us!' Have the gods of any other nations ever saved their people from the
king of Assyria? 19What happened to the gods of Hamath and Arpad? And

36:5 As in Dead Sea Scrolls (see also 2 Kgs 18:20); Masoretic Text reads *Do I think.* 36:11 Hebrew *in the dialect of Judah;* also in 36:13.

what about the gods of Sepharvaim? Did any god rescue Samaria from my
power? 20 What god of any nation has ever been able to save its people from
my power? So what makes you think that the LORD can rescue Jerusalem
from me?"
21 But the people were silent and did not utter a word because Hezekiah
had commanded them, "Do not answer him."
22 Then Eliakim son of Hilkiah, the palace administrator; Shebna the court
secretary; and Joah son of Asaph, the royal historian, went back to Hezekiah.
They tore their clothes in despair, and they went in to see the king and told
him what the Assyrian chief of staff had said.

Hezekiah Seeks the LORD's Help

37 When King Hezekiah heard their report, he tore his clothes and put
on burlap and went into the Temple of the LORD. 2 And he sent Eli-
akim the palace administrator, Shebna the court secretary, and the leading
priests, all dressed in burlap, to the prophet Isaiah son of Amoz. 3 They told
him, "This is what King Hezekiah says: Today is a day of trouble, insults,
and disgrace. It is like when a child is ready to be born, but the mother has
no strength to deliver the baby. 4 But perhaps the LORD your God has heard
the Assyrian chief of staff,* sent by the king to defy the living God, and will
punish him for his words. Oh, pray for those of us who are left!"
5 After King Hezekiah's officials delivered the king's message to Isaiah,
6 the prophet replied, "Say to your master, 'This is what the LORD says: Do
not be disturbed by this blasphemous speech against me from the Assyrian
king's messengers. 7 Listen! I myself will move against him,* and the king will
receive a message that he is needed at home. So he will return to his land,
where I will have him killed with a sword.'"
8 Meanwhile, the Assyrian chief of staff left Jerusalem and went to consult
the king of Assyria, who had left Lachish and was attacking Libnah.
9 Soon afterward King Sennacherib received word that King Tirhakah
of Ethiopia* was leading an army to fight against him. Before leaving to
meet the attack, he sent messengers back to Hezekiah in Jerusalem with
this message:

> 10 "This message is for King Hezekiah of Judah. Don't let your God, in
> whom you trust, deceive you with promises that Jerusalem will not
> be captured by the king of Assyria. 11 You know perfectly well what
> the kings of Assyria have done wherever they have gone. They have
> completely destroyed everyone who stood in their way! Why should you
> be any different? 12 Have the gods of other nations rescued them—such
> nations as Gozan, Haran, Rezeph, and the people of Eden who were in
> Tel-assar? My predecessors destroyed them all! 13 What happened to the
> king of Hamath and the king of Arpad? What happened to the kings of
> Sepharvaim, Hena, and Ivvah?"

14 After Hezekiah received the letter from the messengers and read it, he
went up to the LORD's Temple and spread it out before the LORD. 15 And
Hezekiah prayed this prayer before the LORD: 16 "O LORD of Heaven's Ar-
mies, God of Israel, you are enthroned between the mighty cherubim!

37:4 Or *the rabshakeh;* also in 37:8. 37:7 Hebrew *I will put a spirit in him.* 37:9 Hebrew *of Cush.*

Story Arc 37:14-20

Hezekiah

King Hezekiah offered a glimpse into how to do what is right by turning to the Lord. In the face of trouble, Hezekiah was moved to pray. He praised the power of the Lord and pleaded for God to listen to his requests. Because he humbled himself and prayed, the Lord answered on his behalf (v. 21). What are you facing today that you should give to the Lord in prayer?

Isa 61:1-2 ►

You alone are God of all the kingdoms of the earth. You alone created the
heavens and the earth. 17 Bend down, O LORD, and listen! Open your eyes,
O LORD, and see! Listen to Sennacherib's words of defiance against the
living God.

18 "It is true, LORD, that the kings of Assyria have destroyed all these na-
tions. 19 And they have thrown the gods of these nations into the fire and
burned them. But of course the Assyrians could destroy them! They were not
gods at all—only idols of wood and stone shaped by human hands. 20 Now,
O LORD our God, rescue us from his power; then all the kingdoms of the
earth will know that you alone, O LORD, are God.*"

Isaiah Predicts Judah's Deliverance

21 Then Isaiah son of Amoz sent this message to Hezekiah: "This is what the
LORD, the God of Israel, says: Because you prayed about King Sennacherib
of Assyria, 22 the LORD has spoken this word against him:

"The virgin daughter of Zion
    despises you and laughs at you.
The daughter of Jerusalem
    shakes her head in derision as you flee.

23 "Whom have you been defying and ridiculing?
    Against whom did you raise your voice?
At whom did you look with such haughty eyes?
    It was the Holy One of Israel!
24 By your messengers you have defied the Lord.
    You have said, 'With my many chariots
I have conquered the highest mountains—
    yes, the remotest peaks of Lebanon.
I have cut down its tallest cedars
    and its finest cypress trees.
I have reached its farthest heights
    and explored its deepest forests.
25 I have dug wells in many foreign lands*
    and refreshed myself with their water.
With the sole of my foot,
    I stopped up all the rivers of Egypt!'

26 "But have you not heard?
    I decided this long ago.
Long ago I planned it,
    and now I am making it happen.
I planned for you to crush fortified cities
    into heaps of rubble.
27 That is why their people have so little power
    and are so frightened and confused.
They are as weak as grass,
    as easily trampled as tender green shoots.

37:20 As in Dead Sea Scrolls (see also 2 Kgs 19:19); Masoretic Text reads *you alone are the LORD.* 37:25 As in Dead Sea Scrolls (see also 2 Kgs 19:24); Masoretic Text lacks *in many foreign lands.*

They are like grass sprouting on a housetop,
scorched* before it can grow lush and tall.

28 "But I know you well—
where you stay
and when you come and go.
I know the way you have raged against me.
29 And because of your raging against me
and your arrogance, which I have heard for myself,
I will put my hook in your nose
and my bit in your mouth.
I will make you return
by the same road on which you came."

30 Then Isaiah said to Hezekiah, "Here is the proof that what I say is true:

"This year you will eat only what grows up by itself,
and next year you will eat what springs up from that.
But in the third year you will plant crops and harvest them;
you will tend vineyards and eat their fruit.
31 And you who are left in Judah,
who have escaped the ravages of the siege,
will put roots down in your own soil
and grow up and flourish.
32 For a remnant of my people will spread out from Jerusalem,
a group of survivors from Mount Zion.
The passionate commitment of the LORD of Heaven's Armies
will make this happen!

33 "And this is what the LORD says about the king of Assyria:

"'His armies will not enter Jerusalem.
They will not even shoot an arrow at it.
They will not march outside its gates with their shields
nor build banks of earth against its walls.
34 The king will return to his own country
by the same road on which he came.
He will not enter this city,'
says the LORD.
35 'For my own honor and for the sake of my servant David,
I will defend this city and protect it.'"

36 That night the angel of the LORD went out to the Assyrian camp and
killed 185,000 Assyrian soldiers. When the surviving Assyrians* woke up
the next morning, they found corpses everywhere. 37 Then King Sennacherib
of Assyria broke camp and returned to his own land. He went home to his
capital of Nineveh and stayed there.
38 One day while he was worshiping in the temple of his god Nisroch, his
sons Adrammelech and Sharezer killed him with their swords. They then

37:27 As in Dead Sea Scrolls and some Greek manuscripts (see also 2 Kgs 19:26); most Hebrew manuscripts read *like a terraced field.* 37:36 Hebrew *When they.*

How God is at work here

escaped to the land of Ararat, and another son, Esarhaddon, became the
next king of Assyria.

Hezekiah's Sickness and Recovery

38 About that time Hezekiah became deathly ill, and the prophet Isaiah
son of Amoz went to visit him. He gave the king this message: "This
is what the LORD says: 'Set your affairs in order, for you are going to die. You
will not recover from this illness.'"
2 When Hezekiah heard this, he turned his face to the wall and prayed to
the LORD, 3 "Remember, O LORD, how I have always been faithful to you and
have served you single-mindedly, always doing what pleases you." Then he
broke down and wept bitterly.
4 Then this message came to Isaiah from the LORD: 5 "Go back to Hezekiah
and tell him, 'This is what the LORD, the God of your ancestor David, says:
I have heard your prayer and seen your tears. I will add fifteen years to your
life, 6 and I will rescue you and this city from the king of Assyria. Yes, I will
defend this city.
7 "'And this is the sign from the LORD to prove that he will do as he prom-
ised: 8 I will cause the sun's shadow to move ten steps backward on the sun-
dial* of Ahaz!'" So the shadow on the sundial moved backward ten steps.

Hezekiah's Poem of Praise

9 When King Hezekiah was well again, he wrote this poem:

10 I said, "In the prime of my life,
must I now enter the place of the dead?*
Am I to be robbed of the rest of my years?"
11 I said, "Never again will I see the LORD GOD
while still in the land of the living.
Never again will I see my friends
or be with those who live in this world.
12 My life has been blown away
like a shepherd's tent in a storm.
It has been cut short,
as when a weaver cuts cloth from a loom.
Suddenly, my life was over.
13 I waited patiently all night,
but I was torn apart as though by lions.
Suddenly, my life was over.
14 Delirious, I chattered like a swallow or a crane,
and then I moaned like a mourning dove.
My eyes grew tired of looking to heaven for help.
I am in trouble, Lord. Help me!"

15 But what could I say?
For he himself sent this sickness.
Now I will walk humbly throughout my years
because of this anguish I have felt.
16 Lord, your discipline is good,

38:8 Hebrew *the steps.* 38:10 Hebrew *enter the gates of Sheol?*

for it leads to life and health.
You restore my health
and allow me to live!
17 Yes, this anguish was good for me,
for you have rescued me from death
and forgiven all my sins.
18 For the dead* cannot praise you;
they cannot raise their voices in praise.
Those who go down to the grave
can no longer hope in your faithfulness.
19 Only the living can praise you as I do today.
Each generation tells of your faithfulness to the next.
20 Think of it—the LORD is ready to heal me!
I will sing his praises with instruments
every day of my life
in the Temple of the LORD.

21 Isaiah had said to Hezekiah's servants, "Make an ointment from figs and spread it over the boil, and Hezekiah will recover."

22 And Hezekiah had asked, "What sign will prove that I will go to the Temple of the LORD?"

Envoys from Babylon

39 Soon after this, Merodach-baladan son of Baladan, king of Babylon, sent Hezekiah his best wishes and a gift. He had heard that Hezekiah had been very sick and that he had recovered. 2 Hezekiah was delighted with the Babylonian envoys and showed them everything in his treasure-houses—the silver, the gold, the spices, and the aromatic oils. He also took them to see his armory and showed them everything in his royal treasuries! There was nothing in his palace or kingdom that Hezekiah did not show them.

3 Then Isaiah the prophet went to King Hezekiah and asked him, "What did those men want? Where were they from?"

Hezekiah replied, "They came from the distant land of Babylon."

4 "What did they see in your palace?" asked Isaiah.

"They saw everything," Hezekiah replied. "I showed them everything I own—all my royal treasuries."

5 Then Isaiah said to Hezekiah, "Listen to this message from the LORD of Heaven's Armies: 6 'The time is coming when everything in your palace—all the treasures stored up by your ancestors until now—will be carried off to Babylon. Nothing will be left,' says the LORD. 7 'Some of your very own sons will be taken away into exile. They will become eunuchs who will serve in the palace of Babylon's king.'"

8 Then Hezekiah said to Isaiah, "This message you have given me from the LORD is good." For the king was thinking, "At least there will be peace and security during my lifetime."

Comfort for God's People

40 1 "Comfort, comfort my people,"
says your God.

38:18 Hebrew *Sheol*.

Patterns I see in this text

Question 40:9

Do not be afraid to tell people about the movement of God! People need to know. God is powerful, he is resourceful, and he will care for people like a shepherd, gently and close to his heart. Who could you tell? What message would you share?

2 "Speak tenderly to Jerusalem.
Tell her that her sad days are gone
and her sins are pardoned.
Yes, the LORD has punished her twice over
for all her sins."

3 Listen! It's the voice of someone shouting,
"Clear the way through the wilderness
for the LORD!
Make a straight highway through the wasteland
for our God!
4 Fill in the valleys,
and level the mountains and hills.
Straighten the curves,
and smooth out the rough places.
5 Then the glory of the LORD will be revealed,
and all people will see it together.
The LORD has spoken!"*

6 A voice said, "Shout!"
I asked, "What should I shout?"

"Shout that people are like the grass.
Their beauty fades as quickly
as the flowers in a field.
7 The grass withers and the flowers fade
beneath the breath of the LORD.
And so it is with people.
8 The grass withers and the flowers fade,
but the word of our God stands forever."

9 O Zion, messenger of good news,
shout from the mountaintops!
Shout it louder, O Jerusalem.*
Shout, and do not be afraid.
Tell the towns of Judah,
"Your God is coming!"
10 Yes, the Sovereign LORD is coming in power.
He will rule with a powerful arm.
See, he brings his reward with him
as he comes.
11 He will feed his flock like a shepherd.
He will carry the lambs in his arms,
holding them close to his heart.
He will gently lead the mother sheep
with their young.

40:3-5 Greek version reads *He is a voice shouting in the wilderness, / "Prepare the way for the LORD's coming! / Clear a road for our God! / Fill in the valleys, / and level the mountains and hills. / And then the glory of the LORD will be revealed, / and all people will see the salvation sent from God. / The LORD has spoken!"* Compare Matt 3:3; Mark 1:3; Luke 3:4-6. **40:9** Or *O messenger of good news, shout to Zion from the mountaintops! Shout it louder to Jerusalem.*

The LORD Has No Equal

12 Who else has held the oceans in his hand?
Who has measured off the heavens with his fingers?
Who else knows the weight of the earth
or has weighed the mountains and hills on a scale?
13 Who is able to advise the Spirit of the LORD?*
Who knows enough to give him advice or teach him?
14 Has the LORD ever needed anyone's advice?
Does he need instruction about what is good?
Did someone teach him what is right
or show him the path of justice?

15 No, for all the nations of the world
are but a drop in the bucket.
They are nothing more
than dust on the scales.
He picks up the whole earth
as though it were a grain of sand.
16 All the wood in Lebanon's forests
and all Lebanon's animals would not be enough
to make a burnt offering worthy of our God.
17 The nations of the world are worth nothing to him.
In his eyes they count for less than nothing—
mere emptiness and froth.

18 To whom can you compare God?
What image can you find to resemble him?
19 Can he be compared to an idol formed in a mold,
overlaid with gold, and decorated with silver chains?
20 Or if people are too poor for that,
they might at least choose wood that won't decay
and a skilled craftsman
to carve an image that won't fall down!

21 Haven't you heard? Don't you understand?
Are you deaf to the words of God—
the words he gave before the world began?
Are you so ignorant?
22 God sits above the circle of the earth.
The people below seem like grasshoppers to him!
He spreads out the heavens like a curtain
and makes his tent from them.
23 He judges the great people of the world
and brings them all to nothing.
24 They hardly get started, barely taking root,
when he blows on them and they wither.
The wind carries them off like chaff.

40:13 Greek version reads *Who can know the LORD's thoughts?* Compare Rom 11:34; 1 Cor 2:16.

Make a Difference

40:12–31

(In)formation

Information gives us control. We access and search for information, and that information gives us power. Because we live in an information-driven world, we tend to open the Bible for information, like some archaic, magical Google. We look for information about God, about life, about faith, about a decision, about parenting, about work, about anything else you could think of.

The Bible wasn't written to fill our heads with information, however. Our main goal when approaching the Bible should not be merely to access content. The Bible is not laid out as an instruction manual. It's true that within its pages, the Bible contains some interesting and helpful material. Still, even more than solid information, the Word of God is focused on our formation as God's people. The Bible exists so that we can be shaped and transformed and empowered by God.

Difference Maker

Read prayerfully through these verses from Isaiah a few times. As you do so, ask God how he would like to form you today.

25 "To whom will you compare me?
Who is my equal?" asks the Holy One.

26 Look up into the heavens.
Who created all the stars?
He brings them out like an army, one after another,
calling each by its name.
Because of his great power and incomparable strength,
not a single one is missing.
27 O Jacob, how can you say the LORD does not see your troubles?
O Israel, how can you say God ignores your rights?
28 Have you never heard?
Have you never understood?
The LORD is the everlasting God,
the Creator of all the earth.
He never grows weak or weary.
No one can measure the depths of his understanding.
29 He gives power to the weak
and strength to the powerless.
30 Even youths will become weak and tired,
and young men will fall in exhaustion.
31 But those who trust in the LORD will find new strength.
They will soar high on wings like eagles.
They will run and not grow weary.
They will walk and not faint.

God's Help for Israel

41 1 "Listen in silence before me, you lands beyond the sea.
Bring your strongest arguments.
Come now and speak.
The court is ready for your case.

2 "Who has stirred up this king from the east,
rightly calling him to God's service?
Who gives this man victory over many nations
and permits him to trample their kings underfoot?
With his sword, he reduces armies to dust.
With his bow, he scatters them like chaff before the wind.
3 He chases them away and goes on safely,
though he is walking over unfamiliar ground.
4 Who has done such mighty deeds,
summoning each new generation from the beginning of time?
It is I, the LORD, the First and the Last.
I alone am he."

5 The lands beyond the sea watch in fear.
Remote lands tremble and mobilize for war.
6 The idol makers encourage one another,
saying to each other, "Be strong!"
7 The carver encourages the goldsmith,

and the molder helps at the anvil.
"Good," they say. "It's coming along fine."
Carefully they join the parts together,
then fasten the thing in place so it won't fall over.

8 "But as for you, Israel my servant,
Jacob my chosen one,
descended from Abraham my friend,
9 I have called you back from the ends of the earth,
saying, 'You are my servant.'
For I have chosen you
and will not throw you away.
10 Don't be afraid, for I am with you.
Don't be discouraged, for I am your God.
I will strengthen you and help you.
I will hold you up with my victorious right hand.

11 "See, all your angry enemies lie there,
confused and humiliated.
Anyone who opposes you will die
and come to nothing.
12 You will look in vain
for those who tried to conquer you.
Those who attack you
will come to nothing.
13 For I hold you by your right hand—
I, the LORD your God.
And I say to you,
'Don't be afraid. I am here to help you.
14 Though you are a lowly worm, O Jacob,
don't be afraid, people of Israel, for I will help you.
I am the LORD, your Redeemer.
I am the Holy One of Israel.'
15 You will be a new threshing instrument
with many sharp teeth.
You will tear your enemies apart,
making chaff of mountains.
16 You will toss them into the air,
and the wind will blow them all away;
a whirlwind will scatter them.
Then you will rejoice in the LORD.
You will glory in the Holy One of Israel.

17 "When the poor and needy search for water and
there is none,
and their tongues are parched from thirst,
then I, the LORD, will answer them.
I, the God of Israel, will never abandon them.
18 I will open up rivers for them on the high plateaus.
I will give them fountains of water in the valleys.

Make a Difference **41:10**

With

One of the greatest words in the Bible is the word *with*. Again and again we learn in the Bible that God is with his people. Yahweh, the great I AM, is also Immanuel, who is "God with us." He tells us over and over again throughout the Bible, "I am with you."

This concept of the Lord being so intimate and so near is especially important to the prophet Isaiah. The people of Israel, who at the time had become a scattered and scared nation, needed to know that God was not distant from them. In fact, God spoke, God heard, God loved, God moved, and God dwelled closely. "Everyone!" Isaiah shouted. "Listen to what the Lord says. We are not alone. He is with us. Hold fast!" Knowing that God is near makes everything much more bearable.

Difference Maker

Think of a bold action, something that God has been wanting you to do but that you have been reluctant to tackle. Knowing that God is with you, take a step in the right direction today.

I will fill the desert with pools of water.
  Rivers fed by springs will flow across the parched ground.
19 I will plant trees in the barren desert—
  cedar, acacia, myrtle, olive, cypress, fir, and pine.
20 I am doing this so all who see this miracle
  will understand what it means—
that it is the LORD who has done this,
  the Holy One of Israel who created it.

21 "Present the case for your idols,"
  says the LORD.
"Let them show what they can do,"
  says the King of Israel.*
22 "Let them try to tell us what happened long ago
  so that we may consider the evidence.
Or let them tell us what the future holds,
  so we can know what's going to happen.
23 Yes, tell us what will occur in the days ahead.
  Then we will know you are gods.
In fact, do anything—good or bad!
  Do something that will amaze and frighten us.
24 But no! You are less than nothing and can do nothing at all.
  Those who choose you pollute themselves.

25 "But I have stirred up a leader who will approach from the north.
  From the east he will call on my name.
I will give him victory over kings and princes.
  He will trample them as a potter treads on clay.

26 "Who told you from the beginning
  that this would happen?
Who predicted this,
  making you admit that he was right?
  No one said a word!
27 I was the first to tell Zion,
  'Look! Help is on the way!'*
  I will send Jerusalem a messenger with good news.
28 Not one of your idols told you this.
  Not one gave any answer when I asked.
29 See, they are all foolish, worthless things.
  All your idols are as empty as the wind.

The LORD's Chosen Servant

42 1 "Look at my servant, whom I strengthen.
  He is my chosen one, who pleases me.
I have put my Spirit upon him.
  He will bring justice to the nations.
2 He will not shout
  or raise his voice in public.

41:21 Hebrew *the King of Jacob.* See note on 14:1. **41:27** Or *'Look! They are coming home.'*

3 He will not crush the weakest reed
or put out a flickering candle.
He will bring justice to all who have been wronged.
4 He will not falter or lose heart
until justice prevails throughout the earth.
Even distant lands beyond the sea will wait for
his instruction.*"

5 God, the LORD, created the heavens and stretched them out.
He created the earth and everything in it.
He gives breath to everyone,
life to everyone who walks the earth.
And it is he who says,
6 "I, the LORD, have called you to demonstrate my righteousness.
I will take you by the hand and guard you,
and I will give you to my people, Israel,
as a symbol of my covenant with them.
And you will be a light to guide the nations.
7 You will open the eyes of the blind.
You will free the captives from prison,
releasing those who sit in dark dungeons.

8 "I am the LORD; that is my name!
I will not give my glory to anyone else,
nor share my praise with carved idols.
9 Everything I prophesied has come true,
and now I will prophesy again.
I will tell you the future before it happens."

A Song of Praise to the LORD

10 Sing a new song to the LORD!
Sing his praises from the ends of the earth!
Sing, all you who sail the seas,
all you who live in distant coastlands.
11 Join in the chorus, you desert towns;
let the villages of Kedar rejoice!
Let the people of Sela sing for joy;
shout praises from the mountaintops!
12 Let the whole world glorify the LORD;
let it sing his praise.
13 The LORD will march forth like a mighty hero;
he will come out like a warrior, full of fury.
He will shout his battle cry
and crush all his enemies.

14 He will say, "I have long been silent;
yes, I have restrained myself.
But now, like a woman in labor,
I will cry and groan and pant.

Question 42:5

In what ways does Jesus fulfill the prophecies of this chapter? What difference does that make for everyone who walks the earth?

42:4 Greek version reads *And his name will be the hope of all the world.* Compare Matt 12:21.

15 I will level the mountains and hills
and blight all their greenery.
I will turn the rivers into dry land
and will dry up all the pools.
16 I will lead blind Israel down a new path,
guiding them along an unfamiliar way.
I will brighten the darkness before them
and smooth out the road ahead of them.
Yes, I will indeed do these things;
I will not forsake them.
17 But those who trust in idols,
who say, 'You are our gods,'
will be turned away in shame.

Israel's Failure to Listen and See

18 "Listen, you who are deaf!
Look and see, you blind!
19 Who is as blind as my own people, my servant?
Who is as deaf as my messenger?
Who is as blind as my chosen people,
the servant of the LORD?
20 You see and recognize what is right
but refuse to act on it.
You hear with your ears,
but you don't really listen."

21 Because he is righteous,
the LORD has exalted his glorious law.
22 But his own people have been robbed and plundered,
enslaved, imprisoned, and trapped.
They are fair game for anyone
and have no one to protect them,
no one to take them back home.

23 Who will hear these lessons from the past
and see the ruin that awaits you in the future?
24 Who allowed Israel to be robbed and hurt?
It was the LORD, against whom we sinned,
for the people would not walk in his path,
nor would they obey his law.
25 Therefore, he poured out his fury on them
and destroyed them in battle.
They were enveloped in flames,
but they still refused to understand.
They were consumed by fire,
but they did not learn their lesson.

The Savior of Israel

43 1 But now, O Jacob, listen to the LORD who created you.
O Israel, the one who formed you says,

"Do not be afraid, for I have ransomed you.
I have called you by name; you are mine.
2 When you go through deep waters,
I will be with you.
When you go through rivers of difficulty,
you will not drown.
When you walk through the fire of oppression,
you will not be burned up;
the flames will not consume you.
3 For I am the LORD, your God,
the Holy One of Israel, your Savior.
I gave Egypt as a ransom for your freedom;
I gave Ethiopia* and Seba in your place.
4 Others were given in exchange for you.
I traded their lives for yours
because you are precious to me.
You are honored, and I love you.

5 "Do not be afraid, for I am with you.
I will gather you and your children from east and west.
6 I will say to the north and south,
'Bring my sons and daughters back to Israel
from the distant corners of the earth.
7 Bring all who claim me as their God,
for I have made them for my glory.
It was I who created them.'"

8 Bring out the people who have eyes but are blind,
who have ears but are deaf.
9 Gather the nations together!
Assemble the peoples of the world!
Which of their idols has ever foretold such things?
Which can predict what will happen tomorrow?
Where are the witnesses of such predictions?
Who can verify that they spoke the truth?

10 "But you are my witnesses, O Israel!" says the LORD.
"You are my servant.
You have been chosen to know me, believe in me,
and understand that I alone am God.
There is no other God—
there never has been, and there never will be.
11 I, yes I, am the LORD,
and there is no other Savior.
12 First I predicted your rescue,
then I saved you and proclaimed it to the world.
No foreign god has ever done this.
You are witnesses that I am the only God,"
says the LORD.

43:3 Hebrew *Cush*.

Things to reflect on

Prayer 43:19

Jesus, my Savior, what new thing would you like to do in my life?

13 "From eternity to eternity I am God.
No one can snatch anyone out of my hand.
No one can undo what I have done."

The LORD's Promise of Victory

14 This is what the LORD says—your Redeemer, the Holy One of Israel:

"For your sakes I will send an army against Babylon,
forcing the Babylonians* to flee in those ships they
are so proud of.
15 I am the LORD, your Holy One,
Israel's Creator and King.
16 I am the LORD, who opened a way through the waters,
making a dry path through the sea.
17 I called forth the mighty army of Egypt
with all its chariots and horses.
I drew them beneath the waves, and they drowned,
their lives snuffed out like a smoldering candlewick.

18 "But forget all that—
it is nothing compared to what I am going to do.
19 For I am about to do something new.
See, I have already begun! Do you not see it?
I will make a pathway through the wilderness.
I will create rivers in the dry wasteland.
20 The wild animals in the fields will thank me,
the jackals and owls, too,
for giving them water in the desert.
Yes, I will make rivers in the dry wasteland
so my chosen people can be refreshed.
21 I have made Israel for myself,
and they will someday honor me before the whole world.

22 "But, dear family of Jacob, you refuse to ask for my help.
You have grown tired of me, O Israel!
23 You have not brought me sheep or goats for
burnt offerings.
You have not honored me with sacrifices,
though I have not burdened and wearied you
with requests for grain offerings and frankincense.
24 You have not brought me fragrant calamus
or pleased me with the fat from sacrifices.
Instead, you have burdened me with your sins
and wearied me with your faults.

25 "I—yes, I alone—will blot out your sins for my own sake
and will never think of them again.
26 Let us review the situation together,
and you can present your case to prove your innocence.

43:14 Or *Chaldeans.*

27 From the very beginning, your first ancestor sinned against me;
all your leaders broke my laws.
28 That is why I have disgraced your priests;
I have decreed complete destruction* for Jacob
and shame for Israel.

44 1 "But now, listen to me, Jacob my servant,
Israel my chosen one.
2 The LORD who made you and helps you says:
Do not be afraid, O Jacob, my servant,
O dear Israel,* my chosen one.
3 For I will pour out water to quench your thirst
and to irrigate your parched fields.
And I will pour out my Spirit on your descendants,
and my blessing on your children.
4 They will thrive like watered grass,
like willows on a riverbank.
5 Some will proudly claim, 'I belong to the LORD.'
Others will say, 'I am a descendant of Jacob.'
Some will write the LORD's name on their hands
and will take the name of Israel as their own."

The Foolishness of Idols

6 This is what the LORD says—Israel's King and Redeemer, the LORD of Heaven's Armies:

"I am the First and the Last;
there is no other God.
7 Who is like me?
Let him step forward and prove to you his power.
Let him do as I have done since ancient times
when I established a people and explained its future.
8 Do not tremble; do not be afraid.
Did I not proclaim my purposes for you long ago?
You are my witnesses—is there any other God?
No! There is no other Rock—not one!"

9 How foolish are those who manufacture idols.
These prized objects are really worthless.
The people who worship idols don't know this,
so they are all put to shame.
10 Who but a fool would make his own god—
an idol that cannot help him one bit?
11 All who worship idols will be disgraced
along with all these craftsmen—mere humans—
who claim they can make a god.
They may all stand together,
but they will stand in terror and shame.

43:28 The Hebrew term used here refers to the complete consecration of things or people to the LORD, either by destroying them or by giving them as an offering. 44:2 Hebrew *Jeshurun,* a term of endearment for Israel.

Make a Difference 44:5

Write God's Name on Your Hand

The Lord wants to pour out his Spirit into your life. All he asks is that you be willing to be identified by his name.

Difference Maker

Just like this verse says, write the Lord's name on your hand to remind yourself to live according to his name today.

12 The blacksmith stands at his forge to make
a sharp tool,
pounding and shaping it with all his might.
His work makes him hungry and weak.
It makes him thirsty and faint.
13 Then the wood-carver measures a block of wood
and draws a pattern on it.
He works with chisel and plane
and carves it into a human figure.
He gives it human beauty
and puts it in a little shrine.
14 He cuts down cedars;
he selects the cypress and the oak;
he plants the pine in the forest
to be nourished by the rain.
15 Then he uses part of the wood to make a fire.
With it he warms himself and bakes his bread.
Then—yes, it's true—he takes the rest of it
and makes himself a god to worship!
He makes an idol
and bows down in front of it!
16 He burns part of the tree to roast his meat
and to keep himself warm.
He says, "Ah, that fire feels good."
17 Then he takes what's left
and makes his god: a carved idol!
He falls down in front of it,
worshiping and praying to it.
"Rescue me!" he says.
"You are my god!"

18 Such stupidity and ignorance!
Their eyes are closed, and they cannot see.
Their minds are shut, and they cannot think.
19 The person who made the idol never stops to reflect,
"Why, it's just a block of wood!
I burned half of it for heat
and used it to bake my bread and roast my meat.
How can the rest of it be a god?
Should I bow down to worship a piece of wood?"
20 The poor, deluded fool feeds on ashes.
He trusts something that can't help him at all.
Yet he cannot bring himself to ask,
"Is this idol that I'm holding in my hand a lie?"

Restoration for Jerusalem

21 "Pay attention, O Jacob,
for you are my servant, O Israel.
I, the Lord, made you,
and I will not forget you.

22 I have swept away your sins like a cloud.
I have scattered your offenses like the morning mist.
Oh, return to me,
for I have paid the price to set you free."

23 Sing, O heavens, for the LORD has done this
wondrous thing.
Shout for joy, O depths of the earth!
Break into song,
O mountains and forests and every tree!
For the LORD has redeemed Jacob
and is glorified in Israel.

24 This is what the LORD says—
your Redeemer and Creator:
"I am the LORD, who made all things.
I alone stretched out the heavens.
Who was with me
when I made the earth?
25 I expose the false prophets as liars
and make fools of fortune-tellers.
I cause the wise to give bad advice,
thus proving them to be fools.
26 But I carry out the predictions of my prophets!
By them I say to Jerusalem, 'People will live
here again,'
and to the towns of Judah, 'You will be rebuilt;
I will restore all your ruins!'
27 When I speak to the rivers and say, 'Dry up!'
they will be dry.
28 When I say of Cyrus, 'He is my shepherd,'
he will certainly do as I say.
He will command, 'Rebuild Jerusalem';
he will say, 'Restore the Temple.'"

Question 44:22

What price did God pay to set you free from your sins?

Cyrus, the LORD's Chosen One

45 1 This is what the LORD says to Cyrus, his anointed one,
whose right hand he will empower.
Before him, mighty kings will be paralyzed with fear.
Their fortress gates will be opened,
never to shut again.
2 This is what the LORD says:

"I will go before you, Cyrus,
and level the mountains.*
I will smash down gates of bronze
and cut through bars of iron.
3 And I will give you treasures hidden in the darkness—
secret riches.

45:2 As in Dead Sea Scrolls and Greek version; Masoretic Text reads *the swellings*.

I will do this so you may know that I am the LORD,
the God of Israel, the one who calls you by name.

4 "And why have I called you for this work?
Why did I call you by name when you did not
know me?
It is for the sake of Jacob my servant,
Israel my chosen one.
5 I am the LORD;
there is no other God.
I have equipped you for battle,
though you don't even know me,
6 so all the world from east to west
will know there is no other God.
I am the LORD, and there is no other.
7 I create the light and make the darkness.
I send good times and bad times.
I, the LORD, am the one who does these things.

8 "Open up, O heavens,
and pour out your righteousness.
Let the earth open wide
so salvation and righteousness can sprout up together.
I, the LORD, created them.

9 "What sorrow awaits those who argue with their Creator.
Does a clay pot argue with its maker?
Does the clay dispute with the one who shapes it, saying,
'Stop, you're doing it wrong!'
Does the pot exclaim,
'How clumsy can you be?'
10 How terrible it would be if a newborn baby said
to its father,
'Why was I born?'
or if it said to its mother,
'Why did you make me this way?'"

11 This is what the LORD says—
the Holy One of Israel and your Creator:
"Do you question what I do for my children?
Do you give me orders about the work of my hands?
12 I am the one who made the earth
and created people to live on it.
With my hands I stretched out the heavens.
All the stars are at my command.
13 I will raise up Cyrus to fulfill my righteous purpose,
and I will guide his actions.
He will restore my city and free my captive people—
without seeking a reward!
I, the LORD of Heaven's Armies, have spoken!"

Future Conversion of Gentiles

14 This is what the LORD says:

"You will rule the Egyptians,
the Ethiopians,* and the Sabeans.
They will come to you with all their merchandise,
and it will all be yours.
They will follow you as prisoners in chains.
They will fall to their knees in front of you and say,
'God is with you, and he is the only God.
There is no other.'"

15 Truly, O God of Israel, our Savior,
you work in mysterious ways.
16 All craftsmen who make idols will be humiliated.
They will all be disgraced together.
17 But the LORD will save the people of Israel
with eternal salvation.
Throughout everlasting ages,
they will never again be humiliated and disgraced.

18 For the LORD is God,
and he created the heavens and earth
and put everything in place.
He made the world to be lived in,
not to be a place of empty chaos.
"I am the LORD," he says,
"and there is no other.
19 I publicly proclaim bold promises.
I do not whisper obscurities in some dark corner.
I would not have told the people of Israel* to seek me
if I could not be found.
I, the LORD, speak only what is true
and declare only what is right.

20 "Gather together and come,
you fugitives from surrounding nations.
What fools they are who carry around their wooden idols
and pray to gods that cannot save!
21 Consult together, argue your case.
Get together and decide what to say.
Who made these things known so long ago?
What idol ever told you they would happen?
Was it not I, the LORD?
For there is no other God but me,
a righteous God and Savior.
There is none but me.
22 Let all the world look to me for salvation!
For I am God; there is no other.

45:14 Hebrew *Cushites.* **45:19** Hebrew *of Jacob.* See note on 14:1.

Your thoughts can go here

Question 46:4

If you keep God as your God throughout your lifetime, what do you hope your faith will be like fifty years from now?

23 I have sworn by my own name;
I have spoken the truth,
and I will never go back on my word:
Every knee will bend to me,
and every tongue will declare allegiance to me.*"
24 The people will declare,
"The LORD is the source of all my righteousness and strength."
And all who were angry with him
will come to him and be ashamed.
25 In the LORD all the generations of Israel will be justified,
and in him they will boast.

Babylon's False Gods

46 1 Bel and Nebo, the gods of Babylon,
bow as they are lowered to the ground.
They are being hauled away on ox carts.
The poor beasts stagger under the weight.
2 Both the idols and their owners are bowed down.
The gods cannot protect the people,
and the people cannot protect the gods.
They go off into captivity together.

3 "Listen to me, descendants of Jacob,
all you who remain in Israel.
I have cared for you since you were born.
Yes, I carried you before you were born.
4 I will be your God throughout your lifetime—
until your hair is white with age.
I made you, and I will care for you.
I will carry you along and save you.

5 "To whom will you compare me?
Who is my equal?
6 Some people pour out their silver and gold
and hire a craftsman to make a god from it.
Then they bow down and worship it!
7 They carry it around on their shoulders,
and when they set it down, it stays there.
It can't even move!
And when someone prays to it, there is no answer.
It can't rescue anyone from trouble.

8 "Do not forget this! Keep it in mind!
Remember this, you guilty ones.
9 Remember the things I have done in the past.
For I alone am God!
I am God, and there is none like me.
10 Only I can tell you the future
before it even happens.

45:23 Hebrew *will confess;* Greek version reads *will declare allegiance to God.* Compare Rom 14:11.

Everything I plan will come to pass,
for I do whatever I wish.
11 I will call a swift bird of prey from the east—
a leader from a distant land to come and do my bidding.
I have said what I would do,
and I will do it.

12 "Listen to me, you stubborn people
who are so far from doing right.
13 For I am ready to set things right,
not in the distant future, but right now!
I am ready to save Jerusalem*
and show my glory to Israel.

Prediction of Babylon's Fall

47 1 "Come down, virgin daughter of Babylon, and sit in the dust.
For your days of sitting on a throne have ended.
O daughter of Babylonia,* never again will you be
the lovely princess, tender and delicate.
2 Take heavy millstones and grind flour.
Remove your veil, and strip off your robe.
Expose yourself to public view.*
3 You will be naked and burdened with shame.
I will take vengeance against you without pity."

4 Our Redeemer, whose name is the LORD of Heaven's Armies,
is the Holy One of Israel.

5 "O beautiful Babylon, sit now in darkness and silence.
Never again will you be known as the queen of kingdoms.
6 For I was angry with my chosen people
and punished them by letting them fall into your hands.
But you, Babylon, showed them no mercy.
You oppressed even the elderly.
7 You said, 'I will reign forever as queen of the world!'
You did not reflect on your actions
or think about their consequences.

8 "Listen to this, you pleasure-loving kingdom,
living at ease and feeling secure.
You say, 'I am the only one, and there is no other.
I will never be a widow or lose my children.'
9 Well, both these things will come upon you in a moment:
widowhood and the loss of your children.
Yes, these calamities will come upon you,
despite all your witchcraft and magic.

10 "You felt secure in your wickedness.
'No one sees me,' you said.

46:13 Hebrew *Zion.* 47:1 Or *Chaldea;* also in 47:5. 47:2 Hebrew *Bare your legs; pass through the rivers.*

But your 'wisdom' and 'knowledge' have led you astray,
and you said, 'I am the only one, and there is no other.'
11 So disaster will overtake you,
and you won't be able to charm it away.
Calamity will fall upon you,
and you won't be able to buy your way out.
A catastrophe will strike you suddenly,
one for which you are not prepared.

12 "Now use your magical charms!
Use the spells you have worked at all these years!
Maybe they will do you some good.
Maybe they can make someone afraid of you.
13 All the advice you receive has made you tired.
Where are all your astrologers,
those stargazers who make predictions each month?
Let them stand up and save you from what the future holds.
14 But they are like straw burning in a fire;
they cannot save themselves from the flame.
You will get no help from them at all;
their hearth is no place to sit for warmth.
15 And all your friends,
those with whom you've done business since childhood,
will go their own ways,
turning a deaf ear to your cries.

God's Stubborn People

48 1 "Listen to me, O family of Jacob,
you who are called by the name of Israel
and born into the family of Judah.
Listen, you who take oaths in the name of the LORD
and call on the God of Israel.
You don't keep your promises,
2 even though you call yourself the holy city
and talk about depending on the God of Israel,
whose name is the LORD of Heaven's Armies.
3 Long ago I told you what was going to happen.
Then suddenly I took action,
and all my predictions came true.
4 For I know how stubborn and obstinate you are.
Your necks are as unbending as iron.
Your heads are as hard as bronze.
5 That is why I told you what would happen;
I told you beforehand what I was going to do.
Then you could never say, 'My idols did it.
My wooden image and metal god commanded it to happen!'
6 You have heard my predictions and seen them fulfilled,
but you refuse to admit it.
Now I will tell you new things,
secrets you have not yet heard.

7 They are brand new, not things from the past.
So you cannot say, 'We knew that all the time!'

8 "Yes, I will tell you of things that are entirely new,
things you never heard of before.
For I know so well what traitors you are.
You have been rebels from birth.
9 Yet for my own sake and for the honor of my name,
I will hold back my anger and not wipe you out.
10 I have refined you, but not as silver is refined.
Rather, I have refined you in the furnace of suffering.
11 I will rescue you for my sake—
yes, for my own sake!
I will not let my reputation be tarnished,
and I will not share my glory with idols!

Freedom from Babylon

12 "Listen to me, O family of Jacob,
Israel my chosen one!
I alone am God,
the First and the Last.
13 It was my hand that laid the foundations of the earth,
my right hand that spread out the heavens above.
When I call out the stars,
they all appear in order."

14 Have any of your idols ever told you this?
Come, all of you, and listen:
The LORD has chosen Cyrus as his ally.
He will use him to put an end to the empire of Babylon
and to destroy the Babylonian* armies.

15 "I have said it: I am calling Cyrus!
I will send him on this errand and will help him succeed.
16 Come closer, and listen to this.
From the beginning I have told you plainly what would happen."

And now the Sovereign LORD and his Spirit
have sent me with this message.
17 This is what the LORD says—
your Redeemer, the Holy One of Israel:
"I am the LORD your God,
who teaches you what is good for you
and leads you along the paths you should follow.
18 Oh, that you had listened to my commands!
Then you would have had peace flowing like a gentle river
and righteousness rolling over you like waves in the sea.
19 Your descendants would have been like the sands along the seashore—
too many to count!

Question 48:10

Why is suffering sometimes a necessary part of our lives?

48:14 Or *Chaldean.*

Question 49:6

How does Jesus fulfill this passage? What part do you play in this?

There would have been no need for your destruction,
or for cutting off your family name."

20 Yet even now, be free from your captivity!
Leave Babylon and the Babylonians.*
Sing out this message!
Shout it to the ends of the earth!
The LORD has redeemed his servants,
the people of Israel.*
21 They were not thirsty
when he led them through the desert.
He divided the rock,
and water gushed out for them to drink.
22 "But there is no peace for the wicked,"
says the LORD.

The LORD's Servant Commissioned

49 1 Listen to me, all you in distant lands!
Pay attention, you who are far away!
The LORD called me before my birth;
from within the womb he called me by name.
2 He made my words of judgment as sharp as a sword.
He has hidden me in the shadow of his hand.
I am like a sharp arrow in his quiver.

3 He said to me, "You are my servant, Israel,
and you will bring me glory."

4 I replied, "But my work seems so useless!
I have spent my strength for nothing and to no purpose.
Yet I leave it all in the LORD's hand;
I will trust God for my reward."

5 And now the LORD speaks—
the one who formed me in my mother's womb to
be his servant,
who commissioned me to bring Israel back to him.
The LORD has honored me,
and my God has given me strength.
6 He says, "You will do more than restore the people of Israel to me.
I will make you a light to the Gentiles,
and you will bring my salvation to the ends of the earth."

7 The LORD, the Redeemer
and Holy One of Israel,
says to the one who is despised and rejected by the nations,
to the one who is the servant of rulers:
"Kings will stand at attention when you pass by.
Princes will also bow low

48:20a Or *the Chaldeans.* 48:20b Hebrew *his servant, Jacob.* See note on 14:1.

because of the LORD, the faithful one,
the Holy One of Israel, who has chosen you."

Promises of Israel's Restoration

8 This is what the LORD says:

"At just the right time, I will respond to you.*
On the day of salvation I will help you.
I will protect you and give you to the people
as my covenant with them.
Through you I will reestablish the land of Israel
and assign it to its own people again.
9 I will say to the prisoners, 'Come out in freedom,'
and to those in darkness, 'Come into the light.'
They will be my sheep, grazing in green pastures
and on hills that were previously bare.
10 They will neither hunger nor thirst.
The searing sun will not reach them anymore.
For the LORD in his mercy will lead them;
he will lead them beside cool waters.
11 And I will make my mountains into level paths for them.
The highways will be raised above the valleys.
12 See, my people will return from far away,
from lands to the north and west,
and from as far south as Egypt.*"

13 Sing for joy, O heavens!
Rejoice, O earth!
Burst into song, O mountains!
For the LORD has comforted his people
and will have compassion on them in their suffering.

14 Yet Jerusalem* says, "The LORD has deserted us;
the Lord has forgotten us."

15 "Never! Can a mother forget her nursing child?
Can she feel no love for the child she has borne?
But even if that were possible,
I would not forget you!
16 See, I have written your name on the palms of my hands.
Always in my mind is a picture of Jerusalem's walls in ruins.
17 Soon your descendants will come back,
and all who are trying to destroy you will go away.
18 Look around you and see,
for all your children will come back to you.
As surely as I live," says the LORD,
"they will be like jewels or bridal ornaments for you
to display.

49:8 Greek version reads *I heard you.* Compare 2 Cor 6:2. 49:12 As in Dead Sea Scrolls, which read *from the region of Aswan,* which is in southern Egypt. Masoretic Text reads *from the region of Sinim.* 49:14 Hebrew *Zion.*

19 "Even the most desolate parts of your abandoned land
will soon be crowded with your people.
Your enemies who enslaved you
will be far away.
20 The generations born in exile will return and say,
'We need more room! It's crowded here!'
21 Then you will think to yourself,
'Who has given me all these descendants?
For most of my children were killed,
and the rest were carried away into exile.
I was left here all alone.
Where did all these people come from?
Who bore these children?
Who raised them for me?'"

22 This is what the Sovereign LORD says:
"See, I will give a signal to the godless nations.
They will carry your little sons back to you in their arms;
they will bring your daughters on their shoulders.
23 Kings and queens will serve you
and care for all your needs.
They will bow to the earth before you
and lick the dust from your feet.
Then you will know that I am the LORD.
Those who trust in me will never be put to shame."

24 Who can snatch the plunder of war from the hands of a warrior?
Who can demand that a tyrant* let his captives go?
25 But the LORD says,
"The captives of warriors will be released,
and the plunder of tyrants will be retrieved.
For I will fight those who fight you,
and I will save your children.
26 I will feed your enemies with their own flesh.
They will be drunk with rivers of their own blood.
All the world will know that I, the LORD,
am your Savior and your Redeemer,
the Mighty One of Israel.*"

50 This is what the LORD says:

"Was your mother sent away because I divorced her?
Did I sell you as slaves to my creditors?
No, you were sold because of your sins.
And your mother, too, was taken because of your sins.
2 Why was no one there when I came?
Why didn't anyone answer when I called?
Is it because I have no power to rescue?
No, that is not the reason!

49:24 As in Dead Sea Scrolls, Syriac version, and Latin Vulgate (also see 49:25); Masoretic Text reads *a righteous person.* 49:26 Hebrew *of Jacob.* See note on 14:1.

For I can speak to the sea and make it dry up!
I can turn rivers into deserts covered with dying fish.
3 I dress the skies in darkness,
covering them with clothes of mourning."

The LORD's Obedient Servant

4 The Sovereign LORD has given me his words of wisdom,
so that I know how to comfort the weary.
Morning by morning he wakens me
and opens my understanding to his will.
5 The Sovereign LORD has spoken to me,
and I have listened.
I have not rebelled or turned away.
6 I offered my back to those who beat me
and my cheeks to those who pulled out my beard.
I did not hide my face
from mockery and spitting.

7 Because the Sovereign LORD helps me,
I will not be disgraced.
Therefore, I have set my face like a stone,
determined to do his will.
And I know that I will not be put to shame.
8 He who gives me justice is near.
Who will dare to bring charges against me now?
Where are my accusers?
Let them appear!
9 See, the Sovereign LORD is on my side!
Who will declare me guilty?
All my enemies will be destroyed
like old clothes that have been eaten by moths!

10 Who among you fears the LORD
and obeys his servant?
If you are walking in darkness,
without a ray of light,
trust in the LORD
and rely on your God.
11 But watch out, you who live in your own light
and warm yourselves by your own fires.
This is the reward you will receive from me:
You will soon fall down in great torment.

A Call to Trust the LORD

51 1 "Listen to me, all who hope for deliverance—
all who seek the LORD!
Consider the rock from which you were cut,
the quarry from which you were mined.
2 Yes, think about Abraham, your ancestor,
and Sarah, who gave birth to your nation.

Question 50:8

Compare this section to Romans 8:34-39. How does Jesus make all the difference in our lives?

Abraham was only one man when I called him.
But when I blessed him, he became a great nation."

3 The LORD will comfort Israel* again
and have pity on her ruins.
Her desert will blossom like Eden,
her barren wilderness like the garden of the LORD.
Joy and gladness will be found there.
Songs of thanksgiving will fill the air.

4 "Listen to me, my people.
Hear me, Israel,
for my law will be proclaimed,
and my justice will become a light to the nations.
5 My mercy and justice are coming soon.
My salvation is on the way.
My strong arm will bring justice to the nations.
All distant lands will look to me
and wait in hope for my powerful arm.
6 Look up to the skies above,
and gaze down on the earth below.
For the skies will disappear like smoke,
and the earth will wear out like a piece of clothing.
The people of the earth will die like flies,
but my salvation lasts forever.
My righteous rule will never end!

7 "Listen to me, you who know right from wrong,
you who cherish my law in your hearts.
Do not be afraid of people's scorn,
nor fear their insults.
8 For the moth will devour them as it devours clothing.
The worm will eat at them as it eats wool.
But my righteousness will last forever.
My salvation will continue from generation
to generation."

9 Wake up, wake up, O LORD! Clothe yourself with strength!
Flex your mighty right arm!
Rouse yourself as in the days of old
when you slew Egypt, the dragon of the Nile.*
10 Are you not the same today,
the one who dried up the sea,
making a path of escape through the depths
so that your people could cross over?
11 Those who have been ransomed by the LORD will return.
They will enter Jerusalem* singing,
crowned with everlasting joy.

51:3 Hebrew *Zion;* also in 51:16. 51:9 Hebrew *You slew Rahab; you pierced the dragon.* Rahab is the name of a mythical sea monster that represents chaos in ancient literature. The name is used here as a poetic name for Egypt. 51:11 Hebrew *Zion.*

Sorrow and mourning will disappear,
and they will be filled with joy and gladness.

12 "I, yes I, am the one who comforts you.
So why are you afraid of mere humans,
who wither like the grass and disappear?
13 Yet you have forgotten the LORD, your Creator,
the one who stretched out the sky like a canopy
and laid the foundations of the earth.
Will you remain in constant dread of human oppressors?
Will you continue to fear the anger of your enemies?
Where is their fury and anger now?
It is gone!
14 Soon all you captives will be released!
Imprisonment, starvation, and death will not
be your fate!
15 For I am the LORD your God,
who stirs up the sea, causing its waves to roar.
My name is the LORD of Heaven's Armies.
16 And I have put my words in your mouth
and hidden you safely in my hand.
I stretched out* the sky like a canopy
and laid the foundations of the earth.
I am the one who says to Israel,
'You are my people!'"

17 Wake up, wake up, O Jerusalem!
You have drunk the cup of the LORD's fury.
You have drunk the cup of terror,
tipping out its last drops.
18 Not one of your children is left alive
to take your hand and guide you.
19 These two calamities have fallen on you:
desolation and destruction, famine and war.
And who is left to sympathize with you?
Who is left to comfort you?*
20 For your children have fainted and lie in the streets,
helpless as antelopes caught in a net.
The LORD has poured out his fury;
God has rebuked them.

21 But now listen to this, you afflicted ones
who sit in a drunken stupor,
though not from drinking wine.
22 This is what the Sovereign LORD,
your God and Defender, says:
"See, I have taken the terrible cup from your hands.
You will drink no more of my fury.
23 Instead, I will hand that cup to your tormentors,

51:16 As in Syriac version (see also 51:13); Hebrew reads *planted.* 51:19 As in Dead Sea Scrolls and Greek, Latin, and Syriac versions; Masoretic Text reads *How can I comfort you?*

Reflect on this passage

those who said, 'We will trample you into the dust
and walk on your backs.'"

Deliverance for Jerusalem

52 1 Wake up, wake up, O Zion!
Clothe yourself with strength.
Put on your beautiful clothes, O holy city of Jerusalem,
for unclean and godless people will enter your gates no longer.
2 Rise from the dust, O Jerusalem.
Sit in a place of honor.
Remove the chains of slavery from your neck,
O captive daughter of Zion.
3 For this is what the LORD says:
"When I sold you into exile,
I received no payment.
Now I can redeem you
without having to pay for you."

4 This is what the Sovereign LORD says: "Long ago my people chose to
live in Egypt. Now they are oppressed by Assyria. 5 What is this?" asks the
LORD. "Why are my people enslaved again? Those who rule them shout in
exultation.* My name is blasphemed all day long.* 6 But I will reveal my name
to my people, and they will come to know its power. Then at last they will
recognize that I am the one who speaks to them."

7 How beautiful on the mountains
are the feet of the messenger who brings good news,
the good news of peace and salvation,
the news that the God of Israel* reigns!
8 The watchmen shout and sing with joy,
for before their very eyes
they see the LORD returning to Jerusalem.*
9 Let the ruins of Jerusalem break into joyful song,
for the LORD has comforted his people.
He has redeemed Jerusalem.
10 The LORD has demonstrated his holy power
before the eyes of all the nations.
All the ends of the earth will see
the victory of our God.

11 Get out! Get out and leave your captivity,
where everything you touch is unclean.
Get out of there and purify yourselves,
you who carry home the sacred objects of the LORD.
12 You will not leave in a hurry,
running for your lives.
For the LORD will go ahead of you;
yes, the God of Israel will protect you from behind.

52:5a As in Dead Sea Scrolls; Masoretic Text reads *Those who rule them wail.* 52:5b Greek version reads *The Gentiles continually blaspheme my name because of you.* Compare Rom 2:24. 52:7 Hebrew *of Zion.* 52:8 Hebrew *to Zion.*

Make a Difference 52:7

Beautiful Feet

Feet can be really ugly. Bunions and calluses, hair and veins, nails and knobs–these things can combine to make feet look pretty gross. Add athlete's foot or some dank odor to the equation, and you might need some pretty strong spray to just get through the day.

There might be a chance even for the most stinky, nastiest feet though. The Bible mentions, both in the Old Testament and in the New Testament, that there is a way to make even the lowest part of a person's life look gorgeous. Feet look good when they are used for their proper purpose, which is to carry God's good message to this world. In other words, when you hear that Jesus saves people from sin through his work on the cross, you use your feet to run around and proclaim that good news. This has happened for thousands of years, and God wants you to be a part of his news team.

Difference Maker

To share the good news about what Jesus has done, where do your feet need to go today? (If you need ideas on how to share Jesus with others, search for some ministries that share Jesus.)

The LORD's Suffering Servant

13 See, my servant will prosper;
he will be highly exalted.
14 But many were amazed when they saw him.*
His face was so disfigured he seemed hardly human,
and from his appearance, one would scarcely know he was a man.
15 And he will startle* many nations.
Kings will stand speechless in his presence.
For they will see what they had not been told;
they will understand what they had not heard about.*

53 1 Who has believed our message?
To whom has the LORD revealed his powerful arm?
2 My servant grew up in the LORD's presence like a tender green shoot,
like a root in dry ground.
There was nothing beautiful or majestic about his appearance,
nothing to attract us to him.
3 He was despised and rejected—
a man of sorrows, acquainted with deepest grief.
We turned our backs on him and looked the other way.
He was despised, and we did not care.

4 Yet it was our weaknesses he carried;
it was our sorrows* that weighed him down.
And we thought his troubles were a punishment from God,
a punishment for his own sins!
5 But he was pierced for our rebellion,
crushed for our sins.
He was beaten so we could be whole.
He was whipped so we could be healed.
6 All of us, like sheep, have strayed away.
We have left God's paths to follow our own.
Yet the LORD laid on him
the sins of us all.

7 He was oppressed and treated harshly,
yet he never said a word.
He was led like a lamb to the slaughter.
And as a sheep is silent before the shearers,
he did not open his mouth.
8 Unjustly condemned,
he was led away.*
No one cared that he died without descendants,
that his life was cut short in midstream.*
But he was struck down
for the rebellion of my people.

Question 53:4

When people looked at Jesus, they dismissed him. He wasn't what they expected. They thought he was just another Messiah contestant who would be booed off the stage of history. Even worse, they looked at him and thought he deserved the ridicule and punishment he received. How do people regularly dismiss Jesus today?

Question 53:8

Jesus died for your rebellion. Romans 5:8 says that God showed his great love for you by sending Christ to die for you while you were still a sinner. Have you accepted the salvation that Jesus offers you? If you never have, now is your chance. Turn to the back of this Bible and go through the section called "How to Accept Jesus as Your Lord and Savior."

52:14 As in Syriac version; Hebrew reads *you.* **52:15a** Or *cleanse.* **52:15b** Greek version reads *Those who have never been told about him will see, / and those who have never heard of him will understand.* Compare Rom 15:21. **53:4** Or *Yet it was our sicknesses he carried; / it was our diseases.* **53:8a** Greek version reads *He was humiliated and received no justice.* Compare Acts 8:33. **53:8b** Or *As for his contemporaries, / who cared that his life was cut short in midstream?* Greek version reads *Who can speak of his descendants? / For his life was taken from the earth.* Compare Acts 8:33.

The Difference Isaiah 53 Makes

Make a Difference 53:3

Turned Backs

If you had been in the crowd the day Jesus was crucified, what would you have done? Would you have yelled at him? Would you have denied the miracles that your own eyes had seen him do? Would you have looked at the open slices across his back, and would you have patronized him or felt a pang of pity? When somebody spit on him, would you have laughed, or would you have silently watched it unfold? When he collapsed under the weight of the cross, would you have stepped out of the crowd to help him lift it back up? Perhaps you wouldn't have participated in any of it at all. Maybe you would have fled town, overcome with fear and grief. Afraid or unwilling to honestly confront the rejection absorbed by the Savior, people still turn their backs on Jesus to this day. Ironically, that's why he carried the cross through the crowd.

Difference Maker

Jesus carried your sorrow. What sorrow can you carry for someone today?

Make a Difference 53:5

Beauty Marks

The wounds of Jesus are beauty marks. After his resurrection, Jesus presented himself to one of his followers, a man named Thomas, a man who doubted whether the resurrection had actually happened. To prove who he was, though, Jesus showed Thomas the nail scars in his hands and feet and the spear wound in his side. Not pretty. Certainly terrible. Definitely beautiful.

Even in his resurrected state, Jesus chose to keep his scars. They mean everything to him. His wounds show his story, a story that is woven with more love and intentionality than the world had ever understood before. The Creator of the universe, the one who had been rejected, was crushed to bring life. His scars are evidence of this good news.

Difference Maker

What wounds do you carry today? What healing do you need from Jesus? How can Jesus use your story to reveal the good news of what he can do?

Make a Difference 53:6

Sheep

When people chart their own path, they crisscross and crush one another and create a chaotic, cacophonous confusion in life. God made life so much simpler than that. "Follow me," he said. "Here's how: Listen to my voice. Stay close. If you do that, I'll feed you and take care of you. I'll defend you and give you a home." No, people, like sheep, just feel a magnetic pull to *baa* their way around boulders and into thickets and wander into the jaws of lions. Thankfully, Jesus is the Good Shepherd who knows that his sheep are prone to wander and who is willing to lay down his own life to save them.

Difference Maker

Simplify your life. Get rid of things that complicate your direction or distract you from following Jesus.

Make a Difference 53:7

Quiet Posture

Jesus could have talked back, but he didn't. He didn't retaliate when he was accused of blasphemy and evil. He just took it when he was whipped and beaten and mockingly forced to wear a robe and crown of thorns. He even carried the cross down the crowded road on the way to his own execution.

Why didn't he defend himself? He knew where their anger and hatred were leading. He knew it meant his torture and eventual death. He knew they were about to make him a spectacle of shame. His accusers even mocked him for his quiet posture. "Who hit you?" they screamed. "Why don't you call down your angels to save you?" they shrieked.

Had Jesus reacted in revenge against their rejection, the world would not have been saved. No false accuser would withstand the unrestrained power of almighty God. Jesus, in order to defend and rescue humanity, chose a quiet posture and said nothing.

Difference Maker

In the next twenty-four hours, identify a situation in which you could use quiet restraint to make a difference in someone's life.

Make a Difference 53:9

Uncompromised

Just because you do what is right doesn't mean that you will be treated fairly. In fact, some of the best people in history were mistreated because they were doing what was right. How committed are you to doing right? If the right road gets tough, will you keep going?

In the future, when people talk about you, will they be inspired by your example? Will your story encourage them to live with integrity in the face of opposition? It takes tremendous courage to continue to do what is right in the face of adversity. The world needs uncompromised people who stand for what is right, no matter what.

Jesus pursued the right path and paid a severe price. The world is forever grateful that he didn't join the wrong march but instead chose to walk to the cross. Imagine how pessimistic this Bible would be if he had compromised himself and not gone to the cross!

Difference Maker

Anticipate what difficult situations you might be in today. Pray that Jesus will give you his integrity to do what is right.

Make a Difference

53:10

Good Plan

One of the most startling lines in the Bible is found in Isaiah 53:10. It says that everything that happened to God's Suffering Servant—the crushing and grieving, the carrying of humanity's sin and disdain—was all a part of the Lord's "good plan" for his Son. How is someone—someone innocent—being betrayed, falsely accused, tortured, and executed a good plan? That certainly sounds like a very bad idea, right?

The "good" in the plan, however, is the key. God created everything good, but because death was brought to creation through sin, Jesus took it all upon himself through the cross so that he could offer forgiveness and new life. In other words, God's rescue blueprint called for the terrible things that happened to Jesus in order to restore good to this earth. As a result of what Jesus did, the day of crucifixion became known as Good Friday, and the day of resurrection would prove victory over death.

Difference Maker

On a piece of paper, brainstorm all that is good that Jesus offers through the cross. Which of these things would be life-changing for someone you know?

9 He had done no wrong
and had never deceived anyone.
But he was buried like a criminal;
he was put in a rich man's grave.

10 But it was the LORD's good plan to crush him
and cause him grief.
Yet when his life is made an offering for sin,
he will have many descendants.
He will enjoy a long life,
and the LORD's good plan will prosper in his hands.
11 When he sees all that is accomplished by his anguish,
he will be satisfied.
And because of his experience,
my righteous servant will make it possible
for many to be counted righteous,
for he will bear all their sins.
12 I will give him the honors of a victorious soldier,
because he exposed himself to death.
He was counted among the rebels.
He bore the sins of many and interceded for rebels.

Future Glory for Jerusalem

54 1 "Sing, O childless woman,
you who have never given birth!
Break into loud and joyful song, O Jerusalem,
you who have never been in labor.
For the desolate woman now has more children
than the woman who lives with her husband,"
says the LORD.
2 "Enlarge your house; build an addition.
Spread out your home, and spare no expense!
3 For you will soon be bursting at the seams.
Your descendants will occupy other nations
and resettle the ruined cities.

4 "Fear not; you will no longer live in shame.
Don't be afraid; there is no more disgrace for you.
You will no longer remember the shame of your youth
and the sorrows of widowhood.
5 For your Creator will be your husband;
the LORD of Heaven's Armies is his name!
He is your Redeemer, the Holy One of Israel,
the God of all the earth.
6 For the LORD has called you back from your grief—
as though you were a young wife abandoned by her husband,"
says your God.
7 "For a brief moment I abandoned you,
but with great compassion I will take you back.
8 In a burst of anger I turned my face away for a little while.

But with everlasting love I will have compassion on you,"
says the LORD, your Redeemer.

9 "Just as I swore in the time of Noah
that I would never again let a flood cover the earth,
so now I swear
that I will never again be angry and punish you.
10 For the mountains may move
and the hills disappear,
but even then my faithful love for you will remain.
My covenant of blessing will never be broken,"
says the LORD, who has mercy on you.

11 "O storm-battered city,
troubled and desolate!
I will rebuild you with precious jewels
and make your foundations from lapis lazuli.
12 I will make your towers of sparkling rubies,
your gates of shining gems,
and your walls of precious stones.
13 I will teach all your children,
and they will enjoy great peace.
14 You will be secure under a government that is just and fair.
Your enemies will stay far away.
You will live in peace,
and terror will not come near.
15 If any nation comes to fight you,
it is not because I sent them.
Whoever attacks you will go down in defeat.

16 "I have created the blacksmith
who fans the coals beneath the forge
and makes the weapons of destruction.
And I have created the armies that destroy.
17 But in that coming day
no weapon turned against you will succeed.
You will silence every voice
raised up to accuse you.
These benefits are enjoyed by the servants of the LORD;
their vindication will come from me.
I, the LORD, have spoken!

Invitation to the LORD's Salvation

55 1 "Is anyone thirsty?
Come and drink—
even if you have no money!
Come, take your choice of wine or milk—
it's all free!
2 Why spend your money on food that does not give you strength?
Why pay for food that does you no good?

Prayer **55:1**

Lord God, I am thirsty. Lord, I am poor of spirit. I have come to listen to you today. Amen.

Listen to me, and you will eat what is good.
You will enjoy the finest food.

3 "Come to me with your ears wide open.
Listen, and you will find life.
I will make an everlasting covenant with you.
I will give you all the unfailing love I promised to David.
4 See how I used him to display my power among the peoples.
I made him a leader among the nations.
5 You also will command nations you do not know,
and peoples unknown to you will come running to obey,
because I, the LORD your God,
the Holy One of Israel, have made you glorious."

6 Seek the LORD while you can find him.
Call on him now while he is near.
7 Let the wicked change their ways
and banish the very thought of doing wrong.
Let them turn to the LORD that he may have mercy on them.
Yes, turn to our God, for he will forgive generously.

8 "My thoughts are nothing like your thoughts," says the LORD.
"And my ways are far beyond anything you could imagine.
9 For just as the heavens are higher than the earth,
so my ways are higher than your ways
and my thoughts higher than your thoughts.

10 "The rain and snow come down from the heavens
and stay on the ground to water the earth.
They cause the grain to grow,
producing seed for the farmer
and bread for the hungry.
11 It is the same with my word.
I send it out, and it always produces fruit.
It will accomplish all I want it to,
and it will prosper everywhere I send it.
12 You will live in joy and peace.
The mountains and hills will burst into song,
and the trees of the field will clap their hands!
13 Where once there were thorns, cypress trees will grow.
Where nettles grew, myrtles will sprout up.
These events will bring great honor to the LORD's name;
they will be an everlasting sign of his power and love."

Blessings for All Nations

56 This is what the LORD says:

"Be just and fair to all.
Do what is right and good,
for I am coming soon to rescue you

and to display my righteousness among you.
2 Blessed are all those
who are careful to do this.
Blessed are those who honor my Sabbath days of rest
and keep themselves from doing wrong.

3 "Don't let foreigners who commit themselves to the LORD say,
'The LORD will never let me be part of his people.'
And don't let the eunuchs say,
'I'm a dried-up tree with no children and no future.'
4 For this is what the LORD says:
I will bless those eunuchs
who keep my Sabbath days holy
and who choose to do what pleases me
and commit their lives to me.
5 I will give them—within the walls of my house—
a memorial and a name
far greater than sons and daughters could give.
For the name I give them is an everlasting one.
It will never disappear!

6 "I will also bless the foreigners who commit themselves to the LORD,
who serve him and love his name,
who worship him and do not desecrate the Sabbath day of rest,
and who hold fast to my covenant.
7 I will bring them to my holy mountain of Jerusalem
and will fill them with joy in my house of prayer.
I will accept their burnt offerings and sacrifices,
because my Temple will be called a house of prayer for all nations.
8 For the Sovereign LORD,
who brings back the outcasts of Israel, says:
I will bring others, too,
besides my people Israel."

Sinful Leaders Condemned

9 Come, wild animals of the field!
Come, wild animals of the forest!
Come and devour my people!
10 For the leaders of my people—
the LORD's watchmen, his shepherds—
are blind and ignorant.
They are like silent watchdogs
that give no warning when danger comes.
They love to lie around, sleeping and dreaming.
11 Like greedy dogs, they are never satisfied.
They are ignorant shepherds,
all following their own path
and intent on personal gain.
12 "Come," they say, "let's get some wine and have a party.
Let's all get drunk.

Encouragements from these verses

Then tomorrow we'll do it again
and have an even bigger party!"

57 1 Good people pass away;
the godly often die before their time.
But no one seems to care or wonder why.
No one seems to understand
that God is protecting them from the evil to come.
2 For those who follow godly paths
will rest in peace when they die.

Idolatrous Worship Condemned

3 "But you—come here, you witches' children,
you offspring of adulterers and prostitutes!
4 Whom do you mock,
making faces and sticking out your tongues?
You children of sinners and liars!
5 You worship your idols with great passion
beneath the oaks and under every green tree.
You sacrifice your children down in the valleys,
among the jagged rocks in the cliffs.
6 Your gods are the smooth stones in the valleys.
You worship them with liquid offerings and grain offerings.
They, not I, are your inheritance.
Do you think all this makes me happy?
7 You have committed adultery on every high mountain.
There you have worshiped idols
and have been unfaithful to me.
8 You have put pagan symbols
on your doorposts and behind your doors.
You have left me
and climbed into bed with these detestable gods.
You have committed yourselves to them.
You love to look at their naked bodies.
9 You have gone to Molech*
with olive oil and many perfumes,
sending your agents far and wide,
even to the world of the dead.*
10 You grew weary in your search,
but you never gave up.
Desire gave you renewed strength,
and you did not grow weary.

11 "Are you afraid of these idols?
Do they terrify you?
Is that why you have lied to me
and forgotten me and my words?
Is it because of my long silence
that you no longer fear me?

57:9a Or *to the king.* **57:9b** Hebrew *to Sheol.*

12 Now I will expose your so-called good deeds.
None of them will help you.
13 Let's see if your idols can save you
when you cry to them for help.
Why, a puff of wind can knock them down!
If you just breathe on them, they fall over!
But whoever trusts in me will inherit the land
and possess my holy mountain."

God Forgives the Repentant

14 God says, "Rebuild the road!
Clear away the rocks and stones
so my people can return from captivity."
15 The high and lofty one who lives in eternity,
the Holy One, says this:
"I live in the high and holy place
with those whose spirits are contrite and humble.
I restore the crushed spirit of the humble
and revive the courage of those with repentant hearts.
16 For I will not fight against you forever;
I will not always be angry.
If I were, all people would pass away—
all the souls I have made.
17 I was angry,
so I punished these greedy people.
I withdrew from them,
but they kept going on their own stubborn way.
18 I have seen what they do,
but I will heal them anyway!
I will lead them.
I will comfort those who mourn,
19 bringing words of praise to their lips.
May they have abundant peace, both near and far,"
says the LORD, who heals them.
20 "But those who still reject me are like the restless sea,
which is never still
but continually churns up mud and dirt.
21 There is no peace for the wicked,"
says my God.

True and False Worship

58 1 "Shout with the voice of a trumpet blast.
Shout aloud! Don't be timid.
Tell my people Israel* of their sins!
2 Yet they act so pious!
They come to the Temple every day
and seem delighted to learn all about me.
They act like a righteous nation
that would never abandon the laws of its God.

58:1 Hebrew *Jacob.* See note on 14:1.

What God is saying to us

They ask me to take action on their behalf,
pretending they want to be near me.
3 'We have fasted before you!' they say.
'Why aren't you impressed?
We have been very hard on ourselves,
and you don't even notice it!'

"I will tell you why!" I respond.
"It's because you are fasting to please yourselves.
Even while you fast,
you keep oppressing your workers.
4 What good is fasting
when you keep on fighting and quarreling?
This kind of fasting
will never get you anywhere with me.
5 You humble yourselves
by going through the motions of penance,
bowing your heads
like reeds bending in the wind.
You dress in burlap
and cover yourselves with ashes.
Is this what you call fasting?
Do you really think this will please the LORD?

6 "No, this is the kind of fasting I want:
Free those who are wrongly imprisoned;
lighten the burden of those who work for you.
Let the oppressed go free,
and remove the chains that bind people.
7 Share your food with the hungry,
and give shelter to the homeless.
Give clothes to those who need them,
and do not hide from relatives who need your help.

8 "Then your salvation will come like the dawn,
and your wounds will quickly heal.
Your godliness will lead you forward,
and the glory of the LORD will protect you from behind.
9 Then when you call, the LORD will answer.
'Yes, I am here,' he will quickly reply.

"Remove the heavy yoke of oppression.
Stop pointing your finger and spreading vicious rumors!
10 Feed the hungry,
and help those in trouble.
Then your light will shine out from the darkness,
and the darkness around you will be as bright as noon.
11 The LORD will guide you continually,
giving you water when you are dry
and restoring your strength.

Make a Difference

58:3-7

Treat People Well

Imagine a religious man entering the room, sweat beading down his brow, feverish "fainthood" (false + sainthood = fainthood) in his eyes, declaring dramatically in a dry, raspy voice, "Oh, I am so burdened because I am fasting for the Lord."

God doesn't think it's cool for people to intentionally malnourish themselves to get attention. He looks away in disgust from that kind of theater.

God created you to live altruistically in the patterns of your life. If someone is wronged, give up your own interests to pursue freedom for them. If someone is working too hard on your behalf, take their extra burden upon yourself. If someone needs something that you have in abundance, then give it to them. The bottom line is that we are to give up things on behalf of others because Jesus gave up his life for us.

Difference Maker

Think of somebody in one of the categories listed in Isaiah 58:6. What can you give up today that would help their cause?

Make a Difference

58:10

Feed the Hungry

Jesus is on a mission. He listens for the cry of the hungry and leans into the mess of those who are in trouble. He looks for darkness and pierces it with his brilliance. He searches the rubble for signs of those who are trapped. He works with precision to remove the concrete and rebar and beams crushing them. He attends to wounds and orchestrates restoration efforts.

You will be like a well-watered garden,
like an ever-flowing spring.
12 Some of you will rebuild the deserted ruins of
your cities.
Then you will be known as a rebuilder of walls
and a restorer of homes.

13 "Keep the Sabbath day holy.
Don't pursue your own interests on that day,
but enjoy the Sabbath
and speak of it with delight as the LORD's holy day.
Honor the Sabbath in everything you do on that day,
and don't follow your own desires or talk idly.
14 Then the LORD will be your delight.
I will give you great honor
and satisfy you with the inheritance I promised to your
ancestor Jacob.
I, the LORD, have spoken!"

Warnings against Sin

59 1 Listen! The LORD's arm is not too weak to save you,
nor is his ear too deaf to hear you call.
2 It's your sins that have cut you off from God.
Because of your sins, he has turned away
and will not listen anymore.
3 Your hands are the hands of murderers,
and your fingers are filthy with sin.
Your lips are full of lies,
and your mouth spews corruption.

4 No one cares about being fair and honest.
The people's lawsuits are based on lies.
They conceive evil deeds
and then give birth to sin.
5 They hatch deadly snakes
and weave spiders' webs.
Whoever eats their eggs will die;
whoever cracks them will hatch a viper.
6 Their webs can't be made into clothing,
and nothing they do is productive.
All their activity is filled with sin,
and violence is their trademark.
7 Their feet run to do evil,
and they rush to commit murder.
They think only about sinning.
Misery and destruction always follow them.
8 They don't know where to find peace
or what it means to be just and good.
They have mapped out crooked roads,
and no one who follows them knows a moment's peace.

He patiently heals and persistently rejoices when he sees people find life through his hands.

Difference Maker

There is plenty of rescue work to do. What a privileged calling you have. Make arrangements for some friends to join you at a food-packing agency.

Make a Difference

58:13

Sabbath

Followers of Jesus are asked to do a lot of good things, like treating people well, caring for those in need, and feeding those who are hungry. There is one task that, at first glance, seems out of sync with the rest. Like the others, it's a task that requires great effort, but it is not an exertion of work. It is the pursuit of rest.

This busy, achievement-based culture of our time too often overlooks rest. Rest might be a neglected practice in your own life like it is for many people around you. People make up for missing rest by binging on naps, drinking alcohol, or being lazy. That's not what God wants for us. God wants Sabbath, a day set aside in the rhythm of each week, to focus the heart and mind on God and others. Sabbath is a type of restoration that reorients the soul to be ready to serve in the good work of following Jesus in the six days that follow.

Difference Maker

Pick a day this week to honor the Sabbath.

9 So there is no justice among us,
and we know nothing about right living.
We look for light but find only darkness.
We look for bright skies but walk in gloom.
10 We grope like the blind along a wall,
feeling our way like people without eyes.
Even at brightest noontime,
we stumble as though it were dark.
Among the living,
we are like the dead.
11 We growl like hungry bears;
we moan like mournful doves.
We look for justice, but it never comes.
We look for rescue, but it is far away from us.
12 For our sins are piled up before God
and testify against us.
Yes, we know what sinners we are.
13 We know we have rebelled and have denied the LORD.
We have turned our backs on our God.
We know how unfair and oppressive we have been,
carefully planning our deceitful lies.
14 Our courts oppose the righteous,
and justice is nowhere to be found.
Truth stumbles in the streets,
and honesty has been outlawed.
15 Yes, truth is gone,
and anyone who renounces evil is attacked.

The LORD looked and was displeased
to find there was no justice.
16 He was amazed to see that no one intervened
to help the oppressed.
So he himself stepped in to save them with his
strong arm,
and his justice sustained him.
17 He put on righteousness as his body armor
and placed the helmet of salvation on his head.
He clothed himself with a robe of vengeance
and wrapped himself in a cloak of divine passion.
18 He will repay his enemies for their evil deeds.
His fury will fall on his foes.
He will pay them back even to the ends of the earth.
19 In the west, people will respect the name of the LORD;
in the east, they will glorify him.
For he will come like a raging flood tide
driven by the breath of the LORD.*

20 "The Redeemer will come to Jerusalem
to buy back those in Israel

59:19 Or *When the enemy comes like a raging flood tide, / the Spirit of the LORD will drive him back.*

who have turned from their sins,"*
says the LORD.

21 "And this is my covenant with them," says the LORD. "My Spirit will
not leave them, and neither will these words I have given you. They will be
on your lips and on the lips of your children and your children's children
forever. I, the LORD, have spoken!

Future Glory for Jerusalem

60 1 "Arise, Jerusalem! Let your light shine for all to see.
For the glory of the LORD rises to shine on you.
2 Darkness as black as night covers all the nations
of the earth,
but the glory of the LORD rises and appears over you.
3 All nations will come to your light;
mighty kings will come to see your radiance.

4 "Look and see, for everyone is coming home!
Your sons are coming from distant lands;
your little daughters will be carried home.
5 Your eyes will shine,
and your heart will thrill with joy,
for merchants from around the world will come to you.
They will bring you the wealth of many lands.
6 Vast caravans of camels will converge on you,
the camels of Midian and Ephah.
The people of Sheba will bring gold and frankincense
and will come worshiping the LORD.
7 The flocks of Kedar will be given to you,
and the rams of Nebaioth will be brought for my altars.
I will accept their offerings,
and I will make my Temple glorious.

8 "And what do I see flying like clouds to Israel,
like doves to their nests?
9 They are ships from the ends of the earth,
from lands that trust in me,
led by the great ships of Tarshish.
They are bringing the people of Israel home from far away,
carrying their silver and gold.
They will honor the LORD your God,
the Holy One of Israel,
for he has filled you with splendor.

10 "Foreigners will come to rebuild your towns,
and their kings will serve you.
For though I have destroyed you in my anger,
I will now have mercy on you through my grace.

59:20 Hebrew *The Redeemer will come to Zion / to buy back those in Jacob / who have turned from their sins.* Greek version reads *The one who rescues will come on behalf of Zion, / and he will turn Jacob away from ungodliness.* Compare Rom 11:26.

Drop your brilliant thoughts here

11 Your gates will stay open day and night
to receive the wealth of many lands.
The kings of the world will be led as captives
in a victory procession.
12 For the nations that refuse to serve you
will be destroyed.

13 "The glory of Lebanon will be yours—
the forests of cypress, fir, and pine—
to beautify my sanctuary.
My Temple will be glorious!
14 The descendants of your tormentors
will come and bow before you.
Those who despised you
will kiss your feet.
They will call you the City of the LORD,
and Zion of the Holy One of Israel.

15 "Though you were once despised and hated,
with no one traveling through you,
I will make you beautiful forever,
a joy to all generations.
16 Powerful kings and mighty nations
will satisfy your every need,
as though you were a child
nursing at the breast of a queen.
You will know at last that I, the LORD,
am your Savior and your Redeemer,
the Mighty One of Israel.*
17 I will exchange your bronze for gold,
your iron for silver,
your wood for bronze,
and your stones for iron.
I will make peace your leader
and righteousness your ruler.
18 Violence will disappear from your land;
the desolation and destruction of war will end.
Salvation will surround you like city walls,
and praise will be on the lips of all who enter there.

19 "No longer will you need the sun to shine by day,
nor the moon to give its light by night,
for the LORD your God will be your everlasting light,
and your God will be your glory.
20 Your sun will never set;
your moon will not go down.
For the LORD will be your everlasting light.
Your days of mourning will come to an end.
21 All your people will be righteous.

60:16 Hebrew *of Jacob.* See note on 14:1.

Story Arc **61:1–2**

Jesus

Hundreds of years before Jesus was born, Israel was suffering under the weight of bad decisions and oppressive nations. However, God had good news for them. He would send a Messiah, his servant, who would restore people to freedom. This messianic Servant-King would focus his rule on healing, forgiving, and rebuilding a nation that was released from the chains of oppression. Ultimately, this was fulfilled in the reign of Jesus Christ, but it is also fulfilled in the way that we serve others through the good news of his kingdom. Jesus would later open to this passage, read it aloud, and declare that it was fulfilled (Luke 4:14–21).

Jer 1:1–3 ►

They will possess their land forever,
for I will plant them there with my own hands
in order to bring myself glory.
22 The smallest family will become a thousand people,
and the tiniest group will become a mighty nation.
At the right time, I, the LORD, will make it happen."

Good News for the Oppressed

61 1 The Spirit of the Sovereign LORD is upon me,
for the LORD has anointed me
to bring good news to the poor.
He has sent me to comfort the brokenhearted
and to proclaim that captives will be released
and prisoners will be freed.*
2 He has sent me to tell those who mourn
that the time of the LORD's favor has come,*
and with it, the day of God's anger against their enemies.
3 To all who mourn in Israel,*
he will give a crown of beauty for ashes,
a joyous blessing instead of mourning,
festive praise instead of despair.
In their righteousness, they will be like great oaks
that the LORD has planted for his own glory.

4 They will rebuild the ancient ruins,
repairing cities destroyed long ago.
They will revive them,
though they have been deserted for many generations.
5 Foreigners will be your servants.
They will feed your flocks
and plow your fields
and tend your vineyards.
6 You will be called priests of the LORD,
ministers of our God.
You will feed on the treasures of the nations
and boast in their riches.
7 Instead of shame and dishonor,
you will enjoy a double share of honor.
You will possess a double portion of prosperity in your land,
and everlasting joy will be yours.

8 "For I, the LORD, love justice.
I hate robbery and wrongdoing.
I will faithfully reward my people for their suffering
and make an everlasting covenant with them.
9 Their descendants will be recognized
and honored among the nations.
Everyone will realize that they are a people
the LORD has blessed."

61:1 Greek version reads *and the blind will see.* Compare Luke 4:18. 61:2 Or *to proclaim the acceptable year of the LORD.* 61:3 Hebrew *in Zion.*

Make a Difference 61:3

Transplanted

Trees are meant to be rooted in fertile, well-watered soil, but many trees find themselves stuck in pots that are too small, too shallow, and too dry. What they need is for someone to take them out of the pots and replant them in ground where they can grow.

People need to be planted in a place where they can flourish. They don't need a restricted basin, superficial soil, or bare ground. The good news is that people who are stuck, who are struggling to grow, can be transplanted by Jesus to become strong and flourish. This process is not always easy, and it most certainly costs the planter. Still, it also provides freedom for those with constrained hearts, release for the imprisoned, and beautiful joy for those who yearn for abundant life. It is a powerful message—and it takes root when those who were once stuck begin to find their freedom and identity in Christ.

Difference Maker

Purchase a small plant in a pot. Place it in a window. Take care of it for a few months, making sure it gets adequate water and sunlight. Then, in the spring, plant it in fertile soil.

10 I am overwhelmed with joy in the LORD my God!
For he has dressed me with the clothing of salvation
and draped me in a robe of righteousness.
I am like a bridegroom dressed for his wedding
or a bride with her jewels.
11 The Sovereign LORD will show his justice to the nations
of the world.
Everyone will praise him!
His righteousness will be like a garden in early spring,
with plants springing up everywhere.

Isaiah's Prayer for Jerusalem

62 1 Because I love Zion,
I will not keep still.
Because my heart yearns for Jerusalem,
I cannot remain silent.
I will not stop praying for her
until her righteousness shines like the dawn,
and her salvation blazes like a burning torch.
2 The nations will see your righteousness.
World leaders will be blinded by your glory.
And you will be given a new name
by the LORD's own mouth.
3 The LORD will hold you in his hand for all to see—
a splendid crown in the hand of God.
4 Never again will you be called "The Forsaken City"*
or "The Desolate Land."*
Your new name will be "The City of God's Delight"*
and "The Bride of God,"*
for the LORD delights in you
and will claim you as his bride.
5 Your children will commit themselves to you,
O Jerusalem,
just as a young man commits himself to his bride.
Then God will rejoice over you
as a bridegroom rejoices over his bride.

6 O Jerusalem, I have posted watchmen on your walls;
they will pray day and night, continually.
Take no rest, all you who pray to the LORD.
7 Give the LORD no rest until he completes his work,
until he makes Jerusalem the pride of the earth.
8 The LORD has sworn to Jerusalem by his own strength:
"I will never again hand you over to your enemies.
Never again will foreign warriors come
and take away your grain and new wine.
9 You raised the grain, and you will eat it,
praising the LORD.

62:4a Hebrew *Azubah,* which means "forsaken." 62:4b Hebrew *Shemamah,* which means "desolate." 62:4c Hebrew *Hephzibah,* which means "my delight is in her." 62:4d Hebrew *Beulah,* which means "married."

Within the courtyards of the Temple,
you yourselves will drink the wine you have pressed."

10 Go out through the gates!
Prepare the highway for my people to return!
Smooth out the road; pull out the boulders;
raise a flag for all the nations to see.
11 The LORD has sent this message to every land:
"Tell the people of Israel,*
'Look, your Savior is coming.
See, he brings his reward with him as he comes.'"
12 They will be called "The Holy People"
and "The People Redeemed by the LORD."
And Jerusalem will be known as "The Desirable Place"
and "The City No Longer Forsaken."

Question 62:11

If you have the chance to share with a friend what this "message to every land" was all about, how would you explain it?

Judgment against the LORD's Enemies

63 1 Who is this who comes from Edom,
from the city of Bozrah,
with his clothing stained red?
Who is this in royal robes,
marching in his great strength?

"It is I, the LORD, announcing your salvation!
It is I, the LORD, who has the power to save!"

2 Why are your clothes so red,
as if you have been treading out grapes?

3 "I have been treading the winepress alone;
no one was there to help me.
In my anger I have trampled my enemies
as if they were grapes.
In my fury I have trampled my foes.
Their blood has stained my clothes.
4 For the time has come for me to avenge my people,
to ransom them from their oppressors.
5 I was amazed to see that no one intervened
to help the oppressed.
So I myself stepped in to save them with my strong arm,
and my wrath sustained me.
6 I crushed the nations in my anger
and made them stagger and fall to the ground,
spilling their blood upon the earth."

Praise for Deliverance

7 I will tell of the LORD's unfailing love.
I will praise the LORD for all he has done.

62:11 Hebrew *Tell the daughter of Zion.*

I will rejoice in his great goodness to Israel,
which he has granted according to his mercy and love.
8 He said, "They are my very own people.
Surely they will not betray me again."
And he became their Savior.
9 In all their suffering he also suffered,
and he personally* rescued them.
In his love and mercy he redeemed them.
He lifted them up and carried them
through all the years.
10 But they rebelled against him
and grieved his Holy Spirit.
So he became their enemy
and fought against them.

11 Then they remembered those days of old
when Moses led his people out of Egypt.
They cried out, "Where is the one who brought Israel through the sea,
with Moses as their shepherd?
Where is the one who sent his Holy Spirit
to be among his people?
12 Where is the one whose power was displayed
when Moses lifted up his hand—
the one who divided the sea before them,
making himself famous forever?
13 Where is the one who led them through the bottom of the sea?
They were like fine stallions
racing through the desert, never stumbling.
14 As with cattle going down into a peaceful valley,
the Spirit of the LORD gave them rest.
You led your people, LORD,
and gained a magnificent reputation."

Prayer for Mercy and Pardon

15 LORD, look down from heaven;
look from your holy, glorious home, and see us.
Where is the passion and the might
you used to show on our behalf?
Where are your mercy and compassion now?
16 Surely you are still our Father!
Even if Abraham and Jacob* would disown us,
LORD, you would still be our Father.
You are our Redeemer from ages past.
17 LORD, why have you allowed us to turn from your path?
Why have you given us stubborn hearts so we no longer fear you?
Return and help us, for we are your servants,
the tribes that are your special possession.
18 How briefly your holy people possessed your holy place,
and now our enemies have destroyed it.

63:9 Hebrew *and the angel of his presence.* 63:16 Hebrew *Israel.* See note on 14:1.

19 Sometimes it seems as though we never belonged to you,
as though we had never been known as your people.

64 1*Oh, that you would burst from the heavens and come down!
How the mountains would quake in your presence!
2*As fire causes wood to burn
and water to boil,
your coming would make the nations tremble.
Then your enemies would learn the reason for your fame!
3 When you came down long ago,
you did awesome deeds beyond our highest expectations.
And oh, how the mountains quaked!
4 For since the world began,
no ear has heard
and no eye has seen a God like you,
who works for those who wait for him!
5 You welcome those who gladly do good,
who follow godly ways.
But you have been very angry with us,
for we are not godly.
We are constant sinners;
how can people like us be saved?
6 We are all infected and impure with sin.
When we display our righteous deeds,
they are nothing but filthy rags.
Like autumn leaves, we wither and fall,
and our sins sweep us away like the wind.
7 Yet no one calls on your name
or pleads with you for mercy.
Therefore, you have turned away from us
and turned us over* to our sins.

8 And yet, O LORD, you are our Father.
We are the clay, and you are the potter.
We all are formed by your hand.
9 Don't be so angry with us, LORD.
Please don't remember our sins forever.
Look at us, we pray,
and see that we are all your people.
10 Your holy cities are destroyed.
Zion is a wilderness;
yes, Jerusalem is a desolate ruin.
11 The holy and beautiful Temple
where our ancestors praised you
has been burned down,
and all the things of beauty are destroyed.
12 After all this, LORD, must you still refuse to help us?
Will you continue to be silent and punish us?

64:1 In the Hebrew text this verse is included in 63:19. 64:2 Verses 64:2-12 are numbered 64:1-11 in Hebrew text. 64:7 As in Greek, Syriac, and Aramaic versions; Hebrew reads *melted us.*

Prayer 64:1

Lord, give me a heart that prays like this! Amen.

Question 65:1

The Lord is ready to be found. Are you looking for him?

Judgment and Final Salvation

65 The LORD says,

"I was ready to respond, but no one asked for help.
I was ready to be found, but no one was looking for me.
I said, 'Here I am, here I am!'
to a nation that did not call on my name.*
2 All day long I opened my arms to a rebellious people.*
But they follow their own evil paths
and their own crooked schemes.
3 All day long they insult me to my face
by worshiping idols in their sacred gardens.
They burn incense on pagan altars.
4 At night they go out among the graves,
worshiping the dead.
They eat the flesh of pigs
and make stews with other forbidden foods.
5 Yet they say to each other,
'Don't come too close or you will defile me!
I am holier than you!'
These people are a stench in my nostrils,
an acrid smell that never goes away.

6 "Look, my decree is written out* in front of me:
I will not stand silent;
I will repay them in full!
Yes, I will repay them—
7 both for their own sins
and for those of their ancestors,"
says the LORD.
"For they also burned incense on the mountains
and insulted me on the hills.
I will pay them back in full!

8 "But I will not destroy them all,"
says the LORD.
"For just as good grapes are found among a cluster
of bad ones
(and someone will say, 'Don't throw them all away—
some of those grapes are good!'),
so I will not destroy all Israel.
For I still have true servants there.
9 I will preserve a remnant of the people of Israel*
and of Judah to possess my land.
Those I choose will inherit it,
and my servants will live there.
10 The plain of Sharon will again be filled with flocks

65:1 Or *to a nation that did not bear my name.* 65:1-2 Greek version reads *I was found by people who were not looking for me. / I showed myself to those who were not asking for me. / All day long I opened my arms to them, / but they were disobedient and rebellious.* Compare Rom 10:20-21. 65:6 Or *their sins are written out;* Hebrew reads *it stands written.* 65:9 Hebrew *remnant of Jacob.* See note on 14:1.

for my people who have searched for me,
and the valley of Achor will be a place to pasture herds.

11 "But because the rest of you have forsaken the LORD
and have forgotten his Temple,
and because you have prepared feasts to honor the
god of Fate
and have offered mixed wine to the god of Destiny,
12 now I will 'destine' you for the sword.
All of you will bow down before the executioner.
For when I called, you did not answer.
When I spoke, you did not listen.
You deliberately sinned—before my very eyes—
and chose to do what you know I despise."

13 Therefore, this is what the Sovereign LORD says:
"My servants will eat,
but you will starve.
My servants will drink,
but you will be thirsty.
My servants will rejoice,
but you will be sad and ashamed.
14 My servants will sing for joy,
but you will cry in sorrow and despair.
15 Your name will be a curse word among my people,
for the Sovereign LORD will destroy you
and will call his true servants by another name.
16 All who invoke a blessing or take an oath
will do so by the God of truth.
For I will put aside my anger
and forget the evil of earlier days.

17 "Look! I am creating new heavens and a new earth,
and no one will even think about the old ones anymore.
18 Be glad; rejoice forever in my creation!
And look! I will create Jerusalem as a place of happiness.
Her people will be a source of joy.
19 I will rejoice over Jerusalem
and delight in my people.
And the sound of weeping and crying
will be heard in it no more.

20 "No longer will babies die when only a few days old.
No longer will adults die before they have lived a full life.
No longer will people be considered old at one hundred!
Only the cursed will die that young!
21 In those days people will live in the houses they build
and eat the fruit of their own vineyards.
22 Unlike the past, invaders will not take their houses
and confiscate their vineyards.

Question 66:2-3

Stop for a moment and examine what delights you. Would you be in God's blessed category (66:2) or in God's unaccepted category (66:3)?

For my people will live as long as trees,
and my chosen ones will have time to enjoy their hard-won gains.
23 They will not work in vain,
and their children will not be doomed to misfortune.
For they are people blessed by the LORD,
and their children, too, will be blessed.
24 I will answer them before they even call to me.
While they are still talking about their needs,
I will go ahead and answer their prayers!
25 The wolf and the lamb will feed together.
The lion will eat hay like a cow.
But the snakes will eat dust.
In those days no one will be hurt or destroyed on my holy mountain.
I, the LORD, have spoken!"

66 This is what the LORD says:

"Heaven is my throne,
and the earth is my footstool.
Could you build me a temple as good as that?
Could you build me such a resting place?
2 My hands have made both heaven and earth;
they and everything in them are mine.*
I, the LORD, have spoken!

"I will bless those who have humble and contrite hearts,
who tremble at my word.
3 But those who choose their own ways—
delighting in their detestable sins—
will not have their offerings accepted.
When such people sacrifice a bull,
it is no more acceptable than a human sacrifice.
When they sacrifice a lamb,
it's as though they had sacrificed a dog!
When they bring an offering of grain,
they might as well offer the blood of a pig.
When they burn frankincense,
it's as if they had blessed an idol.
4 I will send them great trouble—
all the things they feared.
For when I called, they did not answer.
When I spoke, they did not listen.
They deliberately sinned before my very eyes
and chose to do what they know I despise."

5 Hear this message from the LORD,
all you who tremble at his words:

66:2 As in Greek, Latin, and Syriac versions; Hebrew reads *these things are.*

"Your own people hate you
and throw you out for being loyal to my name.
'Let the LORD be honored!' they scoff.
'Be joyful in him!'
But they will be put to shame.
6 What is all the commotion in the city?
What is that terrible noise from the Temple?
It is the voice of the LORD
taking vengeance against his enemies.

7 "Before the birth pains even begin,
Jerusalem gives birth to a son.
8 Who has ever seen anything as strange as this?
Who ever heard of such a thing?
Has a nation ever been born in a single day?
Has a country ever come forth in a mere moment?
But by the time Jerusalem's* birth pains begin,
her children will be born.
9 Would I ever bring this nation to the point of birth
and then not deliver it?" asks the LORD.
"No! I would never keep this nation from being born,"
says your God.

10 "Rejoice with Jerusalem!
Be glad with her, all you who love her
and all you who mourn for her.
11 Drink deeply of her glory
even as an infant drinks at its mother's comforting breasts."

12 This is what the LORD says:
"I will give Jerusalem a river of peace and prosperity.
The wealth of the nations will flow to her.
Her children will be nursed at her breasts,
carried in her arms, and held on her lap.
13 I will comfort you there in Jerusalem
as a mother comforts her child."

14 When you see these things, your heart will rejoice.
You will flourish like the grass!
Everyone will see the LORD's hand of blessing on his servants—
and his anger against his enemies.
15 See, the LORD is coming with fire,
and his swift chariots roar like a whirlwind.
He will bring punishment with the fury of his anger
and the flaming fire of his hot rebuke.
16 The LORD will punish the world by fire
and by his sword.
He will judge the earth,
and many will be killed by him.

66:8 Hebrew *Zion's*.

17 "Those who 'consecrate' and 'purify' themselves in a sacred garden
with its idol in the center—feasting on pork and rats and other detestable
meats—will come to a terrible end," says the LORD.
18 "I can see what they are doing, and I know what they are thinking. So I
will gather all nations and peoples together, and they will see my glory. 19 I
will perform a sign among them. And I will send those who survive to be
messengers to the nations—to Tarshish, to the Libyans* and Lydians* (who
are famous as archers), to Tubal and Greece,* and to all the lands beyond the
sea that have not heard of my fame or seen my glory. There they will declare
my glory to the nations. 20 They will bring the remnant of your people back
from every nation. They will bring them to my holy mountain in Jerusalem
as an offering to the LORD. They will ride on horses, in chariots and wagons,
and on mules and camels," says the LORD. 21 "And I will appoint some of them
to be my priests and Levites. I, the LORD, have spoken!

22 "As surely as my new heavens and earth will remain,
so will you always be my people,
with a name that will never disappear,"
says the LORD.
23 "All humanity will come to worship me
from week to week
and from month to month.
24 And as they go out, they will see
the dead bodies of those who have rebelled against me.
For the worms that devour them will never die,
and the fire that burns them will never go out.
All who pass by
will view them with utter horror."

66:19a As in some Greek manuscripts, which read *Put* [that is, *Libya*]; Hebrew reads *Pul.*
66:19b Hebrew *Lud.* **66:19c** Hebrew *Javan.*

Jeremiah Introduction

Jeremiah is called the Weeping Prophet. He cried. A lot. All over the place.

In Jeremiah's day, the Israelites had turned away from God. Then God called Jeremiah to speak up and warn God's people to turn back to him. God wanted his people to humble themselves and seek his will for their lives. For forty years, in Israel and Persia and Egypt, Jeremiah proclaimed God's Word and pleaded for God's people to return to their faith in the Lord, and God's people broke Jeremiah's heart.

Many scholars believe Jeremiah was just a teen when God called him to prophesy. At first, he objected and said he was too young for such a big job. Like us, Jeremiah had to find his confidence in the Lord. God equipped him to do the work of a prophet, to preach to the people and implore them to repent. Jeremiah did the job God called him to do not out of anger but from a compassionate desire to save God's people because God loved them.

This book offers a remarkable insight into the personal nature of God. The Lord longs for people to respond to his invitation and draw close to him. Imagine you are like Jeremiah and spend your entire lifetime preaching that same message over and over again to people who ignore your words of warning. This is the most tragic part of the story—for more than a generation, the Israelites refused to heed Jeremiah's message. They wanted to continue in their arrogant ways instead of following the urgent call of God. Jeremiah's tears over the people of Israel reflect God's own grief when his children decide to distrust and disobey.

Jesus had the same heart. As he approached the gravesite of his friend Lazarus, he wept (John 11:35). As he approached Jerusalem and saw the city, he wept over it (Luke 19:41). The Lord is not some irate, temperamental, unforgiving God. He is compassionate. He is merciful. He stretches his arms wide to carry our sorrows.

As you read this book, respond the way Jeremiah would want you to respond. Turn to the Lord and follow his ways. Weep for the lost and cry out for the rescue of this world.

Story Arcs

- Jeremiah
- Micah
- Baruch
- Ebed-melech

Jeremiah

Question 1:7

Do you think you are too young for God to give you a big calling? Explore your thoughts.

Story Arc 1:1-3

● **Jeremiah**

Jeremiah had longevity. We can be tempted to think that influencing this world involves quick scenarios with rapid results. Sometimes, though, making a difference in this world is more like a marathon. Jeremiah showed a long, consistent faithfulness that stood in contrast to the fickle unfaithfulness of the culture around him. Amid violent governments, frightening cultural storms, and war-torn upheavals, Jeremiah walked faithfully. As enemies bore down on Jerusalem and his people were taken away as captives, Jeremiah fell to his knees with a broken heart. As you read the chapters ahead, consider how Jeremiah found the resolve to continue.

Jer 26:12-24 ►

1 These are the words of Jeremiah son of Hilkiah, one of the priests from
the town of Anathoth in the land of Benjamin. 2 The LORD first gave
messages to Jeremiah during the thirteenth year of the reign of Josiah son
of Amon, king of Judah.* 3 The LORD's messages continued throughout the
reign of King Jehoiakim, Josiah's son, until the eleventh year of the reign of
King Zedekiah, another of Josiah's sons. In August* of that eleventh year the
people of Jerusalem were taken away as captives.

Jeremiah's Call and First Visions

4 The LORD gave me this message:

5 "I knew you before I formed you in your mother's womb.
Before you were born I set you apart
and appointed you as my prophet to the nations."

6 "O Sovereign LORD," I said, "I can't speak for you! I'm too young!"
7 The LORD replied, "Don't say, 'I'm too young,' for you must go wherever
I send you and say whatever I tell you. 8 And don't be afraid of the people, for
I will be with you and will protect you. I, the LORD, have spoken!" 9 Then the
LORD reached out and touched my mouth and said,

"Look, I have put my words in your mouth!
10 Today I appoint you to stand up
against nations and kingdoms.
Some you must uproot and tear down,
destroy and overthrow.
Others you must build up
and plant."

11 Then the LORD said to me, "Look, Jeremiah! What do you see?"
And I replied, "I see a branch from an almond tree."
12 And the LORD said, "That's right, and it means that I am watching,* and
I will certainly carry out all my plans."
13 Then the LORD spoke to me again and asked, "What do you see now?"
And I replied, "I see a pot of boiling water, spilling from the north."
14 "Yes," the LORD said, "for terror from the north will boil out on the
people of this land. 15 Listen! I am calling the armies of the kingdoms of the
north to come to Jerusalem. I, the LORD, have spoken!

1:2 The thirteenth year of Josiah's reign was 627 B.C. 1:3 Hebrew *In the fifth month,* of the ancient Hebrew lunar calendar. A number of events in Jeremiah can be cross-checked with dates in surviving Babylonian records and related accurately to our modern calendar. The fifth month in the eleventh year of Zedekiah's reign occurred within the months of August and September 586 B.C. Also see 52:12 and the note there. 1:12 The Hebrew word for "watching" *(shoqed)* sounds like the word for "almond tree" *(shaqed).*

"They will set their thrones
at the gates of the city.
They will attack its walls
and all the other towns of Judah.
16 I will pronounce judgment
on my people for all their evil—
for deserting me and burning incense to other gods.
Yes, they worship idols made with their own hands!

17 "Get up and prepare for action.
Go out and tell them everything I tell you to say.
Do not be afraid of them,
or I will make you look foolish in front of them.
18 For see, today I have made you strong
like a fortified city that cannot be captured,
like an iron pillar or a bronze wall.
You will stand against the whole land—
the kings, officials, priests, and people of Judah.
19 They will fight you, but they will fail.
For I am with you, and I will take care of you.
I, the LORD, have spoken!"

The LORD's Case against His People

2 The LORD gave me another message. He said, 2"Go and shout this mes-
sage to Jerusalem. This is what the LORD says:

"I remember how eager you were to please me
as a young bride long ago,
how you loved me and followed me
even through the barren wilderness.
3 In those days Israel was holy to the LORD,
the first of his children.*
All who harmed his people were declared guilty,
and disaster fell on them.
I, the LORD, have spoken!"

4Listen to the word of the LORD, people of Jacob—all you families of Is-
rael! 5This is what the LORD says:

"What did your ancestors find wrong with me
that led them to stray so far from me?
They worshiped worthless idols,
only to become worthless themselves.
6 They did not ask, 'Where is the LORD
who brought us safely out of Egypt
and led us through the barren wilderness—
a land of deserts and pits,
a land of drought and death,
where no one lives or even travels?'

2:3 Hebrew *the firstfruits of his harvest.*

7 "And when I brought you into a fruitful land
to enjoy its bounty and goodness,
you defiled my land and
corrupted the possession I had promised you.
8 The priests did not ask,
'Where is the LORD?'
Those who taught my word ignored me,
the rulers turned against me,
and the prophets spoke in the name of Baal,
wasting their time on worthless idols.
9 Therefore, I will bring my case against you,"
says the LORD.
"I will even bring charges against your children's children
in the years to come.

10 "Go west and look in the land of Cyprus*;
go east and search through the land of Kedar.
Has anyone ever heard of anything
as strange as this?
11 Has any nation ever traded its gods for new ones,
even though they are not gods at all?
Yet my people have exchanged their glorious God*
for worthless idols!
12 The heavens are shocked at such a thing
and shrink back in horror and dismay,"
says the LORD.
13 "For my people have done two evil things:
They have abandoned me—
the fountain of living water.
And they have dug for themselves cracked cisterns
that can hold no water at all!

The Results of Israel's Sin

14 "Why has Israel become a slave?
Why has he been carried away as plunder?
15 Strong lions have roared against him,
and the land has been destroyed.
The towns are now in ruins,
and no one lives in them anymore.
16 Egyptians, marching from their cities of Memphis* and Tahpanhes,
have destroyed Israel's glory and power.
17 And you have brought this upon yourselves
by rebelling against the LORD your God,
even though he was leading you on the way!

18 "What have you gained by your alliances with Egypt
and your covenants with Assyria?
What good to you are the streams of the Nile*
or the waters of the Euphrates River?*

2:10 Hebrew *Kittim.* 2:11 Hebrew *their glory.* 2:16 Hebrew *Noph.* 2:18a Hebrew *of Shihor,* a branch of the Nile River. 2:18b Hebrew *the river?*

19 Your wickedness will bring its own punishment.
Your turning from me will shame you.
You will see what an evil, bitter thing it is
to abandon the LORD your God and not to fear him.
I, the Lord, the LORD of Heaven's Armies, have spoken!

20 "Long ago I broke the yoke that oppressed you
and tore away the chains of your slavery,
but still you said,
'I will not serve you.'
On every hill and under every green tree,
you have prostituted yourselves by bowing down to idols.
21 But I was the one who planted you,
choosing a vine of the purest stock—the very best.
How did you grow into this corrupt wild vine?
22 No amount of soap or lye can make you clean.
I still see the stain of your guilt.
I, the Sovereign LORD, have spoken!

Israel, an Unfaithful Wife

23 "You say, 'That's not true!
I haven't worshiped the images of Baal!'
But how can you say that?
Go and look in any valley in the land!
Face the awful sins you have done.
You are like a restless female camel
desperately searching for a mate.
24 You are like a wild donkey,
sniffing the wind at mating time.
Who can restrain her lust?
Those who desire her don't need to search,
for she goes running to them!
25 When will you stop running?
When will you stop panting after other gods?
But you say, 'Save your breath.
I'm in love with these foreign gods,
and I can't stop loving them now!'

26 "Israel is like a thief
who feels shame only when he gets caught.
They, their kings, officials, priests, and prophets—
all are alike in this.
27 To an image carved from a piece of wood they say,
'You are my father.'
To an idol chiseled from a block of stone they say,
'You are my mother.'
They turn their backs on me,
but in times of trouble they cry out to me,
'Come and save us!'
28 But why not call on these gods you have made?

How this passage impacts me

When trouble comes, let them save you if they can!
For you have as many gods
as there are towns in Judah.
29 Why do you accuse me of doing wrong?
You are the ones who have rebelled,"
says the LORD.
30 "I have punished your children,
but they did not respond to my discipline.
You yourselves have killed your prophets
as a lion kills its prey.

31 "O my people, listen to the words of the LORD!
Have I been like a desert to Israel?
Have I been to them a land of darkness?
Why then do my people say, 'At last we are free from God!
We don't need him anymore!'
32 Does a young woman forget her jewelry,
or a bride her wedding dress?
Yet for years on end
my people have forgotten me.

33 "How you plot and scheme to win your lovers.
Even an experienced prostitute could learn from you!
34 Your clothing is stained with the blood of the innocent and the poor,
though you didn't catch them breaking into your houses!
35 And yet you say,
'I have done nothing wrong.
Surely God isn't angry with me!'
But now I will punish you severely
because you claim you have not sinned.
36 First here, then there—
you flit from one ally to another asking for help.
But your new friends in Egypt will let you down,
just as Assyria did before.
37 In despair, you will be led into exile
with your hands on your heads,
for the LORD has rejected the nations you trust.
They will not help you at all.

3 1 "If a man divorces a woman
and she goes and marries someone else,
he will not take her back again,
for that would surely corrupt the land.
But you have prostituted yourself with many lovers,
so why are you trying to come back to me?"
says the LORD.
2 "Look at the shrines on every hilltop.
Is there any place you have not been defiled
by your adultery with other gods?
You sit like a prostitute beside the road waiting for a customer.

You sit alone like a nomad in the desert.
You have polluted the land with your prostitution
and your wickedness.
3 That's why even the spring rains have failed.
For you are a brazen prostitute and completely shameless.
4 Yet you say to me,
'Father, you have been my guide since my youth.
5 Surely you won't be angry forever!
Surely you can forget about it!'
So you talk,
but you keep on doing all the evil you can."

Judah Follows Israel's Example

6 During the reign of King Josiah, the LORD said to me, "Have you seen what
fickle Israel has done? Like a wife who commits adultery, Israel has wor-
shiped other gods on every hill and under every green tree. 7 I thought, 'After
she has done all this, she will return to me.' But she did not return, and her
faithless sister Judah saw this. 8 She saw* that I divorced faithless Israel be-
cause of her adultery. But that treacherous sister Judah had no fear, and now
she, too, has left me and given herself to prostitution. 9 Israel treated it all so
lightly—she thought nothing of committing adultery by worshiping idols
made of wood and stone. So now the land has been polluted. 10 But despite
all this, her faithless sister Judah has never sincerely returned to me. She has
only pretended to be sorry. I, the LORD, have spoken!"

Hope for Wayward Israel

11 Then the LORD said to me, "Even faithless Israel is less guilty than treach-
erous Judah! 12 Therefore, go and give this message to Israel.* This is what
the LORD says:

"O Israel, my faithless people,
come home to me again,
for I am merciful.
I will not be angry with you forever.
13 Only acknowledge your guilt.
Admit that you rebelled against the LORD your God
and committed adultery against him
by worshiping idols under every green tree.
Confess that you refused to listen to my voice.
I, the LORD, have spoken!

14 "Return home, you wayward children,"
says the LORD,
"for I am your master.
I will bring you back to the land of Israel*—
one from this town and two from that family—
from wherever you are scattered.
15 And I will give you shepherds after my own heart,
who will guide you with knowledge and understanding.

3:8 As in Dead Sea Scrolls, one Greek manuscript, and Syriac version; Masoretic Text reads *I saw.* 3:12 Hebrew *toward the north.* 3:14 Hebrew *to Zion.*

Make a Difference 3:6

Confession

One of the major issues Jeremiah had to confront was the astonishing infidelity of Israel's faith. The people had rejected God in favor of other gods and other rulers. If they were ever going to have a chance to get right with God, they would first have to admit their condition. Confession is an essential step in the process of correcting wrongs.

First John 1:9 declares that "if we confess our sins," then God "is faithful and just to forgive us our sins and to cleanse us from all wickedness." That's good news! Even after all we have done, God is more than willing to forgive us and start again.

However, 1 John 1:10 states, "If we claim we have not sinned, we are calling God a liar and showing that his word has no place in our hearts." That's the bad news. If we refuse to admit our condition, then how can God forgive us? It was this sad reality that devastated Jeremiah's heart for years.

Difference Maker

Confess your sins to God. Ask him to forgive you and invite him to cleanse you from everything that goes against his ways.

Question 3:22

These opening chapters of Jeremiah offer a remarkably personal insight into the relational heart of the Lord. It's disarming how personal the Lord is. Looking back over the first three chapters of Jeremiah, what have you learned about God's heart? What aspects of God's heart do you need to develop in your own?

16 "And when your land is once more filled with people," says the LORD, "you
will no longer wish for 'the good old days' when you possessed the Ark of the
LORD's Covenant. You will not miss those days or even remember them, and
there will be no need to rebuild the Ark. 17 In that day Jerusalem will be known
as 'The Throne of the LORD.' All nations will come there to honor the LORD.
They will no longer stubbornly follow their own evil desires. 18 In those days
the people of Judah and Israel will return together from exile in the north.
They will return to the land I gave your ancestors as an inheritance forever.

19 "I thought to myself,
'I would love to treat you as my own children!'
I wanted nothing more than to give you this beautiful land—
the finest possession in the world.
I looked forward to your calling me 'Father,'
and I wanted you never to turn from me.
20 But you have been unfaithful to me, you people of Israel!
You have been like a faithless wife who leaves her husband.
I, the LORD, have spoken."

21 Voices are heard high on the windswept mountains,
the weeping and pleading of Israel's people.
For they have chosen crooked paths
and have forgotten the LORD their God.

22 "My wayward children," says the LORD,
"come back to me, and I will heal your wayward hearts."

"Yes, we're coming," the people reply,
"for you are the LORD our God.
23 Our worship of idols on the hills
and our religious orgies on the mountains
are a delusion.
Only in the LORD our God
will Israel ever find salvation.
24 From childhood we have watched
as everything our ancestors worked for—
their flocks and herds, their sons and daughters—
was squandered on a delusion.
25 Let us now lie down in shame
and cover ourselves with dishonor,
for we and our ancestors have sinned
against the LORD our God.
From our childhood to this day
we have never obeyed him."

4 1 "O Israel," says the LORD,
"if you wanted to return to me, you could.
You could throw away your detestable idols
and stray away no more.
2 Then when you swear by my name, saying,

'As surely as the LORD lives,'
you could do so
with truth, justice, and righteousness.
Then you would be a blessing to the nations of the world,
and all people would come and praise my name."

Coming Judgment against Judah

3 This is what the LORD says to the people of Judah and Jerusalem:

"Plow up the hard ground of your hearts!
Do not waste your good seed among thorns.
4 O people of Judah and Jerusalem,
surrender your pride and power.
Change your hearts before the LORD,*
or my anger will burn like an unquenchable fire
because of all your sins.

5 "Shout to Judah, and broadcast to Jerusalem!
Tell them to sound the alarm throughout the land:
'Run for your lives!
Flee to the fortified cities!'
6 Raise a signal flag as a warning for Jerusalem*:
'Flee now! Do not delay!'
For I am bringing terrible destruction upon you
from the north."

7 A lion stalks from its den,
a destroyer of nations.
It has left its lair and is headed your way.
It's going to devastate your land!
Your towns will lie in ruins,
with no one living in them anymore.
8 So put on clothes of mourning
and weep with broken hearts,
for the fierce anger of the LORD
is still upon us.

9 "In that day," says the LORD,
"the king and the officials will tremble in fear.
The priests will be struck with horror,
and the prophets will be appalled."

10 Then I said, "O Sovereign LORD,
the people have been deceived by what you said,
for you promised peace for Jerusalem.
But the sword is held at their throats!"

11 The time is coming when the LORD will say
to the people of Jerusalem,

4:4 Hebrew *Circumcise yourselves to the LORD, and take away the foreskins of your heart.* 4:6 Hebrew *Zion.*

Prayer 4:19

Lord, break my heart for others who are walking away from you. Give me the courage to sit in that pain so that I will be compelled to cry out to them. Amen.

"My dear people, a burning wind is blowing in from the desert,
and it's not a gentle breeze useful for winnowing grain.
12 It is a roaring blast sent by me!
Now I will pronounce your destruction!"

13 Our enemy rushes down on us like storm clouds!
His chariots are like whirlwinds.
His horses are swifter than eagles.
How terrible it will be, for we are doomed!
14 O Jerusalem, cleanse your heart
that you may be saved.
How long will you harbor
your evil thoughts?
15 Your destruction has been announced
from Dan and the hill country of Ephraim.

16 "Warn the surrounding nations
and announce this to Jerusalem:
The enemy is coming from a distant land,
raising a battle cry against the towns of Judah.
17 They surround Jerusalem like watchmen around a field,
for my people have rebelled against me,"
says the LORD.
18 "Your own actions have brought this upon you.
This punishment is bitter, piercing you to the heart!"

Jeremiah Weeps for His People

19 My heart, my heart—I writhe in pain!
My heart pounds within me! I cannot be still.
For I have heard the blast of enemy trumpets
and the roar of their battle cries.
20 Waves of destruction roll over the land,
until it lies in complete desolation.
Suddenly my tents are destroyed;
in a moment my shelters are crushed.
21 How long must I see the battle flags
and hear the trumpets of war?

22 "My people are foolish
and do not know me," says the LORD.
"They are stupid children
who have no understanding.
They are clever enough at doing wrong,
but they have no idea how to do right!"

Jeremiah's Vision of Coming Disaster

23 I looked at the earth, and it was empty and formless.
I looked at the heavens, and there was no light.
24 I looked at the mountains and hills,
and they trembled and shook.

25 I looked, and all the people were gone.
All the birds of the sky had flown away.
26 I looked, and the fertile fields had become a wilderness.
The towns lay in ruins,
crushed by the LORD's fierce anger.

27 This is what the LORD says:
"The whole land will be ruined,
but I will not destroy it completely.
28 The earth will mourn
and the heavens will be draped in black
because of my decree against my people.
I have made up my mind and will not change it."

29 At the noise of charioteers and archers,
the people flee in terror.
They hide in the bushes
and run for the mountains.
All the towns have been abandoned—
not a person remains!
30 What are you doing,
you who have been plundered?
Why do you dress up in beautiful clothing
and put on gold jewelry?
Why do you brighten your eyes with mascara?
Your primping will do you no good!
The allies who were your lovers
despise you and seek to kill you.

31 I hear a cry, like that of a woman in labor,
the groans of a woman giving birth to her first child.
It is beautiful Jerusalem*
gasping for breath and crying out,
"Help! I'm being murdered!"

The Sins of Judah

5 1 "Run up and down every street in Jerusalem," says the LORD.
"Look high and low; search throughout the city!
If you can find even one just and honest person,
I will not destroy the city.
2 But even when they are under oath,
saying, 'As surely as the LORD lives,'
they are still telling lies!"

3 LORD, you are searching for honesty.
You struck your people,
but they paid no attention.
You crushed them,
but they refused to be corrected.

4:31 Hebrew *the daughter of Zion.*

Make a Difference 5:5

Yoke

A yoke is a bulky, uncomfortable harness placed on animals' shoulders to direct them. In Jeremiah's day, and in ours, people have taken upon themselves heavy, oppressive burdens of life. Jeremiah is shocked when the people of Judah still choose to throw off God's yoke, refusing to be directed by God's ways.

In Matthew 11:28-30, Jesus said, "Come to me, all of you who are weary and carry heavy burdens, and I will give you rest. Take my yoke upon you. Let me teach you, because I am humble and gentle at heart, and you will find rest for your souls. For my yoke is easy to bear, and the burden I give you is light."

Difference Maker

All humans must carry a burden. As a prayerful reflection, spend several minutes writing down the difference between the heavy burden of arrogance and sin and the light burden of following Jesus.

They are determined, with faces set like stone;
they have refused to repent.

4 Then I said, "But what can we expect from the poor?
They are ignorant.
They don't know the ways of the LORD.
They don't understand God's laws.
5 So I will go and speak to their leaders.
Surely they know the ways of the LORD
and understand God's laws."
But the leaders, too, as one man,
had thrown off God's yoke
and broken his chains.
6 So now a lion from the forest will attack them;
a wolf from the desert will pounce on them.
A leopard will lurk near their towns,
tearing apart any who dare to venture out.
For their rebellion is great,
and their sins are many.

7 "How can I pardon you?
For even your children have turned from me.
They have sworn by gods that are not gods at all!
I fed my people until they were full.
But they thanked me by committing adultery
and lining up at the brothels.
8 They are well-fed, lusty stallions,
each neighing for his neighbor's wife.
9 Should I not punish them for this?" says the LORD.
"Should I not avenge myself against such a nation?

10 "Go down the rows of the vineyards and destroy the grapevines,
leaving a scattered few alive.
Strip the branches from the vines,
for these people do not belong to the LORD.
11 The people of Israel and Judah
are full of treachery against me,"
says the LORD.
12 "They have lied about the LORD
and said, 'He won't bother us!
No disasters will come upon us.
There will be no war or famine.
13 God's prophets are all windbags
who don't really speak for him.
Let their predictions of disaster fall on themselves!'"

14 Therefore, this is what the LORD God of Heaven's Armies says:

"Because the people are talking like this,
my messages will flame out of your mouth

and burn the people like kindling wood.
15 O Israel, I will bring a distant nation against you,"
says the LORD.
"It is a mighty nation,
an ancient nation,
a people whose language you do not know,
whose speech you cannot understand.
16 Their weapons are deadly;
their warriors are mighty.
17 They will devour the food of your harvest;
they will devour your sons and daughters.
They will devour your flocks and herds;
they will devour your grapes and figs.
And they will destroy your fortified towns,
which you think are so safe.

18 "Yet even in those days I will not blot you out completely," says the
LORD. 19 "And when your people ask, 'Why did the LORD our God do all this
to us?' you must reply, 'You rejected him and gave yourselves to foreign
gods in your own land. Now you will serve foreigners in a land that is not
your own.'

A Warning for God's People

20 "Make this announcement to Israel,*
and say this to Judah:
21 Listen, you foolish and senseless people,
with eyes that do not see
and ears that do not hear.
22 Have you no respect for me?
Why don't you tremble in my presence?
I, the LORD, define the ocean's sandy shoreline
as an everlasting boundary that the waters cannot cross.
The waves may toss and roar,
but they can never pass the boundaries I set.
23 But my people have stubborn and rebellious hearts.
They have turned away and abandoned me.
24 They do not say from the heart,
'Let us live in awe of the LORD our God,
for he gives us rain each spring and fall,
assuring us of a harvest when the time is right.'
25 Your wickedness has deprived you of these wonderful blessings.
Your sin has robbed you of all these good things.

26 "Among my people are wicked men
who lie in wait for victims like a hunter hiding in a blind.
They continually set traps
to catch people.
27 Like a cage filled with birds,

5:20 Hebrew *to the house of Jacob.* The names "Jacob" and "Israel" are often interchanged throughout the Old Testament, referring sometimes to the individual patriarch and sometimes to the nation.

their homes are filled with evil plots.
And now they are great and rich.
28 They are fat and sleek,
and there is no limit to their wicked deeds.
They refuse to provide justice to orphans
and deny the rights of the poor.
29 Should I not punish them for this?" says the LORD.
"Should I not avenge myself against such a nation?
30 A horrible and shocking thing
has happened in this land—
31 the prophets give false prophecies,
and the priests rule with an iron hand.
Worse yet, my people like it that way!
But what will you do when the end comes?

Jerusalem's Last Warning

6 1 "Run for your lives, you people of Benjamin!
Get out of Jerusalem!
Sound the alarm in Tekoa!
Send up a signal at Beth-hakkerem!
A powerful army is coming from the north,
coming with disaster and destruction.
2 O Jerusalem,* you are my beautiful and delicate daughter—
but I will destroy you!
3 Enemies will surround you, like shepherds camped around the city.
Each chooses a place for his troops to devour.
4 They shout, 'Prepare for battle!
Attack at noon!'
'No, it's too late; the day is fading,
and the evening shadows are falling.'
5 'Well then, let's attack at night
and destroy her palaces!'"

6 This is what the LORD of Heaven's Armies says:
"Cut down the trees for battering rams.
Build siege ramps against the walls of Jerusalem.
This is the city to be punished,
for she is wicked through and through.
7 She spouts evil like a fountain.
Her streets echo with the sounds of violence and destruction.
I always see her sickness and sores.
8 Listen to this warning, Jerusalem,
or I will turn from you in disgust.
Listen, or I will turn you into a heap of ruins,
a land where no one lives."

9 This is what the LORD of Heaven's Armies says:
"Even the few who remain in Israel
will be picked over again,

6:2 Hebrew *Daughter of Zion.*

as when a harvester checks each vine a second time
to pick the grapes that were missed."

Judah's Constant Rebellion

10 To whom can I give warning?
Who will listen when I speak?
Their ears are closed,
and they cannot hear.
They scorn the word of the LORD.
They don't want to listen at all.
11 So now I am filled with the LORD's fury.
Yes, I am tired of holding it in!

"I will pour out my fury on children playing
in the streets
and on gatherings of young men,
on husbands and wives
and on those who are old and gray.
12 Their homes will be turned over to their enemies,
as will their fields and their wives.
For I will raise my powerful fist
against the people of this land,"
says the LORD.
13 "From the least to the greatest,
their lives are ruled by greed.
From prophets to priests,
they are all frauds.
14 They offer superficial treatments
for my people's mortal wound.
They give assurances of peace
when there is no peace.
15 Are they ashamed of their disgusting actions?
Not at all—they don't even know how to blush!
Therefore, they will lie among the slaughtered.
They will be brought down when I punish them,"
says the LORD.

Judah Rejects the LORD's Way

16 This is what the LORD says:
"Stop at the crossroads and look around.
Ask for the old, godly way, and walk in it.
Travel its path, and you will find rest for your souls.
But you reply, 'No, that's not the road we want!'
17 I posted watchmen over you who said,
'Listen for the sound of the alarm.'
But you replied,
'No! We won't pay attention!'

18 "Therefore, listen to this, all you nations.
Take note of my people's situation.

What I want to remember

19 Listen, all the earth!
I will bring disaster on my people.
It is the fruit of their own schemes,
because they refuse to listen to me.
They have rejected my word.
20 There's no use offering me sweet frankincense from Sheba.
Keep your fragrant calamus imported from distant lands!
I will not accept your burnt offerings.
Your sacrifices have no pleasing aroma for me."

21 Therefore, this is what the LORD says:
"I will put obstacles in my people's path.
Fathers and sons will both fall over them.
Neighbors and friends will die together."

An Invasion from the North

22 This is what the LORD says:
"Look! A great army coming from the north!
A great nation is rising against you from far-off lands.
23 They are armed with bows and spears.
They are cruel and show no mercy.
They sound like a roaring sea
as they ride forward on horses.
They are coming in battle formation,
planning to destroy you, beautiful Jerusalem.*"

24 We have heard reports about the enemy,
and we wring our hands in fright.
Pangs of anguish have gripped us,
like those of a woman in labor.
25 Don't go out to the fields!
Don't travel on the roads!
The enemy's sword is everywhere
and terrorizes us at every turn!
26 Oh, my people, dress yourselves in burlap
and sit among the ashes.
Mourn and weep bitterly, as for the loss of an only son.
For suddenly the destroying armies will be upon you!

27 "Jeremiah, I have made you a tester of metals,*
that you may determine the quality of my people.
28 They are the worst kind of rebel,
full of slander.
They are as hard as bronze and iron,
and they lead others into corruption.
29 The bellows fiercely fan the flames
to burn out the corruption.
But it does not purify them,
for the wickedness remains.

6:23 Hebrew *daughter of Zion.* 6:27 As in Greek version; Hebrew reads *a tester of my people a fortress.*

30 I will label them 'Rejected Silver,'
for I, the LORD, am discarding them."

Jeremiah Speaks at the Temple

7 The LORD gave another message to Jeremiah. He said, 2 "Go to the en-
trance of the LORD's Temple, and give this message to the people: 'O Ju-
dah, listen to this message from the LORD! Listen to it, all of you who worship
here! 3 This is what the LORD of Heaven's Armies, the God of Israel, says:
"'Even now, if you quit your evil ways, I will let you stay in your own land.
4 But don't be fooled by those who promise you safety simply because the
LORD's Temple is here. They chant, "The LORD's Temple is here! The LORD's
Temple is here!" 5 But I will be merciful only if you stop your evil thoughts
and deeds and start treating each other with justice; 6 only if you stop exploit-
ing foreigners, orphans, and widows; only if you stop your murdering; and
only if you stop harming yourselves by worshiping idols. 7 Then I will let you
stay in this land that I gave to your ancestors to keep forever.
8 "'Don't be fooled into thinking that you will never suffer because the
Temple is here. It's a lie! 9 Do you really think you can steal, murder, commit
adultery, lie, and burn incense to Baal and all those other new gods of yours,
10 and then come here and stand before me in my Temple and chant, "We are
safe!"—only to go right back to all those evils again? 11 Don't you yourselves
admit that this Temple, which bears my name, has become a den of thieves?
Surely I see all the evil going on there. I, the LORD, have spoken!
12 "'Go now to the place at Shiloh where I once put the Tabernacle that bore
my name. See what I did there because of all the wickedness of my people,
the Israelites. 13 While you were doing these wicked things, says the LORD,
I spoke to you about it repeatedly, but you would not listen. I called out to
you, but you refused to answer. 14 So just as I destroyed Shiloh, I will now
destroy this Temple that bears my name, this Temple that you trust in for
help, this place that I gave to you and your ancestors. 15 And I will send you
out of my sight into exile, just as I did your relatives, the people of Israel.*'

Judah's Persistent Idolatry

16 "Pray no more for these people, Jeremiah. Do not weep or pray for them,
and don't beg me to help them, for I will not listen to you. 17 Don't you see
what they are doing throughout the towns of Judah and in the streets of Je-
rusalem? 18 No wonder I am so angry! Watch how the children gather wood
and the fathers build sacrificial fires. See how the women knead dough and
make cakes to offer to the Queen of Heaven. And they pour out liquid of-
ferings to their other idol gods! 19 Am I the one they are hurting?" asks the
LORD. "Most of all, they hurt themselves, to their own shame."
20 So this is what the Sovereign LORD says: "I will pour out my terrible fury
on this place. Its people, animals, trees, and crops will be consumed by the
unquenchable fire of my anger."
21 This is what the LORD of Heaven's Armies, the God of Israel, says: "Take
your burnt offerings and your other sacrifices and eat them yourselves! 22 When
I led your ancestors out of Egypt, it was not burnt offerings and sacrifices I
wanted from them. 23 This is what I told them: 'Obey me, and I will be your
God, and you will be my people. Do everything as I say, and all will be well!'

Question 7:5-7

If someone were to ask you what God cared about, how would 7:5-7 help you answer their question?

7:15 Hebrew *of Ephraim,* referring to the northern kingdom of Israel.

[24]"But my people would not listen to me. They kept doing whatever they
wanted, following the stubborn desires of their evil hearts. They went back-
ward instead of forward. [25]From the day your ancestors left Egypt until now,
I have continued to send my servants, the prophets—day in and day out.
[26]But my people have not listened to me or even tried to hear. They have been
stubborn and sinful—even worse than their ancestors.
[27]"Tell them all this, but do not expect them to listen. Shout out your warn-
ings, but do not expect them to respond. [28]Say to them, 'This is the nation
whose people will not obey the LORD their God and who refuse to be taught.
Truth has vanished from among them; it is no longer heard on their lips.
[29]Shave your head in mourning, and weep alone on the mountains. For the
LORD has rejected and forsaken this generation that has provoked his fury.'

The Valley of Slaughter

[30]"The people of Judah have sinned before my very eyes," says the LORD. "They
have set up their abominable idols right in the Temple that bears my name,
defiling it. [31]They have built pagan shrines at Topheth, the garbage dump in
the valley of Ben-Hinnom, and there they burn their sons and daughters in
the fire. I have never commanded such a horrible deed; it never even crossed
my mind to command such a thing! [32]So beware, for the time is coming," says
the LORD, "when that garbage dump will no longer be called Topheth or the
valley of Ben-Hinnom, but the Valley of Slaughter. They will bury the bodies
in Topheth until there is no more room for them. [33]The bodies of my people
will be food for the vultures and wild animals, and no one will be left to scare
them away. [34]I will put an end to the happy singing and laughter in the streets
of Jerusalem. The joyful voices of bridegrooms and brides will no longer be
heard in the towns of Judah. The land will lie in complete desolation.

8 "In that day," says the LORD, "the enemy will break open the graves of
the kings and officials of Judah, and the graves of the priests, prophets,
and common people of Jerusalem. [2]They will spread out their bones on the
ground before the sun, moon, and stars—the gods my people have loved,
served, and worshiped. Their bones will not be gathered up again or buried
but will be scattered on the ground like manure. [3]And the people of this evil
nation who survive will wish to die rather than live where I will send them.
I, the LORD of Heaven's Armies, have spoken!

Deception by False Prophets

[4]"Jeremiah, say to the people, 'This is what the LORD says:

"'When people fall down, don't they get up again?
When they discover they're on the wrong road, don't they turn back?
[5] Then why do these people stay on their self-destructive path?
Why do the people of Jerusalem refuse to turn back?
They cling tightly to their lies
and will not turn around.
[6] I listen to their conversations
and don't hear a word of truth.
Is anyone sorry for doing wrong?
Does anyone say, "What a terrible thing I have done"?

No! All are running down the path of sin
as swiftly as a horse galloping into battle!
7 Even the stork that flies across the sky
knows the time of her migration,
as do the turtledove, the swallow, and the crane.*
They all return at the proper time each year.
But not my people!
They do not know the LORD's laws.

8 "'How can you say, "We are wise because we have the word
of the LORD,"
when your teachers have twisted it by writing lies?
9 These wise teachers will fall
into the trap of their own foolishness,
for they have rejected the word of the LORD.
Are they so wise after all?
10 I will give their wives to others
and their farms to strangers.
From the least to the greatest,
their lives are ruled by greed.
Yes, even my prophets and priests are like that.
They are all frauds.
11 They offer superficial treatments
for my people's mortal wound.
They give assurances of peace
when there is no peace.
12 Are they ashamed of these disgusting actions?
Not at all—they don't even know how to blush!
Therefore, they will lie among the slaughtered.
They will be brought down when I punish them,
says the LORD.
13 I will surely consume them.
There will be no more harvests of figs and grapes.
Their fruit trees will all die.
Whatever I gave them will soon be gone.
I, the LORD, have spoken!'

14 "Then the people will say,
'Why should we wait here to die?
Come, let's go to the fortified towns and die there.
For the LORD our God has decreed our destruction
and has given us a cup of poison to drink
because we sinned against the LORD.
15 We hoped for peace, but no peace came.
We hoped for a time of healing, but found only terror.'

16 "The snorting of the enemies' warhorses can be heard
all the way from the land of Dan in the north!
The neighing of their stallions makes the whole land tremble.

8:7 The identification of some of these birds is uncertain.

What God wants people to know

Make a Difference

8:18–9:1

Blessed = Mourn

Jeremiah earned his name as the Weeping Prophet. He dived deeply into his suffering soul. He wept—overcome with grief because people refused to turn to the Lord.

Jesus would later say, "God blesses those who mourn" (Matthew 5:4). How can this be true? Mourning is so difficult because it reflects a severe loss of something vital that is now gone and will never come back. Mourning stems from a deep grief, a death of life and hope. Mourning represents a missing opportunity, a broken dream, a fractured relationship. How could Jesus ever say that those who mourn are blessed?

Difference Maker

Write down the things that make you weep. Do they match God's heart for the lost in this world?

They are coming to devour the land and everything in it—
cities and people alike.
17 I will send these enemy troops among you
like poisonous snakes you cannot charm.
They will bite you, and you will die.
I, the LORD, have spoken!"

Jeremiah Weeps for Sinful Judah

18 My grief is beyond healing;
my heart is broken.
19 Listen to the weeping of my people;
it can be heard all across the land.
"Has the LORD abandoned Jerusalem?*" the people ask.
"Is her King no longer there?"

"Oh, why have they provoked my anger with
their carved idols
and their worthless foreign gods?" says the LORD.

20 "The harvest is finished,
and the summer is gone," the people cry,
"yet we are not saved!"

21 I hurt with the hurt of my people.
I mourn and am overcome with grief.
22 Is there no medicine in Gilead?
Is there no physician there?
Why is there no healing
for the wounds of my people?

9 1*If only my head were a pool of water
and my eyes a fountain of tears,
I would weep day and night
for all my people who have been slaughtered.
2*Oh, that I could go away and forget my people
and live in a travelers' shack in the desert.
For they are all adulterers—
a pack of treacherous liars.

Judgment for Disobedience

3 "My people bend their tongues like bows
to shoot out lies.
They refuse to stand up for the truth.
They only go from bad to worse.
They do not know me,"
says the LORD.

4 "Beware of your neighbor!
Don't even trust your brother!

8:19 Hebrew *Zion?* 9:1 Verse 9:1 is numbered 8:23 in Hebrew text. 9:2 Verses 9:2-26 are numbered 9:1-25 in Hebrew text.

For brother takes advantage of brother,
and friend slanders friend.
5 They all fool and defraud each other;
no one tells the truth.
With practiced tongues they tell lies;
they wear themselves out with all their sinning.
6 They pile lie upon lie
and utterly refuse to acknowledge me,"
says the LORD.

7 Therefore, this is what the LORD of Heaven's Armies says:
"See, I will melt them down in a crucible
and test them like metal.
What else can I do with my people?*
8 For their tongues shoot lies like poisoned arrows.
They speak friendly words to their neighbors
while scheming in their heart to kill them.
9 Should I not punish them for this?" says the LORD.
"Should I not avenge myself against such a nation?"

10 I will weep for the mountains
and wail for the wilderness pastures.
For they are desolate and empty of life;
the lowing of cattle is heard no more;
the birds and wild animals have all fled.

11 "I will make Jerusalem into a heap of ruins," says the LORD.
"It will be a place haunted by jackals.
The towns of Judah will be ghost towns,
with no one living in them."

12 Who is wise enough to understand all this? Who has been instructed by the LORD and can explain it to others? Why has the land been so ruined that no one dares to travel through it?

13 The LORD replies, "This has happened because my people have abandoned my instructions; they have refused to obey what I said.
14 Instead, they have stubbornly followed their own desires and worshiped the images of Baal, as their ancestors taught them.
15 So now, this is what the LORD of Heaven's Armies, the God of Israel, says: Look! I will feed them with bitterness and give them poison to drink.
16 I will scatter them around the world, in places they and their ancestors never heard of, and even there I will chase them with the sword until I have destroyed them completely."

Weeping in Jerusalem

17 This is what the LORD of Heaven's Armies says:
"Consider all this, and call for the mourners.
Send for the women who mourn at funerals.
18 Quick! Begin your weeping!
Let the tears flow from your eyes.

9:7 Hebrew *with the daughter of my people?* Greek version reads *with the evil daughter of my people?*

Question 9:24

In Galatians 6:14, the apostle Paul made this declaration: "As for me, may I never boast about anything except the cross of our Lord Jesus Christ. Because of that cross, my interest in this world has been crucified, and the world's interest in me has also died." How does his bold statement compare to this amazing passage in Jeremiah? In what ways do you need to quit boasting about yourself and start boasting more about God's love?

19 Hear the people of Jerusalem* crying in despair,
'We are ruined! We are completely humiliated!
We must leave our land,
because our homes have been torn down.'"

20 Listen, you women, to the words of the LORD;
open your ears to what he has to say.
Teach your daughters to wail;
teach one another how to lament.
21 For death has crept in through our windows
and has entered our mansions.
It has killed off the flower of our youth:
Children no longer play in the streets,
and young men no longer gather in the squares.

22 This is what the LORD says:
"Bodies will be scattered across the fields like clumps of manure,
like bundles of grain after the harvest.
No one will be left to bury them."

23 This is what the LORD says:
"Don't let the wise boast in their wisdom,
or the powerful boast in their power,
or the rich boast in their riches.
24 But those who wish to boast
should boast in this alone:
that they truly know me and understand that I am the LORD
who demonstrates unfailing love
and who brings justice and righteousness to the earth,
and that I delight in these things.
I, the LORD, have spoken!

25 "A time is coming," says the LORD, "when I will punish all those who
are circumcised in body but not in spirit—26 the Egyptians, Edomites, Am-
monites, Moabites, the people who live in the desert in remote places,* and
yes, even the people of Judah. And like all these pagan nations, the people
of Israel also have uncircumcised hearts."

Idolatry Brings Destruction

10 Hear the word that the LORD speaks to you, O Israel! 2 This is what
the LORD says:

"Do not act like the other nations,
who try to read their future in the stars.
Do not be afraid of their predictions,
even though other nations are terrified by them.
3 Their ways are futile and foolish.
They cut down a tree, and a craftsman carves an idol.

9:19 Hebrew *Zion.* 9:26 Or *in the desert and clip the corners of their hair.*

4 They decorate it with gold and silver
and then fasten it securely with hammer and nails
so it won't fall over.
5 Their gods are like
helpless scarecrows in a cucumber field!
They cannot speak,
and they need to be carried because they cannot walk.
Do not be afraid of such gods,
for they can neither harm you nor do you any good."

6 LORD, there is no one like you!
For you are great, and your name is full of power.
7 Who would not fear you, O King of nations?
That title belongs to you alone!
Among all the wise people of the earth
and in all the kingdoms of the world,
there is no one like you.

8 People who worship idols are stupid and foolish.
The things they worship are made of wood!
9 They bring beaten sheets of silver from Tarshish
and gold from Uphaz,
and they give these materials to skillful craftsmen
who make their idols.
Then they dress these gods in royal blue and purple robes
made by expert tailors.
10 But the LORD is the only true God.
He is the living God and the everlasting King!
The whole earth trembles at his anger.
The nations cannot stand up to his wrath.

11 Say this to those who worship other gods: "Your so-called gods, who
did not make the heavens and earth, will vanish from the earth and from
under the heavens."*

12 But the LORD made the earth by his power,
and he preserves it by his wisdom.
With his own understanding
he stretched out the heavens.
13 When he speaks in the thunder,
the heavens roar with rain.
He causes the clouds to rise over the earth.
He sends the lightning with the rain
and releases the wind from his storehouses.
14 The whole human race is foolish and has no knowledge!
The craftsmen are disgraced by the idols they make,
for their carefully shaped works are a fraud.
These idols have no breath or power.
15 Idols are worthless; they are ridiculous lies!

10:11 The original text of this verse is in Aramaic.

Prayer 10:6

Lord, there is no one like you! You are great, and your name is full of power. Amen.

Make a Difference

10:23-24

Direction

Considering that humans were created to walk with God, they have sure spent a lot of time and energy trying to blaze trails without him. It's remarkable that people are so quick to step off the path that God is on. When people walk away from God, they inevitably get disoriented and lost.

What's even more astonishing, perhaps, is that if these lost people were to stop and listen, they would see God's steps and hear his voice. If they had the sense to look for him, they would discover that God had followed them down that rough trail and had been calling out their name. God leaves his stroll in the garden to save people from the minefield they wandered into and usher them back onto his travel plans.

Difference Maker

Go for a walk. With each step, talk to Jesus about your life, your passions, your goals, and your worries. Confide yourself in him, and he will direct your path to the Father.

On the day of reckoning they will all be destroyed.
16 But the God of Israel* is no idol!
He is the Creator of everything that exists,
including Israel, his own special possession.
The LORD of Heaven's Armies is his name!

The Coming Destruction

17 Pack your bags and prepare to leave;
the siege is about to begin.
18 For this is what the LORD says:
"Suddenly, I will fling out
all you who live in this land.
I will pour great troubles upon you,
and at last you will feel my anger."

19 My wound is severe,
and my grief is great.
My sickness is incurable,
but I must bear it.
20 My home is gone,
and no one is left to help me rebuild it.
My children have been taken away,
and I will never see them again.
21 The shepherds of my people have lost their senses.
They no longer seek wisdom from the LORD.
Therefore, they fail completely,
and their flocks are scattered.
22 Listen! Hear the terrifying roar of great armies
as they roll down from the north.
The towns of Judah will be destroyed
and become a haunt for jackals.

Jeremiah's Prayer

23 I know, LORD, that our lives are not our own.
We are not able to plan our own course.
24 So correct me, LORD, but please be gentle.
Do not correct me in anger, for I would die.
25 Pour out your wrath on the nations that refuse to acknowledge you—
on the peoples that do not call upon your name.
For they have devoured your people Israel*;
they have devoured and consumed them,
making the land a desolate wilderness.

Judah's Broken Covenant

11 The LORD gave another message to Jeremiah. He said, 2"Remind
the people of Judah and Jerusalem about the terms of my covenant
with them. 3Say to them, 'This is what the LORD, the God of Israel, says:
Cursed is anyone who does not obey the terms of my covenant! 4For I said
to your ancestors when I brought them out of the iron-smelting furnace of

10:16 Hebrew *the Portion of Jacob.* See note on 5:20. 10:25 Hebrew *devoured Jacob.* See note on 5:20.

Egypt, "If you obey me and do whatever I command you, then you will be
my people, and I will be your God." 5 I said this so I could keep my promise
to your ancestors to give you a land flowing with milk and honey—the land
you live in today.'"

Then I replied, "Amen, LORD! May it be so."

6 Then the LORD said, "Broadcast this message in the streets of Jerusalem.
Go from town to town throughout the land and say, 'Remember the ancient
covenant, and do everything it requires. 7 For I solemnly warned your ances-
tors when I brought them out of Egypt, "Obey me!" I have repeated this
warning over and over to this day, 8 but your ancestors did not listen or even
pay attention. Instead, they stubbornly followed their own evil desires. And
because they refused to obey, I brought upon them all the curses described
in this covenant.'"

9 Again the LORD spoke to me and said, "I have discovered a conspiracy
against me among the people of Judah and Jerusalem. 10 They have returned
to the sins of their ancestors. They have refused to listen to me and are wor-
shiping other gods. Israel and Judah have both broken the covenant I made
with their ancestors. 11 Therefore, this is what the LORD says: I am going to
bring calamity upon them, and they will not escape. Though they beg for
mercy, I will not listen to their cries. 12 Then the people of Judah and Jerusa-
lem will pray to their idols and burn incense before them. But the idols will
not save them when disaster strikes! 13 Look now, people of Judah; you have
as many gods as you have towns. You have as many altars of shame—altars
for burning incense to your god Baal—as there are streets in Jerusalem.

14 "Pray no more for these people, Jeremiah. Do not weep or pray for them,
for I will not listen to them when they cry out to me in distress.

15 "What right do my beloved people have to come to my Temple,
when they have done so many immoral things?
Can their vows and sacrifices prevent their destruction?
They actually rejoice in doing evil!
16 I, the LORD, once called them a thriving olive tree,
beautiful to see and full of good fruit.
But now I have sent the fury of their enemies
to burn them with fire,
leaving them charred and broken.

17 "I, the LORD of Heaven's Armies, who planted this olive tree, have or-
dered it destroyed. For the people of Israel and Judah have done evil, arous-
ing my anger by burning incense to Baal."

A Plot against Jeremiah

18 Then the LORD told me about the plots my enemies were making against
me. 19 I was like a lamb being led to the slaughter. I had no idea that they were
planning to kill me! "Let's destroy this man and all his words," they said.
"Let's cut him down, so his name will be forgotten forever."

20 O LORD of Heaven's Armies,
you make righteous judgments,
and you examine the deepest thoughts and secrets.

Make a Difference 11:5

Amen!

Jeremiah heard God's plans and declared, "Amen, LORD! May it be so." The word *amen* simply means "let it be so." To say amen means you approach God in a posture of willingness to agree with God. *Amen* means align your own heart and your own preferences in respect to God's preferences. *Amen* means to seek a partnership with God's will.

Difference Maker

Take a moment right now to pray. Examine your motives and plans. Do they show an agreement with God's motives and plans? At the end of your prayer, state, declaratively and with confidence, "Amen, Lord."

Question 12:1

Was it okay for Jeremiah to complain to God? What do you think about his complaint?

Let me see your vengeance against them,
for I have committed my cause to you.

21 This is what the LORD says about the men of Anathoth who wanted
me dead. They had said, "We will kill you if you do not stop prophesying
in the LORD's name." 22 So this is what the LORD of Heaven's Armies says
about them: "I will punish them! Their young men will die in battle, and
their boys and girls will starve to death. 23 Not one of these plotters from
Anathoth will survive, for I will bring disaster upon them when their time
of punishment comes."

Jeremiah Questions the LORD's Justice

12 1 LORD, you always give me justice
when I bring a case before you.
So let me bring you this complaint:
Why are the wicked so prosperous?
Why are evil people so happy?
2 You have planted them,
and they have taken root and prospered.
Your name is on their lips,
but you are far from their hearts.
3 But as for me, LORD, you know my heart.
You see me and test my thoughts.
Drag these people away like sheep to be butchered!
Set them aside to be slaughtered!

4 How long must this land mourn?
Even the grass in the fields has withered.
The wild animals and birds have disappeared
because of the evil in the land.
For the people have said,
"The LORD doesn't see what's ahead for us!"

The LORD's Reply to Jeremiah

5 "If racing against mere men makes you tired,
how will you race against horses?
If you stumble and fall on open ground,
what will you do in the thickets near the Jordan?
6 Even your brothers, members of your own family,
have turned against you.
They plot and raise complaints against you.
Do not trust them,
no matter how pleasantly they speak.

7 "I have abandoned my people, my special possession.
I have surrendered my dearest ones to their enemies.
8 My chosen people have roared at me like a lion of the forest,
so I have treated them with contempt.
9 My chosen people act like speckled vultures,*

12:9 Or *speckled hyenas.*

but they themselves are surrounded by vultures.
Bring on the wild animals to pick their corpses clean!

10 "Many rulers have ravaged my vineyard,
trampling down the vines
and turning all its beauty into a barren wilderness.
11 They have made it an empty wasteland;
I hear its mournful cry.
The whole land is desolate,
and no one even cares.
12 On all the bare hilltops,
destroying armies can be seen.
The sword of the LORD devours people
from one end of the nation to the other.
No one will escape!
13 My people have planted wheat
but are harvesting thorns.
They have worn themselves out,
but it has done them no good.
They will harvest a crop of shame
because of the fierce anger of the LORD."

A Message for Israel's Neighbors

14 Now this is what the LORD says: "I will uproot from their land all the evil
nations reaching out for the possession I gave my people Israel. And I will
uproot Judah from among them. 15 But afterward I will return and have com-
passion on all of them. I will bring them home to their own lands again, each
nation to its own possession. 16 And if these nations truly learn the ways of my
people, and if they learn to swear by my name, saying, 'As surely as the LORD
lives' (just as they taught my people to swear by the name of Baal), then they
will be given a place among my people. 17 But any nation who refuses to obey
me will be uprooted and destroyed. I, the LORD, have spoken!"

Jeremiah's Linen Loincloth

13 This is what the LORD said to me: "Go and buy a linen loincloth and
put it on, but do not wash it." 2 So I bought the loincloth as the LORD
directed me, and I put it on.

3 Then the LORD gave me another message: 4 "Take the linen loincloth you
are wearing, and go to the Euphrates River.* Hide it there in a hole in the
rocks." 5 So I went and hid it by the Euphrates as the LORD had instructed me.

6 A long time afterward the LORD said to me, "Go back to the Euphrates
and get the loincloth I told you to hide there." 7 So I went to the Euphrates
and dug it out of the hole where I had hidden it. But now it was rotting and
falling apart. The loincloth was good for nothing.

8 Then I received this message from the LORD: 9 "This is what the LORD says:
This shows how I will rot away the pride of Judah and Jerusalem. 10 These
wicked people refuse to listen to me. They stubbornly follow their own desires
and worship other gods. Therefore, they will become like this loincloth—good
for nothing! 11 As a loincloth clings to a man's waist, so I created Judah and

Question 13:1–10

As the Lord instructed, Jeremiah had to buy some underwear. God then wanted him to wear it for a while and then go hide it among some rocks along the Euphrates River. After a long time had passed, God wanted Jeremiah to go back to the hiding spot and dig out the underwear. Of course, when Jeremiah did that, he found that the underwear was rotting and falling apart—it "was good for nothing" (v. 7). God gave Jeremiah this crazy, lived-out parable as a metaphor for the spiritual condition of God's people. As you read Jeremiah 13:1-10, what do you learn about God's message in this strange metaphor about underwear?

13:4 Hebrew *Perath;* also in 13:5, 6, 7.

Israel to cling to me, says the LORD. They were to be my people, my pride, my
glory—an honor to my name. But they would not listen to me.
12 "So tell them, 'This is what the LORD, the God of Israel, says: May all
your jars be filled with wine.' And they will reply, 'Of course! Jars are made
to be filled with wine!'
13 "Then tell them, 'No, this is what the LORD means: I will fill everyone
in this land with drunkenness—from the king sitting on David's throne to
the priests and the prophets, right down to the common people of Jerusa-
lem. 14 I will smash them against each other, even parents against children,
says the LORD. I will not let my pity or mercy or compassion keep me from
destroying them.'"

A Warning against Pride

15 Listen and pay attention!
Do not be arrogant, for the LORD has spoken.
16 Give glory to the LORD your God
before it is too late.
Acknowledge him before he brings darkness upon you,
causing you to stumble and fall on the darkening mountains.
For then, when you look for light,
you will find only terrible darkness and gloom.
17 And if you still refuse to listen,
I will weep alone because of your pride.
My eyes will overflow with tears,
because the LORD's flock will be led away into exile.

18 Say to the king and his mother,
"Come down from your thrones
and sit in the dust,
for your glorious crowns
will soon be snatched from your heads."
19 The towns of the Negev will close their gates,
and no one will be able to open them.
The people of Judah will be taken away as captives.
All will be carried into exile.

20 Open up your eyes and see
the armies marching down from the north!
Where is your flock—
your beautiful flock—
that he gave you to care for?
21 What will you say when the LORD takes the allies you have cultivated
and appoints them as your rulers?
Pangs of anguish will grip you,
like those of a woman in labor!
22 You may ask yourself,
"Why is all this happening to me?"
It is because of your many sins!
That is why you have been stripped
and raped by invading armies.

23 Can an Ethiopian* change the color of his skin?
Can a leopard take away its spots?
Neither can you start doing good,
for you have always done evil.

24 "I will scatter you like chaff
that is blown away by the desert winds.
25 This is your allotment,
the portion I have assigned to you,"
says the LORD,
"for you have forgotten me,
putting your trust in false gods.
26 I myself will strip you
and expose you to shame.
27 I have seen your adultery and lust,
and your disgusting idol worship out in the fields and on the hills.
What sorrow awaits you, Jerusalem!
How long before you are pure?"

Judah's Terrible Drought

14 This message came to Jeremiah from the LORD, explaining why he was holding back the rain:

2 "Judah wilts;
commerce at the city gates grinds to a halt.
All the people sit on the ground in mourning,
and a great cry rises from Jerusalem.
3 The nobles send servants to get water,
but all the wells are dry.
The servants return with empty pitchers,
confused and desperate,
covering their heads in grief.
4 The ground is parched
and cracked for lack of rain.
The farmers are deeply troubled;
they, too, cover their heads.
5 Even the doe abandons her newborn fawn
because there is no grass in the field.
6 The wild donkeys stand on the bare hills
panting like thirsty jackals.
They strain their eyes looking for grass,
but there is none to be found."

7 The people say, "Our wickedness has caught up with us, LORD,
but help us for the sake of your own reputation.
We have turned away from you
and sinned against you again and again.
8 O Hope of Israel, our Savior in times of trouble,
why are you like a stranger to us?

13:23 Hebrew *a Cushite.*

Please write on this page!

Why are you like a traveler passing through the land,
stopping only for the night?
9 Are you also confused?
Is our champion helpless to save us?
You are right here among us, LORD.
We are known as your people.
Please don't abandon us now!"

10 So this is what the LORD says to his people:
"You love to wander far from me
and do not restrain yourselves.
Therefore, I will no longer accept you as my people.
Now I will remember all your wickedness
and will punish you for your sins."

The LORD Forbids Jeremiah to Intercede

11 Then the LORD said to me, "Do not pray for these people anymore. 12 When
they fast, I will pay no attention. When they present their burnt offerings
and grain offerings to me, I will not accept them. Instead, I will devour them
with war, famine, and disease."

13 Then I said, "O Sovereign LORD, their prophets are telling them, 'All is
well—no war or famine will come. The LORD will surely send you peace.'"

14 Then the LORD said, "These prophets are telling lies in my name. I did
not send them or tell them to speak. I did not give them any messages. They
prophesy of visions and revelations they have never seen or heard. They
speak foolishness made up in their own lying hearts. 15 Therefore, this is
what the LORD says: I will punish these lying prophets, for they have spoken
in my name even though I never sent them. They say that no war or famine
will come, but they themselves will die by war and famine! 16 As for the people
to whom they prophesy—their bodies will be thrown out into the streets of
Jerusalem, victims of famine and war. There will be no one left to bury them.
Husbands, wives, sons, and daughters—all will be gone. For I will pour out
their own wickedness on them. 17 Now, Jeremiah, say this to them:

"Night and day my eyes overflow with tears.
I cannot stop weeping,
for my virgin daughter—my precious people—
has been struck down
and lies mortally wounded.
18 If I go out into the fields,
I see the bodies of people slaughtered by the enemy.
If I walk the city streets,
I see people who have died of starvation.
The prophets and priests continue with their work,
but they don't know what they're doing."

A Prayer for Healing

19 LORD, have you completely rejected Judah?
Do you really hate Jerusalem?*

14:19 Hebrew *Zion?*

Why have you wounded us past all hope of healing?
We hoped for peace, but no peace came.
We hoped for a time of healing, but found only terror.
20 LORD, we confess our wickedness
and that of our ancestors, too.
We all have sinned against you.
21 For the sake of your reputation, LORD, do not abandon us.
Do not disgrace your own glorious throne.
Please remember us,
and do not break your covenant with us.

22 Can any of the worthless foreign gods send us rain?
Does it fall from the sky by itself?
No, you are the one, O LORD our God!
Only you can do such things.
So we will wait for you to help us.

Judah's Inevitable Doom

15 Then the LORD said to me, "Even if Moses and Samuel stood be-
fore me pleading for these people, I wouldn't help them. Away with
them! Get them out of my sight! 2 And if they say to you, 'But where can we
go?' tell them, 'This is what the LORD says:

"'Those who are destined for death, to death;
those who are destined for war, to war;
those who are destined for famine, to famine;
those who are destined for captivity, to captivity.'

3 "I will send four kinds of destroyers against them," says the LORD. "I will
send the sword to kill, the dogs to drag away, the vultures to devour, and the
wild animals to finish up what is left. 4 Because of the wicked things Manas-
seh son of Hezekiah, king of Judah, did in Jerusalem, I will make my people
an object of horror to all the kingdoms of the earth.

5 "Who will feel sorry for you, Jerusalem?
Who will weep for you?
Who will even bother to ask how you are?
6 You have abandoned me
and turned your back on me,"
says the LORD.
"Therefore, I will raise my fist to destroy you.
I am tired of always giving you another chance.
7 I will winnow you like grain at the gates of your cities
and take away the children you hold dear.
I will destroy my own people,
because they refuse to change their evil ways.
8 There will be more widows
than the grains of sand on the seashore.
At noontime I will bring a destroyer
against the mothers of young men.

Question 15:1

Nope, said the Lord, not "even if Moses and Samuel stood before me pleading." What does this teach you about how the Lord makes decisions?

I will cause anguish and terror
to come upon them suddenly.
9 The mother of seven grows faint and gasps for breath;
her sun has gone down while it is still day.
She sits childless now,
disgraced and humiliated.
And I will hand over those who are left
to be killed by the enemy.
I, the LORD, have spoken!"

Jeremiah's Complaint

10 Then I said,

"What sorrow is mine, my mother.
Oh, that I had died at birth!
I am hated everywhere I go.
I am neither a lender who threatens to foreclose
nor a borrower who refuses to pay—
yet they all curse me."

11 The LORD replied,

"I will take care of you, Jeremiah.
Your enemies will ask you to plead on their behalf
in times of trouble and distress.
12 Can a man break a bar of iron from the north,
or a bar of bronze?
13 At no cost to them,
I will hand over your wealth and treasures
as plunder to your enemies,
for sin runs rampant in your land.
14 I will tell your enemies to take you
as captives to a foreign land.
For my anger blazes like a fire
that will burn forever.*"

15 Then I said,

"LORD, you know what's happening to me.
Please step in and help me. Punish my persecutors!
Please give me time; don't let me die young.
It's for your sake that I am suffering.
16 When I discovered your words, I devoured them.
They are my joy and my heart's delight,
for I bear your name,
O LORD God of Heaven's Armies.
17 I never joined the people in their merry feasts.
I sat alone because your hand was on me.
I was filled with indignation at their sins.

15:14 As in some Hebrew manuscripts (see also 17:4); most Hebrew manuscripts read *will burn against you.*

18 Why then does my suffering continue?
Why is my wound so incurable?
Your help seems as uncertain as a seasonal brook,
like a spring that has gone dry."

19 This is how the LORD responds:

"If you return to me, I will restore you
so you can continue to serve me.
If you speak good words rather than worthless ones,
you will be my spokesman.
You must influence them;
do not let them influence you!
20 They will fight against you like an attacking army,
but I will make you as secure as a fortified wall of bronze.
They will not conquer you,
for I am with you to protect and rescue you.
I, the LORD, have spoken!
21 Yes, I will certainly keep you safe from these wicked men.
I will rescue you from their cruel hands."

Jeremiah Forbidden to Marry

16 The LORD gave me another message. He said, 2 "Do not get married
or have children in this place. 3 For this is what the LORD says about
the children born here in this city and about their mothers and fathers: 4 They
will die from terrible diseases. No one will mourn for them or bury them,
and they will lie scattered on the ground like manure. They will die from war
and famine, and their bodies will be food for the vultures and wild animals."

Judah's Coming Punishment

5 This is what the LORD says: "Do not go to funerals to mourn and show
sympathy for these people, for I have removed my protection and peace from
them. I have taken away my unfailing love and my mercy. 6 Both the great
and the lowly will die in this land. No one will bury them or mourn for
them. Their friends will not cut themselves in sorrow or shave their heads
in sadness. 7 No one will offer a meal to comfort those who mourn for the
dead—not even at the death of a mother or father. No one will send a cup
of wine to console them.

8 "And do not go to their feasts and parties. Do not eat and drink with
them at all. 9 For this is what the LORD of Heaven's Armies, the God of Israel,
says: In your own lifetime, before your very eyes, I will put an end to the
happy singing and laughter in this land. The joyful voices of bridegrooms
and brides will no longer be heard.

10 "When you tell the people all these things, they will ask, 'Why has the
LORD decreed such terrible things against us? What have we done to deserve
such treatment? What is our sin against the LORD our God?'

11 "Then you will give them the LORD's reply: 'It is because your ancestors
were unfaithful to me. They worshiped other gods and served them. They
abandoned me and did not obey my word. 12 And you are even worse than
your ancestors! You stubbornly follow your own evil desires and refuse to

Make a Difference

15:19-20

Influence Others

God wanted Jeremiah to influence the people. God did not want the wicked people to influence him. "You must influence them," God said. "Do not let them influence you!" (v. 19).

You have a calling to share the love and truth of God. In that process, don't let others steer you away from God. Be careful not to copy the patterns of the world (Romans 12:1-2). Be determined to be the one who is proactive. Be sure to be the one who shapes others to follow God's ways.

This is not an easy calling (Jeremiah 15:20). At times you will likely even have people fighting against you. Trust that God will make you strong. Be like Jeremiah!

Difference Maker

Pay attention to Jeremiah's call in your own life. In what ways have you conformed too much to the wickedness around you? In what ways could you be a positive influence on the people around you today? Determine to avoid wicked practices and to pursue life-giving ones today.

listen to me. 13So I will throw you out of this land and send you into a foreign
land where you and your ancestors have never been. There you can worship
idols day and night—and I will grant you no favors!'

Hope despite the Disaster

14"But the time is coming," says the LORD, "when people who are taking an
oath will no longer say, 'As surely as the LORD lives, who rescued the people of
Israel from the land of Egypt.' 15Instead, they will say, 'As surely as the LORD
lives, who brought the people of Israel back to their own land from the land
of the north and from all the countries to which he had exiled them.' For I
will bring them back to this land that I gave their ancestors.

16"But now I am sending for many fishermen who will catch them," says
the LORD. "I am sending for hunters who will hunt them down in the moun-
tains, hills, and caves. 17I am watching them closely, and I see every sin. They
cannot hope to hide from me. 18I will double their punishment for all their
sins, because they have defiled my land with lifeless images of their detest-
able gods and have filled my territory with their evil deeds."

Jeremiah's Prayer of Confidence

19 LORD, you are my strength and fortress,
my refuge in the day of trouble!
Nations from around the world
will come to you and say,
"Our ancestors left us a foolish heritage,
for they worshiped worthless idols.
20 Can people make their own gods?
These are not real gods at all!"

21 The LORD says,
"Now I will show them my power;
now I will show them my might.
At last they will know and understand
that I am the LORD.

Judah's Sin and Punishment

17 1"The sin of Judah
is inscribed with an iron chisel—
engraved with a diamond point on their stony hearts
and on the corners of their altars.
2 Even their children go to worship
at their pagan altars and Asherah poles,
beneath every green tree
and on every high hill.
3 So I will hand over my holy mountain—
along with all your wealth and treasures
and your pagan shrines—
as plunder to your enemies,
for sin runs rampant in your land.
4 The wonderful possession I have reserved for you
will slip from your hands.

I will tell your enemies to take you
as captives to a foreign land.
For my anger blazes like a fire
that will burn forever."

Wisdom from the LORD

5 This is what the LORD says:
"Cursed are those who put their trust in mere humans,
who rely on human strength
and turn their hearts away from the LORD.
6 They are like stunted shrubs in the desert,
with no hope for the future.
They will live in the barren wilderness,
in an uninhabited salty land.

7 "But blessed are those who trust in the LORD
and have made the LORD their hope and confidence.
8 They are like trees planted along a riverbank,
with roots that reach deep into the water.
Such trees are not bothered by the heat
or worried by long months of drought.
Their leaves stay green,
and they never stop producing fruit.

9 "The human heart is the most deceitful of all things,
and desperately wicked.
Who really knows how bad it is?
10 But I, the LORD, search all hearts
and examine secret motives.
I give all people their due rewards,
according to what their actions deserve."

Jeremiah's Trust in the LORD

11 Like a partridge that hatches eggs she has not laid,
so are those who get their wealth by unjust means.
At midlife they will lose their riches;
in the end, they will become poor old fools.
12 But we worship at your throne—
eternal, high, and glorious!
13 O LORD, the hope of Israel,
all who turn away from you will be disgraced.
They will be buried in the dust of the earth,
for they have abandoned the LORD, the fountain of living water.

14 O LORD, if you heal me, I will be truly healed;
if you save me, I will be truly saved.
My praises are for you alone!
15 People scoff at me and say,
"What is this 'message from the LORD' you talk about?
Why don't your predictions come true?"

Question **17:5-8**

The image of a tree is branched all throughout Scripture. See Psalm 1 and Colossians 2:6-7 as examples. How does the illustration in this passage help you understand what it means to live rooted in the hope of the Lord?

Make a Difference

18:1-6

Potter's Hands

You can be confident that God will use you to make a difference in this world because he is at work right now making a difference in you. Every time he chisels a sin out of your life, every time he prunes away a fear, every time he molds your faith into shape, the Lord is preparing you. He asks a lot from you because he knows he can empower you. God trusts himself to generate good work through you. God accepts the fact that he is pretty masterful at producing the right results in your life. He is removing anything false in you so that his truth will be brilliantly evident through all you say and do.

Difference Maker

Buy some modeling clay. Make things out of it all day long. Carry it around and use it as a stress reliever if necessary. As you shape the dough, consider how the Lord is shaping you into the person he wants you to be so that you can do what he wants you to do.

16 LORD, I have not abandoned my job
as a shepherd for your people.
I have not urged you to send disaster.
You have heard everything I've said.
17 LORD, don't terrorize me!
You alone are my hope in the day of disaster.
18 Bring shame and dismay on all who persecute me,
but don't let me experience shame and dismay.
Bring a day of terror on them.
Yes, bring double destruction upon them!

Observing the Sabbath

19 This is what the LORD said to me: "Go and stand in the gates of Jerusalem,
first in the gate where the king goes in and out, and then in each of the
other gates. 20 Say to all the people, 'Listen to this message from the LORD,
you kings of Judah and all you people of Judah and everyone living in Jeru-
salem. 21 This is what the LORD says: Listen to my warning! Stop carrying on
your trade at Jerusalem's gates on the Sabbath day. 22 Do not do your work on
the Sabbath, but make it a holy day. I gave this command to your ancestors,
23 but they did not listen or obey. They stubbornly refused to pay attention
or accept my discipline.

24 "'But if you obey me, says the LORD, and do not carry on your trade at the
gates or work on the Sabbath day, and if you keep it holy, 25 then kings and
their officials will go in and out of these gates forever. There will always be a
descendant of David sitting on the throne here in Jerusalem. Kings and their
officials will always ride in and out among the people of Judah in chariots
and on horses, and this city will remain forever. 26 And from all around Jeru-
salem, from the towns of Judah and Benjamin, from the western foothills*
and the hill country and the Negev, the people will come with their burnt
offerings and sacrifices. They will bring their grain offerings, frankincense,
and thanksgiving offerings to the LORD's Temple.

27 "'But if you do not listen to me and refuse to keep the Sabbath holy, and
if on the Sabbath day you bring loads of merchandise through the gates of
Jerusalem just as on other days, then I will set fire to these gates. The fire will
spread to the palaces, and no one will be able to put out the roaring flames.'"

The Potter and the Clay

18 The LORD gave another message to Jeremiah. He said, 2 "Go down to
the potter's shop, and I will speak to you there." 3 So I did as he told
me and found the potter working at his wheel. 4 But the jar he was making
did not turn out as he had hoped, so he crushed it into a lump of clay again
and started over.

5 Then the LORD gave me this message: 6 "O Israel, can I not do to you as this
potter has done to his clay? As the clay is in the potter's hand, so are you in
my hand. 7 If I announce that a certain nation or kingdom is to be uprooted,
torn down, and destroyed, 8 but then that nation renounces its evil ways, I
will not destroy it as I had planned. 9 And if I announce that I will plant and
build up a certain nation or kingdom, 10 but then that nation turns to evil
and refuses to obey me, I will not bless it as I said I would.

17:26 Hebrew *the Shephelah.*

11 "Therefore, Jeremiah, go and warn all Judah and Jerusalem. Say to them,
'This is what the LORD says: I am planning disaster for you instead of good.
So turn from your evil ways, each of you, and do what is right.'"
12 But the people replied, "Don't waste your breath. We will continue to
live as we want to, stubbornly following our own evil desires."
13 So this is what the LORD says:

"Has anyone ever heard of such a thing,
even among the pagan nations?
My virgin daughter Israel
has done something terrible!
14 Does the snow ever disappear from the mountaintops of Lebanon?
Do the cold streams flowing from those distant mountains ever
run dry?
15 But my people are not so reliable, for they have deserted me;
they burn incense to worthless idols.
They have stumbled off the ancient highways
and walk in muddy paths.
16 Therefore, their land will become desolate,
a monument to their stupidity.
All who pass by will be astonished
and will shake their heads in amazement.
17 I will scatter my people before their enemies
as the east wind scatters dust.
And in all their trouble I will turn my back on them
and refuse to notice their distress."

A Plot against Jeremiah

18 Then the people said, "Come on, let's plot a way to stop Jeremiah. We have
plenty of priests and wise men and prophets. We don't need him to teach the
word and give us advice and prophecies. Let's spread rumors about him and
ignore what he says."

19 LORD, hear me and help me!
Listen to what my enemies are saying.
20 Should they repay evil for good?
They have dug a pit to kill me,
though I pleaded for them
and tried to protect them from your anger.
21 So let their children starve!
Let them die by the sword!
Let their wives become childless widows.
Let their old men die in a plague,
and let their young men be killed in battle!
22 Let screaming be heard from their homes
as warriors come suddenly upon them.
For they have dug a pit for me
and have hidden traps along my path.
23 LORD, you know all about their murderous plots against me.
Don't forgive their crimes and blot out their sins.

Let them die before you.
Deal with them in your anger.

Jeremiah's Shattered Jar

19 This is what the LORD said to me: "Go and buy a clay jar. Then ask
some of the leaders of the people and of the priests to follow you.
2 Go out through the Gate of Broken Pots to the garbage dump in the valley
of Ben-Hinnom, and give them this message. 3 Say to them, 'Listen to this
message from the LORD, you kings of Judah and citizens of Jerusalem! This is
what the LORD of Heaven's Armies, the God of Israel, says: I will bring a ter-
rible disaster on this place, and the ears of those who hear about it will ring!
4 "'For Israel has forsaken me and turned this valley into a place of wicked-
ness. The people burn incense to foreign gods—idols never before acknowl-
edged by this generation, by their ancestors, or by the kings of Judah. And
they have filled this place with the blood of innocent children. 5 They have
built pagan shrines to Baal, and there they burn their sons as sacrifices to
Baal. I have never commanded such a horrible deed; it never even crossed
my mind to command such a thing! 6 So beware, for the time is coming, says
the LORD, when this garbage dump will no longer be called Topheth or the
valley of Ben-Hinnom, but the Valley of Slaughter.
7 "'For I will upset the careful plans of Judah and Jerusalem. I will allow
the people to be slaughtered by invading armies, and I will leave their dead
bodies as food for the vultures and wild animals. 8 I will reduce Jerusalem
to ruins, making it a monument to their stupidity. All who pass by will be
astonished and will gasp at the destruction they see there. 9 I will see to it
that your enemies lay siege to the city until all the food is gone. Then those
trapped inside will eat their own sons and daughters and friends. They will
be driven to utter despair.'
10 "As these men watch you, Jeremiah, smash the jar you brought. 11 Then
say to them, 'This is what the LORD of Heaven's Armies says: As this jar lies
shattered, so I will shatter the people of Judah and Jerusalem beyond all
hope of repair. They will bury the bodies here in Topheth, the garbage dump,
until there is no more room for them. 12 This is what I will do to this place
and its people, says the LORD. I will cause this city to become defiled like
Topheth. 13 Yes, all the houses in Jerusalem, including the palace of Judah's
kings, will become like Topheth—all the houses where you burned incense
on the rooftops to your star gods, and where liquid offerings were poured
out to your idols.'"
14 Then Jeremiah returned from Topheth, the garbage dump where he had
delivered this message, and he stopped in front of the Temple of the LORD.
He said to the people there, 15 "This is what the LORD of Heaven's Armies, the
God of Israel, says: 'I will bring disaster upon this city and its surrounding
towns as I promised, because you have stubbornly refused to listen to me.'"

Jeremiah and Pashhur

20 Now Pashhur son of Immer, the priest in charge of the Temple of
the LORD, heard what Jeremiah was prophesying. 2 So he arrested
Jeremiah the prophet and had him whipped and put in stocks at the Benja-
min Gate of the LORD's Temple.
3 The next day, when Pashhur finally released him, Jeremiah said,

"Pashhur, the LORD has changed your name. From now on you are to be called 'The Man Who Lives in Terror.'* 4 For this is what the LORD says: 'I will send terror upon you and all your friends, and you will watch as they are slaughtered by the swords of the enemy. I will hand the people of Judah over to the king of Babylon. He will take them captive to Babylon or run them through with the sword. 5 And I will let your enemies plunder Jerusalem. All the famed treasures of the city—the precious jewels and gold and silver of your kings—will be carried off to Babylon. 6 As for you, Pashhur, you and all your household will go as captives to Babylon. There you will die and be buried, you and all your friends to whom you prophesied that everything would be all right.'"

Jeremiah's Complaint

7 O LORD, you misled me,
and I allowed myself to be misled.
You are stronger than I am,
and you overpowered me.
Now I am mocked every day;
everyone laughs at me.
8 When I speak, the words burst out.
"Violence and destruction!" I shout.
So these messages from the LORD
have made me a household joke.
9 But if I say I'll never mention the LORD
or speak in his name,
his word burns in my heart like a fire.
It's like a fire in my bones!
I am worn out trying to hold it in!
I can't do it!
10 I have heard the many rumors about me.
They call me "The Man Who Lives in Terror."
They threaten, "If you say anything, we will report it."
Even my old friends are watching me,
waiting for a fatal slip.
"He will trap himself," they say,
"and then we will get our revenge on him."

11 But the LORD stands beside me like a great warrior.
Before him my persecutors will stumble.
They cannot defeat me.
They will fail and be thoroughly humiliated.
Their dishonor will never be forgotten.
12 O LORD of Heaven's Armies,
you test those who are righteous,
and you examine the deepest thoughts and secrets.
Let me see your vengeance against them,
for I have committed my cause to you.
13 Sing to the LORD!
Praise the LORD!

Question 20:7

Does it encourage you or deflate you that Jeremiah suffered from negative self-thoughts? How does his faithfulness to God lead to a sadness of his heart? If faith were always easy, it wouldn't be faith, would it?

20:3 Hebrew *Magor-missabib,* which means "surrounded by terror"; also in 20:10.

For though I was poor and needy,
he rescued me from my oppressors.

14 Yet I curse the day I was born!
May no one celebrate the day of my birth.
15 I curse the messenger who told my father,
"Good news—you have a son!"
16 Let him be destroyed like the cities of old
that the LORD overthrew without mercy.
Terrify him all day long with battle shouts,
17 because he did not kill me at birth.
Oh, that I had died in my mother's womb,
that her body had been my grave!
18 Why was I ever born?
My entire life has been filled
with trouble, sorrow, and shame.

No Deliverance from Babylon

21 The LORD spoke through Jeremiah when King Zedekiah sent Pash-
hur son of Malkijah and Zephaniah son of Maaseiah, the priest, to
speak with him. They begged Jeremiah,
2 "Please speak to the LORD for us and
ask him to help us. King Nebuchadnezzar* of Babylon is attacking Judah.
Perhaps the LORD will be gracious and do a mighty miracle as he has done
in the past. Perhaps he will force Nebuchadnezzar to withdraw his armies."
3 Jeremiah replied, "Go back to King Zedekiah and tell him,
4 'This is what
the LORD, the God of Israel, says: I will make your weapons useless against
the king of Babylon and the Babylonians* who are outside your walls attack-
ing you. In fact, I will bring your enemies right into the heart of this city.
5 I
myself will fight against you with a strong hand and a powerful arm, for I
am very angry. You have made me furious!
6 I will send a terrible plague upon
this city, and both people and animals will die.
7 And after all that, says the
LORD, I will hand over King Zedekiah, his staff, and everyone else in the city
who survives the disease, war, and famine. I will hand them over to King
Nebuchadnezzar of Babylon and to their other enemies. He will slaughter
them and show them no mercy, pity, or compassion.'
8 "Tell all the people, 'This is what the LORD says: Take your choice of life
or death!
9 Everyone who stays in Jerusalem will die from war, famine, or
disease, but those who go out and surrender to the Babylonians will live.
Their reward will be life!
10 For I have decided to bring disaster and not good
upon this city, says the LORD. It will be handed over to the king of Babylon,
and he will reduce it to ashes.'

Judgment on Judah's Kings

11 "Say to the royal family of Judah, 'Listen to this message from the LORD!
12 This is what the LORD says to the dynasty of David:

"'Give justice each morning to the people you judge!
Help those who have been robbed;
rescue them from their oppressors.

21:2 Hebrew *Nebuchadrezzar,* a variant spelling of Nebuchadnezzar; also in 21:7. 21:4 Or *Chaldeans;* also in 21:9.

Otherwise, my anger will burn like an unquenchable fire
because of all your sins.
13 I will personally fight against the people in Jerusalem,
that mighty fortress—
the people who boast, "No one can touch us here.
No one can break in here."
14 And I myself will punish you for your sinfulness,
says the LORD.
I will light a fire in your forests
that will burn up everything around you.'"

A Message for Judah's Kings

22 This is what the LORD said to me: "Go over and speak directly to the
king of Judah. Say to him, 2'Listen to this message from the LORD, you
king of Judah, sitting on David's throne. Let your attendants and your people
listen, too. 3This is what the LORD says: Be fair-minded and just. Do what is
right! Help those who have been robbed; rescue them from their oppressors.
Quit your evil deeds! Do not mistreat foreigners, orphans, and widows. Stop
murdering the innocent! 4If you obey me, there will always be a descendant
of David sitting on the throne here in Jerusalem. The king will ride through
the palace gates in chariots and on horses, with his parade of attendants and
subjects. 5But if you refuse to pay attention to this warning, I swear by my own
name, says the LORD, that this palace will become a pile of rubble.'"

Question 22:3

This is what the Lord wants from leaders. If you were to measure your own leadership qualities up to this standard, how would you rate yourself?

A Message about the Palace

6Now this is what the LORD says concerning Judah's royal palace:

"I love you as much as fruitful Gilead
and the green forests of Lebanon.
But I will turn you into a desert,
with no one living within your walls.
7 I will call for wreckers,
who will bring out their tools to dismantle you.
They will tear out all your fine cedar beams
and throw them on the fire.

8"People from many nations will pass by the ruins of this city and say to
one another, 'Why did the LORD destroy such a great city?' 9And the answer
will be, 'Because they violated their covenant with the LORD their God by
worshiping other gods.'"

A Message about Jehoahaz

10 Do not weep for the dead king or mourn his loss.
Instead, weep for the captive king being led away!
For he will never return to see his native land again.

11For this is what the LORD says about Jehoahaz,* who succeeded his father,
King Josiah, and was taken away as a captive: "He will never return. 12He will
die in a distant land and will never again see his own country."

22:11 Hebrew *Shallum,* another name for Jehoahaz.

Question 22:13-17

Compare and contrast the rule of Jehoiakim (vv. 13-14, 17) with the rule of his father, Josiah (vv. 15-16). What temptations come with power? Why do some people in power stay true to the Lord while others fall away?

Prayer 22:23

Lord, help me be careful with what I want in life. I could end up getting everything I want but fail to get what I need. Let me desire what you desire for my life. Amen.

A Message about Jehoiakim

13 And the LORD says, "What sorrow awaits Jehoiakim,*
who builds his palace with forced labor.*
He builds injustice into its walls,
for he makes his neighbors work for nothing.
He does not pay them for their labor.
14 He says, 'I will build a magnificent palace
with huge rooms and many windows.
I will panel it throughout with fragrant cedar
and paint it a lovely red.'
15 But a beautiful cedar palace does not make a great king!
Your father, Josiah, also had plenty to eat and drink.
But he was just and right in all his dealings.
That is why God blessed him.
16 He gave justice and help to the poor and needy,
and everything went well for him.
Isn't that what it means to know me?"
says the LORD.
17 "But you! You have eyes only for greed and dishonesty!
You murder the innocent,
oppress the poor, and reign ruthlessly."

18 Therefore, this is what the LORD says about Jehoiakim, son of King Josiah:

"The people will not mourn for him, crying
to one another,
'Alas, my brother! Alas, my sister!'
His subjects will not mourn for him, crying,
'Alas, our master is dead! Alas, his splendor is gone!'
19 He will be buried like a dead donkey—
dragged out of Jerusalem and dumped outside
the gates!
20 Weep for your allies in Lebanon.
Shout for them in Bashan.
Search for them in the regions east of the river.*
See, they are all destroyed.
Not one is left to help you.
21 I warned you when you were prosperous,
but you replied, 'Don't bother me.'
You have been that way since childhood—
you simply will not obey me!
22 And now the wind will blow away your allies.
All your friends will be taken away as captives.
Surely then you will see your wickedness and
be ashamed.
23 It may be nice to live in a beautiful palace
paneled with wood from the cedars of Lebanon,
but soon you will groan with pangs of anguish—
anguish like that of a woman in labor.

22:13a The brother and successor of the exiled Jehoahaz. See 22:18. **22:13b** Hebrew *by unrighteousness.* **22:20** Or *in Abarim.*

A Message for Jehoiachin
24 "As surely as I live," says the LORD, "I will abandon you, Jehoiachin* son
of Jehoiakim, king of Judah. Even if you were the signet ring on my right
hand, I would pull you off. 25 I will hand you over to those who seek to kill
you, those you so desperately fear—to King Nebuchadnezzar* of Babylon
and the mighty Babylonian* army. 26 I will expel you and your mother from
this land, and you will die in a foreign country, not in your native land. 27 You
will never again return to the land you yearn for.

28 "Why is this man Jehoiachin like a discarded, broken jar?
Why are he and his children to be exiled to a foreign land?
29 O earth, earth, earth!
Listen to this message from the LORD!
30 This is what the LORD says:
'Let the record show that this man Jehoiachin was childless.
He is a failure,
for none of his children will succeed him on the throne of David
to rule over Judah.'

The Righteous Descendant
23 "What sorrow awaits the leaders of my people—the shepherds of
my sheep—for they have destroyed and scattered the very ones they
were expected to care for," says the LORD.
2 Therefore, this is what the LORD, the God of Israel, says to these shep-
herds: "Instead of caring for my flock and leading them to safety, you have
deserted them and driven them to destruction. Now I will pour out judg-
ment on you for the evil you have done to them. 3 But I will gather together
the remnant of my flock from the countries where I have driven them. I
will bring them back to their own sheepfold, and they will be fruitful and
increase in number. 4 Then I will appoint responsible shepherds who will
care for them, and they will never be afraid again. Not a single one will be
lost or missing. I, the LORD, have spoken!

5 "For the time is coming,"
says the LORD,
"when I will raise up a righteous descendant*
from King David's line.
He will be a King who rules with wisdom.
He will do what is just and right throughout the land.
6 And this will be his name:
'The LORD Is Our Righteousness.'*
In that day Judah will be saved,
and Israel will live in safety.

7 "In that day," says the LORD, "when people are taking an oath, they will
no longer say, 'As surely as the LORD lives, who rescued the people of Israel

22:24 Hebrew *Coniah,* a variant spelling of Jehoiachin; also in 22:28. 22:25a Hebrew *Nebuchadrezzar,* a variant spelling of Nebuchadnezzar. 22:25b Or *Chaldean.* 23:5 Hebrew *a righteous branch.* 23:6 Hebrew *Yahweh Tsidqenu.*

Question 23:5

Does this passage remind you of anyone? How does God's plan of salvation through Jesus help the people Jeremiah was crying out to in his day? What did God want people to hear in this message?

from the land of Egypt.' 8 Instead, they will say, 'As surely as the LORD lives,
who brought the people of Israel back to their own land from the land of the
north and from all the countries to which he had exiled them.' Then they
will live in their own land."

Judgment on False Prophets

9 My heart is broken because of the false prophets,
and my bones tremble.
I stagger like a drunkard,
like someone overcome by wine,
because of the holy words
the LORD has spoken against them.
10 For the land is full of adultery,
and it lies under a curse.
The land itself is in mourning—
its wilderness pastures are dried up.
For they all do evil
and abuse what power they have.

11 "Even the priests and prophets
are ungodly, wicked men.
I have seen their despicable acts
right here in my own Temple,"
says the LORD.
12 "Therefore, the paths they take
will become slippery.
They will be chased through the dark,
and there they will fall.
For I will bring disaster upon them
at the time fixed for their punishment.
I, the LORD, have spoken!

13 "I saw that the prophets of Samaria were terribly evil,
for they prophesied in the name of Baal
and led my people of Israel into sin.
14 But now I see that the prophets of Jerusalem are
even worse!
They commit adultery and love dishonesty.
They encourage those who are doing evil
so that no one turns away from their sins.
These prophets are as wicked
as the people of Sodom and Gomorrah once were."

15 Therefore, this is what the LORD of Heaven's Armies says concerning the
prophets:

"I will feed them with bitterness
and give them poison to drink.
For it is because of Jerusalem's prophets
that wickedness has filled this land."

16This is what the LORD of Heaven's Armies says to his people:

"Do not listen to these prophets when they
prophesy to you,
filling you with futile hopes.
They are making up everything they say.
They do not speak for the LORD!
17 They keep saying to those who despise my word,
'Don't worry! The LORD says you will have peace!'
And to those who stubbornly follow their own desires,
they say, 'No harm will come your way!'

18 "Have any of these prophets been in the LORD's presence
to hear what he is really saying?
Has even one of them cared enough to listen?
19 Look! The LORD's anger bursts out like a storm,
a whirlwind that swirls down on the heads of the wicked.
20 The anger of the LORD will not diminish
until it has finished all he has planned.
In the days to come
you will understand all this very clearly.

21 "I have not sent these prophets,
yet they run around claiming to speak for me.
I have given them no message,
yet they go on prophesying.
22 If they had stood before me and listened to me,
they would have spoken my words,
and they would have turned my people
from their evil ways and deeds.
23 Am I a God who is only close at hand?" says the LORD.
"No, I am far away at the same time.
24 Can anyone hide from me in a secret place?
Am I not everywhere in all the heavens and earth?"
says the LORD.

25"I have heard these prophets say, 'Listen to the dream I had from God
last night.' And then they proceed to tell lies in my name. 26How long will
this go on? If they are prophets, they are prophets of deceit, inventing
everything they say. 27By telling these false dreams, they are trying to get
my people to forget me, just as their ancestors did by worshiping the idols
of Baal.

28 "Let these false prophets tell their dreams,
but let my true messengers faithfully proclaim my every word.
There is a difference between straw and grain!
29 Does not my word burn like fire?"
says the LORD.
"Is it not like a mighty hammer
that smashes a rock to pieces?

Make a Difference

23:18

Time with God

What difference does it make to spend time with God? Many people say they will pray but don't really. Many people say they follow God but spend most of their time following their own pursuits. Many people say they think about God but spend most of their thoughts on other things. What does it mean to be in the Lord's actual presence? What does it mean to hear what God is saying? What does it mean to care enough to listen to God?

Difference Maker

Set an appointment on your calendar every day for the next week for at least fifteen uninterrupted minutes with God.

Question **23:23**

If the Lord is omnipresent, what difference does this make to the way people should live their lives?

Prayer **24:7**

Lord, I want an ongoing, active relationship with you. If I ever stray from you, let me return to you wholeheartedly. Amen.

30“Therefore,” says the LORD, “I am against these prophets who steal
messages from each other and claim they are from me. 31I am against these
smooth-tongued prophets who say, ‘This prophecy is from the LORD!’ 32I am
against these false prophets. Their imaginary dreams are flagrant lies that
lead my people into sin. I did not send or appoint them, and they have no
message at all for my people. I, the LORD, have spoken!

False Prophecies and False Prophets

33“Suppose one of the people or one of the prophets or priests asks you,
‘What prophecy has the LORD burdened you with now?’ You must reply,
‘You are the burden!* The LORD says he will abandon you!’

34“If any prophet, priest, or anyone else says, ‘I have a prophecy from the
LORD,’ I will punish that person along with his entire family. 35You should
keep asking each other, ‘What is the LORD’s answer?’ or ‘What is the LORD
saying?’ 36But stop using this phrase, ‘prophecy from the LORD.’ For people
are using it to give authority to their own ideas, turning upside down the
words of our God, the living God, the LORD of Heaven’s Armies.

37“This is what you should say to the prophets: ‘What is the LORD’s an-
swer?’ or ‘What is the LORD saying?’ 38But suppose they respond, ‘This is a
prophecy from the LORD!’ Then you should say, ‘This is what the LORD says:
Because you have used this phrase, “prophecy from the LORD,” even though
I warned you not to use it, 39I will forget you completely.* I will expel you
from my presence, along with this city that I gave to you and your ancestors.
40And I will make you an object of ridicule, and your name will be infamous
throughout the ages.’”

Good and Bad Figs

24 After King Nebuchadnezzar* of Babylon exiled Jehoiachin* son of
Jehoiakim, king of Judah, to Babylon along with the officials of Ju-
dah and all the craftsmen and artisans, the LORD gave me this vision. I saw
two baskets of figs placed in front of the LORD’s Temple in Jerusalem. 2One
basket was filled with fresh, ripe figs, while the other was filled with bad
figs that were too rotten to eat.

3Then the LORD said to me, “What do you see, Jeremiah?”

I replied, “Figs, some very good and some very bad, too rotten to eat.”

4Then the LORD gave me this message: 5“This is what the LORD, the God
of Israel, says: The good figs represent the exiles I sent from Judah to the land
of the Babylonians.* 6I will watch over and care for them, and I will bring
them back here again. I will build them up and not tear them down. I will
plant them and not uproot them. 7I will give them hearts that recognize me
as the LORD. They will be my people, and I will be their God, for they will
return to me wholeheartedly.

8“But the bad figs,” the LORD said, “represent King Zedekiah of Judah,
his officials, all the people left in Jerusalem, and those who live in Egypt. I
will treat them like bad figs, too rotten to eat. 9I will make them an object of
horror and a symbol of evil to every nation on earth. They will be disgraced
and mocked, taunted and cursed, wherever I scatter them. 10And I will send

23:33 As in Greek version and Latin Vulgate; Hebrew reads *What burden?* **23:39** Some Hebrew manuscripts and Greek version read *I will surely lift you up.* **24:1a** Hebrew *Nebuchadrezzar,* a variant spelling of Nebuchadnezzar. **24:1b** Hebrew *Jeconiah,* a variant spelling of Jehoiachin. **24:5** Or *Chaldeans.*

war, famine, and disease until they have vanished from the land of Israel,
which I gave to them and their ancestors."

Seventy Years of Captivity

25 This message for all the people of Judah came to Jeremiah from
the LORD during the fourth year of Jehoiakim's reign over Judah.*
This was the year when King Nebuchadnezzar* of Babylon began his reign.
2 Jeremiah the prophet said to all the people in Judah and Jerusalem, 3 "For
the past twenty-three years—from the thirteenth year of the reign of Josiah
son of Amon,* king of Judah, until now—the LORD has been giving me his
messages. I have faithfully passed them on to you, but you have not listened.
4 "Again and again the LORD has sent you his servants, the prophets, but
you have not listened or even paid attention. 5 Each time the message was
this: 'Turn from the evil road you are traveling and from the evil things you
are doing. Only then will I let you live in this land that the LORD gave to you
and your ancestors forever. 6 Do not provoke my anger by worshiping idols
you made with your own hands. Then I will not harm you.'
7 "But you would not listen to me," says the LORD. "You made me furious
by worshiping idols you made with your own hands, bringing on yourselves
all the disasters you now suffer. 8 And now the LORD of Heaven's Armies says:
Because you have not listened to me, 9 I will gather together all the armies of
the north under King Nebuchadnezzar of Babylon, whom I have appointed as
my deputy. I will bring them all against this land and its people and against the
surrounding nations. I will completely destroy* you and make you an object of
horror and contempt and a ruin forever. 10 I will take away your happy singing
and laughter. The joyful voices of bridegrooms and brides will no longer be
heard. Your millstones will fall silent, and the lights in your homes will go out.
11 This entire land will become a desolate wasteland. Israel and her neighbor-
ing lands will serve the king of Babylon for seventy years.
12 "Then, after the seventy years of captivity are over, I will punish the king
of Babylon and his people for their sins," says the LORD. "I will make the
country of the Babylonians* a wasteland forever. 13 I will bring upon them
all the terrors I have promised in this book—all the penalties announced by
Jeremiah against the nations. 14 Many nations and great kings will enslave the
Babylonians, just as they enslaved my people. I will punish them in propor-
tion to the suffering they cause my people."

The Cup of the LORD's Anger

15 This is what the LORD, the God of Israel, said to me: "Take from my hand
this cup filled to the brim with my anger, and make all the nations to whom
I send you drink from it. 16 When they drink from it, they will stagger, crazed
by the warfare I will send against them."
17 So I took the cup of anger from the LORD and made all the nations drink
from it—every nation to which the LORD sent me. 18 I went to Jerusalem and
the other towns of Judah, and their kings and officials drank from the cup.
From that day until this, they have been a desolate ruin, an object of hor-
ror, contempt, and cursing. 19 I gave the cup to Pharaoh, king of Egypt, his

25:1a The fourth year of Jehoiakim's reign and the accession year of Nebuchadnezzar's reign was 605 B.C. 25:1b Hebrew *Nebuchadrezzar,* a variant spelling of Nebuchadnezzar; also in 25:9. 25:3 The thirteenth year of Josiah's reign was 627 B.C. 25:9 The Hebrew term used here refers to the complete consecration of things or people to the LORD, either by destroying them or by giving them as an offering. 25:12 Or *Chaldeans.*

Question 25:3

At this point, Jeremiah had been faithfully preaching for twenty-three years in the face of difficulty. What gave him his consistency? How would you do if you were tasked with a calling like his?

attendants, his officials, and all his people, 20 along with all the foreigners liv-
ing in that land. I also gave it to all the kings of the land of Uz and the kings of
the Philistine cities of Ashkelon, Gaza, Ekron, and what remains of Ashdod.
21 Then I gave the cup to the nations of Edom, Moab, and Ammon, 22 and the
kings of Tyre and Sidon, and the kings of the regions across the sea. 23 I gave
it to Dedan, Tema, and Buz, and to the people who live in distant places.* 24 I
gave it to the kings of Arabia, the kings of the nomadic tribes of the desert,
25 and to the kings of Zimri, Elam, and Media. 26 And I gave it to the kings of
the northern countries, far and near, one after the other—all the kingdoms
of the world. And finally, the king of Babylon* himself drank from the cup of
the LORD's anger.

27 Then the LORD said to me, "Now tell them, 'This is what the LORD of
Heaven's Armies, the God of Israel, says: Drink from this cup of my anger.
Get drunk and vomit; fall to rise no more, for I am sending terrible wars
against you.' 28 And if they refuse to accept the cup, tell them, 'The LORD of
Heaven's Armies says: You have no choice but to drink from it. 29 I have begun
to punish Jerusalem, the city that bears my name. Now should I let you go
unpunished? No, you will not escape disaster. I will call for war against all
the nations of the earth. I, the LORD of Heaven's Armies, have spoken!'

30 "Now prophesy all these things, and say to them,

"'The LORD will roar against his own land
from his holy dwelling in heaven.
He will shout like those who tread grapes;
he will shout against everyone on earth.
31 His cry of judgment will reach the ends of the earth,
for the LORD will bring his case against all the nations.
He will judge all the people of the earth,
slaughtering the wicked with the sword.
I, the LORD, have spoken!'"

32 This is what the LORD of Heaven's Armies says:
"Look! Disaster will fall upon nation after nation!
A great whirlwind of fury is rising
from the most distant corners of the earth!"

33 In that day those the LORD has slaughtered will fill the earth from one
end to the other. No one will mourn for them or gather up their bodies to
bury them. They will be scattered on the ground like manure.

34 Weep and moan, you evil shepherds!
Roll in the dust, you leaders of the flock!
The time of your slaughter has arrived;
you will fall and shatter like a fragile vase.
35 You will find no place to hide;
there will be no way to escape.
36 Listen to the frantic cries of the shepherds.
The leaders of the flock are wailing in despair,
for the LORD is ruining their pastures.

25:23 Or *who clip the corners of their hair.* 25:26 Hebrew *of Sheshach,* a code name for Babylon.

37 Peaceful meadows will be turned into a wasteland
by the LORD's fierce anger.
38 He has left his den like a strong lion seeking its prey,
and their land will be made desolate
by the sword* of the enemy
and the LORD's fierce anger.

Jeremiah's Escape from Death

26 This message came to Jeremiah from the LORD early in the reign of
Jehoiakim son of Josiah,* king of Judah. 2“This is what the LORD
says: Stand in the courtyard in front of the Temple of the LORD, and make an
announcement to the people who have come there to worship from all over
Judah. Give them my entire message; include every word. 3Perhaps they will
listen and turn from their evil ways. Then I will change my mind about the
disaster I am ready to pour out on them because of their sins.
4“Say to them, ‘This is what the LORD says: If you will not listen to me and
obey my word I have given you, 5and if you will not listen to my servants,
the prophets—for I sent them again and again to warn you, but you would
not listen to them—6then I will destroy this Temple as I destroyed Shiloh,
the place where the Tabernacle was located. And I will make Jerusalem an
object of cursing in every nation on earth.’”
7The priests, the prophets, and all the people listened to Jeremiah as he
spoke in front of the LORD's Temple. 8But when Jeremiah had finished his
message, saying everything the LORD had told him to say, the priests and
prophets and all the people at the Temple mobbed him. “Kill him!” they
shouted. 9“What right do you have to prophesy in the LORD's name that
this Temple will be destroyed like Shiloh? What do you mean, saying that
Jerusalem will be destroyed and left with no inhabitants?” And all the people
threatened him as he stood in front of the Temple.
10When the officials of Judah heard what was happening, they rushed over
from the palace and sat down at the New Gate of the Temple to hold court.
11The priests and prophets presented their accusations to the officials and
the people. “This man should die!” they said. “You have heard with your own
ears what a traitor he is, for he has prophesied against this city.”
12Then Jeremiah spoke to the officials and the people in his own defense.
“The LORD sent me to prophesy against this Temple and this city,” he said.
“The LORD gave me every word that I have spoken. 13But if you stop your
sinning and begin to obey the LORD your God, he will change his mind about
this disaster that he has announced against you. 14As for me, I am in your
hands—do with me as you think best. 15But if you kill me, rest assured that
you will be killing an innocent man! The responsibility for such a deed will
lie on you, on this city, and on every person living in it. For it is absolutely
true that the LORD sent me to speak every word you have heard.”
16Then the officials and the people said to the priests and prophets, “This
man does not deserve the death sentence, for he has spoken to us in the name
of the LORD our God.”
17Then some of the wise old men stood and spoke to all the people as-
sembled there. 18They said, “Remember when Micah of Moresheth prophe-
sied during the reign of King Hezekiah of Judah. He told the people of Judah,

25:38 As in some Hebrew manuscripts and Greek version; Masoretic Text reads *by the anger.*
26:1 The first year of Jehoiakim's reign was 608 B.C.

Story Arc **26:12-24**

● Micah

Prophets like Jeremiah were being arrested and killed. One prophet, named Uriah, was pursued by King Jehoiakim and killed with a sword (v. 23). When Jeremiah was arrested, it appeared that he would meet the same fate.

Instead, some wise men came to Jeremiah's rescue by reminding people about the story of the prophet Micah. Back in the days of King Hezekiah, Micah had preached a message very similar to Jeremiah's. It was a message calling people to repentance with God. Instead of killing Micah for his alarming prophecies, King Hezekiah listened to him, and the people turned from their sins and worshiped the Lord.

That's what the wise men suggested everyone should do now with Jeremiah's words. One man named Ahikam especially stood up for Jeremiah and persuaded the court not to turn Jeremiah over to the mob to be killed.

Several hundreds of years later, however, the court did not listen to this sort of wise counsel. The mob demanded that Jesus be handed over to death for his message. What do you learn from the history of people's vehement reactions to God's message?

Jer 36:1-32 ►

'This is what the LORD of Heaven's Armies says:
Mount Zion will be plowed like an open field;
  Jerusalem will be reduced to ruins!
A thicket will grow on the heights
  where the Temple now stands.'*

19 But did King Hezekiah and the people kill him for saying this? No, they
turned from their sins and worshiped the LORD. They begged him for mercy.
Then the LORD changed his mind about the terrible disaster he had pro-
nounced against them. So we are about to do ourselves great harm."
20 At this time Uriah son of Shemaiah from Kiriath-jearim was also proph-
esying for the LORD. And he predicted the same terrible disaster against the
city and nation as Jeremiah did. 21 When King Jehoiakim and the army of-
ficers and officials heard what he was saying, the king sent someone to kill
him. But Uriah heard about the plan and escaped in fear to Egypt. 22 Then
King Jehoiakim sent Elnathan son of Acbor to Egypt along with several other
men to capture Uriah. 23 They took him prisoner and brought him back to
King Jehoiakim. The king then killed Uriah with a sword and had him bur-
ied in an unmarked grave.
24 Nevertheless, Ahikam son of Shaphan stood up for Jeremiah and per-
suaded the court not to turn him over to the mob to be killed.

Jeremiah Wears an Ox Yoke

27 This message came to Jeremiah from the LORD early in the reign of
Zedekiah* son of Josiah, king of Judah.
2 This is what the LORD said to me: "Make a yoke, and fasten it on your
neck with leather straps. 3 Then send messages to the kings of Edom, Moab,
Ammon, Tyre, and Sidon through their ambassadors who have come to see
King Zedekiah in Jerusalem. 4 Give them this message for their masters: 'This
is what the LORD of Heaven's Armies, the God of Israel, says: 5 With my great
strength and powerful arm I made the earth and all its people and every ani-
mal. I can give these things of mine to anyone I choose. 6 Now I will give your
countries to King Nebuchadnezzar of Babylon, who is my servant. I have put
everything, even the wild animals, under his control. 7 All the nations will
serve him, his son, and his grandson until his time is up. Then many nations
and great kings will conquer and rule over Babylon. 8 So you must submit
to Babylon's king and serve him; put your neck under Babylon's yoke! I will
punish any nation that refuses to be his slave, says the LORD. I will send
war, famine, and disease upon that nation until Babylon has conquered it.
9 "'Do not listen to your false prophets, fortune-tellers, interpreters of
dreams, mediums, and sorcerers who say, "The king of Babylon will not
conquer you." 10 They are all liars, and their lies will lead to your being driven
out of your land. I will drive you out and send you far away to die. 11 But the
people of any nation that submits to the king of Babylon will be allowed
to stay in their own country to farm the land as usual. I, the LORD, have
spoken!'"
12 Then I repeated this same message to King Zedekiah of Judah. "If you
want to live, submit to the yoke of the king of Babylon and his people. 13 Why
do you insist on dying—you and your people? Why should you choose war,

26:18 Mic 3:12. **27:1** As in some Hebrew manuscripts and Syriac version (see also 27:3, 12); most Hebrew manuscripts read *Jehoiakim*.

famine, and disease, which the LORD will bring against every nation that
refuses to submit to Babylon's king? 14 Do not listen to the false prophets
who keep telling you, 'The king of Babylon will not conquer you.' They are
liars. 15 This is what the LORD says: 'I have not sent these prophets! They are
telling you lies in my name, so I will drive you from this land. You will all
die—you and all these prophets, too.'"

16 Then I spoke to the priests and the people and said, "This is what the
LORD says: 'Do not listen to your prophets who claim that soon the gold
articles taken from my Temple will be returned from Babylon. It is all a lie!
17 Do not listen to them. Surrender to the king of Babylon, and you will live.
Why should this whole city be destroyed? 18 If they really are prophets and
speak the LORD's messages, let them pray to the LORD of Heaven's Armies.
Let them pray that the articles remaining in the LORD's Temple and in the
king's palace and in the palaces of Jerusalem will not be carried away to
Babylon!'

19 "For the LORD of Heaven's Armies has spoken about the pillars in front
of the Temple, the great bronze basin called the Sea, the water carts, and all
the other ceremonial articles. 20 King Nebuchadnezzar of Babylon left them
here when he exiled Jehoiachin* son of Jehoiakim, king of Judah, to Babylon,
along with all the other nobles of Judah and Jerusalem. 21 Yes, this is what the
LORD of Heaven's Armies, the God of Israel, says about the precious things
still in the Temple, in the palace of Judah's king, and in Jerusalem: 22 'They
will all be carried away to Babylon and will stay there until I send for them,'
says the LORD. 'Then I will bring them back to Jerusalem again.'"

Jeremiah Condemns Hananiah

28 One day in late summer* of that same year—the fourth year of the
reign of Zedekiah, king of Judah—Hananiah son of Azzur, a prophet
from Gibeon, addressed me publicly in the Temple while all the priests and
people listened. He said, 2 "This is what the LORD of Heaven's Armies, the
God of Israel, says: 'I will remove the yoke of the king of Babylon from your
necks. 3 Within two years I will bring back all the Temple treasures that King
Nebuchadnezzar carried off to Babylon. 4 And I will bring back Jehoiachin*
son of Jehoiakim, king of Judah, and all the other captives that were taken
to Babylon. I will surely break the yoke that the king of Babylon has put on
your necks. I, the LORD, have spoken!'"

5 Jeremiah responded to Hananiah as they stood in front of all the priests
and people at the Temple. 6 He said, "Amen! May your prophecies come true!
I hope the LORD does everything you say. I hope he does bring back from
Babylon the treasures of this Temple and all the captives. 7 But listen now
to the solemn words I speak to you in the presence of all these people. 8 The
ancient prophets who preceded you and me spoke against many nations,
always warning of war, disaster, and disease. 9 So a prophet who predicts
peace must show he is right. Only when his predictions come true can we
know that he is really from the LORD."

10 Then Hananiah the prophet took the yoke off Jeremiah's neck and broke
it in pieces. 11 And Hananiah said again to the crowd that had gathered, "This

27:20 Hebrew *Jeconiah,* a variant spelling of Jehoiachin. 28:1 Hebrew *In the fifth month,* of the ancient Hebrew lunar calendar. The fifth month in the fourth year of Zedekiah's reign occurred within the months of August and September 593 B.C. Also see note on 1:3.
28:4 Hebrew *Jeconiah,* a variant spelling of Jehoiachin.

Highlights from the text

is what the LORD says: 'Just as this yoke has been broken, within two years I
will break the yoke of oppression from all the nations now subject to King
Nebuchadnezzar of Babylon.'" With that, Jeremiah left the Temple area.
12 Soon after this confrontation with Hananiah, the LORD gave this mes-
sage to Jeremiah: 13 "Go and tell Hananiah, 'This is what the LORD says: You
have broken a wooden yoke, but you have replaced it with a yoke of iron.
14 The LORD of Heaven's Armies, the God of Israel, says: I have put a yoke of
iron on the necks of all these nations, forcing them into slavery under King
Nebuchadnezzar of Babylon. I have put everything, even the wild animals,
under his control.'"
15 Then Jeremiah the prophet said to Hananiah, "Listen, Hananiah! The
LORD has not sent you, but the people believe your lies. 16 Therefore, this is
what the LORD says: 'You must die. Your life will end this very year because
you have rebelled against the LORD.'"
17 Two months later* the prophet Hananiah died.

A Letter to the Exiles

29 Jeremiah wrote a letter from Jerusalem to the elders, priests,
prophets, and all the people who had been exiled to Babylon by King
Nebuchadnezzar. 2 This was after King Jehoiachin,* the queen mother, the
court officials, the other officials of Judah, and all the craftsmen and artisans
had been deported from Jerusalem. 3 He sent the letter with Elasah son of
Shaphan and Gemariah son of Hilkiah when they went to Babylon as King
Zedekiah's ambassadors to Nebuchadnezzar. This is what Jeremiah's letter
said:

4 This is what the LORD of Heaven's Armies, the God of Israel, says to all
the captives he has exiled to Babylon from Jerusalem: 5 "Build homes,
and plan to stay. Plant gardens, and eat the food they produce. 6 Marry
and have children. Then find spouses for them so that you may have
many grandchildren. Multiply! Do not dwindle away! 7 And work for
the peace and prosperity of the city where I sent you into exile. Pray to
the LORD for it, for its welfare will determine your welfare."
8 This is what the LORD of Heaven's Armies, the God of Israel, says:
"Do not let your prophets and fortune-tellers who are with you in the
land of Babylon trick you. Do not listen to their dreams, 9 because they
are telling you lies in my name. I have not sent them," says the LORD.
10 This is what the LORD says: "You will be in Babylon for seventy
years. But then I will come and do for you all the good things I have
promised, and I will bring you home again. 11 For I know the plans
I have for you," says the LORD. "They are plans for good and not for
disaster, to give you a future and a hope. 12 In those days when you pray,
I will listen. 13 If you look for me wholeheartedly, you will find me. 14 I
will be found by you," says the LORD. "I will end your captivity and
restore your fortunes. I will gather you out of the nations where I sent
you and will bring you home again to your own land."
15 You claim that the LORD has raised up prophets for you in
Babylon. 16 But this is what the LORD says about the king who sits
on David's throne and all those still living here in Jerusalem—your

Make a Difference 29:7

Your Community

Stop. Look at your surroundings for a moment. What do you see? Describe the place where you are. Describe the street you are on, the activity level all around you, and the city where you reside. What kind of environment is it? What are the people there like? Think about all the nuances and noises and neighbors around you right now.

You know, where you are is where you represent Jesus. What a privilege that is. *You* get to represent Jesus. You get to do this by caring for all that is around you. You have the opportunity to cherish God's creation, to treasure the rhythms and culture of families and communities, to uplift your city and celebrate its people. You have the incredible honor of praying for everyone around you. You can pray for blessing, for reconciliation, for restoration along with prosperity and peace and joy and freedom and truth and whatever else your loving heart can think to pray. As you fill yourself with the practice of loving your neighbors, the Lord Jesus will honor you.

Difference Maker

Before you do anything else, stop and pray for God to bless your community deeply.

28:17 Hebrew *In the seventh month of that same year.* See 28:1 and the note there. 29:2 Hebrew *Jeconiah,* a variant spelling of Jehoiachin.

relatives who were not exiled to Babylon. 17This is what the LORD of
Heaven's Armies says: "I will send war, famine, and disease upon them
and make them like bad figs, too rotten to eat. 18Yes, I will pursue
them with war, famine, and disease, and I will scatter them around
the world. In every nation where I send them, I will make them an
object of damnation, horror, contempt, and mockery. 19For they refuse
to listen to me, though I have spoken to them repeatedly through the
prophets I sent. And you who are in exile have not listened either," says
the LORD.

20Therefore, listen to this message from the LORD, all you captives
there in Babylon. 21This is what the LORD of Heaven's Armies, the God
of Israel, says about your prophets—Ahab son of Kolaiah and Zedekiah
son of Maaseiah—who are telling you lies in my name: "I will turn
them over to Nebuchadnezzar* for execution before your eyes. 22Their
terrible fate will become proverbial, so that the Judean exiles will curse
someone by saying, 'May the LORD make you like Zedekiah and Ahab,
whom the king of Babylon burned alive!' 23For these men have done
terrible things among my people. They have committed adultery with
their neighbors' wives and have lied in my name, saying things I did not
command. I am a witness to this. I, the LORD, have spoken."

A Message for Shemaiah

24The LORD sent this message to Shemaiah the Nehelamite in Babylon:
25"This is what the LORD of Heaven's Armies, the God of Israel, says: You
wrote a letter on your own authority to Zephaniah son of Maaseiah, the
priest, and you sent copies to the other priests and people in Jerusalem. You
wrote to Zephaniah,

> 26"The LORD has appointed you to replace Jehoiada as the priest in
> charge of the house of the LORD. You are responsible to put into stocks
> and neck irons any crazy man who claims to be a prophet. 27So why
> have you done nothing to stop Jeremiah from Anathoth, who pretends
> to be a prophet among you? 28Jeremiah sent a letter here to Babylon,
> predicting that our captivity will be a long one. He said, 'Build homes,
> and plan to stay. Plant gardens, and eat the food they produce.'"

29But when Zephaniah the priest received Shemaiah's letter, he took it to
Jeremiah and read it to him. 30Then the LORD gave this message to Jeremiah:
31"Send an open letter to all the exiles in Babylon. Tell them, 'This is what the
LORD says concerning Shemaiah the Nehelamite: Since he has prophesied to
you when I did not send him and has tricked you into believing his lies, 32I
will punish him and his family. None of his descendants will see the good
things I will do for my people, for he has incited you to rebel against me. I,
the LORD, have spoken!'"

Promises of Deliverance

30 The LORD gave another message to Jeremiah. He said, 2"This is what
the LORD, the God of Israel, says: Write down for the record every-
thing I have said to you, Jeremiah. 3For the time is coming when I will restore

29:21 Hebrew *Nebuchadrezzar,* a variant spelling of Nebuchadnezzar.

Make a Difference

29:11

The Plans

What a special day this is. It's a day uniquely set aside for you to follow the Lord. A day when you can place your steps on his path. A day when you won't need to fear what will be. This day and all the days to come are in God's hands. He knows what will happen, and he knows what won't happen.

You are incredibly precious to the Lord. He sees his own reflection in your eyes. He hears his own rhythm in your heart. He made you to be with him for the rest of eternity. He has done and will do everything necessary to be with you. While you may not comprehend all that he does, embrace the good that the Lord has for you. Cherish the challenge to trust yourself completely to him today.

Difference Maker

This verse was written to the scattered people of Israel during their exile under King Nebuchadnezzar. In their circumstance, they struggled to see how the Lord was planning good for them. Where do you struggle to see God's good plan in your own life? How can you reconcile this with the Lord's promise?

the fortunes of my people of Israel and Judah. I will bring them home to this land that I gave to their ancestors, and they will possess it again. I, the LORD, have spoken!"

4 This is the message the LORD gave concerning Israel and Judah. 5 This is what the LORD says:

"I hear cries of fear;
  there is terror and no peace.
6 Now let me ask you a question:
  Do men give birth to babies?
Then why do they stand there, ash-faced,
  hands pressed against their sides
  like a woman in labor?
7 In all history there has never been such a time of terror.
  It will be a time of trouble for my people Israel.*
  Yet in the end they will be saved!
8 For in that day,"
  says the LORD of Heaven's Armies,
"I will break the yoke from their necks
  and snap their chains.
Foreigners will no longer be their masters.
9 For my people will serve the LORD their God
and their king descended from David—
  the king I will raise up for them.

10 "So do not be afraid, Jacob, my servant;
  do not be dismayed, Israel,"
  says the LORD.
"For I will bring you home again from distant lands,
  and your children will return from their exile.
Israel will return to a life of peace and quiet,
  and no one will terrorize them.
11 For I am with you and will save you,"
  says the LORD.
"I will completely destroy the nations where I have scattered you,
  but I will not completely destroy you.
I will discipline you, but with justice;
  I cannot let you go unpunished."

12 This is what the LORD says:
"Your injury is incurable—
  a terrible wound.
13 There is no one to help you
  or to bind up your injury.
  No medicine can heal you.
14 All your lovers—your allies—have left you
  and do not care about you anymore.
I have wounded you cruelly,
  as though I were your enemy.

30:7 Hebrew *Jacob;* also in 30:10b, 18. See note on 5:20.

For your sins are many,
and your guilt is great.
15 Why do you protest your punishment—
this wound that has no cure?
I have had to punish you
because your sins are many
and your guilt is great.

16 "But all who devour you will be devoured,
and all your enemies will be sent into exile.
All who plunder you will be plundered,
and all who attack you will be attacked.
17 I will give you back your health
and heal your wounds," says the LORD.
"For you are called an outcast—
'Jerusalem* for whom no one cares.'"

18 This is what the LORD says:
"When I bring Israel home again from captivity
and restore their fortunes,
Jerusalem will be rebuilt on its ruins,
and the palace reconstructed as before.
19 There will be joy and songs of thanksgiving,
and I will multiply my people, not diminish them;
I will honor them, not despise them.
20 Their children will prosper as they did long ago.
I will establish them as a nation before me,
and I will punish anyone who hurts them.
21 They will have their own ruler again,
and he will come from their own people.
I will invite him to approach me," says the LORD,
"for who would dare to come unless invited?
22 You will be my people,
and I will be your God."

23 Look! The LORD's anger bursts out like a storm,
a driving wind that swirls down on the heads of the wicked.
24 The fierce anger of the LORD will not diminish
until it has finished all he has planned.
In the days to come
you will understand all this.

Hope for Restoration

31 "In that day," says the LORD, "I will be the God of all the families
of Israel, and they will be my people. 2This is what the LORD says:

"Those who survive the coming destruction
will find blessings even in the barren land,
for I will give rest to the people of Israel."

30:17 Hebrew *Zion*.

What I will do next

Question 31:3

We were created to be in relationships. First and foremost, we were created to be in a relationship with God. God loves you. He really does. God's love for you is different from any other kind of love anyone else can offer! If you really believed God loves you and delights in you, how would that change the way you live every day?

3 Long ago the LORD said to Israel:
"I have loved you, my people, with an everlasting love.
With unfailing love I have drawn you to myself.
4 I will rebuild you, my virgin Israel.
You will again be happy
and dance merrily with your tambourines.
5 Again you will plant your vineyards on the mountains of Samaria
and eat from your own gardens there.
6 The day will come when watchmen will shout
from the hill country of Ephraim,
'Come, let us go up to Jerusalem*
to worship the LORD our God.'"

7 Now this is what the LORD says:
"Sing with joy for Israel.*
Shout for the greatest of nations!
Shout out with praise and joy:
'Save your people, O LORD,
the remnant of Israel!'
8 For I will bring them from the north
and from the distant corners of the earth.
I will not forget the blind and lame,
the expectant mothers and women in labor.
A great company will return!
9 Tears of joy will stream down their faces,
and I will lead them home with great care.
They will walk beside quiet streams
and on smooth paths where they will not stumble.
For I am Israel's father,
and Ephraim is my oldest child.

10 "Listen to this message from the LORD,
you nations of the world;
proclaim it in distant coastlands:
The LORD, who scattered his people,
will gather them and watch over them
as a shepherd does his flock.
11 For the LORD has redeemed Israel
from those too strong for them.
12 They will come home and sing songs of joy on the heights of Jerusalem.
They will be radiant because of the LORD's good gifts—
the abundant crops of grain, new wine, and olive oil,
and the healthy flocks and herds.
Their life will be like a watered garden,
and all their sorrows will be gone.
13 The young women will dance for joy,
and the men—old and young—will join in the celebration.
I will turn their mourning into joy.
I will comfort them and exchange their sorrow for rejoicing.

31:6 Hebrew *Zion;* also in 31:12. 31:7 Hebrew *Jacob;* also in 31:11. See note on 5:20.

14 The priests will enjoy abundance,
and my people will feast on my good gifts.
I, the LORD, have spoken!"

Rachel's Sadness Turns to Joy

15 This is what the LORD says:

"A cry is heard in Ramah—
deep anguish and bitter weeping.
Rachel weeps for her children,
refusing to be comforted—
for her children are gone."

16 But now this is what the LORD says:
"Do not weep any longer,
for I will reward you," says the LORD.
"Your children will come back to you
from the distant land of the enemy.
17 There is hope for your future," says the LORD.
"Your children will come again to their own land.
18 I have heard Israel* saying,
'You disciplined me severely,
like a calf that needs training for the yoke.
Turn me again to you and restore me,
for you alone are the LORD my God.
19 I turned away from God,
but then I was sorry.
I kicked myself for my stupidity!
I was thoroughly ashamed of all I did in my younger days.'

20 "Is not Israel still my son,
my darling child?" says the LORD.
"I often have to punish him,
but I still love him.
That's why I long for him
and surely will have mercy on him.
21 Set up road signs;
put up guideposts.
Mark well the path
by which you came.
Come back again, my virgin Israel;
return to your towns here.
22 How long will you wander,
my wayward daughter?
For the LORD will cause something new to happen—
Israel will embrace her God.*"

23 This is what the LORD of Heaven's Armies, the God of Israel, says:
"When I bring them back from captivity, the people of Judah and its towns

31:18 Hebrew *Ephraim,* referring to the northern kingdom of Israel; also in 31:20.
31:22 Hebrew *a woman will surround a man.*

Make a Difference

31:33–34

Written on Your Heart

This is a powerful prophecy about a powerful plan. God intended to renew his covenant with his people. Only this time, instead of the law being written on tablets and paper, his instructions would be put deep within people, written on their hearts.

Have you invited God into your heart? He belongs not just in your mind because it is not good to just know *about* God but not actually know God.

Difference Maker

If the Lord were to take a pen to your heart, what would he write? Invite him to live within you and be your God. If you have not ever asked God into your life, go to the back of the Bible and check out the section called "How to Accept Jesus as Your Lord and Savior."

will again say, 'The LORD bless you, O righteous home, O holy mountain!'
24 Townspeople and farmers and shepherds alike will live together in
peace and happiness. 25 For I have given rest to the weary and joy to the
sorrowing."

26 At this, I woke up and looked around. My sleep had been very sweet.
27 "The day is coming," says the LORD, "when I will greatly increase the
human population and the number of animals here in Israel and Judah.
28 In the past I deliberately uprooted and tore down this nation. I overthrew
it, destroyed it, and brought disaster upon it. But in the future I will just as
deliberately plant it and build it up. I, the LORD, have spoken!
29 "The people will no longer quote this proverb:

'The parents have eaten sour grapes,
but their children's mouths pucker at the taste.'

30 All people will die for their own sins—those who eat the sour grapes will
be the ones whose mouths will pucker.
31 "The day is coming," says the LORD, "when I will make a new covenant
with the people of Israel and Judah. 32 This covenant will not be like the one I
made with their ancestors when I took them by the hand and brought them
out of the land of Egypt. They broke that covenant, though I loved them as
a husband loves his wife," says the LORD.
33 "But this is the new covenant I will make with the people of Israel after
those days," says the LORD. "I will put my instructions deep within them,
and I will write them on their hearts. I will be their God, and they will be my
people. 34 And they will not need to teach their neighbors, nor will they need
to teach their relatives, saying, 'You should know the LORD.' For everyone,
from the least to the greatest, will know me already," says the LORD. "And I
will forgive their wickedness, and I will never again remember their sins."

35 It is the LORD who provides the sun to light the day
and the moon and stars to light the night,
and who stirs the sea into roaring waves.
His name is the LORD of Heaven's Armies,
and this is what he says:
36 "I am as likely to reject my people Israel
as I am to abolish the laws of nature!"
37 This is what the LORD says:
"Just as the heavens cannot be measured
and the foundations of the earth cannot be explored,
so I will not consider casting them away
for the evil they have done.
I, the LORD, have spoken!

38 "The day is coming," says the LORD, "when all Jerusalem will be rebuilt
for me, from the Tower of Hananel to the Corner Gate. 39 A measuring line
will be stretched out over the hill of Gareb and across to Goah. 40 And the
entire area—including the graveyard and ash dump in the valley, and all
the fields out to the Kidron Valley on the east as far as the Horse Gate—will
be holy to the LORD. The city will never again be captured or destroyed."

Jeremiah's Land Purchase

32 The following message came to Jeremiah from the LORD in the tenth
year of the reign of Zedekiah,* king of Judah. This was also the eigh-
teenth year of the reign of King Nebuchadnezzar.* 2 Jerusalem was then under
siege from the Babylonian army, and Jeremiah was imprisoned in the courtyard
of the guard in the royal palace. 3 King Zedekiah had put him there, asking
why he kept giving this prophecy: "This is what the LORD says: 'I am about to
hand this city over to the king of Babylon, and he will take it. 4 King Zedekiah
will be captured by the Babylonians* and taken to meet the king of Babylon
face to face. 5 He will take Zedekiah to Babylon, and I will deal with him there,'
says the LORD. 'If you fight against the Babylonians, you will never succeed.'"
6 At that time the LORD sent me a message. He said, 7 "Your cousin Hana-
mel son of Shallum will come and say to you, 'Buy my field at Anathoth. By
law you have the right to buy it before it is offered to anyone else.'"
8 Then, just as the LORD had said he would, my cousin Hanamel came
and visited me in the prison. He said, "Please buy my field at Anathoth in
the land of Benjamin. By law you have the right to buy it before it is offered
to anyone else, so buy it for yourself." Then I knew that the message I had
heard was from the LORD.
9 So I bought the field at Anathoth, paying Hanamel seventeen pieces*
of silver for it. 10 I signed and sealed the deed of purchase before witnesses,
weighed out the silver, and paid him. 11 Then I took the sealed deed and an
unsealed copy of the deed, which contained the terms and conditions of the
purchase, 12 and I handed them to Baruch son of Neriah and grandson of
Mahseiah. I did all this in the presence of my cousin Hanamel, the witnesses
who had signed the deed, and all the men of Judah who were there in the
courtyard of the guardhouse.
13 Then I said to Baruch as they all listened, 14 "This is what the LORD of
Heaven's Armies, the God of Israel, says: 'Take both this sealed deed and the
unsealed copy, and put them into a pottery jar to preserve them for a long
time.' 15 For this is what the LORD of Heaven's Armies, the God of Israel, says:
'Someday people will again own property here in this land and will buy and
sell houses and vineyards and fields.'"

Jeremiah's Prayer

16 Then after I had given the papers to Baruch, I prayed to the LORD:

17 "O Sovereign LORD! You made the heavens and earth by your strong
hand and powerful arm. Nothing is too hard for you! 18 You show
unfailing love to thousands, but you also bring the consequences of one
generation's sin upon the next. You are the great and powerful God,
the LORD of Heaven's Armies. 19 You have all wisdom and do great and
mighty miracles. You see the conduct of all people, and you give them
what they deserve. 20 You performed miraculous signs and wonders in
the land of Egypt—things still remembered to this day! And you have
continued to do great miracles in Israel and all around the world. You
have made your name famous to this day.

32:1a The tenth year of Zedekiah's reign and the eighteenth year of Nebuchadnezzar's reign was 587 B.C. **32:1b** Hebrew *Nebuchadrezzar,* a variant spelling of Nebuchadnezzar; also in 32:28. **32:4** Or *Chaldeans;* also in 32:5, 24, 25, 28, 29, 43. **32:9** Hebrew *17 shekels,* about 7 ounces or 194 grams in weight.

Prayer 32:39

Jesus, give me and the people closest to me discernment to pursue you and you alone. Help us choose what is good from your perspective. Influence us so much that the next generation will be influenced too. Amen.

21 "You brought Israel out of Egypt with mighty signs and wonders,
with a strong hand and powerful arm, and with overwhelming terror.
22 You gave the people of Israel this land that you had promised their
ancestors long before—a land flowing with milk and honey. 23 Our
ancestors came and conquered it and lived in it, but they refused
to obey you or follow your word. They have not done anything you
commanded. That is why you have sent this terrible disaster upon
them.

24 "See how the siege ramps have been built against the city walls!
Through war, famine, and disease, the city will be handed over to the
Babylonians, who will conquer it. Everything has happened just as you
said. 25 And yet, O Sovereign LORD, you have told me to buy the field—
paying good money for it before these witnesses—even though the city
will soon be handed over to the Babylonians."

A Prediction of Jerusalem's Fall

26 Then this message came to Jeremiah from the LORD: 27 "I am the LORD, the
God of all the peoples of the world. Is anything too hard for me? 28 Therefore,
this is what the LORD says: I will hand this city over to the Babylonians and to
Nebuchadnezzar, king of Babylon, and he will capture it. 29 The Babylonians
outside the walls will come in and set fire to the city. They will burn down
all these houses where the people provoked my anger by burning incense
to Baal on the rooftops and by pouring out liquid offerings to other gods.
30 Israel and Judah have done nothing but wrong since their earliest days.
They have infuriated me with all their evil deeds," says the LORD. 31 "From
the time this city was built until now, it has done nothing but anger me, so
I am determined to get rid of it.

32 "The sins of Israel and Judah—the sins of the people of Jerusalem, the
kings, the officials, the priests, and the prophets—have stirred up my anger.
33 My people have turned their backs on me and have refused to return. Even
though I diligently taught them, they would not receive instruction or obey.
34 They have set up their abominable idols right in my own Temple, defiling
it. 35 They have built pagan shrines to Baal in the valley of Ben-Hinnom, and
there they sacrifice their sons and daughters to Molech. I have never commanded such a horrible deed; it never even crossed my mind to command
such a thing. What an incredible evil, causing Judah to sin so greatly!

A Promise of Restoration

36 "Now I want to say something more about this city. You have been saying,
'It will fall to the king of Babylon through war, famine, and disease.' But this
is what the LORD, the God of Israel, says: 37 I will certainly bring my people
back again from all the countries where I will scatter them in my fury. I will
bring them back to this very city and let them live in peace and safety. 38 They
will be my people, and I will be their God. 39 And I will give them one heart
and one purpose: to worship me forever, for their own good and for the
good of all their descendants. 40 And I will make an everlasting covenant with
them: I will never stop doing good for them. I will put a desire in their hearts
to worship me, and they will never leave me. 41 I will find joy doing good
for them and will faithfully and wholeheartedly replant them in this land.

42 "This is what the LORD says: Just as I have brought all these calamities

on them, so I will do all the good I have promised them. 43 Fields will again
be bought and sold in this land about which you now say, 'It has been rav-
aged by the Babylonians, a desolate land where people and animals have all
disappeared.' 44 Yes, fields will once again be bought and sold—deeds signed
and sealed and witnessed—in the land of Benjamin and here in Jerusalem,
in the towns of Judah and in the hill country, in the foothills of Judah* and
in the Negev, too. For someday I will restore prosperity to them. I, the LORD,
have spoken!"

Promises of Peace and Prosperity

33 While Jeremiah was still confined in the courtyard of the guard,
the LORD gave him this second message: 2 "This is what the LORD
says—the LORD who made the earth, who formed and established it,
whose name is the LORD: 3 Ask me and I will tell you remarkable secrets
you do not know about things to come. 4 For this is what the LORD, the
God of Israel, says: You have torn down the houses of this city and even
the king's palace to get materials to strengthen the walls against the siege
ramps and swords of the enemy. 5 You expect to fight the Babylonians,*
but the men of this city are already as good as dead, for I have determined
to destroy them in my terrible anger. I have abandoned them because of
all their wickedness.

6 "Nevertheless, the time will come when I will heal Jerusalem's wounds
and give it prosperity and true peace. 7 I will restore the fortunes of Judah
and Israel and rebuild their towns. 8 I will cleanse them of their sins against
me and forgive all their sins of rebellion. 9 Then this city will bring me joy,
glory, and honor before all the nations of the earth! The people of the world
will see all the good I do for my people, and they will tremble with awe at
the peace and prosperity I provide for them.

10 "This is what the LORD says: You have said, 'This is a desolate land where
people and animals have all disappeared.' Yet in the empty streets of Jerusa-
lem and Judah's other towns, there will be heard once more 11 the sounds of
joy and laughter. The joyful voices of bridegrooms and brides will be heard
again, along with the joyous songs of people bringing thanksgiving offer-
ings to the LORD. They will sing,

'Give thanks to the LORD of Heaven's Armies,
  for the LORD is good.
  His faithful love endures forever!'

For I will restore the prosperity of this land to what it was in the past, says
the LORD.

12 "This is what the LORD of Heaven's Armies says: This land—though it is
now desolate and has no people and animals—will once more have pastures
where shepherds can lead their flocks. 13 Once again shepherds will count
their flocks in the towns of the hill country, the foothills of Judah,* the Negev,
the land of Benjamin, the vicinity of Jerusalem, and all the towns of Judah.
I, the LORD, have spoken!

14 "The day will come, says the LORD, when I will do for Israel and Judah
all the good things I have promised them.

32:44 Hebrew *the Shephelah.* **33:5** Or *Chaldeans.* **33:13** Hebrew *the Shephelah.*

Prayer 33:8

Lord Jesus, let me embrace this truth. Overwhelm me with your presence and cleanse me of sin so that I can bring you joy, glory, and honor. Let the people of the world see all the good you do for your people. Amen.

15 "In those days and at that time
I will raise up a righteous descendant* from King David's line.
He will do what is just and right throughout the land.
16 In that day Judah will be saved,
and Jerusalem will live in safety.
And this will be its name:
'The LORD Is Our Righteousness.'*

17 For this is what the LORD says: David will have a descendant sitting on the
throne of Israel forever. 18 And there will always be Levitical priests to offer
burnt offerings and grain offerings and sacrifices to me."
19 Then this message came to Jeremiah from the LORD: 20 "This is what the
LORD says: If you can break my covenant with the day and the night so that
one does not follow the other, 21 only then will my covenant with my servant
David be broken. Only then will he no longer have a descendant to reign on
his throne. The same is true for my covenant with the Levitical priests who
minister before me. 22 And as the stars of the sky cannot be counted and the
sand on the seashore cannot be measured, so I will multiply the descendants
of my servant David and the Levites who minister before me."
23 The LORD gave another message to Jeremiah. He said, 24 "Have you no-
ticed what people are saying?—'The LORD chose Judah and Israel and then
abandoned them!' They are sneering and saying that Israel is not worthy to
be counted as a nation. 25 But this is what the LORD says: I would no more
reject my people than I would change my laws that govern night and day,
earth and sky. 26 I will never abandon the descendants of Jacob or David, my
servant, or change the plan that David's descendants will rule the descendants
of Abraham, Isaac, and Jacob. Instead, I will restore them to their land and
have mercy on them."

A Warning for Zedekiah

34 King Nebuchadnezzar* of Babylon came with all the armies from the
kingdoms he ruled, and he fought against Jerusalem and the towns
of Judah. At that time this message came to Jeremiah from the LORD: 2 "Go to
King Zedekiah of Judah, and tell him, 'This is what the LORD, the God of Is-
rael, says: I am about to hand this city over to the king of Babylon, and he will
burn it down. 3 You will not escape his grasp but will be captured and taken
to meet the king of Babylon face to face. Then you will be exiled to Babylon.
4 "'But listen to this promise from the LORD, O Zedekiah, king of Judah.
This is what the LORD says: You will not be killed in war 5 but will die peace-
fully. People will burn incense in your memory, just as they did for your
ancestors, the kings who preceded you. They will mourn for you, crying,
"Alas, our master is dead!" This I have decreed, says the LORD.'"
6 So Jeremiah the prophet delivered the message to King Zedekiah of Ju-
dah. 7 At this time the Babylonian army was besieging Jerusalem, Lachish,
and Azekah—the only fortified cities of Judah not yet captured.

Freedom for Hebrew Slaves

8 This message came to Jeremiah from the LORD after King Zedekiah made
a covenant with the people, proclaiming freedom for the slaves. 9 He had

33:15 Hebrew *a righteous branch.* 33:16 Hebrew *Yahweh Tsidqenu.* 34:1 Hebrew *Nebuchadrezzar,* a variant spelling of Nebuchadnezzar.

ordered all the people to free their Hebrew slaves—both men and women.
No one was to keep a fellow Judean in bondage. 10 The officials and all the
people had obeyed the king's command, 11 but later they changed their
minds. They took back the men and women they had freed, forcing them
to be slaves again.
12 So the LORD gave them this message through Jeremiah: 13 "This is what
the LORD, the God of Israel, says: I made a covenant with your ancestors
long ago when I rescued them from their slavery in Egypt. 14 I told them that
every Hebrew slave must be freed after serving six years. But your ancestors
paid no attention to me. 15 Recently you repented and did what was right,
following my command. You freed your slaves and made a solemn covenant
with me in the Temple that bears my name. 16 But now you have shrugged
off your oath and defiled my name by taking back the men and women you
had freed, forcing them to be slaves once again.
17 "Therefore, this is what the LORD says: Since you have not obeyed me
by setting your countrymen free, I will set you free to be destroyed by war,
disease, and famine. You will be an object of horror to all the nations of the
earth. 18 Because you have broken the terms of our covenant, I will cut you
apart just as you cut apart the calf when you walked between its halves to
solemnize your vows. 19 Yes, I will cut you apart, whether you are officials of
Judah or Jerusalem, court officials, priests, or common people—for you have
broken your oath. 20 I will give you to your enemies, and they will kill you.
Your bodies will be food for the vultures and wild animals.
21 "I will hand over King Zedekiah of Judah and his officials to the army
of the king of Babylon. And although they have left Jerusalem for a while,
22 I will call the Babylonian armies back again. They will fight against this
city and will capture it and burn it down. I will see to it that all the towns of
Judah are destroyed, with no one living there."

The Faithful Recabites

35 This is the message the LORD gave Jeremiah when Jehoiakim son of
Josiah was king of Judah: 2 "Go to the settlement where the families
of the Recabites live, and invite them to the LORD's Temple. Take them into
one of the inner rooms, and offer them some wine."
3 So I went to see Jaazaniah son of Jeremiah and grandson of Habazzi-
niah and all his brothers and sons—representing all the Recabite families.
4 I took them to the Temple, and we went into the room assigned to the sons
of Hanan son of Igdaliah, a man of God. This room was located next to the
one used by the Temple officials, directly above the room of Maaseiah son
of Shallum, the Temple gatekeeper.
5 I set cups and jugs of wine before them and invited them to have a drink,
6 but they refused. "No," they said, "we don't drink wine, because our an-
cestor Jehonadab* son of Recab gave us this command: 'You and your de-
scendants must never drink wine. 7 And do not build houses or plant crops
or vineyards, but always live in tents. If you follow these commands, you
will live long, good lives in the land.' 8 So we have obeyed him in all these
things. We have never had a drink of wine to this day, nor have our wives,
our sons, or our daughters. 9 We haven't built houses or owned vineyards or
farms or planted crops. 10 We have lived in tents and have fully obeyed all the

35:6 Hebrew *Jonadab,* a variant spelling of Jehonadab; also in 35:10, 19. See 2 Kgs 10:15.

Encouragements from these verses

Question 35:13

The Recabites stood in stark contrast to a world gone crazy. The Lord used them as an example of how to be faithful. As you read through this chapter of Jeremiah, what lesson did God want people to learn from the Recabites?

commands of Jehonadab, our ancestor. 11But when King Nebuchadnezzar*
of Babylon attacked this country, we were afraid of the Babylonian and Syr-
ian* armies. So we decided to move to Jerusalem. That is why we are here."
12Then the LORD gave this message to Jeremiah: 13"This is what the LORD
of Heaven's Armies, the God of Israel, says: Go and say to the people in Ju-
dah and Jerusalem, 'Come and learn a lesson about how to obey me. 14The
Recabites do not drink wine to this day because their ancestor Jehonadab
told them not to. But I have spoken to you again and again, and you refuse
to obey me. 15Time after time I sent you prophets, who told you, "Turn from
your wicked ways, and start doing things right. Stop worshiping other gods
so that you might live in peace here in the land I have given to you and your
ancestors." But you would not listen to me or obey me. 16The descendants
of Jehonadab son of Recab have obeyed their ancestor completely, but you
have refused to listen to me.'
17"Therefore, this is what the LORD God of Heaven's Armies, the God of
Israel, says: 'Because you refuse to listen or answer when I call, I will send
upon Judah and Jerusalem all the disasters I have threatened.'"
18Then Jeremiah turned to the Recabites and said, "This is what the LORD
of Heaven's Armies, the God of Israel, says: 'You have obeyed your ancestor
Jehonadab in every respect, following all his instructions.' 19Therefore, this
is what the LORD of Heaven's Armies, the God of Israel, says: 'Jehonadab son
of Recab will always have descendants who serve me.'"

Baruch Reads the LORD's Messages

36 During the fourth year that Jehoiakim son of Josiah was king in
Judah,* the LORD gave this message to Jeremiah: 2"Get a scroll, and
write down all my messages against Israel, Judah, and the other nations.
Begin with the first message back in the days of Josiah, and write down every
message, right up to the present time. 3Perhaps the people of Judah will
repent when they hear again all the terrible things I have planned for them.
Then I will be able to forgive their sins and wrongdoings."
4So Jeremiah sent for Baruch son of Neriah, and as Jeremiah dictated all
the prophecies that the LORD had given him, Baruch wrote them on a scroll.
5Then Jeremiah said to Baruch, "I am a prisoner here and unable to go to the
Temple. 6So you go to the Temple on the next day of fasting, and read the
messages from the LORD that I have had you write on this scroll. Read them
so the people who are there from all over Judah will hear them. 7Perhaps even
yet they will turn from their evil ways and ask the LORD's forgiveness before
it is too late. For the LORD has threatened them with his terrible anger."
8Baruch did as Jeremiah told him and read these messages from the LORD
to the people at the Temple. 9He did this on a day of sacred fasting held in
late autumn,* during the fifth year of the reign of Jehoiakim son of Josiah.
People from all over Judah had come to Jerusalem to attend the services at
the Temple on that day. 10Baruch read Jeremiah's words on the scroll to all the
people. He stood in front of the Temple room of Gemariah, son of Shaphan
the secretary. This room was just off the upper courtyard of the Temple, near
the New Gate entrance.

Story Arc 36:1-32

Baruch

Jeremiah had the support of a dedicated friend named Baruch. Jeremiah had a lot of prophecies and a lot of accounts to write down. He needed a scribe to make copies and make sure that the words God had given him were preserved and shared throughout the land.

Baruch was glad to help. He "did as Jeremiah told him" (v. 8). Working with the Weeping Prophet was risky (v. 19) and angered the king (v. 26). Even when the first scroll was destroyed and their lives were threatened, Baruch helped Jeremiah make another one (v. 28). In the process, Baruch embraced the same consistently broken heart that Jeremiah carried (45:1-5).

These men were resilient in the face of hostility. Without them, we would likely not have the profound words of this book today. Partnership in ministry creates a lasting effect.

Jer 38:6-13 ►

35:11a Hebrew *Nebuchadrezzar,* a variant spelling of Nebuchadnezzar. 35:11b Or *Chaldean and Aramean.* 36:1 The fourth year of Jehoiakim's reign was 605 B.C. 36:9 Hebrew *in the ninth month,* of the ancient Hebrew lunar calendar (also in 36:22). The ninth month in the fifth year of Jehoiakim's reign occurred within the months of November and December 604 B.C. Also see note on 1:3.

11 When Micaiah son of Gemariah and grandson of Shaphan heard the messages from the LORD, 12 he went down to the secretary's room in the palace where the administrative officials were meeting. Elishama the secretary was there, along with Delaiah son of Shemaiah, Elnathan son of Acbor, Gemariah son of Shaphan, Zedekiah son of Hananiah, and all the other officials. 13 When Micaiah told them about the messages Baruch was reading to the people, 14 the officials sent Jehudi son of Nethaniah, grandson of Shelemiah and great-grandson of Cushi, to ask Baruch to come and read the messages to them, too. So Baruch took the scroll and went to them. 15 "Sit down and read the scroll to us," the officials said, and Baruch did as they requested.

16 When they heard all the messages, they looked at one another in alarm. "We must tell the king what we have heard," they said to Baruch. 17 "But first, tell us how you got these messages. Did they come directly from Jeremiah?"

18 So Baruch explained, "Jeremiah dictated them, and I wrote them down in ink, word for word, on this scroll."

19 "You and Jeremiah should both hide," the officials told Baruch. "Don't tell anyone where you are!" 20 Then the officials left the scroll for safekeeping in the room of Elishama the secretary and went to tell the king what had happened.

King Jehoiakim Burns the Scroll

21 The king sent Jehudi to get the scroll. Jehudi brought it from Elishama's room and read it to the king as all his officials stood by. 22 It was late autumn, and the king was in a winterized part of the palace, sitting in front of a fire to keep warm. 23 Each time Jehudi finished reading three or four columns, the king took a knife and cut off that section of the scroll. He then threw it into the fire, section by section, until the whole scroll was burned up. 24 Neither the king nor his attendants showed any signs of fear or repentance at what they heard. 25 Even when Elnathan, Delaiah, and Gemariah begged the king not to burn the scroll, he wouldn't listen.

26 Then the king commanded his son Jerahmeel, Seraiah son of Azriel, and Shelemiah son of Abdeel to arrest Baruch and Jeremiah. But the LORD had hidden them.

Jeremiah Rewrites the Scroll

27 After the king had burned the scroll on which Baruch had written Jeremiah's words, the LORD gave Jeremiah another message. He said, 28 "Get another scroll, and write everything again just as you did on the scroll King Jehoiakim burned. 29 Then say to the king, 'This is what the LORD says: You burned the scroll because it said the king of Babylon would destroy this land and empty it of people and animals. 30 Now this is what the LORD says about King Jehoiakim of Judah: He will have no heirs to sit on the throne of David. His dead body will be thrown out to lie unburied—exposed to the heat of the day and the frost of the night. 31 I will punish him and his family and his attendants for their sins. I will pour out on them and on all the people of Jerusalem and Judah all the disasters I promised, for they would not listen to my warnings.'"

32 So Jeremiah took another scroll and dictated again to his secretary, Baruch. He wrote everything that had been on the scroll King Jehoiakim had burned in the fire. Only this time he added much more!

Question 36:25

Elnathan, Delaiah, and Gemariah—the names of these individuals go down in history as having stood up for what was right. They begged the king to listen to the word of the Lord. It's difficult to imagine, but what do you think you would have done if you had been one of these men?

Zedekiah Calls for Jeremiah

37 Zedekiah son of Josiah succeeded Jehoiachin* son of Jehoiakim as
the king of Judah. He was appointed by King Nebuchadnezzar* of
Babylon. 2 But neither King Zedekiah nor his attendants nor the people who
were left in the land listened to what the LORD said through Jeremiah.
3 Nevertheless, King Zedekiah sent Jehucal son of Shelemiah, and Zeph-
aniah the priest, son of Maaseiah, to ask Jeremiah, "Please pray to the LORD
our God for us." 4 Jeremiah had not yet been imprisoned, so he could come
and go among the people as he pleased.
5 At this time the army of Pharaoh Hophra* of Egypt appeared at the
southern border of Judah. When the Babylonian* army heard about it, they
withdrew from their siege of Jerusalem.
6 Then the LORD gave this message to Jeremiah: 7 "This is what the LORD,
the God of Israel, says: The king of Judah sent you to ask me what is going
to happen. Tell him, 'Pharaoh's army is about to return to Egypt, though he
came here to help you. 8 Then the Babylonians* will come back and capture
this city and burn it to the ground.'
9 "This is what the LORD says: Do not fool yourselves into thinking that
the Babylonians are gone for good. They aren't! 10 Even if you were to destroy
the entire Babylonian army, leaving only a handful of wounded survivors,
they would still stagger from their tents and burn this city to the ground!"

Jeremiah Is Imprisoned

11 When the Babylonian army left Jerusalem because of Pharaoh's approach-
ing army, 12 Jeremiah started to leave the city on his way to the territory of
Benjamin, to claim his share of the property among his relatives there.* 13 But
as he was walking through the Benjamin Gate, a sentry arrested him and
said, "You are defecting to the Babylonians!" The sentry making the arrest
was Irijah son of Shelemiah, grandson of Hananiah.
14 "That's not true!" Jeremiah protested. "I had no intention of doing any
such thing." But Irijah wouldn't listen, and he took Jeremiah before the
officials. 15 They were furious with Jeremiah and had him flogged and im-
prisoned in the house of Jonathan the secretary. Jonathan's house had been
converted into a prison. 16 Jeremiah was put into a dungeon cell, where he
remained for many days.
17 Later King Zedekiah secretly requested that Jeremiah come to the palace,
where the king asked him, "Do you have any messages from the LORD?"
"Yes, I do!" said Jeremiah. "You will be defeated by the king of Babylon."
18 Then Jeremiah asked the king, "What crime have I committed? What
have I done against you, your attendants, or the people that I should be im-
prisoned like this? 19 Where are your prophets now who told you the king
of Babylon would not attack you or this land? 20 Listen, my lord the king, I
beg you. Don't send me back to the dungeon in the house of Jonathan the
secretary, for I will die there."
21 So King Zedekiah commanded that Jeremiah not be returned to the
dungeon. Instead, he was imprisoned in the courtyard of the guard in the
royal palace. The king also commanded that Jeremiah be given a loaf of fresh

37:1a Hebrew *Coniah,* a variant spelling of Jehoiachin. **37:1b** Hebrew *Nebuchadrezzar,* a variant spelling of Nebuchadnezzar. **37:5a** Hebrew *army of Pharaoh;* see 44:30. **37:5b** Or *Chaldean;* also in 37:10, 11. **37:8** Or *Chaldeans;* also in 37:9, 13. **37:12** Hebrew *to separate from there in the midst of the people.*

bread every day as long as there was any left in the city. So Jeremiah was put in the palace prison.

Jeremiah in a Cistern

38 Now Shephatiah son of Mattan, Gedaliah son of Pashhur, Jehucal*
son of Shelemiah, and Pashhur son of Malkijah heard what Jeremiah
had been telling the people. He had been saying, 2"This is what the LORD
says: 'Everyone who stays in Jerusalem will die from war, famine, or disease,
but those who surrender to the Babylonians* will live. Their reward will be
life. They will live!' 3The LORD also says: 'The city of Jerusalem will certainly
be handed over to the army of the king of Babylon, who will capture it.'"
4So these officials went to the king and said, "Sir, this man must die! That
kind of talk will undermine the morale of the few fighting men we have left,
as well as that of all the people. This man is a traitor!"
5King Zedekiah agreed. "All right," he said. "Do as you like. I can't stop
you."
6So the officials took Jeremiah from his cell and lowered him by ropes into
an empty cistern in the prison yard. It belonged to Malkijah, a member of the
royal family. There was no water in the cistern, but there was a thick layer of
mud at the bottom, and Jeremiah sank down into it.
7But Ebed-melech the Ethiopian,* an important court official, heard that
Jeremiah was in the cistern. At that time the king was holding court at the
Benjamin Gate, 8so Ebed-melech rushed from the palace to speak with him.
9"My lord the king," he said, "these men have done a very evil thing in put-
ting Jeremiah the prophet into the cistern. He will soon die of hunger, for
almost all the bread in the city is gone."
10So the king told Ebed-melech, "Take thirty of my men with you, and
pull Jeremiah out of the cistern before he dies."
11So Ebed-melech took the men with him and went to a room in the palace
beneath the treasury, where he found some old rags and discarded cloth-
ing. He carried these to the cistern and lowered them to Jeremiah on a rope.
12Ebed-melech called down to Jeremiah, "Put these rags under your armpits
to protect you from the ropes." Then when Jeremiah was ready, 13they pulled
him out. So Jeremiah was returned to the courtyard of the guard—the palace
prison—where he remained.

Zedekiah Questions Jeremiah

14One day King Zedekiah sent for Jeremiah and had him brought to the third
entrance of the LORD's Temple. "I want to ask you something," the king said.
"And don't try to hide the truth."
15Jeremiah said, "If I tell you the truth, you will kill me. And if I give you
advice, you won't listen to me anyway."
16So King Zedekiah secretly promised him, "As surely as the LORD our Cre-
ator lives, I will not kill you or hand you over to the men who want you dead."
17Then Jeremiah said to Zedekiah, "This is what the LORD God of Heaven's
Armies, the God of Israel, says: 'If you surrender to the Babylonian officers,
you and your family will live, and the city will not be burned down. 18But if
you refuse to surrender, you will not escape! This city will be handed over
to the Babylonians, and they will burn it to the ground.'"

38:1 Hebrew *Jucal,* a variant spelling of Jehucal; see 37:3. 38:2 Or *Chaldeans;* also in 38:18, 19, 23. 38:7 Hebrew *the Cushite.*

Story Arc **38:6-13**

● Ebed-melech

Ebed-melech. His name meant "servant of the king." He was an important court official for the king of Judah. He was also Ethiopian, a foreigner in the land either as an emissary or—if this name is a generic indicator of his role—as someone forced to work for the king.

The irony of his name, however, is that Ebed-melech proved himself to be a servant of the King of kings more than a servant of King Zedekiah. Some of Zedekiah's officials had thrown Jeremiah into an empty well in the king's prison yard. This alarmed Ebed-melech to the point that he rushed to Zedekiah to advocate on behalf of the Weeping Prophet.

Zedekiah was moved by Ebed-melech's compassion. He allowed Ebed-melech to set Jeremiah free. Ebed-melech built a harness and organized thirty men to pull Jeremiah to safety. As a result of Ebed-melech's kindness, the Lord later promised to rescue Ebed-melech when the city of Jerusalem was destroyed (39:17).

People of all backgrounds in all situations can serve the Lord. The question is whether they are ready and willing to do so. Look for opportunities today to serve the Lord. Be ready and bold to advocate for people whom the Lord cares about.

Lam 2:13 ►

[19]“But I am afraid to surrender,” the king said, “for the Babylonians may hand me over to the Judeans who have defected to them. And who knows what they will do to me!”

[20]Jeremiah replied, “You won’t be handed over to them if you choose to obey the LORD. Your life will be spared, and all will go well for you. [21]But if you refuse to surrender, this is what the LORD has revealed to me: [22]All the women left in your palace will be brought out and given to the officers of the Babylonian army. Then the women will taunt you, saying,

‘What fine friends you have!
They have betrayed and misled you.
When your feet sank in the mud,
they left you to your fate!’

[23]All your wives and children will be led out to the Babylonians, and you will not escape. You will be seized by the king of Babylon, and this city will be burned down.”

[24]Then Zedekiah said to Jeremiah, “Don’t tell anyone you told me this, or you will die! [25]My officials may hear that I spoke to you, and they may say, ‘Tell us what you and the king were talking about. If you don’t tell us, we will kill you.’ [26]If this happens, just tell them you begged me not to send you back to Jonathan’s dungeon, for fear you would die there.”

[27]Sure enough, it wasn’t long before the king’s officials came to Jeremiah and asked him why the king had called for him. But Jeremiah followed the king’s instructions, and they left without finding out the truth. No one had overheard the conversation between Jeremiah and the king. [28]And Jeremiah remained a prisoner in the courtyard of the guard until the day Jerusalem was captured.

The Fall of Jerusalem

39 In January* of the ninth year of King Zedekiah’s reign, King Nebuchadnezzar* of Babylon came with his entire army to besiege Jerusalem. [2]Two and a half years later, on July 18* in the eleventh year of Zedekiah’s reign, a section of the city wall was broken down. [3]All the officers of the Babylonian army came in and sat in triumph at the Middle Gate: Nergal-sharezer of Samgar, and Nebo-sarsekim,* a chief officer, and Nergal-sharezer, the king’s adviser, and all the other officers of the king of Babylon.

[4]When King Zedekiah of Judah and all the soldiers saw that the Babylonians had broken into the city, they fled. They waited for nightfall and then slipped through the gate between the two walls behind the king’s garden and headed toward the Jordan Valley.*

[5]But the Babylonian* troops chased them and overtook Zedekiah on the plains of Jericho. They captured him and took him to King Nebuchadnezzar of Babylon, who was at Riblah in the land of Hamath. There the king of Babylon pronounced judgment upon Zedekiah. [6]The king of Babylon made

39:1a Hebrew *In the tenth month,* of the ancient Hebrew lunar calendar. A number of events in Jeremiah can be cross-checked with dates in surviving Babylonian records and related accurately to our modern calendar. This event occurred on January 15, 588 B.C.; see 52:4a and the note there. **39:1b** Hebrew *Nebuchadrezzar,* a variant spelling of Nebuchadnezzar; also in 39:5, 11. **39:2** Hebrew *On the ninth day of the fourth month.* This day was July 18, 586 B.C.; also see note on 39:1a. **39:3** Or *Nergal-sharezer, Samgar-nebo, Sarsekim.* **39:4** Hebrew *the Arabah.* **39:5** Or *Chaldean;* similarly in 39:8.

Zedekiah watch as he slaughtered his sons at Riblah. The king of Babylon
also slaughtered all the nobles of Judah. 7Then he gouged out Zedekiah's
eyes and bound him in bronze chains to lead him away to Babylon.
8Meanwhile, the Babylonians burned Jerusalem, including the royal pal-
ace and the houses of the people, and they tore down the walls of the city.
9Then Nebuzaradan, the captain of the guard, took as exiles to Babylon the
rest of the people who remained in the city, those who had defected to him,
and everyone else who remained. 10But Nebuzaradan allowed some of the
poorest people to stay behind in the land of Judah, and he assigned them to
care for the vineyards and fields.

Jeremiah Remains in Judah

11King Nebuchadnezzar had told Nebuzaradan, the captain of the guard, to
find Jeremiah. 12"See that he isn't hurt," he said. "Look after him well, and
give him anything he wants." 13So Nebuzaradan, the captain of the guard;
Nebushazban, a chief officer; Nergal-sharezer, the king's adviser; and the
other officers of Babylon's king 14sent messengers to bring Jeremiah out
of the prison. They put him under the care of Gedaliah son of Ahikam and
grandson of Shaphan, who took him back to his home. So Jeremiah stayed
in Judah among his own people.
15The LORD had given the following message to Jeremiah while he was
still in prison: 16"Say to Ebed-melech the Ethiopian,* 'This is what the LORD
of Heaven's Armies, the God of Israel, says: I will do to this city everything
I have threatened. I will send disaster, not prosperity. You will see its de-
struction, 17but I will rescue you from those you fear so much. 18Because you
trusted me, I will give you your life as a reward. I will rescue you and keep
you safe. I, the LORD, have spoken!'"

40 The LORD gave a message to Jeremiah after Nebuzaradan, the cap-
tain of the guard, had released him at Ramah. He had found Jere-
miah bound in chains among all the other captives of Jerusalem and Judah
who were being sent to exile in Babylon.
2The captain of the guard called for Jeremiah and said, "The LORD your
God has brought this disaster on this land, 3just as he said he would. For
these people have sinned against the LORD and disobeyed him. That is why
it happened. 4But I am going to take off your chains and let you go. If you
want to come with me to Babylon, you are welcome. I will see that you are
well cared for. But if you don't want to come, you may stay here. The whole
land is before you—go wherever you like. 5If you decide to stay, then return
to Gedaliah son of Ahikam and grandson of Shaphan. He has been appointed
governor of Judah by the king of Babylon. Stay there with the people he
rules. But it's up to you; go wherever you like."

Then Nebuzaradan, the captain of the guard, gave Jeremiah some food
and money and let him go. 6So Jeremiah returned to Gedaliah son of Ahikam
at Mizpah, and he lived in Judah with the few who were still left in the land.

Gedaliah Governs in Judah

7The leaders of the Judean military groups in the countryside heard that the
king of Babylon had appointed Gedaliah son of Ahikam as governor over the

39:16 Hebrew *the Cushite.*

Question 39:1-18

As you read chapter 39, imagine the events from Jeremiah's perspective. What did he see? What did he hear? What importance did Nebuchadnezzar give him? What message did he have for Ebed-melech? If you were Jeremiah, what would have been weighing on your heart? What kept him going?

Question **40:9**

How could Gedaliah's instructions serve as guidelines for us living in our society today?

poor people who were left behind in Judah—the men, women, and children
who hadn't been exiled to Babylon. 8So they went to see Gedaliah at Mizpah.
These included: Ishmael son of Nethaniah, Johanan and Jonathan sons of
Kareah, Seraiah son of Tanhumeth, the sons of Ephai the Netophathite, Jez-
aniah son of the Maacathite, and all their men.
9Gedaliah vowed to them that the Babylonians* meant them no harm.
"Don't be afraid to serve them. Live in the land and serve the king of Babylon,
and all will go well for you," he promised. 10"As for me, I will stay at Mizpah
to represent you before the Babylonians who come to meet with us. Settle
in the towns you have taken, and live off the land. Harvest the grapes and
summer fruits and olives, and store them away."
11When the Judeans in Moab, Ammon, Edom, and the other nearby coun-
tries heard that the king of Babylon had left a few people in Judah and that
Gedaliah was the governor, 12they began to return to Judah from the places
to which they had fled. They stopped at Mizpah to meet with Gedaliah and
then went into the Judean countryside to gather a great harvest of grapes
and other crops.

A Plot against Gedaliah

13Soon after this, Johanan son of Kareah and the other military leaders came
to Gedaliah at Mizpah. 14They said to him, "Did you know that Baalis, king
of Ammon, has sent Ishmael son of Nethaniah to assassinate you?" But Ged-
aliah refused to believe them.
15Later Johanan had a private conference with Gedaliah and volunteered
to kill Ishmael secretly. "Why should we let him come and murder you?"
Johanan asked. "What will happen then to the Judeans who have returned?
Why should the few of us who are still left be scattered and lost?"
16But Gedaliah said to Johanan, "I forbid you to do any such thing, for
you are lying about Ishmael."

The Murder of Gedaliah

41 But in midautumn of that year,* Ishmael son of Nethaniah and
grandson of Elishama, who was a member of the royal family and
had been one of the king's high officials, went to Mizpah with ten men to
meet Gedaliah. While they were eating together, 2Ishmael and his ten men
suddenly jumped up, drew their swords, and killed Gedaliah, whom the
king of Babylon had appointed governor. 3Ishmael also killed all the Judeans
and the Babylonian* soldiers who were with Gedaliah at Mizpah.
4The next day, before anyone had heard about Gedaliah's murder, 5eighty
men arrived from Shechem, Shiloh, and Samaria to worship at the Temple
of the LORD. They had shaved off their beards, torn their clothes, and cut
themselves, and had brought along grain offerings and frankincense. 6Ish-
mael left Mizpah to meet them, weeping as he went. When he reached them,
he said, "Oh, come and see what has happened to Gedaliah!"
7But as soon as they were all inside the town, Ishmael and his men killed
all but ten of them and threw their bodies into a cistern. 8The other ten had
talked Ishmael into letting them go by promising to bring him their stores
of wheat, barley, olive oil, and honey that they had hidden away. 9The cistern

40:9 Or *Chaldeans;* also in 40:10. 41:1 Hebrew *in the seventh month,* of the ancient Hebrew lunar calendar. This month occurred within the months of October and November 586 B.C.; also see note on 39:1a. 41:3 Or *Chaldean.*

where Ishmael dumped the bodies of the men he murdered was the large one* dug by King Asa when he fortified Mizpah to protect himself against King Baasha of Israel. Ishmael son of Nethaniah filled it with corpses.

10 Then Ishmael made captives of the king's daughters and the other people who had been left under Gedaliah's care in Mizpah by Nebuzaradan, the captain of the guard. Taking them with him, he started back toward the land of Ammon.

11 But when Johanan son of Kareah and the other military leaders heard about Ishmael's crimes, 12 they took all their men and set out to stop him. They caught up with him at the large pool near Gibeon. 13 The people Ishmael had captured shouted for joy when they saw Johanan and the other military leaders. 14 And all the captives from Mizpah escaped and began to help Johanan. 15 Meanwhile, Ishmael and eight of his men escaped from Johanan into the land of Ammon.

16 Then Johanan son of Kareah and the other military leaders took all the people they had rescued in Gibeon—the soldiers, women, children, and court officials* whom Ishmael had captured after he killed Gedaliah. 17 They took them all to the village of Geruth-kimham near Bethlehem, where they prepared to leave for Egypt. 18 They were afraid of what the Babylonians* would do when they heard that Ishmael had killed Gedaliah, the governor appointed by the Babylonian king.

Warning to Stay in Judah

42 Then all the military leaders, including Johanan son of Kareah and Jezaniah* son of Hoshaiah, and all the people, from the least to the greatest, approached 2 Jeremiah the prophet. They said, "Please pray to the LORD your God for us. As you can see, we are only a tiny remnant compared to what we were before. 3 Pray that the LORD your God will show us what to do and where to go."

4 "All right," Jeremiah replied. "I will pray to the LORD your God, as you have asked, and I will tell you everything he says. I will hide nothing from you."

5 Then they said to Jeremiah, "May the LORD your God be a faithful witness against us if we refuse to obey whatever he tells us to do! 6 Whether we like it or not, we will obey the LORD our God to whom we are sending you with our plea. For if we obey him, everything will turn out well for us."

7 Ten days later the LORD gave his reply to Jeremiah. 8 So he called for Johanan son of Kareah and the other military leaders, and for all the people, from the least to the greatest. 9 He said to them, "You sent me to the LORD, the God of Israel, with your request, and this is his reply: 10 'Stay here in this land. If you do, I will build you up and not tear you down; I will plant you and not uproot you. For I am sorry about all the punishment I have had to bring upon you. 11 Do not fear the king of Babylon anymore,' says the LORD. 'For I am with you and will save you and rescue you from his power. 12 I will be merciful to you by making him kind, so he will let you stay here in your land.'

13 "But if you refuse to obey the LORD your God, and if you say, 'We will not stay here; 14 instead, we will go to Egypt where we will be free from war, the call to arms, and hunger,' 15 then hear the LORD's message to the remnant of

41:9 As in Greek version; Hebrew reads *murdered because of Gedaliah was one.* **41:16** Or *eunuchs.* **41:18** Or *Chaldeans.* **42:1** Greek version reads *Azariah;* compare 43:2.

Make a Difference

42:1-6

Pray for Alignment

Do you know what happens when the tires on a car get out of alignment? They start to wear unevenly, balding on one side, and as a result, the car wants to veer you out of your lane even if you try your best to keep steering straight.

When you let yourself get out of alignment with God, two things happen: first, you begin to work harder to keep yourself from veering off the road, and second, you eventually realize that you can't hold it together anymore.

The military leaders and others left behind in the destruction of Jerusalem were broken people. They approached Jeremiah with a request: "Please pray to the LORD your God for us... Pray that the LORD your God will show us what to do and where to go" (vv. 2-3). They promised to "obey the LORD" whether they liked it or not (v. 6). They realized they needed to be in alignment with the Lord.

Difference Maker

Reach out to a friend right now and ask them to pray that you will be aligned with what God wants for you. Ask them to pray that God will show you what he wants you to do and where he wants you to go.

Question **43:6**

In this chapter, what do you learn about how to discover God's will for your life in moments of big decisions?

Judah. This is what the LORD of Heaven's Armies, the God of Israel, says: 'If
you are determined to go to Egypt and live there, 16the very war and famine
you fear will catch up to you, and you will die there. 17That is the fate await-
ing every one of you who insists on going to live in Egypt. Yes, you will die
from war, famine, and disease. None of you will escape the disaster I will
bring upon you there.'

18"This is what the LORD of Heaven's Armies, the God of Israel, says: 'Just
as my anger and fury have been poured out on the people of Jerusalem, so
they will be poured out on you when you enter Egypt. You will be an object
of damnation, horror, cursing, and mockery. And you will never see your
homeland again.'

19"Listen, you remnant of Judah. The LORD has told you: 'Do not go to
Egypt!' Don't forget this warning I have given you today. 20For you were not
being honest when you sent me to pray to the LORD your God for you. You
said, 'Just tell us what the LORD our God says, and we will do it!' 21And today
I have told you exactly what he said, but you will not obey the LORD your
God any better now than you have in the past. 22So you can be sure that you
will die from war, famine, and disease in Egypt, where you insist on going."

Jeremiah Taken to Egypt

43 When Jeremiah had finished giving this message from the LORD
their God to all the people, 2Azariah son of Hoshaiah and Johanan
son of Kareah and all the other proud men said to Jeremiah, "You lie! The
LORD our God hasn't forbidden us to go to Egypt! 3Baruch son of Neriah has
convinced you to say this, because he wants us to stay here and be killed by
the Babylonians* or be carried off into exile."

4So Johanan and the other military leaders and all the people refused to
obey the LORD's command to stay in Judah. 5Johanan and the other lead-
ers took with them all the people who had returned from the nearby coun-
tries to which they had fled. 6In the crowd were men, women, and children,
the king's daughters, and all those whom Nebuzaradan, the captain of the
guard, had left with Gedaliah. The prophet Jeremiah and Baruch were also
included. 7The people refused to obey the voice of the LORD and went to
Egypt, going as far as the city of Tahpanhes.

8Then at Tahpanhes, the LORD gave another message to Jeremiah. He said,
9"While the people of Judah are watching, take some large rocks and bury
them under the pavement stones at the entrance of Pharaoh's palace here
in Tahpanhes. 10Then say to the people of Judah, 'This is what the LORD of
Heaven's Armies, the God of Israel, says: I will certainly bring my servant
Nebuchadnezzar,* king of Babylon, here to Egypt. I will set his throne over
these stones that I have hidden. He will spread his royal canopy over them.
11And when he comes, he will destroy the land of Egypt. He will bring death
to those destined for death, captivity to those destined for captivity, and war
to those destined for war. 12He will set fire to the temples of Egypt's gods;
he will burn the temples and carry the idols away as plunder. He will pick
clean the land of Egypt as a shepherd picks fleas from his cloak. And he
himself will leave unharmed. 13He will break down the sacred pillars stand-
ing in the temple of the sun* in Egypt, and he will burn down the temples
of Egypt's gods.'"

43:3 Or *Chaldeans.* 43:10 Hebrew *Nebuchadrezzar,* a variant spelling of Nebuchadnezzar.
43:13 Or *in Heliopolis.*

Judgment for Idolatry

44 This is the message Jeremiah received concerning the Judeans living
in northern Egypt in the cities of Migdol, Tahpanhes, and Mem-
phis,* and in southern Egypt* as well: 2“This is what the LORD of Heaven's
Armies, the God of Israel, says: You saw the calamity I brought on Jerusa-
lem and all the towns of Judah. They now lie deserted and in ruins. 3They
provoked my anger with all their wickedness. They burned incense and wor-
shiped other gods—gods that neither they nor you nor any of your ancestors
had ever even known.
4“Again and again I sent my servants, the prophets, to plead with them,
‘Don't do these horrible things that I hate so much.’ 5But my people would
not listen or turn back from their wicked ways. They kept on burning incense
to these gods. 6And so my fury boiled over and fell like fire on the towns of Ju-
dah and into the streets of Jerusalem, and they are still a desolate ruin today.
7“And now the LORD God of Heaven's Armies, the God of Israel, asks you:
Why are you destroying yourselves? For not one of you will survive—not a
man, woman, or child among you who has come here from Judah, not even
the babies in your arms. 8Why provoke my anger by burning incense to the
idols you have made here in Egypt? You will only destroy yourselves and
make yourselves an object of cursing and mockery for all the nations of the
earth. 9Have you forgotten the sins of your ancestors, the sins of the kings
and queens of Judah, and the sins you and your wives committed in Judah
and Jerusalem? 10To this very hour you have shown no remorse or reverence.
No one has chosen to follow my word and the decrees I gave to you and your
ancestors before you.
11“Therefore, this is what the LORD of Heaven's Armies, the God of Israel,
says: I am determined to destroy every one of you! 12I will take this remnant
of Judah—those who were determined to come here and live in Egypt—and
I will consume them. They will fall here in Egypt, killed by war and famine.
All will die, from the least to the greatest. They will be an object of damna-
tion, horror, cursing, and mockery. 13I will punish them in Egypt just as I
punished them in Jerusalem, by war, famine, and disease. 14Of that remnant
who fled to Egypt, hoping someday to return to Judah, there will be no sur-
vivors. Even though they long to return home, only a handful will do so.”
15Then all the women present and all the men who knew that their wives
had burned incense to idols—a great crowd of all the Judeans living in
northern Egypt and southern Egypt*—answered Jeremiah, 16“We will not
listen to your messages from the LORD! 17We will do whatever we want. We
will burn incense and pour out liquid offerings to the Queen of Heaven just
as much as we like—just as we, and our ancestors, and our kings and officials
have always done in the towns of Judah and in the streets of Jerusalem. For
in those days we had plenty to eat, and we were well off and had no troubles!
18But ever since we quit burning incense to the Queen of Heaven and stopped
worshiping her with liquid offerings, we have been in great trouble and have
been dying from war and famine.”
19“Besides,” the women added, “do you suppose that we were burning
incense and pouring out liquid offerings to the Queen of Heaven, and mak-
ing cakes marked with her image, without our husbands knowing it and
helping us? Of course not!”

Question **44:15-17**

To the Judeans who lived in northern Egypt, Jeremiah spoke God's words and judgment for their refusal to obey the Lord. The people responded defiantly and arrogantly. "We will not listen to your messages from the LORD!" they said (v. 16). "We will do whatever we want" (v. 17). What chance do people have when this is their attitude? How can you check your own heart to avoid this sort of stubborn defiance?

44:1a Hebrew *Noph.* **44:1b** Hebrew *in Pathros.* **44:15** Hebrew *in Egypt, in Pathros.*

Question **45:5**

The Lord gave a message of warning to Jeremiah's faithful assistant, Baruch. What was the temptation the Lord was cautioning against? Why is this struggle with pride so difficult for humans?

20 Then Jeremiah said to all of them, men and women alike, who had given
him that answer, 21 "Do you think the LORD did not know that you and your
ancestors, your kings and officials, and all the people were burning incense to
idols in the towns of Judah and in the streets of Jerusalem? 22 It was because the
LORD could no longer bear all the disgusting things you were doing that he
made your land an object of cursing—a desolate ruin without inhabitants—as
it is today. 23 All these terrible things happened to you because you have burned
incense to idols and sinned against the LORD. You have refused to obey him
and have not followed his instructions, his decrees, and his laws."

24 Then Jeremiah said to them all, including the women, "Listen to this
message from the LORD, all you citizens of Judah who live in Egypt. 25 This
is what the LORD of Heaven's Armies, the God of Israel, says: 'You and your
wives have said, "We will keep our promises to burn incense and pour out liquid offerings to the Queen of Heaven," and you have proved by your actions
that you meant it. So go ahead and carry out your promises and vows to her!'

26 "But listen to this message from the LORD, all you Judeans now living
in Egypt: 'I have sworn by my great name,' says the LORD, 'that my name
will no longer be spoken by any of the Judeans in the land of Egypt. None of
you may invoke my name or use this oath: "As surely as the Sovereign LORD
lives." 27 For I will watch over you to bring you disaster and not good. Everyone
from Judah who is now living in Egypt will suffer war and famine until all of
you are dead. 28 Only a small number will escape death and return to Judah
from Egypt. Then all those who came to Egypt will find out whose words are
true—mine or theirs!

29 "'And this is the proof I give you,' says the LORD, 'that all I have threatened will happen to you and that I will punish you here.' 30 This is what the
LORD says: 'I will turn Pharaoh Hophra, king of Egypt, over to his enemies
who want to kill him, just as I turned King Zedekiah of Judah over to King
Nebuchadnezzar* of Babylon.'"

A Message for Baruch

45 The prophet Jeremiah gave a message to Baruch son of Neriah in the
fourth year of the reign of Jehoiakim son of Josiah,* after Baruch had
written down everything Jeremiah had dictated to him. He said, 2 "This is
what the LORD, the God of Israel, says to you, Baruch: 3 You have said, 'I am
overwhelmed with trouble! Haven't I had enough pain already? And now
the LORD has added more! I am worn out from sighing and can find no rest.'

4 "Baruch, this is what the LORD says: 'I will destroy this nation that I
built. I will uproot what I planted. 5 Are you seeking great things for yourself? Don't do it! I will bring great disaster upon all these people; but I will
give you your life as a reward wherever you go. I, the LORD, have spoken!'"

Messages for the Nations

46 The following messages were given to Jeremiah the prophet from
the LORD concerning foreign nations.

Messages about Egypt

2 This message concerning Egypt was given in the fourth year of the reign of
Jehoiakim son of Josiah, the king of Judah, on the occasion of the battle of

44:30 Hebrew *Nebuchadrezzar,* a variant spelling of Nebuchadnezzar. 45:1 The fourth year of Jehoiakim's reign was 605 B.C.

Carchemish* when Pharaoh Neco, king of Egypt, and his army were defeated
beside the Euphrates River by King Nebuchadnezzar* of Babylon.

3 "Prepare your shields,
and advance into battle!
4 Harness the horses,
and mount the stallions.
Take your positions.
Put on your helmets.
Sharpen your spears,
and prepare your armor.
5 But what do I see?
The Egyptian army flees in terror.
The bravest of its fighting men run
without a backward glance.
They are terrorized at every turn,"
says the LORD.
6 "The swiftest runners cannot flee;
the mightiest warriors cannot escape.
By the Euphrates River to the north,
they stumble and fall.

7 "Who is this, rising like the Nile at floodtime,
overflowing all the land?
8 It is the Egyptian army,
overflowing all the land,
boasting that it will cover the earth like a flood,
destroying cities and their people.
9 Charge, you horses and chariots;
attack, you mighty warriors of Egypt!
Come, all you allies from Ethiopia, Libya, and Lydia*
who are skilled with the shield and bow!
10 For this is the day of the Lord, the LORD of Heaven's Armies,
a day of vengeance on his enemies.
The sword will devour until it is satisfied,
yes, until it is drunk with your blood!
The Lord, the LORD of Heaven's Armies, will receive a sacrifice today
in the north country beside the Euphrates River.

11 "Go up to Gilead to get medicine,
O virgin daughter of Egypt!
But your many treatments
will bring you no healing.
12 The nations have heard of your shame.
The earth is filled with your cries of despair.
Your mightiest warriors will run into each other
and fall down together."

46:2a This event occurred in 605 B.C., during the fourth year of Jehoiakim's reign (according to the calendar system in which the new year begins in the spring). **46:2b** Hebrew *Nebuchadrezzar,* a variant spelling of Nebuchadnezzar; also in 46:13, 26. **46:9** Hebrew *from Cush, Put, and Lud.*

13Then the LORD gave the prophet Jeremiah this message about King Neb-
uchadnezzar's plans to attack Egypt.

14 "Shout it out in Egypt!
Publish it in the cities of Migdol, Memphis,* and Tahpanhes!
Mobilize for battle,
for the sword will devour everyone around you.
15 Why have your warriors fallen?
They cannot stand, for the LORD has knocked them down.
16 They stumble and fall over each other
and say among themselves,
'Come, let's go back to our people,
to the land of our birth.
Let's get away from the sword of the enemy!'
17 There they will say,
'Pharaoh, the king of Egypt, is a loudmouth
who missed his opportunity!'

18 "As surely as I live," says the King,
whose name is the LORD of Heaven's Armies,
"one is coming against Egypt
who is as tall as Mount Tabor,
or as Mount Carmel by the sea!
19 Pack up! Get ready to leave for exile,
you citizens of Egypt!
The city of Memphis will be destroyed,
without a single inhabitant.
20 Egypt is as sleek as a beautiful heifer,
but a horsefly from the north is on its way!
21 Egypt's mercenaries have become like fattened calves.
They, too, will turn and run,
for it is a day of great disaster for Egypt,
a time of great punishment.
22 Egypt flees, silent as a serpent gliding away.
The invading army marches in;
they come against her with axes like woodsmen.
23 They will cut down her people like trees," says the LORD,
"for they are more numerous than locusts.
24 Egypt will be humiliated;
she will be handed over to people from the north."

25The LORD of Heaven's Armies, the God of Israel, says: "I will punish Amon,
the god of Thebes,* and all the other gods of Egypt. I will punish its rulers and
Pharaoh, too, and all who trust in him. 26I will hand them over to those who
want them killed—to King Nebuchadnezzar of Babylon and his army. But after-
ward the land will recover from the ravages of war. I, the LORD, have spoken!

27 "But do not be afraid, Jacob, my servant;
do not be dismayed, Israel.

46:14 Hebrew *Noph;* also in 46:19. **46:25** Hebrew *of No.*

For I will bring you home again from distant lands,
and your children will return from their exile.
Israel* will return to a life of peace and quiet,
and no one will terrorize them.
28 Do not be afraid, Jacob, my servant,
for I am with you," says the LORD.
"I will completely destroy the nations to which
I have exiled you,
but I will not completely destroy you.
I will discipline you, but with justice;
I cannot let you go unpunished."

Prayer **46:28**

Lord Jesus, you promised to be with us, even to the end of the age. Give me the sense to be aware of your presence today wherever I may be and in whatever I may be doing. Amen.

A Message about Philistia

47 This is the LORD's message to the prophet Jeremiah concerning the Philistines of Gaza, before it was captured by the Egyptian army.
2 This is what the LORD says:

"A flood is coming from the north
to overflow the land.
It will destroy the land and everything in it—
cities and people alike.
People will scream in terror,
and everyone in the land will wail.
3 Hear the clatter of stallions' hooves
and the rumble of wheels as the chariots rush by.
Terrified fathers run madly,
without a backward glance at their helpless children.

4 "The time has come for the Philistines to be destroyed,
along with their allies from Tyre and Sidon.
Yes, the LORD is destroying the remnant of
the Philistines,
those colonists from the island of Crete.*
5 Gaza will be humiliated, its head shaved bald;
Ashkelon will lie silent.
You remnant from the Mediterranean coast,*
how long will you cut yourselves in mourning?

6 "Now, O sword of the LORD,
when will you be at rest again?
Go back into your sheath;
rest and be still.

7 "But how can it be still
when the LORD has sent it on a mission?
For the city of Ashkelon
and the people living along the sea
must be destroyed."

46:27 Hebrew *Jacob.* See note on 5:20. 47:4 Hebrew *from Caphtor.* 47:5 Hebrew *the plain.*

A Message about Moab

48 This message was given concerning Moab. This is what the LORD of Heaven's Armies, the God of Israel, says:

"What sorrow awaits the city of Nebo;
it will soon lie in ruins.
The city of Kiriathaim will be humiliated and captured;
the fortress will be humiliated and broken down.
2 No one will ever brag about Moab again,
for in Heshbon there is a plot to destroy her.
'Come,' they say, 'we will cut her off from being
a nation.'
The town of Madmen,* too, will be silenced;
the sword will follow you there.
3 Listen to the cries from Horonaim,
cries of devastation and great destruction.
4 All Moab is destroyed.
Her little ones will cry out.*
5 Her refugees weep bitterly,
climbing the slope to Luhith.
They cry out in terror,
descending the slope to Horonaim.
6 Flee for your lives!
Hide* in the wilderness!
7 Because you have trusted in your wealth and skill,
you will be taken captive.
Your god Chemosh, with his priests and officials,
will be hauled off to distant lands!

8 "All the towns will be destroyed,
and no one will escape—
either on the plateaus or in the valleys,
for the LORD has spoken.
9 Oh, that Moab had wings
so she could fly away,*
for her towns will be left empty,
with no one living in them.
10 Cursed are those who refuse to do the LORD's work,
who hold back their swords from shedding blood!

11 "From his earliest history, Moab has lived in peace,
never going into exile.
He is like wine that has been allowed to settle.
He has not been poured from flask to flask,
and he is now fragrant and smooth.
12 But the time is coming soon," says the LORD,
"when I will send men to pour him from his jar.

48:2 *Madmen* sounds like the Hebrew word for "silence"; it should not be confused with the English word *madmen.* **48:4** Greek version reads *Her cries are heard as far away as Zoar.* **48:6** Or *Hide like a wild donkey;* or *Hide like a juniper shrub;* or *Be like* [the town of] *Aroer.* The meaning of the Hebrew is uncertain. **48:9** Or *Put salt on Moab, / for she will be laid waste.*

They will pour him out,
then shatter the jar!
13 At last Moab will be ashamed of his idol Chemosh,
as the people of Israel were ashamed of their gold
calf at Bethel.*

14 "You used to boast, 'We are heroes,
mighty men of war.'
15 But now Moab and his towns will be destroyed.
His most promising youth are doomed to slaughter,"
says the King, whose name is the LORD of Heaven's Armies.
16 "Destruction is coming fast for Moab;
calamity threatens ominously.
17 You friends of Moab,
weep for him and cry!
See how the strong scepter is broken,
how the beautiful staff is shattered!

18 "Come down from your glory
and sit in the dust, you people of Dibon,
for those who destroy Moab will shatter Dibon, too.
They will tear down all your towers.
19 You people of Aroer,
stand beside the road and watch.
Shout to those who flee from Moab,
'What has happened there?'

20 "And the reply comes back,
'Moab lies in ruins, disgraced;
weep and wail!
Tell it by the banks of the Arnon River:
Moab has been destroyed!'
21 Judgment has been poured out on the towns
of the plateau—
on Holon and Jahaz* and Mephaath,
22 on Dibon and Nebo and Beth-diblathaim,
23 on Kiriathaim and Beth-gamul and Beth-meon,
24 on Kerioth and Bozrah—
all the towns of Moab, far and near.

25 "The strength of Moab has ended.
His arm has been broken," says the LORD.
26 "Let him stagger and fall like a drunkard,
for he has rebelled against the LORD.
Moab will wallow in his own vomit,
ridiculed by all.
27 Did you not ridicule the people of Israel?
Were they caught in the company of thieves
that you should despise them as you do?

48:13 Hebrew *ashamed when they trusted in Bethel.* **48:21** Hebrew *Jahzah,* a variant spelling of Jahaz.

Questions I want to ask

28 "You people of Moab,
flee from your towns and live in the caves.
Hide like doves that nest
in the clefts of the rocks.
29 We have all heard of the pride of Moab,
for his pride is very great.
We know of his lofty pride,
his arrogance, and his haughty heart.
30 I know about his insolence,"
says the LORD,
"but his boasts are empty—
as empty as his deeds.
31 So now I wail for Moab;
yes, I will mourn for Moab.
My heart is broken for the men of Kir-hareseth.*

32 "You people of Sibmah, rich in vineyards,
I will weep for you even more than I did for Jazer.
Your spreading vines once reached as far as the Dead Sea,*
but the destroyer has stripped you bare!
He has harvested your grapes and summer fruits.
33 Joy and gladness are gone from fruitful Moab.
The presses yield no wine.
No one treads the grapes with shouts of joy.
There is shouting, yes, but not of joy.

34 "Instead, their awful cries of terror can be heard from Heshbon clear
across to Elealeh and Jahaz; from Zoar all the way to Horonaim and Eglath-
shelishiyah. Even the waters of Nimrim are dried up now.
35 "I will put an end to Moab," says the LORD, "for the people offer sacrifices
at the pagan shrines and burn incense to their false gods. 36 My heart moans
like a flute for Moab and Kir-hareseth, for all their wealth has disappeared.
37 The people shave their heads and beards in mourning. They slash their
hands and put on clothes made of burlap. 38 There is crying and sorrow in
every Moabite home and on every street. For I have smashed Moab like an
old, unwanted jar. 39 How it is shattered! Hear the wailing! See the shame
of Moab! It has become an object of ridicule, an example of ruin to all its
neighbors."
40 This is what the LORD says:

"Look! The enemy swoops down like an eagle,
spreading his wings over Moab.
41 Its cities will fall,
and its strongholds will be seized.
Even the mightiest warriors will be in anguish
like a woman in labor.
42 Moab will no longer be a nation,
for it has boasted against the LORD.

48:31 Hebrew *Kir-heres,* a variant spelling of Kir-hareseth; also in 48:36. 48:32 Hebrew *the sea of Jazer.*

43 "Terror and traps and snares will be your lot,
O Moab," says the LORD.
44 "Those who flee in terror will fall into a trap,
and those who escape the trap will step into a snare.
I will see to it that you do not get away,
for the time of your judgment has come,"
says the LORD.
45 "The people flee as far as Heshbon
but are unable to go on.
For a fire comes from Heshbon,
King Sihon's ancient home,
to devour the entire land
with all its rebellious people.

46 "What sorrow awaits you, O people of Moab!
The people of the god Chemosh are destroyed!
Your sons and your daughters
have been taken away as captives.
47 But I will restore the fortunes of Moab
in days to come.
I, the LORD, have spoken!"

This is the end of Jeremiah's prophecy concerning Moab.

A Message about Ammon

49 This message was given concerning the Ammonites. This is what the LORD says:

"Are there no descendants of Israel
to inherit the land of Gad?
Why are you, who worship Molech,*
living in its towns?
2 In the days to come," says the LORD,
"I will sound the battle cry against your city of Rabbah.
It will become a desolate heap of ruins,
and the neighboring towns will be burned.
Then Israel will take back the land
you took from her," says the LORD.

3 "Cry out, O Heshbon,
for the town of Ai is destroyed.
Weep, O people of Rabbah!
Put on your clothes of mourning.
Weep and wail, hiding in the hedges,
for your god Molech, with his priests and officials,
will be hauled off to distant lands.
4 You are proud of your fertile valleys,
but they will soon be ruined.
You trusted in your wealth,

49:1 Hebrew *Malcam,* a variant spelling of Molech; also in 49:3.

Write your notes in this space

Make a Difference

49:11

I Will Protect

A recurring theme throughout all God's Word is the care for orphans and widows. Even in this prophecy of judgment, where it was revealed that God would destroy a foreign land for its sin, God still promised to protect the orphans and widows. He declared that they could depend upon him.

Difference Maker

Honor God by honoring those God has promised to protect. Contact a local adoption agency or nursing home to see how you could help.

you rebellious daughter,
and thought no one could ever harm you.
5 But look! I will bring terror upon you,"
says the Lord, the LORD of Heaven's Armies.
"Your neighbors will chase you from your land,
and no one will help your exiles as they flee.
6 But I will restore the fortunes of the Ammonites
in days to come.
I, the LORD, have spoken."

Messages about Edom

7 This message was given concerning Edom. This is what the LORD of Heaven's Armies says:

"Is there no wisdom in Teman?
Is no one left to give wise counsel?
8 Turn and flee!
Hide in deep caves, you people of Dedan!
For when I bring disaster on Edom,*
I will punish you, too!
9 Those who harvest grapes
always leave a few for the poor.
If thieves came at night,
they would not take everything.
10 But I will strip bare the land of Edom,
and there will be no place left to hide.
Its children, its brothers, and its neighbors
will all be destroyed,
and Edom itself will be no more.
11 But I will protect the orphans who remain among you.
Your widows, too, can depend on me for help."

12 And this is what the LORD says: "If the innocent must suffer, how much
more must you! You will not go unpunished! You must drink this cup of
judgment! 13 For I have sworn by my own name," says the LORD, "that Bozrah
will become an object of horror and a heap of ruins; it will be mocked and
cursed. All its towns and villages will be desolate forever."

14 I have heard a message from the LORD
that an ambassador was sent to the nations to say,
"Form a coalition against Edom,
and prepare for battle!"

15 The LORD says to Edom,
"I will cut you down to size among the nations.
You will be despised by all.
16 You have been deceived
by the fear you inspire in others
and by your own pride.

49:8 Hebrew *Esau;* also in 49:10.

You live in a rock fortress
and control the mountain heights.
But even if you make your nest among the peaks with the eagles,
I will bring you crashing down,"
says the LORD.

17 "Edom will be an object of horror.
All who pass by will be appalled
and will gasp at the destruction they see there.
18 It will be like the destruction of Sodom and Gomorrah
and their neighboring towns," says the LORD.
"No one will live there;
no one will inhabit it.
19 I will come like a lion from the thickets of the Jordan,
leaping on the sheep in the pasture.
I will chase Edom from its land,
and I will appoint the leader of my choice.
For who is like me, and who can challenge me?
What ruler can oppose my will?"

20 Listen to the LORD's plans against Edom
and the people of Teman.
Even the little children will be dragged off like sheep,
and their homes will be destroyed.
21 The earth will shake with the noise of Edom's fall,
and its cry of despair will be heard all the way to the Red Sea.*
22 Look! The enemy swoops down like an eagle,
spreading his wings over Bozrah.
Even the mightiest warriors will be in anguish
like a woman in labor.

A Message about Damascus

23 This message was given concerning Damascus. This is what the LORD says:

"The towns of Hamath and Arpad are struck with fear,
for they have heard the news of their destruction.
Their hearts are troubled
like a wild sea in a raging storm.
24 Damascus has become feeble,
and all her people turn to flee.
Fear, anguish, and pain have gripped her
as they grip a woman in labor.
25 That famous city, a city of joy,
will be forsaken!
26 Her young men will fall in the streets and die.
Her soldiers will all be killed,"
says the LORD of Heaven's Armies.
27 "And I will set fire to the walls of Damascus
that will burn up the palaces of Ben-hadad."

49:21 Hebrew *sea of reeds.*

A Message about Kedar and Hazor

28 This message was given concerning Kedar and the kingdoms of Hazor, which were attacked by King Nebuchadnezzar* of Babylon. This is what the LORD says:

"Advance against Kedar!
Destroy the warriors from the East!
29 Their flocks and tents will be captured,
and their household goods and camels will be taken away.
Everywhere shouts of panic will be heard:
'We are terrorized at every turn!'
30 Run for your lives," says the LORD.
"Hide yourselves in deep caves, you people of Hazor,
for King Nebuchadnezzar of Babylon has plotted against you
and is preparing to destroy you.

31 "Go up and attack that complacent nation,"
says the LORD.
"Its people live alone in the desert
without walls or gates.
32 Their camels and other livestock will all be yours.
I will scatter to the winds these people
who live in remote places.*
I will bring calamity upon them
from every direction," says the LORD.
33 "Hazor will be inhabited by jackals,
and it will be desolate forever.
No one will live there;
no one will inhabit it."

A Message about Elam

34 This message concerning Elam came to the prophet Jeremiah from the LORD at the beginning of the reign of King Zedekiah of Judah. 35 This is what the LORD of Heaven's Armies says:

"I will destroy the archers of Elam—
the best of their forces.
36 I will bring enemies from all directions,
and I will scatter the people of Elam to the four winds.
They will be exiled to countries around the world.
37 I myself will go with Elam's enemies to shatter it.
In my fierce anger, I will bring great disaster
upon the people of Elam," says the LORD.
"Their enemies will chase them with the sword
until I have destroyed them completely.
38 I will set my throne in Elam," says the LORD,
"and I will destroy its king and officials.

49:28 Hebrew *Nebuchadrezzar,* a variant spelling of Nebuchadnezzar; also in 49:30. **49:32** Or *who clip the corners of their hair.*

39 But I will restore the fortunes of Elam
in days to come.
I, the LORD, have spoken!"

A Message about Babylon

50 The LORD gave Jeremiah the prophet this message concerning Babylon and the land of the Babylonians.* 2 This is what the LORD says:

"Tell the whole world,
and keep nothing back.
Raise a signal flag
to tell everyone that Babylon will fall!
Her images and idols* will be shattered.
Her gods Bel and Marduk will be utterly disgraced.
3 For a nation will attack her from the north
and bring such destruction that no one will live there again.
Everything will be gone;
both people and animals will flee.

Hope for Israel and Judah

4 "In those coming days,"
says the LORD,
"the people of Israel will return home
together with the people of Judah.
They will come weeping
and seeking the LORD their God.
5 They will ask the way to Jerusalem*
and will start back home again.
They will bind themselves to the LORD
with an eternal covenant that will never be forgotten.

6 "My people have been lost sheep.
Their shepherds have led them astray
and turned them loose in the mountains.
They have lost their way
and can't remember how to get back to the sheepfold.
7 All who found them devoured them.
Their enemies said,
'We did nothing wrong in attacking them,
for they sinned against the LORD,
their true place of rest,
and the hope of their ancestors.'

8 "But now, flee from Babylon!
Leave the land of the Babylonians.
Like male goats at the head of the flock,
lead my people home again.
9 For I am raising up an army
of great nations from the north.

50:1 Or *Chaldeans;* also in 50:8, 25, 35, 45. **50:2** The Hebrew term (literally *round things*) probably alludes to dung. **50:5** Hebrew *Zion;* also in 50:28.

Question 50:4

If you've ever been given a second chance, what did you do with it? What advice might Jeremiah's words be giving you here?

They will join forces to attack Babylon,
and she will be captured.
The enemies' arrows will go straight to the mark;
they will not miss!
10 Babylonia* will be looted
until the attackers are glutted with loot.
I, the LORD, have spoken!

Babylon's Sure Fall

11 "You rejoice and are glad,
you who plundered my chosen people.
You frisk about like a calf in a meadow
and neigh like a stallion.
12 But your homeland* will be overwhelmed
with shame and disgrace.
You will become the least of nations—
a wilderness, a dry and desolate land.
13 Because of the LORD's anger,
Babylon will become a deserted wasteland.
All who pass by will be horrified
and will gasp at the destruction they see there.

14 "Yes, prepare to attack Babylon,
all you surrounding nations.
Let your archers shoot at her; spare no arrows.
For she has sinned against the LORD.
15 Shout war cries against her from every side.
Look! She surrenders!
Her walls have fallen.
It is the LORD's vengeance,
so take vengeance on her.
Do to her as she has done to others!
16 Take from Babylon all those who plant crops;
send all the harvesters away.
Because of the sword of the enemy,
everyone will run away and rush back to their own lands.

Hope for God's People

17 "The Israelites are like sheep
that have been scattered by lions.
First the king of Assyria ate them up.
Then King Nebuchadnezzar* of Babylon cracked
their bones."
18 Therefore, this is what the LORD of Heaven's Armies,
the God of Israel, says:
"Now I will punish the king of Babylon and his land,
just as I punished the king of Assyria.
19 And I will bring Israel home again to its own land,
to feed in the fields of Carmel and Bashan,

50:10 Or *Chaldea.* 50:12 Hebrew *your mother.* 50:17 Hebrew *Nebuchadrezzar,* a variant spelling of Nebuchadnezzar.

and to be satisfied once more
in the hill country of Ephraim and Gilead.
20 In those days," says the LORD,
"no sin will be found in Israel or in Judah,
for I will forgive the remnant I preserve.

The LORD's Judgment on Babylon

21 "Go up, my warriors, against the land of Merathaim
and against the people of Pekod.
Pursue, kill, and completely destroy* them,
as I have commanded you," says the LORD.
22 "Let the battle cry be heard in the land,
a shout of great destruction.
23 Babylon, the mightiest hammer in all the earth,
lies broken and shattered.
Babylon is desolate among the nations!
24 Listen, Babylon, for I have set a trap for you.
You are caught, for you have fought against the LORD.
25 The LORD has opened his armory
and brought out weapons to vent his fury.
The terror that falls upon the Babylonians
will be the work of the Sovereign LORD of Heaven's Armies.
26 Yes, come against her from distant lands.
Break open her granaries.
Crush her walls and houses into heaps of rubble.
Destroy her completely, and leave nothing!
27 Destroy even her young bulls—
it will be terrible for them, too!
Slaughter them all!
For Babylon's day of reckoning has come.
28 Listen to the people who have escaped from Babylon,
as they tell in Jerusalem
how the LORD our God has taken vengeance
against those who destroyed his Temple.

29 "Send out a call for archers to come to Babylon.
Surround the city so none can escape.
Do to her as she has done to others,
for she has defied the LORD, the Holy One of Israel.
30 Her young men will fall in the streets and die.
Her soldiers will all be killed,"
says the LORD.

31 "See, I am your enemy, you arrogant people,"
says the Lord, the LORD of Heaven's Armies.
"Your day of reckoning has arrived—
the day when I will punish you.
32 O land of arrogance, you will stumble and fall,
and no one will raise you up.

50:21 The Hebrew term used here refers to the complete consecration of things or people to the LORD, either by destroying them or by giving them as an offering.

Why this matters!

For I will light a fire in the cities of Babylon
that will burn up everything around them."

33 This is what the LORD of Heaven's Armies says:
"The people of Israel and Judah have been wronged.
Their captors hold them and refuse to let them go.
34 But the one who redeems them is strong.
His name is the LORD of Heaven's Armies.
He will defend them
and give them rest again in Israel.
But for the people of Babylon
there will be no rest!

35 "The sword of destruction will strike the Babylonians,"
says the LORD.
"It will strike the people of Babylon—
her officials and wise men, too.
36 The sword will strike her wise counselors,
and they will become fools.
The sword will strike her mightiest warriors,
and panic will seize them.
37 The sword will strike her horses and chariots
and her allies from other lands,
and they will all become like women.
The sword will strike her treasures,
and they all will be plundered.
38 A drought* will strike her water supply,
causing it to dry up.
And why? Because the whole land is filled with idols,
and the people are madly in love with them.

39 "Soon Babylon will be inhabited by desert animals and hyenas.
It will be a home for owls.
Never again will people live there;
it will lie desolate forever.
40 I will destroy it as I* destroyed Sodom and Gomorrah
and their neighboring towns," says the LORD.
"No one will live there;
no one will inhabit it.

41 "Look! A great army is coming from the north.
A great nation and many kings
are rising against you from far-off lands.
42 They are armed with bows and spears.
They are cruel and show no mercy.
As they ride forward on horses,
they sound like a roaring sea.
They are coming in battle formation,
planning to destroy you, Babylon.

50:38 Or *sword;* the Hebrew words for *drought* and *sword* are very similar. **50:40** Hebrew *as God.*

Remember to take notes!

43 The king of Babylon has heard reports about the enemy,
and he is weak with fright.
Pangs of anguish have gripped him,
like those of a woman in labor.

44 "I will come like a lion from the thickets of the Jordan,
leaping on the sheep in the pasture.
I will chase Babylon from its land,
and I will appoint the leader of my choice.
For who is like me, and who can challenge me?
What ruler can oppose my will?"

45 Listen to the LORD's plans against Babylon
and the land of the Babylonians.
Even the little children will be dragged off like sheep,
and their homes will be destroyed.
46 The earth will shake with the shout, "Babylon has been taken!"
and its cry of despair will be heard around the world.

51 1 This is what the LORD says:
"I will stir up a destroyer against Babylon
and the people of Babylonia.*
2 Foreigners will come and winnow her,
blowing her away as chaff.
They will come from every side
to rise against her in her day of trouble.
3 Don't let the archers put on their armor
or draw their bows.
Don't spare even her best soldiers!
Let her army be completely destroyed.*
4 They will fall dead in the land of the Babylonians,*
slashed to death in her streets.
5 For the LORD of Heaven's Armies
has not abandoned Israel and Judah.
He is still their God,
even though their land was filled with sin
against the Holy One of Israel."

6 Flee from Babylon! Save yourselves!
Don't get trapped in her punishment!
It is the LORD's time for vengeance;
he will repay her in full.
7 Babylon has been a gold cup in the LORD's hands,
a cup that made the whole earth drunk.
The nations drank Babylon's wine,
and it drove them all mad.
8 But suddenly Babylon, too, has fallen.
Weep for her.

51:1 Hebrew *of Leb-kamai,* a code name for Babylonia. **51:3** The Hebrew term used here refers to the complete consecration of things or people to the LORD, either by destroying them or by giving them as an offering. **51:4** Or *Chaldeans;* also in 51:54.

Give her medicine.
Perhaps she can yet be healed.
9 We would have helped her if we could,
but nothing can save her now.
Let her go; abandon her.
Return now to your own land.
For her punishment reaches to the heavens;
it is so great it cannot be measured.
10 The LORD has vindicated us.
Come, let us announce in Jerusalem*
everything the LORD our God has done.

11 Sharpen the arrows!
Lift up the shields!*
For the LORD has inspired the kings of the Medes
to march against Babylon and destroy her.
This is his vengeance against those
who desecrated his Temple.
12 Raise the battle flag against Babylon!
Reinforce the guard and station the watchmen.
Prepare an ambush,
for the LORD will fulfill all his plans against Babylon.
13 You are a city by a great river,
a great center of commerce,
but your end has come.
The thread of your life is cut.
14 The LORD of Heaven's Armies has taken this vow
and has sworn to it by his own name:
"Your cities will be filled with enemies,
like fields swarming with locusts,
and they will shout in triumph over you."

A Hymn of Praise to the LORD

15 The LORD made the earth by his power,
and he preserves it by his wisdom.
With his own understanding
he stretched out the heavens.
16 When he speaks in the thunder,
the heavens roar with rain.
He causes the clouds to rise over the earth.
He sends the lightning with the rain
and releases the wind from his storehouses.

17 The whole human race is foolish and has no knowledge!
The craftsmen are disgraced by the idols they make,
for their carefully shaped works are a fraud.
These idols have no breath or power.
18 Idols are worthless; they are ridiculous lies!
On the day of reckoning they will all be destroyed.

51:10 Hebrew *Zion;* also in 51:24. 51:11 Greek version reads *Fill up the quivers.*

19 But the God of Israel* is no idol!
He is the Creator of everything that exists,
including his people, his own special possession.
The LORD of Heaven's Armies is his name!

Babylon's Great Punishment

20 "You* are my battle-ax and sword,"
says the LORD.
"With you I will shatter nations
and destroy many kingdoms.
21 With you I will shatter armies—
destroying the horse and rider,
the chariot and charioteer.
22 With you I will shatter men and women,
old people and children,
young men and young women.
23 With you I will shatter shepherds and flocks,
farmers and oxen,
captains and officers.

24 "I will repay Babylon
and the people of Babylonia*
for all the wrong they have done
to my people in Jerusalem," says the LORD.

25 "Look, O mighty mountain, destroyer of the earth!
I am your enemy," says the LORD.
"I will raise my fist against you,
to knock you down from the heights.
When I am finished,
you will be nothing but a heap of burnt rubble.
26 You will be desolate forever.
Even your stones will never again be used for building.
You will be completely wiped out,"
says the LORD.

27 Raise a signal flag to the nations.
Sound the battle cry!
Mobilize them all against Babylon.
Prepare them to fight against her!
Bring out the armies of Ararat, Minni, and Ashkenaz.
Appoint a commander,
and bring a multitude of horses like swarming locusts!
28 Bring against her the armies of the nations—
led by the kings of the Medes
and all their captains and officers.

29 The earth trembles and writhes in pain,
for everything the LORD has planned against Babylon stands unchanged.

51:19 Hebrew *the Portion of Jacob.* See note on 5:20. 51:20 Possibly Cyrus, whom God used to conquer Babylon. Compare Isa 44:28; 45:1. 51:24 Or *Chaldea;* also in 51:35.

How God is at work here

Prayer 51:36

Jesus, I need you. You are my Advocate. Thank you for standing for me and taking the consequences for me. Thank you for sending your Holy Spirit to fight for me. How could I ever repay you? Amen.

Babylon will be left desolate without a single inhabitant.
30 Her mightiest warriors no longer fight.
They stay in their barracks, their courage gone.
They have become like women.
The invaders have burned the houses
and broken down the city gates.
31 The news is passed from one runner to the next
as the messengers hurry to tell the king
that his city has been captured.
32 All the escape routes are blocked.
The marshes have been set aflame,
and the army is in a panic.

33 This is what the LORD of Heaven's Armies,
the God of Israel, says:
"Babylon is like wheat on a threshing floor,
about to be trampled.
In just a little while
her harvest will begin."

34 "King Nebuchadnezzar* of Babylon has eaten and crushed us
and drained us of strength.
He has swallowed us like a great monster
and filled his belly with our riches.
He has thrown us out of our own country.
35 Make Babylon suffer as she made us suffer,"
say the people of Zion.
"Make the people of Babylonia pay for spilling our blood,"
says Jerusalem.

The LORD's Vengeance on Babylon

36 This is what the LORD says to Jerusalem:

"I will be your lawyer to plead your case,
and I will avenge you.
I will dry up her river,
as well as her springs,
37 and Babylon will become a heap of ruins,
haunted by jackals.
She will be an object of horror and contempt,
a place where no one lives.
38 Her people will roar together like strong lions.
They will growl like lion cubs.
39 And while they lie inflamed with all their wine,
I will prepare a different kind of feast for them.
I will make them drink until they fall asleep,
and they will never wake up again,"
says the LORD.

51:34 Hebrew *Nebuchadrezzar,* a variant spelling of Nebuchadnezzar.

40 "I will bring them down
like lambs to the slaughter,
like rams and goats to be sacrificed.

41 "How Babylon* is fallen—
great Babylon, praised throughout the earth!
Now she has become an object of horror
among the nations.
42 The sea has risen over Babylon;
she is covered by its crashing waves.
43 Her cities now lie in ruins;
she is a dry wasteland
where no one lives or even passes by.
44 And I will punish Bel, the god of Babylon,
and make him vomit up all he has eaten.
The nations will no longer come and worship him.
The wall of Babylon has fallen!

A Message for the Exiles

45 "Come out, my people, flee from Babylon.
Save yourselves! Run from the LORD's fierce anger.
46 But do not panic; don't be afraid
when you hear the first rumor of approaching forces.
For rumors will keep coming year by year.
Violence will erupt in the land
as the leaders fight against each other.
47 For the time is surely coming
when I will punish this great city and all her idols.
Her whole land will be disgraced,
and her dead will lie in the streets.
48 Then the heavens and earth will rejoice,
for out of the north will come destroying armies
against Babylon," says the LORD.
49 "Just as Babylon killed the people of Israel
and others throughout the world,
so must her people be killed.
50 Get out, all you who have escaped the sword!
Do not stand and watch—flee while you can!
Remember the LORD, though you are in a far-off land,
and think about your home in Jerusalem."

51 "We are ashamed," the people say.
"We are insulted and disgraced
because the LORD's Temple
has been defiled by foreigners."

52 "Yes," says the LORD, "but the time is coming
when I will destroy Babylon's idols.
The groans of her wounded people

51:41 Hebrew *Sheshach,* a code name for Babylon.

will be heard throughout the land.
53 Though Babylon reaches as high as the heavens
and makes her fortifications incredibly strong,
I will still send enemies to plunder her.
I, the LORD, have spoken!

Babylon's Complete Destruction

54 "Listen! Hear the cry of Babylon,
the sound of great destruction from the land of the Babylonians.
55 For the LORD is destroying Babylon.
He will silence her loud voice.
Waves of enemies pound against her;
the noise of battle rings through the city.
56 Destroying armies come against Babylon.
Her mighty men are captured,
and their weapons break in their hands.
For the LORD is a God who gives just punishment;
he always repays in full.
57 I will make her officials and wise men drunk,
along with her captains, officers, and warriors.
They will fall asleep
and never wake up again!"
says the King, whose name is
the LORD of Heaven's Armies.

58 This is what the LORD of Heaven's Armies says:
"The thick walls of Babylon will be leveled to the ground,
and her massive gates will be burned.
The builders from many lands have worked in vain,
for their work will be destroyed by fire!"

Jeremiah's Message Sent to Babylon

59 The prophet Jeremiah gave this message to Seraiah son of Neriah and grand-
son of Mahseiah, a staff officer, when Seraiah went to Babylon with King
Zedekiah of Judah. This was during the fourth year of Zedekiah's reign.*
60 Jer-
emiah had recorded on a scroll all the terrible disasters that would soon come
upon Babylon—all the words written here.
61 He said to Seraiah, "When you
get to Babylon, read aloud everything on this scroll.
62 Then say, 'LORD, you
have said that you will destroy Babylon so that neither people nor animals
will remain here. She will lie empty and abandoned forever.'
63 When you have
finished reading the scroll, tie it to a stone and throw it into the Euphrates
River.
64 Then say, 'In this same way Babylon and her people will sink, never
again to rise, because of the disasters I will bring upon her.'"
This is the end of Jeremiah's messages.

The Fall of Jerusalem

52 Zedekiah was twenty-one years old when he became king, and he
reigned in Jerusalem eleven years. His mother was Hamutal, the
daughter of Jeremiah from Libnah.
2 But Zedekiah did what was evil in the

51:59 The fourth year of Zedekiah's reign was 593 B.C.

LORD's sight, just as Jehoiakim had done. 3These things happened because of
the LORD's anger against the people of Jerusalem and Judah, until he finally
banished them from his presence and sent them into exile.
Zedekiah rebelled against the king of Babylon. 4So on January 15,* during
the ninth year of Zedekiah's reign, King Nebuchadnezzar* of Babylon led
his entire army against Jerusalem. They surrounded the city and built siege
ramps against its walls. 5Jerusalem was kept under siege until the eleventh
year of King Zedekiah's reign.
6By July 18 in the eleventh year of Zedekiah's reign,* the famine in the city
had become very severe, and the last of the food was entirely gone. 7Then a
section of the city wall was broken down, and all the soldiers fled. Since the
city was surrounded by the Babylonians,* they waited for nightfall. Then
they slipped through the gate between the two walls behind the king's gar-
den and headed toward the Jordan Valley.*
8But the Babylonian troops chased King Zedekiah and overtook him on
the plains of Jericho, for his men had all deserted him and scattered. 9They
captured the king and took him to the king of Babylon at Riblah in the land
of Hamath. There the king of Babylon pronounced judgment upon Zede-
kiah. 10The king of Babylon made Zedekiah watch as he slaughtered his sons.
He also slaughtered all the officials of Judah at Riblah. 11Then he gouged out
Zedekiah's eyes and bound him in bronze chains, and the king of Babylon
led him away to Babylon. Zedekiah remained there in prison until the day
of his death.

The Temple Destroyed

12On August 17 of that year,* which was the nineteenth year of King Nebu-
chadnezzar's reign, Nebuzaradan, the captain of the guard and an official
of the Babylonian king, arrived in Jerusalem. 13He burned down the Temple
of the LORD, the royal palace, and all the houses of Jerusalem. He destroyed
all the important buildings* in the city. 14Then he supervised the entire Bab-
ylonian* army as they tore down the walls of Jerusalem on every side. 15Then
Nebuzaradan, the captain of the guard, took as exiles some of the poorest
of the people, the rest of the people who remained in the city, the defectors
who had declared their allegiance to the king of Babylon, and the rest of the
craftsmen. 16But Nebuzaradan allowed some of the poorest people to stay
behind to care for the vineyards and fields.
17The Babylonians broke up the bronze pillars in front of the LORD's
Temple, the bronze water carts, and the great bronze basin called the Sea,
and they carried all the bronze away to Babylon. 18They also took all the
ash buckets, shovels, lamp snuffers, basins, dishes, and all the other bronze
articles used for making sacrifices at the Temple. 19The captain of the guard
also took the small bowls, incense burners, basins, pots, lampstands, ladles,
bowls used for liquid offerings, and all the other articles made of pure gold
or silver.

Question 52:1-34

The book of Jeremiah ends in a depressing, crushing blow. It would almost seem that all Jeremiah's prophecies were wasted. It would almost seem like evil won. It would almost seem like God had lost and that his plan for his people, like his temple, was destroyed. How could God ever redeem this loss? How could God fulfill his promises to Abraham and Sarah, to David, to Solomon, and to the prophets? How could God fulfill his promises to you when something so disruptive happens?

52:4a Hebrew *on the tenth day of the tenth month,* of the ancient Hebrew lunar calendar. A number of events in Jeremiah can be cross-checked with dates in surviving Babylonian records and related accurately to our modern calendar. This day was January 15, 588 B.C. **52:4b** Hebrew *Nebuchadrezzar,* a variant spelling of Nebuchadnezzar; also in 52:12, 28, 29, 30. **52:6** Hebrew *By the ninth day of the fourth month* [in the eleventh year of Zedekiah's reign]. This day was July 18, 586 B.C.; also see note on 52:4a. **52:7a** Or *the Chaldeans;* similarly in 52:8, 17. **52:7b** Hebrew *the Arabah.* **52:12** Hebrew *On the tenth day of the fifth month,* of the ancient Hebrew lunar calendar. This day was August 17, 586 B.C.; also see note on 52:4a. **52:13** Or *destroyed the houses of all the important people.* **52:14** Or *Chaldean.*

20 The weight of the bronze from the two pillars, the Sea with the twelve
bronze oxen beneath it, and the water carts was too great to be measured.
These things had been made for the LORD's Temple in the days of King Sol-
omon. 21 Each of the pillars was 27 feet tall and 18 feet in circumference.* They
were hollow, with walls 3 inches thick.* 22 The bronze capital on top of each
pillar was 7½ feet* high and was decorated with a network of bronze pome-
granates all the way around. 23 There were 96 pomegranates on the sides, and
a total of 100 pomegranates on the network around the top.

24 Nebuzaradan, the captain of the guard, took with him as prisoners Se-
raiah the high priest, Zephaniah the priest of the second rank, and the three
chief gatekeepers. 25 And from among the people still hiding in the city, he
took an officer who had been in charge of the Judean army; seven of the
king's personal advisers; the army commander's chief secretary, who was in
charge of recruitment; and sixty other citizens. 26 Nebuzaradan, the captain
of the guard, took them all to the king of Babylon at Riblah. 27 And there at
Riblah, in the land of Hamath, the king of Babylon had them all put to death.
So the people of Judah were sent into exile from their land.

28 The number of captives taken to Babylon in the seventh year of Neb-
uchadnezzar's reign* was 3,023. 29 Then in Nebuchadnezzar's eighteenth
year* he took 832 more. 30 In Nebuchadnezzar's twenty-third year* he sent
Nebuzaradan, the captain of the guard, who took 745 more—a total of 4,600
captives in all.

Hope for Israel's Royal Line

31 In the thirty-seventh year of the exile of King Jehoiachin of Judah, Evil-
merodach ascended to the Babylonian throne. He was kind to* Jehoiachin
and released him from prison on March 31 of that year.* 32 He spoke kindly
to Jehoiachin and gave him a higher place than all the other exiled kings in
Babylon. 33 He supplied Jehoiachin with new clothes to replace his prison
garb and allowed him to dine in the king's presence for the rest of his life.
34 So the Babylonian king gave him a regular food allowance as long as he
lived. This continued until the day of his death.

52:21a Hebrew *18 cubits* [8.3 meters] *tall and 12 cubits* [5.5 meters] *in circumference.* **52:21b** Hebrew *4 fingers thick* [8 centimeters]. **52:22** Hebrew *5 cubits* [2.3 meters]. **52:28** This exile in the seventh year of Nebuchadnezzar's reign occurred in 597 B.C. **52:29** This exile in the eighteenth year of Nebuchadnezzar's reign occurred in 586 B.C. **52:30** This exile in the twenty-third year of Nebuchadnezzar's reign occurred in 581 B.C. **52:31a** Hebrew *He raised the head of.* **52:31b** Hebrew *on the twenty-fifth day of the twelfth month,* of the ancient Hebrew lunar calendar. This day was March 31, 561 B.C.; also see note on 52:4a.

Lamentations Introduction

In every society and every culture, there are moments of grief, despair, and loss that historians have written about. Lamentations is such an account. Lamentations was written sometime between 586 BC and 516 BC by someone (maybe Jeremiah, the Weeping Prophet) who witnessed an enemy nation known as Babylon capture the city of Jerusalem. This army would go on to invade all Judah and destroy most of the city of Jerusalem—including the sacred place, the temple—as well as exile the people of Judah. This was a tragic moment, and the resulting words reflect the truest, deepest grief.

Lamentations was written in poetic form (five poems written in acrostic form, in case you were wondering) and would likely have been read or sung aloud at gatherings like funerals in ancient days. Faithful Jews still read (and pray aloud) from Lamentations at the Western Wall in Jerusalem to this day. One interesting fact about the story line in Lamentations is that it ends tragically. The Lord remained silent throughout the book, and there was no suggestion that there would be restoration—not for the people, not for the temple, and not for the author of the book. Lamentations is a true and pure example of a response to suffering—of remaining in a place of groaning over the sin and pain of the past that has led to present-day consequences.

Lamentations is honest about the fact that the people of Judah were guilty of turning their backs to God, but this book also presents a hope that God will bring mercy. As you read the pages of this lament, sit in the space of suffering with the author, with the people of Judah, and reflect on the hard places in your own life. Don't move beyond them too fast. Instead, allow God to use the lessons that you find in recognizing the pain of a moment to transform you, prayerfully recognizing that God is indeed there in the suffering.

Story Arc

- **Jeremiah**

Lamentations

Sorrow in Jerusalem

1 * 1 Jerusalem, once so full of people,
is now deserted.
She who was once great among the nations
now sits alone like a widow.
Once the queen of all the earth,
she is now a slave.

2 She sobs through the night;
tears stream down her cheeks.
Among all her lovers,
there is no one left to comfort her.
All her friends have betrayed her
and become her enemies.

3 Judah has been led away into captivity,
oppressed with cruel slavery.
She lives among foreign nations
and has no place of rest.
Her enemies have chased her down,
and she has nowhere to turn.

4 The roads to Jerusalem* are in mourning,
for crowds no longer come to celebrate the festivals.
The city gates are silent,
her priests groan,
her young women are crying—
how bitter is her fate!

5 Her oppressors have become her masters,
and her enemies prosper,
for the LORD has punished Jerusalem
for her many sins.
Her children have been captured
and taken away to distant lands.

6 All the majesty of beautiful Jerusalem*
has been stripped away.

1 Each of the first four chapters of this book is an acrostic, laid out in the order of the Hebrew alphabet. The first word of each verse begins with a successive Hebrew letter. Chapters 1, 2, and 4 have one verse for each of the 22 Hebrew letters. Chapter 3 contains 22 stanzas of three verses each. Though chapter 5 has 22 verses, it is not an acrostic. 1:4 Hebrew *Zion;* also in 1:17. 1:6 Hebrew *of the daughter of Zion.*

Please write on this page!

Her princes are like starving deer
searching for pasture.
They are too weak to run
from the pursuing enemy.

7 In the midst of her sadness and wandering,
Jerusalem remembers her ancient splendor.
But now she has fallen to her enemy,
and there is no one to help her.
Her enemy struck her down
and laughed as she fell.

8 Jerusalem has sinned greatly,
so she has been tossed away like a filthy rag.
All who once honored her now despise her,
for they have seen her stripped naked and humiliated.
All she can do is groan
and hide her face.

9 She defiled herself with immorality
and gave no thought to her future.
Now she lies in the gutter
with no one to lift her out.
"LORD, see my misery," she cries.
"The enemy has triumphed."

10 The enemy has plundered her completely,
taking every precious thing she owns.
She has seen foreigners violate her sacred Temple,
the place the LORD had forbidden them to enter.

11 Her people groan as they search for bread.
They have sold their treasures for food to stay alive.
"O LORD, look," she mourns,
"and see how I am despised.

12 "Does it mean nothing to you, all you who pass by?
Look around and see if there is any suffering like mine,
which the LORD brought on me
when he erupted in fierce anger.

13 "He has sent fire from heaven that burns in my bones.
He has placed a trap in my path and turned me back.
He has left me devastated,
racked with sickness all day long.

14 "He wove my sins into ropes
to hitch me to a yoke of captivity.
The Lord sapped my strength and turned me over to my enemies;
I am helpless in their hands.

Question 1:16

Sometimes the most appropriate response to suffering is to weep, mourn, and grieve. It would be wrong to suggest that making a difference in this world always requires your proactive, confident, do-it-yourself attitude. Sometimes the most meaningful posture is to stop and lament. What makes you weep today?

Prayer 1:20

God, help me when I am distressed and point out the things in my life that do not bring you glory. Be with me when I experience loss and give me the ability to be present with those who suffer. Amen.

15 "The Lord has treated my mighty men
with contempt.
At his command a great army has come
to crush my young warriors.
The Lord has trampled his beloved city*
like grapes are trampled in a winepress.

16 "For all these things I weep;
tears flow down my cheeks.
No one is here to comfort me;
any who might encourage me are far away.
My children have no future,
for the enemy has conquered us."

17 Jerusalem reaches out for help,
but no one comforts her.
Regarding his people Israel,*
the LORD has said,
"Let their neighbors be their enemies!
Let them be thrown away like a filthy rag!"

18 "The LORD is right," Jerusalem says,
"for I rebelled against him.
Listen, people everywhere;
look upon my anguish and despair,
for my sons and daughters
have been taken captive to distant lands.

19 "I begged my allies for help,
but they betrayed me.
My priests and leaders
starved to death in the city,
even as they searched for food
to save their lives.

20 "LORD, see my anguish!
My heart is broken
and my soul despairs,
for I have rebelled against you.
In the streets the sword kills,
and at home there is only death.

21 "Others heard my groans,
but no one turned to comfort me.
When my enemies heard about my troubles,
they were happy to see what you had done.
Oh, bring the day you promised,
when they will suffer as I have suffered.

1:15 Hebrew *the virgin daughter of Judah.* 1:17 Hebrew *Jacob.* The names "Jacob" and "Israel" are often interchanged throughout the Old Testament, referring sometimes to the individual patriarch and sometimes to the nation.

22 "Look at all their evil deeds, LORD.
Punish them,
as you have punished me
for all my sins.
My groans are many,
and I am sick at heart."

God's Anger at Sin

2 1 The Lord in his anger
has cast a dark shadow over beautiful
Jerusalem.*
The fairest of Israel's cities lies in the dust,
thrown down from the heights of heaven.
In his day of great anger,
the Lord has shown no mercy even to his Temple.*

2 Without mercy the Lord has destroyed
every home in Israel.*
In his anger he has broken down
the fortress walls of beautiful Jerusalem.*
He has brought them to the ground,
dishonoring the kingdom and its rulers.

3 All the strength of Israel
vanishes beneath his fierce anger.
The Lord has withdrawn his protection
as the enemy attacks.
He consumes the whole land of Israel
like a raging fire.

4 He bends his bow against his people,
as though he were their enemy.
His strength is used against them
to kill their finest youth.
His fury is poured out like fire
on beautiful Jerusalem.*

5 Yes, the Lord has vanquished Israel
like an enemy.
He has destroyed her palaces
and demolished her fortresses.
He has brought unending sorrow and tears
upon beautiful Jerusalem.

6 He has broken down his Temple
as though it were merely a garden shelter.
The LORD has blotted out all memory
of the holy festivals and Sabbath days.

2:1a Hebrew *the daughter of Zion;* also in 2:8, 10, 18. **2:1b** Hebrew *his footstool.* **2:2a** Hebrew *Jacob;* also in 2:3b. See note on 1:17. **2:2b** Hebrew *the daughter of Judah;* also in 2:5. **2:4** Hebrew *on the tent of the daughter of Zion.*

Kings and priests fall together
before his fierce anger.

7 The Lord has rejected his own altar;
he despises his own sanctuary.
He has given Jerusalem's palaces
to her enemies.
They shout in the LORD's Temple
as though it were a day of celebration.

8 The LORD was determined
to destroy the walls of beautiful Jerusalem.
He made careful plans for their destruction,
then did what he had planned.
Therefore, the ramparts and walls
have fallen down before him.

9 Jerusalem's gates have sunk into the ground.
He has smashed their locks and bars.
Her kings and princes have been exiled to distant lands;
her law has ceased to exist.
Her prophets receive
no more visions from the LORD.

10 The leaders of beautiful Jerusalem
sit on the ground in silence.
They are clothed in burlap
and throw dust on their heads.
The young women of Jerusalem
hang their heads in shame.

11 I have cried until the tears no longer come;
my heart is broken.
My spirit is poured out in agony
as I see the desperate plight of my people.
Little children and tiny babies
are fainting and dying in the streets.

12 They cry out to their mothers,
"We need food and drink!"
Their lives ebb away in the streets
like the life of a warrior wounded in battle.
They gasp for life
as they collapse in their mothers' arms.

13 What can I say about you?
Who has ever seen such sorrow?
O daughter of Jerusalem,
to what can I compare your anguish?
O virgin daughter of Zion,

Story Arc **2:13**

Jeremiah

After the overwhelming pain and sorrow of the first chapter and a half of Lamentations, 2:13 is especially moving. Throughout his life, Jeremiah carried the weight of grief for God's hurting people and cried out for a savior. As a result, this verse became a profound glimpse in Scripture of Jesus: a man of sorrows and full of comfort. Through his own deep wounds, he brings healing.

Ezek 1:1-3 ►

how can I comfort you?
For your wound is as deep as the sea.
Who can heal you?

14 Your prophets have said
so many foolish things, false to the core.
They did not save you from exile
by pointing out your sins.
Instead, they painted false pictures,
filling you with false hope.

15 All who pass by jeer at you.
They scoff and insult beautiful Jerusalem,* saying,
"Is this the city called 'Most Beautiful in All the World'
and 'Joy of All the Earth'?"

16 All your enemies mock you.
They scoff and snarl and say,
"We have destroyed her at last!
We have long waited for this day,
and it is finally here!"

17 But it is the LORD who did just as he planned.
He has fulfilled the promises of disaster
he made long ago.
He has destroyed Jerusalem without mercy.
He has caused her enemies to gloat over her
and has given them power over her.

18 Cry aloud* before the Lord,
O walls of beautiful Jerusalem!
Let your tears flow like a river
day and night.
Give yourselves no rest;
give your eyes no relief.

19 Rise during the night and cry out.
Pour out your hearts like water to the Lord.
Lift up your hands to him in prayer,
pleading for your children,
for in every street
they are faint with hunger.

20 "O LORD, think about this!
Should you treat your own people this way?
Should mothers eat their own children,
those they once bounced on their knees?
Should priests and prophets be killed
within the Lord's Temple?

2:15 Hebrew *the daughter of Jerusalem.* 2:18 Hebrew *Their heart cried.*

Question 3:9

Consider the stark contrast of this sense of being blocked by stone and crooked paths to Proverbs 3:5-6. How do both passages represent a deep, resilient faith?

Make a Difference

3:21–26

New Mercies

His mercies are new every morning. Repeat that phrase. *His mercies are new every morning.* It doesn't matter what yesterday was like; his mercies are new every morning. It doesn't matter how you feel about how you did, for his mercies are new every morning. Even if you feel like you blew it, his mercies are new every morning. Whether you feel like you'll never get another chance or it seems like you'll never recover, his mercies are new every morning.

The truth is this: Jesus loves to redeem, and he loves to restore. He loves a fresh, new day because he gets to lift you up again and walk with you. His mercies are new every morning, so don't try to take a twisted advantage of God's mercy, where you sin a little bit while anticipating that he'll forgive you again tomorrow. Instead, take full advantage of his mercy. Live in it! Let it refresh you and change you into a new person who lives in his faithfulness each and every day.

Difference Maker

Be merciful to others today just as God has offered you mercy.

21 "See them lying in the streets—
young and old,
boys and girls,
killed by the swords of the enemy.
You have killed them in your anger,
slaughtering them without mercy.

22 "You have invited terrors from all around,
as though you were calling them to a day
of feasting.
In the day of the LORD's anger,
no one has escaped or survived.
The enemy has killed all the children
whom I carried and raised."

Hope in the LORD's Faithfulness

3 1 I am the one who has seen the afflictions
that come from the rod of the LORD's anger.
2 He has led me into darkness,
shutting out all light.
3 He has turned his hand against me
again and again, all day long.

4 He has made my skin and flesh grow old.
He has broken my bones.
5 He has besieged and surrounded me
with anguish and distress.
6 He has buried me in a dark place,
like those long dead.

7 He has walled me in, and I cannot escape.
He has bound me in heavy chains.
8 And though I cry and shout,
he has shut out my prayers.
9 He has blocked my way with a high stone wall;
he has made my road crooked.

10 He has hidden like a bear or a lion,
waiting to attack me.
11 He has dragged me off the path and torn me in pieces,
leaving me helpless and devastated.
12 He has drawn his bow
and made me the target for his arrows.

13 He shot his arrows
deep into my heart.
14 My own people laugh at me.
All day long they sing their mocking songs.
15 He has filled me with bitterness
and given me a bitter cup of sorrow to drink.

16 He has made me chew on gravel.
He has rolled me in the dust.
17 Peace has been stripped away,
and I have forgotten what prosperity is.
18 I cry out, "My splendor is gone!
Everything I had hoped for from the LORD is lost!"

19 The thought of my suffering and homelessness
is bitter beyond words.*
20 I will never forget this awful time,
as I grieve over my loss.
21 Yet I still dare to hope
when I remember this:

22 The faithful love of the LORD never ends!*
His mercies never cease.
23 Great is his faithfulness;
his mercies begin afresh each morning.
24 I say to myself, "The LORD is my inheritance;
therefore, I will hope in him!"

25 The LORD is good to those who depend on him,
to those who search for him.
26 So it is good to wait quietly
for salvation from the LORD.
27 And it is good for people to submit at an early age
to the yoke of his discipline:

28 Let them sit alone in silence
beneath the LORD's demands.
29 Let them lie face down in the dust,
for there may be hope at last.
30 Let them turn the other cheek to those who strike them
and accept the insults of their enemies.

31 For no one is abandoned
by the Lord forever.
32 Though he brings grief, he also shows compassion
because of the greatness of his unfailing love.
33 For he does not enjoy hurting people
or causing them sorrow.

34 If people crush underfoot
all the prisoners of the land,
35 if they deprive others of their rights
in defiance of the Most High,
36 if they twist justice in the courts—
doesn't the Lord see all these things?

3:19 Or *is wormwood and gall.* **3:22** As in Syriac version; Hebrew reads *of the LORD keeps us from destruction.*

Make a Difference 3:26

Wait

Is there anything more difficult than waiting quietly? Probably. Even so, by the way many of us act when we are supposed to be calm and watch time pass by, you would think we were having a root canal done on our funny bone!

We want God's salvation now, our worries to go away now, evil people to be gone now, our families to be blissful now, our health to be perfect now, and money to fall into our lap now. Perhaps we need to chill out right now, in this instant. We don't think that we can afford to wait any longer. Still, it is good to wait on the Lord.

Difference Maker

Practice waiting today without taking out your phone. Fill the void instead with an active pursuit of God.

Question 3:30

The author of Lamentations made an interesting statement in verse 30 with a scandalous command: turn the other cheek, essentially humbling oneself to take the punishment and humiliation of disgrace. In today's world this is hardly a value. We do everything we can to make sure the world knows we are right about this issue or that issue. How different that sort of thinking is compared to Lamentations 3:30—a full act of humility that relies on God to deal with the situation. In what ways can you turn the other cheek, that is, show patience in situations when it is very difficult to offer this sort of posture?

37 Who can command things to happen
without the Lord's permission?
38 Does not the Most High
send both calamity and good?
39 Then why should we, mere humans, complain
when we are punished for our sins?

40 Instead, let us test and examine our ways.
Let us turn back to the LORD.
41 Let us lift our hearts and hands
to God in heaven and say,
42 "We have sinned and rebelled,
and you have not forgiven us.

43 "You have engulfed us with your anger,
chased us down,
and slaughtered us without mercy.
44 You have hidden yourself in a cloud
so our prayers cannot reach you.
45 You have discarded us as refuse and garbage
among the nations.

46 "All our enemies
have spoken out against us.
47 We are filled with fear,
for we are trapped, devastated, and ruined."
48 Tears stream from my eyes
because of the destruction of my people!

49 My tears flow endlessly;
they will not stop
50 until the LORD looks down
from heaven and sees.
51 My heart is breaking
over the fate of all the women of Jerusalem.

52 My enemies, whom I have never harmed,
hunted me down like a bird.
53 They threw me into a pit
and dropped stones on me.
54 The water rose over my head,
and I cried out, "This is the end!"

55 But I called on your name, LORD,
from deep within the pit.
56 You heard me when I cried, "Listen to
my pleading!
Hear my cry for help!"
57 Yes, you came when I called;
you told me, "Do not fear."

58 Lord, you have come to my defense;
you have redeemed my life.
59 You have seen the wrong they have done to me, LORD.
Be my judge, and prove me right.
60 You have seen the vengeful plots
my enemies have laid against me.

61 LORD, you have heard the vile names they call me.
You know all about the plans they have made.
62 My enemies whisper and mutter
as they plot against me all day long.
63 Look at them! Whether they sit or stand,
I am the object of their mocking songs.

64 Pay them back, LORD,
for all the evil they have done.
65 Give them hard and stubborn hearts,
and then let your curse fall on them!
66 Chase them down in your anger,
destroying them beneath the LORD's heavens.

God's Anger Satisfied

4 1 How the gold has lost its luster!
Even the finest gold has become dull.
The sacred gemstones
lie scattered in the streets!

2 See how the precious children of Jerusalem,*
worth their weight in fine gold,
are now treated like pots of clay
made by a common potter.

3 Even the jackals feed their young,
but not my people Israel.
They ignore their children's cries,
like ostriches in the desert.

4 The parched tongues of their little ones
stick to the roofs of their mouths in thirst.
The children cry for bread,
but no one has any to give them.

5 The people who once ate the richest foods
now beg in the streets for anything they can get.
Those who once wore the finest clothes
now search the garbage dumps for food.

6 The guilt* of my people
is greater than that of Sodom,

4:2 Hebrew *precious sons of Zion.* 4:6 Or *punishment.*

Patterns I see in this text

where utter disaster struck in a moment
and no hand offered help.

7 Our princes once glowed with health—
brighter than snow, whiter than milk.
Their faces were as ruddy as rubies,
their appearance like fine jewels.*

8 But now their faces are blacker than soot.
No one recognizes them in the streets.
Their skin sticks to their bones;
it is as dry and hard as wood.

9 Those killed by the sword are better off
than those who die of hunger.
Starving, they waste away
for lack of food from the fields.

10 Tenderhearted women
have cooked their own children.
They have eaten them
to survive the siege.

11 But now the anger of the LORD is satisfied.
His fierce anger has been poured out.
He started a fire in Jerusalem*
that burned the city to its foundations.

12 Not a king in all the earth—
no one in all the world—
would have believed that an enemy
could march through the gates of Jerusalem.

13 Yet it happened because of the sins of
her prophets
and the sins of her priests,
who defiled the city
by shedding innocent blood.

14 They wandered blindly
through the streets,
so defiled by blood
that no one dared touch them.

15 "Get away!" the people shouted at them.
"You're defiled! Don't touch us!"
So they fled to distant lands
and wandered among foreign nations,
but none would let them stay.

4:7 Hebrew *like lapis lazuli.* 4:11 Hebrew *in Zion.*

16 The LORD himself has scattered them,
and he no longer helps them.
People show no respect for the priests
and no longer honor the leaders.

17 We looked in vain for our allies
to come and save us,
but we were looking to nations
that could not help us.

18 We couldn't go into the streets
without danger to our lives.
Our end was near; our days were numbered.
We were doomed!

19 Our enemies were swifter than eagles in flight.
If we fled to the mountains, they found us.
If we hid in the wilderness,
they were waiting for us there.

20 Our king—the LORD's anointed, the very life
of our nation—
was caught in their snares.
We had thought that his shadow
would protect us against any nation on earth!

21 Are you rejoicing in the land of Uz,
O people of Edom?
But you, too, must drink from the cup of the LORD's anger.
You, too, will be stripped naked in your drunkenness.

22 O beautiful Jerusalem,* your punishment will end;
you will soon return from exile.
But Edom, your punishment is just beginning;
soon your many sins will be exposed.

Prayer for Restoration

5 1 LORD, remember what has happened to us.
See how we have been disgraced!
2 Our inheritance has been turned over to strangers,
our homes to foreigners.
3 We are orphaned and fatherless.
Our mothers are widowed.
4 We have to pay for water to drink,
and even firewood is expensive.
5 Those who pursue us are at our heels;
we are exhausted but are given no rest.
6 We submitted to Egypt and Assyria
to get enough food to survive.

4:22 Hebrew *O daughter of Zion.*

Things to reflect on

Make a Difference **5:17**

An End without Hope?

The book of Lamentations comes to a close with unresolved tension. The author intentionally did not seal it up with a happy feeling. Instead there is a reminder of sadness, as if to say, "This pain must mean something, so don't dismiss it."

As you conclude reading Lamentations, take a moment to think of the world around you. Zoom in and zoom out. Think about your personal situation all the way to a global perspective. It is true that in all our lives, there will be lamenting. Sin, evil, and pain are all too real in our world, and we need the mercy of God. What do you lament in this season in your life? Is it personal? Is it something related to the big picture of the world around you?

God does bring his mercy. We know that, even though the book of Lamentations is open-ended, God does deliver his people and brings salvation through Jesus Christ. Sitting in lamentation is a spiritual practice. May it be an important part of your spiritual life moving forward.

Difference Maker

As you consider these laments, make a prayer list that you can give over to God.

Prayer **5:22**

God, I give you the areas of my life that are in suffering and lamentation. Help me, Lord. Hear the cries of my heart for my life and the people around me. Bring to me your salvation that is found in Jesus Christ and remind me of your presence even in the midst of pain and difficult times. Amen.

7 Our ancestors sinned, but they have died—
and we are suffering the punishment they deserved!

8 Slaves have now become our masters;
there is no one left to rescue us.
9 We hunt for food at the risk of our lives,
for violence rules the countryside.
10 The famine has blackened our skin
as though baked in an oven.
11 Our enemies rape the women in Jerusalem*
and the young girls in all the towns of Judah.
12 Our princes are being hanged by their thumbs,
and our elders are treated with contempt.
13 Young men are led away to work at millstones,
and boys stagger under heavy loads of wood.
14 The elders no longer sit in the city gates;
the young men no longer dance and sing.
15 Joy has left our hearts;
our dancing has turned to mourning.
16 The garlands have* fallen from our heads.
Weep for us because we have sinned.
17 Our hearts are sick and weary,
and our eyes grow dim with tears.
18 For Jerusalem* is empty and desolate,
a place haunted by jackals.

19 But LORD, you remain the same forever!
Your throne continues from generation to generation.
20 Why do you continue to forget us?
Why have you abandoned us for so long?
21 Restore us, O LORD, and bring us back to you again!
Give us back the joys we once had!
22 Or have you utterly rejected us?
Are you angry with us still?

5:11 Hebrew *in Zion.* **5:16** Or *The crown has.* **5:18** Hebrew *Mount Zion.*

Ezekiel Introduction

The book of Ezekiel begins in a setting you may not expect—Babylon. The prophet Ezekiel was in a river of exiles fleeing from Judah. This mass migration of refugees displaced by war had to relocate hundreds of miles east in the land of their conquering enemy. Still, the location and the desperation did not stop God from pouring out his message of strength and new life for his people.

What follows is a series of brain-busting visions, doomsday predictions, frightening punishments, and breath-giving revelations. This book is not for the faint of soul. This book is both a horror show and a heart-lifting adventure. Expect the unexpected.

More than anything, though, the book of Ezekiel wants readers to recognize one primary message from God: "You will know that I am the LORD." God will revive his people and shepherd them home. Don't lose hope in God. In this, the fourth longest book of the Old Testament, the resounding prophetic voice of Ezekiel proclaimed the strength of the Lord against the princes of the world and the hope of faith in God against the hopelessness of false allegiances.

Buckle up for this long tour de force. Put yourself in Ezekiel's mind and heart as you open your imagination but stay rooted to reality. No matter what visions Ezekiel shared, they had real implications for real people experiencing real anguish. Through it all, look for what God is saying to you and your community about knowing the hope of his salvation plan.

Story Arcs

- Ezekiel
- Jesus

Ezekiel

A Vision of Living Beings

1 On July 31* of my thirtieth year,* while I was with the Judean exiles be-
side the Kebar River in Babylon, the heavens were opened and I saw
visions of God. 2 This happened during the fifth year of King Jehoiachin's
captivity. 3 (The LORD gave this message to Ezekiel son of Buzi, a priest, be-
side the Kebar River in the land of the Babylonians,* and he felt the hand of
the LORD take hold of him.)
4 As I looked, I saw a great storm coming from the north, driving before it a
huge cloud that flashed with lightning and shone with brilliant light. There
was fire inside the cloud, and in the middle of the fire glowed something
like gleaming amber.* 5 From the center of the cloud came four living beings
that looked human, 6 except that each had four faces and four wings. 7 Their
legs were straight, and their feet had hooves like those of a calf and shone
like burnished bronze. 8 Under each of their four wings I could see human
hands. So each of the four beings had four faces and four wings. 9 The wings
of each living being touched the wings of the beings beside it. Each one
moved straight forward in any direction without turning around.
10 Each had a human face in the front, the face of a lion on the right side,
the face of an ox on the left side, and the face of an eagle at the back. 11 Each
had two pairs of outstretched wings—one pair stretched out to touch the
wings of the living beings on either side of it, and the other pair covered its
body. 12 They went in whatever direction the spirit chose, and they moved
straight forward in any direction without turning around.
13 The living beings looked like bright coals of fire or brilliant torches,
and lightning seemed to flash back and forth among them. 14 And the living
beings darted to and fro like flashes of lightning.
15 As I looked at these beings, I saw four wheels touching the ground be-
side them, one wheel belonging to each. 16 The wheels sparkled as if made
of beryl. All four wheels looked alike and were made the same; each wheel
had a second wheel turning crosswise within it. 17 The beings could move in
any of the four directions they faced, without turning as they moved. 18 The
rims of the four wheels were tall and frightening, and they were covered
with eyes all around.
19 When the living beings moved, the wheels moved with them. When they
flew upward, the wheels went up, too. 20 The spirit of the living beings was
in the wheels. So wherever the spirit went, the wheels and the living beings
also went. 21 When the beings moved, the wheels moved. When the beings
stopped, the wheels stopped. When the beings flew upward, the wheels rose
up, for the spirit of the living beings was in the wheels.

Story Arc **1:1-3**

● Ezekiel

Ezekiel was thirty years old when God rocked his life. He was in a foreign environment, camped by a river in Babylon, without a home, without a job, without hope for the future. That's when the hand of the Lord took hold of him (v. 3). For the next twenty years, Ezekiel would boldly serve the Lord through an extraordinarily startling ministry (40:1).

Take a moment to scan through the book of Ezekiel. Skim through the many visions and messages that follow these introductory verses. As Ezekiel followed the Lord's lead, what do you think would have been the most difficult part of his life?

Ezek 34:11-24 ►

1:1a Hebrew *On the fifth day of the fourth month,* of the ancient Hebrew lunar calendar. A number of dates in Ezekiel can be cross-checked with dates in surviving Babylonian records and related accurately to our modern calendar. This event occurred on July 31, 593 B.C. **1:1b** Or *in the thirtieth year.* **1:3** Or *Chaldeans.* **1:4** Or *like burnished metal;* also in 1:27.

22 Spread out above them was a surface like the sky, glittering like crystal. 23 Beneath this surface the wings of each living being stretched out to touch the others' wings, and each had two wings covering its body. 24 As they flew, their wings sounded to me like waves crashing against the shore or like the voice of the Almighty* or like the shouting of a mighty army. When they stopped, they let down their wings. 25 As they stood with wings lowered, a voice spoke from beyond the crystal surface above them.

26 Above this surface was something that looked like a throne made of blue lapis lazuli. And on this throne high above was a figure whose appearance resembled a man. 27 From what appeared to be his waist up, he looked like gleaming amber, flickering like a fire. And from his waist down, he looked like a burning flame, shining with splendor. 28 All around him was a glowing halo, like a rainbow shining in the clouds on a rainy day. This is what the glory of the LORD looked like to me. When I saw it, I fell face down on the ground, and I heard someone's voice speaking to me.

Ezekiel's Call and Commission

2 "Stand up, son of man," said the voice. "I want to speak with you." 2 The Spirit came into me as he spoke, and he set me on my feet. I listened carefully to his words. 3 "Son of man," he said, "I am sending you to the nation of Israel, a rebellious nation that has rebelled against me. They and their ancestors have been rebelling against me to this very day. 4 They are a stubborn and hard-hearted people. But I am sending you to say to them, 'This is what the Sovereign LORD says!' 5 And whether they listen or refuse to listen—for remember, they are rebels—at least they will know they have had a prophet among them.

6 "Son of man, do not fear them or their words. Don't be afraid even though their threats surround you like nettles and briers and stinging scorpions. Do not be dismayed by their dark scowls, even though they are rebels. 7 You must give them my messages whether they listen or not. But they won't listen, for they are completely rebellious! 8 Son of man, listen to what I say to you. Do not join them in their rebellion. Open your mouth, and eat what I give you."

9 Then I looked and saw a hand reaching out to me. It held a scroll, 10 which he unrolled. And I saw that both sides were covered with funeral songs, words of sorrow, and pronouncements of doom.

3 The voice said to me, "Son of man, eat what I am giving you—eat this scroll! Then go and give its message to the people of Israel." 2 So I opened my mouth, and he fed me the scroll. 3 "Fill your stomach with this," he said. And when I ate it, it tasted as sweet as honey in my mouth.

4 Then he said, "Son of man, go to the people of Israel and give them my messages. 5 I am not sending you to a foreign people whose language you cannot understand. 6 No, I am not sending you to people with strange and difficult speech. If I did, they would listen! 7 But the people of Israel won't listen to you any more than they listen to me! For the whole lot of them are hard-hearted and stubborn. 8 But look, I have made you as obstinate and hard-hearted as they are. 9 I have made your forehead as hard as the hardest rock! So don't be afraid of them or fear their angry looks, even though they are rebels."

1:24 Hebrew *Shaddai.*

Question **1:26–2:2**

Many have wondered if Ezekiel's vision of a "figure whose appearance resembled a man" refers to preincarnate Jesus (v. 26). The vision certainly had a powerful effect on Ezekiel, who fell to the ground. The scene is reminiscent of Moses with the burning bush (Exodus 3) or the transfiguration of Jesus (Mark 9) or the revelation of John (Revelation 1). What does Ezekiel's reaction reveal about the appropriate response to the presence of God?

Prayer **2:3**

Jesus, let me hear your voice calling me to life today. Amen.

Prayer **2:7**

Dear Jesus, give me the guts to do what you have called me to do. Motivate me to do it, no matter how people respond. Amen.

Make a Difference

3:1-10

Sink into Your Heart

Ezekiel was told to "eat" God's message (vv. 1-3). One of the reasons you are reading these words right now is that you are interested in letting God's Word sink deeply into your own heart. This is your number one calling in life. Before you try to make a difference in the lives of others, first let God make a difference in yours. Let God's words dwell in you. Listen to them carefully for yourself.

Difference Maker

Set aside time every single day to let God's words sink into your heart.

10 Then he added, "Son of man, let all my words sink deep into your own
heart first. Listen to them carefully for yourself. 11 Then go to your people
in exile and say to them, 'This is what the Sovereign LORD says!' Do this
whether they listen to you or not."
12 Then the Spirit lifted me up, and I heard a loud rumbling sound behind
me. (May the glory of the LORD be praised in his place!)* 13 It was the sound
of the wings of the living beings as they brushed against each other and the
rumbling of their wheels beneath them.
14 The Spirit lifted me up and took me away. I went in bitterness and tur-
moil, but the LORD's hold on me was strong. 15 Then I came to the colony of
Judean exiles in Tel-abib, beside the Kebar River. I was overwhelmed and sat
among them for seven days.

A Watchman for Israel

16 After seven days the LORD gave me a message. He said, 17 "Son of man, I have
appointed you as a watchman for Israel. Whenever you receive a message
from me, warn people immediately. 18 If I warn the wicked, saying, 'You are
under the penalty of death,' but you fail to deliver the warning, they will die
in their sins. And I will hold you responsible for their deaths. 19 If you warn
them and they refuse to repent and keep on sinning, they will die in their
sins. But you will have saved yourself because you obeyed me.
20 "If righteous people turn away from their righteous behavior and ignore
the obstacles I put in their way, they will die. And if you do not warn them,
they will die in their sins. None of their righteous acts will be remembered,
and I will hold you responsible for their deaths. 21 But if you warn righteous
people not to sin and they listen to you and do not sin, they will live, and
you will have saved yourself, too."
22 Then the LORD took hold of me and said, "Get up and go out into the
valley, and I will speak to you there." 23 So I got up and went, and there I saw
the glory of the LORD, just as I had seen in my first vision by the Kebar River.
And I fell face down on the ground.
24 Then the Spirit came into me and set me on my feet. He spoke to me and
said, "Go to your house and shut yourself in. 25 There, son of man, you will
be tied with ropes so you cannot go out among the people. 26 And I will make
your tongue stick to the roof of your mouth so that you will be speechless and
unable to rebuke them, for they are rebels. 27 But when I give you a message,
I will loosen your tongue and let you speak. Then you will say to them, 'This
is what the Sovereign LORD says!' Those who choose to listen will listen, but
those who refuse will refuse, for they are rebels.

A Sign of the Coming Siege

4 "And now, son of man, take a large clay brick and set it down in front
of you. Then draw a map of the city of Jerusalem on it. 2 Show the city
under siege. Build a wall around it so no one can escape. Set up the enemy
camp, and surround the city with siege ramps and battering rams. 3 Then
take an iron griddle and place it between you and the city. Turn toward the
city and demonstrate how harsh the siege will be against Jerusalem. This
will be a warning to the people of Israel.
4 "Now lie on your left side and place the sins of Israel on yourself. You

3:12 A possible reading for this verse is *Then the Spirit lifted me up, and as the glory of the LORD rose from its place, I heard a loud rumbling sound behind me.*

are to bear their sins for the number of days you lie there on your side. 5 I am requiring you to bear Israel's sins for 390 days—one day for each year of their sin. 6 After that, turn over and lie on your right side for 40 days—one day for each year of Judah's sin.

7 "Meanwhile, keep staring at the siege of Jerusalem. Lie there with your arm bared and prophesy her destruction. 8 I will tie you up with ropes so you won't be able to turn from side to side until the days of your siege have been completed.

9 "Now go and get some wheat, barley, beans, lentils, millet, and emmer wheat, and mix them together in a storage jar. Use them to make bread for yourself during the 390 days you will be lying on your side. 10 Ration this out to yourself, eight ounces* of food for each day, and eat it at set times. 11 Then measure out a jar* of water for each day, and drink it at set times. 12 Prepare and eat this food as you would barley cakes. While all the people are watching, bake it over a fire using dried human dung as fuel and then eat the bread." 13 Then the LORD said, "This is how Israel will eat defiled bread in the Gentile lands to which I will banish them!"

14 Then I said, "O Sovereign LORD, must I be defiled by using human dung? For I have never been defiled before. From the time I was a child until now I have never eaten any animal that died of sickness or was killed by other animals. I have never eaten any meat forbidden by the law."

15 "All right," the LORD said. "You may bake your bread with cow dung instead of human dung." 16 Then he told me, "Son of man, I will make food very scarce in Jerusalem. It will be weighed out with great care and eaten fearfully. The water will be rationed out drop by drop, and the people will drink it with dismay. 17 Lacking food and water, people will look at one another in terror, and they will waste away under their punishment.

A Sign of the Coming Judgment

5 "Son of man, take a sharp sword and use it as a razor to shave your head and beard. Use a scale to weigh the hair into three equal parts. 2 Place a third of it at the center of your map of Jerusalem. After acting out the siege, burn it there. Scatter another third across your map and chop it with a sword. Scatter the last third to the wind, for I will scatter my people with the sword. 3 Keep just a bit of the hair and tie it up in your robe. 4 Then take some of these hairs out and throw them into the fire, burning them up. A fire will then spread from this remnant and destroy all of Israel.

5 "This is what the Sovereign LORD says: This is an illustration of what will happen to Jerusalem. I placed her at the center of the nations, 6 but she has rebelled against my regulations and decrees and has been even more wicked than the surrounding nations. She has refused to obey the regulations and decrees I gave her to follow.

7 "Therefore, this is what the Sovereign LORD says: You people have behaved worse than your neighbors and have refused to obey my decrees and regulations. You have not even lived up to the standards of the nations around you. 8 Therefore, I myself, the Sovereign LORD, am now your enemy. I will punish you publicly while all the nations watch. 9 Because of your detestable idols, I will punish you like I have never punished anyone before or ever will again. 10 Parents will eat their own children, and children

4:10 Hebrew *20 shekels* [228 grams]. 4:11 Hebrew *1/6 of a hin* [about 1 pint or 0.6 liters].

will eat their parents. I will punish you and scatter to the winds the few
who survive.
11 "As surely as I live, says the Sovereign LORD, I will cut you off completely.
I will show you no pity at all because you have defiled my Temple with your
vile images and detestable sins. 12 A third of your people will die in the city
from disease and famine. A third of them will be slaughtered by the enemy
outside the city walls. And I will scatter a third to the winds, chasing them
with my sword. 13 Then at last my anger will be spent, and I will be satisfied.
And when my fury against them has subsided, all Israel will know that I, the
LORD, have spoken to them in my jealous anger.
14 "So I will turn you into a ruin, a mockery in the eyes of the surrounding
nations and to all who pass by. 15 You will become an object of mockery and
taunting and horror. You will be a warning to all the nations around you.
They will see what happens when the LORD punishes a nation in anger and
rebukes it, says the LORD.
16 "I will shower you with the deadly arrows of famine to destroy you.
The famine will become more and more severe until every crumb of food is
gone. 17 And along with the famine, wild animals will attack you and rob you
of your children. Disease and war will stalk your land, and I will bring the
sword of the enemy against you. I, the LORD, have spoken!"

Judgment against Israel's Mountains

6 Again a message came to me from the LORD: 2 "Son of man, turn and face
the mountains of Israel and prophesy against them. 3 Proclaim this mes-
sage from the Sovereign LORD against the mountains of Israel. This is what the
Sovereign LORD says to the mountains and hills and to the ravines and valleys:
I am about to bring war upon you, and I will smash your pagan shrines. 4 All
your altars will be demolished, and your places of worship will be destroyed.
I will kill your people in front of your idols.* 5 I will lay your corpses in front of
your idols and scatter your bones around your altars. 6 Wherever you live there
will be desolation, and I will destroy your pagan shrines. Your altars will be
demolished, your idols will be smashed, your places of worship will be torn
down, and all the religious objects you have made will be destroyed. 7 The place
will be littered with corpses, and you will know that I alone am the LORD.
8 "But I will let a few of my people escape destruction, and they will be scat-
tered among the nations of the world. 9 Then when they are exiled among
the nations, they will remember me. They will recognize how hurt I am by
their unfaithful hearts and lustful eyes that long for their idols. Then at last
they will hate themselves for all their detestable sins. 10 They will know that
I alone am the LORD and that I was serious when I said I would bring this
calamity on them.
11 "This is what the Sovereign LORD says: Clap your hands in horror, and
stamp your feet. Cry out because of all the detestable sins the people of Israel
have committed. Now they are going to die from war and famine and disease.
12 Disease will strike down those who are far away in exile. War will destroy
those who are nearby. And anyone who survives will be killed by famine. So
at last I will spend my fury on them. 13 They will know that I am the LORD
when their dead lie scattered among their idols and altars on every hill and
mountain and under every green tree and every great shade tree—the places

Question 6:7

There are a couple ways to learn that the Lord alone is God. One way is to discover how good it is to have a committed relationship with God. The other way is to turn against God and pursue other things, only to find that it's the wrong way to go. How does John 14:6 shape the way you think about this major theme in Ezekiel?

6:4 The Hebrew term (literally *round things*) probably alludes to dung; also in 6:5, 6, 9, 13.

where they offered sacrifices to their idols. 14 I will crush them and make their
cities desolate from the wilderness in the south to Riblah* in the north. Then
they will know that I am the LORD."

The Coming of the End

7 Then this message came to me from the LORD: 2 "Son of man, this is what
the Sovereign LORD says to Israel:

"The end is here!
Wherever you look—
east, west, north, or south—
your land is finished.
3 No hope remains,
for I will unleash my anger against you.
I will call you to account
for all your detestable sins.
4 I will turn my eyes away and show no pity.
I will repay you for all your detestable sins.
Then you will know that I am the LORD.

5 "This is what the Sovereign LORD says:
Disaster after disaster
is coming your way!
6 The end has come.
It has finally arrived.
Your final doom is waiting!
7 O people of Israel, the day of your destruction is dawning.
The time has come; the day of trouble is near.
Shouts of anguish will be heard on the mountains,
not shouts of joy.
8 Soon I will pour out my fury on you
and unleash my anger against you.
I will call you to account
for all your detestable sins.
9 I will turn my eyes away and show no pity.
I will repay you for all your detestable sins.
Then you will know that it is I, the LORD,
who is striking the blow.

10 "The day of judgment is here;
your destruction awaits!
The people's wickedness and pride
have blossomed to full flower.
11 Their violence has grown into a rod
that will beat them for their wickedness.
None of these proud and wicked people will survive.
All their wealth and prestige will be swept away.
12 Yes, the time has come;
the day is here!

6:14 As in some Hebrew manuscripts; most Hebrew manuscripts read *Diblah*.

Buyers should not rejoice over bargains,
nor sellers grieve over losses,
for all of them will fall
under my terrible anger.
13 Even if the merchants survive,
they will never return to their business.
For what God has said applies to everyone—
it will not be changed!
Not one person whose life is twisted by sin
will ever recover.

The Desolation of Israel

14 "The trumpet calls Israel's army to mobilize,
but no one listens,
for my fury is against them all.
15 There is war outside the city
and disease and famine within.
Those outside the city walls
will be killed by enemy swords.
Those inside the city
will die of famine and disease.
16 The survivors who escape to the mountains
will moan like doves, weeping for their sins.
17 Their hands will hang limp,
their knees will be weak as water.
18 They will dress themselves in burlap;
horror and shame will cover them.
They will shave their heads
in sorrow and remorse.

19 "They will throw their money in the streets,
tossing it out like worthless trash.
Their silver and gold won't save them
on that day of the LORD's anger.
It will neither satisfy nor feed them,
for their greed can only trip them up.
20 They were proud of their beautiful jewelry
and used it to make detestable idols and
vile images.
Therefore, I will make all their wealth
disgusting to them.
21 I will give it as plunder to foreigners,
to the most wicked of nations,
and they will defile it.
22 I will turn my eyes from them
as these robbers invade and defile my treasured land.

23 "Prepare chains for my people,
for the land is bloodied by terrible crimes.
Jerusalem is filled with violence.

Your thoughts can go here

24 I will bring the most ruthless of nations
to occupy their homes.
I will break down their proud fortresses
and defile their sanctuaries.
25 Terror and trembling will overcome my people.
They will look for peace but not find it.
26 Calamity will follow calamity;
rumor will follow rumor.
They will look in vain
for a vision from the prophets.
They will receive no teaching from the priests
and no counsel from the leaders.
27 The king and the prince will stand helpless,
weeping in despair,
and the people's hands
will tremble with fear.
I will bring on them
the evil they have done to others,
and they will receive the punishment
they so richly deserve.
Then they will know that I am the LORD."

Idolatry in the Temple

8 Then on September 17,* during the sixth year of King Jehoiachin's cap-
tivity, while the leaders of Judah were in my home, the Sovereign LORD
took hold of me. 2 I saw a figure that appeared to be a man.* From what ap-
peared to be his waist down, he looked like a burning flame. From the waist
up he looked like gleaming amber.* 3 He reached out what seemed to be a
hand and took me by the hair. Then the Spirit lifted me up into the sky and
transported me to Jerusalem in a vision from God. I was taken to the north
gate of the inner courtyard of the Temple, where there is a large idol that
has made the LORD very jealous. 4 Suddenly, the glory of the God of Israel
was there, just as I had seen it before in the valley.
5 Then the LORD said to me, "Son of man, look toward the north." So I
looked, and there to the north, beside the entrance to the gate near the altar,
stood the idol that had made the LORD so jealous.
6 "Son of man," he said, "do you see what they are doing? Do you see the
detestable sins the people of Israel are committing to drive me from my
Temple? But come, and you will see even more detestable sins than these!"
7 Then he brought me to the door of the Temple courtyard, where I could see
a hole in the wall. 8 He said to me, "Now, son of man, dig into the wall." So I
dug into the wall and found a hidden doorway.
9 "Go in," he said, "and see the wicked and detestable sins they are com-
mitting in there!" 10 So I went in and saw the walls covered with engrav-
ings of all kinds of crawling animals and detestable creatures. I also saw
the various idols* worshiped by the people of Israel. 11 Seventy leaders of
Israel were standing there with Jaazaniah son of Shaphan in the center.

8:1 Hebrew *on the fifth [day] of the sixth month,* of the ancient Hebrew lunar calendar. This event occurred on September 17, 592 B.C.; also see note on 1:1. 8:2a As in Greek version; Hebrew reads *appeared to be fire.* 8:2b Or *like burnished metal.* 8:10 The Hebrew term (literally *round things*) probably alludes to dung.

Make a Difference 9:4

Marked

Are you vigilant? Some people keep falling into the same traps over and over again because they lose awareness. They repeatedly walk into the same pitfalls and perils, each time just as surprised as the last. "How did this happen?" For some reason they just haven't learned to notice the signals, to scout the land, and to ready the defenses.

Are you like that? Do you get caught unaware, even when you know trouble is brewing, temptation is coming, or someone is trying to undermine your purity, your message, your good work, or your success? You're shrewder than that, right? This world needs you to be. Don't give in to apathy only to be jolted upright by failure. Don't give in to a reactionary life, surprised by the perils that find their way to you. Be ready. Be marked by God as someone who notices the pitfalls and is bothered by sin.

Difference Maker

Examine your world around you. What sins stand out to you? What troubles your soul? What breaks your heart? Lift a cry to the Lord over the sins of this world.

Each of them held an incense burner, from which a cloud of incense rose above their heads.

12 Then the LORD said to me, "Son of man, have you seen what the leaders of Israel are doing with their idols in dark rooms? They are saying, 'The LORD doesn't see us; he has deserted our land!'" 13 Then the LORD added, "Come, and I will show you even more detestable sins than these!"

14 He brought me to the north gate of the LORD's Temple, and some women were sitting there, weeping for the god Tammuz. 15 "Have you seen this?" he asked. "But I will show you even more detestable sins than these!"

16 Then he brought me into the inner courtyard of the LORD's Temple. At the entrance to the sanctuary, between the entry room and the bronze altar, there were about twenty-five men with their backs to the sanctuary of the LORD. They were facing east, bowing low to the ground, worshiping the sun!

17 "Have you seen this, son of man?" he asked. "Is it nothing to the people of Judah that they commit these detestable sins, leading the whole nation into violence, thumbing their noses at me, and provoking my anger? 18 Therefore, I will respond in fury. I will neither pity nor spare them. And though they cry for mercy, I will not listen."

The Slaughter of Idolaters

9 Then the LORD thundered, "Bring on the men appointed to punish the city! Tell them to bring their weapons with them!" 2 Six men soon appeared from the upper gate that faces north, each carrying a deadly weapon in his hand. With them was a man dressed in linen, who carried a writer's case at his side. They all went into the Temple courtyard and stood beside the bronze altar.

3 Then the glory of the God of Israel rose up from between the cherubim, where it had rested, and moved to the entrance of the Temple. And the LORD called to the man dressed in linen who was carrying the writer's case. 4 He said to him, "Walk through the streets of Jerusalem and put a mark on the foreheads of all who weep and sigh because of the detestable sins being committed in their city."

5 Then I heard the LORD say to the other men, "Follow him through the city and kill everyone whose forehead is not marked. Show no mercy; have no pity! 6 Kill them all—old and young, girls and women and little children. But do not touch anyone with the mark. Begin right here at the Temple." So they began by killing the seventy leaders.

7 "Defile the Temple!" the LORD commanded. "Fill its courtyards with corpses. Go!" So they went and began killing throughout the city.

8 While they were out killing, I was all alone. I fell face down on the ground and cried out, "O Sovereign LORD! Will your fury against Jerusalem wipe out everyone left in Israel?"

9 Then he said to me, "The sins of the people of Israel and Judah are very, very great. The entire land is full of murder; the city is filled with injustice. They are saying, 'The LORD doesn't see it! The LORD has abandoned the land!' 10 So I will not spare them or have any pity on them. I will fully repay them for all they have done."

11 Then the man in linen clothing, who carried the writer's case, reported back and said, "I have done as you commanded."

The LORD's Glory Leaves the Temple

10 In my vision I saw what appeared to be a throne of blue lapis lazuli
above the crystal surface over the heads of the cherubim. 2 Then the
LORD spoke to the man in linen clothing and said, "Go between the whirl-
ing wheels beneath the cherubim, and take a handful of burning coals and
scatter them over the city." He did this as I watched.
3 The cherubim were standing at the south end of the Temple when the man
went in, and the cloud of glory filled the inner courtyard. 4 Then the glory of
the LORD rose up from above the cherubim and went over to the entrance of
the Temple. The Temple was filled with this cloud of glory, and the court-
yard glowed brightly with the glory of the LORD. 5 The moving wings of the
cherubim sounded like the voice of God Almighty* and could be heard even
in the outer courtyard.
6 The LORD said to the man in linen clothing, "Go between the cherubim
and take some burning coals from between the wheels." So the man went in
and stood beside one of the wheels. 7 Then one of the cherubim reached out
his hand and took some live coals from the fire burning among them. He
put the coals into the hands of the man in linen clothing, and the man took
them and went out. 8 (All the cherubim had what looked like human hands
under their wings.)
9 I looked, and each of the four cherubim had a wheel beside him, and the
wheels sparkled like beryl. 10 All four wheels looked alike and were made the
same; each wheel had a second wheel turning crosswise within it. 11 The cheru-
bim could move in any of the four directions they faced, without turning as
they moved. They went straight in the direction they faced, never turning
aside. 12 Both the cherubim and the wheels were covered with eyes. The cheru-
bim had eyes all over their bodies, including their hands, their backs, and
their wings. 13 I heard someone refer to the wheels as "the whirling wheels."
14 Each of the four cherubim had four faces: the first was the face of an ox,*
the second was a human face, the third was the face of a lion, and the fourth
was the face of an eagle.
15 Then the cherubim rose upward. These were the same living beings I had
seen beside the Kebar River. 16 When the cherubim moved, the wheels moved
with them. When they lifted their wings to fly, the wheels stayed beside them.
17 When the cherubim stopped, the wheels stopped. When they flew upward,
the wheels rose up, for the spirit of the living beings was in the wheels.
18 Then the glory of the LORD moved out from the entrance of the Temple
and hovered above the cherubim. 19 And as I watched, the cherubim flew with
their wheels to the east gate of the LORD's Temple. And the glory of the God
of Israel hovered above them.
20 These were the same living beings I had seen beneath the God of Israel
when I was by the Kebar River. I knew they were cherubim, 21 for each had four
faces and four wings and what looked like human hands under their wings.
22 And their faces were just like the faces of the beings I had seen at the Kebar,
and they traveled straight ahead, just as the others had.

Judgment on Israel's Leaders

11 Then the Spirit lifted me and brought me to the east gateway of the
LORD's Temple, where I saw twenty-five prominent men of the city.

10:5 Hebrew *El-Shaddai.* **10:14** Hebrew *the face of a cherub;* compare 1:10.

Question 11:5

Ezekiel was instructed to prophesy against wicked leaders. He recounted how the Spirit of the Lord came upon him and told him what to say. Read Luke 12:11-12. What did Jesus say he would do for his followers when they are put before powerful people?

Question 11:16

Ezekiel has a hopeful word mingled into the harsh message: even in exile, the Lord will be a sanctuary. This is the Lord's promise to those who are displaced and feel far from comfort or home. How could you offer this encouraging word to friends or family members who feel this way about their lives right now?

Prayer 11:19

Dear Lord, re-create my heart to beat with yours. Amen.

Among them were Jaazaniah son of Azzur and Pelatiah son of Benaiah, who
were leaders among the people.
2 The Spirit said to me, "Son of man, these are the men who are planning
evil and giving wicked counsel in this city. 3 They say to the people, 'Is it not
a good time to build houses? This city is like an iron pot. We are safe inside
it like meat in a pot.'* 4 Therefore, son of man, prophesy against them loudly
and clearly."
5 Then the Spirit of the LORD came upon me, and he told me to say, "This
is what the LORD says to the people of Israel: I know what you are saying,
for I know every thought that comes into your minds. 6 You have murdered
many in this city and filled its streets with the dead.
7 "Therefore, this is what the Sovereign LORD says: This city is an iron pot
all right, but the pieces of meat are the victims of your injustice. As for you, I
will soon drag you from this pot. 8 I will bring on you the sword of war you so
greatly fear, says the Sovereign LORD. 9 I will drive you out of Jerusalem and
hand you over to foreigners, who will carry out my judgments against you.
10 You will be slaughtered all the way to the borders of Israel. I will execute
judgment on you, and you will know that I am the LORD. 11 No, this city will
not be an iron pot for you, and you will not be like meat safe inside it. I will
judge you even to the borders of Israel, 12 and you will know that I am the
LORD. For you have refused to obey my decrees and regulations; instead, you
have copied the standards of the nations around you."
13 While I was still prophesying, Pelatiah son of Benaiah suddenly died.
Then I fell face down on the ground and cried out, "O Sovereign LORD, are
you going to kill everyone in Israel?"

Hope for Exiled Israel

14 Then this message came to me from the LORD: 15 "Son of man, the people
still left in Jerusalem are talking about you and your relatives and all the
people of Israel who are in exile. They are saying, 'Those people are far away
from the LORD, so now he has given their land to us!'
16 "Therefore, tell the exiles, 'This is what the Sovereign LORD says: Al-
though I have scattered you in the countries of the world, I will be a sanctu-
ary to you during your time in exile. 17 I, the Sovereign LORD, will gather you
back from the nations where you have been scattered, and I will give you the
land of Israel once again.'
18 "When the people return to their homeland, they will remove every
trace of their vile images and detestable idols. 19 And I will give them single-
ness of heart and put a new spirit within them. I will take away their stony,
stubborn heart and give them a tender, responsive heart,* 20 so they will obey
my decrees and regulations. Then they will truly be my people, and I will be
their God. 21 But as for those who long for vile images and detestable idols,
I will repay them fully for their sins. I, the Sovereign LORD, have spoken!"

The LORD's Glory Leaves Jerusalem

22 Then the cherubim lifted their wings and rose into the air with their wheels
beside them, and the glory of the God of Israel hovered above them. 23 Then
the glory of the LORD went up from the city and stopped above the moun-
tain to the east.

11:3 Hebrew *This city is the pot, and we are the meat.* **11:19** Hebrew *a heart of flesh.*

[24]Afterward the Spirit of God carried me back again to Babylonia,* to the people in exile there. And so ended the vision of my visit to Jerusalem. [25]And I told the exiles everything the LORD had shown me.

Signs of the Coming Exile

12 Again a message came to me from the LORD: [2]"Son of man, you live among rebels who have eyes but refuse to see. They have ears but refuse to hear. For they are a rebellious people.

[3]"So now, son of man, pretend you are being sent into exile. Pack the few items an exile could carry, and leave your home to go somewhere else. Do this right in front of the people so they can see you. For perhaps they will pay attention to this, even though they are such rebels. [4]Bring your baggage outside during the day so they can watch you. Then in the evening, as they are watching, leave your house as captives do when they begin a long march to distant lands. [5]Dig a hole through the wall while they are watching and go out through it. [6]As they watch, lift your pack to your shoulders and walk away into the night. Cover your face so you cannot see the land you are leaving. For I have made you a sign for the people of Israel."

[7]So I did as I was told. In broad daylight I brought my pack outside, filled with the things I might carry into exile. Then in the evening while the people looked on, I dug through the wall with my hands and went out into the night with my pack on my shoulder.

[8]The next morning this message came to me from the LORD: [9]"Son of man, these rebels, the people of Israel, have asked you what all this means. [10]Say to them, 'This is what the Sovereign LORD says: These actions contain a message for King Zedekiah in Jerusalem* and for all the people of Israel.' [11]Explain that your actions are a sign to show what will soon happen to them, for they will be driven into exile as captives.

[12]"Even Zedekiah will leave Jerusalem at night through a hole in the wall, taking only what he can carry with him. He will cover his face, and his eyes will not see the land he is leaving. [13]Then I will throw my net over him and capture him in my snare. I will bring him to Babylon, the land of the Babylonians,* though he will never see it, and he will die there. [14]I will scatter his servants and warriors to the four winds and send the sword after them. [15]And when I scatter them among the nations, they will know that I am the LORD. [16]But I will spare a few of them from death by war, famine, or disease, so they can confess all their detestable sins to their captors. Then they will know that I am the LORD."

[17]Then this message came to me from the LORD: [18]"Son of man, tremble as you eat your food. Shake with fear as you drink your water. [19]Tell the people, 'This is what the Sovereign LORD says concerning those living in Israel and Jerusalem: They will eat their food with trembling and sip their water in despair, for their land will be stripped bare because of their violence. [20]The cities will be destroyed and the farmland made desolate. Then you will know that I am the LORD.'"

A New Proverb for Israel

[21]Again a message came to me from the LORD: [22]"Son of man, you've heard that proverb they quote in Israel: 'Time passes, and prophecies come to

Question 12:21

It seems that people had a saying about how prophecies didn't come true. It seems that the people had become complacent. What does the Lord want them to realize?

11:24 Or *Chaldea.* 12:10 Hebrew *the prince in Jerusalem;* similarly in 12:12. 12:13 Or *Chaldeans.*

nothing.’ 23 Tell the people, ‘This is what the Sovereign LORD says: I will
put an end to this proverb, and you will soon stop quoting it.’ Now give
them this new proverb to replace the old one: ‘The time has come for every
prophecy to be fulfilled!’

24 “There will be no more false visions and flattering predictions in Israel.
25 For I am the LORD! If I say it, it will happen. There will be no more delays,
you rebels of Israel. I will fulfill my threat of destruction in your own life-
time. I, the Sovereign LORD, have spoken!”

26 Then this message came to me from the LORD: 27 “Son of man, the people
of Israel are saying, ‘He’s talking about the distant future. His visions won’t
come true for a long, long time.’ 28 Therefore, tell them, ‘This is what the Sov-
ereign LORD says: No more delay! I will now do everything I have threatened.
I, the Sovereign LORD, have spoken!’”

Judgment against False Prophets

13 Then this message came to me from the LORD: 2 “Son of man, proph-
esy against the false prophets of Israel who are inventing their own
prophecies. Say to them, ‘Listen to the word of the LORD. 3 This is what the
Sovereign LORD says: What sorrow awaits the false prophets who are follow-
ing their own imaginations and have seen nothing at all!’

4 “O people of Israel, these prophets of yours are like jackals digging in
the ruins. 5 They have done nothing to repair the breaks in the walls around
the nation. They have not helped it to stand firm in battle on the day of the
LORD. 6 Instead, they have told lies and made false predictions. They say, ‘This
message is from the LORD,’ even though the LORD never sent them. And yet
they expect him to fulfill their prophecies! 7 Can your visions be anything
but false if you claim, ‘This message is from the LORD,’ when I have not even
spoken to you?

8 “Therefore, this is what the Sovereign LORD says: Because what you say is
false and your visions are a lie, I will stand against you, says the Sovereign LORD.
9 I will raise my fist against all the prophets who see false visions and make lying
predictions, and they will be banished from the community of Israel. I will blot
their names from Israel’s record books, and they will never again set foot in
their own land. Then you will know that I am the Sovereign LORD.

10 “This will happen because these evil prophets deceive my people by say-
ing, ‘All is peaceful’ when there is no peace at all! It’s as if the people have built
a flimsy wall, and these prophets are trying to reinforce it by covering it with
whitewash! 11 Tell these whitewashers that their wall will soon fall down. A
heavy rainstorm will undermine it; great hailstones and mighty winds will
knock it down. 12 And when the wall falls, the people will cry out, ‘What hap-
pened to your whitewash?’

13 “Therefore, this is what the Sovereign LORD says: I will sweep away your
whitewashed wall with a storm of indignation, with a great flood of anger,
and with hailstones of fury. 14 I will break down your wall right to its foun-
dation, and when it falls, it will crush you. Then you will know that I am
the LORD. 15 At last my anger against the wall and those who covered it with
whitewash will be satisfied. Then I will say to you: ‘The wall and those who
whitewashed it are both gone. 16 They were lying prophets who claimed peace
would come to Jerusalem when there was no peace. I, the Sovereign LORD,
have spoken!’

Judgment against False Women Prophets

17 "Now, son of man, speak out against the women who prophesy from their
own imaginations. 18 This is what the Sovereign LORD says: What sorrow
awaits you women who are ensnaring the souls of my people, young and
old alike. You tie magic charms on their wrists and furnish them with magic
veils. Do you think you can trap others without bringing destruction on your-
selves? 19 You bring shame on me among my people for a few handfuls of bar-
ley or a piece of bread. By lying to my people who love to listen to lies, you kill
those who should not die, and you promise life to those who should not live.
20 "This is what the Sovereign LORD says: I am against all your magic
charms, which you use to ensnare my people like birds. I will tear them from
your arms, setting my people free like birds set free from a cage. 21 I will
tear off the magic veils and save my people from your grasp. They will no
longer be your victims. Then you will know that I am the LORD. 22 You have
discouraged the righteous with your lies, but I didn't want them to be sad.
And you have encouraged the wicked by promising them life, even though
they continue in their sins. 23 Because of all this, you will no longer talk of
seeing visions that you never saw, nor will you make predictions. For I will
rescue my people from your grasp. Then you will know that I am the LORD."

The Idolatry of Israel's Leaders

14 Then some of the leaders of Israel visited me, and while they were
sitting with me, 2 this message came to me from the LORD: 3 "Son of
man, these leaders have set up idols* in their hearts. They have embraced
things that will make them fall into sin. Why should I listen to their re-
quests? 4 Tell them, 'This is what the Sovereign LORD says: The people of
Israel have set up idols in their hearts and fallen into sin, and then they go
to a prophet asking for a message. So I, the LORD, will give them the kind
of answer their great idolatry deserves. 5 I will do this to capture the minds
and hearts of all my people who have turned from me to worship their de-
testable idols.'

6 "Therefore, tell the people of Israel, 'This is what the Sovereign LORD
says: Repent and turn away from your idols, and stop all your detestable sins.
7 I, the LORD, will answer all those, both Israelites and foreigners, who reject
me and set up idols in their hearts and so fall into sin, and who then come to
a prophet asking for my advice. 8 I will turn against such people and make a
terrible example of them, eliminating them from among my people. Then
you will know that I am the LORD.

9 "'And if a prophet is deceived into giving a message, it is because I, the
LORD, have deceived that prophet. I will lift my fist against such prophets
and cut them off from the community of Israel. 10 False prophets and those
who seek their guidance will all be punished for their sins. 11 In this way, the
people of Israel will learn not to stray from me, polluting themselves with
sin. They will be my people, and I will be their God. I, the Sovereign LORD,
have spoken!'"

The Certainty of the LORD's Judgment

12 Then this message came to me from the LORD: 13 "Son of man, suppose the
people of a country were to sin against me, and I lifted my fist to crush them,

Question **14:6**

The leaders had embraced things that made them (and the people) fall into sin. The Lord wanted them to repent and turn away from those things. There is an old hymn that says, "Turn your eyes upon Jesus and look full in his wonderful face." What happens when you look toward things other than God for your fulfillment?

14:3 The Hebrew term (literally *round things*) probably alludes to dung; also in 14:4, 5, 6, 7.

cutting off their food supply and sending a famine to destroy both people
and animals. 14 Even if Noah, Daniel, and Job were there, their righteousness
would save no one but themselves, says the Sovereign LORD.
15 "Or suppose I were to send wild animals to invade the country, kill the
people, and make the land too desolate and dangerous to pass through. 16 As
surely as I live, says the Sovereign LORD, even if those three men were there,
they wouldn't be able to save their own sons or daughters. They alone would
be saved, but the land would be made desolate.
17 "Or suppose I were to bring war against the land, and I sent enemy
armies to destroy both people and animals. 18 As surely as I live, says the
Sovereign LORD, even if those three men were there, they wouldn't be able
to save their own sons or daughters. They alone would be saved.
19 "Or suppose I were to pour out my fury by sending an epidemic into
the land, and the disease killed people and animals alike. 20 As surely as I
live, says the Sovereign LORD, even if Noah, Daniel, and Job were there, they
wouldn't be able to save their own sons or daughters. They alone would be
saved by their righteousness.
21 "Now this is what the Sovereign LORD says: How terrible it will be when
all four of these dreadful punishments fall upon Jerusalem—war, famine,
wild animals, and disease—destroying all her people and animals. 22 Yet
there will be survivors, and they will come here to join you as exiles in Bab-
ylon. You will see with your own eyes how wicked they are, and then you will
feel better about what I have done to Jerusalem. 23 When you meet them and
see their behavior, you will understand that these things are not being done
to Israel without cause. I, the Sovereign LORD, have spoken!"

Jerusalem—a Useless Vine

15 Then this message came to me from the LORD: 2 "Son of man, how
does a grapevine compare to a tree? Is a vine's wood as useful as the
wood of a tree? 3 Can its wood be used for making things, like pegs to hang
up pots and pans? 4 No, it can only be used for fuel, and even as fuel, it burns
too quickly. 5 Vines are useless both before and after being put into the fire!
6 "And this is what the Sovereign LORD says: The people of Jerusalem are
like grapevines growing among the trees of the forest. Since they are useless,
I have thrown them on the fire to be burned. 7 And I will see to it that if they
escape from one fire, they will fall into another. When I turn against them,
you will know that I am the LORD. 8 And I will make the land desolate because
my people have been unfaithful to me. I, the Sovereign LORD, have spoken!"

Jerusalem—an Unfaithful Wife

16 Then another message came to me from the LORD: 2 "Son of man,
confront Jerusalem with her detestable sins. 3 Give her this message
from the Sovereign LORD: You are nothing but a Canaanite! Your father
was an Amorite and your mother a Hittite. 4 On the day you were born, no
one cared about you. Your umbilical cord was not cut, and you were never
washed, rubbed with salt, and wrapped in cloth. 5 No one had the slightest
interest in you; no one pitied you or cared for you. On the day you were born,
you were unwanted, dumped in a field and left to die.
6 "But I came by and saw you there, helplessly kicking about in your own
blood. As you lay there, I said, 'Live!' 7 And I helped you to thrive like a plant

in the field. You grew up and became a beautiful jewel. Your breasts became
full, and your body hair grew, but you were still naked. 8 And when I passed
by again, I saw that you were old enough for love. So I wrapped my cloak
around you to cover your nakedness and declared my marriage vows. I made
a covenant with you, says the Sovereign LORD, and you became mine.
9 "Then I bathed you and washed off your blood, and I rubbed fragrant oils
into your skin. 10 I gave you expensive clothing of fine linen and silk, beauti-
fully embroidered, and sandals made of fine goatskin leather. 11 I gave you
lovely jewelry, bracelets, beautiful necklaces, 12 a ring for your nose, earrings
for your ears, and a lovely crown for your head. 13 And so you were adorned
with gold and silver. Your clothes were made of fine linen and costly fabric
and were beautifully embroidered. You ate the finest foods—choice flour,
honey, and olive oil—and became more beautiful than ever. You looked like
a queen, and so you were! 14 Your fame soon spread throughout the world
because of your beauty. I dressed you in my splendor and perfected your
beauty, says the Sovereign LORD.
15 "But you thought your fame and beauty were your own. So you gave
yourself as a prostitute to every man who came along. Your beauty was theirs
for the asking. 16 You used the lovely things I gave you to make shrines for
idols, where you played the prostitute. Unbelievable! How could such a thing
ever happen? 17 You took the very jewels and gold and silver ornaments I had
given you and made statues of men and worshiped them. This is adultery
against me! 18 You used the beautifully embroidered clothes I gave you to
dress your idols. Then you used my special oil and my incense to worship
them. 19 Imagine it! You set before them as a sacrifice the choice flour, olive
oil, and honey I had given you, says the Sovereign LORD.
20 "Then you took your sons and daughters—the children you had borne
to me—and sacrificed them to your gods. Was your prostitution not enough?
21 Must you also slaughter my children by sacrificing them to idols? 22 In all
your years of adultery and detestable sin, you have not once remembered
the days long ago when you lay naked in a field, kicking about in your own
blood.
23 "What sorrow awaits you, says the Sovereign LORD. In addition to all
your other wickedness, 24 you built a pagan shrine and put altars to idols in
every town square. 25 On every street corner you defiled your beauty, offering
your body to every passerby in an endless stream of prostitution. 26 Then you
added lustful Egypt to your lovers, provoking my anger with your increas-
ing promiscuity. 27 That is why I struck you with my fist and reduced your
boundaries. I handed you over to your enemies, the Philistines, and even they
were shocked by your lewd conduct. 28 You have prostituted yourself with the
Assyrians, too. It seems you can never find enough new lovers! And after your
prostitution there, you still were not satisfied. 29 You added to your lovers by
embracing Babylonia,* the land of merchants, but you still weren't satisfied.
30 "What a sick heart you have, says the Sovereign LORD, to do such things
as these, acting like a shameless prostitute. 31 You build your pagan shrines
on every street corner and your altars to idols in every square. In fact, you
have been worse than a prostitute, so eager for sin that you have not even
demanded payment. 32 Yes, you are an adulterous wife who takes in strang-
ers instead of her own husband. 33 Prostitutes charge for their services—but

16:29 Or *Chaldea.*

Reflect on this passage

Prayer **16:43**

Lord, help me remember the vibrancy of my faith when I first committed my life to you. Don't allow me to become adulterated in my walk with you as I grow older. Amen.

not you! You give gifts to your lovers, bribing them to come and have sex
with you. 34So you are the opposite of other prostitutes. You pay your lovers
instead of their paying you!

Judgment on Jerusalem's Prostitution

35"Therefore, you prostitute, listen to this message from the LORD! 36This is
what the Sovereign LORD says: Because you have poured out your lust and
exposed yourself in prostitution to all your lovers, and because you have wor-
shiped detestable idols,* and because you have slaughtered your children as
sacrifices to your gods, 37this is what I am going to do. I will gather together
all your allies—the lovers with whom you have sinned, both those you loved
and those you hated—and I will strip you naked in front of them so they can
stare at you. 38I will punish you for your murder and adultery. I will cover you
with blood in my jealous fury. 39Then I will give you to these many nations
who are your lovers, and they will destroy you. They will knock down your
pagan shrines and the altars to your idols. They will strip you and take your
beautiful jewels, leaving you stark naked. 40They will band together in a mob
to stone you and cut you up with swords. 41They will burn your homes and
punish you in front of many women. I will stop your prostitution and end
your payments to your many lovers.

42"Then at last my fury against you will be spent, and my jealous anger
will subside. I will be calm and will not be angry with you anymore. 43But
first, because you have not remembered your youth but have angered me by
doing all these evil things, I will fully repay you for all of your sins, says the
Sovereign LORD. For you have added lewd acts to all your detestable sins.
44Everyone who makes up proverbs will say of you, 'Like mother, like daugh-
ter.' 45For your mother loathed her husband and her children, and so do you.
And you are exactly like your sisters, for they despised their husbands and
their children. Truly your mother was a Hittite and your father an Amorite.

46"Your older sister was Samaria, who lived with her daughters in the
north. Your younger sister was Sodom, who lived with her daughters in the
south. 47But you have not merely sinned as they did. You quickly surpassed
them in corruption. 48As surely as I live, says the Sovereign LORD, Sodom and
her daughters were never as wicked as you and your daughters. 49Sodom's
sins were pride, gluttony, and laziness, while the poor and needy suffered
outside her door. 50She was proud and committed detestable sins, so I wiped
her out, as you have seen.*

51"Even Samaria did not commit half your sins. You have done far more
detestable things than your sisters ever did. They seem righteous compared
to you. 52Shame on you! Your sins are so terrible that you make your sisters
seem righteous, even virtuous.

53"But someday I will restore the fortunes of Sodom and Samaria, and I
will restore you, too. 54Then you will be truly ashamed of everything you
have done, for your sins make them feel good in comparison. 55Yes, your
sisters, Sodom and Samaria, and all their people will be restored, and at that
time you also will be restored. 56In your proud days you held Sodom in con-
tempt. 57But now your greater wickedness has been exposed to all the world,
and you are the one who is scorned—by Edom* and all her neighbors and

16:36 The Hebrew term (literally *round things*) probably alludes to dung. **16:50** As in a few Hebrew manuscripts and Greek version; Masoretic Text reads *as I have seen.* **16:57** As in many Hebrew manuscripts and Syriac version; Masoretic Text reads *Aram.*

by Philistia. 58This is your punishment for all your lewdness and detestable
sins, says the LORD.
59"Now this is what the Sovereign LORD says: I will give you what you de-
serve, for you have taken your solemn vows lightly by breaking your covenant.
60Yet I will remember the covenant I made with you when you were young, and
I will establish an everlasting covenant with you. 61Then you will remember
with shame all the evil you have done. I will make your sisters, Samaria and Sod-
om, to be your daughters, even though they are not part of our covenant. 62And
I will reaffirm my covenant with you, and you will know that I am the LORD.
63You will remember your sins and cover your mouth in silent shame when
I forgive you of all that you have done. I, the Sovereign LORD, have spoken!"

A Story of Two Eagles

17 Then this message came to me from the LORD: 2"Son of man, give
this riddle, and tell this story to the people of Israel. 3Give them this
message from the Sovereign LORD:

"A great eagle with broad wings and long feathers,
covered with many-colored plumage,
came to Lebanon.
He seized the top of a cedar tree
4 and plucked off its highest branch.
He carried it away to a city filled with merchants.
He planted it in a city of traders.
5 He also took a seedling from the land
and planted it in fertile soil.
He placed it beside a broad river,
where it could grow like a willow tree.
6 It took root there and
grew into a low, spreading vine.
Its branches turned up toward the eagle,
and its roots grew down into the ground.
It produced strong branches
and put out shoots.
7 But then another great eagle came
with broad wings and full plumage.
So the vine now sent its roots and branches
toward him for water,
8 even though it was already planted in good soil
and had plenty of water
so it could grow into a splendid vine
and produce rich leaves and luscious fruit.

9 "So now the Sovereign LORD asks:
Will this vine grow and prosper?
No! I will pull it up, roots and all!
I will cut off its fruit
and let its leaves wither and die.
I will pull it up easily
without a strong arm or a large army.

Question 18:4

This chapter is an important message for our culture today. As you read these words, which comments about justice do you think the world needs most?

10 But when the vine is transplanted,
will it thrive?
No, it will wither away
when the east wind blows against it.
It will die in the same good soil
where it had grown so well."

The Riddle Explained

11 Then this message came to me from the LORD: 12 "Say to these rebels of Is-
rael: Don't you understand the meaning of this riddle of the eagles? The king
of Babylon came to Jerusalem, took away her king and princes, and brought
them to Babylon. 13 He made a treaty with a member of the royal family and
forced him to take an oath of loyalty. He also exiled Israel's most influential
leaders, 14 so Israel would not become strong again and revolt. Only by keep-
ing her treaty with Babylon could Israel survive.

15 "Nevertheless, this man of Israel's royal family rebelled against Babylon,
sending ambassadors to Egypt to request a great army and many horses. Can
Israel break her sworn treaties like that and get away with it? 16 No! For as
surely as I live, says the Sovereign LORD, the king of Israel will die in Babylon,
the land of the king who put him in power and whose treaty he disregarded
and broke. 17 Pharaoh and all his mighty army will fail to help Israel when
the king of Babylon lays siege to Jerusalem again and destroys many lives.
18 For the king of Israel disregarded his treaty and broke it after swearing to
obey; therefore, he will not escape.

19 "So this is what the Sovereign LORD says: As surely as I live, I will punish
him for breaking my covenant and disregarding the solemn oath he made in
my name. 20 I will throw my net over him and capture him in my snare. I will
bring him to Babylon and put him on trial for this treason against me. 21 And
all his best warriors* will be killed in battle, and those who survive will be
scattered to the four winds. Then you will know that I, the LORD, have spoken.

22 "This is what the Sovereign LORD says: I will take a branch from the
top of a tall cedar, and I will plant it on the top of Israel's highest mountain.
23 It will become a majestic cedar, sending forth its branches and producing
seed. Birds of every sort will nest in it, finding shelter in the shade of its
branches. 24 And all the trees will know that it is I, the LORD, who cuts the
tall tree down and makes the short tree grow tall. It is I who makes the green
tree wither and gives the dead tree new life. I, the LORD, have spoken, and
I will do what I said!"

The Justice of a Righteous God

18 Then another message came to me from the LORD: 2 "Why do you
quote this proverb concerning the land of Israel: 'The parents have
eaten sour grapes, but their children's mouths pucker at the taste'? 3 As surely
as I live, says the Sovereign LORD, you will not quote this proverb anymore
in Israel. 4 For all people are mine to judge—both parents and children alike.
And this is my rule: The person who sins is the one who will die.

5 "Suppose a certain man is righteous and does what is just and right.
6 He does not feast in the mountains before Israel's idols* or worship them.

17:21 As in many Hebrew manuscripts; Masoretic Text reads *his fleeing warriors*. The meaning is uncertain. 18:6 The Hebrew term (literally *round things*) probably alludes to dung; also in 18:12, 15.

He does not commit adultery or have intercourse with a woman during her
menstrual period. 7 He is a merciful creditor, not keeping the items given as
security by poor debtors. He does not rob the poor but instead gives food
to the hungry and provides clothes for the needy. 8 He grants loans without
interest, stays away from injustice, is honest and fair when judging others,
9 and faithfully obeys my decrees and regulations. Anyone who does these
things is just and will surely live, says the Sovereign LORD.

10 "But suppose that man has a son who grows up to be a robber or mur-
derer and refuses to do what is right. 11 And that son does all the evil things
his father would never do—he worships idols on the mountains, commits
adultery, 12 oppresses the poor and helpless, steals from debtors by refusing
to let them redeem their security, worships idols, commits detestable sins,
13 and lends money at excessive interest. Should such a sinful person live?
No! He must die and must take full blame.

14 "But suppose that sinful son, in turn, has a son who sees his father's
wickedness and decides against that kind of life. 15 This son refuses to wor-
ship idols on the mountains and does not commit adultery. 16 He does not
exploit the poor, but instead is fair to debtors and does not rob them. He
gives food to the hungry and provides clothes for the needy. 17 He helps the
poor,* does not lend money at interest, and obeys all my regulations and
decrees. Such a person will not die because of his father's sins; he will surely
live. 18 But the father will die for his many sins—for being cruel, robbing
people, and doing what was clearly wrong among his people.

19 "'What?' you ask. 'Doesn't the child pay for the parent's sins?' No! For
if the child does what is just and right and keeps my decrees, that child will
surely live. 20 The person who sins is the one who will die. The child will not
be punished for the parent's sins, and the parent will not be punished for
the child's sins. Righteous people will be rewarded for their own righteous
behavior, and wicked people will be punished for their own wickedness.
21 But if wicked people turn away from all their sins and begin to obey my
decrees and do what is just and right, they will surely live and not die. 22 All
their past sins will be forgotten, and they will live because of the righteous
things they have done.

23 "Do you think that I like to see wicked people die? says the Sovereign
LORD. Of course not! I want them to turn from their wicked ways and live.
24 However, if righteous people turn from their righteous behavior and start
doing sinful things and act like other sinners, should they be allowed to
live? No, of course not! All their righteous acts will be forgotten, and they
will die for their sins.

25 "Yet you say, 'The Lord isn't doing what's right!' Listen to me, O people
of Israel. Am I the one not doing what's right, or is it you? 26 When righteous
people turn from their righteous behavior and start doing sinful things, they
will die for it. Yes, they will die because of their sinful deeds. 27 And if wicked
people turn from their wickedness, obey the law, and do what is just and
right, they will save their lives. 28 They will live because they thought it over
and decided to turn from their sins. Such people will not die. 29 And yet the
people of Israel keep saying, 'The Lord isn't doing what's right!' O people of
Israel, it is you who are not doing what's right, not I.

30 "Therefore, I will judge each of you, O people of Israel, according to your

18:17 Greek version reads *He refuses to do evil.*

Question 18:31

How do we find ourselves a new heart and a new spirit?

actions, says the Sovereign LORD. Repent, and turn from your sins. Don't let
them destroy you! 31 Put all your rebellion behind you, and find yourselves
a new heart and a new spirit. For why should you die, O people of Israel? 32 I
don't want you to die, says the Sovereign LORD. Turn back and live!

A Funeral Song for Israel's Kings

19 "Sing this funeral song for the princes of Israel:

2 "What is your mother?
A lioness among lions!
She lay down among the young lions
and reared her cubs.
3 She raised one of her cubs
to become a strong young lion.
He learned to hunt and devour prey,
and he became a man-eater.
4 Then the nations heard about him,
and he was trapped in their pit.
They led him away with hooks
to the land of Egypt.

5 "When the lioness saw
that her hopes for him were gone,
she took another of her cubs
and taught him to be a strong young lion.
6 He prowled among the other lions
and stood out among them in his strength.
He learned to hunt and devour prey,
and he, too, became a man-eater.
7 He demolished fortresses*
and destroyed their towns and cities.
Their farms were desolated,
and their crops were destroyed.
The land and its people trembled in fear
when they heard him roar.
8 Then the armies of the nations attacked him,
surrounding him from every direction.
They threw a net over him
and captured him in their pit.
9 With hooks, they dragged him into a cage
and brought him before the king of Babylon.
They held him in captivity,
so his voice could never again be heard
on the mountains of Israel.

10 "Your mother was like a vine
planted by the water's edge.
It had lush, green foliage
because of the abundant water.

19:7 As in Greek version; Hebrew reads *He knew widows.*

11 Its branches became strong—
strong enough to be a ruler's scepter.
It grew very tall,
towering above all others.
It stood out because of its height
and its many lush branches.
12 But the vine was uprooted in fury
and thrown down to the ground.
The desert wind dried up its fruit
and tore off its strong branches,
so that it withered
and was destroyed by fire.
13 Now the vine is transplanted to the wilderness,
where the ground is hard and dry.
14 A fire has burst out from its branches
and devoured its fruit.
Its remaining limbs are not
strong enough to be a ruler's scepter.

"This is a funeral song, and it will be used in a funeral."

The Rebellion of Israel

20 On August 14,* during the seventh year of King Jehoiachin's captiv-
ity, some of the leaders of Israel came to request a message from the
LORD. They sat down in front of me to wait for his reply. 2Then this message
came to me from the LORD: 3"Son of man, tell the leaders of Israel, 'This is
what the Sovereign LORD says: How dare you come to ask me for a message?
As surely as I live, says the Sovereign LORD, I will tell you nothing!'

4"Son of man, bring charges against them and condemn them. Make
them realize how detestable the sins of their ancestors really were. 5Give
them this message from the Sovereign LORD: When I chose Israel—when I
revealed myself to the descendants of Jacob in Egypt—I took a solemn oath
that I, the LORD, would be their God. 6I took a solemn oath that day that I
would bring them out of Egypt to a land I had discovered and explored for
them—a good land, a land flowing with milk and honey, the best of all lands
anywhere. 7Then I said to them, 'Each of you, get rid of the vile images you
are so obsessed with. Do not defile yourselves with the idols* of Egypt, for
I am the LORD your God.'

8"But they rebelled against me and would not listen. They did not get rid of
the vile images they were obsessed with, or forsake the idols of Egypt. Then I
threatened to pour out my fury on them to satisfy my anger while they were
still in Egypt. 9But I didn't do it, for I acted to protect the honor of my name.
I would not allow shame to be brought on my name among the surrounding
nations who saw me reveal myself by bringing the Israelites out of Egypt. 10So
I brought them out of Egypt and led them into the wilderness. 11There I gave
them my decrees and regulations so they could find life by keeping them.
12And I gave them my Sabbath days of rest as a sign between them and me. It
was to remind them that I am the LORD, who had set them apart to be holy.

20:1 Hebrew *In the fifth month, on the tenth day,* of the ancient Hebrew lunar calendar. This day was August 14, 591 B.C.; also see note on 1:1. **20:7** The Hebrew term (literally *round things*) probably alludes to dung; also in 20:8, 16, 18, 24, 31, 39.

[13]“But the people of Israel rebelled against me, and they refused to obey
my decrees there in the wilderness. They wouldn't obey my regulations even
though obedience would have given them life. They also violated my Sab-
bath days. So I threatened to pour out my fury on them, and I made plans to
utterly consume them in the wilderness. [14]But again I held back in order to
protect the honor of my name before the nations who had seen my power in
bringing Israel out of Egypt. [15]But I took a solemn oath against them in the
wilderness. I swore I would not bring them into the land I had given them,
a land flowing with milk and honey, the most beautiful place on earth. [16]For
they had rejected my regulations, refused to follow my decrees, and violated
my Sabbath days. Their hearts were given to their idols. [17]Nevertheless, I
took pity on them and held back from destroying them in the wilderness.

[18]“Then I warned their children not to follow in their parents' footsteps,
defiling themselves with their idols. [19]‘I am the LORD your God,’ I told them.
‘Follow my decrees, pay attention to my regulations, [20]and keep my Sabbath
days holy, for they are a sign to remind you that I am the LORD your God.’

[21]“But their children, too, rebelled against me. They refused to keep my
decrees and follow my regulations, even though obedience would have given
them life. And they also violated my Sabbath days. So again I threatened to
pour out my fury on them in the wilderness. [22]Nevertheless, I withdrew my
judgment against them to protect the honor of my name before the nations
that had seen my power in bringing them out of Egypt. [23]But I took a solemn
oath against them in the wilderness. I swore I would scatter them among all
the nations [24]because they did not obey my regulations. They scorned my
decrees by violating my Sabbath days and longing for the idols of their ances-
tors. [25]I gave them over to worthless decrees and regulations that would not
lead to life. [26]I let them pollute themselves* with the very gifts I had given
them, and I allowed them to give their firstborn children as offerings to their
gods—so I might devastate them and remind them that I alone am the LORD.

Judgment and Restoration

[27]“Therefore, son of man, give the people of Israel this message from the
Sovereign LORD: Your ancestors continued to blaspheme and betray me, [28]for
when I brought them into the land I had promised them, they offered sacri-
fices on every high hill and under every green tree they saw! They roused my
fury as they offered up sacrifices to their gods. They brought their perfumes
and incense and poured out their liquid offerings to them. [29]I said to them,
‘What is this high place where you are going?’ (This kind of pagan shrine
has been called Bamah—‘high place’—ever since.)

[30]“Therefore, give the people of Israel this message from the Sovereign
LORD: Do you plan to pollute yourselves just as your ancestors did? Do you
intend to keep prostituting yourselves by worshiping vile images? [31]For
when you offer gifts to them and give your little children to be burned as
sacrifices,* you continue to pollute yourselves with idols to this day. Should
I allow you to ask for a message from me, O people of Israel? As surely as I
live, says the Sovereign LORD, I will tell you nothing.

[32]“You say, ‘We want to be like the nations all around us, who serve idols
of wood and stone.’ But what you have in mind will never happen. [33]As
surely as I live, says the Sovereign LORD, I will rule over you with an iron

20:25-26 Or *I gave them worthless decrees and regulations. . . . I polluted them.* **20:31** Or *and make your little children pass through the fire.*

fist in great anger and with awesome power. 34 And in anger I will reach out with my strong hand and powerful arm, and I will bring you back* from the lands where you are scattered. 35 I will bring you into the wilderness of the nations, and there I will judge you face to face. 36 I will judge you there just as I did your ancestors in the wilderness after bringing them out of Egypt, says the Sovereign LORD. 37 I will examine you carefully and hold you to the terms of the covenant. 38 I will purge you of all those who rebel and revolt against me. I will bring them out of the countries where they are in exile, but they will never enter the land of Israel. Then you will know that I am the LORD.

39 "As for you, O people of Israel, this is what the Sovereign LORD says: Go right ahead and worship your idols, but sooner or later you will obey me and will stop bringing shame on my holy name by worshiping idols. 40 For on my holy mountain, the great mountain of Israel, says the Sovereign LORD, the people of Israel will someday worship me, and I will accept them. There I will require that you bring me all your offerings and choice gifts and sacrifices. 41 When I bring you home from exile, you will be like a pleasing sacrifice to me. And I will display my holiness through you as all the nations watch. 42 Then when I have brought you home to the land I promised with a solemn oath to give to your ancestors, you will know that I am the LORD. 43 You will look back on all the ways you defiled yourselves and will hate yourselves because of the evil you have done. 44 You will know that I am the LORD, O people of Israel, when I have honored my name by treating you mercifully in spite of your wickedness. I, the Sovereign LORD, have spoken!"

Judgment against the Negev

45* Then this message came to me from the LORD: 46 "Son of man, turn and face the south* and speak out against it; prophesy against the brushlands of the Negev. 47 Tell the southern wilderness, 'This is what the Sovereign LORD says: Hear the word of the LORD! I will set you on fire, and every tree, both green and dry, will be burned. The terrible flames will not be quenched and will scorch everything from south to north. 48 And everyone in the world will see that I, the LORD, have set this fire. It will not be put out.'"

49 Then I said, "O Sovereign LORD, they are saying of me, 'He only talks in riddles!'"

The LORD's Sword of Judgment

21 1* Then this message came to me from the LORD: 2 "Son of man, turn and face Jerusalem and prophesy against Israel and her sanctuaries. 3 Tell her, 'This is what the LORD says: I am your enemy, O Israel, and I am about to unsheath my sword to destroy your people—the righteous and the wicked alike. 4 Yes, I will cut off both the righteous and the wicked! I will draw my sword against everyone in the land from south to north. 5 Everyone in the world will know that I am the LORD. My sword is in my hand, and it will not return to its sheath until its work is finished.'

6 "Son of man, groan before the people! Groan before them with bitter anguish and a broken heart. 7 When they ask why you are groaning, tell them,

20:34 Greek version reads *I will welcome you.* Compare 2 Cor 6:17. 20:45 Verses 20:45-49 are numbered 21:1-5 in Hebrew text. 20:46 Hebrew *toward Teman.* 21:1 Verses 21:1-32 are numbered 21:6-37 in Hebrew text.

Question 20:49

This was an interesting pushback from Ezekiel. This life of ministry was not an easy role for Ezekiel. What do you find most difficult about following God?

'I groan because of the terrifying news I have heard. When it comes true, the boldest heart will melt with fear; all strength will disappear. Every spirit will faint; strong knees will become as weak as water. And the Sovereign LORD says: It is coming! It's on its way!'"

8 Then the LORD said to me, 9 "Son of man, give the people this message from the Lord:

"A sword, a sword
is being sharpened and polished.
10 It is sharpened for terrible slaughter
and polished to flash like lightning!
Now will you laugh?
Those far stronger than you have fallen beneath its power!*
11 Yes, the sword is now being sharpened and polished;
it is being prepared for the executioner.

12 "Son of man, cry out and wail;
pound your thighs in anguish,
for that sword will slaughter my people and their leaders—
everyone will die!
13 It will put them all to the test.
What chance do they have?*
says the Sovereign LORD.

14 "Son of man, prophesy to them
and clap your hands.
Then take the sword and brandish it twice,
even three times,
to symbolize the great massacre,
the great massacre facing them on every side.
15 Let their hearts melt with terror,
for the sword glitters at every gate.
It flashes like lightning
and is polished for slaughter!
16 O sword, slash to the right,
then slash to the left,
wherever you will,
wherever you want.
17 I, too, will clap my hands,
and I will satisfy my fury.
I, the LORD, have spoken!"

Omens for Babylon's King

18 Then this message came to me from the LORD: 19 "Son of man, make a map
and trace two routes on it for the sword of Babylon's king to follow. Put a
signpost on the road that comes out of Babylon where the road forks into
two—20 one road going to Ammon and its capital, Rabbah, and the other to
Judah and fortified Jerusalem. 21 The king of Babylon now stands at the fork,
uncertain whether to attack Jerusalem or Rabbah. He calls his magicians

21:10 The meaning of the Hebrew is uncertain. 21:13 The meaning of the Hebrew is uncertain.

to look for omens. They cast lots by shaking arrows from the quiver. They
inspect the livers of animal sacrifices. 22The omen in his right hand says, 'Je-
rusalem!' With battering rams his soldiers will go against the gates, shouting
for the kill. They will put up siege towers and build ramps against the walls.
23The people of Jerusalem will think it is a false omen, because of their treaty
with the Babylonians. But the king of Babylon will remind the people of
their rebellion. Then he will attack and capture them.

24"Therefore, this is what the Sovereign LORD says: Again and again you
remind me of your sin and your guilt. You don't even try to hide it! In every-
thing you do, your sins are obvious for all to see. So now the time of your
punishment has come!

25"O you corrupt and wicked prince of Israel, your final day of reckoning
is here! 26This is what the Sovereign LORD says:

"Take off your jeweled crown,
for the old order changes.
Now the lowly will be exalted,
and the mighty will be brought down.
27 Destruction! Destruction!
I will surely destroy the kingdom.
And it will not be restored until the one appears
who has the right to judge it.
Then I will hand it over to him.

A Message for the Ammonites

28"And now, son of man, prophesy concerning the Ammonites and their
mockery. Give them this message from the Sovereign LORD:

"A sword, a sword
is drawn for your slaughter.
It is polished to destroy,
flashing like lightning!
29 Your prophets have given false visions,
and your fortune-tellers have told lies.
The sword will fall on the necks of the wicked
for whom the day of final reckoning has come.

30 "Now return the sword to its sheath,
for in your own country,
the land of your birth,
I will pass judgment upon you.
31 I will pour out my fury on you
and blow on you with the fire of my anger.
I will hand you over to cruel men
who are skilled in destruction.
32 You will be fuel for the fire,
and your blood will be spilled in your own land.
You will be utterly wiped out,
your memory lost to history,
for I, the LORD, have spoken!"

What God is saying to us

Prayer 22:16

God, the theme of Ezekiel's messages was that the people would know that you are the Lord. Please let that be the theme of my life. Amen.

The Sins of Jerusalem

22 Now this message came to me from the LORD: 2"Son of man, are you ready to judge Jerusalem? Are you ready to judge this city of murderers? Publicly denounce her detestable sins, 3and give her this message from the Sovereign LORD: O city of murderers, doomed and damned—city of idols,* filthy and foul—4you are guilty because of the blood you have shed. You are defiled because of the idols you have made. Your day of destruction has come! You have reached the end of your years. I will make you an object of mockery throughout the world. 5O infamous city, filled with confusion, you will be mocked by people far and near.

6"Every leader in Israel who lives within your walls is bent on murder. 7Fathers and mothers are treated with contempt. Foreigners are forced to pay for protection. Orphans and widows are wronged and oppressed among you. 8You despise my holy things and violate my Sabbath days of rest. 9People accuse others falsely and send them to their death. You are filled with idol worshipers and people who do obscene things. 10Men sleep with their fathers' wives and force themselves on women who are menstruating. 11Within your walls live men who commit adultery with their neighbors' wives, who defile their daughters-in-law, or who rape their own sisters. 12There are hired murderers, loan racketeers, and extortioners everywhere. They never even think of me and my commands, says the Sovereign LORD.

13"But now I clap my hands in indignation over your dishonest gain and bloodshed. 14How strong and courageous will you be in my day of reckoning? I, the LORD, have spoken, and I will do what I said. 15I will scatter you among the nations and purge you of your wickedness. 16And when I have been dishonored among the nations because of you,* you will know that I am the LORD."

The LORD's Refining Furnace

17Then this message came to me from the LORD: 18"Son of man, the people of Israel are the worthless slag that remains after silver is smelted. They are the dross that is left over—a useless mixture of copper, tin, iron, and lead. 19So tell them, 'This is what the Sovereign LORD says: Because you are all worthless slag, I will bring you to my crucible in Jerusalem. 20Just as silver, copper, iron, lead, and tin are melted down in a furnace, I will melt you down in the heat of my fury. 21I will gather you together and blow the fire of my anger upon you, 22and you will melt like silver in fierce heat. Then you will know that I, the LORD, have poured out my fury on you.'"

The Sins of Israel's Leaders

23Again a message came to me from the LORD: 24"Son of man, give the people of Israel this message: In the day of my indignation, you will be like a polluted land, a land without rain. 25Your princes* plot conspiracies just as lions stalk their prey. They devour innocent people, seizing treasures and extorting wealth. They make many widows in the land. 26Your priests have violated my instructions and defiled my holy things. They make no distinction between what is holy and what is not. And they do not teach my people the difference between what is ceremonially clean and unclean. They disregard

22:3 The Hebrew term (literally *round things*) probably alludes to dung; also in 22:4. 22:16 As in one Hebrew manuscript and Greek and Syriac versions; Masoretic Text reads *when you have been dishonored among the nations.* 22:25 As in Greek version; Hebrew reads *prophets.*

my Sabbath days so that I am dishonored among them. 27 Your leaders are like
wolves who tear apart their victims. They actually destroy people's lives for
money! 28 And your prophets cover up for them by announcing false visions
and making lying predictions. They say, 'My message is from the Sovereign
LORD,' when the LORD hasn't spoken a single word to them. 29 Even common
people oppress the poor, rob the needy, and deprive foreigners of justice.

30 "I looked for someone who might rebuild the wall of righteousness
that guards the land. I searched for someone to stand in the gap in the wall
so I wouldn't have to destroy the land, but I found no one. 31 So now I will
pour out my fury on them, consuming them with the fire of my anger. I
will heap on their heads the full penalty for all their sins. I, the Sovereign
LORD, have spoken!"

The Adultery of Two Sisters

23

This message came to me from the LORD: 2 "Son of man, once there
were two sisters who were daughters of the same mother. 3 They
became prostitutes in Egypt. Even as young girls, they allowed men to fondle
their breasts. 4 The older girl was named Oholah, and her sister was Oholi-
bah. I married them, and they bore me sons and daughters. I am speaking
of Samaria and Jerusalem, for Oholah is Samaria and Oholibah is Jerusalem.

5 "Then Oholah lusted after other lovers instead of me, and she gave her
love to the Assyrian officers. 6 They were all attractive young men, captains
and commanders dressed in handsome blue, charioteers driving their horses.
7 And so she prostituted herself with the most desirable men of Assyria, wor-
shiping their idols* and defiling herself. 8 For when she left Egypt, she did
not leave her spirit of prostitution behind. She was still as lewd as in her
youth, when the Egyptians slept with her, fondled her breasts, and used
her as a prostitute.

9 "And so I handed her over to her Assyrian lovers, whom she desired so
much. 10 They stripped her, took away her children as their slaves, and then
killed her. After she received her punishment, her reputation was known to
every woman in the land.

11 "Yet even though Oholibah saw what had happened to Oholah, her sis-
ter, she followed right in her footsteps. And she was even more depraved,
abandoning herself to her lust and prostitution. 12 She fawned over all the
Assyrian officers—those captains and commanders in handsome uniforms,
those charioteers driving their horses—all of them attractive young men. 13 I
saw the way she was going, defiling herself just like her older sister.

14 "Then she carried her prostitution even further. She fell in love with
pictures that were painted on a wall—pictures of Babylonian* military of-
ficers, outfitted in striking red uniforms. 15 Handsome belts encircled their
waists, and flowing turbans crowned their heads. They were dressed like
chariot officers from the land of Babylonia.* 16 When she saw these paintings,
she longed to give herself to them, so she sent messengers to Babylonia to
invite them to come to her. 17 So they came and committed adultery with
her, defiling her in the bed of love. After being defiled, however, she rejected
them in disgust.

18 "In the same way, I became disgusted with Oholibah and rejected her,
just as I had rejected her sister, because she flaunted herself before them

23:7 The Hebrew term (literally *round things*) probably alludes to dung; also in 23:30, 37, 39, 49.
23:14 Or *Chaldean*. 23:15 Or *Chaldea;* also in 23:16.

and gave herself to satisfy their lusts. 19 Yet she turned to even greater prostitution, remembering her youth when she was a prostitute in Egypt. 20 She lusted after lovers with genitals as large as a donkey's and emissions like those of a horse. 21 And so, Oholibah, you relived your former days as a young girl in Egypt, when you first allowed your breasts to be fondled.

The LORD's Judgment of Oholibah

22 "Therefore, Oholibah, this is what the Sovereign LORD says: I will send your lovers against you from every direction—those very nations from which you turned away in disgust. 23 For the Babylonians will come with all the Chaldeans from Pekod and Shoa and Koa. And all the Assyrians will come with them—handsome young captains, commanders, chariot officers, and other high-ranking officers, all riding their horses. 24 They will all come against you from the north* with chariots, wagons, and a great army prepared for attack. They will take up positions on every side, surrounding you with men armed with shields and helmets. And I will hand you over to them for punishment so they can do with you as they please. 25 I will turn my jealous anger against you, and they will deal harshly with you. They will cut off your nose and ears, and any survivors will then be slaughtered by the sword. Your children will be taken away as captives, and everything that is left will be burned. 26 They will strip you of your beautiful clothes and jewels. 27 In this way, I will put a stop to the lewdness and prostitution you brought from Egypt. You will never again cast longing eyes on those things or fondly remember your time in Egypt.

28 "For this is what the Sovereign LORD says: I will surely hand you over to your enemies, to those you loathe, those you rejected. 29 They will treat you with hatred and rob you of all you own, leaving you stark naked. The shame of your prostitution will be exposed to all the world. 30 You brought all this on yourself by prostituting yourself to other nations, defiling yourself with all their idols. 31 Because you have followed in your sister's footsteps, I will force you to drink the same cup of terror she drank.

32 "Yes, this is what the Sovereign LORD says:

"You will drink from your sister's cup of terror,
  a cup that is large and deep.
It is filled to the brim
  with scorn and derision.
33 Drunkenness and anguish will fill you,
  for your cup is filled to the brim with distress and desolation,
  the same cup your sister Samaria drank.
34 You will drain that cup of terror
  to the very bottom.
Then you will smash it to pieces
  and beat your breast in anguish.
  I, the Sovereign LORD, have spoken!

35 "And because you have forgotten me and turned your back on me, this is what the Sovereign LORD says: You must bear the consequences of all your lewdness and prostitution."

23:24 As in Greek version; the meaning of the Hebrew is uncertain.

The LORD's Judgment on Both Sisters

36 The LORD said to me, "Son of man, you must accuse Oholah and Oholi-
bah of all their detestable sins. 37 They have committed both adultery and
murder—adultery by worshiping idols and murder by burning as sacrifices
the children they bore to me. 38 Furthermore, they have defiled my Temple
and violated my Sabbath day! 39 On the very day that they sacrificed their
children to their idols, they boldly came into my Temple to worship! They
came in and defiled my house.

40 "You sisters sent messengers to distant lands to get men. Then when
they arrived, you bathed yourselves, painted your eyelids, and put on your
finest jewels for them. 41 You sat with them on a beautifully embroidered
couch and put my incense and my special oil on a table that was spread before
you. 42 From your room came the sound of many men carousing. They were
lustful men and drunkards* from the wilderness, who put bracelets on your
wrists and beautiful crowns on your heads. 43 Then I said, 'If they really want
to have sex with old worn-out prostitutes like these, let them!' 44 And that
is what they did. They had sex with Oholah and Oholibah, these shameless
prostitutes. 45 But righteous people will judge these sister cities for what they
really are—adulterers and murderers.

46 "Now this is what the Sovereign LORD says: Bring an army against them
and hand them over to be terrorized and plundered. 47 For their enemies will
stone them and kill them with swords. They will butcher their sons and
daughters and burn their homes. 48 In this way, I will put an end to lewdness
and idolatry in the land, and my judgment will be a warning to all women
not to follow your wicked example. 49 You will be fully repaid for all your
prostitution—your worship of idols. Yes, you will suffer the full penalty.
Then you will know that I am the Sovereign LORD."

The Sign of the Cooking Pot

24 On January 15,* during the ninth year of King Jehoiachin's captivity,
this message came to me from the LORD: 2 "Son of man, write down
today's date, because on this very day the king of Babylon is beginning his
attack against Jerusalem. 3 Then give these rebels an illustration with this
message from the Sovereign LORD:

"Put a pot on the fire,
and pour in some water.
4 Fill it with choice pieces of meat—
the rump and the shoulder
and all the most tender cuts.
5 Use only the best sheep from the flock,
and heap fuel on the fire beneath the pot.
Bring the pot to a boil,
and cook the bones along with the meat.

6 "Now this is what the Sovereign LORD says:
What sorrow awaits Jerusalem,
the city of murderers!

23:42 Or *Sabeans.* 24:1 Hebrew *On the tenth day of the tenth month,* of the ancient Hebrew lunar calendar. This event occurred on January 15, 588 B.C.; also see note on 1:1.

Drop your brilliant thoughts here

Question 24:13

The Lord had tried to "cleanse" his people, but they had refused. They were like a dog that needs a bath but refuses to get into the tub and then ends up making a bigger mess of the house. Are you like this? Are you ignoring or refusing God's calls to be cleansed?

Question 24:15–27

There are some very difficult chapters to digest in the book of Ezekiel. This section may be the most gut-wrenching. The sin of God's people, the displacement of their lives, and the tragedy of their circumstances culminated personally for Ezekiel in the death of his wife. Even then, the Lord asked Ezekiel to communicate a message through a painfully visible, real-life parable for God's people. What profound struggle of faith and life do you see in these verses?

She is a cooking pot
  whose corruption can't be cleaned out.
Take the meat out in random order,
  for no piece is better than another.
7 For the blood of her murders
  is splashed on the rocks.
It isn't even spilled on the ground,
  where the dust could cover it!
8 So I will splash her blood on a rock
  for all to see,
an expression of my anger
  and vengeance against her.

9 "This is what the Sovereign LORD says:
What sorrow awaits Jerusalem,
  the city of murderers!
  I myself will pile up the fuel beneath her.
10 Yes, heap on the wood!
  Let the fire roar to make the pot boil.
Cook the meat with many spices,
  and afterward burn the bones.
11 Now set the empty pot on the coals.
  Heat it red hot!
  Burn away the filth and corruption.
12 But it's hopeless;
  the corruption can't be cleaned out.
  So throw it into the fire.
13 Your impurity is your lewdness
  and the corruption of your idolatry.
I tried to cleanse you,
  but you refused.
So now you will remain in your filth
  until my fury against you has been satisfied.

14 "I, the LORD, have spoken! The time has come, and I won't hold back. I will not change my mind, and I will have no pity on you. You will be judged on the basis of all your wicked actions, says the Sovereign LORD."

The Death of Ezekiel's Wife

15 Then this message came to me from the LORD: 16 "Son of man, with one blow I will take away your dearest treasure. Yet you must not show any sorrow at her death. Do not weep; let there be no tears. 17 Groan silently, but let there be no wailing at her grave. Do not uncover your head or take off your sandals. Do not perform the usual rituals of mourning or accept any food brought to you by consoling friends."

18 So I proclaimed this to the people the next morning, and in the evening my wife died. The next morning I did everything I had been told to do. 19 Then the people asked, "What does all this mean? What are you trying to tell us?"

20 So I said to them, "A message came to me from the LORD, 21 and I was

told to give this message to the people of Israel. This is what the Sovereign
LORD says: I will defile my Temple, the source of your security and pride, the
place your heart delights in. Your sons and daughters whom you left behind
in Judah will be slaughtered by the sword. 22 Then you will do as Ezekiel
has done. You will not mourn in public or console yourselves by eating the
food brought by friends. 23 Your heads will remain covered, and your sandals
will not be taken off. You will not mourn or weep, but you will waste away
because of your sins. You will groan among yourselves for all the evil you
have done. 24 Ezekiel is an example for you; you will do just as he has done.
And when that time comes, you will know that I am the Sovereign LORD."

25 Then the LORD said to me, "Son of man, on the day I take away their
stronghold—their joy and glory, their heart's desire, their dearest treasure—I
will also take away their sons and daughters. 26 And on that day a survivor from
Jerusalem will come to you in Babylon and tell you what has happened. 27 And
when he arrives, your voice will suddenly return so you can talk to him, and
you will be a symbol for these people. Then they will know that I am the LORD."

A Message for Ammon

25 Then this message came to me from the LORD: 2 "Son of man, turn
and face the land of Ammon and prophesy against its people. 3 Give
the Ammonites this message from the Sovereign LORD: Hear the word of the
Sovereign LORD! Because you cheered when my Temple was defiled, mocked
Israel in her desolation, and laughed at Judah as she went away into exile, 4 I
will allow nomads from the eastern deserts to overrun your country. They will
set up their camps among you and pitch their tents on your land. They will
harvest all your fruit and drink the milk from your livestock. 5 And I will turn
the city of Rabbah into a pasture for camels, and all the land of the Ammonites
into a resting place for sheep and goats. Then you will know that I am the LORD.

6 "This is what the Sovereign LORD says: Because you clapped and danced
and cheered with glee at the destruction of my people, 7 I will raise my fist
of judgment against you. I will give you as plunder to many nations. I will
cut you off from being a nation and destroy you completely. Then you will
know that I am the LORD.

A Message for Moab

8 "This is what the Sovereign LORD says: Because the people of Moab* have
said that Judah is just like all the other nations, 9 I will open up their eastern
flank and wipe out their glorious frontier towns—Beth-jeshimoth, Baal-
meon, and Kiriathaim. 10 And I will hand Moab over to nomads from the
eastern deserts, just as I handed over Ammon. Yes, the Ammonites will no
longer be counted among the nations. 11 In the same way, I will bring my
judgment down on the Moabites. Then they will know that I am the LORD.

A Message for Edom

12 "This is what the Sovereign LORD says: The people of Edom have sinned
greatly by avenging themselves against the people of Judah. 13 Therefore,
says the Sovereign LORD, I will raise my fist of judgment against Edom. I will
wipe out its people and animals with the sword. I will make a wasteland of
everything from Teman to Dedan. 14 I will accomplish this by the hand of my

25:8 As in Greek version; Hebrew reads *Moab and Seir.*

> **Question** 25:17
>
> Go back through the first twenty-five chapters of Ezekiel and look ahead through the rest of the book. How many times did God say: "They will know that I am the LORD." Perhaps you feel a convicting question stemming from this repeated phrase: How many times will God have to say this in your life before you recognize that it is true?

people of Israel. They will carry out my vengeance with anger, and Edom will
know that this vengeance is from me. I, the Sovereign LORD, have spoken!

A Message for Philistia

15 "This is what the Sovereign LORD says: The people of Philistia have acted
against Judah out of bitter revenge and long-standing contempt. 16 There-
fore, this is what the Sovereign LORD says: I will raise my fist of judgment
against the land of the Philistines. I will wipe out the Kerethites and utterly
destroy the people who live by the sea. 17 I will execute terrible vengeance
against them to punish them for what they have done. And when I have
inflicted my revenge, they will know that I am the LORD."

A Message for Tyre

26 On February 3, during the twelfth year of King Jehoiachin's captiv-
ity,* this message came to me from the LORD: 2 "Son of man, Tyre has
rejoiced over the fall of Jerusalem, saying, 'Ha! She who was the gateway to
the rich trade routes to the east has been broken, and I am the heir! Because
she has been made desolate, I will become wealthy!'

3 "Therefore, this is what the Sovereign LORD says: I am your enemy,
O Tyre, and I will bring many nations against you, like the waves of the sea
crashing against your shoreline. 4 They will destroy the walls of Tyre and
tear down its towers. I will scrape away its soil and make it a bare rock! 5 It
will be just a rock in the sea, a place for fishermen to spread their nets, for I
have spoken, says the Sovereign LORD. Tyre will become the prey of many
nations, 6 and its mainland villages will be destroyed by the sword. Then they
will know that I am the LORD.

7 "This is what the Sovereign LORD says: From the north I will bring King
Nebuchadnezzar* of Babylon against Tyre. He is king of kings and brings his
horses, chariots, charioteers, and great army. 8 First he will destroy your main-
land villages. Then he will attack you by building a siege wall, constructing
a ramp, and raising a roof of shields against you. 9 He will pound your walls
with battering rams and demolish your towers with sledgehammers. 10 The
hooves of his horses will choke the city with dust, and the noise of the char-
ioteers and chariot wheels will shake your walls as they storm through your
broken gates. 11 His horsemen will trample through every street in the city.
They will butcher your people, and your strong pillars will topple.

12 "They will plunder all your riches and merchandise and break down your
walls. They will destroy your lovely homes and dump your stones and tim-
bers and even your dust into the sea. 13 I will stop the music of your songs. No
more will the sound of harps be heard among your people. 14 I will make your
island a bare rock, a place for fishermen to spread their nets. You will never
be rebuilt, for I, the LORD, have spoken. Yes, the Sovereign LORD has spoken!

The Effect of Tyre's Destruction

15 "This is what the Sovereign LORD says to Tyre: The whole coastline will
tremble at the sound of your fall, as the screams of the wounded echo in
the continuing slaughter. 16 All the seaport rulers will step down from their

26:1 Hebrew *In the eleventh year, on the first day of the month,* of the ancient Hebrew lunar calendar year. Since an element is missing in the date formula here, scholars have reconstructed this probable reading: *In the eleventh [month of the twelfth] year, on the first day of the month.* This reading would put this message on February 3, 585 B.C.; also see note on 1:1. **26:7** Hebrew *Nebuchadrezzar,* a variant spelling of Nebuchadnezzar.

thrones and take off their royal robes and beautiful clothing. They will sit on the ground trembling with horror at your destruction. 17 Then they will wail for you, singing this funeral song:

"O famous island city,
once ruler of the sea,
how you have been destroyed!
Your people, with their naval power,
once spread fear around the world.
18 Now the coastlands tremble at your fall.
The islands are dismayed as you disappear.

19 "This is what the Sovereign LORD says: I will make Tyre an uninhabited ruin, like many others. I will bury you beneath the terrible waves of enemy attack. Great seas will swallow you. 20 I will send you to the pit to join those who descended there long ago. Your city will lie in ruins, buried beneath the earth, like those in the pit who have entered the world of the dead. You will have no place of respect here in the land of the living. 21 I will bring you to a terrible end, and you will exist no more. You will be looked for, but you will never again be found. I, the Sovereign LORD, have spoken!"

The End of Tyre's Glory

27 Then this message came to me from the LORD: 2 "Son of man, sing a funeral song for Tyre, 3 that mighty gateway to the sea, the trading center of the world. Give Tyre this message from the Sovereign LORD:

"You boasted, O Tyre,
'My beauty is perfect!'
4 You extended your boundaries into the sea.
Your builders made your beauty perfect.
5 You were like a great ship
built of the finest cypress from Senir.*
They took a cedar from Lebanon
to make a mast for you.
6 They carved your oars
from the oaks of Bashan.
Your deck of pine from the coasts of Cyprus*
was inlaid with ivory.
7 Your sails were made of Egypt's finest linen,
and they flew as a banner above you.
You stood beneath blue and purple awnings
made bright with dyes from the coasts of Elishah.
8 Your oarsmen came from Sidon and Arvad;
your helmsmen were skilled men from Tyre itself.
9 Wise old craftsmen from Gebal did the caulking.
Ships from every land came with goods to barter for your trade.

10 "Men from distant Persia, Lydia, and Libya* served in your great army. They hung their shields and helmets on your walls, giving you great honor.

27:5 Or *Hermon*. 27:6 Hebrew *Kittim*. 27:10 Hebrew *Paras, Lud, and Put*.

[11]Men from Arvad and Helech stood on your walls. Your towers were manned
by men from Gammad. Their shields hung on your walls, completing your
beauty.

[12]"Tarshish sent merchants to buy your wares in exchange for silver, iron,
tin, and lead. [13]Merchants from Greece,* Tubal, and Meshech brought slaves
and articles of bronze to trade with you.

[14]"From Beth-togarmah came riding horses, chariot horses, and mules, all
in exchange for your goods. [15]Merchants came to you from Dedan.* Numer-
ous coastlands were your captive markets; they brought payment in ivory
tusks and ebony wood.

[16]"Syria* sent merchants to buy your rich variety of goods. They traded
turquoise, purple dyes, embroidery, fine linen, and jewelry of coral and ru-
bies. [17]Judah and Israel traded for your wares, offering wheat from Minnith,
figs,* honey, olive oil, and balm.

[18]"Damascus sent merchants to buy your rich variety of goods, bringing
wine from Helbon and white wool from Zahar. [19]Greeks from Uzal* came
to trade for your merchandise. Wrought iron, cassia, and fragrant calamus
were bartered for your wares.

[20]"Dedan sent merchants to trade their expensive saddle blankets with
you. [21]The Arabians and the princes of Kedar sent merchants to trade lambs
and rams and male goats in exchange for your goods. [22]The merchants of
Sheba and Raamah came with all kinds of spices, jewels, and gold in ex-
change for your wares.

[23]"Haran, Canneh, Eden, Sheba, Asshur, and Kilmad came with their
merchandise, too. [24]They brought choice fabrics to trade—blue cloth, em-
broidery, and multicolored carpets rolled up and bound with cords. [25]The
ships of Tarshish were your ocean caravans. Your island warehouse was filled
to the brim!

The Destruction of Tyre

26 "But look! Your oarsmen
have taken you into stormy seas!
A mighty eastern gale
has wrecked you in the heart of the sea!

27 Everything is lost—
your riches and wares,
your sailors and pilots,
your ship builders, merchants, and warriors.
On the day of your ruin,
everyone on board sinks into the depths of the sea.

28 Your cities by the sea tremble
as your pilots cry out in terror.

29 All the oarsmen abandon their ships;
the sailors and pilots stand on the shore.

30 They cry aloud over you
and weep bitterly.
They throw dust on their heads
and roll in ashes.

27:13 Hebrew *Javan.* 27:15 Greek version reads *Rhodes.* 27:16 Hebrew *Aram;* some manuscripts read *Edom.* 27:17 The meaning of the Hebrew is uncertain. 27:19 Hebrew *Vedan and Javan from Uzal.* The meaning of the Hebrew is uncertain.

31 They shave their heads in grief for you
and dress themselves in burlap.
They weep for you with bitter anguish
and deep mourning.
32 As they wail and mourn over you,
they sing this sad funeral song:
'Was there ever such a city as Tyre,
now silent at the bottom of the sea?
33 The merchandise you traded
satisfied the desires of many nations.
Kings at the ends of the earth
were enriched by your trade.
34 Now you are a wrecked ship,
broken at the bottom of the sea.
All your merchandise and crew
have gone down with you.
35 All who live along the coastlands
are appalled at your terrible fate.
Their kings are filled with horror
and look on with twisted faces.
36 The merchants among the nations
shake their heads at the sight of you,*
for you have come to a horrible end
and will exist no more.'"

A Message for Tyre's King

28 Then this message came to me from the LORD: 2"Son of man, give the prince of Tyre this message from the Sovereign LORD:

"In your great pride you claim, 'I am a god!
I sit on a divine throne in the heart of the sea.'
But you are only a man and not a god,
though you boast that you are a god.
3 You regard yourself as wiser than Daniel
and think no secret is hidden from you.
4 With your wisdom and understanding you have amassed great wealth—
gold and silver for your treasuries.
5 Yes, your wisdom has made you very rich,
and your riches have made you very proud.

6 "Therefore, this is what the Sovereign LORD says:
Because you think you are as wise as a god,
7 I will now bring against you a foreign army,
the terror of the nations.
They will draw their swords against your marvelous wisdom
and defile your splendor!
8 They will bring you down to the pit,
and you will die in the heart of the sea,

27:36 Hebrew *hiss at you.*

How this passage impacts me

pierced with many wounds.
9 Will you then boast, 'I am a god!'
to those who kill you?
To them you will be no god
but merely a man!
10 You will die like an outcast*
at the hands of foreigners.
I, the Sovereign LORD, have spoken!"

11 Then this further message came to me from the LORD: 12 "Son of man,
sing this funeral song for the king of Tyre. Give him this message from the
Sovereign LORD:

"You were the model of perfection,
full of wisdom and exquisite in beauty.
13 You were in Eden,
the garden of God.
Your clothing was adorned with every precious stone*—
red carnelian, pale-green peridot, white moonstone,
blue-green beryl, onyx, green jasper,
blue lapis lazuli, turquoise, and emerald—
all beautifully crafted for you
and set in the finest gold.
They were given to you
on the day you were created.
14 I ordained and anointed you
as the mighty angelic guardian.*
You had access to the holy mountain of God
and walked among the stones of fire.

15 "You were blameless in all you did
from the day you were created
until the day evil was found in you.
16 Your rich commerce led you to violence,
and you sinned.
So I banished you in disgrace
from the mountain of God.
I expelled you, O mighty guardian,
from your place among the stones of fire.
17 Your heart was filled with pride
because of all your beauty.
Your wisdom was corrupted
by your love of splendor.
So I threw you to the ground
and exposed you to the curious gaze of kings.
18 You defiled your sanctuaries
with your many sins and your dishonest trade.
So I brought fire out from within you,
and it consumed you.

28:10 Hebrew *will die the death of the uncircumcised.* 28:13 The identification of some of these gemstones is uncertain. 28:14 Hebrew *guardian cherub;* similarly in 28:16.

I reduced you to ashes on the ground
in the sight of all who were watching.
19 All who knew you are appalled at your fate.
You have come to a terrible end,
and you will exist no more."

A Message for Sidon
20Then another message came to me from the LORD: 21"Son of man, turn and
face the city of Sidon and prophesy against it. 22Give the people of Sidon this
message from the Sovereign LORD:

"I am your enemy, O Sidon,
and I will reveal my glory by what I do to you.
When I bring judgment against you
and reveal my holiness among you,
everyone watching will know
that I am the LORD.
23 I will send a plague against you,
and blood will be spilled in your streets.
The attack will come from every direction,
and your people will lie slaughtered within your walls.
Then everyone will know
that I am the LORD.
24 No longer will Israel's scornful neighbors
prick and tear at her like briers and thorns.
For then they will know
that I am the Sovereign LORD.

Restoration for Israel
25"This is what the Sovereign LORD says: The people of Israel will again live
in their own land, the land I gave my servant Jacob. For I will gather them
from the distant lands where I have scattered them. I will reveal to the na-
tions of the world my holiness among my people. 26They will live safely in
Israel and build homes and plant vineyards. And when I punish the neigh-
boring nations that treated them with contempt, they will know that I am
the LORD their God."

A Message for Egypt
29 On January 7,* during the tenth year of King Jehoiachin's captivity,
this message came to me from the LORD: 2"Son of man, turn and face
Egypt and prophesy against Pharaoh the king and all the people of Egypt.
3Give them this message from the Sovereign LORD:

"I am your enemy, O Pharaoh, king of Egypt—
you great monster, lurking in the streams of the Nile.
For you have said, 'The Nile River is mine;
I made it for myself.'
4 I will put hooks in your jaws
and drag you out on the land

29:1 Hebrew *On the twelfth day of the tenth month,* of the ancient Hebrew lunar calendar. This event occurred on January 7, 587 B.C.; also see note on 1:1.

Make a Difference

28:25-26

Hope

No matter what circumstances people find themselves in, whether dire or dry or dreaded, Jesus emboldens them to stand strongly with a remarkable joy. People who had been enfolded in the deepest darkness find in Jesus an infusion of light that lifts the heart. God truly does make us joyful despite our circumstances. The Lord promised to restore his people. He promised to give them safety. He promised to give them abundant life. He promised to gather them together and to dwell among them.

Difference Maker

Take a deep breath and smile. Try it. Smile on your own. Smile with others. Exercise the muscles around the mouth all day long. Every time you do, remember that the Lord is dwelling with you, giving you strength and hope and lighthearted joy. Your cheeks will hurt tomorrow, but it will be worth it.

Question **29:21**

Earlier in his ministry, Ezekiel complained about the people making fun of him for his complicated visions and messages. Here, the Lord promised that the people would eventually respect and appreciate Ezekiel's long dedication. What does this teach us about the short-term versus long-term effects of ministry?

with fish sticking to your scales.
5 I will leave you and all your fish
stranded in the wilderness to die.
You will lie unburied on the open ground,
for I have given you as food to the wild animals and birds.
6 All the people of Egypt will know that I am the LORD,
for to Israel you were just a staff made of reeds.
7 When Israel leaned on you,
you splintered and broke
and stabbed her in the armpit.
When she put her weight on you,
you collapsed, and her legs gave way.

8 "Therefore, this is what the Sovereign LORD says: I will bring an army
against you, O Egypt, and destroy both people and animals. 9 The land of
Egypt will become a desolate wasteland, and the Egyptians will know that
I am the LORD.

"Because you said, 'The Nile River is mine; I made it,' 10 I am now the
enemy of both you and your river. I will make the land of Egypt a totally
desolate wasteland, from Migdol to Aswan, as far south as the border of
Ethiopia.* 11 For forty years not a soul will pass that way, neither people nor
animals. It will be completely uninhabited. 12 I will make Egypt desolate, and
it will be surrounded by other desolate nations. Its cities will be empty and
desolate for forty years, surrounded by other ruined cities. I will scatter the
Egyptians to distant lands.

13 "But this is what the Sovereign LORD also says: At the end of the forty
years I will bring the Egyptians home again from the nations to which they
have been scattered. 14 I will restore the prosperity of Egypt and bring its
people back to the land of Pathros in southern Egypt from which they came.
But Egypt will remain an unimportant, minor kingdom. 15 It will be the low-
liest of all the nations, never again great enough to rise above its neighbors.

16 "Then Israel will no longer be tempted to trust in Egypt for help. Egypt's
shattered condition will remind Israel of how sinful she was to trust Egypt
in earlier days. Then Israel will know that I am the Sovereign LORD."

Nebuchadnezzar to Conquer Egypt

17 On April 26, the first day of the new year,* during the twenty-seventh year
of King Jehoiachin's captivity, this message came to me from the LORD:
18 "Son of man, the army of King Nebuchadnezzar* of Babylon fought so hard
against Tyre that the warriors' heads were rubbed bare and their shoulders
were raw and blistered. Yet Nebuchadnezzar and his army won no plunder
to compensate them for all their work. 19 Therefore, this is what the Sovereign
LORD says: I will give the land of Egypt to Nebuchadnezzar, king of Babylon.
He will carry off its wealth, plundering everything it has so he can pay his
army. 20 Yes, I have given him the land of Egypt as a reward for his work, says
the Sovereign LORD, because he was working for me when he destroyed Tyre.

21 "And the day will come when I will cause the ancient glory of Israel to

29:10 Hebrew *from Migdol to Syene as far as the border of Cush.* 29:17 Hebrew *On the first day of the first month,* of the ancient Hebrew lunar calendar. This event occurred on April 26, 571 B.C.; also see note on 1:1. 29:18 Hebrew *Nebuchadrezzar,* a variant spelling of Nebuchadnezzar; also in 29:19.

revive,* and then, Ezekiel, your words will be respected. Then they will know that I am the LORD."

A Sad Day for Egypt

30 This is another message that came to me from the LORD: 2"Son of man, prophesy and give this message from the Sovereign LORD:

"Weep and wail
for that day,
3 for the terrible day is almost here—
the day of the LORD!
It is a day of clouds and gloom,
a day of despair for the nations.
4 A sword will come against Egypt,
and those who are slaughtered will cover the ground.
Its wealth will be carried away
and its foundations destroyed.
The land of Ethiopia* will be ravished.
5 Ethiopia, Libya, Lydia, all Arabia,*
and all their other allies
will be destroyed in that war.

6 "For this is what the LORD says:
All of Egypt's allies will fall,
and the pride of her power will end.
From Migdol to Aswan*
they will be slaughtered by the sword,
says the Sovereign LORD.
7 Egypt will be desolate,
surrounded by desolate nations,
and its cities will be in ruins,
surrounded by other ruined cities.
8 And the people of Egypt will know that I am the LORD
when I have set Egypt on fire
and destroyed all their allies.
9 At that time I will send swift messengers in ships
to terrify the complacent Ethiopians.
Great panic will come upon them
on that day of Egypt's certain destruction.
Watch for it!
It is sure to come!

10 "For this is what the Sovereign LORD says:
By the power of King Nebuchadnezzar* of Babylon,
I will destroy the hordes of Egypt.
11 He and his armies—the most ruthless of all—
will be sent to demolish the land.

29:21 Hebrew *I will cause a horn to sprout for the house of Israel.* 30:4 Hebrew *Cush;* similarly in 30:9. 30:5 Hebrew *Cush, Put, Lud, all Arabia, Cub. Cub* is otherwise unknown and may be another spelling for *Lub* (Libya). 30:6 Hebrew *to Syene.* 30:10 Hebrew *Nebuchadrezzar,* a variant spelling of Nebuchadnezzar.

They will make war against Egypt
until slaughtered Egyptians cover the ground.
12 I will dry up the Nile River
and sell the land to wicked men.
I will destroy the land of Egypt and everything in it
by the hands of foreigners.
I, the LORD, have spoken!

13 "This is what the Sovereign LORD says:
I will smash the idols* of Egypt
and the images at Memphis.*
There will be no rulers left in Egypt;
terror will sweep the land.
14 I will destroy southern Egypt,*
set fire to Zoan,
and bring judgment against Thebes.*
15 I will pour out my fury on Pelusium,*
the strongest fortress of Egypt,
and I will stamp out
the hordes of Thebes.
16 Yes, I will set fire to all Egypt!
Pelusium will be racked with pain;
Thebes will be torn apart;
Memphis will live in constant terror.
17 The young men of Heliopolis and Bubastis* will die in battle,
and the women* will be taken away as slaves.
18 When I come to break the proud strength of Egypt,
it will be a dark day for Tahpanhes, too.
A dark cloud will cover Tahpanhes,
and its daughters will be led away as captives.
19 And so I will greatly punish Egypt,
and they will know that I am the LORD."

The Broken Arms of Pharaoh

20 On April 29,* during the eleventh year of King Jehoiachin's captivity, this
message came to me from the LORD: 21 "Son of man, I have broken the arm of
Pharaoh, the king of Egypt. His arm has not been put in a cast so that it may
heal. Neither has it been bound up with a splint to make it strong enough
to hold a sword. 22 Therefore, this is what the Sovereign LORD says: I am the
enemy of Pharaoh, the king of Egypt! I will break both of his arms—the
good arm along with the broken one—and I will make his sword clatter
to the ground. 23 I will scatter the Egyptians to many lands throughout the
world. 24 I will strengthen the arms of Babylon's king and put my sword in
his hand. But I will break the arms of Pharaoh, king of Egypt, and he will lie
there mortally wounded, groaning in pain. 25 I will strengthen the arms of
the king of Babylon, while the arms of Pharaoh fall useless to his sides. And
when I put my sword in the hand of Babylon's king and he brings it against

30:13a The Hebrew term (literally *round things*) probably alludes to dung. 30:13b Hebrew *Noph;* also in 30:16. 30:14a Hebrew *Pathros.* 30:14b Hebrew *No;* also in 30:15, 16. 30:15 Hebrew *Sin;* also in 30:16. 30:17a Hebrew *of Awen and Pi-beseth.* 30:17b Or *and her cities.* 30:20 Hebrew *On the seventh day of the first month,* of the ancient Hebrew lunar calendar. This event occurred on April 29, 587 B.C.; also see note on 1:1.

the land of Egypt, Egypt will know that I am the LORD. 26 I will scatter the
Egyptians among the nations, dispersing them throughout the earth. Then
they will know that I am the LORD."

Egypt Compared to Fallen Assyria

31 On June 21,* during the eleventh year of King Jehoiachin's captivity,
this message came to me from the LORD: 2 "Son of man, give this
message to Pharaoh, king of Egypt, and all his hordes:

"To whom would you compare your greatness?
3 You are like mighty Assyria,
which was once like a cedar of Lebanon,
with beautiful branches that cast deep forest shade
and with its top high among the clouds.
4 Deep springs watered it
and helped it to grow tall and luxuriant.
The water flowed around it like a river,
streaming to all the trees nearby.
5 This great tree towered high,
higher than all the other trees around it.
It prospered and grew long thick branches
because of all the water at its roots.
6 The birds nested in its branches,
and in its shade all the wild animals gave birth.
All the great nations of the world
lived in its shadow.
7 It was strong and beautiful,
with wide-spreading branches,
for its roots went deep
into abundant water.
8 No other cedar in the garden of God
could rival it.
No cypress had branches to equal it;
no plane tree had boughs to compare.
No tree in the garden of God
came close to it in beauty.
9 Because I made this tree so beautiful,
and gave it such magnificent foliage,
it was the envy of all the other trees of Eden,
the garden of God.

10 "Therefore, this is what the Sovereign LORD says: Because Egypt* be-
came proud and arrogant, and because it set itself so high above the others,
with its top reaching to the clouds, 11 I will hand it over to a mighty nation
that will destroy it as its wickedness deserves. I have already discarded it. 12 A
foreign army—the terror of the nations—has cut it down and left it fallen
on the ground. Its branches are scattered across the mountains and valleys
and ravines of the land. All those who lived in its shadow have gone away
and left it lying there.

31:1 Hebrew *On the first day of the third month,* of the ancient Hebrew lunar calendar. This event occurred on June 21, 587 B.C.; also see note on 1:1. 31:10 Hebrew *you.*

What I want to remember

13 "The birds roost on its fallen trunk,
and the wild animals lie among its branches.
14 Let the tree of no other nation
proudly exult in its own prosperity,
though it be higher than the clouds
and it be watered from the depths.
For all are doomed to die,
to go down to the depths of the earth.
They will land in the pit
along with everyone else on earth.

15 "This is what the Sovereign LORD says: When Assyria went down to the
grave,* I made the deep springs mourn. I stopped its rivers and dried up its
abundant water. I clothed Lebanon in black and caused the trees of the field
to wilt. 16 I made the nations shake with fear at the sound of its fall, for I sent
it down to the grave with all the others who descend to the pit. And all the
other proud trees of Eden, the most beautiful and the best of Lebanon, the ones
whose roots went deep into the water, took comfort to find it there with them in
the depths of the earth. 17 Its allies, too, were all destroyed and had passed away.
They had gone down to the grave—all those nations that had lived in its shade.
18 "O Egypt, to which of the trees of Eden will you compare your strength
and glory? You, too, will be brought down to the depths with all these other
nations. You will lie there among the outcasts* who have died by the sword.
This will be the fate of Pharaoh and all his hordes. I, the Sovereign LORD,
have spoken!"

A Warning for Pharaoh

32 On March 3,* during the twelfth year of King Jehoiachin's captivity,
this message came to me from the LORD: 2 "Son of man, mourn for
Pharaoh, king of Egypt, and give him this message:

"You think of yourself as a strong young lion among the nations,
but you are really just a sea monster,
heaving around in your own rivers,
stirring up mud with your feet.
3 Therefore, this is what the Sovereign LORD says:
I will send many people
to catch you in my net
and haul you out of the water.
4 I will leave you stranded on the land to die.
All the birds of the heavens will land on you,
and the wild animals of the whole earth
will gorge themselves on you.
5 I will scatter your flesh on the hills
and fill the valleys with your bones.
6 I will drench the earth with your gushing blood
all the way to the mountains,
filling the ravines to the brim.

31:15 Hebrew *to Sheol;* also in 31:16, 17. 31:18 Hebrew *among the uncircumcised.* 32:1 Hebrew *On the first day of the twelfth month,* of the ancient Hebrew lunar calendar. This event occurred on March 3, 585 B.C.; also see note on 1:1.

7 When I blot you out,
I will veil the heavens and darken the stars.
I will cover the sun with a cloud,
and the moon will not give you its light.
8 I will darken the bright stars overhead
and cover your land in darkness.
I, the Sovereign LORD, have spoken!

9 "I will disturb many hearts when I bring news of your downfall to dis-
tant nations you have never seen. 10 Yes, I will shock many lands, and their
kings will be terrified at your fate. They will shudder in fear for their lives
as I brandish my sword before them on the day of your fall. 11 For this is what
the Sovereign LORD says:

"The sword of the king of Babylon
will come against you.
12 I will destroy your hordes with the swords of mighty warriors—
the terror of the nations.
They will shatter the pride of Egypt,
and all its hordes will be destroyed.
13 I will destroy all your flocks and herds
that graze beside the streams.
Never again will people or animals
muddy those waters with their feet.
14 Then I will let the waters of Egypt become calm again,
and they will flow as smoothly as olive oil,
says the Sovereign LORD.
15 And when I destroy Egypt
and strip you of everything you own
and strike down all your people,
then you will know that I am the LORD.
16 Yes, this is the funeral song
they will sing for Egypt.
Let all the nations mourn.
Let them mourn for Egypt and its hordes.
I, the Sovereign LORD, have spoken!"

Egypt Falls into the Pit

17 On March 17,* during the twelfth year, another message came to me from
the LORD: 18 "Son of man, weep for the hordes of Egypt and for the other
mighty nations.* For I will send them down to the world below in company
with those who descend to the pit. 19 Say to them,

'O Egypt, are you lovelier than the other nations?
No! So go down to the pit and lie there among
the outcasts.'*

32:17 Hebrew *On the fifteenth day of the month,* presumably in the twelfth month of the ancient Hebrew lunar calendar (see 32:1). This would put this message at the end of King Jehoiachin's twelfth year of captivity, on March 17, 585 B.C.; also see note on 1:1. Greek version reads *On the fifteenth day of the first month,* which would put this message on April 27, 586 B.C., at the beginning of Jehoiachin's twelfth year. 32:18 The meaning of the Hebrew is uncertain. 32:19 Hebrew *the uncircumcised;* also in 32:21, 24, 25, 26, 28, 29, 30, 32.

What God wants people to know

20 The Egyptians will fall with the many who have died by the sword, for the
sword is drawn against them. Egypt and its hordes will be dragged away to
their judgment. 21 Down in the grave* mighty leaders will mockingly wel-
come Egypt and its allies, saying, 'They have come down; they lie among the
outcasts, hordes slaughtered by the sword.'

22 "Assyria lies there surrounded by the graves of its army, those who were
slaughtered by the sword. 23 Their graves are in the depths of the pit, and
they are surrounded by their allies. They struck terror in the hearts of people
everywhere, but now they have been slaughtered by the sword.

24 "Elam lies there surrounded by the graves of all its hordes, those who were
slaughtered by the sword. They struck terror in the hearts of people every-
where, but now they have descended as outcasts to the world below. Now they
lie in the pit and share the shame of those who have gone before them. 25 They
have a resting place among the slaughtered, surrounded by the graves of all
their hordes. Yes, they terrorized the nations while they lived, but now they lie
in shame with others in the pit, all of them outcasts, slaughtered by the sword.

26 "Meshech and Tubal are there, surrounded by the graves of all their
hordes. They once struck terror in the hearts of people everywhere. But
now they are outcasts, all slaughtered by the sword. 27 They are not buried
in honor like their fallen heroes, who went down to the grave* with their
weapons—their shields covering their bodies* and their swords beneath
their heads. Their guilt rests upon them because they brought terror to
everyone while they were still alive.

28 "You too, Egypt, will lie crushed and broken among the outcasts, all
slaughtered by the sword.

29 "Edom is there with its kings and princes. Mighty as they were, they
also lie among those slaughtered by the sword, with the outcasts who have
gone down to the pit.

30 "All the princes of the north and the Sidonians are there with others
who have died. Once a terror, they have been put to shame. They lie there
as outcasts with others who were slaughtered by the sword. They share the
shame of all who have descended to the pit.

31 "When Pharaoh and his entire army arrive, he will take comfort that he
is not alone in having his hordes killed, says the Sovereign LORD. 32 Although
I have caused his terror to fall upon all the living, Pharaoh and his hordes
will lie there among the outcasts who were slaughtered by the sword. I, the
Sovereign LORD, have spoken!"

Ezekiel as Israel's Watchman

33 Once again a message came to me from the LORD: 2 "Son of man, give
your people this message: 'When I bring an army against a country,
the people of that land choose one of their own to be a watchman. 3 When the
watchman sees the enemy coming, he sounds the alarm to warn the people.
4 Then if those who hear the alarm refuse to take action, it is their own fault if
they die. 5 They heard the alarm but ignored it, so the responsibility is theirs.
If they had listened to the warning, they could have saved their lives. 6 But if
the watchman sees the enemy coming and doesn't sound the alarm to warn
the people, he is responsible for their captivity. They will die in their sins,
but I will hold the watchman responsible for their deaths.'

32:21 Hebrew *in Sheol.* 32:27a Hebrew *to Sheol.* 32:27b The meaning of the Hebrew is uncertain.

7 “Now, son of man, I am making you a watchman for the people of Israel.
Therefore, listen to what I say and warn them for me. 8 If I announce that
some wicked people are sure to die and you fail to tell them to change their
ways, then they will die in their sins, and I will hold you responsible for their
deaths. 9 But if you warn them to repent and they don’t repent, they will die
in their sins, but you will have saved yourself.

Question 33:7

How others respond to you is not your responsibility. How you respond to God is your responsibility. Are these statements true?

The Watchman’s Message

10 “Son of man, give the people of Israel this message: You are saying, ‘Our
sins are heavy upon us; we are wasting away! How can we survive?’ 11 As surely
as I live, says the Sovereign LORD, I take no pleasure in the death of wicked
people. I only want them to turn from their wicked ways so they can live.
Turn! Turn from your wickedness, O people of Israel! Why should you die?
12 “Son of man, give your people this message: The righteous behavior of
righteous people will not save them if they turn to sin, nor will the wicked
behavior of wicked people destroy them if they repent and turn from their
sins. 13 When I tell righteous people that they will live, but then they sin, ex-
pecting their past righteousness to save them, then none of their righteous
acts will be remembered. I will destroy them for their sins. 14 And suppose
I tell some wicked people that they will surely die, but then they turn from
their sins and do what is just and right. 15 For instance, they might give back
a debtor’s security, return what they have stolen, and obey my life-giving
laws, no longer doing what is evil. If they do this, then they will surely live
and not die. 16 None of their past sins will be brought up again, for they have
done what is just and right, and they will surely live.
17 “Your people are saying, ‘The Lord isn’t doing what’s right,’ but it is they
who are not doing what’s right. 18 For again I say, when righteous people turn
away from their righteous behavior and turn to evil, they will die. 19 But if
wicked people turn from their wickedness and do what is just and right, they
will live. 20 O people of Israel, you are saying, ‘The Lord isn’t doing what’s
right.’ But I judge each of you according to your deeds.”

Explanation of Jerusalem’s Fall

21 On January 8,* during the twelfth year of our captivity, a survivor from Je-
rusalem came to me and said, “The city has fallen!” 22 The previous evening
the LORD had taken hold of me and given me back my voice. So I was able to
speak when this man arrived the next morning.
23 Then this message came to me from the LORD: 24 “Son of man, the scattered
remnants of Israel living among the ruined cities keep saying, ‘Abraham was
only one man, yet he gained possession of the entire land. We are many; surely
the land has been given to us as a possession.’ 25 So tell these people, ‘This is
what the Sovereign LORD says: You eat meat with blood in it, you worship
idols,* and you murder the innocent. Do you really think the land should be
yours? 26 Murderers! Idolaters! Adulterers! Should the land belong to you?’
27 “Say to them, ‘This is what the Sovereign LORD says: As surely as I live,
those living in the ruins will die by the sword. And I will send wild animals
to eat those living in the open fields. Those hiding in the forts and caves will
die of disease. 28 I will completely destroy the land and demolish her pride.

33:21 Hebrew *On the fifth day of the tenth month,* of the ancient Hebrew lunar calendar. This event occurred on January 8, 585 B.C.; also see note on 1:1. **33:25** The Hebrew term (literally *round things*) probably alludes to dung.

Her arrogant power will come to an end. The mountains of Israel will be
so desolate that no one will even travel through them. 29 When I have com-
pletely destroyed the land because of their detestable sins, then they will
know that I am the LORD.'

30 "Son of man, your people talk about you in their houses and whisper
about you at the doors. They say to each other, 'Come on, let's go hear the
prophet tell us what the LORD is saying!' 31 So my people come pretending
to be sincere and sit before you. They listen to your words, but they have no
intention of doing what you say. Their mouths are full of lustful words, and
their hearts seek only after money. 32 You are very entertaining to them, like
someone who sings love songs with a beautiful voice or plays fine music on
an instrument. They hear what you say, but they don't act on it! 33 But when
all these terrible things happen to them—as they certainly will—then they
will know a prophet has been among them."

The Shepherds of Israel

34 Then this message came to me from the LORD: 2 "Son of man, prophesy
against the shepherds, the leaders of Israel. Give them this message
from the Sovereign LORD: What sorrow awaits you shepherds who feed your-
selves instead of your flocks. Shouldn't shepherds feed their sheep? 3 You drink
the milk, wear the wool, and butcher the best animals, but you let your flocks
starve. 4 You have not taken care of the weak. You have not tended the sick or
bound up the injured. You have not gone looking for those who have wan-
dered away and are lost. Instead, you have ruled them with harshness and cru-
elty. 5 So my sheep have been scattered without a shepherd, and they are easy
prey for any wild animal. 6 They have wandered through all the mountains and
all the hills, across the face of the earth, yet no one has gone to search for them.

7 "Therefore, you shepherds, hear the word of the LORD: 8 As surely as I
live, says the Sovereign LORD, you abandoned my flock and left them to be
attacked by every wild animal. And though you were my shepherds, you
didn't search for my sheep when they were lost. You took care of yourselves
and left the sheep to starve. 9 Therefore, you shepherds, hear the word of the
LORD. 10 This is what the Sovereign LORD says: I now consider these shep-
herds my enemies, and I will hold them responsible for what has happened
to my flock. I will take away their right to feed the flock, and I will stop them
from feeding themselves. I will rescue my flock from their mouths; the sheep
will no longer be their prey.

The Good Shepherd

11 "For this is what the Sovereign LORD says: I myself will search and find my
sheep. 12 I will be like a shepherd looking for his scattered flock. I will find
my sheep and rescue them from all the places where they were scattered
on that dark and cloudy day. 13 I will bring them back home to their own
land of Israel from among the peoples and nations. I will feed them on the
mountains of Israel and by the rivers and in all the places where people live.
14 Yes, I will give them good pastureland on the high hills of Israel. There they
will lie down in pleasant places and feed in the lush pastures of the hills. 15 I
myself will tend my sheep and give them a place to lie down in peace, says
the Sovereign LORD. 16 I will search for my lost ones who strayed away, and I
will bring them safely home again. I will bandage the injured and strengthen

Story Arc **34:11-24**

● **Jesus**

Ezekiel's prophecy compared the bad shepherding of Israel's leaders to the good shepherding of God. It is hard not to see Jesus in this section of Ezekiel. In John 10, Jesus took these words upon himself. He told parables about going out to find the lost sheep. He spoke of how the sheep know his voice. He talked about gathering his flock. He mentioned that he knows his sheep and that they know him (echoing the theme of Ezekiel). Jesus even declared: "I am the good shepherd" (John 10:11).

Then Jesus went even further. As the Good Shepherd, he declared, "I sacrifice my life for the sheep" (v. 15). He stated that in doing so, he would give his sheep "eternal life, and they will never perish" (v. 28).

Do you know Jesus personally? If you have never committed your life to Jesus, turn to the back of this Bible and pray through the section called "How to Accept Jesus as Your Lord and Savior."

Dan 1:8 ►

the weak. But I will destroy those who are fat and powerful. I will feed them,
yes—feed them justice!
17 "And as for you, my flock, this is what the Sovereign LORD says to his
people: I will judge between one animal of the flock and another, separat-
ing the sheep from the goats. 18 Isn't it enough for you to keep the best of the
pastures for yourselves? Must you also trample down the rest? Isn't it enough
for you to drink clear water for yourselves? Must you also muddy the rest
with your feet? 19 Why must my flock eat what you have trampled down and
drink water you have fouled?
20 "Therefore, this is what the Sovereign LORD says: I will surely judge
between the fat sheep and the scrawny sheep. 21 For you fat sheep pushed and
butted and crowded my sick and hungry flock until you scattered them to
distant lands. 22 So I will rescue my flock, and they will no longer be abused. I
will judge between one animal of the flock and another. 23 And I will set over
them one shepherd, my servant David. He will feed them and be a shepherd
to them. 24 And I, the LORD, will be their God, and my servant David will be
a prince among my people. I, the LORD, have spoken!

The LORD's Covenant of Peace

25 "I will make a covenant of peace with my people and drive away the dan-
gerous animals from the land. Then they will be able to camp safely in the
wildest places and sleep in the woods without fear. 26 I will bless my people
and their homes around my holy hill. And in the proper season I will send
the showers they need. There will be showers of blessing. 27 The orchards and
fields of my people will yield bumper crops, and everyone will live in safety.
When I have broken their chains of slavery and rescued them from those
who enslaved them, then they will know that I am the LORD. 28 They will
no longer be prey for other nations, and wild animals will no longer devour
them. They will live in safety, and no one will frighten them.
29 "And I will make their land famous for its crops, so my people will never
again suffer from famines or the insults of foreign nations. 30 In this way, they
will know that I, the LORD their God, am with them. And they will know that
they, the people of Israel, are my people, says the Sovereign LORD. 31 You are
my flock, the sheep of my pasture. You are my people, and I am your God. I,
the Sovereign LORD, have spoken!"

A Message for Edom

35 Again a message came to me from the LORD: 2 "Son of man, turn and
face Mount Seir, and prophesy against its people. 3 Give them this
message from the Sovereign LORD:

"I am your enemy, O Mount Seir,
and I will raise my fist against you
to destroy you completely.
4 I will demolish your cities
and make you desolate.
Then you will know that I am the LORD.

5 "Your eternal hatred for the people of Israel led you to butcher them
when they were helpless, when I had already punished them for all their

Question 34:30

God's main goal was revealed: Know God! Know that God is with you. Know that God is your Good Shepherd. Allow him to find you. Allow his arms to embrace you. Allow Psalm 23 to be true in your life. Allow him to give his own life for yours. Have you allowed Jesus to be your shepherd?

Make a Difference 36:9

I Care about You

"See, I care about you." This was the very message that God's people needed to hear. The worst thing about their exile, the worst thing about their loss of home, was a fear that God didn't notice them anymore. "See, I care about you," God proclaimed. Maybe this is the very word that you need to hear today. Maybe this is the very word that someone you know needs to hear today.

Difference Maker

Surprise a friend by putting together a care package with a note that says, "See, I care about you!" and write "Ezekiel 36:9" on the note.

sins. 6 As surely as I live, says the Sovereign LORD, since you show no distaste
for blood, I will give you a bloodbath of your own. Your turn has come! 7 I
will make Mount Seir utterly desolate, killing off all who try to escape and
any who return. 8 I will fill your mountains with the dead. Your hills, your
valleys, and your ravines will be filled with people slaughtered by the sword.
9 I will make you desolate forever. Your cities will never be rebuilt. Then you
will know that I am the LORD.

10 "For you said, 'The lands of Israel and Judah will be ours. We will take
possession of them. What do we care that the LORD is there!' 11 Therefore, as
surely as I live, says the Sovereign LORD, I will pay back your angry deeds
with my own. I will punish you for all your acts of anger, envy, and hatred.
And I will make myself known to Israel* by what I do to you. 12 Then you
will know that I, the LORD, have heard every contemptuous word you spoke
against the mountains of Israel. For you said, 'They are desolate; they have
been given to us as food to eat!' 13 In saying that, you boasted proudly against
me, and I have heard it all!

14 "This is what the Sovereign LORD says: The whole world will rejoice
when I make you desolate. 15 You rejoiced at the desolation of Israel's terri-
tory. Now I will rejoice at yours! You will be wiped out, you people of Mount
Seir and all who live in Edom! Then you will know that I am the LORD.

Restoration for Israel

36 "Son of man, prophesy to Israel's mountains. Give them this mes-
sage: O mountains of Israel, hear the word of the LORD! 2 This is what
the Sovereign LORD says: Your enemies have taunted you, saying, 'Aha! Now
the ancient heights belong to us!' 3 Therefore, son of man, give the mountains
of Israel this message from the Sovereign LORD: Your enemies have attacked
you from all directions, making you the property of many nations and the
object of much mocking and slander. 4 Therefore, O mountains of Israel,
hear the word of the Sovereign LORD. He speaks to the hills and mountains,
ravines and valleys, and to ruined wastes and long-deserted cities that have
been destroyed and mocked by the surrounding nations. 5 This is what the
Sovereign LORD says: My jealous anger burns against these nations, espe-
cially Edom, because they have shown utter contempt for me by gleefully
taking my land for themselves as plunder.

6 "Therefore, prophesy to the hills and mountains, the ravines and valleys
of Israel. This is what the Sovereign LORD says: I am furious that you have
suffered shame before the surrounding nations. 7 Therefore, this is what the
Sovereign LORD says: I have taken a solemn oath that those nations will soon
have their own shame to endure.

8 "But the mountains of Israel will produce heavy crops of fruit for my
people—for they will be coming home again soon! 9 See, I care about you, and
I will pay attention to you. Your ground will be plowed and your crops planted.
10 I will greatly increase the population of Israel, and the ruined cities will be
rebuilt and filled with people. 11 I will increase not only the people, but also your
animals. O mountains of Israel, I will bring people to live on you once again.
I will make you even more prosperous than you were before. Then you will
know that I am the LORD. 12 I will cause my people to walk on you once again,
and you will be their territory. You will never again rob them of their children.

35:11 Hebrew *to them;* Greek version reads *to you.*

13 “This is what the Sovereign LORD says: The other nations taunt you,
saying, ‘Israel is a land that devours its own people and robs them of their
children!’ 14 But you will never again devour your people or rob them of their
children, says the Sovereign LORD. 15 I will not let you hear those other na-
tions insult you, and you will no longer be mocked by them. You will not be
a land that causes its nation to fall, says the Sovereign LORD.”

16 Then this further message came to me from the LORD: 17 “Son of man,
when the people of Israel were living in their own land, they defiled it by
the evil way they lived. To me their conduct was as unclean as a woman’s
menstrual cloth. 18 They polluted the land with murder and the worship of
idols,* so I poured out my fury on them. 19 I scattered them to many lands to
punish them for the evil way they had lived. 20 But when they were scattered
among the nations, they brought shame on my holy name. For the nations
said, ‘These are the people of the LORD, but he couldn’t keep them safe in his
own land!’ 21 Then I was concerned for my holy name, on which my people
brought shame among the nations.

22 “Therefore, give the people of Israel this message from the Sovereign
LORD: I am bringing you back, but not because you deserve it. I am doing
it to protect my holy name, on which you brought shame while you were
scattered among the nations. 23 I will show how holy my great name is—the
name on which you brought shame among the nations. And when I reveal
my holiness through you before their very eyes, says the Sovereign LORD,
then the nations will know that I am the LORD. 24 For I will gather you up
from all the nations and bring you home again to your land.

25 “Then I will sprinkle clean water on you, and you will be clean. Your
filth will be washed away, and you will no longer worship idols. 26 And I will
give you a new heart, and I will put a new spirit in you. I will take out your
stony, stubborn heart and give you a tender, responsive heart.* 27 And I will
put my Spirit in you so that you will follow my decrees and be careful to
obey my regulations.

28 “And you will live in Israel, the land I gave your ancestors long ago. You
will be my people, and I will be your God. 29 I will cleanse you of your filthy
behavior. I will give you good crops of grain, and I will send no more famines
on the land. 30 I will give you great harvests from your fruit trees and fields,
and never again will the surrounding nations be able to scoff at your land for
its famines. 31 Then you will remember your past sins and despise yourselves
for all the detestable things you did. 32 But remember, says the Sovereign
LORD, I am not doing this because you deserve it. O my people of Israel, you
should be utterly ashamed of all you have done!

33 “This is what the Sovereign LORD says: When I cleanse you from your
sins, I will repopulate your cities, and the ruins will be rebuilt. 34 The fields
that used to lie empty and desolate in plain view of everyone will again be
farmed. 35 And when I bring you back, people will say, ‘This former wasteland
is now like the Garden of Eden! The abandoned and ruined cities now have
strong walls and are filled with people!’ 36 Then the surrounding nations that
survive will know that I, the LORD, have rebuilt the ruins and replanted the
wasteland. For I, the LORD, have spoken, and I will do what I say.

37 “This is what the Sovereign LORD says: I am ready to hear Israel’s prayers
and to increase their numbers like a flock. 38 They will be as numerous as

36:18 The Hebrew term (literally *round things*) probably alludes to dung; also in 36:25.
36:26 Hebrew *a heart of flesh.*

Question 36:22

How does this passage match Romans 6:23?

Make a Difference

36:25-28

Heart Transplant

Jesus scrubs you clean and preps you for major surgery. He has flown in a new heart. He takes out your old, stony, stubborn heart. He gives you a new, tender, responsive heart. Then he puts his Spirit in you to keep that heart pumping forever.

Jesus is hard at work in your life. He doesn't just check in with you when you are afraid and call out to him. He checks in with you constantly. With every heartbeat, he is connected to you and flowing through you.

Therefore, allow him to separate you from your sin and learn the rhythm of this new life in him. Allow him to conform you to his Spirit, to be made like him in the way you think and in what you imagine is possible.

Difference Maker

Listen to the beat of your heart for several minutes and pray that the Lord will continue his re-creative work in you.

the sacred flocks that fill Jerusalem's streets at the time of her festivals. The
ruined cities will be crowded with people once more, and everyone will know
that I am the LORD."

A Valley of Dry Bones

37 The LORD took hold of me, and I was carried away by the Spirit of the
LORD to a valley filled with bones. [2]He led me all around among the
bones that covered the valley floor. They were scattered everywhere across
the ground and were completely dried out. [3]Then he asked me, "Son of man,
can these bones become living people again?"
"O Sovereign LORD," I replied, "you alone know the answer to that."
[4]Then he said to me, "Speak a prophetic message to these bones and say,
'Dry bones, listen to the word of the LORD! [5]This is what the Sovereign LORD
says: Look! I am going to put breath into you and make you live again! [6]I will
put flesh and muscles on you and cover you with skin. I will put breath into
you, and you will come to life. Then you will know that I am the LORD.'"
[7]So I spoke this message, just as he told me. Suddenly as I spoke, there was
a rattling noise all across the valley. The bones of each body came together
and attached themselves as complete skeletons. [8]Then as I watched, muscles
and flesh formed over the bones. Then skin formed to cover their bodies, but
they still had no breath in them.
[9]Then he said to me, "Speak a prophetic message to the winds, son of
man. Speak a prophetic message and say, 'This is what the Sovereign LORD
says: Come, O breath, from the four winds! Breathe into these dead bodies
so they may live again.'"
[10]So I spoke the message as he commanded me, and breath came into their
bodies. They all came to life and stood up on their feet—a great army.
[11]Then he said to me, "Son of man, these bones represent the people of Is-
rael. They are saying, 'We have become old, dry bones—all hope is gone. Our
nation is finished.' [12]Therefore, prophesy to them and say, 'This is what the
Sovereign LORD says: O my people, I will open your graves of exile and cause
you to rise again. Then I will bring you back to the land of Israel. [13]When
this happens, O my people, you will know that I am the LORD. [14]I will put
my Spirit in you, and you will live again and return home to your own land.
Then you will know that I, the LORD, have spoken, and I have done what I
said. Yes, the LORD has spoken!'"

Reunion of Israel and Judah

[15]Again a message came to me from the LORD: [16]"Son of man, take a piece
of wood and carve on it these words: 'This represents Judah and its allied
tribes.' Then take another piece and carve these words on it: 'This represents
Ephraim and the northern tribes of Israel.'* [17]Now hold them together in
your hand as if they were one piece of wood. [18]When your people ask you
what your actions mean, [19]say to them, 'This is what the Sovereign LORD
says: I will take Ephraim and the northern tribes and join them to Judah. I
will make them one piece of wood in my hand.'
[20]"Then hold out the pieces of wood you have inscribed, so the people
can see them. [21]And give them this message from the Sovereign LORD: I will
gather the people of Israel from among the nations. I will bring them home

37:16 Hebrew *This is Ephraim's wood, representing Joseph and all the house of Israel;* similarly in 37:19.

Make a Difference

37:1-14

Dry Bones

God's breath is fresh. Always fresh. It's like he has a constant, eternal supply of mints. God is like the ultimate "Fresh Maker" of heaven and earth. Everything he breathes upon flourishes with life. When God starts the day, his breath is not like yours after a night of snoring. When you wake up and breathe, things wilt and coil back. When God breathes, everything draws closer and opens up for more. God's breath gives abundant life and incredible power.

This chapter is one of the most astonishing pictures in the whole Bible. The Hebrew word for Spirit, *ruach*, also means "breath" or "wind." When God created humans, they stood there as a lump of molded sinew–until God breathed into them. Then they blossomed with relationship and had a lively time, naming things like the platypus and the manatee. When God gave Ezekiel this vision, the dry bones stood there as lumps of reformed sinew–until God breathed onto them the breath of life. Then they lived again! When Jesus commissioned his followers, they stood there as speechless lumps of confused sinew until he breathed onto them and gave them the Holy Spirit, the breath of God. Then they ran through the world changing the air of history (John 20:22; Acts 1).

Difference Maker

Pray this prayer: *Lord Jesus, breathe in me, this unworthy soul. Take this lump of sinew and breathe in me and revive my soul by your Spirit. Amen.*

to their own land from the places where they have been scattered. 22 I will
unify them into one nation on the mountains of Israel. One king will rule
them all; no longer will they be divided into two nations or into two king-
doms. 23 They will never again pollute themselves with their idols* and vile
images and rebellion, for I will save them from their sinful apostasy.* I will
cleanse them. Then they will truly be my people, and I will be their God.

24 "My servant David will be their king, and they will have only one shep-
herd. They will obey my regulations and be careful to keep my decrees.
25 They will live in the land I gave my servant Jacob, the land where their
ancestors lived. They and their children and their grandchildren after them
will live there forever, generation after generation. And my servant David
will be their prince forever. 26 And I will make a covenant of peace with them,
an everlasting covenant. I will give them their land and increase their num-
bers,* and I will put my Temple among them forever. 27 I will make my home
among them. I will be their God, and they will be my people. 28 And when my
Temple is among them forever, the nations will know that I am the LORD,
who makes Israel holy."

Question 37:22-26

In what ways could Ezekiel's vision here (vv. 22-26) be pointing to Jesus?

A Message for Gog

38 This is another message that came to me from the LORD: 2 "Son of
man, turn and face Gog of the land of Magog, the prince who rules
over the nations of Meshech and Tubal, and prophesy against him. 3 Give
him this message from the Sovereign LORD: Gog, I am your enemy! 4 I will
turn you around and put hooks in your jaws to lead you out with your whole
army—your horses and charioteers in full armor and a great horde armed
with shields and swords. 5 Persia, Ethiopia, and Libya* will join you, too, with
all their weapons. 6 Gomer and all its armies will also join you, along with the
armies of Beth-togarmah from the distant north, and many others.

7 "Get ready; be prepared! Keep all the armies around you mobilized, and
take command of them. 8 A long time from now you will be called into ac-
tion. In the distant future you will swoop down on the land of Israel, which
will be enjoying peace after recovering from war and after its people have
returned from many lands to the mountains of Israel. 9 You and all your
allies—a vast and awesome army—will roll down on them like a storm and
cover the land like a cloud.

10 "This is what the Sovereign LORD says: At that time evil thoughts will
come to your mind, and you will devise a wicked scheme. 11 You will say,
'Israel is an unprotected land filled with unwalled villages! I will march
against her and destroy these people who live in such confidence! 12 I will go
to those formerly desolate cities that are now filled with people who have
returned from exile in many nations. I will capture vast amounts of plun-
der, for the people are rich with livestock and other possessions now. They
think the whole world revolves around them!' 13 But Sheba and Dedan and
the merchants of Tarshish will ask, 'Do you really think the armies you have
gathered can rob them of silver and gold? Do you think you can drive away
their livestock and seize their goods and carry off plunder?'

14 "Therefore, son of man, prophesy against Gog. Give him this message

37:23a The Hebrew term (literally *round things*) probably alludes to dung. **37:23b** As in many Hebrew manuscripts and Greek version; Masoretic Text reads *from all their dwelling places where they sinned.* **37:26** Hebrew reads *I will give them and increase their numbers;* Greek version lacks the entire phrase. **38:5** Hebrew *Paras, Cush, and Put.*

from the Sovereign LORD: When my people are living in peace in their land,
then you will rouse yourself.* 15 You will come from your homeland in the
distant north with your vast cavalry and your mighty army, 16 and you will
attack my people Israel, covering their land like a cloud. At that time in the
distant future, I will bring you against my land as everyone watches, and my
holiness will be displayed by what happens to you, Gog. Then all the nations
will know that I am the LORD.

17 "This is what the Sovereign LORD asks: Are you the one I was talking
about long ago, when I announced through Israel's prophets that in the fu-
ture I would bring you against my people? 18 But this is what the Sovereign
LORD says: When Gog invades the land of Israel, my fury will boil over! 19 In
my jealousy and blazing anger, I promise a mighty shaking in the land of
Israel on that day. 20 All living things—the fish in the sea, the birds of the
sky, the animals of the field, the small animals that scurry along the ground,
and all the people on earth—will quake in terror at my presence. Mountains
will be thrown down; cliffs will crumble; walls will fall to the earth. 21 I will
summon the sword against you on all the hills of Israel, says the Sovereign
LORD. Your men will turn their swords against each other. 22 I will punish
you and your armies with disease and bloodshed; I will send torrential rain,
hailstones, fire, and burning sulfur! 23 In this way, I will show my greatness
and holiness, and I will make myself known to all the nations of the world.
Then they will know that I am the LORD.

The Slaughter of Gog's Hordes

39 "Son of man, prophesy against Gog. Give him this message from
the Sovereign LORD: I am your enemy, O Gog, ruler of the nations
of Meshech and Tubal. 2 I will turn you around and drive you toward the
mountains of Israel, bringing you from the distant north. 3 I will knock the
bow from your left hand and the arrows from your right hand, and I will
leave you helpless. 4 You and your army and your allies will all die on the
mountains. I will feed you to the vultures and wild animals. 5 You will fall
in the open fields, for I have spoken, says the Sovereign LORD. 6 And I will
rain down fire on Magog and on all your allies who live safely on the coasts.
Then they will know that I am the LORD.

7 "In this way, I will make known my holy name among my people of Is-
rael. I will not let anyone bring shame on it. And the nations, too, will know
that I am the LORD, the Holy One of Israel. 8 That day of judgment will come,
says the Sovereign LORD. Everything will happen just as I have declared it.

9 "Then the people in the towns of Israel will go out and pick up your small
and large shields, bows and arrows, javelins and spears, and they will use
them for fuel. There will be enough to last them seven years! 10 They won't
need to cut wood from the fields or forests, for these weapons will give them
all the fuel they need. They will plunder those who planned to plunder them,
and they will rob those who planned to rob them, says the Sovereign LORD.

11 "And I will make a vast graveyard for Gog and his hordes in the Valley
of the Travelers, east of the Dead Sea.* It will block the way of those who
travel there, and they will change the name of the place to the Valley of
Gog's Hordes. 12 It will take seven months for the people of Israel to bury
the bodies and cleanse the land. 13 Everyone in Israel will help, for it will be

38:14 As in Greek version; Hebrew reads *then you will know.* **39:11** Hebrew *the sea.*

a glorious victory for Israel when I demonstrate my glory on that day, says the Sovereign LORD.

14“After seven months, teams of men will be appointed to search the land for skeletons to bury, so the land will be made clean again. 15Whenever bones are found, a marker will be set up so the burial crews will take them to be buried in the Valley of Gog's Hordes. 16(There will be a town there named Hamonah, which means ‘horde.’) And so the land will finally be cleansed.

17“And now, son of man, this is what the Sovereign LORD says: Call all the birds and wild animals. Say to them: Gather together for my great sacrificial feast. Come from far and near to the mountains of Israel, and there eat flesh and drink blood! 18Eat the flesh of mighty men and drink the blood of princes as though they were rams, lambs, goats, and bulls—all fattened animals from Bashan! 19Gorge yourselves with flesh until you are glutted; drink blood until you are drunk. This is the sacrificial feast I have prepared for you. 20Feast at my banquet table—feast on horses and charioteers, on mighty men and all kinds of valiant warriors, says the Sovereign LORD.

21“In this way, I will demonstrate my glory to the nations. Everyone will see the punishment I have inflicted on them and the power of my fist when I strike. 22And from that time on the people of Israel will know that I am the LORD their God. 23The nations will then know why Israel was sent away to exile—it was punishment for sin, for they were unfaithful to their God. Therefore, I turned away from them and let their enemies destroy them. 24I turned my face away and punished them because of their defilement and their sins.

Restoration for God's People

25“So now, this is what the Sovereign LORD says: I will end the captivity of my people*; I will have mercy on all Israel, for I jealously guard my holy reputation! 26They will accept responsibility for* their past shame and unfaithfulness after they come home to live in peace in their own land, with no one to bother them. 27When I bring them home from the lands of their enemies, I will display my holiness among them for all the nations to see. 28Then my people will know that I am the LORD their God, because I sent them away to exile and brought them home again. I will leave none of my people behind. 29And I will never again turn my face from them, for I will pour out my Spirit upon the people of Israel. I, the Sovereign LORD, have spoken!”

The New Temple Area

40 On April 28,* during the twenty-fifth year of our captivity—fourteen years after the fall of Jerusalem—the LORD took hold of me. 2In a vision from God he took me to the land of Israel and set me down on a very high mountain. From there I could see toward the south what appeared to be a city. 3As he brought me nearer, I saw a man whose face shone like bronze standing beside a gateway entrance. He was holding in his hand a linen measuring cord and a measuring rod.

4He said to me, “Son of man, watch and listen. Pay close attention to everything I show you. You have been brought here so I can show you many things. Then you will return to the people of Israel and tell them everything you have seen.”

39:25 Hebrew *of Jacob.* **39:26** A few Hebrew manuscripts read *They will forget.* **40:1** Hebrew *At the beginning of the year, on the tenth day of the month,* of the ancient Hebrew lunar calendar. This event occurred on April 28, 573 B.C.; also see note on 1:1.

Question 39:26

How does God's forgiveness change the way you act? "They will accept responsibility..."

The East Gateway

5 I could see a wall completely surrounding the Temple area. The man took a
measuring rod that was 10½ feet* long and measured the wall, and the wall
was 10½ feet* thick and 10½ feet high.
6 Then he went over to the eastern gateway. He climbed the steps and mea-
sured the threshold of the gateway; it was 10½ feet front to back.* 7 There
were guard alcoves on each side built into the gateway passage. Each of these
alcoves was 10½ feet square, with a distance between them of 8¾ feet* along
the passage wall. The gateway's inner threshold, which led to the entry room
at the inner end of the gateway passage, was 10½ feet front to back. 8 He also
measured the entry room of the gateway.* 9 It was 14 feet* across, with sup-
porting columns 3½ feet* thick. This entry room was at the inner end of the
gateway structure, facing toward the Temple.
10 There were three guard alcoves on each side of the gateway passage. Each
had the same measurements, and the dividing walls separating them were
also identical. 11 The man measured the gateway entrance, which was 17½
feet* wide at the opening and 22¾ feet* wide in the gateway passage. 12 In
front of each of the guard alcoves was a 21-inch* curb. The alcoves themselves
were 10½ feet* on each side.
13 Then he measured the entire width of the gateway, measuring the dis-
tance between the back walls of facing guard alcoves; this distance was 43¾
feet.* 14 He measured the dividing walls all along the inside of the gateway up
to the entry room of the gateway; this distance was 105 feet.* 15 The full length
of the gateway passage was 87½ feet* from one end to the other. 16 There were
recessed windows that narrowed inward through the walls of the guard al-
coves and their dividing walls. There were also windows in the entry room.
The surfaces of the dividing walls were decorated with carved palm trees.

The Outer Courtyard

17 Then the man brought me through the gateway into the outer courtyard
of the Temple. A stone pavement ran along the walls of the courtyard, and
thirty rooms were built against the walls, opening onto the pavement.
18 This pavement flanked the gates and extended out from the walls into
the courtyard the same distance as the gateway entrance. This was the lower
pavement. 19 Then the man measured across the Temple's outer courtyard
between the outer and inner gateways; the distance was 175 feet.*

The North Gateway

20 The man measured the gateway on the north just like the one on the east.
21 Here, too, there were three guard alcoves on each side, with dividing walls
and an entry room. All the measurements matched those of the east gateway.

40:5a Hebrew *6 long cubits* [3.2 meters], *each being a cubit* [18 inches or 45 centimeters] *and a handbreadth* [3 inches or 8 centimeters] *in length.* **40:5b** Hebrew *1 rod* [3.2 meters]; also in 40:5c, 7. **40:6** As in Greek version, which reads *1 rod* [3.2 meters] *deep;* Hebrew reads *1 rod deep, and 1 threshold, 1 rod deep.* **40:7** Hebrew *5 cubits* [2.7 meters]; also in 40:48. **40:8** As in many Hebrew manuscripts and Syriac version; other Hebrew manuscripts add *which faced inward toward the Temple; it was 1 rod* [10.5 feet or 3.2 meters] *deep. 9 Then he measured the entry room of the gateway.* **40:9a** Hebrew *8 cubits* [4.2 meters]. **40:9b** Hebrew *2 cubits* [1.1 meters]. **40:11a** Hebrew *10 cubits* [5.3 meters]. **40:11b** Hebrew *13 cubits* [6.9 meters]. **40:12a** Hebrew *1 cubit* [53 centimeters]. **40:12b** Hebrew *6 cubits* [3.2 meters]. **40:13** Hebrew *25 cubits* [13.3 meters]; also in 40:21, 25, 29, 30, 33, 36. **40:14** Hebrew *60 cubits* [31.8 meters]. Greek version reads *20 cubits* [35 feet or 10.6 meters]. The meaning of the Hebrew in this verse is uncertain. **40:15** Hebrew *50 cubits* [26.5 meters]; also in 40:21, 25, 29, 33, 36. **40:19** Hebrew *100 cubits* [53 meters]; also in 40:23, 27, 47.

Please write on this page!

The gateway passage was 87½ feet long and 43¾ feet wide between the back walls of facing guard alcoves. 22The windows, the entry room, and the palm tree decorations were identical to those in the east gateway. There were seven steps leading up to the gateway entrance, and the entry room was at the inner end of the gateway passage. 23Here on the north side, just as on the east, there was another gateway leading to the Temple's inner courtyard directly opposite this outer gateway. The distance between the two gateways was 175 feet.

The South Gateway

24Then the man took me around to the south gateway and measured its various parts, and they were exactly the same as in the others. 25It had windows along the walls as the others did, and there was an entry room where the gateway passage opened into the outer courtyard. And like the others, the gateway passage was 87½ feet long and 43¾ feet wide between the back walls of facing guard alcoves. 26This gateway also had a stairway of seven steps leading up to it, and an entry room at the inner end, and palm tree decorations along the dividing walls. 27And here again, directly opposite the outer gateway, was another gateway that led into the inner courtyard. The distance between the two gateways was 175 feet.

Gateways to the Inner Courtyard

28Then the man took me to the south gateway leading into the inner courtyard. He measured it, and it had the same measurements as the other gateways. 29Its guard alcoves, dividing walls, and entry room were the same size as those in the others. It also had windows along its walls and in the entry room. And like the others, the gateway passage was 87½ feet long and 43¾ feet wide. 30(The entry rooms of the gateways leading into the inner courtyard were 14 feet* across and 43¾ feet wide.) 31The entry room to the south gateway faced into the outer courtyard. It had palm tree decorations on its columns, and there were eight steps leading to its entrance.

32Then he took me to the east gateway leading to the inner courtyard. He measured it, and it had the same measurements as the other gateways. 33Its guard alcoves, dividing walls, and entry room were the same size as those of the others, and there were windows along the walls and in the entry room. The gateway passage measured 87½ feet long and 43¾ feet wide. 34Its entry room faced into the outer courtyard. It had palm tree decorations on its columns, and there were eight steps leading to its entrance.

35Then he took me around to the north gateway leading to the inner courtyard. He measured it, and it had the same measurements as the other gateways. 36The guard alcoves, dividing walls, and entry room of this gateway had the same measurements as in the others and the same window arrangements. The gateway passage measured 87½ feet long and 43¾ feet wide. 37Its entry room* faced into the outer courtyard, and it had palm tree decorations on the columns. There were eight steps leading to its entrance.

Rooms for Preparing Sacrifices

38A door led from the entry room of one of the inner gateways into a side room, where the meat for sacrifices was washed. 39On each side of this entry

40:30 As in 40:9, which reads *8 cubits* [14 feet or 4.2 meters]; here the Hebrew reads *5 cubits* [8¾ feet or 2.7 meters]. Some Hebrew manuscripts and the Greek version lack this entire verse. **40:37** As in Greek version (compare parallels at 40:26, 31, 34); Hebrew reads *Its dividing wall.*

room were two tables, where the sacrificial animals were slaughtered for the burnt offerings, sin offerings, and guilt offerings. 40 Outside the entry room, on each side of the stairs going up to the north entrance, were two more tables. 41 So there were eight tables in all—four inside and four outside—where the sacrifices were cut up and prepared. 42 There were also four tables of finished stone for preparation of the burnt offerings, each 31½ inches square and 21 inches high.* On these tables were placed the butchering knives and other implements for slaughtering the sacrificial animals. 43 There were hooks, each 3 inches* long, fastened all around the foyer walls. The sacrificial meat was laid on the tables.

Rooms for the Priests

44 Inside the inner courtyard were two rooms,* one beside the north gateway, facing south, and the other beside the south* gateway, facing north. 45 And the man said to me, "The room beside the north inner gate is for the priests who supervise the Temple maintenance. 46 The room beside the south inner gate is for the priests in charge of the altar—the descendants of Zadok—for they alone of all the Levites may approach the LORD to minister to him."

The Inner Courtyard and Temple

47 Then the man measured the inner courtyard, and it was a square, 175 feet wide and 175 feet across. The altar stood in the courtyard in front of the Temple. 48 Then he brought me to the entry room of the Temple. He measured the walls on either side of the opening to the entry room, and they were 8¾ feet thick. The entrance itself was 24½ feet wide, and the walls on each side of the entrance were an additional 5¼ feet long.* 49 The entry room was 35 feet* wide and 21 feet* deep. There were ten steps* leading up to it, with a column on each side.

41 After that, the man brought me into the sanctuary of the Temple. He measured the walls on either side of its doorway,* and they were 10½ feet* thick. 2 The doorway was 17½ feet* wide, and the walls on each side of it were 8¾ feet* long. The sanctuary itself was 70 feet long and 35 feet wide.*

3 Then he went beyond the sanctuary into the inner room. He measured the walls on either side of its entrance, and they were 3½ feet* thick. The entrance was 10½ feet wide, and the walls on each side of the entrance were 12¼ feet* long. 4 The inner room of the sanctuary was 35 feet* long and 35 feet wide. "This," he told me, "is the Most Holy Place."

5 Then he measured the wall of the Temple, and it was 10½ feet thick. There was a row of rooms along the outside wall; each room was 7 feet* wide. 6 These side rooms were built in three levels, one above the other, with thirty

40:42 Hebrew *1½ cubits* [80 centimeters] *long and 1½ cubits wide and 1 cubit* [53 centimeters] *high.* **40:43** Hebrew *a handbreadth* [8 centimeters]. **40:44a** As in Greek version; Hebrew reads *rooms for singers.* **40:44b** As in Greek version; Hebrew reads *east.* **40:48** As in Greek version, which reads *The entrance was 14 cubits* [7.4 meters] *wide, and the walls of the entrance were 3 cubits* [1.6 meters] *on each side;* Hebrew lacks *14 cubits wide, and the walls of the entrance were.* **40:49a** Hebrew *20 cubits* [10.6 meters]. **40:49b** As in Greek version, which reads *12 cubits* [21 feet or 6.4 meters]; Hebrew reads *11 cubits* [19¼ feet or 5.8 meters]. **40:49c** As in Greek version; Hebrew reads *There were steps that were.* **41:1a** As in Greek version; the meaning of the Hebrew is uncertain. **41:1b** Hebrew *6 cubits* [3.2 meters]; also in 41:3, 5. **41:2a** Hebrew *10 cubits* [5.3 meters]. **41:2b** Hebrew *5 cubits* [2.7 meters]; also in 41:9, 11. **41:2c** Hebrew *40 cubits* [21.2 meters] *long and 20 cubits* [10.6 meters] *wide.* **41:3a** Hebrew *2 cubits* [1.1 meters]. **41:3b** Hebrew *7 cubits* [3.7 meters]. **41:4** Hebrew *20 cubits* [10.6 meters]; also in 41:4b, 10. **41:5** Hebrew *4 cubits* [2.1 meters].

rooms on each level. The supports for these side rooms rested on exterior
ledges on the Temple wall; they did not extend into the wall. 7 Each level was
wider than the one below it, corresponding to the narrowing of the Temple
wall as it rose higher. A stairway led up from the bottom level through the
middle level to the top level.

8 I saw that the Temple was built on a terrace, which provided a founda-
tion for the side rooms. This terrace was 10½ feet* high. 9 The outer wall of
the Temple's side rooms was 8¾ feet thick. This left an open area between
these side rooms 10 and the row of rooms along the outer wall of the inner
courtyard. This open area was 35 feet wide, and it went all the way around
the Temple. 11 Two doors opened from the side rooms into the terrace yard,
which was 8¾ feet wide. One door faced north and the other south.

12 A large building stood on the west, facing the Temple courtyard. It
was 122½ feet wide and 157½ feet long, and its walls were 8¾ feet* thick.
13 Then the man measured the Temple, and it was 175 feet* long. The court-
yard around the building, including its walls, was an additional 175 feet in
length. 14 The inner courtyard to the east of the Temple was also 175 feet wide.
15 The building to the west, including its two walls, was also 175 feet wide.

The sanctuary, the inner room, and the entry room of the Temple 16 were
all paneled with wood, as were the frames of the recessed windows. The inner
walls of the Temple were paneled with wood above and below the windows.
17 The space above the door leading into the inner room, and its walls inside
and out, were also paneled. 18 All the walls were decorated with carvings
of cherubim, each with two faces, and there was a carving of a palm tree
between each of the cherubim. 19 One face—that of a man—looked toward
the palm tree on one side. The other face—that of a young lion—looked
toward the palm tree on the other side. The figures were carved all along
the inside of the Temple, 20 from the floor to the top of the walls, including
the outer wall of the sanctuary.

21 There were square columns at the entrance to the sanctuary, and the
ones at the entrance of the Most Holy Place were similar. 22 There was an altar
made of wood, 5¼ feet high and 3½ feet across.* Its corners, base, and sides
were all made of wood. "This," the man told me, "is the table that stands in
the LORD's presence."

23 Both the sanctuary and the Most Holy Place had double doorways, 24 each
with two swinging doors. 25 The doors leading into the sanctuary were deco-
rated with carved cherubim and palm trees, just as on the walls. And there
was a wooden roof at the front of the entry room to the Temple. 26 On both
sides of the entry room were recessed windows decorated with carved palm
trees. The side rooms along the outside wall also had roofs.

Rooms for the Priests

42 Then the man led me out of the Temple courtyard by way of the
north gateway. We entered the outer courtyard and came to a
group of rooms against the north wall of the inner courtyard. 2 This struc-
ture, whose entrance opened toward the north, was 175 feet* long and 87½
feet* wide. 3 One block of rooms overlooked the 35-foot* width of the inner

41:8 Hebrew *1 rod, 6 cubits* [3.2 meters]. **41:12** Hebrew *70 cubits* [37.1 meters] *wide and 90 cubits* [47.7 meters] *long, and its walls were 5 cubits* [2.7 meters] *thick.* **41:13** Hebrew *100 cubits* [53 meters]; also in 41:13b, 14, 15. **41:22** Hebrew *3 cubits* [1.6 meters] *high and 2 cubits* [1.1 meters] *across.* **42:2a** Hebrew *100 cubits* [53 meters]; also in 42:8. **42:2b** Hebrew *50 cubits* [26.5 meters]; also in 42:7, 8. **42:3** Hebrew *20[-cubit]* [10.6-meter].

Highlights from the text

courtyard. Another block of rooms looked out onto the pavement of the outer courtyard. The two blocks were built three levels high and stood across from each other. 4 Between the two blocks of rooms ran a walkway 17½ feet* wide. It extended the entire 175 feet of the complex,* and all the doors faced north. 5 Each of the two upper levels of rooms was narrower than the one beneath it because the upper levels had to allow space for walkways in front of them. 6 Since there were three levels and they did not have supporting columns as in the courtyards, each of the upper levels was set back from the level beneath it. 7 There was an outer wall that separated the rooms from the outer courtyard; it was 87½ feet long. 8 This wall added length to the outer block of rooms, which extended for only 87½ feet, while the inner block—the rooms toward the Temple—extended for 175 feet. 9 There was an eastern entrance from the outer courtyard to these rooms.

10 On the south* side of the Temple there were two blocks of rooms just south of the inner courtyard between the Temple and the outer courtyard. These rooms were arranged just like the rooms on the north. 11 There was a walkway between the two blocks of rooms just like the complex on the north side of the Temple. This complex of rooms was the same length and width as the other one, and it had the same entrances and doors. The dimensions of each were identical. 12 So there was an entrance in the wall facing the doors of the inner block of rooms, and another on the east at the end of the interior walkway.

13 Then the man told me, "These rooms that overlook the Temple from the north and south are holy. Here the priests who offer sacrifices to the LORD will eat the most holy offerings. And because these rooms are holy, they will be used to store the sacred offerings—the grain offerings, sin offerings, and guilt offerings. 14 When the priests leave the sanctuary, they must not go directly to the outer courtyard. They must first take off the clothes they wore while ministering, because these clothes are holy. They must put on other clothes before entering the parts of the building complex open to the public."

15 When the man had finished measuring the inside of the Temple area, he led me out through the east gateway to measure the entire perimeter. 16 He measured the east side with his measuring rod, and it was 875 feet long.* 17 Then he measured the north side, and it was also 875 feet. 18 The south side was also 875 feet, 19 and the west side was also 875 feet. 20 So the area was 875 feet on each side with a wall all around it to separate what was holy from what was common.

The LORD's Glory Returns

43 After this, the man brought me back around to the east gateway. 2 Suddenly, the glory of the God of Israel appeared from the east. The sound of his coming was like the roar of rushing waters, and the whole landscape shone with his glory. 3 This vision was just like the others I had seen, first by the Kebar River and then when he came* to destroy Jerusalem. I fell face down on the ground. 4 And the glory of the LORD came into the Temple through the east gateway.

42:4a Hebrew *10 cubits* [5.3 meters]. **42:4b** As in Greek and Syriac versions, which read *Its length was 100 cubits* [53 meters]; Hebrew reads *and a passage 1 cubit* [21 inches or 53 centimeters] *wide.* **42:10** As in Greek version; Hebrew reads *east.* **42:16** As in 45:2 and in Greek version at 42:17, which reads *500 cubits* [265 meters]; Hebrew reads *500 rods* [5,250 feet or 1,590 meters]; similarly in 42:17, 18, 19, 20. **43:3** As in some Hebrew manuscripts and Latin Vulgate; Masoretic Text reads *I came.*

5 Then the Spirit took me up and brought me into the inner courtyard,
and the glory of the LORD filled the Temple. 6 And I heard someone speak-
ing to me from within the Temple, while the man who had been measuring
stood beside me. 7 The LORD said to me, "Son of man, this is the place of my
throne and the place where I will rest my feet. I will live here forever among
the people of Israel. They and their kings will not defile my holy name any
longer by their adulterous worship of other gods or by honoring the rel-
ics of their kings who have died.* 8 They put their idol altars right next to
mine with only a wall between them and me. They defiled my holy name by
such detestable sin, so I consumed them in my anger. 9 Now let them stop
worshiping other gods and honoring the relics of their kings, and I will live
among them forever.

10 "Son of man, describe to the people of Israel the Temple I have shown
you, so they will be ashamed of all their sins. Let them study its plan, 11 and
they will be ashamed* of what they have done. Describe to them all the speci-
fications of the Temple—including its entrances and exits—and everything
else about it. Tell them about its decrees and laws. Write down all these speci-
fications and decrees as they watch so they will be sure to remember and
follow them. 12 And this is the basic law of the Temple: absolute holiness!
The entire top of the mountain where the Temple is built is holy. Yes, this is
the basic law of the Temple.

The Altar

13 "These are the measurements of the altar*: There is a gutter all around the
altar 21 inches deep and 21 inches wide,* with a curb 9 inches* wide around
its edge. And this is the height* of the altar: 14 From the gutter the altar rises
3½ feet* to a lower ledge that surrounds the altar and is 21 inches* wide.
From the lower ledge the altar rises 7 feet* to the upper ledge that is also
21 inches wide. 15 The top of the altar, the hearth, rises another 7 feet higher,
with a horn rising up from each of the four corners. 16 The top of the altar is
square, measuring 21 feet by 21 feet.* 17 The upper ledge also forms a square,
measuring 24½ feet by 24½ feet,* with a 21-inch gutter and a 10½-inch curb*
all around the edge. There are steps going up the east side of the altar."

18 Then he said to me, "Son of man, this is what the Sovereign LORD says:
These will be the regulations for the burning of offerings and the sprinkling
of blood when the altar is built. 19 At that time, the Levitical priests of the
family of Zadok, who minister before me, are to be given a young bull for a
sin offering, says the Sovereign LORD. 20 You will take some of its blood and
smear it on the four horns of the altar, the four corners of the upper ledge,
and the curb that runs around that ledge. This will cleanse and make atone-
ment for the altar. 21 Then take the young bull for the sin offering and burn
it at the appointed place outside the Temple area.

22 "On the second day, sacrifice as a sin offering a young male goat that has
no physical defects. Then cleanse and make atonement for the altar again,

Prayer **43:5**

You are the living God, and I cannot stand before your glory. Thank you for wanting me to be in your presence. Amen.

43:7 Or *kings on their high places.* **43:11** As in Greek version; Hebrew reads *if they are ashamed.* **43:13a** Hebrew *measurements of the altar in long cubits, each being a cubit* [18 inches or 45 centimeters] *and a handbreadth* [3 inches or 8 centimeters] *in length.* **43:13b** Hebrew *a cubit* [53 centimeters] *deep and a cubit wide.* **43:13c** Hebrew *1 span* [23 centimeters]. **43:13d** As in Greek version; Hebrew reads *base.* **43:14a** Hebrew *2 cubits* [1.1 meters]. **43:14b** Hebrew *1 cubit* [53 centimeters]; also in 43:14d. **43:14c** Hebrew *4 cubits* [2.1 meters]; also in 43:15. **43:16** Hebrew *12 [cubits]* [6.4 meters] *long and 12 [cubits] wide.* **43:17a** Hebrew *14 [cubits]* [7.4 meters] *long and 14 [cubits] wide.* **43:17b** Hebrew *a gutter of 1 cubit* [53 centimeters] *and a curb of ½ a cubit* [27 centimeters].

just as you did with the young bull. 23 When you have finished the cleansing ceremony, offer another young bull that has no defects and a perfect ram from the flock. 24 You are to present them to the LORD, and the priests are to sprinkle salt on them and offer them as a burnt offering to the LORD.

25 "Every day for seven days a male goat, a young bull, and a ram from the flock will be sacrificed as a sin offering. None of these animals may have physical defects of any kind. 26 Do this each day for seven days to cleanse and make atonement for the altar, thus setting it apart for holy use. 27 On the eighth day, and on each day afterward, the priests will sacrifice on the altar the burnt offerings and peace offerings of the people. Then I will accept you. I, the Sovereign LORD, have spoken!"

The Prince, Levites, and Priests

44 Then the man brought me back to the east gateway in the outer wall of the Temple area, but it was closed. 2 And the LORD said to me, "This gate must remain closed; it will never again be opened. No one will ever open it and pass through, for the LORD, the God of Israel, has entered here. Therefore, it must always remain shut. 3 Only the prince himself may sit inside this gateway to feast in the LORD's presence. But he may come and go only through the entry room of the gateway."

4 Then the man brought me through the north gateway to the front of the Temple. I looked and saw that the glory of the LORD filled the Temple of the LORD, and I fell face down on the ground.

5 And the LORD said to me, "Son of man, take careful notice. Use your eyes and ears, and listen to everything I tell you about the regulations concerning the LORD's Temple. Take careful note of the procedures for using the Temple's entrances and exits. 6 And give these rebels, the people of Israel, this message from the Sovereign LORD: O people of Israel, enough of your detestable sins! 7 You have brought uncircumcised foreigners into my sanctuary—people who have no heart for God. In this way, you defiled my Temple even as you offered me my food, the fat and blood of sacrifices. In addition to all your other detestable sins, you have broken my covenant. 8 Instead of safeguarding my sacred rituals, you have hired foreigners to take charge of my sanctuary.

9 "So this is what the Sovereign LORD says: No foreigners, including those who live among the people of Israel, will enter my sanctuary if they have not been circumcised and have not surrendered themselves to the LORD. 10 And the men of the tribe of Levi who abandoned me when Israel strayed away from me to worship idols* must bear the consequences of their unfaithfulness. 11 They may still be Temple guards and gatekeepers, and they may slaughter the animals brought for burnt offerings and be present to help the people. 12 But they encouraged my people to worship idols, causing Israel to fall into deep sin. So I have taken a solemn oath that they must bear the consequences for their sins, says the Sovereign LORD. 13 They may not approach me to minister as priests. They may not touch any of my holy things or the holy offerings, for they must bear the shame of all the detestable sins they have committed. 14 They are to serve as the Temple caretakers, taking charge of the maintenance work and performing general duties.

15 "However, the Levitical priests of the family of Zadok continued to

44:10 The Hebrew term (literally *round things*) probably alludes to dung; also in 44:12.

minister faithfully in the Temple when Israel abandoned me for idols. These men will serve as my ministers. They will stand in my presence and offer the fat and blood of the sacrifices, says the Sovereign LORD. 16 They alone will enter my sanctuary and approach my table to serve me. They will fulfill all my requirements.

17 "When they enter the gateway to the inner courtyard, they must wear only linen clothing. They must wear no wool while on duty in the inner courtyard or in the Temple itself. 18 They must wear linen turbans and linen undergarments. They must not wear anything that would cause them to perspire. 19 When they return to the outer courtyard where the people are, they must take off the clothes they wear while ministering to me. They must leave them in the sacred rooms and put on other clothes so they do not endanger anyone by transmitting holiness to them through this clothing.

20 "They must neither shave their heads nor let their hair grow too long. Instead, they must trim it regularly. 21 The priests must not drink wine before entering the inner courtyard. 22 They may choose their wives only from among the virgins of Israel or the widows of the priests. They may not marry other widows or divorced women. 23 They will teach my people the difference between what is holy and what is common, what is ceremonially clean and unclean.

24 "They will serve as judges to resolve any disagreements among my people. Their decisions must be based on my regulations. And the priests themselves must obey my instructions and decrees at all the sacred festivals, and see to it that the Sabbaths are set apart as holy days.

25 "A priest must not defile himself by being in the presence of a dead person unless it is his father, mother, child, brother, or unmarried sister. In such cases it is permitted. 26 Even then, he can return to his Temple duties only after being ceremonially cleansed and then waiting for seven days. 27 The first day he returns to work and enters the inner courtyard and the sanctuary, he must offer a sin offering for himself, says the Sovereign LORD.

28 "The priests will not have any property or possession of land, for I alone am their special possession. 29 Their food will come from the gifts and sacrifices brought to the Temple by the people—the grain offerings, the sin offerings, and the guilt offerings. Whatever anyone sets apart* for the LORD will belong to the priests. 30 The first of the ripe fruits and all the gifts brought to the LORD will go to the priests. The first batch of dough must also be given to the priests so the LORD will bless your homes. 31 The priests may not eat meat from any bird or animal that dies a natural death or that dies after being attacked by another animal.

Division of the Land

45 "When you divide the land among the tribes of Israel, you must set aside a section for the LORD as his holy portion. This piece of land will be 8⅓ miles long and 6⅔ miles wide.* The entire area will be holy. 2 A section of this land, measuring 875 feet by 875 feet,* will be set aside for the Temple. An additional strip of land 87½ feet* wide is to be left empty all

44:29 The Hebrew term used here refers to the complete consecration of things or people to the LORD, either by destroying them or by giving them as an offering. **45:1** As in Greek version, which reads *25,000 [cubits]* [13.3 kilometers] *long and 20,000 [cubits]* [10.6 kilometers] *wide;* Hebrew reads *25,000 [cubits] long and 10,000 [cubits]* [3⅓ miles or 5.3 kilometers] *wide.* Compare 45:3, 5; 48:9. **45:2a** Hebrew *500 [cubits]* [265 meters] *by 500 [cubits], a square.* **45:2b** Hebrew *50 cubits* [26.5 meters].

What I will do next

Make a Difference 45:9

Notice the Need for Justice

We've all seen them—the homeless—huddled up on benches with a piece of cardboard or some newspaper. Still, there is a lot we haven't been willing to see. We haven't seen their hurt and struggles. We haven't seen the families sleeping in cars. We haven't seen the malnourished boy skip gym class because he can't afford running shoes. We haven't seen the runaway daughter trapped in an industry that wants to sell her. We haven't seen the despair and death of an unwanted old woman lost in the alley. Oh, we've seen some problems. We know they're there. Even so, we haven't seen the *people*.

James 2:15-16 poses the question of what good it does if we see people in need and wish them well but don't help them. May the Lord quicken the link between our eyes and our souls so that we will care for our neighbors in need.

Difference Maker

Contact a homeless shelter or food pantry. Ask them when they could use some help and how many people they could use. Then organize a team of people to go and serve.

around it. 3 Within the larger sacred area, measure out a portion of land 8⅓ miles long and 3⅓ miles wide.* Within it the sanctuary of the Most Holy Place will be located. 4 This area will be holy, set aside for the priests who minister to the LORD in the sanctuary. They will use it for their homes, and my Temple will be located within it. 5 The strip of sacred land next to it, also 8⅓ miles long and 3⅓ miles wide, will be a living area for the Levites who work at the Temple. It will be their possession and a place for their towns.*

6 "Adjacent to the larger sacred area will be a section of land 8⅓ miles long and 1⅔ miles wide.* This will be set aside for a city where anyone in Israel can live.

7 "Two special sections of land will be set apart for the prince. One section will share a border with the east side of the sacred lands and city, and the second section will share a border on the west side. Then the far eastern and western borders of the prince's lands will line up with the eastern and western boundaries of the tribal areas. 8 These sections of land will be the prince's allotment. Then my princes will no longer oppress and rob my people; they will assign the rest of the land to the people, giving an allotment to each tribe.

Rules for the Princes

9 "For this is what the Sovereign LORD says: Enough, you princes of Israel! Stop your violence and oppression and do what is just and right. Quit robbing and cheating my people out of their land. Stop expelling them from their homes, says the Sovereign LORD. 10 Use only honest weights and scales and honest measures, both dry and liquid.* 11 The homer* will be your standard unit for measuring volume. The ephah and the bath* will each measure one-tenth of a homer. 12 The standard unit for weight will be the silver shekel.* One shekel will consist of twenty gerahs, and sixty shekels will be equal to one mina.*

Special Offerings and Celebrations

13 "You must give this tax to the prince: one bushel of wheat or barley for every 60* you harvest, 14 one percent of your olive oil,* 15 and one sheep or goat for every 200 in your flocks in Israel. These will be the grain offerings, burnt offerings, and peace offerings that will make atonement for the people who bring them, says the Sovereign LORD. 16 All the people of Israel must join in bringing these offerings to the prince. 17 The prince will be required to provide offerings that are given at the religious festivals, the new moon celebrations, the Sabbath days, and all other similar occasions. He will provide the sin offerings, burnt offerings, grain offerings, liquid offerings, and peace offerings to purify the people of Israel, making them right with the LORD.*

18 "This is what the Sovereign LORD says: In early spring, on the first day of each new year,* sacrifice a young bull with no defects to purify the Temple.

45:3 Hebrew *25,000 [cubits]* [13.3 kilometers] *long and 10,000 [cubits]* [5.3 kilometers] *wide;* also in 45:5. **45:5** As in Greek version; Hebrew reads *They will have as their possession 20 rooms.* **45:6** Hebrew *25,000 [cubits]* [13.3 kilometers] *long and 5,000 [cubits]* [2.65 kilometers] *wide.* **45:10** Hebrew *Use honest scales, an honest ephah, and an honest bath.* **45:11a** The *homer* measures about 50 gallons or 220 liters. **45:11b** The *ephah* is a dry measure; the *bath* is a liquid measure. **45:12a** The *shekel* weighs about 0.4 ounces or 11 grams. **45:12b** Elsewhere the *mina* is equated to 50 shekels. **45:13** Hebrew *⅙ of an ephah from each homer of wheat and ⅙ of an ephah from each homer of barley.* **45:14** Hebrew *the portion of oil, measured by the bath, is ⅒ of a bath from each cor, which consists of 10 baths or 1 homer, for 10 baths are equivalent to a homer.* **45:17** Or *to make atonement for the people of Israel.* **45:18** Hebrew *On the first day of the first month,* of the Hebrew calendar. This day in the ancient Hebrew lunar calendar occurred in March or April.

19 The priest will take blood from this sin offering and put it on the doorposts
of the Temple, the four corners of the upper ledge of the altar, and the gate-
posts at the entrance to the inner courtyard. 20 Do this also on the seventh
day of the new year for anyone who has sinned through error or ignorance.
In this way, you will purify* the Temple.

21 "On the fourteenth day of the first month,* you must celebrate the Pass-
over. This festival will last for seven days. The bread you eat during that
time must be made without yeast. 22 On the day of Passover the prince will
provide a young bull as a sin offering for himself and the people of Israel.
23 On each of the seven days of the feast he will prepare a burnt offering to
the LORD, consisting of seven young bulls and seven rams without defects.
A male goat will also be given each day for a sin offering. 24 The prince will
provide a basket of flour as a grain offering and a gallon of olive oil* with
each young bull and ram.

25 "During the seven days of the Festival of Shelters, which occurs every
year in early autumn,* the prince will provide these same sacrifices for the
sin offering, the burnt offering, and the grain offering, along with the re-
quired olive oil.

46 "This is what the Sovereign LORD says: The east gateway of the inner
courtyard will be closed during the six workdays each week, but it
will be open on Sabbath days and the days of new moon celebrations. 2 The
prince will enter the entry room of the gateway from the outside. Then he
will stand by the gatepost while the priest offers his burnt offering and peace
offering. He will bow down in worship inside the gateway passage and then
go back out the way he came. The gateway will not be closed until evening.
3 The common people will bow down and worship the LORD in front of this
gateway on Sabbath days and the days of new moon celebrations.

4 "Each Sabbath day the prince will present to the LORD a burnt offering of
six lambs and one ram, all with no defects. 5 He will present a grain offering
of a basket of choice flour to go with the ram and whatever amount of flour
he chooses to go with each lamb, and he is to offer one gallon of olive oil* for
each basket of flour. 6 At the new moon celebrations, he will bring one young
bull, six lambs, and one ram, all with no defects. 7 With the young bull he
must bring a basket of choice flour for a grain offering. With the ram he must
bring another basket of flour. And with each lamb he is to bring whatever
amount of flour he chooses to give. With each basket of flour he must offer
one gallon of olive oil.

8 "The prince must enter the gateway through the entry room, and he
must leave the same way. 9 But when the people come in through the north
gateway to worship the LORD during the religious festivals, they must leave
by the south gateway. And those who entered through the south gateway
must leave by the north gateway. They must never leave by the same gateway
they came in, but must always use the opposite gateway. 10 The prince will
enter and leave with the people on these occasions.

11 "So at the special feasts and sacred festivals, the grain offering will be a

45:20 Or *will make atonement for.* **45:21** This day in the ancient Hebrew lunar calendar occurred in late March, April, or early May. **45:24** Hebrew *an ephah* [20 quarts or 22 liters] *of flour . . . and a hin* [3.8 liters] *of olive oil.* **45:25** Hebrew *the festival which begins on the fifteenth day of the seventh month* (see Lev 23:34). This day in the ancient Hebrew lunar calendar occurred in late September, October, or early November. **46:5** Hebrew *an ephah* [20 quarts or 22 liters] *of choice flour . . . a hin* [3.8 liters] *of olive oil;* similarly in 46:7, 11.

basket of choice flour with each young bull, another basket of flour with each
ram, and as much flour as the worshiper chooses to give with each lamb. Give
one gallon of olive oil with each basket of flour. [12]When the prince offers a
voluntary burnt offering or peace offering to the LORD, the east gateway to
the inner courtyard will be opened for him, and he will offer his sacrifices
as he does on Sabbath days. Then he will leave, and the gateway will be shut
behind him.

[13]"Each morning you must sacrifice a one-year-old lamb with no defects
as a burnt offering to the LORD. [14]With the lamb, a grain offering must also
be given to the LORD—about three quarts of flour with a third of a gallon
of olive oil* to moisten the choice flour. This will be a permanent law for
you. [15]The lamb, the grain offering, and the olive oil must be given as a daily
sacrifice every morning without fail.

[16]"This is what the Sovereign LORD says: If the prince gives a gift of land to
one of his sons as his inheritance, it will belong to him and his descendants
forever. [17]But if the prince gives a gift of land from his inheritance to one
of his servants, the servant may keep it only until the Year of Jubilee, which
comes every fiftieth year.* At that time the land will return to the prince. But
when the prince gives gifts to his sons, those gifts will be permanent. [18]And
the prince may never take anyone's property by force. If he gives property
to his sons, it must be from his own land, for I do not want any of my people
unjustly evicted from their property."

The Temple Kitchens

[19]In my vision, the man brought me through the entrance beside the gate-
way and led me to the sacred rooms assigned to the priests, which faced
toward the north. He showed me a place at the extreme west end of these
rooms. [20]He explained, "This is where the priests will cook the meat from
the guilt offerings and sin offerings and bake the flour from the grain offer-
ings into bread. They will do it here to avoid carrying the sacrifices through
the outer courtyard and endangering the people by transmitting holiness
to them."

[21]Then he brought me back to the outer courtyard and led me to each of
its four corners. In each corner I saw an enclosure. [22]Each of these enclosures
was 70 feet long and 52½ feet wide,* surrounded by walls. [23]Along the inside
of these walls was a ledge of stone with fireplaces under the ledge all the
way around. [24]The man said to me, "These are the kitchens to be used by the
Temple assistants to boil the sacrifices offered by the people."

The River of Healing

47 In my vision, the man brought me back to the entrance of the
Temple. There I saw a stream flowing east from beneath the door
of the Temple and passing to the right of the altar on its south side. [2]The man
brought me outside the wall through the north gateway and led me around
to the eastern entrance. There I could see the water flowing out through the
south side of the east gateway.

[3]Measuring as he went, he took me along the stream for 1,750 feet* and
then led me across. The water was up to my ankles. [4]He measured off another

46:14 Hebrew *⅙ of an ephah* [3.7 liters] *of flour with ⅓ of a hin* [1.3 liters] *of olive oil.* **46:17** Hebrew *until the Year of Release;* see Lev 25:8-17. **46:22** Hebrew 40 *[cubits]* [21.2 meters] *long and 30 [cubits]* [15.9 meters] *wide.* **47:3** Hebrew *1,000 cubits* [530 meters]; also in 47:4, 5.

1,750 feet and led me across again. This time the water was up to my knees.
After another 1,750 feet, it was up to my waist. 5Then he measured another
1,750 feet, and the river was too deep to walk across. It was deep enough to
swim in, but too deep to walk through.
6He asked me, "Have you been watching, son of man?" Then he led me
back along the riverbank. 7When I returned, I was surprised by the sight of
many trees growing on both sides of the river. 8Then he said to me, "This
river flows east through the desert into the valley of the Dead Sea.* The waters of this stream will make the salty waters of the Dead Sea fresh and pure.
9There will be swarms of living things wherever the water of this river flows.*
Fish will abound in the Dead Sea, for its waters will become fresh. Life will
flourish wherever this water flows. 10Fishermen will stand along the shores
of the Dead Sea. All the way from En-gedi to En-eglaim, the shores will be
covered with nets drying in the sun. Fish of every kind will fill the Dead Sea,
just as they fill the Mediterranean.* 11But the marshes and swamps will not
be purified; they will still be salty. 12Fruit trees of all kinds will grow along
both sides of the river. The leaves of these trees will never turn brown and fall, and there will always be fruit on their branches. There will be a new crop every month, for they are watered by the river flowing from the Temple. The fruit will be for food and the leaves for healing."

Question 47:6

"Have you been watching?" At the end of this long, detailed vision, God asked Ezekiel if he had noticed what God had shown him. The same question could be posed to you: Have you been watching what the Lord has done? Have you been watching for what the Lord will do? Would you say you have an attitude of expectancy when it comes to what God is doing around you?

Boundaries for the Land

13This is what the Sovereign LORD says: "Divide the land in this way for the
twelve tribes of Israel: The descendants of Joseph will be given two shares
of land.* 14Otherwise each tribe will receive an equal share. I took a solemn
oath and swore that I would give this land to your ancestors, and it will now come to you as your possession.

15"These are the boundaries of the land: The northern border will
run from the Mediterranean toward Hethlon, then on through
Lebo-hamath to Zedad; 16then it will run to Berothah and Sibraim,*
which are on the border between Damascus and Hamath, and finally
to Hazer-hatticon, on the border of Hauran. 17So the northern border
will run from the Mediterranean to Hazar-enan, on the border between Hamath to the north and Damascus to the south.

18"The eastern border starts at a point between Hauran and Damascus and runs south along the Jordan River between Israel and Gilead, past the Dead Sea* and as far south as Tamar.* This will be the eastern border.

19"The southern border will go west from Tamar to the waters of Meribah at Kadesh* and then follow the course of the Brook of Egypt to the Mediterranean. This will be the southern border.

20"On the west side, the Mediterranean itself will be your border from the southern border to the point where the northern border begins, opposite Lebo-hamath.

47:8 Hebrew *the sea.* **47:9** As in Greek and Syriac versions; Hebrew reads *of these two rivers flow.* **47:10** Hebrew *the Great Sea;* also in 47:15, 17, 19, 20. **47:13** It was important to retain twelve portions of land. Since Levi had no portion, the descendants of Joseph's sons, Ephraim and Manasseh, received land as two tribes. **47:15-16** As in Greek version; Masoretic Text reads *then on through Lebo to Zedad;* [16] *then it will run to Hamath, Berothah, and Sibraim.* **47:18a** Hebrew *the eastern sea.* **47:18b** As in Greek version; Hebrew reads *you will measure.* **47:19** Hebrew *waters of Meribath-kadesh.*

21 “Divide the land within these boundaries among the tribes of Israel. 22 Dis-
tribute the land as an allotment for yourselves and for the foreigners who
have joined you and are raising their families among you. They will be like
native-born Israelites to you and will receive an allotment among the tribes.
23 These foreigners are to be given land within the territory of the tribe with
whom they now live. I, the Sovereign LORD, have spoken!

Division of the Land

48 “Here is the list of the tribes of Israel and the territory each is to
receive. The territory of Dan is in the extreme north. Its boundary
line follows the Hethlon road to Lebo-hamath and then runs on to Hazar-
enan on the border of Damascus, with Hamath to the north. Dan’s territory
extends all the way across the land of Israel from east to west.

2 “Asher’s territory lies south of Dan’s and also extends from east to west.
3 Naphtali’s land lies south of Asher’s, also extending from east to west. 4 Then
comes Manasseh south of Naphtali, and its territory also extends from east
to west. 5 South of Manasseh is Ephraim, 6 and then Reuben, 7 and then Judah,
all of whose boundaries extend from east to west.

8 “South of Judah is the land set aside for a special purpose. It will be 8⅓
miles* wide and will extend as far east and west as the tribal territories, with
the Temple at the center.

9 “The area set aside for the LORD’s Temple will be 8⅓ miles long and 6⅔
miles wide.* 10 For the priests there will be a strip of land measuring 8⅓ miles
long by 3⅓ miles wide,* with the LORD’s Temple at the center. 11 This area is
set aside for the ordained priests, the descendants of Zadok who served me
faithfully and did not go astray with the people of Israel and the rest of the
Levites. 12 It will be their special portion when the land is distributed, the
most sacred land of all. Next to the priests’ territory will lie the land where
the other Levites will live.

13 “The land allotted to the Levites will be the same size and shape as that
belonging to the priests—8⅓ miles long and 3⅓ miles wide. Together these
portions of land will measure 8⅓ miles long by 6⅔ miles wide.* 14 None of
this special land may ever be sold or traded or used by others, for it belongs
to the LORD; it is set apart as holy.

15 “An additional strip of land 8⅓ miles long by 1⅔ miles wide,* south
of the sacred Temple area, will be allotted for public use—homes, pasture-
lands, and common lands, with a city at the center. 16 The city will measure
1½ miles* on each side—north, south, east, and west. 17 Open lands will sur-
round the city for 150 yards* in every direction. 18 Outside the city there will
be a farming area that stretches 3⅓ miles to the east and 3⅓ miles to the
west* along the border of the sacred area. This farmland will produce food
for the people working in the city. 19 Those who come from the various tribes
to work in the city may farm it. 20 This entire area—including the sacred
lands and the city—is a square that measures 8⅓ miles* on each side.

48:8 Hebrew *25,000 [cubits]* [13.3 kilometers]. **48:9** As in one Greek manuscript and the Greek reading in 45:1: *25,000 [cubits]* [13.3 kilometers] *long and 20,000 [cubits]* [10.6 kilometers] *wide;* Hebrew reads *25,000 [cubits] long and 10,000 [cubits]* [3⅓ miles or 5.3 kilometers] *wide.* Similarly in 48:13b. Compare 45:1-5; 48:10-13. **48:10** Hebrew *25,000 [cubits]* [13.3 kilometers] *long by 10,000 [cubits]* [5.3 kilometers] *wide;* also in 48:13a. **48:13** See note on 48:9. **48:15** Hebrew *25,000 [cubits]* [13.3 kilometers] *long by 5,000 [cubits]* [2.65 kilometers] *wide.* **48:16** Hebrew *4,500 [cubits]* [2.4 kilometers]; also in 48:30, 32, 33, 34. **48:17** Hebrew *250 [cubits]* [133 meters]. **48:18** Hebrew *10,000 [cubits]* [5.3 kilometers] *to the east and 10,000 [cubits] to the west.* **48:20** Hebrew *25,000 [cubits]* [13.3 kilometers]; also in 48:21.

21 "The areas that remain, to the east and to the west of the sacred lands
and the city, will belong to the prince. Each of these areas will be 8⅓ miles
wide, extending in opposite directions to the eastern and western borders
of Israel, with the sacred lands and the sanctuary of the Temple in the cen-
ter. 22 So the prince's land will include everything between the territories
allotted to Judah and Benjamin, except for the areas set aside for the sacred
lands and the city.

23 "These are the territories allotted to the rest of the tribes. Benjamin's
territory lies just south of the prince's lands, and it extends across the entire
land of Israel from east to west. 24 South of Benjamin's territory lies that of
Simeon, also extending across the land from east to west. 25 Next is the ter-
ritory of Issachar with the same eastern and western boundaries.

26 "Then comes the territory of Zebulun, which also extends across the
land from east to west. 27 The territory of Gad is just south of Zebulun with
the same borders to the east and west. 28 The southern border of Gad runs
from Tamar to the waters of Meribah at Kadesh* and then follows the Brook
of Egypt to the Mediterranean.*

29 "These are the allotments that will be set aside for each tribe's exclusive
possession. I, the Sovereign LORD, have spoken!

The Gates of the City

30 "These will be the exits to the city: On the north wall, which is 1½ miles
long, 31 there will be three gates, each one named after a tribe of Israel. The
first will be named for Reuben, the second for Judah, and the third for Levi.
32 On the east wall, also 1½ miles long, the gates will be named for Joseph,
Benjamin, and Dan. 33 The south wall, also 1½ miles long, will have gates
named for Simeon, Issachar, and Zebulun. 34 And on the west wall, also 1½
miles long, the gates will be named for Gad, Asher, and Naphtali.

35 "The distance around the entire city will be 6 miles.* And from that day
the name of the city will be 'The LORD Is There.'*"

48:28a Hebrew *waters of Meribath-kadesh.* **48:28b** Hebrew *the Great Sea.* **48:35a** Hebrew *18,000 [cubits]* [9.6 kilometers]. **48:35b** Hebrew *Yahweh Shammah.*

Question **48:35**

This book has been about people knowing that the Lord alone is God. To make himself known, the Lord promised through Ezekiel's messages to put new hearts in people, pour out his Spirit on them, breathe on them, and give them life. Now, in this last verse of this long book, the Lord indicated that he would give his people a future city where he himself would reside. The city will be named: "The LORD Is There." If he could, Ezekiel would probably ask you a follow-up question: Is this also a name that your heart could have?

Daniel Introduction

There may not be a more exciting book in all the Bible than Daniel. This book contains stories of some of the most powerful rulers ever to have lived, of heroes getting tossed into fiery furnaces and the lions' den, of a floating human hand scribbling words on a wall, and of intense visions of the past and future, as well as multiple references that look ahead to Jesus.

The book was written by Daniel, who was exiled from Jerusalem to Babylon when King Nebuchadnezzar of Babylon conquered the city and took some of its people hostage. Very quickly, Daniel and three of his friends (whom we know as Shadrach, Meshach, and Abednego) were set apart for special roles, serving the king and bringing glory to God in the process.

Daniel was written at a low time in Israel's history. They were defeated, the enemy had conquered their homeland, many were forced to live as refugees in foreign lands, and the temple in Jerusalem was shut down and gutted. Despite this, through a series of true stories of God's faithfulness (Daniel 1–6) and future stories of God's ultimate victory (Daniel 7–12), the Israelites of that time, and people of all times, have been able to draw hope in difficult moments.

Daniel 12:10 is an excellent summary of the book: "Many will be purified, cleansed, and refined by these trials. But the wicked will continue in their wickedness, and none of them will understand. Only those who are wise will know what it means." In other words, life always has the potential to be difficult, and wicked people and wickedness will be a part of this world. However, even if we are in the minority as followers of God, we can pursue the Lord and trust in his ultimate plan and victory in this world and for all eternity.

Story Arcs

- **Daniel**
- **Shadrach, Meshach, and Abednego**

Daniel

Daniel in Nebuchadnezzar's Court

1 During the third year of King Jehoiakim's reign in Judah,* King Neb-
uchadnezzar of Babylon came to Jerusalem and besieged it. 2The Lord
gave him victory over King Jehoiakim of Judah and permitted him to take
some of the sacred objects from the Temple of God. So Nebuchadnezzar
took them back to the land of Babylonia* and placed them in the treasure-
house of his god.

3Then the king ordered Ashpenaz, his chief of staff, to bring to the palace
some of the young men of Judah's royal family and other noble families, who
had been brought to Babylon as captives. 4"Select only strong, healthy, and
good-looking young men," he said. "Make sure they are well versed in every
branch of learning, are gifted with knowledge and good judgment, and are
suited to serve in the royal palace. Train these young men in the language
and literature of Babylon.*" 5The king assigned them a daily ration of food
and wine from his own kitchens. They were to be trained for three years, and
then they would enter the royal service.

6Daniel, Hananiah, Mishael, and Azariah were four of the young men
chosen, all from the tribe of Judah. 7The chief of staff renamed them with
these Babylonian names:

Daniel was called Belteshazzar.
Hananiah was called Shadrach.
Mishael was called Meshach.
Azariah was called Abednego.

8But Daniel was determined not to defile himself by eating the food and
wine given to them by the king. He asked the chief of staff for permission
not to eat these unacceptable foods. 9Now God had given the chief of staff
both respect and affection for Daniel. 10But he responded, "I am afraid of
my lord the king, who has ordered that you eat this food and wine. If you
become pale and thin compared to the other youths your age, I am afraid the
king will have me beheaded."

11Daniel spoke with the attendant who had been appointed by the chief
of staff to look after Daniel, Hananiah, Mishael, and Azariah. 12"Please test
us for ten days on a diet of vegetables and water," Daniel said. 13"At the end
of the ten days, see how we look compared to the other young men who are
eating the king's food. Then make your decision in light of what you see."
14The attendant agreed to Daniel's suggestion and tested them for ten days.

15At the end of the ten days, Daniel and his three friends looked healthier
and better nourished than the young men who had been eating the food

1:1 This event occurred in 605 B.C., during the third year of Jehoiakim's reign (according to the calendar system in which the new year begins in the spring). 1:2 Hebrew *the land of Shinar.* 1:4 Or *of the Chaldeans.*

Story Arc **1:8**

● Daniel

Daniel was determined that he was going to be faithful to God's law, so he was very careful about what he was supposed to eat and drink, even in a foreign land. By asking for permission not to eat the royal food and wine, Daniel was taking a risk. To stand up for what he believed in, he was boldly going against what almost everyone else was doing.

Like Daniel, Jesus often went against the grain to boldly do what was right. Luke 9:51 tells us that Jesus "resolutely set out for Jerusalem," knowing that his obedience to his Father would lead to his death. Take a moment to celebrate some recent moments of faithfulness to God in your life.

Dan 3:1-30 ►

Make a Difference

1:8–20

Never Waver

Four young men had been displaced by war, removed from their homes, and relocated to the enemy's capital. They were forced to give up their families, change their diets, change their names, and lose much of their heritage. Still, they never wavered in what mattered most: their faithful commitment to the Lord.

These four men had every reason (by the world's standards) to let down their guard and let go of their pursuit of God. Instead, they dedicated themselves to a life of integrity and character and excellence in the ways that God called them to live. When the moment came to use their gifts to influence the world around them, they were ready. The enemy king took notice of the outstanding character and skills of these young men. Before long, God used them to change an empire.

Difference Maker

Think of the limits you would be willing to go to for the Lord to use you. What can you learn from how these four young men were able to hold on to faith in such difficult circumstances?

Question **2:1–28**

Daniel handled this situation with wisdom and discretion. He was cool under pressure! His coolness came from who God is. How can you grow in your knowledge and experience of knowing who God is so that you can trust him even in the crazy moments of life?

assigned by the king. 16 So after that, the attendant fed them only vegetables
instead of the food and wine provided for the others.
17 God gave these four young men an unusual aptitude for understanding
every aspect of literature and wisdom. And God gave Daniel the special ability to interpret the meanings of visions and dreams.
18 When the training period ordered by the king was completed, the chief
of staff brought all the young men to King Nebuchadnezzar. 19 The king
talked with them, and no one impressed him as much as Daniel, Hananiah,
Mishael, and Azariah. So they entered the royal service. 20 Whenever the king
consulted them in any matter requiring wisdom and balanced judgment, he
found them ten times more capable than any of the magicians and enchanters in his entire kingdom.
21 Daniel remained in the royal service until the first year of the reign of
King Cyrus.*

Nebuchadnezzar's Dream

2 One night during the second year of his reign,* Nebuchadnezzar had
such disturbing dreams that he couldn't sleep. 2 He called in his magicians, enchanters, sorcerers, and astrologers,* and he demanded that they
tell him what he had dreamed. As they stood before the king, 3 he said, "I
have had a dream that deeply troubles me, and I must know what it means."
4 Then the astrologers answered the king in Aramaic,* "Long live the king!
Tell us the dream, and we will tell you what it means."
5 But the king said to the astrologers, "I am serious about this. If you don't
tell me what my dream was and what it means, you will be torn limb from
limb, and your houses will be turned into heaps of rubble! 6 But if you tell me
what I dreamed and what the dream means, I will give you many wonderful
gifts and honors. Just tell me the dream and what it means!"
7 They said again, "Please, Your Majesty. Tell us the dream, and we will
tell you what it means."
8 The king replied, "I know what you are doing! You're stalling for time
because you know I am serious when I say, 9 'If you don't tell me the dream,
you are doomed.' So you have conspired to tell me lies, hoping I will change
my mind. But tell me the dream, and then I'll know that you can tell me
what it means."
10 The astrologers replied to the king, "No one on earth can tell the king
his dream! And no king, however great and powerful, has ever asked such
a thing of any magician, enchanter, or astrologer! 11 The king's demand is
impossible. No one except the gods can tell you your dream, and they do
not live here among people."
12 The king was furious when he heard this, and he ordered that all the
wise men of Babylon be executed. 13 And because of the king's decree, men
were sent to find and kill Daniel and his friends.
14 When Arioch, the commander of the king's guard, came to kill them,
Daniel handled the situation with wisdom and discretion. 15 He asked Arioch, "Why has the king issued such a harsh decree?" So Arioch told him all
that had happened. 16 Daniel went at once to see the king and requested more
time to tell the king what the dream meant.

1:21 Cyrus began his reign (over Babylon) in 539 B.C. 2:1 The second year of Nebuchadnezzar's reign was 603 B.C. 2:2 Or *Chaldeans;* also in 2:4, 5, 10. 2:4 The original text from this point through chapter 7 is in Aramaic.

17 Then Daniel went home and told his friends Hananiah, Mishael, and
Azariah what had happened. 18 He urged them to ask the God of heaven
to show them his mercy by telling them the secret, so they would not be
executed along with the other wise men of Babylon. 19 That night the secret
was revealed to Daniel in a vision. Then Daniel praised the God of heaven.
20 He said,

"Praise the name of God forever and ever,
  for he has all wisdom and power.
21 He controls the course of world events;
  he removes kings and sets up other kings.
He gives wisdom to the wise
  and knowledge to the scholars.
22 He reveals deep and mysterious things
  and knows what lies hidden in darkness,
  though he is surrounded by light.
23 I thank and praise you, God of my ancestors,
  for you have given me wisdom and strength.
You have told me what we asked of you
  and revealed to us what the king demanded."

Daniel Interprets the Dream

24 Then Daniel went in to see Arioch, whom the king had ordered to execute
the wise men of Babylon. Daniel said to him, "Don't kill the wise men. Take
me to the king, and I will tell him the meaning of his dream."

25 Arioch quickly took Daniel to the king and said, "I have found one of
the captives from Judah who will tell the king the meaning of his dream!"

26 The king said to Daniel (also known as Belteshazzar), "Is this true? Can
you tell me what my dream was and what it means?"

27 Daniel replied, "There are no wise men, enchanters, magicians, or
fortune-tellers who can reveal the king's secret. 28 But there is a God in heaven
who reveals secrets, and he has shown King Nebuchadnezzar what will hap-
pen in the future. Now I will tell you your dream and the visions you saw
as you lay on your bed.

29 "While Your Majesty was sleeping, you dreamed about coming events.
He who reveals secrets has shown you what is going to happen. 30 And it is
not because I am wiser than anyone else that I know the secret of your dream,
but because God wants you to understand what was in your heart.

31 "In your vision, Your Majesty, you saw standing before you a huge, shin-
ing statue of a man. It was a frightening sight. 32 The head of the statue was
made of fine gold. Its chest and arms were silver, its belly and thighs were
bronze, 33 its legs were iron, and its feet were a combination of iron and baked
clay. 34 As you watched, a rock was cut from a mountain,* but not by human
hands. It struck the feet of iron and clay, smashing them to bits. 35 The whole
statue was crushed into small pieces of iron, clay, bronze, silver, and gold.
Then the wind blew them away without a trace, like chaff on a threshing
floor. But the rock that knocked the statue down became a great mountain
that covered the whole earth.

36 "That was the dream. Now we will tell the king what it means. 37 Your

2:34 As in Greek version (see also 2:45); Hebrew lacks *from a mountain.*

Majesty, you are the greatest of kings. The God of heaven has given you sov-
ereignty, power, strength, and honor. 38 He has made you the ruler over all
the inhabited world and has put even the wild animals and birds under your
control. You are the head of gold.

39 "But after your kingdom comes to an end, another kingdom, inferior to
yours, will rise to take your place. After that kingdom has fallen, yet a third
kingdom, represented by bronze, will rise to rule the world. 40 Following
that kingdom, there will be a fourth one, as strong as iron. That kingdom
will smash and crush all previous empires, just as iron smashes and crushes
everything it strikes. 41 The feet and toes you saw were a combination of iron
and baked clay, showing that this kingdom will be divided. Like iron mixed
with clay, it will have some of the strength of iron. 42 But while some parts
of it will be as strong as iron, other parts will be as weak as clay. 43 This mix-
ture of iron and clay also shows that these kingdoms will try to strengthen
themselves by forming alliances with each other through intermarriage. But
they will not hold together, just as iron and clay do not mix.

44 "During the reigns of those kings, the God of heaven will set up a king-
dom that will never be destroyed or conquered. It will crush all these king-
doms into nothingness, and it will stand forever. 45 That is the meaning of
the rock cut from the mountain, though not by human hands, that crushed
to pieces the statue of iron, bronze, clay, silver, and gold. The great God was
showing the king what will happen in the future. The dream is true, and its
meaning is certain."

Nebuchadnezzar Rewards Daniel

46 Then King Nebuchadnezzar threw himself down before Daniel and wor-
shiped him, and he commanded his people to offer sacrifices and burn sweet
incense before him. 47 The king said to Daniel, "Truly, your God is the greatest
of gods, the Lord over kings, a revealer of mysteries, for you have been able
to reveal this secret."

48 Then the king appointed Daniel to a high position and gave him many
valuable gifts. He made Daniel ruler over the whole province of Babylon, as
well as chief over all his wise men. 49 At Daniel's request, the king appointed
Shadrach, Meshach, and Abednego to be in charge of all the affairs of the
province of Babylon, while Daniel remained in the king's court.

Nebuchadnezzar's Gold Statue

3 King Nebuchadnezzar made a gold statue ninety feet tall and nine feet
wide* and set it up on the plain of Dura in the province of Babylon.
2 Then he sent messages to the high officers, officials, governors, advisers,
treasurers, judges, magistrates, and all the provincial officials to come to the
dedication of the statue he had set up. 3 So all these officials* came and stood
before the statue King Nebuchadnezzar had set up.

4 Then a herald shouted out, "People of all races and nations and lan-
guages, listen to the king's command! 5 When you hear the sound of the
horn, flute, zither, lyre, harp, pipes, and other musical instruments,* bow to
the ground to worship King Nebuchadnezzar's gold statue. 6 Anyone who
refuses to obey will immediately be thrown into a blazing furnace."

3:1 Aramaic *60 cubits* [27 meters] *tall and 6 cubits* [2.7 meters] *wide.* **3:3** Aramaic *the high officers, officials, governors, advisers, treasurers, judges, magistrates, and all the provincial officials.* **3:5** The identification of some of these musical instruments is uncertain.

7 So at the sound of the musical instruments,* all the people, whatever
their race or nation or language, bowed to the ground and worshiped the
gold statue that King Nebuchadnezzar had set up.
8 But some of the astrologers* went to the king and informed on the Jews.
9 They said to King Nebuchadnezzar, "Long live the king! 10 You issued a
decree requiring all the people to bow down and worship the gold statue
when they hear the sound of the horn, flute, zither, lyre, harp, pipes, and
other musical instruments. 11 That decree also states that those who refuse
to obey must be thrown into a blazing furnace. 12 But there are some Jews—
Shadrach, Meshach, and Abednego—whom you have put in charge of the
province of Babylon. They pay no attention to you, Your Majesty. They refuse
to serve your gods and do not worship the gold statue you have set up."
13 Then Nebuchadnezzar flew into a rage and ordered that Shadrach, Me-
shach, and Abednego be brought before him. When they were brought in,
14 Nebuchadnezzar said to them, "Is it true, Shadrach, Meshach, and Abed-
nego, that you refuse to serve my gods or to worship the gold statue I have set
up? 15 I will give you one more chance to bow down and worship the statue I
have made when you hear the sound of the musical instruments.* But if you
refuse, you will be thrown immediately into the blazing furnace. And then
what god will be able to rescue you from my power?"
16 Shadrach, Meshach, and Abednego replied, "O Nebuchadnezzar, we do
not need to defend ourselves before you. 17 If we are thrown into the blazing
furnace, the God whom we serve is able to save us. He will rescue us from
your power, Your Majesty. 18 But even if he doesn't, we want to make it clear
to you, Your Majesty, that we will never serve your gods or worship the gold
statue you have set up."

The Blazing Furnace

19 Nebuchadnezzar was so furious with Shadrach, Meshach, and Abednego
that his face became distorted with rage. He commanded that the furnace be
heated seven times hotter than usual. 20 Then he ordered some of the stron-
gest men of his army to bind Shadrach, Meshach, and Abednego and throw
them into the blazing furnace. 21 So they tied them up and threw them into
the furnace, fully dressed in their pants, turbans, robes, and other garments.
22 And because the king, in his anger, had demanded such a hot fire in the
furnace, the flames killed the soldiers as they threw the three men in. 23 So
Shadrach, Meshach, and Abednego, securely tied, fell into the roaring flames.
24 But suddenly, Nebuchadnezzar jumped up in amazement and ex-
claimed to his advisers, "Didn't we tie up three men and throw them into
the furnace?"
"Yes, Your Majesty, we certainly did," they replied.
25 "Look!" Nebuchadnezzar shouted. "I see four men, unbound, walking
around in the fire unharmed! And the fourth looks like a god*!"
26 Then Nebuchadnezzar came as close as he could to the door of the flam-
ing furnace and shouted: "Shadrach, Meshach, and Abednego, servants of
the Most High God, come out! Come here!"
So Shadrach, Meshach, and Abednego stepped out of the fire. 27 Then the
high officers, officials, governors, and advisers crowded around them and

3:7 Aramaic *the horn, flute, zither, lyre, harp, and other musical instruments.* 3:8 Aramaic *Chaldeans.* 3:15 Aramaic *the horn, flute, zither, lyre, harp, pipes, and other musical instruments.* 3:25 Aramaic *like a son of the gods.*

Story Arc **3:1–30**

Shadrach, Meshach, and Abednego

Even with certain death staring Shadrach, Meshach, and Abednego in the face, they still didn't feel the need to defend themselves before the powerful King Nebuchadnezzar. They believed that their integrity stood for itself. They also believed that God was able to save them even if the king threw them into the fiery furnace.

Hundreds of years later and facing certain death, Jesus let his integrity speak for itself, and he trusted God as his defender as he remained silent before his accusers and Pilate (Mark 15:3-5). Do you live with such integrity and trust in God that it's not really necessary for you to defend yourself?

Hos 1:1 ►

saw that the fire had not touched them. Not a hair on their heads was singed,
and their clothing was not scorched. They didn't even smell of smoke!
28 Then Nebuchadnezzar said, "Praise to the God of Shadrach, Meshach,
and Abednego! He sent his angel to rescue his servants who trusted in him.
They defied the king's command and were willing to die rather than serve
or worship any god except their own God. 29 Therefore, I make this decree: If
any people, whatever their race or nation or language, speak a word against
the God of Shadrach, Meshach, and Abednego, they will be torn limb from
limb, and their houses will be turned into heaps of rubble. There is no other
god who can rescue like this!"
30 Then the king promoted Shadrach, Meshach, and Abednego to even
higher positions in the province of Babylon.

Nebuchadnezzar's Dream about a Tree

4 1*King Nebuchadnezzar sent this message to the people of every race
and nation and language throughout the world:

"Peace and prosperity to you!
2 "I want you all to know about the miraculous signs and wonders the
Most High God has performed for me.

3 How great are his signs,
how powerful his wonders!
His kingdom will last forever,
his rule through all generations.

4*"I, Nebuchadnezzar, was living in my palace in comfort and
prosperity. 5 But one night I had a dream that frightened me; I saw
visions that terrified me as I lay in my bed. 6 So I issued an order calling
in all the wise men of Babylon, so they could tell me what my dream
meant. 7 When all the magicians, enchanters, astrologers,* and fortune-
tellers came in, I told them the dream, but they could not tell me what it
meant. 8 At last Daniel came in before me, and I told him the dream. (He
was named Belteshazzar after my god, and the spirit of the holy gods is
in him.)
9 "I said to him, 'Belteshazzar, chief of the magicians, I know that the
spirit of the holy gods is in you and that no mystery is too great for you
to solve. Now tell me what my dream means.
10 "'While I was lying in my bed, this is what I dreamed. I saw a large
tree in the middle of the earth. 11 The tree grew very tall and strong,
reaching high into the heavens for all the world to see. 12 It had fresh
green leaves, and it was loaded with fruit for all to eat. Wild animals
lived in its shade, and birds nested in its branches. All the world was fed
from this tree.
13 "'Then as I lay there dreaming, I saw a messenger,* a holy one,
coming down from heaven. 14 The messenger shouted,

"Cut down the tree and lop off its branches!
Shake off its leaves and scatter its fruit!

4:1 Verses 4:1-3 are numbered 3:31-33 in Aramaic text. 4:4 Verses 4:4-37 are numbered 4:1-34 in Aramaic text. 4:7 Or *Chaldeans.* 4:13 Aramaic *a watcher;* also in 4:23.

Chase the wild animals from its shade
and the birds from its branches.
15 But leave the stump and the roots in the ground,
bound with a band of iron and bronze
and surrounded by tender grass.
Now let him be drenched with the dew of heaven,
and let him live with the wild animals among the plants of the field.
16 For seven periods of time,
let him have the mind of a wild animal
instead of the mind of a human.
17 For this has been decreed by the messengers*;
it is commanded by the holy ones,
so that everyone may know
that the Most High rules over the kingdoms of the world.
He gives them to anyone he chooses—
even to the lowliest of people."

18"'Belteshazzar, that was the dream that I, King Nebuchadnezzar, had. Now tell me what it means, for none of the wise men of my kingdom can do so. But you can tell me because the spirit of the holy gods is in you.'

Daniel Explains the Dream

19"Upon hearing this, Daniel (also known as Belteshazzar) was overcome for a time, frightened by the meaning of the dream. Then the king said to him, 'Belteshazzar, don't be alarmed by the dream and what it means.'

"Belteshazzar replied, 'I wish the events foreshadowed in this dream
would happen to your enemies, my lord, and not to you! 20The tree you
saw was growing very tall and strong, reaching high into the heavens
for all the world to see. 21It had fresh green leaves and was loaded with
fruit for all to eat. Wild animals lived in its shade, and birds nested in its
branches. 22That tree, Your Majesty, is you. For you have grown strong
and great; your greatness reaches up to heaven, and your rule to the ends of the earth.

23"'Then you saw a messenger, a holy one, coming down from heaven and saying, "Cut down the tree and destroy it. But leave the stump and the roots in the ground, bound with a band of iron and bronze and surrounded by tender grass. Let him be drenched with the dew of heaven. Let him live with the animals of the field for seven periods of time."

24"'This is what the dream means, Your Majesty, and what the Most
High has declared will happen to my lord the king. 25You will be
driven from human society, and you will live in the fields with the wild
animals. You will eat grass like a cow, and you will be drenched with
the dew of heaven. Seven periods of time will pass while you live this
way, until you learn that the Most High rules over the kingdoms of the
world and gives them to anyone he chooses. 26But the stump and roots

4:17 Aramaic *the watchers.*

Encouragements from these verses

Prayer 4:35

Jesus, no matter how you choose to do so, prepare me to serve you today. Amen.

of the tree were left in the ground. This means that you will receive
your kingdom back again when you have learned that heaven rules.
27 "'King Nebuchadnezzar, please accept my advice. Stop sinning and
do what is right. Break from your wicked past and be merciful to the
poor. Perhaps then you will continue to prosper.'

The Dream's Fulfillment

28 "But all these things did happen to King Nebuchadnezzar. 29 Twelve
months later he was taking a walk on the flat roof of the royal palace in
Babylon. 30 As he looked out across the city, he said, 'Look at this great
city of Babylon! By my own mighty power, I have built this beautiful
city as my royal residence to display my majestic splendor.'
31 "While these words were still in his mouth, a voice called down
from heaven, 'O King Nebuchadnezzar, this message is for you! You
are no longer ruler of this kingdom. 32 You will be driven from human
society. You will live in the fields with the wild animals, and you will
eat grass like a cow. Seven periods of time will pass while you live this
way, until you learn that the Most High rules over the kingdoms of the
world and gives them to anyone he chooses.'
33 "That same hour the judgment was fulfilled, and Nebuchadnezzar
was driven from human society. He ate grass like a cow, and he was
drenched with the dew of heaven. He lived this way until his hair was
as long as eagles' feathers and his nails were like birds' claws.

Nebuchadnezzar Praises God

34 "After this time had passed, I, Nebuchadnezzar, looked up to heaven.
My sanity returned, and I praised and worshiped the Most High and
honored the one who lives forever.

His rule is everlasting,
  and his kingdom is eternal.
35 All the people of the earth
  are nothing compared to him.
He does as he pleases
  among the angels of heaven
  and among the people of the earth.
No one can stop him or say to him,
  'What do you mean by doing these things?'

36 "When my sanity returned to me, so did my honor and glory and
kingdom. My advisers and nobles sought me out, and I was restored as
head of my kingdom, with even greater honor than before.
37 "Now I, Nebuchadnezzar, praise and glorify and honor the King of
heaven. All his acts are just and true, and he is able to humble the proud."

The Writing on the Wall

5 Many years later King Belshazzar gave a great feast for 1,000 of his nobles,
and he drank wine with them. 2 While Belshazzar was drinking the wine,
he gave orders to bring in the gold and silver cups that his predecessor,*

5:2 Aramaic *father;* also in 5:11, 13, 18.

Nebuchadnezzar, had taken from the Temple in Jerusalem. He wanted to
drink from them with his nobles, his wives, and his concubines. 3 So they
brought these gold cups taken from the Temple, the house of God in Jerusa-
lem, and the king and his nobles, his wives, and his concubines drank from
them. 4 While they drank from them they praised their idols made of gold,
silver, bronze, iron, wood, and stone.
5 Suddenly, they saw the fingers of a human hand writing on the plaster
wall of the king's palace, near the lampstand. The king himself saw the hand
as it wrote, 6 and his face turned pale with fright. His knees knocked together
in fear and his legs gave way beneath him.
7 The king shouted for the enchanters, astrologers,* and fortune-tellers to
be brought before him. He said to these wise men of Babylon, "Whoever can
read this writing and tell me what it means will be dressed in purple robes
of royal honor and will have a gold chain placed around his neck. He will
become the third highest ruler in the kingdom!"
8 But when all the king's wise men had come in, none of them could read
the writing or tell him what it meant. 9 So the king grew even more alarmed,
and his face turned pale. His nobles, too, were shaken.
10 But when the queen mother heard what was happening, she hurried to
the banquet hall. She said to Belshazzar, "Long live the king! Don't be so pale
and frightened. 11 There is a man in your kingdom who has within him the
spirit of the holy gods. During Nebuchadnezzar's reign, this man was found
to have insight, understanding, and wisdom like that of the gods. Your pre-
decessor, the king—your predecessor King Nebuchadnezzar—made him
chief over all the magicians, enchanters, astrologers, and fortune-tellers of
Babylon. 12 This man Daniel, whom the king named Belteshazzar, has ex-
ceptional ability and is filled with divine knowledge and understanding.
He can interpret dreams, explain riddles, and solve difficult problems. Call
for Daniel, and he will tell you what the writing means."

Daniel Explains the Writing

13 So Daniel was brought in before the king. The king asked him, "Are you
Daniel, one of the exiles brought from Judah by my predecessor, King Neb-
uchadnezzar? 14 I have heard that you have the spirit of the gods within you
and that you are filled with insight, understanding, and wisdom. 15 My wise
men and enchanters have tried to read the words on the wall and tell me their
meaning, but they cannot do it. 16 I am told that you can give interpretations
and solve difficult problems. If you can read these words and tell me their
meaning, you will be clothed in purple robes of royal honor, and you will
have a gold chain placed around your neck. You will become the third high-
est ruler in the kingdom."
17 Daniel answered the king, "Keep your gifts or give them to someone
else, but I will tell you what the writing means. 18 Your Majesty, the Most
High God gave sovereignty, majesty, glory, and honor to your predecessor,
Nebuchadnezzar. 19 He made him so great that people of all races and na-
tions and languages trembled before him in fear. He killed those he wanted
to kill and spared those he wanted to spare. He honored those he wanted to
honor and disgraced those he wanted to disgrace. 20 But when his heart and
mind were puffed up with arrogance, he was brought down from his royal

5:7 Or *Chaldeans;* also in 5:11.

Make a Difference

5:10–12

Legacy

What you do today in integrity and service to God may create a legacy for which God will call upon you again. One victory doesn't mean the end of the season of trials. Daniel had to weather several unexpected tensions and trials, but that didn't mean God wasn't going to use him again at any moment. Daniel's example should prompt you to always be ready for God to use you by living a holy life and by seeking a moment-by-moment dependence on God's Spirit.

Difference Maker

Ask God to search you and show you an area of your life that you could turn over to him in integrity so that he can use you however he wants to use you now and in the future.

throne and stripped of his glory. 21 He was driven from human society. He
was given the mind of a wild animal, and he lived among the wild donkeys.
He ate grass like a cow, and he was drenched with the dew of heaven, until
he learned that the Most High God rules over the kingdoms of the world
and appoints anyone he desires to rule over them.

22 "You are his successor,* O Belshazzar, and you knew all this, yet you have
not humbled yourself. 23 For you have proudly defied the Lord of heaven
and have had these cups from his Temple brought before you. You and your
nobles and your wives and concubines have been drinking wine from them
while praising gods of silver, gold, bronze, iron, wood, and stone—gods that
neither see nor hear nor know anything at all. But you have not honored the
God who gives you the breath of life and controls your destiny! 24 So God has
sent this hand to write this message.

25 "This is the message that was written: MENE, MENE, TEKEL, and PARSIN.
26 This is what these words mean:

Mene means 'numbered'—God has numbered the days of your reign
and has brought it to an end.
27 *Tekel* means 'weighed'—you have been weighed on the balances and
have not measured up.
28 *Parsin** means 'divided'—your kingdom has been divided and given to
the Medes and Persians."

29 Then at Belshazzar's command, Daniel was dressed in purple robes,
a gold chain was hung around his neck, and he was proclaimed the third
highest ruler in the kingdom.
30 That very night Belshazzar, the Babylonian* king, was killed.*
31* And Darius the Mede took over the kingdom at the age of sixty-two.

Daniel in the Lions' Den

6 1* Darius the Mede decided to divide the kingdom into 120 provinces, and
he appointed a high officer to rule over each province. 2 The king also
chose Daniel and two others as administrators to supervise the high officers
and protect the king's interests. 3 Daniel soon proved himself more capable
than all the other administrators and high officers. Because of Daniel's great
ability, the king made plans to place him over the entire empire.

4 Then the other administrators and high officers began searching for
some fault in the way Daniel was handling government affairs, but they
couldn't find anything to criticize or condemn. He was faithful, always
responsible, and completely trustworthy. 5 So they concluded, "Our only
chance of finding grounds for accusing Daniel will be in connection with
the rules of his religion."

6 So the administrators and high officers went to the king and said, "Long
live King Darius! 7 We are all in agreement—we administrators, officials,
high officers, advisers, and governors—that the king should make a law that
will be strictly enforced. Give orders that for the next thirty days any person
who prays to anyone, divine or human—except to you, Your Majesty—will
be thrown into the den of lions. 8 And now, Your Majesty, issue and sign this

5:22 Aramaic *son.* 5:28 Aramaic *Peres,* the singular of *Parsin.* 5:30a Or *Chaldean.* 5:30b The Persians and Medes conquered Babylon in October 539 B.C. 5:31 Verse 5:31 is numbered 6:1 in Aramaic text. 6:1 Verses 6:1-28 are numbered 6:2-29 in Aramaic text.

law so it cannot be changed, an official law of the Medes and Persians that
cannot be revoked." 9 So King Darius signed the law.
10 But when Daniel learned that the law had been signed, he went home
and knelt down as usual in his upstairs room, with its windows open toward
Jerusalem. He prayed three times a day, just as he had always done, giving
thanks to his God. 11 Then the officials went together to Daniel's house and
found him praying and asking for God's help. 12 So they went straight to the
king and reminded him about his law. "Did you not sign a law that for the
next thirty days any person who prays to anyone, divine or human—except
to you, Your Majesty—will be thrown into the den of lions?"

"Yes," the king replied, "that decision stands; it is an official law of the
Medes and Persians that cannot be revoked."
13 Then they told the king, "That man Daniel, one of the captives from Ju-
dah, is ignoring you and your law. He still prays to his God three times a day."
14 Hearing this, the king was deeply troubled, and he tried to think of a way
to save Daniel. He spent the rest of the day looking for a way to get Daniel
out of this predicament.
15 In the evening the men went together to the king and said, "Your Maj-
esty, you know that according to the law of the Medes and the Persians, no
law that the king signs can be changed."
16 So at last the king gave orders for Daniel to be arrested and thrown into
the den of lions. The king said to him, "May your God, whom you serve so
faithfully, rescue you."
17 A stone was brought and placed over the mouth of the den. The king
sealed the stone with his own royal seal and the seals of his nobles, so that
no one could rescue Daniel. 18 Then the king returned to his palace and spent
the night fasting. He refused his usual entertainment and couldn't sleep at
all that night.
19 Very early the next morning, the king got up and hurried out to the
lions' den. 20 When he got there, he called out in anguish, "Daniel, servant of
the living God! Was your God, whom you serve so faithfully, able to rescue
you from the lions?"
21 Daniel answered, "Long live the king! 22 My God sent his angel to shut
the lions' mouths so that they would not hurt me, for I have been found in-
nocent in his sight. And I have not wronged you, Your Majesty."
23 The king was overjoyed and ordered that Daniel be lifted from the den.
Not a scratch was found on him, for he had trusted in his God.
24 Then the king gave orders to arrest the men who had maliciously ac-
cused Daniel. He had them thrown into the lions' den, along with their wives
and children. The lions leaped on them and tore them apart before they even
hit the floor of the den.
25 Then King Darius sent this message to the people of every race and na-
tion and language throughout the world:

"Peace and prosperity to you!
26 "I decree that everyone throughout my kingdom should tremble
with fear before the God of Daniel.

For he is the living God,
and he will endure forever.

Make a Difference

6:10-13

Regular and Bold Faith

When King Darius made the law that a person who prayed to anyone but the king himself would be thrown into the lions' den, Daniel had a choice to make. Either he could keep trusting God and keep praying to God in his regular place and time or he could still pray to God but just keep it a little more secret. If he hid his prayers, no one would know, and his life would be spared, right? Well, when Daniel learned of the law, he went home and prayed "just as he had always done" (v. 10). His prayer time with God was regular (three times a day), and it was bold (where others could see). He didn't compromise his pattern.

Difference Maker

Make two lists. On the first list, record some of the regular things you do because of your faith in God. On the second list, record some of the bold actions you take because of your faith in God. What did you learn about your faith compared to Daniel's, and how can you let God stretch your faith to be bolder and more consistent?

His kingdom will never be destroyed,
and his rule will never end.
27 He rescues and saves his people;
he performs miraculous signs and wonders
in the heavens and on earth.
He has rescued Daniel
from the power of the lions."

28 So Daniel prospered during the reign of Darius and the reign of Cyrus
the Persian.*

Daniel's Vision of Four Beasts

7 Earlier, during the first year of King Belshazzar's reign in Babylon,*
Daniel had a dream and saw visions as he lay in his bed. He wrote down
the dream, and this is what he saw.
2 In my vision that night, I, Daniel, saw a great storm churning the surface
of a great sea, with strong winds blowing from every direction.
3 Then four
huge beasts came up out of the water, each different from the others.
4 The first beast was like a lion with eagles' wings. As I watched, its wings
were pulled off, and it was left standing with its two hind feet on the ground,
like a human being. And it was given a human mind.
5 Then I saw a second beast, and it looked like a bear. It was rearing up on
one side, and it had three ribs in its mouth between its teeth. And I heard a
voice saying to it, "Get up! Devour the flesh of many people!"
6 Then the third of these strange beasts appeared, and it looked like a
leopard. It had four bird's wings on its back, and it had four heads. Great
authority was given to this beast.
7 Then in my vision that night, I saw a fourth beast—terrifying, dreadful,
and very strong. It devoured and crushed its victims with huge iron teeth
and trampled their remains beneath its feet. It was different from any of the
other beasts, and it had ten horns.
8 As I was looking at the horns, suddenly another small horn appeared
among them. Three of the first horns were torn out by the roots to make
room for it. This little horn had eyes like human eyes and a mouth that was
boasting arrogantly.

9 I watched as thrones were put in place
and the Ancient One* sat down to judge.
His clothing was as white as snow,
his hair like purest wool.
He sat on a fiery throne
with wheels of blazing fire,
10 and a river of fire was pouring out,
flowing from his presence.
Millions of angels ministered to him;
many millions stood to attend him.
Then the court began its session,
and the books were opened.

6:28 Or *of Darius, that is, the reign of Cyrus the Persian.* 7:1 The first year of Belshazzar's reign (who was co-regent with his father, Nabonidus) was 556 B.C. (or perhaps as late as 553 B.C.). 7:9 Aramaic *an Ancient of Days;* also in 7:13, 22.

11 I continued to watch because I could hear the little horn's boastful
speech. I kept watching until the fourth beast was killed and its body was
destroyed by fire. 12 The other three beasts had their authority taken from
them, but they were allowed to live a while longer.*
13 As my vision continued that night, I saw someone like a son of man*
coming with the clouds of heaven. He approached the Ancient One and was
led into his presence. 14 He was given authority, honor, and sovereignty over
all the nations of the world, so that people of every race and nation and lan-
guage would obey him. His rule is eternal—it will never end. His kingdom
will never be destroyed.

The Vision Is Explained

15 I, Daniel, was troubled by all I had seen, and my visions terrified me. 16 So
I approached one of those standing beside the throne and asked him what
it all meant. He explained it to me like this: 17 "These four huge beasts rep-
resent four kingdoms that will arise from the earth. 18 But in the end, the
holy people of the Most High will be given the kingdom, and they will rule
forever and ever."
19 Then I wanted to know the true meaning of the fourth beast, the one so
different from the others and so terrifying. It had devoured and crushed its
victims with iron teeth and bronze claws, trampling their remains beneath
its feet. 20 I also asked about the ten horns on the fourth beast's head and the
little horn that came up afterward and destroyed three of the other horns.
This horn had seemed greater than the others, and it had human eyes and a
mouth that was boasting arrogantly. 21 As I watched, this horn was waging
war against God's holy people and was defeating them, 22 until the Ancient
One—the Most High—came and judged in favor of his holy people. Then
the time arrived for the holy people to take over the kingdom.
23 Then he said to me, "This fourth beast is the fourth world power that will
rule the earth. It will be different from all the others. It will devour the whole
world, trampling and crushing everything in its path. 24 Its ten horns are ten
kings who will rule that empire. Then another king will arise, different from
the other ten, who will subdue three of them. 25 He will defy the Most High
and oppress the holy people of the Most High. He will try to change their sa-
cred festivals and laws, and they will be placed under his control for a time,
times, and half a time.
26 "But then the court will pass judgment, and all his power will be taken
away and completely destroyed. 27 Then the sovereignty, power, and great-
ness of all the kingdoms under heaven will be given to the holy people of
the Most High. His kingdom will last forever, and all rulers will serve and
obey him."
28 That was the end of the vision. I, Daniel, was terrified by my thoughts
and my face was pale with fear, but I kept these things to myself.

Daniel's Vision of a Ram and Goat

8 1*During the third year of King Belshazzar's reign, I, Daniel, saw another
vision, following the one that had already appeared to me. 2 In this vi-
sion I was at the fortress of Susa, in the province of Elam, standing beside
the Ulai River.*

7:12 Aramaic *for a season and a time.* 7:13 Or *like a Son of Man.* 8:1 The original text from this point through chapter 12 is in Hebrew. See note at 2:4. 8:2 Or *the Ulai Gate;* also in 8:16.

Question 7:16

How would it make a difference in your life if, when you were troubled (like Daniel was by his vision), instead of worrying, you carried on with your duties and trusted the Lord?

3 As I looked up, I saw a ram with two long horns standing beside the river.*
One of the horns was longer than the other, even though it had grown later
than the other one. 4 The ram butted everything out of his way to the west,
to the north, and to the south, and no one could stand against him or help
his victims. He did as he pleased and became very great.

5 While I was watching, suddenly a male goat appeared from the west,
crossing the land so swiftly that he didn't even touch the ground. This goat,
which had one very large horn between its eyes, 6 headed toward the two-
horned ram that I had seen standing beside the river, rushing at him in a
rage. 7 The goat charged furiously at the ram and struck him, breaking off
both his horns. Now the ram was helpless, and the goat knocked him down
and trampled him. No one could rescue the ram from the goat's power.

8 The goat became very powerful. But at the height of his power, his large
horn was broken off. In the large horn's place grew four prominent horns
pointing in the four directions of the earth. 9 Then from one of the promi-
nent horns came a small horn whose power grew very great. It extended
toward the south and the east and toward the glorious land of Israel. 10 Its
power reached to the heavens, where it attacked the heavenly army, throw-
ing some of the heavenly beings and some of the stars to the ground and
trampling them. 11 It even challenged the Commander of heaven's army by
canceling the daily sacrifices offered to him and by destroying his Temple.
12 The army of heaven was restrained from responding to this rebellion. So
the daily sacrifice was halted, and truth was overthrown. The horn succeeded
in everything it did.*

13 Then I heard two holy ones talking to each other. One of them asked,
"How long will the events of this vision last? How long will the rebellion
that causes desecration stop the daily sacrifices? How long will the Temple
and heaven's army be trampled on?"

14 The other replied, "It will take 2,300 evenings and mornings; then the
Temple will be made right again."

Gabriel Explains the Vision

15 As I, Daniel, was trying to understand the meaning of this vision, someone
who looked like a man stood in front of me. 16 And I heard a human voice
calling out from the Ulai River, "Gabriel, tell this man the meaning of his
vision."

17 As Gabriel approached the place where I was standing, I became so ter-
rified that I fell with my face to the ground. "Son of man," he said, "you
must understand that the events you have seen in your vision relate to the
time of the end."

18 While he was speaking, I fainted and lay there with my face to the
ground. But Gabriel roused me with a touch and helped me to my feet.

19 Then he said, "I am here to tell you what will happen later in the time
of wrath. What you have seen pertains to the very end of time. 20 The two-
horned ram represents the kings of Media and Persia. 21 The shaggy male
goat represents the king of Greece,* and the large horn between his eyes
represents the first king of the Greek Empire. 22 The four prominent horns
that replaced the one large horn show that the Greek Empire will break into
four kingdoms, but none as great as the first.

8:3 Or *the gate;* also in 8:6. **8:11-12** The meaning of the Hebrew for these verses is uncertain.
8:21 Hebrew *of Javan.*

23"At the end of their rule, when their sin is at its height, a fierce king, a
master of intrigue, will rise to power. 24He will become very strong, but not
by his own power. He will cause a shocking amount of destruction and suc-
ceed in everything he does. He will destroy powerful leaders and devastate
the holy people. 25He will be a master of deception and will become arrogant;
he will destroy many without warning. He will even take on the Prince of
princes in battle, but he will be broken, though not by human power.
26"This vision about the 2,300 evenings and mornings* is true. But none
of these things will happen for a long time, so keep this vision a secret."
27Then I, Daniel, was overcome and lay sick for several days. Afterward I
got up and performed my duties for the king, but I was greatly troubled by
the vision and could not understand it.

Daniel's Prayer for His People

9 It was the first year of the reign of Darius the Mede, the son of Ahasue-
rus, who became king of the Babylonians.* 2During the first year of his
reign, I, Daniel, learned from reading the word of the LORD, as revealed to
Jeremiah the prophet, that Jerusalem must lie desolate for seventy years.*
3So I turned to the Lord God and pleaded with him in prayer and fasting. I
also wore rough burlap and sprinkled myself with ashes.
4I prayed to the LORD my God and confessed:

"O Lord, you are a great and awesome God! You always fulfill your
covenant and keep your promises of unfailing love to those who
love you and obey your commands. 5But we have sinned and done
wrong. We have rebelled against you and scorned your commands and
regulations. 6We have refused to listen to your servants the prophets,
who spoke on your authority to our kings and princes and ancestors
and to all the people of the land.
7"Lord, you are in the right; but as you see, our faces are covered
with shame. This is true of all of us, including the people of Judah
and Jerusalem and all Israel, scattered near and far, wherever you have
driven us because of our disloyalty to you. 8O LORD, we and our kings,
princes, and ancestors are covered with shame because we have sinned
against you. 9But the Lord our God is merciful and forgiving, even
though we have rebelled against him. 10We have not obeyed the LORD
our God, for we have not followed the instructions he gave us through
his servants the prophets. 11All Israel has disobeyed your instruction
and turned away, refusing to listen to your voice.

"So now the solemn curses and judgments written in the Law of
Moses, the servant of God, have been poured down on us because of our
sin. 12You have kept your word and done to us and our rulers exactly
as you warned. Never has there been such a disaster as happened in
Jerusalem. 13Every curse written against us in the Law of Moses has
come true. Yet we have refused to seek mercy from the LORD our God by
turning from our sins and recognizing his truth. 14Therefore, the LORD
has brought upon us the disaster he prepared. The LORD our God was
right to do all of these things, for we did not obey him.
15"O Lord our God, you brought lasting honor to your name by

8:26 Hebrew *about the evenings and mornings;* compare 8:14. 9:1 Or *the Chaldeans.* 9:2 See Jer 25:11-12; 29:10.

Prayer 8:27

God, help me to be like Daniel, and when I experience or see things that trouble me, help me to be quick to bring them to you instead of worrying about them. Amen.

Make a Difference 9:2

Read the Word

Daniel was reading Jeremiah! Daniel was reading the Bible for insight into current events and discernment for how he should pray and plan.

You are in a long history of people reading the Word of God. Isn't it wild to think about Daniel reading the same words you can read? Isn't it fascinating to think that Daniel wrote down his own book for you to be reading right now?

Difference Maker

Be like Daniel! Make a regular habit of reading God's Word for discernment and devotion.

Make a Difference

9:2-27

Anguish or Prayer?

As Daniel was reading Jeremiah, he learned that Jerusalem would lie desolate for seventy years (and, in Daniel 9:24, he heard from God that this would actually be "seventy sets of seven" years). This was deeply troubling to Daniel. Despite his distress, instead of allowing anxiety and trouble to rule his mind, Daniel turned his anguish into prayer. This is precisely what Philippians 4:6-7 tells us to do.

Difference Maker

Read Philippians 4:6-7. What anguish are you experiencing? Turn this into prayer.

rescuing your people from Egypt in a great display of power. But we have
sinned and are full of wickedness. 16 In view of all your faithful mercies,
Lord, please turn your furious anger away from your city Jerusalem, your
holy mountain. All the neighboring nations mock Jerusalem and your
people because of our sins and the sins of our ancestors.
17 "O our God, hear your servant's prayer! Listen as I plead. For your
own sake, Lord, smile again on your desolate sanctuary.
18 "O my God, lean down and listen to me. Open your eyes and see our
despair. See how your city—the city that bears your name—lies in ruins.
We make this plea, not because we deserve help, but because of your mercy.
19 "O Lord, hear. O Lord, forgive. O Lord, listen and act! For your own
sake, do not delay, O my God, for your people and your city bear your
name."

Gabriel's Message about the Anointed One

20 I went on praying and confessing my sin and the sin of my people, pleading
with the LORD my God for Jerusalem, his holy mountain. 21 As I was praying,
Gabriel, whom I had seen in the earlier vision, came swiftly to me at the time
of the evening sacrifice. 22 He explained to me, "Daniel, I have come here to
give you insight and understanding. 23 The moment you began praying, a
command was given. And now I am here to tell you what it was, for you are
very precious to God. Listen carefully so that you can understand the meaning of your vision.
24 "A period of seventy sets of seven* has been decreed for your people and
your holy city to finish their rebellion, to put an end to their sin, to atone for
their guilt, to bring in everlasting righteousness, to confirm the prophetic vi-
sion, and to anoint the Most Holy Place.* 25 Now listen and understand! Seven
sets of seven plus sixty-two sets of seven* will pass from the time the command
is given to rebuild Jerusalem until a ruler—the Anointed One*—comes. Jerusa-
lem will be rebuilt with streets and strong defenses,* despite the perilous times.
26 "After this period of sixty-two sets of seven,* the Anointed One will be
killed, appearing to have accomplished nothing, and a ruler will arise whose
armies will destroy the city and the Temple. The end will come with a flood,
and war and its miseries are decreed from that time to the very end. 27 The ruler
will make a treaty with the people for a period of one set of seven,* but after
half this time, he will put an end to the sacrifices and offerings. And as a climax
to all his terrible deeds,* he will set up a sacrilegious object that causes des-
ecration,* until the fate decreed for this defiler is finally poured out on him."

Daniel's Vision of a Messenger

10 In the third year of the reign of King Cyrus of Persia,* Daniel (also
known as Belteshazzar) had another vision. He understood that the
vision concerned events certain to happen in the future—times of war and
great hardship.
2 When this vision came to me, I, Daniel, had been in mourning for three
whole weeks. 3 All that time I had eaten no rich food. No meat or wine crossed
my lips, and I used no fragrant lotions until those three weeks had passed.

9:24a Hebrew *seventy sevens.* **9:24b** Or *the Most Holy One.* **9:25a** Hebrew *Seven sevens plus sixty-two sevens.* **9:25b** Or *an anointed one;* similarly in 9:26. Hebrew reads *a messiah.* **9:25c** Or *and a moat,* or *and trenches.* **9:26** Hebrew *After sixty-two sevens.* **9:27a** Hebrew *for one seven.* **9:27b** Hebrew *And on the wing;* the meaning of the Hebrew is uncertain. **9:27c** Hebrew *an abomination of desolation.* **10:1** The third year of Cyrus's reign was 536 B.C.

4 On April 23,* as I was standing on the bank of the great Tigris River, 5 I
looked up and saw a man dressed in linen clothing, with a belt of pure gold
around his waist. 6 His body looked like a precious gem. His face flashed
like lightning, and his eyes flamed like torches. His arms and feet shone
like polished bronze, and his voice roared like a vast multitude of people.
7 Only I, Daniel, saw this vision. The men with me saw nothing, but they
were suddenly terrified and ran away to hide. 8 So I was left there all alone to
see this amazing vision. My strength left me, my face grew deathly pale, and
I felt very weak. 9 Then I heard the man speak, and when I heard the sound
of his voice, I fainted and lay there with my face to the ground.
10 Just then a hand touched me and lifted me, still trembling, to my hands
and knees. 11 And the man said to me, "Daniel, you are very precious to God,
so listen carefully to what I have to say to you. Stand up, for I have been sent
to you." When he said this to me, I stood up, still trembling.
12 Then he said, "Don't be afraid, Daniel. Since the first day you began to
pray for understanding and to humble yourself before your God, your re-
quest has been heard in heaven. I have come in answer to your prayer. 13 But
for twenty-one days the spirit prince* of the kingdom of Persia blocked my
way. Then Michael, one of the archangels,* came to help me, and I left him
there with the spirit prince of the kingdom of Persia.* 14 Now I am here to
explain what will happen to your people in the future, for this vision con-
cerns a time yet to come."
15 While he was speaking to me, I looked down at the ground, unable to
say a word. 16 Then the one who looked like a man* touched my lips, and I
opened my mouth and began to speak. I said to the one standing in front
of me, "I am filled with anguish because of the vision I have seen, my lord,
and I am very weak. 17 How can someone like me, your servant, talk to you,
my lord? My strength is gone, and I can hardly breathe."
18 Then the one who looked like a man touched me again, and I felt my
strength returning. 19 "Don't be afraid," he said, "for you are very precious
to God. Peace! Be encouraged! Be strong!"

As he spoke these words to me, I suddenly felt stronger and said to him,
"Please speak to me, my lord, for you have strengthened me."
20 He replied, "Do you know why I have come? Soon I must return to fight
against the spirit prince of the kingdom of Persia, and after that the spirit prince
of the kingdom of Greece* will come. 21 Meanwhile, I will tell you what is writ-
ten in the Book of Truth. (No one helps me against these spirit princes except
Michael, your spirit prince.* 11:1 I have been standing beside Michael* to support
and strengthen him since the first year of the reign of Darius the Mede.)

Kings of the South and North

11 2 "Now then, I will reveal the truth to you. Three more Persian kings
will reign, to be succeeded by a fourth, far richer than the others. He
will use his wealth to stir up everyone to fight against the kingdom of Greece.*

Question 10:13

What difference would it make if you were to realize that there is an unseen battle being waged and that God has angels fighting on your behalf?

10:4 Hebrew *On the twenty-fourth day of the first month,* of the ancient Hebrew lunar calendar. This date in the book of Daniel can be cross-checked with dates in surviving Persian records and can be related accurately to our modern calendar. This event occurred on April 23, 536 B.C. **10:13a** Hebrew *the prince;* also in 10:13c, 20. **10:13b** Hebrew *the chief princes.* **10:13c** As in one Greek version; Hebrew reads *and I was left there with the kings of Persia.* The meaning of the Hebrew is uncertain. **10:16** As in most manuscripts of the Masoretic Text; one manuscript of the Masoretic Text and one Greek version read *Then something that looked like a human hand.* **10:20** Hebrew *of Javan.* **10:21** Hebrew *against these except Michael, your prince.* **11:1** Hebrew *him.* **11:2** Hebrew *of Javan.*

3 “Then a mighty king will rise to power who will rule with great authority
and accomplish everything he sets out to do. 4 But at the height of his power,
his kingdom will be broken apart and divided into four parts. It will not be
ruled by the king’s descendants, nor will the kingdom hold the authority it
once had. For his empire will be uprooted and given to others.

5 “The king of the south will increase in power, but one of his own of-
ficials will become more powerful than he and will rule his kingdom with
great strength.

6 “Some years later an alliance will be formed between the king of the
north and the king of the south. The daughter of the king of the south will
be given in marriage to the king of the north to secure the alliance, but she
will lose her influence over him, and so will her father. She will be abandoned
along with her supporters. 7 But when one of her relatives* becomes king
of the south, he will raise an army and enter the fortress of the king of the
north and defeat him. 8 When he returns to Egypt, he will carry back their
idols with him, along with priceless articles of gold and silver. For some years
afterward he will leave the king of the north alone.

9 “Later the king of the north will invade the realm of the king of the south
but will soon return to his own land. 10 However, the sons of the king of the
north will assemble a mighty army that will advance like a flood and carry
the battle as far as the enemy’s fortress.

11 “Then, in a rage, the king of the south will rally against the vast forces
assembled by the king of the north and will defeat them. 12 After the enemy
army is swept away, the king of the south will be filled with pride and will
execute many thousands of his enemies. But his success will be short lived.

13 “A few years later the king of the north will return with a fully equipped
army far greater than before. 14 At that time there will be a general uprising
against the king of the south. Violent men among your own people will join
them in fulfillment of this vision, but they will not succeed. 15 Then the king
of the north will come and lay siege to a fortified city and capture it. The best
troops of the south will not be able to stand in the face of the onslaught.

16 “The king of the north will march onward unopposed; none will be able
to stop him. He will pause in the glorious land of Israel,* intent on destroy-
ing it. 17 He will make plans to come with the might of his entire kingdom
and will form an alliance with the king of the south. He will give him a
daughter in marriage in order to overthrow the kingdom from within, but
his plan will fail.

18 “After this, he will turn his attention to the coastland and conquer many
cities. But a commander from another land will put an end to his insolence
and cause him to retreat in shame. 19 He will take refuge in his own fortresses
but will stumble and fall and be seen no more.

20 “His successor will send out a tax collector to maintain the royal splen-
dor. But after a very brief reign, he will die, though not from anger or in
battle.

21 “The next to come to power will be a despicable man who is not in line
for royal succession. He will slip in when least expected and take over the
kingdom by flattery and intrigue. 22 Before him great armies will be swept
away, including a covenant prince. 23 With deceitful promises, he will make
various alliances. He will become strong despite having only a handful of

11:7 Hebrew *a branch from her roots.* 11:16 Hebrew *the glorious land.*

followers. 24Without warning he will enter the richest areas of the land. Then
he will distribute among his followers the plunder and wealth of the rich—
something his predecessors had never done. He will plot the overthrow of
strongholds, but this will last for only a short while.
25"Then he will stir up his courage and raise a great army against the king
of the south. The king of the south will go to battle with a mighty army, but
to no avail, for there will be plots against him. 26His own household will
cause his downfall. His army will be swept away, and many will be killed.
27Seeking nothing but each other's harm, these kings will plot against each
other at the conference table, attempting to deceive each other. But it will
make no difference, for the end will come at the appointed time.
28"The king of the north will then return home with great riches. On the
way he will set himself against the people of the holy covenant, doing much
damage before continuing his journey.
29"Then at the appointed time he will once again invade the south, but
this time the result will be different. 30For warships from western coastlands*
will scare him off, and he will withdraw and return home. But he will vent
his anger against the people of the holy covenant and reward those who
forsake the covenant.
31"His army will take over the Temple fortress, pollute the sanctuary, put
a stop to the daily sacrifices, and set up the sacrilegious object that causes
desecration.* 32He will flatter and win over those who have violated the cov-
enant. But the people who know their God will be strong and will resist him.
33"Wise leaders will give instruction to many, but these teachers will die
by fire and sword, or they will be jailed and robbed. 34During these perse-
cutions, little help will arrive, and many who join them will not be sincere.
35And some of the wise will fall victim to persecution. In this way, they will
be refined and cleansed and made pure until the time of the end, for the
appointed time is still to come.
36"The king will do as he pleases, exalting himself and claiming to be
greater than every god, even blaspheming the God of gods. He will succeed,
but only until the time of wrath is completed. For what has been determined
will surely take place. 37He will have no respect for the gods of his ancestors,
or for the god loved by women, or for any other god, for he will boast that
he is greater than them all. 38Instead of these, he will worship the god of
fortresses—a god his ancestors never knew—and lavish on him gold, silver,
precious stones, and expensive gifts. 39Claiming this foreign god's help, he
will attack the strongest fortresses. He will honor those who submit to him,
appointing them to positions of authority and dividing the land among
them as their reward.*
40"Then at the time of the end, the king of the south will attack the king
of the north. The king of the north will storm out with chariots, charioteers,
and a vast navy. He will invade various lands and sweep through them like a
flood. 41He will enter the glorious land of Israel,* and many nations will fall,
but Moab, Edom, and the best part of Ammon will escape. 42He will conquer
many countries, and even Egypt will not escape. 43He will gain control over
the gold, silver, and treasures of Egypt, and the Libyans and Ethiopians*
will be his servants.
44"But then news from the east and the north will alarm him, and he will

11:30 Hebrew *from Kittim.* **11:31** Hebrew *the abomination of desolation.* **11:39** Or *at a price.*
11:41 Hebrew *the glorious land.* **11:43** Hebrew *Cushites.*

Questions I want to ask

Prayer 11:45

God, it's amazing that you inspired Daniel to write about events that have happened, are happening, and will happen. Thanks for revealing this knowledge. I trust you with my future. Amen.

Question 12:13

God gave Daniel permission to "rest" (perhaps to die?). God also reassured Daniel that he would rise again to receive the inheritance set aside for him. How does knowing that you have eternal security with God forever give you confidence and peace for today? How does knowing there is an eternal hope change the way you live today?

set out in great anger to destroy and obliterate many. 45He will stop between
the glorious holy mountain and the sea and will pitch his royal tents. But
while he is there, his time will suddenly run out, and no one will help him.

The Time of the End

12 "At that time Michael, the archangel* who stands guard over your
nation, will arise. Then there will be a time of anguish greater than
any since nations first came into existence. But at that time every one of your
people whose name is written in the book will be rescued. 2Many of those
whose bodies lie dead and buried will rise up, some to everlasting life and
some to shame and everlasting disgrace. 3Those who are wise will shine as
bright as the sky, and those who lead many to righteousness will shine like
the stars forever. 4But you, Daniel, keep this prophecy a secret; seal up the
book until the time of the end, when many will rush here and there, and
knowledge will increase."

5Then I, Daniel, looked and saw two others standing on opposite banks
of the river. 6One of them asked the man dressed in linen, who was now
standing above the river, "How long will it be until these shocking events
are over?"

7The man dressed in linen, who was standing above the river, raised both
his hands toward heaven and took a solemn oath by the One who lives for-
ever, saying, "It will go on for a time, times, and half a time. When the shat-
tering of the holy people has finally come to an end, all these things will
have happened."

8I heard what he said, but I did not understand what he meant. So I asked,
"How will all this finally end, my lord?"

9But he said, "Go now, Daniel, for what I have said is kept secret and sealed
until the time of the end. 10Many will be purified, cleansed, and refined by
these trials. But the wicked will continue in their wickedness, and none of
them will understand. Only those who are wise will know what it means.

11"From the time the daily sacrifice is stopped and the sacrilegious object
that causes desecration* is set up to be worshiped, there will be 1,290 days.
12And blessed are those who wait and remain until the end of the 1,335 days!

13"As for you, go your way until the end. You will rest, and then at the end
of the days, you will rise again to receive the inheritance set aside for you."

12:1 Hebrew *the great prince.* 12:11 Hebrew *the abomination of desolation.*

Hosea Introduction

Hosea is a strange book of prophecy and poetry, sex and cheating, forgiveness and true love. It's not the kind of romance you expect to find in the Bible. If you've ever really screwed up, you'll want to explore Hosea.

The book begins by immediately plunging into relationship drama: God tells the prophet Hosea to marry a woman who will cheat on him. This may not be the advice that you'd expect to get from God when you're thinking about marrying someone. In this case, God was trying to teach his people a lesson, and Hosea was willing to help by letting his whole life be used as an example of God's love.

At the time Hosea was written, around the eighth century BC, Israel and Judah (the two kingdoms) were experiencing military strength but spiritual weakness. It was a time of privilege and prosperity that resulted in decadence and selfishness. People were turning away from God and pursuing their own thing. They were in the midst of chaos and injustice, worshiping other gods and only looking out for themselves. They were choosing to ignore God and do whatever they wanted. As frustrating as their behavior was, God continued to love them. When God loves someone, he will do anything to get them back.

God asked Hosea to marry Gomer, to be a flesh-and-blood example of God's love for Israel. Sadly, Gomer's life wasn't like in the movies, where once she found true love, she would change her ways and be forever faithful. No, she kept choosing to cheat despite how much Hosea loved her. God wanted Israel to see that they were behaving like Gomer. It was like God held up a mirror to them and said, "You're just like her! Stop acting out and come back to me, to the one who truly loves you."

Hosea's book is a great example of what happens when we cheat on God and start loving other things more than we love him. God doesn't hesitate to speak the truth—sometimes tough truth—to us when we screw up. Even so, he will always pursue us, always love us, and will always make a way for us to come back to him.

Story Arc

● **Hosea**

HOSEA

Hosea

Question 1:2

God asked Hosea to do something incredibly challenging to bring God's people back to him. Has God ever asked you to do something incredibly challenging that might help your friends see God in a new light?

Story Arc 1:1

● **Hosea**

Hosea's name means "salvation." It's similar to the names Joshua and Jesus. Hosea was a prophet, which means he spoke God's truth, even when it sounded harsh, to get Israel to return to God.

Hosea let his whole life be used as a prophetic message. By marrying Gomer–someone who would cheat on Hosea repeatedly–Hosea demonstrated how God keeps loving his people and will pay a ransom to win them back.

When looking at Hosea's life, it's critical to know that not everything written in the Bible is advice for how to live our lives. In this story, God isn't saying you should marry someone you know will cheat on you. That was God's instruction to Hosea to make a point to all of us–that God will go to great lengths to love you, forgive you, and restore you.

Amos 1:1 ►

1 The LORD gave this message to Hosea son of Beeri during the years when
Uzziah, Jotham, Ahaz, and Hezekiah were kings of Judah, and Jeroboam
son of Jehoash* was king of Israel.

Hosea's Wife and Children

2 When the LORD first began speaking to Israel through Hosea, he said to
him, "Go and marry a prostitute,* so that some of her children will be con-
ceived in prostitution. This will illustrate how Israel has acted like a prosti-
tute by turning against the LORD and worshiping other gods."
3 So Hosea married Gomer, the daughter of Diblaim, and she became preg-
nant and gave Hosea a son. 4 And the LORD said, "Name the child Jezreel, for
I am about to punish King Jehu's dynasty to avenge the murders he com-
mitted at Jezreel. In fact, I will bring an end to Israel's independence. 5 I will
break its military power in the Jezreel Valley."
6 Soon Gomer became pregnant again and gave birth to a daughter. And the
LORD said to Hosea, "Name your daughter Lo-ruhamah—'Not loved'—for
I will no longer show love to the people of Israel or forgive them. 7 But I will
show love to the people of Judah. I will free them from their enemies—not
with weapons and armies or horses and charioteers, but by my power as the
LORD their God."
8 After Gomer had weaned Lo-ruhamah, she again became pregnant and
gave birth to a second son. 9 And the LORD said, "Name him Lo-ammi—'Not
my people'—for Israel is not my people, and I am not their God.
10* "Yet the time will come when Israel's people will be like the sands of the
seashore—too many to count! Then, at the place where they were told, 'You
are not my people,' it will be said, 'You are children of the living God.' 11 Then
the people of Judah and Israel will unite together. They will choose one leader
for themselves, and they will return from exile together. What a day that will
be—the day of Jezreel*—when God will again plant his people in his land.
2:1* "In that day you will call your brothers Ammi—'My people.' And you
will call your sisters Ruhamah—'The ones I love.'

Charges against an Unfaithful Wife

2 2 "But now bring charges against Israel—your mother—
for she is no longer my wife,
and I am no longer her husband.
Tell her to remove the prostitute's makeup from her face
and the clothing that exposes her breasts.
3 Otherwise, I will strip her as naked
as she was on the day she was born.

1:1 Hebrew *Joash,* a variant spelling of Jehoash. 1:2 Or *a promiscuous woman.* 1:10 Verses 1:10-11 are numbered 2:1-2 in Hebrew text. 1:11 *Jezreel* means "God plants." 2:1 Verses 2:1-23 are numbered 2:3-25 in Hebrew text.

I will leave her to die of thirst,
as in a dry and barren wilderness.
4 And I will not love her children,
for they were conceived in prostitution.
5 Their mother is a shameless prostitute
and became pregnant in a shameful way.
She said, 'I'll run after other lovers
and sell myself to them for food and water,
for clothing of wool and linen,
and for olive oil and drinks.'

6 "For this reason I will fence her in with thornbushes.
I will block her path with a wall
to make her lose her way.
7 When she runs after her lovers,
she won't be able to catch them.
She will search for them
but not find them.
Then she will think,
'I might as well return to my husband,
for I was better off with him than I am now.'
8 She doesn't realize it was I who gave her everything she has—
the grain, the new wine, the olive oil;
I even gave her silver and gold.
But she gave all my gifts to Baal.

9 "But now I will take back the ripened grain and new wine
I generously provided each harvest season.
I will take away the wool and linen clothing
I gave her to cover her nakedness.
10 I will strip her naked in public,
while all her lovers look on.
No one will be able
to rescue her from my hands.
11 I will put an end to her annual festivals,
her new moon celebrations, and her Sabbath days—
all her appointed festivals.
12 I will destroy her grapevines and fig trees,
things she claims her lovers gave her.
I will let them grow into tangled thickets,
where only wild animals will eat the fruit.
13 I will punish her for all those times
when she burned incense to her images of Baal,
when she put on her earrings and jewels
and went out to look for her lovers
but forgot all about me,"
says the LORD.

The LORD's Love for Unfaithful Israel

14 "But then I will win her back once again.

Make a Difference 2:23

Names

God used all of Hosea's life as an example to get Israel's attention, even giving his kids specific names. Hosea and Gomar's oldest is Jezreel (1:4). His name was the same as a well-known place that had a bloody battle. The next two may or may not have been Hosea's children. The daughter was named Lo-ruhamah, which means "Not loved" (1:6). Her little brother was Lo-ammi, which means "Not my people" (1:9).

While these names seem harsh, God wanted to get a message to Israel: if you keep going down this road, your nation will fall apart, you won't be loved, and you won't be my people anymore.

Even as God told Israel the hard truth, he offered them a way back to him. In Hosea 2:23, we see that God turned these names around. He made sure Israel knew that if they returned to him, they would be planted (*Jezreel* literally means "God plants"), they would be his people, and he would show them that they were truly "the ones I love" (2:1).

Difference Maker

If you could invent a name that describes your life with God right now, what would it be? How about for the future? Stop right now to pray about God's message through the story of your life.

I will lead her into the desert
and speak tenderly to her there.
15 I will return her vineyards to her
and transform the Valley of Trouble* into a gateway of hope.
She will give herself to me there,
as she did long ago when she was young,
when I freed her from her captivity in Egypt.
16 When that day comes," says the LORD,
"you will call me 'my husband'
instead of 'my master.'*
17 O Israel, I will wipe the many names of Baal from your lips,
and you will never mention them again.
18 On that day I will make a covenant
with all the wild animals and the birds of the sky
and the animals that scurry along the ground
so they will not harm you.
I will remove all weapons of war from the land,
all swords and bows,
so you can live unafraid
in peace and safety.
19 I will make you my wife forever,
showing you righteousness and justice,
unfailing love and compassion.
20 I will be faithful to you and make you mine,
and you will finally know me as the LORD.

21 "In that day, I will answer,"
says the LORD.
"I will answer the sky as it pleads for clouds.
And the sky will answer the earth with rain.
22 Then the earth will answer the thirsty cries
of the grain, the grapevines, and the olive trees.
And they in turn will answer,
'Jezreel'—'God plants!'
23 At that time I will plant a crop of Israelites
and raise them for myself.
I will show love
to those I called 'Not loved.'*
And to those I called 'Not my people,'*
I will say, 'Now you are my people.'
And they will reply, 'You are our God!'"

Hosea's Wife Is Redeemed

3 Then the LORD said to me, "Go and love your wife again, even though
she* commits adultery with another lover. This will illustrate that the
LORD still loves Israel, even though the people have turned to other gods
and love to worship them.*"
2 So I bought her back for fifteen pieces of silver* and five bushels of barley

2:15 Hebrew *valley of Achor.* **2:16** Hebrew *'my baal.'* **2:23a** Hebrew *Lo-ruhamah;* see 1:6. **2:23b** Hebrew *Lo-ammi;* see 1:9. **3:1a** Or *Go and love a woman who.* **3:1b** Hebrew *love their raisin cakes.* **3:2a** Hebrew 15 *[shekels] of silver,* about 6 ounces or 171 grams in weight.

and a measure of wine.* 3 Then I said to her, "You must live in my house for
many days and stop your prostitution. During this time, you will not have
sexual relations with anyone, not even with me.*"

4 This shows that Israel will go a long time without a king or prince, and
without sacrifices, sacred pillars, priests,* or even idols! 5 But afterward the
people will return and devote themselves to the LORD their God and to Da-
vid's descendant, their king.* In the last days, they will tremble in awe of the
LORD and of his goodness.

The LORD's Case against Israel

4 1 Hear the word of the LORD, O people of Israel!
The LORD has brought charges against you, saying:
"There is no faithfulness, no kindness,
no knowledge of God in your land.
2 You make vows and break them;
you kill and steal and commit adultery.
There is violence everywhere—
one murder after another.
3 That is why your land is in mourning,
and everyone is wasting away.
Even the wild animals, the birds of the sky,
and the fish of the sea are disappearing.

4 "Don't point your finger at someone else
and try to pass the blame!
My complaint, you priests,
is with you.*
5 So you will stumble in broad daylight,
and your false prophets will fall with you in the night.
And I will destroy Israel, your mother.
6 My people are being destroyed
because they don't know me.
Since you priests refuse to know me,
I refuse to recognize you as my priests.
Since you have forgotten the laws of your God,
I will forget to bless your children.
7 The more priests there are,
the more they sin against me.
They have exchanged the glory of God
for the shame of idols.*

8 "When the people bring their sin offerings, the priests get fed.
So the priests are glad when the people sin!
9 'And what the priests do, the people also do.'
So now I will punish both priests and people
for their wicked deeds.
10 They will eat and still be hungry.

3:2b As in Greek version, which reads *a homer of barley and a wineskin full of wine;* Hebrew reads *a homer* [5 bushels or 220 liters] *of barley and a lethek* [2.5 bushels or 110 liters] *of barley.* **3:3** Or *and I will live with you.* **3:4** Hebrew *ephod,* the vest worn by the priest. **3:5** Hebrew *to David their king.* **4:4** Hebrew *Your people are like those with a complaint against the priests.* **4:7** As in Syriac version and an ancient Hebrew tradition; Masoretic Text reads *I will turn their glory into shame.*

Question 3:1

God told Hosea to love his wife again even though she cheated on him. Who is someone who hurt you, maybe cheated on you, or betrayed your friendship? What would it take for you to forgive them? Just to be clear, this verse isn't saying that you have to get back together with someone if they cheated on you. That was God's instruction to Hosea. You need to ask God what he is asking you to do.

They will play the prostitute and gain nothing from it,
for they have deserted the LORD
11 to worship other gods.

"Wine has robbed my people
of their understanding.
12 They ask a piece of wood for advice!
They think a stick can tell them the future!
Longing after idols
has made them foolish.
They have played the prostitute,
serving other gods and deserting their God.
13 They offer sacrifices to idols on the mountaintops.
They go up into the hills to burn incense
in the pleasant shade of oaks, poplars, and terebinth trees.

"That is why your daughters turn to prostitution,
and your daughters-in-law commit adultery.
14 But why should I punish them
for their prostitution and adultery?
For your men are doing the same thing,
sinning with whores and shrine prostitutes.
O foolish people! You refuse to understand,
so you will be destroyed.

15 "Though you, Israel, are a prostitute,
may Judah not be guilty of such things.
Do not join the false worship at Gilgal or Beth-aven,*
and do not take oaths there in the LORD's name.
16 Israel is stubborn,
like a stubborn heifer.
So should the LORD feed her
like a lamb in a lush pasture?
17 Leave Israel* alone,
because she is married to idolatry.
18 When the rulers of Israel finish their drinking,
off they go to find some prostitutes.
They love shame more than honor.*
19 So a mighty wind will sweep them away.
Their sacrifices to idols will bring them shame.

The Failure of Israel's Leaders

5 1 "Hear this, you priests.
Pay attention, you leaders of Israel.
Listen, you members of the royal family.
Judgment has been handed down against you.
For you have led the people into a snare
by worshiping the idols at Mizpah and Tabor.

4:15 *Beth-aven* means "house of wickedness"; it is being used as another name for Bethel, which means "house of God." 4:17 Hebrew *Ephraim,* referring to the northern kingdom of Israel. 4:18 As in Greek version; the meaning of the Hebrew is uncertain.

2 You have dug a deep pit to trap them at Acacia Grove.*
But I will settle with you for what you have done.
3 I know what you are like, O Ephraim.
You cannot hide yourself from me, O Israel.
You have left me as a prostitute leaves her husband;
you are utterly defiled.
4 Your deeds won't let you return to your God.
You are a prostitute through and through,
and you do not know the LORD.

5 "The arrogance of Israel testifies against her;
Israel and Ephraim will stumble under their load of guilt.
Judah, too, will fall with them.
6 When they come with their flocks and herds
to offer sacrifices to the LORD,
they will not find him,
because he has withdrawn from them.
7 They have betrayed the honor of the LORD,
bearing children that are not his.
Now their false religion will devour them
along with their wealth.*

8 "Sound the alarm in Gibeah!
Blow the trumpet in Ramah!
Raise the battle cry in Beth-aven*!
Lead on into battle, O warriors of Benjamin!
9 One thing is certain, Israel*:
On your day of punishment,
you will become a heap of rubble.

10 "The leaders of Judah have become like thieves.*
So I will pour my anger on them like a waterfall.
11 The people of Israel will be crushed and broken by my judgment
because they are determined to worship idols.*
12 I will destroy Israel as a moth consumes wool.
I will make Judah as weak as rotten wood.

13 "When Israel and Judah saw how sick they were,
Israel turned to Assyria—
to the great king there—
but he could neither help nor cure them.
14 I will be like a lion to Israel,
like a strong young lion to Judah.
I will tear them to pieces!
I will carry them off,
and no one will be left to rescue them.

5:2 Hebrew *at Shittim.* The meaning of the Hebrew for this sentence is uncertain. 5:7 The meaning of the Hebrew is uncertain. 5:8 *Beth-aven* means "house of wickedness"; it is being used as another name for Bethel, which means "house of God." 5:9 Hebrew *Ephraim,* referring to the northern kingdom of Israel; also in 5:11, 12, 13, 14. 5:10 Hebrew *like those who move a boundary marker.* 5:11 Or *determined to follow human commands.* The meaning of the Hebrew is uncertain.

Question 5:13

Hosea came down hard on leaders. He let them know that God was angry and would not be silent about how they turned to idols instead of worshiping the Lord. Are you in a leadership position? What characteristics do you think God wants you to have so that you're a good leader?

Make a Difference 6:6

Personal Relationship

A close relationship. That's why God created us. God wants to have a close relationship with us. The Lord desires that we know him. Well, do you *know* him? Not just *of* him. Do you *know* him personally?

Please pause everything else in your life for a moment to consider this major point of the book of Hosea: God wants to have a personal relationship with you. Commit yourself to God and don't pursue other things that wreck your personal relationship.

Difference Maker

Turn to the back of this Bible and pray through the section on "How to Accept Jesus as Your Lord and Savior."

15 Then I will return to my place
until they admit their guilt and turn to me.
For as soon as trouble comes,
they will earnestly search for me."

A Call to Repentance

6 1 "Come, let us return to the LORD.
He has torn us to pieces;
now he will heal us.
He has injured us;
now he will bandage our wounds.
2 In just a short time he will restore us,
so that we may live in his presence.
3 Oh, that we might know the LORD!
Let us press on to know him.
He will respond to us as surely as the arrival of dawn
or the coming of rains in early spring."

4 "O Israel* and Judah,
what should I do with you?" asks the LORD.
"For your love vanishes like the morning mist
and disappears like dew in the sunlight.
5 I sent my prophets to cut you to pieces—
to slaughter you with my words,
with judgments as inescapable as light.
6 I want you to show love,*
not offer sacrifices.
I want you to know me*
more than I want burnt offerings.
7 But like Adam,* you broke my covenant
and betrayed my trust.

8 "Gilead is a city of sinners,
tracked with footprints of blood.
9 Priests form bands of robbers,
waiting in ambush for their victims.
They murder travelers along the road to Shechem
and practice every kind of sin.
10 Yes, I have seen something horrible in Ephraim and Israel:
My people are defiled by prostituting themselves with other gods!

11 "O Judah, a harvest of punishment is also waiting for you,
though I wanted to restore the fortunes of my people.

Israel's Love for Wickedness

7 1 "I want to heal Israel, but its* sins are too great.
Samaria is filled with liars.

6:4 Hebrew *Ephraim,* referring to the northern kingdom of Israel. 6:6a Greek version translates this Hebrew term as *to show mercy.* Compare Matt 9:13; 12:7. 6:6b Hebrew *to know God.* 6:7 Or *But at Adam.* 7:1 Hebrew *Ephraim's,* referring to the northern kingdom of Israel; similarly in 7:8, 11.

Thieves are on the inside
    and bandits on the outside!
2 Its people don't realize
    that I am watching them.
Their sinful deeds are all around them,
    and I see them all.

3 "The people entertain the king with their wickedness,
    and the princes laugh at their lies.
4 They are all adulterers,
    always aflame with lust.
They are like an oven that is kept hot
    while the baker is kneading the dough.
5 On royal holidays, the princes get drunk with wine,
    carousing with those who mock them.
6 Their hearts are like an oven
    blazing with intrigue.
Their plot smolders* through the night,
    and in the morning it breaks out like a raging fire.
7 Burning like an oven,
    they consume their leaders.
They kill their kings one after another,
    and no one cries to me for help.

8 "The people of Israel mingle with godless foreigners,
    making themselves as worthless as a half-baked cake!
9 Worshiping foreign gods has sapped their strength,
    but they don't even know it.
Their hair is gray,
    but they don't realize they're old and weak.
10 Their arrogance testifies against them,
    yet they don't return to the LORD their God
    or even try to find him.

11 "The people of Israel have become like silly, witless doves,
    first calling to Egypt, then flying to Assyria for help.
12 But as they fly about,
    I will throw my net over them
and bring them down like a bird from the sky.
    I will punish them for all the evil they do.*

13 "What sorrow awaits those who have deserted me!
    Let them die, for they have rebelled against me.
I wanted to redeem them,
    but they have told lies about me.
14 They do not cry out to me with sincere hearts.
    Instead, they sit on their couches and wail.
They cut themselves,* begging foreign gods for grain and new wine,
    and they turn away from me.

7:6 Hebrew *Their baker sleeps.* 7:12 Hebrew *I will punish them because of what was reported against them in the assembly.* 7:14 As in Greek version; Hebrew reads *They gather together.*

Question 8:6

Why do we drift toward idols? Why are we so easily distracted by things created by our own hands? Why do we so quickly give these things the allegiance of our time and thoughts? It is so obvious that these things are not God, nor could they ever replace God in our lives. What things have snagged your heart that replace God?

15 I trained them and made them strong,
yet now they plot evil against me.
16 They look everywhere except to the Most High.
They are as useless as a crooked bow.
Their leaders will be killed by their enemies
because of their insolence toward me.
Then the people of Egypt
will laugh at them.

Israel Harvests the Whirlwind

8 1 "Sound the alarm!
The enemy descends like an eagle on the people of the LORD,
for they have broken my covenant
and revolted against my law.
2 Now Israel pleads with me,
'Help us, for you are our God!'
3 But it is too late.
The people of Israel have rejected what is good,
and now their enemies will chase after them.
4 The people have appointed kings without my consent,
and princes without my approval.
By making idols for themselves from their silver and gold,
they have brought about their own destruction.

5 "O Samaria, I reject this calf—
this idol you have made.
My fury burns against you.
How long will you be incapable of innocence?
6 This calf you worship, O Israel,
was crafted by your own hands!
It is not God!
Therefore, it must be smashed to bits.

7 "They have planted the wind
and will harvest the whirlwind.
The stalks of grain wither
and produce nothing to eat.
And even if there is any grain,
foreigners will eat it.
8 The people of Israel have been swallowed up;
they lie among the nations like an old discarded pot.
9 Like a wild donkey looking for a mate,
they have gone up to Assyria.
The people of Israel* have sold themselves—
sold themselves to many lovers.
10 But though they have sold themselves to many allies,
I will now gather them together for judgment.
Then they will writhe
under the burden of the great king.

8:9 Hebrew *Ephraim,* referring to the northern kingdom of Israel; also in 8:11.

11 "Israel has built many altars to take away sin,
but these very altars became places for sinning!
12 Even though I gave them all my laws,
they act as if those laws don't apply to them.
13 The people love to offer sacrifices to me,
feasting on the meat,
but I do not accept their sacrifices.
I will hold my people accountable for their sins,
and I will punish them.
They will return to Egypt.
14 Israel has forgotten its Maker and built great palaces,
and Judah has fortified its cities.
Therefore, I will send down fire on their cities
and will burn up their fortresses."

Hosea Announces Israel's Punishment

9 1 O people of Israel,
do not rejoice as other nations do.
For you have been unfaithful to your God,
hiring yourselves out like prostitutes,
worshiping other gods on every threshing floor.
2 So now your harvests will be too small to feed you.
There will be no grapes for making new wine.
3 You may no longer stay here in the LORD's land.
Instead, you will return to Egypt,
and in Assyria you will eat food
that is ceremonially unclean.
4 There you will make no offerings of wine to the LORD.
None of your sacrifices there will please him.
They will be unclean, like food touched by a person in mourning.
All who present such sacrifices will be defiled.
They may eat this food themselves,
but they may not offer it to the LORD.
5 What then will you do on festival days?
How will you observe the LORD's festivals?
6 Even if you escape destruction from Assyria,
Egypt will conquer you, and Memphis* will bury you.
Nettles will take over your treasures of silver;
thistles will invade your ruined homes.

7 The time of Israel's punishment has come;
the day of payment is here.
Soon Israel will know this all too well.
Because of your great sin and hostility,
you say, "The prophets are crazy
and the inspired men are fools!"
8 The prophet is a watchman over Israel* for my God,
yet traps are laid for him wherever he goes.
He faces hostility even in the house of God.

9:6 Memphis was the capital of northern Egypt. 9:8 Hebrew *Ephraim,* referring to the northern kingdom of Israel; also in 9:11, 13, 16.

9 The things my people do are as depraved
as what they did in Gibeah long ago.
God will not forget.
He will surely punish them for their sins.

10 The LORD says, "O Israel, when I first found you,
it was like finding fresh grapes in the desert.
When I saw your ancestors,
it was like seeing the first ripe figs of the season.
But then they deserted me for Baal-peor,
giving themselves to that shameful idol.
Soon they became vile,
as vile as the god they worshiped.
11 The glory of Israel will fly away like a bird,
for your children will not be born
or grow in the womb
or even be conceived.
12 Even if you do have children who grow up,
I will take them from you.
It will be a terrible day when I turn away
and leave you alone.
13 I have watched Israel become as beautiful as Tyre.
But now Israel will bring out her children for slaughter."

14 O LORD, what should I request for your people?
I will ask for wombs that don't give birth
and breasts that give no milk.

15 The LORD says, "All their wickedness began at Gilgal;
there I began to hate them.
I will drive them from my land
because of their evil actions.
I will love them no more
because all their leaders are rebels.
16 The people of Israel are struck down.
Their roots are dried up,
and they will bear no more fruit.
And if they give birth,
I will slaughter their beloved children."

17 My God will reject the people of Israel
because they will not listen or obey.
They will be wanderers,
homeless among the nations.

The LORD's Judgment against Israel

10 1 How prosperous Israel is—
a luxuriant vine loaded with fruit.
But the richer the people get,
the more pagan altars they build.

The more bountiful their harvests,
the more beautiful their sacred pillars.
2 The hearts of the people are fickle;
they are guilty and must be punished.
The LORD will break down their altars
and smash their sacred pillars.
3 Then they will say, "We have no king
because we didn't fear the LORD.
But even if we had a king,
what could he do for us anyway?"
4 They spout empty words
and make covenants they don't intend to keep.
So injustice springs up among them
like poisonous weeds in a farmer's field.

5 The people of Samaria tremble in fear
for their calf idol at Beth-aven,*
and they mourn for it.
Though its priests rejoice over it,
its glory will be stripped away.*
6 This idol will be carted away to Assyria,
a gift to the great king there.
Ephraim will be ridiculed and Israel will be shamed,
because its people have trusted in this idol.
7 Samaria and its king will be cut off;
they will float away like driftwood on an ocean wave.
8 And the pagan shrines of Aven,* the place of Israel's sin, will crumble.
Thorns and thistles will grow up around their altars.
They will beg the mountains, "Bury us!"
and plead with the hills, "Fall on us!"

9 The LORD says, "O Israel, ever since Gibeah,
there has been only sin and more sin!
You have made no progress whatsoever.
Was it not right that the wicked men of Gibeah were attacked?
10 Now whenever it fits my plan,
I will attack you, too.
I will call out the armies of the nations
to punish you for your multiplied sins.

11 "Israel* is like a trained heifer treading out the grain—
an easy job she loves.
But I will put a heavy yoke on her tender neck.
I will force Judah to pull the plow
and Israel* to break up the hard ground.
12 I said, 'Plant the good seeds of righteousness,

Prayer **10:12**

God, sometimes it feels like my heart is as hard as dirt when it comes to you. I keep choosing my way instead of your way. Please make my hard heart soft. I want my life to be one of love. Amen.

10:5a *Beth-aven* means "house of wickedness"; it is being used as another name for Bethel, which means "house of God." **10:5b** Or *will be taken away into exile.* **10:8** *Aven* is a reference to Beth-aven; see 10:5a and the note there. **10:11a** Hebrew *Ephraim,* referring to the northern kingdom of Israel. **10:11b** Hebrew *Jacob.* The names "Jacob" and "Israel" are often interchanged throughout the Old Testament, referring sometimes to the individual patriarch and sometimes to the nation.

Question 11:1–11

Have you ever been in a parking lot and watched a parent call their child to come to them? Perhaps the more they call, the farther the kid runs in the other direction. The parent knows the kid is in danger, but the kid wants to do their own thing. In Hosea 11, Hosea reminded Israel of how deeply God loved them like a parent loves their child, but the more God called to them, the further away Israel moved. Are you running toward God or away from God right now?

and you will harvest a crop of love.
Plow up the hard ground of your hearts,
for now is the time to seek the LORD,
that he may come
and shower righteousness upon you.'

13 "But you have cultivated wickedness
and harvested a thriving crop of sins.
You have eaten the fruit of lies—
trusting in your military might,
believing that great armies
could make your nation safe.
14 Now the terrors of war
will rise among your people.
All your fortifications will fall,
just as when Shalman destroyed Beth-arbel.
Even mothers and children
were dashed to death there.
15 You will share that fate, Bethel,
because of your great wickedness.
When the day of judgment dawns,
the king of Israel will be completely destroyed.

The LORD's Love for Israel

11 1 "When Israel was a child, I loved him,
and I called my son out of Egypt.
2 But the more I called to him,
the farther he moved from me,*
offering sacrifices to the images of Baal
and burning incense to idols.
3 I myself taught Israel* how to walk,
leading him along by the hand.
But he doesn't know or even care
that it was I who took care of him.
4 I led Israel along
with my ropes of kindness and love.
I lifted the yoke from his neck,
and I myself stooped to feed him.

5 "But since my people refuse to return to me,
they will return to Egypt
and will be forced to serve Assyria.
6 War will swirl through their cities;
their enemies will crash through their gates.
They will destroy them,
trapping them in their own evil plans.
7 For my people are determined to desert me.
They call me the Most High,
but they don't truly honor me.

11:2 As in Greek version; Hebrew reads *the more they called to him, the farther he moved from them.*
11:3 Hebrew *Ephraim,* referring to the northern kingdom of Israel; also in 11:8, 9, 12.

8 "Oh, how can I give you up, Israel?
How can I let you go?
How can I destroy you like Admah
or demolish you like Zeboiim?
My heart is torn within me,
and my compassion overflows.
9 No, I will not unleash my fierce anger.
I will not completely destroy Israel,
for I am God and not a mere mortal.
I am the Holy One living among you,
and I will not come to destroy.
10 For someday the people will follow me.
I, the LORD, will roar like a lion.
And when I roar,
my people will return trembling from the west.
11 Like a flock of birds, they will come from Egypt.
Trembling like doves, they will return from Assyria.
And I will bring them home again,"
says the LORD.

Charges against Israel and Judah

12*Israel surrounds me with lies and deceit,
but Judah still obeys God
and is faithful to the Holy One.*

Question 11:9

Sometimes we like to think that God is just like us. He's not. While we can lose our tempers when someone wrongs us, God knows how to contain his anger. Still, we can't forget that God is powerful. Sometimes it's a quiet power. Other times, it's a roaring power! If you've ever experienced God's roaring power, it can have you shaking in your boots. When is a time that you sensed God's power? What about his patience?

12

1*The people of Israel* feed on the wind;
they chase after the east wind all day long.
They pile up lies and violence;
they are making an alliance with Assyria
while sending olive oil to buy support from Egypt.

2 Now the LORD is bringing charges against Judah.
He is about to punish Jacob* for all his deceitful ways,
and pay him back for all he has done.
3 Even in the womb,
Jacob struggled with his brother;
when he became a man,
he even fought with God.
4 Yes, he wrestled with the angel and won.
He wept and pleaded for a blessing from him.
There at Bethel he met God face to face,
and God spoke to him*—
5 the LORD God of Heaven's Armies,
the LORD is his name!
6 So now, come back to your God.
Act with love and justice,
and always depend on him.

11:12a Verse 11:12 is numbered 12:1 in Hebrew text. 11:12b Or *and Judah is unruly against God, the faithful Holy One.* The meaning of the Hebrew is uncertain. 12:1a Verses 12:1-14 are numbered 12:2-15 in Hebrew text. 12:1b Hebrew *Ephraim,* referring to the northern kingdom of Israel; also in 12:8, 14. 12:2 *Jacob* sounds like the Hebrew word for "deceiver." 12:4 As in Greek and Syriac versions; Hebrew reads *to us.*

Make a Difference 13:4

Acknowledge

The story of Hosea is that we should commit ourselves to the Lord and the Lord alone. We were created to be in relationship with God. That's why God is not satisfied when we add other competing commitments to our lives. The truth is that we aren't satisfied when we cheat on him either.

Difference Maker

Ask someone if they'd like to study this Bible with you so that you both can have a deeper relationship with God.

7 But no, the people are like crafty merchants
selling from dishonest scales—
they love to cheat.
8 Israel boasts, "I am rich!
I've made a fortune all by myself!
No one has caught me cheating!
My record is spotless!"

9 "But I am the LORD your God,
who rescued you from slavery in Egypt.
And I will make you live in tents again,
as you do each year at the Festival of Shelters.*
10 I sent my prophets to warn you
with many visions and parables."

11 But the people of Gilead are worthless
because of their idol worship.
And in Gilgal, too, they sacrifice bulls;
their altars are lined up like the heaps of stone
along the edges of a plowed field.
12 Jacob fled to the land of Aram,
and there he* earned a wife by tending sheep.
13 Then by a prophet
the LORD brought Jacob's descendants* out
of Egypt;
and by that prophet
they were protected.
14 But the people of Israel
have bitterly provoked the LORD,
so their Lord will now sentence them to death
in payment for their sins.

The LORD's Anger against Israel

13 1 When the tribe of Ephraim spoke,
the people shook with fear,
for that tribe was important in Israel.
But the people of Ephraim sinned by worshiping Baal
and thus sealed their destruction.
2 Now they continue to sin by making silver idols,
images shaped skillfully with human hands.
"Sacrifice to these," they cry,
"and kiss the calf idols!"
3 Therefore, they will disappear like the morning mist,
like dew in the morning sun,
like chaff blown by the wind,
like smoke from a chimney.

4 "I have been the LORD your God
ever since I brought you out of Egypt.

12:9 Hebrew *as in the days of your appointed feast.* 12:12 Hebrew *Israel.* See note on 10:11b.
12:13 Hebrew *brought Israel.* See note on 10:11b.

You must acknowledge no God but me,
    for there is no other savior.
5 I took care of you in the wilderness,
    in that dry and thirsty land.
6 But when you had eaten and were satisfied,
    you became proud and forgot me.
7 So now I will attack you like a lion,
    like a leopard that lurks along the road.
8 Like a bear whose cubs have been taken away,
    I will tear out your heart.
I will devour you like a hungry lioness
    and mangle you like a wild animal.

9 "You are about to be destroyed, O Israel—
    yes, by me, your only helper.
10 Now where is* your king?
    Let him save you!
Where are all the leaders of the land,
    the king and the officials you demanded of me?
11 In my anger I gave you kings,
    and in my fury I took them away.

12 "Ephraim's guilt has been collected,
    and his sin has been stored up for punishment.
13 Pain has come to the people
    like the pain of childbirth,
but they are like a child
    who resists being born.
The moment of birth has arrived,
    but they stay in the womb!

14 "Should I ransom them from the grave*?
    Should I redeem them from death?
O death, bring on your terrors!
    O grave, bring on your plagues!*
    For I will not take pity on them.
15 Ephraim was the most fruitful of all his brothers,
    but the east wind—a blast from the LORD—
    will arise in the desert.
All their flowing springs will run dry,
    and all their wells will disappear.
Every precious thing they own
    will be plundered and carried away.
16*The people of Samaria
    must bear the consequences of their guilt
    because they rebelled against their God.
They will be killed by an invading army,

13:10 As in Greek and Syriac versions and Latin Vulgate; Hebrew reads *I will be.* **13:14a** Hebrew *Sheol;* also in 13:14b. **13:14b** Greek version reads *O death, where is your punishment? / O grave* [Hades], *where is your sting?* Compare 1 Cor 15:55. **13:16** Verse 16 is numbered 14:1 in Hebrew text.

Prayer 14:4

God, if I'm honest, I've cheated on you. I've chosen to love other things more than I love you. I've decided to walk away from you instead of toward you. Please forgive me. Thank you that there are no limits to your love and forgiveness. Amen.

Question 14:8

Thinking about the story arc of the Bible, why do you think God chose this metaphor to end the book of Hosea?

their little ones dashed to death against the ground,
their pregnant women ripped open by swords."

Healing for the Repentant

14 1*Return, O Israel, to the LORD your God,
for your sins have brought you down.
2 Bring your confessions, and return to the LORD.
Say to him,
"Forgive all our sins and graciously receive us,
so that we may offer you our praises.*
3 Assyria cannot save us,
nor can our warhorses.
Never again will we say to the idols we have made,
'You are our gods.'
No, in you alone
do the orphans find mercy."

4 The LORD says,
"Then I will heal you of your faithlessness;
my love will know no bounds,
for my anger will be gone forever.
5 I will be to Israel
like a refreshing dew from heaven.
Israel will blossom like the lily;
it will send roots deep into the soil
like the cedars in Lebanon.
6 Its branches will spread out like beautiful olive trees,
as fragrant as the cedars of Lebanon.
7 My people will again live under my shade.
They will flourish like grain and blossom like grapevines.
They will be as fragrant as the wines of Lebanon.

8 "O Israel,* stay away from idols!
I am the one who answers your prayers and cares for you.
I am like a tree that is always green;
all your fruit comes from me."

9 Let those who are wise understand these things.
Let those with discernment listen carefully.
The paths of the LORD are true and right,
and righteous people live by walking in them.
But in those paths sinners stumble and fall.

14:1 Verses 14:1-9 are numbered 14:2-10 in Hebrew text. **14:2** As in Greek and Syriac versions, which read *may repay the fruit of our lips;* Hebrew reads *may repay the bulls of our lips.* **14:8** Hebrew *Ephraim,* referring to the northern kingdom of Israel.

Joel Introduction

You know those times when you wake yourself up in the middle of a bad dream? Maybe you're running from something that's trying to devour you, and you just can't go fast enough, and the dream becomes more and more intense. Just when the monster is hot on your heels, right when the creature is about to catch you in its maw, you wake up with a startling feeling—unsettled and shaking in a sweat. The trick with a dream like that is rather simple: change the ending. In your imagination, you can give the horror story you've just dreamed an epic ending in which you defeat the monster and are safe and sound.

This is how God made a difference through the prophet Joel. He gave Joel an imaginative vision of how to change the ending. His people were in the midst of catastrophe, and they were going to be snatched up and destroyed. He told all those who were sleeping and all those without hope to wake up and turn to God. Joel's message from God for the people is this: the story arc will change as God's people change their hearts!

Instead of the destruction of fire, God pours out his Spirit. Instead of having nowhere to run, God's people find sanctuary with God. Instead of destruction from an unforgiving enemy, God's people can experience his open arms of mercy, compassion, forgiveness, and unfailing love. We can make a difference when we can change the ending for people by inviting others to open their hearts to this same gracious God.

Joel

1 The LORD gave this message to Joel son of Pethuel.

Mourning over the Locust Plague

2 Hear this, you leaders of the people.
Listen, all who live in the land.
In all your history,
has anything like this happened before?
3 Tell your children about it in the years to come,
and let your children tell their children.
Pass the story down from generation
to generation.

4 After the cutting locusts finished eating the crops,
the swarming locusts took what was left!
After them came the hopping locusts,
and then the stripping locusts,* too!

5 Wake up, you drunkards, and weep!
Wail, all you wine-drinkers!
All the grapes are ruined,
and all your sweet wine is gone.
6 A vast army of locusts* has invaded my land,
a terrible army too numerous to count.
Its teeth are like lions' teeth,
its fangs like those of a lioness.
7 It has destroyed my grapevines
and ruined my fig trees,
stripping their bark and destroying it,
leaving the branches white and bare.

8 Weep like a bride dressed in black,
mourning the death of her husband.
9 For there is no grain or wine
to offer at the Temple of the LORD.
So the priests are in mourning.
The ministers of the LORD are weeping.
10 The fields are ruined,
the land is stripped bare.
The grain is destroyed,
the grapes have shriveled,
and the olive oil is gone.

1:4 The precise identification of the four kinds of locusts mentioned here is uncertain.
1:6 Hebrew *A nation.*

Question 1:14

Announce a time of fasting. What if you were to get some friends together and fast for one meal? What kind of a difference could you make if you used the energy you would have spent on eating to pray? What kind of a difference could you make if you took the money you would have spent on eating and gave it to a charity?

11 Despair, all you farmers!
Wail, all you vine growers!
Weep, because the wheat and barley—
all the crops of the field—are ruined.
12 The grapevines have dried up,
and the fig trees have withered.
The pomegranate trees, palm trees, and apple trees—
all the fruit trees—have dried up.
And the people's joy has dried up with them.

13 Dress yourselves in burlap and weep, you priests!
Wail, you who serve before the altar!
Come, spend the night in burlap,
you ministers of my God.
For there is no grain or wine
to offer at the Temple of your God.
14 Announce a time of fasting;
call the people together for a solemn meeting.
Bring the leaders
and all the people of the land
into the Temple of the LORD your God,
and cry out to him there.
15 The day of the LORD is near,
the day when destruction comes from the Almighty.
How terrible that day will be!

16 Our food disappears before our very eyes.
No joyful celebrations are held in the house of our God.
17 The seeds die in the parched ground,
and the grain crops fail.
The barns stand empty,
and granaries are abandoned.
18 How the animals moan with hunger!
The herds of cattle wander about confused,
because they have no pasture.
The flocks of sheep and goats bleat in misery.

19 LORD, help us!
The fire has consumed the wilderness pastures,
and flames have burned up all the trees.
20 Even the wild animals cry out to you
because the streams have dried up,
and fire has consumed the wilderness pastures.

Locusts Invade like an Army

2 1 Sound the trumpet in Jerusalem*!
Raise the alarm on my holy mountain!
Let everyone tremble in fear
because the day of the LORD is upon us.

2:1 Hebrew *Zion;* also in 2:15, 23.

Make a Difference

2:12–19

Now Is the Time

The Lord pleaded with his people, "Turn to me now, while there is time" (v. 12).

The Lord was giving an opportunity to his people here. He urged them to seize that chance with the right attitude—an attitude of deep sadness. He expected them to tear their hearts. The Lord is merciful and compassionate, slow to get angry and filled with unfailing love, eager to relent. He let his heart be broken for his wayward people, and he expected his people would have broken hearts to return to him (vv. 13, 15).

Difference Maker

Do you need to turn to God right now? Ask God to remove your sin and come to your rescue. You could use the resource in the back of this Bible called "How to Accept Jesus as Your Lord and Savior" to help you get right with God.

2 It is a day of darkness and gloom,
a day of thick clouds and deep blackness.
Suddenly, like dawn spreading across the mountains,
a great and mighty army appears.
Nothing like it has been seen before
or will ever be seen again.

3 Fire burns in front of them,
and flames follow after them.
Ahead of them the land lies
as beautiful as the Garden of Eden.
Behind them is nothing but desolation;
not one thing escapes.
4 They look like horses;
they charge forward like warhorses.*
5 Look at them as they leap along the mountaintops.
Listen to the noise they make—like the rumbling of chariots,
like the roar of fire sweeping across a field of stubble,
or like a mighty army moving into battle.

6 Fear grips all the people;
every face grows pale with terror.
7 The attackers march like warriors
and scale city walls like soldiers.
Straight forward they march,
never breaking rank.
8 They never jostle each other;
each moves in exactly the right position.
They break through defenses
without missing a step.
9 They swarm over the city
and run along its walls.
They enter all the houses,
climbing like thieves through the windows.
10 The earth quakes as they advance,
and the heavens tremble.
The sun and moon grow dark,
and the stars no longer shine.

11 The LORD is at the head of the column.
He leads them with a shout.
This is his mighty army,
and they follow his orders.
The day of the LORD is an awesome, terrible thing.
Who can possibly survive?

A Call to Repentance

12 That is why the LORD says,
"Turn to me now, while there is time.

2:4 Or *like charioteers.*

Give me your hearts.
Come with fasting, weeping, and mourning.
13 Don't tear your clothing in your grief,
but tear your hearts instead."
Return to the LORD your God,
for he is merciful and compassionate,
slow to get angry and filled with unfailing love.
He is eager to relent and not punish.
14 Who knows? Perhaps he will give you a reprieve,
sending you a blessing instead of this curse.
Perhaps you will be able to offer grain and wine
to the LORD your God as before.

15 Blow the ram's horn in Jerusalem!
Announce a time of fasting;
call the people together
for a solemn meeting.
16 Gather all the people—
the elders, the children, and even the babies.
Call the bridegroom from his quarters
and the bride from her private room.
17 Let the priests, who minister in the LORD's presence,
stand and weep between the entry room to the Temple
and the altar.
Let them pray, "Spare your people, LORD!
Don't let your special possession become an object of mockery.
Don't let them become a joke for unbelieving foreigners who say,
'Has the God of Israel left them?'"

The LORD's Promise of Restoration

18 Then the LORD will pity his people
and jealously guard the honor of his land.
19 The LORD will reply,
"Look! I am sending you grain and new wine and olive oil,
enough to satisfy your needs.
You will no longer be an object of mockery
among the surrounding nations.
20 I will drive away these armies from the north.
I will send them into the parched wastelands.
Those in the front will be driven into the Dead Sea,
and those at the rear into the Mediterranean.*
The stench of their rotting bodies will rise over the land."

Surely the LORD has done great things!
21 Don't be afraid, O land.
Be glad now and rejoice,
for the LORD has done great things.
22 Don't be afraid, you animals of the field,
for the wilderness pastures will soon be green.

Prayer 2:13

Gracious God, I'm easily angered and unreliably loving. As I open my heart to receive your patience, mercy, compassion, and unfailing love, please help me to reflect those same qualities into this world that you love. As your Spirit pours into me, please show me how I can overflow your grace and love to the people I'll encounter today. In Jesus' name, amen.

2:20 Hebrew *into the eastern sea, . . . into the western sea.*

The trees will again be filled with fruit;
fig trees and grapevines will be loaded down once more.
23 Rejoice, you people of Jerusalem!
Rejoice in the LORD your God!
For the rain he sends demonstrates his faithfulness.
Once more the autumn rains will come,
as well as the rains of spring.
24 The threshing floors will again be piled high with grain,
and the presses will overflow with new wine and olive oil.

25 The LORD says, "I will give you back what you lost
to the swarming locusts, the hopping locusts,
the stripping locusts, and the cutting locusts.*
It was I who sent this great destroying army against you.
26 Once again you will have all the food you want,
and you will praise the LORD your God,
who does these miracles for you.
Never again will my people be disgraced.
27 Then you will know that I am among my people Israel,
that I am the LORD your God, and there is no other.
Never again will my people be disgraced.

The LORD's Promise of His Spirit

28*"Then, after doing all those things,
I will pour out my Spirit upon all people.
Your sons and daughters will prophesy.
Your old men will dream dreams,
and your young men will see visions.
29 In those days I will pour out my Spirit
even on servants—men and women alike.
30 And I will cause wonders in the heavens and on the earth—
blood and fire and columns of smoke.
31 The sun will become dark,
and the moon will turn blood red
before that great and terrible* day of the LORD arrives.
32 But everyone who calls on the name of the LORD
will be saved,
for some on Mount Zion in Jerusalem will escape,
just as the LORD has said.
These will be among the survivors
whom the LORD has called.

Judgment against Enemy Nations

3 1*"At the time of those events," says the LORD,
"when I restore the prosperity of Judah and Jerusalem,
2 I will gather the armies of the world
into the valley of Jehoshaphat.*

2:25 The precise identification of the four kinds of locusts mentioned here is uncertain.
2:28 Verses 2:28-32 are numbered 3:1-5 in Hebrew text. 2:31 Greek version reads *glorious.*
3:1 Verses 3:1-21 are numbered 4:1-21 in Hebrew text. 3:2 *Jehoshaphat* means "the LORD judges."

Make a Difference 2:23

Year-Round Hope

The Psalms tell us to look ahead to the future to what God will do. Don't get lost in the calamities that have happened because God will restore all things. He proves it each year by the seasons. Just as the leaves change colors, just as the weather brings rich moisture, he, too, will bring blessing to his people.

Difference Maker

Gather some friends and make plans in whatever season it is to do a practical project that would give someone unexpected hope.

Make a Difference 2:28-32

Connect the Dots

In Acts 2:14-21, Peter had just seen and experienced the Holy Spirit being poured out in amazing ways and connected the dots to this very section of the book of Joel. Peter realized that Joel was talking about the moment that he and his friends were experiencing on Pentecost. When someone does a connect-the-dots activity, a new picture emerges where there was empty space. In a similar way, when we connect the dots of our experiences with God's promises in Scripture, we see a new picture of what God is up to in the world.

Difference Maker

Read the second chapter of the book of Acts. Put yourself in Peter's perspective and connect the dots back to Joel 2:28-32. What picture emerges?

There I will judge them
for harming my people, my special possession,
for scattering my people among the nations,
and for dividing up my land.
3 They threw dice* to decide which of my people
would be their slaves.
They traded boys to obtain prostitutes
and sold girls for enough wine to get drunk.

4 "What do you have against me, Tyre and Sidon and you cities of Philistia?
Are you trying to take revenge on me? If you are, then watch out! I will strike
swiftly and pay you back for everything you have done. 5 You have taken my
silver and gold and all my precious treasures, and have carried them off to
your pagan temples. 6 You have sold the people of Judah and Jerusalem to
the Greeks,* so they could take them far from their homeland.
7 "But I will bring them back from all the places to which you sold them,
and I will pay you back for everything you have done. 8 I will sell your sons
and daughters to the people of Judah, and they will sell them to the people
of Arabia,* a nation far away. I, the LORD, have spoken!"

9 Say to the nations far and wide:
"Get ready for war!
Call out your best warriors.
Let all your fighting men advance for the attack.
10 Hammer your plowshares into swords
and your pruning hooks into spears.
Train even your weaklings to be warriors.
11 Come quickly, all you nations everywhere.
Gather together in the valley."

And now, O LORD, call out your warriors!

12 "Let the nations be called to arms.
Let them march to the valley of Jehoshaphat.
There I, the LORD, will sit
to pronounce judgment on them all.
13 Swing the sickle,
for the harvest is ripe.*
Come, tread the grapes,
for the winepress is full.
The storage vats are overflowing
with the wickedness of these people."

14 Thousands upon thousands are waiting in the valley
of decision.
There the day of the LORD will soon arrive.
15 The sun and moon will grow dark,
and the stars will no longer shine.
16 The LORD's voice will roar from Zion

3:3 Hebrew *They cast lots.* **3:6** Hebrew *to the peoples of Javan.* **3:8** Hebrew *to the Sabeans.*
3:13 Greek version reads *for the harvest time has come.* Compare Mark 4:29.

Prayer 3:20

Lord, you have a vision and plan that lasts through the generations. Give me a faith that doesn't revolve just around my lifetime. Let me see your eternal plan to pardon sin and pour out your Spirit. Amen.

and thunder from Jerusalem,
and the heavens and the earth will shake.
But the LORD will be a refuge for his people,
a strong fortress for the people of Israel.

Blessings for God's People

17 "Then you will know that I, the LORD your God,
live in Zion, my holy mountain.
Jerusalem will be holy forever,
and foreign armies will never conquer her again.
18 In that day the mountains will drip with sweet wine,
and the hills will flow with milk.
Water will fill the streambeds of Judah,
and a fountain will burst forth from the LORD's Temple,
watering the arid valley of acacias.*
19 But Egypt will become a wasteland
and Edom will become a wilderness,
because they attacked the people of Judah
and killed innocent people in their land.

20 "But Judah will be filled with people forever,
and Jerusalem will endure through all generations.
21 I will pardon my people's crimes,
which I have not yet pardoned;
and I, the LORD, will make my home
in Jerusalem* with my people."

3:18 Hebrew *valley of Shittim*. 3:21 Hebrew *Zion*.

Amos Introduction

The book of Amos is an alarmingly depressing book and, therefore, is often an overlooked section of the Old Testament. Wading into the soul-gutting judgments of Amos is a difficult task. Getting past the shocking promises of destruction is a slog. When people mention their favorite parts of the Bible, hardly anyone ever mentions Amos. If they did, you might have reason to be concerned. It is not an enjoyable book.

With its sin and calamity, the book of Amos knocks the wind out of your soul. God accused the people of Tyre of selling whole villages of Israelites into slavery. He accused people from Ammon of ripping "open pregnant women with their swords" (Amos 1:13). Israel itself had been in a violent civil war between the Northern Kingdom (Israel) and the Southern Kingdom (Judah). In this book, it seems that God had had enough.

Amos was an ordinary man living a rather ordinary life. Then God upended his routines, calling him to confront those with whom God was most upset. This scruffy-looking shepherd soon found himself calling down doom and standing before an angry king.

In a day when culture tempts us to be happy but has sabotaged us with anxiety, the book of Amos actually has much to say to us. We have much to learn about who God is, who we are, and the restorative fight that God engages against humanity's worst entrapments of sin. Sometimes being honest and up-front about the most disturbing aspects of our lives is the only way to move toward accepting freedom and hope.

Story Arc

Amos

AMOS

Amos

1 This message was given to Amos, a shepherd from the town of Tekoa in Judah. He received this message in visions two years before the earthquake, when Uzziah was king of Judah and Jeroboam II, the son of Jehoash,* was king of Israel.

2 This is what he saw and heard:

"The LORD's voice will roar from Zion
  and thunder from Jerusalem!
The lush pastures of the shepherds will dry up;
  the grass on Mount Carmel will wither and die."

God's Judgment on Israel's Neighbors

3 This is what the LORD says:

"The people of Damascus have sinned again and again,*
  and I will not let them go unpunished!
They beat down my people in Gilead
  as grain is threshed with iron sledges.
4 So I will send down fire on King Hazael's palace,
  and the fortresses of King Ben-hadad will
    be destroyed.
5 I will break down the gates of Damascus
  and slaughter the people in the valley of Aven.
I will destroy the ruler in Beth-eden,
  and the people of Aram will go as captives to Kir,"
  says the LORD.

6 This is what the LORD says:

"The people of Gaza have sinned again and again,
  and I will not let them go unpunished!
They sent whole villages into exile,
  selling them as slaves to Edom.
7 So I will send down fire on the walls of Gaza,
  and all its fortresses will be destroyed.
8 I will slaughter the people of Ashdod
  and destroy the king of Ashkelon.
Then I will turn to attack Ekron,
  and the few Philistines still left will be killed,"
  says the Sovereign LORD.

Story Arc **1:1**

Amos

Amos was a farmer, shepherd, and arborist (Amos 7:14). He was a rancher of herds of sheep and took care of groves of sycamore-fig trees. He seems to have had a stable, successful career. Then God changed everything. How do you think you would respond if God suddenly called you to speak a bold message about sin and truth to the community around you? What do you think you might need to be willing to give up to do that?

Jon 1:1 ►

1:1 Hebrew *Joash,* a variant spelling of Jehoash. 1:3 Hebrew *have committed three sins, even four;* also in 1:6, 9, 11, 13.

9 This is what the LORD says:

"The people of Tyre have sinned again and again,
and I will not let them go unpunished!
They broke their treaty of brotherhood with Israel,
selling whole villages as slaves to Edom.
10 So I will send down fire on the walls of Tyre,
and all its fortresses will be destroyed."

11 This is what the LORD says:

"The people of Edom have sinned again and again,
and I will not let them go unpunished!
They chased down their relatives, the Israelites, with swords,
showing them no mercy.
In their rage, they slashed them continually
and were unrelenting in their anger.
12 So I will send down fire on Teman,
and the fortresses of Bozrah will be destroyed."

13 This is what the LORD says:

"The people of Ammon have sinned again and again,
and I will not let them go unpunished!
When they attacked Gilead to extend their borders,
they ripped open pregnant women with their swords.
14 So I will send down fire on the walls of Rabbah,
and all its fortresses will be destroyed.
The battle will come upon them with shouts,
like a whirlwind in a mighty storm.
15 And their king* and his princes will go into exile together,"
says the LORD.

2 This is what the LORD says:

"The people of Moab have sinned again and again,*
and I will not let them go unpunished!
They desecrated the bones of Edom's king,
burning them to ashes.
2 So I will send down fire on the land of Moab,
and all the fortresses in Kerioth will be destroyed.
The people will fall in the noise of battle,
as the warriors shout and the ram's horn sounds.
3 And I will destroy their king
and slaughter all their princes,"
says the LORD.

God's Judgment on Judah and Israel

4 This is what the LORD says:

1:15 Hebrew *malcam*, possibly referring to their god Molech. 2:1 Hebrew *have committed three sins, even four*; also in 2:4, 6.

"The people of Judah have sinned again and again,
and I will not let them go unpunished!
They have rejected the instruction of the LORD,
refusing to obey his decrees.
They have been led astray by the same lies
that deceived their ancestors.
5 So I will send down fire on Judah,
and all the fortresses of Jerusalem will be destroyed."

6This is what the LORD says:

"The people of Israel have sinned again and again,
and I will not let them go unpunished!
They sell honorable people for silver
and poor people for a pair of sandals.
7 They trample helpless people in the dust
and shove the oppressed out of the way.
Both father and son sleep with the same woman,
corrupting my holy name.
8 At their religious festivals,
they lounge in clothing their debtors put up as security.
In the house of their gods,*
they drink wine bought with unjust fines.

9 "But as my people watched,
I destroyed the Amorites,
though they were as tall as cedars
and as strong as oaks.
I destroyed the fruit on their branches
and dug out their roots.
10 It was I who rescued you from Egypt
and led you through the desert for forty years,
so you could possess the land of the Amorites.
11 I chose some of your sons to be prophets
and others to be Nazirites.
Can you deny this, my people of Israel?"
asks the LORD.
12 "But you caused the Nazirites to sin by making them
drink wine,
and you commanded the prophets, 'Shut up!'

13 "So I will make you groan
like a wagon loaded down with sheaves of grain.
14 Your fastest runners will not get away.
The strongest among you will become weak.
Even mighty warriors will be unable to save themselves.
15 The archers will not stand their ground.
The swiftest runners won't be fast enough to escape.
Even those riding horses won't be able to save themselves.

2:8 Or *their God.*

16 On that day the most courageous of your fighting men
will drop their weapons and run for their lives,"
says the LORD.

3 Listen to this message that the LORD has spoken against you, O people of Israel—against the entire family I rescued from Egypt:

2 "From among all the families on the earth,
I have been intimate with you alone.
That is why I must punish you
for all your sins."

Witnesses against Guilty Israel

3 Can two people walk together
without agreeing on the direction?
4 Does a lion ever roar in a thicket
without first finding a victim?
Does a young lion growl in its den
without first catching its prey?
5 Does a bird ever get caught in a trap
that has no bait?
Does a trap spring shut
when there's nothing to catch?
6 When the ram's horn blows a warning,
shouldn't the people be alarmed?
Does disaster come to a city
unless the LORD has planned it?

7 Indeed, the Sovereign LORD never does anything
until he reveals his plans to his servants
the prophets.

8 The lion has roared—
so who isn't frightened?
The Sovereign LORD has spoken—
so who can refuse to proclaim his message?
9 Announce this to the leaders of Philistia*
and to the great ones of Egypt:
"Take your seats now on the hills around Samaria,
and witness the chaos and oppression in Israel."

10 "My people have forgotten how to do right,"
says the LORD.
"Their fortresses are filled with wealth
taken by theft and violence.
11 Therefore," says the Sovereign LORD,
"an enemy is coming!
He will surround them and shatter their defenses.
Then he will plunder all their fortresses."

3:9 Hebrew *Ashdod*.

Question 3:1-3

Along with the first two verses of this chapter, the metaphor of verse 3 is incredibly sad. How would you picture the answer to this question?

12 This is what the LORD says:

“A shepherd who tries to rescue a sheep from a lion’s mouth
will recover only two legs or a piece of an ear.
So it will be for the Israelites in Samaria lying on
luxurious beds,
and for the people of Damascus reclining on couches.*

13 “Now listen to this, and announce it throughout all Israel,*” says the
Lord, the LORD God of Heaven’s Armies.

14 “On the very day I punish Israel for its sins,
I will destroy the pagan altars at Bethel.
The horns of the altar will be cut off
and fall to the ground.
15 And I will destroy the beautiful homes of the wealthy—
their winter mansions and their summer
houses, too—
all their palaces filled with ivory,”
says the LORD.

Israel’s Failure to Learn

4 1 Listen to me, you fat cows*
living in Samaria,
you women who oppress the poor
and crush the needy,
and who are always calling to your husbands,
“Bring us another drink!”
2 The Sovereign LORD has sworn this by his holiness:
“The time will come when you will be led away
with hooks in your noses.
Every last one of you will be dragged away
like a fish on a hook!
3 You will be led out through the ruins of the wall;
you will be thrown from your fortresses,*”
says the LORD.

4 “Go ahead and offer sacrifices to the idols at Bethel.
Keep on disobeying at Gilgal.
Offer sacrifices each morning,
and bring your tithes every three days.
5 Present your bread made with yeast
as an offering of thanksgiving.
Then give your extra voluntary offerings
so you can brag about it everywhere!
This is the kind of thing you Israelites love to do,”
says the Sovereign LORD.

3:12 The meaning of the Hebrew in this sentence is uncertain. 3:13 Hebrew *the house of Jacob.* The names “Jacob” and “Israel” are often interchanged throughout the Old Testament, referring sometimes to the individual patriarch and sometimes to the nation. 4:1 Hebrew *you cows of Bashan.* 4:3 Or *thrown out toward Harmon,* possibly a reference to Mount Hermon.

6 "I brought hunger to every city
and famine to every town.
But still you would not return to me,"
says the LORD.

7 "I kept the rain from falling
when your crops needed it the most.
I sent rain on one town
but withheld it from another.
Rain fell on one field,
while another field withered away.
8 People staggered from town to town looking for water,
but there was never enough.
But still you would not return to me,"
says the LORD.

9 "I struck your farms and vineyards with blight and mildew.
Locusts devoured all your fig and olive trees.
But still you would not return to me,"
says the LORD.

10 "I sent plagues on you
like the plagues I sent on Egypt long ago.
I killed your young men in war
and led all your horses away.*
The stench of death filled the air!
But still you would not return to me,"
says the LORD.

11 "I destroyed some of your cities,
as I destroyed* Sodom and Gomorrah.
Those of you who survived
were like charred sticks pulled from a fire.
But still you would not return to me,"
says the LORD.

12 "Therefore, I will bring upon you all the disasters
I have announced.
Prepare to meet your God in judgment, you people of Israel!"

13 For the LORD is the one who shaped the mountains,
stirs up the winds, and reveals his thoughts to mankind.
He turns the light of dawn into darkness
and treads on the heights of the earth.
The LORD God of Heaven's Armies is his name!

A Call to Repentance

5 Listen, you people of Israel! Listen to this funeral song I am singing:

4:10 Or *and slaughtered your captured horses.* **4:11** Hebrew *as when God destroyed.*

Make a Difference

4:1-13

Fat Cows and Vomit Dogs

You've consumed too much, and now you're hovering over the bowl to belch, burp, and barf. You say, "There was so much to take in!" Burp. "So many desirable things!" Belch. "How could I say no to things that make me feel so good?" Barf.

When you stuff your soul with false gratification, your faith won't feel good. You had a craving for pleasure, but you tried to fill it the wrong way. No wonder you turned green with envy and rotten with excess. Gluttony has gotten you nothing but sick. Your stuffed-up life hasn't fulfilled you. Your faith looks more like a "fat cow" being led away with a hook in its nose—full but foolish (4:1-5).

Difference Maker

Whatever false gratification that you would normally return to today, resist it. Instead, do something more proactive that will bring lasting life to your soul.

Prayer **5:4**

Lord God, everything else leaves my soul sick. I want to return to you and live! Thank you for giving me that chance. Amen.

2 "The virgin Israel has fallen,
never to rise again!
She lies abandoned on the ground,
with no one to help her up."

3 The Sovereign LORD says:

"When a city sends a thousand men to battle,
only a hundred will return.
When a town sends a hundred,
only ten will come back alive."

4 Now this is what the LORD says to the family of Israel:

"Come back to me and live!
5 Don't worship at the pagan altars at Bethel;
don't go to the shrines at Gilgal or Beersheba.
For the people of Gilgal will be dragged off into exile,
and the people of Bethel will be reduced to nothing."
6 Come back to the LORD and live!
Otherwise, he will roar through Israel* like a fire,
devouring you completely.
Your gods in Bethel
won't be able to quench the flames.
7 You twist justice, making it a bitter pill for the oppressed.
You treat the righteous like dirt.

8 It is the LORD who created the stars,
the Pleiades and Orion.
He turns darkness into morning
and day into night.
He draws up water from the oceans
and pours it down as rain on the land.
The LORD is his name!
9 With blinding speed and power he destroys the strong,
crushing all their defenses.

10 How you hate honest judges!
How you despise people who tell the truth!
11 You trample the poor,
stealing their grain through taxes and unfair rent.
Therefore, though you build beautiful stone houses,
you will never live in them.
Though you plant lush vineyards,
you will never drink wine from them.
12 For I know the vast number of your sins
and the depth of your rebellions.
You oppress good people by taking bribes
and deprive the poor of justice in the courts.

5:6 Hebrew *the house of Joseph.*

13 So those who are smart keep their mouths shut,
for it is an evil time.

14 Do what is good and run from evil
so that you may live!
Then the LORD God of Heaven's Armies will be your helper,
just as you have claimed.
15 Hate evil and love what is good;
turn your courts into true halls of justice.
Perhaps even yet the LORD God of Heaven's Armies
will have mercy on the remnant of his people.*

16 Therefore, this is what the Lord, the LORD God of Heaven's Armies,
says:

"There will be crying in all the public squares
and mourning in every street.
Call for the farmers to weep with you,
and summon professional mourners to wail.
17 There will be wailing in every vineyard,
for I will destroy them all,"
says the LORD.

Warning of Coming Judgment

18 What sorrow awaits you who say,
"If only the day of the LORD were here!"
You have no idea what you are wishing for.
That day will bring darkness, not light.
19 In that day you will be like a man who runs from a lion—
only to meet a bear.
Escaping from the bear, he leans his hand against a wall
in his house—
and he's bitten by a snake.
20 Yes, the day of the LORD will be dark and hopeless,
without a ray of joy or hope.

21 "I hate all your show and pretense—
the hypocrisy of your religious festivals and
solemn assemblies.
22 I will not accept your burnt offerings and grain offerings.
I won't even notice all your choice peace offerings.
23 Away with your noisy hymns of praise!
I will not listen to the music of your harps.
24 Instead, I want to see a mighty flood of justice,
an endless river of righteous living.

25 "Was it to me you were bringing sacrifices and offerings during the
forty years in the wilderness, Israel? 26 No, you served your pagan gods—
Sakkuth your king god and Kaiwan your star god—the images you made

5:15 Hebrew *the remnant of Joseph.*

Question **5:14-15**

What would need to change in your life to be the kind of person that 5:14-15 is describing?

Make a Difference

6:8–10

The Lord's Name in Vain

Only God can make a promise according to his name. We do not have the right to throw God's name around. We do not have the authority to use the Lord's name in vain. We do not have the permission to invoke the Lord's name to justify our ideas. We cannot control his name. We are not above his name. We cannot use his name in whatever way we please. His name is not a flippant expression. His name is certainly not a cuss word. The Lord cares deeply about his name. We should too. This is one of God's major commandments to us (Deuteronomy 5:11).

Difference Maker

Stop using the Lord's name in vain.

for yourselves. 27 So I will send you into exile, to a land east of Damascus,*"
says the LORD, whose name is the God of Heaven's Armies.

6 1 What sorrow awaits you who lounge in luxury in Jerusalem,*
and you who feel secure in Samaria!
You are famous and popular in Israel,
and people go to you for help.
2 But go over to Calneh
and see what happened there.
Then go to the great city of Hamath
and down to the Philistine city of Gath.
You are no better than they were,
and look at how they were destroyed.
3 You push away every thought of coming disaster,
but your actions only bring the day of judgment closer.
4 How terrible for you who sprawl on ivory beds
and lounge on your couches,
eating the meat of tender lambs from the flock
and of choice calves fattened in the stall.
5 You sing trivial songs to the sound of the harp
and fancy yourselves to be great musicians like David.
6 You drink wine by the bowlful
and perfume yourselves with fragrant lotions.
You care nothing about the ruin of your nation.*
7 Therefore, you will be the first to be led away as captives.
Suddenly, all your parties will end.

8 The Sovereign LORD has sworn by his own name, and this is what he, the
LORD God of Heaven's Armies, says:

"I despise the arrogance of Israel,*
and I hate their fortresses.
I will give this city
and everything in it to their enemies."

9 (If there are ten men left in one house, they will all die. 10 And when a relative
who is responsible to dispose of the dead* goes into the house to carry out
the bodies, he will ask the last survivor, "Is anyone else with you?" When the
person begins to swear, "No, by . . . ," he will interrupt and say, "Stop! Don't
even mention the name of the LORD.")

11 When the LORD gives the command,
homes both great and small will be smashed to pieces.

12 Can horses gallop over boulders?
Can oxen be used to plow them?
But that's how foolish you are when you turn justice into poison

5:26-27 Greek version reads *No, you carried your pagan gods—the shrine of Molech, the star of your god Rephan, and the images you made for yourselves. So I will send you into exile, to a land east of Damascus.* Compare Acts 7:43. 6:1 Hebrew *in Zion.* 6:6 Hebrew *of Joseph.* 6:8 Hebrew *Jacob.* See note on 3:13. 6:10 Or *to burn the dead.* The meaning of the Hebrew is uncertain.

and the sweet fruit of righteousness into bitterness.
13 And you brag about your conquest of Lo-debar.*
You boast, "Didn't we take Karnaim* by our own strength?"

14 "O people of Israel, I am about to bring an enemy nation
against you,"
says the LORD God of Heaven's Armies.
"They will oppress you throughout your land—
from Lebo-hamath in the north
to the Arabah Valley in the south."

A Vision of Locusts

7 The Sovereign LORD showed me a vision. I saw him preparing to send a
vast swarm of locusts over the land. This was after the king's share had
been harvested from the fields and as the main crop was coming up. 2 In my
vision the locusts ate every green plant in sight. Then I said, "O Sovereign
LORD, please forgive us or we will not survive, for Israel* is so small."
3 So the LORD relented from this plan. "I will not do it," he said.

A Vision of Fire

4 Then the Sovereign LORD showed me another vision. I saw him preparing
to punish his people with a great fire. The fire had burned up the depths of
the sea and was devouring the entire land. 5 Then I said, "O Sovereign LORD,
please stop or we will not survive, for Israel is so small."
6 Then the LORD relented from this plan, too. "I will not do that either,"
said the Sovereign LORD.

A Vision of a Plumb Line

7 Then he showed me another vision. I saw the Lord standing beside a wall
that had been built using a plumb line. He was using a plumb line to see if
it was still straight. 8 And the LORD said to me, "Amos, what do you see?"
I answered, "A plumb line."
And the Lord replied, "I will test my people with this plumb line. I will
no longer ignore all their sins. 9 The pagan shrines of your ancestors* will be
ruined, and the temples of Israel will be destroyed; I will bring the dynasty
of King Jeroboam to a sudden end."

Amos and Amaziah

10 Then Amaziah, the priest of Bethel, sent a message to Jeroboam, king of
Israel: "Amos is hatching a plot against you right here on your very doorstep!
What he is saying is intolerable. 11 He is saying, 'Jeroboam will soon be killed,
and the people of Israel will be sent away into exile.'"
12 Then Amaziah sent orders to Amos: "Get out of here, you prophet! Go on
back to the land of Judah, and earn your living by prophesying there! 13 Don't
bother us with your prophecies here in Bethel. This is the king's sanctuary
and the national place of worship!"
14 But Amos replied, "I'm not a professional prophet, and I was never
trained to be one.* I'm just a shepherd, and I take care of sycamore-fig trees.

Question 7:8

What is a "plumb line"? What does God intend to do with it? How does this relate to Romans 3:23?

Question 7:14

In the face of opposition, Amos sticks to his calling and changes the narrative. His confidence is remarkable. Where did he get his resolve?

6:13a *Lo-debar* means "nothing." **6:13b** *Karnaim* means "horns," a term that symbolizes strength. **7:2** Hebrew *Jacob;* also in 7:5. See note on 3:13. **7:9** Hebrew *of Isaac.* **7:14** Or *I'm not a prophet nor the son of a prophet.*

15 But the LORD called me away from my flock and told me, 'Go and prophesy
to my people in Israel.' 16 Now then, listen to this message from the LORD:

"You say,
'Don't prophesy against Israel.
Stop preaching against my people.*'
17 But this is what the LORD says:
'Your wife will become a prostitute in this city,
and your sons and daughters will be killed.
Your land will be divided up,
and you yourself will die in a foreign land.
And the people of Israel will certainly become captives
in exile,
far from their homeland.'"

A Vision of Ripe Fruit

8 Then the Sovereign LORD showed me another vision. In it I saw a bas-
ket filled with ripe fruit. 2 "What do you see, Amos?" he asked.

I replied, "A basket full of ripe fruit."

Then the LORD said, "Like this fruit, Israel is ripe for punishment! I will
not delay their punishment again. 3 In that day the singing in the temple
will turn to wailing. Dead bodies will be scattered everywhere. They will
be carried out of the city in silence. I, the Sovereign LORD, have spoken!"

4 Listen to this, you who rob the poor
and trample down the needy!
5 You can't wait for the Sabbath day to be over
and the religious festivals to end
so you can get back to cheating the helpless.
You measure out grain with dishonest measures
and cheat the buyer with dishonest scales.*
6 And you mix the grain you sell
with chaff swept from the floor.
Then you enslave poor people
for one piece of silver or a pair of sandals.

7 Now the LORD has sworn this oath
by his own name, the Pride of Israel*:
"I will never forget
the wicked things you have done!
8 The earth will tremble for your deeds,
and everyone will mourn.
The ground will rise like the Nile River at floodtime;
it will heave up, then sink again.
9 "In that day," says the Sovereign LORD,
"I will make the sun go down at noon
and darken the earth while it is still day.

7:16 Hebrew *against the house of Isaac.* 8:5 Hebrew *You make the ephah* [a unit for measuring grain] *small and the shekel* [a unit of weight] *great, and you deal falsely by using deceitful balances.* 8:7 Hebrew *the pride of Jacob.* See note on 3:13.

10 I will turn your celebrations into times of mourning
and your singing into weeping.
You will wear funeral clothes
and shave your heads to show your sorrow—
as if your only son had died.
How very bitter that day will be!

11 "The time is surely coming," says the Sovereign LORD,
"when I will send a famine on the land—
not a famine of bread or water
but of hearing the words of the LORD.
12 People will stagger from sea to sea
and wander from border to border*
searching for the word of the LORD,
but they will not find it.
13 Beautiful girls and strong young men
will grow faint in that day,
thirsting for the LORD's word.
14 And those who swear by the shameful idols of Samaria—
who take oaths in the name of the god of Dan
and make vows in the name of the god of Beersheba*—
they will all fall down,
never to rise again."

A Vision of God at the Altar

9 Then I saw a vision of the Lord standing beside the altar. He said,

"Strike the tops of the Temple columns,
so that the foundation will shake.
Bring down the roof
on the heads of the people below.
I will kill with the sword those who survive.
No one will escape!

2 "Even if they dig down to the place of the dead,*
I will reach down and pull them up.
Even if they climb up into the heavens,
I will bring them down.
3 Even if they hide at the very top of Mount Carmel,
I will search them out and capture them.
Even if they hide at the bottom of the ocean,
I will send the sea serpent after them to bite them.
4 Even if their enemies drive them into exile,
I will command the sword to kill them there.
I am determined to bring disaster upon them
and not to help them."

5 The Lord, the LORD of Heaven's Armies,
touches the land and it melts,

8:12 Hebrew *from north to east.* 8:14 Hebrew *the way of Beersheba.* 9:2 Hebrew *to Sheol.*

Write your notes in this space

and all its people mourn.
The ground rises like the Nile River at floodtime,
and then it sinks again.
6 The LORD's home reaches up to the heavens,
while its foundation is on the earth.
He draws up water from the oceans
and pours it down as rain on the land.
The LORD is his name!

7 "Are you Israelites more important to me
than the Ethiopians?*" asks the LORD.
"I brought Israel out of Egypt,
but I also brought the Philistines from Crete*
and led the Arameans out of Kir.

8 "I, the Sovereign LORD,
am watching this sinful nation of Israel.
I will destroy it
from the face of the earth.
But I will never completely destroy the family of Israel,*"
says the LORD.
9 "For I will give the command
and will shake Israel along with the other nations
as grain is shaken in a sieve,
yet not one true kernel will be lost.
10 But all the sinners will die by the sword—
all those who say, 'Nothing bad will happen to us.'

A Promise of Restoration

11 "In that day I will restore the fallen house* of David.
I will repair its damaged walls.
From the ruins I will rebuild it
and restore its former glory.
12 And Israel will possess what is left of Edom
and all the nations I have called to be mine.*"
The LORD has spoken,
and he will do these things.

13 "The time will come," says the LORD,
"when the grain and grapes will grow faster
than they can be harvested.
Then the terraced vineyards on the hills of Israel
will drip with sweet wine!
14 I will bring my exiled people of Israel
back from distant lands,
and they will rebuild their ruined cities
and live in them again.

9:7a Hebrew *the Cushites?* 9:7b Hebrew *Caphtor.* 9:8 Hebrew *the house of Jacob.* See note on 3:13. 9:11a Or *kingdom;* Hebrew reads *tent.* 9:11b-12 Greek version reads *and restore its former glory, / so that the rest of humanity, including the Gentiles— / all those I have called to be mine— might seek me.* Compare Acts 15:16-17.

They will plant vineyards and gardens;
they will eat their crops and drink their wine.
15 I will firmly plant them there
in their own land.
They will never again be uprooted
from the land I have given them,"
says the LORD your God.

Prayer 9:15

Lord Jesus, let me live a life rooted deeply into you so that I may be used to bless others. Amen.

Obadiah Introduction

Follow this for a moment. Jacob outwitted his brother, Esau, and received the blessing of their father, Isaac, as a result. Over hundreds of years, Jacob's descendants became known as the nation of Israel. Esau's descendants became known as the nation of Edom. They were constantly at war.

When Jerusalem was crushed in 586 BC, Edom swooped in and took advantage of their old relatives. Edom was ruthless. They plundered the land of Jacob and gloated over the destruction. Edom puffed itself up with pride while its brother kingdom lay in ruins. Read Psalm 137 and notice how Edom's delighted smirking caught the attention of God's indignation.

Then, God sent Obadiah, alongside a few other prophets, to share some bad news with Edom. Obadiah, whose name means "one who worships the Lord" or "one who serves the Lord," had a message that would undo Edom's pride: Jacob's people will be rescued, and the Lord himself will be their king. You should not have opposed the Lord's people. Now you're going to pay.

This short book offers a dramatic lesson in the perils of pride. Gloating over someone else's misery will only bring calamity upon the puffed-up person. Be careful in rejoicing at the misfortune of others.

Obadiah

This is the vision that the Sovereign LORD revealed to Obadiah concerning the land of Edom.

Edom's Judgment Announced
We have heard a message from the LORD
that an ambassador was sent to the nations to say,
"Get ready, everyone!
Let's assemble our armies and attack Edom!"

2 The LORD says to Edom,
"I will cut you down to size among the nations;
you will be greatly despised.
3 You have been deceived by your own pride
because you live in a rock fortress
and make your home high in the mountains.
'Who can ever reach us way up here?'
you ask boastfully.
4 But even if you soar as high as eagles
and build your nest among the stars,
I will bring you crashing down,"
says the LORD.

5 "If thieves came at night and robbed you
(what a disaster awaits you!),
they would not take everything.
Those who harvest grapes
always leave a few for the poor.
But your enemies will wipe you out completely!
6 Every nook and cranny of Edom*
will be searched and looted.
Every treasure will be found and taken.

7 "All your allies will turn against you.
They will help to chase you from your land.
They will promise you peace
while plotting to deceive and destroy you.
Your trusted friends will set traps for you,
and you won't even know about it.
8 At that time not a single wise person
will be left in the whole land of Edom,"
says the LORD.

6 Hebrew *Esau;* also in 8b, 9, 18, 19, 21.

Question 3

How does pride deceive us into a false sense of security?

Question 15

The Lord himself will be king! What difference does this truth make in your life?

"For on the mountains of Edom
I will destroy everyone who has understanding.
9 The mightiest warriors of Teman
will be terrified,
and everyone on the mountains of Edom
will be cut down in the slaughter.

Reasons for Edom's Punishment

10 "Because of the violence you did
to your close relatives in Israel,*
you will be filled with shame
and destroyed forever.
11 When they were invaded,
you stood aloof, refusing to help them.
Foreign invaders carried off their wealth
and cast lots to divide up Jerusalem,
but you acted like one of Israel's enemies.

12 "You should not have gloated
when they exiled your relatives to distant lands.
You should not have rejoiced
when the people of Judah suffered such misfortune.
You should not have spoken arrogantly
in that terrible time of trouble.
13 You should not have plundered the land of Israel
when they were suffering such calamity.
You should not have gloated over their destruction
when they were suffering such calamity.
You should not have seized their wealth
when they were suffering such calamity.
14 You should not have stood at the crossroads,
killing those who tried to escape.
You should not have captured the survivors
and handed them over in their terrible time of trouble.

Edom Destroyed, Israel Restored

15 "The day is near when I, the LORD,
will judge all godless nations!
As you have done to Israel,
so it will be done to you.
All your evil deeds
will fall back on your own heads.
16 Just as you swallowed up my people
on my holy mountain,
so you and the surrounding nations
will swallow the punishment I pour out on you.
Yes, all you nations will drink and stagger
and disappear from history.

10 Hebrew *your brother Jacob.* The names "Jacob" and "Israel" are often interchanged throughout the Old Testament, referring sometimes to the individual patriarch and sometimes to the nation.

17 "But Jerusalem* will become a refuge for those who escape;
it will be a holy place.
And the people of Israel* will come back
to reclaim their inheritance.
18 The people of Israel will be a raging fire,
and Edom a field of dry stubble.
The descendants of Joseph will be a flame
roaring across the field, devouring everything.
There will be no survivors in Edom.
I, the LORD, have spoken!

19 "Then my people living in the Negev
will occupy the mountains of Edom.
Those living in the foothills of Judah*
will possess the Philistine plains
and take over the fields of Ephraim and Samaria.
And the people of Benjamin
will occupy the land of Gilead.
20 The exiles of Israel will return to their land
and occupy the Phoenician coast as far north as Zarephath.
The captives from Jerusalem exiled in the north*
will return home and resettle the towns of the Negev.
21 Those who have been rescued* will go up to* Mount Zion in Jerusalem
to rule over the mountains of Edom.
And the LORD himself will be king!"

17a Hebrew *Mount Zion.* 17b Hebrew *house of Jacob;* also in 18. See note on 10. 19 Hebrew *the Shephelah.* 20 Hebrew *in Sepharad.* 21a As in Greek and Syriac versions; Hebrew reads *Rescuers.* 21b Or *from.*

Prayer 21

You are my King, Jesus! Lord Jesus, keep me watchful for your kingdom today. Help me find you at work in circumstances that I hadn't considered before. Amen.

Jonah Introduction

Many would say the book of Jonah is a story about a big fish. The truth is that this minor prophet is all about our big God.

God asked Jonah to preach the sermon of his life, a message of judgment against the great Assyrian city of Nineveh. The Assyrians were known for their bloody military campaigns. They were brutal butchers and one of Israel's greatest enemies. God wanted a message of judgment to get to Nineveh not because he wanted to punish them but because he wanted them to turn from their evil ways. Jonah would have loved to preach a sermon of judgment, but knowing God is gracious and compassionate (Jonah 4:2), he feared the people of Nineveh would repent. Jonah believed they deserved punishment, so instead of doing what God asked him to do, he hopped on a boat and took a ride to the edge of the known world. Jonah was literally going as far away as possible.

God wants people who are far from him to draw near to him, and he wants those who are near to him to grow closer and closer to him. Just like God wanted the city of Nineveh to turn around, he also pursued Jonah, wanting Jonah to follow obediently.

Interestingly, the book of Jonah also ends with a question that remains unresolved. Jesus compared himself to Jonah, noting that Jonah *disobeyed* God and ended up in the belly of a great fish for three days before being spit out. Jesus indicated that he himself would be someone who would *obey* God the Father and would spend three days in a grave before being resurrected. The tension of Jonah's story invites us to decide whether we will follow God no matter what God will do and no matter how we will feel about it.

Story Arc

Jonah

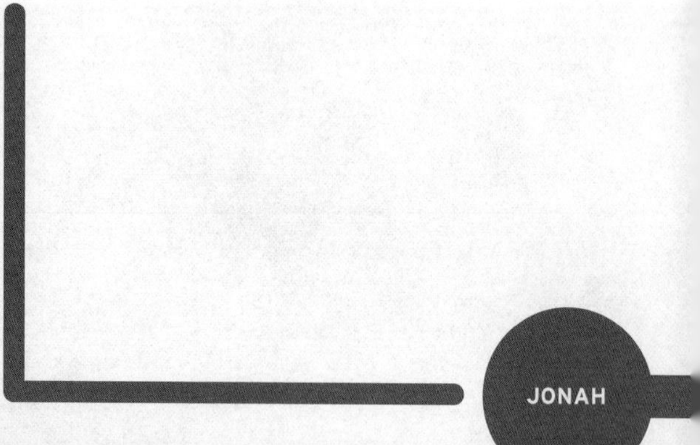

Jonah

Jonah Runs from the LORD

1 The LORD gave this message to Jonah son of Amittai: 2 "Get up and go
to the great city of Nineveh. Announce my judgment against it because
I have seen how wicked its people are."

3 But Jonah got up and went in the opposite direction to get away from
the LORD. He went down to the port of Joppa, where he found a ship leaving
for Tarshish. He bought a ticket and went on board, hoping to escape from
the LORD by sailing to Tarshish.

4 But the LORD hurled a powerful wind over the sea, causing a violent
storm that threatened to break the ship apart. 5 Fearing for their lives, the
desperate sailors shouted to their gods for help and threw the cargo over-
board to lighten the ship.

But all this time Jonah was sound asleep down in the hold. 6 So the captain
went down after him. "How can you sleep at a time like this?" he shouted.
"Get up and pray to your god! Maybe he will pay attention to us and spare
our lives."

7 Then the crew cast lots to see which of them had offended the gods and
caused the terrible storm. When they did this, the lots identified Jonah as
the culprit. 8 "Why has this awful storm come down on us?" they demanded.
"Who are you? What is your line of work? What country are you from? What
is your nationality?"

9 Jonah answered, "I am a Hebrew, and I worship the LORD, the God of
heaven, who made the sea and the land."

10 The sailors were terrified when they heard this, for he had already told
them he was running away from the LORD. "Oh, why did you do it?" they
groaned. 11 And since the storm was getting worse all the time, they asked
him, "What should we do to you to stop this storm?"

12 "Throw me into the sea," Jonah said, "and it will become calm again. I
know that this terrible storm is all my fault."

13 Instead, the sailors rowed even harder to get the ship to the land.
But the stormy sea was too violent for them, and they couldn't make it.
14 Then they cried out to the LORD, Jonah's God. "O LORD," they pleaded,
"don't make us die for this man's sin. And don't hold us responsible for
his death. O LORD, you have sent this storm upon him for your own good
reasons."

15 Then the sailors picked Jonah up and threw him into the raging sea,
and the storm stopped at once! 16 The sailors were awestruck by the LORD's
great power, and they offered him a sacrifice and vowed to serve him.

17 *Now the LORD had arranged for a great fish to swallow Jonah. And
Jonah was inside the fish for three days and three nights.

Question 1:3

What good thing about God makes you run away from him?

Story Arc 1:1

● **Jonah**

We first meet the prophet Jonah in 2 Kings 14:25. At that time, Israel's king listened to "Jonah son of Amittai." Clearly Jonah was familiar with delivering big messages with big consequences to big people during big moments. Here in Jonah 1:1, when "the LORD gave this message to Jonah son of Amittai," Jonah knew what was expected of him.

However, instead of taking this message to Nineveh, around 550 miles from where he was, Jonah decided to flee to Tarshish, about 2,500 miles in the opposite direction. Nineveh was the capital of the Assyrian Empire, and the Assyrians were famous for their crimes. Jonah hated them. Jonah wanted to see the Ninevites pay for their evil ways, so he ran away and refused to deliver the message God gave him. He didn't run from Nineveh because of how evil they were, but he ran from Nineveh because of how compassionate God was. If God's message of judgment caused them to repent, Jonah knew that God would forgive them.

Mic 5:2-4 ►

1:17 Verse 1:17 is numbered 2:1 in Hebrew text.

Prayer 2:9

God, I do not do everything you ask me to do. Even so, you still love me and want me. God, forgive me for all my sins. God, thank you for your rescue. Amen.

Make a Difference 3:1

Second Chances

The Lord spoke to Jonah a second time but with the same message. Have you ever asked God for a second chance? Are you on your third chance or more? God gives second changes because he is "a merciful and compassionate God" (4:2).

Difference Maker

Who is someone who needs a second chance in life with whom you can share and show the love of Jesus? Get up and go and deliver the message God has given you.

Jonah's Prayer

2 [1]*Then Jonah prayed to the LORD his God from inside the fish. [2]He said,

"I cried out to the LORD in my great trouble,
and he answered me.
I called to you from the land of the dead,*
and LORD, you heard me!
3 You threw me into the ocean depths,
and I sank down to the heart of the sea.
The mighty waters engulfed me;
I was buried beneath your wild and stormy waves.
4 Then I said, 'O LORD, you have driven me from your presence.
Yet I will look once more toward your holy Temple.'
5 "I sank beneath the waves,
and the waters closed over me.
Seaweed wrapped itself around my head.
6 I sank down to the very roots of the mountains.
I was imprisoned in the earth,
whose gates lock shut forever.
But you, O LORD my God,
snatched me from the jaws of death!
7 As my life was slipping away,
I remembered the LORD.
And my earnest prayer went out to you
in your holy Temple.
8 Those who worship false gods
turn their backs on all God's mercies.
9 But I will offer sacrifices to you with songs of praise,
and I will fulfill all my vows.
For my salvation comes from the LORD alone."

[10]Then the LORD ordered the fish to spit Jonah out onto the beach.

Jonah Goes to Nineveh

3 Then the LORD spoke to Jonah a second time: [2]"Get up and go to the
great city of Nineveh, and deliver the message I have given you."
[3]This time Jonah obeyed the LORD's command and went to Nineveh, a city
so large that it took three days to see it all.* [4]On the day Jonah entered the city,
he shouted to the crowds: "Forty days from now Nineveh will be destroyed!"
[5]The people of Nineveh believed God's message, and from the greatest to the
least, they declared a fast and put on burlap to show their sorrow.
[6]When the king of Nineveh heard what Jonah was saying, he stepped
down from his throne and took off his royal robes. He dressed himself in
burlap and sat on a heap of ashes. [7]Then the king and his nobles sent this
decree throughout the city:

"No one, not even the animals from your herds and flocks, may eat or
drink anything at all. [8]People and animals alike must wear garments of

2:1 Verses 2:1-10 are numbered 2:2-11 in Hebrew text. 2:2 Hebrew *from Sheol.* 3:3 Hebrew *a great city to God, of three days' journey.*

mourning, and everyone must pray earnestly to God. They must turn
from their evil ways and stop all their violence. 9 Who can tell? Perhaps
even yet God will change his mind and hold back his fierce anger from
destroying us."

10 When God saw what they had done and how they had put a stop to
their evil ways, he changed his mind and did not carry out the destruction
he had threatened.

Jonah's Anger at the LORD's Mercy

4 This change of plans greatly upset Jonah, and he became very angry.
2 So he complained to the LORD about it: "Didn't I say before I left home
that you would do this, LORD? That is why I ran away to Tarshish! I knew
that you are a merciful and compassionate God, slow to get angry and filled
with unfailing love. You are eager to turn back from destroying people.
3 Just kill me now, LORD! I'd rather be dead than alive if what I predicted
will not happen."

4 The LORD replied, "Is it right for you to be angry about this?"

5 Then Jonah went out to the east side of the city and made a shelter to sit
under as he waited to see what would happen to the city. 6 And the LORD God
arranged for a leafy plant to grow there, and soon it spread its broad leaves
over Jonah's head, shading him from the sun. This eased his discomfort, and
Jonah was very grateful for the plant.

7 But God also arranged for a worm! The next morning at dawn the worm
ate through the stem of the plant so that it withered away. 8 And as the sun
grew hot, God arranged for a scorching east wind to blow on Jonah. The
sun beat down on his head until he grew faint and wished to die. "Death is
certainly better than living like this!" he exclaimed.

9 Then God said to Jonah, "Is it right for you to be angry because the plant
died?"

"Yes," Jonah retorted, "even angry enough to die!"

10 Then the LORD said, "You feel sorry about the plant, though you did
nothing to put it there. It came quickly and died quickly. 11 But Nineveh has
more than 120,000 people living in spiritual darkness,* not to mention all
the animals. Shouldn't I feel sorry for such a great city?"

4:11 Hebrew *people who don't know their right hand from their left.*

Make a Difference

3:10–4:4

Fairness Is Overrated

Jonah was filled with anger because, to him, it was not fair that God chose to forgive the Ninevites. The forgiveness God gives to our enemies is the same forgiveness he gives to you. Forgiveness rarely feels fair, and that's what makes compassion like this so courageous.

Difference Maker

Consider writing a letter of encouragement, sharing the hope of Jesus to someone who is not yet a Christian.

Prayer **4:11**

Lord, help me take risks in sharing my faith. Give me compassion for people who need Jesus, eyes to see who they are, and the courage to go unleash the hope we all need. Amen.

Micah Introduction

"You are in trouble!"
"Judgment is coming!"
"I've got a plan, but it is going to hurt first."
"Say you're sorry and mean it."
"It is all going to be okay. I promise."
"I love you."

Hundreds of years before Jesus was born in Bethlehem, the prophet Micah had the responsibility to deliver all these messages from God to the people of Israel. Because he loved them, God wanted to confront and warn his people to stop and repent of their bad actions. He had seen their evil ways. They had been mistreating people, had allowed corrupted leadership, and were worshiping other gods. Now God wanted them to change their ways—or else.

Mingled in this tough message, however, is tremendous hope! Even though the situation seemed bleak, God promised them a Messiah who would be born in Bethlehem (Micah 5:2-4). This Messiah would be a ruler who would shepherd them to restoration to God. If the people would just listen to Micah's words, lament over the things they have done, and confess their sin, they could have the salvation the Lord promised.

Micah's warnings are applicable to us today. We do evil. We do not treat people the way we should. We put other "gods" before God. Just like the people in Micah's day, we are called to confess and lament for the wrongs we have done. Ultimately, we should listen to the challenge of Micah 6:8 "to do what is right, to love mercy, and to walk humbly with your God."

Pray: *God, open my heart to see where I am not pleasing to you in how I treat others, what I idolize, and what evil is in my heart. Create in me a clean heart and remove any sin from me that is separating me from you. Amen.*

Story Arc

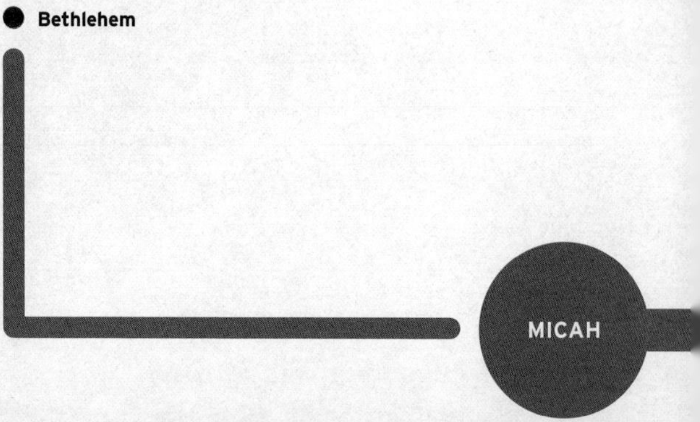

Micah

1 The LORD gave this message to Micah of Moresheth during the years when Jotham, Ahaz, and Hezekiah were kings of Judah. The visions he saw concerned both Samaria and Jerusalem.

Grief over Samaria and Jerusalem

2 Attention! Let all the people of the world listen!
Let the earth and everything in it hear.
The Sovereign LORD is making accusations against you;
the Lord speaks from his holy Temple.
3 Look! The LORD is coming!
He leaves his throne in heaven
and tramples the heights of the earth.
4 The mountains melt beneath his feet
and flow into the valleys
like wax in a fire,
like water pouring down a hill.
5 And why is this happening?
Because of the rebellion of Israel*—
yes, the sins of the whole nation.
Who is to blame for Israel's rebellion?
Samaria, its capital city!
Where is the center of idolatry in Judah?
In Jerusalem, its capital!

6 "So I, the LORD, will make the city of Samaria
a heap of ruins.
Her streets will be plowed up
for planting vineyards.
I will roll the stones of her walls into the valley below,
exposing her foundations.
7 All her carved images will be smashed.
All her sacred treasures will be burned.
These things were bought with the money
earned by her prostitution,
and they will now be carried away
to pay prostitutes elsewhere."

8 Therefore, I will mourn and lament.
I will walk around barefoot and naked.
I will howl like a jackal

Make a Difference 1:2

Gather Round

Imagine after a game, a coach gathers the team to go over everything that went wrong and all the mistakes that contributed to their loss. That's what Micah had to do here. After messing up the game of life, Micah was calling all the people to huddle up and give him their attention.

Now imagine God gathering us into a huddle today. What accusations could the Lord make against you today? What would he say about our society? Just as the players of a team need to listen humbly to the coach, we should humble ourselves and listen to God's observations and guidance.

Difference Maker

Make a list of "wrong plays" or sins you are personally struggling with right now. Now make a list of sins you see in your community. Ask the Lord for forgiveness and ask him to change your heart and the hearts of those in your community. Then ask God to send you back out on the court of life with his playbook.

1:5 Hebrew *Jacob;* also in 1:5b. The names "Jacob" and "Israel" are often interchanged throughout the Old Testament, referring sometimes to the individual patriarch and sometimes to the nation.

Prayer 2:1

Jesus, please keep my mind and heart from creating plans to cause pain and bring hurt to others. When others do things to hurt me, let me respond by not returning their actions with revenge. Amen.

and moan like an owl.
9 For my people's wound
is too deep to heal.
It has reached into Judah,
even to the gates of Jerusalem.

10 Don't tell our enemies in Gath*;
don't weep at all.
You people in Beth-leaphrah,*
roll in the dust to show your despair.
11 You people in Shaphir,*
go as captives into exile—naked and ashamed.
The people of Zaanan*
dare not come outside their walls.
The people of Beth-ezel* mourn,
for their house has no support.
12 The people of Maroth* anxiously wait for relief,
but only bitterness awaits them
as the LORD's judgment reaches
even to the gates of Jerusalem.

13 Harness your chariot horses and flee,
you people of Lachish.*
You were the first city in Judah
to follow Israel in her rebellion,
and you led Jerusalem* into sin.
14 Send farewell gifts to Moresheth-gath*;
there is no hope of saving it.
The town of Aczib*
has deceived the kings of Israel.
15 O people of Mareshah,*
I will bring a conqueror to capture your town.
And the leaders* of Israel
will go to Adullam.

16 Oh, people of Judah, shave your heads in sorrow,
for the children you love will be snatched away.
Make yourselves as bald as a vulture,
for your little ones will be exiled to distant lands.

Judgment against Wealthy Oppressors

2 1 What sorrow awaits you who lie awake at night,
thinking up evil plans.
You rise at dawn and hurry to carry them out,
simply because you have the power to do so.

1:10a *Gath* sounds like the Hebrew term for "tell." **1:10b** *Beth-leaphrah* means "house of dust." **1:11a** *Shaphir* means "pleasant." **1:11b** *Zaanan* sounds like the Hebrew term for "come out." **1:11c** *Beth-ezel* means "adjoining house." **1:12** *Maroth* sounds like the Hebrew term for "bitter." **1:13a** *Lachish* sounds like the Hebrew term for "team of horses." **1:13b** Hebrew *the daughter of Zion.* **1:14a** *Moresheth* sounds like the Hebrew term for "gift" or "dowry." **1:14b** *Aczib* means "deception." **1:15a** *Mareshah* sounds like the Hebrew term for "conqueror." **1:15b** Hebrew *the glory.*

2 When you want a piece of land,
you find a way to seize it.
When you want someone's house,
you take it by fraud and violence.
You cheat a man of his property,
stealing his family's inheritance.

3 But this is what the LORD says:
"I will reward your evil with evil;
you won't be able to pull your neck out of the noose.
You will no longer walk around proudly,
for it will be a terrible time."

4 In that day your enemies will make fun of you
by singing this song of despair about you:
"We are finished,
completely ruined!
God has confiscated our land,
taking it from us.
He has given our fields
to those who betrayed us.*"
5 Others will set your boundaries then,
and the LORD's people will have no say
in how the land is divided.

True and False Prophets

6 "Don't say such things,"
the people respond.*
"Don't prophesy like that.
Such disasters will never come our way!"

7 Should you talk that way, O family of Israel?*
Will the LORD's Spirit have patience with such behavior?
If you would do what is right,
you would find my words comforting.
8 Yet to this very hour
my people rise against me like an enemy!
You steal the shirts right off the backs
of those who trusted you,
making them as ragged as men
returning from battle.
9 You have evicted women from their pleasant homes
and forever stripped their children of all that God would
give them.
10 Up! Begone!
This is no longer your land and home,
for you have filled it with sin
and ruined it completely.

Make a Difference 2:6

Nope

The people did not want to hear it. They did not want to hear what the prophet Micah had to say about their actions or that there would be consequences for them.

Correction is not easy to receive, ever! We often want to respond by saying, "Nope, that's not me. You got the wrong person." Instead, when we humble ourselves and receive correction from God, a parent, a coach, or another trusted adult, we will learn where our blind spots are and how to be better. Are you willing to be a better you? Are you willing to receive correction even when it is uncomfortable? How could helpful feedback help you grow in your faith in Jesus and share with those around you?

Difference Maker

Practice receiving feedback and keeping an open heart. Ask a trusted adult in your life for feedback on how you are doing.

2:4 Or *to those who took us captive.* 2:6 Or *the prophets respond;* Hebrew reads *they prophesy.*
2:7 Hebrew *O house of Jacob?* See note on 1:5a.

Prayer **3:1**

Dear Jesus, today, challenge me to make the right moves, to love being merciful to others, and to walk with your arm wrapped around my shoulders. Amen.

11 Suppose a prophet full of lies would say to you,
"I'll preach to you the joys of wine and alcohol!"
That's just the kind of prophet you would like!

Hope for Restoration

12 "Someday, O Israel, I will gather you;
I will gather the remnant who are left.
I will bring you together again like sheep in a pen,
like a flock in its pasture.
Yes, your land will again
be filled with noisy crowds!
13 Your leader will break out
and lead you out of exile,
out through the gates of the enemy cities,
back to your own land.
Your king will lead you;
the LORD himself will guide you."

Judgment against Israel's Leaders

3 1 I said, "Listen, you leaders of Israel!
You are supposed to know right from wrong,
2 but you are the very ones
who hate good and love evil.
You skin my people alive
and tear the flesh from their bones.
3 Yes, you eat my people's flesh,
strip off their skin,
and break their bones.
You chop them up
like meat for the cooking pot.
4 Then you beg the LORD for help in times of trouble!
Do you really expect him to answer?
After all the evil you have done,
he won't even look at you!"

5 This is what the LORD says:
"You false prophets are leading my people astray!
You promise peace for those who give you food,
but you declare war on those who refuse to
feed you.
6 Now the night will close around you,
cutting off all your visions.
Darkness will cover you,
putting an end to your predictions.
The sun will set for you prophets,
and your day will come to an end.
7 Then you seers will be put to shame,
and you fortune-tellers will be disgraced.
And you will cover your faces
because there is no answer from God."

8 But as for me, I am filled with power—
with the Spirit of the LORD.
I am filled with justice and strength
to boldly declare Israel's sin and rebellion.
9 Listen to me, you leaders of Israel!
You hate justice and twist all that is right.
10 You are building Jerusalem
on a foundation of murder and corruption.
11 You rulers make decisions based on bribes;
you priests teach God's laws only for a price;
you prophets won't prophesy unless you are paid.
Yet all of you claim to depend on the LORD.
"No harm can come to us," you say,
"for the LORD is here among us."
12 Because of you, Mount Zion will be plowed like an open field;
Jerusalem will be reduced to ruins!
A thicket will grow on the heights
where the Temple now stands.

The LORD's Future Reign

4 1 In the last days, the mountain of the LORD's house
will be the highest of all—
the most important place on earth.
It will be raised above the other hills,
and people from all over the world will stream there
to worship.
2 People from many nations will come and say,
"Come, let us go up to the mountain of the LORD,
to the house of Jacob's God.
There he will teach us his ways,
and we will walk in his paths."
For the LORD's teaching will go out from Zion;
his word will go out from Jerusalem.
3 The LORD will mediate between peoples
and will settle disputes between strong nations far away.
They will hammer their swords into plowshares
and their spears into pruning hooks.
Nation will no longer fight against nation,
nor train for war anymore.
4 Everyone will live in peace and prosperity,
enjoying their own grapevines and fig trees,
for there will be nothing to fear.
The LORD of Heaven's Armies
has made this promise!
5 Though the nations around us follow their idols,
we will follow the LORD our God forever and ever.

Israel's Return from Exile

6 "In that coming day," says the LORD,
"I will gather together those who are lame,

Question 3:8

Micah compared himself to the false prophets and checked to make sure that his motives, his message, and his heart were in line with God. What difference does it make to live filled with the power of the Holy Spirit?

Make a Difference 4:5

Road Less Traveled

Whom are you going to serve? Scripture repeatedly presents the idea that we cannot serve two masters. Joshua 24:15 calls us to "choose today whom you will serve." In 1 John 2:15 we learn that "when you love the world, you do not have the love of the Father in you." Jesus said that we can't serve God and money (Matthew 6:24).

What and whom are you following? A lot of people are trying to follow multiple "gods." This might make you feel like choosing God is choosing the road less traveled. Still, in Mark 8:36, Jesus said, "What do you benefit if you gain the whole world but lose your own soul?" It may be a road less traveled, but it has the greatest reward.

Difference Maker

Write down how you spend your free time. Star the areas that help you grow in your faith, like reading the Bible, praying, worshiping, journaling. How many stars did you mark? Finally ask yourself, "If I say I love God, does my free time reflect that I am choosing him daily?"

those who have been exiles,
and those whom I have filled with grief.
7 Those who are weak will survive as a remnant;
those who were exiles will become a
strong nation.
Then I, the LORD, will rule from Jerusalem*
as their king forever."
8 As for you, Jerusalem,
the citadel of God's people,*
your royal might and power
will come back to you again.
The kingship will be restored
to my precious Jerusalem.

9 But why are you now screaming in terror?
Have you no king to lead you?
Have your wise people all died?
Pain has gripped you like a woman in childbirth.
10 Writhe and groan like a woman in labor,
you people of Jerusalem,*
for now you must leave this city
to live in the open country.
You will soon be sent in exile
to distant Babylon.
But the LORD will rescue you there;
he will redeem you from the grip of
your enemies.

11 Now many nations have gathered against you.
"Let her be desecrated," they say.
"Let us see the destruction of Jerusalem.*"
12 But they do not know the LORD's thoughts
or understand his plan.
These nations don't know
that he is gathering them together
to be beaten and trampled
like sheaves of grain on a threshing floor.
13 "Rise up and crush the nations, O Jerusalem!"*
says the LORD.
"For I will give you iron horns and bronze hooves,
so you can trample many nations to pieces.
You will present their stolen riches to the LORD,
their wealth to the Lord of all the earth."

5 1*Mobilize! Marshal your troops!
The enemy is laying siege to Jerusalem.
They will strike Israel's leader
in the face with a rod.

4:7 Hebrew *Mount Zion.* 4:8 Hebrew *As for you, Migdal-eder, / the Ophel of the daughter of Zion.* 4:10 Hebrew *O daughter of Zion.* 4:11 Hebrew *of Zion.* 4:13 Hebrew *"Rise up and thresh, O daughter of Zion."* 5:1 Verse 5:1 is numbered 4:14 in Hebrew text.

A Ruler from Bethlehem

2*But you, O Bethlehem Ephrathah,
are only a small village among all the people
of Judah.
Yet a ruler of Israel,
whose origins are in the distant past,
will come from you on my behalf.
3 The people of Israel will be abandoned to their enemies
until the woman in labor gives birth.
Then at last his fellow countrymen
will return from exile to their own land.
4 And he will stand to lead his flock with the LORD's strength,
in the majesty of the name of the LORD his God.
Then his people will live there undisturbed,
for he will be highly honored around the world.
5 And he will be the source of peace.

When the Assyrians invade our land
and break through our defenses,
we will appoint seven rulers to watch over us,
eight princes to lead us.
6 They will rule Assyria with drawn swords
and enter the gates of the land of Nimrod.
He will rescue us from the Assyrians
when they pour over the borders to invade our land.

The Remnant Purified

7 Then the remnant left in Israel*
will take their place among the nations.
They will be like dew sent by the LORD
or like rain falling on the grass,
which no one can hold back
and no one can restrain.
8 The remnant left in Israel
will take their place among the nations.
They will be like a lion among the animals of the forest,
like a strong young lion among flocks of sheep and goats,
pouncing and tearing as they go
with no rescuer in sight.
9 The people of Israel will stand up to their foes,
and all their enemies will be wiped out.

10 "In that day," says the LORD,
"I will slaughter your horses
and destroy your chariots.
11 I will tear down your walls
and demolish your defenses.
12 I will put an end to all witchcraft,
and there will be no more fortune-tellers.

5:2 Verses 5:2-15 are numbered 5:1-14 in Hebrew text. 5:7 Hebrew *in Jacob;* also in 5:8. See note on 1:5a.

Story Arc **5:2-4**

● Bethlehem

Off to the side, overlooked, small, and poor—this is the picture of the little town of Bethlehem. It is a town of shepherds and families on the outskirts of the real focal point, Jerusalem. Even so, this sheepherding community would become a pivotal difference maker in God's plan. David, the shepherd-king, the champion of Israel, was born there, and the King of kings, the Messiah, the Savior, the World Changer took his first breaths in this same humble town.

Hab 1:1 ►

Make a Difference 6:8

What to Do

Do you know what to do today? Did you know that God has already told you? He has already told everybody, in fact. He has made it pretty clear. God has let the world know what he believes is good—not good as in "I guess that's cool" but good as in God-looked-at-all-he-had-made-and-he-saw-that-it-was-good good. Got that?

Well, what is good in God's eyes? He tells us: Do what is right. Love mercy. Walk humbly with him.

Simple. There's nothing confusing. This was why God created people. Oh, how far from "good" has humanity fallen! What would happen if people set their efforts on restoring these patterns to the earth once again?

Difference Maker

Which of the three requirements do you most need to focus on today? What is one action you could take to pursue that focus?

13 I will destroy all your idols and sacred pillars,
so you will never again worship the work of your own hands.
14 I will abolish your idol shrines with their Asherah poles
and destroy your pagan cities.
15 I will pour out my vengeance
on all the nations that refuse to obey me."

The LORD's Case against Israel

6 Listen to what the LORD is saying:

"Stand up and state your case against me.
Let the mountains and hills be called to witness your complaints.
2 And now, O mountains,
listen to the LORD's complaint!
He has a case against his people.
He will bring charges against Israel.

3 "O my people, what have I done to you?
What have I done to make you tired of me?
Answer me!
4 For I brought you out of Egypt
and redeemed you from slavery.
I sent Moses, Aaron, and Miriam to help you.
5 Don't you remember, my people,
how King Balak of Moab tried to have you cursed
and how Balaam son of Beor blessed you instead?
And remember your journey from Acacia Grove* to Gilgal,
when I, the LORD, did everything I could
to teach you about my faithfulness."

6 What can we bring to the LORD?
Should we bring him burnt offerings?
Should we bow before God Most High
with offerings of yearling calves?
7 Should we offer him thousands of rams
and ten thousand rivers of olive oil?
Should we sacrifice our firstborn children
to pay for our sins?

8 No, O people, the LORD has told you what is good,
and this is what he requires of you:
to do what is right, to love mercy,
and to walk humbly with your God.

Israel's Guilt and Punishment

9 Fear the LORD if you are wise!
His voice calls to everyone in Jerusalem:
"The armies of destruction are coming;
the LORD is sending them.*

6:5 Hebrew *Shittim.* 6:9 Hebrew *"Listen to the rod. / Who appointed it?"*

10 What shall I say about the homes of the wicked
filled with treasures gained by cheating?
What about the disgusting practice
of measuring out grain with dishonest measures?*
11 How can I tolerate your merchants
who use dishonest scales and weights?
12 The rich among you have become wealthy
through extortion and violence.
Your citizens are so used to lying
that their tongues can no longer tell the truth.

13 "Therefore, I will wound you!
I will bring you to ruin for all your sins.
14 You will eat but never have enough.
Your hunger pangs and emptiness will remain.
And though you try to save your money,
it will come to nothing in the end.
You will save a little,
but I will give it to those who conquer you.
15 You will plant crops
but not harvest them.
You will press your olives
but not get enough oil to anoint yourselves.
You will trample the grapes
but get no juice to make your wine.
16 You keep only the laws of evil King Omri;
you follow only the example of wicked King Ahab!
Therefore, I will make an example of you,
bringing you to complete ruin.
You will be treated with contempt,
mocked by all who see you."

Misery Turned to Hope

7 1 How miserable I am!
I feel like the fruit picker after the harvest
who can find nothing to eat.
Not a cluster of grapes or a single early fig
can be found to satisfy my hunger.
2 The godly people have all disappeared;
not one honest person is left on the earth.
They are all murderers,
setting traps even for their own brothers.
3 Both their hands are equally skilled at doing evil!
Officials and judges alike demand bribes.
The people with influence get what they want,
and together they scheme to twist justice.
4 Even the best of them is like a brier;
the most honest is as dangerous as a hedge of thorns.
But your judgment day is coming swiftly now.

6:10 Hebrew *of using the short ephah?* The ephah was a unit for measuring grain.

Your time of punishment is here, a time of confusion.
5 Don't trust anyone—
not your best friend or even your wife!
6 For the son despises his father.
The daughter defies her mother.
The daughter-in-law defies her mother-in-law.
Your enemies are right in your own household!

7 As for me, I look to the LORD for help.
I wait confidently for God to save me,
and my God will certainly hear me.
8 Do not gloat over me, my enemies!
For though I fall, I will rise again.
Though I sit in darkness,
the LORD will be my light.
9 I will be patient as the LORD punishes me,
for I have sinned against him.
But after that, he will take up my case
and give me justice for all I have suffered from my enemies.
The LORD will bring me into the light,
and I will see his righteousness.
10 Then my enemies will see that the LORD is on my side.
They will be ashamed that they taunted me, saying,
"So where is the LORD—
that God of yours?"
With my own eyes I will see their downfall;
they will be trampled like mud in the streets.

11 In that day, Israel, your cities will be rebuilt,
and your borders will be extended.
12 People from many lands will come and honor you—
from Assyria all the way to the towns of Egypt,
from Egypt all the way to the Euphrates River,*
and from distant seas and mountains.
13 But the land* will become empty and desolate
because of the wickedness of those who live there.

The LORD's Compassion on Israel

14 O LORD, protect your people with your shepherd's staff;
lead your flock, your special possession.
Though they live alone in a thicket
on the heights of Mount Carmel,*
let them graze in the fertile pastures of Bashan and Gilead
as they did long ago.

15 "Yes," says the LORD,
"I will do mighty miracles for you,
like those I did when I rescued you
from slavery in Egypt."

7:12 Hebrew *the river.* 7:13 Or *earth.* 7:14 Or *surrounded by a fruitful land.*

Make a Difference

7:7-10

My Posture

God's kindness leads us to turn from sin (Romans 2:4). Because we have sinned against God, we are called to repent and turn from our old ways and receive a new posture. This new posture sees things differently, understands freedom, and experiences the tension of what was and what God has for us in him. This posture is us walking toward God and away from the habits and sins that keep us depressed, in a mindset of poor judgment, and feeling hopeless. This new posture is one of freedom.

Difference Maker

Read 2 Corinthians 5:17-21. What does it look like to see God's righteousness, and what will you change in the way you live?

16 All the nations of the world will stand amazed
at what the LORD will do for you.
They will be embarrassed
at their feeble power.
They will cover their mouths in silent awe,
deaf to everything around them.
17 Like snakes crawling from their holes,
they will come out to meet the LORD our God.
They will fear him greatly,
trembling in terror at his presence.

18 Where is another God like you,
who pardons the guilt of the remnant,
overlooking the sins of his special people?
You will not stay angry with your people forever,
because you delight in showing unfailing love.
19 Once again you will have compassion on us.
You will trample our sins under your feet
and throw them into the depths of the ocean!
20 You will show us your faithfulness and unfailing love
as you promised to our ancestors Abraham and Jacob long ago.

Question 7:18

What does this verse tell us about the character of God? How does God's character demonstrate love for his people? How have you experienced God's character in your own life?

Nahum Introduction

One hundred years after the great fish spit Jonah back onto land, Nineveh had fallen back into sin. Now an unrepentant Assyrian city, Nineveh wanted nothing to do with the God of Israel. This time around, rather than offering mercy, God absolutely ripped into Nineveh.

The book of Nahum is the message Jonah wanted to preach. For the whole book, God is unrelenting in his message of judgment. Nahum is not an uplifting book. Don't spend too much time in this book if you need an easy pick-me-up passage of the Bible. Nahum is not for the faint of heart. Nahum is not for the nice. Nahum is God's all-out, mixed-martial-arts beatdown on a nation that refused to acknowledge his authority and his patterns.

Still, for the follower of God, there is a thread of hope in this frightful vision. Nahum's message for the world was that the Lord would not allow his plan of salvation through the tribe of Judah to be stopped. He would not allow the fruitfulness of Israel to disappear. He would bring good news through this land.

Watch out, O enemies of God, for "there is no healing for your wound; your injury is fatal," declares the Lord (Nahum 3:19).

Nahum

1 This message concerning Nineveh came as a vision to Nahum, who lived in Elkosh.

The LORD's Anger against Nineveh

2 The LORD is a jealous God,
filled with vengeance and rage.
He takes revenge on all who oppose him
and continues to rage against his enemies!
3 The LORD is slow to get angry, but his power is great,
and he never lets the guilty go unpunished.
He displays his power in the whirlwind and the storm.
The billowing clouds are the dust beneath his feet.
4 At his command the oceans dry up,
and the rivers disappear.
The lush pastures of Bashan and Carmel fade,
and the green forests of Lebanon wither.
5 In his presence the mountains quake,
and the hills melt away;
the earth trembles,
and its people are destroyed.
6 Who can stand before his fierce anger?
Who can survive his burning fury?
His rage blazes forth like fire,
and the mountains crumble to dust in his presence.

7 The LORD is good,
a strong refuge when trouble comes.
He is close to those who trust in him.
8 But he will sweep away his enemies*
in an overwhelming flood.
He will pursue his foes
into the darkness of night.

9 Why are you scheming against the LORD?
He will destroy you with one blow;
he won't need to strike twice!
10 His enemies, tangled like thornbushes
and staggering like drunks,
will be burned up like dry stubble in a field.
11 Who is this wicked counselor of yours
who plots evil against the LORD?

Question 1:1

The name *Nahum* means "comfort." Is this a surprise to you? How is this name a contrast with the message he has for Nineveh?

Question 1:7-8

What difference do verses 7 and 8 make in the grand scope of human history?

1:8 As in Greek version; Hebrew reads *sweep away her place.*

12 This is what the LORD says:
"Though the Assyrians have many allies,
they will be destroyed and disappear.
O my people, I have punished you before,
but I will not punish you again.
13 Now I will break the yoke of bondage from your neck
and tear off the chains of Assyrian oppression."

14 And this is what the LORD says concerning the Assyrians
in Nineveh:
"You will have no more children to carry on your name.
I will destroy all the idols in the temples of your gods.
I am preparing a grave for you
because you are despicable!"

15*Look! A messenger is coming over the mountains with good news!
He is bringing a message of peace.
Celebrate your festivals, O people of Judah,
and fulfill all your vows,
for your wicked enemies will never invade your land again.
They will be completely destroyed!

The Fall of Nineveh

2 1*Your enemy is coming to crush you, Nineveh.
Man the ramparts! Watch the roads!
Prepare your defenses! Call out your forces!

2 Even though the destroyer has destroyed Judah,
the LORD will restore its honor.
Israel's vine has been stripped of branches,
but he will restore its splendor.

3 Shields flash red in the sunlight!
See the scarlet uniforms of the valiant troops!
Watch as their glittering chariots move into position,
with a forest of spears waving above them.*
4 The chariots race recklessly along the streets
and rush wildly through the squares.
They flash like firelight
and move as swiftly as lightning.
5 The king shouts to his officers;
they stumble in their haste,
rushing to the walls to set up their defenses.
6 The river gates have been torn open!
The palace is about to collapse!
7 Nineveh's exile has been decreed,
and all the servant girls mourn its capture.
They moan like doves
and beat their breasts in sorrow.

1:15 Verse 1:15 is numbered 2:1 in Hebrew text. 2:1 Verses 2:1-13 are numbered 2:2-14 in Hebrew text. 2:3 Greek and Syriac versions read *into position, / the horses whipped into a frenzy.*

Make a Difference 2:15

Bold Comparison

While Nahum unleashed his vision of destruction upon Nineveh and the Assyrian Empire, he wanted those enemies to take a moment, just a moment, to look up and catch a glimpse of something. A messenger was coming from the mountain! If you were in Nineveh, a kernel of hope might perk up within you, just for a moment until the messenger turned to Judah. The news was good...for Judah. The news was peace...for Judah.

How can this be? Nineveh completely destroyed Judah (2:2)! How can Judah be restored? How can the shattered vine branches of Israel rise again? They didn't realize God would break the oppressive practices and destroy the wicked patterns of Judah's enemies. The process will be alarming. The next two-and-a-half chapters of Nahum are stark. God's messengers offered a bold truth against sin. God would fulfill his promise of salvation. God would not allow his gospel to be destroyed.

Difference Maker

Read Psalm 121. Where does your ultimate help come from? Take several minutes to declare aloud God's hope in the midst of any struggles you face.

8 Nineveh is like a leaking water reservoir!
The people are slipping away.
"Stop, stop!" someone shouts,
but no one even looks back.
9 Loot the silver!
Plunder the gold!
There's no end to Nineveh's treasures—
its vast, uncounted wealth.
10 Soon the city is plundered, empty, and ruined.
Hearts melt and knees shake.
The people stand aghast,
their faces pale and trembling.

11 Where now is that great Nineveh,
that den filled with young lions?
It was a place where people—like lions and their cubs—
walked freely and without fear.
12 The lion tore up meat for his cubs
and strangled prey for his mate.
He filled his den with prey,
his caverns with his plunder.

13 "I am your enemy!"
says the LORD of Heaven's Armies.
"Your chariots will soon go up in smoke.
Your young men* will be killed in battle.
Never again will you plunder conquered nations.
The voices of your proud messengers will be heard
no more."

The LORD's Judgment against Nineveh

3 1 What sorrow awaits Nineveh,
the city of murder and lies!
She is crammed with wealth
and is never without victims.
2 Hear the crack of whips,
the rumble of wheels!
Horses' hooves pound,
and chariots clatter wildly.
3 See the flashing swords and glittering spears
as the charioteers charge past!
There are countless casualties,
heaps of bodies—
so many bodies that
people stumble over them.
4 All this because Nineveh,
the beautiful and faithless city,
mistress of deadly charms,
enticed the nations with her beauty.

2:13 Hebrew *young lions.*

She taught them all her magic,
enchanting people everywhere.

5 "I am your enemy!"
says the LORD of Heaven's Armies.
"And now I will lift your skirts
and show all the earth your nakedness and shame.
6 I will cover you with filth
and show the world how vile you really are.
7 All who see you will shrink back and say,
'Nineveh lies in ruins.
Where are the mourners?'
Does anyone regret your destruction?"

8 Are you any better than the city of Thebes,*
situated on the Nile River, surrounded by water?
She was protected by the river on all sides,
walled in by water.
9 Ethiopia* and the land of Egypt
gave unlimited assistance.
The nations of Put and Libya
were among her allies.
10 Yet Thebes fell,
and her people were led away as captives.
Her babies were dashed to death
against the stones of the streets.
Soldiers threw dice* to get Egyptian officers as servants.
All their leaders were bound in chains.

11 And you, Nineveh, will also stagger like a drunkard.
You will hide for fear of the attacking enemy.
12 All your fortresses will fall.
They will be devoured like the ripe figs
that fall into the mouths
of those who shake the trees.
13 Your troops will be as weak
and helpless as women.
The gates of your land will be opened wide to
the enemy
and set on fire and burned.
14 Get ready for the siege!
Store up water!
Strengthen the defenses!
Go into the pits to trample clay,
and pack it into molds,
making bricks to repair the walls.

15 But the fire will devour you;
the sword will cut you down.

3:8 Hebrew *No-amon;* also in 3:10. 3:9 Hebrew *Cush.* 3:10 Hebrew *They cast lots.*

The enemy will consume you like locusts,
devouring everything they see.
There will be no escape,
even if you multiply like swarming locusts.
16 Your merchants have multiplied
until they outnumber the stars.
But like a swarm of locusts,
they strip the land and fly away.
17 Your guards* and officials are also like swarming locusts
that crowd together in the hedges on a cold day.
But like locusts that fly away when the sun comes up,
all of them will fly away and disappear.

18 Your shepherds are asleep, O Assyrian king;
your princes lie dead in the dust.
Your people are scattered across the mountains
with no one to gather them together.
19 There is no healing for your wound;
your injury is fatal.
All who hear of your destruction
will clap their hands for joy.
Where can anyone be found
who has not suffered from your continual cruelty?

3:17 Or *princes.*

Make a Difference 3:19

What Message?

This chilling final verse is in the present tense. While our focus tends to be on what God is going to do to his enemies, God's focus is on what he is going to do for his people who have been oppressed. The good news here is that the Lord fights for those who are called by his name. The good news is that "the LORD is good, a strong refuge when trouble comes. He is close to those who trust him" (1:7). The Lord is slow to anger, but he will not stand idly by (1:3).

Difference Maker

Look for a friend or family member who has been suffering. Bring them a message of hope by writing an encouraging card. Let them know that the Lord sees their trouble and cares for them. Write "Nahum 1:7" in the card and deliver it today.

Habakkuk Introduction

The book of Habakkuk was written during a time when the people of God were rebelling, which happened and still happens far too often. The book opens with the prophet Habakkuk crying out to God, complaining about all the injustice he saw. He had been waiting for God to do something and wondering why he seemed so silent.

God's silence, though, did not mean he wasn't at work. God eventually answered by saying, "I am doing something in your own day, something you wouldn't believe, even if someone told you about it" (Habakkuk 1:5). Just as God said, Habakkuk was shocked when he learned that God was working to bring correction to his people by raising up a nation that was even more evil than Judah to judge Judah's sinful behavior.

In his limited ability to see and understand the ways of God, Habakkuk learned that God doesn't always seem fair in our eyes, and Habakkuk learned that was actually a good thing. God's plans and timing are beyond our ability to understand fully. God is under no obligation to reveal what he is doing and when he is going to do it. Even so, we can have the confidence that he is always working. We get to observe, be amazed, be humbled, be emboldened, and stand in the awesome wonder of God.

The book of Habakkuk starts with angst and ends with adoration. The prophet moved from worrying to actually worshiping. It's like he was saying, "God, you are not as big as I thought you were. You are much bigger."

Story Arc

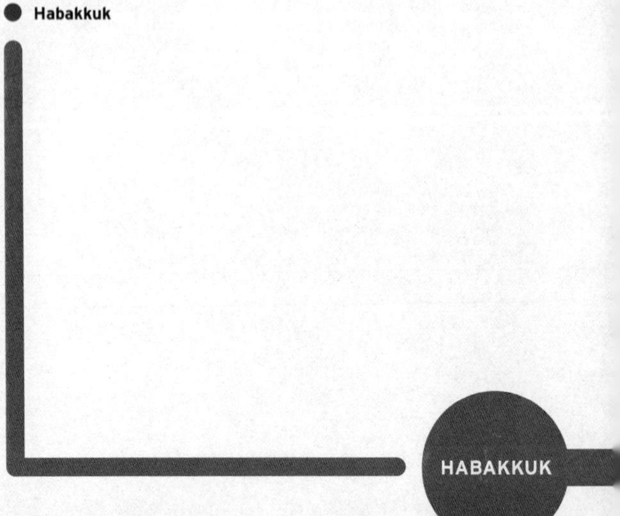

Habakkuk

1 This is the message that the prophet Habakkuk received in a vision.

Habakkuk's Complaint

2 How long, O LORD, must I call for help?
But you do not listen!
"Violence is everywhere!" I cry,
but you do not come to save.
3 Must I forever see these evil deeds?
Why must I watch all this misery?
Wherever I look,
I see destruction and violence.
I am surrounded by people
who love to argue and fight.
4 The law has become paralyzed,
and there is no justice in the courts.
The wicked far outnumber the righteous,
so that justice has become perverted.

The LORD's Reply

5 The LORD replied,

"Look around at the nations;
look and be amazed!*
For I am doing something in your own day,
something you wouldn't believe
even if someone told you about it.
6 I am raising up the Babylonians,*
a cruel and violent people.
They will march across the world
and conquer other lands.
7 They are notorious for their cruelty
and do whatever they like.
8 Their horses are swifter than cheetahs*
and fiercer than wolves at dusk.
Their charioteers charge from far away.
Like eagles, they swoop down to devour their prey.

9 "On they come, all bent on violence.
Their hordes advance like a desert wind,
sweeping captives ahead of them like sand.
10 They scoff at kings and princes

1:5 Greek version reads *Look, you mockers; / look and be amazed and die.* Compare Acts 13:41.
1:6 Or *Chaldeans.* 1:8 Or *leopards.*

Story Arc **1:1**

● Habakkuk

We don't know a lot about Habakkuk. We do know he lived during a difficult time for the people of Israel (likely around the same time as the prophets Jeremiah and Zephaniah), when there was great upheaval and fear. We also know that Habakkuk had struggles just like we do. In the midst of his circumstances, we see his flaws and his questions, and we feel his doubt. He just wanted to see God in action, but God's silence did not mean that God was not at work. As we read, let's imagine ourselves asking the same sorts of questions and discovering the same sort of faith as the prophet Habakkuk.

Zech 1:1 ►

Question 1:12

Have you ever wondered, *God, what are you doing?* What Habakkuk saw happening and what he believed about God were not lining up. How can you grow to trust God when he is not working in the ways you expect him to?

Make a Difference 2:3

Waiting Is Not Wasting

Waiting is hard, and we do not wait well. Waiting on God is a difficult task, but it is a good thing. Waiting on God teaches us to trust him. In our waiting, we learn that his pace and his plans are perfect.

Are you waiting on God to do something in your life? Remember, he may answer, "Yes," and blow your mind, or he may say, "No, that's not for you." He may also be saying, "Not now" or "Not yet," and you get to wait patiently on his plan in his time.

Difference Maker

Write down something big that you are waiting on in your life. Talk to God about it right now but also let him know that if it is his will, you are willing to wait.

and scorn all their fortresses.
They simply pile ramps of earth
against their walls and capture them!
11 They sweep past like the wind
and are gone.
But they are deeply guilty,
for their own strength is their god."

Habakkuk's Second Complaint

12 O LORD my God, my Holy One, you who are eternal—
surely you do not plan to wipe us out?
O LORD, our Rock, you have sent these Babylonians to correct us,
to punish us for our many sins.
13 But you are pure and cannot stand the sight of evil.
Will you wink at their treachery?
Should you be silent while the wicked
swallow up people more righteous than they?

14 Are we only fish to be caught and killed?
Are we only sea creatures that have no leader?
15 Must we be strung up on their hooks
and caught in their nets while they rejoice and celebrate?
16 Then they will worship their nets
and burn incense in front of them.
"These nets are the gods who have made us rich!"
they will claim.
17 Will you let them get away with this forever?
Will they succeed forever in their heartless conquests?

2 1 I will climb up to my watchtower
and stand at my guardpost.
There I will wait to see what the LORD says
and how he* will answer my complaint.

The LORD's Second Reply

2 Then the LORD said to me,

"Write my answer plainly on tablets,
so that a runner can carry the correct message to others.
3 This vision is for a future time.
It describes the end, and it will be fulfilled.
If it seems slow in coming, wait patiently,
for it will surely take place.
It will not be delayed.

4 "Look at the proud!
They trust in themselves, and their lives are crooked.
But the righteous will live by their faithfulness to God.*

2:1 As in Syriac version; Hebrew reads *I.* 2:3b-4 Greek version reads *If the vision is delayed, wait patiently, / for it will surely come and not delay. / 4 I will take no pleasure in anyone who turns away. / But the righteous person will live by my faith.* Compare Rom 1:17; Gal 3:11; Heb 10:37-38.

5 Wealth* is treacherous,
and the arrogant are never at rest.
They open their mouths as wide as the grave,*
and like death, they are never satisfied.
In their greed they have gathered up many nations
and swallowed many peoples.

6 "But soon their captives will taunt them.
They will mock them, saying,
'What sorrow awaits you thieves!
Now you will get what you deserve!
You've become rich by extortion,
but how much longer can this go on?'
7 Suddenly, your debtors will take action.
They will turn on you and take all you have,
while you stand trembling and helpless.
8 Because you have plundered many nations,
now all the survivors will plunder you.
You committed murder throughout the countryside
and filled the towns with violence.

9 "What sorrow awaits you who build big houses
with money gained dishonestly!
You believe your wealth will buy security,
putting your family's nest beyond the reach of danger.
10 But by the murders you committed,
you have shamed your name and forfeited your lives.
11 The very stones in the walls cry out against you,
and the beams in the ceilings echo the complaint.

12 "What sorrow awaits you who build cities
with money gained through murder and corruption!
13 Has not the LORD of Heaven's Armies promised
that the wealth of nations will turn to ashes?
They work so hard,
but all in vain!
14 For as the waters fill the sea,
the earth will be filled with an awareness
of the glory of the LORD.

15 "What sorrow awaits you who make your neighbors drunk!
You force your cup on them
so you can gloat over their shameful nakedness.
16 But soon it will be your turn to be disgraced.
Come, drink and be exposed!*
Drink from the cup of the LORD's judgment,
and all your glory will be turned to shame.
17 You cut down the forests of Lebanon.
Now you will be cut down.

2:5a As in Dead Sea Scroll 1QpHab; other Hebrew manuscripts read *Wine.* 2:5b Hebrew *as Sheol.* 2:16 Dead Sea Scrolls and Greek and Syriac versions read *and stagger!*

Prayer **2:20**

Lord, I want to hear from you, so I will continue to listen. I will listen when I pray, I will listen as I read your Word, and in the times I do not hear you, I will wait in that silence patiently and faithfully. Amen.

Make a Difference **3:2**

Please Be Unfair

Habakkuk asked God to remember mercy in his wrath. Mercy and grace go hand in hand throughout Scripture. Mercy is holding back punishment that one deserves. Grace is receiving a gift that one does not deserve. God sets aside fairness today and replaces it with forgiveness when we openly declare with our mouth that Jesus is Lord and believe in our heart that God raised Jesus from the dead (Romans 10:9). This holds back God's wrath from us and gifts us eternal life with him! When it comes to God's wrath, we all want unfairness to fall in our favor.

Difference Maker

As followers of Jesus, God wants us to extend that level of unfairness to others. Who is someone you know who needs Jesus, and how can you extend grace and mercy to that person this week?

You destroyed the wild animals,
so now their terror will be yours.
You committed murder throughout the countryside
and filled the towns with violence.

18 "What good is an idol carved by man,
or a cast image that deceives you?
How foolish to trust in your own creation—
a god that can't even talk!
19 What sorrow awaits you who say to wooden idols,
'Wake up and save us!'
To speechless stone images you say,
'Rise up and teach us!'
Can an idol tell you what to do?
They may be overlaid with gold and silver,
but they are lifeless inside.
20 But the LORD is in his holy Temple.
Let all the earth be silent before him."

Habakkuk's Prayer

3 This prayer was sung by the prophet Habakkuk*:

2 I have heard all about you, LORD.
I am filled with awe by your amazing works.
In this time of our deep need,
help us again as you did in years gone by.
And in your anger,
remember your mercy.

3 I see God moving across the deserts from Edom,*
the Holy One coming from Mount Paran.*
His brilliant splendor fills the heavens,
and the earth is filled with his praise.
4 His coming is as brilliant as the sunrise.
Rays of light flash from his hands,
where his awesome power is hidden.
5 Pestilence marches before him;
plague follows close behind.
6 When he stops, the earth shakes.
When he looks, the nations tremble.
He shatters the everlasting mountains
and levels the eternal hills.
He is the Eternal One!*
7 I see the people of Cushan in distress,
and the nation of Midian trembling in terror.

8 Was it in anger, LORD, that you struck the rivers
and parted the sea?

3:1 Hebrew adds *according to shigionoth,* probably indicating the musical setting for the prayer. 3:3a Hebrew *Teman.* 3:3b Hebrew adds *selah;* also in 3:9, 13. The meaning of this Hebrew term is uncertain; it is probably a musical or literary term. 3:6 Or *The ancient paths belong to him.*

Were you displeased with them?
No, you were sending your chariots of salvation!
9 You brandished your bow
and your quiver of arrows.
You split open the earth with flowing rivers.
10 The mountains watched and trembled.
Onward swept the raging waters.
The mighty deep cried out,
lifting its hands in submission.
11 The sun and moon stood still in the sky
as your brilliant arrows flew
and your glittering spear flashed.

12 You marched across the land in anger
and trampled the nations in your fury.
13 You went out to rescue your chosen people,
to save your anointed ones.
You crushed the heads of the wicked
and stripped their bones from head to toe.
14 With his own weapons,
you destroyed the chief of those
who rushed out like a whirlwind,
thinking Israel would be easy prey.
15 You trampled the sea with your horses,
and the mighty waters piled high.

16 I trembled inside when I heard this;
my lips quivered with fear.
My legs gave way beneath me,*
and I shook in terror.
I will wait quietly for the coming day
when disaster will strike the people who invade us.
17 Even though the fig trees have no blossoms,
and there are no grapes on the vines;
even though the olive crop fails,
and the fields lie empty and barren;
even though the flocks die in the fields,
and the cattle barns are empty,
18 yet I will rejoice in the LORD!
I will be joyful in the God of my salvation!
19 The Sovereign LORD is my strength!
He makes me as surefooted as a deer,*
able to tread upon the heights.

(For the choir director: This prayer is to be accompanied by stringed instruments.)

3:16 Hebrew *Decay entered my bones.* **3:19** Or *He gives me the speed of a deer.*

Question 3:15–20

God is awesome in the miracles, and he is no less awesome in our messes. In verses 17 and 18, Habakkuk shared a list of what could be excuses for being frustrated with God, but instead he said, "I will rejoice!" What are the "even though" statements that have kept you from a deeper relationship with Jesus? What are your "even though" moments when you need to remember how awesome God is?

Prayer 3:19

Jesus, this world needs you! I place my hope in your salvation today. Amen.

Zephaniah Introduction

The book of Zephaniah is a punch in the gut for those who are apathetic about God. The book of Zephaniah is also an uplifting arm for those who are seeking God's work in their lives.

During the reign of King Josiah in Judah (Jerusalem), the Lord gave this message to Zephaniah, a great-grandson of King Hezekiah. Both kings, Josiah and Hezekiah, tried passionately to redirect people to worship God. To some degree they were each successful. Still, in Josiah's day, people were growing increasingly frightened of the power of surrounding nations and decreasingly aware of the presence of the Lord.

These were frightening times in Judah, yet the hope of the book of Zephaniah is that the Lord will still work his plan of salvation through his people. Despite their stubbornness, despite their sin, God did not forsake them because he would not forsake his gospel promise—that the whole world would be blessed through his people (Zephaniah 3:9). Even though their hearts had left him, God refused to leave his people. The Lord was "still there in the city" (3:5).

God's goal was to refine his people until they were humble. When people let go of their arrogance, they recognize their need for the Savior. When people see their need, they begin to seek and trust in the name of the Lord (3:12). The book of Zephaniah challenges us to examine ourselves and consider which category of faith we fall into: stubborn apathy toward God or humble seeking of God.

Zephaniah

1 The LORD gave this message to Zephaniah when Josiah son of Amon was king of Judah. Zephaniah was the son of Cushi, son of Gedaliah, son of Amariah, son of Hezekiah.

Coming Judgment against Judah

2 "I will sweep away everything
from the face of the earth," says the LORD.
3 "I will sweep away people and animals alike.
I will sweep away the birds of the sky and the fish in the sea.
I will reduce the wicked to heaps of rubble,*
and I will wipe humanity from the face of the earth,"
says the LORD.
4 "I will crush Judah and Jerusalem with my fist
and destroy every last trace of their Baal worship.
I will put an end to all the idolatrous priests,
so that even the memory of them will disappear.
5 For they go up to their roofs
and bow down to the sun, moon, and stars.
They claim to follow the LORD,
but then they worship Molech,* too.
6 And I will destroy those who used to worship me
but now no longer do.
They no longer ask for the LORD's guidance
or seek my blessings."

7 Stand in silence in the presence of the Sovereign LORD,
for the awesome day of the LORD's judgment is near.
The LORD has prepared his people for a great slaughter
and has chosen their executioners.*
8 "On that day of judgment,"
says the LORD,
"I will punish the leaders and princes of Judah
and all those following pagan customs.
9 Yes, I will punish those who participate in pagan
worship ceremonies,
and those who fill their masters' houses with violence
and deceit.

10 "On that day," says the LORD,
"a cry of alarm will come from the Fish Gate

1:3 The meaning of the Hebrew is uncertain. 1:5 Hebrew *Malcam,* a variant spelling of Molech; or it could possibly mean *their king.* 1:7 Hebrew *has prepared a sacrifice and sanctified his guests.*

Question 1:12

Are you guilty of this? Do you keep sinning, thinking that the Lord will never actually do anything about it? Do you keep living life thinking that God won't do anything good for you? What could you do today to notice that God notices you?

and echo throughout the New Quarter of the city.*
And a great crash will sound from the hills.
11 Wail in sorrow, all you who live in the market area,*
for all the merchants and traders will be destroyed.

12 "I will search with lanterns in Jerusalem's darkest corners
to punish those who sit complacent in their sins.
They think the LORD will do nothing to them,
either good or bad.
13 So their property will be plundered,
their homes will be ransacked.
They will build new homes
but never live in them.
They will plant vineyards
but never drink wine from them.

14 "That terrible day of the LORD is near.
Swiftly it comes—
a day of bitter tears,
a day when even strong men will cry out.
15 It will be a day when the LORD's anger is poured out—
a day of terrible distress and anguish,
a day of ruin and desolation,
a day of darkness and gloom,
a day of clouds and blackness,
16 a day of trumpet calls and battle cries.
Down go the walled cities
and the strongest battlements!

17 "Because you have sinned against the LORD,
I will make you grope around like the blind.
Your blood will be poured into the dust,
and your bodies will lie rotting on the ground."

18 Your silver and gold will not save you
on that day of the LORD's anger.
For the whole land will be devoured
by the fire of his jealousy.
He will make a terrifying end
of all the people on earth.*

A Call to Repentance

2 1 Gather together—yes, gather together,
you shameless nation.
2 Gather before judgment begins,
before your time to repent is blown away like chaff.
Act now, before the fierce fury of the LORD falls
and the terrible day of the LORD's anger begins.

1:10 Or *the Second Quarter,* a newer section of Jerusalem. Hebrew reads *the Mishneh.* 1:11 Or *in the valley,* a lower section of Jerusalem. Hebrew reads *the Maktesh.* 1:18 Or *the people living in the land.*

3 Seek the LORD, all who are humble,
and follow his commands.
Seek to do what is right
and to live humbly.
Perhaps even yet the LORD will protect you—
protect you from his anger on that day of destruction.

Judgment against Philistia

4 Gaza and Ashkelon will be abandoned,
Ashdod and Ekron torn down.
5 And what sorrow awaits you Philistines*
who live along the coast and in the land of Canaan,
for this judgment is against you, too!
The LORD will destroy you
until not one of you is left.
6 The Philistine coast will become a wilderness pasture,
a place of shepherd camps
and enclosures for sheep and goats.
7 The remnant of the tribe of Judah will pasture there.
They will rest at night in the abandoned houses
in Ashkelon.
For the LORD their God will visit his people in kindness
and restore their prosperity again.

Judgment against Moab and Ammon

8 "I have heard the taunts of the Moabites
and the insults of the Ammonites,
mocking my people
and invading their borders.
9 Now, as surely as I live,"
says the LORD of Heaven's Armies, the God of Israel,
"Moab and Ammon will be destroyed—
destroyed as completely as Sodom and Gomorrah.
Their land will become a place of stinging nettles,
salt pits, and eternal desolation.
The remnant of my people will plunder them
and take their land."

10 They will receive the wages of their pride,
for they have scoffed at the people of the LORD of
Heaven's Armies.
11 The LORD will terrify them
as he destroys all the gods in the land.
Then nations around the world will worship the LORD,
each in their own land.

Judgment against Ethiopia and Assyria

12 "You Ethiopians* will also be slaughtered
by my sword," says the LORD.

2:5 Hebrew *Kerethites.* **2:12** Hebrew *Cushites.*

Make a Difference 2:3

Seek

This verse is the opposite (the good opposite!) of 1:12. Where that verse speaks of complacent people who didn't think God would ever do anything, this verse speaks of proactive people who are expectantly looking for the Lord in everything they do.

Zephaniah 2:3 sets a good example for you. When you've made mistakes, seek the Lord. Don't pretend your mistakes away and don't avoid the consequences. Be honest, be humble, and have an authentic perspective. Simply put, seek the Lord and do what's right.

Difference Maker

Write this verse on a piece of paper and tape it somewhere that you will see all day today (for example, your mirror, your steering wheel, your locker, or the back of your phone). Let the words of this verse sink into your soul until you are actively in a habit of looking for God in everything you do.

Question 3:2

To be a "disciple" means to be a "learner." What does having a stubborn heart do to a disciple of God?

13 And the LORD will strike the lands of the north with his fist,
destroying the land of Assyria.
He will make its great capital, Nineveh, a desolate wasteland,
parched like a desert.
14 The proud city will become a pasture for flocks and herds,
and all sorts of wild animals will settle there.
The desert owl and screech owl will roost on its ruined columns,
their calls echoing through the gaping windows.
Rubble will block all the doorways,
and the cedar paneling will be exposed to the weather.
15 This is the boisterous city,
once so secure.
"I am the greatest!" it boasted.
"No other city can compare with me!"
But now, look how it has become an utter ruin,
a haven for wild animals.
Everyone passing by will laugh in derision
and shake a defiant fist.

Jerusalem's Rebellion and Redemption

3 1 What sorrow awaits rebellious, polluted Jerusalem,
the city of violence and crime!
2 No one can tell it anything;
it refuses all correction.
It does not trust in the LORD
or draw near to its God.
3 Its leaders are like roaring lions
hunting for their victims.
Its judges are like ravenous wolves at evening time,
who by dawn have left no trace of their prey.
4 Its prophets are arrogant liars seeking their own gain.
Its priests defile the Temple by disobeying God's instructions.
5 But the LORD is still there in the city,
and he does no wrong.
Day by day he hands down justice,
and he does not fail.
But the wicked know no shame.

6 "I have wiped out many nations,
devastating their fortress walls and towers.
Their streets are now deserted;
their cities lie in silent ruin.
There are no survivors—
none at all.
7 I thought, 'Surely they will have reverence for me now!
Surely they will listen to my warnings.
Then I won't need to strike again,
destroying their homes.'
But no, they get up early
to continue their evil deeds.

8 Therefore, be patient," says the LORD.
"Soon I will stand and accuse these evil nations.
For I have decided to gather the kingdoms of the earth
and pour out my fiercest anger and fury on them.
All the earth will be devoured
by the fire of my jealousy.

9 "Then I will purify the speech of all people,
so that everyone can worship the LORD together.
10 My scattered people who live beyond the rivers of Ethiopia*
will come to present their offerings.
11 On that day you will no longer need to be ashamed,
for you will no longer be rebels against me.
I will remove all proud and arrogant people from
among you.
There will be no more haughtiness on my holy mountain.
12 Those who are left will be the lowly and humble,
for it is they who trust in the name of the LORD.
13 The remnant of Israel will do no wrong;
they will never tell lies or deceive one another.
They will eat and sleep in safety,
and no one will make them afraid."

14 Sing, O daughter of Zion;
shout aloud, O Israel!
Be glad and rejoice with all your heart,
O daughter of Jerusalem!
15 For the LORD will remove his hand of judgment
and will disperse the armies of your enemy.
And the LORD himself, the King of Israel,
will live among you!
At last your troubles will be over,
and you will never again fear disaster.
16 On that day the announcement to Jerusalem will be,
"Cheer up, Zion! Don't be afraid!
17 For the LORD your God is living among you.
He is a mighty savior.
He will take delight in you with gladness.
With his love, he will calm all your fears.*
He will rejoice over you with joyful songs."

18 "I will gather you who mourn for the appointed festivals;
you will be disgraced no more.*
19 And I will deal severely with all who have oppressed you.
I will save the weak and helpless ones;
I will bring together
those who were chased away.
I will give glory and fame to my former exiles,
wherever they have been mocked and shamed.

3:10 Hebrew *Cush.* **3:17** Or *He will be silent in his love.* Greek and Syriac versions read *He will renew you with his love.* **3:18** The meaning of the Hebrew for this verse is uncertain.

Make a Difference

3:15-20

So Much

God wants to be with you so much that he would leave the comforts of heaven to walk with you on earth if he could. Oh, wait. He can, and he did! There may not be a greater desire on his heart than to be with you. He wants to talk about news and sports and weather on your way to school. He wants to help you make a sit-down dinner and then throw soapsuds at you when you clean the dishes. He wants to throw a ball in the park and sing you a lullaby at night.

In the Bible, a guy named Zephaniah spoke about how God's joy hit its peak when he was with his people. Much like a parent enamored by their first grader in the Christmas concert or a husband staring into the eyes of his bride on their wedding day or soldiers who would give their lives to save yours, the Lord loves you with an everlasting love.

Difference Maker

Listen to praise music. Join others in singing. Go for a walk and enjoy what God has made. Whatever way you choose to worship, be sure to celebrate God's heart as he celebrates being with you.

20 On that day I will gather you together
and bring you home again.
I will give you a good name, a name of distinction,
among all the nations of the earth,
as I restore your fortunes before their very eyes.
I, the LORD, have spoken!"

Haggai Introduction

The book of Haggai is truly a wake-up call. Haggai was a prophet sent by the Lord to deliver a message to the Israelites in Judah. They were once in captivity and ruins, but when they were released and regaining influence and prosperity, they started to spend all their energy on their finances, lavishly furnished homes, and themselves. Meanwhile, the temple, God's house, hadn't been rebuilt. The self-centered people hadn't bothered to focus on God, so God said, "My house lies in ruins... while all of you are busy building your own fine houses" (Haggai 1:9).

The whole point of the nation of Israel was to glorify God, be a blessing to the world, and honor each other, yet they didn't always live out their calling. Since the people did not put God first in their lives, their work was not fruitful or productive, and their material possessions did not satisfy. The harder the people worked for themselves, the less they had. It was as if their pockets had holes in them and their stomachs were never-ending pits. Similarly, when we do not prioritize our relationship with God, we have no hope of making a difference in the world.

This book of the Bible helps us understand the dire consequences of passivity and ignorance toward God. It also helps us see what happens when the Israelites hear the word of the Lord and rally each other to get to work. Cutting timber in the forest and laying new foundations, they finally move toward God and not away from him.

Through Haggai, God promised that a brighter, more lavish temple of the Lord would come to exist. What would make it more splendid than what the people had known thus far? It would be our Messiah, Jesus.

Haggai

Question 1:14

Is your attention held on your own "fine house," one built on entertainment and pleasures of the world, or on the Lord? How could "sparked enthusiasm" for God change your surroundings?

A Call to Rebuild the Temple

1 On August 29* of the second year of King Darius's reign, the LORD
gave a message through the prophet Haggai to Zerubbabel son of
Shealtiel, governor of Judah, and to Jeshua* son of Jehozadak, the high
priest.
2"This is what the LORD of Heaven's Armies says: The people are saying,
'The time has not yet come to rebuild the house of the LORD.'"
3Then the LORD sent this message through the prophet Haggai: 4"Why
are you living in luxurious houses while my house lies in ruins? 5This is
what the LORD of Heaven's Armies says: Look at what's happening to you!
6You have planted much but harvest little. You eat but are not satisfied.
You drink but are still thirsty. You put on clothes but cannot keep warm.
Your wages disappear as though you were putting them in pockets filled
with holes!
7"This is what the LORD of Heaven's Armies says: Look at what's happen-
ing to you! 8Now go up into the hills, bring down timber, and rebuild my
house. Then I will take pleasure in it and be honored, says the LORD. 9You
hoped for rich harvests, but they were poor. And when you brought your
harvest home, I blew it away. Why? Because my house lies in ruins, says the
LORD of Heaven's Armies, while all of you are busy building your own fine
houses. 10It's because of you that the heavens withhold the dew and the earth
produces no crops. 11I have called for a drought on your fields and hills—a
drought to wither the grain and grapes and olive trees and all your other
crops, a drought to starve you and your livestock and to ruin everything you
have worked so hard to get."

Obedience to God's Call

12Then Zerubbabel son of Shealtiel, and Jeshua son of Jehozadak, the high
priest, and the whole remnant of God's people began to obey the message
from the LORD their God. When they heard the words of the prophet Hag-
gai, whom the LORD their God had sent, the people feared the LORD. 13Then
Haggai, the LORD's messenger, gave the people this message from the LORD:
"I am with you, says the LORD!"
14So the LORD sparked the enthusiasm of Zerubbabel son of Shealtiel,
governor of Judah, and the enthusiasm of Jeshua son of Jehozadak, the high
priest, and the enthusiasm of the whole remnant of God's people. They
began to work on the house of their God, the LORD of Heaven's Armies, 15on
September 21* of the second year of King Darius's reign.

1:1a Hebrew *On the first day of the sixth month,* of the ancient Hebrew lunar calendar. A number of dates in Haggai can be cross-checked with dates in surviving Persian records and related accurately to our modern calendar. This event occurred on August 29, 520 B.C. **1:1b** Hebrew *Joshua,* a variant spelling of Jeshua; also in 1:12, 14. **1:15** Hebrew *on the twenty-fourth day of the sixth month,* of the ancient Hebrew lunar calendar. This event occurred on September 21, 520 B.C.; also see note on 1:1a.

The New Temple's Diminished Splendor

2 Then on October 17 of that same year,* the LORD sent another message through the prophet Haggai. 2"Say this to Zerubbabel son of Shealtiel, governor of Judah, and to Jeshua* son of Jehozadak, the high priest, and to the remnant of God's people there in the land: 3'Does anyone remember this house—this Temple—in its former splendor? How, in comparison, does it look to you now? It must seem like nothing at all! 4But now the LORD says: Be strong, Zerubbabel. Be strong, Jeshua son of Jehozadak, the high priest. Be strong, all you people still left in the land. And now get to work, for I am with you, says the LORD of Heaven's Armies. 5My Spirit remains among you, just as I promised when you came out of Egypt. So do not be afraid.'

6"For this is what the LORD of Heaven's Armies says: In just a little while I will again shake the heavens and the earth, the oceans and the dry land. 7I will shake all the nations, and the treasures of all the nations will be brought to this Temple. I will fill this place with glory, says the LORD of Heaven's Armies. 8The silver is mine, and the gold is mine, says the LORD of Heaven's Armies. 9The future glory of this Temple will be greater than its past glory, says the LORD of Heaven's Armies. And in this place I will bring peace. I, the LORD of Heaven's Armies, have spoken!"

Blessings Promised for Obedience

10On December 18* of the second year of King Darius's reign, the LORD sent this message to the prophet Haggai: 11"This is what the LORD of Heaven's Armies says. Ask the priests this question about the law: 12'If one of you is carrying some meat from a holy sacrifice in his robes and his robe happens to brush against some bread or stew, wine or olive oil, or any other kind of food, will it also become holy?'"

The priests replied, "No."

13Then Haggai asked, "If someone becomes ceremonially unclean by touching a dead person and then touches any of these foods, will the food be defiled?"

And the priests answered, "Yes."

14Then Haggai responded, "That is how it is with this people and this nation, says the LORD. Everything they do and everything they offer is defiled by their sin. 15Look at what was happening to you before you began to lay the foundation of the LORD's Temple. 16When you hoped for a twenty-bushel crop, you harvested only ten. When you expected to draw fifty gallons from the winepress, you found only twenty. 17I sent blight and mildew and hail to destroy everything you worked so hard to produce. Even so, you refused to return to me, says the LORD.

18"Think about this eighteenth day of December, the day* when the foundation of the LORD's Temple was laid. Think carefully. 19I am giving you a promise now while the seed is still in the barn.* You have not yet harvested your grain, and your grapevines, fig trees, pomegranates, and olive trees have not yet produced their crops. But from this day onward I will bless you."

2:1 Hebrew *on the twenty-first day of the seventh month,* of the ancient Hebrew lunar calendar. This event (in the second year of Darius's reign) occurred on October 17, 520 B.C.; also see note on 1:1a. **2:2** Hebrew *Joshua,* a variant spelling of Jeshua; also in 2:4. **2:10** Hebrew *On the twenty-fourth day of the ninth month,* of the ancient Hebrew lunar calendar (similarly in 2:18). This event occurred on December 18, 520 B.C.; also see note on 1:1a. **2:18** Or *On this eighteenth day of December, think about the day.* **2:19** Hebrew *Is the seed yet in the barn?*

Make a Difference

2:4-5

Get to Work

"Now get to work" (v. 4). The people turned the words of God through Haggai into actions. Rarely did a prophet's message get such fast obedience! It was only twenty-three days before the whole remnant of people began rebuilding God's temple.

In our day, we want to be people of prayer, worship, and Bible study. Our intentions are often really good. Still, eventually we have to get out and do the work God has for us. He wants to change the world through us. God has called us to be difference makers where we live, work, study, and play. The time has come to "be strong" and get going because God is with us!

Difference Maker

God provides the resources, but willing hands must do the work. Where's one place this week where your available, willing hands can make a difference for God?

Prayer **2:6**

Lord, thank you that Jesus shook the heavens and the earth by dying on the cross for our sins. Bring me your peace so that I may bring you deserved glory in the world. Amen.

Question 2:23

What does the Lord mean when he said, "I will make you like a signet ring on my finger"?

Promises for Zerubbabel
20On that same day, December 18,* the LORD sent this second message to
Haggai: 21"Tell Zerubbabel, the governor of Judah, that I am about to shake
the heavens and the earth. 22I will overthrow royal thrones and destroy the
power of foreign kingdoms. I will overturn their chariots and riders. The
horses will fall, and their riders will kill each other.
23"But when this happens, says the LORD of Heaven's Armies, I will honor
you, Zerubbabel son of Shealtiel, my servant. I will make you like a signet
ring on my finger, says the LORD, for I have chosen you. I, the LORD of
Heaven's Armies, have spoken!"

2:20 Hebrew *On the twenty-fourth day of the [ninth] month;* see note on 2:10.

Zechariah Introduction

No one makes a difference alone. We all have partners who help us through the challenges of life. Whether those partners are parents, siblings, or best friends, we need the support of others—and they need us to make a difference for and with them as well.

The prophet Zechariah partnered with the prophet Haggai to assist another couple of partners—the governor Zerubbabel and the priest Jeshua (Ezra 5:1-2). The challenge before them was to rebuild the temple that Nebuchadnezzar had completely destroyed seventy years earlier. The job was too big for one person or even one set of partners. A team was needed, and Zechariah made a difference by motivating the people to join in the effort.

Zechariah motivated the people by sharing a series of strange dreams, or night visions. Along the way he cleared up the debated practice of fasting that makes more of a difference than many realize. Finally, he cast a vision with some that would prepare the way for the ultimate difference maker with some clear prophecies of Jesus.

Story Arcs

- **Zechariah**
- **The Branch**

Zechariah

A Call to Return to the LORD

1 In November* of the second year of King Darius's reign, the LORD gave
this message to the prophet Zechariah son of Berekiah and grandson
of Iddo:
2"I, the LORD, was very angry with your ancestors. 3Therefore, say to the
people, 'This is what the LORD of Heaven's Armies says: Return to me, and
I will return to you, says the LORD of Heaven's Armies.' 4Don't be like your
ancestors who would not listen or pay attention when the earlier prophets
said to them, 'This is what the LORD of Heaven's Armies says: Turn from
your evil ways, and stop all your evil practices.'
5"Where are your ancestors now? They and the prophets are long dead.
6But everything I said through my servants the prophets happened to your
ancestors, just as I said. As a result, they repented and said, 'We have received
what we deserved from the LORD of Heaven's Armies. He has done what he
said he would do.'"

A Man among the Myrtle Trees

7Three months later, on February 15,* the LORD sent another message to the
prophet Zechariah son of Berekiah and grandson of Iddo.
8In a vision during the night, I saw a man sitting on a red horse that was
standing among some myrtle trees in a small valley. Behind him were riders
on red, brown, and white horses. 9I asked the angel who was talking with
me, "My lord, what do these horses mean?"

"I will show you," the angel replied.

10The rider standing among the myrtle trees then explained, "They are
the ones the LORD has sent out to patrol the earth."
11Then the other riders reported to the angel of the LORD, who was stand-
ing among the myrtle trees, "We have been patrolling the earth, and the
whole earth is at peace."
12Upon hearing this, the angel of the LORD prayed this prayer: "O LORD
of Heaven's Armies, for seventy years now you have been angry with Jeru-
salem and the towns of Judah. How long until you again show mercy to
them?" 13And the LORD spoke kind and comforting words to the angel who
talked with me.
14Then the angel said to me, "Shout this message for all to hear: 'This is
what the LORD of Heaven's Armies says: My love for Jerusalem and Mount
Zion is passionate and strong. 15But I am very angry with the other nations
that are now enjoying peace and security. I was only a little angry with my
people, but the nations inflicted harm on them far beyond my intentions.

Story Arc 1:1

Zechariah

What difference does a name make? Together the names *Zechariah*, *Berekiah*, and *Iddo* mean "Yahweh will remember, and Yahweh will bless, in time." The names of Zechariah and his ancestors reminded Zechariah's team that making a difference often takes time and always depends on God.

Zech 3:8-9 ▶

1:1 Hebrew *In the eighth month.* A number of dates in Zechariah can be cross-checked with dates in surviving Persian records and related accurately to our modern calendar. This month of the ancient Hebrew lunar calendar occurred within the months of October and November 520 B.C. 1:7 Hebrew *On the twenty-fourth day of the eleventh month, the month of Shebat, in the second year of Darius.* This event occurred on February 15, 519 B.C.; also see note on 1:1.

16 "'Therefore, this is what the LORD says: I have returned to show
mercy to Jerusalem. My Temple will be rebuilt, says the LORD of Heav-
en's Armies, and measurements will be taken for the reconstruction of
Jerusalem.*'
17 "Say this also: 'This is what the LORD of Heaven's Armies says: The towns
of Israel will again overflow with prosperity, and the LORD will again com-
fort Zion and choose Jerusalem as his own.'"

Four Horns and Four Blacksmiths

18 *Then I looked up and saw four animal horns. 19 "What are these?" I asked
the angel who was talking with me.
He replied, "These horns represent the nations that scattered Judah, Is-
rael, and Jerusalem."
20 Then the LORD showed me four blacksmiths. 21 "What are these men
coming to do?" I asked.
The angel replied, "These four horns—these nations—scattered and
humbled Judah. Now these blacksmiths have come to terrify those nations
and throw them down and destroy them."

Future Prosperity of Jerusalem

2 1 *When I looked again, I saw a man with a measuring line in his hand.
2 "Where are you going?" I asked.
He replied, "I am going to measure Jerusalem, to see how wide and how
long it is."
3 Then the angel who was with me went to meet a second angel who was
coming toward him. 4 The other angel said, "Hurry, and say to that young
man, 'Jerusalem will someday be so full of people and livestock that there
won't be room enough for everyone! Many will live outside the city walls.
5 Then I, myself, will be a protective wall of fire around Jerusalem, says the
LORD. And I will be the glory inside the city!'"

The Exiles Are Called Home

6 The LORD says, "Come away! Flee from Babylon in the land of the north,
for I have scattered you to the four winds. 7 Come away, people of Zion, you
who are exiled in Babylon!"
8 After a period of glory, the LORD of Heaven's Armies sent me* against the
nations who plundered you. For he said, "Anyone who harms you harms my
most precious possession.* 9 I will raise my fist to crush them, and their own
slaves will plunder them." Then you will know that the LORD of Heaven's
Armies has sent me.
10 The LORD says, "Shout and rejoice, O beautiful Jerusalem,* for I am com-
ing to live among you. 11 Many nations will join themselves to the LORD on
that day, and they, too, will be my people. I will live among you, and you will
know that the LORD of Heaven's Armies sent me to you. 12 The land of Judah
will be the LORD's special possession in the holy land, and he will once again
choose Jerusalem to be his own city. 13 Be silent before the LORD, all humanity,
for he is springing into action from his holy dwelling."

1:16 Hebrew *and the measuring line will be stretched out over Jerusalem.* 1:18 Verses 1:18-21 are numbered 2:1-4 in Hebrew text. 2:1 Verses 2:1-13 are numbered 2:5-17 in Hebrew text. 2:8a The meaning of the Hebrew is uncertain. 2:8b Hebrew *Anyone who touches you touches the pupil of his eye.* 2:10 Hebrew *O daughter of Zion.*

Question 1:16

In Zechariah's first vision, the people had returned to Jerusalem, but God promised he would also return to Jerusalem and help them rebuild his house—the temple. In other words, God was about to do something big! What do you learn from this about *how* God plans to affect the world?

Prayer 2:5

Lord, I often try to put my own walls up to protect myself, but help me trust you to be my defender. Amen.

Question 2:10-13

How is Zechariah 2:10-13 like Jesus in your life?

Make a Difference

3:1-5

New Clothes

In Zechariah's fourth vision, he saw Jeshua, a key leader in the rebuilding of Jerusalem. God intended to use Jeshua as a living parable of what he would do for his people. Even if Satan himself accuses us or shames us, his accusations cannot destroy God's declaration that we are his new creation. We all stand as Jeshua—in filthy, gross rags of sin and failure—but God clothes us in his righteousness. Our efforts will never make a difference unless we stand in God's power.

Difference Maker

Change into a clean set of clothes. Write down Zechariah 3:4 on a piece of paper and carry it in your pocket all day long.

Story Arc **3:8-9**

● The Branch

Zechariah talked about the Lord's servant, called "the Branch," understood to be the Messiah. This would be the One spoken of throughout Scripture as God's servant who would bring blessing and salvation to the world. In Jeremiah and Isaiah, the Branch, from the line of King David, would rule a forgiven and restored people. This Branch of royalty, Zechariah told us, would "remove the sins" of the people "in a single day" (v. 9). Read 3:8-9 and 6:12-14. How does this deepen your understanding of who Jesus is and what he has done for us?

Mal 3:1 ►

Cleansing for the High Priest

3 Then the angel showed me Jeshua* the high priest standing before the
angel of the LORD. The Accuser, Satan,* was there at the angel's right
hand, making accusations against Jeshua. 2 And the LORD said to Satan, "I,
the LORD, reject your accusations, Satan. Yes, the LORD, who has chosen Jeru-
salem, rebukes you. This man is like a burning stick that has been snatched
from the fire."
3 Jeshua's clothing was filthy as he stood there before the angel. 4 So the
angel said to the others standing there, "Take off his filthy clothes." And
turning to Jeshua he said, "See, I have taken away your sins, and now I am
giving you these fine new clothes."
5 Then I said, "They should also place a clean turban on his head." So they
put a clean priestly turban on his head and dressed him in new clothes while
the angel of the LORD stood by.
6 Then the angel of the LORD spoke very solemnly to Jeshua and said,
7 "This is what the LORD of Heaven's Armies says: If you follow my
ways and carefully serve me, then you will be given authority over my
Temple and its courtyards. I will let you walk among these others stand-
ing here.
8 "Listen to me, O Jeshua the high priest, and all you other priests. You
are symbols of things to come. Soon I am going to bring my servant, the
Branch. 9 Now look at the jewel I have set before Jeshua, a single stone with
seven facets.* I will engrave an inscription on it, says the LORD of Heaven's
Armies, and I will remove the sins of this land in a single day.
10 "And on that day, says the LORD of Heaven's Armies, each of you will
invite your neighbor to sit with you peacefully under your own grapevine
and fig tree."

A Lampstand and Two Olive Trees

4 Then the angel who had been talking with me returned and woke me,
as though I had been asleep. 2 "What do you see now?" he asked.
I answered, "I see a solid gold lampstand with a bowl of oil on top of it.
Around the bowl are seven lamps, each having seven spouts with wicks. 3 And
I see two olive trees, one on each side of the bowl." 4 Then I asked the angel,
"What are these, my lord? What do they mean?"
5 "Don't you know?" the angel asked.
"No, my lord," I replied.
6 Then he said to me, "This is what the LORD says to Zerubbabel: It is
not by force nor by strength, but by my Spirit, says the LORD of Heaven's
Armies. 7 Nothing, not even a mighty mountain, will stand in Zerubbabel's
way; it will become a level plain before him! And when Zerubbabel sets the
final stone of the Temple in place, the people will shout: 'May God bless it!
May God bless it!'*"
8 Then another message came to me from the LORD: 9 "Zerubbabel is the
one who laid the foundation of this Temple, and he will complete it. Then
you will know that the LORD of Heaven's Armies has sent me. 10 Do not de-
spise these small beginnings, for the LORD rejoices to see the work begin, to
see the plumb line in Zerubbabel's hand."

3:1a Hebrew *Joshua,* a variant spelling of Jeshua; also in 3:3, 4, 6, 8, 9. 3:1b Hebrew *The satan;* similarly in 3:2. 3:9 Hebrew *seven eyes.* 4:7 Hebrew *'Grace, grace to it.'*

(The seven lamps* represent the eyes of the LORD that search all around
the world.)
11 Then I asked the angel, "What are these two olive trees on each side of
the lampstand, 12 and what are the two olive branches that pour out golden
oil through two gold tubes?"
13 "Don't you know?" he asked.
"No, my lord," I replied.
14 Then he said to me, "They represent the two anointed ones* who stand
in the court of the Lord of all the earth."

Question 5:2

What did God want people to see with this billboard-sized scroll? What difference did God want to see in the people as a result?

A Flying Scroll

5 I looked up again and saw a scroll flying through the air.
2 "What do you see?" the angel asked.
"I see a flying scroll," I replied. "It appears to be about 30 feet long and
15 feet wide.*"
3 Then he said to me, "This scroll contains the curse that is going out over
the entire land. One side of the scroll says that those who steal will be ban-
ished from the land; the other side says that those who swear falsely will be
banished from the land. 4 And this is what the LORD of Heaven's Armies says:
I am sending this curse into the house of every thief and into the house of
everyone who swears falsely using my name. And my curse will remain in
that house and completely destroy it—even its timbers and stones."

A Woman in a Basket

5 Then the angel who was talking with me came forward and said, "Look up
and see what's coming."
6 "What is it?" I asked.
He replied, "It is a basket for measuring grain,* and it's filled with the
sins* of everyone throughout the land."
7 Then the heavy lead cover was lifted off the basket, and there was a
woman sitting inside it. 8 The angel said, "The woman's name is Wicked-
ness," and he pushed her back into the basket and closed the heavy lid again.
9 Then I looked up and saw two women flying toward us, gliding on the
wind. They had wings like a stork, and they picked up the basket and flew
into the sky.
10 "Where are they taking the basket?" I asked the angel.
11 He replied, "To the land of Babylonia,* where they will build a temple
for the basket. And when the temple is ready, they will set the basket there
on its pedestal."

Four Chariots

6 Then I looked up again and saw four chariots coming from between two
bronze mountains. 2 The first chariot was pulled by red horses, the sec-
ond by black horses, 3 the third by white horses, and the fourth by powerful
dappled-gray horses. 4 "And what are these, my lord?" I asked the angel who
was talking with me.
5 The angel replied, "These are the four spirits* of heaven who stand before

4:10 Or *The seven facets* (see 3:9); Hebrew reads *These seven.* 4:14 Or *two heavenly beings;* Hebrew reads *two sons of fresh oil.* 5:2 Hebrew *20 cubits* [9.2 meters] *long and 10 cubits* [4.6 meters] *wide.* 5:6a Hebrew *an ephah* [20 quarts or 22 liters]; also in 5:7, 8, 9, 10, 11. 5:6b As in Greek version; Hebrew reads *the appearance.* 5:11 Hebrew *the land of Shinar.* 6:5 Or *the four winds.*

Question 6:12–13

As you read verses 12 and 13, what is significant about "the Branch" being a king and a priest at the temple? Read Hebrews 11 and consider this question: In the story arc of Scripture, who else fits this description?

the Lord of all the earth. They are going out to do his work. 6 The chariot with
black horses is going north, the chariot with white horses is going west,* and
the chariot with dappled-gray horses is going south."
7 The powerful horses were eager to set out to patrol the earth. And the
LORD said, "Go and patrol the earth!" So they left at once on their patrol.
8 Then the LORD summoned me and said, "Look, those who went north
have vented the anger of my Spirit* there in the land of the north."

The Crowning of Jeshua

9 Then I received another message from the LORD: 10 "Heldai, Tobijah, and
Jedaiah will bring gifts of silver and gold from the Jews exiled in Babylon.
As soon as they arrive, meet them at the home of Josiah son of Zephaniah.
11 Accept their gifts, and make a crown from the silver and gold. Then put
the crown on the head of Jeshua* son of Jehozadak, the high priest. 12 Tell
him, 'This is what the LORD of Heaven's Armies says: Here is the man called
the Branch. He will branch out from where he is and build the Temple of
the LORD. 13 Yes, he will build the Temple of the LORD. Then he will receive
royal honor and will rule as king from his throne. He will also serve as priest
from his throne,* and there will be perfect harmony between his two roles.'
14 "The crown will be a memorial in the Temple of the LORD to honor
those who gave it—Heldai,* Tobijah, Jedaiah, and Josiah* son of Zephaniah."
15 People will come from distant lands to rebuild the Temple of the LORD.
And when this happens, you will know that my messages have been from
the LORD of Heaven's Armies. All this will happen if you carefully obey what
the LORD your God says.

A Call to Justice and Mercy

7 On December 7* of the fourth year of King Darius's reign, another mes-
sage came to Zechariah from the LORD. 2 The people of Bethel had sent
Sharezer and Regemmelech,* along with their attendants, to seek the LORD's
favor. 3 They were to ask this question of the prophets and the priests at the
Temple of the LORD of Heaven's Armies: "Should we continue to mourn and
fast each summer on the anniversary of the Temple's destruction,* as we have
done for so many years?"
4 The LORD of Heaven's Armies sent me this message in reply: 5 "Say to all
your people and your priests, 'During these seventy years of exile, when you
fasted and mourned in the summer and in early autumn,* was it really for
me that you were fasting? 6 And even now in your holy festivals, aren't you
eating and drinking just to please yourselves? 7 Isn't this the same message
the LORD proclaimed through the prophets in years past when Jerusalem
and the towns of Judah were bustling with people, and the Negev and the
foothills of Judah* were well populated?'"

6:6 Hebrew *is going after them.* 6:8 Hebrew *have given my Spirit rest.* 6:11 Hebrew *Joshua,* a variant spelling of Jeshua. 6:13 Or *There will be a priest by his throne.* 6:14a As in Syriac version (compare 6:10); Hebrew reads *Helem.* 6:14b As in Syriac version (compare 6:10); Hebrew reads *Hen.* 7:1 Hebrew *On the fourth day of the ninth month, the month of Kislev,* of the ancient Hebrew lunar calendar. This event occurred on December 7, 518 B.C.; also see note on 1:1. 7:2 Or *Bethel-sharezer had sent Regemmelech.* 7:3 Hebrew *mourn and fast in the fifth month.* The Temple had been destroyed in the fifth month of the ancient Hebrew lunar calendar (August 586 B.C.); see 2 Kgs 25:8. 7:5 Hebrew *fasted and mourned in the fifth and seventh months.* The fifth month of the ancient Hebrew lunar calendar usually occurs within the months of July and August. The seventh month usually occurs within the months of September and October; both the Day of Atonement and the Festival of Shelters were celebrated in the seventh month. 7:7 Hebrew *the Shephelah.*

8 Then this message came to Zechariah from the LORD: 9 "This is what the
LORD of Heaven's Armies says: Judge fairly, and show mercy and kindness
to one another. 10 Do not oppress widows, orphans, foreigners, and the poor.
And do not scheme against each other.
11 "Your ancestors refused to listen to this message. They stubbornly
turned away and put their fingers in their ears to keep from hearing. 12 They
made their hearts as hard as stone, so they could not hear the instructions or
the messages that the LORD of Heaven's Armies had sent them by his Spirit
through the earlier prophets. That is why the LORD of Heaven's Armies was
so angry with them.
13 "Since they refused to listen when I called to them, I would not listen
when they called to me, says the LORD of Heaven's Armies. 14 As with a whirl-
wind, I scattered them among the distant nations, where they lived as strang-
ers. Their land became so desolate that no one even traveled through it. They
turned their pleasant land into a desert."

Promised Blessings for Jerusalem

8 Then another message came to me from the LORD of Heaven's Armies:
2 "This is what the LORD of Heaven's Armies says: My love for Mount
Zion is passionate and strong; I am consumed with passion for Jerusalem!
3 "And now the LORD says: I am returning to Mount Zion, and I will live
in Jerusalem. Then Jerusalem will be called the Faithful City; the mountain
of the LORD of Heaven's Armies will be called the Holy Mountain.
4 "This is what the LORD of Heaven's Armies says: Once again old men and
women will walk Jerusalem's streets with their canes and will sit together
in the city squares. 5 And the streets of the city will be filled with boys and
girls at play.
6 "This is what the LORD of Heaven's Armies says: All this may seem im-
possible to you now, a small remnant of God's people. But is it impossible
for me? says the LORD of Heaven's Armies.
7 "This is what the LORD of Heaven's Armies says: You can be sure that I
will rescue my people from the east and from the west. 8 I will bring them
home again to live safely in Jerusalem. They will be my people, and I will be
faithful and just toward them as their God.
9 "This is what the LORD of Heaven's Armies says: Be strong and finish
the task! Ever since the laying of the foundation of the Temple of the LORD
of Heaven's Armies, you have heard what the prophets have been saying
about completing the building. 10 Before the work on the Temple began,
there were no jobs and no money to hire people or animals. No traveler was
safe from the enemy, for there were enemies on all sides. I had turned every-
one against each other.
11 "But now I will not treat the remnant of my people as I treated them
before, says the LORD of Heaven's Armies. 12 For I am planting seeds of peace
and prosperity among you. The grapevines will be heavy with fruit. The earth
will produce its crops, and the heavens will release the dew. Once more I will
cause the remnant in Judah and Israel to inherit these blessings. 13 Among
the other nations, Judah and Israel became symbols of a cursed nation. But
no longer! Now I will rescue you and make you both a symbol and a source of
blessing. So don't be afraid. Be strong, and get on with rebuilding the Temple!
14 "For this is what the LORD of Heaven's Armies says: I was determined

Make a Difference

7:7-10

Check Yourself

In a fair court, there is only one person who is ultimately allowed to make the final judgment, and that is the judge. The judge might use a jury occasionally, but even the jury submits to the rules established by the judge.

When people are judgmental against or in favor of someone, justice is skewed. When widows or orphans don't have an advocate, the voice of mercy is silenced. Thankfully, ultimately, judgmental attitudes themselves will be tried and sentenced. Every person will appear before the divine Judge one day, and those who schemed against others will have some pretty tricky explaining to do.

Difference Maker

Prosecute yourself. Make a case against your sin. Then read Romans 5:8 a few times. Consider how your treatment of others today should reflect the generosity of the heavenly Judge.

Question **8:6**

Read Matthew 19:26. What did Jesus think about this idea? How does this change the way you look at obstacles for the future of your life?

to punish you when your ancestors angered me, and I did not change my
mind, says the LORD of Heaven's Armies. 15 But now I am determined to bless
Jerusalem and the people of Judah. So don't be afraid. 16 But this is what you
must do: Tell the truth to each other. Render verdicts in your courts that
are just and that lead to peace. 17 Don't scheme against each other. Stop your
love of telling lies that you swear are the truth. I hate all these things, says
the LORD."

18 Here is another message that came to me from the LORD of Heaven's
Armies. 19 "This is what the LORD of Heaven's Armies says: The traditional
fasts and times of mourning you have kept in early summer, midsummer,
autumn, and winter* are now ended. They will become festivals of joy and
celebration for the people of Judah. So love truth and peace.

20 "This is what the LORD of Heaven's Armies says: People from nations
and cities around the world will travel to Jerusalem. 21 The people of one city
will say to the people of another, 'Come with us to Jerusalem to ask the LORD
to bless us. Let's worship the LORD of Heaven's Armies. I'm determined to
go.' 22 Many peoples and powerful nations will come to Jerusalem to seek the
LORD of Heaven's Armies and to ask for his blessing.

23 "This is what the LORD of Heaven's Armies says: In those days ten men
from different nations and languages of the world will clutch at the sleeve
of one Jew. And they will say, 'Please let us walk with you, for we have heard
that God is with you.'"

Judgment against Israel's Enemies

9 This is the message* from the LORD against the land of Aram* and the
city of Damascus, for the eyes of humanity, including all the tribes of
Israel, are on the LORD.

2 Doom is certain for Hamath,
near Damascus,
and for the cities of Tyre and Sidon,
though they are so clever.
3 Tyre has built a strong fortress
and has made silver and gold
as plentiful as dust in the streets!
4 But now the Lord will strip away Tyre's possessions
and hurl its fortifications into the sea,
and it will be burned to the ground.
5 The city of Ashkelon will see Tyre fall
and will be filled with fear.
Gaza will shake with terror,
as will Ekron, for their hopes will be dashed.
Gaza's king will be killed,
and Ashkelon will be deserted.
6 Foreigners will occupy the city of Ashdod.
I will destroy the pride of the Philistines.

8:19 Hebrew *in the fourth, fifth, seventh, and tenth months.* The fourth month of the ancient Hebrew lunar calendar usually occurs within the months of June and July. The fifth month usually occurs within the months of July and August. The seventh month usually occurs within the months of September and October. The tenth month usually occurs within the months of December and January. 9:1a Hebrew *An Oracle: The message.* 9:1b Hebrew *land of Hadrach.*

7 I will grab the bloody meat from their mouths
and snatch the detestable sacrifices from their teeth.
Then the surviving Philistines will worship our God
and become like a clan in Judah.*
The Philistines of Ekron will join my people,
as the ancient Jebusites once did.
8 I will guard my Temple
and protect it from invading armies.
I am watching closely to ensure
that no more foreign oppressors overrun my people's land.

Zion's Coming King

9 Rejoice, O people of Zion!*
Shout in triumph, O people of Jerusalem!
Look, your king is coming to you.
He is righteous and victorious,*
yet he is humble, riding on a donkey—
riding on a donkey's colt.
10 I will remove the battle chariots from Israel*
and the warhorses from Jerusalem.
I will destroy all the weapons used in battle,
and your king will bring peace to the nations.
His realm will stretch from sea to sea
and from the Euphrates River* to the ends of the earth.*
11 Because of the covenant I made with you,
sealed with blood,
I will free your prisoners
from death in a waterless dungeon.
12 Come back to the place of safety,
all you prisoners who still have hope!
I promise this very day
that I will repay two blessings for each of your troubles.
13 Judah is my bow,
and Israel is my arrow.
Jerusalem* is my sword,
and like a warrior, I will brandish it against the Greeks.*

14 The LORD will appear above his people;
his arrows will fly like lightning!
The Sovereign LORD will sound the ram's horn
and attack like a whirlwind from the southern desert.
15 The LORD of Heaven's Armies will protect his people,
and they will defeat their enemies by hurling
great stones.
They will shout in battle as though drunk with wine.
They will be filled with blood like a bowl,
drenched with blood like the corners of the altar.

9:7 Hebrew *like a leader in Judah.* **9:9a** Hebrew *O daughter of Zion!* **9:9b** Hebrew *and is being vindicated.* **9:10a** Hebrew *Ephraim,* referring to the northern kingdom of Israel; also in 9:13. **9:10b** Hebrew *the river.* **9:10c** Or *the end of the land.* **9:13a** Hebrew *Zion.* **9:13b** Hebrew *the sons of Javan.*

Question 9:9

This is an amazing passage about the king on a donkey. If you compared this chapter in Zechariah with 1 Kings 1:32-40 and Luke 19:28-40, what similarities could you find?

Prayer **10:2**

Lord, please be my shepherd. Amen.

16 On that day the LORD their God will rescue his people,
just as a shepherd rescues his sheep.
They will sparkle in his land
like jewels in a crown.
17 How wonderful and beautiful they will be!
The young men will thrive on abundant grain,
and the young women will flourish on new wine.

The LORD Will Restore His People

10 1 Ask the LORD for rain in the spring,
for he makes the storm clouds.
And he will send showers of rain
so every field becomes a lush pasture.
2 Household gods give worthless advice,
fortune-tellers predict only lies,
and interpreters of dreams pronounce
falsehoods that give no comfort.
So my people are wandering like lost sheep;
they are attacked because they have no shepherd.

3 "My anger burns against your shepherds,
and I will punish these leaders.*
For the LORD of Heaven's Armies has arrived
to look after Judah, his flock.
He will make them strong and glorious,
like a proud warhorse in battle.
4 From Judah will come the cornerstone,
the tent peg,
the bow for battle,
and all the rulers.
5 They will be like mighty warriors in battle,
trampling their enemies in the mud under their feet.
Since the LORD is with them as they fight,
they will overthrow even the enemy's horsemen.

6 "I will strengthen Judah and save Israel*;
I will restore them because of my compassion.
It will be as though I had never rejected them,
for I am the LORD their God, who will hear their cries.
7 The people of Israel* will become like mighty warriors,
and their hearts will be made happy as if by wine.
Their children, too, will see it and be glad;
their hearts will rejoice in the LORD.
8 When I whistle to them, they will come running,
for I have redeemed them.
From the few who are left,
they will grow as numerous as they were before.
9 Though I have scattered them like seeds among the nations,
they will still remember me in distant lands.

10:3 Or *these male goats.* **10:6** Hebrew *save the house of Joseph.* **10:7** Hebrew *of Ephraim.*

They and their children will survive
and return again to Israel.
10 I will bring them back from Egypt
and gather them from Assyria.
I will resettle them in Gilead and Lebanon
until there is no more room for them all.
11 They will pass safely through the sea of distress,*
for the waves of the sea will be held back,
and the waters of the Nile will dry up.
The pride of Assyria will be crushed,
and the rule of Egypt will end.
12 By my power* I will make my people strong,
and by my authority they will go wherever they wish.
I, the LORD, have spoken!"

11 1 Open your doors, Lebanon,
so that fire may devour your cedar forests.
2 Weep, you cypress trees, for all the ruined cedars;
the most majestic ones have fallen.
Weep, you oaks of Bashan,
for the thick forests have been cut down.
3 Listen to the wailing of the shepherds,
for their rich pastures are destroyed.
Hear the young lions roaring,
for their thickets in the Jordan Valley are ruined.

The Good and Evil Shepherds
4 This is what the LORD my God says: "Go and care for the flock that is in-
tended for slaughter. 5 The buyers slaughter their sheep without remorse.
The sellers say, 'Praise the LORD! Now I'm rich!' Even the shepherds have
no compassion for them. 6 Likewise, I will no longer have pity on the people
of the land," says the LORD. "I will let them fall into each other's hands and
into the hands of their king. They will turn the land into a wilderness, and
I will not rescue them."

7 So I cared for the flock intended for slaughter—the flock that was op-
pressed. Then I took two shepherd's staffs and named one Favor and the
other Union. 8 I got rid of their three evil shepherds in a single month.

But I became impatient with these sheep, and they hated me, too. 9 So
I told them, "I won't be your shepherd any longer. If you die, you die.
If you are killed, you are killed. And let those who remain devour each
other!"

10 Then I took my staff called Favor and cut it in two, showing that I had
revoked the covenant I had made with all the nations. 11 That was the end
of my covenant with them. The suffering flock was watching me, and they
knew that the LORD was speaking through my actions.

12 And I said to them, "If you like, give me my wages, whatever I am worth;
but only if you want to." So they counted out for my wages thirty pieces of
silver.

13 And the LORD said to me, "Throw it to the potter*"—this magnificent

10:11 Or *the sea of Egypt,* referring to the Red Sea. 10:12 Hebrew *In the LORD.* 11:13 Syriac version reads *into the treasury;* also in 11:13b. Compare Matt 27:6-10.

Question 12:10

How do all these prophecies of the Lord's Messiah encourage you? How does this surprising and gut-wrenching vision give the hope God intends for the world?

sum at which they valued me! So I took the thirty coins and threw them to
the potter in the Temple of the LORD.
14 Then I took my other staff, Union, and cut it in two, showing that the
bond of unity between Judah and Israel was broken.
15 Then the LORD said to me, "Go again and play the part of a worthless
shepherd. 16 This illustrates how I will give this nation a shepherd who will
not care for those who are dying, nor look after the young, nor heal the in-
jured, nor feed the healthy. Instead, this shepherd will eat the meat of the
fattest sheep and tear off their hooves.

17 "What sorrow awaits this worthless shepherd
who abandons the flock!
The sword will cut his arm
and pierce his right eye.
His arm will become useless,
and his right eye completely blind."

Future Deliverance for Jerusalem

12 This* message concerning the fate of Israel came from the LORD:
"This message is from the LORD, who stretched out the heavens,
laid the foundations of the earth, and formed the human spirit. 2 I will make
Jerusalem like an intoxicating drink that makes the nearby nations stagger
when they send their armies to besiege Jerusalem and Judah. 3 On that day I
will make Jerusalem an immovable rock. All the nations will gather against
it to try to move it, but they will only hurt themselves.
4 "On that day," says the LORD, "I will cause every horse to panic and every
rider to lose his nerve. I will watch over the people of Judah, but I will blind
all the horses of their enemies. 5 And the clans of Judah will say to themselves,
'The people of Jerusalem have found strength in the LORD of Heaven's Ar-
mies, their God.'
6 "On that day I will make the clans of Judah like a flame that sets a wood-
pile ablaze or like a burning torch among sheaves of grain. They will burn
up all the neighboring nations right and left, while the people living in Je-
rusalem remain secure.
7 "The LORD will give victory to the rest of Judah first, before Jerusalem, so
that the people of Jerusalem and the royal line of David will not have greater
honor than the rest of Judah. 8 On that day the LORD will defend the people
of Jerusalem; the weakest among them will be as mighty as King David!
And the royal descendants will be like God, like the angel of the LORD who
goes before them! 9 For on that day I will begin to destroy all the nations that
come against Jerusalem.
10 "Then I will pour out a spirit* of grace and prayer on the family of Da-
vid and on the people of Jerusalem. They will look on me whom they have
pierced and mourn for him as for an only son. They will grieve bitterly for
him as for a firstborn son who has died. 11 The sorrow and mourning in Je-
rusalem on that day will be like the great mourning for Hadad-rimmon in
the valley of Megiddo.
12 "All Israel will mourn, each clan by itself, and with the husbands sepa-
rate from their wives. The clan of David will mourn alone, as will the clan

12:1 Hebrew *An Oracle: This.* 12:10 Or *the Spirit.*

of Nathan, 13 the clan of Levi, and the clan of Shimei. 14 Each of the surviving
clans from Judah will mourn separately, and with the husbands separate
from their wives.

A Fountain of Cleansing

13 "On that day a fountain will be opened for the dynasty of David
and for the people of Jerusalem, a fountain to cleanse them from all
their sins and impurity.
2 "And on that day," says the LORD of Heaven's Armies, "I will erase idol
worship throughout the land, so that even the names of the idols will be
forgotten. I will remove from the land both the false prophets and the spirit
of impurity that came with them. 3 If anyone continues to prophesy, his own
father and mother will tell him, 'You must die, for you have prophesied lies
in the name of the LORD.' And as he prophesies, his own father and mother
will stab him.
4 "On that day people will be ashamed to claim the prophetic gift. No one
will pretend to be a prophet by wearing prophet's clothes. 5 He will say, 'I'm
no prophet; I'm a farmer. I began working for a farmer as a boy.' 6 And if
someone asks, 'Then what about those wounds on your chest?*' he will say,
'I was wounded at my friends' house!'

The Scattering of the Sheep

7 "Awake, O sword, against my shepherd,
  the man who is my partner,"
  says the LORD of Heaven's Armies.
"Strike down the shepherd,
  and the sheep will be scattered,
  and I will turn against the lambs.
8 Two-thirds of the people in the land
  will be cut off and die," says the LORD.
  "But one-third will be left in the land.
9 I will bring that group through the fire
  and make them pure.
I will refine them like silver
  and purify them like gold.
They will call on my name,
  and I will answer them.
I will say, 'These are my people,'
  and they will say, 'The LORD is our God.'"

The LORD Will Rule the Earth

14 Watch, for the day of the LORD is coming when your possessions will
be plundered right in front of you! 2 I will gather all the nations to
fight against Jerusalem. The city will be taken, the houses looted, and the
women raped. Half the population will be taken into captivity, and the rest
will be left among the ruins of the city.
3 Then the LORD will go out to fight against those nations, as he has fought
in times past. 4 On that day his feet will stand on the Mount of Olives, east of
Jerusalem. And the Mount of Olives will split apart, making a wide valley

13:6 Hebrew *wounds between your hands?*

Prayer 13:9

Lord, refine me. Make me pure. Say of me, "This is one of my people." Let me say of you, "The Lord is my God." Amen.

Question 14:20-21

Zechariah ended his book with a declaration that the Lord would cleanse his temple. As you look back at this book, what world-changing story arc do you see threaded throughout its pages?

running from east to west. Half the mountain will move toward the north
and half toward the south. 5You will flee through this valley, for it will reach
across to Azal.* Yes, you will flee as you did from the earthquake in the days
of King Uzziah of Judah. Then the LORD my God will come, and all his holy
ones with him.*

6On that day the sources of light will no longer shine,* 7yet there will be
continuous day! Only the LORD knows how this could happen. There will be
no normal day and night, for at evening time it will still be light.

8On that day life-giving waters will flow out from Jerusalem, half toward
the Dead Sea and half toward the Mediterranean,* flowing continuously in
both summer and winter.

9And the LORD will be king over all the earth. On that day there will be
one LORD—his name alone will be worshiped.

10All the land from Geba, north of Judah, to Rimmon, south of Jerusalem,
will become one vast plain. But Jerusalem will be raised up in its original
place and will be inhabited all the way from the Benjamin Gate over to the
site of the old gate, then to the Corner Gate, and from the Tower of Hananel
to the king's winepresses. 11And Jerusalem will be filled, safe at last, never
again to be cursed and destroyed.

12And the LORD will send a plague on all the nations that fought against
Jerusalem. Their people will become like walking corpses, their flesh rot-
ting away. Their eyes will rot in their sockets, and their tongues will rot in
their mouths. 13On that day they will be terrified, stricken by the LORD with
great panic. They will fight their neighbors hand to hand. 14Judah, too, will
be fighting at Jerusalem. The wealth of all the neighboring nations will be
captured—great quantities of gold and silver and fine clothing. 15This same
plague will strike the horses, mules, camels, donkeys, and all the other ani-
mals in the enemy camps.

16In the end, the enemies of Jerusalem who survive the plague will go up to
Jerusalem each year to worship the King, the LORD of Heaven's Armies, and
to celebrate the Festival of Shelters. 17Any nation in the world that refuses to
come to Jerusalem to worship the King, the LORD of Heaven's Armies, will
have no rain. 18If the people of Egypt refuse to attend the festival, the LORD
will punish* them with the same plague that he sends on the other nations
who refuse to go. 19Egypt and the other nations will all be punished if they
don't go to celebrate the Festival of Shelters.

20On that day even the harness bells of the horses will be inscribed with
these words: HOLY TO THE LORD. And the cooking pots in the Temple of
the LORD will be as sacred as the basins used beside the altar. 21In fact, every
cooking pot in Jerusalem and Judah will be holy to the LORD of Heaven's
Armies. All who come to worship will be free to use any of these pots to boil
their sacrifices. And on that day there will no longer be traders* in the Temple
of the LORD of Heaven's Armies.

14:5a The meaning of the Hebrew is uncertain. **14:5b** As in Greek version; Hebrew reads *with you.* **14:6** Hebrew *the precious ones shall diminish;* or *the precious ones and frost.* The meaning of the Hebrew is uncertain. **14:8** Hebrew *half toward the eastern sea and half toward the western sea.* **14:18** As in some Hebrew manuscripts and Greek and Syriac versions; Masoretic Text reads *will not punish.* **14:21** Hebrew *Canaanites.*

Malachi Introduction

Malachi spoke to troubled people who were struggling with their finances, dealing with disappointment, and feeling skeptical of religion. Sound familiar? Though it may not be the last book written historically in the Old Testament, this was placed as the last prophetic book of the Old Testament. That's intentional. It's a book that looks backward through the story of God's people, confronts their present attitudes, and looks forward to what God would do in the future for his people. This book has such a personal tone from the Lord: "I have always loved you" (Malachi 1:2).

Still, the people who encountered Malachi questioned whether this were true, so Malachi wrote about this tension for the generations to see. As a result, the book of Malachi is power packed, hitting major theological points, practices of religion, politics, societal structures, justice issues, and even prophecies about the Messiah.

One hundred years after their captivity by the Babylonians, many Jewish people were freed and able to return to their homeland to rebuild. You might think that these freed people would be living all out for God, but that was not necessarily the case. Many of those who returned were actually pretty indifferent to God and his laws. They used their worst animals with defects for their sacrifices to God. They held marriage in very low esteem and tossed relationships around without much thought. They basically gave God their leftovers. Malachi's job was to call those unresponsive people not just to return to Israel but, even more importantly, to return to the Lord. Malachi was to remind them that God loved them and was graciously calling them back to himself.

Malachi's name means "messenger" or "messenger of God." His message asked people to look back at what God has done and to look to the future hope that God will provide. The Lord doesn't need human systems to accomplish his work or to bring glory to his name. He will do his work in his way and in his timing. The question is whether we will be on board.

Story Arc

- **John the Baptist**

Malachi

1 This is the message* that the LORD gave to Israel through the prophet
Malachi.*

The LORD's Love for Israel

2"I have always loved you," says the LORD.
But you retort, "Really? How have you loved us?"
And the LORD replies, "This is how I showed my love for you: I loved
your ancestor Jacob, 3but I rejected his brother, Esau, and devastated his hill
country. I turned Esau's inheritance into a desert for jackals."
4Esau's descendants in Edom may say, "We have been shattered, but we
will rebuild the ruins."
But the LORD of Heaven's Armies replies, "They may try to rebuild, but
I will demolish them again. Their country will be known as 'The Land of
Wickedness,' and their people will be called 'The People with Whom the
LORD Is Forever Angry.' 5When you see the destruction for yourselves, you
will say, 'Truly, the LORD's greatness reaches far beyond Israel's borders!'"

Unworthy Sacrifices

6The LORD of Heaven's Armies says to the priests: "A son honors his father,
and a servant respects his master. If I am your father and master, where are
the honor and respect I deserve? You have shown contempt for my name!
"But you ask, 'How have we ever shown contempt for your name?'
7"You have shown contempt by offering defiled sacrifices on my altar.
"Then you ask, 'How have we defiled the sacrifices?*'
"You defile them by saying the altar of the LORD deserves no respect.
8When you give blind animals as sacrifices, isn't that wrong? And isn't it
wrong to offer animals that are crippled and diseased? Try giving gifts like
that to your governor, and see how pleased he is!" says the LORD of Heaven's
Armies.
9"Go ahead, beg God to be merciful to you! But when you bring that
kind of offering, why should he show you any favor at all?" asks the LORD
of Heaven's Armies.
10"How I wish one of you would shut the Temple doors so that these
worthless sacrifices could not be offered! I am not pleased with you," says
the LORD of Heaven's Armies, "and I will not accept your offerings. 11But
my name is honored* by people of other nations from morning till night.
All around the world they offer* sweet incense and pure offerings in honor
of my name. For my name is great among the nations," says the LORD of
Heaven's Armies.
12"But you dishonor my name with your actions. By bringing contempt-
ible food, you are saying it's all right to defile the Lord's table. 13You say, 'It's

1:1a Hebrew *An Oracle: The message.* **1:1b** *Malachi* means "my messenger." **1:7** As in Greek version; Hebrew reads *defiled you?* **1:11a** Or *will be honored.* **1:11b** Or *will offer.*

Question **1:2**

Do you believe God has always loved you?

Make a Difference **1:6**

Respect

Often people who believe they are always right miss out on what is really going on around them. They are so focused on the *doing* that they miss the *being*. Here, God is calling out the religious leaders. He questions their lack of honor and respect. Oblivious and offended, they respond by asking God how they could have ever possibly messed up.

This is very similar to what Jesus said in Matthew 25:41-46, where he called out those who didn't take care of him when he was sick, thirsty, or imprisoned. Like the religious leaders in Malachi, the people in Matthew were oblivious to what was really going on and to what God was really up to.

Difference Maker

In what areas of your life are you prideful? Where might you need to get a better perspective so that you can see what God sees in you?

too hard to serve the LORD,' and you turn up your noses at my commands," says the LORD of Heaven's Armies. "Think of it! Animals that are stolen and crippled and sick are being presented as offerings! Should I accept from you such offerings as these?" asks the LORD.

14"Cursed is the cheat who promises to give a fine ram from his flock but then sacrifices a defective one to the Lord. For I am a great king," says the LORD of Heaven's Armies, "and my name is feared among the nations!

A Warning to the Priests

2 "Listen, you priests—this command is for you! 2Listen to me and make up your minds to honor my name," says the LORD of Heaven's Armies, "or I will bring a terrible curse against you. I will curse even the blessings you receive. Indeed, I have already cursed them, because you have not taken my warning to heart. 3I will punish your descendants and splatter your faces with the manure from your festival sacrifices, and I will throw you on the manure pile. 4Then at last you will know it was I who sent you this warning so that my covenant with the Levites can continue," says the LORD of Heaven's Armies.

5"The purpose of my covenant with the Levites was to bring life and peace, and that is what I gave them. This required reverence from them, and they greatly revered me and stood in awe of my name. 6They passed on to the people the truth of the instructions they received from me. They did not lie or cheat; they walked with me, living good and righteous lives, and they turned many from lives of sin.

7"The words of a priest's lips should preserve knowledge of God, and people should go to him for instruction, for the priest is the messenger of the LORD of Heaven's Armies. 8But you priests have left God's paths. Your instructions have caused many to stumble into sin. You have corrupted the covenant I made with the Levites," says the LORD of Heaven's Armies. 9"So I have made you despised and humiliated in the eyes of all the people. For you have not obeyed me but have shown favoritism in the way you carry out my instructions."

A Call to Faithfulness

10Are we not all children of the same Father? Are we not all created by the same God? Then why do we betray each other, violating the covenant of our ancestors?

11Judah has been unfaithful, and a detestable thing has been done in Israel and in Jerusalem. The men of Judah have defiled the LORD's beloved sanctuary by marrying women who worship idols. 12May the LORD cut off from the nation of Israel* every last man who has done this and yet brings an offering to the LORD of Heaven's Armies.

13Here is another thing you do. You cover the LORD's altar with tears, weeping and groaning because he pays no attention to your offerings and doesn't accept them with pleasure. 14You cry out, "Why doesn't the LORD accept my worship?" I'll tell you why! Because the LORD witnessed the vows you and your wife made when you were young. But you have been unfaithful to her, though she remained your faithful partner, the wife of your marriage vows.

2:12 Hebrew *from the tents of Jacob.* The names "Jacob" and "Israel" are often interchanged throughout the Old Testament, referring sometimes to the individual patriarch and sometimes to the nation.

Question **2:5-9**

As you read verses 5-9, what was God's original purpose for the priests in Israel? What did God want them to do? What benefit were they to bring to the people of Israel? How is this similar to the role of church leaders today? What can we learn from the mistakes of the Levites in this passage?

15 Didn't the LORD make you one with your wife? In body and spirit you are his.* And what does he want? Godly children from your union. So guard your heart; remain loyal to the wife of your youth. 16 "For I hate divorce!"* says the LORD, the God of Israel. "To divorce your wife is to overwhelm her with cruelty,*" says the LORD of Heaven's Armies. "So guard your heart; do not be unfaithful to your wife."

17 You have wearied the LORD with your words.

"How have we wearied him?" you ask.

You have wearied him by saying that all who do evil are good in the LORD's sight, and he is pleased with them. You have wearied him by asking, "Where is the God of justice?"

The Coming Day of Judgment

3 "Look! I am sending my messenger, and he will prepare the way before me. Then the Lord you are seeking will suddenly come to his Temple. The messenger of the covenant, whom you look for so eagerly, is surely coming," says the LORD of Heaven's Armies.

2 "But who will be able to endure it when he comes? Who will be able to stand and face him when he appears? For he will be like a blazing fire that refines metal, or like a strong soap that bleaches clothes. 3 He will sit like a refiner of silver, burning away the dross. He will purify the Levites, refining them like gold and silver, so that they may once again offer acceptable sacrifices to the LORD. 4 Then once more the LORD will accept the offerings brought to him by the people of Judah and Jerusalem, as he did in the past.

5 "At that time I will put you on trial. I am eager to witness against all sorcerers and adulterers and liars. I will speak against those who cheat employees of their wages, who oppress widows and orphans, or who deprive the foreigners living among you of justice, for these people do not fear me," says the LORD of Heaven's Armies.

A Call to Repentance

6 "I am the LORD, and I do not change. That is why you descendants of Jacob are not already destroyed. 7 Ever since the days of your ancestors, you have scorned my decrees and failed to obey them. Now return to me, and I will return to you," says the LORD of Heaven's Armies.

"But you ask, 'How can we return when we have never gone away?'

8 "Should people cheat God? Yet you have cheated me!

"But you ask, 'What do you mean? When did we ever cheat you?'

"You have cheated me of the tithes and offerings due to me. 9 You are under a curse, for your whole nation has been cheating me. 10 Bring all the tithes into the storehouse so there will be enough food in my Temple. If you do," says the LORD of Heaven's Armies, "I will open the windows of heaven for you. I will pour out a blessing so great you won't have enough room to take it in! Try it! Put me to the test! 11 Your crops will be abundant, for I will guard them from insects and disease.* Your grapes will not fall from the vine before they are ripe," says the LORD of Heaven's Armies. 12 "Then all nations will call you blessed, for your land will be such a delight," says the LORD of Heaven's Armies.

2:15 Or *Didn't the one LORD make us and preserve our life and breath?* or *Didn't the one LORD make her, both flesh and spirit?* The meaning of the Hebrew is uncertain. 2:16a Hebrew *For he hates divorcing.* 2:16b Hebrew *to cover one's garment with violence.* 3:11 Hebrew *from the devourer.*

Story Arc 3:1

● John the Baptist

God himself said something remarkable here: "I am sending my messenger, and he will prepare the way before me." Suddenly, God will show up!

Malachi's message echoed the words of Isaiah (Isaiah 40:3) and other prophets who predicted that people should listen for the voice calling in the desert to clear the way for the Lord. Someday, this promised messenger would arrive on the scene to point people to the Lord himself, the Savior of the world.

The messenger whom God is talking about here is John the Baptist (Matthew 3:3; 11:7-10). You can read about John in the first four New Testament books that immediately follow the book of Malachi. In Matthew 3:1-17 and 14:1-12, you can see some of John the Baptist's remarkable story. In Matthew 11:1-19, Jesus called John the Baptist the greatest human to have ever lived. In John 1:6-7, you can read that John the Baptist was sent to tell people about the Light of the World (Jesus) so that everyone might believe.

By revealing his plan in the book of Malachi, God was pointing people to one who would point to him, the bringer of an eternal future and hope.

Matt 1:1-17 ►

13"You have said terrible things about me," says the LORD.
"But you say, 'What do you mean? What have we said against you?'
14"You have said, 'What's the use of serving God? What have we gained
by obeying his commands or by trying to show the LORD of Heaven's Ar-
mies that we are sorry for our sins? 15From now on we will call the arrogant
blessed. For those who do evil get rich, and those who dare God to punish
them suffer no harm.'"

The LORD's Promise of Mercy

16Then those who feared the LORD spoke with each other, and the LORD
listened to what they said. In his presence, a scroll of remembrance was writ-
ten to record the names of those who feared him and always thought about
the honor of his name.
17"They will be my people," says the LORD of Heaven's Armies. "On the
day when I act in judgment, they will be my own special treasure. I will
spare them as a father spares an obedient child. 18Then you will again see
the difference between the righteous and the wicked, between those who
serve God and those who do not."

The Coming Day of Judgment

4 1*The LORD of Heaven's Armies says, "The day of judgment is coming,
burning like a furnace. On that day the arrogant and the wicked will
be burned up like straw. They will be consumed—roots, branches, and all.
2"But for you who fear my name, the Sun of Righteousness will rise with
healing in his wings.* And you will go free, leaping with joy like calves let
out to pasture. 3On the day when I act, you will tread upon the wicked as if
they were dust under your feet," says the LORD of Heaven's Armies.
4"Remember to obey the Law of Moses, my servant—all the decrees and
regulations that I gave him on Mount Sinai* for all Israel.
5"Look, I am sending you the prophet Elijah before the great and dread-
ful day of the LORD arrives. 6His preaching will turn the hearts of fathers to
their children, and the hearts of children to their fathers. Otherwise I will
come and strike the land with a curse."

4:1 Verses 4:1-6 are numbered 3:19-24 in Hebrew text. 4:2 Or *the sun of righteousness will rise with healing in its wings.* 4:4 Hebrew *Horeb,* another name for Sinai.

Prayer 4:2

Lord, thank you for the hope that you give to people who love and follow you. Remind me that my future is filled with joy and righteousness when I am walking through difficult seasons in my life. Amen.

GENESIS
- 3:1-24 Adam and Eve: The First Humans
- 6:1-9 Noah
- 11:29-30 Abram and Sarai
- 14:18-20 Melchizedek
- 29:32-30:24 The Twelve Tribes
- 32:28 Jacob → Israel
- 37:2-36 Joseph

EXODUS
- 2:10 Moses
- 7:1-13 Aaron
- 15:20-21 Miriam
- 17:9 Joshua
- 31:1-11 Bezalel
- 38:22-23 Oholiab

LEVITICUS
- 8:1-15 Aaron

NUMBERS
- 1:1 Moses
- 14:5-30 Joshua and Caleb
- 18:1-32 Aaron
- 21:4-9 Jesus
- 27:12-23 Joshua

DEUTERONOMY
- 3:21-28 Joshua
- 32:48-52 Moses

JOSHUA
- 1:1 Joshua
- 2:1-24 Rahab
- 14:6-15 Caleb

JUDGES
- 3:7-11 Othniel
- 3:12-30 Ehud
- 6:11 Gideon
- 9:1-21 Jotham
- 13:24 Samson → Rescuer!

RUTH
- 2:1-23 Ruth

1 SAMUEL
- 1:2-22 Hannah
- 1:19-28 Samuel
- 13:2 Jonathan
- 16:1-23 David

2 SAMUEL
- 5:7 Zion
- 7:1-17 Nathan
- 11:1-5 Bathsheba

1 KINGS
- 1:1 David
- 1:28-40 Solomon
- 11:29-39 Ahijah
- 17:1 Elijah

2 KINGS
- 1:3 Elijah
- 2:1 Elisha
- 11:1-3 Joash
- 11:4-21 Jehoiada
- 18:1-8 Hezekiah
- 19:5-7 Isaiah
- 22:1-2 Josiah
- 25:27-30 Jesus

1 CHRONICLES
- 1:1-2:15 Adam → David
- 11:1-2 David
- 16:37 Asaph
- 17:1-15 Nathan
- 22:5-19 Solomon

2 CHRONICLES
- 1:1 Solomon
- 3:1 The Mount
- 18:6-27 Micaiah
- 21:12-15 Elijah
- 22:10-12 Jehosheba
- 23:1-11 Jehoiada
- 29:3 Hezekiah
- 32:20 Isaiah
- 34:3 Josiah
- 35:25 Jeremiah

NEHEMIAH
- 1:1-11 Nehemiah
- 8:1-9 Ezra
- 12:1 Zerubbabel and Jeshua

ESTHER
- 2:5-6 Mordecai
- 2:7-20 Esther

JOB
- 1:1-22 Job

PSALMS
- 22:1-31 Jesus
- 51:1-19 David
- 73:1 Asaph

PROVERBS
- 1:1 Solomon

ECCLESIASTES
- 2:11 Solomon

SONG OF SONGS
- 1:1 Solomon

ISAIAH
- 1:1 Isaiah
- 11:1-5 David
- 37:14-20 Hezekiah
- 61:1-2 Jesus

JEREMIAH
- 1:1-3 Jeremiah
- 26:12-24 Micah
- 36:1-32 Baruch
- 38:6-13 Ebed-melech

LAMENTATIONS
- 2:13 Jeremiah

EZEKIEL
- 1:1-3 Ezekiel
- 34:11-24 Jesus

DANIEL
- 1:8 Daniel
- 3:1-30 Shadrach, Meshach, and Abednego

HOSEA
- 1:1 Hosea

AMOS
- 1:1 Amos

JONAH
- 1:1 Jonah

MICAH
- 5:2-4 Bethlehem

Story Arc Index

The NEW TESTAMENT

NEW TESTAMENT INTRODUCTION

These are written so that you may continue to believe that Jesus is the Messiah, the Son of God, and that by believing in him you will have life by the power of his name.

JOHN 20:31

The New Testament introduces the world to Jesus—and Jesus changes everything. Jesus is the most important person you could ever meet. He is your creator. He is your rescuer. He is your judge. He is your healer. He is your friend. He is your Good Shepherd. He is your King. He is the Way. He is your life. He is your truth. Jesus is holy. He is fully man, and he is fully God. Jesus takes away your guilt because he takes away your sin.

Jesus calls you to join his adventure. He gives you an invitation: "Follow me." He gives you power through his Spirit. He gives you the opportunity to know God personally, face-to-face. He gives you the responsibility to love and care for others because he first loved and cared for you. Likewise, he gives you a calling to have a radical effect on this world by making disciples of all nations (Matthew 28:19).

The twenty-seven books that make up the New Testament are comprised of incredibly revealing eyewitness accounts, incredibly articulate theological arguments, incredibly personal letters, and an incredibly vivid apocalyptic revelation. All these were written in a short span of time after Jesus was executed. Something sparked a small group of praying people to multiply a movement across the world within a generation. That epic, nail-biting, soul-plowing, new-creation story of Jesus and his first followers was told through firsthand witnesses in the New Testament.

You may notice that the writers of the New Testament books were heavily invested in what we now call the "Old" Testament. To the New Testament writers, all Scripture was alive and powerful (Hebrews 4:12) because it revealed Jesus. In fact, Jesus said he didn't come to abolish the "law of Moses or the writings of the prophets" but to fulfill them (Matthew 5:17). He told his followers how all the Old Testament pointed to him (Luke 24:27). People like Abraham and Moses, Rahab and Ruth, David and Elijah had set the stage. This is why the New Testament books are steeped with Old Testament verses and characters and story arcs.

As you dive into the final one-third of the Bible, may Jesus open your mind to understand the Old Testament and New Testament Scriptures so that you might know God's personal and compelling call for your life.

Matthew Introduction

Was there a more despised follower of Jesus than Matthew? Simon the Zealot, the violent hater of the Romans, perhaps, but even he had his sympathizers. Judas Iscariot, certainly, but his reputation was ruined only later. All those fishermen, maybe, except that they probably just got some funny looks. Matthew? He was a tax collector. He took money from the Jewish people and gave it to the occupying government—Rome. To make matters worse, he likely added a personal fee on top of every collection. In other words, his own people viewed him as a traitor.

Two simple words made the difference in Matthew's life: "Follow me." Jesus invited Matthew to set aside his scorned life, to leave his betrayals on the table, and to pursue a transformed life. At once, Matthew recounted, he got up and followed Jesus. See Matthew 9:9-13 for Matthew's own account of this story.

"The Gospel according to Matthew," as we often call the first book of the New Testament, is the eyewitness testimony of a radically changed man. The man who had spent his career taking from others now wanted to give the world a gift—the story of Jesus Christ. In the way he wrote, Matthew's skills of accounting and research are evident, his attention to minute details is clear, and his laser-focus descriptions of Jesus are challenging. He wrote as a man forever made different by his encounter with Jesus, and he longed for his readers to find healing, forgiveness, and life with God through their encounters with Jesus in his book.

The question Matthew would want you to answer while you read his account is this: Will you drop everything else in your life so that you, too, can follow Jesus?

Story Arcs

- **Jesus**
- **John the Baptist**
- **Matthew**
- **The Disciples**

Matthew

The Ancestors of Jesus the Messiah

1 This is a record of the ancestors of Jesus the Messiah, a descendant of
David and of Abraham*:

2 Abraham was the father of Isaac.
Isaac was the father of Jacob.
Jacob was the father of Judah and his brothers.
3 Judah was the father of Perez and Zerah
(whose mother was Tamar).
Perez was the father of Hezron.
Hezron was the father of Ram.*
4 Ram was the father of Amminadab.
Amminadab was the father of Nahshon.
Nahshon was the father of Salmon.
5 Salmon was the father of Boaz (whose mother
was Rahab).
Boaz was the father of Obed (whose mother was Ruth).
Obed was the father of Jesse.
6 Jesse was the father of King David.
David was the father of Solomon (whose mother was
Bathsheba, the widow of Uriah).
7 Solomon was the father of Rehoboam.
Rehoboam was the father of Abijah.
Abijah was the father of Asa.*
8 Asa was the father of Jehoshaphat.
Jehoshaphat was the father of Jehoram.*
Jehoram was the father* of Uzziah.
9 Uzziah was the father of Jotham.
Jotham was the father of Ahaz.
Ahaz was the father of Hezekiah.
10 Hezekiah was the father of Manasseh.
Manasseh was the father of Amon.*
Amon was the father of Josiah.
11 Josiah was the father of Jehoiachin* and his brothers
(born at the time of the exile to Babylon).
12 After the Babylonian exile:
Jehoiachin was the father of Shealtiel.
Shealtiel was the father of Zerubbabel.

1:1 Greek *Jesus the Messiah, Son of David and son of Abraham.* 1:3 Greek *Aram,* a variant spelling of Ram; also in 1:4. See 1 Chr 2:9-10. 1:7 Greek *Asaph,* a variant spelling of Asa; also in 1:8. See 1 Chr 3:10. 1:8a Greek *Joram,* a variant spelling of Jehoram; also in 1:8b. See 1 Kgs 22:50 and note at 1 Chr 3:11. 1:8b Or *ancestor;* also in 1:11. 1:10 Greek *Amos,* a variant spelling of Amon; also in 1:10b. See 1 Chr 3:14. 1:11 Greek *Jeconiah,* a variant spelling of Jehoiachin; also in 1:12. See 2 Kgs 24:6 and note at 1 Chr 3:16.

Story Arc 1:1-17

Jesus

The names listed at the beginning of the New Testament are not to be skipped. These names tell the story of salvation that God launched with Abraham a couple thousand years before Jesus was born. Take some time to read through the first sixteen verses of Matthew. Even try to pronounce any awkward names aloud. Go back through the Bible and find moments when God used these people to work out his great plan through Jesus to save people from their sins (Matthew 1:21).

Matt 3:1-17 ►

Make a Difference

2:1-12

Approaching Jesus

The goal of Christmas is that each of us would come to meet Jesus. The Christmas passages, as with the rest of the Bible, share that each of us is to approach Jesus so that we can have an eternal relationship with him. The book of Matthew is full of invitation. In chapter 4, Jesus called out to two brothers, "Come, follow me, and I will show you how to fish for people!" (v. 19). In Matthew 11, Jesus invited everyone: "Come to me, all of you who are weary and carry heavy burdens, and I will give you rest" (v. 28). In Matthew 14, when Peter asked if he could walk out to him on the water, Jesus simply responded, "Yes, come" (v. 29). In chapter 28, after Jesus' resurrection, even the angels got into the action, saying, "Come, see where his body was lying" (v. 6). Jesus has come to meet you. Will you come to meet him today?

Difference Maker

Go meet with Jesus today. Seek him and find him, for he is inviting you to do just that. Set aside some time today just to worship him.

Prayer **2:2**

Jesus, I come to you now and give you my whole life. Amen.

13 Zerubbabel was the father of Abiud.
Abiud was the father of Eliakim.
Eliakim was the father of Azor.
14 Azor was the father of Zadok.
Zadok was the father of Akim.
Akim was the father of Eliud.
15 Eliud was the father of Eleazar.
Eleazar was the father of Matthan.
Matthan was the father of Jacob.
16 Jacob was the father of Joseph, the husband of Mary.
Mary gave birth to Jesus, who is called the Messiah.

17 All those listed above include fourteen generations from Abraham to David, fourteen from David to the Babylonian exile, and fourteen from the Babylonian exile to the Messiah.

The Birth of Jesus the Messiah

18 This is how Jesus the Messiah was born. His mother, Mary, was engaged to be married to Joseph. But before the marriage took place, while she was still a virgin, she became pregnant through the power of the Holy Spirit.
19 Joseph, to whom she was engaged, was a righteous man and did not want to disgrace her publicly, so he decided to break the engagement* quietly.
20 As he considered this, an angel of the Lord appeared to him in a dream. "Joseph, son of David," the angel said, "do not be afraid to take Mary as your wife. For the child within her was conceived by the Holy Spirit. 21 And she will have a son, and you are to name him Jesus,* for he will save his people from their sins."
22 All of this occurred to fulfill the Lord's message through his prophet:

23 "Look! The virgin will conceive a child!
She will give birth to a son,
and they will call him Immanuel,*
which means 'God is with us.'"

24 When Joseph woke up, he did as the angel of the Lord commanded and took Mary as his wife. 25 But he did not have sexual relations with her until her son was born. And Joseph named him Jesus.

Visitors from the East

2 Jesus was born in Bethlehem in Judea, during the reign of King Herod. About that time some wise men* from eastern lands arrived in
Jerusalem, asking, 2 "Where is the newborn king of the Jews? We saw his star as it rose,* and we have come to worship him."
3 King Herod was deeply disturbed when he heard this, as was everyone in Jerusalem. 4 He called a meeting of the leading priests and teachers of religious law and asked, "Where is the Messiah supposed to be born?"
5 "In Bethlehem in Judea," they said, "for this is what the prophet wrote:

1:19 Greek *to divorce her.* 1:21 *Jesus* means "The LORD saves." 1:23 Isa 7:14; 8:8, 10 (Greek version). 2:1 Or *royal astrologers;* Greek reads *magi;* also in 2:7, 16. 2:2 Or *star in the east.*

6 'And you, O Bethlehem in the land of Judah,
are not least among the ruling cities* of Judah,
for a ruler will come from you
who will be the shepherd for my people Israel.'*"

7 Then Herod called for a private meeting with the wise men, and he
learned from them the time when the star first appeared. 8 Then he told
them, "Go to Bethlehem and search carefully for the child. And when you
find him, come back and tell me so that I can go and worship him, too!"
9 After this interview the wise men went their way. And the star they
had seen in the east guided them to Bethlehem. It went ahead of them
and stopped over the place where the child was. 10 When they saw the star,
they were filled with joy! 11 They entered the house and saw the child with
his mother, Mary, and they bowed down and worshiped him. Then they
opened their treasure chests and gave him gifts of gold, frankincense, and
myrrh.
12 When it was time to leave, they returned to their own country by another
route, for God had warned them in a dream not to return to Herod.

The Escape to Egypt

13 After the wise men were gone, an angel of the Lord appeared to Joseph in
a dream. "Get up! Flee to Egypt with the child and his mother," the angel
said. "Stay there until I tell you to return, because Herod is going to search
for the child to kill him."
14 That night Joseph left for Egypt with the child and Mary, his mother,
15 and they stayed there until Herod's death. This fulfilled what the Lord had
spoken through the prophet: "I called my Son out of Egypt."*
16 Herod was furious when he realized that the wise men had outwitted
him. He sent soldiers to kill all the boys in and around Bethlehem who were
two years old and under, based on the wise men's report of the star's first
appearance. 17 Herod's brutal action fulfilled what God had spoken through
the prophet Jeremiah:

18 "A cry was heard in Ramah—
weeping and great mourning.
Rachel weeps for her children,
refusing to be comforted,
for they are dead."*

The Return to Nazareth

19 When Herod died, an angel of the Lord appeared in a dream to Joseph in
Egypt. 20 "Get up!" the angel said. "Take the child and his mother back to
the land of Israel, because those who were trying to kill the child are dead."
21 So Joseph got up and returned to the land of Israel with Jesus and his
mother. 22 But when he learned that the new ruler of Judea was Herod's son
Archelaus, he was afraid to go there. Then, after being warned in a dream,
he left for the region of Galilee. 23 So the family went and lived in a town
called Nazareth. This fulfilled what the prophets had said: "He will be called
a Nazarene."

2:6a Greek *the rulers.* **2:6b** Mic 5:2; 2 Sam 5:2. **2:15** Hos 11:1. **2:18** Jer 31:15.

John the Baptist Prepares the Way

3 In those days John the Baptist came to the Judean wilderness and began preaching. His message was, 2“Repent of your sins and turn to God, for the Kingdom of Heaven is near.*” 3The prophet Isaiah was speaking about John when he said,

“He is a voice shouting in the wilderness,
‘Prepare the way for the LORD’s coming!
Clear the road for him!’”*

4John’s clothes were woven from coarse camel hair, and he wore a leather belt around his waist. For food he ate locusts and wild honey. 5People from Jerusalem and from all of Judea and all over the Jordan Valley went out to see and hear John. 6And when they confessed their sins, he baptized them in the Jordan River.

7But when he saw many Pharisees and Sadducees coming to watch him baptize,* he denounced them. “You brood of snakes!” he exclaimed. “Who warned you to flee the coming wrath? 8Prove by the way you live that you have repented of your sins and turned to God. 9Don’t just say to each other, ‘We’re safe, for we are descendants of Abraham.’ That means nothing, for I tell you, God can create children of Abraham from these very stones. 10Even now the ax of God’s judgment is poised, ready to sever the roots of the trees. Yes, every tree that does not produce good fruit will be chopped down and thrown into the fire.

11“I baptize with* water those who repent of their sins and turn to God. But someone is coming soon who is greater than I am—so much greater that I’m not worthy even to be his slave and carry his sandals. He will baptize you with the Holy Spirit and with fire.* 12He is ready to separate the chaff from the wheat with his winnowing fork. Then he will clean up the threshing area, gathering the wheat into his barn but burning the chaff with never-ending fire.”

The Baptism of Jesus

13Then Jesus went from Galilee to the Jordan River to be baptized by John. 14But John tried to talk him out of it. “I am the one who needs to be baptized by you,” he said, “so why are you coming to me?”

15But Jesus said, “It should be done, for we must carry out all that God requires.*” So John agreed to baptize him.

16After his baptism, as Jesus came up out of the water, the heavens were opened* and he saw the Spirit of God descending like a dove and settling on him. 17And a voice from heaven said, “This is my dearly loved Son, who brings me great joy.”

The Temptation of Jesus

4 Then Jesus was led by the Spirit into the wilderness to be tempted there by the devil. 2For forty days and forty nights he fasted and became very hungry.

3During that time the devil* came and said to him, “If you are the Son of God, tell these stones to become loaves of bread.”

3:2 Or *has come,* or *is coming soon.* 3:3 Isa 40:3 (Greek version). 3:7 Or *coming to be baptized.* 3:11a Or *in.* 3:11b Or *in the Holy Spirit and in fire.* 3:15 Or *for we must fulfill all righteousness.* 3:16 Some manuscripts read *opened to him.* 4:3 Greek *the tempter.*

Story Arc **3:1-17**

John the Baptist

Jesus said that John the Baptist was the greatest human ever to have lived (Matthew 11:10-11) because he was the one the prophets said would prepare the way for the Messiah (Isaiah 40:3; Malachi 3:1). John the Baptist, however, said that he wasn't even worthy to carry Jesus' sandals (Matthew 3:11). John the Baptist preached *repentance*, which means turning away from sin to God, even though it cost him his own life (Matthew 14:1-12).

Matt 9:9-13 ►

[4]But Jesus told him, "No! The Scriptures say,

'People do not live by bread alone,
but by every word that comes from the mouth of God.'*"

[5]Then the devil took him to the holy city, Jerusalem, to the highest point
of the Temple, [6]and said, "If you are the Son of God, jump off! For the Scrip-
tures say,

'He will order his angels to protect you.
And they will hold you up with their hands
so you won't even hurt your foot on a stone.'*"

[7]Jesus responded, "The Scriptures also say, 'You must not test the LORD
your God.'*"
[8]Next the devil took him to the peak of a very high mountain and showed
him all the kingdoms of the world and their glory. [9]"I will give it all to you,"
he said, "if you will kneel down and worship me."
[10]"Get out of here, Satan," Jesus told him. "For the Scriptures say,

'You must worship the LORD your God
and serve only him.'*"

[11]Then the devil went away, and angels came and took care of Jesus.

Question 4:1-11

As you look at Matthew 4:1-11, what do you learn from Jesus about overcoming temptation?

The Ministry of Jesus Begins

[12]When Jesus heard that John had been arrested, he left Judea and returned
to Galilee. [13]He went first to Nazareth, then left there and moved to Ca-
pernaum, beside the Sea of Galilee, in the region of Zebulun and Naphtali.
[14]This fulfilled what God said through the prophet Isaiah:

[15] "In the land of Zebulun and of Naphtali,
beside the sea, beyond the Jordan River,
in Galilee where so many Gentiles live,
[16] the people who sat in darkness
have seen a great light.
And for those who lived in the land where death casts its shadow,
a light has shined."*

[17]From then on Jesus began to preach, "Repent of your sins and turn to
God, for the Kingdom of Heaven is near.*"

The First Disciples

[18]One day as Jesus was walking along the shore of the Sea of Galilee, he saw
two brothers—Simon, also called Peter, and Andrew—throwing a net into
the water, for they fished for a living. [19]Jesus called out to them, "Come,
follow me, and I will show you how to fish for people!" [20]And they left their
nets at once and followed him.
[21]A little farther up the shore he saw two other brothers, James and John,

4:4 Deut 8:3. **4:6** Ps 91:11-12. **4:7** Deut 6:16. **4:10** Deut 6:13. **4:15-16** Isa 9:1-2 (Greek version). **4:17** Or *has come,* or *is coming soon.*

sitting in a boat with their father, Zebedee, repairing their nets. And he called
them to come, too. 22 They immediately followed him, leaving the boat and
their father behind.

Crowds Follow Jesus

23 Jesus traveled throughout the region of Galilee, teaching in the syna-
gogues and announcing the Good News about the Kingdom. And he healed
every kind of disease and illness. 24 News about him spread as far as Syria,
and people soon began bringing to him all who were sick. And whatever
their sickness or disease, or if they were demon possessed or epileptic or
paralyzed—he healed them all. 25 Large crowds followed him wherever he
went—people from Galilee, the Ten Towns,* Jerusalem, from all over Judea,
and from east of the Jordan River.

The Sermon on the Mount

5 One day as he saw the crowds gathering, Jesus went up on the mountain-
side and sat down. His disciples gathered around him, 2 and he began
to teach them.

The Beatitudes

3 "God blesses those who are poor and realize their need for him,*
for the Kingdom of Heaven is theirs.
4 God blesses those who mourn,
for they will be comforted.
5 God blesses those who are humble,
for they will inherit the whole earth.
6 God blesses those who hunger and thirst for justice,*
for they will be satisfied.
7 God blesses those who are merciful,
for they will be shown mercy.
8 God blesses those whose hearts are pure,
for they will see God.
9 God blesses those who work for peace,
for they will be called the children of God.
10 God blesses those who are persecuted for doing right,
for the Kingdom of Heaven is theirs.

11 "God blesses you when people mock you and persecute you and lie about
you and say all sorts of evil things against you because you are my followers.
12 Be happy about it! Be very glad! For a great reward awaits you in heaven.
And remember, the ancient prophets were persecuted in the same way.

Teaching about Salt and Light

13 "You are the salt of the earth. But what good is salt if it has lost its flavor?
Can you make it salty again? It will be thrown out and trampled underfoot
as worthless.

14 "You are the light of the world—like a city on a hilltop that cannot be
hidden. 15 No one lights a lamp and then puts it under a basket. Instead, a
lamp is placed on a stand, where it gives light to everyone in the house. 16 In

4:25 Greek *Decapolis.* **5:3** Greek *poor in spirit.* **5:6** Or *for righteousness.*

the same way, let your good deeds shine out for all to see, so that everyone
will praise your heavenly Father.

Teaching about the Law

17 "Don't misunderstand why I have come. I did not come to abolish the law
of Moses or the writings of the prophets. No, I came to accomplish their
purpose. 18 I tell you the truth, until heaven and earth disappear, not even
the smallest detail of God's law will disappear until its purpose is achieved.
19 So if you ignore the least commandment and teach others to do the same,
you will be called the least in the Kingdom of Heaven. But anyone who obeys
God's laws and teaches them will be called great in the Kingdom of Heaven.
20 "But I warn you—unless your righteousness is better than the righ-
teousness of the teachers of religious law and the Pharisees, you will never
enter the Kingdom of Heaven!

Teaching about Anger

21 "You have heard that our ancestors were told, 'You must not murder. If you
commit murder, you are subject to judgment.'* 22 But I say, if you are even
angry with someone,* you are subject to judgment! If you call someone an
idiot,* you are in danger of being brought before the court. And if you curse
someone,* you are in danger of the fires of hell.*
23 "So if you are presenting a sacrifice* at the altar in the Temple and you
suddenly remember that someone has something against you, 24 leave your
sacrifice there at the altar. Go and be reconciled to that person. Then come
and offer your sacrifice to God.
25 "When you are on the way to court with your adversary, settle your dif-
ferences quickly. Otherwise, your accuser may hand you over to the judge,
who will hand you over to an officer, and you will be thrown into prison.
26 And if that happens, you surely won't be free again until you have paid
the last penny.*

Teaching about Adultery

27 "You have heard the commandment that says, 'You must not commit adul-
tery.'* 28 But I say, anyone who even looks at a woman with lust has already
committed adultery with her in his heart. 29 So if your eye—even your good
eye*—causes you to lust, gouge it out and throw it away. It is better for you
to lose one part of your body than for your whole body to be thrown into
hell. 30 And if your hand—even your stronger hand*—causes you to sin, cut
it off and throw it away. It is better for you to lose one part of your body than
for your whole body to be thrown into hell.

Teaching about Divorce

31 "You have heard the law that says, 'A man can divorce his wife by merely
giving her a written notice of divorce.'* 32 But I say that a man who divorces
his wife, unless she has been unfaithful, causes her to commit adultery. And
anyone who marries a divorced woman also commits adultery.

5:21 Exod 20:13; Deut 5:17. **5:22a** Some manuscripts add *without cause.* **5:22b** Greek uses an Aramaic term of contempt: *If you say to your brother, 'Raca.'* **5:22c** Greek *if you say, 'You fool.'* **5:22d** Greek *Gehenna;* also in 5:29, 30. **5:23** Greek *gift;* also in 5:24. **5:26** Greek *the last kodrantes* [i.e., quadrans]. **5:27** Exod 20:14; Deut 5:18. **5:29** Greek *your right eye.* **5:30** Greek *your right hand.* **5:31** Deut 24:1.

Drop your brilliant thoughts here

The Difference the Beatitudes Make

Make a Difference 5:3

Be Needy

People need God. Every person needs a relationship with the Creator. People need the daily breath and long-term purpose that only God provides. When things fall apart, they cry out to the Lord because he is the one whom they need during those times. When people have God, they have everything they need.

Sometimes people fail to recognize their need for God. Instead of finding their dependency in their Creator, they try to go it alone. While independence from God might puff up the ego and build up a bank account, any get-rich-quick schemes or quick-fix solutions that avoid God are bound to end in ruin.

Being "poor of heart" is an important posture for humans to take. Pride is a false sense of having everything whereas poverty is the desperation of not having enough. Those who realize they need God, that they are desperate without him, will be rewarded with the relationship and royal status that only God can provide.

Difference Maker

Think of something you have in your life that supplants your need for God and discard it.

Make a Difference 5:4

Be Sad

One of the signs of a good heart is a sad heart. In other words, those who don't care don't mourn. In contrast, those who care are willing to feel the pain of loss. There is a remarkable amount of hurt in this world. While it would be great to avoid pain, the alternatives are to become abusive or numb.

Jesus has a good heart. One of the shortest verses in the Bible, and one of the most significant, says, "Jesus wept" (John 11:35). At a funeral, Jesus mourned the loss of his friend, and he carried the heartache of the situation precisely because he was willing to love deeply. He didn't have to care, but he did. Jesus cried with his friends. He wore their burdens. He tended to their wounds. Then he raised them to life once again.

Difference Maker

Grab coffee with or write a note to someone you know who has recently experienced loss and express your sorrow.

Make a Difference 5:5

Be Humble

If anyone ever had a reason to brag, it was Jesus. After listening to some simpleton humans boast about conquering nations or building coliseums or inventing aqueducts, Jesus could have interrupted their grandiosity with a snap of his fingers. "Be still! You don't know squat. You call those tiny buildings 'coliseums'? Ha! I made asteroids bigger than that. What's so great about an aqueduct? Now you can move a little bit of water from one place to the other. Have you ever heard of rivers? Seas? Oh, and have you ever noticed how your heart is beating right now? Yep, that's me. I sustain your life."

No, that is not the Way.

If he wanted to, Jesus could have put humans in their place pretty quickly. If he were tired of conceited humans claiming to be the greatest, he could just snuff out their puffed-up arrogance with one breath. Instead, he served. He listened. He embraced. He healed. He saved. He treasured. He lived among us with humility because he wanted people to share with him all that he had made.

Difference Maker

Be humble like Jesus today. Try to make it through the entire day without using the word *I*. Instead of talking about yourself, take that effort to focus on others.

Make a Difference 5:6

Be Hungry

Jesus wants you to make a difference in the community in which you live. It isn't enough just to feel like people shouldn't be treated unfairly, for instance, or to think that people shouldn't be oppressed. He actually wants you to figure out something to do that will help these people and address the terrible situations they are in.

Jesus hungered and thirsted for justice. He hated it when people were pushed down or overrun. His vision for the world did not include oppression and violence. In one of the most famous and countercultural messages the world has ever heard, Jesus' Sermon on the Mount, he made it clear that God values human life, and he expects people to fight for those whose lives are being stolen. Does your heart break over the wrongs that are committed against the innocent? Does your soul cry for those whose voice has been taken from them? God's does.

Difference Maker

Connect with a local organization or church that seeks to defend those who are being wronged. Ask what kind of support they need and choose a way to respond.

Make a Difference 5:7

Be Merciful

When you are in a position of power, when you are justified to dispense wrath, when you have the opportunity to let loose your fury, what would happen if you chose to withhold it? What if you extended a hand of grace and restoration instead? Mercy recognizes that God is in control, and it acknowledges that the person who deserves judgment is both a fellow child of God and in need of restoration

Not everyone who is offered mercy accepts it or reorients to it. Someone else's response is not your responsibility. Mercy doesn't dictate a person's future; it simply opens it up.

Difference Maker

Here's a gut check: Whom do you judge too easily? Who needs another chance today?

Make a Difference 5:8

Be Pure

To *adulterate* a product is to add an inferior or polluted substance to what may have once been a spotless, wholesome item. It is like secretly adding chemical ingredients to all-natural skin lotion or adding an affair to a marriage.

Purity doesn't imply naivete. To be pure doesn't mean you are inexperienced or ignorant. The world mocks purity because it doesn't understand it and doesn't believe it has survival power. Eventually, the world believes, purity has to be corrupted, right?

Jesus didn't think so. He believed we could live out purity in practical ways. Jesus believed that purity begins in the nature of a person's focus upon God and then it extends into everyday action. He suggested that purity opens the eyes to see in ways that others cannot. In fact, purity expands the paradigm and adventure of life.

Difference Maker

Pick a glaring struggle you have with impurity, then find a friend who struggles with the same issues so you can hold each other faithful in your pursuit of purity.

Make a Difference 5:9

Be Peaceful

Peace is not passive. Peace comes about through incredible strain and sacrifice. Consider the millions of people throughout history who have given their lives so that peace could stand.

There is a war against peace in the world today—ideologically, geographically, culturally, physically, emotionally, and spiritually. There are powers and movements whose goal is the disruption and deterioration and destruction of true peace. Jesus jumped into this same fray when he came to earth. Like a vigilante of justice, Jesus disarmed evil. His effort cost him his life, but it was a cost he decided was worth the outcome.

Jesus is the "Prince of Peace" (Isaiah 9:6), and he exerts himself so that people can have "peace with God" (Romans 5:1). Jesus fought and died to give this world a powerful, proactive peace. When people embrace him and when they choose to become peacemakers themselves, all of heaven celebrates.

Difference Maker

Take a moment to pray. Ask God to show you what steps you need to take to fight for peace in the agitated areas of your life.

Teaching about Vows

33"You have also heard that our ancestors were told, 'You must not break your vows; you must carry out the vows you make to the LORD.'* 34But I say, do not make any vows! Do not say, 'By heaven!' because heaven is God's throne. 35And do not say, 'By the earth!' because the earth is his footstool. And do not say, 'By Jerusalem!' for Jerusalem is the city of the great King. 36Do not even say, 'By my head!' for you can't turn one hair white or black. 37Just say a simple, 'Yes, I will,' or 'No, I won't.' Anything beyond this is from the evil one.

Teaching about Revenge

38"You have heard the law that says the punishment must match the injury: 'An eye for an eye, and a tooth for a tooth.'* 39But I say, do not resist an evil person! If someone slaps you on the right cheek, offer the other cheek also. 40If you are sued in court and your shirt is taken from you, give your coat, too. 41If a soldier demands that you carry his gear for a mile,* carry it two miles. 42Give to those who ask, and don't turn away from those who want to borrow.

Teaching about Love for Enemies

43"You have heard the law that says, 'Love your neighbor'* and hate your enemy. 44But I say, love your enemies!* Pray for those who persecute you! 45In that way, you will be acting as true children of your Father in heaven. For he gives his sunlight to both the evil and the good, and he sends rain on the just and the unjust alike. 46If you love only those who love you, what reward is there for that? Even corrupt tax collectors do that much. 47If you are kind only to your friends,* how are you different from anyone else? Even pagans do that. 48But you are to be perfect, even as your Father in heaven is perfect.

Teaching about Giving to the Needy

6 "Watch out! Don't do your good deeds publicly, to be admired by others, for you will lose the reward from your Father in heaven. 2When you give to someone in need, don't do as the hypocrites do—blowing trumpets in the synagogues and streets to call attention to their acts of charity! I tell you the truth, they have received all the reward they will ever get. 3But when you give to someone in need, don't let your left hand know what your right hand is doing. 4Give your gifts in private, and your Father, who sees everything, will reward you.

Teaching about Prayer and Fasting

5"When you pray, don't be like the hypocrites who love to pray publicly on street corners and in the synagogues where everyone can see them. I tell you the truth, that is all the reward they will ever get. 6But when you pray, go away by yourself, shut the door behind you, and pray to your Father in private. Then your Father, who sees everything, will reward you.

7"When you pray, don't babble on and on as the Gentiles do. They think their prayers are answered merely by repeating their words again and again. 8Don't be like them, for your Father knows exactly what you need even before you ask him! 9Pray like this:

5:33 Num 30:2. 5:38 Greek *the law that says: 'An eye for an eye and a tooth for a tooth.'* Exod 21:24; Lev 24:20; Deut 19:21. 5:41 Greek *milion* [4,854 feet or 1,478 meters]. 5:43 Lev 19:18. 5:44 Some manuscripts add *Bless those who curse you. Do good to those who hate you.* Compare Luke 6:27-28. 5:47 Greek *your brothers.*

Make a Difference

5:33-37

Keep Your Word

Do you marinate your explanations with all kinds of filler words and excuses? A lot of people soak their answers in mazes of confusion and alibis because they are either too afraid to be honest, too afraid to hurt someone's feelings, or just too afraid to make up their minds. From politicians to puppets, confidence and clarity are rare traits of character these days.

Simply let your yes stand for itself and your no be well-defined. Gain your assurance of integrity from your walk with Jesus. Don't compromise your character by pandering to what seems politically correct or presently popular. Don't lie to get out of an uncomfortable situation. Make your responses with clarity, your promises with conviction, and your comments with constructive truth and caring fairness. In the long run, people will trust you and seek your wisdom.

Difference Maker

If someone asks you a direct question today, try answering succinctly and clearly. Give thought and honesty to your words. Don't meander around speaking the truth.

Our Father in heaven,
may your name be kept holy.
10 May your Kingdom come soon.
May your will be done on earth,
as it is in heaven.
11 Give us today the food we need,*
12 and forgive us our sins,
as we have forgiven those who sin against us.
13 And don't let us yield to temptation,*
but rescue us from the evil one.*

14"If you forgive those who sin against you, your heavenly Father will
forgive you. 15But if you refuse to forgive others, your Father will not forgive
your sins.

16"And when you fast, don't make it obvious, as the hypocrites do, for they
try to look miserable and disheveled so people will admire them for their
fasting. I tell you the truth, that is the only reward they will ever get. 17But
when you fast, comb your hair* and wash your face. 18Then no one will notice
that you are fasting, except your Father, who knows what you do in private.
And your Father, who sees everything, will reward you.

Teaching about Money and Possessions

19"Don't store up treasures here on earth, where moths eat them and rust
destroys them, and where thieves break in and steal. 20Store your treasures
in heaven, where moths and rust cannot destroy, and thieves do not break
in and steal. 21Wherever your treasure is, there the desires of your heart will
also be.

22"Your eye is like a lamp that provides light for your body. When your
eye is healthy, your whole body is filled with light. 23But when your eye is
unhealthy, your whole body is filled with darkness. And if the light you think
you have is actually darkness, how deep that darkness is!

24"No one can serve two masters. For you will hate one and love the other;
you will be devoted to one and despise the other. You cannot serve God and
be enslaved to money.

25"That is why I tell you not to worry about everyday life—whether you
have enough food and drink, or enough clothes to wear. Isn't life more than
food, and your body more than clothing? 26Look at the birds. They don't
plant or harvest or store food in barns, for your heavenly Father feeds them.
And aren't you far more valuable to him than they are? 27Can all your worries
add a single moment to your life?

28"And why worry about your clothing? Look at the lilies of the field and
how they grow. They don't work or make their clothing, 29yet Solomon in
all his glory was not dressed as beautifully as they are. 30And if God cares so
wonderfully for wildflowers that are here today and thrown into the fire
tomorrow, he will certainly care for you. Why do you have so little faith?

31"So don't worry about these things, saying, 'What will we eat? What will
we drink? What will we wear?' 32These things dominate the thoughts of
unbelievers, but your heavenly Father already knows all your needs. 33Seek

6:11 Or *Give us today our food for the day;* or *Give us today our food for tomorrow.* **6:13a** Or *And keep us from being tested.* **6:13b** Or *from evil.* Some manuscripts add *For yours is the kingdom and the power and the glory forever. Amen.* **6:17** Greek *anoint your head.*

Make a Difference

6:1-4

Be Anonymous

Every good gift comes from God. We should give donations and offerings in humility of heart and with a grace-filled gratitude. Someone who brags about their good deeds demeans those to whom they give their gifts. To puff up one's own grandeur at the expense of another person's dignity ultimately contributes to a continually oppressive cycle. We should give gifts with a selfless burden to benefit the one who receives. The irony, of course, is that God will know and give honor to the anonymous giver.

Difference Maker

Make a donation to a ministry without letting anyone else know.

Prayer **6:9-13**

"Our Father in heaven, may your name be kept holy. May your Kingdom come soon. May your will be done on earth, as it is in heaven. Give us today the food we need, and forgive us our sins, as we have forgiven those who sin against us. And don't let us yield to temptation, but rescue us from the evil one." Amen.

Prayer **6:27**

Lord, I give my anxiety over to you because it does me no good. Amen.

the Kingdom of God* above all else, and live righteously, and he will give
you everything you need.
34“So don't worry about tomorrow, for tomorrow will bring its own wor-
ries. Today's trouble is enough for today.

Do Not Judge Others

7 “Do not judge others, and you will not be judged. 2For you will be
treated as you treat others.* The standard you use in judging is the
standard by which you will be judged.*
3“And why worry about a speck in your friend's eye* when you have a log
in your own? 4How can you think of saying to your friend,* ‘Let me help you
get rid of that speck in your eye,’ when you can't see past the log in your own
eye? 5Hypocrite! First get rid of the log in your own eye; then you will see
well enough to deal with the speck in your friend's eye.
6“Don't waste what is holy on people who are unholy.* Don't throw your
pearls to pigs! They will trample the pearls, then turn and attack you.

Effective Prayer

7“Keep on asking, and you will receive what you ask for. Keep on seeking,
and you will find. Keep on knocking, and the door will be opened to you.
8For everyone who asks, receives. Everyone who seeks, finds. And to everyone
who knocks, the door will be opened.
9“You parents—if your children ask for a loaf of bread, do you give them
a stone instead? 10Or if they ask for a fish, do you give them a snake? Of
course not! 11So if you sinful people know how to give good gifts to your
children, how much more will your heavenly Father give good gifts to those
who ask him.

The Golden Rule

12“Do to others whatever you would like them to do to you. This is the es-
sence of all that is taught in the law and the prophets.

The Narrow Gate

13“You can enter God's Kingdom only through the narrow gate. The high-
way to hell* is broad, and its gate is wide for the many who choose that way.
14But the gateway to life is very narrow and the road is difficult, and only a
few ever find it.

The Tree and Its Fruit

15“Beware of false prophets who come disguised as harmless sheep but are
really vicious wolves. 16You can identify them by their fruit, that is, by the
way they act. Can you pick grapes from thornbushes, or figs from thistles?
17A good tree produces good fruit, and a bad tree produces bad fruit. 18A good
tree can't produce bad fruit, and a bad tree can't produce good fruit. 19So
every tree that does not produce good fruit is chopped down and thrown into
the fire. 20Yes, just as you can identify a tree by its fruit, so you can identify
people by their actions.

6:33 Some manuscripts do not include *of God*. 7:2a Or *For God will judge you as you judge others.* 7:2b Or *The measure you give will be the measure you get back.* 7:3 Greek *your brother's eye;* also in 7:5. 7:4 Greek *your brother.* 7:6 Greek *Don't give the sacred to dogs.* 7:13 Greek *The road that leads to destruction.*

Make a Difference

7:1-5

Plankineyetis

Plankineyetis is a made-up word that describes a condition that distorts the way people see reality. It diminishes their ability to see themselves with clarity. Plankineyetis attacks the soul through the eyes, and it displays itself when a person sees a splinter in someone else's eye and announces with pride that he or she will help clean it out. This is a monstrous proclamation because what they fail to realize, but what everybody else can easily see, is that the person's judgment is affected by the fact that there is an entire log in their own eye.

As the diseased patient moves around, they cause chaos. People have to duck out of the way. Family and friends begin to avoid eye contact with the one who has contracted plankineyetis. It ruins relationships, leads to blindness of heart, and needs to be cured. Luckily, Jesus tells us the cure.

Difference Maker

Try to catch yourself every time you have a judgmental thought about someone today. When you do have a judgmental thought, cover one eye for one minute.

Make a Difference

7:24-29

Wrap Up

At the end of the most famous sermon in history, Jesus looked back. He had offered world-changing thoughts through beatitudes and teachings on salt and light, anger and adultery, love for enemies, giving to the needy, the Lord's Prayer, ideas on money, and instructions not to worry and not

True Disciples

21 "Not everyone who calls out to me, 'Lord! Lord!' will enter the Kingdom of Heaven. Only those who actually do the will of my Father in heaven will enter. 22 On judgment day many will say to me, 'Lord! Lord! We prophesied in your name and cast out demons in your name and performed many miracles in your name.' 23 But I will reply, 'I never knew you. Get away from me, you who break God's laws.'

Building on a Solid Foundation

24 "Anyone who listens to my teaching and follows it is wise, like a person who builds a house on solid rock. 25 Though the rain comes in torrents and the floodwaters rise and the winds beat against that house, it won't collapse because it is built on bedrock. 26 But anyone who hears my teaching and doesn't obey it is foolish, like a person who builds a house on sand. 27 When the rains and floods come and the winds beat against that house, it will collapse with a mighty crash."

28 When Jesus had finished saying these things, the crowds were amazed at his teaching, 29 for he taught with real authority—quite unlike their teachers of religious law.

Jesus Heals a Man with Leprosy

8 Large crowds followed Jesus as he came down the mountainside. 2 Suddenly, a man with leprosy approached him and knelt before him. "Lord," the man said, "if you are willing, you can heal me and make me clean."

3 Jesus reached out and touched him. "I am willing," he said. "Be healed!" And instantly the leprosy disappeared. 4 Then Jesus said to him, "Don't tell anyone about this. Instead, go to the priest and let him examine you. Take along the offering required in the law of Moses for those who have been healed of leprosy.* This will be a public testimony that you have been cleansed."

The Faith of a Roman Officer

5 When Jesus returned to Capernaum, a Roman officer* came and pleaded with him, 6 "Lord, my young servant* lies in bed, paralyzed and in terrible pain."

7 Jesus said, "I will come and heal him."

8 But the officer said, "Lord, I am not worthy to have you come into my home. Just say the word from where you are, and my servant will be healed. 9 I know this because I am under the authority of my superior officers, and I have authority over my soldiers. I only need to say, 'Go,' and they go, or 'Come,' and they come. And if I say to my slaves, 'Do this,' they do it."

10 When Jesus heard this, he was amazed. Turning to those who were following him, he said, "I tell you the truth, I haven't seen faith like this in all Israel! 11 And I tell you this, that many Gentiles will come from all over the world—from east and west—and sit down with Abraham, Isaac, and Jacob at the feast in the Kingdom of Heaven. 12 But many Israelites—those for whom the Kingdom was prepared—will be thrown into outer darkness, where there will be weeping and gnashing of teeth."

13 Then Jesus said to the Roman officer, "Go back home. Because you believed, it has happened." And the young servant was healed that same hour.

8:4 See Lev 14:2-32. 8:5 Greek *a centurion;* similarly in 8:8, 13. 8:6 Or *child;* also in 8:13.

to judge; he encouraged people to seek and find, keep the Golden Rule, and pass through the narrow gate. He also showed them how to tell who his true followers are. Some of the most famous sayings in history come from the Sermon on the Mount. History would say it was a pretty good message.

Jesus himself thought it was pretty good too. In fact, before he finished, he looked back on it all and encouraged everyone who heard his words to put them into action. If a person applied his teachings, he said, then they would have a stable foundation for life. He wrapped up his words with one of the greatest analogies the world had ever heard.

Difference Maker

Look back through the Sermon on the Mount and highlight some of the difference makers that changed you or those around you, and then choose one of those to repeat today.

Question **8:1-4**

A person with leprosy is shunned by society. Even today, most people would be unwilling to notice a person with leprosy. If they did take a look, they might do so with disapproval or with disgust. Jesus, though, was more than "willing" to notice the man and touch him, to hear his heart, and to heal his soul (v. 3). As a result, Jesus invited this man, whom the world had cast aside, to be a central player in the grand story of God's work to reconcile this world. Why would Jesus want to do this for this man?

Make a Difference

8:16-17

Healer

Jesus came to heal. Our self-dependent culture can overlook that fact sometimes. Jesus came to heal. In just one chapter in Matthew, for instance, he healed a man with leprosy, he healed the paralyzed servant of a centurion, he healed Peter's mother-in-law of her fever (which must have won her son-in-law some brownie points!), he healed several demon-possessed people with a simple command, and he healed many others who were sick. Oh, and he calmed a storm.

That's an impressive chapter indeed. In fact, these sorts of miracles weren't out of the ordinary for Jesus. Matthew wanted us to know that this was what Jesus did. Matthew wrote, "This fulfilled the word of the Lord through the prophet Isaiah, who said, 'He took our sicknesses and removed our diseases'" (v. 17).

Difference Maker

Pray to the Lord for healing, either for yourself or for someone you love. Don't be afraid to ask the Lord for what is honestly on your heart and don't be afraid to gather others to pray with you.

Jesus Heals Many People

14 When Jesus arrived at Peter's house, Peter's mother-in-law was sick in bed
with a high fever. 15 But when Jesus touched her hand, the fever left her. Then
she got up and prepared a meal for him.
16 That evening many demon-possessed people were brought to Jesus. He
cast out the evil spirits with a simple command, and he healed all the sick.
17 This fulfilled the word of the Lord through the prophet Isaiah, who said,

"He took our sicknesses
and removed our diseases."*

The Cost of Following Jesus

18 When Jesus saw the crowd around him, he instructed his disciples to cross
to the other side of the lake.
19 Then one of the teachers of religious law said to him, "Teacher, I will
follow you wherever you go."
20 But Jesus replied, "Foxes have dens to live in, and birds have nests, but
the Son of Man* has no place even to lay his head."
21 Another of his disciples said, "Lord, first let me return home and bury
my father."
22 But Jesus told him, "Follow me now. Let the spiritually dead bury their
own dead.*"

Jesus Calms the Storm

23 Then Jesus got into the boat and started across the lake with his disciples.
24 Suddenly, a fierce storm struck the lake, with waves breaking into the boat.
But Jesus was sleeping. 25 The disciples went and woke him up, shouting,
"Lord, save us! We're going to drown!"
26 Jesus responded, "Why are you afraid? You have so little faith!" Then
he got up and rebuked the wind and waves, and suddenly there was a great
calm.
27 The disciples were amazed. "Who is this man?" they asked. "Even the
winds and waves obey him!"

Jesus Heals Two Demon-Possessed Men

28 When Jesus arrived on the other side of the lake, in the region of the Gad-
arenes,* two men who were possessed by demons met him. They came out
of the tombs and were so violent that no one could go through that area.
29 They began screaming at him, "Why are you interfering with us, Son
of God? Have you come here to torture us before God's appointed time?"
30 There happened to be a large herd of pigs feeding in the distance. 31 So
the demons begged, "If you cast us out, send us into that herd of pigs."
32 "All right, go!" Jesus commanded them. So the demons came out of the
men and entered the pigs, and the whole herd plunged down the steep hill-
side into the lake and drowned in the water.
33 The herdsmen fled to the nearby town, telling everyone what happened
to the demon-possessed men. 34 Then the entire town came out to meet Jesus,
but they begged him to go away and leave them alone.

8:17 Isa 53:4. **8:20** "Son of Man" is a title Jesus used for himself. **8:22** Greek *Let the dead bury their own dead.* **8:28** Other manuscripts read *Gerasenes;* still others read *Gergesenes.* Compare Mark 5:1; Luke 8:26.

Jesus Heals a Paralyzed Man
9 Jesus climbed into a boat and went back across the lake to his own town.
2 Some people brought to him a paralyzed man on a mat. Seeing their
faith, Jesus said to the paralyzed man, "Be encouraged, my child! Your sins
are forgiven."
3 But some of the teachers of religious law said to themselves, "That's blas-
phemy! Does he think he's God?"
4 Jesus knew* what they were thinking, so he asked them, "Why do you
have such evil thoughts in your hearts? 5 Is it easier to say 'Your sins are
forgiven,' or 'Stand up and walk'? 6 So I will prove to you that the Son of
Man* has the authority on earth to forgive sins." Then Jesus turned to the
paralyzed man and said, "Stand up, pick up your mat, and go home!"
7 And the man jumped up and went home! 8 Fear swept through the
crowd as they saw this happen. And they praised God for giving humans
such authority.

Jesus Calls Matthew
9 As Jesus was walking along, he saw a man named Matthew sitting at his
tax collector's booth. "Follow me and be my disciple," Jesus said to him. So
Matthew got up and followed him.
10 Later, Matthew invited Jesus and his disciples to his home as dinner
guests, along with many tax collectors and other disreputable sinners. 11 But
when the Pharisees saw this, they asked his disciples, "Why does your teacher
eat with such scum?*"
12 When Jesus heard this, he said, "Healthy people don't need a doctor—
sick people do." 13 Then he added, "Now go and learn the meaning of this
Scripture: 'I want you to show mercy, not offer sacrifices.'* For I have come
to call not those who think they are righteous, but those who know they
are sinners."

A Discussion about Fasting
14 One day the disciples of John the Baptist came to Jesus and asked him,
"Why don't your disciples fast* like we do and the Pharisees do?"
15 Jesus replied, "Do wedding guests mourn while celebrating with the
groom? Of course not. But someday the groom will be taken away from them,
and then they will fast.
16 "Besides, who would patch old clothing with new cloth? For the new
patch would shrink and rip away from the old cloth, leaving an even bigger
tear than before.
17 "And no one puts new wine into old wineskins. For the old skins would
burst from the pressure, spilling the wine and ruining the skins. New wine
is stored in new wineskins so that both are preserved."

Jesus Heals in Response to Faith
18 As Jesus was saying this, the leader of a synagogue came and knelt before
him. "My daughter has just died," he said, "but you can bring her back to
life again if you just come and lay your hand on her."
19 So Jesus and his disciples got up and went with him. 20 Just then a woman

9:4 Some manuscripts read *saw.* **9:6** "Son of Man" is a title Jesus used for himself. **9:11** Greek *with tax collectors and sinners?* **9:13** Hos 6:6 (Greek version). **9:14** Some manuscripts read *fast often.*

Question 9:1-8

In the face of opposition, the paralyzed man bravely trusted Jesus. As a result, not only did Jesus forgive his sins, but Jesus also enabled him to walk, much to the irritation of the local leaders. Nothing was going to stop the paralyzed man from "jumping" at Jesus' invitation (v. 7). Will you, too, jump at Jesus' invitation? Turn to the back of this Bible and pray through the section on "How to Accept Jesus as Your Lord and Savior."

Story Arc 9:9-13

Matthew

This is Matthew's own account of how his life was entirely turned around. By getting up and following Jesus, Matthew set an example that millions upon millions have imitated for two thousand years.

Matt 10:1-42 ►

who had suffered for twelve years with constant bleeding came up behind
him. She touched the fringe of his robe, 21 for she thought, "If I can just touch
his robe, I will be healed."
22 Jesus turned around, and when he saw her he said, "Daughter, be en-
couraged! Your faith has made you well." And the woman was healed at
that moment.
23 When Jesus arrived at the official's home, he saw the noisy crowd and
heard the funeral music. 24 "Get out!" he told them. "The girl isn't dead;
she's only asleep." But the crowd laughed at him. 25 After the crowd was put
outside, however, Jesus went in and took the girl by the hand, and she stood
up! 26 The report of this miracle swept through the entire countryside.

Jesus Heals the Blind

27 After Jesus left the girl's home, two blind men followed along behind him,
shouting, "Son of David, have mercy on us!"
28 They went right into the house where he was staying, and Jesus asked
them, "Do you believe I can make you see?"
"Yes, Lord," they told him, "we do."
29 Then he touched their eyes and said, "Because of your faith, it will hap-
pen." 30 Then their eyes were opened, and they could see! Jesus sternly warned
them, "Don't tell anyone about this." 31 But instead, they went out and spread
his fame all over the region.
32 When they left, a demon-possessed man who couldn't speak was
brought to Jesus. 33 So Jesus cast out the demon, and then the man began to
speak. The crowds were amazed. "Nothing like this has ever happened in
Israel!" they exclaimed.
34 But the Pharisees said, "He can cast out demons because he is empow-
ered by the prince of demons."

The Need for Workers

35 Jesus traveled through all the towns and villages of that area, teaching in
the synagogues and announcing the Good News about the Kingdom. And he
healed every kind of disease and illness. 36 When he saw the crowds, he had
compassion on them because they were confused and helpless, like sheep
without a shepherd. 37 He said to his disciples, "The harvest is great, but the
workers are few. 38 So pray to the Lord who is in charge of the harvest; ask
him to send more workers into his fields."

Jesus Sends Out the Twelve Apostles

10 Jesus called his twelve disciples together and gave them authority
to cast out evil* spirits and to heal every kind of disease and illness.
2 Here are the names of the twelve apostles:

first, Simon (also called Peter),
then Andrew (Peter's brother),
James (son of Zebedee),
John (James's brother),
3 Philip,
Bartholomew,

10:1 Greek *unclean*.

Story Arc **10:1–42**

The Disciples

How'd you like to have your name immortalized on a team like this one? Did they know what they were getting themselves into when they said yes to following Jesus? How much would they be stretched and tested? What mind-bending miracles would they witness? What soul-lifting words would they hear? What heart-crushing pain would they experience? What world-changing message would they share?

Mark 1:2-3 ►

Thomas,
Matthew (the tax collector),
James (son of Alphaeus),
Thaddaeus,*
4 Simon (the zealot*),
Judas Iscariot (who later betrayed him).

5 Jesus sent out the twelve apostles with these instructions: "Don't go to
the Gentiles or the Samaritans, 6 but only to the people of Israel—God's lost
sheep. 7 Go and announce to them that the Kingdom of Heaven is near.* 8 Heal
the sick, raise the dead, cure those with leprosy, and cast out demons. Give
as freely as you have received!

9 "Don't take any money in your money belts—no gold, silver, or even cop-
per coins. 10 Don't carry a traveler's bag with a change of clothes and sandals
or even a walking stick. Don't hesitate to accept hospitality, because those
who work deserve to be fed.

11 "Whenever you enter a city or village, search for a worthy person and stay
in his home until you leave town. 12 When you enter the home, give it your
blessing. 13 If it turns out to be a worthy home, let your blessing stand; if it
is not, take back the blessing. 14 If any household or town refuses to welcome
you or listen to your message, shake its dust from your feet as you leave. 15 I
tell you the truth, the wicked cities of Sodom and Gomorrah will be better
off than such a town on the judgment day.

16 "Look, I am sending you out as sheep among wolves. So be as shrewd
as snakes and harmless as doves. 17 But beware! For you will be handed over
to the courts and will be flogged with whips in the synagogues. 18 You will
stand trial before governors and kings because you are my followers. But
this will be your opportunity to tell the rulers and other unbelievers about
me.* 19 When you are arrested, don't worry about how to respond or what
to say. God will give you the right words at the right time. 20 For it is not
you who will be speaking—it will be the Spirit of your Father speaking
through you.

21 "A brother will betray his brother to death, a father will betray his own
child, and children will rebel against their parents and cause them to be
killed. 22 And all nations will hate you because you are my followers.* But
everyone who endures to the end will be saved. 23 When you are persecuted
in one town, flee to the next. I tell you the truth, the Son of Man* will return
before you have reached all the towns of Israel.

24 "Students* are not greater than their teacher, and slaves are not greater
than their master. 25 Students are to be like their teacher, and slaves are to be
like their master. And since I, the master of the household, have been called
the prince of demons,* the members of my household will be called by even
worse names!

26 "But don't be afraid of those who threaten you. For the time is coming
when everything that is covered will be revealed, and all that is secret will
be made known to all. 27 What I tell you now in the darkness, shout abroad

10:3 Other manuscripts read *Lebbaeus;* still others read *Lebbaeus who is called Thaddaeus.* **10:4** Greek *the Cananean,* an Aramaic term for Jewish nationalists. **10:7** Or *has come,* or *is coming soon.* **10:18** Or *But this will be your testimony against the rulers and other unbelievers.* **10:22** Greek *on account of my name.* **10:23** "Son of Man" is a title Jesus used for himself. **10:24** Or *Disciples.* **10:25** Greek *Beelzeboul;* other manuscripts read *Beezeboul;* Latin version reads *Beelzebub.*

when daybreak comes. What I whisper in your ear, shout from the housetops
for all to hear!
28“Don’t be afraid of those who want to kill your body; they cannot touch
your soul. Fear only God, who can destroy both soul and body in hell.* 29What
is the price of two sparrows—one copper coin*? But not a single sparrow can
fall to the ground without your Father knowing it. 30And the very hairs on
your head are all numbered. 31So don’t be afraid; you are more valuable to
God than a whole flock of sparrows.
32“Everyone who acknowledges me publicly here on earth, I will also ac-
knowledge before my Father in heaven. 33But everyone who denies me here
on earth, I will also deny before my Father in heaven.
34“Don’t imagine that I came to bring peace to the earth! I came not to
bring peace, but a sword.

35 ‘I have come to set a man against his father,
    a daughter against her mother,
  and a daughter-in-law against her mother-in-law.
36   Your enemies will be right in your own household!’*

37“If you love your father or mother more than you love me, you are not
worthy of being mine; or if you love your son or daughter more than me,
you are not worthy of being mine. 38If you refuse to take up your cross and
follow me, you are not worthy of being mine. 39If you cling to your life, you
will lose it; but if you give up your life for me, you will find it.
40“Anyone who receives you receives me, and anyone who receives me
receives the Father who sent me. 41If you receive a prophet as one who speaks
for God,* you will be given the same reward as a prophet. And if you receive
righteous people because of their righteousness, you will be given a reward
like theirs. 42And if you give even a cup of cold water to one of the least of
my followers, you will surely be rewarded.”

Jesus and John the Baptist

11 When Jesus had finished giving these instructions to his twelve dis-
ciples, he went out to teach and preach in towns throughout the
region.
2John the Baptist, who was in prison, heard about all the things the Mes-
siah was doing. So he sent his disciples to ask Jesus, 3“Are you the Messiah
we’ve been expecting,* or should we keep looking for someone else?”
4Jesus told them, “Go back to John and tell him what you have heard and
seen—5the blind see, the lame walk, those with leprosy are cured, the deaf
hear, the dead are raised to life, and the Good News is being preached to the
poor.” 6And he added, “God blesses those who do not fall away because of me.*”
7As John’s disciples were leaving, Jesus began talking about him to the
crowds. “What kind of man did you go into the wilderness to see? Was he a
weak reed, swayed by every breath of wind? 8Or were you expecting to see a
man dressed in expensive clothes? No, people with expensive clothes live in
palaces. 9Were you looking for a prophet? Yes, and he is more than a prophet.
10John is the man to whom the Scriptures refer when they say,

10:28 Greek *Gehenna.* 10:29 Greek *one assarion* [i.e., one “as,” a Roman coin equal to 1/16 of a denarius]. 10:35-36 Mic 7:6. 10:41 Greek *receive a prophet in the name of a prophet.* 11:3 Greek *Are you the one who is coming?* 11:6 Or *who are not offended by me.*

'Look, I am sending my messenger ahead of you,
and he will prepare your way before you.'*

11 "I tell you the truth, of all who have ever lived, none is greater than John
the Baptist. Yet even the least person in the Kingdom of Heaven is greater
than he is! 12 And from the time John the Baptist began preaching until now,
the Kingdom of Heaven has been forcefully advancing,* and violent people
are attacking it. 13 For before John came, all the prophets and the law of Moses
looked forward to this present time. 14 And if you are willing to accept what I
say, he is Elijah, the one the prophets said would come.* 15 Anyone with ears
to hear should listen and understand!

16 "To what can I compare this generation? It is like children playing a
game in the public square. They complain to their friends,

17 'We played wedding songs,
and you didn't dance,
so we played funeral songs,
and you didn't mourn.'

18 For John didn't spend his time eating and drinking, and you say, 'He's pos-
sessed by a demon.' 19 The Son of Man,* on the other hand, feasts and drinks,
and you say, 'He's a glutton and a drunkard, and a friend of tax collectors and
other sinners!' But wisdom is shown to be right by its results."

Judgment for the Unbelievers

20 Then Jesus began to denounce the towns where he had done so many of
his miracles, because they hadn't repented of their sins and turned to God.
21 "What sorrow awaits you, Korazin and Bethsaida! For if the miracles I did
in you had been done in wicked Tyre and Sidon, their people would have
repented of their sins long ago, clothing themselves in burlap and throwing
ashes on their heads to show their remorse. 22 I tell you, Tyre and Sidon will
be better off on judgment day than you.

23 "And you people of Capernaum, will you be honored in heaven? No, you
will go down to the place of the dead.* For if the miracles I did for you had
been done in wicked Sodom, it would still be here today. 24 I tell you, even
Sodom will be better off on judgment day than you."

Jesus' Prayer of Thanksgiving

25 At that time Jesus prayed this prayer: "O Father, Lord of heaven and earth,
thank you for hiding these things from those who think themselves wise
and clever, and for revealing them to the childlike. 26 Yes, Father, it pleased
you to do it this way!

27 "My Father has entrusted everything to me. No one truly knows the Son
except the Father, and no one truly knows the Father except the Son and
those to whom the Son chooses to reveal him."

28 Then Jesus said, "Come to me, all of you who are weary and carry heavy
burdens, and I will give you rest. 29 Take my yoke upon you. Let me teach
you, because I am humble and gentle at heart, and you will find rest for
your souls. 30 For my yoke is easy to bear, and the burden I give you is light."

11:10 Mal 3:1. 11:12 Or *the Kingdom of Heaven has suffered from violence.* 11:14 See Mal 4:5.
11:19 "Son of Man" is a title Jesus used for himself. 11:23 Greek *to Hades.*

Make a Difference

11:28-30

Pause

You must pause. Your life has been flying by, and you need to catch it. Perhaps the last few weeks have been incredibly rich—full of all the dramatic ups and downs that life has to offer, including tragedies, victories, and frenzies. Because you are tired sometimes, you have been tempted to drift toward mind-numbing laziness.

Be careful! A numbing of the mind leads to a dumbing of the mind, which then leads to a frustration of the soul. You don't need to turn off your brain. What you truly need is a rest. Not just sleep. You need a Sabbath. A restoration. A peace. A pause. A still. A capturing of time. A moment to shut your eyes and dream of what could be, what should be. A reflection of God's image at work and at rest within you. You must pause.

Difference Maker

At a certain point today, put off to the side everything you have planned and take time off. Get away and get alone with God, letting him restore your soul with his peace and rest.

Question **12:9-14**

The Pharisees decided that because Jesus healed this man's hand, Jesus deserved to be killed. If you were this man, whom would you fear more: the Pharisees or Jesus?

A Discussion about the Sabbath

12 At about that time Jesus was walking through some grainfields on
the Sabbath. His disciples were hungry, so they began breaking off
some heads of grain and eating them. 2 But some Pharisees saw them do
it and protested, "Look, your disciples are breaking the law by harvesting
grain on the Sabbath."
3 Jesus said to them, "Haven't you read in the Scriptures what David did
when he and his companions were hungry? 4 He went into the house of God,
and he and his companions broke the law by eating the sacred loaves of bread
that only the priests are allowed to eat. 5 And haven't you read in the law of
Moses that the priests on duty in the Temple may work on the Sabbath? 6 I tell
you, there is one here who is even greater than the Temple! 7 But you would
not have condemned my innocent disciples if you knew the meaning of this
Scripture: 'I want you to show mercy, not offer sacrifices.'* 8 For the Son of
Man* is Lord, even over the Sabbath!"

Jesus Heals on the Sabbath

9 Then Jesus went over to their synagogue, 10 where he noticed a man with a
deformed hand. The Pharisees asked Jesus, "Does the law permit a person
to work by healing on the Sabbath?" (They were hoping he would say yes,
so they could bring charges against him.)
11 And he answered, "If you had a sheep that fell into a well on the Sabbath,
wouldn't you work to pull it out? Of course you would. 12 And how much
more valuable is a person than a sheep! Yes, the law permits a person to do
good on the Sabbath."
13 Then he said to the man, "Hold out your hand." So the man held out his
hand, and it was restored, just like the other one! 14 Then the Pharisees called
a meeting to plot how to kill Jesus.

Jesus, God's Chosen Servant

15 But Jesus knew what they were planning. So he left that area, and many people
followed him. He healed all the sick among them, 16 but he warned them not
to reveal who he was. 17 This fulfilled the prophecy of Isaiah concerning him:

18 "Look at my Servant, whom I have chosen.
He is my Beloved, who pleases me.
I will put my Spirit upon him,
and he will proclaim justice to the nations.
19 He will not fight or shout
or raise his voice in public.
20 He will not crush the weakest reed
or put out a flickering candle.
Finally he will cause justice to be victorious.
21 And his name will be the hope
of all the world."*

Jesus and the Prince of Demons

22 Then a demon-possessed man, who was blind and couldn't speak, was
brought to Jesus. He healed the man so that he could both speak and see.

12:7 Hos 6:6 (Greek version). 12:8 "Son of Man" is a title Jesus used for himself. 12:18-21 Isa 42:1-4 (Greek version for 42:4).

[23]The crowd was amazed and asked, "Could it be that Jesus is the Son of
David, the Messiah?"
[24]But when the Pharisees heard about the miracle, they said, "No won-
der he can cast out demons. He gets his power from Satan,* the prince of
demons."
[25]Jesus knew their thoughts and replied, "Any kingdom divided by civil
war is doomed. A town or family splintered by feuding will fall apart. [26]And
if Satan is casting out Satan, he is divided and fighting against himself. His
own kingdom will not survive. [27]And if I am empowered by Satan, what
about your own exorcists? They cast out demons, too, so they will condemn
you for what you have said. [28]But if I am casting out demons by the Spirit of
God, then the Kingdom of God has arrived among you. [29]For who is powerful
enough to enter the house of a strong man and plunder his goods? Only
someone even stronger—someone who could tie him up and then plunder
his house.
[30]"Anyone who isn't with me opposes me, and anyone who isn't working
with me is actually working against me.
[31]"So I tell you, every sin and blasphemy can be forgiven—except blas-
phemy against the Holy Spirit, which will never be forgiven. [32]Anyone who
speaks against the Son of Man can be forgiven, but anyone who speaks
against the Holy Spirit will never be forgiven, either in this world or in the
world to come.
[33]"A tree is identified by its fruit. If a tree is good, its fruit will be good.
If a tree is bad, its fruit will be bad. [34]You brood of snakes! How could evil
men like you speak what is good and right? For whatever is in your heart
determines what you say. [35]A good person produces good things from the
treasury of a good heart, and an evil person produces evil things from the
treasury of an evil heart. [36]And I tell you this, you must give an account on
judgment day for every idle word you speak. [37]The words you say will either
acquit you or condemn you."

The Sign of Jonah

[38]One day some teachers of religious law and Pharisees came to Jesus and
said, "Teacher, we want you to show us a miraculous sign to prove your
authority."
[39]But Jesus replied, "Only an evil, adulterous generation would demand a
miraculous sign; but the only sign I will give them is the sign of the prophet
Jonah. [40]For as Jonah was in the belly of the great fish for three days and
three nights, so will the Son of Man be in the heart of the earth for three
days and three nights.
[41]"The people of Nineveh will stand up against this generation on judg-
ment day and condemn it, for they repented of their sins at the preaching
of Jonah. Now someone greater than Jonah is here—but you refuse to re-
pent. [42]The queen of Sheba* will also stand up against this generation on
judgment day and condemn it, for she came from a distant land to hear the
wisdom of Solomon. Now someone greater than Solomon is here—but you
refuse to listen.
[43]"When an evil* spirit leaves a person, it goes into the desert, seeking rest
but finding none. [44]Then it says, 'I will return to the person I came from.' So

12:24 Greek *Beelzeboul;* also in 12:27. Other manuscripts read *Beezeboul;* Latin version reads *Beelzebub.* **12:42** Greek *The queen of the south.* **12:43** Greek *unclean.*

it returns and finds its former home empty, swept, and in order. 45Then the
spirit finds seven other spirits more evil than itself, and they all enter the
person and live there. And so that person is worse off than before. That will
be the experience of this evil generation."

The True Family of Jesus

46As Jesus was speaking to the crowd, his mother and brothers stood outside,
asking to speak to him. 47Someone told Jesus, "Your mother and your broth-
ers are standing outside, and they want to speak to you."*
48Jesus asked, "Who is my mother? Who are my brothers?" 49Then he
pointed to his disciples and said, "Look, these are my mother and brothers.
50Anyone who does the will of my Father in heaven is my brother and sister
and mother!"

Parable of the Farmer Scattering Seed

13 Later that same day Jesus left the house and sat beside the lake. 2A
large crowd soon gathered around him, so he got into a boat. Then
he sat there and taught as the people stood on the shore. 3He told many
stories in the form of parables, such as this one:
"Listen! A farmer went out to plant some seeds. 4As he scattered them
across his field, some seeds fell on a footpath, and the birds came and ate
them. 5Other seeds fell on shallow soil with underlying rock. The seeds
sprouted quickly because the soil was shallow. 6But the plants soon wilted
under the hot sun, and since they didn't have deep roots, they died. 7Other
seeds fell among thorns that grew up and choked out the tender plants. 8Still
other seeds fell on fertile soil, and they produced a crop that was thirty, sixty,
and even a hundred times as much as had been planted! 9Anyone with ears
to hear should listen and understand."
10His disciples came and asked him, "Why do you use parables when you
talk to the people?"
11He replied, "You are permitted to understand the secrets* of the King-
dom of Heaven, but others are not. 12To those who listen to my teaching, more
understanding will be given, and they will have an abundance of knowledge.
But for those who are not listening, even what little understanding they have
will be taken away from them. 13That is why I use these parables,

For they look, but they don't really see.
They hear, but they don't really listen or understand.

14This fulfills the prophecy of Isaiah that says,

'When you hear what I say,
you will not understand.
When you see what I do,
you will not comprehend.
15 For the hearts of these people are hardened,
and their ears cannot hear,
and they have closed their eyes—
so their eyes cannot see,

12:47 Some manuscripts do not include verse 47. Compare Mark 3:32 and Luke 8:20.
13:11 Greek *the mysteries.*

and their ears cannot hear,
and their hearts cannot understand,
and they cannot turn to me
and let me heal them.'*

16"But blessed are your eyes, because they see; and your ears, because they
hear. 17I tell you the truth, many prophets and righteous people longed to
see what you see, but they didn't see it. And they longed to hear what you
hear, but they didn't hear it.
18"Now listen to the explanation of the parable about the farmer planting
seeds: 19The seed that fell on the footpath represents those who hear the mes-
sage about the Kingdom and don't understand it. Then the evil one comes
and snatches away the seed that was planted in their hearts. 20The seed on the
rocky soil represents those who hear the message and immediately receive
it with joy. 21But since they don't have deep roots, they don't last long. They
fall away as soon as they have problems or are persecuted for believing God's
word. 22The seed that fell among the thorns represents those who hear God's
word, but all too quickly the message is crowded out by the worries of this life
and the lure of wealth, so no fruit is produced. 23The seed that fell on good soil
represents those who truly hear and understand God's word and produce a
harvest of thirty, sixty, or even a hundred times as much as had been planted!"

Parable of the Wheat and Weeds

24Here is another story Jesus told: "The Kingdom of Heaven is like a
farmer who planted good seed in his field. 25But that night as the work-
ers slept, his enemy came and planted weeds among the wheat, then
slipped away. 26When the crop began to grow and produce grain, the
weeds also grew.
27"The farmer's workers went to him and said, 'Sir, the field where you
planted that good seed is full of weeds! Where did they come from?'
28"'An enemy has done this!' the farmer exclaimed.
"'Should we pull out the weeds?' they asked.
29"'No,' he replied, 'you'll uproot the wheat if you do. 30Let both grow to-
gether until the harvest. Then I will tell the harvesters to sort out the weeds,
tie them into bundles, and burn them, and to put the wheat in the barn.'"

Parable of the Mustard Seed

31Here is another illustration Jesus used: "The Kingdom of Heaven is like a
mustard seed planted in a field. 32It is the smallest of all seeds, but it becomes
the largest of garden plants; it grows into a tree, and birds come and make
nests in its branches."

Parable of the Yeast

33Jesus also used this illustration: "The Kingdom of Heaven is like the yeast
a woman used in making bread. Even though she put only a little yeast in
three measures of flour, it permeated every part of the dough."
34Jesus always used stories and illustrations like these when speaking to
the crowds. In fact, he never spoke to them without using such parables.
35This fulfilled what God had spoken through the prophet:

13:14-15 Isa 6:9-10 (Greek version).

Why this matters!

"I will speak to you in parables.
I will explain things hidden since the creation of the world.*"

Parable of the Wheat and Weeds Explained

36 Then, leaving the crowds outside, Jesus went into the house. His disciples
said, "Please explain to us the story of the weeds in the field."
37 Jesus replied, "The Son of Man* is the farmer who plants the good seed.
38 The field is the world, and the good seed represents the people of the King-
dom. The weeds are the people who belong to the evil one. 39 The enemy who
planted the weeds among the wheat is the devil. The harvest is the end of
the world,* and the harvesters are the angels.
40 "Just as the weeds are sorted out and burned in the fire, so it will be at the
end of the world. 41 The Son of Man will send his angels, and they will remove
from his Kingdom everything that causes sin and all who do evil. 42 And the
angels will throw them into the fiery furnace, where there will be weeping
and gnashing of teeth. 43 Then the righteous will shine like the sun in their
Father's Kingdom. Anyone with ears to hear should listen and understand!

Parables of the Hidden Treasure and the Pearl

44 "The Kingdom of Heaven is like a treasure that a man discovered hidden
in a field. In his excitement, he hid it again and sold everything he owned
to get enough money to buy the field.
45 "Again, the Kingdom of Heaven is like a merchant on the lookout for
choice pearls. 46 When he discovered a pearl of great value, he sold everything
he owned and bought it!

Parable of the Fishing Net

47 "Again, the Kingdom of Heaven is like a fishing net that was thrown
into the water and caught fish of every kind. 48 When the net was full, they
dragged it up onto the shore, sat down, and sorted the good fish into crates,
but threw the bad ones away. 49 That is the way it will be at the end of the
world. The angels will come and separate the wicked people from the righ-
teous, 50 throwing the wicked into the fiery furnace, where there will be
weeping and gnashing of teeth. 51 Do you understand all these things?"
"Yes," they said, "we do."
52 Then he added, "Every teacher of religious law who becomes a disciple in
the Kingdom of Heaven is like a homeowner who brings from his storeroom
new gems of truth as well as old."

Jesus Rejected at Nazareth

53 When Jesus had finished telling these stories and illustrations, he left that
part of the country. 54 He returned to Nazareth, his hometown. When he
taught there in the synagogue, everyone was amazed and said, "Where does
he get this wisdom and the power to do miracles?" 55 Then they scoffed, "He's
just the carpenter's son, and we know Mary, his mother, and his brothers—
James, Joseph,* Simon, and Judas. 56 All his sisters live right here among us.
Where did he learn all these things?" 57 And they were deeply offended and
refused to believe in him.

13:35 Some manuscripts do not include *of the world.* Ps 78:2. 13:37 "Son of Man" is a title Jesus used for himself. 13:39 Or *the age;* also in 13:40, 49. 13:55 Other manuscripts read *Joses;* still others read *John.*

Then Jesus told them, "A prophet is honored everywhere except in his own
hometown and among his own family." 58 And so he did only a few miracles
there because of their unbelief.

The Death of John the Baptist

14 When Herod Antipas, the ruler of Galilee,* heard about Jesus, 2 he
said to his advisers, "This must be John the Baptist raised from the
dead! That is why he can do such miracles."

3 For Herod had arrested and imprisoned John as a favor to his wife He-
rodias (the former wife of Herod's brother Philip). 4 John had been telling
Herod, "It is against God's law for you to marry her." 5 Herod wanted to kill
John, but he was afraid of a riot, because all the people believed John was
a prophet.

6 But at a birthday party for Herod, Herodias's daughter performed a dance
that greatly pleased him, 7 so he promised with a vow to give her anything
she wanted. 8 At her mother's urging, the girl said, "I want the head of John
the Baptist on a tray!" 9 Then the king regretted what he had said; but be-
cause of the vow he had made in front of his guests, he issued the necessary
orders. 10 So John was beheaded in the prison, 11 and his head was brought
on a tray and given to the girl, who took it to her mother. 12 Later, John's dis-
ciples came for his body and buried it. Then they went and told Jesus what
had happened.

Jesus Feeds Five Thousand

13 As soon as Jesus heard the news, he left in a boat to a remote area to be alone.
But the crowds heard where he was headed and followed on foot from many
towns. 14 Jesus saw the huge crowd as he stepped from the boat, and he had
compassion on them and healed their sick.

15 That evening the disciples came to him and said, "This is a remote place,
and it's already getting late. Send the crowds away so they can go to the vil-
lages and buy food for themselves."

16 But Jesus said, "That isn't necessary—you feed them."

17 "But we have only five loaves of bread and two fish!" they answered.

18 "Bring them here," he said. 19 Then he told the people to sit down on
the grass. Jesus took the five loaves and two fish, looked up toward heaven,
and blessed them. Then, breaking the loaves into pieces, he gave the bread
to the disciples, who distributed it to the people. 20 They all ate as much as
they wanted, and afterward, the disciples picked up twelve baskets of left-
overs. 21 About 5,000 men were fed that day, in addition to all the women
and children!

Jesus Walks on Water

22 Immediately after this, Jesus insisted that his disciples get back into the
boat and cross to the other side of the lake, while he sent the people home.
23 After sending them home, he went up into the hills by himself to pray.
Night fell while he was there alone.

24 Meanwhile, the disciples were in trouble far away from land, for a strong
wind had risen, and they were fighting heavy waves. 25 About three o'clock
in the morning* Jesus came toward them, walking on the water. 26 When the

14:1 Greek *Herod the tetrarch.* Herod Antipas was a son of King Herod and was ruler over Galilee.
14:25 Greek *In the fourth watch of the night.*

Remember to take notes!

Question 14:22-33

Jesus questioned why the disciples had "so little faith" (v. 31). What would "big" faith look like?

disciples saw him walking on the water, they were terrified. In their fear, they cried out, "It's a ghost!"

27 But Jesus spoke to them at once. "Don't be afraid," he said. "Take courage. I am here!*"

28 Then Peter called to him, "Lord, if it's really you, tell me to come to you, walking on the water."

29 "Yes, come," Jesus said.

So Peter went over the side of the boat and walked on the water toward Jesus. 30 But when he saw the strong* wind and the waves, he was terrified and began to sink. "Save me, Lord!" he shouted.

31 Jesus immediately reached out and grabbed him. "You have so little faith," Jesus said. "Why did you doubt me?"

32 When they climbed back into the boat, the wind stopped. 33 Then the disciples worshiped him. "You really are the Son of God!" they exclaimed.

34 After they had crossed the lake, they landed at Gennesaret. 35 When the people recognized Jesus, the news of his arrival spread quickly throughout the whole area, and soon people were bringing all their sick to be healed. 36 They begged him to let the sick touch at least the fringe of his robe, and all who touched him were healed.

Jesus Teaches about Inner Purity

15 Some Pharisees and teachers of religious law now arrived from Jerusalem to see Jesus. They asked him, 2 "Why do your disciples disobey our age-old tradition? For they ignore our tradition of ceremonial hand washing before they eat."

3 Jesus replied, "And why do you, by your traditions, violate the direct commandments of God? 4 For instance, God says, 'Honor your father and mother,'* and 'Anyone who speaks disrespectfully of father or mother must be put to death.'* 5 But you say it is all right for people to say to their parents, 'Sorry, I can't help you. For I have vowed to give to God what I would have given to you.' 6 In this way, you say they don't need to honor their parents.* And so you cancel the word of God for the sake of your own tradition. 7 You hypocrites! Isaiah was right when he prophesied about you, for he wrote,

8 'These people honor me with their lips,
  but their hearts are far from me.
9 Their worship is a farce,
  for they teach man-made ideas as commands from God.'*"

10 Then Jesus called to the crowd to come and hear. "Listen," he said, "and try to understand. 11 It's not what goes into your mouth that defiles you; you are defiled by the words that come out of your mouth."

12 Then the disciples came to him and asked, "Do you realize you offended the Pharisees by what you just said?"

13 Jesus replied, "Every plant not planted by my heavenly Father will be uprooted, 14 so ignore them. They are blind guides leading the blind, and if one blind person guides another, they will both fall into a ditch."

14:27 Or *The 'I AM' is here;* Greek reads *I am.* See Exod 3:14. 14:30 Some manuscripts do not include *strong.* 15:4a Exod 20:12; Deut 5:16. 15:4b Exod 21:17 (Greek version); Lev 20:9 (Greek version). 15:6 Greek *their father;* other manuscripts read *their father or their mother.* 15:8-9 Isa 29:13 (Greek version).

15 Then Peter said to Jesus, "Explain to us the parable that says people aren't defiled by what they eat."

16 "Don't you understand yet?" Jesus asked. 17 "Anything you eat passes through the stomach and then goes into the sewer. 18 But the words you speak come from the heart—that's what defiles you. 19 For from the heart come evil thoughts, murder, adultery, all sexual immorality, theft, lying, and slander. 20 These are what defile you. Eating with unwashed hands will never defile you."

The Faith of a Gentile Woman

21 Then Jesus left Galilee and went north to the region of Tyre and Sidon. 22 A Gentile* woman who lived there came to him, pleading, "Have mercy on me, O Lord, Son of David! For my daughter is possessed by a demon that torments her severely."

23 But Jesus gave her no reply, not even a word. Then his disciples urged him to send her away. "Tell her to go away," they said. "She is bothering us with all her begging."

24 Then Jesus said to the woman, "I was sent only to help God's lost sheep—the people of Israel."

25 But she came and worshiped him, pleading again, "Lord, help me!"

26 Jesus responded, "It isn't right to take food from the children and throw it to the dogs."

27 She replied, "That's true, Lord, but even dogs are allowed to eat the scraps that fall beneath their masters' table."

28 "Dear woman," Jesus said to her, "your faith is great. Your request is granted." And her daughter was instantly healed.

Question 15:21-28

This woman relentlessly pursued Jesus even when he tested her resolve. In the end, what impressed Jesus about her "great" faith (v. 28)?

Jesus Heals Many People

29 Jesus returned to the Sea of Galilee and climbed a hill and sat down. 30 A vast crowd brought to him people who were lame, blind, crippled, those who couldn't speak, and many others. They laid them before Jesus, and he healed them all. 31 The crowd was amazed! Those who hadn't been able to speak were talking, the crippled were made well, the lame were walking, and the blind could see again! And they praised the God of Israel.

Jesus Feeds Four Thousand

32 Then Jesus called his disciples and told them, "I feel sorry for these people. They have been here with me for three days, and they have nothing left to eat. I don't want to send them away hungry, or they will faint along the way."

33 The disciples replied, "Where would we get enough food here in the wilderness for such a huge crowd?"

34 Jesus asked, "How much bread do you have?"

They replied, "Seven loaves, and a few small fish."

35 So Jesus told all the people to sit down on the ground. 36 Then he took the seven loaves and the fish, thanked God for them, and broke them into pieces. He gave them to the disciples, who distributed the food to the crowd.

37 They all ate as much as they wanted. Afterward, the disciples picked up seven large baskets of leftover food. 38 There were 4,000 men who were

15:22 Greek *Canaanite.*

fed that day, in addition to all the women and children. 39 Then Jesus sent the people home, and he got into a boat and crossed over to the region of Magadan.

Leaders Demand a Miraculous Sign

16 One day the Pharisees and Sadducees came to test Jesus, demanding that he show them a miraculous sign from heaven to prove his authority.

2 He replied, "You know the saying, 'Red sky at night means fair weather tomorrow; 3 red sky in the morning means foul weather all day.' You know how to interpret the weather signs in the sky, but you don't know how to interpret the signs of the times!* 4 Only an evil, adulterous generation would demand a miraculous sign, but the only sign I will give them is the sign of the prophet Jonah.*" Then Jesus left them and went away.

Yeast of the Pharisees and Sadducees

5 Later, after they crossed to the other side of the lake, the disciples discovered they had forgotten to bring any bread. 6 "Watch out!" Jesus warned them. "Beware of the yeast of the Pharisees and Sadducees."

7 At this they began to argue with each other because they hadn't brought any bread. 8 Jesus knew what they were saying, so he said, "You have so little faith! Why are you arguing with each other about having no bread? 9 Don't you understand even yet? Don't you remember the 5,000 I fed with five loaves, and the baskets of leftovers you picked up? 10 Or the 4,000 I fed with seven loaves, and the large baskets of leftovers you picked up? 11 Why can't you understand that I'm not talking about bread? So again I say, 'Beware of the yeast of the Pharisees and Sadducees.'"

12 Then at last they understood that he wasn't speaking about the yeast in bread, but about the deceptive teaching of the Pharisees and Sadducees.

Peter's Declaration about Jesus

13 When Jesus came to the region of Caesarea Philippi, he asked his disciples, "Who do people say that the Son of Man is?"*

14 "Well," they replied, "some say John the Baptist, some say Elijah, and others say Jeremiah or one of the other prophets."

15 Then he asked them, "But who do you say I am?"

16 Simon Peter answered, "You are the Messiah,* the Son of the living God."

17 Jesus replied, "You are blessed, Simon son of John,* because my Father in heaven has revealed this to you. You did not learn this from any human being. 18 Now I say to you that you are Peter (which means 'rock'),* and upon this rock I will build my church, and all the powers of hell* will not conquer it. 19 And I will give you the keys of the Kingdom of Heaven. Whatever you forbid* on earth will be forbidden in heaven, and whatever you permit* on earth will be permitted in heaven."

20 Then he sternly warned the disciples not to tell anyone that he was the Messiah.

16:2-3 Several manuscripts do not include any of the words in 16:2-3 after *He replied.* 16:4 Greek *the sign of Jonah.* 16:13 "Son of Man" is a title Jesus used for himself. 16:16 Or *the Christ. Messiah* (a Hebrew term) and *Christ* (a Greek term) both mean "anointed one." 16:17 Greek *Simon bar-Jonah;* see John 1:42; 21:15-17. 16:18a Greek *that you are Peter.* 16:18b Greek *and the gates of Hades.* 16:19a Or *bind,* or *lock.* 16:19b Or *loose,* or *open.*

Make a Difference

16:13–19

You Are Peter

At important moments of history, this world has needed people to take a stand for Jesus. When people seize the opportunity to stand for truth, the course of history is stabilized, and healing is distributed to the scattered.

We are perhaps now at one of those moments. We need people bold enough to position their feet as a rock in the rapids, undeterred and unmoved. Then, with loving arms stretched out wide, we need those bold people to catch others before the pressure sweeps them away. As soon as people are caught, they are enabled to catch their breath, steady their stance, and join in the rescue effort.

At one of these pivotal moments in history, Jesus asked Peter, "Who do you say I am?" (v. 15). Peter, against the current, stood boldly and unashamedly and declared, "You are the Messiah, the Son of the living God" (v. 16).

Difference Maker

Peter's original name was Simon. Jesus gave him the name Peter, which means "rock." What would it mean for you to be like a rock for Jesus, standing against the current today?

Jesus Predicts His Death
21 From then on Jesus* began to tell his disciples plainly that it was necessary
for him to go to Jerusalem, and that he would suffer many terrible things at
the hands of the elders, the leading priests, and the teachers of religious law.
He would be killed, but on the third day he would be raised from the dead.
22 But Peter took him aside and began to reprimand him* for saying such
things. "Heaven forbid, Lord," he said. "This will never happen to you!"
23 Jesus turned to Peter and said, "Get away from me, Satan! You are a dan-
gerous trap to me. You are seeing things merely from a human point of view,
not from God's."
24 Then Jesus said to his disciples, "If any of you wants to be my follower,
you must give up your own way, take up your cross, and follow me. 25 If you
try to hang on to your life, you will lose it. But if you give up your life for
my sake, you will save it. 26 And what do you benefit if you gain the whole
world but lose your own soul?* Is anything worth more than your soul? 27 For
the Son of Man will come with his angels in the glory of his Father and will
judge all people according to their deeds. 28 And I tell you the truth, some
standing here right now will not die before they see the Son of Man coming
in his Kingdom."

The Transfiguration
17 Six days later Jesus took Peter and the two brothers, James and John,
and led them up a high mountain to be alone. 2 As the men watched,
Jesus' appearance was transformed so that his face shone like the sun, and
his clothes became as white as light. 3 Suddenly, Moses and Elijah appeared
and began talking with Jesus.
4 Peter exclaimed, "Lord, it's wonderful for us to be here! If you want, I'll
make three shelters as memorials*—one for you, one for Moses, and one
for Elijah."
5 But even as he spoke, a bright cloud overshadowed them, and a voice
from the cloud said, "This is my dearly loved Son, who brings me great joy.
Listen to him." 6 The disciples were terrified and fell face down on the ground.
7 Then Jesus came over and touched them. "Get up," he said. "Don't be
afraid." 8 And when they looked up, Moses and Elijah were gone, and they
saw only Jesus.
9 As they went back down the mountain, Jesus commanded them, "Don't
tell anyone what you have seen until the Son of Man* has been raised from
the dead."
10 Then his disciples asked him, "Why do the teachers of religious law
insist that Elijah must return before the Messiah comes?*"
11 Jesus replied, "Elijah is indeed coming first to get everything ready. 12 But
I tell you, Elijah has already come, but he wasn't recognized, and they chose
to abuse him. And in the same way they will also make the Son of Man suf-
fer." 13 Then the disciples realized he was talking about John the Baptist.

Jesus Heals a Demon-Possessed Boy
14 At the foot of the mountain, a large crowd was waiting for them. A man
came and knelt before Jesus and said, 15 "Lord, have mercy on my son. He has

Question 17:1-9

Two of the greatest figures in history mysteriously appear in person with Jesus. What significance does this moment have in revealing Jesus' purpose?

16:21 Some manuscripts read *Jesus the Messiah.* 16:22 Or *began to correct him.* 16:26 Or *your self?* also in 16:26b. 17:4 Greek *three tabernacles.* 17:9 "Son of Man" is a title Jesus used for himself. 17:10 Greek *that Elijah must come first?*

Question 18:1-7

Do you want to get into the kingdom of heaven? Jesus said you'll need to become like this little child. What was Jesus trying to say?

seizures and suffers terribly. He often falls into the fire or into the water. 16 So
I brought him to your disciples, but they couldn't heal him."
17 Jesus said, "You faithless and corrupt people! How long must I be with
you? How long must I put up with you? Bring the boy here to me." 18 Then
Jesus rebuked the demon in the boy, and it left him. From that moment the
boy was well.
19 Afterward the disciples asked Jesus privately, "Why couldn't we cast
out that demon?"
20 "You don't have enough faith," Jesus told them. "I tell you the truth, if
you had faith even as small as a mustard seed, you could say to this mountain, 'Move from here to there,' and it would move. Nothing would be
impossible.*"

Jesus Again Predicts His Death

22 After they gathered again in Galilee, Jesus told them, "The Son of Man is
going to be betrayed into the hands of his enemies. 23 He will be killed, but
on the third day he will be raised from the dead." And the disciples were
filled with grief.

Payment of the Temple Tax

24 On their arrival in Capernaum, the collectors of the Temple tax* came to
Peter and asked him, "Doesn't your teacher pay the Temple tax?"
25 "Yes, he does," Peter replied. Then he went into the house.
But before he had a chance to speak, Jesus asked him, "What do you think,
Peter?* Do kings tax their own people or the people they have conquered?*"
26 "They tax the people they have conquered," Peter replied.
"Well, then," Jesus said, "the citizens are free! 27 However, we don't want
to offend them, so go down to the lake and throw in a line. Open the mouth
of the first fish you catch, and you will find a large silver coin.* Take it and
pay the tax for both of us."

The Greatest in the Kingdom

18 About that time the disciples came to Jesus and asked, "Who is greatest in the Kingdom of Heaven?"
2 Jesus called a little child to him and put the child among them. 3 Then he
said, "I tell you the truth, unless you turn from your sins and become like
little children, you will never get into the Kingdom of Heaven. 4 So anyone
who becomes as humble as this little child is the greatest in the Kingdom
of Heaven.
5 "And anyone who welcomes a little child like this on my behalf* is welcoming me. 6 But if you cause one of these little ones who trusts in me to fall
into sin, it would be better for you to have a large millstone tied around your
neck and be drowned in the depths of the sea.
7 "What sorrow awaits the world, because it tempts people to sin. Temptations are inevitable, but what sorrow awaits the person who does the tempting. 8 So if your hand or foot causes you to sin, cut it off and throw it away. It's
better to enter eternal life with only one hand or one foot than to be thrown

17:20 Some manuscripts add verse 21, *But this kind of demon won't leave except by prayer and fasting.* Compare Mark 9:29. 17:24 Greek *the two-drachma [tax]*; also in 17:24b. See Exod 30:13-16; Neh 10:32-33. 17:25a Greek *Simon?* 17:25b Greek *their sons or others?* 17:27 Greek *a stater* [a Greek coin equivalent to four drachmas]. 18:5 Greek *in my name.*

into eternal fire with both of your hands and feet. 9 And if your eye causes
you to sin, gouge it out and throw it away. It's better to enter eternal life
with only one eye than to have two eyes and be thrown into the fire of hell.*
10 "Beware that you don't look down on any of these little ones. For I tell
you that in heaven their angels are always in the presence of my heavenly
Father.*

Parable of the Lost Sheep

12 "If a man has a hundred sheep and one of them wanders away, what will
he do? Won't he leave the ninety-nine others on the hills and go out to search
for the one that is lost? 13 And if he finds it, I tell you the truth, he will rejoice
over it more than over the ninety-nine that didn't wander away! 14 In the
same way, it is not my heavenly Father's will that even one of these little
ones should perish.

Correcting Another Believer

15 "If another believer* sins against you,* go privately and point out the of-
fense. If the other person listens and confesses it, you have won that person
back. 16 But if you are unsuccessful, take one or two others with you and go
back again, so that everything you say may be confirmed by two or three
witnesses. 17 If the person still refuses to listen, take your case to the church.
Then if he or she won't accept the church's decision, treat that person as a
pagan or a corrupt tax collector.
18 "I tell you the truth, whatever you forbid* on earth will be forbidden
in heaven, and whatever you permit* on earth will be permitted in heaven.
19 "I also tell you this: If two of you agree here on earth concerning any-
thing you ask, my Father in heaven will do it for you. 20 For where two or three
gather together as my followers,* I am there among them."

Parable of the Unforgiving Debtor

21 Then Peter came to him and asked, "Lord, how often should I forgive some-
one* who sins against me? Seven times?"
22 "No, not seven times," Jesus replied, "but seventy times seven!*
23 "Therefore, the Kingdom of Heaven can be compared to a king who
decided to bring his accounts up to date with servants who had borrowed
money from him. 24 In the process, one of his debtors was brought in who
owed him millions of dollars.* 25 He couldn't pay, so his master ordered that
he be sold—along with his wife, his children, and everything he owned—to
pay the debt.
26 "But the man fell down before his master and begged him, 'Please, be
patient with me, and I will pay it all.' 27 Then his master was filled with pity
for him, and he released him and forgave his debt.
28 "But when the man left the king, he went to a fellow servant who owed
him a few thousand dollars.* He grabbed him by the throat and demanded
instant payment.
29 "His fellow servant fell down before him and begged for a little more

18:9 Greek *the Gehenna of fire.* **18:10** Some manuscripts add verse 11, *And the Son of Man came to save those who are lost.* Compare Luke 19:10. **18:15a** Greek *If your brother.* **18:15b** Some manuscripts do not include *against you.* **18:18a** Or *bind,* or *lock.* **18:18b** Or *loose,* or *open.* **18:20** Greek *gather together in my name.* **18:21** Greek *my brother.* **18:22** Or *seventy-seven times.* **18:24** Greek *10,000 talents* [375 tons or 340 metric tons of silver]. **18:28** Greek *100 denarii.* A denarius was equivalent to a laborer's full day's wage.

Make a Difference

18:20

Get Together

Finding a small group of people to study the Bible with is one of the most important habits you can develop during your lifetime. By meeting with people regularly to focus on Jesus, you'll be encouraged to grow deeper in your faith and make healthy decisions in your life. You'll find people who will support you, care for you, laugh with you, and pray for you. Such a group can become one of those deep gatherings where every word is cherished and treasured, where the surface serves not as a barrier but as an invitation to know what's underneath.

Be sure to intentionally find such a group. It is too easy to fall into hectic schedules or slip into mundane routines of life that usurp an active relationship with God. Don't let that happen to you. Gather others around you to keep you present in relationship with Jesus Christ.

Difference Maker

Be proactive. Contact local ministries or churches, ask friends who are already plugged in somewhere, or gather some people you trust and ask them to start a small group with you.

time. 'Be patient with me, and I will pay it,' he pleaded. 30 But his creditor
wouldn't wait. He had the man arrested and put in prison until the debt
could be paid in full.
31 "When some of the other servants saw this, they were very upset. They
went to the king and told him everything that had happened. 32 Then the king
called in the man he had forgiven and said, 'You evil servant! I forgave you
that tremendous debt because you pleaded with me. 33 Shouldn't you have
mercy on your fellow servant, just as I had mercy on you?' 34 Then the angry
king sent the man to prison to be tortured until he had paid his entire debt.
35 "That's what my heavenly Father will do to you if you refuse to forgive
your brothers and sisters* from your heart."

Discussion about Divorce and Marriage

19 When Jesus had finished saying these things, he left Galilee and
went down to the region of Judea east of the Jordan River. 2 Large
crowds followed him there, and he healed their sick.
3 Some Pharisees came and tried to trap him with this question: "Should
a man be allowed to divorce his wife for just any reason?"
4 "Haven't you read the Scriptures?" Jesus replied. "They record that from
the beginning 'God made them male and female.'*" 5 And he said, "'This
explains why a man leaves his father and mother and is joined to his wife,
and the two are united into one.'* 6 Since they are no longer two but one, let
no one split apart what God has joined together."
7 "Then why did Moses say in the law that a man could give his wife a
written notice of divorce and send her away?"* they asked.
8 Jesus replied, "Moses permitted divorce only as a concession to your hard
hearts, but it was not what God had originally intended. 9 And I tell you this,
whoever divorces his wife and marries someone else commits adultery—un-
less his wife has been unfaithful.*"
10 Jesus' disciples then said to him, "If this is the case, it is better not to
marry!"
11 "Not everyone can accept this statement," Jesus said. "Only those whom
God helps. 12 Some are born as eunuchs, some have been made eunuchs
by others, and some choose not to marry* for the sake of the Kingdom of
Heaven. Let anyone accept this who can."

Jesus Blesses the Children

13 One day some parents brought their children to Jesus so he could lay his
hands on them and pray for them. But the disciples scolded the parents for
bothering him.
14 But Jesus said, "Let the children come to me. Don't stop them! For the
Kingdom of Heaven belongs to those who are like these children." 15 And he
placed his hands on their heads and blessed them before he left.

The Rich Man

16 Someone came to Jesus with this question: "Teacher,* what good deed must
I do to have eternal life?"
17 "Why ask me about what is good?" Jesus replied. "There is only One

18:35 Greek *your brother.* 19:4 Gen 1:27; 5:2. 19:5 Gen 2:24. 19:7 See Deut 24:1. 19:9 Some manuscripts add *And anyone who marries a divorced woman commits adultery.* Compare Matt 5:32. 19:12 Greek *and some make themselves eunuchs.* 19:16 Some manuscripts read *Good Teacher.*

who is good. But to answer your question—if you want to receive eternal
life, keep* the commandments."
18 "Which ones?" the man asked.
And Jesus replied: "'You must not murder. You must not commit adultery.
You must not steal. You must not testify falsely. 19 Honor your father and
mother. Love your neighbor as yourself.'*"
20 "I've obeyed all these commandments," the young man replied. "What
else must I do?"
21 Jesus told him, "If you want to be perfect, go and sell all your posses-
sions and give the money to the poor, and you will have treasure in heaven.
Then come, follow me."
22 But when the young man heard this, he went away sad, for he had many
possessions.
23 Then Jesus said to his disciples, "I tell you the truth, it is very hard for a
rich person to enter the Kingdom of Heaven. 24 I'll say it again—it is easier
for a camel to go through the eye of a needle than for a rich person to enter
the Kingdom of God!"
25 The disciples were astounded. "Then who in the world can be saved?"
they asked.
26 Jesus looked at them intently and said, "Humanly speaking, it is im-
possible. But with God everything is possible."
27 Then Peter said to him, "We've given up everything to follow you. What
will we get?"
28 Jesus replied, "I assure you that when the world is made new* and the
Son of Man* sits upon his glorious throne, you who have been my follow-
ers will also sit on twelve thrones, judging the twelve tribes of Israel. 29 And
everyone who has given up houses or brothers or sisters or father or mother
or children or property, for my sake, will receive a hundred times as much
in return and will inherit eternal life. 30 But many who are the greatest now
will be least important then, and those who seem least important now will
be the greatest then.*

Parable of the Vineyard Workers

20 "For the Kingdom of Heaven is like the landowner who went out
early one morning to hire workers for his vineyard. 2 He agreed to
pay the normal daily wage* and sent them out to work.
3 "At nine o'clock in the morning he was passing through the marketplace
and saw some people standing around doing nothing. 4 So he hired them,
telling them he would pay them whatever was right at the end of the day.
5 So they went to work in the vineyard. At noon and again at three o'clock he
did the same thing.
6 "At five o'clock that afternoon he was in town again and saw some more
people standing around. He asked them, 'Why haven't you been working
today?'
7 "They replied, 'Because no one hired us.'
"The landowner told them, 'Then go out and join the others in my
vineyard.'

19:17 Some manuscripts read *continue to keep.* 19:18-19 Exod 20:12-16; Deut 5:16-20; Lev 19:18. 19:28a Or *in the regeneration.* 19:28b "Son of Man" is a title Jesus used for himself. 19:30 Greek *But many who are first will be last; and the last, first.* 20:2 Greek *a denarius,* the payment for a full day's labor; similarly in 20:9, 10, 13.

Make a Difference

19:16-24

Impoverished

This guy had it all together. He was wealthy. He had influence. He was good. He followed God's patterns. He was as good a man as there is out there. Even so, he felt like he was lacking something.

When he heard Jesus was in town, he went to ask him a question, which was a strange thing to do. Jesus, after all, was not wealthy. He wasn't a businessman. He didn't even own a pillow. Their conversation went something like this:

"It looks like you've got life and faith all figured out," Jesus told the young man.

"Yes, I know it looks that way, but I'm still missing something. What is it?" the rich man asked.

"Well, you lack what you don't have," Jesus answered. "Nothing. You've got everything, but you're possessed by your possessions. To be truly rich, free your heart to follow me."

Difference Maker

Gather any extra stuff that you've accumulated over the years and drop it off at a local thrift store.

8 “That evening he told the foreman to call the workers in and pay them,
beginning with the last workers first. 9 When those hired at five o’clock were
paid, each received a full day’s wage. 10 When those hired first came to get
their pay, they assumed they would receive more. But they, too, were paid
a day’s wage. 11 When they received their pay, they protested to the owner,
12 ‘Those people worked only one hour, and yet you’ve paid them just as much
as you paid us who worked all day in the scorching heat.’

13 “He answered one of them, ‘Friend, I haven’t been unfair! Didn’t you
agree to work all day for the usual wage? 14 Take your money and go. I wanted
to pay this last worker the same as you. 15 Is it against the law for me to do
what I want with my money? Should you be jealous because I am kind to
others?’

16 “So those who are last now will be first then, and those who are first
will be last.”

Jesus Again Predicts His Death

17 As Jesus was going up to Jerusalem, he took the twelve disciples aside pri-
vately and told them what was going to happen to him. 18 “Listen,” he said,
“we’re going up to Jerusalem, where the Son of Man* will be betrayed to the
leading priests and the teachers of religious law. They will sentence him to
die. 19 Then they will hand him over to the Romans* to be mocked, flogged
with a whip, and crucified. But on the third day he will be raised from the
dead.”

Jesus Teaches about Serving Others

20 Then the mother of James and John, the sons of Zebedee, came to Jesus
with her sons. She knelt respectfully to ask a favor. 21 “What is your request?”
he asked.

She replied, “In your Kingdom, please let my two sons sit in places of
honor next to you, one on your right and the other on your left.”

22 But Jesus answered by saying to them, “You don’t know what you are
asking! Are you able to drink from the bitter cup of suffering I am about to
drink?”

“Oh yes,” they replied, “we are able!”

23 Jesus told them, “You will indeed drink from my bitter cup. But I have
no right to say who will sit on my right or my left. My Father has prepared
those places for the ones he has chosen.”

24 When the ten other disciples heard what James and John had asked,
they were indignant. 25 But Jesus called them together and said, “You know
that the rulers in this world lord it over their people, and officials flaunt
their authority over those under them. 26 But among you it will be differ-
ent. Whoever wants to be a leader among you must be your servant, 27 and
whoever wants to be first among you must become your slave. 28 For even
the Son of Man came not to be served but to serve others and to give his life
as a ransom for many.”

Jesus Heals Two Blind Men

29 As Jesus and the disciples left the town of Jericho, a large crowd followed
behind. 30 Two blind men were sitting beside the road. When they heard

20:18 “Son of Man” is a title Jesus used for himself. **20:19** Greek *the Gentiles.*

that Jesus was coming that way, they began shouting, "Lord, Son of David,
have mercy on us!"
31 "Be quiet!" the crowd yelled at them.
But they only shouted louder, "Lord, Son of David, have mercy on us!"
32 When Jesus heard them, he stopped and called, "What do you want me
to do for you?"
33 "Lord," they said, "we want to see!" 34 Jesus felt sorry for them and
touched their eyes. Instantly they could see! Then they followed him.

Jesus' Triumphant Entry

21 As Jesus and the disciples approached Jerusalem, they came to the
town of Bethphage on the Mount of Olives. Jesus sent two of them
on ahead. 2 "Go into the village over there," he said. "As soon as you enter it,
you will see a donkey tied there, with its colt beside it. Untie them and bring
them to me. 3 If anyone asks what you are doing, just say, 'The Lord needs
them,' and he will immediately let you take them."
4 This took place to fulfill the prophecy that said,

5 "Tell the people of Jerusalem,*
'Look, your King is coming to you.
He is humble, riding on a donkey—
riding on a donkey's colt.'"*

6 The two disciples did as Jesus commanded. 7 They brought the donkey
and the colt to him and threw their garments over the colt, and he sat on it.*
8 Most of the crowd spread their garments on the road ahead of him, and
others cut branches from the trees and spread them on the road. 9 Jesus was
in the center of the procession, and the people all around him were shouting,

"Praise God* for the Son of David!
Blessings on the one who comes in the name of the LORD!
Praise God in highest heaven!"*

10 The entire city of Jerusalem was in an uproar as he entered. "Who is
this?" they asked.
11 And the crowds replied, "It's Jesus, the prophet from Nazareth in
Galilee."

Jesus Clears the Temple

12 Jesus entered the Temple and began to drive out all the people buying and
selling animals for sacrifice. He knocked over the tables of the money changers and the chairs of those selling doves. 13 He said to them, "The Scriptures
declare, 'My Temple will be called a house of prayer,' but you have turned it
into a den of thieves!"*
14 The blind and the lame came to him in the Temple, and he healed them.
15 The leading priests and the teachers of religious law saw these wonderful
miracles and heard even the children in the Temple shouting, "Praise God
for the Son of David."

Question 21:1-11

If you had been there, how would you have answered the question the entire city of Jerusalem was asking: "Who is this?" (v. 10).

21:5a Greek *Tell the daughter of Zion.* Isa 62:11. **21:5b** Zech 9:9. **21:7** Greek *over them, and he sat on them.* **21:9a** Greek *Hosanna,* an exclamation of praise that literally means "save now"; also in 21:9b, 15. **21:9b** Pss 118:25-26; 148:1. **21:13** Isa 56:7; Jer 7:11.

But the leaders were indignant. 16 They asked Jesus, "Do you hear what
these children are saying?"
"Yes," Jesus replied. "Haven't you ever read the Scriptures? For they say,
'You have taught children and infants to give you praise.'*" 17 Then he re-
turned to Bethany, where he stayed overnight.

Jesus Curses the Fig Tree

18 In the morning, as Jesus was returning to Jerusalem, he was hungry, 19 and
he noticed a fig tree beside the road. He went over to see if there were any
figs, but there were only leaves. Then he said to it, "May you never bear fruit
again!" And immediately the fig tree withered up.
20 The disciples were amazed when they saw this and asked, "How did the
fig tree wither so quickly?"
21 Then Jesus told them, "I tell you the truth, if you have faith and don't
doubt, you can do things like this and much more. You can even say to this
mountain, 'May you be lifted up and thrown into the sea,' and it will hap-
pen. 22 You can pray for anything, and if you have faith, you will receive it."

The Authority of Jesus Challenged

23 When Jesus returned to the Temple and began teaching, the leading priests
and elders came up to him. They demanded, "By what authority are you
doing all these things? Who gave you the right?"
24 "I'll tell you by what authority I do these things if you answer one ques-
tion," Jesus replied. 25 "Did John's authority to baptize come from heaven,
or was it merely human?"
They talked it over among themselves. "If we say it was from heaven, he
will ask us why we didn't believe John. 26 But if we say it was merely human,
we'll be mobbed because the people believe John was a prophet." 27 So they
finally replied, "We don't know."
And Jesus responded, "Then I won't tell you by what authority I do these
things.

Parable of the Two Sons

28 "But what do you think about this? A man with two sons told the older
boy, 'Son, go out and work in the vineyard today.' 29 The son answered, 'No, I
won't go,' but later he changed his mind and went anyway. 30 Then the father
told the other son, 'You go,' and he said, 'Yes, sir, I will.' But he didn't go.
31 "Which of the two obeyed his father?"
They replied, "The first."*
Then Jesus explained his meaning: "I tell you the truth, corrupt tax col-
lectors and prostitutes will get into the Kingdom of God before you do. 32 For
John the Baptist came and showed you the right way to live, but you didn't
believe him, while tax collectors and prostitutes did. And even when you saw
this happening, you refused to believe him and repent of your sins.

Parable of the Evil Farmers

33 "Now listen to another story. A certain landowner planted a vineyard, built
a wall around it, dug a pit for pressing out the grape juice, and built a lookout

21:16 Ps 8:2 (Greek version). **21:29-31** Other manuscripts read *"The second."* In still other manuscripts the first son says "Yes" but does nothing, the second son says "No" but then repents and goes, and the answer to Jesus' question is that the second son obeyed his father.

tower. Then he leased the vineyard to tenant farmers and moved to another
country. 34 At the time of the grape harvest, he sent his servants to collect his
share of the crop. 35 But the farmers grabbed his servants, beat one, killed one,
and stoned another. 36 So the landowner sent a larger group of his servants
to collect for him, but the results were the same.

37 "Finally, the owner sent his son, thinking, 'Surely they will respect my
son.'

38 "But when the tenant farmers saw his son coming, they said to one an-
other, 'Here comes the heir to this estate. Come on, let's kill him and get the
estate for ourselves!' 39 So they grabbed him, dragged him out of the vineyard,
and murdered him.

40 "When the owner of the vineyard returns," Jesus asked, "what do you
think he will do to those farmers?"

41 The religious leaders replied, "He will put the wicked men to a horrible
death and lease the vineyard to others who will give him his share of the
crop after each harvest."

42 Then Jesus asked them, "Didn't you ever read this in the Scriptures?

'The stone that the builders rejected
    has now become the cornerstone.
This is the LORD's doing,
    and it is wonderful to see.'*

43 I tell you, the Kingdom of God will be taken away from you and given to a
nation that will produce the proper fruit. 44 Anyone who stumbles over that
stone will be broken to pieces, and it will crush anyone it falls on.*"

45 When the leading priests and Pharisees heard this parable, they realized
he was telling the story against them—they were the wicked farmers. 46 They
wanted to arrest him, but they were afraid of the crowds, who considered
Jesus to be a prophet.

Parable of the Great Feast

22 Jesus also told them other parables. He said, 2 "The Kingdom of
Heaven can be illustrated by the story of a king who prepared a great
wedding feast for his son. 3 When the banquet was ready, he sent his servants
to notify those who were invited. But they all refused to come!

4 "So he sent other servants to tell them, 'The feast has been prepared. The
bulls and fattened cattle have been killed, and everything is ready. Come to
the banquet!' 5 But the guests he had invited ignored them and went their
own way, one to his farm, another to his business. 6 Others seized his mes-
sengers and insulted them and killed them.

7 "The king was furious, and he sent out his army to destroy the murder-
ers and burn their town. 8 And he said to his servants, 'The wedding feast is
ready, and the guests I invited aren't worthy of the honor. 9 Now go out to
the street corners and invite everyone you see.' 10 So the servants brought
in everyone they could find, good and bad alike, and the banquet hall was
filled with guests.

11 "But when the king came in to meet the guests, he noticed a man who
wasn't wearing the proper clothes for a wedding. 12 'Friend,' he asked, 'how

21:42 Ps 118:22-23. **21:44** This verse is not included in some early manuscripts. Compare Luke 20:18.

How God is at work here

Prayer **22:38**

Dear Jesus, today, don't let me miss chances to love you by loving others. Amen.

is it that you are here without wedding clothes?' But the man had no reply.
13 Then the king said to his aides, 'Bind his hands and feet and throw him
into the outer darkness, where there will be weeping and gnashing of teeth.'
14 "For many are called, but few are chosen."

Taxes for Caesar

15 Then the Pharisees met together to plot how to trap Jesus into saying some-
thing for which he could be arrested. 16 They sent some of their disciples,
along with the supporters of Herod, to meet with him. "Teacher," they said,
"we know how honest you are. You teach the way of God truthfully. You are
impartial and don't play favorites. 17 Now tell us what you think about this:
Is it right to pay taxes to Caesar or not?"
18 But Jesus knew their evil motives. "You hypocrites!" he said. "Why are
you trying to trap me? 19 Here, show me the coin used for the tax." When
they handed him a Roman coin,* 20 he asked, "Whose picture and title are
stamped on it?"
21 "Caesar's," they replied.
"Well, then," he said, "give to Caesar what belongs to Caesar, and give to
God what belongs to God."
22 His reply amazed them, and they went away.

Discussion about Resurrection

23 That same day Jesus was approached by some Sadducees—religious leaders
who say there is no resurrection from the dead. They posed this question:
24 "Teacher, Moses said, 'If a man dies without children, his brother should
marry the widow and have a child who will carry on the brother's name.'*
25 Well, suppose there were seven brothers. The oldest one married and then
died without children, so his brother married the widow. 26 But the second
brother also died, and the third brother married her. This continued with
all seven of them. 27 Last of all, the woman also died. 28 So tell us, whose wife
will she be in the resurrection? For all seven were married to her."
29 Jesus replied, "Your mistake is that you don't know the Scriptures, and
you don't know the power of God. 30 For when the dead rise, they will neither
marry nor be given in marriage. In this respect they will be like the angels
in heaven.
31 "But now, as to whether there will be a resurrection of the dead—haven't
you ever read about this in the Scriptures? Long after Abraham, Isaac, and
Jacob had died, God said,* 32 'I am the God of Abraham, the God of Isaac, and
the God of Jacob.'* So he is the God of the living, not the dead."
33 When the crowds heard him, they were astounded at his teaching.

The Most Important Commandment

34 But when the Pharisees heard that he had silenced the Sadducees with his
reply, they met together to question him again. 35 One of them, an expert in
religious law, tried to trap him with this question: 36 "Teacher, which is the
most important commandment in the law of Moses?"
37 Jesus replied, "'You must love the LORD your God with all your heart,
all your soul, and all your mind.'* 38 This is the first and greatest command-
ment. 39 A second is equally important: 'Love your neighbor as yourself.'*

22:19 Greek *a denarius.* 22:24 Deut 25:5-6. 22:31 Greek *read about this? God said.* 22:32 Exod 3:6. 22:37 Deut 6:5. 22:39 Lev 19:18.

40The entire law and all the demands of the prophets are based on these two commandments."

Whose Son Is the Messiah?

41Then, surrounded by the Pharisees, Jesus asked them a question: 42"What do you think about the Messiah? Whose son is he?"

They replied, "He is the son of David."

43Jesus responded, "Then why does David, speaking under the inspiration of the Spirit, call the Messiah 'my Lord'? For David said,

44 'The LORD said to my Lord,
Sit in the place of honor at my right hand
until I humble your enemies beneath your feet.'*

45Since David called the Messiah 'my Lord,' how can the Messiah be his son?"

46No one could answer him. And after that, no one dared to ask him any more questions.

Jesus Criticizes the Religious Leaders

23 Then Jesus said to the crowds and to his disciples, 2"The teachers of religious law and the Pharisees are the official interpreters of the law of Moses.* 3So practice and obey whatever they tell you, but don't follow their example. For they don't practice what they teach. 4They crush people with unbearable religious demands and never lift a finger to ease the burden.

5"Everything they do is for show. On their arms they wear extra wide prayer boxes with Scripture verses inside, and they wear robes with extra long tassels.* 6And they love to sit at the head table at banquets and in the seats of honor in the synagogues. 7They love to receive respectful greetings as they walk in the marketplaces, and to be called 'Rabbi.'*

8"Don't let anyone call you 'Rabbi,' for you have only one teacher, and all of you are equal as brothers and sisters.* 9And don't address anyone here on earth as 'Father,' for only God in heaven is your Father. 10And don't let anyone call you 'Teacher,' for you have only one teacher, the Messiah. 11The greatest among you must be a servant. 12But those who exalt themselves will be humbled, and those who humble themselves will be exalted.

13"What sorrow awaits you teachers of religious law and you Pharisees. Hypocrites! For you shut the door of the Kingdom of Heaven in people's faces. You won't go in yourselves, and you don't let others enter either.*

15"What sorrow awaits you teachers of religious law and you Pharisees. Hypocrites! For you cross land and sea to make one convert, and then you turn that person into twice the child of hell* you yourselves are!

16"Blind guides! What sorrow awaits you! For you say that it means nothing to swear 'by God's Temple,' but that it is binding to swear 'by the gold in the Temple.' 17Blind fools! Which is more important—the gold or the Temple that makes the gold sacred? 18And you say that to swear 'by

22:44 Ps 110:1. **23:2** Greek *and the Pharisees sit in the seat of Moses.* **23:5** Greek *They enlarge their phylacteries and lengthen their tassels.* **23:7** *Rabbi,* from Aramaic, means "master" or "teacher." **23:8** Greek *brothers.* **23:13** Some manuscripts add verse 14, *What sorrow awaits you teachers of religious law and you Pharisees. Hypocrites! You shamelessly cheat widows out of their property and then pretend to be pious by making long prayers in public. Because of this, you will be severely punished.* Compare Mark 12:40 and Luke 20:47. **23:15** Greek *of Gehenna;* also in 23:33.

Question 23:1-39

As you consider the alarming tone Jesus used in this chapter, when do you think it is okay to speak out with harsh words?

the altar' is not binding, but to swear 'by the gifts on the altar' is binding. 19 How blind! For which is more important—the gift on the altar or
the altar that makes the gift sacred? 20 When you swear 'by the altar,' you
are swearing by it and by everything on it. 21 And when you swear 'by the
Temple,' you are swearing by it and by God, who lives in it. 22 And when
you swear 'by heaven,' you are swearing by the throne of God and by God,
who sits on the throne.

23 "What sorrow awaits you teachers of religious law and you Pharisees.
Hypocrites! For you are careful to tithe even the tiniest income from your
herb gardens,* but you ignore the more important aspects of the law—
justice, mercy, and faith. You should tithe, yes, but do not neglect the more
important things. 24 Blind guides! You strain your water so you won't accidentally swallow a gnat, but you swallow a camel!*

25 "What sorrow awaits you teachers of religious law and you Pharisees.
Hypocrites! For you are so careful to clean the outside of the cup and the dish,
but inside you are filthy—full of greed and self-indulgence! 26 You blind
Pharisee! First wash the inside of the cup and the dish,* and then the outside
will become clean, too.

27 "What sorrow awaits you teachers of religious law and you Pharisees.
Hypocrites! For you are like whitewashed tombs—beautiful on the outside
but filled on the inside with dead people's bones and all sorts of impurity.
28 Outwardly you look like righteous people, but inwardly your hearts are
filled with hypocrisy and lawlessness.

29 "What sorrow awaits you teachers of religious law and you Pharisees.
Hypocrites! For you build tombs for the prophets your ancestors killed, and
you decorate the monuments of the godly people your ancestors destroyed.
30 Then you say, 'If we had lived in the days of our ancestors, we would never
have joined them in killing the prophets.'

31 "But in saying that, you testify against yourselves that you are indeed
the descendants of those who murdered the prophets. 32 Go ahead and finish
what your ancestors started. 33 Snakes! Sons of vipers! How will you escape
the judgment of hell?

34 "Therefore, I am sending you prophets and wise men and teachers
of religious law. But you will kill some by crucifixion, and you will flog
others with whips in your synagogues, chasing them from city to city. 35 As
a result, you will be held responsible for the murder of all godly people of
all time—from the murder of righteous Abel to the murder of Zechariah
son of Berekiah, whom you killed in the Temple between the sanctuary
and the altar. 36 I tell you the truth, this judgment will fall on this very
generation.

Jesus Grieves over Jerusalem

37 "O Jerusalem, Jerusalem, the city that kills the prophets and stones God's
messengers! How often I have wanted to gather your children together as a
hen protects her chicks beneath her wings, but you wouldn't let me. 38 And
now, look, your house is abandoned and desolate.* 39 For I tell you this, you
will never see me again until you say, 'Blessings on the one who comes in
the name of the LORD!'*"

23:23 Greek *tithe the mint, the dill, and the cumin.* 23:24 See Lev 11:4, 23, where gnats and camels are both forbidden as food. 23:26 Some manuscripts do not include *and the dish.* 23:38 Some manuscripts do not include *and desolate.* 23:39 Ps 118:26.

Jesus Speaks about the Future

24 As Jesus was leaving the Temple grounds, his disciples pointed out
to him the various Temple buildings. 2 But he responded, "Do you
see all these buildings? I tell you the truth, they will be completely demol-
ished. Not one stone will be left on top of another!"
3 Later, Jesus sat on the Mount of Olives. His disciples came to him pri-
vately and said, "Tell us, when will all this happen? What sign will signal
your return and the end of the world?*"
4 Jesus told them, "Don't let anyone mislead you, 5 for many will come in
my name, claiming, 'I am the Messiah.' They will deceive many. 6 And you
will hear of wars and threats of wars, but don't panic. Yes, these things must
take place, but the end won't follow immediately. 7 Nation will go to war
against nation, and kingdom against kingdom. There will be famines and
earthquakes in many parts of the world. 8 But all this is only the first of the
birth pains, with more to come.
9 "Then you will be arrested, persecuted, and killed. You will be hated all
over the world because you are my followers.* 10 And many will turn away from
me and betray and hate each other. 11 And many false prophets will appear and
will deceive many people. 12 Sin will be rampant everywhere, and the love of
many will grow cold. 13 But the one who endures to the end will be saved. 14 And
the Good News about the Kingdom will be preached throughout the whole
world, so that all nations* will hear it; and then the end will come.
15 "The day is coming when you will see what Daniel the prophet spoke
about—the sacrilegious object that causes desecration* standing in the Holy
Place." (Reader, pay attention!) 16 "Then those in Judea must flee to the hills.
17 A person out on the deck of a roof must not go down into the house to
pack. 18 A person out in the field must not return even to get a coat. 19 How
terrible it will be for pregnant women and for nursing mothers in those
days. 20 And pray that your flight will not be in winter or on the Sabbath.
21 For there will be greater anguish than at any time since the world began.
And it will never be so great again. 22 In fact, unless that time of calamity is
shortened, not a single person will survive. But it will be shortened for the
sake of God's chosen ones.
23 "Then if anyone tells you, 'Look, here is the Messiah,' or 'There he is,'
don't believe it. 24 For false messiahs and false prophets will rise up and per-
form great signs and wonders so as to deceive, if possible, even God's chosen
ones. 25 See, I have warned you about this ahead of time.
26 "So if someone tells you, 'Look, the Messiah is out in the desert,' don't
bother to go and look. Or, 'Look, he is hiding here,' don't believe it! 27 For as
the lightning flashes in the east and shines to the west, so it will be when
the Son of Man* comes. 28 Just as the gathering of vultures shows there is a
carcass nearby, so these signs indicate that the end is near.*
29 "Immediately after the anguish of those days,

the sun will be darkened,
  the moon will give no light,
the stars will fall from the sky,
  and the powers in the heavens will be shaken.*

24:3 Or *the age?* 24:9 Greek *on account of my name.* 24:14 Or *all peoples.* 24:15 Greek *the abomination of desolation.* See Dan 9:27; 11:31; 12:11. 24:27 "Son of Man" is a title Jesus used for himself. 24:28 Greek *Wherever the carcass is, the vultures gather.* 24:29 See Isa 13:10; 34:4; Joel 2:10.

30 And then at last, the sign that the Son of Man is coming will appear in
the heavens, and there will be deep mourning among all the peoples of the
earth. And they will see the Son of Man coming on the clouds of heaven with
power and great glory.* 31 And he will send out his angels with the mighty
blast of a trumpet, and they will gather his chosen ones from all over the
world*—from the farthest ends of the earth and heaven.

32 "Now learn a lesson from the fig tree. When its branches bud and its
leaves begin to sprout, you know that summer is near. 33 In the same way,
when you see all these things, you can know his return is very near, right at
the door. 34 I tell you the truth, this generation* will not pass from the scene
until all these things take place. 35 Heaven and earth will disappear, but my
words will never disappear.

36 "However, no one knows the day or hour when these things will happen,
not even the angels in heaven or the Son himself.* Only the Father knows.

37 "When the Son of Man returns, it will be like it was in Noah's day. 38 In
those days before the flood, the people were enjoying banquets and parties
and weddings right up to the time Noah entered his boat. 39 People didn't
realize what was going to happen until the flood came and swept them all
away. That is the way it will be when the Son of Man comes.

40 "Two men will be working together in the field; one will be taken, the
other left. 41 Two women will be grinding flour at the mill; one will be taken,
the other left.

42 "So you, too, must keep watch! For you don't know what day your Lord
is coming. 43 Understand this: If a homeowner knew exactly when a burglar
was coming, he would keep watch and not permit his house to be broken
into. 44 You also must be ready all the time, for the Son of Man will come
when least expected.

45 "A faithful, sensible servant is one to whom the master can give the re-
sponsibility of managing his other household servants and feeding them.
46 If the master returns and finds that the servant has done a good job, there
will be a reward. 47 I tell you the truth, the master will put that servant in
charge of all he owns. 48 But what if the servant is evil and thinks, 'My master
won't be back for a while,' 49 and he begins beating the other servants, party-
ing, and getting drunk? 50 The master will return unannounced and un-
expected, 51 and he will cut the servant to pieces and assign him a place with
the hypocrites. In that place there will be weeping and gnashing of teeth.

Parable of the Ten Bridesmaids

25 "Then the Kingdom of Heaven will be like ten bridesmaids* who
took their lamps and went to meet the bridegroom. 2 Five of them
were foolish, and five were wise. 3 The five who were foolish didn't take
enough olive oil for their lamps, 4 but the other five were wise enough to
take along extra oil. 5 When the bridegroom was delayed, they all became
drowsy and fell asleep.

6 "At midnight they were roused by the shout, 'Look, the bridegroom is
coming! Come out and meet him!'

7 "All the bridesmaids got up and prepared their lamps. 8 Then the five
foolish ones asked the others, 'Please give us some of your oil because our
lamps are going out.'

24:30 See Dan 7:13. **24:31** Greek *from the four winds.* **24:34** Or *this age,* or *this nation.*
24:36 Some manuscripts do not include *or the Son himself.* **25:1** Or *virgins;* also in 25:7, 11.

9 "But the others replied, 'We don't have enough for all of us. Go to a shop and buy some for yourselves.'

10 "But while they were gone to buy oil, the bridegroom came. Then those who were ready went in with him to the marriage feast, and the door was locked. 11 Later, when the other five bridesmaids returned, they stood outside, calling, 'Lord! Lord! Open the door for us!'

12 "But he called back, 'Believe me, I don't know you!'

13 "So you, too, must keep watch! For you do not know the day or hour of my return.

Parable of the Three Servants

14 "Again, the Kingdom of Heaven can be illustrated by the story of a man going on a long trip. He called together his servants and entrusted his money to them while he was gone. 15 He gave five bags of silver* to one, two bags of silver to another, and one bag of silver to the last—dividing it in proportion to their abilities. He then left on his trip.

16 "The servant who received the five bags of silver began to invest the money and earned five more. 17 The servant with two bags of silver also went to work and earned two more. 18 But the servant who received the one bag of silver dug a hole in the ground and hid the master's money.

19 "After a long time their master returned from his trip and called them to give an account of how they had used his money. 20 The servant to whom he had entrusted the five bags of silver came forward with five more and said, 'Master, you gave me five bags of silver to invest, and I have earned five more.'

21 "The master was full of praise. 'Well done, my good and faithful servant. You have been faithful in handling this small amount, so now I will give you many more responsibilities. Let's celebrate together!*'

22 "The servant who had received the two bags of silver came forward and said, 'Master, you gave me two bags of silver to invest, and I have earned two more.'

23 "The master said, 'Well done, my good and faithful servant. You have been faithful in handling this small amount, so now I will give you many more responsibilities. Let's celebrate together!'

24 "Then the servant with the one bag of silver came and said, 'Master, I knew you were a harsh man, harvesting crops you didn't plant and gathering crops you didn't cultivate. 25 I was afraid I would lose your money, so I hid it in the earth. Look, here is your money back.'

26 "But the master replied, 'You wicked and lazy servant! If you knew I harvested crops I didn't plant and gathered crops I didn't cultivate, 27 why didn't you deposit my money in the bank? At least I could have gotten some interest on it.'

28 "Then he ordered, 'Take the money from this servant, and give it to the one with the ten bags of silver. 29 To those who use well what they are given, even more will be given, and they will have an abundance. But from those who do nothing, even what little they have will be taken away. 30 Now throw this useless servant into outer darkness, where there will be weeping and gnashing of teeth.'

25:15 Greek *talents;* also throughout the story. A talent is equal to 75 pounds or 34 kilograms.
25:21 Greek *Enter into the joy of your master* [or *your Lord*]; also in 25:23.

Patterns I see in this text

Make a Difference

25:31-46

Being and Seeing Jesus

You are in a privileged role. You get to represent Jesus today. You! In your unique circumstances, with your unique character and gifts, you can act on behalf of Jesus to others through acts of service. Jesus said that when you follow him, you become part of his body, which is the church. In effect, with the Holy Spirit working through your actions, you become the hands and feet of the Savior.

Not only do you have this great responsibility to be like Jesus to the world, but you also have the calling to see him in others. Jesus wants you to see where he is, what he is doing, and whom he is with. He says repeatedly that he is with those who desperately need him. When you serve people, you are serving Jesus himself. In fact, Jesus identifies himself with the humble, and he empowers you to be humble with him. Look for him today. Be with him. Act with his love.

Difference Maker

Think of someone you know who has one of the needs Jesus mentioned in Matthew 25:35-36. Figure out a way to serve that person today.

Make a Difference

25:41-46

Oops!

"Oops. Didn't know I was supposed to do that." Picture saying that to your teacher after missing something really important.

Then imagine hearing yourself say, "Uh, yeah, it's not really my fault because I didn't even know about it. So...no big deal." Yeah, right.

The Final Judgment

31"But when the Son of Man* comes in his glory, and all the angels with him,
then he will sit upon his glorious throne. 32All the nations* will be gathered
in his presence, and he will separate the people as a shepherd separates the
sheep from the goats. 33He will place the sheep at his right hand and the
goats at his left.

34"Then the King will say to those on his right, 'Come, you who are blessed
by my Father, inherit the Kingdom prepared for you from the creation of the
world. 35For I was hungry, and you fed me. I was thirsty, and you gave me a
drink. I was a stranger, and you invited me into your home. 36I was naked,
and you gave me clothing. I was sick, and you cared for me. I was in prison,
and you visited me.'

37"Then these righteous ones will reply, 'Lord, when did we ever see you
hungry and feed you? Or thirsty and give you something to drink? 38Or a
stranger and show you hospitality? Or naked and give you clothing? 39When
did we ever see you sick or in prison and visit you?'

40"And the King will say, 'I tell you the truth, when you did it to one of the
least of these my brothers and sisters,* you were doing it to me!'

41"Then the King will turn to those on the left and say, 'Away with you,
you cursed ones, into the eternal fire prepared for the devil and his demons.*
42For I was hungry, and you didn't feed me. I was thirsty, and you didn't give
me a drink. 43I was a stranger, and you didn't invite me into your home. I
was naked, and you didn't give me clothing. I was sick and in prison, and
you didn't visit me.'

44"Then they will reply, 'Lord, when did we ever see you hungry or thirsty
or a stranger or naked or sick or in prison, and not help you?'

45"And he will answer, 'I tell you the truth, when you refused to help the
least of these my brothers and sisters, you were refusing to help me.'

46"And they will go away into eternal punishment, but the righteous will
go into eternal life."

The Plot to Kill Jesus

26 When Jesus had finished saying all these things, he said to his dis-
ciples, 2"As you know, Passover begins in two days, and the Son of
Man* will be handed over to be crucified."

3At that same time the leading priests and elders were meeting at the
residence of Caiaphas, the high priest, 4plotting how to capture Jesus secretly
and kill him. 5"But not during the Passover celebration," they agreed, "or
the people may riot."

Jesus Anointed at Bethany

6Meanwhile, Jesus was in Bethany at the home of Simon, a man who had pre-
viously had leprosy. 7While he was eating,* a woman came in with a beautiful
alabaster jar of expensive perfume and poured it over his head.

8The disciples were indignant when they saw this. "What a waste!" they
said. 9"It could have been sold for a high price and the money given to the
poor."

10But Jesus, aware of this, replied, "Why criticize this woman for doing

25:31 "Son of Man" is a title Jesus used for himself. 25:32 Or *peoples.* 25:40 Greek *my brothers.* 25:41 Greek *his angels.* 26:2 "Son of Man" is a title Jesus used for himself. 26:7 Or *reclining.*

such a good thing to me? 11 You will always have the poor among you, but
you will not always have me. 12 She has poured this perfume on me to pre-
pare my body for burial. 13 I tell you the truth, wherever the Good News is
preached throughout the world, this woman's deed will be remembered
and discussed."

Judas Agrees to Betray Jesus

14 Then Judas Iscariot, one of the twelve disciples, went to the leading priests
15 and asked, "How much will you pay me to betray Jesus to you?" And they
gave him thirty pieces of silver. 16 From that time on, Judas began looking
for an opportunity to betray Jesus.

The Last Supper

17 On the first day of the Festival of Unleavened Bread, the disciples came
to Jesus and asked, "Where do you want us to prepare the Passover meal
for you?"

18 "As you go into the city," he told them, "you will see a certain man. Tell
him, 'The Teacher says: My time has come, and I will eat the Passover meal
with my disciples at your house.'" 19 So the disciples did as Jesus told them
and prepared the Passover meal there.

20 When it was evening, Jesus sat down at the table* with the Twelve.
21 While they were eating, he said, "I tell you the truth, one of you will be-
tray me."

22 Greatly distressed, each one asked in turn, "Am I the one, Lord?"

23 He replied, "One of you who has just eaten from this bowl with me will
betray me. 24 For the Son of Man must die, as the Scriptures declared long
ago. But how terrible it will be for the one who betrays him. It would be far
better for that man if he had never been born!"

25 Judas, the one who would betray him, also asked, "Rabbi, am I the one?"
And Jesus told him, "You have said it."

26 As they were eating, Jesus took some bread and blessed it. Then he broke
it in pieces and gave it to the disciples, saying, "Take this and eat it, for this
is my body."

27 And he took a cup of wine and gave thanks to God for it. He gave it to
them and said, "Each of you drink from it, 28 for this is my blood, which
confirms the covenant* between God and his people. It is poured out as a
sacrifice to forgive the sins of many. 29 Mark my words—I will not drink
wine again until the day I drink it new with you in my Father's Kingdom."

30 Then they sang a hymn and went out to the Mount of Olives.

Jesus Predicts Peter's Denial

31 On the way, Jesus told them, "Tonight all of you will desert me. For the
Scriptures say,

'God will strike* the Shepherd,
and the sheep of the flock will be scattered.'

32 But after I have been raised from the dead, I will go ahead of you to Galilee
and meet you there."

26:20 Or *Jesus reclined.* **26:28** Some manuscripts read *the new covenant.* **26:31** Greek *I will strike.* Zech 13:7.

That project was assigned to you, and you were supposed to get it done. Sorry, but your teacher is not going to be very happy with you.

At the end of your life, imagine feeling fine about all the good stuff that you did, but then Jesus informs you that you missed several significant projects. There were some people you passed by whom you could have helped. There were times when you didn't defend someone who was being hurt. There were kind words you could have said, doors you could have held open, and patience you could have given. Oh, and then there was all the time you could have spent praying for people, but you played games instead.

Difference Maker

Be attentive to what you can do for others today.

Question **26:13**

Jesus said that wherever the good news is preached throughout the world, this woman's deeds would be remembered and discussed. Why was Jesus himself so affected by this woman's actions? What does Jesus hope we will learn from discussing her actions?

33 Peter declared, "Even if everyone else deserts you, I will never desert
you."
34 Jesus replied, "I tell you the truth, Peter—this very night, before the
rooster crows, you will deny three times that you even know me."
35 "No!" Peter insisted. "Even if I have to die with you, I will never deny
you!" And all the other disciples vowed the same.

Jesus Prays in Gethsemane

36 Then Jesus went with them to the olive grove called Gethsemane, and he
said, "Sit here while I go over there to pray." 37 He took Peter and Zebedee's
two sons, James and John, and he became anguished and distressed. 38 He
told them, "My soul is crushed with grief to the point of death. Stay here
and keep watch with me."
39 He went on a little farther and bowed with his face to the ground, pray-
ing, "My Father! If it is possible, let this cup of suffering be taken away from
me. Yet I want your will to be done, not mine."
40 Then he returned to the disciples and found them asleep. He said to
Peter, "Couldn't you watch with me even one hour? 41 Keep watch and pray,
so that you will not give in to temptation. For the spirit is willing, but the
body is weak!"
42 Then Jesus left them a second time and prayed, "My Father! If this cup
cannot be taken away* unless I drink it, your will be done." 43 When he returned
to them again, he found them sleeping, for they couldn't keep their eyes open.
44 So he went to pray a third time, saying the same things again. 45 Then
he came to the disciples and said, "Go ahead and sleep. Have your rest. But
look—the time has come. The Son of Man is betrayed into the hands of sin-
ners. 46 Up, let's be going. Look, my betrayer is here!"

Jesus Is Betrayed and Arrested

47 And even as Jesus said this, Judas, one of the twelve disciples, arrived with
a crowd of men armed with swords and clubs. They had been sent by the
leading priests and elders of the people. 48 The traitor, Judas, had given them
a prearranged signal: "You will know which one to arrest when I greet him
with a kiss." 49 So Judas came straight to Jesus. "Greetings, Rabbi!" he ex-
claimed and gave him the kiss.
50 Jesus said, "My friend, go ahead and do what you have come for."
Then the others grabbed Jesus and arrested him. 51 But one of the men
with Jesus pulled out his sword and struck the high priest's slave, slashing
off his ear.
52 "Put away your sword," Jesus told him. "Those who use the sword will
die by the sword. 53 Don't you realize that I could ask my Father for thou-
sands* of angels to protect us, and he would send them instantly? 54 But if I
did, how would the Scriptures be fulfilled that describe what must happen
now?"
55 Then Jesus said to the crowd, "Am I some dangerous revolutionary, that
you come with swords and clubs to arrest me? Why didn't you arrest me in
the Temple? I was there teaching every day. 56 But this is all happening to
fulfill the words of the prophets as recorded in the Scriptures." At that point,
all the disciples deserted him and fled.

26:42 Greek *If this cannot pass.* **26:53** Greek *twelve legions.*

Jesus before the Council
57Then the people who had arrested Jesus led him to the home of Caiaphas, the high priest, where the teachers of religious law and the elders had gathered. 58Meanwhile, Peter followed him at a distance and came to the high priest's courtyard. He went in and sat with the guards and waited to see how it would all end.

59Inside, the leading priests and the entire high council* were trying to find witnesses who would lie about Jesus, so they could put him to death. 60But even though they found many who agreed to give false witness, they could not use anyone's testimony. Finally, two men came forward 61who declared, "This man said, 'I am able to destroy the Temple of God and rebuild it in three days.'"

62Then the high priest stood up and said to Jesus, "Well, aren't you going to answer these charges? What do you have to say for yourself?" 63But Jesus remained silent. Then the high priest said to him, "I demand in the name of the living God—tell us if you are the Messiah, the Son of God."

64Jesus replied, "You have said it. And in the future you will see the Son of Man seated in the place of power at God's right hand* and coming on the clouds of heaven."*

65Then the high priest tore his clothing to show his horror and said, "Blasphemy! Why do we need other witnesses? You have all heard his blasphemy. 66What is your verdict?"

"Guilty!" they shouted. "He deserves to die!"

67Then they began to spit in Jesus' face and beat him with their fists. And some slapped him, 68jeering, "Prophesy to us, you Messiah! Who hit you that time?"

Question 26:62–65

When Jesus confirmed his question, Caiaphas responded not with awe but with horror. Why didn't Caiaphas accept Jesus for who he was?

Peter Denies Jesus
69Meanwhile, Peter was sitting outside in the courtyard. A servant girl came over and said to him, "You were one of those with Jesus the Galilean."

70But Peter denied it in front of everyone. "I don't know what you're talking about," he said.

71Later, out by the gate, another servant girl noticed him and said to those standing around, "This man was with Jesus of Nazareth.*"

72Again Peter denied it, this time with an oath. "I don't even know the man," he said.

73A little later some of the other bystanders came over to Peter and said, "You must be one of them; we can tell by your Galilean accent."

74Peter swore, "A curse on me if I'm lying—I don't know the man!" And immediately the rooster crowed.

75Suddenly, Jesus' words flashed through Peter's mind: "Before the rooster crows, you will deny three times that you even know me." And he went away, weeping bitterly.

Judas Hangs Himself
27 Very early in the morning the leading priests and the elders of the people met again to lay plans for putting Jesus to death. 2Then they bound him, led him away, and took him to Pilate, the Roman governor.

3When Judas, who had betrayed him, realized that Jesus had been

26:59 Greek *the Sanhedrin.* **26:64a** Greek *seated at the right hand of the power.* See Ps 110:1. **26:64b** See Dan 7:13. **26:71** Or *Jesus the Nazarene.*

Question 27:20-25

How can a "mob mentality" catch so many people in a growing swell of misguided decisions and behaviors? If you had been there, what would it have taken for you to avoid getting swept up by the mob?

condemned to die, he was filled with remorse. So he took the thirty pieces
of silver back to the leading priests and the elders. 4 "I have sinned," he de-
clared, "for I have betrayed an innocent man."

"What do we care?" they retorted. "That's your problem."

5 Then Judas threw the silver coins down in the Temple and went out and
hanged himself.

6 The leading priests picked up the coins. "It wouldn't be right to put this
money in the Temple treasury," they said, "since it was payment for mur-
der."* 7 After some discussion they finally decided to buy the potter's field,
and they made it into a cemetery for foreigners. 8 That is why the field is still
called the Field of Blood. 9 This fulfilled the prophecy of Jeremiah that says,

"They took* the thirty pieces of silver—
the price at which he was valued by the people of Israel,
10 and purchased the potter's field,
as the LORD directed.*"

Jesus' Trial before Pilate

11 Now Jesus was standing before Pilate, the Roman governor. "Are you the
king of the Jews?" the governor asked him.

Jesus replied, "You have said it."

12 But when the leading priests and the elders made their accusations
against him, Jesus remained silent. 13 "Don't you hear all these charges they
are bringing against you?" Pilate demanded. 14 But Jesus made no response
to any of the charges, much to the governor's surprise.

15 Now it was the governor's custom each year during the Passover celebra-
tion to release one prisoner to the crowd—anyone they wanted. 16 This year
there was a notorious prisoner, a man named Barabbas.* 17 As the crowds gath-
ered before Pilate's house that morning, he asked them, "Which one do you
want me to release to you—Barabbas, or Jesus who is called the Messiah?"
18 (He knew very well that the religious leaders had arrested Jesus out of envy.)

19 Just then, as Pilate was sitting on the judgment seat, his wife sent him
this message: "Leave that innocent man alone. I suffered through a terrible
nightmare about him last night."

20 Meanwhile, the leading priests and the elders persuaded the crowd to
ask for Barabbas to be released and for Jesus to be put to death. 21 So the gov-
ernor asked again, "Which of these two do you want me to release to you?"

The crowd shouted back, "Barabbas!"

22 Pilate responded, "Then what should I do with Jesus who is called the
Messiah?"

They shouted back, "Crucify him!"

23 "Why?" Pilate demanded. "What crime has he committed?"

But the mob roared even louder, "Crucify him!"

24 Pilate saw that he wasn't getting anywhere and that a riot was develop-
ing. So he sent for a bowl of water and washed his hands before the crowd,
saying, "I am innocent of this man's blood. The responsibility is yours!"

25 And all the people yelled back, "We will take responsibility for his
death—we and our children!"*

27:6 Greek *since it is the price for blood.* 27:9 Or *I took.* 27:9-10 Greek *as the LORD directed me.* Zech 11:12-13; Jer 32:6-9. 27:16 Some manuscripts read *Jesus Barabbas;* also in 27:17. 27:25 Greek *"His blood be on us and on our children."*

26 So Pilate released Barabbas to them. He ordered Jesus flogged with a
lead-tipped whip, then turned him over to the Roman soldiers to be crucified.

The Soldiers Mock Jesus

27 Some of the governor's soldiers took Jesus into their headquarters* and
called out the entire regiment. 28 They stripped him and put a scarlet robe
on him. 29 They wove thorn branches into a crown and put it on his head, and
they placed a reed stick in his right hand as a scepter. Then they knelt before
him in mockery and taunted, "Hail! King of the Jews!" 30 And they spit on
him and grabbed the stick and struck him on the head with it. 31 When they
were finally tired of mocking him, they took off the robe and put his own
clothes on him again. Then they led him away to be crucified.

The Crucifixion

32 Along the way, they came across a man named Simon, who was from Cy-
rene,* and the soldiers forced him to carry Jesus' cross. 33 And they went out
to a place called Golgotha (which means "Place of the Skull"). 34 The soldiers
gave Jesus wine mixed with bitter gall, but when he had tasted it, he refused
to drink it.

35 After they had nailed him to the cross, the soldiers gambled for his
clothes by throwing dice.* 36 Then they sat around and kept guard as he
hung there. 37 A sign was fastened above Jesus' head, announcing the charge
against him. It read: "This is Jesus, the King of the Jews." 38 Two revolutionar-
ies* were crucified with him, one on his right and one on his left.

39 The people passing by shouted abuse, shaking their heads in mockery.
40 "Look at you now!" they yelled at him. "You said you were going to destroy
the Temple and rebuild it in three days. Well then, if you are the Son of God,
save yourself and come down from the cross!"

41 The leading priests, the teachers of religious law, and the elders also
mocked Jesus. 42 "He saved others," they scoffed, "but he can't save himself!
So he is the King of Israel, is he? Let him come down from the cross right now,
and we will believe in him! 43 He trusted God, so let God rescue him now if
he wants him! For he said, 'I am the Son of God.'" 44 Even the revolutionaries
who were crucified with him ridiculed him in the same way.

The Death of Jesus

45 At noon, darkness fell across the whole land until three o'clock. 46 At about
three o'clock, Jesus called out with a loud voice, *"Eli, Eli,* lema sabachthani?"*
which means "My God, my God, why have you abandoned me?"*

47 Some of the bystanders misunderstood and thought he was calling for
the prophet Elijah. 48 One of them ran and filled a sponge with sour wine,
holding it up to him on a reed stick so he could drink. 49 But the rest said,
"Wait! Let's see whether Elijah comes to save him."*

50 Then Jesus shouted out again, and he released his spirit. 51 At that mo-
ment the curtain in the sanctuary of the Temple was torn in two, from top to
bottom. The earth shook, rocks split apart, 52 and tombs opened. The bodies
of many godly men and women who had died were raised from the dead.

27:27 Or *into the Praetorium.* 27:32 *Cyrene* was a city in northern Africa. 27:35 Greek *by casting lots.* A few late manuscripts add *This fulfilled the word of the prophet: "They divided my garments among themselves and cast lots for my robe."* See Ps 22:18. 27:38 Or *criminals;* also in 27:44. 27:46a Some manuscripts read *Eloi, Eloi.* 27:46b Ps 22:1. 27:49 Some manuscripts add *And another took a spear and pierced his side, and out flowed water and blood.* Compare John 19:34.

53 They left the cemetery after Jesus' resurrection, went into the holy city of
Jerusalem, and appeared to many people.
54 The Roman officer* and the other soldiers at the crucifixion were ter-
rified by the earthquake and all that had happened. They said, "This man
truly was the Son of God!"
55 And many women who had come from Galilee with Jesus to care for
him were watching from a distance. 56 Among them were Mary Magdalene,
Mary (the mother of James and Joseph), and the mother of James and John,
the sons of Zebedee.

The Burial of Jesus

57 As evening approached, Joseph, a rich man from Arimathea who had be-
come a follower of Jesus, 58 went to Pilate and asked for Jesus' body. And Pilate
issued an order to release it to him. 59 Joseph took the body and wrapped
it in a long sheet of clean linen cloth. 60 He placed it in his own new tomb,
which had been carved out of the rock. Then he rolled a great stone across the
entrance and left. 61 Both Mary Magdalene and the other Mary were sitting
across from the tomb and watching.

The Guard at the Tomb

62 The next day, on the Sabbath,* the leading priests and Pharisees went to
see Pilate. 63 They told him, "Sir, we remember what that deceiver once said
while he was still alive: 'After three days I will rise from the dead.' 64 So we
request that you seal the tomb until the third day. This will prevent his
disciples from coming and stealing his body and then telling everyone he
was raised from the dead! If that happens, we'll be worse off than we were
at first."
65 Pilate replied, "Take guards and secure it the best you can." 66 So they
sealed the tomb and posted guards to protect it.

The Resurrection

28 Early on Sunday morning,* as the new day was dawning, Mary Mag-
dalene and the other Mary went out to visit the tomb.
2 Suddenly there was a great earthquake! For an angel of the Lord came
down from heaven, rolled aside the stone, and sat on it. 3 His face shone like
lightning, and his clothing was as white as snow. 4 The guards shook with
fear when they saw him, and they fell into a dead faint.
5 Then the angel spoke to the women. "Don't be afraid!" he said. "I know
you are looking for Jesus, who was crucified. 6 He isn't here! He is risen from
the dead, just as he said would happen. Come, see where his body was lying.
7 And now, go quickly and tell his disciples that he has risen from the dead,
and he is going ahead of you to Galilee. You will see him there. Remember
what I have told you."
8 The women ran quickly from the tomb. They were very frightened but
also filled with great joy, and they rushed to give the disciples the angel's
message. 9 And as they went, Jesus met them and greeted them. And they
ran to him, grasped his feet, and worshiped him. 10 Then Jesus said to them,
"Don't be afraid! Go tell my brothers to leave for Galilee, and they will see
me there."

27:54 Greek *The centurion.* 27:62 Or *On the next day, which is after the Preparation.* 28:1 Greek *After the Sabbath, on the first day of the week.*

Make a Difference

28:1–10

Quake

The tomb that held Jesus didn't know what hit it! It was a new tomb, a respectful burial spot offered by a wealthy man near a garden, a peaceful place. Then the earthquake hit. The entrance to the tomb, a huge stone chiseled round, was rolled aside. The new tomb, which had been used, was once again available for rent. Jesus had risen from the dead.

The first people on the scene were guards who had been stationed there to keep things from getting shook up. The tremor, not to mention the angel of the Lord who seemed to be casually sitting on the stone, made the guards quake in their boots. The second group of people on the scene were women who were close followers of Jesus. They spoke to the angel, who informed them that Jesus had been raised from the dead just as he said would happen. Instead of fainting like the guards, they turned their fear into great joy and ran to tell others the good news: Jesus had risen!

Difference Maker

In terms of your awareness of Jesus, do you or the people around you need a quake to shake you up a bit? Use this question as a filter throughout your day.

The Report of the Guard

11 As the women were on their way, some of the guards went into the city and
told the leading priests what had happened. 12 A meeting with the elders
was called, and they decided to give the soldiers a large bribe. 13 They told
the soldiers, "You must say, 'Jesus' disciples came during the night while we
were sleeping, and they stole his body.' 14 If the governor hears about it, we'll
stand up for you so you won't get in trouble." 15 So the guards accepted the
bribe and said what they were told to say. Their story spread widely among
the Jews, and they still tell it today.

The Great Commission

16 Then the eleven disciples left for Galilee, going to the mountain where
Jesus had told them to go. 17 When they saw him, they worshiped him—but
some of them doubted!

18 Jesus came and told his disciples, "I have been given all authority in
heaven and on earth. 19 Therefore, go and make disciples of all the nations,*
baptizing them in the name of the Father and the Son and the Holy Spirit.
20 Teach these new disciples to obey all the commands I have given you. And
be sure of this: I am with you always, even to the end of the age."

28:19 Or *all peoples.*

Make a Difference

28:18-20

Make Disciples

The word *disciple* means "learner," so a disciple of Jesus is a learner of Jesus. No matter how young or old someone is, being a learner of Jesus is the goal of that person's life. A Christian is never a know-it-all; rather, a follower of Jesus is in a continual process of absorbing and practicing the teachings of Rabbi Jesus.

One of the most important things a disciple of Jesus learns is this: disciples make disciples. Learners of Jesus produce more learners of Jesus. This calling to make other disciples has come to be known as the Great Commission. It is the greatest difference-making, history-changing, boundary-breaking strategy this world has ever known. People at all stages of learning have discovered that knowing Jesus is the best thing anyone could possibly do. From generation to generation and geography to geography, people have come to learn about Jesus and passed on their knowledge.

Difference Maker

Be bold. As a learner of Jesus, whom should you influence toward Jesus today?

Mark Introduction

Near the end of the book of Mark, when Jesus was arrested, there was a peculiar comment about a young man who was at the scene. The mob that had led the revolt against Jesus noticed this young man and turned to snare him too. The text says that when they grabbed him, this young man "slipped out of his shirt and ran away naked" (Mark 14:51–52). For almost two thousand years, people have speculated that this naked, young escape artist was Mark.

In that moment, Mark had been in a hurry to run away from the danger of following Jesus. He had been mesmerized by Jesus but had panicked in fear for his life. Now, years later, Mark was in a hurry to tell people the "Good News about Jesus the Messiah, the Son of God" (1:1). Mark's eyewitness version of the life of Jesus is a fast-paced, power-packed rocket ship, fully fueled to launch you into a life-changing relationship with Jesus.

This book is the first of four Gospels (Matthew, Mark, Luke, and John) to have been written. The Gospels are the four books that tell all about the events of the "good news" of Jesus. You might notice that much of Mark's content was used in the framework of two of the other Gospels (Matthew and Luke). Historians also speculate that much of Mark's content is likely to have come from Peter's perspective, offering unique insight into the mind of Jesus' punchiest disciple. Maybe that explains the deep urgency and passionate heart of this book.

Mark presented Jesus as a disruptive force to your unfulfilled life. Jesus spits in your eyes and says, "Look! Why are you going that way? Follow me. You're lost over there. Follow me." The gut-check question you must answer is whether you'll immediately do just that.

Story Arcs

- **Isaiah**
- **The Disciples**
- **God**
- **Simon of Cyrene**

Mark

John the Baptist Prepares the Way

1 This is the Good News about Jesus the Messiah, the Son of God.* It began
2 just as the prophet Isaiah had written:

"Look, I am sending my messenger ahead of you,
and he will prepare your way.*
3 He is a voice shouting in the wilderness,
'Prepare the way for the LORD's coming!
Clear the road for him!'*"

4 This messenger was John the Baptist. He was in the wilderness and preached
that people should be baptized to show that they had repented of their sins
and turned to God to be forgiven. 5 All of Judea, including all the people of
Jerusalem, went out to see and hear John. And when they confessed their
sins, he baptized them in the Jordan River. 6 His clothes were woven from
coarse camel hair, and he wore a leather belt around his waist. For food he
ate locusts and wild honey.

7 John announced: "Someone is coming soon who is greater than I am—so
much greater that I'm not even worthy to stoop down like a slave and untie
the straps of his sandals. 8 I baptize you with* water, but he will baptize you
with the Holy Spirit!"

The Baptism and Temptation of Jesus

9 One day Jesus came from Nazareth in Galilee, and John baptized him in the
Jordan River. 10 As Jesus came up out of the water, he saw the heavens split-
ting apart and the Holy Spirit descending on him* like a dove. 11 And a voice
from heaven said, "You are my dearly loved Son, and you bring me great joy."

12 The Spirit then compelled Jesus to go into the wilderness, 13 where he
was tempted by Satan for forty days. He was out among the wild animals,
and angels took care of him.

14 Later on, after John was arrested, Jesus went into Galilee, where he
preached God's Good News.* 15 "The time promised by God has come at
last!" he announced. "The Kingdom of God is near! Repent of your sins and
believe the Good News!"

The First Disciples

16 One day as Jesus was walking along the shore of the Sea of Galilee, he saw
Simon* and his brother Andrew throwing a net into the water, for they fished
for a living. 17 Jesus called out to them, "Come, follow me, and I will show you
how to fish for people!" 18 And they left their nets at once and followed him.

1:1 Some manuscripts do not include *the Son of God.* 1:2 Mal 3:1. 1:3 Isa 40:3 (Greek version). 1:8 Or *in;* also in 1:8b. 1:10 Or *toward him,* or *into him.* 1:14 Some manuscripts read *the Good News of the Kingdom of God.* 1:16 *Simon* is called "Peter" in 3:16 and thereafter.

Question 1:1

Mark cut straight to the point. This book is about Jesus. What do you learn about Jesus from the titles Mark uses here?

Make a Difference 1:9

Baptism

Baptism is a public demonstration of the forgiveness and new life that we have in Christ. It symbolizes that we are dead to our sin, washed clean of our sin, and raised to new life with Jesus.

Difference Maker

Have you been baptized? If not, talk to your pastor about being baptized to proclaim publicly what Jesus has done for you.

Story Arc 1:2-3

● Isaiah

Isaiah was a prophet who lived seven hundred years before Jesus was born. You can read the book by his name and read about him in several other places in the Old Testament. Why would it be significant that Mark started off his book mentioning this prophet who lived centuries before Jesus?

Mark 3:13-19 ►

Prayer 1:28

Jesus, I pray that news about you would spread quickly throughout the entire region around me. Amen.

Prayer 1:35

Lord, give me the courage to get up before daybreak tomorrow to pray. Amen.

19 A little farther up the shore Jesus saw Zebedee's sons, James and John, in
a boat repairing their nets. 20 He called them at once, and they also followed
him, leaving their father, Zebedee, in the boat with the hired men.

Jesus Casts Out an Evil Spirit

21 Jesus and his companions went to the town of Capernaum. When the Sab-
bath day came, he went into the synagogue and began to teach. 22 The people
were amazed at his teaching, for he taught with real authority—quite unlike
the teachers of religious law.

23 Suddenly, a man in the synagogue who was possessed by an evil* spirit
cried out, 24 "Why are you interfering with us, Jesus of Nazareth? Have you
come to destroy us? I know who you are—the Holy One of God!"

25 But Jesus reprimanded him. "Be quiet! Come out of the man," he or-
dered. 26 At that, the evil spirit screamed, threw the man into a convulsion,
and then came out of him.

27 Amazement gripped the audience, and they began to discuss what had
happened. "What sort of new teaching is this?" they asked excitedly. "It has
such authority! Even evil spirits obey his orders!" 28 The news about Jesus
spread quickly throughout the entire region of Galilee.

Jesus Heals Many People

29 After Jesus left the synagogue with James and John, they went to Simon
and Andrew's home. 30 Now Simon's mother-in-law was sick in bed with a
high fever. They told Jesus about her right away. 31 So he went to her bedside,
took her by the hand, and helped her sit up. Then the fever left her, and she
prepared a meal for them.

32 That evening after sunset, many sick and demon-possessed people were
brought to Jesus. 33 The whole town gathered at the door to watch. 34 So Jesus
healed many people who were sick with various diseases, and he cast out
many demons. But because the demons knew who he was, he did not allow
them to speak.

Jesus Preaches in Galilee

35 Before daybreak the next morning, Jesus got up and went out to an isolated
place to pray. 36 Later Simon and the others went out to find him. 37 When they
found him, they said, "Everyone is looking for you."

38 But Jesus replied, "We must go on to other towns as well, and I will
preach to them, too. That is why I came." 39 So he traveled throughout the
region of Galilee, preaching in the synagogues and casting out demons.

Jesus Heals a Man with Leprosy

40 A man with leprosy came and knelt in front of Jesus, begging to be healed.
"If you are willing, you can heal me and make me clean," he said.

41 Moved with compassion,* Jesus reached out and touched him. "I am will-
ing," he said. "Be healed!" 42 Instantly the leprosy disappeared, and the man
was healed. 43 Then Jesus sent him on his way with a stern warning: 44 "Don't
tell anyone about this. Instead, go to the priest and let him examine you. Take
along the offering required in the law of Moses for those who have been healed
of leprosy.* This will be a public testimony that you have been cleansed."

1:23 Greek *unclean;* also in 1:26, 27. 1:41 Some manuscripts read *Moved with anger.* 1:44 See Lev 14:2-32.

45 But the man went and spread the word, proclaiming to everyone what
had happened. As a result, large crowds soon surrounded Jesus, and he
couldn't publicly enter a town anywhere. He had to stay out in the secluded
places, but people from everywhere kept coming to him.

Jesus Heals a Paralyzed Man

2 When Jesus returned to Capernaum several days later, the news spread
quickly that he was back home. 2 Soon the house where he was staying
was so packed with visitors that there was no more room, even outside the
door. While he was preaching God's word to them, 3 four men arrived car-
rying a paralyzed man on a mat. 4 They couldn't bring him to Jesus because
of the crowd, so they dug a hole through the roof above his head. Then they
lowered the man on his mat, right down in front of Jesus. 5 Seeing their faith,
Jesus said to the paralyzed man, "My child, your sins are forgiven."

6 But some of the teachers of religious law who were sitting there thought
to themselves, 7 "What is he saying? This is blasphemy! Only God can for-
give sins!"

8 Jesus knew immediately what they were thinking, so he asked them,
"Why do you question this in your hearts? 9 Is it easier to say to the paralyzed
man 'Your sins are forgiven,' or 'Stand up, pick up your mat, and walk'? 10 So
I will prove to you that the Son of Man* has the authority on earth to forgive
sins." Then Jesus turned to the paralyzed man and said, 11 "Stand up, pick up
your mat, and go home!"

12 And the man jumped up, grabbed his mat, and walked out through
the stunned onlookers. They were all amazed and praised God, exclaiming,
"We've never seen anything like this before!"

Jesus Calls Levi (Matthew)

13 Then Jesus went out to the lakeshore again and taught the crowds that were
coming to him. 14 As he walked along, he saw Levi son of Alphaeus sitting at
his tax collector's booth. "Follow me and be my disciple," Jesus said to him.
So Levi got up and followed him.

15 Later, Levi invited Jesus and his disciples to his home as dinner guests,
along with many tax collectors and other disreputable sinners. (There were
many people of this kind among Jesus' followers.) 16 But when the teachers
of religious law who were Pharisees* saw him eating with tax collectors and
other sinners, they asked his disciples, "Why does he eat with such scum?*"

17 When Jesus heard this, he told them, "Healthy people don't need a doc-
tor—sick people do. I have come to call not those who think they are righ-
teous, but those who know they are sinners."

A Discussion about Fasting

18 Once when John's disciples and the Pharisees were fasting, some people
came to Jesus and asked, "Why don't your disciples fast like John's disciples
and the Pharisees do?"

19 Jesus replied, "Do wedding guests fast while celebrating with the
groom? Of course not. They can't fast while the groom is with them. 20 But
someday the groom will be taken away from them, and then they will fast.

21 "Besides, who would patch old clothing with new cloth? For the new

2:10 "Son of Man" is a title Jesus used for himself. **2:16a** Greek *the scribes of the Pharisees.*
2:16b Greek *with tax collectors and sinners?*

Question 2:8

How would you answer Jesus' question?

Make a Difference 2:14

Get Up and Follow

Levi (a.k.a. Matthew) was in the middle of doing something that didn't satisfy him. He longed for something better. He went home at night looking for that outlet to numb his feelings, to distract his emptiness, to temporarily help him escape. Then Jesus initiated: "Follow me." Matthew did. He got up and followed Jesus. He left his unfulfillment behind.

What are you doing that doesn't do it for you? What do you pursue that ultimately leaves you feeling empty, disappointed, and frustrated with your life and the direction it's going? Jesus is initiating. He says to you, "Follow me."

Difference Maker

If you have never done so, decide right now to get up and follow Jesus. Turn to the back of this Bible and pray through the section on "How to Accept Jesus as Your Lord and Savior."

patch would shrink and rip away from the old cloth, leaving an even bigger
tear than before.
22 "And no one puts new wine into old wineskins. For the wine would
burst the wineskins, and the wine and the skins would both be lost. New
wine calls for new wineskins."

A Discussion about the Sabbath

23 One Sabbath day as Jesus was walking through some grainfields, his disciples
began breaking off heads of grain to eat. 24 But the Pharisees said to Jesus,
"Look, why are they breaking the law by harvesting grain on the Sabbath?"
25 Jesus said to them, "Haven't you ever read in the Scriptures what David
did when he and his companions were hungry? 26 He went into the house of
God (during the days when Abiathar was high priest) and broke the law by
eating the sacred loaves of bread that only the priests are allowed to eat. He
also gave some to his companions."
27 Then Jesus said to them, "The Sabbath was made to meet the needs of
people, and not people to meet the requirements of the Sabbath. 28 So the
Son of Man is Lord, even over the Sabbath!"

Jesus Heals on the Sabbath

3 Jesus went into the synagogue again and noticed a man with a deformed
hand. 2 Since it was the Sabbath, Jesus' enemies watched him closely. If
he healed the man's hand, they planned to accuse him of working on the
Sabbath.
3 Jesus said to the man with the deformed hand, "Come and stand in front
of everyone." 4 Then he turned to his critics and asked, "Does the law permit
good deeds on the Sabbath, or is it a day for doing evil? Is this a day to save
life or to destroy it?" But they wouldn't answer him.
5 He looked around at them angrily and was deeply saddened by their hard
hearts. Then he said to the man, "Hold out your hand." So the man held out
his hand, and it was restored! 6 At once the Pharisees went away and met with
the supporters of Herod to plot how to kill Jesus.

Crowds Follow Jesus

7 Jesus went out to the lake with his disciples, and a large crowd followed
him. They came from all over Galilee, Judea, 8 Jerusalem, Idumea, from east
of the Jordan River, and even from as far north as Tyre and Sidon. The news
about his miracles had spread far and wide, and vast numbers of people
came to see him.
9 Jesus instructed his disciples to have a boat ready so the crowd would
not crush him. 10 He had healed many people that day, so all the sick people
eagerly pushed forward to touch him. 11 And whenever those possessed by
evil* spirits caught sight of him, the spirits would throw them to the ground
in front of him shrieking, "You are the Son of God!" 12 But Jesus sternly commanded the spirits not to reveal who he was.

Jesus Chooses the Twelve Apostles

13 Afterward Jesus went up on a mountain and called out the ones he wanted
to go with him. And they came to him. 14 Then he appointed twelve of them

3:11 Greek *unclean;* also in 3:30.

and called them his apostles.* They were to accompany him, and he would
send them out to preach, 15 giving them authority to cast out demons. 16 These
are the twelve he chose:

Simon (whom he named Peter),
17 James and John (the sons of Zebedee, but Jesus nicknamed them
"Sons of Thunder"*),
18 Andrew,
Philip,
Bartholomew,
Matthew,
Thomas,
James (son of Alphaeus),
Thaddaeus,
Simon (the zealot*),
19 Judas Iscariot (who later betrayed him).

Jesus and the Prince of Demons

20 One time Jesus entered a house, and the crowds began to gather again.
Soon he and his disciples couldn't even find time to eat. 21 When his family
heard what was happening, they tried to take him away. "He's out of his
mind," they said.

22 But the teachers of religious law who had arrived from Jerusalem said,
"He's possessed by Satan,* the prince of demons. That's where he gets the
power to cast out demons."

23 Jesus called them over and responded with an illustration. "How can
Satan cast out Satan?" he asked. 24 "A kingdom divided by civil war will
collapse. 25 Similarly, a family splintered by feuding will fall apart. 26 And
if Satan is divided and fights against himself, how can he stand? He would
never survive. 27 Let me illustrate this further. Who is powerful enough
to enter the house of a strong man and plunder his goods? Only some-
one even stronger—someone who could tie him up and then plunder
his house.

28 "I tell you the truth, all sin and blasphemy can be forgiven, 29 but anyone
who blasphemes the Holy Spirit will never be forgiven. This is a sin with
eternal consequences." 30 He told them this because they were saying, "He's
possessed by an evil spirit."

The True Family of Jesus

31 Then Jesus' mother and brothers came to see him. They stood outside and
sent word for him to come out and talk with them. 32 There was a crowd sit-
ting around Jesus, and someone said, "Your mother and your brothers* are
outside asking for you."

33 Jesus replied, "Who is my mother? Who are my brothers?" 34 Then
he looked at those around him and said, "Look, these are my mother
and brothers. 35 Anyone who does God's will is my brother and sister and
mother."

3:14 Some manuscripts do not include *and called them his apostles.* 3:17 Greek *whom he named Boanerges, which means Sons of Thunder.* 3:18 Greek *the Cananean,* an Aramaic term for Jewish nationalists. 3:22 Greek *Beelzeboul;* other manuscripts read *Beezeboul;* Latin version reads *Beelzebub.* 3:32 Some manuscripts add *and sisters.*

Question 3:31-35

This is a difficult teaching about whom Jesus defines as family. How does the "family" of God create a new network spanning time, geography, ethnicity, and language?

Story Arc 3:13-19

● The Disciples

Can you imagine being in this group? Some fishermen, some activists, some sold-out government workers, a betrayer, and some hotheaded Sons of Thunder! Challenge yourself to trace the activities and experiences of these first followers of Jesus. What happens to them in the next several books of the Bible? Do some research about what happens to them in the generation after Jesus' resurrection.

Mark 14:62 ►

Parable of the Farmer Scattering Seed

4 Once again Jesus began teaching by the lakeshore. A very large crowd
soon gathered around him, so he got into a boat. Then he sat in the boat
while all the people remained on the shore. 2He taught them by telling many
stories in the form of parables, such as this one:

3"Listen! A farmer went out to plant some seed. 4As he scattered it across
his field, some of the seed fell on a footpath, and the birds came and ate it.
5Other seed fell on shallow soil with underlying rock. The seed sprouted
quickly because the soil was shallow. 6But the plant soon wilted under the
hot sun, and since it didn't have deep roots, it died. 7Other seed fell among
thorns that grew up and choked out the tender plants so they produced
no grain. 8Still other seeds fell on fertile soil, and they sprouted, grew, and
produced a crop that was thirty, sixty, and even a hundred times as much as
had been planted!" 9Then he said, "Anyone with ears to hear should listen
and understand."

10Later, when Jesus was alone with the twelve disciples and with the others
who were gathered around, they asked him what the parables meant.

11He replied, "You are permitted to understand the secret* of the King-
dom of God. But I use parables for everything I say to outsiders, 12so that the
Scriptures might be fulfilled:

'When they see what I do,
they will learn nothing.
When they hear what I say,
they will not understand.
Otherwise, they will turn to me
and be forgiven.'*"

13Then Jesus said to them, "If you can't understand the meaning of this
parable, how will you understand all the other parables? 14The farmer plants
seed by taking God's word to others. 15The seed that fell on the footpath
represents those who hear the message, only to have Satan come at once
and take it away. 16The seed on the rocky soil represents those who hear the
message and immediately receive it with joy. 17But since they don't have deep
roots, they don't last long. They fall away as soon as they have problems or are
persecuted for believing God's word. 18The seed that fell among the thorns
represents others who hear God's word, 19but all too quickly the message is
crowded out by the worries of this life, the lure of wealth, and the desire for
other things, so no fruit is produced. 20And the seed that fell on good soil
represents those who hear and accept God's word and produce a harvest of
thirty, sixty, or even a hundred times as much as had been planted!"

Parable of the Lamp

21Then Jesus asked them, "Would anyone light a lamp and then put it under
a basket or under a bed? Of course not! A lamp is placed on a stand, where its
light will shine. 22For everything that is hidden will eventually be brought
into the open, and every secret will be brought to light. 23Anyone with ears
to hear should listen and understand."

24Then he added, "Pay close attention to what you hear. The closer you

4:11 Greek *mystery.* 4:12 Isa 6:9-10 (Greek version).

listen, the more understanding you will be given*—and you will receive
even more. 25To those who listen to my teaching, more understanding will
be given. But for those who are not listening, even what little understanding
they have will be taken away from them."

Parable of the Growing Seed

26Jesus also said, "The Kingdom of God is like a farmer who scatters seed on
the ground. 27Night and day, while he's asleep or awake, the seed sprouts and
grows, but he does not understand how it happens. 28The earth produces the
crops on its own. First a leaf blade pushes through, then the heads of wheat
are formed, and finally the grain ripens. 29And as soon as the grain is ready,
the farmer comes and harvests it with a sickle, for the harvest time has come."

Parable of the Mustard Seed

30Jesus said, "How can I describe the Kingdom of God? What story should
I use to illustrate it? 31It is like a mustard seed planted in the ground. It is
the smallest of all seeds, 32but it becomes the largest of all garden plants; it
grows long branches, and birds can make nests in its shade."

33Jesus used many similar stories and illustrations to teach the people as
much as they could understand. 34In fact, in his public ministry he never
taught without using parables; but afterward, when he was alone with his
disciples, he explained everything to them.

Jesus Calms the Storm

35As evening came, Jesus said to his disciples, "Let's cross to the other side of
the lake." 36So they took Jesus in the boat and started out, leaving the crowds
behind (although other boats followed). 37But soon a fierce storm came up.
High waves were breaking into the boat, and it began to fill with water.

38Jesus was sleeping at the back of the boat with his head on a cushion.
The disciples woke him up, shouting, "Teacher, don't you care that we're
going to drown?"

39When Jesus woke up, he rebuked the wind and said to the waves, "Si-
lence! Be still!" Suddenly the wind stopped, and there was a great calm.
40Then he asked them, "Why are you afraid? Do you still have no faith?"

41The disciples were absolutely terrified. "Who is this man?" they asked
each other. "Even the wind and waves obey him!"

Jesus Heals a Demon-Possessed Man

5 So they arrived at the other side of the lake, in the region of the Gera-
senes.* 2When Jesus climbed out of the boat, a man possessed by an evil*
spirit came out from the tombs to meet him. 3This man lived in the burial
caves and could no longer be restrained, even with a chain. 4Whenever he was
put into chains and shackles—as he often was—he snapped the chains from
his wrists and smashed the shackles. No one was strong enough to subdue
him. 5Day and night he wandered among the burial caves and in the hills,
howling and cutting himself with sharp stones.

6When Jesus was still some distance away, the man saw him, ran to meet
him, and bowed low before him. 7With a shriek, he screamed, "Why are you

4:24 Or *The measure you give will be the measure you get back.* 5:1 Other manuscripts read *Gadarenes;* still others read *Gergesenes.* See Matt 8:28; Luke 8:26. 5:2 Greek *unclean;* also in 5:8, 13.

Question **4:33-34**

Go to Psalm 78:2. The Bible encourages us to be creative and surprising in the way that we catch people's attention. How do parables (like the ones Jesus uses in Mark 4) help us share God's truth in ways that connect with people and make them think?

Make a Difference

4:35-41

Wake Up

Have you ever wondered how Jesus woke up? Did he startle awake? Did he slowly yawn and stretch out his arms? Did he rub his eyes, grumble his voice, and gruff his shoulders? Do you think he smiled a sly smile, as if he knew something amazing were going to happen? Do you think he wanted to hit his snooze button a few times?

One time Jesus woke up because his disciples frantically awakened him. They were in a boat, and the boat was in the middle of the sea, and the sea was in the middle of a storm. Jesus wasn't worried, however. Maybe he enjoyed the sensation of danger out there on the sea. The Creator of the universe had the opportunity to ride in his own storm. Jesus wasn't shocked by what was going on when he awoke. The chaos didn't overwhelm him. That day, just like any other day, was completely in his control.

Difference Maker

The next time you wake up, trust the circumstances of your day to Jesus.

Question **5:30**

Do you think Jesus really didn't know? Why do you think he asked this question?

interfering with me, Jesus, Son of the Most High God? In the name of God,
I beg you, don't torture me!" 8For Jesus had already said to the spirit, "Come
out of the man, you evil spirit."
9Then Jesus demanded, "What is your name?"
And he replied, "My name is Legion, because there are many of us inside
this man." 10Then the evil spirits begged him again and again not to send
them to some distant place.
11There happened to be a large herd of pigs feeding on the hillside nearby.
12"Send us into those pigs," the spirits begged. "Let us enter them."
13So Jesus gave them permission. The evil spirits came out of the man and
entered the pigs, and the entire herd of about 2,000 pigs plunged down the
steep hillside into the lake and drowned in the water.
14The herdsmen fled to the nearby town and the surrounding country-
side, spreading the news as they ran. People rushed out to see what had
happened. 15A crowd soon gathered around Jesus, and they saw the man
who had been possessed by the legion of demons. He was sitting there fully
clothed and perfectly sane, and they were all afraid. 16Then those who had
seen what happened told the others about the demon-possessed man and
the pigs. 17And the crowd began pleading with Jesus to go away and leave
them alone.
18As Jesus was getting into the boat, the man who had been demon pos-
sessed begged to go with him. 19But Jesus said, "No, go home to your family,
and tell them everything the Lord has done for you and how merciful he has
been." 20So the man started off to visit the Ten Towns* of that region and
began to proclaim the great things Jesus had done for him; and everyone
was amazed at what he told them.

Jesus Heals in Response to Faith

21Jesus got into the boat again and went back to the other side of the lake,
where a large crowd gathered around him on the shore. 22Then a leader of
the local synagogue, whose name was Jairus, arrived. When he saw Jesus,
he fell at his feet, 23pleading fervently with him. "My little daughter is
dying," he said. "Please come and lay your hands on her; heal her so she
can live."
24Jesus went with him, and all the people followed, crowding around him.
25A woman in the crowd had suffered for twelve years with constant bleed-
ing. 26She had suffered a great deal from many doctors, and over the years
she had spent everything she had to pay them, but she had gotten no better.
In fact, she had gotten worse. 27She had heard about Jesus, so she came up
behind him through the crowd and touched his robe. 28For she thought to
herself, "If I can just touch his robe, I will be healed." 29Immediately the
bleeding stopped, and she could feel in her body that she had been healed
of her terrible condition.
30Jesus realized at once that healing power had gone out from him, so he
turned around in the crowd and asked, "Who touched my robe?"
31His disciples said to him, "Look at this crowd pressing around you. How
can you ask, 'Who touched me?'"
32But he kept on looking around to see who had done it. 33Then the fright-
ened woman, trembling at the realization of what had happened to her,

5:20 Greek *Decapolis.*

came and fell to her knees in front of him and told him what she had done.
34 And he said to her, "Daughter, your faith has made you well. Go in peace.
Your suffering is over."
35 While he was still speaking to her, messengers arrived from the home of
Jairus, the leader of the synagogue. They told him, "Your daughter is dead.
There's no use troubling the Teacher now."
36 But Jesus overheard* them and said to Jairus, "Don't be afraid. Just have
faith."
37 Then Jesus stopped the crowd and wouldn't let anyone go with him
except Peter, James, and John (the brother of James). 38 When they came to
the home of the synagogue leader, Jesus saw much commotion and weep-
ing and wailing. 39 He went inside and asked, "Why all this commotion and
weeping? The child isn't dead; she's only asleep."
40 The crowd laughed at him. But he made them all leave, and he took the
girl's father and mother and his three disciples into the room where the girl
was lying. 41 Holding her hand, he said to her, *"Talitha koum,"* which means
"Little girl, get up!" 42 And the girl, who was twelve years old, immediately
stood up and walked around! They were overwhelmed and totally amazed.
43 Jesus gave them strict orders not to tell anyone what had happened, and
then he told them to give her something to eat.

Question 5:21–43

How do you think this twelve-year-old girl described this event to her friends later that week?

Jesus Rejected at Nazareth

6 Jesus left that part of the country and returned with his disciples to
Nazareth, his hometown. 2 The next Sabbath he began teaching in the
synagogue, and many who heard him were amazed. They asked, "Where did
he get all this wisdom and the power to perform such miracles?" 3 Then they
scoffed, "He's just a carpenter, the son of Mary* and the brother of James,
Joseph,* Judas, and Simon. And his sisters live right here among us." They
were deeply offended and refused to believe in him.
4 Then Jesus told them, "A prophet is honored everywhere except in his
own hometown and among his relatives and his own family." 5 And because
of their unbelief, he couldn't do any miracles among them except to place
his hands on a few sick people and heal them. 6 And he was amazed at their
unbelief.

Jesus Sends Out the Twelve Disciples

Then Jesus went from village to village, teaching the people. 7 And he called
his twelve disciples together and began sending them out two by two, giving
them authority to cast out evil* spirits. 8 He told them to take nothing for
their journey except a walking stick—no food, no traveler's bag, no money.*
9 He allowed them to wear sandals but not to take a change of clothes.
10 "Wherever you go," he said, "stay in the same house until you leave town.
11 But if any place refuses to welcome you or listen to you, shake its dust
from your feet as you leave to show that you have abandoned those people
to their fate."
12 So the disciples went out, telling everyone they met to repent of their
sins and turn to God. 13 And they cast out many demons and healed many
sick people, anointing them with olive oil.

5:36 Or *ignored.* 6:3a Some manuscripts read *He's just the son of the carpenter and of Mary.* 6:3b Most manuscripts read *Joses;* see Matt 13:55. 6:7 Greek *unclean.* 6:8 Greek *no copper coins in their money belts.*

Make a Difference 6:31

Restless

Humans are restless creatures. They are busy carrying burdens and are afraid to stop because, if they stop, they might have to think. If they think, they might have to wrestle with their burdens and what is going on inside of them. If they have to wrestle with their burdens, they might get tired. If they get tired, they might need to rest.

Because of this, humans don't stop. Instead, they pride themselves on their activities. They are the most productive and least productive creatures in all of history. They overschedule, overcommit, and overextend themselves and then wish they had time to enjoy themselves. Even God stopped the activity of creation to pause and rest though humans don't. No, they choose pace over peace.

Jesus, the Lord of the Sabbath, is restful. He asks us to stop our scurry long enough to sit down at the table together for a meal.

Difference Maker

Schedule time today to rest. Do something that will rejuvenate your soul. Invite others to come along who will be refreshing for you. Be sure to enjoy God's presence as you pause your pace.

The Death of John the Baptist

14 Herod Antipas, the king, soon heard about Jesus, because everyone was
talking about him. Some were saying,* "This must be John the Baptist raised
from the dead. That is why he can do such miracles." 15 Others said, "He's
the prophet Elijah." Still others said, "He's a prophet like the other great
prophets of the past."
16 When Herod heard about Jesus, he said, "John, the man I beheaded, has
come back from the dead."
17 For Herod had sent soldiers to arrest and imprison John as a favor to
Herodias. She had been his brother Philip's wife, but Herod had married
her. 18 John had been telling Herod, "It is against God's law for you to marry
your brother's wife." 19 So Herodias bore a grudge against John and wanted
to kill him. But without Herod's approval she was powerless, 20 for Herod
respected John; and knowing that he was a good and holy man, he protected
him. Herod was greatly disturbed whenever he talked with John, but even
so, he liked to listen to him.
21 Herodias's chance finally came on Herod's birthday. He gave a party
for his high government officials, army officers, and the leading citizens of
Galilee. 22 Then his daughter, also named Herodias,* came in and performed
a dance that greatly pleased Herod and his guests. "Ask me for anything you
like," the king said to the girl, "and I will give it to you." 23 He even vowed, "I
will give you whatever you ask, up to half my kingdom!"
24 She went out and asked her mother, "What should I ask for?"
Her mother told her, "Ask for the head of John the Baptist!"
25 So the girl hurried back to the king and told him, "I want the head of
John the Baptist, right now, on a tray!"
26 Then the king deeply regretted what he had said; but because of the
vows he had made in front of his guests, he couldn't refuse her. 27 So he
immediately sent an executioner to the prison to cut off John's head and
bring it to him. The soldier beheaded John in the prison, 28 brought his
head on a tray, and gave it to the girl, who took it to her mother. 29 When
John's disciples heard what had happened, they came to get his body and
buried it in a tomb.

Jesus Feeds Five Thousand

30 The apostles returned to Jesus from their ministry tour and told him
all they had done and taught. 31 Then Jesus said, "Let's go off by ourselves
to a quiet place and rest awhile." He said this because there were so many
people coming and going that Jesus and his apostles didn't even have time
to eat.
32 So they left by boat for a quiet place, where they could be alone. 33 But
many people recognized them and saw them leaving, and people from many
towns ran ahead along the shore and got there ahead of them. 34 Jesus saw
the huge crowd as he stepped from the boat, and he had compassion on
them because they were like sheep without a shepherd. So he began teaching them many things.
35 Late in the afternoon his disciples came to him and said, "This is a remote place, and it's already getting late. 36 Send the crowds away so they can
go to the nearby farms and villages and buy something to eat."

6:14 Some manuscripts read *He was saying.* **6:22** Some manuscripts read *the daughter of Herodias herself.*

37 But Jesus said, "You feed them."
"With what?" they asked. "We'd have to work for months to earn enough
money* to buy food for all these people!"
38 "How much bread do you have?" he asked. "Go and find out."
They came back and reported, "We have five loaves of bread and two fish."
39 Then Jesus told the disciples to have the people sit down in groups on
the green grass. 40 So they sat down in groups of fifty or a hundred.
41 Jesus took the five loaves and two fish, looked up toward heaven, and
blessed them. Then, breaking the loaves into pieces, he kept giving the bread
to the disciples so they could distribute it to the people. He also divided the
fish for everyone to share. 42 They all ate as much as they wanted, 43 and after-
ward, the disciples picked up twelve baskets of leftover bread and fish. 44 A
total of 5,000 men and their families were fed.*

Prayer 6:37

Lord, give me the courage and faith to do what you command. Amen.

Jesus Walks on Water

45 Immediately after this, Jesus insisted that his disciples get back into the
boat and head across the lake to Bethsaida, while he sent the people home.
46 After telling everyone good-bye, he went up into the hills by himself to
pray.
47 Late that night, the disciples were in their boat in the middle of the lake,
and Jesus was alone on land. 48 He saw that they were in serious trouble, row-
ing hard and struggling against the wind and waves. About three o'clock in
the morning* Jesus came toward them, walking on the water. He intended
to go past them, 49 but when they saw him walking on the water, they cried
out in terror, thinking he was a ghost. 50 They were all terrified when they
saw him.
But Jesus spoke to them at once. "Don't be afraid," he said. "Take courage!
I am here!*" 51 Then he climbed into the boat, and the wind stopped. They
were totally amazed, 52 for they still didn't understand the significance of the
miracle of the loaves. Their hearts were too hard to take it in.
53 After they had crossed the lake, they landed at Gennesaret. They brought
the boat to shore 54 and climbed out. The people recognized Jesus at once,
55 and they ran throughout the whole area, carrying sick people on mats to
wherever they heard he was. 56 Wherever he went—in villages, cities, or the
countryside—they brought the sick out to the marketplaces. They begged
him to let the sick touch at least the fringe of his robe, and all who touched
him were healed.

Jesus Teaches about Inner Purity

7 One day some Pharisees and teachers of religious law arrived from Je-
rusalem to see Jesus. 2 They noticed that some of his disciples failed to
follow the Jewish ritual of hand washing before eating. 3 (The Jews, especially
the Pharisees, do not eat until they have poured water over their cupped
hands,* as required by their ancient traditions. 4 Similarly, they don't eat
anything from the market until they immerse their hands* in water. This
is but one of many traditions they have clung to—such as their ceremonial
washing of cups, pitchers, and kettles.*)

6:37 Greek *It would take 200 denarii.* A denarius was equivalent to a laborer's full day's wage. **6:44** Some manuscripts read *fed from the loaves.* **6:48** Greek *About the fourth watch of the night.* **6:50** Or *The 'I AM' is here;* Greek reads *I am.* See Exod 3:14. **7:3** Greek *have washed with the fist.* **7:4a** Some manuscripts read *sprinkle themselves.* **7:4b** Some manuscripts add *and dining couches.*

Question 7:19

Why did Jesus make such a gross comment here? What point was he trying to make?

5 So the Pharisees and teachers of religious law asked him, "Why don't your
disciples follow our age-old tradition? They eat without first performing the
hand-washing ceremony."

6 Jesus replied, "You hypocrites! Isaiah was right when he prophesied
about you, for he wrote,

'These people honor me with their lips,
but their hearts are far from me.
7 Their worship is a farce,
for they teach man-made ideas as commands from God.'*

8 For you ignore God's law and substitute your own tradition."

9 Then he said, "You skillfully sidestep God's law in order to hold on
to your own tradition. 10 For instance, Moses gave you this law from God:
'Honor your father and mother,'* and 'Anyone who speaks disrespectfully
of father or mother must be put to death.'* 11 But you say it is all right for
people to say to their parents, 'Sorry, I can't help you. For I have vowed to
give to God what I would have given to you.'* 12 In this way, you let them
disregard their needy parents. 13 And so you cancel the word of God in order
to hand down your own tradition. And this is only one example among
many others."

14 Then Jesus called to the crowd to come and hear. "All of you listen," he
said, "and try to understand. 15 It's not what goes into your body that defiles
you; you are defiled by what comes from your heart.*"

17 Then Jesus went into a house to get away from the crowd, and his dis-
ciples asked him what he meant by the parable he had just used. 18 "Don't
you understand either?" he asked. "Can't you see that the food you put into
your body cannot defile you? 19 Food doesn't go into your heart, but only
passes through the stomach and then goes into the sewer." (By saying this,
he declared that every kind of food is acceptable in God's eyes.)

20 And then he added, "It is what comes from inside that defiles you. 21 For
from within, out of a person's heart, come evil thoughts, sexual immorality,
theft, murder, 22 adultery, greed, wickedness, deceit, lustful desires, envy,
slander, pride, and foolishness. 23 All these vile things come from within;
they are what defile you."

The Faith of a Gentile Woman

24 Then Jesus left Galilee and went north to the region of Tyre.* He didn't
want anyone to know which house he was staying in, but he couldn't keep
it a secret. 25 Right away a woman who had heard about him came and fell at
his feet. Her little girl was possessed by an evil* spirit, 26 and she begged him
to cast out the demon from her daughter.

Since she was a Gentile, born in Syrian Phoenicia, 27 Jesus told her, "First
I should feed the children—my own family, the Jews.* It isn't right to take
food from the children and throw it to the dogs."

28 She replied, "That's true, Lord, but even the dogs under the table are
allowed to eat the scraps from the children's plates."

7:7 Isa 29:13 (Greek version). 7:10a Exod 20:12; Deut 5:16. 7:10b Exod 21:17 (Greek version); Lev 20:9 (Greek version). 7:11 Greek *'What I would have given to you is Corban' (that is, a gift)*. 7:15 Some manuscripts add verse 16, *Anyone with ears to hear should listen and understand.* Compare 4:9, 23. 7:24 Some manuscripts add *and Sidon*. 7:25 Greek *unclean*. 7:27 Greek *Let the children eat first*.

29 "Good answer!" he said. "Now go home, for the demon has left your
daughter." 30 And when she arrived home, she found her little girl lying qui-
etly in bed, and the demon was gone.

Jesus Heals a Deaf Man

31 Jesus left Tyre and went up to Sidon before going back to the Sea of Galilee
and the region of the Ten Towns.* 32 A deaf man with a speech impediment
was brought to him, and the people begged Jesus to lay his hands on the
man to heal him.

33 Jesus led him away from the crowd so they could be alone. He put his
fingers into the man's ears. Then, spitting on his own fingers, he touched
the man's tongue. 34 Looking up to heaven, he sighed and said, "*Ephphatha*,"
which means, "Be opened!" 35 Instantly the man could hear perfectly, and his
tongue was freed so he could speak plainly!

36 Jesus told the crowd not to tell anyone, but the more he told them not
to, the more they spread the news. 37 They were completely amazed and said
again and again, "Everything he does is wonderful. He even makes the deaf
to hear and gives speech to those who cannot speak."

Jesus Feeds Four Thousand

8 About this time another large crowd had gathered, and the people ran
out of food again. Jesus called his disciples and told them, 2 "I feel sorry
for these people. They have been here with me for three days, and they have
nothing left to eat. 3 If I send them home hungry, they will faint along the
way. For some of them have come a long distance."

4 His disciples replied, "How are we supposed to find enough food to feed
them out here in the wilderness?"

5 Jesus asked, "How much bread do you have?"

"Seven loaves," they replied.

6 So Jesus told all the people to sit down on the ground. Then he took the
seven loaves, thanked God for them, and broke them into pieces. He gave
them to his disciples, who distributed the bread to the crowd. 7 A few small
fish were found, too, so Jesus also blessed these and told the disciples to
distribute them.

8 They ate as much as they wanted. Afterward, the disciples picked up
seven large baskets of leftover food. 9 There were about 4,000 men in the
crowd that day, and Jesus sent them home after they had eaten. 10 Immedi-
ately after this, he got into a boat with his disciples and crossed over to the
region of Dalmanutha.

Pharisees Demand a Miraculous Sign

11 When the Pharisees heard that Jesus had arrived, they came and started to
argue with him. Testing him, they demanded that he show them a miracu-
lous sign from heaven to prove his authority.

12 When he heard this, he sighed deeply in his spirit and said, "Why do
these people keep demanding a miraculous sign? I tell you the truth, I will
not give this generation any such sign." 13 So he got back into the boat and
left them, and he crossed to the other side of the lake.

Question **8:11-13**

Jesus had already been healing and performing miracles for eight chapters, so it's shocking that the Pharisees still wanted him to prove himself by giving them a miraculous sign on demand. It's significant that Mark said that, in response, Jesus "got back into the boat and left them" (v. 13). Jesus was not anyone's genie. He was not obligated to do whatever his creatures wanted. The question is this: Will you always want him to prove himself, or will you trust him and notice what he is already doing?

7:31 Greek *Decapolis.*

Make a Difference

8:22-26

See Clearly

Jesus spat. That wasn't even the gross part of it. His spit was directed straight into a man's eyes. The man didn't get mad, though. In fact, he let Jesus do it. He trusted Jesus. He let Jesus form and create and spit on him. He let Jesus ask him questions and put his hands on his eyes. He didn't rub out the spit because he knew that Jesus cared for him.

Jesus might not always do things for you in the way that makes you feel comfortable. Now and then he might even enjoy doing things that are a little messy to focus your eyes and bring about healing within you.

Difference Maker

Be ready to get messy today. Even if it means doing something that is uncomfortable, don't miss an opportunity to help someone see life clearly.

Prayer **8:29**

Jesus, give me the conviction to state this truth in my life: you are the Messiah! You are my Savior! Amen.

Yeast of the Pharisees and Herod

14 But the disciples had forgotten to bring any food. They had only one loaf of
bread with them in the boat. 15 As they were crossing the lake, Jesus warned
them, "Watch out! Beware of the yeast of the Pharisees and of Herod."
16 At this they began to argue with each other because they hadn't brought
any bread. 17 Jesus knew what they were saying, so he said, "Why are you
arguing about having no bread? Don't you know or understand even yet?
Are your hearts too hard to take it in? 18 'You have eyes—can't you see? You
have ears—can't you hear?'* Don't you remember anything at all? 19 When
I fed the 5,000 with five loaves of bread, how many baskets of leftovers did
you pick up afterward?"
"Twelve," they said.
20 "And when I fed the 4,000 with seven loaves, how many large baskets
of leftovers did you pick up?"
"Seven," they said.
21 "Don't you understand yet?" he asked them.

Jesus Heals a Blind Man

22 When they arrived at Bethsaida, some people brought a blind man to Jesus,
and they begged him to touch the man and heal him. 23 Jesus took the blind
man by the hand and led him out of the village. Then, spitting on the man's
eyes, he laid his hands on him and asked, "Can you see anything now?"
24 The man looked around. "Yes," he said, "I see people, but I can't see them
very clearly. They look like trees walking around."
25 Then Jesus placed his hands on the man's eyes again, and his eyes were
opened. His sight was completely restored, and he could see everything
clearly. 26 Jesus sent him away, saying, "Don't go back into the village on
your way home."

Peter's Declaration about Jesus

27 Jesus and his disciples left Galilee and went up to the villages near Caes-
area Philippi. As they were walking along, he asked them, "Who do people
say I am?"
28 "Well," they replied, "some say John the Baptist, some say Elijah, and
others say you are one of the other prophets."
29 Then he asked them, "But who do you say I am?"
Peter replied, "You are the Messiah.*"
30 But Jesus warned them not to tell anyone about him.

Jesus Predicts His Death

31 Then Jesus began to tell them that the Son of Man* must suffer many ter-
rible things and be rejected by the elders, the leading priests, and the teachers
of religious law. He would be killed, but three days later he would rise from
the dead. 32 As he talked about this openly with his disciples, Peter took him
aside and began to reprimand him for saying such things.*
33 Jesus turned around and looked at his disciples, then reprimanded Peter.
"Get away from me, Satan!" he said. "You are seeing things merely from a
human point of view, not from God's."

8:18 Jer 5:21. **8:29** Or *the Christ. Messiah* (a Hebrew term) and *Christ* (a Greek term) both mean "anointed one." **8:31** "Son of Man" is a title Jesus used for himself. **8:32** Or *began to correct him.*

34 Then, calling the crowd to join his disciples, he said, "If any of you wants
to be my follower, you must give up your own way, take up your cross, and
follow me. 35 If you try to hang on to your life, you will lose it. But if you give
up your life for my sake and for the sake of the Good News, you will save it.
36 And what do you benefit if you gain the whole world but lose your own
soul?* 37 Is anything worth more than your soul? 38 If anyone is ashamed of
me and my message in these adulterous and sinful days, the Son of Man will
be ashamed of that person when he returns in the glory of his Father with
the holy angels."

9 Jesus went on to say, "I tell you the truth, some standing here right now
will not die before they see the Kingdom of God arrive in great power!"

The Transfiguration

2 Six days later Jesus took Peter, James, and John, and led them up a high
mountain to be alone. As the men watched, Jesus' appearance was trans-
formed, 3 and his clothes became dazzling white, far whiter than any earthly
bleach could ever make them. 4 Then Elijah and Moses appeared and began
talking with Jesus.

5 Peter exclaimed, "Rabbi, it's wonderful for us to be here! Let's make three
shelters as memorials*—one for you, one for Moses, and one for Elijah."
6 He said this because he didn't really know what else to say, for they were
all terrified.

7 Then a cloud overshadowed them, and a voice from the cloud said, "This
is my dearly loved Son. Listen to him." 8 Suddenly, when they looked around,
Moses and Elijah were gone, and they saw only Jesus with them.

9 As they went back down the mountain, he told them not to tell anyone
what they had seen until the Son of Man* had risen from the dead. 10 So they
kept it to themselves, but they often asked each other what he meant by
"rising from the dead."

11 Then they asked him, "Why do the teachers of religious law insist that
Elijah must return before the Messiah comes?*"

12 Jesus responded, "Elijah is indeed coming first to get everything ready.
Yet why do the Scriptures say that the Son of Man must suffer greatly and
be treated with utter contempt? 13 But I tell you, Elijah has already come, and
they chose to abuse him, just as the Scriptures predicted."

Jesus Heals a Demon-Possessed Boy

14 When they returned to the other disciples, they saw a large crowd sur-
rounding them, and some teachers of religious law were arguing with them.
15 When the crowd saw Jesus, they were overwhelmed with awe, and they
ran to greet him.

16 "What is all this arguing about?" Jesus asked.

17 One of the men in the crowd spoke up and said, "Teacher, I brought my
son so you could heal him. He is possessed by an evil spirit that won't let
him talk. 18 And whenever this spirit seizes him, it throws him violently to
the ground. Then he foams at the mouth and grinds his teeth and becomes
rigid.* So I asked your disciples to cast out the evil spirit, but they couldn't
do it."

8:36 Or *your self?* also in 8:37. **9:5** Greek *three tabernacles.* **9:9** "Son of Man" is a title Jesus used for himself. **9:11** Greek *that Elijah must come first?* **9:18** Or *becomes weak.*

Question 8:31–38

Read verses 8:31-38. What did Jesus mean about taking up your cross?

Question 9:2–29

Compare the awesome mountaintop experience in Mark 9:2-8 with the messy ministry experience in Mark 9:14-29. How does living for Jesus mean accepting a call into both the mountaintops and the valleys of life?

Prayer 9:24

Jesus, I do believe, but help me overcome my unbelief. Amen.

Make a Difference

9:33–37

First

Humility is one of those personal characteristics that is nearly impossible to admit that you have. Right? Once you say you have it, do you still have it? This is the intentionally tricky logic of Jesus. He is shrewd. He knows that we humans love to be recognized for being great, which really makes us not so great, which is why he ensnared his followers with a little teaser about humility. "So," he said, "you'd like to be recognized for being great, huh? Well, then just make sure you treat everyone else as if they are greater than you."

The disciples, learning the secret formula to God's great sauce, must have been excited at first. "Aha! Now we'll be greatest in the kingdom of heaven!" Little did they know that by continuing to serve others, by continuing to make themselves "last," the disciples would be transformed. In the persistence of their good service, they would be changed more and more into the likeness of Jesus.

Difference Maker

Serve people today. Open doors. Wash dishes. Clean up messes. Vacuum. Carry things. Sit down and listen. Make eye contact. Don't interrupt. Let others go first in line. Speak up in defense of someone. Give extra help when needed. Serve people today.

19 Jesus said to them,* "You faithless people! How long must I be with you?
How long must I put up with you? Bring the boy to me."
20 So they brought the boy. But when the evil spirit saw Jesus, it threw
the child into a violent convulsion, and he fell to the ground, writhing and
foaming at the mouth.
21 "How long has this been happening?" Jesus asked the boy's father.
He replied, "Since he was a little boy. 22 The spirit often throws him into
the fire or into water, trying to kill him. Have mercy on us and help us, if
you can."
23 "What do you mean, 'If I can'?" Jesus asked. "Anything is possible if a
person believes."
24 The father instantly cried out, "I do believe, but help me overcome my
unbelief!"
25 When Jesus saw that the crowd of onlookers was growing, he rebuked
the evil* spirit. "Listen, you spirit that makes this boy unable to hear and
speak," he said. "I command you to come out of this child and never enter
him again!"
26 Then the spirit screamed and threw the boy into another violent con-
vulsion and left him. The boy appeared to be dead. A murmur ran through
the crowd as people said, "He's dead." 27 But Jesus took him by the hand and
helped him to his feet, and he stood up.
28 Afterward, when Jesus was alone in the house with his disciples, they
asked him, "Why couldn't we cast out that evil spirit?"
29 Jesus replied, "This kind can be cast out only by prayer.*"

Jesus Again Predicts His Death

30 Leaving that region, they traveled through Galilee. Jesus didn't want
anyone to know he was there, 31 for he wanted to spend more time with his
disciples and teach them. He said to them, "The Son of Man is going to be
betrayed into the hands of his enemies. He will be killed, but three days later
he will rise from the dead." 32 They didn't understand what he was saying,
however, and they were afraid to ask him what he meant.

The Greatest in the Kingdom

33 After they arrived at Capernaum and settled in a house, Jesus asked his
disciples, "What were you discussing out on the road?" 34 But they didn't
answer, because they had been arguing about which of them was the great-
est. 35 He sat down, called the twelve disciples over to him, and said, "Who-
ever wants to be first must take last place and be the servant of everyone
else."
36 Then he put a little child among them. Taking the child in his arms, he
said to them, 37 "Anyone who welcomes a little child like this on my behalf*
welcomes me, and anyone who welcomes me welcomes not only me but also
my Father who sent me."

Using the Name of Jesus

38 John said to Jesus, "Teacher, we saw someone using your name to cast out
demons, but we told him to stop because he wasn't in our group."
39 "Don't stop him!" Jesus said. "No one who performs a miracle in my

9:19 Or *said to his disciples.* **9:25** Greek *unclean.* **9:29** Some manuscripts read *by prayer and fasting.* **9:37** Greek *in my name.*

name will soon be able to speak evil of me. 40 Anyone who is not against us
is for us. 41 If anyone gives you even a cup of water because you belong to the
Messiah, I tell you the truth, that person will surely be rewarded.
42 "But if you cause one of these little ones who trusts in me to fall
into sin, it would be better for you to be thrown into the sea with a large
millstone hung around your neck. 43 If your hand causes you to sin, cut it
off. It's better to enter eternal life with only one hand than to go into the
unquenchable fires of hell* with two hands.* 45 If your foot causes you to
sin, cut it off. It's better to enter eternal life with only one foot than to be
thrown into hell with two feet.* 47 And if your eye causes you to sin, gouge
it out. It's better to enter the Kingdom of God with only one eye than to
have two eyes and be thrown into hell, 48 'where the maggots never die and
the fire never goes out.'*
49 "For everyone will be tested with fire.* 50 Salt is good for seasoning. But if
it loses its flavor, how do you make it salty again? You must have the qualities
of salt among yourselves and live in peace with each other."

Discussion about Divorce and Marriage

10 Then Jesus left Capernaum and went down to the region of Judea
and into the area east of the Jordan River. Once again crowds gath-
ered around him, and as usual he was teaching them.
2 Some Pharisees came and tried to trap him with this question: "Should
a man be allowed to divorce his wife?"
3 Jesus answered them with a question: "What did Moses say in the law
about divorce?"
4 "Well, he permitted it," they replied. "He said a man can give his wife a
written notice of divorce and send her away."*
5 But Jesus responded, "He wrote this commandment only as a conces-
sion to your hard hearts. 6 But 'God made them male and female'* from
the beginning of creation. 7 'This explains why a man leaves his father and
mother and is joined to his wife,* 8 and the two are united into one.'* Since
they are no longer two but one, 9 let no one split apart what God has joined
together."
10 Later, when he was alone with his disciples in the house, they brought
up the subject again. 11 He told them, "Whoever divorces his wife and marries
someone else commits adultery against her. 12 And if a woman divorces her
husband and marries someone else, she commits adultery."

Jesus Blesses the Children

13 One day some parents brought their children to Jesus so he could touch
and bless them. But the disciples scolded the parents for bothering him.
14 When Jesus saw what was happening, he was angry with his disciples.
He said to them, "Let the children come to me. Don't stop them! For the
Kingdom of God belongs to those who are like these children. 15 I tell you
the truth, anyone who doesn't receive the Kingdom of God like a child will
never enter it." 16 Then he took the children in his arms and placed his hands
on their heads and blessed them.

9:43a Greek *Gehenna;* also in 9:45, 47. 9:43b Some manuscripts add verse 44, *'where the maggots never die and the fire never goes out.'* See 9:48. 9:45 Some manuscripts add verse 46, *'where the maggots never die and the fire never goes out.'* See 9:48. 9:48 Isa 66:24. 9:49 Greek *salted with fire;* other manuscripts add *and every sacrifice will be salted with salt.* 10:4 See Deut 24:1. 10:6 Gen 1:27; 5:2. 10:7 Some manuscripts do not include *and is joined to his wife.* 10:7-8 Gen 2:24.

Question 10:13-16

What does Jesus teach us in this passage about letting our faith become adulterated?

Question 10:26

How would you answer the disciples' question here: "Then who in the world can be saved?" How does Jesus answer their question?

Make a Difference

10:32-34

Resolute Faith

Even though Jesus knew what was before him, he was resolute and unwavering in his purpose. Jesus came into this world to save humanity. He went through with the betrayal, the judgment, the ridicule, the torture, and the crucifixion for us. He also went through with it all so that he could "rise again" after three days (v. 34)!

Jesus modeled the grit and commitment and faithfulness that can be reflected in us. He aimed for the cross and asked his followers to serve the world likewise.

Difference Maker

What aim, even if it is difficult or challenging, could you set before you that would help you serve someone this week?

The Rich Man

17 As Jesus was starting out on his way to Jerusalem, a man came running up
to him, knelt down, and asked, "Good Teacher, what must I do to inherit
eternal life?"

18 "Why do you call me good?" Jesus asked. "Only God is truly good. 19 But
to answer your question, you know the commandments: 'You must not
murder. You must not commit adultery. You must not steal. You must not
testify falsely. You must not cheat anyone. Honor your father and mother.'*"

20 "Teacher," the man replied, "I've obeyed all these commandments since
I was young."

21 Looking at the man, Jesus felt genuine love for him. "There is still one thing
you haven't done," he told him. "Go and sell all your possessions and give the
money to the poor, and you will have treasure in heaven. Then come, follow me."

22 At this the man's face fell, and he went away sad, for he had many
possessions.

23 Jesus looked around and said to his disciples, "How hard it is for the rich
to enter the Kingdom of God!" 24 This amazed them. But Jesus said again,
"Dear children, it is very hard* to enter the Kingdom of God. 25 In fact, it is
easier for a camel to go through the eye of a needle than for a rich person to
enter the Kingdom of God!"

26 The disciples were astounded. "Then who in the world can be saved?"
they asked.

27 Jesus looked at them intently and said, "Humanly speaking, it is impos-
sible. But not with God. Everything is possible with God."

28 Then Peter began to speak up. "We've given up everything to follow
you," he said.

29 "Yes," Jesus replied, "and I assure you that everyone who has given up
house or brothers or sisters or mother or father or children or property, for
my sake and for the Good News, 30 will receive now in return a hundred times
as many houses, brothers, sisters, mothers, children, and property—along
with persecution. And in the world to come that person will have eternal life.
31 But many who are the greatest now will be least important then, and those
who seem least important now will be the greatest then.*"

Jesus Again Predicts His Death

32 They were now on the way up to Jerusalem, and Jesus was walking ahead
of them. The disciples were filled with awe, and the people following behind
were overwhelmed with fear. Taking the twelve disciples aside, Jesus once
more began to describe everything that was about to happen to him. 33 "Lis-
ten," he said, "we're going up to Jerusalem, where the Son of Man* will be
betrayed to the leading priests and the teachers of religious law. They will
sentence him to die and hand him over to the Romans.* 34 They will mock
him, spit on him, flog him with a whip, and kill him, but after three days
he will rise again."

Jesus Teaches about Serving Others

35 Then James and John, the sons of Zebedee, came over and spoke to him.
"Teacher," they said, "we want you to do us a favor."

10:19 Exod 20:12-16; Deut 5:16-20. **10:24** Some manuscripts read *very hard for those who trust in riches.* **10:31** Greek *But many who are first will be last; and the last, first.* **10:33a** "Son of Man" is a title Jesus used for himself. **10:33b** Greek *the Gentiles.*

36 “What is your request?” he asked.
37 They replied, “When you sit on your glorious throne, we want to sit in
places of honor next to you, one on your right and the other on your left.”
38 But Jesus said to them, “You don’t know what you are asking! Are you
able to drink from the bitter cup of suffering I am about to drink? Are you
able to be baptized with the baptism of suffering I must be baptized with?”
39 “Oh yes,” they replied, “we are able!”
Then Jesus told them, “You will indeed drink from my bitter cup and
be baptized with my baptism of suffering. 40 But I have no right to say who
will sit on my right or my left. God has prepared those places for the ones
he has chosen.”
41 When the ten other disciples heard what James and John had asked, they
were indignant. 42 So Jesus called them together and said, “You know that the
rulers in this world lord it over their people, and officials flaunt their authority
over those under them. 43 But among you it will be different. Whoever wants to
be a leader among you must be your servant, 44 and whoever wants to be first
among you must be the slave of everyone else. 45 For even the Son of Man came
not to be served but to serve others and to give his life as a ransom for many.”

Jesus Heals Blind Bartimaeus

46 Then they reached Jericho, and as Jesus and his disciples left town, a large
crowd followed him. A blind beggar named Bartimaeus (son of Timaeus) was
sitting beside the road. 47 When Bartimaeus heard that Jesus of Nazareth was
nearby, he began to shout, “Jesus, Son of David, have mercy on me!”
48 “Be quiet!” many of the people yelled at him.
But he only shouted louder, “Son of David, have mercy on me!”
49 When Jesus heard him, he stopped and said, “Tell him to come here.”
So they called the blind man. “Cheer up,” they said. “Come on, he’s call-
ing you!” 50 Bartimaeus threw aside his coat, jumped up, and came to Jesus.
51 “What do you want me to do for you?” Jesus asked.
“My Rabbi,*” the blind man said, “I want to see!”
52 And Jesus said to him, “Go, for your faith has healed you.” Instantly the
man could see, and he followed Jesus down the road.*

Jesus’ Triumphant Entry

11 As Jesus and his disciples approached Jerusalem, they came to the
towns of Bethphage and Bethany on the Mount of Olives. Jesus sent
two of them on ahead. 2 “Go into that village over there,” he told them. “As
soon as you enter it, you will see a young donkey tied there that no one has
ever ridden. Untie it and bring it here. 3 If anyone asks, ‘What are you doing?’
just say, ‘The Lord needs it and will return it soon.’”
4 The two disciples left and found the colt standing in the street, tied out-
side the front door. 5 As they were untying it, some bystanders demanded,
“What are you doing, untying that colt?” 6 They said what Jesus had told
them to say, and they were permitted to take it. 7 Then they brought the colt
to Jesus and threw their garments over it, and he sat on it.
8 Many in the crowd spread their garments on the road ahead of him, and
others spread leafy branches they had cut in the fields. 9 Jesus was in the
center of the procession, and the people all around him were shouting,

10:51 Greek uses the Hebrew term *Rabboni.* 10:52 Or *on the way.*

Question 11:1-33

Look through all of chapter 11 and ask yourself this question: "Why did Jesus curse the fig tree?"

"Praise God!*
Blessings on the one who comes in the name of the LORD!
10 Blessings on the coming Kingdom of our ancestor David!
Praise God in highest heaven!"*

11 So Jesus came to Jerusalem and went into the Temple. After looking
around carefully at everything, he left because it was late in the afternoon.
Then he returned to Bethany with the twelve disciples.

Jesus Curses the Fig Tree

12 The next morning as they were leaving Bethany, Jesus was hungry. 13 He
noticed a fig tree in full leaf a little way off, so he went over to see if he could
find any figs. But there were only leaves because it was too early in the season
for fruit. 14 Then Jesus said to the tree, "May no one ever eat your fruit again!"
And the disciples heard him say it.

Jesus Clears the Temple

15 When they arrived back in Jerusalem, Jesus entered the Temple and began
to drive out the people buying and selling animals for sacrifices. He knocked
over the tables of the money changers and the chairs of those selling doves,
16 and he stopped everyone from using the Temple as a marketplace.* 17 He
said to them, "The Scriptures declare, 'My Temple will be called a house of
prayer for all nations,' but you have turned it into a den of thieves."*

18 When the leading priests and teachers of religious law heard what Jesus
had done, they began planning how to kill him. But they were afraid of him
because the people were so amazed at his teaching.

19 That evening Jesus and the disciples left* the city.

20 The next morning as they passed by the fig tree he had cursed, the dis-
ciples noticed it had withered from the roots up. 21 Peter remembered what
Jesus had said to the tree on the previous day and exclaimed, "Look, Rabbi!
The fig tree you cursed has withered and died!"

22 Then Jesus said to the disciples, "Have faith in God. 23 I tell you the truth,
you can say to this mountain, 'May you be lifted up and thrown into the
sea,' and it will happen. But you must really believe it will happen and have
no doubt in your heart. 24 I tell you, you can pray for anything, and if you
believe that you've received it, it will be yours. 25 But when you are praying,
first forgive anyone you are holding a grudge against, so that your Father in
heaven will forgive your sins, too.*"

The Authority of Jesus Challenged

27 Again they entered Jerusalem. As Jesus was walking through the Temple
area, the leading priests, the teachers of religious law, and the elders came
up to him. 28 They demanded, "By what authority are you doing all these
things? Who gave you the right to do them?"

29 "I'll tell you by what authority I do these things if you answer one ques-
tion," Jesus replied. 30 "Did John's authority to baptize come from heaven, or
was it merely human? Answer me!"

11:9 Greek *Hosanna,* an exclamation of praise that literally means "save now"; also in 11:10. 11:9-10 Pss 118:25-26; 148:1. 11:16 Or *from carrying merchandise through the Temple.* 11:17 Isa 56:7; Jer 7:11. 11:19 Greek *they left;* other manuscripts read *he left.* 11:25 Some manuscripts add verse 26, *But if you refuse to forgive, your Father in heaven will not forgive your sins.* Compare Matt 6:15.

31 They talked it over among themselves. "If we say it was from heaven,
he will ask why we didn't believe John. 32 But do we dare say it was merely
human?" For they were afraid of what the people would do, because every-
one believed that John was a prophet. 33 So they finally replied, "We don't
know."

And Jesus responded, "Then I won't tell you by what authority I do these things."

Parable of the Evil Farmers

12 Then Jesus began teaching them with stories: "A man planted a vineyard. He built a wall around it, dug a pit for pressing out the grape juice, and built a lookout tower. Then he leased the vineyard to tenant farmers and moved to another country.
2 At the time of the grape harvest,
he sent one of his servants to collect his share of the crop.
3 But the farm-
ers grabbed the servant, beat him up, and sent him back empty-handed.
4 The owner then sent another servant, but they insulted him and beat him
over the head.
5 The next servant he sent was killed. Others he sent were
either beaten or killed,
6 until there was only one left—his son whom he
loved dearly. The owner finally sent him, thinking, 'Surely they will respect
my son.'

7 "But the tenant farmers said to one another, 'Here comes the heir to this
estate. Let's kill him and get the estate for ourselves!'
8 So they grabbed him
and murdered him and threw his body out of the vineyard.

9 "What do you suppose the owner of the vineyard will do?" Jesus asked.
"I'll tell you—he will come and kill those farmers and lease the vineyard to
others.
10 Didn't you ever read this in the Scriptures?

'The stone that the builders rejected
has now become the cornerstone.
11 This is the LORD's doing,
and it is wonderful to see.'*"

12 The religious leaders* wanted to arrest Jesus because they realized he was telling the story against them—they were the wicked farmers. But they were afraid of the crowd, so they left him and went away.

Taxes for Caesar

13 Later the leaders sent some Pharisees and supporters of Herod to trap Jesus
into saying something for which he could be arrested.
14 "Teacher," they said,
"we know how honest you are. You are impartial and don't play favorites.
You teach the way of God truthfully. Now tell us—is it right to pay taxes to
Caesar or not?
15 Should we pay them, or shouldn't we?"

Jesus saw through their hypocrisy and said, "Why are you trying to trap
me? Show me a Roman coin,* and I'll tell you."
16 When they handed it to him,
he asked, "Whose picture and title are stamped on it?"

"Caesar's," they replied.

17 "Well, then," Jesus said, "give to Caesar what belongs to Caesar, and give to God what belongs to God."

His reply completely amazed them.

Question 12:17

How does the witty response of Jesus set an example for how you can respond to people in some challenging situations?

12:10-11 Ps 118:22-23. 12:12 Greek *They.* 12:15 Greek *a denarius.*

Question 12:28-34

Jesus said this man was not far from the kingdom of God. What did the man get right, and what did he still need to figure out?

Discussion about Resurrection

18 Then Jesus was approached by some Sadducees—religious leaders who say
there is no resurrection from the dead. They posed this question: 19 "Teacher,
Moses gave us a law that if a man dies, leaving a wife without children, his
brother should marry the widow and have a child who will carry on the
brother's name.* 20 Well, suppose there were seven brothers. The oldest one
married and then died without children. 21 So the second brother married the
widow, but he also died without children. Then the third brother married
her. 22 This continued with all seven of them, and still there were no children.
Last of all, the woman also died. 23 So tell us, whose wife will she be in the
resurrection? For all seven were married to her."

24 Jesus replied, "Your mistake is that you don't know the Scriptures, and
you don't know the power of God. 25 For when the dead rise, they will neither
marry nor be given in marriage. In this respect they will be like the angels
in heaven.

26 "But now, as to whether the dead will be raised—haven't you ever read
about this in the writings of Moses, in the story of the burning bush? Long
after Abraham, Isaac, and Jacob had died, God said to Moses,* 'I am the God
of Abraham, the God of Isaac, and the God of Jacob.'* 27 So he is the God of
the living, not the dead. You have made a serious error."

The Most Important Commandment

28 One of the teachers of religious law was standing there listening to the
debate. He realized that Jesus had answered well, so he asked, "Of all the
commandments, which is the most important?"

29 Jesus replied, "The most important commandment is this: 'Listen, O Is-
rael! The LORD our God is the one and only LORD. 30 And you must love the
LORD your God with all your heart, all your soul, all your mind, and all your
strength.'* 31 The second is equally important: 'Love your neighbor as your-
self.'* No other commandment is greater than these."

32 The teacher of religious law replied, "Well said, Teacher. You have spo-
ken the truth by saying that there is only one God and no other. 33 And I
know it is important to love him with all my heart and all my understanding
and all my strength, and to love my neighbor as myself. This is more im-
portant than to offer all of the burnt offerings and sacrifices required in
the law."

34 Realizing how much the man understood, Jesus said to him, "You are
not far from the Kingdom of God." And after that, no one dared to ask him
any more questions.

Whose Son Is the Messiah?

35 Later, as Jesus was teaching the people in the Temple, he asked, "Why do
the teachers of religious law claim that the Messiah is the son of David?
36 For David himself, speaking under the inspiration of the Holy Spirit,
said,

'The LORD said to my Lord,
Sit in the place of honor at my right hand
until I humble your enemies beneath your feet.'*

12:19 See Deut 25:5-6. 12:26a Greek *in the story of the bush? God said to him.* 12:26b Exod 3:6. 12:29-30 Deut 6:4-5. 12:31 Lev 19:18. 12:36 Ps 110:1.

37Since David himself called the Messiah 'my Lord,' how can the Messiah be
his son?" The large crowd listened to him with great delight.
38Jesus also taught: "Beware of these teachers of religious law! For they
like to parade around in flowing robes and receive respectful greetings as
they walk in the marketplaces. 39And how they love the seats of honor in
the synagogues and the head table at banquets. 40Yet they shamelessly cheat
widows out of their property and then pretend to be pious by making long
prayers in public. Because of this, they will be more severely punished."

The Widow's Offering

41Jesus sat down near the collection box in the Temple and watched as the
crowds dropped in their money. Many rich people put in large amounts.
42Then a poor widow came and dropped in two small coins.*
43Jesus called his disciples to him and said, "I tell you the truth, this poor
widow has given more than all the others who are making contributions.
44For they gave a tiny part of their surplus, but she, poor as she is, has given
everything she had to live on."

Prayer 12:43

Lord, give me the courage to give generously. Amen.

Jesus Speaks about the Future

13 As Jesus was leaving the Temple that day, one of his disciples said,
"Teacher, look at these magnificent buildings! Look at the impressive stones in the walls."
2Jesus replied, "Yes, look at these great buildings. But they will be completely demolished. Not one stone will be left on top of another!"
3Later, Jesus sat on the Mount of Olives across the valley from the Temple.
Peter, James, John, and Andrew came to him privately and asked him, 4"Tell
us, when will all this happen? What sign will show us that these things are
about to be fulfilled?"
5Jesus replied, "Don't let anyone mislead you, 6for many will come in my
name, claiming, 'I am the Messiah.'* They will deceive many. 7And you will
hear of wars and threats of wars, but don't panic. Yes, these things must take
place, but the end won't follow immediately. 8Nation will go to war against
nation, and kingdom against kingdom. There will be earthquakes in many
parts of the world, as well as famines. But this is only the first of the birth
pains, with more to come.
9"When these things begin to happen, watch out! You will be handed
over to the local councils and beaten in the synagogues. You will stand trial
before governors and kings because you are my followers. But this will be
your opportunity to tell them about me.* 10For the Good News must first be
preached to all nations.* 11But when you are arrested and stand trial, don't
worry in advance about what to say. Just say what God tells you at that time,
for it is not you who will be speaking, but the Holy Spirit.
12"A brother will betray his brother to death, a father will betray his own
child, and children will rebel against their parents and cause them to be
killed. 13And everyone will hate you because you are my followers.* But the
one who endures to the end will be saved.
14"The day is coming when you will see the sacrilegious object that causes
desecration* standing where he* should not be." (Reader, pay attention!)

12:42 Greek *two lepta, which is a kodrantes* [i.e., a quadrans]. 13:6 Greek *claiming, 'I am.'* 13:9 Or *But this will be your testimony against them.* 13:10 Or *all peoples.* 13:13 Greek *on account of my name.* 13:14a Greek *the abomination of desolation.* See Dan 9:27; 11:31; 12:11. 13:14b Or *it.*

Question 13:36

What did Jesus mean when he said: "Don't let [the Master] find you sleeping"?

"Then those in Judea must flee to the hills. 15 A person out on the deck of a
roof must not go down into the house to pack. 16 A person out in the field
must not return even to get a coat. 17 How terrible it will be for pregnant
women and for nursing mothers in those days. 18 And pray that your flight
will not be in winter. 19 For there will be greater anguish in those days than
at any time since God created the world. And it will never be so great again.
20 In fact, unless the Lord shortens that time of calamity, not a single person
will survive. But for the sake of his chosen ones he has shortened those days.
21 "Then if anyone tells you, 'Look, here is the Messiah,' or 'There he is,'
don't believe it. 22 For false messiahs and false prophets will rise up and per-
form signs and wonders so as to deceive, if possible, even God's chosen ones.
23 Watch out! I have warned you about this ahead of time!
24 "At that time, after the anguish of those days,

the sun will be darkened,
  the moon will give no light,
25 the stars will fall from the sky,
  and the powers in the heavens will be shaken.*

26 Then everyone will see the Son of Man* coming on the clouds with great
power and glory.* 27 And he will send out his angels to gather his chosen ones
from all over the world*—from the farthest ends of the earth and heaven.
28 "Now learn a lesson from the fig tree. When its branches bud and its
leaves begin to sprout, you know that summer is near. 29 In the same way,
when you see all these things taking place, you can know that his return is
very near, right at the door. 30 I tell you the truth, this generation* will not
pass from the scene before all these things take place. 31 Heaven and earth
will disappear, but my words will never disappear.
32 "However, no one knows the day or hour when these things will happen,
not even the angels in heaven or the Son himself. Only the Father knows. 33 And
since you don't know when that time will come, be on guard! Stay alert*!
34 "The coming of the Son of Man can be illustrated by the story of a man
going on a long trip. When he left home, he gave each of his slaves instruc-
tions about the work they were to do, and he told the gatekeeper to watch for
his return. 35 You, too, must keep watch! For you don't know when the master
of the household will return—in the evening, at midnight, before dawn,
or at daybreak. 36 Don't let him find you sleeping when he arrives without
warning. 37 I say to you what I say to everyone: Watch for him!"

Jesus Anointed at Bethany

14 It was now two days before Passover and the Festival of Unleavened
Bread. The leading priests and the teachers of religious law were
still looking for an opportunity to capture Jesus secretly and kill him. 2 "But
not during the Passover celebration," they agreed, "or the people may riot."
3 Meanwhile, Jesus was in Bethany at the home of Simon, a man who had
previously had leprosy. While he was eating,* a woman came in with a beauti-
ful alabaster jar of expensive perfume made from essence of nard. She broke
open the jar and poured the perfume over his head.

13:24-25 See Isa 13:10; 34:4; Joel 2:10. **13:26a** "Son of Man" is a title Jesus used for himself. **13:26b** See Dan 7:13. **13:27** Greek *from the four winds.* **13:30** Or *this age,* or *this nation.* **13:33** Some manuscripts add *and pray.* **14:3** Or *reclining.*

4 Some of those at the table were indignant. "Why waste such expensive
perfume?" they asked. 5 "It could have been sold for a year's wages* and the
money given to the poor!" So they scolded her harshly.
6 But Jesus replied, "Leave her alone. Why criticize her for doing such a
good thing to me? 7 You will always have the poor among you, and you can
help them whenever you want to. But you will not always have me. 8 She has
done what she could and has anointed my body for burial ahead of time.
9 I tell you the truth, wherever the Good News is preached throughout the
world, this woman's deed will be remembered and discussed."

Prayer 14:9

Lord, even if it costs me everything, let me adore you more than anything else. Amen.

Judas Agrees to Betray Jesus

10 Then Judas Iscariot, one of the twelve disciples, went to the leading priests
to arrange to betray Jesus to them. 11 They were delighted when they heard
why he had come, and they promised to give him money. So he began looking
for an opportunity to betray Jesus.

The Last Supper

12 On the first day of the Festival of Unleavened Bread, when the Passover
lamb is sacrificed, Jesus' disciples asked him, "Where do you want us to go
to prepare the Passover meal for you?"
13 So Jesus sent two of them into Jerusalem with these instructions: "As
you go into the city, a man carrying a pitcher of water will meet you. Follow
him. 14 At the house he enters, say to the owner, 'The Teacher asks: Where is
the guest room where I can eat the Passover meal with my disciples?' 15 He
will take you upstairs to a large room that is already set up. That is where
you should prepare our meal." 16 So the two disciples went into the city and
found everything just as Jesus had said, and they prepared the Passover
meal there.
17 In the evening Jesus arrived with the Twelve. 18 As they were at the table*
eating, Jesus said, "I tell you the truth, one of you eating with me here will
betray me."
19 Greatly distressed, each one asked in turn, "Am I the one?"
20 He replied, "It is one of you twelve who is eating from this bowl with
me. 21 For the Son of Man* must die, as the Scriptures declared long ago. But
how terrible it will be for the one who betrays him. It would be far better for
that man if he had never been born!"
22 As they were eating, Jesus took some bread and blessed it. Then he broke
it in pieces and gave it to the disciples, saying, "Take it, for this is my body."
23 And he took a cup of wine and gave thanks to God for it. He gave it to
them, and they all drank from it. 24 And he said to them, "This is my blood,
which confirms the covenant* between God and his people. It is poured out
as a sacrifice for many. 25 I tell you the truth, I will not drink wine again until
the day I drink it new in the Kingdom of God."
26 Then they sang a hymn and went out to the Mount of Olives.

Jesus Predicts Peter's Denial

27 On the way, Jesus told them, "All of you will desert me. For the Scriptures
say,

14:5 Greek *for 300 denarii.* A denarius was equivalent to a laborer's full day's wage. 14:18 Or *As they reclined.* 14:21 "Son of Man" is a title Jesus used for himself. 14:24 Some manuscripts read *the new covenant.*

Prayer 14:32

Jesus, don't let me miss those opportunities when you want me to pray. Amen.

Question 14:50-52

Many people are convinced that this interesting little note gives us a glimpse into the writer of this gospel. This naked, young man who fled for his life would learn through testing and determination and encouragement to become one of the most meaningful followers of Jesus in history. What can you learn from Mark's lifetime growth from fearful failure to faithful follower?

'God will strike* the Shepherd,
and the sheep will be scattered.'

28 But after I am raised from the dead, I will go ahead of you to Galilee and
meet you there."
29 Peter said to him, "Even if everyone else deserts you, I never will."
30 Jesus replied, "I tell you the truth, Peter—this very night, before the
rooster crows twice, you will deny three times that you even know me."
31 "No!" Peter declared emphatically. "Even if I have to die with you, I will
never deny you!" And all the others vowed the same.

Jesus Prays in Gethsemane

32 They went to the olive grove called Gethsemane, and Jesus said, "Sit here
while I go and pray." 33 He took Peter, James, and John with him, and he be-
came deeply troubled and distressed. 34 He told them, "My soul is crushed
with grief to the point of death. Stay here and keep watch with me."
35 He went on a little farther and fell to the ground. He prayed that, if it
were possible, the awful hour awaiting him might pass him by. 36 "Abba,
Father,"* he cried out, "everything is possible for you. Please take this cup of
suffering away from me. Yet I want your will to be done, not mine."
37 Then he returned and found the disciples asleep. He said to Peter, "Si-
mon, are you asleep? Couldn't you watch with me even one hour? 38 Keep
watch and pray, so that you will not give in to temptation. For the spirit is
willing, but the body is weak."
39 Then Jesus left them again and prayed the same prayer as before. 40 When
he returned to them again, he found them sleeping, for they couldn't keep
their eyes open. And they didn't know what to say.
41 When he returned to them the third time, he said, "Go ahead and sleep.
Have your rest. But no—the time has come. The Son of Man is betrayed into
the hands of sinners. 42 Up, let's be going. Look, my betrayer is here!"

Jesus Is Betrayed and Arrested

43 And immediately, even as Jesus said this, Judas, one of the twelve disciples,
arrived with a crowd of men armed with swords and clubs. They had been
sent by the leading priests, the teachers of religious law, and the elders. 44 The
traitor, Judas, had given them a prearranged signal: "You will know which
one to arrest when I greet him with a kiss. Then you can take him away
under guard." 45 As soon as they arrived, Judas walked up to Jesus. "Rabbi!"
he exclaimed, and gave him the kiss.
46 Then the others grabbed Jesus and arrested him. 47 But one of the men
with Jesus pulled out his sword and struck the high priest's slave, slashing
off his ear.
48 Jesus asked them, "Am I some dangerous revolutionary, that you come
with swords and clubs to arrest me? 49 Why didn't you arrest me in the
Temple? I was there among you teaching every day. But these things are
happening to fulfill what the Scriptures say about me."
50 Then all his disciples deserted him and ran away. 51 One young man fol-
lowing behind was clothed only in a long linen shirt. When the mob tried
to grab him, 52 he slipped out of his shirt and ran away naked.

14:27 Greek *I will strike.* Zech 13:7. **14:36** *Abba* is an Aramaic term for "father."

Jesus before the Council

53 They took Jesus to the high priest's home where the leading priests, the
elders, and the teachers of religious law had gathered. 54 Meanwhile, Peter
followed him at a distance and went right into the high priest's courtyard.
There he sat with the guards, warming himself by the fire.
55 Inside, the leading priests and the entire high council* were trying to
find evidence against Jesus, so they could put him to death. But they couldn't
find any. 56 Many false witnesses spoke against him, but they contradicted
each other. 57 Finally, some men stood up and gave this false testimony: 58 "We
heard him say, 'I will destroy this Temple made with human hands, and in
three days I will build another, made without human hands.'" 59 But even
then they didn't get their stories straight!
60 Then the high priest stood up before the others and asked Jesus, "Well,
aren't you going to answer these charges? What do you have to say for your-
self?" 61 But Jesus was silent and made no reply. Then the high priest asked
him, "Are you the Messiah, the Son of the Blessed One?"
62 Jesus said, "I AM.* And you will see the Son of Man seated in the place of
power at God's right hand* and coming on the clouds of heaven.*"
63 Then the high priest tore his clothing to show his horror and said, "Why
do we need other witnesses? 64 You have all heard his blasphemy. What is
your verdict?"
"Guilty!" they all cried. "He deserves to die!"
65 Then some of them began to spit at him, and they blindfolded him
and beat him with their fists. "Prophesy to us," they jeered. And the guards
slapped him as they took him away.

Peter Denies Jesus

66 Meanwhile, Peter was in the courtyard below. One of the servant girls who
worked for the high priest came by 67 and noticed Peter warming himself
at the fire. She looked at him closely and said, "You were one of those with
Jesus of Nazareth.*"
68 But Peter denied it. "I don't know what you're talking about," he said,
and he went out into the entryway. Just then, a rooster crowed.*
69 When the servant girl saw him standing there, she began telling
the others, "This man is definitely one of them!" 70 But Peter denied it again.
A little later some of the other bystanders confronted Peter and said,
"You must be one of them, because you are a Galilean."
71 Peter swore, "A curse on me if I'm lying—I don't know this man
you're talking about!" 72 And immediately the rooster crowed the sec-
ond time.
Suddenly, Jesus' words flashed through Peter's mind: "Before the rooster
crows twice, you will deny three times that you even know me." And he
broke down and wept.

Jesus' Trial before Pilate

15 Very early in the morning the leading priests, the elders, and the
teachers of religious law—the entire high council*—met to discuss

14:55 Greek *the Sanhedrin.* 14:62a Or *The 'I AM' is here;* or *I am the LORD.* See Exod 3:14.
14:62b Greek *seated at the right hand of the power.* See Ps 110:1. 14:62c See Dan 7:13.
14:67 Or *Jesus the Nazarene.* 14:68 Some manuscripts do not include *Just then, a rooster crowed.*
15:1 Greek *the Sanhedrin;* also in 15:43.

Make a Difference

14:66-72

Peter's Breakdown

When the rooster crowed, Peter broke down and wept. Part of realizing who Jesus is means that we need to face our own sin. Peter tried to cover up his guilt, he tried to ignore it, and he tried to lie about it. When he was exposed, Peter became overwhelmed by his rejection of Jesus. At once, Jesus' words flashed through his mind, and he was undone.

Contrary to our excuse-heavy culture, the Bible encourages us to feel the weight of the consequences of our sin. Meeting Jesus disrupts our pretense and avoidance. Meeting Jesus makes us authentic and honest. Only when we let Jesus' words flash through our minds can our thinking become clear enough to discover the true gift of forgiveness through the cross that Jesus offers.

Difference Maker

Turn to the back of this Bible and pray through the section on "How to Accept Jesus as Your Lord and Savior."

Story Arc 14:62

● God

This is one of the most powerful statements of Jesus. It echoes another passage where Moses asked God for his name (Exodus 3:13-14). This is utterly powerful. The religious leaders understood in an instant what Jesus was claiming. The high priest was so horrified at Jesus' declaration that he tore his clothing and sentenced Jesus to death.

Mark 15:21 ►

Question **15:20**

Look through Isaiah 53. What similarities do you see with the events of Jesus' crucifixion?

Story Arc **15:21**

Simon of Cyrene

Simon of Cyrene just happened to be in the right spot. Imagine how alarming it must have been to return to the city after being out in the countryside all day and to notice a crucifixion crowd. Imagine how alarming it must have been then to have soldiers suddenly point at you and force you to carry the cross of a convicted criminal.

This moment must have forever changed Simon of Cyrene. He must have been compelled to find out about the Man whose cross he carried. He must have sought out other followers of Jesus, learned about Jesus, and put his faith in him fully. Simon of Cyrene must have become someone whom Mark and the early believers grew to know very well. Mark mentioned Simon's name and then added in parentheses "the father of Alexander and Rufus."

Luke 1:3-4 ►

their next step. They bound Jesus, led him away, and took him to Pilate, the
Roman governor.
2 Pilate asked Jesus, "Are you the king of the Jews?"
Jesus replied, "You have said it."
3 Then the leading priests kept accusing him of many crimes, 4 and Pilate
asked him, "Aren't you going to answer them? What about all these charges
they are bringing against you?" 5 But Jesus said nothing, much to Pilate's
surprise.
6 Now it was the governor's custom each year during the Passover cele-
bration to release one prisoner—anyone the people requested. 7 One of the
prisoners at that time was Barabbas, a revolutionary who had committed
murder in an uprising. 8 The crowd went to Pilate and asked him to release
a prisoner as usual.
9 "Would you like me to release to you this 'King of the Jews'?" Pilate
asked. 10 (For he realized by now that the leading priests had arrested Jesus
out of envy.) 11 But at this point the leading priests stirred up the crowd to
demand the release of Barabbas instead of Jesus. 12 Pilate asked them, "Then
what should I do with this man you call the king of the Jews?"
13 They shouted back, "Crucify him!"
14 "Why?" Pilate demanded. "What crime has he committed?"
But the mob roared even louder, "Crucify him!"
15 So to pacify the crowd, Pilate released Barabbas to them. He ordered
Jesus flogged with a lead-tipped whip, then turned him over to the Roman
soldiers to be crucified.

The Soldiers Mock Jesus

16 The soldiers took Jesus into the courtyard of the governor's headquarters
(called the Praetorium) and called out the entire regiment. 17 They dressed
him in a purple robe, and they wove thorn branches into a crown and put
it on his head. 18 Then they saluted him and taunted, "Hail! King of the
Jews!" 19 And they struck him on the head with a reed stick, spit on him, and
dropped to their knees in mock worship. 20 When they were finally tired of
mocking him, they took off the purple robe and put his own clothes on him
again. Then they led him away to be crucified.

The Crucifixion

21 A passerby named Simon, who was from Cyrene,* was coming in from the
countryside just then, and the soldiers forced him to carry Jesus' cross. (Si-
mon was the father of Alexander and Rufus.) 22 And they brought Jesus to
a place called Golgotha (which means "Place of the Skull"). 23 They offered
him wine drugged with myrrh, but he refused it.
24 Then the soldiers nailed him to the cross. They divided his clothes and
threw dice* to decide who would get each piece. 25 It was nine o'clock in the
morning when they crucified him. 26 A sign announced the charge against
him. It read, "The King of the Jews." 27 Two revolutionaries* were crucified
with him, one on his right and one on his left.*
29 The people passing by shouted abuse, shaking their heads in mockery.
"Ha! Look at you now!" they yelled at him. "You said you were going to

15:21 *Cyrene* was a city in northern Africa. 15:24 Greek *cast lots.* See Ps 22:18. 15:27a Or *Two criminals.* 15:27b Some manuscripts add verse 28, *And the Scripture was fulfilled that said, "He was counted among those who were rebels."* See Isa 53:12; also compare Luke 22:37.

destroy the Temple and rebuild it in three days. 30 Well then, save yourself
and come down from the cross!"
31 The leading priests and teachers of religious law also mocked Jesus. "He
saved others," they scoffed, "but he can't save himself! 32 Let this Messiah, this
King of Israel, come down from the cross so we can see it and believe him!"
Even the men who were crucified with Jesus ridiculed him.

The Death of Jesus

33 At noon, darkness fell across the whole land until three o'clock. 34 Then at
three o'clock Jesus called out with a loud voice, *"Eloi, Eloi, lema sabachthani?"*
which means "My God, my God, why have you abandoned me?"*
35 Some of the bystanders misunderstood and thought he was calling for
the prophet Elijah. 36 One of them ran and filled a sponge with sour wine,
holding it up to him on a reed stick so he could drink. "Wait!" he said. "Let's
see whether Elijah comes to take him down!"
37 Then Jesus uttered another loud cry and breathed his last. 38 And the
curtain in the sanctuary of the Temple was torn in two, from top to bottom.
39 When the Roman officer* who stood facing him* saw how he had died,
he exclaimed, "This man truly was the Son of God!"
40 Some women were there, watching from a distance, including Mary
Magdalene, Mary (the mother of James the younger and of Joseph*), and
Salome. 41 They had been followers of Jesus and had cared for him while he
was in Galilee. Many other women who had come with him to Jerusalem
were also there.

The Burial of Jesus

42 This all happened on Friday, the day of preparation,* the day before the
Sabbath. As evening approached, 43 Joseph of Arimathea took a risk and went
to Pilate and asked for Jesus' body. (Joseph was an honored member of the
high council, and he was waiting for the Kingdom of God to come.) 44 Pilate
couldn't believe that Jesus was already dead, so he called for the Roman offi-
cer and asked if he had died yet. 45 The officer confirmed that Jesus was dead,
so Pilate told Joseph he could have the body. 46 Joseph bought a long sheet
of linen cloth. Then he took Jesus' body down from the cross, wrapped it in
the cloth, and laid it in a tomb that had been carved out of the rock. Then
he rolled a stone in front of the entrance. 47 Mary Magdalene and Mary the
mother of Joseph saw where Jesus' body was laid.

The Resurrection

16 Saturday evening, when the Sabbath ended, Mary Magdalene, Mary
the mother of James, and Salome went out and purchased burial
spices so they could anoint Jesus' body. 2 Very early on Sunday morning,*
just at sunrise, they went to the tomb. 3 On the way they were asking each
other, "Who will roll away the stone for us from the entrance to the tomb?"
4 But as they arrived, they looked up and saw that the stone, which was very
large, had already been rolled aside.
5 When they entered the tomb, they saw a young man clothed in a white
robe sitting on the right side. The women were shocked, 6 but the angel said,

15:34 Ps 22:1. 15:39a Greek *the centurion;* similarly in 15:44, 45. 15:39b Some manuscripts add *heard his cry and.* 15:40 Greek *Joses;* also in 15:47. See Matt 27:56. 15:42 Greek *It was the day of preparation.* 16:2 Greek *on the first day of the week;* also in 16:9.

Question **15:34**

Look through Psalm 22. What similarities do you see with the events of Jesus' crucifixion?

Make a Difference

15:37

Take a Deep Breath

God breathed into Adam to give him life. When Adam sinned, it meant that humanity would lose that breath. When Jesus came to this world to breathe among us, he was also deliberately choosing to take the consequence of sin upon his shoulders. Right here, this very moment when Jesus "breathed his last" is the completion of the consequence of sin.

Difference Maker

Don't let the significance of this moment pass you by. Take a deep breath and praise Jesus.

Question **15:39**

One of the Roman officers who was in charge of carrying out the crucifixion of Jesus was startled by Jesus' words, by Jesus' demeanor, and by the dramatic events of his last breath. He stood facing Jesus' dead body and proclaimed a truth the world had been waiting (and needing) to hear: "This man truly was the Son of God!"

What theological significance is there in the fact that the one who put Jesus on the cross came to recognize Jesus' true identity?

Question 16:7

Why do you think the angel asked these women to be the very first people to share the good news that Jesus had risen from the dead?

Make a Difference

16:20

Everywhere

The mashed-up, mixed-up disciples were so emboldened by the resurrection and so empowered by the commissioning of the Spirit that they passionately went "everywhere" to share the good news of Jesus. This is the point of Mark's account. Like the other followers of Jesus, he was transformed from a scared young man into a bold evangelist with an urgent message to share.

Difference Maker

Go back and read the full urgency of all the words of the book of Mark in one sitting. Let Jesus' miracles amaze you. Let Jesus' teachings rock you. Let Jesus' death on the cross undo you. Let Jesus' resurrection ignite you. Let Jesus' Spirit work through you to share his good news.

"Don't be alarmed. You are looking for Jesus of Nazareth,* who was crucified.
He isn't here! He is risen from the dead! Look, this is where they laid his body.
7 Now go and tell his disciples, including Peter, that Jesus is going ahead of
you to Galilee. You will see him there, just as he told you before he died."
8 The women fled from the tomb, trembling and bewildered, and they said
nothing to anyone because they were too frightened.*

[The most ancient manuscripts of Mark conclude with verse 16:8.
Later manuscripts add one or both of the following endings.]

[Shorter Ending of Mark]

Then they briefly reported all this to Peter and his companions. Afterward
Jesus himself sent them out from east to west with the sacred and unfailing
message of salvation that gives eternal life. Amen.

[Longer Ending of Mark]

9 After Jesus rose from the dead early on Sunday morning, the first person
who saw him was Mary Magdalene, the woman from whom he had cast out
seven demons. 10 She went to the disciples, who were grieving and weeping,
and told them what had happened. 11 But when she told them that Jesus was
alive and she had seen him, they didn't believe her.
12 Afterward he appeared in a different form to two of his followers who
were walking from Jerusalem into the country. 13 They rushed back to tell
the others, but no one believed them.
14 Still later he appeared to the eleven disciples as they were eating to-
gether. He rebuked them for their stubborn unbelief because they refused
to believe those who had seen him after he had been raised from the dead.*
15 And then he told them, "Go into all the world and preach the Good
News to everyone. 16 Anyone who believes and is baptized will be saved. But
anyone who refuses to believe will be condemned. 17 These miraculous signs
will accompany those who believe: They will cast out demons in my name,
and they will speak in new languages.* 18 They will be able to handle snakes
with safety, and if they drink anything poisonous, it won't hurt them. They
will be able to place their hands on the sick, and they will be healed."
19 When the Lord Jesus had finished talking with them, he was taken up
into heaven and sat down in the place of honor at God's right hand. 20 And
the disciples went everywhere and preached, and the Lord worked through
them, confirming what they said by many miraculous signs.

16:6 Or *Jesus the Nazarene.* 16:8 The most reliable early manuscripts of the Gospel of Mark end at verse 8. Other manuscripts include various endings to the Gospel. A few include both the "shorter ending" and the "longer ending." The majority of manuscripts include the "longer ending" immediately after verse 8. 16:14 Some early manuscripts add: *And they excused themselves, saying, "This age of lawlessness and unbelief is under Satan, who does not permit God's truth and power to conquer the evil [unclean] spirits. Therefore, reveal your justice now." This is what they said to Christ. And Christ replied to them, "The period of years of Satan's power has been fulfilled, but other dreadful things will happen soon. And I was handed over to death for those who have sinned, so that they may return to the truth and sin no more, and so they may inherit the spiritual, incorruptible, and righteous glory in heaven."* 16:17 Or *new tongues;* some manuscripts do not include *new.*

Luke Introduction

Imagine that four different people get to write about a major event happening today. Each writer uniquely captures it all with precise accuracy, adding their unique angles to the story. Each perspective offers depth and details. When you read each account, you get a rich, full picture of the same story.

The book of Luke is one of four unique accounts of the life of Jesus. Luke's gospel is a brilliantly journaled documentary that shares about the life, ministry, stories, and teachings of Jesus. It was written during a time when Christians had become a target of Rome. The Romans had discovered that Christianity couldn't be labeled as just another religion that they could tolerate in the empire. The followers of Jesus had become a genuinely powerful movement spreading across the world—and it couldn't be ignored. As those in Roman power tried to destroy and discredit Christians, Luke showed how the backstory and ministry of Jesus were legitimate beyond measure. While Rome tried to show itself to be the only culture that mattered, Luke used street language and a scholarly vibe to speak to everyone. By the way, Luke followed this account with a sequel, the book of Acts, where he revealed how Christ's followers began to share his good news all over the Roman Empire.

Don't take this for granted. Luke's gospel offers exclusive details that have formed the most significant stories the world has ever known. From specifics about the birth and death of Jesus that Christians read and remember every Christmas and Easter to powerful descriptions of Jesus' miracles and encounters, this book is meant to change your life.

Story Arcs

- **Theophilus**
- **Simeon and Anna**
- **John the Baptist**
- **Jesus**
- **The Roman Officer**
- **Mary Magdalene**

Luke

Introduction

1 Many people have set out to write accounts about the events that have
been fulfilled among us. 2 They used the eyewitness reports circulating
among us from the early disciples.* 3 Having carefully investigated every-
thing from the beginning, I also have decided to write an accurate account
for you, most honorable Theophilus, 4 so you can be certain of the truth of
everything you were taught.

The Birth of John the Baptist Foretold

5 When Herod was king of Judea, there was a Jewish priest named Zechariah.
He was a member of the priestly order of Abijah, and his wife, Elizabeth, was
also from the priestly line of Aaron. 6 Zechariah and Elizabeth were righteous
in God's eyes, careful to obey all of the Lord's commandments and regula-
tions. 7 They had no children because Elizabeth was unable to conceive, and
they were both very old.
8 One day Zechariah was serving God in the Temple, for his order was on
duty that week. 9 As was the custom of the priests, he was chosen by lot to
enter the sanctuary of the Lord and burn incense. 10 While the incense was
being burned, a great crowd stood outside, praying.
11 While Zechariah was in the sanctuary, an angel of the Lord appeared
to him, standing to the right of the incense altar. 12 Zechariah was shaken
and overwhelmed with fear when he saw him. 13 But the angel said, "Don't
be afraid, Zechariah! God has heard your prayer. Your wife, Elizabeth, will
give you a son, and you are to name him John. 14 You will have great joy and
gladness, and many will rejoice at his birth, 15 for he will be great in the eyes
of the Lord. He must never touch wine or other alcoholic drinks. He will be
filled with the Holy Spirit, even before his birth.* 16 And he will turn many
Israelites to the Lord their God. 17 He will be a man with the spirit and power
of Elijah. He will prepare the people for the coming of the Lord. He will turn
the hearts of the fathers to their children,* and he will cause those who are
rebellious to accept the wisdom of the godly."
18 Zechariah said to the angel, "How can I be sure this will happen? I'm an
old man now, and my wife is also well along in years."
19 Then the angel said, "I am Gabriel! I stand in the very presence of God. It
was he who sent me to bring you this good news! 20 But now, since you didn't
believe what I said, you will be silent and unable to speak until the child is
born. For my words will certainly be fulfilled at the proper time."
21 Meanwhile, the people were waiting for Zechariah to come out of the
sanctuary, wondering why he was taking so long. 22 When he finally did come
out, he couldn't speak to them. Then they realized from his gestures and his
silence that he must have seen a vision in the sanctuary.

Story Arc **1:3-4**

● Theophilus

Two of the most important books ever written were addressed to a man named Theophilus: Luke and Acts. We know very little about him other than the fact that he and Luke must have known one another and that he had previously been taught a bit about Jesus (v. 4). Now, in this account and in Acts, Luke felt compelled to share a full story of Jesus and a full story of the growth of the early church. What would we be missing from our faith if Luke had not written to this man?

Luke 2:25-38 ▸

1:2 Greek *from those who from the beginning were servants of the word.* **1:15** Or *even from birth.* **1:17** See Mal 4:5-6.

23 When Zechariah's week of service in the Temple was over, he returned
home. 24 Soon afterward his wife, Elizabeth, became pregnant and went into
seclusion for five months. 25 "How kind the Lord is!" she exclaimed. "He has
taken away my disgrace of having no children."

The Birth of Jesus Foretold

26 In the sixth month of Elizabeth's pregnancy, God sent the angel Gabriel
to Nazareth, a village in Galilee, 27 to a virgin named Mary. She was engaged
to be married to a man named Joseph, a descendant of King David. 28 Ga-
briel appeared to her and said, "Greetings,* favored woman! The Lord is
with you!*"
29 Confused and disturbed, Mary tried to think what the angel could mean.
30 "Don't be afraid, Mary," the angel told her, "for you have found favor with
God! 31 You will conceive and give birth to a son, and you will name him Jesus.
32 He will be very great and will be called the Son of the Most High. The Lord
God will give him the throne of his ancestor David. 33 And he will reign over
Israel* forever; his Kingdom will never end!"
34 Mary asked the angel, "But how can this happen? I am a virgin."
35 The angel replied, "The Holy Spirit will come upon you, and the power
of the Most High will overshadow you. So the baby to be born will be holy,
and he will be called the Son of God. 36 What's more, your relative Elizabeth
has become pregnant in her old age! People used to say she was barren, but
she has conceived a son and is now in her sixth month. 37 For the word of
God will never fail.*"
38 Mary responded, "I am the Lord's servant. May everything you have said
about me come true." And then the angel left her.

Mary Visits Elizabeth

39 A few days later Mary hurried to the hill country of Judea, to the town
40 where Zechariah lived. She entered the house and greeted Elizabeth. 41 At
the sound of Mary's greeting, Elizabeth's child leaped within her, and Eliz-
abeth was filled with the Holy Spirit.
42 Elizabeth gave a glad cry and exclaimed to Mary, "God has blessed you
above all women, and your child is blessed. 43 Why am I so honored, that the
mother of my Lord should visit me? 44 When I heard your greeting, the baby
in my womb jumped for joy. 45 You are blessed because you believed that the
Lord would do what he said."

The Magnificat: Mary's Song of Praise

46 Mary responded,

"Oh, how my soul praises the Lord.
47 How my spirit rejoices in God my Savior!
48 For he took notice of his lowly servant girl,
and from now on all generations will call me blessed.
49 For the Mighty One is holy,
and he has done great things for me.
50 He shows mercy from generation to generation
to all who fear him.

1:28a Or *Rejoice.* **1:28b** Some manuscripts add *Blessed are you among women.* **1:33** Greek *over the house of Jacob.* **1:37** Some manuscripts read *For nothing is impossible with God.*

Make a Difference 1:28

Hello!

The award for the most awkward hello of all eternity should go to the simply spoken angel Gabriel. Luke revealed that God sent Gabriel to Nazareth to speak to Mary, a young virgin who was engaged to a carpenter named Joseph. Gabriel went to her and politely said, "Greetings." Gabriel then described the reason for his greeting: Mary would conceive and give birth to the Son of God.

Difference Maker

Write an encouraging greeting to someone and share the good news of Jesus with them.

Make a Difference 1:32

Jesus Will Be Very Great

No one could disagree one bit with Gabriel's assessment of Jesus. Jesus simply, no argument, would be great. Not kind of great, he would be the definition of and the very model of greatness. Masterfully great. Awe-inspiringly, knee-shatteringly, jaw-droppingly, arms-raisingly, angel-dumbfoundingly great. Gabriel couldn't have said it any simpler. Never before or since has one uttered such an eternal understatement.

To his credit, Gabriel did elaborate a bit. Besides the fact that Jesus would be great, the angel casually reassured Mary that her son "will be called the Son of the Most High," and, by the way, his kingdom will never end. So, uh, don't be afraid, Mary.

Difference Maker

In celebration of Jesus, no matter what day it is on the calendar, give someone an unexpected gift today.

51 His mighty arm has done tremendous things!
He has scattered the proud and haughty ones.
52 He has brought down princes from their thrones
and exalted the humble.
53 He has filled the hungry with good things
and sent the rich away with empty hands.
54 He has helped his servant Israel
and remembered to be merciful.
55 For he made this promise to our ancestors,
to Abraham and his children forever."

56 Mary stayed with Elizabeth about three months and then went back
to her own home.

The Birth of John the Baptist

57 When it was time for Elizabeth's baby to be born, she gave birth to a son.
58 And when her neighbors and relatives heard that the Lord had been very
merciful to her, everyone rejoiced with her.

59 When the baby was eight days old, they all came for the circumcision
ceremony. They wanted to name him Zechariah, after his father. 60 But Eliz-
abeth said, "No! His name is John!"

61 "What?" they exclaimed. "There is no one in all your family by that
name." 62 So they used gestures to ask the baby's father what he wanted to
name him. 63 He motioned for a writing tablet, and to everyone's surprise
he wrote, "His name is John." 64 Instantly Zechariah could speak again, and
he began praising God.

65 Awe fell upon the whole neighborhood, and the news of what had hap-
pened spread throughout the Judean hills. 66 Everyone who heard about it
reflected on these events and asked, "What will this child turn out to be?"
For the hand of the Lord was surely upon him in a special way.

Zechariah's Prophecy

67 Then his father, Zechariah, was filled with the Holy Spirit and gave this
prophecy:

68 "Praise the Lord, the God of Israel,
because he has visited and redeemed his people.
69 He has sent us a mighty Savior*
from the royal line of his servant David,
70 just as he promised
through his holy prophets long ago.
71 Now we will be saved from our enemies
and from all who hate us.
72 He has been merciful to our ancestors
by remembering his sacred covenant—
73 the covenant he swore with an oath
to our ancestor Abraham.
74 We have been rescued from our enemies
so we can serve God without fear,

1:69 Greek *has raised up a horn of salvation for us.*

75 in holiness and righteousness
for as long as we live.

76 "And you, my little son,
will be called the prophet of the Most High,
because you will prepare the way for the Lord.
77 You will tell his people how to find salvation
through forgiveness of their sins.
78 Because of God's tender mercy,
the morning light from heaven is about to break upon us,*
79 to give light to those who sit in darkness and in the shadow of death,
and to guide us to the path of peace."

80 John grew up and became strong in spirit. And he lived in the wilderness
until he began his public ministry to Israel.

The Birth of Jesus

2 At that time the Roman emperor, Augustus, decreed that a census
should be taken throughout the Roman Empire. 2 (This was the first
census taken when Quirinius was governor of Syria.) 3 All returned to their
own ancestral towns to register for this census. 4 And because Joseph was a de-
scendant of King David, he had to go to Bethlehem in Judea, David's ancient
home. He traveled there from the village of Nazareth in Galilee. 5 He took
with him Mary, to whom he was engaged, who was now expecting a child.
6 And while they were there, the time came for her baby to be born. 7 She
gave birth to her firstborn son. She wrapped him snugly in strips of cloth
and laid him in a manger, because there was no lodging available for them.

The Shepherds and Angels

8 That night there were shepherds staying in the fields nearby, guarding their
flocks of sheep. 9 Suddenly, an angel of the Lord appeared among them, and
the radiance of the Lord's glory surrounded them. They were terrified, 10 but
the angel reassured them. "Don't be afraid!" he said. "I bring you good news
that will bring great joy to all people. 11 The Savior—yes, the Messiah, the
Lord—has been born today in Bethlehem, the city of David! 12 And you will
recognize him by this sign: You will find a baby wrapped snugly in strips of
cloth, lying in a manger."
13 Suddenly, the angel was joined by a vast host of others—the armies of
heaven—praising God and saying,

14 "Glory to God in highest heaven,
and peace on earth to those with whom God is pleased."

15 When the angels had returned to heaven, the shepherds said to each
other, "Let's go to Bethlehem! Let's see this thing that has happened, which
the Lord has told us about."
16 They hurried to the village and found Mary and Joseph. And there was
the baby, lying in the manger. 17 After seeing him, the shepherds told every-
one what had happened and what the angel had said to them about this

1:78 Or *the Morning Light from Heaven is about to visit us.*

Question 2:1-5

God used Caesar Augustus like a puppet. He wasn't concerned about Quirinius complicating things or Herod stopping the show. He had set this plan in motion long before any of those men changed their diapers. A King, the only true King, was going to be born to a humble girl in a lowly corner of the world in the midst of fragility so that the broken people of the world could draw near and embrace their almighty Savior. If God could do this, what can he do in your life?

Make a Difference 2:6-7

Gift

Should we leave Jesus, and our faith, in the manger? That isn't where Jesus stayed. He was wrapped in swaddling cloth and laid in a manger, but later he was wrapped in burial cloths and laid in a tomb. His incarnation is an intense story that encompasses his entire life: the Creator took upon himself blood and body and bones and entered humbly into the world of his created ones to sacrifice himself.

We are inclined to opt for a consumerist faith, selfish in its assumption of undeserved grace and shallow in its apprehension of the humanity of Jesus Christ. That the holy God of the universe would take on the fragility of flesh in this violent, sinful world exposes God's determination to go to the most extreme lengths to love his people. How can we leave Jesus, and our faith, in the manger?

Difference Maker

Wrap up some simple but meaningful gifts and arrange to give them away in a soup kitchen, homeless shelter, prison ministry, nursing home, hospital, or group home.

child. 18 All who heard the shepherds' story were astonished, 19 but Mary kept
all these things in her heart and thought about them often. 20 The shepherds
went back to their flocks, glorifying and praising God for all they had heard
and seen. It was just as the angel had told them.

Jesus Is Presented in the Temple

21 Eight days later, when the baby was circumcised, he was named Jesus, the
name given him by the angel even before he was conceived.
22 Then it was time for their purification offering, as required by the law of
Moses after the birth of a child; so his parents took him to Jerusalem to present
him to the Lord. 23 The law of the Lord says, "If a woman's first child is a boy,
he must be dedicated to the LORD."* 24 So they offered the sacrifice required
in the law of the Lord—"either a pair of turtledoves or two young pigeons."*

The Prophecy of Simeon

25 At that time there was a man in Jerusalem named Simeon. He was righ-
teous and devout and was eagerly waiting for the Messiah to come and res-
cue Israel. The Holy Spirit was upon him 26 and had revealed to him that he
would not die until he had seen the Lord's Messiah. 27 That day the Spirit led
him to the Temple. So when Mary and Joseph came to present the baby Jesus
● to the Lord as the law required, 28 Simeon was there. He took the child in his
arms and praised God, saying,

29 "Sovereign Lord, now let your servant die in peace,
as you have promised.
30 I have seen your salvation,
31 which you have prepared for all people.
32 He is a light to reveal God to the nations,
and he is the glory of your people Israel!"

33 Jesus' parents were amazed at what was being said about him. 34 Then
Simeon blessed them, and he said to Mary, the baby's mother, "This child
is destined to cause many in Israel to fall, and many others to rise. He has
been sent as a sign from God, but many will oppose him. 35 As a result, the
deepest thoughts of many hearts will be revealed. And a sword will pierce
your very soul."

The Prophecy of Anna

36 Anna, a prophet, was also there in the Temple. She was the daughter of
Phanuel from the tribe of Asher, and she was very old. Her husband died
when they had been married only seven years. 37 Then she lived as a widow
to the age of eighty-four.* She never left the Temple but stayed there day
and night, worshiping God with fasting and prayer. 38 She came along just
as Simeon was talking with Mary and Joseph, and she began praising God.
She talked about the child to everyone who had been waiting expectantly
for God to rescue Jerusalem.
39 When Jesus' parents had fulfilled all the requirements of the law of the
Lord, they returned home to Nazareth in Galilee. 40 There the child grew up
healthy and strong. He was filled with wisdom, and God's favor was on him.

2:23 Exod 13:2. 2:24 Lev 12:8. 2:37 Or *She had been a widow for eighty-four years.*

Story Arc 2:25-38

● Simeon and Anna

For two thousand years, people have been celebrating the birth of Jesus. Actually, it has been longer than that because even before Jesus was born, people were anticipating his arrival. The prophet Micah had predicted his arrival in Bethlehem, Isaiah had foreseen his powerful ministry, and Simeon and Anna had waited their whole lives to hold him. Celebrating the birth of the Messiah is one of the greatest and most anticipated traditions of history.

Luke 3:2-20 ►

Jesus Speaks with the Teachers

41 Every year Jesus' parents went to Jerusalem for the Passover festival.
42 When Jesus was twelve years old, they attended the festival as usual. 43 After
the celebration was over, they started home to Nazareth, but Jesus stayed
behind in Jerusalem. His parents didn't miss him at first, 44 because they as-
sumed he was among the other travelers. But when he didn't show up that
evening, they started looking for him among their relatives and friends.

45 When they couldn't find him, they went back to Jerusalem to search for
him there. 46 Three days later they finally discovered him in the Temple, sit-
ting among the religious teachers, listening to them and asking questions.
47 All who heard him were amazed at his understanding and his answers.

48 His parents didn't know what to think. "Son," his mother said to him,
"why have you done this to us? Your father and I have been frantic, search-
ing for you everywhere."

49 "But why did you need to search?" he asked. "Didn't you know that
I must be in my Father's house?"* 50 But they didn't understand what he
meant.

51 Then he returned to Nazareth with them and was obedient to them. And
his mother stored all these things in her heart.

52 Jesus grew in wisdom and in stature and in favor with God and all the
people.

John the Baptist Prepares the Way

3 It was now the fifteenth year of the reign of Tiberius, the Roman em-
peror. Pontius Pilate was governor over Judea; Herod Antipas was ruler*
over Galilee; his brother Philip was ruler* over Iturea and Traconitis; Ly-
sanias was ruler over Abilene. 2 Annas and Caiaphas were the high priests.
At this time a message from God came to John son of Zechariah, who was
living in the wilderness. 3 Then John went from place to place on both sides
of the Jordan River, preaching that people should be baptized to show that
they had repented of their sins and turned to God to be forgiven. 4 Isaiah had
spoken of John when he said,

"He is a voice shouting in the wilderness,
'Prepare the way for the LORD's coming!
Clear the road for him!
5 The valleys will be filled,
and the mountains and hills made level.
The curves will be straightened,
and the rough places made smooth.
6 And then all people will see
the salvation sent from God.'"*

7 When the crowds came to John for baptism, he said, "You brood of
snakes! Who warned you to flee the coming wrath? 8 Prove by the way you
live that you have repented of your sins and turned to God. Don't just say
to each other, 'We're safe, for we are descendants of Abraham.' That means
nothing, for I tell you, God can create children of Abraham from these very

2:49 Or *"Didn't you realize that I should be involved with my Father's affairs?"* 3:1a Greek *Herod was tetrarch.* Herod Antipas was a son of King Herod. 3:1b Greek *tetrarch;* also in 3:1c. 3:4-6 Isa 40:3-5 (Greek version).

Make a Difference 2:51

Fairy-Tale Version?

There's the fairy-tale version of Christmas: A quiet baby laid in a warm manger surrounded by a beautiful young mom and an incredibly gentle adoptive father, graced by humble shepherds and cute, little lambs, all while a star hovered just overhead. Angels sang sweetly o'er the plain while the earth was placid.

Then there's the reality: A screaming baby, held by an unwed teenage mom who had fled her family with her boyfriend, was visited by terrified shepherds on a strange order from angels. The local king demanded the baby's death, so soldiers descended upon the town and murdered every young male child present. The new family frantically escaped to Egypt, where their ancestors had been enslaved years before. Eventually the baby grew, gifted with authority to heal the sick and raise the dead. Crowds clamored for his kingship, but when he refused to incite a revolt, the crowds betrayed him, beat him, and executed him, all while his mother wept at his bloody feet.

No wonder we like the fairy-tale version much better. The sweetness of a carnation is nicer than the shock of the incarnation.

Difference Maker

Take fifteen minutes to consider the raw reality of Jesus' birth.

Story Arc 3:2-20

John the Baptist

Read Luke 1:13-17 and 3:2-20. Can you see why Jesus called John the greatest person to ever have been born (Luke 7:28)?

Luke 3:23-38 ►

stones. 9 Even now the ax of God's judgment is poised, ready to sever the roots
of the trees. Yes, every tree that does not produce good fruit will be chopped
down and thrown into the fire."
10 The crowds asked, "What should we do?"
11 John replied, "If you have two shirts, give one to the poor. If you have
food, share it with those who are hungry."
12 Even corrupt tax collectors came to be baptized and asked, "Teacher,
what should we do?"
13 He replied, "Collect no more taxes than the government requires."
14 "What should we do?" asked some soldiers.
John replied, "Don't extort money or make false accusations. And be con-
tent with your pay."
15 Everyone was expecting the Messiah to come soon, and they were eager
to know whether John might be the Messiah. 16 John answered their ques-
tions by saying, "I baptize you with* water; but someone is coming soon who
is greater than I am—so much greater that I'm not even worthy to be his
slave and untie the straps of his sandals. He will baptize you with the Holy
Spirit and with fire.* 17 He is ready to separate the chaff from the wheat with
his winnowing fork. Then he will clean up the threshing area, gathering the
wheat into his barn but burning the chaff with never-ending fire." 18 John
used many such warnings as he announced the Good News to the people.
19 John also publicly criticized Herod Antipas, the ruler of Galilee,* for
marrying Herodias, his brother's wife, and for many other wrongs he had
done. 20 So Herod put John in prison, adding this sin to his many others.

The Baptism of Jesus

21 One day when the crowds were being baptized, Jesus himself was baptized.
As he was praying, the heavens opened, 22 and the Holy Spirit, in bodily form,
descended on him like a dove. And a voice from heaven said, "You are my
dearly loved Son, and you bring me great joy.*"

The Ancestors of Jesus

23 Jesus was about thirty years old when he began his public ministry.

Jesus was known as the son of Joseph.
Joseph was the son of Heli.
24 Heli was the son of Matthat.
Matthat was the son of Levi.
Levi was the son of Melki.
Melki was the son of Jannai.
Jannai was the son of Joseph.
25 Joseph was the son of Mattathias.
Mattathias was the son of Amos.
Amos was the son of Nahum.
Nahum was the son of Esli.
Esli was the son of Naggai.
26 Naggai was the son of Maath.
Maath was the son of Mattathias.
Mattathias was the son of Semein.

Story Arc 3:23–38

● Jesus

Jesus had a royal lineage. Take a moment to go through the Bible to find some of these key people and discover how their stories fit into God's plan of salvation: Zerubbabel, David, Boaz, Judah, Jacob, Isaac, Abraham, Noah, Methuselah, Enoch, and Adam.

Luke 7:1–10 ►

3:16a Or *in.* 3:16b Or *in the Holy Spirit and in fire.* 3:19 Greek *Herod the tetrarch.* 3:22 Some manuscripts read *my Son, and today I have become your Father.*

Semein was the son of Josech.
Josech was the son of Joda.
27 Joda was the son of Joanan.
Joanan was the son of Rhesa.
Rhesa was the son of Zerubbabel.
Zerubbabel was the son of Shealtiel.
Shealtiel was the son of Neri.
28 Neri was the son of Melki.
Melki was the son of Addi.
Addi was the son of Cosam.
Cosam was the son of Elmadam.
Elmadam was the son of Er.
29 Er was the son of Joshua.
Joshua was the son of Eliezer.
Eliezer was the son of Jorim.
Jorim was the son of Matthat.
Matthat was the son of Levi.
30 Levi was the son of Simeon.
Simeon was the son of Judah.
Judah was the son of Joseph.
Joseph was the son of Jonam.
Jonam was the son of Eliakim.
31 Eliakim was the son of Melea.
Melea was the son of Menna.
Menna was the son of Mattatha.
Mattatha was the son of Nathan.
Nathan was the son of David.
32 David was the son of Jesse.
Jesse was the son of Obed.
Obed was the son of Boaz.
Boaz was the son of Salmon.*
Salmon was the son of Nahshon.
33 Nahshon was the son of Amminadab.
Amminadab was the son of Admin.
Admin was the son of Arni.*
Arni was the son of Hezron.
Hezron was the son of Perez.
Perez was the son of Judah.
34 Judah was the son of Jacob.
Jacob was the son of Isaac.
Isaac was the son of Abraham.
Abraham was the son of Terah.
Terah was the son of Nahor.
35 Nahor was the son of Serug.
Serug was the son of Reu.
Reu was the son of Peleg.
Peleg was the son of Eber.
Eber was the son of Shelah.

3:32 Greek *Sala,* a variant spelling of Salmon; also in 3:32b. See Ruth 4:20-21. 3:33 Some manuscripts read *Amminadab was the son of Aram. Arni* and *Aram* are alternate spellings of Ram. See 1 Chr 2:9-10.

36 Shelah was the son of Cainan.
Cainan was the son of Arphaxad.
Arphaxad was the son of Shem.
Shem was the son of Noah.
Noah was the son of Lamech.
37 Lamech was the son of Methuselah.
Methuselah was the son of Enoch.
Enoch was the son of Jared.
Jared was the son of Mahalalel.
Mahalalel was the son of Kenan.
38 Kenan was the son of Enosh.*
Enosh was the son of Seth.
Seth was the son of Adam.
Adam was the son of God.

The Temptation of Jesus

4 Then Jesus, full of the Holy Spirit, returned from the Jordan River. He
was led by the Spirit in the wilderness,* 2 where he was tempted by the
devil for forty days. Jesus ate nothing all that time and became very hungry.
3 Then the devil said to him, "If you are the Son of God, tell this stone to
become a loaf of bread."
4 But Jesus told him, "No! The Scriptures say, 'People do not live by bread
alone.'*"
5 Then the devil took him up and revealed to him all the kingdoms of the
world in a moment of time. 6 "I will give you the glory of these kingdoms
and authority over them," the devil said, "because they are mine to give to
anyone I please. 7 I will give it all to you if you will worship me."
8 Jesus replied, "The Scriptures say,

'You must worship the LORD your God
and serve only him.'*"

9 Then the devil took him to Jerusalem, to the highest point of the Temple,
and said, "If you are the Son of God, jump off! 10 For the Scriptures say,

'He will order his angels to protect and guard you.
11 And they will hold you up with their hands
so you won't even hurt your foot on a stone.'*"

12 Jesus responded, "The Scriptures also say, 'You must not test the LORD
your God.'*"
13 When the devil had finished tempting Jesus, he left him until the next
opportunity came.

Jesus Rejected at Nazareth

14 Then Jesus returned to Galilee, filled with the Holy Spirit's power. Reports
about him spread quickly through the whole region. 15 He taught regularly
in their synagogues and was praised by everyone.
16 When he came to the village of Nazareth, his boyhood home, he went as

3:38 Greek *Enos,* a variant spelling of Enosh; also in 3:38b. See Gen 5:6. **4:1** Some manuscripts read *into the wilderness.* **4:4** Deut 8:3. **4:8** Deut 6:13. **4:10-11** Ps 91:11-12. **4:12** Deut 6:16.

usual to the synagogue on the Sabbath and stood up to read the Scriptures.
17 The scroll of Isaiah the prophet was handed to him. He unrolled the scroll
and found the place where this was written:

18 "The Spirit of the LORD is upon me,
for he has anointed me to bring Good News to the poor.
He has sent me to proclaim that captives will be released,
that the blind will see,
that the oppressed will be set free,
19 and that the time of the LORD's favor has come.*"

20 He rolled up the scroll, handed it back to the attendant, and sat down.
All eyes in the synagogue looked at him intently. 21 Then he began to speak
to them. "The Scripture you've just heard has been fulfilled this very day!"

22 Everyone spoke well of him and was amazed by the gracious words that
came from his lips. "How can this be?" they asked. "Isn't this Joseph's son?"

23 Then he said, "You will undoubtedly quote me this proverb: 'Physician,
heal yourself'—meaning, 'Do miracles here in your hometown like those
you did in Capernaum.' 24 But I tell you the truth, no prophet is accepted in
his own hometown.

25 "Certainly there were many needy widows in Israel in Elijah's time,
when the heavens were closed for three and a half years, and a severe famine
devastated the land. 26 Yet Elijah was not sent to any of them. He was sent
instead to a foreigner—a widow of Zarephath in the land of Sidon. 27 And
many in Israel had leprosy in the time of the prophet Elisha, but the only
one healed was Naaman, a Syrian."

28 When they heard this, the people in the synagogue were furious. 29 Jump-
ing up, they mobbed him and forced him to the edge of the hill on which the
town was built. They intended to push him over the cliff, 30 but he passed
right through the crowd and went on his way.

Jesus Casts Out a Demon

31 Then Jesus went to Capernaum, a town in Galilee, and taught there in the
synagogue every Sabbath day. 32 There, too, the people were amazed at his
teaching, for he spoke with authority.

33 Once when he was in the synagogue, a man possessed by a demon—an
evil* spirit—cried out, shouting, 34 "Go away! Why are you interfering with
us, Jesus of Nazareth? Have you come to destroy us? I know who you are—
the Holy One of God!"

35 But Jesus reprimanded him. "Be quiet! Come out of the man," he or-
dered. At that, the demon threw the man to the floor as the crowd watched;
then it came out of him without hurting him further.

36 Amazed, the people exclaimed, "What authority and power this man's
words possess! Even evil spirits obey him, and they flee at his command!"
37 The news about Jesus spread through every village in the entire region.

Jesus Heals Many People

38 After leaving the synagogue that day, Jesus went to Simon's home, where he
found Simon's mother-in-law very sick with a high fever. "Please heal her,"

4:18-19 Or *and to proclaim the acceptable year of the* LORD. Isa 61:1-2 (Greek version); 58:6.
4:33 Greek *unclean;* also in 4:36.

Make a Difference

4:16-21

Freedom

These words occur in two places in the Bible. The first time is in Isaiah 61, when Isaiah introduced what the coming Messiah's ministry would be like. The second time, here in Luke 4:18, was when Jesus read those very words from Isaiah 61 in the synagogue.

Jesus opened the Isaiah scroll, read the messianic passage, sat down, and then said, "The Scripture you've just heard has been fulfilled this very day!" (Luke 4:21). Jesus was making a statement: "This is who I am, and this is what I am going to do."

As Christians, we follow Jesus, whose purpose was to share refreshingly good news and to proclaim unexpected release, renewal of sight, and dignity of freedom.

Difference Maker

Think of someone who is experiencing one of the conditions mentioned in the passage that Jesus read. Make a plan to do something on their behalf this week.

Question **4:41**

Why did the demons recognize the identity of Jesus before the people did? What does this tell you about the blindness of the human heart? What does that tell you about the spiritual battle being waged in our world?

Prayer **5:11**

Lord Jesus, give me the courage to consider everything worth dropping in my life so that I may follow you with my whole being. Amen.

everyone begged. 39 Standing at her bedside, he rebuked the fever, and it left
her. And she got up at once and prepared a meal for them.
40 As the sun went down that evening, people throughout the village
brought sick family members to Jesus. No matter what their diseases were,
the touch of his hand healed every one. 41 Many were possessed by demons;
and the demons came out at his command, shouting, "You are the Son of
God!" But because they knew he was the Messiah, he rebuked them and
refused to let them speak.

Jesus Continues to Preach

42 Early the next morning Jesus went out to an isolated place. The crowds
searched everywhere for him, and when they finally found him, they begged
him not to leave them. 43 But he replied, "I must preach the Good News of the
Kingdom of God in other towns, too, because that is why I was sent." 44 So he
continued to travel around, preaching in synagogues throughout Judea.*

The First Disciples

5 One day as Jesus was preaching on the shore of the Sea of Galilee,* great
crowds pressed in on him to listen to the word of God. 2 He noticed two
empty boats at the water's edge, for the fishermen had left them and were
washing their nets. 3 Stepping into one of the boats, Jesus asked Simon,* its
owner, to push it out into the water. So he sat in the boat and taught the
crowds from there.
4 When he had finished speaking, he said to Simon, "Now go out where it
is deeper, and let down your nets to catch some fish."
5 "Master," Simon replied, "we worked hard all last night and didn't catch
a thing. But if you say so, I'll let the nets down again." 6 And this time their
nets were so full of fish they began to tear! 7 A shout for help brought their
partners in the other boat, and soon both boats were filled with fish and on
the verge of sinking.
8 When Simon Peter realized what had happened, he fell to his knees before
Jesus and said, "Oh, Lord, please leave me—I'm such a sinful man."
9 For he was awestruck by the number of fish they had caught, as were the
others with him. 10 His partners, James and John, the sons of Zebedee, were
also amazed.
Jesus replied to Simon, "Don't be afraid! From now on you'll be fishing for
people!" 11 And as soon as they landed, they left everything and followed Jesus.

Jesus Heals a Man with Leprosy

12 In one of the villages, Jesus met a man with an advanced case of leprosy.
When the man saw Jesus, he bowed with his face to the ground, begging to
be healed. "Lord," he said, "if you are willing, you can heal me and make
me clean."
13 Jesus reached out and touched him. "I am willing," he said. "Be healed!"
And instantly the leprosy disappeared. 14 Then Jesus instructed him not to
tell anyone what had happened. He said, "Go to the priest and let him examine
you. Take along the offering required in the law of Moses for those
who have been healed of leprosy.* This will be a public testimony that you
have been cleansed."

4:44 Some manuscripts read *Galilee.* **5:1** Greek *Lake Gennesaret,* another name for the Sea of Galilee. **5:3** *Simon* is called "Peter" in 6:14 and thereafter. **5:14** See Lev 14:2-32.

15 But despite Jesus' instructions, the report of his power spread even
faster, and vast crowds came to hear him preach and to be healed of their
diseases. 16 But Jesus often withdrew to the wilderness for prayer.

Jesus Heals a Paralyzed Man

17 One day while Jesus was teaching, some Pharisees and teachers of religious
law were sitting nearby. (It seemed that these men showed up from every
village in all Galilee and Judea, as well as from Jerusalem.) And the Lord's
healing power was strongly with Jesus.
18 Some men came carrying a paralyzed man on a sleeping mat. They tried
to take him inside to Jesus, 19 but they couldn't reach him because of the
crowd. So they went up to the roof and took off some tiles. Then they lowered
the sick man on his mat down into the crowd, right in front of Jesus. 20 See-
ing their faith, Jesus said to the man, "Young man, your sins are forgiven."
21 But the Pharisees and teachers of religious law said to themselves, "Who
does he think he is? That's blasphemy! Only God can forgive sins!"
22 Jesus knew what they were thinking, so he asked them, "Why do you
question this in your hearts? 23 Is it easier to say 'Your sins are forgiven,' or
'Stand up and walk'? 24 So I will prove to you that the Son of Man* has the
authority on earth to forgive sins." Then Jesus turned to the paralyzed man
and said, "Stand up, pick up your mat, and go home!"
25 And immediately, as everyone watched, the man jumped up, picked up
his mat, and went home praising God. 26 Everyone was gripped with great
wonder and awe, and they praised God, exclaiming, "We have seen amazing
things today!"

Jesus Calls Levi (Matthew)

27 Later, as Jesus left the town, he saw a tax collector named Levi sitting at his
tax collector's booth. "Follow me and be my disciple," Jesus said to him. 28 So
Levi got up, left everything, and followed him.
29 Later, Levi held a banquet in his home with Jesus as the guest of honor.
Many of Levi's fellow tax collectors and other guests also ate with them. 30 But
the Pharisees and their teachers of religious law complained bitterly to Jesus'
disciples, "Why do you eat and drink with such scum?*"
31 Jesus answered them, "Healthy people don't need a doctor—sick people
do. 32 I have come to call not those who think they are righteous, but those
who know they are sinners and need to repent."

A Discussion about Fasting

33 One day some people said to Jesus, "John the Baptist's disciples fast and
pray regularly, and so do the disciples of the Pharisees. Why are your disciples
always eating and drinking?"
34 Jesus responded, "Do wedding guests fast while celebrating with the
groom? Of course not. 35 But someday the groom will be taken away from
them, and then they will fast."
36 Then Jesus gave them this illustration: "No one tears a piece of cloth from
a new garment and uses it to patch an old garment. For then the new garment
would be ruined, and the new patch wouldn't even match the old garment.
37 "And no one puts new wine into old wineskins. For the new wine would

5:24 "Son of Man" is a title Jesus used for himself. **5:30** Greek *with tax collectors and sinners?*

Question 6:6–11

Put yourself into this moment. What attitude would you have had?

burst the wineskins, spilling the wine and ruining the skins. 38 New wine
must be stored in new wineskins. 39 But no one who drinks the old wine
seems to want the new wine. 'The old is just fine,' they say."

A Discussion about the Sabbath

6 One Sabbath day as Jesus was walking through some grainfields, his
disciples broke off heads of grain, rubbed off the husks in their hands,
and ate the grain. 2 But some Pharisees said, "Why are you breaking the law
by harvesting grain on the Sabbath?"
3 Jesus replied, "Haven't you read in the Scriptures what David did when
he and his companions were hungry? 4 He went into the house of God and
broke the law by eating the sacred loaves of bread that only the priests can
eat. He also gave some to his companions." 5 And Jesus added, "The Son of
Man* is Lord, even over the Sabbath."

Jesus Heals on the Sabbath

6 On another Sabbath day, a man with a deformed right hand was in the
synagogue while Jesus was teaching. 7 The teachers of religious law and the
Pharisees watched Jesus closely. If he healed the man's hand, they planned
to accuse him of working on the Sabbath.
8 But Jesus knew their thoughts. He said to the man with the deformed hand,
"Come and stand in front of everyone." So the man came forward. 9 Then Jesus
said to his critics, "I have a question for you. Does the law permit good deeds on
the Sabbath, or is it a day for doing evil? Is this a day to save life or to destroy it?"
10 He looked around at them one by one and then said to the man, "Hold out
your hand." So the man held out his hand, and it was restored! 11 At this, the en-
emies of Jesus were wild with rage and began to discuss what to do with him.

Jesus Chooses the Twelve Apostles

12 One day soon afterward Jesus went up on a mountain to pray, and he prayed
to God all night. 13 At daybreak he called together all of his disciples and
chose twelve of them to be apostles. Here are their names:

14 Simon (whom he named Peter),
Andrew (Peter's brother),
James,
John,
Philip,
Bartholomew,
15 Matthew,
Thomas,
James (son of Alphaeus),
Simon (who was called the zealot),
16 Judas (son of James),
Judas Iscariot (who later betrayed him).

Crowds Follow Jesus

17 When they came down from the mountain, the disciples stood with Jesus
on a large, level area, surrounded by many of his followers and by the crowds.

6:5 "Son of Man" is a title Jesus used for himself.

There were people from all over Judea and from Jerusalem and from as far
north as the seacoasts of Tyre and Sidon. 18They had come to hear him and
to be healed of their diseases; and those troubled by evil* spirits were healed.
19Everyone tried to touch him, because healing power went out from him,
and he healed everyone.

The Beatitudes

20Then Jesus turned to his disciples and said,

"God blesses you who are poor,
for the Kingdom of God is yours.
21 God blesses you who are hungry now,
for you will be satisfied.
God blesses you who weep now,
for in due time you will laugh.

22What blessings await you when people hate you and exclude you and
mock you and curse you as evil because you follow the Son of Man. 23When
that happens, be happy! Yes, leap for joy! For a great reward awaits you in
heaven. And remember, their ancestors treated the ancient prophets that
same way.

Sorrows Foretold

24 "What sorrow awaits you who are rich,
for you have your only happiness now.
25 What sorrow awaits you who are fat and prosperous now,
for a time of awful hunger awaits you.
What sorrow awaits you who laugh now,
for your laughing will turn to mourning and sorrow.
26 What sorrow awaits you who are praised by the crowds,
for their ancestors also praised false prophets.

Love for Enemies

27"But to you who are willing to listen, I say, love your enemies! Do good to
those who hate you. 28Bless those who curse you. Pray for those who hurt you.
29If someone slaps you on one cheek, offer the other cheek also. If someone
demands your coat, offer your shirt also. 30Give to anyone who asks; and
when things are taken away from you, don't try to get them back. 31Do to
others as you would like them to do to you.

32"If you love only those who love you, why should you get credit for that?
Even sinners love those who love them! 33And if you do good only to those
who do good to you, why should you get credit? Even sinners do that much!
34And if you lend money only to those who can repay you, why should you
get credit? Even sinners will lend to other sinners for a full return.

35"Love your enemies! Do good to them. Lend to them without expecting
to be repaid. Then your reward from heaven will be very great, and you will
truly be acting as children of the Most High, for he is kind to those who are
unthankful and wicked. 36You must be compassionate, just as your Father
is compassionate.

6:18 Greek *unclean.*

Make a Difference

6:27-38

Do to Others

The way you treat someone says a lot about you. What erupts out of you reveals what is within you. If you harbor things like apathy or hatred in your soul, then you'll probably act uncaringly toward others. If you have a love for God and a love for others embedded in your heart, then that is what will overflow in your daily practice, even when times get tough.

Difference Maker

Out of God's love, do something profoundly kind today. For instance, when you get to the drive-through window to pay for your meal, pay for the food of the person behind you as well.

Do Not Judge Others

37 “Do not judge others, and you will not be judged. Do not condemn others,
or it will all come back against you. Forgive others, and you will be forgiven.
38 Give, and you will receive. Your gift will return to you in full—pressed
down, shaken together to make room for more, running over, and poured
into your lap. The amount you give will determine the amount you get
back.*”

39 Then Jesus gave the following illustration: “Can one blind person lead
another? Won’t they both fall into a ditch? 40 Students* are not greater than
their teacher. But the student who is fully trained will become like the
teacher.

41 “And why worry about a speck in your friend’s eye* when you have a log
in your own? 42 How can you think of saying, ‘Friend,* let me help you get rid
of that speck in your eye,’ when you can’t see past the log in your own eye?
Hypocrite! First get rid of the log in your own eye; then you will see well
enough to deal with the speck in your friend’s eye.

The Tree and Its Fruit

43 “A good tree can’t produce bad fruit, and a bad tree can’t produce good
fruit. 44 A tree is identified by its fruit. Figs are never gathered from thorn-
bushes, and grapes are not picked from bramble bushes. 45 A good person
produces good things from the treasury of a good heart, and an evil person
produces evil things from the treasury of an evil heart. What you say flows
from what is in your heart.

Building on a Solid Foundation

46 “So why do you keep calling me ‘Lord, Lord!’ when you don’t do what I
say? 47 I will show you what it’s like when someone comes to me, listens to
my teaching, and then follows it. 48 It is like a person building a house who
digs deep and lays the foundation on solid rock. When the floodwaters rise
and break against that house, it stands firm because it is well built. 49 But
anyone who hears and doesn’t obey is like a person who builds a house right
on the ground, without a foundation. When the floods sweep down against
that house, it will collapse into a heap of ruins.”

The Faith of a Roman Officer

7 When Jesus had finished saying all this to the people, he returned to
Capernaum. 2 At that time the highly valued slave of a Roman officer*
was sick and near death. 3 When the officer heard about Jesus, he sent some
respected Jewish elders to ask him to come and heal his slave. 4 So they ear-
nestly begged Jesus to help the man. “If anyone deserves your help, he does,”
they said, 5 “for he loves the Jewish people and even built a synagogue for us.”

6 So Jesus went with them. But just before they arrived at the house, the of-
ficer sent some friends to say, “Lord, don’t trouble yourself by coming to my
home, for I am not worthy of such an honor. 7 I am not even worthy to come
and meet you. Just say the word from where you are, and my servant will be
healed. 8 I know this because I am under the authority of my superior offi-
cers, and I have authority over my soldiers. I only need to say, ‘Go,’ and they
go, or ‘Come,’ and they come. And if I say to my slaves, ‘Do this,’ they do it.”

Story Arc **7:1-10**

The Roman Officer

The enemy of Israel was embodied in a Roman centurion. This military officer commanded a squad of one hundred soldiers whose purpose was to quell and control the Jewish population. The Roman soldiers, don’t forget, would eventually ridicule, torture, and crucify Jesus. It is alarming that this particular man of authority would beg Jesus for help. It is jaw-dropping that this man would place so much trust in Jesus’ word. It is also shocking that Jesus would agree to help him and uphold him as the most faith-filled in all Israel. This should make us wonder what kind of difference we could make in this world if we would approach Jesus with as much deep trust.

Luke 8:1-3 ►

6:38 Or *The measure you give will be the measure you get back.* 6:40 Or *Disciples.* 6:41 Greek *your brother’s eye;* also in 6:42. 6:42 Greek *Brother.* 7:2 Greek *a centurion;* similarly in 7:6.

9 When Jesus heard this, he was amazed. Turning to the crowd that was
following him, he said, "I tell you, I haven't seen faith like this in all Israel!"
10 And when the officer's friends returned to his house, they found the slave
completely healed.

Jesus Raises a Widow's Son

11 Soon afterward Jesus went with his disciples to the village of Nain, and a
large crowd followed him. 12 A funeral procession was coming out as he ap-
proached the village gate. The young man who had died was a widow's only
son, and a large crowd from the village was with her. 13 When the Lord saw
her, his heart overflowed with compassion. "Don't cry!" he said. 14 Then he
walked over to the coffin and touched it, and the bearers stopped. "Young
man," he said, "I tell you, get up." 15 Then the dead boy sat up and began to
talk! And Jesus gave him back to his mother.
16 Great fear swept the crowd, and they praised God, saying, "A mighty
prophet has risen among us," and "God has visited his people today."
17 And the news about Jesus spread throughout Judea and the surrounding
countryside.

Jesus and John the Baptist

18 The disciples of John the Baptist told John about everything Jesus was
doing. So John called for two of his disciples, 19 and he sent them to the Lord
to ask him, "Are you the Messiah we've been expecting,* or should we keep
looking for someone else?"
20 John's two disciples found Jesus and said to him, "John the Baptist sent
us to ask, 'Are you the Messiah we've been expecting, or should we keep
looking for someone else?'"
21 At that very time, Jesus cured many people of their diseases, illnesses,
and evil spirits, and he restored sight to many who were blind. 22 Then he
told John's disciples, "Go back to John and tell him what you have seen
and heard—the blind see, the lame walk, those with leprosy are cured, the
deaf hear, the dead are raised to life, and the Good News is being preached
to the poor." 23 And he added, "God blesses those who do not fall away be-
cause of me.*"
24 After John's disciples left, Jesus began talking about him to the crowds.
"What kind of man did you go into the wilderness to see? Was he a weak
reed, swayed by every breath of wind? 25 Or were you expecting to see a man
dressed in expensive clothes? No, people who wear beautiful clothes and
live in luxury are found in palaces. 26 Were you looking for a prophet? Yes,
and he is more than a prophet. 27 John is the man to whom the Scriptures
refer when they say,

'Look, I am sending my messenger ahead of you,
and he will prepare your way before you.'*

28 I tell you, of all who have ever lived, none is greater than John. Yet even the
least person in the Kingdom of God is greater than he is!"
29 When they heard this, all the people—even the tax collectors—agreed
that God's way was right,* for they had been baptized by John. 30 But the

Question 7:22

What have you seen and heard about Jesus that you could share with others?

7:19 Greek *Are you the one who is coming?* Also in 7:20. 7:23 Or *who are not offended by me.* 7:27 Mal 3:1. 7:29 Or *praised God for his justice.*

Question 7:36–39

Why do you think she was crying? What led her to do this with Jesus? As she did this, what do you think was occurring in her heart?

Pharisees and experts in religious law rejected God’s plan for them, for they
had refused John’s baptism.
31“To what can I compare the people of this generation?” Jesus asked.
“How can I describe them? 32They are like children playing a game in the
public square. They complain to their friends,

‘We played wedding songs,
and you didn’t dance,
so we played funeral songs,
and you didn’t weep.’

33For John the Baptist didn’t spend his time eating bread or drinking wine,
and you say, ‘He’s possessed by a demon.’ 34The Son of Man,* on the other
hand, feasts and drinks, and you say, ‘He’s a glutton and a drunkard, and a
friend of tax collectors and other sinners!’ 35But wisdom is shown to be right
by the lives of those who follow it.*”

Jesus Anointed by a Sinful Woman

36One of the Pharisees asked Jesus to have dinner with him, so Jesus went to
his home and sat down to eat.* 37When a certain immoral woman from that
city heard he was eating there, she brought a beautiful alabaster jar filled
with expensive perfume. 38Then she knelt behind him at his feet, weeping.
Her tears fell on his feet, and she wiped them off with her hair. Then she kept
kissing his feet and putting perfume on them.
39When the Pharisee who had invited him saw this, he said to himself, “If
this man were a prophet, he would know what kind of woman is touching
him. She’s a sinner!”
40Then Jesus answered his thoughts. “Simon,” he said to the Pharisee, “I
have something to say to you.”

“Go ahead, Teacher,” Simon replied.

41Then Jesus told him this story: “A man loaned money to two
people—500 pieces of silver* to one and 50 pieces to the other. 42But neither
of them could repay him, so he kindly forgave them both, canceling their
debts. Who do you suppose loved him more after that?”
43Simon answered, “I suppose the one for whom he canceled the larger debt.”

“That’s right,” Jesus said. 44Then he turned to the woman and said to Si-
mon, “Look at this woman kneeling here. When I entered your home, you
didn’t offer me water to wash the dust from my feet, but she has washed
them with her tears and wiped them with her hair. 45You didn’t greet me
with a kiss, but from the time I first came in, she has not stopped kissing
my feet. 46You neglected the courtesy of olive oil to anoint my head, but she
has anointed my feet with rare perfume.
47“I tell you, her sins—and they are many—have been forgiven, so she has
shown me much love. But a person who is forgiven little shows only little
love.” 48Then Jesus said to the woman, “Your sins are forgiven.”
49The men at the table said among themselves, “Who is this man, that he
goes around forgiving sins?”
50And Jesus said to the woman, “Your faith has saved you; go in peace.”

7:34 “Son of Man” is a title Jesus used for himself. 7:35 Or *But wisdom is justified by all her children.* 7:36 Or *and reclined.* 7:41 Greek 500 *denarii.* A denarius was equivalent to a laborer’s full day’s wage.

Women Who Followed Jesus

8 Soon afterward Jesus began a tour of the nearby towns and villages, preaching and announcing the Good News about the Kingdom of God. He took his twelve disciples with him, 2 along with some women who had been cured of evil spirits and diseases. Among them were Mary Magdalene, from whom he had cast out seven demons; 3 Joanna, the wife of Chuza, Herod's business manager; Susanna; and many others who were contributing from their own resources to support Jesus and his disciples.

Parable of the Farmer Scattering Seed

4 One day Jesus told a story in the form of a parable to a large crowd that had gathered from many towns to hear him: 5 "A farmer went out to plant his seed. As he scattered it across his field, some seed fell on a footpath, where it was stepped on, and the birds ate it. 6 Other seed fell among rocks. It began to grow, but the plant soon wilted and died for lack of moisture. 7 Other seed fell among thorns that grew up with it and choked out the tender plants. 8 Still other seed fell on fertile soil. This seed grew and produced a crop that was a hundred times as much as had been planted!" When he had said this, he called out, "Anyone with ears to hear should listen and understand."

9 His disciples asked him what this parable meant. 10 He replied, "You are permitted to understand the secrets* of the Kingdom of God. But I use parables to teach the others so that the Scriptures might be fulfilled:

'When they look, they won't really see.
When they hear, they won't understand.'*

11 "This is the meaning of the parable: The seed is God's word. 12 The seeds that fell on the footpath represent those who hear the message, only to have the devil come and take it away from their hearts and prevent them from believing and being saved. 13 The seeds on the rocky soil represent those who hear the message and receive it with joy. But since they don't have deep roots, they believe for a while, then they fall away when they face temptation. 14 The seeds that fell among the thorns represent those who hear the message, but all too quickly the message is crowded out by the cares and riches and pleasures of this life. And so they never grow into maturity. 15 And the seeds that fell on the good soil represent honest, good-hearted people who hear God's word, cling to it, and patiently produce a huge harvest.

Parable of the Lamp

16 "No one lights a lamp and then covers it with a bowl or hides it under a bed. A lamp is placed on a stand, where its light can be seen by all who enter the house. 17 For all that is secret will eventually be brought into the open, and everything that is concealed will be brought to light and made known to all.

18 "So pay attention to how you hear. To those who listen to my teaching, more understanding will be given. But for those who are not listening, even what they think they understand will be taken away from them."

8:10a Greek *mysteries.* **8:10b** Isa 6:9 (Greek version).

Question **8:18**

What does Jesus teach us about how to grow as his followers?

Story Arc **8:1-3**

Mary Magdalene

One of Jesus' primary followers was a woman named Mary Magdalene. She got her name from her hometown, Magdala, on the shores of the Sea of Galilee. Mary had a dramatically difficult life until Jesus healed her. She, along with several other women, was part of a remarkably encouraging team that supported Jesus and the disciples during their ministry. Mary goes down as one of the sincerest and most committed followers of Jesus in history. She followed Jesus to the cross, where she watched her Savior breathe his last breaths. She was among the first to go to the tomb on Sunday morning. She was also the first to have her name called by the resurrected Messiah. As you think about Mary's story line, what inspires you the most?

John 1:6-36 ►

Question **8:25**

How would you answer the two questions in this verse?

The True Family of Jesus

19 Then Jesus' mother and brothers came to see him, but they couldn't get to him because of the crowd. 20 Someone told Jesus, "Your mother and your brothers are standing outside, and they want to see you."

21 Jesus replied, "My mother and my brothers are all those who hear God's word and obey it."

Jesus Calms the Storm

22 One day Jesus said to his disciples, "Let's cross to the other side of the lake." So they got into a boat and started out. 23 As they sailed across, Jesus settled down for a nap. But soon a fierce storm came down on the lake. The boat was filling with water, and they were in real danger.

24 The disciples went and woke him up, shouting, "Master, Master, we're going to drown!"

When Jesus woke up, he rebuked the wind and the raging waves. Suddenly the storm stopped and all was calm. 25 Then he asked them, "Where is your faith?"

The disciples were terrified and amazed. "Who is this man?" they asked each other. "When he gives a command, even the wind and waves obey him!"

Jesus Heals a Demon-Possessed Man

26 So they arrived in the region of the Gerasenes,* across the lake from Galilee. 27 As Jesus was climbing out of the boat, a man who was possessed by demons came out to meet him. For a long time he had been homeless and naked, living in the tombs outside the town.

28 As soon as he saw Jesus, he shrieked and fell down in front of him. Then he screamed, "Why are you interfering with me, Jesus, Son of the Most High God? Please, I beg you, don't torture me!" 29 For Jesus had already commanded the evil* spirit to come out of him. This spirit had often taken control of the man. Even when he was placed under guard and put in chains and shackles, he simply broke them and rushed out into the wilderness, completely under the demon's power.

30 Jesus demanded, "What is your name?"

"Legion," he replied, for he was filled with many demons. 31 The demons kept begging Jesus not to send them into the bottomless pit.*

32 There happened to be a large herd of pigs feeding on the hillside nearby, and the demons begged him to let them enter into the pigs.

So Jesus gave them permission. 33 Then the demons came out of the man and entered the pigs, and the entire herd plunged down the steep hillside into the lake and drowned.

34 When the herdsmen saw it, they fled to the nearby town and the surrounding countryside, spreading the news as they ran. 35 People rushed out to see what had happened. A crowd soon gathered around Jesus, and they saw the man who had been freed from the demons. He was sitting at Jesus' feet, fully clothed and perfectly sane, and they were all afraid. 36 Then those who had seen what happened told the others how the demon-possessed man had been healed. 37 And all the people in the region of the Gerasenes begged Jesus to go away and leave them alone, for a great wave of fear swept over them.

8:26 Other manuscripts read *Gadarenes;* still others read *Gergesenes;* also in 8:37. See Matt 8:28; Mark 5:1. 8:29 Greek *unclean.* 8:31 Or *the abyss,* or *the underworld.*

So Jesus returned to the boat and left, crossing back to the other side of
the lake. 38The man who had been freed from the demons begged to go with
him. But Jesus sent him home, saying, 39"No, go back to your family, and tell
them everything God has done for you." So he went all through the town
proclaiming the great things Jesus had done for him.

Jesus Heals in Response to Faith

40On the other side of the lake the crowds welcomed Jesus, because they
had been waiting for him. 41Then a man named Jairus, a leader of the local
synagogue, came and fell at Jesus' feet, pleading with him to come home
with him. 42His only daughter,* who was about twelve years old, was dying.

As Jesus went with him, he was surrounded by the crowds. 43A woman
in the crowd had suffered for twelve years with constant bleeding,* and she
could find no cure. 44Coming up behind Jesus, she touched the fringe of his
robe. Immediately, the bleeding stopped.

45"Who touched me?" Jesus asked.

Everyone denied it, and Peter said, "Master, this whole crowd is pressing
up against you."

46But Jesus said, "Someone deliberately touched me, for I felt healing
power go out from me." 47When the woman realized that she could not stay
hidden, she began to tremble and fell to her knees in front of him. The whole
crowd heard her explain why she had touched him and that she had been
immediately healed. 48"Daughter," he said to her, "your faith has made you
well. Go in peace."

49While he was still speaking to her, a messenger arrived from the home
of Jairus, the leader of the synagogue. He told him, "Your daughter is dead.
There's no use troubling the Teacher now."

50But when Jesus heard what had happened, he said to Jairus, "Don't be
afraid. Just have faith, and she will be healed."

51When they arrived at the house, Jesus wouldn't let anyone go in with
him except Peter, John, James, and the little girl's father and mother. 52The
house was filled with people weeping and wailing, but he said, "Stop the
weeping! She isn't dead; she's only asleep."

53But the crowd laughed at him because they all knew she had died.
54Then Jesus took her by the hand and said in a loud voice, "My child, get
up!" 55And at that moment her life* returned, and she immediately stood up!
Then Jesus told them to give her something to eat. 56Her parents were over-
whelmed, but Jesus insisted that they not tell anyone what had happened.

Jesus Sends Out the Twelve Disciples

9 One day Jesus called together his twelve disciples* and gave them power
and authority to cast out all demons and to heal all diseases. 2Then he
sent them out to tell everyone about the Kingdom of God and to heal the sick.
3"Take nothing for your journey," he instructed them. "Don't take a walking
stick, a traveler's bag, food, money,* or even a change of clothes. 4Wherever
you go, stay in the same house until you leave town. 5And if a town refuses
to welcome you, shake its dust from your feet as you leave to show that you
have abandoned those people to their fate."

Question 9:1-2

Which is more amazing—that the disciples had the ability to cast out demons and heal diseases or that Jesus gave them the power and authority to do so?

8:42 Or *His only child, a daughter.* 8:43 Some manuscripts add *having spent everything she had on doctors.* 8:55 Or *her spirit.* 9:1 Greek *the Twelve;* other manuscripts read *the twelve apostles.* 9:3 Or *silver coins.*

Make a Difference

9:23-25

Imago Ego

Self-image problems began the moment humans rejected *imago Dei* (the belief that we are made in the image of God). Insecurity, embarrassment, frustration, confusion, self-hatred, shame, false thoughts, and self-harm—none of these are characteristics that humans were ever supposed to experience. In the beginning, God created us to have confidence, joy, clarity, innocence, and love. He created us with all the great attributes of God embedded within us.

Instead of being people who represent God, we chose to be creatures who represent ourselves. Ever since, we have suffered with our self-image. We stopped giving attention to God, and we started focusing on ourselves instead. The result, of course, is a broken world full of humans who are self-absorbed and self-destructive. Our world needs people who are brave enough to drop their egos and be re-created by Jesus in the very image of God.

Difference Maker

Look in the mirror and ask yourself, "Whom do others see reflected in me? Whom do I represent today—myself or God?"

6 So they began their circuit of the villages, preaching the Good News and
healing the sick.

Herod's Confusion

7 When Herod Antipas, the ruler of Galilee,* heard about everything Jesus
was doing, he was puzzled. Some were saying that John the Baptist had been
raised from the dead. 8 Others thought Jesus was Elijah or one of the other
prophets risen from the dead.
9 "I beheaded John," Herod said, "so who is this man about whom I hear
such stories?" And he kept trying to see him.

Jesus Feeds Five Thousand

10 When the apostles returned, they told Jesus everything they had done.
Then he slipped quietly away with them toward the town of Bethsaida. 11 But
the crowds found out where he was going, and they followed him. He wel-
comed them and taught them about the Kingdom of God, and he healed
those who were sick.
12 Late in the afternoon the twelve disciples came to him and said, "Send
the crowds away to the nearby villages and farms, so they can find food and
lodging for the night. There is nothing to eat here in this remote place."
13 But Jesus said, "You feed them."
"But we have only five loaves of bread and two fish," they answered. "Or
are you expecting us to go and buy enough food for this whole crowd?" 14 For
there were about 5,000 men there.
Jesus replied, "Tell them to sit down in groups of about fifty each." 15 So
the people all sat down. 16 Jesus took the five loaves and two fish, looked up
toward heaven, and blessed them. Then, breaking the loaves into pieces, he
kept giving the bread and fish to the disciples so they could distribute it to
the people. 17 They all ate as much as they wanted, and afterward, the dis-
ciples picked up twelve baskets of leftovers!

Peter's Declaration about Jesus

18 One day Jesus left the crowds to pray alone. Only his disciples were with
him, and he asked them, "Who do people say I am?"
19 "Well," they replied, "some say John the Baptist, some say Elijah, and
others say you are one of the other ancient prophets risen from the dead."
20 Then he asked them, "But who do you say I am?"
Peter replied, "You are the Messiah* sent from God!"

Jesus Predicts His Death

21 Jesus warned his disciples not to tell anyone who he was. 22 "The Son of
Man* must suffer many terrible things," he said. "He will be rejected by the
elders, the leading priests, and the teachers of religious law. He will be killed,
but on the third day he will be raised from the dead."
23 Then he said to the crowd, "If any of you wants to be my follower, you
must give up your own way, take up your cross daily, and follow me. 24 If you
try to hang on to your life, you will lose it. But if you give up your life for
my sake, you will save it. 25 And what do you benefit if you gain the whole

9:7 Greek *Herod the tetrarch.* Herod Antipas was a son of King Herod and was ruler over Galilee. 9:20 Or *the Christ. Messiah* (a Hebrew term) and *Christ* (a Greek term) both mean "anointed one." 9:22 "Son of Man" is a title Jesus used for himself.

world but are yourself lost or destroyed? [26]If anyone is ashamed of me and
my message, the Son of Man will be ashamed of that person when he returns
in his glory and in the glory of the Father and the holy angels. [27]I tell you
the truth, some standing here right now will not die before they see the
Kingdom of God."

The Transfiguration

[28]About eight days later Jesus took Peter, John, and James up on a mountain
to pray. [29]And as he was praying, the appearance of his face was transformed,
and his clothes became dazzling white. [30]Suddenly, two men, Moses and
Elijah, appeared and began talking with Jesus. [31]They were glorious to see.
And they were speaking about his exodus from this world, which was about
to be fulfilled in Jerusalem.

[32]Peter and the others had fallen asleep. When they woke up, they saw
Jesus' glory and the two men standing with him. [33]As Moses and Elijah were
starting to leave, Peter, not even knowing what he was saying, blurted out,
"Master, it's wonderful for us to be here! Let's make three shelters as me-
morials*—one for you, one for Moses, and one for Elijah." [34]But even as he
was saying this, a cloud overshadowed them, and terror gripped them as
the cloud covered them.

[35]Then a voice from the cloud said, "This is my Son, my Chosen One.*
Listen to him." [36]When the voice finished, Jesus was there alone. They didn't
tell anyone at that time what they had seen.

Jesus Heals a Demon-Possessed Boy

[37]The next day, after they had come down the mountain, a large crowd met
Jesus. [38]A man in the crowd called out to him, "Teacher, I beg you to look
at my son, my only child. [39]An evil spirit keeps seizing him, making him
scream. It throws him into convulsions so that he foams at the mouth. It
batters him and hardly ever leaves him alone. [40]I begged your disciples to
cast out the spirit, but they couldn't do it."

[41]Jesus said, "You faithless and corrupt people! How long must I be with
you and put up with you?" Then he said to the man, "Bring your son here."
[42]As the boy came forward, the demon knocked him to the ground and
threw him into a violent convulsion. But Jesus rebuked the evil* spirit and
healed the boy. Then he gave him back to his father. [43]Awe gripped the people
as they saw this majestic display of God's power.

Jesus Again Predicts His Death

While everyone was marveling at everything he was doing, Jesus said to his
disciples, [44]"Listen to me and remember what I say. The Son of Man is going
to be betrayed into the hands of his enemies." [45]But they didn't know what he
meant. Its significance was hidden from them, so they couldn't understand
it, and they were afraid to ask him about it.

The Greatest in the Kingdom

[46]Then his disciples began arguing about which of them was the greatest.
[47]But Jesus knew their thoughts, so he brought a little child to his side. [48]Then
he said to them, "Anyone who welcomes a little child like this on my behalf*

9:33 Greek *three tabernacles.* **9:35** Some manuscripts read *This is my dearly loved Son.* **9:42** Greek *unclean.* **9:48** Greek *in my name.*

Prayer **9:35**

Lord Jesus, let me listen to you every day of my life. Amen.

Question **9:46-48**

What could you do to welcome a child on behalf of Jesus?

Prayer 10:2

Lord, put me to work! Amen.

welcomes me, and anyone who welcomes me also welcomes my Father who
sent me. Whoever is the least among you is the greatest."

Using the Name of Jesus

49 John said to Jesus, "Master, we saw someone using your name to cast out
demons, but we told him to stop because he isn't in our group."
50 But Jesus said, "Don't stop him! Anyone who is not against you is for
you."

Opposition from Samaritans

51 As the time drew near for him to ascend to heaven, Jesus resolutely set out
for Jerusalem. 52 He sent messengers ahead to a Samaritan village to prepare
for his arrival. 53 But the people of the village did not welcome Jesus because
he was on his way to Jerusalem. 54 When James and John saw this, they said
to Jesus, "Lord, should we call down fire from heaven to burn them up*?"
55 But Jesus turned and rebuked them.* 56 So they went on to another village.

The Cost of Following Jesus

57 As they were walking along, someone said to Jesus, "I will follow you wher-
ever you go."
58 But Jesus replied, "Foxes have dens to live in, and birds have nests, but
the Son of Man has no place even to lay his head."
59 He said to another person, "Come, follow me."
The man agreed, but he said, "Lord, first let me return home and bury
my father."
60 But Jesus told him, "Let the spiritually dead bury their own dead!* Your
duty is to go and preach about the Kingdom of God."
61 Another said, "Yes, Lord, I will follow you, but first let me say good-bye
to my family."
62 But Jesus told him, "Anyone who puts a hand to the plow and then looks
back is not fit for the Kingdom of God."

Jesus Sends Out His Disciples

10 The Lord now chose seventy-two* other disciples and sent them
ahead in pairs to all the towns and places he planned to visit. 2 These
were his instructions to them: "The harvest is great, but the workers are few.
So pray to the Lord who is in charge of the harvest; ask him to send more
workers into his fields. 3 Now go, and remember that I am sending you out
as lambs among wolves. 4 Don't take any money with you, nor a traveler's
bag, nor an extra pair of sandals. And don't stop to greet anyone on the road.
5 "Whenever you enter someone's home, first say, 'May God's peace be on
this house.' 6 If those who live there are peaceful, the blessing will stand; if
they are not, the blessing will return to you. 7 Don't move around from home
to home. Stay in one place, eating and drinking what they provide. Don't
hesitate to accept hospitality, because those who work deserve their pay.
8 "If you enter a town and it welcomes you, eat whatever is set before you.
9 Heal the sick, and tell them, 'The Kingdom of God is near you now.' 10 But

9:54 Some manuscripts add *as Elijah did.* **9:55** Some manuscripts add an expanded conclusion to verse 55 and an additional sentence in verse 56: *And he said, "You don't realize what your hearts are like. 56 For the Son of Man has not come to destroy people's lives, but to save them."* **9:60** Greek *Let the dead bury their own dead.* **10:1** Some manuscripts read *seventy;* also in 10:17.

if a town refuses to welcome you, go out into its streets and say, 11 'We wipe
even the dust of your town from our feet to show that we have abandoned
you to your fate. And know this—the Kingdom of God is near!' 12 I assure
you, even wicked Sodom will be better off than such a town on judgment day.
13 "What sorrow awaits you, Korazin and Bethsaida! For if the miracles I
did in you had been done in wicked Tyre and Sidon, their people would have
repented of their sins long ago, clothing themselves in burlap and throwing
ashes on their heads to show their remorse. 14 Yes, Tyre and Sidon will be
better off on judgment day than you. 15 And you people of Capernaum, will
you be honored in heaven? No, you will go down to the place of the dead.*"
16 **Then he said to the disciples,** "Anyone who accepts your message is also
accepting me. And anyone who rejects you is rejecting me. And anyone who
rejects me is rejecting God, who sent me."
17 **When the seventy-two disciples returned, they joyfully reported to him,
"Lord, even the demons obey us when we use your name!"**
18 "Yes," **he told them,** "I saw Satan fall from heaven like lightning! 19 Look,
I have given you authority over all the power of the enemy, and you can walk
among snakes and scorpions and crush them. Nothing will injure you. 20 But
don't rejoice because evil spirits obey you; rejoice because your names are
registered in heaven."

Jesus' Prayer of Thanksgiving

21 **At that same time Jesus was filled with the joy of the Holy Spirit, and he
said,** "O Father, Lord of heaven and earth, thank you for hiding these things
from those who think themselves wise and clever, and for revealing them to
the childlike. Yes, Father, it pleased you to do it this way.
22 "My Father has entrusted everything to me. No one truly knows the Son
except the Father, and no one truly knows the Father except the Son and
those to whom the Son chooses to reveal him."
23 **Then when they were alone, he turned to the disciples and said,** "Blessed
are the eyes that see what you have seen. 24 I tell you, many prophets and
kings longed to see what you see, but they didn't see it. And they longed to
hear what you hear, but they didn't hear it."

The Most Important Commandment

25 **One day an expert in religious law stood up to test Jesus by asking him this
question: "Teacher, what should I do to inherit eternal life?"**
26 **Jesus replied,** "What does the law of Moses say? How do you read it?"
27 **The man answered, "'You must love the LORD your God with all your
heart, all your soul, all your strength, and all your mind.' And, 'Love your
neighbor as yourself.'"***
28 "Right!" **Jesus told him.** "Do this and you will live!"
29 **The man wanted to justify his actions, so he asked Jesus, "And who is
my neighbor?"**

Parable of the Good Samaritan

30 **Jesus replied with a story:** "A Jewish man was traveling from Jerusalem
down to Jericho, and he was attacked by bandits. They stripped him of his
clothes, beat him up, and left him half dead beside the road.

10:15 Greek *to Hades.* **10:27** Deut 6:5; Lev 19:18.

Question 10:25-37

How did Jesus answer this "expert's" questions?

31 "By chance a priest came along. But when he saw the man lying there,
he crossed to the other side of the road and passed him by. 32 A Temple as-
sistant* walked over and looked at him lying there, but he also passed by
on the other side.
33 "Then a despised Samaritan came along, and when he saw the man, he
felt compassion for him. 34 Going over to him, the Samaritan soothed his
wounds with olive oil and wine and bandaged them. Then he put the man
on his own donkey and took him to an inn, where he took care of him. 35 The
next day he handed the innkeeper two silver coins,* telling him, 'Take care of
this man. If his bill runs higher than this, I'll pay you the next time I'm here.'
36 "Now which of these three would you say was a neighbor to the man
who was attacked by bandits?" Jesus asked.
37 The man replied, "The one who showed him mercy."
Then Jesus said, "Yes, now go and do the same."

Jesus Visits Martha and Mary

38 As Jesus and the disciples continued on their way to Jerusalem, they came
to a certain village where a woman named Martha welcomed him into her
home. 39 Her sister, Mary, sat at the Lord's feet, listening to what he taught.
40 But Martha was distracted by the big dinner she was preparing. She came
to Jesus and said, "Lord, doesn't it seem unfair to you that my sister just sits
here while I do all the work? Tell her to come and help me."
41 But the Lord said to her, "My dear Martha, you are worried and upset
over all these details! 42 There is only one thing worth being concerned about.
Mary has discovered it, and it will not be taken away from her."

Teaching about Prayer

11 Once Jesus was in a certain place praying. As he finished, one of his
disciples came to him and said, "Lord, teach us to pray, just as John
taught his disciples."
2 Jesus said, "This is how you should pray:*

"Father, may your name be kept holy.
May your Kingdom come soon.
3 Give us each day the food we need,*
4 and forgive us our sins,
as we forgive those who sin against us.
And don't let us yield to temptation.*"

5 Then, teaching them more about prayer, he used this story: "Suppose
you went to a friend's house at midnight, wanting to borrow three loaves
of bread. You say to him, 6 'A friend of mine has just arrived for a visit, and I
have nothing for him to eat.' 7 And suppose he calls out from his bedroom,
'Don't bother me. The door is locked for the night, and my family and I are
all in bed. I can't help you.' 8 But I tell you this—though he won't do it for
friendship's sake, if you keep knocking long enough, he will get up and give
you whatever you need because of your shameless persistence.*

10:32 Greek *A Levite.* 10:35 Greek *two denarii.* A denarius was equivalent to a laborer's full day's wage. 11:2 Some manuscripts add additional phrases from the Lord's Prayer as it reads in Matt 6:9-13. 11:3 Or *Give us each day our food for the day;* or *Give us each day our food for tomorrow.* 11:4 Or *And keep us from being tested.* 11:8 Or *in order to avoid shame,* or *so his reputation won't be damaged.*

Make a Difference

11:1-4

Pray like This

When Jesus taught his disciples to pray, he gave them an example, almost like a template to follow. When you pray, Jesus modeled, start with your focus on God the Father. Remember who God is and don't take for granted that he holds the universe that holds you. Give honor and respect to his name, a name that is incomparable to all others.

Next, Jesus said, desire what God desires. Filter all your own thoughts and requests through his will and kingdom. Consider what God wants to have happen in your life and in the world in which you live. Think about what God already is doing and get on board with that. Whatever God desires for his kingdom, desire that for your world, your community, your home, and your life—on earth as it is in heaven.

Difference Maker

Take time to pray, but this time, focus your prayer simply on God's greatness and God's great desire for the world. After a time, ask him how he wants you to respond.

9 "And so I tell you, keep on asking, and you will receive what you ask for.
Keep on seeking, and you will find. Keep on knocking, and the door will be
opened to you. 10 For everyone who asks, receives. Everyone who seeks, finds.
And to everyone who knocks, the door will be opened.
11 "You fathers—if your children ask* for a fish, do you give them a snake
instead? 12 Or if they ask for an egg, do you give them a scorpion? Of course
not! 13 So if you sinful people know how to give good gifts to your children,
how much more will your heavenly Father give the Holy Spirit to those who
ask him."

Jesus and the Prince of Demons

14 One day Jesus cast out a demon from a man who couldn't speak, and when
the demon was gone, the man began to speak. The crowds were amazed,
15 but some of them said, "No wonder he can cast out demons. He gets his
power from Satan,* the prince of demons." 16 Others, trying to test Jesus,
demanded that he show them a miraculous sign from heaven to prove his
authority.
17 He knew their thoughts, so he said, "Any kingdom divided by civil war
is doomed. A family splintered by feuding will fall apart. 18 You say I am em-
powered by Satan. But if Satan is divided and fighting against himself, how
can his kingdom survive? 19 And if I am empowered by Satan, what about
your own exorcists? They cast out demons, too, so they will condemn you for
what you have said. 20 But if I am casting out demons by the power of God,*
then the Kingdom of God has arrived among you. 21 For when a strong man is
fully armed and guards his palace, his possessions are safe—22 until someone
even stronger attacks and overpowers him, strips him of his weapons, and
carries off his belongings.
23 "Anyone who isn't with me opposes me, and anyone who isn't working
with me is actually working against me.
24 "When an evil* spirit leaves a person, it goes into the desert, searching
for rest. But when it finds none, it says, 'I will return to the person I came
from.' 25 So it returns and finds that its former home is all swept and in order.
26 Then the spirit finds seven other spirits more evil than itself, and they all
enter the person and live there. And so that person is worse off than before."
27 As he was speaking, a woman in the crowd called out, "God bless your
mother—the womb from which you came, and the breasts that nursed you!"
28 Jesus replied, "But even more blessed are all who hear the word of God
and put it into practice."

The Sign of Jonah

29 As the crowd pressed in on Jesus, he said, "This evil generation keeps ask-
ing me to show them a miraculous sign. But the only sign I will give them
is the sign of Jonah. 30 What happened to him was a sign to the people of
Nineveh that God had sent him. What happens to the Son of Man* will be a
sign to these people that he was sent by God.
31 "The queen of Sheba* will stand up against this generation on judgment
day and condemn it, for she came from a distant land to hear the wisdom

11:11 Some manuscripts add *for bread, do you give them a stone? Or [if they ask].* 11:15 Greek *Beelzeboul;* also in 11:18, 19. Other manuscripts read *Beezeboul;* Latin version reads *Beelzebub.* 11:20 Greek *by the finger of God.* 11:24 Greek *unclean.* 11:30 "Son of Man" is a title Jesus used for himself. 11:31 Greek *The queen of the south.*

Question 11:33-36

What is the point of a lamp?
How did Jesus say a lamp is
like your faith?

of Solomon. Now someone greater than Solomon is here—but you refuse
to listen. 32 The people of Nineveh will also stand up against this genera-
tion on judgment day and condemn it, for they repented of their sins at
the preaching of Jonah. Now someone greater than Jonah is here—but you
refuse to repent.

Receiving the Light

33 "No one lights a lamp and then hides it or puts it under a basket.* Instead, a
lamp is placed on a stand, where its light can be seen by all who enter the house.
34 "Your eye is like a lamp that provides light for your body. When your
eye is healthy, your whole body is filled with light. But when it is unhealthy,
your body is filled with darkness. 35 Make sure that the light you think you
have is not actually darkness. 36 If you are filled with light, with no dark
corners, then your whole life will be radiant, as though a floodlight were
filling you with light."

Jesus Criticizes the Religious Leaders

37 As Jesus was speaking, one of the Pharisees invited him home for a meal. So
he went in and took his place at the table.* 38 His host was amazed to see that
he sat down to eat without first performing the hand-washing ceremony
required by Jewish custom. 39 Then the Lord said to him, "You Pharisees are
so careful to clean the outside of the cup and the dish, but inside you are
filthy—full of greed and wickedness! 40 Fools! Didn't God make the inside
as well as the outside? 41 So clean the inside by giving gifts to the poor, and
you will be clean all over.
42 "What sorrow awaits you Pharisees! For you are careful to tithe even the
tiniest income from your herb gardens,* but you ignore justice and the love
of God. You should tithe, yes, but do not neglect the more important things.
43 "What sorrow awaits you Pharisees! For you love to sit in the seats of honor
in the synagogues and receive respectful greetings as you walk in the market-
places. 44 Yes, what sorrow awaits you! For you are like hidden graves in a field.
People walk over them without knowing the corruption they are stepping on."
45 "Teacher," said an expert in religious law, "you have insulted us, too, in
what you just said."
46 "Yes," said Jesus, "what sorrow also awaits you experts in religious law!
For you crush people with unbearable religious demands, and you never lift
a finger to ease the burden. 47 What sorrow awaits you! For you build monu-
ments for the prophets your own ancestors killed long ago. 48 But in fact, you
stand as witnesses who agree with what your ancestors did. They killed the
prophets, and you join in their crime by building the monuments! 49 This is
what God in his wisdom said about you:* 'I will send prophets and apostles
to them, but they will kill some and persecute the others.'
50 "As a result, this generation will be held responsible for the murder of
all God's prophets from the creation of the world—51 from the murder of
Abel to the murder of Zechariah, who was killed between the altar and the
sanctuary. Yes, it will certainly be charged against this generation.
52 "What sorrow awaits you experts in religious law! For you remove the
key to knowledge from the people. You don't enter the Kingdom yourselves,
and you prevent others from entering."

11:33 Some manuscripts do not include *or puts it under a basket.* **11:37** Or *and reclined.* **11:42** Greek *tithe the mint, the rue, and every herb.* **11:49** Greek *Therefore, the wisdom of God said.*

53 As Jesus was leaving, the teachers of religious law and the Pharisees be-
came hostile and tried to provoke him with many questions. 54 They wanted
to trap him into saying something they could use against him.

A Warning against Hypocrisy

12 Meanwhile, the crowds grew until thousands were milling about
and stepping on each other. Jesus turned first to his disciples and
warned them, "Beware of the yeast of the Pharisees—their hypocrisy. 2 The
time is coming when everything that is covered up will be revealed, and
all that is secret will be made known to all. 3 Whatever you have said in the
dark will be heard in the light, and what you have whispered behind closed
doors will be shouted from the housetops for all to hear!

4 "Dear friends, don't be afraid of those who want to kill your body; they
cannot do any more to you after that. 5 But I'll tell you whom to fear. Fear
God, who has the power to kill you and then throw you into hell.* Yes, he's
the one to fear.

6 "What is the price of five sparrows—two copper coins*? Yet God does
not forget a single one of them. 7 And the very hairs on your head are all
numbered. So don't be afraid; you are more valuable to God than a whole
flock of sparrows.

8 "I tell you the truth, everyone who acknowledges me publicly here on
earth, the Son of Man* will also acknowledge in the presence of God's angels.
9 But anyone who denies me here on earth will be denied before God's angels.
10 Anyone who speaks against the Son of Man can be forgiven, but anyone
who blasphemes the Holy Spirit will not be forgiven.

11 "And when you are brought to trial in the synagogues and before rulers
and authorities, don't worry about how to defend yourself or what to say,
12 for the Holy Spirit will teach you at that time what needs to be said."

Parable of the Rich Fool

13 Then someone called from the crowd, "Teacher, please tell my brother to
divide our father's estate with me."

14 Jesus replied, "Friend, who made me a judge over you to decide such
things as that?" 15 Then he said, "Beware! Guard against every kind of greed.
Life is not measured by how much you own."

16 Then he told them a story: "A rich man had a fertile farm that produced
fine crops. 17 He said to himself, 'What should I do? I don't have room for all
my crops.' 18 Then he said, 'I know! I'll tear down my barns and build bigger
ones. Then I'll have room enough to store all my wheat and other goods.
19 And I'll sit back and say to myself, "My friend, you have enough stored away
for years to come. Now take it easy! Eat, drink, and be merry!"'

20 "But God said to him, 'You fool! You will die this very night. Then who
will get everything you worked for?'

21 "Yes, a person is a fool to store up earthly wealth but not have a rich
relationship with God."

Teaching about Money and Possessions

22 Then, turning to his disciples, Jesus said, "That is why I tell you not to
worry about everyday life—whether you have enough food to eat or enough

12:5 Greek *Gehenna.* **12:6** Greek *two assaria* [Roman coins equal to 1/16 of a denarius].
12:8 "Son of Man" is a title Jesus used for himself.

Make a Difference

12:22-34

Pocket Protectors

People can be tightfisted, tight-minded tightwads. Even if they were to see another person in need, they might tighten the grip on their wallets, their time, their appearance, their performance, and their stuff. They can desperately keep for themselves whatever precious item they have treasured in their pockets. To let their guard down would be to relinquish control—so without thinking, they might find themselves standing defensively against others who simply need the smallest helping hand.

In contrast, Jesus lived with wide-open arms. He shared his life, kingdom, mercy, and salvation. He offered himself sacrificially, generously, and even scandalously in concern. He reached his hands out in an invitation for the poor and downcast to join him in communion. People were never meant to be stingy, stuffy, or stuck. They were created to treasure Jesus and, as a result, to generously treasure others.

Difference Maker

Offer to buy something for someone in need, leave a larger tip than normal, send a donation to a charity, or volunteer at a soup kitchen. Do something generous today that loosens up your comfort zone.

clothes to wear. 23For life is more than food, and your body more than cloth-
ing. 24Look at the ravens. They don't plant or harvest or store food in barns,
for God feeds them. And you are far more valuable to him than any birds!
25Can all your worries add a single moment to your life? 26And if worry can't
accomplish a little thing like that, what's the use of worrying over bigger
things?

27"Look at the lilies and how they grow. They don't work or make their
clothing, yet Solomon in all his glory was not dressed as beautifully as they
are. 28And if God cares so wonderfully for flowers that are here today and
thrown into the fire tomorrow, he will certainly care for you. Why do you
have so little faith?

29"And don't be concerned about what to eat and what to drink. Don't
worry about such things. 30These things dominate the thoughts of un-
believers all over the world, but your Father already knows your needs. 31Seek
the Kingdom of God above all else, and he will give you everything you need.

32"So don't be afraid, little flock. For it gives your Father great happiness
to give you the Kingdom.

33"Sell your possessions and give to those in need. This will store up trea-
sure for you in heaven! And the purses of heaven never get old or develop
holes. Your treasure will be safe; no thief can steal it and no moth can destroy
it. 34Wherever your treasure is, there the desires of your heart will also be.

Be Ready for the Lord's Coming

35"Be dressed for service and keep your lamps burning, 36as though you were
waiting for your master to return from the wedding feast. Then you will be
ready to open the door and let him in the moment he arrives and knocks.
37The servants who are ready and waiting for his return will be rewarded. I
tell you the truth, he himself will seat them, put on an apron, and serve them
as they sit and eat! 38He may come in the middle of the night or just before
dawn.* But whenever he comes, he will reward the servants who are ready.

39"Understand this: If a homeowner knew exactly when a burglar was
coming, he would not permit his house to be broken into. 40You also must
be ready all the time, for the Son of Man will come when least expected."

41Peter asked, "Lord, is that illustration just for us or for everyone?"

42And the Lord replied, "A faithful, sensible servant is one to whom the
master can give the responsibility of managing his other household servants
and feeding them. 43If the master returns and finds that the servant has done
a good job, there will be a reward. 44I tell you the truth, the master will put
that servant in charge of all he owns. 45But what if the servant thinks, 'My
master won't be back for a while,' and he begins beating the other servants,
partying, and getting drunk? 46The master will return unannounced and
unexpected, and he will cut the servant in pieces and banish him with the
unfaithful.

47"And a servant who knows what the master wants, but isn't prepared and
doesn't carry out those instructions, will be severely punished. 48But some-
one who does not know, and then does something wrong, will be punished
only lightly. When someone has been given much, much will be required in
return; and when someone has been entrusted with much, even more will
be required.

12:38 Greek *in the second or third watch.*

Jesus Causes Division

49 "I have come to set the world on fire, and I wish it were already burning!
50 I have a terrible baptism of suffering ahead of me, and I am under a heavy
burden until it is accomplished. 51 Do you think I have come to bring peace to
the earth? No, I have come to divide people against each other! 52 From now
on families will be split apart, three in favor of me, and two against—or two
in favor and three against.

53 'Father will be divided against son
  and son against father;
mother against daughter
  and daughter against mother;
and mother-in-law against daughter-in-law
  and daughter-in-law against mother-in-law.'*"

54 Then Jesus turned to the crowd and said, "When you see clouds begin-
ning to form in the west, you say, 'Here comes a shower.' And you are right.
55 When the south wind blows, you say, 'Today will be a scorcher.' And it is.
56 You fools! You know how to interpret the weather signs of the earth and
sky, but you don't know how to interpret the present times.
57 "Why can't you decide for yourselves what is right? 58 When you are on
the way to court with your accuser, try to settle the matter before you get
there. Otherwise, your accuser may drag you before the judge, who will hand
you over to an officer, who will throw you into prison. 59 And if that happens,
you won't be free again until you have paid the very last penny.*"

A Call to Repentance

13 About this time Jesus was informed that Pilate had murdered some
people from Galilee as they were offering sacrifices at the Temple.
2 "Do you think those Galileans were worse sinners than all the other people
from Galilee?" Jesus asked. "Is that why they suffered? 3 Not at all! And you
will perish, too, unless you repent of your sins and turn to God. 4 And what
about the eighteen people who died when the tower in Siloam fell on them?
Were they the worst sinners in Jerusalem? 5 No, and I tell you again that un-
less you repent, you will perish, too."

Parable of the Barren Fig Tree

6 Then Jesus told this story: "A man planted a fig tree in his garden and came
again and again to see if there was any fruit on it, but he was always dis-
appointed. 7 Finally, he said to his gardener, 'I've waited three years, and there
hasn't been a single fig! Cut it down. It's just taking up space in the garden.'
8 "The gardener answered, 'Sir, give it one more chance. Leave it another
year, and I'll give it special attention and plenty of fertilizer. 9 If we get figs
next year, fine. If not, then you can cut it down.'"

Jesus Heals on the Sabbath

10 One Sabbath day as Jesus was teaching in a synagogue, 11 he saw a woman
who had been crippled by an evil spirit. She had been bent double for eigh-
teen years and was unable to stand up straight. 12 When Jesus saw her, he

12:53 Mic 7:6. 12:59 Greek *last lepton* [the smallest Jewish coin].

Question 13:18–19

What kind of "kingdom" patterns do you need to have in your life so that you can grow your faith in the years ahead?

called her over and said, "Dear woman, you are healed of your sickness!"
13 Then he touched her, and instantly she could stand straight. How she
praised God!

14 But the leader in charge of the synagogue was indignant that Jesus had
healed her on the Sabbath day. "There are six days of the week for working,"
he said to the crowd. "Come on those days to be healed, not on the Sabbath."

15 But the Lord replied, "You hypocrites! Each of you works on the Sabbath
day! Don't you untie your ox or your donkey from its stall on the Sabbath
and lead it out for water? 16 This dear woman, a daughter of Abraham, has
been held in bondage by Satan for eighteen years. Isn't it right that she be
released, even on the Sabbath?"

17 This shamed his enemies, but all the people rejoiced at the wonderful
things he did.

Parable of the Mustard Seed

18 Then Jesus said, "What is the Kingdom of God like? How can I illustrate it?
19 It is like a tiny mustard seed that a man planted in a garden; it grows and
becomes a tree, and the birds make nests in its branches."

Parable of the Yeast

20 He also asked, "What else is the Kingdom of God like? 21 It is like the yeast
a woman used in making bread. Even though she put only a little yeast in
three measures of flour, it permeated every part of the dough."

The Narrow Door

22 Jesus went through the towns and villages, teaching as he went, always
pressing on toward Jerusalem. 23 Someone asked him, "Lord, will only a few
be saved?"

He replied, 24 "Work hard to enter the narrow door to God's Kingdom, for
many will try to enter but will fail. 25 When the master of the house has locked
the door, it will be too late. You will stand outside knocking and pleading,
'Lord, open the door for us!' But he will reply, 'I don't know you or where
you come from.' 26 Then you will say, 'But we ate and drank with you, and
you taught in our streets.' 27 And he will reply, 'I tell you, I don't know you or
where you come from. Get away from me, all you who do evil.'

28 "There will be weeping and gnashing of teeth, for you will see Abraham,
Isaac, Jacob, and all the prophets in the Kingdom of God, but you will be
thrown out. 29 And people will come from all over the world—from east and
west, north and south—to take their places in the Kingdom of God. 30 And
note this: Some who seem least important now will be the greatest then, and
some who are the greatest now will be least important then.*"

Jesus Grieves over Jerusalem

31 At that time some Pharisees said to him, "Get away from here if you want
to live! Herod Antipas wants to kill you!"

32 Jesus replied, "Go tell that fox that I will keep on casting out demons
and healing people today and tomorrow; and the third day I will accomplish
my purpose. 33 Yes, today, tomorrow, and the next day I must proceed on my
way. For it wouldn't do for a prophet of God to be killed except in Jerusalem!

13:30 Greek *Some are last who will be first, and some are first who will be last.*

34“O Jerusalem, Jerusalem, the city that kills the prophets and stones
God’s messengers! How often I have wanted to gather your children together
as a hen protects her chicks beneath her wings, but you wouldn’t let me.
35And now, look, your house is abandoned. And you will never see me again
until you say, ‘Blessings on the one who comes in the name of the LORD!’*”

Jesus Heals on the Sabbath

14 One Sabbath day Jesus went to eat dinner in the home of a leader of
the Pharisees, and the people were watching him closely. 2There was
a man there whose arms and legs were swollen.* 3Jesus asked the Pharisees
and experts in religious law, “Is it permitted in the law to heal people on the
Sabbath day, or not?” 4When they refused to answer, Jesus touched the sick
man and healed him and sent him away. 5Then he turned to them and said,
“Which of you doesn’t work on the Sabbath? If your son* or your cow falls
into a pit, don’t you rush to get him out?” 6Again they could not answer.

Jesus Teaches about Humility

7When Jesus noticed that all who had come to the dinner were trying to sit
in the seats of honor near the head of the table, he gave them this advice:
8“When you are invited to a wedding feast, don’t sit in the seat of honor. What
if someone who is more distinguished than you has also been invited? 9The
host will come and say, ‘Give this person your seat.’ Then you will be embar-
rassed, and you will have to take whatever seat is left at the foot of the table!

10“Instead, take the lowest place at the foot of the table. Then when your
host sees you, he will come and say, ‘Friend, we have a better place for you!’
Then you will be honored in front of all the other guests. 11For those who
exalt themselves will be humbled, and those who humble themselves will
be exalted.”

12Then he turned to his host. “When you put on a luncheon or a banquet,”
he said, “don’t invite your friends, brothers, relatives, and rich neighbors.
For they will invite you back, and that will be your only reward. 13Instead,
invite the poor, the crippled, the lame, and the blind. 14Then at the resur-
rection of the righteous, God will reward you for inviting those who could
not repay you.”

Parable of the Great Feast

15Hearing this, a man sitting at the table with Jesus exclaimed, “What a bless-
ing it will be to attend a banquet* in the Kingdom of God!”

16Jesus replied with this story: “A man prepared a great feast and sent out
many invitations. 17When the banquet was ready, he sent his servant to tell
the guests, ‘Come, the banquet is ready.’ 18But they all began making excuses.
One said, ‘I have just bought a field and must inspect it. Please excuse me.’
19Another said, ‘I have just bought five pairs of oxen, and I want to try them
out. Please excuse me.’ 20Another said, ‘I just got married, so I can’t come.’

21“The servant returned and told his master what they had said. His mas-
ter was furious and said, ‘Go quickly into the streets and alleys of the town
and invite the poor, the crippled, the blind, and the lame.’ 22After the servant
had done this, he reported, ‘There is still room for more.’ 23So his master said,
‘Go out into the country lanes and behind the hedges and urge anyone you

13:35 Ps 118:26. **14:2** Or *who had dropsy.* **14:5** Some manuscripts read *donkey.* **14:15** Greek *to eat bread.*

Question 14:22-30

What is the cost of discipleship? Why did Jesus say such a difficult thing?

Question 15:11-32

Do you think this parable is more about the younger son, the older son, or the good father? Which of these three do you identify with the most (and why)?

find to come, so that the house will be full. 24 For none of those I first invited
will get even the smallest taste of my banquet.'"

The Cost of Being a Disciple

25 A large crowd was following Jesus. He turned around and said to them,
26 "If you want to be my disciple, you must, by comparison, hate everyone
else—your father and mother, wife and children, brothers and sisters—yes,
even your own life. Otherwise, you cannot be my disciple. 27 And if you do not
carry your own cross and follow me, you cannot be my disciple.
28 "But don't begin until you count the cost. For who would begin con-
struction of a building without first calculating the cost to see if there is
enough money to finish it? 29 Otherwise, you might complete only the foun-
dation before running out of money, and then everyone would laugh at you.
30 They would say, 'There's the person who started that building and couldn't
afford to finish it!'
31 "Or what king would go to war against another king without first sit-
ting down with his counselors to discuss whether his army of 10,000 could
defeat the 20,000 soldiers marching against him? 32 And if he can't, he will
send a delegation to discuss terms of peace while the enemy is still far away.
33 So you cannot become my disciple without giving up everything you own.
34 "Salt is good for seasoning. But if it loses its flavor, how do you make it
salty again? 35 Flavorless salt is good neither for the soil nor for the manure pile.
It is thrown away. Anyone with ears to hear should listen and understand!"

Parable of the Lost Sheep

15 Tax collectors and other notorious sinners often came to listen to
Jesus teach. 2 This made the Pharisees and teachers of religious law
complain that he was associating with such sinful people—even eating with
them!
3 So Jesus told them this story: 4 "If a man has a hundred sheep and one
of them gets lost, what will he do? Won't he leave the ninety-nine others in
the wilderness and go to search for the one that is lost until he finds it? 5 And
when he has found it, he will joyfully carry it home on his shoulders. 6 When
he arrives, he will call together his friends and neighbors, saying, 'Rejoice
with me because I have found my lost sheep.' 7 In the same way, there is more
joy in heaven over one lost sinner who repents and returns to God than over
ninety-nine others who are righteous and haven't strayed away!

Parable of the Lost Coin

8 "Or suppose a woman has ten silver coins* and loses one. Won't she light a
lamp and sweep the entire house and search carefully until she finds it? 9 And
when she finds it, she will call in her friends and neighbors and say, 'Rejoice
with me because I have found my lost coin.' 10 In the same way, there is joy in
the presence of God's angels when even one sinner repents."

Parable of the Lost Son

11 To illustrate the point further, Jesus told them this story: "A man had two
sons. 12 The younger son told his father, 'I want my share of your estate now
before you die.' So his father agreed to divide his wealth between his sons.

15:8 Greek *ten drachmas.* A drachma was the equivalent of a full day's wage.

13“A few days later this younger son packed all his belongings and moved
to a distant land, and there he wasted all his money in wild living. 14About
the time his money ran out, a great famine swept over the land, and he began
to starve. 15He persuaded a local farmer to hire him, and the man sent him
into his fields to feed the pigs. 16The young man became so hungry that
even the pods he was feeding the pigs looked good to him. But no one gave
him anything.

17“When he finally came to his senses, he said to himself, ‘At home even the
hired servants have food enough to spare, and here I am dying of hunger! 18I
will go home to my father and say, “Father, I have sinned against both heaven
and you, 19and I am no longer worthy of being called your son. Please take
me on as a hired servant.”’

20“So he returned home to his father. And while he was still a long way
off, his father saw him coming. Filled with love and compassion, he ran to
his son, embraced him, and kissed him. 21His son said to him, ‘Father, I have
sinned against both heaven and you, and I am no longer worthy of being
called your son.*’

22“But his father said to the servants, ‘Quick! Bring the finest robe in the
house and put it on him. Get a ring for his finger and sandals for his feet.
23And kill the calf we have been fattening. We must celebrate with a feast,
24for this son of mine was dead and has now returned to life. He was lost,
but now he is found.’ So the party began.

25“Meanwhile, the older son was in the fields working. When he returned
home, he heard music and dancing in the house, 26and he asked one of the
servants what was going on. 27‘Your brother is back,’ he was told, ‘and your fa-
ther has killed the fattened calf. We are celebrating because of his safe return.’

28“The older brother was angry and wouldn’t go in. His father came out
and begged him, 29but he replied, ‘All these years I’ve slaved for you and
never once refused to do a single thing you told me to. And in all that time
you never gave me even one young goat for a feast with my friends. 30Yet
when this son of yours comes back after squandering your money on pros-
titutes, you celebrate by killing the fattened calf!’

31“His father said to him, ‘Look, dear son, you have always stayed by me,
and everything I have is yours. 32We had to celebrate this happy day. For
your brother was dead and has come back to life! He was lost, but now he
is found!’”

Parable of the Shrewd Manager

16 Jesus told this story to his disciples: “There was a certain rich man
who had a manager handling his affairs. One day a report came that
the manager was wasting his employer’s money. 2So the employer called him
in and said, ‘What’s this I hear about you? Get your report in order, because
you are going to be fired.’

3“The manager thought to himself, ‘Now what? My boss has fired me. I
don’t have the strength to dig ditches, and I’m too proud to beg. 4Ah, I know
how to ensure that I’ll have plenty of friends who will give me a home when
I am fired.’

5“So he invited each person who owed money to his employer to come and
discuss the situation. He asked the first one, ‘How much do you owe him?’

15:21 Some manuscripts add *Please take me on as a hired servant.*

Make a Difference

16:10-13

Faithful in the Little

If you squander your opportunities, people will struggle to give you another chance. If, however, you work hard and accomplish the task you were given, people will trust you and reward you with even more opportunities in life.

Difference Maker

Be responsible today with the chores you've been given. Go above and beyond and set an example for others in the way you conduct your life.

6 The man replied, 'I owe him 800 gallons of olive oil.' So the manager told
him, 'Take the bill and quickly change it to 400 gallons.*'
7 "'And how much do you owe my employer?' he asked the next man. 'I
owe him 1,000 bushels of wheat,' was the reply. 'Here,' the manager said,
'take the bill and change it to 800 bushels.*'
8 "The rich man had to admire the dishonest rascal for being so shrewd.
And it is true that the children of this world are more shrewd in dealing
with the world around them than are the children of the light. 9 Here's the
lesson: Use your worldly resources to benefit others and make friends. Then,
when your possessions are gone, they will welcome you to an eternal home.*
10 "If you are faithful in little things, you will be faithful in large ones. But
if you are dishonest in little things, you won't be honest with greater respon-
sibilities. 11 And if you are untrustworthy about worldly wealth, who will
trust you with the true riches of heaven? 12 And if you are not faithful with
other people's things, why should you be trusted with things of your own?
13 "No one can serve two masters. For you will hate one and love the other;
you will be devoted to one and despise the other. You cannot serve God and
be enslaved to money."
14 The Pharisees, who dearly loved their money, heard all this and scoffed at
him. 15 Then he said to them, "You like to appear righteous in public, but God
knows your hearts. What this world honors is detestable in the sight of God.
16 "Until John the Baptist, the law of Moses and the messages of the
prophets were your guides. But now the Good News of the Kingdom of God
is preached, and everyone is eager to get in.* 17 But that doesn't mean that the
law has lost its force. It is easier for heaven and earth to disappear than for
the smallest point of God's law to be overturned.
18 "For example, a man who divorces his wife and marries someone else
commits adultery. And anyone who marries a woman divorced from her
husband commits adultery."

Parable of the Rich Man and Lazarus

19 Jesus said, "There was a certain rich man who was splendidly clothed in
purple and fine linen and who lived each day in luxury. 20 At his gate lay a
poor man named Lazarus who was covered with sores. 21 As Lazarus lay there
longing for scraps from the rich man's table, the dogs would come and lick
his open sores.
22 "Finally, the poor man died and was carried by the angels to sit beside
Abraham at the heavenly banquet.* The rich man also died and was buried,
23 and he went to the place of the dead.* There, in torment, he saw Abraham
in the far distance with Lazarus at his side.
24 "The rich man shouted, 'Father Abraham, have some pity! Send Lazarus
over here to dip the tip of his finger in water and cool my tongue. I am in
anguish in these flames.'
25 "But Abraham said to him, 'Son, remember that during your lifetime
you had everything you wanted, and Lazarus had nothing. So now he is
here being comforted, and you are in anguish. 26 And besides, there is a great
chasm separating us. No one can cross over to you from here, and no one can
cross over to us from there.'

16:6 Greek *100 baths . . . 50 [baths].* **16:7** Greek *100 korous . . . 80 [korous].* **16:9** Or *you will be welcomed into eternal homes.* **16:16** Or *everyone is urged to enter in.* **16:22** Greek *to Abraham's bosom.* **16:23** Greek *to Hades.*

27 “Then the rich man said, ‘Please, Father Abraham, at least send him to
my father’s home. 28 For I have five brothers, and I want him to warn them
so they don’t end up in this place of torment.’
29 “But Abraham said, ‘Moses and the prophets have warned them. Your
brothers can read what they wrote.’
30 “The rich man replied, ‘No, Father Abraham! But if someone is sent to
them from the dead, then they will repent of their sins and turn to God.’
31 “But Abraham said, ‘If they won’t listen to Moses and the prophets, they
won’t be persuaded even if someone rises from the dead.’”

Prayer 17:1

Dear Jesus, let me serve you no matter what it costs. Let me stay true no matter what temptations arise. Let me always point others to you and never lead them astray. Amen.

Teachings about Forgiveness and Faith

17 One day Jesus said to his disciples, “There will always be temptations
to sin, but what sorrow awaits the person who does the tempting!
2 It would be better to be thrown into the sea with a millstone hung around
your neck than to cause one of these little ones to fall into sin. 3 So watch
yourselves!
“If another believer* sins, rebuke that person; then if there is repentance,
forgive. 4 Even if that person wrongs you seven times a day and each time
turns again and asks forgiveness, you must forgive.”
5 The apostles said to the Lord, “Show us how to increase our faith.”
6 The Lord answered, “If you had faith even as small as a mustard seed, you
could say to this mulberry tree, ‘May you be uprooted and be planted in the
sea,’ and it would obey you!
7 “When a servant comes in from plowing or taking care of sheep, does his
master say, ‘Come in and eat with me’? 8 No, he says, ‘Prepare my meal, put
on your apron, and serve me while I eat. Then you can eat later.’ 9 And does
the master thank the servant for doing what he was told to do? Of course
not. 10 In the same way, when you obey me you should say, ‘We are unworthy
servants who have simply done our duty.’”

Ten Healed of Leprosy

11 As Jesus continued on toward Jerusalem, he reached the border between
Galilee and Samaria. 12 As he entered a village there, ten men with leprosy
stood at a distance, 13 crying out, “Jesus, Master, have mercy on us!”
14 He looked at them and said, “Go show yourselves to the priests.”* And
as they went, they were cleansed of their leprosy.
15 One of them, when he saw that he was healed, came back to Jesus, shout-
ing, “Praise God!” 16 He fell to the ground at Jesus’ feet, thanking him for
what he had done. This man was a Samaritan.
17 Jesus asked, “Didn’t I heal ten men? Where are the other nine? 18 Has no
one returned to give glory to God except this foreigner?” 19 And Jesus said to
the man, “Stand up and go. Your faith has healed you.*”

The Coming of the Kingdom

20 One day the Pharisees asked Jesus, “When will the Kingdom of God come?”
Jesus replied, “The Kingdom of God can’t be detected by visible signs.*
21 You won’t be able to say, ‘Here it is!’ or ‘It’s over there!’ For the Kingdom
of God is already among you.*”
22 Then he said to his disciples, “The time is coming when you will long to

17:3 Greek *If your brother.* 17:14 See Lev 14:2-32. 17:19 Or *Your faith has saved you.* 17:20 Or *by your speculations.* 17:21 Or *is within you,* or *is in your grasp.*

see the day when the Son of Man returns,* but you won't see it. 23People will
tell you, 'Look, there is the Son of Man,' or 'Here he is,' but don't go out and
follow them. 24For as the lightning flashes and lights up the sky from one
end to the other, so it will be on the day* when the Son of Man comes. 25But
first the Son of Man must suffer terribly* and be rejected by this generation.
26"When the Son of Man returns, it will be like it was in Noah's day. 27In
those days, the people enjoyed banquets and parties and weddings right up
to the time Noah entered his boat and the flood came and destroyed them all.
28"And the world will be as it was in the days of Lot. People went about
their daily business—eating and drinking, buying and selling, farming
and building— 29until the morning Lot left Sodom. Then fire and burn-
ing sulfur rained down from heaven and destroyed them all. 30Yes, it will
be 'business as usual' right up to the day when the Son of Man is revealed.
31On that day a person out on the deck of a roof must not go down into the
house to pack. A person out in the field must not return home. 32Remember
what happened to Lot's wife! 33If you cling to your life, you will lose it, and
if you let your life go, you will save it. 34That night two people will be asleep
in one bed; one will be taken, the other left. 35Two women will be grinding
flour together at the mill; one will be taken, the other left.*"
37"Where will this happen, Lord?"* the disciples asked.
Jesus replied, "Just as the gathering of vultures shows there is a carcass
nearby, so these signs indicate that the end is near."*

Parable of the Persistent Widow

18 One day Jesus told his disciples a story to show that they should
always pray and never give up. 2"There was a judge in a certain city,"
he said, "who neither feared God nor cared about people. 3A widow of that
city came to him repeatedly, saying, 'Give me justice in this dispute with my
enemy.' 4The judge ignored her for a while, but finally he said to himself,
'I don't fear God or care about people, 5but this woman is driving me crazy.
I'm going to see that she gets justice, because she is wearing me out with
her constant requests!'"
6Then the Lord said, "Learn a lesson from this unjust judge. 7Even he
rendered a just decision in the end. So don't you think God will surely give
justice to his chosen people who cry out to him day and night? Will he keep
putting them off? 8I tell you, he will grant justice to them quickly! But when
the Son of Man* returns, how many will he find on the earth who have faith?"

Parable of the Pharisee and Tax Collector

9Then Jesus told this story to some who had great confidence in their own
righteousness and scorned everyone else: 10"Two men went to the Temple
to pray. One was a Pharisee, and the other was a despised tax collector. 11The
Pharisee stood by himself and prayed this prayer*: 'I thank you, God, that I
am not like other people—cheaters, sinners, adulterers. I'm certainly not like
that tax collector! 12I fast twice a week, and I give you a tenth of my income.'
13"But the tax collector stood at a distance and dared not even lift his eyes

17:22 Or *long for even one day with the Son of Man.* "Son of Man" is a title Jesus used for himself. 17:24 Some manuscripts do not include *on the day.* 17:25 Or *suffer many things.* 17:35 Some manuscripts add verse 36, *Two men will be working in the field; one will be taken, the other left.* Compare Matt 24:40. 17:37a Greek *"Where, Lord?"* 17:37b Greek *"Wherever the carcass is, the vultures gather."* 18:8 "Son of Man" is a title Jesus used for himself. 18:11 Some manuscripts read *stood and prayed this prayer to himself.*

to heaven as he prayed. Instead, he beat his chest in sorrow, saying, 'O God, be merciful to me, for I am a sinner.' 14 I tell you, this sinner, not the Pharisee, returned home justified before God. For those who exalt themselves will be humbled, and those who humble themselves will be exalted."

Jesus Blesses the Children

15 One day some parents brought their little children to Jesus so he could touch and bless them. But when the disciples saw this, they scolded the parents for bothering him.

16 Then Jesus called for the children and said to the disciples, "Let the children come to me. Don't stop them! For the Kingdom of God belongs to those who are like these children. 17 I tell you the truth, anyone who doesn't receive the Kingdom of God like a child will never enter it."

Question 18:16

How could you help the next generation come to Jesus? What could you do that would help them grow in their knowledge of God?

The Rich Man

18 Once a religious leader asked Jesus this question: "Good Teacher, what should I do to inherit eternal life?"

19 "Why do you call me good?" Jesus asked him. "Only God is truly good. 20 But to answer your question, you know the commandments: 'You must not commit adultery. You must not murder. You must not steal. You must not testify falsely. Honor your father and mother.'*"

21 The man replied, "I've obeyed all these commandments since I was young."

22 When Jesus heard his answer, he said, "There is still one thing you haven't done. Sell all your possessions and give the money to the poor, and you will have treasure in heaven. Then come, follow me."

23 But when the man heard this he became very sad, for he was very rich.

24 When Jesus saw this,* he said, "How hard it is for the rich to enter the Kingdom of God! 25 In fact, it is easier for a camel to go through the eye of a needle than for a rich person to enter the Kingdom of God!"

26 Those who heard this said, "Then who in the world can be saved?"

27 He replied, "What is impossible for people is possible with God."

28 Peter said, "We've left our homes to follow you."

29 "Yes," Jesus replied, "and I assure you that everyone who has given up house or wife or brothers or parents or children, for the sake of the Kingdom of God, 30 will be repaid many times over in this life, and will have eternal life in the world to come."

Jesus Again Predicts His Death

31 Taking the twelve disciples aside, Jesus said, "Listen, we're going up to Jerusalem, where all the predictions of the prophets concerning the Son of Man will come true. 32 He will be handed over to the Romans,* and he will be mocked, treated shamefully, and spit upon. 33 They will flog him with a whip and kill him, but on the third day he will rise again."

34 But they didn't understand any of this. The significance of his words was hidden from them, and they failed to grasp what he was talking about.

Jesus Heals a Blind Beggar

35 As Jesus approached Jericho, a blind beggar was sitting beside the road.
36 When he heard the noise of a crowd going past, he asked what was

18:20 Exod 20:12-16; Deut 5:16-20. 18:24 Some manuscripts read *When Jesus saw how sad the man was.* 18:32 Greek *the Gentiles.*

> **Question** **19:10**
>
> The Bible tells us that Jesus came to the earth so that he could meet us and have an eternal relationship with us. In what ways did Jesus' comment in this verse sum up the whole point of Scripture?

happening. 37 They told him that Jesus the Nazarene* was going by. 38 So he
began shouting, "Jesus, Son of David, have mercy on me!"
39 "Be quiet!" the people in front yelled at him.
But he only shouted louder, "Son of David, have mercy on me!"
40 When Jesus heard him, he stopped and ordered that the man be brought
to him. As the man came near, Jesus asked him, 41 "What do you want me to
do for you?"
"Lord," he said, "I want to see!"
42 And Jesus said, "All right, receive your sight! Your faith has healed you."
43 Instantly the man could see, and he followed Jesus, praising God. And all
who saw it praised God, too.

Jesus and Zacchaeus

19 Jesus entered Jericho and made his way through the town. 2 There
was a man there named Zacchaeus. He was the chief tax collector
in the region, and he had become very rich. 3 He tried to get a look at Jesus,
but he was too short to see over the crowd. 4 So he ran ahead and climbed a
sycamore-fig tree beside the road, for Jesus was going to pass that way.
5 When Jesus came by, he looked up at Zacchaeus and called him by name.
"Zacchaeus!" he said. "Quick, come down! I must be a guest in your home
today."
6 Zacchaeus quickly climbed down and took Jesus to his house in great
excitement and joy. 7 But the people were displeased. "He has gone to be the
guest of a notorious sinner," they grumbled.
8 Meanwhile, Zacchaeus stood before the Lord and said, "I will give half
my wealth to the poor, Lord, and if I have cheated people on their taxes, I
will give them back four times as much!"
9 Jesus responded, "Salvation has come to this home today, for this man
has shown himself to be a true son of Abraham. 10 For the Son of Man* came
to seek and save those who are lost."

Parable of the Ten Servants

11 The crowd was listening to everything Jesus said. And because he was near-
ing Jerusalem, he told them a story to correct the impression that the King-
dom of God would begin right away. 12 He said, "A nobleman was called away
to a distant empire to be crowned king and then return. 13 Before he left, he
called together ten of his servants and divided among them ten pounds of sil-
ver,* saying, 'Invest this for me while I am gone.' 14 But his people hated him
and sent a delegation after him to say, 'We do not want him to be our king.'
15 "After he was crowned king, he returned and called in the servants to
whom he had given the money. He wanted to find out what their profits
were. 16 The first servant reported, 'Master, I invested your money and made
ten times the original amount!'
17 "'Well done!' the king exclaimed. 'You are a good servant. You have been
faithful with the little I entrusted to you, so you will be governor of ten cities
as your reward.'
18 "The next servant reported, 'Master, I invested your money and made
five times the original amount.'
19 "'Well done!' the king said. 'You will be governor over five cities.'

18:37 Or *Jesus of Nazareth.* **19:10** "Son of Man" is a title Jesus used for himself. **19:13** Greek *ten minas;* one mina was worth about three months' wages.

Question 19:28–44

The people may have realized they needed salvation, but do you think they realized they needed Jesus?

20"But the third servant brought back only the original amount of money
and said, 'Master, I hid your money and kept it safe. 21I was afraid because
you are a hard man to deal with, taking what isn't yours and harvesting
crops you didn't plant.'
22"'You wicked servant!' the king roared. 'Your own words condemn you.
If you knew that I'm a hard man who takes what isn't mine and harvests
crops I didn't plant, 23why didn't you deposit my money in the bank? At least
I could have gotten some interest on it.'
24"Then, turning to the others standing nearby, the king ordered, 'Take
the money from this servant, and give it to the one who has ten pounds.'
25"'But, master,' they said, 'he already has ten pounds!'
26"'Yes,' the king replied, 'and to those who use well what they are given,
even more will be given. But from those who do nothing, even what little they
have will be taken away. 27And as for these enemies of mine who didn't want me
to be their king—bring them in and execute them right here in front of me.'"

Jesus' Triumphant Entry

28After telling this story, Jesus went on toward Jerusalem, walking ahead of
his disciples. 29As he came to the towns of Bethphage and Bethany on the
Mount of Olives, he sent two disciples ahead. 30"Go into that village over
there," he told them. "As you enter it, you will see a young donkey tied there
that no one has ever ridden. Untie it and bring it here. 31If anyone asks, 'Why
are you untying that colt?' just say, 'The Lord needs it.'"
32So they went and found the colt, just as Jesus had said. 33And sure
enough, as they were untying it, the owners asked them, "Why are you un-
tying that colt?"
34And the disciples simply replied, "The Lord needs it." 35So they brought
the colt to Jesus and threw their garments over it for him to ride on.
36As he rode along, the crowds spread out their garments on the road
ahead of him. 37When he reached the place where the road started down the
Mount of Olives, all of his followers began to shout and sing as they walked
along, praising God for all the wonderful miracles they had seen.

38 "Blessings on the King who comes in the name of the LORD!
Peace in heaven, and glory in highest heaven!"*

39But some of the Pharisees among the crowd said, "Teacher, rebuke your
followers for saying things like that!"
40He replied, "If they kept quiet, the stones along the road would burst
into cheers!"

Jesus Weeps over Jerusalem

41But as he came closer to Jerusalem and saw the city ahead, he began to
weep. 42"How I wish today that you of all people would understand the way
to peace. But now it is too late, and peace is hidden from your eyes. 43Before
long your enemies will build ramparts against your walls and encircle you
and close in on you from every side. 44They will crush you into the ground,
and your children with you. Your enemies will not leave a single stone in
place, because you did not recognize it when God visited you.*"

19:38 Pss 118:26; 148:1. **19:44** Greek *did not recognize the time of your visitation,* a reference to the Messiah's coming.

Question 19:48

What do you think Luke meant when he said that the people hung on every word of Jesus? Would this represent the way you live out your faith too?

Jesus Clears the Temple

45 Then Jesus entered the Temple and began to drive out the people selling animals for sacrifices. 46 He said to them, "The Scriptures declare, 'My Temple will be a house of prayer,' but you have turned it into a den of thieves."*

47 After that, he taught daily in the Temple, but the leading priests, the teachers of religious law, and the other leaders of the people began planning how to kill him. 48 But they could think of nothing, because all the people hung on every word he said.

The Authority of Jesus Challenged

20 One day as Jesus was teaching the people and preaching the Good News in the Temple, the leading priests, the teachers of religious law, and the elders came up to him. 2 They demanded, "By what authority are you doing all these things? Who gave you the right?"

3 "Let me ask you a question first," he replied. 4 "Did John's authority to baptize come from heaven, or was it merely human?"

5 They talked it over among themselves. "If we say it was from heaven, he will ask why we didn't believe John. 6 But if we say it was merely human, the people will stone us because they are convinced John was a prophet." 7 So they finally replied that they didn't know.

8 And Jesus responded, "Then I won't tell you by what authority I do these things."

Parable of the Evil Farmers

9 Now Jesus turned to the people again and told them this story: "A man planted a vineyard, leased it to tenant farmers, and moved to another country to live for several years. 10 At the time of the grape harvest, he sent one of his servants to collect his share of the crop. But the farmers attacked the servant, beat him up, and sent him back empty-handed. 11 So the owner sent another servant, but they also insulted him, beat him up, and sent him away empty-handed. 12 A third man was sent, and they wounded him and chased him away.

13 "'What will I do?' the owner asked himself. 'I know! I'll send my cherished son. Surely they will respect him.'

14 "But when the tenant farmers saw his son, they said to each other, 'Here comes the heir to this estate. Let's kill him and get the estate for ourselves!' 15 So they dragged him out of the vineyard and murdered him.

"What do you suppose the owner of the vineyard will do to them?" Jesus asked. 16 "I'll tell you—he will come and kill those farmers and lease the vineyard to others."

"How terrible that such a thing should ever happen," his listeners protested.

17 Jesus looked at them and said, "Then what does this Scripture mean?

'The stone that the builders rejected
has now become the cornerstone.'*

18 Everyone who stumbles over that stone will be broken to pieces, and it will crush anyone it falls on."

19:46 Isa 56:7; Jer 7:11. **20:17** Ps 118:22.

19 The teachers of religious law and the leading priests wanted to arrest
Jesus immediately because they realized he was telling the story against
them—they were the wicked farmers. But they were afraid of the people's
reaction.

Taxes for Caesar

20 Watching for their opportunity, the leaders sent spies pretending to be
honest men. They tried to get Jesus to say something that could be reported
to the Roman governor so he would arrest Jesus. 21 "Teacher," they said, "we
know that you speak and teach what is right and are not influenced by what
others think. You teach the way of God truthfully. 22 Now tell us—is it right
for us to pay taxes to Caesar or not?"

23 He saw through their trickery and said, 24 "Show me a Roman coin.*
Whose picture and title are stamped on it?"

"Caesar's," they replied.

25 "Well then," he said, "give to Caesar what belongs to Caesar, and give to
God what belongs to God."

26 So they failed to trap him by what he said in front of the people. Instead,
they were amazed by his answer, and they became silent.

Discussion about Resurrection

27 Then Jesus was approached by some Sadducees—religious leaders who say
there is no resurrection from the dead. 28 They posed this question: "Teacher,
Moses gave us a law that if a man dies, leaving a wife but no children, his brother
should marry the widow and have a child who will carry on the brother's name.*
29 Well, suppose there were seven brothers. The oldest one married and then
died without children. 30 So the second brother married the widow, but he also
died. 31 Then the third brother married her. This continued with all seven of
them, who died without children. 32 Finally, the woman also died. 33 So tell us,
whose wife will she be in the resurrection? For all seven were married to her!"

34 Jesus replied, "Marriage is for people here on earth. 35 But in the age to
come, those worthy of being raised from the dead will neither marry nor be
given in marriage. 36 And they will never die again. In this respect they will
be like angels. They are children of God and children of the resurrection.

37 "But now, as to whether the dead will be raised—even Moses proved
this when he wrote about the burning bush. Long after Abraham, Isaac, and
Jacob had died, he referred to the Lord* as 'the God of Abraham, the God of
Isaac, and the God of Jacob.'* 38 So he is the God of the living, not the dead,
for they are all alive to him."

39 "Well said, Teacher!" remarked some of the teachers of religious law who
were standing there. 40 And then no one dared to ask him any more questions.

Whose Son Is the Messiah?

41 Then Jesus presented them with a question. "Why is it," he asked, "that
the Messiah is said to be the son of David? 42 For David himself wrote in the
book of Psalms:

'The LORD said to my Lord,
Sit in the place of honor at my right hand

20:24 Greek *a denarius.* **20:28** See Deut 25:5-6. **20:37a** Greek *when he wrote about the bush. He referred to the Lord.* **20:37b** Exod 3:6.

Question 21:1–4

Why did Jesus lift up the poor widow for her example? How would you compare yourself to this woman's commitment to God?

43 until I humble your enemies,
making them a footstool under your feet.'*
44 Since David called the Messiah 'Lord,' how can the Messiah be his son?"
45 Then, with the crowds listening, he turned to his disciples and said,
46 "Beware of these teachers of religious law! For they like to parade around
in flowing robes and love to receive respectful greetings as they walk in the
marketplaces. And how they love the seats of honor in the synagogues and
the head table at banquets. 47 Yet they shamelessly cheat widows out of their
property and then pretend to be pious by making long prayers in public.
Because of this, they will be severely punished."

The Widow's Offering

21 While Jesus was in the Temple, he watched the rich people dropping
their gifts in the collection box. 2 Then a poor widow came by and
dropped in two small coins.*
3 "I tell you the truth," Jesus said, "this poor widow has given more than
all the rest of them. 4 For they have given a tiny part of their surplus, but she,
poor as she is, has given everything she has."

Jesus Speaks about the Future

5 Some of his disciples began talking about the majestic stonework of the
Temple and the memorial decorations on the walls. But Jesus said, 6 "The
time is coming when all these things will be completely demolished. Not
one stone will be left on top of another!"
7 "Teacher," they asked, "when will all this happen? What sign will show
us that these things are about to take place?"
8 He replied, "Don't let anyone mislead you, for many will come in my
name, claiming, 'I am the Messiah,'* and saying, 'The time has come!' But
don't believe them. 9 And when you hear of wars and insurrections, don't
panic. Yes, these things must take place first, but the end won't follow im-
mediately." 10 Then he added, "Nation will go to war against nation, and
kingdom against kingdom. 11 There will be great earthquakes, and there will
be famines and plagues in many lands, and there will be terrifying things
and great miraculous signs from heaven.
12 "But before all this occurs, there will be a time of great persecution. You
will be dragged into synagogues and prisons, and you will stand trial before
kings and governors because you are my followers. 13 But this will be your
opportunity to tell them about me.* 14 So don't worry in advance about how
to answer the charges against you, 15 for I will give you the right words and
such wisdom that none of your opponents will be able to reply or refute you!
16 Even those closest to you—your parents, brothers, relatives, and friends—
will betray you. They will even kill some of you. 17 And everyone will hate
you because you are my followers.* 18 But not a hair of your head will perish!
19 By standing firm, you will win your souls.
20 "And when you see Jerusalem surrounded by armies, then you will know
that the time of its destruction has arrived. 21 Then those in Judea must flee
to the hills. Those in Jerusalem must get out, and those out in the country
should not return to the city. 22 For those will be days of God's vengeance,

20:42-43 Ps 110:1. **21:2** Greek *two lepta* [the smallest of Jewish coins]. **21:8** Greek *claiming, 'I am.'* **21:13** Or *This will be your testimony against them.* **21:17** Greek *on account of my name.*

and the prophetic words of the Scriptures will be fulfilled. 23 How terrible
it will be for pregnant women and for nursing mothers in those days. For
there will be disaster in the land and great anger against this people. 24 They
will be killed by the sword or sent away as captives to all the nations of the
world. And Jerusalem will be trampled down by the Gentiles until the period
of the Gentiles comes to an end.

25 "And there will be strange signs in the sun, moon, and stars. And here
on earth the nations will be in turmoil, perplexed by the roaring seas and
strange tides. 26 People will be terrified at what they see coming upon the
earth, for the powers in the heavens will be shaken. 27 Then everyone will see
the Son of Man* coming on a cloud with power and great glory.* 28 So when all
these things begin to happen, stand and look up, for your salvation is near!"

29 Then he gave them this illustration: "Notice the fig tree, or any other
tree. 30 When the leaves come out, you know without being told that summer
is near. 31 In the same way, when you see all these things taking place, you can
know that the Kingdom of God is near. 32 I tell you the truth, this generation
will not pass from the scene until all these things have taken place. 33 Heaven
and earth will disappear, but my words will never disappear.

34 "Watch out! Don't let your hearts be dulled by carousing and drunken-
ness, and by the worries of this life. Don't let that day catch you unaware,
35 like a trap. For that day will come upon everyone living on the earth. 36 Keep
alert at all times. And pray that you might be strong enough to escape these
coming horrors and stand before the Son of Man."

37 Every day Jesus went to the Temple to teach, and each evening he re-
turned to spend the night on the Mount of Olives. 38 The crowds gathered
at the Temple early each morning to hear him.

Prayer **21:36**

Lord, help my faith to be alert and not dull today. Amen.

Judas Agrees to Betray Jesus

22 The Festival of Unleavened Bread, which is also called Passover, was
approaching. 2 The leading priests and teachers of religious law were
plotting how to kill Jesus, but they were afraid of the people's reaction.

3 Then Satan entered into Judas Iscariot, who was one of the twelve dis-
ciples, 4 and he went to the leading priests and captains of the Temple guard
to discuss the best way to betray Jesus to them. 5 They were delighted, and they
promised to give him money. 6 So he agreed and began looking for an opportu-
nity to betray Jesus so they could arrest him when the crowds weren't around.

The Last Supper

7 Now the Festival of Unleavened Bread arrived, when the Passover lamb is
sacrificed. 8 Jesus sent Peter and John ahead and said, "Go and prepare the
Passover meal, so we can eat it together."

9 "Where do you want us to prepare it?" they asked him.

10 He replied, "As soon as you enter Jerusalem, a man carrying a pitcher of
water will meet you. Follow him. At the house he enters, 11 say to the owner,
'The Teacher asks: Where is the guest room where I can eat the Passover
meal with my disciples?' 12 He will take you upstairs to a large room that is
already set up. That is where you should prepare our meal." 13 They went off
to the city and found everything just as Jesus had said, and they prepared
the Passover meal there.

21:27a "Son of Man" is a title Jesus used for himself. 21:27b See Dan 7:13.

Question 22:7-20

Go back and read Exodus 12. What do you discover about the meaning of this annual celebration and the meaning Jesus was adding to it?

Make a Difference
22:25-28

Serve

As he was preparing for the day ahead, Jesus said something startling. "Normally," he essentially said, "the master sits at the table and is served by his servants but not here! I am your servant." Jesus could have demanded their allegiance. He could have instructed them to bring him some sandals and iced tea (with a lemon slice and one of those little paper umbrellas). He could have called down his angels and waylaid everyone in his path—especially Judas, the guy who was about to betray him. Instead, he attended to their needs, washed their feet, and served them food and drink. Jesus turned the tables upside down.

Difference Maker

Serve someone today. Wash the dishes, pay for gas in their car, buy them lunch, leave them a note, or find some other creative way to do something that shows how much you value them.

14 When the time came, Jesus and the apostles sat down together at the
table.* 15 Jesus said, "I have been very eager to eat this Passover meal with
you before my suffering begins. 16 For I tell you now that I won't eat this meal
again until its meaning is fulfilled in the Kingdom of God."
17 Then he took a cup of wine and gave thanks to God for it. Then he said,
"Take this and share it among yourselves. 18 For I will not drink wine again
until the Kingdom of God has come."
19 He took some bread and gave thanks to God for it. Then he broke it in
pieces and gave it to the disciples, saying, "This is my body, which is given
for you. Do this in remembrance of me."
20 After supper he took another cup of wine and said, "This cup is the new
covenant between God and his people—an agreement confirmed with my
blood, which is poured out as a sacrifice for you.*
21 "But here at this table, sitting among us as a friend, is the man who will
betray me. 22 For it has been determined that the Son of Man* must die. But
what sorrow awaits the one who betrays him." 23 The disciples began to ask
each other which of them would ever do such a thing.
24 Then they began to argue among themselves about who would be the
greatest among them. 25 Jesus told them, "In this world the kings and great
men lord it over their people, yet they are called 'friends of the people.' 26 But
among you it will be different. Those who are the greatest among you should
take the lowest rank, and the leader should be like a servant. 27 Who is more
important, the one who sits at the table or the one who serves? The one who
sits at the table, of course. But not here! For I am among you as one who
serves.
28 "You have stayed with me in my time of trial. 29 And just as my Father
has granted me a Kingdom, I now grant you the right 30 to eat and drink at
my table in my Kingdom. And you will sit on thrones, judging the twelve
tribes of Israel.

Jesus Predicts Peter's Denial

31 "Simon, Simon, Satan has asked to sift each of you like wheat. 32 But I have
pleaded in prayer for you, Simon, that your faith should not fail. So when you
have repented and turned to me again, strengthen your brothers."
33 Peter said, "Lord, I am ready to go to prison with you, and even to die
with you."
34 But Jesus said, "Peter, let me tell you something. Before the rooster crows
tomorrow morning, you will deny three times that you even know me."
35 Then Jesus asked them, "When I sent you out to preach the Good News
and you did not have money, a traveler's bag, or an extra pair of sandals, did
you need anything?"
"No," they replied.
36 "But now," he said, "take your money and a traveler's bag. And if you
don't have a sword, sell your cloak and buy one! 37 For the time has come for
this prophecy about me to be fulfilled: 'He was counted among the rebels.'*
Yes, everything written about me by the prophets will come true."
38 "Look, Lord," they replied, "we have two swords among us."
"That's enough," he said.

22:14 Or *reclined together.* 22:19-20 Some manuscripts do not include 22:19b-20, *which is given for you . . . which is poured out as a sacrifice for you.* 22:22 "Son of Man" is a title Jesus used for himself. 22:37 Isa 53:12.

Jesus Prays on the Mount of Olives

39 Then, accompanied by the disciples, Jesus left the upstairs room and went
as usual to the Mount of Olives. 40 There he told them, "Pray that you will
not give in to temptation."

41 He walked away, about a stone's throw, and knelt down and prayed, 42 "Fa-
ther, if you are willing, please take this cup of suffering away from me. Yet I
want your will to be done, not mine." 43 Then an angel from heaven appeared
and strengthened him. 44 He prayed more fervently, and he was in such agony
of spirit that his sweat fell to the ground like great drops of blood.*

45 At last he stood up again and returned to the disciples, only to find them
asleep, exhausted from grief. 46 "Why are you sleeping?" he asked them. "Get
up and pray, so that you will not give in to temptation."

Jesus Is Betrayed and Arrested

47 But even as Jesus said this, a crowd approached, led by Judas, one of the
twelve disciples. Judas walked over to Jesus to greet him with a kiss. 48 But
Jesus said, "Judas, would you betray the Son of Man with a kiss?"

49 When the other disciples saw what was about to happen, they exclaimed,
"Lord, should we fight? We brought the swords!" 50 And one of them struck
at the high priest's slave, slashing off his right ear.

51 But Jesus said, "No more of this." And he touched the man's ear and
healed him.

52 Then Jesus spoke to the leading priests, the captains of the Temple
guard, and the elders who had come for him. "Am I some dangerous revo-
lutionary," he asked, "that you come with swords and clubs to arrest me?
53 Why didn't you arrest me in the Temple? I was there every day. But this is
your moment, the time when the power of darkness reigns."

Peter Denies Jesus

54 So they arrested him and led him to the high priest's home. And Peter
followed at a distance. 55 The guards lit a fire in the middle of the courtyard
and sat around it, and Peter joined them there. 56 A servant girl noticed him
in the firelight and began staring at him. Finally she said, "This man was
one of Jesus' followers!"

57 But Peter denied it. "Woman," he said, "I don't even know him!"

58 After a while someone else looked at him and said, "You must be one
of them!"

"No, man, I'm not!" Peter retorted.

59 About an hour later someone else insisted, "This must be one of them,
because he is a Galilean, too."

60 But Peter said, "Man, I don't know what you are talking about." And
immediately, while he was still speaking, the rooster crowed.

61 At that moment the Lord turned and looked at Peter. Suddenly, the
Lord's words flashed through Peter's mind: "Before the rooster crows to-
morrow morning, you will deny three times that you even know me." 62 And
Peter left the courtyard, weeping bitterly.

63 The guards in charge of Jesus began mocking and beating him. 64 They
blindfolded him and said, "Prophesy to us! Who hit you that time?" 65 And
they hurled all sorts of terrible insults at him.

22:43-44 Verses 43 and 44 are not included in the most ancient manuscripts.

Make a Difference

22:39–46

The Garden

After Judas betrayed Jesus and just before soldiers came to arrest him, Jesus and his disciples went to the Mount of Olives, to the garden of Gethsemane. He warned his disciples to avoid temptation and sin, but in their emotionally exhausted condition, they chose instead to sleep. Jesus walked "about a stone's throw" away, knelt down, and prayed (v. 41). It was in a garden where humans first tasted sin; it was in a garden where Jesus wrestled with it.

His time of prayer was intense. Sin was not going to die easily. Jesus prayed so fervently, with such agony of spirit, that his sweat became mixed with great drops of blood. This condition is known as hematidrosis, which sometimes occurs when someone is experiencing extreme stress. While the disciples slept through it, Jesus took it upon himself to do the very thing the disciples were unwilling or unable to do.

Difference Maker

After he prayed, Jesus told the disciples to get up and pray so that temptation didn't overpower them. Why not take his words to heart? If possible, find a garden to walk through and pray about overcoming sin through Jesus.

Jesus before the Council

66 At daybreak all the elders of the people assembled, including the lead-
ing priests and the teachers of religious law. Jesus was led before this high
council,* 67 and they said, "Tell us, are you the Messiah?"
But he replied, "If I tell you, you won't believe me. 68 And if I ask you a
question, you won't answer. 69 But from now on the Son of Man will be seated
in the place of power at God's right hand.*"
70 They all shouted, "So, are you claiming to be the Son of God?"
And he replied, "You say that I am."
71 "Why do we need other witnesses?" they said. "We ourselves heard him
say it."

Jesus' Trial before Pilate

23 Then the entire council took Jesus to Pilate, the Roman governor.
2 They began to state their case: "This man has been leading our
people astray by telling them not to pay their taxes to the Roman govern-
ment and by claiming he is the Messiah, a king."
3 So Pilate asked him, "Are you the king of the Jews?"
Jesus replied, "You have said it."
4 Pilate turned to the leading priests and to the crowd and said, "I find
nothing wrong with this man!"
5 Then they became insistent. "But he is causing riots by his teaching wher-
ever he goes—all over Judea, from Galilee to Jerusalem!"
6 "Oh, is he a Galilean?" Pilate asked. 7 When they said that he was, Pilate
sent him to Herod Antipas, because Galilee was under Herod's jurisdiction,
and Herod happened to be in Jerusalem at the time.
8 Herod was delighted at the opportunity to see Jesus, because he had heard
about him and had been hoping for a long time to see him perform a miracle.
9 He asked Jesus question after question, but Jesus refused to answer. 10 Mean-
while, the leading priests and the teachers of religious law stood there shouting
their accusations. 11 Then Herod and his soldiers began mocking and ridiculing
Jesus. Finally, they put a royal robe on him and sent him back to Pilate. 12 (Herod
and Pilate, who had been enemies before, became friends that day.)
13 Then Pilate called together the leading priests and other religious lead-
ers, along with the people, 14 and he announced his verdict. "You brought
this man to me, accusing him of leading a revolt. I have examined him
thoroughly on this point in your presence and find him innocent. 15 Herod
came to the same conclusion and sent him back to us. Nothing this man
has done calls for the death penalty. 16 So I will have him flogged, and then
I will release him."*
18 Then a mighty roar rose from the crowd, and with one voice they
shouted, "Kill him, and release Barabbas to us!" 19 (Barabbas was in prison
for taking part in an insurrection in Jerusalem against the government, and
for murder.) 20 Pilate argued with them, because he wanted to release Jesus.
21 But they kept shouting, "Crucify him! Crucify him!"
22 For the third time he demanded, "Why? What crime has he committed?
I have found no reason to sentence him to death. So I will have him flogged,
and then I will release him."

22:66 Greek *before their Sanhedrin.* 22:69 See Ps 110:1. 23:16 Some manuscripts add verse 17, *Now it was necessary for him to release one prisoner to them during the Passover celebration.* Compare Matt 27:15; Mark 15:6; John 18:39.

23 But the mob shouted louder and louder, demanding that Jesus be cru-
cified, and their voices prevailed. 24 So Pilate sentenced Jesus to die as they
demanded. 25 As they had requested, he released Barabbas, the man in prison
for insurrection and murder. But he turned Jesus over to them to do as they
wished.

The Crucifixion

26 As they led Jesus away, a man named Simon, who was from Cyrene,* hap-
pened to be coming in from the countryside. The soldiers seized him and
put the cross on him and made him carry it behind Jesus. 27 A large crowd
trailed behind, including many grief-stricken women. 28 But Jesus turned
and said to them, "Daughters of Jerusalem, don't weep for me, but weep
for yourselves and for your children. 29 For the days are coming when they
will say, 'Fortunate indeed are the women who are childless, the wombs that
have not borne a child and the breasts that have never nursed.' 30 People will
beg the mountains, 'Fall on us,' and plead with the hills, 'Bury us.'* 31 For
if these things are done when the tree is green, what will happen when it
is dry?*"

32 Two others, both criminals, were led out to be executed with him.
33 When they came to a place called The Skull,* they nailed him to the cross.
And the criminals were also crucified—one on his right and one on his left.

34 Jesus said, "Father, forgive them, for they don't know what they are
doing."* And the soldiers gambled for his clothes by throwing dice.*

35 The crowd watched and the leaders scoffed. "He saved others," they said,
"let him save himself if he is really God's Messiah, the Chosen One." 36 The
soldiers mocked him, too, by offering him a drink of sour wine. 37 They called
out to him, "If you are the King of the Jews, save yourself!" 38 A sign was fas-
tened above him with these words: "This is the King of the Jews."

39 One of the criminals hanging beside him scoffed, "So you're the Mes-
siah, are you? Prove it by saving yourself—and us, too, while you're at it!"

40 But the other criminal protested, "Don't you fear God even when you
have been sentenced to die? 41 We deserve to die for our crimes, but this man
hasn't done anything wrong." 42 Then he said, "Jesus, remember me when
you come into your Kingdom."

43 And Jesus replied, "I assure you, today you will be with me in paradise."

The Death of Jesus

44 By this time it was about noon, and darkness fell across the whole land
until three o'clock. 45 The light from the sun was gone. And suddenly, the
curtain in the sanctuary of the Temple was torn down the middle. 46 Then
Jesus shouted, "Father, I entrust my spirit into your hands!"* And with those
words he breathed his last.

47 When the Roman officer* overseeing the execution saw what had hap-
pened, he worshiped God and said, "Surely this man was innocent.*" 48 And
when all the crowd that came to see the crucifixion saw what had happened,
they went home in deep sorrow.* 49 But Jesus' friends, including the women
who had followed him from Galilee, stood at a distance watching.

23:26 *Cyrene* was a city in northern Africa. 23:30 Hos 10:8. 23:31 Or *If these things are done to me, the living tree, what will happen to you, the dry tree?* 23:33 Sometimes rendered *Calvary,* which comes from the Latin word for "skull." 23:34a This sentence is not included in many ancient manuscripts. 23:34b Greek *by casting lots.* See Ps 22:18. 23:46 Ps 31:5. 23:47a Greek *the centurion.* 23:47b Or *righteous.* 23:48 Greek *went home beating their breasts.*

Make a Difference

23:32-43

Gawking

Crowds gathered at the scene of the horror. They just stood there, entranced by the violence and injustice, hypnotized by the spectacle of it all. When Jesus went to the cross, people just watched—afraid and captivated by the awfulness of the moment. People were ignorant and angry at Jesus. Some were shouting at him while others were silently condemning him to die. Everyone was unable to avert their eyes, yet they were unwilling to truly see what was going on. The cross of Jesus was hideous—so horrific that people couldn't help but stare.

Jesus, in that very moment, as he hung crucified, was looking back at the crowd. He had eyes on the very people who were watching him die. Instead of a look of revenge, Jesus had compassion in his sight. He wanted those gawkers to make eye contact with him so that he could peer into their souls and overcome their judgment and fear with his forgiveness and hope.

Difference Maker

Draw a cross on something that you will see again and again throughout the day. Let it remind you to look Jesus in the eyes.

Question **23:42**

Imagine being the first person who is promised to spend eternity with Jesus. What can you say about why he was saved?

Question 23:53

Go back and read Luke 2:7. How does the "wrapping" of Jesus bookend the story of good news for our world?

Question 24:1-12

Why is the resurrection of Jesus the greatest difference maker in history?

The Burial of Jesus

50 Now there was a good and righteous man named Joseph. He was a member
of the Jewish high council, 51 but he had not agreed with the decision and
actions of the other religious leaders. He was from the town of Arimathea
in Judea, and he was waiting for the Kingdom of God to come. 52 He went
to Pilate and asked for Jesus' body. 53 Then he took the body down from the
cross and wrapped it in a long sheet of linen cloth and laid it in a new tomb
that had been carved out of rock. 54 This was done late on Friday afternoon,
the day of preparation,* as the Sabbath was about to begin.
55 As his body was taken away, the women from Galilee followed and saw
the tomb where his body was placed. 56 Then they went home and prepared
spices and ointments to anoint his body. But by the time they were finished
the Sabbath had begun, so they rested as required by the law.

The Resurrection

24 But very early on Sunday morning* the women went to the tomb,
taking the spices they had prepared. 2 They found that the stone had
been rolled away from the entrance. 3 So they went in, but they didn't find
the body of the Lord Jesus. 4 As they stood there puzzled, two men suddenly
appeared to them, clothed in dazzling robes.
5 The women were terrified and bowed with their faces to the ground.
Then the men asked, "Why are you looking among the dead for someone
who is alive? 6 He isn't here! He is risen from the dead! Remember what he
told you back in Galilee, 7 that the Son of Man* must be betrayed into the
hands of sinful men and be crucified, and that he would rise again on the
third day."
8 Then they remembered that he had said this. 9 So they rushed back from
the tomb to tell his eleven disciples—and everyone else—what had hap-
pened. 10 It was Mary Magdalene, Joanna, Mary the mother of James, and
several other women who told the apostles what had happened. 11 But the
story sounded like nonsense to the men, so they didn't believe it. 12 How-
ever, Peter jumped up and ran to the tomb to look. Stooping, he peered in
and saw the empty linen wrappings; then he went home again, wondering
what had happened.

The Walk to Emmaus

13 That same day two of Jesus' followers were walking to the village of Em-
maus, seven miles* from Jerusalem. 14 As they walked along they were talking
about everything that had happened. 15 As they talked and discussed these
things, Jesus himself suddenly came and began walking with them. 16 But
God kept them from recognizing him.
17 He asked them, "What are you discussing so intently as you walk along?"
They stopped short, sadness written across their faces. 18 Then one of them,
Cleopas, replied, "You must be the only person in Jerusalem who hasn't
heard about all the things that have happened there the last few days."
19 "What things?" Jesus asked.
"The things that happened to Jesus, the man from Nazareth," they said.
"He was a prophet who did powerful miracles, and he was a mighty teacher

23:54 Greek *It was the day of preparation.* 24:1 Greek *But on the first day of the week, very early in the morning.* 24:7 "Son of Man" is a title Jesus used for himself. 24:13 Greek 60 *stadia* [11.1 kilometers].

in the eyes of God and all the people. 20 But our leading priests and other religious leaders handed him over to be condemned to death, and they crucified him. 21 We had hoped he was the Messiah who had come to rescue Israel. This all happened three days ago.

22 "Then some women from our group of his followers were at his tomb early this morning, and they came back with an amazing report. 23 They said his body was missing, and they had seen angels who told them Jesus is alive! 24 Some of our men ran out to see, and sure enough, his body was gone, just as the women had said."

25 Then Jesus said to them, "You foolish people! You find it so hard to believe all that the prophets wrote in the Scriptures. 26 Wasn't it clearly predicted that the Messiah would have to suffer all these things before entering his glory?" 27 Then Jesus took them through the writings of Moses and all the prophets, explaining from all the Scriptures the things concerning himself.

28 By this time they were nearing Emmaus and the end of their journey. Jesus acted as if he were going on, 29 but they begged him, "Stay the night with us, since it is getting late." So he went home with them. 30 As they sat down to eat,* he took the bread and blessed it. Then he broke it and gave it to them. 31 Suddenly, their eyes were opened, and they recognized him. And at that moment he disappeared!

32 They said to each other, "Didn't our hearts burn within us as he talked with us on the road and explained the Scriptures to us?" 33 And within the hour they were on their way back to Jerusalem. There they found the eleven disciples and the others who had gathered with them, 34 who said, "The Lord has really risen! He appeared to Peter.*"

Jesus Appears to the Disciples

35 Then the two from Emmaus told their story of how Jesus had appeared to them as they were walking along the road, and how they had recognized him as he was breaking the bread. 36 And just as they were telling about it, Jesus himself was suddenly standing there among them. "Peace be with you," he said. 37 But the whole group was startled and frightened, thinking they were seeing a ghost!

38 "Why are you frightened?" he asked. "Why are your hearts filled with doubt? 39 Look at my hands. Look at my feet. You can see that it's really me. Touch me and make sure that I am not a ghost, because ghosts don't have bodies, as you see that I do." 40 As he spoke, he showed them his hands and his feet.

41 Still they stood there in disbelief, filled with joy and wonder. Then he asked them, "Do you have anything here to eat?" 42 They gave him a piece of broiled fish, 43 and he ate it as they watched.

44 Then he said, "When I was with you before, I told you that everything written about me in the law of Moses and the prophets and in the Psalms must be fulfilled." 45 Then he opened their minds to understand the Scriptures. 46 And he said, "Yes, it was written long ago that the Messiah would suffer and die and rise from the dead on the third day. 47 It was also written that this message would be proclaimed in the authority of his name to all the nations,* beginning in Jerusalem: 'There is forgiveness of sins for all who repent.' 48 You are witnesses of all these things.

24:30 Or *As they reclined.* **24:34** Greek *Simon.* **24:47** Or *all peoples.*

Make a Difference

24:13-36

Walk of Discovery

Jesus wants to walk with us and talk with us so that we can discover who he is. There is no greater way to change everything in our lives than to spend time in personal conversation with him.

On the Sunday of the resurrection, two of Jesus' followers were walking about seven miles outside of Jerusalem. He suddenly caught up to them, but he kept them from realizing who he was at first. "What are you discussing so intently as you walk along?" he asked them (24:17).

"You must be the only person in Jerusalem who hasn't heard about all the things that have happened there the last few days," they replied (v. 18). They went on to describe to Jesus how they thought he was the Messiah, but the rulers had executed him. Then they shared how his body was no longer in the tomb and how angels declared that Jesus was alive.

Jesus responded in disbelief at their confusion. "You foolish people!" he said (v. 25). "Wasn't it clearly predicted that the Messiah would have to suffer all these things before entering his glory?" (v. 26).

Difference Maker

Get together with some other followers of Jesus and investigate what Jesus might have said on this walk.

49 "And now I will send the Holy Spirit, just as my Father promised. But
stay here in the city until the Holy Spirit comes and fills you with power
from heaven."

The Ascension

50 Then Jesus led them to Bethany, and lifting his hands to heaven, he
blessed them. 51 While he was blessing them, he left them and was taken
up to heaven. 52 So they worshiped him and then returned to Jerusalem
filled with great joy. 53 And they spent all of their time in the Temple, prais-
ing God.

John Introduction

The word *gospel* means "good news."

Near the end of this book, in verse 31 of chapter 20, John explained why he wrote this gospel: so that you may "believe that Jesus is the Messiah, the Son of God, and that by believing in him you will have life by the power of his name." If you miss this, then you miss the whole point of the book.

If you really want to make a difference in this world, the gospel of John provides all the motivation you need. This one book makes a huge mark from start to finish. The very first verses of John echo the first verses of the Bible and point you directly to the astonishing identity of Jesus. John wanted you to know that Jesus is the Word of God and is God! He wanted you to know that Jesus has always existed, that he created the world, that he shines in the darkness, and that he loves you. Remarkably, John also claimed that Jesus "became human and made his home among us" (1:14). John walked with him, ate with him, laughed with him, and wept with him. In other words, John grew to know that Jesus is God in human form and that Jesus is the Savior of the world. This tenet is central to everything about the Christian faith.

That's all in just the first fourteen verses! John's eyewitness storytelling continues with mind-blowing introductions to the good news of Jesus. For instance, John shared how Jesus made several bold claims starting with the words "I am." Jesus said, "I am the bread of life" (6:35); "I am the light of the world" (8:12); "I am the way, the truth, and the life" (14:6); and more! Finally, Jesus said, simply, "I AM" (18:5, 8). This was his way of echoing how the Lord introduced himself to Moses a couple thousand years before: "I AM WHO I AM" (Exodus 3:14).

These claims would be ridiculous if not for the fact that John saw Jesus back up his statements with miracles and power and wisdom beyond imagination. Simply put, Jesus proved his identity through his words and deeds, including his greatest miracle—resurrection from the dead.

Because Jesus lives forever, we can too. This is John's gospel truth. Pass it on.

Story Arcs

- **John the Baptist**
- **Samaritan Woman**
- **Lazarus**

John

Prologue: Christ, the Eternal Word

1 [1] In the beginning the Word already existed.
The Word was with God,
and the Word was God.
[2] He existed in the beginning with God.
[3] God created everything through him,
and nothing was created except through him.
[4] The Word gave life to everything that was created,*
and his life brought light to everyone.
[5] The light shines in the darkness,
and the darkness can never extinguish it.*

[6]God sent a man, John the Baptist,* [7]to tell about the light so that everyone
might believe because of his testimony. [8]John himself was not the light; he
was simply a witness to tell about the light. [9]The one who is the true light,
who gives light to everyone, was coming into the world.
[10]He came into the very world he created, but the world didn't recognize
him. [11]He came to his own people, and even they rejected him. [12]But to all
who believed him and accepted him, he gave the right to become children
of God. [13]They are reborn—not with a physical birth resulting from human
passion or plan, but a birth that comes from God.
[14]So the Word became human* and made his home among us. He was full
of unfailing love and faithfulness.* And we have seen his glory, the glory of
the Father's one and only Son.
[15]John testified about him when he shouted to the crowds, "This is the
one I was talking about when I said, 'Someone is coming after me who is far
greater than I am, for he existed long before me.'"
[16]From his abundance we have all received one gracious blessing after
another.* [17]For the law was given through Moses, but God's unfailing love
and faithfulness came through Jesus Christ. [18]No one has ever seen God. But
the unique One, who is himself God,* is near to the Father's heart. He has
revealed God to us.

The Testimony of John the Baptist

[19]This was John's testimony when the Jewish leaders sent priests and Temple
assistants* from Jerusalem to ask John, "Who are you?" [20]He came right out
and said, "I am not the Messiah."
[21]"Well then, who are you?" they asked. "Are you Elijah?"
"No," he replied.

Question 1:1-5

Compare Genesis 1 with John 1:1-5. What similarities do you see? What does this teach you about what Jesus does?

Prayer 1:12

Jesus, I believe in you! I accept you into my life. Amen.

Make a Difference 1:14

Extraordinary

Jesus came to walk with people in the ordinary moments of their lives. He came to sit in their homes, eat dinner with them, talk about life's issues, and laugh at their jokes. Jesus came to cry with people in times of loss and encourage them to do greater things than they ever could have imagined. He came to heal their wounds and their hearts. He came to challenge their despair and their cynicism. He came because he thought ordinary people were worth far more than they could ever realize.

Difference Maker

Let someone know the extraordinary value that God has placed on their life.

1:3-4 Or *and nothing that was created was created except through him. The Word gave life to everything.* **1:5** Or *and the darkness has not understood it.* **1:6** Greek *a man named John.* **1:14a** Greek *became flesh.* **1:14b** Or *grace and truth;* also in 1:17. **1:16** Or *received the grace of Christ rather than the grace of the law;* Greek reads *received grace upon grace.* **1:18** Some manuscripts read *But the one and only Son.* **1:19** Greek *and Levites.*

"Are you the Prophet we are expecting?"*

"No."

22 "Then who are you? We need an answer for those who sent us. What do you have to say about yourself?"

23 John replied in the words of the prophet Isaiah:

"I am a voice shouting in the wilderness,
'Clear the way for the LORD's coming!'"*

24 Then the Pharisees who had been sent 25 asked him, "If you aren't the Messiah or Elijah or the Prophet, what right do you have to baptize?"

26 John told them, "I baptize with* water, but right here in the crowd is someone you do not recognize. 27 Though his ministry follows mine, I'm not even worthy to be his slave and untie the straps of his sandal."

28 This encounter took place in Bethany, an area east of the Jordan River, where John was baptizing.

Jesus, the Lamb of God

29 The next day John saw Jesus coming toward him and said, "Look! The Lamb of God who takes away the sin of the world! 30 He is the one I was talking about when I said, 'A man is coming after me who is far greater than I am, for he existed long before me.' 31 I did not recognize him as the Messiah, but I have been baptizing with water so that he might be revealed to Israel."

32 Then John testified, "I saw the Holy Spirit descending like a dove from heaven and resting upon him. 33 I didn't know he was the one, but when God sent me to baptize with water, he told me, 'The one on whom you see the Spirit descend and rest is the one who will baptize with the Holy Spirit.' 34 I saw this happen to Jesus, so I testify that he is the Chosen One of God.*"

The First Disciples

35 The following day John was again standing with two of his disciples. 36 As Jesus walked by, John looked at him and declared, "Look! There is the Lamb of God!" 37 When John's two disciples heard this, they followed Jesus.

38 Jesus looked around and saw them following. "What do you want?" he asked them.

They replied, "Rabbi" (which means "Teacher"), "where are you staying?"

39 "Come and see," he said. It was about four o'clock in the afternoon when they went with him to the place where he was staying, and they remained with him the rest of the day.

40 Andrew, Simon Peter's brother, was one of these men who heard what John said and then followed Jesus. 41 Andrew went to find his brother, Simon, and told him, "We have found the Messiah" (which means "Christ"*).

42 Then Andrew brought Simon to meet Jesus. Looking intently at Simon, Jesus said, "Your name is Simon, son of John—but you will be called Cephas" (which means "Peter"*).

43 The next day Jesus decided to go to Galilee. He found Philip and said to

1:21 Greek *Are you the Prophet?* See Deut 18:15, 18; Mal 4:5-6. 1:23 Isa 40:3. 1:26 Or *in;* also in 1:31, 33. 1:34 Some manuscripts read *the Son of God.* 1:41 *Messiah* (a Hebrew term) and *Christ* (a Greek term) both mean "anointed one." 1:42 The names *Cephas* (from Aramaic) and *Peter* (from Greek) both mean "rock."

Question 1:29

Do you know why the label of "Lamb" is an important one for Jesus? Why did John the Baptist say the "Lamb of God" takes away the sin of the world? Has the Lamb taken away your sin?

Question 1:38

These are the first words Jesus spoke in the book of John. What significance do you find in these words?

Question 1:39

What would change in your activities if you spent a whole day with Jesus?

Story Arc 1:6-36

● John the Baptist

Imagine being the cousin of Jesus. Imagine being the prophet who was supposed to introduce the Messiah to the world (Isaiah 40:3; Malachi 4:5-6). Imagine being an outcast who dressed awkwardly and ate poorly. Imagine dedicating every aspect of your life to leading people to repent of sin and to turn to God through baptism. Imagine your life being at risk because you are a nuisance to the authorities. Look for John the Baptist in the Gospels (Matthew, Mark, Luke, and John) and ask yourself what he did to prepare people for Jesus.

John 4:1-42 ►

Prayer **2:5**

Jesus, this is the goal of following you: that I would do whatever you tell me to do. Let this be true of me today. Amen.

him, "Come, follow me." 44 Philip was from Bethsaida, Andrew and Peter's
hometown.
45 Philip went to look for Nathanael and told him, "We have found the very
person Moses* and the prophets wrote about! His name is Jesus, the son of
Joseph from Nazareth."
46 "Nazareth!" exclaimed Nathanael. "Can anything good come from
Nazareth?"
"Come and see for yourself," Philip replied.
47 As they approached, Jesus said, "Now here is a genuine son of Israel—a
man of complete integrity."
48 "How do you know about me?" Nathanael asked.
Jesus replied, "I could see you under the fig tree before Philip found you."
49 Then Nathanael exclaimed, "Rabbi, you are the Son of God—the King
of Israel!"
50 Jesus asked him, "Do you believe this just because I told you I had seen
you under the fig tree? You will see greater things than this." 51 Then he said,
"I tell you the truth, you will all see heaven open and the angels of God
going up and down on the Son of Man, the one who is the stairway between
heaven and earth.*"

The Wedding at Cana

2 The next day* there was a wedding celebration in the village of Cana in
Galilee. Jesus' mother was there, 2 and Jesus and his disciples were also
invited to the celebration. 3 The wine supply ran out during the festivities,
so Jesus' mother told him, "They have no more wine."
4 "Dear woman, that's not our problem," Jesus replied. "My time has not
yet come."
5 But his mother told the servants, "Do whatever he tells you."
6 Standing nearby were six stone water jars, used for Jewish ceremonial
washing. Each could hold twenty to thirty gallons.* 7 Jesus told the servants,
"Fill the jars with water." When the jars had been filled, 8 he said, "Now dip
some out, and take it to the master of ceremonies." So the servants followed
his instructions.
9 When the master of ceremonies tasted the water that was now wine, not
knowing where it had come from (though, of course, the servants knew),
he called the bridegroom over. 10 "A host always serves the best wine first,"
he said. "Then, when everyone has had a lot to drink, he brings out the less
expensive wine. But you have kept the best until now!"
11 This miraculous sign at Cana in Galilee was the first time Jesus revealed
his glory. And his disciples believed in him.
12 After the wedding he went to Capernaum for a few days with his mother,
his brothers, and his disciples.

Jesus Clears the Temple

13 It was nearly time for the Jewish Passover celebration, so Jesus went to
Jerusalem. 14 In the Temple area he saw merchants selling cattle, sheep, and
doves for sacrifices; he also saw dealers at tables exchanging foreign money.
15 Jesus made a whip from some ropes and chased them all out of the Temple.

1:45 Greek *Moses in the law.* 1:51 Greek *going up and down on the Son of Man;* see Gen 28:10-17. "Son of Man" is a title Jesus used for himself. 2:1 Greek *On the third day;* see 1:35, 43. 2:6 Greek *2 or 3 measures* [75 to 113 liters].

He drove out the sheep and cattle, scattered the money changers' coins over
the floor, and turned over their tables. 16Then, going over to the people who
sold doves, he told them, "Get these things out of here. Stop turning my
Father's house into a marketplace!"
17Then his disciples remembered this prophecy from the Scriptures: "Pas-
sion for God's house will consume me."*
18But the Jewish leaders demanded, "What are you doing? If God gave you
authority to do this, show us a miraculous sign to prove it."
19"All right," Jesus replied. "Destroy this temple, and in three days I will
raise it up."
20"What!" they exclaimed. "It has taken forty-six years to build this
Temple, and you can rebuild it in three days?" 21But when Jesus said "this
temple," he meant his own body. 22After he was raised from the dead, his
disciples remembered he had said this, and they believed both the Scriptures
and what Jesus had said.

Jesus and Nicodemus

23Because of the miraculous signs Jesus did in Jerusalem at the Passover cel-
ebration, many began to trust in him. 24But Jesus didn't trust them, because
he knew all about people. 25No one needed to tell him about human nature,
for he knew what was in each person's heart.

3 There was a man named Nicodemus, a Jewish religious leader who was a
Pharisee. 2After dark one evening, he came to speak with Jesus. "Rabbi,"
he said, "we all know that God has sent you to teach us. Your miraculous signs
are evidence that God is with you."
3Jesus replied, "I tell you the truth, unless you are born again,* you cannot
see the Kingdom of God."
4"What do you mean?" exclaimed Nicodemus. "How can an old man go
back into his mother's womb and be born again?"
5Jesus replied, "I assure you, no one can enter the Kingdom of God with-
out being born of water and the Spirit.* 6Humans can reproduce only human
life, but the Holy Spirit gives birth to spiritual life.* 7So don't be surprised
when I say, 'You* must be born again.' 8The wind blows wherever it wants.
Just as you can hear the wind but can't tell where it comes from or where it
is going, so you can't explain how people are born of the Spirit."
9"How are these things possible?" Nicodemus asked.
10Jesus replied, "You are a respected Jewish teacher, and yet you don't
understand these things? 11I assure you, we tell you what we know and have
seen, and yet you won't believe our testimony. 12But if you don't believe me
when I tell you about earthly things, how can you possibly believe if I tell you
about heavenly things? 13No one has ever gone to heaven and returned. But
the Son of Man* has come down from heaven. 14And as Moses lifted up the
bronze snake on a pole in the wilderness, so the Son of Man must be lifted
up, 15so that everyone who believes in him will have eternal life.*
16"For this is how God loved the world: He gave* his one and only Son,
so that everyone who believes in him will not perish but have eternal life.

2:17 Or *"Concern for God's house will be my undoing."* Ps 69:9. 3:3 Or *born from above;* also in 3:7. 3:5 Or *and spirit.* The Greek word for *Spirit* can also be translated *wind;* see 3:8. 3:6 Greek *what is born of the Spirit is spirit.* 3:7 The Greek word for *you* is plural; also in 3:12. 3:13 Some manuscripts add *who lives in heaven.* "Son of Man" is a title Jesus used for himself. 3:15 Or *everyone who believes will have eternal life in him.* 3:16 Or *For God loved the world so much that he gave.*

Question 3:1-21

Imagine asking Jesus the same questions that Nicodemus asked Jesus. How would the answers Jesus gave both satisfy you and challenge you?

Make a Difference 3:16

God Loves You So Much

God has a track record of not giving up on people. When they got lost, he pursued them. When they sinned, he made a plan to rescue them. When they ran away, he actively looked for them. When they were in trouble, he fought for them. When they continued to wander, he continued to seek them. When they cried out, he gave them a Savior. When they turned to him, he embraced them with his creative, unlimited life.

You are a person, are you not? The good news for you today is this: you are so loved by God, the very one who created this world so that he could be in relationship with you. He sent Jesus to find you, to pursue you, to search for you. He will never give up on you. In fact, he is thinking about you right now. He is calling out your name, and he wants you to call out his.

Difference Maker

Turn to the back of this Bible and pray through the section on "How to Accept Jesus as Your Lord and Savior."

Make a Difference

3:19–21

Flashlight

Do you know that moment when you've been in a dark room for a while and somebody suddenly flicks on the light? Your eyes recoil, your face winces and squints, and you inevitably shield your head from the glare of the bright beams. Even with your eyes closed, behind those eyelids of yours, you can somehow see the image of the light burned into your retinas.

Jesus is like that light. When he shines into the darkness of someone's actions or the gloom of someone's soul, the glare can be painfully intense. The light of Jesus is so very good too. It was his light that illuminated the earth at creation. It was his light that led God's people to freedom from slavery. It was his light that represented the greatness and love of God throughout the entire Bible. Jesus created you to walk in his light.

Adjust your eyes to the light of Jesus today. You were made to see his glory, the beauty of his creation, and the worth he gave to every person. Don't recoil back into a shadow of who God made you to be.

Difference Maker

Grab a small flashlight and carry it around with you all day. If you find yourself shrinking back into darkness, shine that light on the floor in front of you.

17 God sent his Son into the world not to judge the world, but to save the
world through him.
18 "There is no judgment against anyone who believes in him. But anyone
who does not believe in him has already been judged for not believing in
God's one and only Son. 19 And the judgment is based on this fact: God's light
came into the world, but people loved the darkness more than the light, for
their actions were evil. 20 All who do evil hate the light and refuse to go near
it for fear their sins will be exposed. 21 But those who do what is right come
to the light so others can see that they are doing what God wants.*"

John the Baptist Exalts Jesus

22 Then Jesus and his disciples left Jerusalem and went into the Judean
countryside. Jesus spent some time with them there, baptizing people.
23 At this time John the Baptist was baptizing at Aenon, near Salim,
because there was plenty of water there; and people kept coming to him
for baptism. 24 (This was before John was thrown into prison.) 25 A debate
broke out between John's disciples and a certain Jew* over ceremonial
cleansing. 26 So John's disciples came to him and said, "Rabbi, the man you
met on the other side of the Jordan River, the one you identified as the
Messiah, is also baptizing people. And everybody is going to him instead
of coming to us."
27 John replied, "No one can receive anything unless God gives it from
heaven. 28 You yourselves know how plainly I told you, 'I am not the Messiah.
I am only here to prepare the way for him.' 29 It is the bridegroom who mar-
ries the bride, and the bridegroom's friend is simply glad to stand with him
and hear his vows. Therefore, I am filled with joy at his success. 30 He must
become greater and greater, and I must become less and less.
31 "He has come from above and is greater than anyone else. We are of the
earth, and we speak of earthly things, but he has come from heaven and is
greater than anyone else.* 32 He testifies about what he has seen and heard,
but how few believe what he tells them! 33 Anyone who accepts his testimony
can affirm that God is true. 34 For he is sent by God. He speaks God's words,
for God gives him the Spirit without limit. 35 The Father loves his Son and has
put everything into his hands. 36 And anyone who believes in God's Son has
eternal life. Anyone who doesn't obey the Son will never experience eternal
life but remains under God's angry judgment."

Jesus and the Samaritan Woman

4 Jesus* knew the Pharisees had heard that he was baptizing and making
more disciples than John 2 (though Jesus himself didn't baptize them—
his disciples did). 3 So he left Judea and returned to Galilee.
4 He had to go through Samaria on the way. 5 Eventually he came to the
Samaritan village of Sychar, near the field that Jacob gave to his son Joseph.
6 Jacob's well was there; and Jesus, tired from the long walk, sat wearily beside
the well about noontime. 7 Soon a Samaritan woman came to draw water, and
Jesus said to her, "Please give me a drink." 8 He was alone at the time because
his disciples had gone into the village to buy some food.
9 The woman was surprised, for Jews refuse to have anything to do with

3:21 Or *can see God at work in what he is doing.* 3:25 Some manuscripts read *some Jews.* 3:31 Some manuscripts do not include *and is greater than anyone else.* 4:1 Some manuscripts read *The Lord.*

Samaritans.* She said to Jesus, "You are a Jew, and I am a Samaritan woman. Why are you asking me for a drink?"

10 Jesus replied, "If you only knew the gift God has for you and who you are speaking to, you would ask me, and I would give you living water."

11 "But sir, you don't have a rope or a bucket," she said, "and this well is very deep. Where would you get this living water? 12 And besides, do you think you're greater than our ancestor Jacob, who gave us this well? How can you offer better water than he and his sons and his animals enjoyed?"

13 Jesus replied, "Anyone who drinks this water will soon become thirsty again. 14 But those who drink the water I give will never be thirsty again. It becomes a fresh, bubbling spring within them, giving them eternal life."

15 "Please, sir," the woman said, "give me this water! Then I'll never be thirsty again, and I won't have to come here to get water."

16 "Go and get your husband," Jesus told her.

17 "I don't have a husband," the woman replied.

Jesus said, "You're right! You don't have a husband— 18 for you have had five husbands, and you aren't even married to the man you're living with now. You certainly spoke the truth!"

19 "Sir," the woman said, "you must be a prophet. 20 So tell me, why is it that you Jews insist that Jerusalem is the only place of worship, while we Samaritans claim it is here at Mount Gerizim,* where our ancestors worshiped?"

21 Jesus replied, "Believe me, dear woman, the time is coming when it will no longer matter whether you worship the Father on this mountain or in Jerusalem. 22 You Samaritans know very little about the one you worship, while we Jews know all about him, for salvation comes through the Jews. 23 But the time is coming—indeed it's here now—when true worshipers will worship the Father in spirit and in truth. The Father is looking for those who will worship him that way. 24 For God is Spirit, so those who worship him must worship in spirit and in truth."

25 The woman said, "I know the Messiah is coming—the one who is called Christ. When he comes, he will explain everything to us."

26 Then Jesus told her, "I AM the Messiah!"*

27 Just then his disciples came back. They were shocked to find him talking to a woman, but none of them had the nerve to ask, "What do you want with her?" or "Why are you talking to her?" 28 The woman left her water jar beside the well and ran back to the village, telling everyone, 29 "Come and see a man who told me everything I ever did! Could he possibly be the Messiah?" 30 So the people came streaming from the village to see him.

31 Meanwhile, the disciples were urging Jesus, "Rabbi, eat something."

32 But Jesus replied, "I have a kind of food you know nothing about."

33 "Did someone bring him food while we were gone?" the disciples asked each other.

34 Then Jesus explained: "My nourishment comes from doing the will of God, who sent me, and from finishing his work. 35 You know the saying, 'Four months between planting and harvest.' But I say, wake up and look around. The fields are already ripe* for harvest. 36 The harvesters are paid good wages, and the fruit they harvest is people brought to eternal life. What joy awaits both the planter and the harvester alike! 37 You know the saying,

4:9 Some manuscripts do not include this sentence. 4:20 Greek *on this mountain.* 4:26 Or *"The 'I AM' is here"*; or *"I am the LORD"*; Greek reads *"I am, the one speaking to you."* See Exod 3:14. 4:35 Greek *white.*

Question **4:10**

Jesus hinted at what the Samaritan woman would do if she knew whom she was speaking to. In the same way, if you know who Jesus is, what does he want you to ask of him?

Story Arc **4:1-42**

Samaritan Woman

When Jesus encountered this woman at Jacob's well, the seeds for what happens in Acts 8 were planted and watered. How did this conversation lead to this woman's unexpected conversion and the astonishing response of an outcast population of people?

John 11:1-44 ►

Question 5:8

Simple command. Simple response. Do you think humans ever overcomplicate things with God?

'One plants and another harvests.' And it's true. 38 I sent you to harvest where
you didn't plant; others had already done the work, and now you will get
to gather the harvest."

Many Samaritans Believe

39 Many Samaritans from the village believed in Jesus because the woman had
said, "He told me everything I ever did!" 40 When they came out to see him,
they begged him to stay in their village. So he stayed for two days, 41 long
enough for many more to hear his message and believe. 42 Then they said
to the woman, "Now we believe, not just because of what you told us, but
because we have heard him ourselves. Now we know that he is indeed the
Savior of the world."

Jesus Heals an Official's Son

43 At the end of the two days, Jesus went on to Galilee. 44 He himself had said
that a prophet is not honored in his own hometown. 45 Yet the Galileans
welcomed him, for they had been in Jerusalem at the Passover celebration
and had seen everything he did there.

46 As he traveled through Galilee, he came to Cana, where he had turned
the water into wine. There was a government official in nearby Capernaum
whose son was very sick. 47 When he heard that Jesus had come from Judea
to Galilee, he went and begged Jesus to come to Capernaum to heal his son,
who was about to die.

48 Jesus asked, "Will you never believe in me unless you see miraculous
signs and wonders?"

49 The official pleaded, "Lord, please come now before my little boy dies."

50 Then Jesus told him, "Go back home. Your son will live!" And the man
believed what Jesus said and started home.

51 While the man was on his way, some of his servants met him with the
news that his son was alive and well. 52 He asked them when the boy had
begun to get better, and they replied, "Yesterday afternoon at one o'clock
his fever suddenly disappeared!" 53 Then the father realized that that was
the very time Jesus had told him, "Your son will live." And he and his entire
household believed in Jesus. 54 This was the second miraculous sign Jesus
did in Galilee after coming from Judea.

Jesus Heals a Lame Man

5 Afterward Jesus returned to Jerusalem for one of the Jewish holy days.
2 Inside the city, near the Sheep Gate, was the pool of Bethesda,* with five
covered porches. 3 Crowds of sick people—blind, lame, or paralyzed—lay on
the porches.* 5 One of the men lying there had been sick for thirty-eight years.
6 When Jesus saw him and knew he had been ill for a long time, he asked him,
"Would you like to get well?"

7 "I can't, sir," the sick man said, "for I have no one to put me into the pool
when the water bubbles up. Someone else always gets there ahead of me."

8 Jesus told him, "Stand up, pick up your mat, and walk!"

9 Instantly, the man was healed! He rolled up his sleeping mat and began

5:2 Other manuscripts read *Beth-zatha;* still others read *Bethsaida.* 5:3 Some manuscripts add an expanded conclusion to verse 3 and all of verse 4: *waiting for a certain movement of the water, [4] for an angel of the Lord came from time to time and stirred up the water. And the first person to step in after the water was stirred was healed of whatever disease he had.*

walking! But this miracle happened on the Sabbath, 10 so the Jewish leaders
objected. They said to the man who was cured, "You can't work on the Sab-
bath! The law doesn't allow you to carry that sleeping mat!"
11 But he replied, "The man who healed me told me, 'Pick up your mat
and walk.'"
12 "Who said such a thing as that?" they demanded.
13 The man didn't know, for Jesus had disappeared into the crowd. 14 But
afterward Jesus found him in the Temple and told him, "Now you are well;
so stop sinning, or something even worse may happen to you." 15 Then the
man went and told the Jewish leaders that it was Jesus who had healed him.

Jesus Claims to Be the Son of God

16 So the Jewish leaders began harassing* Jesus for breaking the Sabbath
rules. 17 But Jesus replied, "My Father is always working, and so am I." 18 So
the Jewish leaders tried all the harder to find a way to kill him. For he not
only broke the Sabbath, he called God his Father, thereby making himself
equal with God.
19 So Jesus explained, "I tell you the truth, the Son can do nothing by him-
self. He does only what he sees the Father doing. Whatever the Father does,
the Son also does. 20 For the Father loves the Son and shows him everything he
is doing. In fact, the Father will show him how to do even greater works than
healing this man. Then you will truly be astonished. 21 For just as the Father
gives life to those he raises from the dead, so the Son gives life to anyone he
wants. 22 In addition, the Father judges no one. Instead, he has given the Son
absolute authority to judge, 23 so that everyone will honor the Son, just as
they honor the Father. Anyone who does not honor the Son is certainly not
honoring the Father who sent him.
24 "I tell you the truth, those who listen to my message and believe in God
who sent me have eternal life. They will never be condemned for their sins,
but they have already passed from death into life.
25 "And I assure you that the time is coming, indeed it's here now, when the
dead will hear my voice—the voice of the Son of God. And those who listen
will live. 26 The Father has life in himself, and he has granted that same life-
giving power to his Son. 27 And he has given him authority to judge everyone
because he is the Son of Man.* 28 Don't be so surprised! Indeed, the time is
coming when all the dead in their graves will hear the voice of God's Son,
29 and they will rise again. Those who have done good will rise to experience
eternal life, and those who have continued in evil will rise to experience
judgment. 30 I can do nothing on my own. I judge as God tells me. Therefore,
my judgment is just, because I carry out the will of the one who sent me,
not my own will.

Witnesses to Jesus

31 "If I were to testify on my own behalf, my testimony would not be valid.
32 But someone else is also testifying about me, and I assure you that every-
thing he says about me is true. 33 In fact, you sent investigators to listen to
John the Baptist, and his testimony about me was true. 34 Of course, I have
no need of human witnesses, but I say these things so you might be saved.
35 John was like a burning and shining lamp, and you were excited for a while

Question **5:24**

Is it the miracle that helps us believe, or is it having Jesus as an active friend?

5:16 Or *persecuting.* **5:27** "Son of Man" is a title Jesus used for himself.

Prayer **5:39**

Jesus, this all points to you. Open my eyes to you every time I open the Bible. Amen.

Question **6:5-6**

How often does Jesus ask us surprising, fun questions like this to test the simplicity of our faith?

Make a Difference **6:27**

Spend Energy

Jesus doesn't want you to waste your energy. He doesn't want you to regret how you spend even one minute of your life. What gives purpose and meaning to all that you do, he says, is himself. Pursuit of him and the life he gives is worth every effort. You will know you are spending your energy wisely when you are seeking after Jesus and filtering all you do through him. Everything in your life will begin to fall into its proper place as you find your priority in Jesus.

Difference Maker

How could you spend your energy searching for the life Jesus offers today?

about his message. 36 But I have a greater witness than John—my teachings
and my miracles. The Father gave me these works to accomplish, and they
prove that he sent me. 37 And the Father who sent me has testified about me
himself. You have never heard his voice or seen him face to face, 38 and you
do not have his message in your hearts, because you do not believe me—the
one he sent to you.

39 "You search the Scriptures because you think they give you eternal life.
But the Scriptures point to me! 40 Yet you refuse to come to me to receive
this life.

41 "Your approval means nothing to me, 42 because I know you don't have
God's love within you. 43 For I have come to you in my Father's name, and you
have rejected me. Yet if others come in their own name, you gladly welcome
them. 44 No wonder you can't believe! For you gladly honor each other, but
you don't care about the honor that comes from the one who alone is God.*

45 "Yet it isn't I who will accuse you before the Father. Moses will accuse
you! Yes, Moses, in whom you put your hopes. 46 If you really believed Moses,
you would believe me, because he wrote about me. 47 But since you don't
believe what he wrote, how will you believe what I say?"

Jesus Feeds Five Thousand

6 After this, Jesus crossed over to the far side of the Sea of Galilee, also
known as the Sea of Tiberias. 2 A huge crowd kept following him wher-
ever he went, because they saw his miraculous signs as he healed the sick.
3 Then Jesus climbed a hill and sat down with his disciples around him. 4 (It
was nearly time for the Jewish Passover celebration.) 5 Jesus soon saw a huge
crowd of people coming to look for him. Turning to Philip, he asked, "Where
can we buy bread to feed all these people?" 6 He was testing Philip, for he
already knew what he was going to do.

7 Philip replied, "Even if we worked for months, we wouldn't have enough
money* to feed them!"

8 Then Andrew, Simon Peter's brother, spoke up. 9 "There's a young boy
here with five barley loaves and two fish. But what good is that with this
huge crowd?"

10 "Tell everyone to sit down," Jesus said. So they all sat down on the grassy
slopes. (The men alone numbered about 5,000.) 11 Then Jesus took the loaves,
gave thanks to God, and distributed them to the people. Afterward he did the
same with the fish. And they all ate as much as they wanted. 12 After everyone
was full, Jesus told his disciples, "Now gather the leftovers, so that nothing is
wasted." 13 So they picked up the pieces and filled twelve baskets with scraps
left by the people who had eaten from the five barley loaves.

14 When the people saw him* do this miraculous sign, they exclaimed,
"Surely, he is the Prophet we have been expecting!"* 15 When Jesus saw that
they were ready to force him to be their king, he slipped away into the hills
by himself.

Jesus Walks on Water

16 That evening Jesus' disciples went down to the shore to wait for him. 17 But
as darkness fell and Jesus still hadn't come back, they got into the boat and

5:44 Some manuscripts read *from the only One.* **6:7** Greek *Two hundred denarii would not be enough.* A denarius was equivalent to a laborer's full day's wage. **6:14a** Some manuscripts read *Jesus.* **6:14b** See Deut 18:15, 18; Mal 4:5-6.

headed across the lake toward Capernaum. 18 Soon a gale swept down upon
them, and the sea grew very rough. 19 They had rowed three or four miles*
when suddenly they saw Jesus walking on the water toward the boat. They
were terrified, 20 but he called out to them, "Don't be afraid. I am here!*"
21 Then they were eager to let him in the boat, and immediately they arrived
at their destination!

Jesus, the Bread of Life

22 The next day the crowd that had stayed on the far shore saw that the dis-
ciples had taken the only boat, and they realized Jesus had not gone with
them. 23 Several boats from Tiberias landed near the place where the Lord had
blessed the bread and the people had eaten. 24 So when the crowd saw that
neither Jesus nor his disciples were there, they got into the boats and went
across to Capernaum to look for him. 25 They found him on the other side of
the lake and asked, "Rabbi, when did you get here?"
26 Jesus replied, "I tell you the truth, you want to be with me because I fed
you, not because you understood the miraculous signs. 27 But don't be so
concerned about perishable things like food. Spend your energy seeking the
eternal life that the Son of Man* can give you. For God the Father has given
me the seal of his approval."
28 They replied, "We want to perform God's works, too. What should we do?"
29 Jesus told them, "This is the only work God wants from you: Believe in
the one he has sent."
30 They answered, "Show us a miraculous sign if you want us to believe
in you. What can you do? 31 After all, our ancestors ate manna while they
journeyed through the wilderness! The Scriptures say, 'Moses gave them
bread from heaven to eat.'*"
32 Jesus said, "I tell you the truth, Moses didn't give you bread from heaven.
My Father did. And now he offers you the true bread from heaven. 33 The
true bread of God is the one who comes down from heaven and gives life
to the world."
34 "Sir," they said, "give us that bread every day."
35 Jesus replied, "I am the bread of life. Whoever comes to me will never be
hungry again. Whoever believes in me will never be thirsty. 36 But you haven't
believed in me even though you have seen me. 37 However, those the Father
has given me will come to me, and I will never reject them. 38 For I have come
down from heaven to do the will of God who sent me, not to do my own will.
39 And this is the will of God, that I should not lose even one of all those he
has given me, but that I should raise them up at the last day. 40 For it is my
Father's will that all who see his Son and believe in him should have eternal
life. I will raise them up at the last day."
41 Then the people* began to murmur in disagreement because he had
said, "I am the bread that came down from heaven." 42 They said, "Isn't this
Jesus, the son of Joseph? We know his father and mother. How can he say, 'I
came down from heaven'?"
43 But Jesus replied, "Stop complaining about what I said. 44 For no one can
come to me unless the Father who sent me draws them to me, and at the last
day I will raise them up. 45 As it is written in the Scriptures,* 'They will all

6:19 Greek *25 or 30 stadia* [4.6 or 5.5 kilometers]. 6:20 Or *The 'I AM' is here;* Greek reads *I am.* See Exod 3:14. 6:27 "Son of Man" is a title Jesus used for himself. 6:31 Exod 16:4; Ps 78:24. 6:41 Greek *Jewish people;* also in 6:52. 6:45 Greek *in the prophets.* Isa 54:13.

Make a Difference 6:29

Believe in Jesus

It would be wrong for you to walk away from the Bible with the impression that somehow your good works are what God ultimately wants from you. God actually wants only one thing from you; he has only one requirement. At the end of your life, as you look back over the years, it would be nice to remember the good things you accomplished or ways you were kind. However, whether you believed in Jesus will be what God ultimately cares about the most. After all, if you believe in Jesus, the good works will come. Good deeds are simply a natural overflow of Jesus being alive within you. There is nothing in life that makes more of a difference than this one thing: believe in the Lord Jesus Christ.

Difference Maker

Turn to the end of this Bible and read through "How to Accept Jesus as Your Lord and Savior."

Make a Difference

6:66-69

Nowhere Else

Many people leave the church simply because they can, feeling like they have a choice in the matter. They don't feel compelled to stay. For whatever reason, many just slip away through the crowd.

There was a time when many people left the crowd that was following Jesus too. They deserted him because they couldn't stomach Jesus' calling on their lives. What Jesus was asking them to do was too radical. Once a few people started wandering away, many others took the easy route too.

Difference Maker

Think of someone you know who has given up on God. Don't let that person walk away from Jesus. How can you invite them to join you in making Jesus the center, not an addition, to life?

be taught by God.' Everyone who listens to the Father and learns from him
comes to me. 46(Not that anyone has ever seen the Father; only I, who was
sent from God, have seen him.)
47"I tell you the truth, anyone who believes has eternal life. 48Yes, I am
the bread of life! 49Your ancestors ate manna in the wilderness, but they all
died. 50Anyone who eats the bread from heaven, however, will never die.
51I am the living bread that came down from heaven. Anyone who eats this
bread will live forever; and this bread, which I will offer so the world may
live, is my flesh."
52Then the people began arguing with each other about what he meant.
"How can this man give us his flesh to eat?" they asked.
53So Jesus said again, "I tell you the truth, unless you eat the flesh of the
Son of Man and drink his blood, you cannot have eternal life within you.
54But anyone who eats my flesh and drinks my blood has eternal life, and I
will raise that person at the last day. 55For my flesh is true food, and my blood
is true drink. 56Anyone who eats my flesh and drinks my blood remains in
me, and I in him. 57I live because of the living Father who sent me; in the
same way, anyone who feeds on me will live because of me. 58I am the true
bread that came down from heaven. Anyone who eats this bread will not die
as your ancestors did (even though they ate the manna) but will live forever."
59He said these things while he was teaching in the synagogue in Capernaum.

Many Disciples Desert Jesus

60Many of his disciples said, "This is very hard to understand. How can anyone accept it?"
61Jesus was aware that his disciples were complaining, so he said to them,
"Does this offend you? 62Then what will you think if you see the Son of Man
ascend to heaven again? 63The Spirit alone gives eternal life. Human effort
accomplishes nothing. And the very words I have spoken to you are spirit
and life. 64But some of you do not believe me." (For Jesus knew from the
beginning which ones didn't believe, and he knew who would betray him.)
65Then he said, "That is why I said that people can't come to me unless the
Father gives them to me."
66At this point many of his disciples turned away and deserted him.
67Then Jesus turned to the Twelve and asked, "Are you also going to leave?"
68Simon Peter replied, "Lord, to whom would we go? You have the words
that give eternal life. 69We believe, and we know you are the Holy One of God.*"
70Then Jesus said, "I chose the twelve of you, but one is a devil." 71He was
speaking of Judas, son of Simon Iscariot, one of the Twelve, who would later
betray him.

Jesus and His Brothers

7 After this, Jesus traveled around Galilee. He wanted to stay out of Judea,
where the Jewish leaders were plotting his death. 2But soon it was time
for the Jewish Festival of Shelters, 3and Jesus' brothers said to him, "Leave
here and go to Judea, where your followers can see your miracles! 4You can't
become famous if you hide like this! If you can do such wonderful things,
show yourself to the world!" 5For even his brothers didn't believe in him.

6:69 Other manuscripts read *you are the Christ, the Holy One of God;* still others read *you are the Christ, the Son of God;* and still others read *you are the Christ, the Son of the living God.*

6 Jesus replied, "Now is not the right time for me to go, but you can go
anytime. 7 The world can't hate you, but it does hate me because I accuse it
of doing evil. 8 You go on. I'm not going* to this festival, because my time
has not yet come." 9 After saying these things, Jesus remained in Galilee.

Jesus Teaches Openly at the Temple

10 But after his brothers left for the festival, Jesus also went, though secretly,
staying out of public view. 11 The Jewish leaders tried to find him at the fes-
tival and kept asking if anyone had seen him. 12 There was a lot of grumbling
about him among the crowds. Some argued, "He's a good man," but others
said, "He's nothing but a fraud who deceives the people." 13 But no one had
the courage to speak favorably about him in public, for they were afraid of
getting in trouble with the Jewish leaders.

14 Then, midway through the festival, Jesus went up to the Temple and
began to teach. 15 The people* were surprised when they heard him. "How
does he know so much when he hasn't been trained?" they asked.

16 So Jesus told them, "My message is not my own; it comes from God who
sent me. 17 Anyone who wants to do the will of God will know whether my
teaching is from God or is merely my own. 18 Those who speak for themselves
want glory only for themselves, but a person who seeks to honor the one who
sent him speaks truth, not lies. 19 Moses gave you the law, but none of you
obeys it! In fact, you are trying to kill me."

20 The crowd replied, "You're demon possessed! Who's trying to kill you?"

21 Jesus replied, "I did one miracle on the Sabbath, and you were amazed.
22 But you work on the Sabbath, too, when you obey Moses' law of circumci-
sion. (Actually, this tradition of circumcision began with the patriarchs, long
before the law of Moses.) 23 For if the correct time for circumcising your son
falls on the Sabbath, you go ahead and do it so as not to break the law of
Moses. So why should you be angry with me for healing a man on the Sab-
bath? 24 Look beneath the surface so you can judge correctly."

Is Jesus the Messiah?

25 Some of the people who lived in Jerusalem started to ask each other, "Isn't
this the man they are trying to kill? 26 But here he is, speaking in public, and
they say nothing to him. Could our leaders possibly believe that he is the
Messiah? 27 But how could he be? For we know where this man comes from.
When the Messiah comes, he will simply appear; no one will know where
he comes from."

28 While Jesus was teaching in the Temple, he called out, "Yes, you know
me, and you know where I come from. But I'm not here on my own. The one
who sent me is true, and you don't know him. 29 But I know him because I
come from him, and he sent me to you." 30 Then the leaders tried to arrest
him; but no one laid a hand on him, because his time* had not yet come.

31 Many among the crowds at the Temple believed in him. "After all," they
said, "would you expect the Messiah to do more miraculous signs than this
man has done?"

32 When the Pharisees heard that the crowds were whispering such things,
they and the leading priests sent Temple guards to arrest Jesus. 33 But Jesus
told them, "I will be with you only a little longer. Then I will return to the

7:8 Some manuscripts read *not yet going.* **7:15** Greek *Jewish people.* **7:30** Greek *his hour.*

Prayer **7:17**

Lord, it's not just about my intellect. It's about my desire to do your will. Grow that desire deep within me. Amen.

Question 7:46

No one has ever heard anyone speak like Jesus because no one has ever spoken like he does. He is the Word of God (John 1:1). His speech created the world. We will spend eternity awed by this question: How astonishing are the words of Jesus?

one who sent me. 34 You will search for me but not find me. And you cannot
go where I am going."
35 The Jewish leaders were puzzled by this statement. "Where is he plan-
ning to go?" they asked. "Is he thinking of leaving the country and going to
the Jews in other lands?* Maybe he will even teach the Greeks! 36 What does
he mean when he says, 'You will search for me but not find me,' and 'You
cannot go where I am going'?"

Jesus Promises Living Water

37 On the last day, the climax of the festival, Jesus stood and shouted to the
crowds, "Anyone who is thirsty may come to me! 38 Anyone who believes in
me may come and drink! For the Scriptures declare, 'Rivers of living water
will flow from his heart.'"* 39 (When he said "living water," he was speaking
of the Spirit, who would be given to everyone believing in him. But the Spirit
had not yet been given,* because Jesus had not yet entered into his glory.)

Division and Unbelief

40 When the crowds heard him say this, some of them declared, "Surely this
man is the Prophet we've been expecting."* 41 Others said, "He is the Mes-
siah." Still others said, "But he can't be! Will the Messiah come from Galilee?
42 For the Scriptures clearly state that the Messiah will be born of the royal
line of David, in Bethlehem, the village where King David was born."* 43 So
the crowd was divided about him. 44 Some even wanted him arrested, but no
one laid a hand on him.
45 When the Temple guards returned without having arrested Jesus, the
leading priests and Pharisees demanded, "Why didn't you bring him in?"
46 "We have never heard anyone speak like this!" the guards responded.
47 "Have you been led astray, too?" the Pharisees mocked. 48 "Is there a
single one of us rulers or Pharisees who believes in him? 49 This foolish crowd
follows him, but they are ignorant of the law. God's curse is on them!"
50 Then Nicodemus, the leader who had met with Jesus earlier, spoke up.
51 "Is it legal to convict a man before he is given a hearing?" he asked.
52 They replied, "Are you from Galilee, too? Search the Scriptures and see
for yourself—no prophet ever comes* from Galilee!"

[*The most ancient Greek manuscripts do not include John 7:53–8:11.*]

53 Then the meeting broke up, and everybody went home.

A Woman Caught in Adultery

8 Jesus returned to the Mount of Olives, 2 but early the next morning he
was back again at the Temple. A crowd soon gathered, and he sat down
and taught them. 3 As he was speaking, the teachers of religious law and the
Pharisees brought a woman who had been caught in the act of adultery. They
put her in front of the crowd.

7:35 Or *the Jews who live among the Greeks?* 7:37-38 Or *"Let anyone who is thirsty come to me and drink. 38 For the Scriptures declare, 'Rivers of living water will flow from the heart of anyone who believes in me.'"* 7:39 Several early manuscripts read *But as yet there was no Spirit.* Still others read *But as yet there was no Holy Spirit.* 7:40 See Deut 18:15, 18; Mal 4:5-6. 7:42 See Mic 5:2. 7:52 Some manuscripts read *the prophet does not come.*

4“Teacher,” they said to Jesus, “this woman was caught in the act of adul-
tery. 5The law of Moses says to stone her. What do you say?”
6They were trying to trap him into saying something they could use
against him, but Jesus stooped down and wrote in the dust with his finger.
7They kept demanding an answer, so he stood up again and said, “All right,
but let the one who has never sinned throw the first stone!” 8Then he stooped
down again and wrote in the dust.
9When the accusers heard this, they slipped away one by one, beginning
with the oldest, until only Jesus was left in the middle of the crowd with the
woman. 10Then Jesus stood up again and said to the woman, “Where are your
accusers? Didn't even one of them condemn you?”
11“No, Lord,” she said.
And Jesus said, “Neither do I. Go and sin no more.”

Jesus, the Light of the World

12Jesus spoke to the people once more and said, “I am the light of the world.
If you follow me, you won't have to walk in darkness, because you will have
the light that leads to life.”
13The Pharisees replied, “You are making those claims about yourself!
Such testimony is not valid.”
14Jesus told them, “These claims are valid even though I make them about
myself. For I know where I came from and where I am going, but you don't
know this about me. 15You judge me by human standards, but I do not judge
anyone. 16And if I did, my judgment would be correct in every respect because
I am not alone. The Father* who sent me is with me. 17Your own law says that
if two people agree about something, their witness is accepted as fact.* 18I am
one witness, and my Father who sent me is the other.”
19“Where is your father?” they asked.
Jesus answered, “Since you don't know who I am, you don't know who my
Father is. If you knew me, you would also know my Father.” 20Jesus made
these statements while he was teaching in the section of the Temple known
as the Treasury. But he was not arrested, because his time* had not yet come.

The Unbelieving People Warned

21Later Jesus said to them again, “I am going away. You will search for me
but will die in your sin. You cannot come where I am going.”
22The people* asked, “Is he planning to commit suicide? What does he
mean, ‘You cannot come where I am going’?”
23Jesus continued, “You are from below; I am from above. You belong to
this world; I do not. 24That is why I said that you will die in your sins; for
unless you believe that I AM who I claim to be,* you will die in your sins.”
25“Who are you?” they demanded.
Jesus replied, “The one I have always claimed to be.* 26I have much to say
about you and much to condemn, but I won't. For I say only what I have
heard from the one who sent me, and he is completely truthful.” 27But they
still didn't understand that he was talking about his Father.

8:16 Some manuscripts read *The One.* 8:17 See Deut 19:15. 8:20 Greek *his hour.* 8:22 Greek *Jewish people;* also in 8:31, 48, 52, 57. 8:24 Greek *unless you believe that I am.* See Exod 3:14. 8:25 Or *Why do I speak to you at all?*

Make a Difference 8:12

Do Something

This world needs you to make a difference. This good world has veered a long way from what God created it to be. God did something about it, and he called you to do something about it with him.

Jesus, the Light of the World, calls you to be the light of the world too. You are a partner with Jesus in his mission on this earth. He wants everyone to see him, and he wants you to help shed some light for them. Jesus wants people to know the way to him. He wants you to offer to light the path. Jesus shines in brilliance. He wants you to shine his radiance upon your family, your friends, and all those you will encounter today.

Difference Maker

Think of someone who is clouded by darkness today. Then take time right now to pray for them. As you do, ask God to let you be a light in their life.

28 So Jesus said, "When you have lifted up the Son of Man on the cross,
then you will understand that I AM he.* I do nothing on my own but say only
what the Father taught me. 29 And the one who sent me is with me—he has
not deserted me. For I always do what pleases him." 30 Then many who heard
him say these things believed in him.

Jesus and Abraham

31 Jesus said to the people who believed in him, "You are truly my disciples
if you remain faithful to my teachings. 32 And you will know the truth, and
the truth will set you free."

33 "But we are descendants of Abraham," they said. "We have never been
slaves to anyone. What do you mean, 'You will be set free'?"

34 Jesus replied, "I tell you the truth, everyone who sins is a slave of sin. 35 A
slave is not a permanent member of the family, but a son is part of the family
forever. 36 So if the Son sets you free, you are truly free. 37 Yes, I realize that you
are descendants of Abraham. And yet some of you are trying to kill me because
there's no room in your hearts for my message. 38 I am telling you what I saw
when I was with my Father. But you are following the advice of your father."

39 "Our father is Abraham!" they declared.

"No," Jesus replied, "for if you were really the children of Abraham, you
would follow his example.* 40 Instead, you are trying to kill me because I told
you the truth, which I heard from God. Abraham never did such a thing.
41 No, you are imitating your real father."

They replied, "We aren't illegitimate children! God himself is our true
Father."

42 Jesus told them, "If God were your Father, you would love me, because I
have come to you from God. I am not here on my own, but he sent me. 43 Why
can't you understand what I am saying? It's because you can't even hear me!
44 For you are the children of your father the devil, and you love to do the evil
things he does. He was a murderer from the beginning. He has always hated
the truth, because there is no truth in him. When he lies, it is consistent with
his character; for he is a liar and the father of lies. 45 So when I tell the truth,
you just naturally don't believe me! 46 Which of you can truthfully accuse
me of sin? And since I am telling you the truth, why don't you believe me?
47 Anyone who belongs to God listens gladly to the words of God. But you
don't listen because you don't belong to God."

48 The people retorted, "You Samaritan devil! Didn't we say all along that
you were possessed by a demon?"

49 "No," Jesus said, "I have no demon in me. For I honor my Father—and
you dishonor me. 50 And though I have no wish to glorify myself, God is going
to glorify me. He is the true judge. 51 I tell you the truth, anyone who obeys
my teaching will never die!"

52 The people said, "Now we know you are possessed by a demon. Even
Abraham and the prophets died, but you say, 'Anyone who obeys my teaching
will never die!' 53 Are you greater than our father Abraham? He died, and so
did the prophets. Who do you think you are?"

54 Jesus answered, "If I want glory for myself, it doesn't count. But it is
my Father who will glorify me. You say, 'He is our God,'* 55 but you don't

8:28 Greek *When you have lifted up the Son of Man, then you will know that I am.* "Son of Man" is a title Jesus used for himself. **8:39** Some manuscripts read *if you are really the children of Abraham, follow his example.* **8:54** Some manuscripts read *You say he is your God.*

even know him. I know him. If I said otherwise, I would be as great a liar as
you! But I do know him and obey him. 56 Your father Abraham rejoiced as he
looked forward to my coming. He saw it and was glad."
57 The people said, "You aren't even fifty years old. How can you say you
have seen Abraham?*"
58 Jesus answered, "I tell you the truth, before Abraham was even born, I
AM!*" 59 At that point they picked up stones to throw at him. But Jesus was
hidden from them and left the Temple.

Question 8:58

Did Jesus use bad grammar here? Why or why not?

Jesus Heals a Man Born Blind

9 As Jesus was walking along, he saw a man who had been blind from
birth. 2 "Rabbi," his disciples asked him, "why was this man born blind?
Was it because of his own sins or his parents' sins?"
3 "It was not because of his sins or his parents' sins," Jesus answered. "This
happened so the power of God could be seen in him. 4 We must quickly carry
out the tasks assigned us by the one who sent us.* The night is coming, and
then no one can work. 5 But while I am here in the world, I am the light of
the world."
6 Then he spit on the ground, made mud with the saliva, and spread the
mud over the blind man's eyes. 7 He told him, "Go wash yourself in the pool
of Siloam" (Siloam means "sent"). So the man went and washed and came
back seeing!
8 His neighbors and others who knew him as a blind beggar asked each
other, "Isn't this the man who used to sit and beg?" 9 Some said he was, and
others said, "No, he just looks like him!"
But the beggar kept saying, "Yes, I am the same one!"
10 They asked, "Who healed you? What happened?"
11 He told them, "The man they call Jesus made mud and spread it over
my eyes and told me, 'Go to the pool of Siloam and wash yourself.' So I went
and washed, and now I can see!"
12 "Where is he now?" they asked.
"I don't know," he replied.
13 Then they took the man who had been blind to the Pharisees, 14 because
it was on the Sabbath that Jesus had made the mud and healed him. 15 The
Pharisees asked the man all about it. So he told them, "He put the mud over
my eyes, and when I washed it away, I could see!"
16 Some of the Pharisees said, "This man Jesus is not from God, for he is
working on the Sabbath." Others said, "But how could an ordinary sinner
do such miraculous signs?" So there was a deep division of opinion among
them.
17 Then the Pharisees again questioned the man who had been blind and
demanded, "What's your opinion about this man who healed you?"
The man replied, "I think he must be a prophet."
18 The Jewish leaders still refused to believe the man had been blind and
could now see, so they called in his parents. 19 They asked them, "Is this your
son? Was he born blind? If so, how can he now see?"
20 His parents replied, "We know this is our son and that he was born blind,

8:57 Some manuscripts read *How can you say Abraham has seen you?* 8:58 Or *before Abraham was even born, I have always been alive;* Greek reads *before Abraham was, I am.* See Exod 3:14. 9:4 Other manuscripts read *I must quickly carry out the tasks assigned me by the one who sent me;* still others read *We must quickly carry out the tasks assigned us by the one who sent me.*

21 but we don't know how he can see or who healed him. Ask him. He is old
enough to speak for himself." 22 His parents said this because they were afraid
of the Jewish leaders, who had announced that anyone saying Jesus was the
Messiah would be expelled from the synagogue. 23 That's why they said, "He
is old enough. Ask him."
24 So for the second time they called in the man who had been blind and
told him, "God should get the glory for this,* because we know this man
Jesus is a sinner."
25 "I don't know whether he is a sinner," the man replied. "But I know this:
I was blind, and now I can see!"
26 "But what did he do?" they asked. "How did he heal you?"
27 "Look!" the man exclaimed. "I told you once. Didn't you listen? Why
do you want to hear it again? Do you want to become his disciples, too?"
28 Then they cursed him and said, "You are his disciple, but we are disciples
of Moses! 29 We know God spoke to Moses, but we don't even know where
this man comes from."
30 "Why, that's very strange!" the man replied. "He healed my eyes, and yet
you don't know where he comes from? 31 We know that God doesn't listen to
sinners, but he is ready to hear those who worship him and do his will. 32 Ever
since the world began, no one has been able to open the eyes of someone born
blind. 33 If this man were not from God, he couldn't have done it."
34 "You were born a total sinner!" they answered. "Are you trying to teach
us?" And they threw him out of the synagogue.

Spiritual Blindness

35 When Jesus heard what had happened, he found the man and asked, "Do
you believe in the Son of Man?*"
36 The man answered, "Who is he, sir? I want to believe in him."
37 "You have seen him," Jesus said, "and he is speaking to you!"
38 "Yes, Lord, I believe!" the man said. And he worshiped Jesus.
39 Then Jesus told him,* "I entered this world to render judgment—to give
sight to the blind and to show those who think they see* that they are blind."
40 Some Pharisees who were standing nearby heard him and asked, "Are
you saying we're blind?"
41 "If you were blind, you wouldn't be guilty," Jesus replied. "But you re-
main guilty because you claim you can see.

The Good Shepherd and His Sheep

10 "I tell you the truth, anyone who sneaks over the wall of a sheepfold,
rather than going through the gate, must surely be a thief and a rob-
ber! 2 But the one who enters through the gate is the shepherd of the sheep.
3 The gatekeeper opens the gate for him, and the sheep recognize his voice
and come to him. He calls his own sheep by name and leads them out. 4 After
he has gathered his own flock, he walks ahead of them, and they follow him
because they know his voice. 5 They won't follow a stranger; they will run
from him because they don't know his voice."
6 Those who heard Jesus use this illustration didn't understand what he

9:24 Or *Give glory to God, not to Jesus;* Greek reads *Give glory to God.* 9:35 Some manuscripts read *the Son of God?* "Son of Man" is a title Jesus used for himself. 9:38-39a Some manuscripts do not include *"Yes, Lord, I believe!" the man said. And he worshiped Jesus. Then Jesus told him.* 9:39b Greek *those who see.*

Question 9:25

After Jesus healed him, the man born blind was confronted by people asking about Jesus. There was a moment of awkwardness, however, because the man didn't really know. However, he did know what Jesus had done for him, so he shared the truth of the difference Jesus had made in his life. What could you say you definitely know about Jesus and about what he has done for you?

Make a Difference

10:1–16

Shepherd

If you know that Jesus supports your cause, then you can be confident to tackle it full on. With Jesus standing behind you, ready to defend you and poised to refresh you, what have you got to lose? He has already laid down his life for you. He made it clear that he wasn't going to let anything snatch you away from his grip. He has absolutely given his whole self for you.

Jesus wants you to learn to be bold for him. There is no need to stand with trepidation; there is no need to let fear or timidity slow you down. Jesus is absolutely good, and Jesus is your Good Shepherd. Because he is the one who guides you and protects you, feeds you and grows you, challenges you and restores you, the calling he has given you is yours to pursue.

Difference Maker

Do something remarkably good for others today, something that you otherwise wouldn't have done, all because Jesus supports you with his life.

meant, 7 so he explained it to them: "I tell you the truth, I am the gate for
the sheep. 8 All who came before me* were thieves and robbers. But the true
sheep did not listen to them. 9 Yes, I am the gate. Those who come in through
me will be saved.* They will come and go freely and will find good pastures.
10 The thief's purpose is to steal and kill and destroy. My purpose is to give
them a rich and satisfying life.

11 "I am the good shepherd. The good shepherd sacrifices his life for the
sheep. 12 A hired hand will run when he sees a wolf coming. He will abandon
the sheep because they don't belong to him and he isn't their shepherd. And
so the wolf attacks them and scatters the flock. 13 The hired hand runs away
because he's working only for the money and doesn't really care about the
sheep.

14 "I am the good shepherd; I know my own sheep, and they know me,
15 just as my Father knows me and I know the Father. So I sacrifice my life
for the sheep. 16 I have other sheep, too, that are not in this sheepfold. I must
bring them also. They will listen to my voice, and there will be one flock
with one shepherd.

17 "The Father loves me because I sacrifice my life so I may take it back
again. 18 No one can take my life from me. I sacrifice it voluntarily. For I have
the authority to lay it down when I want to and also to take it up again. For
this is what my Father has commanded."

19 When he said these things, the people* were again divided in their opin-
ions about him. 20 Some said, "He's demon possessed and out of his mind.
Why listen to a man like that?" 21 Others said, "This doesn't sound like a man
possessed by a demon! Can a demon open the eyes of the blind?"

Jesus Claims to Be the Son of God

22 It was now winter, and Jesus was in Jerusalem at the time of Hanukkah,
the Festival of Dedication. 23 He was in the Temple, walking through the
section known as Solomon's Colonnade. 24 The people surrounded him and
asked, "How long are you going to keep us in suspense? If you are the Mes-
siah, tell us plainly."

25 Jesus replied, "I have already told you, and you don't believe me. The
proof is the work I do in my Father's name. 26 But you don't believe me be-
cause you are not my sheep. 27 My sheep listen to my voice; I know them, and
they follow me. 28 I give them eternal life, and they will never perish. No one
can snatch them away from me, 29 for my Father has given them to me, and
he is more powerful than anyone else.* No one can snatch them from the
Father's hand. 30 The Father and I are one."

31 Once again the people picked up stones to kill him. 32 Jesus said, "At
my Father's direction I have done many good works. For which one are you
going to stone me?"

33 They replied, "We're stoning you not for any good work, but for blas-
phemy! You, a mere man, claim to be God."

34 Jesus replied, "It is written in your own Scriptures* that God said to certain
leaders of the people, 'I say, you are gods!'* 35 And you know that the Scriptures
cannot be altered. So if those people who received God's message were called

10:8 Some manuscripts do not include *before me.* 10:9 Or *will find safety.* 10:19 Greek *Jewish people;* also in 10:24, 31. 10:29 Other manuscripts read *for what my Father has given me is more powerful than anything;* still others read *for regarding that which my Father has given me, he is greater than all.* 10:34a Greek *your own law.* 10:34b Ps 82:6.

Make a Difference

10:27

Ask God about His Day

Have you ever had a one-sided relationship with someone who talked all the time? It's difficult and exhausting. Because you love the person, you put up with him or her, just hoping for the day when the friendship becomes a bit more reciprocal, mutual, or friend-like. The truth is that God wants to chat with you. Like everyone else, you, too, can be too self-absorbed to have a conversation with him. Oh, you probably pray, but you can be tempted to do all the talking.

If you feel like prayer has been too much of a one-sided conversation, try paying attention to God. Ask him what's going on with him. Ask God how he is doing. Silence your life long enough and open your soul wide enough so that you can hear what's on God's heart at that particular moment. In other words, be a friend to God. He has been one to you. It's not that he needs your friendship; rather, it's that he wants it. Perhaps he has something he'd like to say to his friend.

Difference Maker

Stop everything, be still, and listen for God today.

'gods,' 36 why do you call it blasphemy when I say, 'I am the Son of God'? After
all, the Father set me apart and sent me into the world. 37 Don't believe me un-
less I carry out my Father's work. 38 But if I do his work, believe in the evidence
of the miraculous works I have done, even if you don't believe me. Then you
will know and understand that the Father is in me, and I am in the Father."
39 Once again they tried to arrest him, but he got away and left them. 40 He
went beyond the Jordan River near the place where John was first baptizing
and stayed there awhile. 41 And many followed him. "John didn't perform
miraculous signs," they remarked to one another, "but everything he said
about this man has come true." 42 And many who were there believed in Jesus.

The Raising of Lazarus

11 A man named Lazarus was sick. He lived in Bethany with his sisters,
Mary and Martha. 2 This is the Mary who later poured the expensive
perfume on the Lord's feet and wiped them with her hair.* Her brother, Laz-
arus, was sick. 3 So the two sisters sent a message to Jesus telling him, "Lord,
your dear friend is very sick."
4 But when Jesus heard about it he said, "Lazarus's sickness will not end in
death. No, it happened for the glory of God so that the Son of God will receive
glory from this." 5 So although Jesus loved Martha, Mary, and Lazarus, 6 he
stayed where he was for the next two days. 7 Finally, he said to his disciples,
"Let's go back to Judea."
8 But his disciples objected. "Rabbi," they said, "only a few days ago the
people* in Judea were trying to stone you. Are you going there again?"
9 Jesus replied, "There are twelve hours of daylight every day. During the
day people can walk safely. They can see because they have the light of this
world. 10 But at night there is danger of stumbling because they have no
light." 11 Then he said, "Our friend Lazarus has fallen asleep, but now I will
go and wake him up."
12 The disciples said, "Lord, if he is sleeping, he will soon get better!"
13 They thought Jesus meant Lazarus was simply sleeping, but Jesus meant
Lazarus had died.
14 So he told them plainly, "Lazarus is dead. 15 And for your sakes, I'm glad
I wasn't there, for now you will really believe. Come, let's go see him."
16 Thomas, nicknamed the Twin,* said to his fellow disciples, "Let's go,
too—and die with Jesus."
17 When Jesus arrived at Bethany, he was told that Lazarus had already been
in his grave for four days. 18 Bethany was only a few miles* down the road
from Jerusalem, 19 and many of the people had come to console Martha and
Mary in their loss. 20 When Martha got word that Jesus was coming, she went
to meet him. But Mary stayed in the house. 21 Martha said to Jesus, "Lord, if
only you had been here, my brother would not have died. 22 But even now I
know that God will give you whatever you ask."
23 Jesus told her, "Your brother will rise again."
24 "Yes," Martha said, "he will rise when everyone else rises, at the last day."
25 Jesus told her, "I am the resurrection and the life.* Anyone who believes
in me will live, even after dying. 26 Everyone who lives in me and believes in
me will never ever die. Do you believe this, Martha?"

Story Arc **11:1–44**

Lazarus

Resurrection means to "raise from the dead." Two thousand years ago, a man named Lazarus had gotten sick and died. A funeral full of grief was well underway—that is, until Jesus showed up. Imagine Jesus yelling into the tomb, "Lazarus, I want to hang out, bro" (or something to that effect). As anybody would do when Jesus speaks life, Lazarus came out of the tomb walking, much to the astonishment of everyone (except for Jesus, who played it all very cool).

A little later, after, of course, people unwrapped Lazarus's burial cloths, they ate dinner together. For Jesus, this was simply another day of work. Raising people to life is what he does for a living. People didn't know what to think about this situation. They had never seen a resurrected person before. Even though he was no zombie, Lazarus scared them, and this made them scared of Jesus too. The people were challenged to either accept the life-giving power of Jesus or run away.

Acts 1:1–4 ►

11:2 This incident is recorded in chapter 12. **11:8** Greek *Jewish people;* also in 11:19, 31, 33, 36, 45, 54. **11:16** Greek *Thomas, who was called Didymus.* **11:18** Greek *was about 15 stadia* [about 2.8 kilometers]. **11:25** Some manuscripts do not include *and the life.*

27 “Yes, Lord,” she told him. “I have always believed you are the Messiah,
the Son of God, the one who has come into the world from God.” 28 Then she
returned to Mary. She called Mary aside from the mourners and told her,
“The Teacher is here and wants to see you.” 29 So Mary immediately went
to him.

30 Jesus had stayed outside the village, at the place where Martha met him.
31 When the people who were at the house consoling Mary saw her leave so
hastily, they assumed she was going to Lazarus’s grave to weep. So they fol-
lowed her there. 32 When Mary arrived and saw Jesus, she fell at his feet and
said, “Lord, if only you had been here, my brother would not have died.”

33 When Jesus saw her weeping and saw the other people wailing with her,
a deep anger welled up within him,* and he was deeply troubled. 34 “Where
have you put him?” he asked them.

They told him, “Lord, come and see.” 35 Then Jesus wept. 36 The people who
were standing nearby said, “See how much he loved him!” 37 But some said,
“This man healed a blind man. Couldn’t he have kept Lazarus from dying?”

38 Jesus was still angry as he arrived at the tomb, a cave with a stone rolled
across its entrance. 39 “Roll the stone aside,” Jesus told them.

But Martha, the dead man’s sister, protested, “Lord, he has been dead for
four days. The smell will be terrible.”

40 Jesus responded, “Didn’t I tell you that you would see God’s glory if you
believe?” 41 So they rolled the stone aside. Then Jesus looked up to heaven
and said, “Father, thank you for hearing me. 42 You always hear me, but I
said it out loud for the sake of all these people standing here, so that they
will believe you sent me.” 43 Then Jesus shouted, “Lazarus, come out!” 44 And
the dead man came out, his hands and feet bound in graveclothes, his face
wrapped in a headcloth. Jesus told them, “Unwrap him and let him go!”

The Plot to Kill Jesus

45 Many of the people who were with Mary believed in Jesus when they saw
this happen. 46 But some went to the Pharisees and told them what Jesus
had done. 47 Then the leading priests and Pharisees called the high coun-
cil* together. “What are we going to do?” they asked each other. “This man
certainly performs many miraculous signs. 48 If we allow him to go on like
this, soon everyone will believe in him. Then the Roman army will come and
destroy both our Temple* and our nation.”

49 Caiaphas, who was high priest at that time,* said, “You don’t know what
you’re talking about! 50 You don’t realize that it’s better for you that one man
should die for the people than for the whole nation to be destroyed.”

51 He did not say this on his own; as high priest at that time he was led to
prophesy that Jesus would die for the entire nation. 52 And not only for that
nation, but to bring together and unite all the children of God scattered
around the world.

53 So from that time on, the Jewish leaders began to plot Jesus’ death. 54 As
a result, Jesus stopped his public ministry among the people and left Jeru-
salem. He went to a place near the wilderness, to the village of Ephraim, and
stayed there with his disciples.

55 It was now almost time for the Jewish Passover celebration, and many
people from all over the country arrived in Jerusalem several days early so

11:33 Or *he was angry in his spirit.* 11:47 Greek *the Sanhedrin.* 11:48 Or *our position;* Greek reads *our place.* 11:49 Greek *that year;* also in 11:51.

Make a Difference 11:35

Grieve

Too often we are looking for the quick out. When we see someone grieve, we try to make them immediately feel better. Rare is the person who is willing to wait in the pain with someone who is actively hurting. Sometimes, one of the worst things we can do is encourage someone to stop grieving. After all, Jesus wept. He wept for Lazarus and his friends. Jesus wept for Jerusalem. He wept blood from his pores in Gethsemane. Jesus grieved.

Love is the willingness to embrace pain. Yes, it is patient, kind, enduring, and not irritable (1 Corinthians 13:4-7). Each of those attributes requires an intentional willingness to hurt for someone else. Endurance, perseverance, forgiveness, trust—each takes a purposeful step of entering into pain. Blessed are those who mourn. Love is not weakness; it is strength. We have a strong God who loves us, even in the midst of our pain.

Difference Maker

Remember a friend who is hurting today. Do something for them to show that you are by their side in their time of grieving.

Question 12:1-2

Imagine the conversation at dinner that evening. What do you think Lazarus told Jesus he would do with his second chance at life? What would you do if you were Lazarus?

they could go through the purification ceremony before Passover began.
56 They kept looking for Jesus, but as they stood around in the Temple, they
said to each other, "What do you think? He won't come for Passover, will he?"
57 Meanwhile, the leading priests and Pharisees had publicly ordered that
anyone seeing Jesus must report it immediately so they could arrest him.

Jesus Anointed at Bethany

12 Six days before the Passover celebration began, Jesus arrived in Beth-
any, the home of Lazarus—the man he had raised from the dead. 2 A
dinner was prepared in Jesus' honor. Martha served, and Lazarus was among
those who ate* with him. 3 Then Mary took a twelve-ounce jar* of expensive
perfume made from essence of nard, and she anointed Jesus' feet with it,
wiping his feet with her hair. The house was filled with the fragrance.
4 But Judas Iscariot, the disciple who would soon betray him, said, 5 "That
perfume was worth a year's wages.* It should have been sold and the money
given to the poor." 6 Not that he cared for the poor—he was a thief, and since
he was in charge of the disciples' money, he often stole some for himself.
7 Jesus replied, "Leave her alone. She did this in preparation for my burial.
8 You will always have the poor among you, but you will not always have me."
9 When all the people* heard of Jesus' arrival, they flocked to see him and
also to see Lazarus, the man Jesus had raised from the dead. 10 Then the lead-
ing priests decided to kill Lazarus, too, 11 for it was because of him that many
of the people had deserted them* and believed in Jesus.

Jesus' Triumphant Entry

12 The next day, the news that Jesus was on the way to Jerusalem swept
through the city. A large crowd of Passover visitors 13 took palm branches
and went down the road to meet him. They shouted,

"Praise God!*
Blessings on the one who comes in the name of the LORD!
Hail to the King of Israel!"*

14 Jesus found a young donkey and rode on it, fulfilling the prophecy that
said:

15 "Don't be afraid, people of Jerusalem.*
Look, your King is coming,
riding on a donkey's colt."*

16 His disciples didn't understand at the time that this was a fulfillment
of prophecy. But after Jesus entered into his glory, they remembered what
had happened and realized that these things had been written about him.
17 Many in the crowd had seen Jesus call Lazarus from the tomb, raising
him from the dead, and they were telling others* about it. 18 That was the
reason so many went out to meet him—because they had heard about this

12:2 Or *who reclined.* 12:3 Greek *took 1 litra* [327 grams]. 12:5 Greek *worth 300 denarii.* A denarius was equivalent to a laborer's full day's wage. 12:9 Greek *Jewish people;* also in 12:11. 12:11 Or *had deserted their traditions;* Greek reads *had deserted.* 12:13a Greek *Hosanna,* an exclamation of praise adapted from a Hebrew expression that means "save now." 12:13b Ps 118:25-26; Zeph 3:15. 12:15a Greek *daughter of Zion.* 12:15b Zech 9:9. 12:17 Greek *were testifying.*

miraculous sign. 19 Then the Pharisees said to each other, "There's nothing
we can do. Look, everyone* has gone after him!"

Jesus Predicts His Death

20 Some Greeks who had come to Jerusalem for the Passover celebration
21 paid a visit to Philip, who was from Bethsaida in Galilee. They said, "Sir,
we want to meet Jesus." 22 Philip told Andrew about it, and they went to-
gether to ask Jesus.

23 Jesus replied, "Now the time has come for the Son of Man* to enter into
his glory. 24 I tell you the truth, unless a kernel of wheat is planted in the soil
and dies, it remains alone. But its death will produce many new kernels—a
plentiful harvest of new lives. 25 Those who love their life in this world will
lose it. Those who care nothing for their life in this world will keep it for
eternity. 26 Anyone who wants to serve me must follow me, because my ser-
vants must be where I am. And the Father will honor anyone who serves me.

27 "Now my soul is deeply troubled. Should I pray, 'Father, save me from this
hour'? But this is the very reason I came! 28 Father, bring glory to your name."

Then a voice spoke from heaven, saying, "I have already brought glory to
my name, and I will do so again." 29 When the crowd heard the voice, some
thought it was thunder, while others declared an angel had spoken to him.

30 Then Jesus told them, "The voice was for your benefit, not mine. 31 The
time for judging this world has come, when Satan, the ruler of this world,
will be cast out. 32 And when I am lifted up from the earth, I will draw every-
one to myself." 33 He said this to indicate how he was going to die.

34 The crowd responded, "We understood from Scripture* that the Mes-
siah would live forever. How can you say the Son of Man will die? Just who
is this Son of Man, anyway?"

35 Jesus replied, "My light will shine for you just a little longer. Walk in
the light while you can, so the darkness will not overtake you. Those who
walk in the darkness cannot see where they are going. 36 Put your trust in the
light while there is still time; then you will become children of the light."

After saying these things, Jesus went away and was hidden from them.

The Unbelief of the People

37 But despite all the miraculous signs Jesus had done, most of the people
still did not believe in him. 38 This is exactly what Isaiah the prophet had
predicted:

"LORD, who has believed our message?
To whom has the LORD revealed his powerful arm?"*

39 But the people couldn't believe, for as Isaiah also said,

40 "The Lord has blinded their eyes
and hardened their hearts—
so that their eyes cannot see,
and their hearts cannot understand,
and they cannot turn to me
and have me heal them."*

12:19 Greek *the world.* 12:23 "Son of Man" is a title Jesus used for himself. 12:34 Greek *from the law.* 12:38 Isa 53:1. 12:40 Isa 6:10.

Prayer **12:46**

Dear Jesus, help me to stop groping around in the darkness. Call me to walk in your light. Amen.

Make a Difference

13:1–5

So

If you had all the power in the world, what would you do with it? Would you make life comfortable for yourself, hire people to bring you a burrito whenever you felt hungry, or try to become pals with someone famous? The Bible says that Jesus had all the power in the world, but he didn't use his power to serve himself. In fact, right before he was betrayed and arrested, right before he was beaten and ridiculed, right before the soldiers drove nails into his hands and feet, Jesus did something that you wouldn't expect from the most powerful being on earth. John, in his eyewitness account, said that Jesus knew the Father had given him all authority, so he humbly served the disciples.

Difference Maker

Think of a way to bless someone with whatever authority God has blessed you.

41 Isaiah was referring to Jesus when he said this, because he saw the future
and spoke of the Messiah's glory. 42 Many people did believe in him, however,
including some of the Jewish leaders. But they wouldn't admit it for fear
that the Pharisees would expel them from the synagogue. 43 For they loved
human praise more than the praise of God.
44 Jesus shouted to the crowds, "If you trust me, you are trusting not only me,
but also God who sent me. 45 For when you see me, you are seeing the one who
sent me. 46 I have come as a light to shine in this dark world, so that all who put
their trust in me will no longer remain in the dark. 47 I will not judge those who
hear me but don't obey me, for I have come to save the world and not to judge it.
48 But all who reject me and my message will be judged on the day of judgment
by the truth I have spoken. 49 I don't speak on my own authority. The Father
who sent me has commanded me what to say and how to say it. 50 And I know
his commands lead to eternal life; so I say whatever the Father tells me to say."

Jesus Washes His Disciples' Feet

13 Before the Passover celebration, Jesus knew that his hour had come
to leave this world and return to his Father. He had loved his disciples during his ministry on earth, and now he loved them to the very end.*
2 It was time for supper, and the devil had already prompted Judas,* son of
Simon Iscariot, to betray Jesus. 3 Jesus knew that the Father had given him
authority over everything and that he had come from God and would return
to God. 4 So he got up from the table, took off his robe, wrapped a towel
around his waist, 5 and poured water into a basin. Then he began to wash the
disciples' feet, drying them with the towel he had around him.
6 When Jesus came to Simon Peter, Peter said to him, "Lord, are you going
to wash my feet?"
7 Jesus replied, "You don't understand now what I am doing, but someday
you will."
8 "No," Peter protested, "you will never ever wash my feet!"
Jesus replied, "Unless I wash you, you won't belong to me."
9 Simon Peter exclaimed, "Then wash my hands and head as well, Lord,
not just my feet!"
10 Jesus replied, "A person who has bathed all over does not need to wash,
except for the feet,* to be entirely clean. And you disciples are clean, but not
all of you." 11 For Jesus knew who would betray him. That is what he meant
when he said, "Not all of you are clean."
12 After washing their feet, he put on his robe again and sat down and
asked, "Do you understand what I was doing? 13 You call me 'Teacher' and
'Lord,' and you are right, because that's what I am. 14 And since I, your Lord
and Teacher, have washed your feet, you ought to wash each other's feet. 15 I
have given you an example to follow. Do as I have done to you. 16 I tell you
the truth, slaves are not greater than their master. Nor is the messenger more
important than the one who sends the message. 17 Now that you know these
things, God will bless you for doing them.

Jesus Predicts His Betrayal

18 "I am not saying these things to all of you; I know the ones I have chosen.
But this fulfills the Scripture that says, 'The one who eats my food has turned

13:1 Or *he showed them the full extent of his love.* **13:2** Or *the devil had already intended for Judas.*
13:10 Some manuscripts do not include *except for the feet.*

against me.'* 19 I tell you this beforehand, so that when it happens you will
believe that I AM the Messiah.* 20 I tell you the truth, anyone who welcomes
my messenger is welcoming me, and anyone who welcomes me is welcoming
the Father who sent me."
21 Now Jesus was deeply troubled,* and he exclaimed, "I tell you the truth,
one of you will betray me!"
22 The disciples looked at each other, wondering whom he could mean.
23 The disciple Jesus loved was sitting next to Jesus at the table.* 24 Simon
Peter motioned to him to ask, "Who's he talking about?" 25 So that disciple
leaned over to Jesus and asked, "Lord, who is it?"
26 Jesus responded, "It is the one to whom I give the bread I dip in the
bowl." And when he had dipped it, he gave it to Judas, son of Simon Iscar-
iot. 27 When Judas had eaten the bread, Satan entered into him. Then Jesus
told him, "Hurry and do what you're going to do." 28 None of the others at
the table knew what Jesus meant. 29 Since Judas was their treasurer, some
thought Jesus was telling him to go and pay for the food or to give some
money to the poor. 30 So Judas left at once, going out into the night.

Jesus Predicts Peter's Denial

31 As soon as Judas left the room, Jesus said, "The time has come for the Son
of Man* to enter into his glory, and God will be glorified because of him.
32 And since God receives glory because of the Son,* he will give his own
glory to the Son, and he will do so at once. 33 Dear children, I will be with
you only a little longer. And as I told the Jewish leaders, you will search for
me, but you can't come where I am going. 34 So now I am giving you a new
commandment: Love each other. Just as I have loved you, you should love
each other. 35 Your love for one another will prove to the world that you are
my disciples."
36 Simon Peter asked, "Lord, where are you going?"
And Jesus replied, "You can't go with me now, but you will follow me
later."
37 "But why can't I come now, Lord?" he asked. "I'm ready to die for you."
38 Jesus answered, "Die for me? I tell you the truth, Peter—before the
rooster crows tomorrow morning, you will deny three times that you even
know me.

Jesus, the Way to the Father

14 "Don't let your hearts be troubled. Trust in God, and trust also in
me. 2 There is more than enough room in my Father's home.* If this
were not so, would I have told you that I am going to prepare a place for
you?* 3 When everything is ready, I will come and get you, so that you will
always be with me where I am. 4 And you know the way to where I am going."
5 "No, we don't know, Lord," Thomas said. "We have no idea where you
are going, so how can we know the way?"
6 Jesus told him, "I am the way, the truth, and the life. No one can come to

Make a Difference 14:1

In the Trouble

Even in the midst of trouble, Jesus is with you. He is not afraid, and neither should you be. He is in control, even if you feel like you're the only one trying to bail you out or even if you feel alone in your struggle against the current. Likely, Jesus will reveal his posture of peace. That's right. In the middle of what is causing you your greatest panic, Jesus is holding you together. He is amazing. In the end, either he may calm the storm or he may calm you, so in the middle of it, you must remember to trust.

Difference Maker

When your stress level starts to rise, remember that Jesus is not panicking. Take a deep breath and walk confidently through it.

Prayer 14:6

Jesus, I believe that you are the way, the truth, and the life. I believe that you are the only way for me to be saved. I place my trust in you. Amen.

13:18 Ps 41:9. 13:19 Or *that the 'I AM' has come;* or *that I am the LORD;* Greek reads *that I am.* See Exod 3:14. 13:21 Greek *was troubled in his spirit.* 13:23 Greek *was reclining on Jesus' bosom.* The "disciple Jesus loved" was probably John. 13:31 "Son of Man" is a title Jesus used for himself. 13:32 Several early manuscripts do not include *And since God receives glory because of the Son.* 14:2a Or *There are many rooms in my Father's house.* 14:2b Or *If this were not so, I would have told you that I am going to prepare a place for you.* Some manuscripts read *If this were not so, I would have told you. I am going to prepare a place for you.*

the Father except through me. 7If you had really known me, you would know
who my Father is.* From now on, you do know him and have seen him!"
8Philip said, "Lord, show us the Father, and we will be satisfied."
9Jesus replied, "Have I been with you all this time, Philip, and yet you still
don't know who I am? Anyone who has seen me has seen the Father! So why
are you asking me to show him to you? 10Don't you believe that I am in the
Father and the Father is in me? The words I speak are not my own, but my
Father who lives in me does his work through me. 11Just believe that I am
in the Father and the Father is in me. Or at least believe because of the work
you have seen me do.
12"I tell you the truth, anyone who believes in me will do the same works I
have done, and even greater works, because I am going to be with the Father.
13You can ask for anything in my name, and I will do it, so that the Son can
bring glory to the Father. 14Yes, ask me for anything in my name, and I will do it!

Jesus Promises the Holy Spirit

15"If you love me, obey* my commandments. 16And I will ask the Father, and
he will give you another Advocate,* who will never leave you. 17He is the Holy
Spirit, who leads into all truth. The world cannot receive him, because it isn't
looking for him and doesn't recognize him. But you know him, because he
lives with you now and later will be in you.* 18No, I will not abandon you as
orphans—I will come to you. 19Soon the world will no longer see me, but you
will see me. Since I live, you also will live. 20When I am raised to life again,
you will know that I am in my Father, and you are in me, and I am in you.
21Those who accept my commandments and obey them are the ones who
love me. And because they love me, my Father will love them. And I will love
them and reveal myself to each of them."
22Judas (not Judas Iscariot, but the other disciple with that name) said to
him, "Lord, why are you going to reveal yourself only to us and not to the
world at large?"
23Jesus replied, "All who love me will do what I say. My Father will love
them, and we will come and make our home with each of them. 24Anyone
who doesn't love me will not obey me. And remember, my words are not my
own. What I am telling you is from the Father who sent me. 25I am telling you
these things now while I am still with you. 26But when the Father sends the
Advocate as my representative—that is, the Holy Spirit—he will teach you
everything and will remind you of everything I have told you.
27"I am leaving you with a gift—peace of mind and heart. And the peace I
give is a gift the world cannot give. So don't be troubled or afraid. 28Remem-
ber what I told you: I am going away, but I will come back to you again. If you
really loved me, you would be happy that I am going to the Father, who is
greater than I am. 29I have told you these things before they happen so that
when they do happen, you will believe.
30"I don't have much more time to talk to you, because the ruler of this
world approaches. He has no power over me, 31but I will do what the Father
requires of me, so that the world will know that I love the Father. Come,
let's be going.

14:7 Some manuscripts read *If you have really known me, you will know who my Father is.* 14:15 Other manuscripts read *you will obey;* still others read *you should obey.* 14:16 Or *Comforter,* or *Encourager,* or *Counselor.* Greek reads *Paraclete;* also in 14:26. 14:17 Some manuscripts read *and is in you.*

Make a Difference

14:15–18

Never Leave

To obey simply means to listen. Jesus stated the obvious: if you love him, then you'll listen to him. If you listen to him, then the Father will give you his Spirit, who will come to your aid, comfort you, empower you, and stand up for you in every circumstance at any given moment.

Difference Maker

Turn to the back of this Bible and pray through the section on "How to Accept Jesus as Your Lord and Savior."

Make a Difference 14:23

Living Room

Imagine if Jesus walked in and sat down among all the clutter, in the midst of stains, crumbs, filth, dust, and the garbage you'd been putting into your soul. Before you could protest, Jesus gets out the vacuum, the carpet cleaner, the dustrag, and the window cleaner, and he repairs the rip in the couch and throws away the trash and puts his Word out on the coffee table. Then he sits down on the sofa and puts his feet up with a smile. Aah.

Difference Maker

Clean up your room or house today. As you do, think about Jesus making himself at home in you.

Make a Difference

15:1–4

Prune

Pruning is the act of cutting off parts of a plant that are dead and aren't producing fruit. A gardener decides to remove a branch or bud so

Jesus, the True Vine

15 "I am the true grapevine, and my Father is the gardener. 2 He cuts
off every branch of mine that doesn't produce fruit, and he prunes
the branches that do bear fruit so they will produce even more. 3 You have
already been pruned and purified by the message I have given you. 4 Remain
in me, and I will remain in you. For a branch cannot produce fruit if it is
severed from the vine, and you cannot be fruitful unless you remain in me.
5 "Yes, I am the vine; you are the branches. Those who remain in me, and
I in them, will produce much fruit. For apart from me you can do nothing.
6 Anyone who does not remain in me is thrown away like a useless branch
and withers. Such branches are gathered into a pile to be burned. 7 But if you
remain in me and my words remain in you, you may ask for anything you
want, and it will be granted! 8 When you produce much fruit, you are my true
disciples. This brings great glory to my Father.
9 "I have loved you even as the Father has loved me. Remain in my love.
10 When you obey my commandments, you remain in my love, just as I obey
my Father's commandments and remain in his love. 11 I have told you these
things so that you will be filled with my joy. Yes, your joy will overflow!
12 This is my commandment: Love each other in the same way I have loved
you. 13 There is no greater love than to lay down one's life for one's friends.
14 You are my friends if you do what I command. 15 I no longer call you slaves,
because a master doesn't confide in his slaves. Now you are my friends, since I
have told you everything the Father told me. 16 You didn't choose me. I chose
you. I appointed you to go and produce lasting fruit, so that the Father will
give you whatever you ask for, using my name. 17 This is my command: Love
each other.

The World's Hatred

18 "If the world hates you, remember that it hated me first. 19 The world would
love you as one of its own if you belonged to it, but you are no longer part
of the world. I chose you to come out of the world, so it hates you. 20 Do you
remember what I told you? 'A slave is not greater than the master.' Since they
persecuted me, naturally they will persecute you. And if they had listened
to me, they would listen to you. 21 They will do all this to you because of me,
for they have rejected the one who sent me. 22 They would not be guilty if I
had not come and spoken to them. But now they have no excuse for their
sin. 23 Anyone who hates me also hates my Father. 24 If I hadn't done such
miraculous signs among them that no one else could do, they would not be
guilty. But as it is, they have seen everything I did, yet they still hate me and
my Father. 25 This fulfills what is written in their Scriptures*: 'They hated
me without cause.'
26 "But I will send you the Advocate*—the Spirit of truth. He will come to
you from the Father and will testify all about me. 27 And you must also testify
about me because you have been with me from the beginning of my ministry.

16 "I have told you these things so that you won't abandon your faith.
2 For you will be expelled from the synagogues, and the time is com-
ing when those who kill you will think they are doing a holy service for God.
3 This is because they have never known the Father or me. 4 Yes, I'm telling

15:25 Greek *in their law.* Pss 35:19; 69:4. **15:26** Or *Comforter,* or *Encourager,* or *Counselor.* Greek reads *Paraclete.*

that the plant can flourish in times to come.

Jesus promised that those who want to follow God will go through the pruning process too.

Difference Maker

Buy a bonsai tree, learn how to care for it and prune it. Keep it in your room all year as a reminder of the difference God makes in your life.

Make a Difference

15:4-11

Remain

As long as you are fastened to Jesus, whatever you do begins to produce abundance in your life. Your ugly habits begin to disappear because you are securely connected to Jesus, who sanctifies you, and your beautiful habits begin to flourish because you are being grafted into Jesus, who nourishes you.

Difference Maker

Wrap a piece of duct tape around your wrist or finger (not too tightly!). Wear it as a reminder today to be in close relationship with Jesus.

Make a Difference

15:12-17

Give Away Your Faith

You have been entrusted with the good news of Jesus Christ. He has saved you, and he has loved you. Inspire people by the way you live out your faith today. Giving away your faith is one of the most important things you can do today.

Difference Maker

Try sharing your faith with someone else today. Ask Jesus to open the opportunity. Trust him to lead you.

Make a Difference
16:33

Take Heart

If you decide to live for Jesus today, then take heart. It is not easy to decide to go against the flow of the culture, to stand for truth, to rally around those who are outcast, to speak up for those who cannot defend themselves, and to do it with humility and integrity. Following Jesus means not following the patterns in society that are self-serving or peer-pressured or garbage-grabbing. Following Jesus means making a difference in a world that needs someone to make a difference.

That is not easy. Then again, Jesus didn't say it would be easy. He said he would give us peace and strength and that he would fight on our behalf. He said he would empower and embolden us and that he would be with us as we stand for the truth. He said he would enable us to love the unlovable and to fight the good fight of faith.

Jesus wants to change this world. He wants you to change it with him.

Difference Maker

Stand up for Jesus with an emboldened heart today, trusting him for the outcome.

you these things now, so that when they happen, you will remember my
warning. I didn't tell you earlier because I was going to be with you for a
while longer.

The Work of the Holy Spirit

5“But now I am going away to the one who sent me, and not one of you
is asking where I am going. 6Instead, you grieve because of what I've told
you. 7But in fact, it is best for you that I go away, because if I don't, the Ad-
vocate* won't come. If I do go away, then I will send him to you. 8And when
he comes, he will convict the world of its sin, and of God's righteousness,
and of the coming judgment. 9The world's sin is that it refuses to believe
in me. 10Righteousness is available because I go to the Father, and you will
see me no more. 11Judgment will come because the ruler of this world has
already been judged.

12“There is so much more I want to tell you, but you can't bear it now.
13When the Spirit of truth comes, he will guide you into all truth. He will not
speak on his own but will tell you what he has heard. He will tell you about
the future. 14He will bring me glory by telling you whatever he receives from
me. 15All that belongs to the Father is mine; this is why I said, ‘The Spirit will
tell you whatever he receives from me.’

Sadness Will Be Turned to Joy

16“In a little while you won't see me anymore. But a little while after that,
you will see me again.”

17Some of the disciples asked each other, “What does he mean when he
says, ‘In a little while you won't see me, but then you will see me,’ and ‘I am
going to the Father’? 18And what does he mean by ‘a little while’? We don't
understand.”

19Jesus realized they wanted to ask him about it, so he said, “Are you ask-
ing yourselves what I meant? I said in a little while you won't see me, but a
little while after that you will see me again. 20I tell you the truth, you will
weep and mourn over what is going to happen to me, but the world will re-
joice. You will grieve, but your grief will suddenly turn to wonderful joy. 21It
will be like a woman suffering the pains of labor. When her child is born, her
anguish gives way to joy because she has brought a new baby into the world.
22So you have sorrow now, but I will see you again; then you will rejoice, and
no one can rob you of that joy. 23At that time you won't need to ask me for
anything. I tell you the truth, you will ask the Father directly, and he will
grant your request because you use my name. 24You haven't done this before.
Ask, using my name, and you will receive, and you will have abundant joy.

25“I have spoken of these matters in figures of speech, but soon I will stop
speaking figuratively and will tell you plainly all about the Father. 26Then
you will ask in my name. I'm not saying I will ask the Father on your behalf,
27for the Father himself loves you dearly because you love me and believe that
I came from God.* 28Yes, I came from the Father into the world, and now I
will leave the world and return to the Father.”

29Then his disciples said, “At last you are speaking plainly and not figura-
tively. 30Now we understand that you know everything, and there's no need
to question you. From this we believe that you came from God.”

16:7 Or *Comforter,* or *Encourager,* or *Counselor.* Greek reads *Paraclete.* **16:27** Some manuscripts read *from the Father.*

[31] Jesus asked, "Do you finally believe? [32] But the time is coming—indeed
it's here now—when you will be scattered, each one going his own way, leav-
ing me alone. Yet I am not alone because the Father is with me. [33] I have told
you all this so that you may have peace in me. Here on earth you will have
many trials and sorrows. But take heart, because I have overcome the world."

The Prayer of Jesus

17 After saying all these things, Jesus looked up to heaven and said, "Fa-
ther, the hour has come. Glorify your Son so he can give glory back to
you. [2] For you have given him authority over everyone. He gives eternal life
to each one you have given him. [3] And this is the way to have eternal life—to
know you, the only true God, and Jesus Christ, the one you sent to earth. [4] I
brought glory to you here on earth by completing the work you gave me to
do. [5] Now, Father, bring me into the glory we shared before the world began.

[6] "I have revealed you* to the ones you gave me from this world. They were
always yours. You gave them to me, and they have kept your word. [7] Now they
know that everything I have is a gift from you, [8] for I have passed on to them
the message you gave me. They accepted it and know that I came from you,
and they believe you sent me.

[9] "My prayer is not for the world, but for those you have given me, because
they belong to you. [10] All who are mine belong to you, and you have given
them to me, so they bring me glory. [11] Now I am departing from the world;
they are staying in this world, but I am coming to you. Holy Father, you have
given me your name;* now protect them by the power of your name so that
they will be united just as we are. [12] During my time here, I protected them
by the power of the name you gave me.* I guarded them so that not one was
lost, except the one headed for destruction, as the Scriptures foretold.

[13] "Now I am coming to you. I told them many things while I was with
them in this world so they would be filled with my joy. [14] I have given them
your word. And the world hates them because they do not belong to the
world, just as I do not belong to the world. [15] I'm not asking you to take
them out of the world, but to keep them safe from the evil one. [16] They do
not belong to this world any more than I do. [17] Make them holy by your truth;
teach them your word, which is truth. [18] Just as you sent me into the world,
I am sending them into the world. [19] And I give myself as a holy sacrifice for
them so they can be made holy by your truth.

[20] "I am praying not only for these disciples but also for all who will ever
believe in me through their message. [21] I pray that they will all be one, just as
you and I are one—as you are in me, Father, and I am in you. And may they
be in us so that the world will believe you sent me.

[22] "I have given them the glory you gave me, so they may be one as we are
one. [23] I am in them and you are in me. May they experience such perfect
unity that the world will know that you sent me and that you love them as
much as you love me. [24] Father, I want these whom you have given me to be
with me where I am. Then they can see all the glory you gave me because you
loved me even before the world began!

[25] "O righteous Father, the world doesn't know you, but I do; and these
disciples know you sent me. [26] I have revealed you to them, and I will con-
tinue to do so. Then your love for me will be in them, and I will be in them."

17:6 Greek *have revealed your name;* also in 17:26. **17:11** Some manuscripts read *you have given me these [disciples].* **17:12** Some manuscripts read *I protected those you gave me, by the power of your name.*

Make a Difference

17:20

Jesus Had You in Mind

Jesus had you in mind. Right before he was arrested and crucified, Jesus had a strategic time of prayer. He and his disciples had finished their Last Supper and walked to the garden of Gethsemane. Jesus spent his time in the garden praying. He prayed for his disciples, who were about to get scared and scattered. He also prayed for you.

In his prayer, Jesus looked forward to the day when you would be tested as his follower. Would you run and fall, like the disciples would later that night? Would you be restored and empowered to spread his good news, just like the disciples soon would? Jesus prayed in the garden for you. He prayed that you would stand close to him so that the world would be changed through you.

Difference Maker

Be intimate with Jesus through a dedicated time of prayer and reading the Bible and then share his message with someone today.

Prayer **18:4**

Jesus, even though you fully realized all that was going to happen, you still chose to step forward to meet your fate. Your love overwhelms me! Amen.

Question **18:5**

Go back through John's gospel and look for all the "I am" statements Jesus made. What is Jesus trying to tell you about himself?

Jesus Is Betrayed and Arrested

18 After saying these things, Jesus crossed the Kidron Valley with his
disciples and entered a grove of olive trees. 2 Judas, the betrayer, knew
this place, because Jesus had often gone there with his disciples. 3 The leading
priests and Pharisees had given Judas a contingent of Roman soldiers and
Temple guards to accompany him. Now with blazing torches, lanterns, and
weapons, they arrived at the olive grove.

4 Jesus fully realized all that was going to happen to him, so he stepped
forward to meet them. "Who are you looking for?" he asked.

5 "Jesus the Nazarene,"* they replied.

"I AM he,"* Jesus said. (Judas, who betrayed him, was standing with them.)
6 As Jesus said "I AM he," they all drew back and fell to the ground! 7 Once
more he asked them, "Who are you looking for?"

And again they replied, "Jesus the Nazarene."

8 "I told you that I AM he," Jesus said. "And since I am the one you want,
let these others go." 9 He did this to fulfill his own statement: "I did not lose
a single one of those you have given me."*

10 Then Simon Peter drew a sword and slashed off the right ear of Malchus,
the high priest's slave. 11 But Jesus said to Peter, "Put your sword back into its
sheath. Shall I not drink from the cup of suffering the Father has given me?"

Jesus at the High Priest's House

12 So the soldiers, their commanding officer, and the Temple guards arrested
Jesus and tied him up. 13 First they took him to Annas, since he was the father-
in-law of Caiaphas, the high priest at that time.* 14 Caiaphas was the one who
had told the other Jewish leaders, "It's better that one man should die for
the people."

Peter's First Denial

15 Simon Peter followed Jesus, as did another of the disciples. That other dis-
ciple was acquainted with the high priest, so he was allowed to enter the
high priest's courtyard with Jesus. 16 Peter had to stay outside the gate. Then
the disciple who knew the high priest spoke to the woman watching at the
gate, and she let Peter in. 17 The woman asked Peter, "You're not one of that
man's disciples, are you?"

"No," he said, "I am not."

18 Because it was cold, the household servants and the guards had made
a charcoal fire. They stood around it, warming themselves, and Peter stood
with them, warming himself.

The High Priest Questions Jesus

19 Inside, the high priest began asking Jesus about his followers and what
he had been teaching them. 20 Jesus replied, "Everyone knows what I teach.
I have preached regularly in the synagogues and the Temple, where the
people* gather. I have not spoken in secret. 21 Why are you asking me this
question? Ask those who heard me. They know what I said."

22 Then one of the Temple guards standing nearby slapped Jesus across the
face. "Is that the way to answer the high priest?" he demanded.

18:5a Or *Jesus of Nazareth;* also in 18:7. 18:5b Or *"The 'I AM' is here";* or *"I am the LORD";* Greek reads *I am;* also in 18:6, 8. See Exod 3:14. 18:9 See John 6:39 and 17:12. 18:13 Greek *that year.* 18:20 Greek *Jewish people;* also in 18:38.

23 Jesus replied, "If I said anything wrong, you must prove it. But if I'm
speaking the truth, why are you beating me?"
24 Then Annas bound Jesus and sent him to Caiaphas, the high priest.

Peter's Second and Third Denials

25 Meanwhile, as Simon Peter was standing by the fire warming himself, they
asked him again, "You're not one of his disciples, are you?"
He denied it, saying, "No, I am not."
26 But one of the household slaves of the high priest, a relative of the man
whose ear Peter had cut off, asked, "Didn't I see you out there in the olive
grove with Jesus?" 27 Again Peter denied it. And immediately a rooster crowed.

Jesus' Trial before Pilate

28 Jesus' trial before Caiaphas ended in the early hours of the morning. Then
he was taken to the headquarters of the Roman governor.* His accusers didn't
go inside because it would defile them, and they wouldn't be allowed to
celebrate the Passover. 29 So Pilate, the governor, went out to them and asked,
"What is your charge against this man?"
30 "We wouldn't have handed him over to you if he weren't a criminal!"
they retorted.
31 "Then take him away and judge him by your own law," Pilate told them.
"Only the Romans are permitted to execute someone," the Jewish lead-
ers replied. 32 (This fulfilled Jesus' prediction about the way he would die.*)
33 Then Pilate went back into his headquarters and called for Jesus to be
brought to him. "Are you the king of the Jews?" he asked him.
34 Jesus replied, "Is this your own question, or did others tell you about me?"
35 "Am I a Jew?" Pilate retorted. "Your own people and their leading priests
brought you to me for trial. Why? What have you done?"
36 Jesus answered, "My Kingdom is not an earthly kingdom. If it were,
my followers would fight to keep me from being handed over to the Jewish
leaders. But my Kingdom is not of this world."
37 Pilate said, "So you are a king?"
Jesus responded, "You say I am a king. Actually, I was born and came into
the world to testify to the truth. All who love the truth recognize that what
I say is true."
38 "What is truth?" Pilate asked. Then he went out again to the people and
told them, "He is not guilty of any crime. 39 But you have a custom of asking
me to release one prisoner each year at Passover. Would you like me to release
this 'King of the Jews'?"
40 But they shouted back, "No! Not this man. We want Barabbas!" (Barab-
bas was a revolutionary.)

Jesus Sentenced to Death

19 Then Pilate had Jesus flogged with a lead-tipped whip. 2 The soldiers
wove a crown of thorns and put it on his head, and they put a purple
robe on him. 3 "Hail! King of the Jews!" they mocked, as they slapped him
across the face.
4 Pilate went outside again and said to the people, "I am going to bring
him out to you now, but understand clearly that I find him not guilty." 5 Then

18:28 Greek *to the Praetorium;* also in 18:33. 18:32 See John 12:32-33.

Question 19:15

Why would anyone ever
choose someone other than
Jesus to rule over their life?

Jesus came out wearing the crown of thorns and the purple robe. And Pilate
said, "Look, here is the man!"
6When they saw him, the leading priests and Temple guards began shout-
ing, "Crucify him! Crucify him!"
"Take him yourselves and crucify him," Pilate said. "I find him not guilty."
7The Jewish leaders replied, "By our law he ought to die because he called
himself the Son of God."
8When Pilate heard this, he was more frightened than ever. 9He took Jesus
back into the headquarters* again and asked him, "Where are you from?" But
Jesus gave no answer. 10"Why don't you talk to me?" Pilate demanded. "Don't
you realize that I have the power to release you or crucify you?"
11Then Jesus said, "You would have no power over me at all unless it were
given to you from above. So the one who handed me over to you has the
greater sin."
12Then Pilate tried to release him, but the Jewish leaders shouted, "If you
release this man, you are no 'friend of Caesar.'* Anyone who declares himself
a king is a rebel against Caesar."
13When they said this, Pilate brought Jesus out to them again. Then Pilate
sat down on the judgment seat on the platform that is called the Stone Pave-
ment (in Hebrew, *Gabbatha*). 14It was now about noon on the day of prepara-
tion for the Passover. And Pilate said to the people,* "Look, here is your king!"
15"Away with him," they yelled. "Away with him! Crucify him!"
"What? Crucify your king?" Pilate asked.
"We have no king but Caesar," the leading priests shouted back.
16Then Pilate turned Jesus over to them to be crucified.

The Crucifixion

So they took Jesus away. 17Carrying the cross by himself, he went to the place
called Place of the Skull (in Hebrew, *Golgotha*). 18There they nailed him to the
cross. Two others were crucified with him, one on either side, with Jesus
between them. 19And Pilate posted a sign on the cross that read, "Jesus of
Nazareth,* the King of the Jews." 20The place where Jesus was crucified was
near the city, and the sign was written in Hebrew, Latin, and Greek, so that
many people could read it.
21Then the leading priests objected and said to Pilate, "Change it from
'The King of the Jews' to 'He said, I am King of the Jews.'"
22Pilate replied, "No, what I have written, I have written."
23When the soldiers had crucified Jesus, they divided his clothes among
the four of them. They also took his robe, but it was seamless, woven in one
piece from top to bottom. 24So they said, "Rather than tearing it apart, let's
throw dice* for it." This fulfilled the Scripture that says, "They divided my
garments among themselves and threw dice for my clothing."* So that is
what they did.
25Standing near the cross were Jesus' mother, and his mother's sister, Mary
(the wife of Clopas), and Mary Magdalene. 26When Jesus saw his mother
standing there beside the disciple he loved, he said to her, "Dear woman,
here is your son." 27And he said to this disciple, "Here is your mother." And
from then on this disciple took her into his home.

19:9 Greek *the Praetorium.* **19:12** "Friend of Caesar" is a technical term that refers to an ally of the emperor. **19:14** Greek *Jewish people;* also in 19:20. **19:19** Or *Jesus the Nazarene.* **19:24a** Greek *cast lots.* **19:24b** Ps 22:18.

The Death of Jesus

28 Jesus knew that his mission was now finished, and to fulfill Scripture he
said, "I am thirsty."* 29 A jar of sour wine was sitting there, so they soaked
a sponge in it, put it on a hyssop branch, and held it up to his lips. 30 When
Jesus had tasted it, he said, "It is finished!" Then he bowed his head and
gave up his spirit.

31 It was the day of preparation, and the Jewish leaders didn't want the
bodies hanging there the next day, which was the Sabbath (and a very spe-
cial Sabbath, because it was Passover week). So they asked Pilate to hasten
their deaths by ordering that their legs be broken. Then their bodies could
be taken down. 32 So the soldiers came and broke the legs of the two men
crucified with Jesus. 33 But when they came to Jesus, they saw that he was
already dead, so they didn't break his legs. 34 One of the soldiers, however,
pierced his side with a spear, and immediately blood and water flowed out.
35 (This report is from an eyewitness giving an accurate account. He speaks
the truth so that you also may continue to believe.*) 36 These things hap-
pened in fulfillment of the Scriptures that say, "Not one of his bones will
be broken,"* 37 and "They will look on the one they pierced."*

Question **19:30**

These were Jesus' last words before he died. What did he finish? What difference does this make to you?

The Burial of Jesus

38 Afterward Joseph of Arimathea, who had been a secret disciple of Jesus
(because he feared the Jewish leaders), asked Pilate for permission to take
down Jesus' body. When Pilate gave permission, Joseph came and took
the body away. 39 With him came Nicodemus, the man who had come
to Jesus at night. He brought about seventy-five pounds* of perfumed
ointment made from myrrh and aloes. 40 Following Jewish burial cus-
tom, they wrapped Jesus' body with the spices in long sheets of linen
cloth. 41 The place of crucifixion was near a garden, where there was a new
tomb, never used before. 42 And so, because it was the day of preparation
for the Jewish Passover* and since the tomb was close at hand, they laid
Jesus there.

The Resurrection

20 Early on Sunday morning,* while it was still dark, Mary Magdalene
came to the tomb and found that the stone had been rolled away
from the entrance. 2 She ran and found Simon Peter and the other disciple,
the one whom Jesus loved. She said, "They have taken the Lord's body out
of the tomb, and we don't know where they have put him!"

3 Peter and the other disciple started out for the tomb. 4 They were both
running, but the other disciple outran Peter and reached the tomb first.
5 He stooped and looked in and saw the linen wrappings lying there, but he
didn't go in. 6 Then Simon Peter arrived and went inside. He also noticed
the linen wrappings lying there, 7 while the cloth that had covered Jesus'
head was folded up and lying apart from the other wrappings. 8 Then the
disciple who had reached the tomb first also went in, and he saw and
believed—9 for until then they still hadn't understood the Scriptures that
said Jesus must rise from the dead. 10 Then they went home.

19:28 See Pss 22:15; 69:21. **19:35** Some manuscripts read *that you also may believe.* **19:36** Exod 12:46; Num 9:12; Ps 34:20. **19:37** Zech 12:10. **19:39** Greek *100 litras* [32.7 kilograms]. **19:42** Greek *because of the Jewish day of preparation.* **20:1** Greek *On the first day of the week.*

Prayer 20:22

Lord Jesus, breathe the life of your Holy Spirit into me today so that I may serve you and make a difference in those around me. Amen.

Make a Difference

20:30–31

So Much More

We haven't begun to understand all that Jesus has done or all that he will yet do. The Bible only begins to reveal the great works he performed, the great love he shared, and the great hope he restored. Healings and miracles, signs and wonders. He fed, healed, and walked on water. Oh, and he created everything. Jesus is a pretty big deal.

So much more—that's what Jesus did. So much more. He did more than anyone could write about. He did more than his followers would ever be able to explain or share. So much more. That's what Jesus will do for you and for me. So much more. Our greatest desires for change in this world are but a scratch of what Jesus has envisioned. John, his closest follower, who wrote down so much of what we know about Jesus, said it so simply toward the end of his book.

Difference Maker

Pray and look. Pray for the miraculous work of Jesus in the lives of others. Remember all that he has already done and look expectantly for what he will do today.

Jesus Appears to Mary Magdalene

11 Mary was standing outside the tomb crying, and as she wept, she stooped
and looked in. 12 She saw two white-robed angels, one sitting at the head and
the other at the foot of the place where the body of Jesus had been lying.
13 "Dear woman, why are you crying?" the angels asked her.

"Because they have taken away my Lord," she replied, "and I don't know where they have put him."

14 She turned to leave and saw someone standing there. It was Jesus, but
she didn't recognize him. 15 "Dear woman, why are you crying?" Jesus asked
her. "Who are you looking for?"

She thought he was the gardener. "Sir," she said, "if you have taken him away, tell me where you have put him, and I will go and get him."

16 "Mary!" Jesus said.

She turned to him and cried out, "Rabboni!" (which is Hebrew for "Teacher").

17 "Don't cling to me," Jesus said, "for I haven't yet ascended to the Father.
But go find my brothers and tell them, 'I am ascending to my Father and your Father, to my God and your God.'"

18 Mary Magdalene found the disciples and told them, "I have seen the
Lord!" Then she gave them his message.

Jesus Appears to His Disciples

19 That Sunday evening* the disciples were meeting behind locked doors
because they were afraid of the Jewish leaders. Suddenly, Jesus was standing
there among them! "Peace be with you," he said. 20 As he spoke, he showed
them the wounds in his hands and his side. They were filled with joy when
they saw the Lord! 21 Again he said, "Peace be with you. As the Father has sent
me, so I am sending you." 22 Then he breathed on them and said, "Receive
the Holy Spirit. 23 If you forgive anyone's sins, they are forgiven. If you do
not forgive them, they are not forgiven."

Jesus Appears to Thomas

24 One of the twelve disciples, Thomas (nicknamed the Twin),* was not with
the others when Jesus came. 25 They told him, "We have seen the Lord!"
But he replied, "I won't believe it unless I see the nail wounds in his hands, put my fingers into them, and place my hand into the wound in his side."

26 Eight days later the disciples were together again, and this time Thomas
was with them. The doors were locked; but suddenly, as before, Jesus was
standing among them. "Peace be with you," he said. 27 Then he said to
Thomas, "Put your finger here, and look at my hands. Put your hand into the wound in my side. Don't be faithless any longer. Believe!"

28 "My Lord and my God!" Thomas exclaimed.

29 Then Jesus told him, "You believe because you have seen me. Blessed are those who believe without seeing me."

Purpose of the Book

30 The disciples saw Jesus do many other miraculous signs in addition to the
ones recorded in this book. 31 But these are written so that you may continue
to believe* that Jesus is the Messiah, the Son of God, and that by believing in him you will have life by the power of his name.

20:19 Greek *In the evening of that day, the first day of the week.* **20:24** Greek *Thomas, who was called Didymus.* **20:31** Some manuscripts read *that you may believe.*

Epilogue: Jesus Appears to Seven Disciples

21 Later, Jesus appeared again to the disciples beside the Sea of Galilee.*
This is how it happened. 2 Several of the disciples were there—Simon
Peter, Thomas (nicknamed the Twin),* Nathanael from Cana in Galilee, the
sons of Zebedee, and two other disciples.
3 Simon Peter said, "I'm going fishing."
"We'll come, too," they all said. So they went out in the boat, but they
caught nothing all night.
4 At dawn Jesus was standing on the beach, but the disciples couldn't see
who he was. 5 He called out, "Fellows,* have you caught any fish?"
"No," they replied.
6 Then he said, "Throw out your net on the right-hand side of the boat,
and you'll get some!" So they did, and they couldn't haul in the net because
there were so many fish in it.
7 Then the disciple Jesus loved said to Peter, "It's the Lord!" When Simon
Peter heard that it was the Lord, he put on his tunic (for he had stripped for
work), jumped into the water, and headed to shore. 8 The others stayed with
the boat and pulled the loaded net to the shore, for they were only about
a hundred yards* from shore. 9 When they got there, they found breakfast
waiting for them—fish cooking over a charcoal fire, and some bread.
10 "Bring some of the fish you've just caught," Jesus said. 11 So Simon Peter
went aboard and dragged the net to the shore. There were 153 large fish, and
yet the net hadn't torn.
12 "Now come and have some breakfast!" Jesus said. None of the disciples
dared to ask him, "Who are you?" They knew it was the Lord. 13 Then Jesus
served them the bread and the fish. 14 This was the third time Jesus had ap-
peared to his disciples since he had been raised from the dead.
15 After breakfast Jesus asked Simon Peter, "Simon son of John, do you love
me more than these?*"
"Yes, Lord," Peter replied, "you know I love you."
"Then feed my lambs," Jesus told him.
16 Jesus repeated the question: "Simon son of John, do you love me?"
"Yes, Lord," Peter said, "you know I love you."
"Then take care of my sheep," Jesus said.
17 A third time he asked him, "Simon son of John, do you love me?"
Peter was hurt that Jesus asked the question a third time. He said, "Lord,
you know everything. You know that I love you."
Jesus said, "Then feed my sheep.
18 "I tell you the truth, when you were young, you were able to do as you
liked; you dressed yourself and went wherever you wanted to go. But when
you are old, you will stretch out your hands, and others* will dress you and
take you where you don't want to go." 19 Jesus said this to let him know by
what kind of death he would glorify God. Then Jesus told him, "Follow me."
20 Peter turned around and saw behind them the disciple Jesus loved—the
one who had leaned over to Jesus during supper and asked, "Lord, who will
betray you?" 21 Peter asked Jesus, "What about him, Lord?"
22 Jesus replied, "If I want him to remain alive until I return, what is that
to you? As for you, follow me." 23 So the rumor spread among the community

21:1 Greek *Sea of Tiberias,* another name for the Sea of Galilee. 21:2 Greek *Thomas, who was called Didymus.* 21:5 Greek *Children.* 21:8 Greek *200 cubits* [90 meters]. 21:15 Or *more than these others do?* 21:18 Some manuscripts read *and another one.*

Make a Difference

21:25

Jesus

Jesus...
Jesus comes for the sick.
Jesus seeks after the lost.
Jesus searches for runaways.
Jesus finds the hidden.
Jesus heals the broken.
Jesus gives footing to the lame.
Jesus opens the ears of the deaf.
Jesus restores sight to the blind.
Jesus frees the prisoner.
Jesus loves the sinner.
Jesus forgives the repentant.
Jesus strengthens the weak.
Jesus fills the empty.
Jesus dwells with the lonely.
Jesus weeps with the sad, the hurting, and the grieved.
Jesus comforts the mourner.
Jesus breathes into the lifeless.
Jesus lifts up the trampled.
Jesus gathers the displaced.
Jesus feeds the hungry.
Jesus quenches the thirsty.
Jesus puts the last at the front.
Jesus eats with the unsanitary.
Jesus dines with the despised.
Jesus carries the world's sins and burdens.
Jesus dies for his enemies.
Jesus bleeds for his friends.
Jesus stretches out his arms to welcome you home.
"Jesus also did many other things. If they were all written down, I suppose the whole world could not contain the books that would be written."

Difference Maker

What is one thing that he has done that you should put into action today?

of believers* that this disciple wouldn't die. But that isn't what Jesus said at
all. He only said, "If I want him to remain alive until I return, what is that
to you?"
24 This disciple is the one who testifies to these events and has recorded
them here. And we know that his account of these things is accurate.
25 Jesus also did many other things. If they were all written down, I sup-
pose the whole world could not contain the books that would be written.

21:23 Greek *the brothers.*

Acts Introduction

Ever wonder how something goes viral? How does that clip on the internet or that meme on social media go from obscurity to being shared across the world? Something that goes viral speaks to the moment, points to a truth many are unearthing, or is just seriously funny. There's a blueprint and a science behind the spontaneous, organic way that something goes viral.

The book of Acts is Luke's sequel, and it went viral. This is an exciting book—the journeys and heroic moments are nonstop. This is also an eye-popping book—the miracles and wonders are astonishing! This is also an honest book—the persecution for following Jesus is real. This is also a challenging book—the call to make a difference by telling people about Jesus is the call of every believer.

As you jump into the book of Acts, you'll discover ingredients for what makes something go viral. One of the things that makes the book of Acts so powerful is that it isn't just a book that tells you about what happened in the past, but it's also a living story that invites you into what is happening *now.* The book of Acts is more than a viral snapshot in time. It also reveals the blueprint of when and how a global movement started and how to discover your unique place in it.

As you read Luke's sequel to his gospel, put yourself in the story. Be there when the Holy Spirit settled upon the praying community at Pentecost. Be there when thousands were baptized. Be there when Stephen was killed while Saul looked on. Be there when Saul was confronted by the risen Jesus, who gave him a new mission in life. Be there when James was killed and Peter was arrested. Be there when Barnabas stuck up for Paul. Be there when Paul preached in Athens about an "unknown God." Be there when Paul appealed to Caesar. Be there when Paul was shipwrecked on the way to Rome.

Most of all, as you read Luke's sequel, put yourself in the viral trend of God's story. Let his Holy Spirit dwell in you and guide you to discover the power and passion of Jesus Christ.

Story Arcs

- **Luke**
- **Stephen**
- **Paul**
- **Philip**
- **Priscilla and Aquila**
- **Apollos**

Acts of the Apostles

The Promise of the Holy Spirit

1 In my first book* I told you, Theophilus, about everything Jesus began
to do and teach 2until the day he was taken up to heaven after giving his
chosen apostles further instructions through the Holy Spirit. 3During the
forty days after he suffered and died, he appeared to the apostles from time
to time, and he proved to them in many ways that he was actually alive. And
he talked to them about the Kingdom of God.
4Once when he was eating with them, he commanded them, "Do not leave
Jerusalem until the Father sends you the gift he promised, as I told you be-
fore. 5John baptized with* water, but in just a few days you will be baptized
with the Holy Spirit."

The Ascension of Jesus

6So when the apostles were with Jesus, they kept asking him, "Lord, has the
time come for you to free Israel and restore our kingdom?"
7He replied, "The Father alone has the authority to set those dates and
times, and they are not for you to know. 8But you will receive power when
the Holy Spirit comes upon you. And you will be my witnesses, telling people
about me everywhere—in Jerusalem, throughout Judea, in Samaria, and to
the ends of the earth."
9After saying this, he was taken up into a cloud while they were watching,
and they could no longer see him. 10As they strained to see him rising into
heaven, two white-robed men suddenly stood among them. 11"Men of Gal-
ilee," they said, "why are you standing here staring into heaven? Jesus has
been taken from you into heaven, but someday he will return from heaven
in the same way you saw him go!"

Matthias Replaces Judas

12Then the apostles returned to Jerusalem from the Mount of Olives, a dis-
tance of half a mile.* 13When they arrived, they went to the upstairs room of
the house where they were staying.
Here are the names of those who were present: Peter, John, James, Andrew,
Philip, Thomas, Bartholomew, Matthew, James (son of Alphaeus), Simon (the
zealot), and Judas (son of James). 14They all met together and were constantly
united in prayer, along with Mary the mother of Jesus, several other women,
and the brothers of Jesus.
15During this time, when about 120 believers* were together in one place,
Peter stood up and addressed them. 16"Brothers," he said, "the Scriptures had
to be fulfilled concerning Judas, who guided those who arrested Jesus. This
was predicted long ago by the Holy Spirit, speaking through King David.
17Judas was one of us and shared in the ministry with us."

1:1 The reference is to the Gospel of Luke. 1:5 Or *in;* also in 1:5b. 1:12 Greek *a Sabbath day's journey.* 1:15 Greek *brothers.*

Make a Difference **1:8**

Witness

A witness of a crime possesses information valuable to an investigation. A witness of an accident provides important testimony for an insurance company. A witness to a marriage signs a document declaring that the union truly occurred. A witness is someone who confirms that they saw something take place by giving accurate details of the event.

The early followers of Jesus saw him perform miracles, teach crowds, die on a cross, and rise again to life. They confirmed what they had seen by telling people everywhere. Today, followers of Jesus do the same thing.

Difference Maker

On the top of a piece of paper write, "What I have seen Jesus do." Then jot down what you have seen Jesus do in your life and give the paper to someone whom you don't know very well.

Story Arc **1:1-4**

● Luke

Imagine being an eyewitness to the dramatic growth of the early church. Imagine traveling with Paul and navigating Paul's constant trouble with arrests and imprisonments (Colossians 4:14; 2 Timothy 4:11; Philemon v. 24). As you read this sequel to Luke's gospel and see Luke insert himself into the narrative (see "we" in Acts 16:10), imagine what kind of grit the physician Luke (Colossians 4:14) must have had.

Acts 6:2-8 ►

18 (Judas had bought a field with the money he received for his treachery.
Falling headfirst there, his body split open, spilling out all his intestines.
19 The news of his death spread to all the people of Jerusalem, and they gave
the place the Aramaic name *Akeldama,* which means "Field of Blood.")

20 Peter continued, "This was written in the book of Psalms, where it says,
'Let his home become desolate, with no one living in it.' It also says, 'Let
someone else take his position.'*

21 "So now we must choose a replacement for Judas from among the
men who were with us the entire time we were traveling with the Lord
Jesus— 22 from the time he was baptized by John until the day he was taken
from us. Whoever is chosen will join us as a witness of Jesus' resurrection."

23 So they nominated two men: Joseph called Barsabbas (also known as
Justus) and Matthias. 24 Then they all prayed, "O Lord, you know every heart.
Show us which of these men you have chosen 25 as an apostle to replace Ju-
das in this ministry, for he has deserted us and gone where he belongs."
26 Then they cast lots, and Matthias was selected to become an apostle with
the other eleven.

The Holy Spirit Comes

2 On the day of Pentecost* all the believers were meeting together in one
place. 2 Suddenly, there was a sound from heaven like the roaring of a
mighty windstorm, and it filled the house where they were sitting. 3 Then,
what looked like flames or tongues of fire appeared and settled on each
of them. 4 And everyone present was filled with the Holy Spirit and began
speaking in other languages,* as the Holy Spirit gave them this ability.

5 At that time there were devout Jews from every nation living in Jerusa-
lem. 6 When they heard the loud noise, everyone came running, and they
were bewildered to hear their own languages being spoken by the believers.

7 They were completely amazed. "How can this be?" they exclaimed.
"These people are all from Galilee, 8 and yet we hear them speaking in our
own native languages! 9 Here we are—Parthians, Medes, Elamites, people
from Mesopotamia, Judea, Cappadocia, Pontus, the province of Asia,
10 Phrygia, Pamphylia, Egypt, and the areas of Libya around Cyrene, visitors
from Rome 11 (both Jews and converts to Judaism), Cretans, and Arabs. And
we all hear these people speaking in our own languages about the wonderful
things God has done!" 12 They stood there amazed and perplexed. "What can
this mean?" they asked each other.

13 But others in the crowd ridiculed them, saying, "They're just drunk,
that's all!"

Peter Preaches to the Crowd

14 Then Peter stepped forward with the eleven other apostles and shouted to
the crowd, "Listen carefully, all of you, fellow Jews and residents of Jerusa-
lem! Make no mistake about this. 15 These people are not drunk, as some of
you are assuming. Nine o'clock in the morning is much too early for that.
16 No, what you see was predicted long ago by the prophet Joel:

17 'In the last days,' God says,
'I will pour out my Spirit upon all people.

1:20 Pss 69:25; 109:8. **2:1** The Festival of Pentecost came 50 days after Passover (when Jesus was crucified). **2:4** Or *in other tongues.*

Make a Difference

2:1–12

Pentecost

It would be wrong to say that the first followers of Jesus—you know, the ones who changed the entire course of human history—had a great plan. They didn't sit around large conference room tables with the best minds in the industry or the most brilliant political strategists checking popular opinion polls every few minutes.

The truth is that they really didn't know what to do. After his resurrection, Jesus had given them instructions to wait. Jesus said he would send the Holy Spirit, who would empower them to be his witnesses to the ends of the earth. They waited according to his word, spent time praying, and went about their daily routines. They would gather together often and eat and talk about all they had seen Jesus do and all they had heard him say. They waited. Then God showed up.

Difference Maker

Gather some other followers of Jesus to wait with you for God to move. Pray and expect him to do something in your lives.

Question **2:9**

What does this list tell you about the diversity of the early church?

Your sons and daughters will prophesy.
Your young men will see visions,
and your old men will dream dreams.
18 In those days I will pour out my Spirit
even on my servants—men and women alike—
and they will prophesy.
19 And I will cause wonders in the heavens above
and signs on the earth below—
blood and fire and clouds of smoke.
20 The sun will become dark,
and the moon will turn blood red
before that great and glorious day of the
LORD arrives.
21 But everyone who calls on the name of the LORD
will be saved.'*

22"People of Israel, listen! God publicly endorsed Jesus the Nazarene* by
doing powerful miracles, wonders, and signs through him, as you well know.
23But God knew what would happen, and his prearranged plan was carried
out when Jesus was betrayed. With the help of lawless Gentiles, you nailed
him to a cross and killed him. 24But God released him from the horrors of
death and raised him back to life, for death could not keep him in its grip.
25King David said this about him:

'I see that the LORD is always with me.
I will not be shaken, for he is right beside me.
26 No wonder my heart is glad,
and my tongue shouts his praises!
My body rests in hope.
27 For you will not leave my soul among the dead*
or allow your Holy One to rot in the grave.
28 You have shown me the way of life,
and you will fill me with the joy of your presence.'*

29"Dear brothers, think about this! You can be sure that the patriarch Da-
vid wasn't referring to himself, for he died and was buried, and his tomb is
still here among us. 30But he was a prophet, and he knew God had promised
with an oath that one of David's own descendants would sit on his throne.
31David was looking into the future and speaking of the Messiah's resurrec-
tion. He was saying that God would not leave him among the dead or allow
his body to rot in the grave.
32"God raised Jesus from the dead, and we are all witnesses of this. 33Now
he is exalted to the place of highest honor in heaven, at God's right hand.
And the Father, as he had promised, gave him the Holy Spirit to pour out
upon us, just as you see and hear today. 34For David himself never ascended
into heaven, yet he said,

'The LORD said to my Lord,
"Sit in the place of honor at my right hand

2:17-21 Joel 2:28-32. **2:22** Or *Jesus of Nazareth.* **2:27** Greek *in Hades;* also in 2:31.
2:25-28 Ps 16:8-11 (Greek version).

35 until I humble your enemies,
making them a footstool under your feet.’”*

36 “So let everyone in Israel know for certain that God has made this Jesus,
whom you crucified, to be both Lord and Messiah!”
37 Peter’s words pierced their hearts, and they said to him and to the other
apostles, “Brothers, what should we do?”
38 Peter replied, “Each of you must repent of your sins and turn to God,
and be baptized in the name of Jesus Christ for the forgiveness of your sins.
Then you will receive the gift of the Holy Spirit. 39 This promise is to you, to
your children, and to those far away*—all who have been called by the Lord
our God.” 40 Then Peter continued preaching for a long time, strongly urging
all his listeners, “Save yourselves from this crooked generation!”
41 Those who believed what Peter said were baptized and added to the
church that day—about 3,000 in all.

The Believers Form a Community

42 All the believers devoted themselves to the apostles’ teaching, and to
fellowship, and to sharing in meals (including the Lord’s Supper*), and to
prayer.
43 A deep sense of awe came over them all, and the apostles performed
many miraculous signs and wonders. 44 And all the believers met together
in one place and shared everything they had. 45 They sold their property and
possessions and shared the money with those in need. 46 They worshiped
together at the Temple each day, met in homes for the Lord’s Supper, and
shared their meals with great joy and generosity*—47 all the while prais-
ing God and enjoying the goodwill of all the people. And each day the Lord
added to their fellowship those who were being saved.

Peter Heals a Crippled Beggar

3 Peter and John went to the Temple one afternoon to take part in the
three o’clock prayer service. 2 As they approached the Temple, a man
lame from birth was being carried in. Each day he was put beside the Temple
gate, the one called the Beautiful Gate, so he could beg from the people going
into the Temple. 3 When he saw Peter and John about to enter, he asked them
for some money.
4 Peter and John looked at him intently, and Peter said, “Look at us!” 5 The
lame man looked at them eagerly, expecting some money. 6 But Peter said,
“I don’t have any silver or gold for you. But I’ll give you what I have. In the
name of Jesus Christ the Nazarene,* get up and* walk!”
7 Then Peter took the lame man by the right hand and helped him up. And
as he did, the man’s feet and ankles were instantly healed and strengthened.
8 He jumped up, stood on his feet, and began to walk! Then, walking, leaping,
and praising God, he went into the Temple with them.
9 All the people saw him walking and heard him praising God. 10 When
they realized he was the lame beggar they had seen so often at the Beautiful
Gate, they were absolutely astounded! 11 They all rushed out in amazement to
Solomon’s Colonnade, where the man was holding tightly to Peter and John.

2:34-35 Ps 110:1. **2:39** Or *and to people far in the future,* or *and to the Gentiles.* **2:42** Greek *the breaking of bread;* also in 2:46. **2:46** Or *and sincere hearts.* **3:6a** Or *Jesus Christ of Nazareth.* **3:6b** Some manuscripts do not include *get up and.*

Make a Difference 2:42

Devoted

For many people, meals are often eaten on the go, last minute, and alone, but Christians can revive the lost art of the meal. We can relearn that there is a sacredness to eating with others. It’s called *fellowship*, that moment in the practice of everyday life when people who intentionally follow Jesus gather together to share life. In fellowship there is a great reminder that Jesus has drawn us together.

Difference Maker

Invite some people close to you to share a meal today. During the meal, make sure to give thanks, break bread, and drink in remembrance of what Jesus did on the cross for each of you.

Make a Difference 2:44-47

Share

There was so much sharing going on in the early church that everyone had everything they needed. Jesus had gotten such a hold of their lives that they felt they didn’t need to hold on to anything else. The presence of God’s grace in our hearts causes us to be people who share what he has so freely given to us.

Difference Maker

Take extra clothes to a thrift store or homeless shelter.

Question 2:46

On a scale of one to seven, how many days a week are you a follower of Jesus?

Peter Preaches in the Temple

12 Peter saw his opportunity and addressed the crowd. "People of Israel," he
said, "what is so surprising about this? And why stare at us as though we had
made this man walk by our own power or godliness? 13 For it is the God of
Abraham, Isaac, and Jacob—the God of all our ancestors—who has brought
glory to his servant Jesus by doing this. This is the same Jesus whom you
handed over and rejected before Pilate, despite Pilate's decision to release
him. 14 You rejected this holy, righteous one and instead demanded the re-
lease of a murderer. 15 You killed the author of life, but God raised him from
the dead. And we are witnesses of this fact!

16 "Through faith in the name of Jesus, this man was healed—and you
know how crippled he was before. Faith in Jesus' name has healed him be-
fore your very eyes.

17 "Friends,* I realize that what you and your leaders did to Jesus was done
in ignorance. 18 But God was fulfilling what all the prophets had foretold
about the Messiah—that he must suffer these things. 19 Now repent of your
sins and turn to God, so that your sins may be wiped away. 20 Then times of
refreshment will come from the presence of the Lord, and he will again send
you Jesus, your appointed Messiah. 21 For he must remain in heaven until
the time for the final restoration of all things, as God promised long ago
through his holy prophets. 22 Moses said, 'The LORD your God will raise up
for you a Prophet like me from among your own people. Listen carefully to
everything he tells you.'* 23 Then Moses said, 'Anyone who will not listen to
that Prophet will be completely cut off from God's people.'*

24 "Starting with Samuel, every prophet spoke about what is happening
today. 25 You are the children of those prophets, and you are included in
the covenant God promised to your ancestors. For God said to Abraham,
'Through your descendants* all the families on earth will be blessed.' 26 When
God raised up his servant, Jesus, he sent him first to you people of Israel, to
bless you by turning each of you back from your sinful ways."

Peter and John before the Council

4 While Peter and John were speaking to the people, they were confronted
by the priests, the captain of the Temple guard, and some of the Saddu-
cees. 2 These leaders were very disturbed that Peter and John were teaching
the people that through Jesus there is a resurrection of the dead. 3 They ar-
rested them and, since it was already evening, put them in jail until morning.
4 But many of the people who heard their message believed it, so the number
of men who believed now totaled about 5,000.

5 The next day the council of all the rulers and elders and teachers of re-
ligious law met in Jerusalem. 6 Annas the high priest was there, along with
Caiaphas, John, Alexander, and other relatives of the high priest. 7 They
brought in the two disciples and demanded, "By what power, or in whose
name, have you done this?"

8 Then Peter, filled with the Holy Spirit, said to them, "Rulers and elders
of our people, 9 are we being questioned today because we've done a good
deed for a crippled man? Do you want to know how he was healed? 10 Let me
clearly state to all of you and to all the people of Israel that he was healed
by the powerful name of Jesus Christ the Nazarene,* the man you crucified

3:17 Greek *Brothers.* 3:22 Deut 18:15. 3:23 Deut 18:19; Lev 23:29. 3:25 Greek *your seed;* see Gen 12:3; 22:18. 4:10 Or *Jesus Christ of Nazareth.*

but whom God raised from the dead. 11 For Jesus is the one referred to in the
Scriptures, where it says,

'The stone that you builders rejected
has now become the cornerstone.'*

12 There is salvation in no one else! God has given no other name under
heaven by which we must be saved."
13 The members of the council were amazed when they saw the boldness
of Peter and John, for they could see that they were ordinary men with no
special training in the Scriptures. They also recognized them as men who
had been with Jesus. 14 But since they could see the man who had been healed
standing right there among them, there was nothing the council could say.
15 So they ordered Peter and John out of the council chamber* and conferred
among themselves.
16 "What should we do with these men?" they asked each other. "We can't
deny that they have performed a miraculous sign, and everybody in Jerusa-
lem knows about it. 17 But to keep them from spreading their propaganda any
further, we must warn them not to speak to anyone in Jesus' name again."
18 So they called the apostles back in and commanded them never again to
speak or teach in the name of Jesus.
19 But Peter and John replied, "Do you think God wants us to obey you
rather than him? 20 We cannot stop telling about everything we have seen
and heard."
21 The council then threatened them further, but they finally let them go
because they didn't know how to punish them without starting a riot. For
everyone was praising God 22 for this miraculous sign—the healing of a man
who had been lame for more than forty years.

The Believers Pray for Courage
23 As soon as they were freed, Peter and John returned to the other believers
and told them what the leading priests and elders had said. 24 When they
heard the report, all the believers lifted their voices together in prayer to
God: "O Sovereign Lord, Creator of heaven and earth, the sea, and everything
in them—25 you spoke long ago by the Holy Spirit through our ancestor
David, your servant, saying,

'Why were the nations so angry?
Why did they waste their time with futile plans?
26 The kings of the earth prepared for battle;
the rulers gathered together
against the LORD
and against his Messiah.'*

27 "In fact, this has happened here in this very city! For Herod Antipas, Pon-
tius Pilate the governor, the Gentiles, and the people of Israel were all united
against Jesus, your holy servant, whom you anointed. 28 But everything they
did was determined beforehand according to your will. 29 And now, O Lord,
hear their threats, and give us, your servants, great boldness in preaching

4:11 Ps 118:22. 4:15 Greek *the Sanhedrin.* 4:25-26 Or *his anointed one;* or *his Christ.* Ps 2:1-2.

Make a Difference

4:16-22

We Can't Stop

When the authorities ordered Peter and John to "never again" speak or teach in the name of Jesus (v. 18), Peter and John explained, "We cannot stop telling about everything we have seen and heard" (v. 20).

Difference Maker

What is something that you know Jesus has done in your life? Make a point to speak about this in your youth group or share this with a friend during the week.

Question **4:36-37**

Would you be willing to live as generously as Barnabas? Why or why not?

your word. 30 Stretch out your hand with healing power; may miraculous
signs and wonders be done through the name of your holy servant Jesus."
31 After this prayer, the meeting place shook, and they were all filled with
the Holy Spirit. Then they preached the word of God with boldness.

The Believers Share Their Possessions

32 All the believers were united in heart and mind. And they felt that what
they owned was not their own, so they shared everything they had. 33 The
apostles testified powerfully to the resurrection of the Lord Jesus, and God's
great blessing was upon them all. 34 There were no needy people among
them, because those who owned land or houses would sell them 35 and bring
the money to the apostles to give to those in need.
36 For instance, there was Joseph, the one the apostles nicknamed Barnabas
(which means "Son of Encouragement"). He was from the tribe of Levi and
came from the island of Cyprus. 37 He sold a field he owned and brought the
money to the apostles.

Ananias and Sapphira

5 But there was a certain man named Ananias who, with his wife, Sap-
phira, sold some property. 2 He brought part of the money to the apostles,
claiming it was the full amount. With his wife's consent, he kept the rest.
3 Then Peter said, "Ananias, why have you let Satan fill your heart? You
lied to the Holy Spirit, and you kept some of the money for yourself. 4 The
property was yours to sell or not sell, as you wished. And after selling it, the
money was also yours to give away. How could you do a thing like this? You
weren't lying to us but to God!"
5 As soon as Ananias heard these words, he fell to the floor and died.
Everyone who heard about it was terrified. 6 Then some young men got up,
wrapped him in a sheet, and took him out and buried him.
7 About three hours later his wife came in, not knowing what had hap-
pened. 8 Peter asked her, "Was this the price you and your husband received
for your land?"
"Yes," she replied, "that was the price."
9 And Peter said, "How could the two of you even think of conspiring to
test the Spirit of the Lord like this? The young men who buried your husband
are just outside the door, and they will carry you out, too."
10 Instantly, she fell to the floor and died. When the young men came in
and saw that she was dead, they carried her out and buried her beside her
husband. 11 Great fear gripped the entire church and everyone else who heard
what had happened.

The Apostles Heal Many

12 The apostles were performing many miraculous signs and wonders among
the people. And all the believers were meeting regularly at the Temple in the
area known as Solomon's Colonnade. 13 But no one else dared to join them,
even though all the people had high regard for them. 14 Yet more and more
people believed and were brought to the Lord—crowds of both men and
women. 15 As a result of the apostles' work, sick people were brought out into
the streets on beds and mats so that Peter's shadow might fall across some
of them as he went by. 16 Crowds came from the villages around Jerusalem,

bringing their sick and those possessed by evil* spirits, and they were all
healed.

The Apostles Meet Opposition

17 The high priest and his officials, who were Sadducees, were filled with
jealousy. 18 They arrested the apostles and put them in the public jail. 19 But
an angel of the Lord came at night, opened the gates of the jail, and brought
them out. Then he told them, 20 "Go to the Temple and give the people this
message of life!"

21 So at daybreak the apostles entered the Temple, as they were told, and
immediately began teaching.

When the high priest and his officials arrived, they convened the high
council*—the full assembly of the elders of Israel. Then they sent for the
apostles to be brought from the jail for trial. 22 But when the Temple guards
went to the jail, the men were gone. So they returned to the council and
reported, 23 "The jail was securely locked, with the guards standing outside,
but when we opened the gates, no one was there!"

24 When the captain of the Temple guard and the leading priests heard
this, they were perplexed, wondering where it would all end. 25 Then some-
one arrived with startling news: "The men you put in jail are standing in the
Temple, teaching the people!"

26 The captain went with his Temple guards and arrested the apostles,
but without violence, for they were afraid the people would stone them.
27 Then they brought the apostles before the high council, where the high
priest confronted them. 28 "We gave you strict orders never again to teach in
this man's name!" he said. "Instead, you have filled all Jerusalem with your
teaching about him, and you want to make us responsible for his death!"

29 But Peter and the apostles replied, "We must obey God rather than any
human authority. 30 The God of our ancestors raised Jesus from the dead after
you killed him by hanging him on a cross.* 31 Then God put him in the place
of honor at his right hand as Prince and Savior. He did this so the people of
Israel would repent of their sins and be forgiven. 32 We are witnesses of these
things and so is the Holy Spirit, who is given by God to those who obey him."

33 When they heard this, the high council was furious and decided to kill
them. 34 But one member, a Pharisee named Gamaliel, who was an expert in
religious law and respected by all the people, stood up and ordered that the
men be sent outside the council chamber for a while. 35 Then he said to his
colleagues, "Men of Israel, take care what you are planning to do to these
men! 36 Some time ago there was that fellow Theudas, who pretended to
be someone great. About 400 others joined him, but he was killed, and all
his followers went their various ways. The whole movement came to noth-
ing. 37 After him, at the time of the census, there was Judas of Galilee. He
got people to follow him, but he was killed, too, and all his followers were
scattered.

38 "So my advice is, leave these men alone. Let them go. If they are planning
and doing these things merely on their own, it will soon be overthrown.
39 But if it is from God, you will not be able to overthrow them. You may even
find yourselves fighting against God!"

40 The others accepted his advice. They called in the apostles and had them

Prayer **5:29**

Lord, give me, your servant, great boldness in preaching your Word. Amen.

5:16 Greek *unclean.* **5:21** Greek *Sanhedrin;* also in 5:27, 41. **5:30** Greek *on a tree.*

flogged. Then they ordered them never again to speak in the name of Jesus,
and they let them go.
41 The apostles left the high council rejoicing that God had counted them
worthy to suffer disgrace for the name of Jesus.* 42 And every day, in the
Temple and from house to house, they continued to teach and preach this
message: "Jesus is the Messiah."

Seven Men Chosen to Serve

6 But as the believers* rapidly multiplied, there were rumblings of discontent. The Greek-speaking believers complained about the Hebrew-speaking believers, saying that their widows were being discriminated
against in the daily distribution of food.
2 So the Twelve called a meeting of all the believers. They said, "We
apostles should spend our time teaching the word of God, not running a
food program. 3 And so, brothers, select seven men who are well respected
and are full of the Spirit and wisdom. We will give them this responsibility.
4 Then we apostles can spend our time in prayer and teaching the word."
5 Everyone liked this idea, and they chose the following: Stephen (a man
full of faith and the Holy Spirit), Philip, Procorus, Nicanor, Timon, Parmenas, and Nicolas of Antioch (an earlier convert to the Jewish faith). 6 These
seven were presented to the apostles, who prayed for them as they laid their
hands on them.
7 So God's message continued to spread. The number of believers greatly
increased in Jerusalem, and many of the Jewish priests were converted, too.

Stephen Is Arrested

8 Stephen, a man full of God's grace and power, performed amazing miracles
and signs among the people. 9 But one day some men from the Synagogue
of Freed Slaves, as it was called, started to debate with him. They were Jews
from Cyrene, Alexandria, Cilicia, and the province of Asia. 10 None of them
could stand against the wisdom and the Spirit with which Stephen spoke.
11 So they persuaded some men to lie about Stephen, saying, "We heard
him blaspheme Moses, and even God." 12 This roused the people, the elders,
and the teachers of religious law. So they arrested Stephen and brought him
before the high council.*
13 The lying witnesses said, "This man is always speaking against the holy
Temple and against the law of Moses. 14 We have heard him say that this
Jesus of Nazareth* will destroy the Temple and change the customs Moses
handed down to us."
15 At this point everyone in the high council stared at Stephen, because his
face became as bright as an angel's.

Stephen Addresses the Council

7 Then the high priest asked Stephen, "Are these accusations true?"
2 This was Stephen's reply: "Brothers and fathers, listen to me. Our
glorious God appeared to our ancestor Abraham in Mesopotamia before he
settled in Haran.* 3 God told him, 'Leave your native land and your relatives,
and come into the land that I will show you.'* 4 So Abraham left the land of

Story Arc **6:2-8**

● **Stephen**

Stephen had a fire in his soul. He had to tell people about Jesus. Even if it meant danger, even if people got mad, even if he was treated unfairly, he had to tell people about the good news of Jesus Christ. Full of the Holy Spirit, Stephen was a good man who had started serving as one of the key leaders in the early group of believers (Acts 6:5). When he shared about Jesus and performed miracles in Jesus' name, he was arrested and told to explain himself to the rulers. When he eloquently shared the story of salvation through Scripture and how it pointed to Jesus, people grew furious (Acts 7). The mob began to pick up stones and throw them at his head. As he was being pelted to death, blow after blow, Stephen prayed, "Lord Jesus, receive my spirit" (v. 59). Then just like Jesus had prayed on the cross, he added, "Lord, don't charge them with this sin!" (v. 60). Then he died.

Acts 8:1 ►

5:41 Greek *for the name.* 6:1 Greek *disciples;* also in 6:2, 7. 6:12 Greek *Sanhedrin;* also in 6:15. 6:14 Or *Jesus the Nazarene.* 7:2 *Mesopotamia* was the region now called Iraq. *Haran* was a city in what is now called Syria. 7:3 Gen 12:1.

the Chaldeans and lived in Haran until his father died. Then God brought
him here to the land where you now live.
5 "But God gave him no inheritance here, not even one square foot of land.
God did promise, however, that eventually the whole land would belong to
Abraham and his descendants—even though he had no children yet. 6 God
also told him that his descendants would live in a foreign land, where they
would be oppressed as slaves for 400 years. 7 'But I will punish the nation
that enslaves them,' God said, 'and in the end they will come out and wor-
ship me here in this place.'*
8 "God also gave Abraham the covenant of circumcision at that time. So
when Abraham became the father of Isaac, he circumcised him on the eighth
day. And the practice was continued when Isaac became the father of Jacob, and
when Jacob became the father of the twelve patriarchs of the Israelite nation.
9 "These patriarchs were jealous of their brother Joseph, and they sold him
to be a slave in Egypt. But God was with him 10 and rescued him from all his
troubles. And God gave him favor before Pharaoh, king of Egypt. God also
gave Joseph unusual wisdom, so that Pharaoh appointed him governor over
all of Egypt and put him in charge of the palace.

11 "But a famine came upon Egypt and Canaan. There was great misery,
and our ancestors ran out of food. 12 Jacob heard that there was still grain
in Egypt, so he sent his sons—our ancestors—to buy some. 13 The second
time they went, Joseph revealed his identity to his brothers,* and they were
introduced to Pharaoh. 14 Then Joseph sent for his father, Jacob, and all his
relatives to come to Egypt, seventy-five persons in all. 15 So Jacob went to
Egypt. He died there, as did our ancestors. 16 Their bodies were taken to She-
chem and buried in the tomb Abraham had bought for a certain price from
Hamor's sons in Shechem.

17 "As the time drew near when God would fulfill his promise to Abraham,
the number of our people in Egypt greatly increased. 18 But then a new king
came to the throne of Egypt who knew nothing about Joseph. 19 This king
exploited our people and oppressed them, forcing parents to abandon their
newborn babies so they would die.

20 "At that time Moses was born—a beautiful child in God's eyes. His
parents cared for him at home for three months. 21 When they had to aban-
don him, Pharaoh's daughter adopted him and raised him as her own son.
22 Moses was taught all the wisdom of the Egyptians, and he was powerful
in both speech and action.

23 "One day when Moses was forty years old, he decided to visit his rela-
tives, the people of Israel. 24 He saw an Egyptian mistreating an Israelite. So
Moses came to the man's defense and avenged him, killing the Egyptian.
25 Moses assumed his fellow Israelites would realize that God had sent him
to rescue them, but they didn't.

26 "The next day he visited them again and saw two men of Israel fighting.
He tried to be a peacemaker. 'Men,' he said, 'you are brothers. Why are you
fighting each other?'

27 "But the man in the wrong pushed Moses aside. 'Who made you a ruler
and judge over us?' he asked. 28 'Are you going to kill me as you killed that
Egyptian yesterday?' 29 When Moses heard that, he fled the country and lived
as a foreigner in the land of Midian. There his two sons were born.

7:5-7 Gen 12:7; 15:13-14; Exod 3:12. 7:13 Other manuscripts read *Joseph was recognized by his brothers.*

30 "Forty years later, in the desert near Mount Sinai, an angel appeared to Moses in the flame of a burning bush. 31 When Moses saw it, he was amazed at the sight. As he went to take a closer look, the voice of the LORD called out to him, 32 'I am the God of your ancestors—the God of Abraham, Isaac, and Jacob.' Moses shook with terror and did not dare to look.

33 "Then the LORD said to him, 'Take off your sandals, for you are standing on holy ground. 34 I have certainly seen the oppression of my people in Egypt. I have heard their groans and have come down to rescue them. Now go, for I am sending you back to Egypt.'*

35 "So God sent back the same man his people had previously rejected when they demanded, 'Who made you a ruler and judge over us?' Through the angel who appeared to him in the burning bush, God sent Moses to be their ruler and savior. 36 And by means of many wonders and miraculous signs, he led them out of Egypt, through the Red Sea, and through the wilderness for forty years.

37 "Moses himself told the people of Israel, 'God will raise up for you a Prophet like me from among your own people.'* 38 Moses was with our ancestors, the assembly of God's people in the wilderness, when the angel spoke to him at Mount Sinai. And there Moses received life-giving words to pass on to us.*

39 "But our ancestors refused to listen to Moses. They rejected him and wanted to return to Egypt. 40 They told Aaron, 'Make us some gods who can lead us, for we don't know what has become of this Moses, who brought us out of Egypt.' 41 So they made an idol shaped like a calf, and they sacrificed to it and celebrated over this thing they had made. 42 Then God turned away from them and abandoned them to serve the stars of heaven as their gods! In the book of the prophets it is written,

'Was it to me you were bringing sacrifices and offerings
during those forty years in the wilderness, Israel?
43 No, you carried your pagan gods—
the shrine of Molech,
the star of your god Rephan,
and the images you made to worship them.
So I will send you into exile
as far away as Babylon.'*

44 "Our ancestors carried the Tabernacle* with them through the wilderness. It was constructed according to the plan God had shown to Moses. 45 Years later, when Joshua led our ancestors in battle against the nations that God drove out of this land, the Tabernacle was taken with them into their new territory. And it stayed there until the time of King David.

46 "David found favor with God and asked for the privilege of building a permanent Temple for the God of Jacob.* 47 But it was Solomon who actually built it. 48 However, the Most High doesn't live in temples made by human hands. As the prophet says,

49 'Heaven is my throne,
and the earth is my footstool.

7:31-34 Exod 3:5-10. 7:37 Deut 18:15. 7:38 Some manuscripts read *to you.* 7:42-43 Amos 5:25-27 (Greek version). 7:44 Greek *the tent of witness.* 7:46 Some manuscripts read *the house of Jacob.*

Could you build me a temple as good as that?'
asks the LORD.
'Could you build me such a resting place?
50 Didn't my hands make both heaven and earth?'*

51 "You stubborn people! You are heathen* at heart and deaf to the truth.
Must you forever resist the Holy Spirit? That's what your ancestors did, and
so do you! 52 Name one prophet your ancestors didn't persecute! They even
killed the ones who predicted the coming of the Righteous One—the Mes-
siah whom you betrayed and murdered. 53 You deliberately disobeyed God's
law, even though you received it from the hands of angels."

54 The Jewish leaders were infuriated by Stephen's accusation, and they shook
their fists at him in rage.* 55 But Stephen, full of the Holy Spirit, gazed steadily
into heaven and saw the glory of God, and he saw Jesus standing in the place
of honor at God's right hand. 56 And he told them, "Look, I see the heavens
opened and the Son of Man standing in the place of honor at God's right hand!"

57 Then they put their hands over their ears and began shouting. They
rushed at him 58 and dragged him out of the city and began to stone him. His
accusers took off their coats and laid them at the feet of a young man named
Saul.*

59 As they stoned him, Stephen prayed, "Lord Jesus, receive my spirit."
60 He fell to his knees, shouting, "Lord, don't charge them with this sin!"
And with that, he died.

8 Saul was one of the witnesses, and he agreed completely with the kill-
ing of Stephen.

Persecution Scatters the Believers

A great wave of persecution began that day, sweeping over the church in
Jerusalem; and all the believers except the apostles were scattered through
the regions of Judea and Samaria. 2 (Some devout men came and buried Ste-
phen with great mourning.) 3 But Saul was going everywhere to destroy the
church. He went from house to house, dragging out both men and women
to throw them into prison.

Philip Preaches in Samaria

4 But the believers who were scattered preached the Good News about Jesus
wherever they went. 5 Philip, for example, went to the city of Samaria and told
the people there about the Messiah. 6 Crowds listened intently to Philip because
they were eager to hear his message and see the miraculous signs he did. 7 Many
evil* spirits were cast out, screaming as they left their victims. And many who
had been paralyzed or lame were healed. 8 So there was great joy in that city.

9 A man named Simon had been a sorcerer there for many years, amazing
the people of Samaria and claiming to be someone great. 10 Everyone, from
the least to the greatest, often spoke of him as "the Great One—the Power of
God." 11 They listened closely to him because for a long time he had astounded
them with his magic.

12 But now the people believed Philip's message of Good News concerning
the Kingdom of God and the name of Jesus Christ. As a result, many men and

7:49-50 Isa 66:1-2. 7:51 Greek *uncircumcised.* 7:54 Greek *they were grinding their teeth against him.* 7:58 *Saul* is later called Paul; see 13:9. 8:7 Greek *unclean.*

Question **8:5**

Because of the persecution, the early believers in Jesus were scattered. How does God sometimes use difficulties to open up new opportunities for his good news?

Story Arc **8:1**

● Paul

At the moment Stephen was killed, we are introduced to a man named Saul. He had heard what Stephen said. He had seen what Stephen did. He must have thought of that moment for the rest of his life.

Paul, known here by his Jewish name, Saul, was a devout Pharisee. He zealously opposed the followers of Jesus. At the beginning of this chapter, he seemed glad to support all those who were hurling stones at Stephen by holding their coats so their arms could be free. After this moment, Saul became bloodthirsty. He began to hunt down anyone who belonged to Christ. (See Acts 9:1 and Acts 22:20.) Little did he know, however, that Jesus was tracking him and would soon be paying him a visit.

Acts 8:4-40 ►

Question 8:26-34

Go back to read this whole passage in Isaiah (Isaiah 53). What do you imagine Philip said when he told the Ethiopian of the good news about Jesus?

women were baptized. 13 Then Simon himself believed and was baptized. He
began following Philip wherever he went, and he was amazed by the signs
and great miracles Philip performed.
14 When the apostles in Jerusalem heard that the people of Samaria had
accepted God's message, they sent Peter and John there. 15 As soon as they
arrived, they prayed for these new believers to receive the Holy Spirit. 16 The
Holy Spirit had not yet come upon any of them, for they had only been bap-
tized in the name of the Lord Jesus. 17 Then Peter and John laid their hands
upon these believers, and they received the Holy Spirit.
18 When Simon saw that the Spirit was given when the apostles laid their
hands on people, he offered them money to buy this power. 19 "Let me have
this power, too," he exclaimed, "so that when I lay my hands on people, they
will receive the Holy Spirit!"
20 But Peter replied, "May your money be destroyed with you for thinking
God's gift can be bought! 21 You can have no part in this, for your heart is not
right with God. 22 Repent of your wickedness and pray to the Lord. Perhaps
he will forgive your evil thoughts, 23 for I can see that you are full of bitter
jealousy and are held captive by sin."
24 "Pray to the Lord for me," Simon exclaimed, "that these terrible things
you've said won't happen to me!"
25 After testifying and preaching the word of the Lord in Samaria, Peter and
John returned to Jerusalem. And they stopped in many Samaritan villages
along the way to preach the Good News.

Philip and the Ethiopian Eunuch

26 As for Philip, an angel of the Lord said to him, "Go south* down the desert
road that runs from Jerusalem to Gaza." 27 So he started out, and he met the
treasurer of Ethiopia, a eunuch of great authority under the Kandake, the
queen of Ethiopia. The eunuch had gone to Jerusalem to worship, 28 and he
was now returning. Seated in his carriage, he was reading aloud from the
book of the prophet Isaiah.
29 The Holy Spirit said to Philip, "Go over and walk along beside the
carriage."
30 Philip ran over and heard the man reading from the prophet Isaiah.
Philip asked, "Do you understand what you are reading?"
31 The man replied, "How can I, unless someone instructs me?" And he
urged Philip to come up into the carriage and sit with him.
32 The passage of Scripture he had been reading was this:

"He was led like a sheep to the slaughter.
And as a lamb is silent before the shearers,
he did not open his mouth.
33 He was humiliated and received no justice.
Who can speak of his descendants?
For his life was taken from the earth."*

34 The eunuch asked Philip, "Tell me, was the prophet talking about him-
self or someone else?" 35 So beginning with this same Scripture, Philip told
him the Good News about Jesus.

8:26 Or *Go at noon.* 8:32-33 Isa 53:7-8 (Greek version).

36As they rode along, they came to some water, and the eunuch said,
"Look! There's some water! Why can't I be baptized?"* 38He ordered the
carriage to stop, and they went down into the water, and Philip baptized
him.
39When they came up out of the water, the Spirit of the Lord snatched
Philip away. The eunuch never saw him again but went on his way rejoicing.
40Meanwhile, Philip found himself farther north at the town of Azotus. He
preached the Good News there and in every town along the way until he
came to Caesarea.

Saul's Conversion

9 Meanwhile, Saul was uttering threats with every breath and was
eager to kill the Lord's followers.* So he went to the high priest. 2He
requested letters addressed to the synagogues in Damascus, asking for
their cooperation in the arrest of any followers of the Way he found there.
He wanted to bring them—both men and women—back to Jerusalem in
chains.
3As he was approaching Damascus on this mission, a light from heaven
suddenly shone down around him. 4He fell to the ground and heard a voice
saying to him, "Saul! Saul! Why are you persecuting me?"
5"Who are you, lord?" Saul asked.
And the voice replied, "I am Jesus, the one you are persecuting! 6Now get
up and go into the city, and you will be told what you must do."
7The men with Saul stood speechless, for they heard the sound of some-
one's voice but saw no one! 8Saul picked himself up off the ground, but
when he opened his eyes he was blind. So his companions led him by the
hand to Damascus. 9He remained there blind for three days and did not
eat or drink.
10Now there was a believer* in Damascus named Ananias. The Lord spoke
to him in a vision, calling, "Ananias!"
"Yes, Lord!" he replied.
11The Lord said, "Go over to Straight Street, to the house of Judas. When
you get there, ask for a man from Tarsus named Saul. He is praying to me
right now. 12I have shown him a vision of a man named Ananias coming in
and laying hands on him so he can see again."
13"But Lord," exclaimed Ananias, "I've heard many people talk about the
terrible things this man has done to the believers* in Jerusalem! 14And he
is authorized by the leading priests to arrest everyone who calls upon your
name."
15But the Lord said, "Go, for Saul is my chosen instrument to take my
message to the Gentiles and to kings, as well as to the people of Israel. 16And
I will show him how much he must suffer for my name's sake."
17So Ananias went and found Saul. He laid his hands on him and said,
"Brother Saul, the Lord Jesus, who appeared to you on the road, has sent
me so that you might regain your sight and be filled with the Holy Spirit."
18Instantly something like scales fell from Saul's eyes, and he regained his
sight. Then he got up and was baptized. 19Afterward he ate some food and
regained his strength.

8:36 Some manuscripts add verse 37, *"You can," Philip answered, "if you believe with all your heart." And the eunuch replied, "I believe that Jesus Christ is the Son of God."* 9:1 Greek *disciples.* 9:10 Greek *disciple;* also in 9:26, 36. 9:13 Greek *God's holy people;* also in 9:32, 41.

Question 9:4

When Jesus appeared and confronted Saul directly, knocking him to the ground and blinding him, he asked, "Why are you persecuting me?" Why did Jesus say this?

Story Arc 8:4-40

● Philip

Chapter 8 of Acts is an amazing testimony of a man who followed Jesus wherever the Spirit led. Philip found himself running for his life when his good friend Stephen was killed and Saul started the great persecution. This took him to Samaria, a controversial region where Jesus had invested quite a bit of attention and care, where Philip's message released an abundant embrace of the gospel. Philip then was whisked away to a road leading out of Jerusalem toward the African continent where he met an Ethiopian official who just happened to be reading about the Suffering Messiah in Isaiah 53. When the official asked Philip whom this passage was talking about, Philip couldn't help but tell him all about Jesus.

Philip continued to travel around, preaching about Christ, until he eventually settled in Caesarea (Acts 21:8), where he continued to be an evangelist alongside his four prophesying daughters. Do you imagine Philip had any idea what kind of life he would lead when he started serving the early believers in Acts 6:5? What does this teach you about a life of following Jesus?

Acts 18:1-3 ►

Question **9:26-28**

Barnabas, one of the earliest leaders in the growing church (Acts 4:36), showed up again here as his usual encouraging self. Barnabas wasn't just a nice guy; he had a deep conviction that Jesus had converted Saul and called him to preach the good news. What kind of risk did Barnabas take here by advocating to the apostles on Saul's behalf?

Saul in Damascus and Jerusalem

Saul stayed with the believers* in Damascus for a few days. 20 And imme-
diately he began preaching about Jesus in the synagogues, saying, "He is
indeed the Son of God!"
21 All who heard him were amazed. "Isn't this the same man who caused
such devastation among Jesus' followers in Jerusalem?" they asked. "And
didn't he come here to arrest them and take them in chains to the leading
priests?"
22 Saul's preaching became more and more powerful, and the Jews in Da-
mascus couldn't refute his proofs that Jesus was indeed the Messiah. 23 After
a while some of the Jews plotted together to kill him. 24 They were watching
for him day and night at the city gate so they could murder him, but Saul
was told about their plot. 25 So during the night, some of the other believers*
lowered him in a large basket through an opening in the city wall.
26 When Saul arrived in Jerusalem, he tried to meet with the believers,
but they were all afraid of him. They did not believe he had truly become a
believer! 27 Then Barnabas brought him to the apostles and told them how
Saul had seen the Lord on the way to Damascus and how the Lord had spo-
ken to Saul. He also told them that Saul had preached boldly in the name
of Jesus in Damascus.
28 So Saul stayed with the apostles and went all around Jerusalem with
them, preaching boldly in the name of the Lord. 29 He debated with some
Greek-speaking Jews, but they tried to murder him. 30 When the believers*
heard about this, they took him down to Caesarea and sent him away to
Tarsus, his hometown.
31 The church then had peace throughout Judea, Galilee, and Samaria, and
it became stronger as the believers lived in the fear of the Lord. And with the
encouragement of the Holy Spirit, it also grew in numbers.

Peter Heals Aeneas and Raises Dorcas

32 Meanwhile, Peter traveled from place to place, and he came down to visit
the believers in the town of Lydda. 33 There he met a man named Aeneas,
who had been paralyzed and bedridden for eight years. 34 Peter said to him,
"Aeneas, Jesus Christ heals you! Get up, and roll up your sleeping mat!" And
he was healed instantly. 35 Then the whole population of Lydda and Sharon
saw Aeneas walking around, and they turned to the Lord.
36 There was a believer in Joppa named Tabitha (which in Greek is Dorcas*).
She was always doing kind things for others and helping the poor. 37 About
this time she became ill and died. Her body was washed for burial and laid
in an upstairs room. 38 But the believers had heard that Peter was nearby at
Lydda, so they sent two men to beg him, "Please come as soon as possible!"
39 So Peter returned with them; and as soon as he arrived, they took him to
the upstairs room. The room was filled with widows who were weeping and
showing him the coats and other clothes Dorcas had made for them. 40 But
Peter asked them all to leave the room; then he knelt and prayed. Turning
to the body he said, "Get up, Tabitha." And she opened her eyes! When she
saw Peter, she sat up! 41 He gave her his hand and helped her up. Then he
called in the widows and all the believers, and he presented her to them alive.
42 The news spread through the whole town, and many believed in the

9:19 Greek *disciples;* also in 9:26, 38. **9:25** Greek *his disciples.* **9:30** Greek *brothers.* **9:36** The names *Tabitha* in Aramaic and *Dorcas* in Greek both mean "gazelle."

Lord. 43 And Peter stayed a long time in Joppa, living with Simon, a tanner
of hides.

Cornelius Calls for Peter

10 In Caesarea there lived a Roman army officer* named Cornelius, who
was a captain of the Italian Regiment. 2 He was a devout, God-fearing
man, as was everyone in his household. He gave generously to the poor and
prayed regularly to God. 3 One afternoon about three o'clock, he had a vi-
sion in which he saw an angel of God coming toward him. "Cornelius!" the
angel said.

4 Cornelius stared at him in terror. "What is it, sir?" he asked the angel.

And the angel replied, "Your prayers and gifts to the poor have been re-
ceived by God as an offering! 5 Now send some men to Joppa, and summon
a man named Simon Peter. 6 He is staying with Simon, a tanner who lives
near the seashore."

7 As soon as the angel was gone, Cornelius called two of his household
servants and a devout soldier, one of his personal attendants. 8 He told them
what had happened and sent them off to Joppa.

Peter Visits Cornelius

9 The next day as Cornelius's messengers were nearing the town, Peter went
up on the flat roof to pray. It was about noon, 10 and he was hungry. But while
a meal was being prepared, he fell into a trance. 11 He saw the sky open, and
something like a large sheet was let down by its four corners. 12 In the sheet
were all sorts of animals, reptiles, and birds. 13 Then a voice said to him, "Get
up, Peter; kill and eat them."

14 "No, Lord," Peter declared. "I have never eaten anything that our Jewish
laws have declared impure and unclean.*"

15 But the voice spoke again: "Do not call something unclean if God has
made it clean." 16 The same vision was repeated three times. Then the sheet
was suddenly pulled up to heaven.

17 Peter was very perplexed. What could the vision mean? Just then the men
sent by Cornelius found Simon's house. Standing outside the gate, 18 they
asked if a man named Simon Peter was staying there.

19 Meanwhile, as Peter was puzzling over the vision, the Holy Spirit said
to him, "Three men have come looking for you. 20 Get up, go downstairs,
and go with them without hesitation. Don't worry, for I have sent them."

21 So Peter went down and said, "I'm the man you are looking for. Why
have you come?"

22 They said, "We were sent by Cornelius, a Roman officer. He is a devout
and God-fearing man, well respected by all the Jews. A holy angel instructed
him to summon you to his house so that he can hear your message." 23 So Pe-
ter invited the men to stay for the night. The next day he went with them,
accompanied by some of the brothers from Joppa.

24 They arrived in Caesarea the following day. Cornelius was waiting for
them and had called together his relatives and close friends. 25 As Peter en-
tered his home, Cornelius fell at his feet and worshiped him. 26 But Peter
pulled him up and said, "Stand up! I'm a human being just like you!" 27 So
they talked together and went inside, where many others were assembled.

10:1 Greek *a centurion;* similarly in 10:22. 10:14 Greek *anything common and unclean.*

Prayer **10:36**

Thank you, Jesus, that because you are Lord of all, everyone has dignity and everyone, no matter their background or situation, is invited to the table. Amen.

[28]Peter told them, "You know it is against our laws for a Jewish man to
enter a Gentile home like this or to associate with you. But God has shown
me that I should no longer think of anyone as impure or unclean. [29]So I came
without objection as soon as I was sent for. Now tell me why you sent for me."
[30]Cornelius replied, "Four days ago I was praying in my house about
this same time, three o'clock in the afternoon. Suddenly, a man in dazzling
clothes was standing in front of me. [31]He told me, 'Cornelius, your prayer has
been heard, and your gifts to the poor have been noticed by God! [32]Now send
messengers to Joppa, and summon a man named Simon Peter. He is staying
in the home of Simon, a tanner who lives near the seashore.' [33]So I sent for
you at once, and it was good of you to come. Now we are all here, waiting
before God to hear the message the Lord has given you."

The Gentiles Hear the Good News

[34]Then Peter replied, "I see very clearly that God shows no favoritism. [35]In
every nation he accepts those who fear him and do what is right. [36]This is
the message of Good News for the people of Israel—that there is peace with
God through Jesus Christ, who is Lord of all. [37]You know what happened
throughout Judea, beginning in Galilee, after John began preaching his mes-
sage of baptism. [38]And you know that God anointed Jesus of Nazareth with
the Holy Spirit and with power. Then Jesus went around doing good and
healing all who were oppressed by the devil, for God was with him.
[39]"And we apostles are witnesses of all he did throughout Judea and in
Jerusalem. They put him to death by hanging him on a cross,* [40]but God
raised him to life on the third day. Then God allowed him to appear, [41]not
to the general public,* but to us whom God had chosen in advance to be his
witnesses. We were those who ate and drank with him after he rose from the
dead. [42]And he ordered us to preach everywhere and to testify that Jesus is the
one appointed by God to be the judge of all—the living and the dead. [43]He
is the one all the prophets testified about, saying that everyone who believes
in him will have their sins forgiven through his name."

The Gentiles Receive the Holy Spirit

[44]Even as Peter was saying these things, the Holy Spirit fell upon all who were
listening to the message. [45]The Jewish believers* who came with Peter were
amazed that the gift of the Holy Spirit had been poured out on the Gentiles,
too. [46]For they heard them speaking in other tongues* and praising God.
Then Peter asked, [47]"Can anyone object to their being baptized, now that
they have received the Holy Spirit just as we did?" [48]So he gave orders for
them to be baptized in the name of Jesus Christ. Afterward Cornelius asked
him to stay with them for several days.

Peter Explains His Actions

11 Soon the news reached the apostles and other believers* in Judea that
the Gentiles had received the word of God. [2]But when Peter arrived
back in Jerusalem, the Jewish believers* criticized him. [3]"You entered the
home of Gentiles* and even ate with them!" they said.
[4]Then Peter told them exactly what had happened. [5]"I was in the town

10:39 Greek *on a tree.* **10:41** Greek *the people.* **10:45** Greek *The faithful ones of the circumcision.* **10:46** Or *in other languages.* **11:1** Greek *brothers.* **11:2** Greek *those of the circumcision.* **11:3** Greek *of uncircumcised men.*

of Joppa," he said, "and while I was praying, I went into a trance and saw a
vision. Something like a large sheet was let down by its four corners from the
sky. And it came right down to me. 6 When I looked inside the sheet, I saw all
sorts of tame and wild animals, reptiles, and birds. 7 And I heard a voice say,
'Get up, Peter; kill and eat them.'

8 "'No, Lord,' I replied. 'I have never eaten anything that our Jewish laws
have declared impure or unclean.*'

9 "But the voice from heaven spoke again: 'Do not call something unclean
if God has made it clean.' 10 This happened three times before the sheet and
all it contained was pulled back up to heaven.

11 "Just then three men who had been sent from Caesarea arrived at the
house where we were staying. 12 The Holy Spirit told me to go with them and
not to worry that they were Gentiles. These six brothers here accompanied
me, and we soon entered the home of the man who had sent for us. 13 He told
us how an angel had appeared to him in his home and had told him, 'Send
messengers to Joppa, and summon a man named Simon Peter. 14 He will tell
you how you and everyone in your household can be saved!'

15 "As I began to speak," Peter continued, "the Holy Spirit fell on them,
just as he fell on us at the beginning. 16 Then I thought of the Lord's words
when he said, 'John baptized with* water, but you will be baptized with the
Holy Spirit.' 17 And since God gave these Gentiles the same gift he gave us
when we believed in the Lord Jesus Christ, who was I to stand in God's way?"

18 When the others heard this, they stopped objecting and began praising
God. They said, "We can see that God has also given the Gentiles the privilege
of repenting of their sins and receiving eternal life."

The Church in Antioch of Syria

19 Meanwhile, the believers who had been scattered during the persecu-
tion after Stephen's death traveled as far as Phoenicia, Cyprus, and Anti-
och of Syria. They preached the word of God, but only to Jews. 20 However,
some of the believers who went to Antioch from Cyprus and Cyrene began
preaching to the Gentiles* about the Lord Jesus. 21 The power of the Lord
was with them, and a large number of these Gentiles believed and turned
to the Lord.

22 When the church at Jerusalem heard what had happened, they sent Bar-
nabas to Antioch. 23 When he arrived and saw this evidence of God's blessing,
he was filled with joy, and he encouraged the believers to stay true to the
Lord. 24 Barnabas was a good man, full of the Holy Spirit and strong in faith.
And many people were brought to the Lord.

25 Then Barnabas went on to Tarsus to look for Saul. 26 When he found him,
he brought him back to Antioch. Both of them stayed there with the church
for a full year, teaching large crowds of people. (It was at Antioch that the
believers* were first called Christians.)

27 During this time some prophets traveled from Jerusalem to Antioch.
28 One of them named Agabus stood up in one of the meetings and predicted
by the Spirit that a great famine was coming upon the entire Roman world.
(This was fulfilled during the reign of Claudius.) 29 So the believers in Antioch
decided to send relief to the brothers and sisters* in Judea, everyone giving

11:8 Greek *anything common or unclean.* **11:16** Or *in;* also in 11:16b. **11:20** Greek *the Hellenists* (i.e., those who speak Greek); other manuscripts read *the Greeks.* **11:26** Greek *disciples;* also in 11:29. **11:29** Greek *the brothers.*

Make a Difference

11:22-26

Nickname

His real name was Joseph, but the leaders of the early church gave him the nickname "Barnabas," which means "Son of Encouragement" (Acts 4:36). He was a Jewish man from the tribe of Levi and had come to Israel from the island of Cyprus. The book of Acts describes how he had owned a field, had sold it, and had given all the money to the leaders of the church so it could be distributed to those in need (4:37).

Barnabas repeatedly came alongside people who needed support and lavished them with encouragement. Throughout Acts, it becomes evident that Barnabas believed in Paul when few others would have given the former persecutor a chance. Barnabas raised money for the poor, advocated for the outcast, and served with Paul on missionary journeys. It's no wonder that followers of Jesus first earned the nickname "Christians" while Barnabas was around (11:26).

Difference Maker

If people who know you gave you a nickname that reflected the way you live, what would that nickname be? Be proactive to equip people today. Focus on identifying and affirming their God-given qualities.

Question 12:1–5

James and his brother John, the sons of Zebedee, were fishing on the shores of the Sea of Galilee when Jesus first called to them (Mark 1:19-20). Jesus had warned them that they would drink a bitter cup of suffering by following him (Mark 10:39). Sadly, because Herod Agrippa I (the grandson of Herod the Great) held a bloodthirsty anger against the growing church, he had James killed with a sword. Herod's next move was to arrest Peter and further threaten the followers of Jesus. If you had been one of the early Christians, what would you have done in response to this? What can we learn from the way the followers of Jesus responded in Acts 12:12?

as much as they could. 30 This they did, entrusting their gifts to Barnabas and
Saul to take to the elders of the church in Jerusalem.

James Is Killed and Peter Is Imprisoned

12 About that time King Herod Agrippa* began to persecute some believ-
ers in the church. 2 He had the apostle James (John's brother) killed
with a sword. 3 When Herod saw how much this pleased the Jewish people, he
also arrested Peter. (This took place during the Passover celebration.*) 4 Then he
imprisoned him, placing him under the guard of four squads of four soldiers
each. Herod intended to bring Peter out for public trial after the Passover. 5 But
while Peter was in prison, the church prayed very earnestly for him.

Peter's Miraculous Escape from Prison

6 The night before Peter was to be placed on trial, he was asleep, fastened with
two chains between two soldiers. Others stood guard at the prison gate. 7 Sud-
denly, there was a bright light in the cell, and an angel of the Lord stood be-
fore Peter. The angel struck him on the side to awaken him and said, "Quick!
Get up!" And the chains fell off his wrists. 8 Then the angel told him, "Get
dressed and put on your sandals." And he did. "Now put on your coat and
follow me," the angel ordered.

9 So Peter left the cell, following the angel. But all the time he thought it
was a vision. He didn't realize it was actually happening. 10 They passed the
first and second guard posts and came to the iron gate leading to the city,
and this opened for them all by itself. So they passed through and started
walking down the street, and then the angel suddenly left him.

11 Peter finally came to his senses. "It's really true!" he said. "The Lord has
sent his angel and saved me from Herod and from what the Jewish leaders*
had planned to do to me!"

12 When he realized this, he went to the home of Mary, the mother of John
Mark, where many were gathered for prayer. 13 He knocked at the door in the
gate, and a servant girl named Rhoda came to open it. 14 When she recognized
Peter's voice, she was so overjoyed that, instead of opening the door, she ran
back inside and told everyone, "Peter is standing at the door!"

15 "You're out of your mind!" they said. When she insisted, they decided,
"It must be his angel."

16 Meanwhile, Peter continued knocking. When they finally opened the
door and saw him, they were amazed. 17 He motioned for them to quiet down
and told them how the Lord had led him out of prison. "Tell James and the
other brothers what happened," he said. And then he went to another place.

18 At dawn there was a great commotion among the soldiers about what
had happened to Peter. 19 Herod Agrippa ordered a thorough search for him.
When he couldn't be found, Herod interrogated the guards and sentenced
them to death. Afterward Herod left Judea to stay in Caesarea for a while.

The Death of Herod Agrippa

20 Now Herod was very angry with the people of Tyre and Sidon. So they sent
a delegation to make peace with him because their cities were dependent
upon Herod's country for food. The delegates won the support of Blastus,
Herod's personal assistant, 21 and an appointment with Herod was granted.

12:1 Greek *Herod the king.* He was the nephew of Herod Antipas and a grandson of Herod the Great. **12:3** Greek *the days of unleavened bread.* **12:11** Or *the Jewish people.*

When the day arrived, Herod put on his royal robes, sat on his throne, and
made a speech to them. 22 The people gave him a great ovation, shouting,
"It's the voice of a god, not of a man!"
23 Instantly, an angel of the Lord struck Herod with a sickness, because he
accepted the people's worship instead of giving the glory to God. So he was
consumed with worms and died.
24 Meanwhile, the word of God continued to spread, and there were many
new believers.
25 When Barnabas and Saul had finished their mission to Jerusalem, they
returned,* taking John Mark with them.

Barnabas and Saul Are Commissioned

13 Among the prophets and teachers of the church at Antioch of Syria
were Barnabas, Simeon (called "the black man"*), Lucius (from Cy-
rene), Manaen (the childhood companion of King Herod Antipas*), and Saul.
2 One day as these men were worshiping the Lord and fasting, the Holy Spirit
said, "Appoint Barnabas and Saul for the special work to which I have called
them." 3 So after more fasting and prayer, the men laid their hands on them
and sent them on their way.

Paul's First Missionary Journey

4 So Barnabas and Saul were sent out by the Holy Spirit. They went down to
the seaport of Seleucia and then sailed for the island of Cyprus. 5 There, in
the town of Salamis, they went to the Jewish synagogues and preached the
word of God. John Mark went with them as their assistant.
6 Afterward they traveled from town to town across the entire island until
finally they reached Paphos, where they met a Jewish sorcerer, a false prophet
named Bar-Jesus. 7 He had attached himself to the governor, Sergius Paulus, who
was an intelligent man. The governor invited Barnabas and Saul to visit him,
for he wanted to hear the word of God. 8 But Elymas, the sorcerer (as his name
means in Greek), interfered and urged the governor to pay no attention to what
Barnabas and Saul said. He was trying to keep the governor from believing.
9 Saul, also known as Paul, was filled with the Holy Spirit, and he looked
the sorcerer in the eye. 10 Then he said, "You son of the devil, full of every
sort of deceit and fraud, and enemy of all that is good! Will you never stop
perverting the true ways of the Lord? 11 Watch now, for the Lord has laid his
hand of punishment upon you, and you will be struck blind. You will not
see the sunlight for some time." Instantly mist and darkness came over the
man's eyes, and he began groping around begging for someone to take his
hand and lead him.
12 When the governor saw what had happened, he became a believer, for
he was astonished at the teaching about the Lord.

Paul Preaches in Antioch of Pisidia

13 Paul and his companions then left Paphos by ship for Pamphylia, land-
ing at the port town of Perga. There John Mark left them and returned to
Jerusalem. 14 But Paul and Barnabas traveled inland to Antioch of Pisidia.*

Prayer **12:24**

Lord, thank you that despite hostility and obstacles, your Word continues to spread and that many people continue to believe in you. Amen.

Make a Difference

13:1–5

Commissioning

Jesus is the hope for the nations. The Holy Spirit sets some people aside to spread the good news of Jesus. In this chapter, while worshiping with some fascinating believers, Paul and Barnabas were set apart and "commissioned" to travel around the northeast Mediterranean to share about Jesus. The other believers set aside their meals to pray for Paul and Barnabas, and then they "laid their hands on them and sent them on their way" (v. 3). This act of blessing launched what would become the first of several missionary journeys that would forever change the world.

Difference Maker

Start planning to go on a mission trip. When it's time to go, have people fast and pray and lay their hands on you to send you on your way.

12:25 Or *mission, they returned to Jerusalem.* Other manuscripts read *mission, they returned from Jerusalem;* still others read *mission, they returned from Jerusalem to Antioch.* **13:1a** Greek *who was called Niger.* **13:1b** Greek *Herod the tetrarch.* **13:13-14** *Pamphylia* and *Pisidia* were districts in what is now Turkey.

Question **13:33**

Read Psalm 2. How does knowing the Psalms help you know Jesus?

On the Sabbath they went to the synagogue for the services. 15 After the
usual readings from the books of Moses* and the prophets, those in charge
of the service sent them this message: "Brothers, if you have any word of
encouragement for the people, come and give it."
16 So Paul stood, lifted his hand to quiet them, and started speaking. "Men
of Israel," he said, "and you God-fearing Gentiles, listen to me.
17 "The God of this nation of Israel chose our ancestors and made them mul-
tiply and grow strong during their stay in Egypt. Then with a powerful arm
he led them out of their slavery. 18 He put up with them* through forty years
of wandering in the wilderness. 19 Then he destroyed seven nations in Canaan
and gave their land to Israel as an inheritance. 20 All this took about 450 years.
"After that, God gave them judges to rule until the time of Samuel the
prophet. 21 Then the people begged for a king, and God gave them Saul son
of Kish, a man of the tribe of Benjamin, who reigned for forty years. 22 But
God removed Saul and replaced him with David, a man about whom God
said, 'I have found David son of Jesse, a man after my own heart. He will do
everything I want him to do.'*
23 "And it is one of King David's descendants, Jesus, who is God's prom-
ised Savior of Israel! 24 Before he came, John the Baptist preached that all
the people of Israel needed to repent of their sins and turn to God and be
baptized. 25 As John was finishing his ministry he asked, 'Do you think I am
the Messiah? No, I am not! But he is coming soon—and I'm not even worthy
to be his slave and untie the sandals on his feet.'
26 "Brothers—you sons of Abraham, and also you God-fearing Gentiles—
this message of salvation has been sent to us! 27 The people in Jerusalem and
their leaders did not recognize Jesus as the one the prophets had spoken
about. Instead, they condemned him, and in doing this they fulfilled the
prophets' words that are read every Sabbath. 28 They found no legal reason
to execute him, but they asked Pilate to have him killed anyway.
29 "When they had done all that the prophecies said about him, they took
him down from the cross* and placed him in a tomb. 30 But God raised him
from the dead! 31 And over a period of many days he appeared to those who
had gone with him from Galilee to Jerusalem. They are now his witnesses
to the people of Israel.
32 "And now we are here to bring you this Good News. The promise was
made to our ancestors, 33 and God has now fulfilled it for us, their descen-
dants, by raising Jesus. This is what the second psalm says about Jesus:

'You are my Son.
Today I have become your Father.*'

34 For God had promised to raise him from the dead, not leaving him to rot in
the grave. He said, 'I will give you the sacred blessings I promised to David.'*
35 Another psalm explains it more fully: 'You will not allow your Holy One
to rot in the grave.'* 36 This is not a reference to David, for after David had
done the will of God in his own generation, he died and was buried with his
ancestors, and his body decayed. 37 No, it was a reference to someone else—
someone whom God raised and whose body did not decay.

13:15 Greek *from the law.* 13:18 Some manuscripts read *He cared for them;* compare Deut 1:31. 13:22 1 Sam 13:14. 13:29 Greek *from the tree.* 13:33 Or *Today I reveal you as my Son.* Ps 2:7. 13:34 Isa 55:3. 13:35 Ps 16:10.

38*"Brothers, listen! We are here to proclaim that through this man Jesus
there is forgiveness for your sins. 39 Everyone who believes in him is made
right in God's sight—something the law of Moses could never do. 40 Be care-
ful! Don't let the prophets' words apply to you. For they said,

41 'Look, you mockers,
be amazed and die!
For I am doing something in your own day,
something you wouldn't believe
even if someone told you about it.'*"

42 As Paul and Barnabas left the synagogue that day, the people begged
them to speak about these things again the next week. 43 Many Jews and
devout converts to Judaism followed Paul and Barnabas, and the two men
urged them to continue to rely on the grace of God.

Paul Turns to the Gentiles

44 The following week almost the entire city turned out to hear them preach
the word of the Lord. 45 But when some of the Jews saw the crowds, they
were jealous; so they slandered Paul and argued against whatever he said.
46 Then Paul and Barnabas spoke out boldly and declared, "It was neces-
sary that we first preach the word of God to you Jews. But since you have
rejected it and judged yourselves unworthy of eternal life, we will offer it to
the Gentiles. 47 For the Lord gave us this command when he said,

'I have made you a light to the Gentiles,
to bring salvation to the farthest corners of the earth.'*"

48 When the Gentiles heard this, they were very glad and thanked the Lord
for his message; and all who were chosen for eternal life became believers.
49 So the Lord's message spread throughout that region.
50 Then the Jews stirred up the influential religious women and the leaders
of the city, and they incited a mob against Paul and Barnabas and ran them
out of town. 51 So they shook the dust from their feet as a sign of rejection
and went to the town of Iconium. 52 And the believers* were filled with joy
and with the Holy Spirit.

Paul and Barnabas in Iconium

14 The same thing happened in Iconium.* Paul and Barnabas went to
the Jewish synagogue and preached with such power that a great
number of both Jews and Greeks became believers. 2 Some of the Jews, how-
ever, spurned God's message and poisoned the minds of the Gentiles against
Paul and Barnabas. 3 But the apostles stayed there a long time, preaching
boldly about the grace of the Lord. And the Lord proved their message was
true by giving them power to do miraculous signs and wonders. 4 But the
people of the town were divided in their opinion about them. Some sided
with the Jews, and some with the apostles.
5 Then a mob of Gentiles and Jews, along with their leaders, decided to

Prayer 14:3

Lord Jesus, prove our message to be true today. Amen.

13:38 English translations divide verses 38 and 39 in various ways. 13:41 Hab 1:5 (Greek version). 13:47 Isa 49:6. 13:52 Greek *the disciples.* 14:1 *Iconium,* as well as *Lystra* and *Derbe* (14:6), were towns in what is now Turkey.

attack and stone them. [6]When the apostles learned of it, they fled to the region of Lycaonia—to the towns of Lystra and Derbe and the surrounding area. [7]And there they preached the Good News.

Paul and Barnabas in Lystra and Derbe

[8]While they were at Lystra, Paul and Barnabas came upon a man with crippled feet. He had been that way from birth, so he had never walked. He was sitting [9]and listening as Paul preached. Looking straight at him, Paul realized he had faith to be healed. [10]So Paul called to him in a loud voice, "Stand up!" And the man jumped to his feet and started walking.

[11]When the crowd saw what Paul had done, they shouted in their local dialect, "These men are gods in human form!" [12]They decided that Barnabas was the Greek god Zeus and that Paul was Hermes, since he was the chief speaker. [13]Now the temple of Zeus was located just outside the town. So the priest of the temple and the crowd brought bulls and wreaths of flowers to the town gates, and they prepared to offer sacrifices to the apostles.

[14]But when the apostles Barnabas and Paul heard what was happening, they tore their clothing in dismay and ran out among the people, shouting, [15]"Friends,* why are you doing this? We are merely human beings—just like you! We have come to bring you the Good News that you should turn from these worthless things and turn to the living God, who made heaven and earth, the sea, and everything in them. [16]In the past he permitted all the nations to go their own ways, [17]but he never left them without evidence of himself and his goodness. For instance, he sends you rain and good crops and gives you food and joyful hearts." [18]But even with these words, Paul and Barnabas could scarcely restrain the people from sacrificing to them.

[19]Then some Jews arrived from Antioch and Iconium and won the crowds to their side. They stoned Paul and dragged him out of town, thinking he was dead. [20]But as the believers* gathered around him, he got up and went back into the town. The next day he left with Barnabas for Derbe.

Paul and Barnabas Return to Antioch of Syria

[21]After preaching the Good News in Derbe and making many disciples, Paul and Barnabas returned to Lystra, Iconium, and Antioch of Pisidia, [22]where they strengthened the believers. They encouraged them to continue in the faith, reminding them that we must suffer many hardships to enter the Kingdom of God. [23]Paul and Barnabas also appointed elders in every church. With prayer and fasting, they turned the elders over to the care of the Lord, in whom they had put their trust. [24]Then they traveled back through Pisidia to Pamphylia. [25]They preached the word in Perga, then went down to Attalia.

[26]Finally, they returned by ship to Antioch of Syria, where their journey had begun. The believers there had entrusted them to the grace of God to do the work they had now completed. [27]Upon arriving in Antioch, they called the church together and reported everything God had done through them and how he had opened the door of faith to the Gentiles, too. [28]And they stayed there with the believers for a long time.

14:15 Greek *Men.* 14:20 Greek *disciples;* also in 14:22, 28.

The Council at Jerusalem

15 While Paul and Barnabas were at Antioch of Syria, some men from
Judea arrived and began to teach the believers*: "Unless you are
circumcised as required by the law of Moses, you cannot be saved." 2 Paul
and Barnabas disagreed with them, arguing vehemently. Finally, the church
decided to send Paul and Barnabas to Jerusalem, accompanied by some local
believers, to talk to the apostles and elders about this question. 3 The church
sent the delegates to Jerusalem, and they stopped along the way in Phoe-
nicia and Samaria to visit the believers. They told them—much to everyone's
joy—that the Gentiles, too, were being converted.

4 When they arrived in Jerusalem, Barnabas and Paul were welcomed by
the whole church, including the apostles and elders. They reported every-
thing God had done through them. 5 But then some of the believers who
belonged to the sect of the Pharisees stood up and insisted, "The Gentile
converts must be circumcised and required to follow the law of Moses."

6 So the apostles and elders met together to resolve this issue. 7 At the
meeting, after a long discussion, Peter stood and addressed them as follows:
"Brothers, you all know that God chose me from among you some time ago
to preach to the Gentiles so that they could hear the Good News and believe.
8 God knows people's hearts, and he confirmed that he accepts Gentiles by
giving them the Holy Spirit, just as he did to us. 9 He made no distinction
between us and them, for he cleansed their hearts through faith. 10 So why
are you now challenging God by burdening the Gentile believers* with a
yoke that neither we nor our ancestors were able to bear? 11 We believe that
we are all saved the same way, by the undeserved grace of the Lord Jesus."

12 Everyone listened quietly as Barnabas and Paul told about the miracu-
lous signs and wonders God had done through them among the Gentiles.

13 When they had finished, James stood and said, "Brothers, listen to me.
14 Peter* has told you about the time God first visited the Gentiles to take
from them a people for himself. 15 And this conversion of Gentiles is exactly
what the prophets predicted. As it is written:

16 'Afterward I will return
  and restore the fallen house* of David.
I will rebuild its ruins
  and restore it,
17 so that the rest of humanity might seek the LORD,
  including the Gentiles—
  all those I have called to be mine.
The LORD has spoken—
18 he who made these things known so long ago.'*

19 "And so my judgment is that we should not make it difficult for the
Gentiles who are turning to God. 20 Instead, we should write and tell them
to abstain from eating food offered to idols, from sexual immorality, from
eating the meat of strangled animals, and from consuming blood. 21 For these
laws of Moses have been preached in Jewish synagogues in every city on every
Sabbath for many generations."

Prayer **15:11**

Lord Jesus, I don't deserve what you have done for me. Thank you for your forgiveness. Let me live in the freedom you have purchased for me today. Amen.

15:1 Greek *brothers;* also in 15:3, 23, 32, 33, 36, 40. **15:10** Greek *disciples.* **15:14** Greek *Simeon.* **15:16** Or *kingdom;* Greek reads *tent.* **15:16-18** Amos 9:11-12 (Greek version); Isa 45:21.

Question 15:32

What picture does this give you of what church is supposed to be like?

The Letter for Gentile Believers

22 Then the apostles and elders together with the whole church in Jerusalem chose delegates, and they sent them to Antioch of Syria with Paul and Barnabas to report on this decision. The men chosen were two of the church leaders*—Judas (also called Barsabbas) and Silas. 23 This is the letter they took with them:

"This letter is from the apostles and elders, your brothers in Jerusalem. It is written to the Gentile believers in Antioch, Syria, and Cilicia. Greetings!

24 "We understand that some men from here have troubled you and upset you with their teaching, but we did not send them! 25 So we decided, having come to complete agreement, to send you official representatives, along with our beloved Barnabas and Paul, 26 who have risked their lives for the name of our Lord Jesus Christ. 27 We are sending Judas and Silas to confirm what we have decided concerning your question.

28 "For it seemed good to the Holy Spirit and to us to lay no greater burden on you than these few requirements: 29 You must abstain from eating food offered to idols, from consuming blood or the meat of strangled animals, and from sexual immorality. If you do this, you will do well. Farewell."

30 The messengers went at once to Antioch, where they called a general meeting of the believers and delivered the letter. 31 And there was great joy throughout the church that day as they read this encouraging message.

32 Then Judas and Silas, both being prophets, spoke at length to the believers, encouraging and strengthening their faith. 33 They stayed for a while, and then the believers sent them back to the church in Jerusalem with a blessing of peace.* 35 Paul and Barnabas stayed in Antioch. They and many others taught and preached the word of the Lord there.

Paul and Barnabas Separate

36 After some time Paul said to Barnabas, "Let's go back and visit each city where we previously preached the word of the Lord, to see how the new believers are doing." 37 Barnabas agreed and wanted to take along John Mark. 38 But Paul disagreed strongly, since John Mark had deserted them in Pamphylia and had not continued with them in their work. 39 Their disagreement was so sharp that they separated. Barnabas took John Mark with him and sailed for Cyprus. 40 Paul chose Silas, and as he left, the believers entrusted him to the Lord's gracious care. 41 Then he traveled throughout Syria and Cilicia, strengthening the churches there.

Paul's Second Missionary Journey

16 Paul went first to Derbe and then to Lystra, where there was a young disciple named Timothy. His mother was a Jewish believer, but his father was a Greek. 2 Timothy was well thought of by the believers* in Lystra and Iconium, 3 so Paul wanted him to join them on their journey. In deference to the Jews of the area, he arranged for Timothy to be circumcised before

15:22 Greek *were leaders among the brothers.* **15:33** Some manuscripts add verse 34, *But Silas decided to stay there.* **16:2** Greek *brothers;* also in 16:40.

they left, for everyone knew that his father was a Greek. 4 Then they went
from town to town, instructing the believers to follow the decisions made
by the apostles and elders in Jerusalem. 5 So the churches were strengthened
in their faith and grew larger every day.

A Call from Macedonia

6 Next Paul and Silas traveled through the area of Phrygia and Galatia, be-
cause the Holy Spirit had prevented them from preaching the word in the
province of Asia at that time. 7 Then coming to the borders of Mysia, they
headed north for the province of Bithynia,* but again the Spirit of Jesus did
not allow them to go there. 8 So instead, they went on through Mysia to the
seaport of Troas.
9 That night Paul had a vision: A man from Macedonia in northern Greece
was standing there, pleading with him, "Come over to Macedonia and help
us!" 10 So we* decided to leave for Macedonia at once, having concluded that
God was calling us to preach the Good News there.

Lydia of Philippi Believes in Jesus

11 We boarded a boat at Troas and sailed straight across to the island of Sam-
othrace, and the next day we landed at Neapolis. 12 From there we reached
Philippi, a major city of that district of Macedonia and a Roman colony. And
we stayed there several days.
13 On the Sabbath we went a little way outside the city to a riverbank, where
we thought people would be meeting for prayer, and we sat down to speak
with some women who had gathered there. 14 One of them was Lydia from
Thyatira, a merchant of expensive purple cloth, who worshiped God. As she
listened to us, the Lord opened her heart, and she accepted what Paul was
saying. 15 She and her household were baptized, and she asked us to be her
guests. "If you agree that I am a true believer in the Lord," she said, "come
and stay at my home." And she urged us until we agreed.

Paul and Silas in Prison

16 One day as we were going down to the place of prayer, we met a slave girl
who had a spirit that enabled her to tell the future. She earned a lot of money
for her masters by telling fortunes. 17 She followed Paul and the rest of us,
shouting, "These men are servants of the Most High God, and they have
come to tell you how to be saved."
18 This went on day after day until Paul got so exasperated that he turned
and said to the demon within her, "I command you in the name of Jesus
Christ to come out of her." And instantly it left her.
19 Her masters' hopes of wealth were now shattered, so they grabbed Paul
and Silas and dragged them before the authorities at the marketplace. 20 "The
whole city is in an uproar because of these Jews!" they shouted to the city offi-
cials. 21 "They are teaching customs that are illegal for us Romans to practice."
22 A mob quickly formed against Paul and Silas, and the city officials or-
dered them stripped and beaten with wooden rods. 23 They were severely
beaten, and then they were thrown into prison. The jailer was ordered to
make sure they didn't escape. 24 So the jailer put them into the inner dungeon
and clamped their feet in the stocks.

16:6-7 *Phrygia, Galatia, Asia, Mysia,* and *Bithynia* were all districts in what is now Turkey.
16:10 Luke, the writer of this book, here joined Paul and accompanied him on his journey.

Make a Difference

16:16–40

Midnight

Paul and Silas healed a slave girl. They healed her! Her masters got upset because they made a lot of money from her affliction. Because she was now healed, they had lost their ability to profit from her, so the masters grabbed Paul and Silas and incited the authorities against them in the city's marketplace. Because they had disrupted the unjust economic system, a mob formed against them. Paul and Silas were severely beaten and then thrown into prison, where they were chained by their feet to the walls. Then Paul and Silas sang praises to God.

Difference Maker

Plan a time to worship God. At midnight, gather some people together, read through Acts 16:16–40, and have someone lead in singing praises to the Lord.

Make a Difference

17:1–9

Causing Trouble

Paul and Silas kept traveling from town to town and sharing about Jesus. The more they shared, the more they seemed to disrupt the economies and political structures of the regions. When they came to a city called Thessalonica, several people, including a lot of prominent women, gave their lives to Jesus. This upset the local marketplace, which relied upon the corrupt worship system in the local temples, so a mob started a riot. They were so angry that they attacked the home of a man named Jason, where Paul and Silas had been staying. They dragged Jason to the city council, along with some

25 Around midnight Paul and Silas were praying and singing hymns to God, and the other prisoners were listening. 26 Suddenly, there was a massive earthquake, and the prison was shaken to its foundations. All the doors immediately flew open, and the chains of every prisoner fell off! 27 The jailer woke up to see the prison doors wide open. He assumed the prisoners had escaped, so he drew his sword to kill himself. 28 But Paul shouted to him, "Stop! Don't kill yourself! We are all here!"

29 The jailer called for lights and ran to the dungeon and fell down trembling before Paul and Silas. 30 Then he brought them out and asked, "Sirs, what must I do to be saved?"

31 They replied, "Believe in the Lord Jesus and you will be saved, along with everyone in your household." 32 And they shared the word of the Lord with him and with all who lived in his household. 33 Even at that hour of the night, the jailer cared for them and washed their wounds. Then he and everyone in his household were immediately baptized. 34 He brought them into his house and set a meal before them, and he and his entire household rejoiced because they all believed in God.

35 The next morning the city officials sent the police to tell the jailer, "Let those men go!" 36 So the jailer told Paul, "The city officials have said you and Silas are free to leave. Go in peace."

37 But Paul replied, "They have publicly beaten us without a trial and put us in prison—and we are Roman citizens. So now they want us to leave secretly? Certainly not! Let them come themselves to release us!"

38 When the police reported this, the city officials were alarmed to learn that Paul and Silas were Roman citizens. 39 So they came to the jail and apologized to them. Then they brought them out and begged them to leave the city. 40 When Paul and Silas left the prison, they returned to the home of Lydia. There they met with the believers and encouraged them once more. Then they left town.

Paul Preaches in Thessalonica

17 Paul and Silas then traveled through the towns of Amphipolis and Apollonia and came to Thessalonica, where there was a Jewish synagogue. 2 As was Paul's custom, he went to the synagogue service, and for three Sabbaths in a row he used the Scriptures to reason with the people. 3 He explained the prophecies and proved that the Messiah must suffer and rise from the dead. He said, "This Jesus I'm telling you about is the Messiah." 4 Some of the Jews who listened were persuaded and joined Paul and Silas, along with many God-fearing Greek men and quite a few prominent women.*

5 But some of the Jews were jealous, so they gathered some troublemakers from the marketplace to form a mob and start a riot. They attacked the home of Jason, searching for Paul and Silas so they could drag them out to the crowd.* 6 Not finding them there, they dragged out Jason and some of the other believers* instead and took them before the city council. "Paul and Silas have caused trouble all over the world," they shouted, "and now they are here disturbing our city, too. 7 And Jason has welcomed them into his home. They are all guilty of treason against Caesar, for they profess allegiance to another king, named Jesus."

8 The people of the city, as well as the city council, were thrown into

17:4 Some manuscripts read *quite a few of the wives of the leading men.* 17:5 Or *the city council.* 17:6 Greek *brothers;* also in 17:10, 14.

turmoil by these reports. 9 So the officials forced Jason and the other believ-
ers to post bond, and then they released them.

Paul and Silas in Berea

10 That very night the believers sent Paul and Silas to Berea. When they ar-
rived there, they went to the Jewish synagogue. 11 And the people of Berea
were more open-minded than those in Thessalonica, and they listened ea-
gerly to Paul's message. They searched the Scriptures day after day to see if
Paul and Silas were teaching the truth. 12 As a result, many Jews believed, as
did many of the prominent Greek women and men.

13 But when some Jews in Thessalonica learned that Paul was preaching
the word of God in Berea, they went there and stirred up trouble. 14 The be-
lievers acted at once, sending Paul on to the coast, while Silas and Timothy
remained behind. 15 Those escorting Paul went with him all the way to Ath-
ens; then they returned to Berea with instructions for Silas and Timothy to
hurry and join him.

Paul Preaches in Athens

16 While Paul was waiting for them in Athens, he was deeply troubled by all
the idols he saw everywhere in the city. 17 He went to the synagogue to reason
with the Jews and the God-fearing Gentiles, and he spoke daily in the public
square to all who happened to be there.

18 He also had a debate with some of the Epicurean and Stoic philosophers.
When he told them about Jesus and his resurrection, they said, "What's this
babbler trying to say with these strange ideas he's picked up?" Others said,
"He seems to be preaching about some foreign gods."

19 Then they took him to the high council of the city.* "Come and tell us
about this new teaching," they said. 20 "You are saying some rather strange
things, and we want to know what it's all about." 21 (It should be explained
that all the Athenians as well as the foreigners in Athens seemed to spend
all their time discussing the latest ideas.)

22 So Paul, standing before the council,* addressed them as follows: "Men
of Athens, I notice that you are very religious in every way, 23 for as I was
walking along I saw your many shrines. And one of your altars had this in-
scription on it: 'To an Unknown God.' This God, whom you worship without
knowing, is the one I'm telling you about.

24 "He is the God who made the world and everything in it. Since he is Lord
of heaven and earth, he doesn't live in man-made temples, 25 and human
hands can't serve his needs—for he has no needs. He himself gives life and
breath to everything, and he satisfies every need. 26 From one man* he created
all the nations throughout the whole earth. He decided beforehand when
they should rise and fall, and he determined their boundaries.

27 "His purpose was for the nations to seek after God and perhaps feel their
way toward him and find him—though he is not far from any one of us. 28 For
in him we live and move and exist. As some of your* own poets have said,
'We are his offspring.' 29 And since this is true, we shouldn't think of God as
an idol designed by craftsmen from gold or silver or stone.

17:19 Or *the most learned society of philosophers in the city.* Greek reads *the Areopagus.* 17:22 Traditionally rendered *standing in the middle of Mars Hill;* Greek reads *standing in the middle of the Areopagus.* 17:26 Greek *From one;* other manuscripts read *From one blood.* 17:28 Some manuscripts read *our.*

other Christians, and threatened them with treason against the government. How would you respond in this situation? Would you stand tall in faith and love those who falsely accused you, even in the midst of their threats?

Difference Maker

Pray for those who follow Jesus to be loving and bold within their communities.

Make a Difference

17:16-34

Theological Eyes

Through what lens do you see your culture? Do you notice that the good news of Jesus is embedded in the popular stories of your society? Look with theological eyes for a moment. That great story about human survival is so riveting because God created us to live life eternally. That great song about the heartache of a broken relationship is so true because God created us to live in communion with him and with others.

At one point in his life, the apostle Paul walked around the city of Athens. He could have seen everything wrong with the false system of worship there, but instead, as he observed that culture, he found connection points with which to share Jesus. We must learn to view our world through the theological eyes of the Lord.

Difference Maker

The next time you watch a popular movie or listen to a popular song, try to find the theological connection points or the gospel story embedded within.

30“God overlooked people’s ignorance about these things in earlier times,
but now he commands everyone everywhere to repent of their sins and turn
to him. 31 For he has set a day for judging the world with justice by the man
he has appointed, and he proved to everyone who this is by raising him from
the dead.”

32 When they heard Paul speak about the resurrection of the dead, some
laughed in contempt, but others said, “We want to hear more about this
later.” 33 That ended Paul’s discussion with them, 34 but some joined him and
became believers. Among them were Dionysius, a member of the council,* a
woman named Damaris, and others with them.

Paul Meets Priscilla and Aquila in Corinth

18 Then Paul left Athens and went to Corinth.* 2 There he became ac-
quainted with a Jew named Aquila, born in Pontus, who had recently
arrived from Italy with his wife, Priscilla. They had left Italy when Claudius
Caesar deported all Jews from Rome. 3 Paul lived and worked with them, for
they were tentmakers* just as he was.

4 Each Sabbath found Paul at the synagogue, trying to convince the Jews
and Greeks alike. 5 And after Silas and Timothy came down from Macedonia,
Paul spent all his time preaching the word. He testified to the Jews that Jesus
was the Messiah. 6 But when they opposed and insulted him, Paul shook the
dust from his clothes and said, “Your blood is upon your own heads—I am
innocent. From now on I will go preach to the Gentiles.”

7 Then he left and went to the home of Titius Justus, a Gentile who wor-
shiped God and lived next door to the synagogue. 8 Crispus, the leader of the
synagogue, and everyone in his household believed in the Lord. Many others
in Corinth also heard Paul, became believers, and were baptized.

9 One night the Lord spoke to Paul in a vision and told him, “Don’t be
afraid! Speak out! Don’t be silent! 10 For I am with you, and no one will attack
and harm you, for many people in this city belong to me.” 11 So Paul stayed
there for the next year and a half, teaching the word of God.

12 But when Gallio became governor of Achaia, some Jews rose up together
against Paul and brought him before the governor for judgment. 13 They ac-
cused Paul of “persuading people to worship God in ways that are contrary
to our law.”

14 But just as Paul started to make his defense, Gallio turned to Paul’s accusers
and said, “Listen, you Jews, if this were a case involving some wrongdoing or a
serious crime, I would have a reason to accept your case. 15 But since it is merely
a question of words and names and your Jewish law, take care of it yourselves.
I refuse to judge such matters.” 16 And he threw them out of the courtroom.
17 The crowd* then grabbed Sosthenes, the leader of the synagogue, and
beat him right there in the courtroom. But Gallio paid no attention.

Paul Returns to Antioch of Syria

18 Paul stayed in Corinth for some time after that, then said good-bye to the
brothers and sisters* and went to nearby Cenchrea. There he shaved his head
according to Jewish custom, marking the end of a vow. Then he set sail for
Syria, taking Priscilla and Aquila with him.

17:34 Greek *an Areopagite.* 18:1 *Athens* and *Corinth* were major cities in Achaia, the region in the southern portion of the Greek peninsula. 18:3 Or *leatherworkers.* 18:17 Greek *Everyone;* other manuscripts read *All the Greeks.* 18:18 Greek *brothers;* also in 18:27.

Story Arc 18:1–3

● Priscilla and Aquila

This husband-and-wife team became one of the most important difference-making duos in the history of the world. They showed up all over the Roman Empire as leaders, teachers, supporters, equippers, and encouragers for the expanding movement of Christians. They were tentmakers and became Paul’s champions of ministry. Take a moment and look through Paul’s letters in the New Testament for evidence of the effects of Priscilla and Aquila.

Acts 18:24-19:1 ►

19 They stopped first at the port of Ephesus, where Paul left the others
behind. While he was there, he went to the synagogue to reason with the
Jews. 20 They asked him to stay longer, but he declined. 21 As he left, however,
he said, "I will come back later,* God willing." Then he set sail from Ephe-
sus. 22 The next stop was at the port of Caesarea. From there he went up and
visited the church at Jerusalem* and then went back to Antioch.
23 After spending some time in Antioch, Paul went back through Galatia
and Phrygia, visiting and strengthening all the believers.*

Apollos Instructed at Ephesus

24 Meanwhile, a Jew named Apollos, an eloquent speaker who knew the Scrip-
tures well, had arrived in Ephesus from Alexandria in Egypt. 25 He had been
taught the way of the Lord, and he taught others about Jesus with an enthusi-
astic spirit* and with accuracy. However, he knew only about John's baptism.
26 When Priscilla and Aquila heard him preaching boldly in the synagogue,
they took him aside and explained the way of God even more accurately.
27 Apollos had been thinking about going to Achaia, and the brothers
and sisters in Ephesus encouraged him to go. They wrote to the believers in
Achaia, asking them to welcome him. When he arrived there, he proved to
be of great benefit to those who, by God's grace, had believed. 28 He refuted
the Jews with powerful arguments in public debate. Using the Scriptures,
he explained to them that Jesus was the Messiah.

Paul's Third Missionary Journey

19 While Apollos was in Corinth, Paul traveled through the interior
regions until he reached Ephesus, on the coast, where he found
several believers.* 2 "Did you receive the Holy Spirit when you believed?"
he asked them.
"No," they replied, "we haven't even heard that there is a Holy Spirit."
3 "Then what baptism did you experience?" he asked.
And they replied, "The baptism of John."
4 Paul said, "John's baptism called for repentance from sin. But John him-
self told the people to believe in the one who would come later, meaning
Jesus."
5 As soon as they heard this, they were baptized in the name of the Lord
Jesus. 6 Then when Paul laid his hands on them, the Holy Spirit came on
them, and they spoke in other tongues* and prophesied. 7 There were about
twelve men in all.

Paul Ministers in Ephesus

8 Then Paul went to the synagogue and preached boldly for the next three
months, arguing persuasively about the Kingdom of God. 9 But some be-
came stubborn, rejecting his message and publicly speaking against the Way.
So Paul left the synagogue and took the believers with him. Then he held
daily discussions at the lecture hall of Tyrannus. 10 This went on for the next
two years, so that people throughout the province of Asia—both Jews and
Greeks—heard the word of the Lord.
11 God gave Paul the power to perform unusual miracles. 12 When

18:21 Some manuscripts read *"I must by all means be at Jerusalem for the upcoming festival, but I will come back later."* 18:22 Greek *the church.* 18:23 Greek *disciples;* also in 18:27. 18:25 Or *with enthusiasm in the Spirit.* 19:1 Greek *disciples;* also in 19:9, 30. 19:6 Or *in other languages.*

Story Arc **18:24–19:1**

Apollos

One of the most significant champions of the early church was a man named Apollos. He shows up repeatedly in the New Testament. He had considerable skills as a speaker. When Priscilla and Aquila equipped him with a better grasp of the good news of Jesus, Apollos's ministry really took off. What skill sets has God given you, and how could you sharpen them so that God can use you even more effectively?

Rom 4:1 ►

Question 19:21-22

Paul was working with his friends Timothy and Erastus on this world-changing missionary journey. Would you be willing to participate in a missions project with some friends? What could you do? Where could you go? Whom would you ask to work with you?

handkerchiefs or aprons that had merely touched his skin were placed on
sick people, they were healed of their diseases, and evil spirits were expelled.
13 A group of Jews was traveling from town to town casting out evil spirits.
They tried to use the name of the Lord Jesus in their incantation, saying, "I com-
mand you in the name of Jesus, whom Paul preaches, to come out!" 14 Seven sons
of Sceva, a leading priest, were doing this. 15 But one time when they tried it, the
evil spirit replied, "I know Jesus, and I know Paul, but who are you?" 16 Then
the man with the evil spirit leaped on them, overpowered them, and attacked
them with such violence that they fled from the house, naked and battered.
17 The story of what happened spread quickly all through Ephesus, to Jews
and Greeks alike. A solemn fear descended on the city, and the name of the
Lord Jesus was greatly honored. 18 Many who became believers confessed
their sinful practices. 19 A number of them who had been practicing sorcery
brought their incantation books and burned them at a public bonfire. The
value of the books was several million dollars.* 20 So the message about the
Lord spread widely and had a powerful effect.
21 Afterward Paul felt compelled by the Spirit* to go over to Macedonia
and Achaia before going to Jerusalem. "And after that," he said, "I must go
on to Rome!" 22 He sent his two assistants, Timothy and Erastus, ahead to
Macedonia while he stayed awhile longer in the province of Asia.

The Riot in Ephesus

23 About that time, serious trouble developed in Ephesus concerning the
Way. 24 It began with Demetrius, a silversmith who had a large business
manufacturing silver shrines of the Greek goddess Artemis.* He kept many
craftsmen busy. 25 He called them together, along with others employed in
similar trades, and addressed them as follows:
"Gentlemen, you know that our wealth comes from this business. 26 But
as you have seen and heard, this man Paul has persuaded many people that
handmade gods aren't really gods at all. And he's done this not only here
in Ephesus but throughout the entire province! 27 Of course, I'm not just
talking about the loss of public respect for our business. I'm also concerned
that the temple of the great goddess Artemis will lose its influence and that
Artemis—this magnificent goddess worshiped throughout the province of
Asia and all around the world—will be robbed of her great prestige!"
28 At this their anger boiled, and they began shouting, "Great is Artemis of
the Ephesians!" 29 Soon the whole city was filled with confusion. Everyone
rushed to the amphitheater, dragging along Gaius and Aristarchus, who
were Paul's traveling companions from Macedonia. 30 Paul wanted to go in,
too, but the believers wouldn't let him. 31 Some of the officials of the province,
friends of Paul, also sent a message to him, begging him not to risk his life
by entering the amphitheater.
32 Inside, the people were all shouting, some one thing and some another.
Everything was in confusion. In fact, most of them didn't even know why
they were there. 33 The Jews in the crowd pushed Alexander forward and told
him to explain the situation. He motioned for silence and tried to speak.
34 But when the crowd realized he was a Jew, they started shouting again and
kept it up for about two hours: "Great is Artemis of the Ephesians! Great is
Artemis of the Ephesians!"

19:19 Greek *50,000 pieces of silver,* each of which was the equivalent of a day's wage. **19:21** Or *decided in his spirit.* **19:24** *Artemis* is otherwise known as Diana.

35 At last the mayor was able to quiet them down enough to speak. "Cit-
izens of Ephesus," he said. "Everyone knows that Ephesus is the official
guardian of the temple of the great Artemis, whose image fell down to us
from heaven. 36 Since this is an undeniable fact, you should stay calm and
not do anything rash. 37 You have brought these men here, but they have
stolen nothing from the temple and have not spoken against our goddess.

38 "If Demetrius and the craftsmen have a case against them, the courts
are in session and the officials can hear the case at once. Let them make for-
mal charges. 39 And if there are complaints about other matters, they can be
settled in a legal assembly. 40 I am afraid we are in danger of being charged
with rioting by the Roman government, since there is no cause for all this
commotion. And if Rome demands an explanation, we won't know what to
say." 41* Then he dismissed them, and they dispersed.

Paul Goes to Macedonia and Greece

20 When the uproar was over, Paul sent for the believers* and encour-
aged them. Then he said good-bye and left for Macedonia. 2 While
there, he encouraged the believers in all the towns he passed through. Then
he traveled down to Greece, 3 where he stayed for three months. He was pre-
paring to sail back to Syria when he discovered a plot by some Jews against
his life, so he decided to return through Macedonia.

4 Several men were traveling with him. They were Sopater son of Pyrrhus
from Berea; Aristarchus and Secundus from Thessalonica; Gaius from Derbe;
Timothy; and Tychicus and Trophimus from the province of Asia. 5 They
went on ahead and waited for us at Troas. 6 After the Passover* ended, we
boarded a ship at Philippi in Macedonia and five days later joined them in
Troas, where we stayed a week.

Paul's Final Visit to Troas

7 On the first day of the week, we gathered with the local believers to share
in the Lord's Supper.* Paul was preaching to them, and since he was leaving
the next day, he kept talking until midnight. 8 The upstairs room where we
met was lighted with many flickering lamps. 9 As Paul spoke on and on, a
young man named Eutychus, sitting on the windowsill, became very drowsy.
Finally, he fell sound asleep and dropped three stories to his death below.
10 Paul went down, bent over him, and took him into his arms. "Don't worry,"
he said, "he's alive!" 11 Then they all went back upstairs, shared in the Lord's
Supper,* and ate together. Paul continued talking to them until dawn, and
then he left. 12 Meanwhile, the young man was taken home alive and well,
and everyone was greatly relieved.

Paul Meets the Ephesian Elders

13 Paul went by land to Assos, where he had arranged for us to join him, while
we traveled by ship. 14 He joined us there, and we sailed together to Mitylene.
15 The next day we sailed past the island of Kios. The following day we crossed
to the island of Samos, and* a day later we arrived at Miletus.

16 Paul had decided to sail on past Ephesus, for he didn't want to spend
any more time in the province of Asia. He was hurrying to get to Jerusalem,

19:41 Some translations include verse 41 as part of verse 40. 20:1 Greek *disciples.* 20:6 Greek *the days of unleavened bread.* 20:7 Greek *to break bread.* 20:11 Greek *broke the bread.* 20:15 Some manuscripts read *and having stayed at Trogyllium.*

if possible, in time for the Festival of Pentecost. 17 But when we landed at
Miletus, he sent a message to the elders of the church at Ephesus, asking
them to come and meet him.
18 When they arrived he declared, "You know that from the day I set foot
in the province of Asia until now 19 I have done the Lord's work humbly and
with many tears. I have endured the trials that came to me from the plots of
the Jews. 20 I never shrank back from telling you what you needed to hear,
either publicly or in your homes. 21 I have had one message for Jews and
Greeks alike—the necessity of repenting from sin and turning to God, and
of having faith in our Lord Jesus.
22 "And now I am bound by the Spirit* to go to Jerusalem. I don't know
what awaits me, 23 except that the Holy Spirit tells me in city after city that
jail and suffering lie ahead. 24 But my life is worth nothing to me unless I
use it for finishing the work assigned me by the Lord Jesus—the work of
telling others the Good News about the wonderful grace of God.
25 "And now I know that none of you to whom I have preached the King-
dom will ever see me again. 26 I declare today that I have been faithful. If
anyone suffers eternal death, it's not my fault,* 27 for I didn't shrink from
declaring all that God wants you to know.
28 "So guard yourselves and God's people. Feed and shepherd God's flock—
his church, purchased with his own blood*—over which the Holy Spirit has
appointed you as leaders.* 29 I know that false teachers, like vicious wolves, will
come in among you after I leave, not sparing the flock. 30 Even some men from
your own group will rise up and distort the truth in order to draw a following.
31 Watch out! Remember the three years I was with you—my constant watch
and care over you night and day, and my many tears for you.
32 "And now I entrust you to God and the message of his grace that is able
to build you up and give you an inheritance with all those he has set apart
for himself.
33 "I have never coveted anyone's silver or gold or fine clothes. 34 You know
that these hands of mine have worked to supply my own needs and even the
needs of those who were with me. 35 And I have been a constant example of
how you can help those in need by working hard. You should remember the
words of the Lord Jesus: 'It is more blessed to give than to receive.'"
36 When he had finished speaking, he knelt and prayed with them. 37 They
all cried as they embraced and kissed him good-bye. 38 They were sad most
of all because he had said that they would never see him again. Then they
escorted him down to the ship.

Paul's Journey to Jerusalem

21 After saying farewell to the Ephesian elders, we sailed straight to
the island of Cos. The next day we reached Rhodes and then went
to Patara. 2 There we boarded a ship sailing for Phoenicia. 3 We sighted the
island of Cyprus, passed it on our left, and landed at the harbor of Tyre, in
Syria, where the ship was to unload its cargo.
4 We went ashore, found the local believers,* and stayed with them a
week. These believers prophesied through the Holy Spirit that Paul should
not go on to Jerusalem. 5 When we returned to the ship at the end of the

20:22 Or *by my spirit,* or *by an inner compulsion;* Greek reads *by the spirit.* **20:26** Greek *I am innocent of the blood of all.* **20:28a** Or *with the blood of his own [Son].* **20:28b** Or *overseers,* or *bishops.* **21:4** Greek *disciples;* also in 21:16.

Make a Difference

20:24

Align Your Actions

God calls people to make a difference in this world every day they are alive, but people don't always check in with Jesus to get their daily assignments. As a result, they toil and labor, but their work is in vain when it's not something Jesus has set before them. People can play and laze, but their happiness is shallow and empty when it's not on God's radar.

Perhaps much of human dissatisfaction in life comes when people do not do the work Jesus has assigned them to do. What would change in human hearts if people were to present themselves to Jesus ready for work? What if people checked in with him each morning and asked, "Lord, what do you want me to do today?"

Difference Maker

Strive to align all your actions today with the work that Jesus has called you to do.

Make a Difference

20:35

An Example

One reason why Christianity spread so rapidly was because the first followers of Jesus led by example in caring for the poor. They worked tirelessly on behalf of widows and orphans. They started movements to support those suffering from famine, and they constantly addressed the needs of the afflicted. Through these efforts, the world could tell that there was something remarkably genuine and refreshing about those who followed Jesus.

week, the entire congregation, including women* and children, left the city
and came down to the shore with us. There we knelt, prayed, 6 and said our
farewells. Then we went aboard, and they returned home.
7 The next stop after leaving Tyre was Ptolemais, where we greeted the
brothers and sisters* and stayed for one day. 8 The next day we went on to
Caesarea and stayed at the home of Philip the Evangelist, one of the seven
men who had been chosen to distribute food. 9 He had four unmarried
daughters who had the gift of prophecy.
10 Several days later a man named Agabus, who also had the gift of proph-
ecy, arrived from Judea. 11 He came over, took Paul's belt, and bound his own
feet and hands with it. Then he said, "The Holy Spirit declares, 'So shall the
owner of this belt be bound by the Jewish leaders in Jerusalem and turned
over to the Gentiles.'" 12 When we heard this, we and the local believers all
begged Paul not to go on to Jerusalem.
13 But he said, "Why all this weeping? You are breaking my heart! I am
ready not only to be jailed at Jerusalem but even to die for the sake of the
Lord Jesus." 14 When it was clear that we couldn't persuade him, we gave up
and said, "The Lord's will be done."

Paul Arrives at Jerusalem

15 After this we packed our things and left for Jerusalem. 16 Some believers
from Caesarea accompanied us, and they took us to the home of Mnason,
a man originally from Cyprus and one of the early believers. 17 When we
arrived, the brothers and sisters in Jerusalem welcomed us warmly.
18 The next day Paul went with us to meet with James, and all the elders of
the Jerusalem church were present. 19 After greeting them, Paul gave a detailed
account of the things God had accomplished among the Gentiles through
his ministry.
20 After hearing this, they praised God. And then they said, "You know, dear
brother, how many thousands of Jews have also believed, and they all follow
the law of Moses very seriously. 21 But the Jewish believers here in Jerusalem
have been told that you are teaching all the Jews who live among the Gentiles
to turn their backs on the laws of Moses. They've heard that you teach them
not to circumcise their children or follow other Jewish customs. 22 What should
we do? They will certainly hear that you have come.
23 "Here's what we want you to do. We have four men here who have
completed their vow. 24 Go with them to the Temple and join them in the
purification ceremony, paying for them to have their heads ritually shaved.
Then everyone will know that the rumors are all false and that you yourself
observe the Jewish laws.
25 "As for the Gentile believers, they should do what we already told
them in a letter: They should abstain from eating food offered to idols,
from consuming blood or the meat of strangled animals, and from sexual
immorality."

Paul Is Arrested

26 So Paul went to the Temple the next day with the other men. They had
already started the purification ritual, so he publicly announced the date
when their vows would end and sacrifices would be offered for each of them.

21:5 Or *wives.* 21:7 Greek *brothers;* also in 21:17.

Difference Maker

Be an example of how to help those in need. Work hard to organize food and clothing drives, to establish after-school youth drop-in programs, or to arrange a trip to a local rescue mission or food provider. Set the example so that others will join in.

Question 21:19

If you were to greet someone tomorrow, what could you tell them about what God has been doing in your life?

[27]The seven days were almost ended when some Jews from the province
of Asia saw Paul in the Temple and roused a mob against him. They grabbed
him, [28]yelling, "Men of Israel, help us! This is the man who preaches against
our people everywhere and tells everybody to disobey the Jewish laws. He
speaks against the Temple—and even defiles this holy place by bringing in
Gentiles.*" [29](For earlier that day they had seen him in the city with Troph-
imus, a Gentile from Ephesus,* and they assumed Paul had taken him into
the Temple.)

[30]The whole city was rocked by these accusations, and a great riot fol-
lowed. Paul was grabbed and dragged out of the Temple, and immediately
the gates were closed behind him. [31]As they were trying to kill him, word
reached the commander of the Roman regiment that all Jerusalem was in
an uproar. [32]He immediately called out his soldiers and officers* and ran
down among the crowd. When the mob saw the commander and the troops
coming, they stopped beating Paul.

[33]Then the commander arrested him and ordered him bound with two
chains. He asked the crowd who he was and what he had done. [34]Some
shouted one thing and some another. Since he couldn't find out the truth
in all the uproar and confusion, he ordered that Paul be taken to the fortress.
[35]As Paul reached the stairs, the mob grew so violent the soldiers had to lift
him to their shoulders to protect him. [36]And the crowd followed behind,
shouting, "Kill him, kill him!"

Paul Speaks to the Crowd

[37]As Paul was about to be taken inside, he said to the commander, "May I
have a word with you?"

"Do you know Greek?" the commander asked, surprised. [38]"Aren't you the
Egyptian who led a rebellion some time ago and took 4,000 members of the
Assassins out into the desert?"

[39]"No," Paul replied, "I am a Jew and a citizen of Tarsus in Cilicia, which
is an important city. Please, let me talk to these people." [40]The commander
agreed, so Paul stood on the stairs and motioned to the people to be quiet.
Soon a deep silence enveloped the crowd, and he addressed them in their
own language, Aramaic.*

22 "Brothers and esteemed fathers," Paul said, "listen to me as I offer
my defense." [2]When they heard him speaking in their own lan-
guage,* the silence was even greater.

[3]Then Paul said, "I am a Jew, born in Tarsus, a city in Cilicia, and I was
brought up and educated here in Jerusalem under Gamaliel. As his stu-
dent, I was carefully trained in our Jewish laws and customs. I became very
zealous to honor God in everything I did, just like all of you today. [4]And
I persecuted the followers of the Way, hounding some to death, arresting
both men and women and throwing them in prison. [5]The high priest
and the whole council of elders can testify that this is so. For I received
letters from them to our Jewish brothers in Damascus, authorizing me
to bring the followers of the Way from there to Jerusalem, in chains, to
be punished.

[6]"As I was on the road, approaching Damascus about noon, a very

21:28 Greek *Greeks.* **21:29** Greek *Trophimus, the Ephesian.* **21:32** Greek *centurions.* **21:40** Or *Hebrew.* **22:2** Greek *in Aramaic,* or *in Hebrew.*

bright light from heaven suddenly shone down around me. 7 I fell to the
ground and heard a voice saying to me, 'Saul, Saul, why are you perse-
cuting me?'

8 "'Who are you, lord?' I asked.

"And the voice replied, 'I am Jesus the Nazarene,* the one you are perse-
cuting.' 9 The people with me saw the light but didn't understand the voice
speaking to me.

10 "I asked, 'What should I do, Lord?'

"And the Lord told me, 'Get up and go into Damascus, and there you will
be told everything you are to do.'

11 "I was blinded by the intense light and had to be led by the hand to Da-
mascus by my companions. 12 A man named Ananias lived there. He was a
godly man, deeply devoted to the law, and well regarded by all the Jews of
Damascus. 13 He came and stood beside me and said, 'Brother Saul, regain
your sight.' And that very moment I could see him!

14 "Then he told me, 'The God of our ancestors has chosen you to know
his will and to see the Righteous One and hear him speak. 15 For you are to be
his witness, telling everyone what you have seen and heard. 16 What are you
waiting for? Get up and be baptized. Have your sins washed away by calling
on the name of the Lord.'

17 "After I returned to Jerusalem, I was praying in the Temple and fell into
a trance. 18 I saw a vision of Jesus* saying to me, 'Hurry! Leave Jerusalem, for
the people here won't accept your testimony about me.'

19 "'But Lord,' I argued, 'they certainly know that in every synagogue I
imprisoned and beat those who believed in you. 20 And I was in complete
agreement when your witness Stephen was killed. I stood by and kept the
coats they took off when they stoned him.'

21 "But the Lord said to me, 'Go, for I will send you far away to the
Gentiles!'"

22 The crowd listened until Paul said that word. Then they all began to
shout, "Away with such a fellow! He isn't fit to live!" 23 They yelled, threw
off their coats, and tossed handfuls of dust into the air.

Paul Reveals His Roman Citizenship

24 The commander brought Paul inside and ordered him lashed with whips
to make him confess his crime. He wanted to find out why the crowd had
become so furious. 25 When they tied Paul down to lash him, Paul said to
the officer* standing there, "Is it legal for you to whip a Roman citizen who
hasn't even been tried?"

26 When the officer heard this, he went to the commander and asked,
"What are you doing? This man is a Roman citizen!"

27 So the commander went over and asked Paul, "Tell me, are you a Ro-
man citizen?"

"Yes, I certainly am," Paul replied.

28 "I am, too," the commander muttered, "and it cost me plenty!"

Paul answered, "But I am a citizen by birth!"

29 The soldiers who were about to interrogate Paul quickly withdrew when
they heard he was a Roman citizen, and the commander was frightened
because he had ordered him bound and whipped.

Question **22:15**

Go back and read Acts 1:8. For the last twenty-one chapters in the book of Acts, how has the Holy Spirit been fulfilling this promise? For the last two thousand years, how has the Holy Spirit continued to fulfill this promise? For the rest of your life, how could the Holy Spirit continue to fulfill this promise through you?

22:8 Or *Jesus of Nazareth.* 22:18 Greek *him.* 22:25 Greek *the centurion;* also in 22:26.

Question **23:16**

This young man, Paul's nephew, happened to overhear the brutal plans against Paul. What surprises you about the risk he took to warn his uncle? What would it have been like to be a follower of Jesus in those days? How does that compare to how you could live for Jesus today?

Paul before the High Council

30 The next day the commander ordered the leading priests into session with
the Jewish high council.* He wanted to find out what the trouble was all
about, so he released Paul to have him stand before them.

23 Gazing intently at the high council,* Paul began: "Brothers, I have
always lived before God with a clear conscience!"
2 Instantly Ananias the high priest commanded those close to Paul to slap
him on the mouth. 3 But Paul said to him, "God will slap you, you corrupt
hypocrite!* What kind of judge are you to break the law yourself by ordering
me struck like that?"
4 Those standing near Paul said to him, "Do you dare to insult God's high
priest?"
5 "I'm sorry, brothers. I didn't realize he was the high priest," Paul replied,
"for the Scriptures say, 'You must not speak evil of any of your rulers.'*"
6 Paul realized that some members of the high council were Sadducees
and some were Pharisees, so he shouted, "Brothers, I am a Pharisee, as were
my ancestors! And I am on trial because my hope is in the resurrection of
the dead!"
7 This divided the council—the Pharisees against the Sadducees— 8 for the
Sadducees say there is no resurrection or angels or spirits, but the Pharisees
believe in all of these. 9 So there was a great uproar. Some of the teachers of
religious law who were Pharisees jumped up and began to argue forcefully.
"We see nothing wrong with him," they shouted. "Perhaps a spirit or an
angel spoke to him." 10 As the conflict grew more violent, the commander
was afraid they would tear Paul apart. So he ordered his soldiers to go and
rescue him by force and take him back to the fortress.
11 That night the Lord appeared to Paul and said, "Be encouraged, Paul.
Just as you have been a witness to me here in Jerusalem, you must preach
the Good News in Rome as well."

The Plan to Kill Paul

12 The next morning a group of Jews* got together and bound themselves
with an oath not to eat or drink until they had killed Paul. 13 There were more
than forty of them in the conspiracy. 14 They went to the leading priests and
elders and told them, "We have bound ourselves with an oath to eat noth-
ing until we have killed Paul. 15 So you and the high council should ask the
commander to bring Paul back to the council again. Pretend you want to
examine his case more fully. We will kill him on the way."
16 But Paul's nephew—his sister's son—heard of their plan and went to
the fortress and told Paul. 17 Paul called for one of the Roman officers* and
said, "Take this young man to the commander. He has something important
to tell him."
18 So the officer did, explaining, "Paul, the prisoner, called me over and
asked me to bring this young man to you because he has something to tell
you."
19 The commander took his hand, led him aside, and asked, "What is it
you want to tell me?"
20 Paul's nephew told him, "Some Jews are going to ask you to bring Paul

22:30 Greek *Sanhedrin.* 23:1 Greek *Sanhedrin;* also in 23:6, 15, 20, 28. 23:3 Greek *you whitewashed wall.* 23:5 Exod 22:28. 23:12 Greek *the Jews.* 23:17 Greek *centurions;* also in 23:23.

before the high council tomorrow, pretending they want to get some more
information. 21 But don't do it! There are more than forty men hiding along
the way ready to ambush him. They have vowed not to eat or drink any-
thing until they have killed him. They are ready now, just waiting for your
consent."

22 "Don't let anyone know you told me this," the commander warned the
young man.

Paul Is Sent to Caesarea

23 Then the commander called two of his officers and ordered, "Get 200 sol-
diers ready to leave for Caesarea at nine o'clock tonight. Also take 200 spear-
men and 70 mounted troops. 24 Provide horses for Paul to ride, and get him
safely to Governor Felix." 25 Then he wrote this letter to the governor:

> 26 "From Claudius Lysias, to his Excellency, Governor Felix: Greetings!
>
> 27 "This man was seized by some Jews, and they were about to kill
> him when I arrived with the troops. When I learned that he was a
> Roman citizen, I removed him to safety. 28 Then I took him to their high
> council to try to learn the basis of the accusations against him. 29 I soon
> discovered the charge was something regarding their religious law—
> certainly nothing worthy of imprisonment or death. 30 But when I was
> informed of a plot to kill him, I immediately sent him on to you. I have
> told his accusers to bring their charges before you."

31 So that night, as ordered, the soldiers took Paul as far as Antipatris.
32 They returned to the fortress the next morning, while the mounted troops
took him on to Caesarea. 33 When they arrived in Caesarea, they presented
Paul and the letter to Governor Felix. 34 He read it and then asked Paul what
province he was from. "Cilicia," Paul answered.

35 "I will hear your case myself when your accusers arrive," the governor
told him. Then the governor ordered him kept in the prison at Herod's
headquarters.*

Paul Appears before Felix

24 Five days later Ananias, the high priest, arrived with some of the
Jewish elders and the lawyer* Tertullus, to present their case against
Paul to the governor. 2 When Paul was called in, Tertullus presented the
charges against Paul in the following address to the governor:

"You have provided a long period of peace for us Jews and with foresight
have enacted reforms for us. 3 For all of this, Your Excellency, we are very
grateful to you. 4 But I don't want to bore you, so please give me your at-
tention for only a moment. 5 We have found this man to be a troublemaker
who is constantly stirring up riots among the Jews all over the world. He is a
ringleader of the cult known as the Nazarenes. 6 Furthermore, he was trying
to desecrate the Temple when we arrested him.* 8 You can find out the truth
of our accusations by examining him yourself." 9 Then the other Jews chimed
in, declaring that everything Tertullus said was true.

23:35 Greek *Herod's Praetorium.* **24:1** Greek *some elders and an orator.* **24:6** Some manuscripts add an expanded conclusion to verse 6, all of verse 7, and an additional phrase in verse 8: *We would have judged him by our law, 7 but Lysias, the commander of the garrison, came and violently took him away from us, 8 commanding his accusers to come before you.*

Question **24:22**

In those dynamic, early days of faith, Christianity was known as "the Way." Why is this label a really good description of faith in Jesus?

10 The governor then motioned for Paul to speak. Paul said, "I know, sir,
that you have been a judge of Jewish affairs for many years, so I gladly present
my defense before you. 11 You can quickly discover that I arrived in Jerusalem
no more than twelve days ago to worship at the Temple. 12 My accusers never
found me arguing with anyone in the Temple, nor stirring up a riot in any
synagogue or on the streets of the city. 13 These men cannot prove the things
they accuse me of doing.

14 "But I admit that I follow the Way, which they call a cult. I worship the
God of our ancestors, and I firmly believe the Jewish law and everything
written in the prophets. 15 I have the same hope in God that these men have,
that he will raise both the righteous and the unrighteous. 16 Because of this,
I always try to maintain a clear conscience before God and all people.

17 "After several years away, I returned to Jerusalem with money to aid my
people and to offer sacrifices to God. 18 My accusers saw me in the Temple as
I was completing a purification ceremony. There was no crowd around me
and no rioting. 19 But some Jews from the province of Asia were there—and
they ought to be here to bring charges if they have anything against me!
20 Ask these men here what crime the Jewish high council* found me guilty
of, 21 except for the one time I shouted out, 'I am on trial before you today
because I believe in the resurrection of the dead!'"

22 At that point Felix, who was quite familiar with the Way, adjourned the
hearing and said, "Wait until Lysias, the garrison commander, arrives. Then
I will decide the case." 23 He ordered an officer* to keep Paul in custody but
to give him some freedom and allow his friends to visit him and take care
of his needs.

24 A few days later Felix came back with his wife, Drusilla, who was Jew-
ish. Sending for Paul, they listened as he told them about faith in Christ
Jesus. 25 As he reasoned with them about righteousness and self-control and
the coming day of judgment, Felix became frightened. "Go away for now,"
he replied. "When it is more convenient, I'll call for you again." 26 He also
hoped that Paul would bribe him, so he sent for him quite often and talked
with him.

27 After two years went by in this way, Felix was succeeded by Porcius Fes-
tus. And because Felix wanted to gain favor with the Jewish people, he left
Paul in prison.

Paul Appears before Festus

25 Three days after Festus arrived in Caesarea to take over his new re-
sponsibilities, he left for Jerusalem, 2 where the leading priests and
other Jewish leaders met with him and made their accusations against Paul.
3 They asked Festus as a favor to transfer Paul to Jerusalem (planning to am-
bush and kill him on the way). 4 But Festus replied that Paul was at Caesarea
and he himself would be returning there soon. 5 So he said, "Those of you
in authority can return with me. If Paul has done anything wrong, you can
make your accusations."

6 About eight or ten days later Festus returned to Caesarea, and on the
following day he took his seat in court and ordered that Paul be brought in.
7 When Paul arrived, the Jewish leaders from Jerusalem gathered around and
made many serious accusations they couldn't prove.

24:20 Greek *Sanhedrin.* **24:23** Greek *a centurion.*

8 Paul denied the charges. "I am not guilty of any crime against the Jewish
laws or the Temple or the Roman government," he said.
9 Then Festus, wanting to please the Jews, asked him, "Are you willing to
go to Jerusalem and stand trial before me there?"
10 But Paul replied, "No! This is the official Roman court, so I ought to be
tried right here. You know very well I am not guilty of harming the Jews.
11 If I have done something worthy of death, I don't refuse to die. But if I
am innocent, no one has a right to turn me over to these men to kill me. I
appeal to Caesar!"
12 Festus conferred with his advisers and then replied, "Very well! You have
appealed to Caesar, and to Caesar you will go!"
13 A few days later King Agrippa arrived with his sister, Bernice,* to pay
their respects to Festus. 14 During their stay of several days, Festus discussed
Paul's case with the king. "There is a prisoner here," he told him, "whose case
was left for me by Felix. 15 When I was in Jerusalem, the leading priests and
Jewish elders pressed charges against him and asked me to condemn him.
16 I pointed out to them that Roman law does not convict people without
a trial. They must be given an opportunity to confront their accusers and
defend themselves.
17 "When his accusers came here for the trial, I didn't delay. I called the case
the very next day and ordered Paul brought in. 18 But the accusations made
against him weren't any of the crimes I expected. 19 Instead, it was something
about their religion and a dead man named Jesus, who Paul insists is alive. 20 I
was at a loss to know how to investigate these things, so I asked him whether
he would be willing to stand trial on these charges in Jerusalem. 21 But Paul
appealed to have his case decided by the emperor. So I ordered that he be
held in custody until I could arrange to send him to Caesar."
22 "I'd like to hear the man myself," Agrippa said.
And Festus replied, "You will—tomorrow!"

Paul Speaks to Agrippa

23 So the next day Agrippa and Bernice arrived at the auditorium with great
pomp, accompanied by military officers and prominent men of the city. Fes-
tus ordered that Paul be brought in. 24 Then Festus said, "King Agrippa and
all who are here, this is the man whose death is demanded by all the Jews,
both here and in Jerusalem. 25 But in my opinion he has done nothing de-
serving death. However, since he appealed his case to the emperor, I have
decided to send him to Rome.
26 "But what shall I write the emperor? For there is no clear charge against
him. So I have brought him before all of you, and especially you, King
Agrippa, so that after we examine him, I might have something to write.
27 For it makes no sense to send a prisoner to the emperor without specifying
the charges against him!"

26 Then Agrippa said to Paul, "You may speak in your defense."
So Paul, gesturing with his hand, started his defense: 2 "I am for-
tunate, King Agrippa, that you are the one hearing my defense today against
all these accusations made by the Jewish leaders, 3 for I know you are an expert
on all Jewish customs and controversies. Now please listen to me patiently!

25:13 Greek *Agrippa the king and Bernice arrived.*

Make a Difference

25:10–11

We Know Who Is Actually in Charge

Throughout the Bible, God used the most powerful rulers in history to work his plan of salvation. The Lord orchestrated his course of events by using Egyptian Pharaohs, Babylonian and Persian emperors, and all levels of princes and magistrates and governors and officials.

It is fascinating that the most powerful leaders on the planet, the Roman Caesars, became mere pawns in the overarching story of the good news of Jesus. When Jesus was born, Caesar had issued a census. When Jesus was asked a trick question, he told people to give to Caesar what was Caesar's and to God what was God's. Now, here, as a Roman citizen protected by rights, Paul appeals to Caesar so that he can share about Jesus, the almighty King of kings.

Difference Maker

Pray that the Lord will use the powerful leaders of today to spread the good news of Jesus Christ.

Question 26:9-23

You don't have to have a dramatic testimony like Paul's to influence others. You just need to tell your story. If someone asked you how you got to where you are today, what story of Jesus would you tell? How could you make Jesus more and more the center of your story?

4 “As the Jewish leaders are well aware, I was given a thorough Jewish train-
ing from my earliest childhood among my own people and in Jerusalem. 5 If
they would admit it, they know that I have been a member of the Pharisees,
the strictest sect of our religion. 6 Now I am on trial because of my hope in the
fulfillment of God's promise made to our ancestors. 7 In fact, that is why the
twelve tribes of Israel zealously worship God night and day, and they share
the same hope I have. Yet, Your Majesty, they accuse me for having this hope!
8 Why does it seem incredible to any of you that God can raise the dead?

9 “I used to believe that I ought to do everything I could to oppose the
very name of Jesus the Nazarene.* 10 Indeed, I did just that in Jerusalem. Au-
thorized by the leading priests, I caused many believers* there to be sent to
prison. And I cast my vote against them when they were condemned to death.
11 Many times I had them punished in the synagogues to get them to curse
Jesus.* I was so violently opposed to them that I even chased them down in
foreign cities.

12 “One day I was on such a mission to Damascus, armed with the author-
ity and commission of the leading priests. 13 About noon, Your Majesty, as I
was on the road, a light from heaven brighter than the sun shone down on
me and my companions. 14 We all fell down, and I heard a voice saying to me
in Aramaic,* ‘Saul, Saul, why are you persecuting me? It is useless for you to
fight against my will.*’

15 “‘Who are you, lord?’ I asked.

“And the Lord replied, ‘I am Jesus, the one you are persecuting. 16 Now get
to your feet! For I have appeared to you to appoint you as my servant and
witness. Tell people that you have seen me, and tell them what I will show
you in the future. 17 And I will rescue you from both your own people and
the Gentiles. Yes, I am sending you to the Gentiles 18 to open their eyes, so
they may turn from darkness to light and from the power of Satan to God.
Then they will receive forgiveness for their sins and be given a place among
God's people, who are set apart by faith in me.’

19 “And so, King Agrippa, I obeyed that vision from heaven. 20 I preached
first to those in Damascus, then in Jerusalem and throughout all Judea, and
also to the Gentiles, that all must repent of their sins and turn to God—and
prove they have changed by the good things they do. 21 Some Jews arrested me
in the Temple for preaching this, and they tried to kill me. 22 But God has pro-
tected me right up to this present time so I can testify to everyone, from the
least to the greatest. I teach nothing except what the prophets and Moses said
would happen—23 that the Messiah would suffer and be the first to rise from
the dead, and in this way announce God's light to Jews and Gentiles alike.”

24 Suddenly, Festus shouted, “Paul, you are insane. Too much study has
made you crazy!”

25 But Paul replied, “I am not insane, Most Excellent Festus. What I am
saying is the sober truth. 26 And King Agrippa knows about these things. I
speak boldly, for I am sure these events are all familiar to him, for they were
not done in a corner! 27 King Agrippa, do you believe the prophets? I know
you do—”

28 Agrippa interrupted him. “Do you think you can persuade me to become
a Christian so quickly?”*

26:9 Or *Jesus of Nazareth.* 26:10 Greek *many of God's holy people.* 26:11 Greek *to blaspheme.* 26:14a Or *Hebrew.* 26:14b Greek *It is hard for you to kick against the oxgoads.* 26:28 Or *“A little more, and your arguments would make me a Christian.”*

29 Paul replied, "Whether quickly or not, I pray to God that both you and
everyone here in this audience might become the same as I am, except for
these chains."
30 Then the king, the governor, Bernice, and all the others stood and left.
31 As they went out, they talked it over and agreed, "This man hasn't done
anything to deserve death or imprisonment."
32 And Agrippa said to Festus, "He could have been set free if he hadn't
appealed to Caesar."

Prayer 26:29

Lord, I pray that everyone around me would recognize you as their Savior and invite you into their lives. Amen.

Paul Sails for Rome

27 When the time came, we set sail for Italy. Paul and several other pris-
oners were placed in the custody of a Roman officer* named Julius, a
captain of the Imperial Regiment. 2 Aristarchus, a Macedonian from Thessa-
lonica, was also with us. We left on a ship whose home port was Adramyttium
on the northwest coast of the province of Asia;* it was scheduled to make
several stops at ports along the coast of the province.
3 The next day when we docked at Sidon, Julius was very kind to Paul and
let him go ashore to visit with friends so they could provide for his needs.
4 Putting out to sea from there, we encountered strong headwinds that made
it difficult to keep the ship on course, so we sailed north of Cyprus between
the island and the mainland. 5 Keeping to the open sea, we passed along the
coast of Cilicia and Pamphylia, landing at Myra, in the province of Lycia.
6 There the commanding officer found an Egyptian ship from Alexandria
that was bound for Italy, and he put us on board.
7 We had several days of slow sailing, and after great difficulty we finally
neared Cnidus. But the wind was against us, so we sailed across to Crete
and along the sheltered coast of the island, past the cape of Salmone. 8 We
struggled along the coast with great difficulty and finally arrived at Fair
Havens, near the town of Lasea. 9 We had lost a lot of time. The weather was
becoming dangerous for sea travel because it was so late in the fall,* and Paul
spoke to the ship's officers about it.
10 "Men," he said, "I believe there is trouble ahead if we go on—shipwreck,
loss of cargo, and danger to our lives as well." 11 But the officer in charge of
the prisoners listened more to the ship's captain and the owner than to Paul.
12 And since Fair Havens was an exposed harbor—a poor place to spend the
winter—most of the crew wanted to go on to Phoenix, farther up the coast
of Crete, and spend the winter there. Phoenix was a good harbor with only
a southwest and northwest exposure.

The Storm at Sea

13 When a light wind began blowing from the south, the sailors thought
they could make it. So they pulled up anchor and sailed close to the shore of
Crete. 14 But the weather changed abruptly, and a wind of typhoon strength
(called a "northeaster") burst across the island and blew us out to sea. 15 The
sailors couldn't turn the ship into the wind, so they gave up and let it run
before the gale.
16 We sailed along the sheltered side of a small island named Cauda,* where

27:1 Greek *centurion;* similarly in 27:6, 11, 31, 43. 27:2 *Asia* was a Roman province in what is now western Turkey. 27:9 Greek *because the fast was now already gone by.* This fast was associated with the Day of Atonement (*Yom Kippur*), which occurred in late September or early October. 27:16 Some manuscripts read *Clauda.*

with great difficulty we hoisted aboard the lifeboat being towed behind us.
17 Then the sailors bound ropes around the hull of the ship to strengthen it.
They were afraid of being driven across to the sandbars of Syrtis off the Af-
rican coast, so they lowered the sea anchor to slow the ship and were driven
before the wind.

18 The next day, as gale-force winds continued to batter the ship, the crew
began throwing the cargo overboard. 19 The following day they even took
some of the ship's gear and threw it overboard. 20 The terrible storm raged
for many days, blotting out the sun and the stars, until at last all hope was
gone.

21 No one had eaten for a long time. Finally, Paul called the crew together
and said, "Men, you should have listened to me in the first place and not left
Crete. You would have avoided all this damage and loss. 22 But take courage!
None of you will lose your lives, even though the ship will go down. 23 For last
night an angel of the God to whom I belong and whom I serve stood beside
me, 24 and he said, 'Don't be afraid, Paul, for you will surely stand trial before
Caesar! What's more, God in his goodness has granted safety to everyone
sailing with you.' 25 So take courage! For I believe God. It will be just as he
said. 26 But we will be shipwrecked on an island."

The Shipwreck

27 About midnight on the fourteenth night of the storm, as we were being
driven across the Sea of Adria,* the sailors sensed land was near. 28 They
dropped a weighted line and found that the water was 120 feet deep. But a
little later they measured again and found it was only 90 feet deep.* 29 At this
rate they were afraid we would soon be driven against the rocks along the
shore, so they threw out four anchors from the back of the ship and prayed
for daylight.

30 Then the sailors tried to abandon the ship; they lowered the lifeboat as
though they were going to put out anchors from the front of the ship. 31 But
Paul said to the commanding officer and the soldiers, "You will all die un-
less the sailors stay aboard." 32 So the soldiers cut the ropes to the lifeboat
and let it drift away.

33 Just as day was dawning, Paul urged everyone to eat. "You have been so
worried that you haven't touched food for two weeks," he said. 34 "Please eat
something now for your own good. For not a hair of your heads will perish."
35 Then he took some bread, gave thanks to God before them all, and broke off
a piece and ate it. 36 Then everyone was encouraged and began to eat—37 all
276 of us who were on board. 38 After eating, the crew lightened the ship
further by throwing the cargo of wheat overboard.

39 When morning dawned, they didn't recognize the coastline, but they
saw a bay with a beach and wondered if they could get to shore by running
the ship aground. 40 So they cut off the anchors and left them in the sea. Then
they lowered the rudders, raised the foresail, and headed toward shore. 41 But
they hit a shoal and ran the ship aground too soon. The bow of the ship stuck
fast, while the stern was repeatedly smashed by the force of the waves and
began to break apart.

42 The soldiers wanted to kill the prisoners to make sure they didn't swim
ashore and escape. 43 But the commanding officer wanted to spare Paul, so

27:27 The *Sea of Adria* includes the central portion of the Mediterranean. **27:28** Greek *20 fathoms . . . 15 fathoms* [37 meters . . . 27 meters].

he didn't let them carry out their plan. Then he ordered all who could swim
to jump overboard first and make for land. 44 The others held on to planks or
debris from the broken ship.* So everyone escaped safely to shore.

Paul on the Island of Malta

28 Once we were safe on shore, we learned that we were on the island
of Malta. 2 The people of the island were very kind to us. It was cold
and rainy, so they built a fire on the shore to welcome us.
3 As Paul gathered an armful of sticks and was laying them on the fire, a
poisonous snake, driven out by the heat, bit him on the hand. 4 The people of
the island saw it hanging from his hand and said to each other, "A murderer,
no doubt! Though he escaped the sea, justice will not permit him to live."
5 But Paul shook off the snake into the fire and was unharmed. 6 The people
waited for him to swell up or suddenly drop dead. But when they had waited
a long time and saw that he wasn't harmed, they changed their minds and
decided he was a god.
7 Near the shore where we landed was an estate belonging to Publius, the
chief official of the island. He welcomed us and treated us kindly for three
days. 8 As it happened, Publius's father was ill with fever and dysentery. Paul
went in and prayed for him, and laying his hands on him, he healed him.
9 Then all the other sick people on the island came and were healed. 10 As a
result we were showered with honors, and when the time came to sail, people
supplied us with everything we would need for the trip.

Paul Arrives at Rome

11 It was three months after the shipwreck that we set sail on another ship
that had wintered at the island—an Alexandrian ship with the twin gods*
as its figurehead. 12 Our first stop was Syracuse,* where we stayed three days.
13 From there we sailed across to Rhegium.* A day later a south wind began
blowing, so the following day we sailed up the coast to Puteoli. 14 There we
found some believers,* who invited us to spend a week with them. And so
we came to Rome.
15 The brothers and sisters* in Rome had heard we were coming, and they
came to meet us at the Forum* on the Appian Way. Others joined us at The
Three Taverns.* When Paul saw them, he was encouraged and thanked God.
16 When we arrived in Rome, Paul was permitted to have his own private
lodging, though he was guarded by a soldier.

Paul Preaches at Rome under Guard

17 Three days after Paul's arrival, he called together the local Jewish leaders.
He said to them, "Brothers, I was arrested in Jerusalem and handed over
to the Roman government, even though I had done nothing against our
people or the customs of our ancestors. 18 The Romans tried me and wanted
to release me, because they found no cause for the death sentence. 19 But
when the Jewish leaders protested the decision, I felt it necessary to appeal to
Caesar, even though I had no desire to press charges against my own people.
20 I asked you to come here today so we could get acquainted and so I could

27:44 Or *or were helped by members of the ship's crew.* **28:11** The *twin gods* were the Roman gods Castor and Pollux. **28:12** *Syracuse* was on the island of Sicily. **28:13** *Rhegium* was on the southern tip of Italy. **28:14** Greek *brothers.* **28:15a** Greek *brothers.* **28:15b** *The Forum* was about 43 miles (70 kilometers) from Rome. **28:15c** *The Three Taverns* was about 35 miles (57 kilometers) from Rome.

Question 28:20

Jesus, the hope of Israel, the Messiah, came to this earth so that all nations could receive salvation and be restored to relationship with God. Do you know Jesus personally? Turn to the back of the Bible and pray through the section called "How to Accept Jesus as Your Lord and Savior."

Question 28:30-31

How does Jesus want you to boldly proclaim the kingdom of God where you are?

explain to you that I am bound with this chain because I believe that the
hope of Israel—the Messiah—has already come."
21 They replied, "We have had no letters from Judea or reports against you
from anyone who has come here. 22 But we want to hear what you believe,
for the only thing we know about this movement is that it is denounced
everywhere."
23 So a time was set, and on that day a large number of people came to
Paul's lodging. He explained and testified about the Kingdom of God and
tried to persuade them about Jesus from the Scriptures. Using the law of
Moses and the books of the prophets, he spoke to them from morning until
evening. 24 Some were persuaded by the things he said, but others did not
believe. 25 And after they had argued back and forth among themselves, they
left with this final word from Paul: "The Holy Spirit was right when he said
to your ancestors through Isaiah the prophet,

26 'Go and say to this people:
When you hear what I say,
you will not understand.
When you see what I do,
you will not comprehend.
27 For the hearts of these people are hardened,
and their ears cannot hear,
and they have closed their eyes—
so their eyes cannot see,
and their ears cannot hear,
and their hearts cannot understand,
and they cannot turn to me
and let me heal them.'*

28 So I want you to know that this salvation from God has also been offered
to the Gentiles, and they will accept it."*
30 For the next two years, Paul lived in Rome at his own expense.* He wel-
comed all who visited him, 31 boldly proclaiming the Kingdom of God and
teaching about the Lord Jesus Christ. And no one tried to stop him.

28:26-27 Isa 6:9-10 (Greek version). 28:28 Some manuscripts add verse 29, *And when he had said these words, the Jews departed, greatly disagreeing with each other.* 28:30 Or *in his own rented quarters.*

Romans Introduction

Romans is half-encouraging, half-convicting, and half-offensive. Yep—three halves. That's because Romans contains more of each of these three components than most books ever written. Romans is a fully prepared meal. It asks that we sit down with others at the table and dine. There is more in Romans than a person can fully digest about God, about our motivations, about our desires, about our nature, and about our networks. There is just so much that is good, so much that is challenging, and so much that is hard to swallow.

As a result, a lot of people only read the parts of Romans they like (verses like Romans 5:3; 8:1; 8:31-39; 12:2) and overlook the parts they don't like (perhaps Romans 1:18; all chapter 2; 6:15; 8:13; 9:31; 12:9, 12; 14:1). It's a bit like picking ripe fruit from a market and rejecting the entire production process from seed to nurture to harvest. Fruit comes from context. Sadly, Romans is often picked at by biased, selfish, hurried consumers.

There is a remarkable human element to Romans. Paul wrote this book to real people (see chapter 16) at a real time (AD 55-57) in a real place (Rome). There are dramatic, intense stories to each of the dozens of individuals named in this book-letter. The list of names in the final chapter of Romans is one of the most authentic moments in all the Bible because it proves the words of salvation authentic and tangible.

Romans demands our attention, but our attention spans aren't used to diving into a book like Romans. Romans is really one solid argument all the way through, so don't just pick at it. Perhaps our current culture is too immediate, too localized, too shortsighted, too fast-foodish to appreciate the huge scale of God's work that so profoundly affects the little surroundings in which we find ourselves.

Story Arcs

- **Abraham**
- **Adam**
- **Moses**
- **The Roman Church Network**

Romans

Greetings from Paul

1 1 This letter is from Paul, a slave of Christ Jesus, chosen by God to be an apostle and sent out to preach his Good News. 2 God promised this Good News long ago through his prophets in the holy Scriptures. 3 The Good News is about his Son. In his earthly life he was born into King David's family line, 4 and he was shown to be* the Son of God when he was raised from the dead by the power of the Holy Spirit.* He is Jesus Christ our Lord. 5 Through Christ, God has given us the privilege* and authority as apostles to tell Gentiles everywhere what God has done for them, so that they will believe and obey him, bringing glory to his name.

6 And you are included among those Gentiles who have been called to belong to Jesus Christ. 7 I am writing to all of you in Rome who are loved by God and are called to be his own holy people.

May God our Father and the Lord Jesus Christ give you grace and peace.

God's Good News

8 Let me say first that I thank my God through Jesus Christ for all of you, because your faith in him is being talked about all over the world. 9 God knows how often I pray for you. Day and night I bring you and your needs in prayer to God, whom I serve with all my heart* by spreading the Good News about his Son.

10 One of the things I always pray for is the opportunity, God willing, to come at last to see you. 11 For I long to visit you so I can bring you some spiritual gift that will help you grow strong in the Lord. 12 When we get together, I want to encourage you in your faith, but I also want to be encouraged by yours.

13 I want you to know, dear brothers and sisters,* that I planned many times to visit you, but I was prevented until now. I want to work among you and see spiritual fruit, just as I have seen among other Gentiles. 14 For I have a great sense of obligation to people in both the civilized world and the rest of the world,* to the educated and uneducated alike. 15 So I am eager to come to you in Rome, too, to preach the Good News.

16 For I am not ashamed of this Good News about Christ. It is the power of God at work, saving everyone who believes—the Jew first and also the Gentile.* 17 This Good News tells us how God makes us right in his sight. This is accomplished from start to finish by faith. As the Scriptures say, "It is through faith that a righteous person has life."*

God's Anger at Sin

18 But God shows his anger from heaven against all sinful, wicked people who suppress the truth by their wickedness.* 19 They know the truth about

1:4a Or *and was designated.* **1:4b** Or *by the Spirit of holiness;* or *in the new realm of the Spirit.* **1:5** Or *the grace.* **1:9** Or *in my spirit.* **1:13** Greek *brothers.* **1:14** Greek *to Greeks and barbarians.* **1:16** Greek *also the Greek.* **1:17** Or *"The righteous will live by faith."* Hab 2:4. **1:18** Or *who, by their wickedness, prevent the truth from being known.*

Question 1:1

Why did Paul call himself a "slave of Christ Jesus"?

Question 1:3–4

In verses 3–4, the good news of Jesus is described. Do you personally know this good news enough to share it with someone?

Make a Difference 1:16

Ashamed?

For some reason, though, the world tricks us into thinking that we cannot, or should not, feel the same way about Jesus. If we see God doing something great, it's as if we're encouraged to suppress our wonder or make our faith a private matter. This is ridiculous. Jesus dying on the cross for our sins to give us abundant life is better than anything. Let it be known today what God has done in and through you.

Difference Maker

When the opportunity arises today, be proud that you know Jesus.

God because he has made it obvious to them. [20]For ever since the world was created, people have seen the earth and sky. Through everything God made, they can clearly see his invisible qualities—his eternal power and divine nature. So they have no excuse for not knowing God.

[21]Yes, they knew God, but they wouldn't worship him as God or even give him thanks. And they began to think up foolish ideas of what God was like. As a result, their minds became dark and confused. [22]Claiming to be wise, they instead became utter fools. [23]And instead of worshiping the glorious, ever-living God, they worshiped idols made to look like mere people and birds and animals and reptiles.

[24]So God abandoned them to do whatever shameful things their hearts desired. As a result, they did vile and degrading things with each other's bodies. [25]They traded the truth about God for a lie. So they worshiped and served the things God created instead of the Creator himself, who is worthy of eternal praise! Amen. [26]That is why God abandoned them to their shameful desires. Even the women turned against the natural way to have sex and instead indulged in sex with each other. [27]And the men, instead of having normal sexual relations with women, burned with lust for each other. Men did shameful things with other men, and as a result of this sin, they suffered within themselves the penalty they deserved.

[28]Since they thought it foolish to acknowledge God, he abandoned them to their foolish thinking and let them do things that should never be done. [29]Their lives became full of every kind of wickedness, sin, greed, hate, envy, murder, quarreling, deception, malicious behavior, and gossip. [30]They are backstabbers, haters of God, insolent, proud, and boastful. They invent new ways of sinning, and they disobey their parents. [31]They refuse to understand, break their promises, are heartless, and have no mercy. [32]They know God's justice requires that those who do these things deserve to die, yet they do them anyway. Worse yet, they encourage others to do them, too.

God's Judgment of Sin

2 You may think you can condemn such people, but you are just as bad, and you have no excuse! When you say they are wicked and should be punished, you are condemning yourself, for you who judge others do these very same things. [2]And we know that God, in his justice, will punish anyone who does such things. [3]Since you judge others for doing these things, why do you think you can avoid God's judgment when you do the same things? [4]Don't you see how wonderfully kind, tolerant, and patient God is with you? Does this mean nothing to you? Can't you see that his kindness is intended to turn you from your sin?

[5]But because you are stubborn and refuse to turn from your sin, you are storing up terrible punishment for yourself. For a day of anger is coming, when God's righteous judgment will be revealed. [6]He will judge everyone according to what they have done. [7]He will give eternal life to those who keep on doing good, seeking after the glory and honor and immortality that God offers. [8]But he will pour out his anger and wrath on those who live for themselves, who refuse to obey the truth and instead live lives of wickedness. [9]There will be trouble and calamity for everyone who keeps on doing what is evil—for the Jew first and also for the Gentile.* [10]But there will be glory

Question **2:4**

Repeat the questions of this verse to yourself. If you were honest, how would you answer these questions right now?

2:9 Greek *also for the Greek;* also in 2:10.

Question **2:29**

This is a challenging section of Romans. From this verse, what would you say is God's simple goal for his people?

and honor and peace from God for all who do good—for the Jew first and also for the Gentile. 11 For God does not show favoritism.

12 When the Gentiles sin, they will be destroyed, even though they never had God's written law. And the Jews, who do have God's law, will be judged by that law when they fail to obey it. 13 For merely listening to the law doesn't make us right with God. It is obeying the law that makes us right in his sight. 14 Even Gentiles, who do not have God's written law, show that they know his law when they instinctively obey it, even without having heard it. 15 They demonstrate that God's law is written in their hearts, for their own conscience and thoughts either accuse them or tell them they are doing right. 16 And this is the message I proclaim—that the day is coming when God, through Christ Jesus, will judge everyone's secret life.

The Jews and the Law

17 You who call yourselves Jews are relying on God's law, and you boast about your special relationship with him. 18 You know what he wants; you know what is right because you have been taught his law. 19 You are convinced that you are a guide for the blind and a light for people who are lost in darkness. 20 You think you can instruct the ignorant and teach children the ways of God. For you are certain that God's law gives you complete knowledge and truth.

21 Well then, if you teach others, why don't you teach yourself? You tell others not to steal, but do you steal? 22 You say it is wrong to commit adultery, but do you commit adultery? You condemn idolatry, but do you use items stolen from pagan temples?* 23 You are so proud of knowing the law, but you dishonor God by breaking it. 24 No wonder the Scriptures say, "The Gentiles blaspheme the name of God because of you."*

25 The Jewish ceremony of circumcision has value only if you obey God's law. But if you don't obey God's law, you are no better off than an uncircumcised Gentile. 26 And if the Gentiles obey God's law, won't God declare them to be his own people? 27 In fact, uncircumcised Gentiles who keep God's law will condemn you Jews who are circumcised and possess God's law but don't obey it.

28 For you are not a true Jew just because you were born of Jewish parents or because you have gone through the ceremony of circumcision. 29 No, a true Jew is one whose heart is right with God. And true circumcision is not merely obeying the letter of the law; rather, it is a change of heart produced by the Spirit. And a person with a changed heart seeks praise* from God, not from people.

God Remains Faithful

3 Then what's the advantage of being a Jew? Is there any value in the ceremony of circumcision? 2 Yes, there are great benefits! First of all, the Jews were entrusted with the whole revelation of God.*

3 True, some of them were unfaithful; but just because they were unfaithful, does that mean God will be unfaithful? 4 Of course not! Even if everyone else is a liar, God is true. As the Scriptures say about him,

"You will be proved right in what you say,
and you will win your case in court."*

2:22 Greek *do you steal from temples?* 2:24 Isa 52:5 (Greek version). 2:29 Or *receives praise.* 3:2 Greek *the oracles of God.* 3:4 Ps 51:4 (Greek version).

5"But," some might say, "our sinfulness serves a good purpose, for it helps
people see how righteous God is. Isn't it unfair, then, for him to punish us?"
(This is merely a human point of view.) 6Of course not! If God were not en-
tirely fair, how would he be qualified to judge the world? 7"But," someone
might still argue, "how can God condemn me as a sinner if my dishonesty
highlights his truthfulness and brings him more glory?" 8And some people
even slander us by claiming that we say, "The more we sin, the better it is!"
Those who say such things deserve to be condemned.

All People Are Sinners

9Well then, should we conclude that we Jews are better than others? No, not
at all, for we have already shown that all people, whether Jews or Gentiles,*
are under the power of sin. 10As the Scriptures say,

"No one is righteous—
not even one.
11 No one is truly wise;
no one is seeking God.
12 All have turned away;
all have become useless.
No one does good,
not a single one."*
13 "Their talk is foul, like the stench from an open grave.
Their tongues are filled with lies."
"Snake venom drips from their lips."*
14 "Their mouths are full of cursing and bitterness."*
15 "They rush to commit murder.
16 Destruction and misery always follow them.
17 They don't know where to find peace."*
18 "They have no fear of God at all."*

19Obviously, the law applies to those to whom it was given, for its purpose
is to keep people from having excuses, and to show that the entire world is
guilty before God. 20For no one can ever be made right with God by doing
what the law commands. The law simply shows us how sinful we are.

Christ Took Our Punishment

21But now God has shown us a way to be made right with him without keep-
ing the requirements of the law, as was promised in the writings of Moses*
and the prophets long ago. 22We are made right with God by placing our
faith in Jesus Christ. And this is true for everyone who believes, no matter
who we are.

23For everyone has sinned; we all fall short of God's glorious standard.
24Yet God, in his grace, freely makes us right in his sight. He did this through
Christ Jesus when he freed us from the penalty for our sins. 25For God pre-
sented Jesus as the sacrifice for sin. People are made right with God when
they believe that Jesus sacrificed his life, shedding his blood. This sacrifice
shows that God was being fair when he held back and did not punish those
who sinned in times past, 26for he was looking ahead and including them

3:9 Greek *or Greeks.* 3:10-12 Pss 14:1-3; 53:1-3 (Greek version). 3:13 Pss 5:9 (Greek version); 140:3. 3:14 Ps 10:7 (Greek version). 3:15-17 Isa 59:7-8. 3:18 Ps 36:1. 3:21 Greek *in the law.*

Make a Difference 3:23

Falling Short

One of the great tortures of life is receiving grades on papers and tests. Sometimes those all-night cram sessions just don't cut it. Those practice questions and study groups might help a bit, but they don't solve every problem. The standard is 100 percent—and we all know that no one gets 100 percent 100 percent of the time.

The greatest achievements are not enough to sustain any human being forever. Eventually everyone succumbs to a less than perfect score. Often by mistake and regularly even by deliberate choice, humans fail to measure up to God's pattern. We never hit the 100 percent mark.

Difference Maker

Anytime some pride creeps into your judgment today, keep it in check. A humble heart is an essential characteristic for a person God wants to use to serve others.

Question 3:25

What does it mean not to be right with God? How is a person made right with God?

Question **3:27**

In the presence of Jesus, can you truly boast about anything?

in what he would do in this present time. God did this to demonstrate his
righteousness, for he himself is fair and just, and he makes sinners right in
his sight when they believe in Jesus.
27 Can we boast, then, that we have done anything to be accepted by God?
No, because our acquittal is not based on obeying the law. It is based on faith.
28 So we are made right with God through faith and not by obeying the law.
29 After all, is God the God of the Jews only? Isn't he also the God of the
Gentiles? Of course he is. 30 There is only one God, and he makes people right
with himself only by faith, whether they are Jews or Gentiles.* 31 Well then,
if we emphasize faith, does this mean that we can forget about the law? Of
course not! In fact, only when we have faith do we truly fulfill the law.

The Faith of Abraham

4 Abraham was, humanly speaking, the founder of our Jewish nation.
What did he discover about being made right with God? 2 If his good
deeds had made him acceptable to God, he would have had something to
boast about. But that was not God's way. 3 For the Scriptures tell us, "Abra-
ham believed God, and God counted him as righteous because of his faith."*
4 When people work, their wages are not a gift, but something they have
earned. 5 But people are counted as righteous, not because of their work,
but because of their faith in God who forgives sinners. 6 David also spoke of
this when he described the happiness of those who are declared righteous
without working for it:

7 "Oh, what joy for those
whose disobedience is forgiven,
whose sins are put out of sight.
8 Yes, what joy for those
whose record the LORD has cleared of sin."*

9 Now, is this blessing only for the Jews, or is it also for uncircumcised
Gentiles?* Well, we have been saying that Abraham was counted as righteous
by God because of his faith. 10 But how did this happen? Was he counted as
righteous only after he was circumcised, or was it before he was circumcised?
Clearly, God accepted Abraham before he was circumcised!
11 Circumcision was a sign that Abraham already had faith and that God
had already accepted him and declared him to be righteous—even before
he was circumcised. So Abraham is the spiritual father of those who have
faith but have not been circumcised. They are counted as righteous because
of their faith. 12 And Abraham is also the spiritual father of those who have
been circumcised, but only if they have the same kind of faith Abraham had
before he was circumcised.
13 Clearly, God's promise to give the whole earth to Abraham and his
descendants was based not on his obedience to God's law, but on a right
relationship with God that comes by faith. 14 If God's promise is only for those
who obey the law, then faith is not necessary and the promise is pointless.
15 For the law always brings punishment on those who try to obey it. (The
only way to avoid breaking the law is to have no law to break!)
16 So the promise is received by faith. It is given as a free gift. And we are all

Story Arc **4:1**

● Abraham

Now is a good chance to go back through all the Bible and see how Abraham's story plays into the entire story of the good news of Jesus.

Rom 5:12-21 ►

3:30 Greek *whether they are circumcised or uncircumcised.* 4:3 Gen 15:6. 4:7-8 Ps 32:1-2 (Greek version). 4:9 Greek *is this blessing only for the circumcised, or is it also for the uncircumcised?*

certain to receive it, whether or not we live according to the law of Moses, if
we have faith like Abraham's. For Abraham is the father of all who believe.
17 That is what the Scriptures mean when God told him, "I have made you
the father of many nations."* This happened because Abraham believed in
the God who brings the dead back to life and who creates new things out
of nothing.

18 Even when there was no reason for hope, Abraham kept hoping—
believing that he would become the father of many nations. For God had said
to him, "That's how many descendants you will have!"* 19 And Abraham's
faith did not weaken, even though, at about 100 years of age, he figured his
body was as good as dead—and so was Sarah's womb.

20 Abraham never wavered in believing God's promise. In fact, his faith
grew stronger, and in this he brought glory to God. 21 He was fully convinced
that God is able to do whatever he promises. 22 And because of Abraham's
faith, God counted him as righteous. 23 And when God counted him as righ-
teous, it wasn't just for Abraham's benefit. It was recorded 24 for our benefit,
too, assuring us that God will also count us as righteous if we believe in him,
the one who raised Jesus our Lord from the dead. 25 He was handed over to
die because of our sins, and he was raised to life to make us right with God.

Faith Brings Joy

5 Therefore, since we have been made right in God's sight by faith, we have
peace* with God because of what Jesus Christ our Lord has done for us.
2 Because of our faith, Christ has brought us into this place of undeserved
privilege where we now stand, and we confidently and joyfully look forward
to sharing God's glory.

3 We can rejoice, too, when we run into problems and trials, for we know
that they help us develop endurance. 4 And endurance develops strength of
character, and character strengthens our confident hope of salvation. 5 And
this hope will not lead to disappointment. For we know how dearly God loves
us, because he has given us the Holy Spirit to fill our hearts with his love.

6 When we were utterly helpless, Christ came at just the right time and
died for us sinners. 7 Now, most people would not be willing to die for an
upright person, though someone might perhaps be willing to die for a per-
son who is especially good. 8 But God showed his great love for us by send-
ing Christ to die for us while we were still sinners. 9 And since we have been
made right in God's sight by the blood of Christ, he will certainly save us
from God's condemnation. 10 For since our friendship with God was restored
by the death of his Son while we were still his enemies, we will certainly be
saved through the life of his Son. 11 So now we can rejoice in our wonderful
new relationship with God because our Lord Jesus Christ has made us friends
of God.

Adam and Christ Contrasted

12 When Adam sinned, sin entered the world. Adam's sin brought death, so
death spread to everyone, for everyone sinned. 13 Yes, people sinned even
before the law was given. But it was not counted as sin because there was not
yet any law to break. 14 Still, everyone died—from the time of Adam to the
time of Moses—even those who did not disobey an explicit commandment

4:17 Gen 17:5. 4:18 Gen 15:5. 5:1 Some manuscripts read *let us have peace*.

Make a Difference 5:6

Helpless

We often can't help ourselves. We see something tempting, and we can't resist it. This sickness fuels our thirst for even more. It is a perpetually spiraling cycle: craving and conquest and loss, craving and conquest and loss, craving and conquest and loss.

"No matter how much we see, we are never satisfied," Solomon reminded us (Ecclesiastes 1:8). The fleeting pleasures we have sought cannot satisfy our deep thirst for wholeness. Only Jesus can help us. He is able to give us what we cannot grasp by our own power and strength. Christ alone can give us the fulfillment we were created to have.

Difference Maker

Instead of buying something new today, get rid of something you already have. Simplify your attachments so that you can be ready to receive satisfaction in Jesus alone.

Story Arc 5:12-21

Adam

Remember this guy? He and Eve are responsible for our need for salvation. Why did Adam's sin bring death to everyone? In verses 12–21, what is the contrast between Adam and Jesus?

Story Arc 5:14

Moses

How did Moses help teach people what sin was? Hint: go back and look at Deuteronomy 5.

Rom 16:1-27 ►

Prayer 6:12

Lord, help me stop offering myself to sin. Instead, help me offer myself to you. Amen.

of God, as Adam did. Now Adam is a symbol, a representation of Christ,
who was yet to come. [15]But there is a great difference between Adam's sin
and God's gracious gift. For the sin of this one man, Adam, brought death
to many. But even greater is God's wonderful grace and his gift of forgive-
ness to many through this other man, Jesus Christ. [16]And the result of
God's gracious gift is very different from the result of that one man's sin.
For Adam's sin led to condemnation, but God's free gift leads to our being
made right with God, even though we are guilty of many sins. [17]For the sin
of this one man, Adam, caused death to rule over many. But even greater is
God's wonderful grace and his gift of righteousness, for all who receive it
will live in triumph over sin and death through this one man, Jesus Christ.
[18]Yes, Adam's one sin brings condemnation for everyone, but Christ's one
act of righteousness brings a right relationship with God and new life for
everyone. [19]Because one person disobeyed God, many became sinners. But
because one other person obeyed God, many will be made righteous.
[20]God's law was given so that all people could see how sinful they were.
But as people sinned more and more, God's wonderful grace became more
abundant. [21]So just as sin ruled over all people and brought them to death,
now God's wonderful grace rules instead, giving us right standing with God
and resulting in eternal life through Jesus Christ our Lord.

Sin's Power Is Broken

6 Well then, should we keep on sinning so that God can show us more and
more of his wonderful grace? [2]Of course not! Since we have died to sin,
how can we continue to live in it? [3]Or have you forgotten that when we were
joined with Christ Jesus in baptism, we joined him in his death? [4]For we died
and were buried with Christ by baptism. And just as Christ was raised from
the dead by the glorious power of the Father, now we also may live new lives.
[5]Since we have been united with him in his death, we will also be raised to
life as he was. [6]We know that our old sinful selves were crucified with Christ
so that sin might lose its power in our lives. We are no longer slaves to sin.
[7]For when we died with Christ we were set free from the power of sin. [8]And
since we died with Christ, we know we will also live with him. [9]We are sure
of this because Christ was raised from the dead, and he will never die again.
Death no longer has any power over him. [10]When he died, he died once to
break the power of sin. But now that he lives, he lives for the glory of God.
[11]So you also should consider yourselves to be dead to the power of sin and
alive to God through Christ Jesus.
[12]Do not let sin control the way you live;* do not give in to sinful desires.
[13]Do not let any part of your body become an instrument of evil to serve sin.
Instead, give yourselves completely to God, for you were dead, but now you
have new life. So use your whole body as an instrument to do what is right
for the glory of God. [14]Sin is no longer your master, for you no longer live
under the requirements of the law. Instead, you live under the freedom of
God's grace.
[15]Well then, since God's grace has set us free from the law, does that mean
we can go on sinning? Of course not! [16]Don't you realize that you become the
slave of whatever you choose to obey? You can be a slave to sin, which leads
to death, or you can choose to obey God, which leads to righteous living.

6:12 Or *Do not let sin reign in your body, which is subject to death.*

17 Thank God! Once you were slaves of sin, but now you wholeheartedly obey
this teaching we have given you. 18 Now you are free from your slavery to sin,
and you have become slaves to righteous living.
19 Because of the weakness of your human nature, I am using the illustra-
tion of slavery to help you understand all this. Previously, you let yourselves
be slaves to impurity and lawlessness, which led ever deeper into sin. Now
you must give yourselves to be slaves to righteous living so that you will
become holy.
20 When you were slaves to sin, you were free from the obligation to do
right. 21 And what was the result? You are now ashamed of the things you
used to do, things that end in eternal doom. 22 But now you are free from the
power of sin and have become slaves of God. Now you do those things that
lead to holiness and result in eternal life. 23 For the wages of sin is death, but
the free gift of God is eternal life through Christ Jesus our Lord.

No Longer Bound to the Law

7 Now, dear brothers and sisters*—you who are familiar with the law—
don't you know that the law applies only while a person is living? 2 For
example, when a woman marries, the law binds her to her husband as long
as he is alive. But if he dies, the laws of marriage no longer apply to her. 3 So
while her husband is alive, she would be committing adultery if she married
another man. But if her husband dies, she is free from that law and does not
commit adultery when she remarries.
4 So, my dear brothers and sisters, this is the point: You died to the power
of the law when you died with Christ. And now you are united with the one
who was raised from the dead. As a result, we can produce a harvest of good
deeds for God. 5 When we were controlled by our old nature,* sinful desires
were at work within us, and the law aroused these evil desires that produced
a harvest of sinful deeds, resulting in death. 6 But now we have been released
from the law, for we died to it and are no longer captive to its power. Now
we can serve God, not in the old way of obeying the letter of the law, but in
the new way of living in the Spirit.

God's Law Reveals Our Sin

7 Well then, am I suggesting that the law of God is sinful? Of course not! In
fact, it was the law that showed me my sin. I would never have known that
coveting is wrong if the law had not said, "You must not covet."* 8 But sin
used this command to arouse all kinds of covetous desires within me! If there
were no law, sin would not have that power. 9 At one time I lived without
understanding the law. But when I learned the command not to covet, for
instance, the power of sin came to life, 10 and I died. So I discovered that the
law's commands, which were supposed to bring life, brought spiritual death
instead. 11 Sin took advantage of those commands and deceived me; it used
the commands to kill me. 12 But still, the law itself is holy, and its commands
are holy and right and good.
13 But how can that be? Did the law, which is good, cause my death? Of
course not! Sin used what was good to bring about my condemnation to
death. So we can see how terrible sin really is. It uses God's good commands
for its own evil purposes.

7:1 Greek *brothers;* also in 7:4. 7:5 Greek *When we were in the flesh.* 7:7 Exod 20:17; Deut 5:21.

Make a Difference 6:23

Emergency Rescue Effort

God created humanity to walk with him in a close relationship. We can think of sin as anything we do that lets go of his hand and steps away from him. Sin is a "work" of our heart that leads us away from the life God created humans to have. Since God is the author of all life, the consequence of the refusal to walk with God is to miss out on God's life. We all get paid for our work. If the work is sin, however, then the paycheck is death.

Even after humans walked away and found themselves in serious peril, God went on a dramatic rescue mission. He sent his Son, Jesus, the greatest emergency response expert the world has ever seen, to save people who wandered away from life. He reaches out to those who get lost, extends his arms just as their lives hang in the balance, and urges them, "Grab my hand!"

Difference Maker

Accept the rescuing arms of Jesus Christ today. Accept his free gift of life and reject sin. Turn to the back of this Bible and pray through the section on "How to Accept Jesus as Your Lord and Savior."

Struggling with Sin

14 So the trouble is not with the law, for it is spiritual and good. The trouble
is with me, for I am all too human, a slave to sin. 15 I don't really understand
myself, for I want to do what is right, but I don't do it. Instead, I do what I hate.
16 But if I know that what I am doing is wrong, this shows that I agree that the
law is good. 17 So I am not the one doing wrong; it is sin living in me that does it.
18 And I know that nothing good lives in me, that is, in my sinful nature.* I
want to do what is right, but I can't. 19 I want to do what is good, but I don't.
I don't want to do what is wrong, but I do it anyway. 20 But if I do what I
don't want to do, I am not really the one doing wrong; it is sin living in me
that does it.
21 I have discovered this principle of life—that when I want to do what
is right, I inevitably do what is wrong. 22 I love God's law with all my heart.
23 But there is another power* within me that is at war with my mind. This
power makes me a slave to the sin that is still within me. 24 Oh, what a miser-
able person I am! Who will free me from this life that is dominated by sin and
death? 25 Thank God! The answer is in Jesus Christ our Lord. So you see how
it is: In my mind I really want to obey God's law, but because of my sinful
nature I am a slave to sin.

Life in the Spirit

8 So now there is no condemnation for those who belong to Christ Jesus.
2 And because you belong to him, the power* of the life-giving Spirit
has freed you* from the power of sin that leads to death. 3 The law of Moses
was unable to save us because of the weakness of our sinful nature.* So God
did what the law could not do. He sent his own Son in a body like the bodies
we sinners have. And in that body God declared an end to sin's control over
us by giving his Son as a sacrifice for our sins. 4 He did this so that the just
requirement of the law would be fully satisfied for us, who no longer follow
our sinful nature but instead follow the Spirit.
5 Those who are dominated by the sinful nature think about sinful things,
but those who are controlled by the Holy Spirit think about things that
please the Spirit. 6 So letting your sinful nature control your mind leads to
death. But letting the Spirit control your mind leads to life and peace. 7 For
the sinful nature is always hostile to God. It never did obey God's laws, and
it never will. 8 That's why those who are still under the control of their sinful
nature can never please God.
9 But you are not controlled by your sinful nature. You are controlled by
the Spirit if you have the Spirit of God living in you. (And remember that
those who do not have the Spirit of Christ living in them do not belong to
him at all.) 10 And Christ lives within you, so even though your body will die
because of sin, the Spirit gives you life* because you have been made right
with God. 11 The Spirit of God, who raised Jesus from the dead, lives in you.
And just as God raised Christ Jesus from the dead, he will give life to your
mortal bodies by this same Spirit living within you.
12 Therefore, dear brothers and sisters,* you have no obligation to do what
your sinful nature urges you to do. 13 For if you live by its dictates, you will
die. But if through the power of the Spirit you put to death the deeds of

7:18 Greek *my flesh;* also in 7:25. 7:23 Greek *law;* also in 7:23b. 8:2a Greek *the law;* also in 8:2b. 8:2b Some manuscripts read *me.* 8:3 Greek *our flesh;* similarly in 8:4, 5, 6, 7, 8, 9, 12. 8:10 Or *your spirit is alive.* 8:12 Greek *brothers;* also in 8:29.

Make a Difference
7:14–25

Be Real

One of the most impressive things about the Bible is its raw honesty. Even the heroes of faith, like Moses, David, and Paul, were real people with real issues and real problems. In fact, their problems were absolutely astonishing at times. Each of those guys was a murderer, each of them had blatant public sins, and each of them had to make dramatic U-turns in life. No fake celebrities here. Perhaps you can relate to these guys?

Difference Maker

Examine the way you present yourself on social media. Do you present a glamorized version of yourself, or do you reveal God at work in the true you?

Question **8:1**

In such a judgmental world, what could this verse mean for the people around you?

Prayer **8:9**

Lord, let me follow you and not myself. Amen.

Question **8:10**

Christ lives in you. How does this truth change you?

your sinful nature,* you will live. 14 For all who are led by the Spirit of God
are children* of God.
15 So you have not received a spirit that makes you fearful slaves. Instead,
you received God's Spirit when he adopted you as his own children.* Now
we call him, "Abba, Father."* 16 For his Spirit joins with our spirit to affirm
that we are God's children. 17 And since we are his children, we are his heirs.
In fact, together with Christ we are heirs of God's glory. But if we are to share
his glory, we must also share his suffering.

The Future Glory

18 Yet what we suffer now is nothing compared to the glory he will reveal to
us later. 19 For all creation is waiting eagerly for that future day when God
will reveal who his children really are. 20 Against its will, all creation was
subjected to God's curse. But with eager hope, 21 the creation looks forward
to the day when it will join God's children in glorious freedom from death
and decay. 22 For we know that all creation has been groaning as in the pains
of childbirth right up to the present time. 23 And we believers also groan, even
though we have the Holy Spirit within us as a foretaste of future glory, for we
long for our bodies to be released from sin and suffering. We, too, wait with
eager hope for the day when God will give us our full rights as his adopted
children,* including the new bodies he has promised us. 24 We were given
this hope when we were saved. (If we already have something, we don't need
to hope* for it. 25 But if we look forward to something we don't yet have, we
must wait patiently and confidently.)
26 And the Holy Spirit helps us in our weakness. For example, we don't
know what God wants us to pray for. But the Holy Spirit prays for us with
groanings that cannot be expressed in words. 27 And the Father who knows
all hearts knows what the Spirit is saying, for the Spirit pleads for us believ-
ers* in harmony with God's own will. 28 And we know that God causes every-
thing to work together* for the good of those who love God and are called
according to his purpose for them. 29 For God knew his people in advance,
and he chose them to become like his Son, so that his Son would be the first-
born* among many brothers and sisters. 30 And having chosen them, he called
them to come to him. And having called them, he gave them right standing
with himself. And having given them right standing, he gave them his glory.

Nothing Can Separate Us from God's Love

31 What shall we say about such wonderful things as these? If God is for us,
who can ever be against us? 32 Since he did not spare even his own Son but
gave him up for us all, won't he also give us everything else? 33 Who dares
accuse us whom God has chosen for his own? No one—for God himself
has given us right standing with himself. 34 Who then will condemn us? No
one—for Christ Jesus died for us and was raised to life for us, and he is sitting
in the place of honor at God's right hand, pleading for us.
35 Can anything ever separate us from Christ's love? Does it mean he no
longer loves us if we have trouble or calamity, or are persecuted, or hungry,
or destitute, or in danger, or threatened with death? 36 (As the Scriptures say,

8:13 Greek *deeds of the body.* **8:14** Greek *sons;* also in 8:19. **8:15a** Greek *you received a spirit of sonship.* **8:15b** *Abba* is an Aramaic term for "father." **8:23** Greek *wait anxiously for sonship.* **8:24** Some manuscripts read *wait.* **8:27** Greek *for God's holy people.* **8:28** Some manuscripts read *And we know that everything works together.* **8:29** Or *would be supreme.*

Question 8:26

Good thing you've got weaknesses then, right?

Make a Difference 8:28

In Context

If this verse were removed from this chapter about sin and suffering and trials, how could people misuse it? You know, Paul never meant for this book to be a collection of proverbs or nice quotations for motivational posters. Paul saw this letter as a solid whole, an argument sharing God's plan of salvation in history for all creation. Romans is an explanation that flows together, feeds itself, networks itself, supports itself, and informs itself.

Difference Maker

With this in mind, consider your current struggles and circumstances. What purpose is God working toward in you?

Question 8:35

Well, how would you answer this question?

"For your sake we are killed every day; we are being slaughtered like sheep."*)
37 No, despite all these things, overwhelming victory is ours through Christ,
who loved us.
38 And I am convinced that nothing can ever separate us from God's love.
Neither death nor life, neither angels nor demons,* neither our fears for
today nor our worries about tomorrow—not even the powers of hell can
separate us from God's love. 39 No power in the sky above or in the earth
below—indeed, nothing in all creation will ever be able to separate us from
the love of God that is revealed in Christ Jesus our Lord.

God's Selection of Israel

9 With Christ as my witness, I speak with utter truthfulness. My con-
science and the Holy Spirit confirm it. 2 My heart is filled with bitter
sorrow and unending grief 3 for my people, my Jewish brothers and sisters.*
I would be willing to be forever cursed—cut off from Christ!—if that would
save them. 4 They are the people of Israel, chosen to be God's adopted chil-
dren.* God revealed his glory to them. He made covenants with them and
gave them his law. He gave them the privilege of worshiping him and receiv-
ing his wonderful promises. 5 Abraham, Isaac, and Jacob are their ancestors,
and Christ himself was an Israelite as far as his human nature is concerned.
And he is God, the one who rules over everything and is worthy of eternal
praise! Amen.*
6 Well then, has God failed to fulfill his promise to Israel? No, for not all
who are born into the nation of Israel are truly members of God's people!
7 Being descendants of Abraham doesn't make them truly Abraham's chil-
dren. For the Scriptures say, "Isaac is the son through whom your descen-
dants will be counted,"* though Abraham had other children, too. 8 This
means that Abraham's physical descendants are not necessarily children
of God. Only the children of the promise are considered to be Abraham's
children. 9 For God had promised, "I will return about this time next year,
and Sarah will have a son."*
10 This son was our ancestor Isaac. When he married Rebekah, she gave
birth to twins.* 11 But before they were born, before they had done anything
good or bad, she received a message from God. (This message shows that
God chooses people according to his own purposes; 12 he calls people, but
not according to their good or bad works.) She was told, "Your older son will
serve your younger son."* 13 In the words of the Scriptures, "I loved Jacob,
but I rejected Esau."*
14 Are we saying, then, that God was unfair? Of course not! 15 For God said
to Moses,

"I will show mercy to anyone I choose,
and I will show compassion to anyone I choose."*

16 So it is God who decides to show mercy. We can neither choose it nor work
for it.
17 For the Scriptures say that God told Pharaoh, "I have appointed you

8:36 Ps 44:22. 8:38 Greek *nor rulers.* 9:3 Greek *my brothers.* 9:4 Greek *chosen for sonship.* 9:5 Or *May God, the one who rules over everything, be praised forever. Amen.* 9:7 Gen 21:12. 9:9 Gen 18:10, 14. 9:10 Greek *she conceived children through this one man.* 9:12 Gen 25:23. 9:13 Mal 1:2-3. 9:15 Exod 33:19.

for the very purpose of displaying my power in you and to spread my fame
throughout the earth."* 18 So you see, God chooses to show mercy to some,
and he chooses to harden the hearts of others so they refuse to listen.

19 Well then, you might say, "Why does God blame people for not responding? Haven't they simply done what he makes them do?"

20 No, don't say that. Who are you, a mere human being, to argue with God?
Should the thing that was created say to the one who created it, "Why have
you made me like this?" 21 When a potter makes jars out of clay, doesn't he
have a right to use the same lump of clay to make one jar for decoration and
another to throw garbage into? 22 In the same way, even though God has the
right to show his anger and his power, he is very patient with those on whom
his anger falls, who are destined for destruction. 23 He does this to make the
riches of his glory shine even brighter on those to whom he shows mercy,
who were prepared in advance for glory. 24 And we are among those whom
he selected, both from the Jews and from the Gentiles.

25 Concerning the Gentiles, God says in the prophecy of Hosea,

"Those who were not my people,
  I will now call my people.
And I will love those
  whom I did not love before."*

26 And,

"Then, at the place where they were told,
  'You are not my people,'
there they will be called
  'children of the living God.'"*

27 And concerning Israel, Isaiah the prophet cried out,

"Though the people of Israel are as numerous as the sand of the
    seashore,
  only a remnant will be saved.
28 For the LORD will carry out his sentence upon the earth
  quickly and with finality."*

29 And Isaiah said the same thing in another place:

"If the LORD of Heaven's Armies
  had not spared a few of our children,
we would have been wiped out like Sodom,
  destroyed like Gomorrah."*

Israel's Unbelief

30 What does all this mean? Even though the Gentiles were not trying to follow God's standards, they were made right with God. And it was by faith
that this took place. 31 But the people of Israel, who tried so hard to get right
with God by keeping the law, never succeeded. 32 Why not? Because they were

9:17 Exod 9:16 (Greek version). 9:25 Hos 2:23. 9:26 Greek *sons of the living God.* Hos 1:10.
9:27-28 Isa 10:22-23 (Greek version). 9:29 Isa 1:9 (Greek version).

Things to reflect on

Question 9:33

How does Jesus make people stumble? Why does God intentionally want that to happen?

Prayer 10:9

Heavenly Father, I openly declare that Jesus is Lord, and I believe in my heart that you have raised Jesus from the dead. Thank you for saving me. Amen.

Make a Difference

10:13

You Are in God's Plans

Jesus created this world so that he could hang out with you. There is also a second truth that is just as remarkable: God doesn't give up on his plans. No matter what you are experiencing today, no matter what you are facing in this moment, it just so happens that you are in the blueprint of God's plans for this planet. That is good news indeed. Good news is what Jesus is all about.

Turn to the Lord today. Call on his name. Ask him to re-create things around you and in you. This is what he wants for your life. It's why he created you in the first place. It is why he came for you, and it is why he called out on your behalf on the cross. It is why he conquered sin and death. Jesus made you, loves you, and plans to do great things through you. Call on Jesus today.

Difference Maker

What desires has he placed on your heart that can make a positive mark on this world?

trying to get right with God by keeping the law* instead of by trusting in
him. They stumbled over the great rock in their path. 33 God warned them
of this in the Scriptures when he said,

"I am placing a stone in Jerusalem* that makes people stumble,
a rock that makes them fall.
But anyone who trusts in him
will never be disgraced."*

10 Dear brothers and sisters,* the longing of my heart and my prayer to
God is for the people of Israel to be saved. 2 I know what enthusiasm
they have for God, but it is misdirected zeal. 3 For they don't understand
God's way of making people right with himself. Refusing to accept God's
way, they cling to their own way of getting right with God by trying to keep
the law. 4 For Christ has already accomplished the purpose for which the
law was given.* As a result, all who believe in him are made right with God.

Salvation Is for Everyone

5 For Moses writes that the law's way of making a person right with God
requires obedience to all of its commands.* 6 But faith's way of getting right
with God says, "Don't say in your heart, 'Who will go up to heaven?' (to bring
Christ down to earth). 7 And don't say, 'Who will go down to the place of the
dead?' (to bring Christ back to life again)." 8 In fact, it says,

"The message is very close at hand;
it is on your lips and in your heart."*

And that message is the very message about faith that we preach: 9 If you
openly declare that Jesus is Lord and believe in your heart that God raised
him from the dead, you will be saved. 10 For it is by believing in your heart
that you are made right with God, and it is by openly declaring your faith
that you are saved. 11 As the Scriptures tell us, "Anyone who trusts in him
will never be disgraced."* 12 Jew and Gentile* are the same in this respect.
They have the same Lord, who gives generously to all who call on him. 13 For
"Everyone who calls on the name of the LORD will be saved."*

14 But how can they call on him to save them unless they believe in him?
And how can they believe in him if they have never heard about him? And
how can they hear about him unless someone tells them? 15 And how will
anyone go and tell them without being sent? That is why the Scriptures say,
"How beautiful are the feet of messengers who bring good news!"*

16 But not everyone welcomes the Good News, for Isaiah the prophet said,
"LORD, who has believed our message?"* 17 So faith comes from hearing, that
is, hearing the Good News about Christ. 18 But I ask, have the people of Israel
actually heard the message? Yes, they have:

"The message has gone throughout the earth,
and the words to all the world."*

9:32 Greek *by works.* 9:33a Greek *in Zion.* 9:33b Isa 8:14; 28:16 (Greek version). 10:1 Greek *Brothers.* 10:4 Or *For Christ is the end of the law.* 10:5 See Lev 18:5. 10:6-8 Deut 30:12-14. 10:11 Isa 28:16 (Greek version). 10:12 Greek *and Greek.* 10:13 Joel 2:32. 10:15 Isa 52:7. 10:16 Isa 53:1. 10:18 Ps 19:4.

19 But I ask, did the people of Israel really understand? Yes, they did, for even in the time of Moses, God said,

"I will rouse your jealousy through people who are not even a nation.
I will provoke your anger through the foolish Gentiles."*

20 And later Isaiah spoke boldly for God, saying,

"I was found by people who were not looking for me.
I showed myself to those who were not asking for me."*

21 But regarding Israel, God said,

"All day long I opened my arms to them,
but they were disobedient and rebellious."*

God's Mercy on Israel

11 I ask, then, has God rejected his own people, the nation of Israel? Of
course not! I myself am an Israelite, a descendant of Abraham and a
member of the tribe of Benjamin.
2 No, God has not rejected his own people, whom he chose from the very
beginning. Do you realize what the Scriptures say about this? Elijah the
prophet complained to God about the people of Israel and said, 3 "LORD,
they have killed your prophets and torn down your altars. I am the only one
left, and now they are trying to kill me, too."*
4 And do you remember God's reply? He said, "No, I have 7,000 others who
have never bowed down to Baal!"*
5 It is the same today, for a few of the people of Israel* have remained
faithful because of God's grace—his undeserved kindness in choosing
them. 6 And since it is through God's kindness, then it is not by their good
works. For in that case, God's grace would not be what it really is—free
and undeserved.
7 So this is the situation: Most of the people of Israel have not found the
favor of God they are looking for so earnestly. A few have—the ones God has
chosen—but the hearts of the rest were hardened. 8 As the Scriptures say,

"God has put them into a deep sleep.
To this day he has shut their eyes so they do not see,
and closed their ears so they do not hear."*

9 Likewise, David said,

"Let their bountiful table become a snare,
a trap that makes them think all is well.
Let their blessings cause them to stumble,
and let them get what they deserve.
10 Let their eyes go blind so they cannot see,
and let their backs be bent forever."*

10:19 Deut 32:21. 10:20 Isa 65:1 (Greek version). 10:21 Isa 65:2 (Greek version). 11:3 1 Kgs 19:10, 14. 11:4 1 Kgs 19:18. 11:5 Greek *for a remnant.* 11:8 Isa 29:10; Deut 29:4. 11:9-10 Ps 69:22-23 (Greek version).

11 Did God's people stumble and fall beyond recovery? Of course not! They
were disobedient, so God made salvation available to the Gentiles. But he
wanted his own people to become jealous and claim it for themselves. 12 Now
if the Gentiles were enriched because the people of Israel turned down God's
offer of salvation, think how much greater a blessing the world will share
when they finally accept it.

13 I am saying all this especially for you Gentiles. God has appointed me
as the apostle to the Gentiles. I stress this, 14 for I want somehow to make the
people of Israel jealous of what you Gentiles have, so I might save some of
them. 15 For since their rejection meant that God offered salvation to the rest
of the world, their acceptance will be even more wonderful. It will be life for
those who were dead! 16 And since Abraham and the other patriarchs were
holy, their descendants will also be holy—just as the entire batch of dough
is holy because the portion given as an offering is holy. For if the roots of the
tree are holy, the branches will be, too.

17 But some of these branches from Abraham's tree—some of the people
of Israel—have been broken off. And you Gentiles, who were branches from
a wild olive tree, have been grafted in. So now you also receive the blessing
God has promised Abraham and his children, sharing in the rich nourish-
ment from the root of God's special olive tree. 18 But you must not brag about
being grafted in to replace the branches that were broken off. You are just
a branch, not the root.

19 "Well," you may say, "those branches were broken off to make room for
me." 20 Yes, but remember—those branches were broken off because they
didn't believe in Christ, and you are there because you do believe. So don't
think highly of yourself, but fear what could happen. 21 For if God did not
spare the original branches, he won't* spare you either.

22 Notice how God is both kind and severe. He is severe toward those who
disobeyed, but kind to you if you continue to trust in his kindness. But if
you stop trusting, you also will be cut off. 23 And if the people of Israel turn
from their unbelief, they will be grafted in again, for God has the power to
graft them back into the tree. 24 You, by nature, were a branch cut from a
wild olive tree. So if God was willing to do something contrary to nature by
grafting you into his cultivated tree, he will be far more eager to graft the
original branches back into the tree where they belong.

God's Mercy Is for Everyone

25 I want you to understand this mystery, dear brothers and sisters,* so that
you will not feel proud about yourselves. Some of the people of Israel have
hard hearts, but this will last only until the full number of Gentiles comes
to Christ. 26 And so all Israel will be saved. As the Scriptures say,

"The one who rescues will come from Jerusalem,*
  and he will turn Israel* away from ungodliness.
27 And this is my covenant with them,
  that I will take away their sins."*

28 Many of the people of Israel are now enemies of the Good News, and
this benefits you Gentiles. Yet they are still the people he loves because he

11:21 Some manuscripts read *perhaps he won't.* **11:25** Greek *brothers.* **11:26a** Greek *from Zion.*
11:26b Greek *Jacob.* **11:26-27** Isa 59:20-21; 27:9 (Greek version).

chose their ancestors Abraham, Isaac, and Jacob. 29 For God's gifts and his
call can never be withdrawn. 30 Once, you Gentiles were rebels against God,
but when the people of Israel rebelled against him, God was merciful to you
instead. 31 Now they are the rebels, and God's mercy has come to you so that
they, too, will share* in God's mercy. 32 For God has imprisoned everyone in
disobedience so he could have mercy on everyone.

33 Oh, how great are God's riches and wisdom and knowledge! How im-
possible it is for us to understand his decisions and his ways!

34 For who can know the LORD's thoughts?
Who knows enough to give him advice?*
35 And who has given him so much
that he needs to pay it back?*

36 For everything comes from him and exists by his power and is intended
for his glory. All glory to him forever! Amen.

A Living Sacrifice to God

12 And so, dear brothers and sisters,* I plead with you to give your bod-
ies to God because of all he has done for you. Let them be a living
and holy sacrifice—the kind he will find acceptable. This is truly the way
to worship him.* 2 Don't copy the behavior and customs of this world, but
let God transform you into a new person by changing the way you think.
Then you will learn to know God's will for you, which is good and pleasing
and perfect.

3 Because of the privilege and authority* God has given me, I give each of
you this warning: Don't think you are better than you really are. Be honest
in your evaluation of yourselves, measuring yourselves by the faith God has
given us.* 4 Just as our bodies have many parts and each part has a special
function, 5 so it is with Christ's body. We are many parts of one body, and we
all belong to each other.

6 In his grace, God has given us different gifts for doing certain things well.
So if God has given you the ability to prophesy, speak out with as much faith
as God has given you. 7 If your gift is serving others, serve them well. If you
are a teacher, teach well. 8 If your gift is to encourage others, be encouraging.
If it is giving, give generously. If God has given you leadership ability, take
the responsibility seriously. And if you have a gift for showing kindness to
others, do it gladly.

9 Don't just pretend to love others. Really love them. Hate what is wrong.
Hold tightly to what is good. 10 Love each other with genuine affection,* and
take delight in honoring each other. 11 Never be lazy, but work hard and serve
the Lord enthusiastically.* 12 Rejoice in our confident hope. Be patient in
trouble, and keep on praying. 13 When God's people are in need, be ready to
help them. Always be eager to practice hospitality.

14 Bless those who persecute you. Don't curse them; pray that God will
bless them. 15 Be happy with those who are happy, and weep with those who

11:31 Other manuscripts read *will now share;* still others read *will someday share.* **11:34** Isa 40:13 (Greek version). **11:35** See Job 41:11. **12:1a** Greek *brothers.* **12:1b** Or *This is your spiritual worship;* or *This is your reasonable service.* **12:3a** Or *Because of the grace;* compare 1:5. **12:3b** Or *by the faith God has given you;* or *by the standard of our God-given faith.* **12:10** Greek *with brotherly love.* **12:11** Or *but serve the Lord with a zealous spirit;* or *but let the Spirit excite you as you serve the Lord.*

Prayer 11:33

Jesus, how much greater are your resources than mine! I turn to you for all I need. Amen.

Question 12:1-2

In what ways would your lifestyle change if every day you practiced being "a living and holy sacrifice" to God (v. 1)?

Make a Difference
12:3-8

Use Your Gift

When a basketball player releases a jump shot from the three-point line and gives the ball a perfect arc on the release with thousands of fans watching the ball swish straight through the hoop, nothing but net, it's one of those moments when everything seems to slow down, harmony and precision combine in wonder, and life just seems to make sense. Unless we are mistaken, those moments only come from a player's dedicated commitment to improving their skill over a period of years. Investment. Hard work. Study. Joy.

Difference Maker

Make a long-term plan to become even better at the skills God has given you.

Prayer 12:11

Kick me out of my laziness and motivate me to do something good for you today, Lord. Amen.

weep. [16]Live in harmony with each other. Don't be too proud to enjoy the
company of ordinary people. And don't think you know it all!
[17]Never pay back evil with more evil. Do things in such a way that everyone
can see you are honorable. [18]Do all that you can to live in peace with everyone.
[19]Dear friends, never take revenge. Leave that to the righteous anger of
God. For the Scriptures say,

"I will take revenge;
I will pay them back,"*
says the LORD.

[20]Instead,

"If your enemies are hungry, feed them.
If they are thirsty, give them something to drink.
In doing this, you will heap
burning coals of shame on their heads."*

[21]Don't let evil conquer you, but conquer evil by doing good.

Respect for Authority

13 Everyone must submit to governing authorities. For all authority
comes from God, and those in positions of authority have been
placed there by God. [2]So anyone who rebels against authority is rebelling
against what God has instituted, and they will be punished. [3]For the authori-
ties do not strike fear in people who are doing right, but in those who are
doing wrong. Would you like to live without fear of the authorities? Do what
is right, and they will honor you. [4]The authorities are God's servants, sent
for your good. But if you are doing wrong, of course you should be afraid,
for they have the power to punish you. They are God's servants, sent for the
very purpose of punishing those who do what is wrong. [5]So you must submit
to them, not only to avoid punishment, but also to keep a clear conscience.
[6]Pay your taxes, too, for these same reasons. For government workers need
to be paid. They are serving God in what they do. [7]Give to everyone what you
owe them: Pay your taxes and government fees to those who collect them,
and give respect and honor to those who are in authority.

Love Fulfills God's Requirements

[8]Owe nothing to anyone—except for your obligation to love one another.
If you love your neighbor, you will fulfill the requirements of God's law.
[9]For the commandments say, "You must not commit adultery. You must not
murder. You must not steal. You must not covet."* These—and other such
commandments—are summed up in this one commandment: "Love your
neighbor as yourself."* [10]Love does no wrong to others, so love fulfills the
requirements of God's law.
[11]This is all the more urgent, for you know how late it is; time is running
out. Wake up, for our salvation is nearer now than when we first believed.
[12]The night is almost gone; the day of salvation will soon be here. So remove
your dark deeds like dirty clothes, and put on the shining armor of right

12:19 Deut 32:35. **12:20** Prov 25:21-22. **13:9a** Exod 20:13-15, 17. **13:9b** Lev 19:18.

living. 13 Because we belong to the day, we must live decent lives for all to
see. Don't participate in the darkness of wild parties and drunkenness, or
in sexual promiscuity and immoral living, or in quarreling and jealousy.
14 Instead, clothe yourself with the presence of the Lord Jesus Christ. And
don't let yourself think about ways to indulge your evil desires.

The Danger of Criticism

14 Accept other believers who are weak in faith, and don't argue with
them about what they think is right or wrong. 2 For instance, one
person believes it's all right to eat anything. But another believer with a
sensitive conscience will eat only vegetables. 3 Those who feel free to eat
anything must not look down on those who don't. And those who don't eat
certain foods must not condemn those who do, for God has accepted them.
4 Who are you to condemn someone else's servants? Their own master will
judge whether they stand or fall. And with the Lord's help, they will stand
and receive his approval.

5 In the same way, some think one day is more holy than another day,
while others think every day is alike. You should each be fully convinced that
whichever day you choose is acceptable. 6 Those who worship the Lord on a
special day do it to honor him. Those who eat any kind of food do so to honor
the Lord, since they give thanks to God before eating. And those who refuse
to eat certain foods also want to please the Lord and give thanks to God.
7 For we don't live for ourselves or die for ourselves. 8 If we live, it's to honor
the Lord. And if we die, it's to honor the Lord. So whether we live or die, we
belong to the Lord. 9 Christ died and rose again for this very purpose—to be
Lord both of the living and of the dead.

10 So why do you condemn another believer*? Why do you look down on
another believer? Remember, we will all stand before the judgment seat of
God. 11 For the Scriptures say,

"'As surely as I live,' says the LORD,
'every knee will bend to me,
and every tongue will declare allegiance to God.*'"

12 Yes, each of us will give a personal account to God. 13 So let's stop condemning
each other. Decide instead to live in such a way that you will not cause another
believer to stumble and fall.

14 I know and am convinced on the authority of the Lord Jesus that no food,
in and of itself, is wrong to eat. But if someone believes it is wrong, then for that
person it is wrong. 15 And if another believer is distressed by what you eat, you
are not acting in love if you eat it. Don't let your eating ruin someone for whom
Christ died. 16 Then you will not be criticized for doing something you believe is
good. 17 For the Kingdom of God is not a matter of what we eat or drink, but of
living a life of goodness and peace and joy in the Holy Spirit. 18 If you serve Christ
with this attitude, you will please God, and others will approve of you, too. 19 So
then, let us aim for harmony in the church and try to build each other up.

20 Don't tear apart the work of God over what you eat. Remember, all foods
are acceptable, but it is wrong to eat something if it makes another person
stumble. 21 It is better not to eat meat or drink wine or do anything else if it

14:10 Greek *your brother;* also in 14:10b, 13, 15, 21. 14:11 Or *declare praise for God.* Isa 49:18; 45:23 (Greek version).

Make a Difference

13:11-14

Clothe Yourself

Look at yourself in a mirror. What are you wearing? Did you have trouble deciding what to put on this morning? How do you feel about how you look? Are you happy with the fashion option you chose? Isn't it hard to stand in front of the mirror day after day and think that what you are wearing is perfect? Some people change multiple times before heading out of their room.

In this culture, what you wear reflects who you are in many ways. Remember that there is one set of clothes that never fades, never looks bad, and never makes you feel below average. When you put on Jesus, you feel like a million bucks—or more. Jesus may not always be "in style," but he always looks great on you.

Difference Maker

If you were to wear Jesus, what sort of "clothing" would you put on? How can you motivate yourself to put him on and keep him on all day long?

Question **14:8**

How could this thought free people from living anxiously?

might cause another believer to stumble.* 22 You may believe there's nothing
wrong with what you are doing, but keep it between yourself and God. Blessed
are those who don't feel guilty for doing something they have decided is right.
23 But if you have doubts about whether or not you should eat something, you
are sinning if you go ahead and do it. For you are not following your convic-
tions. If you do anything you believe is not right, you are sinning.*

Living to Please Others

15 We who are strong must be considerate of those who are sensitive
about things like this. We must not just please ourselves. 2 We should
help others do what is right and build them up in the Lord. 3 For even Christ
didn't live to please himself. As the Scriptures say, "The insults of those who
insult you, O God, have fallen on me."* 4 Such things were written in the
Scriptures long ago to teach us. And the Scriptures give us hope and encour-
agement as we wait patiently for God's promises to be fulfilled.

5 May God, who gives this patience and encouragement, help you live in
complete harmony with each other, as is fitting for followers of Christ Jesus.
6 Then all of you can join together with one voice, giving praise and glory to
God, the Father of our Lord Jesus Christ.

7 Therefore, accept each other just as Christ has accepted you so that God
will be given glory. 8 Remember that Christ came as a servant to the Jews* to
show that God is true to the promises he made to their ancestors. 9 He also
came so that the Gentiles might give glory to God for his mercies to them.
That is what the psalmist meant when he wrote:

> "For this, I will praise you among the Gentiles;
> I will sing praises to your name."*

10 And in another place it is written,

> "Rejoice with his people,
> you Gentiles."*

11 And yet again,

> "Praise the LORD, all you Gentiles.
> Praise him, all you people of the earth."*

12 And in another place Isaiah said,

> "The heir to David's throne* will come,
> and he will rule over the Gentiles.
> They will place their hope on him."*

13 I pray that God, the source of hope, will fill you completely with joy and
peace because you trust in him. Then you will overflow with confident hope
through the power of the Holy Spirit.

14:21 Some manuscripts read *to stumble or be offended or be weakened.* 14:23 Some manuscripts place the text of 16:25-27 here. 15:3 Greek *who insult you have fallen on me.* Ps 69:9. 15:8 Greek *servant of circumcision.* 15:9 Ps 18:49. 15:10 Deut 32:43. 15:11 Ps 117:1. 15:12a Greek *The root of Jesse.* David was the son of Jesse. 15:12b Isa 11:10 (Greek version).

Make a Difference 15:13

Overflow

Could God ever be depleted of his resources? How many times can we keep asking for more? If we keep pulling up to God's station to fill up our tanks, will God eventually run out of energy? Will he finally say, "Enough! I can't take the pressure! Please ask somebody else"?

If God wanted to fill you, don't you think he could? The fact is that he does want to fill you and he is totally able to do so. In fact, he has got more than you can ever bear. When he fills you up, it's not one of those leave-some-room-on-the-top-so-I-won't-spill sorts of fills. No, God fills to overflowing. All his unending hope, unlimited joy, and unrelenting peace are available in abundance for you. Perhaps the true question is this: Do you want him to fill you?

Difference Maker

Go outside and enjoy what God has made. Jesus, who fills the entire creation with his presence, is the same one who fills you with his vast love.

Paul's Reason for Writing

[14]I am fully convinced, my dear brothers and sisters,* that you are full of
goodness. You know these things so well you can teach each other all about
them. [15]Even so, I have been bold enough to write about some of these points,
knowing that all you need is this reminder. For by God's grace, [16]I am a spe-
cial messenger from Christ Jesus to you Gentiles. I bring you the Good News
so that I might present you as an acceptable offering to God, made holy by
the Holy Spirit. [17]So I have reason to be enthusiastic about all Christ Jesus has
done through me in my service to God. [18]Yet I dare not boast about anything
except what Christ has done through me, bringing the Gentiles to God by
my message and by the way I worked among them. [19]They were convinced
by the power of miraculous signs and wonders and by the power of God's
Spirit.* In this way, I have fully presented the Good News of Christ from Je-
rusalem all the way to Illyricum.*

[20]My ambition has always been to preach the Good News where the name
of Christ has never been heard, rather than where a church has already been
started by someone else. [21]I have been following the plan spoken of in the
Scriptures, where it says,

"Those who have never been told about him will see,
  and those who have never heard of him will understand."*

[22]In fact, my visit to you has been delayed so long because I have been preach-
ing in these places.

Paul's Travel Plans

[23]But now I have finished my work in these regions, and after all these long
years of waiting, I am eager to visit you. [24]I am planning to go to Spain, and
when I do, I will stop off in Rome. And after I have enjoyed your fellowship
for a little while, you can provide for my journey.

[25]But before I come, I must go to Jerusalem to take a gift to the believers*
there. [26]For you see, the believers in Macedonia and Achaia* have eagerly
taken up an offering for the poor among the believers in Jerusalem. [27]They
were glad to do this because they feel they owe a real debt to them. Since the
Gentiles received the spiritual blessings of the Good News from the believ-
ers in Jerusalem, they feel the least they can do in return is to help them
financially. [28]As soon as I have delivered this money and completed this good
deed of theirs, I will come to see you on my way to Spain. [29]And I am sure
that when I come, Christ will richly bless our time together.

[30]Dear brothers and sisters, I urge you in the name of our Lord Jesus Christ
to join in my struggle by praying to God for me. Do this because of your love
for me, given to you by the Holy Spirit. [31]Pray that I will be rescued from
those in Judea who refuse to obey God. Pray also that the believers there will
be willing to accept the donation* I am taking to Jerusalem. [32]Then, by the
will of God, I will be able to come to you with a joyful heart, and we will be
an encouragement to each other.

[33]And now may God, who gives us his peace, be with you all. Amen.*

15:14 Greek *brothers;* also in 15:30. **15:19a** Other manuscripts read *the Spirit;* still others read *the Holy Spirit.* **15:19b** *Illyricum* was a region northeast of Italy. **15:21** Isa 52:15 (Greek version). **15:25** Greek *God's holy people;* also in 15:26, 31. **15:26** *Macedonia* and *Achaia* were the northern and southern regions of Greece. **15:31** Greek *the ministry;* other manuscripts read *the gift.* **15:33** Some manuscripts do not include *Amen.* One very early manuscript places 16:25-27 here.

Paul Greets His Friends

16 I commend to you our sister Phoebe, who is a deacon in the church in Cenchrea. 2 Welcome her in the Lord as one who is worthy of honor among God's people. Help her in whatever she needs, for she has been helpful to many, and especially to me.

3 Give my greetings to Priscilla and Aquila, my co-workers in the ministry of Christ Jesus. 4 In fact, they once risked their lives for me. I am thankful to them, and so are all the Gentile churches. 5 Also give my greetings to the church that meets in their home.

Greet my dear friend Epenetus. He was the first person from the province of Asia to become a follower of Christ. 6 Give my greetings to Mary, who has worked so hard for your benefit. 7 Greet Andronicus and Junia,* my fellow Jews,* who were in prison with me. They are highly respected among the apostles and became followers of Christ before I did. 8 Greet Ampliatus, my dear friend in the Lord. 9 Greet Urbanus, our co-worker in Christ, and my dear friend Stachys.

10 Greet Apelles, a good man whom Christ approves. And give my greetings to the believers from the household of Aristobulus. 11 Greet Herodion, my fellow Jew.* Greet the Lord's people from the household of Narcissus. 12 Give my greetings to Tryphena and Tryphosa, the Lord's workers, and to dear Persis, who has worked so hard for the Lord. 13 Greet Rufus, whom the Lord picked out to be his very own; and also his dear mother, who has been a mother to me.

14 Give my greetings to Asyncritus, Phlegon, Hermes, Patrobas, Hermas, and the brothers and sisters* who meet with them. 15 Give my greetings to Philologus, Julia, Nereus and his sister, and to Olympas and all the believers* who meet with them. 16 Greet each other with a sacred kiss. All the churches of Christ send you their greetings.

Paul's Final Instructions

17 And now I make one more appeal, my dear brothers and sisters. Watch out for people who cause divisions and upset people's faith by teaching things contrary to what you have been taught. Stay away from them. 18 Such people are not serving Christ our Lord; they are serving their own personal interests. By smooth talk and glowing words they deceive innocent people. 19 But everyone knows that you are obedient to the Lord. This makes me very happy. I want you to be wise in doing right and to stay innocent of any wrong. 20 The God of peace will soon crush Satan under your feet. May the grace of our Lord Jesus* be with you.

21 Timothy, my fellow worker, sends you his greetings, as do Lucius, Jason, and Sosipater, my fellow Jews.

22 I, Tertius, the one writing this letter for Paul, send my greetings, too, as one of the Lord's followers.

23 Gaius says hello to you. He is my host and also serves as host to the whole church. Erastus, the city treasurer, sends you his greetings, and so does our brother Quartus.*

25 Now all glory to God, who is able to make you strong, just as my Good

16:7a *Junia* is a feminine name. Some late manuscripts accent the word so it reads *Junias,* a masculine name; still others read *Julia* (feminine). **16:7b** Or *compatriots;* also in 16:21. **16:11** Or *compatriot.* **16:14** Greek *brothers;* also in 16:17. **16:15** Greek *all of God's holy people.* **16:20** Some manuscripts read *Lord Jesus Christ.* **16:23** Some manuscripts add verse 24, *May the grace of our Lord Jesus Christ be with you all. Amen.* Still others add this sentence after verse 27.

Make a Difference 16:16

Get Connected

The book of Romans is a soaring theological argument. For fifteen chapters, the apostle Paul explained humanity's history with God. He summarized profound truths with memorable phrases and simple language. He wrote things like, "We all fall short of God's glorious standard" (3:23); "The wages of sin is death, but the free gift of God is eternal life through Christ Jesus our Lord" (6:23); "Nothing can ever separate us from God's love" (8:38); and "Don't copy the behavior and customs of this world, but let God transform you" (12:2).

With all this amazing clarity, many people overlook the last chapter. After all, instead of eloquent rhetoric, there is just a bunch of people Paul wrote to and about. He listed dozens by name and hundreds, perhaps thousands, of people by reference. Some were famous (like the apostles) whereas others were obscure (like Junia, Nereus and his sister, or Rufus's dear mom). Romans 16 should not be overlooked, however, because in this real-life network of people is the real-life theological truth of Romans. What Paul talked about actually works in the everyday fabric of people's lives. Jesus unites people in a growing network that changes everything in this world.

Difference Maker

Contact a local ministry group so that you get plugged in.

News says. This message about Jesus Christ has revealed his plan for you
Gentiles, a plan kept secret from the beginning of time. 26 But now as the
prophets* foretold and as the eternal God has commanded, this message
is made known to all Gentiles everywhere, so that they too might believe
and obey him. 27 All glory to the only wise God, through Jesus Christ, for-
ever. Amen.*

16:26 Greek *the prophetic writings.* 16:25-27 Various manuscripts place the doxology (shown here as 16:25-27) after 14:23 or after 15:33 or after 16:23.

Story Arc **16:1-27**

● The Roman Church Network

Nowhere is the real-life drama and community of Christianity revealed like it is in the letter of Romans. Unfortunately, many people miss it. This New Testament book is so power-packed full of memorable verses that it can be easy to find inspiration or challenge by just revisiting old favorites (perhaps 1:16; 3:23; 5:8; 6:23; 8:1; 8:35; 12:1). The theological argument that runs from chapter 1 through the middle of chapter 15 is so good that the personal greetings at the end of the letter almost seem out of place.

There is a treasure to be found at the end of Romans. The sixteenth chapter proves the powerful arguments of the first fifteen chapters are true. It is precisely because this letter is lived out in the real lives of real people embedded in the reality of a real geography during a hinge-point period of history that the grand theological teachings of Romans can be embraced as real. Following Jesus, in other words, is a real movement. Take a moment to read through all the names included in chapter 16 and try to trace where else they show up in the New Testament.

The early churches were made up of people woven together into networks of Jesus followers. Go back through this book to see the unique people mentioned and consider how they got involved in God's world-changing movement.

1 Cor 3:21-23 ►

The Roman Church Network

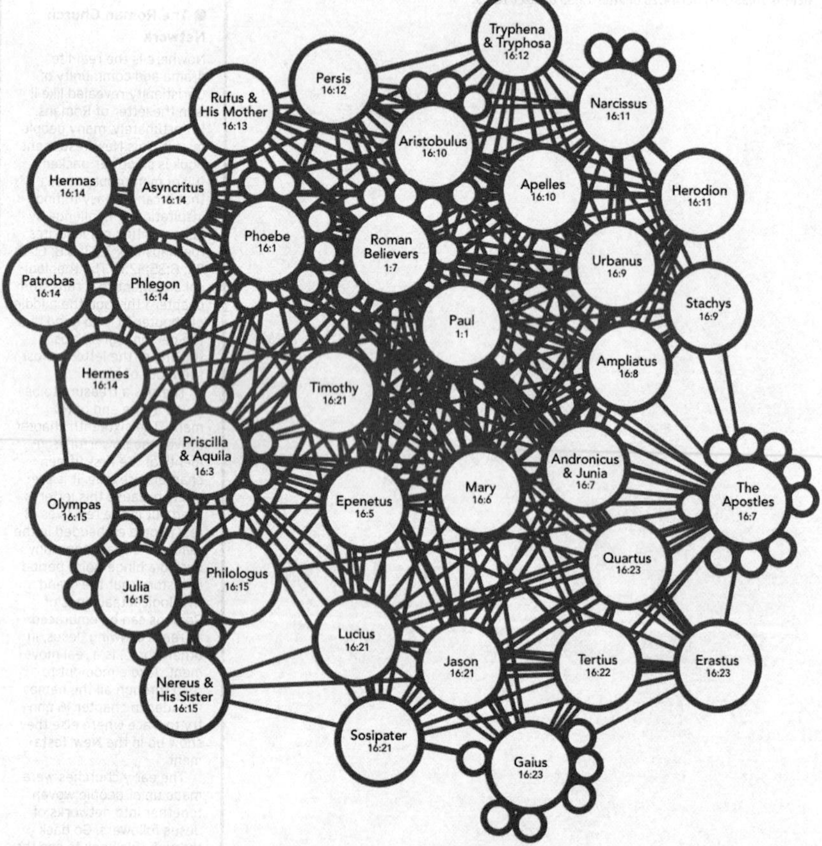

1 Corinthians Introduction

This first letter that Paul wrote to the church in Corinth is strangely comforting. In Corinth, there was a collection of people who loved Jesus and knew the truth of the gospel, but they had some serious problems to work through.

Your church might have a few of the problems the Corinthians had, but the Corinthians had *all* the problems. Paul wrote to help them work through some deep issues of sin. This church had issues with rampant sexual sin (1 Corinthians 5:1–2), lawsuits against each other (6:1–11), people of wealth not sharing communion meals with the poor in their congregation (11:17–22), members comparing spiritual gifts to see who was "best" (12:1–13:3), and that's not even the full list!

Despite this church functioning like a reality show, God loved each one of these people. God envisioned a future for them and used Paul to remind them of what they already knew to be true: Christ died for their sins, was buried, and was raised on the third day so that they could have new life! There is hope even in the midst of dysfunction and imperfection.

Odds are that your situation isn't perfect either. Maybe there are sinful things happening around you; maybe you're even participating in those things. The surprising comfort of 1 Corinthians is that Jesus is still with those who are struggling. That means he is still there for you. There is a path toward him and toward true life even during tough times.

Story Arc

● **Early Church Leaders**

The 1 Corinthians Church Network

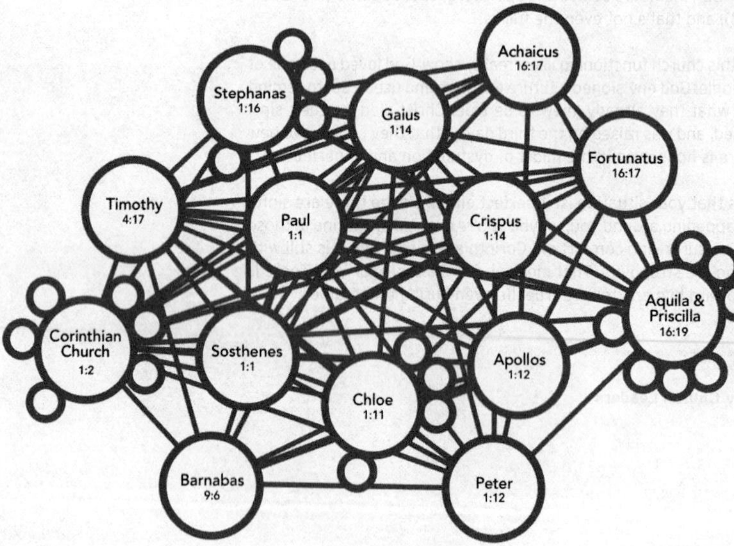

1 Corinthians

Greetings from Paul

1 This letter is from Paul, chosen by the will of God to be an apostle of
Christ Jesus, and from our brother Sosthenes.
2 I am writing to God's church in Corinth,* to you who have been called by
God to be his own holy people. He made you holy by means of Christ Jesus,*
just as he did for all people everywhere who call on the name of our Lord
Jesus Christ, their Lord and ours.
3 May God our Father and the Lord Jesus Christ give you grace and peace.

Paul Gives Thanks to God

4 I always thank my God for you and for the gracious gifts he has given you,
now that you belong to Christ Jesus. 5 Through him, God has enriched your
church in every way—with all of your eloquent words and all of your knowl-
edge. 6 This confirms that what I told you about Christ is true. 7 Now you have
every spiritual gift you need as you eagerly wait for the return of our Lord
Jesus Christ. 8 He will keep you strong to the end so that you will be free from
all blame on the day when our Lord Jesus Christ returns. 9 God will do this,
for he is faithful to do what he says, and he has invited you into partnership
with his Son, Jesus Christ our Lord.

Divisions in the Church

10 I appeal to you, dear brothers and sisters,* by the authority of our Lord
Jesus Christ, to live in harmony with each other. Let there be no divisions in
the church. Rather, be of one mind, united in thought and purpose. 11 For
some members of Chloe's household have told me about your quarrels, my
dear brothers and sisters. 12 Some of you are saying, "I am a follower of Paul."
Others are saying, "I follow Apollos," or "I follow Peter,*" or "I follow only
Christ."
13 Has Christ been divided into factions? Was I, Paul, crucified for you?
Were any of you baptized in the name of Paul? Of course not! 14 I thank God
that I did not baptize any of you except Crispus and Gaius, 15 for now no
one can say they were baptized in my name. 16 (Oh yes, I also baptized the
household of Stephanas, but I don't remember baptizing anyone else.) 17 For
Christ didn't send me to baptize, but to preach the Good News—and not
with clever speech, for fear that the cross of Christ would lose its power.

The Wisdom of God

18 The message of the cross is foolish to those who are headed for destruc-
tion! But we who are being saved know it is the very power of God. 19 As the
Scriptures say,

1:2a *Corinth* was the capital city of Achaia, the southern region of the Greek peninsula. **1:2b** Or *because you belong to Christ Jesus.* **1:10** Greek *brothers;* also in 1:11, 26. **1:12** Greek *Cephas.*

Question **1:1-3**

There are a lot of people mentioned in this letter. Go through every chapter and circle the names mentioned. What can you discover about why Paul mentioned these people and what difference Jesus had made in their lives?

Question **1:8**

In what areas of your life do you feel weak? Paul suggested that Jesus can keep you strong. How can Jesus do that?

Prayer **1:18**

Lord, how I wish people didn't think the message of the cross was foolish. I pray for those who don't know you. In your power, help them find your salvation through the cross of Christ. Amen.

Question 2:2

Does this verse reflect the way you interact with others?

"I will destroy the wisdom of the wise
and discard the intelligence of the intelligent."*

20 So where does this leave the philosophers, the scholars, and the world's
brilliant debaters? God has made the wisdom of this world look foolish.
21 Since God in his wisdom saw to it that the world would never know him
through human wisdom, he has used our foolish preaching to save those
who believe. 22 It is foolish to the Jews, who ask for signs from heaven. And
it is foolish to the Greeks, who seek human wisdom. 23 So when we preach
that Christ was crucified, the Jews are offended and the Gentiles say it's all
nonsense.

24 But to those called by God to salvation, both Jews and Gentiles,* Christ
is the power of God and the wisdom of God. 25 This foolish plan of God is
wiser than the wisest of human plans, and God's weakness is stronger than
the greatest of human strength.

26 Remember, dear brothers and sisters, that few of you were wise in the
world's eyes or powerful or wealthy* when God called you. 27 Instead, God
chose things the world considers foolish in order to shame those who think
they are wise. And he chose things that are powerless to shame those who
are powerful. 28 God chose things despised by the world,* things counted as
nothing at all, and used them to bring to nothing what the world considers
important. 29 As a result, no one can ever boast in the presence of God.

30 God has united you with Christ Jesus. For our benefit God made him to
be wisdom itself. Christ made us right with God; he made us pure and holy,
and he freed us from sin. 31 Therefore, as the Scriptures say, "If you want to
boast, boast only about the LORD."*

Paul's Message of Wisdom

2 When I first came to you, dear brothers and sisters,* I didn't use lofty
words and impressive wisdom to tell you God's secret plan.* 2 For I
decided that while I was with you I would forget everything except Jesus
Christ, the one who was crucified. 3 I came to you in weakness—timid and
trembling. 4 And my message and my preaching were very plain. Rather than
using clever and persuasive speeches, I relied only on the power of the Holy
Spirit. 5 I did this so you would trust not in human wisdom but in the power
of God.

6 Yet when I am among mature believers, I do speak with words of wisdom,
but not the kind of wisdom that belongs to this world or to the rulers of this
world, who are soon forgotten. 7 No, the wisdom we speak of is the mystery
of God*—his plan that was previously hidden, even though he made it for
our ultimate glory before the world began. 8 But the rulers of this world have
not understood it; if they had, they would not have crucified our glorious
Lord. 9 That is what the Scriptures mean when they say,

"No eye has seen, no ear has heard,
and no mind has imagined
what God has prepared
for those who love him."*

1:19 Isa 29:14. **1:24** Greek *and Greeks.* **1:26** Or *high born.* **1:28** Or *God chose those who are low born.* **1:31** Jer 9:24. **2:1a** Greek *brothers.* **2:1b** Greek *God's mystery;* other manuscripts read *God's testimony.* **2:7** Greek *But we speak God's wisdom in a mystery.* **2:9** Isa 64:4.

10 But* it was to us that God revealed these things by his Spirit. For his
Spirit searches out everything and shows us God's deep secrets. 11 No one
can know a person's thoughts except that person's own spirit, and no one
can know God's thoughts except God's own Spirit. 12 And we have received
God's Spirit (not the world's spirit), so we can know the wonderful things
God has freely given us.

13 When we tell you these things, we do not use words that come from
human wisdom. Instead, we speak words given to us by the Spirit, using the
Spirit's words to explain spiritual truths.* 14 But people who aren't spiritual*
can't receive these truths from God's Spirit. It all sounds foolish to them and
they can't understand it, for only those who are spiritual can understand
what the Spirit means. 15 Those who are spiritual can evaluate all things, but
they themselves cannot be evaluated by others. 16 For,

"Who can know the LORD's thoughts?
Who knows enough to teach him?"*

But we understand these things, for we have the mind of Christ.

Paul and Apollos, Servants of Christ

3 Dear brothers and sisters,* when I was with you I couldn't talk to you as
I would to spiritual people.* I had to talk as though you belonged to this
world or as though you were infants in Christ. 2 I had to feed you with milk,
not with solid food, because you weren't ready for anything stronger. And
you still aren't ready, 3 for you are still controlled by your sinful nature. You
are jealous of one another and quarrel with each other. Doesn't that prove
you are controlled by your sinful nature? Aren't you living like people of the
world? 4 When one of you says, "I am a follower of Paul," and another says, "I
follow Apollos," aren't you acting just like people of the world?

5 After all, who is Apollos? Who is Paul? We are only God's servants through
whom you believed the Good News. Each of us did the work the Lord gave
us. 6 I planted the seed in your hearts, and Apollos watered it, but it was God
who made it grow. 7 It's not important who does the planting, or who does
the watering. What's important is that God makes the seed grow. 8 The one
who plants and the one who waters work together with the same purpose.
And both will be rewarded for their own hard work. 9 For we are both God's
workers. And you are God's field. You are God's building.

10 Because of God's grace to me, I have laid the foundation like an expert
builder. Now others are building on it. But whoever is building on this foun-
dation must be very careful. 11 For no one can lay any foundation other than
the one we already have—Jesus Christ.

12 Anyone who builds on that foundation may use a variety of materials—
gold, silver, jewels, wood, hay, or straw. 13 But on the judgment day, fire will re-
veal what kind of work each builder has done. The fire will show if a person's
work has any value. 14 If the work survives, that builder will receive a reward.
15 But if the work is burned up, the builder will suffer great loss. The builder
will be saved, but like someone barely escaping through a wall of flames.

Make a Difference

3:5–9

Work Together

Your ability to work with others is much like the hand and the mouth working together. When the hand and mouth refuse to bless one another as a team, eating dinner is really dysfunctional. When the hand uses its gift to grab on to that carnitas burrito and when the mouth uses its giftedness to open up wide and take a gargantuan bite, the whole of the body benefits and praises the Lord.

The church is an amazing team of great people who are uniquely gifted and uniquely flawed and who are ready to work together to bring good to this world through faith in Jesus. Practically, this means that you should live your life within a network of others who are striving to follow Jesus and make a difference in this world too. While you use your gifts to bless others, others use their gifts to bless you. No one has a monopoly on God's calling.

Difference Maker

If you are not involved already in a vibrant church or ministry group, start taking the risk to do so. If you already are involved, then invite others into your group so that they can be built up too.

2:10 Some manuscripts read *For.* 2:13 Or *explaining spiritual truths in spiritual language,* or *explaining spiritual truths to spiritual people.* 2:14 Or *who don't have the Spirit;* or *who have only physical life.* 2:16 Isa 40:13 (Greek version). 3:1a Greek *Brothers.* 3:1b Or *to people who have the Spirit.*

16 Don't you realize that all of you together are the temple of God and that
the Spirit of God lives in* you? 17 God will destroy anyone who destroys this
temple. For God's temple is holy, and you are that temple.
18 Stop deceiving yourselves. If you think you are wise by this world's stan-
dards, you need to become a fool to be truly wise. 19 For the wisdom of this
world is foolishness to God. As the Scriptures say,

"He traps the wise
in the snare of their own cleverness."*

20 And again,

"The LORD knows the thoughts of the wise;
he knows they are worthless."*

21 So don't boast about following a particular human leader. For everything
belongs to you—22 whether Paul or Apollos or Peter,* or the world, or life and
death, or the present and the future. Everything belongs to you, 23 and you
belong to Christ, and Christ belongs to God.

Story Arc **3:21-23**

Early Church Leaders

You may recognize the names of Paul and Peter here, but you may not be as familiar with this person named Apollos. It turns out that Apollos, along with the two famous apostles, played a significant role in the faith of the Corinthian church and was an important part of the dynamic spread of Christianity in the first century AD. There were others too! The book of 1 Corinthians also mentions key leaders like Sosthenes, Crispus, Gaius, Stephanas, Timothy, Barnabas, Fortunatus, Achaicus, Aquila, and Priscilla. Christ so profoundly affected these people, from all kinds of backgrounds and experiences, that they went on to make a difference across thousands of miles and among thousands of people. Throughout history, God has raised up people to share the good news of his gospel. Maybe you're next? Are you ready for God to tap you on the shoulder and invite you to join his world-changing movement?

2 Cor 7:5-7 ►

Paul's Relationship with the Corinthians

4 So look at Apollos and me as mere servants of Christ who have been
put in charge of explaining God's mysteries. 2 Now, a person who is
put in charge as a manager must be faithful. 3 As for me, it matters very
little how I might be evaluated by you or by any human authority. I don't
even trust my own judgment on this point. 4 My conscience is clear, but
that doesn't prove I'm right. It is the Lord himself who will examine me
and decide.
5 So don't make judgments about anyone ahead of time—before the Lord
returns. For he will bring our darkest secrets to light and will reveal our pri-
vate motives. Then God will give to each one whatever praise is due.
6 Dear brothers and sisters,* I have used Apollos and myself to illustrate
what I've been saying. If you pay attention to what I have quoted from the
Scriptures,* you won't be proud of one of your leaders at the expense of an-
other. 7 For what gives you the right to make such a judgment? What do you
have that God hasn't given you? And if everything you have is from God,
why boast as though it were not a gift?
8 You think you already have everything you need. You think you are al-
ready rich. You have begun to reign in God's kingdom without us! I wish
you really were reigning already, for then we would be reigning with you.
9 Instead, I sometimes think God has put us apostles on display, like prisoners
of war at the end of a victor's parade, condemned to die. We have become a
spectacle to the entire world—to people and angels alike.
10 Our dedication to Christ makes us look like fools, but you claim to be so
wise in Christ! We are weak, but you are so powerful! You are honored, but
we are ridiculed. 11 Even now we go hungry and thirsty, and we don't have
enough clothes to keep warm. We are often beaten and have no home. 12 We
work wearily with our own hands to earn our living. We bless those who
curse us. We are patient with those who abuse us. 13 We appeal gently when

3:16 Or *among.* **3:19** Job 5:13. **3:20** Ps 94:11. **3:22** Greek *Cephas.* **4:6a** Greek *Brothers.*
4:6b Or *If you learn not to go beyond "what is written."*

evil things are said about us. Yet we are treated like the world's garbage, like
everybody's trash—right up to the present moment.
[14]I am not writing these things to shame you, but to warn you as my be-
loved children. [15]For even if you had ten thousand others to teach you about
Christ, you have only one spiritual father. For I became your father in Christ
Jesus when I preached the Good News to you. [16]So I urge you to imitate me.
[17]That's why I have sent Timothy, my beloved and faithful child in the
Lord. He will remind you of how I follow Christ Jesus, just as I teach in all
the churches wherever I go.
[18]Some of you have become arrogant, thinking I will not visit you again.
[19]But I will come—and soon—if the Lord lets me, and then I'll find out
whether these arrogant people just give pretentious speeches or whether
they really have God's power. [20]For the Kingdom of God is not just a lot of
talk; it is living by God's power. [21]Which do you choose? Should I come with
a rod to punish you, or should I come with love and a gentle spirit?

Paul Condemns Spiritual Pride

5 I can hardly believe the report about the sexual immorality going on
among you—something that even pagans don't do. I am told that a
man in your church is living in sin with his stepmother.* [2]You are so proud
of yourselves, but you should be mourning in sorrow and shame. And you
should remove this man from your fellowship.
[3]Even though I am not with you in person, I am with you in the Spirit.*
And as though I were there, I have already passed judgment on this man
[4]in the name of the Lord Jesus. You must call a meeting of the church.* I
will be present with you in spirit, and so will the power of our Lord Jesus.
[5]Then you must throw this man out and hand him over to Satan so that his
sinful nature will be destroyed* and he himself* will be saved on the day
the Lord* returns.
[6]Your boasting about this is terrible. Don't you realize that this sin is like
a little yeast that spreads through the whole batch of dough? [7]Get rid of the
old "yeast" by removing this wicked person from among you. Then you will
be like a fresh batch of dough made without yeast, which is what you really
are. Christ, our Passover Lamb, has been sacrificed for us.* [8]So let us celebrate
the festival, not with the old bread* of wickedness and evil, but with the new
bread* of sincerity and truth.
[9]When I wrote to you before, I told you not to associate with people who
indulge in sexual sin. [10]But I wasn't talking about unbelievers who indulge
in sexual sin, or are greedy, or cheat people, or worship idols. You would
have to leave this world to avoid people like that. [11]I meant that you are not
to associate with anyone who claims to be a believer* yet indulges in sexual
sin, or is greedy, or worships idols, or is abusive, or is a drunkard, or cheats
people. Don't even eat with such people.
[12]It isn't my responsibility to judge outsiders, but it certainly is your re-
sponsibility to judge those inside the church who are sinning. [13]God will
judge those on the outside; but as the Scriptures say, "You must remove the
evil person from among you."*

5:1 Greek *his father's wife.* **5:3** Or *in spirit.* **5:4** Or *In the name of the Lord Jesus, you must call a meeting of the church.* **5:5a** Or *so that his body will be destroyed;* Greek reads *for the destruction of the flesh.* **5:5b** Greek *and the spirit.* **5:5c** Other manuscripts read *the Lord Jesus;* still others read *our Lord Jesus Christ.* **5:7** Greek *has been sacrificed.* **5:8a** Greek *not with old leaven.* **5:8b** Greek *but with unleavened [bread].* **5:11** Greek *a brother.* **5:13** Deut 17:7.

Question **4:16**

Do you have anyone in your life who sets a good example of faith that you want to imitate? Are you setting an example of faith that you want others to imitate?

Prayer **4:20**

Lord, never let me treat your kingdom as just a thought. Let me be changed daily by your very real presence and activity in my life. Amen.

Question **6:18-20**

The temple in Jerusalem was to be the house where the presence of the Lord would reside. The prophets in the Old Testament made it clear, however, that someday the Lord would reside within people. When we invite Jesus into our lives, we are asking him to move in and even remodel. This is an amazing thing! With this in mind, what could you do to take better care of your whole self so that Jesus feels at home in you?

Avoiding Lawsuits with Christians

6 When one of you has a dispute with another believer, how dare you file a lawsuit and ask a secular court to decide the matter instead of taking it to other believers*! 2 Don't you realize that someday we believers will judge the world? And since you are going to judge the world, can't you decide even these little things among yourselves? 3 Don't you realize that we will judge angels? So you should surely be able to resolve ordinary disputes in this life. 4 If you have legal disputes about such matters, why go to outside judges who are not respected by the church? 5 I am saying this to shame you. Isn't there anyone in all the church who is wise enough to decide these issues? 6 But instead, one believer* sues another—right in front of unbelievers!

7 Even to have such lawsuits with one another is a defeat for you. Why not just accept the injustice and leave it at that? Why not let yourselves be cheated? 8 Instead, you yourselves are the ones who do wrong and cheat even your fellow believers.*

9 Don't you realize that those who do wrong will not inherit the Kingdom of God? Don't fool yourselves. Those who indulge in sexual sin, or who worship idols, or commit adultery, or are male prostitutes, or practice homosexuality, 10 or are thieves, or greedy people, or drunkards, or are abusive, or cheat people—none of these will inherit the Kingdom of God. 11 Some of you were once like that. But you were cleansed; you were made holy; you were made right with God by calling on the name of the Lord Jesus Christ and by the Spirit of our God.

Avoiding Sexual Sin

12 You say, "I am allowed to do anything"—but not everything is good for you. And even though "I am allowed to do anything," I must not become a slave to anything. 13 You say, "Food was made for the stomach, and the stomach for food." (This is true, though someday God will do away with both of them.) But you can't say that our bodies were made for sexual immorality. They were made for the Lord, and the Lord cares about our bodies. 14 And God will raise us from the dead by his power, just as he raised our Lord from the dead.

15 Don't you realize that your bodies are actually parts of Christ? Should a man take his body, which is part of Christ, and join it to a prostitute? Never! 16 And don't you realize that if a man joins himself to a prostitute, he becomes one body with her? For the Scriptures say, "The two are united into one."* 17 But the person who is joined to the Lord is one spirit with him.

18 Run from sexual sin! No other sin so clearly affects the body as this one does. For sexual immorality is a sin against your own body. 19 Don't you realize that your body is the temple of the Holy Spirit, who lives in you and was given to you by God? You do not belong to yourself, 20 for God bought you with a high price. So you must honor God with your body.

Instruction on Marriage

7 Now regarding the questions you asked in your letter. Yes, it is good to abstain from sexual relations.* 2 But because there is so much sexual immorality, each man should have his own wife, and each woman should have her own husband.

6:1 Greek *God's holy people;* also in 6:2. 6:6 Greek *one brother.* 6:8 Greek *even the brothers.* 6:16 Gen 2:24. 7:1 Or *to live a celibate life;* Greek reads *It is good for a man not to touch a woman.*

3The husband should fulfill his wife's sexual needs, and the wife should
fulfill her husband's needs. 4The wife gives authority over her body to her
husband, and the husband gives authority over his body to his wife.
5Do not deprive each other of sexual relations, unless you both agree to re-
frain from sexual intimacy for a limited time so you can give yourselves more
completely to prayer. Afterward, you should come together again so that
Satan won't be able to tempt you because of your lack of self-control. 6I say
this as a concession, not as a command. 7But I wish everyone were single, just
as I am. Yet each person has a special gift from God, of one kind or another.
8So I say to those who aren't married and to widows—it's better to stay
unmarried, just as I am. 9But if they can't control themselves, they should
go ahead and marry. It's better to marry than to burn with lust.
10But for those who are married, I have a command that comes not from
me, but from the Lord.* A wife must not leave her husband. 11But if she does
leave him, let her remain single or else be reconciled to him. And the hus-
band must not leave his wife.
12Now, I will speak to the rest of you, though I do not have a direct com-
mand from the Lord. If a fellow believer* has a wife who is not a believer and
she is willing to continue living with him, he must not leave her. 13And if
a believing woman has a husband who is not a believer and he is willing to
continue living with her, she must not leave him. 14For the believing wife
brings holiness to her marriage, and the believing husband* brings holiness
to his marriage. Otherwise, your children would not be holy, but now they
are holy. 15(But if the husband or wife who isn't a believer insists on leaving,
let them go. In such cases the believing husband or wife* is no longer bound
to the other, for God has called you* to live in peace.) 16Don't you wives realize
that your husbands might be saved because of you? And don't you husbands
realize that your wives might be saved because of you?
17Each of you should continue to live in whatever situation the Lord has
placed you, and remain as you were when God first called you. This is my
rule for all the churches. 18For instance, a man who was circumcised before
he became a believer should not try to reverse it. And the man who was un-
circumcised when he became a believer should not be circumcised now. 19For
it makes no difference whether or not a man has been circumcised. The im-
portant thing is to keep God's commandments.
20Yes, each of you should remain as you were when God called you. 21Are
you a slave? Don't let that worry you—but if you get a chance to be free, take
it. 22And remember, if you were a slave when the Lord called you, you are now
free in the Lord. And if you were free when the Lord called you, you are now
a slave of Christ. 23God paid a high price for you, so don't be enslaved by the
world.* 24Each of you, dear brothers and sisters,* should remain as you were
when God first called you.

25Now regarding your question about the young women who are not yet
married. I do not have a command from the Lord for them. But the Lord in
his mercy has given me wisdom that can be trusted, and I will share it with
you. 26Because of the present crisis,* I think it is best to remain as you are. 27If
you have a wife, do not seek to end the marriage. If you do not have a wife,
do not seek to get married. 28But if you do get married, it is not a sin. And if

7:10 See Matt 5:32; 19:9; Mark 10:11-12; Luke 16:18. **7:12** Greek *a brother.* **7:14** Greek *the brother.* **7:15a** Greek *the brother or sister.* **7:15b** Some manuscripts read *us.* **7:23** Greek *don't become slaves of people.* **7:24** Greek *brothers;* also in 7:29. **7:26** Or *the pressures of life.*

Question 8:6

This is perhaps one of the oldest hymns in Christianity. If you were to memorize this "hymn," repeating it daily, what would change in the way you look at this world?

a young woman gets married, it is not a sin. However, those who get married
at this time will have troubles, and I am trying to spare you those problems.
29 But let me say this, dear brothers and sisters: The time that remains is
very short. So from now on, those with wives should not focus only on their
marriage. 30 Those who weep or who rejoice or who buy things should not
be absorbed by their weeping or their joy or their possessions. 31 Those who
use the things of the world should not become attached to them. For this
world as we know it will soon pass away.

32 I want you to be free from the concerns of this life. An unmarried man
can spend his time doing the Lord's work and thinking how to please him.
33 But a married man has to think about his earthly responsibilities and how
to please his wife. 34 His interests are divided. In the same way, a woman who
is no longer married or has never been married can be devoted to the Lord
and holy in body and in spirit. But a married woman has to think about her
earthly responsibilities and how to please her husband. 35 I am saying this for
your benefit, not to place restrictions on you. I want you to do whatever will
help you serve the Lord best, with as few distractions as possible.

36 But if a man thinks that he's treating his fiancée improperly and will
inevitably give in to his passion, let him marry her as he wishes. It is not
a sin. 37 But if he has decided firmly not to marry and there is no urgency
and he can control his passion, he does well not to marry. 38 So the person
who marries his fiancée does well, and the person who doesn't marry does
even better.

39 A wife is bound to her husband as long as he lives. If her husband dies,
she is free to marry anyone she wishes, but only if he loves the Lord.* 40 But in
my opinion it would be better for her to stay single, and I think I am giving
you counsel from God's Spirit when I say this.

Food Sacrificed to Idols

8 Now regarding your question about food that has been offered to idols.
Yes, we know that "we all have knowledge" about this issue. But while
knowledge makes us feel important, it is love that strengthens the church.
2 Anyone who claims to know all the answers doesn't really know very much.
3 But the person who loves God is the one whom God recognizes.*

4 So, what about eating meat that has been offered to idols? Well, we all
know that an idol is not really a god and that there is only one God. 5 There
may be so-called gods both in heaven and on earth, and some people actually
worship many gods and many lords. 6 But for us,

There is one God, the Father,
by whom all things were created,
and for whom we live.
And there is one Lord, Jesus Christ,
through whom all things were created,
and through whom we live.

7 However, not all believers know this. Some are accustomed to thinking
of idols as being real, so when they eat food that has been offered to idols,
they think of it as the worship of real gods, and their weak consciences are

7:39 Greek *but only in the Lord.* 8:3 Some manuscripts read *the person who loves has full knowledge.*

violated. [8]It's true that we can't win God's approval by what we eat. We don't
lose anything if we don't eat it, and we don't gain anything if we do.
[9]But you must be careful so that your freedom does not cause others with
a weaker conscience to stumble. [10]For if others see you—with your "superior
knowledge"—eating in the temple of an idol, won't they be encouraged to
violate their conscience by eating food that has been offered to an idol? [11]So
because of your superior knowledge, a weak believer* for whom Christ died
will be destroyed. [12]And when you sin against other believers* by encourag-
ing them to do something they believe is wrong, you are sinning against
Christ. [13]So if what I eat causes another believer to sin, I will never eat meat
again as long as I live—for I don't want to cause another believer to stumble.

Paul Gives Up His Rights

9 Am I not as free as anyone else? Am I not an apostle? Haven't I seen Jesus
our Lord with my own eyes? Isn't it because of my work that you belong
to the Lord? [2]Even if others think I am not an apostle, I certainly am to you.
You yourselves are proof that I am the Lord's apostle.
[3]This is my answer to those who question my authority.* [4]Don't we have
the right to live in your homes and share your meals? [5]Don't we have the
right to bring a believing wife* with us as the other apostles and the Lord's
brothers do, and as Peter* does? [6]Or is it only Barnabas and I who have to
work to support ourselves?
[7]What soldier has to pay his own expenses? What farmer plants a vineyard
and doesn't have the right to eat some of its fruit? What shepherd cares for
a flock of sheep and isn't allowed to drink some of the milk? [8]Am I express-
ing merely a human opinion, or does the law say the same thing? [9]For the
law of Moses says, "You must not muzzle an ox to keep it from eating as
it treads out the grain."* Was God thinking only about oxen when he said
this? [10]Wasn't he actually speaking to us? Yes, it was written for us, so that
the one who plows and the one who threshes the grain might both expect
a share of the harvest.
[11]Since we have planted spiritual seed among you, aren't we entitled to a
harvest of physical food and drink? [12]If you support others who preach to
you, shouldn't we have an even greater right to be supported? But we have
never used this right. We would rather put up with anything than be an
obstacle to the Good News about Christ.
[13]Don't you realize that those who work in the temple get their meals from
the offerings brought to the temple? And those who serve at the altar get a
share of the sacrificial offerings. [14]In the same way, the Lord ordered that
those who preach the Good News should be supported by those who benefit
from it. [15]Yet I have never used any of these rights. And I am not writing this
to suggest that I want to start now. In fact, I would rather die than lose my
right to boast about preaching without charge. [16]Yet preaching the Good
News is not something I can boast about. I am compelled by God to do it.
How terrible for me if I didn't preach the Good News!
[17]If I were doing this on my own initiative, I would deserve payment.
But I have no choice, for God has given me this sacred trust. [18]What then is
my pay? It is the opportunity to preach the Good News without charging
anyone. That's why I never demand my rights when I preach the Good News.

8:11 Greek *brother;* also in 8:13. **8:12** Greek *brothers.* **9:3** Greek *those who examine me.*
9:5a Greek *a sister a wife.* **9:5b** Greek *Cephas.* **9:9** Deut 25:4.

Prayer 9:25

Jesus, discipline my routines and my focus so that I can exercise my faith today. Amen.

Make a Difference

10:12-13

Endure

Every day you will have opportunity to flail and fall and flop. There will always be chances for you to be sidetracked or sideswiped or blindsided.

You also have the opportunity to stand every day. There will always be chances for you to remain strong in the face of fear or to resist the trap of temptation. In the throes of an alluring choice that you know is wrong, you have the authority to choose freedom. You do not have to relent. You can endure. You are not alone.

God wants to walk with you and empower you to do what is right. He does not expect it will be easy for you, but he does expect you, just as he expects everyone else, to follow him through every struggle, every day. You can endure with his help and his empowerment. The temptations in your life are no different from what others experience. God is faithful.

Difference Maker

You know yourself. What traps are waiting for you today? Identify them by name. Don't let them catch you off guard. How might God be leading you to avoid them or overcome them?

[19]Even though I am a free man with no master, I have become a slave to all people to bring many to Christ. [20]When I was with the Jews, I lived like a Jew to bring the Jews to Christ. When I was with those who follow the Jewish law, I too lived under that law. Even though I am not subject to the law, I did this so I could bring to Christ those who are under the law. [21]When I am with the Gentiles who do not follow the Jewish law,* I too live apart from that law so I can bring them to Christ. But I do not ignore the law of God; I obey the law of Christ.

[22]When I am with those who are weak, I share their weakness, for I want to bring the weak to Christ. Yes, I try to find common ground with everyone, doing everything I can to save some. [23]I do everything to spread the Good News and share in its blessings.

[24]Don't you realize that in a race everyone runs, but only one person gets the prize? So run to win! [25]All athletes are disciplined in their training. They do it to win a prize that will fade away, but we do it for an eternal prize. [26]So I run with purpose in every step. I am not just shadowboxing. [27]I discipline my body like an athlete, training it to do what it should. Otherwise, I fear that after preaching to others I myself might be disqualified.

Lessons from Israel's Idolatry

10 I don't want you to forget, dear brothers and sisters,* about our ancestors in the wilderness long ago. All of them were guided by a cloud that moved ahead of them, and all of them walked through the sea on dry ground. [2]In the cloud and in the sea, all of them were baptized as followers of Moses. [3]All of them ate the same spiritual food, [4]and all of them drank the same spiritual water. For they drank from the spiritual rock that traveled with them, and that rock was Christ. [5]Yet God was not pleased with most of them, and their bodies were scattered in the wilderness.

[6]These things happened as a warning to us, so that we would not crave evil things as they did, [7]or worship idols as some of them did. As the Scriptures say, "The people celebrated with feasting and drinking, and they indulged in pagan revelry."* [8]And we must not engage in sexual immorality as some of them did, causing 23,000 of them to die in one day.

[9]Nor should we put Christ* to the test, as some of them did and then died from snakebites. [10]And don't grumble as some of them did, and then were destroyed by the angel of death. [11]These things happened to them as examples for us. They were written down to warn us who live at the end of the age.

[12]If you think you are standing strong, be careful not to fall. [13]The temptations in your life are no different from what others experience. And God is faithful. He will not allow the temptation to be more than you can stand. When you are tempted, he will show you a way out so that you can endure.

[14]So, my dear friends, flee from the worship of idols. [15]You are reasonable people. Decide for yourselves if what I am saying is true. [16]When we bless the cup at the Lord's Table, aren't we sharing in the blood of Christ? And when we break the bread, aren't we sharing in the body of Christ? [17]And though we are many, we all eat from one loaf of bread, showing that we are one body. [18]Think about the people of Israel. Weren't they united by eating the sacrifices at the altar?

[19]What am I trying to say? Am I saying that food offered to idols has some

9:21 Greek *those without the law.* **10:1** Greek *brothers.* **10:7** Exod 32:6. **10:9** Some manuscripts read *the Lord.*

significance, or that idols are real gods? 20 No, not at all. I am saying that
these sacrifices are offered to demons, not to God. And I don't want you to
participate with demons. 21 You cannot drink from the cup of the Lord and
from the cup of demons, too. You cannot eat at the Lord's Table and at the
table of demons, too. 22 What? Do we dare to rouse the Lord's jealousy? Do
you think we are stronger than he is?
23 You say, "I am allowed to do anything"*—but not everything is good
for you. You say, "I am allowed to do anything"—but not everything is beneficial.
24 Don't be concerned for your own good but for the good of others.
25 So you may eat any meat that is sold in the marketplace without raising
questions of conscience. 26 For "the earth is the LORD's, and everything in it."*
27 If someone who isn't a believer asks you home for dinner, accept the
invitation if you want to. Eat whatever is offered to you without raising
questions of conscience. 28 (But suppose someone tells you, "This meat was
offered to an idol." Don't eat it, out of consideration for the conscience of
the one who told you. 29 It might not be a matter of conscience for you, but
it is for the other person.) For why should my freedom be limited by what
someone else thinks? 30 If I can thank God for the food and enjoy it, why
should I be condemned for eating it?
31 So whether you eat or drink, or whatever you do, do it all for the glory of
God. 32 Don't give offense to Jews or Gentiles* or the church of God. 33 I, too,
try to please everyone in everything I do. I don't just do what is best for me;
I do what is best for others so that many may be saved. 11:1 And you should
imitate me, just as I imitate Christ.

> **Prayer** 11:1
>
> *Lord Jesus, let me imitate you so well that I can be confident to ask others to imitate me. Amen.*

Instructions for Public Worship

11 2 I am so glad that you always keep me in your thoughts, and that you
are following the teachings I passed on to you. 3 But there is one thing
I want you to know: The head of every man is Christ, the head of woman is
man, and the head of Christ is God.* 4 A man dishonors his head* if he covers
his head while praying or prophesying. 5 But a woman dishonors her head* if
she prays or prophesies without a covering on her head, for this is the same
as shaving her head. 6 Yes, if she refuses to wear a head covering, she should
cut off all her hair! But since it is shameful for a woman to have her hair cut
or her head shaved, she should wear a covering.*
7 A man should not wear anything on his head when worshiping, for man
is made in God's image and reflects God's glory. And woman reflects man's
glory. 8 For the first man didn't come from woman, but the first woman came
from man. 9 And man was not made for woman, but woman was made for
man. 10 For this reason, and because the angels are watching, a woman should
wear a covering on her head to show she is under authority.*
11 But among the Lord's people, women are not independent of men, and
men are not independent of women. 12 For although the first woman came
from man, every other man was born from a woman, and everything comes
from God.
13 Judge for yourselves. Is it right for a woman to pray to God in public
without covering her head? 14 Isn't it obvious that it's disgraceful for a man

10:23 Greek *All things are lawful;* also in 10:23b. **10:26** Ps 24:1. **10:32** Greek *or Greeks.* **11:3** Or *to know: The source of every man is Christ, the source of woman is man, and the source of Christ is God.* Or *to know: Every man is responsible to Christ, a woman is responsible to her husband, and Christ is responsible to God.* **11:4** Or *dishonors Christ.* **11:5** Or *dishonors her husband.* **11:6** Or *should have long hair.* **11:10** Greek *should have an authority on her head.*

Question 11:17-34

The Lord's Supper is sometimes called Communion or the Eucharist. It is that time when believers in Jesus gather to remember that he died for us on the cross. When you have the opportunity to participate in the Lord's Supper, are you more likely to appreciate the experience or to be flippant about it? What guidance did Paul give in this chapter for the kind of attitude you should have during this time together?

to have long hair? 15And isn't long hair a woman's pride and joy? For it has
been given to her as a covering. 16But if anyone wants to argue about this,
I simply say that we have no other custom than this, and neither do God's
other churches.

Order at the Lord's Supper

17But in the following instructions, I cannot praise you. For it sounds as if
more harm than good is done when you meet together. 18First, I hear that
there are divisions among you when you meet as a church, and to some ex-
tent I believe it. 19But, of course, there must be divisions among you so that
you who have God's approval will be recognized!

20When you meet together, you are not really interested in the Lord's Sup-
per. 21For some of you hurry to eat your own meal without sharing with
others. As a result, some go hungry while others get drunk. 22What? Don't
you have your own homes for eating and drinking? Or do you really want
to disgrace God's church and shame the poor? What am I supposed to say?
Do you want me to praise you? Well, I certainly will not praise you for this!

23For I pass on to you what I received from the Lord himself. On the night
when he was betrayed, the Lord Jesus took some bread 24and gave thanks to
God for it. Then he broke it in pieces and said, "This is my body, which is
given for you.* Do this in remembrance of me." 25In the same way, he took the
cup of wine after supper, saying, "This cup is the new covenant between God
and his people—an agreement confirmed with my blood. Do this in remem-
brance of me as often as you drink it." 26For every time you eat this bread and
drink this cup, you are announcing the Lord's death until he comes again.

27So anyone who eats this bread or drinks this cup of the Lord unworthily
is guilty of sinning against* the body and blood of the Lord. 28That is why you
should examine yourself before eating the bread and drinking the cup. 29For
if you eat the bread or drink the cup without honoring the body of Christ,*
you are eating and drinking God's judgment upon yourself. 30That is why
many of you are weak and sick and some have even died.

31But if we would examine ourselves, we would not be judged by God in
this way. 32Yet when we are judged by the Lord, we are being disciplined so
that we will not be condemned along with the world.

33So, my dear brothers and sisters,* when you gather for the Lord's Supper,
wait for each other. 34If you are really hungry, eat at home so you won't bring
judgment upon yourselves when you meet together. I'll give you instruc-
tions about the other matters after I arrive.

Spiritual Gifts

12 Now, dear brothers and sisters,* regarding your question about the
special abilities the Spirit gives us. I don't want you to misunder-
stand this. 2You know that when you were still pagans, you were led astray
and swept along in worshiping speechless idols. 3So I want you to know that
no one speaking by the Spirit of God will curse Jesus, and no one can say Jesus
is Lord, except by the Holy Spirit.

4There are different kinds of spiritual gifts, but the same Spirit is the
source of them all. 5There are different kinds of service, but we serve the

11:24 Greek *which is for you;* other manuscripts read *which is broken for you.* 11:27 Or *is responsible for.* 11:29 Greek *the body;* other manuscripts read *the Lord's body.* 11:33 Greek *brothers.* 12:1 Greek *brothers.*

same Lord. 6 God works in different ways, but it is the same God who does
the work in all of us.
7 A spiritual gift is given to each of us so we can help each other. 8 To one
person the Spirit gives the ability to give wise advice*; to another the same
Spirit gives a message of special knowledge.* 9 The same Spirit gives great
faith to another, and to someone else the one Spirit gives the gift of healing.
10 He gives one person the power to perform miracles, and another the ability
to prophesy. He gives someone else the ability to discern whether a message
is from the Spirit of God or from another spirit. Still another person is given
the ability to speak in unknown languages,* while another is given the ability
to interpret what is being said. 11 It is the one and only Spirit who distributes
all these gifts. He alone decides which gift each person should have.

One Body with Many Parts

12 The human body has many parts, but the many parts make up one whole
body. So it is with the body of Christ. 13 Some of us are Jews, some are Gen-
tiles,* some are slaves, and some are free. But we have all been baptized into
one body by one Spirit, and we all share the same Spirit.*
14 Yes, the body has many different parts, not just one part. 15 If the foot
says, "I am not a part of the body because I am not a hand," that does not
make it any less a part of the body. 16 And if the ear says, "I am not part of the
body because I am not an eye," would that make it any less a part of the body?
17 If the whole body were an eye, how would you hear? Or if your whole body
were an ear, how would you smell anything?
18 But our bodies have many parts, and God has put each part just where he
wants it. 19 How strange a body would be if it had only one part! 20 Yes, there
are many parts, but only one body. 21 The eye can never say to the hand, "I
don't need you." The head can't say to the feet, "I don't need you."
22 In fact, some parts of the body that seem weakest and least important
are actually the most necessary. 23 And the parts we regard as less honorable
are those we clothe with the greatest care. So we carefully protect those parts
that should not be seen, 24 while the more honorable parts do not require
this special care. So God has put the body together such that extra honor
and care are given to those parts that have less dignity. 25 This makes for
harmony among the members, so that all the members care for each other.
26 If one part suffers, all the parts suffer with it, and if one part is honored,
all the parts are glad.
27 All of you together are Christ's body, and each of you is a part of it. 28 Here
are some of the parts God has appointed for the church:

first are apostles,
second are prophets,
third are teachers,
then those who do miracles,
those who have the gift of healing,
those who can help others,
those who have the gift of leadership,
those who speak in unknown languages.

12:8a Or *gives a word of wisdom.* **12:8b** Or *gives a word of knowledge.* **12:10** Or *in various tongues;* also in 12:28, 30. **12:13a** Greek *some are Greeks.* **12:13b** Greek *we were all given one Spirit to drink.*

Question **12:7**

How has the Lord uniquely gifted you, and how does he want you to use your gifts?

Make a Difference

12:12-31

One Body, Many Parts

Church means "gathering" or "assembly." The church is a gathering of people who are compelled to find Jesus and be forever changed by him. Church changes the world because Jesus changes those in the church. It is a gathering where uniquely gifted individuals discover that together they are a part of something greater. It's where people with unique backgrounds and passions are united through the mission of Jesus Christ.

Followers of Jesus are never competing against one another or putting others down. There is no place for that in the body of Christ. Each person is equally valuable to Jesus.

Difference Maker

If you are not already a part of a good church or ministry group, find one where you can serve with others on mission with Jesus. Invite some others to join you.

Question **12:31**

In the chapter that follows this verse, what did Paul say is the way of life that is best of all?

Question **13:4-7**

What practical examples could you give for each attribute of 13:4-7?

29 Are we all apostles? Are we all prophets? Are we all teachers? Do we all have the power to do miracles? 30 Do we all have the gift of healing? Do we all have the ability to speak in unknown languages? Do we all have the ability to interpret unknown languages? Of course not! 31 So you should earnestly desire the most helpful gifts.

But now let me show you a way of life that is best of all.

Love Is the Greatest

13 If I could speak all the languages of earth and of angels, but didn't love others, I would only be a noisy gong or a clanging cymbal. 2 If I had the gift of prophecy, and if I understood all of God's secret plans and possessed all knowledge, and if I had such faith that I could move mountains, but didn't love others, I would be nothing. 3 If I gave everything I have to the poor and even sacrificed my body, I could boast about it;* but if I didn't love others, I would have gained nothing.

4 Love is patient and kind. Love is not jealous or boastful or proud 5 or rude. It does not demand its own way. It is not irritable, and it keeps no record of being wronged. 6 It does not rejoice about injustice but rejoices whenever the truth wins out. 7 Love never gives up, never loses faith, is always hopeful, and endures through every circumstance.

8 Prophecy and speaking in unknown languages* and special knowledge will become useless. But love will last forever! 9 Now our knowledge is partial and incomplete, and even the gift of prophecy reveals only part of the whole picture! 10 But when the time of perfection comes, these partial things will become useless.

11 When I was a child, I spoke and thought and reasoned as a child. But when I grew up, I put away childish things. 12 Now we see things imperfectly, like puzzling reflections in a mirror, but then we will see everything with perfect clarity.* All that I know now is partial and incomplete, but then I will know everything completely, just as God now knows me completely.

13 Three things will last forever—faith, hope, and love—and the greatest of these is love.

Tongues and Prophecy

14 Let love be your highest goal! But you should also desire the special abilities the Spirit gives—especially the ability to prophesy. 2 For if you have the ability to speak in tongues,* you will be talking only to God, since people won't be able to understand you. You will be speaking by the power of the Spirit,* but it will all be mysterious. 3 But one who prophesies strengthens others, encourages them, and comforts them. 4 A person who speaks in tongues is strengthened personally, but one who speaks a word of prophecy strengthens the entire church.

5 I wish you could all speak in tongues, but even more I wish you could all prophesy. For prophecy is greater than speaking in tongues, unless someone interprets what you are saying so that the whole church will be strengthened.

6 Dear brothers and sisters,* if I should come to you speaking in an unknown language,* how would that help you? But if I bring you a revelation or

13:3 Some manuscripts read *sacrificed my body to be burned.* 13:8 Or *in tongues.* 13:12 Greek *see face to face.* 14:2a Or *in unknown languages;* also in 14:4, 5, 13, 14, 18, 22, 26, 27, 28, 39. 14:2b Or *speaking in your spirit.* 14:6a Greek *brothers;* also in 14:20, 26, 39. 14:6b Or *in tongues;* also in 14:19, 23.

some special knowledge or prophecy or teaching, that will be helpful. 7 Even
lifeless instruments like the flute or the harp must play the notes clearly, or
no one will recognize the melody. 8 And if the bugler doesn't sound a clear
call, how will the soldiers know they are being called to battle?
9 It's the same for you. If you speak to people in words they don't under-
stand, how will they know what you are saying? You might as well be talking
into empty space.
10 There are many different languages in the world, and every language
has meaning. 11 But if I don't understand a language, I will be a foreigner
to someone who speaks it, and the one who speaks it will be a foreigner to
me. 12 And the same is true for you. Since you are so eager to have the special
abilities the Spirit gives, seek those that will strengthen the whole church.
13 So anyone who speaks in tongues should pray also for the ability to in-
terpret what has been said. 14 For if I pray in tongues, my spirit is praying,
but I don't understand what I am saying.
15 Well then, what shall I do? I will pray in the spirit,* and I will also pray
in words I understand. I will sing in the spirit, and I will also sing in words
I understand. 16 For if you praise God only in the spirit, how can those who
don't understand you praise God along with you? How can they join you in
giving thanks when they don't understand what you are saying? 17 You will
be giving thanks very well, but it won't strengthen the people who hear you.
18 I thank God that I speak in tongues more than any of you. 19 But in a
church meeting I would rather speak five understandable words to help
others than ten thousand words in an unknown language.
20 Dear brothers and sisters, don't be childish in your understanding of
these things. Be innocent as babies when it comes to evil, but be mature in
understanding matters of this kind. 21 It is written in the Scriptures*:

"I will speak to my own people
through strange languages
and through the lips of foreigners.
But even then, they will not listen to me,"*
says the LORD.

22 So you see that speaking in tongues is a sign, not for believers, but for un-
believers. Prophecy, however, is for the benefit of believers, not unbelievers.
23 Even so, if unbelievers or people who don't understand these things come
into your church meeting and hear everyone speaking in an unknown lan-
guage, they will think you are crazy. 24 But if all of you are prophesying, and
unbelievers or people who don't understand these things come into your
meeting, they will be convicted of sin and judged by what you say. 25 As they
listen, their secret thoughts will be exposed, and they will fall to their knees
and worship God, declaring, "God is truly here among you."

A Call to Orderly Worship

26 Well, my brothers and sisters, let's summarize. When you meet together,
one will sing, another will teach, another will tell some special revelation
God has given, one will speak in tongues, and another will interpret what is
said. But everything that is done must strengthen all of you.

Question **14:20**

Compare this verse to what Jesus says in Matthew 10:16. What's going on here?

14:15 Or *in the Spirit;* also in 14:15b, 16. **14:21a** Greek *in the law.* **14:21b** Isa 28:11-12.

Make a Difference

15:3-4

Resurrection

The cross and empty tomb go together—it is a double event. The cross demonstrated God's verdict against sin, a punishment that Jesus took in our place, whereas the empty tomb proclaimed hope after judgment, the power of death rolled away by the life and authority of Jesus. We need both. On the cross, Jesus took our sin to its grave, but we need the empty tomb because, from it, Jesus offers us life after death.

This is the central truth of Christianity. Without it, everything churchy is just good (or bad) religion that actually offers false hope. The Bible points to the crux of history in Jesus. He came to bring God's wrath against humanity for its sin and to offer forgiveness. Jesus came as a human, took the wrath upon himself, and offered new life that gracefully dances upon the ashes of judgment.

Difference Maker

How can you live practically in the double event of the cross and the empty tomb? How will forgiveness and new life in Jesus affect the way you interact with others today?

27 No more than two or three should speak in tongues. They must speak one at a time, and someone must interpret what they say. 28 But if no one is present who can interpret, they must be silent in your church meeting and speak in tongues to God privately.

29 Let two or three people prophesy, and let the others evaluate what is said. 30 But if someone is prophesying and another person receives a revelation from the Lord, the one who is speaking must stop. 31 In this way, all who prophesy will have a turn to speak, one after the other, so that everyone will learn and be encouraged. 32 Remember that people who prophesy are in control of their spirit and can take turns. 33 For God is not a God of disorder but of peace, as in all the meetings of God's holy people.*

34 Women should be silent during the church meetings. It is not proper for them to speak. They should be submissive, just as the law says. 35 If they have any questions, they should ask their husbands at home, for it is improper for women to speak in church meetings.*

36 Or do you think God's word originated with you Corinthians? Are you the only ones to whom it was given? 37 If you claim to be a prophet or think you are spiritual, you should recognize that what I am saying is a command from the Lord himself. 38 But if you do not recognize this, you yourself will not be recognized.*

39 So, my dear brothers and sisters, be eager to prophesy, and don't forbid speaking in tongues. 40 But be sure that everything is done properly and in order.

The Resurrection of Christ

15 Let me now remind you, dear brothers and sisters,* of the Good News I preached to you before. You welcomed it then, and you still stand firm in it. 2 It is this Good News that saves you if you continue to believe the message I told you—unless, of course, you believed something that was never true in the first place.*

3 I passed on to you what was most important and what had also been passed on to me. Christ died for our sins, just as the Scriptures said. 4 He was buried, and he was raised from the dead on the third day, just as the Scriptures said. 5 He was seen by Peter* and then by the Twelve. 6 After that, he was seen by more than 500 of his followers* at one time, most of whom are still alive, though some have died. 7 Then he was seen by James and later by all the apostles. 8 Last of all, as though I had been born at the wrong time, I also saw him. 9 For I am the least of all the apostles. In fact, I'm not even worthy to be called an apostle after the way I persecuted God's church.

10 But whatever I am now, it is all because God poured out his special favor on me—and not without results. For I have worked harder than any of the other apostles; yet it was not I but God who was working through me by his grace. 11 So it makes no difference whether I preach or they preach, for we all preach the same message you have already believed.

The Resurrection of the Dead

12 But tell me this—since we preach that Christ rose from the dead, why are some of you saying there will be no resurrection of the dead? 13 For if there is

14:33 The phrase *as in all the meetings of God's holy people* could instead be joined to the beginning of 14:34. **14:35** Some manuscripts place verses 34-35 after 14:40. **14:38** Some manuscripts read *If you are ignorant of this, stay in your ignorance.* **15:1** Greek *brothers;* also in 15:31, 50, 58. **15:2** Or *unless you never believed it in the first place.* **15:5** Greek *Cephas.* **15:6** Greek *the brothers.*

no resurrection of the dead, then Christ has not been raised either. 14 And if
Christ has not been raised, then all our preaching is useless, and your faith
is useless. 15 And we apostles would all be lying about God—for we have said
that God raised Christ from the grave. But that can't be true if there is no
resurrection of the dead. 16 And if there is no resurrection of the dead, then
Christ has not been raised. 17 And if Christ has not been raised, then your faith
is useless and you are still guilty of your sins. 18 In that case, all who have died
believing in Christ are lost! 19 And if our hope in Christ is only for this life,
we are more to be pitied than anyone in the world.

20 But in fact, Christ has been raised from the dead. He is the first of a great
harvest of all who have died.

21 So you see, just as death came into the world through a man, now the
resurrection from the dead has begun through another man. 22 Just as every-
one dies because we all belong to Adam, everyone who belongs to Christ
will be given new life. 23 But there is an order to this resurrection: Christ was
raised as the first of the harvest; then all who belong to Christ will be raised
when he comes back.

24 After that the end will come, when he will turn the Kingdom over to
God the Father, having destroyed every ruler and authority and power. 25 For
Christ must reign until he humbles all his enemies beneath his feet. 26 And
the last enemy to be destroyed is death. 27 For the Scriptures say, "God has
put all things under his authority."* (Of course, when it says "all things are
under his authority," that does not include God himself, who gave Christ his
authority.) 28 Then, when all things are under his authority, the Son will put
himself under God's authority, so that God, who gave his Son authority over
all things, will be utterly supreme over everything everywhere.

29 If the dead will not be raised, what point is there in people being bap-
tized for those who are dead? Why do it unless the dead will someday rise
again?

30 And why should we ourselves risk our lives hour by hour? 31 For I swear,
dear brothers and sisters, that I face death daily. This is as certain as my
pride in what Christ Jesus our Lord has done in you. 32 And what value was
there in fighting wild beasts—those people of Ephesus*—if there will be
no resurrection from the dead? And if there is no resurrection, "Let's feast
and drink, for tomorrow we die!"* 33 Don't be fooled by those who say such
things, for "bad company corrupts good character." 34 Think carefully about
what is right, and stop sinning. For to your shame I say that some of you
don't know God at all.

The Resurrection Body

35 But someone may ask, "How will the dead be raised? What kind of bodies
will they have?" 36 What a foolish question! When you put a seed into the
ground, it doesn't grow into a plant unless it dies first. 37 And what you put
in the ground is not the plant that will grow, but only a bare seed of wheat
or whatever you are planting. 38 Then God gives it the new body he wants it
to have. A different plant grows from each kind of seed. 39 Similarly there are
different kinds of flesh—one kind for humans, another for animals, another
for birds, and another for fish.

40 There are also bodies in the heavens and bodies on the earth. The glory

15:27 Ps 8:6. **15:32a** Greek *fighting wild beasts in Ephesus.* **15:32b** Isa 22:13.

of the heavenly bodies is different from the glory of the earthly bodies. 41 The
sun has one kind of glory, while the moon and stars each have another kind.
And even the stars differ from each other in their glory.
42 It is the same way with the resurrection of the dead. Our earthly bodies
are planted in the ground when we die, but they will be raised to live forever.
43 Our bodies are buried in brokenness, but they will be raised in glory. They
are buried in weakness, but they will be raised in strength. 44 They are buried
as natural human bodies, but they will be raised as spiritual bodies. For just
as there are natural bodies, there are also spiritual bodies.
45 The Scriptures tell us, "The first man, Adam, became a living person."*
But the last Adam—that is, Christ—is a life-giving Spirit. 46 What comes
first is the natural body, then the spiritual body comes later. 47 Adam, the first
man, was made from the dust of the earth, while Christ, the second man,
came from heaven. 48 Earthly people are like the earthly man, and heavenly
people are like the heavenly man. 49 Just as we are now like the earthly man,
we will someday be like* the heavenly man.
50 What I am saying, dear brothers and sisters, is that our physical bodies
cannot inherit the Kingdom of God. These dying bodies cannot inherit what
will last forever.
51 But let me reveal to you a wonderful secret. We will not all die, but we
will all be transformed! 52 It will happen in a moment, in the blink of an eye,
when the last trumpet is blown. For when the trumpet sounds, those who
have died will be raised to live forever. And we who are living will also be
transformed. 53 For our dying bodies must be transformed into bodies that
will never die; our mortal bodies must be transformed into immortal bodies.
54 Then, when our dying bodies have been transformed into bodies that
will never die,* this Scripture will be fulfilled:

"Death is swallowed up in victory.*
55 O death, where is your victory?
O death, where is your sting?*"

56 For sin is the sting that results in death, and the law gives sin its power.
57 But thank God! He gives us victory over sin and death through our Lord
Jesus Christ.
58 So, my dear brothers and sisters, be strong and immovable. Always work
enthusiastically for the Lord, for you know that nothing you do for the Lord
is ever useless.

The Collection for Jerusalem

16 Now regarding your question about the money being collected for
God's people in Jerusalem. You should follow the same procedure I
gave to the churches in Galatia. 2 On the first day of each week, you should
each put aside a portion of the money you have earned. Don't wait until
I get there and then try to collect it all at once. 3 When I come, I will write
letters of recommendation for the messengers you choose to deliver your
gift to Jerusalem. 4 And if it seems appropriate for me to go along, they can
travel with me.

15:45 Gen 2:7. 15:49 Some manuscripts read *let us be like.* 15:54a Some manuscripts add *and our mortal bodies have been transformed into immortal bodies.* 15:54b Isa 25:8. 15:55 Hos 13:14 (Greek version).

Make a Difference

15:54-59

In a Mess

There are some troubles that are massive in scale—like war, terror, disease, and death. Some of the troubles we see appear to be less intense, but they are the seeds that spawn disruption in our lives, such as hate, pride, jealousy, and selfishness. These things interfere with the amazing vision God has for his creation.

This is where you come into play. First, God wants you to know something powerfully life-changing: the problems of this world will one day fade away. Jesus is taking care of them. Second, God wants your words and actions to stand in contrast to the disruptive troubles of this world.

Live today in the freedom and power of Jesus. Don't allow the troubles around you to control your mind or your heart. Turn yourself toward your Creator today, knowing that he is taking care of all things.

Difference Maker

Jesus cleaned up a big human mess. Try this: if you see a mess today, clean it up. Just do it, whether someone notices or not.

Paul's Final Instructions

5 I am coming to visit you after I have been to Macedonia,* for I am planning
to travel through Macedonia. 6 Perhaps I will stay awhile with you, possibly
all winter, and then you can send me on my way to my next destination.
7 This time I don't want to make just a short visit and then go right on. I want
to come and stay awhile, if the Lord will let me. 8 In the meantime, I will be
staying here at Ephesus until the Festival of Pentecost. 9 There is a wide-open
door for a great work here, although many oppose me.

10 When Timothy comes, don't intimidate him. He is doing the Lord's
work, just as I am. 11 Don't let anyone treat him with contempt. Send him
on his way with your blessing when he returns to me. I expect him to come
with the other believers.*

12 Now about our brother Apollos—I urged him to visit you with the other
believers, but he was not willing to go right now. He will see you later when
he has the opportunity.

13 Be on guard. Stand firm in the faith. Be courageous.* Be strong. 14 And
do everything with love.

15 You know that Stephanas and his household were the first of the harvest
of believers in Greece,* and they are spending their lives in service to God's
people. I urge you, dear brothers and sisters,* 16 to submit to them and others
like them who serve with such devotion. 17 I am very glad that Stephanas,
Fortunatus, and Achaicus have come here. They have been providing the
help you weren't here to give me. 18 They have been a wonderful encourage-
ment to me, as they have been to you. You must show your appreciation to
all who serve so well.

Paul's Final Greetings

19 The churches here in the province of Asia* send greetings in the Lord, as do
Aquila and Priscilla* and all the others who gather in their home for church
meetings. 20 All the brothers and sisters here send greetings to you. Greet
each other with a sacred kiss.

21 HERE IS MY GREETING IN MY OWN HANDWRITING—PAUL.

22 If anyone does not love the Lord, that person is cursed. Our Lord, come!*

23 May the grace of the Lord Jesus be with you.

24 My love to all of you in Christ Jesus.*

16:5 *Macedonia* was in the northern region of Greece. 16:11 Greek *with the brothers;* also in 16:12. 16:13 Greek *Be men.* 16:15a Greek *in Achaia,* the southern region of the Greek peninsula. 16:15b Greek *brothers;* also in 16:20. 16:19a *Asia* was a Roman province in what is now western Turkey. 16:19b Greek *Prisca.* 16:22 From Aramaic, *Marana tha.* Some manuscripts read *Maran atha,* "Our Lord has come." 16:24 Some manuscripts add *Amen.*

Make a Difference

16:8-9

Open Door

Have you ever walked into a sliding glass door? You thought it was open, but it actually wasn't. Bam! It took you a moment to figure out that (1) there was a door there and (2) the door was closed. The worst part was probably that all your friends or family were laughing at you. You just had to roll with it. You smiled and maybe chuckled a bit, but ouch, your face hurt!

To find the open door, you must use all the resources God has given to you—sight, hearing, and other senses. You must search for it. Ask God to lead you. Listen for his Spirit's guidance and ask for wisdom. Stay close to Jesus so that you aren't led the wrong way. He wouldn't lead you the wrong way. Jesus wouldn't trick you and laugh at you when you smash into a closed door.

The apostle Paul wrote about a wide-open door God had opened for him as well. He didn't assume everything would be easy or perfect because the door was open, but he knew God was giving him an opportunity to make a big difference in the world in which he lived.

Difference Maker

Every time you walk through a door today, remember to look for opportunities God is giving you to serve him and others.

2 Corinthians Introduction

Paul's letters are typically overflowing with humility. He said he was an unworthy apostle (1 Corinthians 15:9), the least of all God's people (Ephesians 3:8), and the worst sinner (1 Timothy 1:15). This is what makes the book of 2 Corinthians so interesting—Paul was forced to defend himself and his ministry so that the people in Corinth would continue to follow his teaching. False teachers had arrived in Corinth, spread lies about him robbing churches (2 Corinthians 11:7–8), and tried to discredit his reputation and achievements (11:21–27). In his first letter to the Corinthians, it is clear there were already some serious struggles within the community. Now, in this second letter, Paul had to respond to some troublemakers who were hurling accusations at him.

Throughout the book, Paul defended his effective ministry while also making sure the readers knew that it was God working through him the entire time (4:7). There is hope that comes from knowing Jesus here on earth (1:3–5) and in future glory (5:1–5). Paul's confidence in this letter came from knowing that the gospel couldn't be squashed by the harsh realities of his life (4:8) or the constant bothering ("thorn") in his side (12:7–9). Paul decided to boast in what God had done through him and his companions instead of taking the credit or slandering his opponents.

Today, 2 Corinthians gives you a model of what faithfulness looks like. Even when you are mistreated, even when you have every right to retaliate, the world-changing power of Jesus helps you live a world-changing life of integrity and character.

Story Arc

- **Titus**

The 2 Corinthians Church Network

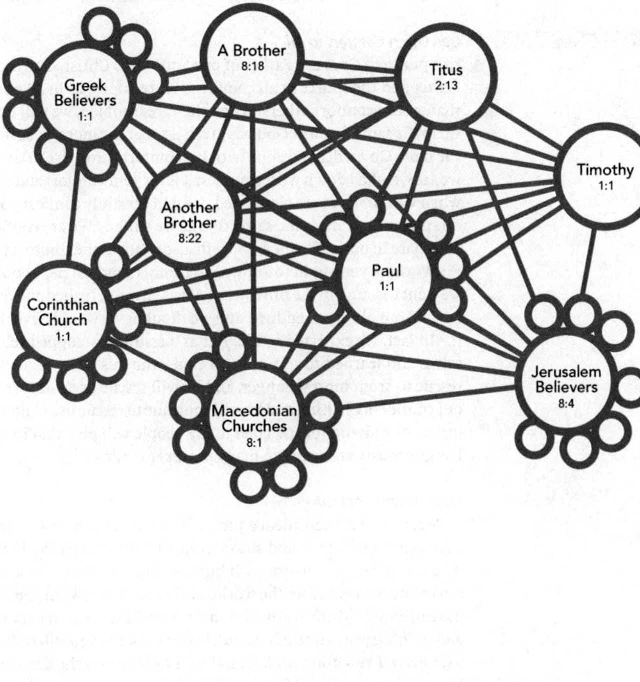

2 Corinthians

Prayer 1:3

Lord, thank you for being the source of my comfort. Help me to be bold enough to trust you for my well-being. Amen.

Greetings from Paul

1 This letter is from Paul, chosen by the will of God to be an apostle of
Christ Jesus, and from our brother Timothy.
I am writing to God's church in Corinth and to all of his holy people
throughout Greece.*
2May God our Father and the Lord Jesus Christ give you grace and peace.

God Offers Comfort to All

3All praise to God, the Father of our Lord Jesus Christ. God is our merciful
Father and the source of all comfort. 4He comforts us in all our troubles so
that we can comfort others. When they are troubled, we will be able to give
them the same comfort God has given us. 5For the more we suffer for Christ,
the more God will shower us with his comfort through Christ. 6Even when
we are weighed down with troubles, it is for your comfort and salvation! For
when we ourselves are comforted, we will certainly comfort you. Then you
can patiently endure the same things we suffer. 7We are confident that as
you share in our sufferings, you will also share in the comfort God gives us.
8We think you ought to know, dear brothers and sisters,* about the trouble
we went through in the province of Asia. We were crushed and overwhelmed
beyond our ability to endure, and we thought we would never live through
it. 9In fact, we expected to die. But as a result, we stopped relying on our-
selves and learned to rely only on God, who raises the dead. 10And he did
rescue us from mortal danger, and he will rescue us again. We have placed
our confidence in him, and he will continue to rescue us. 11And you are help-
ing us by praying for us. Then many people will give thanks because God
has graciously answered so many prayers for our safety.

Paul's Change of Plans

12We can say with confidence and a clear conscience that we have lived with
a God-given holiness* and sincerity in all our dealings. We have depended
on God's grace, not on our own human wisdom. That is how we have con-
ducted ourselves before the world, and especially toward you. 13Our letters
have been straightforward, and there is nothing written between the lines
and nothing you can't understand. I hope someday you will fully understand
us, 14even if you don't understand us now. Then on the day when the Lord
Jesus* returns, you will be proud of us in the same way we are proud of you.
15Since I was so sure of your understanding and trust, I wanted to give
you a double blessing by visiting you twice—16first on my way to Macedo-
nia and again when I returned from Macedonia.* Then you could send me
on my way to Judea.

1:1 Greek *Achaia,* the southern region of the Greek peninsula. **1:8** Greek *brothers.* **1:12** Some manuscripts read *honesty.* **1:14** Some manuscripts read *our Lord Jesus.* **1:16** *Macedonia* was in the northern region of Greece.

17 You may be asking why I changed my plan. Do you think I make my plans
carelessly? Do you think I am like people of the world who say "Yes" when
they really mean "No"? 18 As surely as God is faithful, our word to you does
not waver between "Yes" and "No." 19 For Jesus Christ, the Son of God, does
not waver between "Yes" and "No." He is the one whom Silas,* Timothy, and
I preached to you, and as God's ultimate "Yes," he always does what he says.
20 For all of God's promises have been fulfilled in Christ with a resounding
"Yes!" And through Christ, our "Amen" (which means "Yes") ascends to God
for his glory.

21 It is God who enables us, along with you, to stand firm for Christ. He
has commissioned us, 22 and he has identified us as his own by placing the
Holy Spirit in our hearts as the first installment that guarantees everything
he has promised us.

23 Now I call upon God as my witness that I am telling the truth. The reason
I didn't return to Corinth was to spare you from a severe rebuke. 24 But that
does not mean we want to dominate you by telling you how to put your faith
into practice. We want to work together with you so you will be full of joy,
for it is by your own faith that you stand firm.

2 So I decided that I would not bring you grief with another painful visit.
2 For if I cause you grief, who will make me glad? Certainly not someone
I have grieved. 3 That is why I wrote to you as I did, so that when I do come,
I won't be grieved by the very ones who ought to give me the greatest joy.
Surely you all know that my joy comes from your being joyful. 4 I wrote that
letter in great anguish, with a troubled heart and many tears. I didn't want
to grieve you, but I wanted to let you know how much love I have for you.

Forgiveness for the Sinner

5 I am not overstating it when I say that the man who caused all the trouble
hurt all of you more than he hurt me. 6 Most of you opposed him, and that
was punishment enough. 7 Now, however, it is time to forgive and comfort
him. Otherwise he may be overcome by discouragement. 8 So I urge you now
to reaffirm your love for him.

9 I wrote to you as I did to test you and see if you would fully comply with
my instructions. 10 When you forgive this man, I forgive him, too. And when
I forgive whatever needs to be forgiven, I do so with Christ's authority for
your benefit, 11 so that Satan will not outsmart us. For we are familiar with
his evil schemes.

12 When I came to the city of Troas to preach the Good News of Christ,
the Lord opened a door of opportunity for me. 13 But I had no peace of mind
because my dear brother Titus hadn't yet arrived with a report from you. So
I said good-bye and went on to Macedonia to find him.

Ministers of the New Covenant

14 But thank God! He has made us his captives and continues to lead us along
in Christ's triumphal procession. Now he uses us to spread the knowledge
of Christ everywhere, like a sweet perfume. 15 Our lives are a Christ-like fra-
grance rising up to God. But this fragrance is perceived differently by those
who are being saved and by those who are perishing. 16 To those who are

Prayer **1:20**

Lord Jesus, you are so good. Let me live in the satisfaction and power of your promises. Amen.

Question **2:5–11**

What did Paul say could happen if the Corinthians refused to forgive and comfort this man? In other words, what difference can forgiveness make in people's lives?

1:19 Greek *Silvanus.*

Make a Difference 3:17

The Suffix *-dom*

A suffix at the end of a lot of words is *-dom*, which refers to a "realm" or "rank." For example, a king*dom* is the realm of the king, star*dom* is the realm of a popular person (a "star"), and bore*dom* is hopefully not the realm you have just entered because of this grammatical study.

Free*dom* is the realm where a person can act or speak without hinderance. When someone is free, they can do what they'd like and know that it is good. Freedom is not hedonism, where people choose to ignore the consequences and do whatever feels good (only to be forced to deal with their bad decisions later). Rather, freedom is being able to walk where you need to go, say what you need to say, laugh when you need to laugh, and cry when you need to cry. Freedom is being able to wander with friends, dine with family, and enjoy what God has made. To truly enter the domain of freedom, people must turn to the Spirit of the Lord, for "wherever the Spirit of the Lord is, there is freedom."

Difference Maker

Connect with a friend who is weighed down by his or her bad decisions. Invite them to turn to the Lord and walk in freedom today.

perishing, we are a dreadful smell of death and doom. But to those who are
being saved, we are a life-giving perfume. And who is adequate for such a
task as this?
17 You see, we are not like the many hucksters* who preach for personal
profit. We preach the word of God with sincerity and with Christ's authority,
knowing that God is watching us.

3 Are we beginning to praise ourselves again? Are we like others, who need
to bring you letters of recommendation, or who ask you to write such
letters on their behalf? Surely not! 2 The only letter of recommendation we
need is you yourselves. Your lives are a letter written in our* hearts; everyone
can read it and recognize our good work among you. 3 Clearly, you are a let-
ter from Christ showing the result of our ministry among you. This "letter"
is written not with pen and ink, but with the Spirit of the living God. It is
carved not on tablets of stone, but on human hearts.
4 We are confident of all this because of our great trust in God through
Christ. 5 It is not that we think we are qualified to do anything on our own.
Our qualification comes from God. 6 He has enabled us to be ministers of
his new covenant. This is a covenant not of written laws, but of the Spirit.
The old written covenant ends in death; but under the new covenant, the
Spirit gives life.

The Glory of the New Covenant

7 The old way,* with laws etched in stone, led to death, though it began with
such glory that the people of Israel could not bear to look at Moses' face. For his
face shone with the glory of God, even though the brightness was already fad-
ing away. 8 Shouldn't we expect far greater glory under the new way, now that
the Holy Spirit is giving life? 9 If the old way, which brings condemnation, was
glorious, how much more glorious is the new way, which makes us right with
God! 10 In fact, that first glory was not glorious at all compared with the over-
whelming glory of the new way. 11 So if the old way, which has been replaced,
was glorious, how much more glorious is the new, which remains forever!
12 Since this new way gives us such confidence, we can be very bold. 13 We
are not like Moses, who put a veil over his face so the people of Israel would
not see the glory, even though it was destined to fade away. 14 But the people's
minds were hardened, and to this day whenever the old covenant is being
read, the same veil covers their minds so they cannot understand the truth.
And this veil can be removed only by believing in Christ. 15 Yes, even today
when they read Moses' writings, their hearts are covered with that veil, and
they do not understand.
16 But whenever someone turns to the Lord, the veil is taken away. 17 For the
Lord is the Spirit, and wherever the Spirit of the Lord is, there is freedom.
18 So all of us who have had that veil removed can see and reflect the glory of
the Lord. And the Lord—who is the Spirit—makes us more and more like
him as we are changed into his glorious image.

Treasure in Fragile Clay Jars

4 Therefore, since God in his mercy has given us this new way,* we never
give up. 2 We reject all shameful deeds and underhanded methods. We

2:17 Some manuscripts read *the rest of the hucksters.* 3:2 Some manuscripts read *your.* 3:7 Or *ministry;* also in 3:8, 9, 10, 11, 12. 4:1 Or *ministry.*

don't try to trick anyone or distort the word of God. We tell the truth before
God, and all who are honest know this.
3 If the Good News we preach is hidden behind a veil, it is hidden only from
people who are perishing. 4 Satan, who is the god of this world, has blinded
the minds of those who don't believe. They are unable to see the glorious
light of the Good News. They don't understand this message about the glory
of Christ, who is the exact likeness of God.
5 You see, we don't go around preaching about ourselves. We preach that
Jesus Christ is Lord, and we ourselves are your servants for Jesus' sake. 6 For
God, who said, "Let there be light in the darkness," has made this light shine
in our hearts so we could know the glory of God that is seen in the face of
Jesus Christ.
7 We now have this light shining in our hearts, but we ourselves are like
fragile clay jars containing this great treasure.* This makes it clear that our
great power is from God, not from ourselves.
8 We are pressed on every side by troubles, but we are not crushed. We are
perplexed, but not driven to despair. 9 We are hunted down, but never aban-
doned by God. We get knocked down, but we are not destroyed. 10 Through
suffering, our bodies continue to share in the death of Jesus so that the life
of Jesus may also be seen in our bodies.
11 Yes, we live under constant danger of death because we serve Jesus, so
that the life of Jesus will be evident in our dying bodies. 12 So we live in the
face of death, but this has resulted in eternal life for you.
13 But we continue to preach because we have the same kind of faith the
psalmist had when he said, "I believed in God, so I spoke."* 14 We know that
God, who raised the Lord Jesus,* will also raise us with Jesus and present us
to himself together with you. 15 All of this is for your benefit. And as God's
grace reaches more and more people, there will be great thanksgiving, and
God will receive more and more glory.
16 That is why we never give up. Though our bodies are dying, our spirits
are* being renewed every day. 17 For our present troubles are small and won't
last very long. Yet they produce for us a glory that vastly outweighs them and
will last forever! 18 So we don't look at the troubles we can see now; rather, we
fix our gaze on things that cannot be seen. For the things we see now will
soon be gone, but the things we cannot see will last forever.

New Bodies

5 For we know that when this earthly tent we live in is taken down (that is,
when we die and leave this earthly body), we will have a house in heaven,
an eternal body made for us by God himself and not by human hands. 2 We
grow weary in our present bodies, and we long to put on our heavenly bod-
ies like new clothing. 3 For we will put on heavenly bodies; we will not be
spirits without bodies.* 4 While we live in these earthly bodies, we groan and
sigh, but it's not that we want to die and get rid of these bodies that clothe
us. Rather, we want to put on our new bodies so that these dying bodies
will be swallowed up by life. 5 God himself has prepared us for this, and as a
guarantee he has given us his Holy Spirit.
6 So we are always confident, even though we know that as long as we live
in these bodies we are not at home with the Lord. 7 For we live by believing

4:7 Greek *We now have this treasure in clay jars.* **4:13** Ps 116:10. **4:14** Some manuscripts read *who raised Jesus.* **4:16** Greek *our inner being is.* **5:3** Greek *we will not be naked.*

Make a Difference 4:7

Treasure

It is in your broken heart where God has room to act. It is in the midst of your weakness that God's light and strength and power can do their glorious work. When you embrace the treasure of Jesus in your life, you quickly recognize that you cannot contain him. You are much too fragile to be the living container of almighty God, yet in you is precisely where Jesus wants to live. He wants to take up residence in your life and use you to bring his light to others.

Difference Maker

Turn to the back of this Bible and pray through the section on "How to Accept Jesus as Your Lord and Savior."

Make a Difference 4:8

Garbage Compactor

Sometimes, pressures close in on us like a trash compactor. No matter what creative options we devise to wrangle free, no amount of personal effort can offer rescue forever. Only Jesus is freedom. Even in overwhelming circumstances, Jesus enables people to escape from being crushed so they can keep on fighting.

Difference Maker

Throughout the day, press your fingers together hard for thirty seconds and then release them. Each time you do this, remember that Jesus offers rescue.

and not by seeing. 8 Yes, we are fully confident, and we would rather be away
from these earthly bodies, for then we will be at home with the Lord. 9 So
whether we are here in this body or away from this body, our goal is to please
him. 10 For we must all stand before Christ to be judged. We will each receive
whatever we deserve for the good or evil we have done in this earthly body.

We Are God's Ambassadors

11 Because we understand our fearful responsibility to the Lord, we work hard
to persuade others. God knows we are sincere, and I hope you know this,
too. 12 Are we commending ourselves to you again? No, we are giving you a
reason to be proud of us,* so you can answer those who brag about having a
spectacular ministry rather than having a sincere heart. 13 If it seems we are
crazy, it is to bring glory to God. And if we are in our right minds, it is for your
benefit. 14 Either way, Christ's love controls us.* Since we believe that Christ
died for all, we also believe that we have all died to our old life.* 15 He died for
everyone so that those who receive his new life will no longer live for them-
selves. Instead, they will live for Christ, who died and was raised for them.
16 So we have stopped evaluating others from a human point of view. At
one time we thought of Christ merely from a human point of view. How
differently we know him now! 17 This means that anyone who belongs to
Christ has become a new person. The old life is gone; a new life has begun!
18 And all of this is a gift from God, who brought us back to himself
through Christ. And God has given us this task of reconciling people to him.
19 For God was in Christ, reconciling the world to himself, no longer count-
ing people's sins against them. And he gave us this wonderful message of
reconciliation. 20 So we are Christ's ambassadors; God is making his appeal
through us. We speak for Christ when we plead, "Come back to God!" 21 For
God made Christ, who never sinned, to be the offering for our sin,* so that
we could be made right with God through Christ.

6 As God's partners,* we beg you not to accept this marvelous gift of God's
kindness and then ignore it. 2 For God says,

> "At just the right time, I heard you.
> On the day of salvation, I helped you."*

Indeed, the "right time" is now. Today is the day of salvation.

Paul's Hardships

3 We live in such a way that no one will stumble because of us, and no one will
find fault with our ministry. 4 In everything we do, we show that we are true
ministers of God. We patiently endure troubles and hardships and calamities
of every kind. 5 We have been beaten, been put in prison, faced angry mobs,
worked to exhaustion, endured sleepless nights, and gone without food.
6 We prove ourselves by our purity, our understanding, our patience, our
kindness, by the Holy Spirit within us,* and by our sincere love. 7 We faith-
fully preach the truth. God's power is working in us. We use the weapons
of righteousness in the right hand for attack and the left hand for defense.

5:12 Some manuscripts read *proud of yourselves.* 5:14a Or *urges us on.* 5:14b Greek *Since one died for all, then all died.* 5:21 Or *to become sin itself.* 6:1 Or *As we work together.* 6:2 Isa 49:8 (Greek version). 6:6 Or *by our holiness of spirit.*

Make a Difference 5:17

New Person

Imagine waking up knowing that God has some pretty great ideas for your day. Imagine living in such a way that you seek to please him rather than seeking to please others. Imagine being able to speak the truth in love because you aren't tempted cave to what others want to hear. Imagine having the courage to face your shortcomings because God empowers you. Imagine being so secure in God that you are able to love your family, your friends, and your coworkers selflessly. Imagine finding your identity in God so that no matter what turmoil happens, you will not be able to lose yourself.

Difference Maker

Because God has a purpose for you, do something bold today that you would not otherwise have done.

Make a Difference 5:20

Ambassador

An ambassador is a person who is sent by the leader of a government as an official representative. Because of this, it is important that the ambassador does and speaks only what their leader would want them to do and say.

Jesus has asked you to be his ambassador. He wants you to represent him. As you interact with others, Jesus has given you his authority to share his words and customs. It's as if you were a citizen of heaven and have been sent to your family, your friends, your workplace, and your community to let others know what God is like.

Difference Maker

What can you speak on God's behalf today?

8 We serve God whether people honor us or despise us, whether they slander
us or praise us. We are honest, but they call us impostors. 9 We are ignored,
even though we are well known. We live close to death, but we are still alive.
We have been beaten, but we have not been killed. 10 Our hearts ache, but we
always have joy. We are poor, but we give spiritual riches to others. We own
nothing, and yet we have everything.
11 Oh, dear Corinthian friends! We have spoken honestly with you, and our
hearts are open to you. 12 There is no lack of love on our part, but you have
withheld your love from us. 13 I am asking you to respond as if you were my
own children. Open your hearts to us!

The Temple of the Living God

14 Don't team up with those who are unbelievers. How can righteousness
be a partner with wickedness? How can light live with darkness? 15 What
harmony can there be between Christ and the devil*? How can a believer
be a partner with an unbeliever? 16 And what union can there be between
God's temple and idols? For we are the temple of the living God. As God said:

"I will live in them
  and walk among them.
I will be their God,
  and they will be my people.*
17 Therefore, come out from among unbelievers,
  and separate yourselves from them, says the LORD.
Don't touch their filthy things,
  and I will welcome you.*
18 And I will be your Father,
  and you will be my sons and daughters,
  says the LORD Almighty.*"

7 Because we have these promises, dear friends, let us cleanse ourselves
from everything that can defile our body or spirit. And let us work to-
ward complete holiness because we fear God.
2 Please open your hearts to us. We have not done wrong to anyone, nor
led anyone astray, nor taken advantage of anyone. 3 I'm not saying this to
condemn you. I said before that you are in our hearts, and we live or die
together with you. 4 I have the highest confidence in you, and I take great
pride in you. You have greatly encouraged me and made me happy despite
all our troubles.

Paul's Joy at the Church's Repentance

5 When we arrived in Macedonia, there was no rest for us. We faced conflict
from every direction, with battles on the outside and fear on the inside. 6 But
God, who encourages those who are discouraged, encouraged us by the ar-
rival of Titus. 7 His presence was a joy, but so was the news he brought of the
encouragement he received from you. When he told us how much you long
to see me, and how sorry you are for what happened, and how loyal you are
to me, I was filled with joy!

6:15 Greek *Beliar;* various other manuscripts render this proper name of the devil as *Belian, Beliab,* or *Belial.* 6:16 Lev 26:12; Ezek 37:27. 6:17 Isa 52:11; Ezek 20:34 (Greek version). 6:18 2 Sam 7:14.

Story Arc **7:5-7**

● Titus

You may have noticed that the young man named in verse 6 has a book of the Bible named after him. Paul spoke of Titus as being someone who encouraged him and whose "presence was a joy" (v. 7). Here are two challenges: (1) read the book of Titus (a few books after this one) to learn more about this young man; (2) consider whether others could say about you what Paul said about Titus here.

Gal 3:6-9 ►

8 I am not sorry that I sent that severe letter to you, though I was sorry at
first, for I know it was painful to you for a little while. 9 Now I am glad I sent
it, not because it hurt you, but because the pain caused you to repent and
change your ways. It was the kind of sorrow God wants his people to have, so
you were not harmed by us in any way. 10 For the kind of sorrow God wants
us to experience leads us away from sin and results in salvation. There's no
regret for that kind of sorrow. But worldly sorrow, which lacks repentance,
results in spiritual death.

11 Just see what this godly sorrow produced in you! Such earnestness, such
concern to clear yourselves, such indignation, such alarm, such longing to
see me, such zeal, and such a readiness to punish wrong. You showed that
you have done everything necessary to make things right. 12 My purpose,
then, was not to write about who did the wrong or who was wronged. I wrote
to you so that in the sight of God you could see for yourselves how loyal you
are to us. 13 We have been greatly encouraged by this.

In addition to our own encouragement, we were especially delighted to
see how happy Titus was about the way all of you welcomed him and set
his mind* at ease. 14 I had told him how proud I was of you—and you didn't
disappoint me. I have always told you the truth, and now my boasting to
Titus has also proved true! 15 Now he cares for you more than ever when he
remembers the way all of you obeyed him and welcomed him with such fear
and deep respect. 16 I am very happy now because I have complete confidence
in you.

A Call to Generous Giving

8 Now I want you to know, dear brothers and sisters,* what God in his
kindness has done through the churches in Macedonia. 2 They are being
tested by many troubles, and they are very poor. But they are also filled with
abundant joy, which has overflowed in rich generosity.

3 For I can testify that they gave not only what they could afford, but far
more. And they did it of their own free will. 4 They begged us again and
again for the privilege of sharing in the gift for the believers in Jerusalem.*
5 They even did more than we had hoped, for their first action was to give
themselves to the Lord and to us, just as God wanted them to do.

6 So we have urged Titus, who encouraged your giving in the first place, to
return to you and encourage you to finish this ministry of giving. 7 Since you
excel in so many ways—in your faith, your gifted speakers, your knowledge,
your enthusiasm, and your love from us*—I want you to excel also in this
gracious act of giving.

8 I am not commanding you to do this. But I am testing how genuine your
love is by comparing it with the eagerness of the other churches.

9 You know the generous grace of our Lord Jesus Christ. Though he was
rich, yet for your sakes he became poor, so that by his poverty he could make
you rich.

10 Here is my advice: It would be good for you to finish what you started a
year ago. Last year you were the first who wanted to give, and you were the
first to begin doing it. 11 Now you should finish what you started. Let the
eagerness you showed in the beginning be matched now by your giving. Give
in proportion to what you have. 12 Whatever you give is acceptable if you give

7:13 Greek *his spirit.* 8:1 Greek *brothers.* 8:4 Greek *for God's holy people.* 8:7 Some manuscripts read *your love for us.*

it eagerly. And give according to what you have, not what you don't have. 13 Of course, I don't mean your giving should make life easy for others and hard for yourselves. I only mean that there should be some equality. 14 Right now you have plenty and can help those who are in need. Later, they will have plenty and can share with you when you need it. In this way, things will be equal. 15 As the Scriptures say,

"Those who gathered a lot had nothing left over,
and those who gathered only a little had enough."*

Titus and His Companions

16 But thank God! He has given Titus the same enthusiasm for you that I have. 17 Titus welcomed our request that he visit you again. In fact, he himself was very eager to go and see you. 18 We are also sending another brother with Titus. All the churches praise him as a preacher of the Good News. 19 He was appointed by the churches to accompany us as we take the offering to Jerusalem*—a service that glorifies the Lord and shows our eagerness to help.

20 We are traveling together to guard against any criticism for the way we are handling this generous gift. 21 We are careful to be honorable before the Lord, but we also want everyone else to see that we are honorable.

22 We are also sending with them another of our brothers who has proven himself many times and has shown on many occasions how eager he is. He is now even more enthusiastic because of his great confidence in you. 23 If anyone asks about Titus, say that he is my partner who works with me to help you. And the brothers with him have been sent by the churches,* and they bring honor to Christ. 24 So show them your love, and prove to all the churches that our boasting about you is justified.

The Collection for Christians in Jerusalem

9 I really don't need to write to you about this ministry of giving for the believers in Jerusalem.* 2 For I know how eager you are to help, and I have been boasting to the churches in Macedonia that you in Greece* were ready to send an offering a year ago. In fact, it was your enthusiasm that stirred up many of the Macedonian believers to begin giving.

3 But I am sending these brothers to be sure you really are ready, as I have been telling them, and that your money is all collected. I don't want to be wrong in my boasting about you. 4 We would be embarrassed—not to mention your own embarrassment—if some Macedonian believers came with me and found that you weren't ready after all I had told them! 5 So I thought I should send these brothers ahead of me to make sure the gift you promised is ready. But I want it to be a willing gift, not one given grudgingly.

6 Remember this—a farmer who plants only a few seeds will get a small crop. But the one who plants generously will get a generous crop. 7 You must each decide in your heart how much to give. And don't give reluctantly or in response to pressure. "For God loves a person who gives cheerfully."* 8 And God will generously provide all you need. Then you will always have everything you need and plenty left over to share with others. 9 As the Scriptures say,

8:15 Exod 16:18. 8:19 See 1 Cor 16:3-4. 8:23 Greek *are apostles of the churches.* 9:1 Greek *about the offering for God's holy people.* 9:2 Greek *in Achaia,* the southern region of the Greek peninsula. *Macedonia* was in the northern region of Greece. 9:7 See footnote on Prov 22:8.

Prayer **9:6**

Lord Jesus, you have asked me to be like you, radically committed to openhandedness. Lead me to an opportunity to practice generous living today. Amen.

Question **10:3-4**

Paul said that Christians don't "wage war as humans do." If this is true, what kind of "weapons" do followers of Jesus use?

"They share freely and give generously to the poor.
Their good deeds will be remembered forever."*

10 For God is the one who provides seed for the farmer and then bread to
eat. In the same way, he will provide and increase your resources and then
produce a great harvest of generosity* in you.
11 Yes, you will be enriched in every way so that you can always be generous.
And when we take your gifts to those who need them, they will thank God.
12 So two good things will result from this ministry of giving—the needs of
the believers in Jerusalem* will be met, and they will joyfully express their
thanks to God.
13 As a result of your ministry, they will give glory to God. For your generos-
ity to them and to all believers will prove that you are obedient to the Good
News of Christ. 14 And they will pray for you with deep affection because of
the overflowing grace God has given to you. 15 Thank God for this gift* too
wonderful for words!

Paul Defends His Authority

10 Now I, Paul, appeal to you with the gentleness and kindness of
Christ—though I realize you think I am timid in person and bold
only when I write from far away. 2 Well, I am begging you now so that when
I come I won't have to be bold with those who think we act from human
motives.
3 We are human, but we don't wage war as humans do. 4 *We use God's
mighty weapons, not worldly weapons, to knock down the strongholds of
human reasoning and to destroy false arguments. 5 We destroy every proud
obstacle that keeps people from knowing God. We capture their rebellious
thoughts and teach them to obey Christ. 6 And after you have become fully
obedient, we will punish everyone who remains disobedient.
7 Look at the obvious facts.* Those who say they belong to Christ must
recognize that we belong to Christ as much as they do. 8 I may seem to be
boasting too much about the authority given to us by the Lord. But our au-
thority builds you up; it doesn't tear you down. So I will not be ashamed of
using my authority.
9 I'm not trying to frighten you by my letters. 10 For some say, "Paul's letters
are demanding and forceful, but in person he is weak, and his speeches are
worthless!" 11 Those people should realize that our actions when we arrive in
person will be as forceful as what we say in our letters from far away.
12 Oh, don't worry; we wouldn't dare say that we are as wonderful as these
other men who tell you how important they are! But they are only comparing
themselves with each other, using themselves as the standard of measure-
ment. How ignorant!
13 We will not boast about things done outside our area of authority. We
will boast only about what has happened within the boundaries of the work
God has given us, which includes our working with you. 14 We are not reach-
ing beyond these boundaries when we claim authority over you, as if we had
never visited you. For we were the first to travel all the way to Corinth with
the Good News of Christ.

9:9 Ps 112:9. **9:10** Greek *righteousness.* **9:12** Greek *of God's holy people.* **9:15** Greek *his gift.* **10:4** English translations divide verses 4 and 5 in various ways. **10:7** Or *You look at things only on the basis of appearance.*

15 Nor do we boast and claim credit for the work someone else has done.
Instead, we hope that your faith will grow so that the boundaries of our
work among you will be extended. 16 Then we will be able to go and preach
the Good News in other places far beyond you, where no one else is working.
Then there will be no question of our boasting about work done in some-
one else's territory. 17 As the Scriptures say, "If you want to boast, boast only
about the LORD."*
18 When people commend themselves, it doesn't count for much. The im-
portant thing is for the Lord to commend them.

Question 10:18

For you, what is the most difficult aspect of this truth?

Paul and the False Apostles

11 I hope you will put up with a little more of my foolishness. Please
bear with me. 2 For I am jealous for you with the jealousy of God
himself. I promised you as a pure bride* to one husband—Christ. 3 But I fear
that somehow your pure and undivided devotion to Christ will be corrupted,
just as Eve was deceived by the cunning ways of the serpent. 4 You happily put
up with whatever anyone tells you, even if they preach a different Jesus than
the one we preach, or a different kind of Spirit than the one you received, or
a different kind of gospel than the one you believed.
5 But I don't consider myself inferior in any way to these "super apostles"
who teach such things. 6 I may be unskilled as a speaker, but I'm not lacking
in knowledge. We have made this clear to you in every possible way.
7 Was I wrong when I humbled myself and honored you by preaching
God's Good News to you without expecting anything in return? 8 I "robbed"
other churches by accepting their contributions so I could serve you at no
cost. 9 And when I was with you and didn't have enough to live on, I did
not become a financial burden to anyone. For the brothers who came from
Macedonia brought me all that I needed. I have never been a burden to you,
and I never will be. 10 As surely as the truth of Christ is in me, no one in all of
Greece* will ever stop me from boasting about this. 11 Why? Because I don't
love you? God knows that I do.
12 But I will continue doing what I have always done. This will undercut
those who are looking for an opportunity to boast that their work is just like
ours. 13 These people are false apostles. They are deceitful workers who dis-
guise themselves as apostles of Christ. 14 But I am not surprised! Even Satan
disguises himself as an angel of light. 15 So it is no wonder that his servants
also disguise themselves as servants of righteousness. In the end they will
get the punishment their wicked deeds deserve.

Paul's Many Trials

16 Again I say, don't think that I am a fool to talk like this. But even if you do,
listen to me, as you would to a foolish person, while I also boast a little. 17 Such
boasting is not from the Lord, but I am acting like a fool. 18 And since others
boast about their human achievements, I will, too. 19 After all, you think you
are so wise, but you enjoy putting up with fools! 20 You put up with it when
someone enslaves you, takes everything you have, takes advantage of you,
takes control of everything, and slaps you in the face. 21 I'm ashamed to say
that we've been too "weak" to do that!
But whatever they dare to boast about—I'm talking like a fool again—I

10:17 Jer 9:24. 11:2 Greek *a virgin.* 11:10 Greek *Achaia,* the southern region of the Greek peninsula.

Question 11:30

Why would Paul rather boast about his weaknesses? What did he mean?

Make a Difference

12:5-10

Grace Is Not Wishful Thinking

Wishful thinking. That's how we treat grace. It's almost like how we treat unicorns. Unicorns are magical and pretty. They can fly and roast marshmallows from their horns. They seem so nice. Did you know that a group of unicorns is even called a "blessing"? For real, if someone said to you, "Blessings on you," would that be a good thing? What if a stampeding herd of unicorns descended on you as these words left their mouth? They could trample you, hee-haw with terror, skewer you, and leave you covered in burnt sparkly marshmallows.

Thankfully, the difference between unicorns and grace is that grace is real. Don't ever treat grace as wishful thinking, like it is a pretend thing that would be nice to have but is elusive and mythical. No, grace has the power to change lives for real. It is all-sufficient for your life, so accept the power of grace through Jesus in your life.

Difference Maker

Remind someone who feels weak of the reality of God's grace through an act of extreme kindness.

dare to boast about it, too. 22 Are they Hebrews? So am I. Are they Israelites?
So am I. Are they descendants of Abraham? So am I. 23 Are they servants of
Christ? I know I sound like a madman, but I have served him far more! I have
worked harder, been put in prison more often, been whipped times without
number, and faced death again and again. 24 Five different times the Jewish
leaders gave me thirty-nine lashes. 25 Three times I was beaten with rods.
Once I was stoned. Three times I was shipwrecked. Once I spent a whole
night and a day adrift at sea. 26 I have traveled on many long journeys. I have
faced danger from rivers and from robbers. I have faced danger from my own
people, the Jews, as well as from the Gentiles. I have faced danger in the cities,
in the deserts, and on the seas. And I have faced danger from men who claim
to be believers but are not.* 27 I have worked hard and long, enduring many
sleepless nights. I have been hungry and thirsty and have often gone without
food. I have shivered in the cold, without enough clothing to keep me warm.
28 Then, besides all this, I have the daily burden of my concern for all the
churches. 29 Who is weak without my feeling that weakness? Who is led
astray, and I do not burn with anger?
30 If I must boast, I would rather boast about the things that show how
weak I am. 31 God, the Father of our Lord Jesus, who is worthy of eternal
praise, knows I am not lying. 32 When I was in Damascus, the governor under
King Aretas kept guards at the city gates to catch me. 33 I had to be lowered in
a basket through a window in the city wall to escape from him.

Paul's Vision and His Thorn in the Flesh

12 This boasting will do no good, but I must go on. I will reluctantly
tell about visions and revelations from the Lord. 2 I* was caught up
to the third heaven fourteen years ago. Whether I was in my body or out of
my body, I don't know—only God knows. 3 Yes, only God knows whether I
was in my body or outside my body. But I do know 4 that I was caught up* to
paradise and heard things so astounding that they cannot be expressed in
words, things no human is allowed to tell.
5 That experience is worth boasting about, but I'm not going to do it. I
will boast only about my weaknesses. 6 If I wanted to boast, I would be no
fool in doing so, because I would be telling the truth. But I won't do it, be-
cause I don't want anyone to give me credit beyond what they can see in my
life or hear in my message, 7 even though I have received such wonderful
revelations from God. So to keep me from becoming proud, I was given a
thorn in my flesh, a messenger from Satan to torment me and keep me from
becoming proud.
8 Three different times I begged the Lord to take it away. 9 Each time he
said, "My grace is all you need. My power works best in weakness." So now
I am glad to boast about my weaknesses, so that the power of Christ can
work through me. 10 That's why I take pleasure in my weaknesses, and in
the insults, hardships, persecutions, and troubles that I suffer for Christ.
For when I am weak, then I am strong.

Paul's Concern for the Corinthians

11 You have made me act like a fool. You ought to be writing commendations
for me, for I am not at all inferior to these "super apostles," even though I am

11:26 Greek *from false brothers.* 12:2 Greek *I know a man in Christ who.* 12:3-4 Greek *But I know such a man, [4]that he was caught up.*

nothing at all. 12 When I was with you, I certainly gave you proof that I am an apostle. For I patiently did many signs and wonders and miracles among you. 13 The only thing I failed to do, which I do in the other churches, was to become a financial burden to you. Please forgive me for this wrong!

14 Now I am coming to you for the third time, and I will not be a burden to you. I don't want what you have—I want you. After all, children don't provide for their parents. Rather, parents provide for their children. 15 I will gladly spend myself and all I have for you, even though it seems that the more I love you, the less you love me.

16 Some of you admit I was not a burden to you. But others still think I was sneaky and took advantage of you by trickery. 17 But how? Did any of the men I sent to you take advantage of you? 18 When I urged Titus to visit you and sent our other brother with him, did Titus take advantage of you? No! For we have the same spirit and walk in each other's steps, doing things the same way.

19 Perhaps you think we're saying these things just to defend ourselves. No, we tell you this as Christ's servants, and with God as our witness. Everything we do, dear friends, is to strengthen you. 20 For I am afraid that when I come I won't like what I find, and you won't like my response. I am afraid that I will find quarreling, jealousy, anger, selfishness, slander, gossip, arrogance, and disorderly behavior. 21 Yes, I am afraid that when I come again, God will humble me in your presence. And I will be grieved because many of you have not given up your old sins. You have not repented of your impurity, sexual immorality, and eagerness for lustful pleasure.

Question 13:5

On a scale of one to ten, how would you score on the genuineness of your faith?

Paul's Final Advice

13 This is the third time I am coming to visit you (and as the Scriptures say, "The facts of every case must be established by the testimony of two or three witnesses"*). 2 I have already warned those who had been sinning when I was there on my second visit. Now I again warn them and all others, just as I did before, that next time I will not spare them.

3 I will give you all the proof you want that Christ speaks through me. Christ is not weak when he deals with you; he is powerful among you. 4 Although he was crucified in weakness, he now lives by the power of God. We, too, are weak, just as Christ was, but when we deal with you we will be alive with him and will have God's power.

5 Examine yourselves to see if your faith is genuine. Test yourselves. Surely you know that Jesus Christ is among you*; if not, you have failed the test of genuine faith. 6 As you test yourselves, I hope you will recognize that we have not failed the test of apostolic authority.

7 We pray to God that you will not do what is wrong by refusing our correction. I hope we won't need to demonstrate our authority when we arrive. Do the right thing before we come—even if that makes it look like we have failed to demonstrate our authority. 8 For we cannot oppose the truth, but must always stand for the truth. 9 We are glad to seem weak if it helps show that you are actually strong. We pray that you will become mature.

10 I am writing this to you before I come, hoping that I won't need to deal severely with you when I do come. For I want to use the authority the Lord has given me to strengthen you, not to tear you down.

13:1 Deut 19:15. **13:5** Or *in you.*

Prayer 13:11

Lord Jesus, may your Spirit live in me so that I can live in harmony with others. Let me represent you today in everything I say and everything I do. Amen.

Paul's Final Greetings

11 Dear brothers and sisters,* I close my letter with these last words: Be joyful.
Grow to maturity. Encourage each other. Live in harmony and peace. Then
the God of love and peace will be with you.
12 Greet each other with a sacred kiss. 13 All of God's people here send you
their greetings.
14 *May the grace of the Lord Jesus Christ, the love of God, and the fellowship of the Holy Spirit be with you all.

13:11 Greek *Brothers.* 13:14 Some English translations include verse 13 as part of verse 12, and then verse 14 becomes verse 13.

Galatians Introduction

From the moment you were born, those around you celebrated your achievements. When you took your first step, everyone cheered. When you said your first word, your parents were amazed. When you made your first finger-painted masterpiece, your grandmother hung it front and center on the refrigerator. As you have gotten older, your value as a person seems to have gotten all tied up in the grades you get, the teams you're on, and the paths you have chosen. If you're not careful, you could easily let achievement define you.

Tying our value to our achievements certainly could become an issue that affects how we view our relationship with Jesus. This is the kind of mentality that Paul was addressing within the church in Galatia. Paul had always taught that we are justified, or made right in God's sight, through Jesus' life, death, and resurrection, but the Galatian church had started slipping back into teaching that works or good deeds are the means to salvation. They were living their faith with an achievement mentality.

Paul pointed out that when you put your faith in Jesus, the Holy Spirit produces a fruitfulness in your life. In other words, you are not ultimately the one who does the work of achievement in your own life. In reality, Jesus has already done all the important work on the cross. When you put your faith in Jesus, you receive the benefit of a celebration with God. Because of what Jesus has done and because of all the Holy Spirit will be doing, letting God work in you is the greatest achievement you could ever accomplish in your life.

Story Arc

- **Abraham**

Galatians

Question 1:4

What difference does this truth make in the everyday meaning of your life?

Question 1:10

Would you call yourself a "people pleaser"? What did Paul say should be our goal?

Greetings from Paul

1 This letter is from Paul, an apostle. I was not appointed by any group of
people or any human authority, but by Jesus Christ himself and by God
the Father, who raised Jesus from the dead.
2 All the brothers and sisters* here join me in sending this letter to the
churches of Galatia.
3 May God the Father and our Lord Jesus Christ* give you grace and peace.
4 Jesus gave his life for our sins, just as God our Father planned, in order to
rescue us from this evil world in which we live. 5 All glory to God forever
and ever! Amen.

There Is Only One Good News

6 I am shocked that you are turning away so soon from God, who called you
to himself through the loving mercy of Christ.* You are following a different
way that pretends to be the Good News 7 but is not the Good News at all. You
are being fooled by those who deliberately twist the truth concerning Christ.
8 Let God's curse fall on anyone, including us or even an angel from heaven,
who preaches a different kind of Good News than the one we preached to
you. 9 I say again what we have said before: If anyone preaches any other Good
News than the one you welcomed, let that person be cursed.
10 Obviously, I'm not trying to win the approval of people, but of God. If
pleasing people were my goal, I would not be Christ's servant.

Paul's Message Comes from Christ

11 Dear brothers and sisters, I want you to understand that the gospel mes-
sage I preach is not based on mere human reasoning. 12 I received my message
from no human source, and no one taught me. Instead, I received it by direct
revelation from Jesus Christ.*
13 You know what I was like when I followed the Jewish religion—how
I violently persecuted God's church. I did my best to destroy it. 14 I was far
ahead of my fellow Jews in my zeal for the traditions of my ancestors.
15 But even before I was born, God chose me and called me by his marvelous
grace. Then it pleased him 16 to reveal his Son to me* so that I would proclaim
the Good News about Jesus to the Gentiles.
When this happened, I did not rush out to consult with any human being.*
17 Nor did I go up to Jerusalem to consult with those who were apostles be-
fore I was. Instead, I went away into Arabia, and later I returned to the city
of Damascus.
18 Then three years later I went to Jerusalem to get to know Peter,* and I
stayed with him for fifteen days. 19 The only other apostle I met at that time

1:2 Greek *brothers;* also in 1:11. **1:3** Some manuscripts read *God our Father and the Lord Jesus Christ.* **1:6** Some manuscripts read *through loving mercy.* **1:12** Or *by the revelation of Jesus Christ.* **1:16a** Or *in me.* **1:16b** Greek *with flesh and blood.* **1:18** Greek *Cephas.*

was James, the Lord's brother. 20 I declare before God that what I am writing
to you is not a lie.
21 After that visit I went north into the provinces of Syria and Cilicia. 22 And
still the churches in Christ that are in Judea didn't know me personally. 23 All
they knew was that people were saying, "The one who used to persecute us
is now preaching the very faith he tried to destroy!" 24 And they praised God
because of me.

The Apostles Accept Paul

2 Then fourteen years later I went back to Jerusalem again, this time
with Barnabas; and Titus came along, too. 2 I went there because God
revealed to me that I should go. While I was there I met privately with those
considered to be leaders of the church and shared with them the message I
had been preaching to the Gentiles. I wanted to make sure that we were in
agreement, for fear that all my efforts had been wasted and I was running
the race for nothing. 3 And they supported me and did not even demand that
my companion Titus be circumcised, though he was a Gentile.*
4 Even that question came up only because of some so-called believers
there—false ones, really*—who were secretly brought in. They sneaked
in to spy on us and take away the freedom we have in Christ Jesus. They
wanted to enslave us and force us to follow their Jewish regulations. 5 But
we refused to give in to them for a single moment. We wanted to preserve
the truth of the gospel message for you.
6 And the leaders of the church had nothing to add to what I was preach-
ing. (By the way, their reputation as great leaders made no difference to me,
for God has no favorites.) 7 Instead, they saw that God had given me the re-
sponsibility of preaching the gospel to the Gentiles, just as he had given
Peter the responsibility of preaching to the Jews. 8 For the same God who
worked through Peter as the apostle to the Jews also worked through me as
the apostle to the Gentiles.
9 In fact, James, Peter,* and John, who were known as pillars of the church,
recognized the gift God had given me, and they accepted Barnabas and me
as their co-workers. They encouraged us to keep preaching to the Gentiles,
while they continued their work with the Jews. 10 Their only suggestion was
that we keep on helping the poor, which I have always been eager to do.

Paul Confronts Peter

11 But when Peter came to Antioch, I had to oppose him to his face, for what
he did was very wrong. 12 When he first arrived, he ate with the Gentile believ-
ers, who were not circumcised. But afterward, when some friends of James
came, Peter wouldn't eat with the Gentiles anymore. He was afraid of criti-
cism from these people who insisted on the necessity of circumcision. 13 As a
result, other Jewish believers followed Peter's hypocrisy, and even Barnabas
was led astray by their hypocrisy.
14 When I saw that they were not following the truth of the gospel mes-
sage, I said to Peter in front of all the others, "Since you, a Jew by birth, have
discarded the Jewish laws and are living like a Gentile, why are you now
trying to make these Gentiles follow the Jewish traditions?
15 "You and I are Jews by birth, not 'sinners' like the Gentiles. 16 Yet we

2:3 Greek *a Greek.* 2:4 Greek *some false brothers.* 2:9 Greek *Cephas;* also in 2:11, 14.

know that a person is made right with God by faith in Jesus Christ, not by
obeying the law. And we have believed in Christ Jesus, so that we might be
made right with God because of our faith in Christ, not because we have
obeyed the law. For no one will ever be made right with God by obeying
the law."*
17 But suppose we seek to be made right with God through faith in Christ
and then we are found guilty because we have abandoned the law. Would
that mean Christ has led us into sin? Absolutely not! 18 Rather, I am a sinner
if I rebuild the old system of law I already tore down. 19 For when I tried to
keep the law, it condemned me. So I died to the law—I stopped trying to
meet all its requirements—so that I might live for God. 20 My old self has
been crucified with Christ.* It is no longer I who live, but Christ lives in me.
So I live in this earthly body by trusting in the Son of God, who loved me
and gave himself for me. 21 I do not treat the grace of God as meaningless.
For if keeping the law could make us right with God, then there was no
need for Christ to die.

The Law and Faith in Christ

3 Oh, foolish Galatians! Who has cast an evil spell on you? For the mean-
ing of Jesus Christ's death was made as clear to you as if you had seen
a picture of his death on the cross. 2 Let me ask you this one question: Did
you receive the Holy Spirit by obeying the law of Moses? Of course not! You
received the Spirit because you believed the message you heard about Christ.
3 How foolish can you be? After starting your new lives in the Spirit, why are
you now trying to become perfect by your own human effort? 4 Have you
experienced* so much for nothing? Surely it was not in vain, was it?
5 I ask you again, does God give you the Holy Spirit and work miracles
among you because you obey the law? Of course not! It is because you believe
the message you heard about Christ.
6 In the same way, "Abraham believed God, and God counted him as righ-
teous because of his faith."* 7 The real children of Abraham, then, are those
who put their faith in God.
8 What's more, the Scriptures looked forward to this time when God would
make the Gentiles right in his sight because of their faith. God proclaimed
this good news to Abraham long ago when he said, "All nations will be
blessed through you."* 9 So all who put their faith in Christ share the same
blessing Abraham received because of his faith.
10 But those who depend on the law to make them right with God are
under his curse, for the Scriptures say, "Cursed is everyone who does not ob-
serve and obey all the commands that are written in God's Book of the Law."*
11 So it is clear that no one can be made right with God by trying to keep the
law. For the Scriptures say, "It is through faith that a righteous person has
life."* 12 This way of faith is very different from the way of law, which says,
"It is through obeying the law that a person has life."*
13 But Christ has rescued us from the curse pronounced by the law. When
he was hung on the cross, he took upon himself the curse for our wrong-
doing. For it is written in the Scriptures, "Cursed is everyone who is hung

2:16 Some translators hold that the quotation extends through verse 14; others through verse 16; and still others through verse 21. 2:20 Some English translations put this sentence in verse 19. 3:4 Or *Have you suffered.* 3:6 Gen 15:6. 3:8 Gen 12:3; 18:18; 22:18. 3:10 Deut 27:26. 3:11 Hab 2:4. 3:12 Lev 18:5.

Make a Difference 2:20

No Longer I

We know, in hindsight of the resurrection, that the crucifixion of Jesus is beautiful terror...or terrible beauty. It wasn't just the beatings–as wretched as they were–nor the insults–as hideous as they were. It wasn't even the nails–as horribly awful as they were. It was also the asphyxiation–the very breath that Jesus gave to us at the creation of the world stolen from him. He couldn't keep leveraging his legs to push himself up enough to catch air in his lungs. Still, he mustered enough strength, swallowed more pride than all humanity combined, and spoke out those resoundingly refreshing words, "Father, forgive them" (Luke 23:34).

Difference Maker

Speak to some people today about the hope of the cross. As you risk your pride and comfort, invite them into deeper relationship with God through the loving work of Jesus.

Story Arc 3:6-9

Abraham

Go back into the book of Genesis and look for the overarching difference-making story of Abraham. What does Father Abraham have to do with belonging to Christ?

Phil 2:19-23 ►

on a tree."* 14 Through Christ Jesus, God has blessed the Gentiles with the
same blessing he promised to Abraham, so that we who are believers might
receive the promised* Holy Spirit through faith.

The Law and God's Promise

15 Dear brothers and sisters,* here's an example from everyday life. Just as
no one can set aside or amend an irrevocable agreement, so it is in this case.
16 God gave the promises to Abraham and his child.* And notice that the
Scripture doesn't say "to his children,*" as if it meant many descendants.
Rather, it says "to his child"—and that, of course, means Christ. 17 This is
what I am trying to say: The agreement God made with Abraham could not
be canceled 430 years later when God gave the law to Moses. God would be
breaking his promise. 18 For if the inheritance could be received by keeping
the law, then it would not be the result of accepting God's promise. But God
graciously gave it to Abraham as a promise.

19 Why, then, was the law given? It was given alongside the promise to show
people their sins. But the law was designed to last only until the coming of
the child who was promised. God gave his law through angels to Moses, who
was the mediator between God and the people. 20 Now a mediator is helpful
if more than one party must reach an agreement. But God, who is one, did
not use a mediator when he gave his promise to Abraham.

21 Is there a conflict, then, between God's law and God's promises?* Ab-
solutely not! If the law could give us new life, we could be made right with
God by obeying it. 22 But the Scriptures declare that we are all prisoners of
sin, so we receive God's promise of freedom only by believing in Jesus Christ.

God's Children through Faith

23 Before the way of faith in Christ was available to us, we were placed under
guard by the law. We were kept in protective custody, so to speak, until the
way of faith was revealed.

24 Let me put it another way. The law was our guardian until Christ came;
it protected us until we could be made right with God through faith. 25 And
now that the way of faith has come, we no longer need the law as our guardian.

26 For you are all children* of God through faith in Christ Jesus. 27 And all
who have been united with Christ in baptism have put on Christ, like put-
ting on new clothes.* 28 There is no longer Jew or Gentile,* slave or free, male
and female. For you are all one in Christ Jesus. 29 And now that you belong
to Christ, you are the true children* of Abraham. You are his heirs, and God's
promise to Abraham belongs to you.

4 Think of it this way. If a father dies and leaves an inheritance for his
young children, those children are not much better off than slaves until
they grow up, even though they actually own everything their father had.
2 They have to obey their guardians until they reach whatever age their fa-
ther set. 3 And that's the way it was with us before Christ came. We were
like children; we were slaves to the basic spiritual principles* of this world.

4 But when the right time came, God sent his Son, born of a woman, subject

3:13 Deut 21:23 (Greek version). **3:14** Some manuscripts read *the blessing of the.* **3:15** Greek *Brothers.* **3:16a** Greek *seed;* also in 3:16c, 19. See notes on Gen 12:7 and 13:15. **3:16b** Greek *seeds.* **3:21** Some manuscripts read *and the promises?* **3:26** Greek *sons.* **3:27** Greek *have put on Christ.* **3:28** Greek *Jew or Greek.* **3:29** Greek *seed.* **4:3** Or *powers;* also in 4:9.

Prayer 4:7

Lord Jesus, thank you for dying on the cross to set me free. Let your forgiveness sink to the very core of who I am so that I don't fall back into the trap of my old self. Amen.

to the law. 5God sent him to buy freedom for us who were slaves to the law,
so that he could adopt us as his very own children.* 6And because we* are his
children, God has sent the Spirit of his Son into our hearts, prompting us
to call out, "Abba, Father."* 7Now you are no longer a slave but God's own
child.* And since you are his child, God has made you his heir.

Paul's Concern for the Galatians

8Before you Gentiles knew God, you were slaves to so-called gods that do
not even exist. 9So now that you know God (or should I say, now that God
knows you), why do you want to go back again and become slaves once more
to the weak and useless spiritual principles of this world? 10You are trying to
earn favor with God by observing certain days or months or seasons or years.
11I fear for you. Perhaps all my hard work with you was for nothing. 12Dear
brothers and sisters,* I plead with you to live as I do in freedom from these
things, for I have become like you Gentiles—free from those laws.

You did not mistreat me when I first preached to you. 13Surely you re-
member that I was sick when I first brought you the Good News. 14But even
though my condition tempted you to reject me, you did not despise me or
turn me away. No, you took me in and cared for me as though I were an angel
from God or even Christ Jesus himself. 15Where is that joyful and grateful
spirit you felt then? I am sure you would have taken out your own eyes and
given them to me if it had been possible. 16Have I now become your enemy
because I am telling you the truth?

17Those false teachers are so eager to win your favor, but their intentions
are not good. They are trying to shut you off from me so that you will pay
attention only to them. 18If someone is eager to do good things for you, that's
all right; but let them do it all the time, not just when I'm with you.

19Oh, my dear children! I feel as if I'm going through labor pains for you
again, and they will continue until Christ is fully developed in your lives.
20I wish I were with you right now so I could change my tone. But at this
distance I don't know how else to help you.

Abraham's Two Children

21Tell me, you who want to live under the law, do you know what the law actu-
ally says? 22The Scriptures say that Abraham had two sons, one from his slave
wife and one from his freeborn wife.* 23The son of the slave wife was born in
a human attempt to bring about the fulfillment of God's promise. But the
son of the freeborn wife was born as God's own fulfillment of his promise.

24These two women serve as an illustration of God's two covenants. The
first woman, Hagar, represents Mount Sinai where people received the law
that enslaved them. 25And now Jerusalem is just like Mount Sinai in Ara-
bia,* because she and her children live in slavery to the law. 26But the other
woman, Sarah, represents the heavenly Jerusalem. She is the free woman,
and she is our mother. 27As Isaiah said,

"Rejoice, O childless woman,
you who have never given birth!

4:5 Greek *sons;* also in 4:6. **4:6a** Greek *you.* **4:6b** *Abba* is an Aramaic term for "father." **4:7** Greek *son;* also in 4:7b. **4:12** Greek *brothers;* also in 4:28, 31. **4:22** See Gen 16:15; 21:2-3. **4:25** Greek *And Hagar, which is Mount Sinai in Arabia, is now like Jerusalem;* other manuscripts read *And Mount Sinai in Arabia is now like Jerusalem.*

Break into a joyful shout,
you who have never been in labor!
For the desolate woman now has more children
than the woman who lives with her husband!"*

28 And you, dear brothers and sisters, are children of the promise, just like
Isaac. 29 But you are now being persecuted by those who want you to keep
the law, just as Ishmael, the child born by human effort, persecuted Isaac,
the child born by the power of the Spirit.
30 But what do the Scriptures say about that? "Get rid of the slave and her
son, for the son of the slave woman will not share the inheritance with the
free woman's son."* 31 So, dear brothers and sisters, we are not children of the
slave woman; we are children of the free woman.

Freedom in Christ

5 So Christ has truly set us free. Now make sure that you stay free, and
don't get tied up again in slavery to the law.
2 Listen! I, Paul, tell you this: If you are counting on circumcision to make
you right with God, then Christ will be of no benefit to you. 3 I'll say it again.
If you are trying to find favor with God by being circumcised, you must obey
every regulation in the whole law of Moses. 4 For if you are trying to make
yourselves right with God by keeping the law, you have been cut off from
Christ! You have fallen away from God's grace.
5 But we who live by the Spirit eagerly wait to receive by faith the righ-
teousness God has promised to us. 6 For when we place our faith in Christ
Jesus, there is no benefit in being circumcised or being uncircumcised. What
is important is faith expressing itself in love.
7 You were running the race so well. Who has held you back from fol-
lowing the truth? 8 It certainly isn't God, for he is the one who called you to
freedom. 9 This false teaching is like a little yeast that spreads through the
whole batch of dough! 10 I am trusting the Lord to keep you from believing
false teachings. God will judge that person, whoever he is, who has been
confusing you.
11 Dear brothers and sisters,* if I were still preaching that you must be
circumcised—as some say I do—why am I still being persecuted? If I were
no longer preaching salvation through the cross of Christ, no one would be
offended. 12 I just wish that those troublemakers who want to mutilate you
by circumcision would mutilate themselves.*
13 For you have been called to live in freedom, my brothers and sisters.
But don't use your freedom to satisfy your sinful nature. Instead, use your
freedom to serve one another in love. 14 For the whole law can be summed
up in this one command: "Love your neighbor as yourself."* 15 But if you are
always biting and devouring one another, watch out! Beware of destroying
one another.

Living by the Spirit's Power

16 So I say, let the Holy Spirit guide your lives. Then you won't be doing what
your sinful nature craves. 17 The sinful nature wants to do evil, which is just
the opposite of what the Spirit wants. And the Spirit gives us desires that

4:27 Isa 54:1. 4:30 Gen 21:10. 5:11 Greek *Brothers;* similarly in 5:13. 5:12 Or *castrate themselves,* or *cut themselves off from you;* Greek reads *cut themselves off.* 5:14 Lev 19:18.

Prayer **5:16**

Jesus, just as you gave your life for me, I give my life to you. As I imitate you, may people be drawn to you, and may they find forgiveness and peace, salvation and hope. Guide me by your Holy Spirit. Amen.

Make a Difference

5:16–6:10

Reaping

Sometimes the difference you make in this world is immediate. Perhaps you called someone on their birthday, and they were greatly encouraged. Good job—you made a difference in their life. Quick response. Lives changed. Keep doing it! Other times, however, the difference you make in this world isn't always immediately evident. Perhaps you started getting rid of some bad habits in your life, but they keep rearing their ugly head and trying to drag you down. The battle is still there. It isn't fixed, and it isn't clear if anything good is coming out of it.

God's Word encourages us again and again to persist. Keep going. Don't give up pursuing Jesus and the life he has for you. Don't quit doing what he wants you to do. Don't stop changing the patterns of your life and the lives of those around you in the long-term direction of Jesus. You will reap a harvest if you don't give up.

Difference Maker

Write down five goals for your life that you would like to have accomplished five years from now. Put this somewhere that you will occasionally revisit to remind yourself not to give up.

are the opposite of what the sinful nature desires. These two forces are con-
stantly fighting each other, so you are not free to carry out your good inten-
tions. 18 But when you are directed by the Spirit, you are not under obligation
to the law of Moses.

19 When you follow the desires of your sinful nature, the results are very
clear: sexual immorality, impurity, lustful pleasures, 20 idolatry, sorcery, hos-
tility, quarreling, jealousy, outbursts of anger, selfish ambition, dissension,
division, 21 envy, drunkenness, wild parties, and other sins like these. Let me
tell you again, as I have before, that anyone living that sort of life will not
inherit the Kingdom of God.

22 But the Holy Spirit produces this kind of fruit in our lives: love, joy,
peace, patience, kindness, goodness, faithfulness, 23 gentleness, and self-
control. There is no law against these things!

24 Those who belong to Christ Jesus have nailed the passions and desires
of their sinful nature to his cross and crucified them there. 25 Since we are
living by the Spirit, let us follow the Spirit's leading in every part of our
lives. 26 Let us not become conceited, or provoke one another, or be jealous
of one another.

We Harvest What We Plant

6 Dear brothers and sisters, if another believer* is overcome by some sin,
you who are godly* should gently and humbly help that person back
onto the right path. And be careful not to fall into the same temptation your-
self. 2 Share each other's burdens, and in this way obey the law of Christ.
3 If you think you are too important to help someone, you are only fooling
yourself. You are not that important.

4 Pay careful attention to your own work, for then you will get the satisfac-
tion of a job well done, and you won't need to compare yourself to anyone
else. 5 For we are each responsible for our own conduct.

6 Those who are taught the word of God should provide for their teachers,
sharing all good things with them.

7 Don't be misled—you cannot mock the justice of God. You will always
harvest what you plant. 8 Those who live only to satisfy their own sinful na-
ture will harvest decay and death from that sinful nature. But those who live
to please the Spirit will harvest everlasting life from the Spirit. 9 So let's not
get tired of doing what is good. At just the right time we will reap a harvest of
blessing if we don't give up. 10 Therefore, whenever we have the opportunity,
we should do good to everyone—especially to those in the family of faith.

Paul's Final Advice

11 NOTICE WHAT LARGE LETTERS I USE AS I WRITE THESE CLOSING WORDS IN
MY OWN HANDWRITING.

12 Those who are trying to force you to be circumcised want to look good to
others. They don't want to be persecuted for teaching that the cross of Christ
alone can save. 13 And even those who advocate circumcision don't keep the
whole law themselves. They only want you to be circumcised so they can
boast about it and claim you as their disciples.

14 As for me, may I never boast about anything except the cross of our
Lord Jesus Christ. Because of that cross,* my interest in this world has been

6:1a Greek *Brothers, if a man.* 6:1b Greek *spiritual.* 6:14 Or *Because of him.*

Make a Difference

5:22-25

In Step

Have you ever tried to brush your teeth without using a toothbrush—or toothpaste for that matter? Likewise, have you ever tried to make a bowl of cereal without a bowl or without cereal?

Why would you try to live today without using the Spirit for your every step and breath? If you want an abundant life, why not walk with God, the one who gives abundant life? If you need direction for major decisions in your life today, why not walk with the one who provides all wisdom and truth? If you need hope in a time of despair, why not make the effort to walk with the one who gives comfort and counsel?

It can be tempting to complicate something so simple. If you want to truly live, then walk in step with the Spirit. You were created to walk with God, so do what you were created to do.

Difference Maker

Go for a walk with someone. Allow your strides to fall into rhythm together, then talk about how we are to walk with God just like that.

Question **6:14**

What would happen today if you boasted about Jesus? What if, instead of bragging about your own accomplishments or calling attention to your own problems, you spoke boldly and favorably about what Jesus did on the cross? What would you say if you chose to do this?

crucified, and the world's interest in me has also died. 15 It doesn't matter
whether we have been circumcised or not. What counts is whether we have
been transformed into a new creation. 16 May God's peace and mercy be upon
all who live by this principle; they are the new people of God.*
17 From now on, don't let anyone trouble me with these things. For I bear
on my body the scars that show I belong to Jesus.
18 Dear brothers and sisters,* may the grace of our Lord Jesus Christ be
with your spirit. Amen.

6:16 Greek *this principle, and upon the Israel of God.* 6:18 Greek *Brothers.*

The Galatian Church Network

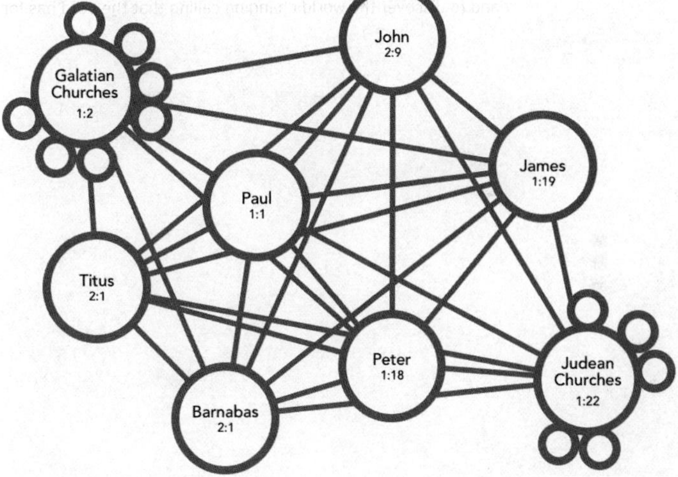

Ephesians Introduction

Have you ever sat in class and wondered, *When am I ever going to use this in everyday life?* Maybe you've even felt that way about the Bible at times.

There are a lot of great stories in the Bible, and through those stories, we get to see the powerful love that God has for his people and how he cared so much about them that he sent Jesus, his Son, to die as a payment for the sin that separated them from himself. Sometimes we find ourselves asking, "Okay, but now what? How do I use this in my everyday life? What does it look like to follow Jesus?"

In Paul's letter to the church in Ephesus, he laid out the fact that the gospel, the good news of Jesus, changes every aspect of how we live. It changes how we view ourselves, how we view others, and how we view God himself. It explains that in this journey of following Jesus, we actively need to pursue knowing Jesus more and more every day. Paul showed how joining others in the journey through finding strong Christian friends is of the utmost importance. Ultimately, Paul's purpose for writing to the Ephesians wasn't to fix a problem but to encourage them to find practical ways to protect against spiritual attacks, to overcome divisiveness, and to discover the world-changing calling that the Lord has for them.

Ephesians

Greetings from Paul

1 This letter is from Paul, chosen by the will of God to be an apostle of
Christ Jesus.

I am writing to God's holy people in Ephesus,* who are faithful followers
of Christ Jesus.

2 May God our Father and the Lord Jesus Christ give you grace and peace.

Spiritual Blessings

3 All praise to God, the Father of our Lord Jesus Christ, who has blessed us
with every spiritual blessing in the heavenly realms because we are united
with Christ. 4 Even before he made the world, God loved us and chose us in
Christ to be holy and without fault in his eyes. 5 God decided in advance to
adopt us into his own family by bringing us to himself through Jesus Christ.
This is what he wanted to do, and it gave him great pleasure. 6 So we praise
God for the glorious grace he has poured out on us who belong to his dear
Son.* 7 He is so rich in kindness and grace that he purchased our freedom with
the blood of his Son and forgave our sins. 8 He has showered his kindness on
us, along with all wisdom and understanding.

9 God has now revealed to us his mysterious will regarding Christ—which
is to fulfill his own good plan. 10 And this is the plan: At the right time he
will bring everything together under the authority of Christ—everything
in heaven and on earth. 11 Furthermore, because we are united with Christ,
we have received an inheritance from God,* for he chose us in advance, and
he makes everything work out according to his plan.

12 God's purpose was that we Jews who were the first to trust in Christ
would bring praise and glory to God. 13 And now you Gentiles have also heard
the truth, the Good News that God saves you. And when you believed in
Christ, he identified you as his own* by giving you the Holy Spirit, whom
he promised long ago. 14 The Spirit is God's guarantee that he will give us the
inheritance he promised and that he has purchased us to be his own people.
He did this so we would praise and glorify him.

Paul's Prayer for Spiritual Wisdom

15 Ever since I first heard of your strong faith in the Lord Jesus and your love
for God's people everywhere,* 16 I have not stopped thanking God for you. I
pray for you constantly, 17 asking God, the glorious Father of our Lord Jesus
Christ, to give you spiritual wisdom* and insight so that you might grow
in your knowledge of God. 18 I pray that your hearts will be flooded with
light so that you can understand the confident hope he has given to those he
called—his holy people who are his rich and glorious inheritance.*

1:1 The most ancient manuscripts do not include *in Ephesus.* 1:6 Greek *to us in the beloved.* 1:11 Or *we have become God's inheritance.* 1:13 Or *he put his seal on you.* 1:15 Some manuscripts read *your faithfulness to the Lord Jesus and to God's people everywhere.* 1:17 Or *to give you the Spirit of wisdom.* 1:18 Or *called, and the rich and glorious inheritance he has given to his holy people.*

Make a Difference **1:5**

Adoption

One of the places on this planet where God can most be understood is in a loving orphanage. The sickness of the world has left too many children alone, but there are places—homes—where orphaned babies are bathed in warm water, wrapped in blankets, nourished to health, sung to sleep, and cherished as precious people with a great destiny. God is a God who rescues. Jesus came to this earth just so that people could be brought home into the family of God.

Difference Maker

How could you use your future career to support an orphanage or adoption ministry?

Prayer **1:16**

Lord, thank you for my friends who have a strong faith in you. Give them deep insight and flood them with hope. Let them understand your incredible power living within them. Amen.

Question **2:8**

Your good actions do not save you. God saves you when you believe in what Jesus has done for you. Have you placed your faith in Jesus? If you'd like to receive Jesus as your Savior right now, go to the "How to Accept Jesus as Your Lord and Savior" section at the back of this Bible.

19 I also pray that you will understand the incredible greatness of God's
power for us who believe him. This is the same mighty power 20 that raised
Christ from the dead and seated him in the place of honor at God's right
hand in the heavenly realms. 21 Now he is far above any ruler or authority
or power or leader or anything else—not only in this world but also in the
world to come. 22 God has put all things under the authority of Christ and
has made him head over all things for the benefit of the church. 23 And the
church is his body; it is made full and complete by Christ, who fills all things
everywhere with himself.

Made Alive with Christ

2 Once you were dead because of your disobedience and your many sins.
2 You used to live in sin, just like the rest of the world, obeying the
devil—the commander of the powers in the unseen world.* He is the spirit at
work in the hearts of those who refuse to obey God. 3 All of us used to live that
way, following the passionate desires and inclinations of our sinful nature.
By our very nature we were subject to God's anger, just like everyone else.
4 But God is so rich in mercy, and he loved us so much, 5 that even though
we were dead because of our sins, he gave us life when he raised Christ from
the dead. (It is only by God's grace that you have been saved!) 6 For he raised
us from the dead along with Christ and seated us with him in the heavenly
realms because we are united with Christ Jesus. 7 So God can point to us in all
future ages as examples of the incredible wealth of his grace and kindness to-
ward us, as shown in all he has done for us who are united with Christ Jesus.
8 God saved you by his grace when you believed. And you can't take credit
for this; it is a gift from God. 9 Salvation is not a reward for the good things
we have done, so none of us can boast about it. 10 For we are God's master-
piece. He has created us anew in Christ Jesus, so we can do the good things
he planned for us long ago.

Oneness and Peace in Christ

11 Don't forget that you Gentiles used to be outsiders. You were called "un-
circumcised heathens" by the Jews, who were proud of their circumcision,
even though it affected only their bodies and not their hearts. 12 In those
days you were living apart from Christ. You were excluded from citizenship
among the people of Israel, and you did not know the covenant promises
God had made to them. You lived in this world without God and without
hope. 13 But now you have been united with Christ Jesus. Once you were far
away from God, but now you have been brought near to him through the
blood of Christ.

14 For Christ himself has brought peace to us. He united Jews and Gentiles
into one people when, in his own body on the cross, he broke down the wall
of hostility that separated us. 15 He did this by ending the system of law with
its commandments and regulations. He made peace between Jews and Gen-
tiles by creating in himself one new people from the two groups. 16 Together
as one body, Christ reconciled both groups to God by means of his death on
the cross, and our hostility toward each other was put to death.

17 He brought this Good News of peace to you Gentiles who were far away
from him, and peace to the Jews who were near. 18 Now all of us can come to

2:2 Greek *obeying the commander of the power of the air.*

the Father through the same Holy Spirit because of what Christ has done
for us.

A Temple for the Lord

19 So now you Gentiles are no longer strangers and foreigners. You are citi-
zens along with all of God's holy people. You are members of God's family.
20 Together, we are his house, built on the foundation of the apostles and
the prophets. And the cornerstone is Christ Jesus himself. 21 We are carefully
joined together in him, becoming a holy temple for the Lord. 22 Through
him you Gentiles are also being made part of this dwelling where God lives
by his Spirit.

God's Mysterious Plan Revealed

3 When I think of all this, I, Paul, a prisoner of Christ Jesus for the benefit
of you Gentiles* . . . 2 assuming, by the way, that you know God gave me
the special responsibility of extending his grace to you Gentiles. 3 As I briefly
wrote earlier, God himself revealed his mysterious plan to me. 4 As you read
what I have written, you will understand my insight into this plan regarding
Christ. 5 God did not reveal it to previous generations, but now by his Spirit
he has revealed it to his holy apostles and prophets.

6 And this is God's plan: Both Gentiles and Jews who believe the Good
News share equally in the riches inherited by God's children. Both are part of
the same body, and both enjoy the promise of blessings because they belong
to Christ Jesus.* 7 By God's grace and mighty power, I have been given the
privilege of serving him by spreading this Good News.

8 Though I am the least deserving of all God's people, he graciously gave
me the privilege of telling the Gentiles about the endless treasures available
to them in Christ. 9 I was chosen to explain to everyone* this mysterious
plan that God, the Creator of all things, had kept secret from the beginning.
10 God's purpose in all this was to use the church to display his wisdom
in its rich variety to all the unseen rulers and authorities in the heavenly
places. 11 This was his eternal plan, which he carried out through Christ Jesus
our Lord.

12 Because of Christ and our faith in him,* we can now come boldly and
confidently into God's presence. 13 So please don't lose heart because of my
trials here. I am suffering for you, so you should feel honored.

Paul's Prayer for Spiritual Growth

14 When I think of all this, I fall to my knees and pray to the Father,* 15 the
Creator of everything in heaven and on earth.* 16 I pray that from his glorious,
unlimited resources he will empower you with inner strength through his
Spirit. 17 Then Christ will make his home in your hearts as you trust in him.
Your roots will grow down into God's love and keep you strong. 18 And may
you have the power to understand, as all God's people should, how wide,
how long, how high, and how deep his love is. 19 May you experience the
love of Christ, though it is too great to understand fully. Then you will be
made complete with all the fullness of life and power that comes from God.

3:1 Paul resumes this thought in verse 14: "When I think of all this, I fall to my knees and pray to the Father." **3:6** Or *because they are united with Christ Jesus.* **3:9** Some manuscripts do not include *to everyone.* **3:12** Or *Because of Christ's faithfulness.* **3:14** Some manuscripts read *the Father of our Lord Jesus Christ.* **3:15** Or *from whom every family in heaven and on earth takes its name.*

Prayer **3:16**

Lord Jesus, you created this world, and you want to empower me to do extraordinary things in it. Let me take that seriously today. Amen.

Make a Difference **3:17**

Moving In

Jesus just showed up with his moving truck. Think quick: What would Jesus need to do to make your heart his home? Having Jesus make himself comfortable in your life might not be such a comforting thought. Even so, it is the best possible scenario. It might mean some disruption to your old habits and routines, but those didn't bring you confidence or peace anyway. The new daily routines with Jesus are going to be so much more fulfilling than what you have been doing.

Difference Maker

What is one thing you can do to show Jesus he is welcome in your heart today?

Prayer **3:18**

Lord Jesus, I pray that you will give me the power to understand how much your love covers me. Amen.

Prayer 4:1

Jesus, let me never give up my pursuit of how you want to use me in this world. Amen.

Make a Difference 4:7

Gifted on Purpose

God uniquely gifts you on purpose. He gave you specific talents, experiences, and passions so that you can make a difference in the world in which you live. Your unique set of gifts can help others live according to their God-given giftedness too. God has planned to use you to do good things in this world.

Remember that God also exceptionally wired others so that they could encourage and equip people like you to do what he has called you to do. God has put everyone on the same playing field. Each person is a recipient of this radical generosity so that each person can serve the Lord with his or her whole heart.

Difference Maker

Pick a talent that God has given to you, and then combine it with someone else's giftedness.

Make a Difference 4:11-13

Work for Everyone

People have assumed that it is the pastor's job to visit a sick person in the hospital, to pray before a meal, or to do the Bible teaching on Wednesday night. After all, it's what the pastor was hired for, right? Well, this is true to a degree but just to a degree. Ultimately, the pastor's job is to shepherd (*pastor* means "shepherd") people to a closer relationship with Jesus so that Jesus can empower them to do good work.

20 Now all glory to God, who is able, through his mighty power at work
within us, to accomplish infinitely more than we might ask or think. 21 Glory
to him in the church and in Christ Jesus through all generations forever and
ever! Amen.

Unity in the Body

4 Therefore I, a prisoner for serving the Lord, beg you to lead a life worthy
of your calling, for you have been called by God. 2 Always be humble and
gentle. Be patient with each other, making allowance for each other's faults
because of your love. 3 Make every effort to keep yourselves united in the
Spirit, binding yourselves together with peace. 4 For there is one body and
one Spirit, just as you have been called to one glorious hope for the future.

5 There is one Lord, one faith, one baptism,
6 one God and Father of all,
who is over all, in all, and living through all.

7 However, he has given each one of us a special gift* through the generos-
ity of Christ. 8 That is why the Scriptures say,

"When he ascended to the heights,
he led a crowd of captives
and gave gifts to his people."*

9 Notice that it says "he ascended." This clearly means that Christ also de-
scended to our lowly world.* 10 And the same one who descended is the one
who ascended higher than all the heavens, so that he might fill the entire
universe with himself.

11 Now these are the gifts Christ gave to the church: the apostles, the
prophets, the evangelists, and the pastors and teachers. 12 Their responsibil-
ity is to equip God's people to do his work and build up the church, the body
of Christ. 13 This will continue until we all come to such unity in our faith
and knowledge of God's Son that we will be mature in the Lord, measuring
up to the full and complete standard of Christ.

14 Then we will no longer be immature like children. We won't be tossed
and blown about by every wind of new teaching. We will not be influenced
when people try to trick us with lies so clever they sound like the truth.
15 Instead, we will speak the truth in love, growing in every way more and
more like Christ, who is the head of his body, the church. 16 He makes the
whole body fit together perfectly. As each part does its own special work, it
helps the other parts grow, so that the whole body is healthy and growing
and full of love.

Living as Children of Light

17 With the Lord's authority I say this: Live no longer as the Gentiles do, for
they are hopelessly confused. 18 Their minds are full of darkness; they wander
far from the life God gives because they have closed their minds and hard-
ened their hearts against him. 19 They have no sense of shame. They live for
lustful pleasure and eagerly practice every kind of impurity.

4:7 Greek *a grace.* 4:8 Ps 68:18. 4:9 Some manuscripts read *to the lower parts of the earth.*

[20]But that isn't what you learned about Christ. [21]Since you have heard
about Jesus and have learned the truth that comes from him, [22]throw off
your old sinful nature and your former way of life, which is corrupted by lust
and deception. [23]Instead, let the Spirit renew your thoughts and attitudes.
[24]Put on your new nature, created to be like God—truly righteous and holy.
[25]So stop telling lies. Let us tell our neighbors the truth, for we are all parts
of the same body. [26]And "don't sin by letting anger control you."* Don't let
the sun go down while you are still angry, [27]for anger gives a foothold to
the devil.
[28]If you are a thief, quit stealing. Instead, use your hands for good hard
work, and then give generously to others in need. [29]Don't use foul or abusive
language. Let everything you say be good and helpful, so that your words
will be an encouragement to those who hear them.
[30]And do not bring sorrow to God's Holy Spirit by the way you live. Re-
member, he has identified you as his own,* guaranteeing that you will be
saved on the day of redemption.
[31]Get rid of all bitterness, rage, anger, harsh words, and slander, as well
as all types of evil behavior. [32]Instead, be kind to each other, tenderhearted,
forgiving one another, just as God through Christ has forgiven you.

Living in the Light

5 Imitate God, therefore, in everything you do, because you are his dear
children. [2]Live a life filled with love, following the example of Christ. He
loved us* and offered himself as a sacrifice for us, a pleasing aroma to God.
[3]Let there be no sexual immorality, impurity, or greed among you. Such
sins have no place among God's people. [4]Obscene stories, foolish talk, and
coarse jokes—these are not for you. Instead, let there be thankfulness to
God. [5]You can be sure that no immoral, impure, or greedy person will in-
herit the Kingdom of Christ and of God. For a greedy person is an idolater,
worshiping the things of this world.
[6]Don't be fooled by those who try to excuse these sins, for the anger of
God will fall on all who disobey him. [7]Don't participate in the things these
people do. [8]For once you were full of darkness, but now you have light from
the Lord. So live as people of light! [9]For this light within you produces only
what is good and right and true.
[10]Carefully determine what pleases the Lord. [11]Take no part in the worth-
less deeds of evil and darkness; instead, expose them. [12]It is shameful even
to talk about the things that ungodly people do in secret. [13]But their evil
intentions will be exposed when the light shines on them, [14]for the light
makes everything visible. This is why it is said,

"Awake, O sleeper,
rise up from the dead,
and Christ will give you light."

Living by the Spirit's Power

[15]So be careful how you live. Don't live like fools, but like those who are
wise. [16]Make the most of every opportunity in these evil days. [17]Don't act
thoughtlessly, but understand what the Lord wants you to do. [18]Don't be

4:26 Ps 4:4. 4:30 Or *has put his seal on you.* 5:2 Some manuscripts read *loved you.*

In other words, the pastor's role is to equip everyone to work for Jesus.

Difference Maker

Pick one of these ministry tasks to accomplish today: visit someone who is sick, pray aloud before dinner, do a house project for an older person, or volunteer for a ministry role in church this weekend.

Make a Difference 5:1-2

Mimic

Imitating God is like the moment when a little boy, after watching his dad shaving in the mirror, puts shaving cream on his face, picks up a razor (with the cap still on, of course!), and begins to practice the strokes up and down his face. Every father who has experienced this moment can't help but smile.

When we imitate God, we watch God, and we learn to do what he does. When we follow his actions, his words, and his heart, we tend to put his movements into practice. In this way, when we mimic God, a smile spreads across his face, for we are becoming more and more like him.

Difference Maker

Think about your favorite characteristic of God. Then think of a way you can put that same characteristic into practical action today.

Prayer 5:15

Dear Jesus, first, let me seek to love you in everything I do. Second, let me seek to be a loving light for others in a darkened world. Give me creativity and discernment as to how to be a loving witness to my friends and neighbors today. Amen.

Prayer 5:20

Jesus, I can't do this on my own for very long before I get distracted and start to complain about something again. Please help me be saturated in who you are today so that I can learn to be truly thankful. Amen.

Question 6:1-3

What is the hardest thing for you about 6:1-3?

Question 6:10-18

After reading 6:10-18, draw every piece of armor described in these verses. As you think about this "armor" of God, which piece of armor is the strongest of your faith? Which is the weakest? What could you do to become even stronger to "stand firm" (v. 11) and "resist the enemy" (v. 13)?

drunk with wine, because that will ruin your life. Instead, be filled with the
Holy Spirit, 19 singing psalms and hymns and spiritual songs among your-
selves, and making music to the Lord in your hearts. 20 And give thanks for
everything to God the Father in the name of our Lord Jesus Christ.

Spirit-Guided Relationships: Wives and Husbands

21 And further, submit to one another out of reverence for Christ.
22 For wives, this means submit to your husbands as to the Lord. 23 For a
husband is the head of his wife as Christ is the head of the church. He is the
Savior of his body, the church. 24 As the church submits to Christ, so you wives
should submit to your husbands in everything.
25 For husbands, this means love your wives, just as Christ loved the
church. He gave up his life for her 26 to make her holy and clean, washed
by the cleansing of God's word.* 27 He did this to present her to himself as a
glorious church without a spot or wrinkle or any other blemish. Instead, she
will be holy and without fault. 28 In the same way, husbands ought to love
their wives as they love their own bodies. For a man who loves his wife actu-
ally shows love for himself. 29 No one hates his own body but feeds and cares
for it, just as Christ cares for the church. 30 And we are members of his body.
31 As the Scriptures say, "A man leaves his father and mother and is joined
to his wife, and the two are united into one."* 32 This is a great mystery, but
it is an illustration of the way Christ and the church are one. 33 So again I say,
each man must love his wife as he loves himself, and the wife must respect
her husband.

Children and Parents

6 Children, obey your parents because you belong to the Lord,* for this
is the right thing to do. 2 "Honor your father and mother." This is the
first commandment with a promise: 3 If you honor your father and mother,
"things will go well for you, and you will have a long life on the earth."*
4 Fathers,* do not provoke your children to anger by the way you treat
them. Rather, bring them up with the discipline and instruction that comes
from the Lord.

Slaves and Masters

5 Slaves, obey your earthly masters with deep respect and fear. Serve them
sincerely as you would serve Christ. 6 Try to please them all the time, not just
when they are watching you. As slaves of Christ, do the will of God with all
your heart. 7 Work with enthusiasm, as though you were working for the
Lord rather than for people. 8 Remember that the Lord will reward each one
of us for the good we do, whether we are slaves or free.
9 Masters, treat your slaves in the same way. Don't threaten them; remem-
ber, you both have the same Master in heaven, and he has no favorites.

The Whole Armor of God

10 A final word: Be strong in the Lord and in his mighty power. 11 Put on all of
God's armor so that you will be able to stand firm against all strategies of the
devil. 12 For we* are not fighting against flesh-and-blood enemies, but against

5:26 Greek *washed by water with the word.* 5:31 Gen 2:24. 6:1 Or *Children, obey your parents who belong to the Lord;* some manuscripts read simply *Children, obey your parents.* 6:2-3 Exod 20:12; Deut 5:16. 6:4 Or *Parents.* 6:12 Some manuscripts read *you.*

evil rulers and authorities of the unseen world, against mighty powers in
this dark world, and against evil spirits in the heavenly places.
13 Therefore, put on every piece of God's armor so you will be able to resist
the enemy in the time of evil. Then after the battle you will still be standing
firm. 14 Stand your ground, putting on the belt of truth and the body armor of
God's righteousness. 15 For shoes, put on the peace that comes from the Good
News so that you will be fully prepared.* 16 In addition to all of these, hold
up the shield of faith to stop the fiery arrows of the devil.* 17 Put on salvation
as your helmet, and take the sword of the Spirit, which is the word of God.
18 Pray in the Spirit at all times and on every occasion. Stay alert and be
persistent in your prayers for all believers everywhere.*
19 And pray for me, too. Ask God to give me the right words so I can boldly
explain God's mysterious plan that the Good News is for Jews and Gentiles
alike.* 20 I am in chains now, still preaching this message as God's ambassador.
So pray that I will keep on speaking boldly for him, as I should.

Final Greetings

21 To bring you up to date, Tychicus will give you a full report about what I
am doing and how I am getting along. He is a beloved brother and faithful
helper in the Lord's work. 22 I have sent him to you for this very purpose—to
let you know how we are doing and to encourage you.
23 Peace be with you, dear brothers and sisters,* and may God the Father
and the Lord Jesus Christ give you love with faithfulness. 24 May God's grace
be eternally upon all who love our Lord Jesus Christ.

6:15 Or *For shoes, put on the readiness to preach the Good News of peace with God.* **6:16** Greek *the evil one.* **6:18** Greek *all of God's holy people.* **6:19** Greek *explain the mystery of the Good News;* some manuscripts read simply *explain the mystery.* **6:23** Greek *brothers.*

Philippians Introduction

If you were put in prison because of your faith in Jesus, what message would you write to some of your closest friends? This is exactly what had happened to Paul when he wrote this letter to his friends in Philippi. Paul was most likely in prison in Rome, waiting to go to court. He could even have been sentenced to death because he believed that Jesus is Lord instead of Caesar, the Roman ruler.

Therefore, Paul talked about real-life decisions of ultimate importance and how to make a difference by following the example of Jesus. One main message of this friendship letter is that the Philippians, like Jesus, would most likely suffer for their faith. Additionally, he called them to stay unified as they followed Christ.

Throughout this letter Paul shared how thankful he was for their partnership with him in sharing the good news about Jesus. Their city was geographically in a strategic place in the world at that time. Therefore, he called them to shine "like bright lights" (Philippians 2:15) as they put their faith in the true God, Jesus, so that they could influence the world travelers who found themselves in Philippi.

Paul, while in prison, asked his friends to live a life filled with joy, to pray continuously, and, especially, to focus on Jesus. Of the 104 verses of Philippians, Jesus is specifically mentioned in 51 of them!

Consider how it might have felt for the people in Philippi to read this letter. How would you have felt? What do you think surprised them? How do you think they acted after hearing from their dear friend during his time of suffering? What would you tell your friends in order to encourage them to make a difference for Christ in the world?

Story Arcs

- **Timothy**
- **Epaphroditus**

The Philippian Church Network

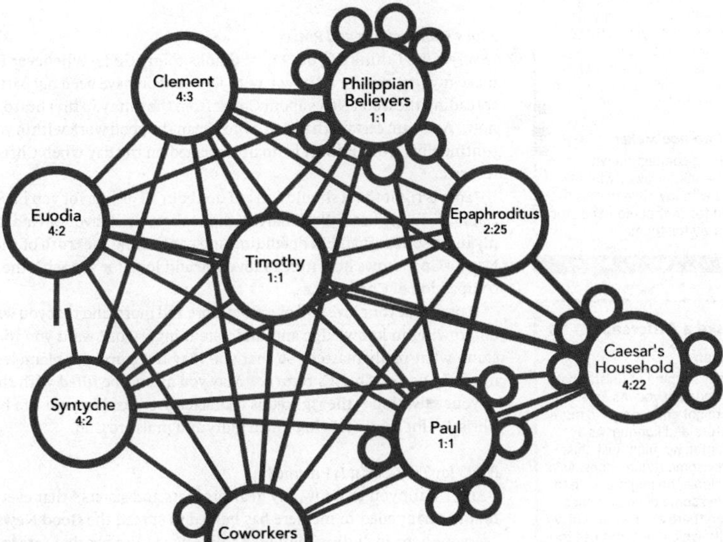

Philippians

Greetings from Paul

1 This letter is from Paul and Timothy, slaves of Christ Jesus.
I am writing to all of God's holy people in Philippi who belong to
Christ Jesus, including the church leaders* and deacons.
2 May God our Father and the Lord Jesus Christ give you grace and peace.

Paul's Thanksgiving and Prayer

3 Every time I think of you, I give thanks to my God. 4 Whenever I pray, I
make my requests for all of you with joy, 5 for you have been my partners in
spreading the Good News about Christ from the time you first heard it until
now. 6 And I am certain that God, who began the good work within you, will
continue his work until it is finally finished on the day when Christ Jesus
returns.
7 So it is right that I should feel as I do about all of you, for you have a spe-
cial place in my heart. You share with me the special favor of God, both in
my imprisonment and in defending and confirming the truth of the Good
News. 8 God knows how much I love you and long for you with the tender
compassion of Christ Jesus.
9 I pray that your love will overflow more and more, and that you will keep
on growing in knowledge and understanding. 10 For I want you to under-
stand what really matters, so that you may live pure and blameless lives
until the day of Christ's return. 11 May you always be filled with the fruit
of your salvation—the righteous character produced in your life by Jesus
Christ*—for this will bring much glory and praise to God.

Paul's Joy That Christ Is Preached

12 And I want you to know, my dear brothers and sisters,* that everything
that has happened to me here has helped to spread the Good News. 13 For
everyone here, including the whole palace guard,* knows that I am in chains
because of Christ. 14 And because of my imprisonment, most of the believers*
here have gained confidence and boldly speak God's message* without fear.
15 It's true that some are preaching out of jealousy and rivalry. But others
preach about Christ with pure motives. 16 They preach because they love
me, for they know I have been appointed to defend the Good News. 17 Those
others do not have pure motives as they preach about Christ. They preach
with selfish ambition, not sincerely, intending to make my chains more
painful to me. 18 But that doesn't matter. Whether their motives are false or
genuine, the message about Christ is being preached either way, so I rejoice.
And I will continue to rejoice. 19 For I know that as you pray for me and the
Spirit of Jesus Christ helps me, this will lead to my deliverance.

1:1 Or *overseers,* or *bishops.* **1:11** Greek *with the fruit of righteousness through Jesus Christ.* **1:12** Greek *brothers.* **1:13** Greek *including all the Praetorium.* **1:14a** Greek *brothers in the Lord.* **1:14b** Some manuscripts read *speak the message.*

Make a Difference 1:3-5

Think Thanks

When Paul wrote his letter to some friends in a city called Philippi, he couldn't help but gush all over the papyrus. He absolutely loved these fellow difference makers. Whenever he thought of his Philippian friends, Paul gave thanks to God.

Difference Maker

Make a connection with someone far away who fills you with joy. Give thanks to God for that person and stop to pray for them.

Make a Difference 1:6

Finish

Jesus is going to finish what he began in you. As an artist, he might choose to add more texture and lighting. As a sculptor, he might just chisel away some rough edges. As a gardener, he might decide to prune some dead branches. Then there are his carpentry skills, which he might use to measure and cut and hammer and sand for a while—sometimes a long while. Whatever he needs to do, he is going to continue creating in you until he is finished with his work. He won't give up until he can step back and look at all he has made and say, "Very good!"

Difference Maker

Think of a project that has been hanging over your head. Move it toward completion today.

Paul's Life for Christ

[20]For I fully expect and hope that I will never be ashamed, but that I will
continue to be bold for Christ, as I have been in the past. And I trust that my
life will bring honor to Christ, whether I live or die. [21]For to me, living means
living for Christ, and dying is even better. [22]But if I live, I can do more fruitful
work for Christ. So I really don't know which is better. [23]I'm torn between
two desires: I long to go and be with Christ, which would be far better for
me. [24]But for your sakes, it is better that I continue to live.
[25]Knowing this, I am convinced that I will remain alive so I can continue
to help all of you grow and experience the joy of your faith. [26]And when I
come to you again, you will have even more reason to take pride in Christ
Jesus because of what he is doing through me.

Live as Citizens of Heaven

[27]Above all, you must live as citizens of heaven, conducting yourselves in a
manner worthy of the Good News about Christ. Then, whether I come and
see you again or only hear about you, I will know that you are standing to-
gether with one spirit and one purpose, fighting together for the faith, which
is the Good News. [28]Don't be intimidated in any way by your enemies. This
will be a sign to them that they are going to be destroyed, but that you are
going to be saved, even by God himself. [29]For you have been given not only
the privilege of trusting in Christ but also the privilege of suffering for him.
[30]We are in this struggle together. You have seen my struggle in the past, and
you know that I am still in the midst of it.

Have the Attitude of Christ

2 Is there any encouragement from belonging to Christ? Any comfort
from his love? Any fellowship together in the Spirit? Are your hearts
tender and compassionate? [2]Then make me truly happy by agreeing whole-
heartedly with each other, loving one another, and working together with
one mind and purpose.
[3]Don't be selfish; don't try to impress others. Be humble, thinking of
others as better than yourselves. [4]Don't look out only for your own interests,
but take an interest in others, too.
[5]You must have the same attitude that Christ Jesus had.

6 Though he was God,*
he did not think of equality with God
as something to cling to.
7 Instead, he gave up his divine privileges*;
he took the humble position of a slave*
and was born as a human being.
When he appeared in human form,*
8 he humbled himself in obedience to God
and died a criminal's death on a cross.

9 Therefore, God elevated him to the place of
highest honor
and gave him the name above all other names,

2:6 Or *Being in the form of God.* **2:7a** Greek *he emptied himself.* **2:7b** Or *the form of a slave.*
2:7c Some English translations put this phrase in verse 8.

Question 2:3

If the choice is between saving his own life or saving yours, Jesus would save yours. In fact, that's exactly what he has already done. He gave himself up on your behalf. What is the proper response to this astonishing truth? (Hint: see verses 5 and 10-11.)

Make a Difference 2:5-11

Jesus Gave Up

To say that Jesus gave up is alarming, but it is also true. Jesus had everything. As the Creator, he owned everything—he was in charge of everything—but then he simply gave up everything. He gave himself up so that we can capture him. He surrendered his greatness so that we can embrace him. He let down his power so that we can enclose around him. Because we were unable to see him in all his brilliant glory, he chose to lay aside his power so that we can know him personally once again.

Jesus doesn't ask us to do anything that he is unwilling to do himself. Rather, he asks us to follow his example, to do what he does, and to be reflections of his attitude and actions on the earth today. He loves others so much that he willingly gave himself up so they—and we—could have life.

Difference Maker

What will you give up today that is more about you than God?

10 that at the name of Jesus every knee should bow,
in heaven and on earth and under the earth,
11 and every tongue declare that Jesus Christ is Lord,
to the glory of God the Father.

Shine Brightly for Christ

12 Dear friends, you always followed my instructions when I was with you.
And now that I am away, it is even more important. Work hard to show the
results of your salvation, obeying God with deep reverence and fear. 13 For
God is working in you, giving you the desire and the power to do what
pleases him.

14 Do everything without complaining and arguing, 15 so that no one can
criticize you. Live clean, innocent lives as children of God, shining like bright
lights in a world full of crooked and perverse people. 16 Hold firmly to the
word of life; then, on the day of Christ's return, I will be proud that I did not
run the race in vain and that my work was not useless. 17 But I will rejoice even
if I lose my life, pouring it out like a liquid offering to God,* just like your
faithful service is an offering to God. And I want all of you to share that joy.
18 Yes, you should rejoice, and I will share your joy.

Paul Commends Timothy

19 If the Lord Jesus is willing, I hope to send Timothy to you soon for a visit.
Then he can cheer me up by telling me how you are getting along. 20 I have
no one else like Timothy, who genuinely cares about your welfare. 21 All the
others care only for themselves and not for what matters to Jesus Christ.
22 But you know how Timothy has proved himself. Like a son with his father,
he has served with me in preaching the Good News. 23 I hope to send him to
you just as soon as I find out what is going to happen to me here. 24 And I have
confidence from the Lord that I myself will come to see you soon.

Paul Commends Epaphroditus

25 Meanwhile, I thought I should send Epaphroditus back to you. He is a true
brother, co-worker, and fellow soldier. And he was your messenger to help
me in my need. 26 I am sending him because he has been longing to see you,
and he was very distressed that you heard he was ill. 27 And he certainly was
ill; in fact, he almost died. But God had mercy on him—and also on me, so
that I would not have one sorrow after another.

28 So I am all the more anxious to send him back to you, for I know you will
be glad to see him, and then I will not be so worried about you. 29 Welcome
him in the Lord's love* and with great joy, and give him the honor that people
like him deserve. 30 For he risked his life for the work of Christ, and he was at
the point of death while doing for me what you couldn't do from far away.

The Priceless Value of Knowing Christ

3 Whatever happens, my dear brothers and sisters,* rejoice in the Lord.
I never get tired of telling you these things, and I do it to safeguard
your faith.

2 Watch out for those dogs, those people who do evil, those mutilators who
say you must be circumcised to be saved. 3 For we who worship by the Spirit

2:17 Greek *I will rejoice even if I am to be poured out as a liquid offering.* 2:29 Greek *in the Lord.*
3:1 Greek *brothers;* also in 3:13, 17.

Story Arc 2:19-23

● Timothy

There are two books of the Bible with Timothy's name on them. Search through the New Testament and learn more about this amazing companion of Paul.

Story Arc 2:25-30

● Epaphroditus

Epaphroditus was one of Paul's most encouraging champions of the faith. Epaphroditus probably delivered this letter to Philippi for Paul. To discover more about him, read Philippians 2:25-30 and 4:18.

Col 1:7-8 ►

of God* are the ones who are truly circumcised. We rely on what Christ Jesus
has done for us. We put no confidence in human effort, 4though I could have
confidence in my own effort if anyone could. Indeed, if others have reason
for confidence in their own efforts, I have even more!

5I was circumcised when I was eight days old. I am a pure-blooded citizen
of Israel and a member of the tribe of Benjamin—a real Hebrew if there ever
was one! I was a member of the Pharisees, who demand the strictest obedi-
ence to the Jewish law. 6I was so zealous that I harshly persecuted the church.
And as for righteousness, I obeyed the law without fault.

7I once thought these things were valuable, but now I consider them
worthless because of what Christ has done. 8Yes, everything else is worthless
when compared with the infinite value of knowing Christ Jesus my Lord. For
his sake I have discarded everything else, counting it all as garbage, so that I
could gain Christ 9and become one with him. I no longer count on my own
righteousness through obeying the law; rather, I become righteous through
faith in Christ.* For God's way of making us right with himself depends on
faith. 10I want to know Christ and experience the mighty power that raised
him from the dead. I want to suffer with him, sharing in his death, 11so that
one way or another I will experience the resurrection from the dead!

Pressing toward the Goal

12I don't mean to say that I have already achieved these things or that I have
already reached perfection. But I press on to possess that perfection for which
Christ Jesus first possessed me. 13No, dear brothers and sisters, I have not
achieved it,* but I focus on this one thing: Forgetting the past and looking
forward to what lies ahead, 14I press on to reach the end of the race and re-
ceive the heavenly prize for which God, through Christ Jesus, is calling us.

15Let all who are spiritually mature agree on these things. If you disagree
on some point, I believe God will make it plain to you. 16But we must hold
on to the progress we have already made.

17Dear brothers and sisters, pattern your lives after mine, and learn from
those who follow our example. 18For I have told you often before, and I say it
again with tears in my eyes, that there are many whose conduct shows they
are really enemies of the cross of Christ. 19They are headed for destruction.
Their god is their appetite, they brag about shameful things, and they think
only about this life here on earth. 20But we are citizens of heaven, where the
Lord Jesus Christ lives. And we are eagerly waiting for him to return as our
Savior. 21He will take our weak mortal bodies and change them into glorious
bodies like his own, using the same power with which he will bring every-
thing under his control.

4 Therefore, my dear brothers and sisters,* stay true to the Lord. I love
you and long to see you, dear friends, for you are my joy and the crown
I receive for my work.

Words of Encouragement

2Now I appeal to Euodia and Syntyche. Please, because you belong to the
Lord, settle your disagreement. 3And I ask you, my true partner,* to help

3:3 Some manuscripts read *worship God in spirit;* one early manuscript reads *worship in spirit.* 3:9 Or *through the faithfulness of Christ.* 3:13 Some manuscripts read *not yet achieved it.* 4:1 Greek *brothers;* also in 4:8. 4:3 Or *loyal Syzygus.*

Make a Difference

3:7-8

Skubala

You could call it "garbage" (v. 8). If you are British, perhaps you'd like to call it "rubbish." Literally, when he wrote it in Greek, the word the apostle Paul used was *skubala*. Dung. Excrement. Waste.

Paul had come to a point in his life where the things that he once held as most important he now considered *skubala*. All his ambitions and work, all his pride and achievements, were worth a pile of waste when compared to the surpassing greatness of knowing Jesus. Compared to knowing Jesus, everything else is *skubala*.

Difference Maker

The next time you go to the bathroom, think about those things that you've given more value in your life than Jesus and, in a manner of speaking, flush them down.

Question **3:20**

What if we were to invest our time and heart and energy into our local communities and schools and neighborhoods because Jesus wants us to be his ambassadors representing our true home in heaven? What if we began to long for our true home?

Make a Difference
4:6-7

Instead

Twist the intent of worry to your advantage. Every time apprehension hits your heart, take the opportunity to deflect it over to God. Use your anxiousness to help you trust Jesus more and more today. The more you worry, the more you can ask God for help. Don't forget to thank him when he lifts it off your shoulders.

Difference Maker

Commit these two verses to memory. Each time you grow anxious, pray and entrust it to Jesus.

Make a Difference **4:8**

Fix Your Thoughts

One of the benefits of knowing Jesus is that he is a great mechanic. If your thoughts are breaking down or need a tune-up, Jesus is your guy. He is honest and tells you clearly what's wrong. Then–and this is the really good part–he can take your broken thoughts and fix them, and he can fix them onto what is good.

Difference Maker

Stretch your mind for a moment. What are those things that you should fix your mind on? Write down at least five things you believe Jesus would like you to be thinking about today.

these two women, for they worked hard with me in telling others the Good
News. They worked along with Clement and the rest of my co-workers,
whose names are written in the Book of Life.
4 Always be full of joy in the Lord. I say it again—rejoice! 5 Let everyone see
that you are considerate in all you do. Remember, the Lord is coming soon.*
6 Don't worry about anything; instead, pray about everything. Tell God
what you need, and thank him for all he has done. 7 Then you will experi-
ence God's peace, which exceeds anything we can understand. His peace will
guard your hearts and minds as you live in Christ Jesus.
8 And now, dear brothers and sisters, one final thing. Fix your thoughts on
what is true, and honorable, and right, and pure, and lovely, and admirable.
Think about things that are excellent and worthy of praise. 9 Keep putting
into practice all you learned and received from me—everything you heard
from me and saw me doing. Then the God of peace will be with you.

Paul's Thanks for Their Gifts

10 How I praise the Lord that you are concerned about me again. I know you
have always been concerned for me, but you didn't have the chance to help
me. 11 Not that I was ever in need, for I have learned how to be content with
whatever I have. 12 I know how to live on almost nothing or with everything.
I have learned the secret of living in every situation, whether it is with a full
stomach or empty, with plenty or little. 13 For I can do everything through
Christ,* who gives me strength. 14 Even so, you have done well to share with
me in my present difficulty.
15 As you know, you Philippians were the only ones who gave me financial
help when I first brought you the Good News and then traveled on from
Macedonia. No other church did this. 16 Even when I was in Thessalonica you
sent help more than once. 17 I don't say this because I want a gift from you.
Rather, I want you to receive a reward for your kindness.
18 At the moment I have all I need—and more! I am generously supplied
with the gifts you sent me with Epaphroditus. They are a sweet-smelling
sacrifice that is acceptable and pleasing to God. 19 And this same God who
takes care of me will supply all your needs from his glorious riches, which
have been given to us in Christ Jesus.
20 Now all glory to God our Father forever and ever! Amen.

Paul's Final Greetings

21 Give my greetings to each of God's holy people—all who belong to Christ
Jesus. The brothers who are with me send you their greetings. 22 And all the
rest of God's people send you greetings, too, especially those in Caesar's
household.
23 May the grace of the Lord Jesus Christ be with your spirit.*

4:5 Greek *the Lord is near.* **4:13** Greek *through the one.* **4:23** Some manuscripts add *Amen.*

Colossians Introduction

Paul, being the difference maker he was, wrote this letter while in prison (Colossians 1:24–25). It was his preaching of the whole truth of the gospel that landed him in trouble. He wrote this letter to his friends in the city of Colosse to share a few goals: to encourage and pray for them, to combat false teachings, to clarify the truth of Christ, and to share the freedom of new life.

Paul loved to stress the supremacy of Christ. This is how Paul fought against so many of the nonsense ideas and empty philosophies blowing around in culture. There are no rules that can make you good enough, kind enough, or controlled enough to conquer the effects of sin. Paul wrote this letter to assure his friends, and you today, that "Christ is all that matters" (3:11).

Our relationship with Christ transforms our lives. Paul shared some of the signs of the new life Christ gives Christians. When Jesus lives in you, you keep your sights in the heavenly places, you get rid of sin, and you put on your new self. These signs have less to do with swearing off sin and have everything to do with Christ and the new life he gives you.

The truth of Christ and what he has done on your behalf should not remain in your mind but be expressed in your life. Only by being connected to Christ by faith can anyone have eternal life. Only through a continuing connection with him can anyone have power for living. The difference maker in you is found solely in the transforming power of being made new in Christ.

Story Arcs

- **Epaphras**
- **The Colossian Church Network**

Colossians

Make a Difference

1:3-6

Always Pray

Paul prayed perhaps more than he did anything else because he wanted so much to participate in what God and his friends were doing in the world.

Difference Maker

Use social media to your advantage today. Scroll through your contacts and stop to pray with thankfulness for people as God gets hold of your heart.

Question **1:15-20**

Colossians 1:15-20 is one of the clearest and boldest depictions of the deity of Christ in all the Bible. Read through these verses and stop at each line to consider the fullness of Christ. Which one stands out to you the most?

Story Arc **1:7-8**

● Epaphras

There are few people in the Bible spoken of as well as Epaphras. Take a moment to read about him in the following verses: 1:7-8 and 4:12-13 and verse 23 of Philemon. What set him apart?

Col 4:7-18 ►

Greetings from Paul

1 This letter is from Paul, chosen by the will of God to be an apostle of
Christ Jesus, and from our brother Timothy.
2 We are writing to God's holy people in the city of Colosse, who are faithful
brothers and sisters* in Christ.
May God our Father give you grace and peace.

Paul's Thanksgiving and Prayer

3 We always pray for you, and we give thanks to God, the Father of our Lord
Jesus Christ. 4 For we have heard of your faith in Christ Jesus and your love
for all of God's people, 5 which come from your confident hope of what God
has reserved for you in heaven. You have had this expectation ever since you
first heard the truth of the Good News.
6 This same Good News that came to you is going out all over the world.
It is bearing fruit everywhere by changing lives, just as it changed your
lives from the day you first heard and understood the truth about God's
wonderful grace.
7 You learned about the Good News from Epaphras, our beloved co-
worker. He is Christ's faithful servant, and he is helping us on your behalf.*
8 He has told us about the love for others that the Holy Spirit has given you.
9 So we have not stopped praying for you since we first heard about you. We
ask God to give you complete knowledge of his will and to give you spiritual
wisdom and understanding. 10 Then the way you live will always honor and
please the Lord, and your lives will produce every kind of good fruit. All the
while, you will grow as you learn to know God better and better.
11 We also pray that you will be strengthened with all his glorious power
so you will have all the endurance and patience you need. May you be filled
with joy,* 12 always thanking the Father. He has enabled you to share in the
inheritance that belongs to his people, who live in the light. 13 For he has
rescued us from the kingdom of darkness and transferred us into the King-
dom of his dear Son, 14 who purchased our freedom* and forgave our sins.

Christ Is Supreme

15 Christ is the visible image of the invisible God.
He existed before anything was created and is supreme over
all creation,*
16 for through him God created everything
in the heavenly realms and on earth.
He made the things we can see
and the things we can't see—

1:2 Greek *faithful brothers.* **1:7** Or *he is ministering on your behalf;* some manuscripts read *he is ministering on our behalf.* **1:11** Or *all the patience and endurance you need with joy.* **1:14** Some manuscripts add *with his blood.* **1:15** Or *He is the firstborn of all creation.*

such as thrones, kingdoms, rulers, and authorities in the unseen world.
Everything was created through him and for him.
17 He existed before anything else,
and he holds all creation together.
18 Christ is also the head of the church,
which is his body.
He is the beginning,
supreme over all who rise from the dead.*
So he is first in everything.
19 For God in all his fullness
was pleased to live in Christ,
20 and through him God reconciled
everything to himself.
He made peace with everything in heaven and on earth
by means of Christ's blood on the cross.

21 This includes you who were once far away from God. You were his en-
emies, separated from him by your evil thoughts and actions. 22 Yet now he
has reconciled you to himself through the death of Christ in his physical
body. As a result, he has brought you into his own presence, and you are holy
and blameless as you stand before him without a single fault.
23 But you must continue to believe this truth and stand firmly in it. Don't
drift away from the assurance you received when you heard the Good News.
The Good News has been preached all over the world, and I, Paul, have been
appointed as God's servant to proclaim it.

Paul's Work for the Church

24 I am glad when I suffer for you in my body, for I am participating in the
sufferings of Christ that continue for his body, the church. 25 God has given
me the responsibility of serving his church by proclaiming his entire mes-
sage to you. 26 This message was kept secret for centuries and generations
past, but now it has been revealed to God's people. 27 For God wanted them
to know that the riches and glory of Christ are for you Gentiles, too. And
this is the secret: Christ lives in you. This gives you assurance of sharing
his glory.
28 So we tell others about Christ, warning everyone and teaching every-
one with all the wisdom God has given us. We want to present them to God,
perfect* in their relationship to Christ. 29 That's why I work and struggle so
hard, depending on Christ's mighty power that works within me.

2 I want you to know how much I have agonized for you and for the
church at Laodicea, and for many other believers who have never met
me personally. 2 I want them to be encouraged and knit together by strong
ties of love. I want them to have complete confidence that they understand
God's mysterious plan, which is Christ himself. 3 In him lie hidden all the
treasures of wisdom and knowledge.
4 I am telling you this so no one will deceive you with well-crafted argu-
ments. 5 For though I am far away from you, my heart is with you. And I re-
joice that you are living as you should and that your faith in Christ is strong.

1:18 Or *the firstborn from the dead.* **1:28** Or *mature.*

Question 2:6

Would you like to do this? Turn to the back of this Bible and pray through the section on "How to Accept Jesus as Your Lord and Savior."

Make a Difference 2:7

Rooted

You've been told that you are supposed to be an adult. What a ridiculous pressure that is! Society is already too full of grown-ups. Many of them are ungrounded and more childish than the most tantrum-crazed kids. "Mine!" or "I need this!" or "I deserve this!" are common mantras for today's adults.

People who keep adding other things to their lives in pursuit of fulfillment are never satisfied. That's why the Bible suggests a different way to grow: down in Jesus. Root yourself in him. Build your life in him. Draw from him all the nourishment you'll need for each day. Then overflow with gratitude for his abundance within you.

Difference Maker

What have you added to your life that doesn't fit with a life rooted in Jesus?

Prayer 3:1–4

God, help me to get my head out of the gutters of this earth and focus my thoughts on the things of heaven today. Amen.

Make a Difference

3:8–15

Laundry

Keep your faith fresh. Don't put on lazy-heart clothes with stained grudges,

Freedom from Rules and New Life in Christ

6 And now, just as you accepted Christ Jesus as your Lord, you must continue
to follow him. 7 Let your roots grow down into him, and let your lives be built
on him. Then your faith will grow strong in the truth you were taught, and
you will overflow with thankfulness.
8 Don't let anyone capture you with empty philosophies and high-
sounding nonsense that come from human thinking and from the spiritual
powers* of this world, rather than from Christ. 9 For in Christ lives all the
fullness of God in a human body.* 10 So you also are complete through your
union with Christ, who is the head over every ruler and authority.
11 When you came to Christ, you were "circumcised," but not by a physical
procedure. Christ performed a spiritual circumcision—the cutting away
of your sinful nature.* 12 For you were buried with Christ when you were
baptized. And with him you were raised to new life because you trusted the
mighty power of God, who raised Christ from the dead.
13 You were dead because of your sins and because your sinful nature was
not yet cut away. Then God made you alive with Christ, for he forgave all
our sins. 14 He canceled the record of the charges against us and took it away
by nailing it to the cross. 15 In this way, he disarmed* the spiritual rulers and
authorities. He shamed them publicly by his victory over them on the cross.
16 So don't let anyone condemn you for what you eat or drink, or for not
celebrating certain holy days or new moon ceremonies or Sabbaths. 17 For
these rules are only shadows of the reality yet to come. And Christ himself is
that reality. 18 Don't let anyone condemn you by insisting on pious self-denial
or the worship of angels,* saying they have had visions about these things.
Their sinful minds have made them proud, 19 and they are not connected to
Christ, the head of the body. For he holds the whole body together with its
joints and ligaments, and it grows as God nourishes it.
20 You have died with Christ, and he has set you free from the spiritual
powers of this world. So why do you keep on following the rules of the world,
such as, 21 "Don't handle! Don't taste! Don't touch!"? 22 Such rules are mere
human teachings about things that deteriorate as we use them. 23 These rules
may seem wise because they require strong devotion, pious self-denial, and
severe bodily discipline. But they provide no help in conquering a person's
evil desires.

Living the New Life

3 Since you have been raised to new life with Christ, set your sights on
the realities of heaven, where Christ sits in the place of honor at God's
right hand. 2 Think about the things of heaven, not the things of earth. 3 For
you died to this life, and your real life is hidden with Christ in God. 4 And
when Christ, who is your* life, is revealed to the whole world, you will share
in all his glory.
5 So put to death the sinful, earthly things lurking within you. Have noth-
ing to do with sexual immorality, impurity, lust, and evil desires. Don't be
greedy, for a greedy person is an idolater, worshiping the things of this
world. 6 Because of these sins, the anger of God is coming.* 7 You used to do

2:8 Or *the spiritual principles;* also in 2:20. 2:9 Or *in him dwells all the completeness of the Godhead bodily.* 2:11 Greek *the cutting away of the body of the flesh.* 2:15 Or *he stripped off.* 2:18 Or *or worshiping with angels.* 3:4 Some manuscripts read *our.* 3:6 Some manuscripts read *is coming on all who disobey him.*

these things when your life was still part of this world. 8But now is the time
to get rid of anger, rage, malicious behavior, slander, and dirty language.
9Don't lie to each other, for you have stripped off your old sinful nature
and all its wicked deeds. 10Put on your new nature, and be renewed as you
learn to know your Creator and become like him. 11In this new life, it doesn't
matter if you are a Jew or a Gentile,* circumcised or uncircumcised, barbaric,
uncivilized,* slave, or free. Christ is all that matters, and he lives in all of us.
12Since God chose you to be the holy people he loves, you must clothe
yourselves with tenderhearted mercy, kindness, humility, gentleness, and
patience. 13Make allowance for each other's faults, and forgive anyone who
offends you. Remember, the Lord forgave you, so you must forgive others.
14Above all, clothe yourselves with love, which binds us all together in perfect
harmony. 15And let the peace that comes from Christ rule in your hearts. For as
members of one body you are called to live in peace. And always be thankful.
16Let the message about Christ, in all its richness, fill your lives. Teach and
counsel each other with all the wisdom he gives. Sing psalms and hymns
and spiritual songs to God with thankful hearts. 17And whatever you do or
say, do it as a representative of the Lord Jesus, giving thanks through him
to God the Father.

Instructions for Christian Households

18Wives, submit to your husbands, as is fitting for those who belong to the
Lord.
19Husbands, love your wives and never treat them harshly.
20Children, always obey your parents, for this pleases the Lord. 21Fathers,
do not aggravate your children, or they will become discouraged.
22Slaves, obey your earthly masters in everything you do. Try to please
them all the time, not just when they are watching you. Serve them sincerely
because of your reverent fear of the Lord. 23Work willingly at whatever you
do, as though you were working for the Lord rather than for people. 24Re-
member that the Lord will give you an inheritance as your reward, and that
the Master you are serving is Christ.* 25But if you do what is wrong, you will
be paid back for the wrong you have done. For God has no favorites.

4 Masters, be just and fair to your slaves. Remember that you also have a
Master—in heaven.

An Encouragement for Prayer

2Devote yourselves to prayer with an alert mind and a thankful heart. 3Pray
for us, too, that God will give us many opportunities to speak about his mys-
terious plan concerning Christ. That is why I am here in chains. 4Pray that I
will proclaim this message as clearly as I should.
5Live wisely among those who are not believers, and make the most of
every opportunity. 6Let your conversation be gracious and attractive* so that
you will have the right response for everyone.

Paul's Final Instructions and Greetings

7Tychicus will give you a full report about how I am getting along. He is a
beloved brother and faithful helper who serves with me in the Lord's work.

3:11a Greek *a Greek.* **3:11b** Greek *Barbarian, Scythian.* **3:24** Or *and serve Christ as your Master.* **4:6** Greek *and seasoned with salt.*

a nasty chip on your shoulder, and frayed emotions on your sleeves. Strip off any of your old, stinky perspectives and, instead, put on a fresh outlook, washed in Jesus Christ. When you wake up in the morning, the first thing you should do is cover yourself with the Holy Spirit. Then, piece by piece, put on the character and love of your Savior. Those around you will thank you.

Difference Maker

Do your laundry. Take a shower. Brush your teeth. Put on fresh clothes. When someone asks you why you smell so good, tell them it's because of Jesus. Then see what happens.

Make a Difference

4:2-4

Paced

When people are paced by prayer, they develop a growing sense of gratitude because they become increasingly aware of all Jesus is doing. Prayer forms an alert mind and cultivates a thankful heart. It provides wisdom for decisions, reassurance for apprehension, strength for trials, and unity with God's plans.

This is one of the reasons Jesus prayed so much. He surprised people by how often he retreated from busy moments to spend time with the Father. At the height of his popularity, he withdrew from the crowds and spent time in prayer. In the midst of his darkest moments, he prayed. When alone and tempted, he prayed. Before gathering with others, he prayed. His life was paced by prayer, not hectic activity.

Difference Maker

At least twice today, set aside time to pray.

[8]I have sent him to you for this very purpose—to let you know how we are
doing and to encourage you. [9]I am also sending Onesimus, a faithful and
beloved brother, one of your own people. He and Tychicus will tell you every-
thing that's happening here.
[10]Aristarchus, who is in prison with me, sends you his greetings, and so
does Mark, Barnabas's cousin. As you were instructed before, make Mark
welcome if he comes your way. [11]Jesus (the one we call Justus) also sends his
greetings. These are the only Jewish believers among my co-workers; they
are working with me here for the Kingdom of God. And what a comfort
they have been!
[12]Epaphras, a member of your own fellowship and a servant of Christ
Jesus, sends you his greetings. He always prays earnestly for you, asking God
to make you strong and perfect, fully confident that you are following the
whole will of God. [13]I can assure you that he prays hard for you and also for
the believers in Laodicea and Hierapolis.
[14]Luke, the beloved doctor, sends his greetings, and so does Demas.
[15]Please give my greetings to our brothers and sisters* at Laodicea, and to
Nympha and the church that meets in her house.
[16]After you have read this letter, pass it on to the church at Laodicea so they
can read it, too. And you should read the letter I wrote to them.
[17]And say to Archippus, "Be sure to carry out the ministry the Lord gave
you."
[18]HERE IS MY GREETING IN MY OWN HANDWRITING—PAUL.
Remember my chains.
May God's grace be with you.

4:15 Greek *brothers.*

Story Arc 4:7-18

The Colossian Church Network

True Christian ministry involves not a few but all followers of Jesus. Each person works in concert to use their gifts and calling to pursue God and to share him with the world. The true church, therefore, is one in which the body of Christ works in unity through the unique equipping of every person. The letter that Paul wrote to the church in Colosse is a great example of the partnership nature of true ministry.

In total, Colossians mentions twelve people by name, along with multiple house groups and churches in multiple cities. Even though we are tempted to lift up Paul as a super-apostle, Paul didn't believe in a lone-ranger or "hero" approach to ministry. He practiced an every-person, hub-networked, coworker concept.

Are you a part of a mission-minded network like this? You need to be!

The early churches were made up of people woven together into networks of Jesus followers. Go back through this book to see the unique people mentioned and consider how they got involved in God's world-changing movement.

1 Thes 3:1-13 ▶

The Colossian Church Network

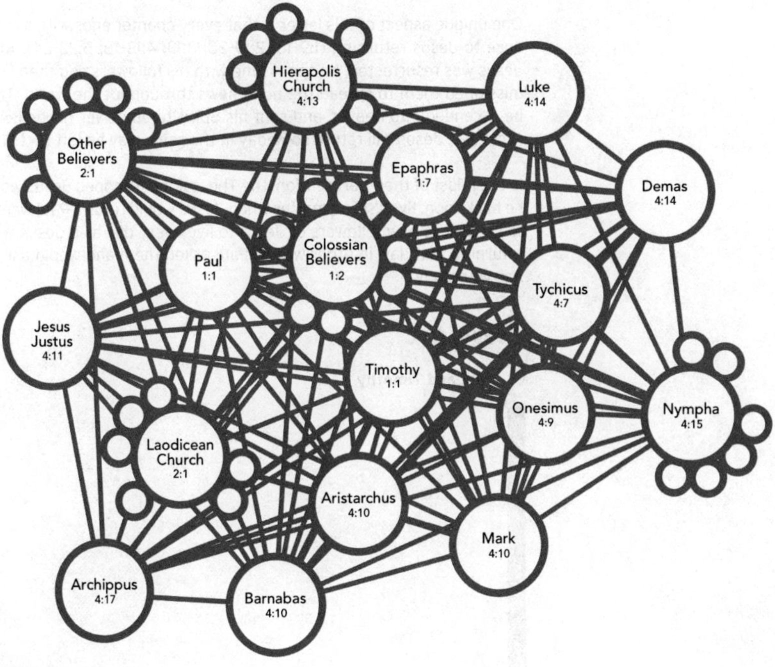

1 Thessalonians Introduction

Paul was on the move. He had to leave Thessalonica quickly (Acts 17:5-10) after a rather short stay in this area. Those who had become followers of Jesus while he was there did not have a lot of support, and they began to be persecuted (1 Thessalonians 1:6).

Paul's purpose in writing this letter was to encourage these new followers of Jesus. It was a difficult letter to write. Without Paul, the Thessalonians faced lots of difficulty in their town (3:3-5). Paul, therefore, wanted to coach them to live for Jesus (4:1-12) and to give them courage even in the face of death (4:13-18).

One unique aspect of this letter is that every chapter ends with a reference to Jesus returning (1:9-10; 2:19-20; 3:13; 4:13-18; 5:23-24). After Jesus was resurrected, he spent time with his followers and then commissioned them to spread the good news throughout the world. Then he ascended into heaven and sent his Spirit to empower his believers (Acts 1-2). Jesus will return someday in the same way he left (Acts 1:11).

In the midst of their persecution, the Thessalonians hoped Jesus would be back soon. Even so, no matter when Jesus would return, Paul wanted to help these new followers of Jesus to live every day as if Jesus were returning that day. In other words, Paul asked them and would ask us: Are you ready?

Story Arc

Paul and Timothy

The 1 Thessalonians Church Network

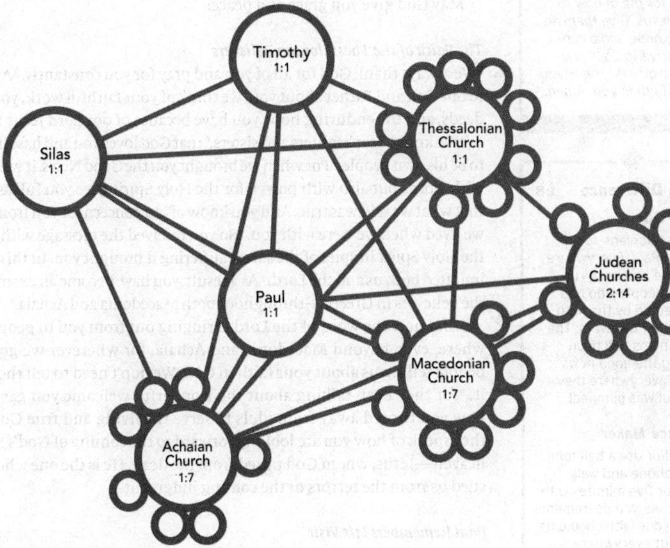

1 Thessalonians

Greetings from Paul

1 This letter is from Paul, Silas,* and Timothy.
We are writing to the church in Thessalonica, to you who belong to
God the Father and the Lord Jesus Christ.
May God give you grace and peace.

The Faith of the Thessalonian Believers

2 We always thank God for all of you and pray for you constantly. 3 As we pray
to our God and Father about you, we think of your faithful work, your loving
deeds, and the enduring hope you have because of our Lord Jesus Christ.
4 We know, dear brothers and sisters,* that God loves you and has chosen you
to be his own people. 5 For when we brought you the Good News, it was not only
with words but also with power, for the Holy Spirit gave you full assurance*
that what we said was true. And you know of our concern for you from the way
we lived when we were with you. 6 So you received the message with joy from
the Holy Spirit in spite of the severe suffering it brought you. In this way, you
imitated both us and the Lord. 7 As a result, you have become an example to all
the believers in Greece—throughout both Macedonia and Achaia.*
8 And now the word of the Lord is ringing out from you to people every-
where, even beyond Macedonia and Achaia, for wherever we go we find
people telling us about your faith in God. We don't need to tell them about
it, 9 for they keep talking about the wonderful welcome you gave us and
how you turned away from idols to serve the living and true God. 10 And
they speak of how you are looking forward to the coming of God's Son from
heaven—Jesus, whom God raised from the dead. He is the one who has res-
cued us from the terrors of the coming judgment.

Paul Remembers His Visit

2 You yourselves know, dear brothers and sisters,* that our visit to you
was not a failure. 2 You know how badly we had been treated at Phi-
lippi just before we came to you and how much we suffered there. Yet our
God gave us the courage to declare his Good News to you boldly, in spite of
great opposition. 3 So you can see we were not preaching with any deceit or
impure motives or trickery.
4 For we speak as messengers approved by God to be entrusted with the
Good News. Our purpose is to please God, not people. He alone examines
the motives of our hearts. 5 Never once did we try to win you with flattery,
as you well know. And God is our witness that we were not pretending to
be your friends just to get your money! 6 As for human praise, we have never
sought it from you or anyone else.

Prayer 1:2

Lord, I am so thankful for the people in my life who set an example for me of how to live for Jesus. Give them an enduring hope and a continuing drive to do loving things for others. Thank you for their faith in you. Amen.

Make a Difference 1:8

Ringing Out

The Thessalonians so encouraged Paul. Everywhere he went he had been running into people who had been affected by the faith of these new believers. The Thessalonians had been spreading the good news of Jesus everywhere they went. Paul was pumped!

Difference Maker

Get a bell or use a bell tone on your phone and walk around for five minutes with it ringing. As you do, remember that your faith should be ringing out everywhere you go.

Question 2:5–6

If the message of Jesus is true, should you need to do anything special (like use flattery) when you share it?

1:1 Greek *Silvanus,* the Greek form of the name. 1:4 Greek *brothers.* 1:5 Or *with the power of the Holy Spirit, so you can have full assurance.* 1:7 *Macedonia* and *Achaia* were the northern and southern regions of Greece. 2:1 Greek *brothers;* also in 2:9, 14, 17.

7 As apostles of Christ we certainly had a right to make some demands of
you, but instead we were like children* among you. Or we were like a mother
feeding and caring for her own children. 8 We loved you so much that we
shared with you not only God's Good News but our own lives, too.
9 Don't you remember, dear brothers and sisters, how hard we worked
among you? Night and day we toiled to earn a living so that we would not be
a burden to any of you as we preached God's Good News to you. 10 You your-
selves are our witnesses—and so is God—that we were devout and honest
and faultless toward all of you believers. 11 And you know that we treated each
of you as a father treats his own children. 12 We pleaded with you, encour-
aged you, and urged you to live your lives in a way that God would consider
worthy. For he called you to share in his Kingdom and glory.
13 Therefore, we never stop thanking God that when you received his mes-
sage from us, you didn't think of our words as mere human ideas. You ac-
cepted what we said as the very word of God—which, of course, it is. And
this word continues to work in you who believe.
14 And then, dear brothers and sisters, you suffered persecution from your
own countrymen. In this way, you imitated the believers in God's churches
in Judea who, because of their belief in Christ Jesus, suffered from their own
people, the Jews. 15 For some of the Jews killed the prophets, and some even
killed the Lord Jesus. Now they have persecuted us, too. They fail to please
God and work against all humanity 16 as they try to keep us from preaching
the Good News of salvation to the Gentiles. By doing this, they continue
to pile up their sins. But the anger of God has caught up with them at last.

Timothy's Good Report about the Church

17 Dear brothers and sisters, after we were separated from you for a little while
(though our hearts never left you), we tried very hard to come back because
of our intense longing to see you again. 18 We wanted very much to come to
you, and I, Paul, tried again and again, but Satan prevented us. 19 After all,
what gives us hope and joy, and what will be our proud reward and crown
as we stand before our Lord Jesus when he returns? It is you! 20 Yes, you are
our pride and joy.

3 Finally, when we could stand it no longer, we decided to stay alone
in Athens, 2 and we sent Timothy to visit you. He is our brother and
God's co-worker* in proclaiming the Good News of Christ. We sent him to
strengthen you, to encourage you in your faith, 3 and to keep you from being
shaken by the troubles you were going through. But you know that we are
destined for such troubles. 4 Even while we were with you, we warned you
that troubles would soon come—and they did, as you well know. 5 That is
why, when I could bear it no longer, I sent Timothy to find out whether your
faith was still strong. I was afraid that the tempter had gotten the best of you
and that our work had been useless.
6 But now Timothy has just returned, bringing us good news about your
faith and love. He reports that you always remember our visit with joy and that
you want to see us as much as we want to see you. 7 So we have been greatly en-
couraged in the midst of our troubles and suffering, dear brothers and sisters,*

2:7 Some manuscripts read *we were gentle.* 3:2 Other manuscripts read *and God's servant;* still others read *and a co-worker,* or *and a servant and co-worker for God,* or *and God's servant and our co-worker.* 3:7 Greek *brothers.*

Question **2:13**

If the message of Jesus was simply a bunch of human ideas, would it last? What difference does it make that the good news of Jesus would be the very Word of God?

Story Arc **3:1-13**

Paul and Timothy

Paul trusted Timothy to run some pretty big errands for him. In this situation, Paul sent Timothy to Thessalonica while he stayed in Athens. Paul wanted to hear about how they were doing as people grew hostile to Christianity in their town, so Paul sent Timothy right into the middle of the trouble to find out if their faith was still strong. What range of emotions must Paul have felt when Timothy returned with his update?

1 Tim 3:1-13 ►

because you have remained strong in your faith. 8It gives us new life to know
that you are standing firm in the Lord.
9How we thank God for you! Because of you we have great joy as we enter
God's presence. 10Night and day we pray earnestly for you, asking God to let
us see you again to fill the gaps in your faith.
11May God our Father and our Lord Jesus bring us to you very soon. 12And
may the Lord make your love for one another and for all people grow and
overflow, just as our love for you overflows. 13May he, as a result, make your
hearts strong, blameless, and holy as you stand before God our Father when
our Lord Jesus comes again with all his holy people. Amen.

Live to Please God

4 Finally, dear brothers and sisters,* we urge you in the name of the Lord
Jesus to live in a way that pleases God, as we have taught you. You live
this way already, and we encourage you to do so even more. 2For you remem-
ber what we taught you by the authority of the Lord Jesus.
3God's will is for you to be holy, so stay away from all sexual sin. 4Then
each of you will control his own body* and live in holiness and honor—5not
in lustful passion like the pagans who do not know God and his ways. 6Never
harm or cheat a fellow believer in this matter by violating his wife,* for the
Lord avenges all such sins, as we have solemnly warned you before. 7God has
called us to live holy lives, not impure lives. 8Therefore, anyone who refuses
to live by these rules is not disobeying human teaching but is rejecting God,
who gives his Holy Spirit to you.
9But we don't need to write to you about the importance of loving each
other,* for God himself has taught you to love one another. 10Indeed, you
already show your love for all the believers* throughout Macedonia. Even
so, dear brothers and sisters, we urge you to love them even more.
11Make it your goal to live a quiet life, minding your own business and
working with your hands, just as we instructed you before. 12Then people
who are not believers will respect the way you live, and you will not need
to depend on others.

The Hope of the Resurrection

13And now, dear brothers and sisters, we want you to know what will happen
to the believers who have died* so you will not grieve like people who have
no hope. 14For since we believe that Jesus died and was raised to life again,
we also believe that when Jesus returns, God will bring back with him the
believers who have died.
15We tell you this directly from the Lord: We who are still living when the
Lord returns will not meet him ahead of those who have died.* 16For the Lord
himself will come down from heaven with a commanding shout, with the
voice of the archangel, and with the trumpet call of God. First, the believers
who have died* will rise from their graves. 17Then, together with them, we
who are still alive and remain on the earth will be caught up in the clouds to
meet the Lord in the air. Then we will be with the Lord forever. 18So encour-
age each other with these words.

4:1 Greek *brothers;* also in 4:10, 13. 4:4 Or *will know how to take a wife for himself;* or *will learn to live with his own wife;* Greek reads *will know how to possess his own vessel.* 4:6 Greek *Never harm or cheat a brother in this matter.* 4:9 Greek *about brotherly love.* 4:10 Greek *the brothers.* 4:13 Greek *those who have fallen asleep;* also in 4:14. 4:15 Greek *those who have fallen asleep.* 4:16 Greek *the dead in Christ.*

Prayer 3:12–13

Lord Jesus, I don't know how, but give me the mind and heart to live these verses out today. Amen.

Make a Difference

4:9–10

Others Focused

The first person on our mind in the morning is often ourselves, and the last person in our thoughts at the end of each night is often ourselves too. The primary person we're concerned about throughout the events of each day is often ourselves. Do you see a pattern here?

Do you want to change the world? Then try to think less about yourself and more about others. Consider what a friend is thinking about. Put yourself in your parents' shoes. Look at a situation through a hurting person's eyes. You see, Jesus calls us to be others focused. He doesn't want us to be so self-absorbed that we miss what is happening in the lives of our friends and family. He created us to be like him and to follow his example. Because he loves others and gave himself up for others, so should we.

Difference Maker

Pick an important person in your life and, before you do anything else, call them or text them with a note of encouragement.

5 Now concerning how and when all this will happen, dear brothers and
sisters,* we don't really need to write you. 2For you know quite well that
the day of the Lord's return will come unexpectedly, like a thief in the night.
3When people are saying, "Everything is peaceful and secure," then disaster
will fall on them as suddenly as a pregnant woman's labor pains begin. And
there will be no escape.
4But you aren't in the dark about these things, dear brothers and sisters,
and you won't be surprised when the day of the Lord comes like a thief.* 5For
you are all children of the light and of the day; we don't belong to darkness
and night. 6So be on your guard, not asleep like the others. Stay alert and be
clearheaded. 7Night is the time when people sleep and drinkers get drunk.
8But let us who live in the light be clearheaded, protected by the armor of
faith and love, and wearing as our helmet the confidence of our salvation.
9For God chose to save us through our Lord Jesus Christ, not to pour out
his anger on us. 10Christ died for us so that, whether we are dead or alive
when he returns, we can live with him forever. 11So encourage each other
and build each other up, just as you are already doing.

Paul's Final Advice

12Dear brothers and sisters, honor those who are your leaders in the Lord's
work. They work hard among you and give you spiritual guidance. 13Show
them great respect and wholehearted love because of their work. And live
peacefully with each other.
14Brothers and sisters, we urge you to warn those who are lazy. Encour-
age those who are timid. Take tender care of those who are weak. Be patient
with everyone.
15See that no one pays back evil for evil, but always try to do good to each
other and to all people.
16Always be joyful. 17Never stop praying. 18Be thankful in all circum-
stances, for this is God's will for you who belong to Christ Jesus.
19Do not stifle the Holy Spirit. 20Do not scoff at prophecies, 21but test
everything that is said. Hold on to what is good. 22Stay away from every
kind of evil.

Paul's Final Greetings

23Now may the God of peace make you holy in every way, and may your
whole spirit and soul and body be kept blameless until our Lord Jesus Christ
comes again. 24God will make this happen, for he who calls you is faithful.
25Dear brothers and sisters, pray for us.
26Greet all the brothers and sisters with a sacred kiss.
27I command you in the name of the Lord to read this letter to all the
brothers and sisters.
28May the grace of our Lord Jesus Christ be with you.

5:1 Greek *brothers;* also in 5:4, 12, 14, 25, 26, 27. 5:4 Some manuscripts read *comes upon you as if you were thieves.*

Prayer **5:14**

Lord Jesus, let me be more like you today by noticing the feelings and needs of others. Push me to do things for others that will give them encouragement and hope. Amen.

Make a Difference

5:16-18

Impossible Instructions?

Two thousand years ago, the apostle Paul said we should "always be joyful" and "never stop praying" (vv. 16-17). He also said that God's people should always "be thankful," no matter what they were going through (v. 18).

Are these instructions practical? Is it realistic to think that anyone could truly do these things? If life absolutely stinks (absolutely, repulsively, horribly stinks), is it possible to "be thankful in all circumstances" (v. 18)? Are these instructions from Paul just pleasant "Christianese" phrases similar to "keep your chin up" or "it'll all be okay"?

These must be more than just empty commands. Perhaps in our fallen human strength, these are impossible, but in the power of Jesus, there is potential to live these out. In Jesus, people can be captured by joy, be caught up in conversation with God, and be overwhelmed to overflowing with his grace.

Difference Maker

Pick one of the three instructions in verses 16-18 and write it on your hand to remind yourself throughout the day what Jesus wants within you.

2 Thessalonians Introduction

Like his first letter to the church in a city called Thessalonica, Paul tried to encourage the followers of Jesus there. These Christians were being persecuted for their faith in Jesus, but they were also getting confused about some of the details of their faith. Paul had to be gentle and caring, but he also had to be bold and direct. Paul had to correct some misunderstandings concerning when Jesus would return for the second time (2 Thessalonians 2:1–12), and he needed to offer encouragement to the church to keep living for Jesus in the meantime (2:13–15).

This letter is a personal one. Paul was so proud of this group of believers. He knew them. He missed them. He prayed for them. He was inspired by them. As a result, he challenged them because he believed they could endure in the truth of Jesus Christ.

No matter what you are facing today, read this letter through Paul's heart. Imagine him writing these words in his own handwriting (3:17) and pouring his heart out with each phrase. Let these words encourage you to live boldly for Jesus, strong and resilient in your faith.

The 2 Thessalonians Church Network

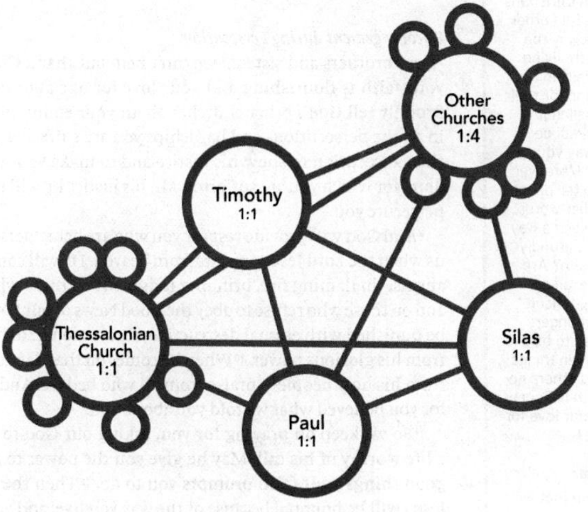

2 Thessalonians

Make a Difference

1:3-4

Are You Inspiring?

The Thessalonian Christians inspired Paul. He told other people about the way the Thessalonians were living for Jesus, especially in the face of persecution for their faith. Here's a challenging question: Would Paul be inspired by the way you are living your faith? Moreover, would he want to tell people about you? In other words, are you living in such a way that people would proudly talk about your faith? Are you an inspiring example for others during difficult times? Would a younger person be inspired to be like you, especially when things get tough? Would others notice that your faith is flourishing and that your love for people is evident?

Difference Maker

Do something bold that will help your faith to flourish today.

Prayer 1:12

Lord, help me to honor you in the way I live. Help me to glorify you with my life. Help me to receive your grace and give your grace to others. Amen.

Greetings from Paul

1 This letter is from Paul, Silas,* and Timothy.
We are writing to the church in Thessalonica, to you who belong to
God our Father and the Lord Jesus Christ.
2 May God our Father* and the Lord Jesus Christ give you grace and peace.

Encouragement during Persecution

3 Dear brothers and sisters,* we can't help but thank God for you, because
your faith is flourishing and your love for one another is growing. 4 We
proudly tell God's other churches about your endurance and faithfulness
in all the persecutions and hardships you are suffering. 5 And God will use
this persecution to show his justice and to make you worthy of his King-
dom, for which you are suffering. 6 In his justice he will pay back those who
persecute you.
7 And God will provide rest for you who are being persecuted and also for
us when the Lord Jesus appears from heaven. He will come with his mighty
angels, 8 in flaming fire, bringing judgment on those who don't know God
and on those who refuse to obey the Good News of our Lord Jesus. 9 They will
be punished with eternal destruction, forever separated from the Lord and
from his glorious power. 10 When he comes on that day, he will receive glory
from his holy people—praise from all who believe. And this includes you,
for you believed what we told you about him.
11 So we keep on praying for you, asking our God to enable you to live
a life worthy of his call. May he give you the power to accomplish all the
good things your faith prompts you to do. 12 Then the name of our Lord
Jesus will be honored because of the way you live, and you will be honored
along with him. This is all made possible because of the grace of our God
and Lord, Jesus Christ.*

Events prior to the Lord's Second Coming

2 Now, dear brothers and sisters,* let us clarify some things about the
coming of our Lord Jesus Christ and how we will be gathered to meet
him. 2 Don't be so easily shaken or alarmed by those who say that the day of
the Lord has already begun. Don't believe them, even if they claim to have
had a spiritual vision, a revelation, or a letter supposedly from us. 3 Don't
be fooled by what they say. For that day will not come until there is a great
rebellion against God and the man of lawlessness* is revealed—the one who
brings destruction.* 4 He will exalt himself and defy everything that people
call god and every object of worship. He will even sit in the temple of God,
claiming that he himself is God.

1:1 Greek *Silvanus,* the Greek form of the name. **1:2** Some manuscripts read *God the Father.* **1:3** Greek *Brothers.* **1:12** Or *of our God and our Lord Jesus Christ.* **2:1** Greek *brothers;* also in 2:13, 15. **2:3a** Some manuscripts read *the man of sin.* **2:3b** Greek *the son of destruction.*

5 Don't you remember that I told you about all this when I was with you? 6 And you know what is holding him back, for he can be revealed only when his time comes. 7 For this lawlessness is already at work secretly, and it will remain secret until the one who is holding it back steps out of the way. 8 Then the man of lawlessness will be revealed, but the Lord Jesus will slay him with the breath of his mouth and destroy him by the splendor of his coming.

9 This man will come to do the work of Satan with counterfeit power and signs and miracles. 10 He will use every kind of evil deception to fool those on their way to destruction, because they refuse to love and accept the truth that would save them. 11 So God will cause them to be greatly deceived, and they will believe these lies. 12 Then they will be condemned for enjoying evil rather than believing the truth.

Believers Should Stand Firm

13 As for us, we can't help but thank God for you, dear brothers and sisters loved by the Lord. We are always thankful that God chose you to be among the first* to experience salvation—a salvation that came through the Spirit who makes you holy and through your belief in the truth. 14 He called you to salvation when we told you the Good News; now you can share in the glory of our Lord Jesus Christ.

15 With all these things in mind, dear brothers and sisters, stand firm and keep a strong grip on the teaching we passed on to you both in person and by letter.

16 Now may our Lord Jesus Christ himself and God our Father, who loved us and by his grace gave us eternal comfort and a wonderful hope, 17 comfort you and strengthen you in every good thing you do and say.

Paul's Request for Prayer

3 Finally, dear brothers and sisters,* we ask you to pray for us. Pray that the Lord's message will spread rapidly and be honored wherever it goes, just as when it came to you. 2 Pray, too, that we will be rescued from wicked and evil people, for not everyone is a believer. 3 But the Lord is faithful; he will strengthen you and guard you from the evil one.* 4 And we are confident in the Lord that you are doing and will continue to do the things we commanded you. 5 May the Lord lead your hearts into a full understanding and expression of the love of God and the patient endurance that comes from Christ.

An Exhortation to Proper Living

6 And now, dear brothers and sisters, we give you this command in the name of our Lord Jesus Christ: Stay away from all believers* who live idle lives and don't follow the tradition they received* from us. 7 For you know that you ought to imitate us. We were not idle when we were with you. 8 We never accepted food from anyone without paying for it. We worked hard day and night so we would not be a burden to any of you. 9 We certainly had the right to ask you to feed us, but we wanted to give you an example to follow. 10 Even while we were with you, we gave you this command: "Those unwilling to work will not get to eat."

11 Yet we hear that some of you are living idle lives, refusing to work and

2:13 Some manuscripts read *chose you from the very beginning.* 3:1 Greek *brothers;* also in 3:6, 13. 3:3 Or *from evil.* 3:6a Greek *from every brother.* 3:6b Some manuscripts read *you received.*

Prayer **2:15**

Lord, give me the strength to stand firm in you and hold fast to what you teach in the Bible. Help me not to stray away from what you have taught me today. Amen.

Make a Difference

3:1–2

Ask for Prayer

Paul believed in prayer. He asked this church in Thessalonica to pray for him as he shared with others about the life, death, and resurrection of Jesus. He knew that God needed to open hearts and minds to listen to who Jesus really was, and he longed for the Thessalonian Christians to lift him to God in prayer.

Difference Maker

Reach out right now and ask someone to pray for you to have open doors, the right words, and opportunities to share about Jesus with others.

Question 3:13

What would it look like for you to never get tired of doing good? Think through your plans for tomorrow and consider how your day might look different if you never got tired of doing good.

Question 3:16

Because you know Jesus wants to always give you peace, what could you do to pause and rest in the peace he is giving you today?

meddling in other people's business. 12We command such people and urge
them in the name of the Lord Jesus Christ to settle down and work to earn
their own living. 13As for the rest of you, dear brothers and sisters, never get
tired of doing good.

14Take note of those who refuse to obey what we say in this letter. Stay
away from them so they will be ashamed. 15Don't think of them as enemies,
but warn them as you would a brother or sister.*

Paul's Final Greetings

16Now may the Lord of peace himself give you his peace at all times and in
every situation. The Lord be with you all.

17HERE IS MY GREETING IN MY OWN HANDWRITING—PAUL. I DO THIS IN
ALL MY LETTERS TO PROVE THEY ARE FROM ME.

18May the grace of our Lord Jesus Christ be with you all.

3:15 Greek *as a brother.*

1 Timothy Introduction

The book of 1 Timothy is the first of three Pastoral Letters. Alongside 2 Timothy and Titus, this section of the Bible is concerned with helping Christians work out their faith practically, particularly as they do life together in the church. When we buy some flat-packed furniture, we get an instruction manual to help us build the product properly. When a coach leads practice for his team, he is carrying his playbook in his hands. First Timothy is a pastoral playbook, an instruction manual to help this new community live faithfully and fruitfully in the world.

As new groups of people were assembling in Christian communities, pastors and elders needed help and guidance from Jesus' first followers, the apostles. First Timothy is a set of guidance notes the experienced Pastor Paul, the apostle, shared with his young apprentice pastor, Timothy. This letter includes wisdom for choosing the right people to lead churches, advice for navigating false teaching and false teachers, and some helpful directions for leading worship services.

While this letter was written from one pastor to another, it contains helpful lessons for all Christians for all time. As you read these six chapters, look out for practical takeaways for your journey with Jesus. First Timothy can teach us about prayer, handling money, and showing respect to older people. It will also inspire us to be bold and courageous in our faith and to worship Jesus as King of kings and Lord of lords.

Story Arc

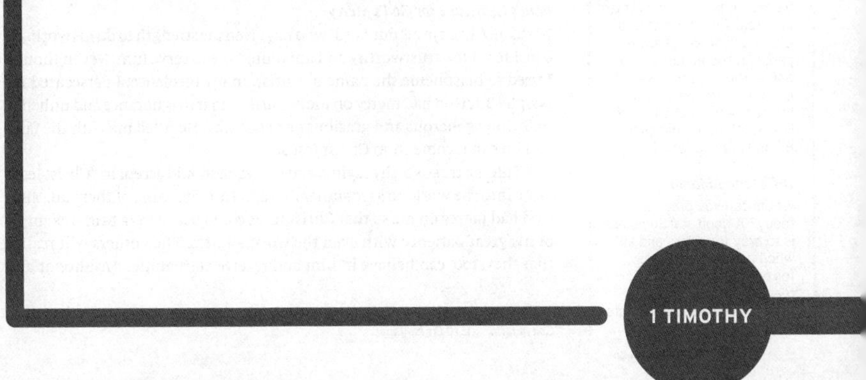

1 Timothy

Greetings from Paul

1 This letter is from Paul, an apostle of Christ Jesus, appointed by the com-
mand of God our Savior and Christ Jesus, who gives us hope.
2 I am writing to Timothy, my true son in the faith.
May God the Father and Christ Jesus our Lord give you grace, mercy, and
peace.

Warnings against False Teachings

3 When I left for Macedonia, I urged you to stay there in Ephesus and stop
those whose teaching is contrary to the truth. 4 Don't let them waste their
time in endless discussion of myths and spiritual pedigrees. These things
only lead to meaningless speculations,* which don't help people live a life
of faith in God.*
5 The purpose of my instruction is that all believers would be filled with
love that comes from a pure heart, a clear conscience, and genuine faith. 6 But
some people have missed this whole point. They have turned away from
these things and spend their time in meaningless discussions. 7 They want
to be known as teachers of the law of Moses, but they don't know what they
are talking about, even though they speak so confidently.
8 We know that the law is good when used correctly. 9 For the law was not
intended for people who do what is right. It is for people who are lawless
and rebellious, who are ungodly and sinful, who consider nothing sacred
and defile what is holy, who kill their father or mother or commit other
murders. 10 The law is for people who are sexually immoral, or who practice
homosexuality, or are slave traders,* liars, promise breakers, or who do any-
thing else that contradicts the wholesome teaching 11 that comes from the
glorious Good News entrusted to me by our blessed God.

Paul's Gratitude for God's Mercy

12 I thank Christ Jesus our Lord, who has given me strength to do his work. He
considered me trustworthy and appointed me to serve him, 13 even though
I used to blaspheme the name of Christ. In my insolence, I persecuted his
people. But God had mercy on me because I did it in ignorance and unbelief.
14 Oh, how generous and gracious our Lord was! He filled me with the faith
and love that come from Christ Jesus.
15 This is a trustworthy saying, and everyone should accept it: "Christ Jesus
came into the world to save sinners"—and I am the worst of them all. 16 But
God had mercy on me so that Christ Jesus could use me as a prime example
of his great patience with even the worst sinners. Then others will realize
that they, too, can believe in him and receive eternal life. 17 All honor and

1:4a Greek *in myths and endless genealogies, which cause speculation.* 1:4b Greek *a stewardship of God in faith.* 1:10 Or *kidnappers.*

Question **1:5**

What was Paul's purpose in writing this letter to Timothy? Who in your life provides this kind of instruction for you?

Prayer **1:17**

Dear God, all honor and glory are yours forever and ever. You are the eternal King, the unseen one who never dies. You alone are God! Amen.

Make a Difference

2:1-4

Pray like It Matters Because It Does

You can make a difference right now! In fact, according to 2:1-4, you can change the world today. When we pray, not only is God pleased, but he is also moved, and he responds to our prayers. Paul told Timothy that God is in the business of saving people through Jesus, and one of the ways that we get in on the action is by bowing our hearts, bending our knees, lifting our hands (v. 8), and praying for all people.

Difference Maker

Whom can you pray for today? A good starting place is to pray for rulers and all who have authority. Pray for politicians and pray for teachers at your school. Pray for your church leaders

glory to God forever and ever! He is the eternal King, the unseen one who
never dies; he alone is God. Amen.

Timothy's Responsibility

18 Timothy, my son, here are my instructions for you, based on the prophetic
words spoken about you earlier. May they help you fight well in the Lord's
battles. 19 Cling to your faith in Christ, and keep your conscience clear. For
some people have deliberately violated their consciences; as a result, their
faith has been shipwrecked. 20 Hymenaeus and Alexander are two examples.
I threw them out and handed them over to Satan so they might learn not
to blaspheme God.

Instructions about Worship

2 I urge you, first of all, to pray for all people. Ask God to help them;
intercede on their behalf, and give thanks for them. 2 Pray this way for
kings and all who are in authority so that we can live peaceful and quiet
lives marked by godliness and dignity. 3 This is good and pleases God our
Savior, 4 who wants everyone to be saved and to understand the truth. 5 For,

> There is one God and one Mediator who can reconcile God and
> humanity—the man Christ Jesus. 6 He gave his life to purchase freedom
> for everyone.

This is the message God gave to the world at just the right time. 7 And I have
been chosen as a preacher and apostle to teach the Gentiles this message
about faith and truth. I'm not exaggerating—just telling the truth.

8 In every place of worship, I want men to pray with holy hands lifted up
to God, free from anger and controversy.

9 And I want women to be modest in their appearance.* They should wear
decent and appropriate clothing and not draw attention to themselves by
the way they fix their hair or by wearing gold or pearls or expensive clothes.
10 For women who claim to be devoted to God should make themselves at-
tractive by the good things they do.

11 Women should learn quietly and submissively. 12 I do not let women
teach men or have authority over them.* Let them listen quietly. 13 For God
made Adam first, and afterward he made Eve. 14 And it was not Adam who
was deceived by Satan. The woman was deceived, and sin was the result.
15 But women will be saved through childbearing,* assuming they continue
to live in faith, love, holiness, and modesty.

Leaders in the Church

3 This is a trustworthy saying: "If someone aspires to be a church leader,*
he desires an honorable position." 2 So a church leader must be a man
whose life is above reproach. He must be faithful to his wife.* He must ex-
ercise self-control, live wisely, and have a good reputation. He must enjoy
having guests in his home, and he must be able to teach. 3 He must not be a
heavy drinker* or be violent. He must be gentle, not quarrelsome, and not

2:9 Or *to pray in modest apparel.* 2:12 Or *teach men or usurp their authority.* 2:15 Or *will be saved by accepting their role as mothers,* or *will be saved by the birth of the Child.* 3:1 Or *an overseer,* or *a bishop;* also in 3:2, 6. 3:2 Or *must have only one wife,* or *must be married only once;* Greek reads *must be the husband of one wife;* also in 3:12. 3:3 Greek *must not drink too much wine;* similarly in 3:8.

and pray for your parents or guardians. You can make a difference today. It is as simple as lifting your hands and beginning with the words "Dear God, I pray for…"

Question 2:5-6

This is one of the most important truths about Jesus. If you were to explain what this means, what would you say?

Question 3:2

Could someone describe you this way: as above reproach?

Story Arc 3:1-13

● Timothy

Pastor Paul was trying to teach Pastor Timothy that, when it comes to being a leader in the movement of Jesus, it is less about what you can do, your gifts and talents and personality, and more about the person you are now and the person you are becoming in Christ. It is about character! Take some time to reflect on the passage in 3:1-13, where the apostle sets out the qualifications for leaders in the Christian community. Let these descriptions serve as a job description and ask the Holy Spirit to show you things that God might want to do in your life to shape you as a leader.

2 Tim 1:3-5 ►

love money. 4 He must manage his own family well, having children who
respect and obey him. 5 For if a man cannot manage his own household, how
can he take care of God's church?
6 A church leader must not be a new believer, because he might become
proud, and the devil would cause him to fall.* 7 Also, people outside the
church must speak well of him so that he will not be disgraced and fall into
the devil's trap.
8 In the same way, deacons must be well respected and have integrity. They
must not be heavy drinkers or dishonest with money. 9 They must be com-
mitted to the mystery of the faith now revealed and must live with a clear
conscience. 10 Before they are appointed as deacons, let them be closely ex-
amined. If they pass the test, then let them serve as deacons.
11 In the same way, their wives* must be respected and must not slander
others. They must exercise self-control and be faithful in everything they do.
12 A deacon must be faithful to his wife, and he must manage his chil-
dren and household well. 13 Those who do well as deacons will be rewarded
with respect from others and will have increased confidence in their faith
in Christ Jesus.

The Truths of Our Faith

14 I am writing these things to you now, even though I hope to be with you
soon, 15 so that if I am delayed, you will know how people must conduct
themselves in the household of God. This is the church of the living God,
which is the pillar and foundation of the truth.
16 Without question, this is the great mystery of our faith*:

Christ* was revealed in a human body
 and vindicated by the Spirit.*
He was seen by angels
 and announced to the nations.
He was believed in throughout the world
 and taken to heaven in glory.

Warnings against False Teachers

4 Now the Holy Spirit tells us clearly that in the last times some will turn
away from the true faith; they will follow deceptive spirits and teachings
that come from demons. 2 These people are hypocrites and liars, and their
consciences are dead.*
3 They will say it is wrong to be married and wrong to eat certain foods.
But God created those foods to be eaten with thanks by faithful people who
know the truth. 4 Since everything God created is good, we should not reject
any of it but receive it with thanks. 5 For we know it is made acceptable* by
the word of God and prayer.

A Good Servant of Christ Jesus

6 If you explain these things to the brothers and sisters,* Timothy, you will
be a worthy servant of Christ Jesus, one who is nourished by the message of

Make a Difference

4:6–10

Train Hard, Play Harder

The apostle Paul loved to use metaphors from the gym when he wrote his letters. Athletes train hard so that they can play hard. In New Testament times, sports and athletics were central to culture, a lot like today. The gym in Ephesus was a center for learning and creating (arts, theater, etc.) and also training.

Being a Christian is similar to being an athlete. We need to be in training, getting ready for whatever event comes next, whether that is a wrestling match, an endurance race, or a chariot ride. Practice and training are an important part of preparation.

For the Christian, our most important resource, making us stronger and equipping us, is God's Word. You are already making a difference today by choosing to dig into the Bible. It is making you stronger for the life of faith. It is good to train your body in the gym, but it is even better to train your soul in God's truth.

Difference Maker

Get down on the floor right now and do some push-ups or sit-ups. As you do, repeat these athletic metaphors to yourself again and again.

3:6 Or *he might fall into the same judgment as the devil.* **3:11** Or *the women deacons.* The Greek word can be translated *women* or *wives.* **3:16a** Or *of godliness.* **3:16b** Greek *He who;* other manuscripts read *God.* **3:16c** Or *in his spirit.* **4:2** Greek *are seared.* **4:5** Or *made holy.* **4:6** Greek *brothers.*

faith and the good teaching you have followed. [7]Do not waste time arguing over godless ideas and old wives' tales. Instead, train yourself to be godly. [8]"Physical training is good, but training for godliness is much better, promising benefits in this life and in the life to come." [9]This is a trustworthy saying, and everyone should accept it. [10]This is why we work hard and continue to struggle,* for our hope is in the living God, who is the Savior of all people and particularly of all believers.

[11]Teach these things and insist that everyone learn them. [12]Don't let anyone think less of you because you are young. Be an example to all believers in what you say, in the way you live, in your love, your faith, and your purity. [13]Until I get there, focus on reading the Scriptures to the church, encouraging the believers, and teaching them.

[14]Do not neglect the spiritual gift you received through the prophecy spoken over you when the elders of the church laid their hands on you. [15]Give your complete attention to these matters. Throw yourself into your tasks so that everyone will see your progress. [16]Keep a close watch on how you live and on your teaching. Stay true to what is right for the sake of your own salvation and the salvation of those who hear you.

Advice about Widows, Elders, and Slaves

5 Never speak harshly to an older man,* but appeal to him respectfully as you would to your own father. Talk to younger men as you would to your own brothers. [2]Treat older women as you would your mother, and treat younger women with all purity as you would your own sisters.

[3]Take care of* any widow who has no one else to care for her. [4]But if she has children or grandchildren, their first responsibility is to show godliness at home and repay their parents by taking care of them. This is something that pleases God.

[5]Now a true widow, a woman who is truly alone in this world, has placed her hope in God. She prays night and day, asking God for his help. [6]But the widow who lives only for pleasure is spiritually dead even while she lives. [7]Give these instructions to the church so that no one will be open to criticism.

[8]But those who won't care for their relatives, especially those in their own household, have denied the true faith. Such people are worse than unbelievers.

[9]A widow who is put on the list for support must be a woman who is at least sixty years old and was faithful to her husband.* [10]She must be well respected by everyone because of the good she has done. Has she brought up her children well? Has she been kind to strangers and served other believers humbly?* Has she helped those who are in trouble? Has she always been ready to do good?

[11]The younger widows should not be on the list, because their physical desires will overpower their devotion to Christ and they will want to remarry. [12]Then they would be guilty of breaking their previous pledge. [13]And if they are on the list, they will learn to be lazy and will spend their time gossiping from house to house, meddling in other people's business and talking about things they shouldn't. [14]So I advise these younger widows to marry again, have children, and take care of their own homes. Then the enemy will not be

Make a Difference

4:12–15

Countercultural

Jesus has called you to be a radical person. He wants to empower you to stand rooted in him against the winds of a culture that tries to make everybody look the same. Too many people conform to the patterns of this world, giving in to pursuits that are not good for them. Jesus wants you to be an example of a more audacious path.

The apostle Paul told a young leader this very same thing a long time ago. While culture expected Timothy to conform, Paul challenged him to rise to the occasion and make a difference with the people around him.

Difference Maker

What kind of a role model could you be for those around you? What could you do as an example of countercultural living that would encourage others to make the right decisions too?

Question **4:16**

On a scale of one (loose) to ten (tight), how well do you keep a watch on the truthfulness of your behavior?

4:10 Some manuscripts read *continue to suffer.* **5:1** Or *an elder.* **5:3** Or *Honor.* **5:9** Greek *was the wife of one husband.* **5:10** Greek *and washed the feet of God's holy people?*

Question **5:25**

Does this verse concern you? Why or why not?

able to say anything against them. 15 For I am afraid that some of them have already gone astray and now follow Satan.

16 If a woman who is a believer has relatives who are widows, she must take care of them and not put the responsibility on the church. Then the church can care for the widows who are truly alone.

17 Elders who do their work well should be respected and paid well,* especially those who work hard at both preaching and teaching. 18 For the Scripture says, "You must not muzzle an ox to keep it from eating as it treads out the grain." And in another place, "Those who work deserve their pay!"*

19 Do not listen to an accusation against an elder unless it is confirmed by two or three witnesses. 20 Those who sin should be reprimanded in front of the whole church; this will serve as a strong warning to others.

21 I solemnly command you in the presence of God and Christ Jesus and the highest angels to obey these instructions without taking sides or showing favoritism to anyone.

22 Never be in a hurry about appointing a church leader.* Do not share in the sins of others. Keep yourself pure.

23 Don't drink only water. You ought to drink a little wine for the sake of your stomach because you are sick so often.

24 Remember, the sins of some people are obvious, leading them to certain judgment. But there are others whose sins will not be revealed until later. 25 In the same way, the good deeds of some people are obvious. And the good deeds done in secret will someday come to light.

6 All slaves should show full respect for their masters so they will not bring shame on the name of God and his teaching. 2 If the masters are believers, that is no excuse for being disrespectful. Those slaves should work all the harder because their efforts are helping other believers* who are well loved.

False Teaching and True Riches

Teach these things, Timothy, and encourage everyone to obey them. 3 Some people may contradict our teaching, but these are the wholesome teachings of the Lord Jesus Christ. These teachings promote a godly life. 4 Anyone who teaches something different is arrogant and lacks understanding. Such a person has an unhealthy desire to quibble over the meaning of words. This stirs up arguments ending in jealousy, division, slander, and evil suspicions. 5 These people always cause trouble. Their minds are corrupt, and they have turned their backs on the truth. To them, a show of godliness is just a way to become wealthy.

6 Yet true godliness with contentment is itself great wealth. 7 After all, we brought nothing with us when we came into the world, and we can't take anything with us when we leave it. 8 So if we have enough food and clothing, let us be content.

9 But people who long to be rich fall into temptation and are trapped by many foolish and harmful desires that plunge them into ruin and destruction. 10 For the love of money is the root of all kinds of evil. And some people, craving money, have wandered from the true faith and pierced themselves with many sorrows.

5:17 Greek *should be worthy of double honor.* 5:18 Deut 25:4; Luke 10:7. 5:22 Greek *about the laying on of hands.* 6:2 Greek *brothers.*

Paul's Final Instructions

[11]But you, Timothy, are a man of God; so run from all these evil things. Pur-
sue righteousness and a godly life, along with faith, love, perseverance, and
gentleness. [12]Fight the good fight for the true faith. Hold tightly to the eter-
nal life to which God has called you, which you have declared so well before
many witnesses. [13]And I charge you before God, who gives life to all, and
before Christ Jesus, who gave a good testimony before Pontius Pilate, [14]that
you obey this command without wavering. Then no one can find fault with
you from now until our Lord Jesus Christ comes again. [15]For,

At just the right time Christ will be revealed from heaven by the blessed
and only almighty God, the King of all kings and Lord of all lords. [16]He
alone can never die, and he lives in light so brilliant that no human can
approach him. No human eye has ever seen him, nor ever will. All honor
and power to him forever! Amen.

[17]Teach those who are rich in this world not to be proud and not to trust
in their money, which is so unreliable. Their trust should be in God, who
richly gives us all we need for our enjoyment. [18]Tell them to use their money
to do good. They should be rich in good works and generous to those in
need, always being ready to share with others. [19]By doing this they will be
storing up their treasure as a good foundation for the future so that they
may experience true life.

[20]Timothy, guard what God has entrusted to you. Avoid godless, fool-
ish discussions with those who oppose you with their so-called knowledge.
[21]Some people have wandered from the faith by following such foolishness.
May God's grace be with you all.

Prayer **6:11**

Lord, help me run away from the love of money and stuff and instead move toward a life of serving you in faith, love, patience, and gentleness. Amen.

Make a Difference

6:11–12

The Good Fight

When you were a child, did adults tell you not to fight? Did you know that whoever told you that was wrong? You are supposed to fight at times. You aren't supposed to just let the world crumble around you. You are supposed to stand up for what is right and repel what harms the people of this planet. You are supposed to join in the struggle, the resistance movement, the revolution that refuses to allow evil to have its way.

You are supposed to pick up the weapons of Jesus' powerful grace and mercy and wield his enduring love. You may, at first, find that others are afraid to stand with you or afraid to understand why you take risks to represent Jesus. Despite their fear, hold tight to this calling and don't hesitate to call others to unite with you in the fight.

Difference Maker

Find other followers of Jesus and start a weekly prayer meeting for the revival of your community.

2 Timothy Introduction

The book of 2 Timothy is one of three Pastoral Letters. Alongside 1 Timothy and Titus, this section of the Bible is concerned with helping Christians stay connected to the good news about Jesus. Lots of organizations start out as one thing and then become something else. When this does not happen on purpose, it is called *mission drift*. For example, the YMCA, which is now a great place to take swimming lessons, go to a spin class, or get childcare, was actually set up to share the good news about Jesus with young men.

Every generation of Christians and every generation of the church is at risk of mission drift. Cultural forces are always pushing and pulling us and trying to get us to change direction. When the apostle Paul wrote this letter to Timothy, just one generation after the events of the New Testament Gospels, the local church was already at risk of drifting off course. This letter reminds readers about the mission of the local and global church. Our business is good news business!

In each of the four chapters of this letter, Paul reminded young Pastor Timothy of what it means to be a good news pastor in a good news church. Firstly, Timothy had to safeguard the gospel, making sure that nobody tried to change the message. Secondly, Paul reminded Timothy to suffer for the gospel. Thirdly, Paul reminded the church in Ephesus to continue in the gospel. That meant that they were to let the good news shape everything that they did and everything that they were. Finally, Paul instructed Timothy that the work to which he was called, to which we are all called, was to preach the gospel.

As you embark on this section of Scripture, get ready, for you are about to be called to action. If you hear the commanding officer King Jesus and follow him, you will make a difference!

Story Arc

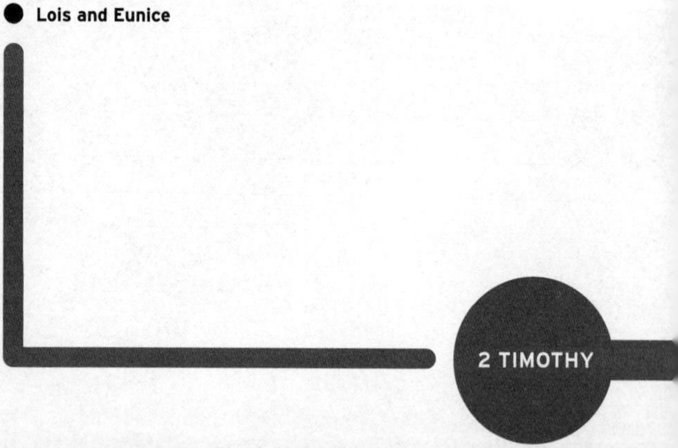

The 2 Timothy Church Network

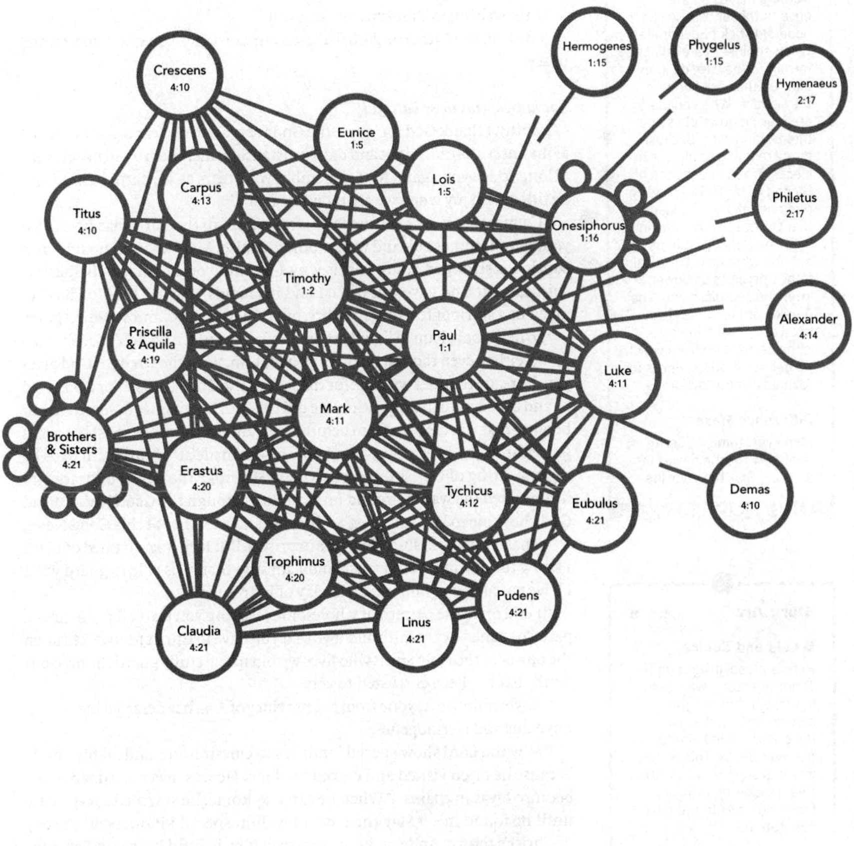

2 Timothy

Greetings from Paul

1 This letter is from Paul, chosen by the will of God to be an apostle of
Christ Jesus. I have been sent out to tell others about the life he has
promised through faith in Christ Jesus.
2 I am writing to Timothy, my dear son.
May God the Father and Christ Jesus our Lord give you grace, mercy, and
peace.

Encouragement to Be Faithful

3 Timothy, I thank God for you—the God I serve with a clear conscience, just
as my ancestors did. Night and day I constantly remember you in my prayers.
4 I long to see you again, for I remember your tears as we parted. And I will
be filled with joy when we are together again.
5 I remember your genuine faith, for you share the faith that first filled
your grandmother Lois and your mother, Eunice. And I know that same faith
continues strong in you. 6 This is why I remind you to fan into flames the
spiritual gift God gave you when I laid my hands on you. 7 For God has not
given us a spirit of fear and timidity, but of power, love, and self-discipline.
8 So never be ashamed to tell others about our Lord. And don't be ashamed
of me, either, even though I'm in prison for him. With the strength God gives
you, be ready to suffer with me for the sake of the Good News. 9 For God saved
us and called us to live a holy life. He did this, not because we deserved it, but
because that was his plan from before the beginning of time—to show us his
grace through Christ Jesus. 10 And now he has made all of this plain to us by
the appearing of Christ Jesus, our Savior. He broke the power of death and
illuminated the way to life and immortality through the Good News. 11 And
God chose me to be a preacher, an apostle, and a teacher of this Good News.
12 That is why I am suffering here in prison. But I am not ashamed of it, for
I know the one in whom I trust, and I am sure that he is able to guard what
I have entrusted to him* until the day of his return.
13 Hold on to the pattern of wholesome teaching you learned from me—a
pattern shaped by the faith and love that you have in Christ Jesus. 14 Through
the power of the Holy Spirit who lives within us, carefully guard the precious
truth that has been entrusted to you.
15 As you know, everyone from the province of Asia has deserted me—even
Phygelus and Hermogenes.
16 May the Lord show special kindness to Onesiphorus and all his family
because he often visited and encouraged me. He was never ashamed of me
because I was in chains. 17 When he came to Rome, he searched everywhere
until he found me. 18 May the Lord show him special kindness on the day
of Christ's return. And you know very well how helpful he was in Ephesus.

1:12 Or *what has been entrusted to me.*

Make a Difference 1:6–7

Turn Up the Heat

Nothing makes a difference to the landscape like a good old stick of dynamite! When engineers are leveling terrain for new roads, they blow up the rock beneath the surface. When builders are tearing down old structures, stand clear because they are going to blast it to pieces. When Paul began his second letter to Timothy, he reminded the young leader that God's Spirit resided in him. The Holy Spirit in us is not one who makes us afraid; rather, he gives us power, love, and self-discipline. The Greek word *dunamis*, translated as "power" in verse 7, is the same word from which we get our modern words for "dynamic" and "dynamite."

Difference Maker

Stop everything and pray right now for the power of the Holy Spirit in your life.

Story Arc 1:3–5

● Lois and Eunice

Here is a cool insight into Timothy's story. We learn in verse 5 that his grandmother and mother were the ones who led him to discover Jesus. This is the way it is supposed to work! One generation proclaims the good news to the next generation.

Titus 1:4 ►

A Good Soldier of Christ Jesus

2 Timothy, my dear son, be strong through the grace that God gives you in
Christ Jesus. [2]You have heard me teach things that have been confirmed
by many reliable witnesses. Now teach these truths to other trustworthy
people who will be able to pass them on to others.
[3]Endure suffering along with me, as a good soldier of Christ Jesus. [4]Sol-
diers don't get tied up in the affairs of civilian life, for then they cannot please
the officer who enlisted them. [5]And athletes cannot win the prize unless they
follow the rules. [6]And hardworking farmers should be the first to enjoy the
fruit of their labor. [7]Think about what I am saying. The Lord will help you
understand all these things.
[8]Always remember that Jesus Christ, a descendant of King David, was
raised from the dead. This is the Good News I preach. [9]And because I preach
this Good News, I am suffering and have been chained like a criminal. But
the word of God cannot be chained. [10]So I am willing to endure anything if it
will bring salvation and eternal glory in Christ Jesus to those God has chosen.
[11]This is a trustworthy saying:

If we die with him,
  we will also live with him.
12 If we endure hardship,
  we will reign with him.
If we deny him,
  he will deny us.
13 If we are unfaithful,
  he remains faithful,
  for he cannot deny who he is.

[14]Remind everyone about these things, and command them in God's pres-
ence to stop fighting over words. Such arguments are useless, and they can
ruin those who hear them.

An Approved Worker

[15]Work hard so you can present yourself to God and receive his approval.
Be a good worker, one who does not need to be ashamed and who correctly
explains the word of truth. [16]Avoid worthless, foolish talk that only leads
to more godless behavior. [17]This kind of talk spreads like cancer,* as in the
case of Hymenaeus and Philetus. [18]They have left the path of truth, claiming
that the resurrection of the dead has already occurred; in this way, they have
turned some people away from the faith.
[19]But God's truth stands firm like a foundation stone with this inscrip-
tion: "The LORD knows those who are his,"* and "All who belong to the LORD
must turn away from evil."*
[20]In a wealthy home some utensils are made of gold and silver, and some
are made of wood and clay. The expensive utensils are used for special occa-
sions, and the cheap ones are for everyday use. [21]If you keep yourself pure,
you will be a special utensil for honorable use. Your life will be clean, and
you will be ready for the Master to use you for every good work.
[22]Run from anything that stimulates youthful lusts. Instead, pursue

2:17 Greek *gangrene*. 2:19a Num 16:5. 2:19b See Isa 52:11.

Make a Difference
2:3-4

Jesus above All

At the time of writing, many of the soldiers from Paul and Timothy's world were mercenaries. They were paid to fight, and that often led to soldiers being disloyal. Historians have documented battles during which entire battalions of soldiers changed sides in the middle of the fight after having received a better financial offer.

As a Christian, we can be tempted to think that we might find a better deal somewhere else. Timothy was to remember that his job was to show up ready for duty and willing to follow the orders from his commander in chief, Jesus Christ, and to be loyal.

Difference Maker

Name one specific "active duty" command from Jesus that you will follow today.

Make a Difference 2:22

Run

Life is a lot like a marathon. Learning how to run over a long distance is the key to finishing well. You can't just wake up one day and go out and run a marathon. You need to build stamina for long-distance running.

Many runners have gotten derailed over the years. Sadly, they have missed the opportunity to pursue their full potential. Jesus created you to run the marathon of life. Run as if it were the only thing you had to do. Run from the things that mess you up and run toward the things that build you up.

Difference Maker

Go for a run today and pray through this verse.

Make a Difference 3:16

Better Than a Snooze Button

When that alarm goes off, say at 6:15 in the morning, do you hit the snooze button with a bad attitude? Do you ask God to help get your mind in the right frame for the next nine minutes? When the alarm goes off again at 6:24, do you feel any more refreshed than when it went off nine minutes earlier? Did those minutes rid you of your grumpiness? Or do those problems in the world, including your own flaws and festering worries, continue to mock you and make you want to stay in bed?

When that alarm goes off, you may not feel like you are ready for what's ahead, but God believes you can do good work today. All he asks is that you give him your attention. He gave you his Word to help you prepare for your day. Nine minutes in the Bible can be much more effective than hitting the snooze button and getting nine more minutes of sleep.

Difference Maker

Instead of hitting the snooze button tomorrow morning, use those extra minutes to read 2 Timothy.

Prayer 3:17

Lord, thank you for your Word. As I read it and obey it, train me to serve you and be ready for every good work. Amen.

righteous living, faithfulness, love, and peace. Enjoy the companionship of
those who call on the Lord with pure hearts.
23 Again I say, don't get involved in foolish, ignorant arguments that only
start fights. 24 A servant of the Lord must not quarrel but must be kind to
everyone, be able to teach, and be patient with difficult people. 25 Gently
instruct those who oppose the truth. Perhaps God will change those people's
hearts, and they will learn the truth. 26 Then they will come to their senses
and escape from the devil's trap. For they have been held captive by him to
do whatever he wants.

The Dangers of the Last Days

3 You should know this, Timothy, that in the last days there will be very
difficult times. 2 For people will love only themselves and their money.
They will be boastful and proud, scoffing at God, disobedient to their par-
ents, and ungrateful. They will consider nothing sacred. 3 They will be un-
loving and unforgiving; they will slander others and have no self-control.
They will be cruel and hate what is good. 4 They will betray their friends, be
reckless, be puffed up with pride, and love pleasure rather than God. 5 They
will act religious, but they will reject the power that could make them godly.
Stay away from people like that!
6 They are the kind who work their way into people's homes and win the
confidence of* vulnerable women who are burdened with the guilt of sin
and controlled by various desires. 7 (Such women are forever following new
teachings, but they are never able to understand the truth.) 8 These teach-
ers oppose the truth just as Jannes and Jambres opposed Moses. They have
depraved minds and a counterfeit faith. 9 But they won't get away with this
for long. Someday everyone will recognize what fools they are, just as with
Jannes and Jambres.

Paul's Charge to Timothy

10 But you, Timothy, certainly know what I teach, and how I live, and what my
purpose in life is. You know my faith, my patience, my love, and my endur-
ance. 11 You know how much persecution and suffering I have endured. You
know all about how I was persecuted in Antioch, Iconium, and Lystra—but
the Lord rescued me from all of it. 12 Yes, and everyone who wants to live a
godly life in Christ Jesus will suffer persecution. 13 But evil people and impos-
tors will flourish. They will deceive others and will themselves be deceived.
14 But you must remain faithful to the things you have been taught. You
know they are true, for you know you can trust those who taught you. 15 You
have been taught the holy Scriptures from childhood, and they have given
you the wisdom to receive the salvation that comes by trusting in Christ
Jesus. 16 All Scripture is inspired by God and is useful to teach us what is true
and to make us realize what is wrong in our lives. It corrects us when we are
wrong and teaches us to do what is right. 17 God uses it to prepare and equip
his people to do every good work.

4 I solemnly urge you in the presence of God and Christ Jesus, who
will someday judge the living and the dead when he comes to set up
his Kingdom: 2 Preach the word of God. Be prepared, whether the time is

3:6 Greek *and take captive.*

favorable or not. Patiently correct, rebuke, and encourage your people with good teaching.

3 For a time is coming when people will no longer listen to sound and wholesome teaching. They will follow their own desires and will look for teachers who will tell them whatever their itching ears want to hear. 4 They will reject the truth and chase after myths.

5 But you should keep a clear mind in every situation. Don't be afraid of suffering for the Lord. Work at telling others the Good News, and fully carry out the ministry God has given you.

6 As for me, my life has already been poured out as an offering to God. The time of my death is near. 7 I have fought the good fight, I have finished the race, and I have remained faithful. 8 And now the prize awaits me—the crown of righteousness, which the Lord, the righteous Judge, will give me on the day of his return. And the prize is not just for me but for all who eagerly look forward to his appearing.

Paul's Final Words

9 Timothy, please come as soon as you can. 10 Demas has deserted me because he loves the things of this life and has gone to Thessalonica. Crescens has gone to Galatia, and Titus has gone to Dalmatia. 11 Only Luke is with me. Bring Mark with you when you come, for he will be helpful to me in my ministry. 12 I sent Tychicus to Ephesus. 13 When you come, be sure to bring the coat I left with Carpus at Troas. Also bring my books, and especially my papers.*

14 Alexander the coppersmith did me much harm, but the Lord will judge him for what he has done. 15 Be careful of him, for he fought against everything we said.

16 The first time I was brought before the judge, no one came with me. Everyone abandoned me. May it not be counted against them. 17 But the Lord stood with me and gave me strength so that I might preach the Good News in its entirety for all the Gentiles to hear. And he rescued me from certain death.* 18 Yes, and the Lord will deliver me from every evil attack and will bring me safely into his heavenly Kingdom. All glory to God forever and ever! Amen.

Paul's Final Greetings

19 Give my greetings to Priscilla and Aquila and those living in the household of Onesiphorus. 20 Erastus stayed at Corinth, and I left Trophimus sick at Miletus.

21 Do your best to get here before winter. Eubulus sends you greetings, and so do Pudens, Linus, Claudia, and all the brothers and sisters.*

22 May the Lord be with your spirit. And may his grace be with all of you.

4:13 Greek *especially the parchments.* **4:17** Greek *from the mouth of a lion.* **4:21** Greek *brothers.*

Prayer 4:7

Lord, at the end of this day, let me be able to say, "I have fought the good fight." Amen.

Titus Introduction

The book of Titus is one of three Pastoral Letters. Alongside 1 and 2 Timothy, this section of the Bible is concerned with helping Christians live as authentic and faithful witnesses. This life that Paul described for his young protégé Titus is full of joy, freedom, and hope. Our journey into this Jesus-centered life is by grace. Difference makers have encountered grace, and it is the source of their significance in the world.

Titus had remained on the island of Crete to continue the gospel work that he, Paul, and other members of their missionary team had started. Like an elite operative on a special forces team, this young pastor had been tasked with staying behind and holding the fort. The rest of the team had to move forward and keep advancing the kingdom of God through mission and evangelism. Equally important was Titus's work. He was coming along behind the apostle Paul, building infrastructure and support systems to ensure that their good work was not wasted. Titus's priority was the training and deployment of future leaders.

The gospel is always moved forward, and the church is always built through the development of godly, Jesus-centered, Spirit-filled young people. As you dig into these three chapters and think about making a difference in the world, imagine yourself, like Titus, on a mission with a special assignment.

Story Arc

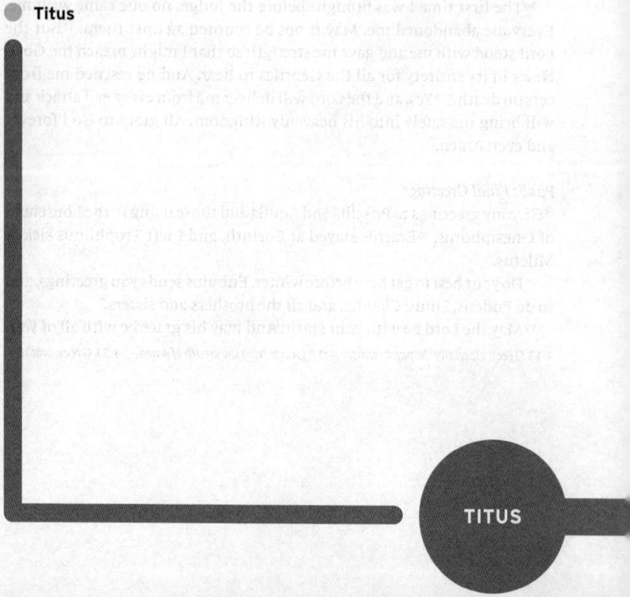

Titus

Greetings from Paul

1 This letter is from Paul, a slave of God and an apostle of Jesus Christ. I
have been sent to proclaim faith to* those God has chosen and to teach
them to know the truth that shows them how to live godly lives. 2 This truth
gives them confidence that they have eternal life, which God—who does
not lie—promised them before the world began. 3 And now at just the right
time he has revealed this message, which we announce to everyone. It is by
the command of God our Savior that I have been entrusted with this work
for him.
4 I am writing to Titus, my true son in the faith that we share.

May God the Father and Christ Jesus our Savior give you grace and peace.

Titus's Work in Crete

5 I left you on the island of Crete so you could complete our work there and
appoint elders in each town as I instructed you. 6 An elder must live a blame-
less life. He must be faithful to his wife,* and his children must be believers
who don't have a reputation for being wild or rebellious. 7 A church leader*
is a manager of God's household, so he must live a blameless life. He must
not be arrogant or quick-tempered; he must not be a heavy drinker,* violent,
or dishonest with money.
8 Rather, he must enjoy having guests in his home, and he must love what
is good. He must live wisely and be just. He must live a devout and disci-
plined life. 9 He must have a strong belief in the trustworthy message he was
taught; then he will be able to encourage others with wholesome teaching
and show those who oppose it where they are wrong.
10 For there are many rebellious people who engage in useless talk and de-
ceive others. This is especially true of those who insist on circumcision for
salvation. 11 They must be silenced, because they are turning whole families
away from the truth by their false teaching. And they do it only for money.
12 Even one of their own men, a prophet from Crete, has said about them,
"The people of Crete are all liars, cruel animals, and lazy gluttons."* 13 This
is true. So reprimand them sternly to make them strong in the faith. 14 They
must stop listening to Jewish myths and the commands of people who have
turned away from the truth.
15 Everything is pure to those whose hearts are pure. But nothing is pure to
those who are corrupt and unbelieving, because their minds and consciences
are corrupted. 16 Such people claim they know God, but they deny him by
the way they live. They are detestable and disobedient, worthless for doing
anything good.

1:1 Or *to strengthen the faith of.* 1:6 Or *must have only one wife,* or *must be married only once;* Greek reads *must be the husband of one wife.* 1:7a Or *An overseer,* or *A bishop.* 1:7b Greek *must not drink too much wine.* 1:12 This quotation is from Epimenides of Knossos.

Question 1:8

Why would these guidelines be good suggestions for those who would like to be leaders in a church?

Story Arc 1:4

Titus

Paul was trying to teach Titus that the good news transforms us. The people of Crete had a reputation for laziness, gluttony, and wastefulness. They had received the gift of grace, but they were not allowing that grace to do its life-transforming work. The gospel of Jesus makes us into new people. According to Paul's letter to Titus, this grace saves us, washes us clean, and makes us right with God. That is really good news. If you ever feel like you have lost your way, lost your heart, or lost your purpose, find your way back to Crete and join Titus on his mission, and when you do, you will encounter the good news about Jesus all over again.

Phlm 10-16 ►

Promote Right Teaching

2 As for you, Titus, promote the kind of living that reflects wholesome
teaching. 2Teach the older men to exercise self-control, to be worthy of
respect, and to live wisely. They must have sound faith and be filled with
love and patience.
3Similarly, teach the older women to live in a way that honors God. They
must not slander others or be heavy drinkers.* Instead, they should teach
others what is good. 4These older women must train the younger women to
love their husbands and their children, 5to live wisely and be pure, to work
in their homes,* to do good, and to be submissive to their husbands. Then
they will not bring shame on the word of God.
6In the same way, encourage the young men to live wisely. 7And you your-
self must be an example to them by doing good works of every kind. Let every-
thing you do reflect the integrity and seriousness of your teaching. 8Teach
the truth so that your teaching can't be criticized. Then those who oppose us
will be ashamed and have nothing bad to say about us.
9Slaves must always obey their masters and do their best to please them.
They must not talk back 10or steal, but must show themselves to be entirely
trustworthy and good. Then they will make the teaching about God our
Savior attractive in every way.
11For the grace of God has been revealed, bringing salvation to all people.
12And we are instructed to turn from godless living and sinful pleasures. We
should live in this evil world with wisdom, righteousness, and devotion to
God, 13while we look forward with hope to that wonderful day when the
glory of our great God and Savior, Jesus Christ, will be revealed. 14He gave
his life to free us from every kind of sin, to cleanse us, and to make us his
very own people, totally committed to doing good deeds.
15You must teach these things and encourage the believers to do them.
You have the authority to correct them when necessary, so don't let anyone
disregard what you say.

Do What Is Good

3 Remind the believers to submit to the government and its officers. They
should be obedient, always ready to do what is good. 2They must not
slander anyone and must avoid quarreling. Instead, they should be gentle
and show true humility to everyone.
3Once we, too, were foolish and disobedient. We were misled and became
slaves to many lusts and pleasures. Our lives were full of evil and envy, and
we hated each other. 4But—

> When God our Savior revealed his kindness and love, 5he saved us,
> not because of the righteous things we had done, but because of
> his mercy. He washed away our sins, giving us a new birth and new
> life through the Holy Spirit.* 6He generously poured out the Spirit
> upon us through Jesus Christ our Savior. 7Because of his grace he
> made us right in his sight and gave us confidence that we will inherit
> eternal life.

2:3 Greek *be enslaved to much wine.* 2:5 Some manuscripts read *to care for their homes.* 3:5 Greek *He saved us through the washing of regeneration and renewing of the Holy Spirit.*

Make a Difference **2:11**

Grace to the Rescue!

Paul wanted to remind young leaders not to forget the good news about Jesus. If you forget the gospel, you will lose your way and lose your heart. At the center of the gospel is the beautiful idea of grace. Grace is God's incredible generosity to people who don't deserve it. God expressed that generosity in the sending of our Savior, Jesus Christ. He has generously given himself to free us from all our sin. We don't deserve that kind of love. That is grace. Grace is God's way of making a difference.

Difference Maker

Grace is also our way of making a difference. Because we have received grace, we can be vehicles of grace to the world around us. We can be generous even when people don't deserve it. Pick someone and then pick a way to give them grace today.

Make a Difference

3:3-7

Life Preserver

Out of his loving-kindness the Lord saved us. We had fallen off the boat into the raging sea because we didn't listen to his commands to stay off the deck during the storm. We thought that was unfair. After yelling at him for being too constrictive, we pounded up the stairs to play outside on the deck. It wasn't long before we slipped off. God, always keeping a loving eye on us, called out our name, jumped in the torrent with a life preserver, put it around us, and pulled us back into the cabin of the boat. It was his kindness that saved us, not because of what we have done but only because of his great mercy.

8 This is a trustworthy saying, and I want you to insist on these teachings
so that all who trust in God will devote themselves to doing good. These
teachings are good and beneficial for everyone.
9 Do not get involved in foolish discussions about spiritual pedigrees* or
in quarrels and fights about obedience to Jewish laws. These things are use-
less and a waste of time. 10 If people are causing divisions among you, give
a first and second warning. After that, have nothing more to do with them.
11 For people like that have turned away from the truth, and their own sins
condemn them.

Paul's Final Remarks and Greetings

12 I am planning to send either Artemas or Tychicus to you. As soon as one of
them arrives, do your best to meet me at Nicopolis, for I have decided to stay
there for the winter. 13 Do everything you can to help Zenas the lawyer and
Apollos with their trip. See that they are given everything they need. 14 Our
people must learn to do good by meeting the urgent needs of others; then
they will not be unproductive.
15 Everybody here sends greetings. Please give my greetings to the
believers—all who love us.

May God's grace be with you all.

3:9 Or *spiritual genealogies.*

Difference Maker

Think of a friend who needs someone to throw a life preserver out to them in the middle of a storm. Reach out to that person today.

Prayer 3:9

Lord, help me not to waste my words today. I want my words and actions to be full of grace. Protect me from arguments. Empower me with truth and trustworthiness. Amen.

Make a Difference

3:12-14

Be Helpful

If you want to make a difference today, look for small opportunities to do little things. God always seems pleased to make the biggest difference through the smallest of gestures and efforts.

At the end of Paul's letter to Titus, the apostle wrapped up by giving Titus some really mundane, unexciting administrative tasks to do. Titus was to get practical. Some other team members needed help. Perhaps they needed some food to eat, some laundry done, a place to stay, or some medical care.

The good news people of the New Testament were people like you and me. They needed encouragement and prayer, a coffee and a muffin and a note to say, "Keep up the great work." Titus was an incredibly important leader, yet he was not too important to do simple and small kingdom tasks.

Difference Maker

Choose a boring but helpful chore and just do it in the name of Jesus.

Philemon Introduction

Jesus challenges people to be better humans. He sets a pretty high bar, but the path is ripe with forgiveness, restoration, and new starts. Jesus' goal is to encourage people from different backgrounds to work in concert to share God's life-changing presence with the world. He does not expect that his followers will always be perfect or, more practically, pretend to be perfect. He does expect that they will pursue perfection in him and, as a result, will be people who are allowing God to transform them.

At twenty-five total verses, this letter to Philemon is one of the shortest books in the New Testament. Even with its small size, it is scrappy, multilayered, and very meaningful. It is like the "meme" of the New Testament. This letter to Philemon packs an unexpected sucker punch.

This personal letter written by Paul is a great example of this high calling. It gives a real-life example of how one man was radically turned around and given a new status as a partner in life and ministry. It also challenges another man, and an entire culture, to rise to the occasion and accept the God-ordained dignity of this man. In this short letter, which likely accompanied his letter to the Colossians, Paul gently pointed to the high bar as he boldly defended Onesimus, a runaway slave, as a fully accepted coworker in Christ.

Paul drew his friends (Philemon, Apphia, and Archippus) into his arms with kind words and heartfelt, flowing flatteries. Then he turned to Philemon and caught him unsuspectingly with a left hook out of nowhere. In effect, Paul said, "I'm so thankful for how good a person you are, Philemon. You're my friend. You are a good person, right, Philemon? You are my friend, right, Philemon? Yes? Good. That's why I'm boldly going to ask for something."

Story Arcs

- **Onesimus**
- **Philemon's Church Network**

Philemon

Greetings from Paul
This letter is from Paul, a prisoner for preaching the Good News about Christ
Jesus, and from our brother Timothy.
I am writing to Philemon, our beloved co-worker, 2 and to our sister
Apphia, and to our fellow soldier Archippus, and to the church that meets
in your* house.
3 May God our Father and the Lord Jesus Christ give you grace and peace.

Paul's Thanksgiving and Prayer
4 I always thank my God when I pray for you, Philemon, 5 because I keep hear-
ing about your faith in the Lord Jesus and your love for all of God's people.
6 And I am praying that you will put into action the generosity that comes
from your faith as you understand and experience all the good things we
have in Christ. 7 Your love has given me much joy and comfort, my brother,
for your kindness has often refreshed the hearts of God's people.

Paul's Appeal for Onesimus
8 That is why I am boldly asking a favor of you. I could demand it in the name
of Christ because it is the right thing for you to do. 9 But because of our love,
I prefer simply to ask you. Consider this as a request from me—Paul, an old
man and now also a prisoner for the sake of Christ Jesus.*
10 I appeal to you to show kindness to my child, Onesimus. I became his
father in the faith while here in prison. 11 Onesimus* hasn't been of much
use to you in the past, but now he is very useful to both of us. 12 I am sending
him back to you, and with him comes my own heart.
13 I wanted to keep him here with me while I am in these chains for preach-
ing the Good News, and he would have helped me on your behalf. 14 But
I didn't want to do anything without your consent. I wanted you to help
because you were willing, not because you were forced. 15 It seems you lost
Onesimus for a little while so that you could have him back forever. 16 He is no
longer like a slave to you. He is more than a slave, for he is a beloved brother,
especially to me. Now he will mean much more to you, both as a man and
as a brother in the Lord.
17 So if you consider me your partner, welcome him as you would welcome
me. 18 If he has wronged you in any way or owes you anything, charge it to
me. 19 I, PAUL, WRITE THIS WITH MY OWN HAND: I WILL REPAY IT. AND I WON'T
MENTION THAT YOU OWE ME YOUR VERY SOUL!
20 Yes, my brother, please do me this favor* for the Lord's sake. Give me
this encouragement in Christ.
21 I am confident as I write this letter that you will do what I ask and even

2 Throughout this letter, *you* and *your* are singular except in verses 3, 22, and 25. 9 Or *a prisoner of Christ Jesus.* 11 *Onesimus* means "useful." 20 Greek *onaimen,* a play on the name Onesimus.

Question 6

Notice how Paul prayed for Philemon. If you were to stop to pray for someone right now, whom would you pray for, and how would you pray?

Story Arc 10-16

● Onesimus

Paul understood that Jesus frees people from the indignity of caste systems and oppression. Knowing this, Paul wrote this letter as an appeal to Philemon, the former "master," to receive Onesimus as a brother on equal footing. Read what Paul said about him in verses 15-16.

Phim 23-24 ►

more! 22 One more thing—please prepare a guest room for me, for I am hop-
ing that God will answer your prayers and let me return to you soon.

Paul's Final Greetings

23 Epaphras, my fellow prisoner in Christ Jesus, sends you his greetings. 24 So
do Mark, Aristarchus, Demas, and Luke, my co-workers.
25 May the grace of the Lord Jesus Christ be with your spirit.

Story Arc 23-24

● Philemon's Church Network

To add significance to his partnership argument, this little letter reminded Philemon that he was part of a larger movement. In all, this letter mentions ten people specifically by name, along with a church and house group. These are letter-closing, human-packed verses that reflect a truth evident in all Paul's writings: Paul didn't believe in a lone ranger or "hero" approach to ministry. He practiced an every-person, hub-networked, coworker concept.

The early churches were made up of people woven together into networks of Jesus followers. Go back through this book to see the unique people mentioned and consider how they got involved in God's world-changing movement.

Heb 3:1-6 ►

Philemon's Church Network

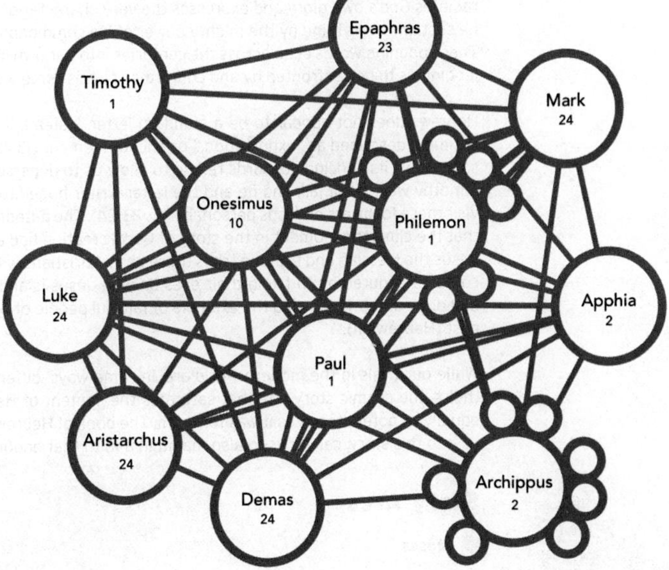

Hebrews Introduction

It is usually not a good idea to jump to an episode halfway into a streaming video series without watching the episodes that lead up to it. Without the beginning, we lose too much of the story to understand what is happening. In many ways, the same is true of Hebrews.

The book opens by transporting us into the past: "Long ago God spoke many times and in many ways to our ancestors through the prophets" (Hebrews 1:1). Throughout the rest of Hebrews, the author brings forward important moments from the distant past to illuminate the present. Something remarkable has happened. Like a burst of X-ray vision, the stories of the past and present have been exposed by a new light: "Now in these final days, he has spoken to us through his Son...[who] radiates God's own glory and expresses the very character of God, and he sustains everything by the mighty power of his command" (vv. 2-3). These opening words echo across the centuries into our own lives, challenging us to be confronted by and conformed to this same Son, Jesus.

Hebrews does not appear to be a standard letter. Instead, its content is simply described as "exhortation," or encouragement (13:22). At the same time, its concluding words refuse to allow us to depersonalize it: Timothy was out of jail, and he and the letter writer hoped to come to visit these followers of Jesus personally (vv. 23-24). The author believed that the climactic moment in the story of God's creation had arrived in Jesus the Messiah and that the trials these early Christians were facing could be endured by (1) fixing their eyes on who Jesus is and what he had done and (2) following the example of faithful people of God in the past (Hebrews 11).

While our trials in the modern world are, in some ways, different from theirs, the cosmic story line that saturates the content of Hebrews is equally as potent for us as it was for them. The book of Hebrews invites us into this story, calling us to also maintain a faith that endures.

Story Arcs

- **Moses**
- **Melchizedek**
- **Hall of Difference Makers**

The Hebrews Church Network

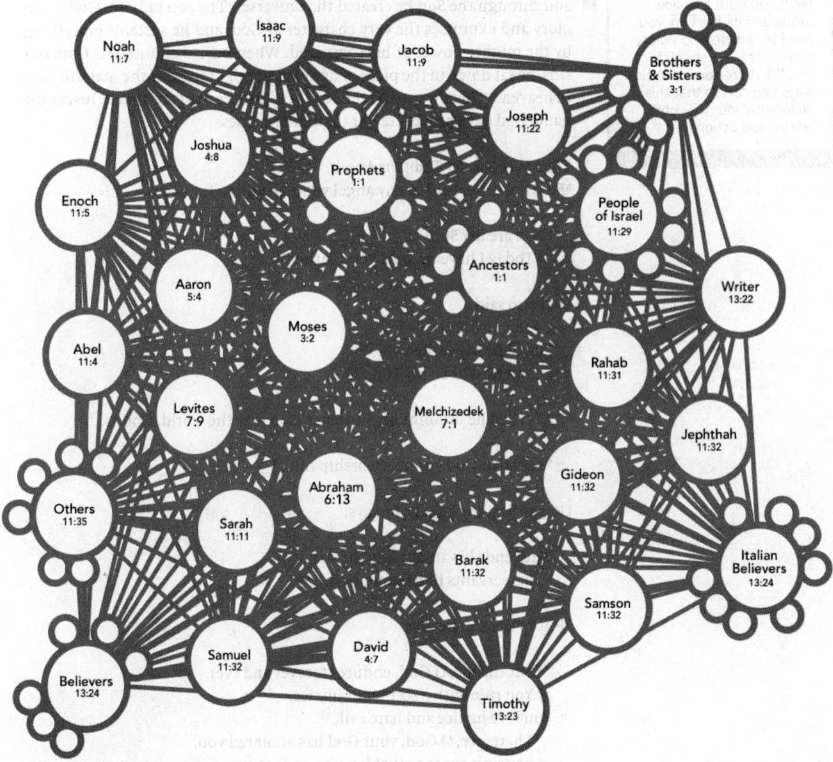

Hebrews

Question 1:3

Jesus radiates God's glory and expresses God's character. If you want to follow Jesus and be like him, you need to radiate God's glory and express his character too. What are some practical ways you can do that this week with your thoughts, words, and actions?

Jesus Christ Is God's Son

1 Long ago God spoke many times and in many ways to our ancestors
through the prophets. 2 And now in these final days, he has spoken to
us through his Son. God promised everything to the Son as an inheritance,
and through the Son he created the universe. 3 The Son radiates God's own
glory and expresses the very character of God, and he sustains everything
by the mighty power of his command. When he had cleansed us from our
sins, he sat down in the place of honor at the right hand of the majestic God
in heaven. 4 This shows that the Son is far greater than the angels, just as the
name God gave him is greater than their names.

The Son Is Greater Than the Angels

5 For God never said to any angel what he said to Jesus:

"You are my Son.
Today I have become your Father.*"

God also said,

"I will be his Father,
and he will be my Son."*

6 And when he brought his supreme* Son into the world, God said,*

"Let all of God's angels worship him."*

7 Regarding the angels, he says,

"He sends his angels like the winds,
his servants like flames of fire."*

8 But to the Son he says,

"Your throne, O God, endures forever and ever.
You rule with a scepter of justice.
9 You love justice and hate evil.
Therefore, O God, your God has anointed you,
pouring out the oil of joy on you more than on
anyone else."*

1:5a Or *Today I reveal you as my Son.* Ps 2:7. **1:5b** 2 Sam 7:14. **1:6a** Or *firstborn.* **1:6b** Or *when he again brings his supreme Son* [or *firstborn Son*] *into the world, God will say.* **1:6c** Deut 32:43. **1:7** Ps 104:4 (Greek version). **1:8-9** Ps 45:6-7.

10 He also says to the Son,

"In the beginning, Lord, you laid the foundation of the earth
and made the heavens with your hands.
11 They will perish, but you remain forever.
They will wear out like old clothing.
12 You will fold them up like a cloak
and discard them like old clothing.
But you are always the same;
you will live forever."*

13 And God never said to any of the angels,

"Sit in the place of honor at my right hand
until I humble your enemies,
making them a footstool under your feet."*

14 Therefore, angels are only servants—spirits sent to care for people who will inherit salvation.

A Warning against Drifting Away

2 So we must listen very carefully to the truth we have heard, or we may
drift away from it. 2 For the message God delivered through angels has
always stood firm, and every violation of the law and every act of disobedi-
ence was punished. 3 So what makes us think we can escape if we ignore this
great salvation that was first announced by the Lord Jesus himself and then
delivered to us by those who heard him speak? 4 And God confirmed the
message by giving signs and wonders and various miracles and gifts of the
Holy Spirit whenever he chose.

Jesus, the Man

5 And furthermore, it is not angels who will control the future world we are
talking about. 6 For in one place the Scriptures say,

"What are mere mortals that you should think about them,
or a son of man* that you should care for him?
7 Yet for a little while you made them a little lower than the angels
and crowned them with glory and honor.*
8 You gave them authority over all things."*

Now when it says "all things," it means nothing is left out. But we have not
yet seen all things put under their authority. 9 What we do see is Jesus, who
for a little while was given a position "a little lower than the angels"; and
because he suffered death for us, he is now "crowned with glory and honor."
Yes, by God's grace, Jesus tasted death for everyone. 10 God, for whom and
through whom everything was made, chose to bring many children into
glory. And it was only right that he should make Jesus, through his suffering,
a perfect leader, fit to bring them into their salvation.

11 So now Jesus and the ones he makes holy have the same Father. That

1:10-12 Ps 102:25-27. 1:13 Ps 110:1. 2:6 Or *the Son of Man.* 2:7 Some manuscripts add *You gave them charge of everything you made.* 2:6-8 Ps 8:4-6 (Greek version).

Question **2:14**

Have you wondered why Jesus became a man who walked on this earth? How does this section help you comprehend who Jesus is and what he has done for us?

Prayer **2:18**

Jesus, thank you that you understand what I'm going through right now, and thank you that you want to help. Please remind me that I don't have to struggle through this on my own. I need your mercy. I need your joy. I need your strength, Lord. Amen.

Story Arc **3:1-6**

Moses

Jesus is greater than Moses. That is saying a lot! Go and read about Moses in the book of Exodus and consider Jesus being exponentially greater.

Heb 7:1-28 ►

is why Jesus is not ashamed to call them his brothers and sisters.* 12For he
said to God,

"I will proclaim your name to my brothers and sisters.
I will praise you among your assembled people."*

13He also said,

"I will put my trust in him,"
that is, "I and the children God has given me."*

14Because God's children are human beings—made of flesh and blood—
the Son also became flesh and blood. For only as a human being could he
die, and only by dying could he break the power of the devil, who had* the
power of death. 15Only in this way could he set free all who have lived their
lives as slaves to the fear of dying.
16We also know that the Son did not come to help angels; he came to
help the descendants of Abraham. 17Therefore, it was necessary for him to
be made in every respect like us, his brothers and sisters,* so that he could
be our merciful and faithful High Priest before God. Then he could offer
a sacrifice that would take away the sins of the people. 18Since he himself
has gone through suffering and testing, he is able to help us when we are
being tested.

Jesus Is Greater Than Moses

3 And so, dear brothers and sisters who belong to God and* are partners
with those called to heaven, think carefully about this Jesus whom we
declare to be God's messenger* and High Priest. 2For he was faithful to God,
who appointed him, just as Moses served faithfully when he was entrusted
with God's entire* house.
3But Jesus deserves far more glory than Moses, just as a person who builds
a house deserves more praise than the house itself. 4For every house has a
builder, but the one who built everything is God.
5Moses was certainly faithful in God's house as a servant. His work was
an illustration of the truths God would reveal later. 6But Christ, as the Son,
is in charge of God's entire house. And we are God's house, if we keep our
courage and remain confident in our hope in Christ.*
7That is why the Holy Spirit says,

"Today when you hear his voice,
8 don't harden your hearts
as Israel did when they rebelled,
when they tested me in the wilderness.
9 There your ancestors tested and tried my patience,
even though they saw my miracles for forty years.
10 So I was angry with them, and I said,
'Their hearts always turn away from me.
They refuse to do what I tell them.'

2:11 Greek *brothers;* also in 2:12. 2:12 Ps 22:22. 2:13 Isa 8:17-18. 2:14 Or *has.* 2:17 Greek *like the brothers.* 3:1a Greek *And so, holy brothers who.* 3:1b Greek *God's apostle.* 3:2 Some manuscripts do not include *entire.* 3:6 Some manuscripts add *faithful to the end.*

11 So in my anger I took an oath:
'They will never enter my place of rest.'"*

12 Be careful then, dear brothers and sisters.* Make sure that your own hearts
are not evil and unbelieving, turning you away from the living God. 13 You
must warn each other every day, while it is still "today," so that none of you
will be deceived by sin and hardened against God. 14 For if we are faithful to
the end, trusting God just as firmly as when we first believed, we will share
in all that belongs to Christ. 15 Remember what it says:

"Today when you hear his voice,
don't harden your hearts
as Israel did when they rebelled."*

16 And who was it who rebelled against God, even though they heard his
voice? Wasn't it the people Moses led out of Egypt? 17 And who made God
angry for forty years? Wasn't it the people who sinned, whose corpses lay in
the wilderness? 18 And to whom was God speaking when he took an oath that
they would never enter his rest? Wasn't it the people who disobeyed him?
19 So we see that because of their unbelief they were not able to enter his rest.

Promised Rest for God's People

4 God's promise of entering his rest still stands, so we ought to tremble
with fear that some of you might fail to experience it. 2 For this good
news—that God has prepared this rest—has been announced to us just as
it was to them. But it did them no good because they didn't share the faith
of those who listened to God.* 3 For only we who believe can enter his rest.
As for the others, God said,

"In my anger I took an oath:
'They will never enter my place of rest,'"*

even though this rest has been ready since he made the world. 4 We know it
is ready because of the place in the Scriptures where it mentions the seventh
day: "On the seventh day God rested from all his work."* 5 But in the other
passage God said, "They will never enter my place of rest."*

6 So God's rest is there for people to enter, but those who first heard this
good news failed to enter because they disobeyed God. 7 So God set another
time for entering his rest, and that time is today. God announced this
through David much later in the words already quoted:

"Today when you hear his voice,
don't harden your hearts."*

8 Now if Joshua had succeeded in giving them this rest, God would not have
spoken about another day of rest still to come. 9 So there is a special rest*
still waiting for the people of God. 10 For all who have entered into God's
rest have rested from their labors, just as God did after creating the world.

3:7-11 Ps 95:7-11. 3:12 Greek *brothers.* 3:15 Ps 95:7-8. 4:2 Some manuscripts read *they didn't combine what they heard with faith.* 4:3 Ps 95:11. 4:4 Gen 2:2. 4:5 Ps 95:11. 4:7 Ps 95:7-8. 4:9 Or *a Sabbath rest.*

Question **3:15**

How might you be hardening your heart to God? Is there a private sin you give in to repeatedly? Maybe there's something you know God's calling you to do, but you're not trusting him enough to follow him. Whatever it is, what are the dangers of hardening your heart?

11 So let us do our best to enter that rest. But if we disobey God, as the people of Israel did, we will fall.

12 For the word of God is alive and powerful. It is sharper than the sharpest two-edged sword, cutting between soul and spirit, between joint and marrow. It exposes our innermost thoughts and desires. 13 Nothing in all creation is hidden from God. Everything is naked and exposed before his eyes, and he is the one to whom we are accountable.

Christ Is Our High Priest

14 So then, since we have a great High Priest who has entered heaven, Jesus the Son of God, let us hold firmly to what we believe. 15 This High Priest of ours understands our weaknesses, for he faced all of the same testings we do, yet he did not sin. 16 So let us come boldly to the throne of our gracious God. There we will receive his mercy, and we will find grace to help us when we need it most.

5 Every high priest is a man chosen to represent other people in their dealings with God. He presents their gifts to God and offers sacrifices for their sins. 2 And he is able to deal gently with ignorant and wayward people because he himself is subject to the same weaknesses. 3 That is why he must offer sacrifices for his own sins as well as theirs.

4 And no one can become a high priest simply because he wants such an honor. He must be called by God for this work, just as Aaron was. 5 That is why Christ did not honor himself by assuming he could become High Priest. No, he was chosen by God, who said to him,

"You are my Son.
Today I have become your Father.*"

6 And in another passage God said to him,

"You are a priest forever in the order of Melchizedek."*

7 While Jesus was here on earth, he offered prayers and pleadings, with a loud cry and tears, to the one who could rescue him from death. And God heard his prayers because of his deep reverence for God. 8 Even though Jesus was God's Son, he learned obedience from the things he suffered. 9 In this way, God qualified him as a perfect High Priest, and he became the source of eternal salvation for all those who obey him. 10 And God designated him to be a High Priest in the order of Melchizedek.

A Call to Spiritual Growth

11 There is much more we would like to say about this, but it is difficult to explain, especially since you are spiritually dull and don't seem to listen. 12 You have been believers so long now that you ought to be teaching others. Instead, you need someone to teach you again the basic things about God's word.* You are like babies who need milk and cannot eat solid food. 13 For someone who lives on milk is still an infant and doesn't know how to do what is right. 14 Solid food is for those who are mature, who through training have the skill to recognize the difference between right and wrong.

Make a Difference 4:12

The Word of God

Let the Word of God cut straight through all your walls, all your fluff, all your burdens, and all your defenses. Let the Word of God expose your innermost thoughts, your secret desires, your darkest hurts, and your deepest longings. Let the Word of God help you become exactly who God created you to be, for the Lord already knows you. He gave you his Word so you could learn to know yourself.

Difference Maker

This is not a quiet-time Bible. This is a loud-time Bible. It is meant to change you! Set a time every day to be changed by the living and powerful Word of God.

Prayer 5:12

Jesus, thank you for putting people in my life who taught me about the joys of following you. I want to make a difference like that in the lives of others. Please put specific people on my heart, give me opportunities to talk with them, and give me your words. Amen.

5:5 Or *Today I reveal you as my Son.* Ps 2:7. 5:6 Ps 110:4. 5:12 Or *about the oracles of God.*

6 So let us stop going over the basic teachings about Christ again and
again. Let us go on instead and become mature in our understanding.
Surely we don't need to start again with the fundamental importance of
repenting from evil deeds* and placing our faith in God. 2You don't need
further instruction about baptisms, the laying on of hands, the resurrec-
tion of the dead, and eternal judgment. 3And so, God willing, we will move
forward to further understanding.
4For it is impossible to bring back to repentance those who were once
enlightened—those who have experienced the good things of heaven and
shared in the Holy Spirit, 5who have tasted the goodness of the word of God
and the power of the age to come—6and who then turn away from God. It
is impossible to bring such people back to repentance; by rejecting the Son
of God, they themselves are nailing him to the cross once again and holding
him up to public shame.
7When the ground soaks up the falling rain and bears a good crop for the
farmer, it has God's blessing. 8But if a field bears thorns and thistles, it is
useless. The farmer will soon condemn that field and burn it.
9Dear friends, even though we are talking this way, we really don't be-
lieve it applies to you. We are confident that you are meant for better things,
things that come with salvation. 10For God is not unjust. He will not forget
how hard you have worked for him and how you have shown your love to
him by caring for other believers,* as you still do. 11Our great desire is that
you will keep on loving others as long as life lasts, in order to make certain
that what you hope for will come true. 12Then you will not become spiritu-
ally dull and indifferent. Instead, you will follow the example of those who
are going to inherit God's promises because of their faith and endurance.

God's Promises Bring Hope

13For example, there was God's promise to Abraham. Since there was no one
greater to swear by, God took an oath in his own name, saying:

14 "I will certainly bless you,
and I will multiply your descendants beyond number."*

15Then Abraham waited patiently, and he received what God had promised.
16Now when people take an oath, they call on someone greater than them-
selves to hold them to it. And without any question that oath is binding.
17God also bound himself with an oath, so that those who received the prom-
ise could be perfectly sure that he would never change his mind. 18So God has
given both his promise and his oath. These two things are unchangeable be-
cause it is impossible for God to lie. Therefore, we who have fled to him for ref-
uge can have great confidence as we hold to the hope that lies before us. 19This
hope is a strong and trustworthy anchor for our souls. It leads us through the
curtain into God's inner sanctuary. 20Jesus has already gone in there for us. He
has become our eternal High Priest in the order of Melchizedek.

Melchizedek Is Greater Than Abraham

7 This Melchizedek was king of the city of Salem and also a priest of God
Most High. When Abraham was returning home after winning a great

6:1 Greek *from dead works.* **6:10** Greek *for God's holy people.* **6:14** Gen 22:17.

Make a Difference 6:1-3

Saturate

Keep growing in your understanding of what it means to follow Jesus. Did you know you have permission to grow in your faith? True adventure happens when you keep learning to saturate all your activities with Jesus. Your pursuits become more exhilarating because every aspect produces praise from your heart. Your education or work becomes more rewarding because you practice faithfulness and integrity while preparing for your future. Your ministry projects become more fulfilling because they become regular features to your weekly routines.

Don't segregate the growth of your faith from your practical life. Faith doesn't grow that way, and life doesn't truly work that way either. Integrate faith and life with one another, for then you'll see your life reflecting Jesus more and more in this world.

Difference Maker

Do something to move forward in your understanding of what it means to follow Jesus.

Question 6:11

Who's one person in your life who needs love but who's maybe not the most natural person for you to give love to?

battle against the kings, Melchizedek met him and blessed him. 2Then Abra-
ham took a tenth of all he had captured in battle and gave it to Melchizedek.
The name Melchizedek means "king of justice," and king of Salem means
"king of peace." 3There is no record of his father or mother or any of his
ancestors—no beginning or end to his life. He remains a priest forever, re-
sembling the Son of God.

4Consider then how great this Melchizedek was. Even Abraham, the great
patriarch of Israel, recognized this by giving him a tenth of what he had
taken in battle. 5Now the law of Moses required that the priests, who are
descendants of Levi, must collect a tithe from the rest of the people of Israel,*
who are also descendants of Abraham. 6But Melchizedek, who was not a de-
scendant of Levi, collected a tenth from Abraham. And Melchizedek placed
a blessing upon Abraham, the one who had already received the promises of
God. 7And without question, the person who has the power to give a blessing
is greater than the one who is blessed.

8The priests who collect tithes are men who die, so Melchizedek is greater
than they are, because we are told that he lives on. 9In addition, we might
even say that these Levites—the ones who collect the tithe—paid a tithe
to Melchizedek when their ancestor Abraham paid a tithe to him. 10For al-
though Levi wasn't born yet, the seed from which he came was in Abraham's
body when Melchizedek collected the tithe from him.

11So if the priesthood of Levi, on which the law was based, could have
achieved the perfection God intended, why did God need to establish a dif-
ferent priesthood, with a priest in the order of Melchizedek instead of the
order of Levi and Aaron?*

12And if the priesthood is changed, the law must also be changed to permit
it. 13For the priest we are talking about belongs to a different tribe, whose
members have never served at the altar as priests. 14What I mean is, our Lord
came from the tribe of Judah, and Moses never mentioned priests coming
from that tribe.

Jesus Is like Melchizedek

15This change has been made very clear since a different priest, who is like
Melchizedek, has appeared. 16Jesus became a priest, not by meeting the
physical requirement of belonging to the tribe of Levi, but by the power of
a life that cannot be destroyed. 17And the psalmist pointed this out when
he prophesied,

> "You are a priest forever in the order of Melchizedek."*

18Yes, the old requirement about the priesthood was set aside because it was
weak and useless. 19For the law never made anything perfect. But now we
have confidence in a better hope, through which we draw near to God.

20This new system was established with a solemn oath. Aaron's descen-
dants became priests without such an oath, 21but there was an oath regarding
Jesus. For God said to him,

> "The LORD has taken an oath and will not break his vow:
> 'You are a priest forever.'"*

Story Arc 7:1-28

● Melchizedek

A brief encounter with Abraham helped Melchizedek become one of the most important characters of the entire Bible (Genesis 14:17-20). Melchizedek's name means "king of justice." He was both the king and the high priest of Salem, the site upon which Jerusalem was established. It was also the site where God provided Abraham with a sacrifice in place of his son, Isaac. It was also the site where David established his throne and where the temple was built. It was, of course, also the site where Jesus established his righteous kingdom by offering his own life as a perfect sacrifice. Psalm 110 predicted that the future Messiah would be a Priest-King in the order of Melchizedek. In what ways did the writer of Hebrews want you to see the comparison between Melchizedek and Jesus? Why does this matter?

Heb 11:1-38 ►

7:5 Greek *from their brothers.* 7:11 Greek *the order of Aaron?* 7:17 Ps 110:4. 7:21 Ps 110:4.

22 Because of this oath, Jesus is the one who guarantees this better covenant
with God.
23 There were many priests under the old system, for death prevented
them from remaining in office. 24 But because Jesus lives forever, his priest-
hood lasts forever. 25 Therefore he is able, once and forever, to save* those
who come to God through him. He lives forever to intercede with God on
their behalf.
26 He is the kind of high priest we need because he is holy and blameless,
unstained by sin. He has been set apart from sinners and has been given
the highest place of honor in heaven.* 27 Unlike those other high priests, he
does not need to offer sacrifices every day. They did this for their own sins
first and then for the sins of the people. But Jesus did this once for all when
he offered himself as the sacrifice for the people's sins. 28 The law appointed
high priests who were limited by human weakness. But after the law was
given, God appointed his Son with an oath, and his Son has been made the
perfect High Priest forever.

Christ Is Our High Priest

8 Here is the main point: We have a High Priest who sat down in the place
of honor beside the throne of the majestic God in heaven. 2 There he
ministers in the heavenly Tabernacle,* the true place of worship that was
built by the Lord and not by human hands.
3 And since every high priest is required to offer gifts and sacrifices, our
High Priest must make an offering, too. 4 If he were here on earth, he would
not even be a priest, since there already are priests who offer the gifts re-
quired by the law. 5 They serve in a system of worship that is only a copy, a
shadow of the real one in heaven. For when Moses was getting ready to build
the Tabernacle, God gave him this warning: "Be sure that you make every-
thing according to the pattern I have shown you here on the mountain."*
6 But now Jesus, our High Priest, has been given a ministry that is far supe-
rior to the old priesthood, for he is the one who mediates for us a far better
covenant with God, based on better promises.
7 If the first covenant had been faultless, there would have been no need
for a second covenant to replace it. 8 But when God found fault with the
people, he said:

"The day is coming, says the LORD,
 when I will make a new covenant
 with the people of Israel and Judah.
9 This covenant will not be like the one
 I made with their ancestors
when I took them by the hand
 and led them out of the land of Egypt.
They did not remain faithful to my covenant,
 so I turned my back on them, says the LORD.
10 But this is the new covenant I will make
 with the people of Israel on that day,* says the LORD:
I will put my laws in their minds,
 and I will write them on their hearts.

7:25 Or *is able to save completely.* 7:26 Or *has been exalted higher than the heavens.* 8:2 Or *tent;* also in 8:5. 8:5 Exod 25:40; 26:30. 8:10 Greek *after those days.*

Prayer 8:10

God, can I be honest? Sometimes obedience is frustrating, but I know that your laws are there to protect me and lead me to real joy. Please help me not only to know your commands in my head but also to truly trust them in my heart. Amen.

Prayer 9:11

Jesus, thank you for entering the Most Holy Place for me and allowing me into the place of ultimate closeness and intimacy with God, the place I could never enter on my own due to my sin. Thank you that through my relationship with you, Jesus, I can enter into God's presence with confidence. Amen.

I will be their God,
and they will be my people.
11 And they will not need to teach their neighbors,
nor will they need to teach their relatives,*
saying, 'You should know the LORD.'
For everyone, from the least to the greatest,
will know me already.
12 And I will forgive their wickedness,
and I will never again remember their sins."*

13 When God speaks of a "new" covenant, it means he has made the first one obsolete. It is now out of date and will soon disappear.

Old Rules about Worship

9 That first covenant between God and Israel had regulations for worship
and a place of worship here on earth. 2 There were two rooms in that
Tabernacle.* In the first room were a lampstand, a table, and sacred loaves of bread on the table. This room was called the Holy Place. 3 Then there was
a curtain, and behind the curtain was the second room* called the Most Holy
Place. 4 In that room were a gold incense altar and a wooden chest called the Ark of the Covenant, which was covered with gold on all sides. Inside the Ark were a gold jar containing manna, Aaron's staff that sprouted leaves,
and the stone tablets of the covenant. 5 Above the Ark were the cherubim
of divine glory, whose wings stretched out over the Ark's cover, the place of atonement. But we cannot explain these things in detail now.
6 When these things were all in place, the priests regularly entered the first
room* as they performed their religious duties. 7 But only the high priest
ever entered the Most Holy Place, and only once a year. And he always offered blood for his own sins and for the sins the people had committed in
ignorance. 8 By these regulations the Holy Spirit revealed that the entrance
to the Most Holy Place was not freely open as long as the Tabernacle* and the system it represented were still in use.
9 This is an illustration pointing to the present time. For the gifts and sacrifices that the priests offer are not able to cleanse the consciences of the
people who bring them. 10 For that old system deals only with food and drink and various cleansing ceremonies—physical regulations that were in effect only until a better system could be established.

Christ Is the Perfect Sacrifice

11 So Christ has now become the High Priest over all the good things that
have come.* He has entered that greater, more perfect Tabernacle in heaven, which was not made by human hands and is not part of this created world.
12 With his own blood—not the blood of goats and calves—he entered the Most Holy Place once for all time and secured our redemption forever.
13 Under the old system, the blood of goats and bulls and the ashes of a
heifer could cleanse people's bodies from ceremonial impurity. 14 Just think
how much more the blood of Christ will purify our consciences from sinful deeds* so that we can worship the living God. For by the power of the eternal

8:11 Greek *their brother.* 8:8-12 Jer 31:31-34. 9:2 Or *tent;* also in 9:11, 21. 9:3 Greek *second tent.* 9:6 Greek *first tent.* 9:8 Or *the first room;* Greek reads *the first tent.* 9:11 Some manuscripts read *that are about to come.* 9:14 Greek *from dead works.*

Spirit, Christ offered himself to God as a perfect sacrifice for our sins. 15 That
is why he is the one who mediates a new covenant between God and people,
so that all who are called can receive the eternal inheritance God has prom-
ised them. For Christ died to set them free from the penalty of the sins they
had committed under that first covenant.

16 Now when someone leaves a will,* it is necessary to prove that the person
who made it is dead.* 17 The will goes into effect only after the person's death.
While the person who made it is still alive, the will cannot be put into effect.

18 That is why even the first covenant was put into effect with the blood
of an animal. 19 For after Moses had read each of God's commandments to
all the people, he took the blood of calves and goats,* along with water,
and sprinkled both the book of God's law and all the people, using hyssop
branches and scarlet wool. 20 Then he said, "This blood confirms the cov-
enant God has made with you."* 21 And in the same way, he sprinkled blood
on the Tabernacle and on everything used for worship. 22 In fact, according
to the law of Moses, nearly everything was purified with blood. For without
the shedding of blood, there is no forgiveness.

23 That is why the Tabernacle and everything in it, which were copies of
things in heaven, had to be purified by the blood of animals. But the real
things in heaven had to be purified with far better sacrifices than the blood
of animals.

24 For Christ did not enter into a holy place made with human hands,
which was only a copy of the true one in heaven. He entered into heaven
itself to appear now before God on our behalf. 25 And he did not enter heaven
to offer himself again and again, like the high priest here on earth who enters
the Most Holy Place year after year with the blood of an animal. 26 If that had
been necessary, Christ would have had to die again and again, ever since the
world began. But now, once for all time, he has appeared at the end of the
age* to remove sin by his own death as a sacrifice.

27 And just as each person is destined to die once and after that comes
judgment, 28 so also Christ was offered once for all time as a sacrifice to take
away the sins of many people. He will come again, not to deal with our sins,
but to bring salvation to all who are eagerly waiting for him.

Christ's Sacrifice Once for All

10 The old system under the law of Moses was only a shadow, a dim pre-
view of the good things to come, not the good things themselves. The
sacrifices under that system were repeated again and again, year after year,
but they were never able to provide perfect cleansing for those who came to
worship. 2 If they could have provided perfect cleansing, the sacrifices would
have stopped, for the worshipers would have been purified once for all time,
and their feelings of guilt would have disappeared.

3 But instead, those sacrifices actually reminded them of their sins year
after year. 4 For it is not possible for the blood of bulls and goats to take away
sins. 5 That is why, when Christ* came into the world, he said to God,

"You did not want animal sacrifices or sin offerings.
  But you have given me a body to offer.

9:16a Or *covenant;* also in 9:17. **9:16b** Or *Now when someone makes a covenant, it is necessary to ratify it with the death of a sacrifice.* **9:19** Some manuscripts do not include *and goats.* **9:20** Exod 24:8. **9:26** Greek *the ages.* **10:5** Greek *he;* also in 10:8.

6 You were not pleased with burnt offerings
or other offerings for sin.
7 Then I said, 'Look, I have come to do your will, O God—
as is written about me in the Scriptures.'"*

8 First, Christ said, "You did not want animal sacrifices or sin offerings or
burnt offerings or other offerings for sin, nor were you pleased with them"
(though they are required by the law of Moses). 9 Then he said, "Look, I have
come to do your will." He cancels the first covenant in order to put the second
into effect. 10 For God's will was for us to be made holy by the sacrifice of the
body of Jesus Christ, once for all time.
11 Under the old covenant, the priest stands and ministers before the altar
day after day, offering the same sacrifices again and again, which can never
take away sins. 12 But our High Priest offered himself to God as a single sac-
rifice for sins, good for all time. Then he sat down in the place of honor at
God's right hand. 13 There he waits until his enemies are humbled and made
a footstool under his feet. 14 For by that one offering he forever made perfect
those who are being made holy.
15 And the Holy Spirit also testifies that this is so. For he says,

16 "This is the new covenant I will make
with my people on that day,* says the LORD:
I will put my laws in their hearts,
and I will write them on their minds."*

17 Then he says,

"I will never again remember
their sins and lawless deeds."*

18 And when sins have been forgiven, there is no need to offer any more
sacrifices.

A Call to Persevere

19 And so, dear brothers and sisters,* we can boldly enter heaven's Most Holy
Place because of the blood of Jesus. 20 By his death,* Jesus opened a new and
life-giving way through the curtain into the Most Holy Place. 21 And since
we have a great High Priest who rules over God's house, 22 let us go right into
the presence of God with sincere hearts fully trusting him. For our guilty
consciences have been sprinkled with Christ's blood to make us clean, and
our bodies have been washed with pure water.
23 Let us hold tightly without wavering to the hope we affirm, for God
can be trusted to keep his promise. 24 Let us think of ways to motivate one
another to acts of love and good works. 25 And let us not neglect our meeting
together, as some people do, but encourage one another, especially now that
the day of his return is drawing near.
26 Dear friends, if we deliberately continue sinning after we have received
knowledge of the truth, there is no longer any sacrifice that will cover these
sins. 27 There is only the terrible expectation of God's judgment and the

10:5-7 Ps 40:6-8 (Greek version). 10:16a Greek *after those days.* 10:16b Jer 31:33a.
10:17 Jer 31:34b. 10:19 Greek *brothers.* 10:20 Greek *Through his flesh.*

Question **10:17**

God doesn't just promise to forgive our sins. He promises to forget them. What's a sin you've committed that you're especially glad God has both forgiven and forgotten? How does it change your perception of yourself, knowing that when God looks at you, he doesn't remember any of your sins?

Prayer **10:23**

Lord Jesus, help me overcome my hesitations to do what you want me to do. Give me a new boldness of heart and hands today. Amen.

Make a Difference

10:24

Motivate Good

Jesus celebrates when we spur one another on to do things he wants us to do. When you give a sudden display of kindness to someone, others notice and eventually do likewise. Your good works can pay it forward to someone else.

When you are creative about your good deeds, your influence increases even more. Your creativity in serving others shows your commitment to love others. It shows that you are thinking of the unique needs and personalities of other people. When you take the time to care uniquely for someone, you display God's love by treasuring and cherishing who they are. Keep doing good. Keep making a difference. Keep blessing this world with the blessing of Jesus.

Difference Maker

Think of two new "acts of love" or "good works."

raging fire that will consume his enemies. 28 For anyone who refused to obey
the law of Moses was put to death without mercy on the testimony of two
or three witnesses. 29 Just think how much worse the punishment will be
for those who have trampled on the Son of God, and have treated the blood
of the covenant, which made us holy, as if it were common and unholy, and
have insulted and disdained the Holy Spirit who brings God's mercy to us.
30 For we know the one who said,

"I will take revenge.
I will pay them back."*

He also said,

"The LORD will judge his own people."*

31 It is a terrible thing to fall into the hands of the living God.
32 Think back on those early days when you first learned about Christ.*
Remember how you remained faithful even though it meant terrible suffer-
ing. 33 Sometimes you were exposed to public ridicule and were beaten, and
sometimes you helped others who were suffering the same things. 34 You suf-
fered along with those who were thrown into jail, and when all you owned
was taken from you, you accepted it with joy. You knew there were better
things waiting for you that will last forever.
35 So do not throw away this confident trust in the Lord. Remember the
great reward it brings you! 36 Patient endurance is what you need now, so
that you will continue to do God's will. Then you will receive all that he
has promised.

37 "For in just a little while,
the Coming One will come and not delay.
38 And my righteous ones will live by faith.*
But I will take no pleasure in anyone who turns away."*

39 But we are not like those who turn away from God to their own destruction.
We are the faithful ones, whose souls will be saved.

Great Examples of Faith

11 Faith shows the reality of what we hope for; it is the evidence of
things we cannot see. 2 Through their faith, the people in days of old
earned a good reputation.
3 By faith we understand that the entire universe was formed at God's com-
mand, that what we now see did not come from anything that can be seen.
4 It was by faith that Abel brought a more acceptable offering to God than
Cain did. Abel's offering gave evidence that he was a righteous man, and God
showed his approval of his gifts. Although Abel is long dead, he still speaks
to us by his example of faith.
5 It was by faith that Enoch was taken up to heaven without dying—"he
disappeared, because God took him."* For before he was taken up, he was

10:30a Deut 32:35. 10:30b Deut 32:36. 10:32 Greek *when you were first enlightened.* 10:38 Or *my righteous ones will live by their faithfulness;* Greek reads *my righteous one will live by faith.* 10:37-38 Hab 2:3-4. 11:5 Gen 5:24.

Practice one of these ways yourself and encourage someone else to practice the other. Then be sure to connect in the next twenty-four hours to celebrate what happened.

Story Arc 11:1-38

Hall of Difference Makers

The writer of Hebrews provided one of the greatest overviews of the story arc of God's salvation plan. Take a few moments (or a whole lifetime!) to go over the names of the individuals mentioned in this chapter. Go through the Bible and review their stories. Don't forget about those who were mentioned in 11:35-38, even though they didn't get their names revealed. As you go through these people in chapter 11, which names surprise you? Whose stories stand out the most to you? How did all these heroes show faith to be "the reality of what we hope for" and the "evidence of things we cannot see" (v. 1)?

Jas 1:1 ►

known as a person who pleased God. 6 And it is impossible to please God
without faith. Anyone who wants to come to him must believe that God
exists and that he rewards those who sincerely seek him.

7 It was by faith that Noah built a large boat to save his family from the
flood. He obeyed God, who warned him about things that had never hap-
pened before. By his faith Noah condemned the rest of the world, and he
received the righteousness that comes by faith.

8 It was by faith that Abraham obeyed when God called him to leave home
and go to another land that God would give him as his inheritance. He went
without knowing where he was going. 9 And even when he reached the land
God promised him, he lived there by faith—for he was like a foreigner, living
in tents. And so did Isaac and Jacob, who inherited the same promise. 10 Abra-
ham was confidently looking forward to a city with eternal foundations, a
city designed and built by God.

11 It was by faith that even Sarah was able to have a child, though she was
barren and was too old. She believed* that God would keep his promise.
12 And so a whole nation came from this one man who was as good as dead—a
nation with so many people that, like the stars in the sky and the sand on the
seashore, there is no way to count them.

13 All these people died still believing what God had promised them. They
did not receive what was promised, but they saw it all from a distance and
welcomed it. They agreed that they were foreigners and nomads here on
earth. 14 Obviously people who say such things are looking forward to a coun-
try they can call their own. 15 If they had longed for the country they came
from, they could have gone back. 16 But they were looking for a better place,
a heavenly homeland. That is why God is not ashamed to be called their God,
for he has prepared a city for them.

17 It was by faith that Abraham offered Isaac as a sacrifice when God was
testing him. Abraham, who had received God's promises, was ready to sac-
rifice his only son, Isaac, 18 even though God had told him, "Isaac is the son
through whom your descendants will be counted."* 19 Abraham reasoned
that if Isaac died, God was able to bring him back to life again. And in a sense,
Abraham did receive his son back from the dead.

20 It was by faith that Isaac promised blessings for the future to his sons,
Jacob and Esau.

21 It was by faith that Jacob, when he was old and dying, blessed each of
Joseph's sons and bowed in worship as he leaned on his staff.

22 It was by faith that Joseph, when he was about to die, said confidently
that the people of Israel would leave Egypt. He even commanded them to
take his bones with them when they left.

23 It was by faith that Moses' parents hid him for three months when he
was born. They saw that God had given them an unusual child, and they
were not afraid to disobey the king's command.

24 It was by faith that Moses, when he grew up, refused to be called the son
of Pharaoh's daughter. 25 He chose to share the oppression of God's people
instead of enjoying the fleeting pleasures of sin. 26 He thought it was better
to suffer for the sake of Christ than to own the treasures of Egypt, for he was
looking ahead to his great reward. 27 It was by faith that Moses left the land
of Egypt, not fearing the king's anger. He kept right on going because he

11:11 Or *It was by faith that he [Abraham] was able to have a child, even though Sarah was barren and he was too old. He believed.* **11:18** Gen 21:12.

kept his eyes on the one who is invisible. 28 It was by faith that Moses com-
manded the people of Israel to keep the Passover and to sprinkle blood on
the doorposts so that the angel of death would not kill their firstborn sons.
29 It was by faith that the people of Israel went right through the Red Sea
as though they were on dry ground. But when the Egyptians tried to follow,
they were all drowned.
30 It was by faith that the people of Israel marched around Jericho for seven
days, and the walls came crashing down.
31 It was by faith that Rahab the prostitute was not destroyed with the
people in her city who refused to obey God. For she had given a friendly
welcome to the spies.
32 How much more do I need to say? It would take too long to recount the
stories of the faith of Gideon, Barak, Samson, Jephthah, David, Samuel, and all
the prophets. 33 By faith these people overthrew kingdoms, ruled with justice,
and received what God had promised them. They shut the mouths of lions,
34 quenched the flames of fire, and escaped death by the edge of the sword. Their
weakness was turned to strength. They became strong in battle and put whole
armies to flight. 35 Women received their loved ones back again from death.
But others were tortured, refusing to turn from God in order to be set free.
They placed their hope in a better life after the resurrection. 36 Some were
jeered at, and their backs were cut open with whips. Others were chained
in prisons. 37 Some died by stoning, some were sawed in half,* and others
were killed with the sword. Some went about wearing skins of sheep and
goats, destitute and oppressed and mistreated. 38 They were too good for this
world, wandering over deserts and mountains, hiding in caves and holes in
the ground.
39 All these people earned a good reputation because of their faith, yet
none of them received all that God had promised. 40 For God had something
better in mind for us, so that they would not reach perfection without us.

God's Discipline Proves His Love

12 Therefore, since we are surrounded by such a huge crowd of wit-
nesses to the life of faith, let us strip off every weight that slows
us down, especially the sin that so easily trips us up. And let us run with
endurance the race God has set before us. 2 We do this by keeping our eyes
on Jesus, the champion who initiates and perfects our faith.* Because of the
joy* awaiting him, he endured the cross, disregarding its shame. Now he is
seated in the place of honor beside God's throne. 3 Think of all the hostility
he endured from sinful people;* then you won't become weary and give up.
4 After all, you have not yet given your lives in your struggle against sin.
5 And have you forgotten the encouraging words God spoke to you as his
children?* He said,

"My child,* don't make light of the LORD's discipline,
  and don't give up when he corrects you.
6 For the LORD disciplines those he loves,
  and he punishes each one he accepts as his child."*

11:37 Some manuscripts add *some were tested.* 12:2a Or *Jesus, the originator and perfecter of our faith.* 12:2b Or *Instead of the joy.* 12:3 Some manuscripts read *Think of how people hurt themselves by opposing him.* 12:5a Greek *sons;* also in 12:7, 8. 12:5b Greek *son;* also in 12:6, 7. 12:5-6 Prov 3:11-12 (Greek version).

Make a Difference 12:1

Run Free

Today you might have found that you have a problem. Like many others, you carry burdens that hinder your speed and strength, that weigh down your ability to run faithfully. You may have attached yourself to some baggage, things that God did not place in your arms, which burden and slow down your faith. When God asks you to do something, go somewhere, help someone, or spend faithful time alone with him, you want to respond well, but you can't. You are entangled.

The race of faith is a daily endurance run. It demands freedom, not baggage, which is why the writer of Hebrews said to get rid of the stuff that distracts you.

Difference Maker

What is weighing you down and tripping you up? What is keeping you from running the race God has set for you? What do you need to do to loosen those entanglements today?

Question 12:2

Have you focused the gaze of your soul upon Jesus? Jesus is initiating a relationship with you. He is looking at you and calling you to run. If you haven't invited Jesus into your life, turn to the back of this Bible and pray through the section on "How to Accept Jesus as Your Lord and Savior."

7 As you endure this divine discipline, remember that God is treating you
as his own children. Who ever heard of a child who is never disciplined by
its father? 8 If God doesn't discipline you as he does all of his children, it
means that you are illegitimate and are not really his children at all. 9 Since
we respected our earthly fathers who disciplined us, shouldn't we submit
even more to the discipline of the Father of our spirits, and live forever?*
10 For our earthly fathers disciplined us for a few years, doing the best they
knew how. But God's discipline is always good for us, so that we might share
in his holiness. 11 No discipline is enjoyable while it is happening—it's pain-
ful! But afterward there will be a peaceful harvest of right living for those
who are trained in this way.

12 So take a new grip with your tired hands and strengthen your weak
knees. 13 Mark out a straight path for your feet so that those who are weak
and lame will not fall but become strong.

A Call to Listen to God

14 Work at living in peace with everyone, and work at living a holy life, for
those who are not holy will not see the Lord. 15 Look after each other so that
none of you fails to receive the grace of God. Watch out that no poisonous
root of bitterness grows up to trouble you, corrupting many. 16 Make sure
that no one is immoral or godless like Esau, who traded his birthright as the
firstborn son for a single meal. 17 You know that afterward, when he wanted
his father's blessing, he was rejected. It was too late for repentance, even
though he begged with bitter tears.

18 You have not come to a physical mountain,* to a place of flaming fire,
darkness, gloom, and whirlwind, as the Israelites did at Mount Sinai. 19 For
they heard an awesome trumpet blast and a voice so terrible that they begged
God to stop speaking. 20 They staggered back under God's command: "If
even an animal touches the mountain, it must be stoned to death."* 21 Moses
himself was so frightened at the sight that he said, "I am terrified and
trembling."*

22 No, you have come to Mount Zion, to the city of the living God, the
heavenly Jerusalem, and to countless thousands of angels in a joyful gath-
ering. 23 You have come to the assembly of God's firstborn children, whose
names are written in heaven. You have come to God himself, who is the judge
over all things. You have come to the spirits of the righteous ones in heaven
who have now been made perfect. 24 You have come to Jesus, the one who
mediates the new covenant between God and people, and to the sprinkled
blood, which speaks of forgiveness instead of crying out for vengeance like
the blood of Abel.

25 Be careful that you do not refuse to listen to the One who is speaking.
For if the people of Israel did not escape when they refused to listen to
Moses, the earthly messenger, we will certainly not escape if we reject the
One who speaks to us from heaven! 26 When God spoke from Mount Si-
nai his voice shook the earth, but now he makes another promise: "Once
again I will shake not only the earth but the heavens also."* 27 This means
that all of creation will be shaken and removed, so that only unshakable
things will remain.

28 Since we are receiving a Kingdom that is unshakable, let us be thankful

12:9 Or *and really live?* 12:18 Greek *to something that can be touched.* 12:20 Exod 19:13.
12:21 Deut 9:19. 12:26 Hag 2:6.

and please God by worshiping him with holy fear and awe. 29 For our God
is a devouring fire.

Concluding Words

13 Keep on loving each other as brothers and sisters.* 2 Don't forget to
show hospitality to strangers, for some who have done this have
entertained angels without realizing it! 3 Remember those in prison, as if
you were there yourself. Remember also those being mistreated, as if you
felt their pain in your own bodies.
4 Give honor to marriage, and remain faithful to one another in mar-
riage. God will surely judge people who are immoral and those who com-
mit adultery.
5 Don't love money; be satisfied with what you have. For God has said,

"I will never fail you.
I will never abandon you."*

6 So we can say with confidence,

"The LORD is my helper,
so I will have no fear.
What can mere people do to me?"*

7 Remember your leaders who taught you the word of God. Think of all the
good that has come from their lives, and follow the example of their faith.
8 Jesus Christ is the same yesterday, today, and forever. 9 So do not be at-
tracted by strange, new ideas. Your strength comes from God's grace, not
from rules about food, which don't help those who follow them.
10 We have an altar from which the priests in the Tabernacle* have no right
to eat. 11 Under the old system, the high priest brought the blood of animals
into the Holy Place as a sacrifice for sin, and the bodies of the animals were
burned outside the camp. 12 So also Jesus suffered and died outside the city
gates to make his people holy by means of his own blood. 13 So let us go out
to him, outside the camp, and bear the disgrace he bore. 14 For this world is
not our permanent home; we are looking forward to a home yet to come.
15 Therefore, let us offer through Jesus a continual sacrifice of praise to
God, proclaiming our allegiance to his name. 16 And don't forget to do good
and to share with those in need. These are the sacrifices that please God.
17 Obey your spiritual leaders, and do what they say. Their work is to watch
over your souls, and they are accountable to God. Give them reason to do this
with joy and not with sorrow. That would certainly not be for your benefit.
18 Pray for us, for our conscience is clear and we want to live honorably in
everything we do. 19 And especially pray that I will be able to come back to
you soon.

20 Now may the God of peace—
who brought up from the dead our Lord Jesus,
the great Shepherd of the sheep,
and ratified an eternal covenant with his blood—

13:1 Greek *Continue in brotherly love.* 13:5 Deut 31:6, 8. 13:6 Ps 118:6. 13:10 Or *tent.*

Question 13:8-9

Why would we keep looking for the next new thing to bring satisfaction to our lives?

Question 13:16

Who's one person in your life who's in need? Their needs might be emotional, like the need for acceptance. They might be spiritual, like the need for the gospel. They might be tangible, like the need for food. How can you help share your resources with them this week?

Prayer 13:20-21

Lord, may you equip me with all I need to do your will. May you produce in me, through the power of Jesus Christ, every good thing that is pleasing to you. All glory to you forever and ever! Amen.

[21] may he equip you with all you need
for doing his will.
May he produce in you,*
through the power of Jesus Christ,
every good thing that is pleasing to him.
All glory to him forever and ever! Amen.

[22] I urge you, dear brothers and sisters,* to pay attention to what I have written in this brief exhortation.

[23] I want you to know that our brother Timothy has been released from jail. If he comes here soon, I will bring him with me to see you.

[24] Greet all your leaders and all the believers there.* The believers from Italy send you their greetings.

[25] May God's grace be with you all.

13:21 Some manuscripts read *in us.* 13:22 Greek *brothers.* 13:24 Greek *all of God's holy people.*

James Introduction

Perseverance is a terrible word. *Per* means "through," and *severance* means "to get cut off." Therefore, *perseverance* means going through a time of getting cut off. Those who have had to persevere through terrible circumstances understand the near-devastating process of long-suffering, especially when the suffering is caused by someone else or, perhaps, when it means saying no to a tempting desire or cheap escape.

James knew something about perseverance. Most scholars believe he was the half brother of Jesus (Matthew 13:55; Galatians 1:19). Because of his relationship to Jesus, he had to endure all kinds of struggles over the course of his life. On the one hand, he disagreed with Jesus about how Jesus should go about doing his ministry (John 7:1–5). On the other hand, after committing himself to his brother as his Lord and Savior, James experienced persecution for his faith. At times, it would have been so tempting to take the easy way out, to disassociate with Jesus. Nevertheless, James learned to put into practice the blessed reality of following the "glorious Lord Jesus Christ" (James 2:1).

Here James wrote primarily to Jewish Christians who had been scattered around the Roman Empire following Stephen's death in Acts 11:19. These first Christians were persecuted simply for following Jesus. They had to learn to persevere through some terrible treatment and some harsh realities. They had to face fear and threats and loss and pain. It must have been tempting at times to wonder about giving up and pursuing a path that would help them fit in better with the world around them. Still, they endured. Their trials proved their perseverance, displaying miraculous character that changed the world.

Gritty perseverance for following Jesus does not come from a mild, passive commitment to faith. It comes only from a daily put-into-practice devotion to Christ. The question James poses to the reader is simple: Will you choose to draw close to God and live out your faith today...and then do it again tomorrow...no matter what comes your way?

Story Arc

- **James**

JAMES

James

Greetings from James

1 This letter is from James, a slave of God and of the Lord Jesus Christ.
I am writing to the "twelve tribes"—Jewish believers scattered abroad.
Greetings!

Faith and Endurance

2 Dear brothers and sisters,* when troubles of any kind come your way, con-
sider it an opportunity for great joy. 3 For you know that when your faith is
tested, your endurance has a chance to grow. 4 So let it grow, for when your
endurance is fully developed, you will be perfect and complete, needing
nothing.
5 If you need wisdom, ask our generous God, and he will give it to you. He
will not rebuke you for asking. 6 But when you ask him, be sure that your
faith is in God alone. Do not waver, for a person with divided loyalty is as un-
settled as a wave of the sea that is blown and tossed by the wind. 7 Such people
should not expect to receive anything from the Lord. 8 Their loyalty is divided
between God and the world, and they are unstable in everything they do.
9 Believers who are* poor have something to boast about, for God has hon-
ored them. 10 And those who are rich should boast that God has humbled
them. They will fade away like a little flower in the field. 11 The hot sun rises
and the grass withers; the little flower droops and falls, and its beauty fades
away. In the same way, the rich will fade away with all of their achievements.
12 God blesses those who patiently endure testing and temptation. After-
ward they will receive the crown of life that God has promised to those who
love him. 13 And remember, when you are being tempted, do not say, "God
is tempting me." God is never tempted to do wrong,* and he never tempts
anyone else. 14 Temptation comes from our own desires, which entice us and
drag us away. 15 These desires give birth to sinful actions. And when sin is
allowed to grow, it gives birth to death.
16 So don't be misled, my dear brothers and sisters. 17 Whatever is good
and perfect is a gift coming down to us from God our Father, who created
all the lights in the heavens.* He never changes or casts a shifting shadow.*
18 He chose to give birth to us by giving us his true word. And we, out of all
creation, became his prized possession.*

Listening and Doing

19 Understand this, my dear brothers and sisters: You must all be quick to lis-
ten, slow to speak, and slow to get angry. 20 Human anger* does not produce
the righteousness* God desires. 21 So get rid of all the filth and evil in your

1:2 Greek *brothers;* also in 1:16, 19. 1:9 Greek *The brother who is.* 1:13 Or *God should not be put to a test by evil people.* 1:17a Greek *from above, from the Father of lights.* 1:17b Some manuscripts read *He never changes, as a shifting shadow does.* 1:18 Greek *we became a kind of firstfruit of his creatures.* 1:20a Greek *A man's anger.* 1:20b Or *the justice.*

Prayer 1:12-15

Lord Jesus, I don't have the strength in me unless you enable it. Please give me the motivation to never quit. Amen.

Prayer 1:19

Lord Jesus, let my words be few and my ears be wide open. Amen.

Story Arc 1:1

James

Imagine knowing Jesus as your brother. After Jesus was born, Mary had other children (Matthew 12:46; 13:55-56; Mark 3:31-32; 6:3; Galatians 1:19). At first, it seems, they struggled to trust Jesus' mission. Eventually though, James, along with another brother, Jude, became leaders in the early church, and both wrote letters that bear their names in the New Testament. At the start of his letter, James called himself a "slave of God and of the Lord Jesus Christ." What do you think happened in James's understanding of his half brother to make him speak something so daring?

1 Pet 1:1 ►

lives, and humbly accept the word God has planted in your hearts, for it has
the power to save your souls.
22But don't just listen to God's word. You must do what it says. Otherwise,
you are only fooling yourselves. 23For if you listen to the word and don't obey,
it is like glancing at your face in a mirror. 24You see yourself, walk away, and
forget what you look like. 25But if you look carefully into the perfect law that
sets you free, and if you do what it says and don't forget what you heard, then
God will bless you for doing it.
26If you claim to be religious but don't control your tongue, you are fool-
ing yourself, and your religion is worthless. 27Pure and genuine religion in
the sight of God the Father means caring for orphans and widows in their
distress and refusing to let the world corrupt you.

A Warning against Prejudice

2 My dear brothers and sisters,* how can you claim to have faith in our
glorious Lord Jesus Christ if you favor some people over others?
2For example, suppose someone comes into your meeting* dressed in
fancy clothes and expensive jewelry, and another comes in who is poor and
dressed in dirty clothes. 3If you give special attention and a good seat to the
rich person, but you say to the poor one, "You can stand over there, or else sit
on the floor"—well, 4doesn't this discrimination show that your judgments
are guided by evil motives?
5Listen to me, dear brothers and sisters. Hasn't God chosen the poor in this
world to be rich in faith? Aren't they the ones who will inherit the Kingdom
he promised to those who love him? 6But you dishonor the poor! Isn't it the
rich who oppress you and drag you into court? 7Aren't they the ones who
slander Jesus Christ, whose noble name* you bear?
8Yes indeed, it is good when you obey the royal law as found in the Scrip-
tures: "Love your neighbor as yourself."* 9But if you favor some people over
others, you are committing a sin. You are guilty of breaking the law.
10For the person who keeps all of the laws except one is as guilty as a
person who has broken all of God's laws. 11For the same God who said,
"You must not commit adultery," also said, "You must not murder."* So
if you murder someone but do not commit adultery, you have still broken
the law.
12So whatever you say or whatever you do, remember that you will be
judged by the law that sets you free. 13There will be no mercy for those who
have not shown mercy to others. But if you have been merciful, God will be
merciful when he judges you.

Faith without Good Deeds Is Dead

14What good is it, dear brothers and sisters, if you say you have faith but don't
show it by your actions? Can that kind of faith save anyone? 15Suppose you
see a brother or sister who has no food or clothing, 16and you say, "Good-bye
and have a good day; stay warm and eat well"—but then you don't give that
person any food or clothing. What good does that do?
17So you see, faith by itself isn't enough. Unless it produces good deeds,
it is dead and useless.
18Now someone may argue, "Some people have faith; others have good

2:1 Greek *brothers;* also in 2:5, 14. 2:2 Greek *your synagogue.* 2:7 Greek *slander the noble name.* 2:8 Lev 19:18. 2:11 Exod 20:13-14; Deut 5:17-18.

Make a Difference 1:27

Pure Religion

When Christianity is at its best, it is undeniably beneficial for the world. The irony, however, is that Christianity is at its best when it is countercultural. Spending yourself on behalf of people who cannot pay you back goes against the give-and-receive culture in which we live.

Difference Maker

Contact a nursing home or an orphanage today. Ask them if you can visit to see what opportunities they have.

Make a Difference

2:1-13

Seat of Honor

The human heart is full of so much potential. It was made to reflect the love that God has for every person, yet in its corruption are the ingredients for all kinds of hatred and cruelty. The person who discriminates against people incriminates himself in twisted ambitions. Each person, no matter their life circumstance, is valuable in the eyes of God. Jesus is calling you to restore to a godly pattern the way you treat people.

Difference Maker

Whenever you have the opportunity, give dignity ("the seat of honor") to someone whom society doesn't readily recognize as being worthy.

Prayer 2:17

Lord Jesus, don't let me treat you like an add-on to my life. Amen.

deeds." But I say, "How can you show me your faith if you don't have good deeds? I will show you my faith by my good deeds."

19 You say you have faith, for you believe that there is one God.* Good for you! Even the demons believe this, and they tremble in terror. 20 How foolish! Can't you see that faith without good deeds is useless?

21 Don't you remember that our ancestor Abraham was shown to be right with God by his actions when he offered his son Isaac on the altar? 22 You see, his faith and his actions worked together. His actions made his faith complete. 23 And so it happened just as the Scriptures say: "Abraham believed God, and God counted him as righteous because of his faith."* He was even called the friend of God.* 24 So you see, we are shown to be right with God by what we do, not by faith alone.

25 Rahab the prostitute is another example. She was shown to be right with God by her actions when she hid those messengers and sent them safely away by a different road. 26 Just as the body is dead without breath,* so also faith is dead without good works.

Controlling the Tongue

3 Dear brothers and sisters,* not many of you should become teachers in the church, for we who teach will be judged more strictly. 2 Indeed, we all make many mistakes. For if we could control our tongues, we would be perfect and could also control ourselves in every other way.

3 We can make a large horse go wherever we want by means of a small bit in its mouth. 4 And a small rudder makes a huge ship turn wherever the pilot chooses to go, even though the winds are strong. 5 In the same way, the tongue is a small thing that makes grand speeches.

But a tiny spark can set a great forest on fire. 6 And among all the parts of the body, the tongue is a flame of fire. It is a whole world of wickedness, corrupting your entire body. It can set your whole life on fire, for it is set on fire by hell itself.*

7 People can tame all kinds of animals, birds, reptiles, and fish, 8 but no one can tame the tongue. It is restless and evil, full of deadly poison. 9 Sometimes it praises our Lord and Father, and sometimes it curses those who have been made in the image of God. 10 And so blessing and cursing come pouring out of the same mouth. Surely, my brothers and sisters, this is not right! 11 Does a spring of water bubble out with both fresh water and bitter water? 12 Does a fig tree produce olives, or a grapevine produce figs? No, and you can't draw fresh water from a salty spring.*

True Wisdom Comes from God

13 If you are wise and understand God's ways, prove it by living an honorable life, doing good works with the humility that comes from wisdom. 14 But if you are bitterly jealous and there is selfish ambition in your heart, don't cover up the truth with boasting and lying. 15 For jealousy and selfishness are not God's kind of wisdom. Such things are earthly, unspiritual, and demonic. 16 For wherever there is jealousy and selfish ambition, there you will find disorder and evil of every kind.

17 But the wisdom from above is first of all pure. It is also peace loving,

2:19 Some manuscripts read *that God is one;* see Deut 6:4. 2:23a Gen 15:6. 2:23b See Isa 41:8. 2:26 Or *without spirit.* 3:1 Greek *brothers;* also in 3:10. 3:6 Or *for it will burn in hell* (Greek *Gehenna*). 3:12 Greek *from salt.*

Make a Difference 2:26

Lifeless

No pulse. DOA (dead on arrival). That's how the Bible describes faith that fails to show any evidence through good works. It's a dramatic statement, but the point is valid. Faith inhales and then exhales the very breath of God. A faith with no indication of dynamic activity is no faith at all. Don't let the coroner be called out to comment on your faith. No, be alive with Jesus. Let him kick-start your heart and motivate your hands to action in this world. Let others see a living faith, pulsating with the life of the Creator of the universe.

Difference Maker

Notice your breathing. Each time you inhale and exhale, think about the living, breathing relationship you have with Jesus.

Make a Difference 3:1–12

Tame

We have figured out how to train elephants to stand on buckets. Also, for some reason, we have persuaded lions to let us stick our heads between their open jaws. We have figured out how to make seals clap, dolphins wave, and killer whales belly flop, all on command. We have even convinced snakes to dance to music, tigers to jump through hoops, and bears to wear tutus and tiaras. Even so, none of us have yet to figure out how to control that little muscle in our mouths.

Difference Maker

To remind yourself of this passage, draw a smiley face with a tongue sticking out (on your hand or arm) and write "James 3" next to it.

gentle at all times, and willing to yield to others. It is full of mercy and the
fruit of good deeds. It shows no favoritism and is always sincere. 18 And
those who are peacemakers will plant seeds of peace and reap a harvest of
righteousness.*

Drawing Close to God

4 What is causing the quarrels and fights among you? Don't they come
from the evil desires at war within you? 2 You want what you don't have,
so you scheme and kill to get it. You are jealous of what others have, but you
can't get it, so you fight and wage war to take it away from them. Yet you
don't have what you want because you don't ask God for it. 3 And even when
you ask, you don't get it because your motives are all wrong—you want only
what will give you pleasure.
4 You adulterers!* Don't you realize that friendship with the world makes
you an enemy of God? I say it again: If you want to be a friend of the world,
you make yourself an enemy of God. 5 Do you think the Scriptures have no
meaning? They say that God is passionate that the spirit he has placed within us
should be faithful to him.* 6 And he gives grace generously. As the Scriptures say,

"God opposes the proud
but gives grace to the humble."*

7 So humble yourselves before God. Resist the devil, and he will flee from
you. 8 Come close to God, and God will come close to you. Wash your hands,
you sinners; purify your hearts, for your loyalty is divided between God and
the world. 9 Let there be tears for what you have done. Let there be sorrow
and deep grief. Let there be sadness instead of laughter, and gloom instead
of joy. 10 Humble yourselves before the Lord, and he will lift you up in honor.

Warning against Judging Others

11 Don't speak evil against each other, dear brothers and sisters.* If you criti-
cize and judge each other, then you are criticizing and judging God's law.
But your job is to obey the law, not to judge whether it applies to you. 12 God
alone, who gave the law, is the Judge. He alone has the power to save or to
destroy. So what right do you have to judge your neighbor?

Warning about Self-Confidence

13 Look here, you who say, "Today or tomorrow we are going to a certain
town and will stay there a year. We will do business there and make a profit."
14 How do you know what your life will be like tomorrow? Your life is like the
morning fog—it's here a little while, then it's gone. 15 What you ought to say
is, "If the Lord wants us to, we will live and do this or that." 16 Otherwise you
are boasting about your own pretentious plans, and all such boasting is evil.
17 Remember, it is sin to know what you ought to do and then not do it.

Warning to the Rich

5 Look here, you rich people: Weep and groan with anguish because of
all the terrible troubles ahead of you. 2 Your wealth is rotting away, and

Prayer **4:8**

Lord Jesus, thank you for creating me to have relationship with you. Turn my eyes from worthless things. Amen.

Make a Difference
4:7-10

Humbled

Humility is such an elusive, ironic beauty. The moment we think we have it, haven't we lost it? Could anyone ever accurately say, "I am humble"? Yes. Someone could. Jesus could. In fact, he is the only one who was qualified to do so. Jesus is the ultimate King, and he is the ultimate Servant. Although he is greater than the greatest greatness that could ever be, he humbled himself to the point of dying on a cross for our sake. He voluntarily gave up all his glory so that we could live. No one can ever be as truly great as Jesus or as truly humble as Jesus. That fact should humble us even further.

Difference Maker

Today, don't ask God to honor your plans or to do something for you. Instead, consider how you might honor the Lord through your words and actions.

Question **4:17**

What good thing should you be doing that you have been avoiding?

3:18 Or *of good things,* or *of justice.* 4:4 Greek *You adulteresses!* 4:5 Or *They say that the spirit God has placed within us is filled with envy;* or *They say that the Holy Spirit, whom God has placed within us, opposes our envy.* 4:6 Prov 3:34 (Greek version). 4:11 Greek *brothers.*

your fine clothes are moth-eaten rags. 3 Your gold and silver are corroded.
The very wealth you were counting on will eat away your flesh like fire. This
corroded treasure you have hoarded will testify against you on the day of
judgment. 4 For listen! Hear the cries of the field workers whom you have
cheated of their pay. The cries of those who harvest your fields have reached
the ears of the LORD of Heaven's Armies.

5 You have spent your years on earth in luxury, satisfying your every desire.
You have fattened yourselves for the day of slaughter. 6 You have condemned
and killed innocent people,* who do not resist you.*

Patience and Endurance

7 Dear brothers and sisters,* be patient as you wait for the Lord's return.
Consider the farmers who patiently wait for the rains in the fall and in the
spring. They eagerly look for the valuable harvest to ripen. 8 You, too, must
be patient. Take courage, for the coming of the Lord is near.

9 Don't grumble about each other, brothers and sisters, or you will be
judged. For look—the Judge is standing at the door!

10 For examples of patience in suffering, dear brothers and sisters, look at
the prophets who spoke in the name of the Lord. 11 We give great honor to
those who endure under suffering. For instance, you know about Job, a man
of great endurance. You can see how the Lord was kind to him at the end, for
the Lord is full of tenderness and mercy.

12 But most of all, my brothers and sisters, never take an oath, by heaven
or earth or anything else. Just say a simple yes or no, so that you will not sin
and be condemned.

The Power of Prayer

13 Are any of you suffering hardships? You should pray. Are any of you happy?
You should sing praises. 14 Are any of you sick? You should call for the elders
of the church to come and pray over you, anointing you with oil in the name
of the Lord. 15 Such a prayer offered in faith will heal the sick, and the Lord
will make you well. And if you have committed any sins, you will be forgiven.

16 Confess your sins to each other and pray for each other so that you may
be healed. The earnest prayer of a righteous person has great power and
produces wonderful results. 17 Elijah was as human as we are, and yet when
he prayed earnestly that no rain would fall, none fell for three and a half
years! 18 Then, when he prayed again, the sky sent down rain and the earth
began to yield its crops.

Restore Wandering Believers

19 My dear brothers and sisters, if someone among you wanders away from
the truth and is brought back, 20 you can be sure that whoever brings the sin-
ner back from wandering will save that person from death and bring about
the forgiveness of many sins.

5:6a Or *killed the Righteous One.* **5:6b** Or *Don't they resist you?* or *Doesn't God oppose you?* or *Aren't they now accusing you before God?* **5:7** Greek *brothers;* also in 5:9, 10, 12, 19.

Prayer **5:9**

Lord Jesus, change my grumbling heart into a fulfilled one. Amen.

Make a Difference **5:16**

Accountability

When you mess up, simply admit it. Don't let the mess fester. Free yourself from the self-imposed shackles of your sin. Let it off your heart. Share it with someone you can trust and who will help you take the next steps toward freedom. It would be good to find someone to hold you accountable—a friend who will follow up with you and encourage you and watch where you step, a friend who will pray for your healing and change.

Difference Maker

Ask someone you trust to be your accountability partner.

Make a Difference **5:19-20**

Reach Out

One of the most gut-wrenching things in life is a friend who wanders away from a relationship with God and with you. Don't give up on your friend. Reach out. Extend a loving invitation back into a relationship. Organize people in your church community to show love, forgiveness, and joy. Don't try to push or trick your friend. Simply and vigilantly, keep watch for the moment of restoration.

Difference Maker

Think of a friend you have not seen for a while who has slowly wandered away. Invite them to grab a coffee or to hang out with you sometime.

1 Peter Introduction

Peter was a central character in the Gospels and one of the people closest to Jesus during his time on earth. In fact, Jesus told Peter he would use him as the starting point for the entire Christian church. That's a big deal!

Despite his costarring role in the story of Jesus, only two short books in the Bible were written by him. Still, just as Jesus said, Peter's words are valuable for the entire church, for Jesus followers everywhere, and his words come at just the right time.

Being a Christian is hard, and it is getting even harder. With all the challenges that are happening, many Christians are starting to wonder if it is worth it. If following Jesus is really the best choice, why do so many things seem to go wrong? Modern Christians are asking if it is really worth it to be resilient and go through all the hard stuff.

Peter passionately argued that yes, it is worth it. He said that even the struggles are a chance to experience God's love in new ways and to help others discover the hope that Jesus offers. Following Jesus isn't the easiest, but it's the best.

In 1 Peter, we are reminded that God is still working even when things go wrong. Life is unfair, and sometimes being a Christian means accepting unfair or hard circumstances because that's what Jesus did, and it's how we can make the biggest difference.

Story Arc

- **Peter**

1 Peter

Greetings from Peter

1 This letter is from Peter, an apostle of Jesus Christ.

I am writing to God's chosen people who are living as foreigners in the provinces of Pontus, Galatia, Cappadocia, Asia, and Bithynia.* 2 God the Father knew you and chose you long ago, and his Spirit has made you holy. As a result, you have obeyed him and have been cleansed by the blood of Jesus Christ.

May God give you more and more grace and peace.

The Hope of Eternal Life

3 All praise to God, the Father of our Lord Jesus Christ. It is by his great mercy that we have been born again, because God raised Jesus Christ from the dead. Now we live with great expectation, 4 and we have a priceless inheritance—an inheritance that is kept in heaven for you, pure and undefiled, beyond the reach of change and decay. 5 And through your faith, God is protecting you by his power until you receive this salvation, which is ready to be revealed on the last day for all to see.

6 So be truly glad.* There is wonderful joy ahead, even though you must endure many trials for a little while. 7 These trials will show that your faith is genuine. It is being tested as fire tests and purifies gold—though your faith is far more precious than mere gold. So when your faith remains strong through many trials, it will bring you much praise and glory and honor on the day when Jesus Christ is revealed to the whole world.

8 You love him even though you have never seen him. Though you do not see him now, you trust him; and you rejoice with a glorious, inexpressible joy. 9 The reward for trusting him will be the salvation of your souls.

10 This salvation was something even the prophets wanted to know more about when they prophesied about this gracious salvation prepared for you. 11 They wondered what time or situation the Spirit of Christ within them was talking about when he told them in advance about Christ's suffering and his great glory afterward.

12 They were told that their messages were not for themselves, but for you. And now this Good News has been announced to you by those who preached in the power of the Holy Spirit sent from heaven. It is all so wonderful that even the angels are eagerly watching these things happen.

A Call to Holy Living

13 So prepare your minds for action and exercise self-control. Put all your hope in the gracious salvation that will come to you when Jesus Christ is revealed to the world. 14 So you must live as God's obedient children. Don't slip back into your old ways of living to satisfy your own desires. You didn't

Story Arc 1:1

● Peter

Peter, along with his dear friends Silas and Mark, wrote this letter to Christians living in what is now called Türkiye (Turkey). Peter is a changed man from his early, brash days as a hotheaded fisherman. Jesus changed him. The cross changed him. The empty tomb changed him. As a result, he couldn't stop telling people all over the world about being "born again" (1:3) because of Jesus. By writing this letter, Peter hoped that these new believers would be encouraged to stand firm in Christ (5:12-13).

2 Pet 3:15-16 ►

1:1 *Pontus, Galatia, Cappadocia, Asia,* and *Bithynia* were Roman provinces in what is now Turkey.
1:6 Or *So you are truly glad.*

know any better then. 15 But now you must be holy in everything you do,
just as God who chose you is holy. 16 For the Scriptures say, "You must be
holy because I am holy."*

17 And remember that the heavenly Father to whom you pray has no
favorites. He will judge or reward you according to what you do. So you
must live in reverent fear of him during your time here as "temporary
residents." 18 For you know that God paid a ransom to save you from the
empty life you inherited from your ancestors. And it was not paid with
mere gold or silver, which lose their value. 19 It was the precious blood of
Christ, the sinless, spotless Lamb of God. 20 God chose him as your ran-
som long before the world began, but now in these last days he has been
revealed for your sake.

21 Through Christ you have come to trust in God. And you have placed
your faith and hope in God because he raised Christ from the dead and gave
him great glory.

22 You were cleansed from your sins when you obeyed the truth, so now
you must show sincere love to each other as brothers and sisters.* Love each
other deeply with all your heart.*

23 For you have been born again, but not to a life that will quickly end. Your
new life will last forever because it comes from the eternal, living word of
God. 24 As the Scriptures say,

"People are like grass;
their beauty is like a flower in the field.
The grass withers and the flower fades.
25 But the word of the Lord remains forever."*

And that word is the Good News that was preached to you.

Question 1:23

If you knew you had the rest of *eternity* to pursue your goals in life, would it change the sort of goals you would pursue? Think about the long-term goals you have for your life. If you had all the time in the universe, would those goals be big enough?

2 So get rid of all evil behavior. Be done with all deceit, hypocrisy, jealousy,
and all unkind speech. 2 Like newborn babies, you must crave pure spiri-
tual milk so that you will grow into a full experience of salvation. Cry out
for this nourishment, 3 now that you have had a taste of the Lord's kindness.

Living Stones for God's House

4 You are coming to Christ, who is the living cornerstone of God's temple. He
was rejected by people, but he was chosen by God for great honor.

5 And you are living stones that God is building into his spiritual temple.
What's more, you are his holy priests.* Through the mediation of Jesus
Christ, you offer spiritual sacrifices that please God. 6 As the Scriptures say,

"I am placing a cornerstone in Jerusalem,*
chosen for great honor,
and anyone who trusts in him
will never be disgraced."*

7 Yes, you who trust him recognize the honor God has given him.* But for
those who reject him,

1:16 Lev 11:44-45; 19:2; 20:7. **1:22a** Greek *must have brotherly love.* **1:22b** Some manuscripts read *with a pure heart.* **1:24-25** Isa 40:6-8. **2:5** Greek *holy priesthood.* **2:6a** Greek *in Zion.* **2:6b** Isa 28:16 (Greek version). **2:7a** Or *Yes, for you who believe, there is honor.*

Make a Difference

2:11-12

How You Live

People don't learn about Jesus just from going to church. In fact, most people learn about Jesus through everyday, regular life encounters with his followers. This means that if people regularly go to the grocery store, then they will repeatedly run into followers of Jesus who also naturally go to the grocery store. If people regularly sit down for meals, spend hours at work, hang out at school, or watch a baseball game, it is very likely that followers of Jesus will be there too.

While good behavior at church is noteworthy, it could be argued that what is significantly more important is how followers of Jesus live the other six days of the week in the regular routines of everyday life. It makes a difference what kind of words they use on Monday. It matters how they speak about others on Tuesday, how they stand in a long line on Wednesday, whether they are trustworthy at work on Thursday, how they spend their money on Friday, and if they are reliable as neighbors on Saturday.

Difference Maker

Next time you are not at church but still find that you are with people, consider how important it is to follow Jesus right in that moment.

Prayer **2:15**

Dear Jesus, let my talk and my walk be so saturated in you today that others will see you in me. Amen.

"The stone that the builders rejected
has now become the cornerstone."*

8 And,

"He is the stone that makes people stumble,
the rock that makes them fall."*

They stumble because they do not obey God's word, and so they meet the fate that was planned for them.

9 But you are not like that, for you are a chosen people. You are royal priests,* a holy nation, God's very own possession. As a result, you can show others the goodness of God, for he called you out of the darkness into his wonderful light.

10 "Once you had no identity as a people;
now you are God's people.
Once you received no mercy;
now you have received God's mercy."*

11 Dear friends, I warn you as "temporary residents and foreigners" to keep
away from worldly desires that wage war against your very souls. 12 Be care-
ful to live properly among your unbelieving neighbors. Then even if they accuse you of doing wrong, they will see your honorable behavior, and they will give honor to God when he judges the world.*

Respecting People in Authority

13 For the Lord's sake, submit to all human authority—whether the king as
head of state, 14 or the officials he has appointed. For the king has sent them
to punish those who do wrong and to honor those who do right.
15 It is God's will that your honorable lives should silence those igno-
rant people who make foolish accusations against you. 16 For you are free,
yet you are God's slaves, so don't use your freedom as an excuse to do
evil. 17 Respect everyone, and love the family of believers.* Fear God, and
respect the king.

Slaves

18 You who are slaves must submit to your masters with all respect.* Do what
they tell you—not only if they are kind and reasonable, but even if they are
cruel. 19 For God is pleased when, conscious of his will, you patiently endure
unjust treatment. 20 Of course, you get no credit for being patient if you are
beaten for doing wrong. But if you suffer for doing good and endure it patiently, God is pleased with you.

21 For God called you to do good, even if it means suffering, just as Christ suffered* for you. He is your example, and you must follow in his steps.

22 He never sinned,
nor ever deceived anyone.*

2:7b Ps 118:22. 2:8 Isa 8:14. 2:9 Greek *a royal priesthood.* 2:10 Hos 1:6, 9; 2:23. 2:12 Or *on the day of visitation.* 2:17 Greek *love the brotherhood.* 2:18 Or *because you fear God;* Greek reads *in all fear.* 2:21 Some manuscripts read *died.* 2:22 Isa 53:9.

23 He did not retaliate when he was insulted,
nor threaten revenge when he suffered.
He left his case in the hands of God,
who always judges fairly.
24 He personally carried our sins
in his body on the cross
so that we can be dead to sin
and live for what is right.
By his wounds
you are healed.
25 Once you were like sheep
who wandered away.
But now you have turned to your Shepherd,
the Guardian of your souls.

Wives

3 In the same way, you wives must accept the authority of your husbands. Then, even if some refuse to obey the Good News, your godly lives will speak to them without any words. They will be won over 2 by observing your pure and reverent lives.

3 Don't be concerned about the outward beauty of fancy hairstyles, expensive jewelry, or beautiful clothes. 4 You should clothe yourselves instead with the beauty that comes from within, the unfading beauty of a gentle and quiet spirit, which is so precious to God. 5 This is how the holy women of old made themselves beautiful. They put their trust in God and accepted the authority of their husbands. 6 For instance, Sarah obeyed her husband, Abraham, and called him her master. You are her daughters when you do what is right without fear of what your husbands might do.

Husbands

7 In the same way, you husbands must give honor to your wives. Treat your wife with understanding as you live together. She may be weaker than you are, but she is your equal partner in God's gift of new life. Treat her as you should so your prayers will not be hindered.

All Christians

8 Finally, all of you should be of one mind. Sympathize with each other. Love each other as brothers and sisters.* Be tenderhearted, and keep a humble attitude. 9 Don't repay evil for evil. Don't retaliate with insults when people insult you. Instead, pay them back with a blessing. That is what God has called you to do, and he will grant you his blessing. 10 For the Scriptures say,

"If you want to enjoy life
and see many happy days,
keep your tongue from speaking evil
and your lips from telling lies.
11 Turn away from evil and do good.
Search for peace, and work to maintain it.

3:8 Greek *Show brotherly love.*

Make a Difference

3:3-4

Beauty Within

Who you are on the inside is much more important than who you make yourself to be on the outside. Skin will wrinkle, muscle will weaken, and hair will gray. While it is right and healthy to take care of your body, it is even more valuable to invest in those things that can mature and strengthen over time, such as wisdom and skills, character and reliability, loving relationships and faith in Jesus.

These verses are directed to wives who, because of the culture's misguided standards, tried to impress their husbands in all the wrong ways. Peter's words could apply to most everyone in our society today.

Difference Maker

Go a full day without looking in the mirror.

Make a Difference **3:9**

Keep Calm And...

Just because people do awful things to you doesn't mean that you can do awful things in return. Keep calm and respond with gentleness. In your responses, be shrewdly aware of the creative way that Jesus would like to work through you. Instead of repaying with retribution, try reimbursing someone's nasty deposit with a blessing. Surprise them in your dignity and graciousness.

Difference Maker

When you feel anger and retribution welling up within you, pray for the person who has upset you.

12 The eyes of the LORD watch over those who do right,
and his ears are open to their prayers.
But the LORD turns his face
against those who do evil."*

Suffering for Doing Good

13 Now, who will want to harm you if you are eager to do good? 14 But even if you
suffer for doing what is right, God will reward you for it. So don't worry or be
afraid of their threats. 15 Instead, you must worship Christ as Lord of your life.
And if someone asks about your hope as a believer, always be ready to explain
it. 16 But do this in a gentle and respectful way.* Keep your conscience clear.
Then if people speak against you, they will be ashamed when they see what a
good life you live because you belong to Christ. 17 Remember, it is better to suf-
fer for doing good, if that is what God wants, than to suffer for doing wrong!
18 Christ suffered* for our sins once for all time. He never sinned, but he
died for sinners to bring you safely home to God. He suffered physical death,
but he was raised to life in the Spirit.*
19 So he went and preached to the spirits in prison—20 those who disobeyed
God long ago when God waited patiently while Noah was building his boat.
Only eight people were saved from drowning in that terrible flood.* 21 And
that water is a picture of baptism, which now saves you, not by removing
dirt from your body, but as a response to God from* a clean conscience. It is
effective because of the resurrection of Jesus Christ.
22 Now Christ has gone to heaven. He is seated in the place of honor next
to God, and all the angels and authorities and powers accept his authority.

Living for God

4 So then, since Christ suffered physical pain, you must arm yourselves
with the same attitude he had, and be ready to suffer, too. For if you have
suffered physically for Christ, you have finished with sin.* 2 You won't spend
the rest of your lives chasing your own desires, but you will be anxious to
do the will of God. 3 You have had enough in the past of the evil things that
godless people enjoy—their immorality and lust, their feasting and drunk-
enness and wild parties, and their terrible worship of idols.
4 Of course, your former friends are surprised when you no longer plunge
into the flood of wild and destructive things they do. So they slander you.
5 But remember that they will have to face God, who stands ready to judge
everyone, both the living and the dead. 6 That is why the Good News was
preached to those who are now dead*—so although they were destined to
die like all people,* they now live forever with God in the Spirit.*
7 The end of the world is coming soon. Therefore, be earnest and disci-
plined in your prayers. 8 Most important of all, continue to show deep love
for each other, for love covers a multitude of sins. 9 Cheerfully share your
home with those who need a meal or a place to stay.
10 God has given each of you a gift from his great variety of spiritual gifts.
Use them well to serve one another. 11 Do you have the gift of speaking? Then
speak as though God himself were speaking through you. Do you have the

3:10-12 Ps 34:12-16. **3:16** Some English translations put this sentence in verse 15. **3:18a** Some manuscripts read *died.* **3:18b** Or *in spirit.* **3:20** Greek *saved through water.* **3:21** Or *as an appeal to God for.* **4:1** Or *For the one* [or *One*] *who has suffered physically has finished with sin.* **4:6a** Greek *preached even to the dead.* **4:6b** Or *so although people had judged them worthy of death.* **4:6c** Or *in spirit.*

Question **3:14-17**

If someone were to ask you, "Where do you get your hope?" what kind of answer would you like to hear yourself say?

Question **4:9**

Do you know someone who needs a clean bed or a warm meal, new clothes or house supplies, or a used vehicle or transportation to a job? How could you offer to help them?

Make a Difference
4:10-11

Unique Gifts

If every person got every gift every year, this earth would become a miserably boring and overstuffed planet. If everybody got the same thing, then no one would get anything exceptional.

God blesses people abundantly with uniqueness. Each person is gifted differently by God's design. He has the resources to give whatever he wants in whatever quantity and quality he desires, and he selects each gift precisely for each person.

The gifts God has given to you are intentional. He wants you to use your specific gifts so that you can bless others in extraordinary ways. You don't have everything, so you can't boast in arrogance, but you do have something that no one else has. Your mix of talent, passion, experience, context, and timing is unlike the gift mix given to anyone else. As a result, God has some very important work he wants you to do.

gift of helping others? Do it with all the strength and energy that God sup-
plies. Then everything you do will bring glory to God through Jesus Christ.
All glory and power to him forever and ever! Amen.

Suffering for Being a Christian

12 Dear friends, don't be surprised at the fiery trials you are going through,
as if something strange were happening to you. 13 Instead, be very glad—for
these trials make you partners with Christ in his suffering, so that you will
have the wonderful joy of seeing his glory when it is revealed to all the world.
14 If you are insulted because you bear the name of Christ, you will be
blessed, for the glorious Spirit of God* rests upon you.* 15 If you suffer, how-
ever, it must not be for murder, stealing, making trouble, or prying into
other people's affairs. 16 But it is no shame to suffer for being a Christian.
Praise God for the privilege of being called by his name! 17 For the time has
come for judgment, and it must begin with God's household. And if judg-
ment begins with us, what terrible fate awaits those who have never obeyed
God's Good News? 18 And also,

> "If the righteous are barely saved,
> what will happen to godless sinners?"*

19 So if you are suffering in a manner that pleases God, keep on doing what
is right, and trust your lives to the God who created you, for he will never
fail you.

Advice for Elders and Young Men

5 And now, a word to you who are elders in the churches. I, too, am an
elder and a witness to the sufferings of Christ. And I, too, will share in
his glory when he is revealed to the whole world. As a fellow elder, I appeal
to you: 2 Care for the flock that God has entrusted to you. Watch over it will-
ingly, not grudgingly—not for what you will get out of it, but because you
are eager to serve God. 3 Don't lord it over the people assigned to your care,
but lead them by your own good example. 4 And when the Great Shepherd
appears, you will receive a crown of never-ending glory and honor.
5 In the same way, you who are younger must accept the authority of the
elders. And all of you, dress yourselves in humility as you relate to one an-
other, for

> "God opposes the proud
> but gives grace to the humble."*

6 So humble yourselves under the mighty power of God, and at the right
time he will lift you up in honor. 7 Give all your worries and cares to God,
for he cares about you.
8 Stay alert! Watch out for your great enemy, the devil. He prowls around
like a roaring lion, looking for someone to devour. 9 Stand firm against him,
and be strong in your faith. Remember that your family of believers* all over
the world is going through the same kind of suffering you are.

4:14a Or *for the glory of God, which is his Spirit.* **4:14b** Some manuscripts add *On their part he is blasphemed, but on your part he is glorified.* **4:18** Prov 11:31 (Greek version). **5:5** Prov 3:34 (Greek version). **5:9** Greek *your brotherhood.*

Difference Maker

What could you do for someone today according to the unique way God has wired you?

Make a Difference 5:7

Give Your Worries to God

Imagine a bus sitting on top of you. Now imagine that the bus is one of those rusty, yellow hulks of metal belching out smoke and overflowing with sugar-crazed elementary school kids screaming and yelling and pushing and shoving. Imagine that the driver just keeps turning the radio up louder and louder in a futile attempt to drown out the cacophony, and the station just keeps playing the same annoying pop song that always gets stuck in your head on repeat. Repeat. Repeat. Repeat.

Life can feel like this sometimes. Pressing. Heavy. Anxious and crushing. Loads of concern piled on chaotic demands shrieking for your immediate attention. Your burdens need to be lifted off you somehow or else your heart will struggle to beat. The cares need to be taken off you sometime, or your mind will struggle to think.

Who is able to lift your burdens for you?

Difference Maker

Write down your concerns on a piece of paper. Once your list is complete, on the top of the paper write, "Jesus can have these now." Pray. Then crumple up the paper and throw it in the trash.

10 In his kindness God called you to share in his eternal glory by means of
Christ Jesus. So after you have suffered a little while, he will restore, support,
and strengthen you, and he will place you on a firm foundation. 11 All power
to him forever! Amen.

Peter's Final Greetings

12 I have written and sent this short letter to you with the help of Silas,* whom
I commend to you as a faithful brother. My purpose in writing is to encour-
age you and assure you that what you are experiencing is truly part of God's
grace for you. Stand firm in this grace.
13 Your sister church here in Babylon* sends you greetings, and so does my
son Mark. 14 Greet each other with a kiss of love.
Peace be with all of you who are in Christ.

5:12 Greek *Silvanus.* **5:13** Greek *The elect one in Babylon.* Babylon was probably symbolic for Rome.

The 1 Peter Church Network

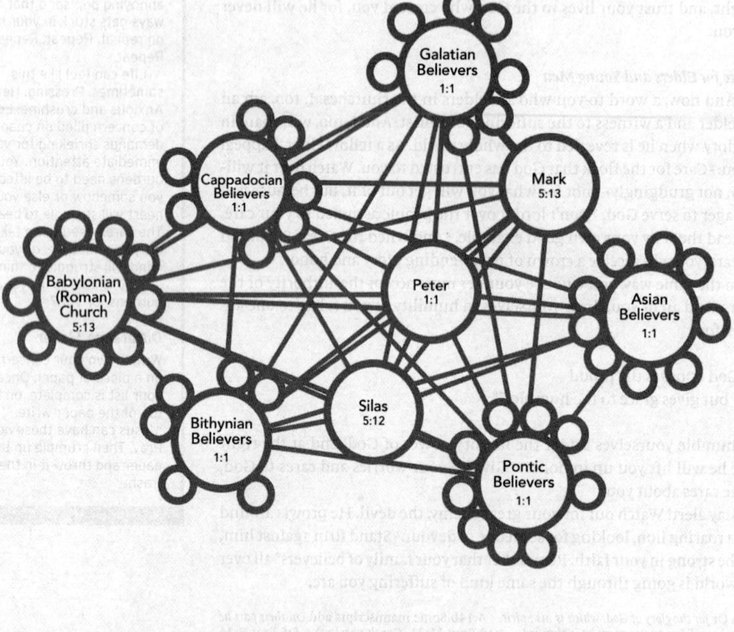

2 Peter Introduction

Do you ever set reminders in your phone? In 2 Peter, the apostle Peter was basically writing a reminders app for Christians everywhere. He was setting reminders for them of what to expect as they followed Jesus.

Some of those reminders are about how Christians are supposed to live. Peter pointed out that Jesus had shown us how to be responsible for our actions, have self-control, and support those around us. Peter also pointed out that those who don't live like Jesus can't call themselves followers of Jesus.

Other reminders are about the importance of Scripture. God has spoken through many men and women, and a lot of those words have been recorded. Studying what God has said over thousands of years helps us understand him more. Second Peter reminds Christians to try to see the big picture and reminds them that reading God's Word is the best way to expand our view.

The entire middle section of Peter's letter is a reminder that not everyone who says they follow God is telling the truth. As soon as people started following Jesus, some evil people saw an opportunity to take advantage of it. Peter revealed that there would always be people who "make up clever lies to get hold of your money" (2 Peter 2:3). These people act like Christians, but their hearts are focused on selfishness and loving themselves instead of loving others.

The last reminder that Peter gave his people was that in the end, God will make everything right. It will be hard until then, and we need to be wise about how we live and whom we listen to, but Christians can look forward to a time when the hard parts of life will be a fading memory and when the goodness of being connected with God will be all that is left.

Story Arc

- **Peter and Paul**

2 Peter

Greetings from Peter

1 This letter is from Simon* Peter, a slave and apostle of Jesus Christ.
I am writing to you who share the same precious faith we have. This
faith was given to you because of the justice and fairness* of Jesus Christ,
our God and Savior.
2 May God give you more and more grace and peace as you grow in your
knowledge of God and Jesus our Lord.

Growing in Faith

3 By his divine power, God has given us everything we need for living a godly
life. We have received all of this by coming to know him, the one who called
us to himself by means of his marvelous glory and excellence. 4 And because
of his glory and excellence, he has given us great and precious promises.
These are the promises that enable you to share his divine nature and escape
the world's corruption caused by human desires.
5 In view of all this, make every effort to respond to God's promises.
Supplement your faith with a generous provision of moral excellence, and
moral excellence with knowledge, 6 and knowledge with self-control, and
self-control with patient endurance, and patient endurance with godliness,
7 and godliness with brotherly affection, and brotherly affection with love
for everyone.
8 The more you grow like this, the more productive and useful you will be
in your knowledge of our Lord Jesus Christ. 9 But those who fail to develop in
this way are shortsighted or blind, forgetting that they have been cleansed
from their old sins.
10 So, dear brothers and sisters,* work hard to prove that you really are
among those God has called and chosen. Do these things, and you will never
fall away. 11 Then God will give you a grand entrance into the eternal King-
dom of our Lord and Savior Jesus Christ.

Paying Attention to Scripture

12 Therefore, I will always remind you about these things—even though
you already know them and are standing firm in the truth you have been
taught. 13 And it is only right that I should keep on reminding you as long
as I live.* 14 For our Lord Jesus Christ has shown me that I must soon leave
this earthly life,* 15 so I will work hard to make sure you always remember
these things after I am gone.
16 For we were not making up clever stories when we told you about the
powerful coming of our Lord Jesus Christ. We saw his majestic splendor with
our own eyes 17 when he received honor and glory from God the Father. The
voice from the majestic glory of God said to him, "This is my dearly loved

Question 1:5-8

Which qualities from the last three verses (vv. 5-7) do you have? Which ones do you struggle with?

Make a Difference
1:9-12

Benign Neglect

Are you one of the growing number of people who need a swift kick in the backside to get you going today? There is a mentality in society today known as "benign neglect." Basically, it means that people feel like they can put off the normal responsibilities of life until some other time in the future. They feel like they can extend their adolescence for years, even into their thirties or forties, and that "real life" begins later, when they feel more ready. It is "benign" because it doesn't "feel bad" (at first), but over time it can be neglectful of a person's potential and gifts and calling in life. Now is not the time to put off doing what you need to do. Don't fall into the pit of this off-putting, chronic illness. Don't give in to benign neglect. Rather, work hard to prove that God has made you alive by his Spirit.

Difference Maker

What is something that you should strive to accomplish but have been putting off? What do you need to do to get going once again?

1:1a Greek *Simeon.* **1:1b** Or *to you in the righteousness.* **1:10** Greek *brothers.* **1:13** Greek *as long as I am in this tent* [or *tabernacle*]. **1:14** Greek *I must soon put off my tent* [or *tabernacle*].

Son, who brings me great joy."* 18 We ourselves heard that voice from heaven when we were with him on the holy mountain.

19 Because of that experience, we have even greater confidence in the message proclaimed by the prophets. You must pay close attention to what they wrote, for their words are like a lamp shining in a dark place—until the Day dawns, and Christ the Morning Star shines* in your hearts. 20 Above all, you must realize that no prophecy in Scripture ever came from the prophet's own understanding,* 21 or from human initiative. No, those prophets were moved by the Holy Spirit, and they spoke from God.

The Danger of False Teachers

2 But there were also false prophets in Israel, just as there will be false teachers among you. They will cleverly teach destructive heresies and even deny the Master who bought them. In this way, they will bring sudden destruction on themselves. 2 Many will follow their evil teaching and shameful immorality. And because of these teachers, the way of truth will be slandered. 3 In their greed they will make up clever lies to get hold of your money. But God condemned them long ago, and their destruction will not be delayed.

4 For God did not spare even the angels who sinned. He threw them into hell,* in gloomy pits of darkness,* where they are being held until the day of judgment. 5 And God did not spare the ancient world—except for Noah and the seven others in his family. Noah warned the world of God's righteous judgment. So God protected Noah when he destroyed the world of ungodly people with a vast flood. 6 Later, God condemned the cities of Sodom and Gomorrah and turned them into heaps of ashes. He made them an example of what will happen to ungodly people. 7 But God also rescued Lot out of Sodom because he was a righteous man who was sick of the shameful immorality of the wicked people around him. 8 Yes, Lot was a righteous man who was tormented in his soul by the wickedness he saw and heard day after day. 9 So you see, the Lord knows how to rescue godly people from their trials, even while keeping the wicked under punishment until the day of final judgment. 10 He is especially hard on those who follow their own twisted sexual desire, and who despise authority.

These people are proud and arrogant, daring even to scoff at supernatural beings* without so much as trembling. 11 But the angels, who are far greater in power and strength, do not dare to bring from the Lord* a charge of blasphemy against those supernatural beings.

12 These false teachers are like unthinking animals, creatures of instinct, born to be caught and destroyed. They scoff at things they do not understand, and like animals, they will be destroyed. 13 Their destruction is their reward for the harm they have done. They love to indulge in evil pleasures in broad daylight. They are a disgrace and a stain among you. They delight in deception* even as they eat with you in your fellowship meals. 14 They commit adultery with their eyes, and their desire for sin is never satisfied. They lure unstable people into sin, and they are well trained in greed. They live under God's curse. 15 They have wandered off the right road and followed the

1:17 Matt 17:5; Mark 9:7; Luke 9:35. 1:19 Or *rises.* 1:20 Or *is a matter of one's own interpretation.* 2:4a Greek *Tartarus.* 2:4b Some manuscripts read *in chains of gloom.* 2:10 Greek *at glorious ones,* which are probably evil angels. 2:11 Other manuscripts read *to the Lord;* still others do not include this phrase at all. 2:13 Some manuscripts read *in fellowship meals.*

Prayer **1:19–21**

God, help me to read the Bible as a direct message from you. Amen.

Question **2:3**

How can you test if something you're being taught is true or made-up?

Make a Difference
2:4–9

Tough Surroundings

It can be possible to do everything right and still feel like everything is going wrong. Noah, Lot, and many other biblical characters experienced very hard and painful circumstances in their life.

When life is hard, it doesn't mean we did something wrong. It might mean we're the one person doing what's right. Staying connected to God through prayer, Scripture study, and godly living is how we can know if our hard times are because of our mistakes or because we are following God.

Difference Maker

What hard thing are you facing right now? Is it hard because you are ignoring Jesus or because you are following him?

Prayer 3:9

God, help me to be patient when I feel like you aren't responding. Help me to trust that you have a reason for what you are doing. Amen.

Question 3:14

Would you consider yourself peaceful, pure, and blameless with God? If not, what are areas you need to examine in your life?

Story Arc 3:15–16

Peter and Paul

These verses are a cool little window into the story of Peter and Paul. They weren't too sure of each other early on. After all, before Paul became a Christian, Paul oversaw the arrests and murders of some of Peter's best friends. Even so, here Peter gave an incredible reference for Paul. Peter said that Paul's writing came from the wisdom of God, and while his letters are sometimes difficult, they are just like other parts of Scripture (v. 16). It is amazing to see how God can so radically change two hotheaded people and bring them together to spread the glory of Jesus Christ.

Rev 4:1-11 ►

footsteps of Balaam son of Beor,* who loved to earn money by doing wrong.
16 But Balaam was stopped from his mad course when his donkey rebuked
him with a human voice.
17 These people are as useless as dried-up springs or as mist blown away by
the wind. They are doomed to blackest darkness. 18 They brag about them-
selves with empty, foolish boasting. With an appeal to twisted sexual desires,
they lure back into sin those who have barely escaped from a lifestyle of
deception. 19 They promise freedom, but they themselves are slaves of sin
and corruption. For you are a slave to whatever controls you. 20 And when
people escape from the wickedness of the world by knowing our Lord and
Savior Jesus Christ and then get tangled up and enslaved by sin again, they
are worse off than before. 21 It would be better if they had never known the
way to righteousness than to know it and then reject the command they
were given to live a holy life. 22 They prove the truth of this proverb: "A dog
returns to its vomit."* And another says, "A washed pig returns to the mud."

The Day of the Lord Is Coming

3 This is my second letter to you, dear friends, and in both of them I have
tried to stimulate your wholesome thinking and refresh your memory.
2 I want you to remember what the holy prophets said long ago and what our
Lord and Savior commanded through your apostles.
3 Most importantly, I want to remind you that in the last days scoffers will
come, mocking the truth and following their own desires. 4 They will say,
"What happened to the promise that Jesus is coming again? From before the
times of our ancestors, everything has remained the same since the world
was first created."
5 They deliberately forget that God made the heavens long ago by the
word of his command, and he brought the earth out from the water and
surrounded it with water. 6 Then he used the water to destroy the ancient
world with a mighty flood. 7 And by the same word, the present heavens
and earth have been stored up for fire. They are being kept for the day of
judgment, when ungodly people will be destroyed.
8 But you must not forget this one thing, dear friends: A day is like a thou-
sand years to the Lord, and a thousand years is like a day. 9 The Lord isn't
really being slow about his promise, as some people think. No, he is being
patient for your sake. He does not want anyone to be destroyed, but wants
everyone to repent. 10 But the day of the Lord will come as unexpectedly as
a thief. Then the heavens will pass away with a terrible noise, and the very
elements themselves will disappear in fire, and the earth and everything on
it will be found to deserve judgment.*
11 Since everything around us is going to be destroyed like this, what holy
and godly lives you should live, 12 looking forward to the day of God and hur-
rying it along. On that day, he will set the heavens on fire, and the elements
will melt away in the flames. 13 But we are looking forward to the new heav-
ens and new earth he has promised, a world filled with God's righteousness.
14 And so, dear friends, while you are waiting for these things to happen,
make every effort to be found living peaceful lives that are pure and blame-
less in his sight.
15 And remember, our Lord's patience gives people time to be saved. This

2:15 Some manuscripts read *Bosor.* 2:22 Prov 26:11. 3:10 Other manuscripts read *will be burned up;* one early manuscript reads *will be found destroyed.*

is what our beloved brother Paul also wrote to you with the wisdom God
gave him—16 speaking of these things in all of his letters. Some of his com-
ments are hard to understand, and those who are ignorant and unstable have
twisted his letters to mean something quite different, just as they do with
other parts of Scripture. And this will result in their destruction.

Peter's Final Words

17 You already know these things, dear friends. So be on guard; then you will
not be carried away by the errors of these wicked people and lose your own
secure footing. 18 Rather, you must grow in the grace and knowledge of our
Lord and Savior Jesus Christ.

All glory to him, both now and forever! Amen.

1 John Introduction

Have you ever doubted God's work in your life? Have you ever wondered where you will go when you die? Have you ever questioned whether God has really forgiven you and loves you? The readers of this letter had these same questions, and these early believers were hearing all kinds of false answers. This little letter was circulated among many of the first churches to answer these very serious questions and to correct some of the untruths that were being taught.

As one of Jesus' disciples, John had the perfect vantage point to answer many of the questions these early believers were asking. In fact, he had wrestled with the same things (John 16:29–30). As an eyewitness of Jesus' miracles (6:19), to Jesus' teaching (3:16), to Jesus' claims (8:58), and to Jesus' death and resurrection (19:26; 20:3), John longed for his readers to embrace the truth of the forgiveness and love that Jesus offers.

In this book, John gave an inside look into how the love of God could transform a person's life. There is no narrative more compelling than the absolute love of a holy God for sinful people (1 John 3:1). Written by someone who called himself "the disciple Jesus loved" (John 21:7), 1 John's message to you is that God loves you, too, and is ready to forgive you if you just ask (1 John 1:9). Imagine the difference that receiving true forgiveness can make to change the narrative of your life. If you wonder what that looks like, read on as John shared with every person how they could know that they have eternal life (5:13).

1 John

Introduction

1 We proclaim to you the one who existed from the beginning,* whom we have heard and seen. We saw him with our own eyes and touched him with our own hands. He is the Word of life. 2 This one who is life itself was revealed to us, and we have seen him. And now we testify and proclaim to you that he is the one who is eternal life. He was with the Father, and then he was revealed to us. 3 We proclaim to you what we ourselves have actually seen and heard so that you may have fellowship with us. And our fellowship is with the Father and with his Son, Jesus Christ. 4 We are writing these things so that you may fully share our joy.*

Living in the Light

5 This is the message we heard from Jesus* and now declare to you: God is light, and there is no darkness in him at all. 6 So we are lying if we say we have fellowship with God but go on living in spiritual darkness; we are not practicing the truth. 7 But if we are living in the light, as God is in the light, then we have fellowship with each other, and the blood of Jesus, his Son, cleanses us from all sin.

8 If we claim we have no sin, we are only fooling ourselves and not living in the truth. 9 But if we confess our sins to him, he is faithful and just to forgive us our sins and to cleanse us from all wickedness. 10 If we claim we have not sinned, we are calling God a liar and showing that his word has no place in our hearts.

2 My dear children, I am writing this to you so that you will not sin. But if anyone does sin, we have an advocate who pleads our case before the Father. He is Jesus Christ, the one who is truly righteous. 2 He himself is the sacrifice that atones for our sins—and not only our sins but the sins of all the world.

3 And we can be sure that we know him if we obey his commandments. 4 If someone claims, "I know God," but doesn't obey God's commandments, that person is a liar and is not living in the truth. 5 But those who obey God's word truly show how completely they love him. That is how we know we are living in him. 6 Those who say they live in God should live their lives as Jesus did.

A New Commandment

7 Dear friends, I am not writing a new commandment for you; rather it is an old one you have had from the very beginning. This old commandment—to love one another—is the same message you heard before. 8 Yet it is also new. Jesus lived the truth of this commandment, and you also are living it. For the darkness is disappearing, and the true light is already shining.

9 If anyone claims, "I am living in the light," but hates a fellow believer,*

1:1 Greek *What was from the beginning.* 1:4 Or *so that our joy may be complete;* some manuscripts read *your joy.* 1:5 Greek *from him.* 2:9 Greek *hates his brother;* also in 2:11.

Question 1:6

Where is your lifestyle out of alignment with your faith? What one deliberate step could you take to practice alignment in your life today?

Prayer 1:9

Jesus, I confess my sins to you. Forgive me and cleanse me. Amen.

Make a Difference 2:1-2

Advocate

Someone who committed a crime and appears in court could try to plead their own case. They could pour out their heart with apologies and ask the court for compassion. Even so, the judge is in a no-win situation. That unfortunate thing still happened, damage was done, and someone still needs to pay for it and restore it.

At the end of their life, every person will appear before God. They will plead and pour out. God will want to grant mercy, but who, then, will pay for the damage that has been done? That's when Jesus will stand up and say, "I will stand in this person's place."

Difference Maker

The biggest difference you could ever make is to accept Jesus Christ as your Savior. If you'd like to do that, turn to the back of this Bible and read "How to Accept Jesus as Your Lord and Savior."

that person is still living in darkness. 10 Anyone who loves a fellow believer*
is living in the light and does not cause others to stumble. 11 But anyone who
hates a fellow believer is still living and walking in darkness. Such a person
does not know the way to go, having been blinded by the darkness.

12 I am writing to you who are God's children
because your sins have been forgiven through Jesus.*
13 I am writing to you who are mature in the faith*
because you know Christ, who existed from the beginning.
I am writing to you who are young in the faith
because you have won your battle with the evil one.
14 I have written to you who are God's children
because you know the Father.
I have written to you who are mature in the faith
because you know Christ, who existed from the beginning.
I have written to you who are young in the faith
because you are strong.
God's word lives in your hearts,
and you have won your battle with the evil one.

Do Not Love This World

15 Do not love this world nor the things it offers you, for when you love the
world, you do not have the love of the Father in you. 16 For the world offers
only a craving for physical pleasure, a craving for everything we see, and
pride in our achievements and possessions. These are not from the Father,
but are from this world. 17 And this world is fading away, along with every-
thing that people crave. But anyone who does what pleases God will live
forever.

Warning about Antichrists

18 Dear children, the last hour is here. You have heard that the Antichrist is
coming, and already many such antichrists have appeared. From this we
know that the last hour has come. 19 These people left our churches, but they
never really belonged with us; otherwise they would have stayed with us.
When they left, it proved that they did not belong with us.
20 But you are not like that, for the Holy One has given you his Spirit,* and
all of you know the truth. 21 So I am writing to you not because you don't
know the truth but because you know the difference between truth and lies.
22 And who is a liar? Anyone who says that Jesus is not the Christ.* Anyone
who denies the Father and the Son is an antichrist.* 23 Anyone who denies
the Son doesn't have the Father, either. But anyone who acknowledges the
Son has the Father also.
24 So you must remain faithful to what you have been taught from the
beginning. If you do, you will remain in fellowship with the Son and with
the Father. 25 And in this fellowship we enjoy the eternal life he promised us.
26 I am writing these things to warn you about those who want to lead you
astray. 27 But you have received the Holy Spirit,* and he lives within you, so
you don't need anyone to teach you what is true. For the Spirit* teaches you

2:10 Greek *loves his brother.* 2:12 Greek *through his name.* 2:13 Or *to you fathers;* also in 2:14. 2:20 Greek *But you have an anointing from the Holy One.* 2:22a Or *not the Messiah.* 2:22b Or *the antichrist.* 2:27a Greek *the anointing from him.* 2:27b Greek *the anointing.*

Make a Difference

2:20-27

Discernment

Have you noticed how some older and wiser people don't waste their words? It's as if they have learned to measure what they say in order to have the maximum effect with their message.

When the apostle John chose to write a letter to the early Christians, he didn't want to waste words either. As an older person, he wanted his "children" to live freely in the eternal truth of Jesus and not get caught up in the trends of culture that ebb and flow throughout history. He wasn't going to throw away words and ink and papyrus on people who weren't going to listen. He knew that these early followers of Jesus would be strengthened by his message.

Difference Maker

Connect with an older person whom you know has some wisdom to pass on to you. Consider asking him or her to become a mentor to you in life and in faith.

Question **2:26**

Scan the day ahead. What potential obstacles might you face? Develop a plan to remain resolute in the things God would have you do.

everything you need to know, and what he teaches is true—it is not a lie. So
just as he has taught you, remain in fellowship with Christ.

Living as Children of God

28 And now, dear children, remain in fellowship with Christ so that when he
returns, you will be full of courage and not shrink back from him in shame.
29 Since we know that Christ is righteous, we also know that all who do
what is right are God's children.

3 See how very much our Father loves us, for he calls us his children, and
that is what we are! But the people who belong to this world don't recog-
nize that we are God's children because they don't know him. 2 Dear friends,
we are already God's children, but he has not yet shown us what we will be
like when Christ appears. But we do know that we will be like him, for we
will see him as he really is. 3 And all who have this eager expectation will keep
themselves pure, just as he is pure.
4 Everyone who sins is breaking God's law, for all sin is contrary to the law
of God. 5 And you know that Jesus came to take away our sins, and there is no
sin in him. 6 Anyone who continues to live in him will not sin. But anyone
who keeps on sinning does not know him or understand who he is.
7 Dear children, don't let anyone deceive you about this: When people
do what is right, it shows that they are righteous, even as Christ is righ-
teous. 8 But when people keep on sinning, it shows that they belong to the
devil, who has been sinning since the beginning. But the Son of God came
to destroy the works of the devil. 9 Those who have been born into God's
family do not make a practice of sinning, because God's life* is in them. So
they can't keep on sinning, because they are children of God. 10 So now we
can tell who are children of God and who are children of the devil. Anyone
who does not live righteously and does not love other believers* does not
belong to God.

Love One Another

11 This is the message you have heard from the beginning: We should love
one another. 12 We must not be like Cain, who belonged to the evil one and
killed his brother. And why did he kill him? Because Cain had been doing
what was evil, and his brother had been doing what was righteous. 13 So don't
be surprised, dear brothers and sisters,* if the world hates you.
14 If we love our brothers and sisters who are believers,* it proves that we
have passed from death to life. But a person who has no love is still dead.
15 Anyone who hates another brother or sister* is really a murderer at heart.
And you know that murderers don't have eternal life within them.
16 We know what real love is because Jesus gave up his life for us. So we
also ought to give up our lives for our brothers and sisters. 17 If someone has
enough money to live well and sees a brother or sister* in need but shows
no compassion—how can God's love be in that person?
18 Dear children, let's not merely say that we love each other; let us show
the truth by our actions. 19 Our actions will show that we belong to the truth,
so we will be confident when we stand before God. 20 Even if we feel guilty,
God is greater than our feelings, and he knows everything.

3:9 Greek *because his seed.* 3:10 Greek *does not love his brother.* 3:13 Greek *brothers.* 3:14 Greek *the brothers;* similarly in 3:16. 3:15 Greek *hates his brother.* 3:17 Greek *sees his brother.*

Question **3:5**

Why did Jesus show up? What did he want to accomplish? What difference did he want to make in your life?

Prayer **3:16**

Jesus, thank you for showing me what real love is. Help me to really love my friends and family with the same passion. Amen.

Question 4:9

How does this verse make all the difference in the world?

21 Dear friends, if we don't feel guilty, we can come to God with bold con-
fidence. 22 And we will receive from him whatever we ask because we obey
him and do the things that please him.
23 And this is his commandment: We must believe in the name of his Son,
Jesus Christ, and love one another, just as he commanded us. 24 Those who
obey God's commandments remain in fellowship with him, and he with
them. And we know he lives in us because the Spirit he gave us lives in us.

Discerning False Prophets

4 Dear friends, do not believe everyone who claims to speak by the Spirit.
You must test them to see if the spirit they have comes from God. For
there are many false prophets in the world. 2 This is how we know if they
have the Spirit of God: If a person claiming to be a prophet* acknowledges
that Jesus Christ came in a real body, that person has the Spirit of God. 3 But
if someone claims to be a prophet and does not acknowledge the truth about
Jesus, that person is not from God. Such a person has the spirit of the Anti-
christ, which you heard is coming into the world and indeed is already here.
4 But you belong to God, my dear children. You have already won a victory
over those people, because the Spirit who lives in you is greater than the
spirit who lives in the world. 5 Those people belong to this world, so they
speak from the world's viewpoint, and the world listens to them. 6 But we
belong to God, and those who know God listen to us. If they do not belong to
God, they do not listen to us. That is how we know if someone has the Spirit
of truth or the spirit of deception.

Loving One Another

7 Dear friends, let us continue to love one another, for love comes from God.
Anyone who loves is a child of God and knows God. 8 But anyone who does
not love does not know God, for God is love.
9 God showed how much he loved us by sending his one and only Son
into the world so that we might have eternal life through him. 10 This is
real love—not that we loved God, but that he loved us and sent his Son as a
sacrifice to take away our sins.
11 Dear friends, since God loved us that much, we surely ought to love each
other. 12 No one has ever seen God. But if we love each other, God lives in us,
and his love is brought to full expression in us.
13 And God has given us his Spirit as proof that we live in him and he in
us. 14 Furthermore, we have seen with our own eyes and now testify that the
Father sent his Son to be the Savior of the world. 15 All who declare that Jesus
is the Son of God have God living in them, and they live in God. 16 We know
how much God loves us, and we have put our trust in his love.
God is love, and all who live in love live in God, and God lives in them.
17 And as we live in God, our love grows more perfect. So we will not be afraid
on the day of judgment, but we can face him with confidence because we live
like Jesus here in this world.
18 Such love has no fear, because perfect love expels all fear. If we are afraid,
it is for fear of punishment, and this shows that we have not fully experi-
enced his perfect love. 19 We love each other* because he loved us first.
20 If someone says, "I love God," but hates a fellow believer,* that person

4:2 Greek *If a spirit;* similarly in 4:3. 4:19 Greek *We love.* Other manuscripts read *We love God;* still others read *We love him.* 4:20 Greek *hates his brother.*

is a liar; for if we don't love people we can see, how can we love God, whom
we cannot see? 21 And he has given us this command: Those who love God
must also love their fellow believers.*

Faith in the Son of God

5 Everyone who believes that Jesus is the Christ* has become a child of
God. And everyone who loves the Father loves his children, too. 2 We
know we love God's children if we love God and obey his commandments.
3 Loving God means keeping his commandments, and his commandments
are not burdensome. 4 For every child of God defeats this evil world, and we
achieve this victory through our faith. 5 And who can win this battle against
the world? Only those who believe that Jesus is the Son of God.

6 And Jesus Christ was revealed as God's Son by his baptism in water and
by shedding his blood on the cross*—not by water only, but by water and
blood. And the Spirit, who is truth, confirms it with his testimony. 7 So we
have these three witnesses*—8 the Spirit, the water, and the blood—and all
three agree. 9 Since we believe human testimony, surely we can believe the
greater testimony that comes from God. And God has testified about his Son.
10 All who believe in the Son of God know in their hearts that this testimony
is true. Those who don't believe this are actually calling God a liar because
they don't believe what God has testified about his Son.

11 And this is what God has testified: He has given us eternal life, and this
life is in his Son. 12 Whoever has the Son has life; whoever does not have God's
Son does not have life.

Conclusion

13 I have written this to you who believe in the name of the Son of God, so
that you may know you have eternal life. 14 And we are confident that he
hears us whenever we ask for anything that pleases him. 15 And since we
know he hears us when we make our requests, we also know that he will
give us what we ask for.

16 If you see a fellow believer* sinning in a way that does not lead to death,
you should pray, and God will give that person life. But there is a sin that
leads to death, and I am not saying you should pray for those who commit
it. 17 All wicked actions are sin, but not every sin leads to death.

18 We know that God's children do not make a practice of sinning, for God's
Son holds them securely, and the evil one cannot touch them. 19 We know that
we are children of God and that the world around us is under the control
of the evil one.

20 And we know that the Son of God has come, and he has given us under-
standing so that we can know the true God.* And now we live in fellowship
with the true God because we live in fellowship with his Son, Jesus Christ.
He is the only true God, and he is eternal life.

21 Dear children, keep away from anything that might take God's place
in your hearts.*

4:21 Greek *The one who loves God must also love his brother.* **5:1** Or *the Messiah.* **5:6** Greek *This is he who came by water and blood.* **5:7** A few very late manuscripts add *in heaven—the Father, the Word, and the Holy Spirit, and these three are one. And we have three witnesses on earth.* **5:16** Greek *a brother.* **5:20** Greek *the one who is true.* **5:21** Greek *keep yourselves from idols.*

Make a Difference

5:1-5

God's Patterns

Many people look at the commandments in the Bible as a negative list of don'ts—what they are not supposed to do. God's patterns, however, are more about living according to his original blueprint for life on this earth. Like a good parent trying to raise children for successful living, God's instructions provide the right framework for a relationship with him, relationships with others, and responsibility on the earth.

Difference Maker

Read the Ten Commandments in Exodus 20:1-17, not from a mindset of don'ts but from a perspective of potential: What if people followed these commands? How would things improve? What damage could be avoided? What good could be done?

Question **5:13**

Why did John write this letter? What difference did he want to make?

2 John Introduction

"Church" is not a building but a body of people. A church is any gathering of followers of Jesus who are together for the purpose of loving one another, reading God's Word, adhering to the truth of God's Word, worshiping, and living out the commands of Jesus. This letter helps us understand the primary characteristic of a loving church. A loving church adheres to the truth of the Scriptures and obeys the commands of Jesus faithfully.

John saw Jesus. He talked with him and traveled with him. Now, as an old man, he longed for people to embrace the truth that he knew so well: God's most loving act was sending his Son, Jesus, to earth. John 3:16 says, "This is how God loved the world: He gave his one and only Son, so that everyone who believes in him will not perish but have eternal life."

Because of this, the most loving thing any church can do is ensure that others receive a chance to believe that Jesus was a real man in the flesh who, being fully God, came to forgive all people of their sin and help them be reunited with God forever.

Sometimes, being a difference maker means standing up for the truth that the Bible teaches even when it is not culturally popular in the world around you and especially if it starts to become unpopular even within a church. We adhere to biblical truth not only because it's right but because it's the most loving thing we can do for other people.

2 John

Greetings
This letter is from John, the elder.*
I am writing to the chosen lady and to her children,* whom I love in the
truth—as does everyone else who knows the truth—2because the truth lives
in us and will be with us forever.
3Grace, mercy, and peace, which come from God the Father and from Jesus
Christ—the Son of the Father—will continue to be with us who live in truth
and love.

Live in the Truth
4How happy I was to meet some of your children and find them living ac-
cording to the truth, just as the Father commanded.
5I am writing to remind you, dear friends,* that we should love one
another. This is not a new commandment, but one we have had from the
beginning. 6Love means doing what God has commanded us, and he has
commanded us to love one another, just as you heard from the beginning.
7I say this because many deceivers have gone out into the world. They
deny that Jesus Christ came* in a real body. Such a person is a deceiver and
an antichrist. 8Watch out that you do not lose what we* have worked so hard
to achieve. Be diligent so that you receive your full reward. 9Anyone who
wanders away from this teaching has no relationship with God. But any-
one who remains in the teaching of Christ has a relationship with both the
Father and the Son.
10If anyone comes to your meeting and does not teach the truth about
Christ, don't invite that person into your home or give any kind of encour-
agement. 11Anyone who encourages such people becomes a partner in their
evil work.

Conclusion
12I have much more to say to you, but I don't want to do it with paper and
ink. For I hope to visit you soon and talk with you face to face. Then our joy
will be complete.
13Greetings from the children of your sister,* chosen by God.

1a Greek *From the elder.* 1b Or *the church God has chosen and its members.* 5 Greek *I urge you, lady.* 7 Or *will come.* 8 Some manuscripts read *you.* 13 Or *from the members of your sister church.*

Prayer 6

Jesus, let me be known for my love of other people. Give me strength to live a life obedient to your commandments. Amen.

Make a Difference 10-11

Standing Up for the Truth

Sometimes we have to speak up for what is true. If the truth is being attacked, we may need to take action to protect and defend the truth. We do this, first of all, because we don't want anything to compromise our friendship with God. Second, we defend the truth because we don't want harm to come to our friends who know Jesus. Third, we defend the truth because the truth is how people who don't yet know Jesus will come to discover that they can have friendship with God. The truth of the gospel is the only way for any of us to be fully reunited with God through Jesus.

Difference Maker

Encourage a friend who is doubting some of the truths of God by finding passages that address their issues. Share the truth with them in person.

3 John Introduction

In ancient Near East culture, hospitality, the ability to welcome strangers and give them food, shelter, and conversation, was then and is today a dominant value. Back then, there were no hotels, inns, or travel plazas. Travelers were dependent on the hospitality and willingness of total strangers to invite them into their homes so they could stay safe on the road, and it became a defining characteristic of the early church. They welcomed everyone and treated them just like Jesus would have. Their hospitality was the difference maker in many people's lives.

Even more so, the church showed above-and-beyond hospitality to other Christians. They viewed one another as family, often calling each other "brother" and "sister." No one in this culture would ever close the door on family. As the church was growing in hospitality, one church in particular was sticking out like a sore thumb. One of their leaders, Diotrephes, was harming the work of his church by closing the door on his church family and other strangers. He was unwilling to share his food or home, and he was kicking people out of his church who dared to confront him on his inhospitable actions.

In contrast, Gaius decided to take a stand and act in such a way as to restore the reputation of their church. His actions reinstated this value in their church, and he was commended by John for the Jesus-like love he showed everyone who came into his home.

The 3 John Church Network

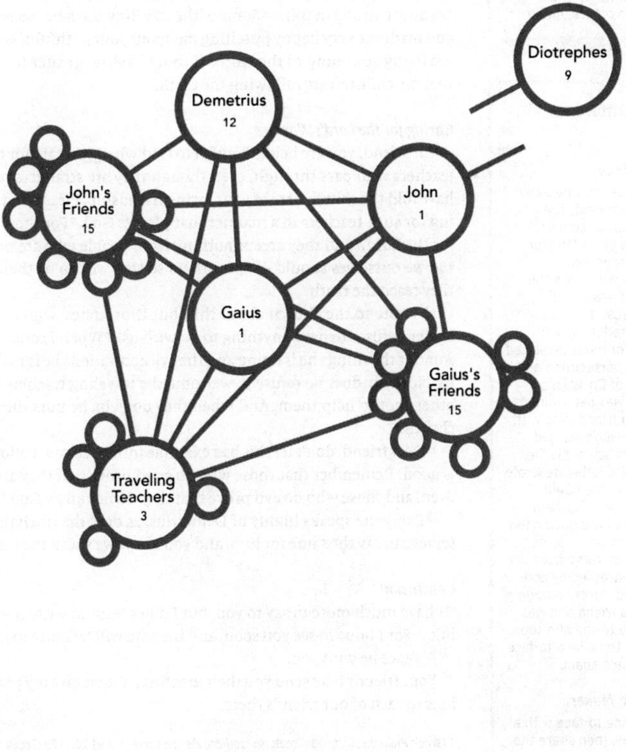

3 John

Greetings

This letter is from John, the elder.*
I am writing to Gaius, my dear friend, whom I love in the truth.
2Dear friend, I hope all is well with you and that you are as healthy in body
as you are strong in spirit. 3Some of the traveling teachers* recently returned
and made me very happy by telling me about your faithfulness and that you
are living according to the truth. 4I could have no greater joy than to hear
that my children are following the truth.

Caring for the Lord's Workers

5Dear friend, you are being faithful to God when you care for the traveling
teachers who pass through, even though they are strangers to you. 6They
have told the church here of your loving friendship. Please continue provid-
ing for such teachers in a manner that pleases God. 7For they are traveling
for the Lord,* and they accept nothing from people who are not believers.*
8So we ourselves should support them so that we can be their partners as
they teach the truth.
9I wrote to the church about this, but Diotrephes, who loves to be the
leader, refuses to have anything to do with us. 10When I come, I will report
some of the things he is doing and the evil accusations he is making against
us. Not only does he refuse to welcome the traveling teachers, he also tells
others not to help them. And when they do help, he puts them out of the
church.
11Dear friend, don't let this bad example influence you. Follow only what
is good. Remember that those who do good prove that they are God's chil-
dren, and those who do evil prove that they do not know God.*
12Everyone speaks highly of Demetrius, as does the truth itself. We our-
selves can say the same for him, and you know we speak the truth.

Conclusion

13I have much more to say to you, but I don't want to write it with pen and
ink. 14For I hope to see you soon, and then we will talk face to face.
15*Peace be with you.
Your friends here send you their greetings. Please give my personal greet-
ings to each of our friends there.

1 Greek *From the elder.* 3 Greek *the brothers;* also in verses 5 and 10. 7a Greek *They went out on behalf of the Name.* 7b Greek *from Gentiles.* 11 Greek *they have not seen God.* 15 Some English translations combine verses 14 and 15 into verse 14.

Prayer 6

Dear Jesus, let me be known for my hospitality and kindness to others. Amen.

Make a Difference

13–14

Face-to-Face

It wasn't easy for the early church to connect. The Roman Empire regularly threatened Christians for gathering together.

One guy who knew this reality well was one of Jesus' closest disciples, a man named John. For decades, John was displaced due to the persecution and scattering of Christians. Still, John was determined to carry on friendships with those with whom he had shared so much of his life.

In his third letter, he wrote to a friend named Gaius. Gaius was a key figure in the spread of the good news about Jesus. John, somehow now separated from him and distressed by conflict, missed the encouragement of his friend and was determined to see him soon. He wanted to be face-to-face with him once again.

Difference Maker

Sit down face-to-face with a friend today, then share the peace of Jesus as you remember old times and old stories together.

Jude Introduction

If you've ever thought, *What I do against God isn't that big of a deal. After all, he'll forgive me,* Jude is a must read. This false mindset had become quite popular in Jude's day. Jude was so troubled by this that he felt compelled to write an urgent letter to warn God's people about those who were secretly slipping in and presenting these false ideas about God's grace. Jude was worried that these false beliefs and teachings were causing people to deny Jesus Christ himself.

Jude was one of Jesus' own brothers. Their brother James was also mentioned in here (Jude v. 1). That seems weird, doesn't it? After Jesus was born, it seems that Mary and Joseph had many other children (Matthew 13:55–56). You can imagine James and Jude struggling to fathom who their brother was, but sometime after the resurrection, they both came to believe that Jesus was their Savior and Lord (Jude vv. 1, 25). That's quite a thing to say about your brother!

The book of Jude is one of only five books of the Bible with just one chapter. Despite its short length, Jude packs a punch. There is an urgency to his tone, a concern to his focus.

Interestingly, this one short book is jam-packed with references from Old Testament stories. There are three warnings of the seriousness of abusing God's grace (vv. 5–7). There are also three examples of people in the Old Testament who corrupted others (v. 11). You can go back and read some of these stories to see how it turned out for them. Spoiler alert: not well!

Perhaps surprisingly, Jude gave instructions on how we are to treat these false teachers. We should show them mercy and seek to rescue them. However, we are to do this with great caution while steering clear of the sin in their lives.

As the book closes, we're reminded of God's majesty, power, and authority to keep us from falling away even when surrounded by attractive false teaching. As with each story of God's Word, God is the hero and center focus of our lives.

Jude

Make a Difference 1-2

Greet Well

How we greet each other says a lot about how we think about each other. The way that the writers of the New Testament greeted people reveals an incredible attitude of blessing. Greeting people well prioritizes our hearts, gets us out of our shells, and prayerfully encourages others.

Paul began all his letters with some form of this greeting: "May God our Father and the Lord Jesus Christ give you grace and peace." Peter launched his letters with these words: "May God give you more and more grace and peace" (1 Peter 1:2; 2 Peter 1:2). John started his third letter with a remarkable greeting to his friend Gaius: "To Gaius, my dear friend, whom I love in the truth" (3 John v. 1). Jude also began his letter with his unique greeting.

Difference Maker

Say something more profound than hello today. Put thought into a simple prayer of blessing to say when you greet people.

Greetings from Jude

This letter is from Jude, a slave of Jesus Christ and a brother of James.
I am writing to all who have been called by God the Father, who loves you
and keeps you safe in the care of Jesus Christ.*
2 May God give you more and more mercy, peace, and love.

The Danger of False Teachers

3 Dear friends, I had been eagerly planning to write to you about the salvation
we all share. But now I find that I must write about something else, urging
you to defend the faith that God has entrusted once for all time to his holy
people. 4 I say this because some ungodly people have wormed their way into
your churches, saying that God's marvelous grace allows us to live immoral
lives. The condemnation of such people was recorded long ago, for they have
denied our only Master and Lord, Jesus Christ.
5 So I want to remind you, though you already know these things, that
Jesus* first rescued the nation of Israel from Egypt, but later he destroyed
those who did not remain faithful. 6 And I remind you of the angels who
did not stay within the limits of authority God gave them but left the place
where they belonged. God has kept them securely chained in prisons of dark-
ness, waiting for the great day of judgment. 7 And don't forget Sodom and
Gomorrah and their neighboring towns, which were filled with immorality
and every kind of sexual perversion. Those cities were destroyed by fire and
serve as a warning of the eternal fire of God's judgment.
8 In the same way, these people—who claim authority from their dreams—
live immoral lives, defy authority, and scoff at supernatural beings.* 9 But even
Michael, one of the mightiest of the angels,* did not dare accuse the devil of
blasphemy, but simply said, "The Lord rebuke you!" (This took place when
Michael was arguing with the devil about Moses' body.) 10 But these people
scoff at things they do not understand. Like unthinking animals, they do
whatever their instincts tell them, and so they bring about their own destruc-
tion. 11 What sorrow awaits them! For they follow in the footsteps of Cain,
who killed his brother. Like Balaam, they deceive people for money. And like
Korah, they perish in their rebellion.
12 When these people eat with you in your fellowship meals commemorating
the Lord's love, they are like dangerous reefs that can shipwreck you.* They are
like shameless shepherds who care only for themselves. They are like clouds
blowing over the land without giving any rain. They are like trees in autumn
that are doubly dead, for they bear no fruit and have been pulled up by the roots.
13 They are like wild waves of the sea, churning up the foam of their shameful
deeds. They are like wandering stars, doomed forever to blackest darkness.

1 Or *keeps you for Jesus Christ.* 5 Other manuscripts read *[the] Lord,* or *God,* or *God Christ.* 8 Greek *at glorious ones,* which are probably evil angels. 9 Greek *Michael, the archangel.* 12 Or *they are contaminants among you;* or *they are stains.*

14 Enoch, who lived in the seventh generation after Adam, prophesied
about these people. He said, "Listen! The Lord is coming with countless
thousands of his holy ones 15 to execute judgment on the people of the world.
He will convict every person of all the ungodly things they have done and for
all the insults that ungodly sinners have spoken against him."*
16 These people are grumblers and complainers, living only to satisfy their
desires. They brag loudly about themselves, and they flatter others to get
what they want.

A Call to Remain Faithful

17 But you, my dear friends, must remember what the apostles of our Lord
Jesus Christ predicted. 18 They told you that in the last times there would
be scoffers whose purpose in life is to satisfy their ungodly desires. 19 These
people are the ones who are creating divisions among you. They follow their
natural instincts because they do not have God's Spirit in them.
20 But you, dear friends, must build each other up in your most holy faith,
pray in the power of the Holy Spirit,* 21 and await the mercy of our Lord Jesus
Christ, who will bring you eternal life. In this way, you will keep yourselves
safe in God's love.
22 And you must show mercy to* those whose faith is wavering. 23 Rescue
others by snatching them from the flames of judgment. Show mercy to still
others,* but do so with great caution, hating the sins that contaminate their
lives.*

A Prayer of Praise

24 Now all glory to God, who is able to keep you from falling away and will
bring you with great joy into his glorious presence without a single fault.
25 All glory to him who alone is God, our Savior through Jesus Christ our
Lord. All glory, majesty, power, and authority are his before all time, and in
the present, and beyond all time! Amen.

14-15 The quotation comes from intertestamental literature: Enoch 1:9. **20** Greek *pray in the Holy Spirit.* **22** Some manuscripts read *must reprove.* **22-23a** Some manuscripts have only two categories of people: (1) those whose faith is wavering and therefore need to be snatched from the flames of judgment, and (2) those who need to be shown mercy. **23b** Greek *with fear, hating even the clothing stained by the flesh.*

Prayer **18**

Lord, even if people mock me, let my faith in you never waver. Amen.

Make a Difference

24-25

Eternal Hope

This little book, which is only twenty-five verses long, has an underlying intensity of hope. It begins in love and joy, addresses a frigid concern, and then springs back to love and joy at the end.

The last verses of Jude thaw the cold and bloom freshness into the soul. Arms once huddled close to the chest are suddenly spread wide open! God's Word sings hope. When the season seems most somber, the eternal song of Jesus brings out the Bermuda shorts and points to the refreshing life that is to come.

Difference Maker

Do something whimsical that will give you and others around you a refreshing reminder of hope.

Revelation Introduction

J. R. R. Tolkien's third volume in *The Lord of the Rings* series is called *The Return of the King*. In the story, the prophesied rescuer, Aragorn, returns to the land of Gondor, fights victoriously against evil forces, and is joyously crowned king. As a result, the land is restored, those fighting the battle return home, and refreshing peace reigns over the land.

Tolkien had Jesus in mind as he penned this story. The prophecies in the Bible speak about Jesus' coming to launch his rescue mission, but they also promise he would return to fight an apocalyptic battle to destroy evil and complete his restorative work.

Jesus is called "the Alpha and the Omega—the beginning and the end" (Revelation 1:8). What he starts, he will finish. He has promised to return to gather us—all of us—to him once again (John 14:1-3). Having once carried our sin, he has promised to return to save us, absolutely and finally, from it (Hebrews 9:28). He wants us to watch for him (Matthew 24:44) because he has promised to fight for those who look for him (John 6:39-40).

Read this book with anticipation! As you do, look for Jesus today. Look for glimpses of his coming and anticipate the stirring of his Spirit. Be aware of his work. Don't miss him.

Story Arcs

- **Jesus**
- **The Word, the King, Jesus**
- **Jesus, the Promised King**

Revelation

Prologue

1 This is a revelation from* Jesus Christ, which God gave him to show
his servants the events that must soon* take place. He sent an angel to
present this revelation to his servant John, 2 who faithfully reported every-
thing he saw. This is his report of the word of God and the testimony of
Jesus Christ.
3 God blesses the one who reads the words of this prophecy to the church,
and he blesses all who listen to its message and obey what it says, for the
time is near.

Prayer **1:7**

Jesus, when you return, let me not be caught looking for something other than you. Amen.

John's Greeting to the Seven Churches

4 This letter is from John to the seven churches in the province of Asia.*
Grace and peace to you from the one who is, who always was, and who is
still to come; from the sevenfold Spirit* before his throne; 5 and from Jesus
Christ. He is the faithful witness to these things, the first to rise from the
dead, and the ruler of all the kings of the world.
All glory to him who loves us and has freed us from our sins by shedding
his blood for us. 6 He has made us a Kingdom of priests for God his Father.
All glory and power to him forever and ever! Amen.

7 Look! He comes with the clouds of heaven.
  And everyone will see him—
  even those who pierced him.
And all the nations of the world
  will mourn for him.
Yes! Amen!

8 "I am the Alpha and the Omega—the beginning and the end,"* says the
Lord God. "I am the one who is, who always was, and who is still to come—
the Almighty One."

Vision of the Son of Man

9 I, John, am your brother and your partner in suffering and in God's King-
dom and in the patient endurance to which Jesus calls us. I was exiled to the
island of Patmos for preaching the word of God and for my testimony about
Jesus. 10 It was the Lord's Day, and I was worshiping in the Spirit.* Suddenly,
I heard behind me a loud voice like a trumpet blast. 11 It said, "Write in a
book* everything you see, and send it to the seven churches in the cities of
Ephesus, Smyrna, Pergamum, Thyatira, Sardis, Philadelphia, and Laodicea."
12 When I turned to see who was speaking to me, I saw seven gold

1:1a Or *of.* 1:1b Or *suddenly,* or *quickly.* 1:4a *Asia* was a Roman province in what is now western Turkey. 1:4b Greek *the seven spirits.* 1:8 Greek *I am the Alpha and the Omega,* referring to the first and last letters of the Greek alphabet. 1:10 Or *in spirit.* 1:11 Or *on a scroll.*

Question 1:17-18

What were the key things Jesus wanted John to know about him, and why do these things make all the difference in our lives?

Question 2:4

How have your feelings for Jesus shifted since reading this letter? Can you identify the time and circumstances in your life that have influenced your feelings for Jesus?

lampstands. [13]And standing in the middle of the lampstands was someone
like the Son of Man.* He was wearing a long robe with a gold sash across his
chest. [14]His head and his hair were white like wool, as white as snow. And his
eyes were like flames of fire. [15]His feet were like polished bronze refined in a
furnace, and his voice thundered like mighty ocean waves. [16]He held seven
stars in his right hand, and a sharp two-edged sword came from his mouth.
And his face was like the sun in all its brilliance.

[17]When I saw him, I fell at his feet as if I were dead. But he laid his right
hand on me and said, "Don't be afraid! I am the First and the Last. [18]I am the
living one. I died, but look—I am alive forever and ever! And I hold the keys
of death and the grave.*

[19]"Write down what you have seen—both the things that are now happen-
ing and the things that will happen.* [20]This is the meaning of the mystery of
the seven stars you saw in my right hand and the seven gold lampstands: The
seven stars are the angels* of the seven churches, and the seven lampstands
are the seven churches.

The Message to the Church in Ephesus

2 "Write this letter to the angel* of the church in Ephesus. This is the message from the one who holds the seven stars in his right hand, the one who walks among the seven gold lampstands:

[2]"I know all the things you do. I have seen your hard work and your
patient endurance. I know you don't tolerate evil people. You have
examined the claims of those who say they are apostles but are not.
You have discovered they are liars. [3]You have patiently suffered for me
without quitting.

[4]"But I have this complaint against you. You don't love me or each
other as you did at first!* [5]Look how far you have fallen! Turn back to
me and do the works you did at first. If you don't repent, I will come
and remove your lampstand from its place among the churches. [6]But
this is in your favor: You hate the evil deeds of the Nicolaitans, just as
I do.

[7]"Anyone with ears to hear must listen to the Spirit and understand
what he is saying to the churches. To everyone who is victorious I will
give fruit from the tree of life in the paradise of God.

The Message to the Church in Smyrna

[8]"Write this letter to the angel of the church in Smyrna. This is the message
from the one who is the First and the Last, who was dead but is now alive:

[9]"I know about your suffering and your poverty—but you are rich! I
know the blasphemy of those opposing you. They say they are Jews,
but they are not, because their synagogue belongs to Satan. [10]Don't be
afraid of what you are about to suffer. The devil will throw some of you
into prison to test you. You will suffer for ten days. But if you remain
faithful even when facing death, I will give you the crown of life.

1:13 Or *like a son of man.* See Dan 7:13. "Son of Man" is a title Jesus used for himself. **1:18** Greek *and Hades.* **1:19** Or *what you have seen and what they mean—the things that have already begun to happen.* **1:20** Or *the messengers.* **2:1** Or *the messenger;* also in 2:8, 12, 18. **2:4** Greek *You have lost your first love.*

11 "Anyone with ears to hear must listen to the Spirit and understand
what he is saying to the churches. Whoever is victorious will not be
harmed by the second death.

The Message to the Church in Pergamum

12 "Write this letter to the angel of the church in Pergamum. This is the message from the one with the sharp two-edged sword:

13 "I know that you live in the city where Satan has his throne, yet
you have remained loyal to me. You refused to deny me even when
Antipas, my faithful witness, was martyred among you there in
Satan's city.

14 "But I have a few complaints against you. You tolerate some
among you whose teaching is like that of Balaam, who showed Balak
how to trip up the people of Israel. He taught them to sin by eating
food offered to idols and by committing sexual sin.
15 In a similar way,
you have some Nicolaitans among you who follow the same teaching.
16 Repent of your sin, or I will come to you suddenly and fight against
them with the sword of my mouth.

17 "Anyone with ears to hear must listen to the Spirit and understand
what he is saying to the churches. To everyone who is victorious I will
give some of the manna that has been hidden away in heaven. And I will
give to each one a white stone, and on the stone will be engraved a new
name that no one understands except the one who receives it.

The Message to the Church in Thyatira

18 "Write this letter to the angel of the church in Thyatira. This is the message from the Son of God, whose eyes are like flames of fire, whose feet are like polished bronze:

19 "I know all the things you do. I have seen your love, your faith, your
service, and your patient endurance. And I can see your constant
improvement in all these things.

20 "But I have this complaint against you. You are permitting that
woman—that Jezebel who calls herself a prophet—to lead my servants
astray. She teaches them to commit sexual sin and to eat food offered
to idols.
21 I gave her time to repent, but she does not want to turn away
from her immorality.

22 "Therefore, I will throw her on a bed of suffering,* and those who
commit adultery with her will suffer greatly unless they repent and
turn away from her evil deeds.
23 I will strike her children dead. Then all
the churches will know that I am the one who searches out the thoughts
and intentions of every person. And I will give to each of you whatever
you deserve.

24 "But I also have a message for the rest of you in Thyatira who have
not followed this false teaching ('deeper truths,' as they call them—
depths of Satan, actually). I will ask nothing more of you
25 except
that you hold tightly to what you have until I come.
26 To all who are
victorious, who obey me to the very end,

2:22 Greek *a bed.*

To them I will give authority over all the nations.
27 They will rule the nations with an iron rod
and smash them like clay pots.*

28 They will have the same authority I received from my Father, and
I will also give them the morning star!
29 "Anyone with ears to hear must listen to the Spirit and understand
what he is saying to the churches.

The Message to the Church in Sardis

3 "Write this letter to the angel* of the church in Sardis. This is the message from the one who has the sevenfold Spirit* of God and the seven stars:

"I know all the things you do, and that you have a reputation for being
alive—but you are dead. 2 Wake up! Strengthen what little remains, for
even what is left is almost dead. I find that your actions do not meet the
requirements of my God. 3 Go back to what you heard and believed at
first; hold to it firmly. Repent and turn to me again. If you don't wake
up, I will come to you suddenly, as unexpected as a thief.
4 "Yet there are some in the church in Sardis who have not soiled their
clothes with evil. They will walk with me in white, for they are worthy.
5 All who are victorious will be clothed in white. I will never erase their
names from the Book of Life, but I will announce before my Father and
his angels that they are mine.
6 "Anyone with ears to hear must listen to the Spirit and understand
what he is saying to the churches.

The Message to the Church in Philadelphia

7 "Write this letter to the angel of the church in Philadelphia.

This is the message from the one who is holy and true,
the one who has the key of David.
What he opens, no one can close;
and what he closes, no one can open:*

8 "I know all the things you do, and I have opened a door for you that
no one can close. You have little strength, yet you obeyed my word
and did not deny me. 9 Look, I will force those who belong to Satan's
synagogue—those liars who say they are Jews but are not—to come
and bow down at your feet. They will acknowledge that you are the
ones I love.
10 "Because you have obeyed my command to persevere, I will protect
you from the great time of testing that will come upon the whole world
to test those who belong to this world. 11 I am coming soon.* Hold on to
what you have, so that no one will take away your crown. 12 All who are
victorious will become pillars in the Temple of my God, and they will
never have to leave it. And I will write on them the name of my God,
and they will be citizens in the city of my God—the new Jerusalem that

2:26-27 Ps 2:8-9 (Greek version). **3:1a** Or *the messenger;* also in 3:7, 14. **3:1b** Greek *the seven spirits.* **3:7** Isa 22:22. **3:11** Or *suddenly,* or *quickly.*

Make a Difference 3:20

Provocative

You were created to live a radical life. You were made to be deeply alive, stretched to your fullest, and passionately involved in this world. It is no wonder, then, that you are attracted to the provocative.

Provocative simply means to "call forward." It recognizes your God-created thirst for activity and purpose. You were created to be called and called to be creative. You were formed so that you could step forward in the shaping of how life is lived on this planet. Jesus didn't make you to squander your days; rather, he made you to live them.

Both Jesus and Satan employ the provocative. Let your ninja-like reflexes be aware that Satan also calls you forward, but his is an enticement to eat from a cornucopia of carnage, using you for his own self-serving survival and scheming plans. On the other hand, Jesus calls you forward, and his is an invitation to dinner shared with friends, empowering you as his partner to give life to others.

Difference Maker

Pray for someone who could use a positive nudge. Then call that person on the phone. Invite them to step forward in faith today by starting a Bible study with you, doing a service project, or praying with you.

comes down from heaven from my God. And I will also write on them
my new name.
13 “Anyone with ears to hear must listen to the Spirit and understand
what he is saying to the churches.

The Message to the Church in Laodicea
14 “Write this letter to the angel of the church in Laodicea. This is the message
from the one who is the Amen—the faithful and true witness, the begin-
ning* of God's new creation:

15 “I know all the things you do, that you are neither hot nor cold. I
wish that you were one or the other! 16 But since you are like lukewarm
water, neither hot nor cold, I will spit you out of my mouth! 17 You
say, 'I am rich. I have everything I want. I don't need a thing!' And you
don't realize that you are wretched and miserable and poor and blind
and naked. 18 So I advise you to buy gold from me—gold that has been
purified by fire. Then you will be rich. Also buy white garments from
me so you will not be shamed by your nakedness, and ointment for your
eyes so you will be able to see. 19 I correct and discipline everyone I love.
So be diligent and turn from your indifference.
20 “Look! I stand at the door and knock. If you hear my voice and open
the door, I will come in, and we will share a meal together as friends.
21 Those who are victorious will sit with me on my throne, just as I was
victorious and sat with my Father on his throne.
22 “Anyone with ears to hear must listen to the Spirit and understand
what he is saying to the churches.”

Worship in Heaven
4 Then as I looked, I saw a door standing open in heaven, and the same
voice I had heard before spoke to me like a trumpet blast. The voice said,
“Come up here, and I will show you what must happen after this.” 2 And
instantly I was in the Spirit,* and I saw a throne in heaven and someone sit-
ting on it. 3 The one sitting on the throne was as brilliant as gemstones—like
jasper and carnelian. And the glow of an emerald circled his throne like a
rainbow. 4 Twenty-four thrones surrounded him, and twenty-four elders sat
on them. They were all clothed in white and had gold crowns on their heads.
5 From the throne came flashes of lightning and the rumble of thunder. And
in front of the throne were seven torches with burning flames. This is the
sevenfold Spirit* of God. 6 In front of the throne was a shiny sea of glass,
sparkling like crystal.
In the center and around the throne were four living beings, each covered
with eyes, front and back. 7 The first of these living beings was like a lion; the
second was like an ox; the third had a human face; and the fourth was like an
eagle in flight. 8 Each of these living beings had six wings, and their wings
were covered all over with eyes, inside and out. Day after day and night after
night they keep on saying,

“Holy, holy, holy is the Lord God, the Almighty—
the one who always was, who is, and who is still to come.”

3:14 Or *the ruler*, or *the source*. 4:2 Or *in spirit*. 4:5 Greek *They are the seven spirits*.

Story Arc **4:1-11**

● Jesus
In Luke 1:46-55, Mary, the mother of Jesus, sang a song after finding out she would give birth to the Son of God, the Savior of the world. Notice the words in her song and compare them to the words sung by the angels here in Revelation 4. This section also echoes Isaiah 6:3, where angels sing a similar song. Throughout the Bible, every created being who encounters the living God cannot help but praise the holiness of the Lord and declare a song of victory. The rest of this book of Revelation is a victorious declaration of how God will redeem the world once and for all through his Son, Jesus.

Rev 19:13 ►

Question 5:1-14

Why is this chapter in Revelation one of the most powerful and majestic moments in all the Bible?

9 Whenever the living beings give glory and honor and thanks to the one sitting on the throne (the one who lives forever and ever), 10 the twenty-four elders fall down and worship the one sitting on the throne (the one who lives forever and ever). And they lay their crowns before the throne and say,

11 "You are worthy, O Lord our God,
to receive glory and honor and power.
For you created all things,
and they exist because you created what you pleased."

The Lamb Opens the Scroll

5 Then I saw a scroll* in the right hand of the one who was sitting on the
throne. There was writing on the inside and the outside of the scroll,
and it was sealed with seven seals. 2 And I saw a strong angel, who shouted
with a loud voice: "Who is worthy to break the seals on this scroll and open
it?" 3 But no one in heaven or on earth or under the earth was able to open
the scroll and read it.
4 Then I began to weep bitterly because no one was found worthy to open
the scroll and read it. 5 But one of the twenty-four elders said to me, "Stop
weeping! Look, the Lion of the tribe of Judah, the heir to David's throne,* has
won the victory. He is worthy to open the scroll and its seven seals."
6 Then I saw a Lamb that looked as if it had been slaughtered, but it was
now standing between the throne and the four living beings and among
the twenty-four elders. He had seven horns and seven eyes, which represent
the sevenfold Spirit* of God that is sent out into every part of the earth. 7 He
stepped forward and took the scroll from the right hand of the one sitting
on the throne. 8 And when he took the scroll, the four living beings and the
twenty-four elders fell down before the Lamb. Each one had a harp, and they
held gold bowls filled with incense, which are the prayers of God's people.
9 And they sang a new song with these words:

"You are worthy to take the scroll
and break its seals and open it.
For you were slaughtered, and your blood has ransomed
people for God
from every tribe and language and people and nation.
10 And you have caused them to become
a Kingdom of priests for our God.
And they will reign* on the earth."

11 Then I looked again, and I heard the voices of thousands and millions
of angels around the throne and of the living beings and the elders. 12 And
they sang in a mighty chorus:

"Worthy is the Lamb who was slaughtered—
to receive power and riches
and wisdom and strength
and honor and glory and blessing."

5:1 Or *book;* also in 5:2, 3, 4, 5, 7, 8, 9. 5:5 Greek *the root of David.* See Isa 11:10. 5:6 Greek *which are the seven spirits.* 5:10 Some manuscripts read *they are reigning.*

13 And then I heard every creature in heaven and on earth and under the
earth and in the sea. They sang:

"Blessing and honor and glory and power
belong to the one sitting on the throne
and to the Lamb forever and ever."

14 And the four living beings said, "Amen!" And the twenty-four elders fell
down and worshiped the Lamb.

The Lamb Breaks the First Six Seals

6 As I watched, the Lamb broke the first of the seven seals on the scroll.*
Then I heard one of the four living beings say with a voice like thunder,
"Come!" 2 I looked up and saw a white horse standing there. Its rider carried
a bow, and a crown was placed on his head. He rode out to win many battles
and gain the victory.
3 When the Lamb broke the second seal, I heard the second living being
say, "Come!" 4 Then another horse appeared, a red one. Its rider was given a
mighty sword and the authority to take peace from the earth. And there was
war and slaughter everywhere.
5 When the Lamb broke the third seal, I heard the third living being say,
"Come!" I looked up and saw a black horse, and its rider was holding a pair
of scales in his hand. 6 And I heard a voice from among the four living beings
say, "A loaf of wheat bread or three loaves of barley will cost a day's pay.* And
don't waste* the olive oil and wine."
7 When the Lamb broke the fourth seal, I heard the fourth living being say,
"Come!" 8 I looked up and saw a horse whose color was pale green. Its rider
was named Death, and his companion was the Grave.* These two were given
authority over one-fourth of the earth, to kill with the sword and famine and
disease* and wild animals.
9 When the Lamb broke the fifth seal, I saw under the altar the souls of all
who had been martyred for the word of God and for being faithful in their
testimony. 10 They shouted to the Lord and said, "O Sovereign Lord, holy and
true, how long before you judge the people who belong to this world and
avenge our blood for what they have done to us?" 11 Then a white robe was
given to each of them. And they were told to rest a little longer until the full
number of their brothers and sisters*—their fellow servants of Jesus who
were to be martyred—had joined them.
12 I watched as the Lamb broke the sixth seal, and there was a great
earthquake. The sun became as dark as black cloth, and the moon became
as red as blood. 13 Then the stars of the sky fell to the earth like green
figs falling from a tree shaken by a strong wind. 14 The sky was rolled
up like a scroll, and all of the mountains and islands were moved from
their places.
15 Then everyone—the kings of the earth, the rulers, the generals, the
wealthy, the powerful, and every slave and free person—all hid themselves
in the caves and among the rocks of the mountains. 16 And they cried to the
mountains and the rocks, "Fall on us and hide us from the face of the one

Question 6:15–17

Which kind of people are in hiding from God's wrath, and what do you think they could have done during their lifetime to avoid God's wrath?

6:1 Or *book.* **6:6a** Greek *A choinix* [1 quart or 1 liter] *of wheat for a denarius, and 3 choinix of barley for a denarius.* A denarius was equivalent to a laborer's full day's wage. **6:6b** Or *harm.* **6:8a** Greek *was Hades.* **6:8b** Greek *death.* **6:11** Greek *their brothers.*

who sits on the throne and from the wrath of the Lamb. [17]For the great day
of their wrath has come, and who is able to survive?"

God's People Will Be Preserved

7 Then I saw four angels standing at the four corners of the earth, hold-
ing back the four winds so they did not blow on the earth or the sea, or
even on any tree. [2]And I saw another angel coming up from the east, car-
rying the seal of the living God. And he shouted to those four angels, who
had been given power to harm land and sea, [3]"Wait! Don't harm the land
or the sea or the trees until we have placed the seal of God on the foreheads
of his servants."

[4]And I heard how many were marked with the seal of God—144,000 were
sealed from all the tribes of Israel:

[5] from Judah 12,000
from Reuben 12,000
from Gad 12,000
[6] from Asher 12,000
from Naphtali 12,000
from Manasseh 12,000
[7] from Simeon 12,000
from Levi 12,000
from Issachar 12,000
[8] from Zebulun 12,000
from Joseph 12,000
from Benjamin 12,000

Praise from the Great Crowd

[9]After this I saw a vast crowd, too great to count, from every nation and tribe
and people and language, standing in front of the throne and before the
Lamb. They were clothed in white robes and held palm branches in their
hands. [10]And they were shouting with a great roar,

"Salvation comes from our God who sits
on the throne
and from the Lamb!"

[11]And all the angels were standing around the throne and around the
elders and the four living beings. And they fell before the throne with their
faces to the ground and worshiped God. [12]They sang,

"Amen! Blessing and glory and wisdom
and thanksgiving and honor
and power and strength belong to our God
forever and ever! Amen."

[13]Then one of the twenty-four elders asked me, "Who are these who are
clothed in white? Where did they come from?"

[14]And I said to him, "Sir, you are the one who knows."

Make a Difference

7:9-17

Savior

In the middle of the Bible is an important question: "I look up to the mountains—does my help come from there?" (Psalm 121:1).

The concept of salvation can be difficult to understand for someone who has never felt in need of rescue. People who have lived fairly comfortably postpone discomfort and, as a result, can struggle to comprehend the desperation caused by trouble. It's one reason Jesus said that it's harder for the rich to get into heaven than for a camel to fit through the eye of a needle (Matthew 19:24).

Eventually, though, everyone's temporary comfort gives way to the need to be rescued. Something inevitably breaks through the coziness: sin, evil, sickness, death, or separation from God. Something eventually urges everyone to cry out for Jesus. Those who choose to look up and ask for his help will be saved and shout with joy.

Difference Maker

If you have never stopped to accept salvation from Jesus, recognize your need, look to him now, and ask for it. Go to the back of this Bible for a prayer that you can use to accept Jesus as your Lord and Savior!

Then he said to me, "These are the ones who died in* the great tribulation.* They have washed their robes in the blood of the Lamb and made them white.

15 "That is why they stand in front of God's throne
and serve him day and night in his Temple.
And he who sits on the throne
will give them shelter.
16 They will never again be hungry or thirsty;
they will never be scorched by the heat of the sun.
17 For the Lamb on the throne*
will be their Shepherd.
He will lead them to springs of life-giving water.
And God will wipe every tear from their eyes."

The Lamb Breaks the Seventh Seal

8 When the Lamb broke the seventh seal on the scroll,* there was silence
throughout heaven for about half an hour. 2 I saw the seven angels who
stand before God, and they were given seven trumpets.
3 Then another angel with a gold incense burner came and stood at the
altar. And a great amount of incense was given to him to mix with the prayers
of God's people as an offering on the gold altar before the throne. 4 The smoke
of the incense, mixed with the prayers of God's holy people, ascended up to
God from the altar where the angel had poured them out. 5 Then the angel
filled the incense burner with fire from the altar and threw it down upon
the earth; and thunder crashed, lightning flashed, and there was a terrible
earthquake.

The First Four Trumpets

6 Then the seven angels with the seven trumpets prepared to blow their
mighty blasts.
7 The first angel blew his trumpet, and hail and fire mixed with blood were
thrown down on the earth. One-third of the earth was set on fire, one-third
of the trees were burned, and all the green grass was burned.
8 Then the second angel blew his trumpet, and a great mountain of fire
was thrown into the sea. One-third of the water in the sea became blood,
9 one-third of all things living in the sea died, and one-third of all the ships
on the sea were destroyed.
10 Then the third angel blew his trumpet, and a great star fell from the sky,
burning like a torch. It fell on one-third of the rivers and on the springs of
water. 11 The name of the star was Bitterness.* It made one-third of the water
bitter, and many people died from drinking the bitter water.
12 Then the fourth angel blew his trumpet, and one-third of the sun was
struck, and one-third of the moon, and one-third of the stars, and they became dark. And one-third of the day was dark, and also one-third of the
night.
13 Then I looked, and I heard a single eagle crying loudly as it flew through
the air, "Terror, terror, terror to all who belong to this world because of what
will happen when the last three angels blow their trumpets."

7:14a Greek *who came out of.* **7:14b** Or *the great suffering.* **7:17** Greek *on the center of the throne.* **8:1** Or *book.* **8:11** Greek *Wormwood.*

Question **8:3**

Incense is a combination of spices that, when burned, produces a wonderfully pleasing aroma. Do you think it's awesome or strange that all your prayers are a pleasing scent to God, and how could this knowledge shift the way you pray?

Question 9:20

Why do you think people are slow to turn away from their sin even when their sin is causing such great pain?

The Fifth Trumpet Brings the First Terror

9 Then the fifth angel blew his trumpet, and I saw a star that had fallen to
earth from the sky, and he was given the key to the shaft of the bottom-
less pit.* [2]When he opened it, smoke poured out as though from a huge
furnace, and the sunlight and air turned dark from the smoke.
[3]Then locusts came from the smoke and descended on the earth, and they
were given power to sting like scorpions. [4]They were told not to harm the grass
or plants or trees, but only the people who did not have the seal of God on their
foreheads. [5]They were told not to kill them but to torture them for five months
with pain like the pain of a scorpion sting. [6]In those days people will seek
death but will not find it. They will long to die, but death will flee from them!
[7]The locusts looked like horses prepared for battle. They had what looked
like gold crowns on their heads, and their faces looked like human faces. [8]They
had hair like women's hair and teeth like the teeth of a lion. [9]They wore armor
made of iron, and their wings roared like an army of chariots rushing into
battle. [10]They had tails that stung like scorpions, and for five months they had
the power to torment people. [11]Their king is the angel from the bottomless
pit; his name in Hebrew is *Abaddon,* and in Greek, *Apollyon*—the Destroyer.
[12]The first terror is past, but look, two more terrors are coming!

The Sixth Trumpet Brings the Second Terror

[13]Then the sixth angel blew his trumpet, and I heard a voice speaking from
the four horns of the gold altar that stands in the presence of God. [14]And the
voice said to the sixth angel who held the trumpet, "Release the four angels
who are bound at the great Euphrates River." [15]Then the four angels who
had been prepared for this hour and day and month and year were turned
loose to kill one-third of all the people on earth. [16]I heard the size of their
army, which was 200 million mounted troops.
[17]And in my vision, I saw the horses and the riders sitting on them. The
riders wore armor that was fiery red and dark blue and yellow. The horses
had heads like lions, and fire and smoke and burning sulfur billowed from
their mouths. [18]One-third of all the people on earth were killed by these
three plagues—by the fire and smoke and burning sulfur that came from
the mouths of the horses. [19]Their power was in their mouths and in their
tails. For their tails had heads like snakes, with the power to injure people.
[20]But the people who did not die in these plagues still refused to repent
of their evil deeds and turn to God. They continued to worship demons and
idols made of gold, silver, bronze, stone, and wood—idols that can neither
see nor hear nor walk! [21]And they did not repent of their murders or their
witchcraft or their sexual immorality or their thefts.

The Angel and the Small Scroll

10 Then I saw another mighty angel coming down from heaven, sur-
rounded by a cloud, with a rainbow over his head. His face shone like
the sun, and his feet were like pillars of fire. [2]And in his hand was a small
scroll* that had been opened. He stood with his right foot on the sea and his
left foot on the land. [3]And he gave a great shout like the roar of a lion. And
when he shouted, the seven thunders answered.
[4]When the seven thunders spoke, I was about to write. But I heard a voice

9:1 Or *the abyss,* or *the underworld;* also in 9:11. **10:2** Or *book;* also in 10:8, 9, 10.

from heaven saying, "Keep secret* what the seven thunders said, and do not
write it down."
5 Then the angel I saw standing on the sea and on the land raised his right
hand toward heaven. 6 He swore an oath in the name of the one who lives
forever and ever, who created the heavens and everything in them, the earth
and everything in it, and the sea and everything in it. He said, "There will
be no more delay. 7 When the seventh angel blows his trumpet, God's mys-
terious plan will be fulfilled. It will happen just as he announced it to his
servants the prophets."
8 Then the voice from heaven spoke to me again: "Go and take the open
scroll from the hand of the angel who is standing on the sea and on the land."
9 So I went to the angel and told him to give me the small scroll. "Yes, take
it and eat it," he said. "It will be sweet as honey in your mouth, but it will
turn sour in your stomach!" 10 So I took the small scroll from the hand of
the angel, and I ate it! It was sweet in my mouth, but when I swallowed it, it
turned sour in my stomach.
11 Then I was told, "You must prophesy again about many peoples, nations,
languages, and kings."

The Two Witnesses

11 Then I was given a measuring stick, and I was told, "Go and measure
the Temple of God and the altar, and count the number of worship-
ers. 2 But do not measure the outer courtyard, for it has been turned over
to the nations. They will trample the holy city for 42 months. 3 And I will
give power to my two witnesses, and they will be clothed in burlap and will
prophesy during those 1,260 days."
4 These two prophets are the two olive trees and the two lampstands that
stand before the Lord of all the earth. 5 If anyone tries to harm them, fire
flashes from their mouths and consumes their enemies. This is how anyone
who tries to harm them must die. 6 They have power to shut the sky so that
no rain will fall for as long as they prophesy. And they have the power to turn
the rivers and oceans into blood, and to strike the earth with every kind of
plague as often as they wish.
7 When they complete their testimony, the beast that comes up out of the
bottomless pit* will declare war against them, and he will conquer them and
kill them. 8 And their bodies will lie in the main street of Jerusalem,* the city
that is figuratively called "Sodom" and "Egypt," the city where their Lord was
crucified. 9 And for three and a half days, all peoples, tribes, languages, and na-
tions will stare at their bodies. No one will be allowed to bury them. 10 All the
people who belong to this world will gloat over them and give presents to each
other to celebrate the death of the two prophets who had tormented them.
11 But after three and a half days, God breathed life into them, and they
stood up! Terror struck all who were staring at them. 12 Then a loud voice
from heaven called to the two prophets, "Come up here!" And they rose to
heaven in a cloud as their enemies watched.
13 At the same time there was a terrible earthquake that destroyed a tenth
of the city. Seven thousand people died in that earthquake, and everyone else
was terrified and gave glory to the God of heaven.
14 The second terror is past, but look, the third terror is coming quickly.

Make a Difference

10:9-10

Can You Stomach God's Message?

You are near the end of the Bible. Hopefully, you have read a lot of it. If so, you have an important role to play in sharing the story of Jesus! Still, like John, the thought of sharing the gospel may be putting knots in your stomach. You know this story is good; you know it is sweet! You have tasted and seen the goodness of the message of Jesus, but that might not change how you feel about speaking it aloud. To get over your fear, just imagine the sweet joy of seeing lives transformed by the story of God's love for all people.

Difference Maker

Get a copy of this Bible and give it to a friend who has yet to taste how sweet the love of Jesus can be. Highlight all your favorite Difference Maker challenges and share with your friend the difference Jesus has made in your life.

10:4 Greek *Seal up.* **11:7** Or *the abyss,* or *the underworld.* **11:8** Greek *the great city.*

Prayer 11:15

Lord Jesus, you will reign forever and ever! Amen.

The Seventh Trumpet Brings the Third Terror

15 Then the seventh angel blew his trumpet, and there were loud voices shout-
ing in heaven:

"The world has now become the Kingdom of our Lord
and of his Christ,*
and he will reign forever and ever."

16 The twenty-four elders sitting on their thrones before God fell with their
faces to the ground and worshiped him. 17 And they said,

"We give thanks to you, Lord God, the Almighty,
the one who is and who always was,
for now you have assumed your great power
and have begun to reign.
18 The nations were filled with wrath,
but now the time of your wrath has come.
It is time to judge the dead
and reward your servants the prophets,
as well as your holy people,
and all who fear your name,
from the least to the greatest.
It is time to destroy
all who have caused destruction on the earth."

19 Then, in heaven, the Temple of God was opened and the Ark of his cov-
enant could be seen inside the Temple. Lightning flashed, thunder crashed
and roared, and there was an earthquake and a terrible hailstorm.

The Woman and the Dragon

12 Then I witnessed in heaven an event of great significance. I saw a
woman clothed with the sun, with the moon beneath her feet, and
a crown of twelve stars on her head. 2 She was pregnant, and she cried out
because of her labor pains and the agony of giving birth.
3 Then I witnessed in heaven another significant event. I saw a large red
dragon with seven heads and ten horns, with seven crowns on his heads. 4 His
tail swept away one-third of the stars in the sky, and he threw them to the
earth. He stood in front of the woman as she was about to give birth, ready
to devour her baby as soon as it was born.
5 She gave birth to a son who was to rule all nations with an iron rod. And
her child was snatched away from the dragon and was caught up to God
and to his throne. 6 And the woman fled into the wilderness, where God had
prepared a place to care for her for 1,260 days.
7 Then there was war in heaven. Michael and his angels fought against the
dragon and his angels. 8 And the dragon lost the battle, and he and his angels
were forced out of heaven. 9 This great dragon—the ancient serpent called
the devil, or Satan, the one deceiving the whole world—was thrown down
to the earth with all his angels.
10 Then I heard a loud voice shouting across the heavens,

11:15 Or *his Messiah.*

"It has come at last—
salvation and power
and the Kingdom of our God,
and the authority of his Christ.*
For the accuser of our brothers and sisters*
has been thrown down to earth—
the one who accuses them
before our God day and night.
11 And they have defeated him by the blood of the Lamb
and by their testimony.
And they did not love their lives so much
that they were afraid to die.
12 Therefore, rejoice, O heavens!
And you who live in the heavens, rejoice!
But terror will come on the earth and the sea,
for the devil has come down to you in great anger,
knowing that he has little time."

13 When the dragon realized that he had been thrown down to the earth,
he pursued the woman who had given birth to the male child. 14 But she was
given two wings like those of a great eagle so she could fly to the place pre-
pared for her in the wilderness. There she would be cared for and protected
from the dragon* for a time, times, and half a time.
15 Then the dragon tried to drown the woman with a flood of water that
flowed from his mouth. 16 But the earth helped her by opening its mouth
and swallowing the river that gushed out from the mouth of the dragon.
17 And the dragon was angry at the woman and declared war against the rest
of her children—all who keep God's commandments and maintain their
testimony for Jesus.
18 Then the dragon took his stand* on the shore beside the sea.

The Beast out of the Sea

13 Then I saw a beast rising up out of the sea. It had seven heads and
ten horns, with ten crowns on its horns. And written on each head
were names that blasphemed God. 2 This beast looked like a leopard, but it
had the feet of a bear and the mouth of a lion! And the dragon gave the beast
his own power and throne and great authority.
3 I saw that one of the heads of the beast seemed wounded beyond
recovery—but the fatal wound was healed! The whole world marveled at
this miracle and gave allegiance to the beast. 4 They worshiped the dragon
for giving the beast such power, and they also worshiped the beast. "Who is
as great as the beast?" they exclaimed. "Who is able to fight against him?"
5 Then the beast was allowed to speak great blasphemies against God.
And he was given authority to do whatever he wanted for forty-two
months. 6 And he spoke terrible words of blasphemy against God, slan-
dering his name and his dwelling—that is, those who dwell in heaven.*
7 And the beast was allowed to wage war against God's holy people and to

Question 12:17

How do you feel knowing that following Jesus is going to gain you an enemy? How can you prepare for the spiritual battle being waged in this world?

12:10a Or *his Messiah.* 12:10b Greek *brothers.* 12:14 Greek *the serpent;* also in 12:15. See 12:9. 12:18 Greek *Then he took his stand;* some manuscripts read *Then I took my stand.* Some translations put this entire sentence into 13:1. 13:6 Some manuscripts read *and his dwelling and all who dwell in heaven.*

Question 13:8

God designed people to worship, but these people were worshiping the beast. What do you think this beast represents? Why would people tend to worship it?

Make a Difference

14:1-5

High Praise

Have you ever thought about the legacy you want to leave behind? These 144,000 in verses 1-5 are a reminder that a life lived for Jesus will leave an enduring legacy.

These people made a difference on earth because they had such a high view of Jesus in their life. They walked by faith, were blameless in their actions, and never allowed a lie to leave their mouths. It was so honoring to Jesus that he gives them the honor of being able to sing a worship song only they would ever know. How cool is that to have a secret song with Jesus?

Difference Maker

Consider a few friends you deeply admire who follow Jesus. Create a legacy paragraph on their behalf. Write down what you will always remember about them and give it to them as a reminder to keep a high view of Jesus in their life.

conquer them. And he was given authority to rule over every tribe and
people and language and nation.
8 And all the people who belong to this
world worshiped the beast. They are the ones whose names were not written in the Book of Life that belongs to the Lamb who was slaughtered before the world was made.*

9 Anyone with ears to hear
should listen and understand.
10 Anyone who is destined for prison
will be taken to prison.
Anyone destined to die by the sword
will die by the sword.

This means that God's holy people must endure persecution patiently and remain faithful.

The Beast out of the Earth

11 Then I saw another beast come up out of the earth. He had two horns like
those of a lamb, but he spoke with the voice of a dragon.
12 He exercised all
the authority of the first beast. And he required all the earth and its people
to worship the first beast, whose fatal wound had been healed.
13 He did
astounding miracles, even making fire flash down to earth from the sky
while everyone was watching.
14 And with all the miracles he was allowed to
perform on behalf of the first beast, he deceived all the people who belong
to this world. He ordered the people to make a great statue of the first beast,
who was fatally wounded and then came back to life.
15 He was then permitted to give life to this statue so that it could speak. Then the statue of the
beast commanded that anyone refusing to worship it must die.
16 He required everyone—small and great, rich and poor, free and slave—
to be given a mark on the right hand or on the forehead.
17 And no one could
buy or sell anything without that mark, which was either the name of the
beast or the number representing his name.
18 Wisdom is needed here. Let
the one with understanding solve the meaning of the number of the beast,
for it is the number of a man.* His number is 666.*

The Lamb and the 144,000

14 Then I saw the Lamb standing on Mount Zion, and with him were
144,000 who had his name and his Father's name written on their
foreheads.
2 And I heard a sound from heaven like the roar of mighty ocean
waves or the rolling of loud thunder. It was like the sound of many harpists
playing together.
3 This great choir sang a wonderful new song in front of the throne of
God and before the four living beings and the twenty-four elders. No one
could learn this song except the 144,000 who had been redeemed from the
earth.
4 They have kept themselves as pure as virgins,* following the Lamb
wherever he goes. They have been purchased from among the people on the
earth as a special offering* to God and to the Lamb.
5 They have told no lies;
they are without blame.

13:8 Or *not written in the Book of Life before the world was made—the Book that belongs to the Lamb who was slaughtered.* **13:18a** Or *of humanity.* **13:18b** Some manuscripts read 616. **14:4a** Greek *They are virgins who have not defiled themselves with women.* **14:4b** Greek *as firstfruits.*

The Three Angels
6 And I saw another angel flying through the sky, carrying the eternal Good
News to proclaim to the people who belong to this world—to every nation,
tribe, language, and people. 7 "Fear God," he shouted. "Give glory to him.
For the time has come when he will sit as judge. Worship him who made the
heavens, the earth, the sea, and all the springs of water."
8 Then another angel followed him through the sky, shouting, "Babylon
is fallen—that great city is fallen—because she made all the nations of the
world drink the wine of her passionate immorality."
9 Then a third angel followed them, shouting, "Anyone who worships
the beast and his statue or who accepts his mark on the forehead or on the
hand 10 must drink the wine of God's anger. It has been poured full strength
into God's cup of wrath. And they will be tormented with fire and burn-
ing sulfur in the presence of the holy angels and the Lamb. 11 The smoke of
their torment will rise forever and ever, and they will have no relief day or
night, for they have worshiped the beast and his statue and have accepted
the mark of his name."
12 This means that God's holy people must endure persecution patiently,
obeying his commands and maintaining their faith in Jesus.
13 And I heard a voice from heaven saying, "Write this down: Blessed are
those who die in the Lord from now on. Yes, says the Spirit, they are blessed
indeed, for they will rest from their hard work; for their good deeds follow
them!"

The Harvest of the Earth
14 Then I saw a white cloud, and seated on the cloud was someone like the
Son of Man.* He had a gold crown on his head and a sharp sickle in his hand.
15 Then another angel came from the Temple and shouted to the one sit-
ting on the cloud, "Swing the sickle, for the time of harvest has come; the
crop on earth is ripe." 16 So the one sitting on the cloud swung his sickle over
the earth, and the whole earth was harvested.
17 After that, another angel came from the Temple in heaven, and he also
had a sharp sickle. 18 Then another angel, who had power to destroy with
fire, came from the altar. He shouted to the angel with the sharp sickle,
"Swing your sickle now to gather the clusters of grapes from the vines of the
earth, for they are ripe for judgment." 19 So the angel swung his sickle over
the earth and loaded the grapes into the great winepress of God's wrath.
20 The grapes were trampled in the winepress outside the city, and blood
flowed from the winepress in a stream about 180 miles* long and as high
as a horse's bridle.

The Song of Moses and of the Lamb
15 Then I saw in heaven another marvelous event of great significance.
Seven angels were holding the seven last plagues, which would bring
God's wrath to completion. 2 I saw before me what seemed to be a glass sea
mixed with fire. And on it stood all the people who had been victorious over
the beast and his statue and the number representing his name. They were
all holding harps that God had given them. 3 And they were singing the song
of Moses, the servant of God, and the song of the Lamb:

14:14 Or *like a son of man.* See Dan 7:13. "Son of Man" is a title Jesus used for himself.
14:20 Greek *1,600 stadia* [300 kilometers].

Prayer **15:3–4**

Great and marvelous are your works, O Lord God, the Almighty. Amen.

Question 16:5

How does reading these expressions of God's justice inspire you to pray for the world?

"Great and marvelous are your works,
O Lord God, the Almighty.
Just and true are your ways,
O King of the nations.*
4 Who will not fear you, Lord,
and glorify your name?
For you alone are holy.
All nations will come and worship before you,
for your righteous deeds have been revealed."

The Seven Bowls of the Seven Plagues

5 Then I looked and saw that the Temple in heaven, God's Tabernacle, was
thrown wide open. 6 The seven angels who were holding the seven plagues
came out of the Temple. They were clothed in spotless white linen* with
gold sashes across their chests. 7 Then one of the four living beings handed
each of the seven angels a gold bowl filled with the wrath of God, who lives
forever and ever. 8 The Temple was filled with smoke from God's glory and
power. No one could enter the Temple until the seven angels had completed
pouring out the seven plagues.

16 Then I heard a mighty voice from the Temple say to the seven angels,
"Go your ways and pour out on the earth the seven bowls containing
God's wrath."

2 So the first angel left the Temple and poured out his bowl on the earth,
and horrible, malignant sores broke out on everyone who had the mark of
the beast and who worshiped his statue.

3 Then the second angel poured out his bowl on the sea, and it became like
the blood of a corpse. And everything in the sea died.

4 Then the third angel poured out his bowl on the rivers and springs, and
they became blood. 5 And I heard the angel who had authority over all water
saying,

"You are just, O Holy One, who is and who always was,
because you have sent these judgments.
6 Since they shed the blood
of your holy people and your prophets,
you have given them blood to drink.
It is their just reward."

7 And I heard a voice from the altar,* saying,

"Yes, O Lord God, the Almighty,
your judgments are true and just."

8 Then the fourth angel poured out his bowl on the sun, causing it to
scorch everyone with its fire. 9 Everyone was burned by this blast of heat,
and they cursed the name of God, who had control over all these plagues.
They did not repent of their sins and turn to God and give him glory.

10 Then the fifth angel poured out his bowl on the throne of the beast, and

15:3 Some manuscripts read *King of the ages.* 15:6 Other manuscripts read *white stone;* still others read *white [garments] made of linen.* 16:7 Greek *I heard the altar.*

his kingdom was plunged into darkness. His subjects ground their teeth* in
anguish, 11 and they cursed the God of heaven for their pains and sores. But
they did not repent of their evil deeds and turn to God.
12 Then the sixth angel poured out his bowl on the great Euphrates River,
and it dried up so that the kings from the east could march their armies
toward the west without hindrance. 13 And I saw three evil* spirits that
looked like frogs leap from the mouths of the dragon, the beast, and the
false prophet. 14 They are demonic spirits who work miracles and go out to
all the rulers of the world to gather them for battle against the Lord on that
great judgment day of God the Almighty.

15 "Look, I will come as unexpectedly as a thief! Blessed are all who are
watching for me, who keep their clothing ready so they will not have
to walk around naked and ashamed."

16 And the demonic spirits gathered all the rulers and their armies to a
place with the Hebrew name *Armageddon*.*
17 Then the seventh angel poured out his bowl into the air. And a mighty
shout came from the throne in the Temple, saying, "It is finished!" 18 Then
the thunder crashed and rolled, and lightning flashed. And a great earth-
quake struck—the worst since people were placed on the earth. 19 The great
city of Babylon split into three sections, and the cities of many nations fell
into heaps of rubble. So God remembered all of Babylon's sins, and he made
her drink the cup that was filled with the wine of his fierce wrath. 20 And
every island disappeared, and all the mountains were leveled. 21 There was a
terrible hailstorm, and hailstones weighing as much as seventy-five pounds*
fell from the sky onto the people below. They cursed God because of the ter-
rible plague of the hailstorm.

The Great Prostitute

17 One of the seven angels who had poured out the seven bowls came
over and spoke to me. "Come with me," he said, "and I will show
you the judgment that is going to come on the great prostitute, who rules
over many waters. 2 The kings of the world have committed adultery with
her, and the people who belong to this world have been made drunk by the
wine of her immorality."
3 So the angel took me in the Spirit* into the wilderness. There I saw a
woman sitting on a scarlet beast that had seven heads and ten horns, and
blasphemies against God were written all over it. 4 The woman wore purple
and scarlet clothing and beautiful jewelry made of gold and precious gems
and pearls. In her hand she held a gold goblet full of obscenities and the
impurities of her immorality. 5 A mysterious name was written on her fore-
head: "Babylon the Great, Mother of All Prostitutes and Obscenities in the
World." 6 I could see that she was drunk—drunk with the blood of God's holy
people who were witnesses for Jesus. I stared at her in complete amazement.
7 "Why are you so amazed?" the angel asked. "I will tell you the mystery
of this woman and of the beast with seven heads and ten horns on which
she sits. 8 The beast you saw was once alive but isn't now. And yet he will
soon come up out of the bottomless pit* and go to eternal destruction. And

16:10 Greek *gnawed their tongues.* **16:13** Greek *unclean.* **16:16** Or *Harmagedon.* **16:21** Greek *1 talent* [34 kilograms]. **17:3** Or *in spirit.* **17:8** Or *the abyss,* or *the underworld.*

Make a Difference 17:1

Do Justice

God is about to do something about the injustice in this world. He is coming to make right everything that has gone wrong. Is that something you look forward to? The hard truth is that we want justice, but we really want justice according to what we perceive is right. After all, we have justice movements and a system of justice in most governments, but usually, these are only moderately restorative. God's justice, however, is complete. It fully restores his people, his kingdom, and his intended order, and as a result, there will one day be complete justice for all people.

Difference Maker

Discover what justice ministries exist in your area or through a local church that align closely with God's heart. Find out if there is a way that you can get involved and help people experience a small part of the justice Jesus wants to bring to the world.

the people who belong to this world, whose names were not written in the
Book of Life before the world was made, will be amazed at the reappearance
of this beast who had died.
9 "This calls for a mind with understanding: The seven heads of the beast
represent the seven hills where the woman rules. They also represent seven
kings. 10 Five kings have already fallen, the sixth now reigns, and the seventh
is yet to come, but his reign will be brief.
11 "The scarlet beast that was, but is no longer, is the eighth king. He is like
the other seven, and he, too, is headed for destruction. 12 The ten horns of the
beast are ten kings who have not yet risen to power. They will be appointed
to their kingdoms for one brief moment to reign with the beast. 13 They will
all agree to give him their power and authority. 14 Together they will go to
war against the Lamb, but the Lamb will defeat them because he is Lord of
all lords and King of all kings. And his called and chosen and faithful ones
will be with him."
15 Then the angel said to me, "The waters where the prostitute is ruling
represent masses of people of every nation and language. 16 The scarlet beast
and his ten horns all hate the prostitute. They will strip her naked, eat her
flesh, and burn her remains with fire. 17 For God has put a plan into their
minds, a plan that will carry out his purposes. They will agree to give their
authority to the scarlet beast, and so the words of God will be fulfilled. 18 And
this woman you saw in your vision represents the great city that rules over
the kings of the world."

The Fall of Babylon

18 After all this I saw another angel come down from heaven with great
authority, and the earth grew bright with his splendor. 2 He gave a
mighty shout:

"Babylon is fallen—that great city is fallen!
  She has become a home for demons.
She is a hideout for every foul* spirit,
  a hideout for every foul vulture
  and every foul and dreadful animal.*
3 For all the nations have fallen*
  because of the wine of her passionate immorality.
The kings of the world
  have committed adultery with her.
Because of her desires for extravagant luxury,
  the merchants of the world have grown rich."

4 Then I heard another voice calling from heaven,

"Come away from her, my people.
  Do not take part in her sins,
  or you will be punished with her.
5 For her sins are piled as high as heaven,
  and God remembers her evil deeds.

18:2a Greek *unclean;* also in each of the two following phrases. **18:2b** Some manuscripts condense the last two lines to read *a hideout for every foul [unclean] and dreadful vulture.* **18:3** Some manuscripts read *have drunk.*

6 Do to her as she has done to others.
Double her penalty* for all her evil deeds.
She brewed a cup of terror for others,
so brew twice as much* for her.
7 She glorified herself and lived in luxury,
so match it now with torment and sorrow.
She boasted in her heart,
'I am queen on my throne.
I am no helpless widow,
and I have no reason to mourn.'
8 Therefore, these plagues will overtake her in
a single day—
death and mourning and famine.
She will be completely consumed by fire,
for the Lord God who judges her is mighty."

9 And the kings of the world who committed adultery with her and en-
joyed her great luxury will mourn for her as they see the smoke rising from
her charred remains. 10 They will stand at a distance, terrified by her great
torment. They will cry out,

"How terrible, how terrible for you,
O Babylon, you great city!
In a single moment
God's judgment came on you."

11 The merchants of the world will weep and mourn for her, for there is
no one left to buy their goods. 12 She bought great quantities of gold, silver,
jewels, and pearls; fine linen, purple, silk, and scarlet cloth; things made of
fragrant thyine wood, ivory goods, and objects made of expensive wood;
and bronze, iron, and marble. 13 She also bought cinnamon, spice, incense,
myrrh, frankincense, wine, olive oil, fine flour, wheat, cattle, sheep, horses,
wagons, and bodies—that is, human slaves.

14 "The fancy things you loved so much
are gone," they cry.
"All your luxuries and splendor
are gone forever,
never to be yours again."

15 The merchants who became wealthy by selling her these things will
stand at a distance, terrified by her great torment. They will weep and cry
out,

16 "How terrible, how terrible for that great city!
She was clothed in finest purple and scarlet linens,
decked out with gold and precious stones and pearls!
17 In a single moment
all the wealth of the city is gone!"

18:6a Or *Give her an equal penalty.* **18:6b** Or *brew just as much.*

Your thoughts can go here

Question 19:1

Which song do you identify with most: the one in Revelation 18 or this one in chapter 19? Is it appropriate to feel loss and joy at the same time?

And all the captains of the merchant ships and their passengers and sail-
ors and crews will stand at a distance. 18 They will cry out as they watch the
smoke ascend, and they will say, "Where is there another city as great as
this?" 19 And they will weep and throw dust on their heads to show their
grief. And they will cry out,

"How terrible, how terrible for that great city!
The shipowners became wealthy
by transporting her great wealth on the seas.
In a single moment it is all gone."

20 Rejoice over her fate, O heaven
and people of God and apostles and prophets!
For at last God has judged her
for your sakes.

21 Then a mighty angel picked up a boulder the size of a huge millstone.
He threw it into the ocean and shouted,

"Just like this, the great city Babylon
will be thrown down with violence
and will never be found again.
22 The sound of harps, singers, flutes, and trumpets
will never be heard in you again.
No craftsmen and no trades
will ever be found in you again.
The sound of the mill
will never be heard in you again.
23 The light of a lamp
will never shine in you again.
The happy voices of brides and grooms
will never be heard in you again.
For your merchants were the greatest in the world,
and you deceived the nations with your sorceries.
24 In your* streets flowed the blood of the prophets and
of God's holy people
and the blood of people slaughtered all over
the world."

Songs of Victory in Heaven

19 After this, I heard what sounded like a vast crowd in heaven shout-
ing,

"Praise the LORD!*
Salvation and glory and power belong to our God.
2 His judgments are true and just.
He has punished the great prostitute
who corrupted the earth with her immorality.
He has avenged the murder of his servants."

18:24 Greek *her.* 19:1 Greek *Hallelujah;* also in 19:3, 4, 6. *Hallelujah* is the transliteration of a Hebrew term that means "Praise the LORD."

[3]And again their voices rang out:

"Praise the LORD!
The smoke from that city ascends forever and ever!"

[4]Then the twenty-four elders and the four living beings fell down and
worshiped God, who was sitting on the throne. They cried out, "Amen! Praise
the LORD!"
[5]And from the throne came a voice that said,

"Praise our God,
all his servants,
all who fear him,
from the least to the greatest."

[6]Then I heard again what sounded like the shout of a vast crowd or the
roar of mighty ocean waves or the crash of loud thunder:

"Praise the LORD!
For the Lord our God,* the Almighty, reigns.
[7] Let us be glad and rejoice,
and let us give honor to him.
For the time has come for the wedding feast of the Lamb,
and his bride has prepared herself.
[8] She has been given the finest of pure white linen to wear."
For the fine linen represents the good deeds of God's holy people.

[9]And the angel said to me, "Write this: Blessed are those who are invited
to the wedding feast of the Lamb." And he added, "These are true words
that come from God."
[10]Then I fell down at his feet to worship him, but he said, "No, don't wor-
ship me. I am a servant of God, just like you and your brothers and sisters*
who testify about their faith in Jesus. Worship only God. For the essence of
prophecy is to give a clear witness for Jesus.*"

The Rider on the White Horse

[11]Then I saw heaven opened, and a white horse was standing there. Its rider
was named Faithful and True, for he judges fairly and wages a righteous
war. [12]His eyes were like flames of fire, and on his head were many crowns.
A name was written on him that no one understood except himself. [13]He
wore a robe dipped in blood, and his title was the Word of God. [14]The armies
of heaven, dressed in the finest of pure white linen, followed him on white
horses. [15]From his mouth came a sharp sword to strike down the nations.
He will rule them with an iron rod. He will release the fierce wrath of God,
the Almighty, like juice flowing from a winepress. [16]On his robe at his thigh*
was written this title: King of all kings and Lord of all lords.
[17]Then I saw an angel standing in the sun, shouting to the vultures fly-
ing high in the sky: "Come! Gather together for the great banquet God has
prepared. [18]Come and eat the flesh of kings, generals, and strong warriors;

19:6 Some manuscripts read *the Lord God.* 19:10a Greek *brothers.* 19:10b Or *is the message confirmed by Jesus.* 19:16 Or *On his robe and thigh.*

Question **19:9**

"Blessed are those who are invited to the wedding feast of the Lamb." Threaded throughout Scripture, the image of a wedding and the visual of the lamb both point people to God's plan of salvation. Can you go through the whole Bible and tell God's story using these two illustrations?

Story Arc **19:13**

The Word, the King, Jesus

In John 1, we read that Jesus is "the Word" who spoke the world into being and then became human and made his dwelling among us. Here in Revelation 19, we see Jesus coming again to reign permanently as the King of his creation. This is the real return of the King!

Rev 20:6 ►

of horses and their riders; and of all humanity, both free and slave, small
and great."

19 Then I saw the beast and the kings of the world and their armies gathered
together to fight against the one sitting on the horse and his army. 20 And the
beast was captured, and with him the false prophet who did mighty miracles
on behalf of the beast—miracles that deceived all who had accepted the mark
of the beast and who worshiped his statue. Both the beast and his false prophet
were thrown alive into the fiery lake of burning sulfur. 21 Their entire army
was killed by the sharp sword that came from the mouth of the one riding
the white horse. And the vultures all gorged themselves on the dead bodies.

The Thousand Years

20 Then I saw an angel coming down from heaven with the key to
the bottomless pit* and a heavy chain in his hand. 2 He seized the
dragon—that old serpent, who is the devil, Satan—and bound him in chains
for a thousand years. 3 The angel threw him into the bottomless pit, which
he then shut and locked so Satan could not deceive the nations anymore
until the thousand years were finished. Afterward he must be released for
a little while.

4 Then I saw thrones, and the people sitting on them had been given the
authority to judge. And I saw the souls of those who had been beheaded
for their testimony about Jesus and for proclaiming the word of God. They
had not worshiped the beast or his statue, nor accepted his mark on their
foreheads or their hands. They all came to life again, and they reigned with
Christ for a thousand years.

5 This is the first resurrection. (The rest of the dead did not come back to
life until the thousand years had ended.) 6 Blessed and holy are those who
share in the first resurrection. For them the second death holds no power,
but they will be priests of God and of Christ and will reign with him a thou-
sand years.

The Defeat of Satan

7 When the thousand years come to an end, Satan will be let out of his prison.
8 He will go out to deceive the nations—called Gog and Magog—in every
corner of the earth. He will gather them together for battle—a mighty army,
as numberless as sand along the seashore. 9 And I saw them as they went
up on the broad plain of the earth and surrounded God's people and the
beloved city. But fire from heaven came down on the attacking armies and
consumed them.

10 Then the devil, who had deceived them, was thrown into the fiery lake
of burning sulfur, joining the beast and the false prophet. There they will
be tormented day and night forever and ever.

The Final Judgment

11 And I saw a great white throne and the one sitting on it. The earth and sky
fled from his presence, but they found no place to hide. 12 I saw the dead, both
great and small, standing before God's throne. And the books were opened,
including the Book of Life. And the dead were judged according to what they
had done, as recorded in the books. 13 The sea gave up its dead, and death and

Story Arc 20:6

● Jesus, the Promised King

Jesus is going to be the King forever; this is just his first thousand years. This will be a season of joy, peace, and restoration for all humankind. It's part of God's direct promise to David (1 Chronicles 28:4-7) that one of his descendants would be the king who sits on the throne forever.

20:1 Or *the abyss,* or *the underworld;* also in 20:3.

the grave* gave up their dead. And all were judged according to their deeds.
14Then death and the grave were thrown into the lake of fire. This lake of
fire is the second death. 15And anyone whose name was not found recorded
in the Book of Life was thrown into the lake of fire.

The New Jerusalem

21 Then I saw a new heaven and a new earth, for the old heaven and the
old earth had disappeared. And the sea was also gone. 2And I saw the
holy city, the new Jerusalem, coming down from God out of heaven like a
bride beautifully dressed for her husband.
3I heard a loud shout from the throne, saying, "Look, God's home is now
among his people! He will live with them, and they will be his people. God him-
self will be with them.* 4He will wipe every tear from their eyes, and there will
be no more death or sorrow or crying or pain. All these things are gone forever."
5And the one sitting on the throne said, "Look, I am making everything
new!" And then he said to me, "Write this down, for what I tell you is trust-
worthy and true." 6And he also said, "It is finished! I am the Alpha and the
Omega—the Beginning and the End. To all who are thirsty I will give freely
from the springs of the water of life. 7All who are victorious will inherit all
these blessings, and I will be their God, and they will be my children.
8"But cowards, unbelievers, the corrupt, murderers, the immoral, those
who practice witchcraft, idol worshipers, and all liars—their fate is in the
fiery lake of burning sulfur. This is the second death."
9Then one of the seven angels who held the seven bowls containing the
seven last plagues came and said to me, "Come with me! I will show you the
bride, the wife of the Lamb."
10So he took me in the Spirit* to a great, high mountain, and he showed
me the holy city, Jerusalem, descending out of heaven from God. 11It shone
with the glory of God and sparkled like a precious stone—like jasper as clear
as crystal. 12The city wall was broad and high, with twelve gates guarded by
twelve angels. And the names of the twelve tribes of Israel were written on
the gates. 13There were three gates on each side—east, north, south, and
west. 14The wall of the city had twelve foundation stones, and on them were
written the names of the twelve apostles of the Lamb.
15The angel who talked to me held in his hand a gold measuring stick to
measure the city, its gates, and its wall. 16When he measured it, he found it
was a square, as wide as it was long. In fact, its length and width and height
were each 1,400 miles.* 17Then he measured the walls and found them to be
216 feet thick* (according to the human standard used by the angel).
18The wall was made of jasper, and the city was pure gold, as clear as glass.
19The wall of the city was built on foundation stones inlaid with twelve pre-
cious stones:* the first was jasper, the second sapphire, the third agate, the
fourth emerald, 20the fifth onyx, the sixth carnelian, the seventh chrysolite,
the eighth beryl, the ninth topaz, the tenth chrysoprase, the eleventh jacinth,
the twelfth amethyst.
21The twelve gates were made of pearls—each gate from a single pearl!
And the main street was pure gold, as clear as glass.
22I saw no temple in the city, for the Lord God Almighty and the Lamb are its

20:13 Greek *and Hades;* also in 20:14. 21:3 Some manuscripts read *God himself will be with them, their God.* 21:10 Or *in spirit.* 21:16 Greek *12,000 stadia* [2,220 kilometers]. 21:17 Greek *144 cubits* [65 meters]. 21:19 The identification of some of these gemstones is uncertain.

Make a Difference

21:3-7

Return to Normal

Broken bones, sickness, hunger, poverty, disease, heartache, loss, loneliness, and death were never a part of God's original creation. Your day-to-day life is one characterized by the strange and hurtful effects of sin. It's weird that we have to live in this mess, but we have become so used to it that it's hard to imagine anything different. Jesus affirmed that his kingdom will be a return to normal, a place where there are no tears and no suffering. It's so awesomely normal that it sounds unbelievable, but without a doubt, it's the normal we long for.

Difference Maker

Comfort a hurting friend. Take them a small gift or call them and pray for them. Participate with Jesus in returning things to normal now so people can have a small taste of what the kingdom will look like when the King makes all things new and normal again.

Question 22:3-5

Check out Numbers 6:24-26. It's a blessing for all God's people. What do you think your first reaction will be when you look upon the face of Jesus and experience the fulfillment of this blessing for the first time?

Make a Difference

22:20

Lasting Prayer

The first book of the Bible, Genesis, launches our understanding of God's purpose in creating the world. The last book of the Bible, Revelation, has us calling for God to come back and re-create. We long to be fully restored to the relationship that God intended us to have in the world that God intended for us to live in.

John, the writer of Revelation, could hardly wait for God's promised restoration. As he wrote what would become the very last words of the Bible, he was filled with awe and anticipation. He chose to respond to Jesus with a few wonderful words that captured his heart: "Come, Lord Jesus!" John knew of no better way to conclude than this thought for his readers. The greatest blessing he could give to the world would be a prayer for Jesus to come back once again.

Difference Maker

Gather some good friends or family and celebrate your experiences together and look ahead to the experiences you are yet to have. Then add a twist. Stop to pray for Jesus' return so that the world will be remade as it was intended to be.

temple. 23 And the city has no need of sun or moon, for the glory of God illumi-
nates the city, and the Lamb is its light. 24 The nations will walk in its light, and
the kings of the world will enter the city in all their glory. 25 Its gates will never
be closed at the end of day because there is no night there. 26 And all the nations
will bring their glory and honor into the city. 27 Nothing evil* will be allowed to
enter, nor anyone who practices shameful idolatry and dishonesty—but only
those whose names are written in the Lamb's Book of Life.

22 Then the angel showed me a river with the water of life, clear as
crystal, flowing from the throne of God and of the Lamb. 2 It flowed
down the center of the main street. On each side of the river grew a tree of
life, bearing twelve crops of fruit,* with a fresh crop each month. The leaves
were used for medicine to heal the nations.

3 No longer will there be a curse upon anything. For the throne of God and
of the Lamb will be there, and his servants will worship him. 4 And they will
see his face, and his name will be written on their foreheads. 5 And there will
be no night there—no need for lamps or sun—for the Lord God will shine
on them. And they will reign forever and ever.

6 Then the angel said to me, "Everything you have heard and seen is trust-
worthy and true. The Lord God, who inspires his prophets,* has sent his
angel to tell his servants what will happen soon.*"

Jesus Is Coming

7 "Look, I am coming soon! Blessed are those who obey the words
of prophecy written in this book.*"

8 I, John, am the one who heard and saw all these things. And when I heard
and saw them, I fell down to worship at the feet of the angel who showed
them to me. 9 But he said, "No, don't worship me. I am a servant of God,
just like you and your brothers the prophets, as well as all who obey what is
written in this book. Worship only God!"

10 Then he instructed me, "Do not seal up the prophetic words in this book,
for the time is near. 11 Let the one who is doing harm continue to do harm; let
the one who is vile continue to be vile; let the one who is righteous continue
to live righteously; let the one who is holy continue to be holy."

12 "Look, I am coming soon, bringing my reward with me to repay all
people according to their deeds. 13 I am the Alpha and the Omega, the
First and the Last, the Beginning and the End."

14 Blessed are those who wash their robes. They will be permitted to enter
through the gates of the city and eat the fruit from the tree of life. 15 Outside
the city are the dogs—the sorcerers, the sexually immoral, the murderers,
the idol worshipers, and all who love to live a lie.

16 "I, Jesus, have sent my angel to give you this message for the churches.
I am both the source of David and the heir to his throne.* I am the
bright morning star."

21:27 Or *ceremonially unclean.* 22:2 Or *twelve kinds of fruit.* 22:6a Or *The Lord, the God of the spirits of the prophets.* 22:6b Or *suddenly,* or *quickly;* also in 22:7, 12, 20. 22:7 Or *scroll;* also in 22:9, 10, 18, 19. 22:16 Greek *I am the root and offspring of David.*

17 The Spirit and the bride say, "Come." Let anyone who hears this say,
"Come." Let anyone who is thirsty come. Let anyone who desires drink freely
from the water of life. 18 And I solemnly declare to everyone who hears the
words of prophecy written in this book: If anyone adds anything to what is
written here, God will add to that person the plagues described in this book.
19 And if anyone removes any of the words from this book of prophecy, God
will remove that person's share in the tree of life and in the holy city that
are described in this book.

20 He who is the faithful witness to all these things says, "Yes, I am coming soon!"

Amen! Come, Lord Jesus!

21 May the grace of the Lord Jesus be with God's holy people.*

22:21 Other manuscripts read *be with all;* still others read *be with all of God's holy people.* Some manuscripts add *Amen.*

Make a Difference

22:21

Invite Jesus into Your Life

There is no better way to know the grace of the Lord Jesus than to invite him into your life.

Difference Maker

If you have never done so, turn to the back of this Bible and pray through the section on "How to Accept Jesus as Your Lord and Savior."

APPENDIXES

How to Accept Jesus as Your Lord and Savior

Throughout the entire Bible, we see God's heart in relationship with people. This has been his intention from the beginning. One of the most helpful ways of outlining this is by using the acrostic "GOSPEL" (Gospel means "good news"):

God created us to be with him.

- "Acknowledge that the LORD is God! He made us, and we are his" (Psalm 100:3).
- *You were made with a purpose: to know God.*

Our sins separate us from God.

- "Everyone has sinned; we all fall short of God's glorious standard" (Romans 3:23).
- *Only God is perfect. We all have a sinful nature. Even one disobedient step leads to imperfection and disruption of our relationship with God.*

Sins cannot be removed by good deeds.

- "When we display our righteous deeds, they are nothing but filthy rags" (Isaiah 64:6).
- *No amount of doing good can cover up the wrong we have done. We cannot get back to our purpose of a relationship with God by our own strength.*

Paying the price for sin, Jesus died and rose again.

- "God showed his great love for us by sending Christ to die for us while we were still sinners" (Romans 5:8).
- *Jesus took what we deserved. Like being sentenced in a court of law, we have been found guilty, and as a result, we deserve the punishment of death. Even though Jesus was sinless and not guilty, he took the penalty for our sin upon himself on the cross, and he died in our place.*
- *Then he rose from the grave, coming back to life, conquering sin, Satan, and death.*

Everyone who trusts in him alone has eternal life.

- "This is how God loved the world: He gave his one and only Son, so that everyone who believes in him will not perish but have eternal life" (John 3:16).
- *The focus is not on you trying to please God. It's on you trusting in what Jesus did on the cross. When we trust in Jesus, we are welcomed into the family of God, and we are given a new identity as sons and daughters of the King of kings.*

Life with Jesus starts now and lasts forever.

- "This is the way to have eternal life—to know you, the only true God, and Jesus Christ, the one you sent to earth" (John 17:3).
- *True life can only be found in Jesus, and you don't have to wait until the end of your life to experience it. Fullness of life can start now.*

START TODAY

In the same way you sit on a chair and trust that it will hold you up, you can trust in Jesus Christ, in him alone, and you can experience the fullness of life. It would be ridiculous to believe a chair will hold you up but never put your trust in the chair by actually sitting on it. In the same way, Jesus invites you to put your trust in him to save you from your sin and give you life:

- **Past:** save you from the penalty of sin
- **Present:** save you from the power of sin
- **Future:** one day he will save you fully from the presence of sin

You are invited to place your faith and trust in Jesus. If you do that, you can express your trust in Jesus by saying a prayer. Right now, you can pray:

God, I thank you for sending your one and only Son to live a perfect life, the life that I could never live. God, I thank you for sending your Son to die on the cross, taking my place and dying as a payment for the penalty of my sin. Thank you, God, that you did not abandon Jesus to death but that you brought him back to life when you resurrected him from the dead. I confess that Jesus is God and that he is my only hope for forgiveness of sins, my only hope for freedom from the power of sin in life, and my only hope for future victory over death itself when I will be united with you, God, one day. I receive the gift of life you have given through Jesus. Please come into my life by your Holy Spirit. In Jesus' name, amen.

ACTION

You are saved not by a prayer but by trusting in Jesus Christ. If this is true, then you have just been given new life! This new life is called the Christian life, the greatest adventure in all of life. This is an adventure in growing daily to be more like Jesus as you get to know him through prayer, his Word (the Bible), his church, and his mission as you share your new relationship with Jesus with others. In fact, it would be good to tell at least one person right now. Call or text a friend, talk to the person who gave you this Bible, or tell someone else about the decision you just made to trust Jesus. Let the adventure begin!

dare 2 share

Why Jesus Makes All the Difference

Around two thousand years ago God deliberately entered his creation, and nothing has ever been the same since. After all, Jesus did not come just to tweak things or shift ideas. He came to change this world at its core.

First, Jesus showed up and lived a perfect life. His life was completely without sin and wrongdoing (Hebrews 4:15). In that way, Jesus shows you that living well is possible—because he was a human in the same way you are. By following his life, your daily life is changed forever.

Second, Jesus went to the cross to die for people's sin. In doing so, he paid the debt all people owed (2 Corinthians 5:21). Now, without that debt of sin hanging over you, you are free to explore the type of life God designed and desires for you to live. By knowing Jesus, your whole life is changed forever.

Third, Jesus rose from the grave. His resurrection proves that Jesus truly is the One with power over death (1 Corinthians 15:55–57). This means that when he promises that you'll be with him in heaven, he actually has the ability and authority to make it happen. By trusting Jesus, your eternal life is changed forever!

In these actions, the reason Jesus makes all the difference in your life becomes clear: he is your example of perfect living, he frees you to live a life like his, and he has the power to bring you to glory with him in heaven.

Still, there is more. Don't ever forget that he does all this by loving you more than anyone else ever could (1 John 4:9–10).

Love Your Neighbor

To know how to love your neighbor, there are three questions you need to answer: Who? What? How?

Who: To know how to love your neighbor, you must first know who your neighbor is. When the Bible talks about your neighbor, it's talking about anyone you may interact with during the day (Luke 10:25–37). You interact with people every day, and you have the choice to treat them with respect or not.

What: When you think about what it looks like to love your neighbor, two words come to mind: *respect* and *kindness*. When you love your neighbors, you treat them with respect and the way you would want to be treated (Mark 12:29–31). If you wouldn't want to be laughed at after dropping something in front of a crowd, you shouldn't laugh and make fun of others either. You can get caught up in the "it's all about me" attitude and forget that being kind to others is evidence of how Jesus has been kind to you.

How: The way that you love your neighbors can be a hard thing to figure out. This is when you put your faith into action. To love others well, you need to view them as being more important than yourself. Jesus set the example by coming to serve others not by being served by others (Matthew 20:28). You need to serve others as you encounter people throughout the day. You can do this in many ways, such as holding doors open for others, allowing others in line before you, doing your chores without complaining, or helping pick up what someone may have dropped. These are all ways you can love your neighbor. When you allow yourself to be inconvenienced for a second, you can change the lives of those around you. You can make a dramatic difference in this world by loving your neighbors, just as Jesus commanded.

Develop Difference-Making Habits

Here are some tips to help you develop some new difference-making habits in your life.

Plan: Your first step to developing a habit is to plan. Set the goal of what you want to accomplish. Do you want to read the Bible more? Pray more? Help others? Stop using bad language? Get a job? What is the goal of the habit you want to make? Write down your goal here:

Prepare: Preparation is usually the most-skipped step in developing a new habit, but a lack of thoughtfulness can easily lead to failure. For instance, if you want to read your Bible more, prepare by picking a time, finding a place, removing distractions, and setting a reminder. When you block out the time, you keep other things from getting in the way. When you find a place for your reading (like a special chair or corner where you can spend undisturbed time in God's Word), it will help you remove outside interruptions. Once you have your location, be sure to remove those things that can easily distract you. For instance, set your cell phone aside or turn off the notifications. This will help keep your mind focused. Finally, setting a reminder will help you stay on track and keep you accountable. Write down your preparations for your new difference-making habit:

Begin: Start working on your plan and your preparation. Count down the days of your targeted goal. Work toward that end. Also, be sure to allow yourself some grace. If you miss a day, get back to the plan the next. Don't get discouraged. Just keep working your plan. You've got this!

School Survival Skills

Survival is defined as "the act or fact of surviving, especially under adverse or unusual circumstances."[1] School can be an adverse or unusual circumstance to live through, right? What do you need to put in your backpack to survive during your school years?

Survival Item #1: Shoes

Survival tactic #1: Run from temptation.

Having a good pair of shoes helps you to be nimble and fast on your feet. If the zombies of this world try to get you, you'll need to make a quick getaway! The Bible teaches us that we should run to God and run from temptation. Compare this list:

RUN TO GOD	RUN FROM SIN
Hebrews 12:1-2	2 Timothy 2:22
Proverbs 18:10	1 Corinthians 6:18
2 Timothy 4:7	James 4:7 * (This verse has an interesting twist.)
Isaiah 40:31	Job 20:22
Psalm 143:9	1 Timothy 6:11
1 Corinthians 9:24-27	1 Corinthians 10:14

Even though there are common struggles all teenagers have, areas of temptation can vary from student to student. You need to identify your area of temptation and learn to avoid and run from that temptation. If you can take the time and honestly identify your areas of temptation and make a plan to run when that kind of temptation comes near, you will be so far beyond your peers in maturity!

Survival Item #2: Gloves

Survival tactic #2: Choose friends who are givers.

What do you think is the opposite of a "giver"? A "taker"! Some of us have way more takers in our lives than givers. It's no wonder we often feel like we're walking on eggshells—trying to keep our friends happy, listening to them, counseling them, sacrificing for them—yet it seems that some of them just keep taking and taking.

[1] *Dictionary.com*, s.v. "survival," accessed March 3, 2022, https://www.dictionary.com/browse/survival.

Friendship is supposed to be a two-way street. Friendship is supposed to be mutually beneficial. A friend is someone who gives and receives. First Thessalonians 5:11 says that we should "encourage each other and build each other up, just as you are already doing." A friend in Jesus is going to be someone who gives you encouragement, gives you their time, gives you their effort, gives you their kindness, and gives you their honest feedback.

If you want to survive through your school years, identify the givers and takers in your life. Be sure to nurture the relationships with the givers and caution yourself from most of the takers.

Survival Item #3: The Bible

Survival tactic #3: The Bible is my source for life.

Sometimes we need a kick to head in the best, healthiest direction in our lives. That kick comes from the Bible. Second Timothy 3:16 says, "All Scripture is inspired by God and is useful to teach us what is true and to make us realize what is wrong in our lives. It corrects us when we are wrong and teaches us to do what is right."

Sometimes life during your school years can feel dark. God's Word will shine light for you to see your way! Psalm 119:105 says, "Your word is a lamp to guide my feet and a light for my path."

Sometimes life during your school years can feel lonely. God's Word will remind you that God is near. Zephaniah 3:17 says, "The LORD your God is living among you. He is a mighty savior. He will take delight in you with gladness. With his love, he will calm all your fears. He will rejoice over you with joyful songs." Psalm 34:18 says, "The LORD is close to the brokenhearted; he rescues those whose spirits are crushed."

These three items in your backpack (shoes, gloves, and the Bible) will enable you to survive your school years. In fact, you might thrive as Jesus calls you to represent him and influence those around you. Go and make a difference today!

Bible Reading Plan

There are nearly 450 Difference Maker entries connected to verses in the *Make a Difference Youth Bible*. In the list below, 365 entries have been selected for a daily devotional reading plan. Over the course of a year, if you were to read one of these entries a day, you would develop a solid grasp of what it means to follow Jesus and make a difference in this world.

WEEK	DAY	DIFFERENCE MAKER
1	1.	Genesis 1:1-31
	2.	Genesis 1:26-28
	3.	Genesis 7:6-18
	4.	Genesis 9:1-7
	5.	Genesis 13:1-12
	6.	Genesis 15:9
	7.	Genesis 22:1-18
2	8.	Genesis 25:27-34
	9.	Genesis 35:19
	10.	Genesis 39:1-6
	11.	Genesis 40:23-41:57
	12.	Genesis 43:34
	13.	Genesis 47:9
	14.	Genesis 50:20
3	15.	Exodus 3:1-6
	16.	Exodus 4:1-17
	17.	Exodus 12:1-30
	18.	Exodus 20:1-21
	19.	Exodus 35:30-35
	20.	Leviticus 1:1-4
	21.	Leviticus 19:14
4	22.	Leviticus 19:32
	23.	Leviticus 27:30
	24.	Numbers 5:6-8
	25.	Numbers 6:22-27
	26.	Numbers 11:1-14
	27.	Numbers 12:3
	28.	Deuteronomy 4:1-2
5	29.	Deuteronomy 5:11
	30.	Deuteronomy 5:16
	31.	Deuteronomy 6:5-9
	32.	Deuteronomy 7:6
	33.	Deuteronomy 30:1-10
	34.	Joshua 4:1-8
	35.	Joshua 8:30-32

WEEK	DAY	DIFFERENCE MAKER
6	36.	Joshua 24:29-31
	37.	Judges 2:10
	38.	Judges 4:4
	39.	Judges 15:16
	40.	Judges 16:28
	41.	Judges 17:1-6
	42.	Ruth 1:16
7	43.	Ruth 4:11-22
	44.	1 Samuel 3:1-21
	45.	1 Samuel 7:12
	46.	1 Samuel 12:23
	47.	1 Samuel 16:1-13
	48.	1 Samuel 17:12-22
	49.	1 Samuel 23:15-18
8	50.	2 Samuel 6:16-22
	51.	2 Samuel 9:1-13
	52.	2 Samuel 19:31-40
	53.	2 Samuel 22:1-51
	54.	1 Kings 14:1-18
	55.	2 Kings 15:1-5
	56.	1 Chronicles 12:32
9	57.	1 Chronicles 16:7-36
	58.	1 Chronicles 16:34
	59.	1 Chronicles 28:7-10
	60.	2 Chronicles 7:11-22
	61.	2 Chronicles 10:16-19
	62.	2 Chronicles 17:3-6
	63.	Ezra 2:70
10	64.	Ezra 5:2
	65.	Ezra 10:1-17
	66.	Nehemiah 2:1-8
	67.	Nehemiah 4:1-5
	68.	Nehemiah 10:28-29
	69.	Esther 4:1-14
	70.	Esther 4:15-5:8

WEEK	DAY	DIFFERENCE MAKER
11	71.	Esther 7:1-8
	72.	Esther 9:20-32
	73.	Job 6:26
	74.	Job 32:1-5
	75.	Job 40:3
	76.	Psalm 1:3
	77.	Psalm 4:4
12	78.	Psalm 8:3-8
	79.	Psalm 9:1
	80.	Psalm 13:6
	81.	Psalm 19:1-6
	82.	Psalm 19:14
	83.	Psalm 23:1
	84.	Psalm 23:2
13	85.	Psalm 23:3
	86.	Psalm 23:4
	87.	Psalm 23:5
	88.	Psalm 23:6
	89.	Psalm 27:14
	90.	Psalm 33:6-9
	91.	Psalm 37:1-7
14	92.	Psalm 37:7
	93.	Psalm 46:3
	94.	Psalm 69:1-36
	95.	Psalm 78:4
	96.	Psalm 78:5-7
	97.	Psalm 88:1-18
	98.	Psalm 92:12-14
15	99.	Psalm 100:3
	100.	Psalm 100:4
	101.	Psalm 104:1-35
	102.	Psalm 107:1-43
	103.	Psalm 111:2
	104.	Psalm 113:9
	105.	Psalm 118:5

WEEK	DAY	DIFFERENCE MAKER
16	106.	Psalm 119:11
	107.	Psalm 119:37
	108.	Psalm 119:96
	109.	Psalm 133:1-3
	110.	Psalm 139:1
	111.	Psalm 139:3
	112.	Psalm 139:11
17	113.	Psalm 139:13
	114.	Psalm 139:15
	115.	Psalm 139:23
	116.	Psalm 145:8
	117.	Psalm 145:18
	118.	Proverbs 3:5-6
	119.	Proverbs 4:25
18	120.	Proverbs 10:17
	121.	Proverbs 11:17
	122.	Proverbs 11:25
	123.	Proverbs 11:30
	124.	Proverbs 12:1
	125.	Proverbs 14:29
	126.	Proverbs 16:3
19	127.	Proverbs 19:2
	128.	Proverbs 28:13
	129.	Proverbs 28:19
	130.	Proverbs 31:8
	131.	Ecclesiastes 1:1-11
	132.	Ecclesiastes 4:9-12
	133.	Ecclesiastes 5:18-20
20	134.	Ecclesiastes 11:4
	135.	Ecclesiastes 12:13
	136.	Song of Songs 8:6
	137.	Isaiah 1:17
	138.	Isaiah 6:1-8
	139.	Isaiah 7:14
	140.	Isaiah 9:6a
21	141.	Isaiah 9:6b
	142.	Isaiah 9:6c
	143.	Isaiah 9:6d
	144.	Isaiah 9:6e
	145.	Isaiah 9:6f
	146.	Isaiah 12:4
	147.	Isaiah 44:5
22	148.	Isaiah 52:7
	149.	Isaiah 53:3
22	150.	Isaiah 53:5
	151.	Isaiah 53:6
	152.	Isaiah 53:7
	153.	Isaiah 53:9
	154.	Isaiah 53:10
23	155.	Isaiah 58:3-7
	156.	Isaiah 58:10
	157.	Isaiah 58:13
	158.	Isaiah 61:3
	159.	Jeremiah 3:6
	160.	Jeremiah 10:23-24
	161.	Jeremiah 18:1-6
24	162.	Jeremiah 23:18
	163.	Jeremiah 29:7
	164.	Jeremiah 31:33-34
	165.	Lamentations 5:17
	166.	Ezekiel 3:1-10
	167.	Ezekiel 9:4
	168.	Ezekiel 28:25-26
25	169.	Ezekiel 36:9
	170.	Ezekiel 36:25-28
	171.	Ezekiel 37:1-14
	172.	Ezekiel 45:9
	173.	Daniel 1:8-20
	174.	Daniel 5:10-12
	175.	Daniel 6:10-13
26	176.	Daniel 9:2
	177.	Daniel 9:2-27
	178.	Hosea 6:6
	179.	Hosea 13:4
	180.	Joel 2:12-19
	181.	Joel 2:23
	182.	Amos 6:8-10
27	183.	Jonah 3:1
	184.	Jonah 3:10-4:4
	185.	Micah 1:2
	186.	Micah 2:6
	187.	Micah 4:5
	188.	Micah 6:8
	189.	Nahum 3:19
28	190.	Habakkuk 2:3
	191.	Zephaniah 2:3
	192.	Zephaniah 3:15-20
	193.	Haggai 2:4-5
28	194.	Zechariah 3:1-5
	195.	Zechariah 7:7-10
	196.	Malachi 1:6
29	197.	Matthew 2:1-12
	198.	Matthew 5:3
	199.	Matthew 5:4
	200.	Matthew 5:5
	201.	Matthew 5:6
	202.	Matthew 5:7
	203.	Matthew 5:8
30	204.	Matthew 5:9
	205.	Matthew 5:33-37
	206.	Matthew 6:1-4
	207.	Matthew 7:1-5
	208.	Matthew 7:24-29
	209.	Matthew 8:16-17
	210.	Matthew 11:28-30
31	211.	Matthew 16:13-19
	212.	Matthew 18:20
	213.	Matthew 19:16-24
	214.	Matthew 25:31-46
	215.	Matthew 25:41-46
	216.	Matthew 28:1-10
	217.	Matthew 28:18-20
32	218.	Mark 1:9
	219.	Mark 2:14
	220.	Mark 4:35-41
	221.	Mark 6:31
	222.	Mark 8:22-26
	223.	Mark 9:33-37
	224.	Mark 10:32-34
33	225.	Mark 14:66-72
	226.	Mark 15:37
	227.	Mark 16:20
	228.	Luke 1:28
	229.	Luke 1:32
	230.	Luke 2:6-7
	231.	Luke 2:51
34	232.	Luke 4:16-21
	233.	Luke 6:27-38
	234.	Luke 9:23-25
	235.	Luke 11:1-4
	236.	Luke 12:22-34

WEEK	DAY	DIFFERENCE MAKER
34	237.	Luke 16:10-13
	238.	Luke 22:25-28
35	239.	Luke 22:39-46
	240.	Luke 23:32-43
	241.	Luke 24:13-36
	242.	John 1:14
	243.	John 3:16
	244.	John 3:19-21
	245.	John 6:27
36	246.	John 6:29
	247.	John 6:66-69
	248.	John 8:12
	249.	John 10:1-16
	250.	John 10:27
	251.	John 11:35
	252.	John 13:1-5
37	253.	John 14:1
	254.	John 14:15-18
	255.	John 14:23
	256.	John 15:1-4
	257.	John 15:4-11
	258.	John 15:12-17
	259.	John 16:33
38	260.	John 17:20
	261.	John 20:30-31
	262.	John 21:25
	263.	Acts 1:8
	264.	Acts 2:1-12
	265.	Acts 2:42
	266.	Acts 2:44-47
39	267.	Acts 4:16-22
	268.	Acts 11:22-26
	269.	Acts 13:1-5
	270.	Acts 16:16-40
	271.	Acts 17:1-9
	272.	Acts 17:16-34
	273.	Acts 20:24
40	274.	Acts 20:35
	275.	Acts 25:10-11
	276.	Romans 1:16
	277.	Romans 3:23
	278.	Romans 5:6
	279.	Romans 6:23
	280.	Romans 7:14-25

WEEK	DAY	DIFFERENCE MAKER
41	281.	Romans 8:28
	282.	Romans 10:13
	283.	Romans 12:3-8
	284.	Romans 13:11-14
	285.	Romans 15:13
	286.	Romans 16:16
	287.	1 Corinthians 3:5-9
42	288.	1 Corinthians 10:12-13
	289.	1 Corinthians 12:12-31
	290.	1 Corinthians 15:3-4
	291.	1 Corinthians 15:54-59
	292.	1 Corinthians 16:8-9
	293.	2 Corinthians 3:17
	294.	2 Corinthians 4:7
43	295.	2 Corinthians 4:8
	296.	2 Corinthians 5:17
	297.	2 Corinthians 5:20
	298.	2 Corinthians 12:5-10
	299.	Galatians 2:20
	300.	Galatians 5:16-6:10
	301.	Galatians 5:22-25
44	302.	Ephesians 1:5
	303.	Ephesians 3:17
	304.	Ephesians 4:7
	305.	Ephesians 4:11-13
	306.	Ephesians 5:1-2
	307.	Philippians 1:3-5
	308.	Philippians 1:6
45	309.	Philippians 2:5-11
	310.	Philippians 3:7-8
	311.	Philippians 4:6-7
	312.	Philippians 4:8
	313.	Colossians 1:3-6
	314.	Colossians 2:7
	315.	Colossians 3:8-15
46	316.	Colossians 4:2-4
	317.	1 Thessalonians 1:8
	318.	1 Thessalonians 4:9-10
	319.	1 Thessalonians 5:16-18
	320.	2 Thessalonians 1:3-4
	321.	2 Thessalonians 3:1-2
	322.	1 Timothy 2:1-4
47	323.	1 Timothy 4:6-10
	324.	1 Timothy 4:12-15

WEEK	DAY	DIFFERENCE MAKER
47	325.	1 Timothy 6:11-12
	326.	2 Timothy 1:6-7
	327.	2 Timothy 2:3-4
	328.	2 Timothy 2:22
	329.	2 Timothy 3:16
48	330.	Titus 2:11
	331.	Titus 3:3-7
	332.	Titus 3:12-14
	333.	Hebrews 4:12
	334.	Hebrews 6:1-3
	335.	Hebrews 10:24
	336.	Hebrews 12:1
49	337.	James 1:27
	338.	James 2:1-13
	339.	James 2:26
	340.	James 3:1-12
	341.	James 4:7-10
	342.	James 5:16
	343.	James 5:19-20
50	344.	1 Peter 2:11-12
	345.	1 Peter 3:3-4
	346.	1 Peter 3:9
	347.	1 Peter 4:10-11
	348.	1 Peter 5:7
	349.	2 Peter 1:9-12
	350.	2 Peter 2:4-9
51	351.	1 John 2:1-2
	352.	1 John 2:20-27
	353.	1 John 5:1-5
	354.	2 John 1:10-11
	355.	3 John 1:13-14
	356.	Jude 1:1-2
	357.	Jude 1:24-25
52	358.	Revelation 3:20
	359.	Revelation 7:9-17
	360.	Revelation 10:9-10
	361.	Revelation 14:1-5
	362.	Revelation 17:1
	363.	Revelation 21:3-7
	364.	Revelation 22:20
	365.	Revelation 22:21

JESUS

Tyndale Verse Finder

APPEARANCE

ARGUMENTS

ASSURANCE

ATTITUDE

BELIEF

BIBLE

BIRTH

CARING

CHURCH

COMFORT

COMPLAIN

COMPROMISE

CONFESSION OF SIN

SEE ALSO REPENTANCE

CONSCIENCE

ROMANS 9:1 • pg 1578

Keep your conscience clear
1 TIMOTHY 1:18-19 • pg 1671

Church leaders must have clear consciences
1 TIMOTHY 3:9 • pg 1672

Consciences can be destroyed
1 TIMOTHY 4:2 • pg 1672

Jesus' forgiveness clears our conscience
HEBREWS 9:14 • pg 1700

A clear conscience helps us live a God-honoring life
1 PETER 3:16 • pg 1720

COURAGE

God gives us victory
PSALM 112:8 • pg 818

Jesus' strength gives us courage
JOHN 16:33 • pg 1513

Courage helps us boldly represent Christ
ACTS 4:31 • pg 1528

Christians should be courageous
1 CORINTHIANS 16:13 • pg 1611

Pray for courage
EPHESIANS 6:19-20 • pg 1643

Christians can pray to God with confidence
HEBREWS 4:16 • pg 1696

CREATION

God the Holy Spirit was involved in Creation
GENESIS 1:1-2 • pg 3

God created people
GENESIS 1:27 • pg 4

God created the world good
GENESIS 1:31 • pg 4

God the Father was involved in Creation
PSALM 33:6 • pg 736

God rules over his creation
PSALM 89:11 • pg 793

God created every angel
PSALM 148:2-5 • pg 850

God created everything
JEREMIAH 10:16 • pg 1064

Creation reveals God's greatness
AMOS 4:13 • pg 1273

Jesus was involved in Creation
COLOSSIANS 1:16 • pg 1652

God the Creator is worthy of worship
REVELATION 4:11 • pg 1748

God will make a new heaven and new earth
REVELATION 21:1-4 • pg 1765

CRITICISM

Take care of your own problems before criticizing others
MATTHEW 7:3-5 • pg 1362

Criticism should help people deepen their relationship with God
LUKE 17:3-5 • pg 1469

Criticism should be given with a loving attitude
1 CORINTHIANS 13:4-5 • pg 1606

Harsh criticism can destroy rather than help
GALATIANS 5:15 • pg 1633

DARKNESS, SPIRITUAL

God's Word enlightens us
PSALM 119:105 • pg 827

The way of wicked people is darkness
PROVERBS 4:19 • pg 858

Jesus brings light to darkened lives
JOHN 1:5 • pg 1486

Living without God is living in spiritual darkness
ACTS 26:17-18 • pg 1562

Christians do not live in spiritual darkness
EPHESIANS 5:8 • pg 1641

God rescued us from eternal darkness
COLOSSIANS 1:13 • pg 1652

There is no darkness in Jesus
1 JOHN 1:5 • pg 1729

Sinners' eternal punishment will be in darkness
JUDE 1:4-13 • pg 1740

DEATH

Death is a result of sin
GENESIS 3:17-19 • pg 6

Life is short
JOB 7:6-7 • pg 661

Every person will face death
PSALM 89:48 • pg 795

Death of Christians is precious
PSALM 116:15 • pg 820

Christians enter perfect peace at death
ISAIAH 57:1-2 • pg 1024

God has power over death
JOHN 14:19 • pg 1510

The death of Christians brings fellowship with Jesus
ACTS 7:59 • pg 1533

God provides eternal life
ROMANS 6:23 • pg 1575

Jesus will raise everyone who has died
1 CORINTHIANS 15:20-23 • pg 1609

Living in heaven is better than living on earth
2 CORINTHIANS 5:6-7 • pg 1617

Death is not the end of a person
1 THESSALONIANS 4:13-14 • pg 1662

Prepare your spiritual life for death
HEBREWS 9:27-28 • pg 1701

We don't know how long we'll live
JAMES 4:13-14 • pg 1713

God will destroy death
REVELATION 21:4 • pg 1765

DECISIONS

Pray before making decisions
NEHEMIAH 1:4 • pg 621

Decide to do things that honor God
JOB 1:8 • pg 654

God's Word helps us make decisions
PSALM 119:105 • pg 827

Get good advice before making decisions
PROVERBS 18:15 • pg 881

Ask God for wisdom before making decisions
JAMES 1:2-8 • pg 1710

DEPRESSION

Depression can follow exhausting times
JUDGES 15:18 • pg 333

God can encourage hurting people
2 SAMUEL 22:29-31 • pg 422

Depression can follow success
1 KINGS 19:3-4 • pg 461

God helps those who feel crushed

ENCOURAGEMENT

ETERNAL LIFE

EVIL

FAITH

FAMILY

FEAR

FOOLISHNESS

2 PETER 3:13 • pg 1726

God is the focus of attention in heaven
REVELATION 7:17 • pg 1751

There will not be any sadness in heaven
REVELATION 21:4 • pg 1765

People in heaven will walk with God
REVELATION 22:5 • pg 1766

HELL

God will deliver his children from hell
PSALM 86:13 • pg 791

Hell is a place of weeping
MATTHEW 8:12 • pg 1363

Hell was prepared for Satan and demons
MATTHEW 25:41 • pg 1394

Wicked people will receive punishment
ROMANS 1:18-20 • pg 1568

God will punish those who do not turn from their sin
2 PETER 2:4-9 • pg 1725

Hell is a place of eternal fire
JUDE 1:7 • pg 1740

God will send to hell those who do not believe in him
REVELATION 21:8 • pg 1765

HOLY SPIRIT

The Holy Spirit was involved in Creation
GENESIS 1:2 • pg 3

The Holy Spirit empowers leaders
JUDGES 3:10 • pg 314

The Holy Spirit teaches us
JOHN 14:26 • pg 1510

The Holy Spirit guides us
JOHN 16:13 • pg 1512

The Holy Spirit empowers us to be witnesses
ACTS 1:8 • pg 1522

The Holy Spirit lives within us
ROMANS 8:11 • pg 1576

The Holy Spirit sanctifies us
ROMANS 15:16 • pg 1587

The Holy Spirit opens our spiritual eyes
1 CORINTHIANS 2:10 • pg 1595

The Holy Spirit is involved in salvation
TITUS 3:5 • pg 1684

HONESTY

Honesty is commanded by God
EXODUS 20:16 • pg 98

Only honest people can worship God
PSALM 24:3-4 • pg 728

God is truth and desires truth
PSALM 51:6 • pg 756

God hates lies
PROVERBS 6:16-17 • pg 860

Be honest
PROVERBS 19:1 • pg 882

Christians should be known by their honesty
MATTHEW 5:37 • pg 1360

Lies make someone unclean before God
MATTHEW 15:18-20 • pg 1377

Christians should put away dishonesty from their lives
EPHESIANS 4:25 • pg 1641

HOPE

God gives hope to the needy
PSALM 9:18 • pg 714

Hope gives us confidence
PSALM 25:3 • pg 729

The Bible gives us hope
PSALM 119:43 • pg 824

Christians always have hope
ROMANS 8:28 • pg 1577

Hope comes from the Holy Spirit
ROMANS 15:13 • pg 1586

Jesus' resurrection gives us hope
1 CORINTHIANS 6:14 • pg 1598

We have hope in Jesus
1 CORINTHIANS 15:19 • pg 1609

We have confidence of eternal life
TITUS 1:1-2 • pg 1683

HOSPITALITY

Christians should take care of those in need
MATTHEW 25:34-40 • pg 1394

Hospitality brings heavenly reward
MARK 9:41 • pg 1419

Christians should be hospitable
ROMANS 12:13 • pg 1583

Christians should be hospitable to people they do not know well
HEBREWS 13:2 • pg 1707

Be cheerful about being hospitable
1 PETER 4:9-11 • pg 1720

Hospitality reflects God's love
3 JOHN 1:5-8 • pg 1738

HUMILITY

God humbles us for our own good
DEUTERONOMY 8:16 • pg 241

God hears the prayers of the humble
2 CHRONICLES 7:14 • pg 566

God saves those who are humble
PSALM 18:27 • pg 720

God preserves the lives of humble people
PSALM 147:6 • pg 849

Those who are humble become wise
PROVERBS 11:2 • pg 867

God cares for the humble
ISAIAH 66:2 • pg 1038

God will exalt the humble
LUKE 18:14 • pg 1471

Be humble in dealing with others
PHILIPPIANS 2:1-11 • pg 1647

Humble yourself before God
JAMES 4:10 • pg 1713

HYPOCRISY

Do not associate with hypocrites
PSALM 26:4 • pg 730

God hates hypocrisy in worship
ISAIAH 29:13 • pg 975

Hypocrites pretend to be devoted to God
EZEKIEL 33:31-32 • pg 1198

God finds hypocrites repulsive
MATTHEW 23:27-28 • pg 1390

Beware of hypocrisy in your life
LUKE 12:1-2 • pg 1461

God will punish hypocrisy
LUKE 20:46-47 • pg 1476

Hypocrites are worthless
TITUS 1:16 • pg 1683

Get rid of hypocrisy
1 PETER 2:1 • pg 1717

IDOLATRY

We should have no other gods
EXODUS 20:3 • pg 97

Do not be devoted to anyone or anything more than God
DEUTERONOMY 4:23 • pg 235

Devote your heart to God
JOSHUA 24:14 • pg 308

Look to God for your security
JUDGES 10:13-16 • pg 327

We give in to idolatry when we forget God
PSALM 106:19-22 • pg 810

God will not share his glory with anything else
ISAIAH 42:8 • pg 997

Christians cannot serve both God and the things of this world
LUKE 16:13 • pg 1468

IMMORALITY

Compromises can lead to immorality
JUDGES 3:1-11 • pg 314

Stay away from immoral Christians
1 CORINTHIANS 5:9-11 • pg 1597

Practicing immorality treats God lightly
1 CORINTHIANS 6:19-20 • pg 1598

Immorality should have no place among Christians
EPHESIANS 4:17-19 • pg 1640

INTEGRITY

Leaders should have integrity
PSALM 78:72 • pg 784

Integrity takes effort
PSALM 101:3-8 • pg 803

Leaders in the church should be full of integrity
TITUS 1:7 • pg 1683

Maintain integrity in teaching others
TITUS 2:7 • pg 1684

JEALOUSY

God doesn't want to share our devotion
DEUTERONOMY 4:24 • pg 235

Jealousy can destroy someone
JOB 5:2 • pg 658

Do not envy those who do wrong
PSALM 37:1 • pg 740

Do not be jealous of wicked people
PSALM 73:2-3 • pg 776

Jealousy steals away peace
PROVERBS 14:30 • pg 874

Jealousy is a powerful enemy
PROVERBS 27:4 • pg 896

Jealousy is foolish
ECCLESIASTES 4:4 • pg 910

Jealousy can cause rash behavior
ACTS 7:9 • pg 1531

We should not be jealous of other Christians
GALATIANS 5:26 • pg 1634

Jealousy has no place in a Christian's life
TITUS 3:3-5 • pg 1684

JESUS CHRIST

Jesus is all-powerful
ISAIAH 9:6 • pg 944

Jesus has authority over demons
MARK 1:27 • pg 1404

Jesus is the Son of God
LUKE 1:35 • pg 1435

Jesus is God
JOHN 1:1-5 • pg 1486

Jesus is the Messiah
JOHN 4:25-26 • pg 1491

Jesus is the Judge
JOHN 5:22 • pg 1493

Jesus gives life
JOHN 10:10 • pg 1503

Jesus is the Good Shepherd
JOHN 10:11 • pg 1503

Jesus is the only way to God
JOHN 14:6 • pg 1509

Jesus is the author of life
ACTS 3:15 • pg 1526

Jesus is the wisdom of God
1 CORINTHIANS 1:21-24 • pg 1594

Jesus is the head of the church
EPHESIANS 5:23 • pg 1642

Jesus is the highest authority
PHILIPPIANS 2:9-10 • pg 1647

Jesus is the Creator
COLOSSIANS 1:15-16 • pg 1652

Jesus is faithful
2 TIMOTHY 2:13 • pg 1679

Jesus is coming again
TITUS 2:13 • pg 1684

Jesus is sinless
HEBREWS 4:15 • pg 1696

Jesus is holy
HEBREWS 7:26 • pg 1699

Jesus is the King of the ages
REVELATION 15:3 • pg 1757

Jesus is the Lamb of God
REVELATION 21:22 • pg 1765

JUDGMENT

God is able to judge
JOB 34:23 • pg 694

God is the ultimate authority
PSALM 9:7 • pg 713

God will judge all people
ECCLESIASTES 3:17 • pg 909

God will judge people for their actions
ECCLESIASTES 11:9 • pg 916

God will judge everything done in secret
ECCLESIASTES 12:14 • pg 917

God will rule that wicked people are guilty
MALACHI 3:5 • pg 1342

God will judge the words we speak
MATTHEW 12:36 • pg 1371

God does not judge by appearances
JOHN 7:21-24 • pg 1497

God will judge Christians
ROMANS 14:10 • pg 1585

God will judge Christians for their actions
2 CORINTHIANS 5:10 • pg 1618

God will judge all people
HEBREWS 9:27 • pg 1701

People whose names are in God's Book of Life will enter heaven
REVELATION 20:11-15 • pg 1764

JUSTICE

Justice should not be influenced by a crowd
EXODUS 23:2 • pg 101

Protect the poor
EXODUS 23:6 • pg 102

Do not hold back justice
DEUTERONOMY 27:19 • pg 262

God loves justice
PSALM 11:7 • pg 715

Jesus' death was justice for sin
ROMANS 3:25-26 • pg 1571

God is concerned about our loneliness
GENESIS 2:18 • pg 5
God encourages the lonely
1 KINGS 19:14-18 • pg 462
God takes care of lonely people
PSALM 68:6 • pg 769
Friends help in times of loneliness
ECCLESIASTES 4:10-11 • pg 910
God remains with us
MATTHEW 28:20 • pg 1401

LOVE

Love in marriage is strong
SONG OF SONGS 8:6-7 • pg 928
Love your enemies
MATTHEW 5:43-44 • pg 1360
Loving God is the most important command
MARK 12:29-30 • pg 1424
Christians must love each other
JOHN 13:34 • pg 1509
We cannot be separated from Jesus' love
ROMANS 8:35-39 • pg 1577
Love must be genuine
ROMANS 12:9 • pg 1583
Love never quits
1 CORINTHIANS 13:4-8 • pg 1606
God's love for us is beyond our understanding
EPHESIANS 3:18 • pg 1639
Love helps you look past offenses
1 PETER 4:8 • pg 1720
God is love
1 JOHN 4:16 • pg 1732
We must be known for our love
2 JOHN 1:5 • pg 1735

LOYALTY

Friends are loyal
PROVERBS 17:17 • pg 880
We cannot divide our loyalty
MATTHEW 6:24 • pg 1361
There must be loyalty in marriage
HEBREWS 13:4 • pg 1707

LUST

Lustful thoughts are sinful
MATTHEW 5:28 • pg 1357
Christians should not give in to lust
COLOSSIANS 3:5 • pg 1654
Christians should avoid lust
1 THESSALONIANS 4:3-5 • pg 1662
Godless people enjoy immorality
1 PETER 4:3 • pg 1720

LYING *SEE DISHONESTY*

MARRIAGE

SEE ALSO RELATIONSHIPS

God hates divorce
MALACHI 2:16 • pg 1342
Two people become one through marriage
MARK 10:2-12 • pg 1419
Angels do not get married
MARK 12:25 • pg 1424
Married partners should meet each other's needs
1 CORINTHIANS 7:2-5 • pg 1598
Married partners are united to each other for life
1 CORINTHIANS 7:39 • pg 1600
A Christian wife can witness to her non-Christian husband
1 PETER 3:1-6 • pg 1719

MERCY

God requires that we show mercy
MICAH 6:8 • pg 1298
People who show mercy to others will be rewarded
MATTHEW 5:7 • pg 1356
We should imitate God's mercy
LUKE 6:36 • pg 1447
Jesus is merciful
1 TIMOTHY 1:2 • pg 1670
Mercy is from God
2 TIMOTHY 1:2 • pg 1678

MIND

Keep away from mental sins
MATTHEW 5:27-30 • pg 1357
A Christian's thoughts should be holy
ROMANS 12:2 • pg 1583
Our fellowship with God helps us make decisions
1 CORINTHIANS 2:6-16 • pg 1594
Christians should please God with their thoughts
PHILIPPIANS 4:8 • pg 1650

MONEY

Greed brings trouble
PROVERBS 15:27 • pg 876
Do not make money the most important part of your life
MATTHEW 6:19 • pg 1361
Money can distract people from God
MARK 10:17-24 • pg 1420
You cannot serve both God and money
LUKE 16:13 • pg 1468
Christians should share their resources with those in need
ACTS 2:42-45 • pg 1525
Christians should not be lovers of money
1 TIMOTHY 3:3 • pg 1671
We should look to God for security, not money
1 TIMOTHY 6:17-19 • pg 1675
Do not love money
HEBREWS 13:5 • pg 1707
Be careful to treat rich and poor equally
JAMES 2:1-9 • pg 1711

MURDER

God has forbidden murder
DEUTERONOMY 5:17 • pg 237
Hateful anger is the same in God's eyes as murder
MATTHEW 5:21-22 • pg 1357

OBEDIENCE

Obeying is better than saying, "I'm sorry"
1 SAMUEL 15:22 • pg 369
People who obey God's Word will be blessed
LUKE 11:28 • pg 1459
Christians should obey the government
ROMANS 13:1-4 • pg 1584
Children should obey their parents
EPHESIANS 6:1 • pg 1642
Christians obey God
1 JOHN 2:3 • pg 1729

PAIN

God cares for his people
DEUTERONOMY 7:9 • pg 239

Christ's resurrection is a historical fact
MATTHEW 28:5-10 • pg 1400

All people will be resurrected
JOHN 5:24-30 • pg 1493

Jesus promised to raise his followers
JOHN 6:38-40 • pg 1495

We know we will be resurrected
JOHN 11:24-26 • pg 1504

We will experience resurrection
ROMANS 6:3-11 • pg 1574

Jesus' resurrection is the foundation of Christianity
1 CORINTHIANS 15:12-21 • pg 1608

Our resurrected bodies will be eternal bodies
1 CORINTHIANS 15:51-53 • pg 1610

REVENGE

God's people should not seek revenge
LEVITICUS 19:18 • pg 155

Do not pay back evil for evil
PROVERBS 24:29 • pg 892

Believers ought to resist revenge
MATTHEW 5:38-42 • pg 1360

Leave revenge in God's hands
ROMANS 12:19 • pg 1584

Desire for revenge is not compatible with the Christian life
1 THESSALONIANS 5:15 • pg 1663

Jesus is our example
1 PETER 2:21-23 • pg 1718

RIGHTEOUS/ RIGHTEOUSNESS

God is completely righteous
ISAIAH 45:21-24 • pg 1005

We cannot attain righteousness on our own
ISAIAH 64:6 • pg 1035

Human nature is the opposite of righteousness
ROMANS 3:10-18 • pg 1571

Righteousness is not attained by works
ROMANS 4:18-25 • pg 1573

Strict legalism cannot make us righteous
GALATIANS 3:11-21 • pg 1630

Our God-given righteousness is armor against Satan's attacks
EPHESIANS 6:14 • pg 1643

We become righteous through faith in Christ
PHILIPPIANS 3:9 • pg 1649

Studying God's Word helps us grow in righteousness
2 TIMOTHY 3:16 • pg 1680

Righteousness ought to characterize each believer's life
1 PETER 2:24 • pg 1719

SADNESS *SEE GRIEF, SORROW*

SALVATION

Those who receive salvation become God's children
JOHN 1:12-13 • pg 1486

Salvation is a work of the Holy Spirit in a person's life
JOHN 3:1-16 • pg 1489

Belief and trust in Jesus Christ are the only way to be saved
JOHN 14:6 • pg 1509

Salvation includes gaining a relationship with God
JOHN 17:1-5 • pg 1513

Receiving salvation means we must turn from our sins
ACTS 2:37-38 • pg 1525

Salvation cannot be earned; it is a gift of God
ROMANS 6:23 • pg 1575

Receiving salvation is simple and personal
ROMANS 10:8-10 • pg 1580

Salvation is by God's grace alone
EPHESIANS 2:1-9 • pg 1638

Salvation rescues us from Satan's dominion
COLOSSIANS 1:13-14 • pg 1652

Our salvation was obtained by Jesus' blood
1 PETER 1:18-19 • pg 1717

SATAN

Satan is under God's authority
JOB 1:6-12 • pg 654

Satan will tempt Jesus' followers
MATTHEW 4:1-11 • pg 1354

Satan is completely evil
JOHN 8:44 • pg 1500

Satan is the temporary ruler over this world
EPHESIANS 2:1-2 • pg 1638

Satan and his demons are spiritual
EPHESIANS 6:12 • pg 1642

Satan works through an army of demons
1 TIMOTHY 4:1 • pg 1672

Believers have the authority to resist Satan
JAMES 4:1-10 • pg 1713

Satan is an enemy to Christians
1 PETER 5:8 • pg 1721

Jesus destroyed Satan's work with his death on the cross
1 JOHN 3:7-8 • pg 1731

Satan is a defeated enemy
REVELATION 20:10 • pg 1764

SECOND COMING OF CHRIST

We do not know when Jesus will return
MATTHEW 24:36 • pg 1392

Christ's return will be unmistakable
MARK 13:26-27 • pg 1426

Christ's return will be joyous for those who are ready
LUKE 12:35-40 • pg 1462

The Second Coming will be a time of judgment on unbelievers
JOHN 12:37-50 • pg 1507

At Christ's second coming we will be with him forever
JOHN 14:1-3 • pg 1509

The promise of Christ's return
ACTS 1:10-11 • pg 1522

Believers will be resurrected and given glorious bodies
1 CORINTHIANS 15:51-57 • pg 1610

Christ's return will be visible and glorious
1 THESSALONIANS 4:16 • pg 1662

At Christ's return, Christians who are dead and alive will rise to meet him
1 THESSALONIANS 4:16-17 • pg 1662

Continue to serve God as you await the Second Coming
1 PETER 4:7-8 • pg 1720

Patiently await Christ's return

2 PETER 3:8-13 • pg 1726
Jesus is coming soon
REVELATION 22:20-21 • pg 1767

SELF-ESTEEM
SEE ALSO PRIDE

We are made in God's image
GENESIS 1:26-27 • pg 4
We are a little lower than the angels
PSALM 8:3-5 • pg 712
God took special care to create us
PSALM 139:1-18 • pg 840
We have been formed by God's loving hands
ISAIAH 64:8 • pg 1035
We are of great value to God
LUKE 12:4-12 • pg 1461
God gave his Son for us
JOHN 3:16 • pg 1489
Our self-esteem is affected by our relationship with Christ
ROMANS 12:1-8 • pg 1583
Our self-esteem is based on God's approval
2 CORINTHIANS 10:12-18 • pg 1622
We should not overestimate ourselves
GALATIANS 6:3-5 • pg 1634

SEX

Sex is God's gift to married people
PROVERBS 5:15-21 • pg 859
Sex outside of marriage is foolish
PROVERBS 6:23-35 • pg 861
Sex within marriage is meant to be a delight
SONG OF SONGS 4:1-16 • pg 922
Sexual sin begins in the mind
MATTHEW 5:27-30 • pg 1357
Sex is a powerful bond not meant to be taken lightly
1 CORINTHIANS 6:13-20 • pg 1598
Sexual immorality has no place among Christians
EPHESIANS 5:1-3 • pg 1641
We are to have nothing to do with sexual immorality
COLOSSIANS 3:5 • pg 1654
God wants us to live in holiness, not lustful passion
1 THESSALONIANS 4:1-8 • pg 1662
Sex in marriage is honorable and pure
HEBREWS 13:4 • pg 1707

SICKNESS

God cares for the sick
PSALM 41:1-13 • pg 746
A cheerful spirit can act as good medicine against sickness
PROVERBS 17:22 • pg 880
Jesus can heal sickness
MATTHEW 4:23-25 • pg 1356
Believers ought to have compassion on the sick
MATTHEW 25:34-40 • pg 1394
It is better to be physically crippled than spiritually crippled
MARK 9:43-48 • pg 1419
Paul had an infirmity that God would not remove
2 CORINTHIANS 12:7-10 • pg 1624

SIN

Sin has consequences
GENESIS 3:1-19 • pg 5
God must punish sin
EXODUS 32:34 • pg 115
Our consciences can identify sin
2 SAMUEL 24:10-15 • pg 426
We should humbly confess our sins to God
EZRA 9:5-15 • pg 616
We should ask God to forgive our sins
PSALM 51:1-10 • pg 755
Stay away from people who lead you to sin
PROVERBS 1:10-19 • pg 853
Sin begins in the mind
MATTHEW 5:27-28 • pg 1357
All people have sinned
ROMANS 3:23 • pg 1571
Sin leads to eternal death
ROMANS 6:23 • pg 1575
Jesus takes the penalty of our sin on himself
ROMANS 8:1-2 • pg 1576
Sin begins with temptation
JAMES 1:15 • pg 1710
We can sin by avoiding something we should do
JAMES 4:17 • pg 1713
God is willing to forgive our sins
1 JOHN 1:8-9 • pg 1729

SORROW *SEE ALSO GRIEF*

Sorrow is often a necessary part of repentance
JUDGES 2:4-5 • pg 313
Weeping will be followed by joy
PSALM 30:5 • pg 733
Jesus understands sorrow
ISAIAH 53:3-9 • pg 1017
God promises comfort to those who experience sorrow
MATTHEW 5:4 • pg 1356
God may use sorrow to point out sin and draw us back to him
2 CORINTHIANS 7:10-11 • pg 1620
We sorrow over believers who die, but one day we will meet again
1 THESSALONIANS 4:13-18 • pg 1662
Sorrow will not exist in God's Kingdom
REVELATION 21:3-4 • pg 1765

SOUL

People cannot destroy your soul
MATTHEW 10:28 • pg 1368
We are to love God with our whole being—heart, soul, and mind
MATTHEW 22:36-40 • pg 1388
It is of no value to gain the world but lose your soul
MARK 8:34-38 • pg 1417
We can place our soul under Christ's protection
JOHN 10:27-29 • pg 1503
Believers are assured of immortality
1 CORINTHIANS 15:46-53 • pg 1610

SPIRITUAL GIFTS

God expects us to use our gifts
ROMANS 12:3-8 • pg 1583
God gives us our spiritual gifts
1 CORINTHIANS 12:4-11 • pg 1604
Spiritual gifts build up the body of Christ
EPHESIANS 4:11-13 • pg 1640
Spiritual gifts ought not be denied nor overemphasized
1 THESSALONIANS 5:19-22 • pg 1663

God distributes spiritual gifts according to his will
HEBREWS 2:4 • pg 1693

STRESS

Delegating work can alleviate stress
EXODUS 18:13-26 • pg 95

God is a refuge in times of stress
PSALM 62:1-8 • pg 764

Pray to God in times of stress
PSALM 69:1-36 • pg 771

Wait upon the Lord
ISAIAH 40:30-31 • pg 994

God is always with us
ROMANS 8:31-39 • pg 1577

God cares about our stress
2 CORINTHIANS 4:8-12 • pg 1617

Don't let stress cause you to worry
PHILIPPIANS 4:4-9 • pg 1650

SUFFERING

Those who suffer need encouragement
JOB 16:1-6 • pg 672

Christ's followers will face suffering
MATTHEW 16:21-26 • pg 1379

Our suffering helps us comfort others who are suffering
2 CORINTHIANS 1:3-7 • pg 1614

Our suffering will end in glory
2 CORINTHIANS 4:17-18 • pg 1617

Jesus can help us through suffering
HEBREWS 2:11-18 • pg 1693

Christ showed how to handle suffering
1 PETER 2:21-24 • pg 1718

There will be no suffering in Christ's Kingdom
REVELATION 21:4 • pg 1765

TEACHING

SEE ALSO WITNESSING

Parents must teach their children about the Lord
DEUTERONOMY 6:4-9 • pg 238

Believers teach each other
2 TIMOTHY 2:2 • pg 1679

Qualities of a good teacher
2 TIMOTHY 2:22-26 • pg 1679

Instruction to those who teach God's Word
TITUS 2:1-15 • pg 1684

TEMPTATION

Temptation comes from Satan
GENESIS 3:1-6 • pg 5

How to avoid temptation
PROVERBS 7:1-5 • pg 861

How to respond when tempted
MATTHEW 4:1-11 • pg 1354

God will provide a way of escape from every temptation
1 CORINTHIANS 10:13 • pg 1602

Run from temptation
2 TIMOTHY 2:22 • pg 1679

Christ can help us, for he, too, has faced temptation
HEBREWS 4:15-16 • pg 1696

God never tempts people to sin
JAMES 1:13-15 • pg 1710

THANKFULNESS

Thank the Lord because he is good
PSALM 107:1-3 • pg 812

Be thankful for answers to prayer
PSALM 138:1-5 • pg 839

Be thankful for salvation
EPHESIANS 2:4-10 • pg 1638

Our prayers should include words of thankfulness
PHILIPPIANS 4:6 • pg 1650

Our life should be characterized by thankfulness to God
COLOSSIANS 3:15-17 • pg 1655

We are called to give thanks in all circumstances
1 THESSALONIANS 5:16-18 • pg 1663

TRUST *SEE FAITH*

TRUTH

God wants us to be true and righteous
PSALM 51:1-6 • pg 755

Truth never changes
PROVERBS 12:19 • pg 870

Truth sets us free
JOHN 8:31-32 • pg 1500

Truth is found in Jesus Christ
JOHN 14:6 • pg 1509

God's Word is truth
JOHN 17:17 • pg 1513

We must not only believe the truth but also live by it
1 JOHN 1:5-7 • pg 1729

UNITY

Unity among believers pleases God
PSALM 133:1 • pg 836

Christians are not supposed to live in isolation
JOHN 17:11 • pg 1513

Unity includes bearing one another's joys and burdens
ROMANS 12:9-16 • pg 1583

Believers must seek unity in all essentials
1 CORINTHIANS 1:10 • pg 1593

There can be great unity even in great diversity
EPHESIANS 4:3-13 • pg 1640

The love Christ commanded should create unity among believers
PHILIPPIANS 1:3-11 • pg 1646

Unity ought to be a distinctive mark among Christians
PHILIPPIANS 2:1-2 • pg 1647

WISDOM

The fear of God is the beginning of wisdom
PROVERBS 1:7 • pg 853

To find wisdom, first find God
PROVERBS 2:6-12 • pg 855

Wise people accept advice
PROVERBS 13:10 • pg 871

Wise people boast not in their wisdom but in knowing God
JEREMIAH 9:23-24 • pg 1062

The wise understand God's ways and follow his guidance
HOSEA 14:9 • pg 1258

Wise people build on the solid foundation of God and his Word
MATTHEW 7:24-27 • pg 1363

God's wisdom is different from the world's wisdom
1 CORINTHIANS 2:1-16 • pg 1594

God will give us wisdom if we ask for it
JAMES 1:5 • pg 1710

Jesus in the Old Testament

Luke 24:27

WHAT DID JESUS CLAIM ABOUT HIMSELF?

IMAGINE THIS DISCUSSION

Then Jesus took them through the writings of Moses and all the prophets, explaining from all the Scriptures the things concerning himself.

What did Jesus explain on that road?

Luke 24:27

HOW CREATION REVEALS HIM
HOW NOAH SERVED HIM
HOW ABRAHAM OBEYED HIM
HOW JOSEPH POINTED TO HIM
HOW ISRAEL EMBODIED HIM
HOW JUDAH SET THE STAGE FOR HIM
HOW MOSES SPOKE FOR HIM
HOW THE PASSOVER LAMB DEPICTED HIM
HOW JOSHUA REPRESENTED HIM
HOW THE JUDGES FORESHADOWED HIM
HOW RUTH GREAT-GRANDMOTHERED HIM
HOW DAVID TRUSTED HIM
HOW ELIJAH BATTLED FOR HIM
HOW ISAIAH PROPHESIED ABOUT HIM
HOW EZEKIEL ENVISIONED HIM
HOW HOSEA SUFFERED FOR HIM
HOW DANIEL STOOD UP FOR HIM
HOW NEHEMIAH WAS DEDICATED TO HIM
HOW MALACHI FORESAW HIM
HOW JOHN THE BAPTIST PREPARED A WAY FOR HIM
HOW HE CREATED EVERYTHING THERE IS
HOW HE EXISTED BEFORE ABRAHAM EVER WAS
HOW HE IS THE PLAN OF SALVATION
HOW HE IS THE PROMISED ONE
HOW HE IS THE SAVIOR
HOW HE IS THE REDEEMER
HOW HE IS THE MEDIATOR
HOW HE IS THE TRUE JUDGE
HOW HE IS THE SON OF GOD
HOW HE IS THE PROPHESIED KING
HOW HE IS THE HEIR TO DAVID'S THRONE
HOW HE IS THE GOOD SHEPHERD
HOW HE IS THE BREAD OF LIFE
HOW HE IS THE WORD OF GOD
HOW HE IS THE PROMISED MESSIAH
HOW HE IS THE LIVING WATER
HOW HE IS THE WAY, THE TRUTH, THE LIFE
HOW HE IS THE FORGIVER OF SIN
HOW HE IS THE LION OF JUDAH
HOW HE IS THE LAMB OF GOD
HOW HE WILL RE-CREATE EVERYTHING

Noticing Jesus in the Old Testament

MAKES A DIFFERENCE IN HOW YOU READ THE BIBLE

GENESIS 49:9–10

Judah, my son, is a young lion
that has finished eating its prey.
Like a lion he crouches and lies down;
like a lioness—who dares to rouse him?
The scepter will not depart from Judah,
nor the ruler's staff from his descendants,
until the coming of the one to whom it belongs,
the one whom all nations will honor.

REVELATION 5:5

Stop weeping! Look, the Lion of the tribe of Judah, the heir to David's throne, has won the victory.

Noticing Jesus in the Old Testament
MAKES A DIFFERENCE IN HOW YOU READ THE BIBLE

ISAIAH 61:1–2

The Spirit of the Sovereign Lord is upon me,
for the Lord has anointed me
to bring good news to the poor.
He has sent me to comfort the brokenhearted
and to proclaim that captives will be released
and prisoners will be freed...
that the time of the Lord's favor has come.

LUKE 4:18–21

"The Spirit of the Lord is upon me,
for he has anointed me to bring Good News to the poor.
He has sent me to proclaim that captives will be released,
that the blind will see,
that the oppressed will be set free,
and that the time of the Lord's favor has come."

He rolled up the scroll...Then he began to speak to them. "The Scripture you've just heard has been fulfilled this very day!"

Noticing Jesus in the Old Testament
MAKES A DIFFERENCE IN HOW YOU READ THE BIBLE

GENESIS 1:1–3

In the beginning God created the heavens and the earth. The earth was formless and empty, and darkness covered the deep waters. And the Spirit of God was hovering over the surface of the waters.

Then God said, "Let there be light," and there was light.

JOHN 1:1–5

In the beginning the Word already existed.
The Word was with God,
and the Word was God.
He existed in the beginning with God.
God created everything through him,
and nothing was created except through him.
The Word gave life to everything that was created,
and his life brought light to everyone.
The light shines in the darkness,
and the darkness can never extinguish it.

Noticing Jesus in the Old Testament
MAKES A DIFFERENCE IN HOW YOU READ THE BIBLE

PSALM 22:1, 16, 18

My God, my God, why have you abandoned me?...

My enemies surround me like a pack of dogs;
an evil gang closes in on me.
They have pierced my hands and feet...

They divide my garments among themselves
and throw dice for my clothing.

MATTHEW 27:46

At about three o'clock, Jesus called out with a loud voice, *"Eli, Eli, lema sabachthani?"* which means "My God, my God, why have you abandoned me?"

MARK 15:24

Then the soldiers nailed him to the cross. They divided his clothes and threw dice to decide who would get each piece.

about the Bible

WHAT WERE THE FIRST WORDS OF JESUS RECORDED IN THE BOOK OF JOHN?

a. Hey, fam. Be holy.
b. Verily, verily, verily, verily, life is but a dream.
c. Man, it stinks down here.
d. I made you—and I can unmake you.
e. What do you want?

THE ANSWER

"WHAT DO YOU WANT?"
JOHN 1:38

QUESTIONS

COMMON CONCERNS PEOPLE HAVE ABOUT THE BIBLE

Is the Bible even relevant anymore?
Who told you it wasn't? There is more relevance and practical guidance in these pages than in any other resource you'll find anywhere else today.

Are the ethics of the Bible wrong?
Or could it be instead that some of the ethics of our culture are wrong? Challenging a society that creates its own ethical systems can make the Bible seem countercultural at times. The radical truth in the Bible actually is the foundation upon which our definitions for right and wrong are to be built.

Isn't the wording of the Bible too old-fashioned?
Have you read this Bible yet? One of the reasons we use the New Living Translation is so that readers can understand the Bible in English. The Bible was originally written in Hebrew and Greek (and a little bit of Aramaic), so the words have been translated into English so that people who can't read those languages can understand what was written. You might find some things that are difficult to comprehend at first. But that just reveals that you are engaging with a big story that spreads over a big history across a big geography.

QUESTIONS

COMMON CONCERNS PEOPLE HAVE ABOUT THE BIBLE

Is the Bible boring?

Please read the book of Judges and see if you still think the Bible is boring.

Do you need to be a Bible geek to enjoy the Bible?

You only need interest.

What about all the weird stories, like Noah or Jonah?

They're amazing, aren't they? Just dig in and discover!

Isn't the Bible just a bunch of rules?

Thou shalt not think this. The Bible is so much more than an instruction manual. Just start reading the book of Mark or the story of Esther.

Is God different in the Old and New Testament?

Nope. Same God in both. That's one of the things that makes Jesus so fascinating and so life-changingly challenging.

WHAT OTHER QUESTIONS DO YOU THINK PEOPLE HAVE?

How We Got the Bible

ONE GENERATION SHARING IT WITH THE NEXT

Old Testament

Thirty-nine books written in Hebrew over a period of 1500+ years before Jesus.

New Testament

Twenty-seven books written in Greek during the first generation after Jesus.

Translations & Copies

Thousands of copies made over the early centuries. Eventually people made translations into their own unique languages, including English.

Global Reach

Multiplying the Word of God into thousands of languages all across the globe. Now 98 percent of people have access to a Bible.

The Story Arc of Scripture

YOU CAN ENTER THE STORY ANYWHERE IN THE BIBLE AND STEP INTO A HUGE, MULTILAYERED, EYE-OPENING, INTRIGUE-PACKED, WORLD-SAVING ADVENTURE. AND ALL OF IT ORBITS JESUS.

Creation

In the beginning, God created. His Spirit hovered. His Word spoke. And it was very good.

People

Sin brought death to humankind. But by using ordinary people to share an extraordinary message, God prepared the way for salvation. For God so loved the world.

Miracles

From the parting of the sea and the calming of the storm to the raising of the dead and the healing of the sick, God has always demonstrated his reconciling work in this world.

Prophecies

From beginning to end, God's message has been the same: prepare the way for the Lord, the Savior, the Suffering Servant, the baby to be born in Bethlehem, the Lion of Judah, the Lamb of God, for he will change the world.

2 TIMOTHY 3:16–17

All Scripture is inspired by God and is useful to teach us what is true and to make us realize what is wrong in our lives. It corrects us when we are wrong and teaches us to do what is right. God uses it to prepare and equip his people to do every good work.

The Word of God

WHAT DOES THE BIBLE CLAIM ABOUT ITSELF?

The **Bible** claims to be the very **Word of God**. The Bible also proclaims that **Jesus is the Word of God** (John 1:1–18). And Jesus claims that the whole of Scripture points to him (John 5:31–47, Luke 24, and more).

Hebrews 4:12

For the word of God is alive and powerful. It is sharper than the sharpest two-edged sword, cutting between soul and spirit, between joint and marrow. It exposes our innermost thoughts and desires.

John 5:39

You search the Scriptures because you think they give you eternal life. But the Scriptures point to me!

Parables and Illustrations of Jesus

	Matthew	Mark	Luke	John
Nature and farming				
Lilies of the field	6:25-34		12:22-31	
Trees and their fruit	7:15-20		6:43-45	
The farmer scattering seed	13:1-23	4:1-29	8:4-15	
Barren fig tree			13:6-9	
Weeds	13:24-43			
Mustard seed	13:31-32	4:30-32	13:18-19	
Lost sheep	18:10-14		15:1-7	
Vineyard workers	20:1-16			
Evil farmers	21:33-46	12:1-12	20:9-19	
Fig tree	24:32-35	13:28-31	21:29-33	
Sheep and goats	25:31-46			
Harvest				4:35-38
The good shepherd				10:1-18
Kernel of wheat				12:20-26
The true vine				15:1-17
Everyday objects of Bible times				
Water				4:5-14
Salt of the earth	5:13			
Light of the world	5:14-16	4:21-22	8:16-18	12:35-36
Bread of life				6:25-35
New wine	9:17	2:22	5:37-39	
Yeast	13:33		13:20-21	
Pearls	13:45-46			
Fishing net	13:47-50			
Lost coin			15:8-10	
Daily life				
Children playing	11:16-19		7:31-35	
Forgiving	18:21-35			
Two sons	21:28-32			
The wedding banquet	22:1-14		14:15-24	
The ten bridesmaids	25:1-13			
The silver	25:14-30		19:11-27	
House builders	7:24-27		6:46-49	
Patching clothes	9:16	2:21	5:36	
The two debtors			7:41-47	
The good Samaritan			10:25-37	
Friend in need			11:5-13	
The rich fool			12:16-21	
Watchful servants		13:33-37	12:35-40	
Counting the cost			14:25-33	
The prodigal son			15:11-32	
The shrewd manager			16:1-13	
The rich man and Lazarus			16:19-31	
A servant's duty			17:7-10	
The persistent widow			18:1-8	
The Pharisee and the tax collector			18:9-14	

The Miracles of Jesus

	Matthew	Mark	Luke	John
Healing people				
Official's son				4:46-54
Sick man at Bethesda				5:1-15
Man with evil spirit		1:21-28	4:31-37	
Man with leprosy	8:1-4	1:40-45	5:12-14	
Roman officer's servant	8:5-13		7:1-10	
Raising widow's son			7:11-15	
Peter's mother-in-law	8:14-15	1:29-31	4:38-39	
Man with legion		5:1-20	8:26-39	
Man who was paralyzed	9:1-7	2:1-12	5:17-26	
Woman with constant bleeding	9:20-22	5:25-34	8:43-48	
Raising Jairus' daughter	9:18-26	5:21-43	8:40-56	
Possessed man who couldn't speak	9:32-34			
Man with deformed hand	12:9-14	3:1-6	6:6-11	
Possessed man	12:22		11:14	
Gentile woman's daughter	15:21-28	7:24-30		
Deaf man with speech impediment		7:31-37		
Blind man at Bethsaida		8:22-26		
Afflicted boy	17:14-18	9:17-29	9:37-43	
Blind Bartimaeus		10:46-52	18:35-43	
Woman with bowed back			13:10-17	
Man with swollen limbs			14:1-6	
Man blind from birth				9:1-41
Raising Lazarus				11:1-44
Slave's ear			22:47-51	
Healing groups				
Sick people in Capernaum	8:16-17	1:32-34	4:40-41	
Two blind men	9:27-31			
Sick people in Galilee		3:7-12		
Sick people on hillside	15:29-31			
Ten men with leprosy			17:11-19	
Control over nature				
Water changed to wine				2:1-11
Draught of fish			5:1-11	
Stilling a storm	8:23-27	4:35-41	8:22-25	
Feeding 5,000	14:13-21	6:32-44	9:10-17	6:1-13
Walking on water	14:22-33	6:45-52		6:16-21
Feeding 4,000	15:32-38	8:1-10		
A fish to pay temple tax	17:24-27			
Barren fig tree	21:18-22	11:12-24		
Great catch of fish				21:1-11

Archaeological Discoveries

1.

Peter's House, Capernaum

Archaeologists uncovered a simple first-century AD home in Capernaum that Jesus may have lived in while he was ministering in Galilee. It later became a place for gatherings linked with Jesus and the apostle Peter.

2.

The Siloam Pool, Jerusalem

In 2004, archaeologists excavated part of this monumental pool south of Jerusalem's Temple Mount. This is where Jesus restored the sight of a blind man, according to John's gospel.

3.

The Dead Sea Scrolls

This hugely important library of more than eight hundred manuscripts, dating from between around 250 BC and AD 68, was discovered in 1947 by a Bedouin shepherd in caves near the Dead Sea. It throws unique light on Jewish religion, culture, and the Bible.

4.

Jerusalem Siege Tower

In the 1970s, archaeologists discovered a twenty-two-foot tower, with walls twelve feet thick, which formed part of Jerusalem's defenses against the Babylonian invasion of 586 BC in the city's Jewish quarter. A thick layer of charred wood, ashes, and soot around the base of the tower shows there was a fire during the Babylonian destruction.

5.

The Siloam Inscription, Hezekiah's Tunnel, Jerusalem

This unique inscription was discovered in 1880 by two local boys who had been playing in the tunnel. The text describes the moment when quarrymen from each end met in the middle of the tunnel and throws light on 2 Kings 20:20, which describes King Hezekiah's preparations to defend the city from attack by Sennacherib of Assyria.

6.

Ain Dara Temple

This temple, discovered by archaeologists in northern Syria, is very similar in structure to Solomon's Temple, as described in the Bible. Its plan, size, date, and details are typical of temple buildings of this region and period, supporting the truth of the Bible's description.

7.

Tel Dan Stela

This is a ninth-century BC inscription from northern Israel that gives us the first evidence for King David outside the pages of the Bible.

8.

Pilate Inscription

An inscription dating to AD 30 discovered at Caesarea, Israel, mentions Pontius Pilate, the governor of Judah who sentenced Jesus to death.

9.

Galilee Boat

The remains of a wooden fishing vessel were discovered in 1986 on the seabed of Galilee. The boat dates to first century BC or first century AD and is similar to the fishing boats used by the fishermen whom Jesus called to follow him.

10.

Black Obelisk of Shalmaneser III

This stone obelisk, dated to 841 BC, depicts and mentions the Israelite King Jehu, who appears in the Old Testament in 2 Kings.

So What?

GOD THINKS THE BIBLE IS MORE THAN RELEVANT FOR YOUR LIFE. SO THE REAL QUESTION IS THIS: DO YOU?

The Bible won't be relevant or powerful for you if you don't spend time in it.

So start opening it up and digging into its pages. If you don't understand something, investigate it. Jesus said, "Keep on asking, and you will receive what you ask for. Keep on seeking, and you will find. Keep on knocking, and the door will be opened to you" (Matthew 7:7). Ask! Seek! Knock!

The Bible won't be relevant or powerful for you if you don't want God in your life.

A heart thirsty for God will draw you to Jesus in the Bible.

The Bible won't be relevant or powerful for you or your friends if you don't let God change you.

If you allow, the Holy Spirit will speak to you as you read the Bible. Jesus often said, "Anyone with ears to hear should listen and understand!" (e.g., Matthew 11:15). But if you close yourself off from God's work, his Word falls on deaf ears. Then how will you grow in your walk with God, and how will you be able to show your friends that the good news found in the Bible is true?

you're made for this

I'm not asking you to take them out of the world, but to keep them safe from the evil one. They do not belong to this world any more than I do. Make them holy by your truth; teach them your word, which is truth. Just as you sent me into the world, I am sending them into the world. And I give myself as a holy sacrifice for them so they can be made holy by your truth.

John 17:15–19

Three Truths that Change the World

TRUTH #1

REJOICING REQUIRES ENDURANCE.

TRUTH #2

CHARACTER AVOIDS CUTTING CORNERS.

TRUTH #3

HOPE COMES FROM CONFIDENCE IN GOD.

ROMANS 5:3–8

We can rejoice, too, when we run into problems and trials, for we know that they help us develop endurance. And endurance develops strength of character, and character strengthens our confident hope of salvation. And this hope will not lead to disappointment. For we know how dearly God loves us, because he has given us the Holy Spirit to fill our hearts with his love.

When we were utterly helpless, Christ came at just the right time and died for us sinners. Now, most people would not be willing to die for an upright person, though someone might perhaps be willing to die for a person who is especially good. But God showed his great love for us by sending Christ to die for us while we were still sinners.

Jesus Prompts You to Make a Decision about Him

CHOICE 1

Jesus is difficult to understand. You don't get everything about him, and it scares you to surrender your life. So you walk away and pursue what you want.

CHOICE 2

Jesus is difficult to understand...but you think there might be truth in him. So you decide to stay interested.

This is a good start, but eventually you will be faced with making choice 1 or choice 3.

CHOICE 3

Yes, living for Jesus is difficult, but it is also amazing. So you commit to always learn, always grow, and always live resilient in the life he provides for you.

* TURN TO THE BEGINNING OF THE APPENDIXES AND PRAY THE PRAYER IN THE SECTION TITLED "HOW TO ACCEPT JESUS AS YOUR LORD AND SAVIOR."

DON'T UNDERESTIMATE THE POWER OF THE

PRESENCE

OF GOD IN THE FELLOWSHIP OF HIS PEOPLE.

All the believers devoted themselves to the apostles' teaching, and to fellowship, and to sharing in meals (including the Lord's Supper), and to prayer.

A deep sense of awe came over them all, and the apostles performed many miraculous signs and wonders. And all the believers met together in one place and shared everything they had. They sold their property and possessions and shared the money with those in need. They worshiped together at the Temple each day, met in homes for the Lord's Supper, and shared their meals with great joy and generosity— all the while praising God and enjoying the goodwill of all the people. And each day the Lord added to their fellowship those who were being saved.

Acts 2:42–47

SPEND YOUR ENERGY SEEKING THE ETERNAL LIFE THAT THE SON OF MAN CAN GIVE YOU.

JOHN 6:27

Unless you are

born again,

you cannot

see

the Kingdom of

God.

JOHN 3:3

THE TWO-STEP GUIDE TO JUMP-START A PURE HEART

STEP 1:
Get right with God.

STEP 2:
Do what God does.

PSALM 51:10–12

CREATE IN ME A CLEAN HEART, O GOD.
  RENEW A LOYAL SPIRIT WITHIN ME.
DO NOT BANISH ME FROM YOUR PRESENCE,
  AND DON'T TAKE YOUR HOLY SPIRIT FROM ME.

RESTORE TO ME THE JOY OF YOUR SALVATION,
  AND MAKE ME WILLING TO OBEY YOU.

So we are Christ's ambassadors; God is making his appeal through us. We speak for Christ when we plead, "Come back to God!"

2 CORINTHIANS 5:20

••• THINK ABOUT JESUS.

AND NOW, DEAR BROTHERS AND SISTERS, ONE FINAL THING. FIX YOUR THOUGHTS ON WHAT IS TRUE, AND HONORABLE, AND RIGHT, AND PURE, AND LOVELY, AND ADMIRABLE. THINK ABOUT THINGS THAT ARE EXCELLENT AND WORTHY OF PRAISE.

PHILIPPIANS 4:8

In John 6, Jesus Is a...

Crowd Feeder 6:1–14
Water Walker 6:16–21
Soul Provider 6:22–40
Eternity Giver 6:41–52
Thought Challenger 6:53–59
Decision Prompter 6:60–66
Life Saver 6:68–69

JESUS CHALLENGES THIS WORLD TO CHANGE

Amid displaying his power over food, over nature, over souls, and over eternity, Jesus revealed what God really wants from humans (in John 6:29): "Jesus told them, 'This is the only work God wants from you: Believe in the one he has sent.'"

Do you believe in Jesus? No one can escape this life without accepting him. Too often, people struggle to receive his simple invitation. The saddest verse in the entire Bible might be John 6:66: "At this point many of his disciples turned away and deserted him."

Thankfully, this verse is quickly followed by Peter's bold statement in John 6:68–69: "Simon Peter replied, 'Lord, to whom would we go? You have the words that give eternal life. We believe, and we know you are the Holy One of God.'"

If you have never done so, please accept Jesus as the Lord of your life right now. You can turn to the beginning of the appendixes and pray the prayer in the section titled "How to Accept Jesus as Your Lord and Savior."

Do you want what God wants for you?

SEEK THE KINGDOM OF GOD ABOVE ALL ELSE, AND LIVE RIGHTEOUSLY, AND HE WILL GIVE YOU EVERYTHING YOU NEED.
MATTHEW 6:33

TAKE DELIGHT IN THE LORD, AND HE WILL GIVE YOU YOUR HEART'S DESIRES.
PSALM 37:4

THE LORD IS MY SHEPHERD; I HAVE ALL THAT I NEED.
PSALM 23:1

AND THIS SAME GOD WHO TAKES CARE OF ME WILL SUPPLY ALL YOUR NEEDS FROM HIS GLORIOUS RICHES, WHICH HAVE BEEN GIVEN TO US IN CHRIST JESUS.
PHILIPPIANS 4:19

THIS IS THE ONLY WORK GOD WANTS FROM YOU: BELIEVE IN THE ONE HE HAS SENT.
JOHN 6:29

PSALM 119:105

Your word is a lamp to
guide my feet
and a light for my path.

JESUS,

EVERY
ACTION
OF
MINE
IS
YOURS
TO
USE.

AMEN.

Do not conform.

Let God transform you.

Don't copy the behavior and customs of this world, but let God transform you into a new person by changing the way you think. Then you will learn to know God's will for you, which is good and pleasing and perfect.

Romans 12:2

you're made for this